The Oxford Companion to
Philosophy

The Oxford Companion to
Philosophy

Second Edition

Edited by Ted Honderich

OXFORD
UNIVERSITY PRESS

OXFORD
UNIVERSITY PRESS

Great Clarendon Street, Oxford OX2 6DP

Oxford University Press is a department of the University of Oxford.
It furthers the University's objective of excellence in research, scholarship,
and education by publishing worldwide in

Oxford New York

Auckland Cape Town Dar es Salaam Hong Kong Karachi
Kuala Lumpur Madrid Melbourne Mexico City Nairobi
New Delhi Shanghai Taipei Toronto

With offices in

Argentina Austria Brazil Chile Czech Republic France Greece
Guatemala Hungary Italy Japan South Korea Poland Portugal
Singapore Switzerland Thailand Turkey Ukraine Vietnam

Oxford is a registered trade mark of Oxford University Press
in the UK and in certain other countries

Published in the United States
by Oxford University Press Inc., New York

© Oxford University Press 1995, 2005

The moral rights of the author have been asserted
Database right Oxford University Press (maker)

First edition 1995
New edition 2005

British Library Cataloguing in Publication Data

Data available

Library of Congress Cataloging in Publication Data

The Oxford companion to philosophy / edited by Ted Honderich.
Includes bibliographical references and index.
1. Philosophy—Encyclopedias. I. Honderich, Ted.
B51.094 1995 100—dc20 94–36914

ISBN 0–19–926479–1

10 9 8 7 6 5 4 3 2 1

Typeset in Dante by
Jayvee, Trivandrum, India
Printed in Great Britain
on acid-free paper by
Biddles Ltd,
King's Lynn, Norfolk

To Bee, Ingrid, John, Kiaran, and Rina, with love

Preface

THE brave, large aim of this book has been to bring philosophy together between two covers better than ever before. That is not a job for one man, or one woman, or a few, or a team, although it is tried often enough. So 249 of us joined forces joined forces ten years ago for the first edition. We have now been reinforced by forty-two more contributors for this second edition. To the 1,932 entries in the first edition, about 300 more have been added. Also, many of the entries in the first edition have been considerably lengthened and revised. Many others have been updated. The list of contemporary philosophers in the first edition has been adjusted in order to reflect what McTaggart denied, that time is real.

The philosophy brought together includes, first of all, the work of the great philosophers. As that term is commonly used, there are perhaps twenty of them. By anyone's reckoning, this pantheon of philosophy includes Plato, Aristotle, Aquinas, Hobbes, Descartes, Spinoza, Leibniz, Locke, Berkeley, the blessed Hume, Kant, Hegel, and Nietzsche. These, together with others who stand a bit less solidly in the pantheon, are the subjects of long essays in this book.

Philosophy as this book conceives it, secondly, includes all of its history in the English language, a history mainly of British and American thinkers. In this history there are many figures not so monumental as Locke, Berkeley, and Hume. Among them, if they are not admitted to the pantheon, are John Stuart Mill, Charles Sanders Peirce, Bertrand Russell, and, if an Austrian can be counted in this particular history, and should be, Ludwig Wittgenstein. They also include Jonathan Edwards, Thomas Reid, William James, and F. H. Bradley.

Thirdly, if the book cannot include all of the histories of philosophy in languages other than English, it does attend to them. It attends to more than the great leaders of the philosophies in these languages. Thus Descartes is joined by such of his countrymen and countrywomen as Simone de Beauvoir, Henri Bergson, and Auguste Comte. Kant and Hegel are joined by J. G. Fichte, Jürgen Habermas, Karl Jaspers, and others. There are also general entries on each of the national philosophies, from Australian to Croatian to Japanese to Russian.

A fourth part of the book, not an insignificant one, consists in about 150 entries on contemporary philosophers, the largest groups being American and British. It would have been an omission to leave out contemporaries, and faint-hearted. Philosophy thrives. Its past must not be allowed to exclude its present. It is true, too, that one of these contemporaries may one day stand in the pantheon.

What has now been said of four subject-matters within philosophy as the book conceives it can be said differently. These subject-matters can be regarded less in terms of individual thinkers and more in terms of ideas, arguments, theories, doctrines, world-views, schools, movements, and traditions. This contributes to another characterization of the book, more complete and at least as enlightening, perhaps more enlightening. In particular, it brings out more of the great extent to which the book is about contemporary philosophy rather than the subject's history.

There are perhaps a dozen established parts of philosophy: epistemology, metaphysics, moral philosophy, political philosophy, philosophical logic, logic, the philosophy of mind, aesthetics, and so on. In the case of each of these, the book contains a long essay on its history and another on its problems as they now are, by contributors not at all new to them.

In the case of each of these established parts of philosophy, more light is shed by very many additional entries—for a start, by the aforementioned entries on the great philosophers, on their lesser companions in English-language history and other-language histories, and on contemporaries now carrying on the struggle.

In the case of each of the established parts of philosophy, there are also very many subordinate entries not about individual philosophers. They are quite as important and perhaps take up more of the book. They range from shorter essays down to definitions. To glance at subordinate entries just in the philosophy of mind, the two long essays go with such shorter entries as *actions, animalism in personal identity, anomalous monism, body, Brentano, bundle theory of the self, cognitive architecture, cognitive science,* and *determinism, double-mindedness, dualism,* and *duck-rabbit.* That is but a very small start on the philosophy of mind.

I have now said something of the philosophy which it is the aim of the 2,230 entries of this book to bring into clear view. But whose clear view? The book is for all those who want authoritative enlightenment, judgement by good judges. Thus it is directed partly to general readers for whom philosophy has a fascination greater than, or at least as great as, any other part of our intellectual and cultural existence, and who want accounts of it that they can trust. The book is also directed to those who study and practise the subject, and are scrupulous about their guides. If it did not also have the second aim, it could not have the first. No accounts of a subject can be authoritative for the general reader if they do not also attract and aim to survive the scrutiny of its experts.

If that is one description of the two classes of intended readers of this book, there is another quite as important. There are different ways of reading. The general readers and the experts can be taken together and then divided into two other classes of readers. The first class has in it readers who are on the job, the second those who are not. Not even your most conscientious postgraduate, or your academic of truly careerist inclination, or your zealous autodidact, is always attending to duty. Reading is not always work. Fortunately, it is more often not work. It is not done to get answers to pre-existing questions, to pass exams or write essays, to get promoted to full Professor. It is not done out of a stern determination to become informed, to pursue truth. To read is often to browse, dally, and meander. It is to satisfy curiosity, or a curiosity owed just to a page that falls open. It is to be intrigued by the sight of *affirming the consequent,*

*agglomeration, American philosophy today, arthritis in the thigh, Baudrillard, beati-
tude's kiss, closure, feminist philosophy of science, quantum logic, slime, slingshot arguments, tarot, tarwater, Thrasymachus, vague objects,* or *the new Wittgenstein.*

A Companion, then, in what there is excuse to call the correct sense of that
sometimes abused word, is not only a book for diligent readers, to be studied
and perhaps laboured over. It is not only a complete reference book. It is more
amiable than that. It diverts. It suits a Sunday morning. Hence, not all that is in
it was chosen by the high principle of nose to the grindstone. There are entries
in it, as already noticed, that are owed to their intrinsic interest rather than their
proven place in a sterner editor's list of headwords.

Only three things remain to be said in this Preface, the first of them about the
nature of philosophy and hence of the book. Isaiah Berlin, one of the contributors, once characterized philosophy not only as lacking answers to many questions but also as lacking an agreed method for the finding of answers. (He may
have had in mind a contrast with science, perhaps a contrast not dear, albeit for
different reasons, to a fellow contributor or two, say Paul Feyerabend or W. V.
Quine.) Certainly it is true that philosophy, no doubt because of the peculiar difficulty of its questions, is at least as much given to disagreement and dispute as
any other kind of inquiry. In fact it may be more given to disagreement and dispute than any other inquiry. It has the hardest questions.

As a result, this book cannot be wholly consistent. Even with fewer than 291
contributors, if they were as committed to their views as philosophers usually
are, and no doubt should be, there would be disagreement. There would be disagreement if the book was limited to the thirty-four Oxford philosophers in it,
or, say, the various Californians. As it is, there are entries, occasionally cheek by
jowl, that fight among themselves, or at any rate jostle. As an editor, I have not
tried too hard to subdue or get between my colleagues, but only succumbed to
a thought or two about *unlikely philosophical propositions.* (Nor have I bullied my
colleagues about what sort of thing to put into the bibliographies at the ends of
their entries, or ruthlessly excluded an entry whose subject is also treated,
somewhat differently, somewhere else.) To do so would have produced more
decorum but less truth about philosophy. It would also have touched what I
hope is another recommendation of the book: it has not only different views
but different voices in it.

That brings to mind a second matter, that of the 150 contemporary philosophers on whom there are entries in the book. The aim was to give to the reader,
mainly the general reader, a sense of the philosophical enterprise as it is now
being carried forward. (Philosophy, as already remarked, is not a dead or dying
subject, but one whose vigour—I am tempted to say its youth—is as great as
ever it has been. It is only the sciences and the superstitions that come and go.)
Another editor, quite as sane, would have looked around at his cohorts, contemplated a reputation or two, no doubt mused on the fact of philosophical
fashion, and chosen somewhat differently.

For the first edition, a list of contemporaries was initially drawn up mainly by
me. The list was subsequently the subject of a kindly suggestion or two from
possible contributors to the book who laid eye on it, and perhaps a letter or two
of hurt pride or disbelief. Notice was taken of these pleas, in a certain way. The
initial list of contemporaries was submitted to a jury of a dozen distinguished

philosophers from all parts and inclinations of the subject. They agreed about the large and indisputable core of the list, but not much more. They did not much agree about their proposed additions to the rest of the list, or their proposed deletions from it. No proposed inclusion or deletion got more than two votes from the twelve good philosophers and true. Any contemporary who did get two votes was added in. No deletions were made.

For this second edition, opinions were taken from thirty philosophers, of all or anyway various persuasions, as to how to make the contemporaries in the book representative of the new millennium well under way. The results of this poll contained some biffs to my loyalties and sensibilities. But, being a true as against merely a hierarchic democrat, I acted on the advice. Should you be certain, reader, that this little anointing is a very serious matter, remember David Hume, Saint David, the greatest of British philosophers. He did not get elected to professorships at Edinburgh and Glasgow, which accolades went instead to Mr Cleghorn and Mr Clow.

Finally, my gratitude, of which there is a lot. I am grateful to many people, first the 291 contributors. They did not do too much satisficing. Contributors to the first edition put up with a change of mind about entry lengths. Many of them put up with a lot more, including a lot of letters about revising their work or making new starts. Some were stalwarts who did a goodly number of entries very well. They rush to mind, and produce glows of gratitude there. Some were philosophical about the sad fact that their prize entry, say the Frankfurt School or the indeterminacy of translation, did not get into the book because the editor had blundered and earlier assigned it to someone else. Some contributors and others were decent or anyway silent when their proposed entries, say *marital act* and *Ayn Rand*, did not penetrate my fortress of philosophical principle.

My special thanks to Peter Momtchiloff, doyen of the world's philosophy editors, the Philosophy Editor of Oxford University Press. This book is almost as much his doing as mine, despite my sole responsibility for errors, infelicities, and one or two judgements with which he is not in absolute agreement. I am also grateful to the following fourteen philosophers who read all or parts of the first manuscript and issued proposals for its improvement: Christopher Kirwan, David Hamlyn, and Jonathan Lowe, above all, and also Simon Blackburn, Alexander Broadie, Jonathan Cohen, Ross Harrison, Ronald Hepburn, Michael Inwood, Nicola Lacey, David Miller, Richard Norman, Anthony O'Hear, and Richard Swinburne.

My thanks as well to the jury of distinguished philosophers who cast an eye over the initial list of their contemporaries, and then to the thirty advisers in this matter for the second edition.

Thanks too to all of these: Ingrid Coggin Honderich; Jane O'Grady; Alan Lacey, who did the Chronological Table of Philosophy and the Maps of Philosophy; John Allen of the library at University College London; Helen Betteridge, Vivien Crew, and Ann Wooldridge for some secretarial assistance; Tim Barton, Laurien Berkeley, Angela Blackburn, and Frances Morphy of Oxford University Press, all of whom were fortitudinous, and almost always right.

T.H.

Contents

List of Portraits

Contributors

Almost all the contributors are or were members of the departments, faculties or sub-faculties of philosophy at the mentioned universities.

A.C.A. Dr Alison Ainley
University College, Dublin

E.B.A. Prof. Edwin B. Allaire
University of Texas, Austin

H.E.A. Prof. Henry E. Allison
Boston University

M.A. Dr Miloš Arsenijević
University of Heidelberg

M.M.A. Prof. Marilyn McCord Adams
University of Oxford

S.R.A. Dr Sophie Allen
University of Oxford

W.E.A. Prof. William E. Abraham
University of California, Santa Cruz

A.B. Prof. Akeel Bilgrami
Columbia University

A.Bel. Mr Andrew Belsey
University of Wales, Cardiff

A.Bre. Prof. Andrew Brennan
University of Western Australia

A.Bro. Prof. Alexander Broadie
University of Glasgow

D.B. Mr David Bostock
University of Oxford

D.Bak. Prof. David Bakhurst
Queen's University, Ontario

D.Ber. Prof. David Berman
Trinity College, Dublin

G.B. Prof. George Bozonis
University of Athens

G.H.B. Prof. Graham Bird
University of Manchester

H.A.B. Prof. Hugo Adam Bedau
Tufts University

H.I.B. Prof. Harold I. Brown
Northern Illinois University

I.B. Sir Isaiah Berlin
University of Oxford

J.B.B. Prof. James Bogen
Pitzer College

J.Ber. Prof. Jose Bermudez
Washington University, St Louis

J.Bish. Dr John Bishop
University of Auckland

J.Bro. Prof. Justin Broackes
Brown University

J.W.B. *See* Alvin Goldman

K.B. Prof. Kent Bach
San Francisco State University

K.Ber. *See* Pauza

L.W.B. Prof. Lewis W. Beck
University of Rochester

M.B. Prof. Myles Brand
Indiana University

N.B. Prof. Ned Block
New York University

R.L.B. Prof. Robert Bernasconi
Memphis State University

R.P.B. Prof. Richard Bellamy
University of Reading

S.B. Prof. Sissela Bok
Harvard University

S.W.B. Prof. Simon Blackburn
University of Cambridge

T.L.B. Prof. Tom L. Beauchamp
Georgetown University

T.R.B. Prof. Thomas Baldwin
University of York

W.B.	Prof. Dr Wilhelm Baumgartner University of Würzburg		T.C.	Prof. Tim Crane University College London
A.C.	Prof. Arindam Chakrabarti University of Delhi		T.Car.	Prof. Terrell Carver University of Bristol
A.Car.	Prof. Alisa Carse Georgetown University		T.Chi.	*See* Cartwright
B.J.C.	Prof. Jack Copeland University of Canterbury, New Zealand		W.C.	Mr William Charlton University of Edinburgh
			D.D.	Prof. Donald Davidson University of California, Berkeley
C.A.J.C.	Prof. C. A. J. Coady University of Melbourne		F.D.	Prof. Fred Dretske Stanford University
C.C.	Prof. Charles Crittenden California State University, Northridge		J.D.	Prof. Jonathan Dancy University of Reading
			M.D.	Sir Michael Dummett University of Oxford
D.C.	Dr David Charles University of Oxford		N.C.D.	Mr N. C. Denyer University of Cambridge
D.E.C.	Prof. David E. Cooper University of Durhan		N.J.H.D.	Prof. Nicholas Dent University of Birmingham
F.C.	Prof. Frank Cioffi University of Essex		R.D.	Prof. Ronald Dworkin University College London
F.Chr.	Prof. Ferrell Christensen University of Alberta		R.De G.	Prof. Richard T. De George University of Kansas
J.C.	Prof. James Cargile University of Virginia		R.S.D.	Prof. R. S. Downie University of Glasgow
J.Cot.	Prof. John Cottingham University of Reading		W.A.D.	Prof. Wayne A. Davis Georgetown University
L.J.C.	Mr L. Jonathan Cohen University of Oxford		D.E.	Prof. Dorothy Edgington University of Oxford
M.C.	Mr Michael Cohen University of Wales, Swansea		J.D.G.E.	Prof. J. D. G. Evans Queen's University, Belfast
M.J.C.	Prof. Max Cresswell Victoria University, Wellington		P.E.	Prof. Paul Edwards Brooklyn College
N.C.	Prof. Nancy Cartwright London School of Economics and Political Science		E.J.F.	Dr Elizabeth Frazer University of Oxford
	Associate contributors		J.M.F.	Prof. John Finnis University of Oxford
	T.Chi. Timothy Childers R.F.H. Robin Findlay Hendry T.U. Thomas E. Uebel		N.F.	Prof. Nicholas G. Fotion Emory University
N.S.C.	Prof. Norman S. Care Oberlin College		O.F.	Prof. Owen Flanagan Duke University
Q.C.	Prof. Quassim Cassam University College London		P.K.F.	Prof. Paul K. Feyerabend University of California, Berkeley
R.Clif.	Prof. Robert Clifton University of Western Ontario		P.R.F.	Prof. Philippa Foot University of Oxford
R.Cri.	Dr Roger Crisp University of Oxford			
S.C.	Prof. Steven Coutinho Towson University		A.C.G.	Dr Anthony Grayling Birkbeck College, London
S.R.L.C.	Prof. Stephen Clark University of Liverpool		A.Gew.	Prof. Alan Gewirth University of Chicago

A.Gom.   Dr Antoni Gomila
University of Salamanca

A.Gup.   Prof. Anil Gupta
Indiana University

A.H.G.   Prof. Alan Goldman
University of Miami

A.I.G.   Prof. Alvin Goldman
Rutgers University

Associate contributor
J.W.B.   Prof. John Bender

B.G.   Prof. Bernard Gert
Dartmouth College

D.G.   Prof. Don Gustafson
University of Cincinnati

G.G.   Prof. Gary Gutting
University of Notre Dame

J.C.A.G.   Prof. J. C. A. Gaskin
Trinity College, Dublin

J.C.B.G.   Mr J. C. B. Gosling
University of Oxford

J.G.   Prof. Jorge J. E. Gracia
State University of New York, Buffalo

Associate contributors
M. G.   Michael German
E. M.   Elizabeth Millan

J.Gar.   Dr James Garvey
Royal Institute of Philosophy

J.O.G.   Prof. James O. Grunebaum
Buffalo State College

J.P.G.   Prof. James P. Griffin
University of Oxford

L.E.G.   Prof. Lenn E. Goodman
Vanderbilt University

L.P.G.   Prof. Lloyd P. Gerson
St Michael's College, Toronto

M.D.G.   Dr Marcus Giaquinto
University College London

M.G.   *See* Gracia

P.G.   Prof. Paul Gilbert
University of Hull

P.Good.   Prof. Peter Goodrich
Birkbeck College, London

P.G.-S.   Prof. Peter Godfrey-Smith
Australian National University

P.L.G.   Mr Patrick Gardiner
University of Oxford

R.G.   Prof. Reinhardt Grossmann
Indiana University

R.M.G.   Prof. Richard M. Gale
University of Pittsburgh

R.P.G.   Prof. Robert P. George
Princeton University

S.A.G.   Prof. S. A. Grave
University of Western Australia

S.G.   Dr Stefan Gosepath
Hochschule der Künste, Berlin

S.Gard.   Prof. Sebastian Gardner
University College, London

S.Gau.   Prof. Stephen Gaukroger
University of Sydney

A.H.   Prof. Alastair Hannay
University of Oslo

B.H.   Prof. Brad Hooker
University of Reading

C.H.   Prof. Colin Howson
London School of Economics and Political Science

C.J.H.   Prof. C. J. Hookway
University of Sheffield

D.W.H.   Prof. D. W. Hamlyn
Birkbeck College, London

D.W.Has.   Prof. D. W. Haslett
University of Delaware

E.L.H.   Mr E. L. Hussey
University of Oxford

G.P.H.   Mr Geoffrey Hawthorn
University of Cambridge

I.C.H.   Ingrid Coggin Honderich
Royal Institute of Philosophy

J.Hal.   Prof. John Haldane
University of St Andrews

J.Heil   Prof. John Heil
Washington University, St Louis

J.Horn.   Prof. Jennifer Hornsby
Birkbeck College, London

K.H.   Prof. Karen Hanson
Indiana University

K.J.J.H.   Prof. Jaakko Hintikka
Boston University

P.H.   Prof. Paul Humphreys
University of Virginia

P.H.H.   Prof. Peter H. Hare
State University of New York, Buffalo

P.M.S.H.   Dr Peter Hacker
University of Oxford

R.B.H.   Prof. R. Baine Harris
Old Dominion University

R.F.H.   *See* Cartwright

R.H.   Dr Ross Harrison
University of Cambridge

R.Har.	Prof. Russell Hardin New York University	S.T.K.	Prof. Steven T. Kuhn Georgetown University
R.J.H.	Mr R. J. Hawkins University of Oxford	W.K.	Prof. Will Kymlicka Queen's University, Ontario
R.W.H.	Prof. R. W. Hepburn University of Edinburgh	A.J.L.	Mr Ardon Lyon City University, London
V.H.	Mr Vincent Hope University of Edinburgh	A.R.L.	Dr Alan Lacey King's College London
W.A.H.	Prof. Wilfrid Hodges Queen Mary and Westfield College, London	B.L.	Prof. Brian Leiter University of Texas, Austin
M.J.I.	Mr M. J. Inwood University of Oxford	E.J.L.	Prof. E. J. Lowe University of Durham
C.J.	Prof. C. Janaway University of Southampton	H.L.	Dr Hallvard Lillehammer University of Cambridge
E.R.J.	Dr Roger Jones Berea College, Kentucky	J.L.	Dr James Logue University of Oxford
M.D.J.	Prof. Mark D. Jordan University of Notre Dame	J.Lac.	Prof. John Lachs Vanderbilt University
O.R.J.	Mr O. R. Jones University of Wales, Aberystwyth	J.Lev.	Prof. Jerrold Levinson University of Maryland, College Park
P.F.J.	Prof. Paul F. Johnson St Norbert College	K.-S.L.	Prof. Kwang-Sae Lee Kent State University
S.J.	Stuart Jeffries *The Guardian*	M.L.	Prof. Margaret Little Georgetown University
S.P.J.	Dr Simon James University of Durham	N.L.	Prof. Noa Latham University of Calgary
A.J.P.K.	Sir Anthony Kenny University of Oxford	N.M.L.	Prof. Nicola Lacey London School of Economics
C.A.K.	Mr Christopher Kirwan University of Oxford	O.L.	Prof. Oliver Leaman University of Kentucky
C.H.K.	Prof. C. H. Koch University of Copenhagen	R.Le P.	Prof. Robin Le Poidevin University of Leeds
H.-H.K.	Prof. Hans-Herbert Kögler University of Illinois, Urbana–Champaign	W.G.L.	Prof. William G. Lycan University of North Carolina, Chapel Hill
J.A.K.	Dr Jill Kraye Warburg Institute, London	A.M.	Prof. Adam Morton University of Alberta
J.J.K.	Prof. Joel J. Kupperman University of Connecticut	A.MacI.	Prof. Alasdair MacIntyre University of Notre Dame
J.K.	Prof. Jaegwon Kim Brown University	A.R.M.	Prof. Alfred R. Mele Florida State University
J.Kek.	Prof. John Kekes State University of New York, Albany	B.M.	Dr Benjamin Morison University of Oxford
L.K.	Prof. Leszek Kolakowski University of Oxford	C.McK.	Prof. Catherine McKeen SUNY Brockport
M.K.	Dr Martha Klein University of Oxford	D.M.	Dr Derek Matravers Open University
P.K.	Prof. Peter King University of Toronto	D.McL.	Prof. David McLellan University of Kent, Canterbury
R.K.	Prof. Robert Kirk University of Nottingham	D.McN.	Dr Mike McNamee University of Wales, Swansea

E.J.M. Dr Elinor Mason
University of Edinburgh

E.M. *See* Gracia

F.MacB. Dr Fraser MacBride
Birkbeck College,
London

G.B.M. Prof. Gareth B. Matthews
University of Massachusetts,
Amherst

G.F.M. Prof. Gregory Mellema
Calvin College

G.I.M. Prof. George I. Mavrodes
University of Michigan,
Ann Arbor

G.W.McC. Prof. Gregory McCulloch
University of Nottingham

J.J.M. Prof. Jack Macintosh
University of Calgary

J.M. Prof. Joseph Margolis
Temple University

J.McM. Prof. Jeff McMahan
Rutgers University

K.M. Dr Kevin Magill
University of Wolverhampton

M.G.F.M. Prof. Michael Martin
University College London

N.M. Prof. Nenad Miščevič
Central European University

P.J.M. Dr Penelope Mackie
University of Nottingham

P.N.M. Mr Peter Momtchiloff
Oxford University Press

R.B.M. Prof. Ruth Barcan Marcus
Yale University

R.D.M. Prof. Ronald D. Milo
University of Arizona

S.M. Prof. Susan Mendus
University of York

S.McC. Prof. Storrs McCall
McGill University

S.M.-G. Dr Saladin Meckled-Garcia
University College London

C.N. Prof. Christopher Norris
University of Wales, Cardiff

H.W.N. Prof. Harold Noonan
University of Nottingham

J.N. Prof. Jan Narveson
University of Waterloo

P.J.P.N. Dr Paul Noordhof
University of Nottingham

R.J.N. Prof. Richard Norman
University of Kent, Canterbury

S.N. Dr Svante Nordin
University of Lund

T.N. Prof. Thomas Nagel
New York University

A.D.O. Dr Alexander D. Oliver
University of Cambridge

A.O'H. Prof. Anthony O'Hear
University of Buckingham

J.O'G. Ms Jane O'Grady
Fine Arts College, London

D.P. Prof. David Papineau
King's College London

D.Pri. Dr D. H. Pritchard
University of Stirling

G.P. Prof. Graham Priest
University of Melbourne

G.R.P. Prof. Graham Parkes
University of Hawaii, Manoa

I.S.P. Prof. Ingmar Persson
University of Lund

L.P. Dr Letizia Panizza
Royal Holloway College,
London

M.J.P. Prof. M. J. Petry
Erasmus University

M.P. Dr Miroslav Pauza
Institute of Philosophy, Prague

Associate contributors
K.Ber. Prof. Karel Berka
V.S. Dr Vera Soudilova

M.Pot. Prof. Matjaž Potrč
University of Ljubljana

O.P. Dr Oliver Pooley
University of Oxford

P.P. Prof. Philip Pettit
Princeton University

S.P. Mr Stephen Priest
University of Oxford

T.P. Dr Thomas Pink
King's College London

A.Q. The Rt. Hon. Lord Quinton
University of Oxford

P.L.Q. Prof. Philip L. Quinn
University of Notre Dame

W.V.Q. Prof. W. V. Quine
Harvard University

B.B.R. Mr Bede Rundle
University of Oxford

M.R.	Prof. Michael Ruse Florida State University	R.M.S.	Prof. Mark Sainsbury University of Texas, Austin
N.R.	Prof. Nicholas Rescher University of Pittsburgh	R.S.	Prof. Richard Schacht University of Illinois, Urbana–Champaign
P.R.	Prof. Peter Railton University of Michigan, Ann Arbor	R.W.S.	Prof. R. W. Sharples University College London
S.D.R.	Dr Sarah Richmond University College London	S.S.	Prof. Stewart Shapiro Ohio State University
S.L.R.	Dr Stephen Read University of St Andrews	T.S.	Prof. Timothy Schroeder University of Manitoba
B.C.S.	Dr Barry C. Smith Birkbeck College, London	T.L.S.S.	Prof. T. L. S. Sprigge University of Edinburgh
D.H.S.	Prof. David H. Sanford Duke University	V.S.	*See* Pauza
E.S.	Prof. Ernest Sosa Brown University	V.Such.	Dr Victor Suchar Bath Royal Literary and Scientific Institute
E.T.S.	Prof. Edward Sankowski University of Oklahoma	B.T.	Prof. Bergeth Tregenza California State University, Northridge
J.E.R.S.	Mr Roger Squires University of St Andrews	C.C.W.T.	Prof. C. C. W. Taylor University of Oxford
J.M.S.	Prof. John Skorupski University of St Andrews	G.M.T.	Prof. G. M. Tamas Hungarian Academy of Sciences
J.P.S.	Prof. James P. Sterba University of Notre Dame	I.T.	Prof. Ivo Tretera Charles University, Prague
J.R.S.	Prof. John Searle University of California, Berkeley	L.S.T.	Prof. Larry S. Temkin Rutgers University
J.S.	Dr Jeremy Stangroom *The Philosophers' Magazine*	R.E.T.	Prof. Robert Tully St Michael's College, Toronto
K.-l. S.	Prof. Kwong-loi Shun University of California, Berkeley	R.P.L.T.	Dr Roger Teichmann University of Oxford
L.F.S.	Mr Leslie F. Stevenson University of St Andrews	T.U.	*See* Cartwright
L.S.	Prof. Lawrence Sklar University of Michigan, Ann Arbor	R.V.	Mr. Ruediger Vaas University of Giessen
M.S.	Prof. Michael Slote University of Miami	A.D.W.	Mr Andrew Williams University of Reading
P.F.S.	Professor Paul Snowdon University College London	A.W.W.	Prof. Allen Wood Stanford University
P.S.	Prof. Peter Singer Princeton University	Cath.W.	Prof. Catherine Wilson University of British Columbia
R.A.K.S.	Dr Rowland Stout University College, Dublin	C.J.F.W.	Prof. C. J. F. Williams University of Bristol
R.A.S.	Prof. Robert Sharpe University of Wales, Lampeter	C.W.	Mr Colwyn Williamson University of Wales, Swansea
R.C.Sle.	Prof. R. C. Sleigh, Jr. University of Massachusetts, Amherst	D.N.W.	Prof. Douglas Walton University of Winnipeg
R.C.Sol.	Prof. Robert C. Solomon University of Texas, Austin	G.J.W.	Sir Geoffrey Warnock University of Oxford
R.G.S.	Prof. R. G. Swinburne University of Oxford	I.P.W.	Prof. John White Institute of Education, London
		J.Wol.	Prof. Jan Woleński Jagiellonian University, Cracow

J.Woo.	Prof. John Woods University of British Columbia	P.W.	Ms Patricia Walsh King's College London
K.W.	Prof. Kwasi Wiredu University of South Florida	R.C.W.	Prof. Roy C. Weatherford University of South Florida
K.Wuch.	Prof. Dr Kurt Wuchterl University of Stuttgart	R.S.W.	Prof. Roger Woolhouse University of York
M.W.	Prof. Michael Wreen Marquette University	S.W.	Dr Sybil Wolfram University of Oxford
M.Walz.	Prof. Michael Walzer Institute for Advanced Study, Princeton	T.W.	Prof. Timothy Williamson University of Oxford
M.Warn.	Baroness Warnock University of Cambridge	H.Z.	Prof. Hossein Ziai University of California, Los Angeles

On Using the Book

In one way there is little need for an entry in this book to contain cross-references to other entries. This is so since the reader can safely assume that almost every philosophical term which is used for an idea or doctrine or whatever also has an entry to itself. The same is true of almost every philosopher who is mentioned. That is not all. Entries can be counted on for very many subjects which fall under such common terms as 'beauty', 'causation', 'democracy', 'guilt', 'knowledge', 'mind', and 'time'—all such subjects which get philosophical attention.

Still, it seems a good idea to provide occasional reminders of the general possibility of having more lights shed on something by turning elsewhere. And there is often a good reason for prompting or directing a reader to look elsewhere, a reason of which a reader may be unaware.

So occasionally a term in an entry is preceded by an asterisk, indicating that it is the heading or the first word of the heading of another entry. For the same reason an asterisked term or terms may appear on a line at the end of an entry. In some cases the latter references are to related or opposed ideas or the like. In order not to have the book littered with asterisks, they have very rarely been put on the names of philosophers. But it is always a good idea to turn to the entries on the mentioned philosophers.

The cross-references are more intended for the browsing reader than the reader at work. For the reader at work, there is an Index and List of Entries at the back of the book. The Index and List of Entries usually gives references to more related entries than are given by cross-references in and at the end of an entry. It is also possible to look up all the entries on, say, aesthetics or American philosophy or applied ethics.

The book is alphabetized by the whole headings of entries, as distinct from the first word of a heading. Hence, for example, *abandonment* comes before *a priori and a posteriori*. It is wise to look elsewhere if something seems to be missing.

At the end of the book there is also a useful appendix on *Logical Symbols* as well as the appendices *A Chronological Table of Philosophy* and *Maps of Philosophy*.

A

abandonment. A rhetorical term used by existentialist philosophers such as Heidegger and Sartre to describe the absence of any sources of ethical authority external to oneself. It suggests that one might have expected to find such an authority, either in religion or from an understanding of the natural world, and that the discovery that there is none leads one to feel 'abandoned'. For existentialists such as Sartre, however, this sense of abandonment is only a prelude to the recognition that ethical values can be grounded from within a reflective understanding of the conditions under which individuals can attain *authenticity in their lives. Thus the conception of abandonment is essentially an existentialist dramatization of Kant's rejection of heteronomous conceptions of value in favour of the *autonomy of the good will.   T.R.B.

*existentialism; despair.

J.-P. Sartre, *Existentialism and Humanism*, tr. P. Mairet (London, 1948).

abduction. Abductive reasoning accepts a conclusion on the grounds that it explains the available evidence. The term was introduced by Charles Peirce to describe an inference pattern sometimes called 'hypothesis' or '*inference to the best explanation'. He used the example of arriving at a Turkish seaport and observing a man on horseback surrounded by horsemen holding a canopy over his head. He inferred that this was the governor of the province since he could think of no other figure who would be so greatly honoured. In his later work, Peirce used the word more widely: the logic of abduction examines all of the norms which guide us in formulating new hypotheses and deciding which of them to take seriously. It addresses a wide range of issues concerning the 'logic of discovery' and the economics of research.   C.J.H.

*induction.

C. S. Peirce, *Collected Papers*, vii (Cambridge, Mass., 1958), 89–164.

Abelard, Peter (1079–1142). Most widely known for his love affair with Héloïse, about which we learn a good deal from his letters to her as well as from his *Historia Calamitatum*. He was also one of the great controversialists of his era. After studying under Roscelin (*c*.1095) and William of Champeaux (*c*.1100), he established himself as a master in

his own right, and one to whom students flocked throughout his career. In the dispute about the nature of *universals he was in the nominalist camp, holding that universals are utterances (*voces*) or mental terms, not things in the real world. The universality of a universal derives from the fact that it is predicable of many things. Nevertheless, unless a number of things are in the same state, the one universal term cannot be predicated of them. Hence although universals are not themselves real things, it is a common feature of real things that justifies the predication of a universal of them.

In his *Dialectica* Abelard takes up, among numerous other topics, the question, widely discussed in the Middle Ages, of the relation between human freedom and divine providence. If God, who is omniscient, knows that we are going to perform a given act, is it not necessary that we perform it, and in that case how can the act be free? Abelard's answer is that we do indeed act freely and that it is not merely our acts but our *free* acts that come under divine providence. God's foreknowing them carries no implication that we are not free to avoid performing them.   A.BRO.

*Héloïse complex; properties; qualities.

Abelard, *Dialectica*, ed. L. M. de Rijk (Assen, 1970).
J. Marenbon, *The Philosophy of Peter Abelard* (Cambridge, 2002).

ableism. Prejudice against people with disabilities, which can take many forms. It can take the form of a prejudice against using sign language with those who are deaf even when only a small percentage of them can master the alternatives of lipreading and speaking. It also shows itself as a prejudice against the use of Braille with the blind or visually impaired even when this makes them less efficient readers than they might be. In general, it is a prejudice against performing activities in ways that are better for disabled people.   J.P.S.

*disability and morality.

Anita Silvers, 'People with Disabilities', in Hugh LaFollette (ed.), *The Oxford Handbook of Practical Ethics* (Oxford, 2003).

abortion. Human beings develop gradually inside women's bodies. The death of a newly fertilized human egg does not seem the same as the death of a person. Yet there is no obvious line that divides the gradually developing foetus from the adult. Hence abortion poses a difficult ethical issue.

Those who defend women's rights to abortion often refer to themselves as 'pro-choice' rather than as 'pro-abortion'. In this way they seek to bypass the issue of the moral status of the foetus, and instead make the right to abortion a question of individual liberty. But it cannot simply be *assumed* that a woman's right to have an abortion is a question of individual liberty, for it must first be established that the aborted foetus is not a being worthy of protection. If the foetus is worthy of protection, then laws against abortion do not create 'victimless crimes' as laws against homosexual relations between consenting adults do. So the question of the moral status of the foetus cannot be avoided.

The central argument against abortion may be put like this:

It is wrong to kill an innocent human being.
A human foetus is an innocent human being.
Therefore it is wrong to kill a human foetus.

Defenders of abortion usually deny the second premiss of this argument. The dispute about abortion then becomes a dispute about whether a foetus is a human being, or, in other words, when a human life begins. Opponents of abortion challenge others to point to any stage in the gradual process of human development that marks a morally significant dividing-line. Unless there is such a line, they say, we must either upgrade the status of the earliest embryo to that of the child, or downgrade the status of the child to that of the foetus; and no one advocates the latter course.

The most commonly suggested dividing-lines between the fertilized egg and the child are birth and viability. Both are open to objection. A prematurely born infant may well be *less* developed in these respects than a foetus nearing the end of its normal term, and it seems peculiar to hold that we may not kill the premature infant, but may kill the more developed foetus. The point of viability varies according to the state of medical technology, and, again, it is odd to hold that a foetus has a right to life if the pregnant woman lives in London, but not if she lives in New Guinea.

Those who wish to deny the foetus a right to life may be on stronger ground if they challenge the first, rather than the second, premiss of the argument set out above. To describe a being as 'human' is to use a term that straddles two distinct notions: membership of the species *Homo sapiens*, and being a person, in the sense of a rational or self-conscious being. If 'human' is taken as equivalent to 'person', the second premiss of the argument, which asserts that the foetus is a human being, is clearly false; for one cannot plausibly argue that a foetus is either rational or self-conscious. If, on the other hand, 'human' is taken to mean no more than 'member of the species *Homo sapiens*', then it needs to be shown why mere membership of a given biological species should be a sufficient basis for a

right to life. Rather, the defender of abortion may wish to argue, we should look at the foetus for what it is—the actual characteristics it possesses—and value its life accordingly.   P.S.

*applied ethics; double effect.

D. Boonin, *A Defense of Abortion* (Cambridge, 2002).
Rosalind Hursthouse, *Beginning Lives* (Oxford, 1987).
Judith Jarvis Thomson, 'A Defense of Abortion', in Peter Singer (ed.), *Applied Ethics* (Oxford, 1986).
Michael Tooley, *Abortion and Infanticide* (Oxford, 1983).

Absolute, the. That which has an unconditioned existence, not conditioned by, relative to, or dependent upon anything else. Usually deemed to be the whole of things, conceived as unitary, as spiritual, as self-knowing (at least in part via the human mind), and as rationally intelligible, as finite things, considered individually, are not. The expression was introduced into philosophy by Schelling and Hegel. In the English speaking world it became the key concept of such absolute idealists as Josiah Royce and F. H. Bradley.   T.L.S.S.

*idealism, philosophical.

J. N. Findlay, *Ascent to the Absolute* (London, 1970).
T. L. S. Sprigge, *The Vindication of Absolute Idealism* (Edinburgh, 1983).

absolutism, moral. The view that certain kinds of actions are *always* wrong or are *always* obligatory, whatever the consequences. Typical candidates for such absolute principles would be that it is always wrong deliberately to kill an innocent human being, or that one ought always to tell the truth or to keep one's promises. Absolutism is to be contrasted with *consequentialism, the view that the rightness or wrongness of actions is determined solely by the extent to which they lead to good or bad consequences. A consequentialist could maintain, for example, that *killing is normally wrong because it creates a great deal of grief and suffering and deprives the person who is killed of the future happiness which he/she would have experienced, but that since, in some cases, a refusal to kill may lead to even more suffering and loss of happiness, it may sometimes be right even to kill the innocent.

Moral absolutism is linked to, but not synonymous with, a *deontological position in ethics. The latter is the view that certain kinds of actions are *intrinsically* right or wrong—right or wrong simply because they are that kind of action—independently of the consequences to which they may lead. Killing the innocent, for instance, may be thought to be wrong *just because it is the killing of the innocent*, quite apart from the suffering and loss of happiness to which it will normally lead. A deontological position obviously contrasts with a consequentialist one, and may appear to be the same as absolutism, but in fact the two are distinct. One may hold that killing the innocent is intrinsically wrong, but also accept that in certain extreme circumstances the intrinsic wrongness of killing the innocent may itself be overridden by the appalling consequences which will occur if one refuses to kill. Absolutism builds on a deontological position but adds a stronger claim—not only is the action intrinsically wrong, but its wrongness can never be overridden by any consideration of consequences.

The absolutist position corresponds to common traditional views of morality, particularly of a religious kind—what might be called the 'Ten Commandments' idea of morality. Nevertheless, when detached from appeals to religious authority absolutism may appear to be vulnerable to rational criticism. Is it not perverse to maintain that a certain kind of action is simply ruled out, even when the refusal to perform it will lead to even worse consequences? Why insist on *never* killing the innocent, for instance, if in certain circumstances a refusal to do so will mean that more innocent people will die? To be plausible, absolutism needs to be supplemented with some further distinction between different ways in which consequences may come about, such as the distinction between *acts and omissions, or the doctrine of *double effect. The absolutist who refuses to condone the killing of the innocent, even though more innocent people will die as a result of not doing so, can then say that though the loss of innocent lives is a terrible thing; nevertheless, letting innocent people die, or bringing about innocent deaths as an unintended side-effect, is not ruled out by an absolute prohibition in the same way as is the intentional killing of the innocent. Whether this is a sufficient defence of absolutism remains a matter for debate.   R.J.N.

　*ideals, moral; lying.

G. E. M. Anscombe, 'War and Murder', in *Collected Philosophical Papers*, iii (Oxford, 1981).

Jonathan Bennett, 'Whatever the Consequences', in *Analysis* (1966).

Thomas Nagel, 'War and Massacre', in *Mortal Questions* (Cambridge, 1979).

abstract entities. The dichotomy between the abstract and the concrete is supposed to effect a mutually exclusive and jointly exhaustive ontological classification. The dichotomy is, however, too naïve to be of theoretical use. There are many different ways, themselves vague, to mark the distinction: abstract entities are not perceptible, cannot be pointed to, have no causes or effects, have no spatio-temporal location, are necessarily existent. Nor is there agreement about whether there are any abstract entities, and, if so, which sorts of entity are abstract. Abstract entities, conceived as having no causal powers, are thought problematic for epistemological reasons: how can we refer to or know anything about entities with which we have no causal commerce? Hence the existence of nominalists, who try to do without abstract entities.   A.D.O.

　*universals; nominalism; proposition.

B. Hale, *Abstract Objects* (Oxford, 1987).

abstract ideas: *see* ideas.

abstraction. A putative psychological process for the acquisition of a *concept *x* either by attending to the features common to all and only *x*s or by disregarding just the spatio-temporal locations of *x*s. The existence of abstraction is endorsed by Locke in the *Essay Concerning Human Understanding* (esp. II. xi. 9 and 10 and III. iii. 6 ff.) but rejected by Berkeley in *The Principles of Human Knowledge* (esp. paras. 6 ff. and paras. 98, 119, and 125). For Locke the capacity to abstract distinguishes human beings from animals. It enables them to think in abstract ideas and hence use language. Berkeley argues that the concept of an abstract *idea is incoherent because it entails both the inclusion and the exclusion of one and the same property. This in turn is because any such putative idea would have to be general enough to subsume all *x*s yet precise enough to subsume only *x*s. For example, the abstract idea of triangle 'is neither oblique nor rectangular, equilateral nor scalenon, but all and none of these at once' (*The Principles of Human Knowledge*, Introduction, para. 13).   S.P.

George Berkeley, *A Treatise Concerning the Principles of Human Knowledge* (1710).

John Locke, *An Essay Concerning Human Understanding* (1689).

Stephen Priest, *The British Empiricists* (London, 1990).

abstract particulars: *see* properties, individual.

absurd, the. A term used by existentialists to describe that which one might have thought to be amenable to reason but which turns out to be beyond the limits of rationality. For example, in Sartre's philosophy the 'original choice' of one's fundamental project is said to be 'absurd', since, although choices are normally made for reasons, this choice lies beyond reason because all reasons for choice are supposed to be grounded in one's fundamental project. Arguably, this case in fact shows that Sartre is mistaken in supposing that reasons for choice are themselves grounded in a choice; and one can argue that other cases which are supposed to involve experience of the 'absurd' are in fact a *reductio ad absurdum* of the assumptions which produce this conclusion. The 'absurd' does not in fact play an essential role within existentialist philosophy; but it is an important aspect of the broader cultural context of existentialism, for example in the 'theatre of the absurd', as exemplified by the plays of Samuel Beckett.
                T.R.B.

　*abandonment; existentialism.

A. Camus, *The Myth of Sisyphus* (London, 1955).

J.-P. Sartre, *Being and Nothingness*, tr. H. Barnes (London, 1958), 479.

academic freedom. An integral aspect of open societies, academic freedom is the right of teachers in universities and other sectors of education to teach and research as their subject and conscience demands. This right, though, may not be unproblematically applicable, even in free societies. Should academic freedom be extended to those perceived by others as using it to interfere with the rights of others, or to pursue morally objectionable research? Like other *freedoms, in practice academic freedom is constrained by often tacit conventions regarding its limits. One should never underestimate the ingenuity of academics themselves in justifying denials of academic freedom to their colleagues.   A.O'H.

*persecution of philosophers; teaching and indoctrinating.

C. Russell, *Academic Freedom* (London, 1993).

Academy, the. The educational institution founded by Plato, probably around 387 BC, so-called because of its location at a site sacred to the hero Academus. It is fanciful to call the Academy a 'university' or 'college'. The best idea we have of the subjects studied there comes from Plato's dialogues themselves and Aristotle's testimony. When Plato died, the leadership of the Academy passed to his nephew Speusippus. About 275 the so-called Middle Academy came to be dominated by *Sceptics under the leadership of Arcesilaus. This dominance continued through the middle of the second century when Carneades founded the New Academy. In 87/6 Antiochus of Ascalon broke away from the sceptical tradition of Platonic interpretation to try to recover what he regarded as a more authentic form of Platonism. Since the physical structures of the original Academy had been destroyed with the fall of Athens in 88, Antiochus' Academic leadership was more notional than real. Though the Academy was revived in the later fourth century AD, it was destroyed finally by Justinian in 529.   L.P.G.

*philosophy, history of centres and departments of.

J. Dillon, *The Heirs of Plato: A Study of the Old Academy 347–274 BC* (Oxford, 2003).
—— *The Middle Platonists 80 BC to AD 220* (Ithaca, NY, 1977).

access, privileged: *see* privileged access.

accident. The term 'accident' in philosophy has two main uses, both stemming from Aristotle. In the first an accident is a quality which is not essential to the kind of thing (or in later philosophers, to the individual) in question. 'Being musical' is accidental to Socrates, 'being rational' and 'being an animal' are not. Which *qualities, if any, are essential or non-accidental is a controversial matter in contemporary philosophy. In the second main use, the term 'accident' is a way of allowing chance and causality to coexist: digging for truffles I turn up some treasure. The digging was not an accident, and since the treasure was there all along, my finding it if I dug there was determined; none the less, my finding of it was accidental, since my digging was a digging for truffles, not for treasure. Typically, events which are accidental under one description are determined under another. In non-philosophical contexts the term often connotes *harmful* accidents.   J.J.M.

*properties, general.

J. L. Austin, 'A Plea for Excuses', in *Philosophical Papers* (Oxford, 1961).

Irving Copi, 'Essence and Accident', in Stephen P. Schwartz (ed.), *Naming, Necessity, and Natural Kinds* (Ithaca, NY, 1977).

Achilles paradox. A paradox of motion, due to Zeno of Elea. In a race, Achilles can never catch the tortoise, if the tortoise is given a head start. For while Achilles closes the initial gap between them, the tortoise will have created a new gap, and while Achilles is closing that one, the tortoise will have created another. However fast Achilles runs, all that the tortoise has to do, in order not to be beaten, is make some progress in the time it takes Achilles to close the previous gap. Standard responses include claiming that the argument misconceives the implicit ideas of infinite series and their limits; alternatively, that space is not adequately described in purely mathematical terms. Zeno's own response is not documented. One hypothesis is that he took the conclusion at face value, as part of a general scepticism concerning matter, space, and motion.   R.M.S.

*infinity.

Mark Sainsbury, *Paradoxes* (New York, 1988), ch. 1.

acquaintance and description. A distinction between two kinds of knowledge, crucial to Russell's philosophy, and analogous to that between *connaître* and *savoir*. We are not acquainted with Sir Walter Scott, so we know him only by description, for example as *the author of Waverley*. By contrast, we can know one of our experiences 'by acquaintance', that is, without the intermediary of any definite description. More generally, to know a thing by description is to know that there is something uniquely thus and so; to know a thing by acquaintance is for it to come before the mind without the intermediary of any description. Knowledge by description involves knowledge of truths, whereas knowledge by acquaintance does not: it is knowledge of things.

For Russell, acquaintance is basic on two counts: all understanding rests upon acquaintance (with what the word or concept stands for); and all knowledge of truths depends upon acquaintance with those things which the truths concern.   R.M.S.

*descriptions, theory of.

B. Russell, 'Knowledge by Acquaintance and Knowledge by Description', in *The Collected Papers of Bertrand Russell*, vi (London, 1992); first pub. in *Proceedings of the Aristotelian Society* (1911).
—— *The Problems of Philosophy* (London, 1912), ch. 5.

action. An action is sometimes defined as someone's doing something intentionally. The phenomenon of human action owes its importance both to questions about *agents' metaphysical status, and to ethical and legal questions about human *freedom and *responsibility. Recently many philosophers have thought that an account of action (the phenomenon) should proceed via an account of actions (events). When an action is defined as someone's doing something intentionally, actions are taken to be a species of event, and events are taken to be particulars which can be described in different ways. On this account, Jane's moving of her fingers against the keyboard, where it results in sounds of piano playing, *is* Jane's playing of the piano. Thus Jane does two things—move her fingers and play the piano—although there is only one action here. Typically someone who does something does several 'linked' things, each one being done *by* or *in* doing some other. (*Basic action.) According to the definition, for there to be an action a person only has to have done intentionally one (at least) of the things she did. So Jane's waking up the neighbours could be an action, even though she didn't intentionally wake them: it would be, if it were also her playing of the piano, and she did play the piano intentionally.

When this definition is combined with the thought that it is *by* moving her body that a person does anything, the claim that actions are bodily movements is made: every action is an event of a person's moving (the whole or a part of) her body.

The definition is not uncontroversial. Some philosophers (such as Goldman) deny that a person's doing one thing can be the same as her doing another; they believe that events should be 'finely individuated', not 'coarsely', so that only some actions, not all of them, are bodily movements. Other philosophers deny that actions are events at all: either they think that there are no such things as particular events, or they allow that there are events but say that actions are not among them.

Even a proponent of the definition will acknowledge that it does not cover all of the ground where attributions of responsible agency can be made. (1) A person may be said to have done something when she keeps perfectly still—when, apparently, no event occurs. In such cases, it seems intuitively right that to say there is an instance of action only if the person *intentionally* kept still. Thus it may still be thought that 'doing something intentionally' marks out action: the original definition can be seen to be basically right, but it has to be conceded that there is not always an event when there is an instance of action, and that no fully general link can be made between action and bodily movement. (2) A person may be answerable for doing something that she didn't intentionally do: for instance, when she starts a fire by idly throwing away her lighted cigarette. To cover cases like this, more resources than the word 'intentionally' are needed. But further elucidation of 'intentionally' may uncover a range of concepts which can in turn illuminate a broad conception of responsible agency.

A person's doing of something intentionally, it may be argued, always results from that person's believing something and her desiring something, which jointly constitute her having a reason to do the thing. The definition of actions, then, may be part of a view according to which a certain sort of causal history distinguishes actions from other events. Such a view fell from philosophical favour in the 1950s and 1960s, but has by now been largely restored to credibility. The view has many variants. In a traditional empiricist version, each action is caused by a *volition. In some quarters, the traditional version has been supplanted by the thesis that each action is itself an event of someone's *trying to do something: the suggestion is that a person's having a reason to do something leads her to attempt to do it, and then, when her attempt actually has the effects she wants, as usually it does, it is her doing the thing intentionally.

Giving someone's reasons is a matter of saying *why* she did what she did, so that the idea of a distinctive kind of explanation—action explanation—enters the picture when an action is seen to result from someone's having a reason. (*Reasons and causes.) Also introduced is the idea of a distinctive kind of thinking from which action issues— *practical reason, or deliberation, an account of which requires understanding of (at least) *belief, desire, valuing, *intention, and choice.　　　　　　　　　J.HORN.

*choosing and deciding; mental causation.

D. Davidson, *Essays on Actions and Events* (Oxford, 1980).
A. I. Goldman, *A Theory of Human Action* (Princeton, NJ, 1970).
J. Hornsby, *Actions* (London, 1980).
A. Mele (ed.), *The Philosophy of Action* (Oxford, 1997).

action, basic: *see* basic action.

action at a distance. That one event could have direct causal influence on another spatially separated from it without causation being propagated continuously from point to point has often been met with scepticism. In the nineteenth century field theories 'filled in' the causation between particles with spatially continuous fields. But field theories have their own problems, especially with the interaction of the source particle of the field with its own generated field. These have led to contemporary action at a distance theories of interaction. In order to conform to the observed facts and to relativity, these must posit a time delay between cause and spatially distant effect. In order to account for the behaviour of the source, both retarded and advanced effects must be posited. While the denial of action at a distance is built into quantum field theory and into many accounts of causation (Hume, Reichenbach, Salmon), the famous space-like correlations of *quantum mechanics are a difficulty for those who deny action at a distance.　　　　　　　　　　　　　　L.S.

*causality.

P. Davies, *The Physics of Time Asymmetry* (Berkeley, Calif., 1974), sect. 5.8.
J. Earman, *A Primer of Determinism* (Dordrecht, 1986), ch. 4, sects. 7, 8.

active and passive intellects. Two powers relating to conceptual thought associated with Aristotelian philosophy. In *De anima* Aristotle distinguishes between the *mind as a capacity for conceptual thinking (the passive intellect), and another power (the active intellect) which forms concepts and activates the latent capacity for thought. The interpretation of these notions has been a matter of controversy since antiquity and remains unresolved today. Some medieval Arabic commentators regarded the active intellect as a single immaterial principle to which all thinkers are related; other medievals held this to be so in respect of *both* intellects. Aquinas argued instead that the two intellects are simply powers of the mind of each thinker. Conceived in this way the distinction corresponds to that recurrent in cognitive psychology between concept-forming and concept-employing capacities. It also bears upon the debate between nativism and abstractionism in relation to the source of *ideas.   J.HAL.

*acts, mental.

Z. Kuksewicz, 'The Potential and the Agent Intellect', in N. Kretzmann, A. Kenny, and J. Pinborg (eds.), *The Cambridge History of Later Medieval Philosophy* (Cambridge, 1982).

acts and omissions. The moral distinction between acts and omissions amounts to the claim that there is a morally significant difference between a particular action and a corresponding failure to act, even though they have the same outcomes. Thus, it is said that there is a moral difference between, for example, lying and not telling the truth, hindering and failing to help, and between *killing and letting die, even though, in each case, the consequences of the action and the omission may be the same.

There is undoubtedly some obscurity about the distinction. Understanding it is complicated by the somewhat untidy concept of an omission. Roughly speaking, an omission of mine may be said to occur when I fail to do something which I might reasonably have been expected to do. Such an omission may or may not be a matter of moral censure, depending on what duties I have and what expectations they give rise to.

However, since the fact that something is an omission *settles* no moral questions, it is mistaken to interpret the acts–omissions distinction as straightforwardly differentiating between what we are obliged not to do and what we are allowed to do. Hence it is not the claim that killing, for instance, is morally forbidden while letting die is morally permissible. Nor does it seem helpful to see the distinction as hanging on a difference in intention, for, clearly, *both* a case of killing *and* a case of letting die would have to be intentional, as opposed to accidental, to raise serious moral questions. The point of the distinction seems rather to be to assert that there are prima-facie differences in gravity in the moral logic of the two areas, i.e. that cases of positive commission require reasons that are morally weightier than, and perhaps different in kind from, those that would justify an omission. Thus not killing and not lying, for example, are held to be morally more basic than saving lives and telling the truth, even though the latter are also a matter of moral duty.

As a cornerstone of *deontological ethics, the acts–omissions distinction is vulnerable to the usual criticisms by *consequentialism and its proponents. But some of these criticisms are misguided: utilitarian dismissals of the distinction are often based on the idea that it amounts to,

for instance, a denial of the duty to save life. Yet one does not have to refute the distinction to establish the moral duty to save lives. If we can be held just as responsible for the things we fail to do as for the things we do, we need not deny what the distinction asserts—that there is a difference between the moral ground we should be able to take for granted and the moral ground we have to struggle continuously to gain.   P.W.

*absolutism, moral.

E. D'Arcy, *Human Acts* (Oxford, 1963).

acts, linguistic: *see* linguistic acts.

acts, mental. (1) Mental actions; or, less commonly, (2) *mental events in general. Mental events that are not mental actions include suddenly remembering where one left one's keys and noticing that it is raining. Paradigmatic mental actions include adding numbers in one's head, deliberating, and (one some views) choosing and trying. The precise difference between mental events that are actions and those that are not is a vexed question (sometimes examined under the rubric 'activity versus passivity'). Whether there is a single concept of action that includes both mental actions and actions essentially involving peripheral bodily movement is controversial. The promising idea that actions are analysable as events with 'the right sort' of psychological–causal history may provide the key to both questions, provided that the right sort of history does not itself essentially include actions.   A.R.M.

*active and passive intellects; mental states; volitions.

B. O'Shaughnessy, *The Will: A Dual Aspect Theory* (Cambridge, 1980).

Adams, Marilyn McCord (1943–   ). American philosopher (at Michigan, UCLA, Yale, and Oxford) who has written particularly on medieval philosophy and in philosophy of religion. She is the author, *inter alia*, of numerous papers on various topics, and of a monumental two-volume study of William of Ockham (1987). She has written on the problems of *evil. For example, in 'Horrendous Evils and the Goodness of God', considering 'evils the participation in (the doing or suffering of) which gives one reason prima facie to doubt whether one's life could . . . be a great good to one on the whole', she argues that 'the how of God's victory' can be rendered intelligible for Christians 'by integrating participation in horrendous evils into a person's relationship with God'. Her work often offers solutions for believers using terms internal to Christian tradition. Arguably, it also clarifies religious views for non-believers. Spouse of R. Adams.

E.T.S.

*Anselm.

Marilyn McCord Adams, 'Horrendous Evils and the Goodness of God', in Marilyn McCord Adams and Robert Merrihew Adams (eds.), *The Problem of Evil* (Oxford, 1990).

Adams, Robert M. (1937–). American philosopher (at Michigan, UCLA, Yale, and Oxford) who has done work in philosophy of religion, ethics, metaphysics, and the history of philosophy. His book *The Virtue of Faith* incorporates diverse aspects of his views in philosophy of religion, with references. Another example of his writing is the paper 'Involuntary Sins' (*Philosophical Review* (1985)), in which Adams argues that persons may be responsible for emotions and attitudes such as anger even if these are not voluntary (subject to direct or indirect control by the will). This paper draws on concepts with a religious history, but has also challenged philosophers who have non-religious interests in the ethics of emotion and in action theory. Adams has, in addition, done influential work on a modified *divine command theory of ethics, and on the problem of *evil, among other topics. Spouse of M. Adams.   E.T.S.

*Sin.

Robert M. Adams, *The Virtue of Faith* (Oxford, 1987).
——*Leibniz: Determinist, Theist, Idealist* (New York, 1994).
——*Finite and Infinite Goods* (New York, 1999).

***ad hominem* argument.** For Aristotle, a *fallacy in which 'persons direct their solutions against the man, not against his arguments' (*Sophistical Refutations*, 178^{b}17). Locke sees it as a 'way to press a man with consequences drawn from his own principles or concessions' (*Essay Concerning Human Understanding*, IV. xvii. 21). Locke's *ad hominem*, though he does not describe it as a fallacy, is not a proof 'drawn from any of the foundations of knowledge or probability'.   J.WOO.

*risus sophisticus.

John Woods and Douglas Walton, *Fallacies: Selected Papers, 1972–1982* (Dordrecht, 1989), chs. 5 and 7.

Adorno, Theodor Wiesengrund (1903–69). German philosopher, sociologist, and musicologist, who was the most brilliant and versatile member of the *Frankfurt School. He studied philosophy, music, and sociology at Frankfurt and music in Vienna under Alban Berg. In 1934 he was forced to emigrate, first to Oxford, then in 1938 to New York.

His thought was permanently marked by the rise of fascism, and by the failure of *Marxism both in the West and in the Soviet Union. Political defeat accounts for the survival of philosophy, against Marx's expectations: 'Philosophy, which once seemed obsolete, lives on because the moment to realize it was missed.' He and Horkheimer diagnose the ills of modernity in *Dialectic of the Enlightenment* (1947; tr. New York, 1972).

Another factor shaping Adorno's thought is *existentialism, which was in part a 'movement of rebellion against the dehumanization of man in industrial society' (Tillich) and a response to the failure of Marx's and Hegel's solutions to it. Despite his criticisms of the existentialists, Adorno shared many of their concerns: Kierkegaard's reinstatement of subjectivity against Hegel's supposedly panlogistic and historicist system, Heidegger's antipathy to technology, and so on. (Adorno's 1933 habilitation thesis on Kierkegaard appeared as *Kierkegaard: Construction of the Aesthetic* in 1965.) He criticizes them from a (considerably modified) Hegelian–Marxist viewpoint, arguing that they, like more traditional philosophies, misrepresent social and political relations and thereby provide an ideological justification for domination. Even to ignore sociopolitical relations is to justify them, by suggesting, for example, that the individual is more autonomous than he is: 'If thought is not measured by the extremity that eludes the concept, it is from the outset of the nature of the musical accompaniment with which the SS liked to drown the screams of its victims.' But he also subjects them to 'immanent' philosophical criticism, applying 'Hegel's dictum that in dialectics an opponent's strength is absorbed and turned against him.'

In *Against Epistemology: A Metacritique* (1956; but written in Oxford, 1934–7; tr. Oxford, 1982) he applied these methods to Husserl's half-hearted idealism, arguing that 'one cannot both derive advantage from this solipsistic approach and transcend its limit' and that 'phenomenologically speaking, [the fact that it is done] "with the eyes" belongs to the sense of seeing and is not only [the result of] causal reflection and theoretical explanation'. Adorno invokes Hegel's belief that everything is mediated against Husserl's attempt to find an indubitable beginning or foundation for philosophy: 'The insistence on the mediatedness of everything immediate is the model of dialectical thinking as such, and also of materialistic thinking, insofar as it ascertains the social preformation of contingent, individual experience.'

In *The Jargon of Authenticity* (1965; tr. London, 1973), besides censuring what he saw as Heidegger's obfuscating and ideological jargon, Adorno criticized him both on a philosophical level ('In view of our potential, and growing, control over organic processes, we cannot dismiss *a fortiori* the thought of the elimination of death. This may be very unlikely; but we can entertain a thought, which, according to existential ontology, should be unthinkable') and on a political level: 'Heidegger's dignity is again the shadow of such a borrowed ideology; the subject who based his dignity on the (albeit questionable) Pythagorean claim that he is a good citizen of a good state, gives way to the respect due to him merely because he, like everyone else, must die. In this respect Heidegger is a reluctant democrat.'

Negative Dialectics (1966; tr. New York, 1973) gives a general account of Adorno's thought. Like Socrates and the early Plato, he wields a negative dialectic and does not, like Hegel and the later Plato, derive a positive result, let alone an all-encompassing system or a philosophy of 'identity', from his critique of other philosophers and of social institutions. His aim is to dissolve conceptual forms before they harden into lenses which distort our vision of, and impair our practical engagements with, reality. Reality is not transparent to us; there is a 'totally other', a 'nonidentical', that eludes our concepts.

When concepts fail us, *art comes to our aid. Aesthetic illusion sustains the hope for an ideology-free utopia that neither theory nor political activity can secure: 'In illusion there is a promise of freedom from illusion.' Art, especially music, is relatively autonomous of repressive social structures and thus represents a demand for freedom and a critique of society. This is to be discerned in the formal properties of particular works. Art is 'concentrated social substance'. Even music commercially mass-produced by the 'culture industry' has a social meaning: the repressive irrationality of capitalism.   M.J.I.

M. Jay, *The Dialectical Imagination* (London, 1973).

G. Rose, *The Melancholy Science* (London, 1979).

L. Zuidervaart, *Adorno's Aesthetic Theory: The Redemption of Illusion* (Cambridge, Mass., 1991).

aesthetic attitude. The aesthetic attitude is supposedly a particular way of experiencing or attending to objects. It is said to be an attitude independent of any motivations to do with utility, economic value, moral judgement, or peculiarly personal emotion, and concerned with experiencing the object 'for its own sake'. At the limit, the observer's state would be one of pure detachment, marked by an absence of all desires directed to the object. It could be conceived of as an episode of exceptional elevation wholly beyond our ordinary understanding of empirical reality (as in Schopenhauer), or simply as a state of heightened receptiveness in which our perception of the object is more disengaged than usual from other desires and motivations which we have. The term 'disinterested' is often applied to such an attitude.

Commonly, proponents of the aesthetic attitude think that it can be directed as much to nature as to works of art, and, for some thinkers, it is important that we may adopt an aesthetic attitude towards any object without restriction. However, it is questionable whether we can always abandon our instrumental, moral, or emotional attitudes. For a range of different cases to test this question, think of buildings which we live in, war atrocities which we see on film, and the naked human body. The two questions are whether we can, and whether we ever should, adopt a purely aesthetic attitude to these things. In the case of art, an aesthetic attitude theory can support the idea that certain kinds of response are privileged, others discountable on the grounds of failing to take the 'correct' attitude towards the object concerned. This assumes that the point of *art is wholly aesthetic. The notion of an aesthetic attitude deserves to be treated with some scepticism, as it has been in recent philosophy.   C.J.

    *aesthetic concepts; aesthetic judgement.

G. Dickie, 'The Myth of the Aesthetic Attitude', *American Philosophical Quarterly* (1964); repr. in J. Hospers (ed.), *Introductory Readings in Aesthetics* (New York, 1969).

A. Schopenhauer, *The World as Will and Representation*, i, tr. E. F. J. Payne (New York, 1964), Third Book.

aesthetic concepts. Term introduced into aesthetic theory in Frank Sibley's landmark 1959 essay of that name.

According to Sibley, aesthetic concepts, such as *balanced, delicate, anguished*, differ from non-aesthetic ones, such as *orange, rough, square*, in being strongly non-condition-governed, that is, not applicable according to a rule going from non-aesthetic concepts to aesthetic concepts. Aesthetic concepts, Sibley insisted, were strongly perceptual ones—their presence must be experienced, not inferred—but unlike non-aesthetic perceptual concepts, they require taste, not merely functioning senses, for their discernment, and they are of a higher order than and dependent on non-aesthetic perceptual concepts. Sibley's claim is plainly related to the Kantian notion that the judgement of beauty is not subject to rule.

It is important to see that Sibley's claim is, in terms suggested by Monroe Beardsley, a denial of application conditions for aesthetic concepts, not a denial of occurrence conditions for them. And one piece of evidence for the correctness of Sibley's claim concerning the non-condition-governedness of the aesthetic is how finely dependent on the non-aesthetic complexion of an object the application of an aesthetic term appears to be, very small differences in non-aesthetic complexion being able to induce large differences in the aesthetic terms that apply. Nevertheless, Sibley's thesis came under attack early on from philosophers such as Ted Cohen, who maintained that the aesthetic/non-aesthetic distinction was untenable, and Peter Kivy, who held that aesthetic terms were in fact condition-governed after all.

In more recent discussion, talk of aesthetic concepts has usually been replaced by talk of aesthetic properties, and Sibley's claim of dependence has been transmuted into talk of the supervenience of aesthetic properties on non-aesthetic properties, including those relating to an object's appreciative context. Current debate about aesthetic concepts turns on the issue of how to delineate clearly the class of such concepts, the issue of whether such concepts essentially involve a normative or evaluative component, and the issue of the defensibility of realism with respect to such concepts.   J.LEV.

    *aesthetic attitude.

E. Brady and J. Levinson (eds.), *Aesthetic Concepts: Essays After Sibley* (Oxford, 2001).

J. Levinson, 'Aesthetic Supervenience', in *Music, Art, and Metaphysics* (Ithaca, NY, 1990).

Frank Sibley, *Approach to Aesthetics: Collected Papers*, ed. J. Benson, B. Redfern, and J. R. Cox (Oxford, 2001).

aesthetic distance. In one version of *'aesthetic attitude' theory, aesthetic responses are alleged to occur when people 'distance' themselves from an object they perceive, suspending their desires and other feelings, and leaving the mere experience of contemplating it. 'Distancing' is also thought of as a feature in understanding artistic representations. Someone whose own emotions became engaged in an experience of full-blown pity or contempt for a fictional character would be 'under-distanced.'   C.J.

E. Bullough, 'Psychical Distance as a Factor in Art and an Aesthetic Principle', in *Aesthetics: Lectures and Essays* (London, 1957).

aesthetic imagination: *see* imagination, aesthetic.

aestheticism. A term sometimes used pejoratively for a view about the value of *art. More often presupposed than argued for, it is the idea that works of art have value to the extent that they can be appreciated for their aesthetic merits, and that such appreciation requires no justification by reference to anything outside itself. Aestheticism presupposes both that there is distinctively aesthetic value, and that such value is not derivative from any other kind. An alternative to aestheticism would be instrumentalism, the view that art is valuable, if at all, because it is a means to some end, such as moral improvement, knowledge (say, of human psychology or history), or a more cohesive society. For aestheticism, by contrast, art belongs securely in the realm of the aesthetic, and that realm has a wholly autonomous value.   c.j.

W. Pater, *The Renaissance: Studies in Art and Poetry*, in W. E. Buckler (ed.), *Walter Pater: Three Major Texts* (New York, 1986).
L. Tolstoy, *What is Art?*, tr. A Maude (Indianapolis, 1960).

aesthetic judgement. An aesthetic judgement attributes a form of aesthetic value to a thing, of whatever kind. (For most philosophers, not all aesthetic judgements are about art, and not all judgements about art are aesthetic judgements.) Kant's influential theory provides a starting point for analysing such judgements. For Kant, aesthetic judgements are distinguished both from the expression of subjective likes and dislikes, and from judgements that ascribe an objective property to the thing that is judged. Like subjective preferences, they must be made on the basis of an experience of *pleasure; but like property-ascribing judgements, they make a claim with which other subjects are expected to agree. Other views would assimilate aesthetic judgements more closely to truth claims about a thing's properties, or place more emphasis on subjective response, and less on the notion of agreement or correctness.   c.j.

  *aesthetic attitude.

I. Kant, *Critique of Judgement*, tr. J. C. Meredith (Oxford, 1969).

aesthetics, history of. Aesthetics, conceived as a distinct discipline or sub-discipline dealing with philosophical questions concerning *art and aesthetic value, is a modern invention, originating in the eighteenth century. Ancient and medieval writers gave consideration to *beauty, artistic representation, the *sublime, and the value of the arts, and among these discussions those of Plato (especially in the *Republic*) and Aristotle (in the *Poetics*) have been vastly influential and are still studied by aestheticians today. Later writings by, for example, Plotinus, Augustine, and Aquinas are of historical importance for the philosophy of art. However, this sketch will concentrate on major lines of thought concerning art and the aesthetic on the part of philosophers in the modern period, from roughly 1700 onwards.

  Philosophical aesthetics owes much to German philosophy of the eighteenth and nineteenth centuries,

including its name (Alexander Baumgarten coined the term in 1735, taking it from the Greek *aisthesis*, meaning sensation or perception), but also, thanks to Kant, Hegel, and their contemporaries, its first definitive book, its arrival as a systematic discipline, and its period of greatest intellectual fervour. However, the earliest recognizable practitioners of aesthetics were philosophers in the British empiricist tradition. The most important work here is that of David Hume; other figures are Joseph Addison, Francis Hutcheson, Edmund Burke, Alexander Gerard, Lord Kames, and Archibald Alison. These thinkers are broadly in the wake of Locke's empiricism, but worked on problems of *taste, beauty, and critical judgement in a way that Locke had not. Locke's contemporary Shaftesbury addressed such issues prominently, and has sometimes been considered the founder of aesthetics, though he never achieves the separation from ethical questions which allows the aesthetic to emerge as an area of investigation in its own right. The work often credited with developing the first independent notion of aesthetic response is Hutcheson's *Inquiry into the Original of Our Ideas of Beauty and Virtue* (1725). Hutcheson attempts to explain the source of our pleasure in beauty, and assigns it to an 'internal sense' in addition to the five familiar senses. We are caused by some objects to have ideas of beauty, but their occurring in us is neither determined by knowledge we have of the object, nor attended by any desire or interest towards it. This effectively sets the stage for many later theories of aesthetic response.

  A concise early discussion of the problem of *aesthetic judgements is Hume's essay 'Of the Standard of Taste' (1757), regarded today as the most important contribution to aesthetics before Kant. Hume starts from an apparent contradiction. Judgements of taste, which in this context are critical judgements about the arts, are founded upon sentiments of beauty, but sentiments make no reference to states of affairs in the world and are merely subjective, so judgements of taste, which are frequently found to be in conflict with one another, might all seem equally 'right'. Yet there are some judgements which we would regard as clearly wrong, absurd or ridiculous (such as the assertion of 'an equality of genius between Ogilby and Milton'). How to explain the rightness or greater authoritativeness of some critical judgements, while acknowledging them to be based upon subjective responses? Hume proposes that there must be some standard of taste to settle aesthetic disputes. He mentions the idea of general principles of taste, though what they are and how they are applied is less clear. He adduces the fact that certain works of classical literature are universally regarded as paradigms. Finally he suggests that some human beings can be found who are 'true judges' and whose responses are more authoritative than those of others. These true judges would be characterized by 'strong sense, united to delicate sentiment, improved by practice, perfected by comparison, and cleared of all prejudice'. Though it remains difficult to see how such judges are to be identified and why we should assume that their judgements will agree with one another, Hume's essay is a clear exposition of the issues surrounding aesthetic judgement.

The now familiar concept of art also has its roots in the eighteenth century. In the work of such French authors as Dubos and especially Batteux there formed the concept of the *beaux arts*: *music, *poetry, painting, sculpture, and dance. New at this time was the separation of the arts as such from other human accomplishments, notably the sciences, and the idea that there were systematic resemblances that united all the arts. In Germany, where rationalist philosophy predominated, Baumgarten's innovation was to claim that the sense experience provided by a poetic work could be analysed as having its own kind of perfection, a perfection that must be distinguished from that of intellectual thinking. He thus showed the way to theorize the arts as human attainments distinct from science and rational thought. The *Enlightenment figures Moses Mendelssohn and Lessing were much influenced by this. The grouping of the arts under a single heading allowed also for work on the differences between them, of which a striking example is Lessing's analysis of representation in poetry and the visual arts in his essay *Laokoön*.

Immanuel Kant's *Critique of Judgement* (1790) begins by pursuing essentially the same question as Hume, though in different terminology. Kant's central notion is that of judgements of taste, or judgements of some particular object's beauty, which he is concerned to demarcate from judgements of the good or judgements of the merely agreeable. Judgements of taste, though similar to these other judgements in being associated with pleasure, have distinct characteristics: the pleasure they are founded upon is disinterested, they claim universal assent but without basing that claim upon concepts, they arise out of a consciousness of purposiveness in the object without its being assigned any determinate purpose, and they regard pleasure in the object as necessary for all judging subjects. The central question is: How can such judgements be justified in claiming universal assent, when their basis is a subjective pleasure? Kant's answer relies on his theory that ordinary perception involves a joint operation of the imagination and the understanding. The pleasure in something's beauty engages these cognitive capacities in 'free play', where we are conscious of a 'formal' harmoniousness in our experience, or a unity of the same kind as when we judge something under a concept, but without the determinate content a concept provides. Kant argues that since we can assume the same cognitive faculties in all, we can rightfully expect them all to experience the same pleasure.

Kant has often been interpreted as putting forward a theory of art which is formalist and centred around the notion of a pure aesthetic encounter with the art object. But this is to some degree an anachronistic reading, answering to later views of the nature of art. Kant's own theory of art requires a distinction between 'pure' aesthetic judgements and other judgements of beauty in which we take into account the object's purpose and its perfection in answering to that purpose. Even more importantly, Kant characterizes art from the productive viewpoint as the work of genius, a natural capacity for forming original images rich in suggestions of thought that cannot be conveyed directly in language or concepts. He has a lively sense of the connections between the aesthetic and the ethical, saying that beauty symbolizes morality, that an interest in natural beauty is the mark of a moral character, and that the cultivation of taste and that of moral feeling go hand in hand. A connection with his ethics is also evident in Kant's treatment of feelings of the *sublime, which occur when some object is either too vast for us to comprehend or so powerful that it can destroy us. Our capacity to tolerate these limitations gives pleasure because it acquaints us with our existence as free moral agents who are not wholly exhausted by our empirical natures.

The period immediately after Kant was fertile for aesthetics. For Friedrich Schiller (1759–1805) art has an exalted role in human life because of its *freedom from constraints of moral duty and physical need. Human beings have two essential drives, the material and the formal, and these are united in a 'play drive', manifest in art which in its freedom succeeds in uniting form and matter. An emphasis on freedom, *autonomy, spontaneity, runs through the main movements of the day: early romanticism and German idealism. Art was seen as the prime arena for human self-expression and as important in the quest for a problematic union with nature and with society. In the early philosophical work of F. W. J. von Schelling (1775–1854) art is seen as uniquely unifying the conscious productivity of mind and the unconscious productivity of nature. But the most substantial and enduring contribution to aesthetics from this period of German idealism was the work of G. W. F. Hegel, principally in his *Lectures on Aesthetics* delivered in the 1820s. Art has a cognitive value for Hegel: it does what religion and ultimately philosophy do more perfectly, that is allow humans to attain self-understanding as freely self-determining conscious beings. Art's distinctive manner of achieving this is via the making of sensous material objects. Hegel is much concerned with beauty, though unlike Kant he excludes from consideration the beauty of nature, because for him philosophy studies the development of the human mind or reason through history. Hegel's pronouncement that his topic is 'the beauty of art' fixes in place the confluence of interests that defined but also bedevilled philosophical aesthetics long afterwards.

For Hegel beauty in art is conceived neither in terms of mere form nor principally in terms of its giving pleasure: rather it is 'sensuous appearance of the idea', a manifestation of truth through some experienceable medium. Hegel not only gives a thorough systematic account of architecture, sculpture, painting, music and poetry, but provides a unified history of the development of the arts, embracing a wide range of epochs and cultures (including non-Western ones). This historical approach has been vastly influential on the practice of art history and criticism, and indeed on the practice of the arts to this day.

Hegel divided the history of art into a pre-classical 'symbolic' phase, then the classical phase of the ancient Greeks, which he regarded as superior because of its attainment of unity between content and sensory medium, and a third phase of romanticism which embraced medieval Christian art and the art of modernity. Art had already declined in the modern period, and must end, according to Hegel, superseded by religion and philosophy.

Two further German philosophers of the nineteenth century produced original aesthetic theories of lasting interest: Schopenhauer and Nietzsche. In *The World as Will and Representation* (1818) Schopenhauer developed one of the earliest *'aesthetic attitude' theories. Aesthetic experience is for him a suspension of the will, allowing the subject to enter a higher state of consciousness, freed from desire or interest towards the object of contemplation, and free of the suffering that attends willing. This state of peaceful elevation is of peculiar value to Schopenhauer because of his philosophical pessimism, the view that human individuals must strive and suffer without attaining any lasting or redeeming goals. Aesthetic experience is a temporary relief from the misery of an existence we would prefer not to have if we understood it properly. But Schopenhauer also attaches to the aesthetic state a supreme cognitive value, in that by freeing ourselves of will we free ourselves of subjective forms and achieve a purer knowledge, which he says is of *Ideas, conceived in a Platonic manner. Art—treated here in a resolutely ahistorical manner—is of special value because through the work of a genius, who can suspend individual willing and merely perceive, we are enabled to experience reality more objectively. Schopenhauer gives accounts of the distinctive value of the different art forms. Of special note is his theory of music, which he says dispenses with representation of Platonic Ideas and copies directly the movements of the will, of which, according to his metaphysics, the whole of reality consists.

In his early period Nietzsche was influenced by Schopenhauer, but he took seriously the more Hegelian emphasis on the historical development of the arts, imbued his theory with scholarship of the ancient world, and sought to promote the recent œuvre of Richard Wagner as a model art form. The result of this mixture was Nietzsche's first book *The Birth of Tragedy* (1872). Nietzsche's central opposition here is between two Greek deities, Apollo and Dionysus, who have complex symbolic significance. Apollo is associated with sun, light, appearance, and clarity, Dionysus with trance, abandon, and ritual dance. Nietzsche takes them to symbolize natural forces or drives whose key-words are *dream* and *intoxication*. We have drives to immerse ourselves in an alternative world of appearance and beauty, and to lose our sense of self in a drunken transport or trance in which we become conscious of an identity with nature as a whole. The plastic arts and music respectively answer to these drives in their purest forms. But Nietzsche's central claim is that in tragic drama of the classical age in Athens these two creative drives became fused so as to create the perfect art form. *Tragedy represents the individual in image, but uses the music and dance of the chorus to provide an identification with a greater unity, a viewpoint from which the suffering and destruction of the individual can be witnessed with fulfilment and joy. Nietzsche pronounces that 'it is only as an aesthetic phenomenon that existence and the world are eternally justified', in part because of a pessimism similar to Schopenhauer's: life itself is brief, painful and ultimately without point, so that only when transfigured by art is it something we can celebrate.

Nietzsche's narrative concludes with the claim that philosophy brought about the death of tragedy through the figure of Socrates, who held an optimistic view of human happiness and devalued anything for which there was not a rational explanation. Nietzsche's unorthodox book, which he himself more or less disowned in later years, was influential in revealing the expressive and irrational in Greek culture. More recently it has attained great resonance in postmodernist critiques of traditional philosophy and its treatment of the arts. The later Nietzsche was preoccupied with a critique of post-Christian culture, including its morality, metaphysics, and conception of truth. He produced no other systematic work in aesthetics, but regarded artistic creativity, with its licence to form fictions that disregard truth but affirm life, as paradigmatic of autonomous agency and value formation, so that in a sense his moral psychology and theory of value are at the same time contributions to the philosophy of art.

German philosophy continued its tradition of aesthetic theorizing into the twentieth century, where it emerged variously in the form of *phenomenology, *hermeneutics and Marxism. A unique body of work arising out of phenomenology is that of Martin Heidegger, whose 1936 essay 'The Origin of the Work of Art' is his most studied work in the philosophy of art. Heidegger was influenced by Hegel and Nietzsche, and by his reading of the poet Hölderlin. A preoccupation with art as revelatory of truth and frequent reference to Greek paradigms show continuity with Hegel, but Heidegger invents a quite new way of describing the work of art and what it does. It is for him a fundamental mistake characteristic of modernity to regard the work of art as a thing present in the world; rather, for Heidegger a work of art 'opens up a world' and is a 'happening of truth'. The being of things in our experience is 'unconcealed' by an art work: for example, a Van Gogh painting of peasant shoes allegedly 'lets us know what shoes are in truth'. Heidegger makes rich, quasi-poetic use of the concepts 'world' and 'earth', to convey that which opens itself to us in our experience of using 'equipment', and the firm but concealed basis on which human lives are lived. Art is a uniquely revelatory form of *poeisis* or 'bringing forth', for Heidegger, and fundamentally challenges traditional *ontology and the technological conception of things that he criticizes in modernity. Hans-Georg Gadamer, a pupil of Heidegger, is the principal exponent of the tradition of hermeneutics, or theory of interpretation, in the German tradition. His *Truth and*

Method (1960) seeks a conception of 'experience of truth' which is absent from traditional Kantian conceptions of aesthetic experience, and which sees the experience of art works as transformatory of our own self-understanding.

The most discussed writers in Marxist theoretical aesthetics are Walter Benjamin, whose essay 'The work of art in the age of mechanical reproduction' (1936) is especially widely read, and Theodor Adorno, whose later work is woven from many influences apart from Marxism, including Kant, Hegel, Nietzsche, twentieth-century music—in which he was expert and on which he wrote sophisticated criticism—and aesthetic modernism more generally. Adorno analysed art works as commodities within Western capitalism, but also saw art as having the potential for an autonomy which enabled 'truth content' and a critical standpoint towards society. In his *Aesthetic Theory* (published posthumously in 1970) he adopts a complex dialectical approach, multiplying pairs of opposed concepts to describe art works from many perspectives.

In the English-speaking world the late nineteenth and early twentieth century saw the prevalence of *aestheticism and *formalism. Aestheticism arose out of specific artistic preoccupations in Victorian Britain, and is sloganized as the 'art for art's sake' movement, with Oscar Wilde one of its notable proponents. Formalism was championed by Clive Bell, who in his book *Art* (1914) wrote that art was characterized by 'significant form', or 'a combination of lines and colours that moves me aesthetically'. These theories mirrored modernist developments in the various art forms, and reflected a tendency to secure autonomy for art by linking it with a conception of pure aesthetic experience. Such theories had their opponents, most notably perhaps Leo Tolstoy in *What is Art?* (1898) and the American pragmatist John Dewey in *Art as Experience* (1934). Tolstoy rejected much of the celebrated art of his day because it did not fulfil his preferred criterion of communicating moral feeling between human beings. Dewey also accentuated the role of communication and opposed the notion of the single detached subject of aesthetic experience. In a highly developed though recently rather neglected theory, he sought a more comprehensive conception of art, opposing the separation of art from the rest of human experience, and viewing art—conceived more broadly than the traditional fine arts—as an activity productive of consummatory experience.

In *The Principles of Art* (1938) R. G. Collingwood, influenced by the Italian aesthetician Benedetto Croce with whom he is often linked, presents the view that 'art proper' is the expression of emotion. Some activities that are called art Collingwood relegates to the categories of amusement and 'magic', the latter being the arousal of emotions with social usefulness such as solidarity and religious allegiance, while amusement is the arousal of emotions for the sake simply of enjoying them. Collingwood opposes the conception of art as a craft or techinque of arousing emotions by making representations, and regards representation as inessential to art. Expressing an emotion is quite distinct from arousing it; expression involves the authentic realization, through an artistic medium, of the emotion that one is feeling, and independently of this there can be no adequate characterization of what the expressed emotion is.

After the Second World War there began what could be called the first phase of analytical aesthetics in the English-speaking world, influenced by the ordinary language philosophy of the day and by Wittgenstein. The latter's work issued in scepticism about the possibility of defining art. 'Art' was perhaps a family-resemblance concept, whose use did not depend on necessary and sufficient conditions. In the 1960s this dovetailed with an awareness of the rapid change occurring especially in the visual arts, and gave rise to an anti-essentialist view that art was not by essence representation, or pure form, or expression, but an open-ended and liberating set of activities with no clear boundaries. Much debate ensued about what is to be included under the heading of art. In a period when a well known article was entitled 'The Dreariness of Aesthetics', work that stands out as of enduring value is that of Frank Sibley on the relation of aesthetic and non-aesthetic concepts, and Nelson Goodman's proposal to view art as a set of symbol-systems analogous to but importantly distinct from language.

Other influential trends in aesthetics in the second half of the twentieth century could be grouped under the heading of *post-modernism, stemming from work by a number of French philosophers, of whom Nietzsche is often, with some justification, invoked as a precursor. Some of the approaches now labelled as post-modernism are foreshadowed in the work of Michel Foucault. Others occur in, for example, Roland Barthes and Jacques Derrida. Characteristic ideas of post-modernism are the plurality and arbitrariness of interpretations of art works, the unavailability of stable truth or meaning, the inability of language to refer to a reality beyond itself, the historical constructedness of the interpreter's own standpoint, and the 'death of the author', which supposedly leaves texts interpretable in an unregulated 'play' of multiple readings. Such work challenges many presuppositions about the traditional subject-matter of aesthetics, throwing into question the notions of the autonomy of art, of art as a single coherent category, of the subject of aesthetic experience, of privileged or correct interpretation of art works, and of there being any truth for art to reveal.

These ideas have been highly influential on literary and art theory, and where they have influenced philosophers they have tended to break down the distinction between philosophy and other disciplines. Similar characteristics are found in feminist aesthetics, which has recently emerged as a recognizable strand of thought. Taking a lead from feminist cultural criticism, philosophers have questioned the extent to which art and the concepts in which it is described are gendered. Kant is often a focus for feminist critique, as indeed he is in much twentieth-century aesthetics. In this case, the notion of the disinterested spectator of an object of beauty is argued to reflect a privileged 'male gaze' (a term first used in film theory by

Laura Mulvey) for which women are the prime object. Christine Battersby has argued that the concept of genius too has been constructed in the modern period so as to embody a peculiarly male set of characteristics.

A later phase of aesthetics in the analytic tradition has seen an increased diversity of enquiry, somewhat less isolation of aesthetics from other areas of philosophy, and some degree of interest in questions raised by the so-called continental strains of philosophy. One aspect of recent analytical work has been a decisive, though not uncontested, move away from the assumption that the aesthetic is definitive of art. The work of George Dickie attacked the aesthetic attitude, and he and Arthur Danto argued, in different ways, that art must be defined and interpreted in the context of the history and institutions of art and of its specific history of production. Monroe Beardsley championed a more traditional definition of art as designed to arouse aesthetic response, a view which would exclude many of the broadly 'conceptual' works that impressed other theorists. More recently analytical aesthetics has been alive to a widening range of questions, including the ontology of art, art's relation to mental states such as emotions and beliefs, the nature of pictorial representation (where Richard Wollheim's work has been prominently discussed), musical expressiveness, the value of tragedy, narrative, film, popular art, the relation between aesthetics and ethics, and the distinctiveness of the appreciation of nature. If towards the end of its three-hundred-year history aesthetics is expanding in sophistication and varying its repertoire of questions, that has been accompanied in all of its traditions by increasing uncertainty as to whether aesthetic experience has any role in accounting for art, or indeed whether art is anything of which a unitary account can be given.   C.J.

*performing arts.

B. Gaut and D. M. Lopes (eds.), *The Routledge Companion to Aesthetics* (London, 2001).

I. Kant, *Critique of the Power of Judgment*, tr. P. Guyer and E. Matthews (Cambridge, 2000).

R. Kearney and D. Rasmussen (eds.), *Continental Aesthetics: Romanticism to Postmodernism: An Anthology* (Oxford, 2001).

M. Kelly (ed.), *Encyclopedia of Aesthetics*, 4 vols. (Oxford, 1998).

P. Kristeller, 'The Modern System of the Arts: A Study in the History of Aesthetics', *Journal of the History of Ideas* vol. 12 (1951), 496–527 and vol. 13 (1952), 17–46.

aesthetics, problems of. Aesthetics is that branch of philosophy which deals with the arts, and with other situations that involve aesthetic experience and aesthetic value. Thus only part of aesthetics is the philosophy of art. The rest, which might be termed the philosophy of the aesthetic, centres on the nature of aesthetic responses and judgements. The philosophy of art and the philosophy of the aesthetic overlap, without either being clearly subordinate to the other. Contemporary aesthetics is a rich and challenging part of philosophy, marked by a high level of disagreement even about what its basic problems are. Faced with a field of diverse subject matter, aesthetics often looks to stable reference points in its own history, as well as calling on knowledge of the various arts and a sensibility to wider philosophical issues.

Philosophy of the Aesthetic. Many different kinds of thing are regarded as having aesthetic value. If we think of pieces of music, poems, paintings, cinematography, bird song, stretches of countryside, cathedrals, flowers, clothes, cars, and the presentation of food, the aesthetic seems to be one pervasive dimension of our lives. A central task will be to examine what 'having aesthetic value' amounts to.

Are we talking about *beauty? Truth, beauty, and the good may be the traditional staples of philosophy, but contemporary aestheticians would not necessarily accept that the second item in the trinity is the predominant concern of their subject. To many, beauty does not even appear to be a single quality, let alone the summation of everything aesthetic. When we think in particular of the arts, it is debatable whether beauty is *the* quality which gives them value. There has been some interest recently in the notion of the *sublime as an alternative. All in all, it may be safer to talk about 'aesthetic value' in a more general way, while noting that some philosophers regard 'beauty' as the best name for aesthetic value.

The big, obvious question about *aesthetic value is whether it is ever 'really in' the objects it is attributed to. This issue parallels *realism–anti-realism debates elsewhere in philosophy—though there is little reason to assume that aesthetic value will behave in just the same way as, for example, moral value. An extreme realist would say that aesthetic values reside in an object as properties independent of any observer's responses, and that if we make the judgement 'That is a beautiful flower', or 'This painting is aesthetically good', what we say is true or false— true if the flower or painting has the property, false if it does not. We will tend to like the object if we recognize the aesthetic value in it, but, for the realist, whether we recognize it and whether it is there are two separate questions.

Departing from this realist starting point one may suggest various ways in which aesthetic value is less than fully objective. Most people would agree that to have aesthetic value is to be prone to bring about certain responses in observers. Aesthetic value is closely linked with a kind of satisfaction which we may feel when we perceive the thing in question. So whether a cathedral is beautiful depends on whether people who look at it in the right way are liable to enjoy what they see. This does not in itself mean that aesthetic judgements are not true or false. But if they are true or false, what they say about an object is that perception of it is likely to bring about a kind of satisfaction in an observer.

Consequently, much work in aesthetics has gone into trying to specify the nature of aesthetic experience or aesthetic response. One factor is pleasure, satisfaction, or liking. The second is experience: the response we are looking for must be a way of attending to the object itself. In the case of music, it must be a response to perceived patterns of sound, in the case of cinematography, a response to the experience of seeing something on the screen. If you merely describe a piece of music or a sequence of images to me, I am not yet in a position to respond in the kind of way which is peculiarly relevant to aesthetic value. The third factor in aesthetic response is often thought to be 'disinterestedness'. The idea is that the pleasurable experience of attending to something in perception should not consist in liking a thing only because it fulfils some definite function, satisfies a desire, or lives up to a prior standard or principle.

One paradigmatic view of aesthetic response in recent philosophical aesthetics runs as follows. There are subjective responses which we are justified in demanding from others: these are not idiosyncratic likes and dislikes, but deeply rooted in our common nature as experiencing subjects, and founded on a pleasurable response to the form of the object as it is presented in perception. This means, among other things, that aesthetic value cannot be enshrined in learnable principles—there are no genuine aesthetic principles because to find aesthetic value we must (as Kant put it) 'get a look at the object with our own eyes'. Aesthetic judgements are founded upon the slender basis of one's own feeling of pleasure, but can justifiably claim universal agreement if the subjective response in question is one which *any* properly equipped observer would have.

Proponents of this line contend that agreement in aesthetic judgement is agreement in one's subjective responses. We thus seem to move further away from the idea that aesthetic value is a property residing in objects. If an aesthetic judgement can be made only by someone who undergoes the right sort of aesthetic experience, then we have to accept the following as a consequence: if someone tells me that an object which I have not seen is ten feet tall, black, and made of steel (non-aesthetic properties), I am usually in a position to form the belief that it has these properties; but if someone merely tells me that the same thing is beautiful or has high aesthetic value, I am not yet in a position to make my own aesthetic judgement on it. This is a puzzling result, which should incline us to examine the notion of aesthetic judgement in more depth.

Another line is taken by *aesthetic attitude theories, which hold that we may approach whatever comes before us in a contemplative frame of mind, submerging or disengaging our desires and extraneous motivations. Historically the clearest and most extreme instance is Schopenhauer's theory of the suspension of the will, in which the mind supposedly becomes temporarily empty of everything except the contemplated object. Aesthetic attitude theories are sometimes conducive to the idea that the value in aesthetic situations resides not in the object perceived but in our entering a particularly liberating and receptive state of mind. Recent critics of the aesthetic attitude have, however, doubted whether any such state of mind exists, or whether, if it does, it is anything more important than simply concentrating fully on what one is looking at or listening to.

The aesthetic attitude approach suggests that any kind of thing may be the occasion of an aesthetically valuable experience, which provokes a query with wider resonance: in trying to explain aesthetic value and aesthetic experience, should we treat *art* with any special privilege? Some philosophers contend that the true home of aesthetic judgements is the artistic sphere, and that we would scarcely think of judging nature aesthetically if we did not inhabit a culture which produced art. If we believe them, then the main focus for a theory of the aesthetic should be judgements of, and responses to, art. But aesthetic responses to art usually depend to some extent upon knowledge of such matters as the style and genre which a piece is in, the identity and intentions of the artist, or at least the historical period and the cultural possibilities available. There is such a thing as understanding a work of art: how does such understanding relate to aesthetic judgements of art? On the one hand, the uninformed observer seems entitled to aesthetic judgements based on his or her responses; on the other, there must be room in principle for right and wrong aesthetic judgements, whose possibility tends to be assumed by ordinary aesthetic discourse.

The aesthetic as a phenomenon, and theories about aesthetic value, can also be studied from a sociological or historical point of view. It is quite fashionable to claim that the practices of aesthetic judgement carried out by particular classes in society, and the very idea of the aesthetic as a realm of self-contained value, have a political or ideological function. But we should avoid the dubious assumption that such claims, if true, would show the whole notion of aesthetic value to be somehow spurious. To use an analogy, the practice of attending football matches may, from a sociological point of view, serve some function of preserving class identities; but this does not alter the fact that people judge matches and players as better or worse. Similarly, it is a fact that aesthetic judgements occur, and that they purport to be about aesthetic value. Whatever their social roles (and these may be quite diverse), we can still ask what aesthetic judgement and aesthetic value are.

Philosophy of Art. Sometimes it is assumed that the prime interest in art is aesthetic. But that assumption bears some examination. Unless 'aesthetic' stretches to cover everything conceivable that is of value in art (making it a very impoverished term), art may have values which are not aesthetic. For example, it might have therapeutic value, or give us moral insights, or help us to understand epochs in history or points of view radically unlike our own. We might admire a work for its moral integrity, or despise it for its depravity or political untruthfulness. Are all these a matter of aesthetic value? If not, then *aestheticism gives too narrow a view of the value of art. Without succumbing to the instrumentalist view that art's point is always as a means to some end outside itself, we should concede that works of art have a great variety of values. Plato's well known hostility to certain artistic practices was largely based on the idea that one should demand from the artist a concern for truth and appropriate moral paradigms of behaviour. It is too simple to say that he missed the point of art altogether.

Much contemporary philosophy of art does not address what might be called Art with a capital A, which to many writers seems an outdated an unmanageable notion. It is debatable whether there is any reason beyond historical circumstance why music, painting, architecture, drama, novels, dance, films, and other things should all have come to be called *art. Although the attempt to define art is certainly within the brief of aesthetics, it is not always the most fruitful initial approach. Many, including the present writer, have felt that the more exciting definitions of art ('art as expression of emotion', 'art as significant form') tend to be too narrow, while recent alternatives which are wide enough to include everything fail to tell us why art is important. Prominent among these is the much-discussed institutional definition, which links something's status as art to the role it plays within the practices of the 'artworld'.

Philosophically productive work on art in today's aesthetics is often more narrowly focused, looking at a specific art form and posing of it a specific question. For example, How does music express emotion? What makes a painting a picture *of* something? What happens when we imagine characters in novels, plays, or films? What characterizes metaphorical uses of language? How is one literary work distinguished from another? (*Expression; *fiction; *forgery; *imagination; *metaphor; *music; *tragedy; *representation in art.) In addressing these questions, the philosopher of art will often call on philosophical conceptions of identity, meaning, intention, and other mental states such as belief, emotion, and imagination. Parts of aesthetics are also parts of the philosophy of mind and metaphysics.

When dealing with the arts, we are by and large concerned with intentionally produced artefacts. Having said this, there are differences in kind between them. A symphony is not a physical object, nor are other things which may have multiple instantiations (such as a short story or a film). A painting seems more likely to be physical object, although thinking about the means by which the image in a painting can be reproduced gives one a taste for the problems of identity which works of art can throw up. Is the work of art the thing on the wall of a certain gallery, or is it the image which you also find in art books and on the postcard you take home with you? Performing arts raise more complexities: all performances of a particular play or opera could be failures, while yet the play is one of the greatest ever written. This suggests that the play is not identical with its performances—but what is it then? Only a plunge into metaphysics will take this much further—a plunge which today's aestheticians are often willing to take.

Artworks are, nevertheless, usually intentionally produced things. They are also things with characteristic modes of reception or consumption. Paintings are placed where we can see them in a certain way, music is enjoyed or analysed mostly by being heard. This pattern of production and reception gives rise to two recurring general questions in the philosophy of art: What relation does the work bear to the mind that produced it? And what relation does it bear to the mind that perceives and appreciates it? As an example, we may take emotion and *music. We say that music has, or expresses, some emotional character. Since emotions are mental states, we may think that the emotion gets into the sounds by first being present in the mind of the composer or performer. Or we may think that the listener's emotional reactions are somehow projected back on to the sounds. Neither of these approaches has great plausibility, however, so that a fresh question emerges: The music all by itself somehow seems to point to, or stand for, emotions—how? Aesthetics has yet to come to terms with this tantalizing problem. There is a similar pattern in the case of artistic representation. In the question of what a picture depicts, what role is played by the artist's intentions, and what by the interpretations which an observer may conjure up? Or does the painting itself have a meaning by standing in symbolic relations to items in the world? If the latter, how similar, and how dissimilar, are depiction and linguistic representation?

There have been widely differing views about the role played by the mind of the artist in determining the identity of an artwork. At one extreme stands the theory of Croce and Collingwood, according to which the artwork is an expression of emotion by the artist, and exists primarily in the artist's mind. At the other end have been a number of views in literary theory, including the notion of the *intentional fallacy and the *death-of-the author thesis. For different reasons, these views hold that the work of art, or text, can and should be interpreted without any reference to the supposed mind of the author that lies behind it. The philosophical issues here are complex. It may, for example, be an illusion that interpreting the text and interpreting the author's mind are entirely separable. We have to engage with the philosophy of mind, to decide how people generally become aware of mental states such as intentions, and whether interpreting a text can be assimilated to interpreting a person's action as informed by their intentions. But we also have to be careful not to depart too much from the practice of ordinary readers. For many people, their interpretation of a novel will be crucially affected by their beliefs about the author; it will matter, for example, whether the author is male or female, European or African. Who shall prescribe that such readers are wrong?

Critical discourse about the arts (that is, literary criticism, music criticism, or criticism of the visual arts) provides another important topic for the philosophy of art. Until very recently the philosophical conception of *art criticism has seen it either as a form of expert evaluative judgement which enables others to find aesthetic value in a work, or as an interpretative exercise in search of a meaning which the work may bear. Criticism in the various fields has its own traditions, and its own ways of theorizing about itself, and the philosophy of criticism should be informed by knowledge of these. However, the question of what criticism stands to gain from philosophy is not an easy one to answer. Those who retain faith in the philosophical enterprise will be confident that the clearer the account given of the nature of aesthetic value, perception, meaning, intention, identity, and so forth, the better the description of discourse about the arts.

Ranged against such a view, however, are those closer to recent developments in criticism itself, who claim to deconstruct any notions of stable meaning or value, do not accept the terms in which philosophers tend to ask about the identity of work or author, and are at best ambivalent towards the notion of the aesthetic. The philosophy of criticism therefore faces a dilemma: either to engage in debate with theories that arise from criticism itself, and become involved in a protracted attempt to justify its own methodology, or to carry on its own task of clarification, at the risk of producing an idealized account of art criticism which may be only tenuously related to actual critical practices.

Plato spoke of an 'ancient quarrel between philosophy and poetry'. His conception of philosophy as rational inquiry into truth and the good was built on the claim that it was distinct from and superior to the arts. *Poetry was no guide to truth, and could not be relied upon to set its own standards. Some recent philosophers have alleged that the philosophy of art has tacitly operated on much the same assumption ever since, and that when the value of the arts is at issue, philosophy's own right to call the tune should also be questioned. Once it starts to address problems at this level, the philosophy of art starts to concern the nature of philosophy as a whole.   c.j.

N. Carroll, *Philosophy of Art: A Contemporary Introduction* (London, 1999).

R. G. Collingwood, *The Principles of Art* (Oxford, 1938).

A. C. Danto, *The Transfiguration of the Commonplace: A Philosophy of Art* (Cambridge, Mass., 1981).

J. Levinson (ed.), *The Oxford Handbook of Aesthetics* (Oxford, 2003).

A. Neill and A. Ridley (eds.), *Arguing about Art: Contemporary Philosophical Debates* (London, 2002).

R. Wollheim, *Art and its Objects* (Cambridge, 1980).

aesthetic value: *see* value, aesthetic.

aeterni patris: *see* neo-Thomism.

affirmative action. This term refers to positive steps taken to rank, admit, hire, or promote persons who are members of groups previously and/or currently discriminated against. The term has been understood both narrowly and broadly. The original meaning was minimalist: it referred to plans to safeguard equal opportunity, to protect against *discrimination, to advertise positions openly, to create scholarship programmes to ensure recruitment from specific groups, and the like. Controversy today centres on expanded meanings associated with quotas and preferential policies that target specific groups, especially underrepresented minority groups and women.

Policies of affirmative action are often said to have their foundations in the principle of compensatory *justice, which requires that if an injustice has been committed, just compensation or reparation is owed to the injured person(s). Everyone agrees that if *individuals* have been injured by past discrimination, they should be compensated, but controversy has arisen over whether past discrimination against *groups* such as women and minorities justifies compensation for current members of the group.   T.L.B.

G. Ezorsky, *Racism and Justice: The Case for Affirmative Action* (Ithaca, NY, 1991).

R. K. Fullinwider, *The Reverse Discrimination Controversy* (Totowa, NJ, 1980).

affirmative and negative propositions. Given any proposition *p*, it is possible to form its negation, not-*p*. Since not-*p* is itself a proposition, it in turn has its negation, not-not-*p*, which in classical logic is just equivalent to *p*. On some theories of propositions, indeed, *p* and not-not-*p*, being logically equivalent, are not distinct propositions. This casts some doubt on the idea that some propositions are intrinsically negative and others affirmative.

A *sentence* used to express a proposition may be negative, in that it contains a negative particle—for example, 'This is *not* red' or 'He is *un*happy'. But it is easy enough to express the same proposition using a sentence which does not contain a negative particle—for example, 'This lacks redness' or 'He is sad'. The latter sentences are, grammatically speaking, affirmative. So it does not appear that one can satisfactorily define a negative proposition to be a proposition expressible by means of, or only by means of, a negative sentence, where a negative sentence is understood as one containing a negative particle. Nor is it particularly plausible to maintain that certain *concepts, such as the concept of sadness, are intrinsically 'negative', being definable as the negations of supposedly more fundamental 'positive' concepts—in this case, the concept of happiness.

Rather than try to set up such fruitless divisions, it is better simply to see (classical) negation as a logical *operation which, applied to any proposition, transforms a truth into a falsehood and vice versa. At the same time, it is important to distinguish between the *speech-acts of affirmation and denial on the one hand and the propositional content of an assertion on the other, for we can concede the legitimacy of such a distinction between speech-acts while rejecting the idea that propositions themselves are intrinsically affirmative or negative.   E.J.L.

A. J. Ayer, 'Negation', in *Philosophical Essays* (London, 1954).

M. Dummett, *Frege: Philosophy of Language*, 2nd edn. (London, 1981).

G. Frege, 'Negation', in *Translations from the Philosophical Writings of Gottlob Frege*, ed. P. Geach and M. Black, 2nd edn. (Oxford, 1960).

affirming the antecedent. In a hypothetical proposition 'If *p*, then *q*', *p* is the antecedent, *q* the consequent.

Asserting *p*, so that *q* may be inferred, is called affirming the antecedent; the inference is said to be in the **modus ponens*. Knowing that if it lacks a watermark, the note is counterfeit, I affirm the antecedent when I discover that it lacks a watermark, concluding that it is counterfeit. The corresponding fallacy is **affirming the consequent*. c.w.

H. W. B. Joseph, *An Introduction to Logic*, 2nd edn. (Oxford, 1916), ch. 15.

affirming the consequent. To reason that, because he opposes the status quo and communists oppose the status quo, John must be a communist, is to commit this fallacy. In the **traditional logic of terms, inferences like 'If *A* is *B*, it is *C*; it is *C*; therefore it is *B*' illustrated the fallacy. In **propositional calculus, any inference of the form 'If *p* then *q*, and *q*; therefore *p*' affirms the consequent. c.w.

   **affirming the antecedent.

C. L. Hamblin, *Fallacies* (London, 1970), 35–7.

African philosophy has its roots in an oral tradition of speculative thought stretching as far back as African culture itself. In many parts of Africa south of the Sahara the written phase of that tradition emerges mainly as a response to the exigencies of the anti-colonial struggle and the challenges of post-colonial reconstruction. On the continent as a whole, however, written philosophy reaches back in time to Pharaonic Egypt and runs through the epochs of Greek and Roman interaction with North Africa which produced many intellectual luminaries, among whom the best known is St Augustine. Similarly, Arabic records reveal a tradition of Islamic philosophy in parts of northern, western and eastern Africa extending from the second half of the medieval period to the nineteenth century. Home also to a long, if not profuse, tradition of written philosophy is Ethiopia whose Zar'a Ya'eqob, for an illustrious example, propounded an original, rationalistically inclined, philosophy in the seventeenth century.

In the contemporary era a sizeable body of philosophical literature emerged in the 1960s and early 1970s from the efforts of the first wave of post-colonial rulers in Africa, who, having led their peoples to independence, felt the need to articulate the theoretical foundations of their programmes for socio-economic development and cultural renewal. With rare exceptions they argued for forms of socialism based on first principles deriving from traditional African communalism. The African provenance of their philosophies was clearest in the 'Ujamaa' (Familyhood) socialism of Nyerere of Tanzania and the 'Zambian humanism' of Kaunda, who both steered studiously clear of foreign ideological admixtures. More indebted to foreign philosophies, specifically to Marxism-Leninism, though no less sincere in their pursuit of African authenticity, were the 'scientific' socialisms of Nkrumah of Ghana and Sékou Touré of Guinea. In between these philosopher-kings was Senghor of Senegal, poet, statesman, scholar, and philosopher of 'Negritude', whose writings display more scholarly appreciation for Marx than ideological commitment to him.

Academic, professionalized philosophy is, by and large, a post-colonial phenomenon in many parts of Africa south of the Sahara. That discipline has been intensely methodological, seeking to define its African identity as part of the general post-independence quest for intellectual self-definition on the continent. In brass tacks, the issue reduces to the question of how contemporary African philosophers may best synthesize the insights obtainable from indigenous resources of philosophy with any from the Western philosophical tradition within which their institutional education has come to be situated by the force of historical circumstances. In the resulting literature an unmistakable tension has developed between the more and the less traditionalist approaches to the issue.

Nevertheless, there is no dispute about the richness of African traditional thought. A study of that system of thought, moreover, discloses conceptual options that contrast in philosophically instructive ways with many of those embedded in Western philosophy. Thus, although no continental unanimity is assumed, traditional African conceptions of the cosmos in many instances involve homogeneous ontologies that cut across the natural/supernatural opposition in Western philosophy. God is conceived as a cosmic architect of the world order rather than its *ex nihilo* creator, and mind as a capacity rather than an entity. The associated conception of human personality, though postulating a life principle not fully material, is still devoid of any sharp dualism of body and spirit. That conception also has a normative dimension which incorporates a communalist and humanistic (as distinct from a religious) notion of moral responsibility into the very definition of a person. At the level of the state this went along naturally with a consensual philosophy of politics based on kinship representation under a kingship dispensation. How to adapt this understanding of politics to current African conditions is one of the severest challenges facing African philosophy today.

Some recent attempts to meet this challenge have taken the form of an exploration of alternatives to the majoritarian democracies current in Britain and the USA and exported to Africa with questionable results. The suggestion has been that a democracy based on co-operation rather than competition among political associations (as distinct from political parties) would better reflect African traditions of consensus in political decision making and also better cohere with the ethnic stratification of contemporary African states. This notion is rife with conceptual issues currently receiving attention. k.w.

   **black philosophy; negritude.

K. Gyekye, *Tradition and Modernity: Philosophical Reflections on the African Experience* (New York, 1997), chs. 2 and 4.

Gideon-Cyrus M. Mutiso and S. W. Rohio (eds.), *Readings in African Political Thought* (London, 1975).

Claude Sumner (ed.), *Classical Ethiopian Philosophy* (Los Angeles, 1994).

Kwasi Wiredu, *Cultural Universals and Particulars: An African Perspective* (Bloomington, Ind., 1996).

agapē. Used originally to refer to the love feast of the early Christians intended to promote Christian fellowship, the word has come to mean brotherly or selfless *love. The Latin translation was *caritas*, whence 'charity' as in 1 Cor. 13, where it vaunteth not itself, suffereth long, and is kind. It is one of C. S. Lewis's four loves in his book of that title, the others being affection, friendship, and eros. At root, it comprises a deep cherishing care for each individual as such as a being of intrinsic worth. Kant's notion of practical love approximates to *agapē*.   N.J.H.D.

G. Outka, *Agapē* (New Haven, Conn., 1972) contains a useful discussion.

agent. A person (or other being) who is the subject when there is *action. A long history attaches to thinking of the property of being an agent as (i) possessing a capacity to choose between options and (ii) being able to do what one chooses. Agency is then treated as a causal power. Some such treatment is assumed when 'agent-causation' is given a prominent role to play in the elucidation of action.

In recent times, a doctrine of agent-causation is associated with Chisholm, who thinks that no concept of event-causality is adequate for understanding human beings' agency. Ryle's attack on *volitions had the effect of distracting philosophers from the *experience* of agency. But whatever Ryle may have shown, it seems undeniable that bodily action has a first-person aspect. Some recent writing attempts to rehabilitate the phenomenology of agency. Brian O'Shaughnessy's 'dual aspect theory' brings out the importance of achieving a view of action in which a third-person and first-person perspective are both incorporated but neither is exaggerated.

A range of philosophical theses hold that the concept of agency, which human beings acquire in their experience of agency, is prior (in one or another sense) to the concept of *causality. Collingwood claimed that the primitive notion of cause was derived from agency. And in the pre-modern world, causation in the absence of human action was typically construed either as divine action, or as the action of an object whose nature it was to realize certain ends. Reid claimed that the idea of cause and effect in nature must be arrived at by analogy, from the relation between an active power (of which human agency is a species) and its products.   J.HORN.

*intention; mental causation.

Alan Donagan, *Choice: The Essential Element in Human Action* (London, 1987).
Alfred R. Mele, *Motivation and Agency* (Oxford, 2003).
Brian O'Shaughnessy, *The Will*, 2 vols. (Cambridge, 1980).

agent causation. A direct causal relation between agents and actions that is irreducible to causation by events and states. Advocates of agent causation usually argue that it is required for free will and moral responsibility because both an action's being uncaused and its being caused (solely) by events and states—whether deterministically or indeterministically—preclude the control needed for free, morally responsible action. The agent causal power is said to be the power to exert direct control over one's actions. What this control power is supposed to be, whether agent causation is conceptually possible, and whether, if it is conceptually possible, our universe is likely to have a place for it, are vexed questions.   A.R.M.

*freedom, determinism.

T. O'Connor, *Persons and Causes* (New York, 2000).

agent-relative moralities. Typical agent-relative moral principles forbid us from committing one murder even if by not doing so we permit five to occur, and allow us to spend income on our friends rather than famine relief. Such principles characteristically either require or permit different individuals to pursue distinct ultimate aims. They may require that agents not perform a prohibited act *themselves* even if their doing so would reduce the performance of such acts. They may also permit each agent to devote attention to their own particular concerns in a manner disproportionate to their value considered from an impartial perspective. Much of contemporary moral philosophy is concerned with the content, justification, and interrelationship of agent-relative principles. Although such principles are central to ordinary moral thought, they appear difficult to reconcile with at least one widely held moral theory—*consequentialism—since it standardly claims that each agent should pursue the common aim of promoting the best outcome considered from an impartial perspective.   A.D.W.

T. Nagel, *The View from Nowhere* (New York, 1986), ch. 9.
S. Scheffler (ed.), *Consequentialism and its Critics* (Oxford, 1988).
B. Williams, 'A Critique Of Utilitarianism', sect. 5 in J. J. C. Smart and B. Williams, *Utilitarianism: For and Against* (Cambridge, 1987).

agglomeration. A term coined by Bernard Williams for the principle that 'I ought to do *a*' and 'I ought to do *b*' together imply 'I ought to do *a* and *b*'. It has since been generalized to other properties or operations where a property or operator is said to agglomerate if it can be factored out of a conjunction, as, for example, in 'Necessarily *P* and necessarily *Q*' implies 'Necessarily, *P* and *Q*'. It has been argued that an agent may be obliged to do *a* and be obliged to do *b* but on the assumption that 'ought implies can', may not be obliged to do both and hence agglomeration fails.   R.B.M.

B. Williams, 'Ethical Consistency' (first pub. 1965), in *Problems of the Self* (Cambridge, 1973).

agnosticism: *see* atheism and agnosticism.

agreement, method of: *see* method of agreement.

Ajdukiewicz, Kazimierz (1890–1963), Polish philosopher and logician, author of a radically anti-empiricist theory of meaning. Studied in Lvov and Göttingen. Professor at Lvov, Warsaw, and Poznan. Ajdukiewicz was an eminent representative of the Polish variety of analytical philosophy. In a series of studies published in *Erkenntnis* in 1934–5 (*Sprache und Sinn, Das Weltbild und die Begriffsapparatur, Die wissenschaftliche Welt-perspektive*) he elaborated a formal theory of coherent and closed languages which, unless they are exact copies of each other, are utterly untranslatable, so that no proposition accepted in one of them can be either accepted or denied in the other; in terms of this 'radical *conventionalism' an indefinite number of independent and untranslatable world-descriptions can be built on the basis of the same empirical data. Later on, Ajdukiewicz shifted to a more empiricist approach and argued that even analytical propositions in some cases require empirical premisses. He tried to translate traditional metaphysical and epistemological problems into semantic questions, analytically soluble.   L.K.

*translation, indeterminacy of.

Kazimierz Ajdukiewicz, *Język i Poznanie* (Language and Knowledge), 2 vols. (Warsaw, 1960–5).
H. Skolimowski, *Polish Analytical Philosophy* (1967).

akrasia. Socrates questioned whether one could ever deliberately, when able to follow either course, choose the worse, because overcome by fear, pleasure, etc.—i.e. whether *akrasia* could occur. In his view any deliberate agent must consider that what they are doing best fits their objectives (what they take to be their good). If seriously *overcome*, they would not be acting deliberately. What we deliberate (reason practically) about is always what we consider will be the best way to achieve our good. The apparent conflict between *reason and *passion is rejected: passions are unstable, untutored judgements about what is best; knowledge is necessary and sufficient for bringing stability to our judgements. This set the problem as (i) how can we act against what reason dictates? And (ii) how can we act against our view of what we take as good? Socrates answered that we cannot.

Aristotle and others following him thought Socrates ignored the obvious facts. They contrasted reason and pursuit of the good with motivation by passion. This involved denying the Socratic view that all deliberate action is aimed at what the agent considers best: I can take a meringue because I want it, without thinking taking one the best thing for me to do. There grew up a tendency to ally virtue with the exercise of reason, in opposition to passion with its relatively short-term considerations: and to see *akrasia* as a moral problem, the question of its possibility as one for ethics.

In the Middle Ages account had to be given of how the Devil, without passion, could deliberately go wrong. Aquinas tried to account for this as an error of reason, Scotus saw it as a case of the will freely choosing a good, but

one which it should not choose. Passion-free *akrasia* was on the map.

In the twentieth century R. M. Hare saw a problem arising because he considered that in their primary use moral judgements express the agent's acceptance of a guiding principle of *action: if they are not acted on, how are they guiding? To account for *akrasia* he tried to devise a notion of psychological compulsion compatible with blame. Donald Davidson sees the problem as more generally one in philosophy of action: can we give an account of intentional or deliberate behaviour which allows of deliberate choice of an action contrary to what deliberation, whether moral or not, favours? The limitations to morality and conflict with passion have been dropped, but the contrast of reason with something less long-term or comprehensive retained.

Davidson retains the assumption that akratic behaviour is irrational in being contrary to what in some sense the agent considers at the time that reason requires—contrary to an all-things-considered or better judgement—and in contravention of a principle of practical reason, which he calls the principle of continence, which enjoins us always to act on such judgements. These judgements, which always have 'more reason' on their side, also are generally seen as contrasted with a narrower and more short-term view. Attempts to characterize such judgements have not been successful. There are insuperable problems with all-things-considered judgements; but talk of better judgement only secures the tie with reason if it collapses into talk of all-things-considered judgement.

In fact the puzzle, if there is one, arises even where a contrast between reason and something else is hard to make out: Hamlet is an interesting case. It arises because the agent seems in a way to favour a course which he then does not take, without apparently ceasing to favour it. Neither passion nor short-term considerations are an essential factor. What is puzzling is unforced action against apparently sincere declarations of opposition to it.

The views mentioned earlier treat the problem as one of how we can act against reason. A difference between animals and humans has been thought to be that the latter have a natural tendency towards what they reason to be their good, enabling them to resist passion. This is a rational faculty, the *will, which is either always responsive to reason, in which case weakness is always a defect of reason; or always aims at some good, but is able to reject the one reason proffers, in which case *akrasia* is seen as weakness of *will*.

That reason does not always dictate intentional action seems to follow from the fact that if there is no common standard for judging between two objectives, or there is, but reason cannot determine that one is to be preferred to the other by that standard, then the agent (the will) must be free to choose either way. If, in the case of wrongdoing, there is no overarching standard for choosing between the moral good and some other objective, then the will has to choose between standards, without the help of reason. The will may be overcome by passion (be weak), but in the absence of passion is just evil when it chooses the worse course.

This view of the will can be de-moralized by attaching it to long-term objectives generally, or to reflective choice. Yet there are many problems in the whole project of postulating such a rational faculty, which is an unstable structure built too rapidly on some familiar idioms and supposed requirements of experience.   J.C.B.G.

*reason as the slave of the passions.

William Charlton, *Weakness of Will* (Oxford, 1988).
Donald Davidson, *Problems of Rationality* (Oxford, 2004).
Justin Gosling, *Weakness of the Will* (London, 1990).
R. M. Hare, *Freedom and Reason* (Oxford, 1963).
A. Mele, *Autonomy, Self-Control and Weakness of Will* (New York, 2002).
B. O'Shaughnessy, *The Will* (Cambridge, 1980).
S. Stroud and C. Tappolet (eds.), *Weakness of Will and Practical Irrationality* (Oxford, 2003).

Albert the Great (*c.*1206–80). Born in the German town of Lauingen, he studied briefly at Padua, becoming a Dominican in 1223. He was a regent master at Paris (1242–8), during which time Aquinas was one of his students, and in 1248 the two men became colleagues at Cologne. He was known as *doctor universalis* because of his encyclopedic knowledge displayed in his voluminous writings. He wrote extensively on scientific matters, and also on theology and philosophy, where he was heavily influenced by the works of Aristotle then reaching the Christian West accompanied by the commentaries of Muslim philosophers, in particular al-Fārābī and Avicenna. He was one of the earliest to realize that it was vital to work out a means of squaring Aristotelian philosophy with Christianity, for Aristotle had highly persuasive arguments for his doctrines, and those who would be persuaded by the arguments had to be shown that they could assent to the doctrines without in so doing implying the falsity of the faith. More than anyone it was Aquinas who carried out the task that Albert had recognized to be so necessary.   A.BRO.

*Aristotelianism.

J. Weisheipl (ed.), *Albertus Magnus and the Sciences: Commemorative Essays* (Toronto, 1980).

Albo, Joseph (*c.*1360–1444?). Jewish philosopher of Castile, author of *Sefer ha-Ikkarim* (The Book of Principles, 1425). A student of Crescas, well versed in mathematics, medicine, Islamic, Christian, and Jewish philosophy, and biblical and rabbinical learning, Albo spoke in the Tortosa Disputation of 1413–14. Against a backdrop of anti-Jewish polemic, he sought to forge a philosophically defensible Jewish creed centred on God, revelation, and requital, de-emphasizing the Messianic idea, the sorest point of Christian–Jewish polemics. From Aquinas Albo adopted the idea of natural law, arguing, with Maimonides, that the superiority of divine legislation lay in its (credal) provision for spiritual felicity, not just temporal welfare. Grotius and Richard Simon admired him, but Jewish thinkers often resented the idea of a formal creed and fault his lack of originality.   L.E.G.

Joseph Albo, *Sefer ha-Ikkarim*, ed. and tr. Isaac Husik, 5 vols. (Philadelphia, 1929–30; first printed ed. Soncino, 1485).

Alcmaeon of Croton (*fl. c.*450 BC). Medical theorist. He originated the influential quasi-political theory of medicine, one version of which was developed into the 'four humours' pathology which, through Galen, dominated medieval and early modern medicine. In Alcmaeon's version, four opposed 'powers' (hot, cold, wet, dry) are naturally in balance (because their strengths are everywhere in the right proportion) in the healthy body. A disturbance of the balance in any way means a damaging preponderance of one or more powers, and causes conflict. This is disease; the variety of diseases, and their different natures, are to be explained by the variety of ways and places in which the right proportion can be disturbed.   E.L.H.

J. Mansfeld, 'Alcmaeon: "Physikos" or Physician?', in *Kephalaion: Studies in Greek Philosophy and its Continuation Offered to Professor C. J. de Vogel* (Assen, 1975).

alethic concepts: *see* deontic logic.

Alexander, Samuel (1859–1938). Australian-born, Oxford-educated, Alexander spent his career at Manchester University. Trying always to keep abreast of developments in modern science, particularly psychology and biology, Alexander is best known for his theory of 'emergent evolution', which he expounded in his *Space, Time and Deity* (1920). His claim was that existence is hierarchically ordered, and that there is an ongoing evolutionary process with the emergence of ever-higher levels of existence. Through time, therefore, new qualities come into being, although Alexander would have thought of these as principles of organization rather than entities akin to the Bergsonian *élan vital*. As a man for whom his Jewishness was a significant factor, from his combating prejudice at Oxford to being close to prominent Zionists in Manchester, Alexander felt a keen affinity to Spinoza. Like the earlier philosopher, Alexander saw mind as at one with material substance, making itself manifest in the course of evolution. The next and ultimate emergent, Alexander supposed, would be God. One presumes that, at this point, he had left behind the constraints of science, although apparently he carried with him not a few eminent men of science.   M.R.

*evolution.

S. Alexander, *Space, Time and Deity* (London, 1920).

al-Fārābī: *see* Fārābī.

algebra, Boolean: *see* Boolean algebra.

al-Ghazali: *see* Ghazali.

algorithm. An algorithm is a mechanical procedure for determining the value of a function for any argument from a specified *domain. For example, addition is a function which maps pairs of natural numbers on to a natural number (the sum of the pair). The simple paper-and-pencil rules for determining the sum of any two numbers are an algorithm for the addition function. A mechanical procedure for deciding whether a given object has a particular property is also called an algorithm. So, for example, the *truth-table test for deciding whether a formula of the propositional calculus is a tautology is an algorithm. A mechanical procedure can be given as a finite set of instructions which are executed in a stepwise manner, without appeal to random processes or ingenuity. A *function is effectively computable if and only if there is an algorithm for computing it.   A.D.O.

H. Rogers, *Theory of Recursive Functions and Effective Computability* (New York, 1967), ch. 1.

alienation. A psychological or social evil, characterized by one or another type of harmful separation, disruption or fragmentation, which sunders things that belong together. People are alienated from the political process when they feel separated from it and powerless in relation to it; this is alienation because in a democratic society you belong in the political process, and as a citizen it ought to belong to you. Reflection on your beliefs, values, or social order can also alienate you from them. It can undermine your attachment to them, cause you to feel separated from them, no longer identified with them, yet without furnishing anything to take their place; they are yours, *faute de mieux*, but no longer truly yours: they are yours, but you are alienated from them.

The term 'alienation' gained currency through Marxian theory, and is used with special prominence in Marx's manuscripts of 1844 (which were first published in 1930). Marx derived the terms *Entäusserung* and *Entfremdung* from Hegel, who used them to portray the 'unhappy consciousness' of the Roman world and the Christian Middle Ages, when individuals under the Roman Empire, deprived of the harmonious social and political life prevailing in pagan antiquity, turned inward and directed their aspirations toward a transcendent Deity and his other-worldly kingdom. For Hegel, the unhappy consciousness is divided against itself, separated from its 'essence', which it has placed in a 'beyond'.

Marx used essentially the same notion to portray the situation of modern individuals—especially modern wage labourers—who are deprived of a fulfilling mode of life because their life-activity as socially productive agents is devoid of any sense of communal action or satisfaction and gives them no ownership over their own lives or their products. In modern society, individuals are alienated in so far as their common human essence, the actual co-operative activity which naturally unites them, is powerless in their lives, which are subject to an inhuman power—created by them, but separating and dominating them instead of being subject to their united will. This is the power of the market, which is 'free' only in the sense that it is beyond the control of its human creators, enslaving them by separating them from one another, from their activity, and from its products.

The German verbs *entäussern* and *entfremden* are reflexive, and in both Hegel and Marx alienation is always fundamentally *self*-alienation. Fundamentally, to be alienated is to be separated from one's own essence or nature; it is to be forced to lead a life in which that nature has no opportunity to be fulfilled or actualized. In this way, the experience of 'alienation' involves a sense of a lack of self-worth and an absence of meaning in one's life. Alienation in this sense is not fundamentally a matter of whether your conscious desires are satisfied, or how you experience your life, but instead of whether your life objectively actualizes your nature, especially (for both Marx and Hegel) your life with others as a social being on the basis of a determinate course of historical development. Their view that alienation, so conceived, can nevertheless have historical consequences, and even be a lever for social change, clearly involves some sort of realism about the human good: it makes a difference, psychologically and socially, whether people actualize their nature, and when they do not, this fact explains what they think, feel, and do, and it can play a decisive role in historical change.   A.W.W.

*capitalism.

Raymond Geuss, *The Idea of a Critical Theory* (Cambridge, 1981).
Istvan Meszaros, *Marx's Theory of Alienation* (New York, 1972).
Bertell Ollman, *Alienation*, 2nd edn. (Cambridge, 1976).
John Plamenatz, *Karl Marx's Philosophy of Man* (Oxford, 1975).

al-Kindī: *see* Kindī.

all: *see* universal proposition.

Alston, William P. (1921–). Although he has contributed to other areas of philosophy, his main interests lie in the areas of epistemology and philosophy of religion. His work on *epistemic justification has been particularly influential, and he has published extensive discussions of religious language. In *Perceiving God* (1991), these two interests come together in a detailed account of the epistemology of religious experience. Alston argues that *religious experiences which are taken by their subjects to be direct non-sensory experiences of God are perceptual in character because they involve a presentation or appearance to the subject of something that the subject identifies as God. He defends the view that such mystical perception is a source of prima facie justified beliefs about divine manifestations by arguing for the practical rationality of engaging in a belief-forming practice that involves reliance on mystical perception.   P.L.Q.

*God and the philosophers.

W. P. Alston, *Divine Nature and Human Language* (Ithaca, NY, 1989).
—— *Epistemic Justification: Essays in the Theory of Knowledge* (Ithaca, NY, 1989).

Althusser, Louis (1918–90). The most influential Marxist philosopher in the 1960s and 1970s, Althusser produced a novel form of Marxism by attempting to integrate into it the dominant ideas of *structuralism. Born in Algeria and spending most of his life lecturing at the élite Collège de France, Althusser and his disciples were much influenced by the leading currents of Parisian intellectual life.

Althusser's version of Marxism was in sharp contrast to the Hegelian and humanist interpretations of Marx that had gained prominence in the two decades after the Second World War. As regards Marx himself, Althusser saw a sharp epistemological break between the earlier humanist writings and the later scientific texts: each was governed by a different problematic or theoretical framework which determined what questions could be asked on what presuppositions. In his view, the young Marx propounded an ideological view of humanity's *alienation and eventual self-recovery, strongly influenced by Hegel; whereas the later Marx disclosed a science, a theory of social formations and their structural determination.

This later Marx, according to Althusser, had inaugurated a new type of philosophy which underlay his social scientific analysis. This *dialectical materialism was above all a theory of knowledge. In a distinctly neo-Kantian vein, Althusser saw the task of philosophy as the creation of concepts which were a pre-condition for knowledge. He insisted on the strict separation of the object of thought from the real object. Knowledge working on its own object was a specific form of practice, theoretical practice, of which Marxist philosophy was the theory.

When applied to society, the result of this epistemology was the science of historical materialism. Each of the instances of society—economics, politics, ideology—was a structure united within a structure of structures. The complex and uneven relationship of the instances to each other at a specific time was called by Althusser a 'conjuncture'. Every conjuncture was said to be 'overdetermined' in that each of the levels contributed to determining the structure as well as being determined by it: determination was always complex. This structured causality resulted in a reading of history as process without a subject—as opposed to the tendency of, for example, Sartre or the early Marx to see human beings as the active subjects of the historical process.

Althusser's account of Marx, in particular its concept of the problematic and its insistence on the relative autonomy of the sciences, was a good antidote both to all types of reductionism and to extreme forms of Hegelian Marxism. But it does contain severe weaknesses which have been re-emphasized by the superficiality of his approach revealed in his autobiography. Its status as an interpretation of what Marx actually said is dubious; since any recourse to a real object is ruled out, it is difficult to see what the criterion of scientificity could be; and, finally, since the science of dialectical materialism is cut off from the social formation, Althusser can offer no satisfactory account of the relation of theory to practice.   D.McL.

L. Althusser, *For Marx* (London, 1965).
G. Elliott, *Althusser: The Detour of Theory* (London, 1987).

—— (ed.), *Althusser: A Critical Reader* (Oxford, 1994).
E. P. Thompson, *The Poverty of Theory* (London, 1978).

altruism: *see* egoism and altruism.

ambiguity. A word, expression, or sentence is ambiguous if it has two or more distinct meanings, e.g. 'can', 'poor violinist', 'Everyone loves a sailor'. In particular contexts it may be clear with which of its meanings a word etc. is used, e.g. 'can' in 'I can do it', or 'poor violinist' when what is under discussion is the merits of orchestral players.   s.w.

*vagueness; vague objects.

Trudy Govier, *A Practical Study of Argument*, 3rd edn. (Belmont, Calif., 1992).
S. Wolfram, *Philosophical Logic* (London, 1989), ch. 2. 1.

ambiguous middle, fallacy of. A categorical syllogism contains two premisses, a conclusion, and three terms. The premisses contain two occurrences of one of the terms, the middle term. It is by virtue of relations of the other two terms to the middle term that the conclusion, containing the other two terms, follows, given other constraints. Where the middle term is ambiguous, with each occurrence differing in meaning, the syllogism is fallacious, and falls under the fallacy of *four terms. An example of the fallacy is the inference of:

Bees receive government subsidies.

from the premisses

Bees are producers of honey.
Producers of honey receive government subsidies.
                                                        R.B.M.

C. Hamblin, *Fallacies* (London, 1970).

American philosophy. Philosophizing in the United States has developed apace over the past century and has never been in as flourishing a condition as today, with philosophy firmly established as a subject of instruction in thousands of institutions of higher learning. However, the nature of the philosophical enterprise is changing, with the earlier heroic phase of a small group of important thinkers giving way to a phase of dis-aggregated production in a scattered industry of diversified contributors.

Already in colonial times there were various writers who treated philosophical subjects: theologians like Jonathan Edwards and philosophically inclined statesmen like Benjamin Franklin or Thomas Jefferson. But such talented amateurs exerted no influence on other identifiable philosophers. More systematic developments had to await the growth of the university system in the nineteenth century, when academic philosophy was imported from Europe, with idealists dominant at Harvard and Scottish thought dominant at Princeton, while Kantians were prominent in Chicago, Hegelians in St Louis, and Thomists at the Catholic institutions. But even late into the nineteenth century America's most significant philosophers operated outside the academic system, where eccentric thinkers like R. W. Emerson, John Fiske, C. S. Peirce, and Orestes Brownson never managed to obtain a secure foothold. However, with the rising importance of the natural sciences, philosophy became the linchpin that linked them to the liberal arts. The Harvard of James and Palmer and such distinguished imports as Santayana and Münsterberg was a harbinger of this, with philosophy here closely joined to psychology. The influx of the scientifically trained philosopher-refugees who crossed the Atlantic after the rise of Nazism greatly intensified this linkage of philosophy to the sciences.

The era between the two world wars saw a flourishing in American academic philosophy, with people like John Dewey, C. I. Lewis, R. B. Perry, W. P. Montague, A. O. Lovejoy, Ernest Nagel, and many others making substantial contributions throughout the domain. And after the Second World War there was an enormous burgeoning of the field. Numerous important contributors to philosophy were now at work in America, and the reader will find individual articles on dozens of them in this Companion.

However, no characteristically American school or style of philosophizing has developed, excepting one, namely *pragmatism as originated by C. S. Peirce and popularized by William James. The pragmatists saw the validity of standards of meaning, truth, and value as ultimately rooted in consideration of practical efficacy—of 'what works out in practice'. Though highly influential at home, this approach met with a very mixed reception abroad. Bertrand Russell, for example, objected that beliefs can be useful but plainly false. And various continental philosophers have disapprovingly seen in pragmatism's concern for practical efficacy—for 'success' and 'paying off'—the expression of characteristically American social attitudes: crude materialism and naïve democratic populism. Pragmatism was thus looked down upon as reflecting a quintessentially crass American tenor of thought—a philosophical expression of the American go-getter spirit with its success-orientated ideology, and a manifestation of a populist reaction against the chronic ideological controversies of European philosophizing—epistemological *rationalism versus *empiricism, ontological *materialism versus *idealism, etc. (Americans, de Tocqueville wrote, seek to 'échapper à l'esprit de système'.)

With pragmatism as a somewhat special case, American philosophers past and present have, as a group, been thoroughly eclectic and have drawn their inspiration for style and substance from across the entire spectrum of philosophizing. In consequence, American philosophizing as a whole reflects the world, with its contributors drawing their inspiration from materialism and idealism, from Aristotle and Kant, from ancient *scepticism and modern *phenomenology, etc. What is distinctive about contemporary American philosophizing is not so much its *ideas* (which, taken individually, could have issued from the minds and pens of non-Americans), but rather *the enterprise as a whole*, viewed as a productive industry of sorts.

Perhaps the most striking feature of present-day professional philosophy in North America is its scope and scale. The American Philosophical Association, to which most US academic practitioners of the discipline belong, currently has more than 8,000 members, and the comprehensive *Directory of American Philosophers* for 2002–3 lists well over 12,000 philosophers affiliated to colleges and universities in the USA and Canada. North American philosophers are extraordinarily gregarious by standards prevailing anywhere else. Apart from the massive American Philosophical Association, there presently exist well over 1,000 different philosophical societies in the USA and Canada, most of them with well over 100 members. In part because of the 'publish or perish' syndrome of their academic base, American philosophers are extraordinarily productive. They publish well over 200 books per annum nowadays. And issue by issue they fill up the pages of over 175 journals. Almost 4,000 philosophical publications (books or articles) and a roughly similar number of symposium papers and conference presentations appear annually in North America. The comparatively secure place of philosophy in the 'liberal arts' tradition of American collegiate education assures it a numerical size that makes for such professional health. (It is this statistical fact rather than anything coherent in the traditions themselves that has led to the ascendancy of American over British philosophy: as with industrial production, America's intellectual production is of preponderant volume.)

To be sure, this variation of philosophical approaches brings conflict in its wake, with each methodological camp and each school of thought convinced that it alone is doing competent work and the rest are at best misguided and probably pernicious. Few philosophers are sufficiently urbane to see philosophical disagreement and controversy as a form of collaboration. Internecine conflict is particularly acute between the analytic tradition, which looks to science as the cognitive model, and those who march to the drum of continental thinkers who—like Nietzsche, Heidegger, Foucault, Derrida, and co.—take not 'reality' but cultural artefacts (particularly literature and even philosophy itself) as the prime focus of philosophical concern. (Since deep-rooted values are at stake, there is no easy compromise here, although in intellectual as in social matters there is much to be said for live and let live.)

The total number of doctorates awarded by institutions of higher learning in the USA has been relatively stable at around 100,000 per annum since 1960. But the production of *philosophy* doctorates has declined substantially (along with that of humanities Ph.D.s in general), sinking from some 1,200 for 1970–5 to less than 600 by the end of the century. But even this meagre replenishment rate still enables the profession to maintain itself at a very substantial level.

Given the scale of the enterprise, it is only natural and to be expected that such unity as American philosophy affords is that of an academic industry, not that of a single doctrinal orientation or school. The size and scope of the academic establishment exerts a crucial formative influence on the nature of contemporary American philosophy. It means that two different—and sometimes opposed—tendencies are at work to create a balance of countervailing forces. The one is an impetus to separateness and differentiation—the desire of individual philosophers to 'do their own thing', to have projects of their own and not be engaged in working on just the same issues as everyone else. The other is an impetus to togetherness—the desire of philosophers to find companions, to be able to interact with others who share their interest to the extent of providing them with conversation partners and with a readership of intellectual cogeners. The first, centrifugal tendency means that philosophers will fan out across the entire reach of the field—that most or all of the 'ecological niches' within the problem-domain will be occupied. The second, centripetal tendency means that most or all of these problem-subdomains will be multiply populated—that group or networks of kindred spirits will form so that the community as a whole will be made up of subcommunities united by common *interests* (more prominently than by common opinions), with each group divided from the rest by different priorities as to what 'the really interesting and important issues' are. Accordingly, the most striking aspect of contemporary American philo-sophy is its fragmentation. The scale and complexity of the enterprise is such that if one seeks in contemporary American philosophy for a consensus on the problem-agenda, let alone for agreement on the substantive issues, then one is predestined to look in vain. Here theory diversity and doctrinal dissonance are the order of the day, and the only interconnection is that of geographic proximity. Such unity as American philosophy affords is that of an academic industry, not that of a single doctrinal orientation or school. Every doctrine, every theory, every approach finds its devotees somewhere within the overall community. On most of the larger issues there are no dominant majorities. To be sure, some uniformities are apparent at the localized level. (In the San Francisco Bay area one's philosophical discussions might well draw on model theory, in Princeton possible worlds would be brought in, in Pittsburgh pragmatic themes would be prominent, and so on.) But in matters of method and doctrine there is a proliferation of schools and tendencies, and there are few if any all-pervasively dominant trends. Balkanization reigns supreme.

The extent to which significant, important, and influential work is currently produced by academics outside the high-visibility limelight has not been sufficiently recognized. For better or for worse, in the late twentieth century we entered a new philosophical era where what counts is not just a dominant élite but a vast host of lesser mortals. Great kingdoms are thus notable by their absence, and the scene is more like that of medieval Europe—a collection of small territories ruled by counts-palatine and prince-bishops. Scattered here and there in separated castles, a prominent individual philosophical knight gains a local following of loyal vassals or dedicated enemies. But no one among the academic philosophers of today manages to impose their agenda on more than a minimal fraction of the larger, internally diversified community. Given that well over 10,000 academic philosophers are at work in North America alone, even the most influential of contemporary American philosophers is simply yet another—somewhat larger—fish in a very populous sea.

As regards those 'big names', the fact is that those bigger fish do not typify what the sea as a whole has to offer. Matters of philosophical history aside, salient themes and issues with which American philosophers are grappling at the present time include: ethical issues in the professions, the epistemology of information processing, the social implications of medical technology (abortion, euthanasia, right to life, medical research issues, informed consent), feminist issues, distributive justice, human rights, truth and meaning in mathematics and formalized languages, the merits and demerits of relativism regarding knowledge and morality, the nature of personhood and the rights and obligations of persons, and many more. None of these topics was put on the problem-agenda of present concern by any one particular philosopher. They blossomed forth like the leaves of a tree in springtime, appearing in many places at once under the formative impetus of the *Zeitgeist* of societal concern. Accordingly, philosophical innovation in America today is generally not the response to the preponderant effort of pace-setting individuals but a genuinely collective effort.

So much for the question of issues. But what of methodology and style? Pragmatism and applied philosophy apart, all of the dominant styles of American philosophy in the twentieth century—analytic philosophy, scientistic and logicist philosophizing, neo-Kantianism, phenomenology and 'Continental' philosophizing at large—originated in Europe. As far as philosophical approaches are concerned, Emerson's idea of an America moving beyond the dominance of European tendencies and traditions of thought has not been realized, and—given currently pervasive intellectual globalization—may never be. The extent to which American philosophy rests on European antecedents is graphically reflected in the great divide in the American Philosophical Association between the 'Analysts' and the 'Pluralists'. To all intents and purposes this split mirrored the opposition in the Germany of the 1920s between the followers of Reichenbach and Carnap, on the one side, and those of Heidegger and Gadamer, on the other, the one looking for inspiration and example to science (especially mathematics and physics), the other to humanistic studies (especially literature and philology)—a duality of perspective which itself had deep roots in the philosophizing of nineteenth-century Germany with its opposed allegiances, respectively to the *Naturwissenschaften* (Fries, Bolzano, Haeckel) and the *Geisteswissenschaften* (Schleiermacher, Nietzsche, Dilthey).

A century ago, the historian Henry Adams lamented the end of the predominance of an oligarchy of the great and the good in American politics—as it had been in the days of the Founding Fathers. He regretted the emergence

JOHN DEWEY represented a distinctively American no-nonsense naturalism in philosophy. He was born in Schopenhauer's lifetime and outlived Wittgenstein.

RUDOLF CARNAP had established himself at the forefront of European philosophy when he left Prague for America in 1935. His works exemplify the technical skill and scientific approach of Logical Positivism.

W. V. QUINE, the doyen of American philosophy in the late twentieth century, inherited and promulgated his mentor Carnap's view that philosophy should be pursued as part of natural science.

NELSON GOODMAN: a continuing aim of his work was to examine how language relates to experience, from scientific enquiry to artistic appreciation.

of a new order based on the dominance of the masses and their often self-appointed and generally plebeian representatives. Control of the political affairs of the nation had slipped from the hands of a cultural élite into that of the unimposing, albeit vociferous, representatives of ordinary people. In short, democracy was setting in. Precisely this same transformation from the pre-eminence of great figures to the predominance of mass movements is now, 100 years on, the established situation in even so intellectual an enterprise as philosophy. (Not that a sizeable percentage of people-at-large take any interest in philosophy; in this regard the democratization of the field is something quite different from its popularization.) In its present configuration, American philosophy reflects that 'revolt of the masses' which Ortega y Gasset thought characteristic of our era. This phenomenon manifests itself not only in politics and social affairs, but even in intellectual culture, including philosophy, where Ortega himself actually did not expect it, since 'its perfect uselessness protects it'. For what the past century's spread of affluence and education has done through its expansion of cultural literacy is to broaden the social base of creative intellectual efforts beyond the imaginings of any earlier time. A cynic might characterize the current situation as a victory of the troglodytes over the giants. In the Anglo-Saxon world, at any rate, cultural innovation in philosophy as elsewhere is nowadays a matter of trends and fashions set by substantial constituencies that go their own way without seeking the guidance of agenda-controlling individuals. This results in a state of affairs that calls for description on a statistical rather than a biographical basis. (It is ironic to see the partisans of political correctness in academia condemning philosophy as an élitist discipline at the very moment when professional philosophy itself has abandoned élitism and succeeded in reinventing itself in a populist reconstruction. American philosophy has now well and truly left 'the genteel tradition' behind.)

And so the heroic age of American philosophy, in which the work of a few 'big names' towered over the philosophical landscape like a great mountain range, is now over. One sign of this is that the topical anthology has in recent years gained a position of equality with, if not preponderance over, the monographic philosophical text. Another sign is that philosophers nowadays are not eccentric geniuses working in obscure isolation, but work-aday members of the academic bourgeoisie (even if not, as in continental Europe, civil servants).

The rapid growth of 'applied philosophy'—that is, philosophical reflection about detailed issues in science, law, business, social affairs, computer use, and the like—is a particularly striking structural feature of contemporary American philosophy. In particular, the past three decades have seen a great proliferation of narrowly focused philosophical investigations of particular issues in areas such as economic justice, social welfare, ecology, abortion, population policy, military defence, and so on. This situation illustrates the most characteristic feature of much of contemporary English-language philosophizing: the emphasis on detailed investigation of special issues and themes. For better or for worse, anglophone philosophers in recent years have tended to stay away from large-scale abstract matters of wide and comprehensive scope, characteristic of the earlier era of Whitehead or Dewey, and generally address their investigations to issues of small-scale detail.

In line with the increasing specialization and division of labour, American philosophy has become increasingly technical in character. Contemporary American philosophical investigations generally make increasingly extensive use of the formal machinery of philosophical semantics, modal logic, computation theory, psychology, learning theory, etc. Unfortunately, this increasing technicalization of philosophy has been achieved at the expense of its wider accessibility—and indeed even of its accessibility to members of the profession. No single thinker commands the whole range of knowledge and interests that characterizes present-day American philosophy, and indeed no single university department is so large as to have on its faculty specialists in every branch of the subject. The field has outgrown the capacity not only of its practitioners but even of its institutions.

Do American philosophers exert influence? Here the critical question is: Upon whom? Certainly as far as the wider society is concerned, it must be said that the answer is emphatically negative. American philosophers are not opinion-shapers: they do not have access to the media, to the political establishment, to the 'think tanks' that seek to mould public opinion. In so far as they exert an external influence at all, it is confined to *academics* of other fields. Professors of government may read John Rawls, professors of literature Richard Rorty, professors of linguistics W. V. Quine. But the writings of such important American philosophers exert no influence outside the academy. It was otherwise earlier in the century—in the era of philosophers like William James, John Dewey, and George Santayana—when the writings of individual philosophers set the stage for at least some discussions and debates among a wider public. But it is certainly not so in the America of today. American society today does not reflect the concerns of philosophers; the very reverse is the case—where 'relevant' at all, the writings of present-day American philosophers reflect the concerns of the society.   N.R.

*American philosophy today; Canadian philosophy; philosophy, influence of; Harvard philosophy; English philosophy; continental philosophy; analytic philosophy.

Elizabeth Flower and Murray G. Murphey, *A History of Philosophy in America*, 2 vols. (New York, 1977).

Bruce Kuklick, *The Rise of American Philosophy* (New Haven, Conn., 1977).

—— *A History of Philosophy in America: 1720–2000* (Oxford, 2001).

Nicholas Rescher, *American Philosophy Today* (Totowa, NJ, 1994).

Interesting perspectives from a continental standpoint are provided in:

Gérard Deledalle, *La Philosophie américaine* (Lausanne, 1983).

L. Marcuse, *Amerikanisches philosophieren* (Hamburg, 1959).

American philosophy today. Harvard's W. V. Quine (1908–2000) has had a more profound impact on the shape of *American philosophy in recent decades than any other single figure, even if no history of the period would be complete without attention to philosophers like Wilfrid Sellars (1912–89), David Lewis (1941–2001), Donald Davidson (1917–2003), Jerry Fodor (b. 1936), Saul Kripke (b. 1940), and, in moral and political philosophy, Quine's colleague John Rawls (1921–2002).

Quine's attack on the distinction between 'analytic' statements (those true in virtue of meaning) and 'synthetic' statements (those true in virtue of empirical fact) cast doubt on the idea that there was a domain of truths ('analytic' or 'conceptual' truths) that philosophers were uniquely suited to analyse. Quine recommended a radical *naturalization* of philosophy, such that philosophy would be continuous with empirical science, as its slightly more abstract and reflective branch. Versions of such a programme have been influential in epistemology (Alvin Goldman and Stephen Stich at Rutgers in New Brunswick) and philosophy of mind (Patricia and Paul Churchland at the University of California at San Diego, Robert Cummins at the University of California at Davis, Fodor at Rutgers), and, more recently, in ethics (Gilbert Harman at Princeton, Peter Railton at the University of Michigan at Ann Arbor). Cummins, for example, runs a 'philosophical lab' under the slogan 'no armchair philosophy allowed', while Harman and Railton argue that ethics had better attend to what we learn from empirical psychology about the role of character in the explanation of action. With few exceptions, American philosophers of mind take themselves to have an obligation to attend to the findings of psychologists and neuroscientists about the brain and mental life.

The interdisciplinary and naturalistic turns in philosophy launched by Quine have had other consequences. Philosophers of science, for example, now routinely have expertise in one of the special sciences (physics and biology are the most popular), and, indeed, often publish and participate in debates in the cognate field (David Malament at the University of California at Irvine and Elliott Sober at the University of Wisconsin at Madison are leading examples). Philosophers of language (such as the University of Southern California's James Higginbotham) now attend with care to developments in linguistics. Philosophers in almost all fields feel the need to explain how their subject-matter—morality, meaning, free will, consciousness—can be reconciled with a scientific picture of the world.

The Quinean attack on analytic truths and conceptual analysis has also had an unintended, and somewhat ironic, consequence: by contributing to the demise of Logical Positivism, which viewed metaphysical inquiries as nonsensical, Quine inadvertently opened the door to a new wave of metaphysical theorizing. Quine's student, David Lewis, led the way in returning metaphysical inquiry to philosophical respectability (though Lewis, unlike some who followed him, took the findings of empirical science as a constraint on metaphysical claims). Philosophers like Lewis and Kripke offered accounts of *modal* concepts—such as 'necessity' and 'possibility'—which could then be deployed in understanding a range of traditional metaphysical questions about the nature of causation, free will, meaning, and reference. Metaphysical theorizing about classic questions relating to time, material objects, substance, and change has also flourished. The return to metaphysics has been a prominent feature at several leading American philosophy departments besides Princeton, including those at Rutgers (where it coexists with the naturalistic turn, though partly divided along generational lines), MIT (Robert Stalnaker, Stephen Yablo), and Notre Dame (Alvin Plantinga, Peter van Inwagen, and others).

A more minor theme in post-Quinean American philosophy has reflected the influence of the later Wittgenstein's quietism: his view that philosophical questions were predicated on confusions about language, and so could be dissolved or neutralized. The American pragmatist philosopher Richard Rorty (b. 1931) popularized (some would say vulgarized) Wittgensteinian, Quinean, and Sellarsian ideas, and reached a large audience outside academic philosophy with his message that philosophy, as traditionally conceived, was over. This, unfortunately, ignored the revival of metaphysical inquiry and the naturalized approach to philosophical questions which most philosophers took to be Quine's legacy.

The naturalistic and metaphysical developments in American philosophy in recent decades have coincided with a revival of systematic inquiries in moral and political philosophy. Rawls's 1971 book *A Theory of Justice* is usually identified as the turning-point away from the mid-twentieth-century view that the only philosophical questions about values were questions about the meaning of evaluative language. Oddly, Rawls never responded directly to mid-century doubts about the objectivity of morality, but his book gave rise, none the less, to a lively literature on timely questions about distributive justice, the nature of rights, equality and freedom, and related topics. Beginning in the late 1970s, naturalistically minded philosophers began returning to the old 'meta-ethical' questions (questions about the meaning and objectivity of moral judgements), with Allan Gibbard (University of Michigan at Ann Arbor) breathing new life into the 'non-cognitivist' view that normative judgements are really expressive of certain attitudes, rather than descriptive of the world; while the so-called Cornell realists argued, conversely, that the objectivity of moral judgements could be reconciled with a scientific view of the world.

The largesse and largeness of the American university system—with more than 100 doctoral programmes, turning out hundreds of Ph.D.s each year—has made it possible for there to be specialists in every conceivable topic (from medieval logic to Heidegger's aesthetics), and for departments not in the top ranks of the profession to carve out riches of great distinction. This may go some distance towards explaining the explosion of work in the history of philosophy in recent decades, work that strives to understand figures in their historical context, while also engaging with them as philosophers, and not simply museum pieces from the history of ideas. (Julia Annas at the University of Arizona, who writes on ancient Greek philosophers, and the late Margaret Wilson of Princeton, who wrote on philosophers of the early modern period, have been influential figures.) Of particular note is the way in which figures outside the English-speaking traditions of philosophy have been incorporated into those traditions, from Allen Wood (Stanford University) on Kant, Hegel, and Marx, to Hubert Dreyfus (University of California at Berkeley) on Heidegger and Husserl. German philosophy of the nineteenth and twentieth centuries is increasingly a part of philosophical dialogue and debate in American philosophy at the dawn of the twenty-first century.   B.L.

S. Freeman (ed.), *The Cambridge Companion to Rawls* (Cambridge, 2002).

C. Hookway, *Quine: Language, Experience, and Reality* (Stanford, Calif., 1988).

H. Kornblith (ed.), *Naturalizing Epistemology*, 2nd edn. (Cambridge, Mass., 1994).

R. Rorty, *Philosophy and the Mirror of Nature* (Princeton, NJ, 1979).

P. van Inwagen, *Metaphysics*, 2nd edn. (Boulder, Colo., 2002).

amorality. Sometimes but incorrectly used to mean extreme immorality or wickedness, amorality more properly signifies the absence, in a person, of any understanding of or concern for moral standards or decencies. In this sense all babies and small children are amoral, but it is usually expected of adults that they should not be. If they are, they will probably commit horrible acts, hence the confusion of meanings noted at the start. But whether amorality is significant will depend on how we understand the nature of moral demands and their role in regulating human conduct; often simple good-naturedness is as effective as a sense of duty in promoting peace among persons. Amoralists are often depicted as monsters, but the example just given suggests this is not necessarily so. What is true is that they are uncommon. Less dramatically, certain acts or choices are amoral, i.e. involve no moral factors, such as choosing cabbage rather than carrots for lunch.   N.J.H.D.

*evil.

B. A. O. Williams, *Morality* (Cambridge, 1976) contains a brief discussion.

amphiboly. That kind of *ambiguity in which the linguistic context allows an expression to be taken in more than one way. There are several types, and writers differ over which to include out of: ambiguous grouping or *scope ('He had wanted to stand on the top of Everest *for ten years*'), linkage ('When a horse approaches a car, *it* should engage low gear'), denotation ('Catherine disliked Rachel biting *her* nails'), and part of speech ('Save soap and *waste* paper').   C.A.K.

C. A. Kirwan, 'Aristotle and the So-called Fallacy of Equivocation', *Philosophical Quarterly* (1979).

analogy, argument from, for the existence of God: *see* teleological argument for the existence of God.

analysis is the philosophical method, or set of methods, characteristic of much twentieth-century anglophone philosophy, of the type which describes itself as 'analytic' to express allegiance to rigour and precision, science, logical techniques, and—perhaps most distinctively of all—careful investigation of language as the best means of investigating concepts.

Analysis is pre-eminently a style, not a body of doctrine. It is piecemeal and particular in its interests. Some of its practitioners have professed hostility to 'metaphysics', by which they meant system-building efforts of the kind associated with Spinoza and Hegel, whose philosophizing might be called synthetic, in that it ventures to construct inclusive explanations of the universe. In sharp contrast, philosophical analysis is best understood by analogy with analysis in chemistry, as being a process of investigation into the structure, functioning, and connections of a particular matter under scrutiny.

Although analytic philosophers look back to Aristotle and the British Empiricists, especially Hume, as major influences on their tradition, it is the work of Bertrand Russell and G. E. Moore at the beginning of the twentieth century which is the proximate source of analysis so called.

Moore conceived the philosopher's task to be a quest for *definitions as a way of clarifying philosophical claims. This involves finding a definition of the concept or proposition (not merely the words used to express them) under discussion. One begins with a concept in need of definition (the analysandum) and looks for another concept or concepts (the analysans) which will explain or elucidate it. Indeed Moore made the more stringent demand that analysans and analysandum should be strictly equivalent.

Russell's conception of analysis derived from his work in logic. On his view, the surface forms of language can mislead us philosophically, as when the grammatical similarity of 'the table is brown' and 'the complexity of the situation is growing' leads us to think that tables and complexities exist in the same way. We must therefore penetrate to the underlying logical structure to clarify what is being said. The classic example is provided by Russell's theory of *descriptions. Suppose someone now asserts 'The present King of France is wise'. Is the sentence false, or neither true nor false? Russell argued that it is a concealed three-part conjunction asserting that there is a king of France, that there is only one such thing ('the' implies uniqueness), and that it is wise. Since the first conjunct is false, the whole is so.

These early techniques of analysis were soon extended and varied into practices not restricted either to the giving of definitions or to the attempt to unearth underlying logical structure. Some philosophers who would standardly be classified as belonging to the analytic tradition—a broad church—have explicitly repudiated both the claim that language has a hidden logical structure (the later Wittgenstein) and the idea that the chief task of the philosopher is to state definitions. It has indeed been argued that this latter view is in any case inapt, for if definiens and definiendum are strictly equivalent, analysis is trivial; but if not, it is incorrect.

Analysis has sometimes been claimed to involve *reduction of one kind of item—in the linguistic mode, a statement or proposition, or set of them; in the material mode, entities of given sorts—to items of another kind. For example, *phenomenalists argue that statements about physical objects are to be analysed into (translated into) statements about sense-data. In the philosophy of mind, *physicalists claim that mental phenomena can be exhaustively analysed in terms of physical phenomena in central nervous systems. This second kind of reductive analysis is eliminative, unlike the first, in holding that it is the reducing class of phenomena which is real or fundamental, and that talk of phenomena in the reduced class is merely a *façon de parler* or a function of ignorance.

Other conceptions of analysis have been influential. On Michael Dummett's view, analysis consists on elucidating the nature of thought by investigation of language. The idea is that to get a philosophical understanding of ourselves and the world, we have to proceed by way of what we think about these matters; but our chief and perhaps only access to what we think is what we say; so analysis comes down to the philosophical study of meaning. For P. F. Strawson analysis is the descriptive task of tracing connections between the concepts in our scheme of thought, with a view among other things to seeing what order of dependence obtains among them, thereby helping us to see why, for example, various forms of scepticism need not trouble us.

These remarks show that the concept of analysis is not univocal; there is no one method or set of methods which can be claimed as definitive of it. Philosophers in the analytic tradition have in practice agreed with the celebrated dictum of Deng Xiaoping concerning methodology, that 'it does not matter whether a cat is black or white so long as it catches mice'. But although there is no defining *method* of analysis, there can be said to be a defining *manner*, embodied in the ideal characterized in the opening paragraph above as any careful, detailed, and rigorous approach which throws light on the nature and implications of our concepts, characteristically revealed by the way we employ them in discourse.   A.C.G.

*analytic philosophy.

A. Flew (ed.), *Essays in Conceptual Analysis* (London, 1956).
F. Jackson, *From Metaphysics to Ethics: A Defence of Conceptual Analysis* (Oxford, 1998).
G. E. Moore, 'Replies to my Critics', *The Philosophy of G. E. Moore*, ed. P. A. Schilpp (Evanston, Ill., 1942).
Bertrand Russell, *Essays in Analysis*, ed. D. Lackey (London, 1973), esp. 'On Denoting'.

analytic and synthetic statements. According to Kant, an analytic statement (or judgement) is one in which the concept of the predicate is already contained, or thought, in the concept of the subject—an example would be the statement that a vixen is a female fox—whereas a synthetic statement is one in which this is not so, for instance, the statement that foxes are carnivorous. The *Logical Positivists, adopting the linguistic turn, held that an analytic statement is one which is true or false purely in virtue of the meanings of the words used to make it and the grammatical rules governing their combination. This definition has the advantages that it does not have application only to statements of subject–predicate form and avoids either reliance on the obscure notion of 'containment' or appeal to psychological considerations. Both Kant and the Logical Positivists assumed that true analytic statements must express necessary truths knowable *a priori, though Kant also held that some synthetic statements express such truths, including mathematical statements like '7 plus 5 equals 12' and metaphysical statements like 'Every event has a cause'. The Logical Positivists, by contrast, held mathematical truths to be analytic, and metaphysical statements to be nonsensical or meaningless.

Most contemporary philosophers are very wary of appearing to endorse the analytic–synthetic distinction following W. V. Quine's devastating onslaught upon it (though Grice and Strawson subsequently mounted a vigorous rearguard defence of its validity). Quine argues that this supposed distinction cannot be defined save (circularly) in terms which already presuppose it and that, in any case, it depends upon an untenable view of meaning. The positivists had adopted a verificationist theory of *meaning according to which there is a sharp distinction to be drawn amongst meaningful statements between those which can only be known to be true on the evidence of experience (synthetic statements) and those which are verifiable independently of any possible experience and which are therefore immune to empirical falsification (analytic statements). Quine, however, contends that no such sharp distinction can in principle be drawn, because our statements are not answerable to the court of experience *individually*, but only *collectively*—and *any* statement, even a supposed 'law' of logic, is potentially revisable in the light of experience, though some revisions will have more far-reaching implications than others for the rest of our presumed knowledge.   E.J.L.

H. P. Grice and P. F. Strawson, 'In Defence of a Dogma', *Philosophical Review* (1956).
W. V. Quine, 'Two Dogmas of Empiricism', in *From a Logical Point of View*, 2nd edn. (Cambridge, Mass., 1961).

analytic philosophy began with the arrival of Wittgenstein in Cambridge in 1912 to study with Russell and, as it turned out, significantly to influence him. Between the wars, through the influence of Russell's writings and Wittgenstein's own *Tractatus Logico-Philosophicus* (1922), analytic philosophy came to dominate British philosophy. In the 1930s the ideas of Russell and Wittgenstein were taken up and put forward more radically and systematically by the Logical Positivists of the *Vienna Circle and Reichenbach's circle in Berlin. There were sympathetic groups in Poland and Scandinavia and some scattered but distinguished adherents in the United States (to which many of the European positivists fled from Hitler), such as Nagel and Quine. The very different ideas of the later Wittgenstein, who came back to Cambridge in 1929, closer to those of Russell's original ally G. E. Moore, became increasingly influential and, under the label *'linguistic philosophy', prevailed in most of the English-speaking world from 1945 until about 1960. In the post-positivist era from then until the present English-speaking philosophy has been mainly analytic in the older, pre-linguistic sense, but with large variations of method and doctrine.

There had been some anticipations of analytic philosophy before Russell achieved philosophical maturity. The first is possibly Bernard Bolzano, a brilliant, isolated, and largely neglected Czech. Gottlob Frege, W. K. Clifford, Karl Pearson, Ernst Mach, and Henri Poincaré were all serious mathematicians, several of them highly creative and original, and they wrote philosophy, as did their more self-consciously analytic successors, in something of the style of a mathematical treatise: impersonal and objective, with terms explicitly defined and arguments formally and rigorously set out. That distinguishes them from the great fellow-travellers of analytic philosophy, Hume and J. S. Mill.

Russell and Moore emerged as original thinkers in the first decade of the century when they broke demonstratively away from the kind of Bradleian idealism which they had been taught. They argued against the view that reality is both an undissectable unity and spiritual in nature, that it is a plurality made up of an indefinite multiplicity of things, and that these things are of fundamentally different kinds—material and abstract as well as mental. They fatally undermined the idealist theory that all relations are internal or essential to the things they relate and, less persuasively, that the direct objects of perception are subjective contents of consciousness.

In the first decade of the twentieth century Moore was the leader, Russell being fully engaged in his work in mathematical logic. Moore's immensely methodical work had a quasi-mathematical quality, and he was perhaps the first to describe it as analysis. What he meant by that was the careful elaboration in the most lucid possible way of the precise meaning of the problematic assertions he was discussing, to make them available for critical scrutiny. That entangled him in the toils of the so-called paradox of analysis (if analysis reveals A to be identical to BC, how can 'A = BC' amount to more than the empty truism 'A = A'?).

During this decade Russell's main work was in logic. He defined the basic concepts of mathematics in purely logical terms and attempted, less successfully as it turned out, to deduce the fundamental principles of mathematics from purely logical laws. In his theory of descriptions he provided a new kind of definition, a definition in use or contextual definition, which did not equate synonym with synonym but gave a rule for replacing sentences in which the word to be defined occurred with sentences in which it

did not. This was described by F. P. Ramsey as the 'paradigm of philosophy'.

Working in conjunction with Wittgenstein between 1912 and 1914 Russell elaborated the *'logical atomism' set out rather casually in his *Our Knowledge of the External World* (1914) and *Philosophy of Logical Atomism* (1918) and more systematically, but obscurely, in Wittgenstein's *Tractatus*. All our significant thought and discourse, they held, can be analysed into elementary propositions which directly picture states of affairs, the complexes analysed being composed by the relations symbolized by the logical terms 'not', 'and', 'or', 'if', and, perhaps, 'all' (Russell thought it irreducible, Wittgenstein did not). The truth, or falsity, of the complex propositions was unequivocally determined by the way in which truth and falsity were distributed among their elementary components. Some complexes were true whatever the truth-value of their elementary components. These were the truths of logic and mathematics.

Both believed that the true logical content of complex propositions is concealed by ordinary language and can be made clear only by their kind of reductive analysis. Propositions which cannot be analysed into elementary statements of fact are 'metaphysical', for example those of morals and religion. They also held that elementary propositions represented the world as it really is. But the ontological conclusions they drew from this were different. Wittgenstein took it to reveal the general form of the world. Russell, giving elementary propositions an empiricist interpretation as the immediate deliverances of sense, arrived at the neutral monist conclusion that only experiential events really exist; the minds which have the experiences and the physical things to which the experiences attest are merely constructions out of experience, not independently existent things. He drew here on the analyses of material particles, points in space, and instants of time, put forward in the early 1920s by A. N. Whitehead, the collaborator in his early logico-mathematical work.

The Vienna Circle, led by Carnap and Schlick, took over the conception of philosophy as reductive logical analysis and the doctrine of the analytic (purely formal, factually empty) character of logic and mathematics. They followed Russell in taking elementary propositions to be reports of immediate experience and developed from this the principle that verifiability in experience is the criterion of meaningfulness. Deprived of significance by this criterion, judgements of value are imperatives (or expressions of emotion) not statements and the affirmations of the metaphysician or theologian are at best a kind of poetry. But they rejected the analytic ontologies of their predecessors. Against Wittgenstein they contended that language is conventional, not pictorial. Against Russell they maintained that bodies and minds are no less really existent than events, despite being constructions rather than elements.

*Logical Positivism was memorably introduced to the English-speaking world in A. J. Ayer's *Language, Truth and Logic* (1936). But as it became the height of philosophical fashion a new tendency was in the making in Wittgenstein's fairly esoteric circle. Language, he came to hold, in his new philosophical incarnation, is not simply descriptive or fact-stating, it has a multiplicity of uses and its meaning consists in the way it is used. It does not have a logical essence which it is the business of analysis to reveal; it has, rather, a natural history which it is the therapeutic, puzzlement-alleviating task of philosophy to describe. Our beliefs, about the mental states of other people for example, cannot be analysed into the evidence we have for them; that evidence is more loosely related to the beliefs as 'criteria' of their truth. This mood of acceptance, rather than large-scale reconstruction or reinterpretation, of ordinary discourse, has some affinity with the resolute pedestrianism about common sense and ordinary language which Moore had been practising for a long time. It took a different form in post-war Oxford: breezily definite with Ryle, scrupulously lexicographic with J. L. Austin. This is the linguistic philosophy which, centred at Oxford, was dominant in the English-speaking world from 1945 to about 1960, when it disappeared in its original form almost without trace.

Philosophical analysis, in a more or less Russellian spirit, but in a considerable variety of forms, has continued from its revival around 1960 to the present day. Quine's famous essay 'Two Dogmas of Empiricism' (1951) seemed to undermine the whole analytic project. He claimed that there was no theoretically adequate way of distinguishing identity of meaning from identity of reference, on the ground that there is no scientifically respectable 'criterion of synonymy'. The alleged findings of philosophical analysis, therefore, are no more than general factual beliefs we are specially unwilling to abandon in the face of apparently contrary evidence. Quine's view was received with great respect and was very little criticized, but philosophers went on very much as before. Quine's own philosophy is analytic in tone. His argument is not obviously convincing. Is a scientific criterion of sameness of meaning really needed? The verificationist theory of meaning was widely criticized, for the most part as self-refuting, by no one more effectively, perhaps, than by Popper, who based a new account of the nature of science on the thesis that falsifiability is a criterion, not of meaning, but of scientific status. The two most notable specimens of reductive analysis (the phenomenalist conception of material things as systems of appearances, actual and possible, and the behaviourist theory of states of mind as dispositions of human bodies to behave in certain ways in particular circumstances) were generally discarded, most thoroughly in the work of various Australian materialists, for instance D. M. Armstrong and J. J. C. Smart. They held that we have direct, if inherently fallible, awareness of material things and that the mental states of which we are aware in self-consciousness are in fact identical with brain-states which cause behaviour.

There is not much literal analysis in the work of prominent late twentieth-century practitioners of analytic philosophy such as Putnam and Nozick. But they think and write in the analytic spirit, respectful of science, both as a paradigm of reasonable belief and in conformity with its argumentative rigour, its clarity, and its determination to be objective.   A.Q.

*analysis; British philosophy today; verification principle; Oxford philosophy; reductionism.

Brand Blanshard, *Reason and Analysis* (London, 1962).
M. Dummett, *Origins of Analytic Philosophy* (Cambridge, Mass., 1994).
John Passmore, *Recent Philosophers* (London, 1985).
Bertrand Russell, *The Philosophy of Logical Atomism* (London, 1918).
Anders Wedberg, *History of Philosophy*, iii (Oxford, 1984).

analytic, transcendental: *see* transcendental analytic; Kant.

anamnesis. Recollection (Greek). Plato argued that some knowledge could have been acquired only by our immortal souls' acquaintance with the *Forms before our birth and not through sense-experience. 'Learning' is therefore anamnesis. In *Meno*, Socrates elicits geometrical knowledge from a slave-boy, while in *Phaedo* he argues that knowledge of concepts like equality, which are always imperfectly instantiated in this world, could come only from anamnesis.   R.CRI.

*memory.

anarchism. In its narrower meaning anarchism is a theory of society without state rule. In its broader meaning it is a theory of society without any coercive authority in any area—government, business, industry, commerce, religion, education, the family. Although some of its advocates trace its roots back to Greek thinkers—such as the Stoics, especially Zeno (336–264 BC)—or to the Bible, the modern work generally recognized as presenting the first articulation and defence of anarchism is William Godwin's *An Inquiry Concerning Political Justice and its Influence on General Virtue and Happiness* (1793). Pierre Joseph Proudhon (1809–65) is credited with being the first person to call himself an anarchist. There is no single defining position that all anarchists hold, and those considered anarchists at best share certain family resemblances.

Anarchist positions can be total, dealing with society as a whole and calling for a violent *revolution, or more restrictive in their views, dealing with smaller units or advocating piecemeal change. They also vary from the radical individualism of Max Stirner to the anarchist communism of Kropotkin, with the positions of Proudhon, Bakunin, and the anarcho-syndicalists falling in between.

Max Stirner (1806–56) is the most individualistic and 'egoistic' of the anarchist thinkers. For him the freedom of the individual is absolutely sovereign, and any infringement on that freedom is unjustifiable. He attacks not only the *State, government, law, and *private property, but also religion, the family, ethics, and love—all of which impose limits on individual action. He does not preclude human interaction but all associations are to be completely free and individuals enter them only for their own reasons and benefit. Leo Tolstoy (1828–1910), another somewhat atypical anarchist, adopted a type of religious anarchism, using the Bible to attack the rule of one person over another and the legitimacy of secular power. He finds in the Gospels a doctrine of peace and love that is sufficient for the organization of society and that is violated by governments, laws, police, armies, and private property. Proudhon's anarchism advocated a society based on small enterprises and skilled craftsmen who organized to form a co-operative community of equals. Michael Bakunin (1814–76), who favoured violent overthrow of the state, envisaged replacing it with a federation built from below on the basis of voluntary associations. Anarcho-syndicalism focused on trade unions, or syndicates, as the engine of change in society, for syndicates championed the interests of the workers and could serve as the basis for social organization after a successful revolution had overthrown the existing state structures. Peter Kropotkin (1842– 1921), as an anarcho-communist, held that the individual is essentially a social being who can fully develop only in a communist-type society, which precluded authoritarian rule and the special interests of dominant groups. Like other communists he advocated the abolition of private property and the development of a society built on common ownership of the means of production. For him the commune is the basic social unit, and communal needs are balanced with individual needs.

Despite their differences the proponents of anarchism generally tend to: (1) affirm freedom as a basic value; some add other values as well, such as justice, equality, or human well-being; (2) attack the state as inconsistent with freedom (and/or the other values); and (3) propose a programme for building a better society without the state. Most of the literature on anarchism considers the state an instrument of oppression, typically run by its leaders for their own benefit. Government is often, though not always, similarly attacked, as are exploitative owners of the means of production in a capitalistic system, despotic teachers, and over-dominant parents. By extension anarchists hold as unjustifiable any form of authoritarianism, which is the use of one's position of power for one's own benefit rather than for the benefit of those subject to authority. The anarchist emphasis on *freedom, *justice, and human *well-being springs from a positive view of human nature. Human beings are seen as for the most part capable of rationally governing themselves in a peaceful, co-operative, and productive manner.

Whereas the traditional role of the political theorist is to justify the existing structures of society, the role of the anarchist is to challenge these structures and to demand their justification prior to accepting them. In accord with the anarchists' view of the state as an instrument of oppression in the hands of a ruling class, they see law as simply the means by which that class defends its self-interest, and armies and police as the means the rulers use to enforce their will. The state so conceived has injustice built into it and hence is in principle unjustifiable. More-

over, the state is the major perpetrator of violence, and the cause of much of the oppression, social disorder, and other ills suffered by society. The anarchists differ on how to rid society of the state, violent revolution being the most drastic, and piecemeal change from below, often through education, the least radical.

The good society which forms part of the positive anarchist project is similarly an issue on which there is considerable disagreement. But most advocates of anarchism envisage a society to which the members voluntarily belong, which they are able to leave if they wish, and in which the members agree to the rules under which they live. Size and levels of complexity are not major issues, although the emphasis is usually on beginning with smaller units of self-determination and building on those.

Thus, anarchism does not preclude social organization, social order or rules, the appropriate delegation of authority, or even of certain forms of government, as long as this is distinguished from the state and as long as it is administrative and not oppressive, coercive, or bureaucratic. Anarchism maintains that all those who hold authority should exercise it for the benefit of those below them, and if they hold offices of authority they are accountable to those below them and recallable by them. The abolition of the state precludes not the organization of things but the domination of people. Most, though not all, anarchists acknowledge the importance of the moral law as the proper guide for social interaction, providing this is envisaged as compatible with the autonomy of the individual. Most anarchists accept a kind of democracy in which people are self-governed at all levels. The details of social organization are not to be set out in advance but are in part to be decided by those who are subject to them.

Although anarchists were politically active in Spain, Italy, Belgium, and France especially in the 1870s and in Spain during the Spanish Civil War, and although anarchists formed an anarcho-syndicalist union in the United States in 1905, there have been no significant, successful anarchist communities of any size.

Anarchism enjoyed a renaissance for a period in the 1960s and early 1970s in the writings of such proponents as Paul Goodman (1911–72), perhaps best known for his writings on education, and Daniel Guérin (1904–88), who develops a communitarian type of anarchism that builds on but goes beyond nineteenth-century anarchosyndicalism, which is now out of date.

As a political theory anarchism is not at present widely held; but it continues to serve as an important basis for the critique of authoritarianism and as a continuing reminder of the need to justify existing institutions.   R.DE G.

D. Guérin, *Anarchism*, tr. Mary Klopper (New York, 1970).
J. Joll, *The Anarchists*, 2nd edn. (London, 1979).
G. Woodcock, *Anarchism* (Harmondsworth, 1986).

Anaxagoras (500–428 BC). *Pre-Socratic philosopher. A native of Clazomenae in Asia Minor, he lived most of his life at Athens, where he was a friend of the democratic statesman Pericles. Rather unreliable sources say that he was ultimately exiled from Athens after a prosecution for impiety (his statement that the sun was a large lump of metal was allegedly the basis of the charge).

Like his contemporaries the early Atomists (Leucippus and Democritus), Anaxagoras re-thought the Milesian cosmological enterprise in the light of Eleatic methods and arguments, but without any wholesale acceptance of them.

On two cardinal points Anaxagoras went the opposite way to Atomism. (1) He postulated a material continuum (without void) with infinitely complex micro-structure. There were infinitely many fundamental kinds of matter, not further reducible and not interchangeable. *All* of these kinds of matter were present in *every* spatially continuous portion of matter, however small. Hence there were no places in which any type of matter existed unmixed with all the others. There was 'a portion of everything in everything'. This was in effect a 'field theory' (as opposed to the Atomists' 'particle theory'), exploiting the possibilities of arbitrarily small scales of size. The details are obscure and controversial. (2) His universe was dominated by teleology. The ordering of things was planned and initiated by Mind (*Nous*), which was conceived of both as a unified cosmic intelligence and as an explanation of human and animal intelligence. Both Plato and Aristotle praised Anaxagoras for his explicit assertion of the rule of Mind (Aristotle said 'he showed up like a sober man, as compared with his wild-talking predecessors'), but both complained that he gave only mechanistic explanations of particular phenomena.   E.L.H.

*atomism, physical; teleological explanation.

M. Schofield, *An Essay on Anaxagoras* (Cambridge, 1980).

Anaximander of Miletus (*fl. c.*550 BC). Associate of Thales and one of the three Milesian 'natural philosophers'. (*Pre-Socratic philosophy.) His monistic cosmology was based on the self-transformations of 'the Infinite', an infinitely extended being, living and intelligent. In his explanations, biological and legal analogies are used, and there is a striking appeal to symmetry (the earth stays at rest because it is symmetrically placed in the cosmos; so there is no reason why it should move in one direction rather than another).   E.L.H.

C. H. Kahn, *Anaximander and the Origins of Greek Cosmology* (New York, 1960).

Anaximenes of Miletus (*fl. c.*550 BC). The third of the troika of Milesian 'natural philosophers' (*Pre-Socratic philosophy). He proposed a cosmological theory in which the whole of the universe consisted of air in different degrees of density—the first attested attempt to explain qualitative differences in terms of quantitative ones, and one backed up by an appeal to everyday experience (air breathed from an open mouth feels warm, air breathed through pursed lips feels cold).   E.L.H.

J. Barnes, *The Presocratic Philosophers*, i (London, 1979), 38–47.

ancestral relation. A relation obtained through the following logical transformation of a given relation: The ancestral of a relation R holds between objects x and y if and only if either x bears R to y, or x bears R to some z_1 that itself bears R to y, or x bears R to some z_2 that bears R to a z_1 that bears R to y, or . . . Thus, 'ancestor' is the ancestral of 'parent', and 'less than' (restricted to natural numbers) is the ancestral of 'immediate predecessor'. Frege showed that the ancestral of a *relation can be explicitly defined, without ellipsis, within second-order logic.   A.GUP.

G. Boolos, 'Reading the *Begriffsschrift*', *Mind* (1985).

ancient philosophy. 'Ancient philosophy' is the conventional title, in Europe and the English-speaking academy, for the philosophical activities of the thinkers of the Graeco-Roman world. It includes a succession of philosophers who operated over a 1,000-year period from the middle of the first millennium BC to the middle of the first millennium AD—from Thales and the earliest Pre-Socratics to late Neoplatonists and Aristotelian commentators, such as Simplicius and Philoponus. Later thinkers in Europe (e.g. Scotus Eriugena) are normally assigned to the category *'medieval', as are Arabic philosophers such as Avicenna and Averroës, and also Jewish philosophers such as Gabriol and Maimonides. Contemporary philosophers from other cultures (e.g. Confucius, Buddha) are also not included.

Traditionally ancient philosophy is divided into four main periods: the *Pre-Socratic philosophers, Plato, Aristotle, the post-Aristotelian philosophers. Recently there has been a tendency to divide the last by adding a fifth phase of Christian and Neo-platonist philosophers. The most important of the ancient philosophers are Plato and Aristotle; and even though there has been a considerable shift of interest in the past thirty years in favour of the post-Aristotelians, it remains the case that the two fourth-century BC philosophers are the primary focus of interest, both to specialists and to students and the wider philosophical community. This is partly because their writings survive in extensive and accessible form, so that they can be studied and assessed for the quality of their argumentation as well as for their conclusions; it is also a recognition of the superior nature of their philosophical work.

In their different ways Plato and Aristotle look both backwards and forwards in philosophy. Each constructs his theorizing so as to encapsulate leading elements in the earlier tradition: Plato does this with impressionistic flair, Aristotle perhaps with more precision and historical accuracy. This retrospective work is intended to supersede the insights of preceding philosophers; and it largely succeeds in this. Thus the available options in ontology are summarized in Plato's *Sophist* as monism, dualism, or pluralism, and a commitment to the primacy either of perceptible body or of intelligible ideas. Aristotle discovers in earlier thought confused but recoverable traces of four distinct kinds of explanation, which correspond to his four kinds of cause—material, formal, efficient, and final. In these and many other ways Plato and Aristotle absorb what is philosophically valuable in Pre-Socratic thought, and they transmute it into something which has endured with greater vitality in the later philosophical tradition.

None the less, there are certain Pre-Socratic themes which Plato and Aristotle undervalue and which have been emphasized by contemporary philosophers. Heraclitus and Parmenides, in particular, were clearly very much concerned with the relations between language and thought and the world. Philosophers in the contemporary hermeneutical tradition (but also many others before them) have been interested in Parmenides' comments on the limits of the expressible; and Marxists and paraconsistent logicians have sought to develop Heraclitus' aphorisms on the contradictoriness of truth. Empedocles and Anaxagoras are scrutinized to see how they connected chemical analysis with mental causation.

While the concerns of Plato and Aristotle also exert great influence on the work of post-Aristotelian philosophers, these latter also develop a number of new themes. For example, there were substantial advances in propositional and modal logic, in speculation about the natural basis of epistemology, and in the philosophies of physics and of law. They also supplied important clarification of the philosophical issues involved in the debate over determinism and freedom. In ethics they were concerned with appropriate attitudes to animal suffering and to human death, in ways which anticipate recent themes in applied philosophy.

What are the main features of ancient philosophy? This 1,000-year period of Graeco-Roman philosophy has bequeathed certain central themes for later thinkers. It is incumbent on all philosophers to be aware of the precise way in which these problems were introduced into the subject, even though the later course of debate may have injected new directions or emphases. The key themes are these: the ontological specification of non-perceptible items (e.g. numbers, gods, universal kinds); the isolation of objective causes in the non-animate sphere of nature; the analysis and evaluation of patterns of reasoning and argument; the importance of understanding in the pursuit of the good life; the need to analyse the nature of the human person; the importance of the concept of justice in defining the nature of a political system; critical self-awareness regarding the content and manner of philosophical utterance; and many more.

The ancient philosophers created and laid much of the groundwork for later philosophical debate in the fields of ontology, epistemology, logic, hermeneutics, ethics, and political philosophy. They also established the crucial features of philosophical method—open-mindedness as to the agenda of problems, and rational progress through argument and debate.

While much of ancient philosophy runs with common sense, it also contains paradoxes and eccentricities. Among these are to be counted Plato's theory of Forms, according to which universal kinds or properties are actually separate from their instances, Aristotle's conception of God as concerned only with his own essence, and the Stoics' absolutist distinctions between good and bad.

Some themes are prominent in ancient philosophy which have become less so in the more recent history of the subject, while in the case of others it has been claimed that they were unknown or ignored by the ancient thinkers and only came to the fore in philosophy in the period since Descartes. Examples of the former are the significance of form in relation to the stuff of which a thing is made, and the idea that the most effective strategy for explaining natural change is through end-results (teleology). On the other hand, the modern philosophical themes of personal identity, the distinction between mind and body, and the contrast between first and second-order questions—in ethics and elsewhere—seem to be missing from the agenda of ancient philosophy. But these idiosyncrasies can be exaggerated. It would be prudent to assume that on these, as on other, topics there will be further research which reopens debate between ancient philosophers and their successors.

One of the most fertile fields of ancient philosophy was ethics. Here a central figure is Socrates, whose intellectually profound and persistent interest in the nature of the good life led him to penetrating comment on human knowledge and rationality. The constructive scepticism of Socrates has been a major determinant of subsequent philosophical method. Socrates has always been an emblem of the true philosopher; and this iconic tendency has become more pronounced in recent years. (It is sometimes reinforced by the fact that Socrates, who published nothing, could not have been 'assessed' by current league table methods). Aristotle's ethical work was strongly influenced by Socrates. He reacted against Socrates by emphasizing the importance of character and, as such, has inspired a recent revival of what is now called 'virtue ethics'. His theory of the ethical mean is particularly interesting to value-pluralists, who strive to avoid oversimplification in moral theory. Ancient moral philosophy reinforces the contemporary philosophical interest in applying ethical analysis to real life problems. The ancient philosophers always saw their theoretical interest as directed on practical matters. Their ethics is, therefore, applied as well as being theoretical.

A further way in which the habits of ancient philosophical thought connect with modern interests comes from the concept of dialectic. Contemporary philosophers are rediscovering the connection between analytical and dialectical philosophical styles. The roots of both lie in ancient philosophy, whose leading thinkers placed high value both on the pursuit of philosophical dialogue and on the analysis of complex and potentially ambiguous concepts. Philosophers who are concerned with hermeneutics have recently rediscovered the literary complexity of Plato's compositions; they have found philosophical significance in the ways in which different characters are portrayed as presenting the truth. This method has been applied to some of the most 'analytical' of his works, such as *Sophist*. Attention to the works of the major ancient

PLATO's status as the father of Western philosophy is owed not just to the fortunate preservation of his entire *œuvre* (unusual for an ancient philosopher) but to the exceptional richness, subtlety, breadth, and beauty of his writings.

ARISTOTLE first came to Plato's Academy as a teenager, and thirty years later founded a new school in Athens, the Lyceum, where he taught and wrote on all subjects: philosophy, logic, politics, rhetoric, literature, and the sciences. He was still regarded as the authority on these subjects 1,500 years later.

EPICURUS taught that pleasure is the only good, but the life of pleasure that he advocated was a sober one, guided by wisdom.

PLOTINUS, probably a Hellenic Egyptian by birth, settled in Rome in middle age, and spent the rest of his life teaching philosophy through informal discussion groups.

thinkers is an excellent antidote to the division of philosophy into sectarian factions which is still urged in some quarters.

The study of ancient philosophy is an important element in philosophy, which needs to be sustained at a level of suitable scholarly rigour. But there is a declining complement of qualified specialist academic staff, and a personnel crisis.   J.D.G.E.

*Aristotelianism; Neoplatonism; Platonism; Roman philosophy; Stoicism; Sceptics, ancient; Epicureanism; footnotes to Plato.

The nature of current work in ancient philosophy can be assessed from the following rather different kinds of material:

J. Barnes, *The Toils of Scepticism* (Cambridge, 1990).
W. K. C. Guthrie, *A History of Greek Philosophy*, 6 vols. (Cambridge, 1962–81).
T. H. Irwin, *Aristotle's First Principles* (Oxford, 1988).
M. M. McCabe, *Plato and his Predecessors* (Cambridge, 2000).
M. Nussbaum, *The Fragility of Goodness* (Cambridge, 1986).
R. Sorabji, *Animal Minds and Human Morals* (London, 1993).

ancient philosophy, relevance to contemporary philosophy: *see* footnotes to Plato.

and: *see* conjunction and disjunction.

Anderson, John (1893–1962). Anderson had more influence than anyone else on Australian philosophy, and the philosophy he taught was unlike anyone else's. (Heraclitus and Alexander were influences.) It put everything on one level: no God, no atomic ultimates, no substantial selves; everything just 'a set of interacting situations' occupying a region of space and time. Correspondingly, all truth is of one kind: there is no necessary truth; there is just being so.

Andersonian realism asserts the independence of knower and known, whatever the known. To regard a relation as at all constitutive of anything is a form of 'relativistic' confusion. Anderson is always hunting down relativistic confusion. He finds it, for example, in the obligatory. This is generated when a relation with one term suppressed—a requirer—is seen as a quality—requirement—of an action. The demolishing questions are: Who does the requiring? and What is his policy?   S.A.G.

John Anderson, *Studies in Empirical Philosophy* (Sydney, 1962) includes most of Anderson's writing.
J. L. Mackie, 'The Philosophy of John Anderson', *Australasian Journal of Philosophy* (1962).

Anderson and Belnap. Alan Ross Anderson (1925–73) and Nuel D. Belnap, Jr. (b. 1930) came together at Yale University in the late 1950s, the former as teacher, the latter as student. Belnap had returned from study in Europe with Robert Feys, who had interested him in Wilhelm Ackermann's seminal paper on '*strenge Implikation*' in the *Journal of Symbolic Logic* for 1956; Anderson was delighted to find a fellow enthusiast, and between them they began (little knowing what it would become) a programme of research into **'relevance logic'*.

Anderson's other work in modal logic, deontic logic, and philosophy of mind should not be forgotten; nor his dry wit and felicitous style. Equally, remember Belnap's short but seminal paper on 'Tonk, Plonk and Plink' (*Analysis* (1962)) giving the beginnings of an answer to Prior on whether logical connectives can be defined by the inferences they make valid; and his work on the logic of questions. Both men have worked effectively in joint research with a range of colleagues. Last but not least, we should not overlook the effect of both men as inspiring teachers, grandfathers of late twentieth-century philosophical logic through the influence of their pupils.   S.L.R.

A. R. Anderson, N. D. Belnap *et al.*, *Entailment: The Logic of Relevance and Necessity*, 2 vols. (Princeton, NJ, 1975, 1992).

Angst. A recurrent state of disquiet concerning one's life which Existentialists interpret as evidence that human life has a dimension which a purely naturalistic psychology cannot comprehend. The term was introduced by Kierkegaard, who held that *Angst* (usually translated here as 'dread') concerning the contingencies of fortune should show us that we can only gain a secure sense of our identity by taking the leap of faith and entering into a relationship with God. Heidegger uses the same term (here usually translated as 'anxiety') to describe a sense of unease concerning the structure of one's life which, because it does not arise from any specific threat, is to be diagnosed as a manifestation of our own responsibility for this structure. Sartre uses the term *angoisse* (usually translated as 'anguish') for much the same phenomenon as Heidegger describes.   T.R.B.

*existentialism; despair.

M. Heidegger, *Being and Time*, tr. J. MacQuarrie and E. Robinson (Oxford, 1962), sects. 40, 53.

animal consciousness. Whether animals have consciousness is a question that naturally arises in modern philosophy, which has been dominated in one way or another by Cartesian dualism. In my own case, it is suggested, I know that the bodily movements observed by others are accompanied by a mental life, that is hidden from them; but when I observe their 'behaviour', I can't be certain that they've got minds. Animals (and nowadays computers) appear to generate the same problem, except that denying them consciousness is felt to be less of an outrage to common sense.

Animals are of very different kinds, their behaviour varies, and some have lives closely interwoven with ours. Philosophers who treat animal consciousness as problematic are happy to say that their own dogs want taking for walks, or look guilty because they've been on the furniture. Descartes himself, however, steadfastly maintained that his dog was merely an elaborate clock-like mechanism. But he didn't actually take the dog apart to prove this.   C.W.

M. Bekoff and D. Jamieson (eds.), *Readings in Animal Cognition* (Cambridge, Mass., 1996).
Descartes, *Discourse on Method*, Part V.

animalism in personal identity. Animalists maintain that a human *person just *is* (identical with) a living human organism or human animal, in opposition to those philosophers who, because they believe that the persistence conditions of persons are psychological rather than biological in character, hold that a person is distinct from his or her living body. In defence of their position, animalists urge the plausibility of the view that I existed, as a human embryo, some weeks before I was the subject of any conscious mental states, and may well go on existing for a time after I cease to be such a subject. Against the animalist, it may be urged that if my intact and functioning brain were to be transplanted into the evacuated cranium of another human animal, I would acquire a new body rather than someone else acquiring a new brain. However, the animalist may perhaps agree, saying that in this case the animal that I am is first reduced to the size of its brain and is then supplied with a new set of body parts. E.J.L.

*personal identity.

E. Olson, *The Human Animal* (Cambridge, 1997).

animals. In Western ethics, non-human animals were until quite recent times accorded a very low moral status. In the first chapter of Genesis, God gives human beings dominion over the animals. In the Hebrew Bible, this dominion was moderated by some injunctions towards kindness—for example, to rest one's oxen on the sabbath. The Christian scriptures, however, are devoid of such suggestions, and Paul even reinterprets the injunction about resting one's oxen, insisting that the command is intended only to benefit humans. Augustine followed this interpretation, adding that Jesus caused the Gadarene swine to drown in order to demonstrate that we have no duties to animals. Aquinas denied that we have any duty of charity to animals, adding that the only reason for us to avoid cruelty to them is the risk that cruel habits might carry over into our treatment of human beings.

Descartes's views were even more hostile to animals than those of his Christian predecessors. He regarded them as machines like clocks, which move and emit sounds, but have no feelings. This view was rejected by most philosophers, but Kant went back to a view similar to that of Aquinas when he held that animals, not being rational or autonomous, were not ends in themselves, and so the only reason for being kind to them is to train our dispositions for kindness toward humans. It was not until Bentham that a major figure in Western ethics advocated the direct inclusion of the interests of animals in our ethical thinking.

The debate over the moral status of animals remained peripheral to philosophical thinking until the 1970s, when a spate of books and articles led to a vigorous and continuing debate. Peter Singer compared speciesism with racism and sexism, and urged that there is no good reason for refusing to extend the basic principle of equality—the principle of equal consideration of interests—to non-human animals. Singer argued specifically against factory farming and animal experimentation, and urged that, where there are nutritionally adequate alternatives to eating meat, the pleasures of our palate cannot outweigh the suffering inflicted on animals by the standard procedures of commercial farming; hence *vegetarianism is the only ethically acceptable diet. On animal experimentation, Singer urged that, in considering whether a given experiment is justifiable, we ask ourselves whether we would be prepared to perform it on an orphaned human being at a mental level similar to that of the proposed animal subject. Only if the answer was affirmative could we claim that our readiness to use the animal was not based on a speciesist prejudice against giving the interests of non-human animals a similar weight to the interests of members of our own species.

Other contemporary philosophers have reached similar, or even more uncompromising, conclusions on a different philosophical basis. Tom Regan, for example, argued that all animals—or at least mammals above a certain age—are 'subjects of a life' and therefore have basic *rights. Eating animals and performing harmful experiments on them are, he holds, violations of these rights.

In addition to giving rise to a heated philosophical debate, these writings are unique in modern academic philosophy in that they have sparked and continue to influence a popular movement. Major animal liberation and animal rights organizations have developed in many countries, taking their inspiration from the writings of academic philosophers like Singer and Regan, and have made many people more aware of the ethical issues involved in our relations with animals. P.S.

Ted Benton, *Natural Relations: Ecology, Animal Rights, and Social Justice* (London, 1993).

R. G. Frey, *Interests and Rights: The Case Against Animals* (Oxford, 1980).

D. Jamieson, *Morality's Progress: Essays on Humans, Other Animals, and the Rest of Nature* (Oxford, 2003).

Tom Regan, *The Case for Animal Rights* (Berkeley, Calif., 1983).

—— and Peter Singer (eds.), *Animal Rights and Human Obligations* (Englewood Cliffs, NJ, 1989).

Peter Singer, *Animal Liberation* (New York, 1975; 2nd edn. 1990).

animal souls. For Aristotle souls are general modes of functioning. A plant will have a soul because it feeds and reproduces; the soul of an animal will also cover the capacity to move and sense, and that of a person the capacity to think. Descartes substituted the idea of an immaterial *soul whose essence is abstract thought, excluding non-humans. So, he concludes, animals are machines with no feelings. (So for humans but not animals there is a chance of immortality.) But even if there are such souls it does not follow that non-humans do not feel, and thus that they lack souls in Aristotle's more reasonable sense. A.M.

Mary Midgley, *Beast and Man* (London, 1980).

Peter Singer, *Animal Liberation*, 2nd edn. (New York, 1990).

animal spirits. There is nothing spiritual about Descartes's animal spirits. In Cartesian physiology, they are the purely material medium for the transmission of nervous impulses in humans and animals. 'All the movements of the muscles and likewise all sensations, depend on the nerves, which are like little threads or tubes coming from the brain, and containing, like the brain itself, a certain very fine air or wind, which is called the "animal spirits" (*les esprits animaux*)' (*Passions of the Soul* (1649), art. 7). For the relationship between these pneumatic events and sensory awareness, Descartes had recourse to the pineal gland.   J.COT.

John Cottingham, *Descartes* (Oxford, 1986), ch. 5.

anima mundi. Latin for 'world-soul', an idea stemming from Plato's *Timaeus*, where the world is a living organism, endowed with a soul by the Demiurge. It explains the harmonious celestial motions and is a model for the restoration of harmony in the human soul. The idea was adopted by Stoicism and Plotinus, and later by Bruno, Goethe, Herder, and Schelling. It is akin to the 'world-spirit' (e.g. of Hegel), but this is more intellectual and is not (as the world-soul often is) distinct from, and subordinate to, God.   M.J.I.

F. M. Cornford, *Plato's Cosmology* (London, 1937).
F. A. Yates, *Giordano Bruno and the Hermetic Tradition* (Chicago, 1964).

anomalous monism. The view that the mental and the physical are two irreducibly different ways of describing and explaining the same objects and events. The position, like that of Spinoza, combines ontological *monism with conceptual *dualism. It holds that mental concepts, though supervenient on physical concepts, cannot be fully analysed or defined in physical terms, and claims that there are no strict *psychophysical laws.   D.D.

*supervenience; identity theory of mind.

D. Davidson, 'Mental Events', in *Essays on Actions and Events* (Oxford, 1980).

anomie. Breakdown of the conventions of everyday life; weakening of a society's collective self-image or social laws. The term derives from the Greek *nomos* (strictly, 'anything assigned or apportioned', 'that which one has in use or possession', but, derivatively, 'law', 'usage', 'custom'); so its etymology is suggestive of 'absence of law'. Anomic terror is the psychological state of individuals stripped of the mores which socially legitimate their death to self and other. *Durkheim argues that suicide rates increase during periods of anomie. The raising of philosophical questions arguably calls into question established world-views and partly deconditions the individual. If so, philosophy is partly conducive to anomie.   S.P.

Peter L. Berger and Thomas Luckmann, *The Social Construction of Reality* (Harmondsworth, 1967).
Emile Durkheim, *The Rules of Sociological Method*, tr. W. D. Halls, ed. Stephen Lukes (London, 1982).

Anscombe, G. E. M. (1919–2001). A distinguished pupil of Wittgenstein and one of his literary executors, responsible for editing and translating many of his posthumous publications. Her *Introduction to Wittgenstein's* Tractatus (1959) shed light on his first masterpiece. But Elizabeth Anscombe was also, in her own right, one of the most influential philosophers of the late twentieth century. Her 1957 book *Intention* initiated extensive discussion of intentional action and its explanation, and her 1958 essay 'Modern Moral Philosophy' reset the agenda for that subject. Her ethical writings, critical of contemporary trends, are informed by dogmatic Catholicism. Her numerous essays on metaphysics and philosophy of mind are critical of empiricism, challenging, for example, received views of causality and of the first-person pronoun. She was a tutor at Oxford, and later a professor at Cambridge, and was married to the philosopher Peter Geach.   P.M.S.H.

G. E. M. Anscombe, *Collected Philosophical Papers*, 3 vols. (Oxford, 1981).

Anselm of Canterbury, St (1033–1109). Benedictine monk, second Norman Archbishop of Canterbury, and philosophical theologian dubbed 'the Father of *Scholasticism'. Anselm is justly famous for his distinctive method ('faith seeking understanding'), his '*ontological' argument(s), and his classic articulation of the satisfaction theory of the *atonement. Better suited to philosophy and contemplation than to politics, Anselm possessed a subtlety and originality that rank him among the most penetrating medieval thinkers (along with Augustine, Aquinas, Duns Scotus, and William of Ockham) and explain the perennial fascination with his ideas.

Like Augustine a Christian Platonist in metaphysics, Anselm centres his proofs of God's existence around the value theory intuition that something is too good not to be real! In *Monologion*, he offers *cosmological arguments that the single source of all goods is Good through Itself (*per se*) and hence supremely good. It exists through itself and is the self-sufficient source of everything else. In *Proslogion*, Anselm reasons that a being greater than which is inconceivable exists in the intellect because even a fool understands the phrase when he hears it; but if it existed in the intellect alone, a greater could be conceived which existed in reality. This supremely valuable object is essentially whatever it is better to be—other things being equal—than not to be, and so living, wise, powerful, true, just, blessed, immaterial, immutable, eternal, even the paradigm of sensory goods—beauty, harmony, sweetness, and pleasing texture! Yet, *God is not compounded from a plurality of excellences, but supremely simple, 'wholly and uniquely, entirely and solely good' (*omne et unum, totum et solum bonum*), a being more delightful than which is inconceivable.

Not only is God the efficient cause of the being and well-being of everything else, but also the exemplar of all created natures, whose value depends upon their degree of similarity to the Supreme Good. Hence, it is better to be human than horse, to be horse than wood, even though every creature is 'almost nothing' in comparison with God. As fundamentally ways of striving into God, created natures have a *teleological structure, a that-for-which-they-were-made (*ad quod factum est*) and for which their powers were given by God. Anselm explains in *De veritate* how teleology gives rise to *obligation: since creatures *owe* their being and well-being to their divine cause, so they *owe* it to God to praise him by being the most excellent handiwork (truest instances of their kinds) they can. Obstacles aside, non-rational creatures fulfil this obligation and 'act rightly' by natural necessity; rational creatures, freely and spontaneously when they exercise their powers of reason and will to conform to God's purpose in creating them. Thus, the goodness of an individual creature depends upon its natural end (i.e. what sort of imitation of divine nature it aims for), and its rightness (in exercising its natural powers to pursue its end). By contrast, God as absolutely independent owes nothing to anything and so has no obligations to creatures.

Anselm advertises the optimism of his *ontology in *De casu diaboli* by arguing that since the Supreme Good and Supreme Being are identical, every being is good and every good a being. Corollary to this, because all genuine (metaphysically basic) powers are given to enable a being to pursue its natural *telos* and so to be the best being it can, all genuine powers are optimific, essentially aim at goods, while *evils are metaphysically marginalized as merely incidental side-effects of their operation, involving some lack of co-ordination among powers or between them and the surrounding context. Accordingly, divine omnipotence properly speaking excludes corruptibility, passibility, or the 'ability' to lie, because the latter involve defects and/or powers in other things to obstruct the flourishing of the corruptible, passible, or potential liar. Ultimately, Anselm qualifies the other Augustinian thesis—that evil is a privation of being, the absence of good in something that properly ought to have it (e.g. blindness in normally sighted animals, injustice in humans or angels)—by recognizing certain disadvantages (e.g. pain and suffering) as positive beings.

Anselm's innovative *action theory begins teleologically with the observation that rational creatures were made for a happy immortality enjoying God and to that end given the powers of reason to make accurate value judgements and will to love accordingly. While freedom and imputability of choice are essential and permanent features of all rational beings, freedom cannot be defined as the power to sin and the power not to sin because sin is an evil at which no metaphysically basic power can aim. Rather, for Anselm, freedom is the power to preserve *justice for its own sake. Only spontaneous actions that have their source in the agent itself are imputable. Since creatures do not have their natures from themselves but from God, they cannot act spontaneously by the necessity of their natures. To make it possible for them to become just *somehow* of themselves, God endows them with two motivational drives towards goodness—an affection for the advantageous (*affectio commodi*) or tendency to will things

for the sake of their benefit to the agent itself; and an affection for justice (*affectio iustitiae*) or tendency to will things because of their own intrinsic value—which they can co-ordinate (by letting the latter temper the former) or not. The good angels, who upheld justice by not willing some advantage possible for them but forbidden by God for that time, can no longer sin by willing more advantage than God wills for them, because God wills their maximum as a reward. Moreover, because they now know (what couldn't have been predicted apart from experience or revelation) that God punishes sin, willing more happiness than God wills them to will can no longer even *appear* advantageous. Creatures who sin by willing advantage inordinately lose both uprightness of will and their affection for justice, and hence the ability to temper their pursuit of advantage or to will the best goods. Anselm holds that it would be unjust to restore justice to angels who desert it. But animality both makes human nature weaker and opens the possibility of redemption.

Anselm's argument for the necessity of the Incarnation plays out the dialectic of justice and mercy featured in *Proslogion*, chs. 9–11, and characteristic of his prayers. God is the heavenly patron-king, who awards all creatures the status of clients. Justice requires that humans make all of their choices and actions conform to his will. Failure to render what is owed insults God's honour and makes the offender liable to satisfaction. Since dishonouring God is worse than destroying countless worlds, the satisfaction due for even the smallest sin is incommensurate with any created good. Because it would be maximally indecent for God to overlook such a great offence, and only God can do or be immeasurably deserving, depriving the creature of its honour (through eternal frustration of its end) seems the only way to balance the scales. Yet, justice also forbids that God's purposes be thwarted through created resistance, while divine mercy destined humans for immortal beatific intimacy with God. Moreover, biological nature (lacked by angels) makes humans come in families, and justice permits an offence by one family member to be compensated by another. Anselm assumes that all actual humans descended from Adam and Eve, and concludes that Adam's race can make satisfaction for sin, if God becomes a family member and discharges the debt.

Anselm's method reflects his estimate of *human nature and integrates the dynamics of monastic prayer with anticipations of the scholastic *quaestio*. If human destiny is beatific intimacy with God, ante-mortem human vocation is to strive into God with all of our powers—reason as well as emotions and will. Because the subject matter—God—is too difficult for us, permanently partially beyond reach, and because human powers have been damaged by sin, our task presupposes considerable education. The holistic discipline of faith tutors us, training our souls away from 'stupid', 'silly' questions for right-headed fruitful inquiry. In the intellectual dimension, human duty is not the passive appropriation of authority, but faith seeking to understand what it believes through questions, objections, measuring contrasting positions with arguments. Likewise noteworthy are Anselm's sharp attention to proper versus improper linguistic usage and his subtle treatments of metaphysical and deontological modalities. Where logic and semantics are concerned, Anselm was as up to date as it was possible for an eleventh-century European to be. But his own philosophy subsumes both school-book discussions and his own innovations under metaphysical value theory, accords them significance within his larger project of probing the semantics of the Divine Word, Truth Itself!   M.M.A.

*teleological explanation.

Anselm of Canterbury, *The Major Works*, ed. B. Davies and G. Evans (Oxford, 1998).
G. R. Evans, *Anselm and Talking about God* (Oxford, 1978).
D. P. Henry, *The Logic of Saint Anselm* (Oxford, 1967).
F. S. Schmitt, *Sancti Anselmi Opera Omnia*, 6 vols. (Edinburgh, 1946–61).
R. W. Southern, *Saint Anselm: A Portrait in a Landscape* (Cambridge, 1990).

anthropic principle. A principle asserting that the universe must have certain features given that human observers exist. In *cosmology the weak anthropic principle asserts that we can observe only universes that allow the development of cognitive agents similar to humans. The weak principle is not trivial; for example, it places limits on how young the universe can be. More controversially, the strong anthropic principle asserts that various coincidences in the values of physical constants are explained by the fact that those values are essential for the existence of humans. Anthropic principles have played an important role in alternatives to theological arguments from design, but they have also exposed how improbable are the coincidences required for human life.   P.H.

John D. Barrow and Frank J. Tipler, *The Anthropic Cosmological Principle* (Oxford, 1986).

anthropology, philosophical. Anthropology, the 'study of man', goes back to the beginnings of philosophy. The term 'anthropology' was also used by, for example, Kant and Hegel to denote a specific field of philosophy. Kant's *Anthropology from a Pragmatic Point of View* (1798; tr. The Hague, 1974) deals not with physiological anthropology, the study of 'what nature makes of man', but with pragmatic anthropology, with 'what man as a freely acting entity makes of himself or can and should make of himself'. Hegel applies the term 'anthropology' to the study of the 'soul', the subrational aspects of the human psyche that do not yet involve awareness of external objects. But philosophical anthropology came into its own only in the wake of German idealism. For '*anthrōpos*', 'man', contrasts, in this context, not only with 'God', but also with 'soul', 'mind', 'spirit', 'thought', 'consciousness', words denoting the mental (or transcendental) and intellectual aspect of man that the idealists tended to stress. Anthropology is to study not some favoured aspect of man, but man as such, man as a whole biological, acting, thinking,

etc. being. It was in this spirit that Feuerbach called his own philosophy 'anthropology'.

The term 'philosophical anthropology' (in contrast to the empirical sciences of 'physical' and 'cultural' anthropology) was used by Scheler to describe his enterprise at a time when his allegiance to *phenomenology was waning. The new discipline is given urgency, Scheler argued, by the variety of apparently incommensurable conceptions of man now available to us. These are: (1) the Judaeo-Christian account of man in terms of original sin and the fall from paradise; (2) the Greek and Enlightenment conception of man as a creature qualitatively distinguished from all other animals by his divine spark of reason; (3) the modern scientific conception of man as no more than a highly developed animal. Scheler also mentions two other variants: (4) man is a biological dead-end, his life and vitality sapped by 'spirit', science, and technology (Klages and Nietzsche), and (5) once relieved of the suffocating tutelage of God, man can take his fate into his own hands and rise to the heights of a superman (Nicolai Hartmann and again Nietzsche). In his main work on anthropology, *Man's Place in Nature* (1928; tr. New York, 1961), Scheler gives an account of the biological, intellectual, and religious aspects of man ('life' and 'spirit'), attempting to combine what is true in all earlier conceptions. Philosophical anthropology should, he argues, show how all the 'works of man—language, conscience, tools, weapons, the state, leadership, the representational function of art, myths, religion, science, history, and social life—arise from the basic structure of human nature'. In *Man and History* (1926), he argued that different conceptions of man give rise to different conceptions of history, but that one of the tasks of anthropology is to give (in part to liberate ourselves from inherited preconceptions about man) a 'history of man's self-consciousness', that is, a history of man's ways of conceiving man. He did not live to complete more than a fraction of these tasks, but Helmuth Plessner, beginning with his *Man and the Stages of the Organic* (1929), attempted to give a similarly comprehensive and unitary account of man, both as a biological and as a rational creature.

Scheler regarded anthropology as an essential foundation for the social, historical, and psychological sciences. To this extent he is at odds with Husserl's phenomenology, which purports to provide *the* foundation for all science. It is less clear that Husserl was correct in associating anthropology with psychologism, the attempt to justify logical and mathematical laws by regarding them as generalizations about human psychology. (Husserl's 1931 lecture 'Phenomenology and Anthropology' mentions only Dilthey by name, but is also directed against Scheler and Heidegger.) For firstly, Scheler's anthropology is not much concerned with *epistemology*, the justification of our beliefs, and secondly, he argued that values are wholly objective, regardless of the historical and cultural variations in the degree and mode of our access to them. (A more recent philosophical anthropologist, Arnold Gehlen (1904–76), regards values and truth as cultural products.)

Heidegger has a close affinity to Scheler's anthropology, but apart from (officially, at least) rejecting the presupposition-laden term 'man' (*Mensch*) in favour of *Dasein*, his central question is not 'What is man?' and 'What is man's place in the nature of things?' but 'What is being?' He argued that the nature and scope of philosophical anthropology and the grounds for assigning it a central place in philosophy are wholly unclear. These matters can be clarified not within philosophical anthropology, but only in a more fundamental discipline, namely 'fundamental ontology'.   M.J.I.

A. Gehlen, *Der Mensch: seine Natur und seine Stellung in der Welt* (Leipzig, 1940).

M. Heidegger, *Kant and the Problem of Metaphysics*, tr. J. S. Churchill (Bloomington, Ind., 1962).

H. Plessner, *Laughter and Weeping*, tr. J. S. Churchill and M. Grene (Evanston, Ill., 1970).

anti-communism. *Communism aims for a situation in which every individual will be free to fulfil his or her potential, and to live on an equal footing with everyone else. But its chosen means is the centralized control of the means of production, distribution, and much else besides. Anti-communism points to the inevitable tension amounting at times to a contradiction between *freedom and organization, and particularly to the manifold abuses of organizational power and to the lack of any compensating material or moral success in actually existing forms of communism. Given that philosophy never flourished freely under communist rule, communism has nevertheless been surprisingly well received by philosophers, as by other intellectuals. The strident and illiberal anti-communism of Senator McCarthy and his Un-American Activities Committee, which offended liberals as well as those who were socialists by conviction, may be part of the explanation, though communism also appeals to the perennial temptation of intellectuals to seek to create a rationally ordered society from scratch. There have been notable exceptions. Bertrand Russell recommended using the atomic bomb on the Soviet Union in the 1940s. During the same period Popper and Hayek mounted impressive intellectual critiques of communism, showing that communistic regimes were bound to be oppressive and inefficient, however admirable their intentions. Their writings were politically influential in the Reagan–Thatcher years in stiffening Western anti-communist resolve.   A.O'H.

*liberty and equality; persecution of philosophers; conservatism; liberalism.

F. A. Hayek, *The Road to Serfdom* (London, 1944).

K. R. Popper, *The Open Society and its Enemies* (London, 1945).

anti-individualism: *see* externalism; individualism.

antilogism. Christine Ladd-Franklin's term for the inconsistent triad consisting of the premises and negated conclusion of a valid syllogism. Any two of the three will validly yield the contradictory of the third. Indirect reduction of other figures of the syllogism to the first uses the negated conclusion with one of the original premises to yield a valid first-figure syllogism whose conclusion is the contradictory of the remaining original premiss. The antilogism from the second-figure syllogism 'All philosophers are mendacious, some scientists are not mendacious; so some scientists are not philosophers' is the first two sentences plus 'All scientists are philosophers'. But 'All philosophers are mendacious' and 'All scientists are philosophers' are the premises of a valid first-figure syllogism whose conclusion is 'All scientists are mendacious'—the negation of the remaining sentence in our antilogism. Thus the second-figure syllogism (Baroco) is valid if the corresponding first-figure syllogism (Barbara) is.   J.J.M.

*Barbara, Celarent.

R. Sylvan and J. Norman, 'Routes in Relevant Logic', in R. Sylvan and J. Norman (eds.), *Directions in Relevant Logic* (Dordrecht, 1989).

antinomies. An antinomy—literally 'conflict of laws'—is usually described as a *contradiction or as a *paradox (from the Greek meaning 'contrary to opinion'), though both these general senses are now probably outdated.

Within philosophy, the term is most commonly used to refer to the apparent contradictions which Kant found in speculative *cosmology—our thought about the world as a whole. In the *Critique of Pure Reason*, Kant set out the antinomies as four pairs of propositions, each consisting of a thesis, and its supposed contradictory, or antithesis. In each case there are, he thinks, apparently compelling reasons for accepting both thesis and antithesis.

The thesis of the first antinomy is that the world has a beginning in time and is spatially limited. The thesis of the second is that every composite substance consists of simple substances. The thesis of the third is that there is a kind of causality related to free will and independent of the causality of laws of nature; its antithesis is that freedom is an illusion. The thesis of the fourth is that there exists either as part of the world or as its cause an absolutely necessary being.

Kant draws a distinction between the first two antinomies, which he calls 'mathematical', and the second two, which he calls 'dynamical'. The feature common to the first two is the idea of *infinity: each presents us with arguments purporting to show that the world is in a certain respect finite (in size, in age, in divisibility) together with arguments purporting to show that it cannot be. The dynamical antinomies involve the notion of causality.

In Kant's view the antinomies are not genuine contradictions: he describes the opposition between thesis and antithesis as dialectical (the opposition between genuine contradictions he calls analytical). The antinomies arise from the way in which answering a certain type of question—for example, by citing a phenomenon as the cause of phenomenon—generates a further question of the same type: in this case, the question what is the cause of the cause? We appear driven, by what Kant calls 'the demand of reason for the unconditioned', to seek an answer for which the further question does not arise. But, Kant says, nothing in our experience could provide us with that kind of answer.

How does Kant resolve the problem? This is what he says about the first antinomy: 'Since the world does not exist in itself, independently of the regressive series, it exists *in itself* neither as an *infinite* whole nor as a *finite* whole.' The suggestion may be that the antinomies arise from our thinking of the world as an object, of which it would make sense to ask how big it is or where it comes from. But—not clearly distinguished from this by Kant— is the idea that the antinomies arise from our attributing to the world 'in itself' features which are properly seen as determined by our thought. Seen in this way, the antinomies underpin his transcendental idealism.

Kant says that this diagnosis of the first antinomy— which requires that both thesis and antithesis be false— applies to the others. But he also suggests that in the case of the dynamical antinomies both thesis and antithesis may be *true*. In the case of the third antinomy the fact that the causality involved in free action is, as Kant thinks, beyond any possible experience does not mean that the idea of such causality is senseless, a doctrine which he admits is 'bound to appear extremely subtle and obscure' when stated in this abstract way.

More recently Quine has defined an antinomy as a paradox which 'produces a self-contradiction by accepted ways of reasoning. It establishes that some tacit and trusted pattern of reasoning must be made explicit and henceforward be avoided or revised.' Such revision, Quine says, involves 'nothing less than a repudiation of part of our conceptual heritage'.   M.C.

J. F. Bennett, *Kant's Dialectic* (Cambridge, 1974).
I. Kant, *Critique of Pure Reason*, tr. N. Kemp Smith (London, 1929).
W. V. Quine, *The Ways of Paradox* (New York, 1966), ch. 1.
P. F. Strawson, *The Bounds of Sense* (London, 1966).

Antiochus of Ascalon (*c*.130 BC–68/67 BC). Precursor of the movement in philosophy that became known as Middle Platonism. Born in the Palestinian town of Ascalon, Antiochus travelled to Athens around 110 BC to study with Philo of Larisa, head of the New *Academy. After a long period of discipleship Antiochus rejected Philo's scepticism in favour of a constructive interpretation of Plato. The basis for Antiochus' defence of the possibility of knowledge was Stoic epistemology. Since, however, Stoic epistemology is rooted in materialism, Antiochus was led to the conflation of Stoic and Platonic accounts in physics, theology, and psychology. Later Platonists, inspired by Antiochus' efforts to recover Platonic authentic teaching, were nevertheless largely unimpressed by the Stoicizing of Plato.

Cicero attended Antiochus' lectures in Athens in 79/78 BC. His own view of ancient Greek philosophy is greatly influenced by Antiochus' syncretic approach. His writings are our principal source for Antiochus' own doctrines.
          L.P.G.

*Stoicism.

John Dillon, *The Middle Platonists 80 BC to AD 220* (Ithaca, NY, 1977).

anti-realism: *see* realism.

anti-Semitism is sometimes treated as a continuous history of prejudice and *discrimination extending from the desecration of the Second Temple in 135 BC through to the Holocaust. But in Hellenistic times the Gentiles, who were engaged in commerce, persecuted the Jews, who were farmers. As the official religion of medieval Europe, Christianity, originally a Jewish sect, legitimated a pattern of persecution by reclassifying the Jews as 'usurers' and 'Christ murderers'. Modern anti-Semitism has underwritten the political vision of movements portraying themselves as the enemies of both capitalism and communism, which are equally 'Jewish'. This is why Bebel called anti-Semitism the 'socialism of fools', a simple-minded alternative to the politics of class. The great logician Frege thought it 'a misfortune that there are so many Jews in Germany', but that legislating against them is difficult without a 'distinguishing mark by which one can recognise a Jew for certain'. Thus anti-Semitism, like racism generally, maintains its grip on those who cannot even be sure whom they hate.   C.W. and M.C.

*race.

J.-P. Sartre, *Réflexions sur la Question Juive* (Paris, 1946); tr. G. J. Becker under the title *Anti-Semite and Jew* (New York, 1962).

Antisthenes (5th–4th century BC). He was an independent-minded philosopher, a pupil of Socrates and a near-contemporary of Plato, who exercised influence on Diogenes the Cynic. Despite much speculation, little is known about his philosophical ideas. He was interested in the relation between names and things, and he argued against the possibility of contradiction. It has been conjectured that he contributed to the riddles about error which troubled Plato. Information about his writings and ideas are collected in F. D. Caizzi, *Antisthenis Fragmenta* (Varese, 1966).   J.D.G.E.

*Cynics.

antitheism. Attitude of opposition or metaphysical revolt against God, conceived as personal, omnipotent, and omniscient, as in traditional theism. This rebellion is mostly literary or symbolic, sometimes articulated as fictitious myths or representations of nightmares. It is based on hurt, pride, moral outrage, and a desire for self-determination and conceptual autonomy. Antitheism can be regarded as a transition to agnosticism, atheism, as well as tragic individualism. It is more common in French and German philosophy than in the Anglo-American tradition.   R.V.

A. Camus, *The Myth of Sisyphus and Other Essays*, tr. J. O'Brien (New York, 1991).

antithesis: *see* thesis and antithesis.

apeiron. The earliest known philosophical term. Literally 'without limit', it is used by Anaximander for the material out of which everything arises. Plato in the *Philebus* applies it to things signified by words which, like 'hot' and 'large', admit of comparatives, but these for him play the same material role. Aristotle, followed by Hellenistic writers, uses it to express the notions of infinite quantity and infinite progression.   w.c.

J.C.B. Gosling, *Plato's* Philebus (Oxford, 1975).

apodeictic. Literally, demonstrative. Traditionally applied to propositions, whether or not used in a *demonstration, that are marked with a sign of necessity or impossibility, especially in connection with Aristotle's modal syllogistic; e.g. 'π is *necessarily* irrational', 'What's blue *must* be coloured', 'Spring *can't* follow summer', 'If it's a giraffe, it's *bound* to have a long neck'.   c.a.k.

    *necessity, logical.

H. W. B. Joseph, *An Introduction to Logic*, 2nd edn. (Oxford, 1916).

apodosis: *see* protasis.

Apollonian: *see* Dionysian and Apollinian.

aporia, or 'apory' in English, is the cognitive perplexity posed by a group of individually plausible but collectively inconsistent propositions. For example, in Pre-Socratic times, philosophers were involved with the following incompatible beliefs: (1) Physical *change occurs. (2) Something persists unaffected throughout physical change. (3) Matter does not persist unaffected through change. (4) Matter (in its various guises) is all there is. There are four ways out of this inconsistency: (1-denial) Change is a mere illusion (Zeno and Parmenides). (2-denial) Nothing whatever persists unaffected through physical change (Heraclitus). (3-denial) Matter does persist unaffected throughout physical change, albeit only in *the small*—in its 'atoms' (the Atomists). (4-denial) Matter is not all there is; there is also *form* by way of geometric structure (Pythagoras), or arithmetical proportion (Anaxagoras), or abstract form (Plato). To overcome aporetic inconsistency, we must give up at least one of the theses involved in the inconsistency. There will always be different alternatives here and logic as such can enforce no resolution. The pervasiveness of apories throughout human inquiry has led sceptics ancient and modern to propose abandoning the entire cognitive enterprise, preferring cognitive vacuity to risk of error.   n.r.

    *inconsistent triad; Pyrrhonism; Sceptics, ancient.

G. Matthews, *Socratic Perplexity and the Nature of Philosophy* (Oxford, 1999).
Nicholas Rescher, *The Strife of Systems* (Pittsburgh, 1985).
Sextus Empiricus, *Outlines of Pyrrhonism.*

appearance and reality. The conviction that it must be possible to make the distinction between appearance and reality drives constructive and critical projects not only in epistemology, metaphysics, and philosophy of science, where the adequacy of our representations and our ability to distinguish between the veridical and the illusory is in question, but in also ethics and political philosophy, where true and apparent good, justice and its semblance, are in question. Though philosophers have occasionally tried to argue that *all is *illusion* or that *there are only appearances*, this line of argument becomes quickly mired in paradox.

The appearance–reality problem is supported to a large extent by a single argument, the 'argument from illusion', which points to the subjective indistinguishability of states of cognitive or perceptual illusion and veridical perception or knowledge. The problem then becomes one of determining a truth-conferring criterion, e.g. coherence or intersubjectivity, or conceding that all appearances are equally veridical (*phenomenalism). Other arguments, such as the variability of perceptual qualities and their evident dependence on the state and health of the observer's nervous system, have been thought to lead to the conclusion that reality in itself can be neither perceived nor known. But this conclusion is scarcely acceptable in light of (*a*) the causal nature of perception and belief; (*b*) the existence of reasonably habile procedures for testing perceptions and beliefs; and (*c*) the likelihood that perception and cognition are evolutionary adaptations to the real world. For some time it was believed—under the influence of J. L. Austin's *Sense and Sensibilia* (1962)—that careful attention to the contexts of use of various locutions involving 'seeming', 'looking', and 'appearing' would reveal that no profound philosophical problem involving appearance and reality could be formulated. But these hopes have not been rewarded. No such taxonomizing can prevent the formulation of such unanswerable questions as 'At what distance must an object be from a perceiver in order for its appearance to equal its real size?'

The internal, private, conditioned nature of appearances can be reconciled with the external, public, unconditioned nature of reality, H. J. Robinson has proposed, only if 'theoretical perception', the process involving lightwaves and anatomical structures such as the retina and layers of brain cells, is distinguished from 'empirical perception'—our immediate apprehension of objects, qualities, and relations. Perceivers, Robinson argues, must each possess two bodies, one real and one apparent. Real bodies—human as well as non-human—which are strictly speaking imperceptible—are the cause of apparent bodies, which alone can be empirically perceived and which represent them.

Historically, the appearance–reality distinction has been understood as having moral/theological overtones: this was pointed out by Nietzsche, who found all otherworldliness 'decadent'. The intuition that what we call the real world is only a dim reflection, or a shadow, a semblance of the real world, is in any case an old one, associated in Western philosophy with the name of Plato and with ascetic philosophies of the East. F. H. Bradley in *Appearance and Reality* (1893) argued in keeping with this tradition that the appearances of time, space, and matter are riddled with inconsistencies, while reality is coherent and one. Meanwhile, the notion that appearances are a dim and confused reflection of something more robust and contradiction-free which is above, beneath, or behind them has suffered somewhat in modern philosophy. From Descartes onwards, the real or noumenal world is thought of as the colourless and largely qualityless source from which the world we experience emanates. Kant's 'thing-in-itself' is a mere place-holder, which allows him nevertheless to distinguish, in the *Critique of Pure Reason*, between those appearances which have 'objective reality' and furnish the subject-matter of our empirical knowledge and the mere appearances which we decry as illusion. CATH.W.

J. J. Gibson, *The Perception of the Visual World* (Boston, 1950).
M. K. Munitz, *The Question of Reality* (Princeton, NJ, 1990).
H. J. Robinson, *Renascent Rationalism* (Toronto, 1975).

apperception. Leibniz's term for inner awareness or *self-consciousness. Leibniz held that it was possible to perceive without thereby being conscious, and that it is the exercise of apperception which marks the difference between conscious awareness and unconscious perception. Kant draws a distinction between inner sense, or empirical apperception, and what he calls 'the transcendental unity of apperception'. Where the former involves the actual exercise of introspection, the latter is the interconnectedness of all thought which is, according to Kant, the formal pre-condition of any thought or experience of an objective world, and also of empirical apperception itself. M.G.F.M.

   *introspection.

Paul Guyer, *Kant and the Claims of Knowledge* (Cambridge, 1987).

applied ethics. Since the 1960s academic work in ethics dealing with practical or 'applied' questions has become a major part of both teaching and research in ethics. This development is a revival of an ancient tradition. Greek and Roman philosophers discussed how we are to live, and die, in quite concrete terms. Medieval writers were concerned with whether it is always wrong to kill, *abortion, and when going to *war is justifiable. Hume wrote an essay defending suicide, and Kant was interested in finding a means to perpetual peace. In the nineteenth century all the major Utilitarian philosophers—Bentham, Mill, and Sidgwick— wrote extensively in applied ethics.

It is, then, the first part of twentieth-century ethics that was aberrant in disregarding applied ethics, rather than the later part which took up the field with enthusiasm. In part, the earlier reluctance to deal with applied issues was due to the influence of *Logical Positivism, with its implication that ethical statements were nothing more than the evincing of emotions. The role of the moral philosopher was therefore restricted to the meta-ethical task of analysing the meaning of the moral terms. This view was finally rejected only when the students of the 1960s demanded courses that were more relevant to the great issues of the day, which in the United States included the civil rights movement and the war in Vietnam. Hence racial equality, the justifiability of war, and *civil disobedience were among the first issues in applied ethics to be discussed by academic philosophers. Sexual equality and *environmental ethics followed soon after, as the women's liberation movement and the environmental movement gained strength. Interestingly, in the case of the animal liberation movement, the direction of causation ran the other way: it was the writings of academic philosophers on the ethics of our treatment of animals that triggered the rise of the modern animal liberation movement.

Applied ethics has now developed several separate areas of specialization, each with its own centres for research and teaching, specialized journals, and a rapidly growing literature. Perhaps the most prominent is *bioethics, which deals with ethical questions arising in the biological sciences and in the field of health care. This includes both perennial issues like *euthanasia and new questions such as *fertilization *in vitro*. Whereas thirty years ago very few medical or nursing undergraduates took courses in ethics, today such courses are widespread.

The moral status of *animals has been an important topic in recent applied ethics, with ramifications for farming, animal experimentation, and the fur industry. Similarly, increasing concern with the environment has led many to ask if traditional Western ethics is so deeply 'human chauvinist' that it needs to be replaced with an ethic that takes all living things, and perhaps even ecological systems, as the bearers of value. Attempts to develop such ethics have led to lively debates in which new questions have been raised about the limits of ethics.

*Business ethics is another area of applied ethics that has found a receptive audience, and is now taught in many institutions where no ethics courses were to be found a short time ago. Many large corporations, having been caught out in dubious activities such as bribing overseas officials, or infringing regulations for trading in securities, now perceive a need for greater ethical sensitivity among their employees.

There are, of course, still some who doubt the value of applied ethics. They may be sceptical about ethics in general. Often they deny that reason has a role to play in ethics. Yet anyone reading the literature in applied ethics will have to concede that at least some of these works are fine examples of applying reason to practical problems; and since many of these problems are unavoidable, it seems clear that it is better for us to reason about them, to the best of our ability, than not to reason at all. P.S.

   *vegetarianism.

H. LaFollette (ed.), *The Oxford Handbook of Practical Ethics* (Oxford, 2003).
Peter Singer (ed.), *Applied Ethics* (Oxford, 1986).

applied ethics, autonomy in: *see* autonomy in applied ethics.

a priori and a posteriori. These are terms primarily used to describe two species of propositional knowledge but also, derivatively, two classes of *propositions or *truths, namely, those that are knowable a priori and a posteriori respectively. Knowledge is said to be a priori when it does not depend for its authority upon the evidence of experience, and a posteriori when it does so depend.

Whether knowledge is a priori is quite a different question from whether it is *innate. Mathematics provides the most often cited examples of a priori knowledge, but most of our mathematical knowledge is no doubt *acquired* through experience even though it is *justifiable* independently of experience. Kant and others have held that a priori knowledge concerns only necessary truths while a posteriori knowledge concerns only contingent truths, but Kripke has challenged this assumption.   E.J.L.

P. Boghossian and C. Peacocke (eds.), *New Essays on the A Priori* (Oxford, 2000).

P. K. Moser (ed.), *A Priori Knowledge* (Oxford, 1987).

Aquinas, St Thomas (1224/5–74). The greatest of the *medieval philosopher-theologians. After centuries of neglect by thinkers outside the Catholic Church, his writings are increasingly studied by members of the wider philosophical community and his insights put to work in present-day philosophical debates in the fields of philosophical logic, metaphysics, epistemology, philosophy of mind, moral philosophy, and the philosophy of religion.

He was born in Roccasecca in the Kingdom of Naples and sent at the age of 5 to the Abbey of Monte Cassino, from where in his mid-teens he progressed to the University of Naples. In 1242 or the following year he entered the Order of Preachers (the Dominican Order), and spent the rest of his life exemplifying the Order's commitment to study and preaching. In 1256 he received from the University of Paris his licence to teach, and subsequently taught also at Orvieto, Rome, and Naples, all the while developing and refining a vast intellectual system which has come to acquire in the Church an authority unrivalled by the system of any other theologian. That authority was not, however, immediately forthcoming. His canonization in 1323 puts in perspective the fact that a number of propositions he defended were condemned by Church leaders in Paris and Oxford in 1277 shortly after his death.

His written output is vast, 8 million words at a conservative estimate, the more remarkable as he died aged no more than 50. Many of his works are in the form of commentaries, especially upon the Gospels, upon Aristotelian treatises, several of which had only recently reached the Christian West, and upon the *Sentences* of Peter Lombard, the main vehicle in the Middle Ages for the teaching of theology. He also conducted a number of disputations, dealing with questions on truth, on the power of God, on the soul, and on evil, and these disputations were duly committed to paper. Finally, and most famously, he wrote two *Summae* (Summations) of theology. The first, *On the Truth of the Catholic Faith against the Gentiles*, known as the *Summa contra Gentiles*, may have been written as a handbook for those seeking to convert others, in particular Muslims, to the Catholic faith. The second, his chief masterpiece, is the *Summa Theologiae* (Summation of Theology), left unfinished at his death. On 6 December 1273 he underwent an experience during Mass, and thereafter wrote nothing. His reported explanation for the cessation was: 'All that I have written seems to me like straw compared to what has now been revealed to me.' He died four months after the revelation.

That Aquinas wrote commentaries on several of Aristotle's books is indicative of the fact that Aquinas recognized the necessity of showing that Aristotle's system could be squared, more or less, with Christianity. Aristotle had constructed a system of immense range and persuasive power; persuasive not because of the rhetorical skill of the author but by virtue of his remorseless application of logic to propositions that all people of sound mind would accept. Aquinas was not the first to recognize the need to determine the extent to which Aristotle's system was compatible with Christian teaching, and to wonder how the latter teaching was to be defended in those cases where Aristotle clashed with it. But Aquinas more than anyone else rose to the challenge, and produced what must be as nearly the definitive resolution as any that we shall ever have. The resolution is the system of Christian Aristotelian philosophy which was most fully expounded in the *Summa Theologiae*. There we find Aristotelian metaphysics, philosophy of mind, and moral philosophy forming a large part of an unmistakably Christian vision of the created world and of *God.

Aquinas draws a sharp distinction between two routes to knowledge of God. One is revelation and the other is human reason. There are many things it is better for us to know than not to know, for example that God exists and that he is one and incorporeal, and in general our reason is a less sure guide than is revelation to the acquisition of this valuable knowledge. Nevertheless, Aquinas believes that it is possible for us to reach these truths without the aid of revelation, by arguing, in particular on the basis of the facts of common experience, such as the existence of motion in the world. To argue to the foregoing propositions about God on such a basis and by rigorous logic is to do philosophy; it is not to do theology, and even less is it simply to rely on revelation. Such exercises of logic are to be found scattered throughout Aquinas's writings, and for this reason he is to be considered a philosopher even in those contexts where he is dealing with overtly religious matters such as the existence and nature of God.

Aquinas is compelled to seek a *demonstration of God's existence because he recognizes that the proposition 'God exists' is not self-evident to us, though it is self-evidence in itself. A demonstration can proceed in either of two directions: from consideration of a cause we can infer its effect, and from an effect we can infer its cause. Aquinas presents five proofs of God's existence, the *quinque viae* (five ways), each of which starts with an effect of a divine act and argues back to its cause. In Aquinas's view no demonstration can start from God and work to his effects, for such a procedure would require us to have insight into God's nature, and in fact we cannot naturally have such a thing—we know of God *that* he is but not *what*.

Aquinas argues first from the fact that things move in this world to the conclusion that there must be a first mover which is not moved by anything, 'and everyone thinks of this as God'. The second way starts from the fact that we find in the world an order of efficient causes, and the conclusion drawn is that there must be some efficient cause, which everyone calls 'God', which is first in the chain of such causes. Thirdly, Aquinas begins with the fact that we find things that have the possibility of both being and not being, for they are things that are generated and will be destroyed. And, arguing that not everything can be like that, he concludes that there must exist something, called 'God' by everyone, which is necessary of itself and does not have a cause of its necessity outside itself. The fourth way starts from the fact that we find gradations in things, for some things are more good, some less, some more true, some less, and so on; and concludes that there must be something, which we call 'God', which is the cause of being, and goodness, and every perfection in things. And finally Aquinas notes that things in nature act for the sake of an end even though they lack awareness, and concludes that there must be an intelligent being, whom we call 'God', by whom all natural things are directed to an end. It has been argued that several of these arguments are fatally flawed by their reliance upon an antiquated physics, though other modern commentators have raised doubts about this line of criticism.

Aquinas's belief that we do not have an insight into God's nature forced him to deal with the problem of how we are to understand the terms used in the Bible to describe God. What do terms such as 'good', 'wise', and 'just' mean when predicated of God? Their meaning is otherwise than when predicated of human beings, for if not we would indeed have insight into God's nature. Should the terms therefore be understood merely negatively, as meaning 'not wicked', 'not foolish', and so on? This solution, especially associated with Maimonides (1135–1204), was rejected by Aquinas because this is not what people intend when they use such words. Aquinas's own answer is that the terms are used analogically of God. Since we cannot have an adequate conception of God, that is, since our idea of him falls short of reality, we have to recognize that the qualities that the terms for the perfections normally signify exist (or 'pre-exist') in God in a higher way than in us. It is not that God is not really, or in the fullest sense, good, wise, just, and so on. On the contrary, he has these perfections in the fullest way possible, and it is we creatures who fall short in respect of these perfections.

Among the divine perfections to which Aquinas attends is that of knowledge. God knows everything knowable. As regards his knowledge of the created world he does not know it as a spectator knows an object he happens upon. God, as absolute first cause, is not dependent upon anything for anything. His knowledge of things is therefore not dependent upon the prior existence of the things he knows. On the contrary, it is the act of knowing that brings the things into existence. We can, thinks Aquinas, get a small glimpse into the nature of such knowledge by thinking of it as the kind of knowledge an architect has of a house before he has built it, as compared with the knowledge that a passer-by has of it. It is because of the conception of the house in the architect's mind that the house comes into existence, whereas it is because the house already exists that the passer-by comes to form a conception of it.

Since God knows everything knowable, he must know every act that any human being will ever perform, which raises the notorious problem of whether human beings are free if God is indeed omniscient. In tackling this problem Aquinas offers us a metaphor. A man standing on top of a hill sees simultaneously all the travellers walking along the path that goes round the hillside even though the travellers on the path cannot see each other. Likewise the eternal God sees simultaneously everything past, present, and future, for 'eternity includes all time'. And just as my present certain knowledge of the action you are performing before my eyes does not imply that your action is unfree, so also God's timelessly present knowledge of our acts, past, present, and future, does not imply that our acts are unfree. One prominent problem associated with this solution concerns the fact, mentioned earlier, that Aquinas does not believe God's knowledge of the world to be like that of a spectator but instead to be more like the knowledge an agent has of what he makes. If the history of the world is to be seen as the gradual unfolding of a divinely ordained plan then it is indeed difficult to see in what sense, relevant at least to morality, human acts can be free. Aquinas's solution is still the subject of intense debate.

Given the close relation at many levels between knowledge and truth, Aquinas recognizes that his exposition of the nature of knowledge would be incomplete without a discussion of truth—a concept in which he is in any case bound to be interested given the biblical assertion 'I am the truth'. Truth is to be sought either in the knowing mind or in the things which are known, and Aquinas sees point to accepting both alternatives, so long as distinctions are made. He builds on a comparison with goodness. We use the term 'good' to refer to that to which our desire tends and use 'true' to refer to that to which our intellect tends. But whereas our desire directs us outward to the thing desired, our intellect directs us inward to the truth which is in our mind. In that sense desire and intellect point in opposite directions, and they do so in a further sense also, for in the case of desire we say that the thing desired is good, but then the desire itself is said to be good in so far as what is desired is good. And likewise, though the knowledge in our mind is primarily true, the outer object is said to be true in virtue of its relation to the truth in the mind.

As regards the relation between the inner truth and the outer, a distinction has to be made because something can have either an essential or an accidental relation to the knowing mind. If the thing known depends for its existence upon the knowing mind then the relation between it and the mind is essential. Thus the relation that something planned has to the plan is an essential relation. The house would not have had the features it has if the architect had not planned it that way, and those features are therefore related essentially to the idea in the architect's mind. Likewise as regards natural things, they are essentially related to the mind of God, who created them, since they depend for their existence upon the idea which he had of them. This contrasts with the relation between an object and a passer-by. The relation in which the house stands to the mind of the passer-by is accidental, for the house does not depend upon the passer-by. In making this distinction Aquinas is developing the concept now known as 'direction of fit'. It is primarily the idea in the mind of the architect that is true and the house built according to his plan is said to be true only derivatively. If the house constructed by the builder does not correspond to the architect's plan then the builder has made a mistake—the house is not true to the architect's plan. It is not that the plan does not fit the house but that the house does not fit the plan. On the other hand if the passer-by does not form an accurate idea of the house then it is his idea that does not fit the house—it is not true to the house.

This distinction enables Aquinas to say that *truth is, though in different ways, in both the mind and in that to which the mind is directed. Or if the thing is essentially related to the knowing mind then truth is primarily in the mind and secondarily in the thing, whereas if the thing is accidentally related to the knowing mind then truth is primarily in the thing and secondarily in the mind that knows it. In each case what is said is determined by the order of dependency. Truth is secondarily in that which is dependent.

The truth of the house lies in its conformity to the plan, and the truth of the passer-by's idea of the house lies in its conformity to the house. In each case there is truth where there is a form shared by an intellect and a thing. In view of this Aquinas affirms that truth is defined as conformity of intellect and thing. But for there to be such a conformity does not imply that the knowing mind knows also that the conformity exists. That knowledge involves a further stage in which the intellect judges that the thing has a given form or that it does not have a given form. Here we are dealing not merely with a concept corresponding to an outer thing, we are dealing instead with a judgement in which two concepts are related affirmatively or negatively. And it is such truth, the truth as known, that Aquinas identifies as the perfection of the intellect.

Aquinas is impelled thereafter to describe ways in which something can be false, for otherwise he might be thought to hold that falsity cannot exist. A central doctrine

in the *Summa Theologiae* is that truth is a transcendental term, that is, it is truly predicable of all things. In short, whatever exists is true. It is clear why Aquinas maintains this, for truth lies in the conformity between a thing and an intellect, and everything conforms with some intellect, whether human or divine. But if everything is true there is no room for falsity. Aquinas's conclusions concerning truth dictate his principal doctrines concerning falsity. Since truth and falsity are opposites, falsity is to be found where it is natural for truth to be. It occupies the space reserved for truth. That space is primarily in the intellect, and secondarily in things related to an intellect. A natural thing, as produced by an act of the divine will, will not be false to God's idea of it, but a human artefact is false in so far as it does not conform to the artificer's plan. But both divinely and humanly made things may be called false in a qualified way, in so far as they have a natural tendency to produce in us false opinions about them. Thus tin is called 'false silver' because of its deceptive appearance, and a confidence-trickster is a false person because of the plausibility of his self-presentation. In a sense there must on Aquinas's account be more, infinitely more, truth in the world than falsity, for the truths about the created order known by God are infinite, unlike the false opinions which we creatures have, which though numerous are nothing as compared with the truth which God has.

Aquinas had a great deal to say about the human soul. He had inherited from Aristotle the doctrine that every living thing, whether plant, dumb animal, or human being, has a soul. In the first case the soul is nutritive, in the second nutritive and sensitive, and in the third nutritive and sensitive and rational. Since in each case there is a body which has the soul, a question arises concerning how the soul relates to the body. Is it perhaps a corporeal part of the body it vivifies? Aquinas's answer is this. The soul is the 'first principle of life in things which live amongst us'. No body is alive merely in virtue of being corporeal, for otherwise every body would be alive. A body is alive in virtue of being a body of such and such a kind. Aquinas uses the term 'substantial form' to signify that by which something is the kind of thing it is, and hence the soul of a particular body is the substantial form of that body. And it is plain that a substantial form of a body cannot itself be corporeal, any more than the circularity of a rose window, which is the window's geometrical form, can be corporeal. The window is corporeal, but its circularity is not.

Turnips and tortoises, though having souls, are not spiritual beings. Humans are spiritual in virtue of having specifically rational souls. Unlike vegetables and dumb animals we have intellect. Aquinas held, following Aristotle, that human knowledge involves the non-material assimilation of the knower's mind to the thing known, thus becoming in a sense identical with that thing. Our intellect has two functions, one active and one passive. The intellect *qua* active abstracts from 'phantasms', that is, from our sense-experience. What is abstracted is stored in the intellect *qua* passive, and is available so that even when corporeal objects are not present to our senses we can none the less think about them.

The bodies we experience with our senses are compounds of matter and form. 'Abstraction' is the metaphor Aquinas uses to signify that the form of the body sensorily experienced becomes also the form of the knower's intellect. The form in the intellect does not, however, have the same mode of existence as the form in the body known. In the latter case the form is said to have 'natural existence' and in the former 'intentional existence'. The knowledge of the object gained by this abstractive act is universal in the sense that it is not the object itself in its individuality that is being thought about, but rather the nature of the object. Such universal knowledge is available only to creatures with intellect, and not to creatures whose highest faculty is that of sense.

The rational soul of a human being has two parts. It is intellect plus will. As is to be expected, the concept of will plays a large role in Aquinas's extensive examination, in the *Summa Theologiae*, of morality. That examination is systematically related to the long discussion which precedes it concerning God, his knowledge and powers, and the world considered precisely as a created thing. For human beings have, according to Aquinas, a twin status as coming from God, in the sense that we owe to him our existence, and also as turned towards him as the end to which we are by nature directed. Indeed the concepts of *exitus* and *reditus*, departure from and return to God, not only define our status but also give the fundamental structuring principle of the *Summa Theologiae*. Building upon Aristotle's teaching, particularly the *Nicomachean Ethics* III and VI, Aquinas gives a detailed analysis of human acts, focusing upon voluntariness, intention, choice, and deliberation, and argues that these features have to be present if an act is to be human, and not merely, like sneezing or twitching, an act which might as truly be said to happen to us as to be something we do, and which could equally happen to a non-human animal. Human acts are those that we see ourselves as having a reason for performing, our reason being the value that we attach to something which is therefore the end in relation to our act. Aquinas argues that beyond all the subsidiary ends at which we might aim, there is an ultimate end, happiness, which we cannot reject, though through ignorance or incompetence we may in fact act in such a way as to put obstacles in the way of our achieving it. However, the fundamental practical principle 'Eschew evil and do good' is built into all of us in such a way that no person can be ignorant of it. This practical principle and others following from it form, in the *Summa Theologiae*, a full and detailed system of natural law which has had a major impact on modern discussions in the philosophy of law.

In this area as in others the discussions that Aquinas's writings have provoked in modern times are as much between, and with, secular-minded philosophers as between Christian theologians, and in that sense the title *doctor communis*, by which he used to be known, applies now as never before.   A.BRO.

*God and the philosophers; God, arguments for the existence of; God, arguments against existence of.

Thomas Aquinas, *Summa Theologiae*, ed. Thomas Gilby (London, 1963–75), 60 vols.
—— *Aquinas: Selected Philosophical Writings*, ed. Timothy McDermott (Oxford, 1993).
Brian Davies, *The Thought of Thomas Aquinas* (Oxford, 1992).
Anthony Kenny, *Aquinas* (Oxford, 1980).
—— (ed.), *Aquinas: A Collection of Critical Essays* (London, 1969).
Norman Kretzmann and Eleonore Stump (eds.), *The Cambridge Companion to Aquinas* (Cambridge, 1993).
Christopher Martin (ed.), *Thomas Aquinas: Introductory Readings* (London, 1988).

Arabic philosophy: *see* Islamic philosophy.

Arcesilaus of Pitane (*c.*315–240 BC). Head of the *Academy from about 273, who advocated scepticism as the true teaching of Socrates and Plato. He did not argue for the doctrine that we can know nothing, but recommended suspension of judgement on everything. His method was to direct *ad hominem* arguments against any doctrine proposed to him. He attacked, for instance, the Stoics' belief that some sense-impressions could not be false (i.e. could be known for certain to represent reality). Even if some impressions are true, he argued, they cannot be distinguished qualitatively from others that are false. So any impression could turn out to be false. Since the Stoics themselves proposed suspension of judgement about anything that was not certain, they should, on their own principles, be sceptical about sense-impressions. Arcesilaus left no writings.   R.J.H.

*Sceptics, ancient; stoicism

A. A. Long and D. N. Sedley, *The Hellenistic Philosophers*, i (Cambridge, 1987), 438–60.

archetype: *see* Jung.

architectonic. Architectonic studies the systematic structure of our knowledge. For Kant, 'Human reason is by nature architectonic' because 'it regards all our knowledge as belonging to a possible system'. Many Kantian philosophers, such as Peirce, insist that we shall only know how philosophical knowledge is possible when we can understand its place within a unified system of *knowledge.   C.J.H.

I. Kant, *Critique of Pure Reason*, tr. N. Kemp Smith (London, 1968), 'The Architectonic of Pure Reason'.

Arendt, Hannah (1906–75). Originator of a broad political theory and analyst of the major historical events of her times, Arendt was a student of Jaspers and Heidegger and one of the first to apply the phenomenological method to politics. She rejected the Western political tradition from Plato through Marx, arguing in *The Human Condition* (1958) that the apex of human achievement is not thought but the active life. This divides into labour (repetitive but sustaining life), work (creating objects and a human world), and particularly action (new, especially political, activity involving shared enterprises). Her account of Eichmann's trial (1963) presented the idea of the 'banality of *evil—Eichmann simply drifted with the times and refused to think critically about his actions. Her unfinished *Life of the Mind* analyses thinking, willing, and judging as conditions for moral responsibility. c.c.

Leah Bradshaw, *Acting and Thinking: The Political Thought of Hannah Arendt* (Toronto, 1989).

P. Hansen, *Hannah Arendt: Politics, History and Citizenship* (Stanford, Calif., 1993).

aretē. Normally translated *'virtue', the Greek term in fact signifies excellence, i.e. a quality the possession of which either constitutes the possessor as, or causes it to be, a good instance of its kind. Thus sharpness is an *aretē* of a knife, strength an *aretē* of a boxer, etc. Since in order to be a good instance of its kind an object normally has to possess several excellences, the term may designate each of those excellences severally or the possession of them all together—overall or total excellence. Much Greek ethical theory is concerned with the investigation of the nature of human excellence overall, and of human excellences severally; the possession of the excellences is constitutive of being a good human being, i.e. of achieving a good human life (*eudaimonia*). c.c.w.t.

A. W. H. Adkins, *Merit and Responsibility* (Oxford, 1960), esp. chs. 3–4.

argument. The word has three main senses.

1. A quarrel, as when the neighbours across a courtyard argued from opposite premises.

2. In the most important sense for philosophy an argument is a complex consisting of a set of propositions (called its premises) and a proposition (called its conclusion). You can use an argument by asserting its premises and drawing or inferring its conclusion. The conclusion must be marked, for example by putting 'because' or the like before the premises ('It must be after six, because it's summer and the sun has set'), or 'therefore', 'consequently', 'so', or the like before the conclusion ('Souls are incorporeal; therefore they have no location'). An argument is valid when its conclusion follows from its premisses (other descriptions are 'is deducible from' or 'is entailed by'). It can be a good argument even when not valid, if its premises support its conclusion in some non-deductive way, for example inductively.

The reasons why bad arguments give no or weak support to their conclusions are too various to survey. But here are some examples: 'Jim and Bill are not both teetotallers; Jim isn't; so Bill is', 'Ann can't ride a bicycle, because she's in the bath and you can't ride a bicycle in the bath', 'Most con men are smooth-talking; so that smooth-talker is probably a con man', 'Most con men are good-looking; so that scar-faced con man is probably good-looking', 'Every number is a number or its successor; every number or its successor is even; so every number is even' (due to Geach), 'Grass is green; so snow is white'. And here are some good arguments (good in the sense that they are valid, or otherwise support their conclusions effectively): 'Everything indescribable is describable as indescribable; so everything is describable', 'Since there have only been a finite number of humans, some human had no human mother', 'God can do anything; so God can commit suicide', 'London must be south of Messina, for it's south of Rome, and Rome is south of Messina', 'It's heavier than air; so it won't fly far without power'.

Some of these examples show that a good argument can have an untrue conclusion, and a bad argument can have true premises and a true conclusion. An ideal *method* of argument will never lead from true premises to an untrue conclusion (it will be, in the jargon, truth-preserving), but only deduction attains that ideal. Other methods, such as induction, are worth using provided they are usually truth-preserving. For *proving* a conclusion you need more than a good argument to it. The premises from which the proof starts must also be true (the word 'sound' is sometimes reserved for valid arguments with true premises) and must be already 'given'—i.e. accepted or acceptable at a stage when the conclusion is not (you cannot, for example, prove a true conclusion from *itself*, even though you would be arguing soundly). (*Begging the question.)

As the examples also suggest, an argument can be made stronger by adding extra premises. In fact any argument 'P_1 . . . so Q', however bad, can be converted into a valid argument by adding the extra premise 'If P_1 and . . . then Q'. But of course, if the original argument was a bad one, this extra premiss will be untrue and so no help in the project of proving the conclusion. *Some* extra premises may weaken an argument, if it is non-deductive; for example 'It's a lake' supports 'It's fresh' more strongly than 'It's a lake with no outflow' does.

3. In mathematical parlance an argument of a *function is an input to it, or what it is applied to; and the output, for a given argument, is called the value. For example the function *father of*, or *being x's father*, has value David for argument Solomon, and the function *minus*, or $x - y$, has value 3 for arguments 17, 14, in that order. c.a.k.

*arguments, types of; deduction; induction; inference; validity.

P. T. Geach, *Reason and Argument* (Oxford, 1976).

C. A. Kirwan, *Logic and Argument* (London, 1978).

R. M. Sainsbury, *Logical Forms* (Oxford, 1991).

argument from design: *see* design.

arguments, types of. An *argument is a set of propositions, one of which, the conclusion, is subject to dispute or questioning, and the others, the premises, provide a basis, actually or potentially, for resolving the dispute or removing the questioning. This definition is a little narrow, because it is possible for an argument to have several conclusions, i.e. in the case of a sequence of argumentation, where the conclusion of one subargument functions also as a premiss in another. But it is also a little wide, in relation to a sense of 'argument' commonly used in philosophy, where the term refers to a complex of propositions (usually a quite small and specific set) designated as premisses and a conclusion.

Also, the definition above can be implemented somewhat differently in different conversational contexts, for several types of dispute can be involved. One common sense of 'argument' is that of a quarrelsome exchange of verbal attacks and counter-attacks. This is one conversational context of argument, but another context is the more orderly type of exchange where each party has the goal of justifying his or her own thesis, and questioning or refuting the other party's thesis, by reasoned means, using accepted standards of evidence. Argument of this kind, used to resolve an initial conflict of opinions, takes place in a critical discussion (van Eemeren and Grootendorst, *Argumentation, Communication and Fallacies*). In contrast, argument to bargain over goods or services takes place in a negotiation. But basically, in an argument, some key proposition is held to be in doubt, in contrast to an explanation, for example, where the proposition to be explained is generally taken as granted, or at least not subject to doubt or questioning, as far as the purpose of the explanation is concerned.

In a *deductively valid argument*, the link between the premisses and the conclusion is *strict* in the sense that the conclusion must be true in every case in which the premisses are true, barring any exception. In such an argument, the conclusion follows from the premisses by logical necessity. A traditional example is: 'All men are mortal; Socrates is a man; therefore Socrates is mortal'. The premisses don't have to be true, but if they are, the conclusion has to be true.

In an *inductively strong argument*, the link between the premisses and the conclusion is based on probability, so that if the premisses are true, then it can be said that the conclusion is true with a degree of probability (usually measured as a fraction between 0 and 1, the latter being the value assigned to a deductively valid argument, the limiting case).

In a *presumptively *plausible argument*, the link between the premisses and the conclusion is based on *burden of proof*, meaning that it is not known whether the conclusion is true or not, but if the premisses are true, that is enough of a provisional, practical basis for acting as though the conclusion were true, in the absence of evidence showing it to be false. Presumptively plausible arguments are species of arguments from ignorance that should be treated with caution, because of their provisional nature, making them subject to default, and even in some cases fallacious (Walton, *Plausible Argument in Everyday Conversation*).

Presumptively plausible arguments are very common in everyday conversation, and their abuse or erroneous use is associated with many of the traditional informal fallacies, familiar in logic textbooks. A few of the more common types of presumptively plausible arguments are noted below, along with some traditional types of argument and fallacy.

Argument from sign derives a conclusion that some feature of a situation is present, based on some other observed feature that generally indicates its presence. For example, 'Here are (what appear to be) some bear tracks in the snow; therefore a bear passed this way'.

Argument from expert opinion creates a presumption that a proposition is true, based on an appeal to the opinion of a suitably qualified expert who has claimed that it is true. More broadly, arguments are often based on appeals to authority of one kind or another, e.g. judicial authority, other than that of expertise. Locke (in his *Essay Concerning Human Understanding*) identified a type of argument he called *argumentum ad verecundiam* (argument from respect or modesty), which is 'to allege the opinions of men whose parts, learning, eminency, power, or some other cause has gained a name and settled their reputation in the common esteem with some kind of authority', and use this allegation to support one's own opinion. Locke does not say this is a fallacy, but he indicates how it could be used as a fallacy by someone who portrays anyone who disagrees with the appeal as insolent or immodest, having insufficient respect for authority.

Argument from ethos puts forward a proposition as being more plausible on the ground that it was asserted by a person with good character. The negative version of this is the abusive or personal *ad hominem* argument, which claims that an argument is not plausible on the ground that the arguer who advocated it has a bad character (typically bad character for veracity is emphasized). In the *Essay* Locke defined the **argumentum ad hominem* as the tactic of pressing someone 'with consequences drawn from his own principles or concessions'. This description is closer to the variant usually called the *circumstantial ad hominem* argument, where a person's argument is questioned or refuted on the grounds that his personal circumstances are inconsistent with what he advocates in his argument. For example, if a politician argues for wage cuts in the public sector, but is unwilling to cut his own high salary, a critic may attack his argument by citing the ostensible inconsistency.

Argumentum ad ignorantiam (argument to ignorance) is the argument that because a particular proposition has not been proved true (false), we may conclude that it is false (true). This is sometimes a legitimate kind of argumentation based on burden of proof. For example, in a criminal trial, if it is not proved that the defendant is guilty, it is concluded that she is not guilty. However, if pressed ahead too aggressively, it can be used as a sophistical tactic. For example, in the McCarthy hearings in the 1950s, absence of any disproof of communist connections was taken as evidence to show that some people were guilty of being communist sympathizers.

Argumentum ad populum is the use of appeal to popular opinion to support a conclusion. It may take the form of appeal to group loyalties, popular trends of one kind or another, or to customary ways of doing things. This type of argumentation is reasonable in many cases, but it can be used as a sophistical tactic to bring pressure against an opponent in argument, or to appeal to group interests or loyalties in an emotional way, in lieu of presenting stronger forms of evidence that should be provided.

Argumentum ad misericordiam is the use of appeal to pity to support one's conclusion. Such appeals are sometimes appropriate, but too often they are used as sophistical tactics to evade a burden of proof by diverting the line of argument away from the real issue. D.N.W.

> *deduction; induction; methods, Mill's; slingshot, arguments; testimony.

Charles L. Hamblin, *Fallacies* (London, 1970).
John Locke, *An Essay Concerning Human Understanding* (1690), ed. P. H. Nidditch (Oxford, 1975).
Frans H. van Eemeren and Rob Grootendorst, *Argumentation, Communication and Fallacies* (Hillsdale, NJ, 1992).
Douglas N. Walton, *Plausible Argument in Everyday Conversation* (Albany, NY, 1992).

Aristippus (5th century BC). An associate of Socrates, celebrated as a defender and exemplar of a life of sensual pleasure. His advocacy of pleasure was taken up by the Cyrenaic school (named after Aristippus' native city of Cyrene in North Africa), reputedly founded by his grandson, also called Aristippus. The Cyrenaics maintained that the supreme good is the pleasure of the moment, which they identified with a physical process, a 'smooth motion of the flesh'. They supported their hedonism by the argument that all creatures pursue pleasure and avoid pain. This concentration on immediate pleasure reflected a general scepticism, according to which only immediate sensations could be known. Concern with past or future caused uncertainty and anxiety, and should therefore be avoided. (*Ataraxia.) C.C.W.T.

E. Mannebach, *Aristippi et Cyrenaicorum Fragmenta* (Leiden, 1961).

aristocracy, natural. Rule by the members of a long-established ruling class distinguished by ability, property, and a privileged education which instils a high sense of honour, responsibility, and public duty.

Aristocracy is one of the three basic types of government noted by the Greeks, the others being monarchy (rule by one) and democracy (rule by the people). Aristocracies can be based on heredity, wealth (oligarchy), or merit (meritocracy). Some thinkers, especially Burke, believe in the natural aristocracy of those whose place in the social fabric has been established by stable hierarchical values hallowed by time. Such a view finds a friendly environment in some forms of *conservatism and can be seen as the expression of a belief in the value of an *organic society. It is easy for critics on the left to make fun of the idea because it can be depicted as the expression of entrenched privilege and arbitrary power with no rational basis. Nevertheless, the belief in a natural aristocracy can be combined with constitutional safeguards (as in Burke) and its systematic destruction over the last fifty years by the egalitarianism of the left and the managerialism of the right has not ushered in a glorious new era of public service. R.S.D.

E. Burke, *Reflections on the Revolution in France* (1790), ed. Conor Cruise O'Brien (Harmondsworth, 1968).

Aristotelianism. Aristotle's philosophical influence spans the period from his death in 322 BC to today. It has led to a wide range of different philosophical viewpoints, as his work has been interpreted and reinterpreted to fit different programmes and serve differing goals. His thought has influenced the terminology of *philosophy itself: 'syllogism', 'premiss', 'conclusion', 'substance', 'essence', 'accident', 'metaphysics', 'species', 'genera', 'potentiality', 'categories', '*akrasia*', 'dialectic', and 'analytic' are all terms taken over from Aristotle. Many contemporary philosophers working on ethics, philosophy of mind and action, political philosophy, and metaphysics claim that their views are influenced by, or even derived from, Aristotle's own writings. Still others define their own position by their rejection of Aristotle's views on essentialism, metaphysics, and natural science. And this situation is not merely an artefact of current philosophical interests; it is one which has obtained through nearly the whole period of Western philosophy since Aristotle's death.

The history of Aristotelianism has many phases. Immediately after his death, his school (the Lyceum) remained a centre for scientific and philosophical study. Theophrastus succeeded him as its head, expanded on his biological researches by a study of botany, and also wrote a history of physical theories and cosmology, while Eudemus composed the first history of mathematics and Aristoxenus wrote on music. Theophrastus and the next head of the Lyceum, Strato, were independent thinkers, prepared to criticize Aristotle's views, and to develop their own theories on basic issues. There were sometimes as many as 2,000 students during this period, and internal debate flourished. Zeno of Citium, the founder of the Stoa, said that Theophrastus' chorus was larger than his own, but that the voices in his own chorus were in greater harmony. However, in the third century BC, other philosophical schools emerged—the *Epicureans, *Stoics, and *Sceptics—and took centre-stage, rejecting some of Aristotle's views and modifying others, and the influence of the Lyceum itself diminished.

In the first century BC, Aristotle's manuscripts were edited by Andronicus and his writings were widely studied. Between the second and sixth centuries AD a series of scholarly commentators studied Aristotle's work with care and ingenuity, paying particular attention to his writings on logical, physical, and metaphysical topics. Alexander of Aphrodisias (second century AD), Porphyry (third century AD), and Philoponus and Simplicius (sixth century AD) were amongst the most distinguished contributors to this tradition. Some aimed not only to interpret Aristotle's views, but also to criticize them. Philoponus, in particular, developed a series of fundamental objections to Aristotle's dynamics and attempted to develop his own account of change and movement. This first renaissance of Aristotelianism declined after Justinian closed the schools of philosophy at Athens in AD 529, although Aristotle was actively studied in Constantinople for a longer period.

The second great renaissance of Aristotelian thought in western Europe began in the twelfth century AD, and was prompted initially by Syrian and Arabic scholar-philosophers who had discussed and developed Aristotle's scientific and metaphysical works. Of these, the best known are Avicenna (Ibn Sīnā) and Averroës (Ibn Rushd), 'the Commentator', who produced commentaries on nearly all of the works of Aristotle which we now possess. Averroës himself believed that Aristotle both initiated and perfected the study of logic, natural science, and metaphysics. Latin translations of Arabic texts and commentaries on Aristotle began to reach Europe (via Spain) in this period, and provoked widespread interest. Initially, Aristotle was seen as a threat to Christian orthodoxy, and in 1210 the Council of Paris banned the study of his natural philosophy and threatened to excommunicate anyone who studied it. However, the study of his writings flourished under mild persecution, and was further stimulated by the Crusaders' discovery in Constantinople of many of Aristotle's manuscripts (as handed down from the Greek commentators), which subsequently were skilfully translated into Latin and made more generally available. Within a few generations, Aristotle's writings became one of the mainstays of university life in Europe. This was due mainly to the enthusiasm and ability of two Dominicans, Albert the Great (c.1200–80) and Thomas Aquinas (1224/5–74), who sought to present the basic principles of Aristotle's philosophy in a systematic fashion and to integrate it (as far as possible) with Christian and contemporary scientific thought. Albertus aimed to give an account of the whole of nature in Aristotelian terms, to capture what Aristotle would have said had he been alive and well-informed in the thirteenth century AD. Aquinas's goal was to distinguish what was fundamentally sound in Aristotle's philosophical writings from certain of the conclusions which he actually drew. For example, while Aquinas (as a Christian) wished to reject Aristotle's view that the world had no beginning, he argued that it was by revelation alone that one could know the relevant facts. Thus, he upheld Aristotle's criticism of his predecessors' theories that the world had a beginning on the grounds that no philosophical argument could establish what had in fact occurred. Aquinas aimed to reconcile religion and philosophy, and to produce a wide-ranging synthesis of Aristotelian philosophy, Christianity, and the current scientific thinking of his day.

The success of Aquinas's synthesis ensured that for a time Aristotle held the pre-eminent position in Western philosophy. He was regarded for several centuries as the supreme philosopher, 'the master of those who know', as Dante called him. However, the effect of this synthesis was in many ways pernicious. After the thirteenth century Aristotle came to represent the status quo in philosophy and science, and to be identified with dogmatic resistance

to further speculation and scientific discovery. Naturally, critics arose: in Oxford, William of Ockham and, in Paris, Jean Buridan and Albert of Saxony amongst others. By the end of the fourteenth century, they had (like Philoponus before them) criticized Aristotle's dynamics and the astronomical theories constructed on this basis. The way was open for Copernicus and Galileo to undermine these parts of Aristotle's physical theories. Perhaps the nadir of this form of Aristotelianism was reached when Cremonini, a leading Aristotelian in Padua, refused to look through Galileo's telescope because he suspected that what he saw would conflict with his own theories. In the seventeenth century, Francis Bacon, Galileo, and Boyle developed more general attacks against Aristotelianism, accusing it of a resistance to scientific method and empirical observation. Hobbes complained of Aristotle's continuing influence with considerable vehemence. 'I believe that scarce anything can be more absurdly said in natural philosophy, than that which is now called Aristotle's *Metaphysics* . . . nor more ignorantly, than a great part of his *Ethics*' (*Leviathan*, IV. xlvi).

It is something of a paradox that Aristotle was criticized by John Locke and Francis Bacon for lack of interest in scientific method and empirical observation. He had, after all, pioneered the empirical science of biology, and had written at length about the importance of ensuring that one's theories are true to appearances and consistent with the reputable opinions of the relevant experts. His reputation in natural science suffered because of the narrow-minded attempts of the Aristotelians of the seventeenth century to defend every aspect of his physical theory. Their ultra-conservative approach prompted a radical rejection of central contentions of Aristotle's metaphysics and epistemology. A century later, Bishop Berkeley noted judiciously: 'In these free-thinking times, many an empty head is shook at Aristotle and Plato, as well as at Holy Scriptures. And the writings of those celebrated ancients are by most men treated on a foot with the dry and barbarous lucubrations of the Schoolmen.' In this way, the successful criticism of the most speculative features of Aristotle's dynamics prompted a major sea-change in the development of Western philosophy. The starting-point for philosophical thinking after Descartes came to be subjective experience and the challenge of scepticism, rather than man understood as a distinctive species of animal in a world of substances, essences, and natural kinds with their own causal powers. Indeed, from a post-Cartesian viewpoint many of Aristotle's central concepts appeared ungrounded or epistemologically insecure.

Aristotle's influence was not undermined in all areas. At a time when his metaphysical doctrines were under sustained attack, the German educationalist Philip Melanchthon (1497–1560) referred to the *Ethics* as a seminal document, and made it essential reading in German universities. Later in the German philosophical tradition, Hegel and Marx were enthusiastic students of Aristotle. Indeed, Marx was sometimes described as a left-wing Aristotelian.

Aristotle's *Poetics* exercised a powerful influence on the seventeenth-century French dramatists Corneille and Racine, who attempted to construct tragedies according to his precepts. Corneille went so far as to say that Aristotle's dramatic principles were valid 'for all peoples and for all times'. In nineteenth-century biology, Darwin was so deeply impressed with Aristotle's biological observations and theories that he remarked that while 'Linnaeus and Cuvier have been my gods, they were mere schoolboys to old Aristotle'. However, these remarks were exceptions to an intellectual climate in which Aristotle's central claims about scientific explanation, metaphysics, and logic were rejected either in whole or in part. Indeed, Darwin's own work appeared to undermine the need for Aristotle's style of teleological explanation of biological phenomena.

The last two centuries have seen several major developments in Aristotelian studies. In the nineteenth century, scholars sought to establish a secure text of his surviving books, culminating in the Berlin edition, published from 1831 onwards. Later writers tended to see Aristotle not as propounding one finished philosophical system, but as developing and modifying his views throughout the treatises. Others focused with increasing rigour on Aristotle's discussion of particular issues in his *Ethics* or *Metaphysics*, or more recently his biological works, without assuming that they all fit perfectly into one package of ideas. There has been, in these respects, an attempt to formulate clear and precise accounts of Aristotle's views, rather than to rest content with the 'Aristotle of legend'. It is perhaps no accident in this context that the last few years have seen renewed scholarly interest in the Greek commentators of the first Aristotelian renaissance.

What is the current position of 'Aristotelianism' in modern philosophy? In several areas, his influence remains strong and alive. I shall only comment on two.

1. *Philosophy of Action, Moral Psychology.* Many contemporary philosophers have been influenced directly by Aristotle's pioneering discussions of a variety of issues. The philosophy of *action contains a variety of questions: What counts as *an* action? How are actions individuated? What is to count as an *intentional* action or a *rational* action? Can there be intentional but irrational actions (*akrasia)? Further issues concern the explanation of intentional action: Is it to be explained causally, or in a distinctive manner (rational explanation)? Are the explanantia desires or beliefs, and which are explanatorily more basic? How are such psychological states related to underlying physical states? On each of these issues, Aristotle has a distinctive and interesting answer. Philosophers as diverse as Austin, Anscombe, von Wright, and Davidson, who reopened these issues in the late twentieth century, have found much to use in Aristotle's discussions. But his sustained and detailed analysis of these problems repays study on its own account.

His interest in ontological issues led him to develop an account of the nature and identity of processes, states, activities, and actions which differs from the alternatives canvassed in modern debates. In analysing intentional action, he gave an important role to efficient causation, but saw this as fully consistent with the recognition of the role of agents' knowledge and teleological (or rational) explanation. Where modern discussions represent these as rival explanatory schemes, Aristotle portrayed them as complementary. His discussion of *akrasia* focuses on the issue of how akratic action is possible and how it is to be explained—whether in terms of a failure of intellect or imagination, or in terms of desires not fully integrated into one's picture of well-being. This discussion stands comparison with even the best modern work. Aristotle is aiming to account for a wide range of cases (some involving failure of intellect, others separate failures of motivation) in a way which does justice to the variety of the phenomena of ordinary experience. But at the same time he seeks to develop a theory of practical reasoning and virtue which shows how the akratic is irrational and to be censured. The range and subtlety of Aristotle's account is evident throughout his discussion of virtue and self-control, which has received considerable attention from contemporary philosophers (such as John McDowell and Philippa Foot). Similar claims can be made for his discussions of the interconnection between psychological and physical states. Aristotle is engaging with precisely the issues which concern contemporary opponents of materialist reduction who wish to avoid (Platonic or Cartesian) *dualism. In these areas, Aristotle not only initiated philosophical discussion but provided a framework within which much contemporary work can be located and better understood.

2. *Metaphysical Issues.* Contemporary discussion, mainly prompted by two American philosophers, Saul Kripke and Hilary Putnam, has done much to refocus attention on to the Aristotelian issues of *substance, *essence, and *natural kinds. Kripke and Putnam share a range of assumptions with Aristotle. Terms such as 'man' or 'gold' have their significance because they signify a distinct natural kind whenever they are coherently uttered. They could not retain their significance and apply to a different object or kind. Aristotle accepted this as a consequence of his account of signification in which the thoughts (with which these terms are conventionally correlated) are 'likened' to objects or kinds in the world. But what makes these kinds and objects the same whenever they were specified? At this point, Aristotle developed his metaphysical theory of substance and essence to answer this question and thus to underwrite and legitimize his account of names. Modern authors have highlighted the linguistic and semantic data from which Aristotle began his account; but few (if any) have attempted to present such a systematic metaphysical basis for their semantic claims. In this respect, his project is at least as detailed and developed as those currently on offer. At the very least it indicates what a systematic theory of essence would be like.

Aristotle advanced his metaphysical claims apparently untroubled by sceptical doubts of the kind which undermined the first great period of Aristotelianism (in third-century BC Athens) and the third (in western Europe in the seventeenth century AD). Perhaps it was because he was so little concerned by *scepticism that he was able to develop his metaphysical theory in the way he did. However, from a modern perspective, this may not seem the major mistake it was once taken to be. Aristotle was not disturbed by global scepticism because (in his view) we had to be in cognitive contact with the world for our basic terms (such as 'man' or 'gold') to make sense. Our thoughts had to be 'likened' to objects and kinds in the world for them to be the thoughts they are, or for our terms to make sense to us. From the Aristotelian standpoint, global scepticism seems something of a trick: it assumes that we understand terms with meanings which they could only have if we were in reliable cognitive contact with the world, and then proceeds to raise sceptical doubts about the reliability of that cognitive contact. This anti-sceptical feature of Aristotle's thinking made it unappealing in an earlier age when philosophers raised sceptical doubts with scant concern for the question how our thoughts can have the content they do. But it is precisely this aspect of Aristotle's philosophy, together with its attendant interest in metaphysical issues, which makes it strikingly relevant today. In these areas, Aristotle's influence on contemporary philosophy appears stronger and more benign today than it has been at any time since the anti-Aristotelian revolution of the seventeenth century.   D.C.

D. Charles, *Aristotle's Philosophy of Action* (London, 1984).

G. E. R. Lloyd, *Aristotle: The Growth and Structure of his Thought* (Cambridge, 1968).

R. Sorabji, *Time, Creation and the Continuum* (London, 1983).

J. L. Stocks, *Aristotelianism* (Boston, 1925).

Aristotle (384–322 BC). Aristotle was born at Stagira in Chalcidice in northern Greece. His father was a doctor whose patients included Amyntas, King of Macedonia. At the age of 17, Aristotle went to Athens to study under Plato, and remained at the *Academy for nearly twenty years until Plato's death in 348/7. When Speusippus succeeded Plato as its head, Aristotle left Athens, lived for a while in Assos and Mytilene, and then was invited to return to Macedonia by Philip to tutor Alexander. Aristotle returned to Athens in 335 at the age of 49, and founded his own philosophical school. He worked there for twelve years until Alexander's death in 323, when the Athenians in strongly anti-Macedonian mood brought a formal charge of impiety against him. Aristotle escaped with his life to Chalcis, but died there in the following year at the age of 62. He married twice, and had a son, Nicomachus, by his second wife.

Aristotle's philosophical interests covered an extremely wide area. He composed major studies of logic, ethics, and metaphysics, but also wrote on epistemology, physics, biology, meteorology, dynamics, mathematics, psychology, rhetoric, dialectic, aesthetics, and politics. Many of his treatises constitute an attempt to see the topics studied through the perspective of one set of fundamental concepts and ideas. All reflect similar virtues: a careful weighing of arguments and considerations, acute insight, a sense of what is philosophically plausible, and a desire to separate and classify distinct issues and phenomena. They also exhibit considerable reflection on the nature of philosophical activity and the goals of philosophy itself.

Aristotle's philosophical development is difficult to determine chronologically. He probably worked on a range of concerns simultaneously, and did not always see clearly how far his thinking on logic or philosophy of science fitted with his current work on (for example) metaphysics or biology. He may have returned more than once to similar topics, and added to existing drafts in a piecemeal fashion at different times. It is, in general, more fruitful to inquire how far different elements in his thinking cohere rather than what preceded what. Further, many of his extant works read more like notebooks of work in progress or notes for discussion than books finished and ready for publication. His writings (like Wittgenstein's) reflect the activity of thinking itself, uncluttered by rhetoric or stylistic affectation. Their consequent freshness of tone should make one cautious of accepting over-regimented accounts of his overall project: for it may well have been developing as he proceeded.

In what follows, I shall aim to introduce a few of Aristotle's leading ideas in three areas only: logic and philosophy of science, ethics, and metaphysics. While these subjects differ widely, there is considerable overlap of concerns and interests between them.

Logic and Philosophy of Science. Aristotle was the first to develop the study of deductive inference. He defined the *syllogism as a 'discourse in which certain things having been stated, something else follows of necessity from their being so'. Syllogisms are deductively valid arguments, and include both arguments of the form:

> All *a*s are *b*,
> All *b*s are *c*,
> All *a*s are *c*,

and

> *a*s are red,
> *a*s are coloured.

Both these arguments are *perfect* syllogisms since nothing needs to be added to make clear what necessarily follows. By contrast, arguments form *imperfect* syllogisms when more needs to be added beyond the premises to make clear that the conclusion follows of necessity. It is a distinctive feature of Aristotle's account that it takes as its starting-point the notion of 'following of necessity', which is not itself defined in formal or axiomatic terms. If this notion has a further basis, it lies in Aristotle's semantical account of the predicate as what affirms that a given property belongs to a substance (and so rests on his metaphysics of substance and property).

Aristotle focused on perfect syllogisms which share a certain form involving three terms: two premises and a conclusion. Examples of such syllogisms are (reading downwards):

All *as* are *b*,	All *as* are *b*,	Some *as* are *b*,	Some *as* are *b*,
All *bs* are *c*,	No *bs* are *c*,	All *bs* are *c*,	No *bs* are *c*,
All *as* are *c*.	No *a* is *c*.	Some *as* are *c*.	Not all *as* are *c*.

He claimed that other syllogisms with a similar form and the same crucial terms ('all', 'some', 'none', 'not all') could be expressed using one of these perfect cases if one adds three conversion rules:

From No *bs* are *a*	infer	No *as* are *b*.
From All *bs* are *a*	infer	Some *as* are *b*.
From Some *bs* are *a*	infer	Some *as* are *b*.

Finally, he proposed that any deductively valid argument can be expressed in one of the four obvious perfect syllogisms specified above or reduced to these by means of the conversion rules. If so, any such argument can be reformulated as one of the basic cases of perfect syllogisms in which the conclusion obviously follows of necessity.

Aristotle was interested in this logical system in part because he was interested in explanation (or demonstration). Every *demonstration is a syllogism, but not every syllogism is a demonstration. In a demonstration, the aim is to explain why the conclusion is true. Thus, if the conclusion states that (for example) trees of a given type are deciduous, the premiss of the relevant demonstration will state this is so because their sap solidifies. If no further explanation can be given of why their leaves fall, this premiss states the basic nature of their shedding leaves. Premisses in demonstrations are absolutely prior, when no further explanation can be offered of why they are true. These constitute the starting-points for explanation in a given area.

Aristotle's ideas about the nature of valid inference and explanation form the basis of his account of the form a successful science should take. In terms of these, he outlined an account of what each thing's essence is (the feature which provides the fundamental account of its other genuine properties), of how things should be defined (in terms of their basic explanatory features), and of the ideal of a complete science in which a set of truths is represented as a sequence of consequences drawn from a few basic postulates or common principles. These ideas, which underlie his *Analytics*, determined the course of logic and philosophy of science, and to some extent that of science itself, for two millennia.

Aristotle's system has its own shortcomings and idiosyncrasies. His treatment of the syllogistic does not exhaust all of logic, and not all arguments of a developed science can be formulated into the favoured Aristotelian form. His system was a pioneering one which required supplementation. It was unfortunate, not least for his own subsequent reputation, that it came to be regarded as the complete solution to all the problems it raised.

It is important to note that Aristotle's logical project was directly connected with his metaphysical goals. His aim was to develop a logical theory for a natural language capable of describing the fundamental types of object required for a full understanding of reality (individual substances, species, processes, states, etc.). He had no interest in artificial languages, which speak of entities beyond his favoured metaphysical and epistemological theory. His goal was rather to develop a logical theory 'of a piece' with his philosophical conception of what exists in the world and how it can be understood. In this respect, his goals differ markedly from those of metalogicians since Frege, who speak of artificial as well as natural languages, and domains of objects unconstrained by any privileged metaphysics.

Ethics and Politics. Aristotle's *Ethics* contains several major strands.

1. It aims to give a reflective understanding of *well-being or the good life for humans.

2. It suggests that well-being consists in excellent activity such as intellectual contemplation and virtuous actions stemming from a virtuous character. Virtuous action is what the person with practical wisdom would choose; and the practically wise are those who can deliberate successfully towards well-being. This might be termed the *Aristotelian circle*, as the key terms (well-being, virtue, and practical wisdom) appear to be interdefined.

3. It develops a theory of virtue (*aretē) which aims to explain the fact that what is good seems so to the virtuous. Aristotle examines the characteristic roles of desire, goals, imagination, emotion, and intuition in the choices and intentional actions of the virtuous, and explains in these terms how virtue differs from self-control, incontinence (*akrasia), and self-indulgence. This is a study in moral psychology and epistemology, involving detailed discussion of particular virtues involved in the good life.

Each of these is important but controversial, and Aristotle's own viewpoint is far from clear. Sometimes it appears that the self-sufficient contemplation (of truth) by the individual sage constitutes the ideal good life, but elsewhere man is represented as a 'political animal' who needs friendship and other-directed virtues (such as courage, generosity, and justice) if he is to achieve human well-being. On occasion, Aristotle seems to found his account of the good life on background assumptions about human nature, but elsewhere bases his account of human nature on what it is good for humans to achieve. He remarks that the virtuous see what is good, but elsewhere writes that what is good is so because it appears good to the virtuous.

One way (there are many) to fit these strands together runs as follows. The paradigm case of activity which manifests well-being is intellectual contemplation, and everything else that is an element in the good life is in some relevant way like intellectual contemplation. Practical wisdom is akin to theoretical activity: both are excellences of the rational intellect, both involve a proper grasp of first principles and the integration of relevant psychological states, and both require a grasp of truth in their respective areas. Intellectual contemplation is the activity which best exemplifies what is good for humans; anything else which is good for us in some way resembles it.

But what counts as truth in practical matters? Is this is to be understood merely as what seems to be the case to the virtuous agent? Alternatively, practical truth might be taken as a basic notion. Or perhaps the virtuous agent is the proper judge because the virtue she possesses, when allied with practical wisdom, constitutes part of well-being. On this view, the interconnections between virtue and well-being would explain why her practical reasoning is as it is (in a way consistent with reputable and well-established opinion). This preserves the analogy with truth in theoretical matters, where inter-connections between kinds, essences, and causal powers explain why our theoretical reasoning is as it is (in a way consistent with reputable opinion). While the third of these interpretations captures substantial parts of Aristotle's discussion, he proceeds with characteristic caution and appears reluctant to commit himself finally on this issue.

Aristotle wrote his *Ethics* as a prolegomenon to his study of *Politics*. This too reflects his interest in virtue and well-being, but also contains several other major themes. Thus Aristotle holds the following theses.

1. A city state has as its goal well-being, and the ideal constitution is one in which every citizen achieves well-being.

2. In practice, *democracy is preferable to oligarchy because it is more stable and its judgements are likely to be wiser since individuals when grouped together have more wisdom than a few.

3. The practice of slavery, with regard to both 'natural' and 'non-natural' slaves required to till the soil and maintain the state (1330ᵃ32–3), is justifiable.

4. Plato's 'communist' society of guardians in the *Republic* is to be condemned because it leads to social disturbances, undermines private property and friendship, 'which is the greatest safeguard against revolution', and is unobtainable.

What holds these diverse views together? Sometimes, Aristotle writes as if his aim is for each citizen to achieve the perfectionist goals set out in the *Ethics*. However, his commitment to this ideal is mitigated by other factors including the need for stability and social harmony. When these conflict (as in his discussion of non-natural slaves), he does not give authority to perfectionist values in a direct or systematic way. It may be that Aristotle thought that there would be more excellent activity in the long run if considerations of harmony and stability were taken seriously. But he fails to spell this out or to specify in detail the distributional policies which are to be implemented by the wise rulers who hold power in his preferred constitution. While the *Politics* contains many influential remarks, such as those condemning the practice of lending money for profit and analysing the nature of revolutions, it is incomplete as a work of political theory. It also exhibits some of the less attractive aspects of perfectionist theory: if people lack the abilities required for a life of excellence, they are natural slaves rightfully deprived of the basic freedoms enjoyed by those with higher-grade capacities. Similarly, if children are born with serious physical handicaps, they are to be left to die. Aristotle does not seriously address the intuitions of liberty or equality of treatment which run contrary to the demands of perfectionist theory in these cases.

Metaphysics and Biology. Aristotle's metaphysical proposals have a number of different sources. Three of them can be summarized as follows.

1. Aristotle's logical system (as set out above) required a metaphysical underpinning—an account of species, substances, and essences—to underwrite his treatment of logical necessity and demonstration. The same was true of his semantical discussion of the signification of names and the principle of non-contradiction. Names signify (in his view) substances with essences. 'Man' has the significance it does because it signifies the same species on all occasions when it is used. But what makes this the same species is that it possesses a distinctive essence which it cannot lack. The kind occupies its own slot in the intelligible structure of the world in virtue of its possession of this essence. The *essence is the fundamental feature which makes the *substance what it is, and explains the other properties of the substance. Aristotle was faced with two problems: he required a metaphysical account of substances, species, and essence to sustain this view, and a psychological account of how we grasp these substances and kinds. (The latter issue is addressed in *De anima*, where Aristotle proposed that our thoughts and perceptions are of objects and kinds when we are in appropriate causal contact with them, and are thus 'likened' to them.)

2. Aristotle was convinced that *teleological explanation was the key to the proper study of natural organisms. What determined a thing's nature was what counted as its successful operation: its achieving what it is good for it to achieve (as is implicit in his ethical writings). These goals, and being organized so as to achieve them, is what makes the species the one it is. Some goals are extrinsic; the goal of an axe is to cut wood, and this explains the arrangement of the metal in the axe. But the teleological goal of man is to live a life of a given kind (e.g. of rational activity), and the rest of his nature is designed so as to achieve this intrinsic goal. The distinctive goal of each biological kind is what determines its respective essence.

3. Aristotle's critical study of Plato's theory of *universals had convinced him that universals could not exist by themselves, but only in particular things. Since substances must be capable of independent existence, it appears that they cannot be universals but must be particulars. However, this generated a dilemma since Aristotle also believed that only universals were definable and the objects of scientific knowledge (in the *Analytics* model). Thus if substances are knowable, they cannot be particulars. But now it looks as if substances cannot exist at all since they cannot be either universals or particulars. Aristotle's dilemma arises because he was tempted to regard

particular substances as ontologically primary, while (at the same time) insisting that understanding and definition are of universals. The latter thought he shared with Plato; but the former is very much his own, and one which led to a fundamentally different account of numbers and universals than the one Plato offered.

In addressing the first two issues, Aristotle needed to represent the essences of substances in a way which respected two ideas: (*a*) that each substance has one fundamental feature which causes its other features to be as they are, (*b*) this feature is teleologically basic. *Form* is the candidate proposed as the relevant essence of substances, composed of form and matter. But is the form particular or universal? How is it related to matter? Is it itself *one* unitary thing? These questions dominate Aristotle's reflections in the *Metaphysics*, and parts of his account of the soul in *De anima* and natural kinds in the biological writings.

Aristotle's discussion of these issues has generated several major scholarly controversies. First, did he take the notion of one unified substance as basic, and regard its matter and form as abstractions from this basic notion? Or did he regard form and matter as independent starting-points which, when related in a given way, yield a unified substance? Second, if each individual substance's form is unique, how is the form itself individuated? Is its identity fixed independently of the matter (or the composite) it informs? Or is it rather a distinct form precisely because it is the result of a general form informing certain quantities of matter? Third, did Aristotle regard general forms as abstractions from the forms of particular substances, which served as his basic case? Or is the order of explanation reversed, general forms taken as explanatorily prior and forms of particular substances derived from general forms enmattered in particular quantities of matter?

One approach (there are again many) takes general forms as explanatorily basic, and construes particular forms as the result of their instantiation in different quantities of matter. On this view, Aristotle regards form and matter as prior to the composite substance, while maintaining as a separate thesis that universals cannot exist uninstantiated. Composites such as humans are to be understood as the result of the operation of form on matter. They are composed from arms and legs, composed in turn from flesh and blood, themselves composed from basic elements. At each level above the lowest, the relevant entities are defined by representing the matter as serving certain teleological goals. While matter is described as potentiality, this means no more than that it can be informed in favourable conditions. This perspective is at work in *The Parts of Animals* and *De anima*, yielding a distinctive picture of the soul and of animal. The teleological operations which introduce such phenomena as desire or perception are not definable in terms of efficient causation, but refer essentially to the creature's own goals, such as well-being or survival. Nor can they be defined as 'whatever plays a given role in a system of explanation', as they are genuine entities in their own

right with their own causal powers and essential features. On this view, Aristotle is neither offering a reductive account of psychological states, nor regarding them as inexplicable or mysterious (as in Platonic dualism).

These scholarly issues remain highly controversial, and are at the centre of current debate. Other more general problems are raised by Aristotle's discussion. First, is it possible to explain the unity or identity of a particular substance at all? Second, what is the nature of a metaphysical explanation which Aristotle is seeking? He appears to offer a constructive account of higher-order states, in some way intermediate between reductionism and dualism. But is this a genuine alternative, and how is the relevant construction itself constrained? Third, is there always one teleologically basic feature which explains the presence and nature of the other genuine properties of substances?

As already indicated, Aristotle made substantial progress with each of these questions in his treatises on psychology and biology. Indeed, much of their philosophical interest lies in tracing how far he succeeded in explaining the nature of the relevant phenomena in terms of his central concepts and favoured methodology. The results, particularly in his psychological writings, are often exciting and compelling but sometimes inconclusive. Aristotle encountered serious difficulties in his study of biological natural kinds. He did not succeed in finding one basic feature to explain the remainder of their genuine properties (as required by the *Analytics* model). Thus, he saw that fish are so constituted as to fulfil a range of diverse functions—swimming, feeding, reproducing, living in water—which cannot all easily be unified in a unitary essence of the type proposed in the *Analytics*. The model he had developed to analyse physical pheno-mena (such as thunder) could not be applied without major changes to central aspects of the biological world. Aristotle's commitment to teleological explanation generated results apparently contrary to the guiding idea of non-complex unifying forms proposed in the *Metaphysics*. It is not clear whether he believed that these problems could be overcome, or concluded that the model of explanation which applied elsewhere could not successfully analyse biological kinds. He did not succeed in integrating all his beliefs into a complete and unified theory.

Aristotle's writings in metaphysics, morals, biology, and psychology are unified by common interests in *natural kinds, teleology, and essence, but they are not parts of the seamless web of a perfectly unified and finished theory. Aristotle was too cautious and scrupulous a thinker to carry through a 'research programme' without constant refinement and attention to recalcitrant detail. In this respect his writings seem to reflect the nature of intellectual contemplation itself.   D.C.

*logic, traditional.

J. L. Ackrill, *Aristotle the Philosopher* (Oxford, 1981).
J. Barnes (ed.), *The Complete Works of Aristotle*, i and ii (Princeton, NJ, 1984).
—— (ed.), *The Cambridge Companion to Aristotle* (Cambridge, 1995).

A. Gotthelf and J. Lennox (eds.), *Philosophical Issues in Aristotle's Biology* (Cambridge, 1987).

T. H. Irwin, *Aristotle's First Principles* (Oxford, 1988).

R. Sorabji, *Necessity, Cause and Blame* (London, 1980).

W. D. Ross, *Aristotle* (Oxford, 1923).

arithmetic, foundations of. Arithmetic is the study of the natural numbers—0, 1, 2, 3, and so on. A foundation for arithmetic can serve three interconnected interests: an interest in rigorous axiomatization, an epistemological interest in the source and justification of our knowledge of the *numbers, and an ontological interest in the nature of the numbers.

Dedekind, and, following him, Peano, dissected the concept of the progression of the natural numbers and formulated an axiomatic foundation for arithmetic, now known, unfairly, as the Peano axioms. The idea behind an axiomatic foundation is to set down a small number of axioms, expressed using a small number of primitive, non-logical terms, from which other sentences can be deduced. The primitive terms used are '0' (0 is the first natural number), 'successor' (the successor of 0 is 1, the successor of 1 is 2, etc.) and 'natural number', and the five axioms are:

1. 0 is a natural number.
2. The successor of any natural number is a natural number.
3. No two natural numbers have the same successor.
4. 0 is not the successor of any natural number.
5. For any property P, if (i) 0 has P and (ii) the successor of any natural number which has P also has P, then every natural number has P (the principle of mathematical induction).

This informal axiomatic foundation organizes and regiments arithmetical truths within an economical system. It can be formalized by translating the axioms into a formal language from which theorems can be deduced via rigorous proofs (though Gödel's *incompleteness theorem limits the success of any such formal axiomatization).

How is our knowledge of arithmetical truths to be explained? An axiomatic foundation provides a partial answer: assuming that the axioms are known, then knowledge of theorems is logical knowledge of the logical consequences of the axioms. The outstanding question is: how do we know the axioms? According to the Euclidean paradigm, we know the axioms because they are self-evident, but this is an unsatisfactory answer because judgements of self-evidence are notoriously fallible. Rather than appeal to self-evidence right away, Frege developed his *logicism. The logicist project has three parts: define the vocabulary of arithmetic solely in terms of the vocabulary of logic, identify the natural numbers with 'logical objects', and deduce Peano's axioms as the logical consequences of logical axioms. Thus the logicist project grounds knowledge of arithmetical truth on knowledge of logical axioms which Frege held to be self-evident. This explanation was ripped apart by *Russell's

paradox which demonstrated that Frege's logic is inconsistent and which initiated the vigorous foundational research of the early twentieth century.

The very idea of an epistemological foundation for arithmetic can be questioned; for example, '2 + 2 = 4' is more obvious and certain than any recondite set of axioms of logic or set theory from which it may be deduced. Nevertheless, an account of the ontological foundation of arithmetic is compulsory. Prima facie, arithmetical truths are truths about objects—the numbers. What sort of objects are they? They do not seem to be either physical or mental objects because there might not be enough of those to serve as the numbers and because the numbers are thought to be necessary existents unlike physical or mental objects. Thus the numbers appear to be *abstract entities, as the Platonist would have us believe: either a *sui generis* progression or one drawn from a more extensive kind of abstract object such as sets, but in each case having no causal powers. Now epistemological problems resurface since there is no agreed account of how our knowledge of abstract objects is possible. A.D.O.

P. Benacerraf and H. Putnam (eds.), *Philosophy of Mathematics*, 2nd edn. (Cambridge, 1983).

G. Frege, *The Foundations of Arithmetic*, tr. J. L. Austin, 2nd edn. (Oxford, 1953).

I. Lakatos, 'Infinite Regress and the Foundations of Mathematics', in *Mathematics, Science and Epistemology*, ed. J. Worral and G. Currie (Cambridge, 1978).

M. Potter, *Reason's Nearest Kin: Philosophies of Arithmetic from Kant to Carnap* (Oxford, 2002).

arkhē. A 'first thing from which something is, or comes to be, or is known' (Aristotle, *Metaphysics* v. 1013[a] 18–19). Applied to materials which do not arise out of anything more primitive, to causes of change, to propositions fundamental in deductive systems, by teleologists to benefits and beneficiaries, and, colloquially, since they are sources of initiatives in states, to governments. Kinds of *arkhē* are as numerous as ways of explaining or senses of 'understand'. W.C.

*first cause argument.

Armstrong, D. M. (1926–). Australian philosopher, Officer of the Order of Australia, and one of the dominant figures in the school sometimes known as Australian materialism. Armstrong was one of the first to advocate *functionalism as a theory of the mind, and to combine that view with *materialism. In metaphysics, he has defended a distinctive version of realism about *universals. Armstrong's view is that there are philosophical reasons for believing in the existence of universals, but universals do not exist independently of the particulars that instantiate them, and which universals exist is an empirical question. This view has been in the background of his later work on scientific laws, and on the nature of modality. Armstrong's metaphysical realism, his vigorous defence of empirical metaphysics, and his clear, argument-based philosophical style show the influence of John

Anderson—of whom Gilbert Ryle reputedly said 'he thinks there are only brass tacks'.   T.C.

D. M. Armstrong, *A Materialist Theory of the Mind* (London, 1968).
—— *A World of States of Affairs* (Cambridge, 1997).

Arnauld, Antoine (1612–94). A brilliant philosophical controversialist, Arnauld exerted a powerful influence on the development of seventeenth-century thought. When still under 30 he composed a devastating critique of Descartes's arguments for the distinctness of mind and body, casting doubt on the logical completeness and adequacy of the Cartesian conception of a pure thinking substance (Fourth Set of Objections to the *Meditations*, 1641). A defender, despite his criticisms, of many aspects of the Cartesian system, he went on to write, with Pierre Nicole, the celebrated *La Logique, ou L'Art de penser*—the so-called Port-Royal Logic—in 1662. In his early seventies, Arnauld published a detailed refutation of Nicolas Malebranche's theory of perception in the *Traité des vraies et fausses idées* (1683). A few years later, in a famous exchange of letters with Leibniz, he argued that the Leibnizian theory of individual substance eradicates genuine contingency and leads to universal fatalism.   J.COT.

*Cartesianism; mind–body problem; Port-Royalists.

S. M. Nadler, *Arnauld and the Cartesian Philosophy of Ideas* (Manchester, 1989).
R. C. Sleigh, *The Leibniz–Arnauld Correspondence* (New Haven, Conn., 1990).

Arrow, Kenneth Joseph (1921–). Leading theorist of social choice, winner of a Nobel Prize in 1972. In *Social Choice and Individual Values* (1951), Arrow studied the determination of rational choice at the collective level for cases where this choice is to be a function of the preferences of the individuals making up the collective. In this study he proved the general impossibility theorem, which gives rise to *Arrow's paradox. Assuming that any acceptable function must meet a small number of intuitive conditions, Arrow proved that there is no consistent function from individual preferences to collective choice. With Debreu, Arrow also made a major contribution to general equilibrium theory. (In an economy in competitive *equilibrium* all markets clear simultaneously: there is a balance of supply and demand in all markets.)   T.P.

C. C. von Weizsacker, 'Kenneth Arrow's Contributions to Economics', *Scandinavian Journal of Economics* (1972).

Arrow's paradox. A paradox in social choice theory. Why not devise a function which orders options for a society in terms of the preferences of its individual members? Such a function would have to meet certain conditions on reasonableness—such as that (*a*) an ordering could be obtained from any logically possible set of individuals' preferences, (*b*) if everyone prefers a given *A* to a *B*, then that *A* should be ordered above that *B*, (*c*) no individual can dictate the social ordering—there can be no individual such that whenever he prefers an *A* to a *B*, then that *A* must

be ordered above that *B*, and (*d*) the ordering of any *A* and *B* depends on individuals' preferences between that *A* and that *B* alone. *Arrow proved that there was no consistent function which met all the conditions.   T.P.

*voting paradox.

K. J. Arrow, *Social Choice and Individual Values* (New Haven, Conn., 1951).

art. The idea that various activities such as painting, sculpture, architecture, music, and poetry have something essential in common belongs to a particular period beginning only in the eighteenth century. It was then that the 'fine arts' became separated off from scientific disciplines and more mundane exercises of skill. Later, during the eras of romanticism and modernism, this became transmuted into the single notion of *art*. Contemporary philosophers have inherited the notion, but are no longer entirely sure what to do with it.

One problem is the difficulty of defining art. Consider what is usually treated as the earliest definition: art as mimesis, or the reproduction of the world in images. For a long time painting and literature could be united under this heading (and a precedent cited in Greek thought). However, if art is to include music and architecture, as well as the non-figurative visual forms of the twentieth century, this definition will not easily suffice. Two notable definitions from the early part of this century built on the rejection of representation as a defining feature of art: art as significant form, and art as the expression of emotion. Both play down the artwork's relation to reality, in favour of perceptible aesthetic qualities of the art object itself, or of the relation between the work and the creative mind in which it originated. Earlier intimations of both can be found in the ideas of *beauty and *genius in Kant's theory of art. Both object-centred and artist-centred definitions of art could be used to discriminate that which was 'properly' art from that which was not, and such ideas helped in their day to explain the value of many progressive forms of art. But each is at best one-sided as a comprehensive definition.

Successive waves of the avant-garde, together with increasing knowledge of different cultures, have shown how society's institutions accommodate radical change in what is recognized as art. It has even been suggested that the very point of the concept of art lies in its open-ended capacity to accept change. Some have offered what is called an institutional definition of art, prompted by the thought that the only common feature among artworks is just their being recognized as art by certain institutions in particular societies. It would presumably be left to history to show what these institutions were, and the various functions or values which the things called art have had within them. While there must remain appropriate standards by which one work can be judged superior to another, it would be hard to deny that the inclusion and exclusion of different activities from the status of art has served other functions in society, such as fostering élitism or class-distinction.

One drawback of an institutional theory is that it cannot easily be used, as earlier theories were, to persuade us of what is peculiarly valuable about art. Sometimes it is assumed that art is a good thing to the extent that it has purely aesthetic value, as distinct from moral or cognitive or utility value. Others think, surely rightly, that art is also important as a way of gaining understanding of human behaviour, and that what value art-products have cannot be divorced from issues of truth and morality. Ideas which have had currency in past theories and which have spread into popular thinking—that art achieves a unique insight into 'higher' truths, or provides an elevated form of human self-realization—should not be dismissed, but in philosophy they require cautious investigation. Few philosophers, one suspects, would be quick to nominate any one value as that possessed by everything which is called art.   C.J.

*aesthetics, history of; aesthetics, problems of; emotion and art.

R. G. Collingwood, *The Principles of Art* (Oxford, 1938).
G. Dickie, *Art and the Aesthetic* (Ithaca, NY, 1974).
R. Wollheim, *Art and its Objects*, 2nd edn. (Cambridge, 1980).

art, contemporary. Contemporary art-making practices from 1945 to the present can be intelligibly viewed as 'working' the medium: a sensuous and intellectual experimentation not just with the physicality of the constituents—the paint, the graphic line, the colour field—but with that set of conventions specific to the art world at a particular time—the particular techniques, procedures, and standards, both articulated and implicit, that discipline and define an art practice. Abstract Expressionists worked with space and form within a single plane to establish complex part-by-part relations that collapsed illusionistic space while still maintaining 'the opticality of matter' (Clement Greenberg). The Minimalists eliminated the optical focus of spatial art using 'obdurate masses' (Donald Judd) that were aggressively tactile; they reduced the bare canvas to a limiting frame, expanding the framing function of painting by constructing installation works that brought the spectator literally into the work. Using mixed media, their works borrowed 'the look of non-art' (Michael Fried). Together with Pop artists, they extended the plastic arts into the temporal by working serially. In the period of neo-avant-gardes that included Fluxus, Conceptual, Situationist, Process, and Performance art, a series of cross-overs took place between sculpture and architecture, painting and popular culture, and art, music, film with performance. This shift did not lead to another style, but to a fully transformed conception of art founded on alternative theoretical premises. Contemporary art is often characterized by the dematerialization of the art object into untraditional and often temporary forms, which include video, performance, installation, and film art. Contemporary artists today, whether sculpture-based, painting-based, installation, or post studio, operate within 'a Post Medium Convention' (Robert Gero). Here there is no longer a concern with specificity, purity, or the limits of painting *qua* painting, but only an artistic concern with the painterly, the sculptural, the architectural, as well as the use of artefacts of Pop culture, as a varied means to actualize contents. The new canon is Duchampian: anything has the potential to be art. Today, artworks are often barely recognizable as 'art'. For example some contemporary artists have built houses, cooked dinners, planted gardens, or parked cars at the museum as artworks. This merging with the world is one way of making artworks critically relevant to a fluid culture that is ahistorically adrift in a virtual space of promiscuous signifiers.   B.T.

Arthur Danto, *The Transfiguration of the Commonplace* (Cambridge, 1983).
C. Freeland, *Art Theory: A Very Short Introduction* (Oxford, 2003).
Charles Harrison and Paul Wood (eds.), *Art in Theory 1900–1990: An Anthology of Changing Ideas* (Oxford, 1992).

art, philosophy of: *see* aesthetics.

art, representation in: *see* representation in art.

art, science, and religion: *see* science, art, and religion.

art, suspect. There are two important areas in which art comes under suspicion. First, a work of art can embody a view that challenges the prevailing beliefs of a society, such as Manet's *Olympia* (which challenged views of female sexuality). In the Thirties both the Nazis and the Soviet Union made life difficult for any artist not affirming the official line in an academic, classical style. In philosophical parlance, dominant ideologies will be suspicious of works of art in which challenges to that dominance are exercised. The second area of suspicion concerns the general public's suspicion of art (broadly referred to as 'the avant-garde') which repudiates sources of value such as beauty, profundity, or technical skill without drawing (in any way that is obvious) on alternative sources of value. If one cannot tell by looking whether an object is or is not art (as with much 'found art'), there will always be the suspicion that a fraud is being perpetuated.   D.M.

Stanley Cavell, *Must We Mean What We Say?* (Cambridge, 1976).

art and morality. Argument in this area tends to cluster around either of two poles: one seeing the relation between art and morality as close and harmonious, the other more keenly aware of conflicts and tensions between them.

1. *Art is taken as vital to moral health. It brings into play, expresses, 'purges' emotions and energies that, in real-life situations, could be harmful and destructive. It allows us, without risk, to explore in depth the essential nature and outworking of endless types of human character and social interaction—in plays and novels.

If art appreciation is essentially contemplative, attentive to the individuality of its objects, and respecting and loving them for what they are in themselves, these aesthetic attitudes are close neighbours to the morally desirable attitudes of respect for persons and moral attentiveness to their individual natures and needs.

Again, art can enlarge the scope of individual *freedom, by expanding awareness of our options for action and for forms of human relationship, beyond those options that are immediately apparent in everyday society. More broadly, the arts enhance human vitality through teaching a keener, more vivid perception of the colours, forms, and sounds of a world of which we are normally only dimly aware, and a more intense and clarified awareness of values.

2. Nevertheless, art has also been seen as morally dubious or harmful. At the level of theory, the Kantian and post-Kantian accounts of a disinterested, calmly contemplative *aesthetic attitude have recently been facing critical challenge. It is claimed, furthermore, that art stimulates emotions better not aroused; encourages the imagination to realize in detail, and to enjoy, morally deplorable activity, thereby making that more likely to be acted out in life.

If freedom can be enhanced by art, it can also be diminished—by artworks that present current stereotypes, fashions in attitudes and action, farouche or degraded visions of human nature, as if these alone were the 'available' models for life-responses. There can be little ground for confidence that the sometimes desperate search for the innovative and 'different' in art (and the role of the complex of interested promoters of particular arts—the 'artworld') reliably leads to morally serious and wise interpretations of human problems.   R.W.H.

    *aesthetics, history of; aesthetics, problems of; moral philosophy, history of; moral philosophy, problems of.

J. Levinson (ed.), *Aesthetics and Ethics* (Cambridge, 1998).
Iris Murdoch, *The Fire and the Sun: Why Plato Banished the Artists* (Oxford, 1977).
J. Passmore, *Serious Art* (London, 1991), ch. 8.

art and truth. There are two main philosophical issues concerning art and truth. First, in representational art, is truthfulness, accuracy, or realism a criterion of value, or at least relevant to the artistic value an artwork possesses? Second, is art, representational or not, the source of a sort of truth other than that which can be attained outside of art and which can be stated propositionally?

It seems clear that the answer to the first question is that it depends on the art-form and, even more, on the specific genre involved. With realistic paintings and novels, a high degree of truth-to-life is generally a virtue, since it is in tune with the aesthetic aims of such works. With expressionist paintings or fantasy novels or avant-garde films, a high degree of truth-to-life is neither sought nor desirable, given what such works are about aesthetically. It is sometimes held, however, that even in such cases works are better, the truer they somehow are to the fundamental facts of human nature, even if taking leave of the outward forms and appearances of human life.

Positive answers to the second question have usually looked to what art expresses or exemplifies or illustrates, as opposed to represents or denotes or describes, as loci of truth of a non-propositional sort, and to forms of intuitive, perceptual, or experiential knowing as modes of access to such truth that the appreciation of art may involve. Among the more plausible claims of this stripe are ones concerning insights into the nature of emotional life that engagement with expressive music might afford, and insights into the nature of moral values that engagement with imaginative literature or cinema might afford. Many such claims turn on the idea that the experience of art can reveal truths to us that are not manifested in ordinary experience, or that the experience of art can cognitively affect us in certain ways that are unparalleled in extra-artistic experience.   J.LEV.

Monroe Beardsley, *Aesthetics: Problems in the Philosophy of Criticism*, 2nd edn. (Indianapolis, 1981).
Nelson Goodman, *Languages of Art*, 2nd edn. (Indianapolis, 1976).
Martha Nussbaum, *Love's Knowledge: Essays on Philosophy and Literature* (New York, 1990).

art criticism. Critical discourse about the various arts is enormously diverse in nature and intent. The versions of criticism which philosophical aesthetics puts forward tend to be idealized rather than practical accounts. Some criticism is subsumed under the notion of *aesthetic judgement: an evaluation of (say) a novel or musical performance, which professes to state truths about its degree of success, based on the critic's response, and which may enable other spectators to respond similarly. Criticism is also conceived as an interpretative exercise, seeking to construct, by scrutiny of the work, or by using historical evidence, a meaning which the work will bear. Whether a literary work or a painting thus interpreted permits conflicting readings, and whether there can be any privileged interpretation which approximates to the 'artist's meaning', are matters of great contention.   C.J.

M. C. Beardsley, *The Possibility of Criticism* (Detroit, 1970).

arthritis in the thigh was the subject of the following thought experiment. Someone who believes that he or she has arthritis in the thigh believes something false. But, arguably, a physical duplicate of that individual with the same physical history in a possible world in which the word 'arthritis' covers ailments in the thigh as well would, in comparable circumstances, have a different, true, belief. So, it is said, the mental fact of the intentional content of propositional attitudes is partly determined by facts concerning an individual's socio-linguistic environment.   P.J.P.N.

    *externalism; anti-individualism.

T. Burge, 'Individualism and the Mental', in P. French, T. Uehling, and H. Wettstein (eds.), *Midwest Studies in Philosophy*, iv (Minneapolis, 1979).

artificial intelligence. A relatively new discipline which studies the programming and performance of computers used both for problem-solving across a wide range of intellectual, engineering, and operational tasks, and as a tool in psychology for modelling mental abilities. Originally inspired by Alan Turing's 1950 paper 'Computing Machinery and Intelligence', in which he replaced the question whether machines can think by the question whether we would attribute intelligence to a device that performed (in written questions and answers) as well as a human (i.e. was indistinguishable). The aim of much work in AI has been to pass this Turing test by building devices that perform certain tasks as well as we do, such as playing chess and constructing proofs. Some, however, use AI techniques to build machines that perform better than we do, or to perform tasks we cannot perform, whether these are intellectual tasks such as theorem-proving, the large-scale storage and use of knowledge about a particular domain, or physical tasks best performed by robots. The first two kinds of task present problems of representation for programmers, who must secure access to information and reliable inferences in a large search space and within a realistic time-scale. The search problem is tackled by using both *algorithms and *heuristics. The former are effective procedures that produce specified results in a principled way; the latter are less reliable, but useful, rules of thumb.

Although AI research in robotics, theorem-proving, and the kind of knowledge-based systems used for diagnosing medical and engineering problems may lack psychological relevance, the related fields of vision, logic programming, and knowledge representation are of psychological relevance. Typical examples of links with psychology include work on 3D representation in vision, deductive and analogical reasoning, parsing of natural-language sentences, conversions between orthographic and phonetic forms, cognitive maps of the position of objects in a bounded environment.

Investigations into the nature of computation itself are part of AI and can be found in Turing's work. According to the Church–Turing hypothesis, every calculation is computable and each computation is a procedure which computes an input–output function. These can be described by Turing machines—abstract devices which make moves according to a table of instructions and a tape divided into squares on which symbols can be written or erased. Each move consists of reading a symbol on the tape, deleting or rewriting it, and/or moving to another part of the tape. By repeated applications of these moves and with an infinitely long tape, it is possible in principle to create a Turing machine to compute any input–output function. Universal Turing machines are devices that can mimic the input–output function of any particular Turing machine. To model human intelligence requires a device with the power of a universal Turing machine, although the limits of formalization shown by Gödel's *incompleteness result suggest to many that this may not be sufficient since there are propositions that humans can understand which cannot be represented formally in a machine; AI could model only some but not all human intelligence. If correct, this result would tell against those who claim that AI not only simulates but replicates thinking. According to this strong AI thesis, a suitably programmed computer would qualify as having mental states. Some argue this is because its program would reproduce human psychological processes. John Searle has vigorously opposed this thesis, claiming that a human in a room could carry out programming instructions to convert inputs to outputs written in Chinese characters to the satisfaction of those on the outside without thereby understanding anything about Chinese. Since *computers are just formal symbol-manipulators they cannot tell us anything about understanding or thought, and so cannot qualify for mental ascription. Many replies have been offered to Searle's argument (in M. Boden (ed.), *The Philosophy of Artificial Intelligence*).

AI researcher David Marr laid the foundations for psychologically realistic computational modelling, in his theory of vision, by describing a hierarchy of levels to be found in any theory of computational psychology. Level 1 describes what is to be computed and why. Level 2 analyses different representations and algorithms for computing that function. And Level 3 describes how any given algorithm is to be implemented in the hardware.   B.C.S.

*Chinese room argument; consciousness, its irreducibility; mind, syntax, and semantics.

M. Boden, *Artificial Intelligence and Natural Man*, 2nd edn. (Cambridge, Mass., 1987).
—— (ed.), *The Philosophy of Artificial Intelligence* (Oxford, 1990); includes Alan Turing, 'Computing Machinery and Intelligence'.
J. Haugeland (ed.), *Mind Design* (Cambridge, Mass., 1981).
D. Marr, *Vision* (San Francisco, 1982).
A. Turing, *The Essential Turing*, ed. B. J. Copeland (Oxford, 2004).

artificial language. All *language is man-made, but artificial languages are made systematically for some particular purpose. They take many forms, from mere adaptations of an existing writing system (numerals), through completely new notations (sign language), to fully expressive systems of speech devised for fun (Tolkien) or secrecy (Poto and Cabenga) or learnability (Esperanto). Logicians' artificial symbolic languages are none of these, for although they typically contain some new vocabulary (logical *constants) and syntax designed to avoid *ambiguity and *vagueness, they also largely consist of schemata intended to be open to an inexhaustible range of interpretations, and are therefore not available for ordinary linguistic purposes such as assertion (you can't use '*P*' or '(*P* → *Q*)', or even '(*P* → *P*)', to *say* anything). Their purpose is to present *forms* into which natural-language utterances may be artificially squeezed; their value is as aids for appraising reasoning, and in the philosophical study of reasoning.   C.A.K.

*Formal language.

S. Guttenplan, *The Languages of Logic* (Oxford, 1986).

artworld: *see* aesthetics, history of.

asceticism. Principally a doctrine or way of life in which the enjoyment of bodily *pleasures, comfort, and ease is forsworn for moral, spiritual, or religious reasons. Enjoyment of such pleasures and comforts may be held to tempt to sin; to prevent contemplation of or dedication to higher things; to tie one to the illusory world of matter and false goods; and so on. Such doctrines and practices enjoy little popularity these days, but history records some notable ascetics such as St Simeon Stylites (*c*.390–459), who lived on the top of his pillar and attracted many imitators.

N.J.H.D.

P. Rousseau, *Ascetics, Authority and the Church in the Age of Jerome and Cassian* (Oxford, 1978).
The Sayings of the Desert Fathers, tr. B. Ward (London, 1975).

A-series and B-series. These are terms introduced by J. M. E. McTaggart to describe two different ways in which events can be thought of as being ordered in *time. Events are ordered in the A-series as being past, present, or future, whereas in the B-series they are ordered as being earlier or later than one another. Thus the battle of Hastings is past and the destruction of earth is future, and the former is earlier than the latter. However, events do not change their B-series relations over time, whereas they do change in respect of being past, present, or future. The battle of Hastings was once a future event and the destruction of earth will in time become a past event, but those two events always have stood and always will stand in the same earlier–later relation to one another.

E.J.L.

D. H. Mellor, *Real Time* (Cambridge, 1981).

as if: *see* Vaihinger.

aspects. Ways of appearing; what appears in ways of appearing; in Wittgenstein's philosophy, what is seen in *'seeing as'. *Wittgenstein distinguishes the 'continuous seeing' of an aspect from the 'dawning' of an aspect, suggests that the concept of an aspect is like the concept of a (re)presentation (*Vorstellung*), and says that 'aspect-blindness' is like the lack of a 'musical ear'. According to Wittgenstein, seeing aspects is 'subject to the will', but does not entail the existence of any 'private object'. In a change of aspect, paradoxically, there seems to be a new perception, yet what is presented remains unchanged.

In German phenomenology, aspects are the phenomenological appearances known as *Abschattungen*, through which spatial items such as shapes and colours are given directly in perception. *Husserl thinks physical objects are presented through *Abschattungen*, but that non-spatial items, notably mental processes, are not.

S.P.

Ludwig Wittgenstein, *Philosophical Investigations*, tr. G. E. M. Anscombe (Oxford, 1953), esp. 194–6, 206–8, 210, 213–14, 536.
Edmund Husserl, *Ideas Pertaining to a Pure Phenomenology and to a Phenomenological Philosophy*, first book, tr. F. Kersten (The Hague, 1983), esp. §§ 41, 44, 97.

ass, Buridan's. Since the Middle Ages this ass, associated with the name of Buridan though not referred to in his extant writings, has been invoked in discussions concerning *free will and *determinism. The hungry animal stood between two haystacks which were indistinguishable in respect of their delectability and accessibility. Unable to decide from which stack to feed, the ass starved to death.

A.BRO.

assertion. A type of linguistic act (act performed by the utterance of a sentence): in making an assertion, the speaker claims that a *proposition is true (contrast issuing a command, asking a question). Crucially, the proposition asserted by uttering, for example, 'He fell', can also occur unasserted, as part of another assertion, for example 'If he fell, he died'. Otherwise we could not conclude from these two assertions that he died; and we would have no account of the meaning of complex sentences in terms of their parts. Frege held that a perspicuous language would have an 'assertion sign' to indicate when a proposition is being asserted. In languages like ours, the indicative mood of the main verb conventionally (though defeasibly) indicates that an utterance of the sentence (not as a part of a longer sentence) is an assertion.

D.E.

*statements and sentences.

Michael Dummett, *Frege: Philosophy of Language*, 2nd edn. (London, 1981), ch. 10.

associationism. A theory of the nature and sources of ideas and the relations among sensations and ideas in the mind. British associationism is a school of philosophy and psychology which flourished during the eighteenth and nineteenth centuries. The theory of *ideas was largely derived from John Locke, with contributions to the principles of association made by David Hartley, David Hume, James Mill and John Stuart Mill, and Alexander Bain, among others. These philosophers, and many of their predecessors and contemporaries, British and continental (for instance, Thomas Hobbes, Revd J. Gay, Étienne Condillac), were impressed with such facts as that differences in ideas seem tied to differences in sense-experience, so that the theory of innate ideas is implausible; that the presence of something to the mind—the sensible idea of the sun, say—often continues beyond the presence of the object, the sun itself; and that some ideas seem ineluctably tied to others, so that one comes to mind immediately after the other. These facts could best be explained by principles relating to how sensations, ideas of sensations, and ideas themselves are associated one with another.

David Hartley's *Observations on Man, his Frame, his Duty, and his Expectations* (1749) contains perhaps the first systematic account of the associationist doctrine; it appears to have been developed independently of David Hume's version. Hume's writing and that of other British contributors to associationism, e.g. James Mill's *Analysis of the Phenomena of the Human Mind* (1829) and Alexander Bain's

The Senses and the Intellect (1855), *Emotion and Will* (1859), and *Mind and Body* (1872) insisted that the primary form of association is the mere contiguity of ideas of sensation in experience. (Bain was the founder of *Mind*, in 1876.) Hartley's earlier version traces the character of types of ideas of sensations to the physical, 'vibratory' motions in the brain and to the kind, locality, and line of directions of influences from the brain. Later associationists abandon the physiological account.

James Mill described the 'train of feelings, of which our lives consist' as arising by a 'general law of the Association of Ideas which is nothing but an order of occurrence, both successive and synchronous'. Individual sensible ideas do not arise in the mind, one from another, by virtue of logical connections among them. Nor do they arise in the mind by virtue of some mental power of the mind. James Mill, like Hume before him, rejected a distinctive law of association of the form of causes and effects, since such an association reduces to contiguity of ideas. Similarity among ideas, too, is not a law apart from the regular or habitual association of ideas, due merely to their contiguity or co-occurrence.

Bain further systematized associative laws, added an articulation of psychophysical parallelism, and expanded the physiological basis of psychological processes first introduced in Hartley's account of association of ideas as a special instance of Newton's theory of vibrations.

From its sources in Locke's use of the phrase 'association of ideas' (in a discussion of the intellectual errors and sources of biased belief due to illogical, merely associative relations among our ideas), associationism developed into an account of the dynamic relations in the 'stream of consciousness' and mental activity generally. Historians of psychology credit associationism as the beginning of experimental psychology, in contrast to speculative, philosophical psychology. In philosophy, associationism was vigorously criticized by the British thinkers influenced by Kant and then Hegel (e.g. T. H. Green, F. H. Bradley, Bernard Bosanquet, and others). However, in recent philosophy of psychology inspired by the connectionist or *parallel distributed processing model of the functioning of the mind–brain, some principles of mental activity with very strong echoes of associationism have been noted and, perhaps, exploited.   D.G.

E. B. de Condillac, *Traité des sensations* (1754).

Revd J. Gay, 'Dissertation on the Fundamental Principle of Virtue', preface to Archbishop King, *Origin of Evil*, tr. Archdeacon Law (*c*.1731).

John Stuart Mill, *System of Logic, Ratiocinative and Inductive* (1843).

astrology. Up to the seventeenth century astrology overlapped with astronomy and *cosmology. All studied the movements of heavenly bodies, assuming a Ptolemaic model of a finite universe composed of concentric circles with a motionless earth (neither rotating nor revolving) at the centre. Astrology is associated mainly with theories of celestial influences, understood as causal forces literally flowing down on to the static earth and bringing about all aspects of meteorological and biological change—winds, tides, and seasons, and generation, growth, corruption, and death. Astrology found a place in the deterministic view of nature woven into ancient philosophical systems—Aristotelian, Platonic, and Stoic—and their medieval and Renaissance derivatives. From antiquity, astrological practice supported *fatalism, especially with the entry into medieval western Europe of Arabic sources. Casting horoscopes and 'fortune-telling', with its claims to relate a detailed pattern of the heavenly bodies at birth to all future events of one's life, was accused of denying *free will, but condemnations did little to lessen astrology's popularity. Once the earth was shown to be a rotating and revolving planet, once an infinite universe replaced a finite one, and once genetics placed the causes for biological diversity and specificity within the organism rather than in the stars, there could be no scientific foundation for astrology whatsoever.   L.P.

J. D. North, *Stars, Minds and Fate* (London, 1989).

D. Pingree, 'Astrology', *Dictionary of the History of Ideas* (New York, 1973).

ataraxia. Freedom from trouble or anxiety. In Epicurean theory, one of the two constituents of *eudaimonia*, the other being freedom from bodily pain. Since for Epicurus the absence of pain or distress was the highest form of pleasure, this conception of *eudaimonia* was not merely negative. The elimination of anxiety, in particular of the fear of death and the afterlife, was for *Epicureans the principal motivation for the study of philosophy. It was also adopted as their end by the *Sceptics, who held that it was to be attained by suspension of judgement.

C.C.W.T.

A. A. Long and D. N. Sedley, *The Hellenistic Philosophers* (Cambridge, 1987).

atheism and agnosticism. Atheism is ostensibly the doctrine that there is no God. Some atheists support this claim by arguments. But these arguments are usually directed against the Christian concept of God, and are largely irrelevant to other possible gods. Thus much Western atheism may be better understood as the doctrine that the Christian God does not exist.

Agnosticism may be strictly personal and confessional— 'I have no firm belief about God'—or it may be the more ambitious claim that no one ought to have a positive belief for or against the divine existence. Perhaps only the ambitious version invites an argument. A promising version might combine something like William Clifford's dictum that no one ought to hold a belief on insufficient evidence with the claim that the existence of God is evidentially indeterminable. Both of these claims, of course, have been strongly contested.   G.I.M.

*God, arguments against the existence of; God and the philosophers; religion, scepticism about; religion, history of the philosophy of; religion, problems of the philosophy of.

William Clifford, 'The Ethics of Belief', in Antony Flew (ed.), *The Presumption of Atheism* (London, 1976).
Bertrand Russell, *Why I am not a Christian* (New York, 1957).

atomism, logical. A phrase used by Russell (in his paper 'Analytic Realism' (1911), 135) for a position he most fully characterized in 1918: the world is made up of logical atoms, 'little patches of colour or sounds, momentary things . . . predicates or relations and so on' ('Lectures on the Philosophy of Logical Atomism' (1918), 179), together with the facts composed of these atoms. Atomism as a theory of matter dates back to the ancients. Hume's atomism is psychological: the ultimate constituents of the world are perceptions (impressions and ideas). Russell calls his atoms logical because they have the logical, but not the metaphysical, features of substances: they are the ultimate simple subjects of predication, but they do not endure through time. He calls the process of discovering the atoms 'logical analysis'. Reflection shows that Piccadilly is not an ultimate simple, and that judgements apparently about it are really about its simple constituents. Another reason which Russell might have had for calling his atomism logical is that logical techniques are involved in constructing the complexes out of the simples: complex facts are constructed out of atomic facts, and complex things are classes constructed out of the atoms.

Russell's atomic things are *sense-data, and as short-lived as Hume's perceptions. Yet Russell denies that one can infer from this that they are mental. In the 1918 account, he speaks sympathetically, though without fully committing himself, of neutral monism, the theory that the atoms are neither mental nor physical, the distinction emerging only through the different kinds of ways in which the atoms are combined into complexes. Logical atomism has no commitment to idealism.

An atomic fact is one properly expressed by a sentence in which there are no logical connectives. Thus 'This is red', if true, states an atomic fact, whereas 'This is red or green' does not. Sentence form alone cannot be relied upon. Thus 'Tom is married' does not state an atomic fact, since it really means 'Tom is married *to someone*', and this is a general fact, involving existential quantification. Hence logical atomism is associated with the need for philosophical analysis: in order that the real nature of facts can be seen, sentences have to be analysed into their logical form.

The purest atomistic vision concerning facts is provided in Wittgenstein's *Tractatus*, and is the view that all facts, or all basic facts, are atomic, and every atomic facts independent of every other. For example, there are not really any disjunctive facts, facts of the form: p or q. For 'p or q', if true, is made true by the fact that p or by the fact that q. There is no need to posit any further fact, over and above the fact that p or the fact that q, to make 'p or q' true. Problems for this view include: the independence of atomic facts, the nature of negative facts, and whether general facts and facts of propositional attitude are reducible to atomic facts.

Wittgenstein himself abandoned the Tractarian vision because he felt that the best candidates for atomic facts were not independent. Thus *this is red* and *this is green* are incompatible, but apparently atomic. Russell argued that universally general facts are *sui generis*, contradicting Wittgenstein's view that all facts, or all basic facts, are atomic. Even if we were to enumerate all the atomic facts, we would have left something out if we did not add that these are *all* the facts there are, and this further fact is not atomic. Russell also argued that facts of *propositional attitude, for example the fact that John believes that this is red, are not atomic (since they include a complete sentence, here 'This is red'), and are also not reducible to atomic facts.   R.M.S.

B. Russell, 'Analytic Realism', in *The Collected Papers of Bertrand Russell*, vi (London, 1992), 133–46; first pub. as 'Le Réalism analytique', *Bulletin de la Société Française de Philosophie* (1911).
—— 'Lectures on the Philosophy of Logical Atomism', in *Bertrand Russell: Logic and Knowledge: Essays 1901–1950*, ed. R. C. Marsh (London, 1965), 178–281; first pub. in *Monist* (1918, 1919).
L. Wittgenstein, 'Elementary Propositions' (1932), in R. Rhees (ed.), *Philosophical Grammar*, tr. A. Kenny (Oxford, 1974), 210–14.
—— *Tractatus Logico-Philosophicus* (1921), tr. D. F. Pears and Brian McGuinness (London, 1961).

atomism, physical. A theory of the physical world, according to which it is constituted by an infinite number of indivisible corpuscles moving randomly in an infinite void. Initiated in the fifth century BC by Leucippus and Democritus, it was adopted by Epicurus, and via the rediscovery of *Epicureanism in the Renaissance developed into the 'corpuscular philosophy' of the seventeenth century.   C.C.W.T.

*Diodorus Cronus.

C. Bailey, *The Greek Atomists and Epicurus* (Oxford, 1928).

atomism, psychological. The view that the ultimate contents of the mind consist in self-standing items owing their significance to no other mental items. The psychological atoms are arrived at by breaking down complex thoughts into their simpler parts. This is achieved by psychological discrimination not logical analysis. (*Logical atomism.) When the thinker can distinguish no further separation of parts what remains are the atomic simples.   B.C.S.

D. Hume, *A Treatise of Human Nature*, ed. P. H. Nidditch, 2nd edn. (Oxford, 1978), I. i. 1.

atonement. According to this Christian doctrine, the life and death of Jesus make an important contribution to reuniting human sinners with *God. Various theological accounts of this contribution have invoked the motifs of a victory in battle over personal or impersonal forces of evil, ransom paid to liberate sinners from the devil, payment of a debt of punishment sinners cannot pay, a sacrifice sinners can offer God, and an example of love that inspires repentance. Human wrongdoers may and often should make atonement to their victims.   P.L.Q.

*forgiveness.

R. Swinburne, *Responsibility and Atonement* (Oxford, 1989).

attention. As William James says, 'consciousness goes away from where it is not needed,' and it seems an everyday truth that one can selectively consider, concentrate, or focus on some aspect of the world or of one's inner life. Searle draws a distinction between the centre and the periphery within the field of consciousness, arguing that there are different levels of attention—from the full attention I pay to my feet when putting on my shoes to the marginal attention due to them the rest of the day. How attention stands *vis-à-vis* a clear conception of consciousness, though, is a matter of debate. It seems possible to be conscious of something without attending to it. One might be conscious of the background murmurings at a party, for example, while attending exclusively to the host's speech. Despite this, the term is often used as a synonym for 'consciousness' in what can only be incomplete functional, cognitive scientific, or psychological accounts of consciousness.   J.GAR.

attitude. In a broad sense, any mental state with propositional content. Attitudes, in this sense, include beliefs, desires, hopes, and wishes. On one view, the content of any attitude is a traditional (declarative) *proposition, or a corresponding mental *representation. A person may *believe* that AIDS is curable, *desire* that AIDS is curable, *hope* that AIDS is curable, and so on. In each case, the content is the same. On another view, some different kinds of attitudes have different kinds of content. The contents of desires, for example, might be 'optative propositions' (e.g. 'Would that AIDS were curable'), whereas the contents of beliefs are declarative in form. Some accounts of attitudes replace propositions with situations. Attitudes are sometimes characterized, more narrowly, as thoughts or feelings possessing an affective tone and encompassing desire.   A.R.M.

*emotion and feeling.

J. Fodor, *Psychosemantics* (Cambridge, Mass., 1987).

attitude, aesthetic: *see* aesthetic attitude.

attribute: *see* substance and attribute.

Augustine, St (354–430). Bishop of Hippo Regius (now Annaba, Algeria), Doctor of the Western Church. His enormous influence on the doctrines of Western Christianity owes much to his skill and perseverance as a philosopher. In the history of philosophy itself he is a secondary figure, partly because he didn't have the taste or leisure to acquire more than a scrappy knowledge of the 800-year tradition preceding him.

As a young student at Carthage he formed the ambition, according to his *Confessions* (397–400), to lead a philosophical life pursuing truth. The opportunity to fulfil this ambition came when, aged 31, he resumed his childhood Christianity at Milan (386) and gave up his career as a schoolmaster. With some friends he spent a winter at Cassiciacum by the north Italian lakes, discussing philosophy and composing dialogues on scepticism, the happy life, and the soul's immortality. Returning from there (388) to his birthplace Thagaste in Numidia (Souk-Ahras, Algeria), he set up a community of young disciples and wrote on the problem of *evil, order, prosody, and language and learning. But that life soon ended, when the Catholic congregation at Hippo on the Numidian coast prevailed on him in 391 to become their presbyter and later bishop. From then on he was never free of pastoral business. He by no means stopped writing (his written output, nearly all of which survives, is bulkier than from any other ancient author), but the subject-matter became mainly polemical, against schismatics and heretics. Even his masterpieces, the *Confessions* and *City of God* (413–26), have a pastoral purpose, the one being a public meditation on his own slow road to Catholic Christianity, and the other an attack (which was to have important historical effect) on the pretensions of pagans to possess a valuable independent culture. At the end of his life he catalogued and reviewed ninety-three of his works, excluding the numerous sermons and letters, in his *Retractationes* (426–7).

In spite of his hostility to the pagan past, Augustine was formed by classicism (all through Latin—he hardly read Greek), and he commended its contributions to knowledge, and helped to transmit some of its flavour to the Western Middle Ages. In philosophy the chief influence on him was Platonist.

The *Platonism came from Plotinus. For Augustine, as for the circle from whom he imbibed it during the Milan years (384–7), it was a route to Christianity, rescuing him from Cicero's scepticism and from the materialism and good–evil dualism of the Manichees, whose sect he had joined at Carthage. Now he could agree with 'the Platonic philosophers, who said that the true God is at once the author of things, the illuminator of truth, and the giver of happiness' (*City of God*, 8.5). He could believe that there are three 'natures' or kinds of substance: bodies, mutable in time and place; souls, incorporeal but mutable in time; and *God, incorporeal and immutable (*De Genesi ad Litteram* (c.410), 8. 20. 39). God makes everything, and all that he makes is good. Badness arises from the tendency of things to decay: 'for a thing to be bad is for it to fall away from being (*deficere ab essentia*) and tend to a state in which it is not' (*De Moribus Manichaeorum* (388), 2. 2). The 'ordinary course of nature' is the regular and planned unfolding of causal or 'seminal' reasons, which date from the creation when God 'completed' his work (*De Genesi ad Litteram*, 9. 17. 32, 6. 11. 18–19).

Like Plato's *Form of the Good, Augustine's God is not only the cause of things' being but the cause of our knowing them. God illuminates truths as the sun illuminates visible things. The senses do not supply knowledge, because their objects are mutable (*Soliloquia* (386–7), 1. 3. 8).

But understanding (which is the actualization of knowledge) can be *compared* to vision as the successful exercise, like successful looking, of the faculty of reason, which is like sight, in the presence of God or wisdom, which is like light (*Soliloquia*, 1. 6. 12–15). This analogy with one of the five senses was enough to convince Augustine that knowledge is enlightenment by God, the only teacher who can do more than provide an occasion for learning (*De Magistro*, 389).

Platonism also helped to shape Augustine's views about the relation of men and other animals to their souls (*animae*), at least to the extent of persuading him that souls are incorporeal, against the *Stoic influence that had been felt by some earlier Christians. Soul, he thought, is a nature, or substance (*De Trinitate* (400–20), 2. 8. 14), and he was content to believe that until the general resurrection the souls of the dead will 'live' without bodies (*City of God*, 13. 19). But confronting the question whether a man not yet dead 'is both [a body and a soul], or only a body, or only a soul' (*De Moribus Catholicae Ecclesiae* (388), 4. 6) he chose the first answer, while also confessing that 'the *way* in which spirits adhere to bodies and become animals is altogether mysterious' (*City of God*, 21. 10. 1). The adherence may be like mixture of light with air, but perhaps should not be called mixture at all (*Epistulae*, 137.7.11).

In brooding on scepticism Augustine gradually came to think that even the tough 'criterion' of knowledge that had been agreed, seven centuries before, between Stoics and their adversaries the Academic *Sceptics could be satisfied by assent to 'I exist' and 'I am alive'. In scattered passages of his works we can see developing an argument that finds final, Descartes-anticipating form at *City of God*, 11.26: 'if I am wrong, I exist (*si fallor, sum*)'—hence one's own existence is something one cannot believe in erroneously.

Augustine made some casual remarks about language-learning in the *Confessions*, but also discussed language quite thoroughly elsewhere. He accepted the standard view that speech 'signifies', not only in the sense of *indicating* thoughts (and perhaps things) but also, apparently, in the sense of *representing* the structure of thoughts in its own verbal structure, each unit of thought being itself a word 'that we say in the heart' (*De Trinitate*, 15. 10. 19), not in any language. The theme of such inner words seemed to him important enough to be gently and lucidly expounded in more than one sermon.

Among the Christian controversies which he entered into with great zest and skill were some that involved the major philosophical themes of *time and *free will. Both Manichees and pagans had mocked the Genesis story of Creation. In *Confessions*, and *City of God*, 11–12, Augustine met the pagan challenge 'Why did God create *then*?' with a response inherited from Philo Judaeus that God made time too. It then follows—or at any rate Augustine asserted—that God himself, being beginningless, must be outside time: his years do not pass but 'stand simultaneously' (*Confessions*, 11. 13. 16). Augustine proceeded to treat Aristotle's puzzle how times can exist, seeing that all

of them are past or future or durationless. Starting from the insight that we measure times by memorizing their length (as when, in reciting the long syllables of the hymn 'Deús creátor ómniúm', we remember the duration of the short syllables and double it), he speculates whether times are affections of the mind (*Confessions*, 11. 27. 36).

Augustine saw human free will—more exactly free decision, or perhaps free control, of the will, *liberum voluntatis arbitrium*—as essential to Catholic theology because otherwise an almighty God, exempt from the limitations of Manichaean dualism, could not be justified in tolerating ill deeds and punishing ill-doers. The latter requires original guilt, *originalis reatus*, so that the sin we inherit from Adam must be 'penal' (*De Peccatorum Meritis* (411), 1. 37. 68); and both require the two-way power of acting and not acting, a 'movement of the mind free both for doing and for not doing' (*De Duabus Animabus* (392–3), 12. 17). In *De Libero Arbitrio* (391–5) and *City of God*, 5, Augustine made useful moves towards reconciling such freedom of decision with divine foreknowledge.

By the 390s he also believed, and later against Pelagius felt obliged to proclaim, that men are not able to 'fulfil the divine commands' without God's aid (*De Gratia et Libero Arbitrio* (426), 15. 31), nor even to 'will and believe' aright without God's 'acting' (*De Spiritu et Littera* (412), 34. 60). To those who receive them these benefits come as grace, unmerited, and God's will in bringing them 'cannot be resisted' (*De Corruptione et Gratia* (426), 14. 45). Yet it seems that what cannot be resisted is not received freely and—in one mood—Augustine at last confessed that though 'I tried hard to maintain the free decision of the human will, the grace of God was victorious' (*Retractationes*, 2. 1).

In one of his two works about lying Augustine criticized *consequentialism as a decision procedure on the ground of its neutrality between doing ill oneself and acquiescing in the ill deeds of others. He advised that a Christian in penal times threatened with sexual abuse unless he sacrificed to pagan gods 'more ought' to avoid 'his own sin than somebody else's, and a lesser sin of his own than a graver sin of somebody else's' (*De Mendacio* (396), 9. 14). Although this is not a licence to 'wash your hands', it does mean that sins cannot be exculpated by their good consequences. Augustine doggedly inferred that lies, being sinful, are never justified. But like St Paul disavowing 'Let us do ill that good may come' (Romans 3: 8), he did not pause to ask how sins or ill deeds are to be recognized: homicide, for example, he thought only sometimes sinful, because it is permitted to properly authorized soldiers (*Contra Faustum* (400), 22. 70) and executioners (*City of God*, 1. 21).

Augustine shared the *asceticism common among Christian and pagan intellectuals of his time. In particular sexual activity, and therefore marriage, would not fit well with philosophy. In his twenties he lived with a woman (he never names her), the mother of his son; and he says in the *Confessions* that what chiefly held him back from the plunge into Christianity was desire for a woman's arms (6. 11. 20). As a bishop he commended to others the partnership of marriage, but even more highly he commended marital continence and virginity. There was something inescapably *low* about sex.

Beginning as a champion of religious toleration, Augustine was gradually drawn into a campaign by the Catholics of north Africa to encourage state coercion of the schismatic Donatist Church, a popular and turbulent movement in the area. His chief motive may have been the same as later persuaded English liberals like Locke to stop short of advocating toleration of Roman Catholics: civil peace. His attitude to the Roman imperial power, Christian since forty years before his birth, was compliant. No one should despise the services it continued to render in increasingly 'barbarian times', while release from its evils must await the end of life's pilgrimage in this 'earthly city' and the home-coming of the saved to heaven.   C.A.K.

A. H. Armstrong (ed.), *The Cambridge History of Later Greek and Early Medieval Philosophy* (Cambridge, 1967), chs. 21–7.
P. R. L. Brown, *Augustine of Hippo: A Biography* (London, 1967).
H. Chadwick, *Augustine*, Past Masters (Oxford, 1986).
C. A. Kirwan, *Augustine*, Arguments of the Philosophers (London, 1989).
J. M. Rist, *Augustine: Ancient Thought Baptized* (Cambridge, 1994).
E. Stump and N. Kretzmann (eds.), *The Cambridge Companion to Augustine* (Cambridge, 2001).

Aurelius, Marcus (AD 121–80). Roman Emperor AD 161–80, and the last great Stoic writer of antiquity. His *Meditations*, twelve books of unsystematic private reflections on life, death, conduct, and the cosmos, appear to have survived fortuitously. Their unique value is to show us what it would be for a man at the apex of human power to live honourably, deliberately, and sensitively in accordance with the world-view and moral principles of *Stoicism: that the All is one great natural system having order and excellence as a whole; that man should seek to understand this order, should accept what is inevitable for himself, and should act with understanding and integrity towards others. The *Meditations* are immensely readable at any point of entry. They are available in numerous English translations. There is no hint in them that Stoic thought was about to be overwhelmed by superstition and its ethic absorbed into the Christian tradition.
   J.C.A.G.

A. R. Birley, *Marcus Aurelius*, 2nd edn. (Dordrecht, 1987).
F. W. Bussell, *Marcus Aurelius and the Later Stoics* (Edinburgh, 1910).

Aurobindo, Ghose (1872–1950). Cambridge educated Indian nationalist, sent to prison for anti-British 'terrorism'. In prison he had life-transforming mystical experiences. His voluminous English writings on Hindu philosophy and Indian culture deeply influenced understanding of India's spiritual traditions in terms of European thought. He combines traditional elements of the theistic philosophy of *Bhagavadgītā, contemporary science, and his own mystical encounter with God, into an original teleological or evolutionary metaphysics which

can be summarized as follows. The evolution of matter into life and mind suggests that the individual 'psyche' too can further elevate itself, through 'integral yoga', into an 'overmind'. This overmind can then commune with the 'supermind', eventually merging with Existence–Consciousness–Bliss, the Ultimate Reality called 'Brahman' in Sanskrit. The present world with all its distinctions and disharmonies is real, but awaits the compensating descent of divine life which will gradually lead to spiritual perfection for every individual. The empirically inscrutable 'logic of the infinite' ensures that this supramental descent will make all life 'beatitude's kiss'.   A.C.

*Indian philosophy.

Sri Aurobindo, *Life Divine* (Pondicherry, 1983).

Austin, John (1790–1859). Lawyer and first Professor of Jurisprudence at London University, his lectures on the philosophy of law gave wide and long-lasting currency to Bentham's *legal positivism.

Austin wanted his leading terms to have the simplicity, fewness, and definiteness of geometry's, so that political theory, like the distinct utilitarian 'science of legislation', could be popularly understood. Acknowledging Hobbes, he therefore defined positive law as commands of sovereigns (supreme political superiors habitually obeyed in independent political societies)—observing more clearly than Bentham the definition's unwelcome entailments: e.g. much constitutional law is merely 'positive morality' (distinguished in his useful terminology from 'critical morality'), and sovereigns have no legal rights. Hart's critique attributes to oversight or muddle much that Austin understood well but was obliged, by his (vulnerable) method and definitions, to exclude from 'analytical jurisprudence'.   J.M.F.

*law, philosophy of; law, positive.

John Austin, *The Province of Jurisprudence Determined*, ed. and intro. H. L. A. Hart (London, 1954).

Austin, John Langshaw (1911–60). Philosopher reputed to have led a movement giving rise in the 1950s and 1960s to *'linguistic philosophy'. Austin's career was in Oxford, where he held a Chair from 1952 until his death at the age of 48. (This was the White's Chair of Moral Philosophy, although that was not a subject in which he had a particular interest.) Austin held no general theories about language or philosophy or method; his reputation is owed to his concern sometimes to approach philosophical problems through an examination of the resources of 'ordinary language', to his characteristic style of writing (at once plain and witty), and to his great influence on his contemporaries. His approach to philosophical problems is illustrated in his idea that 'much . . . of the amusement, and of the instruction, comes in drawing the coverts of the microglot, in hounding down the minutiae': he believed that a good treatment of a topic began with a taxonomy. Austin's overall views on philosophical subjects are robustly realist, and, in epistemology at least, he was inclined to think of problems as manufactured by philosophers.

Three books appeared posthumously. *Philosophical Papers* (Oxford, 1961; 2nd edn. 1970) is a collection, which covers some epistemology, metaphysics, and philosophy of action. *Sense and Sensibilia* (Oxford, 1962) argues that a series of alleged problems about perception are bogus. *How to Do Things with Words* (Oxford, 1961) is the revised text of the William James Lectures that he gave at Harvard in 1955; this gave rise to the theory of speech-acts, which has a continuing influence in philosophy, in linguistics, and in literary studies.   J. HORN.

*Oxford philosophy; linguistic acts.

G. L. Warnock, *J. L. Austin* (London, 1989).

Australian philosophy. New South Wales was claimed for Britain by Captain Cook in 1770, and a penal colony established there in 1788. Ninety-eight years later, the first chair in philosophy was established in the new colony of Victoria at the University of Melbourne. While there have been recent attempts by feminist theorists and some moral philosophers to address the issues of justice for indigenous people and to call for recognition of the special relationship the first peoples have with the land, the continent's philosophical development owed most of its inspiration to links with Britain and Europe, later with the United States. Contemporary Australian work has a strongly 'analytic' flavour and robust academic links with New Zealand philosophy.

John Anderson's arrival in Sydney in 1927 ended forty years of idealist dominance in Australian philosophy. Obstinately realist, Anderson's thought was hostile to many of the conventional views of the age, championing an idiosyncratic form of 'empiricism' (one excluding both sense-data and ideas). Few others had such an influence on the subject's Australian development, although, thanks to invitations arranged by J. J. C. Smart, two visitors to the country had a more recent influence: first, Donald Davidson, and subsequently, David Lewis, the latter making no less than twenty-five visits to Australia from the Seventies onwards. While Anderson's influence was local, the dominant figures in Australian philosophy of the second half of the twentieth century—including J. J. C. Smart, David Armstrong, Frank Jackson, and Philip Pettit—held sway not only at home but also world-wide.

Anderson's views, however polemical, were always cast in systematic form. Poised against his system building was Sydney's historic rival, Melbourne. Stranded there during the Second World War, George Paul fuelled the competition between the two centres by spreading the doctrine of the later Wittgenstein, a task continued by Douglas Gasking, who even translated Wittgensteinian doctrine 'into Sydney' to facilitate its dissemination. By the early Fifties, some thought that the Sydney conception of philosophy as a systematic investigation into the nature of things was finished.

In 1950 Smart was appointed to the chair of philosophy at Adelaide. In turn, Smart appointed U. T. Place and C. B. Martin. Place converted Smart from a Rylean to a materialist view, and was the first to publish—in 1956—an account of the new 'identity theory of mind' (often called 'Australian materialism'). The new theory was not only championed by Smart, but later developed, under Armstrong, into a fully-fledged 'central-state materialism' claiming that all mental processes are simply physical processes in the brain. Martin, who introduced into Australia the concept of truth-maker (that, whatever it is, in virtue of which a proposition, or other truth-bearer, is true), favoured a double-aspect view of the mental in preference to straight reductionism. The Adelaide-based arguments about materialism constituted a golden age in the development of Australian metaphysical realism—a position that still pervades much of contemporary Australian writing. Place left Australia in 1956, but not until 1982 did the most significant Australian objection to the reduction of the mental to the physical appear, in Jackson's appealing thought experiment. Mary—a scientist with normal colour vision who has lived since birth in a black and white world—knows everything about the physics and physiology of colour perception, yet still, Jackson argued, she does not know what it is like to sense red.

While Anderson's use of logic was restricted to a version of syllogistic reasoning, Melbourne had been largely indifferent to formal logic altogether. However, from the Seventies onwards, a number of distinctive approaches to logic developed, focusing particularly on the fields of relevance and paraconsistent logic. Several of the leading contributors to this logical turn included migrants—Richard Routley (later Sylvan) from New Zealand, Len Goddard and Graham Priest from the United Kingdom, and Bob Meyer from the United States. Alongside this interest in logic, history and philosophy of science has also found a central place in both teaching and research in Australia, with recent studies in philosophy of biology by Kim Sterelny and Paul Griffiths complementing the focus on physics and problems of space and time of an earlier generation of writers such as Graham Nerlich. The history of philosophy itself has received careful attention in the writings of John Passmore, Stephen Gaukroger, and Stewart Candlish.

Work on moral and political philosophy was shaped to an extent by migrant influence, though some of the best-known work in this area was carried out by Australians who chose to live overseas—for example, J. L. Mackie, famous for his defence of the 'error theory' of value in his 1977 book on *Ethics*. Before then, Kurt Baier had defended a robust moral objectivism, D. H. Monro had defended moral subjectivism, and Julius Kovesi had queried the 'fact-value gap'. Many of the works on ethical and political theory originating from Australia after the Seventies championed forms of utilitarianism and consequentialism (in the hands, for example, of Smart, Pettit, and Robert Goodin), with C. L. Ten and Robert Young standing apart from this general trend. Engagement with meta-ethical theory continued when in 1994 Michael Smith published *The Moral Problem*, an attempt at reconciling a form of moral rationalism with a Humean approach to motivation.

A different way of approaching philosophical, political, and moral problems, incorporating psychological and sociological perspectives, has inspired a distinctive school of Australian feminist philosophy, in the hands of Moira Gatens, Elizabeth Grosz, and others, whose writing intersects to an extent with a developing interest in, and indeed resurgence of, European philosophy in both Australia and New Zealand. Matching the synthesis of analytic and European styles of philosophizing championed by Hubert Dreyfus and Richard Rorty in the United States, a similar convergence has characterized recent Australian writing by Max Deutscher, Jeff Malpas, Paul Redding, and a few others. Applied ethics has lately received recognition, and large-scale financial support, in keeping with earlier Australian pioneering studies in environmental philosophy by Routley, Passmore, Val Routley (later Plumwood), Robert Elliot, and others. Debates on social and political justice, poverty, abortion, bioethics, and biomedical ethics have been subject to philosophically informed scrutiny by writers like Michael Tooley, Genevieve Lloyd, Peter Singer, Freya Mathews, Janna Thompson, and Rai Gaita. While some of these arguments have taken on a life of their own, disengaged from technical issues within philosophy itself, the emergence of intellectual debate at home and overseas featuring these and other thinkers is a powerful testimony to the continuing vigour and influence of Australian philosophy.   A.BRE.

*New Zealand philosophy; women in philosophy.

C. A. J. Coady, 'Australia, Philosophy in', in E. Craig (ed.), *Routledge Encyclopedia of Philosophy* (London, 1998).

S. A. Grave, *A History of Philosophy in Australia* (St Lucia, Queensland, 1984).

J. T. J. Srzednicki and D. Wood (eds.), *Essays on Philosophy in Australia* (Dordrecht, 1992).

authenticity. The condition of those, according to Heidegger, who understand the existential structure of their lives. Heidegger held that each of us acquires an identity from our situation—our family, culture, etc. Usually we just absorb this identity uncritically, but to let one's values and goals remain fixed without critical reflection on them is 'inauthentic'. The 'authentic' individual, who has been aroused from everyday concerns by *Angst*, takes responsibility for their life and thereby 'chooses' their own identity. But Heidegger also holds that some degree of inauthenticity is unavoidable: the critical assessment of values presupposes an uncritical acceptance of them, and the practical necessities of life give a priority to unreflective action over critical deliberation. So, as Heidegger makes clear, authenticity is like Christian salvation: a state which 'fallen' individuals cannot guarantee by their own efforts.   T.R.B.

M. Heidegger, *Being and Time*, tr. J. MacQuarrie and E. Robinson (Oxford, 1962), sects. 38, 41, 61–6.

authority. An authority is a person or group having a right to do or to demand something, including the right to demand that other people do something.

Authority is invariably and justifiably discussed alongside *power. The joint discussion is justifiable not only because the concepts overlap in confusing ways but also because both are essential for an adequate analysis of political and legal systems.

Authority is of course used in contexts other than the legal and political. We speak in various contexts of people being 'in authority', 'having authority', and 'being authorized'. What is common to all these usages is the essential idea of having some sort of right or entitlement to behave in the way indicated, or that the behaviour is in some way 'legitimate' (another concept essentially related to authority).

This analysis applies also to Max Weber's account of authority, which has exerted a large influence on sociological theory. Weber distinguishes three kinds of authority: rational–legal, traditional, and charismatic. In rational–legal authority the right to give orders or to act in certain ways derives from an office or role held within a set of rules setting out rights and duties. Traditional authority exists because those accepting the authority see it as deriving from a long and hallowed tradition of obedience to a leader. Charismatic authority exists where exceptional abilities cause a person to be followed or obeyed, and the exceptional ability is perceived as conferring a right to lead. (We must add the last clause or charismatic authority will become simply charismatic power.)

If authority is to be effective the person in authority must also possess power. But the two are distinct: a government in exile may be legitimate or be in authority or be *de jure*, whereas the *de facto* rulers may have power while lacking the authority. But while that is true as far as it goes the situation is more complex than that neat distinction suggests. A schoolteacher may be in authority, but have no authority with his pupils. This means not just that he lacks power to influence them; it also means that in some sense they do not regard him as legitimate. The same situation could happen politically. The explanation of the paradox lies in a separation which has taken place between two sorts of legitimization: in terms of rules and in terms of popular approval. A second complication in distinguishing authority from power is that for some people or groups the source of their power lies in the fact that they are in authority. We could then say that authority is their 'power-base' (as it is sometimes called), just as wealth, military might, or physical beauty might be power-bases. If we stress this line of thought, then it would be possible to make 'power' the dominant concept and authority would become a subset of power, and some political theorists and sociologists might take this line. But it is more usual, and probably it is philosophically preferable, to contrast authority as a *de jure* or normative concept with power as a *de facto* or causal concept, and allow that in some cases there can be overlap. No consistent distinction between the two can be derived from ordinary usage or political and legal discourse, and some measure of stipulation is inevitable.

We are left with one sense of 'authority' to fit in—where we speak of a person as being (say) an authority on birds or the seventeenth century. But this sense can be accommodated into our analysis: the authority has passed recognized examinations, published in the journals, and written the books which entitle or give the right to pronounce on the subject. R.S.D.

A. de Crespigny and A. Wertheimer (eds.), *Contemporary Political Theory* (London, 1970).

C. J. Friedrich (ed.), *Authority: Nomos*, i (New York, 1958).

J. Raz (ed.), *Authority* (Oxford, 1990).

Max Weber, *The Theory of Social and Economic Organization*, tr. A. M. Henderson and Talcott Parsons (New York, 1947).

autobiography, philosophical. The role and aims of autobiography have changed in fundamental ways in the course of the history of philosophy. Marcus Aurelius, author of a quasi-autobiographical *Meditations*, noted that nothing is as morally uplifting and joyful as meditating on a virtuous life, and this provided a rationale for autobiography from antiquity up to the modern era. Descartes, in the autobiographical sections of his *Discourse on Method* (1637), was not so much concerned to register how he felt and worked, but rather with how someone in this position should have felt and worked: the story he tells is designed to be morally and intellectually uplifting, and would doubtless have seen the kind of aims that have guided nineteenth- and twentieth-century autobiography as mere self-indulgence and an amoral form of narcissism, a genre useless for moral or personal guidance. Hume and Rousseau, writing in the eighteenth century, presented their lives—the first briefly, the second at length—as virtuous and blameless, although in Rousseau's case this did not prevent him from revealing personal and sexual details.

The idea of a person having a history other than that which typifies a particular aspect of some general human condition receives its first expression in the late sixteenth century in the *Essays* of Montaigne. Montaigne initiated his project of self-exploration with the traditional aim of discovering a universal human nature, but what he ended up doing was something completely different: he discovered himself, his thoughts, feelings, emotions. Although biography continued primarily within a didactic genre up to the end of the nineteenth century, Montaigne initiated an understanding of subjectivity which—in the hands of Descartes, Rousseau, Kant, and others—fostered a notion of the self as a centralized locus of subjectivity. This philosophical understanding of subjectivity gradually changed what was possible at the biographical level.

From the end of the nineteenth century, developments in areas such as psychoanalysis allowed a deepening of the way in which affective states were thought of, and this had a very significant impact on the genre of biography, encouraging the inclusion of detailed material which would have been thought irrelevant or inappropriate in earlier conceptions of the genre. It also had a reductive effect, however, levelling differences between the philosopher, the politician, and the artist, for example, so that individual psychology now became the focus of biography.

One of the main values of philosophical autobiography is that it can show us the struggle to develop philosophical theories—a struggle which involves hestitations, mistakes, and uncertainties—that helps demystify claims to special access to truth. Another is providing a context for philosophical views—this is especially the case in J. S. Mill's autobiography—which enables us to see how they arose out of general political and economic concerns, for example, giving us a sense of how philosophers have elucidated particularly intractable problems by translating them into a philosophical form. However, like any other form of autobiography, philosophers can use the genre to obfuscate or to rationalize their beliefs or behaviour. Descartes, for example, was keen for his readers to believe that he never rose before midday and spent little time on philosophy, for this was how he saw the behaviour of a gentleman, whereas in fact he spent the whole of his day on philosophical and related questions. Russell intimated in his autobiography that his shift of interest from philosophy to social questions in the early 1920s was the result of his experiences in the First World War, but as more recent biographical and autobiographical work has shown, the shift derives rather from his meeting with D. H. Lawrence, whom he later came to regard as a proto-Fascist and whose influence he disowned.

Few philosophical autobiographies stand out as great works of literature, but the autobiographical writings of Augustine, Rousseau, Mill, and Simone de Beauvoir (many would also include at least the first volume of Russell's autobiography in this list) stand out as classics, and are likely to be read as long as philosophy exists. S.G.

Augustine, *Confessions*, tr. H. Chadwick, (Oxford, 1991).

Simone de Beauvoir, *Memoirs of a Dutiful Daughter* (Harmondsworth, 2001).

—— *Force of Circumstance* (New York, 1994).

—— *Prime of Life* (Harmondsworth, 1965).

R. Descartes, *Discourse on Method and Related Writings*, tr. D. Clarke (Harmondsworth, 1999).

M. de Montaigne, *The Complete Essays of Montaigne*, tr. D. Frame (Stanford, Calif., 1965).

J.-J. Rousseau, *Confessions* (1782) (Harmondsworth, 1953).

B. Russell, *Autobiography* (London, 1967).

autonomy and heteronomy. Correlative terms, developed by Kant, of very wide applicability to moral theory. Autonomy (Greek 'self' + 'law') understands the moral imperative as the moral agent's own freely and rationally adopted moral policy. As moral agents, we are all subject to the moral law, but we repudiate all maxims (personal policies of action) which 'cannot accord with the will's own enactment of universal law' (*Groundwork*, ch. 2). All alternative accounts, where moral law is commanded from without, are heteronomous (the law of 'another').

Among heteronomous theories are those that see moral imperatives as commands of the state or of society, or even as the commands of a deity. No less heteronomous is a theory that identifies the source of morality with some contingent drive or sentiment in one's empirical psychology. For a Kantian moralist, moral maturity crucially involves the recognition of autonomy. There is an important link here with *freedom. Heteronomy, in any form, entails that we are passive under some command or impulsion which we do not, can not, initiate. In contrast, if we autonomously recognize and endorse a moral value, make it our own, we are acting (when we obey it) as we have most deeply and freely resolved to act.

What autonomy amounts to, however, has been interpreted in radically different ways: by some as the discerning and 'enacting'—through common rational procedures—of a common moral law. This was Kant's own position. As reworked by certain Existentialists, analytical philosophers, and radical educationalists, autonomy has amounted to the individual's total sovereignty over his or her 'choice' of moral values and self-construction, a view that accords a unique importance to *'authenticity', freedom from 'mauvaise foi'. This extreme version of autonomy is seriously and dangerously flawed. It is hard or impossible, for one thing, to justify in its own terms the place it gives to the virtue of authenticity itself. Again, it would seem to imply that any value-claim whatever ('maximize suffering', say) is vindicated so long as it stems from individual, 'autonomous' decision. In practice, such implications tend to be masked by smuggling into a theory basic, common judgements of value not at all derived from individual decision.   R.W.H.

*autonomy in applied ethics; bad faith.

H. E. Allison, *Kant's Theory of Freedom* (Cambridge, 1990).
I. Kant, *Groundwork of the Metaphysic of Morals*, in H. J. Paton (ed.), *The Moral Law* (London, 1948).
Charles Taylor, 'Responsibility for Self', in G. Watson (ed.), *Free Will* (Oxford, 1982).

autonomy in applied ethics. The concept of personal autonomy, used in a broad sense which goes beyond its Kantian origins, has been much invoked in recent writing on issues in *applied ethics. It has been suggested, for instance, that the wrongness of *killing rests, in part, on the fact that to deprive someone of their life is normally to violate their autonomy. This account carries the implication that the moral prohibition of taking life would not apply in a case where someone wished their life to be ended—for instance, in the case of voluntary *euthanasia. On the contrary, respect for the person's autonomy would then require one to comply with their wishes. Another application of the concept in *medical ethics is the suggestion that the importance of 'informed consent' in relations between the patient and the medical practitioner rests on respect for personal autonomy.

In political philosophy, the idea of persons as autonomous agents underlies liberal theories of *justice such as that of Rawls, as well as liberal defences of more

specific political values such as *freedom of speech and expression. And in the philosophy of education, the promotion of personal autonomy has been identified as one of the principal aims of education.

These various uses of the concept have prompted attempts at a more precise account of what autonomy is. Our idea of the autonomous person seems to involve more than just the capacity to act on particular desires and choices. It suggests a more general capacity to be self-determining, to be in control of one's own life. At this point some writers have found helpful the distinction between first-order desires and second-order desires; the autonomous person is one who is able to assess his or her own first-order desires, to reject or modify some of them and to endorse others, and to act upon these second-order preferences.   R.J.N.

*freedom; autonomy and heteronomy; autonomy, personal.

Gerald Dworkin, *The Theory and Practice of Autonomy* (Cambridge, 1988).
Richard Lindley, *Autonomy* (London, 1986).

Avecebrol: *see* Ibn Gabirol.

Avenarius, Richard (1843–96). German positivist and empiricist philosopher who argues for the elimination of cognitive preconceptions which generate metaphysical dualisms and obscure the findings of 'pure experience'. Avenarius holds that prima facie mutually inconsistent philosophies presuppose a 'natural realism' entailing the existence of physical objects and other minds. Avenarius' 'empirio-criticism' putatively exposes metaphysics as a spurious branch of philosophy and urges its replacement by the natural sciences, which have an empirical justification in the findings of pure experience. Avenarius may be thought of as an empiricist neo-Kantian whose 1888–90 work *Kritik der Reinen Erfahrung* (Critique of Pure Experience) anticipates in important respects the empiricism of James and the Logical Positivists and the phenomenology of Husserl. Avenarius' work was influential in Russia and was one of the targets of Lenin's book *Materialism and Empirio-Criticism* (1908).   S.P.

*neo-Kantianism; positivism.

Richard Avenarius, *Kritik der Reinen Erfahrung*, 2 vols. (Leipzig, 1891).
—— *Der Menschliche Weltbegriff* (Leipzig, 1891).
Friedrich Raab, *Die Philosophie von Richard Avenarius* (Leipzig, 1912).

Averroës (*c*.1126–98). Andalusian philosopher acclaimed as the greatest Aristotelian commentator, though his work had little impact in the East. His principal works, surviving in Hebrew and Latin and studied in the West to the mid-seventeenth century, consist of commentaries on Aristotelian texts and on Plato's *Republic*. His text, *The Incoherence of the Incoherence*, written in response to al-Ghazālī's attack on philosophy, illustrates Averroës's contention that theologians are incapable of reaching the highest demonstrative knowledge and are thus unfit to interpret divine law correctly. His Aristotelian commentaries principally sought: (1) to cleanse the Islamic philosophical corpus from Neoplatonist emanationist views; (2) to separate pure philosophy from theological arguments by al-Fārābī and Avicenna, among others; and thus (3) to recover 'pure' Aristotelian thought. H.Z.

*Aristotelianism.

Averroës, *The Incoherence of the Incoherence*, tr. S. Van den Bergh (Oxford, 1954).

Avicenna (980–1037). Persian philosopher, scientist, and physician, widely called 'The Supreme Master'; he held an unsurpassed position in *Islamic philosophy. His works, including the *Canon of Medicine*, are cited throughout most medieval Latin philosophical and medical texts. The subject of more commentaries, glosses, and superglosses than any other Islamic philosopher, they have inspired generations of thinkers, including Persian poets. His philosophical works—especially *Healing: Directives and Remarks*, and *Deliverance*—define Islamic Peripatetic philosophy, one of the three dominant schools of Islamic philosophy.

His contributions to science and philosophy are extraordinary in scope. He is thought to be the first logician to clearly define temporal modalities in propositions, to diagnose and identify many diseases, and to identify a specific number of pulse beats in diagnosis. His best-known philosophical formulations are: (1) the ontological distinction between essence and existence, in which the essences of existing entities cannot be explained as actualized forms of their material potentialities without an existing cause whose existence, while coexistent with the caused and perceived essence, is prior in rank (later designated 'primary of existence over essence' and redefined by Mollā Ṣadrā); (2) the ontological distinctions of possible, impossible, and necessary being—i.e. the Avicennan constructed whole of reality consisting of ranked and ordered ontic entities, each the cause of the existence of the one ranking below it. Since infinity is impossible in this system, every entity is a distinct being and must be contingent, except for the top of the ontological chain, which is necessary. This is because existence is observed and vacuum is proven impossible; therefore the Necessary Being's essence and existence are identical, so It is self-existent and the cause of all other existent entities. This philosophical existence proof, denoted in Latin texts as Avicennan, is generally considered novel within the history of philosophy. H.Z.

L. Goodman, *Avicenna* (London, 1992).
G. M. Wickens (ed.), *Avicenna, Scientist and Philosopher: A Millenary Symposium* (London, 1952).

awareness, sense. *Perception of objects and conditions by means of the senses. Normally taken to include proprioception—awareness of the position and movement of one's own limbs, for example—and to exclude (because not a form of *sense* awareness) *introspection of mental states. Sensory awareness of external objects is mediated by particular bodily organs (eyes, nose, etc.) and gives rise to distinctive types of experience (visual, olfactory, etc.). F.D.

*sense-data.

M. Perkins, *Sensing the World* (Indianapolis, 1983).

axiological ethics. That portion of ethics that is concerned specifically with *values. Unlike the portions concerned with morality and with social justice, axiological ethics does not focus directly on what we should do. Instead it centres on questions of what is worth pursuing or promoting and what should be avoided, along with issues of what such questions mean and of whether and how there is any way of arriving at answers to them that constitute knowledge. Many philosophers have offered systematic accounts of what is of value without much indication of how their answers are justified or of why they should be taken as having some kind of objective validity. But much of the current philosophical interest in axiological ethics centres on the epistemology (if any) of values.

The issue of justification arises whether or not a set of values is systematic. If it is, then we may ask whether whatever organizes the system has any validity. If it is not, then one wants to know whether the diverse value judgements represent merely personal (or societal) invention or preference, or instead have something more objective to be said for them. G. E. Moore's answer, 'intuition', is no longer regarded by many people as satisfactory.

A possible outcome always is that there is no justification for values beyond the dictates or preferences of particular persons or societies. This amounts to a value anti-realism (a denial that judgements of value can have any objective validity), parallel to, but distinct from, moral anti-realism. Indeed it looks possible to be a moral anti-realist but to hold that some things or styles of life really are better than others, and Nietzsche sometimes sounds as if he has this combination of views. Conversely, moral realists who lean toward a contractual view of moral validity sometimes sound unwilling to affirm any objective values apart from those of a certain kind of political or social order.

One promising line is to regard judgements of value as characteristically rooted in emotions. John Stuart Mill held, for example, that desire has the same relation to knowledge about what is desirable as our senses and introspection have to knowledge about the world. Everyone desires pleasure and only pleasure, he held, which gives some kind of objective validity to the judgement that pleasure is the *good. Other philosophers, not so ready to make claims about the uniformity of the human sense of value, have suggested that values are rooted in particular preferences, or in approval, or in responses such as delight, admiration, repugnance, or disgust. A judgement of value could be justifiable if the emotion at its root is justified.

There also are interesting questions concerning how values are related to self and to sense of self. Much modern discussion of values has treated them in the context of our deciding what things to have or not to have in our lives. There may be an influence of consumerism in this: the focus is on things, relationships, and states of mind to be had rather than on the nature of the person who might have them. But there is psychological evidence that what is broadly the same kind of thing or relationship can have different impacts on the lives of different people, and also that *happiness (which is often treated as a cluster of major values) has a close link with self-esteem, and more generally with sense of self. It is instructive that in both Plato's and Aristotle's accounts of values the process of becoming a particular kind of person is treated as paramount.   J.J.K.

*well-being; right action.

J. N. Findlay, *Axiological Ethics* (London, 1970).
James Griffin, *Well-Being* (Oxford, 1986).
G. E. Moore, *Principia Ethica* (Cambridge, 1903).
J. Raz *et al.*, *The Practice of Value* (Oxford, 2003).

axiom. An axiom is one of a select set of propositions, presumed true by a system of logic or a theory, from which all other propositions which the system or theory endorses as true are deducible—these derived propositions being called *theorems of the system or theory. Thus, Pythagoras' theorem is deducible from the axioms of Euclidean geometry. The axioms and theorems of a system of logic—for instance, of the *propositional calculus—are regarded as being true of logical *necessity.
                                                           E.J.L.
*axiomatic method; deduction.

W. V. Quine, *Methods of Logic*, 3rd edn. (London, 1974).

axiomatic method. Thinkers in a tradition including Euclid, Newton, Hilbert, Peano, Whitehead and Russell, and others have used the axiomatic method to present different subject-matters as formal and coherent theories, all propositions of which are deducible from a clearly specified set of initial assumptions. A fully formalized axiomatic system contains (i) primitive symbols, (ii) rules of formation distinguishing well-formed from ill-formed expressions, (iii) definitions, (iv) *axioms, and (v) rules of inference establishing how theorems are proved. It is a formal *calculus which must be distinguished carefully from its interpretation, the latter being a semantic notion associating the system with the models of which it holds true. Desirable characteristics of axiomatic systems are consistency (freedom from contradiction), completeness (sufficient strength to enable all semantically true propositions to be proved), and independence of axioms. Unsuccessful attempts to show the independence of Euclid's parallel postulate led in the nineteenth century to the discovery of non-Euclidean geometries.   S.McC.

R. Blanché, *Axiomatics* (London, 1962).

Ayer, Alfred Jules (1910–89). British philosopher, published his first book *Language, Truth and Logic* in 1936. It remains the classic statement in English of *Logical Positivism. Its central doctrine is that there are just two sorts of cognitively meaningful statement, those which are, in principle, empirically verifiable (observationally testable) and those which are analytic (true simply in virtue of linguistic rules). Scientific statements and statements of ordinary fact belong to the first class, while statements of mathematics and of logic belong to the second. Religious and metaphysical statements, such as that God exists (or, indeed, that he does not), or that there is a realm of things in themselves behind phenomena, are meaningless, because they belong to neither class. Basic ethical statements are regarded similarly as factually meaningless but are allowed an emotive meaning (that is, they express emotional attitudes). That Ayer is not disfavouring them as such, as he is the religious and metaphysical ones, is made clearer in later works. As for philosophy, its task is logical clarification of the basic concepts of science, not the attempt to say how things truly are.

His later works move steadily away from doctrinaire Logical Positivism, but much of its spirit is retained, in particular the view that religion is nonsense whenever it is not simply false. Ayer saw himself as essentially advocating an *empiricism in the tradition of Hume, rendered more forceful by the devices of modern logic. Metaphysics is treated with more respect in so far as conceptual clarification is seen as itself illuminating the world to which our concepts apply.

Certain themes are recurrent in his substantial later *œuvre*, such as the meaning and justification of statements about other minds, about personal identity, and above all about the nature of our knowledge of the physical world. While he was originally a phenomenalist, his later view is that physical objects are posits in a theory, the point of which is to enable us to predict our sense-data, but which is not reducible to facts about them. He also wrote importantly on probability and induction. Ethically he espoused a qualified utilitarianism, though interpreting the *greatest happiness principle as the expression of an optional fundamental attitude.

Perhaps his finest book is *The Problem of Knowledge* (1956). This sees epistemology as primarily an effort to justify ordinary claims to *knowledge against philosophical scepticism. One knows that *p* if and only if one believes that *p*, has a right to be sure on the matter, and is, in fact, right that *p* is so. *Scepticism arises when there appears to be a logical gap between our only possible evidence for the existence and character of things of a certain sort and our ordinary confident claims to knowledge about them. For example, our access to the physical world seems to be only via our own sense-data, to the minds of others via their behaviour, and to the past via our memories. There are four types of possible solution. (1) Naïve realism holds that the problematic things are, after all, directly given to us, so that we somehow directly perceive physical objects, other minds, or the past, without the intermediary of any sense-data, behaviour, or memories which are mere representations of them. (2) Reductionism reduces the existence of the problematic things to the holding of suitable patterns among the evidential data, e.g. sense-data, behaviour, or memory images and historical records. (3) The scientific approach tries to show that after all the inference from the evidence to the conclusion has a scientifically respectable inductive character. The difficulty here is that there can be no inductive grounds for moving from Xs to Ys, if we have no possible access to the latter except by the former. (4) The method of descriptive analysis, largely favoured by Ayer (though somewhat modified later) simply describes how we do, in fact, base our beliefs on the evidence and shows that the complaint that these are not well based is unreasonable as making an impossible demand.

In spite of his iconoclasm Ayer had no truck with some of the wilder assaults upon traditional philosophical thought, such as ordinary-language philosophy on the one hand, and behaviourism and physicalism on the other.

T.L.S.S.

*London philosophy; Oxford philosophy; verification principle; tender- and tough-minded.

A. J. Ayer, *Perception and Identity*, ed. G. F. Macdonald (London, 1979).

L. E. Hahn (ed.), *The Philosophy of A. J. Ayer*, The Library of Living Philosophers, xxi (La Salle, Ill., 1992).

John Foster, *A. J. Ayer*, The Arguments of the Philosophers (London, 1985).

A. Phillips Griffiths (ed.) *A. J. Ayer: Memorial Essays* (London, 1991).

B

Babbage–Chambers paradox. Charles Babbage (1791–1871), mathematician and almost-inventor of the digital computer, observed in his *Ninth Bridgwater Thesis* (1838) that his calculating engine could produce the series of natural numbers from 1 to 100,000,000, and then—without any interference— produce 100,000,001; 100,010,002; 100,030,003; 100,060,004; 'and so on' for many hundred terms, till yet another rule came into play. This realization, that the same process might suddenly reveal another law (and so that *miracles could not be ruled out), was further developed by Robert Chambers (1802–71) to explain the differences between successive geological eras: the 'same process' operated by different laws to produce unpredictable changes. As an account of *evolution, or of miracles, the story proved unpopular. As an anticipation of Goodman's problem with grue, and Wittgenstein's with the notion of rule-following, it retains its interest: no finite string of observations or operations can identify what rule is being followed, or what its correct application might require in the future.   s.r.l.c.

Robert Chambers, *Vestiges of Creation* (Edinburgh, 1844).
Doron Swade, *The Cogwheel Brain: Charles Babbage and the Quest to Build the First Computer* (London, 2001).

Bachelard, Gaston (1884–1962). Bachelard's studies of the emergence of scientific *objectivity anticipated some of the conclusions of Popper and Kuhn without exerting any direct influence. His reputation depends, however, less on his anti-positivism and his discovery of 'epistemological ruptures' than on his studies of poetic language, daydream, and phenomenology, and their application to episodes in the history of science. Like Bacon, Bachelard regarded the projection of subjective values and interests into the experience of the physical world as impediments to knowledge. In *Le Nouvel Esprit scientifique* (1938), which he described as a 'psychoanalysis of knowledge', he showed how the emergence of an objective and quantified science required depersonalization and abstraction, emotional restraint, and 'taciturnity'. His intention was not thereby to discredit subjectivity. Rather, he placed the capacity for reverie, which he saw as the source of great poetry as well as of abject sentimentality and imaginary physical theories, at the centre of his theory of the human mind, and he understood that affective engagement with

'things' was a condition of scientific productivity. 'Psychoanalysis', in Bachelard's terms, did not refer to the Freudian study of sublimated drives of the individual, but to the disclosure of *archetypes, which Jung's studies on alchemy of the early 1930s had first shown to have a bearing on the interpretation of early chemical theories and the practice of alchemy. In his study of eighteenth-century experiments with fire, *La Psychanalyse du feu* (1938), Bachelard showed how the phenomenology of fire as painful, dangerous, soothing, purifying, destructive, and a symbol of life and passion, determined scientific discourse. Other studies on air, water, and earth, which, like fire, have since been deconstituted as subjects of scientific inquiry, showed how they too were 'dreamt' by the eighteenth century. Bachelard's influence on the early work of Foucault and other French theorists of his generation is significant.

                                                              cath.w.

C. G. Christofides, 'Gaston Bachelard and the Imagination of Matter', *Revue internationale de philosophie* (1963).
P. Quillet, *Bachelard: Présentation, choix de textes, bibliographie* (Paris, 1964).
Mary Tiles, *Gaston Bachelard: Science and Objectivity* (Cambridge, 1984).

backgammon. Board game for two players, renowned among philosophers as one of Hume's methods of recovery from philosophical melancholy and *scepticism. 'I dine, I play a game of backgammon, I converse, and am merry with my friends; and when after three or four hour's amusement, I wou'd return to these speculations, they appear so cold, and strain'd, and ridiculous, that I cannot find in my heart to enter into them any farther' (*A Treatise of Human Nature*, I. iv. 7). If we may follow Adam Smith's account of Hume in later life, however, the philosopher's favourite game was actually whist.   j.bro.

background. The previously acquired understanding or knowledge that allows utterances, beliefs, and actions to have explicit meaning for us. The problem of the background has recently received philosophical attention with respect to meaning in language, knowledge in science, and objectivity in interpretation. Words and utterances presuppose an implicit and a holistic understanding of beliefs and practices. Observation and justification in the sciences function only against the background of shared paradigms of understanding acquired in scientific socialization. And the necessary reliance of any interpreter on her own prior understanding rules out the possibility of any neutral perspective in cultural interpretation. There is disagreement about whether the background is basically conceptual and symbolic in nature—and thus in principle explicable—or whether it is mainly practical and prepropositional—and therefore can never be captured fully in theory.   H.-H.K.

   *hermeneutics; holism.

H. Dreyfus, 'Holism and Hermeneutics', *Review of Metaphysics* (1981).

backwards causation. This is the idea that a cause may be later in time than its effect. In the case of physical processes and human actions we naturally assume that the direction of causation is from earlier to later time. The play in a football match causes the final result; it would be absurd to believe that the result could cause the earlier play. On the other hand, people do sometimes suppose that prayer or more overt religious rituals might have causal influence on what has happened at an earlier time. Aristotle argued extensively in favour of a different mode of backward, or *teleological*, causation, with the following examples: the goal (e.g. health) as the cause of purposive activity (e.g. physical exercise), or a developed natural product (e.g. an oak) as the cause of the process which culminates in it (the developing acorn). A thorough discussion of the issue is provided by Michael Dummett, 'Can an Effect Precede its Cause?' and 'Bringing about the Past', in *Truth and Other Enigmas* (London, 1978).   J.D.G.E.

   *causality; teleological explanation.

Bacon, Francis (1561–1626). Lawyer, politician, and philosopher at the Courts of Elizabeth Tudor and her successor James Stuart. Bacon had two great ambitions. One was political, where he was helped initially by his kinship with the Cecil family; and at the summit of his career he held the office of Lord Chancellor for four years before being gaoled on an unfair charge of corruption. His other ambition was philosophical—to refound human knowledge on the basis of a systematic methodology for scientific inquiry.

   Part of this methodology was institutional, in that Bacon saw the advancement of science as a social activity. So he wished to set up a college for the purpose, equipped with all necessary research facilities—laboratories, botanical and zoological gardens, specialist technicians, etc. Though he failed to secure royal support for this venture in his own lifetime, he was widely credited later in the seventeenth century with having inspired the foundation of the Royal Society.

   But Bacon's methodology also proposed, within an overall framework for the reclassification of the sciences, a distinctively inductive structure for the study of nature. He advocated in his *Novum Organum* (London, 1620) that scientists interrogate nature by their *experiments in order to be able to tabulate both the various circumstances in which instances of the phenomenon under investigation have been found to be present and also the circumstances under which they have been found to be absent. For example, Bacon found heat present in the sun's rays, in flame, and in boiling liquids, but absent in the moon's and stars' rays, in phosphorescence, and in natural liquids. Moreover, scientists should concentrate in their investigations on certain important kinds of experimentally reproducible situation, which Bacon called 'prerogative instances'. To the extent that scientists thus discover a circumstance which correlates uniquely with the phenomenon—i.e. is always present when it is present and always absent when it is absent—they have discovered its proximate *explanation (or 'form') and have acquired power to reproduce it at will. But the investigator should also aim to make a gradual ascent to more and more comprehensive laws, and will acquire greater and greater certainty as he or she moves up the pyramid of laws. At the same time each law that is reached should lead him to new kinds of experiment, that is, to kinds of experiment over and above those that led to the discovery of the law.

   Bacon insisted that his methodology, like Aristotle's syllogistic, is just as applicable to normative as to factual issues. He held that it has a role in *jurisprudence, for example, as well as in natural science, because legal maxims in English common law, just like the axioms of nature in science, are grounded on induction from individual cases and then, once formulated, are applied back to determine new particulars. Bacon was therefore keen to emphasize that good legal reports were as valuable for jurisprudential induction as good reports of experimental results were for scientific induction. By the former we reduce uncertainty about our legal rights and duties: by the latter we reduce uncertainty about what is the case in nature. And negative instances, he held (anticipating Popper), are of primary importance in both inquiries, in order to eliminate false propositions. This is because there is only a limited number of ultimate forms, and so falsificatory evidence, by conclusively excluding incorrect hypotheses, permits firmer progress than verificatory evidence does towards identifying the correct hypothesis. Correspondingly Bacon repudiated as 'childish' the method of *induction by simple enumeration, whereby a generalization that is as yet unfalsified is supposed to acquire support that varies in strength with the number of known instances that verify it.

   But Bacon cautioned that his new method of induction would not get properly under way unless those trying to practise it repudiated four kinds of intellectual *idol—perceptual illusions ('idols of the tribe'), personal biases ('idols of the cave'), linguistic confusions ('idols of the market-place'), and dogmatic philosophical systems ('idols of the theatre').   L.J.C.

   *hypothetico-deductive method.

Francis Bacon, *Novum Organum*, ed. M. Silverthorne and L. Jardine (Cambridge, 2000).
—— *The Major Works*, ed. B. Vickers (Oxford, 2002).
M. Hesse, 'Francis Bacon', in D. J. O'Connor (ed.), *A Critical History of Western Philosophy* (New York, 1964).
M. Pentenon (ed.), *The Cambridge Companion to Bacon* (Cambridge, 1996).
P. Urbach, *Francis Bacon's Philosophy of Science* (La Salle, Ill., 1987).

Bacon, Roger (*c*.1220–*c*.1292). A student and a teacher at both Oxford and Paris, he devoted many years to the study of science, especially optics and alchemy. Bacon, a member of the Franciscan Order, wrote extensively in the fields of philosophy, theology, and science.

He was in many ways an independent thinker, though he was undoubtedly deeply influenced by his teacher Robert Grosseteste, and of course by Aristotle, whose writings were reaching Christian Europe via the Arab commentators. Of the latter, Bacon had an especial admiration for Avicenna and Averroës. Although during the Middle Ages he was perhaps chiefly known for his alchemical works, it is his epistemology that now attracts greatest attention, and especially as that relates to his writings on optics. In particular he was interested in light and visual perception. If something is at a distance from us, how can we be aware of it? The answer given is that similitudes or images, or species, emanate from the object, pass through the intervening space, and strike the eye. Without this multiplicity of species in the medium seeing could not occur. Questions concerning the metaphysical and epistemological status of species occupied Bacon and were to occupy many who followed him; questions such as whether species take up space, and whether they are visible, or instead are partial causes, and no more than that, of the visibility of the things from which they emanate. Bacon believed that there are also species corresponding to non-visual accidents in things, but his main work was in the field of visual perception.   A.BRO.

S. Easton, *Roger Bacon and his Search for a Universal Science* (Oxford, 1952).

bad faith. Sartre's conception of *self-deception. According to Sartre, bad faith involves the deliberate creation in myself of the appearance of a belief which I in fact know to be false. Sartre claims that we are able to play this trick on ourselves because of ambiguities in our nature, because we are not 'in-ourselves' what we are 'for-ourselves', and so on. In his view, in bad faith we exploit these ambiguities in reflection upon ourselves to avoid facing up to painful facts about ourselves. Sartre imagines a homosexual denying his homosexuality on the ground that he is not 'in himself' a homosexual. These ambiguities, Sartre holds, enable one to account for self-deception without postulating an unconscious self that controls the conscious one: the phenomenon exemplifies the complexity of our reflexive structures, not the agency of a secret self.   T.R.B.

J.-P. Sartre, *Being and Nothingness*, tr. H. Barnes (London, 1958), pt. I, ch. 2.

Bain, Alexander (1818–1903). A weaver's son, he was born in Aberdeen and studied at Marischal College. He anticipates *pragmatism. In *The Senses and the Intellect* (London, 1855) he says that perception depends on a muscular sense and on distinguishing one's body from the world. There is one substance with two sets of properties, mental and physical. In *The Emotions and the Will* (London, 1859) he says that belief belongs with agency and is for action. He was variously professorial assistant, public lecturer, journalist, civil servant (sanitation reform in London), and Professor of Logic and Rhetoric in Aberdeen. He was friendly with J. S. Mill and radical Utilitarian circles in London, and personally knew Darwin, Comte, Herschel, Faraday, and Wundt. Much of his writing was deflationary as he tried to promote the union of physiology, psychology, and philosophy, for which he founded the philosophical journal *Mind*.   V.H.

*associationism; Scottish philosophy.

Bakhtin, Mikhail Mikhailovich (1895–1975). Russian philosopher of language and literature, famous for his concepts of dialogism and 'heteroglossia'. For Bakhtin, the basic linguistic act is the utterance. Utterances acquire meaning only in dialogue, which is always situated in a social–cultural context where a multiplicity of different languages intersect (political, technical, literary, interpersonal, etc.). From this emerges a conception of personhood where we author ourselves in dialogue with others and subject to the reinterpretations they give us. Bakhtin's writings on the novel as the literary embodiment of heteroglossia have been very influential, particularly his work on Dostoevsky's 'polyphonic' novel, and many find in his dialogism a critique of totalitarianism. Significant also are his early works on linguistics and psychology, Marxist in orientation and published under names of other members of Bakhtin's circle (though authorship of these works is disputed). Bakhtin lived in Vitebsk and Leningrad before being exiled to Kazakhstan from 1929 to 1934. He later taught literature for many years at the Mordovian Pedagogical Institute in Saransk.   D.BAK.

*Russian philosophy.

M. M. Bakhtin, *The Dialogic Imagination*, tr. Caryl Emerson and Michael Holquist (Austin, Tex., 1981).
—— *Problems of Dostoevsky's Poetics*, tr. Caryl Emerson (Minneapolis, 1984).

Bakunin, Mikhail Alexandrovich (1814–76). Russian revolutionist, the moving spirit of nineteenth-century *anarchism. Although remembered mostly for his revolutionary passion, he was learned, intelligent, and philosophically reflective. In moments of intermittent recess from insurrection and imprisonment he wrote influential formulations of anarchist philosophy and incisive and insightful criticisms of Marxism. He maintained that political power was intrinsically oppressive whether wielded by the bourgeoisie or the proletariat. Real freedom was possible only after the destruction of the status quo. But the individual's freedom was so bound up with that of society that nothing short of 'collectivism', a non-governmental system based on voluntary co-operation without private property and with reward according to contribution, was required. In philosophical outlook he was a voluntaristic determinist, respectful of the authority of science but sharply critical of the authority of scientists. A keen materialist, he was ferociously anti-theological.

K.W.

G. P. Maximoff (ed.), *The Political Philosophy of Bakunin: Scientific Anarchism* (London, 1953).

bald man paradox. Suppose a man has a full head of hair: if he loses one hair he will still have a full head of hair. But if he loses enough hairs he will become bald. Clearly, though, there is no particular number of hairs whose loss marks the transition to baldness. How can a series of changes, each of which makes no difference to his having a full head of hair, make a difference to his having a full head of hair? This is an example of an ancient paradox called **sorites* (from the Greek word meaning 'heaped'), after a well-known variant which involves the removal of grains of sand from a heap of sand. M.C.

*vagueness.

See R. M. Sainsbury, *Paradoxes* (Cambridge, 1988) for *sorites*.

Barbara, Celarent. The opening of an 800-year-old hexameter verse incorporating the mnemonic names of valid *syllogisms. Described by De Morgan as 'magic words . . . more full of meaning than any that ever were made', and by Jevons as 'barbarous and wholly unscientific'. The vowels signify *quantity and quality, but most of the remaining letters are also logically important, especially regarding 'reduction', the derivation of some syllogistic forms from others. C.W.

*logic, traditional.

W. S. Jevons, *Elementary Lessons in Logic* (London, 1897), lesson XVII.
A. Kenny, *Medieval Philosophy* (Oxford, 2005), ch. 3.

barber paradox. The barber in a certain village is *a man who shaves all and only those men in the village who do not shave themselves*. Is he a man who shaves himself? If he is then he isn't, and if he isn't then he is. It follows that he is a man who both does and does not shave himself. This contradiction shows that the apparently innocent italicized description can apply to no one. Formally, the paradox resembles *Russell's paradox of the class of all classes which are not members of themselves. The latter though is not so easy to dispose of, since it is generated by an assumption—that every predicate determines a class—which cannot simply be abandoned. M.C.

M. Clark, *Paradoxes from A to Z* (London, 2002).

Barcan formula. A principle which says, roughly, that if it is possible that something *A*s (or has *A*) then there is something that possibly *A*s (or has *A*). In the first formalization

of quantified *modal logic, R. C. Barcan (later Marcus) introduced such an axiom schema:

$$\text{BF. } \Diamond(\exists \alpha)\, A \dashv 3 \, (\exists \alpha)\Diamond A.$$

The principle BF, provable equivalents of BF, and some schemata from which BF was deducible came to be designated as the 'Barcan formula'.

The plausibility of BF was questioned. Marcus sketched a model-theoretic proof of BF's validity on the assumption that domains of alternative possible 'interpretations' (worlds) were coextensive. Saul Kripke showed that on his semantics for modality, where coextensive domains are not assumed, neither BF nor its converse is valid. R.B.M.

R. Barcan Marcus, *Journal of Symbolic Logic* (1946, 1947); *Synthese* (1961).
—— *Modalities* (Oxford, 1993).

Barnes, Jonathan (1942–). Professor of Ancient Philosophy at the Sorbonne in Paris, formerly at Oxford and Geneva. Although Barnes's contributions to the understanding of ancient philosophy are both philosophy and history, historical reconstruction never overrides the attempt to solve philosophical problems by reference to ancient texts. Notably, Barnes is the author of the two-volume work *The Presocratic Philosophers* (1979), and studies of Aristotle, ranging from the translation and commentary on Aristotle's *Posterior Analytics* (1975) to *Aristotle* (1982) and many papers. Barnes is also one of the editors of the series of volumes Articles on Aristotle and the editor of *Early Greek Philosophy* (1987). His early work *The Ontological Argument* (1972) is a rigorous examination of that putative proof of the existence of God. S.P.

*ontological argument for the existence of God.

Barry, Brian (1936–). Among the leaders of the move in recent decades to make moral and political philosophy relevant to public policy and current political debates. As an intellectual descendant of the Scottish Enlightenment project, Barry addresses the intersection of moral, political, and economic issues and arguments. He violates the norms of twentieth-century moral and political philosophy by grounding his arguments in unwashed data rather than fanciful examples. His major concern has been with *justice, arguing that the best theories are grounded in mutual advantage, or fairness, or both. He has also written on democracy, voting, ethnic conflict, welfare policy, communitarianism, legal theory, future generations, migration, and economic and sociological theories of collective behaviour. R.HAR.

Brian Barry, *Theories of Justice* (Berkeley, Calif., 1989).
—— *Justice as Impartiality* (Oxford, 1995).
—— *Culture and Equality* (Cambridge, Mass., 2001).

Barth, Karl (1886–1968). Swiss theologian and biblical scholar, notable particularly for his early polemical work on the Epistle to the Romans (1919) and later for 9,000 pages of *Church Dogmatics*. Philosophically Barth is interesting because he adopts a form of extreme realism regarding *God and God's transcendence. He had been sickened by the course of theology and New Testament study in the nineteenth century. To Barth, it reduced God and his self-revelation in Christ to the merely human, the narrowly rational, the comfortably liberal. Barth saw himself as standing in the tradition of Kierkegaard, Luther, Calvin, Paul, and Jeremiah, prophetic figures for whom 'man is made to serve God and not God man'. Religion and piety were castigated by Barth along with natural theo-logy as misguided, as attempts on the part of fallen man to tame the otherness of God and to 'bolt and bar himself against revelation'.

God, for Barth, is wholly other, inaccessible to human thought and reason, who yet in Christ broke into the human world 'vertically from above'. It is at this point that philosophers will want to press Barth. How is it that without some natural theology or initial inkling of God on our part we can recognize Christ's revelation as divine? And how, in any case, could the Wholly Other express himself in the human person who lived in Galilee two millennia ago? Barth's own logic forbids a direct answer to these questions. He appeals rather to the Pauline doctrine of election by grace: that through divine grace and not through any effort of ours some are brought (correctly) to see the Word of God in the New Testament. He calls this the humiliation of the Gospel; it might equally be called the humiliation of reason.

Barth's searching critique of *Enlightenment rationalism is refreshing, and not only in the theological field; but it was followers of Barth who later went on to proclaim the death of God from within the theological world.

A.O'H.

*God is dead.

H. Hartwell, *The Theology of Karl Barth: An Introduction* (London, 1964).

T. F. Torrance, *Karl Barth: An Introduction to his Early Theology 1910–1931* (London, 1962).

J. Webster (ed.), *The Cambridge Companion to Karl Barth* (Cambridge, 2000).

Barthes, Roland (1915–1980). French literary and cultural critic, elected chair of literary semiology at the Collège de France in 1976, he appropriated and destabilized the critical methodologies of the linguist Ferdinand de Saussure and the psychoanalyst Jacques Lacan in the course of his systematic investigation of signs and signifying systems. For him, language (and culture) is structured, but 'off-centred without closure', since signs are not mere denotative units but polysemous, operating in a moving play of signifiers that can generate meaning in relation to other signifiers. The text is then no static work but a rich, dynamic field of explosive scraps of code capable of 'the infinite deferment of the signified'. Reading, then is, not reductive deciphering but a productive activity analogous to playing from a musical score. This eliminates the possibility of any privileged interpretation, authorial or critical, but makes it possible to participate in a 'hedonistic textuality', a paradoxical *jouissance*, where the psychically

split reader is at once lost and merged within a sea of cross-pollinating signs.

B.T.

Roland Barthes, *S/Z* (Paris, 1970).

—— *Image–Music–Text*, tr. Stephen Heath (New York, 1977).

Michael Payne, *Reading Knowledge: An Introduction to Barthes, Foucault and Althusser* (Oxford, 1997).

base and superstructure. According to the *historical materialism of Marx and Engels, the social 'base' is the ensemble of social relations or the economic structure of society; politics, law, morality, religion, and art constitute the social 'superstructure'. In some writings, the term 'superstructure' is used to refer solely to people's thoughts about their social relations (*'ideology'), while in others it refers also to non-economic social institutions. The primary relation asserted in Marxian theory between the base and the superstructure is one of explanatory dependence: 'superstructural' phenomena are to be explained materialistically through their dependence on the economic base. According to Marx, phenomena in the base can be understood with scientific precision, whereas superstructural phenomena are comparatively contingent, and admit of rigorous treatment only to the degree that they exhibit dependence on the economic base. There is no coherent history of politics, law, religion, or art as such; people's real history is economic.

The reasoning behind these Marxian claims, and even their meaning, has been a matter of dispute among Marxian scholars and Marxian theorists. One reading, usually proposed by critics rather than proponents of Marxism, takes what is 'superstructural' to be 'epiphenomenal'; that is, superstructural phenomena exhibit causal dependence on eco-nomic facts, but exercise no causal influence on the economic realm. This implausible interpretation of historical materialism was rejected by Engels, who insisted that although the dependent spheres of life 'react' on the economic realm, it is always the economic 'driving forces' which are determining 'in the last instance'. But this leaves unexplained why economic forces should be thought always to be decisively determining in causal interactions which are admittedly reciprocal.

The Marxian theory is perhaps best understood if we take the primacy of the economic to be an assertion not about causal influences but about historical tendencies. The Marxian theory holds that human history makes the most sense if we understand it in terms of certain fundamental tendencies, operating at the economic level: the tendency of productive powers to grow over time and of the economic structure of society to adjust so as to facilitate new productive powers. The claim that forces of production are primary amounts to the claim that history makes most sense if we proceed from a pattern of explanation proceeding from the tendency to growth in productive forces; the explanations in question are functional or *teleological, not causal, in form, though they do involve causal mechanisms through which the basic tendencies operate: the tendency of productive forces to grow and the tendency of production relations (and, along with them, superstructural phenomena) to adjust to that growth.

The mechanism of such adjustments is the *class struggle; that class is victorious whose ascendancy is most conducive to the employment and further development of the growing powers of production. Superstructural phenomena are then to be explained functionally by the way in which they serve the prevailing economic structure, or the interests of contending classes. Clearly they could not serve this function or these interests without exercising some influence on the economic realm, and so they cannot be merely 'epiphenomenal'. Their historical development, however, is best understood in relation to the fundamental tendencies of human society, which are economic.

A.W.W.

G. A. Cohen, *Karl Marx's Theory of History* (Princeton, NJ, 1978).
Jon Elster, *Making Sense of Marx* (Cambridge, 1985).
Ted Honderich, 'Against Teleological Historical Materialism', *Inquiry* (1982).

basic action. An idea introduced in the philosophy of action. A person may do one thing *by* doing another, e.g. vote by raising her arm. Then raising her arm is said to be *more basic* (or *primitive*) *than* voting. That than which nothing is more basic—i.e. that which is not done by doing something else—is the *basic* thing. Variants on this idea have been introduced, sometimes to protect accounts of action from regress, sometimes to cast light on different kinds of relation between different things agents do.

If an action is a particular (an event such as Jane's raising of her arm at time *t*), and such particulars are coarsely individuated, then 'more basic than' and 'basic' do not really apply to actions themselves: they apply to things done when there are actions, things such as raising the arm or voting (which are sometimes called acts).   J.HORN.

*action.

Jennifer Hornsby, *Actions* (London, 1980), chs. 5 and 6.

basic statements. A statement, *P*, is a basic statement if and only if *P*'s truth-value determines that of at least one further statement, *Q*, but there is no statement *R* such that *R* determines the truth-value of *P*.

Paradigmatically, but not essentially, if *P* is a basic statement then *P*'s truth-value is determined by the obtaining or non-obtaining of some empirical state of affairs. *Empiricism about meanings logically entails the existence of basic statements but not vice versa.

Neurath's *protocol statements (*Protokollsätze*), Wittgenstein's elementary propositions (*Elementarsätze*), and Russell's atomic propositions are basic statements, but we owe the expression 'basic statement' to Ayer.   S.P.

A. J. Ayer, *Philosophical Essays* (London, 1959).

bat, what it is like to be a: *see* Nagel, Thomas.

Baudrillard, Jean (1929–). French social theorist who came to prominence in the early 1980s. Baudrillard, whose message is that the subject is dominated by the object, sees consumption as the prime mover in the social order, and takes our behaviour, language, and perceptual experience to be increasingly formed by media-propagated ideals and images. As a result, we live in a world of signs removed from any external reality that might help us to keep account of what we take to be signified. In this 'hyper-reality' the real and the 'televisual' merge, and fantasy institutionally replaces reality. Since the historical and causal contexts are lost to view too, the real distinctions, social, economic, etc., that the images might represent also disappear, and political life with them. Baudrillard's perspective owes much to his Continental predecessors from Marx onwards, with debts to J. K. Galbraith and Marshall McLuhan. He marches under the same anti-meta-narrative banner as *Lyotard, but, nevertheless, consistently with his thought-provoking (or, as he might claim, thought-liberating) reversals of established ideas, denies that he is a *post-modernist.   A.H.

J. Baudrillard, *Fatal Strategies*, tr. P. Beitchman and W. G. J. Niesluchowski (London, 1990).
M. Poster (ed.), *Jean Baudrillard: Selected Writings* (Stanford, Calif., 1988).

Bauer, Bruno (1809–82). German theologian, philosopher, and historian, who was a leading Left Hegelian. He attended Hegel's lectures on religion, and contributed his notes for the posthumous edition of the lectures. He began his career with a Right Hegelian attack on D. F. Strauss's *Life of Jesus* (1835–6), which saw the Gospels as myth rather than history. But in 1842 his conversion to religious radicalism lost him his professorship at Bonn. He now argued that Christ was a fiction, and interpreted Hegel as an atheist and revolutionary, who deified human self-consciousness, notably that of the enlightened critic in contrast to the docile masses—a view more akin to the pre-Hegelian romanticism of Friedrich Schlegel than to Hegel himself. Marx contested this and other doctrines of Bauer in *The Holy Family* (1845).   M.J.I.

*Hegelianism; Romanticism.

L. S. Stepelevich (ed.), *The Young Hegelians: An Anthology* (Cambridge, 1983).

Bayesian confirmation theory. The most influential attempt in the logical positivist tradition to provide a uniform, general account of scientific knowledge. Bayesians identify the epistemic support *evidence confers on a hypothesis with *probability, usually understood in terms of dispositions to take risks whose outcome would depend on the correctness of the hypothesis of interest. They suppose that background beliefs and expectations which may vary among investigators determine the extent to which any given evidence supports a hypothesis. Someone who evaluates a hypothesis (*H*) on the basis of evidence (*E*) brings to its assessment (1) a prior degree of confidence in *H*, (2) prior expectations concerning whether *E* should occur if *H* is correct, and (3) a prior degree of confidence that E should (or shouldn't) occur regardless of whether H is true. If B are the investigator's background beliefs which determine these expectations, Bayes's theorem says the probability of H, given E, should vary directly with (1) and (2), and inversely with (3). In symbols,

$$Pr(H \mid E \& B) \text{ [the probability of } H, \text{ given } B \text{ and } E]$$
$$= \frac{Pr(E \mid H \& B) \times Pr(H \mid B)}{Pr(E \mid B)}$$

where $Pr(H \mid B)$ corresponds to (1), $Pr(E \mid H \& B)$ corresponds to (2), and $Pr(E \mid B)$ corresponds to (3).

Bayesianism has its attractions: it avoids technical difficulties which beset its rivals; it treats epistemic support quantitatively; it seems to shed light on disagreements (emphasized by Kuhn) among scientists over the epistemic bearing of evidence. It applies to reasoning from uncertain evidence.

The following are among Bayesianism's problems: its applications to real world cases are clouded by the apparent arbitrariness of its assignments of numbers to prior degrees of confidence (1, 2, and 3 above). And it has trouble explaining how a theory can be tested against old evidence already accepted with certainty. For such evidence, priors (1) and (3) above are identical to 1 (complete confidence) and therefore, by Bayes's theorem, the probability of the hypothesis, given the evidence, can be no different from its prior probability. What makes this a problem is that old evidence can have great epistemic significance, as illustrated by the support the general theory of relativity received from facts about Mercury's perihelion that were firmly established before Einstein proposed the theory.   J.B.B.

*Logical Positivism.

L. Bovens and S. Hartmann, *Bayesian Epistemology* (Oxford, 2003).

John Earman, *Bayes or Bust?* (Cambridge, Mass., 1992) thoroughly examines strengths and weaknesses.

Alan Franklin, *Experiment, Right or Wrong* (Cambridge, 1990) applies Bayesianism to examples from physics.

Colin Howson and Peter Urbach, *Scientific Reasoning: The Bayesian Approach* (La Salle, Ill., 1989) is the standard exposition.

Bayle, Pierre (1647–1706). French scholar and controversialist, best known for his *Historical and Critical Dictionary* (1697). Through painstaking research into the lives and thought of hundreds of biblical and historical figures, Bayle subjected countless philosophical and religious doctrines to critical scrutiny, and demonstrated, with scathing wit and dialectical virtuosity, that none of them had any legitimate claim to the status of final truth. He argued, in direct opposition to the rationalist philosophers, that reason was too feeble an instrument to be relied upon in the pursuit of truth, but that religious faith, while crucial to our support, had need of constraint and modesty in advancing its own claims. Bayle exerted a powerful influence upon the eighteenth-century *philosophes, who admired his intellectual courage, the rigour of his scholarly methods, and his passionate commitment to the cause of religious toleration.   P.F.J.

Elisabeth Labrousse, *Bayle*, tr. Denys Potts (Oxford, 1983).

'be': *see* 'to be', the verb.

beatitude's kiss: *see* Aurobindo, Ghose.

beauty. Despite its ancient aura as one of the supreme values in human life and in the cosmos, some philosophers give beauty short shrift. They remind us that discussions of aesthetic matters often do not use the words 'beauty' or 'beautiful', and that, on the other hand, discussions involving these words are often not aesthetic. If we call a person beautiful, is that always an aesthetic judgement? Presumably not, if desires towards the person are material to the judgement. So beauty is and is not something aesthetic. It can seem merely a vague way of praising something: whether we have a beautiful time at a wonderful party, or vice versa, makes little difference.

Philosophical aesthetics has tried to rescue the concept of beauty, suggesting that it is the best general concept of *aesthetic value. The idea is that beauty applies to any kind of thing, whether an artefact or a part of nature, and that to judge anything beautiful is always the highest form of aesthetic praise. If ethics is an investigation of the good (despite the vagaries of the word 'good'), then aesthetics is an investigation of the beautiful. However, are not some great works of art ugly? We must be careful here. A work which depicts scenes that are gruesome and harrowing, such as the blinding of Gloucester in *King Lear*, may loosely be said to be ugly. But whether the play depicts pleasant and beautiful things, and whether it succeeds aesthetically, are obviously questions at two different levels. A similar point could apply to a piece of music which was discordant and unsettling to listen to. Though not beautiful by conventional standards, such works acquire this epithet according to the theory that aesthetic worth is beauty.

Aquinas's definition of beauty as 'that which pleases in the very apprehension of it' still commands some respect—provided that we can expand a little on what 'pleases' and 'apprehension' mean. Taking pleasure in the perception of visible forms and colours, or combinations of sound, are the most obvious candidates. Beauty that is not perceptible is harder to accept, although this raises doubts about 'a beautiful idea' or 'a beautiful mathematical proof'. To rule these out as expressions of approval which are not proper cases of aesthetic judgement seems an unhappy solution. Are grasping the structure of a mathematical proof and the structure of a piece of music in sonata form so vastly different that one must be 'aesthetic beauty' while the other is not?

Another problem is what to say about the case of literature, whose form is not strictly perceptible. If literature may be aesthetically good (whatever point may ultimately attach to judging it so), and if 'beauty' is the term for aesthetic value, then we have to acknowledge that a novel or short story can be beautiful, however strange that may sound outside aesthetic theory. Few would deny that art of any form can be beautiful, but the idea that art should be prized especially for its beauty, or that a purely aesthetic way of regarding it is somehow privileged, may be questioned. Surely we care not only about beauty, but also about such matters as whether a work has integrity, whether it presents a view of the world that is honest or enlightening rather than trivializing or lazy. The view that beauty alone matters in art is apt to be derided as an assumption of *aestheticism. On the other hand, if absolutely any value that an artwork can have is included in its being beautiful, then beauty really becomes a vacuous idea for philosophical purposes.   C.J.

*ugliness.

I. Kant, *Critique of Judgement*, tr. J. C. Meredith (Oxford, 1969).
M. Mothersill, *Beauty Restored* (Oxford, 1984).
Plato, *Symposium*, tr. W. Hamilton (Harmondsworth, 1972).

beauty above beauty: *see* Plotinus.

Beauvoir, Simone de: *see* de Beauvoir, Simone.

becoming: *see* change; process; time.

***Bedeutung* :** *see* sense and reference; Frege.

beetle in the box. An example in Wittgenstein's *Philosophical Investigations*, § 293. If one wrongly construes the grammar of sensation words on the model of name and designated object, then the sensation drops out as irrelevant. It would be like an object called 'beetle' in a private box, which no one else could ever see, and hence could play no role in explaining what the word means. Instead, Wittgenstein argued that to say that '*S*' is the name of a sensation is to say that the utterance 'I have *S*' is the *expression* of a sensation. The logical grammar of sensation words is fundamentally different from that of names of objects or perceptual properties.   P.M.S.H.

*Grammar, autonomy of.

P. M. S. Hacker, *An Analytical Commentary on the* Philosophical Investigations, iii: *Wittgenstein: Meaning and Mind* (Oxford, 1990), 206–8.

begging the question, or *petitio principii.* Literally, requesting what is sought, or at issue. So, requesting an opponent to grant what the opponent seeks a proof of. So, by extension, assuming what is to be proved. A traditional *fallacy. Assuming has to be distinguished from entailing, or all valid proofs would beg the question (as J. S. Mill thought). But the boundary is sometimes hazy: for example, does an argument of the form 'Even if not *P*, *Q*; so at any rate *Q*' assume '*Q*'? (The expression is sometimes misused: it does not mean '*raise* the question', or 'assume *without argument*'.)   C.A.K.

J. S. Mill, *A System of Logic* (London, 1843), II. iii.

behaviourism. A family of doctrines united by metaphysical worries about dualism and epistemic worries about the status of mental terms (even when not undergirded by a dualistic metaphysic). *Operationalism, *positivism, and behaviourism were mutually inspiring doctrines designed, in the case of psychology, to make it scientifically respectable. Psychology, traditionally conceived as the science of mind, became conceived as the science of behaviour, where behaviour was understood to include only the 'observable' activities of an organism, or, in the version B. F. Skinner dubbed 'radical behaviourism', where behaviour was conceived of expansively so that 'private events' like thinking, feeling, and so on, although not directly observable were taken to be kinds of behaviour subject to the same laws as more public, conspicuous behaviour. Every type of behaviourism involved some sort of challenge to 'mental realism', to our ordinary way(s) of thinking of mind and mentality. Some of the more interesting behaviouristic doctrines include the following:

Operationalistic behaviourism. The meaning of a mental term is *exhausted* by the observable operations that determine its use. So '*P* is thirsty' means *P* says she is thirsty if asked, drinks water if given the chance, and so on.

Logical behaviourism. Mental terms are disposition terms. To say that '*P* is thirsty' is to imply, among other things, that *P* will probably say she is thirsty if asked, will drink if given the chance, and so on. The difference between the first and second doctrine is that the first denies any 'surplus meaning' to the concept of 'thirst' beyond that entailed by the observations used in the determination to use it; whereas the second allows that the concept of 'thirst' is only partially reduced to the observable events that justify its use, and thus that it maintains a legitimate surplus meaning referring to a 'state' inside the organism, the qualitative state, say, of 'being thirsty'.

Methodological behaviourism. Despite the fact that there are private psychological events, 'psychology', conceived as the science of behaviour, can avoid talking about them, and thereby retain its scientific credentials. The basic idea was pointed out by B. F. Skinner in *Science and Human Behavior* (1953) and was picked up and elaborated on by Carl Hempel, who called it the 'Theoretician's Dilemma'. Assuming that unobservable private events serve to link stimuli and responses in lawlike ways, we can, for purposes of psychology, treat the mind as a black box, observing the effects of the environment on behaviour, and predicting and explaining behaviour on that basis.

Radical behaviourism. The doctrine that behaviour can be observable or unobservable (from the third-person point of view) but that both can be analysed within the substantive framework of behaviouristic psychology. In 'Behaviorism at 50' (1964), Skinner writes: 'It is especially important that a science of behavior face the problem of privacy. It may do so without abandoning the basic position of behaviorism. Science often talks about things it cannot see or measure . . . The skin is not that important a boundary.' With the advent of radical behaviourism, one sees the attempt on Skinner's part to argue for the thesis that all behaviour, public or private, is governed by the laws of classical conditioning (as articulated by Pavlov and Watson) or operant conditioning (as articulated by Thorndike and himself). Skinner argued that thinking, choosing, and deciding—things about which more draconian forms of behaviourism vowed silence—could be analysed as private behaviours with characteristic causal relations to overt behaviour and as subject to the basic principles of operant conditioning. Despite this expansiveness, Skinner remained unimpressed until his dying day with the rising tide of cognitive psychology, thinking it lacked epistemic discipline and was rudely ignorant of the contributions of the substantive doctrines of classical and operant behaviourism. Although no version of behaviourism is a live position within the philosophy of mind, most philosophers still think that mental terms typically get at least part of their meaning from links to observable causes and effects.   O.F.

*functionalism; psychology and philosophy.

Gilbert Ryle, *The Concept of Mind* (London, 1949).
B. F. Skinner, *Science and Human Behavior* (New York, 1953).
—— *About Behaviorism* (New York, 1974).
L. D. Smith, *Behaviorism and Logical Positivism* (Stanford, Calif., 1986).

being is the subject matter of *ontology. According to long tradition, there are *kinds* of being and *modes* of being. The kinds of being may be subdivided in various ways: for instance, into *universals and particulars and into concrete beings and abstract beings. Another term for 'being' in this sense is 'entity' or *'thing'. In a second sense, being is what all real entities possess—in other words, *existence. Being in this second sense has various modes. Thus the being of concrete physical objects is spatio-temporal while that of abstract mathematical entities like numbers is eternal and non-spatial. Again, the being of some entities (for instance, qualities) is logically dependent upon that of others, whereas the being of substances is logically independent.

Connected with some of these traditional categorial distinctions are certain grammatical distinctions concerning the verb 'to be'. The use of 'is' as a copula may be interpreted in a variety of ways. 'This ring is yellow' features the 'is' of attribution, since it ascribes a quality to a substantial particular. 'This ring is golden' involves the 'is' of constitution, as it states what kind of material that particular is made of. 'This ring is my grandmother's wedding-ring' features the 'is' of identity. Finally, 'This object is a ring' involves the 'is' of instantiation, since it states what kind of thing the object in question is an instance of. Thus, although being yellow, being golden, being my grandmother's wedding-ring, and being a ring are all properties of this ring, they are properties of very different natures. Moreover, none of these properties constitutes the being of this ring, in the sense of constituting its exist-ence. 'This ring *is* (exists)' apparently involves a sense of 'is' distinct from any in which 'is' functions merely as a copula.

What is it to be a being or entity? Here we must distinguish between the question what it is for an entity of any given kind to exist and the question what is the distinguishing feature of entityhood. The famous dictum of W. V. Quine, To be is to be the value of a variable, is potentially confusing on this score. It might be better phrased, 'To be accounted amongst the entities recognized as existing by a given theory is to belong to the domain assigned to the variables of quantification of that theory according to its standard interpretation'. But another well-known dictum of Quine's, 'No entity without identity', goes nearer to the heart of our second question, suggesting that the crucial feature of entityhood is the possession of determinate identity-conditions.

In a special, restricted sense the term 'being' is commonly used to denote a subject of consciousness (or self), and thus a kind of entity to be contrasted with mere 'objects'. Such entities are often supposed to enjoy a special *mode* of being inasmuch as they are conscious of their own existence and possess a capacity freely to determine its course—a view elaborated in the existentialist doctrine that, for such entities, 'existence precedes essence' (Sartre). The contrast between being (in the sense of existence) and *essence is itself an ancient one, rooted in the distinction between accidental and essential properties. Traditionally, God is an entity whose essence includes existence, making God a necessary being, and indeed the only such being in the restricted sense in which this signifies a subject as opposed to an object. But this doctrine seems to require one to think of existence as a property of individual beings, contrary to the now dominant view of existence developed by Frege and Russell.   E.J.L.

*necessary and contingent existence; 'to be', the verb.

E. J. Lowe, *Kinds of Being* (Oxford, 1989).
W. V. Quine, *Ontological Relativity and Other Essays* (New York, 1969).
J.-P. Sartre, *Being and Nothingness*, tr. H. Barnes (London, 1957).

being-in-the-world (*In-der-Welt-sein*) is, for Heidegger, the 'determining character' or 'basic state' of *Dasein (the kind of being which humans have). The hyphens signal that it is a 'unitary phenomenon', for world (human) being and the relation of 'being-in' are only 'provisionally' distinguishable. Human beings cannot be understood apart from a world that, in turn, is intelligible only as what they are 'in'. The world, in this 'primary' sense, is not the spatio-temporal one of physics, but a 'totality of significance' which we are 'in', not as peas in a pod, but as meaningfully and practically engaged with. (Compare 'He's in the world of motor-racing'.) Heidegger's characterization of our being challenges the view held by Descartes and many later philosophers that we are, in essence, 'thinking things' logically independent of a world of material, spatial substances. It registers the conviction, shared by other *phenomenologists such as Merleau-Ponty, that human beings must be 'primordially' seen as immersed, through their meaning-giving 'projects', in a world whose contours and articulation are themselves a function of those projects.   D.E.C.

H. L. Dreyfus, *Being-in-the-World: Commentary on Heidegger's* Being and Time, *Division I* (Cambridge, Mass., 1991).

M. Heidegger, *Being and Time*, tr. J. Macquarrie and E. Robinson (Oxford, 1962).

belief. A mental state, representational in character, taking a proposition (either true or false) as its content and involved, together with motivational factors, in the direction and control of voluntary behaviour. (*Thinking; *propositional attitude; *representation.) Belief (thought) is often (especially in the philosophy of mind) taken to be the primary cognitive state; other cognitive and conative states (e.g. knowledge, perception, memory, intention) being some combination of belief and other factors (such as truth and justification in the case of knowledge).

In referring to beliefs—to Ted's belief that snow is white, for instance—one may be referring to either a particular mental state occurring in the believer (a state that has content) or the propositional content itself—something more like a meaning that is not locatable *in* the believer. In the first case, Ted's belief that snow is white is not the same as Tom's belief that snow is white. They occur in different heads. In the second sense, they are the same belief: that snow is white. What Ted and Tom believe (i.e. the propositional content of their belief) is the same.

Beliefs involve the deployment of *concepts: one cannot believe that something is a cow unless one understands what a cow is and, in this sense, has the concept cow (one needn't, of course, understand the word 'cow'). One can, to be sure, have beliefs about cows (these are called *de re or demonstrative beliefs) without knowing what a cow is. One can, for instance, believe that *that* animal, the one you see, is spotted. If that animal happens to be a cow, one believes of the cow that it is spotted and, thus, has a belief about a cow. But one cannot believe of the cow (or of anything else for that matter) that it is a cow (the word 'cow' here appears in what is called an oblique or referentially opaque position) without understanding what a cow is. Since concepts can remain distinct even when their reference is the same, belief descriptions are *intensional in character.

Some beliefs (called 'core' beliefs) are at the forefront of consciousness—things one is, at the moment, actually thinking about. Others are not. Even if you thought about it once (when you learned geography), you were not consciously thinking, a moment ago, that San Francisco is in California. None the less, it seems correct to say that you believed it even when you weren't actively thinking about it. Other beliefs seem even more remote from consciousness, even more part of the background. Even if you *never* consciously thought about whether turtles wear pyjamas, it seems right to say that you none the less believed they did not wear pyjamas before your attention was ever called to the fact.

Beliefs, together with other mental states (desires, fears, intentions) function as *reasons for action. Thus,

beliefs are to be distinguished from a variety of other internal representations that control reflexes and other non-intentional behaviours. There is a difference between closing your eyes as a reflexive response to a sudden movement (a response that is controlled by an internal representation of nearby events) and closing your eyes purposely, because you have certain desires (to avoid eye injury) and beliefs (that someone's finger is headed for your eye).

There are two broadly contrasting views about the nature of belief content. Individualists (sometimes called solipsists) maintain that the content of belief (what it is we believe when we believe something) supervenes on the neurobiology of the believer. If two individuals are physically indistinguishable, then they are psychologically indistinguishable. They must, therefore, have the same beliefs. Non-individualists, on the other hand, hold that belief content is, at least in part, determined by the believer's environment. Two individuals that are physically identical could have different beliefs. A version of non-individualism maintains that a person's social—including linguistic—context helps fix the content of what they believe.   F.D.

> *belief and desire; judgement; mental causation; norms, epistemic;.virtues, doxastic.

L. R. Baker, *Saving Belief* (Princeton, NJ, 1987).
A. Phillips Griffiths (ed.), *Knowledge and Belief* (Oxford, 1967).
A. Woodfield (ed.), *Thought and Object* (Oxford, 1982).

belief, ethics of. A set of rules used in evaluating doxastic states (beliefs, doubts, etc.) in ways similar to the evaluation of acts (murder, lying, etc.) by ordinary moral rules. An assumption is made that doxastic states are voluntary in at least a weak sense. Proponents of the ethics of belief are of two types: (1) epistemicists, who hold that the rules should refer only to epistemic considerations (sensory evidence, logical consistency, etc.), and (2) pragmatists, who hold that non-epistemic considerations (e.g. saving a person's life) are also relevant. Among epistemicists, W. K. Clifford holds the extreme view that we never have a right to believe a proposition without adequate evidence. Among moderate epistemicists, R. M. Chisholm holds that we have a right to believe a proposition unless its contradictory is evident.

Pragmatists also advocate more or less moderate views. Pragmatic considerations should: (1) determine belief choice only when epistemic considerations are balanced pro and con or evidence is lacking, or (2) sometimes override a preponderance of evidence. W. James defended both types of pragmatic ethics of belief on different occasions.   P.H.H.

> *norms, epistemic; virtue, doxastic.

R. Chisholm, *The Foundations of Knowing* (Minneapolis, 1982).
W. Clifford, *The Ethics of Belief and Other Essays*, ed. T. Madigan (Amherst, NY, 1999).

belief and desire. Familiar states of mind that do much theoretical work in some philosophical spheres and are topics of philosophical analysis. A popular way of understanding belief, desire, and the differences between them features the notion of direction of fit. It is said that the defining aim of belief is to fit the world, whereas that of desire is to get the world to fit it. According to a notion of satisfaction and a notion of content that apply to beliefs and desires, a belief that *p* and a desire that *p* have the same satisfaction condition—its being the case that *p*—and the same content, *p*. Philosophers who favour these notions see beliefs and desires as differing in their respective orientations toward their content. Whereas many desires are functionally fit to contribute to their own satisfaction, relatively few beliefs are: potentially self-fulfilling beliefs are the exception, not the norm. Philosophers often distinguish occurrent from dispositional beliefs and desires. Where is New York City? Now that the issue has been raised, you have an occurrent belief that NYC is in the USA; before the issue was raised, you had a dispositional belief that it is. The same distinction applies to desires. 'Sam desires a career in philosophy' is true even while he is wholly absorbed in a tennis match or dreamlessly sleeping. When Sam's supervisor, Sue, finds herself about to tell a prospective employer that he definitely desires a career in philosophy, she need not phone Sam to see whether he is awake before she can be confident that she will be speaking truly. The quoted sentence is also true when Sam is writing a cover letter for his job applications. In the latter case, but not the former, Sam has an occurrent desire for a career in philosophy. Beliefs come with degrees of confidence, and desires with degrees of strength. Both Sam and Sue believe that he will get a philosophy job this year, but she is more confident about that than he; and Sam's desire for a career in philosophy is much stronger than his desire to eat the sandwich he is holding.   A.R.M.

*simulation.

J. Searle, *Intentionality* (Cambridge, 1983).

belief-in. There are two main varieties of 'belief-in', neither of which is translatable in terms of 'belief-that'. In the first, 'belief-in' has a commendatory function (we do not, save ironically, *believe in* someone's incompetence, disloyalty, etc.). In the case of entities (though not of abstractions such as ideal states) this use of 'believe in' requires the existence of the believed-in entity. In the second, 'believe in' simultaneously notes and rejects a claim to existence: 'Children often believe in Santa Claus', 'James I believed in witches', etc. Religion apart, first-person uses of this sense of 'believe in' are rare, and carry with them an acceptance of the need to justify the embedded existence-claim. The very terminology in which *belief in God is claimed seems to reveal the need for a justification of the belief.   J.J.M.

H. H. Price, *Belief* (London, 1969).

believe, will to: *see* will to believe.

Belnap: *see* Anderson and Belnap.

Bell's theorem. Quantum mechanics (QM) predicts that various correlations will be observed between the outcomes of measurements on special types of two-component systems. Bell's theorem shows that these correlations are incompatible with a particular type of deterministic theory, one that seeks to explain the outcomes of the measurements in terms of local causal mechanisms. The theorem also rules out local indeterministic theories.

The typical experimental set-up involves a physical system that consists of two, spatially separated subsystems, *A* and *B*. One is to measure some property of subsystem *A* and simultaneously to measure some property of subsystem *B*. If the system is deterministic, the (possibly unknown) state of the total system before the experiment will determine the result of every such joint measurement. *Locality* is the assumption that, given the state of the total system, the outcome of the measurement of a particular property of subsystem *A* does not depend on which property of *B* is measured, or on the outcome of the measurement on *B*.

In 1964 John Bell showed that the assumptions of determinism and locality together imply that various inequalities should hold between the probabilities of certain outcomes of various joint measurements. The probabilities predicted by QM violate these inequalities. It follows that any deterministic theory that recovers the statistical predictions of QM will violate locality and will thus involve 'action at a distance'. (Bohm's 'hidden-variable' interpretation of QM is an example of such a non-local deterministic theory.) Bell and others later generalized the result to show that indeterministic theories (so-called stochastic hidden-variable theories) that satisfy an appropriate locality condition are equally incompatible with the predictions of QM. These predictions have since been verified, most famously by Alain Aspect and collaborators in 1982. Whether this shows that nature itself is non-local remains controversial.   O.P.

*Einstein, Podolsky, and Rosen paradox; quantum theory and philosophy.

J. S. Bell, *Speakable and Unspeakable in Quantum Mechanics* (Cambridge, 1987).
J. T. Cushing and E. McMullin (eds.), *Philosophical Consequences of Quantum Theory* (Notre Dame, Ind., 1989).

benevolence. To be benevolent is to be possessed by a desire for the good of others and a willingness to forward that good actively. Since the good of others takes many different forms it requires a range of different responses. Benevolence, therefore, may take the form of compassion, mercy, kindness, or generosity.

While benevolence is quite properly understood as a general attitude of goodwill towards others and as the specific forms such goodwill might take, the term has also come to be used more recently in a much narrower sense, to refer to acts of charity. An act of charity occurs when some benefit is freely bestowed by one individual with a surplus on another who is in need. This narrowing of the meaning of benevolence means what was initially a term used to describe an uncontroversially desirable attitude to others has come to be used, perhaps, to put a good face on the largess of the better-off to the worse-off. It thereby introduces doubts about the moral value of benevolence.

The question of the moral importance of benevolence is often addressed by way of a comparison with the alternative major 'other-regarding' virtue, *justice. Benevolence is said to depend, for instance, on the agent's *feeling* concern for others, while the demands of justice are recognized by reason and are thus independent of the vagaries of individual emotional capacity. This particular contrast owes a great deal to Hume's influential account of benevolence as a natural and essentially sentiment-based virtue, which has led some to conclude that it is inadequate to meet the demands of morality because it is neither impartial nor, ultimately, open to rational assessment. There are, however, other conceptions of benevolence which evade these criticisms. *Utilitarianism, for example, may be described as a theory of universal benevolence, which refuses any necessary connection between feeling and right action. Nevertheless, its highly stipulative definition of benevolence is challenged by the Humean recommendation that we ought to assess and be critical of our moral relationships from the point of view of sentiment. A second possible contrast between justice and benevolence consists in the assertion that, because it is by definition concerned with what is strictly *due* to others, justice marks the boundaries of what we are morally *obliged* to do, while benevolence consists in morally desirable, but in the final analysis *optional*, actions. However, this view merely reflects the largely unargued assertion that justice is of overriding moral importance.

To conceive of justice and benevolence as independent and mutually exclusive in this way may be mistaken: the two notions seem rather to be logically correlative and, therefore, they cannot be explicated independently of each other. And if they are logically correlative, i.e. related not only at the level of certain particular conceptions of each, but in all and any full and coherent conceptions of either, then fully to understand a conception, or to achieve a proper conception, of either justice or benevolence requires making explicit the conception of the other that it implies and from which it partly derives.   P.W.

D. Hume, *A Treatise of Human Nature*, ii.
T. A. Roberts, *The Concept of Benevolence* (London, 1973).

Benjamin, Walter (1892–1940). German philosopher and literary and social critic, who was a member of the *Frankfurt School. He went into exile in Paris when the Nazis came to power in 1933. After the fall of France he headed for Spain, but was denied entry and killed himself.

His cryptic, ambiguous, ironical writings owe as much to messianic and kabbalistic Judaism as to Marxism and surrealism. Art serves theological, philosophical, and political ends. His essay 'The Work of Art in the Age of Mechanical Reproduction' (1936) defends photography and cinema, as a way of 'politicizing' aesthetics, against

the 'aura' of traditional art—to the annoyance of Adorno, who saw greater critical power in autonomous art than in the mass media. Benjamin championed the revolutionary epic theatre of his friend Brecht. He was a practitioner of 'immanent criticism': theoretical principles are to emerge from the work studied, not brought to it from outside. He despised Heidegger, but such pieces as 'On Language as Such and on the Language of Man' and 'Fate and Character', in *One-Way Street* (1928; tr. London, 1979), have a Heideggerian rather than a Marxian flavour: 'The enslavement of language in prattle is joined by the enslavement of things in folly' and 'Fate is the guilt context of the living'.   M.J.I.

W. Benjamin, *Illuminations* (New York, 1969).
—— *Reflections* (New York, 1986).
G. Smith (ed.), *Benjamin: Philosophy, Aesthetics, History* (Chicago, 1989).

Bennett, Jonathan F. (1930–). Historian of philosophy, philosopher of language, and metaphysician, noted for his work on Kant, Spinoza, and the British Empiricists, as well as on rationality, linguistic convention, conditionals, and the ontology of actions and events. He rejects the widely assumed distinction between subjunctive and indicative *conditionals and has challenged aspects of David Lewis's work on counterfactuals. He criticizes Davidson's account of the individuation of actions and events and defends a role for both events and facts as admissible relata of causal relations. His work on the act–omission distinction has had an important impact on the debate over active versus passive *euthanasia and the distinction between *killing and letting die. Bennett is perhaps most renowned for his highly individual interpretations of major early modern philosophers, which have sometimes provoked controversy on account of his ahistorical approach to classic texts.   E.J.L.

J. Bennett, *Events and their Names* (Oxford, 1988).
—— *Learning from Six Philosophers: Descartes, Spinoza, Leibniz, Locke, Berkeley, Hume*, 2 vols. (Oxford, 2001).
—— *A Philosophical Guide to Conditionals* (Oxford, 2003).

Bentham, Jeremy (1748–1832). English philosopher who dreamed at a young age of founding a sect of philosophers called utilitarians and who lived to see his dream fulfilled. He also planned that his body when he died should be made into what he called an 'auto-icon' (that is, a representation of itself) so that it could be used as a monument to the founder of the sect. This intention was also fulfilled, so that to this day meetings of Benthamites sometimes take place in the actual presence of Bentham himself (who spends the rest of his time sitting in a glass box in University College London).

Bentham was the son and grandson of lawyers working in the City of London and was intended by his father to follow and surpass them as a practising lawyer. However, while following his legal studies, Bentham became disgusted with the current state of English law and so, rather than making money by the practice of the law as it is, he turned instead to a study of what the law might be. This study formed the centre of his long life, during which he wrote an enormous amount of manuscript material on law, economics, politics, and the philosophy which naturally arises from these subjects.

In his earlier years Bentham turned some of this manuscript into books, such as his *Fragment on Government* of 1776, or his *Introduction to the Principles of Morals and Legislation* of 1789 (although, as the titles indicate, both of these were in fact only parts of projected works). Later on, even the fragments tended not to be published by him and were left for others to edit. In this manner, the first work which made his name was produced in French and published in Paris by his disciple Étienne Dumont of Geneva (the *Traités de législation civile et pénale* of 1802). Dumont subsequently edited other works; these were translated into English by disciples, who also edited others directly. Therefore much of the published text of Bentham has passed through the hands of others, and also sometimes been translated or retranslated prior to its publication. In fact, Bentham's greatest work on the philosophy of law was not published until the present century (in its latest version, edited by H. L. A. Hart, under the title *Of Laws in General*).

Bentham's grand project was for legislation: the exploration and theoretical foundations of a perfect system of law and government. For this he needed a measure of perfection, or of value; and this for Bentham was the principle of *utility, otherwise known as the *greatest happiness principle. In his already mentioned *Introduction* to the subject, Bentham starts chapter 1 with the rousing declaration that 'Nature has placed mankind under the governance of two sovereign masters, *pain* and *pleasure.*' This first paragraph ends with the statement that 'the *principle of utility* recognises this subjection, and assumes it for the foundation of that system, the object of which is to rear the fabric of felicity by the hands of reason and of law'. Bentham's aim is to produce felicity, happiness. The means to be employed are 'reason and law': the right law will produce happiness, and the right law is one in accordance with reason. This means one in accordance with the principle of utility. In Bentham's draft codes of law, each particular law was attached to a 'commentary of reasons on this law'. The commentary demonstrated its value and also, Bentham hoped, improved its effect. For, as he says elsewhere, 'power gives reason to law for the moment, but it is upon reason that it must depend for its stability'.

Bentham explicitly says in the *Introduction* that by 'utility' he means 'that property in any object, whereby it tends to produce benefit, advantage, pleasure, good, or happiness . . . or . . . to prevent the happening of mischief, pain, evil, or unhappiness'. The rightness of actions depends on their utility; and the utility is measured by the consequences which the actions tend to produce. Of all these varying terms describing the consequences, the most important for Bentham are the ones with which he began the *Introduction*, pleasure and pain. For Bentham thinks that these are clear, easily understandable terms,

which can therefore be used to give precise sense to the others. So the good, for Bentham, is the maximization of pleasure and the minimization of pain. Otherwise, as he puts it in the *Introduction*, we would be dealing 'in sounds instead of sense, in caprice instead of reason, in darkness instead of light'. For Bentham the principle of utility, interpreted in terms of pleasure and pain, is the only appropriate measure of value because it is the only comprehensible one.

Bentham's aim of increasing happiness is a practical one; and he had many purely practical proposals, such as for trains of carts between London and Edinburgh, or a Panama canal, or the freezing of peas. But the most famous and important of these particular practical proposals was for a prison which he called the 'panopticon'. It was to be circular so that the warders could sit in the centre and observe all the prisoners. It was also going to be privately run, by contract management with Bentham as its manager. Bentham therefore not only intended to produce what he called a 'mill for grinding rogues honest' but also to make money in the process. In fact, blocked by the interests of the landowners whose property abutted the site of the proposed prison (now occupied by the Tate Britain Gallery on Millbank in London), he lost both money and time until, after twenty years' struggle, he was compensated by Parliament. Bentham took his winnings, rented a house in Devon, and instead of grinding rogues chopped logic, producing his most profound work on the philosophy of language.

In his more general theory of government, just as in his more particular prison proposals, Bentham needed to rely on a psychology. This is that people tend to act in their own interests, where these are again understood in terms of pleasure and pain. People are understood to be seekers after pleasure and avoiders of pain. Given this knowledge of people's psychology, the benign legislator can so arrange his system of law that people, seeking only their own interests, will in fact be led into doing what they are meant to do, which is to promote the general interest (or the greatest happiness for all).

From this follows the Benthamite theory of *punishment. It is a deterrent account. The proper aim of punishment, as of anything else, is to produce pleasure and prevent pain. Now all punishment is in itself a pain. Therefore, for Bentham, all punishment is in itself a harm. Therefore it can only be justified if this particular pain is outbalanced by the reduction in pain (or increase of pleasure) it causes. If people are deterred by punishment from doing things which would produce more pain (such, for example, as rape, theft, or murder), then the punishment will be justified. If not, not: there is no point in punishment or retribution for its own sake. This defence of punishment not only justifies punishment but also enables in principle the precise calculation of how much punishment is appropriate. It is that amount whose pain is outweighed by the pains of the actions it deters.

Bentham's general account of law and punishment and his use of the principle of utility as a means of providing reasons for his particular codes of law is constant through his life. However, his ideas about the particular political system which should be the source of this law developed. At the start he thought that he only needed to appeal to enlightened governments for such obviously beneficial arrangements to be put into effect. When he found that this did not happen (or that he was blocked in his own proposals, such as that for the panopticon), he became a supporter of democracy. Not just the law had to be changed but also the system of government. He was accordingly active in the movement for the extension of the parliamentary franchise, which finally came into effect in the year he died (although Bentham wanted something considerably more radical than the extension which actually happened: he wanted one man, one vote; and a secret ballot).

Such democratic proposals were in any case much more in accord with his general theories. If, according to the psychological theory, everyone acts in their own interests, so also do governments or governors. The classic eighteenth-century figure of the benevolent, semi-divine legislator has to be dispensed with. Dictators (supposedly enlightened or otherwise), kings, oligarchies can not be trusted. The appropriate end of government, popularly sloganized by Bentham as 'the greatest happiness of the greatest number', is only safe in the hands of the greatest number themselves. If the people as a whole are granted political power, they will, merely by following their own interests, promote what is also the appropriate end. Just as in the right system of law, so in the right system of politics or government, actual and appropriate action will coincide.

It can be seen that Bentham's project was centrally a project of clarification. He wanted to clarify values, to show at what we ought to aim. He wanted to clarify psychology, to show at what people actually do aim. He wanted to devise the appropriate systems of government, law, or punishment so that these two things could be placed in step. However, his interest in clarification went further. He also wanted to clarify the very idea of law; both as a whole and also in its central terms. It was in this project that he was led into his most original thought.

Understanding the law involves understanding such things as *rights and duties. In the empiricist tradition, to which Bentham was loosely attached, understanding is provided by perception. Locke and, following him, Hume made a distinction between simple and complex ideas which allowed them to understand things which were not directly perceived. Complex ideas, such as that of a golden mountain, can be understood because they can be analysed into their simple constituents, of which we have experience. However, this technique does not work for the terms which Bentham wished to analyse, such as obligation or right. So here he was forced into a wholly new technique, which he called 'paraphrasis'.

This technique anticipates twentieth-century methods of analysis as does Bentham's related claim that the primary unit of significance is a sentence rather than a word.

His idea in paraphrasis is not to translate the problematic word into other words. Rather, 'some whole sentence of which it forms a part is translated into another sentence'. So in the analysis of what Bentham called 'fictional entities' (such as right, duty, property, obligation, immunity, privilege—the whole language of the law), he uses his technique of paraphrasis to place these terms in sentences for which he then gives substitute sentences not containing the offending term. For example, sentences about rights are explained by Bentham in terms of sentences about duties. A particular right is for him the benefit which is conferred on someone by the imposition of duties on others. With duties we still, of course, have fictional entities. But these, in turn, can be placed in sentences which are translated into sentences about the threat of punishment. Punishment is, for Bentham, the threat of the imposition of pain. So here, at last, we reach what Bentham calls real entities. We reach clear, simple ideas, which can be directly understood by perception. As Bentham says in the *Fragment on Government*, 'pain and pleasure at least are words which a man has no need, we may hope, to go to a Lawyer to know the meaning of'. With them the law can be clarified; for lawyers and others. The ultimate clarifier of value, of what the law should be, will also work as a clarifier of what the law actually is.

These projects are projects for change: current conditions are criticized. However, although Bentham's goals were the same as many of the contemporary movements for change, his foundations were not. Bentham was on the side not just of the struggle for reform of the franchise in England but also of the American and French Revolutions. The central contemporary justification for these revolutions was in terms of natural rights. However, Bentham was consistently opposed to the use of natural rights and he therefore criticized the rhetorical justification of both of these revolutions.

Bentham thinks that a *natural right is a 'contradiction in terms'. He thinks that they are 'nonsense', fictitious entities. However, as has been seen, Bentham produced a new engine of analysis in his technique of paraphrasis precisely to make sense of fictitious entities. So it might be thought that he could make sense in the same way of natural rights. However, comparing a natural right with a legal right exposes the difference. Both can be analysed in terms of corresponding duties. However, as seen, Bentham analyses a legal duty in terms of the law (or threat of punishment) which creates it. There is no corresponding law, he holds, with respect to supposed natural duties. Hence he holds that natural rights are just imaginary rights by contrast with the real rights produced by actually existing systems of law. As he puts it, 'from real law come real rights . . . from imaginary laws come imaginary ones'. The so-called rights of man are in fact merely 'counterfeit rights'.

Bentham's most famous slogan expressing this view is *'nonsense on stilts'. This comes from his critical analysis of the French Declaration of the Rights of Man and Citizen in a work usually known as *Anarchical Fallacies* (which, in fact, is Dumont's title). Bentham's claim is that language which looks as if it is describing what rights there actually are is in fact suggesting what rights there ought to be. That is, instead of citing existing rights, the French Declaration is giving reasons why there ought to be rights. As Bentham puts it in *Anarchical Fallacies*, 'a reason for wishing that a certain right were established, is not that right; want is not supply; hunger is not bread'. So to suppose that such rights actually exist is nonsense. Even worse is to suppose that we can be sure that the correct rights have been found for all time. For Bentham is a promoter of experimentation. We have to keep seeing what utility is actually produced by particular systems of rights. Hence it is an additional mistake to think that any rights are unalterable (indefeasible, imprescriptible). This mistake was also made by the French. Hence the famous slogan. The complete remark from which it comes is 'natural rights is simple nonsense: natural and imprescriptible rights, rhetorical nonsense, nonsense upon stilts'.

Natural rights was one attempted answer to the question of the source of obedience to the state and the conditions for legitimate revolution. Another attempted answer also popular in Bentham's day was the original or social contract. This device, founding obedience on agreement, was used by the leading contemporary defender of British law William Blackstone. Bentham ridicules such a defence in his *Fragment on Government*. For Bentham, justification of obedience to government depends upon utility, that is upon calculation of whether the 'probable mischiefs of obedience are less than the probable mischiefs of resistance'.

A contract will not work here for Bentham because, just like rights, all real contracts are legal contracts. Hence they are produced by law and government; and cannot therefore be used to provide a foundation for law and government. Even if its force is not supposed to be the force of a proper contract but merely that of a promise, or agreement, this again will not help to provide justification. For whether someone (government or people) should keep their agreements has, again, for Bentham to be tested by the calculation of utility. Yet if utility is to be the ultimate justification of promise-keeping, it would have been better to have started there in the first place, rather than (like Blackstone) traversing a tortuous path through contracts, original contracts, and largely fictional agreements. Again Bentham designates the supposed alternative source of justification to be merely a fiction and, as he puts it in the *Fragment*, 'the indestructible prerogatives of mankind have no need to be supported upon the sandy foundation of a fiction'.

Although all justification comes from utility, this does not mean that Bentham can not support secondary ends; that is, things which, if promoted, will normally tend to increase utility. He lays down four such intermediate ends which should be promoted by the right system of law and government: subsistence, abundance, security, equality. These form two pairs so that subsistence (the securing to people of the means to life) takes precedence over abun-

dance; and securing people's expectations takes precedence over equality. The utilitarian argument for this depends upon the psychological claim that deprivation of the former member of each pair causes more pain than the latter.

Psychological assumptions also lie behind Bentham's promotion of *equality. He claims that (in general) equal increments of a good will not produce equal increments of utility. (That is, he claims that there is diminishing marginal utility.) Therefore, in general, provision of a particular good will provide more utility for those who already have less than those who already have more; hence a general tendency towards providing goods for the less well-off; or equality.

Bentham's is a consequentialist ethic. It looks towards actual and possible future states of affairs for justification of right action, not to what happened in the past. (For example, punishment is not retribution for past action, but prevention of future harms; obedience to the state is not because of some past promise, but to prevent future harms.) This is for Bentham the right, indeed the only possible, way of thinking correctly about these matters. It explains his central stance with regard to reform of the law. The law he found was common law, made by judges, based on precedent and custom. It came from history. For this he wanted to substitute statute law, made by democratic parliaments, and founded on reason. These reasons would be independent of history and would be in terms of future benefit.   R.H.

*consequentialism; utilitarianism.

J. Dinwiddy, *Bentham* (Oxford, 1989).
Ross Harrison, *Bentham* (London, 1983).
H. L. A. Hart, *Essays on Bentham* (Oxford, 1982).
David Lyons, *In the Interest of the Governed* (Oxford, 1991).
Gerald J. Postema, *Bentham and the Common Law Tradition* (Oxford, 1989).
Frederick Rosen, *Jeremy Bentham and Representative Democracy* (Oxford, 1983).

bent stick in water: *see* oar in water.

Berdyaev, Nikolai Alexandrovich (1874–1948). Influential Russian religious philosopher who, after a youthful flirtation with Marxism of neo-Kantian persuasion, developed a form of Russian idealism sometimes called 'Christian existentialism'. According to Berdyaev, what truly exists is spirit, conceived as a creative process: every existent, including God, is a self-determining subjectivity engaged in the realization of value. Human beings attain personhood only if they realize their creative essence, which they may do in a society which embodies true community (*sobornost'*) and which aspires to identity of purpose with God. Berdyaev opposed his vision of 'personal socialism' to both bourgeois individualism and any collectivism that subordinates the individual to the community. A perceptive critic of totalitarianism, he was expelled from the USSR in 1922 and settled in Paris. Since the demise of the Soviet Union, Berdyaev's writings have enjoyed renewed popularity in Russia.   D.BAK.

N. A. Berdyaev, *The End of Our Time*, tr. D. Attwater (London, 1933).
—— *Solitude and Society*, tr. G. Reavey (London, 1938).
—— *Dream and Reality*, tr. K. Lampert (London, 1950).

Bergmann, Gustav (1906–87). Austrian-born American philosopher, who taught at the University of Iowa for forty years, Bergmann disdained all versions of *materialism, though he did defend methodological *behaviourism. A member of the Vienna Circle and influenced by Moore, Russell, and Wittgenstein, Bergmann wrote extensively on individuation, universals, and intentionality, often setting out his views by contrasting them with those of others: Meinong, Brentano, Husserl, Quine, Strawson, and so on. As an ideal-language philosopher, Bergmann tried to design a formalism which allows for the analytic–synthetic distinction and the syntactical features of which point to solutions to the ontological problems. Bergmann's most striking contribution emerges in his attempt to show that the truth-bearers of thoughts are mental states which, though simple, have truth-makers that are are complex.   E.B.A.

*materialism.

Gustav Bergmann, *Logic and Reality* (Madison, Wis., 1964).

Bergson, Henri-Louis (1859–1941). French philosopher of Anglo-Polish extraction who worked mainly at the Collège de France in Paris. Bergson is famous for two main doctrines, those of duration and the *élan vital*. In a letter written in 1915 he speaks of 'the intuition of duration' as 'the core of the doctrine' which any summary of his views must start from and constantly return to. Duration is time at its most timelike, as we might put it. For the scientist time is a homogeneous medium which can be divided into periods of equal length, and treated for the purposes of the calculus as analysable at the limit into an infinity of instants with no length. None of this holds for duration, which is heterogeneous, ever-changing without repeating itself, and cannot be divided into instants (though one interpretation sees Bergson as led to duration by reflecting on the calculus in terms of Newton's doctrine of 'fluxions'). Duration is *time as experienced by consciousness, and perhaps Bergson's most important insight is that we do not experience the world moment by moment but in a fashion essentially continuous, illustrated by the way we hear a melody, which cannot consist simply in hearing a succession of disjointed notes. Past, present, and future cannot be so separated that it becomes impossible for us to know of the past because only the present is ever present to experience. It is perhaps rather strange that of the two main philosophers of time of the late nineteenth and early twentieth centuries, Bergson and McTaggart, neither seems to have paid any attention to the other. Bergson wrote his main relevant works before McTaggart's famous 1908 article, but he never overtly reacted to it and shows no signs of being influenced by it in his later writings (despite being fluent in English and having lectured in England).

Born in the year of *The Origin of Species* Bergson was familiar enough with the conflict between evolutionism and religion. His book *Creative Evolution*, introducing the *élan vital* as a sort of life force, probably owed its popularity partly to his attempt, backed by scientific as well as philosophical arguments, to develop a non-Darwinian evolutionism that made room for religion, albeit not for orthodox Christianity. He envisaged a process of constant change and development, irreversible and unrepeatable (so that biology is a fundamentally different science from physics), and governed by the *élan*, which uses effort and subtlety to overcome the resistance of matter (an echo of the divine Craftsman in Plato's *Timaeus*?), but is not drawn by some pre-envisaged end, for that would be a mere 'inverted mechanism'.

Later in life Bergson turned his attention to morality. Just as duration could never be generated from time considered as isolated moments (an argument he also used against Zeno's paradoxes of motion), so, he claimed, universal benevolence could never be achieved by starting with group loyalties and making the groups ever wider. Group loyalty always required a contrasting out-group, and could be transcended only by a qualitative leap of the sort taken by mystics in their love of all mankind.

Another application Bergson makes of his general philosophy comes in his treatment of *laughter in the short book of that name. Man is a spiritual outgrowth in a world which works, along with his body, on mechanical principles, and laughter arises when he is seen as reverting to the mechanical level, primitively when he slips on a banana skin, sophisticatedly when his conscious actions unconsciously mimic the mechanical.   A.R.L.

*evolution.

H.-L. Bergson, *The Creative Mind* (New York, 1946; French original 1934). Good starting-point.
L. Kolakowski, *Bergson* (London, 1985). Brief introduction.
A. R. Lacey, *Bergson* (London, 1989). General critique of Bergson's philosophy.

Berkeley, George (1685–1753). Berkeley is a most striking and even unique phenomenon in the history of philosophy. There have been many philosophers who have constructed bold and sweeping, often strange and astonishing, metaphysical systems. Some, particularly in the English tradition—for example, Thomas Reid in the eighteenth century or G. E. Moore in the twentieth—have been devoted to the clarification and defence of 'common sense'. And some have made it their chief concern to defend religious faith and doctrine against their perceived enemies. It is the peculiar achievement of Berkeley that, with high virtuosity and skill, he contrived to present himself in all these roles at once. His readers have differed in their assessments of the relative weights to be accorded to these not clearly compatible concerns. It is easy to read him as primarily a fantastic metaphysician—a line taken, to his baffled chagrin, by almost all his own contemporaries. More recently some, by reaction against this, have perhaps tended to overstress his credentials as the champion of *common sense. His religious apologetics, if scarcely his dominant interest, were unquestionably sincere. But mainly one should try to see how, not merely temperamentally but as a lucid theorist, he really did contrive to make a coherent whole of his diverse concerns.

The works on which Berkeley's fame securely rests were written when he was a very young man. Born and educated in Ireland, he first visited England in 1713, when he was 28, and his *Three Dialogues between Hylas and Philonous* was published in that year. But he had by then already published his *Essay towards a New Theory of Vision* (1709) and his major work *A Treatise Concerning the Principles of Human Knowledge* (1710). His later philosophical writings do little more than defend, amplify, and in one or two respects amend the comprehensive views thus early arrived at. It is, in fact, evident from his correspondence that in his later years concern with philosophical issues was for long periods wholly displaced by other interests. In this respect he differs markedly from John Locke—the chief target of his criticism—whose *Essay Concerning Human Understanding* (1690), long meditated and much revised, did not appear till its author was nearly 60. The young Berkeley was apt to commend Locke's thoughts, not without irony, as quite creditable for one so far advanced in years.

A major motive of Locke's philosophy—with which Berkeley was well acquainted in his student days—was to work out the implications of the great achievements of seventeenth-century science. It had been established beyond all question, he took it, that the material universe was really, essentially a system of bodies mechanically interacting in space—bodies 'made', so to speak, of matter, and really possessing just those qualities (*primary* qualities) required for their mechanical mode of operation—'solidity, figure, extension, motion or rest, and number'. This was the bedrock of Locke's position. These bodies operate on, among other things, the sense-organs of human beings—either through actual contact with the 'external object' or, as in vision, by 'insensible particles' emitted or reflected from it. This mechanical stimulation in due course reaches the brain, and thereupon causes *'ideas' to arise in the mind; and these are the items of which the observer is really aware. In some respects these ideas faithfully represent to the mind the actual character of the 'external world'—bodies really do have 'solidity', etc.—but in others not; ideas of, for instance, sound, colour, and smell have no real counterparts in physical reality, but are merely modes in which a suitably constituted observer is affected by the appropriate mechanical stimuli.

Berkeley came very early to regard this picture of the world as at once absurd, dangerous, and repulsive. It was absurd, he argued, because it implied a fantastic *scepticism, plainly intolerable to good common sense. For how could an observer, aware only of his own ideas, know *anything* of Locke's 'external world'? Locke himself had insisted that colour, for example, is only an apparent, not a real, feature of that world; but how, in fact, could he know

that our ideas correctly represent to us, in any respect, the world's actual character? A sceptic has only to suggest that our ideas perhaps mislead us not merely in some ways, but in every way, and it is evident that Locke is left helpless before that suggestion—unable, indeed, even to assure himself that any 'external' world actually exists. That is surely, for any person of good sense, an intolerable position.

But it is also dangerous, Berkeley holds. For—besides this general leaning towards an absurd scepticism—the *'scientism', as one may perhaps call it, of Locke's doctrine seemed to lead naturally towards materialism and, by way of universal causal determinism, to atheism also, and therefore, in Berkeley's view, to the subversion of all morality. God is brought in by Locke as the designer, creator, and starter of the great Machine; but could he show that matter itself was not eternal, with no beginning and no creator? Might God turn out to be superfluous? Again, though Locke himself had made the supposition that minds are 'immaterial substances' and no doubt hoped to sustain a Christian view of the soul, he had confessed that he could not disprove the counter-suggestion that consciousness might be merely one of the properties of matter, and so wholly dependent on the maintenance of certain purely physical conditions. Thus Locke's theories at best permit, at worst positively encourage, denial of God's existence and the soul's immortality; with that denial religion falls and, in Berkeley's view, drags morality after it.

Finally, it is clear from, though less explicit in, Berkeley's words that he was simply oppressed and repelled by the notion of the universe as a vast machine. Locke loved mechanisms. He delighted in metaphors of *clocks and engines, springs, levers, and wheels, and indeed took mechanics to be the paradigm of satisfactory intelligibility. All this Berkeley detested. God's creation, he was sure, could not really be like that—particularly if, in order to maintain that it is, we have to assert that its actual appearance is delusive, that 'the visible beauty of creation' is to be regarded as nothing but 'a false imaginary glare'. Why, to embrace such a nightmare, should we deny the evidence of our senses?

What then was to be done? Berkeley thought that the solution of all these perplexities was obvious, luminously simple, and ready to hand. As he wrote in his notebook, 'I wonder not at my sagacity in discovering the obvious though amazing truth, I rather wonder at my stupid inadvertency in not finding it out before.' The solution was *to deny the existence of *matter.*

First, Berkeley insists, this odd-looking denial is wholly supportive of common sense. On Locke's own admission we are never actually aware of anything but our own ideas; to deny the existence, then, of his 'external objects', material bodies, is not to take away anything that has ever entered into our experience. But not only so; it must also put an end to all sceptical questioning. For Locke was obliged to concede to the sceptic that our ideas might mislead us about the real character of things, precisely because he had regarded things as something other than, merely 'represented' by, our ideas. But if, eliminating the supposed material body, we adopt the view that the ordinary objects of experience simply *are* 'collections of ideas', it will be plainly impossible to suggest that things may not be as they appear to us—even more so, to suggest that their very existence might be doubted. If an apple is not an 'external' material body, but a collection of ideas, then I may be entirely certain—as of course, Berkeley says, any person of good sense actually is—both that it exists, and that it really has the colour, taste, texture, and aroma that I find in it. Doubt on so simple a matter could only seem to arise as a result of the quite needless assertion that things exist, distinct from and in superfluous addition to the ideas we have.

But surely, it may be objected, our ideas have causes. We do not generate our own ideas just as we please; they plainly come to us from some independent source; and what could this be, if not the 'external world'? But this point redounds wholly, Berkeley claims, to his own advantage. For to cause is to *act*; and nothing is genuinely active but the will of an intelligent being. Locke's inanimate material bodies, therefore, could not be true causes of anything; that ideas occur in our minds as they do, with such admirable order, coherence, and regularity, must be by the will of an intelligent being. And of course we know that there is such a Being—God, eternal, omnipresent, omnipotent, 'in whom we live, and move, and have our being', 'who works all in all, and by whom all things consist'. Berkeley wonders at the 'stupidity and inattention' of men who, though every moment 'surrounded with such clear manifestations of the Deity, are yet so little affected by them, that they seem as it were blinded with excess of light' (*Principles*, para. 149).

Finally—and certainly, for Berkeley, most satisfactorily—he finds himself in a position to put the physical scientist firmly in his place. For if there is no matter, no material bodies, there are no 'corpuscles', no 'insensible particles'; that whole corpus of mechanistic physical theorizing in which Locke delighted cannot possibly be true, for there is simply nothing for it to be true *of*. At first, in his early (though major) work the *Principles*, Berkeley embraced this position in the most unqualified form. There is a modest role for the scientist, he there argued, in observation and description of the objects of experience, in the search for true generalizations about the course of our ideas, that is, of natural phenomena; but all reference to items supposedly 'underlying'—supposedly explanatory of, and according to Locke more 'real' than—human experience, must be dismissed as moonshine, the product of mere confusion. But later—regarding, perhaps, as over-drastic this wholesale dismissal of not only Locke but also, for example, Gassendi, Newton, and Boyle—he devised a strikingly ingenious variant position in which, though running hopelessly against the main tendency of his age, he foreshadowed the ideas of many contemporary philosophers of science. In his pamphlet *De Motu* of 1721, he still maintained that corpuscular theories of matter, for

example, or the particle theory of light could not be true; but they may nevertheless be allowed, not indeed as truths, but as useful fictions. The 'theory' of the corpuscular structure of matter makes possible the exact mathematical expression of formulae, by which we can make very valuable calculations and predictions; but there is no need to make the supposition that the corpuscles and particles of that theory actually exist. So long as it is useful to us to speak and to calculate *as if* they exist, let us so speak and calculate. Such intellectual dodges 'serve the purpose of mechanical science and reckoning; but to be of service to reckoning and mathematical demonstrations is one thing, to set forth the nature of things is another'. It is Locke's concession, one might say, to the physical scientist of metaphysical *authority* that Berkeley, at every stage, implacably opposes.

Two of Berkeley's later works may be mentioned briefly. His *Alciphron* (1732) is a long work in dialogue form, in which the tenets of Anglican orthodoxy are defended against various types of 'free-thinking' and *deism. Though able enough, it suffers from the artificiality of the convention, and has limited interest now that the controversies which prompted it are moribund. His last work was *Siris* (1744), a very strange, even baffling production, in which a most uncharacteristically rambling, ponderous, and speculative statement of some part of his earlier opinions leads on to an inquiry into the virtues of *tar-water, a medicine which Berkeley made popular, and for the promotion of which he worked in his later years with surprising zeal.

Berkeley's main work was slow to exert any influence on philosophy, though his limited early *Essay* on vision became fairly well known. His criticism of Locke, though not always ideally fair, was for the most part powerful and well taken; and the transition to his own remarkable doctrine of a wholly non-material, theocentric universe, whose *esse* was *percipi*, and in which human 'spirits' were conceived of as conversing directly with the mind of God, was at least a feat of dazzling ingenuity. But this doctrine was too extraordinary to be taken quite seriously. The fact that, so far as the course of actual experience went, he could insist that it coincided with the customary views of ordinary life was felt, rightly, to be not enough to make it actually the same—he was far indeed from being accepted as the friend of common sense. His strikingly original philosophy of science—really *the* fundamental area in which he dissented from Locke—was also much less persuasive then than it would be if it were propounded today. In the early eighteenth century it was still possible, even natural, to regard physical theory as merely a kind of extension of ordinary observation, offering—or at any rate aiming at—literal truths of just the same kind, and couched in much the same terms, as those of everyday experience. Today the sophistication of physical theory has made this difficult, or indeed impossible, to believe; but to deny it then was probably felt not only to be perverse and unnecessary, but also—entirely rightly, in Berkeley's case—to constitute an attempt to undermine the physicist's prestige. It was his misfortune that he opposed, even hated, the 'scientific world-view' at a time when that view was in the first flush of its general ascendancy.

Berkeley was born near Kilkenny, and educated at Kilkenny College and, from 1700, at Trinity College, Dublin. He was a Fellow of that college—though often absent—from 1707 to 1724. Ordained in 1709, he was appointed Dean of Derry in 1724, and Bishop of Cloyne in 1734. He married in 1728, and died at his lodgings in Holywell Street, Oxford, in 1753, while overseeing the introduction of his son George to Christ Church. Berkeley's life, apart from his philosophical writings, is remarkable chiefly for his curious attempt in middle life to establish a college in Bermuda. The purpose of this project was mainly missionary. Berkeley's hope was to attract to his college both the colonial settlers of America and the indigenous American Indians, so that they would in due course return to their communities as ministers of religion and purveyors of enlightenment. As Dean of Derry he devoted to this scheme his considerable energies, powers of persuasion, and personal charm, and at first succeeded in securing for it both private and official backing. He was granted a charter, raised substantial funds by private subscription, and was even promised an ample parliamentary grant. But the scheme was really impracticable, and was in the end recognized to be so. Bermuda—as he was perhaps not clearly aware—is far too distant from the American mainland to have been an attractive location for his institution. Berkeley himself set out boldly for America in 1728, but in his absence doubts and hesitations began to prevail in London. He waited nearly three years for his promised grant to be paid over, but in 1731 the Prime Minister, Walpole, discreetly indicated that there was no prospect that his hopes would be gratified. The house at Newport, Rhode Island, which Berkeley built and inhabited is still preserved.   G.J.W.

*empiricism; Irish philosophy; *esse est percipi*.

George Berkeley, *Works*, ed. A. A. Luce and T. E. Jessop, 9 vols. (London, 1949–57).
J. Foster and H. Robinson (eds.), *Essays on Berkeley* (Oxford, 1985).
G. W. Pitcher, *Berkeley* (London, 1977).
I. C. Tipton, *The Philosophy of Immaterialism* (London, 1974).
G. J. Warnock, *Berkeley* (London, 1953; reissued Oxford, 1982).
K. Winkler, *Berkeley: An Interpretation* (Oxford, 1989).

Berlin, Isaiah (1909–97). Berlin was born in Riga, Latvia, into a Jewish family that migrated to England in 1919 in the wake of the Bolshevik Revolution. He studied at Oxford and taught philosophy there in the 1930s, becoming a significant part of the movement that developed into 'ordinary language' philosophy, and publishing influential papers on the logic of counterfactual conditionals. He wrote his first book in 1939, on Karl Marx. During the war, he had diplomatic postings in Washington and, briefly, Moscow ('one week's work in an embassy—that is my experience—is less of a strain than one day's teaching at Oxford') and met outstanding Russian writers such as Pasternak and Akhmatova. Back in Oxford, Berlin's inter-

ests shifted more to the history of ideas with particular reference to political thought, and in 1957 he was knighted and appointed to the Chair of Social and Political Theory at Oxford. He was the first President of Wolfson College, Oxford (1966–75), and President of the British Academy from 1974 to 1978.

Berlin was rare amongst historians of thought and philosophy in being himself a substantial philosopher, and it is this, plus considerable powers of empathy and a wide range of learning, that gives his explorations of the work and impact of thinkers as diverse as Vico and de Maistre, Machiavelli and Herder, such power and fascination. A lifelong secular liberal, Berlin's writings on liberal theory have had a lasting impression on contemporary political philosophy, his discussions of the concepts of negative and positive liberty being his best-known contribution. Equally significant, however, has been his passionate advocacy of the view that the ends of life cannot form a unified whole.

Although his concerns and heroes were eclectically European, Berlin's method and intellectual temper were rooted in English philosophical tradition with its stress on clarity, argument, and vigorous debate.   C.A.J.C.

*liberty.

I. Berlin, *Against the Current* (New York, 1980).
—— *Four Essays on Liberty* (Oxford, 1969), reissued with a fifth essay as *Liberty* (Oxford, 2002).

Bernoulli's theorem. The theorem is named after the Swiss mathematician who first proved it, Jakob Bernoulli. It is also known as the 'weak law of large numbers', and was historically the first of a cluster of famous limit theorems of mathematical *probability. It states that if successive outcomes, A and not-A, of a sequence of n trials are independent, and the probability of A at each trial is p, then the probability that the relative frequency of As in the n trials differs from p by more than an arbitrarily small number tends to 0 as n increases. The relation between probabilities and frequencies established by the theorem led many people, including Bernoulli, to believe that probabilities could be inferred from observed frequencies. Whether such an inference is possible is still unresolved.
                                                              C.H.

W. Feller, *An Introduction to Probability Theory and its Applications* (New York, 1950).

Berry's paradox is credited to G. G. Berry by Bertrand Russell. The phrase 'the least integer not nameable in fewer than nineteen syllables' consists of eighteen syllables. Thus the assumption that there is an 'integer not nameable . . . ' etc., and that the phrase names it, is contradictory. Russell claimed that the phrase 'denotes' 111,777, thus involving himself in the contradiction. The truth is that 111,777 *can* be named such things as 'Russell's Berry example number' or even 'Joe'. (Nameability in zero syllables raises some interesting questions which, fortunately, needn't be discussed to justify dismissing Berry's puzzle as not deeply paradoxical.) Both the assumptions leading to the *paradox are false. Read aloud, '111,777' has nineteen syllables, but being named in some way must not be confused with being name*able*. J.C.

Bertrand Russell and A. N. Whitehead, *Principia Mathematica* (Cambridge, 1961), 61.

Bertrand's paradox, due to Joseph Bertrand, brings out an inconsistency in certain *a priori ways of calculating *probability. What is the probability that the length k of a 'randomly selected' chord to a given circle is less than the length l of a side of an equilateral triangle inscribed in the circle? Viewing the chord as determined by a line through a point p on the circumference, $k < l$ if and only if the angle between the chord and a tangent at p is either $< 60°$ or $> 120°$. This is ⅔ the possible angles, which suggests that the probability that $(k < l) = ⅔$. But one of many other possibilities is to view the chord as determined by a perpendicular to a radius. $k < l$ if and only if the perpendicular intersects the radius over half-way between the mid-point of the circle and the circumference, suggesting the probability that $(k < l) = ½$. The 'a priorist' technique of finding a 'random' method to generate the chord and then dividing the possibilities for that method to get the probability thus seems to lead to inconsistency, unless some method can be shown to be the 'right' one. J.C.

Joseph Bertrand, *Calcul des probabilités* (1889), 4–5; cited by William Kneale, *Probability and Induction* (Oxford, 1952).

Bhagavadgītā. 'Song of God', a part of the ancient (fifth to second century BC) epic *Mahābhārata*. In the *Bhagavadgītā* a brave but conscientious prince weakens and turns pacifist in the wake of a fratricidal civil war. A philosophical discourse by Krishna, who is the Hindu God-in-human form, is designed to goad him back to his soldierly duty and to his 'own nature'. It runs to 650 Sanskrit verses, commented upon for over 1,000 years by Indian philosophers of various persuasions. It is famous for metaphysical arguments for the immortality of the soul, the doctrine of a Supreme Person (God), transcending but ontologically supporting both individual consciousness and matter, and a subtle moral psychology of action *vis-à-vis* inaction. It teaches spiritual detachment even in the midst of constant commitment to the most violent of professions. Synthesizing work, worship, and wisdom, the ensuing ethics of moderation, desirelessness, and equality have a Kantian deontological ring. There is the overarching theme of a blissful liberation from the cycle of rebirths. A.C.

*Vedānta; deontological ethics; Hindu philosophy; Indian philosophy.

Śrī Aurobindo, *Essays on the Gītā* (Pondicherry, 1987).

biconditional. A conditional proposition is of the form: If P then Q. The conditional which is its converse is of the form: If Q then P. A biconditional, P if and only if Q, is equivalent to the conjunction of a conditional and its converse. In notations of the propositional calculus a biconditional is represented as $P \equiv Q$ or often $P \leftrightarrow Q$. In the standard propositional calculus (the system of material implication) $P \equiv Q$ holds where P and Q have the same truth value. Where $P \equiv Q$ is a *tautology, P and Q are taken to be logically equivalent. R.B.M.

*equivalence, logical.

B. Mates, *Elementary Logic* (Oxford, 1972).

bioethics is the study of the moral and social implications of developments in the biological sciences and the related technology. This entails considering the value that is or should be accorded to various forms of life. Are human beings morally entitled to use other living things, plants or animals, in any way that they choose? Is there a special 'sacredness' or 'dignity' attached to human life? If so, does the stage of development that a human life has reached nevertheless make a difference to the morality of destroying it? Such questions as these are the concern of bioethics. It is a subject that grew enormously in the late twentieth century, and most universities now have professional bioethicists among their members, whether interested in broadly environmental and ecological issues or in medical applications of the new technologies.

Bioethics is concerned, for example, with the rights and wrongs of the genetic manipulation of crops and animals, including human animals (and at this point there is an overlap between bioethics and Green political theory). How are possible advantages to impoverished countries of genetically modified crops, designed to resist drought or flooding, to be weighed against the possible exploitation of the poor by chemical or pharmaceutical companies? Is there, in any case, something inherently wrong with the genetic modification of crops or cattle, different in kind from the taking of cuttings or the selective breeding that has been part of horticulture and agriculture for ages past? Is the manipulation of human genes to prevent a child's being born with a devastating monogenetic disease, such as Tay-Sachs's disease or Duchenne's Muscular Distrophy, different in kind from surgical intervention, or intervention by drugs, which doctors have always practised in pursuit of their professional goal to alleviate suffering? Some regard genetic intervention as uniquely sinister; it is thought to contravene the laws of nature by artificially speeding up the kinds of changes properly brought about by the slow processes of evolution and natural selection. Debate about what is or is not 'natural' is curiously emotive. Part of the work of bioethics is to analyse and evaluate such appeals to Nature.

Of particular importance at the beginning of the twenty-first century have been the questions raised about embryonic stem cell research, or therapeutic cloning. This is a process by which embryos are produced, not by normal conception, the fertilization of female eggs by male sperm, but by cell nuclear transfer, where the nucleus of an egg is removed and replaced by that of another; after the application of an electric current, the egg with its new nucleus can develop into an embryo. This is the first part of the process of cloning a whole animal, or reproductive cloning. If a whole animal is to be reproduced, the newly formed embryo is placed in the uterus of a surrogate animal and brought to term. Thus Dolly the sheep was cloned at the end of the twentieth century. But the purpose of therapeutic cloning would be frustrated if an embryo were allowed to develop beyond its very first stages. For at the beginning of its life the cells of the embryo are 'totipotent'; that is, each may develop in any direction, to become any of the 120 or so types of cell that make up the body, or indeed may become part not of the embryo itself, but of the placenta or umbilical cord. The purpose of the research is to discover how to direct these cells (embryonic stem cells) to develop in specific ways, to become, let us say, cells belonging to the spinal cord, or the brain, or the skin. The ultimate aim is to produce banks of cells of particular types that may be used for cell transplant rather than whole organ transplant. This would have enormous advantages, in that parts of the body, including the brain, could receive transplants, and damaged cells would renew themselves permanently. All this is far in the future; but the possible ethical objections to such procedures, especially centred on the fact that embryos would be created and then destroyed when their use was over, are already among the issues to be argued by bioethicists.

In fact, at the core of much of their philosophical concern is the status that should be accorded to the human embryo. In the UK human embryos may be used for research up to fourteen days after their creation (whether by fertilization etc. or by nuclear transfer). The Human Fertilization and Embryology Act (1990) enshrined that principle in law. At that time, embryos might be used only for research into issues concerned with fertility, infertility, and contraception. Later, regulations were introduced through Parliament which permitted their use in research into therapeutic cloning, but the fourteen-day limit remained. The reason for this cut-off point was physiological. Until fourteen or fifteen days from the beginning of its life, the embryo, however it was brought into being, has no vestige of a central nervous system, and therefore can have no conscious experiences of any kind. It is impossible to cause such an embryo pain. Though its genetic identity has been fixed, it cannot be regarded as an individual person; indeed, it may yet divide and become twins or quadruplets. Using it for research is therefore more akin to using human tissue than using a child or an adult experimentally.

Such considerations fell, and still fall, to be considered by bioethicists. For despite the largely evidence-based arguments of those who supported the 1990 law, there are many people who dispute the moral acceptability of the law, and would like to see it changed so that from the moment it comes into existence an embryo is protected from being used for research and then destroyed. These people uphold the principle of the sanctity of human life, at all its stages.

This principle is strongly supported by most members of the Roman Catholic Church, and this partly explains the difference, on bioethical issues, between different countries, within Europe and beyond. There was a period when the Roman Catholic Church, following Thomas Aquinas (himself following Aristotle), held that a human foetus becomes a full human being, acquiring a soul, at about forty or ninety days from conception, depending on its gender. However, in the nineteenth century the Church decided, rightly, that there could be no certainty about when the soul entered the body, and that therefore even the earliest embryo should be given the benefit of the doubt. It was therefore deemed that immediately after conception the embryo had, or probably had, a soul, and was effectively a human person, so that to destroy it was murder.

Against this there is the argument put forward by, among others, John Habgood, an eminent bioethicist, a biologist turned churchman who became archbishop of York, which holds that we must, as post-Darwinians, take a developmental view of the human embryo, as we do of the human race itself. There is no one moment when the human person springs into existence. The further the collection of cells which forms the human embryo develops, the more we are properly inclined to accord it the status of a person, and the higher the value we attach to its life and life-chances. It was such arguments as these that prevailed in the UK in 1990. But the arguments continue, and the issue still dominates bioethics in at least one of its branches.

Questions raised by the new techniques do not depend on wholly new moral principles. But they involve applying moral principles to sometimes wholly new possibilities; and this in turn involves taking a newly long-term view of possible consequences for society. How would it be if people could choose the sex of their babies, or, more startling, choose to alter their genetic make-up before birth? Could society tolerate a world in which the mixture of genes a child was born with was no longer a matter of chance but could be 'designed' deliberately? What, if any, is the fundamental moral objection to the cloning of human beings, supposing such a thing were ever to become safe enough to try? Such questions, which used to be strictly a matter of science fiction, now seem nearer to reality, and it is the fear of such a reality that causes bioethicists to be in increasing demand. Their task is to help people to think clearly about how, in the light of our new knowledge, we value, or ought to value, life in all its form, and at all stages of development. M.WARN.

John C. Avise, *The Genetic Gods* (Cambridge, Mass., 1998).
John Habgood, *Being a Person* (London, 1998).
Arlene Klotzko (ed.), *The Cloning Sourcebook* (Oxford, 2001).
Onora O'Neill, *Autonomy and Trust in Bioethics* (Cambridge, 2002).
Steven Rose, *Lifelines* (Harmondsworth, 1998).
Gregory Stock, *Redesigning Humans* (London, 2002).
Mary Warnock, *Making Babies* (Oxford, 2002).

biological naturalism. The view that mental phenomena such as *consciousness and *intentionality are natural biological phenomena on a par with growth, digestion, or photosynthesis. Biological naturalism is defined by two main theses: (1) all mental phenomena from pains, tickles, and itches to the most abstruse thoughts are caused by lower-level neurobiological processes in the brain; (2) mental phenomena are higher-level features of the brain.

Mental phenomena are thus 'emergent' in the sense that they are causally explained by the behaviour of lower-level elements which do not in themselves individually have these features. Thus, according to biological naturalism, the brain is conscious and consciousness is caused by the behaviour of lower-level elements such as neurons even though no single neuron is conscious. Formally speaking, relations of this sort are common and unmysterious in nature. For example, a whole system can be in a liquid state, and the liquid behaviour can be caused by the behaviour of the molecules even though no single molecule is liquid. Biological naturalism does not deny that alternative forms of chemistry might be able to cause consciousness but insists that since mental phenomena are in fact caused by brain processes any other system that caused mental phenomena would have to have causal powers equivalent to brains.   J.R.S.

*anomalous monism; cloning; mind; mind–body problem.

John R. Searle, *Intentionality: An Essay in the Philosophy of Mind* (Cambridge, 1983).
—— *Minds, Brains, and Science* (Cambridge, Mass., 1984).
—— *The Rediscovery of the Mind* (Cambridge, Mass., 1992).

biology, philosophical problems of. The most distinctive feature of biology, from a philosophical point of view, is its characteristic use of *functional* or *teleological explanations*. These are explanations in which some biological trait is explained by showing how it is useful for the organism in question. For example, the function of the polar bear's white fur is to camouflage it; the function of human sweating is to lower body temperature; and so on. The philosophically interesting aspect of these explanations is their apparent commitment to teleology: they seem to explain items (the whiteness, the sweating) in terms of their consequences (the camouflage, the cooling). By contrast, normal causal explanations run in the other direction, and account for consequences in terms of their causes.

Until fairly recently most philosophers of biology took these explanations at face value, and argued that the parts of integrated systems, like biological organisms, can legitimately be explained in terms of their contribution to the well-being of the whole. In particular, Carl Hempel argued that such explanations were a subspecies of covering-law explanations. This approach is now widely rejected, however. Most contemporary philosophers of biology now hold that functional explanations in biology are in fact disguised *causal* explanations, which explain biological traits not by looking forward to *future* beneficial results, but by looking backwards to the *past* evolutionary his-tories in which such results led to the natural selection

of the traits in question. Thus the functional explanation of the polar bear's whiteness does not refer to the future camouflaging of the bears, but to the fact that their past camouflaging led to the natural selection of their whiteness.

The centrality of the Darwinian theory of *evolution by natural selection to biological thinking raises a number of further philosophical issues. An initial question is whether the theory has any real predictive content, or whether the thesis of 'the survival of the fittest' simply collapses into the empty truism that 'whatever survives, survives'. However, there are ways of formulating the theory so that 'fit' acquires a meaning which is independent of survival.

A related charge is 'adaptationism': does not the theory of evolution by natural selection simply invent evolutionary 'just so stories' in order to portray all biological traits as having some selective benefit? In response, supporters of the theory will admit that some biological traits are accidents that serve no function, but will insist that there is genuine evidence to show that many other traits have been selected because of their effects, and that this process of selection has been crucial to the evolution of species.

At a more detailed level, there is controversy about which 'units of selection' are involved in Darwinian processes. Should we think of natural selection as operating primarily on groups, or individuals, or genes? Some progress with this knotty issue has been made by distinguishing 'replicators', in the form of the genes which embody the lasting effects of selection, from 'vehicles', such as individuals and groups, whose survival is usually the prerequisite for gene survival.

Work on the logic of natural selection has led to the development of sociobiology, which seeks to understand animal social behaviour as the genetically based product of natural selection. Critics of sociobiology object that much behaviour is non-genetic, especially in higher animals and humans. Some sociobiologists deny this claim. Others respond that, even if environmental influences on behaviour are also important, it is still valuable to understand the evolutionary pressures on those genes which do affect behaviour.

Biology, along with other special sciences like psychology, geology, meteorology, and so on, raises the issue of *reductionism. Most contemporary philosophers of biology are reductionists at least to the extent of denying 'vital spirits' or other emergent biological substances, and accepting the *supervenience of biological properties on physical properties. Far fewer, however, are reductionists in the stricter sense of believing that all biological laws can be explained by physical laws. Instead they hold that there are *sui generis* biological laws, patterns which are common to biological systems with different physical make-ups, and which therefore cannot be explained in terms of physical law alone.   D.P.

*causality.

D. Hull and M. Ruse (eds.), *Philosophy of Biology* (Oxford, 1998).
P. Kitcher, *Vaulting Ambition* (Cambridge, Mass., 1985).

A. Rosenberg, *The Structure of Biological Science* (Cambridge, 1985).

E. Sober, *The Nature of Selection* (Cambridge, Mass., 1984).

K. Sterelny and P. Griffiths, *Sex and Death: An Introduction to Philosophy of Biology* (Chicago, 1999).

bivalence. Semantic principle to the effect that every statement is either true or false. Intuitionists refuse to affirm this, since for them it would amount to affirming that every statement can either be proved or disproved, which no one believes. Three familiar putative counter-examples are: (1) *vagueness: perhaps 'This is red' is neither true nor false of a borderline case; (2) the *liar paradox sentence: 'This sentence is not true'; (3) *reference failure: if there is no elephant present 'That elephant has a lean and hungry look' is arguably neither true nor false. Defenders of bivalence tend to urge that putative counter-examples are not genuine *statements*.　　　R.M.S.

*intuitionism.

W. Kneale and M. Kneale, *The Development of Logic* (Oxford, 1962).

Black, Max (1909–88). Influential for contributions to philosophy of language, philosophy of mathematics and science, philosophy of art, conceptual analysis, and interpretative studies of figures such as Wittgenstein and Frege.

Born in Baku, Azerbaijan, he was educated in England and emigrated to the United States in 1940. In 1977 he retired as professor at Cornell University but continued in the programme on science, technology, and society.

There are over 200 items in Black's bibliography. His first book critically explores the formalist, logicist, and intuitionist accounts of mathematics. It remains a staple. Black was no system-builder. His preoccupation was with conceptual clarity and sound argument directed toward well-delineated questions or puzzles concerning, *inter alia*, meaning, rules, vagueness, choice, and metaphor. Throughout his work he showed an uncommon appreciation of common language and common sense.　　R.B.M.

Max Black, *Language and Philosophy* (Ithaca, NY, 1949).

—— *Models and Metaphors* (Ithaca, NY, 1962).

—— *The Nature of Mathematics* (London, 1933).

—— *The Prevalence of Humbug* (Ithaca, NY, 1983).

black box. A black box is a system whose internal workings are unknown or irrelevant to current purposes. The computer model of the mind treats the mind as a system that itself is composed of interacting systems, which themselves may be composed of further interacting systems, and so on. The bottom-level *primitive* processors, the black boxes that cognitive science leaves unopened, are understood behaviouristically: what they do (their input–output function) is in the domain of cognitive science, but how they do it is not. (How they do it is in the domain of electronics or neurophysiology, etc.) Via the hierarchy of systems, cognitive science explains intelligence, by reducing the capacities of an intelligent system to the interactions among the capacities of unintelligent systems, grounded in the bottom-level black boxes. But the model does not explain *intentionality in this way since the bottom-level black boxes are themselves intentional systems.　　　N.B.

N. Block, 'The Computer Model of the Mind', in D. Osherson and E. Smith (eds.), *An Invitation to Cognitive Science*, iii: *Thinking* (Cambridge, Mass., 1990).

Blackburn, Simon (1944–). Professor at Cambridge, formerly at Oxford and North Carolina, known for his defence of *quasi-realism about items whose reality has been much disputed—e.g. values, causes, numbers. As to values, he argues that the impact of the perceived world on the mind, together with the beliefs formed thereby, generate habits, emotions, sentiments, and attitudes which come to be projected on to the world and to be regarded as real properties of that world; so commitments of approval or disapproval become judgements with truth-values. And rightly so, for values supervene on natural properties. Thus, such judgements are neither mere expressions of subjective sentiments nor truths which obtain independently of human attitudes. And we should be neither anti-realist nor realist about values; the right stance is quasi-realism. Blackburn has also published a successful popular introduction to philosophy, *Think* (1999).

O.R.J.

*language, history of the philosophy of; language, problems of the philosophy of; realism and anti-realism; philosophy of language.

Simon Blackburn, *Spreading the Word* (Oxford, 1984).

—— *Essays in Quasi-Realism* (Oxford, 1993).

—— *Ruling Passions* (Oxford, 1999).

black philosophy today takes two principal forms. In one form, it is a hermeneutic enterprise, offering explications, interpretations, and exploitations of the traditional wisdom of African societies through the concepts and terminology of contemporary Western philosophy. The topics typically include the general nature of being, the numinous, the nature of human society and the place of human beings in it, causality and agency, and action. An offshoot of this instead exploits insights and nuances available in African *languages* to enrich philosophical analyses of concepts dealt with in Western philosophy. In its other form, black philosophy employs the analytical tools of contemporary philosophizing in order to characterize the social history and problems of peoples of African descent to the extent that these are either peculiar to their experience or peculiarly exacerbated in their experience.

The first form is enmeshed in a vigorous debate about the proper classification of the material, and in consequence its possible usefulness. One camp proposes to treat it as no more than ethnographic material, invaluable in clarifying self-concepts of Africans. This camp, notwithstanding the practice of elders gathering in conversation, regards the material a priori as lacking in individual contributions or modifications and critical debate, principally because it was originally unscripted; for this camp proposes scripted authorship and critical debate as *sine qua non* tests for the rubric of philosophy. It describes the hermeneutic account as *ethnophilosophy*.

A second camp postulates that the tradition is an evolving result of the collaboration of individual elders whose discussions and debates are submerged, by the nature of the case, in the tenets of the oral tradition. It is noted that, even in the case of the literate early Pythagoreans, critical debate does not appear to have been permitted, and it remains a highly speculative thing to impute a specific view to any of them. Indeed, all their accepted views seem to have been ascribed to Pythagoras himself, even well after his death, irrespective of their actual source.

In fact, the idea of philosophy, like that of any discipline, is quite variable, and there is hardly ever a single overriding paradigm sufficiently protean to fit philosophy or any other discipline at every stage in its history. For example, much of what is admired today as ancient Greek philosophy does not satisfy contemporary notions of philosophy, and some did not satisfy even Aristotle's! It would be equally pointless to try to bring the diversity of today's philosophical practices under a single paradigm.

A broader view can discern philosophy at different points in its evolutionary tree, and can penetrate the density of the idiom of African philosophy and recognize the philosophical aspects of its preoccupation and content, and thereby avoid the superficiality of an inflexible equation of idiom with myth. It thus becomes clear, for example, that of two West African peoples, the Diola proposed corporeally expressed force as a cosmological principle, denied it a temporal beginning, and made it inexhaustible, indestructible, and all-encompassing. General quantitative variations in it were taken to express its creative energy, and the actualizations of these variations constitute the diversity of natural forms. Different orders of being come about through a progressive lessening in its expressiveness. By contrast, the celebrated Dogon people postulated an extremely dense body for their cosmological principle, and, by appeal to concepts of prefiguration and specific motions, sought to explain principal and determinative categories of nature, the four elemental natural masses of air, fire, water, and earth, as well as consciousness and human society, etc. Data like the above enjoy a cultural and historical centrality, but their hermeneutic explication and its tools are transcultural and transhistorical. In its variety of versions, the above kind of black philosophy (or African philosophy) is today supported by a rapidly growing literature.

The other form of black philosophy is an independent movement and not a direct development from African philosophy. It is the more vigorous, the more fully established, and the clearer in its aims and methods. It is centred in the United States. Avoiding metaphysical issues, it concentrates on the development of normative concepts of the identity and emancipation beyond sheer liberty of the black peoples of the Americas and on strategies for their application towards social reconstruction of American societies. Issues of race and moral attitudes and actions become dominant in it. The discussion of race, however, is, only now overcoming a remarkable denial of the reality of race which merely confused the *factitious* with the *fictitious*. This form of black philosophy uses techniques of analytical philosophy to re-cluster and redefine concepts relating to issues of social identity, social and economic emancipation and justice, and relations between cultures. It uses the re-clustered and redefined concepts to direct the critique of phenomena relating to them. It calls to its aid the categories and syntheses of the European continental tradition in philosophy in the endeavour to develop and illuminate strategies for the existential grounding of historical readings and the elimination of reifying processes and bad faith in the continuance of racist displays.

It has reinvigorated its topics by making the black experience salient as a modifier of the intuitions, ideals, common sense, and persuasiveness of argumentation in the social and normative domain. In this way, it has shed considerable light on its topics, especially those of social discrimination, affirmative action, and the underclass. Its intention, however, is not the mere clarification of concepts, but the promotion of emancipation beyond liberty.

W.E.A.

*negritude.

Gordon R. Lewis (ed.), *Existence in Black: An Anthology of Black Existential Philosophy* (New York, 1997).

Henry O. Oruka, 'Sage Philosophy', in R. H. Coetzee and A. P. J. Roux (eds.), *The African Philosophy Reader* (London, 1998).

Kwasi Wiredu, 'How not to Compare African Thought with Western Thought', in R. Wright (ed.), *African Philosophy: An Introduction* (Washington, DC, 1979).

George Yancy (ed.), 'Lewis R. Gordon', in *African-American Philosophers* (New York, 1998).

bladders of philosophy

> Reason, an Ignis fatuus, in the Mind,
> Which leaving light of Nature, sense behind;
> Pathless and dang'rous wandring ways it takes,
> Through errors Fenny—Boggs, and Thorny Brakes;
> Whilst the misguided follower, climbs with pain,
> Mountains of Whimseys, heap'd in his own Brain:
> Stumbling from thought to thought, falls headlong down,
> Into doubts boundless Sea, where like to drown,
> Books bear him up awhile, and make him try,
> To swim with Bladders of Philosophy . . .
>
> (John Wilmot, Earl of Rochester,
> 'Satyr on Mankind', lines 12–21)

Rochester derides the tendency of philosophers and others to elevate 'Reason, which Fifty times for one does err' over 'certain instinct'. He declares *reason a 'cheat', because it first 'frames deep Mysteries, then finds them out'. The doubts it stirs up make 'Cloysterd Coxcombs' follow formulas, not appetites, and drove Diogenes to abandon the world for a tub. As Rochester implies, when the reasoning mind is made indubitable starting point and final arbiter, everything else, including its body, becomes the external world, whose nature, and even existence, is forever doubtful, perhaps mind-dependent. Yet, as Thomas Reid put it, 'reason's light' and the senses' corollary dimness 'both came out of the same shop', so each is likely to be as faulty—or effective—as the other.   J.O'G.

Blanshard, Brand (1892–1987). American, educated partly in England as a Rhodes Scholar, who defended *rationalism and *idealism during an era in which they had few defenders. He taught at the University of Michigan, Swarthmore, Columbia, and for most of his career at Yale University. He argued against the doctrine of Hume that causation is merely the constant conjunction of events and the view of *Logical Positivism that a priori statements are merely consequences of linguistic conventions. There are, Blanshard said, genuine 'necessary connections' in the world. A naturalist in ethics, Blanshard held that 'to call an experience intrinsically good *is* to say that it is fulfilling and satisfying'. Since he granted 'that the word "good" has [in addition] an aura of emotional and associative meaning', he could 'keep emotive meaning and also keep it in its place'. A naturalist in religion too, he took 'the service of reason' as his religion. 'That service calls for the use of one's reason to embrace as much as one can of the reason implicit in the universe, and its use at the same time to define and harmonize the ends of practical life.' Blanshard's personal demeanour was one of extraordinary graciousness.   P.H.H.

P. A. Schilpp (ed.), *The Philosophy of Brand Blanshard* (La Salle, Ill., 1980).

blindsight. Absence of visual awareness despite the presence of visual capacity. Some brain-damaged humans retain discriminative capacities in portions of the visual field—manifested, for example, in correct 'guesses' concerning what is there—in which they report they can see nothing. (Removal of the visual cortex in the rhesus monkey also apparently induces blindsight.) Philosophical interest arises because the phenomenon casts doubt on the relation usually assumed between *consciousness and *perception.   J.HORN.

L. Weiskrantz, *Blindsight: A Case Study and Implications* (Oxford, 1986).

Bloch, Ernst (1885–1977). Bloch believed that reality is an ongoing 'mediation' between object and subject. This somewhat baffling claim should be read in the light of the fact that, although his reputation in the West was as a leading Marxist philosopher, in respects Bloch's debts were to the deeper and more ancient roots of *Natur-philosophie. Apparently, the basic stuff of existence (*Urgrund*) has a kind of teleological drive towards the end of the life process (*Endziel*). Causally, this is all driven by a fundamental cosmic force—'hunger'—which Bloch saw as translatable into 'hope' in our own species. Politically,

the end-point translates into a utopia where the exploitation of humans by fellow humans has ceased.   M.R.

E. Bloch, *Das Prinzip Hoffnung* (Berlin, 1954–9).
W. Hudson, *The Marxist Philosophy of Ernst Bloch* (London, 1982).

Block, Ned (1942–). American philosopher, best known for his work on *images and his inventive objections to *behaviourism and *functionalism. Consider a chess-playing computer in which every possible position has been stored in memory, together with a good move which it makes automatically if that position turns up. Its high standard of play could hardly be ascribed to its intelligence. Block describes an analogous program (even more remote from practical possibility) for a robot. It would have the behavioural capacities of an intelligent person, but 'the intelligence of a toaster'. If its practical impossibility may be disregarded, it looks like a counter-example to behaviourism. Against functionalism Block uses similarly ingenious examples to emphasize the problems posed by the alleged possibilities of transposed and absent *'qualia'. Functionalists reply that his reasoning begs the question.   R.K.

N. Block, 'Troubles with Functionalism', excerpt repr. in *Mind and Cognition*, ed. W. G. Lycan (Cambridge, Mass., 1990).

boat, Neurath's. 'We are like sailors who have to rebuild their ship on the open sea, without ever being able to dismantle it in dry-dock and reconstruct it from the best components.' Originated by Neurath and later adopted by Quine, this simile depicts anti-*foundationalism and *naturalism. For Neurath, the simile goes beyond epistemology. His pragmatism encompasses the social sciences and extends to society and politics: knowledge and life are built without foundations.   N.C.
                                                         T.U.

N. Cartwright, K. Fleck, J. Cat, and T. Uebel, *On Neurath's Boat* (Cambridge, 1994).
Otto Neurath, 'Protokollsätze', *Erkenntnis* (1932–3), repr. as 'Protocol Statements', in Otto Neurath, *Philosophical Papers 1913–1946*, ed. and tr. R. S. Cohen and M. Neurath (Dordrecht, 1983).

Bobbio, Norberto (1909–2004). Leading Italian philosopher of politics and law, who taught in the university of his native Turin and became a life senator in 1984. His aim was a synthesis of the liberal concern with individual liberty, rights, and the rule of law with the socialist concern with equality and social justice. Bobbio's main contribution was to democratic theory. On the one hand, he criticized participatory theorists for concentrating on who holds power to the neglect of the moral and practical issue of how power is exercised. He believed that a liberal constitutionalist democracy, including social along with civil and political rights, to be the only feasible and legitimate form of democratic rule in modern societies. On the other hand, he believed that democratic decision-making can and should be extended over a far greater range of centres of power than simply central government. He contended that battles over where you can vote have now replaced the debates over who can vote as the key area for democratic advance. R.P.B.

*Italian philosophy.

Richard Bellamy, *Modern Italian Social Theory* (Cambridge, 1987), ch. 8.

Bodin, Jean (1530–96). French political theorist celebrated for *Six livres de la république* (1576). Like Hobbes, with whom he has some ideas in common, Bodin feared civil war. His *Republic* was inspired by that feeling, and he belonged to a group known as the Politiques, who wished to support royal power as the safeguard of peace. He regarded the natural grouping of the family as the mainstay of social order, and made the principle of absolute sovereignty the defining principle of the state. He allowed that the state, based solely on sovereign power, might be monarchical or democratic, but argued that the only really well-ordered state was one with undivided power, a monarchy. His advocacy of undivided sovereign power was not consistently combined with his belief in constitu-tionalism. R.S.D.

*conservatism.

G. H. Sabine, *A History of Political Theory* (London, 1937).

body. One of the most fundamental concepts in philosophy because of the role it plays in the picture of an 'external world' composed of three-dimensional entities which we perceive. Generally contrasted in this sense with *space*, the medium containing these entities, bodies are also contrasted with *minds* (except in the thinking of materialists like Hobbes) because the external world containing bodies is not external to my own body; it is rather that my body is itself one of them. Once this picture holds sway, two great problems emerge. One is that, if my knowledge of reality is confined to my own perceptions, how can I be certain what the world is really like, or even that it exists at all? Almost all the great philosophers have regarded these as difficult questions, some concluding that there is no external world, some that we can't know what it is like. This is not surprising: given the picture of perceptual experience which generates such questions, they are unanswerable. If my perceptions are private mental phenomena, the gap between them and the 'physical' world is unbridgeable.

The other great problem is that I appear in this scheme of things to have a special and peculiar relationship with one of the entities in the physical world, which is my body. But it is difficult to say why I believe, as it is generally claimed I do, that it belongs to me. Descartes was inclined to think that I regard it as mine because it always accompanies me, which might be called the 'stray dog' conception of ownership. It ought to be clear, however, that any such account is confused: it relies on describing me, and where I am, in terms that are ruled out by the picture which generates the problem. If I am, as Descartes thought, a mind, a non-spatial entity, it makes no sense to

say where I am, and hence no sense to suggest that my body might be in the same place or close by.

Both these alleged problems, then, have tormented philosophers endlessly precisely because they are generated by a metaphysical picture which makes them insoluble. C.W.

M. Proudfoot (ed.), *The Philosophy of Body* (Oxford, 2003).

C. Williamson, 'Attitudes Towards the Body: Philosophy and Common Sense', *Philosophical Quarterly*, 40, no. 161 (1990).

body and mind: *see* mind–body problem.

Boethius, Anucius Manlius Severinus (*c*.480–*c*.526). Roman patrician, Master of the Offices under the Italian king Theodoric, later accused of treason and magic, imprisoned at Pavia, tortured and executed; an early eminence in the tradition of Latin philosophy stretching forward to Kant. Besides commentaries on Cicero, Porphyry, and Aristotle, essays on logic, and short treatises on the Trinity, we still have from him textbooks on his 'quadrivium' of geometry, arithmetic, astronomy, and music, intended for his own darkening times but destined to serve all the Latin Middle Ages. Their tone is Platonist, their aim not practice but understanding of the cosmos as befits a 'liberal' education. In prison he wrote the incomparable *Consolation of Philosophy*, which contains (at 5. 6) a famous definition of *eternity as 'perfect possession all at the same time of endless life', and perhaps the first clear statement of the difference between conditional and simple necessity (the necessity that he's-walking-if-you-know-he-is does not—when added to the fact that you know he is—'drag with it' the necessity that he's-walking). For many centuries Aristotle was known in the West only from two of Boethius' translations. C.A.K.

*Platonism.

H. Chadwick, *Boethius: The Consolations of Music, Logic, Theology, and Philosophy* (Oxford, 1981).

J. Marenbon, *Boethius* (Oxford, 2003).

Bogdanov, Alexandr Alexandrovich (1873– 1928), real name Malinovsky. Bolshevik philosopher and ideologist who developed 'empirio-monism', a combination of Marxism and the positivist *'empirio-criticism' of Mach and Ave-narius. Empirio-monism advances an extreme collectivism where reality is 'socially organized experience' and the distinction between individual minds (i.e. between individual ways of organizing experience) will dissolve once social conflict is eradicated by communism.

Bogdanov was a significant leader of the Bolshevik faction until 1909, when Lenin condemned Russian empirio-criticism as a revisionist heresy. Thereafter Bogdanov's political star declined, though he continued to develop his ideas, first in science fiction, then in the 'general organizational science' of *tektology*. After the 1917 revolution, Bogdanov was influential in the 'proletarian culture' movement. He died in the service of his collectivist ideals after performing upon himself an experiment in blood transfusion designed to promote 'the comradely exchange of life'.   D.BAK.

A. A. Bogdanov, *Empiriomonizm*, 3 vols. (Moscow, 1904–6).
—— *Essays in Tektology*, tr. George Gorelik (Seaside, Calif., 1980).

Bohr, Niels (1885–1962). Danish physicist and Nobel prize-winner (1922). Bohr made important contributions to atomic theory and nuclear physics (the liquid drop model) and, indirectly, influenced the rise of molecular biology. Much to his surprise he found that his early (1910) belief that experience is basically ambiguous was supported by 'hard and solid' scientific evidence: concepts firmly grounded in facts divide into mutually exclusive or 'complementary' groups all of which are needed for stating what we know, though the use of any particular group rules out the use of the rest. According to Bohr different cultures, different concepts or attitudes within a particular culture (truth and clarity, love and justice), and different methodological approaches (mechanicism and teleology in the life sciences) are related in a similar way. Bohr believed that the problems created by the paradoxical status of human beings—they are part of the world and yet put themselves outside of it when claiming to possess knowledge—are resolved by using complementarity descriptions instead of a single 'objective' frame.   P.K.F.

A. Pais, *Niels Bohr's Times in Physics, Philosophy and Polity* (Oxford, 1991). Literature, analysis, and biography.

Boltzmann, Ludwig (1844–1906). As philosopher of science Boltzmann emphasized, against the positivist phenomenalists (Mach, Duhem), the role of invented hypotheses and the importance of posited unobservable theoretical entities and properties. He defended atomism in a period in which it was under sceptical attack. Along with J. C. Maxwell he is the inventor of modern statistical mechanics, his contributions including the Boltzmann equation, the *H*-theorem allegedly proving irreversible approach to equilibrium, and the ergodic hypothesis. His was also the discovery of the association of entropy with the probability of the micro-states of a system. He introduced the first 'anthropic' argument into physics in his discussion of the place of non-equilibrium in an (allegedly) mostly equilibrium universe and originated the claim that entropic increase in time is the ground of all of our intuitive distinctions between past and future.   L.S.

*theory.

E. Broda, *Ludwig Boltzmann* (Vienna, 1955).

Bolzano, Bernard (1781–1848). Bohemian philosopher, mathematician, and logician; a late follower of Leibnizian rationalism and a critic of Kant's philosophy of mathematics. Bolzano developed a special logico-ontological atomism directed against radical scepticism and subjectivism. The objectivity of knowledge had to be secured by the existence of non-linguistic entities (ideas, propositions, and truths) independent of human beings and prior to cog-

nition. As mathematician Bolzano helped to establish the foundations of analysis (for example, the Bolzano–Weierstrass theorem), attempted to elaborate mathematical method, and anticipated some basic ideas of Cantor's set theory. His major work, *Wissenschaftslehre* (1837), contains various contributions to logic and semantics concerning the relations of compatibility, derivability, and con-sequence, the deduction theorem, and the logic of classes, entailment, and probability. He was also influential as a social moralist.   M.P.
                                                                         K.B.

J. Sebestik, *Logique et mathématique chez Bernard Bolzano* (Paris, 1992).

Bonaventure, St (1221–74). A native of Tuscany, he joined the Franciscan Order, and subsequently studied at Paris under Alexander of Hales, who influenced him strongly. He later became Professor of Theology at Paris, before being appointed Minister-General of the Franciscans (1257), and Cardinal in the year before his death. His writings are in the Augustinian tradition but he did not ignore the writings of Aristotle. Bonaventure, always more a theologian than a philosopher, rejected important parts of Aristotle's system, for that system failed to take account of central truths such as the divinity of Christ and the triunity of God. Amongst other doctrines he rejected Aristotle's teaching on the eternity of the world. Bonaventure's great contemporary Aquinas had argued, contrary to Aristotle, that reason alone could not settle the issue whether the world was eternal, but Bonaventure rejected Aquinas's position also, and held instead that Aristotle's doctrine was impossible, for if the world had indeed lasted for an infinite time the infinite must be getting bigger because each new day is a further period of time added to an infinitely long period; yet there cannot be two infinites one of which is bigger than the other. It is therefore a matter of reason and not of faith that the world has not existed from all eternity.   A.BRO.

E. Gilson, *The Philosophy of Bonaventure* (London, 1938).

Bonhoeffer, Dietrich (1906–45). German Lutheran theologian martyred by the Nazis. His 'non-religious interpretation of biblical concepts' has been misunderstood as a kind of secularism. In fact, Bonhoeffer thinks that the growth of scientific atheism in the West provides an opportunity to dispense with God as an empty intellectual postulate, and return to the living *God who suffers as Christ: the self-revelation that essentially distinguishes Christianity from other religions. This 'theology of the cross' is apparent as early as the dissertation *Akt und Sein* (1931), his most overtly philosophical work. The cost of discipleship argued for in *Nachfolge* (1937) is the death of the old worldly self in submission to Christ. Nazism shows that human beings are not naturally religious, and Hitler is the anti-Christ. Theologically, Bonhoeffer's thought emphasizes the immanence rather than the *transcendence of God. In this it is arguably consistent with some twentieth-century positivist, materialist, and naturalist attacks on the possibility of metaphysics. s.p.

Dietrich Bonhoeffer, *Act and Being* (*Akt und Sein*), tr. Bernard Noble (London, 1963).

—— *The Cost of Discipleship* (*Nachfolge*), tr. R. H. Fuller with revisions by Irmgard Booth and a forward by Bishop G. K. A. Bell (London, 1971).

—— *Letters and Papers from Prison*, ed. E. Bethge (London, 1971).

boo–hoorah theory. Apt nickname for crude version of *emotivism. The theory states that we use ethical words to express our feelings or attitudes and to evoke similar feelings or attitudes in other people. Hence, '. . . is wrong' or '. . . is right' amount only to 'Boo!' or 'Hoorah!' This provides only an embryonic theory of moral language, involving a sharp distinction between facts and values. The theory was developed into more subtle versions of emotivism. R.S.D.

*emotive theory of ethics.

A. J. Ayer, *Language, Truth and Logic* (London, 1936), ch. 6.

Boole, George (1815–64). Mathematician, born in Lincoln and died while Professor of Mathematics at Queen's College, Cork. In 1847 Boole proposed a *calculus for proving *syllogisms; it involved translating each syllogism into arithmetical notation and then eliminating a variable with the help of the laws of arithmetic (such as $x + y = y + x$) together with the new law $x^2 = x$. Boole's creatively chaotic ideas led directly to the invention of *propositional calculus and *Boolean algebras, after tidying up by W. S. Jevons, C. S. Peirce, and others. Boole gave several different interpretations of his calculus, interpreting the variables either as propositions or as classes, or even as periods of time. With hindsight we can see Boole's suggested correspondences between these interpretations as early steps in *formal semantics. w.a.h.

George Boole, *An Investigation of the Laws of Thought on which are Founded the Mathematical Theories of Logic and Probabilities* (London, 1854; repr. New York, 1958).

Boolean algebra. A simple and elegant type of algebraic structure. In 1847 George Boole gave the structure its first unrefined description as part of his development of an algebra of logic. His aim was to translate sentences expressing logical relations into algebraic equations which were then to be manipulated according to algebraic laws to determine what can be deduced from the original sentences. The algebraic laws can be thought of as axioms governing the operations they mention. Boole saw that the axioms do not have a unique subject matter but rather characterize a type of structure. This generalizing move enabled the Boolean structure to be discerned in a wide variety of domains; for example, there are Boolean algebras of propositions, sets, and switching-circuits.

In formal terms, a Boolean algebra is a structure containing a set B, two binary functions $\wedge$ (intersection or meet) and $\vee$ (union or join) on B, one unary function $'$ (complementation) on B, and two distinguished elements 0 (the null-element) and 1 (the unit-element) of B, satisfying the following axioms, for all $x, y, z \in B$:

1. $x \vee (y \vee z) = (x \wedge y) \vee z$ and $x \wedge (y \wedge z) = (x \wedge y) \wedge z$.
2. $x \vee y = y \vee x$ and $x \wedge y = y \wedge x$.
3. $x \vee (y \wedge z) = (x \vee y) \wedge (x \vee z)$ and $x \wedge (y \vee z) = (x \wedge y) \vee (x \wedge z)$.
4. $x \vee x' = 1$ and $x \wedge x' = 0$.
5. $x \vee 0 = x$ and $x \wedge 1 = x$.

A binary relation $\leq$ on B is defined as $x \leq y \leftrightarrow x \wedge y = x$; $\leq$ partially orders B. To see that the algebra of sets is a Boolean algebra let B be the power set of any set S, $\wedge$ be set-theoretic intersection, $\vee$ be set-theoretic union, $'$ be complementation with respect to S, 0 be the null set, and 1 be S. Then $\leq$ is set-theoretic inclusion. a.d.o.

R. R. Stoll, *Set Theory and Logic* (San Francisco, 1961), ch. 6.

bootstrapping. An anti-holist account of theory-testing designed to show how *evidence can count for or against a single hypothesis instead of the entire theory it belongs to. Bootstrapping construes the confirmation of a hypothesis, H, by evidence, E, as depending upon whether an instance of H can be deductively or probabilistically derived from E together with other hypotheses ('bootstraps') from the theory H belongs to. Unlike *hypothetico-deductive accounts, bootstrapping does not have as a consequence that evidence which supports any hypothesis equally supports any consistent conjunction of that hypothesis and any irrelevant propositions you choose. j.b.b.

Clark Glymour, *Theory and Evidence* (Princeton, NJ, 1980).

Bosanquet, Bernard (1848–1923). British philosopher who, influenced by T. H. Green, was, along with F. H. Bradley, one of the chief promoters of Hegelian, or absolute, *idealism in late nineteenth-century England. He taught for a while at Oxford (and more briefly later at St Andrews) but spent most of his life as a writer and engaged in the politics of charity. Less sceptical and more purely Hegelian than Bradley, he wrote on metaphysics and logic: *Knowledge and Reality* (1885); *Logic; or, The Morphology of Knowledge* (1888). Probably his best work is *The Philosophical Theory of the State* (1899; 4 edns.; frequently repr.). In it he identifies the individual's real will with the state and hence holds that 'the common self or moral person of society is more real than the apparent individual'. Given this great importance of the state as 'the fly-wheel of our life', he easily constructs a retributive theory of punishment in which punishment is someone's 'right, of which he must not be defrauded'. r.h.

A. J. M. Milne, *The Social Philosophy of English Idealism* (London, 1962).

bourgeoisie and proletariat. In Marxian theory, the two most historically influential social classes in modern capitalist society, which is fundamentally characterized by the *class struggle. The bourgeoisie are those who privately own the means of production and live from the profits and interest on capital; the proletariat is the class of wage-labourers hired and exploited by capital. Marx credits the bourgeoisie with creating the productive forces which are the foundation of modern society; but he thinks the potential of these forces to serve humanity will be actualized only after the social order has been revolutionized by the proletariat.   A.W.W.

*dictatorship of the proletariat.

Harry Braverman, *Labor and Monopoly Capital* (New York, 1974).

G. A. Cohen, 'Bourgeoisie and Proletarians', in S. Avineri (ed.), *Marxist Socialism* (New York, 1973).

E. P. Thompson, *The Making of the English Working Class* (Harmondsworth, 1968).

Boyle, Robert (1627–91). Boyle is well known as a scientist but underrated as a philosopher. He wrote interestingly, lengthily, and with more philosophical sophistication than the admiring Locke on topics such as atheism, atomism, epistemology, God's existence, miracles, natural laws, qualities, and scientific method. Emphasizing experiment over theory Boyle refused, as Leibniz complained to Huygens, to construct global theories. Boyle's universe involved God at every stage as creator, designer, sustainer, and frequent intervener. For example, God 'almost every moment in the day' works 'Physical Miracles' by forming 'Animals of such a Compounded nature, as the . . . Laws of matter & motion, would not wthout a peculiar interposition of God, be able to produce'. None the less, in science appeal to God was inappropriate: all 'intelligible' explanations must be in terms of minute corpuscles of matter and their motions.   J.J.M.

Michael Hunter (ed.), *Robert Boyle Reconsidered* (Cambridge, 1993).

bracketing. An essential part of Husserl's so-called phenomenological reduction. According to Husserl, and some of his followers, we can describe the objects of our minds *as phenomena* only after we have bracketed their existence. By bracketing the objective world, one *suspends* judgement about the existence of the things around us. The botanist, for example, takes for granted that there are trees and studies their characteristics. The phenomenologist does not deny that the botanist is right, but he puts the existence assumption in brackets, and tries to describe the phenomena precisely as they present themselves to him. For example, the phenomenologist may study the object of a mental act of seeing a tree, the precise *what* of what he is seeing at that moment, irrespective of whether his perception is correct, of whether there are trees, or even of whether there are any perceptual objects at all.   R.G.

*phenomenology.

For Husserl's description of bracketing see Edmund Husserl, *Ideas*, tr. W. R. Boyce Gibson (New York, 1962), 96–101.

Bradley, Francis Herbert (1846–1924). British philosopher, fellow of Merton College, Oxford. Bradley is indisputably the greatest British philosopher between J. S. Mill and Bertrand Russell. His philosophy is a late example of the movement of British philosophers away from the tradition of British *empiricism towards German *idealism, in particular Hegel. However, despite himself, he was much nearer to British Empiricism than other British idealists of the period such as T. H. Green and Bernard Bosanquet.

Ethical Studies (1876) was his most Hegelian work. Contending that a moral outlook must be justified by the form of 'self-realization' it offers, Bradley examines a series of moral systems which in turn rectify each other's contradictions.

*Hedonism, whether individualist or universalist, presents itself initially as the most attractively down to earth of moral theories. But the maximization of pleasure provides no genuine form of self-realization for anyone. The pleasures of different times form no real totality, since they never exist together, and can never constitute a state of affairs of which anyone can say: 'Here I have that which I was seeking'.

Bradley now turns to the sharply opposed Kantian ideal of 'duty for duty's sake'. Here the good is identified with sheer rationality; one is to behave only in a way which one could will universalized without contradiction. This advances on hedo-nism in recognizing the self as somehow a 'universal' rather than as a series of 'perishing particulars'. But its purely formal notion of morality provides neither a definite guide nor any proper human satisfaction.

Next comes the vastly superior Hegelian morality of 'my station and its duties'. Here the demands of morality are no longer those of a remote logical abstraction, with no appeal for flesh and blood, but those of a role in a concrete historical community such as provides a satisfying life for the real empirical man. Much more satisfactory as is this social ethic than the two preceding, it cannot be the final truth. For the community itself may be rotten with a morality to be transcended; moreover, full self-realization need not be purely social.

These limitations push us on to what Bradley calls 'ideal morality'. The basic injunction here is to realize everywhere the best self, and our idea of our best self, though it must arise from the ideals we learn in the family and in life in the community, may develop beyond it to take account of values learnt from other societies or based on internal criticisms of our own society. The basic test for the adequacy of an ideal morality is that it satisfies the individual as a 'concrete universal', that is as an individual whose life is a unity, resting on his unity with his kind, rather than, like the other three theories respectively, as a mere series of experiences, or as some abstract pure ego, or as being entirely socially conditioned.

In his next great work, *The Principles of Logic* (1883), the Empiricists' psychologistic approach to logic is criticized in a manner not unlike Husserl, but, like Husserl, he includes the examination of strictly necessary features of thinking within its remit. A main theme is the inadequacies of the traditional Aristotelian analysis of judgements into subject and predicate. There are many propositions (e.g. existential and relational ones) and related forms of inference which escape this net.

Ultimately every judgement ascribes a single (normally complex) idea as predicate to Reality as subject. Reality is that greater whole of which the perceptual manifold presents itself as an incomplete fragment. There are intriguing similarities and contrasts between Bradley's position here and that of Bertrand Russell, whose theory of definite *descriptions (talking of the King of France where Bradley talks of the King of Utopia) as belonging logically to the predicate owes somewhat to him, as does his account of existential (also universal) propositions. For Russell the most basic factual propositions concern particulars with which we are acquainted; those whose grammatical subjects are only identified by description are logically derivative. Bradley is even more insistent that it is only because our access to Reality is not entirely conceptual that we get beyond the circle of our own ideas in thought and treats demonstratives quite similarly, though holding that they must be dropped in fundamental theory.

*Inference is the construction of a larger mental representation put together from those which constitute the premisses, and reading off a conclusion from the holistic character it turns out to possess (oddly anticipative, though without any whiff of materialism, of suggestions by some current 'cognitive scientists').

Appearance and Reality (1893) is the main statement of his metaphysics. Book I, *Appearance*, argues that most ordinary things (e.g. things and their qualities, time and space, causation, the self, even things-in-themselves) are merely appearances, while book II, *Reality*, strains to characterize, with more final truth, the Reality they so usefully misrepresent to us, namely the *Absolute, a single cosmic experience of which we (so far as we truly are at all) are components.

In calling something an appearance Bradley means, primarily, that the concept of it only gives a pragmatically useful way of thinking about some aspect of the world of which, being incoherent, it cannot give us a finally satisfactory grasp. Something in the Absolute, for example, corresponds to Time, but it is so unlike Time, as we ordinarily conceive it, that thus conceived it is ultimately an illusion. However, reality (as predicate) is a matter of degree, that is, our concepts are true (and conversely false) of reality (as thing) in different degrees. The concept of the Absolute is more adequate than that of *time, but both are just our way of grappling with what the intellect cannot finally grasp. This is established by two main lines of argument, firstly, that reality must have a unitary togetherness which cannot be captured by the ordinary conception of many distinct things in relation, secondly, that all concrete reality must somehow be psychical in its nature. Reality is somehow one vast eternal self-experiencing many-in-one. Though often presented somewhat sophistically, there is a vein of powerful argument to back this conclusion up.

The most famous feature of the first line of argument is his attempt to show that the idea that the world consists in a multiplicity of distinct things standing in various relations to each other is incoherent. For when two terms stand in a certain relation, we must either think of the relation as a separable component in the total state of affairs or in some other way. (1) If you think of it as some kind of *separable component*, then it seems to require to be related to its terms by fresh relations, and these to be related to those relations and their terms by further ones, and so on in an impossible regress. (2) To avoid this you may treat the relation as an aspect of one or other of the terms, or divide it into two aspects one pertaining to each of the terms. But in either case the terms are apparently left apart, each simply possessing a feature which does not bring it together with the other one. (3) Finally, you may treat the relation as an aspect of the terms taken together as constituting a unit. But that betrays the very notion of a relation by merging the terms between which they hold into a single thing; moreover, their togetherness does not seem particularly due to the relation since they have already (logically speaking) to be together to provide a home for it. In effect, Bradley's position is that relational thought allows us to shift between thinking of a thing as something conceivable independently of how it stands to other things and thinking of it as a mere aspect of some larger whole they jointly help to constitute, two ways of conceiving it which militate against each other.

Bradley's solution is that for one thing to be (as we would ordinarily somewhat distortingly put it) related to another is in the end always a matter of their being aspects of some more comprehensive and more genuinely concrete individual, conceived apart from which they are necessarily to some extent misconceived. If so, and since everything is somehow related (as we would ordinarily put it) to everything else, there must be some maximally comprehensive and concrete individual (the Absolute) from which everything else is an abstraction.

That this ultimate individual must be a single cosmic experience including everything is established by the second line of argument according to which we can form no genuine conception of an unexperienced reality. An application of this principle at the level of finite existence shows that it consists ultimately of myriad finite centres of experience and their presentations on the basis of which they construct the world of common sense, while the monistic argument shows that these centres must pertain to a Whole conceived apart from which they are partly misconceived.

In some respects his form of absolute idealism receives a better presentation in his *Essays on Truth and Reality* (1914). This also contains the classic statement of a *coherence theory of truth and knowledge. His contention that there are no basic judgements beyond revision, and that the whole system of our thought continually faces experience as a whole, has strong affinities with aspects of the work of W. V. Quine. Nicholas Rescher has derived much of his own elaborate coherence theory of truth from Bradley.   T.L.S.S.

L. McHenry, *Whitehead and Bradley: A Comparative Analysis* (Albany, NY, 1992).

A. Manser, *Bradley's Logic* (Oxford, 1983).

——and Guy Stock (eds.), *The Philosophy of F. H. Bradley* (Oxford, 1984).

Nicholas Rescher, *The Coherence Theory of Truth* (Oxford, 1973).

T. L. S. Sprigge, *James and Bradley: American Truth and British Reality* (La Salle, Ill., 1993).

Richard Wollheim, *F. H. Bradley* (Harmondsworth, 1959).

brain in a vat. Contemporary counterpart of Descartes's hypothesis that one's beliefs are induced by an evil genius.

Used within a premiss in arguments for scepticism, the hypothesis says that nothing exists except one's brain—in a vat, in order that its electrochemical activity should be sustained—so that whatever may seem to one to be the case, its seeming so is accounted for by such activity alone. The sceptic invites one to say 'For all I know, I am a brain in a vat, and there is no external world'.

Brains in vats are introduced also in philosophy of mind in connection with the idea that a person's psychological faculties require nothing but a brain's operations. The idea may be questioned, and will be by the supporters of *anti-individualism and others.   J.HORN.

*malin génie.

Hilary Putnam, *Reason, Truth and History* (Cambridge, 1981), ch. 1.

Braithwaite, Richard Bevan (1900–90). Professor of Philosophy at Cambridge, mainly known for his staunchly empiricist views within philosophy of science. Thus he followed Hume in believing that laws of nature do not embody any kind of necessity but are, objectively, merely constant correlations. Braithwaite also attempted to apply the mathematical theory of games within moral philosophy, and to reinterpret religious statements as declarations of intention to accept particular moral ways of living.

Rather than considering scientific assertions in their rough-and-tumble variety of uses within scientific communities, in *Scientific Explanation* Braithwaite described uninterpreted formal systems, and how a tough empiricist might give them meaning as scientific statements. Within this basic framework he discussed the standard problems of theoretical terms, models, probability, induction, laws, causation, and explanation.   A.J.L.

*Cambridge philosophy; empiricism.

R. B. Braithwaite, *Scientific Explanation* (Cambridge, 1955).

Brandom, Robert B. (1950–). Distinguished Service Professor at the University of Pittsburgh, working largely in the philosophy of language, but also in metaphysics and the history of philosophy. His prominent book *Making it Explicit* defends and develops an inferentialist, as opposed to a representationalist, approach to the relationship between language and the world. This approach starts by explaining the *pragmatics of language in terms of the inferences which language-users should accept and the attitudes other language-users should have to those inferences; so the norms of language use must be understood in social terms. *Semantics is then explained in terms of pragmatics; according to Brandom, the meanings of words depend on their roles in inference. By understanding the way those inferences allow certain substitutions, Brandom claims to explain the representational language of truth and reference. His work is influenced by *pragmatism, in particular the *neo-pragmatism of *Sellars, as well as by *Hegel's construction of objectivity out of the process of dialectic.   R.A.K.S.

R. Brandom, *Making it Explicit* (Cambridge, Mass., 1994).

——*Tales of the Mighty Dead: Historical Essays in the Metaphysics of Intentionality* (Cambridge, Mass., 2002).

Brentano, Franz (1838–1917). German philosopher educated at Würzburg, Munich, Berlin, and Münster Universities. He was awarded his Ph.D. at Tübingen University *in absentia* in 1862. Two years later he was ordained a priest. In 1866 he wrote his habilitation thesis and was appointed *Privatdozent* at the University of Würzburg. His best-known book, *Psychology from an Empirical Standpoint* (tr. London, 1973), appeared first in Leipzig, in 1874. Brentano was called the same year to the University of Vienna as full Professor of Philosophy. After he left the Catholic Church and got married in 1879 he had to resign the professorship, but continued to serve as *Privatdozent* at Vienna University until 1894. He spent the following years mostly in Florence, and finally in Zurich, where he died.

The Background: The Philosophy of Aristotle. Franz Brentano's work was inspired by the philosophy of Aristotle, whom he regarded as a 'man for all times'. Much of Brentano's work, although critical in spirit, is dedicated to Aristotelian issues. His doctoral dissertation *The Several Senses of Being in Aristotle* (Freiburg im Breisgau, 1862; tr. Berkeley, Calif., 1981) and his habilitation thesis on *The Psychology of Aristotle* (Mainz, 1867; tr. Berkeley, Calif., 1977) focus on Brentano's chief preoccupations, psychology and *ontology. Brentano also investigates these topics in his lectures on metaphysics which began in 1867.

Metaphysics, says Brentano, in order to be established as a strict science, has first to seek for a basis in certainty. Scientific knowledge has to show itself either as evident, and therefore true, or at least as highly probable. Immediately evident thoughts, for Brentano, are the 'Archimedean points' of all our knowledge and arguments, and of all sciences (*The True and the Evident* (tr. London, 1966)). Secondly, metaphysics has to deal with ontological questions, (*a*) in a narrow sense, where it is *'phenomenology of mind', and (*b*) in a wider sense, where it is the ontology of things other than ourselves: the world, God (*On the Existence of God* (tr. The Hague, 1987)), the cosmos.

The Ontology of Mind: Psychology and Phenomenology.
Brentano's psychology starts from an empirical standpoint. Empirical psychology, in his view, is to be defined as the science of inner experience or awareness. This conscious awareness, considered in itself, presents itself as being (*a*) intentionally related to external entities, and (*b*) reflexively related to itself. Brentano analyses both relations in order to describe the ultimate elements of the experienced, intentional structure of the mind. This he does in his theory of *intentionality. He sets out to analyse the epistemic status of these phenomena in his *Descriptive Psychology* (Hamburg, 1982; tr. London, 1994), which he also called 'descriptive phenomenology' or 'phenomenognosis'. His aim is 'to define the elements of the human consciousness and of their interconnections (as far as possible) in an exhaustive manner, in order to give us a general notion of the entire human consciousness' (ibid. 1–2). Brentano gives a 'pure description' of the facts of consciousness, rather than a consideration of the physiological genesis of our conscious phenomena, since such a genetic psychology must rest on a descriptive psychology. In order to give a complete description ('microscopic analysis') of the phenomena of the human mind, philosophical psychology must first and foremost examine 'mental phenomena', 'functions', or 'acts' (*The Psychology of Aristotle* and *Psychology from an Empirical Standpoint*). Thus Brentano became known as the founder of 'act psychology'.

All the data of our consciousness, according to Brentano, are divided into two classes: the class of physical phenomena and the class of mental phenomena. A mental phenomenon is, for instance,

[e]very idea or presentation which we acquire either through sense perception or imagination . . . By presentation I do not mean that which is presented, but rather the act of presentation . . . Furthermore, every judgement . . . is a mental phenomenon. Also to be included under this term is every emotion . . . the term 'mental phenomena' applies to presentations as well as to all the phenomena which are based upon presentations . . . This act of presentation forms the foundation not merely of the act of judging but also of desiring and of every other mental act. Nothing can be judged, desired, hoped or feared, unless one has a presentation of that thing . . . Examples of physical phenomena, on the other hand, are a color, a figure, a landscape which I see; a chord which I hear; warmth, cold, odor which I sense; as well as similar images which appear in the imagination. (*Psychology from an Empirical Standpoint*, 78–80)

The characteristic common positive property of each mental phenomenon is what was

called the intentional (or mental) inexistence of an object, and what we might call, though not wholly unambiguously, reference to a content, direction towards an object (which is not to be understood here as meaning a thing), or immanent objectivity . . . We can therefore define mental phenomena by saying that they are those phenomena which contain an object intentionally within themselves. (Ibid. 88–9.)

The characteristics of mental phenomena stated by Brentano here and elsewhere can be summarized under three headings.

1. There are three classes of them: presentations, judgements, and emotive phenomena. They are either acts of presenting which serve as a basis for all other mental acts, i.e. these other acts necessarily contain presentations as 'parts' and are dependent on presentations, which are the 'fundaments' or 'motifs' for the other 'superposed' acts. This implies that the science of judgements, i.e. logic (*The Theory of Correct Judgement*; German edn. *Die Lehre vom richtigen Urteil* (Bern, 1956)), and the science of emotive phenomena, i.e. ethics (*The Origin of Our Knowledge of Right and Wrong* (tr. Westminster, 1902; repr. London, 1969); *The Foundation and Construction of Ethics* (tr. London, 1973)), relies on *fundamental* psychological observations of modes of presentations. In a correct judgement, some presentation, or a part of it, is either affirmed or denied if the categories true or false are evidently applicable. Analogously, in a correct act of emotion, something is either loved or hated correctly, or preferred correctly, motivated by the goodness of what is presented. Yet acts of judgements and of emotions differ fundamentally from acts of presentation (*a*) because there is no inner difference in presentations—they are all positive; (*b*) because a judgement as well as an act of emotion is not just a connection or separation of presentations but an additional judging or emotive act, respectively, on the ground of what is presented.

2. Mental phenomena (*a*) are or have an intentional relation towards a 'content' (a thought) or an 'immanent object' (an object thought of); (*b*) are conscious and reflexive mental acts. To any conscious act there essentially belongs a relation. And as in any relation, there are two inseparable correlates. The one correlate is the conscious mental act itself (the 'fundament' of a relation), the other correlate is that (the 'terminus' of a relation) to which it is directed. The conscious act is always the real correlate; that about which it thinks is not necessarily a real adjunct of the act of thinking. I may think about a unicorn as my thought content. My thinking about it is real, the unicorn is not. It is a thinker who has mental phenomena or properties: only individuals, persons, can have psychical properties. Structures or abstract systems cannot have them. If a psychical state is to be exemplified, then it can be exemplified only in an individual.

3. Mental phenomena show a 'twofold energy'. Each act, whilst directed towards something, at the same time and in passing is reflexively directed towards itself. Being presented with a physical or 'primary' object, e.g. a sound, we are aware of being presented with it. In a mental phenomenon as such, the consciousness of itself, the 'secondary object of perception', is included. This 'secondary inner perception' is a true, self-referential, evident perception in the strict sense. When an intentional phenomenon occurs to us, we know that it occurs; and in knowing this we grasp its essential nature. When we judge, we know what the property of judging is and what is logically required if an individual is to have such a property.

Ontology of Things. In his philosophy of mind, or psychology, Brentano deals mainly with inner experience and sets aside the objects of outer experience.

In the metaphysical context, he argues for the value and the validity of our mediate, indirect knowledge of bodily substances and their properties, with properties of all beings, of God and the world. This ontology in the broader sense presupposes the ontology of mind, which thus forms a foundational, integral part of the ontology of things. So, as the phenomena of human consciousness essentially are characterized as being 'intentionally directed', the 'outer world' analogously is seen as characterized by its teleological structure.

In his description of mental phenomena and their structural interrelation Brentano aims at a 'microscopic' analysis, as remarked earlier, but in his macroscopic cosmology he sees 'the whole as end of the parts'. His ontology of things develops what he had envisaged in his doctoral dissertation, where he attempted a description of Aristotle's theory of categories. Brentano differentiates the categories into (1) objective ('*reelle*') concepts of the kinds (genera) of being, and (2) semantic ('*logische*') modes (predicaments) of speaking about being. This differentiation is to be seen not as a fundamental discrepancy, but as a change of aspects in a description theory of being. Brentano goes on to emphasize that only real things, '*res*', or individuals, not concepts of things, or universals, are the proper objects of description.

Brentano's Influence. Brentano's empirically motivated philosophy was designed in analogy to the method of natural science: 'The adequate method of philosophy is that of natural science.' This was the thesis of his habilitation colloquium and Carl Stumpf, who was then studying under Brentano, reports that it attracted many students to him. Among them were Stumpf himself, known for his *Tonpsychologie*; Anton Marty (and students of his in the Prague Linguistic Circle, such as Franz Kafka and Max Brod), known for his descriptive philosophy of language; Sigmund Freud; the 'Graz School' around Alexius Meinong, known for its 'object theory'; Christian von Ehrenfels, for his '*Gestalt* theory'; Edmund Husserl, for his phenomenology; Tadeusz Kotarbinski, for his 'reism'; Thomas G. Masaryk, for his 'concretism'; George F. Stout and his students Bertrand Russell and G. E. Moore; the Würzburg School centred around Oswald Külpe, known for its experimental psychology of thinking; Max Scheler, known for his ethics; and Martin Heidegger. Quite a number of more recent influential thinkers, such as Roderick M. Chisholm, admit Brentano's influence, and there is good reason to call him the 'grandfather of phenomenology' (Gilbert Ryle) and '*terminus a quo* of Austrian philosophy' (Rudolf Haller).   w.b.

Wilhelm Baumgartner, Franz-Peter Burkard, and Franz Wiedmann (eds.), *Brentano Studien. An International Yearbook of Franz Brentano Forschung* (Würzburg, 1988–). Each volume dedicated to a special topic in the tradition of phenomenological and analytic philosophy.

Roderick M. Chisholm, *Brentano and Meinong Studies* (Amsterdam, 1982).
D. Jacquette (ed.), *The Cambridge Companion to Brentano* (Cambridge, 2004).
Linda L. McAlister (ed.), *The Philosophy of Brentano* (London, 1976). Collection of first-class papers on Brentano, and bibliography.

Brentano's thesis: *see* intentionality.

Bridgman, Percy William (1882–1962). Distinguished as a physicist, Bridgman has had considerable impact on the philosophy of science in the twentieth century, with his insistence that the work and results of science, especially physics, are 'operational'. Much impressed by Einstein's work on relativity and its seemingly paradoxical conclusions about time, Bridgman argued that the only recourse is a fairly stringent form of instrumentalism, whereby the concepts of science are reduced or replaced by the operations necessary to achieve or measure them.

Many professional philosophers have found Bridgman's thinking simplistic, arguing that science simply has to be 'open-ended', reaching beyond its empirical base, making claims which transcend anything reducible to operations. Bridgman himself conceded that sometimes the connection in science between concepts and operations is 'indirect'. In the opinion of critics, however, being 'indirectly operational' is somewhat on a par with being 'a little bit pregnant'.   M.R.

*instrumentalism.

P. Bridgman, *The Logic of Modern Physics* (New York, 1927).
—— *The Way Things Are* (Cambridge, Mass., 1959).
P. Frank, *The Validation of Scientific Theories* (Boston, 1959).

Brightman, Edgar Sheffield (1884–1953). American exponent at Boston University of personalistic *idealism, who held that *God created out of a chaotic, irrational 'Given', not *ex nihilo*. The Given's relation to God is left somewhat ambiguous, however. Brightman's attempts to make his account self-consistent by distinguishing different senses of 'internal to God' are not entirely convincing. None the less, Brightman unequivocally stated that God, finite in power, is growing in perfection through effort in time. Such a religious metaphysics has affinities with the process theism of Whitehead and Hartshorne as well as with the mature views of Royce. Characteristic of one strain of American philosophical theology is a desire to cling to the essentials of monotheism while conceiving of God as a quasi-democratic leader who heroically struggles to perfect himself and the world, just as he asks lesser persons to do.   P.H.H.

Andrew J. Reck, *Recent American Philosophy: Studies of Ten Representative Thinkers* (New York, 1964).

Brillat-Savarin, Jean Anthelme (1755–1826). A judge of appeal and amateur philosopher. He upstaged the aestheticians by treating *taste simply as the sense by which we discern flavours. The charm of personality that carried him unscathed through a lifetime of revolutionary violence still makes his gastronomic meditations delightful reading. He does for eating all that Izaak Walton did for angling, and more. Cooking, which Plato had despised as a mere 'routine', is transmuted into philosophy out of office hours. In the Meditations 'On Dreams' and 'On the End of the World' he shames, respectively, Descartes and Kant; and we can all profit from his opening Aphorisms, for instance 'The discovery of a new dish does more for the happiness of mankind than the discovery of a star'.

W.C.

J. A. Brillat-Savarin, *The Physiology of Taste; or, Meditations on Transcendental Gastronomy* (1825), tr. Peter Davies with biographical note (New York, 1926).

British philosophy today. Most (although not all) of the philosophy practised in Britain today is firmly within the tradition of analytic philosophy, a tradition shared with North America, South Africa, and Australia (and certain European countries, especially Germany and Austria). It would be hard to argue that there was any longer a characteristically British way of doing philosophy. Certainly, there are no movements peculiar to the country that are as readily identifiable as that of British empiricism in the seventeenth and eighteenth centuries, or the 'ordinary language' philosophy of 1950s Oxford. In addition, the influence of North American philosophers has been very substantial, and the initial stimulus for some research programmes has come from them. (One indication of this influence is the number of British university chairs taken up by—or at least offered to—American philosophers in recent years.) However, any country has its own distinctive intellectual history, even if philosophical problems and methods are international. The following therefore attempts to identify in a necessarily very selective way some trends in the development of philosophy in Britain since 1970, and some of the key personalities in that development, rather than describe in detail any particular set of problems.

The legacy of Logical Positivism. Following A. J. Ayer's vigorous application of the principles of verificationism to statements that appear to refer to a reality that is beyond immediate appearances—statements about the past, for example, Michael Dummett articulated a more circumspect *anti-realism* concerning such statements. This project has been extended by Crispin Wright, who has developed a detailed account of what is at issue in disputes concerning the reality of certain kinds of object. A position intended to be intermediate between *realism and anti-realism, 'quasi-realism', has been articulated by Simon Blackburn (now back in Britain after an extended stay in the USA).

Philosophy of language and mind. Greatly influenced by the American philosophers Saul Kripke and Donald Davidson, work in the philosophy of language in the 1970s (especially in Oxford) placed the issues of truth and reference centre stage, representing them as key to a number of debates. The two prominent questions were: Can the meaning of sentences be given by an account of what would make them true? and How do singular terms succeed in referring to particular objects? Since then, and partly as a result of the work of Gareth Evans (d. 1980), there has been a shift of focus towards mental representation, the corresponding questions being: What determines the content of a thought? and How does a thought succeed in being about a particular object? This second question is sometimes referred to as the problem of *intentionality. There has also been work on specific forms of mental representation—for example, spatial representation. Interest in the relationship between language and mind led to the foundation in 1985 of a new British-based journal, *Mind and Language*.

Philosophy of mind, on both sides of the Atlantic, was dominated in the 1970s and 1980s by two aspects of Davidson's work: the analysis of intentional *action and the defence of *physicalism (although action had already been the subject of studies by Stuart Hampshire and Elizabeth Anscombe). The worry was expressed, however, that Davidson's own brand of physicalism (anomalous monism) was unstable—specifically, that it collapsed into *epiphenomenalism. In the 1990s, enthusiasm for physicalism waned somewhat with the emergence of doubts as to whether a non-trivial form of physicalism could be articulated. These doubts were quite independent of any renewed enthusiasm for dualistic accounts of the mind. Among other developments could be mentioned the interest in computational models of the mind and the mechanisms underlying ascription of mental states to others.

Metaphysics. Britain in the 1950s and 1960s was not particularly congenial to metaphysics, although the appearance in 1959 of P. F. Strawson's enormously influential *Individuals: An Essay in Descriptive Metaphysics* was an honourable exception. The last twenty years, however, has seen a remarkable resurgence of interest. There has been increasing confidence in the power of language to capture substantial truths about the structure of the world, as opposed to the logical form of sentences, and a greater willingness to take certain kinds of statement at face value, as positing the existence of things that are independent of our conceptual schemes. (Perhaps one can identify the Australian influence here, through the work of such philosophers as David Armstrong and J. J. C. Smart, but a major stimulus has been, once again, American, particularly in the form of David Lewis (d. 2001).) Two debates might be mentioned as illustrative. (a) *Realism concerning abstract entities.* Work in the philosophy of mathematics has involved a reconstruction of Frege's work on the existence of numbers as objects, and the articulation and defence of a mathematical 'Platonist' (i.e. realist) position, and its extension to abstract entities generally. What is distinctive about British work in the area is the attention given to the epistemological problems raised by Platonism, especially the question of whether it can be reconciled with the causal theory of knowledge. (b) *Vagueness*. A brief but provocative paper by Gareth Evans ('Can There Be Vague Objects?'), which appeared in 1978, inspired a considerable amount of work on the question whether vagueness was simply a feature of language or knowledge or also of the world itself. There has been a flowering of work on traditional ontological issues, concerning *causality, *identity, *modality, *time, *properties, and *particulars.

Ethics. Three important developments should be mentioned. (a) The work of Bernard Williams, Alasdair MacIntyre (based in the USA since 1972), and Derek Parfit has highlighted the central place of the self, and ideas of the self, in ethics. Parfit in particular has questioned our ordinary view of the self as retaining its numerical identity through time, and shown how his alternative view breaks down the boundaries between persons and so undermines *egoism. (b) John Mackie's influential critique of moral *objectivism (*Ethics: Inventing Right and Wrong*, published in 1977) has provoked two kinds of critical response. One is a defence of objectivism, or realism, championed by Jonathan Dancy, John McDowell (based in the USA since 1986), and David McNaughton. Although realism has its American proponents, the British version rejects *ethical naturalism (the view that moral properties are reducible to non-moral properties). The other response, offered by Simon Blackburn is 'quasi-realism' or 'projectivism', which takes ethical values to be real, though mind-dependent, qualities. (c) British moral philosophers have also played in influential role in the revival of interest in two central ideas in ethics: *consequentialism and the *virtues. Here we should name, on the one hand, R. M. Hare (arguably the father of contemporary moral theory (d. 2002)), and on the other, Elizabeth Anscombe (d. 2001), and Phillipa Foot.

Philosophy of science. Perhaps the most striking development in philosophy of science in recent years has been the detailed engagement with the philosophical and metaphysical implications of quantum physics, pioneered by Michael Redhead and Nancy Cartwright (based in the UK since 1991), and pursued notably in Oxford, London, Cambridge, and Leeds.

Engagement with continental philosophy. *Continental philosophy is, by definition, not British in its origins, aims, and methods. Nevertheless, a significant feature of the national scene in recent years has been the increasing interest and specialization in continental philosophy within British departments. Traditionally, analytic philosophy has been hostile to the continental style, culminating in the publicly voiced objections to the award in 1992 of an honorary degree to Jacques Derrida by Cambridge University. Recent work, however, has attempted something of a *rapprochement*.

Philosophers and public debate. Although much philosophical work is conducted within academic institutions, prominent philosophers have from time to time been appointed to leading roles on Government committees, especially on ethical matters. Examples of this contribution of philosophers to the formulation of policy include Bernard Williams's chairing of the Committee on Obscenity and Film Censorship, Mary Warnock's chairing of the Committee of Inquiry into Human Fertilization, which produced the much discussed Warnock Report in 1984, and Anthony O'Hear's work as a government adviser on education. A recent high-profile discussion was Onora O'Neill's 2002 BBC Reith Lectures, *A Question of Trust*, on accountability, deception, and freedom of the press.

Political constraints. The 1980s was a time of crisis for philosophy in Britain, in economic, rather than intellectual, terms. University cut-backs saw the freezing of posts and the closure of some departments. The overall situation improved during the 1990s, and with the increasing popularity of philosophy as a university subject, some departments have actually expanded. However, one significant determinant of the fortunes of individual departments has been the five-yearly national Research Assessment Exercise, instituted in 1991, which rates quality of research output, with corresponding implications for the research funding allocation to universities. Partly, but not wholly, as a result of this, there has been a significant increase in productivity (as measured by publications), and research activity is now widespread rather than concentrated in a few dominant departments.   R.LE P.

*Cambridge philosophy; English philosophy; London philosophy; Oxford philosophy; Scottish philosophy; Wittgensteinians.

Julian Baggini and Jeremy Stangroom (eds.), *New British Philosophy: The Interviews* (London, 2002).

Margaret Little, 'Recent Work on Moral Realism II: Non-Naturalism', *Philosophical Books* (1995).

Bryan Magee, *Talking Philosophy: Dialogues with Fifteen Leading Philosophers* (Oxford, 2001).

Andrew Pyle, *Key Philosophers in Conversation: The Cogito Interviews* (London, 1999).

G. J. Warnock, *English Philosophy since 1900* (Oxford, 1969).

Broad, Charles Dunbar (1887–1971). Judicious and witty Cambridge philosopher, author of many thorough works on science, mind, ethics, and psychical research. Broad's typical method was an elaborately exhaustive classification of all possible answers to some carefully clarified question, a judicious weighing-up of the pros and cons of each, and a tentative suggestion for the most plausible. He believed that in *perception we are presented with 'sensa', whose occurrence is the effect of events in the brain in virtue of a peculiar kind of causation, that these sensa are not literally spatio-temporal parts of the perceived objects but provide literally true information about their spatio-temporal character and relations, and that physical objects must also have other characteristics which provide their qualitative filling. He developed a notion of absolute becoming to explain the greater reality of past than future and postulated a ψ component which combined with the brain to produce consciousness. He judged the empirical evidence on our survival of *death finely balanced.   T.L.S.S.

C. D. Broad, *An Examination of McTaggart's Philosophy* (Cambridge, 1933, 1938).
P. Schilpp, (ed.), *The Philosophy of C. D. Broad* (La Salle, Ill., 1959).

Brouwer, L. E. J. (1881–1966). Dutch mathematician known to philosophers as the founder of *intuitionism as a philosophy of mathematics. This owes something to the philosophy of Kant, but more to the paradoxes and contradictions that beset logic and mathematics in the early 1900s. Brouwer thought that these arose because familiar principles of reasoning were being blindly applied to an unsuitable subject-matter, i.e. to infinite totalities. In his view only a 'potential' infinity can be understood, and consequently a statement about all numbers can be counted as true only if we have a method of proving it for any arbitrary number. Since there are many statements about all numbers which we can neither prove nor disprove, Brouwer inferred that the law of excluded middle does not hold in mathematics.   D.B.

*intuitionist logic; constructivism.

A. Heyting, *Intuitionism*, 3rd edn. (Amsterdam, 1971).
P. Mancosu (ed.), *From Hilbert to Brouwer: The Debate on the Foundations of Mathematics in the 1920s* (Oxford, 1988).

Brownson, Orestes Augustus (1803–76). New England social critic, political advocate, religious controversialist, philosopher, and journalist, Brownson was for a time an effective advocate of *New England Transcendentalism. He was perhaps the most socially astute transcendentalist, arguing in 'The Laboring Classes' (published in his *Boston Quarterly Review* in 1840) that the wage system exploited the many in favour of the few and that reform could result only from changing the *system* and not simply from individual moral improvement (the standard transcendentalist solution to social problems). His most radical reform proposal was for the abolition of hereditary property: at death one's property reverts to the state, which is to distribute it fairly. His conversion in 1844 to Roman Catholicism caused dismay among his former transcendentalist compatriots; as a Catholic Brownson was as creative, outspoken, and controversial as he had been as a transcendentalist.   C.C.

Arthur M. Schlesinger Jr., *Orestes A. Brownson: A Pilgrim's Progress* (Boston, 1939).

Bruno, Giordano (1548–1600). Italian philosopher who sought to overthrow Aristotelianism and replace it with his own eclectic and often self-contradictory philosophical system. Combining the astronomy of Copernicus with the metaphysics of Nicholas of Cusa and the atomism of Lucretius, he believed in an infinite universe which contained an infinite number of inhabited worlds, moving within an uncentred space and composed of minimal particles. He rejected *hylomorphism in favour of a *monism in which the universal, infinite, and eternal substance was identical with both God and nature. Having been excommunicated by the Catholic, Lutheran, and Calvinist Churches on account of his unconventional religious views and undisciplined behaviour, he was finally burned at the stake by the Inquisition. He died a heretic, but in the nineteenth century he was transformed into a martyr to free philosophical inquiry.   J.A.K.

*persecution of philosophers.

P. Michel, *The Cosmology of Giordano Bruno* (Paris, 1973).

Brunschvicg, Léon (1869–1944). French idealist philosopher who provides a sustained neo-Hegelian answer to the Kantian question: How is knowledge possible? Rejecting the Kantian project of a transcendental deduction of the categories, Brunschvicg construes philosophy as the historical reflection of consciousness on consciousness. This reveals 'the progress of consciousness' (*le progrès de la conscience*) typified by the emergence of the natural sciences, the findings of which, Brunschvicg argues, are consistent with his own idealism.

Brunschvicg is also known for his scholarly treatments of Descartes and Pascal and for the extension of his historical idealism to the ethics of conscience.   S.P.

*idealism; Hegelianism.

Leon Brunschvicg, *La Philosophie de Léon Brunschvicg* (Paris, 1949).
—— *Le Progrès de la conscience dans la philosophie occidentale*, 2 vols. (Paris, 1927).

brute fact. Two related uses of this idea feature in contemporary analytical philosophy. The first and more common one signifies the terminus of a series of explanations which is not itself further explicable. Thus, for example, it is often said that while the behaviour of matter can be explained by reference to laws of nature the existence and character of those laws is itself a 'brute fact'. The second and more technical use indicates an underlying situation partly constitutive of the truth of a claim. The expression was first used in this sense by Anscombe to characterize the status of facts relative to higher-level descriptions. A set of facts S is 'brute' relative to a description D when the truth of D is constituted by the holding of those facts in a certain context and under normal conditions. Thus, the *fact that I inscribed a piece of paper, in a context constituted by banking conventions, is brute relative to the description 'J.H. signed a cheque', and the fact so described may itself, in a given context, be brute relative to the description 'J.H. ran into debt'. Hence the status of brute and non-brute facts is a relative one.   J.HAL.

G. E. M. Anscombe, 'On Brute Facts', *Analysis* (1958).

Buber, Martin (1878–1965). Jewish philosopher born in Vienna and raised in the Ukraine in the home of his grandfather, the Midrash scholar Solomon Buber. Martin Buber studied in Vienna with Dilthey and Simmel and became a Zionist leader in the 1890s, advocating cultural and educational activism. Attracted to the Hasidism of Naḥman of Bratslav, whose tales he adapted in German, he wrote novels of the Hasidic milieu and urged formation of a *Gemeinschaft* in Palestine that would include Arabs and Jews. His teaching cut off by Nazi edicts, Buber settled in Palestine in 1938 and became a prominent advocate of a binational (Arab–Jewish) state. His *I and Thou* (1923) grounds ethics and theology in a dialogical encounter: our fundamental attitudes of turning-toward or leaning-back demarcate the basic relations of I–It and *I–Thou, which constitute both self and other in radically different ways, objectively, in terms of uses, causes, effects, and challenges to be overcome; or intersubjectively, and personally, that is, morally, even aesthetically. Authenticity, responsiveness, even genuine presentness (and thus freedom) are attained only in the I–Thou relationship. The objectivity of the I–It is fixed in the past. *God is the eternal Thou, never transformed into an It by spiritual ennui or fatigue, but glimpsed through our encounters with others, with nature and with works of art. It is when we speak to him, not of him, that we encounter the living God. Even those who hate God's name can do this, when they address their lives in terms of a subjecthood that cannot be limited by another. Revelation is humanity's continuing response to the eternal Thou, epitomized in God's covenant with Israel.   L.E.G.

P. A. Schilpp and M. Friedman (eds.), *The Philosophy of Martin Buber* (La Salle, Ill., 1967).

Buddha, the (*fl.* fifth century BC). The Sanskrit word 'buddha' refers to any enlightened person, but '*The* Buddha' refers specifically to Siddhārtha Gautama, son of a ruler of Sākya in what is now Nepal. Modern scholarship places him rather later than the traditional dates of *c.*560–480. The Buddha founded a non-theistic religion and articulated the foundations of *Buddhist philosophy—the Four Noble Truths concerning suffering, its causes and its cessation, the theory of 'dependent origination', and the denial of substantial selfhood.

According to tradition, the twenty-nine-year-old Gautama, troubled by the sickness and death he witnessed, left Sākya in search of an understanding of suffering. After several unsuccessful years of ascetic and spiritual practice, he found enlightenment, at thirty-five, while meditating beneath a fig-tree. He then delivered the first of many discourses (*suttas*) that, after centuries of oral transmission, were recorded in the Pali Canon. The Buddha was a man of great physical presence, compassion, and serenity. This, allied to his dialectical skills, ensured that before his painful but dignified death he had already gained a large following of monks and lay people.

Unlike the founders of other religions, the Buddha grounded his teachings on rational reflection, not divine revelation, and adumbrated a philosophically sophisticated account of reality, mind, and the human condition. His philosophical temper was decidedly *empiricist, for 'right view' is vouchsafed by clear-headed experience of the world and oneself. He criticizes Brahmanism for postulating such transcendent entities as an absolute Self (*ātman*), and rejects so-called unanswered questions

(e.g. 'Is the world eternal?'), not only because they are irrelevant to obtaining 'release' from suffering, but because, enquiring beyond the limits of experience, they are senseless. The truths he himself advances are available to anyone fully 'mindful' of the world around him and the workings of his own mind. Indeed, mindful experience is essential to proper understanding of these truths. One who grasps that there is only 'not-self', for example, does not simply assent to the Buddha's propositions, but experiences the world and himself in a new key. The Buddha's moral philosophy is equally empiricist in character, experientially based reflections on the integral role of such virtues as compassion and equanimity in a life liberating itself from the causes of suffering.   D.E.C.

M. Carrithers, *The Buddha* (Oxford, 1983).
S. Hamilton, *Early Buddhism: A New Approach* (Richmond, Surrey, 2000).

Buddhism: *see* Buddhist philosophy.

Buddhist philosophy. Ethical, metaphysical, and epistemological views held by an Indian prince turned ascetic, Siddhārtha Gautama (said to have been born 563 BC), and by subsequent schools of thought claiming allegiance to him. Siddhārtha was called 'Buddha', which means 'the awakened one'.

Buddha's teachings. Facing the fragility of life, and the facts of disease, decay, and death, young Siddhārtha left his family in search of peace and enlightenment, which came not through extreme austerity or philosophical wrangling but through meditating along 'the middle way'. On finally becoming 'awakened' he preached Four Noble Truths:

1. Life is suffering.
2. Suffering involves a chain of causes.
3. Suffering can cease.
4. There is a path to such cessation.

The first truth, equating existence with suffering, was buttressed by a reductionist metaphysics of universal impermanence and soullessness. We suffer because we expect a substantial core in things, when in fact there is none either inside or outside us. Apparent *substances are reducible to groups of ephemeral parts, *persons to streams of causally interdependent collections of five psychophysical aggregates, an 'essence' like *catness* to mere exclusion from the mixed set of non-feline individuals. Since selves and things are so unstable and essenceless, our inborn wish to retain our identity and to cling to an essence of what we desire leads to frustration. The truth of universal pain ultimately becomes an evaluative rather than descriptive judgement. Buddha urges that life *should* be looked upon as agony through and through.

The second truth concerning the cause of suffering was fleshed out as the twelve-link causal chain of dependent arising: ignorance → karma-propensities → embryonic sentience → body and psychoses → five senses plus an introspective faculty → sense–object contact → experience → thirst → clinging → rebirth → decay → death.

This, called the 'Wheel of Becoming', obviously connects with the *karma-based theory of metempsychosis. But if there is no self, what is reborn? In answer, Buddha draws a Ryle-like analogy between 'The individual gets reborn' and 'The news travels'. It is ignorance to think of *the news* as an entity doing the travelling. To conceive a continuing agent is equally mistaken, and propels us towards egoistic actions—we find ourselves enmeshed in the causal chain of becoming. The so-called person is in fact just a bundle of five psychophysical factors. These five aggregates (physical forms, sensations, feelings, judgements, and latent dispositions) constituting the individual at the dying moment cause another, subtler, fivefold replica, which causes yet another—and so on until the new physical form of a foetus is produced, to which all the cravings, traces, and the illusory sense of identity of the dying bundle have been bequeathed. 'The soul' is the name of a causally bound bundle which spans countless deaths and births. This reductionist set-and-series concept of a person, called the doctrine of *anattā* in Pali, has recently received some publicity among English-speaking philosophers through the work of Derek Parfit.

The third noble truth sets up *nirvana as the final liberation from the pain of repeated embodiment, which can only happen if the ignorance of regarding oneself as a substantial permanent ego is dispelled. Ultimate and unending calm is attained when all cravings—even the craving for extinction—cease without leaving behind any seed. Since such a state is attainable by every thinking being, irrespective of class, gender, caste, or even species, Buddhism is not pessimistic or discriminatory.

Finally, the fourth noble truth of the way to the *summum bonum* of nirvana gives the ethics. This is the eightfold path: ethically correct views, right resolutions, right speech, right action, right livelihood, right effort, proper mindfulness, and regular practice of concentration. These intellectual, social, and meditational virtues promote the overarching moral qualities of clarity, desirelessness, universal friendliness, and compassion. Suffering ceases through *selflessness*, metaphysical and moral. Using a universalizability criterion the Buddha preached: 'All men tremble at punishment, all men fear death. Likening others to oneself, one should neither slay nor cause to slay.'

The Subsequent Schools. Although all Buddhists owed allegiance to the three scriptural 'baskets' into which the doctrines, codes of conduct, and philosophical utterances of Buddha were collected, there arose a major theoretical rift between the so-called 'Lesser Vehicle' (Hīnayāna) and 'Greater Vehicle' (Mahāyāna) within 200 years of the Master's death. The former faction now survives in Sri Lanka and Burma, and the latter in Tibet, China, Korea, and Japan. The latter faction of Buddhism may have been called 'greater' because in it the aim of life is not only to end one's own suffering but to strive, even after one's own personal nirvana, for the enlightenment and happiness of others. Hence the ideal of an altruistic enlightened man who caringly resolves 'May the fruits of my austerities and meditations alleviate the sufferings of all sentient creatures, even of women giving birth!' This is supra-moral kindness.

The Lesser Vehicle. The Lesser Vehicle itself branched into two schools, the first being the realist Vaibhāṣika. Postulating some seventy-two types of composite elements and even a few eternal entities like space and the state of perennial painlessness, this school earned the title 'the everything-exists school'. Some members offered detailed accounts of how atoms combine to form directly perceivable matter. Acute in-house debates regarding the reality of the past and the future led to observations like this: 'Past', 'present', 'future' are equally objective descriptions of the same bit of reality, just as the same woman is correctly described as 'mother', 'wife', and 'daughter'.

The second school of the Lesser Vehicle, representationalist–realist Sautrāntika, criticized the first for eternalist heresies and gave the following sorts of argument for strict impermanence: If A endures for more than a moment, say over t_1, t_2, t_3, then, given the Buddhist definition of reality, it can be real only by being *causally productive* at t_1, t_2, and t_3. Now, either A produces some effect at each moment or it lies capable but fallow at t_1 and t_2 and actually fructifies at t_3, when operating auxiliary conditions join A. If it produces effects at each moment, then it must have three different effects because the same effect cannot be produced thrice. Accordingly A disintegrates into three momentary realities, corresponding to three distinct causal capacities. If it remains fallow at t_1 and t_2 waiting for some auxiliary conditions, as the seed in the granary waits for soil and rain, it is only the terminal entity A-at-t_3 which qualifies as real, the previous temporal parts being non-entities, or distinct entities, one generating the other. This is the heart of the famous doctrine of momentariness.

Given such strict momentariness, the really real is accessible only to pure sensation, which grasps these instantaneous propertyless particulars. Sautrāntika epistemology is thus at best a critical realism about tables and chairs where the macroscopic world is a construction of inference. Any verbalizable perception invoking classificatory concepts is analysed as inference and imagination.

Later Sautrāntika Buddhists like Jñānaśrī attack all word-generated awareness as fiction-loaded. Words refer to objects through modes of presentations which are generalities—they never capture particular objects in their vivid singularity. This goes by the name of the exclusion theory of meaning, which is at the heart of Buddhist nominalism. Even an expression like 'that cow' serves only to distinguish the referent from dogs, horses, asses, and other cows further away. Apart from this network of mind-made distinctions, there is no natural kind called 'the cow'.

The Greater Vehicle. This nominalistic representationalism of Sautrāntika inevitably led to a Berkeleian idealism of the first school of the Greater Vehicle. Yogācāra, also named 'the mind-only school' seeks to refute atomists and critical realists by four major arguments.

1. Many intricate considerations are put forward against the existence of bodies in space. If, as the realistic Vaibhāṣika school maintained, six atoms join the seventh from six sides, either the central atom falls into six parts, which goes against its indivisibility, or the contacts all happen at one point, which fails to explain any increase of size. So the very idea of extension is incoherent.

2. No external object—macroscopic or atomic—has both the causal and phenomenological features of a real object of awareness. That which both *causes* and bears the manifest *form* of a piece of awareness can count as its real object. If I see glistening water but my seeing is caused by hot air refracting sunlight, I call that a mirage. But, upon the critical realist theory, the actual cause and the phenomenological content of perception fall apart. Awareness is caused by imperceptible atoms while it assumes the felt form of chairs and cherry blossoms.

3. Thus, as awarenesses, wakeful and veridical ones are indistinguishable from dream and erroneous ones, and equally devoid of any extra-mental object.

4. Finally, if *x* and *y* are not the same they could be isolated from each other, but blue can never be isolated from awareness of blue; hence they must be the same.

These idealistic arguments offered by Vasubandhu (fifth century AD) were vigorously attacked by realists of the Jaina, Mīmāṃsā, and Nyāya schools. Even Śaṅkara, himself an absolute idealist, scoffed at the mind-only Buddhist: 'If externality is such an impossibility, how come things even appear to be external? No one is even *mistaken* for a barren woman's son!' Anticipating G. E. Moore, philosophers of the Nyāya school appealed to *common sense, and isolated formless awareness as the common element in awareness *of* blue and awareness *of* yellow, thereby questioning the inseparability of objects and perception. Jaina opponents of Yogācāra claimed that perception itself points to the act–object distinction, but Yogācāra stuck to treating the 'of' of intentionality after the fashion of 'City of Rome', as if the distinction was verbal and spurious.

The last and currently most influential school of the Greater Vehicle—thanks to the present Dalai Lama—is Voidism or Mādhyamika, which was fully developed by *Nāgārjuna with the help of such sceptical arguments as the following. The reliable means of knowledge are established by appeal to the reality of the objects they make us know; but the reality of the objects, in turn, is established upon the authority of the means of knowledge. Since the criterion of knowledgehood itself is so hopelessly circular, how can anything be known to have this or that determinate nature? Excelling in negative dialectics, anti-realism reaches its mystical climax in Voidism. This mysticism, of course, has nothing to do with faith in God. In chapter 10 of his *Twelve-Gate Treatise* Nāgārjuna argued,

God could not be our father because children should have some resemblance with their father, but in our suffering we are most ungodly. Being self-existent, God should also have no needs, yet obviously he needed to create, otherwise he would be whimsical like an infant. As omnipotent, God should not have any obstacles to his desire, so what explains the gradual unfolding of creation

instead of creation of everything all at once? Finally, if God is the maker there should be no evil or ugliness in things, but obviously there is.

Suffering, causation, and temporal succession are all shown to be uncharacterizable in any determinate manner, because all characterizations are equally empty. It is this insistence on the emptiness of all things which makes Nāgārjuna a 'Voidist'. Since all things are empty, so is the doctrine of emptiness. Far from being self-refuting, such absolute *epochē* is said to be irrefutable. 'If I had a view I could have had a flaw, but, emptied of all views, I am flawless.' So says the Voidist, enjoying tranquillity.   A.C.

*Indian philosophy; Hindu philosophy.

M. Carrithers, *The Buddha: A Very Short Introduction* (Oxford, 2001).

A. K. Chatterjee, *The Yogacara Idealism* (Benares, 1976).

E. Conze, *Buddhist Thought in India* (Ann Arbor, Mich., 1970).

S. Mookherjee, *The Buddhist Philosophy of Universal Flux* (Delhi, 1980).

T. Stcherbatsky, *Buddhist Logic*, 2 vols. (Paris, 1958).

Bultmann, Rudolf (1884–1976). German theologian who gives a Heideggerian interpretation of the New Testament which is both anti-metaphysical and existentialist. Bultmann argues that it is the awareness of death as an immediate possibility which produces the need for Christianity, and claims that a life without Christ is inauthentic but a life lived in Christ is authentic. His 'demythologizing' of the New Testament construes its historical and theological doctrines as descriptions of the human condition in so far as this is a condition of need for God. Bultmann's readings are controversial because they might be logically consistent with atheism.   S.P.

*existentialism; authenticity.

Rudolf Bultmann, *Theologie des Neuen Testaments* (Tübingen, 1948–53); tr. as *Theology of the New Testament*, 2 vols. (New York, 1952).

Ronald W. Hepburn, 'Demythologizing and the Problem of Validity', in A. G. N. Flew and A. MacIntyre (eds.), *New Essays in Philosophical Theology* (London, 1955).

bundle theory of the self. Empiricist theory of *personal identity particularly associated with David Hume. Hume's view—that we are never aware of our *self as a substance, but only as a 'bundle or collection of different perceptions'—has been interpreted as a sceptical denial of personal identity. More plausibly, Hume can be taken to be meaning that the peculiarly complex unity or identity of the self should be interpreted in terms of constantly changing causal relations, more like the identity of a complex play than a simple material object. A Humean theory of the self was developed by William James.   R.S.D.

David Hume, *A Treatise of Human Nature*, I. iv. 6.

William James, *The Principles of Psychology* (New York, 1890).

Burali-Forti's paradox, due to Cesare Burali-Forti, arises from the assumption that there is a series S_1 consisting of all ordinal numbers and that this series is well-ordered.

From this it follows that S_1 has an ordinal number X. From this it follows that there is a series S_2 of ordinals up to and including X which has the ordinal number $X + 1$. This contradicts the assumption that S_1 has all the ordinal numbers. This contradiction about ordinals is not usually taken up in popular discussions because the notion of a transfinite ordinal is more difficult to explain than that of a trans-finite cardinal. In this sense all transfinite ordinals are inaccessible.   J.C.

*number.

Cesare Burali-Forti, 'Una questione sui numeri transfiniti', *Rendiconti di Palermo* (1897); Eng. tr. in J. van Heijenoort (ed.), *Source Book in Mathematical Logic 1879–1931* (Cambridge, Mass., 1964).

Burckhardt, Jakob Christoph (1818–97). A historian who lived for most of his life in his native Basle. Although a pupil of Ranke, he was less concerned to discover objective facts than to explore European *'culture' (one of the three great 'forces', along with religion and the state, that govern history), often by way of an anecdote that enabled him to 'discern and feel the general in the particular'. His influential works include *The Age of Constantine the Great* (1852; tr. London, 1949) and *The Culture of the Renaissance in Italy* (1860; tr. London, 1878). His main philosophical work, consisting of lectures (which Nietzsche attended) at Basle between 1868 and 1871, was published as *Reflections on History* (1906; tr. London, 1943). Like Schopenhauer (whom, to Nietzsche, he called 'our philosopher'), he despised Hegel's rationalist and teleological view of history; denied that man makes significant progress, and thus preferred to focus on what is 'recurrent, constant and typical'; and regarded democracy and industrialization as threats to liberty and culture.   M.J.I.

K. Löwith, *Jakob Burckhardt: Der Mensch inmitten der Geschichte* (Lucerne, 1936).

Burge, Tyler (1946–). American philosopher based at the University of California, Los Angeles. Burge has worked largely in the philosophies of mind, language, and logic. His earlier work on singular terms and demonstratives was within the context of Davidson's theory of meaning. He is also known for a series of papers, beginning in 1979, in which he argues for *anti-individualism: the thesis that the contents of thinkers' intentional states cannot be fixed by facts about those thinkers taken in isolation from the rest of their community. Burge argues for this through an ingenious variation on Putnam's Twin Earth thought experiment (*arthritis in the thigh). Burge claims that only by appreciating the social determination of the contents of thinkers' thoughts can we account for the irreducibly normative character of intentional mental states.   T.C.

*externalism.

Tyler Burge, 'Individualism and the Mental', *Midwest Studies in Philosophy*, iv (1979).

Buridan, John (*c.*1295/1300–*c.*1360). Student, and then teacher, at Paris, he was twice rector of the university, in 1328 and 1340. Generally classified as a nominalist, he was one of the great logicians of the Middle Ages, but also a philosopher and theologian. He wrote commentaries on a number of works by Aristotle, his Commentary on the *Physics* of Aristotle being particularly well known for its discussion of impetus, in which Buridan attempts to explain how it happens that when a projectile leaves the projector (for example, when a stone leaves the thrower's hand) it does not promptly fall to earth as a heavy object surely would but instead continues upward. Buridan solves the problem by arguing that the projector imparts an impulse, or impetus, to the projectile, and that it is the impetus that maintains the projectile in motion until countervailing forces, in particular air resistance and the projectile's weight, prevail and the body finally falls to earth. In the course of his discussion Buridan develops the concept of inertia at least in respect of celestial bodies and in so doing makes a clean break with Aristotelian physics.   A.BRO.

*ass, Buridan's; Aristotelianism.

E. A. Moody, 'Jean Buridan', in *Studies in Medieval Philosophy, Science and Logic: Collected Papers 1933–1969* (Berkeley, Calif., 1975).

Burke, Edmund (1729–97). Irish-born political writer noted for literary style, and English MP believed to be an important source of *conservatism.

In describing the work of Burke it is accurate to call him a 'political writer' rather than a political theorist or philosopher. He was suspicious of the abstract and his writings predominantly exemplify rhetoric at the expense of reasoned argument. He was a master of prose style, although he was never noted for skill in oratory, and some of his best speeches were said to have emptied the House of Commons. Burke is not and would not have wanted to be considered a great political philosopher, but he satisfies one criterion of greatness—his thought appeals to successive generations of political thinkers.

For one who was later to dismiss abstract philosophizing with some contempt Burke rather oddly began his literary career with two successful works in that genre. The first was *A Vindication of Natural Society* (1756; 2nd edn. 1757), in which he attacked social philosophy, especially that of Rousseau. In 1757 he published a second philosophical essay which, like the first, was very successful—*A Philosophical Enquiry into the Origin of our Ideas of the Sublime and Beautiful*. As a result of his success he was taken up by the literary and artistic circles of London, and was encouraged by his publisher to try his hand at history. His historical work was not published in his lifetime. Thereafter began his political life, in which he was to continue until his death in 1797.

In his political life he devoted himself (as he says) to five 'great, just and honourable causes': the emancipation of the House of Commons from the control of George III and the 'King's friends'; the emancipation of the American colonies; the emancipation of Ireland; the emancipation of India from the misgovernment of the East India Company; and opposition to the atheistical Jacobinism shown in the French Revolution. Successive generations have reacted in different ways to Burke's position on all these questions, if indeed he has a consistent position. For example, his stand against the French Revolution was attacked by the early Utilitarians such as Paine, Bentham, and James Mill, on the ground that he had betrayed his earlier championship of political *liberty. He himself regarded his defence of the Indian people against the East India Company as his greatest achievement, yet it has been argued that he was lacking in historical knowledge of India and that he did not really understand the difficulties facing Warren Hastings in dealing with a totally different social order. His greatest contribution to political thought is summed up by Wordsworth in *The Prelude*. Wordsworth says of Burke that he 'declares the vital power of social ties Endeared by custom'. In other words, Burke thought of all political power as a trust, and in the case of Britain politicians were entrusted with the preservation of a traditional hierarchical social and political order.

Burke's belief that society depends on what he called 'prejudice', that is, on instinctive feelings of love and loyalty, plus his rejection of the central place which revolutionary thinkers had given to reason, led to his critique of natural law and natural rights. Basically he seems to be saying that communities are held together not by self-interest but by the feeling that we are members one of another; communal feeling is everything and reason is insignificant. Hence, he rejected the appeal made by the revolutionaries to abstract individual rights. For Burke the important contrast is not between repressive governments and the abstract rights of the rational individual, but between the beautiful order of society bonded by loyalties and 'prejudice', and 'a disbanded race of deserters and vagabonds'. In rejecting natural law he shared the conservatism of Hume, but his reverential attitude to the state is much more like Rousseau than Hume.   R.S.D.

*sublime; revolution.

Edmund Burke, *Reflections on the Revolution in France* (1790), ed. Conor Cruise O'Brien (Harmondsworth, 1968).
—— *Pre-Revolutionary Writings*, ed. I. Harris (Cambridge, 1993).
C. B. Macpherson, *Burke* (Oxford, 1980).

Burnyeat, Myles Frederic (1939–). Laurence Professor of Ancient Philosophy, University of Cambridge in the 1980s and 1990s, thereafter Fellow of All Souls College, Oxford. Noted chiefly but not solely for his work on the history of epistemology, he has produced important studies of Plato, and has played a significant role in the redirection of scholarly attention to *Hellenistic philosophy, in particular to the ideas of the *Sceptics.   N.C.D.

Myles Burnyeat, *The* Theaetetus *of Plato* (Indianapolis, 1990).
——(ed.), *The Skeptical Tradition* (Berkeley, Calif., 1983).
——(co-ed.), *Doubt and Dogmatism: Studies in Hellenistic Epistemology* (Oxford, 1980).
——(co-ed.), *Science and Speculation: Studies in Hellenistic Theory and Practice* (Cambridge, 1982).

business ethics. One of the areas of *applied ethics. Although the application of morality to business is as old as business and morality themselves, the rise of business ethics as an identifiable subject of study took place in the 1970s in the United States, and since the late 1980s in Europe, Australia, and a number of countries in Asia, Africa, and South America.

Business ethics as an academic area is defined by the interaction of business and ethics, and the set of related problems thus generated. At its broadest, it studies the moral justification of economic systems, whether national or international. Within a given system it studies the moral justification of the system's structures and practices. Since corporations are a dominant feature of the free-enterprise system, a good deal of work has focused on the structures, governance, responsibilities, and activities of corporations. Within the corporation business ethics deals with the moral responsibilities and rights of individual managers and employees—the more traditional focus of previous work on ethics in business.

Those who work in business ethics tend to engage in four types of activity. The first and most common is the development and discussion of case-studies that raise some moral issue in business. These are used to sensitize students, those in business, and the general public to the need for ethical considerations in business. Although at first these cases tended to illustrate unethical behaviour on the part of large corporations, in recent years there has also been a growing literature on positive cases presenting exemplary corporate or individual activity. Cases-studies in turn have led to the investigation of the morality of particular practices, to the responsibility of corporations with respect to consumers and the public, product safety, the rights of workers, environmental degradation, and similar issues. A third kind of research considers how corporations might be structured so as to reinforce ethical behaviour and discourage unethical behaviour on the part of both workers and managers. A fourth kind of activity can be called meta-ethical. This looks at the appropriateness of applying moral language to entities other than human beings, e.g. to corporations, corporate structures, economic systems. There has been lively discussion of whether corporations can rightly be said to have moral *obligations or responsibilities. Terms such as *'responsibility', *'conscience', *'rights', *'virtue', mean something different when applied to corporations than when applied to human individuals, as do notions of praise and blame, reward and punishment.

The importance of international business has led to discussions of international business ethics and to a reconsideration of moral and cultural relativism, which take on special significance when considering doing business in societies with corrupt governments and in the absence of many traditional restraints. Work in international business ethics has called into question whether Western-type approaches to ethical theory actually enjoy the universality which they claim or to which they aspire. The primary focus of international business ethics has been on the actions of multinational corporations from developed countries operating in less developed countries. Issues include bribery, the use of child labour, the degradation of the environment, the exploitation of workers, and the increasing gap between rich and poor countries. Global issues involve the justice or fairness of policies of global institutions such as the World Trade Organization and the World Bank, the depletion of the ozone layer, and the appropriate role of corporations and nations in halting or reversing the process, and the depletion of non-renewable natural resources. The growth of the Internet as a medium of commerce that easily crosses national boundaries has also generated new concerns about the ethical dimensions of privacy violations by businesses, control of commercial pornography, and protection of intellectual property available in digitalized form.

Business ethics has developed into a significant area of research and teaching with its own texts, journals, and professional societies. But it has gone beyond the academic setting in which it developed. It has become something of a movement, in which corporations have adopted codes of conduct or statements of values and beliefs, have introduced the position of corporate-ethics officer, instituted in-house training programmes in ethics, established ethics hotlines, and appointed ethical ombudsmen. The corporate movement is mixed: sometimes salutary, providing positive promotion and reinforcement of ethical norms; sometimes self-serving, emphasizing ethics for employees towards the corporation, but exempting the corporation itself (and its top officers) from ethical assessment; and sometimes negative, serving simply as 'window-dressing' to mask amoral corporate activity. The movement can be distinguished from the academic area with which it is related, but which continues to have a critical (although not necessarily antagonistic) component with respect to business, and which interacts with standard normative and meta-ethical theory.   R.DE G.

*capitalism; markets and the public good; professional ethics.

Tom L. Beauchamp and Norman E. Bowie (eds.), *Ethical Theory and Business*, 6th edn. (Upper Saddle River, NJ, 2001).

Richard T. De George, *Business Ethics*, 5th edn. (Upper Saddle River, NJ, 1999).

—— *Business Ethics Quarterly*, 10, no. 1 (2000).

G. Enderle (ed.), *International Business Ethics: Challenges and Approaches* (Notre Dame, Ind., 1999).

Butler, Joseph (1692–1752). Anglican divine, Bishop of Durham. His *Fifteen Sermons* (1726), perhaps the finest ethical work in English, brilliantly attacks psychological and ethical *hedonism and provides a *via media* between a moral-sense approach to ethics and a rationalist one. Since pleasure is the satisfaction of an impulse, the desire to maximize one's own (self-love) requires impulses with other objects, e.g. particular passions (like hunger) and *benevolence. Self-love is not peculiarly 'natural'. Life is 'natural' when the influence of each motive accords with its intrinsic authority. *Conscience* should adjudicate

between the two high-level principles of self-love and benevolence and these should control the particular passions. Butler's book *The Analogy of Religion* (1736) defends Christianity against *deism. The analogy is between the Bible and nature, which bear the marks of the same author. In a famous appendix Butler defends the absoluteness of *personal identity against Locke's empiricist treatment.

                                                        T.L.S.S.

Austin Duncan-Jones, *Butler's Moral Philosophy* (Harmondsworth, 1952).

Terence Penelhum, *Butler* (London, 1985).

Butler, Samuel (1835–1902). Satirist, novelist, metaphysical biologist, anti-Christian. *Erewhon* (1872), and *Erewhon Revisited* (1901), satirize Victorian values. In Erewhon ('nowhere' backwards—almost) there are two currencies, one issued by commercial banks and used for all practical purposes (the decencies of ordinary and business life) and another issued with great solemnity in magnificent buildings, but commercially useless (Christianity). Erewhonian thought also includes elements of his own striking speculations, for example on machines as extensions of the human organism which may threaten us by a rival evolution of their own and on the invalidity of a distinction between an individual and his influence (so that there is a genuine afterlife as long as this continues). In several anti-Darwinian works Butler propounds his Lamarckian theory of creative *evolution by inherited memory, as he does also in his novel of generational change *The Way of All Flesh* (1903). His satirical (and sometimes perversely persuasive) defence of the Resurrection in *The Fair Haven* (1873) was quoted in pulpits until its disguised authorship was discovered.   T.L.S.S.

Peter Raby, *Samuel Butler: A Biography* (London, 1991).

Byzantine philosophy. 'Byzantine philosophy' would seem to refer, straightforwardly, to philosophy written in the Byzantine Empire. In fact the reference is anything but straightforward. There is, for example, no clear chronological line separating late ancient from Byzantine philosophy. There is, again, no responsible way to extricate Byzantine philosophy from Byzantine theology or Byzantine literature. The best that can be done is to depict some features in authors who have as good a claim as any to the label 'Byzantine'.

The most obvious feature is a continuity of learning. Byzantine writers who disagreed about much else understood themselves to share at least two kinds of tradition. They shared a tradition of Greek literacy, including a legacy of Greek philosophical texts considerably larger than that available in Latin translation before the Renaissance. Byzantine writers shared next a set of theological authorities. These authorities included the seven ecumenical councils of the Church (325–787), but also Christian writers who combined fervent piety with formidable learning in Greek letters, including philosophy and natural science. Chief among these were Gregory Nazianzen

(323–89), Basil of Caesarea (c.330–79) and his brother Gregory of Nyssa (c.335–95), and John Chrysostom (347–407). Later Byzantine writers looked back to these four, and especially to Basil and John, as the 'fathers' of right belief and holy practice.

Byzantine writers were further able to appropriate the last works of non-Christian Greek philosophy. The intricate *Neoplatonism of Proclus (c.410–85) was taken over by a Syrian who took as pseudonym 'Dionysius the Areopagite'. The writings of this pseudo-Dionysius (active c.500) present a thoroughly Christian adaptation of Procline philosophy to questions about the intelligibility and accessibility of God. In the same years, Proclus' pagan successors in Athens continued his reinvigoration of the old practices of philosophical commentary. Among their most remarkable expositions were the extensive commentaries on Aristotle by Simplicius. The fact of expert Aristotelian commentaries by Neoplatonists illustrated another kind of adaptation, as it seemed to fulfil the ancient wish for a reconciliation of Plato and Aristotle.

The shared sources, Christian and pagan, and the models of adaptation inspired various Byzantine works in or about what seems to us philosophy. John Damascene (died c.751) composed a *Fount of Knowing* that contains: (1) a dictionary of technical terms ranging from Aristotelian logic to Trinitarian theology, (2) a critical history and doctrinal analysis of Christian heresies, and (3) a compendium of orthodox theology comprising, among much else, elementary lessons in Aristotelian and Galenic natural philosophy. Michael Psellos (1018–c.1096) wrote a *Teaching of All Sorts* that displays an unusual knowledge of pagan Neoplatonism and even an interest in philosophical

astrology and magic. By contrast, the *Philosophy* of George Pachymeres (1242–1307) is a sequential paraphrase of the principal works of Aristotle, from the *Categories* to the *Nicomachean Ethics*.

Of course, the simultaneous inheritance of pagan and Christian sources brought deep tensions. Even those friendliest to ancient philosophy, such as Psellos, were careful to note its discrepancies with Christianity. Other Byzantine authors viewed these discrepancies as evidence for the bankruptcy of pagan learning. So, for example, the *150 Chapters* of Gregory Palamas (1296–1359) rejects the errors of prideful reason, and especially the errors of Plato and Aristotle, in favour of Christian revelation grasped by the prayer of the heart.

No one can know how these controversies would have developed if Byzantine life had not been disrupted by the fall of Constantinople in 1453. What can be known is the influence of visiting or exiled Byzantine scholars on Western Europe. George Gemistos Plethon (1355/60–1452), for example, electrified Florentine humanists with his teaching of Plato. John Bessarion (1403–72), who died a Roman cardinal, not only defended Plato against the attacks of Aristotelians, he left his valuable Greek library to the Venetians. Much of *Renaissance philosophy is the afterlife of Byzantine philosophy.   M.D.J.

Milton V. Anastos, *The Mind of Byzantium* (New York, 1966).

K. Ierodiakonou (ed.), *Byzantine Philosophy and its Ancient Sources* (Oxford, 2002).

G. Podskalsky, *Theologie und Philosophie in Byzanz* (Munich, 1977).

Basile Tatakis, *La Philosophie byzantine* (Paris, 1949; English translation, Indianapolis, 2004).

C

cabbala: *see* Kabbalah.

Cajetan, Cardinal Thomas de Vio (1468–1534). General of the Dominicans and, as Cardinal-legate to the Empire in 1518–19, involved in unsuccessful dialogue with Luther, Cajetan was an influential commentator on Aristotle and Aquinas. More pessimistic of the powers of human reason than previous Thomists, Cajetan denied in particular that the immortality of the soul could be established independently of revelation. Cajetan also developed the Thomist theory of analogy, and so of how terms such as 'good' could be applied without equivocation both to *God and to finite creatures. Cajetan argued that when we describe both God and finite creatures as good, we employ an analogy of proportionality: the same quality is attributed to God as is attributed to creatures—but proportionately to their differing natures.   T.P.

*Thomism.

M. McCandles, 'Univocalism in Cajetan's Doctrine of Analogy', *New Scholasticism* (1968).

calculus. A calculus is a formal language and rules for manipulating expressions of the language. For example, by applying *algorithms to arabic numerals one can determine the values of arithmetical functions. A logical calculus is used to construct valid *arguments. It can be described as the syntax of a logic where syntax has to do only with the shapes and structure of expressions, not their meanings.

The syntax of a logic has two parts: the grammar and the deductive system. The grammar is a list of symbols or rules for constructing symbols of the logical language, and a specification of which finite strings of symbols are to count as sentences or well-formed formulae. The deductive system of a logic consists of axioms and rules of inference which are used to construct proofs of sentences of the logical language. Axioms can be written at any line of a proof and do not rest on any premisses; rules of inference permit the writing of a sentence at a line of a proof given that appropriate conditions are met. A deductive system must have at least one rule of inference but need not have any axioms; a deductive system is an axiomatic system if it contains axioms, a natural deduction system if it does not.

A proof of a sentence A from a set of premisses Γ is a finite, non-empty sequence of sentences such that the last member of the sequence is A and each member of the sequence is either a member of Γ or an axiom or follows according to a rule of inference from one or more sentences that precede it. One can mechanically determine whether any given finite sequence of sentences is a proof.

Although logical calculuses can be objects of study in their own right, it is their application to the construction and criticism of arguments that gives calculuses their original point. An argument in English is valid just in case it is not possible for all the premisses to be true and the conclusion false. Valid arguments can be grouped according to their shapes or form. For example, it is easy to see that the following arguments share their form, despite their different content or subject-matter. If Wales wins, then England loses; Wales wins; therefore, England loses. If John is tall, then John is heavy; John is tall; therefore, John is heavy. Logical calculuses differ according as they concentrate on different kinds of valid argument forms. For example, the *propositional calculus is concerned with arguments, such as the pair just given, which depend for their validity on the meanings of the truth-functional connectives, here the meaning of 'if . . . then'.

Arguments in English are often hard to make out. Better to translate English arguments into a logical calculus which is brief and unambiguous and then determine whether the translation is a *proof or can be made into a proof by inserting extra steps. For example, we can translate the simple argument that establishes the defeat of England into the propositional calculus: let 'P' represent 'Wales wins', 'Q' represent 'England loses', and '$P \rightarrow Q$' represent 'If Wales wins, then England loses'. Then we can make a proof of the translated argument by employing the rule of inference known as *modus ponendo ponens*, which permits the move from a pair of sentences of the form A and $A \rightarrow B$ to the sentence of the form B and, hence, justifies the move from 'P' and '$P \rightarrow Q$' to 'Q' in our translated argument.

To guarantee that the existence of a proof entails that the original English argument is valid the rules of inference must be truth-preserving. A semantics for the calculus explicates, using the notion of an interpretation, the idea of a possible situation in which sentences are true or false. An argument of the calculus is defined to be valid just in case in any interpretation in which all the premises are true, the conclusion is also true. Then the minimum requirement for the rules of inference is that they be sound: if there is a proof of A from a set Γ, then the argument with the members of Γ as premises and A as conclusion is valid.   A.D.O.

A. Church, *Introduction to Mathematical Logic* (Princeton, NJ, 1956), i introduction, sect. 7.

W. Kneale and M. Kneale, *The Development of Logic* (Oxford, 1962), ch. 9.

E. J. Lemmon, *Beginning Logic* (London, 1965).

calculus, predicate: *see* predicate calculus.

calculus, propositional: *see* propositional calculus.

Calvin, John (Jean) (1509–64). French theologian. Reformer active in Geneva. A principal founder of Protestantism, his main theological doctrine is absolute predestination, which entails the inevitability of the eternal salvation of the elect and the eternal damnation of the unchosen, irrespective of perceived desert but according to the will of God. The inamissibility of *grace is a logical consequence of absolute predestination (because F is inamissible if and only if F is not liable to be lost). Calvin's theology entails the Lutheran doctrines that Scripture is the only guide to faith, there is human free will before but not after the Fall of Adam, and the distinguishing of the righteous from the sinful is by faith alone (*sola fide*), not works. Calvinism is characterized by a strong emphasis on the omnipotence of God and human sin, rather than God's benevolence and human freedom. *Barth's arguments against the possibility of *natural theology and insistence on the unique importance of God's self-revelation in Christ lend support to Calvinism.   S.P.

*Calvinism.

John Calvin, *The Institutes of Christian Religion* (Grand Rapids, Mich., 1987).

Paul Helm, *John Calvin's Ideas* (Oxford, 2004).

Alister E. McGrath (ed.), *The Christian Theology Reader* (Oxford, 2002), pp. 425–6.

Calvinism. Based primarily upon the teachings of John Calvin (1509–64), Calvinism has a doctrinal side and a cultural side. The former stresses the sovereignty of God, the goodness of his creation, the sinfulness of human creatures, the sole authority of Scripture, and (though not as centrally as commonly believed) the predestination of his creatures to eternal life made possible by Christ's redemptive work. The latter (built on the theme of the goodness of creation) stresses an approach to culture which emphasizes involvement, hard work, and material success rather than withdrawal and other-worldly flight. Often characterized as deterministic, the teachings of Calvinism are perfectly compatible with the *freedom of the will, as (non-compatibilist) philosophers understand this notion. Thus, for example, the doctrine of pre-destination entails that one's final state is determined, but it does not entail that one is unfree with respect to all of the numerous decisions one makes over the course of one's life. Unlike Lutheranism, Calvinism has evolved out of the teachings of more than one individual; besides Calvin, these include Zwingli, Melanchthon, and Bucer.   G.F.M.

*compatibilism and incompatibilism.

P. Helm, *John Calvin's Ideas* (Oxford, 2004).

J. T. McNeill, *History and Character of Calvinism* (Oxford, 1954).

Cambridge change. If a predicate is true of an object x at a time t, but not true of x at a later time, then x has undergone what P. T. Geach has called a 'Cambridge change'. Many philosophers believe that Cambridge change is necessary but not sufficient for genuine *change. For example, when my brother grows taller than me, I become shorter than him. I have undergone a Cambridge change, but not a genuine change.   T.C.

Sydney Shoemaker, 'Causality and Properties', in *Identity, Cause and Mind* (Cambridge, 1984).

Cambridge philosophy. In the Middle Ages Cambridge was a good deal smaller than Oxford and produced no philosopher to compare with Oxford's Duns Scotus or Ockham. Francis Bacon was the first important philosopher to study at Cambridge, although he, like Hobbes, Locke, and Bentham at Oxford, thought little of the instruction he had received at his university. The first significant teachers of philosophy at Cambridge were the mid-seventeenth-century Cambridge Platonists, especially Cudworth and Henry More. For the most part members of the strongly Calvinist Emmanuel College, they were hostile to all kinds of fanatical enthusiasm and argued for the rationality of religion against Calvinism, Laudian High Anglicanism, and the Erastianism of Hobbes. They sought to found morality on reason, not will, whether of God or king, and, against Descartes's mechanism argued that the world as a whole is a unity, animated throughout by purpose.

Samuel Clarke, writing in the early years of the eighteenth century, was the most mathematically minded of philosopher-theologians and very much a product of Newton's Cambridge, although he did not teach there. He defended, against Leibniz, Newton's theory of space as absolute. His abstract lucidities were echoed, towards the end of the century, in the ethics and theology of William Paley, Christian utilitarian and authoritative expounder of the 'evidences' of Christianity.

A lonely figure in the unphilosophical Cambridge of the mid-nineteenth century was William Whewell. His account of scientific thinking as *hypothetico-deductive, with hypothesis being prior to observation, was unfairly criticized, and unreasonably obliterated, by J. S. Mill. Whewell's views, unlike Mill's, were based on wide experience of scientific work and profound knowledge of the history of science. John Grote revived philosophy in Cambridge later in the century, and by the end of it the subject

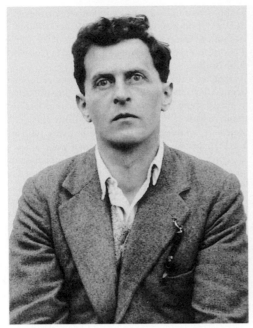

LUDWIG WITTGENSTEIN: his influence coursed twice through Western philosophy, first via Logical Positivism in the 1930s and 1940s, then through a diaspora of disciples in the 1950s and 1960s. The open texture and vatic style of his writings allow endless discovery and reinterpretation.

BERTRAND RUSSELL transcended the successive influences of Bradley, Moore, Frege, and Wittgenstein to emerge as the most widely read British philosopher of the twentieth century.

G. E. MOORE defended the value of common sense and clarity in philosophy and inspired a generation of British intellectuals with his ethical writings.

R. G. COLLINGWOOD, the last bastion of idealism in interwar Oxford, stressed the historical nature of the philosophical enterprise.

was pursued there with distinction by the idealists James Ward and J. M. E. McTaggart—the second of whom derived extra-ordinary conclusions with seemingly rigorous logic from self-evident premises in crystalline prose—and the utilitarian moral philosopher Henry Sidgwick, an inspiring example of intellectual scrupulousness.

Bertrand Russell and G. E. Moore, who were to overwhelm the prevailing idealist consensus, were pupils of these three. In the first decade of this century Russell, with A. N. Whitehead, produced *Principia Mathematica*, expanding the range and increasing the systematic character of logic and purporting to derive mathematics from it. He brought the topic of meaning to the centre of philosophy and, with his theory of descriptions, supplied an exemplary instance of how it should be analysed. Moore set about the doctrines of other philosophers, whether idealists or utilitarians, with stolid but acute literalness. Russell and Moore agreed that there are many different things, of different fundamental kinds, in the world and that reality is not, as the idealists had concluded, one all-inclusive mental or spiritual thing.

Wittgenstein came to Cambridge to learn from Russell and soon reversed the relationship. There is nothing of Moore in the *Tractatus*, in which the topics he and Russell had worked on together are oracularly set out: an intensely abstract account of the ultimate logical constituents of the world and of our thought and speech about it. Absent from 1914 to 1929, he came back with a point of view closer to Moore, at least in taking ordinary language to be in need, not of replacement, but of a fuller, deeper understanding. Ramsey, the only disciple he seems to have respected intellectually, was, like him and Russell, a mathematician. Dying at 26, he showed enormous promise. Wittgenstein dominated Cambridge philosophy until his death in 1953 and for a considerable time afterwards. But since about 1960 Cambridge philosophy, much like that of Oxford, has largely lost its distinctive flavour, perhaps because of the reversal by the philosophy of the United States of its former colonial dependence on that of Britain.   A.Q.

*London philosophy; Oxford philosophy; English philosophy; British philosophy today.

Cambridge Platonists
A school of seventeenth-century English philosophers who found in Platonism a way of criticizing Hobbes and of defending Christianity against the fanaticism of Puritans, Calvinists, and Prelatists.

The Cambridge Platonists included Ralph Cudworth (1617–80), who is perhaps best known, John Smith (1618–52), Benjamin Whichcote (1609–83), and Nathaniel Culverwell (1618–50). All these thinkers were from Emmanuel College, and to these we can add Henry More (1614–87) who was from Christ's College. Ralph Cudworth eventually became Master of Christ's (for over thirty years) and Professor of Hebrew in the University. His major work *The True Intellectual System of the Universe* (1678) was conceived as a systematic refutation of

Hobbes, and indeed it was a major work of seventeenth-century philosophical thought. What follows is an account of the main lines of argument of the Cambridge Platonists, especially as these are found in Cudworth and John Smith.

Hobbes's account of the mind was reductivist—he argued that it consisted of motions in the substance of the brain. Perception consisted of a passive registration by the sense-organs of vibrations received from outside, 'apparitions' or 'seemings', as Hobbes calls them. John Smith in his *Discourse Concerning the Immortality of the Soul* points out, probably following Plotinus, that Hobbes has not distinguished between the motions of material particles and our awareness of the motions. He is maintaining, in other words, that Hobbes lacks an account of *consciousness. Smith argues that there must be some incorporeal substance through which we become aware of the 'seemings' and by means of which we can interpret and correct them. For Smith, then, the senses presuppose a mind as their co-ordinating principle. In a similar sort of way Cudworth presents a theory of knowledge which anticipates Kant: mind is not secondary and derivative but 'senior to the world, and the architect thereof'.

The doctrine of the eternal and immutable character of *morality is the most characteristic doctrine of the Cambridge Platonists. Things, including morality, are as they are by nature and independently of our wills. They have been created by a God whose will is subject to his wisdom and goodness. The mind of man is derivative from the divine mind, which is itself antecedent to all corporeal things. When human ideas are true they are readings of the divine thoughts. In other words, there is a realm of intelligible ideas to which 'good' or 'just' belong, every bit as much as geometrical truths. These intelligible and changeless ideas are rational patterns in the mind of God and are accessible to human minds through the use of right reason. It is clear from this that in their metaphysics and moral philosophy the Cambridge Platonists (influenced by Plato, Plotinus, and Descartes) totally reject Hobbes.

In their philosophy of religion they reject *Calvinism, and in particular they reject both the doctrine of the total depravity of man since the Fall, and also the doctrine of predestination. They believed in the power of each person by the light of reason to move towards perfection. It is also interesting to note that the Cambridge Platonists were themselves Puritans by origin and education. Their Puritan dislike of ritual, vestments, and stained glass was of course supported by their belief in Platonism. But they were mild and tolerant in their views and were sometimes called the 'latitude men'. Their position had something in common with that of Milton, and pointed towards *deism and the moral sense theory of Shaftesbury.   R.S.D.

*latitudinarianism.

S. Hutton, 'The Cambridge Platonists', in S. Nadler (ed.), *A Companion to Early Modern Philosophy* (Oxford, 2002).

Basil Willey, *The Seventeenth Century Background* (London, 1953).

Campanella, Tommaso (1568–1639). A highly prolific Italian philosopher imprisoned for years by the Inquisition for his *libertinism, Campanella was a contemporary of fellow Dominican Giordano Bruno, defender of Galileo Galilei, and correspondent of the French libertines Gabriel Naudé and François de La Mothe le Vayer. In *Atheismus Trionfatus* (1631), Campanella claimed to expose the arguments for atheism in order to refute them—the triumph over atheism of the title. But because he proposed a form of *deism, discoverable by the light of reason alone, of which Christianity was just one manifestation and Christ a preacher of a natural morality, the book was denounced as proclaiming 'atheism triumphant', and pillaged for a more decidedly atheistic tract, *Theophrastus Redivivus*. In Campanella's utopian *City of the Sun*, investigation of nature would benefit mankind, whether by means of political and ethical laws or by technology. Rulers would use natural philosophy and scientific astrology, purged of superstition, to control and transform the world.   L.P.

G. Ernst, *Religione, ragione e natura: Studi su T. Campanella* (Milan, 1991).

F. Yates, *Giordano Bruno and the Hermetic Tradition* (London, 1964).

Campbell, John (1956–). British metaphysician and philosopher of mind, at Berkeley, formerly at Oxford. Campbell's distinctive approach to metaphysics and the philosophy of mind aims to reconcile a broadly Kantian investigation of the structure of self-conscious thought about an objective world with the results of empirical enquiry into the nature of cognition. *Past, Space and Self* (1994) undertakes to map out the central conceptual skills making up the human capacity for self-conscious thought and distinguishing human beings from other animals. These conceptual skills involve capacities to think not just about oneself, but also about space and time and the nature of physical objects. *Reference and Consciousness* (2002) explores the functional role of conscious experience. Campbell sees conscious attention to objects as playing a foundational role in thought and action—a foundational role that we can only understand through the complex interactions between conscious attention and the subpersonal information-processing mechanisms that solve the binding problem.   J.BER.

Camus, Albert (1913–60). Algerian French philosopher who is best known for his concept of 'the *absurd', which he described as 'a widespread sensitivity of our times' and defined as a confrontation between our demands for rationality and justice and the 'indifferent universe'. He explored this idea in novels, *The Stranger* (1942), *The Plague* (1947), and *The Fall* (1956), as well as philosophical essays, *The Myth of Sisyphus* (1942) and *The Rebel* (1951). He was born and grew up in war-torn north Africa, and memories of the bitter civil war and his experiences under the Nazi occupation permeated his philosophy. Like his one-time philosophical friend and colleague Jean-Paul Sartre, he was obsessed with questions of responsibility, innocence, and guilt in the face of overwhelming tragedy. In *The Plague*, for example, he pits his characters against an invisible, unpredictable, lethal enemy in order to explore the vicissitudes of responsibility in a situation for which no one can be blamed. Nevertheless, there are heroes and there are cads. In his early novel *The Stranger*, by contrast, Camus introduces us to a character who is utterly innocent, despite the fact that he violates virtually all of the dictates of 'decent' society, including the prohibition against murder.

Camus's notion of 'the absurd' is best exemplified by the Greek mythological hero Sisyphus, who was condemned by the gods to the endless, futile task of rolling a rock up a mountain. Nevertheless, Camus assures us, Sisyphus is happy. He accepts his futile fate, but he also 'rebels' by scorning the gods. In *The Stranger*, by contrast, the protagonist had simply accepted the absurdity of life, 'opening up his heart to the benign indifference of the universe'. But Camus, like Sartre, also displays a deep appreciation of what we might call 'original' guilt, guilt that is inherent in our very existence as human beings. In *The Fall*, a particularly perverse character named Jean-Baptiste Clamence, who was once a lawyer, makes the conflation of guilt and innocence a matter of philosophical principle. How could one be innocent in a world that is absurd? Camus won the Nobel Prize for Literature in 1957.   R.C.SOL.

*existentialism.

D. Sprintzen, *Camus: A Critical Examination* (Philadelphia, 1988).

Canadian philosophy. Something of Canada's national character is reflected in the philosophical effort of three centuries. Starting from 1665 with the teaching of the Ratio Studiorum at the Jesuit Collège in Quebec, emphasis was placed on the writings of Aristotle and Aquinas which were thought to serve the higher objectives of theology. From early in the nineteenth century, the philosophical programme of French Canada was to resist the attractions of the Protestant Reformation and the Enlightenment. In due course, efforts were made to articulate a positive Catholic philosophy which, as it emerged, underwrote the ultramontanism which prevailed in French Canada until the 1960s. In English Canada philosophy originated with the founding of the first universities in Maritimes in the eighteenth century. In most cases, the university had a religious affiliation, and it is natural that there should have been a preoccupation with the philosophical foundations of religion. Canada's harsh climate also called forth a serious interest in the philosophy of nature, and her emerging social pluralism issued in the philosophical analysis of politics.

Genuine philosophical ability was widely scattered across the country, and no English-speaking university could represent itself as the centre of philosophical effort in the late nineteenth and early twentieth centuries; but Toronto began in the early 1920s to achieve a hegemony that would endure for nearly fifty years. In 1929 the Institute of Mediaeval Studies (later the Pontifical Institute) was established in that city, and it is to this day one of the world's leading centres for such work. George Brett and later Fulton H. Anderson shaped the philosophy department at the University of Toronto into one of the foremost places for the study of the history of philosophy.

Canada had made substantial and internationally recognized contributions to medieval studies and the history of philosophy generally, but in the 1960s the Quiet Revolution was under way in Quebec, and everywhere Sputnik worked its magic. Canada came to know unprecedented expansion of its universities, in both size and number. In Quebec philosophy became more vigorously secular and made significant contributions to the intellectual foundations of her own social transformation. Anglophone philosophers were turning their attention away from the history of philosophy and from cultural self-examination, and were positioning themselves in research programmes set elsewhere, chiefly those of the analytic philosophers of Cambridge, of positivism and its critics, mainly in the United States, of Oxford linguistic philosophy, and of postwar phenomenology and existentialism in France and Germany.

The University of Western Ontario assembled an internationally recognized team of philosophers of science, and a monograph series was launched. The Canadian Philosophical Association originated its official journal, *Dialogue*, in 1961, and this was followed ten years later by the *Canadian Journal of Philosophy* and *Russell: The Journal of the Bertrand Russell Archives* (based at McMaster University). In the same year the Society for Exact Philosophy came into being. *Laval théologique et philosophique* was born in 1945, and *Philosophiques* in 1974.

After the transformations of the 1960s it may be said that professional Canadian philosophy lost much of the discernibly Canadian character that it had had previously. Canadian researchers now work on specialized problems, and employ methods to do so, which resist narrowly national definition. Even so, there are exceptions to this trend. George Grant's *Lament for a Nation* (1965) and *Technology and Empire* (1969) had an influence well beyond the universities, and did much to underwrite a resurgence of Canadian cultural nationalism in the 1960s and 1970s.

Grant's work was in the main greeted unsympathetically by academically based philosophers. They found its arguments unrigorous and its Platonized anglicanism over-sentimental. Thus, while several Canadians, both at home and abroad, are in the forefront of various branches of philosophical enquiry, less amply exemplified are concentrations of 'analytically approved' research accomplishment that have a recognizably Canadian 'signature'. In the case of Australia, one tends to think of materialism; present-day Oxford calls to mind neo-Kantianism; and so on. In some areas, Canadians have achieved dominance, whether in Gauthier's work on contractarian ethics, van Fraassen's promotion of constructive empiricism, the Woods–Walton approach to fallacy theory, or the development of preservationist variations of paraconsistent logic by Peter Schotch, R. E. Jennings, and Bryson Brown. In only one area, however, can there be said to exist a professionally well-respected signature that reflects a distinctively Canadian philosophical character. This is the philosophy of multiculturalism, typified by the works of Will Kymlicka. Leslie Armour has also provided the estimable service of showing how deep is the Canadian intellectual preoccupation with multiculturalism, which pre-dates by generations Quebec's Quiet Revolution. So Kymlicka (and certain of his critics, such as Edward Andrew) are building upon a thick analytical foundation.

In the Canadian tradition, a just citizenship must respect a fundamental difference between the rights of immigrants and the constitutionally protected distinctiveness of aboriginals and Québécois. While all immigrants must have the right to acquire citizenship, neither Canadian policy nor practice favours an open border. So there is a problem about what ethno-cultural justice requires in the case of illegals, or 'metrics' as Kymlicka calls them. Both Charles Taylor and Kymlicka reflect in their writings the Canadian openness to ethnic diversity. Taylor sees religion as essential to 'deep diversity'. Kymlicka concedes the impossibility of separating culture and politics, but favours the expungement of the religious from the political. Canadian multicultural politics is an accommodation of cleavages both ethnic and linguistic. It is not surprising, therefore, that her leading political philosophers should emphasize the Canadian confederal state as the appropriate governing structure. Some critics see in these arrangements the loss of Canada's former distinctiveness, its replacement by a timorous and unconfident new nationalism of the affirmative of otherness, and a misappropriation of the founding rationale of confederation.   j.woo.

*American philosophy; Australian philosophy.

Dialogue: The Canadian Philosophical Review (1986): vol. 25 mainly devoted to philosophy in Canada.

Leslie Armour, *The Idea of Canada and the Crisis of Community* (Ottawa, 1981).

Will Kymlicka and Magda Opalski (eds.), *Can Liberal Pluralism be Exported? Western Political Theory and Ethnic Relations in Eastern Europe* (Oxford, 2002).

Cantor, Georg (1845–1918). Cantor created the mathematics of the *infinite as well as effectively creating *set theory. A set has the *same* number of members as another if each member of either set can be paired with a unique member of the other. If a set can be put into such a one-to-one correspondence with the integers it is said to be denumerable. Cantor demonstrated the denumerability of algebraic numbers (roots of polynomial equations with integer coefficients), and the *non*-denumerability of the real numbers, numbers whose decimal expansion need not repeat or terminate (1873, diagonal proof 1891). Cantor's continuum hypothesis (there is no set intermediate in size between the integers and the real numbers) was proved by P. J. Cohen (1963), following a partial result by Gödel (1938), to be consistent with but underivable from normal set theory.   j.j.m.

Joseph Warren Dauben, *Georg Cantor: His Mathematics and Philosophy of the Infinite* (Cambridge, Mass., 1979).

Cantor's paradox. How many points are there in a line segment? As Cantor's diagonal proof reveals, infinitely more than there are integers. And in the infinite plane? Just as many as there are in the line segment. Indeed and in general, precisely as many as there are in a space of *n* dimensions, $n \geq 1$. 'I see it,' Cantor wrote to Dedekind, 'but I don't believe it.' Is this infinite number of points, then, the highest degree of *infinity available? No. Cantor also proved that for any set, a set with more members (the original set's *power set*, consisting of all its subsets) is constructible. Thus there is no greatest set. Hence also (Cantor's paradox) there is not a set of all sets, since such a supposed total set would at once yield a larger one.

J.J.M.

M. M. Zuckerman, *Sets and Transfinite Numbers* (New York, 1974).

capacity. A capacity is a *power or ability (either natural or acquired) of a *thing or person, and as such one of its real (because causally effective) properties. The natural capacities of inanimate objects, such as the capacity of copper to conduct electricity, are dispositional properties whose ascription entails the truth of corresponding subjunctive conditionals, such as that an electric current would flow in a copper wire if a potential difference were applied to its ends. But the capacities of persons the exercise of which is subject to their voluntary control, such as a person's capacity to speak English, do not sustain such a pattern of entailments and are consequently not strictly *dispositions. Ascribing to something a capacity to F is not the same as saying that it is naturally possible for that thing to F, since circumstances can obtain in which a thing's capacity to F cannot be exercised.

E.J.L.

*causality; propensity; potentiality.

R. Tuomela (ed.), *Dispositions* (Dordrecht, 1978).

capitalism. The modern, market-based, commodity-producing economic system controlled by 'capital', that is, purchasing-power used to hire labour for wages. The term was first used prominently, and pejoratively, by Marx, but for defenders of the system it has become a term of praise.

Marx sees the origins of capitalism in the forcible expropriation of European peasants and small artisans during the later Middle Ages, leading to a separation between the *bourgeoisie or capitalist class, who privately own the means of production, and the proletariat or working class. Possessing no such means, proletarians can live only by selling their labour power to members of the bourgeoisie. Ownership of the means of production gives the bourgeoisie a decisive bargaining advantage over the proletariat, which shows itself in the form of the profit and interest on capital, resulting from the *exploitation of wage labour. One central claim of Marxian economics is that capitalism has been responsible for a colossal growth in humanity's productive capabilities. Another is that capital has an inherent tendency to accumulate, concentrating social power in the hands of the capitalist class and

bringing the exploited working class more and more under its economic domination. The potential for a higher society and a better life which capitalism has made possible can be realized for the vast majority only if the workers are emancipated from the domination of capital.

Defenders of capitalism deny the charge that wage labourers are exploited, citing the indispensable economic functions performed by capitalists, such as managerial and supervisory labour, saving, and the assumption of risks. Critics of capitalism respond that in principle there is no reason why these functions must be performed by capitalists. Workers need not be supervised by those who represent interests antagonistic to theirs; capitalists typically bear fewer burdens of deprivation than workers do for the sake of social saving, and if capitalists are rewarded for risk-taking, the system offers no similar rewards to workers, who nevertheless risk losing their livelihood when an enterprise fails. They see capitalists as 'rewarded' for performing these functions only because the system gives them greater control over production, saving, and risk-taking, hence putting them in a position to reap the fruits of economic co-operation, accumulation, and good fortune. Profit and interest on capital are not rewards for managing, saving, and risk-taking, but rather consequences of capital's social power to exploit labour.

To this defenders of capitalism will reply that the failure of the Soviet system reveals capitalism to be the most efficient way yet discovered to manage a modern economic system. To grant this point, however, is not in the least to concede that capitalism is not exploitative, only that we have yet to find an efficient modern economic system which does not exploit workers. It is doubtless a troubling fact that we have not, but this fact provides us with no reason for feeling any loyalty to the capitalist system and leaves untouched the basic Marxian reason to seek an alternative to capitalism.

A.W.W.

*anti-communism; democracy and capitalism; globalization, morality, and politics.

Harry Braverman, *Labor and Monopoly Capital* (New York, 1974).
Milton Friedman, *Capitalism and Freedom* (Chicago, 1982).
Karl Marx, *Capital*, tr. Ben Fowkes and David Fernbach (London, 1976).
Alec Nove, *The Economics of Feasible Socialism* (London, 1983).
Joseph Schumpeter, *Capitalism, Socialism and Democracy* (New York, 1951).
Paul Sweezy, *Theory of Capitalist Development* (London, 1962).

capital punishment. The question whether it is morally permissible for the state to execute any of its citizens and, if so, under what circumstances, has been debated by philosophers, sociologists, and politicians ever since the middle of the eighteenth century. The arguments supporting capital punishment have usually been divided into those based on 'justice', which in this context simply means retribution, and those based on 'utility'. The appeal to *justice usually takes the following form: people deserve to suffer for wrongdoing. In the case of criminal wrongdoing the suffering takes the form of legal *punishment; and justice requires that the most severe crimes, especially murder, be punished with the severest penalty—death. It should be emphasized that somebody who reasons in this way is not committed to a defence of the *lex talionis—the principle of 'an eye for an eye'.

There are four major utilitarian arguments favouring the death penalty. It is said to deter, and to prevent the executed criminals from repeating their crimes, it is less cruel than life imprisonment (and hence should be welcomed by the criminal), and it brings a measure of satisfaction to the family and friends of the victim as well as to other citizens outraged by the crime.

Of the arguments against capital punishment by far the most important is that sooner or later innocent persons are certain to be executed. The only way to avoid this is to abolish capital punishment altogether. Another argument is that capital punishment lowers the 'tone' of the society in which it is practised. Civilized societies do not tolerate the torture of prisoners and they would not do so even if torture could be shown to have a deterrent effect. It has also been argued by Dostoevsky and Camus that capital punishment is unjust on retributionist assumptions because the anticipatory suffering of the person who is to be executed is immeasurably greater than that of his victim. Finally, Arthur Koestler and Clarence Darrow have argued that capital punishment must be unjust because human beings never act freely and hence should not be blamed and punished for even the most terrible acts. Koestler did not see that this argument would undermine all punishment. Darrow saw this and favoured the abolition of punishment altogether (as distinct from detention for purposes of social protection).

By way of commentary it should be mentioned that statistical studies in all parts of the world have shown that capital punishment does not deter, or rather that its deterrent effect is no greater than that of life imprisonment. If anything, capital punishment tends to inflame certain disturbed individuals and thus leads to an increase in murder. This fact, together with what is known about the fallibility of witnesses and juries and the bias and even corruption of prosecutors, has convinced many educated persons throughout the world, regardless of their political affiliation, that there is no place for capital punishment in a civilized society.   P.E.

H. A. Bedau (ed.), *The Death Penalty in America*, 4th edn. (New York, 1988).
—— 'Capital Punishment', in H. LaFollette (ed.), *The Oxford Handbook to Practical Ethics* (Oxford, 2003).
Thorsten Sellin (ed.), *Capital Punishment* (New York, 1967).

care, ethics of. This term refers to a group of moral reflections about the moral emotion and virtue of care that emerged from feminist theory. The hypothesis that 'women speak in a different voice'—'the voice of care'—rose to prominence in Carol Gilligan's book *In a Different Voice* (1982). Through empirical research, she claimed to discover a female voice stressing empathic association with others and a sense of being responsible and caring.

Gilligan thus identified two modes of relationship and two modes of moral thinking: an ethic of care and an ethic of rights.

Allied developments then occurred in philosophical ethics. For example, Annette Baier argued that the reasoning and methods of women in ethical theory is noticeably different from traditional theories. She found in them the same different voice that Gilligan heard. She criticizes the near-exclusive emphasis in traditional moral philosophy on universal rules and principles, to the neglect of sympathy with and concern for others. The ethics of care therefore promotes traits in intimate personal relationships, such as sympathy, compassion, fidelity, discernment, love, and trustworthiness.   T.L.B.

*feminism; feminist philosophy.

A. Baier, *Moral Prejudices* (Cambridge, Mass., 1994).

Carnap, Rudolf (1891–1970). German empiricist philosopher and logician who moved to the United States in 1935. Carnap was a pupil of Frege and much influenced by him, as well as by Russell and Wittgenstein. He was a prominent member of the *Vienna Circle and a leading exponent of *Logical Positivism before the Second World War. Technical rigour was a hallmark of his important contributions to formal semantics, the philosophy of science, and the foundations of inductive *probability.

Carnap's most important early work was *Der logische Aufbau der Welt* (1928), translated under the title *The Logical Structure of the World* (1967). This attempted to spell out in some detail the radical empiricist programme of reconstructing human knowledge of the social and physical world and other minds on the basis of individual experience, using as the sole starting-point the relation of remembered similarity between experiences. Carnap originally believed that all meaningful physical concepts were definable in terms of experience, in accordance with a strong version of the principle of *verifiability. Later he moderated this view to accommodate the fact that the language of physics is not exhaustively translatable into the language of sense experience. He also came to put more emphasis on his belief that the method of construction used in the *Aufbau* could with equal legitimacy be used to construct individual psychology on a physicalist basis.

In *The Logical Syntax of Language* (1934; Eng. tr. 1937), Carnap deployed his technical skills to develop a rigorous formal account of the structure of any possible language, seeing this as a necessary preliminary to the pursuit of the only form of philosophical inquiry deemed legitimate by him—logical analysis. In the foreword of that book he memorably states his view that 'Philosophy is to be replaced by the logic of science [and] the logic of science is nothing other than the logical syntax of the language of science' (p. xiii). Later, however, Carnap became more concerned with the *semantics of natural and formal languages, doing work which culminated in his important and influential book *Meaning and Necessity* (1947), which laid the foundations of much subsequent work in the semantics of *modal logic. In that book Carnap argues in favour of an alternative to Frege's theory of *sense and reference, called by him the 'method of extension and intension'. Carnap held that this method provided the most economical account of the logical behaviour of expressions in modal contexts—for instance, the expressions '9' and '7' in the sentence '9 is necessarily greater than 7'. His criticism of Frege involved a rejection of the traditional category of *names, conceived as a class of expressions each of which stood for a unique thing.

After the Second World War, Carnap's energies were increasingly devoted to the development of inductive logic as a branch of probability theory, resulting in his magisterial volume *Logical Foundations of Probability* (1950) and many subsequent publications. This interest was continuous with his earlier ones, since his concern was to put on a rigorous footing the notion, central to scientific method, of the confirmation of a hypothesis by empirical evidence. Although he had abandoned a strong form of the principle of verifiability, he continued to adhere to a fundamentally empiricist theory of meaning which required scientific hypotheses to be susceptible to empirical confirmation. He also, in consequence, adhered to the *analytic–synthetic distinction, notwithstanding the strictures of W. V. Quine—though their differences on this issue were perhaps less substantial than they appeared to be, since Carnap was always insistent that logical principles themselves are always a matter for freely chosen convention, to be justified on pragmatic grounds. In all matters of logic and mathematics, Carnap espoused what he called the principle of tolerance: 'It is not our business to set up prohibitions, but to arrive at conventions' (*Logical Syntax*, 51).   E.J.L.

*confirmation; formal and material mode.

R. Carnap, *The Logical Structure of the World and Pseudoproblems in Philosophy*, tr. R. A. George (London, 1967).
—— *Meaning and Necessity: A Study in Semantics and Modal Logic*, 2nd edn. (Chicago, 1956).
P. A. Schilpp (ed.), *The Philosophy of Rudolf Carnap* (La Salle, Ill., 1963).

Carneades (214–129 BC). Head of Plato's *Academy, who followed Arcesilaus in emphasizing the sceptical rather than the dogmatic elements in Plato's legacy. Carneades scandalized Cato the Elder by arguing in favour of justice and against it on successive days. Holding that certainty is impossible and that we should always suspend judgement, he nevertheless claimed that we should be guided by the 'probable' (in the sense of 'approvable' or persuasive, not of statistical likelihood). Criticizing both Stoic and Epicurean views in the debate on freedom and determinism, he anticipated Gilbert Ryle on the truth of future contingents and Richard Taylor on agent causation; but whether he himself did, or as a Sceptic consistently could, assert a libertarian position is controversial.
                                    R.W.S.

A. A. Long, *Hellenistic Philosophy* (London, 1974).

—— and D. N. Sedley (eds.), *The Hellenistic Philosophers* (Cambridge, 1987). Texts and commentary.

Carroll, Lewis (1832–98). Pseudonym of the Revd Charles Lutwidge Dodgson, a mathematics don at Christ Church, Oxford. Best known for his Alice stories, which brim over with logical puzzles and absurdities and have been duly pillaged by philosophers. Coming at the tail-end of the degenerating programme of Aristotelian logic, his contributions to formal logic are inevitably insignificant, their only lasting value being their testimony to his inimitable talent for devising extraordinary syllogisms. Carroll's most important philosophical article is the characteristically quaint and deceptively light 'What the Tortoise Said to Achilles' (*Mind* (1895)). He hints at a deep problem about the epistemology of valid inference, demonstrating that the acceptance of a rule of inference cannot be identified with the acceptance of a conditional proposition.
                                    A.D.O.

J. Fisher (ed.), *The Magic of Lewis Carroll* (London, 1973).
Special centenary issue of the journal *Mind* (1995), including the original 1895 article.

Cartesianism. Name given to the movement inaugurated by René Descartes (after 'Cartesius', the Latin version of his name); it shaped the philosophical landscape of the early modern period, and its influence, even today, is by no means entirely exhausted. In the decades following Descartes's death, Cartesianism was seen primarily as a new programme for physical science, based on mathematical principles. Descartes had defined matter as *res extensa*, or 'extended substance', that is to say, whatever has length, breadth, and height. The Cartesian programme was to exhibit all physical phenomena as explicable in terms of the 'modes' or modifications of extension; in effect, this meant showing how all the apparent complexity and diversity of matter could be accounted for simply by reference to the size, shape, and motion of the particles of which it was composed. 'I freely acknowledge', Descartes had written in his *Principles of Philosophy* (1644) 'that I recognize no matter in corporeal *things apart from that which the geometers call quantity, and take as the object of their demonstrations, i.e. that to which every kind of division shape and motion is applicable' (pt. II, art. 64).

The appeal of the Cartesian approach in the latter half of the seventeenth century undoubtedly owed much to its rejection of occult forms and qualities, and its insistence that physics should invoke only the 'clearly and distinctly perceivable' properties of mathematics. A growing body of critics, however, pointed out that mere extension in three dimensions could yield only an inert and passive universe. To generate *motion in the system, the Cartesians had to have recourse to God, whom Descartes had described as 'the primary cause of motion, who in the beginning created matter along with its motion and rest, and now preserves the same amount of motion as he put there in the beginning' (*Principles*, pt. II, art. 36). Though this may seem to be a piece of *ad hoc* metaphysics, the cash value of the appeal to immutable and continuous divine action in the Cartesian system was the rejection of the Aristotelian assumption that all matter tended 'naturally' to come to rest, and its replacement with the Cartesian principle of the persistence of motion in a straight line (what has subsequently come to be known as the law of inertia). The idea of the conservation of motion was highly influential for the subsequent development of physics. In later Newtonian physics, however, what is conserved is mass times velocity, and neither of these notions is to be found in Descartes; as the working-out of Descartes's 'rules of impact' make clear, what is conserved is 'quantity of motion', measured simply as the product of size (volume) and speed (the latter factor, unlike the more modern notion of velocity, is not held to be affected by a change in direction of motion).

Although, from a scientific point of view, the eventual downfall of Cartesian physics was a result of Isaac Newton's formulating mathematical covering laws of far greater predictive power than anything Descartes had been able to devise, many of the philosophical debates over Cartesianism centred on its denial of any inherent power or force in matter. To some, notably Descartes's deviant disciple Nicolas Malebranche, this was a positive advantage: if *causality involves the necessitating of effects, only God has the requisite power to count as a genuine causal agent; matter is, of itself, wholly inert— mere 'extended stuff'. For G. W. Leibniz, by contrast, it is a violation of the *principle of sufficient reason to see physics as merely a series of arbitrary, divinely decreed covering laws; the behaviour of matter must proceed from something inherent in its nature, and hence (*contra* the Cartesians), some recourse must be had to the notion of force or power in things. Such debates indicate the extent to which the 'new' Cartesian physics opened up serious questions about the nature of causation in the late seventeenth and early eighteenth century, paving the way for David Hume's eventual radical critique of the very idea of causal power.

Among philosophers today, the main feature of Cartesianism which remains of interest is its theory of the mind. Descartes, in the celebrated theory known as *dualism, had maintained that the mind is an entirely separate substance from the body, and, moreover, that its nature is wholly distinct from the nature of anything physical: it is an incorporeal, indivisible, non-spatial, unextended thing, which is 'entirely distinct from the body, and would not fail to be what it is even if the body did not exist' (*Discourse on the Method*, pt. IV). The Cartesian view of the mind as a *'ghost in the machine' of the body (to use Gilbert Ryle's celebrated phrase) has few takers nowadays. To begin with, its view of the nature of the mind remains essentially obscure: we are simply told what the mind is *not* (not extended, not divisible), but are not given any explanatorily satisfying account of what it is. Moreover, even granted the existence of such supposed purely spiritual substance, it is far from clear how it could interact with the

mechanism of the body in the required way. When I decide to go for a walk my legs move, but if the chain of impulses generating the requisite muscle movements is traced back through the nervous system to the brain, the causal process is somehow mysteriously initiated by a ghostly *'volition' whose nature, and relationship to the observed physical events, remains beyond the reach of explanatory science. The form of Cartesianism proposed by Descartes's disciples in the late seventeenth century was content to leave mind–body correlations as irreducible regularities decreed by God: God obligingly ordains that the required bodily movements occur when I decide to go for a walk; conversely, he ordains that sensations of an appropriate kind (e.g. of pain or of colour) should 'arise' in the soul when the organs of the body are stimulated. Cartesianism thus typically leads to an *'occasionalism' with respect to the relation between mind and body: bodily events are the 'occasion' for the production of mental events and vice versa, but such productivity remains beyond the reach of human science—not just something we cannot so far explain, but something that no scientific account, however sophisticated, could ever in principle explain.

Cartesian attempts to resolve this puzzle tended to generate further obscurities. Descartes himself sometimes seems to have viewed the mind or soul as a kind of nonphysical 'homunculus' dwelling inside the brain (he identified the *pineal gland or conarion as the 'principal seat' of the soul). Some scholastic philosophers had argued for the existence of a common sensorium where the data from the five specialized senses are integrated (a notion canvassed by Aristotle (see *De anima*, bk. III, ch. 1, 425^{a}14)). One might have expected Descartes to have rejected this idea, both in the light of his resolute hostility to received scholastic doctrine, and also because of his conception of the mind as an incorporeal substance; in fact, however, he not only accepted it, but incorporated it into his own theory of mind–body interaction. The pineal gland receives data (via the nerves) from all parts of the body, and it is only after the data have been integrated in the gland into a unitary signal or impression that any sensory awareness can occur. 'The mind', Descartes wrote in the Sixth Meditation, 'is not immediately affected by all parts of the body, but only by the brain, or perhaps just by one small part of the brain, namely the part containing the "common sense".' In his later work, *The Passions of the Soul*, Descartes observes that 'there must necessarily be some place where the two images coming through the two eyes, or the two impressions coming from a single object through the double organs of any other sense, can come together in a single image or impression before reaching the soul, so that they do not present to it two objects instead of one' (art. 32). The argument is a curious one, since it is not at first sight apparent why a unitary image in the conscious mind requires a unitary signal or impression in the brain. Writing to Mersenne on 24 December 1640, Descartes reflected that 'the only alternative is to suppose that the soul is not joined immediately to any solid part of the body, but only to the animal spirits which are in its concavities, and which enter or leave it continually like the water of a river. That would certainly be thought too absurd.' The suggestion seems far from absurd to the modern reader, accustomed to the notion that *consciousness arises from just such a shifting and elusive interplay of electrical activity in the cerebral cortex. But to have contemplated the possibility that consciousness could arise from purely physical processes would have taken Descartes away from dualism entirely, and have made the notion of a separate substance called the mind or soul redundant—a step the Cartesians were not prepared to take, since they followed Descartes in insisting that the complexities of conscious thought could never be explained by the operations of 'mere matter'.

The reason that the Cartesian approach to the mind is not yet extinct is that some philosophers continue to maintain that there is something about consciousness that eludes the explanatory apparatus of physical science. Here a further feature of Cartesianism has been very influential, namely its stress on the subjective or 'first-personal' aspects of human experience. The Cartesian search for knowledge starts from the private meditations of the solitary thinker; and in the course of those meditations Descartes rapidly arrives at the doctrine of the perfect 'transparency' of the mind—the view that I have direct and privileged access to the contents of my mind, and that I know my own nature as a conscious being better than that of any 'external' objects. From here, Descartes moves on to the conclusion that my own experiences (e.g. of hunger, thirst, pleasure, and pain) have a phenomenal character that is vividly accessible 'from the inside', but which necessarily lacks the kind of objective clarity and distinctness that belongs to the quantitative language of physical science. This notion of the essential privacy of our conscious experience has been attacked in our own century, notably by Ludwig Wittgenstein, but still retains a hold. Thus the contemporary philosopher Thomas Nagel has argued that the character of experience, 'what it is like' for the experiencing organism, cannot be captured by any physicalist account of the world. Such a perspective may not inappropriately be called 'Cartesian' even though its advocates tend to reject Descartes's doctrine of a non-physical separable substance called 'the mind', since it continues to be held that certain aspects of the mental are *sui generis* and not reducible to the objective descriptions of physics. Although it is too early to say whether such residual Cartesianism will retain a permanent philosophical foothold, its present survival, over 300 years after the death of its founder, is testimony to the enduring appeal of Descartes's approach to the complex problem of consciousness and its relation to the physical word.   J.COT.

*light of nature.

D. M. Clarke, *Occult Powers and Hypotheses* (Oxford, 1989).

T. M. Lennon *et al.* (eds.), *Problems of Cartesianism* (Kingston, 1982).

L. E. Loeb, *From Descartes to Hume* (Ithaca, NY, 1981).

S. Nadler, *Causation in Early Modern Philosophy* (Pennsylvania, 1993).

T. Schmaltz, *Radical Cartesianism* (Cambridge, 2002).

R. A. Watson, *The Breakdown of Cartesian Metaphysics* (Atlantic Highlands, NJ, 1987).

Cartwright, Nancy (1943–). American philosopher (at Stanford and the London School of Econoics) who views the higher-level laws of physics as instruments of explanation and prediction which are not true, and whose predictive and explanatory value does not require them to be true. Unlike many instrumentalists, she is a realist about the causal factors mentioned by the *laws—including so-called 'theoretical entities' generally considered unobservable. The phenomena that physicists try to explain, she says, are produced by interactions of non-Humean causal factors which are too numerous, whose interactions are too complicated, and whose influences differ too much from one physical setting to another for the phenomena they produce to be systematically explained or predicted without recourse to simplifications, idealizations, and unrealistic generalizations. The falsity of the laws, simplifications, and idealizations are the price physicists must pay for useful and cognitively manageable pictures of the physical universe. Cartwright has written extensively on scientific explanation, the epistemology of science, and problems in the philosophy of quantum physics. She was married to Stuart Hampshire.   J.B.B.

*methodology.

Nancy Cartwright, *How the Laws of Physics Lie* (Oxford, 1983).

—— *The Dappled World: A Study of the Boundaries of Science* (Cambridge, 1999).

Cassirer, Ernst (1874–1945). German philosopher who was a neo-Kantian, but differed from Kant in two respects. First, while he agreed that we need some a priori *categories to organize experience, these are not, as Kant believed, the same at all times: our categories develop over history. Second, his early researches in the philosophy of science, especially on the mathematization of physics, led him beyond Kant's central focus on scientific knowledge to a consideration of all symbolizing activities—language, myth, religion, etc.—which are, on his view, the distinguishing feature of man and are all, along with science, of equal status.

His *Philosophy of Symbolic Forms* (1923–31; tr. New Haven, Conn., 1953–7) attempts to give a unified account of 'symbolic representation'. Our systems of symbols constitute the world, since there is no reality in itself apart from our symbolizations. Conversely, man himself is essentially the source of various symbolizing activities. The philosopher's task is thus to describe man's symbolizing activities, and the categories involved in them, throughout history.   M.J.I.

*neo-Kantianism.

P. A. Schilpp (ed.), *The Philosophy of Ernst Cassirer* (New York, 1949).

casuistry. The art of resolving problems of *conscience. The starting-point for the exercise of casuistry is the individual case (*casus*) of conscience, and characteristically involves answering the question whether an act that an agent wishes to perform does or does not conflict with a law. The art, which was particularly associated with priests exercising pastoral care, fell into disrepute partly because of the multiplication of fine distinctions that began to be made as ways were sought of so describing the act in question that it did not conflict with a law with which it could otherwise be seen plainly to be in conflict. Such justificatory exercises were regarded as pandering to the vice of laxity. The art of casuistry, shorn of its laxist associations, is beginning to flourish again today within the field of professional, particularly *medical, ethics.   A.BRO.

Edmund Leites (ed.), *Conscience and Casuistry in Early Modern Europe* (Cambridge, 1988).

cat, Schrödinger's. A *quantum mechanical system supposedly exists in a superposition of states until a measurement or observation is made, whereupon the system will be found to exist in just one of those states—though it is impossible to predict with certainty which state that will be. As long as this picture is only held to apply to microphysical states, it may not appear unacceptably paradoxical. But the following *thought experiment suggests that the threat is not so easily contained.

Imagine a cat confined to a box containing a bottle of poisonous gas which will break, killing the cat, if and only if a device connected to it registers the radioactive decay of a radium atom. If the atom, device, and cat together constitute a quantum system, then it seems that this system will exist in a superposition of states unless and until an observer tries to determine which state it is in, by seeing whether or not the cat is dead. But this implies that in the absence of such an observation the cat is neither determinately dead nor determinately alive, which seems absurd.

This thought experiment was conceived by Erwin Schrödinger (1887–1961), an eminent Austrian physicist who was one of the founders of quantum mechanics. He also had philosophical interests.   E.J.L.

M. Lockwood, *Mind, Brain and the Quantum* (Oxford, 1989).
E. Schrödinger, *What is Life? and Mind and Matter* (Cambridge, 1944).

categorical imperative. The formal moral law in Kantian ethics, based on reason. It is opposed to hypothetical imperatives, which depend upon desires, e.g. 'Catch the 9.15—*if* you want to arrive by noon'. In its most famous formulation, it states that the 'maxim' implied by a proposed action must be such that one can will that it become a universal law of nature. I consider *lying to you so that you will lend me some money, my maxim therefore being 'Whenever I can gain something from it, I shall lie'. Can I will this to become a universal law of nature? No, for the practices of communication on which lying depends would break down. This is Kant's conception of *universalizability, based ultimately on fairness: why am I entitled to *free-ride on the honesty of others?   R.CRI.

C. D. Broad, *Five Types of Ethical Theory* (London, 1930), ch. 5.
I. Kant, *The Groundwork of the Metaphysic of Morals*, ed. H. Paton (New York, 1964).

categorical judgement. In traditional logic, categorical judgements affirm or deny a predicate of all or some of a subject, as in 'No coins are bent'. They are contrasted both with modal judgements, which express necessity (*apodeictic) or possibility (*problematic), as in 'Some coins are not necessarily bent', and also with complex judgements, in which two or more predicates or propositions are combined, as in 'Every coin is bent or shiny', 'If some coins are bent, some coin-makers are busy'.   C.A.K.

I. M. Copi, *Symbolic Logic* (New York, 1978), ch. 5.

categoricity. Informally, a *theory is categorical if it describes, or characterizes, only one structure. The idea is that all the models of the theory are notational variants of each other. Technically, two interpretations, M, N, of the same formal language are 'isomorphic' if there is a one-to-one function f from the domain of M on to the domain of N which preserves the structure. For example, if R is a binary predicate in the language, then for any elements x, y in the domain of M, R holds of the pair $\langle x, y \rangle$ in M if and only if R holds of the pair $\langle f(x), f(y) \rangle$ in N. A theory T is *categorical* if any two structures that satisfy T are isomorphic.   S.S.

John Corcoran, 'Categoricity', *History and Philosophy of Logic* (1980).

categories. The most fundamental divisions of some subject-matter. In the fifth century BC various philosophers, following Parmenides, decided that anything that was real could not come to be or go out of existence. But many *things, indeed most of the things around us, manifestly did both. Therefore they could not be in the fullest sense real. In fact some of them, like red or sweet, seemed not only to be intermittent but to depend for their existence on human or animal perception. Evidently they were things of a radically different kind from those which satisfied the requirements for full-blooded reality (Democritean atoms in this case).

This was probably the start of the idea that fundamental divisions can be made among things, and it was reinforced a little later when paradoxes arose in the nascent philosophy of language: if you try to treat the predicate of a sentence in exactly the same way as the subject you will end up by first naming the subject and then just naming the predicate, so that you won't have connected the predicate to the subject and won't have said anything *about* the subject at all. Evidently predicates were radically different kinds of things from subjects. The realization of this was one of the points brought out by Plato in his late dialogue the *Sophist*, where he caricatures as 'late learners' those who constructed paradoxes which depended on not realizing this point (251a).

The word 'category' comes from a word meaning 'accuse', and thence (in philosophy) 'predicate', perhaps via some sense like 'mark out as the relevant item for consideration' (cf. also 'accusative case' in grammar). Aristotle's *Categories* was the first attempt that survives at a division into fundamental kinds, and what it divides is predicates, which Aristotle treated as 'things', not as mere linguistic items. He can therefore be seen as embodying both the motifs discussed in the last two paragraphs. His own list of categories extends to ten, but he does not emphasize the number, and in one place (end of ch. 8) even seems to allow categories to overlap. The most important ones were the first four, substance, quantity, relation, quality, but more important still was the distinction between substance and the rest.

Various other philosophers have engaged in the enterprise of making grand divisions in things, notably the Stoics, who provided a list of four (substrate, qualified, disposed, relatively disposed) and Kant, who picked out certain concepts in terms of which any mind recognizably like the human mind would have to view reality if it was to make sense of it. It would, for instance, have to think in terms of *things* which had *properties*, and were *one* or *many*. Kant provided a structured list of twelve categories, in four groups of three, but his scheme has been treated as rather artificial and factitious, and of much less importance than the general idea that some such list must exist and governs our thinking. Hegel used the term rather more broadly for general divisions of thought and reality, which his system tended to fuse together.

In the twentieth century, theories of logical *types have arisen in answer to the logical paradoxes, but outside logic and its technical requirements attention has turned more to how far such grand overall classifications are possible. There is some danger of introducing so many categories that the enterprise becomes vacuous, a danger facing Ryle, though others (notably Sommers) have been more optimistic and have offered criteria for classifications of things that remain fundamental and do not run riot. But it seems doubtful that any scheme both simple and satisfying will be possible, and for the moment at any rate interest in the topic seems to have abated.   A.R.L.

*ontology.

F. Sommers, 'Types and Ontology', *Philosophical Review* (1963).
P. F. Strawson, 'Categories', in O. P. Wood and G. Pitcher (eds.), *Ryle* (London, 1970).

category mistake. The error of ascribing to something of one *category a feature attributable only to another (e.g. colour to sounds, truth to questions) or otherwise misrepresenting the category to which something belongs. (Ryle supposes we or some of us misrepresent the category to which the facts of mental life belong. We take them to be inner, ghostly events.) Metaphorical uses of a term may allow sentences to be true that would, if the term were used literally, embody a category mistake. For example, 'Time crawled'.   S.W.

G. Ryle, *The Concept of Mind* (London, 1949).

catharsis. Literally 'purgation' or 'purification', whether medical or religious. Aristotle's statement that *tragedy 'produces through pity and fear a catharsis of such *emotions' (*or* 'happenings'—the Greek can mean either) has usually been understood as indicating a purifying or release of pity and fear, in reply to Plato, who had attacked tragedy for encouraging them. For some recent interpreters, however, there is no direct reference to Plato or to the spectators' emotions, and Aristotle's primary claim is that drama clarifies or resolves the events it portrays. As so often, Aristotle's compressed and allusive way of writing makes the question impossible to decide.   R.W.S.

A. O. Rorty (ed.), *Essays on Aristotle's Poetics* (Princeton, NJ, 1992).

causal asymmetry. Causation seems to be an antisymmetrical relation, meaning that if an event a is a *cause of another event b, then b is not also a cause of a. But 'if and only if' is a symmetrical relation, so given two events causally related to one another, such that one happens if and only if the other happens, what determines which is the cause and which the effect? Some philosophers hold that the cause is always the earlier of the two events, and the effect the later, which presupposes that an effect cannot either precede its cause or be simultaneous with it. However, *backwards causation is thought by other philosophers to be at least metaphysically possible, not least because they think that *time-travel is metaphysically possible and would have to involve it. Alternatively, then, it may be suggested that the asymmetry of causation is grounded in the asymmetry of *explanation: causes *explain* their effects, but effects do not explain their causes. Explanation, it would seem, must be asymmetrical, because otherwise circular explanations would be legitimate.   E.J.L.

D. M. Hausman, *Causal Asymmetries* (Cambridge, 1998).

causality. The relation between two items one of which is a cause of the other; alternatively 'causation'. 'Causality' or 'causation' can also refer to a group of topics including the nature of the causal relation, causal explanation, and the status of causal laws.

In modern philosophy (as in modern usage in general) the notion of cause is associated with the idea of something's producing or bringing about something else (its effect); a relation sometimes called 'efficient causation'. Historically, the term 'cause' has a broader sense, equivalent to 'explanatory feature'. This usage survives in the description of Aristotle as holding 'the doctrine of the four causes'. The members of Aristotle's quartet, the material, formal, efficient, and *final cause, correspond to four kinds of explanation. But only the efficient cause is unproblematically a candidate for a cause that produces something distinct from itself.

Modern discussions tend to treat causality as exclusively or primarily a relation between *events. On this approach, examples of paradigmatic *singular* causal statements are 'The explosion caused the fire' and 'Her pressing of the button caused the opening of the door'. Paradigmatic *general* causal statements will be ones like 'Droughts cause famines'. Recasting ordinary causal statements in such forms is a Procrustean enterprise. The second example sentence is an awkward paraphrase of 'She opened the door by pressing the button', which does not *overtly* report a relation between events at all. The interpretation of ordinary causal talk is the subject of dispute. One contentious issue concerns the apparent commitment of ordinary language to *facts, as well as events, as causes. While this fact leads some philosophers to recognize a relation of fact causation, others (notably Davidson) argue that facts cannot, strictly speaking, be causes, although they are relevant to causal explanation.

What is distinctive of pairs of events related as cause and effect? Obviously, it is not *sufficient*, for an event to cause another, that the second happen after the first. (*Post hoc, ergo propter hoc.*) Further, it has been argued that this is not even necessary, and that both simultaneous causation and 'backwards causation' (effects preceding their causes) are at least conceptually possible. This poses a problem. Causality appears to be an *asymmetric* relation (if *a* caused *b*, then *b* did not cause *a*). But if temporal order cannot be relied on to explain the asymmetrical 'direction of causation', what can? Another difficulty is that of explaining what differentiates cause–effect pairs from effects of a common cause. It is no accident that the kettle switched itself off after it started to whistle: what, then, makes it false that the whistling caused the switching?

One important suggestion (which may or may not overcome these problems) is that causes *necessitate* the events that are their effects. (Rather confusingly, this can also be described as the idea that causes are sufficient for their effects (*necessary and sufficient conditions).) This proposal takes a variety of forms. In one version, it asserts that a relation of causal necessity holds between particular events, making one an inevitable consequence of another. Thus, when I heat the water, it *must* evaporate; when the first billiard-ball hits the second, the second ball *has to* move. Hume is famous for a sceptical attack on this notion of a necessitating tie between cause and effect.

However, the idea that causes necessitate (are sufficient for) their effects has another interpretation, congenial to 'Humean' empiricists, who refuse to countenance a relation of causal necessity. Under this interpretation, the necessity for the second billiard-ball to move when the first hits it is only a *hypothetical* or *conditional* necessity: necessity 'given the laws of nature'. Roughly, to say that event *a* necessitated event *b* need be to say no more than that it is a consequence of the laws of nature that when *a* occurred, so did *b*. (*Covering-law model; *explanation.) If—as empiricists standardly hold—the laws of nature are contingent, rather than necessary truths, necessity-given-the-laws is not in danger of reintroducing the necessitating ties between events discussed in the previous paragraph. If there had been different laws of nature—as, on this empiricist view, there could have been—perhaps water need not have evaporated when heated, even though the

actual laws entail that it invariably does so. (The empiricist theory of causation just described is a species of what is known as a 'regularity theory'. On the anti-empiricist view that laws of nature are necessary truths, what is necessary-given-the-laws will be itself necessary. This is perhaps how some ratio-nalist philosophers saw the necessity of causal connections (*laws, natural or scientific).)

It has been argued that if a particular event is the effect of a combination of causes, it may be false that any of these causes necessitated the effect. (Suppose that Smith's early morning swim caused his heart attack, but only in conjunction with his champagne breakfast.) One response to this is the proposal (inspired by J. S. Mill) that a cause is an *element* in a set of conditions that *jointly* necessitate (are sufficient for) its effect. J. L. Mackie's treatment (in 1965) of causes as 'INUS conditions' ('Insufficient but Necessary parts of Unnecessary but Sufficient conditions') is a version of this approach. Another problem is that 'necessitation' accounts of causation require that causality be deterministic. They must therefore be abandoned, or at least modified, if (as some contemporary philosophers suppose) causality can be fundamentally probabilistic. (*Determinism.)

One notable rival to the accounts of the causal relation mentioned so far is David Lewis's *counterfactual analysis of event-causation. This ingeniously exploits the idea that effects are typically 'counterfactually dependent' on their causes: if the announcement caused the riot, it seems to follow that if the announcement had not occurred, neither would the riot.

Many theories of causation involve a principle that Davidson calls 'the nomological character of causality': where there is causality, there is causal law. However, some philosophers believe that there are species of causality independent of causal law. This claim is most commonly made about human agency. (The issues here are complex: *action; *agent; *reasons and causes; *teleological explanation; also *social science; *laws, natural or scientific.)

The 'regularity theory' mentioned earlier is a descendant of one of Hume's definitions of cause: 'an object, followed by another, and where all the objects similar to the first are followed by objects similar to the second'. According to a standard interpretation, Hume argued that nothing in the world deserves the name of causal necessity. At most there are certain *constant conjunctions—exceptionless regularities—between events. We are conditioned, by regularities in our experience, to form an idea of causal necessity, and thus to suppose that the second billiard ball not only *will*, but *must*, move when the first one strikes it. But *this* idea of causal necessity—being, as Kant put it, 'a bastard of the imagination, impregnated by experience'—has no legitimate application to the world.

This account of Hume's views is so well established that regularity theories of causation (denying causal necessity, and analysing causality in terms of (contingent) constant conjunctions) are standardly described as 'Humean'. However, this traditional interpretation is under attack, and several recent commentators argue that Hume did not deny the existence of genuine causal necessity.   P.J.M.

*necessity, nomic.

D. Hume, *A Treatise of Human Nature* (1739), ed. L. A. Selby-Bigge and P. H. Nidditch (Oxford, 1978), I. iii.
—— *An Enquiry Concerning Human Understanding* (1748), ed. L. A. Selby-Bigge and P. H. Nidditch (Oxford, 1975), sect. VII.
E. Sosa and M. Tooley (eds.), *Causation* (Oxford, 1993).
J. L. Mackie, 'Causes and Conditions', *American Philosophical Quarterly* (1965); repr. in *The Cement of the Universe: A Study of Causation* (Oxford, 1974).

causa sui. This Latin phrase means 'cause of itself'. Some theologians maintain that *God is self-caused, but this claim is quite problematic. Any exercise of causal power presupposes the cause's existence, and so its existence cannot be the result of such an exercise. Even an omnipotent being cannot bootstrap itself into existence. For this reason, God is more commonly thought of as the uncaused cause of the existence of all contingent things, and God's existence is supposed to need no cause because it is necessary.   P.L.Q.

D. Braine, *The Reality of Time and the Existence of God: The Project of Proving God's Existence* (Oxford, 1988).

causation, backwards: *see* backwards causation.

causation, downwards. The alleged causal influence of higher-level phenomena on lower-level processes, a notable example being the supposed causation of the physical by the mental. Although Cartesian *dualism may seem to provide the most obvious case, the question of downward causation more properly arises in the case of *monistically conceived structures arranged hierarchically. Science since the seventeenth century typically holds that higher-level features, including the kind we call mental, can be explained in terms of the features and behaviour of the more basic elements and structures of which the systems are composed. Reductive *physicalism denies that there are higher-level systems with causal powers of their own, while non-reductive physicalists and emergentists claim that higher-level structures, with properties uninferrable from those of their constitutive parts, can influence the presence or absence of properties both at the same level (same-level causation) and at a lower level (e.g. mental-to-physical). Some philosophers argue that with consciousness and reason at the top, downwards causation provides for a notion of *free will.   A.H.

*emergent properties.

John Heil, *The Nature of True Minds* (Cambridge, 1992), ch. 4.
John R. Searle, *Rationality in Action* (Boston, 2001).

causation, mnemic: *see* mnemic causation.

cause: *see* causality; backwards causation; causal deviance; constant conjunction; final causes; laws, natural or scientific; mnemic causation; necessity, nomic; reasons and causes; plurality of causes; *post hoc ergo propter hoc*; thinking causes.

causes, final: *see* final causes.

causes and reasons: *see* reasons and causes.

cave, analogy of. In *Republic* VII Plato represents the philosophically unenlightened as prisoners chained from birth in an underground cave, able to see nothing but moving shadows, which they take to be the whole of reality. The world outside the cave represents the *Forms and the escape of the prisoners from the cave the process of philosophical enlightenment.   C.C.W.T.

*appearance and reality.

J. Annas, *An Introduction to Plato's Republic* (Oxford, 1981), ch. 10.

Cavell, Stanley (1926–). American philosopher (at Harvard) who has written in such diverse areas as aesthetics, ethics, philosophy of mind, and epistemology. Cavell's earlier work is perhaps best known for its sympathetic presentation of 'ordinary-language philosophy' and its interpretation and extension of the philosophy of the later Wittgenstein. Throughout his career, Cavell has also written much about philosophically traditional and non-traditional aesthetic topics, including the ontology of *film, Hollywood comedy, television, and so on. This work is often simultaneously philosophy, art criticism, and cultural criticism. His interdisciplinary tendency, his stylistic flair, his interest in authors and topics neglected in most contemporary Anglo-American philosophy, all test the boundaries of the discipline, while his depth in dealing with basic philosophical problems such as scepticism should persuade even the most academically conservative of philosophers (if such persuasion were necessary) of Cavell's primary identity as a philosopher.   E.T.S.

Stanley Cavell, *Must We Mean What We Say?* (New York, 1969).

cement of the universe. Hume's description of resemblance, contiguity, and causation—the three relations which induce people to associate ideas, and hence to build up their picture of the world. 'As it is by means of thought only that any thing operates upon our passions, and as these are the only ties of our thoughts, they are really *to us* the cement of the universe, and all the operations of the mind must, in a great measure, depend on them' (*An Abstract of A Treatise of Human Nature*).

The Cement of the Universe, J. L. Mackie's fine study of causation, takes its title from Hume, as well as sharing his empiricist perspective and his general conviction that causal necessity is 'upon the whole . . . something, that exists in the mind, not in objects' (*Treatise*, I. iii. 14).   J.BRO.

*causality.

J. L. Mackie, *The Cement of the Universe* (Oxford, 1974).

central-state materialism. A theory of mind which came into its own as the weaknesses of Ryle's *behaviourism became evident—especially its inability to provide for non-vacuous explanation of action. According to Ryle, for Jones to believe that aspirin relieves headaches is for it to be true that whenever Jones has a headache he takes aspirin. But this means that explaining why Jones takes aspirin when he has a headache, by saying that he believed aspirin relieves headaches, is exactly the same as explaining it by saying that Jones takes aspirin whenever he has a headache. Ryle's account must be wrong since it implies that what is obviously a substantial explanation is mere repetition of words. The central state theorists, chiefly Smart and Armstrong, maintained that there are inner mental states which are responsive to external stimuli and causally explain consequent behaviour. These states, they argued, are material states of the central nervous system. The theory was empirical, holding that identification of the mental with the material is to be a matter of future discovery, rather like the way lightning has been discovered to be an electrical discharge, or water to be a collection of H_2O molecules. However, the idea that types of mental states identify with types of material states later gave way to a token *identity theory.   O.R.J.

D. M. Armstrong, *A Materialist Theory of Mind* (London, 1968).

certainty. A proposition is said to be certain when it is indubitable. A person is certain of a proposition when he or she cannot *doubt it. It is thus possible that someone may be certain of something (or feel certain of it) when it can in fact be doubted. In his First Meditation, Descartes suggested that much that we normally take to be certain is in fact dubitable, and he held the controversial view that *scepticism will be defeated only if genuine certainty is available.   C.J.H.

A. R. White, *Modal Thinking* (Oxford, 1975), ch. 5.

ceteris paribus. 'Other things being equal.' Certain scientific *laws are not true without some qualification to the effect that nothing interferes or that all else remains the same. For example, if the supply of some good is constant and demand increases, then the price of that good will increase too—but only if the shopkeepers are rational, they are not distracted by a fire in the shop, they are interested in increased profits instead of, say, unloading stolen merchandise, and so on. Such laws, it seems, are subject to the following dilemma. Either the law is left without proviso, in which case it seems false, or a proviso is added, rendering the law trivial—price increases unless, for some reason, it does not. Whether the problem affects just the soft sciences or goes all the way down to physics is a matter of debate.
                                                    J.GAR.

C. G. Hempel, 'Provisos: A Problem Concerning the Inferential Function of Scientific Laws', in A. Grünbaum and W. Salmon (eds.), *The Limits of Deductivism* (Berkeley, Calif., 1988).
M. Lange, 'Natural Laws and the Problem of Provisos', *Erkenntnis* (1993).

Chalmers, David (1966–). In his book *The Conscious Mind* (1996), David Chalmers has written probably the lengthiest and certainly the most sophisticated defence of the possibility of *zombies and how we should face up to them. These are not the undead inhabitants of horror movies but, rather, benighted creatures physically identical to us but with one great lack. There is nothing it is like to be them: no ouchiness of their pain or panginess of their hunger (philosophers call these properties 'phenomenal properties'). If zombies are possible, *physicalism is false. The key move in Chalmers's defence stems from his insistence that, if physicalism were true, there should be a priori necessary *truths detailing the connection between physical and phenomenal properties. But, he argues, there aren't. So phenomenal properties aren't physical. It turns out that they are worse than that. Since there will always be a complete physical explanation of the workings of our brain and bodily movements, phenomenal properties turn out to be entirely inefficacious. Chalmers explains how this result is not vitiated by the fact that he has written and published a book seemingly stimulated by the existence of these inefficacious features of the world.
                                                    P.J.P.N.

David Chalmers, *The Conscious Mind* (New York, 1996).

chance. In ordinary use, this term is interchangeable with 'probability' in 'The chance of heads is ½' but not in 'Shall we take a chance and hire him?' Among experts, however, there are more distinctions, or attempted distinctions, between 'chance', 'probability', 'degree of belief', 'relative frequency', 'propensity', 'likelihood', and some others. For a given coin-tossing device, we may think of (1) the actual frequency of heads in a given series of tosses, (2) the betting-rate a given person would offer on heads for a prospective toss, (3) what the frequency would be for some prospective 'long' run, (4) the dispositional condition of the device to produce heads, and other related things. We may come to disagree over whether we are identifying something definite and whether to call it 'chance'.

A traditional question in philosophy concerns the view that nothing ever really happens merely 'by chance'. On this view, even though the probability or chance of heads for a single toss may be explained in various theories as being ½, it will none the less be true that the outcome of the toss was causally determined in advance. In this discussion 'mere chance' is seen by its proponents as a feature of events that, contrary to metaphysical *determinism, are not completely caused by antecedent events, and, contrary to metaphysical *libertarianism, are not caused by 'free agents' either.   J.C.

Ian Hacking, *The Emergence of Probability: A Philosophical Study of Early Ideas about Probability, Induction and Statistical Inference* (Cambridge, 1975).
K. R. Popper, 'The Propensity Interpretation of Probability', *British Journal of the Philosophy of Science* (1959).

change. Alteration, change of size, rotation, and translation are unimpeachable varieties of change. Russell counted it sufficient for change that the same thing should be true at one time and false at another; on this conception (sometimes called the 'Cambridge' conception), something's arising out of nothing could be a change. Others want to distinguish change from replacement and debate whether, for this purpose, we must suppose that throughout any change there is something (the thing it befalls) that remains in existence, or can allow one thing to pass away into another. Whether change really occurs becomes problematic for some philosophers of time, for instance those who deny there is any real difference between the past and the future. Another problem is whether we need distinct categories of changes that occur and objects that exist and have properties. Certainly we speak differently of objects and changes; objects are conceivable and describable, changes reportable and understandable; and whether objects can be reduced to changes or conversely has been debated for as long as the analogous question about the physical and the psychological. Davidson is an object–change dualist, but most philosophers from Heraclitus to Russell prefer just one sort of basic entity. w.c.

*process; Cambridge change.

Donald Davidson, *Essays on Action and Events* (Oxford, 1980), essay 6.

chaos. The opposite of order. Some schools of Greek *cosmogony sought to explain the origin and existence of the orderly world or universe (cosmos) by distinguishing between an unformed primordial chaos and the cosmos produced by the imposition on chaos of an order, or regular arrangement. In politics there is a dogma, denied only by anarchists and classical Marxists, that unless imposed by the *State, social order will collapse into chaos. A.BEL.

Gregory Vlastos, *Plato's Universe* (Oxford, 1975).

chaos theory. The theory of apparently random behaviour within a deterministic system, such as the weather. The unpredictability of a chaotic system is not due to any lack of governing laws but to the outcome being sensitive to minute, unmeasurable variations in the initial conditions. An example is the 'butterfly effect': the idea that the mere flap of a butterfly's wing can make the difference between a hurricane occurring and not occurring. A.BEL.

*determinism, scientific.

Ian Stewart, *Does God Play Dice? The New Mathematics of Chaos*, 2nd edn. (Oxford, 2002).

character. A person's moral nature. Moral philosophy after the rejection of Aristotelianism concentrated on discrete acts, not on the character of moral agents. Since the recent revival of interest in the *virtues by Anscombe and others, character has re-emerged. Cultivation of good character is seen as pivotal to moral life, and an understanding of character provides a standpoint for ethical criticism of oneself and others. Some have said that such understanding comes more from novels than philosophy.

Aristotle, however, has much to say about virtuous and vicious character and personality. The virtues of character are stable dispositions to feel and to act at the right time, towards the right people, etc. (this is Aristotle's 'doctrine of the *mean'). A virtuous character develops out of the reflective performance of virtuous acts. R.CRI.

*duty; integrity; loyalty.

G. E. M. Anscombe, 'Modern Moral Philosophy', *Philosophy* (1958).
Aristotle, *Nicomachean Ethics* II–IV.

characteristic: *see* attribute; qualities; properties.

characteristica universalis. Artificial written *language, intended to express ideas rather than represent speech-sounds. Inspired by Chinese ideograms, it was envisaged by Francis Bacon solely as a medium for international communication, but by Descartes, Leibniz, and others as also a way of achieving the systematization and completion of scientific knowledge. George Dalgarno and John Wilkins were leading authors of such languages. Leibniz wanted his language to function additionally as a logical calculus.

While many *artificial languages, such as Esperanto, have been used for international communication, and many others have been coined for logical or mathematical investigation or for taxonomic purposes, these projects seem to be too different from one another to have been ever usefully combined in a single linguistic system. L.J.C.

L. J. Cohen, 'On the Project of a Universal Character', *Mind* (1954).

charismatic authority: *see* authority.

charity, principle of. A principle of interpretation. In its simplest form, it holds that (other things being equal) one's interpretation of another speaker's words should minimize the ascription of false beliefs to that speaker. For example, it suggests that, given the choice between translating a speaker of a foreign language as expressing the belief that elephants have wings and as expressing the belief that elephants have tusks, one should opt for the latter translation. Several variants of the principle have been proposed; for example, that translation should (*ceteris paribus*) minimize the ascription of *inexplicable* error. The principle is prominent in the work of Davidson, who adopts it as a generalization of a maxim proposed by Quine. (Quine takes the label 'principle of charity' from a principle about reference formulated by N. L. Wilson.) P.J.M.

*radical interpretation

D. Davidson, *Inquiries into Truth and Interpretation* (Oxford, 1984).

cheating, in the paradigm case, involves intentionally violating the rules of a game in order to achieve its built-in goal, but the violation cannot be incorporated into the game. It is unlike fouling in basketball, which has set penalties and is often done openly. Although cheating is closely related to both breaking a promise and deceiving, it is distinct from both. Cheating is not playing the game as the rules require. Promises, even implicit promises, are always made to a particular person or group of persons. Cheating depends on a social institution rather than on personal interaction. It necessarily involves violating the rules of an activity that no one participating in that activity is allowed to violate. That is why cheating normally involves deception. However, when a boss plays golf with his subordinates, he may sometimes cheat quite openly, e.g., not count missed strokes, or remove the ball from the rough without taking a penalty. Cheating requires neither deception nor breaking a promise.   B.G.

B. Gert, *Morality: Its Nature and Justification*, ch. 8 (Oxford, 1998).

chemistry, philosophy of. Perhaps the most contentious issue in the philosophy of chemistry is whether there is such a subject. That various episodes and concepts in the history of chemistry may be used to illustrate or explore philosophical positions is not in doubt: 'phlogiston' has been used as an example of a theoretical term that appears to have *meaning even though it lacks *reference, and Mendeleev's use of the Periodic Table has been used to assess the role of prediction in the *epistemology of scientific *theory. But the phrase 'philosophy of chemistry' implies a set of philosophical problems peculiar to chemistry, and this is threatened by the assumption, widely held amongst philosophers, that chemistry is somehow reducible to physics. This may explain why, apart from the odd, isolated article, a self-conscious body of literature on the philosophy of chemistry has emerged only in the last twenty years.

Challenging the assumption of *reductionism is, not surprisingly, a preoccupation of a number of recent champions of this new and expanding field, though not to the exclusion of other issues. The reduction of chemistry to physics may take one of two forms: (a) *theoretical* (otherwise *epistemological* or *conceptual*) reduction, in which the *laws and concepts of chemistry are derived from those of physics, and (b) *ontological* reduction, in which chemical properties are held to supervene upon more basic physical ones. The main focus of debate has been (a) rather than (b), although (b), mirroring as it does a similar, and much-disputed, *super-venience thesis in the *philosophy of mind, should not be taken for granted. Under (a), relevant issues include the definition of chemistry itself—should we characterize it in macro-physical terms as the study of substances and their transformation into other substances, or in micro-physical terms as the study of atoms, molecules, and their interaction? What is it for two things to be of the same (chemical) substance? Is this something definable only at the molecular, or sub-molecular level? What is a chemical 'law'?—Is it exceptionless? Does it involve *natural kinds? Should we adopt *realism about its terms?

The neglect of chemistry in traditional analytic philosophy may have had a significant effect on the course of certain debates. We might reasonably ask, for instance, how the nature of *causality would have been represented if chemical, rather than mechanical, interaction had been taken as the paradigm; or how plausible the direct realist account of *perception would have seemed if the paradigm sense had been, not vision, but the chemical senses of smell and taste.   R.LE P.

*kind, natural; laws, natural or scientific, reductionism; supervenience.

Nalini Bhushan and Stuart Rosenfeld (eds.), *Of Minds and Molecules: New Philosophical Perspectives on Chemistry* (Oxford, 2000).
Eric Scerri (ed.), *Synthese* issue on philosophy of chemistry, vol. 111 (1997).

children and philosophy. Although Collingwood and Popper both say that they first became interested in philosophical questions around the age of eight, such precocity seems rare. But could things be otherwise? In some educational circles there is growing enthusiasm for introducing children, sometimes very young ones, to philosophical thinking. A pioneer since the early 1970s has been Matthew Lipman of Montclair State College, New Jersey, whose Philosophy for Children programme has become influential globally. Based partly on philosophical novels specially written for children, it engages school classes from age nine upwards, or even earlier, in elementary discussions about such things as knowledge, personhood, and moral values.

The idea that young children can philosophize may seem counterintuitive, owing to the capacity for abstract, or higher-order, thinking that philosophizing requires. It has drawn criticism, for instance, from Piagetians who hold that young children are still at the stage of concrete rather than formal cognitive operations. On the other hand, children not uncommonly wonder whether numbers go on for ever or where space ends. Does this in itself show a capacity for philosophizing? Or would a more adequate test be whether or how far they proceed beyond such wonderings into engagement with the hard philosophical thinking about infinity and the nature of numbers and of space which seeks answers and does not stop at questions?

Much turns in these debates on what counts as philosophizing. The strangeness of the notion of children's philosophizing—which brings it much attention from the media and from educationalists—derives from the thought that children must be doing much the same sort of thing as fully fledged philosophers, only in a more embryonic form. There is far less counterintuitiveness in the idea that children can *think about* things—the material they study in school, for instance, or how they ought to behave. Lipman *et al.* say that 'Children begin to think philosophically when they begin to ask why'. (Is this true? Not all 'why' questions are philosophical in the usual sense.) The work of those involved in teaching children philosophy—and teaching teachers to teach it to them—seems sometimes to operate at this sub-philosophical level as judged by the more stringent criterion.   I.P.W.

M. Lipman, *et al.*, *Philosophy in the Classroom*, 2nd edn. (Philadelphia, 1980).

G. Matthews, *Philosophy and the Young Child* (Cambridge, Mass., 1980).

J. White, 'The Roots of Philosophy', in A. P. Griffiths, (ed.), *The Impulse to Philosophise* (Cambridge, 1992).

See also *http://plato.stanford.edu/entries/children/*

Chinese philosophy. Philosophical thought in China has a predominantly practical character, being motivated primarily by a concern with the ideal way of life for human beings and, for some schools of thought, also by a concern to maintain social and political order. This predominantly practical orientation is, however, also coupled with a reflectivity which has led to the development of views about such subjects as the use of language and ways of assessing doctrines, the nature of human beings and their place in the cosmic order, or the basic constituents of the universe and the explanation of differentiation and change. The following provides a historical sketch of the development of major movements of thought in China.

Chinese philosophical thought is often supposed to have originated and blossomed in the last few hundred years of the Chou dynasty (mid-eleventh century to 249 BC), before the unification of the country by Ch'in (221–206 BC). Philosophical movements of this 'classical' period were classified, retrospectively after the end of the period, into schools of thought, many of which were driven by a concern to seek a remedy for the social and political disorder of the times and a way to conduct oneself amidst the disorder. The Confucian school, represented by Confucius (sixth to fifth century BC), Mencius (fourth century BC), and Hsün Tzǔ (third century BC), diagnosed the disorder as due to the disintegration of traditional values and norms which underlie the social hierarchy, and advocated the restoration of such values and norms as a remedy. It emphasized cultivation of the self to embody such values as loyalty and filial piety, and regarded the attractive and transforming powers of moral examples as ideally the basis for government. Mencius and Hsün Tzǔ differ in their understanding of human nature and the self-cultivation process. While Mencius regarded human nature as 'good' in that human beings have certain incipient ethical inclinations which should be nurtured for one to become virtuous, Hsün Tzǔ, in rhetorical opposition to Mencius, described human nature as 'evil' in that human beings are born with self-regarding desires that need to be transformed for one to become virtuous.

The Mohist school, originating with Mo Tzǔ (fifth century BC), diagnosed the disorder as stemming from strife and contention which were due to a partial concern for oneself, one's family, or one's state. As a remedy, it advocated an equal concern for everyone, as opposed to the kind of graded affective concern advocated by Confucians. Another point of opposition was the Mohist rejection of traditional practices advocated by Confucians, such as elaborate funerals and musical activities, which the Mohists regarded as detrimental to the material well-being of the common people. The Yangist school, associated with Yang Chu (fifth to fourth century BC), diagnosed the disorder as stemming from the preoccupation of individuals, especially those in office, with power and material possessions, even to the detriment of one's bodily well-being. It advocated a concern with one's own bodily well-being as a way of steering attention away from power and material possessions; order will be restored if those in office, including the ruler, all share such an outlook. Yangist thought is sometimes regarded as a precursor to Taoist thought, represented by Chuang Tzǔ (fourth century BC) and the text *Lao Tzǔ* (date uncertain). The Taoist school diagnosed the ills of the times as due to striving after worldly goals, adherence to social conventions and moral teachings, and other artificial impositions preventing human beings from functioning in a way continuous with the natural order. It advocated a life free from such impositions, one which is supposed to lead to both personal fulfilment and orderly coexistence.

Some schools of the period did not share such broader ethical concerns. Legalist thought, with Han Fei Tzǔ (third century BC) as a major exponent, was directed primarily to the ruler and concerned how a ruler can maintain effective government. Unlike Confucians, who emphasized moral examples and education in government, the Legalists emphasized the need for the ruler to build up prestige and to institute a clearly propagated system of laws enforced strictly by punishment. Hui Shih and Kung-sun Lung of the fourth century BC, associated with the School of Names, were interested in the mechanisms of argumentation and how they can be deployed to yield paradoxical conclusions, such as the well-known proposal by Kung-sun Lung that a white horse is not a horse. The Yin–yang school was interested in cosmology, and portrayed the operation of the world as involving the interplay between two forces or elements, yin, which is negative, passive, and weak, and yang, which is positive, active, and strong.

A number of major thinkers of the Han dynasty (206 BC–AD 220) were self-professed Confucians and defended the Confucian ideal, though they also drew on Taoist and yin–yang cosmological ideas. For example, the Confucian Tung Chung-shu (second century BC) regarded the operation of the human realm and that of the natural realm as regulated by the same forces and hence as corresponding to each other. Just as the operation of the natural order involves yin and yang, yin being subordinated to yang in its operation, human beings are born with bad and good elements, and should subsume the former to the latter. In the political realm, just as the natural order operates in a cyclical fashion as illustrated by the change of seasons, political changes in history also proceed in a cyclical fashion. Tung's view on human nature drew upon the views of both Mencius and Hsün Tzǔ, and Han Confucian thought was often characterized by the interplay of ideas drawn from both of these two classical Confucian thinkers.

Philosophical thought in the Wei (220–65) and Chin (265–420) dynasties involved divergent developments of

Taoist thought, yielding an important commentary on the *Lao Tzǔ* by Wang Pi (226–49) and one on the *Chuang Tzǔ* by Kuo Hsiang (d. 312), who either borrowed from or built on a commentary by Hsiang Hsiu (*fl.* 250). While some thinkers of the period lived a life of disregard for social conventions and values, Wang Pi and Kuo Hsiang viewed the Taoist ideal as compatible with the more traditional ways of life advocated by the Confucians. They even interpreted Confucius as someone who had attained the highest Taoist ideal and manifested it in his daily life without having to discourse on it, unlike Lao Tzǔ and Chuang Tzǔ, who still had to discourse on the Taoist ideal because they had not personally attained it.

Chinese translations of Buddhist scriptures from India were known to have existed as early as the second century AD, and the influence of Buddhism grew until it reached its peak during the Sui (581–618) and T'ang (618–907) dynasties. While some Chinese schools of Buddhism were further developments of existing schools in India, others were innovative interpretations of Buddhist thought, such as the T'ien-t'ai, Hua-yen, and Ch'an (Zen) schools, which were influential among intellectuals. Buddhist ideas had influence on the later development of Confucian thought, such as its metaphysical orientation and the view held by some schools that all human beings have a pure Buddha nature which has become defiled by erroneous thoughts and clingings; such defilement is the source of suffering, and its elimination will restore the original purity of the Buddha nature.

Confucian thinkers at the end of the T'ang, such as Han Yü (768–824) and Li Ao (eighth to ninth century), opposed Buddhism, criticizing it for neglecting familial, social, and political responsibilities. Han Yü regarded Mencius as the true transmitter of Confucius' teachings, and Li Ao interpreted the Mencian idea that human nature is good to mean that human beings have a perfectly good nature which has been obscured. Both ideas became generally accepted among Confucian thinkers of the Sung (960–1279) and Ming (1368–1644) dynasties, who showed a degree of interest in metaphysical speculations that was absent in classical Confucian thought. The most prominent and influential Confucian thinkers of the period were Chu Hsi (1130–1200) and Wang Yang-ming (1472–1529), who, while sharing the view that human beings are born with a perfectly good nature which has been obscured by distortive desires and thoughts, were opposed on a number of issues. For example, while Chu regarded knowledge as ideally guiding action, Wang held the view that knowledge ideally accompanies but does not guide action. Also, while Chu emphasized the examination of daily affairs and the study of classics and historical records as part of the process of self-cultivation, Wang emphasized one's attending directly to the mind, constantly watching out for and eliminating distortive desires and thoughts. Confucian thought of the Sung–Ming period, often referred to as 'Neo-Confucianism', made significant contributions to our understanding of the subtle workings of the mind and the methods of self-transformation.

Confucians at the end of the Ming and during the Ch'ing dynasties (1644–1912) regarded Sung– Ming Confucians as influenced by Taoist and especially Buddhist ideas in their interpretation of Confucian thought. For example, while Mencius regarded human nature as good in the sense that human beings share certain incipient ethical inclinations which will develop into a fully virtuous disposition with adequate nourishment, Sung–Ming Confucians interpreted the Mencian position in terms of the idea that human beings have a perfectly good nature which has been obscured by distortive desires and thoughts. This idea they even illustrate with analogies drawn from Taoist and Buddhist texts, such as that of the sun being obscured by clouds or the mirror being obscured by dust. Ch'ing Confucians, the best known of whom include Wang Fuchih (1619–92), Yen Yüan (1635–1704), and Tai Chen (1724–77), distanced themselves from metaphysical speculations and instead sought to recover the true meaning of Confucian thought via careful and critical study of the Confucian classics, with attention to philological and textual details. Though the idea that Mencius was the true transmitter of Confucius' teachings had become part of Confucian orthodoxy by this time, some Confucian scholars of this period, such as Tai Chen, also drew heavily on Hsün Tzǔ's teachings.

Western philosophical and political ideas were introduced and some works translated into Chinese at and after the end of the Ch'ing, and this, along with increasing knowledge of scientific and technological advances of the West, led to debates about the extent to which traditional Chinese culture, which is predominantly Confucian in character, should be retained, discarded, or transformed. Social and political ideas, such as Marxist and democratic ideas, had impact in the political realm, while exposure to Western philosophical ideas led to reconstitutions of Chinese philosophical systems. While Marxist thought was expounded and developed in mainland China, development of Confucian thought which takes into account recent Western scientific, philosophical, and democratic ideas was a vital intellectual movement in Hong Kong, Taiwan, and overseas Chinese communities. This revitalized interest in Confucian thought has now also gained attention in mainland China as well as in Western countries such as the United States.

K.-L.S.

*Confucianism; Taoism; Buddhist philosophy; Japanese philosophy; Korean philosophy.

A Source Book in Chinese Philosophy, tr. and ed. Wing-tsit Chan (Princeton, NJ, 1963).

Encyclopedia of Chinese Philosophy, ed. Antonio S. Cua (London, 2003).

Fung Yu-lan, *A History of Chinese Philosophy*, tr. D. Bodde, 2 vols. (Princeton, NJ, 1952–3).

Journal of Chinese Philosophy (Oxford).

Philosophy East and West (Honolulu).

Sources of Chinese Tradition, tr. and ed. W. Theodore De Bary, Wing-tsit Chan, and Burton Watson (New York, 1960).

Chinese room. A thought experiment invented by John Searle to establish that nothing could think simply by being a computer. Imagine yourself in a room with two windows, and a large book of instructions. Through one window come pieces of paper with marks on them; you follow the instructions and match the pieces of paper with others which you pass out through the other window. Searle says this is analogous to the set-up inside a computer: you are simply producing output in response to input according to certain rules. But suppose that the input to the room really consists of questions in Chinese, and the output consists of answers. You do not understand Chinese; yet you do all that a computer does. So nothing could understand Chinese simply by manipulating symbols according to 'formal' rules. As Searle puts it, 'syntax is not sufficient for semantics'.   T.C.

*functionalism; consciousness, its irreducibility; mind, syntax, and semantics.

J. Preston and M. Bishop (eds.), *Views into the Chinese Room: New Essays on Searle and Artificial Intelligence* (Oxford, 2002).
John Searle, 'Minds, Brains and Programs', in John Haugeland (ed.), *Mind Design* (Cambridge, Mass., 1981).

Chisholm, Roderick (1916–99). American philosopher at Brown University who was influential particularly in the areas of metaphysics, philosophy of mind, epistemology, and ethics. Apart from his purely philosophical work, he was known as a scholar of the Austrian philosopher Franz Brentano, whose work he translated into English.

In metaphysics Chisholm is open and precise about his ontological commitments, which, according to his later writings, include only attributes and individual things. On this basis, Chisholm characterizes the distinction between *mind and body in terms of the differing identity-conditions of the two. Following Bishop Butler, he maintains that persons persist through time in a 'strict and philosophical' sense whereas that in which bodies persist through time is merely 'loose and popular'. He consequently holds that a person is distinct from his body and is either a monad—an individual having no proper parts—or a microscopic piece of matter located within the body, probably in the brain.

In epistemology Chisholm was an influential *foundationalist. His notion of the epistemic enterprise is that it is an attempt to answer the Socratic questions 'What do I know?' and 'What can I know?' It presupposes that the inquirer can find out the answer to these questions, that *knowledge is justified true belief, and that a belief may be justified and yet not true, and true and yet not justified. Chisholm's commitment to the second of these presuppositions caused him to devote a great deal of time to the 'Gettier problem'. His commitment to the third led him to reject externalist accounts of justification in terms of reliability.   H.W.N.

*counter-example, philosophy by; foundationalism.

Roderick Chisholm, *Person and Object* (London, 1976).
—— *Theory of Knowledge* (Englewood Cliffs, NJ, 1987).

choice, axiom of. A set, roughly, is a collection of things, which may themselves be sets. Consider, for example, an infinite set of (non-empty) sets, no two of which have a common member. Must there be a way of choosing just one member from each of these sets? 'Yes' is what the axiom of choice says. Many apparently diverse mathematical principles turn out to be equivalent to it. None the less its use aroused controversy. In some cases we may be unable to *define* such a way of choosing (known as a *choice function*), hence use of the axiom was rejected by those who held that, for sets and functions, to be is to be definable.   M.D.G.

A. Fraenkel, Y. Bar Hillel, and A. Levy, *Foundations of Set Theory* (Amsterdam, 1973), ch. 2, sect. 4.

Chomsky, Noam (1928–). American linguist and philosopher whose pioneering work on language, *Syntactic Structures* (1957), and devastating 'Review of B. F. Skinner's *Verbal Behaviour*' (in *Language* (1959)) led to the cognitive revolution, and the demise of behaviourism, in psychology. Languages are largely identified by their structure, so, for Chomsky, *linguistics is the study of the structure of human languages. He also argues that the theory of language is the theory of a speaker's knowledge of language—knowledge represented in the mind of the individual. So linguistic theory becomes the study of those linguistic structures represented in the minds of speakers which constitute their knowledge of language. Thus linguistics is a branch of cognitive psychology which studies the mental structures responsible for linguistic competence. Linguistic competence is just one of the interacting components which contribute to the production of linguistic behaviour, so the latter can provide only a rough guide to the speaker's linguistic knowledge. A theory of competence aims to factor it out from the performance data of language use by eliciting judgements from speakers about which strings of words belong to their language (i.e. which strings they find grammatical), then constructing a *grammar that generates all and only those grammatical strings.

Chomsky uses the term 'grammar' to mean both the theory formulated by the linguist and an internal component of the speaker–hearer's mind. This is legitimate so long as the grammar provides a model of the speaker–hearer's competence: a finite means for generating the potential infinity of linguistic forms a speaker–hearer can produce or recognize. Part of the task in explaining what the speaker knows is to account for this creativity: that by the age of 4 most children can produce and recognize a huge range of sentences they have never heard before, by rearranging familiar words into new but legitimate configurations. The best available hypothesis is that they have mastered a system of grammatical knowledge which it is the task of the linguist to describe. Because the grammatical rules or principles are not consciously known and cannot be explicitly stated by the speaker–hearer, Chomsky infers that they must be unconsciously, or tacitly, known. This mentalist hypothesis serves to explain why speaker–hearers conform to complex generalizations that go beyond what could be picked up from the available linguistic evidence.

The philosopher Quine has criticized Chomsky's position claiming that all we have to go on is behavioural dispositions of speakers, and that these do not discriminate between different descriptively adequate grammars speakers could be using to assign structure to sentences they recognize as belonging to their language. But although the evidence is behavioural, the theoretical constructs posited to explain it do not have to be. By postulating the grammars that underlie linguistic behaviour, Chomsky can formulate generalizations which explain speakers' linguistic judgements and use, including the gaps we find in the data.

Another task is to explain how children with such different cultural backgrounds, intelligence, and experience learn, without explicit training, and at much the same age, to speak their native language. How do speakers acquire knowledge of language? In Chomsky's view, a large part of this knowledge is innate, a matter of a biological endowment specific to humans. Speakers move from an initial state of the language faculty, which they share, to an attained state, which they develop on exposure to the primary linguistic data. The initial state is characterized by the principles of *universal grammar: a finite set of interactive principles which allow for parametric variation within a certain range. The variety of human languages is explained by the different vocabularies and parameter settings of the universal principles which characterize the attained states of the language faculty in different speakers. Chomsky distinguishes E-language—the common notion of languages like Dutch, English, German—which is hopelessly vague, and I-language—the internal language of an individual speaker–hearer— which is the proper object of scientific study.

In addition to his work in linguistics, Chomsky has been an active critic on the left of the political spectrum and has published far-reaching criticisms of US domestic and foreign policy.   B.C.S.

*indeterminacy of meaning; heredity and environment; minimalism.

N. Chomsky, *Deterring Democracy* (London, 1992).
—— *Knowledge of Language: Its Nature, Origin and Use* (New York, 1986).
—— *The Minimalist Program* (Cambridge, Mass., 1995).
—— *New Horizons in the Study of Language and Mind* (Cambridge, 2000).
A. George (ed.), *Reflections on Chomsky* (Oxford, 1989).
W. V. Quine, 'Methodological Reflections on Current Linguistic Theory', in D. Davidson and G. Harman (eds.), *Semantics of Natural Language* (Dordrecht, 1972).

choosing and deciding. These have most often been taken by philosophers to be mental events or processes that may issue in ordinary actions, but sometimes choices are identified with the ordinary actions themselves. There are fundamental similarities between choices and decisions. One is that both involve selecting from a range of options, or at least between two options. Another is that neither a choice nor a decision, as against a belief, is true or false. A third is that both may be bound up with intentions.

However, there are some differences between choices and decisions. It seems that I can choose without deliberating, but not decide without deliberating. I can choose out of habit, but can I decide out of habit? Also, it is at least more natural to speak of deciding and not choosing what is true.

Choosing and deciding form a philosophical problem of their own, indicated above. Are they things that precede ordinary bodily *actions—and if so, are they acts themselves—or are they parts of or bound up with or identical to those ordinary actions themselves? (Choosing and deciding, after all, are things we *do*. Not only traditional behaviourists have identified choices with ordinary actions.) If they are taken as mental acts which precede ordinary actions, and are needed to make bodily movements into actions, must they themselves be preceded by other acts? If so, we seem to have an infinite regress. How, exactly, do choosing and deciding relate to intentions? It may be supposed, for example, that they often consist in the formings of intentions.

Choosing and deciding come into a number of larger philosophical problems. When taken as *mental events, they are part of the problem of the nature of those events: for example, whether they are different from or identical with brain events. Choosing and deciding are also central to certain moralities, and to the dispute between those who focus morally on the antecedents of actions and those, often called consequentialists, who focus on the consequences of actions. Above all, choosing and deciding enter into the debate about freedom and determinism. Here libertarians assert that freedom requires choices or decisions which are originations, as distinct from effects of previous causes. Others assert that free choices or decisions are events quite consistent with determinism.   R.C.W.

*behaviourism; intention; freedom and determinism; volition; will; compatibilism and incompatibilism.

A. Donagan, *Choice: The Essential Element in Human Action* (London, 1987).
T. Honderich, *How Free Are You?* 2nd edn. (Oxford, 2002).
Gilbert Ryle, *The Concept of Mind* (London, 1949).

Chrysippus (*c.*280–207 BC). Third head of the Stoic school and formalizer of its doctrines, said to have written over 700 works; 'without Chrysippus there would have been no Stoa', i.e. no Stoic school. He invented propositional logic as a formal system. Unruly emotions he interpreted as false judgements, refusing to allow a conflict between rational and irrational parts of the psyche, and interpreting the experience of being torn between alternatives as an oscillation, too rapid to be perceived, between different judgements of what is best. Drawing on contemporary scientific ideas, he developed the explanation of divine agency in terms of a 'breath' (spirit, *pneuma*) penetrating all things, and also contributed to the theory of causation. He devoted much energy to arguing for the universality of divine providence and the compatibility of responsibility and determinism.   R.W.S.

*Stoicism.

A. A. Long, *Hellenistic Philosophy* (London, 1974).
—— and D. N. Sedley (eds.), *The Hellenistic Philosophers* (Cambridge, 1987). Texts and commentary.

Chuang Tzŭ (4th century BC). Master Chuang was a Chinese Taoist thinker often described as espousing a kind of scepticism or relativism. His full name was Chuang Chou, and his teachings are probably recorded in the first seven chapters (the inner chapters) of the text *Chuang Tzŭ*. The text highlights the observation that there is no neutral ground for adjudicating between opposing judgements made from different perspectives. Realization of this is supposed to lead to a relaxation of the importance one attaches to social institutions and conventions, and to such distinctions as those between right and wrong, self and others, and life and death. This results in a lessened emotional involvement in such things, and ideally one is supposed to respond spontaneously to situations one is confronted with, with no preconceived goals or preconceptions of what is right or proper.   K.-L.S.

*Confucianism; Taoism.

Chuang Tzŭ: The Inner Chapters, tr. A. C. Graham (London, 1981).

Chu Hsi (1130–1200). Confucian thinker in China best known for having developed an elaborate Confucian philosophy which synthesizes ideas from earlier thinkers. He drew heavily on Ch'eng I's (1033–1107) teachings, and scholars often refer to his teachings and their later developments as the Ch'eng–Chu school. He regarded things as composed of pattern–principle, which is incorporeal and unchanging, and ether–material-force which is physical and changeable. Human beings are born with insight into pattern–principle by virtue of which they are fully virtuous, but the endowment of ether–material-force can be impure, involving distortive desires and thoughts which obscure such insight. Self-cultivation requires one's examining daily affairs and studying classics and historical records to regain the insight into pattern–principle which has been obscured.   K.-L.S.

*Confucianism; Taoism.

Reflections on Things at Hand: The Neo-Confucian Anthology Compiled by Chu Hsi and Lü Tsu-ch'ien, tr. Wing-tsit Chan (New York, 1967).

Church, Alonzo (1903–95). One of the most significant figures in the development of mathematical logic, Alonzo Church is credited with two major discoveries. First, making use of his ingenious notion of lambda-definability, which he employed to capture the intuitive concept of 'effectively calculable', Church was able to demonstrate that for a large number of formal systems, even simple arithmetic, there are no effective decision procedures for the provable well-formed formulae. This means that it is not possible to construct, even theoretically, a computing machine that would identify the valid sentences of simple arithmetic. Second, Church discovered that the mathematical notion of recursiveness as defined by Gödel coincides exactly with what is lambda-definable and thus formulated the hypothesis, which textbooks refer to as *Church's thesis, that the informal notion of effective computability is characterized by recursiveness and various other equivalent notions. While the first discovery was generally regarded as somewhat startling, the second confirmed what had been widely believed but unproven. Both results were discovered by Church during the 1930s. In 1944 Church published his landmark text *Introduction to Mathematical Logic*, a work which was subsequently revised and enlarged in later editions. Much later in life Church turned his attention to the philosophy of language and eventually produced a remarkably detailed logic of sense and denotation.   G.F.M.

A. Church, *Introduction to Mathematical Logic* (Princeton, NJ, 1956).
—— 'Outline of a Revised Formulation of the Logic of Sense and Denotation', 2 parts, *Nous* (1973).

Churchland, Paul (1942–), who currently teaches at the University of California, San Diego, is most closely associated with a form of materialism known as *'eliminativism', a movement which has its roots in the aftermath of Logical Positivism. He believes that the explanations of human mental processes in terms of intentions, desires, motives, and reasons are explanations of human behaviour which belong to what is described, pejoratively, as *'folk psychology' (a term which is now very widely used). Folk psychology is primitive science. It has not progressed and developed in the way that pukka natural sciences have. Eliminativism states that its terms can be expected to fall into desuetude as we increasingly explain human behaviour in terms of the concepts of neuro-science.
                                                           R.A.S.

Paul Churchland, 'Eliminative Materialism and Propositional Attitudes', *Journal of Philosophy* (1981).
—— *The Engine of Reason, the Seat of the Soul* (Cambridge, Mass., 1995).

Church's thesis. A number-theoretic *function is computable if there is an *algorithm, or mechanical procedure, that computes it. The procedure should specify what is to be done at each step, as a function of the input only, without involving any creativity on the part of the agent. Computability is an informal, or pre-formal, notion in that it has meaning independently of, and prior to, its formal development. In contrast, recursiveness, Turing-computability, and lambda-definability are rigorously defined properties of number-theoretic functions, which were formulated in the mid 1930s, as part of different programs in logic. A function is recursive, for example, if its values can be derived from a fixed set of equations in a certain form. These technical notions were shown to be coextensive. It is reasonably clear that every recursive function is computable, since an algorithm can be 'read off' a recursive derivation or a Turing machine. Church's thesis is the assertion that a function is computable if and only if it is recursive, Turing-computable, etc. Thus, Church's thesis identifies the extension of a pre-formal notion with that of an explicitly defined rigorous notion.   s.s.

*logic, history of.

Martin Davis (ed.), *The Undecidable* (New York, 1965).
Hartly Rogers, *Theory of Recursive Functions and Effective Computability* (New York, 1967).

Cicero, Marcus Tullius (106–43 BC). Roman statesman, orator, and prolific writer, over-annotated by classical scholars and underestimated by recent philosophers. Educated at Athens, his Latin expositions of *Hellenistic philosophy, mostly written between February 45 and November 44 BC, are the source for otherwise lost Stoic, Epicurean, and Academic arguments. Often in dialogue form, always clearly and fairly presented, his philosophical writings include *De finibus* and *De officiis* on ethics; *De natura deorum* and *De divinatione* on the philosophy of religion; and *Academica* on sceptical epistemology. *De legibus* and *De republica* are justly famous for their assertion of human rights and the brotherhood of man. The latter contains the influential account of natural law (III. xxii. 33): universal because based upon the common nature of man, and binding because part of the divine reason and order permeating all that is. *De legibus* includes Cicero's affirmation of the equality of all men (I. x. 28–32). Cicero's influence on European thought from *natural-law theorists down to and beyond Hume's *Dialogues Concerning Natural Religion* is incalculably great.   J.C.A.G.

T. A. Dorey (ed.), *Cicero* (London, 1965).
P. MacKendrick, *The Philosophical Books of Cicero* (London, 1989).
J. Powell (ed.), *Cicero the Philosopher* (Oxford, 1995).

circle, Cartesian: *see* Descartes.

circle, vicious: *see* vicious circle.

circle, virtuous: *see* virtuous circle.

circularity. A sequence of *reasoning is circular if one of the premisses depends on, or is even equivalent to, the conclusion. Circularity is not always fallacious, but can be a defect in an argument where the conclusion is doubtful and the premisses are supposed to be a less doubtful basis for proving the conclusion. Normally an argument is used in such a way that the line of support goes from the premisses to the conclusion:

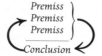

But if it is required that the conclusion be used to support one of the premisses, the resulting circle destroys the purpose of the argument. Circularity is not always obvious, or on the surface of a text of discourse. In some cases, it takes quite a bit of analysis of the argument to expose the circle in the reasoning. Circularity can also be a problem, in some cases, in explanations and definitions.   D.N.W.

*vicious circle; virtuous circle.

Douglas N. Walton, *Begging the Question: Circular Reasoning as a Tactic of Argumentation* (New York, 1991).

citizenship. Within political philosophy, citizenship refers not only to a legal status, but also to a normative ideal—that the governed should be full and equal participants in the political process. As such, it is a distinctively democratic ideal. People who are governed by monarchs or military dictators are subjects, not citizens. In Aristotle, citizenship was viewed primarily in terms of duties— citizens were legally obliged to take their turn in public office, and sacrificed part of their private life to do so. In the modern world, influenced by *liberalism, citizenship is increasingly viewed as a matter of *rights—citizens have the right to participate in public life, but also the right to place private commitments ahead of political involvement. Republican philosophers, following Rousseau, worry that contemporary democracies have focused too much on rights, and not enough on civic duties.   W.K.

*democracy.

Paul A. B. Clarke (ed.), *Citizenship: A Reader* (London, 1993).
W. Kymlicka, *Multicultural Citizenship* (Oxford, 1995).

civil disobedience. Unlawful public conduct designed to appeal to the sense of justice of the majority, in order to change the law without rejecting the rule of law. Thus non-violence and non-revolutionary intent, as well as a willingness to accept lawful punishment, are often treated as defining conditions of civil disobedience. The term itself was apparently coined by the American naturalist Henry David Thoreau (1817–62), in reference to his refusal to pay a state poll tax enacted to finance enforcement of the Fugitive Slave Law (and thus southern chattel slavery).

As in Thoreau's case, civil disobedience may be indirect; the law violated may not itself be the target of protest. As a form of non-violent mass protest, civil disobedience was made famous by Mohandas K. Gandhi (1869–1948) as one tactic among several intended to relieve India of British rule. It played an important albeit less revolutionary role in the United States's civil rights movement during the 1960s.

Civil disobedience may be usefully contrasted with lawful protest (boycotts, picketing), unlawful violent disobedience (for some, non-violence is part of the very definition of civil disobedience), conscientious objection or passive obedience (a willingness to accept lawful punishment rather than comply with an unjust law, without any intention of changing the law), and with testing the constitutionality of a law (which typically requires a plaintiff whose standing to protest is gained by a nominal violation of the law).

Civil disobedience may well be a futile tactic in any society whose government is indifferent to the rule of law. In a constitutional democracy, it is justified to the extent that the remedies provided by law have been tried but to no avail, that it is aimed at protesting a basic injustice, and that it holds out a reasonable prospect of success without grave costs to society. If the law being protested is of dubious constitutionality, prosecution and punishment of the protesters must take this into account.   H.A.B.

*political violence; rule of law; terrorism.

H. A. Bedau (ed.), *Civil Disobedience in Focus* (London, 1991).
Vinit Haksar, *Civil Disobedience, Threats and Offers: Gandhi and Rawls* (Delhi, 1986).
Peter Singer, *Democracy and Disobedience* (Oxford, 1973).

civil liberties. Freedom of speech, press, assembly, and worship ('conscience') are central among the privileges and immunities claimed as civil liberties. Liberal political philosophies accord them the highest priority, regard them as valuable both instrumentally and intrinsically, and seek to extend them equally to all persons. To protect them against abuse from popular majorities and the government, they are often enshrined in a constitution (as in the Bill of Rights of the US Constitution of 1791); their day-to-day defence can be secured only through an independent bar and judiciary. There is no exhaustive and exclusive list of civil liberties, nor is there any standard criterion that demarks them from civil or human *rights.
                                                                                      H.A.B.

*liberalism; liberty.

Richard L. Perry (ed.), *Sources of Our Liberties* (New York, 1952).

civil society. From Aristotle's *koinōnia politikē* down to Locke's 'political or civil society' and Ferguson's 'civil society', this term indicated civilized, political society in contrast to barbarism, paternal authority, and the state of nature. It was translated into German as *bürgerliche Gesellschaft*, which also suggests 'bourgeois society', and thus came, in Hegel, to indicate economic and social arrangements in contrast to both the state and the family. Civil society in this sense did not become apparent before the emergence of an economy transcending the household and of centralized monarchical or revolutionary states clearly distinct from the social and economic life of their subjects. For Hegel civil society was an inevitable and valuable aspect of modern life. Marx disparaged it as benefiting primarily the bourgeoisie and operating outside conscious, i.e. political, control. For liberals, a thriving civil society is an obstacle to 'totalitarian' attempts to absorb all social life into the political realm and provides a training ground for democratic politics. Radical liberals such as Hayek contrast the free interactions of civil society with the coercion of the state, and advocate the minimization of the state's sphere of activity.   M.J.I.

Adam Ferguson, *An Essay on the History of Civil Society 1767* (Edinburgh, 1966).
G. W. F. Hegel, *Elements of the Philosophy of Right* (Cambridge, 1991).
F. A. von Hayek, *The Road to Serfdom* (London, 1944).

Clarke, Samuel (1675–1729). English rationalist philosopher and theologian; champion of Newton, admired by Voltaire, sacked as chaplain for unorthodoxy.

Clarke's main writings on moral philosophy and natural theology are contained in his Boyle lectures, which he delivered in 1704 and 1705. In the first set he uses a mathematical method to prove the existence of God, and in the second he argues (against Hobbes and others) that *moral judgements can be as certain as those in mathematics: gratitude (for example) is fitting to a situation in which we have been done a favour just as triangles can be shown to be congruent. 'Iniquity is the very same in action, as falsity or contradiction in theory; and the same cause which makes one absurd, makes the other unreasonable.' In 1706 he translated Newton's *Opticks* and in 1717 published a correspondence, *The Leibniz–Clarke Correspondence*, in which he defended Newtonianism (with Newton's approval) against the criticisms of Leibniz.   R.S.D.

The Leibniz–Clarke Correspondence, ed. H. Alexander, with intro. and notes (Manchester, 1956).

class. The term 'class' is often used interchangeably with 'set' to denote what might loosely be called a collection of things, these things being the members of the class. The members of a class may be specified either by means of a list or by reference to a *property which all and only the members of the class possess. The identity of a class is entirely determined by the identity of its members.

Some writers on *set theory reserve the term 'proper class' to denote collections which are not sets because they are allegedly 'too big' to be themselves members of sets. The thought that there can or must be such collections arises from the threat of *paradox which ensues from supposing that certain properties—such as the property of being a set—can serve to specify the membership, and thus the existence, of corresponding sets, such as a set of all sets.
                                                                                      E.J.L.

W. V. Quine, *Set Theory and its Logic* (Cambridge, Mass., 1969).

class struggle. In the *historical materialism of Marx, the chief mechanism of historical change and development. Social relations of production divide people into groups with a common situation and common economic interests. These groups are classes potentially, and become so actually through social consciousness and a political movement representing the class's objective interest in achieving and maintaining a set of production relations in which the class is dominant. That class tends to be dominant whose rule at that time best promotes the use and further development of the productive powers of society. Marx's analysis of modern society identifies a number of classes, including the feudal nobility, the peasantry, and the petty bourgeoisie, but it views the antagonism between *bourgeoisie and proletariat the principal class struggle which will be decisive for the historical future of modern society.   A.W.W.

*progress.

Hal Draper, *Karl Marx's Theory of Revolution*, ii: *The Politics of Social Classes* (New York, 1978).

John Roemer, *A General Theory of Exploitation and Class* (Cambridge, Mass., 1982).

E. P. Thompson, *The Making of the English Working Class* (Harmondsworth, 1968).

clear and distinct ideas. Rationalists make use of the notion in formulating theories of cognitive error, establishing standards of evidence, characterizing some mental life, and identifying and describing the principal axioms of their systems, among much else. Clear ideas, for Descartes, are perceptions present and manifest to an attentive mind, cognitive analogues to objects strongly and clearly presented in vision. Distinct ideas are perceptions delineated from all others, containing nothing but that which is clear. For Descartes, we avoid error by assenting only to those things which we clearly and distinctly perceive.   J.GAR.

Descartes, *Meditations* IV, in J. Cottingham, R. Stoothoff and D. Murdoch (eds.), *The Philosophical Writings of Descartes* (Cambridge, 1985).

Clifford, William Kingdon (1845–79). A British philosopher and mathematician who died young from tuberculosis, Clifford was one of the first *'evolutionary epistemologists', in that he tried to marry the Kantian philosophy about a priori knowledge with Darwinian evolutionary theory, arguing that what is ontogenetically innate may be phylo-genetically learned. Our ancestors may have had to work through various geometries by trial and error, whereas we can now know them instinctively.

Emboldened by this sensible epistemological conclusion, Clifford then gave full rein to his metaphysical imagination, arguing that as well as 'objects', things we perceive, there are also 'ejects', *things we know of without perception. Apparently these latter involve minds, and Clifford concluded by arguing that ultimately all existence involves mind, which makes itself manifest through evolution. This Spinozistic world-view was the forerunner of many such theories of 'creative evolution', popular at the beginning of this century.   M.R.

*evolutionary epistemology.

W. K. Clifford, *The Common Sense of the Exact Sciences* (London, 1885).

—— *The Ethics of Belief and Other Essays*, ed. T. Madigan (Amherst, NY, 1999).

A. S. Eddington, *The Nature of the Physical World* (Cambridge, 1929).

clip an angel's wings

Do not all charms fly
At the mere touch of cold philosophy?
There was an awful rainbow once in heaven:

We know her woof, her texture; she is given
In the dull catalogue of common things.
Philosophy will clip an Angel's wings,
Conquer all mysteries by rule and line,
Empty the haunted air, and gnomed mine—
Unweave a rainbow.
          (John Keats, 'Lamia', pt. ii, lines 229–37)

Keats's Romantic anti-intellectualism continually undermines the moral of his story, certainly as it was originally recounted by Philostratus and in Burton's *Anatomy of Melancholy*. The philosopher Apollonius saves his handsome pupil Lycius from marrying a woman-seeming snake. Arriving uninvited at their wedding-feast, he transfixes her with his eyes and shouts her name, until, her illusion unmasked, she vanishes with a frightful shriek. Keats of course loves the enchanting cheat, loathes the philosopher who exposes her.   J.O'G.

clocks, known in Europe in the thirteenth century, improved much in the seventeenth century. They provided the imagery for three memorable philosophical views.

Descartes left unsolved a problem about the relation of mind and body. If the mind and body are substances of different kinds, how can they affect each other, as they seem to do in action and perception? The 'two clocks' theory, suggested by Geulincx, and enthusiastically embraced by Leibniz, was that the mind and body do not in fact interact at all: they merely run in parallel, like two clocks that go through corresponding movements, though each is independent of the other.

To illustrate his distinction between real and nominal *essence, Locke refers to the great Strasbourg clock of 1547. In addition to showing the time and the day of the week, this clock had a marvellous series of moving forms, to represent Death, Christ, the planets, the four periods of life, and the gods that gave their names to the seven days of the week. The 'gazing Country-man' who only observes the 'outward appearances' of the clock has a very different idea of the clock from the expert who knows 'all the Springs and Wheels, and other contrivances within' (*Essay Concerning Human Understanding*, III. vi. 3, 9). The country-man knows the nominal essence, but not the real essence from which the outward appearances flow. In the face of hidden complexities of plants, animals, and even minerals and metals, all of us are in the position of the gazing Country-man, and therefore cannot hope to classify these things according to their real essences.

On the third usage of the image, the whole world is regarded as a clock or watch. Like these artefacts it operates according to pure mechanical principles; as a watch requires a watchmaker, however, the world must also be the creation of a Creator, though (unless the watch is thought to need winding up) it evolves independently of the Creator once it has been brought into existence. The classic objections to this kind of natural theology are found in Hume's *Dialogues Concerning Natural Religion*.   J.BRO.

*parallelism; God.

G. W. Leibniz, 'New System of Nature' (1695), Postscript to Letter to Basnage to Beauval (1696).

R. S. Woolhouse, *Locke* (Brighton, 1983), sect. 11.

cloning. The technique of 'nuclear transfer' or 'cloning' involves removing the nucleus of an unfertilized egg (human or animal) and substituting a nucleus taken from the cell of another individual. The donor cell determines almost all of the genetic characteristics of the embryo. There are two possible purposes of cloning by nuclear transfer: research and reproduction. Research here offers the possibility of studying a range of genetic diseases, such as motor neurone disease. Ethical objections can only be from those who oppose any kind of research on the embryo. Objections to reproductive cloning are of two main kinds. First, the desire to produce a genotype of oneself, or a dead child, seems an unsatisfactory basis for child rearing. Secondly, the desire to create a clone of oneself as a bank of spare organs for possible transplant seems to be a paradigm of treating another human being solely as a means. For these reasons reproductive cloning is illegal in the UK.   R.S.D.

John Harris, *Clones, Genes and Immortality* (Oxford, 1998).

——and Soren Holm (eds.), *The Future of Human Reproduction* (Oxford, 1998).

closure. As used in philosophy, a domain of objects is closed with respect to some relation just in case the relation never holds between sets of objects some of which are inside the domain and some outside. One of the most common applications is to causal closure: physicalists hold that physical events are closed under causation— nothing physical is caused by anything non-physical such as mental events, nor do physical phenomena cause mental phenomena. In logic, a domain is closed under a set of operations if the result of applying any of those operations to a member of the domain results in something that is itself in the domain. Thus, the integers are closed under the operations of addition, subtraction, and multiplication, but not under division.   P.H.

coercion occurs if one party intentionally and successfully influences another by presenting a credible threat of unwanted and avoidable harm so severe that the person is unable to resist acting to avoid it. For the threat to be credible, either both parties must know that the person making the threat can make good on it, or the one making the threat must successfully deceive the person threatened into so believing. A mere perception of coercion is not sufficient for coercion.

Sometimes 'coercion' is used in a broader, and more judgemental, sense to designate forms of pressure or influence that take unfair advantage or inappropriately compromise the quality of autonomy. This account is overly broad and introduces an improper moral judgement into the meaning of the term.

Coercion itself should be distinguished from so-called coercive situations. These situations involve *non-intentional*

situations of control—e.g. situations of illness and economic necessity—in which persons feel controlled by the situation rather than by the design of another person.
                                                      T.L.B.

J. Feinberg, *Harm to Others*, vol. 1 of *The Moral Limits of the Criminal Law* (New York, 1984).

R. Nozick, 'Coercion', in S. Morgenbesser, P. Suppes, and M. White (eds.), *Philosophy, Science and Method: Essays in Honor of Ernest Nagel* (New York, 1969).

Cogito ergo sum. Perhaps the most celebrated philosophical dictum of all time, Descartes's 'I am thinking, therefore I exist' is the starting-point of his system of knowledge. In his *Discourse on the Method* (1637) Descartes observes that the proposition *je pense, donc je suis* is 'so firm and sure that the most extravagant suppositions of the sceptics [are] incapable of shaking it'. The dictum, in its better-known Latin version, also occurs in the *Principles of Philosophy* (1644). In the *Meditations* (1641), the canonical phrase does not occur, but Descartes argues instead that 'I am, I exist is certain as often as it is put forward or conceived in the mind.' Descartes later observed that the meditator's indubitable awareness of his own existence was 'recognized as self-evident by a simple intuition of the mind'. There is a partial anticipation of Descartes's Cogito in Augustine, *De Civitate Dei*, 11. 26.   J.COT.

*certainty; doubt; scepticism.

P. Markie, 'The Cogito and its Importance', in J. Cottingham (ed.), *The Cambridge Companion to Descartes* (Cambridge, 1992).

cognition. Traditionally this has been regarded as the domain of thought and inference, marking the contrast with perceptual experiences and other mental phenomena such as pains and itches. Sensations, perceptions, and feelings are all distinguished from episodes of cognition since they provide input to the domain of thinking and reasoning but are not thoughts themselves.

More recently, cognition has been conceived as the domain of representational states and processes studied in cognitive psychology and *cognitive science. These are phenomena involved in thinking about the world, using a language, guiding and controlling behaviour. The new definition embraces some aspects of sensory perception where this involves representations of a spatial world and the intelligent processing of sensory input.

Theories of cognition can span occurrent conscious events like seeing, thinking, and reasoning, dispositional states such as intentions, beliefs, and desires, and nonconscious states which occur in the early stages of visual and linguistic processing. The domain of cognitive theory is broader than the realm of the propositional attitudes, regarded by many philosophers as the space of reasons. Cognitive states lying beyond the space of reasons will not be governed by the norms of rationality which tell us what we ought to think, given what we believe, and what we ought to do, given our intentions and desires. Instead, they will be governed by computational or causal laws of cognitive psychology which may or may not be sensitive to the intentionality or 'aboutness' of the cognitive states to which they apply.

It has been argued that states lying outside the space of reasons can have no representational content since they are not presented to a subject of experience, but belong instead to a thinker's subsystems. However, empirical psychology has enjoyed considerable success in explaining many of our mental activities by using generalizations framed in terms of the contents of states of our cognitive subsystems. Typical examples include: Chomsky's views about the mental representation of linguistic knowledge; research into the processes the visual system employs to construct 3D representations of objects from 2D retinal images; the processes which facilitate the recognition of faces, or visual word recognition. Sceptics about the representational contents of states of these cognitive systems must provide some alternative means to explain these findings.

Due to these successes cognitivism has largely replaced *behaviourism in scientific psychology. Instead of explaining human activities by means of stimulus and response, intellectual capacities are now to be explained by postulating inner mental states which combine semantic content and causal powers to affect behaviour. The ambition of cognitive science in developing a naturalistic theory of mind is to provide a satisfactory and unifying treatment of these two properties for the vast range of our cognitive states. It hopes to do this by treating mental processes as computational processes. (*Computers.) Transitions between representational states are defined as computations, performed on the representational vehicles of those contents. Syntactic processes that explain the causal transitions between mental representations run parallel to the inferential relations between their contents.

Opposition to this computational hypothesis takes many forms. Some accept that the laws of psychology are computational but argue that, since they are syntactic and formal, mental states and processes can be scientifically explained only if they are syntactically explained. The syntactic theory of mind retains the causal power of cognitive states while jettisoning their contents. Other critics seek to limit the ambition of cognitive science, claiming that the realm of propositional attitudes (*folk psychology) and the phenomenon of consciousness resist scientific explanations of the type which account for cognitive subsystems. Others still consider psychological explanations in terms of belief and desire to be instrumentalistic, and claim that for genuine explanations of intelligent behaviour we must resort to the details of micro-cognition.

Cognitive theories will impose different architectures on the domain of cognition, but most accept a broad division between the states of a person involving in experience and reasoning, and informational states of subpersonal processing systems. Whether this boundary is drawn in terms of consciousness, or conceptual and non-conceptual content, it marks an important place for collaboration between philosophers and psychologists. One such example is Jerry Fodor's theory of *cognitive architecture, which sees the mind as modular, comprising several perceptual input systems that supply information to the central domain of thinking and reasoning. Fodor argues that the central system must make use of sentence-like structures in a *language of thought. Opponents in psychology and computer science propose rival cognitive architectures, including some that reject the symbolic representation entirely.   B.C.S.

> *consciousness, its irreducibility; content, nonconceptual; frame problem; thinking; reasoning; perception; parallel distributed processing.

A. Clark, *Microcognition* (Cambridge, Mass., 1989).
M. Davies, 'Thinking Persons and Cognitive Science', in *AI and Society*, vol. 4 (1990).
J. A. Fodor, *The Modularity of Mind* (Cambridge, Mass., 1983).
S. Stich, *From Folk Psychology to Cognitive Science* (Cambridge, Mass., 1985).

cognitive architecture. A term used in theories of cognition to describe the functional organization of the mind into component parts. Human cognition is seldom studied as an undifferentiated whole. Rather, it is subdivided into specific domains of information (e.g. visual, auditory, linguistic information), or into distinctive tasks accomplished by the cognitive mind (e.g. face recognition, speech processing, reasoning). Various cognitive architectures have been proposed to explain our capacities to respond to such information or to perform such tasks. Faculties are posited that encode domain-specific information of a visual or linguistic kind, and dedicated cognitive mechanisms are postulated that perform the operations required to complete specific tasks. The overall organization of faculties or interaction of mechanisms is the architecture of the cognitive mind. On one view, the mind is a collection of modules—where a module is a cognitive mechanism that works in isolation from other modules on a restricted range of inputs and outputs. On another, the mind has a connectionist architecture where processing is global, taking place across a network of connected and active nodes. Competing claims about the mind's capacities and limitations are thought to flow from the choice of cognitive architecture.   B.C.S.

J. A. Fodor, *The Mind Doesn't Work That Way: The Scope and Limits of Computational Psychology* (Cambridge, Mass., 2000).

cognitive meaning. An element of *meaning which accounts for an expression's not just standing for something but representing it in a particular way. This explains how a speaker can attach different significance to two words for the same thing. Expressions share the same cognitive meaning when and only when a speaker who understands those expressions regards them as synonymous. Whether different speakers can share the same cognitive meaning to an expression depends on whether their judgements concerning the sameness and difference in meaning for this and other related expressions coincide.   B.C.S.

> *emotive and descriptive meaning.

M. Dummett, *Frege: Philosophy of Language* (London, 1973), ch. 19.

cognitive science is the interdisciplinary investigation of *cognition by psychology, linguistics, neuroscience, artificial intelligence (AI), and philosophy. Cognitive science treats reasoning, perception, and other cognitive processes as information-processing, involving the manipulation of mental representations. Cognitive scientists also hold either that these mental processes can be modelled by computers, or that these processes actually are computational processes (i.e. that the mind is a computer). One dominant ('classical') approach in cognitive science treats the computational processes as defined over a representational system in which the symbols have semantic and syntactic properties. Jerry Fodor's 'language of thought' hypothesis is the theoretical paradigm for this approach. An alternative approach, which emerged in the mid-1980s, is known as 'connectionism', and denies that mental representations have syntactic structure. According to connectionists, mental representations are processed in parallel, and their representational content is holistically distributed across entire networks of simple representational units. While connectionists claim that their approach is more biologically realistic than the classical approach—their models are sometimes called 'neural networks'—critics of connectionism have argued that it cannot do justice to the fact that cognition is systematic: for example, the fact that thinkers who can think that A loves B can also entertain the thought that B loves A. The need to integrate the science of cognition with the developing theories of the human brain has led to the development of *cognitive neuroscience*, which has attempted to integrate data provided by brain-imaging technology into a better understanding of how the brain underpins mental faculties.   T.C.

*artificial intelligence; Chinese room; connectionism; neuroscience; parallel distributed processing.

Ernest Lepore and Zenon Pylyshyn (eds.), *What is Cognitive Science?* (Oxford, 1999).
Robert A. Wilson and Frank Keil (eds.), *The MIT Encyclopedia of the Cognitive Sciences* (Cambridge, Mass., 1999).
'The Philosophy of Neuroscience' and 'Cognitive Science', in *The Stanford Encyclopedia of Philosophy*, http://plato.stanford.edu

cognitivism: *see* non-cognitivism.

Cohen, G. A. (1941–). Canadian political philosopher who has specialized in the study of *Marxism. He is a leading proponent of 'analytical Marxism'—the view that the traditional doctrines of Marxism should be understood and evaluated using the methods of Anglo-American analytical philosophy. Cohen has attempted to reformulate Marx's doctrines of *alienation, exploitation, and *historical materialism, culminating in his *Karl Marx's Theory of History: A Defence* (1978). His aim has been described as the 'demystification' of Marxism, by clarifying or eliminating the metaphysical and teleological concepts which Marx inherited from Hegel. Since then, he has worked on broader issues of justice, focusing in particular on contemporary liberal and libertarian attempts to justify private property and economic inequality. Cohen is currently the Chichele Professor of Social and Political Theory at the University of Oxford.   W.K.

G. A. Cohen, *History, Labour and Freedom: Themes from Marx* (Oxford, 1988).

Cohen, Hermann (1842–1918). Philosopher of Judaism, founder of the Marburg school of Kantian philosophy. Son of a cantor and son-in-law of the liturgical composer Lewandowski, Cohen studied at Jewish and secular institutions, winning his Marburg chair after brilliantly defending Kant's a priori time and space. He went on to argue that all principles of knowledge are *a priori: all objects are mental constructs; Kantian *things-in-themselves, untenable. Newtonian physics demonstrates the reality of science and so the possibility of a priori judgements. But science progresses. It is never complete. Supplementing Kant's ethics with Aristotelian and biblical ideas of virtue and justice, Cohen championed universal human dignities and rebutted the anti-Semitic historian Treitschke, defending the loyalty of German Jews by appeal to the Kantian respect for moral subjects implicit in Jewish ethics. On his retirement, Marburg snubbed his chosen successor, Ernst Cassirer, and appointed Paul Natorp. Bitterly disappointed, Cohen moved to Berlin, exploring the theology of the biblical fellow man in *Religion of Reason out of the Sources of Judaism* (1919). God was the backstop of moral fairness and generosity, orientating human progress toward a community of free individuals. Philosophy cannot prove that progress inevitable or demonstrate the reality of the divine Comforter of those who suffer in its long unfolding. Here personal conviction stands alone.   L.E.G.

*Jewish philosophy; Kantianism.

Hermann Cohen, *Religion of Reason out of the Sources of Judaism*, tr. Simon Kaplan (New York, 1972).

Cohen, L. Jonathan (1923–). Oxford philosopher who, after early work on political philosophy, has contributed widely to the philosophy of science, of induction and probability, and of language, among other areas. One central preoccupation of his has been with generalizing modal logic to provide a basis for an inductive logic where inductive support is quite independent of mathematical probability. This 'Baconianism' about induction led him to a pluralist view of probability, seen as a generalization of provability: from different types of provability, different types of probability—relative frequency, personalist, propensity etc.—are generated. Perhaps his most radical and controversial claim is that types of *probability can be generated which do not conform to the standard mathematical calculus, and, moreover, that these are not mere theoretical constructs but fundamental to judicial decision-making as well as inductive and scientific inference.   J.L.

L. J. Cohen, *The Probable and the Provable* (Oxford, 1977).

coherence. *p* and *q* are coherent if and only if the possible *truth of *p* does not preclude the possible truth of *q* and the possible truth of q does not preclude the possible truth of p. It follows that the concept of coherence presupposes the concept of truth, so truth cannot be explained in terms of coherence without circularity. Nevertheless, coherence is necessary for truth because if $\{p, q\}$ form an incoherent set, then at least one of p and q is false. Coherence also provides a test for truth because if it can be shown that $\{p, q\}$ form an incoherent set, and it is known that one of p, q is true, then it follows that the other is false, and if it can be known which is true, then it can be known which is false. However, coherence is not sufficient for truth because the coherence of $\{p, q\}$ is consistent with the falsity of both p and q.   S.P.

*coherence theory of truth.

Sybil Wolfram, *Philosophical Logic* (London, 1989).

coherence theory of truth. A theory of *truth according to which a statement is true if it 'coheres' with other statements—false if it does not. Some criticisms focus on what 'cohere' means—'is consistent with' appears too weak, 'entails and is entailed by', too strong. Other criticisms have to do with the fact that it seems that some statements must be assigned a truth-value independently if others are to be assessed by way of their coherence. Although the theory is more plausible for axiomatic systems where 'coherence' can take the definite form of being derivable from the axioms, the theory is extended to contingent statements. This is often owed to the conviction that the truth or falsity of individual statements can never, or only rarely, be conclusively established. It is sometimes owed to the conviction that there may be several sets of cohering statements with equal claim to describe the world correctly.   S.W.

*realism and anti-realism.

A. C. Grayling, *An Introduction to Philosophical Logic* (Brighton, 1982), ch. 5.
S. Wolfram, *Philosophical Logic* (London, 1989), ch. 4.3.

coherentism: *see* epistemic justification; epistemology, problems of.

Coleridge, Samuel Taylor (1772–1834). Poet and conversationalist rather than professional philosopher, Coleridge was, nevertheless, fascinated by philosophy. In early life a believer in Berkeley's *idealism, he was then converted to the philosophy of Kant, Schelling, and Fichte. He came to be regarded as a 'sage', and had a profound effect on nineteenth-century thought, religious, literary, and political. His most original work was on language, which he regarded as an evolving, flexible, personal tool for the construction of an intelligible world. His notebooks contain profound insights into the nature of perception and the functions of the imagination. His distinction between Imagination and Fancy (*Biographia Literaria* (1817), ch. 4) is his best-known contribution to the theory of *imagination, but was more concerned with style than with the philosophy of mind. His early thoughts

on the subject are impossible to disentangle from those of Wordsworth. Later, he was largely responsible for the introduction of German philosophy into English academic life.   M.WARN.

John Stuart Mill, *Mill on Bentham and Coleridge*, intro. F. R. Leavis (London, 1971).
M. A. Perkins, *Coleridge's Philosophy* (Oxford, 1994).

collective responsibility is *responsibility that can be assigned to some group or organization. A focus on moral blame or punishment (e.g. of the German people for the Nazi period), although not exhaustive of this concept, is common. In this sense, collective responsibility contributes to the generating of many questions. We can ask, *inter alia*, about similarities and differences between individual and collective responsibility; whether either one undermines the other; whether either one is preferable in moral assessment in some context. We may particularly ask when there ought to be collective responsibility. Arguably there should be collective responsibility (as fault) when a group or organization intends or causes harm, and the group or organization has or had the capacity to understand the wrongness of the intention or the causing of harm, and to modify or avoid these. This account does not fit no-fault collective responsibility, an enormously important, but complex, concept, which is also indispensable in modern societies.   E.T.S.

*business ethics; corporate responsibility.

Larry May, *Sharing Responsibility* (Chicago, 1992).

Colletti, Lucio (1924–2001). Professor of Philosophy at La Sapienza University in Rome, he came to fame as the principal Italian Marxist theorist of his generation, although he ultimately abandoned Marxism in the late 1970s. A pupil of Galvano Della Volpe, his distinctiveness in the Italian context arose from his rejection of the dominant school of Hegelian Marxism associated with Gramsci. Drawing on Kant, he argued for a form of transcendental realism that insisted on the independent reality of the material world from the knowing subject as a presupposition of an intersubjectively valid empirical science. He interpreted the Marxist project as the formulation of empirically verifiable scientific laws of economic development, an endeavour in which *Capital* was central. This thesis led him to stress the need for the empirical study of *capitalism with the object of reformulating Marx's own analysis whilst remaining true to his approach.   R.P.B.

*Marxism.

Richard Bellamy, *Modern Italian Social Theory* (Cambridge, 1987), ch. 8.

Collingwood, Robin George (1889–1943). R. G. Collingwood was Waynflete Professor of Metaphysical Philosophy in Oxford from 1935 to 1941, and also an archaeologist and historian of Roman Britain. His dominant interest was in the *imagination, especially as exercised by the historian, who interpreted historical data to reconstruct the thoughts of past people, and by the creative artist. He held that true *art, as opposed to mere entertainment, constructs an 'imaginary object' which can be shared, as an idea can be, by the artist with his public. In looking at a painting or listening to a symphony, like the historian we must imaginatively reconstruct the artist's own creative thought. His influence on practising historians has been considerable. In aesthetics, his somewhat austere theory applies well to *music. He was a considerable musician himself.   M.W.

*history, problems of the philosophy of; history, history of the philosophy of.

A full annotated bibliography is published by David Pole, *Aesthetics, Form and Emotion* (London, 1983). Collingwood's major works: *The Idea of History* (mainly 1936); *The Principles of Art* (1938); *An Essay on Metaphysics* (1940).

Collins, Anthony (1676–1729). Educated at Eton and Cambridge, he was a close friend of Locke, who seems to have regarded him as his intellectual heir. Collins is important philosophically for his materialist theory of mind, developed most fully in his *Answer* to Clarke (1708), and his much-applauded *Philosophical Inquiry* (1717), a work which unites Hobbes's metaphysical determinism and Locke's psychic determinism. Collins's *Discourse of Free-Thinking* (1713), which defends freedom of expression, is probably his best-known work. His position is generally thought to be deistic; however, there is strong external and internal evidence that he was a covert atheist. According to Berkeley, Collins claimed to have a proof for the non-existence of God; and many of his published statements seem to hint at, or imply, atheism. T. H. Huxley described him as the 'Goliath of Freethought', but he can also be seen as the most notable British philosopher between Locke and Berkeley, drawing on Hobbes, Spinoza, and Bayle, but chiefly on the rationalistic and materialistic side of Locke's thought.   D.BER.

*deism.

D. Berman, *A History of Atheism in Britain* (London, 1988).
J. O'Higgins, *Anthony Collins: The Man and his Works* (The Hague, 1970).

colours. These are part of the perceptible world, and accounts of them are consequently bound up with theories of mind and perception. Much work is influenced by the doctrine that they fall on the secondary side of the *primary- and secondary-quality distinction. This is the view that whereas primary qualities such as shape, size, and weight are intrinsic to material objects, secondary qualities such as colour, taste, and smell are not. It often involves the claim that in subjective awareness, colours are analogous to bodily *sensations like pains. But although this approach to secondary qualities may be promising for senses like touch and taste, which do involve sensations, it is unfaithful to the character of colour experience to suppose that normal vision involves one in being aware of the eyes or other part of the body.

Other approaches identify colours with objective properties of surfaces. However, there is no simple correlation between these and perceived colour, and philosophy awaits a theory which satisfactorily combines colour's subjective and objective aspects.   G.W.McC.

A. Byrne and D. Hilbert (eds.), *Readings on Color*, 2 vols. (Cambridge, Mass., 1997).
C. L. Hardin, *Colour for Philosophers* (Cambridge, 1988).

comedy. Events, situations, insights, narratives—in reality or fiction—which prompt feelings of relief or delight, often through the exposing of the ridiculous, the absurd or foolishly inappropriate in human life.

As a moral and social corrective, the comic shows up disparities between lofty profession and squalid performance: it works towards the sharpening of self-knowledge and self-criticism, checks the blurring of fantasy and fact, levels by exhibiting a common, highly fallible humanity.

Theories of the comic have (variously) taken as central a sense of superiority at that spectacle of human foibles and obsessions, or the offer of temporary release from constricting norms, or delight in discerning the incongruous. Language itself is a favoured domain for the comic—in nonsense verse, riddles, and puns.

The comic in philosophy is often an exposure of irrationality, or the showing-up of a theory as over-ambitious, pretentious, and ill-grounded. Deflationary philosophy, however, must take care not to fall into the opposite error—diminishing its subject-matter through being excessively reductionist.   R.W.H.

*laughter; tragedy; humour.

H. Bergson, *Le Rire* (Paris, 1900); tr. as *Laughter* (London, 1911).
D. H. Monro, *Argument of Laughter* (Cambridge, 1951).
R. Scruton, *The Aesthetic Understanding* (Manchester, 1983), ch. 12.

Comenius: *see* Komenský.

common sense. Philosophers tend to divide sharply in their attitudes to common sense. Amongst the founding fathers, Aristotle is a respecter of common sense and Plato a disdainer, and the contrasting attitudes can be seen in their metaphysics, ethics, and political theory. Consider only their theories about *universals or about the ideal construction of the family. Later, Reid and Moore are respecters, Hegel and McTaggart lofty disdainers. Of course, this is too simplistic, for the respecters are not usually worshippers and the flouters never entirely disregard some constraints of common sense. But what is common sense and why should it exercise *any* constraints over the creative intellect?

It seems likely that common sense defies definition; certainly no one has succeeded in giving a satisfactory definition, and very few have tried. To define it may be a self-defeating enterprise like codifying an ideology of that anti-ideology, *conservatism. Yet this indefiniteness, though it has certain strengths, makes it difficult to address such important questions as whether common sense is itself implicitly theoretical and whether or to what degree it is changeable. Without answering these questions, we may none the less make headway by sketching the rough location of common sense in the landscape of philosophical inquiry.

It is clear that the creative intellect needs some constraints other than logic since the conclusions of metaphysical thought need tests of acceptability other than consistency, and sheer intellectual intuition is unlikely to provide enough. Moreover, in spite of the excitement of esoteric theory, philosophers have always hoped that their thinking had important connections with ordinary life, and theories that entirely flout common sense tend to forfeit such connections. There is a sort of bad faith involved in acknowledging and living by certain beliefs in day-to-day life and denying these beliefs in the study. Even so extravagant an advocate of bewildering idealism as Bishop Berkeley claimed to be speaking on behalf of the vulgar.

Thomas Reid, a staunch apostle of a strong role for common sense in philosophy, treated the invocation of common sense as ultimately an appeal to certain innate principles of human nature that are partly constitutive of what it is to reason. Reid used his understanding of common sense to attack various sceptical or reductionist views in metaphysics and morality. But he does not rely solely upon appeal to self-evidence or general consensus, since it is an important part of his argument that those who ignore the commonsense principles in building their metaphysics find their reductive constructions built upon sand. It can, he thinks, be shown that Hume's metaphysics rests upon his theory of *ideas and this theory is not only incompatible with the cognitive practices of ordinary people, but makes it impossible for Hume to reach conclusions that his own position requires.

Descartes said that good sense or good judgement was so widely distributed amongst people that no one ever thought they needed more of it. This touches on a crucial idea behind the appeal of common sense in philosophy. The most brilliant and abstract theorist is none the less part of a community of thought and inherits a network of concepts that is pinned to the judgements and practices of that community (and of the species at large) in myriad ways. This is most evident in the shared language that supports the intelligibility of the boldest speculations. In the twentieth century, notably in the work of Wittgenstein and, in a different way, in J. L. Austin, the appeal to common sense was often transformed into an appeal to the common language. This appeal survives in a great deal of contemporary *'analytic' philosophy though not in as direct a way as was common with philosophers like Ryle and Austin. It may well account for the admirable capacity that its practitioners have for discussing and criticizing each other instead of merely proclaiming different world-views.   C.A.J.C.

*Scottish philosophy; empiricism; nationalism.

S. A. Grave, *The Scottish Philosophy of Common Sense* (Oxford, 1960).

G. E. Moore, 'A Defence of Common Sense', *Philosophical Papers* (London, 1959).

Thomas Reid, *An Inquiry into the Human Mind* (Chicago, 1970).

—— *Essays on the Intellectual Powers of Man* (Cambridge, Mass., 1969).

communication. The act of meaning something, of conveying a *propositional attitude (belief, desire, intention, regret, etc.) to an audience, by linguistic or other means. On the intuitive code or message model, endorsed, for example, by Locke, to communicate is simply a matter of encoding a thought in a form that one's audience can decipher. However, communication is more complex a matter than (in the linguistic case) just putting one's thoughts into words and hoping one's audience will reverse the process. As Grice discovered, the speaker's intention is distinctively *reflexive*: the speaker intends to produce a certain effect on his listeners partly by way of their recognizing his intention to produce it. The effect specific to communication is understanding, which consists in their recognition of that intention—inducing belief or action is a further effect. Communication is, in short, the act of expressing an attitude with a reflexive intention whose fulfilment consists in its recognition.   K.B.

*language; meaning.

Kent Bach and Robert M. Harnish, *Linguistic Communication and Speech Acts* (Cambridge, Mass., 1979).

communism. Any system of social organization in which property is held in common by members of a community rather than being owned privately by individuals. Since the early twentieth century the term has been associated with the name of Marx and with self-professed Marxist economic systems (such as the Soviet Union). Marx, however, used the term to refer to a movement which he thought would emancipate the working class from *capitalism. Marx thought it was premature to define the social arrangements which this movement would create; his writings contain nothing like a precise or detailed account of what a future 'communist' social system would be like.   A.W.W.

*anti-communism; conservatism.

Shlomo Avineri (ed.), *Marxist Socialism* (New York, 1973).

Alec Nove, *The Economics of Feasible Socialism* (London, 1983).

communitarianism. The thesis that the *community, rather than the individual, the state, the nation, or any other entity, is and should be at the centre of our analysis and our value system. Although it is an influential strand in political philosophy, it has not been systematized—as liberalism has, for example by Rawls, as *utilitarianism has, or as Marxists have developed 'grand theory'. Nevertheless, certain key themes are clear.

Primarily, communitarians emphasize the social nature of life, identity, relationships, and institutions.

They emphasize the embedded and embodied status of the individual person, by contrast with central themes in particular in contemporary liberal thought which are taken to focus on an abstract and disembodied individual. They tend to emphasize the value of specifically communal and public goods, and conceive of values as rooted in communal practices, again by contrast with liberalism, which stresses individual rights and conceives of the individual as the ultimate originator and bearer of value. The centrality of the real, historical, individual person in communitarian theory, though, distances it equally from certain varieties of *Marxism—specifically strong varieties of historical determinism and those varieties of state socialism where power is highly centralized.

Communitarians can be understood to be conducting a straightforwardly *prescriptivist* argument: human life will go better if communitarian, collective, and public values guide and construct our lives. There is also a *descriptive* thesis: that the communitarian conception of the embodied and embedded individual is a truer and more accurate model, a better conception of reality, than, say, liberal individualism or atomism, or structuralist Marxism. The descriptive and prescriptive levels of analysis can be fused—communitarians argue that given the state of the world, certain social, political, and normative arrangements and values are unviable. For example, a society which understands itself to be constituted by atomistic and autonomous discrete individuals, and which makes that kind of autonomy its highest value, will not work. Similarly, a top–down imposition of values (as in Stalinism) or the attempt completely to subordinate the individual to the state (as in modern fascism) will fail (as well as being morally repellent and indefensible).

Another important distinction within communitarianism is that between *social constructionism* and *value communitarianism*. Social constructionism refers to the claim that social reality is contingent upon social relations and human practices, rather than given. Value communitarianism refers to two things. First, the commitment to collective values, for example, reciprocity, trust, solidarity. These cannot be enjoyed by individuals as such—each person's enjoyment depends on others' enjoyment. In other words, they depend on a threshold recognition of 'intersubjectivity'. Second, the commitment to public goods—facilities and practices designed to help members of the community develop their common and hence their personal lives. Theorists suggest that a commitment to such collective values would engender a political practice which realized a range of public goods. Whether social constructionism and value communitarianism imply one another is a matter for dispute.

Communitarianism has often been criticized for its *conservative social and political implications—because theorists like MacIntyre uphold the integrity and value of tradition and established practice. However, social constructionism and value communitarianism feature in *socialism, Marxism, and *feminism. Certain communitarian themes—notably a form of social constructionism, and some community values like reciprocity—have been affirmed by liberal thinkers like Rawls and Dworkin. Theorists like Charles Taylor, who have been dubbed communitarian, on the other hand, have affirmed their commitment to the values of *liberalism.   E.J.F.

*individualism.

Shlomo Avineri and Avner de-Shalit (eds.), *Individualism and Communitarianism* (Oxford, 1992).

Elizabeth Frazer and Nicola Lacey, *The Politics of Community: A Feminist Critique of the Liberal–Communitarian Debate* (Hemel Hempstead, 1993).

S. Mulhall and A. Swift (eds.), *Liberals and Communitarians*, 2nd edn. (Oxford, 1996).

Charles Taylor, 'Cross Purposes: The Liberal Communitarian Debate', in N. Rosenblum (ed.), *Liberalism and the Moral Life* (Cambridge, Mass., 1989).

community. Group of people living a common life through reciprocal relationships. Communities are contrasted with associations organized for specific purposes in accordance with enforceable rules. Thus there is controversy over whether social life is fundamentally communal or, as Hobbes thought, the product of an association to maintain order. More generally communitarians see individuals as embedded in communities, rather than the independent atoms that compose them.
                                                      P.G.

*fraternity.

W. Kymlicka, *Liberalism, Community and Culture* (Oxford, 1989).

compatibilism and incompatibilism. Compatibilism is a view about *determinism and freedom that claims we are sometimes free and morally responsible even though all events are causally determined. Incompatibilism says that we cannot be free and responsible if determinism is true. The compatibilist defends his view by arguing that the contrary of 'free' is not 'caused' but 'compelled' or 'coerced'. A free act is one where the agent could have done otherwise *if* she had chosen otherwise, and in such acts the agent is morally responsible even if determined. The incompatibilist defends his view by arguing that a free act must involve more than this—the freedom to choose called origination. Honderich has argued that both sides, embattled for centuries, misconceive the problem. There is not one true definition of 'free'. There are two entrenched sets of attitudes at war here—within as well as between individuals. The two attitudes involve two conceptions of freedom.   R.C.W.

*freedom and determinism; responsibility.

T. Honderich, *A Theory of Determinism: The Mind, Neuroscience, and Life-Hopes* (Oxford, 1988).

R. Kane (ed.), *The Oxford Handbook of Free Will* (Oxford, 2001).

P. van Inwagen, *An Essay on Free Will* (Oxford, 1983).

completeness. A formal system of logic is semantically complete where all semantically valid formulae are derivable as *theorems. A semantically valid formula of a formal system of logic is one which, given a specified interpretation of the logical operators, is true on any interpretation of the non-logical terms. For example, $(P \lor \sim P)$ is semantically valid and is also derivable as a theorem in the propositional calculus. The *propositional and *predicate calculuses are complete in this sense.

A stronger sense of completeness (d-completeness) is defined syntactically. A system is d-complete where if a non-derivable formula is added as an axiom, a contradiction is derivable. The propositional but not the predicate calculus is d-complete.   R.B.M.

*validity; incompleteness.

B. Mates, *Elementary Logic* (Oxford, 1972).

complex idea: *see* ideas.

complexity theory. Computational complexity theory is the branch of computer science/mathematics that deals with the resources required to solve problems—as distinct from the theory of *computability, which deals with whether problems can be solved at all. An important resource in problem solving is time. Complexity theorists distinguish the class of decision problems P that can be *solved* by a deterministic *Turing machine in polynomial time (i.e. where the time required is determined by the size of the input raised to a certain power) from the class of decision problems NP that can be *verified* by a deterministic *Turing machine in polynomial time. One of the outstanding questions of complexity theory is whether $P = NP$.   J.BER.

M. Sipser, *Introduction to the Theory of Computation* (Boston, 1997).

composite idea: *see* ideas.

composition and division, fallacies of. If I reason 'Every member of the team is strong; therefore the team is strong', I am committing the fallacy of composition—it is possible for the premiss to be true and the conclusion false. If I reason 'The rope is strong; therefore the threads of which the rope is made are strong', I am committing the fallacy of division. These are fallacies not because every inference from parts to whole or whole to parts is invalid, but because some are.   J.BER.

*fallacy.

C. L. Hamblin, *Fallacies* (London, 1970).

computability. A mathematical *function determines a unique numerical output for any appropriate numerical input. A function is computable just if there is a procedure that can be carried out in a finite number of steps by a human being or a computer following a finite number of exact instructions for calculating the output for any given input. Computability theorists have made this informal notion precise in a variety of ways. According to *Church's thesis, the set of computable functions coincides with the set of functions that can be calculated by a universal *Turing machine.   J.BER.

*Church's thesis; computers; function; Turing machine.

G. S. Boolos and R. C. Jeffrey, *Computability and Logic*, 2nd edn. (Cambridge, 1980).

computers. Devices in which formal computations are performed automatically. A computation is a inference-like operation which is defined over a set of representational structures, and results from the manipulation of those structures in accordance with a fixed set of rules. Particular applications of the rules can create, transform, or erase symbolic structures at any given stage of processing. The modern digital computer performs these tasks when guided by a *program which contains instructions to carry out particular operations in a given sequence. If the instructions specified in a given programming language fail to correspond directly to the basic operations of the machine they must be converted into, or interpreted in, another programming language whose operations do directly correspond, or which are themselves converted into, or interpreted in, a language which corresponds more closely to the basic workings of the machine. Finally, we reach the level of machine code, whose commands are executed by the electronic functions of machine hardware. This is called the implementation hierarchy; and for any high-level programming language implemented in the levels below, we can imagine a computer operating directly in accordance with its commands: this is called a virtual machine.

Philosophers of mind like Jerry Fodor and Daniel Dennett appeal to computational mechanisms in providing theories of mind, and many have supposed the software–hardware distinction can illuminate the mind–body problem. Psychologists have claimed that many of our mental abilities and capacities can be explained computationally; and researchers in *artificial intelligence have supposed that by suitable programming it is possible to build a machine that thinks. Each of these claims relies on the notion of computational explanation. To give a computational account of a physical system is to explain its outward behaviour by reference to certain functionally defined interpretable inner states and processes. A computational process P arises when a processor Q manipulates a field of symbolic structures with a certain behavioural result (i.e. running a program). The operation of the processor can itself be seen as a process, call it P', internal to P, which is the result of an interior processor Q' manipulating *its* field of symbolic structures. Within each process we can define an ingredient processor and its field of application until we reach a processor which simply performs the hardwired electronic functions of the machine. This is called serial reduction. It provides a means whereby complex procedures can be broken down into sequences of simpler tasks until we reach the ground-level operations of the machine. Dennett takes this model to show how to dispense with homunculi: intelligent behaviour could be the upshot of an assembly of relatively 'dumb' processing units carrying out simpler tasks; the level of conscious mental life would be a virtual machine implemented in the neural hardware. In contrast, Fodor sees the laws of intentional psychology as implemented by computational laws which govern real belief–desire states of an internal behaviour-causing mechanism. Beliefs, for Fodor, are computational relations to mental representations: structures in a *language of thought which have both a syntax and a semantics. Desires are different behaviour-causing computational relations to just such mental representations. Psychological processes can be regarded as computational processes if they can be formally defined in terms of sequences of operations for manipulating interpretable symbols.

The crucial remaining difference between ourselves and machines is that whereas we have to attribute semantic content to the machine's representations, or data structures, semantics arises in us without external attribution. What computational explanations do show is the possibility of a level of organization within a system which can be implemented (multiply realized) in a variety of ways. Thus creatures with different neurophysiological states can share the same computational states and processes. Rules and representations at each level can be defined independently of their physical realizations: their 'semantics does not cross implementation boundaries' (Brian Cantwell Smith). So to establish a distinct computational level in a creature is to establish that it has states with certain semantically interpretable contents. (For the limits of computability see the entry on artificial intelligence.)

B.C.S.

*complexity theory; mind, syntax, and semantics.

D. Dennett, *Consciousness Explained* (New York, 1991).
J. A. Fodor, *Representations* (Brighton, 1981).
Z. Pylyshyn, *Computation and Cognition* (Cambridge, Mass., 1985).
Brian Cantwell Smith, 'Reflection and Semantics in a Procedural Language' (MIT Ph.D. dissertation and technical report LCS/TR-272, 1982).

Comte, Isidore Auguste Marie François Xavier (1798–1857). The father of French *positivism was much influenced by the *philosophes, as well as by Saint-Simon, to whom he served as secretary for several years. At the same time, although he repudiated formal religious belief at an early age, he showed a respect for Catholicism quite alien to those earlier thinkers. An appallingly miserable life, of which misery he was the chief author, came to an end as Comte strove to found his own non-theistic religion, complete with a catalogue of secular saints and observances.

Comte's major contribution to thought—part philosophical, part historical, part sociological—was expressed in his law of the three-part nature of human societal development. Apparently, societies are fated to go through the *theological*, the *metaphysical*, and the *positive* stages of existence. And, although it is certainly not the case that every later event is better than every earlier event—Comte showed a deep distaste for the Protestant Reformation, even to the point of refusing to recognize its contributions

to science—the overall effect of change up through the stages is *progressive*.

Looking therefore at the history of the West—Comte had as little sympathy for non-Europeans as any of his contemporaries—we see a three-part upwards rise. In the theological stage (the medieval period), one had beliefs in gods and spirit forces. It was not so much that this was wrong—in fact Comte argued that it was a necessary part of growth—but that it was immature. Then, in the metaphysical stage (the Scientific Revolution), one moved on to beliefs in unseen forces and the like. Finally, in the positive stage (which Comte cherished and at whose birth he saw himself as helping), one moves to a purer form of understanding, where one confines explanation to the expression of verifiable and measurable correlations between phenomena.

Comte argued that this forward movement of *society is reflected into each area of science, and that here also one sees progress through three stages. Comte was strongly anti-reductionist, inasmuch as each branch of science supposedly has its own peculiar methods—this includes 'sociology', thus justifying Comte's own existence! But more than this. Apparently, there is an ordering of science taken as a whole, and the prior forms of science must start out on their paths before the lower forms can get started. It is because of this that we find that, taking the sciences in order—mathematics, astronomy, physics, chemistry, biology, and sociology—only the first two have achieved a purely positive status, and that theological and metaphysical thinking exists in major force in the others.

It is easy to laugh at a man who founds a religion with Frederick the Great and Adam Smith among its canon of saints. However, one should not underestimate the influence of Comte on individuals, like John Stuart Mill, or on fields of study, like education, with his claim that the individual, like society, must learn in one inevitable fixed pattern. Nor should one neglect the fact that there is an identifiable chain from Comte down to the positivists of various kinds in this century. At the moment, given the influence of constructivism, positivist philosophies of science are not very popular; but, for those of us who incline to a cyclical philosophy of history rather than a unidirectional progressivist one, the possibility remains real that Auguste Comte and his philosophy will ride again.

M.R.

A. Comte, *The Positive Philosophy of August Comte* (London, 1853).
H. Gouhier, *La Jeunesse d'Auguste Comte et la formation du positivisme* (Paris, 1931).
F. Manuel, *The Prophets of Paris* (Cambridge, Mass., 1962).

conation: *see* intention; trying; will.

conceivability. Admissibility by the mind. Thinkability. If imagination entails the generation of mental imagery, then everything imaginable is conceivable, but not everything conceivable is imaginable. Something is conceivable if and only if it is possible to form a concept of it, but a concept need not involve an image.

Logical possibility is necessary for conceivability, so logical impossibilities are inconceivable, but conceivability is not what logical possibility consists in. A putative state of affairs is logically impossible if and only if every description of it entails a contradiction, logically possible if it has at least one consistent description. A putative state of affairs is conceivable if and only if it can be thought. Nevertheless, conceivability without contradiction is important to the epistemology of logical possibility.

On some empiricist views, if I have experience of *a* and experience of *b*, then I can conceive of some new item, *c*, composed of *a* and *b*, but not of any item I have neither experienced nor experienced the constituents of.

On some materialist views, if I think I am thinking of something non-physical, say spiritual or abstract, I have in fact only succeeded in thinking of something physical. On this view, to conceive of something is to think of it as possessing at least some primary qualities.   S.P.

T. Gendler and J. Hawthorne (eds.), *Conceivability and Possibility* (Oxford, 2002).

concept. The term is the modern replacement for the older term *idea, stripped of the latter's imagist associations, and thought of as more intimately bound up with language. How intimately? There are innumerable concepts which, on any view, lie quite beyond the attainments of a languageless creature, as a quick inspection of any technical volume, such as a computer manual, makes plain: concepts such as *format*, *debug*, and *backup* are light-years away from a place in the brightest of chimpanzees' repertoires. On the other hand, the use of *language which shows a person to have such and such a concept will not occur in a vacuum, but there will be underlying abilities, notably those of a broadly recognitional or discriminatory character, which give substance, as it were, to the word usage, and in many cases it will make sense to ascribe comparable abilities to animals.

But is this enough to warrant speaking of the grasp of a *concept*? We do not have, in addition, to assure ourselves that some form of abstract, internal representation has occurred in the simian mind, but it is true that we have focused on one aspect only of concept possession, the fully developed case presenting us with a *cluster* of capacities: not merely the ability to respond differentially to things which fall under the concept, as can be realized in a non-language-user, but also the ability to apply or indeed to misapply a concept, to extend it to new cases, to abandon it in favour of an alternative concept, to invoke the concept in the absence of things to which it applies, and so forth. In the absence of a word or other *sign to which the concept might be annexed, it is difficult to make sense of these possibilities, difficult to say that non-language-users can possess concepts in anything more than an extended sense.   B.B.R.

*thinking; meaning; image.

P. T. Geach, *Mental Acts* (London, 1957).
E. Margolis and S. Laurence (eds.), *Concepts: Core Readings* (Cambridge, Mass., 1999).
G. Ryle, *Thinking and Meaning* (Louvain, 1962).

concepts, thick and thin. Thin evaluative concepts are those such as 'ought', 'right', 'wrong', 'good', 'bad', 'duty', 'obligation', and 'rights'. These are the concepts used in final moral decisions about how to act. Thick concepts lie between these and the non-evaluative concepts below them; examples are 'brave', 'tactful', 'lewd', and 'insensitive'. The idea is that there is a sort of layer-cake of concepts, with the non-evaluative at the bottom and the thin at the top. Thick concepts are distinctive in being a sort of mix of evaluation and description; there is a debate about whether that mix is a combination of two separate parts.

                                                                J.D.

S. Blackburn, 'Morality and Thick Concepts', *Proceedings of the Aristotelian Society*, suppl. vol. 66 (1992), 285–99.

conceptual analysis. The attempt to solve philosophical problems, or exhibit them as illusory, by defining words or being clear about how concepts are used. In practice, conceptual analysis involves logical deduction, because it requires showing the entailments of definitions. The logical status of true sentences of philosophy is then 'analytic'. In so far as conceptual analysis is the method of philosophy (as it was widely held to be for much of the twentieth century), philosophy is a second-order subject, because it is about language, not the world or what language is about. However, the philosophical results of solving problems of the form 'What is the definition of "x"?' are not independent of those obtained from answering 'What is x?' or 'What is the essence of x?'

Some concepts seem recalcitrant to analysis, or, to put it another way, some words seem resistant to verbal definition. 'Red' is hard to define if construed phenomenologically, even though readily definable in terms of physics. 'Exists' resists definition, at least once we realize that being *F* is not sufficient for being.

Conceptual analysis, if not under that name, has been practised intermittently in philosophy at least since Plato. For example, it is recognizable in the work of Aquinas, Hobbes, Leibniz, and Kant. In the last century it was the philosophical method advocated by the Logical Positivists.

The later Wittgenstein argues that, for at least some concepts, there are no necessary and sufficient conditions for being *F*, because there is nothing that all and only those items truly called '*F*' have in common. Rather than engage in definition, then, philosophers should attend to the vast diversity of linguistic use.

The idea that non-linguistic reality is too changing, too phenomenological, or too paradoxical to be realistically depicted by terms admitting of precise definition is as old as Heraclitus, but also salient in the thought of Hegel and Nietzsche. In philosophy, though, we should be as clear as we can for as long as we can if we are to begin to understand its problems. If we define our terms as clearly as we are able, we can avoid beginning by arguing past one another. A philosopher should be concerned about definition in the way that a historian is concerned about putting dates in the right order.   S.P.

*analytic philosophy; Ayer; family resemblance; implicature; Wittgenstein.

A. J. Ayer, *Language, Truth and Logic*, 2nd edn. (Harmondsworth, 1976).

John Hospers, *An Introduction to Philosophical Analysis* (London, 1997).

Ludwig Wittgenstein, *Philosophical Investigations* (Oxford, 1953).

conceptual scheme. A set of concepts and propositions that provide a framework for describing and explaining items of some subject-matter along with criteria for recognizing which phenomena are to be considered deviant and in need of explanation. For example, ancient astronomers thought of planets as moving in circular paths at constant speed and attempted to reduce observed non-circular motions to systems of underlying circular motions that appear non-circular from our perspective. Newton introduced a new conceptual scheme that viewed physical objects as moving in straight lines unless acted on by some force. Planetary orbits were then explained as resulting from the interaction of straight-line motion and gravitational forces. In epistemology Quine has sought to eliminate the traditional conceptual scheme that treats every proposition as either *analytic or synthetic.   H.I.B.

D. Davidson, 'On the Very Idea of a Conceptual Scheme' (1974), repr. in *Inquiries into Truth and Interpretation*, 2nd edn. (Oxford, 2001).

W. V. Quine, 'Two Dogmas of Empiricism' (1951), repr. in *From a Logical Point of View* (Cambridge, Mass., 1953).

concomitant variations, method of: *see* method of concomitant variations.

concrete universal. One standard meaning for 'concrete' is 'particular', and in a tradition based on Aristotle, only particulars can be genuine subjects, while only *universals can be predicated of subjects, and universals cannot themselves be subjects of predication. 'Socrates is wise' would predicate the universal, wisdom, of the particular, Socrates, and 'Wisdom is a characteristic of Socrates' would be a grammatically misleading way of predicating that same universal of that same particular, while 'Wisdom is a primary virtue' would be a grammatically misleading way of saying that any person having wisdom has a primary virtue. In that system of usage, 'concrete universal' would be an inconsistent phrase. However, in the philosophy of Plato, universals can themselves be genuine subjects of predication, just as much as any particular (and in fact are regarded as *superior* subjects).

Aristotle regarded universals as grasped by a mental process of abstraction, so that, at least as grasped by us, universals are abstract entities (another difference from Plato, who regards universals as more clearly mind-independent). Since another use of 'concrete' is as an opposite to *'abstract', this would be another source of tension in the phrase, from an Aristotelian, but not a Platonic, viewpoint. Locke's version of universals was 'abstract general ideas'—which tends toward the

Aristotelian side, but he also held that 'Everything that exists is particular'. This would make possible another reading (besides the Platonic one) of 'concrete universal' which would make it consistent, namely, 'particular abstract general idea'. So the two meanings for 'concrete', namely 'particular' and 'non-abstract', should not be run together.

The deliberate use of the idea of a concrete universal is due to Hegel, for whom the 'I', the 'now', the 'spirit of a free people', etc. are either both concrete and universal or in some sort of transition in between. Hegel would not have minded a reading of 'concrete' and of 'universal' which would make the phrase combine logically conflicting ideas. This would be part of his theme of the dialectical combining of opposites.   J.C.

Herbert Marcuse, *Hegel's Ontology and the Theory of Historicity* (Cambridge, Mass., 1987).

concupiscence. Literally, the state of desiring or coveting something with great ardour, but used more particularly to signify sexual or other strong bodily desire. It is used in a related sense by St Thomas Aquinas, in the *Summa Theologiae*, with respect to bodily desires generically, or the capacity or faculty for having such desires. He referred to our 'concupiscible powers'. It is his equivalent term for the Greek *epithumia*, as used in the division of the powers of the active soul by Plato and Aristotle (with the 'irascible powers' corresponding to the Greek *thumos*). The term is archaic, and only found outside academic discussion in coy descriptions of sexual congress. Different *virtues are said to pertain to these different powers, enabling us to find a pattern within the range of human excellences.   N.J.H.D.

*sex; sexual conduct.

Aquinas, *Summa Theologiae*, Ia. 2ae, QQ. 22–30, 56.

Condillac, Étienne Bonnot de (1715–80). French philosopher who attempted to formulate a rigorous epistemology as the theoretical basis for the enlightened agenda of the eighteenth-century *philosophes. He combined elements of Locke's 'sensationalist' theory of knowledge with the scientific methodology of Newton, and mixed in a small portion of Cartesian tough-minded doubt to produce a sort of empiricist foundationalism that was quite serviceable for the broader aims and intentions of the *Enlightenment intellectuals, though deeply problematic and unstable from the very start. Condillac devoted careful attention to questions surrounding the origins and nature of language, and enhanced contemporary awareness of the importance of the use of language as a scientific instrument. He began the work of constructing a science of ideas, 'idéologie' in the parlance of later thinkers who were influenced by him.   P.F.J.

Isabel F. Knight, *The Geometric Spirit: The Abbé de Condillac and the French Enlightenment* (New Haven, Conn., 1968).

conditional probability. The *probability that a card drawn at random from a deck is a heart is ¼; the conditional probability that it's a heart, given that it's red, is ½; the conditional probability that it's a spade, given that it's red is 0. The conditional probability of an event *E* given an event *F*—in symbols, $p(E|F)$—is defined as $p(E \& F)/p(F)$, where $p(E \& F)$ is the probability that both *E* and *F* occur; where $p(F) = 0$, $p(E|F)$ is undefined. If $p(E|F) = p(E)$, then *E* and *F* are said to be independent.   M.C.

conditionals. Traditionally, any sentence of the form *If A (then) B*. *A* is called the antecedent, *B* the consequent. Here are three examples:

(a) If there was a run on sterling, interest rates rose.
(b) If there had been a run on sterling, interest rates would have risen.
(c) If there is a run on sterling, interest rates will rise.

(*a*) and (*c*) are usually classed together as indicatives. (*b*) is called subjunctive or *counterfactual.

Philosophers have generally conceived their problem to be that of explaining in what conditions a conditional is true. There is a widespread assumption that *A* and *B* must be propositions—true or false—and, under the influence of formal logic, a certain presumption in favour of the view that the conditions for the truth of the conditional are those of so-called material implication, where *A* materially implies *B* just in case *A* is false or *B* true.

On this interpretation, arguments generally accounted valid *are* valid; unfortunately, so are arguments which appear quite eccentric. Thus, interpreting 'if' as material implication, the argument whose premiss is 'I did not raise my arm' and whose conclusion is 'If I raised my arm the world came to an end' is valid. Some philosophers have argued that this does not defeat the presumption, showing not that the conditional is false, but only that it is misleading to assert it. To assert it suggests (though the conditional does not entail) something false—that, for example, there is a connection between my raising my arm and the world's coming to an end.

Another approach appeals to *possible worlds: the truth of a conditional is the truth-value of its consequent at the possible world most similar to the actual world in which its antecedent is true. Our example is false even if I do not raise my arm, because (presumably) in the possible world most like the actual world in which I do raise my arm, the world doesn't come to an end.

A third approach centres on acceptability (defined in terms of probability) rather than truth: *If A then B* is acceptable provided that the *conditional probability of B given A* is sufficiently high. One objection to this approach is that the law of contraposition—*If A then B* entails *If not-B then not-A*—fails. But contraposition works unambiguously only with examples like (*a*): what is usually described as the contrapositive of (*c*)—'If interest rates don't rise, there will be no run on sterling' is logically unrelated to it. *Grammatically*, though, it's not clear that this should be called the contrapositive of (*c*), nor is it obvious what the contrapositive of (*b*) is.

This suggests that there is an important distinction between (*a*) on the one hand and (*b*) and (*c*) on the other, a view taken by V. H. Dudman. Unlike most theorists, Dudman's work is marked by close attention to grammar, in particular to tense in conditionals. On Dudman's view (*b*) and (*c*) are conditionals. But conditionals are not propositions compounded of propositions. They are what Dudman calls simple messages: they have a subject and their conditional clauses are constituents of their predicates, rather than propositions. They represent verdicts on 'fantasies' where we are 'envisioning the unfolding of a causally continuous sequence of events', (*b*) placing in the past what (*c*) puts in the future; they are not propositions, true or false. (*a*), on the other hand, is a compound message. It is a hypothetical, a kind of condensed argument; hence its obedience to logical laws. But again it is not a proposition. It would seem that Dudman's aim of 'deflating truth' has a philosophical significance not confined to 'if' sentences.   M.C.

J. Bennett, *A Philosophical Guide to Conditionals* (Oxford, 2003).
F. Jackson (ed.), *Conditionals* (Oxford, 1991).
J. L. Mackie, *Truth, Probability and Paradox* (London, 1973).
D. Sanford, *'If P, then Q': Theories of Conditionals Past and Present* (London, 1988).

Condorcet, Marie-Jean-Antoine-Nicolas Caritat, Marquis de (1743–94). French philosopher, mathematician, political theorist, and a moderate revolutionary who died in prison. He developed 'social mathematics', applying mathematics and probability theory to social and political affairs. He analysed complex decisions, such as an election between three candidates, where the candidate selected by a simple majority may not be preferred by the voters when they compare each candidate with every other candidate. Complex decisions should thus be reduced to a series of simple decisions and should be taken by an enlightened élite capable of such reduction. Condorcet was a feminist, arguing that women should have the same rights as men, political as well as civil, and an education enabling them to exercise their rights. His *Sketch for a Historical Picture of the Progress of the Human Mind* (1793) presented society as developing by stages from primitive hunters and gatherers down to the French republic, and predicted indefinite progress in science, technology, and (guided by social mathematics) social organization.   M.J.I.

Condorcet, *Selected Writings*, ed. K. M. Baker (Indianapolis, 1976).

conduct: *see* right action.

confectionery fallacy. The confectionery fallacy (so named by Ray Jennings) is found mainly (and frequently) in elementary logic texts whose authors are desperate for a convincing example of an 'exclusive "or"' (either *p* or *q*, but not both). Numerous writers offer examples such as the following. A parent says to a child, 'You may have pie or cake if you eat your vegetables'. In fact, the consequent of this conditional is not *any* kind of *disjunction. It is a *conjunction: 'You may have pie and you may have cake'. (It does not of course follow from this that the child may have *both*.) If it were really an exclusive disjunction the child would have a 50 per cent chance of opting for the *unpermitted* alternative. The mistake seems to arise from confusing 'Permissibly~*p* and permissibly~*q*' with 'Permissibly~(*p* and *q*)'.   J.J.M.

R. E. Jennings, 'The Punctuational Sources of the Truth-Functional "Or"', *Philosophical Studies* (1986).

confirmation. The relation, in Carnap's kind of inductive logic, between evidence and hypothesis. Confirmation-judgements, according to Carnap, assess the probability of a specified hypothesis, on specified *evidence, in either classificatory, comparative, or quantitative terms. They have a truth-value that is determined a priori by the rules of the language in which they are formulated, and they are thus to be distinguished from those assessments of *probability that measure the empirically given relative frequency of one kind of outcome among another kind.

In effect Carnap analysed the extent to which, in a given language, a sentence *e* confirms a sentence *h*—written '*c*(*h*,*e*)'—as the ratio of the quantity of logically possible worlds in which both *e* and *h* are true to the quantity of logically possible worlds in which *e* is true. (Earlier, but much sketchier, versions of this analysis may be found in the writings of Leibniz, Wittgenstein, and Waismann.) Carnap recognized, however, that a language can supply a non-denumerably infinite variety of possible measures for quantities of possible worlds and that a correspondingly non-denumerable infinity of different confirmation-*functions can be made available. So, first, he concentrated his attention on those confirmation-functions that treat all individuals alike—allowing any uniform, difference-preserving replacement of one individual's name by another's. Secondly, out of all those confirmation-functions he favoured use of one that assigns a fundamental equality to each of the different structures that are possible in a world, where one structure differs from another if it involves the instantiation of a different pattern of predicates. And, thirdly, he favoured use of the one such confirmation-function that within any particular structure assigns a fundamental equality to each possible distribution of individuals. Carnap's chosen measure for quantities of possible worlds then ensured that *a*'s having the property *F* will always be better confirmed by the evidence that both *b* and *c* have *F* than just by the evidence that *b* has *F*, and better confirmed by the evidence that there are *n* + 1 different kinds from which the new instances are taken than by the evidence that there are just *n* different kinds.

Unfortunately, however, this choice of function fails to distinguish between the project of constructing a measure for the validity that an experimental result derives from its replicability in similar circumstances, and the project of constructing a measure for the strength of inductive support that depends on the thoroughness with which the experiment tests the performance of the hypothesis under variation of relevant circumstances. Nor does Carnap's system provide any methodology for selecting an appropriate language, or for selecting which particular kinds of circumstances describable within the language are known to be especially relevant for testing which particular kind of hypothesis. The system also assigns a very small degree of confirmation to any hypothesized law, whatever the evidence, when the supposed number of individuals is very large, and assigns zero confirmation when this number is infinite. So, although predictions can enjoy a plausible degree of confirmation (because they concern individuals), explanatory laws cannot.

Hintikka's system of confirmation theory eliminates the difficulty about measuring the confirmation of laws, as distinct from the confirmation of predictions about individuals, but remains vulnerable to the other criticisms.   L.J.C.

*induction.

R. Carnap, *Logical Foundation of Probability* (Chicago, 1950).
L. J. Cohen, *An Introduction to the Philosophy of Induction and Probability* (Oxford, 1989).
J. Hintikka, 'Towards a Theory of Inductive Generalisation', in Y. Bar-Hillel (ed.), *Proceedings of the 1964 Congress for Logic, Methodology and Philosophy of Science* (Amsterdam, 1965).

Confucianism. Major school of thought in China which defends an ethical and political ideal that has been a dominant influence on the way of life of the Chinese. Members of the school are motivated by social and political concerns, and many take part in government at some stage of their careers, with some attaining influential official positions. They regard cultivation of the self as the basis of social and political order, and many of them are also influential teachers devoted to bettering themselves and their pupils. This predominantly practical orientation is coupled with a reflectivity that has led to the development of elaborate metaphysical views, theories of human nature, and accounts of the human psychology. Their discussion of such issues as the cultivation of character, forms of integrity, the nature of emotions and desires, and the relation between knowledge and action has important implications for the contemporary study of moral psychology and ethics in general.

The origin of the school can be traced to a social group in early China whose members, referred to as *Ju* (a term probably with basic meaning of weakling), were ritualists and sometimes also teachers by profession. Confucius (sixth to fifth century BC) belonged to the group but, although he retained the interest in rituals, he was also concerned with a search for remedy for the social and political disorder of the times, which he believed to lie with the restoration of traditional values and norms. Later thinkers who professed to be followers of Confucius shared such concern and belief, and developed Confucius' teachings in different directions. The school of thought comprising these thinkers has traditionally been referred to as 'Ju-chia' (the school of *Ju*), a term often translated as 'Confucianism'. Confucius' thinking was given divergent developments by Mencius (fourth century BC) and Hsün

Tzǔ (third century BC), and different kinds of Confucian thought continued to evolve in the early period, yielding such major thinkers as Tung Chung-shu (second century BC). After a period in which it was overshadowed by Buddhism, a revival of interest in Confucianism was seen among such thinkers as Han Yü (768–824), Shao Yung (1011–77), Chou Tun-i (1017–73), Chang Tsai (1020–77), Ch'eng Hao (1032–85), and Ch'eng I (1033–1107), marking the beginning of a movement often referred to as *'neo-Confucianism'. Han Yü's view that Mencius was the true transmitter of Confucius' teachings became generally accepted largely through the efforts of Chu Hsi (1130–1200), who put together the *Lun Yü* (Analects) of Confucius, *Meng Tzǔ* (Mencius), *Ta Hsüeh* (Great Learning), and *Chung Yung* (Doctrine of the Mean) as the Four Books. The Mencian branch of Confucian thought continued to be developed in different ways, leading to differences between the Ch'eng–Chu school of Ch'eng I and Chu Hsi, and the Lu–Wang school of Lu Hsiang-shan (1139–93) and Wang Yang-ming (1472–1529). Further development occurred among later thinkers such as Wang Fu-chih (1619–92), Yen Yüan (1635–1704), and Tai Chen (1724–77), and new forms of Confucian thought continue to evolve up to the present.

Two important concepts in Confucian thought are *tao* (the Way) and *te* (virtue, moral power, potency). Originally meaning 'road' or 'way', 'tao' came to be used to refer to the ideal way of life as well as teachings about that way of life. 'Te' originally referred to that by virtue of which a ruler has the authority to rule; it referred to both a quality involving proper religious sacrifice and such attributes as self-sacrificial generosity and humility, as well as a psychic power of attraction and transformation associated with that quality. It came to be used of human beings generally, referring to the quality or power by virtue of which one can tread the Way. The two concepts have been used by other schools (such as Taoism) in connection with different ideals, but Confucians further explain their conception of *tao* and *te* in terms of *jen*, *li*, and *yi*.

'Jen' (humanity, goodness, benevolence) has either the basic meaning of kindness, or the basic meaning of a quality distinctive of certain aristocratic clans. It is used in Confucian texts sometimes to refer to the all-encompassing ethical ideal and sometimes to refer specifically to an affective concern for all living things. Distinctive of Confucian thought and opposed by Mohist opponents is the view that the nature of such concern should vary according to one's relation to such things. Later Confucians also explain *jen* in terms of one's forming one body with, and hence one's being sensitive to the well-being of, all things.

'Li' (rites, rituals, propriety), originally referring to sacrificial rites, gradually came to refer more generally to all norms governing ceremonious behaviour and the responsibilities one has by virtue of one's social position. Just as performance of sacrificial rites should ideally be accompanied by reverence for spirits, observance of *li* in dealing with other people should ideally be accompanied by reverence for others; the attitude behind *li* is described in some Confucian texts as lowering oneself and elevating others. The emphasis on *li* is another distinctive feature of Confucian thought, setting it in opposition to Mohist and Taoist opponents.

To avoid its leading to improper behaviour, an affective concern for others has to be regulated by a sense of what is right, and departure from *li* in unusual circumstances or proper conduct in circumstances not covered by *li* also calls for an assessment of what is right. Confucians therefore also emphasize the importance of *yi* (rightness, duty, fittingness), the character 'yi' probably having the earlier meaning of a sense of honour before coming to refer to the fitting or right way of conducting oneself. Confucians emphasize that *yi* is not determined by fixed rules of conduct, but requires the proper weighing of relevant considerations in any context of action. The ideal form of courage involves a firm commitment to *yi*, as well as the absence of fear or uncertainty if one realizes upon self-examination that one is in the right.

Confucian thinkers emphasize gradual cultivation of the self to embody the attributes just described. In the political realm, although some Confucian thinkers, such as Hsün Tzǔ and Tung Chung-shu, also advocate the use of law and punishment as secondary measures, Confucian thinkers are generally agreed that moral examples and education should ideally be the basis for government. A ruler who embodies the attributes described will care about and provide for the common people, who will be attracted to him, and the moral example he sets will have a transforming effect on the people.

Though sharing a roughly common ideal, Confucian thinkers disagree about the justification of the ideal and the metaphysics underlying it. The disagreement has in large part to do with their different conceptions of *hsing* (nature). Originally derived from a character meaning 'life' or 'to grow', 'hsing' came to mean the direction of development that a thing will realize if unobstructed. Mencius believed that human beings share certain incipient ethical inclinations which are fully realized in the Confucian ideal; *hsing* is constituted by the direction of development of such inclinations and is good in that it has an ethical direction. Hsün Tzǔ regarded the *hsing* of human beings as comprising primarily self-regarding desires that human beings have by birth; *hsing* is evil in that unregulated pursuit of satisfaction of such desires leads to strife and disorder. Thus, while Mencius defended traditional social distinctions and norms on the ground that they make possible full realization of shared incipient ethical inclinations, Hsün Tzǔ defended them on the ground that they help to transform and regulate the pursuit of satisfaction of desires, thereby making possible social order and maximal satisfaction of human desires.

Different views of *hsing* continued to evolve within the Confucian tradition, such as Tung Chung-shu's view that human beings are born with both good and bad elements, and that *hsing* in the broad sense includes the bad elements and cannot be described as good. Along with the acceptance of the view that Mencius was the true transmitter of

Confucius' teachings, Confucian thinkers came to agree that *hsing* is good. But this Mencian idea was also reinterpreted in terms of the metaphysics of *li*.

For example, Chu Hsi, following Ch'eng I, regarded all things as composed of *li* (principle, pattern) and *ch'i* (ether, material force). While the term had the earlier meaning of 'good order' or 'inner structure', *li* came to be regarded as something incorporeal and unchanging that runs through everything, explaining why things are as they are. It is also that to which the behaviour of things should conform; in the human realm, it includes all norms of human conduct. *Ch'i* is the concrete stuff of which things are composed, and is freely moving and active. According to Chu, *hsing* is constituted by the *li* in human beings, which is identical with the Confucian virtues; so, *hsing* is good in that human beings are born fully virtuous. While the mind originally had insight into *li*, this has been obscured by distortive desires and thoughts which are due to impure *ch'i*. While de-emphasizing the metaphysics of *li* and *ch'i*, Wang Yang-ming shared the view that human beings are already fully virtuous by virtue of the *li* present in them and that ethical failure is due to the obscuring effect of distortive desires and thoughts. However, while Chu regarded *li* as also residing in all things, Wang held the view that *li* ultimately resides in the way the mind responds to situations when not obscured, a point he put by saying that there is no *li* outside the mind.

Thus, unlike Mencius, who viewed self-cultivation as a process of developing shared incipient ethical inclinations, Chu and Wang viewed it as a process of making fully manifest the *li* in human beings which has been obscured by distortive desires and thoughts. Later Confucian thinkers regarded this as a reinterpretation of Mencian thought under Buddhist influence, and sought to recapture what they regarded as the true meaning of classical Confucianism. For example, Tai Chen regarded *li* not as a distinct metaphysical entity, but as the proper ordering of human desires and emotions which are due to *ch'i*. By applying a form of golden rule, one can know how one's own and other people's desires can be appropriately satisfied and emotions appropriately expressed, and this constitutes a grasp of *li*. *Hsing* is good not in the sense that human beings are already fully virtuous, but in the sense that being virtuous involves an ordering of desires and emotions natural to human beings.

Different views of *hsing* and of the underlying metaphysics have implications for ethical and political practices. For example, the view that there are bad elements in *hsing* tends to be coupled with some degree of advocacy of restrictive measures in politics—both Hsün Tzǔ and Tung Chung-shu advocated laws and punishment as secondary measures to restrain the bad elements in *hsing*. As another example, Chu Hsi's and Wang Yang-ming's different views of *li* led to different accounts of self-cultivation. Since Chu Hsi regarded *li* as present in all things, he regarded self-cultivation as involving to an important extent examining daily affairs and studying classics and historical records to regain the insight into *li* that one

originally had. However, given his view that *li* does not reside outside the mind, Wang regarded the method of cultivation advocated by Chu as misguided; instead, self-cultivation should involve one's attending to the mind, constantly watching out for and eliminating distortive desires and thoughts.

Thus, while Confucian thought is given unity by a roughly common ethical and political ideal and eventually by a set of canonical texts, it includes a rich variety of metaphysical views as well as conceptions of human nature and of self-cultivation. New advances and developments continue to be made up to the present, and Confucianism continues to exert great influence not just on Chinese intellectuals, but also on the social and political order as well as on the daily life of the Chinese up to the present century.   K.-L.S.

*Chinese philosophy; neo-Confucianism.

A Source Book in Chinese Philosophy, tr. and ed. Wing-tsit Chan (Princeton, NJ, 1963).
Confucius: The Analects, tr. D. C. Lau (Harmondsworth, 1979).
Hsün Tzǔ: Basic Writings, tr. Burton Watson (New York, 1963).
Mencius, tr. D. C. Lau (Harmondsworth, 1970).
Reflections on Things at Hand: The Neo-Confucian Anthology Compiled by Chu Hsi and Lü Tsu-ch'ien, tr. Wing-tsit Chan (New York, 1967).
Wang Yang-ming, *Instructions for Practical Living and Other Neo-Confucian Writings*, tr. Wing-tsit Chan (New York, 1963).

Confucius (sixth to fifth century BC). Chinese thinker regarded by many as a sage and worshipped in temples in certain parts of China. In intellectual circles, he is usually regarded as the founder of the Confucian school of thought. His full name was K'ung Ch'iu or K'ung Chung-ni, and he was also known as K'ung Fu-tzǔ (Master K'ung), latinized as 'Confucius'. He advocated restoring traditional values and norms as a remedy for the social and political disorder of his times, and sought political office in an attempt to put this ideal into practice. He never attained an influential position in government, and was much more influential as a teacher. His teachings are recorded in the *Analects* (*Lun Yü*), a collection of sayings by him and by his disciples, and of conversations between him and his disciples.

His ethical ideal includes a general affective concern for others (involving a preparedness to refrain from doing to others what one would not have wished done to oneself), certain desirable attributes within familial, social, and political institutions (such as filial piety and loyalty to rulers), as well as other traits such as courage and trustworthiness. It also includes the observance of various traditional norms governing both ceremonious behaviour (such as sacrificial rites, marriage ceremonies, reception of guests) as well as the responsibilities one has in virtue of one's social positions (such as the responsibilities of a son or an official). Those who have approximated the ideal will have a non-coercive transformative power on others; others will admire and be attracted to them, and will be inspired to emulate their way of life. This transformative power should ideally be the basis for government. Edicts and punishment can at best secure behavioural conformity but, if a ruler has approximated the ideal, he will care about and provide for the people, who will be attracted to him and be inspired to reform themselves.   K.-L.S.

*Confucianism; Chinese philosophy.

Confucius: The Analects, tr. D. C. Lau (Harmondsworth, 1979).

conjunction. A proposition (*P* and *Q*) is a conjunction where *P* and *Q* are each propositions. The English connective 'and' conjoining propositions is sometimes ambiguous. For example, temporal succession may or may not be implicit in 'Sally arrived late and Jane scolded her'.

In the *propositional calculus a conjunction (*P*·*Q*) is true if and only if each conjunct is true. Alternative notations for '·' are '&', '∧', and juxtaposition.

The inference of (*P*·*Q*) from premiss *P* and premiss *Q* is known as the rule of conjunction.   R.B.M.

*truth-function.

W. V. Quine, *Methods of Logic*, 4th edn. (Cambridge, Mass., 1982).

connectionism. An approach in *artificial intelligence and *cognitive science aimed at producing biologically realistic models of the brain and of mental processing; sometimes called PDP (*parallel distributed processing).

In 'old-fashioned' (or cognitivist) accounts, the brain is viewed as a symbol manipulator. In PDP (or connectionist) accounts, the brain is viewed as a complex weave of multilayered networks. The units of a network (which may be compared to the brain's neurons) are simple processors, and the connections between them, of which there are massively many, have different strengths. Information-processing is parallel, i.e. much is carried on simultaneously; and it is distributed, i.e. any individual connection participates in the storage of many different items of information.

There is controversy about the exact significance of this new approach, and about its repercussions for debates in the philosophy of mind.   J.HORN.

K. Plunkett, 'Connectionism Today', *Synthese*, 129/2 (2001).
William Ramsey, Stephen P. Stich, and David E. Rumelhart (eds.), *Philosophy and Connectionist Theory* (Hillsdale, NJ, 1991).

connective. A word or sequence of words which forms a complex indicative sentence when joined with an indicative sentence or sentences. For example, the English connective 'and' joins two sentences to make a more complex sentence. Connectives are classified according to the number of sentences with which they combine: 'it is not the case that' is a one-place connective and 'and' is two-place. Connectives also divide into the truth-functional and non-truth-functional. A connective is truth-functional if the truth-value(s) of the sentence(s) with which the connective combines completely determines the truth-value of the sentence formed through the combination; otherwise it is non-truth-functional. The '&' of the propositional

calculus is truth-functional: '*p* & *q*' is true if and only if *p* and *q* are both true.   A.D.O.

*truth-function.

R. M. Sainsbury, *Logical Forms* (Oxford, 1991), ch. 2.

connotation: *see* denotation.

conscience. By 'conscience' is meant the sense of *right and wrong in an individual; described variously by philosophers as a reflection of the voice of God, as a human faculty, as the voice of reason, or as a special *moral sense. The most famous modern discussion is in the work of Joseph Butler, who insisted on conscience's claim to 'authority' over other sources of motivation. In moral epistemology Butler combined the rationalist and moral sense theories of the eighteenth century, describing conscience as 'a sentiment of the understanding or a perception of the heart'. He underestimated the moral problem of the erring conscience, treated explicitly in Aquinas's *Summa Theologiae* (1a. 2ae, Q. 19, arts. 5 and 6). Aquinas pointed out that one acts badly in doing what is in fact bad, but also in going against conscience; so that unless he 'put away his error' someone of evil conscience cannot act well.   P.R.F.

Charles A. Baylis, 'Conscience', in Paul Edwards (ed.), *The Encyclopedia of Philosophy* (New York, 1967).

consciousness exists, but it resists definition. There are some criteria for saying of some organism or state that it is conscious. Consciousness involves experience or awareness. Human mental life has a phenomenal side, a subjective side that the most sophisticated information-processing system might lack. To paraphrase Thomas Nagel, there is something it is like to be in a conscious *mental state, something it is like for the organism itself. Conscious mental states are heterogeneous in phenomenal kind. Sensations, moods, emotions, dreams, propositional thought, self-awareness all occur consciously—perhaps some of these states only occur consciously.

For Descartes, all thinking is conscious; conscious thought is the essence of mind; humans have privileged and incorrigible access to their own conscious states; and the mind is a non-physical substance. The modern naturalistic consensus is that only some mental processes are conscious and that all mental events and processes are physical. That is, all mental states have neural *realizations in *Homo sapiens*. The best way to think about consciousness involves as a first step thinking in terms of conscious mental states and not in terms of consciousness as a unified faculty. Despite the widespread but by no means unanimous commitment to a naturalistic metaphysic of consciousness, there is heated debate over what exactly consciousness is; whether, and if so how, it can be studied; what if anything its causal role is; and whether, despite the fact that it is so far always realized in biological systems, it must be so realized. The fact that consciousness has a subjective, uniquely first-personal side has led some to maintain allegiance to the Cartesian view that consciousness is as consciousness seems. On this view, first-person phenomenology is the method for studying consciousness. The problem with this sort of view is that while it may be true that there is direct and privileged access to one's own conscious states, it does not follow that this access is incorrigible. First, even first-person phenomenology is ambivalent about the claim that we are always in perfect touch with whatever conscious state(s) we are in. Furthermore, even if we do have privileged and incorrigible access, the latter being stronger than the former, to the subjective aspects of consciousness, it does not follow that we have either sort of access to all the aspects of consciousness. If, as most naturalists think, consciousness has depth and hidden structure, then first-person phenomenology will hardly be capable of yielding a complete theory of consciousness. *Naturalism implies that conscious mental states supervene on certain neural states. What neural state my experience of red supervenes on is something to which there is no first-personal access.

Some philosophers are pessimistic about joining the subjective and objective sides of the story. Others are hopeful that we can yoke together the phenomenological, psychological, and neural analyses of conscious mental life to yield a more complete theory, a theory that gives the way things seem its due and which at the same time deepens our understanding of how conscious mental events are realized and what causal roles they play. The question of causal role is pressing. There is at present no widely accepted theory of why consciousness evolved. It seems to many that a merely informationally sensitive system, such as a community of ants and bees, may be, or could be, as well adapted as equivalent experientially sensitive systems. There is no doubt that we are conscious, but because the adaptive value of being conscious is not well understood, epiphenomenalism, the view that consciousness is a side-effect of more causally significant processes, remains a live, and much discussed, possibility in contemporary philosophy of mind and cognitive science. Another area of lively research and debate is on the relation of conscious states and intentional states. The dominant view is that many conscious states are not intentional. Some conscious states, such as moods, do not appear to be 'of' or 'about' anything. Relatedly, there is the question of whether unconscious mental states exist. If there are unconscious mental states, then the door is open for unconscious intentional states, for example, Freudian beliefs and desires. John Searle, despite advocating *'biological naturalism', thinks that Descartes was right in thinking that all bona fide mental states are conscious. On Searle's view there are no *unconscious mental states at all: all mental states are conscious states; beyond that there are just non-conscious neural states, events, and processes.   O.F.

*consciousness, its irreducibility; mind, syntax, and semantics; for-itself and in-itself; Honderich; intentionality; dualism; content of consciousness zombies.

D. Chalmers, *The Conscious Mind* (New York, 1996).
Daniel C. Dennett, *Consciousness Explained* (New York, 1991).
Owen Flanagan, *Consciousness Reconsidered* (Cambridge, Mass., 1992).
Thomas Nagel, 'What is it Like to Be a Bat?', in *Mortal Questions* (Cambridge, 1979).
John Searle, *The Rediscovery of Mind* (Cambridge, Mass., 1992).
Q. Smith and A. Jokic (eds.), *Consciousness: New Philosophical Perspectives* (Oxford, 2003).

consciousness, false: *see* false consciousness.

consciousness, its irreducibility. Many efforts have been made to identify consciousness with some other feature such as behaviour, functional states, or neurobiological states described solely in third-person neurobiological terms. All of these fail because consciousness has an irreducible subjective character which is not identical with any third-person objective features. Consciousness is irreducibly subjective in the sense that conscious states are experienced by and accessible to the individual who has them in a way that they are not experienced by or accessible to other individuals. To understand this point it is essential to distinguish between the epistemic sense of the distinction between objectivity and *subjectivity and the ontological sense. In the epistemic sense, objectivity is a matter of propositions being ascertainable by any competent observer as opposed to subjective matters which are relative to individual tastes and preferences. But in the ontological sense of the objective–subjective distinction, there are certain phenomena which are intrinsically subjective and other phenomena which are intrinsically objective. Such matters as mass, force, and gravitational attraction are ontologically objective, but, in this sense, consciousness is ontologically subjective. Subjectivity in this case is not a matter of the epistemology by way of which we find out about consciousness but a matter of its ontological status. The objection, then, to any form of *reductionism is that it is bound to fail because the ontologically subjective cannot be reduced to the ontologically objective.   J.R.S.

*behaviourism; artificial intelligence; cognition; functionalism; cognitive science.

F. Jackson, 'Epiphenomenal Qualia', *Philosophical Quarterly* (1982).
T. Nagel, 'What is it Like to Be a Bat?', in *Mortal Questions* (Cambridge, 1979).
J. R. Searle, *The Rediscovery of the Mind* (Cambridge, Mass., 1992).

consciousness, neural correlates of. Activities, states, or parts of central nervous systems which are directly related to the occurrence of conscious perceptions, feelings, thoughts, and intentions, maybe under certain environmental or bodily conditions. A central philosophical and also scientific question is whether the correlates are sufficient or just necessary for consciousness, and whether this is a matter of nomic connection or something else. How explanatory or predictive are they? Correlation, at least until more is said, is consistent with both dualistic theories of causal connection between mind and brain and also mind–brain identity theories. In fact, the existence of neural correlates is compatible with most of the different philosophical theories of mind–body relationship. When correlates are taken as being only necessary conditions for consciousness, they are compatible with the doctrine of externalism, to the effect that conscious states depend on extra-cranial facts. Still, the ongoing discovery of correlations has strengthened naturalistic views of the mind rather than any others.   R.V.

T. Metzinger (ed.), *Neural Correlates of Consciousness* (Cambridge, 2000).

consciousness, stream of: *see* stream of consciousness.

consent. The standard way of establishing *political obligation, and so binding citizens to obey the laws of the state, in liberal thought and, putatively at least, in liberal practice. Consent in the political realm is modelled on the private promise and subject to the same qualifications: it is morally binding only in so far as it is voluntary, undertaken with full knowledge, after deliberation. (The only exception to this rule is the act of surrender in war, where the implicit or explicit commitment not to renew the combat, made under extreme duress, is morally binding none the less.) The pre-liberal practice of exacting oaths of allegiance to new rulers (especially usurpers and conquerors, who had reason to worry about their legitimacy) suggests that the idea of consent has practical as well as theoretical value. As obviously or mysteriously as the promise, political consent generates a strong sense of being bound. Hence it provides a foundation for the claims made on individuals by established regimes and for the charge of criminal disobedience, rebellion, or treason if these claims are ignored or refused.

But explicit consent is relatively rare in political life. Oaths are commonly demanded only from notables, office-holders, and aliens in the process of naturalization. Or, they are ritually recited (as American schoolchildren recite the Pledge of Allegiance) under conditions that don't meet the requirements of rational agreement. In order to save the theory of obligation by consent, two different strategies have been adopted. The first is embodied in the idea of the social *contract as an act of hypothetical consent by imaginary men and women negotiating with one another (or engaged in solitary deliberation) in the artificial conditions of the *State of nature or the *original position. Real men and women are invited to recognize themselves in their imaginary fellows and to accept the conclusions they reach. The second strategy involves the redescription of certain ordinary acts and omissions as signs of tacit consent to the established form of political rule. These strategies might appear to cripple consent and render it unable to play any sort of foundational role, and yet they are compatible with radical claims: hence Hobbes's suggestion that rebels and traitors have consented to their own punishment—either because as

rational individuals they must have consented, or because as actual citizens they have tacitly consented, to the authority of the sovereign.

The leading candidates for strategic redescription are, in ascending order of plausibility, the failure to leave the country upon coming of age, the acceptance of whatever benefits the regime or, more generally, the ongoing system of political co-operation provides, and the decision to participate in certain political practices (voting, campaigning, protesting governmental policies). It is an interesting question whether redescription 'works' by virtue of being plausible, so that reasonable people ought to acknowledge its force, or only by virtue of being widely accepted as plausible, acknowledged in fact by actual people. The second view might well require the conclusion that consent doesn't 'work' at all, not at least in the way liberal writers hoped it would, since most people, if asked, would not be able to recognize their own putative agreements. They would probably declare themselves bound none the less, loyal and obedient citizens, but that kind of inward consent is as real in authoritarian as in liberal regimes.

Perhaps the strongest grounds for taking consent as the foundation of liberal democracy is the guaranteed right of dissent. If avenues of political protest and oppositional politics are genuinely open and widely used in particular cases, then the survival of the organized system of political co-operation might be a sign that people really value it and in that sense consent to its continuation.   M.WALZ.

*democracy; liberalism.

John Dunn, 'Consent in the Political Theory of John Locke', in *Political Obligation in its Historical Context* (Cambridge, 1980).
P. H. Partridge, *Consent and Consensus* (New York, 1971).
J. P. Plamenatz, *Consent, Freedom and Political Obligation*, 2nd edn. (Oxford, 1968).

consequentialism determines the rightness or wrongness of an act, either solely by comparing the act's consequences with the consequences of alternative acts, or solely by comparing the consequences of rules or practices or motives that allow the act with the consequences of rules or practices or motives that prohibit the act.

The term 'consequentialism' first appeared in Elizabeth Anscombe's article 'Modern Moral Philosophy' (*Philosophy*, 1958). Anscombe espoused a kind of moral *absolutism according to which some kinds of act (e.g. intentionally killing the innocent) are wrong in any circumstances, i.e. no matter how bad the consequences would be of not doing the act. She used the term 'consequentialism' to refer to any moral theory that rejected such absolutism. On the meaning Anscombe gave to 'consequentialism', the simple view that *only* consequences matter qualifies as a kind of consequentialism. But so does the view (espoused by many *moral pluralists) that, while consequences are only one among a plurality of moral factors, consequences are a factor of sufficient importance to make it the case that any kind of act can be morally right if it has good enough consequences or avoids bad enough consequences. Few philosophers now use 'consequential-ism' so broadly.

There is controversy, however, over whether the term 'consequentialism' should or should not extend so far as to allow the goodness of consequences to be *agent-relative. If each agent is required to produce the best available set of consequences, but the goodness of consequences is rela-tive to the agent who produces them, then different agents will be required to produce different sets of conse-quences. An extreme example of agent-relative conse-quentialism is the kind of egoism that claims an act is right if and only if it produces the best available consequences *for the agent*. This kind of egoism can reach different con-clusions about the rightness of an act that makes Jill worse off but produces the best available consequences for Jack. If Jack did this act, this kind of egoism judges the action to be right. If instead Jill did this act, this kind of egoism judges it to be wrong.

Another controversy over how broadly to take the term 'consequentialism' concerns the relation between acts and consequences. Perhaps the most natural reading of 'consequences' assumes that, apart from exceptional cases, an act is not part of its consequences. (This is not to deny that some of an act's consequences may be part of the act: killing Jones necessarily has the consequence that Jones goes from alive to dead. Perhaps in the special case of an act that produces the best consequences, all of the act's consequences are part of the act. But we can think that an act is not part of its consequences even if we admit that some or all of the act's consequences are part of the act.) If an act is not part of its consequences, then any intrinsic value in the act itself will not be included in the value of the consequences. So, if an act is not part of its consequences, and if consequentialism evaluates an act by its consequences, then consequentialist evaluation of acts ignores any intrinsic value in the act itself.

Examples of acts that have been thought to contain intrinsic value are acts of promise keeping, of loyalty to friends and family, of gratitude, of reparation to those whom one has wronged, and acts of developing one's own talents and capacities. Examples of acts that have been thought to contain intrinsic disvalue are acts of harming the innocent, of stealing, of promise breaking, of disloyalty, of threatening to infringe others' rights, of lying, and acts of taking pleasure in the misfortune or suffering of others. However, whether these or any other acts have intrinsic value or disvalue is controversial. So is whether to use the term 'consequentialism' so broadly as to include theories that attribute intrinsic value or disvalue to acts.

Also controversial is the question of how much a con-sequentialist theory can take facts about the past to be morally pivotal. It might seem that, if acts or rules or prac-tices or motives are evaluated solely in terms of their con-sequences, this evaluation ignores any relation an outcome might have with the past. However, many who have called themselves consequentialists ascribe intrinsic value to equal distributions among currently existing people over their whole lives (as opposed to during each time slice). Since currently existing lives are partly in the past, this kind of egalitarianism takes that past to be morally relevant. Another group who think of themselves as consequentialists evaluate outcomes wholly or partly in terms of whether agents get what they deserve. This approach also takes facts about the past to be morally piv-otal, since what people deserve presumably depends on their past.

So some philosophers use the term 'consequentialism' broadly enough to allow for the inclusion of agent-relativity. Some use 'consequentialism' broadly enough to allow for inclusion of whatever intrinsic value or disvalue acts have. And some use 'consequentialism' broadly enough to allow facts about the past to be morally relevant. However, if the borders of 'consequentialism' are pushed out so far in all three directions, then 'conse-quentialism' acquires such a wide meaning that virtually every moral theory could be formulated as a kind of con-sequentialism. The term 'consequentialism' should not be stretched so far as to trivialize it.

Moreover, there is a good reason for consequentialists specifically not to allow agent-relativity into the founda-tional level of their theory. This reason derives from the very close association of morality with *impartiality. Much of the appeal of the most philosophically prominent forms of consequentialism derives from their aspiration to substantive impartiality at the foundational level of their theory.

There is also a good reason for consequentialists not to allow intrinsic value for acts, intrinsic disvalue for acts, or desert into the foundational level of their theory. What a theory assumes, it does not explain. So if consequential-ism starts by assuming that such-and-such kinds of behav-iour deserve reward and so-and-so kinds of behaviour deserve punishment, then consequentialism is not explaining why there should be practices of reward and punishment. Likewise, if consequentialism starts by assuming that such-and-such kinds of act have intrinsic value and so-and-so kinds have intrinsic disvalue, then consequentialism is positing rather than explaining the value of such acts. Theories become less interesting the more they posit rather than try to explain. Many conse-quentialists have thus eschewed assumptions about desert and the intrinsic value or intrinsic disvalue of acts.

The most philosophically prominent form of conse-quentialism has been the combination of the commitment to impartiality with the commitment to pleasure as the single intrinsic value. The classic *utilitarians—Jeremy Bentham, J. S. Mill, and Henry Sidgwick—held that the consequences that matter ultimately are increases or decreases in aggregate *happiness, which they took to consist in pleasure. In the twentieth century, however, many philosophers and economists were persuaded that what people rationally want for themselves can extend beyond pleasure and indeed beyond any other introspect-ively discernible state. In the name of preference auton-omy, many philosophers moved from thinking that the fundamental value is pleasure or happiness to thinking that it is more broadly the fulfilment of people's desires.

Other consequentialists have been impressed by the thought that people can desire things for themselves that are in fact worthless. Some of these consequentialists have held that a good life for us is one in which we both get or achieve certain things and desire these things. Examples of what these things might be are autonomy, knowledge, friendship, achievement, beauty, and the perfection of our natures (intellectual and physical). But there is disagreement among consequentialists (as well as among other philosophers) whether, in addition to pleasure, these other things have intrinsic value.

There is also disagreement among consequentialists about what view of distribution to take. The classical utilitarians held that what matters is the amount of aggregate good, where this is calculated by impartially adding together everyone's good (i.e. with equal weighting). Later consequentialists held that it matters not only how much aggregate good is produced but also how equally this good is distributed. *Equality as an aim in distribution has come under attack because of its acceptance of 'levelling down'. Instead of aiming for equality, many consequentialists have advocated *prioritarianism, the view that gains in the well-being of the worse off are morally more important than the same size gains for the better off. Whether such priority for the worst off is compatible with substantive impartiality, however, is uncertain.

A more general dispute between consequentialists concerns the common sort of situation where consequences cannot be known with certainty in advance. Some consequentialists frame their theory in terms of *actual* value: that is, the value of the outcome that would *in fact* result. Other consequentialists frame their theory in terms of the *expected* value. Expected value is calculated by multiplying the values of each possible outcome by the probability of that outcome's occurring and then adding together the products of these multiplications.

Especially since the 1950s, consequentialists have taken a variety of views about the connection between (actual or expected) good and moral rightness. Three of the most prominent consequentialist views have been maximizing act-consequentialism, satisficing act-consequentialism, and rule-consequentialism.

Maximizing act-consequentialism holds that an act is morally right if and only if that particular act maximizes (expected) impartial value. This is a view about morally right action. It is not the view that the agent's standard decision procedure should consist of trying to calculate the expected values of the alternative possible actions and then choosing the one with the highest expected value. Very few (if any) maximizing act-consequentialists think agents should have such a decision procedure. Agents frequently lack the information needed to calculate the expected good. Even if they had the information, they would frequently miscalculate. Even if they didn't miscalculate, there is the cost in time and attention of doing the calculations. Furthermore, there are 'expectation effects'.

If people could not confidently predict that others would behave in certain ways (e.g. not attack others, not steal, not break their promises, not lie, etc.) without having to wait for the endorsement of consequentialist calculations, there would be a disastrous breakdown of trust in society.

For these and other reasons, most maximizing act-consequentialists hold that the decision procedure that agents should have for day-to-day moral thinking is made up of rules such as 'Don't harm others', 'Don't steal', 'Keep your promises', 'Tell the truth', 'Look out for the welfare of your friends and family', and so on. Maximizing act-consequentialism therefore agrees to a considerable extent with agent-relative moralities and *deontological ethics about how agents should decide what to do. But opponents of maximizing act-consequentialism hold that acts of intentionally injuring others, stealing, promise breaking, and other infringements of moral rights can be morally wrong even when the acts maximize impartial good.

Impartial maximizing act-consequentialism is also persistently attacked for unreasonably making relentless demands on ordinary people to sacrifice their own good in order to help needy strangers. A version of consequentialism that tries to accommodate that objection is satisficing act-consequentialism, a theory developed by Michael Slote. According to this theory, an act is morally permissible if and only if its consequences are good enough. Obviously, satisficing act-consequentialism may have difficulty specifying what counts as 'good enough'. Tim Mulgan's *Demands of Consequentialism* (2001) put forward other devastating objections to satisficing act-consequentialism. One is that satisficing act-consequentialism is even more permissive with respect to acts of intentionally injuring others, stealing, promise breaking, and so on than maximizing act-consequentialism is. The other objection is that, where the cost to the agent and others of producing the best consequences is no more than that of producing less good consequences, satisficing act-consequentialism seems mistaken to allow the agent to choose the less good consequences.

Rule-consequentialism calls for the code of rules whose general acceptance has the greatest expected value, impartially considered. The theory then judges the rightness or wrongness of acts by that code. No kind of impartial act-consequentialism does as well as rule-consequentialism at agreeing with agent-relative moralities and deontological ethics about which acts are right and which wrong. But rule-consequentialism disagrees with agent-relative moralities and deontological ethics (and of course with every other rival theory) over the fundamental explanation of why certain acts are right and others wrong. Since the 1960s, rule-consequentialism has repeatedly been attacked as an unstable or incoherent compromise between deontology and act-consequentialism.   B.H.

*absolutism, moral; agent-relative moralities; deontological ethics; unlikely philosophical propositions.

F. Feldman, *Utilitarianism, Hedonism, and Desert* (New York, 1997).

B. Hooker, *Ideal Code, Real World: A Rule-Consequentialist Theory of Morality* (Oxford, 2000).

D. McNaughton and P. Rawling, 'On Defending Deontology', *Ratio* (1998).

D. Parfit, *Reasons and Persons*, part 2 (Oxford, 1984).

P. Pettit, 'The Consequentialist Perspective', in M. Baron, P. Pettit, and M. Slote (eds.), *Three Methods of Ethics* (Oxford, 1997).

S. Scheffler, *Consequentialism and its Critics* (Oxford, 1988).

conservatism. An approach to political and social questions which was mapped out initially by Burke, though drawing on earlier lines of thought dating back to Hobbes and even to Aristotle, and subsequently developed by many writers, including, notably, Oakeshott and, in his later years, Hayek. The conservative approach is empirical as opposed to rationalistic, cautiously sceptical rather than dogmatic, and, in certain circumstances, seeks to preserve the status quo rather than engage in wholesale revolution or overthrow existing institutions. It is a matter of judgement how far so-called conservative political parties are conservative in the wider, philosophical sense. Nor would a philosophical conservative seek to preserve an apparently orderly political set-up simply for the sake of preserving order if that set-up were based on principles antithetical to conservatism (as was the case in Eastern Europe during the Cold War).

Recognizably conservative thinkers have held a large variety of views on such matters as religion, ethics, and the concept of *human nature. But, unlike liberals and socialists, they have all possessed a keen sense of the darker, more egoistic sides of human beings. For the conservative, the main defence against the Hobbesian war of all against all is not the naked might of the sovereign. Naked power over others, whether vested in a hereditary tyrant, a central party committee, or an elected legislature, would actually be a form of the war of all against all. Life in such a society, as in Eastern Europe under communism, would be characterized by mutual fear and suspicion.

For the conservative, egoism, power, and mutual suspicion need what Burke referred to as 'the decent drapery of life', 'pleasing illusions . . . to make power gentle, and obedience liberal'. Without institutions and forms to temper and channel the energy and rapacity of the strong, and to commend the allegiance of the ruled, we will have a society which is dominated either by terror or by continual litigiousness, and neither state is conducive to peace or enjoyment.

Where, though, are civilizing and allegiance-provoking institutions and forms to come from? Here again the conservative differs significantly from liberals and socialists. F. H. Bradley echoes Hegel in saying that 'the man into whose essence his community with others does not enter, who does not include relations to others in his very being, is a fiction'; the individual is who he is because of the relationships and the *society into which he is born. Individuality being situated in this way implies the existence of duties and roles not chosen by the individual, binding on him and constitutive of his identity. His relationship to his

society and its institutions is not first and foremost a contractual one, as liberals would maintain. Whether, in practice, the relationship is oppressive or genial will depend on the decency or indecency of the drapery of particular societies.

Ideally, for a conservative each society's forms and institutions will have evolved steadily over generations. Such steady evolution will have two beneficial consequences. First, it will enable today's individuals to see themselves as linked to earlier centuries, reinforcing their own sense of identity and culture. Secondly, in evolving over time, institutions will be shaped in accordance with the demands made on them; their defects and unintended consequences will become apparent and, under pressure for reform, reshaped.

Far from being opposed to *reform, a principle of reform is central to conservatism. For conservatives are sceptical of the ability of planners to know the consequences of policies or, indeed, of anyone to be able to survey everything going on in a large society. Rulers must legislate, but there must be means of counterbalancing and ameliorating the effects of their policies. In the end, by trial and error, institutions and forms develop, often in ways undreamt of by their founders but often in ways which do serve the needs of those involved in them. They thus embody a kind of tacit wisdom. Because of his admitted ignorance about the ways in which things work and about the effects of change, the conservative, though open to reform, will be cautious about large-scale disturbance of things which are running reasonably well. He will also seek to uncover the wisdom latent in ancient institutions and traditions.

Our ignorance of the effects of policies and of the nature of society makes the conservative favour limited government, autonomous institutions (such as the family, the army, churches, and schools), and individual *freedom. Conservatism, with its hesitations about human perfectibility and its sense of the corrupting effect of power, would prefer government to focus on its basic tasks of upholding security and a framework of law in which individual decisions and transactions can be made. Despite what is sometimes claimed, there is, in fact, no conflict between conservatism and the free *market, once markets are understood as simply the most efficient way we know of enabling individuals to pursue their own ends, and once it is realized that markets depend for their proper running on an antecedent framework of law and morality.

Those who see the state of their society as riddled with defects and inequities are likely to be impatient with conservatism for what appears to be its complacency. Surely, it will be urged, and not only by those moved by what conservatives would call the *hermeneutics of suspicion, we must be able to reorganize things in a new and better way, so as to eliminate whatever serious social and political problems we are confronted with.

Conservatism, then, looks like little more than self-interest without the support of moral principle. Moreover, the conservative stress on human ignorance, the concomitant hostility to reason in political planning, and the counterbalancing appeal to the wisdom of generations is not just depressing of human endeavour and good intention; it would, its critics say, not be given a hearing in any other sphere, particularly not in the scientific, where such principles would doubtless license creationism and flat-earthism.

Is conservatism based on nothing more than self-interest bolstered up by a fine-sounding but ultimately shifty obscurantism? It is true that conservatism, as exemplified by Burke, say, will in certain circumstances tend to uphold hierarchies and distinctions in a society. To that extent, it is a position which, from a functional point of view, is acting in the interests of those hierarchies, and will doubtless earn for the conservative the disapproval of moralists such as Matthew Arnold. What the moralist needs to ask himself, though, is whether (in Maurice Cowling's words) 'the freedom, discipline and social solidarity of modern societies' would be possible at all without 'the inequalities, sufferings and alienations consequent upon ideological hegemony'. Burke's point would, of course, be that the inequalities etc. consequent upon the French and Russian Revolutions were certainly no less than those of before, while the freedoms were a great deal less. And as far as socialism or its opposite are concerned in basically democratic societies, the right balance between inequality and freedom is always a difficult one to find. Experience at least has shown that it cannot be assumed that centralized attempts either to increase freedom or reduce inequality will actually have the desired effects. The conservative tendency will always be to defend the tolerable and even the tolerably bad against what he fears will be immeasurably worse.

In any case, the Burkian conservative would not defend any sort of hierarchy just because it is hierarchical. In particular, he would not defend a hierarchical society in which all important institutions are in the hands of the state. As part of his ignorance thesis, the conservative must support autonomous institutions and the freedom of individuals to make their own way through life and to form and develop their own little platoons. He will also deny, in distinction to natural science, that there are any special experts in morality or politics, asserting that the experience of the whole of mankind over time is the main source of moral knowledge, against which should be balanced the pretensions of any particular set of people to moral expertise, however intelligent they are in particular fields.

Upholding the right of individuals to make their own way through life and to benefit (or not) from the results of their efforts, as the conservative does, is to say that individuals are the best judges of their own interests. It is not to say, as critics claim the conservative is saying, that individuals should be motivated only by selfishness. The conservative, indeed, stresses the importance of the traditional *virtues of individuals providing for their dependants and also of charity, and would emphasize the problems, social and individual, which arise when all such matters are placed in the hands of the state.

While the conservative does not find *inequality *per se* objectionable, and will claim that there is no reason beyond resentment why anyone should, the value the conservative puts on both social cohesion and individual self-reliance must push him some way in the direction of economic redistribution, in order to ensure that no one starts so far behind the rest as to be unable to make his or her own way through life. The conservative is neither an anarchist nor a *laissez-faire* liberal.

In practice, in democratic societies the difference over redistribution between 'one nation' conservatives and welfarist socialists will tend to be one of degree. The conservative, though, will be more resistant to centralized controls and blueprints than his opponents on the left. This resistance arises not out of sheer obscurantism nor out of failure to recognize the need for limited social interventions. It is rather because the conservative is more sensitive than his opponents to the unintended consequences of such plans, to their potential for bureaucratic bossiness and interference, to the self-serving characteristic of bureaucracies, and to the way centralized planning cramps individual initiative, undermining the intuitive sense individuals have of their right to keep the rewards of their efforts, talents, and luck. Attacking this intuition by a policy of bureaucratic egalitarianism will seem to the conservative likely to sap whatever enterprise or energy exists in a society, and it cannot be said that history has shown him to be wrong.

The issue between conservatism and political rationalism, whether of a liberal or a socialist cast, is in the end an empirical one. Have those societies which have had autonomous traditions and unplanned institutions done better socially and economically than those in which radical and centralizing planning have been attempted? And, in the developing world, have countries which have modelled themselves and their institutions on a conservative free-market model proved more successful than those governed by rationalistic attempts to impose new types of order on their peoples? If the facts of history suggest that a conservative approach to politics produces greater *liberty and *well-being for individuals than rationalist approaches, conservatives can rebut the charge that they are merely advocating self-interest, and that their scepticism about politics is sheerly obscurantist.

With their emphasis on learning from experience and their mistrust of a priori reasoning in social and political matters, conservatives might welcome a broadly empirical approach to these questions. They would, though, do well to temper any triumphalism the answers might tempt them to. No country in the modern world has as limited a government as, in their different ways Burke, Hayek, or Oakeshott would see as compatible with true conservatism.   A.O'H.

*anti-communism; liberalism; socialism; Marxism; Marxist philosophy.

E. Burke, *Reflections on the Revolution in France* (1790).
F. A. Hayek, *The Fatal Conceit* (London, 1988).

G. W. F. Hegel, *The Philosophy of Right* (1833).

T. Honderich, *Conservatism* (London, 1990).

M. Oakeshott, *Rationalism in Politics* (London, 1962).

R. Scruton, *The Meaning of Conservatism* (London, 1980).

conservatism and Romanticism. Romanticism was a reaction against *Enlightenment rationalism, stressing the importance of non-rational or even irrational aspects of human nature. Conservatism, too, is critical of what it takes as the shallowness of rationalism. Not surprisingly, therefore, some important conservative thinkers manifest Romantic tendencies, and vice versa. Examples would be the defence of the wisdom contained in spontaneous custom and tradition in Edmund Burke, the cultural organicism of J. G. Herder, the mystical attitude to authority and monarchy of Louis de Bonald and Joseph de Maistre, and Thomas Carlyle's exaltation of the hero as genius and type. However, following strains of thought in Rousseau, the predominant tendency of the Romantic Movement emphasized the natural, the free, and the unconventional. If you suspect the workings of *reason, one possible response will be to replace the rational and the conventional with the spontaneous and the *natural, and, even, like the German Romantics, to attempt to break down all existing categories of thought and language. The conservative, though, schooled in Hobbes and in history, is too aware of the destination of unconstrained freedom, and relies rather on a strong social and cultural order, buttressed by tradition. Thus, Burke, Bonald, and de Maistre, though certainly anti-Enlightenment Romantics in their attitude to tradition and to authority, would have none of the free-booting insouciance of a Byron, nor of the antinomianism of a Novalis or an E. T. A. Hoffmann.   A.O'H.

I. Berlin, *The Crooked Timber of Humanity* (London, 1992).

A. O. Lovejoy, *Essays in the History of Ideas* (Baltimore, 1948).

consilience. According to Whewell, consilience occurs when inductive explanations of two or more different kinds of phenomena are discovered separately, but unexpectedly lead scientists to the same underlying cause. For example, universal gravitation explained both the perturbations of the planets and the precession of the equinoxes. Such discoveries corroborate one another in proportion to the number of explanations thus connected, as do independent testimonies to the same fact in a legal trial.

L.J.C.

*induction.

W. Whewell, *The Philosophy of the Inductive Sciences* (London, 1847), ii. 65–8.

consistency proofs. A set of *axioms is said to be *consistent* if no contradiction can be derived from the set by logical reasoning. This notion is best confined to axioms in a precisely defined formal language with given rules of inference; otherwise the logical *paradoxes might make any set of axioms inconsistent. By the *completeness theorem, a set of first-order axioms is consistent if and only if some interpretation makes it true. Hilbert's programme proposed a goal for the foundations of mathematics, namely to prove the consistency of axioms for arithmetic, using only finitary methods. *Gödel's incompleteness theorem showed that this is impossible if 'finitary methods' consist of syntactic operations on finite strings of symbols (as Hilbert probably intended); but Gödel also gave a consistency proof for first-order Peano arithmetic, using only finite mental constructions.   W.A.H.

G. T. Kneebone, *Mathematical Logic and the Foundations of Mathematics* (London, 1963), chs. 7 and 8.

constant. In the *propositional calculus, a constant is a truth-functional operator, such as 'not', 'and', or 'or'. The truth-value of 'p and q', for instance, is a *function* of the truth-values of 'p' and 'q': it's true if they are both true, false if either is false. 'Variable' was originally applied, by contrast, to sentence-letters 'p', 'q', etc. The specific role of a constant can be given by a *truth-table, or by its introduction and elimination rules (the basic rules governing its involvement in logical inferences). Beyond the confines of the propositional calculus, other symbols with fixed meanings can also be called constants, e.g. the symbols for 'all', 'some', and 'is the same as' (in predicate logic), and for 'necessarily' and 'possibly' (in *modal logic).   R.P.L.T.

W. Hodges, *Logic* (Harmondsworth, 1977), sect. 17.

constant conjunction. Term used by Hume to describe the relation between two events one of which invariably accompanies the other. If catching influenza is always followed by fever, these events are 'constantly conjoined'; if there is no smoke without fire, there is a constant conjunction between the production of smoke and burning. Hume regarded our experience of constant conjunctions as the principal source of our idea of *causality. Many interpreters have held that he also proposed an *analysis* of causality in terms of constant conjunction.   P.J.M.

D. Hume, *A Treatise of Human Nature* (1739), ed. L. A. Selby-Bigge and P. H. Nidditch (Oxford, 1978), I. iii. 6 and 15.

Constant de Rebecque, Henri Benjamin (1767–1830). Although Swiss-born, Constant came to play a leading role in the politics and development of liberal ideology in France. His *liberalism grew out of a critique of the ideas of his compatriot Rousseau that was sparked off by their employment by the Jacobins during the French Revolution. Drawing on the arguments of the Scottish *Enlightenment, which he had picked up during a brief period at the University of Edinburgh, he contended that the advent of commercial society had radically changed the character of *liberty and the political mechanisms needed to secure it. In the ancient republics that inspired Rousseau's works, freedom had been understood primarily in collective terms and had involved participation in the life of the polity in order to secure it. Within modern societies, in contrast, liberty was essentially individualistic in nature. The division of labour had destroyed any notion of a common good or *general will. The public welfare could only be promoted by protecting the ability of individuals to pursue their private ends and accumulate property by freely contracting and exchanging with each other in the *market. This goal was best achieved not through direct forms of participatory democracy, since unrestricted popular sovereignty could prove as tyrannous as an unrestricted monarch, but via liberal constitutional mechanisms such as representative democracy, the separation of powers, and a bill of rights.   R.P.B.

   *conservatism.

B. Constant, *Political Writings*, tr. and ed. Biancamaria Fontana (Cambridge, 1988).
S. Holmes, *Benjamin Constant and the Making of Modern Liberalism* (New Haven, Conn., 1984).

constatives. Class of 'fact-stating' utterances considered in the work of J. L. Austin. He initially distinguished constative uses of speech, where a speaker *states* something, from performative uses, where a speaker *does* something. But he came to doubt his own distinction, realizing that stating is a species of doing, and that stating, like other speech-acts that may use performative formulas, should be classified as *illocutionary.   J.HORN.

   *linguistic acts.

J. L. Austin, *How to Do Things with Words* (Oxford, 1961).

constitutionalism relates to both the foundation and the regulation of governments. As a foundationalist doctrine, it finds expression in the constitutional conventions that have not only served to establish new political regimes, as occurred in many European states after the Second World War, but have also led to the formation of states, as in the case of the United States. As a regulative doctrine, it consists of formal conventions, rules, and procedures, such as voting by majority rule, and more substantive norms, such as those embodied in written bills of rights or assumed prerogatives and entitlements, which serve to define legitimate political activity. Whilst conservatives have generally interpreted constitutionalism in terms of the practices that have evolved over time and favour the unwritten constitution of tradition and custom, liberals associate it with the limitation of government and usually favour a written constitution. Constitutionalism harbours a paradox, however, that is particularly problematic for the liberal view. For in both its foundationalist and regulative guises it seeks to lie outside politics, providing its grounding and framework, and yet can only achieve these ends by political means. As a result, constitutions come to be objects of political debate and consequently are within the very politics they claim to create and control.   R.P.B.

   *conservatism; liberalism.

S. Elkin and K. E. Soltan (eds.), *A New Constitutionalism: Designing Political Institutions for a Good Society* (Chicago, 1993).
C. H. McIlwain, *Constitutionalism Ancient and Modern* (New York, 1940).

constructivism. The thesis of the programme is that an assertion that there exists a mathematical object (such as a number) with a given property is an assertion that one knows how to find, or construct, such an object. Philosophical opponents of constructivism include realists, who hold that since mathematical objects exist independent of the mind of the mathematician, one can establish the existence of an object without showing how to find it. Most constructivists hold that principles of reasoning concerning ordinary, finite domains do not apply to mathematics. For example, if one proves that not all natural numbers lack a certain property, one cannot conclude that there is a number that has the property, because the indicated proof need not provide a method for constructing such a number. Similarly, the laws of *excluded middle and double negation are also rejected. The technique of *reductio ad absurdum* can only be used to establish a negative formula. Constructivism can result from reflection either on the nature of mathematics (Brouwer) or on the learnability of mathematical language (Dummett).   s.s.

   *intuitionism; intuitionistic logic; mathematics, problems of the philosophy of; mathematics, history of the philosophy of.

C. Chihara, *Constructibility and Mathematical Existence* (Oxford, 1990).
Erret Bishop, *Foundations of Constructive Analysis* (New York, 1967).

constructivism in ethics. The term 'constructivism' was first applied to ethical theories by *John Rawls. The basic idea is that a system of moral obligations can be constructed using an uncontroversial procedure, and starting from uncontroversial premises about human nature. Thus the constructivist approach is supposed to yield a moral theory that has no odd metaphysical commitments, and is demonstrably true (or at the very least, reasonable). Rawls's own view developed over his lifetime, but remained broadly constructivist in its form: if a group of people situated in a certain way would choose a set of principles, then those principles are legitimate. When Rawls introduced the term, he intended it in a fairly narrow sense: to apply to views that, like his, started from premises about choices that rational beings would make in certain circumstances. These days the term is used more broadly, to include views such as Korsgaard's that start from premises about our nature more generally.   E.J.M.

consumerist ethics. The ethics of consumerism partly derives from the *rights-based approach to morality which was a marked feature of the second half of the twentieth century, and partly has been encouraged by those who advocate belief in the efficacy and essential righteousness of a free-market economy. The main concepts in consumer ethics are *access* to, *choice* of, and *information* about goods and services, *competition* beween suppliers, *safety regulations*, and *redress* in the event of faulty goods or services. Consumerism can be seen as a specific outcome of nineteenth-century *laissez-faire* individualism, and it is therefore opposed to any form of paternalism and to professional perceptions of social need in the supply of goods and services.   R.S.D.

P. N. Stearms, *Consumerism in World History: The Global Transformation of Desire* (London, 2001).

content, non-conceptual. Theorists of non-conceptual mental content hold that some mental states can represent the world and be true or false even though the bearer of those mental states does not possess the *concepts required to specify how they represent the world (to specify their content). This basic idea has been used to try to do justice to the differences between how the world is represented in perceptual experience and how it is represented in belief, as well as to elucidate the representational content of subpersonal computational states, such as those appealed to in information-processing accounts of vision. On some accounts of what it is to possess a concept, the representational states of non-linguistic creatures such as human infants and non-human animals have non-conceptual content. Not all of these developments and applications are consistent with each other, but each offers a challenge to the widely held view that the way in which a creature can represent the world is determined by its conceptual capacities.   J.BER.

*cognition; perception.

Y. H. Gunther (ed.), *Essays on Nonconceptual Content* (Cambridge, Mass., 2003).

content of consciousness. That which one is, or seems to be, conscious of. The content of *consciousness is to be contrasted with one's consciousness of it. The consciousness is always mental, the content may (e.g. a toothache) or may not (a sunset) be mental. Contents come in two distinct flavours: sensory and propositional. In seeing (or hallucinating) a spotted cow, the content of sensory consciousness is either the spotted cow, if there is one, or (on some theories of perception) a mental image (*percept, *sense-datum, appearance) of a spotted cow. In either case, spottedness is a feature of the content, of *what* one is conscious of. The content of propositional awareness, on the other hand, is a *proposition, what it is one consciously knows or believes, judges or thinks. Believing that there are spotted cows, for example, is a mental state that has as its content the (possibly false) proposition that there are spotted cows or that one is seeing a spotted cow. Propositions, even propositions about spotted cows, are not themselves spotted.   F.D.

C. McGinn, *Mental Content* (Oxford, 1989).
C. Peacocke, *Sense and Content* (Oxford, 1983).

contextual definition. Definition of an expression by explaining systematically how to paraphrase all sentences in which the expression is to be used. It is far more widely applicable than direct definition, which paraphrases the expression in isolation. It supports the view that sentences rather than words are the basic vehicles of meaning.

In 1813 Bentham propounded contextual definition, or 'definition by paraphrasis', as a way of accommodating convenient expressions without commitment to fictitious objects to which they seem to refer. Thirty years later Boole applied the idea in mathematics, instituting a so-called method of operators. Familiar operators are the minus sign, the square-root sign, the prefix 'log' for logarithm, the 'sin' and 'cos' of trigonometry. Boole simulated multiplication, as if '$-x$', '$\sqrt{x}$', '$\log x$', and the rest were numerical products like '$5x$', subject to the usual algebraic manipulations. He applied the idea to operators in the differential and integral calculus, where it became standard procedure.

Russell's account (1905) of singular *descriptions as 'incomplete symbols' is a celebrated contextual definition, prompted, he wrote, by the method of operators. He wanted to make sense of '*the* object x such that Fx', symbolically '$(\imath x)Fx$', irrespective of there being such a unique object. Where '$G(\imath x)Fx$' represents an innermost context of '$(\imath x)Fx$', hence an innermost sentence about that purported object, Russell defined '$G(\imath x)Fx$' as

There is something y such that Gy and such that anything x is identical with y if and only if Fx.   W.V.Q.

Bertrand Russell, 'On Denoting', *Mind* (1905); repr. in R. C. Marsh (ed.), *Bertrand Russell: Logic and Knowledge* (London, 1965).

contextualism. The dependence of important features of language (or thought) on the surroundings in language or reality; also called token-reflexiveness, of which egocentricity is one species. Any linguistic expression can be used many times—e.g. there is only one English word 'mother' (the word-type), and one sentence 'Today is her birthday' (the sentence-type), but many utterances of them (word-tokens and sentence-tokens). The *referents of singular terms, the truth-values of sentences, and the illocutionary force of an utterance often depend on the context of use. Who 'she' refers to depends on the linguistic or perceptual context of utterance, who 'my mother' refers to depends on who is speaking; the truth of 'Today is her birthday' depends on the date, and the point of saying this (e.g. as an excuse for rejecting an invitation) will depend on other features of the context. The meaning of an ambiguous word or sentence is also context-dependent (e.g. 'He went to the bank', 'Flying planes can be dangerous'). According to some theorists such as Charles Travis, some kind of contextualism, occasion-sensitivity, or *externalism affects *all* language use. A contextualist theory of *meaning would try to make all this explicit, giving rules by which meaning, reference, truth-value, and linguistic act can be determined from sentence-type and context of use.   L.F.S.

*egocentric particulars.

R. M. Gale, 'Indexical Reference, Egocentric Particulars, and Token-Reflexive Words', in P. Edwards (ed.), *Encyclopedia of Philosophy* (New York, 1967).
G. Preyer (ed.), *Contextualism in Philosophy* (Oxford, 2005).

continental philosophy. The phrase 'continental philosophy' acquired its current meaning only after the Second World War when a process of increasing mutual exclusion of the English-speaking philosophical world and that of the continent of Europe, which had been going on since early in the century, was finally recognized to be as deep as it was. In the Middle Ages philosophy, expressed in the universal learned language of Latin, was practised by philosophers who, whatever their place of birth, were constantly in movement from one centre of learning to another. This unity survived the Renaissance and even the initiation of writing philosophy in the vernacular by Bacon and Descartes. The vernacular came later to Germany, primarily as the vehicle of Kant's three *Critiques*. His earlier writings had been in Latin, as had been those of Leibniz, when they were not in French. The latter's disciple Christian Wolff, in whose school of thought Kant had been brought up, published his work in both Latin and German versions.

Locke, whose writings were so influential in France, was himself influenced by Descartes and Gassendi and studied Malebranche. Hume, who woke Kant from his 'dogmatic slumber', read Bayle (and was accused by Samuel Johnson of writing like a Frenchman). The Scottish philosophy of common sense was a central element in the official eclecticism of Victor Cousin in the period of the Orleanist monarchy. Mill studied Comte and wrote about him. Green, Bradley, and the absolute idealists of England and Scotland studied Kant and Hegel closely and were enthusiastic about Lotze. But English-speaking philosophers showed little interest in the prevailing neo-Kantianism of late nineteenth-century Germany or in the 'spiritualist' French philosophers of that period. Russell and Moore respectively studied Frege and Brentano, the two main sources of Husserl's thinking, but that led neither them nor their compatriots to Husserl himself. William James read Renouvier and Bergson. But by the end of the First World War the rupture between the philosophies of continental Europe and of Britain and America was fairly fully established.

It was not complete until the time of the Second World War. Bergson had a brief cult among some British philosophers and Russell took him seriously enough to criticize him at some length. The fashion for Croce was even shorter-lived, although he had one distinguished disciple, R. G. Collingwood, who only vestigially acknowledged him. There was a minute current of interest in Husserl, but the other philosophical luminaries of Europe in the interwar years were ignored: Brunschvicg, Nicolai Hartmann (one peripheral book was translated), Dilthey (who died in 1911 but whose fame was largely posthumous), Scheler. Gilson and Cassirer attracted attention from those interested in the history of philosophy; Maritain from Catholics; Mach, Poincaré, and Duhem, to go a bit further back, from philosophers of science (Russell acknowledges a debt to Mach and Poincaré in the preface to *Our Knowledge of the External World*).

The discovery of Sartre at the time of the liberation of France brought *existentialism and the *phenomenology, with which it was associated, to general notice. Heidegger was not absolutely unknown. Ryle had written with respect and an element of suspicion about his *Sein und Zeit* in 1928 and four years later, in a more sharply critical spirit, about phenomenology, but by then there was little British interest in phenomenology for him to repel. In the 1930s the only living philosophers from continental Europe to be at all closely read were the members of the Vienna Circle, most of whom came to settle in the English-speaking world. There was some awareness of like-minded groups in Poland and Scandinavia, although Twardowski and Hägerström, Kotarbinski and Marc Wogau were little more than names to most British philosophers.

Since 1945 the originally minute group of English-speaking philosophers interested in continental philosophy has slowly enlarged. There have been a few French and German philosophers who have associated themselves with one or another brand of *analytic philosophy in the Anglo-American style. But there is really no perceptible convergence between the two philosophical worlds. Existentialism, structuralism, and critical theory are very different from each other. The first exalts the human individual as the creator of meaning in a world itself meaningless; the second proclaims the death of man, attributing his human characteristics to the objective mental structures, especially language, which define what he is and does; the third seeks to rescue consciousness, in a fairly abstract form, from the 'social existence' in which orthodox Marxism immerses it. But all, in varying degrees, rely on dramatic, even melodramatic, utterance rather than sustained rational argument.

Existentialism has a long and distinguished ancestry. On one side it descends from Kierkegaard and Nietzsche, the first affirming the irreducibility of the particular individual and the unintelligibility and inescapability of God, the second maintaining that the human intellect is a weapon in the struggle for existence or power, not a contemplative means for the discovery of objective truth. The Existentialists attached these large cosmic gestures to the phenomenology of Husserl. He had applied his technique of the direct, presuppositionless inspection of consciousness mainly to cognitive activities. They applied it to man as an agent and as the bearer of emotions and desires. Heidegger, after bringing these two things together in his *Sein und Zeit*, moved to a meditative point of view in which the philosopher must passively await the intimations of itself that Being may provide him with. Sartre added some literary spice and a French urban sensibility to the ideas of the early Heidegger. Merleau-Ponty usefully reinstated the Cartesian self to the body of which it is continually aware and without which it cannot perceive and act.

*Structuralism has a humbler and more recent family background. It was born in the Geneva of the linguist de Saussure, came to France with the anthropologist Lévi-Strauss, and went on to inform the literary criticism of Barthes, the psychiatry of Lacan, and the Marxism of

EDMUND HUSSERL invented the term 'phenomenology' and was himself the most rigorous and perhaps the greatest phenomenologist. He inaugurated the modern philosophical obsession with consciousness.

JOSÉ ORTEGA Y GASSETT examined with distaste the role of 'the masses' in modern society, and saw truth and reality as founded in the perspective of the individual.

GOTTLOB FREGE, the greatest modern logician, was 'discovered' in his fifties by Russell and by Husserl. He argued that mathematics could be founded upon formal logic (for which he invented a new notation) and attempted to explain logic without reference to the mental or the material world.

MARTIN HEIDEGGER transformed the Kantian and Romantic inheritance of European philosophy into a daunting metaphysics of Being, with deep roots in the history of Christian thought.

Althusser. It may be said to have culminated with Foucault and to have transcended itself, shooting off into outer intellectual space, with Derrida. De Saussure held that language is not an accumulation of independent conventions but an interlocking system in which every element is what it is by virtue of its relations to everything else in the system. In the hands of Lévi-Strauss that led to the conclusion that there is nothing truly primitive about what have been supposed to be primitive languages and the supposedly primitive people who speak them. Foucault saw the human mind as dominated in successive ages by different ways of representing the world, each of which was an impersonal Nietzschean stratagem by which some could exercise power over others.

*Critical theory was inspired by Georg Lukács's rejection of the orthodox Marxist doctrine that men's ideas and beliefs are wholly determined by socio-economic circumstances. The critical theorists proper—Horkheimer, Adorno, Marcuse, and, in the second generation, Habermas—dismissed the positivist identification of rationality with the exercise of scientific method, at least in application to man and society. In that domain they believed it essential to grasp things, in the manner of Hegel, in their totality, not in abstracted fragments. There is a link with Nietzsche in the critical theorists' contention that language and ideas can serve as instruments of domination, as creators of 'false consciousness'.

There was some affinity between the Existentialists' ethics of decision and the non-cognitive ethical theories of many analytic philosophers, at least in the more iconoclastic versions of the latter. Chomsky's structural linguistics had a certain amount in common with de Saussure's, but, unlike de Saussure's followers, he combined it with an uncomplicated radical extremism in morals and politics. The evident political intentions of the critical theorists ruled out any interest on the part of analytic philosophers, committed to neutrality. In no case was there enough connection on which to build any sort of *rapprochement*. Derrida's *deconstructionism, for which everything is text, freely, endlessly interpretable, seemed to analytic philosophers a *reductio ad absurdum* of philosophy since it allowed for no standards of truth, evidence, or logical consistency. It made philosophy not only a game, but a game without rules.

During the closing decades of the twentieth century Britain became more and more involved with the European mainland, politically and economically, and complete absorption seemed imminent. This inspired a certain impatience with the expression 'continental philosophy'. But philosophy in Britain is still almost entirely unrelated to that of the European mainland, neither influenced by it nor interested in it. An indication of the gulf is the fact that there is only one notable and productive European-type philosopher in the English-speaking world, the American Richard Rorty. He began as an able analytic philosopher, and traces of that earlier allegiance endure in his incorporation of William James, Dewey, and Wittgenstein in his pantheon. His dismissal of the pursuit of objective truth in favour of 'edifying conversation' was caused by his denial of any correspondence between our thoughts or beliefs and an independently existing reality. We cannot compare our beliefs with a reality outside thought. In British philosophy, that of continental Europe is the object of occasional startled observation, like that of a nasty motor accident viewed from a passing car. Where it has lodged itself in English-speaking universities is in departments of literature and social studies, partly as a result of failure of methodological self-confidence, partly from a desire to liberate ideological affirmation from the constraints of logic and evidence.   A.Q.

*'continental' and 'analytic'; Marxist philosophy; English philosophy; American philosophy.

David Cooper, *Existentialism* (Oxford, 1990).
S. Critchley, *Continental Philosophy: A Very Short Introduction* (Oxford, 2001).
P. Gorner, *Twentieth-Century German Philosophy* (Oxford, 2000).
R. Kearney, *Modern Movements in European Philosophy* (Manchester, 1986).
E. Matthews, *Twentieth-Century French Philosophy* (Oxford, 1996).
J. A. Passmore, *Recent Philosophers* (London, 1985).
J. Sturrock (ed.), *Structuralism and Since* (Oxford, 1979).
David West, *An Introduction to Continental Philosophy* (London, 1996).

'continental' and 'analytic'. Although books, journals, courses, degrees, faculties, and departments rely upon this distinction, it enshrines several confusions and considerable historical naïveté. The distinction can be exposed methodologically, geographically, and historically.

Methodologically, philosophy since Kant can be rightly, but not cleanly or exhaustively, divided into the following movements: idealism, Marxism, pragmatism, existentialism, phenomenology, structuralism, Logical Positivism, linguistic analysis, post-structuralism, post-modernism.

Geographically and historically, every one of these movements in modern philosophy is Austrian or German in its modern genesis and in its major practitioners. Indeed, future historians will regard the nineteenth and twentieth centuries as an essentially Austrian period in philosophy. Wittgenstein was Austrian. The Logical Positivists of the Vienna Circle were Austrian and German. The opponent of Logical Positivism, Karl Popper, was Austrian. The 'father' of phenomenology, Edmund Husserl, was Austrian. (His province of Moravia was part of the Austro-Hungarian Empire when he was born there in 1859.) The mathematical logician *Gödel was Austrian. (The German-speaking part of what is now the Czech Republic was part of the Austro-Hungarian Empire when he was born there in 1906.) Philosophy is no exception to an explosion of ideas from Austria. Without the Austrian Freud there is no psychoanalysis. Without the Austrian Hitler there is no Nazism, no Holocaust, no Second World War, at least as we know them. Arguably, the greatest lacuna in the history of ideas is the Austrian Century.

The modern movements in philosophy that are not Austrian are German in genesis. Hegel, Nietzsche,

Brentano, Frege, Einstein, and Heidegger were German, although sometimes affiliated to German-speaking countries outside Germany: Nietzsche wrote in Switzerland, Brentano taught at Vienna, Einstein studied at Zurich.

Modern French philosophy is derived from German and Austrian philosophy. It is historically impossible that Sartre and Merleau-Ponty could have produced the existential phenomenology of *L'Être et le néant* and *Phénoménologie de la perception* without Nietzsche, Husserl, and Heidegger. The philosophical content of Derrida's writing is in Hegel, Nietzsche, and Heidegger. Despite his protestations, Derrida is engaged in a Freudian psychoanalysis of philosophy. Indeed, much twentieth-century French philosophy reads as a summary of its German and Austrian influences.

Modern British philosophy is derivative from German and Austrian philosophy. The idealism of Bradley, Green, Bosanquet, and McTaggart would have been impossible without the system of Hegel. Logical atomism is the metaphysics of Wittgenstein's *Tractatus*. *Ayer visited the Vienna Circle and returned with the ideas for *Language, Truth and Logic*, which is a summary of Logical Positivism. Ryle's *The Concept of Mind* is Wittgensteinian philosophy of mind. Hare's *The Language of Morals* is Wittgensteinian ethics. J. L. Austin's *How to Do Things with Words* is Wittgensteinian philosophy of language. Peter Winch's *The Idea of a Social Science* is Wittgensteinian social philosophy. T. D. Weldon's *The Vocabulary of Politics* is Wittgensteinian political philosophy. If the expression 'modern continental philosophy' makes sense at all, modern British philosophy is a part of modern continental philosophy.

American pragmatism is essentially Hegelian. It was Hegel who criticized Kant for inspecting categories in abstraction from their real applications. Peirce, Dewey, and James are implementing that Hegelian project. In Kantian terms, the findings of pragmatism are *regulative*, not *constitutive*. The scientific philosophy practised in America since 1945 has been influenced by Austrian and German emigrés from Nazism such as Carl Hempel, if not by members of the Frankfurt School, such as Marcuse and Horkheimer. *Rorty's pragmatic post-modern relativism is essentially Derridian, but those components of Derrida's writing are anticipated in turn by Nietzsche's 'perspectivism'.

'Continental philosophy' has become a name for doing exegesis on the texts (or, more usually, the translations) of existentialism, phenomenology, structuralism, or post-structuralism. 'Analytical philosophy' has become a collective name for Frege's philosophy, Logical Positivism, Wittgensteinian and neo-Wittgensteinian linguistic philosophy, and the use of philosophical and mathematical logic to clarify philosophical problems. The philosophical disagreements between, say, Logical Positivism and the later Wittgenstein, or the methodological divergences between, say, Frege and Ryle, make it hard to give 'analytical philosophy' clear sense or reference. In so far as the expression 'analytical philosophy' means anything, it is methodologically and genetically Austrian and German.

Analytical philosophy is part of modern continental philosophy.

The methodological and doctrinal differences between those movements grouped together as 'continental' are at least as conspicuous and difficult to resolve as those between them and the movements grouped together as 'analytical'. Nietzsche, Husserl, Heidegger, Sartre, Merleau-Ponty, Lacan, Foucault, Derrida *et al.* disagree with one another (biographically and as a matter of problematic) as much as they do with Frege, Wittgenstein, the Vienna Circle, and Popper. Therefore there is no good philosophical ground for grouping some post-Kantian movements as 'continental' and others as 'analytical'.

Because the two expressions are in common usage, there are *self-styled* practitioners of 'both kinds of philosophy'. A sort of historically retrospective bifurcation between two 'traditions' is being created by footnoting. Europe contains both kinds of footnoter, and the English-speaking universities contain both kinds of footnoter.

Indeed, although this might bring a *frisson* of terror to those who believe in two kinds of philosophy, methodological similarities might obtain between putatively 'analytical' and 'continental' movements. For example, both Logical Positivism and pure, or Husserlian, phenomenology have the following tenets in common: metaphysics is impossible; there is something 'given' in experience upon which all knowledge is founded or grounded; philosophy should have the rigour of science; philosophy needs to be begun afresh. Structuralism and logical atomism are both formal a priori inquiries into our fundamental conceptual scheme. In linguistic philosophy and in post-structuralism there is a reaction against this a priorism. 'Our' conceptual scheme, impressionistic and shifting, resists formal analysis and Aristotelian definition. Besides, who are 'we'? The ethical and political commitments of existentialism are later paralleled by an emphasis on practical issues of abortion, capital punishment, animal liberation, philosophy, and public affairs in English-speaking moral philosophy. When the devotees of two philosophical movements barely recognize one another as doing philosophy, this is paradoxically a sign that they are similar in method and doctrine.

If modern continental philosophy, including French and British philosophy, is geographically and historically Austrian and German, methodologically it is neo-Kantian. In Kant's *Critique of Pure Reason* *conceptual analysis is practised in the 'Transcendental Analytic'. Structuralism is apparent in the list of categories and judgement forms and the thesis that perception is organized conceptually. Hegelian and Marxist dialectic is anticipated in the triadic organization of the table of categories, the 'Third Antinomy', and (although this would have horrified Kant) throughout the 'Transcendental Dialectic'. As Husserl points out, Kant was the first to engage in phenomenology, in 'The Transcendental Deduction'. Heidegger rightly saw in the schematism the anticipation of his own fundamental ontology. The thesis of the Logical Positivists and Derrida that metaphysics is impossible but difficult to avoid is a salient lesson of the *Critique of Pure Reason*.

It is sometimes assumed by those who think they are practising 'continental philosophy' that it is in some way radical or left-wing. It is true that Sartre was a Marxist political activist, Althusser a structuralist Marxist, and Merleau-Ponty a Marxist until his break with Sartre over what he saw as the latter's 'ultrabolshevism'. However, the relativism entailed by post-structuralism and post-modernism has been part of the ideology of global capitalism during its liberal (but, of course, still anti-socialist) period 1968–2001. What formerly belonged to the intellectual left was successfully recuperated by capitalist liberalism during that historical period.

The term 'continental philosophy' is, I suspect, British in origin. In Britain 'the Continent' is used to denote that part of Europe that does not include Britain and Ireland, even though if Britain is part of a continent, it is part of Europe. So 'continental' is a geographical predicate. 'Analytical' is a methodological predicate. If the expressions 'continental' and 'analytical' did mark a distinction, it could only be between philosophy done in a certain place and philosophy done in a certain way. This would be a muddled distinction, like that between fighting using firearms and fighting in Africa, or two kinds of chemical, one found in Australia and one that dissolves in water.

It is not unusual for philosophers to self-righteously align themselves with 'continental philosophy' or with 'analytical philosophy', sometimes with the evangelical zeal of the convert ('I had to learn a whole new way of thinking ...'). There are even self-appointed ambassadors who think they are transmitting ideas from one camp to another or who think they can do 'both kinds of philosophy'. It is high time the whole terminology was dropped, and the anti-metaphysical Kantian orthodoxy broken.

S.P.

Franz Brentano, *Psychology from an Empirical Standpoint*, tr. A. C. Rancurello, D. B. Terrell, and L. L. McAlister (London, 1973).

Jacques Derrida, *Speech and Phenomena*, tr. David B. Allison (Evanston, Ill., 1973).

—— *Writing and Difference*, tr. Alan Bass (London, 1978).

Martin Heidegger, *Being and Time*, tr. J. Macquarrie and E. Robinson (Oxford, 1973).

Christina Howells, *Derrida* (Oxford, 1998).

Edmund Husserl, *Logical Investigations*, tr. J. N. Findlay, 2 vols. (New York, 1970).

—— *Ideas Pertaining to a Pure Phenomenology and to a Phenomenological Philosophy*, first book, tr. F. Kersten (The Hague, 1982).

—— *Ideas Pertaining to a Pure Phenomenology and to a Phenomenological Philosophy*, second book, tr. R. Rojcewicz and A. Schuwer (Dordrecht, 1989).

Michael Inwood, *A Heidegger Dictionary* (Oxford, 1999).

—— *Heidegger* (Oxford, 2000).

Immanuel Kant's Critique of Pure Reason, tr. Norman Kemp-Smith (London, 1978).

Jacques Lacan, *The Four Fundamental Concepts of Psychoanalysis*, tr. Alan Sheridan (London, 1973).

Maurice Merleau-Ponty, *Phenomenology of Perception*, tr. Colin Smith (London, 1962).

—— *The Visible and the Invisible*, tr. Alphonso Lingis (Evanston, Ill., 1968).

Stephen Mulhall, *Heidegger and* Being and Time (London, 1996).

Stephen Priest, *Theories of the Mind* (London, 1990), esp. ch. 7: 'The Phenomenological View'.

—— *The Subject in Question: Sartre's Critique of Husserl in 'The Transcendence of the Ego'* (London, 2000).

—— *Merleau-Ponty* (London, 2003).

Jean-Paul Sartre, *Being and Nothingness*, tr. Hazel Barnes (London, 1972).

—— *Basic Writings* (London, 2002).

Ferdinand de Saussure, *Course in General Linguistics*, tr. W. Baskin (New York, 1959).

continental philosophy of law: *see* law and continental philosophy.

contingent and necessary existence: *see* necessary and contingent existence.

contingent and necessary statements. A necessary statement (or proposition) is one which *must* be true—where this 'must' may be understood as being expressive of logical necessity or (less commonly) some other kind of modality, such as *epistemic, physical, or metaphysical necessity. A contingent statement is one which *may* be true and *may* be false—that is, which *need not* be false and *need not* be true. Thus, if a statement is contingent, neither it nor its *negation is necessary.

E.J.L.

*necessity, logical; necessity, metaphysical.

A. Plantinga, *The Nature of Necessity* (Oxford, 1974).

continuum problem. What is the number of points on a continuous line? Cantor conjectured that it is the second smallest infinite cardinal number, having proved it greater than the first. An instance of a general enigma about infinite cardinality, this problem was shown by Gödel and Cohen to be unsolvable on the basis of all currently accepted axioms. This raises the puzzling possibility that Cantor's conjecture (that the number of points on a line is the second infinite cardinal number) and related propositions are neither true nor false.

M.D.G.

*infinity; number.

K. Gödel, 'What is Cantor's Continuum Problem?', in P. Benacerraf and H. Putnam (eds.), *Philosophy of Mathematics* (Cambridge, 1983).

contract, social. The imaginary device through which equally imaginary individuals, living in solitude (or, perhaps, in nuclear families), without government, without a stable division of labour or dependable exchange relations, without parties, leagues, congregations, assemblies, or associations of any sort, come together to form a society, accepting obligations of some minimal kind to one another and immediately or very soon thereafter binding themselves to a political sovereign who can enforce those obligations. The contract is a philosophical fiction developed by early modern theorists to show how *political obligation rests on individual *consent—that is, on the consent that rational individuals would give were they ever to experience life without obligation and authoritative rule. To make this fictional consent plausible, the theorist must tell a story about what is commonly called the *state of nature, the asocial condition of humankind before or without political authority. Commonly, the more harrowing the story (Thomas Hobbes's 'war of all against all' is the limiting case), the more authoritarian the political order established by the contract—for rational men and women cannot be imagined to consent to tyranny or absolute rule except to escape something worse. They accept the rule of the lion only in order to avoid an anarchy of wolves. A more liberal or democratic politics follows from a more benign story (as in John Locke's *Second Treatise of Government*) or from no story at all: John Rawls's rational decision-makers in the *original position are denied any knowledge of their actual interests and so of their past competition or co-operation. But the assumption that they are not adventurers or risk-takers probably serves the same purpose as a benign story.

Social contract theory was first worked out in the seventeenth century, and it undoubtedly owes something to the religious culture of that time. Renewed interest in the Hebrew Bible and the political and theological usefulness of the biblical covenant to Protestant writers together gave currency to the idea of a founding agreement. Most of the theoretical problems of the contract are first addressed in covenant theology. Is the covenant made between each individual and God (a series of vertical agreements) or is it made between each individual and every other, to obey God's law (a much larger series of horizontal agreements)? What are God's stipulations, if he is a party? Is the covenant conditional or unconditional? What actions are warranted by God's or man's non-performance? In secular form, these questions generate arguments about who is bound by the contract, what they are bound to do, what constitutes a violation, and how and by whom the contract is to be enforced.

Perhaps the most significant claim of social contract theory is that political society is a human construct—even if men and women are driven to the construction by necessities arising in the state of nature, hence by 'natural' necessities—and not an organic growth. There is no body politic but only this artefact, made in (fictional) time and in principle open to remaking. Mixed metaphors of design and structure replace the metaphor of the body. Hobbes first suggests the twofold character of contract theory when he writes that man is both the 'maker' and the 'matter' of the commonwealth. He is the maker because the social contract depends upon his willing agreement, and he is the matter because the content of the contract, the social and political arrangements it establishes, are designed (by whom?) to shape and control his behaviour. Jean-Jacques Rousseau's version of the argument is similar: the members of the newly created polity are sovereign (citizens) and subjects, simultaneously ruling and being ruled.   M.WALZ.

*Scanlon.

Thomas Hobbes, *Leviathan* (1651).
John Locke, *Two Treatises of Government* (1690).
John Rawls, *A Theory of Justice* (Cambridge, Mass., 1971).
Jean-Jacques Rousseau, *The Social Contract* (1762).

contractarianism. Suppose right actions are those that accord with moral principles. One thought is that we should act according to principles that can be rationally endorsed as having universal sway (Kant), or which no one else can reasonably reject (Scanlon). A different thought is that each of us should act as if we have agreed to the principles that maximize (or at least satisfice) individual self-interest (Gauthier, inspired by Hobbes). How to determine the relevant principles in each case? Contractarians propose the following answer. Suppose we imagine a state (like Hobbes's 'state of nature') in which there are as yet no agreed political or moral standards. As writers like John Rawls argue, the principles for a good society can be inferred by envisaging the contract that might be freely and voluntarily forged in the imagined state. Hume long ago pointed out that even if there had been an original, historical contract, it would be up to us now to determine whether it should have any present authority. If not an empirical thesis, is contractarianism a conceptual tool for uncovering the principles that might bind ideally rational agents? In this case, the contractarian has to explain how circularity is avoided, so that the conditions of the imagined contract are not just chosen in a way that produces the principles the theorist desires to endorse.   A.BRE.

D. Gauthier, *Moral Dealing: Contract, Ethics and Reason* (Ithaca, NY, 1990).
D. Hume, 'Of the Original Contract', in *Essays, Moral, Political and Literary* (original edn. 1777, rev. edn. ed. E. F. Miller (Indianapolis, 1987)).
T. M. Scanlon, *What We Owe to Each Other* (Cambridge, 1998).

contradiction. The conjunction of a proposition and its denial. In the *propositional and *predicate calculus a sentence of the form $(\phi \cdot \sim \phi)$ is formally contradictory and always takes the value false. (*Truth-table.) Where ϕ, ψ, are such that each entails the negation of the other, their conjunction is also designated as a contradiction. See, for example, the pairs A,O and E,I of the *square of opposition in the *traditional logic of the syllogism.   R.B.M.

B. Mates, *Elementary Logic* (Oxford, 1972).

contradictions, material: *see* material contradictions.

contradictories. Two propositions are contradictories when one must be true, the other false. Specifying its contradictory sometimes clarifies the meaning of a proposition. Consider 'Everybody loves somebody'. 'Nobody is loved by everybody' would be its contradictory if it meant that everybody loves the same person; otherwise its contradictory is 'Somebody loves nobody'.   C.W.

*contrapositives; contraries.

P. T. Geach, 'Contradictories and Contraries', in *Logic Matters* (Oxford, 1972).

contraposition. In traditional logic the contrapositive of a proposition is obtained by negating both its terms and reversing their order. Thus 'All rabbits are herbivores' ('All *S* are *P*') becomes 'Everything which isn't a herbivore isn't a rabbit' ('All non-*P* are non-*S*'). The inference from a proposition to its contrapositive is valid for the 'All *S* are *P*' and 'Some *S* are not *P*' forms considered by traditional logic; invalid for the 'No *S* are *P*' and 'Some *S* are *P*' forms. In *modern logic 'contraposition' characterizes the relation between conditionals of the forms 'If *p*, then *q*' and 'If not *q*, then not *p*'.   c.w.

*logic, traditional.

J. N. Keynes, *Formal Logic*, 4th edn. (London, 1906), ch. 4.

contraries. Two propositions *p* and *q* are contraries when, as with 'The number of the unemployed is five million' and 'The number of the unemployed is three million', they cannot both be true but can both be false, so that each entails, but is not entailed by, the negation of the other. Traditionally 'All *S* are *P*' and 'No *S* are *P*' were called contraries.   c.w.

*contradictories; square of opposition.

P. T. Geach, 'Contradictories and Contraries', in *Logic Matters* (Oxford, 1972).

contrary-to-fact conditional: *see* conditionals; counterfactuals.

convention. This is usually understood as involving some form of human agreement (either explicit or, more interestingly, implicit) to facilitate a common end. The topic is intriguing in itself and important for its wider philosophical relevance. One of the deepest issues in metaphysics is that of the degree to which 'our' agreements determine how 'the world' of fact, science, or value is. Here, the idea of convention has been used to analyse mathematical truth and moral fact as basically matters of communally agreed decision. Likewise, some have seen *political obligation and the requirements of *justice as entirely grounded in convention. By contrast, realists claim that nature or 'independent' reality itself plays a major part in determining at least some such matters. Yet the character of convention remains unclear, with respect to both the sort of agreement it involves and the ways in which it should be contrasted with either nature or reason.   c.a.j.c.

*consent.

D. K. Lewis, *Convention* (Cambridge, Mass., 1969).

conventionalism. A convention is a principle or proposal which is adopted by a group of people, either by explicit choice, as in Sweden's decision to drive on the right-hand side of the road, or as a matter of custom, whose origins are unknown and unplanned, as in the convention of placing forks on the left and knives on the right. The crucial point, though, is that conventions are not forced on us by nature and could, if we collectively wished, be changed. In

a certain sense, then, conventions are manifestations of human freedom.

Conventionalism is a view about the status of theories in science. Linked to *instrumentalism and *positivism, it urges us to regard deep-level theories about the nature of the world as chosen by us from among many possible alternative ways of explaining the observable phenomena. Theories such as Newton's laws or quantum theory which purport to reveal the underlying structure of the world are not directly provable or disprovable by observation or experiment. They are freely chosen conventions, which may be maintained in the face of apparent counterevidence. If we wish to move to a new theory of the relevant domain, it will not in the final analysis be because the evidence forces us to do so, but because a new theory (or 'convention') is simpler, easier to apply, more aesthetic, or for some other non-epistemic reason.

Following the scientific revolutions of this century most philosophers of science would now admit an element of decision or convention in the initial acceptance of an explanatory theory in science and in adherence to it through continuing vicissitudes, but the key conventionalist text is Henri Poincaré's *Science and Hypothesis* of 1905. Poincaré argued that Newton's three laws are definitions and, as such, unrevisable. He thought that such deep-lying principles in science are similar to particular sets of geometrical axioms, in that they are chosen to fit a particular range of phenomena. For Poincaré the choice of scientific principles, as of geometrical axioms, could be justified on grounds of their usefulness or convenience in application to the actual world, about whose regularities we could learn a great deal by experiment and observation. We would not, then, be moved to accept a set of principles like Newton's laws did they not mesh easily with the experimental laws we formulate in observing empirical regularities. To this extent, then, Poincaré, in common with subsequent conventionalists, admits a degree of empirical constraint on the choice of hypothesis.

Where conventionalists differ from their opponents is not so much on the element of choice in scientific theorizing, or, if it is, it turns out to be only a matter of degree. The difference is that so-called realists will insist that the most useful set of scientific principles is not just a useful convention we adopt: it is also true. Realists will profess horror at Poincaré's admission that contradictory scientific principles can be maintained so long as they are applied in different areas of experience; certainly if scientific theories are regarded as describing the mechanisms underlying the world, we should search for theories which are mutually consistent, and not merely adequate for a limited domain of data. Nevertheless, the conventionalist might regard the realist's insistence on the truth and reality of scientific principles as so much thumping the table, when he sees how even the most real 'conventions' (such as Newton's principles) have been abandoned in favour of other explanatory schemes. The relationship between experimental (or observational) laws and theoretical principles in science is no clearer now than it was when Poincaré wrote, as, in different ways, the works of Quine, van Fraassen, and Hacking testify.   A.O'H.

I. Hacking, *Representing and Intervening* (Cambridge, 1983).

W. V. Quine, 'Two Dogmas of Empiricism', in *From a Logical Point of View* (Cambridge, Mass., 1953).

B. van Fraassen, *The Scientific Image* (Oxford, 1980).

conversion. Reversing the order of terms in a proposition. Thus 'The idle are unemployed' is converted (invalidly) to 'The unemployed are idle'. Valid in traditional logic for 'No S are P' and 'Some S are P', invalid for 'All S are P' and 'Some S are not P'. The (valid) move from 'All S are P' to 'Some P are S' is called 'conversion *per accidens*'.   C.W.

*logic, traditional.

J. N. Keynes, *Formal Logic*, 4th edn. (London, 1906), ch. 4.

Conway, Anne Finch (1631–79). Conway's philosophical work was much admired by Leibniz and by her friend and frequent correspondent Henry More. In *The Principles of the Most Ancient and Modern Philosophy* (a posthumous partial transcription from a notebook, now lost, which was probably written in the early 1670s, published 1690) she argued that God's necessary creativity must produce a universe infinite in all its aspects: infinite in space and time (both past and future), and infinite in the number and types of creatures, with each creature 'contain[ing] an Infinity of entire Creatures'. In this infinitely plenist universe 'every Body may be turned into a Spirit, and a Spirit into a Body'. Moreover, 'all Creatures . . . are inseparably united' and consequently may 'act one upon another at the greatest distance'. Conway became a Quaker shortly before her death.   J.J.M.

*women in philosophy.

Anne Finch Conway, *The Principles of the Most Ancient and Modern Philosophy*, ed. Peter Loptson (The Hague, 1982).

Cook Wilson, John (1849–1915). British realist philosopher. After a brilliant undergraduate career at Oxford, where he got double firsts in both classics and mathematics, Cook Wilson taught philosophy there for more than forty years, becoming professor of logic in 1889. A fertile and original thinker, he was slow in breaking away from the idealism in which he had been brought up. He wrote a good deal, but published next to nothing. The posthumous *Statement and Inference* (1926) collects some of his output, as well as a wonderful account of his comical eccentricity in its introductory memoir. He rejected Bradley's view that all thinking is 'judgement', since not all thinking is assertive and since judgement, as ordinarily understood, is a particular, reflective attitude of mind. His best-known thesis—that knowledge is indefinable—is parallel to G. E. Moore's claim about the indefinability of goodness. His teaching has had a considerable influence on the course of philosophy in Oxford up to the present day. A group of his disciples—H. A. Prichard, H. W. B. Joseph, W. D. Ross—were dominant there until the late 1930s. But there are many audible echoes later. His stress

on the philosophical significance of the ordinary meaning of words was carried to new heights by J. L. Austin. His criticisms of both formal and idealistic logic foreshadow the early work of P. F. Strawson, particularly his denial that universal affirmatives (all A are B) are really hypothetical (if anything is A, it is B). His insistence that knowledge is indefinable resurfaces in Timothy Williamson's account of the topic.   A.Q.

Richard Robinson, *The Province of Logic* (London, 1931).

Copernicus, Nicolaus (1473–1543). Polish astronomer who revolutionized *cosmology by transferring the centre of the universe from the earth to the sun. Like all scientists, Copernicus believed that a theory must agree with the facts and also conform to certain privileged ideas—*simplicity being a good example. For Copernicus the ideal was uniform circular motion. Earth-centred systems of astronomy based on uniform circular motion did not agree with the observed facts; earth-centred systems agreeing with the facts were not based on uniform circular motion. Therefore, argued Copernicus, a sun-centred system which met both conditions was justified. This episode shows that developments in science can be revolutionary without being correct (Copernicus's picture of a circular, sun-centred universe was not particularly accurate), and provides evidence for a philosophy of science that attributes to science a large 'philosophical' component—a useful corrective to purely empiricist accounts of science.   A.BEL.

Robert S. Westman (ed.), *The Copernican Achievement* (Berkeley, Calif., 1975).

corollary. A corollary is a proposition of significance which can be demonstrated to follow from another proposition which has previously been established as true. In mathematics and formal logic this previously established proposition is known as a theorem, and the *proof of the corollary is based upon the proof of the theorem. It must be possible to show that the corollary follows from the theorem in a relatively straightforward manner.   G.F.M.

R. Wilder, *Introduction to the Foundations of Mathematics* (New York, 1952).

corporate responsibility is the responsibility of a corporate person, which we might define as an association of individuals bound together by a common purpose and governed by agreed rules or a charter. Corporate responsibility is closely connected to *collective responsibility, but whereas collective responsibility is typically a convenient fiction to refer to the individual responsibilities of those who make up the collective, corporate responsibility seems an indivisible form of responsibility, as in Cabinet responsibility. Corporate responsibility can be a valid legal concept, but it is less clear that it can be a moral concept, since the corporate person seems not to be individually divisible, as required for moral responsibility. A solution might be to say that a corporate person is divisible into functional roles defined in terms of the purposes and rules of the corporation. In this way it is possible to combine corporate decisions—the agreed decisions emerging from the relevant roles—and moral responsibility, since individuals occupy the roles. To the extent that a chief executive, or head of a corporation, endorses these decisions, he or she will become responsible for the decisions of the corporation.   R.S.D.

Larry May and Stacy Hoffman (eds.), *Collective Responsibility: Five Decades of Debate* (Savage, Md., 1998).

corpuscularianism. In the work of Italian philosophers such as Telesio in the sixteenth century, there is a revival of the Epicurean doctrine that physical processes are to be explained by the behaviour of the internal material constituents of macroscopic bodies. We can define 'corpuscularianism' as the doctrine that the fundamental constituents of the world are inert corpuscles making up and determining the behaviour of macroscopic bodies. It takes a variety of forms, depending on whether those properties of the corpuscles that do the explanatory work are restricted to mechanical properties such as speed/ velocity and size/weight (as in Descartes), or whether they have macroscopically modelled properties like shape, which are invoked in explaining macroscopic effects such as taste, as in traditional Epicureanism (as in Gassendi). The latter view is properly called atomism, and is consonant with the traditional view that physical properties are due simply to the material constitution of bodies, whereas the former was often allied to mechanical explanations and did not even have to be formulated in terms of discrete bits of matter moving in a void. The most significant development of corpuscularianism in the seventeenth century was in the work of Robert Boyle. After the seventeenth century, mass points in mechanics and atoms in chemistry came to replace the generic idea of corpuscles, although disputes over the nature of light tended to be pursued in terms of waves versus corpuscles in a generic sense.   S.GAU.

P. Alexander, *Ideas, Qualities and Corpuscles* (Cambridge, 1985).

A. Pyle, *Atomism and its Critics* (Bristol, 1995).

corrective justice. Diorthotic *justice (*Nicomachean Ethics* v. 4; 1132ª25), also called remedial or rectificatory justice, is one of Aristotle's two species of particular justice (the other being dianemetic, or distributive, justice). It aims to repair an injustice arising from a private transaction (voluntary or involuntary) between persons in which one has gained unfairly, or otherwise caused harm or loss, at the expense of another. Although translators sometimes render as a 'penalty' what Aristotle says the judge takes from the former in order to give to the latter, corrective justice does not include retribution, or deserved *punishment for crimes. Instead, it awards compensation for what we would call violations of contract (which the wronged party had entered voluntarily) and torts (which stem from no voluntary act by the wronged party).   H.A.B.

Max Hamburger, *Morals and Law: The Growth of Aristotle's Legal Theory* (New Haven, Conn., 1950).

correspondence theory of truth. Whether what is said about the world is true surely must depend on how the world is. This simple observation appears to offer strong intuitive support to one of the major philosophical accounts of *truth, the correspondence theory, according to which propositions are true if and only if they correspond with the facts. However, despite its immediate appeal, the account has met with a number of objections, both the conception of facts as worldly items, and the construal of truth as a relation, drawing criticism.

The theory maintains that the truth of a proposition p requires the following two conditions to be met: (1) it is a *fact that p, and (2) the proposition corresponds to that fact. Attention may now shift to the relation of correspondence—e.g. must a proposition mirror the structure of the fact?—but such an enquiry can reasonably be short-circuited, since condition (2) is surely superfluous: p being true if and only if it is a fact that p, all that is required by way of correspondence is that for each true proposition there should *be* a fact. Still, the reduced equivalence remains of significance if, as the theory would have it, the association of a true proposition with a fact is an association of words with world.

But now, if facts are in the world, it should make sense to ask where they are to be found, yet such questions as 'Where is the fact that the recession is over?' seem to admit of no answer. Moreover, other attributes associated with worldly items have no application to facts, which do not take up space or act upon anything, cannot be measured, dissected, or destroyed. Is 'fact', as is often supposed, equivalent simply to 'true proposition'? This suggestion in turn meets with difficulties—propositions can be mistranslated or misattributed, not facts—so it is beginning to look as if facts are neither in the world nor in language. And perhaps that is, however unexpectedly, their true status. Perhaps the term 'fact' does not have a role in which it is true of anything whatsoever. In stating, 'It is a fact that insulin is a hormone' we are not describing something named by the clause, 'that insulin is a hormone', but the contribution which 'fact' makes could equally be channelled through an adverbial phrase, as with 'Insulin is in fact a hormone'. The correspondence theorist's claim would then reduce to affirming a series of trivialities after the pattern of ' "Insulin is a hormone" is true if and only if insulin is, in fact, a hormone', or—final ignominy—' "Insulin is a hormone" is true if and only if insulin is indeed a hormone'.

The idea that truth consists in a relation between words and world is, however, unlikely to be abandoned, even if 'fact' is not suited to providing one of the terms of this relation. What other form might that relation take? There is no denying that our words latch on to worldly items in various ways, but what is suspect is the idea of a relation over and above any that the given proposition might present as a matter of its own internal structure. Thus, suppose it is said that 'Insulin is a hormone' presents us with a relation of predication, 'is a hormone' being predicated of what is named by 'insulin'. Then, of course, the proposition is true if and only if the relation holds; that is, if and only if insulin—a substance to be found in the world—*is* a hormone. Anything the supposed relation of correspondence might achieve has already been provided for without going beyond the relation which is affirmed with the affirmation of the proposition itself. There is no call to single out a mysterious complex on to which the proposition as a whole can be mapped.   B.B.R.

  *coherence theory of truth; realism and anti-realism; redundancy theory of truth.

J. L. Austin, 'Truth', *Philosophical Papers* (Oxford, 1961).

R. Fumerton, *Realism and the Correspondence Theory of Truth* (Lanham, Md., 2004).

B. Rundle, *Wittgenstein and Contemporary Philosophy of Language* (Oxford, 1990).

P. F. Strawson, *Logico-Linguistic Papers* (London, 1971).

corroboration. Introduced as a technical term in philosophy of science by Popper. A theory's degree of corroboration is measured by *'the severity of the various tests* to which the hypothesis in question can be, and has been, subjected' (*The Logic of Scientific Discovery*). Since stronger—more falsifiable—theories can be subjected to severer tests than weaker ones, degree of corroboration is not *probability. A high degree of corroboration makes no promises about the theory's future performance.   M.C.

A. O'Hear, *Karl Popper* (London, 1980).

cosmogony. A cosmogony is an account of the origin or *creation of the universe. The account may be mythological or anthropomorphic, as in early Greek and Near Eastern thought. It may be theological, as in the Judaeo-Christian tradition. Or it may be scientific, for example the big bang theory. In the latter case scientific experiments, using instruments such as very high-speed particle accelerators, attempt to replicate the initial stages of the universe in order to understand how its development occurred.   M.B.

G. S. Kirk, S. E. Raven, and M. Schofield, *The Presocratic Philosophers*, 2nd edn. (Cambridge, 1983), ch. 1, for a review of Pre-Socratic cosmogony.

cosmological argument. A line of theistic argument appealing to very general contingent facts, e.g. the existence of caused things. There must be some sufficient explanation for these contingent facts. Each such fact may be explained by some other contingent fact, but this series of explanations cannot be infinite. It must terminate (or begin) with something whose existence needs no further explanation, i.e. God.

  The first three of St Thomas Aquinas's set of five theistic arguments are versions of the cosmological argument. The most puzzling element is the claim that a certain series of causes etc. cannot be infinite, especially since Thomas himself appears to hold that a series of finite causes without a *temporal* beginning cannot be ruled out on philosophical grounds. One might also wish for a further clarification of the idea of a being whose existence calls for no explanation.   G.I.M.

St Thomas Aquinas, *Summa Theologiae*, ed. Thomas Gilby *et al.* (London, 1964).

Alvin Plantinga, *God and Other Minds* (Ithaca, NY, 1967).

William Rowe, *The Cosmological Argument* (Princeton, NJ, 1975).

cosmology. Traditionally a branch of metaphysics dealing with features of the world as a whole, though the term can also be synonomous with speculative philosophy in its widest sense. But since the advent of Einstein's general theory of relativity, the term has almost exclusively referred to the endeavours of physicists to understand the large-scale *space-time structure of the universe on the basis of that theory. Far from curtailing philosophical discussion, their work has breathed new life into long-standing debates about the origin and uniqueness of the universe.

  Newton thought that space and time were separate and immutable, space invariably obeying the axioms of Euclidean geometry. But general relativity abandons observer-dependent notions of length and temporal duration in favour of space-time, and links its geometry to the matter distribution in the universe via Einstein's field equations. Given that different matter distributions inserted into these equations yield different space-time geometries, which geometry best describes *our* universe?

  The first proposal was Einstein's. Assuming, as Newton did, that the universe is static and contains an essentially uniform distribution of matter, Einstein obtained a solution to his equations which delivered a vast, spatially spherical universe that is temporally infinite.

  This illustrates how Euclidean geometry can be abandoned. If we *did* live on the surface of a sphere, straight lines specifying the shortest distance between two points would correspond to circles drawn on its surface with centres that coincide with the centre of the sphere (think of the equator or any line of longitude on the earth). This means that straight lines always intersect (e.g. lines of longitude intersect at the North Pole), and that triangles drawn with such lines always have angles that sum to more than 180° (e.g. take the triangle with *two* right angles formed by two lines of longitude and the Equator). Of course, if in our portion of the universe we were confined to a small patch on the surface of some cosmic sphere, then these deviations from Euclidean geometry would never show up in everyday experience.

  To ensure his spherical universe was static, Einstein actually had to do some fiddling with his equations. Since Newton, it was well known that an initially static universe would soon have to collapse under its own weight; so an extra term—the so-called cosmological constant—was put into the equations to counteract this effect. The artificiality of this manœuvre suggested that perhaps the universe is not static after all: maybe the predictions of the field equations (*sans* cosmological constant) should be taken at face value.

  This was first done by Friedman, and later Robertson and Walker, who proved that if—as observational evidence suggests—the universe looks roughly the same in all directions from any point of view, then it must be either expanding or contracting. About the same time, and using the same method (the Doppler effect) by which we can tell whether an ambulance is moving towards or away from us, namely from the pitch of its siren, Hubble verified that distant galaxies are receding from the earth. One might think Hubble's observation suggests that the focal point of the universe's expansion must be somewhere near the earth, and therefore that the universe is *not* the same from any point of view. But if the earth's location is like a point on a uniformly expanding sphere (say, an inflating balloon), then from any other standpoint *on the sphere* one would have to observe the very same expansion.

There are in fact three general relativistic scenarios compatible with Hubble's observation. The first extreme is that the universe started expanding so slowly that at a certain point in our future gravitational forces are going to take over and cause it to collapse back on itself. The second extreme is that the universe started out expanding so quickly that gravitational forces will never hold it back and it will go on expanding for ever. Finally, there is a middle way: the universe started off with *just enough* expansion to allow it to *just escape* eventual collapse. None of these scenarios has yet been totally ruled out (though, curiously, something like the middle way looks to be the best candidate). But they all require that the universe began in a highly compressed 'big bang' state following an initial singularity, i.e. a point at which physical laws break down.

All this has revived two old bones of contention: whether the universe needs a creator, and whether its unique features are evidence of design.

To avoid the need for divine intervention at the big bang, some physicists modified general relativity to produce a 'steady state' model of the universe. In this model, the universe has always existed, and new matter is continually being created to fill the gaps left behind by expanding galaxies, ensuring that the overall matter density of the universe remains constant. However, there are empirical reasons for rejecting this model—not least, Penzias and Wilson's discovery that the earth is being showered from all directions by microwave radiation as a by-product of the big bang. Moreover, Hawking and Penrose proved that, under minimal, very reasonable conditions (e.g. supposing that matter is attractive), we should *expect* a big bang singularity to exist in any *classical* relativistic model of the universe. On the other hand, Hawking and Hartle have recently found a *quantum mechanical* model of an expanding space-time which doesn't begin in a singularity, and so no longer has any natural point through which a creator could intervene.

As evidence of design, some point to things like the fact that to avoid our universe collapsing back on itself in the early stages of the big bang, yet prevent it from expanding so fast that galaxy formation would have been impossible, the rate of expansion at early instants needed to be 'fine-tuned' to within one part in 10^{55}. Others respond that many causally disjoint universes *actually* exist, each initially

expanding at different rates (e.g. each could be a different cycle in an infinite sequence of big bangs and big crunches). With so many universes around, it would then be no surprise to find ourselves in one of the very few hospitable to life. R.CLI.

*anthropic principle; cosmology and religious belief.

A. Grünbaum, 'The Pseudo-Problem of Creation in Physical Cosmology', *Philosophy of Science* (1989).

S. Hawking, *A Brief History of Time: From the Big Bang to Black Holes* (London, 1988).

J. Leslie, *Universes* (London, 1989).

cosmology and religious belief. It is fundamental to Christian belief that *God is held to exist in a cosmos-transcending mode, however much he is seen also as immanent in the world. God creates and continues to give actuality to the world; otherwise it would lapse into non-being. No rival cosmological principles or powers share God's dominion, his sovereignty over the universe.

The metaphysical difficulties attending that cosmological dimension have prompted its abandonment by some religious writers; and Christian discourse may then be taken to be essentially and solely moral (or existential) discourse. The language of divine creation, command, and judgement is understood as parable or myth, giving imaginative vividness and urgency to a style of life centred on neighbour-love and moral accountability. Such a view, however, is not a clarification of Christian belief, but, rather, a drastic revision.

Both types of religious orientation have their defenders among philosophers of religion today: some having confidence in reworkings of *cosmological and *design arguments for a transcendent God; others developing conceptions of religion as a 'Way', or a discipline of attention, imagination and will, with worthwhile moral and aesthetic goals. R.W.H.

*cosmology; religion, history of the philosophy of; religion, problems of the philosophy of.

Richard M. Gale, *On the Nature and Existence of God* (Cambridge, 1991).

Germain Grisez, *Beyond the New Theism* (Notre Dame, Ind., 1975).

John Polkinghorne, *Science and Creation* (London, 1988).

could have done otherwise: *see* freedom and determinism.

counselling, philosophical. The remedial use of philosophical discussion (in a very wide sense of the term) to help individuals reflect on their lives and deal with 'personal problems' such as relationship issues and career dilemmas. As with other one-to-one psychotherapies, the objects of the activity are to generate fees for the counsellor and to alleviate the mental anxiety or intellectual imbalance of the counselled. Modern (post-1980) counselling thus differs from the *Socratic method, to which it is sometimes compared, where the objective is the disinterested pursuit of truth and/or the exposure of simplistic claims to have the truth. The saying of Epicurus, 'Vain is the word of a philosopher which healeth not the sufferings of man', might seem to associate him with the interested purposes of counselling, but *Epicureanism (like *Stoicism) was held to be a universal truth commended by valid reasons and good evidence, not merely or mainly a therapy for individuals. Objectives apart, a main question about philosophical counselling is whether, and how, a learnt, critical, academic discipline such as philosophy can be used with integrity as a form of treatment for those with no critical training in, or academic awareness of, the issues.   J.C.A.G.

Journal: *Practical Philosophy*.

counter-example, philosophy by. A strategy for showing that a philosophical assertion is false and generating data to be taken into account in working toward true assertions on the topic. A counter-example to the claim that all A's are B's is an example of an A that is not a B. A counter-example to the claim that something is an A if and only if it is a B is an example of an A that is not a B or an example of a B that is not an A. When something is asserted to be necessarily true, as in conceptual analysis, mere possibilities may serve as counter-examples. Suppose it is claimed that, necessarily, a case in which my arm rises is a case in which I raise it if and only if the rising has my intention to raise it as a cause. A logically possible scenario in which, unbeknownst to me, mind-reading Martians respond to my intention by levitating my arm is a counter-example. Edmund Gettier produced well-known counter-examples to the assertion that knowledge is to be analysed as justified, true belief. His examples feature people who have a justified, true belief that *p* but do not know that *p*. Philosophy by counter-example has both a negative side—showing that a philosophical assertion is false—and a positive side. Counter-examples to attempted conceptual analyses typically motivate revised analyses designed to yield, among other things, the correct pronouncement about those examples. If a new counter-example falsifies a revised analysis, the process typically continues. Some philosophers attempt to motivate their own conceptual analyses by starting with a suggestive analysis they deem false and producing counter-examples to it and to revised versions until they arrive at an analysis that seems to them to be immune to counter-examples. Roderick Chisholm was well known for this practice. In many of Plato's dialogues, Socrates offers a counter-example to a character's attempted analysis of a concept (e.g. justice or knowledge), the analysis is revised to handle the counter-example, Socrates produces a counter-example to the revised analysis, and the process of revision and counter-example continues until Socrates' conversation partners run out of steam. It has been said that philosophical conversations without counter-examples are like ham and cheese omelettes without eggs.   A.R.M.

R. Sorensen, *Thought Experiments* (Oxford, 1992).

counterfactuals. A counterfactual is a *conditional whose antecedent is false (typically, in philosophical practice, *known* to be false). The term is usually reserved for those (non-truth-functional) counterfactuals which are *not* true in virtue simply of their antecedent's falsity. Lawlike generalizations support counterfactuals: 'Sugar dissolves in water' licenses 'If this sugar cube were dropped in water it would dissolve'; but 'All coins in my pocket are silver' does not yield 'If this penny were in my pocket it would be silver'.   J.J.M.

N. Goodman, *Fact, Fiction and Forecast*, 4th edn. (Cambridge, Mass., 1983).

counterpart theory. According to some theories of *possible worlds, an individual object which exists in this world—the actual world—can be identical with one which exists in another possible world. Such identity across possible worlds, or transworld identity, is rejected by counterpart theorists like David Lewis, who insist that no individual can exist in more than one possible world. For the counterpart theorist, each possible world is simply an aggregate of spatio-temporally interrelated individuals, and the individuals of one world stand in no spatial or temporal relation to the individuals of any other. While a transworld identity theorist would interpret a modal proposition such as 'Napoleon could have died young' as meaning 'There is some possible world in which Napoleon dies young', the counterpart theorist interprets it as meaning 'There is some possible world in which a counterpart of Napoleon dies young'. Napoleon's counterpart in another possible world, if he has one, is the individual in that world that is most similar to Napoleon in every relevant respect.   E.J.L.

D. Lewis, *On the Plurality of Worlds* (Oxford, 1986).

counting. To determine the numerical size, or cardinality, of any but a very small group of objects we count them. Distinguish the process of counting from the product of that process. The transitive process of counting consists in establishing a one-to-one correspondence between the members of an uttered sequence of number-words, 'one, two, three', and the members of the set counted. The product of the process is a cardinality judgement, 'This set has three members', with the number of the set being the number denoted by the last number-word uttered. For a set with finitely many members, the order in which we pair off the members with the number-words does not affect the cardinality judgement. In intransitive counting, we just say the number-words in their order, perhaps to send us to sleep.   A.D.O.

*numbers.

R. L. Goodstein, *Essays in the Philosophy of Mathematics* (Leicester, 1965), ch. 4.

count noun. Noun in connection with which 'how many?' is appropriate; alternatively, one that provides a principle for counting items to which it applies. Thus defined, the notion is not purely grammatical, but a rough test is whether the noun takes plural forms and (in languages that have one) the indefinite article. 'Shoe', 'ship', and 'walrus' are count nouns; 'sand', 'butter', 'greed', and 'sunlight' are not; nor are proper *names (as standardly used, but cf. 'some mute inglorious Milton'). Some deny that 'thing' is a count noun, on the grounds that there is no principle for counting *things* as such. Words with both count-noun and non-count-noun senses include 'wine', 'philosophy', 'misery'.   P.J.M.

*sortal; number.

V. C. Chappell, 'Stuff and Things', *Proceedings of the Aristotelian Society* (1970–1).

courage. A *virtue indispensable to the good life: a readiness to persist in a valued project, despite risk of harm, injury, death, censure, or loss of personal standing. Given the nature of the human life-world, few worthwhile enterprises are possible for those who will take no avoidable risks: such a policy would entail (at the everyday level) no parenthood, little travel, few ventures in work or play; and (in extreme situations) no standing up to tyranny, no speaking out against injustice. For an act to be courageous, as distinct from reckless, or stubborn, or obstinate, the risks must be reasonable in relation to the goal, and the goal itself soundly appraised.   R.W.H.

Peter Geach, *The Virtues* (Cambridge, 1977).

Couturat, Louis (1868–1914). A French philosopher-logician with a central interest in the concept of the infinite, he was especially influenced by Leibniz. In his first major work, *L'Infinie mathématique* (1896), he argued, against the prevailing current, in support of the doctrine that there must be an actual, and not a merely possible, infinite. Leibniz also had devoted himself to mathematical and philosophical questions concerning the infinite, and Couturat's interest in Leibniz's work resulted in publication by him of an edition of a number of writings by Leibniz which had until then lain unpublished. Leibniz had had an abiding interest in the possibility of a universal language and, as further indication of his debt to Leibniz, Couturat devoted much of his short life to the development of such a language. The monthly journal *Progreso*, which he founded, was written in his language (Ido). The subsequent history of Ido suggests, however, that the language, or at least its supporters, did not have the resources to withstand the hostility of the Esperanto lobby.   A.BRO.

*infinity.

André Lalande, 'L'Œuvre de Louis Couturat', *Revue de métaphysique* (1914).

covering-law model. According to this model of scientific *explanation, developed by Carl Hempel, a statement of particular or general fact is explained if and only if it is *deduced* from other statements which include at least one general scientific law. For particular facts, this model implies a symmetry between explanation and prediction: if an event can be explained, it could have been predicted, and vice versa. The covering-law model has close affinities with David Hume's equation of causation with *constant conjunction, and accordingly faces similar difficulties about causal priority and indeterministic causation.   D.P.

*causality.

C. Hempel, *Aspects of Scientific Explanation* (New York, 1965).

Craig's theorem. A result in mathematical logic that has been used to argue for the in-principle dispensability of theoretical terms. Suppose T is a formal axiomatic theory of the usual sort (for instance T may be a formalization of physics). Suppose O is a restricted part of T's vocabulary (perhaps O contains just the 'observational' terms). Craig's theorem states that there is a formal axiomatic theory T^* such that (i) the axioms of T^* contain only terms in O and (ii) T and T^* imply the same O-sentences, i.e. sentences built out of terms in O.   A.GUP.

For a proof of the theorem see W. Craig, 'On Axiomatizability within a System', *Journal of Symbolic Logic* (1953).

Cratylus (*fl. c.*400 BC). A self-declared follower of Heraclitus, who maintained that all sensible particulars are changing in every respect all the time. According to Aristotle (*Metaphysics* 987^{a}32–^{b}1), this doctrine influenced the young Plato. Also according to Aristotle (*Metaphysics* 1010^{a}10–15), Cratylus drew radical conclusions about the impossibility of reference to things in the perceptible world: he 'rebuked Heraclitus for saying that you cannot step twice into the same river; he himself [Cratylus] thought you cannot even step into it once'; and 'in the end he thought that one should not say anything at all, and merely moved his finger'. This position seems to be included in the 'Heraclitean' doctrines of *'flux' which are severely criticized by Plato in his dialogue *Theaetetus*. It is this dialogue if anything which may give further insight into Cratylus' thinking. (Plato's dialogue *Cratylus* represents Cratylus as developing a theory of the Greek language, involving a system of non-conventional correspondences between (parts of) words and the world.)
                                   E.L.H.

M. Burnyeat, *The* Theaetetus *of Plato*, tr. M. J. Levett (Indianapolis, 1990), 7–65.

creation. The bringing of something into existence. In Christian *cosmology creation often means the bringing of the universe into existence *ex nihilo* by God. A contrasting conception of a much longer ancestry and of a wider spread in the world is the conception of creation as the fashioning of the cosmos out of a pre-existing indeterminate stuff by some divine being or principle. Apart from other grave problems, it is not clear how *ex nihilo* creation coheres with the principle *ex nihilo nihil fit* embraced by most classical Christian philosophers. Nor are the prospects of intelligibility rosy for the notion of a presumably absolutely indeterminate and therefore unconceptualizable original stuff. Such are some of the problems created by creation. In recent times some fallacious interpretations of the big bang theory have sought to boost *ex nihilo* creation.   K.W.

John Leslie (ed.), *Physical Cosmology and Philosophy* (New York, 1990), esp. Adolf Grünbaum, 'The Pseudo-Problem of Creation in Physical Cosmology' and Paul Davies, 'What Caused the Big Bang?'.

Creationism is the American Protestant movement that takes the early chapters of Genesis as literally true accounts of the origin of the universe, including our globe, of the plants and animals that inhabit the earth, and of the human species. Also known as fundamentalism, it climaxed in 1925 in the so-called Scopes trial, when a young Tennessee schoolteacher was tried and convicted for teaching that there were humans before the time when Adam is supposed to have lived. By the 1960s, the movement adopted the term 'Creation science', arguing that the best scientific evidence points to a young earth (about 6,000 years old), the miraculous arrival of all living beings, and shortly thereafter a world-wide deluge (Noah's Flood). The most recent manifestation now goes under the title of 'Intelligent Design'. Its supporters argue that the organic world shows irreducible complexity, and this can be explained only by reference to causes out of the usual course of nature—causes that imply intelligence. Critics point out that Creationism judged as science is simply false. Physics points to a universe that is about 20 (American) billion years old and an earth that is 4½ billion years old. Life has been evolving here on earth for nearly 4 billion years. As significantly, Creationism is bad religion. Since the days of St Augustine (AD 400), it has been agreed by mainstream Christians that Genesis is not a scientific account of origins, and must be interpreted metaphorically to understand the relationship of humans to their Creator.   M.R.

R. L. Numbers, *The Creationists: The Evolution of Scientific Creationism* (New York, 1992).
M. Ruse (ed.), *But is it Science? The Philosophical Question in the Creation/Evolution Controversy* (Buffalo, 1988).

credo quia absurdum est ('I believe because it is absurd'). This is an inexact quotation from Tertullian's *De carne Christi*, a diatribe against the gnostic Marcion, who had sought to remove the apparent contradiction in believing that God became man. Tertullian responded, angrily, that the very impossibility of the incarnation was the mark of divine agency.

The saying is often used, unsympathetically, to express the idea that religious belief is irrational.   G.B.M.

   *reductio ad absurdum.

Bernard Williams, 'Tertullian's Paradox', in A. Flew and A. MacIntyre (eds.), *New Essays in Philosophical Theology* (New York, 1955).

credo ut intelligam. This means 'I believe so that I may understand'. The words come in the first chapter of St Anselm's *Proslogion*, the book which contains his famous proof, commonly called *'ontological', of the existence of

God. Anselm adds that, without faith, understanding is impossible. This doctrine has appealed to those, like Karl Barth, who regard reason, unassisted by God's grace, as unable to discover anything about God.   C.J.F.W.

Karl Barth, *Anselm: Fides Quaerens Intellectum* (London, 1960).

Crescas, Ḥasdai ibn (1340–*c*.1412). Jewish philosopher, born in Barcelona. Imprisoned for 'desecrating the host', Crescas became a courtier in Aragon and was charged by the Crown with rehabilitating Spanish Jewry after the anti-Jewish riots of 1391, in which he lost his son. His *Light of the Lord* (1410; printed in Ferrara, 1555) criticized Maimonidean *Aristotelianism, which seemed to shelter would-be apostates: Maimonides wrongly treated belief in God as a commandment; rather, it is presupposed by any divine commandment. Aristotelian *cosmology, as outlined by Maimonides, is systematically refuted. There is no contradiction in the idea of empty space or an infinite magnitude; all bodies have weight, not a natural tendency upward or downward. Citing the Talmudic view that God governs 18,000 worlds, Crescas suggests that worlds may be infinite, each providing its own 'centre' for the heaviness of falling objects. Many of these views are welcomed by Spinoza.   L.E.G.

Harry Wolfson, *Crescas' Critique of Aristotle* (first pub. 1929; Cambridge, Mass., 1971).

criterion. A standard by which to judge something; a feature of a thing by which it can be judged to be thus and so. In the writings of the later Wittgenstein it is used as a quasi-technical term. Typically, something counts as a criterion for another thing if it is necessarily good evidence for it. Unlike inductive evidence, criterial support is determined by convention and is partly constitutive of the *meaning of the expression for whose application it is a criterion. Unlike *entailment, criterial support is characteristically defeasible. Wittgenstein argued that behavioural expressions of the 'inner', e.g. groaning or crying out in pain, are neither inductive evidence for the mental (Cartesianism), nor do they entail the instantiation of the relevant mental term (behaviourism), but are defeasible criteria for its application.   P.M.S.H.

P. M. S. Hacker, *An Analytical Commentary on the* Philosophical Investigations, iii: *Wittgenstein: Meaning and Mind* (Oxford, 1990), 545–70.

Critical Realism. American Critical Realism was a collaborative effort to oppose American *New Realism. Critical Realists opposed the New Realists' epistemological monism, the assertion of identity of the contents of consciousness and its object. Critical Realists held the theory of epistemological dualism, which maintained that content and object were ontologically different. They divided on how to move from content to object without recourse to a Lockean theory, which would lead to *idealism. Most of the Critical Realists were also psychophysical dualists and assigned a greater role to mental activity than was allowed by New Realism, which thereby showed itself incapable of solving the problem of sensory illusion. Beyond insisting upon the two dualisms the Critical Realists could agree on little else, and the movement shortly lost its coherence. The most important Critical Realists were George Santayana, R. W. Sellars, and A. O. Lovejoy.

L.W.B.

Durant Drake, A. O. Lovejoy, *et al.*, *Essays in Critical Realism: A Cooperative Study of the Problem of Knowledge* (London, 1920).
A. O. Lovejoy, *The Revolt against Dualism* (La Salle, Ill., 1960).

critical theory: *see* Frankfurt School.

critical thinking: *see* informal logic.

Croatian philosophy. The earliest contact Croatians had with philosophy was in the ninth century, with the stay of the German philosopher-theologian Gottschalk at the Court of the Croatian duke Trpimir, but the first figure of importance was Hermann of Dalmatia (twelfth century), pupil of Thierry de Chartres, translator of Euclid and of Arabic astronomic treatises, and author of the work *De Essentiis*.

The golden age of Croatian philosophy was the Renaissance and the Baroque period. At this time several philosophers chose to present their opinions through commentaries on Aristotle, notably Aristotelians like Antun Medo (1530–1603), who inclined towards nominalism, and Juraj of Dubrovnik (1579–1622), whose tone was more conservative. Franjo Petrić (1529–97) was a critic of Aristotle, and the author of a Neoplatonic synthesis, *Nova de Universis Philosophia*. Other philosophers of Neoplatonist leanings were Frederik Grisogono (1472–1538), Nikola Vito Gučetić (1549–1610), and Miho Monaldi (1540–92).

The early Protestant theologian and philosopher Matija Vlačić Ilirik (1520–75) made an important contribution to hermeneutics. Other distinguished names are the theologians Benedikt Benković and Juraj Dragišćić (fifteenth century). Dragišćić was active in Florence; his best-known work is a defence of Savonarola entitled *Prophetic Solutions*. On the more scientific side were the scientist-theologians M. A. de Dominis and F. Vrančić (sixteenth and seventeenth century), both working on logic and methodology of science.

At the beginning of the seventeenth century in the wave of Counter-Reformation, several important church schools were founded (such as the Jesuit Academy in Zagreb in 1606 and the Croatian Collegium in Vienna 1624) in which philosophy was taught and studied.

The most famous Croatian scientist and philosopher was Ruđer Bosčković (1711–87), whose dynamic theories of space and matter inspired Faraday and Maxwell and anticipated modern physics.

Throughout the eighteenth and nineteenth centuries Croatian philosophers actively and swiftly followed philosophical developments in Europe. Kant's philosophy, for example, was commented upon critically by J. B. Horvath at the close of the eighteenth century, and approvingly by Simeon Čuccić in 1815. Andrija Dorotić (1764–1837), who taught philosophy in Rome, wrote, among others, on philosophical anthropology (*Philosophicum Specimen de Homine* (1795)) and on history of philosophy. Philosophy of language was discussed by two Dalmatians, F. Bottura (1779–1861) and J. Pulić (1816–83). The early reception of mathematical logic (of Peano and Schröder) was in the work of Albin Nađ (1866–1901). The best-known nineteenth-century author was the aesthetician Franjo Marković (1845–1914). His aesthetics was a pioneering work in Croatian philosophy, although somewhat conservative and over-formalistic when viewed in the European context. For him, beauty resides in harmony or unity-in-plurality, in the 'final harmonic reconciliation which resolves temporary historical dissonances', and then in clarity, vividness, and completeness. Djuro Arnold, a pupil of H. Lotze, developed a metaphysical system of spiritualist kind, inspired in part by Leibniz.

The most original philosopher in the first part of the twentieth century was Pavao Vuk-Pavlović, the author of *Knowledge and the Theory of Knowledge* (1926). He argued against the possibility of epistemology: knowledge does not form a unitary domain, since it encompasses both cognitive processes, which are the province of psychology, and the objects of cognition, which are the province of metaphysics. Important historians of philosophy were Albert Bazala and Vladimir Filipović. In the period after the Second World War the most important group was the Praxis group, or Zagreb school of Marxism (the late Gajo Petrović, then Milan Kangrga, Branko Bošnjak, and others), defending a humanistic Marxism with idealistic and Heideggerian overtones. Analytical philosophy is represented by the Zadar-Rijeka school and by Neven Sesardić, author of a book on physicalism.   N.M.

*Serbian philosophy; Slovene philosophy.

The most authoritative sources are publications of the Department for the History of Philosophy of the Institute for History at Zagreb University, notably the review *Prilozi za istraživanje hrvatske filozofske baš tine*, which has begun to appear also in English and German versions. The Institute also publishes a series of monographs (all in Croatian). A publication in English and German is the issue on *Croatian Philosophy* of the review *Synthesis philosophica* (1993).

Croce, Benedetto (1866–1952). Italian philosopher influenced by Vico, Francesco de Sanctis, an Italian literary critic and historian, and German idealism. Croce defines art as *intuizione*, or lyrical intuition, the presentation of images that are beautiful or well expressed. Image production *simpliciter* is not necessarily the manufacture of art: images assembled randomly, juxtaposed, copied, or mechanically distorted may reveal an artist's boredom or competitiveness, but are not articulated, coherent unities unless 'animated' by intense feeling. Nor are there artworks in passionate artists' heads which are not yet translated into external form. Artworks are individualized universals: the poem is 'born' in *these* words, *that* rhythm. 'Heroism and meditation on death are in the faultless blank-verse hendecasyllables of Foscolo.' An artwork is an aesthetic a priori synthesis of image and feeling in intuition, so each artwork is original, untranslatable, and unclassifiable in artistic genres and categories. But artworks are not physical facts, nor are artists making assertions about reality: Dante's *Francesca* is immune to moral censure, fire, and critical evaluation.   B.T.

Benedetto Croce, *Breviario di estetica: quattro lezioni*, 12th edn. (Bari, 1954).

crucial experiment. An *experiment whose result enables us to decide between two opposing scientific theories. The idea is that when two theories predict contrary results for an experimental situation, the crucial experiment will decide in favour of one theory against the other. According to Francis Bacon such an experiment is sometimes decisive. Popper argued that the most such an experiment can do is falsify one of the theories. Others, e.g. Lakatos, held that they are never, in themselves, finally decisive.   O.R.J.

Karl Popper, *Conjectures and Refutations* (London, 1963).

Cudworth, Ralph (1617–80). Belonged to the *Cambridge Platonists, a school which drew on Plato to assert the primacy of mind as 'senior to the world, and the architect thereof'. Cudworth's major work was *The True Intellectual System of the Universe* (1678). It was conceived as a refutation of Hobbes, but it incorporates many ideas which are anticipations of twentieth-century philosophy. For example, there is an interesting anticipation of one of G. E. Moore's (dubious) arguments for the autonomy of morality: ' . . . the nature of things [is] that which it is, and nothing else . . . '. In other words, any quality of an object or situation is what it is by reason of its own nature—justice is justice and whiteness is whiteness—and cannot be made that quality by any command, even God's. The general thrust of Cudworth's arguments is against any sort of reductivism, whether of mind to brain or of morality to command.   R.S.D.

A. N. Prior, *Logic and the Basis of Ethics* (Oxford, 1956).

culture. The word may be used in a wide sense to describe all aspects characteristic of a particular form of human life, or in a narrow sense to denote only the system of values implicit in it. Understanding culture in the wide sense is one typical concern of historical, anthropological, and sociological studies. The study of culture in the narrow sense is the province of the humanities, whose aim is to interpret and transmit to future generations the system of values in terms of which participants in a *form of life find meaning and purpose. In either of its senses, culture may be thought of as a causal agent that affects the evolutionary process by uniquely human means. For it permits the self-conscious evaluation of human possibilities in the light of a system of values that reflect prevailing ideals about what human life ought to be. Culture is thus an indispensable device for increasing human control over the direction in which our species changes.   J.K.

C. Geertz, *The Interpretation of Cultures* (New York, 1973) explores the implications of the evolutionary influence of culture.

E. Hatch, *Theories of Man and Culture* (New York, 1973) is a survey of anthropological theories of culture.

R. Williams, *Culture and Society* (London, 1958) traces the development of the idea of culture in the history of ideas.

curve-fitting problem. If finitely many data connecting two quantities (e.g. temperature and pressure) are plotted on a graph, infinitely many curves can be drawn passing through them all, each representing a theory. Which curve represents the best theory? The simplest? (But which is the simplest?) Or perhaps a still simpler one passing near but not through them? The problem is of fundamental importance for any attempt to solve the problem of *induction.   A.R.L.

*grue.

D. Stalker (ed.), *Grue! The New Riddle of Induction* (Chicago, 1994).

custom: *see* convention.

cybernetics. The study of artificial or natural systems which store information and use feedback mechanisms to guide and control their behaviour. Such devices have a fixed behavioural repertoire and thus lack the flexibility of modern programmable *computers. The notion of information is precisely mathematically specified in a branch of electrical engineering called communication theory. The notion of feedback has been studied widely in biology. Both of these disciplines have studied such systems. The interest for philosophers resides in the complex patterns of behaviour that can emerge from compounds of such relatively simple components.   B.C.S.

K. Sayre, *Cybernetics and the Philosophy of Mind* (London, 1976).

Cynics. The major assault on 'civilized values' in the ancient world, as being no true values, was mounted by the Cynics. One of Socrates' disciples, Antisthenes, was later reckoned the first of that order, but it was Diogenes, whom Plato described as Socrates run mad, that fixed the type. Many a Cynic, literally 'doggish', was doubtless no more than a tramp—but every age and nation but our own has recognized that many a tramp may be a wandering sage. Diogenes, formerly of Sinope but long resident in Corinth (404–323 BC), is known, like other philosophers of the time, through anecdotes: as that, asked by a momentarily respectful Alexander what he, Alexander, could do to help, he replied 'Get out of my light' (a request that could have had a larger meaning than the literal). Like *Pyrrho, he seems to have identified animals as admirable: the mouse running unafraid about the house to find its food. At first he kept a cup as well as a cloak and knapsack, but seeing a boy drink from cupped hands, threw away the cup. Being sold into slavery, he pointed out a potential purchaser with the words, 'Sell me to him: he needs a master', and devoted himself to bringing up his owner's children in good health and spirits. He is said eventually to have died from eating a raw octopus (in an attempt to prove a point about the unnaturalness of cooking). Many of the anecdotes concerning him are crude (found masturbating in the market-place, he remarked that it was a pity hunger could not be assuaged so easily). Many are by now incomprehensible. What survives is the image of intransigent devotion to the 'natural life'. Amongst his followers was Crates, who had abandoned a rich inheritance to live the Cynic's life (accompanied by a similarly devoted wife, Hipparchia). He left his fortune in trust, with instructions that if his sons were ordinary men, they should have the money, and if they were philosophers, it should be given to the people, as his sons would have no need of it. He wrote popular verse extolling the natural life, devoid of luxury, pride, or malice. A merchant from Citium in Cyprus, *Zeno, happened on Xenophon's account of *Socrates at an Athenian bookstall and asked where he could find such a man: the bookseller pointed to Crates, and Zeno abandoned trade for good, eventually establishing himself in the Painted Portico, the Stoa.

Those early *Stoics, his followers, were almost as shameless as the Cynics, acknowledging no merit in traditional distinctions and taboos. Why not have sex in temples, eat one's dead parents, and reckon other people's property one's own? The gods, after all, own everything; friends have everything in common, and only the wise are really friends of the gods: so the wise own what they please, though being wise they will not use it to satisfy escapable desires. Cynics put more of this into practice than the Stoics did, and despised the cosmological and logical enquiries of Stoics and the Academy. What we need to know is only how to live here-now, reducing our wants to what can easily be achieved, and entertaining no opinions about how things happen. This antinomian detachment, unexpectedly, has echoes in the sermons of another sect of wanderers, whom we now identify as Christian missionaries. These would have seemed to most of their contemporaries just another sort of Cynic. There are indeed many echoes of Cynic conversation in the Gospels (as one might expect from natives of a heavily Hellenized Galilee). The Cynics' rule was, as it were, to take up their knapsack and follow Heracles, identified as one who pursues the rugged path of laborious virtue rather than of pleasure, despite the shame that others see in this.

The history of the term since Hellenistic days is curious. Diogenes and the rest may have despised the intellectual and political currency of their day: Diogenes was indeed said to have been exiled from Sinope for (literally) defacing the coinage. But they were dedicated moralists, not nihilists. 'Cynic' once meant 'one who lives a dog's life: shamelessly, and without any settled home'. Now, drawing on an anecdote of Diogenes' searching in daylight with a lantern for a genuinely 'just' man, cynics despise all moral or altruistic claims. Some part of this derives from the poor reputation of Cynics during the early centuries AD, described by such satirists as Lucian. But the major explanation lies in the natural assumption that those who despise *our* values must despise all values. Cynics, like

early Christians, were reckoned misanthropes because they preached against class division, greed, and enmity, and showed their own vulgarity by not being as ashamed as others thought they should be of their lack of honour.

S.R.L.C.

Diogenes Laertius, *Lives of the Philosophers*, tr. R. D. Hicks, Loeb Classical Library (London, 1925).

F. Gerald Downing, *Christ and the Cynics* (Sheffield, 1988).

D. R. Dudley, *A History of Cynicism* (London, 1937).

F. Sayre, *The Greek Cynics* (Baltimore, 1948).

Cyrenaics: *see* Aristippus.

Czech philosophy. The first central European university, which owed much to the Czech cultural tradition of orientation to the West, was founded by the emperor Charles IV in Prague in 1348. This French-educated sovereign gathered around him representatives of early *humanism whom the spiritual father of the school, Petrarch, described as being as significant and gentle as if they had been born in ancient Athens. One was the religious reformer, a rector of the university, Jan Hus (1370/1–1415). His injunction was 'Seek the truth, love the truth, nurture the truth, cling to the truth, defend the truth'.

The thought of Amos Komenský—Comenius (1592–1670)—the Czech counterpart of Descartes, tended to humanism, toleration, non-violence, and a harmonic coexistence with the order of nature. The outstanding figure of a later age was Bernard Bolzano (1781–1848), whose work on logic later influenced Husserl, Tarski, and others. Subsequently, followers of the German philosopher J. F. Herbart came to the fore in Prague University. Although tedious, the Herbartians made Czech thought more factual, sober, and precise, and prepared the ground for a later *positivism.

It was T. G. Masaryk (1850–1937), the great Czech philosopher and statesman, who played a key role in reorientating Czech thought away from German to English and French models. 'Courage and honesty' was his life's model. He was elected the first president of the Czechoslovak republic in 1918. Another remarkable figure of this period was Ladislav Klíma (1878–1927), who built on the thought of Schopenhauer and Nietzsche, and anticipated both *existentialism and *phenomenology. Russell and Bergson were the foreign philosophers most translated into Czech at this time.

The pro-Western orientation was badly affected by the Munich Agreement. In the struggle against the Nazi occupation, earlier Russophile and pan- Slavic moods emerged again. Many intellectuals spontaneously accepted Marxism. Only after the Communist coup in 1948 were illusions dispelled.

After the failed hopes of the Prague Spring of 1968, there emerged a dissident movement bringing together critical neo-Marxists with liberals and Christians. The leading Czech philosopher of the twentieth century, Jan Patočka (1907–77), Husserl's pupil and himself a phenomenologist, became a leading personality in this opposition. His various works, including *The Natural World as a Philosophical Problem*, developed the thought of his teacher in a distinctive way.

The Velvet Revolution in 1989 brought about a renewal of free philosophical life. Formerly persecuted dissidents returned to the university, as did exiles from abroad. The new head of state, Vaclav Havel (1936–), was the second Czech philosopher-king. In the footsteps of Masaryk he strove to base his policy consistently on ethics.   I.T.

E. Kohák, *Jan Patočka* (Chicago, 1989).

T. G. Masaryk, *Masaryk on Thought and Life: Conversations with Karel Capek*, ed. and tr. M. and R. Weatherall (New York, 1971).

—— *The Meaning of Czech History* (Chapel Hill, NC, 1974).

D

d'Alembert, Jean le Rond (1717–83). Leading mathematician and co-editor, with Diderot, of the *Encyclopédie*. D'Alembert composed the *Discours préliminaire de l'Encyclopédie* (1751) in which, influenced by Bacon, Newton, and Locke, he defended the reliability of the senses, and the basis they provided for all our knowledge. D'Alembert was, however, strongly rationalist, making mathematics the ideal form of knowledge, and physics the basic science. He insisted that all truth was derivable from a single ultimate principle, could we but know what it was. Diderot, by contrast, took biology to be the basic science and thought d'Alembert's emphasis on mathematics outmoded. These and personal differences led d'Alembert to resign as an editor. Initially a deist, d'Alembert denied that mere matter could produce intelligence; but he later became an atheist and materialist.   T.P.

*deism; materialism; Encyclopaedists.

J. d'Alembert, *Discours préliminaire de l'Encyclopédie*, ed. P. Picavet (Paris, 1912)

Danish philosophy. The philosophical tradition in Denmark has always been a part of mainstream European philosophy. In the late thirteenth century Danish philosophers co-operated in the revival of Aristotelian philosophy in France, and contributed to the development of speculative grammar. In the late sixteenth century Danish philosophy and theology were influenced by Melanchthon's Aristotelian school of philosophy and that of its opponent Ramism, the intellectual and pedagogical movement inspired by the critique of Aristotelianism by the French philosopher Petrus Ramus. The attempt to establish Lutheran orthodoxy within the Danish Church led to the elimination of Ramism, and to the dominance of *Aristotelianism, which, later in the seventeenth century, combined with *Cartesianism.

In the first half of the eighteenth century the teaching of philosophy in Denmark was strongly influenced by Wolffianism, which was based on the German philosopher Christian Wolff's Leibnizian systematization of human knowledge (in particular metaphysics, logic, and ethics). Jens Kraft (1720–65), an undogmatic pupil of Wolff, tried to give Newtonian physics a Leibnizian metaphysical foundation, diverging from Wolff in rejecting the possibility of metaphysical knowledge of individual substances, in that respect anticipating Kant.

Later in the century *Kantianism caused a considerable debate among Danish intellectuals. The philosophers Johannes Boye (1756–1830) and Niels Treschow (1751–1833) both rejected Kant. Boye opposed Kantian ethics from a position influenced by English and Scottish philosophy, especially that of Adam Smith. Treschow, who opposed Kantianism from a nominalist and empiricist point of view, also rejected romantic philosophy and Hegelianism, ultimately turning to a kind of *Neoplatonism. The natural philosopher H. C. Ørsted (1777–1851) was originally inspired by Kant. Later he turned to Schelling. His brother, the lawyer A. S. Ørsted (1778–1860), first subscribed to Kantian ethics, but was later convinced by Fichte that the principles of ethics differ from those of jurisprudence.

Intellectuals at the turn of the eighteenth century were introduced to German romantic philosophy by the Norwegian philosopher and naturalist H. Steffens (1773–1845), but the next generation was turning to Hegelianism. By about 1840 a whole generation of students was under the spell of Hegelian speculative theology. However, one of their number, Søren Kierkegaard (1813–55), soon reacted against the reduction of faith to knowledge he found in Hegelianism. Kierkegaard's impact on Danish philosophy was mainly indirect. His stern interpretation of Christianity, and the strictures he passed on the Danish Church, caused several Danish philosophers to break with Christianity. Thus Kierkegaard paved the way for the separation of theology and philosophy, and his irrationalism may have indirectly promoted the influence of positivism and naturalism in the late nineteenth century.

F. C. Sibbern (1785–1872) and P. M. Møller (1794–1838), with whom Kierkegaard had studied philosophy, had also attacked Hegelianism. They maintained that philosophy always presupposes and is limited by human existence, with all the latter's uncertainties. Kierkegaard repeats this in his dictum that human existence cannot be confined within a philosophical system.

In about 1870 French *positivism and English *empiricism were introduced by the literary critic George Brandes (1842–1927) and the philosopher Harald Høffding (1843–1931). Høffding's broad humanistic and positivist approach made a great impact on Danish culture in the first half of the twentieth century. Høffding's pupil the logical positivist J. Jørgensen (1894–1969) maintained his antimetaphysical, empiricist attitude. After the Second World War academic philosophy took a linguistic turn, while the philosophizing theologians and poets were influenced by *existentialism, *phenomenology, and German *hermeneutics. The nuclear physicist Niels Bohr's (1885–1962) philosophical thoughts have also left their mark on Danish philosophy.

Now, at the beginning of the twenty-first century, a broad spectrum of competing trends exists, as in other European countries. Analytical philosophy still enjoys some support in academic philosophy, but modern French and German philosophy have made a strong impact on both popular philosophical discussion and academic philosophy. Perhaps this ability and readiness to receive and adopt philosophical movements from abroad is the distinctive character of Danish philosophy.   C.H.K.

*Norwegian philosophy; Swedish philosophy.

J. Hartnack, 'Scandinavian Philosophy', in P. Edwards (ed.), *The Encyclopedia of Philosophy* (New York, 1967).
S. E. Stybe, 'Trends in Danish Philosophy', *Journal of the British Society for Phenomenology* (1973).

Dante Alighieri (1265–1321). Italian poet and political philosopher famed for his visionary poem *The Divine Comedy*, a daunting moral philosophical apologetic of individual freedom and responsibility, and their divine retribution and reward. Dante's most rigorously argued treatise is *Monarchia*, which proposes, in contrast to his contemporary Marsilius of Padua, a strong universal monarchy as the only solution to the ruinous Italian factionalism of his day. But Dante's most original theories cleanly separate the spheres of influence of Church and State. Human society is directed to its end of happiness by two, not one, divinely appointed authorities, Emperor and Pope, each independent of the other. The Church, by means of divine revelation and the theological virtues, confers heavenly beatitude on the immortal soul; but the State, by means of (mainly moral) philosophy and the natural virtues, confers earthly happiness on mankind. Temporal authority descends directly from God to the Emperor, and is not mediated by the Pope, as medieval canon lawyers fiercely argued.   L.P.

*Italian philosophy.

E. Gilson, *Dante and Philosophy* (London, 1948).
G. Holmes, *Dante* (Oxford, 1980).

Danto, Arthur C. (1924–). American philosopher, at Columbia University, who has contributed to many areas of philosophy, including philosophy of history and epistemology; but, with the exception of a seminal paper defining the idea of a *basic action (an action which we perform without doing anything else to bring it about), his major work has been in aesthetics, where he is largely responsible for bringing the idea of the 'artworld' into prominence. For Danto, works of *art are only recognized and understood as such if they are located within a context which constitutes the artworld, involving, *inter alia*, the works of other artists and the practices of critics. Art is surrounded by an 'atmosphere of theory'. We cannot separate work and interpretation.   R.A.S.

A. C. Danto, *The Transfiguration of the Commonplace* (Cambridge, Mass., 1981).

Darwinism. In a general sense the term Darwinism is taken to refer to any view which sees the development of species, including the human species, as the result of competition among and within species, which weeds out the less fit. The mechanism fuelling this process is that of the selective retention by the environment of those individuals who have particular genetically based features which give them competitive advantage over their fellows. They then transmit these features to their offspring. Since in nature genetically based variations within species arise randomly, Darwinism is a non-teleological theory of order: the variations chosen by the environment and which fit it were not designed to do so, nor did they arise in direct response to environmental pressure (*contra* Lamarck). The absence of *teleological explanation means that it cannot be applied directly to developments in human society or culture.   A.O'H.

*evolution; social Darwinism.

J. Dupre, *Darwin's Legacy: What Evolution Means Today* (Oxford, 2003).

Dasein. German compound from *da* ('there, here') and *sein* ('to be'), thus literally 'to be there' and, as a substantival infinitive, 'being there'. In Kant, Hegel, etc. it is 'determinate being', especially in space and time, but also the 'existence' of God. It often amounts to a person's 'life'. For Nicolai Hartmann it is the *Dasssein* of something ('the fact *that* it is, its existence'), in contrast to its *Sosein* ('essence, being thus'). Heidegger uses it for 'the entity which each of us himself is' and 'the being of man'. He does so for several reasons. *Dasein* is a neutral term: it does not commit us to viewing man as a biological entity, as consciousness (*Bewusstsein*, a formation parallel to *Dasein*), or as essentially rational. *Dasein* has no determinate essence; its being consists in its possibilities, in what it can make itself be: for *Dasein*, 'To be or not to be, that is the question'. It is 'there' in the world. But it is not confined to a particular place (or time); it 'transcends' and is 'there' alongside others or past events. It is the 'there' or locus of 'being': without *Dasein* there would be beings, but no being as such.   M.J.I.

*German philosophy.

M. Heidegger, *The Metaphysical Foundations of Logic*, tr. M. Heim (Bloomington, Ind., 1984).

Davidson, Donald (1917–2003). American philosopher who developed a widely admired and influential theory of mind and language. Davidson's deepest influence was

Quine, with whom he shared a commitment to the fundamental importance of standard logic to metaphysics, and a consequent suspicion of 'intensional' entities like meanings, propositions, and properties or attributes. (*Extensionality; *intension and extension.)

Quine thinks that the language of first-order logic is adequate to 'limn the true and ultimate structure of reality'. Given this commitment, what happens to those mental states whose ascriptions exhibit *intensionality, such as beliefs and desires? The problem here is that the language which we use to attribute these states does not obey the principles of extensional logic. For example, Leibniz's law—the principle that if $x = y$ then whatever is true of x is true of y—can fail when talking about beliefs and desires. If I believe that Cary Grant starred in *Notorious*, it does not follow that I believe that Archibald Leach starred in *Notorious*, since I may not know that Cary Grant is Archibald Leach. Since such intensionality is plausibly essential to descriptions of belief and desires, how can we accommodate these states within a Quinean theory of the world?

Quine's own response to this is to adopt a form of eliminativism about the mental: mental categories are not suitable for science and should therefore be dispensed with. Davidson's approach is different. He agrees with Quine that the intensionality of mental descriptions renders mental categories irreducible as a whole to physical categories. But he rejects Quine's behaviourism, and in 'Mental Events' (1970) he uses the irreducibility of the mental as a premiss in an argument for a version of the *identity theory of mind, *anomalous monism.

Davidson argues for his identity theory by making the plausible assumption that all mental events causally interact with physical events. He also assumes that wherever there is causal interaction, there is a strict law of nature encompassing the interacting events. This would seem to imply that there are psychophysical laws: laws linking mental and physical events. But if there were, then the mental would be reducible to the physical, which Davidson denies.

Davidson's theory of causation gives him a way out of this conflict: for him, causation is an extensional relation between individual *events. It is extensional in the sense that if '*a* caused *b*' is true, then it remains true regardless of how we describe *a* and *b*—so 'The cause of *b* caused *b*' is as good a statement of causation as '*a* caused *b*'. It is not, however, a good causal *explanation*, and this is where laws come in. Laws relate events only in so far as the events are described in a certain way. So an event may instantiate a law under some descriptions but not under others. With this distinction in mind, Davidson argues ingeniously as follows: since mental and physical events causally interact, they must instantiate a law. But they can't instantiate a psychophysical law, since there aren't any—so they must instantiate a physical law. But to instatiate a physical law, the mental events must have a physical description, and to have a physical description is to be a physical event. So all mental events are physical events.

But if explanation of mental phenomena is not a matter of describing them in terms of laws of nature, what is it? Davidson's claim is that it is a form of normative rationalizing explanation: in describing how someone is mentally, we are describing them as rational beings, subject to the norms of logic and good reasoning. Davidson developed these ideas as part of his theory of radical interpretation. (*Translation.) His influential theory of meaning attempts to elucidate meaning in terms of the idea of truth, conceived more or less along the lines of a formal theory like Tarski's, and then to apply theories of truth to individual speakers, appropriately constrained by the principles of interpretation.   T.C.

*deflationary theories of truth; externalism; meaning; triangulation.

Davidson's essays are collected in five volumes:
Essays on Actions and Events (Oxford, 1980).
Inquiries into Truth and Interpretation (Oxford, 1984).
Subjective, Intersubjective, Objective (Oxford, 2001).
Problems of Rationality (Oxford, 2004).
Truth, Language, and History (Oxford, 2005).

death. Apart from trying to avoid it for as long as possible the philosopher has two main problems concerning death: What is it? And why does it matter? Death is the end of life, or at least of our earthly life, but when does that occur? If I render someone permanently unconscious, but his body goes on functioning till its natural term, have I murdered him? If I am decapitated, but a scientist rushes in announcing a new technique of sewing heads back on, as they now do hands, am I brought back from the dead, or did I never die? Is it worth ordering my body to be preserved for generations, in case such advances should occur (as apparently some Americans are actually doing)?

Is death always bodily death? Might we not one day swap bodies as we already swap hearts? Questions of *personal identity loom here. Suppose the 'teleportation' of science fiction became real, so that when I want to visit Mars a complete molecule-for-molecule scan of my brain is radioed to Mars and there fed into a suitable synthesized body, which then comes to life complete with all my mental characteristics and memories, and feeling as though waking from an anaesthetic. The return journey is similar, landing me up either in my old body, deep-frozen, or in a new one. The complication that my earth-brain might survive the scan and continue normally on earth without disintegrating or being deep-frozen probably makes us say the Martian 'me' is a mere duplicate, so that *I* die whenever my earth-body perishes. But this takes us towards our second question: Suppose the scanning does destroy my earth-body; why should I mind, since all my projects and memories etc. will continue? If such travel became common, but with just one duplicate of me existing at any time, public life could continue as now. Might we not eventually accept the situation, just as we accept that the 'me' that will wake tomorrow is the same, or as good, as the 'me' that falls asleep ('dies'?) tonight? Perhaps I want my non-material soul to survive. But why should that be tied to the body? Why would it not be teleported?

Perhaps it is unclear what counts as surviving. But there are further problems too. Firstly, some, notably Heidegger, have seen problems about envisaging one's own death (though not, apparently, about envisaging one's own birth), and have wondered whether 'death' means the same when used of ourselves and of others. Secondly, why do we want to survive, or fear annihilation, since, as Epicurus said, where death is I am not; where I am death is not; so we never meet? Is it an irrational fear, developed by evolution—though *evolution, here as in other cases, could only account for its development and not for its appearance in the first place? Or is annihilation a real deprivation, so that the fear of it is rational enough? Epicurus' argument suggests that the fear of death is irrational because death is something we cannot experience; but if it is rational to fear the loss of what is valuable this argument may not work, for it can be argued that experiences are not, and indeed cannot be, the only things of value or disvalue. (*Life, meaning of.) A related question is why we worry about future non-existence but not about past non-existence. Fear, it is true, concerns only the future, but we do not seem to regret those past aeons.

A final thought for those (including the writer) who fear annihilation: is the thought of *everlasting* life any less disconcerting?   A.R.L.

*immortality; mortalism; reincarnation.

T. Nagel, *Mortal Questions* (Cambridge, 1979), esp. ch. 1: 'Annihilation'.

D. Parfit, *Reasons and Persons* (London, 1984), pt. 3: 'Teleportation' etc.

A. O. Rorty (ed.), *The Identities of Persons* (Berkeley, Calif., 1976). Includes a version of Parfit and discussions of him.

B. A. O. Williams, *Problems of the Self* (Cambridge, 1973).

death instinct: *see* Freud.

death-of-the-author thesis. This approach to the interpretation of literature originates in contemporary French thought, and has been influential in the philosophy of literary criticism. It proclaims that 'text' is a prior concept to 'author', and jettisons the latter as a mere construct. A text emerges as an 'interplay of signs' in which 'meanings proliferate', without any privileged author's meaning. A liberating idea for literary critics, it is regarded sceptically by many philosophers.   C.J.

R. Barthes, 'The Death of the Author', in *Image–Music–Text*, tr. S. Heath (London, 1977).

deaths of philosophers. The first philosopher known to us as an individual person is also the first to die an interesting and dramatic death. Socrates, condemned to death by the Athenian state for, among other things, corrupting the young, drank hemlock amongst his friends, as memorably recounted in Plato's *Phaedo*. Lucretius is alleged to have killed himself after being driven mad by taking a love philtre. Seneca opened his veins in the bath after falling

out with Nero. Boethius was strangled on the orders of the Ostrogoth king Theodoric. Peter of Spain, having been pope for a year as John XXI, was killed by the collapse of a roof. Simon Magus, expecting a miracle, had himself buried alive and died of it. Peter Ramus was killed on St Bartholomew's night in 1572. Giordano Bruno was burnt by the Inquisition, as was Vanini, after horrible tortures. Uriel da Costa, after being flogged and trampled over by the Jewish community he had offended, went home and shot himself. Thomas More was beheaded. Francis Bacon died of a cold contracted while stuffing snow into a chicken as an experiment in refrigeration. Descartes was similarly afflicted through rising early to instruct Queen Christina of Sweden. Hume died cheerfully, after fending off the pressing inquiries of Boswell about an atheist's attitude to death. Hegel died in a cholera epidemic. Jevons was drowned while bathing. Gentile was murdered by communist partisans for his involvement with Mussolini's fascist regime. Simone Weil starved herself to death for the sake of solidarity with her compatriots in occupied France. Richard Montague was beaten to death by a piece of rough trade he had brought home. But for the most part, as might have been expected, philosophers have died in their beds.   A.Q.

*autobiography, philosophical; persecution of philosophers.

Paul Edwards (ed.), *Encyclopedia of Philosophy* (New York, 1967), biographies of individual philosophers.

de Beauvoir, Simone (1908–86). French existentialist philosopher, perhaps better known as feminist theoretician and novelist, and as the lover and companion of Jean-Paul Sartre, with whom she had a famously open lifelong relationship. She billed herself as one of his disciples and often cites his works in her own, but she in turn greatly influenced him, both through discussion and in the criticism which it was her expected role to produce of each of his writings.

De Beauvoir is best known for *The Second Sex* (1949), a pioneering examination along existentialist lines of the female condition. Sartre's Hegel-derived model of the struggle between subjective consciousnesses—each seeking to avoid objectification and to be looker rather than looked-at—is adapted to describe male–female relations. Men compel women to assume the status of the *Other. Thus the standard human (the *for-itself self-transcender) is implicitly defined as male, woman dismissed as mere in-itself embodiment. De Beauvoir proposes historical reasons for this oppressive objectification, and deconstructs the myth of the feminine, including its perpetration by five major male authors. She also examines the contemporary Western woman's roles as girl, wife, mother, lesbian, prostitute, in the light of her central analysis.

But influential, now invisibly, as this analysis is, it seems inadvertently to endorse what it condemns, which is a problem endemic in any attempt to existentialize an essentialism. 'One is not born, but rather becomes, a woman', intended to be liberatingly anti-deterministic, implies that femaleness is indeed optional and subhuman, and maleness the slipped-from standard. Feminists have criticized her tendency to talk as if women should re-create themselves in the image of men, rather than reorientating a male-skewed world. Few, however, would deny the central truth of de Beauvoir's diagnosis, and its importance.

De Beauvoir was not a feminist before writing *The Second Sex*, nor, until after 60, did she profess to be one. According to her notion of existential *freedom, women were largely responsible for their oppression, abdicating transcendence for security. But she later regretted the overly idealist, insufficiently materialist underpinning of the book, for she gradually softened her original extreme Sartrean stance on freedom and responsibility, shifting from almost-solipsist severity to a view that the individual is importantly the product of his or her background and social context. In discussion with Sartre she objected, against his theories on absolute unlimited freedom ('the slave in chains is as free as his master'), that the prisoner in cell or harem lacked it. And in her essays *Pyrrhus et Cinéas* (1944) and *The Ethics of Ambiguity* (1947) she attempted to reconcile her less extreme view with Sartre's by distinguishing two sorts of freedom: the ability to transcend and alter the circumstances in which one finds oneself, and the ability to dominate and utilize them to the fullest possible extent. She thus introduced into Sartrean existentialism the notion of freedom in the context of situation, and of the 'concrete possibilities' which may impede people from actually transcending their circumstances. She also, before Sartre did, reconciled with existentialist subjectivity the position that personal freedom is ineluctably bound up with that of others. However, like him, she was unable ever convincingly to give content to the idea of freedom as a moral ideal, or, logically, to escape the admission that the Sartrean existentialist has no grounds for preferring one project to another.

As well as her long essays on ethics (a subject Sartre promised, but failed, to write on), de Beauvoir explored existentialism in shorter essays and a two-volume autobiography, and, as he did, through novels and plays. *Old Age*, which she called 'the counterpart' to *The Second Sex*, is more political, blaming poverty and exploitation for worsening the aged's plight. With Sartre, Merleau-Ponty, and Aron, de Beauvoir headed the editorial board of the left-wing magazine *Les Temps modernes*, which consistently took a controversial stand on the Algerian War, feminism, and other issues, but also condemned the invasions of Hungary and Czechoslovakia.   J.O'G.

*existentialism; Héloïse complex; women in philosophy.

C. Card (ed.), *The Cambridge Companion to Simone de Beauvoir* (Cambridge, 2003).
E. Grosholz (ed.), *The Legacy of Simone de Beauvoir* (Oxford, 2004).
T. Keefe, *Simone de Beauvoir: A Study of her Writings* (London, 1983).
C. Savage Brosman, *Simone de Beauvoir Revisited* (Boston, 1991).
A. Whitmarsh, *Simone de Beauvoir and the Limits of Commitment* (Cambridge, 1981).

decidability. A set is decidable with respect to a given property if there is a finite procedure with explicit terminus for determining membership. The set need not be finite. For example, the set of even numbers is decidable. Frequent focus in logic is on decidability for (1) the set of theorems or (2) the set of semantically valid propositions of a formal system. Propositions (or sentences) of the propositional calculus are decidable in both senses. (*Decision procedure; tautology.) Not so for the predicate calculus. Although there is a specifiable proof-procedure for the latter, there is no specifiable *terminus* for the procedure and hence the set of theorems is undecidable.

Gödel showed that in a system which accommodates axioms for arithmetic there will be some sentences of arithmetic which are not provable and nor are their negations. Given *bivalence there are therefore undecidable true sentences of arithmetic. Gödel produced one such sentence which on the assumption of consistency is plausibly true but not provable.   R.B.M.

B. Mates, *Elementary Logic* (Oxford, 1972).

deciding: *see* choosing and deciding.

decision procedure. A specifiable terminating procedure (algorithm) for determining whether something has a given property. In logic one focus has been on procedures for determining for a formal system whether or not a *well-formed formula is a theorem, i.e. is provable. One procedure for identifying the set of *theorems in the propositional calculus is the method of *truth-tables since it is demonstrable that the set of theorems and the set of *tautologies are coextensive. No decision procedure is available for determining the set of theorems of the predicate calculus but there are decision procedures for certain subsets of formulae with quantifiers.

Another focus is on procedures for the determination of semantic validity, i.e. whether a well-formed formula is true under any interpretation. In the *propositional calculus, truth-tables provide a decision procedure for semantic validity.   R.B.M.

B. Mates, *Elementary Logic* (Oxford, 1972).

decision theory. The abstract (or 'formal', or mathematical) theory of decision-making, or more precisely of rational decision-making. The decision-maker is assumed to have a range of objectives, measurable at least in terms of their rank order, though it is theorized that we can also talk of their 'utility' or relative degree of preferredness; but it is *not* assumed that one agent's utility may be directly compared with another's. Of special interest are decisions under various kinds of limited knowledge of outcomes of possible actions, such as those in which probabilities are known, and especially those in which even they are not known (termed 'uncertainty'). Of very special interest are those cases involving interaction with other decision-makers; these are called 'games'. Investigation of such 'games' as *Prisoner's Dilemma, Co-ordination, and Chicken inform much recent social, political, and moral philosophy. Decision theory is mathematically orientated, but many results are philosophically disputable. An example that is not: in two-person zero-sum games, one does best with a minimax strategy.   J.N.

*game theory.

R. Duncan Luce and Howard Raiffa, *Games and Decisions* (New York, 1957) is the classic in the field.

Michael D. Resnik, *Choices* (Minneapolis, 1987) is one of many excellent texts for the novice.

deconstruction. Introduced into philosophy by the French philosopher Jacques Derrida in the late 1960s, the term 'deconstruction' is now chiefly associated, despite the disclaimers of its originator, with a school of literary criticism. Derrida's disclaimers present a major obstacle to any attempt, this one included, to encapsulate his thought. He tells us that deconstruction is neither an analytical nor a critical tool; neither a method, nor an operation, nor an act performed on a text by a subject; that it is, rather, a term that resists both definition and translation. To make matters worse, he adds that 'All sentences of the type "deconstruction is X" or "deconstruction is not X" miss the point, which is to say that they are at the least false' ('Letter to a Japanese Friend'). The following elucidatory remarks, which I shall nevertheless offer, are perhaps especially compromised by their subject-matter.

Deconstruction can be illuminated by considering two major intellectual influences on Derrida: the philosophy of Heidegger and *structuralism. Derrida's term alludes, deliberately, to Heidegger's project of the destruction (*Destruktion*) of the history of *ontology. In this reappraisal of Western philosophy, Heidegger argued that a particular tense—the present—had continually been awarded priority in accounts of the nature of being. To correct this prejudice philosophy needed to reconsider the problem of time. Derrida's deconstruction, also a response to the 'metaphysics of presence', is distinguished by its central concern with the treatment of *language* in Western thought. In his 'classic' period (1967–72), at least, the texts Derrida deconstructs take language as their theme: Plato's *Phaedrus*, Rousseau's *Essay on the Origin of Languages*, and Saussure's *Course in General Linguistics*, among others. Derrida suggests that the idea of presence lies behind the traditional ranking of speech above writing. This tradition holds speech to be the direct expression of thought or *logos*, contemporaneous with its meaning, while writing enters the scene subsequently, a dangerous substitute for speech in which the speaker's intentions, no longer 'present', are likely to be betrayed. Derrida's strategy is to demonstrate that the logic of the texts that promote this picture invites its own refutation. (It is this strategy—the turning of a text against itself—that has become the hallmark of deconstructive literary criticism.) Derrida's

reading of Saussure, for example, argues that the properties that purportedly distinguish writing from speech are ones that Saussure's own theory must commit him to ascribe equally to speech: spoken signs, like written ones, are arbitrary, material, and system-relative. The primacy of the voice rests on an entrenched philosophical illusion.

Derrida inherits from structuralist theory the idea that signification must be explained in terms of the system that governs it and the oppositions mobilized by that system. Just as the structuralist anthropologist Lévi-Strauss used the opposition between the raw and the cooked to illuminate cultural practices concerning food, so Derrida's readings of philosophical texts begin by identifying the fundamental conceptual oppositions they rely on: speech–writing, soul–body, intelligible–sensible, literal–metaphorical, natural–cultural, masculine–feminine. Derrida's post-structuralist credentials come from his next steps: first, as we have seen, to subject these oppositions to an internal critique that destabilizes them; then, to raise the Kantian question of what makes these oppositions possible. This last question, Derrida believes, takes thought and language to their limits. His response is to generate a set of terms, many neologistic, and all avowedly inadequate and self-defeating, for the reader to struggle with. We are offered archi-writing, *différance*, textuality, the trace—terms that appear to be ultimate but that necessarily presuppose already established linguistic structures. Derrida thus condemns the structuralist hope of delineating closed systems to be for ever unfulfilled.

                                        S.D.R.

David Wood and Robert Bernasconi (eds.), *Derrida and Différance* (Coventry, 1985).

Jonathan Culler, *On Deconstruction: Theory and Criticism after Structuralism* (Ithaca, NY, 1982).

Jacques Derrida, 'Différance', in *Margins of Philosophy* (Chicago, 1982).

Dedekind, J. W. R. (1831–1916). German mathematician, who made two important contributions to the foundations of mathematics. The first showed how the theory of the real *numbers could be freed from any reliance on geometrical intuition by being constructed instead from the theory of the rational numbers. Dedekind's basic idea here was that each real number corresponds to a 'cut' in the rationals, i.e. a separation of all rationals into two non-empty sets, with all in the one set being less than all in the other. The second contribution was a set of axioms for the natural numbers, which in effect are those known today as *'Peano's postulates'. Dedekind proved that these axioms do exactly characterize the structure of the number series. Both these contributions are conveniently translated in J. W. R. Dedekind, *Essays on the Theory of Numbers* (New York, 1963).   D.B.

H. Wang, 'The Axiomatisation of Arithmetic', *Journal of Symbolic Logic* (1957).

de dicto: see *de re* and *de dicto*.

deduction. A species of *argument or *inference where from a given set of premisses the conclusion must follow. For example, from the premisses P_1, P_2 the conclusion P_1 and P_2 is deducible. The set consisting of the premisses and the negation of the conclusion is inconsistent. An argument advanced as deductive where the foregoing fails is invalid. If deducibility holds between a conclusion and premisses, the conclusion is also described as a logical consequence of the premisses.

In the standard *propositional calculus, it is provable that if Q is deducible from a set of premisses P_1, P_2, ..., P_n then $P_n \supset Q$ is deducible from P_1, P_2, ..., P_{n-1}. Where $n = 1$, $P_1 \supset Q$ is a theorem. This result is known as the deduction theorem.   R.B.M.

*horseshoe; induction.

B. Mates, *Elementary Logic* (Oxford, 1972).

deduction, natural: *see* natural deduction.

defeasible. A defeasible property, relation, or judgement is subject to defeat (nullification, termination, or substantial revision) by further considerations (e.g. later facts or evidence).

Lawyers' English has always known defeasible estates, titles, transactions. Hart introduced the term into his first essay in philosophy of *law, arguing that legal concepts do not describe (for example) actions, but ascribe responsibility or liability, ascriptions defeasible on proof of exceptions (e.g. duress, infancy). Hart soon abandoned this thesis, and the word. But legal philosophers debate law's defeasible (presumptive, prima facie) moral obligatoriness. And concepts of defeasibility have seen wide service in epistemology and semantics. For example, some explanations of an assertion's sense refer to what would give the assertion evidential or inferential warrant (and even certainty), albeit a warrant defeasible by further evidence or considerations.
                                                            J.M.F.

G. P. Baker, 'Defeasibility and Meaning', in P. M. S. Hacker and
    J. Raz (eds.), *Law, Morality and Society* (Oxford, 1977).

de Finetti, Bruno (1906–85). Italian mathematician and theorist of *probability whose technically sophisticated, if philosophically somewhat underdeveloped, work laid the foundations for the modern subjectivist interpretation of probabilities as the partial beliefs of a judging agent, intermediate between full belief and full disbelief. Such views seem to flout our intuitions that probabilities are more objective than this. De Finetti's achievement was to show that, from imposing the single minimal constraint on an agent's judgements of *coherence* (a generalization of consistency), two results follow: initially different sets of judgements will converge as the probabilities are adjusted in the light of incoming evidence; and, in the contexts of most interest to science, they must converge on to the observed relative frequency of the outcomes of repeated trials. Hence, subjectivist theory can find room for the objective concepts of consensus and relative frequency.   J.L.

B. de Finetti, *Theory of Probability*, 2 vols. (New York, 1974).

definist fallacy. The definist fallacy is the tactic in argumentation of defining a term so that it is friendly to your own side of a dispute, or unfriendly to the opposed side, without leaving any room for questioning the definition or considering alternatives. For example, a pro-life advocate in an abortion dispute may insist rigidly on defining abortion as the act of murdering an unborn baby. The expression 'definist fallacy' has also been used in ethics (G. E. Moore) to exclude the practice of defining one ethical property by means of another (supposedly) identical property. But it is not clear that this is a *fallacy.   D.N.W.

*definition.

Douglas N. Walton, *Informal Logic* (Cambridge, 1991).

definite descriptions: *see* descriptions, theory of.

definition. Explanation of the meaning of a word or expression, either as established in a language ('dictionary definition') or as it is to be used ('stipulative definition').

Traditionally, the definition of a word properly consisted of expressions naming the genus (wider class) to which something belonged and differentia (distinguishing features). Thus 'triangle' was defined as 'a plane figure (genus) bounded by three straight sides (differentia)'. The expression supplying the definition (definiens) was taken as synonymous with and capable of being substituted for the term being defined (definiendum). However, there are many types of words whose meaning is capable of precise explanation, which, for one reason or another, cannot be defined in this sense. Some of the reasons were given by Locke in *An Essay Concerning Human Understanding* (1690).

1. An explanatory equivalent may require more than the traditional two terms for genus and differentia. 'Languages are not always so made, according to the Rules of Logick, that every term can have its signification exactly and clearly expressed by two others' (*Essay*, III. iii. 10).

2. Some words cannot be defined by means of other words: 'For if the Terms of one Definition, were still to be defined by another, Where at last should we stop?' (ibid. III. iv. 5). Locke restricted definitions to explanations of meaning by other words, and held that the names of simple ideas, e.g. 'blue', whose meaning can be explained but only by pointing out examples, 'are incapable of being defined' (ibid. III. iv. 7). Explanation via examples, however, is now included as a type of definition: ostensive, as opposed to verbal, definition.

A dictionary definition, since it claims to describe the established meaning of a word, may be inaccurate. It may be too narrow, excluding things that ought to be included, e.g. ' "queen" = the wife of a king', or too broad, including things that ought to be excluded, e.g. ' "king" = the sovereign of a country', or simply wrong, e.g. ' "princess" = the wife of a king'. Stipulative definitions, which merely specify the proposed use of a word, new or old, cannot in this sense be inaccurate, although divergence from established meanings may be open to other criticisms, such as that the new use is confusing or, in some legal contexts, that it has adverse practical effects. Suggested definitions of either kind may have the defect of being insufficiently explanatory: e.g. obscure, circular, or, with ostensive definitions, leaving more than one possibility open.

Definitions dubbed 'persuasive' by C. L. Stevenson, generally purport to describe the 'true' or 'real' existing meaning of a term (e.g. true democracy, real freedom) while in fact stipulating a particular or an altered use. Definitions are commonly thought of as given for the purposes of clarification, but someone who gives a persuasive definition usually has the different object of inducing acceptance of some view, e.g. that only some particular system is democratic. In the same vein, there are 'legal' or 'coercive' definitions, which have the object or effect of creating or altering rights, duties, or crimes.   s.w.

Trudy Govier, *A Practical Study of Argument*, 3rd edn. (Belmont, Calif., 1992), ch. 4.
J. Locke, *An Essay Concerning Human Understanding* (London, 1690); 4th edn. of 1700, ed. P. H. Nidditch (Oxford, 1975).
C. L. Stevenson, *Ethics and Language* (New Haven, Conn., 1944).

definition, contextual: *see* contextual definition.

definition, ostensive: *see* ostensive definition.

definitions, explicit and implicit. An explicit definition of a term t (the *definiens*) provides necessary and sufficient conditions (the *definiendum*) for the correct employment of t, usually in terms of previously understood vocabulary. Thus the explicit definition 'For all x, x is a triangle if and only if x is a three-sided polygon' provides semantically equivalent conditions for using the expression 'is a triangle'. A key feature of explicit definitions is that they allow the elimination of the *definiens* from sentences in which it occurs and its replacement by the *definiendum* without change in truth-value. Implicit definitions place constraints on the use of a term, usually in the form of a theory, such that any term satisfying the constraints falls under the definition. So, *probability theory implicitly defines what 'probability' means. Implicitly defined terms are not eliminable, and the associated concept is underdetermined in the sense that there is never a unique concept satisfying the implicit definition—hence the multiple meanings of 'probability'.   p.h.

Paul Horwich, *Meaning* (Oxford, 1998).

deflationary theories of truth. A theory of *truth is deflationary if it declares that truth is a concept that is easily shown to be dispensable, or is no more than technically useful. The simplest deflationary theories are *redundancy theories, which observe that 'It is true that' or 'It is a fact that', when appended to a sentence, add nothing but emphasis. Frank Ramsey, who made this observation,

also noticed that reference to truth is not so easily removed from sentences like 'Everything he says is true', but this was a problem he thought could be solved. Deflationists who treat truth as a property of sentences or utterances rather than of propositions note that Tarski has shown how to eliminate the words 'is true' when predicated of sentences of certain formalized languages. They consider that this shows that the concept of truth is not metaphysically deep, and so does not require appeal to such notions as correspondence to reality, coherence, or success of one sort or another in coping.   d.d.

P. F. Strawson, 'Truth', *Proceedings of the Aristotelian Society*, supp. vol. (1950).

deism. Philosophical belief in a god established by reason and evidence (notably by the design argument) without acceptance of the special information supposedly revealed in, for example, the Bible or Koran. Hence deism involves belief in a creator who has established the universe and its processes but does not respond to human prayer or need. In the eighteenth century the word was applied to positions as far apart as the positive religious rationalism of Samuel Clarke and the negative quasi-atheism of Anthony Collins. The archetypal deist is Voltaire.   j.c.a.g.

*atheism and agnosticism.

Peter Byrne, *Natural Religion and the Nature of Religion* (London, 1989).
Peter Gay, *Deism: An Anthology* (New York, 1968).

Deleuze, Gilles (1925–95). French philosopher whose earliest books included studies of Spinoza, Hume, Kant, and Bergson, each written from an angle sharply at odds with the received exegetical wisdom. Deleuze reads always with an eye to those 'heretic' doctrines—like Spinoza's ontology of bodily affects and forces or Hume's radical empiricism—which retain their power to provoke and disconcert. Hence also his attraction to Nietzsche (the subject of another expository *tour de force*). In *Différence et répétition* and *Logique du sens* he came as near as possible to offering a full-scale programmatic statement of this postphilosophical, anti-systematic, ultra-nominalist or resolutely 'non-totalizing' mode of thought.

Deleuze subsequently produced a number of works in collaboration with Félix Guattari, a political theorist and close cousin to the late 1960s 'anti-psychiatry' movement. Best known of these is their joint diatribe entitled the *Anti-Oedipus*. This is a vast, chaotic rag-bag of a book which attacks Freudian *psychoanalysis (along with its Lacanian post-structuralist offshoot) as a mechanism for channelling or policing the flows of vagrant 'molecular' desire, and thus reinforcing the 'molar' dictates of capitalist socio-political order. Spinoza and Nietzsche are still the great heroes, standing as they do—or as these authors read them—for a counter-tradition of sceptical, affirmative, non-subject-centred, instinctually driven 'desiring-production'.   c.n.

Ronald Bogue, *Deleuze and Guattari* (London, 1989).

de Maistre, Joseph Marie (1753–1821). De Maistre is now known chiefly as a proponent of monarchical government and of the Christian foundations of civil society. He espoused these doctrines originally in diagnosing the causes of the French Revolution, which he regarded as divine punishment for France's embrace of the anti-Christian *Enlightenment. He urged the doctrines more generally in *On the Pope* (*Du pape* (1819)), in which he argued that an infallible papacy is the unique source not only for Christian orthodoxy, but for all legitimate political power and for the progress of universal civilization. De Maistre wrote further both an extended vindication of divine providence (*Soirées de Saint-Pétersbourg* (1821)) and a polemical refutation of the *materialism of Francis Bacon (*L'Examen de la philosophie de Bacon* (1826)).

M.D.J.

*conservatism.

Richard A. Lebrun, *Joseph de Maistre: An Intellectual Biography* (Kingston, Ont., 1988).

demandingness of morality. Morality presupposes certain tests, criteria, or requirements that actions must meet in order to be morally acceptable. Failure with respect to living up to moral norms is considered to diminish one's standing as a human being in a way that failure to meet other achievement norms allegedly does not. Most moralists, including modern Kantians and consequentialists, hold that morality is specially demanding and that moral tests are difficult for the ordinary person to pass on an ongoing basis, in so far as morality requires the suppression of self-interest and inclination. Moral failure is not always excused by situational or psychological reasons for poor performance, or compensated for by the attainment of non-moral goods. Critics of this demandingness favour greater concessions to human weakness and partiality. They may insist that the meta-ethical notion of an ineluctable and universally binding moral requirement has not been adequately grounded. Moral considerations can sometimes be justifiably overruled by non-moral considerations, or even ignored on occasion. Moral rules, on their view, correspond, like most other norms, to defeasible ought-statements.

CATH.W.

Bernard Williams, *Ethics and the Limits of Philosophy* (London, 1993).

demiurge. The ancient Greek word means 'craftsman' or 'artisan'. Plato, in the *Timaeus*, uses the word for the maker of the universe. Plato says of this maker that he is unreservedly good and so desired that the world should be as good as possible. The reason why the world is not better than it is is that the demiurge had to work on pre-existing chaotic matter. Thus, the demiurge is not an omnipotent creator. Early Christian philosophers were quick to claim that the demiurge represented pagan philosophy's anticipation of the God of revealed religion.

L.P.G.

*cosmogony.

F. M. Cornford, *Plato's Cosmology: The Timaeus of Plato*, tr. with running commentary (London, 1937).

democracy. Government by the people. Until recently, democracies counted very few persons among 'the people'. Now they include all adult citizens, including, in many nations, recent immigrants, and democracy is virtually universally revered as the best or the right form of government. In the democratic upsurges in Eastern Europe in 1989, a rallying-cry from crowds in the street was '*We* are the people'. Every chanter, every listener, knew what that meant, and most of them presumably thought it a claim of morality, of right.

In its simplest form, democracy entails having all citizens participate in voting on policies. In large states this is not sensible or even possible and participation takes place in sequential forms. First, representatives are chosen and then they decide on policies. It is widely believed that different structures for representation could produce substantially different outcomes. Hence, there is no simple formula for democracy that relates popular preferences to political outcomes in large polities.

Because the general character of democracy is widely understood, we may focus discussion most acutely by beginning with its difficulties. Contemporary public choice theory began in the analysis of two critical problems for democratic decision. (1) The economist Kenneth Arrow showed that orderly individual preferences do not generally aggregate into orderly collective preferences, which may be ill-defined. This result is essentially a generalization of a long-ignored result of C. L. Dodgson (Lewis Carroll). (2) The economists Anthony Downs and Mancur Olson argued that individual motivations for action are incompatible with collective preferences even when the latter are well defined. The logic of democracy is doubly flawed. One might respond to the first result by saying that democracy need not be determinate even though individual preferences might be. Of course democracy will be a mess when the society is a mess. The second result is not so easy to accommodate. It includes the sad conclusion that the individual need not even have motivation to know enough about public life to make intelligent decisions. Self-interest leads to public ignorance. Hence, democracy can be a mess even when the society is not. The perverse logic of its motivation may undermine justifications for democracy.

Among the major contemporary justifications of democracy are that it serves interests by bringing them into decision procedures, that democratic participation enhances autonomy, that democracy is the best form of government for political *equality, and that it is the natural form for consent through deliberation. In order, it serves welfare, autonomy, equality, and agreement. *Consent plays a role in all of these, but the role is largely causal for welfare and equality, and constitutive for autonomy and agreement. A grudging, negative justification is that democracy is better than other forms of government at blocking particularly bad results from continuing (this is often, but not always, a welfarist claim). A final justification, which may be merely a historically specific variant of justification from *autonomy, is that changing to democratic forms can be enlivening and fulfilling for the generation that makes a change. For this to be true, some other justification must generally be believed.

The first four—positive—justifications are, in their own terms, less compelling than they might be just because they founder on the two perverse logics of democracy. They founder both conceptually and empirically. The negative claim for democracy is a variant of Winston Churchill's quip that democracy is the worst form of government other than all the other forms we know. This sounds like a strictly empirical claim, but it requires some sense of the notion 'better', which may make no sense under the perverse logics of democracy. And the claim for the beauty of changing to democracy is a claim about the facts of actual experiences, such as in the United States two centuries ago, Spain recently, and Eastern Europe today. There are contrary experiences, such as in France after the Revolution, Germany between the wars, and Algeria and Iran more recently.

Welfarist justifications of democracy reached their height in the work of the Utilitarians, especially John Stuart Mill. In the twentieth century, they turned increasingly negative: democracy is more valuable for what it prevents than for what it creates. The lesson of the collapse of socialism in the 1980s will likely be invoked for generations to support the welfarist value of democracy, which may be too readily associated with the *market in Western thought. An early and still arguably the most articulate welfarist justification of a form of government was Thomas Hobbes's defence of extreme autocracy. The twentieth century provided vicious counter-examples to Hobbes's vision. Apart from empirical concerns, there is also a deep conceptual problem in the definition of welfare, especially as compared across individuals.

Justifications of democracy that turn on equality are still in their infancy. One might look to equality of outcomes, such as economic results, or to equality of political power or opportunities for participation. Democracy may tend to produce welfare policies that elevate the condition of the very poor and thereby enhance equality of outcomes, but the data are quite ambiguous and the causal theory of why this should happen is very thin. Equality of political power is perhaps the more compelling justification, but it lacks conceptual clarity. How do we measure power to equate it?

Deliberation is especially associated with Jürgen Habermas. Critics argue that the appeal of deliberation is the appeal of the intellectual salon with a dozen or so erudite and witty discussants. Deliberation was not even very good much of the time in Athens, with its extraordinarily supportive conditions. It has little chance in a nation of 50 or 200 million adult citizens. Perhaps therefore, much of the argument in favour of deliberation has the flavour of rationalist, rather than genuinely procedural, justification.

Rationalist debate is, of course, carried out by theorists, not by peoples. Indeed, the salon model of deliberation is an oddly élitist vision of democracy.

Autonomy, whether in the tradition of Immanuel Kant or of Mill, has similar problems. First, if autonomy depends on the efficacy of participation, we should hope few have it, because life in which tens or hundreds of millions of people are effective in imposing their idiosyncratic views on us would be horrendous. The movie *Dr Strangelove*, which has too few lunatics, understates how horrendous such a world would be. Quite possibly, we must conclude that Downs's world, in which few have incentive to participate seriously, is a good world, and that it is a world in which autonomy cannot depend very much on democratic participation. Second, if autonomy depends on the benefits that come from participation, then it is contingent on whatever good motivates participation. Most people cannot sensibly think they benefit from participation that does not have effects on government policy.

Democratic theory is in the throes of a revolution of creative energies and ideas, especially from interdisciplinary borrowings and insights and from current, remarkable experience. When have political theorists previously had the luxury of quoting the latest issue of *The Times* to undergird their arguments? As is true of many intellectual enterprises, clarification regularly uncovers difficulties, often grievous difficulties, for our understanding of democracy. As a result, democratic theory thrives while theoretically democracy looks more shambling than ever. Though democracy may not be a good example of deliberation, its theory often is. Debates are beautiful, wide-ranging, insightful, and, unusually for philosophy, increasingly grounded in empirical cases. There is no call for science fiction or contrived examples in democratic theory.   R.HAR.

*anti-communism; voting paradox.

Charles Beitz, *Political Equality* (Princeton, NJ, 1989).

John W. Chapman (ed.), *NOMOS 32: Majorities and Minorities* (New York, 1990).

David Copp, Jean Hampton, and John E. Roemer (eds.), *The Idea of Democracy* (Cambridge, 1993).

R. A. Dahl, *A Preface to Democratic Theory* (Chicago, 1956).

——*Dilemmas of Pluralist Democracy* (New Haven, Conn., 1982).

——*A Preface to Economic Democracy* (Cambridge, 1985).

Anthony Downs, *An Economic Theory of Democracy* (New York, 1957).

democracy and capitalism. Democracy is a form of government where political power is exercised on behalf of the people as a whole; capitalism is an economic system whereby goods and services are produced and distributed for profit.

Classical liberal theory conceives of democracy and capitalism as independent systems, with disparate goals, requirements, and types of influence. Democracy restricts economic processes only to protect basic rights; it does not limit wealth, and so allows the profit motive to stimulate innovation and mass production which can benefit society. However, capitalism creates a large wage-dependent class lacking the goods, opportunities, and political power of the wealthy. Secondly, unrestricted global capitalism has created international, non-democratic bodies able to override domestic democratically enacted environmental or labour restrictions. And democracy requires citizens who can think critically; capitalism needs consumers easily influenced by advertising.

Social democracy extends citizens' rights to include health care, housing, transportation, education, welfare programmes, union and work-place protection, and a minimum wage. It includes progressive taxation and restricts financial influence on political processes.   c.c.

E. M. Wood, *Democracy against Capitalism: Renewing Historical Materialism* (Cambridge, 1995).

democratic violence. Political violence, according to some, is necessarily undemocratic since it involves force rather than democratic process. Others argue that it is admissible, but only against undemocratic states. If closer attention is given to the real operation of democracy and the intent of political violence, however, some violence may be considered democratic in virtue of features it shares with democratic practice. If, for example, violence falls short of literally forcing obedience, it can be considered as a way of bringing persuasive pressure to bear and therefore akin to procedures of persuasion that are intrinsic to democracies. Violence can, in addition, be aimed at rectifying the undemocratic influence of wealth and position, and may bring about more democracy. That acts of violence can be considered to be democratic would be import-ant in determining whether they are justified, but neither sufficient nor necessary for it.   k.m.

J. Hoffman, *The Gramscian Challenge* (Oxford, 1984).

T. Honderich, *Terrorism for Humanity: Inquiries in Political Philosophy* (London, 2004).

Democritus (*c*.460–*c*.370 BC). Co-founder with Leucippus of the theory of *atomism. His exact relation to Leucippus is obscure. Aristotle and his school agree in treating Leucippus as the originator of the theory, but also in assigning its basic principles to both, while later sources treat the theory as the work of Democritus alone.

Very little is known about his life. His works, none of which survive, included a complete account of the physical universe, and works on astronomy and other natural sciences, mathematics, literature, epistemology, and ethics. Ancient sources preserve almost 300 purported quotations, the great majority on ethics; the authenticity of the ethical fragments is disputed. Sextus Empiricus preserves some important quotations on epistemology. For our knowledge of the physical doctrines we are reliant on the doxographical tradition stemming ultimately from Aristotle, who discusses atomism extensively.

According to Aristotle, the Atomists attempted to reconcile the observable data of plurality, motion, and change with the denial by the *Eleatics of the possibility of coming to be or ceasing to be. Accordingly they postulated as primary substances an infinity of unchanging physical corpuscles in eternal motion in empty space, and explained apparent generation and corruption as the formation and dissolution of aggregates of those. These corpuscles were physically indivisible (whence the term *atomon*, lit. 'uncuttable'), not merely in fact, but in principle. Empty space was postulated as required for motion, but was characterized as 'what is not', thus violating the Eleatic principle that what is not cannot be. We have no evidence of how the Atomists met the accusation of outright self-contradiction.

Democritus seems to have been the first to recognize the observer-dependence of the secondary qualities. Perception of the secondary qualities reveals merely how things seem to us, as opposed to how they really are. According to some sources, he used this contrast to show the unreliability of the senses, but then faced the problem of the justification of his theory, which was founded on sensory data. It is disputed whether he responded to this problem by espousing scepticism.

The ethical fragments, if genuine, show that Democritus was one of the first philosophers to maintain a form of enlightened hedonism, and that he had a strong commitment to social cohesion and the rule of law.   c.c.w.t.

*primary and secondary qualities.

D. Furley, *The Greek Cosmologists*, i (Cambridge, 1987), chs. 8–14.

W. K. C. Guthrie, *A History of Greek Philosophy*, ii (Cambridge, 1965), ch. 8.

demonstration. Proof. Something is demonstrably true if you can prove it, demonstrably false if you can give a *proof that it is false. Deductive proof is usually meant here. A demonstration will generally consist of true premisses, followed by logical steps to a conclusion. Wittgenstein thought that genuine proofs in logic or mathematics were surveyable—i.e. could be taken in. The term 'demonstration' ('showing') might be thought to embody this principle. If a 'number-crunching' calculator churns out the solution to an equation, we will accept it, of course—but the solution won't have been demonstrated.   r.p.l.t.

P. T. Geach, *Reason and Argument* (Oxford, 1976).

De Morgan, Augustus (1806–71). British mathematician who also played a useful part in the development of logic. He was one of those who realized that much valid reasoning could not be forced into the mould of Aristotelian syllogistic, giving examples such as: 'Horses are animals; therefore the head of a horse is the head of an animal.' As a logician he is remembered now by two laws named after him, namely

'Not (*P* and *Q*)' is equivalent to 'Not-*P* or not-*Q*'
'Not (*P* or *Q*)' is equivalent to 'Not-*P* and not-*Q*'

(As stated here, these are laws of propositional logic. In De Morgan's own formulation they would belong rather to the algebra of classes.) D.B.

*Boolean algebra; logic, history of.

Dennett, Daniel C. (1942–). Dennett's guiding idea is that of the 'intentional stance'. We take the intentional stance towards a system—a person, a bat, a computer—when we attribute rationality to the system and predict what the system will do given the beliefs and desires ascribed. There is an abiding controversy about whether the intentional stance captures the way things really are or whether the stance is merely a heuristic, an instrumentally useful way of conceiving mind, which awaits the more accurate analyses to be offered from the neurophysiological level (the physical stance) or the subpersonal cognitive psychology level (the design stance). Dennett tries to avoid realism or *instrumentalism, dubbing himself a 'mild realist'. Following Ryle (and Reichenbach) he holds that there are different senses of 'exist': the marks on this paper exist and so, in a different sense, do the Equator and the self. Dennett is a realist about 'representations', since our best science tells us that we are intentional systems; folk psychological notions like 'belief' and 'desire' pick out 'real patterns', but it is doubtful whether they do so in the most perspicuous manner. O.F.

*folk psychology; homunculus; intentionality; Lexicon, Philosophical.

D. C. Dennett, *The Intentional Stance* (Cambridge, Mass., 1987).
——'Self-Portrait', in S. Guttenplan (ed.), *Blackwell Companion to the Philosophy of Mind* (Oxford, 1994).

denotation and connotation. A distinction introduced by J. S. Mill. The denotation of a term, e.g. 'woman', is all the individuals to which it correctly applies, e.g. Mrs Smith, Prince Charles, etc. The connotation of the term consists in the attributes by which it is defined, e.g. being human, adult, female. A term's connotation determines its denotation. In Mill connotation is taken to be meaning. Terms like proper names, e.g. 'Charles', which have denotation, since there is someone so called, but no connotation, since no attributes define 'Charles', are taken to lack meaning. S.W.

*sense and reference.

J. S. Mill, *A System of Logic* (London, 1843).

denying the antecedent. To reason that, because Nazis hate Jews and John is not a Nazi, he cannot be an anti-Semite, is to commit this fallacy. In the traditional logic of terms, inferences like 'If *A* is *B*, it is *C*; it is not *A*; therefore it is not *C*' illustrate the fallacy. In *propositional calculus, any inference of the form 'If *p* then *q*, and not *p*; therefore not *q*' denies the antecedent. C.W.

*denying the consequent.

C. L. Hamblin, *Fallacies* (London, 1970).

denying the consequent. In a hypothetical proposition 'If *p*, then *q*', *p* is the antecedent, *q* the consequent. Asserting that *q* is false, so that the falsity of *p* may be inferred, is denying the consequent; the inference is in the *modus tollens*. When a man who is patently not Dutch says 'If the Queen cannot afford to pay taxes, I'm a Dutchman', he means us to deny the consequent and conclude that the Queen is patently wealthy. The corresponding fallacy is *denying the antecedent. C.W.

H. W. B. Joseph, *An Introduction to Logic*, 2nd edn. (Oxford, 1916), ch. 15.

deontic logic. The study of principles of reasoning pertaining to obligation, permission, prohibition, moral commitment, and other normative matters. Although often described as a branch of logic, deontic logic lacks the 'topic-neutrality' characteristic of logic proper. It is better viewed as an application of logic to ethical concepts, in much the same way as formal geometry is an application of logic to spatial concepts. Likewise, although hopes have been expressed that deontic logic might help to systematize the *practical* reasoning whereby we infer from general principles and observed facts what we ought to do, the most studied systems of deontic logic comprise mainly *theoretical* principles, expressing inferential relations among various ethical concepts.

Several principles prominent in the current literature were noted by various medieval philosophers, and again by Leibniz and by Jeremy Bentham, but focused and sustained thought in the field is a twentieth-century phenomenon, kindled largely by the writings of G. H. von Wright. Early work was motivated by analogies between the deontic concepts of obligation, permission, and prohibition, and the alethic concepts of necessity, possibility, and impossibility. The first analogies to be noted concerned 'interchange' principles. If $\square$ and $\Diamond$ represent necessity and possibility, for example, then the formula $\neg \square A \leftrightarrow \Diamond \neg A$ says that to deny *A* is necessary is to assert not-*A* is possible. If they represent obligation and permission it says (equally plausibly) that to deny *A* is obligatory is to assert not-*A* is permitted. Similarly, $\neg \Diamond A \leftrightarrow \square \neg A$ and $\neg IA \leftrightarrow \Diamond A$ (where I is either 'impossible' or 'forbidden') have equally plausible alethic and deontic readings. The development of complete formal systems of necessity led naturally to an effort to see how far the analogy can be extended. The weakest system in which $\square$ can plausibly be regarded as expressing some form of alethic necessity is the system T, which contains, in addition to the interchange principles, principles of distribution ($\square (A \& B) \rightarrow \square A \& \square B$) and reflexivity ($\square A \rightarrow A$). Of these, reflexivity is obviously false under the deontic interpretation. Replacing it by the weaker formula $\square A \rightarrow \Diamond A$ (what is obligatory is permitted), yields what is sometimes called the standard system of deontic logic. The system T is known to be characterized by an interpretation according to which $\square A$ is true at a world *w* exactly when *A* is true at all worlds that are *possible* relative to *w*, i.e. at all worlds at which all the necessary truths of *w* are true. It follows that the standard system of deontic logic is characterized by an interpretation according to which $\square A$ is true at w exactly when A is true in all worlds 'deontically accessible' from w, i.e. all worlds in which all the obligations of w are fulfilled.

Much of the contemporary work in deontic logic has been inspired by the deontic paradoxes, a collection of puzzle cases that have seemed to highlight deficiencies in the standard system. For example, according to a version of Chisholm's paradox, the following clauses should be mutually independent and jointly consistent: Dr Jones ought to administer anaesthesia if she operates; she ought not to if she doesn't; she has an obligation to operate, which she fails to meet. But attempts to represent these sentences within the standard system yield inconsistencies or redundancies. According to a version of the good Samaritan paradox, Smith's repenting of a murder logically implies his committing the murder, but his obligation to repent does not imply his obligation to have committed it. Yet in the standard system, the provability of $A \rightarrow B$ implies the provability of $\square A \rightarrow \square B$. One reaction to examples like these has been to take sentences like 'Jones should administer anaesthesia if she operates' as exemplifying an irreducibly dyadic relation of conditional obligation. 'A is obligatory given B' has been interpreted, for example, as saying that B is true in the 'best' of the worlds in which A is. Another reaction has been to eschew the operator 'It is obligatory that . . . ' which attaches to sentences in favour of a predicate of obligation which attaches only to names of actions. This approach eliminates altogether awkward formulae like $\square A \rightarrow \square\square A$, though it also risks eliminating formulae like $\square (\square A \rightarrow A)$ which have been thought to express important truths. It raises interesting questions about the nature of combined actions like 'a or b' and about the relations between general deontic statements ('Smoking is prohibited') and their instances ('Smith's smoking here now is prohibited'). In recent years, there has been considerable discussion about the plausibility of the schema $\neg(\square A \wedge \square\neg A)$, which is provable in the standard system. The issue is whether there is a phenomenon of moral experience, ruled out by the schema, in which an agent is faced with irresolvable and tragic moral 'dilemma' or 'conflict'. It has also been suggested that some of the shortcomings of the standard system can be remedied by a closer attention to the ways in which obligation and permission depend on time, and that there might be fruitful connections among deontic logic, formal epistemology and logics for the verification of computer *programs.   s.t.k.

L. Åqvist, 'Deontic Logic', in D. Gabbay and F. Guenthner (eds.), *Handbook of Philosophical Logic*, ii (Dordrecht, 1984).

C. Gowans (ed.), *Moral Dilemmas* (Oxford, 1987).

R. Hilpinen (ed.), *Deontic Logic: Introductory and Systematic Readings* (Dordrecht, 1971).

——(ed.), *New Studies in Deontic Logic: Norms, Actions and the Foundations of Ethics* (Dordrecht, 1981).

deontological ethics. Moral theories according to which certain acts must or must not be done, regardless to some

extent of the consequences of their performance or nonperformance (the Greek *dei* = one must). According to teleology or *consequentialism, as commonly understood, the rightness or wrongness of any act depends entirely upon its consequences. Deontology is seen in opposition to consequentialism in various ways.

1. According to deontology, certain acts are right or wrong *in themselves*. Deontologists tend to concentrate on those acts which are wrong. So, according to deontologists such as Kant or Ross, promise-breaking is wrong independently of its consequences. Its wrongness does not depend solely on any bad effects promise-breaking may have. A consequentialist—in particular an act-consequentialist—will tend to claim that one should act in whatever way will bring about the best state of affairs. Ross would suggest that it is counter-intuitive to argue that one ought to break a promise for a very small gain in overall good. Note that deontology is not the same as absolutism, according to which certain acts are wrong *whatever the consequences*. Ross could allow that in exceptional circumstances it is not wrong to break a promise.

Two immediate problems for deontology as so described are, first, the difficulty of describing how we know which acts are wrong, and, second, the difficulty of drawing a sharp distinction between acts and omissions.

2. Deontologists such as Nozick argue that there are deontological constraints on our actions. We may have a reason to maximize the overall good, but in certain cases this reason disappears or its force is overridden. I should not, for example, kill an innocent person to save two others from death, since this would be to violate that innocent person's *rights. Indeed I should not kill the person even to prevent the killing of the two others by someone else. Deontology tells *me* not to kill, and is in this sense *agent-relative*. The main difficulty here is to explain this agent-relativity. If killing is bad, why should I not act so as to minimize the number of killings, even if that involves my killing?

3. Rawls's distinction between deontological and teleological or consequentialist theories has become influential in recent years. It concerns the relation between the *right* and the *good*. A teleological theory defines the good independently from the right, and the right is then defined as that which maximizes the good. Deontological theories either do not specify the good independently from the right or do not interpret the right as maximizing the good.

All of the above attempts to distinguish deontology from consequentialism face the difficulty that a theory such as *utilitarianism, which is usually taken to be the paradigm consequentialist theory, can be expressed as deontological. (1) The act of maximizing utility can be said to be right in itself, and that of failing to maximize utility as wrong, independently of consequences. (2) It can be said to be a constraint on our acting in any way that we must maximize the good. (3) An ideal utilitarian such as Rashdall may argue that the good is partly constituted by the right and so cannot be defined independently of it. Of course, straightforward utilitarianism does not deny that the right consists in maximizing the good. But it *can* suggest that the right is indeed prior to the good, in the sense that utilitarians can state that it is right to maximize the good, whatever the good turns out to be. Finally, the agent-relative–agent-neutral distinction which is now commonly used in attempts to distinguish deontology and consequentialism cuts across any deontology–consequentialism distinction, since there can be agent-relative forms of consequentialism. Philosophical effort would be better spent on working out exactly what various moral theories actually say rather than in attempts to clarify what appears likely to be a dubious distinction.   R.CRI.

*absolutism, moral.

John Broome, *Weighing Goods* (Oxford, 1991), ch. 1.
Samuel Scheffler, Introduction, in *Consequentialism and its Critics* (Oxford, 1988).

departments of philosophy: *see* philosophy, history of centres and departments of.

de re **and** *de dicto.* The distinction between *de re* and *de dicto* necessity (necessity of *things* versus necessity of *words*) seems to have first surfaced explicitly in Abelard, though there are hints of it in Aristotle. By the time of Aquinas it is being treated as a handy but familiar conceptual tool, occurring in two main forms: picking out the difference between a sentential operator and a predicate operator, between '*necessarily (Fa)*' and '*a is (necessarily-F)*' on the one hand, and on the other as a way of highlighting the scope fallacy involved in treating *necessarily* (if *p* then *q*) as if it were (if *p* then *necessarily-q*). Similarly we have *de re* or *de dicto* beliefs. Believing, *of God*, that he is benevolent is different from believing that God is benevolent.   J.J.M.

*necessity, logical.

W. V. Quine, 'Quantifiers and Propositional Attitudes', in L. Linsky (ed.), *Reference and Modality* (Oxford, 1971).

Derrida, Jacques (1930–2004). French philosopher who came to prominence in the late 1960s. Derrida's influence within philosophy has been largely confined to the continental tradition, while in the English-speaking world his impact has been mainly in the area of literary criticism.

Born and raised in a Jewish family in Algeria, Derrida went to Paris to complete his secondary education before studying philosophy at the École Normale Supérieure. The philosophy of Husserl, the founder of *phenomenology, was an important element in Derrida's training, and exercised a strong influence on his early writings. Other acknowledged influences are Nietzsche, Heidegger, Freud, and Levinas. Derrida's early research attempted to formulate a phenomenological theory of literature. His first major publication (1962) was a French translation, accompanied by a long introductory essay, of Husserl's *The Origin of Geometry*. Between 1967 and 1972 Derrida published his most influential works, an extensive series of

commentaries on texts by key thinkers in the Western tradition, in which he developed the approach to texts which became known as *deconstruction. A particular concern of Derrida's is with the relationship between philosophy and language. Many of his essays examine philosophical theories of language, demonstrating, by close attention to the letter of the text, the ways in which language outwits philosophers. To this end Derrida emphasizes aspects of language that philosophy has often neglected, such as ambiguity, indeterminacy, pun, and metaphor. Later works by Derrida are increasingly 'playful' in their own right, importing a performative dimension to his meditations on language: *Glas* (1974) and *The Post Card* (1980), for example, exhibit a fragmentation and reliance on graphic effect that generate a style quite unlike classic philosophy. From the mid-1980s Derrida's work addressed ethical and political questions, in particular the implications, for concepts like responsibility and rights, of his challenge to humanism.

Assessment of Derrida's contribution to philosophy remains controversial: an impassioned dispute in Cambridge University preceded the award of an honorary doctorate in 1992. *Analytical philosophy continues on the whole to ignore Derrida, despite undeniable parallels between his thought and that of Davidson, Quine, and Wittgenstein.   S.D.R.

Christopher Norris, *Derrida* (London, 1987).

Descartes, René (1596–1650). Beyond question, Descartes was the chief architect of the seventeenth-century intellectual revolution which destabilized the traditional doctrines of medieval and Renaissance *scholasticism, and laid down the philosophical foundations for what we think of as the 'modern' scientific age. As a small boy Descartes was sent to the newly founded college of La Flèche in Anjou, where he received from the Jesuits a firm grounding in the very scholastic philosophy he was subsequently to challenge. 'I observed with regard to philosophy', he later wrote, 'that despite being cultivated for many centuries by the best minds, it contained no point which was not disputed and hence doubtful' (*Discourse on the Method*, pt. I). In his early adulthood Descartes came to see in the methods and reasoning of mathematics the kind of precision and certainty which traditional philosophy lacked: 'those long chains, composed of very simple and easy reasonings, which geometers customarily use to arrive at their most difficult demonstrations, gave me occasion to suppose that all the things which fall within the scope of human knowledge are interconnected in the same way' (*Discourse*, pt. II).

Much of Descartes's early work as a 'philosopher' was what we should now call scientific. His *Le Monde* (The World, or The Universe), composed in the early 1630s, was a treatise on physics and cosmology, which resolutely avoided the old scholastic apparatus of 'substantial forms' and 'real qualities', and instead offered a comprehensive explanatory schema invoking only simple mechanical principles. A cornerstone of Descartes's approach was that the matter throughout the universe was of essentially the same type; hence there was no difference in principle between 'terrestrial' and 'celestial' phenomena, and the earth was merely one part of a homogeneous universe obeying uniform physical laws. In the climate of the mid-seventeenth century such views could still be dangerous, and Descartes cautiously withdrew his *World* from publication in 1633 on hearing of the condemnation of Galileo by the Roman Inquisition for advocating the heliocentric hypothesis (which Descartes too supported). But in 1637 he ventured to release to the public (anonymously) a sample of his work, the *Geometry*, *Optics*, and *Meteorology*. Prefaced to these three 'specimen essays', was what was to become an acknowledged philosophical classic—the *Discourse on the Method of Rightly Conducting Reason and Reaching the Truth in the Sciences*. The *Discourse* is part intellectual biography, part summary of the author's scientific views (including a presentation of some central themes from the earlier suppressed treatise *Le Monde*). But the book's fame rests on the short central section where Descartes discusses the foundations of knowledge, the existence of God, and the distinction between mind and body. The metaphysical arguments contained here, and greatly expanded in Descartes's philosophical masterpiece, the *Meditations on First Philosophy* constitute the philosophical core of the Cartesian system. The *Meditations* were published in Latin in 1641, along with a six sets of detailed Objections by various well-known philosophers, plus Descartes's Replies (a seventh set of Objections with the author's Replies was added in the second edition of 1642).

It is often said that Descartes inaugurated modern philosophy by making questions about the validation of knowledge the first questions to be dealt with in the subject. But while he certainly aimed in the *Discourse* and the *Meditations* to establish epistemically reliable foundations for his new system, it is a distortion to see his interests as primarily epistemological in the modern academic sense. The Descartes who is often presented in today's textbooks is a philosopher obsessively preoccupied with questions like 'How do I know I am really awake?', or 'Could the whole of reality be a dream?' But although the sixteenth-century revival of interest in classical problems about scepticism certainly influenced the framework within which Descartes chose to present his arguments, he was not chiefly interested in contributing to these debates. 'The purpose of my arguments', he wrote in the Synopsis to the *Meditations*, 'is not that they prove what they establish—that there really is a world and that human beings have bodies and so on—since no one has ever seriously doubted these things.' Descartes's main aim was to show how the world of physics, the mathematically describable world, could be reliably mapped out independently of the often vague and misleading deliverances of our sensory organs.

Descartes begins his project of 'leading the mind away from the senses' by observing that 'the senses deceive from time to time, and it is prudent never to trust wholly those who have deceived us even once' (First Meditation). No examples are given of such 'deception', but Descartes later cited standard cases like that of the straight stick which looks bent in water: visual appearances may be misleading. But in some situations, Descartes goes on to concede, such doubts would be absurd: no amount of evidence on the supposed unreliability of my sense-organs could lead me to doubt that I am now sitting by the fire holding a piece of paper in my hands. At this stage, Descartes introduces his famous 'dreaming argument': 'there are no certain marks to distinguish being awake from being asleep', and hence my belief that I am sitting by the fire could turn out to be false (I might be asleep in bed). As first presented, the dreaming argument impugns only particular judgements I may make about what I am doing, or what I think is in front of me; but Descartes goes on to raise more radical doubts about the existence of whole classes of external objects. In their most exaggerated or 'hyperbolical' form (to use Descartes's own epithet), these doubts are expressed in the deliberately conjured up supposition of a 'malicious demon of the utmost power and cunning' bent on deceiving me in every possible way. Perhaps 'the sky, the earth, colours, shapes, sounds and all external things' are merely 'the delusions of dreams which he has devised to ensnare my judgement' (end of First Meditation).

The first truth to emerge unscathed from this barrage of doubt is the meditator's certainty of his own existence. 'Let the demon deceive me as much as he may . . . *I am, I exist* is certain, so long as it is put forward by me or conceived in my mind' (Second Meditation). This is often known as the Cogito argument, from the Latin phrase *Cogito ergo sum* ('I am thinking, therefore I exist'). The certainty of the Cogito is, for Descartes, a curiously temporary affair: I can be sure of my existence only for as long as I am thinking. But from this fleeting and flickering insight, Descartes attempts to reconstruct a whole system of reliable knowledge. The route outwards from subjective certainty to objective science depends on the meditator's being able to prove the existence of a perfect God who is the source of all truth. In a much criticized causal argument, Descartes reasons that the representative content of the idea of infinite perfection which he finds within himself is so great that he could not have constructed it from the resources of his own mind; the cause of an idea containing so much perfection must itself be perfect, and hence the idea must have been placed in his mind ('like the mark of the craftsman stamped on his work') by an actually existing perfect being—God (Third Meditation). Later Descartes supplements this proof by a version of what has come to be known as the 'ontological argument': since God is, by definition, the sum of all perfections, and since existence is itself a perfection, it follows that 'existence can no more be separated from the essence of God than the fact that its angles equal two right angles can be separated from the essence of a triangle' (Fifth Meditation).

The central importance of *God in Descartes's system lies in the deity's role as guarantor of the reliability of human cognition. Humans often go astray in their think-ing, but this is because they rashly jump in and give their assent to propositions whose truth is not clear. But pro-vided they use their God-given power of reason correctly, assenting only to what they clearly and distinctly perceive, they can be sure of avoiding error (Fourth Meditation). One problem with this argument was seized on by one of Descartes's contemporary critics, *Antoine Arnauld: if we need to prove God's existence in order to underwrite the reliability of the human mind, how can we be sure of the reliability of the reasoning needed to establish his exist-ence in the first place?

Descartes's attempts to extricate himself from this 'Cartesian circle' have been the subject of endless discus-sion; roughly, his starting position seems to be that there are certain basic truths whose content is so simple and self-evident that we can be sure of them even prior to proving God's existence, and hence the circle can be broken. Truths such as the Cogito—that I must exist so long as I am thinking—are of this kind. The idea of self-standing truths guaranteed merely by their extreme simplicity of content has a certain attraction. But the problem remains—raised indeed by Descartes himself—that it seems possible to imagine that our grasp of such truths could be systematically distorted. The First Meditation had raised the nightmarish doubt that an omnipotent creator might make me able to go wrong 'every time I add two and three or count the sides of a square, or in some even simpler matter if that is imaginable'. If the most funda-mental intuitions of the intellect are called into question, then the circle seems to remain as an insoluble puzzle: the intellect cannot without circularity be used to validate its own intuitions. In so far as Descartes got to grips with this problem, he apparently maintained that the irresistible psychological certainty of such elementary truths dispels any reasonable doubt that could be raised: 'If a conviction is so firm that it is impossible for us ever to have any rea-son for doubting what we are convinced of, then there are no further questions for us to ask; we have everything we could reasonably want' (Second Set of Replies to Objections to the *Meditations*). On one possible interpret-ation of this much discussed passage, Descartes is in effect retreating from the claim to provide guaranteed and unshakeably validated foundations for knowledge, and moving towards a position which in some respects anticipates that of *David Hume a century later: human beings have to rest content with what their nature irre-sistibly inclines them to believe; there are no 'absolute' guarantees.

Whatever the solution to the vexed problem of the foundations of Descartes's system, and their epistemic sta-tus, Descartes himself clearly believed that if he could get as far as establishing the existence of God, 'in whom all the wisdom of the sciences lies hid' (Fourth Meditation, para-phrasing Colossians 2: 3), he could proceed to establish a systematic physical science, covering 'the whole of that corporeal nature which is the subject matter of pure math-ematics' (Fifth Meditation). The resulting system of 'mathematicized' science was developed most fully by Descartes in his mammoth *Principles of Philosophy* (pub-lished in Latin in 1644). Matter is defined as that which has extension (length, breadth, and height), and all observed phenomena explained simply in terms of the various modi-fications (or 'modes') of this extended stuff—namely the size and shape of the various particles into which it is divided (cf. *Principles of Philosophy*, pt. II. art. 64). While this quantitative approach to physics clearly constituted an extremely fruitful advance (it remains the basis of our modern scientific outlook), Descartes had problems in accounting for all the properties of the universe as simple modes of extended substance. Even the fact that the mat-ter of the universe is in *motion* seems to take us beyond mere extension in three dimensions (*see* *Cartesianism)— something which leads Descartes to invoke the power of the Deity: 'in the beginning God created matter, along with its motion and rest, and now . . . he conserves the same quantity of motion in the universe as he put there in the beginning'. From the uniformity and constancy of God, Descartes proceeds to deduce important general principles such as the law of the conservation of rectilinear motion; he also arrives at seven mathematical rules for calculating the results of impacts between bodies, all of which presuppose that the quantity of motion (measured as size times speed) is conserved. Although Descartes is often described as an apriorist in science, and although the main structural principles of his physics are arrived at independently of experience, Descartes nevertheless insists that at a lower level reason alone cannot determine which of the various hypotheses consistent with these general principles is in fact correct: 'here I know of no other way than to seek various observations whose out-comes vary according to which is the correct explanation' (*Discourse*, pt. VI).

Descartes's general ambitions in philosophy / science were unificatory: the whole of philosophy, he observed, is like a tree of which the roots are metaphysics, the trunk physics, and the branches the specific sciences, reducible to three principal subjects—medicine, mechanics, and morals. Descartes had originally planned to extend the *Principles of Philosophy* to include a complete account of plant and animal physiology, all based on purely mechan-ical principles; and he later wrote a *Description of the Human Body* (1647) which argued that complex biological functions such as nutrition, digestion, and growth, as well as reflexes and non-voluntary movements, can all be explained mechanically, without the need to introduce any such notions as the 'nutritive' or 'locomotive' soul of traditional Aristotelian biology: 'we have no more reason to suppose that a soul produces such movements than we have reason to believe that there is a soul in a clock which makes it tell the time.'

But the Cartesian vision of a comprehensive and uni-fied system of knowledge abruptly disintegrates when it comes to the phenomenon of thought. For a variety of reasons—theological, metaphysical, and scientific— Descartes believed that mind, or 'thinking substance' (*res cogitans), was wholly distinct from the world of matter. Matter was extended, divisible, spatial; mind unextended, indivisible, and non-spatial. The result is the theory known as Cartesian dualism—the view that the mind or soul (Descartes makes no distinction between these two terms) is 'entirely distinct from the body, and would not fail to be what it is even if the body did not exist' (*Discourse*, pt. IV). Some of Descartes's arguments for the incorporeality of the mind are decidedly weak: in the *Discourse* he baldly concludes, from his (alleged) ability to think of himself existing without a body, that the body is not necessary to his essence as a thinking thing. Other arguments are more interesting: in part v of the *Discourse* he notes that the ability to reason, and to use language, involves the capacity to respond in indefinitely complex ways to 'all the contingencies of life', and that this power goes beyond anything that could be generated by a mere stimulus–response device. The utterances of animals are not genuine language, but simply automatic responses to external and internal stimuli.

In describing animals as 'automata' (self-moving devices), Descartes aimed to show how all their functions could be accounted for in mechanistic terms; but although Descartes is often accused of reducing higher animals to the status of 'mere machines', it is not entirely clear whether he aimed to explain away, as opposed to merely explain, their complex cognitive and affective responses. The case of animal sensation is particularly sensitive, since critics of Descartes's approach have frequently castigated him for implying that animals cannot feel genuine pain.

The nature of sensation turns out to be something of a problem for Descartes, even in the case of human beings. If the essential self is a pure incorporeal mind, wholly distinct from the body, then it is hard to account for the character of our ordinary feelings and sensations, which seem intimately bound up with our bodily nature as creatures of flesh and blood. A pure spirit, like an angel, could hardly have a tummy-ache—indeed, Descartes himself remarks that such an incorporeal soul would not have sensations like us, 'and so would be different from a genuine human being' (letter to Regius of January 1642). Descartes observes in the Sixth Meditation that 'nature teaches me by these sensations of hunger, thirst, pleasure and pain that I am not merely present in the body like a sailor in a ship, but that I am very closely conjoined and intermingled with it so that I and the body form a unit'. But the difficulty is to see how two utterly alien and incompatible substances, mind and body, can be united in this way. Descartes wrote in correspondence with Princess Elizabeth of Bohemia that whereas the distinction between mind and body could be grasped by our reason, the 'substantial union' between them just had to be experienced. Yet this seems tantamount to admitting that what we experience undermines the distinction which reason (allegedly) perceives.

The relation between mind and body is sometimes explained by Descartes in a way which suggests a causal flow between the two (and Descartes even specified a place where the mind receives and transmits data to the body, namely the *conarion* or *pineal gland in the brain (*Passions of the Soul*, art. 31)). This has given rise to what is sometimes called the problem of 'Cartesian interactionism': how can mind and body, being two utterly distinct substances, one material and one immaterial, causally interact in such a way? Descartes himself, however, declared that this objection was based on a supposition— that heterogeneous substances cannot interact—which he saw no reason to accept (letter to Clerselier of 12 January 1646). But alongside the model of two quite distinct substances interacting, Descartes also continued to insist that mind and body are really and substantially united so as to form a 'genuine human being'. There is thus a divergence between the metaphysical conception of himself as a pure incorporeal substance that Descartes arrives at through his dualistic arguments in the *Discourse* and the *Meditations*—the conception that *Gilbert Ryle was later famously to stigmatize as the 'doctrine of the ghost in the machine'—and the real embodied creature that is the subject of Descartes's ethics and psychology. The sensory and affective part of our nature (including the having of bodily sensations such as pain and emotional states such as fear) is for Descartes irreducibly psycho-physical: such sensations and states always involve both physiological activity and conscious awareness. In explaining how we have sensory and emotional awareness when our bodies and brains are stimulated in certain ways, Descartes sometimes appeals to a 'natural' or divinely instituted predisposition: 'our mind is [innately] capable of representing to itself the idea of pain, colours, sounds and the like on the occasion of certain corporeal motions' (*Comments on a Certain Broadsheet*, 1648). Such passages can be interpreted as containing the germ of the later doctrine known as '*occasionalism', according to which God directly causes certain sensory states in the human mind on the 'occasion' of bodily happenings (see *Malebranche).

The distinction between, on the one hand, the purely mental part of us, comprising understanding and volition, and, on the other hand, the sensory and affective part of us, which is always 'contaminated', as it were, with the happenings in the body, gives rise to some important issues in Descartes's philosophical psychology. The ideal mental state, as presented in the *Meditations*, is one of 'clear and distinct perception': here the mind's contents are, as it were, completely open and transparent to consciousness, so that we have a direct and unproblematic awareness of what we are thinking and willing. In the case of sensations and emotions, however, although there is something that is immediately (and often urgently) present to the mind, Descartes insists that the resulting ideas are necessarily 'obscure and confused', as a result of the body's involvement. This obscurity has important implications for ethics, for the confusions inherent in our affective nature mean that the passions may often mislead us about the importance or value of a particular object of desire or aversion (letter of 1 September 1645).

In his last work, the *Passions of the Soul*, composed shortly before his ill-fated visit to Sweden in the winter of 1649–50 (where he contracted pneumonia and died just short of his fifty-fourth birthday), Descartes examines the physiological basis for our feelings and sensations. Although the mechanisms of the body are no part of our nature as 'thinking beings', Descartes none the less maintains that there is a regular pattern whereby physiological events automatically generate certain psychological responses; learning about these responses, and about the conditioning process which can allow us to modify them in certain cases, is the key to controlling the passions 'so that the evils they cause become bearable and even a source of joy' (*Passions*, art. 212). Descartes thus holds out the hope that a proper understanding of our nature as human beings will yield genuine benefits for the conduct of life—a hope which accords with the early ambition, which he had voiced in the *Discourse*, to replace the 'speculative' philosophy of scholasticism with a practical philosophy that would improve the human lot.

For all his ambitions to ameliorate the human condition, Descartes's account of that condition as depending on a mysterious fusion of incorporeal self and mechanical body remains deeply unsatisfying. But the so-called *mind–body problem which continues to engage the attention of philosophers today bears witness to the compelling nature of the issues with which Descartes wrestled. The relationship between the physical world, as described in the objective language of mathematical physics, and the inner world of the mind, of which each of us has a peculiarly direct and intimate awareness, involves difficulties which even now we seem far from being able to resolve. But the reason why these problems so fascinate us is precisely that they represent the ultimate test case for that all-embracing model of scientific understanding which Descartes himself so spectacularly and so successfully inaugurated.   J.COT.

C. Adam and P. Tannery (eds.), *Œuvres de Descartes*, rev. edn., 12 vols. (Paris, 1964–76).

J. Cottingham, R. Stoothoff, and D. Murdoch (eds.), *The Philosophical Writings of Descartes*, 2 vols. (Cambridge, 1985); vol. iii of the preceding, by the same translators and Anthony Kenny (Cambridge, 1991).

——*Descartes* (Oxford, 1986).

——(ed.), *The Cambridge Companion to Descartes* (Cambridge, 1992).

D. Garber, *Descartes' Metaphysical Physics* (Chicago, 1992).

S. Gaukroger, *Descartes: An Intellectual Biography* (Oxford, 1995).

B. Williams, *Descartes, The Project of Pure Inquiry* (Harmondsworth, 1978).

M. Wilson, *Descartes* (London, 1978).

description, knowledge by: *see* acquaintance and description, knowledge by.

descriptions. According to Russell, a *definite description* is a phrase of the form 'the so-and-so' (e.g. 'the author of *Waverley*'), an *indefinite description* a phrase of the form 'a

so-and-so' (e.g. 'a man'). (Where 'description' is used without qualification, the definite variety is usually intended.) Russell thought that indefinite descriptions should be understood in terms of the existential quantifier ('There is at least one thing which . . . '), definite descriptions in terms of the uniqueness quantifier ('There is exactly one thing which . . . '). In both cases, Russell treated expressions that might be thought to be referring expressions not as having this role, but as quantifier phrases. Thus there is no reference to a man in 'I met a man', for this is equivalent to 'Something human was met by me'. Nor is there any reference to Scott in 'The author of *Waverley* is prolific', for this sentence is really general and quantificational, saying that there is exactly one author of *Waverley*, and whoever wrote *Waverley* is prolific. To see in each case that the proper semantic functioning of these sentences does not require reference (to a man, to Scott), it is helpful to imagine each of these sentences to be false. (Russell thought that one way for the second sentence to be false is for *Waverley* to have been a team production, rather than having had a unique author.)

Russell favoured his account of definite descriptions for the following reasons: (1) It enabled him to account for true negative existential judgements. Thus 'The golden mountain does not exist' does not have to be understood as saying, absurdly, *of* something that *it* does not exist, but can be understood as saying that there is not exactly one golden mountain. (2) It enabled him to see a sentence like 'Scott is the author of *Waverley*' as something other than an identity sentence (since it does not consist in two referring expressions separated by the 'is' of identity), which enabled him to explain how 'George IV wanted to know whether Scott was the author of *Waverley*' could be true yet 'George IV wanted to know whether Scott was Scott' false. (3) It enabled him to allow that either a sentence or its negation must be true. One might think this fails, for it might seem that neither (*a*) 'The present King of France is bald' nor (*b*) 'The present King of France is not bald' is true. Russell argued that (*b*) is ambiguous between being the negation of (*a*), and thus entailing truly that there is not exactly one present King of France, and being, not the negation of (*a*), but rather equivalent to 'There is exactly one present King of France and whoever is the King of France is not bald', which, like (*a*) is false. (4) He thought that the only difference between indefinite and definite descriptions was that the latter entail uniqueness.

Russell held that his view about definite descriptions had important consequences, both for theory of knowledge (explaining how one could know things with which one had no *acquaintance) and for logic (paving the way, supposedly, for the dissolution of *Russell's paradox). In addition to its intrinsic importance, it has been held up as a model of 'philosophical analysis' or of 'philosophical logic' (a term invented by Russell to describe his project of formalizing English sentences).

New work on definite descriptions takes Russell as a starting-point, and the question, famously raised by Strawson, is whether descriptions at least sometimes function as *referring expressions. Thus an utterance in the terraces of 'The man with the ball knows how to play' seems equivalent to 'That man with the ball knows how to play'; and many would unhesitatingly classify the latter as involving reference to *that man*.   R.M.S.

S. Neale, *Descriptions* (Oxford, 1992).

M. Reimer and A. Bezuidenhout (eds.), *Descriptions and Beyond* (Oxford, 2004).

B. Russell, *Introduction to Mathematical Philosophy* (London, 1918), ch. 16.

——'On Denoting', *Mind* (1905); repr. in R. C. Marsh (ed.), *Bertrand Russell: Logic and Knowledge. Essays 1901–1950* (London, 1965).

P. F. Strawson, 'On Referring', *Mind* (1950).

descriptive meaning: *see* emotive meaning and descriptive meaning.

descriptive metaphysics, by contrast with *revisionary metaphysics, describes, according to P. F. Strawson, 'the actual structure of our thought about the world' rather than projecting an alternative preferred version of the world itself. A variety of conceptual analysis, it does not address itself merely to the uses of terms and the entailments of propositions, but to our cognitive apparatus. Thus Kant found that a certain minimal spatio-temporal and causal structure in our representations of external objects was a necessary condition of ordinary experience and scientific theorizing. Strawson finds that 'bodies' and 'persons' are the fundamental terms of our ontology, and proposes conditions governing their identification and re-identification and the possibility of framing meaningful subject–predicate propositions about them.

The possibility of a descriptive *metaphysics is threatened first by the claims of a cognitive science free of the a priori, second, by the suspicion that all a priori investigation harbours revisionary content.   CATH.W.

S. Haack, 'Descriptive and Revisionary Metaphysics', *Philosophical Studies* (1979).

P. F. Strawson, *Individuals: An Essay in Descriptive Metaphysics* (London, 1959).

descriptivism is a term sometimes used to characterize theories which hold that judgements made in a particular area are descriptive; that is, that they refer to and are true of something. Distinguishing theories in this way only has point as a way of contrasting them with rival theories which hold that the judgements being considered are not descriptive. For example, some theories about evaluative judgements claim that they do not describe independent facts, but are merely expressions of attitude or emotion. A theory which denies this can be called descriptivist.   R.H.

*emotivism; prescriptivism; moral realism.

R. M. Hare, *Moral Thinking* (Oxford, 1981), ch. 4.

desert. It is a belief fundamental to morality that people ought to get what they deserve. What they deserve are benefits and harms made appropriate by some past fact about the recipients. The benefits are reward for achievement or compensation for injury, while the harms are *punishment for wrongdoing or deprivation stemming from culpable deficiency. Deserved benefits and harms may be understood in terms of the presence or absence of tangible goods, like money, or intangible goods, such as opportunities, status, appreciation, or advancement. Benefits and harms are deserved depending on some action, characteristic, state, or relationship that is correctly ascribed to individuals. The claim that something is deserved is, therefore, partly backward- and partly forward-looking because the morally significant fact in an individual's past dictates that the individual ought or ought not to receive some benefit or harm in the future.

Underlying the *ought* involved in desert is the notion of a moral equilibrium: the state in which the benefits and harms an individual receives are proportional to what is warranted by the significant fact in the individual's past. One central aim of morality is to maintain this equilibrium by distributing benefits and harms according to desert and by correcting the disequilibrium that occurs when benefits and harms are received undeservedly.

Legitimate claims of desert may or may not create an institutional or personal obligation to honour them. There is undeserved good and bad fortune, benefiting or harming people, whose occurrence is not attributable to human agency. The contingency of life and the scarcity of resources may upset the moral equilibrium just as much as immorality does, but there may be nothing anyone can do to correct the former. Legitimate claims of desert create obligations, therefore, only if institutional or personal culpability can be reasonably assigned for causing the disequilibrium. Perhaps there are good reasons to intervene and reverse instances of naturally occurring undeserved fortune or misfortune, but whatever these reasons may be, they cannot be based on some wrong that a person or an institution has done.

What actually it is that people deserve and what the significant facts are that create legitimate claims of desert are controversial questions at the centre of current moral and political debates. The most often favoured candidates as appropriate bases of desert are universal human *needs or wants, human or contractual *rights, genuine interests, and moral merits. What one bases desert on, how one proposes to distribute benefits and harms, and how one aims to correct past distribution will strongly influence one's view of justice, and that, in turn, will influence what position one occupies on the political continuum extending between *Left and *Right.

How basic desert is supposed to be in morality will also influence the kind of moral theory that is found acceptable. The more basic desert is supposed to be, the less egalitarian the resulting moral theory will be, since the greater moral importance is attributed to desert, the more the distribution of benefits and harms will have to be made proportional to the differing moral merits of their recipients. Similarly, the more egalitarian moral theories are, the less importance they will attribute to desert. It is a sign of the prevalence of egalitarianism in our times that little attention is paid to desert by most contemporary moral theories. Regardless of whether the tendency to ignore moral merit in the distribution of benefits and harms is an achievement or a failure, it is a characteristic of the moral and political sensibility that prevails at least in the Western world.   J.KEK.

M. Henberg, *Retribution* (Philadelphia, 1990).

T. Honderich, *Punishment: The Supposed Justifications* (Harmondsworth, 1984).

J. Kekes, *Facing Evil* (Princeton, NJ, 1990).

S. Olsaretti (ed.), *Desert and Justice* (Oxford, 2003).

G. Sher, *Desert* (Princeton, NJ, 1987).

design, argument from, for the existence of God: *see* God, arguments for; teleological argument for the existence of God.

desire. That mental state motivating voluntary behaviour and opening its bearer to feelings of both pleasure and displeasure. Desires, like *beliefs, take a proposition as their content: what is desired (the content of the desire) is always that some state of affairs obtain.

Philosophers generally think of the term 'desire' as covering two distinct things. In the broader use of the term, a desire is any mental state capable of being fulfilled, carried out, or acted upon, or for which such notions are appropriate. (The term 'pro attitude' is also used to denote these mental states.) In this broad use, one's will counts as a desire, as do one's intentions, plans, goals, preferences, wishes, whims, decisions, and (perhaps) beliefs about what is reasonable or good. In the narrower use, desires are a more restricted set of mental states: they are those mental states to which we normally attach the terms 'desire' (the desire that you and I have a sexual affair, say) and 'want' (wanting that there be peace on earth, that the movers not damage the piano, and so on). Many philosophers hold that desires, in the narrower sense, are the basic mental states in terms of which all desires, in the broader sense, are to be explained: that willing is simply being moved by one's strongest current (narrow) desire, that intending is simply (narrowly) desiring to do something and believing one will do it, and so on.

There is an important distinction to make between desires for things wanted merely as means to some further end (instrumental desires) and desires for things wanted for their own sakes (intrinsic desires). A person who wants to own yellow paint, for example, typically desires the paint only as a means to some other goal, such as having a cheerfully coloured kitchen, and in this case the desire is clearly instrumental. Intrinsic desires are a more controversial matter. According to psychological hedonists, only pleasure (or the absence of displeasure) is desired for its own sake. Others take the view that many things are intrinsically desired: that the home team win, that my father enjoy a happy retirement, and so on.

A desire is said to be conscious when one is vividly aware that one has the desire; hunger and thirst are paradigmatic examples, but one can also be vividly aware of one's desire to strangle the boss or to help an injured bird. Desires can also influence consciousness without being conscious desires. For instance, a woman might be completely unaware that she desires acceptance by her professional subordinates, and yet, upon finding she has their acceptance, she might be very pleased—precisely as a consequence of her desire.

There are two principal, long-standing theories of the nature of desire. According to the more widely held motivational theory of desire, to desire some end is simply to tend to be motivated to bring it about. (A variant of the theory holds that it is to contain an inner representation of that end, which tends to make one motivated to produce the end.) According to the less widely held hedonic theory of desire, to desire some end is to tend toward feeling pleasure if one comes to believe that one's end is achieved, and/or to tend toward feeling displeasure if one comes to believe that it is not. Of course, desires are held by almost everyone to have both motivational and emotional features as a general rule: the question is which feature, if either, is the sole essential feature of desire.

An important controversy surrounding desire is the relation between desiring some end and having a reason to pursue that end. Humeans (*see* *David Hume) generally hold that desiring an end is necessary and sufficient for having at least some reason to pursue it; others deny either the necessity of desiring, the sufficiency, or both. The importance of the controversy is highlighted by moral considerations: does one have a reason to do what is moral even if one does not desire to act morally? In addition, there are ongoing discussions about the relation of one's desires to the praise- or blameworthiness of one's actions, the virtuousness of one's character, and one's status as an agent with *free will.   T.S.

*belief and desire; mental states; propositional attitude; reason; action; sex, philosophy of.

J. Marks (ed.), *Ways of Desire* (Chicago, 1986).

G. F. Schueler, *Desire* (Cambridge, Mass., 1994).

despair. A term in Kierkegaard's moral psychology to characterize life-styles rather than singular biographical events. In *The Sickness unto Death* to despair is to shun a goal of spiritual satisfaction, either by preventing that goal from coming to consciousness or, failing that, by trying to replace or remove the self that can neither ignore nor face up to it. The latter two expedients are vain projects because any attempt to gainsay the goal presupposes it. Suicide would fail because death encompasses only the finite and the self already grasps itself as more. The most basic form of despair is open defiance of the self's essential relationship to God. As in German, the root of the Danish *Fortvivlelse* is 'doubt' (*Tvivl*). For Kierkegaard despair is sin and its opposite is faith. The earlier *Either/Or* had advocated despair as freeing one from the superficialities of the aesthetic way of life and thus opening the way to acceptance of the self.   A.H.

*abandonment; existentialism; *Angst*.

S. Kierkegaard, *The Sickness unto Death* (Harmondsworth, 1989).

destiny. Fixed and inevitable future. Etymologically, that which is ordained or appointed. Whether identified with the *Moira* or Fate of the Greeks, the divinely pre-ordained salvation or damnation of Luther and Calvin, or what is to come according to the clocklike causal regularity of Newton's universe, one's destiny is inescapable. *Fatalism claims that no action can affect this future for good or ill. *Determinism also says the future is fixed, but that our present actions (themselves determined by the past) will affect or bring about what it turns out to be. *Libertarianism denies that we have destinies. Our futures, because of our intrinsic freedom, are not settled.   R.C.W.

A. W. H. Adkins, *Merit and Responsibility* (Oxford, 1960).

detachment. In various writings in *Indian philosophy and religions, detachment is the attitude to one's actions towards which one should aim, sometimes described as impartiality to success and failure. In action this is manifest when one does something purely as a matter of sacred duty, as ritual, or for a deity, not aiming to satisfy an independent desire, such as for sensory pleasure or social rewards. It has its source in understanding that there is something illusory about the belief that an individual person is an agent. Someone in the grip of such an illusion fails to see that everything that happens is determined by nature. Freed from this illusion, people accept their own success or failure in an attitude of equanimity. This has some affinity with Spinoza's account of the emotional effects of grasping the necessity of the divine nature.

                                                            N.L.

*Indian philosophy.

Bhagavadgītā, esp. chs. 2 and 3.

determinables and determinates. The terms were employed by W. E. Johnson to indicate a relation between the more general and the more particular which is different from that between genus and species. Thus colour and shape are determinables in relation to such terms as red and circular. Determinates ('red', 'blue', etc.) under the same determinables ('colour') exclude each other, but are not co-ordinate in such a way that they can be distinguished from each other by a single differentia. Some may be determinables in relation to shades of red: 'scarlet', 'vermilion', etc.   S.W.

W. E. Johnson, *Logic*, i (Cambridge, 1921).

determinism. It is often taken as the very general thesis about the world that all events without exception are effects—events necessitated by earlier events. Hence any event of any kind is an effect of a prior series of effects, a causal chain with every link solid. The thesis is fundamentally simple. The ideas which it contains, notably those of events and causal connection, are certainly open to

definition. If the thesis cannot be expressed in terms of some part of science or theory in it, some determinists say, the shortcoming is not in the thesis.

If the thesis is true, future events are as fixed and unalterable as the past is fixed and unalterable. One graphic expression of determinism is in terms of what William James called 'the iron block universe': 'those parts of the universe already laid down,' he wrote, 'appoint and decree what other parts shall be. The future has no ambiguous possibilities hidden in its womb: the part we call the present is compatible with only one totality. Any other future complement than the one fixed from eternity is impossible. The whole is in each and every part, and welds it with the rest into an absolute unity, an iron block, in which there can be no equivocation or shadow of turning.' If this is the way the world is, then only what actually happens in it could possibly have happened. There are no genuine alternatives to be realized.

Philosophers and scientists have been concerned with the question of whether determinism conceived in this general and all-inclusive way is true. The problem is ancient in its origins. The Homeric Fates were enigmatically described as having power over the future. Early forms of atomism were more clearly deterministic, so disturbingly so that Epicurus found it necessary to hypothesize an uncaused 'swerve' of the atoms as they fell through the void. Hobbes and Hume, and many great and not so great philosophers after them, have been determinists.

But philosophers have been more concerned with what is to many of us the most compelling part of that general question: whether we ourselves, persons, are subject to the same sort of causal necessity. Philosophers have cared less about whether or not the rest of the universe is determined—what they have cared more about is whether or not our lives are determined. Indeed, determinism has often been taken as the more limited thesis that all our choices, decisions, intentions, other mental events, and our actions are no more than effects of other equally necessitated events. The problem of determinism in this second sense is pretty well identical with the problem of freedom, or the free will problem.

When philosophers have worried about this limited thesis in the past, they have typically focused on what it would mean for our concept of *moral responsibility. But Strawson led us to see that more is at stake than that, including many human attitudes such as resentment and gratitude. Honderich has raised the stakes higher. Determinism puts in doubt all 'life-hopes, personal feelings, knowledge, moral responsibility, the rightness of actions, and the moral standing of persons'. And van Inwagen has suggested that if determinism were known to be true, no one could ever rationally deliberate about any type of action. Deliberation, it is said, makes sense only if genuine alternatives are available to us. If I deliberate about whether or not to raise my arm, my deliberation is rational only if I am able either to raise it or not to raise it. If determinism is true, only one course is genuinely open to me. So, it is alleged, my deliberation is irrational.

But, as remarked, the most important issue historically has been moral responsibility. And what can be said about it applies in a general way to the other implications of determinism. Typically we believe that agents are morally responsible only for those acts that are freely chosen and within the power of the agent to decide. We are guilty only if we could have done otherwise. But if determinism is true, then in some sense we *never* could have done otherwise. Thus many philosophers have concluded that determinism and holding people responsible are incompatible. Others have strongly disagreed. We will not address this issue here—it is developed more fully in the entries on *freedom and determinism and *compatibilism and incompatibilism.

To return to the general thesis of determinism—which of course is not really to leave the limited human thesis—some of its most important forms have been scientific determinisms. After Newton propounded his laws of gravitation and mechanics, Laplace pointed out that if a powerful intellect (usually called Laplace's demon) possessed an understanding of Newton's laws, and had a description of the current position and momentum of each particle in the universe, and the requisite mathematical ability, that powerful intellect could predict and retrodict every event in the history of the universe. This 'clockwork universe' came to dominate the physical theory of the next two centuries, causing great consternation among theologians and most moral philosophers.

Recently, however, *quantum mechanics and relativity theory have generally displaced Newtonian mechanics, and various proofs of them have been claimed. Many scientists and not a few philosophers believe that the dragon of determinism has been slain. Some, as a result, go on to believe that the world has been made safe for the freedom of the will and responsibility.

But, first, as Einstein himself argued, quantum mechanics may be just another way-station on the route to a true, complete, and deterministic physical theory. It is surely arrogance, despite some experimental results, to believe that we possess the final truth about reality. There is reason to say that the only permanent truth with respect to science, or that among the permanent truths, is the truth that science changes.

And, secondly, quantum mechanics may be replaced by something conceptually far better than quantum mechanics as it is interpreted. There has never been agreement about making sense of how the theory, even if it works, actually applies to the world. This is what really matters.

Thirdly, the randomness and uncertainty taken as implied by quantum mechanics operates primarily at the micro-particle level. As more and more particles enter the calculations, a statistical smoothing occurs. Thus, while the theory implies that there is some chance that all the particles in a table will simultaneously and randomly happen to move upwards, so that the table will levitate, the odds against such an occurrence are so astronomical that it is not reasonable to expect an event of this sort even once in the entire history of the universe. In terms of the number of particles involved, the brain, and even an individual neuron, is an enormous object for which no such deviation from 'expected' behaviour is likely to occur. Thus even if quantum mechanics as interpreted is true, the bodies of human beings are so near to deterministic as makes no difference.

Finally, so far as we know, the indeterminism involved in quantum mechanics is pure randomness, real chance. But if my actions are saved from determinism only by becoming random, how does that get back to the moral responsibility sought by libertarians? Which would you rather be, a clock or the ball on a roulette wheel? Or rather, the ball on a roulette wheel so far unconstructed, which does involve real chance and not just practical unpredictability? A pure chance event in you would not be anything that got you moral credit.   R.C.W.

*agent causation; causality; determinism, scientific; Diodorus Cronus; necessity, nomic; Quantum Theory and philosophy.

T. Honderich, *A Theory of Determinism: The Mind, Neuroscience, and Life-Hopes* (Oxford, 1988).

K. R. Popper and J. C. Eccles, *The Mind and its Brain* (Berlin, 1977).

P. F. Strawson, 'Freedom and Resentment', in *Studies in the Philosophy of Thought and Action* (Oxford, 1968).

P. van Inwagen, *An Essay on Free Will* (Oxford, 1983).

R. Weatherford, *The Implications of Determinism* (London, 1991).

determinism, economic: *see* base and superstructure.

determinism, historical. A conception of human affairs according to which the historical process conforms to developmental patterns or laws that render its constitutive events necessary or inevitable. Doctrines affirming such a position exhibit wide variations. While those of an earlier vintage frequently involved providential or *teleological assumptions, ones of later date have tended instead to presuppose the causal principle that whatever occurs in history is explicable as a law-governed consequence of empirically specifiable antecedent conditions. Views of the latter kind are sometimes endorsed on the grounds that they reflect a presumption fundamental to history conceived as an essentially explanatory form of inquiry. Against this, however, it has been maintained that a theoretical commitment to *determinism is hard to reconcile with the practice of historians, *libertarian convictions about human agency being integral to the historical studies as actually pursued.   P.L.G.

I. Berlin, 'Historical Inevitability', in *Four Essays on Liberty* (Oxford, 1969).

determinism, logical. Whether or not God or anyone or anything else knows the future, it is alleged, there must *be* a true description of the future, a set of true statements about it. The conjunction of all the true statements about the future we will call The Book. Now The Book must contain either the statement 'John Doe gets married on 20 June 2145' or the statement 'John Doe does not get married on 20 June 2145'. Whichever alternative The Book contains is true. Thus, it is alleged, whether or not Mr Doe will get married is already settled. So with every other future event. Logical determinism of this sort is not to be confused with *determinism, since it includes no causal story about the future, but is rightly associated with *fatalism—the attitude that it makes no difference what we do because the future is unaffected by our present actions.   R.C.W.

*destiny.

R. Taylor, *Metaphysics*, 3rd edn. (Englewood Cliffs, NJ, 1983).

determinism, scientific. The best examples of *determinism, or the lack of it, are found in the theories of physics. At first glance, we might say that such a theory is deterministic whenever the state of a system at some initial time plus the laws of the theory fix that system's state at any later time. But we need to take account of the fact that in relativistic (as opposed to Newtonian) *space-time theories, the notions of 'at some initial time' or 'at any later time' are inapplicable to spatially extended systems, due to the relativity of simultaneity. Also, it could be the case that an entire segment of a system's history is needed before its future behaviour gets fixed, or that only a portion of its future behaviour will be fixed. And we might want to distinguish fixing a system's future behaviour from fixing its past history as well (though in most physical theories the two go hand-in-hand, since laws remain the same when the direction of time is reversed). Finally, we want a definition adaptable to systems of any size or kind, from electrons to the entire universe.

Therefore the following revised definition suggests itself. Let R_1 and R_2 be any two regions of space-time, perhaps including two distinct segments of an electron's history, or events surrounding the big bang and the rest of the universe. Then a physical theory is deterministic with respect to R_1 and R_2 just in case the state it assigns to R_2 is fixed by the theory's laws and the state it assigns to R_1; more precisely, just in case any two models of the theory (i.e. possible states of the world, according to the theory's laws) that agree on R_1 also agree on R_2. Clearly, the bigger the 'determining' region R_1 needs to be—relative to the 'determined' region R_2—in order for a theory to satisfy this definition, the weaker the form of determinism at issue.

We now need to see this definition in action. Two paradigm examples will be offered: one of extreme determinism, the other of extreme indeterminism.

First, consider a Newtonian world composed of point particles moving under their mutual gravitational attraction, with each particle satisfying Newton's second law (force impressed on it = its mass × its acceleration). Working through the resulting equations, one finds that the positions plus velocities of all the particles at any moment completely fix all their past and future positions and velocities. So we have a nice strong instance of

determinism: R_1 can be a mere slice through Newtonian space-time picking out any set of absolutely simultaneous events, with the result that R_2 will be the whole of space-time containing the complete trajectories of the particles.

However, this 'paradigm' example only works if we ignore collisions; for, since gravitational attraction between two bodies is inversely proportional to the square of their separation, that attraction becomes infinite when point particles collide, leading to a breakdown in the applicability of Newton's laws. And, perhaps more seriously, our example had to ignore 'space-invaders': a particle that, after a finite time, can fly into the vicinity of our particles from spatial infinity! Incredible though it sounds, Newtonian physics does not forbid this; unlike Einstein's *relativity, it imposes no upper limit on speeds. Thus, space-invaders can upset determinism by failing to leave a calling-card on some initial time slice R_1 so that the particles' state on R_1, because it contains no record of the presence of the space-invader and its gravitational influence, will no longer fix their future trajectories. (This picture also helps to see why determinism can fail even in relativistic space-times: for example, the analogue of a space-invader can jump out of a nearby 'naked' singularity without ever having registered its presence on any time slice that precedes it.)

The second paradigm example, this time of extreme indeterminism, is *quantum mechanics; though it too doesn't quite fit with its popular reputation as an indeterministic theory. To be sure, the quantum state associated with any space-time region R_1, no matter how big, does not (in general) fix the outcomes of measurements performed in other regions R_2 but, at best, only their probabilities. Nevertheless, the Schrödinger equation ensures that quantum states *themselves* evolve deterministically in time, at least in the absence of measurements. In fact, this curious mix of determinism with indeterminism is at the heart of the 'paradox' of Schrödinger's cat—when and how does indeterminism take over during a measurement to produce a definite outcome out of a superposition?

Determinism is an *ontological* doctrine about a feature of the world which, if it obtains, need not imply that the states of systems are predictable, which is also a question of *epistemology*. Two examples will illustrate this distinction.

First, in the space-time of special relativity, the state of the world at any time (relative to any observer!) fixes the whole of events throughout the space-time. But the fact that information cannot be transmitted faster than light guarantees that no observer will ever be able to gather up all the data they would need for predicting an event before it actually occurs.

Second, returning to Newtonian mechanics, a system can be deterministic yet 'chaotic'. This means that no matter how precisely we specify its initial state for the purposes of predicting its final state, there will always be a small range of possible initial states that the system could still be in which will very quickly evolve into drastically different final states. Since we can never empirically discriminate between alternative initial states with *absolute* precision, we lose the ability to predict the future behaviour of such a system.   R.CLI.

*chaos theory; cat, Schrödinger's.

J. Earman, *A Primer on Determinism* (Dordrecht, 1986).
J. Gleick, *Chaos: Making a New Science* (New York, 1987).
R. Montague, 'Deterministic Theories', in R. H. Thomason (ed.), *Formal Philosophy* (New Haven, Conn., 1974).

determinism and freedom: *see* freedom and determinism.

Deus sive Natura: *see* Spinoza.

development ethics. The 1987 Brundtland Report emphasized 'sustainable development' for the future welfare of humanity. If 'development' means economic growth, this can bring benefits for some and disbenefits for others (e.g., unemployment and displacement due to new forms of industrialization). Development ethics recognizes that policy-makers, aid donors, corporations, and agencies like the World Bank, confront moral questions when planning socio-economic changes, particularly in the world's poorest countries. The International Development Ethics Association was established in 1984 to encourage critical reflection on issues of poverty, globalization, and world development.   A.BRE.

W. Aiken and H. LaFollette (eds.), *World Hunger and Morality* (Englewood Cliffs, NJ, 1996).

deviance, causal. An abnormal causal connection between one event or state and another. Causal deviance is potentially problematic for causal theories of such things as intentional action and perception. For example, a crude causal theory might hold that *S intentionally* does an action *A* if *S* intends to do *A* and *S*'s so intending is a cause of *S*'s doing *A*. Imagine that *S* intends to phone her uncle, but mistakenly dials her mother's number instead. If her uncle happens to answer, *S*'s intention is a cause of her phoning him; but her phoning him is too coincidental to be intentional. In a popular example, *S*'s intention to break an expensive vase so unnerves him that the vase falls from his trembling hands to the hard floor. However, it may be doubted that *S*'s 'breaking the vase' was an action. A.R.M.

*mental causation.

C. Peacocke, *Holistic Explanation* (Oxford, 1979).

Dewey, John (1859–1952). American philosopher who developed a systematic *pragmatism addressing the central questions of epistemology, metaphysics, ethics, and aesthetics. In a manner consistent with, in fact driven by, his philosophical views, Dewey was also deeply involved in the social issues of his day, especially with reform of American schools, but also with matters of national and international politics.

He began his philosophic career under the tutelage of Hegelians, and his lifelong rejection of dualisms, his

search for mediating ideas, is sometimes traced to the remnants of that influence. He rejected not only the *dualism of mind and body, but also any but a functional or contextual distinction between fact and value, means and ends, thought and action, organism and environment, man and nature, individual and society. He early and firmly abandoned Hegelian idealism, however, and the evolutionary character of his developed philosophy was biologically based, grounded on Darwinian theory and committed to scientific experimentalism.

Dewey advanced a philosophy interested in the question of how life should be lived, and he argued that addressing that question required bridging the gap between morals and science. His work in all areas of philosophy, including in the logical studies to which he turned both early and late in his career, was particularly devoted to securing the continuity he discerned between philosophy and social and biological psychology. His logic was a theory of inquiry, a general account of how thought functions, not in an abstract or purely formal mode, but in the inquiries of successful science and in the problem-solving of ordinary daily life. Dewey's *'instrumentalism' defined inquiry as the transformation of a puzzling, indeterminate situation into one that is sufficiently unified to enable warranted assertion or coherent action; and the knowledge that is the object of inquiry is, Dewey insisted, just as available in matters of morals and politics as in matters of physics and chemistry. What is required in all cases is the application of intelligent inquiry, the self-correcting method of experimentally testing hypotheses created and refined from our previous experience. What counts as 'testing' may vary with the 'felt difficulty' in need of resolution—testing may occur in a chemistry laboratory, in imaginative rehearsal of conflicting habits of action, in legislation that changes some functions of a government—but in all cases there is a social context, mediating both the terms of the initial problem and its solution, and being in turn transformed by the inquiry.

Dewey's epistemological and moral *fallibilism—his view that no knowledge-claim, no moral rule, principle, or ideal is ever certain, immune from all possible criticism and revision—was yet allied with an optimistic progressivism. The realization of progress requires, however, the cultivation of intelligent habits in individuals and the maintenance of social structures that encourage continuous inquiry. Thus Dewey focused on the nature and practical improvement of education, arguing that children cannot be understood as empty vessels, passively awaiting the pouring-in of knowledge, but must rather be seen as active centres of impulse, shaped by but also shaping their environment. Children will develop habits of one sort or another in the course of their interactions with their social and physical surroundings, so if we want those habits to be flexible, intelligent, we must do our best to structure an environment that will allow and indeed provoke the operations of intelligent inquiry. It was this sort of environment that Dewey sought concretely to provide in the Laboratory School he established at the University of

Chicago. Dewey's goal for children, as for adults, was 'growth'—growth in powers, in capacities for experience. Growth, he claimed, is really 'the only moral "end"', for it is not, quite plainly, a real end, but always a means.

*Democracy, Dewey's other guiding ideal, is likewise both a goal and a means. The continuity of change that characterizes our world—its natural evolution, for example, and the replacement of one generation by another—implies what Dewey understood as a 'continual rhythm of disequilibrations and recoveries of equilibrium'. We need the best thoughts and actions of the entire community in order to reconstruct our equilibrium, not only because the community sets the conditions for recovery, but also because we have no antecedent assurance of the source or nature of the required reconstruction. It is always experimental, and Dewey took democracy both to be and to further that grand experiment.   K.H.

*American philosophy.

Sidney Morgenbesser (ed.), *Dewey and his Critics* (New York, 1977).

Israel Scheffler, *Four Pragmatists* (London, 1974).

Robert B. Westbrook, *John Dewey and American Democracy* (Ithaca, NY, 1991).

dialectic. In ancient Greece, dialectic was a form of reasoning that proceeded by question and answer, used by Plato. In later antiquity and the Middle Ages, the term was often used to mean simply logic, but Kant applied it to arguments showing that principles of science have contradictory aspects. Hegel thought that all logic and world history itself followed a dialectical path, in which internal contradictions were transcended, but gave rise to new contradictions that themselves required resolution. Marx and Engels gave Hegel's idea of dialectic a material basis; hence *dialectical materialism.   P.S.

Peter Singer, *Hegel* (Oxford, 1983), ch. 5.

dialectical materialism. The official name given to Marxist philosophy by its proponents in the Soviet Union and their affiliates elsewhere. The term was never used by either Marx or Engels, though the latter did favourably contrast both 'materialist dialectics' with the 'idealist dialectics' of Hegel and also the German idealist tradition, and the 'dialectical' outlook of Marxism with the 'mechanistic' or 'metaphysical' standpoint of other nineteenth-century materialists. The source of the main doctrines of dialectical materialism is the writings of Engels, especially *Anti-Dühring* (1878) and *Dialectics of Nature* (1875–82, published posthumously, 1927).

According to dialectical materialism, the fundamental question of all philosophy is: 'Which is primary, matter or consciousness?' The question of 'primacy' is also described as 'Which, matter or consciousness, is the source of the other?' *Materialism holds to the primacy of matter, idealism to the primacy of consciousness. Theism, which maintains that matter was created by a supernatural consciousness, is taken to be the chief form of *idealism;

under the title 'objective idealism' this is sometimes distinguished from 'subjective idealism', the view that the material world exists only for the individual mind. Though these two versions of idealism do not appear to make consciousness the 'source' of matter in the same sense, it is even less clear in what way materialism takes matter to be the 'source' of consciousness. Because it is often claimed that the results of modern science support materialism against idealism, dialectical materialists apparently mean to endorse whatever account of mind results from scientific investigation, but think that we already know enough to be confident that the resulting theory will suffice to exclude theism or other idealist accounts. Yet dialectical materialists also insist that thought bears a certain determinate relation to matter, serving as its 'image' or 'reflection'; the world of consciousness is the material world 'translated into forms of thought'. The point of this last phrase seems to be that thought is given in certain determinate forms, which bear determinate relationships (especially developmental ones) to each other, whose subject-matter is 'dialectics'.

The 'primacy of matter over consciousness' is sometimes also given an epistemological interpretation. Idealists are charged with a tendency to scepticism concerning knowledge of the material world, whereas materialists maintain that the material world is knowable through empirical science. This confidence is often supported by appeal to the practical successes of empirical science, by which is meant both the results of experimentation (which involve the experimenter's practical interaction with the world) and the technological fruits of empirical science. Practice is asserted to be the sole criterion of *truth. Doubts and questions which cannot be given a practical significance are to be dismissed; the sceptical doubts of idealistic philosophy are held to be refutable in this way.

If the opposition of idealism and materialism concerns the fundamental question of philosophy, the opposition between metaphysics and dialectics concerns the fundamental issue of method. The 'metaphysical' method is identified with the mechanistic programme of early modern science, which is taken to have been discredited by such nineteenth-century discoveries as electromagnetic field theory. But, following Engels, dialectical materialism upholds (at least a modified version of) the critique of early modern science presented by German idealism and its 'philosophy of nature', which opposes formalism and reductionism and emphasizes phenomena of organic interconnection and qualitative emergence. Thus the commonest charges against metaphysical materialism are that it ignores the fundamentally developmental nature of matter, that it tries to reduce all change to quantitative change, and that it fails to recognize internal contradictions in the nature of material things as the fundamental source of change. The antidote is to recognize the dialectical laws of thought, which are sometimes summarized as

1. The unity of opposites. The nature of everything involves internal opposition of contradiction.

2. Quantity and quality. Quantitative change always eventually leads to qualitative change or development.
3. Negation of the negation. Change negates what is changed, and the result is in turn negated, but this second negation leads to a further development and not a return to that with which we began.

(This last idea is sometimes presented by expositors of *'dialectic' in the jargon of 'thesis–antithesis–synthesis'; this jargon, however, is not characteristic of dialectical materialists. Since it was never used by Hegel, and was used by Marx only once, solely for the purpose of ridicule, it is easy to understand why its use is nearly always a sign of either ignorance of or hostility to dialectical thinking—usually both at once.)

As the official Soviet philosophy, dialectical materialism was always doomed to be shallow and sterile because any impulse to creativity or critical thinking on the part of its practitioners was smothered by authoritarianism, political repression, and fear. Ironically, a philosophy whose spirit was to challenge traditional religious authority and to exalt the fact of qualitative novelty and ceaseless progressive development has become our century's most notorious example of ossified dogmatism, incapable either of internal development or of response to ongoing changes in science and philosophy, often reduced to nothing but the mechanical repetition of empty phrases borrowed from an earlier century. However, this easily obscures the important fact that the basic aims and principles of dialectical materialism remain very much in harmony with the fundamental spirit of progressive, rational scientific thought, which continues to perceive a fundamental opposition between scientific theories and religious myths, to address the scientific challenges posed by the failure of the seventeenth- and eighteenth-century mechanistic programme, and to seek a scientific metaphysics as the basis for an enlightened view of the world.

A.W.W.

V. G. Afanasyev, *Marxist Philosophy*, 4th edn. (Moscow, 1980).
Maurice Cornforth, *Dialectical Materialism* (New York, 1971).
Friedrich Engels, *Anti-Dühring* (Moscow, 1962).
——*Dialectics of Nature* (New York, 1973).
David Ruben, *Marxism and Materialism*, 2nd edn. (Brighton, 1979).

dialectics, negative: *see* Adorno.

dialeth(e)ism. A *dialetheia* (a neologism indicating 'two-way truth', and pronounced di/aletheia) is a true contradiction: that is, a pair of propositions, A, $\neg A$ such that both are true (where $\neg$ is negation). Hence *dialetheism* (alternatively, *dialethism*) is the view that some contradictions are true. There have been dialetheists in the history of Western philosophy (arguably, Hegel is one such), but the law of *non-contradiction, which rules out dialetheias, has been the orthodox view since Aristotle's defence of the view. Contemporary dialetheists, such as Priest and Routley, appeal, amongst other things, to paradoxes of

self-reference, such as the *liar paradox. They endorse the correctness of a paraconsistent logic.   G.P.

G. Priest, *In Contradiction* (Dordrecht, 1987).

dichotomy. In logic, a division of a whole into two parts, as with a class into two mutually exclusive and jointly exhaustive subclasses, or a *genus into two likewise disjoint species. Usually called 'division by dichotomy', this procedure is sometimes also known as 'dichotomy by contradiction' because the resulting binary classification may be defined by 'contradictory marks', as when we say 'Everything must be red or not red'.

One major application of the concept is to *'definition by division', in which an entity is classified by differentiation of genus and species. Aristotle criticized the procedure for lacking the apodeictic certainty of syllogistic deduction, on the grounds that since one cannot be sure that the right differentiae have been selected, one cannot be sure that the resulting division is exhaustive.

Zeno of Elea's 'paradox of the *stadium' is sometimes called 'The Dichotomy', 'dichotomy' in this connection meaning arithmetical or geometrical division. The paradox is that one cannot cross a given space because to do so one must first get half-way, and before that half-way to the half-way point, and so on *ad infinitum*; but we cannot traverse an infinite number of such points in a finite time.   A.C.G.

Aristotle, *Physics*, bk. 6, ch. 8, for Zeno.
——*Posterior Analytics*, bk. 1, ch. 31; bk. 2, ch. 5.

dictatorship of the proletariat. According to Marx, the forceful use of state power by the working class against its enemies during the passage from capitalism to communism. Since Marx regarded all political states—parliamentary democracies just as much as one-person autocracies—as class dictatorships, in the sense of forcefully furthering the interests of one class at the expense of others, the concept does not imply dictatorship in the ordinary sense.   K.M.

*Marxism.

K. Marx, Letter to Weydemeyer, 5 Mar. 1852, in D. McLellan (ed.), *Karl Marx: Selected Writings* (Oxford, 1977).

dictionaries and encyclopaedias of philosophy. Philosophical dictionaries began before encyclopaedias in general, and certainly before philosophical encyclopaedias. The first is the small but pregnant fifth book (Δ) of the *Metaphysics* of Aristotle, the original organizer and professionalizer of philosophy. In this 'philosophical lexicon' the senses of some thirty crucial terms are distinguished and defined. On the whole, important and original thinkers have left dictionary-making to those who are, comparatively speaking, drudges. The principal exceptions are Pierre Bayle's *Dictionnaire historique et critique* (1697), a cunningly indirect assault on metaphysics and theology, and Voltaire's *Dictionnaire philosophique* (1764), a more openly sceptical attack on Christianity and revealed religion in general. There is also one fine recent instance: W. V. Quine's highly entertaining *Quiddities* (1987), which is more strictly philosophical (and logico-mathematical) in scope.

Notable among medieval dictionaries are one based on Avicenna's writings and the *Compendium Philosophiae* (*c.*1327), which derives from Aristotle and Albertus Magnus. Numerous dictionaries of the seventeenth century in Latin are of limited interest. J. G. Walch's *Philosophisches Lexicon* (1726) achieved a new level of comprehensiveness and vitality. Kant's successor at Königsberg, W. T. Krug, produced an *Allgemeines Handwörterbuch der Philosophischen Wissenschaften* (1827–9) which stands out from other German efforts of its period. In France the *Dictionnaire des sciences philosophiques*, edited by A. Franck, a disciple of Victor Cousin, is comparably eminent. An unprecedented level of technical competence was attained by Rudolf Eisler's massive *Wörterbuch* of 1899.

The *Dictionary of Philosophy and Psychology* (1899), edited by J. M. Baldwin, with contributions from William James, G. E. Moore, and many other distinguished philosophers, is the first serious philosophical dictionary in English. The *Dictionary of Philosophy* (1942), edited by Dagobert D. Runes, also had some impressive contributors, several of whom united to condemn the editor's handling of their contributions. Subsequent dictionaries in English, such as those of A. R. Lacey (1976) and A. G. N. Flew (1979), have been modest, useful, and short. A remarkable production somewhere between dictionary and encyclopaedia is the *Synopticon* (1952), in which essays by Mortimer G. Adler on 102 'great ideas' lead into careful analyses of the internal articulation of the ideas treated, which, in their turn, serve as the framework for a vast array of references to the works of major writers. By no means wholly philosophical in content, the work is throughout philosophical in spirit. Adler's essays have been published as a single volume: *The Great Ideas* (1992).

The first real encyclopaedias are medieval: the compendia of Cassiodorus (sixth century), Isidore of Seville (seventh century), and Vincent of Beauvais (thirteenth century). Bacon's *Instauratio Magna* (early seventeenth century) was the sketch of a co-operative encyclopaedia which was realized by the compilers, in particular Diderot, of the famous *Encyclopédie* (1751–72). Later, general encyclopaedias have followed it with extensive coverage of philosophical topics: the *Britannica* (from 1768 to the present), *Brockhaus* (1796 to the present), *Larousse* (1866 to the present).

The first works explicitly claiming to be encyclopaedias of philosophy were those of Hegel and Herbart in the early nineteenth century: they were essentially systematic surveys of their authors' ideas. An ambitious project of Windelband and Ruge, begun in 1912, never got beyond a distinguished first volume on logic. The first really serious encyclopaedia of philosophy is the four-volume Italian *Enciclopedia filosofica* of 1957, which was unprecedented in its scope, completeness, and scholarly quality. J. O. Urmson's *Concise Encyclopaedia of Western Philosophy and Philosophers* (1960) contained many lively and authoritative

contributions but too closely reflected the prevailing interests and loyalties of British philosophy at its moment of publication. Superior in every way to all its predecessors was the *Encyclopaedia of Philosophy* (1967), edited by Paul Edwards in eight volumes. There was nothing since to compare with it until 1998, when the 10-vol. *Routledge Encyclopaedia of Philosophy* appeared, edited by Edward Craig.   A.Q.

*Encyclopaedists; journals of philosophy; Lexicon, Philosophical.

Diderot, Denis (1713–84). One of the *philosophes whose thought typifies the scientistic secularism of the French Enlightenment. Diderot became editor of the *Encyclopédie* in 1750, and contributed articles to it in the field of moral and social philosophy. His vividly entertaining dialogue *Le Neveu de Rameau* (begun in the early 1760s) raises disturbing questions about the relationship between the life of *genius and the demands of conventional morality. In several of his philosophical essays, including *Pensées sur l'interprétation de la nature* (1754), he argued for a form of materialistic reductionism, which would account even for complex phenomena such as sensation without reference to anything over and above matter in motion. In his views on human knowledge and the importance of observation and experiment as against abstract speculation, he was broadly influenced by the ideas of John Locke (some of whose writings he translated into French). In the area of biological theory, he put forward the suggestion that all living things pass through stages of development, in this respect anticipating some of the evolutionary thinking of the following century.

J.COT.

G. Bremner, *Order and Change: The Pattern of Diderot's Thought* (Cambridge, 1983).

différance. Neologism coined by the philosopher of *deconstruction Jacques Derrida through a punning play on the French verb 'différer', meaning both 'to differ' and 'to defer'. The term figures chiefly in his reading of Husserl, and refers to the perpetual slippage of meaning from sign to sign (or from moment to moment) in the linguistic chain. The result of this—so Derrida argues—is the strict *impossibility* of achieving what Husserl set out to achieve, that is to say, a rigorously theorized account of the structures and modalities of internal time-consciousness, or of the relation between utterer's meaning and language as a network of differential signs. There is no way of reducing or judging this endless play of differing-deferral—no 'transcendental signified' or 'logocentric' anchor-point in consciousness, meaning, or truth.   C.N.

Jacques Derrida, *'Speech and Phenomena' and Other Essays on Husserl's Theory of Signs*, tr. David B. Allison (Evanston, Ill., 1973).

difference, method of: *see* method of difference.

difference principle. The principle, proposed by John Rawls, that economic and social advantages for the better-off members of a society are justified only if they benefit the worst-off. For example, differences in income, wealth, and status among different professions and social groups can be defended as just only if they are produced by a system of incentives, market forces, and capital accumulation whose productivity makes even unskilled labourers better off than they would be in a more equal system. Rawls argues that the more fortunate cannot be said to morally deserve either their inherited wealth or the natural talents that enable them to command higher pay in the labour market, so the justification for an economic system which rewards people unequally must come from its benefits to everyone. This is a strongly egalitarian principle, which doesn't permit inequalities even if the advantage to the better-off is greater than the disadvantage to the worst-off. It also denies that people are naturally entitled to the product of their natural abilities. The principle has therefore drawn resistance both from utilitarians and from those who believe that inequalities resulting from natural endowments are not morally arbitrary, and require no further justification.   T.N.

*equality; inequality; justice.

J. Rawls, *A Theory of Justice* (Cambridge, Mass., 1971).

dilemma. As used informally, a person is in a dilemma when he is confronted with difficult choices as in the case of moral obligations which conflict. Adapting an example from Plato:

> If I return John's gun then he will inflict harm.
> If I don't return John's gun I will have broken a promise.
> I return it or I don't return it.
> Therefore someone will be harmed or I will have broken a promise.

On a formal account, traditional logic characterized as dilemmas some arguments consisting of a conjunction of two *conditionals and a *disjunction. Singled out were four valid arguments which can be represented in the *propositional calculus.

Dilemma		Premiss 1	Premiss 2	Conclusion
Constructive	Complex	$(P \supset Q) \cdot (R \supset S)$	$(P \vee R)$	$(Q \vee S)$
	Simple	$(P \supset Q) \cdot (R \supset Q)$	$(P \vee R)$	Q
Destructive	Complex	$(P \supset Q) \cdot (R \supset S)$	$(\sim Q \vee \sim S)$	$(\sim P \vee \sim R)$
	Simple	$(P \supset Q) \cdot (P \supset S)$	$(\sim Q \vee \sim S)$	$\sim P$

Dilemmas can have rhetorical force when used, for example, to persuade that the disjunctive premiss has an unacceptable conclusion.   R.B.M.

C. W. Gowans (ed.), *Moral Dilemmas* (Oxford, 1987).

Dilthey, Wilhelm (1833–1911). German philosopher who developed *hermeneutics and extended Kant's method to the cultural sciences (*Geisteswissenschaften*). These sciences rest on 'lived experience (*Erlebnis*), expression, and understanding (*Verstehen*)'. History, art, religion, law, etc. express the spirit of their authors. We understand them by grasping this spirit. Such understanding involves our lived experience of our own culture. The continuity and unity of all cultures—life (*Leben*)—enables us to relive (*nacherleben*), and thus understand, the past. The historian employs categories, such as 'meaning, value, purpose, development, ideal', which are not a priori, but 'lie in the nature of life itself'. Life has no single meaning: our idea of its meaning is always changing, and the 'purpose which we set for the future conditions our account of the meaning of the past'. World-views (*Weltanschauungen) are relative to cultures, but by studying them and life in general, man approaches (but never attains) objective self-knowledge. Knowledge involves life, not only reason: we affirm an external world because our will meets resistance.   M.J.I.

*Verstehen.

H. P. Rickman, *Dilthey Today: A Critical Appraisal of the Contemporary Relevance of his Work* (London, 1988).

Ding-an-sich: *see* thing-in-itself.

Diodorus Cronus (d. 284 BC) is most notable for his advocacy of atomism and determinism. In response to Aristotle's argument that the continuous motion of partless things is inconceivable, Diodorus maintained that motion is discontinuous: something is in one place at one instant and in a different place at the very next instant. In defending this view, he seems to have contemplated not only an atomistic view of matter but also a spatial and temporal atomism, whereby space and time are not continuous magnitudes but comprise smallest minimal parts. Diodorus' defence of determinism falls within a class of temporal symmetry arguments, whereby it is argued that the future is like the past, which is fixed and unchangeable, because the fixed nature of events cannot change simply as a result of whether we consider an event to be past or future, depending on where we imagine ourselves to be on the time line. Note however that he says nothing to refute the possible claim that temporal symmetry also holds the other way: one might equally argue that the past is like the future, namely open and undetermined. His distinct-ive argument is that what is past is true and necessary, and that only what is or will be true is possible.   S.GAU.

R. Sorabji, *Time, Creation and the Continuum* (London, 1983).
J. Vuillemin, *Necessity or Contingency* (Stanford, Calif., 1996).

Diogenes the Cynic (404–323 BC). Greek philosopher who seems to have held that only the distinction between virtue and vice matters, and that other conventionally acknowledged distinctions (e.g. between public and private, Greek and barbarian, raw and cooked, yours and mine) should therefore be disdained. He propagated these views, occasionally by argument ('All things belong to the gods; the gods are friends to the wise; friends hold in common what belongs to them; so all things belong to the wise'), but much more frequently by action: a characteristic anecdote records that he once masturbated in the market-place, remarking to passers-by 'If only it were as easy to get rid of hunger by rubbing my stomach'. His flamboyantly disgusting actions and savage repartee earned him the nickname 'Dog'; his followers were called *'Cynics', or 'Doggies'.   N.C.D.

Socratis et Socraticorum Reliquiae, ed. Gabriele Giannantoni (Naples, 1990), ii. 227–509 (= *Elenchos*, vol. XVIII**).

Diogenes Laertius (probably 3rd century AD). Author of *Lives and Opinions of Eminent Philosophers*. This is an uncritical scissors-and-paste work on Greek philosophers from Thales to the *Sceptics of the third century AD. Diogenes took his material from hundreds of earlier works of very variable quality. Where his sources are reliable, Diogenes provides some important evidence, notably on the philosophy of Epicurus and some of the Pre-Socratic philosophers. But on others, such as Aristotle, his accounts are unreliable, and sometimes incoherent. He had a taste for anecdote and paradox, but no talent for philosophical exposition. Nothing is known of his life, and, as he presents many different philosophical views with evident approval, it is hard to detect any distinct philosophical position of his own.   R.J.H.

Diogenes Laertius, tr. R. D. Hicks, intro. H. S. Long (Cambridge, Mass., 1972).

Dionysian and Apollinian (or Apollonian). Nietzsche's designations of two different Greek art forms and artistic tendencies, reflecting two fundamental human and natural impulses. He invoked the names of the gods Apollo and Dionysus to identify and distinguish them in his discussion of the origin of the tragic art and culture of the Greeks (which he traced to their confluence), associating Apollo with order, lawfulness, perfected form, clarity, precision, self-control, and individuation, and Dionysus with change, creation and destruction, movement, rhythm, ecstasy, and oneness. (See *The Birth of Tragedy* (1872), sects. 1–5; *The Will to Power* (1901), sects. 1049–52.)   R.S.

*tragedy.

Richard Schacht, *Nietzsche* (London, 1983), ch. 8.

direct realism: *see* naïve realism.

dirty hands. In Jean-Paul Sartre's 1948 play *Dirty Hands*, Hoederer speaks of having hands dirty up to his elbows, having plunged them in filth and blood: 'So what? Do you think one can govern innocently?'

Under the heading of 'dirty hands', contemporary thinkers debate whether actions that violate ordinary moral principles can be excused on grounds that they are undertaken for the sake of the greater good; and what degree of guilt such violations impose on those who perpetrate them. How seriously should they take the analogy implied by the proverbial saying 'He that touches pitch shall be defiled therewith' (Ecclesiasticus 13: 1)?

In the practice of politics, the metaphor of dirty hands is often invoked by public officials hoping to brush aside accusations of wrongdoing by claiming to have acted strictly in the public's best interest. Some take a more categorical stand: they argue that it would be naïve to imagine that politicians could ever truly serve the public's best interests without violating fundamental moral principles.

This view has long antecedents. In *The Prince*, Machiavelli maintains that rulers who cling to moral principles such as those prohibiting dishonesty, breaches of faith, and the killing of innocent persons invariably end up defeated by adversaries who lack such scruples. Max Weber, in 'Politics as a Vocation', holds that the tasks of politics can be accomplished only by means of violence, and that deceit and breaches of faith are needed for such purposes as well.

Conversely, Erasmus, in *The Education of a Christian Prince*, and Kant, in 'Perpetual Peace', consider such views untenable not only in principle but in practice, and bound to victimize innocents, corrupt agents, and destroy trust. Often charged with naïvety, they take it to reside, rather, in ignoring the destructive role that faith in the dirty-hands rationale, by whatever name, plays in politics.   S.B.

*consequentialism.

Dennis Thompson, 'Democratic Dirty Hands', in *Political Ethics and Public Office* (Cambridge, Mass., 1987).
Michael Walzer, 'Political Action: The Problem of Dirty Hands', *Philosophy and Public Affairs* (1973).

disability and morality. 'Disability' principally implies permanent or long-term missing physical capacities but often includes mental capacities too. Yet, whilst we can compare the result of illness or injury to a set of capacities owned originally, it is controversial what set of capacities a person should have to begin with. One view proposes that any account will presuppose an essence or ideal type of human form and functioning, against which we can compare individuals. Individual variations, even quite significant ones, exist in all species, however. Unless one is committed to vulgar evolutionary reductionism, there is no plausible reason for according any one of these priority or value over the others.

Permanent conditions do exist which prevent a person from enjoying a full life; medical impairments can inherently produce pain and suffering, or render lives unviable. However, many so-called disabilities are not like this. Often incapacity is due to the way society has structured its environment and the encouragement and rewards it gives to projects requiring certain traits and abilities. Wheelchair users are 'disabled' by how we organize access, rather than having an inherent incapacity or 'disability'. Yet, this view faces a problem. Whilst some traits are not inherently disabling, society may nevertheless be unable to correct for them if, say, doing so will place unreasonable burdens on others, or is simply unfeasible. Thus, a notion of disability which is not medical, nor purely social, can still be sketched.

Given the equal value of persons, irrespective of such variation, two central issues emerge. First, where society does not correct for people's inability to make choices they could make, were things differently arranged, is there a responsibility to compensate these people? Secondly, in a technological era where choices can be made by selecting future offspring with different features, how should choices be informed by our understanding of disability? Choosing not to have a deaf or a blind child might seem legitimate. But if it is, those championing diversity will argue that it is equally legitimate to choose to have blind or deaf children. This raises further questions as to whether such choices harm the child, given that she would not exist without the choice being made, and also to what extent lack of social accommodation for a trait should feature in such a choice.   S.M.-G.

*ableism; justice; evolutionary ethics.

M. Oliver, *Understanding Disability: From Theory to Practice* (London, 1996).
S. Smith, 'The Social Construction of Talent: A Defence of Justice as Reciprocity', *Journal of Political Philosophy* (2001).
J. Feinberg, 'Wrongful Life and the Counterfactual Element in Harming', in his *Freedom and Fulfilment* (Princeton, NJ, 1992).

discourse. According to Émile Benveniste, 'discourse' is language in so far as it can be interpreted with reference to the speaker, to his or her spatio-temporal location, or to other such variables that serve to specify the localized context of utterance. The study of discourse thus includes the personal pronouns (especially 'I' and 'you'), deictics of place ('here', 'there', etc.), and temporal markers ('now', 'today', 'last week'), in the absence of which the speech-act in question would lack determinate sense.

More often, 'discourse' signifies any piece of language longer (or more complex) than the individual sentence. Discourse analysis therefore operates at the supra-grammatical level where sentences can be shown to hang together through relationships of entailment, presupposition, contextual implicature, argumentative coherence, real-world and speaker-related knowledge, etc. In philosophical terms it is of interest chiefly to thinkers in the field of logico-semantic analysis, as well as those who adopt (after Quine) a more holistic view of the issues that arise for any theory of meaning—or 'radical translation'—allowing for the fact of ontological relativity, or the existence of widely varying conceptual schemes.   C.N.

Nikolas Coupland (ed.), *Styles of Discourse* (London, 1988).
Émile Benveniste, *Problems in General Linguistics*, tr. M. E. Meek (Coral Gables, Fla., 1971).

discrimination. In one familiar sense simply the act of distinguishing between different things. The notion, though not the word itself, has a central role in philosophy, because the 'application of a concept' consists in distinguishing those objects which 'fall under' it from those which don't. One tradition sees 'concept formation' as a process in which words are used to mark the natural resemblances and differences imposed on our minds by objects themselves—what Plato called 'carving nature at the joints'. Another stresses that language is social, and that the words we inherit impose distinctions on the objects of our perception.

In a different but equally familiar sense, 'discrimination' is pejorative, signifying unfair treatment on grounds of, for example, race or gender. The two senses are curiously interwoven in the writings of those social psychologists who argue that, because all thinking requires generalization, prejudices and stereotypes are the 'natural' products of the human mind.   C.W.

*ableism; affirmative action.

G. M. Allport, *The Nature of Prejudice* (Boston, 1954).

disjunction. A proposition (P or Q), where P and Q are propositions, is a disjunction. In English 'or' is ambiguous; especially as between an inclusive use, i.e. ((P or Q) or both) and an exclusive use, i.e. ((P or Q) and not both). In the *propositional calculus, an inclusive disjunction is standardly represented by ($P \lor Q$). It is true except where both P and Q are false. No further relation as between the content of P and Q is required. (*Truth-function.) An exclusive disjunction can be given by (($P \lor Q) \cdot \sim (P \cdot Q)$). The inference of Q from ($P \lor Q$) and $\sim P$, known as the disjunctive syllogism, is valid for the propositional calculus. Its validity has been challenged by alternative systems of logic.   R.B.M.

*logic, relevance; configuration.

W. V. Quine, *Methods of Logic*, 4th edn. (Cambridge, Mass., 1982).

disposition. A *capacity, tendency, *potentiality, or *'power' to act or be acted on in a certain way. Obvious examples include irascibility, fragility, and being poisonous. Non-dispositional properties (e.g. a person's age) are sometimes called 'intrinsic' or 'categorical' properties. Many concepts that are not overtly dispositional have been given dispositional analyses, including mental concepts such as belief and desire. (*Ryle; *behaviourism; *identity theory of mind.) *Secondary qualities such as redness have also been treated as dispositions, as have moral virtues such as courage. Some hold that dispositional properties cannot be fundamental, arguing that every disposition must depend on other properties that provide its ground or basis (as the solubility of a sugar cube depends on its chemical properties). However, it has also been suggested that the fundamental properties of matter may be dispositional.   P.J.M.

*causality; conditionals.

D. M. Armstrong, D. H. Mellor, and U. T. Place, *A Debate on Dispositions*, ed. T. Crane (London, 1996).
J. L. Mackie, *Truth, Probability, and Paradox* (Oxford, 1973), ch. 4.
S. Mumford, *Dispositions* (Oxford, 1998).

disquotation. We use quotation marks to form a name of a linguistic expression. Disquotation can be thought of as the inverse of quotation—that is, as the cancellation of quotation marks. The truth-predicate 'is true' obeys the following disquotational principle or schema: '*p*' is true if and only if *p* (where *p* may be replaced by any English sentence—the *liar sentence apart!). For example, 'Snow is white' is true if and only if snow is white. The principle tells us that we should be prepared to assert a sentence if and only if we are prepared to assert its truth. But this amounts to little more than a truism, rather than conveying the nature of *truth itself.   E.J.L.

*redundancy theory of truth.

W. V. Quine, *Pursuit of Truth* (Cambridge, Mass., 1990).

distribution of terms. The subjects of 'All *S* are *P*' and 'No *S* are *P*', and the predicates of 'No *S* are *P*', and 'Some *S* are not *P*' were traditionally said to be 'distributed'; and this was supposed to explain why certain inferences are valid, others invalid. A term, said Keynes, is 'distributed' when reference is made to *all* the individuals denoted by it'. This theory is obscure, and the traditional rules are flawed.   C.W.

*inversion.

P. T. Geach, *Reference and Generality*, 2nd edn. (Ithaca, NY, 1968).

distributism. A social philosophy propounded in England by Hilaire Belloc and G. K. Chesterton in the early part of the twentieth century. Although primarily a political–economic doctrine, it included ideas about art, culture, and spirituality. A version of *communitarianism, it was strongly opposed to *laissez-faire* *capitalism, and to centralized collectivism, which it associated with welfare *liberalism and state *socialism. The core element, elaborated most effectively in Chesterton's writings, was a view of persons as value-orientated, affective agents whose happiness can only be self-determined. This personalist anthropology (admired by several central European phenomenologists) led to an emphasis on social liberty and individual ownership from which the name derives.
                    J.HAL.

Q. Laurer, *G. K. Chesterton: Philosopher without Portfolio* (New York, 1988).

distributive justice: *see* justice.

divine command ethics. This ethical theory holds that all moral requirements derive from God's commands. One way of articulating the basic idea goes as follows. (1) An action is morally forbidden (wrong) just in case and because God commands that it not be performed. (2) An action is morally permitted (right) just in case and because it is not the case that God commands that it not be performed. (3) An action is morally obligatory just in case and because God commands that it be performed. A consequence of these claims is that, if there is no God, nothing is morally forbidden, nothing is morally obligatory, and everything is morally permitted.

This conception of morality has a distinguished pedigree. In the Middle Ages, it figured prominently in the writings of Ockham and his disciples. It is found in works by Locke and Berkeley. More recently it has been endorsed by Kierkegaard and Barth. It coheres with scriptural portraits of God. The Hebrew Bible is full of stories of God imposing requirements by fiat. In the Gospels Jesus teaches his ethics of love in the form of commands to love God and to love one's neighbour as oneself (Matthew 22: 37–40).

But the theory has also attracted philosophical suspicion ever since Plato. Adapting a question from his *Euthyphro*, one asks: Is torturing the innocent wrong because God forbids it, or does God forbid it because it is wrong? In the latter case, torture is wrong independent of divine commands. In the former, torture would be right if God were not to forbid it, though intuitively torture seems to be necessarily wrong. However, if God necessarily forbids torture, then according to the theory it is necessarily wrong. So some contemporary divine command theorists argue for an account of divine sovereignty in which necessary moral truths depend on necessary divine commands.
                    P.L.Q.

J. M. Idziak (ed.), *Divine Command Morality: Historical and Contemporary Readings* (New York, 1980).

P. L. Quinn, *Divine Commands and Moral Requirements* (Oxford, 1978).

divine philosophy

> How charming is divine philosophy!
> Not harsh, and crabbed as dull fools suppose,
> But musical as is Apollo's lute,
> And a perpetual feast of nectared sweets,
> Where no crude surfeit reigns.
>
>   (Milton, *Comus*, lines 475–9)

Milton's *Comus*, a masque in which Comus, son of Circe and Bacchus, tries to seduce the innocent Lady, was mainly a debate on the importance of virginity. The little speech above follows a far-from-charming diatribe against 'carnal sensuality', said to clot the soul with contagion in this life and draw it to charnel-houses afterwards. Milton is invoking Plato's claim, in *Phaedo*, that unless the soul is free of the body's 'contamination' it will be weighed down by earthiness and dragged back into the visible world after death.   J.O'G.

divorce: *see* marriage.

Dodgson, Charles Lutwidge: *see* Carroll, Lewis.

Dōgen Kigen (1200–53). A *Zen master regarded by the Japanese Sōtō school as its spiritual founder, Dōgen was a gifted nature poet as well as a profound thinker, whose ideas about the 'Buddha-nature' of all things would exemplify in the West a religious *panpsychism. His monumental *Shōbōgenzō* (Treasury of the True Dharma Eye), densely poetic in style, is one of the most brilliant gems of

Japanese philosophy. In accord with the Mahāyāna Buddhist insight that the world of enlightenment (*nirvana*) is not different from the world of impermanence (*saṃsāra*), Dōgen understands all things as being basically already enlightened. Thus Zen practice is to be understood as itself a manifestation of—rather than a means to—enlightenment. Dōgen developed a sophisticated philosophy of temporality, in which everything in the world 'generates' its own time (and with some remarkable parallels to ideas in Kierkegaard, Nietzsche, and Heidegger). G.R.P.

William R. LaFleur (ed.), *Dōgen Studies* (Honolulu, 1985).

dogma. A term that is generally applied to religious doctrines that are accepted irrespective of reason or evidence, usually on scriptural or ecclesiastical authority. It is now used pejoratively, because it sanctions not only belief unjustified by reason, but also intolerance, i.e. the punishment of false belief. However, McTaggart revives the original positive sense, suggesting that the definition should be widened to include any proposition which has metaphysical significance, whether or not it is based on reason. D.BER.

J. M. E. McTaggart, *Some Dogmas of Religion* (London, 1906).

dogmatists: *see* scepticism, history of.

domain. (1) A domain of discourse, or universe of discourse, is the class of things being talked about on a given occasion. For example, 'the baby' will be understood only if the domain includes one (and not more than one) baby. (2) A domain of quantification is the class of things covered by a *quantifier. For example, '*Every* native of this town speaks Arabic' presumably means to exclude non-humans, infants, the dead, etc. Context, or meaning (e.g. 'some*one*'), may indicate that the domain of a quantifier is narrower than the current domain of discourse. (3) The domain of a binary relation is the class of things that have that relation to something; and the converse domain, or range, is the class of things to which something has it (the domain of *R* is the class *x*: ∃*yRxy*, and the range is the class *x*: ∃*yRyx*). (4) Similarly the domain of a *function is the class from which its *arguments are drawn. C.A.K.

double aspect theory. The view, derived from Spinoza, that certain states of living creatures have both mental and physical aspects. Perception and thought, for example, are processes in the brain, but not just physical processes, because some brain processes have experiential or cognitive aspects which are inseparable from their neurophysiological character. Double aspect theory therefore attempts to identify the mental and the physical without analysing either in terms of the other, thus avoiding both *dualism and *materialism. If true, it would explain how the causes of our actions can be simultaneously physical and mental. However, it is obscure how such apparently different things could really be aspects of one thing. A related modern view is Donald Davidson's *'anomalous monism', according to which every mental event is identical to a physical event, but mental properties cannot be analysed in physical terms. T.N.

*Identity theory; mind–body problem.

Spinoza, *Ethics*, pt. II.

double effect. The 'doctrine of double effect' is a thesis in the philosophy of action which is put to use in moral choice and moral assessment. In many actions we may identify the central, directly intended goal or objective for the principal sake of which the action is selected and done. However, there will normally also be side-effects of the process of achieving that objective or of its accomplishment, which may be known prior to taking the action. The doctrine of double effect maintains that it may be permissible to perform a good act with the knowledge that bad consequences will ensue, but that it is always wrong intentionally to do a bad act for the sake of good consequences that will ensue. Sometimes moral problems may arise, or be resolved, by thus considering whether something bad is the direct effect, or the side-effect, of some intention or action. That someone dies as the result of your action is in any case bad, but directly to intend their death appears worse than directly to intend some benefit, but with the knowledge that death may be hastened by this. Administering pain-relieving drugs which shorten life expectancy is a standard example. The extension of this pattern of reasoning to (for example) *killing in self-defence or operating to save a pregnant woman's life but causing foetal death is controversial. N.J.H.D.

*Abortion; consequentialism; deontological ethics.

There is useful discussion in Philippa Foot, 'The Problem of Abortion and the Doctrine of the Double Effect', in *Virtues and Vices* (Oxford, 1978); and in Jonathan Glover, *Causing Deaths and Saving Lives* (Harmondsworth, 1977).

double-mindedness. Adapted by Kierkegaard from James 4: 8, 'purify your hearts ye double-minded', to capture failures to do the moral thing due to subordinating the latter to extra-moral goals (e.g. a reward for doing it or the avoidance of punishment for not doing it). It includes doing the good thing on condition of its being done by oneself, and even doing it with pride that this is not the case. Purity of heart, or to 'will one thing', is to be able to conceive of one's deed as embodying that state of spiritual satisfaction which, in double-mindedness, is conceived as an end to be achieved, here or in the hereafter, by means of the deed. A.H.

S. Kierkegaard, *Purity of Heart is to Will One Thing* (New York, 1958).

double truth. The doctrine of double truth posits the existence of two distinct realms of discourse, the philosophical and the theological, which give different but non-conflicting answers to the same questions, e.g. the immortality of the soul, the eternality of the world, the perfectibility of the individual human life. The doctrine originated in the encounter between the rationalism of Greek philosophy and the theology of omnipotence and inscrutability in Islam and was associated with Averroës, who, in his *Decisive Treatise*, tried to justify a double standard of truth for the masses and truth for the philosopher. This earned him the ire of Islamic and Christian theologians and led to the Paris Condemnations of Bishop Tempier of 1270 and 1277 in which Boethius was centrally involved, and to the attempts of St Thomas Aquinas to produce a coherent synthesis of pagan philosophy and Christian theology. The moral and intellectual privilege of the philosopher is a prominent theme in Spinoza (*Ethics*, proposition 41, Scholium).   c.w.

*subjective truth.

G. F. Hourani, *Averroës on the Harmony of Religion and Philosophy* (London, 1961).

doubt. When we doubt a proposition, we neither believe nor disbelieve it: rather, we suspend judgement, regarding it as an open question whether it is true. Doubt can thus be a sceptical attitude: one form of *scepticism holds that any cognitive attitude other than doubt is irrational or illegitimate—rationality requires a general suspension of judgement. The arguments employed by sceptics (for example, Pyrrhonists such as Sextus Empiricus) are thus designed to induce doubt, to shake our beliefs and certainties, and to force us to suspend judgement.

Descartes made doubt the cornerstone of a philosophical method: in order to place our knowledge on foundations which are genuinely secure, we should try to doubt all of our beliefs, retaining them only if they are absolutely indubitable. Ordinary empirical beliefs are threatened by the possibility that I am dreaming; as are even logical principles because I might be deceived by an evil demon. Unless I can eliminate these possibilities, I cannot escape the suspicion that all my beliefs are infected by unnoticed error. Few have been convinced by Descartes's claims about when doubt is impossible, and many have questioned his claims about the desirability of trying to extend doubt as far as possible.

A problem emerges because Descartes's arguments do not produce a genuine doubt: the possibility that I might be dreaming or deceived by a demon does not touch my everyday confidence that I will be supported when I sit down or my ordinary reliance upon elementary arithmetic. Descartes acknowledged that the doubt induced by hypothesizing an evil demon is 'very slight, and so to speak metaphysical': we can acknowledge the abstract possibility or appropriateness of doubt but we feel no live doubt. But many of his critics have claimed that he relied upon an inadequate, excessively 'intellectual' understanding of doubt and certainty.

*Common-sense philosophers have questioned the apparent assumption that if we can conceive a possible situation incompatible with the truth of some everyday claim, then, unless we have independent grounds for ruling out that possibility, our everyday certainty is unwarranted.

There are kinds of certainty (and indubitability) falling short of the absolute certainty criticized by sceptics. In 1675 John Wilkins defended our certainty that there was such a man as Henry VIII and that there are such places as America and China. And John Tillotson insisted that 'It is possible that the sun may not rise to Morrow morning; and yet, for all this, I suppose that no Man has the least Doubt but that it will.' We do not hesitate to accept standards of rationality which underwrite such certainties; and it is unreasonable to follow sceptics in disregarding these standards. Doubt is made to appear a neurotic and unreasonable fear which leads us to doubt things because they cannot receive kinds of proofs which it is unreasonable to expect them to receive. They may not be beyond all possible doubt, but they are beyond all *reasonable* doubt. Similar arguments against the Cartesian use of the method of doubt are found in thinkers like Thomas Reid.

Alongside this claim that sceptical doubts are unreasonable, we find the suggestion that they are unreal, that they are a pretence. The way in which I confidently trust that the chair will take my weight suggests that I entertain no real possibility that it is not there. Philosophers like Wittgenstein have insisted that these 'practical certainties', things we do not doubt 'in deed', form the true foundations of our knowledge: the Cartesian method of doubt misconstrues this distinctive kind of certainty as a form of intellectual assent.   c.j.h.

*certainty.

R. Descartes, *Meditations*, in *The Philosophical Writings of Descartes*, tr. J. Cottingham *et al.* (Cambridge, 1985).
M. J. Ferreira, *Scepticism and Reasonable Doubt* (Oxford, 1986).

doxa. A Greek word signifying opinions, beliefs, conjectures, estimates. A very important notion in Aristotle's philosophical methodology, where it means the 'things that are said' by the many or the wise regarding some problem or issue which any adequate philosophical assessment must take into account justly and properly. The *'intuitions' often appealed to in modern moral philosophy, or in John Rawls's method of *'reflective equilibrium', are all *doxa*, but it is not obvious that philosophical theorizing need be constrained by such things.   n.j.h.d.

A notable treatment is given by G. E. L. Owen in '*Tithenai ta phainomena*', in *Logic, Science, and Dialectic* (Ithaca, NY, 1986).

doxastic virtues: *see* virtues, doxastic.

dread: see *Angst*.

dreams. Hallucinations in sleep? Philosophers have concerned themselves with dreams in three ways.

(1) *Dream scepticism*. The effectiveness of any self-applied waking-or-dreaming test presupposes that you did not merely dream you carried it out. Does it follow that you know neither that you are not dreaming nor any of those many things you think you know provided you are awake?

(2) *The interpretation of dreams.* Freud said dreams are the (disguised) fulfilment of a (repressed) wish. Are such explanations causal, purposive, or something else? And what would vindicate or refute them? Or is the point to change dreamers rather than to understand them?

(3) *The concept of dreams.* Given that most of what is reported as dreamt belongs to Cloud-cuckoo-land, is this remembering at all? If so, of what? And what would count as misremembering? Do dreams occur during sleep or are our waking impressions memory illusions?   J.E.R.S.

*psychoanalysis, philosophical problems of.

C. E. M. Dunlop (ed.), *Philosophical Essays on Dreaming* (Ithaca, NY, 1977).

Dretske, Fred I. (1932–). American philosopher, who has made significant contributions to epistemology, metaphysics, and the philosophy of mind. In the philosophy of perception he defended the idea that there is a 'non-epistemic' variety of visual experience—the sense of seeing an object that is attributable in purely extensional sentences. (*intentionality.) In epistemology he was one of the pioneers of the 'relevant alternatives' approach to *knowledge. In recent work, Dretske has offered a reductive account of the intentionality of mental states in terms of the notion of *information*—reliable lawlike correlation between types of phenomena. Clouds are reliably correlated with rain. There is a sense therefore in which clouds carry information about the presence of rain: they are 'reliable indicators' of rain. Dretske argues that intentionality can ultimately be reduced to such reliable indication.   T.C.

*perception; experience.

Fred I. Dretske, *Knowledge and the Flow of Information* (Oxford, 1981).
—— *Naturalizing the Mind* (Cambridge, Mass., 1995).

dualism. The theory that mind and matter are two distinct things. Its most famous defender is Descartes, who argues that as a subject of conscious thought and experience, he cannot consist simply of spatially extended matter. His essential nature must be non-material, even if in fact he (his soul) is intimately connected with his body. The main argument for dualism is that facts about the objective external world of particles and fields of force, as revealed by modern physical science, are not facts about how things appear from any particular point of view, whereas facts about subjective experience are precisely about how things are from the point of view of individual conscious subjects. They have to be described in the first person as well as in the third person.

Descartes argued that the separate existence of mind and body is conceivable; therefore it is possible; but if it is possible for two things to exist separately, they cannot be identical. A modern form of this argument has been presented by Saul Kripke, against recent forms of scientific materialism which claim that the relation of mental states to brain states is like the relation of water to H_2O. What happens in the mind clearly depends on what happens in

the brain, but facts about the physical operation of the brain don't seem to be capable of adding up to subjective experiences in the way that hydrogen and oxygen atoms can add up to water. Theoretical identifications of which both terms are physical and objective don't provide a model for identifications where one term is physical and the other is mental and subjective. However, while there are problems with the identification of mind and brain, it is not clear what other kind of entity could have subjective states and a point of view, either.

Substance dualism holds that the mind or soul is a separate, non-physical entity, but there is also *double aspect theory or property dualism, according to which there is no soul distinct from the body, but only one thing, the person, that has two irreducibly different types of properties, mental and physical. Substance dualism leaves room for the possibility that the soul might be able to exist apart from the body, either before birth or after death; property dualism does not. Property dualism allows for the compatibility of mental and physical causation, since the cause of an action might under one aspect be describable as a physical event in the brain and under another aspect as a desire, emotion, or thought; substance dualism usually requires causal interaction between the soul and the body. Dualistic theories at least acknowledge the serious difficulty of locating consciousness in a modern scientific conception of the physical world, but they really give metaphysical expression to the problem rather than solving it.

The desire to avoid dualism has been the driving motive behind much contemporary work on the mind–body problem. Gilbert Ryle made fun of it as the theory of 'the *ghost in the machine', and various forms of *behaviourism and *materialism are designed to show that a place can be found for thoughts, sensations, feelings, and other mental phenomena in a purely physical world. But these theories have trouble accounting for *consciousness and its subjective *qualia. Neither dualism nor materialism seems likely to be true, but it isn't clear what the alternatives are.   T.N.

*identity theory; mind–body problem.

René Descartes, *Meditations*.
S. Kripke, *Naming and Necessity* (Cambridge, Mass., 1980).
C. McGinn, *The Character of Mind* (Oxford, 1982).

Ducasse, Curt John (1881–1969). A French-born American philosopher who taught at Brown University and was an advocate and practitioner of *analytical philosophy before it became the dominant mode in the English-speaking world. In contrast to most analytical philosophers, however, Ducasse had a comprehensive philosophical system.

'When any philosophically pure-minded person sees a brick strike a window and the window break', Ducasse said in his attack on Hume on *causation, 'he judges that the impact of the brick was the cause of the breaking, *because* he believes that impact to have been the only change which took place then in the immediate environment of the window.' According to his adverbial view of sensing (influential on the epistemology of his student Chisholm), when we sense a red colour, the red colour is not a substantive but refers to a way of sensing—'I see redly'. Ducasse was also celebrated for his lifelong fascination with psychical research.   P.H.H.

P. H. Hare and Edward H. Madden, *Causing, Perceiving and Believing: An Examination of the Philosophy of C. J. Ducasse* (Dordrecht, 1975).

duck-rabbit. A visually ambiguous drawing, introduced by J. Jastrow. It can be perceived either as a duck or as a rabbit, but not both simultaneously. It constitutes the starting-point for Wittgenstein's study, in *Philosophical Investigations*, II. ix, of aspect perception. It exemplifies the concept-laden character of some forms of *perception, and provides a connecting link to examination of the perception of speech and writing.   P.M.S.H.

   *illusion.

S. Mulhall, *On Being in the World: Wittgenstein and Heidegger on Seeing Aspects* (London, 1990), 1–52.

Duhem, Pierre (1861–1916). French physicist, philosopher, and historian of science most famous for Quine's use of his thesis that theories cannot enjoy empirical consequences of their own, but only in complexes. Duhem's stated position varied from the thoroughgoing *instrumentalism of *To Save the Phenomena* to a *conventionalism tinged with what has been interpreted as structural realism in *Aim and Structure*. Whether any properties of the world can be inferred from the success of a physical theory, the power responsible for these successes was, for Duhem, the mathematical structure beloved of 'French' minds, rather than the strings and pulleys of English atomism. Thus Duhem was enamoured of—and contributed to—phenomenological thermodynamics as expressed in abstract differential equations.   N.C.
                                                         R.F.H.

   *holism.

P. M. M. Duhem, *To Save the Phenomena*, tr. E. Doland and C. Maschler (Chicago, 1969).
—— *The Aim and Structure of Physical Theory*, tr. P. Wiener (Princeton, NJ, 1982).

Dühring, Eugen (1833–71). A prominent socialist intellectual, Dühring was originally trained as a lawyer and came to teach philosophy and economics at the University of Berlin. Building on Feuerbach's materialism, Dühring developed an atheistic optimism allied to a fairly mechanistic sort of *positivism. From this he constructed proposals for the reform of society which were distinctly utopian. In 1875 he became the object of a polemic by Engels, entitled *Anti-Dühring*, in which Engels counterposed his own, and allegedly Marx's, *dialectical materialism to the supposedly cruder *materialism of Dühring.
                                                         D.McL.

Dummett, Michael (1925–). British philosopher of language, logic, and mathematics, noted for his exposition of Frege's philosophy and defence of *anti-realism. Dummett characterizes anti-realism in terms of a denial of the principle of *bivalence—the principle requiring that any assertoric sentence is either true or false. To hold that this principle fails for sentences concerning a given domain of discourse—such as past events, other minds, or mathematics—is to be, in Dummettian terms, an anti-realist with respect to that domain. Dummett's anti-realism stems from his approach to the theory of *meaning, and has affinities with verificationism. Like Davidson, Dummett believes that a learnable language must have a compositional semantics, but rather than associate sentence-meaning with realist truth-conditions Dummett associates it with assertibility-conditions, because whereas a child can be taught to recognize circumstances in which evidence suffices to justify the assertion of a sentence, it cannot be taught to grasp circumstances in which a sentence would be true independently of any evidence that might bear upon its truth. Consequently, if a sentence about (say) the past is such that neither it nor its negation is justifiably assertible, we can have, it seems, no genuine grasp of what it would be for that sentence to be true and its negation false, or vice versa.

   Dummett's views on anti-realism and the theory of meaning are intimately related to his work in logic and the philosophy of mathematics, especially his sympathetic treatment of *intuitionism. Yet at the same time he has perhaps done more than any other commentator to promote interest in Frege's philosophy of language and mathematics and to elevate Frege ahead of Russell, Moore, and Whitehead as founder of modern analytic philosophy—all this despite Frege's strong Platonist leanings, which run quite counter to intuitionist precepts.   E.J.L.

   *normalization; Tarot.

M. Dummett, *Frege: Philosophy of Language*, 2nd edn. (London, 1981).
—— *Truth and Other Enigmas* (London, 1978).
—— *The Seas of Language* (Oxford, 1993).
—— *Truth and the Past* (New York, 2004).

Duns Scotus, John (*c.*1266–1308). Scholastic philosopher, the 'Subtle Doctor', the original 'dunce', and, for Gerard Manley Hopkins, 'Of realty the rarest-veined unraveller', who was one of the great Christian *medieval philosophers. His critical attitude to Aquinas led to Ockham's more radical criticism.

   The details of Scotus' life are uncertain. He was born in Scotland and became a Franciscan. He did not live to revise his writings, and they are only now being properly edited and disentangled from spurious works. His genius lies not only in the novelty of his doctrines but also in his meticulous exposition and dissection of arguments, even when he accepted their conclusions. He believed, for example, in the immortality of the soul but regarded none of the arguments for it as conclusive; and, in discussing the proofs of God's existence, he took pains to distinguish those cases in which an infinite regress of causes is vicious (and thus needs to be curtailed by the postulation of an uncaused entity) from those in which it is not.

In his discussions of theological questions, he elaborated several doctrines that diverge from *Thomism. (He rarely mentions Aquinas, however, but attacks less eminent opponents such as Henry of Ghent.) He rejects negative theology, since 'negation is only known through affirmation'. Being (the subject of metaphysics), and other terms predicated of both God and creatures, are univocal. I may be certain that something, e.g. God, *is*, or is wise, but uncertain whether he is finite or infinite, created or uncreated; but my concept of being or of wisdom will be the same whichever of these alternatives is true. (This argument is open to an objection: If I overhear someone saying 'That's too hard', I may be certain that something is too hard, and that the speaker believes it to be so, while being uncertain whether what is referred to is a chair or a question; but it does not follow that 'hard' is univocal as applied to chairs and to questions. Analogously, the fact that we can believe God to be, while remaining uncertain of his categorial status, does not demonstrate the (otherwise plausible) conclusion that 'being' applies univocally to entities in different categories.) Moreover, concepts are derived from our acquaintance with creatures. If the concepts applied to God are not the *same* concepts, we can neither give a sense to them nor validly argue from premisses about creatures to truths about God.

He criticized a position close to Ockham's nominalism, arguing that things have 'common natures', e.g. the humanity common to Socrates and Plato. But he rejected the Aristotelian–Thomist view that individual things are distinguished by their (designated) matter and are thus not truly intelligible. Tweedledum is distinct from Tweedledee in virtue of his *haecceitas* or thisness, a formal feature intelligible to God and angels if not to fallen humanity: 'the ultimate specific difference is simply to be different from everything else'. The distinction between an entity's common nature, its *haecceity, and its existence is intermediate between a real and a conceptual distinction, namely, an 'objective formal distinction' (*distinctio formalis a parte rei*).

This type of distinction also obtains between the divine attributes, the powers of the soul, etc. The will, both of God and of man, is distinct from the intellect and not determined by it. The will does not necessarily choose the *summum bonum* even when it discerns it intellectually. Will, not intellect, plays the main part in our free ascent from worldly perfection to beatitude, the love of God. God too is free, and the world does not emanate from him by intelligible necessity, but results from his freely given love. By freely willing the moral law God makes it binding on us: 'To command pertains only to the appetite or will'. But the *content* of the primary precepts, e.g. that one should not worship other gods, is not determined by God's will; God wills them because they are intrinsically self-evident, and we cannot be dispensed from them. There are, however, secondary precepts which, though in harmony with

the primary, are neither derivable from them nor self-evident, and their content as well as their obligatoriness depends on God's will; from these he can dispense us. Scotus is half-way between Thomism and Ockham's view that all law stems from the will of God alone.

He was less fond than Aquinas of Aristotle's proof of God's existence from the occurrence of motion, not because the proof is invalid, but because God transcends the physical realm: 'it is a more perfect and immediate knowledge of the first being to know it as first or necessary being than to know it as first mover'. Proofs of God's existence must be a posteriori. But Anselm's *ontological argument is a 'probable persuasion', if not a demonstrative proof, as long it is appropriately 'coloured'. That is, Scotus (like Leibniz) added the premiss that the most perfect being is possible, i.e. can be 'thought without contradiction', but held that we cannot prove that it contains no contradiction from our inability to detect one.

His immense influence extends to Peirce and Heidegger as well as to his medieval followers.   M.J.I.

F. Copleston, *A History of Philosophy*, ii: *Mediaeval Philosophy*, pt. 2: *Albert the Great to Duns Scotus* (Westminster, Md., 1950).

R. Cross, *Duns Scotus* (New York, 1999).

E. Gilson, *Jean Duns Scot: Introduction à ses positions fondamentales* (Paris, 1952).

T. Williams (ed.), *The Cambridge Companion to Duns Scotus* (Cambridge, 2003).

A. B. Wolter, *The Philosophical Theology of John Duns Scotus* (Ithaca, NY, 1990).

Durkheim, Émile (1858–1917). From a French rabbinical family, he started his career teaching secondary-school philosophy, then sociology at the Universities of Bordeaux and Paris. He claimed that societies are irreducible entities, the laws governing which could not be derived from biology or psychology. 'Collective representations' of a society, such as social traits, customs, legal systems, languages, and 'group emotions' are said to 'exist outside the individual consciousness', on which they have an effect greater than the mere sum of the effects of other individuals. So sociology is a distinctive science with a distinctive subject-matter (which happily prevents sociologists being redundant).

What is 'normal' is relative to particular stages of society. Lack of social norms, or conflict between them, produces 'anomie', a moral lawlessness. Durkheim attempted functional explanations of the division of labour, primitive religions, etc. in terms of societies' (not individuals') needs.   A.J.L.

*anomie; society.

Émile Durkheim, *The Rules of Sociological Method*, tr. W. D. Halls, ed. Stephen Lukes (London, 1982).

Dutch book. A Dutch book has been made against you if you accept odds and make bets in such a way that you lose regardless of the outcome. For example, suppose you bet $4 at 5–2 that the Canadiens will win the Stanley Cup, and $4 at 5–2 that the Nordiques will win. Hedging, you then bet $7 at even odds that neither will win. Whoever wins, you lose: Dutch book!   J.J.M.

B. Skyrms, *Choice and Chance*, 3rd edn. (Belmont, Calif., 1986).

Dutch philosophy: *see* Netherlands philosophy.

duty. Along with the concepts of *'ought' and *'obligation', the concept of duty expresses moral action as *demanded* or *required*. 'The moral law', wrote Kant, is, for us, 'a law of duty, of moral constraint.' How is this cluster of concepts related to the contrasting cluster centring upon 'good' and the realization of value? For some moralists (including Kant again), 'Duty and obligation are the *only* names' for 'our relation to the moral law' (*Critique of Practical Reason*). For others, our duties, though not reducible to different terms, make sense only as regulating human life so as best to achieve good ends and to respect rational and sentient beings.

Certain performances, such as promise-making, generate duties to act in quite specific ways: other duties result from special relationships—parent to child, doctor to patient: others again are owed to living beings simply on the ground of their sentience or their rational, personal status.   R.W.H.

*supererogation.

D. P. Gautier, *Practical Reasoning* (Oxford, 1963).

I. Kant, *Critique of Practical Reason* (1788); tr. L. W. Beck (Chicago, 1949).

O. O'Neill, *Constructions of Reason* (Cambridge, 1989).

Dworkin, Ronald (1931–). American Professor of Jurisprudence at Oxford then London, whose explicitly liberal theory of law radically extends Hart's 'internal viewpoint' by treating philosophy of law as a primarily normative contribution to political, particularly judicial, deliberation. Moral, political, and legal theory should be not goal or duty-based but *rights-based, upholding principles (rights) over policies (collective goals), so as to respect everyone's right to equality of concern and respect (*Taking Rights Seriously* (1977)). This fundamental right requires that governments be neutral about worthwhile or worthless forms of life, and support even suicidal individual self-determination (*Life's Dominion* (1993)). Such principles are already part of the law; 'creative interpretation' (*Law's Empire* (1986)), seeking to make the law the best it can be, legally authorizes substantial transformations of 'settled law' by judges duty-bound to apply only law.   J.M.F.

*law and morals; law, philosophy of; moral scepticism.

Ronald Dworkin, *A Matter of Principle* (Cambridge, Mass., 1985).
Stephen Guest, *Ronald Dworkin* (Edinburgh, 1992).

dyadic: *see* relations.

E

earliest known philosophical term: see *apeiron*.

Earman, John (1942–). American philosopher, a member of the History and Philosophy of Science department at the University of Pittsburgh. He is best known for his work in the history and philosophy of modern physics. An early proponent of casting philosophical problems about space and time as conjectures within the mathematical language of space-time structure, he has probed, in the words of an early paper, the 'thicket of problems growing out of the intersection of mathematics, physics, and metaphysics'. He has explored this thicket in books on determinism, absolute and relational theories of space and time, and acausal space-time structure. Alongside books on Bayesian inference, and more recently on Hume's argument against miracles, he has maintained his technical expertise with work on inflationary cosmologies and quantum field theories.   E.R.J.

John Earman, *A Primer on Determinism* (Dordrecht, 1986).
—— *World Enough and Spacetime* (Cambridge, Mass., 1989).

ecological morality: *see* environmental ethics.

economic determinism: *see* base and superstructure.

economics, philosophy of. The philosophy of economics may be taken as the *philosophy of social science run with economic examples, in which case there is not much to be said specifically about it. Or it may be taken to designate a more or less distinct area of inquiry: one which overlaps with the philosophy of social science, as it is bound to do, but which is motivated by distinctively economic concerns. I shall take it here in the latter sense. Economics is a highly distinctive approach to social theory, and the philosophical problems which it raises are cast in nice perspective by contrasting it with other social disciplines of thought. I will consider the contrasts it displays with sociology, psychology, and politics.

The most striking contrast between economics and sociology—economics in the dominant neoclassical sense and sociology in the traditional, Durkheimian mould—is that economics is individualistic, sociology not. (*Social philosophy.) The individualist thinks that none of the aggregate patterns and pressures revealed in social science—or revealed otherwise—gives the lie to our general sense of the individual human agent, while the non-individualist denies this. The individualist holds that human agents conform to our commonplace folk psychology, being more or less rational in the attitudes they form and the choices they make. The non-individualist believes that individuals take second place, in a manner inconsistent with common sense, to the sorts of social regularities that social science is well equipped to reveal. For example, he may say that there are social regularities that are predetermined or predestined to obtain, in such a way that individuals are bound to act as the regularities require: they are bound to have the attitudes that lead by ordinary psychology to suitable actions; or they are bound, at whatever cost to their attitudinal coherence— they may 'go on the blink'—to display the behaviour involved.

The debate between *individualism and non-individualism does not have much prominence in the philosophy of economics, because individualism reigns almost unquestioned; unlike certain sorts of sociology, economics has never suggested that it has a new and iconoclastic image of the human being to offer. But a related, methodological question does often figure in current debates. Assuming that economics is individualistic in the more or less ontological sense explicated, does this mean that it must also be methodologically individualistic? Does it mean that economics must deny validity and interest to *explanations that relate events or patterns to aggregate antecedents: say, that it must reject as ill-conceived the sort of explanation that traces a rise in crime to a rise in unemployment or a decrease in religious practice to growing urbanization? This question is of particular relevance, because many so-called macro-economic explanations appear to be aggregate in character.

Whether or not economics can countenance such aggregate-level explanations, it is associated in practice with a style of individual-level explanation that marks a contrast with the explanations preferred in traditional sociology. This style of explanation involves two elements, one psychological, the other institutional. The psychological element suggests that given a certain circumstance or change or whatever, it is unsurprising that people should generally—or at least in significant numbers—come to behave in a certain way. The institutional element then goes on to show that given this shift in overall behaviour, there are bound to be certain consequences—in all likelihood, unintended consequences—that make for an aggregate change. If the consequences are thought of as beneficial, then the pattern identified in the explanation is traditionally described, in a phrase of Adam Smith's, as an invisible hand; if they are thought of as harmful, it is sometimes described as an invisible backhand or an invisible foot. Invisible hand and invisible backhand explanations are the very stuff of economic theorizing in the received, neoclassical mould.

So much for the contrast between economics and sociology. A second contrast that points us towards distinctive features of economics is that with psychology. Here there are a number of things to notice. Economics has traditionally been more or less behaviouristic in orientation, preferring to build a picture of the human subject out of actions displayed rather than on a reflective or introspective basis. Again, economics has traditionally been not just behaviouristic, but also rationalistic. It has assumed that decision theory is on the right tracks in seeking to explain human behaviour by reference to the maximization of expected utility: the maximization of expected preference-satisfaction. And, finally, economics has tended, at least in practice, to be egocentrically reductionistic, assuming that the preferences which human agents seek to satisfy are, on the whole, self-concerned or egoistic desires. These features of economics put it in contrast with many traditions of psychological theorizing and they even create tensions with our commonplace psychology. Economic psychology may not reject commonplace psychology in the manner of non-individualistic theories, but it gives a controversial gloss to much that that psychology contains. (Michael Bacharach and Susan Hurley (eds.), *Essays in the Foundations of Decision Theory*.)

The status of the psychological assumptions that economics makes is a matter at the core of the philosophy of economics: there is much discussion both of the necessity for such assumptions and of the plausibility of the assumptions made. The questions raised have been greatly sharpened with the increasing application of economic method, not just in the explanation of market and related behaviour, but also in the explanation of behaviour outside the market: for example, in the explanation of social interaction, as in so-called exchange theory, and in the explanation of political behaviour, as in what is known as the theory of public choice. Is it really reasonable to treat social and political agents as hard-headed and hard-hearted calculators of the kind that economics projects into the market-place? Some have thought that it is, on the grounds that human beings are always unconsciously of this cast of mind. Others have sought less dramatic means of vindicating the contribution that economics can make in non-economic domains. (Philip Pettit, *The Common Mind*, ch. 5.)

The final contrast that I want to mention is between economics and politics. Traditional political thinking, especially normative political thinking, is characterized by two features. First, a willingness to contemplate exogenous ideals—say, ideals of equality or liberty or solidarity—in the assessment of social and political institutions. And second, a tendency to assume that the main task in normative thought is just to argue for the ideals introduced and to provide a sense of what their institutionalization would involve. Economics breaks with both of these dispositions, being associated with quite a different sense of how normative thinking should go. (Geoffrey Brennan, 'The Economic Contribution'.)

Perhaps the main assumption of normative thinking in traditional economic circles—an assumption now frequently questioned (Amartya Sen, *Choice, Welfare and Measurement*; John Broome, *Weighing Goods*)—is that it is inappropriate to judge the institutions of a society except by reference to the preferences of the people they affect. This assumption is broadly utilitarian in character—unsurprisingly, since the history of economic thought was closely tied up with the utilitarian movement in the last century—but economics has given its own distinctive twist to the utilitarian thought. Arguing that we cannot compare preference-satisfaction across individuals and therefore cannot compute the level of total preference-satisfaction in a society—the exercise is not epistemologically feasible—economics has explored other ways of developing the preference-based idea. A development that gained momentum in the 1930s yielded the Pareto-criterion, according to which one arrangement is better than another if and only if it satisfies the preferences of some and does not frustrate the preferences of any. This criterion has been at the centre of what came to be known as welfare economics. Another, more recent development, and one which has made for a connection with philosophical discussions, suggests that one arrangement is better than another if and only if it would be preferred by suitable parties in a suitable collective choice. This contractarian development is of great contemporary importance.

But not only is economics distinguished by the role it gives to preferences in normative thinking, it is also marked off from traditional normative thought by the emphasis it places on feasibility. It is not enough, so economics suggests, to be able to identify a plausible ideal and to describe what it would institutionally require. What is also necessary is to be able to show that the institutionalization in question represents a feasible way of realizing the ideal: one that is currently accessible and one that would remain in place, if once established. There are many products of this concern with feasibility, among them the minimalist approach of F. A. Hayek, which argues that the information that good government would require in a more-than-minimal state is never going to be reliably available. Public choice theory and social choice theory are also products of this concern and they have had a major influence on contemporary political philosophy. (Iain McLean, *Public Choice*.)

The public choice theorist argues that it is silly to prescribe a form of government, or to allocate certain responsibilities to those in government, unless one has reason to believe that the arrangement is institutionally robust: at the least, it won't lead to worst results than would otherwise ensue. Public choice theory is meant to enable us to deal with the problem raised: to give us an idea of what to expect from those in government under this or that institutional amendment. The social choice theorist, on the other hand, is concerned with more abstract matters. He argues that there are many ways of aggregating individual preferences into a social preference-ordering—many ways of moving from what you want and what I want to what we should prefer as a group—that cannot simultaneously satisfy various attractive conditions; the most famous result in the area is Kenneth Arrow's impossibility theorem. Social choice theory castigates traditional theory for being over-relaxed about such matters and tries to explore questions about the aggregation of preferences in a systematic manner.

P.P.

*psychology and philosophy; capitalism; rational choice theory.

Michael Bacharach and Susan Hurley (eds.), *Essays in the Foundations of Decision Theory* (Oxford, 1991).
Geoffrey Brennan, 'The Economic Contribution', in R. E. Goodin and Philip Pettit (eds.), *A Companion to Contemporary Political Philosophy* (Oxford, 1993).
John Broome, *Weighing Goods* (Oxford, 1991).
Iain McLean, *Public Choice* (Oxford, 1987).
Philip Pettit, *The Common Mind* (New York, 1993).
Amartya Sen, *Choice, Welfare and Measurement* (Oxford, 1982).

economics and morality. All societies must make moral decisions on how their resources are to be distributed. But for every resource allocation that brings benefits, conditions of scarcity mean that there are associated burdens, or costs. The discipline of economics offers a method of analysis for comparing alternative distributions by clarifying what is at stake, in terms of the burdens associated with the benefits. However, the relationship between economics and morality is not straightforward. Neo-classical (Welfare) Economics (NCE), by far the most influential modern school, is based on a number of theoretical presuppositions that raise moral questions.

Though economists may seek a value-free analytic technique, specific value commitments underpin the way they conceptualize benefits and burdens. They employ a metric of comparison for alternative distributions, within which burdens can be counted against benefits. Yet, in order to do this in a 'value-neutral' framework, they make benefit gains relative to each person's own conception of value. This they do predominantly by adopting the metric of individual welfare, understood as the maximisation of preference satisfaction (although some alternatives have been offered).

To this individualized notion of welfare, economists add the principle that distributions which optimize welfare gains across individuals, according to the Pareto improvement and optimality theorems, are economically superior. Accordingly, the institution of the market is central to NCE. Under ideal conditions, a market is 'efficient' in its allocation of resources because, free, preference-based exchanges optimally maximize welfare (preference satisfaction).

These basic principles of individual welfare maximization, aggregation, the imperative to optimize gains, and market efficiency are not morally neutral; nor is it clear that they are compatible with important moral values. Trivially, distributions which satisfy these conditions may fail to respect rights or uphold communally important values, such as equality and fairness, unless one falsely identifies optimizing welfare allocations with fairness, or assumes that they respect rights. Less trivially, the idea that well-being can be understood in terms of maximizing preference satisfaction is controversial, as is claiming superiority for set-ups which optimally maximize it across individuals. Some goods, such as health or personal freedom, for example, may not be commensurable with other preference-satisfiers which can be exchanged on a market.

So even asking people to consider goods, like the environment or human relationships, solely in terms of preferences, especially those which can be expressed in market exchanges, seems morally distorting. Nor is it obviously ethically acceptable to treat persons in terms of one 'snapshot' of their preferences. These can change over time, and, more importantly, they can be responsive to reasons. Yet the value of political participation—influencing communal decisions through argument and discussion—is not itself expressible in terms of preferences in the market-place. Nevertheless, might not NCE help us with choices where all other morally relevant factors are taken into account? Whilst there is nothing wrong with reducing burdens, a moral problem remains for NCE. What counts as a burden, that which is costly, and what costs it is appropriate to associate with a choice, are questions themselves sensitive to moral judgement. It seems wrong, for example, to see the discharge of a moral duty as something for which one could be compensated.

NCE also employs a theory of rationality for individuals (rational choice theory) and for collectives (social choice theory). This aims both to explain actual states of affairs and to evaluate choices. The theory has a normative core which characterizes rational agent motivations as maximizing preference satisfaction and supplies axioms for ordering preferences. As a comprehensive description of rationality, then, the view places conditions on moral reasoning. For some philosophers, it even forms the basis of an account of morality. One response is that a plausible notion of good and bad reasons exists which is independent of actual preferences. It is not obviously rational for someone to act on their strong preferences for harming others, even if they can do so with impunity. The conclusions of rational choice theory, then, may sometimes compete with moral reasoning.

The productive successes of market economies, and paucity of viable alternatives to NCE, pose a different moral problem. Can we retain market benefits, without

NCE's theoretical presuppositions? It seems possible to do this by retaining the market, within a morally determined regulatory framework. However, this leaves us in need of a principle for determining to what degree personal choice (preference), versus moral duties to others, can legitimately play a role in setting economic priorities.   S. M-G.

*economics and philosophy; justice.

E. Anderson, *Value in Ethics and Economics* (Cambridge, Mass., 1993).

D. M. Hausman and M. S. McPherson, *Economic Analysis and Moral Philosophy* (Cambridge, 1996).

A. Sen, *On Ethics and Economics* (Oxford, 1989).

education, history of the philosophy of. A problem confronting anyone writing on the history of the philosophy of education is that many of the names mentioned in standard treatments of the topic, such as Pestalozzi, Froebel, and Hebart, are unlikely to be mentioned in standard histories of philosophy. Conversely, many if not most of the great philosophers have had little directly to say on the subject of education, and sometimes, as with Locke, when they do say something directly it is of little consequence. Nevertheless, despite this mismatch between philosophy and educational thinking, the topic of education does raise important philosophical issues. In concentrating on philosophers of importance *and* topics central to education, my account may be found somewhat revisionary.

The starting-point, though, must, as always, be Plato, whose *Republic*, though not exclusively that, is the first and greatest work in the philosophy of education. In the *Republic*, Plato is concerned with educating people in such a way that a just society is the outcome. Many would find this an extraordinary overestimation of the powers of education, and indeed it would be were education conceived in terms acceptable to a liberal democracy and did not involve, as Plato advocates, a form of child-farming. Plato is not concerned with the liberal ideal of individuals pursuing their own tastes and interests. He rejects the family and private property, at least for the rulers. For Plato, the good life is characterized rather by a general turning towards what is good and true outside of us and independently of us. Although this external good has left its traces deep within us, it is hidden and needs to be recovered by a process of externally directed discipline and thought. Each individual is born destined to play a particular type of role in a society which aims at the good, and will be happy when his own powers are so arranged as to enable him to fulfil this role. In such a society the rulers will possess the wisdom to guide the rest in the light of the good and the true.

In the good city there will be all the usual trades and crafts, and the majority of citizens should be trained to perform them, presumably learning reading, writing, counting, and the particular skills appropriate to their trade. But educators will notice that some youths are suited by temperament to guard and guide the city; those singled out need to be both brave and gentle. To produce soldiers of the right disposition, those selected will receive an education in music and gymnastics, based on the traditional classical Greek models. Music, which includes literature, will have to be uplifting and moral, rather than effeminate or disorderly. Poetry which shows the gods behaving disreputably and music which is barbaric or effete are ruled out. Gymnastics will train both bodies and characters.

The most selfless and steadfast of the guardians are to be educated further to become rulers of the city. For this, they will need to become philosophers, lovers of wisdom, skilled in science and reasoning (or what Plato calls dialectic). Both rulers and soldiers are to be brought into what is in effect an armed camp within the city, and taken away from their parents. For the rest of their lives they will possess everything in common, including wives and children. The presumption is that the offspring of the initial guardians will share their qualities and form the next generation of guardians.

Within the camp no one will know who his or her parents are. There will also be no distinction between the sexes, women being selected as guardians as much as men, and educated in the same way. Future generations of guardians will be told that they have been bred for the city. Their philosophizing is not for their own satisfaction only, but is so that they can rule and instruct the rest.

Simply to recount Plato's proposals may seem to have little philosophical point. There are, though, certain themes which have recurred in educational thinking since Plato's time: the idea that education and individual lives are ideally for the sake of the state, not for the sake of the individual alone; the idea that education is as much about the building of character as of intelligence in our sense (which is the case even with the rulers' philosophizing, which is all directed towards a type of static wisdom which is coterminous with moral goodness); and the idea that education is capable of transforming individual minds and characters so as to produce acceptance of a revolutionary communist project.

Plato's doubtless exaggerated assessment of the power of education nevertheless leads him to write scathingly and brilliantly of forms of education of which he disapproves. He writes of the schoolmaster in a democratic society who 'fears and flatters his pupils' and the pupils who consequently despise him, of old men who, ridiculously, condescend to the young, 'imitating their juniors in order to avoid the appearance of being sour or despotic'. For Plato, although education is communistic, it cannot be democratic or, in the modern sense, child-centred. Even though within us there are the seeds or traces of wisdom, wisdom eludes the grasp of the young, who are wayward and blind and who have to be trained over many years to have the right dispositions and thoughts. Education then cannot proceed on the basis of the current interests of the young. The philosophers, indeed, have a duty, which is painful for them, of descending into the *cave metaphorically occupied by the unenlightened, so as to instruct and rule them. And wisdom is fixed and one. So a pluralistic approach to value or education is rejected.

Like much else in philosophy, philosophy of education continually rehearses Platonic themes: authoritarian or child-centred? dictatorial or pluralistic? collectivistic or individualistic? And there is also continual worrying at the relationship between what is already inside the child and what is to be received from without. Of course, strange transmogrifications have happened on the way. The train of thought now known as liberal education, as reflected in the writings of Michael Oakeshott, say, would agree with Plato in rejecting child-centredness, but disagree with him on the fixity of knowledge and on the nature of the state. It would agree with Plato on the importance of learning what has been discovered, but disagree with him on the closure of traditions of thought. And while it would give some thought to the importance of moral education, it would tend to view education in far more intellectualist terms than Plato, claiming that intellectual disciplines and their content are worth learning for themselves irrespective of any moral improvement they bring.

We have no systematic treatise by Aristotle on education, but he would have shared Plato's suspicion of teachers who are afraid to appear despotic. He also made some suggestive remarks about the need to inculcate the right dispositions in the young before encouraging them to reflect on morality and politics. (Otherwise their reasoning will be clever rather than wise.) And he endorsed the classical stress on music and gymnastics in terms similar to Plato. But, although he saw the happy individual as playing a role in public affairs, he saw the gaining of knowledge by individuals as an end in itself and not to be justified in terms of the contribution this might enable an educated individual to make to the state. For Aristotle men have intrinsic desire to know and understand, which it is part of their nature to pursue. Here Aristotle was close to Socrates' dictum that the unexamined life is not worth living. He was also closer to the individualism of Socrates than to the Plato of the *Republic*.

During the Christian era, Platonic themes resurface, notably in the writings of St Augustine. Human nature needs to be turned to the light because of original sin and its enmeshment in body. The young are not yet rational. They need instruction in the basic subjects. The content of what is taught is censored, and the aim of elementary education will be the prevention of idleness. Only in the higher stages, with the study of philosophy and theology, will anything like full rationality be possible. Augustine sees God as the source of all truth and analyses learning quasi-Platonically as a form of opening ourselves to an inner divine illumination, an opening which, as with Plato, does not preclude didactic teaching methods.

While not accepting Augustine's Platonic view of knowledge, most Christian writers on education up to the time of Luther and St Ignatius of Loyola saw education in terms of the salvifically necessary transmission of truths established and revealed. Even with the recovery of pagan learning in the Renaissance the stress is on imparting to the young what has been learned. There is, though, something of a sea-change, in the seventeenth century, with its dismissal of past authority, and stress on individual experience. Thus Francis Bacon, who believed that the truth about nature would be manifest to the individual who engaged in presuppositionless observation, opposed the foundation of Charterhouse school on the grounds that its curriculum was to be based on the ancient classics. He wrote: 'what happiness it would be to throw myself into the river Lethe, to erase completely from my soul the memory of all knowledge, all art, all poetry; what happiness it would be to reach the opposite shore, naked like the first man.' Education should, therefore proceed by the learner making his own observations and discoveries, without external direction. Locke was not so sanguine as Bacon about the possibility of learning much about the world through the senses, although he believed with Bacon that we have no other access to the world. Locke, accordingly, emphasized the moral aspects of education, at the expense of the intellectual and scientific. But he agreed with Bacon's thoroughly utilitarian approach to knowledge and to education, both, in Bacon's terms, to be directed to 'the relief of man's estate'.

Throughout the seventeenth and eighteenth centuries, schools and universities went on traditionally. The new philosophies of Bacon and Descartes which stressed individual discovery and reasoning and which downplayed didactic instruction had little effect on curriculum or pedagogy. It is indeed doubtful that *any* philosophy had any significant effect on the practice of education prior to the beginning of the nineteenth century, when the ideas of Rousseau and his followers Pestalozzi and Froebel began to make an impact.

Rousseau's *Émile* (1762), in common with many of his other writings, is a sustained criticism of civilization as it existed in Rousseau's time. Although, in Rousseau's words at the start of *Émile*: 'God made all things good, man meddles with them and they become evil.' We are born free, but live in chains. Our first natural impulses are always right, yet society, by encouraging envy and vanity, makes us into civilized monsters, suffering and causing suffering. The child, moreover, is not a miniature adult, but a creative being with its own particular needs and desires, which should be allowed to 'indulge its sports, its pleasures, its delightful instincts'. *Émile* was a heady brew, combining nature-worship, child-centredness, an emphasis on doing and discovery at the expense of reading and being taught, and a pervasive hatred of the existing order of things, from which the child must be protected. Its actual proposal, to allow each Émile to develop 'naturally' and in isolation from society, under the exclusive tutelage of a Rousseauian guide or, in today's terms, 'facilitator', is as impracticable as Plato's. Nevertheless despite an ineradicable lack of clarity about what Rousseau means by nature and uncertainty about the benefit to be gained by following nature's impulses, *Émile*'s influence can be seen in every primary school in the Anglo-Saxon world. (France, perhaps surprisingly, has so far remained somewhat immune.) Rousseau's work can also be seen as the start of a pervasive interest in the details of child development in educational thought, even if the details of the work of such as Piaget and Kohlberg owe more to the category-based philosophical psychology of Kant than to Rousseau himself.

Despite differing radically on the beneficence of an unreformed nature, Plato and Rousseau were at one in seeing education as part of an overarching political and social project. So, indeed, did Dewey, whose philosophy of education combines Rousseauian child-centredness and hostility to traditional learning with a pragmatic socialism. Throughout his long and active life, Dewey was involved with experimental schools and educational reform. He linked meaningful education with the child's own attempts to solve problems arising from its own fundamentally social experience. The 'full meaning' of studies is secured only when they become 'integral parts of the child's conduct and character . . . as organic parts of his present needs and aims—which in turn are social'. Traditional education produces only barren symbols and flat residues of real knowledge. In addition it reinforces and perpetuates *élitism and social divisions. The classroom should be 'a social enterprise in which all individuals have an opportunity to contribute', in which 'all are engaged in communal projects', a sort of democracy in miniature in which the teacher himself is not an 'external boss or dictator', imposing curricular standards alien to the pupils' lives and experiences, but rather the 'leader of group activities', who gives the group not 'cast-iron' results, but rather starting-points to be developed through the contributions of all involved.

Dewey hopes that children will discover everything which it is useful for them to know by working on projects suggested by objects and materials from their everyday life. If this means that they never get round to studying the history and classics prescribed by the traditional curriculum, so much the better. Dewey shares Rousseau's hostility to all that. He is, in addition, Baconian in his hostility to an inner life which is not generally shared and shareable, and also to any form of study not clearly directed to practical problem-solving.

There will be little need to emphasize the way in which Dewey's educational ideas are, like Rousseau's, live. Dewey reinforces Rousseau's child-centredness with the Baconian thought that what the child should be centring on are problems and practice. Dewey would obliterate any distinction between training (in what conduces to the pursuit of practical problem-solving) and education (in what it is good to know in and for itself).

Education, in this sense, is a thoroughly classical concept, which since the time of Socrates and Aristotle has never entirely disappeared in institutions of learning. Even in medieval times, the minority who studied philosophy and theology strove to understand the rationale for what the rest believed, and perhaps only a minority will ever be capable of rationality in that sense. Similarly, even the most Baconian and Deweyesque programmes of study have never succeeded entirely in quenching the desire of some for a more liberal education. Nor has the notion of liberal learning as an end in itself lacked vocal and eloquent defenders, whenever it has been under threat.

Thus, in the nineteenth century Matthew Arnold and Cardinal Newman both preached the virtues of an education in which the pupil would, in Arnold's words, be inducted into 'the best that has been thought and said'. Arnold, the school inspector, hoped that a kingdom in which such an education prevailed would be bathed in sweetness and light. His ideas owe something to Schiller, who hoped for a similar result from aesthetic education, and something to Coleridge, who wrote of a non-religious clerisy, an educated élite who would leaven the rest of society. Newman is notable for his insistence on a rounded education, the aim of which was not narrow specialism, but development of the capacity to see all things in relation to each other. Whether Newman thought this was a possibility in schooling prior to the university education about which he actually wrote is unclear, but the tenor of his thought is undoubtedly in the tradition of Socrates and Aristotle.

But does a liberal education of the sort envisaged by Arnold and Newman produce the results they wanted? Can it? As we have already seen, Rousseau and Dewey, in their different ways, argue that an education based on authority and cultural canons may alienate, produce only inert knowledge, and be socially divisive to boot. Nietzsche, too, wrote of the grammar school education from which he profited as producing only pedants and old maids. More radically, in his deconstructive moods, he questioned whether what we claimed to know and value was either true or valuable as opposed to a mask for power relations and (not entirely consistently) whether the scientific quest to discover the truth about nature and ourselves was not, in a deep sense, life-denying. And, today, those who see education in terms of the transmission of the best that has been thought and known are haunted by the image of the Goethe-reading camp commandant and Hitler's enthusiasm for Beethoven's Ninth Symphony.

My own feeling is that since Plato philosophers have expected too much and often the wrong things from education. Education should indeed touch the soul, and turn it, though it is a moot point whether it should turn it inward, as suggested, though in rather different ways, by both Plato and Rousseau. It should involve the formation of habits of behaviour and learning, habits which, *contra* Rousseau, are not in any obvious sense natural. But even the best moral education cannot guarantee a moral response, nor, *contra* Plato, Rousseau, and Dewey, an improved society. And the recommendations of Rousseau and Dewey are educationally harmful if they direct educators away from what education can and ought to do: namely to introduce the young to what their elders believe is the best that has been done in the various forms of knowledge and experience that have been developed.

Doing that, even successfully, is no guarantee against wickedness, individual or social. But there are forms of barbarism other than those of the tyrant; and a society which, in the spirit of Bacon and Dewey, makes no distinction between education and training for problem-solving is one.   A.O'H.

M. Arnold, *Culture and Anarchy* (London, 1869).

D. E. Cooper, *Authenticity and Learning* (London, 1983).

J. Dewey, *Democracy and Education* (New York, 1916).

M. Oakeshott, *The Voice of Liberal Learning* (New Haven, Conn., 1989).

A. O'Hear, *Education, Society and Human Nature* (London, 1981).

R. S. Peters, *Essays on Educators* (London, 1981).

education, problems of the philosophy of. An area where philosophical understanding is applied to the illumination of issues in education—where this notion covers upbringing within the family as well as learning in schools and other institutions. Systematic studies of this kind began in the USA in the mid-twentieth-century and slightly later in Britain and its commonwealth. To begin with, much work was done on investigating concepts like education, teaching, and indoctrination, on the assumption that to be a regular, respectable branch of philosophy like aesthetics or philosophy of religion, philosophy of education required its own puzzling concepts paralleling the concepts of art or god. Over time, however, work on these notions proved to be not so much puzzling as unbearably dull. Most philosophers of education in Britain, Holland, and Canada, as well as in more enlightened corners of the USA and Australasia, began to reconstrue their discipline as a form of applied philosophy, whose task is to clarify the aims, content, methods, and distribution of education appropriate to contemporary society. As such, philosophy of education in some ways resembles *medical ethics, which brings moral philosophy and philosophy of mind to bear on dilemmas faced by health care professionals. The philosophical horizons of philosophy of education are, however, wider, covering—as we shall see—issues drawn from virtually every area of general philosophy.

Hirstian liberal education. A major preoccupation over the past three decades has been with an education, parental or institutional, suitable for a liberal society. Paul Hirst's early and influential account of liberal education saw it as the development of the student's rational mind, consisting in an induction into logically distinct patterns of reasoning and imagining found in various 'forms of knowledge'—mathematics, physical science, human science, history, philosophy, literature and the fine arts, moral knowledge, and (possibly) religion—each with its own unique concepts and tests for truth.

A liberal education in this sense was all about acquiring these forms of knowledge for their own sake—as contrasted with some extrinsic purpose as when studying physics to become an engineer. The theory was popular with educational reformers up to government level wishing to extend to the many the rigorous intellectual education hitherto enjoyed only by the few.

But it ran into difficulties. These were partly specific—about whether, for instance, there are unique concepts in history, or whether literature and the fine arts constitute a form of *knowledge. But there was also a more general problem about why the central aim should be the pursuit of knowledge for its own sake. Hirst's Kantian or 'transcendental' defence, found also in Peters, that one cannot sensibly ask why knowledge should be pursued because the questioner is already committed to its pursuit, proved unconvincing—partly because a sceptical questioner is clearly *not* so committed.

Educational aims in a liberal society. It became clear that one had to start further back than Hirst, with a comprehensive assessment of educational aims. This, in turn, demanded some picture of the kind of society within which these aims would operate. In the last thirty years work on aims and content has usually been conducted within a liberal-democratic framework and has been, and continues to be, strongly influenced by ideas in general philosophy on *liberalism and liberal values.

Much of the recent history of philosophy of education can be read as an attempt to formulate a defensible account of an education suitable for a liberal society and to detach this from more problematic versions. Already the Peters–Hirst version of liberal education had drawn the fire of some Marxists and other left-wingers who saw the pursuit of knowledge for its own sake as an ideal suitable only to a leisured élite.

Many writers have located a more universally applicable aim in the cultivation of personal *autonomy. The basic notion here is that everyone should be equipped to determine his or her own major goals in life and not have these paternalistically imposed, whether by custom, parents, teachers, or political leaders. This is not, of course, to rule out aims to do with expanding knowledge, since in order to be autonomous one needs a good understanding of options available to one, as well as of the social world within which one chooses one's goals. But the focus is now less exclusively than with Hirst on the pursuit of knowledge for its own sake.

Quite what the autonomy ideal should include beyond this bare statement has been the topic of much dispute, some invoking the notion of following a life plan, others rejecting this, some putting what others see as excessive weight on rationality, and so on. Personal autonomy has also had to be distinguished from the more general notion of personal well-being. In tradition-directed societies those responsible for children's upbringing seek to promote their well-being, but hardly their autonomy, given that goals are ascribed by custom and not chosen. The practical import of this is clear as soon as one reflects on the multicultural nature of British or American society and the duties which religions may impose upon parents and communities to bring up their children in values at odds with personal autonomy. Should the liberal state favour aims to do with self-determination, or should it be neutral for all but commonly agreed values? Should it prevent parents and non-state schools from bringing children up in non-liberal values? Much will turn in these discussions on how terms like 'liberal', 'autonomy', and 'neutrality' are interpreted.

Further issues arise about the nature of personal *well-being. If this is in part to do with the achievement of one's major goals, then are there limits on what these can consist in? An educator will certainly want to rule out goals which harm other people. In general philosophy the claim that personal flourishing necessarily involves altruistic or moral concern has been constantly disputed since Thrasymachus' challenge to Socrates in book 1 of *Plato's Republic. From the educator's point of view, however, there seems every reason to bring children up to see their own good as inextricably intermeshed with others'.

On this view, moral education would not be, as it is often taken to be, a separate area of education. Yet whatever its status, there are differences in its conception. Commonly it has had to do with bringing about behaviour in accordance either with moral codes or with higher-order rational moral principles. But recent work on virtue ethics has called this rules-based approach into question, suggesting that we should rather think first of how to bring children up to be kind, courageous, friendly, co-operative, loyal. (*Virtues.) This is a far from being an ivory-tower matter: it has implications, for instance, for the way we think about teacher-training—as well as about parental education and the role of the media in the formation and deformation of character.

Another uncertainty over the notion of personal well-being is whether what John Stuart Mill called the 'higher' *pleasures—intellectual and aesthetic enjoyments—must form a part of a child's future goal-structures, or whether, say, a life of well-being could consist wholly in sex, drinking Budweiser, watching TV, and playing computer games. Have parents and teachers any responsibility to steer children towards the more exalted alternative, or would the true liberal leave things wholly open?

Of course, in promoting autonomy educators will in any case want to open up intellectual and aesthetic activities as possible options, but there may be grounds for them to do more than this. Suppose we take experience of the arts. If the theory is true that this constitutes an autonomous world of its own, so that listening to music is docketed as a leisure pursuit on all fours with pumping iron or bass-fishing, educators may have to be content with the 'options' position. But if aesthetic experience has deeper contributions to make to human well-being—as a form of social bonding, for instance, or as a way of promoting self-understanding or psychic harmony—parents and teachers may well be justified in encouraging pupils to adopt a way of life in which the arts occupy an important place. (*Aesthetics, problems of.)

At the root of many of these issues about personal well-being is the question whether this notion is to be understood in terms of the satisfaction of major informed preferences or in some other way. On the preference-satisfaction account, the education system and the market for consumer goods and services, so often seen as at odds over their values, could be seen as working hand in hand, each having the function of revealing and supplying possible intrinsic ends—further study of science, say, in the first case, and personalized number-plates on the other. Another view of personal well-being sees this not as a function of individual desire, but in terms of the attainment of such goods as intimacy, self-knowledge, autonomy, aesthetic activity, physical pleasures—although there are still unresolved issues about whether these goods are derivable in some way from human nature or culturally generated. On the second view of well-being, education has a role *distinct* from that of the market—in revealing these goods to learners and disposing them to value them. Further work on the aims of education depends on the resolution of this central issue, which has now become a major focus of debate in general ethics.

Education and politics. Vocational aims lie outside a Hirstian account of liberal education, but other accounts which stress personal autonomy will seek to equip pupils with an understanding of a wide range of vocational as well as non-vocational options. There are also wider issues about what attitudes parents, teachers, and other educators should encourage towards work in general. Is there still room for some version of the traditional 'work-ethic', or is this a jettisonable remnant from a more religious culture? What place does work play in personal well-being, intrinsically as well as instrumentally? Does only 'meaningful work' count? Should education be for a Work Society or for an Activity Society?

Education for work, in its turn, is inextricable from education for citizenship, about which there are, again, different variants, partly depending on one's view of a liberal society. Leaner ones focus only on the knowledge required for informed political decisions, while others add to this the dispositions, or political virtues, demanded of the citizen. Should the education system have a hand in nurturing such qualities as tolerance, a sense of justice, political courage, and civic friendship? Or when it transcends the aim of mere understanding and begins to shape young people's characters in a certain direction, is it becoming a vehicle of indoctrination?

What place among political virtues should there be for attachment to one's national community? Is education for patriotism at odds with liberal values, since it favours the interests of a particular community rather than those of human beings more generally? Some philosophers have argued that we should think more in terms of education for global citizenship—while others have claimed that patriotism is not the same as chauvinism and that imbuing a love of country need not bring with it the idea that that country is somehow superior to others.

So much for aims of education, closely intertwined as they are. One task of philosophy of education is to explore interrelationships between them in the interests of a coherent, synoptic, and defensible account. The content of aims apart, there is also the question of who should determine them. While some other countries have recently loosened state control in favour of schools and teachers, England and Wales moved in 1988 from professional to political determination of the curriculum. Many of us would applaud political control in principle, holding that there are good reasons for it in the democratic right of every citizen—as distinct from sectional groups like teachers or parents—to participate in major decisions shaping the social future. At the same time there are good liberal reasons why teachers should be given considerable autonomy in implementing these decisions. Political control of aims and curricula should be far from heavy-handed. Whether the detailed, test-led, minutely prescriptive, and incoherent provisions of the 1988 National Curriculum met this requirement is not a matter on which a philosopher should pronounce. In 2000 the English and Welsh school curriculum was provided—for the first time in its history, remarkably enough—with an extensive set of general aims. In so far as these are adequate, they provide a touchstone for assessing how much of the traditional content of school education needs to be retained. Is there still a place for religious education? What weight should be placed on acquiring a foreign language? What room is there for contemporary history in schools? Why learn maths? How justified is the traditional weight on theoretical enquiry as compared with practical activity and rationality? At the more school-focused end of their work, philosophers of education in several countries are now working with policy-makers on questions like these.

That the state should play *any* role in determining the curriculum would be rejected by some libertarian thinkers about education. The content of schooling, like its provision, is, on their view, ideally a matter for the private sector. Their views overlap with those of some religious thinkers anxious to preserve and enlarge the domain of private faith schools. The assumption in both views is that parents should have the right to determine what the aims and content of their children's education should be. (We are talking of moral rights. That they have legal rights in many contexts is uncontestable.) This is often asserted, but the grounds for it are dubious. Parents do not own their children, so no right can be based on this. But neither are they in a privileged position to know what is in the best interest of their children, as individuals and as citizens. While parents have rights arising from their responsibilities—e.g. the right to exclude a busybody neighbour from interfering with their child's upbringing—it is not at all clear whether they have any other kind of moral right.

Over the last three decades the force of Aristotle's insistence that education must begin from a political framework has become increasingly evident. Here the distribution of education has been much discussed. Would it be fairer to give all children a common education in the same schools? Or to divide them by school and curriculum according to their IQ, giftedness, specialist talents, parents' religious and other preferences, parents' ability to pay for private education? To egalitarians, arguments for

division often appear flaky rationalizations of an élitist, class-based system. Are intelligence and giftedness, as claimed, largely innate (see below)? What is giftedness, anyway? Is the 'equality of opportunity' on which arguments for selection often rely another vehicle of rationalization?

Some see a stronger argument for a selective system in the claim that giving able students special provision is in the general interest, since this will help to maximize the benefits they are likely to bestow on society and the economy—or, following *Rawls's 'difference principle', in the claim that this is likely to improve the well-being of the most disadvantaged. Are these arguments more solid? Is there too much obsession with selection, as some would say, at the cost of doing more, and more immediately, for the educationally deprived?

Children's minds and learning. 'Child-centred' education can mean different things, including—defensibly—an education which puts children's flourishing first and school subjects second. It can also refer to a conception of education as a process of biological development akin to the growth of plants or animal bodies. It is doubtful whether the notions of mental or moral development—found, for instance, in theories like Piaget's—make logical sense. If development is always development towards a biologically given mature state (such as the fully grown tree or human body), it might seem that nothing could count as this in the non-physical areas just mentioned. An assumption in developmentalism, shared with other psychological theories applied to education, like those of Chomsky and Skinner, is that learning is a matter of an individual's causal interactions with the environment, whether or not these are also powered by developmental forces from within.

These psychological viewpoints bring us back again to the wider issue of what education is appropriate for a liberal society. One conception of this, reflected in the theories just mentioned, starts, as classical liberalism in general started, from a picture of pupils as atomic individuals. On an alternative model, heavily influenced by Wittgensteinian arguments against the possibility of private conceptual schemes, learning is essentially a social enterprise, involving the induction of the pupil into publicly agreed rules, practices, and values. This second view lies behind the 'forms of knowledge' approach to the curriculum, as well as behind broader and more recent conceptions, in some ways more Deweyan in outlook, stressing induction into a wider range of co-operative social activities and institutions, including, as well as intellectual and aesthetic activities, occupations, sports and leisure, family life, and attachments to local or national communities.

Whether a liberal account of education can accommodate these more collective purposes is central to the increasingly embattled debates between liberal and communitarian thinkers in the field. If liberalism is tied, as some claim, to atomistic notions of the person, to the hegemony of the free market, and to the privileging of egoism over altruism, are its days not rightly numbered? Or are those right who say that a liberal education can encompass and celebrate the idea that individuals are social beings and should cherish their interpersonal attachments, whether at the level of intimate relationships or more widely at the level of the nation or other forms of community?

Underlying any account of education must lie some kind of conception of *human nature. The relative weight to be placed on biological and on social aspects of this is a central issue in the field. It emerges, for instance, in discussions of whether concepts can be acquired by abstraction from experience—a topic which links Locke directly with the child-centred nursery. It is at the root of controversies about the nature of intelligence and the IQ, concepts which in their Galtonian form interestingly share the assumption in biological developmentalism that there are ceilings (of the mature tree) beyond which individuals cannot move. The political significance of such an assumption should be plain. If many children possess low intellectual ceilings, there seems a powerful reason for providing them with a different, less demanding form of education than the more able. This is one of the arguments for a selective system, already mentioned. But what justification is there for the view that we all have our individually differing mental ceilings? Is it verifiable? Is it falsifiable? Or is it, as some would say, as untestable as beliefs at the heart of other ideological systems, like the belief in the existence of God?

More generally, differences over human nature lie behind the broad division among those philosophies of education, often of *Kantian inspiration, like those of Peters and the early Hirst, which see education above all as developing (in the transitive sense) forms of rationality; and those, often influenced by *Aristotle, which, while still attached to rationality, especially practical rationality, pay more attention to the ways in which our biologically given desires and feelings are shaped into virtues, activities, attitudes, and reactions necessary to our flourishing. (Hirst, in his more recent writings, has forsaken the first for the second camp.)

The topic of the education of *emotion and feeling illustrates this division. On one view, found in Peters, emotion is a form of passivity which can obstruct the rational life: children need to learn how to control and canalize it and bring it under the sway of reason. On another, emotions have also a more positive, active role, fear, anger, and sympathy, for instance, being the bases of children's acquisition of the virtues of courage, self-control, and altruistic virtues like friendliness and benevolence. The educative role of the arts, especially literature, in such a refinement of the emotions brings us back to the place of aesthetic activities in the good life and the liberal curriculum.

These are some of the ways in which philosophers have investigated children's minds. Another area of interest has been in thinking skills. Governments across the world have recently promoted these in school curricula, often in the belief that teaching generalizable skills of logical, creative, and critical thinking is an antidote to the regime of fact learning and rote recall which plagues educational systems from Nanjing to Nantucket. But do general thinking skills exist? In what way can the critical thinking developed in history lessons be transferred to the mathematics classroom? Are there logically different kinds of imagining and reasoning found in epistemologically different areas—a claim we saw embedded in the Hirstian form of liberal education?

There is much in this brief account which has had to be omitted—work, for instance, on the cultivation of the imagination, higher education, lifelong learning, the nature of mathematical education, the teaching of history, the Internet, and a host of other specific topics—to say nothing of more grandiose abstract inquiries into the challenges and perils of something called *post-modernism.　　J.P.W.

*teaching philosophy.

E. Callan, *Creating Citizens* (Oxford, 1997).
D. E. Cooper (ed.), *Education, Values and Mind* (London, 1986).
D. W. Hamlyn, *Experience and the Growth of Understanding* (London, 1978).
P. Hirst, *Knowledge and the Curriculum* (London, 1974).
J. Kleinig, *Philosophical Issues in Education* (London, 1982).
R. S. Peters (ed.), *The Philosophy of Education* (Oxford, 1973).
K. Strike, *Liberty and Learning* (Oxford, 1982).
J. White, *The Child's Mind* (London, 2002).

Edwards, Jonathan (1703–58). Perhaps the foremost of Puritan theologians and philosophers, Edwards, after graduating from Yale in 1720, held a series of pastorates and ministerial posts in the American colonies. This left him time to compose the writings in which he systematizes and justifies the Puritan theme of the utter dependence of humanity and nature on God.

Edwards argues from the unthinkability of the notion of absolute nothingness to the eternal existence of being; this necessary eternal being must be infinite and omnipresent and cannot be solid. It can only be space, or God. Furthermore, consciousness and being are the same since it is unthinkable that something could exist from all eternity and nothing be conscious of it.

There is another route to this same idealistic conclusion. Edwards agrees with the view often attributed to Locke that secondary qualities such as colour and taste exist not in objects but in the mind. But Edwards holds that *primary qualities have a similar existence: solidity is just resistance, shape is the termination of resistance, and motion is the communication of resistance from space to space. Yet 'resistance is nothing else but the actual exertion of God's power'; so resistance exists in God's mind and 'the world is therefore an ideal one', existing in God's mind through his free act of creation and in our minds through God's communicating it to us in a series of regular ideas. These claims, reminiscent of Berkeley, were probably arrived at without any knowledge of Berkeley's reasoning.

As the world is entirely dependent on God's continued creation of it, so our wills are entirely dependent on the causes that God has predestined for them. The Arminians of Edwards's time believed that human choices were spontaneous and self-determined. This violates the principle of universal causality that Edwards took from Newton; thus an act of will is determined by its strongest motives. Further, to say that in a *free act a free choice determines the will involves an infinite regress, for on this characterization that free choice must be determined by a prior free choice, and so on.

The solution is to deny any meaningfulness to talk of a free will—rather freedom is something that belongs to a *person* when not hindered in doing what one wills. How one comes to perform this act of willing has no bearing on its freedom; thus Edwards can hold that choices can be entirely predestined by God and nevertheless that an agent not prevented from carrying them out is free. Indeed Edwards can reconcile freedom not only with *Calvinism but with Newtonian science, which sees nature as entirely determined.

Moral judgements are based on sentiment and not on reason: by a sense of beauty one perceives the beauty of heart, or virtuous motive, in a virtuous act. There are two kinds of *beauty—there is benevolence or love of being in general, which is the only true, spiritual, or divine beauty, and which is relished by a divine sense activated by God only in the few he has elected to heaven. The other kind of beauty consists in harmony, proportion, and uniformity in variety; this is a secondary, natural, inferior beauty perceived by a natural sense. Although nothing is approved by the one sense not approved by the other, true virtue consists in acting according to the former beauty. Only the saint whose inner motives have been entirely changed by God is capable of acting without the taint of self-love found even in the most just or altruistic but non-saintly individuals. Once again Edwards unifies his religious commitments with secular thought: an ethics of sainthood is reconciled with an account of ordinary ethical belief.   C.C.

Norman Fiering, *Jonathan Edwards' Moral Thought in its British Context* (Chapel Hill, NC, 1981).
Sang Hyun Lee, *The Philosophical Theology of Jonathan Edwards* (Princeton, NJ, 1988).
John E. Smith, *Jonathan Edwards: Puritan, Preacher, Philosopher* (Notre Dame, Ind., 1993).

Edwards, Paul (1923–). American philosopher who is mixed one part analytic philosopher to one part *philosophe. Although Edwards is best known as the editor-in-chief of the *Encyclopedia of Philosophy* (8 vols., 1967), a massive Enlightenment work with a notable analytic sensibility, his own widely discussed work focuses on such traditional philosophical issues as God, free will, immortality, induction, and the nature of value-judgements. Articles and books by him include: 'Bertrand Russell's Doubts about Induction' (1949), *The Logic of Moral Discourse* (1955), 'Hard and Soft Determinism' (1958),

'The Cosmological Argument' (1959), 'Atheism' (1967), *Buber and Buberism* (1970), *Heidegger on Death* (1979), 'The Case against Reincarnation' (1986–7, in four parts), *Voltaire* (1989), and *Immortality* (1992). A deep respect for science and common sense mark Edwards's writings, and he is well known for his use of humour as a lethal weapon against philosophers whom he regards as pompous purveyors of platitudes, especially Heidegger and Tillich.
                                                M.W.

*capital punishment; God and the philosophers.

'Heidegger's Quest for Being', *Philosophy* (1989) captures the distinctive flavour of Edwards's work.

effect: *see* causality.

egalitarianism: *see* equality; inequality; justice; liberty and equality; socialism; well-being.

ego. What 'I' stands for, the subject's essence. Plato and Descartes thought a person could exist disembodied. Locke imagined that a prince could swap bodies with a cobbler. It is hard to see how these stories could be intelligible (not to say true) without conceding the existence of an incorporeal ego, a subject for thinking, feeling, and willing, which makes each person who they are. But Hume sought in vain to *observe* his core *self, and contemporaries who share Hobbes's hostility to mysterious non-physical substances wonder whether the stories make sense after all! It needs to be explained, however, why ghost stories at least *seem* to make sense for people, whereas we can make nothing of disembodied trees, and the thought that the Lada should swap identities with the Mercedes Benz (there being no physical change) strikes us immediately as absurd.   J.E.R.S.

J. Glover, *I: The Philosophy and Psychology of Personal Identity* (Harmondsworth, 1988).

egocentric particulars. The referents of some words—notably pronouns and demonstrative expressions like 'this', 'here', and 'now'—depend in a systematic way on who utters them, when, where, and with what pointing gestures or referential intentions. The particulars (people, objects, events, places, times) thus referred to have been described as 'egocentric' (in a purely logical sense of the word, i.e. context-dependent).   L.F.S.

*contextual definition.

B. Russell, *An Inquiry into Meaning and Truth* (London, 1940), ch. 7.

egocentric predicament. This name was given by Ralph Barton Perry to Berkeley's argument that anything supposed by an opponent of *idealism to be a thing 'without the mind' is, by virtue of that supposition, just another idea 'within the mind' whose *esse est percipi. Berkeley believed, in Perry's words, that 'One cannot conceive things to exist apart from consciousness because to conceive is *ipso facto* to bring within consciousness.' The predicament, Perry says, does nothing to prove there are no things without the mind, which is what Berkeley was trying to prove in setting up the argument. Neither the idealist nor the realist can use this predicament to prove his point about unperceived objects.   L.W.B.

Ralph Barton Perry, *Present Philosophical Tendencies* (New York, 1925), 129 ff.

egoism, psychological. The theory that all human actions are motivated by self-interest. Taken as a factual claim based on observation, this is obviously false: people are often motivated by emotions like anger, love, or fear, by altruism or pride, by the desire for knowledge or the hatred of injustice. However, egoism can seem true on the basis of a general argument which shows that all these apparently distinct motives, if properly analysed, are really examples of self-interest after all—that any motive must be. The argument is that every voluntary act is something the person on balance wants to do, something he does because he desires to do it; therefore, he does it in order to satisfy his desire to do it; therefore, the act is really self-interested. Even if it seems to sacrifice the person's interests, its aim is to satisfy his predominant desires.

This argument has several things wrong with it. First, as Joseph Butler pointed out, the motive of self-interest would have nothing to aim at unless the person had other motives as well. For example, if you are hungry it is in your interest to eat. But hunger is a desire whose object is eating, and not your interests. Self-interest is a different, second-order desire that has as its object the satisfaction of other, first-order desires, like hunger, which also motivate us directly. And some first-order desires are for things quite apart from oneself. If you donate money to famine relief, your motive is that you don't want other people to starve; your motive is not that you want to satisfy your desire that other people not starve. You may feel good if you donate the money and bad if you don't, but that's because you already think there's a reason to donate: the feelings don't explain the motive, rather the motive explains the feelings.

Another problem with the argument is that it considers only the influence of present desires on choice. But even if an act aimed at the greatest possible satisfaction of present desires, that would not make it self-interested, because a self-interested action must take into account all one's interests, future as well as present. So if someone refuses a cholera inoculation during an epidemic, out of fear of the needle, and later contracts cholera, the refusal may have satisfied his strongest desire at the time, but it was not self-interested. Psychological egoism should not be confused with ethical egoism, the view that each person *ought* to do what will best advance his own interests.   T.N.

*Mandeville.

F. H. Bradley, *Ethical Studies*, essay VII: 'Selfishness and Self-Sacrifice'.
Joseph Butler, *Fifteen Sermons*, esp. 11 and 12: 'On the Love of our Neighbor'.

David Hume, *An Enquiry Concerning the Principles of Morals*, app. II: 'Of Self-Love'.

egoism and altruism. Does morality require a person to act for the good of others, or can its requirements be consistently seen as means to self-fulfilment for the moral agent? If the latter, some egoists will argue that only the thought of benefit or gratification to myself can in any case motivate me to action (*egoism psychological); others, 'ethical egoists', claim that although I could aim at the good of another, the moral life is in fact the life that maximizes good-for-me, if not always in the shorter term, then reliably over a lifetime. It is a highly challengeable—indeed unconvincing—claim: situations arise, e.g. when some virtually undetectable injustice offers a person great reward and no deterrents. On such a theory, not even conscience would deter. Central to the very notion of a moral imperative is the idea that it has authority to override all other considerations, self-interest notably among them, and to rule out the thought of calculating and quantifying the balance for and against advantage to self on particular occasions of moral obligation. Again, if as an egoist I propose an ethical theory that *everyone should understand the object of moral endeavour to be the pursuit of his or her individual good*, the proposing of such a universal policy must itself conflict with my own pursuit of my individual good. I cannot really *want* others to attend to their good, as distinct from my own! But if I simply assert, as a personal manifesto (or, indeed, write it secretly in my diary), 'I am going to pursue my own fulfilment only, and I understand morality as precisely a means to that'—then I achieve consistency—but express no public moral theory.

It is not true that everything we can be said to 'want' or 'desire' is an enhancement or fulfilment of the self. We may want to give way to irrational rage or to wayward sexual desire, to hurt another or indeed to help another—without manifesting 'self-love' in any of these instances. My rage or aggression may in fact be self-destructive. The beginning of altruism is the realization that not all good and bad are good-for-me and bad-for-me: that certain others—my close friends, say—have joys and sufferings distinct from mine, but for which I have a sympathetic concern—and for their sake, not my own. I may then acknowledge that others beyond the small circle of my friends are not fundamentally different—and so reach the belief that there are objective goods and bads as such. As one self among the others I cannot claim special privileges simply for being the individual that I am! If it is neither impossible nor irrational to act simply for the sake of another, the occurrence of satisfaction or 'good conscience' when we have done so is not sufficient ground for the egoist to claim that it was only for these 'rewards' that the acts were performed.

Nor on the other hand does the possibility of altruism mean that it is a constant moral necessity: an altruist can allow that in most circumstances I can act far more effectively on my own behalf than can any other person. A simple but crucial step separates a broken-backed ethical egoism from a minimally acceptable and consistent *moral* theory. It involves the recognition of others as more than instrumental to my fulfilment. I may promote my own interests and personal fulfilment, so long as I do not encroach upon the pursuit by others of their fulfilment. That is to recognize other persons as limits to my action: altruism may, of course, go beyond that in seeking positively to advance their good.   R.W.H.

D. P. Gauthier (ed.), *Morality and Rational Self-Interest* (Princeton, NJ, 1970).
J. Hospers, *Human Conduct* (London, 1961).

eidetic imagery. Enjoyed by those who can imagine or recall something as if it were in front of their eyes. Unlike hallucinators, they remain in control of what they 'see', even (as in the extraordinary case reported by Luria) to the extent of improving the lighting! The philosophical challenge is that an inner-perception story looks unavoidable, despite threatened regressive and sceptical arguments that have made imagist accounts of ordinary perception unpopular.   J.E.R.S.

*image; perception.

A. R. Luria, *The Mind of a Mnemonist* (New York, 1968).

eidetic reduction: *see* Husserl.

Eightfold Path: *see* Buddhist philosophy.

Einfühlung: *see* empathy.

Einstein, Albert (1879–1955). German physicist most famous for founding relativity theory on the basis of two simple, empirically well-confirmed principles: that the laws of physics should be the same for all observers regardless of their state of motion, and that all such observers will measure the speed of light to be the same. As a consequence of these principles, he dramatically departed from traditional conceptions of substance and time by proving the equivalence of mass and energy, $E = mc^2$, and deducing that the spatio-temporal coordinates used by two observers in relative motion to express the laws of physics must be related so that their judgements differ over which events occur simultaneously. Einstein is also remembered for his opposition to the orthodox interpretation of *quantum mechanics— though his oft-quoted quip 'God does not play with dice' does little justice to his other main criticism that the interpretation fails to deliver a determinate, measurement-independent description of physical reality. Among Einstein's numerous other contributions to physics, two stand out: his hypothesis that light is composed of tiny discrete packets of energy called photons (for which he officially won his Nobel Prize); and his analysis of the curved trajectory of a body under gravity as, in fact, 'straight line' motion occurring in a curved *space-time that has a shape fashioned by the distribution of matter within it.   R.CLI.

*determinism.

A. Pais, '*Subtle is the Lord . . .*': *The Science and Life of Albert Einstein* (Oxford, 1982).

Einstein, Podolsky, and Rosen paradox. In general, quantum mechanics (QM) provides only probabilistic information about the possible results of measurements. The question arises whether this is because the world is genuinely indeterministic and, prior to measurement, the physical system measured does not possess determinate properties corresponding to the measurement outcomes, or whether it is because QM gives an *incomplete* description of a fully deterministic world. Might the QM description of a system be supplemented, so that the augmented description fully determines the results of measurements?

In 1935, Einstein, Podolsky, and Rosen argued that QM is incomplete. They considered a system of two spatially separated particles, A and B, in a particular quantum state, Ψ. Ψ does not determine the results of measuring the positions of A and B but, *given the result obtained on measuring A's position*, it does allow one to predict B's position with certainty. It therefore seems that B has a determinate position immediately *after* A's position is measured. But because A and B are spatially separated, B's position cannot be made determinate as a result of the measurement of A's position without there being some sort of 'action at a distance'. In order to uphold a principle of locality (that there can be no action at a distance), EPR conclude that B must have had a determinate position all along and that QM is thus incomplete. However, *Bell's theorem shows that regarding QM as incomplete is not sufficient to save locality.   O.P.

*quantum theory and philosophy.

A. Einstein, B. Podolsky, and N. Rosen, 'Can Quantum-mechanical Description of Physical Reality be Considered Complete?', *Physical Review* (1935).
A. Fine, *The Shaky Game: Einstein, Realism and the Quantum Theory*, 2nd edn. (Chicago, 1996).

élan vital. The key concept in the theory of 'creative evolution' proposed by the French philosopher Henri Bergson (1859–1941). Much influenced by Darwin and (even more) by Herbert Spencer, Bergson nevertheless felt that a purely materialistic approach to *evolution is unable to capture both the origination of new complex organs and the general rise of life up the order of being. He therefore argued that there is a kind of vital spirit (*élan vital*) which powers organic evolution. Bergson denied that he was painting an end-directed picture; but, as in such pictures, Bergson's scheme left humans in a familiar place, namely at the top.   M.R.

H. Bergson, *L'Évolution créatrice* (Paris, 1907); tr. as *Creative Evolution* (London, 1911).

Eleatics. A collective name for three philosophers active in the early to mid-fifth century BC: Parmenides, Zeno of Elea, and Melissus; after Elea (now Velia) in Southern Italy, the native city of the first two. Nothing is known of any other philosophers who may have been active at Elea or shared the Eleatic approach (but Plato, *Sophist* 242c–d suggests there may have been some), apart from the Sophist Gorgias (see below), and, according to a dubious tradition, Xenophanes. There is no evidence of any formal 'school', nor even of personal contact between Melissus and the other two. Grouping the Eleatics together is justified by the similarities of method, arguments, and results found in the extant remains of their writings and in other testimony. (For individual details: *Parmenides; *Zeno of Elea; *Melissus.)

Common to the Eleatics was a rejection of sense experience as a way to truth, and the acceptance of mathematical standards of clarity and necessity in argument. Parmenides and Melissus claimed to start from premisses indubitable to reason, and to argue deductively from these. Zeno, with destructive intent, took only the premisses of opponents and claimed to deduce contradictions from them. His weapon, frequently used by the others too, is *reductio ad absurdum* of the contrary thesis.

The influence of the Eleatics was immediate, deep, and lasting. They raised the standards of reasoning all round, and intensified the demand for sharply defined objects of knowledge. Both the later Pre-Socratics and Aristotle, who rejected their conclusions, took their arguments seriously, and were driven to take up positions on the metaphysical questions they raised. Gorgias (one of the *Sophists) argued in Eleatic style to sceptical conclusions in his work 'On Nature or What Is Not'. Plato's acknowledgement to them is made in his scene-setting in the *Parmenides* and in the role of the 'Eleatic Stranger' in the *Sophist* and *Politicus*. Most subsequent philosophical analysis in the ancient period, particularly of logical and mathematical concepts, is ultimately indebted to their techniques and insights.   E.L.H.

J. Barnes, *The Presocratic Philosophers*, i (London, 1979), chs. 9–14.

elenchus. A Greek word, signifying questioning someone with a view to testing or examining the cogency or credibility of what they have said. Such questioning was wholly central to Socrates' method of examining the ideas of others, as depicted in Plato's early dialogues (such as the *Protagoras*). In his hands, this examination was almost always intended to show up confusions, inconsistencies, or other flaws in his opponents' positions, so *elenchus* came to signify a refutation or disproval of some point of view. Accompanied by his noted *irony, Socrates' fondness for refuting views won him no friends.   N.J.H.D.

Richard Robinson, *Plato's Earlier Dialectic* (Oxford, 1953) is a central text for this.

eliminativism. Extreme materialist doctrine advocating the elimination of everyday psychological concepts in favour of neuroscientific ones.

The doctrine is sometimes cast in the claim that *folk psychology is false. This seems incredible: if it were correct, then (*belief* being a state of folk psychology) it could not be true that anyone believed it.

The doctrine is usually premissed on (*a*) a metaphysical thesis purporting to show the need to reduce commonsense categories to categories of some mature science (*reductionism), (*b*) a purported demonstration that our commonsense psychological categories are not such as to match up with those that could be used in any scientific account.   J.HORN.

Paul Churchland, 'Eliminative Materialism and the Propositional Attitudes', *Journal of Philosophy* (1981).

élitism. The belief that in any society there exist or ought to exist groups of those pre-eminent in any given field, including the political. In the Seventh Letter (326a–b) Plato wrote. 'The human race will not see better days until either the stock of those who rightly and genuinely follow philosophy acquire political authority, or else the class who have political control be led by some dispensation of providence to become real philosophers.' Plato thus holds both that it is possible to identify individuals who are by nature or grace specially fitted to rule, and that those so identified should rule. Both tenets will be questioned, the first by those dubious that there is a special identifiable talent for political leadership, and the second by those who want political power diffused rather than concentrated in the hands of a demarcated élite. However, even rule by 'the people' in practice often becomes rule by a new political élite: perhaps the most prudent course is to follow Karl Popper, for whom the most important political question is not *who* should rule, but rather how rulers can be regularly and peacefully got rid of by the ruled. Popper's position tacitly admits the likelihood of political élites and sets about devising the means to control them.

While the term 'élitist' has lately become a term of abuse, the existence of élites in various areas of life is an inevitable consequence of the unequal distribution of human powers combined with a degree of social mobility and division of labour, which enables some of those who excel in a valued field to devote themselves to the development of their talent. To object to this in itself seems, as Nietzsche urged, to be little more than a symptom of envy on the part of the untalented. What is more questionable in Nietzsche is the claim that 'the good of humanity' lies 'only in its highest specimens'. If members of élites behave as though they believed Nietzsche, they will doubtless provoke in their fellows expression of the resentful egalitarianism to which Nietzsche himself took such strong objection.

If élitism is, at least on the surface, to be distinguished from egalitarianism, it must also be distinguished from a belief in the virtues of an hereditary class system. Those who owe their position to birth are not necessarily talented in any sphere, and so do not, in the strict sense of the term, count as part of an élite. One of the objections to rule by a political élite chosen because of its members' administrative or political skills is that such people may have little sense of the duties which go or ought to go with rule.

The magnanimity of *noblesse oblige* often eludes the meritocrat, who lacks that sense of responsibility to the underdog which in good times should be part of the upbringing of the aristocrat.

Élitism, then, is one of the marks of that type of classless society in which the talented are allowed to rise from any starting position. A thoroughgoing élitism, indeed, while not ostensibly egalitarian, would have to embody a principle of *equality of opportunity whereby everyone in a society was free to rise where his or her talents led. In practice, such a principle may lead to a constant levelling-off of outcomes, and to preventing members of élites from giving advantages to their children. Élitism then, if not tempered with a right of parents to give special advantages to their children, will drift towards the very egalitarianism it set out to oppose. There may also be worries about the effect the rapid social mobility implied by a society structured on achievement rather than on class would have on culture and social continuity more generally.   A.O'H.

*conservatism; inequality; justice; socialism.

T. S. Eliot, *Notes towards the Definition of Culture* (London, 1948).
K. Mannheim, *Man and Society in an Age of Reconstruction* (London, 1940).
V. Pareto, *The Mind and Society* (London, 1935).

Elster, Jon (1940–). Norwegian social and political theorist who has taught in Norway, France, and the United States. In his prolific and lively writings, which focus on social theory and rationality, Elster employs a wide range of conceptual tools drawn from philosophy, logic, game theory, economics, and psychology. His critical examination of Marx's social theories formed a cornerstone of so-called analytical *Marxism, while his insistence on the need to look for the micro-foundations of social change, together with the light his analyses of problems in theories of rational action throw on the many faces of irrationality, and the role of emotion, have provided a multidisciplinary resource for the detailed explanation of complex and large-scale social phenomena.   A.H.

Jon Elster, *Sour Grapes: Studies in the Subversion of Rationality* (Cambridge, 1983).

embodiment. The doctrine in aesthetics and elsewhere that all and only cultural entities and phenomena (persons, artworks, actions) exhibit indissolubly complex properties that are at once material and intentional. The intentional features signify the collective linguistic, semiotic, and institutional aspects of societal life. On the argument, the mind–body problem proves to be a restricted form of a more general culture–nature problem. The thesis is taken to provide the minimal metaphysics of the human sciences, the arts, morality, and the like, that is, those inquiries that admit intrinsically interpretable phenomena. The admission entails the non-reductive *sui generis* nature of cultural emergence relative to physical nature.   J.M.

*intentionality.

Joseph Margolis, *Art and Philosophy* (Atlantic Highlands, NJ, 1980).
——*Culture and Cultural Entities* (Dordrecht, 1984).

embraced and reluctant desires. Reluctant desires are those desires we would prefer not to have and act on. Embraced desires are first-order desires, perhaps constituting life-hopes, which we actually desire to have. Reluctant desires operate in frustrating or obstructing circumstances (a weary writer's watching television), embraced desires in satisfying or enabling ones (the writer's keenness to complete her promising novel). Acting-out of embraced desires is having a freedom consistent with determinism; what is inconsistent with it is another kind of freedom we want—one having to do not with either kind of desire but with origination.   J.O'G.

H. Frankfurt, 'Freedom of the Will and the Concept of a Person', *Journal of Philosophy* (1971).
T. Honderich, *A Theory of Determinism: The Mind, Neuroscience and Life-Hopes* (Oxford, 1988), ch. 7.

emergence. In the philosophy of mind, emergentism is the view that conscious mental states are not reducible to neurological states of the brain, even though they first came into existence only as a result of the evolution of increasing levels of neurological complexity in higher animals. The emergentist may accept that conscious states, such as thoughts and perceptions, need somehow to be 'realized by' or 'grounded in' underlying neurological states of the subject's brain, but will typically contend that conscious states make a contribution to the causal explanation of animal and human behaviour over and above any explanation that can be provided by neurological states alone. Whether this should be taken to imply that supposedly emergent phenomena like consciousness introduce into the world genuinely novel causal powers is a disputed matter, turning in part on contested issues in the philosophy of causation and causal explanation. Mental phenomena are not the only ones that have been claimed to be emergent, even if they provide the most frequently cited examples.   E.J.L.

A. Beckermann, H. Flohr, and J. Kim (eds.), *Emergence or Reduction?* (Berlin, 1992).

emergent properties. A property of a complex system is said to be 'emergent' just in case, although it arises out of the properties and relations characterizing its simpler constituents, it is neither predictable from, nor reducible to, these lower-level characteristics. According to emergentism, which flourished during the first half of this century, many properties of wholes are emergent in that sense, and hence 'genuinely novel' features of the world in which these wholes have evolved. For example, the transparency of water was held to be emergent on the ground that it could not be inferred from the properties of the hydrogen and oxygen atoms of which water is composed. Emergent properties were contrasted with 'additive' or 'resultant' properties, e.g. the mass of an object, which could be inferred from the properties of the parts.

The particular claim about the transparency of water may be disputable. However, an emergentist view of mentality is still influential, and survives in the doctrine of non-reductive *physicalism, a leading position on the *mind–body problem, according to which psychological characteristics, although they occur only under appropriate physical–biological conditions, are irreducibly distinct from them. The ultimate coherence of the notion of an emergent property remains controversial, however.   J.K.

A. Beckermann, H. Flohr, and J. Kim (eds.), *Emergence or Reduction?* (Berlin, 1992).

C. Lloyd Morgan, *Emergent Evolution* (London, 1923).

Emerson, Ralph Waldo (1803–82). American philosopher and poet, one of the central figures of *New England Transcendentalism. His Romantic treatment of the problems of *scepticism suggested knowledge of the self as the crucial epistemological and moral imperative. His counsel in 'Self-Reliance'—'Nothing is at last sacred but the integrity of your own mind'—was coupled with the assurance that 'in yourself is the law of all nature . . . in yourself slumbers the whole of Reason' ('The American Scholar'). An important influence on Bergson and, especially, Nietzsche, some of whose aphorisms can be seen as virtual translations of Emerson's prose, Emerson's writings were also of considerable interest to James and Dewey.   K.H.

Stanley Cavell, 'The Philosopher in American Life', 'Emerson, Coleridge, Kant', and 'Being Odd, Getting Even', in *In Quest of the Ordinary* (Chicago, 1988).

emotion and art. There are many philosophical problems raised by the phenomenon of emotion in art, only some of which can be sketched here. There is (a) the problem of the arousal of emotions by art; (b) the problem of the expression of emotions by art; (c) the problem of the nature and range of the emotions expressed by art; (d) the problem of emotion and fiction; and (e) the problem of art and negative emotion; and (f) the problem of the value of artistic expression.

Under (a) philosophers have asked whether artworks truly arouse, or evoke, emotions in appreciators and, if so, which artworks and which emotions. How such evocation might be a source of art's value for appreciators has been pondered, as has the question of how the evocation of emotions, if those of everyday life, is compatible with maintenance of an appropriately aesthetic attitude toward the works involved. Under (b) philosophers have sought to understand how it is that artworks, which are non-sentient human constructions, can express emotions, and whether this is to be analysed in terms of the power works have to arouse emotions or related states in audiences, the emotional appearances that works can wear, the emotions that works invite us to attribute to their implied utterers, or the emotions that works induce us to imagine they are the expression of. In addition, there is the

question of how a work's expression of emotion—what is often called its *expressiveness*—relates to the artist's expression of emotion through the work. Under (c) it has been asked whether art is capable of expressing the full range of emotions experienced in life, and whether what is expressed are always full-fledged emotions rather than, say, feelings or moods.

Under (d) the main focus of discussion has been the paradox of fiction, turning on the fact that, when engaged with fiction, we appear to have emotions of a robust, belief-presupposing sort for people and situations we know do not exist. Under (e) the main focus of discussion has been the paradox of tragedy, turning on the fact that we do not shy away from, but instead seem to relish or find satisfaction in, the experience of negative emotions from tragedy, emotions such as pity, sorrow, and fear. Under (f) the main issue is to illuminate how expression in art can be of aesthetic value when the corresponding expression in life—that is, via human behaviour—would not be.   J.LEV.

Mette Hjort and Sue Laver (eds.), *Emotion and the Arts* (Oxford, 1997).

Peter Kivy, *Sound Sentiment* (Philadelphia, 1989).

Kendall Walton, *Mimesis as Make-Believe* (Cambridge, Mass., 1990).

emotion and feeling. The initially obvious view of an emotion is that it is a mental item like a sensation, which is infallibly classifiable in the having of it. But versions of this 'feeling theory', originally formulated by Descartes, fail to explain how, if emotions are only accessible to *introspection, we all learn to speak of them more or less uniformly and can unreflectively assume knowledge of other people's, while occasionally having to discover or deduce our own. According to various philosophical views, not only is it possible for a person to be mistaken about the emotion she feels, but to have an emotion without feeling it.

William James persuasively argued that without palpable 'bodily symptoms' emotion would merely be detached observation, and thus not emotion at all. He considered emotions to be sensations of the physiological disturbances caused by perceptions (of external events)—we are sad because we cry, angry because we strike, rather than crying because we are sad, or striking because we are angry. His, and other, bodily-upset theories are in fact more physically orientated versions of feeling theories, and fail to remedy their main problems.

They apply only to occurrent emotions, not dispositional or lasting ones, and, in making emotion an involuntary process (whether mental or physical), they assign it only a contingent, empirical connection with its associated causes, circumstances, behaviours, or expression—as if anger, jealousy, or suspicion, for instance, can occur irrespective of context. All sorts of unlikely candidates thereby count as emotions, including drug-induced anxiety states or other bodily perturbations which the experiencer himself perceives in a detached way and discounts as merely physiological. That we often regard emotions as being justified or unjustified, rational or irrational, realistic or unrealistic, is made inexplicable.

Theories of *behaviourism, such as those held by Watson and Skinner, hold, at their most extreme, that an emotion is nothing more than engaging, or being liable to engage, in certain sorts of behaviour. These accounts at least contain the public, shared aspect of emotion which feeling theories neglect, though at the expense of omitting what they capture: that emotion is also importantly private (and concealable). And, like the Jamesian theories that influenced them, behaviourisms ignore that behaviours cannot be minutely charted and matched to the complex specificity of emotions: an angry person may exhibit any or none of a range of behaviours, and by behaviour alone it would be hard to discriminate indignation from resentment or either from irritation.

Emotion theories of a fourth type (including those of Aristotle and Aquinas which Descartes disparaged) make cognition, motivation, or evaluation central. Such theories vary as to whether emotions themselves are cognitions, or are caused by cognitions, or even, in emotivism, *cause* cognitions, or are part of a motivational process—what causes us to apprehend things in certain ways and act accordingly. If there are necessary connections between knowledge and emotion, emotions can be seen as rational ways of perceiving and inter-acting with the world, rather than random, self-enclosed psychic or physical sensations. The assumption initiated by Plato that emotions distort or obscure the true way of seeing the world, because they conflict with reason, can be replaced by the view that they complement reason and open up the realms of moral, aesthetic, and religious values.

Against this connecting of emotion and knowledge, it must be said that fears can be phobias, and that anger's extent, and even occurrence, can depend as much on its experiencer's temperament as on its objective validity. Psychoanalytic theories make emotion a matter of reacting to something in our unconscious, not something in reality. Similarly, Sartre saw emotion as a way we 'live' the world (through perception and muscular reaction) 'as though the relations between things were governed not by deterministic processes but by magic'. He considered even a 'rational' emotion, like fear which spurs flight, as 'magical transformation'—ersatz elimination of the object fled from.

Unfortunately for cognition theories, it seems more a matter of stipulation than of logical necessity that specific sorts of cognition (which is in principle nakedly cerebral and impartial) intrinsically involve emotion (which is in principle something over and above cognition). Two people may have the same perceptual evaluation of a situation and make the same response, yet each have different emotional responses. They may both, for instance, realize they have been cheated and both take steps to remedy this, but one may be indignant, the other amused.

A comprehensive (but unspelled-out) theory of emotion is sometimes recommended, one that will combine all the above-mentioned features, and avoid the mistakes of their each being taken too much in isolation. J.O'G.

*passion and emotion in the history of philosophy.

W. P. Alston, 'Emotion', in P. Edwards (ed.), *Encyclopedia of Philosophy* (New York, 1967).
C. Calhoun and R. Solomon (eds.), *What is an Emotion?* (Oxford, 1984).
P. Goldie, *The Emotions: A Philosophical Exploration* (Oxford, 2000).
W. Lyons, *Emotion* (Cambridge, 1980).

emotions, James–Lange theory of: *see* James–Lange theory.

emotive and descriptive meaning. The emotive meaning of words is their power to express a speaker's emotions, and to evoke the emotions of a hearer. Descriptive meaning is the cognitive role of language, in determining belief and understanding. Expressions in moral discourse have descriptive and emotive meaning in combination—though these components are capable of independent variation. Opponents of the *emotive theory of ethics can hardly deny any of this: but they do deny that the emotive component is the more fundamental to moral judgement. R.W.H.

C. L. Stevenson, *Ethics and Language* (New Haven, Conn., 1944).

emotive theory of ethics. That moral responses and judgements have an emotional *aspect* is allowed by very different moral theories, and can hardly be reasonably denied. The emotive theory, however, argues that the emotive element is the ultimate basis of appraisal. *'Reason' examines the situation to be appraised, and discerns the alternatives for action. Reason, however, is inert; it cannot provide the equally necessary dynamic, action-initiating component: only *emotion can. The language of moral judgement expresses the speaker's emotion and evokes the hearer's.

The philosophy of mind and action on which the theory relies was enunciated clearly by Hume, and has had immense influence. It attracted numerous twentieth-century philosophers with positivistic, non-cognitivist leanings. A distinction was made between analyses that equated moral judgement with a 'report' on the subject's inner feelings (but thereby making moral disagreement enigmatic), and those that saw it as an essentially emotive reaction, non-propositional expression analogous to exclamation (hence the nickname 'Boo! Hoorah!' theory). It was readily claimed, in addition, that beliefs about the context of action, and disagreement over beliefs, entered essentially into moral deliberation and dispute. In other versions, 'emotion' shaded into 'attitude'—basically 'approval' and 'disapproval'. Analyses on clear-cut emotivist lines tended to be displaced (particularly under the influence of R. M. Hare) by 'prescriptivist' accounts.

In its simplest forms, the emotive theory omits (or dismisses) far too much of its subject-matter. Moral judgements are not in fact discrete explosions of feeling: they have logical linkages. Emotions can be responses to already discriminated moral properties; and, crucially, they can (and ought) themselves be judged morally appropriate or perverse. The theory cannot properly distinguish moral reasoning from rhetoric; nor can it give an intelligible account of how a perplexed moral agent who lacks initially any definite, unambiguous reaction to a moral challenge can think his way responsibly towards a moral position.

Notable among critics of that general theory of motivation which hinges on a dichotomy of reason–feeling or belief–desire—the theory from which emotivism and other forms of non-cognitivism spring—are some contemporary 'moral realists', e.g. Jonathan Dancy, in his *Moral Reasons* (Oxford, 1993).　　　　R.W.H.

　*emotive and descriptive meaning; prescriptivism; non-cognitivism.

C. L. Stevenson, *Ethics and Language* (New Haven, Conn., 1944).
J. O. Urmson, *The Emotive Theory of Ethics* (London, 1968).

empathy. State of mind in which someone shares the feelings or outlook of another, sometimes prompted by imaginative exercises such as 'stepping into someone's shoes'. The English word was introduced initially, early in the twentieth century, to render the German *Einfühlung*. This early usage was within aesthetics: a spectator was said to appreciate a work of art empathically, by projecting his personality into it. In its broader, current meaning, empathy—distinguished from sympathy—features in discussions of moral psychology, the imagination, and the simulation/theory debate.　　　　S.D.R.

Stephen Darwall, 'Empathy, Sympathy, Care', *Philosophical Studies*, 89 (1998).
Alvin I. Goldman, 'Empathy, Mind, and Morals', reprinted in Martin Davies and Tony Stone (eds.), *Mental Simulation* (Oxford, 1995).

Empedocles (*c*.495–435 BC). A pluralist from Sicily, who by legend leapt to his death into the crater of Etna, he maintained that earth, air, fire, and water are the four elements ('roots') of all material reality. Aristotle agreed, and gave the idea widespread currency, though he further analysed these elements into the combinations possible among hot, cold, wet, and dry.

The surviving fragments of Empedocles' two poems *On Nature* and *Purifications* are the most extensive writings we have from any Pre-Socratic philosopher. *On Nature* tells of cosmic evolution driven by the force of, first, love, and then strife. At one stage, anatomical parts stick to each other in random configurations (e.g. 'man-faced oxprogeny'), some of which are well adapted for survival. Empedocles thus anticipated Darwin, but without an account of how well-adapted organisms can reproduce their type.
　　　　G.B.M.

G. S. Kirk, J. E. Raven, and M. Schofield, *The Presocratic Philosophers*, 2nd edn. (Cambridge, 1990).

empirical. Based on experience. An idea or concept is empirical if it is derived ultimately from the five senses, to which introspection is sometimes added. It need not be derived from any one sense alone, and the data supplied by the senses may need to be processed by the mind, and indeed may not count as data at all until some activity by the mind has taken place; it is controversial whether there are such things as 'raw data' which the mind simply receives before acting on them. (*Empiricism.) A statement, proposition, or judgement is empirical if we can only know its truth or falsity by appealing to experience, but it can contain empirical concepts without being itself empirical. *Red* is an empirical concept, but 'Red is a colour' is not empirical: we do not find its truth by looking.　　　　A.R.L.

G. Ryle, 'Epistemology', in J. O. Urmson (ed.), *The Concise Encyclopedia of Western Philosophy and Philosophers* (London, 1960), brings out some of the complications in the traditional contrast between empiricism and rationalism.

empiricism. Any view which bases our knowledge, or the materials from which it is constructed, on experience through the traditional five senses. What might be called the classical empiricist view is associated especially with Locke, the first of the so-called British Empiricists, though elements of it go back much earlier. It found itself in a running battle with *scepticism, which led it to become more extreme, especially in Locke's successors Berkeley and Hume, with echoes early in the twentieth century. This in turn led to a critical reappraisal and severe reining-in of empiricism by Kant, and later, after the twentieth-century revival, by Wittgenstein. A more sober empiricism, however, is much more widespread, though its very sobriety puts it in some danger of losing its distinctive nature as empiricism. What follows is intended to fill out this picture, ending with a few miscellaneous points and distinctions.

Empiricism has its roots in the idea that all we can know about the world is what the world cares to tell us; we must observe it neutrally and dispassionately, and any attempt on our part to mould or interfere with the process of receiving this information can only lead to distortion and arbitrary imagining. This gives us a picture of the mind as a 'blank tablet' (*tabula rasa) on which information is imprinted by the senses in the form of *'sense-data', to use a technical term invented in the nineteenth century and not to be confused with the wider and vaguer term 'the data of the senses'. Previously the term *'idea' had been used in this sense, though confusingly in others as well. Sense-data were therefore the 'given', prior to all interpretation, and the mind, which now and only now became active, manipulated these sense-data in various ways, combining them or abstracting from them, to form the great bulk of our ideas and concepts, and then went on to discover relations between these ideas, or to observe further manifestations of them in experience and relations between these manifestations.

This in varying versions is the classical empiricist view. It leads straight off to problems involving scepticism, for if

THOMAS HOBBES was a European as much as an English philosopher: he takes his place at the beginning of the European Enlightenment between Galileo and Leibniz, alongside Descartes. Leibniz called Hobbes 'that profoundest examiner of basic principles in all matters'.

JOHN LOCKE trained as a physician but found in middle age, under the patronage of the Earl of Shaftesbury and the influence of Descartes, that he had more to contribute to politics and philosophy than to science and medicine.

GEORGE BERKELEY published three classic works of empiricism in his twenties, and thereafter sought to benefit humanity mainly in other ways.

DAVID HUME was the greatest and most radical of modern empiricists, but his philosophical works overtook his historical, political, and economic writings in the public estimation only after his death.

the mind is limited in this way and must rely entirely on these ideas or sense-data, how can it ever know anything beyond them? They are supposed to 'represent' an outer world, but how can the mind know that they do any such thing? Indeed how can it know what is meant by talking of an 'outer world' at all? Locke himself, at least as traditionally interpreted, seems not to have taken these problems very seriously, but they come fully to the fore in his successors, especially Berkeley and Hume.

Empiricism becomes more extreme when it abandons the claim to know an outer world at all, and insists that what we call the outer world is simply a construction by our minds, indistinguishable from a real outer world in practice. But can this view be coherently stated at all? If we have no knowledge whatever of anything beyond our own experiences, how can we even envisage the possibility of something beyond them in order to contrast them with it? How would we understand what it was we were envisaging? This is an example of a move very common in philosophy, whereby a theory is accused of being unable, on its own terms, to state itself coherently. It is developed, in various ways, both by Kant and by Wittgenstein.

There is another objection too to this extreme kind of empiricism, because it is not obvious that sense-data of the kind required by the theory can exist. They are usually supposed to be things that are exactly as they appear. Since their being just consists in their appearing to some mind they can have no hidden depths that that mind could fail to know about, and they cannot fail to have whatever properties they appear to have. Our knowledge of them must be incorrigible, i.e. it does not make sense to say that we might be wrong about them (about those that appear to ourselves, that is; we might go wrong in our guesses about those that appear to other people, but it is not clear how we could know of the existence of other people). We can, and of course do, have sensory experiences, but what is not clear is that what these are of is certain objects which we cannot go wrong about. As Wittgenstein claimed, and surely with some plausibility, what we cannot go wrong about we cannot go right about either; there is simply no room for anything that could be called judgement or knowledge. An image can exist on a camera plate, but the camera does not 'know' the image, and can no more be right about it than wrong about it. Of course when presented with a brightly coloured object I can hardly in practice go wrong if I claim 'This is red'. But I could in principle be confused about just what counts as being red—and might be confused in practice if I ventured as far as 'This is scarlet'. Such confusion need not be merely linguistic, or about the meaning of the word 'scarlet'; I might well become persuaded that the thing I called scarlet had not in fact really appeared to me in the same way as things I had previously called scarlet. We may remember too the difficulty aspiring painters have in 'seeing things as they really look'; if taken literally this would be an illusory goal to seek (Gombrich).

Extreme empiricism of this sort then seems to be incoherent. By insisting that we know *everything* through experience it makes us start from a position of total isolation from the world, and then it becomes miraculous that we could ever escape from there. We are locked into a castle surrounded by a moat, and the ideas or sense-data that we hoped to use to bridge the moat turn into a drawbridge and fly up in our face. Evidently we must start from within the world itself, which means that in some sense we must already know some things, without having to find them out. It is not that we must have some magical armchair access to the world—that would be to put us behind the moat again but supplied now with a magical bridge across it. Rather we must come to the world armed with certain ways of looking at it, and without insisting that our knowledge must always start with something we can know incorrigibly (a view known as *foundationalism*). The mind must be active not just, as Locke thought, in manipulating and building on an experience already received passively, but also in receiving that experience itself.

This at any rate is the sort of reaction to extreme empiricism that we find in writers like Kant and Wittgenstein. But so far we have only been concerned with empiricism taken to its limits. Many philosophers and many features of a philosophy, or approaches to a question, can be called empiricist without involving this whole story. Empiricists may, for instance, confine themselves to opposing the more extreme forms of *rationalism*. Or they may allow that the mind is active in the way mentioned above, but insist that there are no a priori truths, i.e. truths that can be known without recourse to experience; apparent exceptions such as the truths of mathematics and logic they will regard as not really truths in any substantive sense at all, but more like rules of procedure, so that 'Twice two is four' means something like 'When confronted with two things and two things assume you have four things'. Probably most philosophers would regard themselves as empiricists to some degree, if only because refusing to do so might suggest adherence to an extreme form of rationalism. But the distinction between empiricism and rationalism is wearing thin for reasons connected with the challenges recently mounted against the analytic–synthetic distinction, and one motive for refusing to call oneself an empiricist (or a rationalist for that matter) is that it suggests that one accepts that distinction. But even with regard to the older philosophers the traditional contrast between 'British empiricists' and 'continental rationalists' cannot be regarded as anything but a rough label of convenience, however true it may be that, as explained above, empiricism in particular reached a zenith among the former.

Also one should distinguish between empiricism as a psychological doctrine of how the mind acquires the contents it has and empiricism as a doctrine of justification, about how we can justify our various claims to knowledge. However, these questions are often run together, especially in older writers, and indeed they have not always been kept apart in the present article. Furthermore though the two questions are conceptually distinct, and for much of the twentieth century in particular the distinction was rigorously insisted on, more recently the tendency has been revived, though this time overt and acknowledged, to run the questions together, or else to assert that the latter (concerning justification) cannot be answered and must be replaced by the former (concerning origins and development).

One further sphere in which the relevance of empiricism may be mentioned is ethics. If we cast cheerfully aside the bogy represented by the *naturalistic fallacy, we might define 'good' in terms of something like 'catering for certain interests', and then perhaps define 'right' as something like 'tending to maximize good'. If we insist that this is what the terms *mean*, so that the definitions are simply a matter of semantics, we can then claim that ethics has become an empirical subject, assuming at any rate that it is an empirical matter what things count as interests and for whom. Of course whether we should take this line is another question.

Various types of empiricism have been singled out from time to time and given special names. *Logical Positivism is a type of empiricism, and indeed is one of the main forms that extreme empiricism has taken in its revival during the twentieth century. Because it concerns the meanings of words or sentences it has sometimes been called *logical empiricism, just as Logical Positivism itself is so called for that reason. One Logical Positivist in particular, Moritz Schlick, dignified his own version of the theory with the name 'consistent empiricism'. One philosophy with some kinship to empiricism is *pragmatism, and William James called his own version of empiricism 'radical empiricism', though, distinguishing it from pragmatism. Constructive empiricism is the view, associated with Bas van Fraassen, that science should aim to construct a theory which will be 'empirically adequate', i.e. will imply the truth of all that we find to be true when we observe entities that can be observed. The theory may make statements purporting to claim the existence of unobservable entities (electrons etc.) and such statements must be taken literally, not analysed as 'really' saying something different and innocuous; but we can treat it as a good theory, and *accept* it for scientific purposes, without *believing* it.   A.R.L.

*naturalism.

E. H. Gombrich, *Art and Illusion* (London, 1968) is useful on how things 'really look'.

D. Odegard, 'Locke as an Empiricist', *Philosophy* (1965) includes discussion of senses of 'empiricism'.

B. van Fraassen, *The Scientific Image* (Oxford, 1980). Constructive empiricism.

L. Wittgenstein, *Philosophical Investigations* (London, 1953). His main relevant work.

empiricism, logical. A programme for the study of science that combined traditional *empiricism with symbolic logic. Logical empiricists held that all scientific claims must be evaluated on the basis of empirical evidence. They attempted to develop a formal inductive logic, modelled on deductive logic, to assess the empirical justification of scientific hypotheses. This inductive logic would be established a priori and provide norms for evaluating hypotheses against the evidence. They also sought to make clear the logical structure of scientific explanation and prediction. Logical empiricists attempted to show that all scientific concepts derive their meaning from their relation to experience. This proved particularly difficult in the case of concepts such as electron or gene; attempts to establish the empirical basis of such concepts provided a major research problem throughout the history of logical empiricism. Logical empiricism, as originally formulated, has been superseded, but its spirit continues in those philosophers who use formal semantics for the analysis of scientific theories and who seek an inductive logic built on *Bayes's theorem.   H.I.B.

*Logical Positivism.

J. J. Joergensen, *The Development of Logical Empiricism* (Chicago, 1951).

empiricism, radical: *see* James.

empirio-criticism. A theory of the knowledge of nature promoted by the German positivist Richard Avenarius and associated with the Austrian physicist and philosopher Ernst Mach. It eliminates all scientific notions not directly or indirectly verifiable in sense experience. The theory marks a meeting-point between German *idealism and British *empiricism, and the inherent *phenomenalism of the position led to Lenin's criticism of it in *Materialism and Empirio-criticism* as a form of Berkeleian idealism.   A.H.

R. Avenarius, *Kritik der reinen Erfahrung* (Critique of Pure Experience), 2 vols. (Leipzig, 1888–90)).

enantiomorph: *see* incongruent counterparts.

Encyclopaedists. A group of eighteenth-century European scholars, scientists, writers, and artists who collaborated in a massive effort to bring the fruits of human learning together into a single publication. Under the editorship of Denis Diderot and Jean d'Alembert, this 'encyclopaedia' was intended as both a concise summation of all theoretical knowledge, and a practical manual of concrete 'how-to-do-it' advice of use to every worker in his shop. It also contained, through a complex system of ironic, and often irreverent, 'cross-references', a surreptitious challenge to the traditional authority of the Catholic Church, and to the political establishment as well. Publication was intermittently suspended by the authorities, but eventually permitted to see completion. The final edition of the work appeared in 1772, and comprised a total of seventeen volumes of text and eleven volumes of technical, illustrative plates.   P.F.J.

*dictionaries and encyclopaedias of philosophy.

John Viscount Morley, *Diderot and the Encyclopaedists*, 2 vols. (first pub. 1923; Ann Arbor, Mich., 1971).

ends and means. It is a common philosophical assumption that all actions can be analysed as *means* to the achievement of some *end* or goal or purpose. With this goes the idea that the end of a particular action may in turn be a means to some further end, and perhaps also (though this does not necessarily follow) that all sequences of means and ends terminate in some one ultimate end—for example, happiness. Thus I may go for a walk, this activity being a means to the end of taking some exercise, which in turn is a means to the end of improving my health—and this, perhaps, is a means to the ultimate end of my happiness.

A natural objection would then be that though some actions are performed for the sake of an end, others are not. My going for a walk may not be with the aim of taking exercise and improving my health—I may simply like going for a walk. The defender of the 'ends–means' analysis can then say, however, that if the action is not a means to an end, then it is an end in itself; every action must still, therefore, be either an end or a means.

There is no doubt that all actions *can* be fitted into this ends–means framework. It may nevertheless be misleading, for what it naturally suggests is a division between *actions* as means and something like *states of affairs* as ends. This way of thinking becomes particularly contentious when applied to the moral assessment of actions. It leads easily to the view that actions can be assessed as right or wrong simply by reference to their effectiveness in bringing about desirable ends. Such a view of morality is referred to as a 'teleological' view or *consequentialism. A classic example is *utilitarianism.

This kind of moral position can perhaps be argued to be a correct one, but it is not just self-evidently correct. A traditional criticism has been that morality is not just a matter of ends, it also imposes certain moral *constraints* on the way in which we pursue our ends; whatever we are aiming at, we ought not to try to achieve it by killing innocent people, by torturing or enslaving people, by lying or deceiving. Such actions are said to be wrong in themselves, whatever ends they may or may not achieve. This position is sometimes called a *deontology, and if the constraints are thought of as ones to which there can be no exception, it may be called a form of 'absolutism'. It is not refuted simply by asserting that the ends–means analysis necessarily applies to all actions, for this would be a misleading application of that claim.

The point can be illustrated by the use that is made of the dictum 'The end justifies the means'. Strictly interpreted, it may be unexceptionable, for what else could justify something *as a means* if not the fact that it will effectively achieve its end? However, it does not follow that all actions can be justified only in this way, as the teleological moralists would assert. All the more dangerous is the use of the maxim 'The end justifies the means' to suggest that because some particular end is thought to be supremely important—the triumph of a particular religious creed, or the capture of political power by a particular party—the use of any means whatever is morally acceptable.   R.J.N.

*instrumental value.

Jonathan Glover, *Causing Death and Saving Lives* (Harmondsworth, 1977), chs. 6–7.

J. L. Mackie, *Ethics* (Harmondsworth, 1977), ch. 7.
Samuel Scheffler (ed.), *Consequentialism and its Critics* (Oxford, 1988).

endurance and perdurance. In order for something to persist over time, it must—somehow or other—exist at different times. Endurance and perdurance theories offer contrasting accounts of persistence, of how something may succeed in existing in this way. According to a perdurance theory, a thing persists by virtue of 'perduring': this means the thing has different temporal parts that exist at different times. (Note that the definition of perdurance does not require that the different temporal parts that make up a thing exist at continuous times.) According to an endurance theory, a thing persists by virtue of 'enduring': this means that the thing is wholly present at different times. It is contentious, however, just what the notion of being wholly present really amounts to.   F.MacB.

David Lewis, *On the Plurality of Worlds* (Oxford, 1986), 202–4.

energy. Early work on statics indicated that the product of force times distance, later called work, was an essential organizing concept. The capacity of something to produce or generate work became known as energy. It was also clear as early as Aristotle that the motion of an object contributed to its ability to generate work.

In the heroic days of the Scientific Revolution, the question arose how properly to measure the 'quantity of motion' or 'vis viva'. The Cartesians suggested that it was proportionate to mass times velocity and Leibniz that it was proportionate to mass times the square of velocity. In all collision phenomena the former quantity is conserved. In collisions involving appropriately hard objects the latter is conserved as well. Only later was it realized that both momentum and kinetic energy are important separately conserved dynamical quantities.

The disappearance of energy of motion which is 'stored' in some state of the system but recoverable as energy of motion led to the notion of latent or potential energy. Examples include the energy stored when an object is raised in a gravitational field that can be reconverted to energy of motion by allowing the object to fall, the energy stored in the elastic distortion of a solid, or the energy stored in a electromagnetic field. This potential energy becomes distinguished from the energy of motion, itself later called kinetic energy. The discovery that heat could be treated as energy of hidden motions of the microcomponents of systems and that the gain or loss of overt energy was matched by a compensating loss or gain of heat content when combined with the recoverability of energy of motion from potential energy led finally to the full conservation of energy principle.

Work culminating in that of Emma Noether led to the realization that dynamical conservation was intimately related to symmetry in space and time. Conservation of energy follows from the invariance of system behaviour under time translation, as conservation of momentum does from invariance under spatial translation and conservation of angular momentum from invariance under rotation.

With the advent of special relativistic *space-time, energy and momentum become unified as components of a four-vector. There had been earlier philosophical speculation that matter could just be considered, in some sense, a centre of force or some sort of 'congealed energy'. Such speculations increased as the field concept of the nineteenth century led to an expanded notion of substance as being spatially dispersed and having as its essential nature the ability to carry causal influence over distance and time. The relativistic discovery of the proportionality of inertial mass to energy content leads to the conception of energy as 'quantity of substance' rather than as mere feature of matter. With general relativity comes the possibility of space-times that are not homogeneous or isotropic. With this loss of symmetry energy conservation in the global sense goes as well. The concept of energy in general relativity is a subtle one. For example, although energy can go from matter into the gravitational field, i.e. the curvature structure of space-time, the very localization of such gravitational energy is undetermined.   L.S.

*relativity theory.

P. Duhem, *The Evolution of Mechanics* (Germantown, Md., 1980).
E. Hiebert, *Historical Roots of the Principle of the Conservation of Energy* (Madison, Wis., 1962).
M. Jammer, 'Energy', in P. Edwards (ed.), *The Encyclopedia of Philosophy* (New York, 1967).

enforcement of morals. The view that morality should be enforced by the criminal law.

The disentanglement of distinctively moral norms from legal norms has taken several centuries and is still controversial. Moreover, even those who allow that law and morality can be independently identified may still argue about the extent to which the criminal law should be used to sanction morality. Clearly, all must agree that some moral rules should be sanctioned, such as those against unjustifiable killing, assault, theft, fraud, the protection of minors from exploitation, and so on. But should the criminal law be brought into such matters as prostitution and *homosexuality? Those who think that it should can argue that society may use the law to preserve morality in the same way as it uses it to safeguard anything else that is essential to its existence.

This thesis was put in an extreme form by the nineteenth-century jurist Sir James Fitzjames Stephen, who argued that the enforcement of morality is good in itself, and in a more moderate form by Lord Patrick Devlin in the twentieth century, who argued that the enforcement of morals was good as a means because morality is the cement of society. The opposition came from J. S. Mill in the nineteenth century and H. L. A. Hart in the twentieth. They argue that the law should be used only to protect individuals from demonstrable harm from others, and that any more extensive use of the criminal law is unjustifiable legal paternalism. The controversy continues over

such matters as legalizing the use of cannabis, censorship, and so on.   R.S.D.

*liberty; public morality; public–private distinction.

Patrick Devlin, *The Enforcement of Morals* (Oxford, 1965).
H. L. A. Hart, *Law, Liberty and Morality* (Oxford, 1963).

Engels, Friedrich (1820–95). German social theorist, working-class organizer, and philosopher. Son of a textile manufacturer, his hopes for a career in literature were crossed by his father, who insisted that he work in the family business. He was already an adherent of the Young Hegelian and radical working-class movements when he first made the acquaintance of Karl Marx in Berlin in November 1842. It was not until nearly two years later in Paris that the two men became friends, beginning a lifetime of extraordinarily close collaboration. It was Engels who introduced Marx both to the working-class movement and to the study of political economy. After participating in the unsuccessful revolution of 1848, Engels moved to Manchester, where until 1869 he worked in the family business. Until Marx's death in 1883 he produced a series of writings on history, politics, and philosophy, devoting the last ten years of his life to the posthumous publication of the second and third volumes of Marx's *Capital*.

Always acknowledging Marx's mind to be more original and profound than his own, Engels nevertheless was an able writer of encyclopaedic learning, whose writings cover a much broader range of topics than Marx's. Because Engels popularized the thought of his friend and extended it to the realms of science and philosophy, the philosophy of *dialectical materialism owes far more to his writings than to Marx's. Some of the principal doctrines with which Marxism is identified are more Engels's doctrines than Marx's. Chief among such doctrines are that Marxian socialism is *scientific*, in contrast to the 'utopian' socialism of earlier theorists, and that the world outlook based on materialist dialectics should view nature as operating according to dialectical laws.   A.W.W.

*anti-communism.

K. Marx and F. Engels, *Selected Works* (London, 1942, 1951).
G. Lichtheim, *Marxism* (London, 1964).

English philosophy. It is not easy to distinguish English philosophy strictly so called from philosophy in the English language. It is even harder to disentangle it from British philosophy. American philosophy, even in the colonial period, has always been reasonably distinctive; that of Australasia and Canada less so, since many of the chief practitioners came from either England or Scotland (Anderson, Brett) or settled there (Alexander, Mackie). Of the Irish philosophers, one, the eighth-century Neoplatonist John Scotus Eriugena, had no English connection whatever. Berkeley came to live, and die, in England, and Burke spent most of his active life there. Hume was the greatest member of a substantially independent Scottish tradition, but the movement of philosophers, and their ideas, between England and Scotland was on too large a scale to allow the exclusion of Scottish philosophers from any survey of English philosophy that aims to avoid eccentricity.

In the space available it will not be possible to mention all the leading philosophers and give an informative account of their opinions. What follows is a general survey of tendencies. English philosophy proper began with Adelard of Bath (c.1080–c.1145), expositor of Arab science, translator of Euclid, and author of a treatise on the problem of universals. The topic had been installed at the centre of philosophical discussion by the Frenchmen William of Champeaux, Roscellinus, and Abelard. With John of Salisbury (1115–80) the impact of the rediscovered writings of Aristotle was registered.

The harmonization of the doctrines of Aristotle with Christian beliefs became a dominating project for *medieval philosophers, a daunting one since Aristotle thought the world had no beginning, and so was not created, and that only the 'active reason', a small, impersonal part of the soul, survived death. The planned reconciliation was carried to a gloriously systematic completion by Aquinas in the third quarter of the thirteenth century. A conservative attachment to the opposed and more spiritual Neoplatonic philosophy of Augustine was almost universal in England during this period: in Alexander of Hales (c.1178–1245), the teacher of Bonaventure, who led the anti-Aristotelian movement in France, Robert Grosseteste (c.1175–1273), the first major Oxford philosopher, who made large contributions to natural science, and his wayward pupil Roger Bacon (1220–92), who saw experiment and mathematics as essential for natural knowledge.

Grosseteste, one of Oxford's first chancellors, initiated the unchallenged dominance by the Franciscans of Oxford, and consequently of English, philosophy at that time, in the thirteenth and fourteenth centuries. That effectively excluded the Thomism of the Dominicans, which never got a hold in England. Starting from the proposition 'God said led there be light', he understood knowledge as divine illumination and saw God's creation of nature as the endowment of prime matter with extension by means of light. His pupil Roger Bacon went on to develop an optical theory according to which 'species' convey the nature of external objects to the perceiving mind.

With Duns Scotus (c.1266–1308) and William of Ockham (c.1285–1349) the Franciscans moved from resisting the Aristotelianism of Dominicans like Aquinas to actively undermining it. Both insisted on the inadequacy of reason in the supernatural realm of theology, which must rest on faith in revelation. Scotus was a realist about universals, but Ockham held that generality is a feature of language, not of the world. Ockham was a precursor of empiricism, maintaining that all natural knowledge comes from direct sensory awareness. That led his French followers towards some brilliant anticipations of the mathematical physics of the seventeenth century, but in England the main effect was the inspiration of a productive group of

mathematicians and logicians. One way in which Scotus and Ockham limited the scope of reason was by affirming the absolute freedom of God's infinitely powerful will. The morally right is simply what God commands. Some English philosophers (the Pelagians) applied this by analogy to man and were vehemently resisted by the Augustinian determinist Thomas Bradwardine (1290–1349). Ockham was the first English philosopher to acquire a large European reputation. He had no notable followers in England, but European universities soon divided into groups supporting the old and the new Ockhamite logic. His firm defence of Franciscan poverty led to his condemnation by the Pope. He managed to escape from this to the protection of Ludwig of Bavaria, repaying his benefactor with copious writings on the necessity of separating church and state.

After a century and a half of remarkable vitality English philosophy sank into inertia and repetitiveness for 200 years. John Wyclif (c.1320–84), who began as a rationalistic philosopher, helped to bring this about by his subsequent ecclesiastical and political excesses of opinion, which amounted to a kind of protestantism. Rendered suspect to the authorities, philosophy fell silent through the fifteenth century and the religious strife of the first, pre-Elizabethan half of the Tudor period was equally unpropitious for independent thought. The circle of humanists around Erasmus in early sixteenth-century Oxford soon disintegrated. The Platonic theology of John Colet and Thomas More's *Utopia* (1516) were its main fruits.

The absence of interesting philosophy in England between the metaphysics of the young Wyclif (*Summa de Ente, c.1370*) and the emergence of Francis Bacon in the early seventeenth century calls for explanation. The Black Death is one possible factor; another is the Great Schism (1378–1415), which exposed English thinkers to more direct and local ecclesiastical control. Furthermore, the Hundred Years War broke the previously invigorating connections with the universities of the Continent. Perhaps, like the roughly contemporaneous period of drought in English poetry between Chaucer (d. 1400) and Wyatt and Spenser over a century later, it is just a brute fact.

Francis Bacon (1561–1626) may have profited from some renewed philosophical life in Elizabethan Cambridge, however scornful he may have been about his official course of studies. He projected a giant scheme of philosophical renovation and carried three parts of it to something like completion: his critique of false philosophies—scholastic, humanistic, and occult—and of obstacles in human nature to the acquisition of real knowledge; his detailed survey and classification of all actual and possible intellectual disciplines; and his technique for acquiring genuine scientific knowledge by eliminative induction. The elaborate formal apparatus of 'tables', qualified by a thick encrustation of 'prerogative instances', was taken over two centuries later by J. S. Mill with little improvement and even less acknowledgement. Less well known

FRANCIS BACON attempted to found a new programme and method for scientific enquiry, to replace the ancient Greek models which he rejected.

THOMAS REID propounded a philosophy founded on common sense, with which faculty he sought to dispel the doubts and difficulties thrown up by the empiricists.

HENRY SIDGWICK offered in the late nineteenth century a utilitarian moral theory whose central principle was universal hedonism.

F. H. BRADLEY: his appetite for pedagogy was reputedly satisfied by one brief tutorial at Merton College, Oxford; he concentrated thereafter on his own flamboyantly original work. His fellowship at Merton was tenable until marriage, which deliverance Bradley never sought.

is Bacon's materialist philosophy of nature, largely derived from Telesio.

Thomas Hobbes (1588–1679) was equally independent and systematic and more uncompromisingly materialist than Bacon. For him everything is matter in motion, including man (his mental life consists of small movements in the head) and human society, the subject of *Leviathan*. There he maintained that reason, in the service of the supreme value of bodily security, dictates obedience to an unlimited sovereign. All men are equally liable to death at the hands of others, so all have the same interest in the establishment of a supreme power that can protect them against it. The only circumstance in which obedience to the state can be rationally withheld is its failure to provide that protection. Hobbes saw the civil war as the outcome of the unfettered exercise of a supposed right to private judgement in matters of belief. He concluded that the church should be wholly subordinate to the state, which alone should authorize its doctrines.

Bacon was quietly and Hobbes noisily irreligious. Hobbes's excesses were countered by Lord Herbert of Cherbury (1583–1648) and directly attacked by the Cambridge Platonists, of whom the most important was Ralph Cudworth (1617–88). Herbert boiled religion down to five large principles (God exists and should be worshipped etc.) taken to be intuitively self-evident. Cudworth argued that mind is wholly distinct from matter and is prior to it in being constructively essential to our knowledge of it.

The ideas of Herbert underlay the long eighteenth-century episode of deism. Deism denied the personality of God and the claims of Christ or anybody else to be the incarnation of God. Deism was espoused by Voltaire, but had no philosophically distinguished exponents in England, although it was defended by many vigorous and intelligent controversialists. Bolingbroke, who infuriated Samuel Johnson and Burke, was at least a major public figure and a brilliant writer. A less extreme form of latitudinarianism was inspired by John Locke (1632–1704), as intimated by the title of his book *The Reasonableness of Christianity*. Even more important and influential were his *Two Treatises of Government*, whose ideas were communicated to the *philosophes by Voltaire and were central to the thoughts and actions of the Founding Fathers of the United States. Locke's political theory is more a moderate version of Hobbes's than wholly opposed to it. Both contend that government is a human contrivance set up to serve certain human purposes and to be obeyed only to the extent that it succeeds in serving them. Locke differs from Hobbes over what the relevant purposes are, adding liberty and property to Hobbes's life.

Philosophically, however, Locke is important for making the theory of knowledge the heart of the subject, under the influence of Descartes. Nearly all our knowledge of matters of fact comes from our *'ideas' or private sense-impressions. We infer from them external, material causes which we may conclude resemble them as far as the measurable qualities of interest to physics are concerned. We can infer God from the evident existence of intelligence in the world. We can form abstract ideas, but no abstract universals correspond to them, only resemblances. Of most matters of fact we do not have certain knowledge, only probable opinion.

The theory of knowledge of the Irish George Berkeley (1685–1753) is largely a critical commentary on that of Locke, which accepts Locke's first, empiricist principle. The inference Locke proposes from 'ideas' to objects is unacceptable. The involuntariness of their occurrence shows that they have a cause outside us, but it can only be spiritual, that is to say God, who, as well as administering to us those we perceive, sustains in his own mind the ideas unperceived by us whose existence is suggested by continuity.

The Scottish David Hume (1711–76) is conventionally seen as carrying on directly from Locke and Berkeley, though there were other influences on him—his Scottish predecessor Francis Hutcheson (1694–1746) and the French sceptic and apostle of tolerance Pierre Bayle. Impressions are all that we really know and all inferences from them to other modes of being, whether material as in Locke or spiritual as in Berkeley, are unjustifiable. Of particular importance is his view that our belief in causal connection, assumed unquestioningly by Locke and confined to the spiritual realm by Berkeley, is an unjustifiable inference from the intimations of regularity that we actually perceive. For Hume our beliefs in objects, minds, and causes can be explained but not validated; they are the outcome of habit, of instinct rather than intellect. Hume's scepticism was less offensive to his contemporaries than his attacks on religion. The argument from design was classically demolished in his *Dialogues Concerning Natural Religion* (1779). Miracles were disposed of by the consideration that the falsity of the testimony on which they were based was much more probable that that of the well-attested laws of nature which they flouted.

From the end of the Middle Ages philosophy had been pursued by independent men of letters rather than teachers in universities. The universities of Scotland came to life in the eighteenth century, as they were doing in Germany. In England they remained intellectually torpid until the nineteenth century was fairly well advanced. Before then there were some philosophically active clergymen, such as Samuel Clarke (1675–1729), who sought to establish the existence and nature of God by rigorous, quasi-mathematical deduction, and Joseph Butler (1692–1752), who used an effective critique of Hobbes's narrowly egoistic account of human motivation to support a theory that moral truth is discovered by rational intuition, as had been less persuasively affirmed by Cudworth, Clarke, and, rather furtively, Locke.

A casual remark of Locke that God might have attached the power of thinking to material substance led, by way of David Hartley's (1705–57) resolute *associationism and the belief that the mind is dependent on the brain, to the full-blooded materialism and *determinism of Joseph Priestley (1733–1804). Locke's clerical critics were of less importance than these independent-minded developers of his thought. A leading theme of eighteenth-century ethical theory had been the doctrine of a moral sense, understood in an almost aesthetically contemplative way by Lord Shaftesbury (1671–1713). His ideas were taken up by Hutcheson, who parenthetically took the greatest good of the greatest number to be the common element of the actions approved by the moral sense. The same idea is presented more forcefully in Hume. He took the sentiment of approval arising from disinterested contemplation of conduct to be the actual basis of moral judgments, but then went on to say that what in fact secures approval is conduct which is useful or agreeable to the agent or others, a short step from making general utility the criterion of right conduct. A more explicit utilitarianism is to be found in Priestley, in Hartley's disciple Abraham Tucker (1705–74), and, above all, in William Paley (1743–1805).

As well as his materialist theory of the mind and his utilitarian ethics (from which Bentham derived his fundamental principle), Priestley developed a radically democratic theory of government, arguing that only in a democratic system do the rulers have an immediate motive for pursuing the general good. Other friends of the American and French Revolutions agreed with him, notably Burke's critic Thomas Paine and Shelley's disreputable father-in-law, William Godwin. Burke, the great conservative opponent of the French, but not of the American, Revolution, based his opposition on a general theory of the intrinsic complexity of human society which makes it inaccessible to the elementary moral arithmetic of the radicals. He had begun his intellectual career (after an ironical piece about Bolingbroke) an an aesthetician, his *Philosophical Enquiry into the Origin of our Ideas of the Sublime and Beautiful* being the first truly philosophical aesthetic treatise in English.

Hume's best critics were his compatriots of the Scottish school of *common sense, all, like Hutcheson, professors. Thomas Reid (1710–96) saw Hume's apparently desperate scepticism as the inevitable consequence of his subjectively empiricist starting-point. Perception, he held, is not the same thing as sensation. He took what were for Hume imaginative habits to be the expression of self-evident principles. His ideas were sonorously elaborated by Dugald Stewart (1753–1828), tricked out with a great deal of rather unconvincing scholarship by Sir William Hamilton (1788–1856), and imported to Oxford by the stylish H. L. Mansel (1820–71). The last two of these constituted the 'school of intuition' against whom J. S. Mill represented his own 'school of experience'.

Hume's ideas, particularly his associationist theory of mind and his utilitarian theory of value, came into their own as publicly influential through the agency of Jeremy Bentham (1748–1832) and the 'philosophical radicals' who followed him. James Mill (1773–1836), father of J.S., took charge of association (and supplied a simple, potent argument for democracy on utilitarian grounds); Bentham set to work with the principle of utility, attacking the Lockean certainties of Blackstone about law and the state, designing legal and penal codes, and defending the principle

itself. John Stuart Mill (1806–73), loyal to his utilitarian inheritance, gave the principle its best-known defence, with qualifications that laid it open to criticism. He had earlier renovated Bacon's account of *induction and, in the guise of an attack on Hamilton and Mansel, put forward a reductive view of objects and minds that was to be carried further by his secular godson Russell. In the wider world he supplied a rather marginally utilitarian defence for his belief in extensive liberty and relied more on justice than utility in his attack on the subjection of women.

By the early nineteenth century, the ancient English universities were coming to, after a long period of torpor. J. H. Newman had to educate himself philosophically, but did so to some purpose, as shown by his *University Sermons* (1841), and *Grammar of Assent* (1870). A recognizably professorial professionalism first appears with H. L. Mansel's *Metaphysics* (1857). Apart from his general philosophy, what made him well known in his own time was his almost Ockhamist rejection of positive theology in the interest of faith and revelation. The publication of *The Origin of Species* in 1859 caused a turmoil of intellectual activity spreading far beyond the domain of zoology. Herbert Spencer (1820–1903) applied the evolutionary principle to a large range of topics but nowhere very incisively, least of all in philosophy. T. H. Huxley (1825–95) was more impressive, but he was only an occasional philosopher, as was the brilliant, short-lived W. K. Clifford (1845–79), a kind of English Ernst Mach in whom ideas like Mill's were stiffened with much mathematics and some biology.

By the time of his death in the 1870s the small trickle of German *idealism introduced in the early years of the century by S. T. Coleridge (1772–1834) had swelled to a tide that was soon to engulf the universities and, with the retreat of the amateur, the philosophy of England, Scotland, and the English-speaking world generally. T. H. Green (1836–82) introduced it to Oxford, where it was most memorably, and aggressively, expounded by F. H. Bradley (1846–1924). In Cambridge a milder version of idealism was introduced by John Grote (1813–66). J. M. E. McTaggart (1866–1925), the most talented and systematic of later Cambridge idealists, was anything but mild, holding that, in the end, all that exists are individual souls timelessly related by love. Green and Bradley held that matter, space, time, and in Bradley's case the self were unreal, internally inconsistent abstractions which the understanding carved out of reality for practical purposes, leaving it to philosophic reason to represent things as a unified whole. Idealism had edifying consequences for religion and politics, eliminating superstitious literalism from the one and supporting the more Platonic aspects of the status quo in the other.

It was in this body of ideas that Russell and Moore were brought up and from which they reacted into a pluralism which insisted that reality is composed not only of many things but of things of several different ultimate kinds: material, mental, abstract. As a byproduct of his herculean effort to devise a logic strong and flexible enough to derive mathematics from, Russell acquired the intellectual machinery for the analysis that the plurality of the world made legitimate. The arrival of Wittgenstein in Cambridge led to the joint invention by him and Russell of logical atomism. Respectable philosophers shied away from this. C. D. Broad (1887–1971), for example, did not move far from the positions held by Russell and Moore in 1910: a Lockean theory of matter, a Cartesian theory of mind, and a Kantian theory of necessary truth.

The younger English philosophers of the 1930s, influenced by the local *logical atomism and by the positivists of the *Vienna Circle, saw matter as a system or family of sense-impressions, actual and possible, mind as a sequence of experiences, and necessary truth as analytic or definitional. This was the body of ideas audaciously put forward by A. J. Ayer (1910–89) and steadily watered down by him over the following half-century. He rejected metaphysics more vehemently than Russell, or even Wittgenstein, and scandalized many by his denial of meaning to judgements of value. The passage of time has led to the recognition that his accounts of both meaning and value are self-refuting.

A realism at Oxford parallel to that of Russell and Moore in Cambridge derived from John Cook Wilson. He had been brought up in Bradleyan idealism but very gradually, and (as it turned out with the posthumous publication of his writings) very copiously, broke away. His main theme, the necessary independence of the object known from the mind that knows it, was elaborated in a refined and somewhat paradoxical way, by his most gifted pupil, H. A. Prichard. Most Oxford philosophers from the Edwardian decade to the present are, whether aware of it or, as is more usual, not, Cook Wilsonians. In some eminent cases, such as H. H. Price and Gilbert Ryle, other influences have been importantly at work, largely from Cambridge. But J. L. Austin was very plainly a product of the school. There is a marked Cook Wilsonian flavour to P. F. Strawson's early critique of formal logic.

Metaphysics did not lie down dead under the attack of Russell, Wittgenstein, and their followers. Samuel Alexander (1859–1938) produced one large system of an evolutionary kind, A. N. Whitehead (1861–1947) another. They fell on stony ground, flowered briefly, and then forfeited attention. R. G. Collingwood (1889–1943), a late-Hegelian idealist, not influenced, as Alexander and Whitehead had been, by recent developments in natural science, avoided a system, but had some powerful ideas about art, religion, history, and even the history of science.

By 1945 and the end of the war idealism had a vestigial presence on a few Scottish chairs. British, Russellian positivism was well entrenched, but was taking on a new inflexion. On the one hand Wittgenstein's later, informal, puzzlement-relieving doctrines were seeping, against his wishes, from Cambridge. (Ryle took them up in Oxford in his own breezy, even peremptory, manner.) On the other J. L. Austin (1911–60), with great brilliance, turned a local, Oxonian practice of lexicographic exactitude

(parallel to that of Moore in Cambridge) into an enthralling, if only occasionally philosophical, technique.

The influence of Quine and some other American philosophers turned English philosophy away from the painstaking analysis of ordinary language after Austin's death. The year before, P. F. (now Sir Peter) Strawson (1919–) had produced *Individuals*, a large book on a very large subject. Its predominant theme is that if there is to be coherent discourse, objects that are located in space and endure through time must be presupposed. This broadly Kantian notion was brought to bear in Strawson's remarkable work of Kant interpretation, in which, if much of Kant is jettisoned, much remains. Since then the style, if not the doctrine, of Russell and the early Wittgenstein and of logically, and often scientifically, sophisticated American philosophers under their influence, has obliterated linguistic philosophy. The most admired, if not best-understood, English philosopher at the end of the twentieth century was Michael Dummett (1925–), close student of the great logician Frege, pertinacious questioner of the law of excluded middle. Comparably gifted, if less sharply focused, was the imaginative moral philosopher Bernard Williams (1929–2003), who doubted the possibility of giving a fully rational foundation to our moral beliefs and practices. Along with many of the best of currently active English philosophers he departed (in his case only partially) to the United States. Perhaps the history of English philosophy, as distinct from English-language philosophy, is drawing to its close. If so, it is on terms that few would have expected as little as thirty years ago.   A.Q.

*American philosophy; Irish philosophy; Scottish philosophy; Oxford philosophy; Cambridge philosophy; London philosophy.

M. H. Carré, *Phases of Thought in England* (Oxford, 1949).
J. H. Muirhead, *The Platonic Tradition in Anglo-Saxon Philosophy* (London, 1931).
J. Seth, *English Philosophers and Schools of Philosophy* (London, 1912).
W. R. Sorley, *A History of English Philosophy* (Cambridge, 1920).

Enlightenment. 'Enlightenment', and its equivalents in other European languages, denotes an intellectual movement which began in England in the seventeenth century (Locke and the deists), and developed in France in the eighteenth century (Bayle, Voltaire, Diderot, and other Encyclopaedists) and also (especially under the impetus of the rationalist philosophy of Christian Wolff) in Germany (Mendelssohn, Lessing). But virtually every European country, and every sphere of life and thought, was affected by it. The age in which the movement predominated is known as the Age of Enlightenment or the Age of Reason.

'Enlightenment' contrasts with the darkness of irrationality and superstition that supposedly characterized the Middle Ages, but it is not easy to define in a general way. Kant, one of the last, as well as the greatest, of Enlightenment thinkers, said that enlightenment is the 'emergence of man from his self-imposed infancy. Infancy is the inability to use one's reason without the guidance of another. It is self-imposed, when it depends on a deficiency, not of reason, but of the resolve and courage to use it without external guidance. Thus the watchword of enlightenment is: *Sapere aude!* Have the courage to use one's own reason!' Thus the leading doctrines of the Enlightenment, shared by many, if not all, of its spokesmen, are these:

1. *Reason is man's central capacity, and it enables him not only to think, but to act, correctly.

2. Man is by nature rational and good. (Kant endorsed the Christian view of a 'radical evil' in human nature, but held that it must be possible to overcome it.)

3. Both an individual and humanity as a whole can progress to perfection.

4. All men (including, on the view of many, women) are equal in respect of their rationality, and should thus be granted equality before the law and individual liberty.

5. Tolerance is to be extended to other creeds and ways of life. (Lessing conveyed this message in his play *Nathan the Wise* (1779).)

6. Beliefs are to be accepted only on the basis of reason, not on the authority of priests, sacred texts, or tradition. Thus Enlightenment thinkers tended to atheism, or at most to a purely natural or rational *deism, shorn of supernatural and miraculous elements and designed primarily to support an enlightened moral code and, in some cases, to account for the fact that the universe is a rational system, wholly accessible to human reason.

7. The Enlightenment devalues local 'prejudices' and customs, which owe their development to historical peculiarities rather than to the exercise of reason. What matters to the Enlightenment is not whether one is French or German, but that one is an individual man, united in brotherhood with all other men by the rationality one shares with them.

8. In general, the Enlightenment plays down the non-rational aspects of human nature. Works of art, for example, should be regular and instructive, the product of taste rather than genius. Education should impart knowledge rather than mould feelings or develop character.

The Enlightenment is in one sense 'unhistorical', holding that all men are at all times (and in all places) fundamentally the same in nature and that differences between them that have arisen over history are superficial and dispensable. But it nevertheless had a considerable influence on historiography. In his *Essai sur les mœurs et l'esprit des nations*, Voltaire (who coined the phrase 'philosophie de l'histoire') presents the standard Enlightenment view: history is man's progressive struggle for rational culture. The Encyclopaedist Montesquieu anticipated post-Enlightenment developments by attempting to explain the laws of a nation in terms of its natural and historical circumstances.

From its beginnings, but especially from the late eighteenth century on, the Enlightenment was subjected to powerful criticism. Its suggestion that medieval philosophers accepted their beliefs on authority alone will not withstand a reading of their works. Its wholesale rejection of traditional beliefs and institutions is vulnerable to Burke's (and, with regard to language, J. L. Austin's) response that the accumulated wisdom of past generations is more likely to be correct than the ideas of an individual philosopher. Its demand that an individual should subject *all* his beliefs to criticism, and accept *nothing* on authority (a claim still endorsed in J. S. Mill's *On Liberty*), is thwarted by the gulf between any given individual's meagre first-hand experience and the range of knowledge now available to him. Its depreciation of the non-rational aspects of man and of the differences between cultures, in favour of a narrowly defined rationality, met with criticism from later thinkers, the best of whom (such as Hegel) attempted to combine the individualist rationalism of the Enlightenment with the requirements of a cohesive, stable community. But some opponents of the Enlightenment, such as Nietzsche, rejected its doctrines over a wide front, its egalitarianism and belief in progress, as well as the primacy of reason.

Many of these criticisms have force and are the subject of continuing debate. But the benefits of the Enlightenment to, for example, historiography, cannot be denied. Even its critics have little choice but to pay the Enlightenment the compliment of turning its own weapons against it: the limits of reason can be discerned only by reason itself.

If it is clear enough when the Age of Enlightenment began, it is less clear when, or whether, it ended. In one sense, it seems to end with the French Revolution, which was in part the result of the Enlightenment and which, despite its apparent defeat, established the Enlightenment ideals of popular sovereignty, equality before the law, and liberalism. It thereby identified the whole people with the nation, and reinforced nationalism, something less agreeable to most enlightened tastes. In 1947 Adorno and Horkheimer argued that the very reason which the Enlightenment used as a weapon against myth, religion, and illusion has, in modern technocratic societies, turned against itself and become self-destructive. But in fairness to the Enlightenment, it should be added that, if this is so, reason's self-destruction relies on the co-operation of pre-Enlightenment values.   M.J.I.

*Enlightenment philosophy.

T. W. Adorno and M. Horkheimer, *Dialectic of the Enlightenment*, tr. J. Cumming (New York, 1972).

E. Cassirer, *The Philosophy of the Enlightenment* (Princeton, NJ, 1951).

P. J. Gay, *The Enlightenment: An Interpretation*, 2 vols. (London, 1973).

——*The Party of Humanity: Studies in the French Enlightenment* (London, 1964).

Enlightenment philosophy. There is no set of philosophical doctrines common to all and only those thinkers usually subsumed under the label *'Enlightenment'. However, most of Diderot, Voltaire, D'Alembert, Condorcet, Holbach, Hume, and Kant share a scepticism about the metaphysical powers of reason but an optimism about its power to yield knowledge about the natural, including the human, world. Enlightenment philosophy is paradigmatically atheistic or agnostic, anti-theological and sometimes anticlerical. It often entails a liberal scepticism about the value and legitimacy of the institutions of state. Enlightenment philosophy characteristically rejects authority and advocates intellectual and moral self-reliance.

In his essay 'An Answer to the Question *What is Enlightenment?*' Kant says that Enlightenment is essentially opposed to humanity's 'immaturity', where '*Immaturity* is the inability to use one's own understanding without the guidance of another'. The obstacles to Enlightenment are political and economic, because 'I need not think so long as I can pay; others will soon enough take that tiresome task over for me'; and 'The guardians who have kindly taken upon themselves the work of supervision will soon see to it that by far the largest part of mankind (including the entire fair sex) should consider the step forward to maturity not only as difficult but also as highly dangerous' (p. 54). The motto of the Enlightenment, *sapere aude*, 'dare to know', implies that learning requires risk.

The English Enlightenment pre-dated the French, German, and Scottish Enlightenments and made them possible. Without the thought of *Bacon, *Locke, and *Newton, there could have been no Voltaire, Hume, or Kant. The English empiricists' reliance on science, rather than the authority of Aristotle and the Church, and the advocating of religious, intellectual, and political toleration were models for *les philosophes* and the *Aufklärung*.

Much Enlightenment writing is not philosophy but political polemics, anticlerical tracts, and literary essays. Hume and Kant are the two philosophical giants of the Enlightenment. Hume's philosophy is best understood as motivated by a limit he perceives in empiricism. Famously, Hume maintains that there are no ideas without impressions: concepts have an empirical origin in sense perception. However, several concepts prima facie essential to the intelligibility of experience seem exceptions to this empiricism. Causation, identity (including personal identity), the self, God, morality, private property, and physical objects have no clear empirical origin in the way, for example, that 'red' seems to. Hume's radicalism as an Enlightenment philosopher is his questioning the legitimacy of these concepts, even if their application is finally given diverse justifications.

In the *Critique of Pure Reason* (1781, 1787) Kant argues that there is no persuasive proof for the existence of God and the immortality of the soul. Transcendent metaphysics is impossible, because the attempt to use categories outside our experience of the spatio-temporal world leads to contradictions or nonsense. In the *Critique of Practical Reason* (1788), however, God and immortality are reinstated as objects of faith, or 'postulates of pure practical reason'. He means that we have to postulate God and immortality, as well as the free will that was admitted in the *Critique of Pure Reason*, as necessary conditions for our moral lives making sense. Kant writes on the cusp of ambiguity. On one reading, he criticized reason only to make room for faith. Free will is then Christian. This Kant is like Aquinas. On another reading, he reduced God and the soul to mere fictions. We humans *postulate* God and the soul, but there is no God, and there is no immortality, and the ethical life they presuppose is without theological or metaphysical foundation. Freedom is then existential. This Kant is like Nietzsche.

Historically, Enlightenment philosophy is a product of the decline of the medieval theocentric world picture. The religious conflicts of the sixteenth and seventeenth centuries caused a reactive desire for religious toleration. The methods of the new science required an openness to intellectual enquiry. Religious and intellectual toleration required some political freedom, at first, in each state, for intellectuals, artists, writers, and the bourgeoisie, but then for a wider population. In Locke's political philosophy, legitimate government is only by the consent of the governed, so is forfeited by the violation of the natural rights of the governed. That legitimacy was seen to be lost by James II in 1688, George III in 1776, and Louis XVI in 1789.

The putatively anti-Enlightenment writing found in post-structuralism and post-modernism rests on a mistake. Those movements do not go beyond orthodox Kantian doctrines: there is no metaphysical truth, but a recurrent propensity to try to find it using something called 'reason'; there is no truth or reality accessible independently of a conceptual scheme; philosophical problems depend upon binary oppositions which resist synthesis; there is no unconstituted metaphysical subject.

S.P.

Carl L. Becker, *The Heavenly City of the Eighteenth-Century Philosophers* (New Haven, Conn., 1932).

Ernst Cassirer, *The Philosophy of the Enlightenment*, 2nd edn., tr. F. C. A. Koelln and J. P. Pettegrove (Boston, 1955).

Immanuel Kant, 'An Answer to the Question *What is Enlightenment?*', in Hans Reiss (ed.), *Kant: Political Writings* (Cambridge, 1991).

Stephen Priest, *The British Empiricists* (Harmondsworth, 1990).

entailment. A set of propositions (or statements, or sentences) entails a proposition (etc.) when the latter follows necessarily (logically, deductively) from the former, i.e. when an *argument consisting of the former as premises and the latter as conclusion is a valid *deduction. The criterion of this is contentious. The classical criterion identifies entailment with strict *implication, where 'Set Γ strictly implies A' means: it is impossible for all members of Γ to be true without A being true. A variant is: the argument from Γ to A has a certain form, and no argument of that form combines true premises with an untrue conclusion. The classical criterion has the consequences that an impossibility entails everything and a necessary truth is entailed by everything (the paradoxes of strict implication). Accordingly some logicians search for a different criterion, to escape the paradoxes and more generally to respect the feeling that a set of propositions should be required to have some 'relevance' to what it entails. (*Logic, relevance.)   C.A.K.

S. Haack, *Philosophy of Logics* (Cambridge, 1978), 198–203.
C. A. Kirwan, *Logic and Argument* (London, 1978), 55–8.

entelechy. Hans Driesch (1867–1941), this century's leading neovitalist, was much impressed with his discovery that, despite extreme interference in the early stages of embryological development, some organisms nevertheless develop into perfectly formed adults. In a thoroughly Aristotelian fashion, therefore, he became convinced that there is some life-element, transcending the purely material, controlling and promoting such development. Denying that this 'entelechy' is a force in the usual sense, Driesch openly argued that it is end-directed. In his later writings, Driesch moved beyond his Greek influences, starting to sound more Hegelian, as he argued that all life culminates ultimately in a 'supra-personal whole'.   M.R.

   *vitalism.

H. Driesch, *The History and Theory of Vitalism* (London, 1914).

enthusiasm. Used as a term of opprobrium in the seventeenth and eighteenth centuries to describe the irrationalism and behavioural excesses of latter-day prophets, religious mystics, utopian social reformers, and other visionaries. Enthusiasm was the subject of numerous critical treatises, pamphlets, and essays, including those by Meric Casaubon (1655); Henry More (1662); and by John Locke in the fourth edition of the *Essay Concerning Human Understanding* (1700), all of whom emphasized the importance of 'temperance, humility, and reason', and especially tradition, and attempted to discredit conclusions reached in agitated states of inner illumination. Kant's extreme distaste for *Schwärmerei* is an important determinant of his 'critical' philosophy of religion. From its appearance in Plato's *Ion*, where the poet is described as 'a light and winged thing, and holy', but as not possessing knowledge, enthusiasm has been 'the other of reason' which philosophy can neither ignore nor incorporate.
                                                            CATH.W.

R. Knox, *Enthusiasm: A Chapter in the History of Religion with Special Reference to the Seventeenth and Eighteenth Centuries* (Oxford, 1950).

enthymeme. Aristotle applied this term to reasoning from a premiss that is only probably true. Perhaps because he gave abbreviated examples, it soon came to mean a *syllogism with an unstated premiss. Thus 'Dolphins are mammals, so they suckle their young' is an enthymeme if it is granted that mammals suckle their young. But it is difficult to be sure that a hidden premiss is 'really there', and any silly argument may be turned into a valid one by arbitrary additions.   C.W.

H. W. B. Joseph, *An Introduction to Logic*, 2nd edn. (Oxford, 1916), 350–2.

entity: *see* things.

entropy. A measure of *unavailable* *energy in a physical system. Since usable energy is lost in irreversible energy transfers, entropy increases in closed systems (the second law of thermodynamics). Entropy is defined in two complementary ways: as the ratio of heat change to absolute temperature; and as proportional to the statistical probability of the system's state. The word also labels information theory's average information per symbol, which is defined by a formally similar probability function.   J.J.M.

J. H. Weaver (ed.), *The World of Physics*, 3 vols. (New York, 1987), vol. i, ch. 1.

enumerative induction. Confirmation of a generalization by observation of particular instances. Noticing that all the snowflakes I have ever seen are hexagonal, I might conclude that all are. Enumerative *induction is usually distinguished from eliminative induction, which places weight not on the number of confirming instances, but on their variety: but given that any pair of snowflakes differs in *some* way, the distinction requires an account of which variations are supposed to matter.   M.C.

L. J. Cohen, *An Introduction to the Philosophy of Induction and Probability* (Oxford, 1989).

environmental and ecological philosophy. Environmental philosophy encompasses all philosophical reflection on the relations between human beings and the non-human environment. Since the discipline grew out of concerns with how humans ought to behave towards the natural world, it has been dominated by discussions of *environmental ethics. In the face of this hegemony, some writers refer to 'environmental philosophy' rather than 'environmental ethics' in order to make the point that they are not primarily concerned with questions of applied ethics. The reasoning here is that while applied ethics seeks to bring familiar ethical theories such as utilitarianism to bear on practical issues, environmental philosophy is inherently sceptical of attempts to apply traditional philosophical theories to environmental issues. This scepticism is born of a belief that the dominant tendencies of Western philosophical thought are inherently 'anthropocentric' or perniciously human-centred, and hence inimical to environmental concern. For these writers, the proper aim of environmental philosophy is to develop a new, non-anthropocentric account of the relation between humans and the natural world, which, it is hoped, will provide a metaphysical basis for ethical concern for the non-human environment.

Ecological philosophers hold that the science of ecology provides an appropriate model for such a non-anthropocentric position. The focus here is not on the array of technical concepts employed in modern ecological science but on the generally holistic standpoint associated with the discipline. Ecology is applauded for showing, in its accounts of energy cycles, food webs, and the like, that any part of the natural world must be understood as a function of its relations to other parts. Accordingly, an ecological metaphysics is seen as one that rejects the Judaeo-Christian and 'Cartesian' assumption that humans are separate from and superior to the natural world, and replaces it with a conception of the unity of humans and nature. To corroborate their claims, ecological philosophers, and in particular 'deep ecologists', look not just to ecology, but also to other areas: quantum mechanics and relativity theory, for instance; appropriately holistic Western philosophies, such as those developed by Spinoza, Heidegger, and Whitehead; non-Western philosophies such as Advaita Vedānta, Buddhism, and Taoism; and the world-views of indigenous peoples such as Native Americans.   S.P.J.

*environmental ethics; holism.

C. Belshaw, *Environmental Philosophy: Reason, Nature and Human Concern* (Teddington, 2001).
W. Fox, *Toward a Transpersonal Ecology: Developing New Foundations for Environmentalism* (Boston, 1990).
F. Mathews, *The Ecological Self* (London, 1991).

environmental ethics. The attempt to expand the moral framework to *nature and counter human chauvinism by showing that feathers, fur, species membership, and even inorganic composition are not barriers to the range of ethical consideration. Peter Singer uses *utilitarian theory to support equality of consideration for all sentient life-forms. To act morally in dealing with sentient creatures requires imaginative empathy, a sense of what it is like to be a creature of that sort. Tom Regan extends *rights talk to non-human animals, increasing human duties and obligations without regarding other animals as moral agents under reciprocal nets of obligation. Using Kantian ethical theory, Paul Taylor defends the adoption of a bio-centric ethical attitude of respect for nature. He grounds this attitude in the intelligibility of regarding each living entity as striving to realize its own good and as having the same inherent worth within a network of teleological centres of life. Holmes Rolston III argues against preferring the integrated autonomy of a short-lived individual to the dynamic life-form of its species, genetically persisting through millions of years. Species live in biotic communities: there is no right to life for a species apart from the continued existence of the ecosystem with which it evolves. Humans have duties to ecosystems themselves. Recent developments include hostile critiques of any attempt to enlarge the moral community by using either utilitarian or *deontological ethical theory. Also under attack is the shared presupposition of both capitalist and socialist economic systems that nature has value only when transformed by human agency. Ecofeminists hold that an adequate environmental ethics must recognize important connections between the oppression of nature and the oppression of women. Karen J. Warren sees this as based on a patriarchal conceptual framework mediated by a logic of domination that legitimates the manipulation and domestication of the natural. Ecofeminism replaces negative evaluations of nature and of women by a care-sensitive ethics based on the ability to care for oneself and human and non-human others, including 'earth Others'—animals, forests, and the land.   B.T.

*environmental and ecological philosophy.

Holmes Rolston III, *Environmental Ethics: Duties to and Values in the Natural World* (Philadelphia, 1988).
K. J. Warren, *Ecofeminist Philosophy: A Western Perspective on What it is and Why it Matters* (New York, 2000).

Epictetus (*c.*55–*c.*135 AD). Originally a slave belonging to one of the Emperor Nero's freedmen, and a major Stoic moralist, he is said to have endured his master's physical abuse without complaint, treating his body merely as a garment. Freed after Nero's death, he was later exiled by Domitian to Nicopolis in north-western Greece. His lectures, or *Discourses*, were recorded by his pupil Arrian.

He did not wholly neglect physics and logic, the other two parts of *Stoic thought, but concentrated on ethics. The task of philosophy, he said, is to become like *Socrates, indifferent to bodily comfort or social applause, in order to think and act as a citizen of the world, a part of a larger whole—which should not make us forget that we are also members of families and ordinary cities, with more particular duties. When we kiss our child, he warned, we should be reminding ourselves that this too is mortal: a piece of advice that some have found disturbing. The indifference, or *apatheia*, that he preached is not a lack of love—on the contrary, as is best understood through his comments on a distraught father, confessedly unable to tend to his sick son because the sight upset him. This, said Epictetus, showed how little he loved his son: *apatheia* is the opposite of being, literally, pathetic, and essential for any genuinely loving action. What he meant by 'philosophy' has fixed the popular meaning of the term ever since, though not the professional: the lessons that philosophers ought to rehearse, he said, to write down daily and to put into practice, are the primacy of individual moral choice, the relative unimportance of body, rank, and estate, and the knowledge of what is truly their own and what is permitted them. One who pretends to 'teach philosophy' without the knowledge, virtue, and the strength of soul to cope with distressed and corrupted souls, 'and above all the counsel of God advising him to occupy this office' is a vulgarizer of the mysteries, a quack doctor.

> The affair is momentous, it is full of mystery, not a chance gift, nor given to all comers. You are opening up a doctor's office although you possess no equipment other than drugs, but when or how these drugs are applied you neither know nor have ever taken the trouble to learn. Why do you play at hazard in matters of the utmost moment? If you find the principles of philosophy entertaining sit down and turn them over in your mind all by yourself, but don't ever call yourself a philosopher.

He did not even claim to be a philosopher himself, nor what he called 'a dyed-in-the-wool Jew', willingly obedient to God's command.

It is not clear how he reconciled the fervour of his insistence that we all have choices to make with the Stoic belief in absolute *determinism. Perhaps the reconciliation is a merely practical one: what is the case we must accept as God's inexorable will; what might be the case (as being an apparent option for us here-now) must be judged as if we could do other than we shall. A further tension in his thought concerns our relationship with animal nature: on the one hand, our affections and impulses are ones we share with animals, and our superiority lies only in our duty to be aware of those affections; on the other, vice exactly is becoming like an animal in ways that he deplores. He was at any rate too gentle a philosopher to draw the usual Stoic, and Spinozistic, conclusion that people were entitled to treat animals exactly as they pleased.   S.R.L.C.

*Stoics.

E. V. Arnold, *Roman Stoicism* (Cambridge, 1911).

Epictetus, *Discourses and Encheiridion*, tr. W. A. Oldfather (London, 1926).

A. A. Long, *Epictetus: A Stoic and Socratic Guide to Life* (Oxford, 2002).

——and D. N. Sedley (eds.), *The Hellenistic Philosophers* (Cambridge, 1987).

Epicureanism. Epicureanism consisted of a way of life directed at worldly *happiness and an atomistic account of the exclusively material nature of reality. *Atomism, it was argued, was true. Hence the way pointed out by Epicurus could be presented as not merely psychologically satisfying, but in accord with the true nature of things.

Epicurus established his school of philosophy in 306 BC just outside the walls of Athens where he purchased a house for accommodation and a garden in which teaching took place. He himself was the leader of the community 'the Garden' until his death in about 270 when he was succeeded first by Hermarchus and then, in about 250, by Polystratus. The Garden was still in existence 450 years later. But references to Epicureans at Tyre, Sidon, Alexandria, Gadara (in Syria), and elsewhere in the Hellenistic world before 30 BC indicate active dissemination of Epicureanism.

In Italy, during the period c.100–c.50 BC, a thriving and cultured Epicurean community was established in Naples by Siro and, at nearby Herculaneum, Philodemus of Gadara (poet and author of fragmentarily surviving Greek expositions of Epicurus) was 'house philosopher' to the father-in-law of Julius Caesar. In Rome, Amafinius and others were circulating popular over-simplifications (now lost) of Epicureanism in Latin, and in the 50s BC Lucretius completed his full and sophisticated account for Latin readers. In 45–44 BC Cicero gave the Epicureans considerable but unsympathetic attention in his expositions of Greek philosophy. But 100 years later Epicureanism, true to its precept 'live unnoticed', had yielded place to *Stoicism as the philosophy favoured by influential Romans. Nevertheless, Epicurus is much referred to by Seneca (c.5 BC–AD 65), Plutarch (c.46–c.120) and others. Epicurus' rational humanism was enlisted by Lucian about 180 in 'Alexander the False Prophet' and, towards

the end of the second century, Diogenes Flavianus caused a vast account of Epicurean teaching to be inscribed on the colonnade of his city Oenoanda (about a quarter, c.5,000 words, has been unearthed). Not long after, Diogenes Laertius cited Epicurus' works as 'the beginning of happiness'. Thereafter we hear little from the Epicureans on their own behalf and in AD 361 Julianus Caesar wrote 'indeed the gods have already in their wisdom destroyed their works so that most of their books have ceased to be'.

Epicurean atomism attracted the opposition of the Stoics (who had a different materialistic philosophy) and the criticism of Academic philosophers. But the Epicureans were always more anxious to preserve and make known their revered master's life-enhancing teaching than to adjust it or its atomistic basis in the light of philosophical criticism. Thus Epicureanism remained substantially the same over five centuries.

It encouraged withdrawal from the political and administrative service of the state into sheltered communities of like-minded people ruled by friendship and by a common allegiance to Epicurus. Contrary to social convention, it admitted men and women, rich and poor, and even slaves on terms of equality. Its central purpose was happiness: a mind free from disturbance and a body free from pain. As a consequence it gained a reputation for attracting voluptuaries. But Epicurus' own words make it abundantly clear that his 'hedonism', theoretically permissive, is in reality very austere, and Seneca's judgement is probably about right: Epicureanism 'has a bad name, is of ill repute, and yet undeservedly' (*De vita beata* xiii. 1–2).

To Christians the *naturalism of the Epicureans, their total rejection of active supernatural powers, and their humanism was anathema. After the fifth century AD, caricatured as an embodiment of Antichrist, Epicureanism retained a tenuous existence in a few manuscripts. It was rediscovered in the sixteenth and seventeenth centuries and became a major influence upon modern science and humanism.   J.C.A.G.

*Epicurus; ancient philosophy.

D. J. Furley, *Two Studies in Greek Atomists* (Princeton, NJ, 1967).

Howard Jones, *The Epicurean Tradition* (London, 1992).

A. A. Long and D. N. Sedley (eds.), *The Hellenistic Philosophers*, i (Cambridge, 1987).

Epicurean objection, the. According to Epicurus, a man who says that all things come to pass by necessity cannot criticize one who denies it, for he admits that this too happens of necessity. This can be taken as the first in an intriguing (if elusive) run of philosophical arguments purporting to show that belief in *determinism is self-invalidating. Since necessitation of a belief does not exclude one's having good reasons for it, Epicurus' argument remains unclear. A recent suggestion is that the true force of the argument is in the consequence of determinism that our beliefs are owed to our being caused to make some discoveries and not others. In that case, however, the argument would still lack force, since indeterminism would not only have the consequence of making possible discoveries that determinism closes off, but also that we might miss out on discoveries that determinism necessitates.   K.M.

K. Magill, 'Epicurus, Determinism, and the Security of Knowledge', *Theoria* 58 (1992).
T. Honderich, *A Theory of Determinism* (Oxford, 1988).

Epicurus (*c*.341–270 BC). Athenian philosopher who adopted Democritus' atomism, possibly emended it in the light of Aristotle's criticisms, developed a related ethic, and established the Garden— the Epicurean school.

Epicurus was an extremely prolific writer. But apart from his reputedly most important work, *On Nature*, fractions of which still have a precarious existence in badly damaged rolls from Herculaneum, almost all that survives is in Diogenes Laertius' *Lives of the Eminent Philosophers*, book x (second century AD). Diogenes preserves the following: 'Letter to Herodotus' on the physical universe, sense perception, and life; 'Letter to Pythocles' on astronomy and meteorology; 'Letter to Menoeceus' on moral teachings; and forty 'Principal Sayings'. Other sayings are in Cicero, Seneca, Plutarch, and elsewhere, but by far the most complete and faithful account of Epicurus' teachings is in the great Latin didactic poem *De rerum natura* by Lucretius (*c*.100–55 BC).

Epicurus argues: (*a*) The universe consists of matter and void. This fundamental thesis establishes a vast gulf between Epicureanism and Platonism, Christianity, Cartesianism, or any other variety of matter–spirit dualism. (*b*) Matter consists of indestructible and indivisible particles ('atoms') having a variety of shapes and sizes which, in clusters, make up all things that exist. (*c*) Atoms *and their movement* are a single ultimate fact about the way things are, but each atom is susceptible to unpredictable 'swerves' that result in overall random movements. (*d*) No atom is ever brought into being or put out of existence by divine or any other power. (*e*) The universe is eternal and infinitely extended. (*f*) All agglomerates of atoms are fortuitous and of finite duration. (*g*) Hence, from (*e*) and (*f*), there are more worlds than this and this will eventually disperse. (*h*) Life is a complex of particularly fine atoms which form both body and mind in a single natural entity whose death is irrevocable dispersal of the person. (*i*) The gods are inactive and far off, 'blessed' and long enduring, but from whom 'we nothing have to hope and nothing fear'. (*j*) In such a universe man is delivered from superstitious fear: death is literally nothing to him. (*k*) The good life is secured by kindness and friendship with those about you, and by moderation of appetite so that, although nothing is forbidden, he who measures his desires by the utilitarian standard and needs least has the firmest grasp on happiness.

The logical progression of theses (*a*) to (*k*) is not merely affirmed by the Epicureans as a life-enhancing credo. It is accompanied by a philosophy of language and an epistemology affirming the veridical nature of perception, and it is commended by detailed arguments. For example

(*e*) is supported by the thought experiment of 'the javelin argument': go to what you suppose to be the limit of space and throw a javelin in a geometrically straight line. If it hits nothing, space continues. If it hits something, (occupied) space continues. Hence the universe is not finite in any direction (Lucretius, book I, lines 958–83). Similarly (*h*) is supported by a formidable and still usable array of arguments for mind–body identity and mutual death in Lucretius, book III, and in Epicurus' 'Letter to Herodotus'.

Widespread but mildly disapproved of in antiquity because of its self-sufficient privacy, its acceptance of slaves and women into its communities, and its professed concern with happiness and the good life, Epicureanism was anathema to Christianity. It denied a provident God, affirmed the value of life and the values of this world, denied immortality, and advocated an account of the universe wholly at variance with the Christian. The account was revived in the seventeenth century to become the basis of modern science; but the world shaped by modern science has never seemed able to accept in full the world-view and ethic that gave Epicurus' system a reasonable claim to be complete, consistent, and livable.   J.C.A.G.

*Epicureanism.

C. Bailey, *The Greek Atomists and Epicurus* (Oxford, 1928).
D. J. Furley, *The Greek Cosmologists*, i: *The Formation of the Atomic Theory and its Earliest Critics* (Cambridge, 1987).
J. C. A. Gaskin (ed.), *The Epicurean Philosophers* (London, 1994).
A. A. Long, *Hellenistic Philosophy* (London, 1974).

epiphenomenalism. Group of doctrines about mental–physical causal relations, which view some or all aspects of mentality as byproducts of the physical goings-on in the world.

The classic definition (e.g. in C. D. Broad, *The Mind and its Place in Nature* (1925)) ensures that epiphenomenalism is a species of *dualism. Whereas Descartes, an interactionist, held that mental things both cause and are caused by physical things, the epiphenomenalist holds that mental things do not cause physical things although they are caused by them. The epiphenomenalist then can accept that there are no causal influences on physical events besides other physical events, and thus can escape one objection sometimes raised against dualism. But the epiphenomenalist's picture of mental events as tacked on to the physical world, having no causal influence there, is unappealing: she would seem to think that mental things feature in the world as accompanying shadows of the physical—in the realm of 'pure experience'.

Some non-dualist positions are accused of commitment to epiphenomenalism. The idea is that the mental is not caught in the physical causal net, but now not because mental *things* aren't caught there, but because mental *properties* of things aren't caught there, these not being causally relevant properties. The picture again is one in which mentality appears causally idle.

Two contemporary physicalist doctrines are alleged to have specific epiphenomenalist consequences. The first is *functionalism, which holds that types of mental states are definable in terms of the causal roles played by their tokens in an interconnected network. An objection has it that a causal account omits something crucial to some mental states—namely the intrinsic nature of those states, which is accessible only from a first-person perspective. Some functionalists concede the objection, and say that although the mental can be circumscribed by way of its operation in the causal world, none the less subjective features of experience, sometimes called qualia, must be acknowledged, and these indeed are epiphenomenal.

Davidson's *anomalous monism is the other physicalist position attacked on grounds of supposed epiphenomenalist commitments. Davidson holds that explanations which introduce terms like 'believe' and 'desire' are causal explanations; and he argues that beliefs and desires are physical by arguing that vocabulary used in stating physical laws applies to them. An objection claims that because the real causal power of any state which has a mental property must be seen, from Davidson's perspective, to reside in some lawlike physical property that it has, mental properties must be acknowledged by Davidson to be not genuinely causally relevant, but rather epiphenomenal, inefficacious. An answer may be that, since there are two different sorts of causal explanation, some events simply do possess two different properties each of which has causal relevance. But a problem may remain: it seems that conceiving of mental events in the physical terms in which causal laws are framed, it can be hard to persist in thinking that our talk of them using mental terms can offer genuinely causal explanations of what happens.

The objection made to Davidson might be made against any materialist who allows a gap between, on the one hand, the metaphysics of mental causation, which concentrates on properties characterized in the physical sciences, and, on the other hand, what we actually know about the nature and existence of mental causation, which derives from everyday explanations of people and their doings.   J.HORN.

*mental indispensability.

Jerry Fodor, 'Making Mind Matter More', *Philosophical Topics* (1989).

John Heil and Alfred Mele (eds.), *Mental Causation* (Oxford, 1993).

Frank Jackson, 'Epiphenomenal Qualia', *Philosophical Quarterly* (1982).

epistemic. Like 'epistemological', an adjective derived from 'epistēmē', a Greek word for knowledge. Anything thus described has some relation to knowledge (or at least to the justification for belief), or to the general theory of these (epistemology). A proposition is epistemic if and only if it has some implication for what, in some circumstances, is rationally worthy of belief.   L.F.S.

R. Chisholm, *Theory of Knowledge* (Englewood Cliffs, NJ, 1966), ch. 1.

epistemological relativism: *see* relativism, epistemological.

epistemology, feminist. Feminist philosophers have criticized common-sense, philosophical, and scientific knowledge both as regards content (e.g. the alleged fact that women are less rational than men) and more importantly as regards structure. The perpetration of absurd but socially powerfully 'knowledge' in such fields as social theory and social science is interpreted by feminist philosophers as bound up with the tendency for Western philosophers and scientists to see the world dualistically. Invariably, one side of each duality has been privileged over the other—objective knowledge is superior to subjective opinion, masculinity to femininity, science to other forms of knowledge and theory, reason to emotion, the mind to the body, and so on. Further, such oppositions are systematically linked, so that objectivity, masculinity, reason, and science seem to be bound up with one another. Thus the conception of knowledge, and epistemology itself, participates in a structure of inequality which is gendered.

What sense might we make of 'feminist epistemology'? Philosophers have developed a variety of options. First, that 'knowledge' is actually constructed and understood from a particular social standpoint. The dualistic tendency identified is not a matter of stupidity or malice, but is determined by a social standpoint and the corresponding network of meanings and values. We must therefore consider the implications of thinking about knowledge from alternative standpoints. Second, that we should focus on relations between *subjectivity and *objectivity, or *reason and *emotion, not see them as oppositions. Third, that we take seriously the place—which has tended to be erased in conventional epistemology—of emotion, subjectivity, and the body in knowledge. Fourth, that we cease to think of reason and emotion as normatively the province of men and women respectively. Fifth, some feminist epistemologists have concentrated on revaluing the 'feminine' sides of the dualisms—e.g. denigrating abstract reason and valorizing the role of emotion—arguing in effect that 'women's knowledge' is of a higher quality.   E.J.F.

*feminist philosophy.

Ann Garry and Marilyn Pearsall (eds.), *Women, Knowledge and Reality: Explorations in Feminist Philosophy* (London, 1989).

Kathleen Lennon and Margaret Whitford (eds.), *Knowing the Difference: Feminist Perspectives on Epistemology* (London, 1994).

Genevieve Lloyd, *The Man of Reason: 'Male' and 'Female' in Western Philosophy* (London, 1984).

epistemology, genetic. Term originally coined by James Mark Baldwin to characterize an account of the acquisition of knowledge and understanding in developmental terms. It was taken over by Jean Piaget to describe his own general, and biological, theory of the development of knowledge and intelligence in the individual. Piaget thought that genetic epistemology could be distinguished from developmental psychology, but the distinction, as he made it, was not clear. It might be argued, however, that just as the prime concern of ordinary *epistemology is to show how knowledge is possible, so the aim of genetic epistemology should be to show how the acquisition and growth of knowledge is possible. This is a matter for genuine philosophical concern. The first instance of such a philosophical theory, only partially successful, is to be found in the last chapter of Aristotle's *Posterior Analytics* and is a response to an argument in Plato's *Meno* that *learning and the acquisition of new knowledge is impossible.   D.W.H.

D. W. Hamlyn, *Experience and the Growth of Understanding* (London, 1978).

epistemology, history of.
Epistemology, or the theory of knowledge, is that branch of philosophy concerned with the nature of knowledge, its possibility, scope, and general basis. It has been a major interest of many philosophers almost from the beginnings of the subject. Often, but not always, these philosophers have had as their main preoccupation the attempt to provide a general basis which would ensure the possibility of knowledge. For this reason it is sometimes said that the seventeenth and eighteenth centuries were *the* age of epistemology, in that Descartes then introduced what is sometimes termed the 'search for certainty', seeking a sure foundation for knowledge, and was followed in this by other philosophers of the period. To this end Descartes employed his 'method of doubt', a form of systematic *scepticism, in order to ascertain what could not be doubted. He found this in his notorious proposition *'Cogito ergo sum' ('I think, therefore I am'), which, he thought, established the existence of the self as a thinking thing (although it seems, on the face of it, to imply only that a thought must have a thinker, and what that thinker must be like is another matter, as is the question whether 'I think' itself can be doubted). Given the thoughts of that self as he construed it, he then sought to derive from them the existence of God and thereafter that of the external world, as it came to be called (the world being external to the mind, the only thing to which, it was thought, we have direct access).

There was in Descartes's time a renewed interest in scepticism, though it is arguable that his systematic scepticism went further than any previous form in that he was prepared to consider the application of doubt to himself and not merely to other things. The interest in scepticism was *renewed* in that, much earlier, in the period of post-Aristotelian philosophy, a school of sceptical philosophy had been founded by Pyrrho. The Greek Sceptics maintained that they were inquirers, refusing to acknowledge claims to knowledge unless a 'criterion of truth', as it was called, could be produced. The rival philosophical schools, particularly the *Stoics and *Epicureans, tried to produce such a criterion, something in experience that had the mark of certain truth, in what appears to have

been a running debate between them and the Sceptics and members of Plato's *Academy who were influenced by scepticism. The search for a criterion of truth is obviously a version of the search for certainty.

Plato himself had had little of such concerns, although he was interested in the nature of knowledge, and *Republic* 477e6 seems to suggest that the title of knowledge should be reserved for that over which there cannot be error. By and large, however, Plato was more concerned with the question what distinguishes knowledge from belief (*doxa*), construed as having something simply before the mind, and considered as true or false. In his middle period, he seems to have been so influenced by metaphysical considerations as to be inclined to distinguish knowledge by confining it to a particular realm of entities, his Forms or Ideas. Later, however, particularly in his dialogue the *Theaetetus*, he seems to revert to an idea put forward in the early dialogue the *Meno*, that correct belief can be turned into knowledge by fixing it by means of a reason or cause. The *Theaetetus* gives good reasons for thinking that knowledge is more than true belief, but fails to find an adequate account of what the extra thing required can amount to. (He supposes that it might be some interpretation of the term *logos*—speech, enumeration of the parts of a thing, or the determination of the thing's identity—but finds all three objectionable.) Nevertheless, Plato seems throughout to have in mind by knowledge a state of mind related to an object, and the question is what that state and that relation can be.

Aristotle has similar preconceptions, and is hardly at all concerned with the justification of knowledge-claims. He says repeatedly that we think we have knowledge proper (*epistēmē*) of something when we know its reason or cause. In his view that reason is brought out when the subject-matter can be ordered in terms of a demonstrative syllogism (where the premisses and conclusions state essential or necessary truths about something), the middle term of which (what the two premisses have in common) gives that reason. Knowledge proper, therefore, entails bringing its object within a context of explanatory and reason-giving propositions, which amounts to science as Aristotle conceived it. He thus thought that knowledge of a thing involved understanding it in terms of the reasons for it. (Some recent scholars have said that by 'knowledge' Aristotle *meant* understanding, but that is not quite right.) There is no concern here about exactly what it is to know that such and such is the case, so-called propositional knowledge, and even less with the attempt to base knowledge-claims on something absolutely certain. That came in only when the Sceptics, who thought that freedom from care resulted from it, pressed their scepticism. The rival schools such as the Stoics had a similar motivation to some extent in seeking a source of certainty in a 'criterion of truth'.

Although Plato thought, at any rate at one time, that knowledge was reserved for the Forms, and also suggested in his 'Theory of Recollection', put forward in his *Meno* and *Phaedo*, that we are born with such knowledge but have to be reminded of it by particular experiences, he put forward otherwise no general theory about the source of our knowledge. It is often said that Aristotle thought that all the materials of knowledge, all the concepts which it involves, are derived from experience. In my opinion, there is some doubt about that, although he did think that the acquisition of knowledge depended in one way or another on experience. On the other hand, Thomas Aquinas, the great medieval Aristotelian, certainly thought that all the materials for knowledge are derived from experience, although he certainly did not claim that all knowledge as such is derived from experience (as his theological concerns indicate). The distinction between knowledge and its materials (the concepts presupposed by it) is important and it became crucial in the eighteenth century. Apart from this, the philosophers of the Middle Ages contributed little to epistemology that was not available from the Greeks. It is perhaps worth noting, however, that Augustine was near enough to the post-Aristotelians to be influenced by scepticism and produced a kind of pre-echo of Descartes's 'Cogito ergo sum' in his own 'Si fallor sum' ('If I err, I exist').

One thing that was novel about the kind of philosophy that Descartes introduced was its first-person approach. The general basis for justification of claims to knowledge was to be found in the individual's own mind, and the 'I think' is, for Descartes, the basis for any confidence an individual can have in believing himself to have knowledge. The possibility of any further knowledge must be derived from that. Descartes also introduced the 'way of ideas' as part of that programme. What we are given is ideas of one kind or another and the problem is how we can justifiably use them as a basis for belief in a world which is outside our minds. Perception is just as much a matter of having ideas as is any other operation of the mind, and the problem is therefore what kind of justification we have for believing that our ideas are representative of anything. This approach was characteristic of seventeenth- and eighteenth-century philosophy, and although it is conventional to divide the philosophers of the time between those who were rationalists (in emphasizing the part played by reason in it) and empiricists (in emphasizing the part played by experience) they were not fundamentally at odds in that general approach.

Descartes did not think that all our ideas are derived from experience, and the rationalists who followed him, particularly Leibniz, maintained the possibility of innate ideas, or at least ideas which are independent of experience or a priori (a term which goes back to Aristotle's distinction between knowledge derived from truths which are prior to demonstration and truths which are posterior in that they are as yet undemonstrated and may be arrived at by induction from experience). In fact an a priori idea or truth does not have to be innate, as Kant was to emphasize in saying that while all knowledge begins with experience it does not follow that it all arises out of experience. Thus the thesis that some knowledge is a priori is quite compatible with the thesis that no knowledge is innate.

Nevertheless, the rationalists tended to assert the possibility of innate, and not merely a priori, knowledge, as in effect did Plato when, in putting forward his 'Theory of Recollection', he claimed that experience reminds us of knowledge with which we are born. Such knowledge might be either knowledge of truths or the knowledge which we may have in having a genuine idea of something.

Locke, the first of the so-called British Empiricists, argued vehemently that all our ideas arise from experience, but he did not think, as did some later empiricists, including J. S. Mill, that all knowledge of truths was derived from experience. Some such knowledge, he thought, rests on intuition and some on demonstration. Locke did think, however, that experience is the foundation for knowledge in that the simple ideas of sense are the origin of everything else in the understanding. That thought was taken further by Berkeley and Hume. The main epistemological concerns of these philosophers were, thus, the limits and extent of the human understanding, as typified by the central claim of Hume's empiricism—that all ideas are derived from impressions of sense, every simple idea being a copy of a corresponding impression. The problem for Hume, given this, is what justifies us in going from one impression to another, and thus, since he thought that belief consisted of a lively idea related to or associated with a present impression, what justifies us in belief about anything beyond a present impression. What justifies us, in particular, in belief in causality and in a world apart from present impressions? Hume thought, sceptically, that there was no such justification; we can explain only what, psychologically, makes us have those beliefs. This is a matter of custom, producing a determination of the mind, as is involved in the principles of the association of ideas.

Apart from what they thought about ideas none of these philosophers thought that knowledge of all *truths* was derived solely from experience, although the empiricists tended to suggest that what were in effect a priori truths were confined to what Hume called 'relations of ideas'. Kant made a systematic distinction between analytic judgements, the truth of which is a priori in depending on the relations between the ideas involved, and synthetic judgements which go beyond what is implicit in the ideas involved. An empiricist would have no problems about such truths provided that the latter class of judgements are confined to what can be justified by reference to experience, and are thus a posteriori. But Kant thought that there were, in addition, synthetic a priori truths—necessary but more than analytic truths involved in mathematics and in the presuppositions of the sciences and of objective knowledge generally. He also thought, however, that it was impossible to go beyond what was so presupposed in human understanding, despite what some philosophers had claimed, and what Hegel, for example, claimed after him, could be achieved by pure reason. Kant argued that the attempt to use pure reason in that way inevitably led to antinomies and other forms of contradiction; Hegel thought that such apparent logical obstacles could be transcended in higher forms of rationality. The issues can be no more than hinted at here; in Hegelian philosophy epistemology tends to be swallowed up in a certain style of metaphysics.

There were almost immediate reactions against Hegel, but most of them were metaphysically orientated. Schopenhauer, who reacted to Hegel in a very bad-tempered and abusive way, urged a return, as far as epistemology was concerned, to Kant, although he thought that the principles of objective knowledge which Kant had argued for could be reduced to one of four forms of the *principle of sufficient reason, a principle due originally to Leibniz. Nietzsche, who was influenced in some ways by Schopenhauer, even if he misinterpreted him, maintained the doctrine of the subjectivity of truth—truth is in effect power. This is a difficult doctrine, to say the least, but it has had considerable influence on recent continental philosophy. None of this, however, is, strictly speaking, epistemology for its own sake.

Outside neo-Kantianism, epistemology in the nineteenth century remained almost exclusively an Anglo-Saxon phenomenon. J. S. Mill, as already indicated, argued for an extreme empiricism, maintaining that knowledge of all truths was derived from experience, thus putting a great deal of weight on the role of induction in arriving at general truths of all kinds. The end of the century saw the rise of American *pragmatism, initially in the claim by C. S. Peirce that the meaningfulness of our ideas is a function of their contribution to rational conduct. This notion was misleadingly extended to truth by William James. Because knowledge entails truth, this inevitably affected conceptions of knowledge on the part of these philosophers and their pragmatist descendants. Perhaps the main epistemological tenet inherited from Peirce, however, is that of *'fallibilism', the idea that we may always be wrong and that, from the point of view of knowledge, truth is simply an ideal limit. This idea has been extremely influential, although if it is taken to imply that we cannot be certain of anything it seems quite wrong.

Twentieth-century empiricism, the main subsequent movement in epistemology, tended to be a kind of reversion to Hume without the psychological dress. It was concerned, however, less with the basis of our ideas than with the scope and certainty of our knowledge of truths. Logical Positivists, such as A. J. Ayer, asserted that all knowable truths are either analytic or empirical—there is no room for the synthetic a priori. At the same time the problem of our knowledge of the external world remains because all that is 'given' is to be found in the individual's experience, particularly in what have become known as *sense-data (a notion which is close, at any rate in status, to Hume's impressions). Sense-data propositions are indubitable, if anything is (and Ayer himself vacillated on that point), But there is then a problem about the relation between sense-data and so-called material objects—a problem which generated various epistemological theories of perception, particularly phenomenalism, the doctrine that material objects are either bundles of actual and possible sense-data or what came to be known, following Russell, as logical constructions from these. The whole notion of the *'given' has subsequently come under criticism from many sources. But does knowledge need, in any case, an indubitable basis? Knowledge may entail belief and the truth of what is believed, but, whatever else it entails, it is not evident that it is that such truth must be indubitable.

Philosophers have thus, for good reason, most often ceased to invoke sense-data as perceptual foundations for knowledge. Interest in that kind of approach to epistemology has thereby declined. What has remained of considerable interest for philosophers is perhaps twofold. First, there is the question what knowledge is, what exhaustive account one is to give of that concept. A short paper by Edmund Gettier on whether knowledge amounts to justified true belief (a theory which he supposed was espoused by Plato), arguing that there could be justified true belief which did not amount to knowledge, has generated a whole industry of attempts to give the necessary and sufficient truth-conditions for any proposition of the form 'X knows that p'. This, it has been suggested, may be achieved either by adding further conditions apart from those involved in speaking of justified true belief or by eschewing reference to justification and substituting reference to something like a causal relation between what is known and the belief involved. Pursuit of the industry continues with no firm resolution, although it is clear that, whatever else is entailed, the possibility that the belief is true by chance must be ruled out.

Second, there is the question, pursued most indefatigably by some American philosophers, about the general foundations for our system of beliefs—whether there is such a foundation, whether it is all a matter of the coherence of our beliefs, or what. So the desire that knowledge should have foundations in some way is still alive. A question that remains open is whether that desire is based on an illusion concerning the nature of knowledge (whether, that is, it requires foundations, or whether the appeal to that architectural image is just a misleading metaphor) or whether the failure to provide sure foundations is a reason for despair about the whole idea of knowledge. So the two problems are in fact connected—as they always have been, though not equally for every philosopher, as we have seen.   D.W.H.

*epistemology, problems of.

Jonathan Dancy, *Introduction to Contemporary Epistemology* (Oxford, 1985).

Stephen Everson (ed.), *Epistemology: Companions to Ancient Thought*, i (Cambridge, 1990).

D. W. Hamlyn, *The Theory of Knowledge* (London, 1971).

——*The Penguin History of Western Philosophy* (London, 1987).

R. H. Popkin, *The History of Scepticism* (1960; 3rd edn. New York, 2003).

Richard Rorty, *Philosophy and the Mirror of Nature* (Princeton, NJ, 1980).

B. A. O. Williams, *Descartes: The Project of Pure Enquiry* (London, 1978).

epistemology, problems of. Epistemology is the study of our right to the beliefs we have. More generally, we start from what we might call our cognitive stances, and ask whether we do well to have those stances. Cognitive stances include both our beliefs and (what we take to be) our knowings; and in another dimension they include our attitudes towards the various strategies and methods we use to get new beliefs and filter out old ones, as well as the products of those strategies and methods. Epistemology, on this showing, is explicitly *normative*; it is concerned with whether we have acted well or badly (responsibly or irresponsibly) in forming the beliefs we have.

In pursuing this enquiry, we do not, of course, ask only about the beliefs and strategies we find ourselves with at the beginning. We also ask whether there are not others which we would do better to have, and whether there are not others which we should have if we have these ones to start off with. The hope is to end up with a full account of how a responsible cognitive agent should behave, with some assurance that we do not fall too far short of that ideal.

1. Justification. We can distinguish between two sorts of belief: the mediated and the unmediated. Mediated beliefs are those which we reach by some strategy which starts from other beliefs we have. Inference is such a strategy (but not the only one); we infer that it will rain soon from our separate beliefs that it is mid-morning and that it is growing very dark outside. Mediated beliefs raise the question of whether the strategy we adopt is one to which we have a right—one we do well to use. Unmediated beliefs are those which we adopt without moving to them from other beliefs we already have. These raise different problems, which concern the *source* of our right to believe. I open my eyes and, because of what I see, immediately believe that there is a book in front of me. If I do well in adopting that belief, it is justified (or I am justified in adopting it). This focus on justification is one way of expressing the idea that epistemology is normative. What makes it the case, then, that this belief is justified?

Various answers suggest themselves. One is the *reliabilist answer: that the belief is justified because it is the result of a reliable process. Another is the *coherentist answer: that this belief is justified because my world is more coherent with it than it would be without it. A third is the *foundationalist claim (at least in its classical form) that this belief is not in fact unmediated, but inferred from a belief about how things seem to me just now. If this last were true, we are thrown back to two questions. The first is whether, and how, the belief about how things seem to me just now is justified. The second is whether the inference from that belief is justified. We might ask what principle of inference is employed. Suppose it is this: that if things seem to me that way, they probably are that way. What makes it the case that we do well to use this principle?

2. The structure of justification. This brings us to one particular question about justification, which has received much attention. Suppose that we give the justification of a mediated belief *A* which appeals to its relation to some other belief *B*. This belief, *B*, justifies that one, *A*; my belief that it is Sunday justifies my belief that there will be no mail today. There is a very strong intuition that *B* can only transmit justification to *A* if it is itself justified. So the question whether *A* is justified has not yet been answered, when we appealed to *B*, but only shelved. Whether it is justified depends on whether *B* is. What justified *B*? We might appeal to some further belief *C*, but then the problem will simply recur. We have here the beginnings of an infinite regress. The first belief in the series is not justified unless the last one is. But will there ever be a last belief in the series?

This is the infinite regress of justification. Foundationalism takes this regress seriously, and tries to find 'basic beliefs' that are capable of stopping it. Promising ways of doing this include the idea that basic beliefs are justified by their *source* (they are the immediate products of the sense, perhaps), or by their subject-matter (they concern the nature of the believer's current sensory states). *Empiricism, in this connection, wants in some way to ground basic beliefs in experience. Foundationalism concerns itself with the structure of this empiricist programme.

So a concern with the regress of justification is a concern with the *structure* of justification. Coherentism tries to show that a justified set of beliefs need not have the form of a superstructure resting on a base; the idea here is that the foundationalist programme is bound to fail, so that the 'base' is left groundless, resting on nothing. If this were the result, and if foundationalists were right about the structure of a justified belief set, the only possible conclusion would be the sceptical one that none of our beliefs are in fact justified.

Coherentists reject the base/superstructure distinction; there are no beliefs which are intrinsically grounds, and none which are intrinsically superstructure. Beliefs about experience can be supported by appeal to theory (which would be going upwards in terms of the foundationalist model), as well as vice versa (theories need the support of experience). The whole thing is much more of a mess, and cannot be sorted neatly into layers.

3. Knowledge. Epistemology, as so far explained, focuses on justification. There is a second focus, on knowledge. Someone whose belief is justified does well. But justification comes in degrees, and so does our epistemic status (determined by how well we are doing). The top status is that of knowledge. Someone who *knows* that p could not be doing better (at least with respect to p). There is a natural interest in this top status. Two main questions arise: what is the most we can hope for, and in what areas do we get it? The traditional attempts to define knowledge focus on the first of these. These attempts come in two main families. The first tries to see knowledge as some clever form of belief; the best-known form of this view is the 'tripartite definition', which takes knowledge to be (1) belief which is both (2) justified and (3) true. The second family of views takes knowledge to start where belief gives out. Plato's version of this was that belief is concerned with the changing (especially the material world), and knowledge with the unchanging (e.g. mathematics). Other versions might suggest that we can have knowledge of our surroundings, but only when some physical thing is directly present to the mind. On this approach, knowledge is a direct relation, while belief is conceived as an indirect relation to the thing believed.

The second question about knowledge, namely what areas we can get it in, introduces us to the distinction between global and local. In some areas, we might say, knowledge is available, and in others it is not—or at least less freely available. It is common to hear people say that we have no knowledge of the future, of God, or of right and wrong, while allowing that there is at least some scientific knowledge and some knowledge of the past (in memory). Similarly, in discussing the justification of belief, we might say that our beliefs about our present surroundings are on firm ground, as firm as that which supports our (rather different) central theoretical beliefs in science, while our beliefs about God and about the future are *intrinsically* less well supported.

4. Scepticism. Scepticism about knowledge comes in both global and local forms. The knowledge-sceptic holds that we cannot achieve knowledge, and this claim could be made in general (the global variety) or only in certain areas such as those mentioned above (the local form). The belief-sceptic is generally held to be more interesting. This person, in global form, holds that we have no right to any of our beliefs; none are better than others, and none are good enough to count as justified. More locally, a belief-sceptic might say that while we do well in some of our beliefs about things presently hidden from us (e.g. what is in the cupboard), we have no right to any beliefs about right and wrong. Someone who said this would be a moral sceptic, and the difficulty in that position is to make sure that the reasons that underlie one's moral scepticism do not spread over into other areas. If, for instance, one's objection to beliefs about moral matters is that they lie beyond the reach of observation, one would have to make the same objection to scientific beliefs about matters too small to be observed.

So there is a distinction between local and global scepticism, both in the theory of justified belief and in that of knowledge. Both sorts of scepticism need to be supported by argument, and one main problem of epistemology is the attempt to assess and rebut such arguments as they appear. This is one important way in which we can work to establish our right to our beliefs.

There have been two classic strands of sceptical argument in the history of epistemology, the Pyrrhonist and the Cartesian. *Pyrrhonism (named after its leading figure, Pyrrho of Elis (*c.*365–270 BC)) focuses on the justification of belief, while the scepticism we inherit from Descartes starts with knowledge and attempts to move to belief from there. Descartes argued that we cannot know

something if we are unable to distinguish the case where it is true from the case where, though false, it seems to be true. For if we cannot distinguish, then though it may here be true, for all we know it isn't; this case might, for all we can tell, be one where the appearances are deceiving us, and if so, we can hardly claim to know that they are not. Though persuasive enough as an argument for knowledge-scepticism, this approach cannot easily be extended to support belief-scepticism; for the fact that I cannot tell when appearances are deceiving me does little to show that I have no (or insufficient) reason for my beliefs. Matters are different with the Pyrrhonist tradition. This is explicitly aimed at showing that the reasons on one side are never better than they are on the other. If so, we would be forced to allow that there is no such thing as a belief that is favoured by the balance of the reasons, and so to admit that we cannot defend our right to our beliefs in the only way available to us, namely that of showing that the evidence supports them. Pyrrhonism focuses on the criteria by which we distinguish between the true and the false and argues in various ways that we have no right to those criteria, and so that they cannot be rationally defended. One classic move here is to ask what criteria we can use to evaluate our criteria; if we are to appeal to the very criteria that are under consideration, we beg the question, and we have no further criteria to appeal to. Pyrrhonism is here attacking our cognitive strategies, arguing that none of them can be defended. Hume's argument attacking the rationality of induction is the classic instance.

*5. *Naturalism in epistemology.* Being normative, epistemology is concerned with evaluation—the evaluation of strategies and their products (beliefs). Among the strategies it evaluates are those of science. So conceived, epistemology sits in judgement on all other areas of human enquiry; it counts as *First Philosophy. (The sceptical question above asks how epistemology can succeed in evaluating itself.) Quine attempted to reverse this position, and to conceive of epistemology as part of science, looking to the results of science to answer the questions of epistemology. This enterprise, called naturalizing epistemology, is not impossible. Science does sometimes succeed in evaluating its own strategies, just as it evaluates its own instruments. So science is sometimes normative; it may not only examine our perceptual processes, but also pronounce on their reliability. But some of the questions of epistemology seem to resist naturalization, e.g. those which concern reason rather than observation.

To say that science is sometimes normative, and that traditional epistemology is a large part of its normative element, might indeed reverse the relation between epistemology and natural science and thereby 'naturalize' it. But this alone would not be enough for many determined naturalizers. I have been presenting epistemology as a normative enterprise, whether or not it is placed within the sphere of natural science. But there are many who suppose that if normative claims and assertions make genuine sense and are capable of being true or false, they must be somehow identical with natural claims, ones from which the normativity has been removed. The worry here is that if normative facts are not identical with natural facts, we will find ourselves landed with two realms, the realm of nature (where we find such things as particles, electricity, and gravity) and the realm of the normative (where we find such things as duties, responsibilities, and rights), without there being any way of understanding how those two realms are co-present in one and the same world. More aggressively, the question becomes how there is any room for distinct normative facts in a natural world, the world that can be studied by science. If we want normative epistemological facts, then, we will have to show that those facts are *also* natural. If we succeeded in doing that, we would have naturalized epistemology in a much more dramatic sense.

6. *Special areas*. There are traditionally four sources of knowledge (or of justified belief): the senses, *memory, *introspection, and *reason. Each of these has its epistemology. The study of perceptual knowledge asks how perception manages to yield knowledge of our material surroundings. To answer this question one obviously needs to know a certain amount about how the senses actually work. But that knowledge seems to be not enough on its own (so perhaps the epistemology of the senses cannot be naturalized either). There are difficulties to be faced here which cannot be solved with a bit more scientific information. One is the sceptical difficulty sometimes called the *veil of perception. If our senses only reveal knowledge about how things *seem*, how can we hope to use them to find out how things really *are*? The appearances, on this showing, are obstructing rather than helping us in our attempts to discern the nature of reality; perception casts a veil over the world rather than revealing it to us. Another sceptical difficulty here derives from the *argument from illusion.

At the other extreme is the epistemology of reason. The activities of reason are twofold. First there is inference, in which we move from old knowledge to new knowledge. The strongest form of this is valid deductive inference, which occurs when it is not possible that our premises (what we are moving from) are true if our conclusion (what we are moving to) is false. One question here is how such inference could ever yield *new* knowledge. Surely the conclusion must be somehow already contained in the premises, if the premises cannot be true where the conclusion is false. The second supposed activity of reason is the direct discovery of new truths. A truth that can be discovered by the activity of reason alone is called an *a priori truth, and knowledge of it is a priori knowledge. One of the great questions in epistemology is how a priori knowledge is possible, and what sorts of truth can be known in this way. Some propositions are true in virtue of their meaning alone, e.g. that all bachelors are people. We know this truth, and not by appeal to the senses, to introspection, or to memory. So we know it by reason. But propositions of this sort (often called analytic) are

trivial. They give us no substantial knowledge. Can reason give us substantial knowledge of anything, or is all a priori knowledge analytic and (therefore) trivial? For example, if mathematical knowledge is the product of reason, can it be substantial? Are mathematical truths merely analytic? We appear to be torn between saying that mathematical truths are important and saying that we know them by the activity of reason alone. It was the attempt to avoid this dilemma that led to Kant's first *Critique*.

7. *The place of epistemology*. Where does epistemology come on the philosophical map? I see it as a chapter in the more general enterprise which is called the philosophy of mind; it is the evaluative side of that enterprise. In the philosophy of mind we ask about the nature of mental states, in particular (for present purposes) about the nature of belief. Our views in epistemology are sensitive to our answers to that question, just as they are sensitive to scientific results about the nature of perceptual processes. For instance, our account of the relation between knowledge and belief will depend crucially on the way in which we conceive of belief. Is it a *closed* state, in which we are aware merely of representations of things rather than of things themselves (the veil of belief)? If so, is knowledge to be merely the best form of such a state—the thinnest veil? Or is knowledge to be conceived quite differently?

The other philosophical area to which epistemology is tightly tied is the theory of meaning. The question whether we are able to know propositions of a certain sort is sensitive to our account of what those propositions mean. For instance, if we take statements about a material world to be a disguised form of statement about experience, and if we think that our knowledge of experiences is secure from sceptical attack, we may hope to emerge with a defence of our ability to know the nature of the material world. This hope is the hope that *phenomenalism will solve some of our epistemological problems for us.   J.D.

*epistemology, history of; epistemic justification; epistemology, genetic; evolutionary epistemology; feminist epistemology; naturalized epistemology; relativism, epistemological; knowledge.

R. B. Brandom, 'Insights and Blindspots of Reliabilism', in *Articulating Reasons: An Introduction to Inferentialism* (Cambridge, Mass., 2000).

R. M. Chisholm, *Theory of Knowledge*, 2nd edn. (Englewood Cliffs, NJ, 1977).

J. Dancy, *Introduction to Contemporary Epistemology* (Oxford, 1985).

A. Goldman, *Epistemology and Cognition* (Cambridge, Mass., 1986).

W. V. Quine, 'Epistemology Naturalised', in *Ontological Relativity* (New York, 1969).

W. F. Sellars, 'Empiricism and the Philosophy of Mind', in *Science, Perception and Reality* (London, 1963).

L. Wittgenstein, *On Certainty* (Oxford, 1969).

epistemology and psychology. The divorce of philosophy and psychology is a relatively recent affair. Histories of psychology read like histories of philosophy until the mid-nineteenth century, when the methods and preoccupations of philosophers and psychologists began to diverge, and psychologists came to regard themselves as engaged in a fully fledged science emancipated from its empirically feeble predecessors. In 1879, Wilhelm Wundt established the first psychological laboratory at the University of Leipzig. Not until well into the twentieth century, however, did professional associations and university departments of philosophy and psychology become distinct. The disciplines have resisted reconciliation and maintained a respectful distance ever since.

Academic departmental boundaries aside, W. V. Quine convinced many philosophers that distinctions between scientific and philosophical endeavours are tenuous; in particular, 'epistemology . . . is a chapter of psychology'. Traditionally, epistemology sought an unassailable foundation for subsequent empirical theorizing: philosophical investigation must be independent of, and prior to, empirical inquiry. The goal was to demonstrate that knowledge of the world around us could be inferred from sensory experiences that mediate access to that world. The grounds for such an inference have proved remarkably difficult to locate, however. Hume demonstrated that they were not to be found in reason alone. One possibility is that talk of a mind-independent world is misplaced: sentences about physical bodies might be reducible to, or translatable into, sentences concerning sense experiences. Quine argues against this possibility, and concludes that the relation we bear to the physical world is best comprehended by empirical psychology. It is not that epistemology is to be replaced by psychology, only that we must cease to regard epistemology as operating in the classical mode, prior to and independently of psychology and the natural sciences.

Inspired by Quine, some philosophers have turned to empirical psychological findings in support of conclusions concerning traditional philosophical matters. Stephen Stich, taking the dark view, argues that work in psychology undermines philosophers' time-honoured trust in reason as a vehicle, if not a source, of truth. P. M. Churchland, in dismissing belief and reason as being on a par with ghosts and devils, favours the replacement of theories of mind with a properly hard-nosed neuroscience, leaving little for philosophers to work with. D. C. Dennett finds answers to age-old philosophical questions about conscious experience and belief in cutting-edge work of psychologists and neuroscientists.

In a more moderate vein, A. I. Goldman, a proponent of the 'naturalizing' of epistemology and metaphysics, argues that philosophy begins, but does not end, with the consideration of 'folk theories', conceptions of ourselves and our world embodied in our language and everyday patterns of thought. Having mapped these folk conceptions, we turn to psychologists, anthropologists, and others for an explanation of their deployment. Suppose, for instance, that our folk scheme treats colours as objective features of objects on a par with shapes. We might learn from psychology and neurobiology that perceived colours are better regarded as artefacts arising from the operation of our visual apparatus. Having accepted this, we would be in a position both to explain and to revise our naïve 'pre-theoretical' conception of colour. We would do so, not on the basis of a priori reflection, however, but by way of an explicit appeal to what we took to be empirical fact.

It is by no means universally accepted that philosophy can, or must, be naturalized in any of these ways. Even so, many philosophers now concede it is a mistake to assume that philosophical inquiry could be altogether insulated from empirical findings in psychology and elsewhere, hence the emergence of 'cognitive science', a disciplinary hybrid comprising psychologists, computer scientists, linguists, philosophers, and others, striving to understand the mind and its place in the natural order. Whether this represents an investigatory advance remains to be seen. While on the whole laudable, interdisciplinary co-operation can serve to blur the focus of research. Philosophers are prone to forget that empirical theories of mind can incorporate substantive philosophical commitments with shadowy credentials. These may be recycled back into philosophy, though in a way that disguises their character. Loosely paraphrasing Wittgenstein: philosophers nowadays risk taking on board conceptual confusions disguised as experimental methods.   J.HEIL.

P. M. Churchland, *The Engine of Reason, the Seat of the Soul* (Cambridge, Mass., 1995).

D. C. Dennett, *Kinds of Minds* (New York, 1996).

A. I. Goldman, *Liaisons: Philosophy Meets the Cognitive and Social Sciences* (Cambridge, Mass., 1991).

W. V. Quine, 'Epistemology Naturalized', in *Ontological Relativity and Other Essays* (New York, 1969).

S. P. Stich, *The Fragmentation of Reason* (Cambridge, Mass., 1990).

epochē. 'Withholding' of assent and dissent, i.e. suspense of judgement. Ancient *scepticism combined a thesis, 'There is no knowledge', with a prescription, 'Practise *epochē*'. The one leads to the other via a view shared by some non-sceptics that it is stupid to assent to what you do not know. And the outcome is delightful: 'Freedom from disturbance follows like a shadow' (Diogenes Laertius on Pyrrho). But there was, and is, controversy whether general *epochē* is a practicable option.   C.A.K.

M. F. Burnyeat, 'Can the Sceptic Live his Scepticism?', in M. Schofield, M. F. Burnyeat, and J. Barnes (eds.), *Doubt and Dogmatism* (Oxford, 1980); repr. in M. F. Burnyeat (ed.), *The Skeptical Tradition* (Berkeley, Calif., 1983).

equality. Currently the most controversial of the great social ideals. In the abstract, it means that people who are similarly situated in morally relevant respects should be treated similarly; but everything depends on what kinds of similarity count as relevant, and what constitutes similar treatment. Is a society equal enough if it guarantees all its citizens the same basic political and legal rights, or should it try to foster a much more general equality of condition? Complete equality among persons being impossible, the real meaning of the idea is reduction or amelioration of *inequality.

Possible interpretations include equality before the law, equality of political power, equality of opportunity for social and economic advancement, equality of resources, equality of welfare, equality of freedom, and equality of respect. Merely abolishing aristocracy and giving everybody the vote is compatible with huge inequalities in social condition and political influence. By now it is relatively uncontroversial in Western societies that governments should not discriminate on the basis of race, religion, sex, or national origin, and that they should discourage such discrimination by private parties. Controversy arises over the extent to which governments should also aim at greater social and economic equality through policies of collective social provision, public health and education, and redistribution of income or wealth, and whether they should employ policies of affirmative action to produce greater equality among groups if there has been discrimination in the past.

The main issue is whether we should regard certain human inequalities and their consequences as natural, and only be concerned not to impose further artificial ones, or whether we should base social policy on the assumption that all persons are equally deserving of a good life, and that their society should try to make it possible for them to have it. This latter goal of positive equality will not be realized through mere equality of opportunity, since equal opportunity combined with unequal ability and luck produce very unequal results.

An important alternative view is that equality has no value in itself, but is significant only for its effects. *Utilitarianism, for example, holds that society should be arranged to maximize the total happiness of its members, without regard to how benefits and disadvantages are distributed, except as this affects the total. However, economic equality is likely to have instrumental value, because of the principle of diminishing marginal utility: a given sum transferred from rich to poor will enhance the welfare of the latter more than it will decrease the welfare of the former. But too strong an effort toward equality can have economic effects which diminish utility.   T.N.

*liberty and equality; justice; well-being.

R. Dworkin, *A Matter of Principle* (Cambridge, Mass., 1985).
T. Nagel, *Equality and Partiality* (New York, 1991).
M. Walzer, *Spheres of Justice* (New York, 1983).

equipollence. The theory of equipollence developed by some medieval logicians, e.g. Peter of Spain (c.1215–77), concerned the equivalences that result from inserting a negation sign before or after a sign of quantity, e.g. 'Not every A is B', 'Every A is not B'. 'Equipollence' later became synonymous with *equivalence in general. Tarski, though, defines as 'equipollent' two systems of sentences such that any sentence in one can be derived from the sentences in the other.   C.W.

A. Tarski, *Introduction to Logic* (New York, 1965), 32–3.

equivalence. Relation between two statements p and q when p implies q and q implies p. Material equivalence, in line with *material implication (p implies q unless p is true and q false; q implies p unless q is true and p false), holds between p and q if and only if they have the same truth-value. But equivalence is also often interpreted to require necessary identity of truth-value and/or identity of content and/or identity of meaning.   S.W.

*equivalence relation.

S. Wolfram, *Philosophical Logic* (London, 1989), ch. 4. 1.

equivalence relation. An equivalence relation is a binary, i.e. two-term, relation that is *transitive, *symmetric, and (strongly) *reflexive; for example, *being the same age as* is an equivalence relation, relative to the domain of things with age.   C.A.K.

*equivalence of statements.

W. Hodges, *Logic* (Harmondsworth, 1977).

equivalences of the form T: *see* snow is white.

equivocation: *see* ambiguity.

equivocation, fallacy of. You equivocate when you mean two things by one or more occurrences of a single word or phrase. Often this is innocuous, as in puns. But it will lead to faulty reasoning when an *argument requires one such meaning in order to entail the intended conclusion, another in order to have true premisses. Usually the fault is not deceptive, but sometimes it is thought-provoking, as in: What you are able to do or not do, you are *free* not to do; you are able to pay or not pay taxes; so you are *free* not to pay them.   C.A.K.

*ambiguity.

C. L. Hamblin, *Fallacies* (London, 1970).

Erasmus, Desiderius (1466–1536). Born in poor circumstances in Rotterdam, he attended the University of Paris where he came into contact with many who were due to play a crucial role in the new humanist movement. He rose to become a key figure in *Renaissance humanism, active as a critic of the Church and of contemporary mores, and active also as an editor of major writings from an earlier age, such as the works of the early Fathers of the Church, and above all the Greek text of the New Testament. His edition of the New Testament, though inadequate in many ways, was a major advance on anything available in the Middle Ages. Many of his writings, such as *In Praise of Folly*, a powerful satire on society both ecclesiastical and lay, argue the case for a return to a form of Christian pietism. Though he attacked many abuses committed by the Church, abuses which in due course it tried to stamp out, he was unsympathetic to the Reformation then under way, as is made clear by his attack on Luther. It is an irony of history that his works were placed on the Index by the Council of Trent.   A.BRO.

Roland H. Bainton, *Erasmus of Rotterdam* (London, 1969).

Eriugena, John Scotus (*c*.810–*c*.877) from Ireland, lived for years in France where he worked at the Court of Charles the Bald. He translated a number of works, including some by pseudo-Dionysius, from Greek into Latin, and in addition wrote treatises of his own, in particular *On the Division of Nature*, the first great philosophical system of the Middle Ages. The *Division*, which was heavily influenced by the Neoplatonism of pseudo-Dionysius, is presented as a system of Christian thought, but there is room for dispute over whether it avoids an un-Christian *pantheism. He considers nature under four heads: nature which creates and is uncreated, nature which is created and creates, nature which is created and does not create, and nature which neither creates nor is created. Since God is said to fall under the first heading, it might well seem that there is a pantheistic philosophy here, but the distinction that Eriugena draws between uncreated creator and all else is sufficient to convince some commentators that he has found his own way to develop a position which is not far removed from Christian orthodoxy.   A.BRO.

John J. O'Meara, *Eriugena* (Oxford, 1988).

error theory of value is the label given by J. L. Mackie to a position he promoted about the nature of *value. According to Mackie, although moral judgements in their meaning aim at something objective, there are in fact no objective values. Hence our normal moral judgements involve an error.   R.H.

J. L. Mackie, *Ethics* (Harmondsworth, 1977), ch. 1.

eschatology. That branch of theology concerned with 'the last things'—death, what follows it for each individual, and the final fate of the universe. According to traditional Christian theology, death is followed by resurrection of the dead, God's judgement on their past life, and their apportionment to heaven or hell. 'Realized eschatology' is the view that states analogous to the traditional after-death states occur in our present life—e.g. God's judgement on the past is a feature of life on earth. Scholars have found strains of realized eschatology, as well as traditional eschatology, in the New Testament; a few very radical theologians defend only realized eschatology.   R.G.S.

R. Swinburne, *Responsibility and Atonement* (Oxford, 1989), ch. 12.

esoteric. 'Inner'. A word coined in the second century AD to refer to Aristotle's more difficult works, as contrasted with his accessible *'exoteric' ones. The esoteric works were intended for more advanced pupils. Their obscurity gave rise to the story that they concealed Aristotle's true doctrines, which were a secret to be revealed only to disciples. The word was later applied with the sense 'secret', e.g. to the doctrines of Pythagoras' inner circle.   R.J.H.

*Pythagoreanism.

I. Düring, *Aristotle in the Ancient Biographical Tradition* (Göteborg, 1957), 426–43.

ESP phenomena, philosophical implications of. ESP (extrasensory perception), the supposed ability to receive information about the world without the use of the recognized senses, raises questions about various aspects of the physicalistic world-view that dominates current philosophical thinking. Apparent occurrences of ESP, while often extremely convincing to participants, are difficult to investigate applying standard scientific canons of repeatability, independence of observation, and applicability of quantitative measurement. Thus such occurrences, if genuine, question the universality of these canons. Events supposedly learned of by ESP include ones at great distances or even of future events; this would violate known causal relations and so undermine causal theories of perception (how can future events cause the perception of such events in the present?). More generally, ESP, if it exists, would appear to be non-physical: ESP is disanalogous to the familiar senses (no known organ of sensation, no known physical link with events perceived) and so explanations, perhaps purely mentalistic, outside the current physicalistic paradigm seem required.   G.C.

J. R. Smythies (ed.), *Science and ESP* (London, 1967).

esse est percipi. 'To be is to be perceived.' Berkeley, in his *Treatise Concerning the Principles of Human Knowledge* (1710), asserts (para. 3) of 'unthinking things' that 'their *esse* is *percipi*, nor is it possible they should have any existence, out of the minds or thinking things which perceive them'—on the ground that unthinking things, 'sensible objects', are *'ideas or sensations'. Note that he affirms this only of 'unthinking' things.   G.J.W.

A. A. Luce, *The Dialectic of Immaterialism* (London, 1963), ch. 6.

essence. There are four grades of *essentialism. According to *grade 1*, a thing *x* is allowed to have a property ϕ essentially only relative to some other (implicitly or explicitly) singled-out property that *x* has (or kind to which it belongs). Such a property ϕ is thus a 'relativistic' essence, and the acceptance of such essences requires only acceptance of *de dicto* necessity: that is, it presupposes only the sort of necessary truth that applies to general propositions such as the proposition that if something is square then it has a shape. Locke's doctrine of 'nominal essence' belongs with this grade of essentialism.

According to *grade 2*, in addition to such *de dicto* necessity there is also fundamental *de re* necessity. According to this grade, moreover, it is a necessary truth that any property possessed essentially by anything is possessed essentially by everything that possesses it. Thus, necessarily if something is a body, then it is necessarily a body. Note well: it is not just necessarily a body relative to some property of it that entails its being a body, it is not just necessarily a body 'under some description' that yields its being a body. No, the thing itself that is a body has that property not just contingently but necessarily. In a sense essentiality is, for this intermediate grade, fundamentally a feature of properties. Some properties are essential properties; and, most would say, some are not. Properties that are thus essential are in a sense 'absolute essences', since *whatever* has them must have them essentially.

But there is a higher grade of essentialism, *grade 3*, according to which in addition to properties had essentially in the relativistic fashion of the lowest grade and in the absolute and *de re* necessary fashion of the second grade, there are properties had essentially by some things while they are had but not essentially by other things. Thus a snowball may be said to be round and necessarily so (it is of the essence of a snowball, part of its essential nature, that it be round), but the constituent piece of snow is round yet not necessarily so. This might be called 'particularistic' essentialism, since one and the same property might be of the essence of one particular while it is had by another particular without being of *its* essence.

Finally, a higher-yet grade of essentialism, *grade 4*, requires that each particular have a property that *only it could possibly have had*, in any possible world: its 'thisness' or *haecceity. Roundness is a sort of essence that, as we have seen, is distinctively of the essence of some (only) of those particulars that have it. A thing's haecceity, on the other hand, is in a more extreme fashion distinctively of the essence of something: for it is a property that is necessarily possessed by that thing in whatever possible world it might have existed, and one that could not possibly have been possessed by any other thing.

The higher grades of essentialism give rise to puzzling conundrums. For example, it seems very plausible that if a thing has a differential modal property (one that not everything has or need have), then there must be some actual (non-modal) property of that thing to explain why it has that modal property. But this gives rise to a problem concerning any property that is not only differentially but also 'distinctively' essential, it being possible that something have it essentially while something else has it also but not essentially. Take the roundness of a snowball, which it shares with its constituent piece of snow, even though one, the snowball, has it essentially, and the other, the constituent snow, has it also but not essentially. Given the extent and nature of the similarity in actual properties, including roundness, between the snowball and the constituent snow, it is hard to see what could possibly explain the possession of that modal property by that snowball. Whatever property of the snowball we might appeal to in order to explain its *essential* possession of roundness would seem to be shared by the constituent snow, which is supposed to have roundness only *accidentally*. So what could possibly explain this difference between them, that one has roundness essentially while the other has it only accidentally? E.S.

S. Kripke, *Naming and Necessity* (Cambridge, Mass., 1972).
M. Loux (ed.), *The Possible and the Actual* (Ithaca, NY, 1979).
A. Plantinga, *The Nature of Necessity* (Oxford, 1974).
W. V. Quine, *From a Logical Point of View* (Cambridge, Mass., 1953; 2nd edn. 1961).

essence, individual: *see* haecceity.

essentialism. The essentialist claims that we can draw an objective distinction between an object's *essential* and *accidental* properties, which is not simply a reflection of how we choose to describe the object. An essential property of an object is one that it possesses in every *possible world in which it exists—or, if one favours *counterpart theory, it is one that is possessed by every counterpart of the object in other possible worlds. For example, it may be urged that it was an essential property of Napoleon that he was a human being, but only an accidental property of him that he was Emperor of France. Some supposedly essential properties of objects, such as Napoleon's property of being human, are shared by other objects of the same kind, but there may also be essential properties that are unique to the object possessing them—and these are said to constitute that object's individual *essence. In the case of a human being like Napoleon, one such property may be his property of having originated from the fusion of a particular sperm and egg. E.J.L.

E. J. Lowe, *A Survey of Metaphysics* (Oxford, 2002).

essentially contested concepts. It is sometimes claimed that the enduring diversity of opinion over, e.g., moral, political, or religious issues reveals that such questions lie beyond the domain of rational enquiry. In the 1950s, W. B. Gallie challenged this claim, arguing that disputes about concepts like 'art', 'democracy', and 'social justice' are not merely semantic or attitudinal in character, but often involve arguments that aspire to be, and sometimes are, rationally persuasive. None the less, the internal complexity of such concepts ensures that dispute is always prone to break out. Thus, from the fact that such concepts are 'essentially contested', we should not conclude that their use defies rational assessment. D.BAK.

W. B. Gallie, 'Essentially Contested Concepts', *Proceedings of the Aristotelian Society*, 56 (1955/6).

eternal recurrence. An ancient cosmological idea, seized upon by Nietzsche, to the effect that everything that happens is part of an endlessly repeating cycle or sequence of events. While Nietzsche entertained this idea as an actual cosmological hypothesis, he first introduced it and chiefly employed it hypothetically as a kind of test. One who is able to affirm life even on this supposition will have what it takes to endure and flourish in the aftermath of all disillusionment. (See e.g. *The Gay Science*, sect. 341; *Thus Spoke Zarathustra*, pt. 3; *The Will to Power*, sect. 1066.) R.S.

*cosmology.

John Stambaugh, *Nietzsche's Thought of Eternal Return* (Baltimore, 1972).

eternity. Sometimes used to mean simply the whole of *time; but more usually used to mean a timeless realm (with no past or future) in which God lives. Boethius defined it as the 'total and perfect possession at once of an endless life'. It seemed unthinkable that for God there should be a 'no longer' and a 'not yet'. Most Christian thinkers since the fourth century (unlike the authors of the Bible) held that God exists outside time, but in his timeless realm simultaneously acts at and knows about every moment of time. It is, however, doubtful if this is a coherent claim—if God sees some event in 500 BC as it happens and sees some other event in 2000 AD as it happens and all divine seeings are simultaneous with each other, then 500 BC must be the same year as 2000 AD—which is absurd.   R.G.S.

N. Pike, *God and Timelessness* (London, 1970).

ethical formalism. A type of ethical theory which defines *moral judgements in terms of their logical form (for example, as 'laws' or 'universal prescriptions') rather than their content (for example, as judgements about what actions will best promote human well-being). The term often also carries critical connotations. Kant, for example, has been criticized for defining morality in terms of the formal feature of being a 'universal law', and then attempting to derive from this formal feature various concrete moral duties.   R.J.N.

   *prescriptivism.

Immanuel Kant, *Groundwork of the Metaphysic of Morals*, various edns., e.g. tr. H. J. Paton (London, 1948).
G. J. Warnock, *Contemporary Moral Philosophy* (London, 1967).

ethical naturalism: *see* naturalism, ethical.

ethical objectivism: *see* objectivism and subjectivism, ethical.

ethical relativism: *see* relativism, ethical.

ethical subjectivism: *see* objectivism and subjectivism, ethical.

ethical voluntarism: *see* voluntarism, ethical.

ethics: *see* moral philosophy.

ethics, applied: *see* applied ethics.

ethics, axiological: *see* axiological ethics.

ethics, bio-: *see* bioethics.

ethics, business: *see* business ethics.

ethics, Chinese: *see* Chinese philosophy; Confucianism.

ethics, deontological: *see* deontological ethics.

ethics, divine command: *see* divine command ethics.

ethics, emotive theory of: *see* emotive theory of ethics.

ethics, environmental: *see* environmental ethics.

ethics, evolutionary: *see* evolutionary ethics.

ethics, feminist: *see* feminist ethics.

ethics, Japanese: *see* Japanese philosophy.

ethics, Kantian: *see* Kantian ethics.

ethics, medical: *see* medical ethics.

ethics, naturalistic: *see* naturalism, ethical.

ethics and aesthetics. The two traditional branches of the theory of value. Aesthetics understood as value theory concerns itself with the value of perceptual and imaginative experiences to be had from engagement with objects, both natural and man-made, or with the value inherent in those objects in relation to human lives. More broadly, aesthetics as value theory may be said to be concerned with intrinsic value generally. Ethics as value theory concerns itself with the evaluation of human conduct, with how human beings ought fundamentally to behave, particularly in relation to one another. Ethics and aesthetics are thus connected, in that part of the answer to the broader question ethics asks most likely involves an answer to the narrower question aesthetics asks, regarding what is worthwhile experiencing for its own sake, or what sorts of things enrich human lives. Furthermore, issues about the reality and objectivity of ethical and aesthetic values are more or less parallel.

   Certain ethical theories, most notably virtue ethics of either an Aristotelian or Nietzschean sort, seem to make an aesthetic appeal at base, valorizing characters or actions or lives that display unity, balance, or grace, and making holistic grasp of situations in their concrete detail, rather than formulaic application of rules, the *sine qua non* of sound moral judgement. Even Kantian moral theory, with its emphasis on the good will as the ultimate source of value, might be seen as grounding morality in something's having a certain form or structure, an arguably aesthetic notion.

   On the other hand, most accounts of aesthetic evaluation, and more particularly, the evaluation of art, allow that ethical considerations play a genuine role in such evaluation, one more or less central according the sort of artwork involved. Thus the ethical perspective embodied in, or conveyed by, a novel or film can be held to be ineliminably relevant to its evaluation as art, because appreciation of the work requires sharing or entering into that perspective to some extent, and yet such engagement might not be merited or justified. The moral dimension of artistic evaluation is most prominent with representational works having sexual, violent, or racist content, but it can be argued that even pure instrumental music has an artistically relevant moral aspect, turning on the character of the mind one engages with in listening.   J.LEV.

*art and morality.

José Luis Bermúdez and Sebastian Gardner (eds.), *Art and Morality* (London, 2003).
Noël Carroll, 'Art and Ethical Criticism: An Overview', *Ethics* (2000).
Jerrold Levinson (ed.), *Aesthetics and Ethics: Essays at the Intersection* (Cambridge, 1998).

ethics and morality. 'Morality' and 'ethics' are terms often used as synonyms: an ethical issue just is a moral issue. Increasingly, however, the term 'ethics' is being used to apply to specialized areas of morality, such as medicine, business, the environment, and so on. Where professions are involved, a governing body will typically draw up a code of ethics for its members. 'Ethics' in this sense can be thought of as a subset of morality, being that aspect of morality concerned with the moral obligations pertaining to the practice of a profession. On the other hand, some philosophers, from Socrates to Bernard Williams, use 'ethics' in a broad sense to refer to reflective answers to the question 'How should I live?'. If we accept this broad sense of 'ethics', then morality becomes a subset of ethics, being that aspect of ethics concerned with obligation.   R.S.D.

Brenda Almond and Donald Hill (eds.), *Applied Philosophy: Morals and Metaphysics in Contemporary Debate* (London, 1991).
Bernard Williams, *Ethics and the Limits of Philosophy* (London, 1985).

ethics of belief: *see* belief, ethics of.

ethics of care: *see* care, ethics of.

eudaimonia. Literally 'having a good guardian spirit', i.e. the state of having an objectively desirable life, universally agreed by ancient philosophical theory and popular thought to be the supreme human good. This objective character distinguishes it from the modern concept of *happiness, i.e. of a subjectively satisfactory life. Much ancient theory concerns the question of what constitutes the good life, e.g. whether virtue is sufficient for it, as Socrates and the Stoics held, or whether external goods such as good fortune are also necessary, as Aristotle maintained. Immoralists such as Thrasymachus (in Plato's *Republic*) sought to discredit morality by arguing that it prevents the achievement of *eudaimonia*, while its defenders (including Plato) argued that it is necessary and/or sufficient. The Kantian conception of morality binding on rational beings independently of their well-being was absent from Greek thought.   C.C.W.T.

*well-being.

J. Annas, *The Morality of Happiness* (New York, 1993).
T. H. Irwin, 'Stoic and Aristotelian Conceptions of Happiness', in M. Schofield and G. Striker (eds.), *The Norms of Nature* (Cambridge, 1986).

euthanasia. Originally, the word 'euthanasia' was derived from two Greek roots meaning 'good death'. The term subsequently came to have two distinct meanings: (1) the act or practice of painlessly putting to death those who suffer from terminal conditions (active euthanasia); (2) intentionally not preventing death in those who suffer from terminal conditions (passive euthanasia). The second meaning came into usage when technological advances in medicine made it possible to prolong the lives of persons without hope of recovery. Eventually, the requirement of a 'terminal condition' was dropped in many proposed definitions.

Perhaps the most accurate general meaning today is that euthanasia occurs if and only if: (1) the death is intended by at least one other person who is either the cause of *death or a causally relevant condition of the death; (2) the person put to death is either acutely suffering or irreversibly comatose (or soon will be), and this is the reason for intending the person's death; and (3) the means chosen to produce the death must be as painless as possible, or there must be a sufficient moral justification for a more painful method.

If a person requests the termination of his or her life, the action is called voluntary euthanasia (and often also assisted *suicide). If the person is not mentally competent to make an informed request, the action is called nonvoluntary euthanasia. Both forms should be distinguished from involuntary euthanasia, which involves a person capable of making an informed request, but who has not done so. Involuntary euthanasia is universally condemned and plays no role in current moral controversies. A final set of distinctions appeals to the active–passive distinction: passive euthanasia involves letting someone die from a disease or injury, whereas active euthanasia involves taking active steps to end a person's life. All of these distinctions suffer from borderline cases and various forms of unclarity.

The centre of recent public and philosophical controversy has been over voluntary active euthanasia (VAE), especially physician-assisted suicide. Supporters of VAE argue that there are cases in which relief from suffering supersedes all other consequences and that respect for autonomy obligates society to respect the decisions of those who elect euthanasia. If competent patients have a legal and moral right to refuse treatment that brings about their deaths, there is a similar right to enlist the assistance of physicians or others to help patients cause their deaths by an active means. Proponents of VAE primarily look to circumstances in which (1) a condition has become overwhelmingly burdensome for a patient, (2) pain management for the patient is inadequate, and (3) only a physician seems capable of bringing relief.

The laws of most nations and the codes of medical and research ethics from the Hippocratic corpus to today's major professional codes strictly prohibit VAE (and all forms of merciful hastened death), even if a patient has a good reason for wanting to die. Although courts have often defended the rights of patients in cases of passive euthanasia, courts have rarely allowed any form of what they judged to be VAE.

Those who defend laws and medical traditions opposed to VAE often appeal to either (1) professional-role obligations that prohibit killing or (2) the social consequences that would result from changing these traditions. The first argument is straightforward: *killing patients is inconsistent with the roles of nursing, care-giving, and healing. The second argument is more complex and has been at the centre of many discussions. This argument is referred to as the wedge argument or the *slippery slope argument, and proceeds roughly as follows: although particular acts of active termination of life are sometimes morally justified, the social consequences of sanctioning such practices of killing would run serious risks of abuse and misuse and, on balance, would cause more harm than benefit. The argument is not that these negative consequences will occur immediately, but that they will grow incrementally over time, with an ever-increasing risk of unjustified termination.   T.L.B.

T. L. Beauchamp and R. M. Veatch (eds.), *Ethical Issues in Death and Dying* (Upper Saddle River, NJ, 1997).

Baruch A. Brody (ed.), *Suicide and Euthanasia: Historical and Contemporary Themes* (Dordrecht, 1989).

G. Dworkin, R. G. Frey, and S. Bok, *Euthanasia and Physician-Assisted Suicide: For and Against* (New York, 1998).

James Rachels, *The End of Life: Euthanasia and Morality* (Oxford, 1986).

Euthyphro problem. Euthyphro, in the Platonic dialogue named after him, attempts to define 'the pious' as 'the god-loved'. Socrates responds with the famous question: 'Is the pious loved by the gods because it is pious, or is it pious because they love it?' (*Euthyphro* 10a).

The general point behind the discussion that follows seems to be this: No normative term (such as 'the pious' or 'the *right') can be defined satisfactorily as what some rational authority, such as God or the gods, loves or commands, unless we suppose that the command or approval is without rational justification. Alternatively, if we suppose the approval or command to be rationally justified, then it is to that justification, rather than to the action or attitude of the authority, that we must look for the meaning of the normative term.   G.B.M.

S. Marc Cohen, 'Socrates on the Definition of Piety', in G. Vlastos (ed.), *The Philosophy of Socrates* (Garden City, NY, 1971).

evaluation: *see* value.

Evans, Gareth (1946–80). Evans was part of a post-1970 flowering of work in Oxford on mind and language, influenced by the American Donald Davidson (see also Dummett, McDowell, Peacocke, Crispin Wright). His posthumous book *The Varieties of Reference* develops McDowell's idea that aspects of mind such as thinking about individual objects are forms of embeddedness in an environment. This departs radically from *Cartesianism,

according to which thinking is a process that takes place essentially independently of the nature or even existence of an environment. Evans has been particularly influential in stressing that thinking is grounded in bodily capacities and abilities, and this work continues the Oxford Kantian tradition, associated with Strawson, of laying down the conditions for the objectivity of thought. His very early death was, like Ramsey's, a serious loss for British philosophy.   G.W.McC.

*reference.

G. Evans, *Collected Papers* (Oxford, 1985).

event. Roughly, a happening, occurrence, or episode: for example, the General Strike, the sinking of the *Titanic*, the arrival of the guests, the local jumble sale. Events need not be momentous: the fall of a sparrow is as much an event as the fall of the Roman Empire.

According to most accounts, events need not be instantaneous, nor even of brief duration. Ordinary language attempts to distinguish events from processes, but most modern theories of events show no interest in this distinction. An event is sometimes defined as a change (for example, the loss or acquisition of a property by something) or composite of changes. However, many theories of events include *states* that consist in things' having (or retaining) properties (e.g. the lawn's staying wet) as well as changes that consist in their acquiring or losing them (e.g. the lawn's becoming dry). On this liberal view, a rest may be as good as a change as a candidate for an event.

'An event' is ambiguous: it may mean a particular event, occurring only once, with a particular duration and location (e.g. the *1992* Grand National), or a 'type-event' that can occur repeatedly (e.g. the Grand National that is a famous annual event). Events in the first sense are sometimes described as 'concrete particulars' (also *'tokens' as opposed to 'types'); events in the second sense as *'universals' and as 'abstract'. Most contemporary theorists (Chisholm was an exception) are primarily concerned with events as particulars.

What distinguishes particular events from 'things'? We speak of events as *occurring*, but we do not say this of material objects like tortoises, books, and pebbles. And we seem to think that the *whole* of a tortoise or a rock is there at any time in its existence, whereas (excepting instantaneous events) only part of an event is present at any one time. However, many are unimpressed by these facts. 'A thing . . . is simply a long event [with certain characteristics]', wrote C. D. Broad (*Scientific Thought*, 393), and many philosophers have reduced material objects to series of events. (*Identity; mereology.) On the other hand, Aristotle, Strawson, and others have held that at least some material objects belong to an ontological *category distinct from, and prior to, that of events. (*Substance; *things; *ontology.)

The category of events is the focus of much recent discussion of *action, the *mind–body problem, and *causality, especially in work influenced by Davidson. Davidson has emphasized the significance of questions about the *individuation* of events. When do we have one event rather than two? When do different descriptions pick out the same event? Could a mental occurrence (e.g. one of my decisions) be identical with some physical event in my brain? Was Oedipus' marriage to Jocasta the same event as his marriage to his mother? If my hammering woke the cat next door and also caused the fall of the vase, was my hammering the same event as my waking of the cat, with the consequence (if causality is a genuine *relation* between events) that my waking of the cat caused the fall of the vase? (*Extensionality.) These are not mere conundrums: satisfactory answers are needed if we are to give coherent accounts of *mentality, *intention, *responsibility, and causation. (*Reasons and causes; *fact.)

Davidson's answers to these puzzles appear to be independent of his much-criticized criterion for the identity of events: that events are identical if and only if they have exactly the same causes and effects. (Indeed, this criterion does not appear to help us to answer substantive questions about event identity such as our question whether the hammering was the waking of the cat.) Davidson subsequently abandoned his 'causal' criterion in favour of the principle (also held by Quine) that events are identical just in case they occupy exactly the same places at the same times. Yet another criterion (proposed by Jaegwon Kim) is that events are identical when they consist in the same objects' having the same properties at the same times.

Another issue concerns the identity of events in different possible circumstances. Would it have been the same death if it had been a shooting rather than a stabbing? If it had happened at a different time or location? (*Essence.) Such questions must be addressed by theories that appeal to *counterfactual conditionals when assigning causes to, or attributing responsibility for, particular events.

P.J.M.

*process.

J. Bennett, *Events and their Names* (Indianapolis, 1988).
C. D. Broad, *Scientific Thought* (Paterson, NJ, 1959).
D. Davidson, *Essays on Actions and Events* (Oxford, 1980).
P. F. Strawson, *Individuals* (London, 1959).

evidence. That body of belief, often of an observational sort, which supports some less well-established hypothesis. Doubtless the wise man should apportion his belief to the evidence he has, but problems lie in formalizing the notion of evidential support. Logically 'All ravens are black' is equivalent to 'All non-black things are non-ravens', and if logically equivalent statements are confirmed by the same evidence, an irrelevant green violin is evidence for all ravens being black. Equally troubling is the fact that a black raven seen today logically supports mankind's belief that all ravens are black, but also a Martian's contrary belief that all ravens are blite (= black if observed before the year 2000, and otherwise white). In practice these philosophically well-known dilemmas trouble us not; in life we assess how some evidence bears on a *theory against a background of shared but unformalizable assumptions about the nature of the world and degrees of evidential support.   A.O'H.

*confirmation; induction; grue.

N. Goodman, *Fact, Fiction, and Forecast*, 4th edn. (1983).

evil, human. The suffering which results from morally wrong human choices, especially when the moral wrong is of an extreme kind. Moral evil can be contrasted with natural evil, such as the suffering and death caused by earthquakes or other natural disasters. Whereas natural evil creates a problem for theology, moral evil creates one for secular moral philosophy.

The first of these problems is whether evil is a predicate primarily applicable to human agents or to the effects of human choices. It is certainly true that there can be evil effects which follow from sincerely held beliefs, such as political ideologies or religious fundamentalism. This is the evil of fanaticism. But to the extent that the common thread in all fanaticism is the belief that individual suffering is unimportant compared to the righteousness of the cause, the sincerity of the beliefs cannot exonerate the perpetrators from the charge of evil. A second source of evil is self-interest. The pursuit of self-interest at the expense of others is a common form of moral wrongdoing, but when the others are made to suffer in outstandingly bad ways, then we enter the sphere of moral evil. This is the evil of Macbeth. A third sort of moral evil lies in the enjoyment which many people seem to obtain from the infliction of suffering for its own sake. Closely related to this evil in human agency is the way in which some people try to compensate for their own feelings of inadequacy by dominating and humiliating their captives. Of course, evil desires of the sort mentioned could not be expressed unless the social and political conditions of a regime encouraged or at least permitted them. Hence, a fourth root for the growth of moral evil lies in the will of political rulers. Sometimes regimes actively encourage terror, and sometimes they remain silent for political reasons in the face of known perpetrators of evil.

A fifth source of moral evil lies in a failure in moral imagination. It is well known that a psychopath is unable to imagine the sufferings he will cause, but the same can be true on a large scale at the political level. An example here is the use of napalm or nuclear weapons. Since the victims are remote, it is easy to fail to imagine their sufferings. Of course, this failure of the moral imagination happens more easily if the enemy has already been humiliated or can be depicted in some impersonal sort of way as subhuman, as happened at the Amritsar Massacre in 1919, or to the Jews in Nazi Germany, or to the Vietcong in the Vietnam War. R. L. Stevenson in 'Dr Jekyll and Mr Hyde' brings out in fiction the chilling truth that we have a dual nature, and that all of us may be capable of moral evil in certain circumstances. Perhaps the upsurge of pressure from advocates of human rights can help a little to combat moral evil, although there is a risk that human rights will be trivialized by their use in minor legal grievances.   R.S.D.

*evil, problem of.

Jonathan Glover, *Humanity: A Moral History of the Twentieth Century* (London, 2001).

Brian Keenan, *An Evil Cradling* (London, 1992).

F. Nietzsche, *The Genealogy of Morals*, in *The Complete Works of Friedrich Nietzsche*, vol. 13, ed. Oscar Levy (Edinburgh, 1910).

evil, the problem of. In Christianity and other Western religions, God is supposed to be omnipotent (i.e. able to do anything logically possible), omniscient (i.e. to know everything logically possible to know), and perfectly good; yet manifestly there is evil (e.g. pain and other suffering) in the world. Atheists have argued that since an omnipotent being could prevent evil if he chose, an omniscient being would know how to do so and a perfectly good being would always choose to do so, there is no *God of the kind supposed. The problem of evil has always been the most powerful objection to traditional theism. The usual response of theists to this 'problem' is to deny that a perfectly good being will always choose to prevent evil, claiming that allowing some evils may make possible greater goods. If God is to allow evil to occur, it must not be logically possible to bring about the greater goods by any better route. Some theists have held that, being only human, we cannot be expected to know for which greater goods the evils of our world are needed. But it seems unreasonable to believe that there are any such goods without some demonstration as to what they are, i.e. without a *'theodicy'. Central to most theodicies is the 'freewill defence'. This claims that the greater good of humans having a free choice between good and evil involves no one, not even God, preventing them from bringing about evil. Theodicy needs one or more further defences to explain why God allows evil of kinds for which humans are not responsible, such as the pain of currently unpreventable disease. The 'higher-order goods defence' claims that such evils give humans opportunities to perform, in response to them, heroic actions of showing courage, patience, and sympathy, opportunities which they would not otherwise have. This does still leave the problem of what justifies God in allowing some (e.g. battered babies) to suffer for the benefit of others (e.g. parents, social workers, etc. having free choices). The theist may argue in reply that God who gives us life has the right to allow some to suffer for a limited time, that it is a privilege to be used by God for a useful purpose, and that there is always the possibility of compensation in an afterlife. The crux of the problem is whether such defences are adequate for dealing with the kinds and amount of evil we find around us.   R.G.S.

*evil, human.

M. M. Adams and R. M. Adams (eds.), *The Problem of Evil* (Oxford, 1990).

A. Plantinga, *God, Freedom and Evil* (London, 1975), pt. 1a.

R. Swinburne, *The Existence of God* (Oxford, 1979), chs. 9–11.

evil demon, evil spirit: see *malin génie*.

evolution. Evolution, the idea that the world and its contents—particularly organisms—have developed from primitive beginnings through natural processes, is a child of the *Enlightenment. Until that time, the Christian story of Creation combined with the essentialist thought of the Greeks, prevented people from thinking of origins in such a non-miraculous manner. What the Scientific Revolution started, with its successful subsumption of so much to natural regularity and material cause, was finished by the rise of hopes and beliefs in progress, the ideology of upward change and improvement in the human lot, encouraged by an ever-increasing knowledge and control of nature's processes. In France particularly, but also in Britain and Germany, people moved easily from a belief in social and cultural *progress to an analogous belief in upward development in the world of life, which latter development was then taken as confirmation of their social beliefs!

Most notorious of the early evolutionists was the Frenchman Jean-Baptiste de Lamarck, whose *Philosophie zoologique* (1809) offered the first full-length treatment of the subject. Interestingly, the inheritance of acquired characteristics, the mechanism to which Lamarck gave his name, played only a minor role in his thinking, which was much more dominated by a desire to turn the static Chain of Being into an ever-moving escalator. More influential, perhaps, were the German *Naturphilosophs, who saw repeated patterns running through nature, and who linked this belief naturally with one of the unity of the organic world. Not that most of these thinkers or those sympathetic to them (such as Goethe) became full-blown evolutionists. In the spirit of the time, the idea was always more significant than the reality.

It was therefore to be the middle of the nineteenth century before the picture of all-embracing development—now known as evolution and distinguished from the development of the individual organism—became an established doctrine and entered the halls of respectable science. Credit for this is due to the English naturalist Charles Darwin, who presented his theory of evolution through natural selection in his *On the Origin of Species* (1859). Starting with the Malthusian struggle for existence, Darwin argued that successful organisms in life's battles will tend to differ from the unsuccessful. There will thus be a 'natural selection' of the 'fittest'—the successful giraffe will have a longer neck than the unsuccessful giraffe. It was Darwin's claim that, over time, this will lead to significant permanent change. Darwin, however, had no adequate theory of heredity. This gap was filled in the twentieth century by the new science of genetics, which itself dates back to the middle of the nineteenth century and the ideas of Darwin's then unknown contemporary, the monk Gregor Mendel.

Evolution raises questions of considerable philosophical interest and much controversy. Most obviously, there are matters to do with the science itself. Is it, as critics often claim, 'just a theory and not a fact'? Comments of this ilk play on an equivocation on the word *theory. If one is asking whether evolution as such is well established, then this is a matter beyond reasonable doubt. Palaeontology, bio-geography, embryology, anatomy, and more all point to evolutionary origins. But if one is asking about a particular theory, then serious debate continues. Darwinian selection speaks to the fact that organisms seem well designed—they are 'adapted'. Critics argue either that Darwinism is inadequate to account for this phenomenon, or (taking the counter tack) that the fit between organisms and their world is nowhere like as tight as the Darwinian supposes. In either case, other mechanisms must be sought.

As pressing, there is the question whether our thinking on evolution can profitably be applied to the traditional problems of philosophy, especially epistemology and ethics. Traditional philosophers, most notably, in recent years, Wittgenstein, tend to rear back from such suggestions like vampires before garlic. But, thanks especially to the enthusiasm of Herbert Spencer, there has always been a steady stream of biological thinkers who extend their thinking to philosophy. Complementing them, there have generally been a few philosophers who suspect that the fact that we humans are the product of a long, slow natural process of evolution rather than the miraculous products of a Good God working on the Sixth Day may indeed be significant. *Evolutionary epistemology and *evolutionary ethics are hardly yet respectable, but today—thanks especially to some who think that perhaps evolution can be brought to work in conjunction with the insights and achievements of traditional philosophy rather that as a replacing rival—they thrive and offer new directions as never before.   M.R.

*evolution and philosophy.

J. Dupré, *Darwin's Legacy: What Evolution Means Today* (Oxford, 2003).
R. Richards, *The Meaning of Evolution* (Chicago, 1991).
M. Ruse, *The Darwinian Revolution* (Chicago, 1979).
—— *Monad to Man: The Concept of Progress in Evolutionary Biology* (Cambridge, Mass., 1996).

evolution and philosophy. *Evolution is the belief that the organic world, including our own species, is the product of a long, slow, natural process of development from forms very different, extremely simple, and probably themselves the result of natural processes that turned the inorganic into the living. There have been many causal theories of evolution, but the dominant one today dates to the *Origin of Species*, published in 1859, by the English naturalist Charles Darwin. He pointed to the struggle for existence that rules universally in the living world, and argued that this leads to a natural selection of the fitter over the less fit, with consequent ongoing change.

Many philosophers, most famously Ludwig Wittgenstein, have argued that evolution has no implications at all for philosophy. Others, starting with Darwin himself, disagree, thinking that the natural evolutionary origins of human beings has to make a difference to our thinking about knowledge (epistemology), as well as to our thinking about morality (ethics). Some philosophers indeed—notably the American pragmatists—have thought that

evolution must be one of the basic starting-points of any attempt to understand human nature and how it functions in the world.

Applying evolution—selection theory in particular—to problems of knowledge ('*evolutionary epistemology') usually takes one of two forms. The first is to argue analogically from the biological situation to the cultural world. There is a struggle for existence among organisms leading to a natural selection; so, likewise, there is a struggle for existence among ideas leading to a selection of the best, which then survive and rule for a while. The philosopher Karl Popper argued that this is precisely what he was referring to when he spoke of the need of scientific theories to be falsifiable—always ready to battle out their claims in the intellectual struggle for survival. The second approach is to take a literal position, pointing to the fact that the way in which humans think is itself moulded by selection. In other words, as was argued by W. V. Quine, our beliefs about causation and the virtues of such epistemic notions as prediction are beliefs that we have because they served well the ends of our would-be ancestors. There is therefore no ultimate justification for thinking causally. It is just that those proto-humans who learned to associate fire with burning survived and reproduced, and those that did not, did not.

Applying evolution—again selection theory in particular—to problems of morality ('*evolutionary ethics') likewise takes one of two forms. The first, due especially to Darwin's contemporary Herbert Spencer, goes from the processes of evolution to the way that things ought to be—notoriously from the struggle for existence to the promotion of *laissez-faire* socio-economics. More recent exponents have been the English biologist Julian Huxley, who argued for large-scale public works in the name of Darwinism, and today the American biologist Edward O. Wilson, who thinks that the evolutionary process justifies conservation. Famously, this whole line of thinking was severely criticized by G. E. Moore in his *Principia Ethica*, where it was claimed that such an approach to morality (often called 'Social Darwinism') commits the naturalistic fallacy, a version of the illicit move noted by David Hume, where one goes without cause or reason from statements of fact to statements of obligation.

The second approach to evolutionary ethics parallels the second approach to evolutionary epistemology, in this case arguing that human moral thought and behaviour is a result of evolution, particularly of the fact that in the struggle co-operation (what biologists call 'altruism') is often a better strategy than outright warfare. Better to share a cake than to run the risk of getting no cake at all. At the normative level of ethics (What should I do?), there has been much recent interest in evolutionary strategies (often based on principles of game theory) that might generate the norms that we hold dear. In his *Theory of Justice*, John Rawls argued for a contractarian theory of ethics (justice as fairness), suggesting that the original contract was not one put in place by conscious human intention but a result of the genes as chosen by natural selection. At the meta-ethical level of discussion (Why should I do what I should do?), there is still considerable disagreement. Some think, as in epistemology, that because a feature like morality is adaptive, this does not preclude its giving a true picture of reality. There may well be objective or real moral norms. Others are less sure, and incline to scepticism, thinking that perhaps in some sense the whole of (normative) morality is an illusion put in place by our genes to make us good social co-operators.

Recently, there has been much interest by philosophers of mind in the implications of evolutionary thought for a full understanding of the mind's operating and functioning. If indeed selection cares not about truth but about success—Patricia Churchland speaks of the 4-F imperatives, Feeding, Fighting, Fleeing, and Reproduction—can we possibly expect that the mind receives a true account of external reality? Some, notably Popper (following the ethologist Konrad Lorenz), think that this is no major problem. Others, notably the Christian philosopher Alvin Plantinga, think it spells the end of any approach to understanding using Darwinian evolution. Most, like philosopher Ruth Millikan, take a middle line. One can be mistaken, but evolutionary theory itself dictates the sorts of times when one might be mistaken—for instance, when there are no selective advantages in having the truth. If a fast train is bearing down on one, then the strong presumption is that selection is not about to deceive—there are no obvious reasons why one should be deceived into thinking it exists if it does not, and very good reasons why one should not be deceived if it does exist.   M.R.

R. Millikan, *White Queen Psychology and Other Essays for Alice* (Cambridge, Mass., 1993).
K. R. Popper, *Unended Quest: An Intellectual Autobiography* (LaSalle, Ill., 1976).
M. Ruse, *Taking Darwin Seriously: A Naturalistic Approach to Philosophy*, 2nd edn. (Buffalo, 1998).
E. O. Wilson, *The Diversity of Life* (Cambridge, Mass., 1992).

evolutionary epistemology. This is an approach to the theory of knowledge claiming that the very fact that we humans are the end-product of a natural process of *evolution must be a significant factor in the ways in which we know and understand the world. Part of an overall contemporary move towards a naturalized epistemology, it comes in two main forms. One argues that the growth of knowledge, especially scientific knowledge, is akin to the evolutionary growth of organisms. Everything is in flux, forever moving towards some new level. Moreover, just as there is a struggle for existence in the organic world, so also is there a struggle in the world of concepts, with the consequent selection of the 'fittest'. There is, of course, a major disanalogy, in that the raw stuff of *biology— 'mutations'—are random, in the sense of not occurring according to need, whereas the raw stuff of science—'discoveries'—generally come in response to need and are directed to such need. Hence, the growing popularity of the other form of evolutionary epistemology, which claims that all knowledge is shaped and informed by

certain innate principles (like the laws of logic and mathematics, as well as such epistemic norms as a preference for simplicity) which have selected into human thought because of their adaptive value. Controversial is the question whether these principles represent the necessary conditions of rational thought (that is, the synthetic a priori) or are merely contingent and non-unique, and could well have been quite different. Is the logic on Andromeda as different from that of Aristotle as the slithering of the snake is different from the walking of the human? Equally controversial is the question whether such a philosophy points to the conclusion that knowledge is a generally faithful mapping of a real (human-perception-independent) world, or whether one is pointed towards some sort of pragmatic or coherence theory of truth.   M.R.

*evolutionary ethics; evolution and philosophy.

M. Ruse, *Taking Darwin Seriously: A Naturalistic Approach to Philosophy* (Oxford, 1986).

evolutionary ethics. This is a body of theory which seeks to locate moral institutions within the main ideas of evolutionary biology. The general thesis is that we value things and persons in accordance with their capacity to sustain and maintain survival in evolutionary terms. For example, it may be thought that friendship and altruism are valued because they preserve members of the human species against violence. Objections to this approach come, partly, from those who reject its strategy of deriving values from facts about human nature, and partly from those who accuse it of over-simplifying factual issues about what strategies actually ensure survival. As an example of the latter kind of difficulty, it has been objected that even if a certain practice has been successful, its previous environment may be unstable; so it would be bad practice, despite its evolutionary success.   J.D.G.E.

*evolutionary epistemology.

M. Ruse, *Sociobiology: Sense or Nonsense?* (Dordrecht, 1979) contains a sympathetic but critical account of the subject.

examination paradox. The teacher says that some time next week there will be an unexpected examination: on the morning of the relevant day, the students will not know it will happen on that day. The students reason that the teacher cannot set the examination on the last day of the week, for when that day comes they would expect it. He cannot set it on the penultimate day, for when that day comes, and knowing from the previous reasoning that it cannot be held on the last day, they would expect it on the penultimate day. And so on for each possible day. So there cannot be an unexpected examination!   R.M.S.

*prediction paradox.

Mark Sainsbury, *Paradoxes* (New York, 1988), ch. 4.

excluded middle, law of. The oldest principle so called is Aristotle's 'There is nothing between asserting and denying', i.e. 'If neither "yes" nor "no" truly answers the question "Is it the case that P?", nothing does'. This can slide into 'Either "P" or "not-P" is true', and further into 'Every proposition is true or false' (more properly called the law of *bivalence). In modern logic the law usually called excluded middle is '"P or not-P" is valid', i.e. true on all interpretations of 'P'. C.A.K.

W. V. Quine, *Philosophy of Logic* (Englewood Cliffs, NJ, 1970), 83–5.

existence. 'Existence', a key term of *ontology, in one sense refers to the sum total of reality—everything that exists—and in another to the elusive characteristic of *being, which differentiates real *things from fictional ones. But whether there really is such a characteristic is debatable, because it is often held that 'exist' is not a first-level predicate. What this means is that 'exist' does not express a property of objects, as verbs like 'shine' and 'fall' do. According to Frege and Russell, 'exist' is a *second*-level predicate, expressing a property of properties. Thus 'God exists' does not have the same logical form as 'Sirius shines', predicating a property of a particular object. Rather, it is equivalent to 'Godhood is instantiated', asserting that the property of being divine has at least one instance, or that there is at least one thing possessing that property. According to Frege and Russell, in a tradition reaching back to Kant, Anselm's *ontological argument for God's existence is vitiated by its failure to grasp this point.

W. V. Quine's famous dictum 'To be is to be the value of a variable' takes the Frege–Russell account of existence as its inspiration, and implies that the entities to whose existence a theory is committed are precisely those which need to be invoked to interpret the quantified sentences of the theory. But this controversially assumes an 'objectual' rather than a 'substitutional' interpretation of the quantifiers. According to the latter, 'There is at least one thing which is F' is true just in case there is some true sentence of the form 'a is F', where 'a' is a singular term. Thus, if 'Pegasus is identical with Pegasus' is deemed true despite the non-existence of Pegasus, 'There is at least one thing which is identical with Pegasus' must likewise be deemed true, whence adherents of this account must repudiate Quine's dictum.

The thought that fictional entities like Pegasus have some reality despite lacking full-blooded existence is a tempting one, often associated with Meinong. But according to David Lewis's more recent doctrine of modal realism, Pegasus and other possible but non-actual objects do have full-blooded existence, and differ from actual objects only in residing in other *possible worlds. This doctrine requires one to distinguish sharply between existence and actuality, treating the latter as an indexical notion akin to those of being here and now. On Lewis's view, Pegasus is just as 'actual' in the worlds in which it exists as Julius Caesar is in 'our' world, and the objects existing in a world are all actual to its inhabitants in just the way that all moments of time are present or 'now' to those experiencing them. Such a view may, however, be accused of grossly inflating existence, understood as the sum total of reality.

Perhaps the biggest metaphysical problem concerning existence is why anything should exist at all—why there

should be something rather than nothing. Physicists can maybe tell us why matter exists, adverting to conditions obtaining shortly after the Big Bang; perhaps they can even explain the existence of time and space, if this is as intimately linked to the existence of matter and energy as modern cosmologists suggest. But the metaphysical question clearly goes beyond such merely empirical considerations. One response is to say that the question is absurd, because it erroneously presupposes that we can make sense of the idea of absolute nothingness as a genuine alternative to the existence of at least *something*. On this view, we mistake the contingency of the things that do exist for a contingency in the fact that anything whatever exists. However, while it may indeed be impossible to *imagine* a world in which nothing exists, the notion of a wholly empty world does not seem obviously incoherent. E.J.L.

*'to be', the verb.

D. Lewis, *On the Plurality of Worlds* (Oxford, 1986).
W. V. Quine, 'On What There Is', in *From a Logical Point of View* (Cambridge, Mass., 1953).
Bede Rundle, *Why There Is Something Rather Than Nothing* (Oxford, 2004).
C. J. F. Williams, *What is Existence?* (Oxford, 1981).

existence, contingent and necessary: *see* contingent and necessary existence.

existence precedes essence. An existentialist formula which signifies that we make ourselves the individuals we are. Heidegger uses the formula to indicate that for each *'Dasein*', its 'being' or 'essence' is the way in which it shapes its life, its manner of 'existence' (in his special sense). Sartre interprets the formula in the light of his emphasis upon free choice: we are what we 'choose' ourselves to be. T.R.B.

*existentialism.

J.-P. Sartre, *Existentialism and Humanism*, tr. P. Mairet (London, 1948).

existentialism. 'Existentialism' is a loose term for the reaction, led by Kierkegaard, against the abstract rationalism of Hegel's philosophy. As against Hegel's conception of 'absolute consciousness' within which all oppositions are supposedly reconciled, Kierkegaard insisted on the irreducibility of the subjective, personal dimension of human life. He characterized this in terms of the perspective of the 'existing individual', and it is from this special use of the term 'existence' to describe a distinctively human mode of being that existentialism gets its name. Kierkegaard's successors include the German philosophers Heidegger and Jaspers and the French philosophers Sartre and Marcel (who actually coined the term 'existentialism'). I shall concentrate here only on aspects of the works of Heidegger and Sartre in addition to those of Kierkegaard.

Kierkegaard rejected the claim, which he took (perhaps unfairly) to be Hegel's, that we can look forward to a time

JEAN-PAUL SARTRE became the archetype of the French intellectual: deep and difficult, against convention, politically committed, with a recognized role as a critic of culture and society, in a café, with a cigarette.

SIMONE DE BEAUVOIR brought to existentialist morality, which exalted freedom, awareness of the importance of the social context of choice, and in particular of the power-relations between the sexes.

MICHEL FOUCAULT, in his histories of madness, sexuality, and punishment, examined how societies control discourse and knowledge and thus power.

LOUIS ALTHUSSER offered, in the 1960s, a new Marxist approach to social and cultural theory, rejecting the principle of reductive explanation in terms of economic factors.

when the different interests and concerns of people can be satisfied through their comprehension within an all-embracing objective understanding of the universe. For, according to Kierkegaard, no such synthesis can do justice to an individual's concern for their own life; hence, he argues, even though Kantian epistemology correctly implies that we should recognize that our own subjective perceptions are just the manifestation of our objective situation in the world, we cannot similarly resolve ethical questions by subjecting our moral consciousness to an impersonal deliberative perspective. For ethical questions essentially concern ourselves; in asking ourselves how we are to lead our lives, we deceive ourselves if we pretend that the adoption of an objective, impersonal understanding of our situation will by itself provide an answer.

Kierkegaard takes it that this relationship between ethics and subjectivity is a two-way relationship. Not only are ethical questions essentially first-person, the 'real subject' is also 'the ethically existing subject', as he puts it. He also holds, however, that we should not think of our existence as 'real subjects' as a feature of our lives which we can just take for granted (comparable, say, to our embodiment). Instead (and here he remains to some degree Hegelian) he thinks that it is an aspect of our lives that needs to be developed if we are to achieve our full potential as individuals; the fact of our 'existence' implies that we cannot avoid first-person practical questions, but we may well lack a coherent conception of ourselves by reference to which we can begin to answer them. How, then, is such a conception to be acquired? How is one to 'become an individual'? Not, certainly, by acquiring more knowledge of the world. Instead we have to engage the will: it is by making choices and commitments (such as marriage) which enable us to develop long-term interests that we give our lives an ethical structure. When Kierkegaard writes that 'it is impossible to exist without passion', he means that it is only by entering into engagements whose fate can arouse the passions that we gain a sense of our own identity and in that way become an 'existing individual'.

Nothing so far explicitly implies that in becoming such an individual one becomes a virtuous one. But Kierkegaard takes it that the good life for a person is one that fulfils the requirement that that person live as an individual. The basic idea here is that one is able to make sense of one's life as a whole only through personal conduct and relationships with others which manifest the virtues. This may not seem persuasive. In Kierkegaard's case, however, this thesis is presented in the context of the further belief that no one can create a life for themselves which will survive the vicissitudes of fortune without making 'the leap of faith', a personal commitment to the kind of life lived by Jesus Christ, i.e. without becoming 'Christlike'. What stands behind this belief is the experience of *'Angst'—variously translated as 'dread' or 'anxiety'. Kierkegaard's claim is both that this experience reveals to us the unsatisfactory nature of a life that depends on the contingencies

of success or human love, and that we are thereby motivated to commit ourselves to an 'ethico-religious' life which offers a salvation that is not dependent upon such contingencies because it rests upon a relationship with God.

Heidegger follows Kierkegaard in using the term *Existenz* to describe the mode of being that is distinctive of human life (or *Dasein*, as Heidegger would put it), and he explicitly contrasts this mode of being with that of the everyday objects which we categorize in terms of their use (the *Zuhandenheit*) and that of those objects which we think of as altogether independent of us (the *Vorhandenheit*). Heidegger also holds that the distinctive feature of human existence arises from the irreducibility of the practical concern we each face concerning our lives: for each of us 'our own being is an issue', and the way in which we face up to this issue determines the nature of our existence. There is no fixed human essence which gives a structure to human life that is independent of the engagements and goals which, by giving us a sense of our own practical identity, fill out our existence.

Where Heidegger differs from Kierkegaard is in assigning this 'existential' thesis an absolutely fundamental role in general metaphysics. He maintains that the answer to the question of being in general is to be found by a line of inquiry which commences with an inquiry into the 'existential' constitution of *Dasein*, i.e. human life. Since, as we have seen, *Dasein's* existence involves a practical concern for itself, it is not surprising that a metaphysics which builds out from this has many similarities with pragmatism. So when Heidegger proceeds to develop his account of *Dasein's* 'existence' as 'being-in-the-world', he makes it clear that our fundamental mode of being-in-the-world is action (rather than, say, contemplative perception), and that we basically understand the world in terms of the categories which enter into the explanation of our actions. So, for example, although Heidegger endorses Kant's claim that spatiality is an essential element of our experience of the world, he argues that we should not think of this spatiality in terms of the space of physical theory (as Kant did); instead, we should think of it as the 'existential space' of everyday life, that spatiality which is conceived in essentially egocentric and practical terms.

Heidegger's 'existential pragmatism' goes beyond Kierkegaard's existentialism, and in other respects, too, he modifies important aspects of Kierkegaard's conception of existence. Where Kierkegaard linked the 'passionate' nature of human existence directly to the will, to the subject's chosen commitments, Heidegger argues that our emotions characteristically reflect cares and concerns that we have not chosen, since they arise from involvements which we just find ourselves 'thrown' into (e.g. our country, our family, and, more fundamentally, those aspects of our world which simply record our everyday needs). Heidegger then argues that these involvements provide an essential background for the practical undertakings of everyday life whereby we seek to meet our needs and answer the demands that arise from our unchosen involvements. So although these practical undertakings manifest an existential concern with the world, Heidegger argues that they do not arise from the will if that is conceived in terms of the self-conscious adoption of a project. Thus Heidegger's account of the existential structure of human life is basically worked out at an un-self-conscious level, which is also fundamental to the conception of the 'lived world' implied by his existential pragmatism.

Heidegger does not of course deny that there is a level of self-conscious deliberation and decision, and it is in the context of this feature of human life that he employs his distinction between 'inauthenticity' and 'authenticity'. Heidegger's discussion here looks back to Kierkegaard's thesis that it is an achievement to become an individual, and he deliberately invokes religious terminology to describe his position, though without Kierkegaard's explicit invocation of religious faith. The basic idea is that those whose understanding of themselves is not informed by a grasp of the true nature of their individual existence, who think of themselves, say, as just complicated animals, are said to have only an inauthentic existence; whereas those who have internalized the truth of Heidegger's conception of their existence and are able to conduct their lives in accordance with it are said to have attained authenticity. According to Heidegger, we always start out with an inauthentic conception of ourselves, since our pre-reflective involvements with the world and others lead us to think of ourselves as not significantly different from them. What then motivates us to become authentic is the experience of *Angst*, which Heidegger interprets as an awareness of the precariousness of a life whose goals and values are not understood as arising from the structure of one's own existence. *Angst*, therefore, recalls us to ourselves, and by making the existential structure of our life available to us, helps to bring us to an authentic recognition of our freedom. Heidegger connects this experience of *Angst* with one's attitude to one's own death: this attitude is typically one of *Angst*, and because a correct understanding of death as the end of one's existence reveals to us the structure of our own existence, an authentic life is 'an impassioned freedom towards death'.

Heidegger's existentialism is essentially metaphysical. He even denies that the authentic-inauthentic distinction has any ethical content, although his actual language betrays him here. Sartre, by contrast, explicitly presents existentialism as an ethical doctrine. He largely takes his existentialist starting-point from Heidegger, except that where Heidegger clearly separates human existence from the exercise of choice, Sartre reformulates the position as one in which the role of choice in human life is absolutely fundamental. He argues that we choose our emotions as much as any other aspect of our life, and that the basic goals of our lives cohere around a fundamental project which is itself the product of an 'original choice'—a choice which, since it provides us with all the motivations we have, must itself be unmotivated, or **'absurd'.

This unattractive line of thought goes back to Kant. In Kant's case the implied threat of ethical nihilism is supposed to be averted by the requirements of the categorical imperative. Sartre's ethical theory is basically similar: although he celebrates the 'absurdity' of existentialist freedom, he actually only commends those exercises of this freedom which manifest respect for the freedom of others. It is not clear what basis Sartre's existentialism can offer for this value-judgement, but it looks as though he holds both that the existentialist's values must meet the requirement that they be the values of someone whose life is, in Heidegger's sense, authentic, and that authenticity can only be attained within a community which practises mutual respect. This leads to the principle Sartre endorses, but it should be noted that the price Sartre has had to pay in order to provide some social content to his existentialist ethic is an important qualification of the emphasis on the situation of the isolated individual which is so prominent in Kierkegaard's writings.

Sartre was the last significant existentialist philosopher. But existentialism lives on, primarily in attempts to combine the basic structure of Heidegger's metaphysics with other, less theoretical, doctrines: thus we still have 'existential Marxism', 'existential sociology', 'existential psychoanalysis', 'existential theology', and so on. The general feature of these hybrids is an emphasis on the irreducibility of the perspective of human agents, whose activities, emotions, and thoughts, it is supposed, are to be understood in terms of their aspiration to 'become an individual', as Kierkegaard would have put it.   T.R.B.

*existence precedes essence.

M. Heidegger, *Being and Time*, tr. J. MacQuarrie and E. Robinson (Oxford, 1962).

S. Kierkegaard, *Concluding Unscientific Postscript*, tr. D. Swenson (Princeton, NJ, 1941).

J.-P. Sartre, *Existentialism and Humanism*, tr. P. Mairet (London, 1948).

T. Sprigge, *Theories of Existence* (London, 1984).

existential proposition. An existential proposition (or statement) is one affirming the *existence of some *thing or kind of things—for instance, 'The yeti exists' or 'Unicorns exist'. Problems arise over the interpretation of *negative* existential statements, especially singular ones like 'The yeti does not exist', because the singular term which functions as the grammatical subject of such a statement seems to make reference to an object which, if the statement is true, does not exist.   E.J.L.

W. V. Quine, 'On What There Is', in *From a Logical Point of View*, 2nd edn. (Cambridge, Mass., 1961).

existential quantifier: *see* quantifier.

exoteric. 'External' (Greek, *exoterikos*). A word used by Aristotle to refer to well-known or published works or arguments of his own, and perhaps of others. Later commentators distinguished his 'exoteric' works, which were easy enough for non-specialists and written in a polished style, from the more difficult works (sometimes called *esoteric) intended for his own pupils. The former were mainly in dialogue form and survive only in fragments.

R.J.H.

I. Düring, *Aristotle in the Ancient Biographical Tradition* (Göteborg, 1957), 426–43.

experience. Direct, observational knowledge of the world. More narrowly, experience is sometimes restricted to the sensory basis (*sensation) of this knowledge. In the first sense, one's experience includes whatever one has come to know or believe about the world by direct observation and without inference. If you read a book and watch a movie about baboons, you may learn a lot about baboons, but such knowledge would not be counted as part of your experience. Your experience would be limited to books and movies—that a certain book *said* that baboons were primates and that a movie *depicted* them as having doglike muzzles.

In the second, narrower, sense, experience is distinguished from belief or knowledge. It refers to the sensory events (e.g. visual and auditory sensations) on which beliefs about the world are typically based. In observing an event—a robbery, say—one's experience of this event would be the sensations caused in one by the robbery. One might experience a robbery in this second sense of the term without ever coming to know or believe that a robbery was taking place—without, that is, experiencing the robbery *as a* robbery. Should this occur, one would have robbery experiences (in the narrow sense of this term), but no experience (i.e. knowledge) of robberies in the broader sense.

It is this second, narrower, sense of the term that is at issue in epistemological debates about whether all knowledge is ultimately empirical—i.e. based on experience. (*Empiricism.*) If knowledge is to be based on experience, as it seems reasonable to think that observational knowledge is, one's beliefs about the world must somehow be derived from, or justified by, one's sense experience of the world. It is a problem, however, to understand how it is possible for experience to lend support to, or justify, the beliefs it gives rise to. If one thinks (as some philosophers do) of experience as itself belief-like in character, as having propositional content, a content that can (like the content of a belief) be false, then a question can be asked about what justifies the experience. What guarantee (or even justification) is there that the experience (its content) is true? If, on the other hand, experience is understood as non-propositional (as it usually is), as something without (a possibly false) content, then there is a problem about how experience can justify the beliefs based on it. Beliefs justify other beliefs by standing in appropriate logical and explanatory relationships to them, relations that require the possession of content. If experiences are not themselves belief-like in character, if they have no propositional content, they cannot imply, cannot explain or be explained by, anything. How, then, can they function as *reasons* to believe anything? This problem has encouraged coherence theories of justification to locate justification (and, hence, knowledge), not in a belief's relationship to experience, but in a belief's relationships to (its coherence with) the rest of one's beliefs. According to such a view, our experience of the world may be a cause of, but it is not a justification for, the beliefs we have about the world.

Other theories of justification (*reliabilism*), however, locate justification (for observational beliefs) in the way that beliefs can be made to covary (reliably) with the world by the perceptual systems whose functioning produce such beliefs. Such theories, unlike coherence theories, give experience both a causal and a justificatory role (as carriers of information) in cognition.

F.D.

*consciousness; perception.

L. Bonjour, *The Structure of Empirical Knowledge* (Cambridge, Mass., 1985).
F. Dretske, *Knowledge and the Flow of Information* (Cambridge, Mass., 1981), ch. 6.
A. Goldman, *Epistemology and Cognition* (Cambridge, Mass., 1986).

experiment. Science aims to understand the world of experience. One puts its ideas to the test through experiment, where one manipulates phenomena in such a way that answers can be given to specific questions. A much-discussed subset of experiments contains those labelled *'crucial', in the sense that they decide authoritatively between rival hypotheses. Historians argue that frequently, as in the case of Young's double slit experiment, supposedly deciding between the wave and the particle theories of light, the use of the word 'crucial' is a victory roll by the winners after the event.

Some experiments are 'natural', in the sense that unplanned circumstances simulate what the purposeful experimenter might have attempted. In dealing with human subjects or vast scales of time and space, these are often the only possible ways of testing nature. Here, as in all experiments, what may have started as an attempt to test ends as a voyage of discovery, as the results suggest new lines of inquiry. Charles Darwin used the practices of animal breeders primarily as experimental evidence for his evolutionary speculations, but they proved also to have great heuristic value, even to the point of leading him to his mechanism of natural selection.

Various theorists, from John Stuart Mill with his well-known *methods for distinguishing real from apparent causes to those today who sell computer programs of statistical techniques, have offered prescriptions for the proper performance of experiments. However, while there is certainly a craft to be learnt—for instance, in ways of using controls to avoid reading out prior expectations which one has previously read in—and while today the growth of 'Big Science' means that one might have literally hundreds of researchers and an army of technicians working on the same project, ultimately in science the great experimenter is as gifted and unique as the great theoretician.

M.R.

*evolution; thought experiment.

I. Hacking, *Representing and Intervening* (Cambridge, 1983).
M. Ruse, *The Darwinian Revolution* (Chicago, 1979).

experiment, crucial: *see* crucial experiment.

explanation. That which produces understanding how or why something is as it is. In ancient Greek thought a distinction gradually emerged between explanatory theories and theories about the nature of explanation. Thus whereas Thales, Empedocles, Anaxagoras, and others proposed explanations of natural phenomena, Plato's theory of Forms offered at the same time both a systematic explanation of things and also a connected epistemology of explanation. Aristotle, however, seems to have been the first thinker to differentiate explicitly between investigating what causes what and investigating the very nature of causation. On his view the latter investigation revealed four different kinds of cause that an explanation of physical phenomena could cite. The formal cause is that in virtue of which a thing is the type of thing that it is; the material cause is the stuff, whatever it may be, that is typed by the formal cause; the efficient cause is what produces a thing; and the final cause is the purpose for which something is produced.

Medieval philosophy mostly echoed Aristotle's ideas about explanation. Indeed his concept of final causes supplied a convenient foundation for religiously orientated teleology.

It was Francis Bacon who took the decisive step of segregating *teleological explanation from scientific explanation. At the same time Bacon treated the form correlated with an observable characteristic as the law in accordance with which that characteristic occurs or can be made to occur, and within the hierarchy of these laws he supposed that the more comprehensive the explanation that a law achieves, the more certainty it has.

Hume held that such causal laws state merely the constancy with which one particular type of observable phenomenon succeeds another, and argued that the feeling that this succession occurs necessarily should be explained as being merely the outcome of a mental association between the idea of the earlier phenomenon and the idea of the later one. Whether or not Hume is right about this, the dominant model for explanation in the natural sciences seems to require the citation of one or more laws which, when conjoined with the statement of relevant facts, entail occurrences of the phenomenon or uniformity that is to be explained.

Russell argued that such laws should specify not a causal process but the correlation of one natural variable with one or more others. But, wherever we want to derive a technology from scientific knowledge, we shall need to know what causes a desired effect. So we need to distinguish between different levels of explanation, in that while, for example, the disappearance of a patient's infection may be causally explained by his antibiotic injection, the operation of that causal process is in its turn to be explained by correlational laws of biochemistry. And for

discovering this kind of deeper and more comprehensive explanation it will often be necessary to devise appropriate new terminology. Moreover, it should also be noted that some scientific explanations cite statistical probabilities rather than determinate laws.

Further questions arise, especially in the social sciences, about the explanation of specifically human behaviour. For example, Hempel held that in historical inquiry the pattern of explanation to be sought accords with the same *covering-law model that applies in the natural sciences. Collingwood argued, however, that the historian achieves understanding of other people's actions by the reenactment of their thoughts in his own experience. And in any case we cannot overlook the fact that people's rational acts need to be explained teleologically—that is, in terms of what their aims are and what they regard as appropriate means. But even in those cases what has to do the explaining is temporally prior to, or concurrent with, what has to be explained. It is the present thought, not the future satisfaction, of our aims that helps to explain what we are doing to achieve them: one should not think of teleological explanation as a kind of influence exerted on the present by the future.   L.J.C.

*causality.

P. Achinstein, *The Nature of Explanation* (Oxford, 1983).
The Philosophy of C. G. Hempel, ed. J. Fetzer (New York, 2001).
D.-H. Ruben (ed.), *Explanation* (Oxford, 1993).
W. C. Salmon, *Statistical Explanation and Statistical Relevance* (London, 1971).

explanation, historical: *see* history, problems of the philosophy of.

explanation, inference to the best: *see* inference to the best explanation; explanationism.

explanation, levels of. Any natural phenomenon can be studied in a range of different ways. A living organism, for example, can be studied as a collection of particles, as a structure with a complex chemical composition, as a biological entity, and as a member of a social grouping. Each of these can be considered a separate level of explanation, where a level of explanation is characterized in terms of a distinctive vocabulary and distinctive explanatory principles (generalizations that may or may not be law-like). The natural question to ask is how different levels of explanation fit together. According to proponents of the *unity of science, in addition to principles holding at a single level, there are law-like vertical connections between different levels of explanation, so that science forms a hierarchical structure with physics at its base. The issue of the relation between different levels of explanation is central to the philosophy of *mind, where one of the most pressing questions is how our ordinary *folk-psychological understanding of each other is related to subpersonal explanations of *cognition in information-processing terms.   J.BER.

*reductionism, mental.

D. Charles and K. Lennon (eds.), *Reduction, Explanation, and Realism* (Oxford, 1992).

explanation, teleological: *see* teleological explanation.

explanatory gap. The phrase 'explanatory gap' was introduced by Joseph Levine to label the apparent lack of an intelligible or explanatory relationship between neural properties of the brain and the phenomenal properties of experience (e.g. what it's like to feel pain). Scientists explain the macro-feature of solidity in terms of micro-properties concerning the lack of free movement of atoms. By contrast, it seems that nothing we could know about the nature of neural processing, and interaction with the environment, would explain the nature of phenomenal properties in similar fashion. There is no consensus over whether the gap holds merely for phenomenal properties or more widely for, at least, some intentional properties as well. P.J.P.N.

Joseph Levine, *Purple Haze* (Oxford, 2001).

explanation and stories: *see* stories and explanation.

explanation by samples: *see* samples, explanation by.

explanationism. This slightly barbarous term was first applied by James Cornman to, roughly, the doctrine that what justifies an ampliative inference—or more generally the formation of any new belief—is that the doxastic move increases the explanatory coherence of one's overall set of beliefs. In particular, the explanationist holds that some beliefs are justified by **'inference to the best explanation', the inference from a set of data to the available hypothesis that best explains those data, where 'best' is to be understood in terms of the pragmatic virtues, such as *simplicity, explanatory power, and fruitfulness. Explanationism derives ultimately from Peirce and Dewey, by way of Quine and Wilfrid Sellars. But Harman (in 'The Inference to the Best Explanation', 1965) was the first to articulate it and defend it against better-entrenched competing epistemologies. It has since received support from Paul Thagard and from Lycan (*Judgement and Justification*, 1988).

One must distinguish between at least three grades of explanationism. We may call them respectively 'weak', 'sturdy', and 'ferocious'. Weak explanationism is the modest claim that explanatory inference *can* epistemically justify a conclusion. (That claim is disputed by Bas van Fraassen, by Nancy Cartwright, and by Ian Hacking.) Sturdy explanationism adds that explanatory inference can do its justifying intrinsically, i.e. without being *derived* from some other form of ampliative inference, such as probability theory, taken as more basic. (That claim is disputed by Cornman and by Keith Lehrer.) Ferocious explanationism adds that no other form of ampliative inference is basic; all are derived from explanatory inference. (That claim is disputed by almost everyone.) Interestingly, Harman originally defended ferocious explanationism,

ignoring the weak–sturdy–ferocious distinction, by trying to exhibit various common forms of inductive inference as enthymematic instances of explanatory inference (see also Lycan, *Judgement and Justification*, ch. 9). Harman's mature explanationist view of all reasoning is given in his *Change in View*. W.G.L.

**explanation.

G. Harman, *Change in View* (Cambridge, Mass., 1986).
——'The Inference to the Best Explanation', *Philosophical Review* (1965).
P. Lipton, *Inference to the Best Explanation* (London, 1991).
W. Lycan, *Judgement and Justification* (Cambridge, 1988).
——'Explanation and Epistemology', in Paul Moser (ed.), *The Oxford Handbook of Epistemology* (Oxford, 2002).

exploitation. To exploit someone or something is to make use of him, her, or it for your own ends by playing on some weakness or vulnerability in the object of your exploitation. Most dictionaries define 'exploitation' as 'making use of someone or something unjustly or unethically'; but they are wrong. If exploitation is judged unjust or unethical, that is not a matter of definition but is due to positive—and controversial—ethical commitments on the part of those who judge it.

In the first instance, it is always some weakness or vulnerability which is the object of exploitation. A manipulative friend, lover, or parent exploits someone's feelings of guilt or need for affection; a loan shark exploits a debtor's financial emergency. A tabloid exploits a celebrity's messy divorce and also the public's prurient tastes in reading about it; we speak of exploitation here because we take the divorce to be a point of vulnerability in the celebrity, and prurient tastes to be a weakness in the public, and we see the tabloid using these weaknesses for its own profit. To exploit a *person* is to use a weakness in order to gain substantial control over the person's life or labour.

Is exploitation necessarily wrong or unethical? Few think it is wrong or unethical for a chess-player to exploit her opponent's inattention in order to win the game, or for a lawyer to exploit the weaknesses in her opponent's case in order to win a (just) judgement for her client. Where we do think exploitation is wrong or unethical, this is because we think that it is wrong or unethical to use those weaknesses of a person to gain your ends. If we think it is wrong to exploit a *person*, that is only because we think that someone's vulnerability should not be used to bring his or her life or labour under another's control. Yet some—such as Nietzsche, or Callicles in Plato's *Gorgias*—have held in general that it is entirely ethical—indeed, it is only natural justice—for the strong to exploit the weak. Such views cannot be cogently refuted by citing dictionary definitions of 'exploitation'.

Views like Nietzsche's and Callicles' are more widespread than people will admit. In capitalist society it is quite commonly believed just and right for people to buy and sell commodities—including one another's labouring capacities—at whatever prices the free *market will bear. Since the rate of wages is largely determined to the advantage of employers by the fact that ownership of the means of production puts them in a strong bargaining position, while propertylessness puts wage labourers in a weaker bargaining position, the resulting bargain is clearly exploitative; nevertheless it is commonly judged by loyal defenders of the capitalist system to be perfectly fair and ethical. Those who accept this judgement together with the standard dictionary definition of 'exploitation' are then able to deny that wage labour is exploitative, since they hold that it is just and ethical. Here we see that the standard definition of exploitation is not an innocent error, but a pernicious ruse to protect people from having to admit the similarity of their views to those of more honest defenders of exploitation such as Nietzsche and Callicles.

Of course the thesis that wage labour is exploitative is now associated chiefly with the name of Karl Marx, who gave the name 'rate of exploitation' to the ratio of the labour time in which the worker produces the capitalist's surplus to the labour time in which the worker produces his own wages. Following what they think is Marx's lead, economists often provide some technical definition of 'exploitation'—such as that of John Roemer, according to which you are exploited if the goods you receive embody less labour than you perform—and then use clever (and utterly fictional) counter-examples to show that intuitively there need be nothing in any way objectionable about exploitation as such (so defined). But since the counter-examples never involve anyone's turning another's weaknesses to account, what they really show is that the technical definition is not a good definition of exploitation.

Marx, of course, thought that in the real world surplus labour is extracted from workers through the fact that their propertylessness puts them in a position of vulnerability; so he really did think they were exploited. But he did not hold that capitalist exploitation is unjust, because he thought that since it harmonizes completely with the system of capitalist production, it must harmonize too with the only standards of right and justice which can be rationally applied to that system. For Marx the point of unmasking capitalist exploitation is to drive home to the working class that the capitalist economic system is founded on their condition of vulnerability, which it also perpetuates through the use which the capitalist class makes of it. Whether or not someone's exploitation of you is just, the fact that he exploits you shows that you are vulnerable and that someone is turning your vulnerability to account. In such a case you have good reason to do whatever it takes to protect yourself from the exploiter, even if doing this requires you to overthrow the entire social order and establish one in which you are strong enough not to be able to be exploited.   A.W.W.

*business ethics; capitalism; invisible hand.

Richard Arneson, 'What's Wrong with Exploitation?', *Ethics* (1981).
G. A. Cohen, 'The Structure of Proletarian Unfreedom', in John Roemer (ed.), *Analytical Marxism* (Cambridge, 1986).
Karl Marx, *Capital*, i, tr. Ben Fowkes (London, 1976).
John Roemer, 'Should Marxists be Interested in Exploitation?', in John Roemer (ed.), *Analytical Marxism* (Cambridge, 1986).

exportation. A principle which supports inferring 'If *P* then if *Q* then *R*' from 'If *P* and *Q*, then *R*'. In the *propositional calculus, it is represented as the inference of $(P \supset (Q \supset R))$ from the premiss $((P \cdot Q) \supset R)$. This rule of exportation is reflected in the theorem $((P \cdot Q) \supset R) \supset (P \supset (Q \supset R))$. Since the converse of the latter is also a theorem $((P \cdot Q) \supset R) \equiv (P \supset (Q \supset R))$ is sometimes designated the principle of exportation. There are systems with stronger conditionals such as *strict implication and *entailment where unrestricted exportation fails for those conditionals.

R.B.M.

R. Barcan Marcus, 'A Functional Calculus of First Order Based on Strict Implication', *Journal of Symbolic Logic* (1946).
B. Mates, *Elementary Logic* (Oxford, 1972).

expression. Expression is a key concept in aesthetic theory—especially Romantic theory: most systematically elaborated by Croce and Collingwood. Where expression is given the chief explanatory role, artworks do not merely describe or represent emotions, they more directly communicate an artist's highly specific moods and feelings, and enable the appreciator to experience them also. For Collingwood, the artist typically starts with a confused notion of what he feels: his creative work clarifies and stabilizes it.

The communication and arousal of emotion, however, are by no means essential to appreciation. What is true in the theory is that works of art are certainly bearers of subtly discriminated emotional qualities, the 'feel' of human life as lived—i.e. they are 'expressive': and that is partly why we treasure them. But not all such qualities interest us, and not all in art that interests us is expression. The values of form are distinct and different: so too the disclosure of alternative ways of seeing the common world.   R.W.H.

R. G. Collingwood, *The Principles of Art* (Oxford, 1938).
M. Mothersill, *Beauty Restored* (Oxford 1984), ch. 12, sect. 46.

expressivism in ethics. A theory about what is going on when people make moral judgements. Basically, the view is that people are expressing their attitudes to certain features of the world. Usually, these attitudes are understood as some species of emotion, though contemporary expressivists, notably *Blackburn (who calls the view quasi-realism, and applies it beyond morality) and *Gibbard, have argued that the attitude in question should not be understood as 'mere' emotion. In this they depart from cruder forms of *emotivism and *non-cognitivism. Most importantly, they argue that there are standards of correctness for our value judgements, and that we are thus entitled to use value judgements in arguments and in embedded linguistic contexts. Gibbard argues that the attitude we express is acceptance of a norm for behaviour. The other crucial feature of contemporary expressivism is that the attitudes that we are expressing have an essentially practical nature: we are not merely expressing our dislikes, but legislating for ourselves and others.   E.J.M.

*moral realism; prescriptivism.

Simon Blackburn, *Ruling Passions* (Oxford, 2000).
Allan Gibbard, *Wise Choices, Apt Feelings* (Cambridge, Mass., 1990).

extensionality. The extension of a term is roughly the thing or set of things to which it refers. The extension of 'Socrates' is Socrates, of 'human', the set of human beings.

The standard semantics of the *predicate calculus is characterized as extensional. Given a fixed domain of individuals (D), assigned to each individual constant is a member of D, to each n-adic predicate a set constructed from elements of D which is its extension, and to each sentence a truth-value. There is no further account of meaning for the non-logical terms. Properties are identified with the set of things which satisfy the property.

Some controversial consequences follow for non-purely mathematical applications of such extensional systems of logic. Suppose 'featherless biped' and 'rational animal' have the same extension. Given the assumption that coextensive classes (sets) are identical (the axiom of extensionality) those predicates should be interchangeable *salva veritate*, but there are contexts, often designated as indirect or opaque, where the substitution fails.

Languages with such failures are characterized as *intensional. Modal languages have been so characterized but that may be misleading. There are some interpretations of modal systems where the only departures from the standard semantics is that predicates are assigned different *extensions* in different worlds. There is still a reduction of properties to *extensions*.   R.B.M.

*referential opacity.

R. Barcan Marcus, 'Extensionality', *Mind* (1960).
W. V. Quine, *From a Logical Point of View* (Cambridge, Mass., 1953).

externalism. One of a number of views that hold that what is thought or said (content) depends in part on factors external to the mind of the thinker or speaker. One variety of externalism holds that content is tied to how experts use words ('the linguistic division of labour', Hilary Putnam); another contends that social usage more generally determines meaning (*'individualism and anti-individualism', Tyler Burge). Kripke's interpretation of Wittgenstein makes social usage the source of the possibility of content. In addition to these forms of social externalism there are views that make the perception of objects or events, or other causal relations to them, conditions for thinking and talking about such things. Kripke's theory of the reference of proper names is an example; so are Burge's and Davidson's versions of perceptual externalism.   D.D.

P. Ludlow and N. Martin (eds.), *Externalism and Self-Knowledge* (Stanford, Calif., 1998).

H. Putnam, 'The Meaning of "Meaning" ', in *Philosophical Papers*, ii: *Mind, Language, and Reality* (Cambridge, 1975).

external relations: *see* internal and external relations; relations.

external world. External to what? To the mind? But that does not give us a contrast in which 'external' applies literally, as when some medicinal preparation can be used externally but is not to be taken internally. The mind is here being thought of as a space or place, but in any normal space things can be variously disposed, some to the left, some to the right, some in front of others, some below. No such orderings are possible for anything that occurs in the mind; the 'in' here is purely figurative. This is not to say that a contrast cannot be drawn between 'in the mind' and 'in the world', but there is nothing to which the world is literally external. The world just is the domain within which external–internal distinctions apply.

But perhaps, without placing too great a weight on the term 'external', it is possible none the less to specify the problem which the existence of the external world has traditionally been thought to present. Thus, our knowledge being held to extend to no more than our immediate experiences, we are supposedly afforded no secure basis for affirming the reality of abiding, public, bodies. Such *scepticism is nowadays less common, but something of the position is preserved in the pragmatist's claim that the existence of physical bodies is at best a useful hypothesis, a matter of theory rather than fact. Could this be the truth that remains when the misconceived parallels are set aside?

There is a problem only to the extent that we are supposed to be given something less than the external world to begin with. Why should this be conceded? In the first place, there is some difficulty in attaching a clear sense to some of the terms which, like *'sense-datum' or 'impression', are enlisted in characterizing what is presented to us in experience. Secondly, we do not in any event argue to the physical from anything, but the external world seems to have the status of a starting-point.

The sceptic might seek to meet the first point by switching to the term *'sensation'. Most discussions of the problem start with the deliverances of sight, and terms such as 'sense-datum' may be questionable in this connection, but it would seem that touch is at least as important in telling us of the character of the physical—a blind man is not left in any doubt about the substantiality of objects he touches—and the language already has in 'sensation' an appropriate and meaningful term geared to that sense.

However, the second point is more troublesome for the sceptic. There are occasions when it would be rash to repose any confidence in a judgement made about a physical object—as when we try to make out something at a distance and in poor light—but there are also circumstances in which we have no realistic grounds for doubt about the modest claims in question. Moreover, in such circumstances it would normally be reckoned in order to judge *directly* of the existence and character of the bodies about us, and pointless to settle for anything less. It is not as if we were taking a hazardous plunge in proceeding in this way; on the contrary, we are dealing with a category of judgement which has stood the test of time as well as any. Nor is there any pressure to retreat to pragmatism, to regard the existence of material bodies as nothing more than a useful hypothesis. That standing does not suit a proposition which has everything to be said in its favour and nothing against. We may speak of *theory* to acknowledge the possibility of invoking a different range of concepts in describing the world, but this offers no threat to the factual character of our actual descriptions. No less than the sceptic, the pragmatist confronts a formidable task in persuading us that the line between fact and non-fact is to be redrawn at his chosen point.   R.B.R.

*body; existence; appearance and reality.

A. J. Ayer, *The Central Problems of Philosophy* (London, 1973).
B. Rundle, *Facts* (London, 1993).
L. Wittgenstein, *On Certainty* (Oxford, 1969).

F

fact. A fact is, traditionally, the worldly correlate of a true proposition, a state of affairs whose obtaining makes that proposition true. Thus a fact is an actual state of affairs. Facts possess internal structure, being complexes of objects and properties or relations (though facts themselves are abstract even when their constituents are not). Thus the fact that Brutus stabbed Caesar contains the objects Brutus and Caesar standing to one another (in that order) in the relation of stabbing. It is the actual obtaining of this state of affairs that makes it true that Brutus stabbed Caesar. Difficulties for this approach do, however, arise concerning the existence of negative, disjunctive, modal, and moral facts. For instance, should we say that what makes the proposition that Caesar did *not* stab Brutus true is the fact that he did not, or rather the non-obtaining of the state of affairs that he did?   E.J.L.

*brute fact.

S. Neale, *Facing Facts* (Oxford, 2001).
B. Taylor, *Modes of Occurrence* (Oxford, 1985).

facts, social: *see* social facts.

fact–value distinction. This distinction, which is crucial to moral theories of the middle and late twentieth century such as those of A. J. Ayer, C. L. Stevenson, and R. M. Hare depends on the idea that 'good', like 'other evaluative terms', has a special function in language. According to Ayer and Stevenson it expresses *feelings and attitudes, and according to Hare signals the acceptance of a special kind of imperative. On this basis a contrast was drawn between these 'evaluative' uses of language and 'descriptions of the world'; the latter, but not the former, being supposed to 'state facts'. Some utterances were indeed said to be partly descriptive and partly evaluative, so treating both of *fact and *value, but the factual and the evaluative elements in any word could in principle always be factored out. There was therefore a 'logical gap' between 'fact' and 'value', and this was taken to explain and support the idea (derived from Hume) that no 'ought' can be deduced from an 'is'. (*'Is' and 'ought'.)

Very many modern writers on moral philosophy believe that it must be possible to describe a distinction between fact and value such as was insisted on by Ayer, Stevenson, and Hare, but it has no place in the work of neo-Aristotelian moral philosophers such as G. E. M. Anscombe. Critics have challenged the account of evaluation on which the distinction draws, and doubts have also been raised about whether *value* stands in opposition to any clear notion of *fact*.   P.R.F.

*emotivism; prescriptivism; naturalistic fallacy.

A. J. Ayer, *Language, Truth and Logic* (London, 1949).
P. R. Foot, 'Moral Beliefs', *Proceedings of the Aristotelian Society* (1958–9); repr. in P. R. Foot (ed.), *Theories of Ethics* (Oxford, 1967).
R. M. Hare, *The Language of Morals* (Oxford, 1952).
C. L. Stevenson, *Facts and Values* (New Haven, Conn., 1963).
D. Wiggins, 'Truth, Invention and the Meaning of Life', in *Needs, Values, Truth* (Oxford, 1987).

fairness. Formal fairness precludes bias or inconsistency in the application of rules. However, rules can be applied fairly without being substantively fair. As Henry Sidgwick observed (*Methods of Ethics* (1907), p. 267) a rule requiring only red-haired men to serve in the army would be substantively unfair, even if this rule were always applied fairly.

One popular view about substantive fairness is that it is constituted by reciprocity. If one set of people (e.g. red-haired men) are required to provide benefits (e.g. national defence) for other people without getting proportional benefits in return, the arrangement is substantively unfair. But whether substantive fairness is limited to reciprocity seems dubious.

Suppose you have benefited from a communal practice. Suppose the benefit you received was greater than the cost you are now being asked to pay in order to sustain the practice. Still, you may not be morally obligated to contribute to the practice. It matters morally whether, when you accepted the benefits, you *consented* to reciprocate. If you didn't know when you accepted the benefits that the other party conceived of your accepting the benefits as the first stage of an exchange, then you are not required to pay up, since you didn't actually agree to the exchange. On this view, fairness does not require all mutually beneficial exchanges, but only those to which the parties actually agreed.

A further difficulty with limiting substantive fairness to reciprocity is that fairness may require agents to do things for others who will never be able to reciprocate. And even where all the relevant agents can do things for one another, suppose these agents begin with very unequal resources. Focusing on reciprocity may obscure the unfairness of that initial inequality.

Fairness is often closely associated with *equality. Fairness in its broadest sense requires that any two individuals be treated equally unless there is some morally relevant distinction between them. If the distinction between the harder-working and the less hard-working is morally relevant, then a fair arrangement will be sensitive to that distinction. Because the distinction between red-haired people and others is not morally relevant, fairness condemns the rule requiring only the red-haired to serve in the army.

Fairness as the consistent, unbiased application of all and only morally relevant distinctions does not indicate which distinctions are morally relevant.   B.H.

*economics and morality; justice.

C. L. Carr, *On Fairness* (Burlington, Vt., 2000).
J. Rawls, *Justice as Fairness: A Restatement* (Cambridge, Mass., 2001).
N. Rescher, *Fairness* (New Brunswick, NJ, 2002).

faith and reason. Each has been regarded as an independent source of truth, faith by virtue of what is reputedly given to a state of conviction voluntarily produced, reason by virtue of the outcome of compelling argument. For certain kinds of truth, access through faith rather than reason has been claimed the proper course. *Fideism regards religious truths in this way. Reason conceived as a source of knowledge has also been thought capable of arriving at divine truth (as in *arguments, types of). But in classic Catholic and Protestant thought, access to divine truth requires a combination of faith and reason: while faith itself is belief in revealed truth, reason is required to demonstrate that revelation actually occurs. That reason can be a source of factual truth at all is denied by *Kant, who with regard to truths previously accepted on faith insisted that they could be accredited only to the extent that they agree with ideals that can be rationally shown to be embodied in moral experience. In our own time, reason, following *Kierkegaard, *Nietzsche, and the *positivists, relieved of its truth-finding role becomes just one natural ability among others, paradigmatically the ability to choose means for given ends and to calculate risk. Faith then becomes an irrational refusal to abandon a means which reason tells us will not produce a desired result, or else a calculated willingness to ignore the risk that it may not do so. Some claim that, with beliefs held with certainty, faith is required even where reason proclaims the *likelihood* of their truth. Actions actually entered upon can be a *de facto* case in point, but also sincerely held religious beliefs, since anything short of certainty will cause a doubt which only a conscious leap of faith can erase. *Wittgen-steinians claim that reason as the tool of a fact-finding discourse has no place in the devotional language and practice of religion. Against the presumption that this is a return to fideism, they may argue that there is a religious form of reason(ing), employing its own criteria to distinguish, say, properly religious beliefs from mere superstition. A secularized form of faith freed from the strains involved in subjecting religious belief to the tests of reason has been proposed, which allows the more heroic forms of religious belief to be aligned with the latter.   A.H.

A. Hannay, 'Faith and Probability', in his *Kierkegaard and Philosophy* (London, 2003).
S. Mulhall, *Faith and Reason* (London, 1994).
G. Vattimo, *Belief*, tr. L. D'Isanto and D. Webb (Cambridge, 1999).

fallacy. In logic, (1) an invalid *argument* with the appearance of validity, or (2) a *form* of argument with some invalid instances. Fallacy is plainest when the argument, or some instance of the form (called a counter-example), combines true premises with an untrue conclusion. An argument that has a fallacious form need not itself be fallacious (this is because every argument has many forms, each displaying its structure in greater or lesser detail, and some of them are bound to be fallacious). Nevertheless, accusing an argument's champion of relying on a fallacious form that it has ('You might as well argue that . . . ') is often effective. More widely, (3) a fallacy is any prevalent fault of *proof*, such as *begging the question or *ignoratio elenchi*, which do not involve invalidity.   C.A.K.

*composition and division.

C. L. Hamblin, *Fallacies* (London, 1970).

fallibilism. A philosophical doctrine regarding natural science—most closely associated with C. S. Peirce—which maintains that our scientific knowledge-claims are invariably vulnerable and may turn out to be false. On this view, scientific theories cannot be asserted as true categorically, but can only be maintained as having some probability of being true. Accordingly, Peirce, and Karl Popper after him, insisted that we must acknowledge an inability to attain the final and definitive truth in the theoretical concerns of natural science—in particular at the level of theoretical physics. Present-day science cannot plausibly claim to deliver a definitive picture of physical reality, regardless of the present at issue. We would like to think of our science as 'money in the bank'—as something safe, solid, and reliable—but the history of science itself militates decisively against this comfortable view of our scientific theorizing. We should come to terms with the fact that—at any rate, at the scientific level of generality and precision—*each* of our accepted beliefs *may* turn out to be false, and *many* of our accepted beliefs *will* turn out to be false.

For Peirce, fallibilism represents a deep-rooted and far-ranging epistemological attitude: 'I used for myself to collect my [logical] ideas under the designation *fallibilism*; and indeed the first step toward *finding out* is to acknowledge that you do not satisfactorily know already; so that no blight can so surely arrest all intellectual growth as the blight of cocksureness' (*Collected Papers*, vol. i, sect. 1.13).

As fallibilism sees the matter, we have no assurance that our scientific theories or systems are definitely true; they are simply the best we can do here and now to resolve our question regarding nature's *modus operandi*. New knowledge does not just supplement but generally upsets our knowledge-in-hand. Any scientific theory or system is the product of human contrivance, and like any such contrivance—be it a house, a dam, or a knowledge-claim—it is fragile and impermanent. Every structure, be it material or cognitive, is thus ultimately likely to encounter conditions that its constructors did not anticipate—and could not have anticipated. And this circumstance renders its ultimate failure likely. The processes of change that come with time always involve chance eventuations that bring new, unforeseen, and unforeseeable circumstances to the fore. Changed social conditions destabilize social systems; changed physical conditions destabilize physical structures; changed experiential (i.e. experimental and observational) conditions—changed scientific technology, if you will—destabilize scientific theories. Rational inquiry links the products of our understanding to the experienced conditions of a world in which chance and chaos play an ineliminable role, so that there will always be new relations that ultimately threaten our rational contrivances. (Of course, while we can safely predict *that* our scientific theories will fail—will have to be replaced or modified—we cannot foresee *how* these replacements and modifications will be configured.)

There is much in this picture of the cognitive situation that rings true. The fact is that the equilibrium achieved by natural science at *any* given stage of its development is always an unstable one. The subject's history indicates that scientific theories have a finite life-span; they come to be modified or replaced under various innovative pressures, in particular the enhancement of observational and experimental evidence (through improved techniques of experimentation, more powerful means of observation and detection, superior procedures for data-processing, etc.).

The striking fact is that fallibilism is a more plausible doctrine with respect to *scientific* knowledge than with respect to the less demanding *'knowledge'* of everyday life, such as 'In the normal course of things humans have one head and two hands'. Such a statement has all sorts of implied safeguards, such as 'more or less', 'in ordinary circumstances', 'by and large', 'normally', 'if all things are equal', and so on. They are thus so well hedged that it is unthinkable that contentions such as these should be overthrown. In science, however, we willingly accept greater cognitive risks because we ask much more of the project. Here objectives are primarily theoretical and governed by the aims of disinterested inquiry. Hence the claims of informativeness— of generality, exactness, and precision—are paramount. We deliberately court risk by aiming at maximal definiteness and thus at maximal informativeness and testability. Aristotle's view that terrestrial science deals with what happens ordinarily and in the normal course of things has long ago been left by the wayside. The theories of modern natural science have little interest in what happens generally or by and large; they seek to transact their explanatory business in terms of strict universality—in terms of what happens always and everywhere and in all kinds of circumstances. We therefore have little choice but to acknowledge the vulnerability of our scientific statements, subject to the operation of the security-definiteness trade-off. Ironically, then, the *'common sense'* information of everyday life is securer than the 'well-established knowledge' science.

Some philosophers (Peirce included) see fallibilism as having ethical implications. They project an ethics of belief according to which we have *no right* to claim definitive truth for our current scientific claims, a view which they combine with a purported duty for the community of inquirers to pursue inquiry to the greatest extent realizable in the circumstances. Accordingly, they insist that the fallibilism of our cognitive endeavours must emphatically *not* be construed as an open invitation to a sceptical abandonment of the scientific enterprise. Instead, it is an incentive to do the very best we can. In human inquiry, the cognitive ideal is correlative with the quest for truth. And this is an ideal that, like other ideals, is worthy of pursuit despite the fact that we must recognize that its satisfactory attainment lies beyond our grasp.   N.R.

*Science, history of the philosophy of; science, problems of the philosophy of.

C. S. Peirce, *Collected Papers of C. S. Peirce*, ed. C. Hartshorne and P. Weiss, i: *Principles of Philosophy* (Cambridge, Mass., 1931); see esp. sect. 1.120: 'The Uncertainty of Scientific Results'.

K. R. Popper, *The Logic of Scientific Discovery* (New York, 1959).

N. Rescher, *The Limits of Science* (Berkeley, Calif., 1984).

false consciousness. A Marxian term, meaning a social awareness mystified by *ideology and ignorant of its own class basis. The term actually occurs only once in the writings of Marxism's founders, in a late letter of Engels: 'Ideology is a process accomplished by the so-called thinker, but with a false consciousness. The real motive forces impelling him remain unknown to him; otherwise it simply would not be an ideological process' (letter to Franz Mehring of 14 July 1893).   A.W.W.

D. Meyerson, *False Consciousness* (Oxford, 1991).

falsifiability. A property of a theory that, according to Karl Popper, provides a demarcation criterion between the scientific and the non-scientific. A theory is falsifiable just in case it is open to empirical test and there are possible empirical data that would, if observed, show the theory to be false. Scientific generalizations, including laws, are falsifiable but not confirmable. Unfalsifiable statements may be disreputable, such as those of pseudo-science, or of good intellectual standing, as with much philosophy. Falsifiability leads to *fallibilism, the position that nothing, including observation statements, can be known with certainty. This requires that certain observational statements are taken as basic by general agreement, a feature that is the Achilles' heel of falsificationism.   P.H.

Karl R. Popper, *The Logic of Scientific Discovery* (London, 1959).

family, ethics and the. The ethics of the family concerns, first, problems *within* a family, such as the extent to which children should be allowed to make their own decisions, and how far parents should be held responsible for their children's behaviour, and secondly, problems *about* the family, such as what constitutes a family, and how far a family unit should be kept together despite dysfunctional parents or children. The first set of issues has come to the forefront because there has been more emphasis in contemporary morality on children's rights. But the language of rights fits awkwardly into the context of the family, which is basically a kind of mutually supporting community, ideally providing security for the development of children. This is why (to move to the second set of issues) social workers and others go to some lengths to try to keep a family unit together. Those who stress 'family values' have in mind married heterosexual parents and two children, but one-parent families and families with same-sex parents are now common. Since the idea of 'the family' carries many moral implications, it is perhaps less discriminatory to think of the social unit as a 'household' rather than a family.   R.S.D.

J. Blustein, *Parents and Children: The Ethics of the Family* (New York, 1982).
Lainie Friedman Ross, *Children, Families, and Health Care Decision-Making* (Oxford, 1998).

family resemblance. Quasi-technical Wittgensteinian term. Wittgenstein denied that all definables must be explained by an analytic definition specifying necessary and sufficient conditions for the application of the definiendum. The members of the extension of a concept-word may be united not by essential common characteristics, but by family resemblance, i.e. by a network of overlapping but discontinuous similarities, like the fibres in a rope, or the facial features of members of a family. A family resemblance *concept, e.g. 'game', is explained by a series of paradigmatic examples with the rider: 'and other similar things'. The empirical discovery of common characteristics would not show that the concept in question was not a family resemblance concept; what is decisive is the existing practice of explaining the expression. Wittgenstein argued that many concepts central to philosophy are family resemblance ones, e.g. proposition, name, number, proof, language, and so too are many psychological concepts. In such cases, the search for an analytic definition is futile, and proposing one may distort the existing concept.   P.M.S.H.

G. P. Baker and P. M. S. Hacker, *An Analytic Commentary on the Philosophical Investigations*, i: *Wittgenstein: Understanding and Meaning* (Oxford, 1980), 320–43.

Fanon, Frantz (1925–61). Martinican psychiatrist who, as a proponent of Algerian Independence and Third World Revolution, developed a philosophy of *violence. *Black Skin, White Masks* (1952) explored the extensive effects of colonialism and *racism and indicated that extreme means would be necessary to purge Blacks of those effects in a 'collective catharsis'. Hence in *The Wretched of the Earth* (1961) Fanon insisted on the necessity of violence to promote justice and, primarily, psychic liberation. This was not a celebration of violence for violence's sake as some critics charged, but a conclusion drawn from an analysis of the violence endemic to the colonial situation and for the sake of a radical transformation of society. Although the colonized would initially tend to be violent against each other, violence against the oppressor would liberate them from despair and from a conception of humanity proposed by a discredited Europe.   R.L.B.

H. A. Bulhan, *Frantz Fanon and the Psychology of Oppression* (New York, 1985).

Fārābī, Abū Naṣr al- (c.872–950). Islamic Neo-platonist, philosopher of language, culture, and society, called 'the Second Teacher' for his achievements in logic. Of Turkic origin, al-Fārābī studied under Christian thinkers. He settled in Baghdad, travelled in Byzantium, and died in Damascus. His Arabic commentary on Aristotle's *De interpretatione* argues that divine omniscience does not imply *determinism, since the necessary implication of a fact by the corresponding knowledge is not transferred to the fact itself. This division of intrinsic from relational (hypothetical) necessity undergirds Avicenna's essence–existence distinction and his central claim that nature is contingent in itself, although necessary in relation to its causes. Al-Fārābī found the logic of Koranic promises and threats by seeing prophets in the role Plato had assigned to poets: naturalizing higher truths through imagery and legislation.   L.E.G.

Al-Fārābī, *Commentary and Short Treatise on Aristotle's* De Interpretatione, tr. F. W. Zimmermann (Oxford, 1981).
—— *On the Perfect State*, ed. and tr. R. Walzer (Oxford, 1985).

fascism. Political doctrine combining ethnic *nationalism with the totalitarian view that the state should control all aspects of social life. Fascism is thus opposed both to *liberalism—individual liberty and fulfilment being held to be relative to the nation's, rather than vice versa—and to *communism—class-identity and aspirations being held to threaten national unity. Fascism has presented itself as a tempting conclusion from three apparently plausible premises: the relativity of values to a culture; the rootedness of culture in the social life of a nation; and the role of the state as the upholder of values. Political and cultural authority are assimilated and identified with a national will articulated by a national leader, who conceives his task (compare *conservatism) as arresting national decline. The observed results constitute a *reductio ad absurdum* of the doctrine.   P.G.

*totalitarianism; anti-communism; racism.

N. O'Sullivan, *Fascism* (London, 1983).

fashion in philosophy. In the history of philosophy there have been constant changes in styles of philosophizing and in what are taken as givens in philosophical argument. Many of such changes have had nothing to do with rational considerations, but often with factors external to philosophy and sometimes simply with changes of fashion within philosophy. Whether *philosophy is more prey to fashion than other subjects are is hard to estimate, but in the present century at least the effect of fashion is very evident for anyone who has been a philosopher for a long time. It is not only styles of philosophizing that have changed, and with that current conceptions of who are the leading figures in the business, but even such things as conceptions of what constitutes a good argument. What seemed quite evident to those involved in *linguistic philosophy in Oxford in the 1950s, for example, may now seem quite bizarre.

In the present century some of the effects of fashion may arise from the institutional arrangements for the practice of philosophy. In most countries philosophy is now the province of the universities alone, and these function in competitive circumstances. The enthusiasms of the up-and-coming student may have something to do with what are simply features of personality—who is seen as the personification of philosophy at the time. The slant of journals and the influences of those who affect what gets published gives the impression to those coming into philosophy that that is how it must be done.

One can exaggerate the place of fashion in philosophy, but it is undeniable that changes which are, arguably, the result of fashion can be dramatic. The reputation of the greatest philosophers may perhaps survive such changes, but in a subject in which rationality is supposed to be the main consideration, it is sad that fashion exerts such power. If it is a by-product of institutional factors which also bring benefits, it nevertheless behoves philosophers to be aware of it.   D.W.H.

D. W. Hamlyn, *Being a Philosopher: The History of a Practice* (London, 1993).

fatalism. The belief, not to be confused with causal *determinism, that deliberation and action are pointless because the future will be the same no matter what we do. According to the famous 'idle argument' of antiquity, 'If it is fated for you to recover from this illness, you will recover whether you call in a doctor or not; similarly, if it is fated for you not to recover from this illness, you will not recover whether you call in a doctor or not; and either your recovery or non-recovery is fated; therefore there is no point in calling in a doctor.' Thus all actions and choices are 'idle' because they cannot affect the future.

Determinists reject fatalism on the grounds that it may be determined that we can be cured only by calling the doctor.   R.C.W.

*determinism, logical; many-valued logics.

R. Taylor, *Metaphysics*, 3rd edn. (Englewood Cliffs, NJ, 1983).

fear. A particularly distressing emotion aroused by impending danger, which plays a profound role in a number of central philosophical texts and theses. Fear of the consequences of our actions suggests a readily available motive for refraining from wrong, from Plato's Glaucon to some contemporary utilitarians. In Aristotle, on the other hand, how one manages fear is the measure of courage—not too much, not too little, which result in cowardice and foolhardiness, respectively. In Thomas Hobbes, it is the fear of each other and later fear of the sovereign that brings us into society. In G. W. F. Hegel's parable of *'master and slave', it is the loser's fear that results in servitude and, according to some interpretations of the *Phenomenology*, drives the dialectic through the remaining stages of self-consciousness. True religious belief, according to Søren Kierkegaard, is marked by 'fear and trembling', and so on. But fear also plays a central role in the philosophy of emotions and cognitive science. Fear turns out not to be a mere 'feeling' but necessarily exhibits *'intentionality', requires a 'formal object' (i.e. something fearful) and therefore can be said to have a cognitive 'structure'.

R.C.SOL.

R. Gordon, *The Structure of Emotion* (Cambridge, 1988).

feeling: *see* emotion and feeling.

Feinberg, Joel (1926–2004). American philosopher (at Princeton, Rockefeller, Arizona) noted for his papers and books in ethics, action theory, philosophy of law, and political philosophy. Feinberg's writing is notable for its distinctions reflecting common sense and ordinary language, but also for its systematicity. In his reformulation of a version of liberalism, two topics which, besides responsibility, are among the many Feinberg has treated are *autonomy and *paternalism. Feinberg sees the exercise of autonomy as closely connected with making major individual life choices. He seems less concerned with autonomy as exercised in contributing one's due influence to the formation of very basic societal ground-rules. Feinberg sees autonomy and paternalism as tending to conflict, but tolerates some 'paternalism' where the individual's choice is not fully voluntary or intervention is necessary to determine if it is voluntary.   E.T.S.

Joel Feinberg, *The Moral Limits of the Criminal Law*, i: *Harm to Others*, ii: *Offense to Others*, iii: *Harm to Self*, iv: *Harmless Wrongdoing* (Oxford, 1984–8).

felicific calculus: *see* hedonic calculus.

feminism. This is a term with many nuances of meaning. In a narrow sense it refers to attempts to attain equal legal and political rights for women, while in its broadest sense it refers to any theory which sees the relationship between the sexes as one of inequality, subordination, or oppression, and which aims to identify and remedy the sources of that oppression.

The term 'feminism' has its origins in the French word *féminisme*, which was coined by the utopian socialist Charles Fourier. The first recorded use in English was in the 1890s, when the word was used to indicate support for women's equal legal and political rights with men. However, many earlier writers may be said to be feminist in the sense that they too identified and opposed the subordination of women. Thus, Mary Wollstonecraft's *A Vindication of the Rights of Woman*, published in 1792, is an extended defence of woman as a rational being, capable of benefiting from education and of performing the duties of a citizen. Wollstonecraft's feminism, however, does not extend to the claim that men and women should be equal in terms of political participation, and indeed she defends a differential conception of citizenship according to which women may properly fulfil their duties as citizens from within the home.

But if earlier feminists did not invariably see equality of roles as necessary for feminism, many modern feminists have argued that such equality is insufficient as a response to women's oppression. On their account, feminism involves more than a simple demand for legal and political equality; it involves the identification and removal of all aspects of women's subordination, whether political or social. This raises two distinct difficulties for our understanding of feminism: the first is whether such a broad definition can be useful; the second is whether feminism, so understood, is a belief system or a political movement.

On the first point, some have argued that the broader definition is simply a 'catch-all' and that, as such, it allows any woman to label herself feminist irrespective of her political beliefs. Against this, however, we might wonder why political affiliation need disqualify: if feminism consists essentially in an attempt to alleviate women's oppression, then it should be open to the idea that there are different sources of oppression, and different ways of responding to them. Feminism, so understood, can be a broad church, and indeed some have argued that there is not one single doctrine of feminism, but a variety of feminisms, each with its own distinctive account of the sources of and remedies for oppression. Thus, within the broad, general category of feminism, we will find liberal feminists, socialist feminists, Marxist feminists, radical feminists, and many others who are united in their belief that there is much that is wrong with society's treatment of women, but who differ in their diagnosis of the problem and in their proposals for change.

This broader interpretation of feminism draws our attention to the second question, which is whether feminism is a philosophical doctrine or a political movement. On the narrower definition, and the definition which informed the organized women's movements in the nineteenth century, feminism was understood as essentially concerned with the equality of woman and man, and with the attempt to attain equal legal and political rights for women. It is in this sense of the term that writers such as John Stuart Mill and William Thompson are described as feminist, since they deny the existence of natural differences between men and women, or at any rate deny that those differences are such as to warrant according differential legal and political rights to men and women. This understanding of feminism as essentially concerned with the attainment of legal and political equality fits well with the conception of it as a political movement. However, as the definition broadens to include not merely the pursuit of legal and political equality, but also the removal of the much more general social and economic causes of women's oppression, it becomes progressively more difficult to construe feminism as a single political movement which can unite all women. This for the simple reason that different analyses of the sources of women's oppression will dictate different, and possibly conflicting, political responses.

The difficulty is compounded by the fact that even a demand for political and legal *equality is open to different interpretations. As we have seen, Mary Wollstonecraft asserted the equality of men and women as rational beings, but she believed this equality to be compatible with conceptions of citizenship which were different as between men and women. By contrast, modern liberal feminists have insisted that the equality of women as rational beings dictates a single, undifferentiated conception of citizenship which makes no distinction between women and men in respect of their legal and political rights. But this too is a controversial claim, for it is argued that by their emphasis on human beings as fundamentally rational, liberal feminists neglect the important biological and social differences which undermine women's ability to make equal use of their political and legal rights. Thus, even if we accept that men and women are, by nature, equal in respect of their rationality, it is still far from clear that women's subordination may be remedied simply by the institution of formally equal legal and political rights, since the value of those rights may be far less in the case of women than of men.

Additionally, and yet more controversially, some feminists have questioned the appeal to rationality as a justification for equal treatment. The claim that women and men are essentially rational beings is, it is argued, a gendered claim and one which does not reflect a universal truth, but only the preoccupations of Enlightenment philosophers. By conceding its importance, and arguing for equality on the basis of women's status as rational beings, feminists in effect argue for a woman's right to be like a man.

The debate about the meaning and significance of rationality draws attention to one of the ways in which feminism may constitute an important challenge to those forms of philosophy which have their origins in Enlightenment thought. Feminism has been characterized as a response, or set of responses, to the oppression of women in all its forms. This oppression, however, springs in part from the belief that men and women have a different nature—that men are rational whereas women are emotional, or that men are logical whereas women are intuitive. This belief (or some variation on it) is common in the history of philosophy, and may be found in the writings of Aristotle, Kant, Hegel, Rousseau, and many others, and it prompts the suspicion that rationality is a gendered concept, one which applies primarily to men and only derivatively, if at all, to women.

There are two distinct reponses to this emphasis on the importance of rationality: the response associated with Mary Wollstonecraft, with John Stuart Mill, and with early feminists generally, takes the form of a denial that women have a different nature from men and an assertion that, properly educated, women may be just as rational as men. However, in more modern philosophy, a more radical response has been evident. This concedes that woman's nature is different from man's, but goes on to advocate a form of feminism which rejoices in that difference, and which argues for the revaluing of 'women's qualities'—qualities of emotion and intuition—above the 'male' value of rationality. More subtly, it also argues for a reinterpretation of our understanding of rationality, one which recognizes that being rational is not a matter of denying emotional responses, but rather of including them as an important component of rationality itself.

Clearly, this debate about the meaning and significance of rationality has consequences for moral and political philosophy. In political philosophy, the injunction to pay less attention to the dictates of universal reason, and more attention to the context and narrative of specific situations, has led to criticism of modern political philosophy's emphasis on universal concepts such as *justice and equality. Yet more radically, it has prompted reflection on whether it is possible to be rational independent of specific circumstances and contexts, and this turn to a more 'narrative' and contextual approach now extends beyond explicitly feminist writers and constitutes one of the major ways in which feminist thought has influenced 'mainstream' political philosophy.

In moral philosophy, too, feminist emphasis on the importance of emotion has been highly influential and has prompted reconsideration of the reason–emotion dichotomy itself, a return to discussion of Humean themes in morality, specifically the claim that reason is the slave of the passions, and a re-examination of the dilemmas of impartialist moral theory. Yet more generally, feminist arguments have called into question the universalizing pretensions of epistemology, metaphysics, and philosophy of science. One of the most important consequences of these feminist preoccupations has been an increasing doubt about the concepts of objectivity, rationality, and universality characteristically associated with the philosophers of the Enlightenment.

There is, perhaps, an irony in the fact that feminism, which was itself born of Enlightenment thinking, now constitutes one of the main sources of criticism of it, and this irony has implications for feminism itself, which is often accused of abandoning its own intellectual heritage when it voices suspicion of universal concepts such as equality and justice. It was, after all, appeal to these concepts that gave intellectual force to women's claims for suffrage and for equal legal and political rights with men. Against that background, the rejection of them in favour of a vocabulary of care and concern, of difference, or of contextualization, may appear a dangerous strategy for feminists to pursue. Indeed, some have seen in the appeal to difference an abandonment of feminism's traditional concern for equality, whether that is understood narrowly as political and legal equality, or more broadly as including social and economic equality.

Unsurprisingly, therefore, one of the main concerns of modern feminism is with the question of how to understand difference, and how to attain a political order which will properly reflect differences between men and women. More specifically, one of the main concerns of modern feminism is to explain how differences between men and women are to be identified, and how equality can be attained through the recognition, rather than the removal, of those differences. Chastened by the allegation that liberal feminism purchases equality only by the denial of difference and that it requires women to become like men, modern feminism seeks to establish equality while acknowledging difference. Here, too, feminist thought has informed philosophy more widely, and feminist approaches to the problem of reconciling equality and difference have been adopted by philosophers concerned with problems of racism, multiculturalism, and ethnicity, for they, too, seek to establish a political order that recognizes differences between people, and sees those differences as both ineradicable and desirable.

Feminism, however, faces a distinctive problem in its attempts to attain equality through difference. This problem arises from the fact that much political philosophy, and liberal political philosophy especially, draws an important distinction between the *public and the private, where 'public' signifies the area in which political intervention is legitimate, while 'private' refers to those areas of life over which the state has no legitimate power, and where people should be left free from government interference. The problem here is that, both philosophically and in practice, women are identified with the private sphere and, as such, they occupy a realm that is, or is held to be, beyond the reach of state intervention. What seems to follow from this, however, is that the sources of inequality and oppression which are most likely to afflict women do not admit of any political remedy. Domestic violence and marital rape have traditionally been considered 'private' matters, but in so far as they are (or are deemed to be) private, they are beyond the reach of the state, and indeed fall outside the scope of theories of justice. The recognition that some of the most serious sources of women's oppression are purely personal matters and lie outside the scope of theories of justice has prompted the famous feminist claim 'the personal is political', and has also prompted the feminist reflection that the public–private distinction is the most important distinction for feminism, and indeed that it is what feminism is all about.

The importance of this last claim is that it draws attention to the link between the two definitions of feminism mentioned at the outset. If justice and equality have application primarily in the public or political realm, and if women in fact spend the greater part of their lives outside that realm, then political life, and the concepts of equality and justice which political philosophy emphasizes, are themselves significant factors in the subordination of women. It may therefore be that the very distinction between a narrow and a broad definition of feminism itself contains questionable assumptions, notably the assumption that legal and political equalities are not contributory factors in the subordination of women in so far as they imply a conception of equality which disregards important differences between men's and women's lives.   S.M.

*feminist philosophy; feminism, radical; well-being; women in philosophy; masculism; sex, philosophy of.

Carol Gilligan, *In a Different Voice* (Cambridge, Mass., 1982).
Will Kymlicka, *Contemporary Political Philosophy: An Introduction* (Oxford, 2002), ch. 9.
J. S. Mill, *The Subjection of Women* (London, 1983).
Anne Phillips, *Democracy and Difference* (Cambridge, 1993).
Harriet Taylor, *The Enfranchisement of Women* (London, 1983).
Mary Wollstonecraft, *A Vindication of the Rights of Woman* (Harmondsworth, 1978).

feminism, lesbian: *see* lesbian feminism.

feminism, radical. The 'radical' in radical *feminism refers not only to the degree of militancy advocated by this theory. Rather, radical feminism purports to analyse the roots of oppression (from the Latin *radicalis*, having roots). In particular, radical feminists hold that dominant political and social systems are founded on oppression. One might elaborate on this claim as follows: dominant political and social systems are organized on an ethos of inclusion–exclusion which dictates that some group of people must be 'outsiders' and which thus encourages the oppression of these people. Some radical feminists believe that the oppression of women is the model for all other forms of oppression. Others simply hold that various oppressions (e.g. class oppression, race oppression) are closely linked.   C.McK.

*racism; lesbian feminism.

Marilyn Frye, *The Politics of Reality* (Trumansburg, NY, 1983).
Adrienne Rich, *On Lies, Secrets and Silences* (New York, 1979).

feminist epistemology: *see* epistemology, feminist.

feminist ethics focuses on the questions what people do and should value, with specific reference to gender and sexual relations, and with a normative orientation to the liberation of women from sexual injustice. Feminist ethics thus flows into social philosophy: it conceptualizes relations between the sexes to be such that they can and must alter.

Feminists argue that historically dominant ethical conceptions of equality, justice, rights, liberty, autonomy, etc. have been more or less sublimated portrayals of a distinctively masculine (not a gender-neutral) mode of being. Some ethical theories, like Hobbes's and Rawls's, begin with the methodological injunction to consider individuals as if they are a-social and atomized. From this starting-point a philosopher can reason to a justification of co-operation between persons and even of care for others. However, the methodological premiss makes puzzling and problematic what is, from an alternative social point of view, not puzzling at all. Hence, an exaggerated individualism and voluntarism can forsake its role as a methodological premise and reappear in the guise of an ethical ideal.

Heteronomy, the capacity for and value of care, and the value of unconditional love, have frequently been judged outwith the ambit of truly ethical life. The differential impact this has on the ethical standing of women as opposed to men need not be laboured. Feminist ethics ranges between two alternative responses to this. First, there are attempts to pick out and revalue what is distinctive about women's lives and has traditionally been denigrated. Second, feminists keep a critical theoretical eye on the social processes by which it comes about that in a given context ethical qualities and virtues are associated more with one sex than another.

These problems raise the question of the nature of sexual or gender neutrality. The reclamation of 'feminine virtue' logically implies the continuation of 'masculine virtue'. A single ethical system could encompass the whole possible range of gender positions. Or, ethics could take as its objects human individuals as such and the relations between them. Once again, the indissolubility of the relationship between ethics and social theory or philosophical anthropology is emphasized.   E.J.F.

*feminism; feminist philosophy.

Elizabeth Frazer, Jennifer Hornsby, and Sabina Lovibond (eds.), *Ethics: A Feminist Reader* (Oxford, 1992).
Virginia Held (ed.), *Justice and Care: Essential Readings in Feminist Ethics* (London, 1995).
Catriona McKenzie and Natalie Stoljar (eds.), *Relational Autonomy: Feminist Perspectives on Autonomy* (Oxford, 2000).

feminist philosophy. Although women have been active philosophers for many centuries, the development of a specifically feminist viewpoint in the context of philosophy has gained credence only comparatively recently; partly as a result of more widespread debates about sexual politics in recent years, and partly as a result of social and economic changes in the status of women. The strands of feminist thinking in relation to philosophy have been and continue to be diverse and do not necessarily present a unified point of view. Feminist approaches to philosophy can take place at a number of levels and from different perspectives, and indeed this has been identified as a notable strength. For example, feminists have presented philosophical critiques of philosophers' images of women, political critiques of the organization of the discipline of philosophy, critiques of philosophy as masculine, historical research into the work of past women philosophers whose work may have been unjustly disregarded, and positive contributions to philosophy from a feminist perspective. Feminist philosophers may take some or all of these approaches to be important, but, generally speaking, feminist philosophy will assume the question of sexual difference to be a philosophical issue at some level and, depending on the point of departure, produce very different ways of theorizing about this question. Although women tend to work in this area, not all women philosophers are necessarily feminist philosophers (although there may be feminist implications in their work).

One central question for feminist philosophers has been the extent to which philosophy is biased towards a masculine viewpoint, when the majority of past philosophers have been men. Can philosophy be trusted to be neutral on the question of sexual difference? It may be a historical accident that philosophy has been an activity associated with men. If, however, it is more deeply permeated with masculine values, feminists have asked whether such values are indelibly or contingently imprinted into the practice of philosophy. Such questions implicate the basis of philosophy itself. Notions of reason, truth, and knowledge, and the way that philosophical inquiries often seem to fall into distinctions of mind–body, order–chaos, or rely on hierarchies of terms, are called into question. Feminists also point out that such distinctions often map on to, or presuppose, sexual difference, aligning masculinity with reason and order.

This issue is of significance because it has bearing on topics such as personhood or identity and epistemology. If the association of reason with masculinity is reinforced by social structures, then it would seem that a particular type of experience is being validated at the expense of other possible viewpoints, and, as far as possible, that such a bias should be corrected. But problems arise in trying to assess where exactly the bias lies: which aspects of experience belong to which sex; to what extent such differences, if identified, belong contingently or properly to each sex; whether men and women see the world very differently, and, if so, whether they are very different persons. These issues are often expressed in terms of a distinction between *sex and *gender, where sex is the biologically invariant factor and gender is comprised of various socially, culturally, or historically variable components. Other ways in which the division has been expressed are as nature–culture, or male–masculine and female–feminine. But making such distinctions does not necessarily resolve all the problems.

In the past it has been argued that sex creates or causes gender, i.e. that biology shapes cultural perceptions of difference. But this view has been objected to if it seems to result in a deterministic account of identity which cannot allow for the transformation of perceptions of difference, or attributes essentially different identities or ways of thinking to men and women. Essential difference is not necessarily a problem, but differences may be given unequal value such that women are seen as 'the weaker sex'. A milder version of the above argument would allow that biological difference contributes to perceptions of difference but is not the only factor, and so cannot be wholly determining. Differences could then be minimized and some equality established. Difference would not disappear altogether, but, with equality of opportunity, would not be used prejudicially against one sex. Thinkers such as Mill and de Beauvoir suggest this approach. However, ideas of equality may already have been shaped in a particular way, based on notions of freedom and self-determination which are not automatically neutral. Or the argument might lead to a form of neutrality on the question which disregards women's specificity, differences *between* women, or implicitly tries to make women more like men. Rousseau's and Plato's discussions of sexual difference illustrate some of the problems discussed above. Feminists working on political philosophy (for example, Carole Pateman) discuss issues such as equality, rights, and social organization in this context.

Other feminists such as Carol Gilligan have suggested that difference is significant in that it leads to quite different experiences of the world. Women's experience has largely featured caring, nurturing, and motherhood in the past, and so, it is suggested, could form the basis for a different model of ethical relations, an 'ethics of care'. But the validation of difference connected to sex here (and specifically women's role in reproduction) may reinforce a model of different world-views and essential difference, which makes it difficult to see how such an ethical model could be generalized for both sexes.

With Foucault and some Marxist theorists, some feminists have argued that sex itself is a social or cultural construct, suggesting that sex differences are an effect of power relations and of meaning. As such they may be open to social and cultural transformation. But if these meanings are inherited from a past which has shaped power in particular ways, again it may seem that women have to relinquish their specificity to escape restrictive identities, or else accept more limited transformations.

Others have tried to re-evaluate difference without reinforcing sex–gender connections, arguing that the symbolic and experiential differences which already exist can be used to enrich existing conceptions of personhood or identity, ethics, and epistemology. Thinkers such as Irigaray, Cixous, and Kristeva have used notions of difference strategically to point out how philosophy has excluded 'the feminine' as symbolically other to reason. French feminists draw upon *structuralism and psychoanalysis as resources to account for sexuality, identity, and difference. With this approach, difference can lead to plurality without a necessary loss of embodiment or of the specificity of women.

In addition to raising questions of sexual difference in the context of philosophy, feminist philosophers also raise questions about the connection (or lack of it) between theory and practice or lived experience. How well do theories of personhood or identity, equality and ethics, correspond to the diversity of lives in the contemporary world? How are such theories manifest, for example, in hiring-policies? Such issues as pornography, rape, and medical ethics (e.g. reproductive technologies) are also currently under examination by feminists working in philosophy.   A.C.A.

*feminism; Héloïse complex; women in philosophy; ethics, feminist; law, feminist philosophy of; science, feminist philosophy of; epistemology, feminist; masculism.

Judith Butler, *Gender Trouble: Feminism and the Subversion of Identity* (London, 1990).
Simone de Beauvoir, *The Second Sex* (Harmondsworth, 1984).
Genevieve Lloyd, *The Man of Reason: 'Male' and 'Female' in Western Philosophy* (London, 1984).
Toril Moi (ed.), *French Feminist Thought: A Reader* (Oxford, 1988).
Carole Pateman, *The Sexual Contract* (Cambridge, 1988).
J. Saul, *Feminism: Issues and Arguments* (Oxford, 2003).

feminist philosophy of law: *see* law, feminist philosophy of.

feminist philosophy of science: *see* science, feminist philosophy of.

feminist political philosophy. A diverse field of theoretical inquiry marked by the systematic study of historical conditions, conceptual schemas, and social practices that manufacture and legitimate gender inequality. The multiplicity of positions is a function of the presence of different liberatory strategies grounded in different analyses of female subordination. Some feminists locate institutionalized male privilege as an artefact of kinship systems that create social bonds between men through the ritualized circulation of women. Such feminists seek to graph new social structures, new 'Oedipal phases', into the existing socialization trajectory that processes 'raw' infants into 'cooked' or socialized humans. On this view, the forms of life that define and enshrine cultural standards for child care and child rearing are irreducibly political. Other feminists want to see female reproductive systems technologically altered so that all humans can be equally positioned with respect to procreation and full autonomous activity. Other feminists claim that men must be changed or females must escape from a male culture structured around the eroticization of domination and the destruction of life. Other feminists want 'women' to break free of male-dependent identities by destroying the category of woman, a destruction presumably commenced by the recognition that this category is only political and not a natural kind. Other feminists feel that political revolution is possible only if the oppressed restructure their own subjectivities through creative invention of a new triumphant imaginary or deliberate subversion of the daily, nearly invisible performance of gender. Other feminists, while rejecting any ahistorical stance that 'woman' refers to some common nature persisting through, and underlying

every possible human social system, still insist that unified political action requires that an essentialist category of woman be deployed provisionally. Other feminists engage in a feminist reconstructing of such core concepts as contract, power, justice, consent, obligation, and rights, which have been used to legitimate the classical liberal ideology.

No matter how diverse the methodological tactics, feminist political theorists have together forced classical political theory to encompass what was once considered apolitical—the family, child-rearing practices, gender, the body, sexuality, and human relationships. In the process, the revolutionary schemas of Karl Marx and Sigmund Freud in particular have each been meticulously reworked, refined, and appropriated to fuel a new refiguring of the individual and the state.   B.T.

Nancy Hirschmann and Christine Di Stefano (eds.), *Revisioning the Political: Feminist Reconstructions of Traditional Concepts in Western Political Theory* (Boulder, Colo., 1996).
Mary Lyndon Shanley and Carole Pateman (eds.), *Feminist Interpretations and Political Theory* (University Park, Pa., 1991).

Ferguson, Adam (1723–1816). Hailed from Perthshire, studied at St Andrews, and held various chairs at Edinburgh, achieving international prominence with his *Essay on the History of Civil Society* (1767; ed. and intro. D. Forbes (Edinburgh, 1966)). This broke decisively with speculation about human origins and development, in favour of known facts and historical evidence. In a sweeping review of the transition from rudeness to civilization Ferguson describes the *human being as a 'progressive animal', liable to luxurious corruption, who combines sociableness with an instinctive relish for fighting. In his moral philosophy he expounded man 'as he ought to be', not as he is. All the virtues are benevolent. He disagreed with Hume's utilitarianism and Smith's theory of moral sympathy: sympathy can be misplaced. His idea that social *progress was natural but neither inevitable nor irreversible was superseded by Hegelianism and Marxism.   V.H.

Ferrater-Mora, José (1912–91). Spanish philosopher exiled in 1939, after the Civil War. Heir to the existentialist philosophy of Unamuno and Ortega, Ferrater-Mora was concerned with how those things that make human life special—namely, reason and morality—are not opposed to, but continuous with, the natural world. To this extent, he proposes an ontology with different levels of reality—physical, biological, neural–mental, biological–social, and social–cultural—each stemming from, but not reducible to, the previous, more basic, one.

He calls this view 'integrationism', by which he means two things. First, he wants to overcome the traditional opposition of irreducible concepts—e.g.: nature–reason, causality–freedom, is–ought—by integrating them in a continuous ontology. Second, he intends to work out a methodological approach that is at the same time analytical, critical, and speculative, thus combining the virtues of different philosophical traditions. The outcome is a robust form of normative *naturalism.   A.GOM.

*Spanish philosophy.

J. Ferrater-Mora, 'Fictions, Universals and Abstract Entities', *Philosophy and Phenomenological Research* (1977).

fertilization *in vitro*. '*In vitro*' means, literally, 'in glass', but *in vitro* fertilization, or IVF, is the standard term used for the technique of fertilizing an egg outside the body, and transferring the resulting embryo to the womb of a female recipient. This procedure was first successfully carried out with human beings in 1978 in Britain, by Robert Edwards and Patrick Steptoe. The birth of Louise Brown ushered in a new era of artificial reproduction, with concomitant ethical and legal dilemmas.

Several distinct ethical objections have been made to the use of IVF. Initially, there was concern about the risk that the children born as a result of this procedure would be abnormal. Now that there are tens of thousands of children who were conceived outside the body, these fears can be seen to be unjustified. On the other hand, objections on the basis of the cost of the procedure remain serious, especially where the resources are drawn from a limited national health budget. Because the rate of births per cycle of treatment remains low, generally around 15 per cent, the cost of each child produced is considerable. In addition, there is a human cost for those couples whose hopes of overcoming infertility are raised by reading headlines about IVF, but find that they do not achieve a pregnancy. Many reasonably ask if adoption, including overseas adoption, would not be a better solution to the needs of infertile couples.

The Roman Catholic Church objects to fertilization *in vitro* on several grounds. These include the fact that to obtain the sperm requires masturbation, which in the eyes of the Church is inherently sinful, even when it is the only way to bring children to a marriage. The Church objects to the division that the technique introduces between procreation and the sexual act, believing that this weakens the marital relationship. Finally, the Church condemns the loss of embryonic human life involved both in research directed towards improving IVF, and in the procedure itself.

The development of artificial reproduction has met with a mixed response from feminists, some anticipating its coming as a means of liberating women from biological inequality, while others see it as one more form of male domination over women's bodies. They see women being used as subjects of medical experimentation, and suggest that the end-result may be to remove women's control over pregnancy and childbirth.

During the 1980s fertilization *in vitro* ceased to be an experimental technique, and became a standard treatment for some forms of infertility. The ethical debate then moved on to further applications of IVF. The existence of a viable human embryo outside the human body provides an opportunity for various forms of interference. These include: using the embryo for research purposes; freezing the embryo for long-term storage (raising the possibility that the couple may divorce or die); donating the embryo to another infertile couple; contracting with another woman to gestate the embryo and return it to the genetic parents; and screening the embryo to determine its genetic characteristics (including its sex) before deciding whether to proceed with implantation.

In many countries, government commissions have considered fertilization *in vitro*. Philosophers such as Mary Warnock and Jonathan Glover have played key roles in these commissions, which have generally approved the practice of IVF under specified conditions.
                                                                P.S.

*applied ethics; feminism.

Congregation for the Doctrine of the Faith, *Instruction on Respect for Human Life in its Origin and on the Dignity of Procreation* (Rome, 1987).

Jonathan Glover and others, *Fertility and the Family* (London, 1989).

J. Harris and S. Holm (eds.), *The Future of Human Reproduction* (Oxford, 1998).

Report of the Committee of Enquiry into Human Fertilisation and Embryology (The Warnock Report) (London, 1984).

Peter Singer and Deane Wells, *The Reproduction Revolution* (Oxford, 1984).

M. Warnock, *Making Babies* (Oxford, 2003).

Feuerbach, Ludwig Andreas (1804–72). German philosopher, who was a leading Left Hegelian. He originally studied Protestant theology at Heidelberg but soon moved to Berlin where for two years he studied philosophy with Hegel. In 1830 he published *Thoughts on Death and Immortality* (tr. Berkeley, Calif., 1980), arguing against personal immortality and the transcendence, if not the existence, of God. This established him as a leading member of the Left or Young Hegelians. (The Right or Old Hegelians tended to endorse immortality and divine transcendence.) But it also lost him his post at Erlangen, and ended his academic career. He withdrew into private life, and made only one more public appearance, when he was invited to lecture at Heidelberg in the revolutionary upheaval of 1848.

Until 1839 Feuerbach's public persona was that of an innovative and independent-minded Hegelian. His Erlangen lectures, on logic and the history of philosophy, were thoroughly Hegelian. But with the publication in 1839 of *Towards a Critique of Hegel's Philosophy*, he became a critic of Hegel, as well as an interpreter. He rejects Hegel's tendency to downgrade perceptible reality in favour of conceptual thought, criticizing, for example, his argument (in the *Phenomenology of Spirit*) that words such as 'this' and 'here' cannot be used to refer to perceptible individuals and also his claim (in the *Science of Logic*) that being becomes nothing: 'Hegel starts from being, i.e. the notion of being or abstract being. Why should I not be able to start from being itself, i.e. real being?' While agreeing with Hegel that men are capable of abstract thought, he denies that thought is man's central capacity and insists that a thinker, an 'I', is an embodied being who essentially requires a 'you': 'The truth lies only in the unification of "I" and "you"'. (He later saw this as rooted in the biological fact of sexual differentiation.)

Feuerbach proposes a naturalistic *humanism. Philosophy is the science of reality in its truth and totality. The totality of reality is nature, and this can be known only by sense-perception. This does not mean that philosophy is to be abandoned in favour of such specialized sciences as physics, physiology, and psychology. These too consider merely abstract aspects of the complete human being. Thus philosophy needs to become anthropology, a science of the human being as a whole. For Feuerbach, as much as for Hegel, man stands at the centre of the world: 'The being of man is no longer particular and subjective, but a universal being, for man has the whole universe as the object of his drive for knowledge. Only a cosmopolitan being can have the cosmos as its object.' In later years, his philosophy declined into a physiological *materialism, epitomized by his punning dictum 'Man is (ist) what he eats (isst)'.

Hegel had argued that 'speculative' philosophy has the same 'content' as the Christian religion, but presents it in a conceptual form rather than in pictorial imagery. Feuerbach believed this to be true of Hegelian philosophy: 'The "absolute spirit" is the "departed spirit" of theology, a ghost still haunting the Hegelian philosophy.' Feuerbach's new earthly naturalism is as hostile to religion as to Hegelianism. Thus in his most celebrated work, The Essence of Christianity (1841), translated by George Eliot in 1853, Feuerbach directed anthropology against religion. Indeed, an examination of religion is, on his view, an essential requirement for discovering what man is. Polytheistic religions, he argues, express man's dependence on nature and personify natural forces. But the Christian *God is in fact the essence of man himself, abstracted from individual, embodied men, and objectified and worshipped as a distinct entity. Man attributes to God his own highest feelings, thoughts, and hopes. Thus God is held to be almighty, merciful, and loving. What this really means is that omnipotence, mercy, and love are divine. Belief in immortality too is no more than a projection of our ideals into another world. It does not follow that religion is nothing but a regrettable error. Without religion man would not have become aware either of nature as a unified system or of his own essence. (Feuerbach agrees with Hegel that education involves alienation.) But now that this work is done, religion impedes the earthly realization of the ideals that it implicitly acknowledges by projecting them into heaven. We need to heal the fissure between heaven and earth, to replace love of God by love of man, and faith in God by faith in man, to recognize that man's fate depends on man alone and not on supernatural forces, before we can devote our collective energies to the wholehearted pursuit of human welfare, to the realization of the essence of man on earth. In a later work, On the Essence of Faith in Luther's Sense (1844; tr. New York, 1967), he argued that his humanization of theology is already implicit in Protestantism. Quoting Luther's claim 'If God sat all alone in heaven, like a bump on a log, he would not be God', Feuerbach infers that God exists only in so far as he is an object of our faith.

Feuerbach differs from Hegel in two general respects. First, Hegel attempts, with a good measure of success, to present not one particular philosophy among others, but the universal philosophy, to integrate into a coherent whole what is true in all reasonable philosophies. (A similarly conciliatory spirit is found in J. S. Mill, in contrast to the more combative Bentham: Mill wants to combine what is true in both Bentham and Coleridge.) Feuerbach, for all his claims to totality, is more exclusive: he wants to exorcise the 'ghosts' of theology and idealism rather than domesticate them. Secondly, Hegel condemns proposals (and predictions) with regard to the future. Philosophers at least must confine themselves to understanding the past and the present. Feuerbach proposes plans for the reform of philosophy—Provisional Theses for the Reformation of Philosophy (1843) and Principles of the Philosophy of the Future (1843)—plans which were largely unrealized. He has high hopes for the future of humanity. The dissolution of Protestantism will make way for a democratic republican state. Like Hegel, he believed the nation state to be the ideal human community and had no sympathy for any larger political organization. He made little attempt to reconcile this with his insistence on the unity of the human species and on universal love.

Some of Feuerbach's best ideas, however, are already to be found in Hegel, especially in the Phenomenology of Spirit. Hegel was familiar with the ideas that the 'unhappy consciousness' of medieval Christianity projects its own essence on to the other-worldly being before which it abases itself, and that Lutheranism tends to the humanization of religion. Hegel knew as well as Feuerbach that a person, or 'I', requires another, a 'you', to sustain and confirm his self-consciousness. Even in those cases where his criticisms—of Hegel's treatment of 'this', for example, and of being—have since become commonplace, we feel that he is making points of which Hegel was already aware, that he has not descended to the depths of Hegel's thought, and that he has therefore not fully emerged from it. His main achievement is his explanation (if not demolition) of religion. But even this is impaired by the abstract vagueness of his concept of man, and the naïve sentimentality of his belief that what primarily unites men is love. This comes close to the young Hegel of the early theological writings and represents a step back in comparison to the mature Hegel's historically and conceptually differentiated account of man or 'spirit'. Feuerbach's importance lies not so much in his own thought as in the impetus that he gave to that of Marx and Engels.   M.J.I.

*Hegelianism.

W. B. Chamberlain, Heaven wasn't his Destination: The Philosophy of Ludwig Feuerbach (London, 1941).

E. Kamenka, The Philosophy of Ludwig Feuerbach (London, 1970).

K. Löwith, From Hegel to Nietzsche (New York, 1946).

L. S. Stepelevich (ed.), *The Young Hegelians: An Anthology* (Cambridge, 1983).

M. Wartofsky, *Feuerbach* (Cambridge, 1977).

Feyerabend, Paul (1924–94). Austrian-American philosopher of science who argued for the abolition of his subject. The early Feyerabend stressed the importance—for Popperian reasons—of theory proliferation and identified *and rationalized* historical exceptions to methodological theses. In debate with Lakatos he argued that no set of methodological rules could do justice to the complexity of the history of science. A *methodology which was *not* historically laughable would be empty of normative content. If there is no rationalization for science, there is nothing to privilege scientific beliefs over, say, voodoo. On the contrary, an examination of the 'material basis' of voodoo could 'enrich, and perhaps even . . . revise' physiology. From this heuristic thesis he moved finally to the relativity of knowledge-claims.   N.C.
                                                                T.CHI.
                                                                R.F.H.

*science, history of the philosophy of.

Paul Feyerabend, *Philosophical Papers*, i and ii (Cambridge, 1981).

—— *Against Method*, rev. edn. (London, 1988).

Fichte, Johann Gottlieb (1762–1814). German philosopher who was the first of the great post-Kantian idealists. In his first book, *Attempt at a Critique of All Revelation* (1792; tr. Cambridge, 1978), he argued, in a thoroughly Kantian manner, that revealed religion is an important element in the moral education of imperfect humanity. The publisher omitted Fichte's name from the book, and Kant was thus widely assumed to be its author. (Kant's own work on the subject, *Religion within the Limits of Pure Reason*, did not appear until the following year.) Fichte rose to fame when he revealed his authorship, and secured a professorship at Jena in 1793. He lost this post in 1799 owing to a controversy over his supposed atheism (he regarded God not as a person, but as the moral order of the world), a controversy exacerbated by his uncompromising temperament and by his support of the French Revolution. He then moved to Berlin, the capital of Prussia, where he associated, and later quarrelled, with Friedrich Schlegel and the Romantic circle. (The Romantics admired Fichte, but did not share his moral ardour.) His popular lectures in Berlin (and at Erlangen, where from 1805 he held a chair) increased his fame, especially his *Addresses to the German Nation* (1807–8), in which, after the French victories over Prussia at Jena and Auerstadt, he urged the moral regeneration of Germany (primarily through educational reforms) and thereby of humanity as a whole. In 1809 he became professor, and in 1811–12 Rector, of the new university of Berlin. He was buried in Berlin, and Hegel was later buried next to him.

Fichte saw himself as a loyal Kantian, but there were several features of Kant's system, or at least of Kant's exposition of it, that he was unable to accept. In particular, Kant had implied that there are things-in-themselves, unknowable to us, which are responsible for the sensory element in our knowledge, a sensory element which is thus quite distinct from the conceptual element. Moreover, Kant is, on Fichte's view, insufficiently systematic. Not only does he inadequately explain the relationship between sensations and concepts; he does not supply an adequate derivation of the categories that inform all our knowledge of phenomena. Kant's theoretical and practical philosophies appear in distinct works, with no satisfactory link between them. To remedy these defects Fichte proposed to begin not, as Kant had done, with an examination of our knowledge, to discover what is involved in it, but with a consideration of the pure I or ego, that is, the 'I think', which, on Kant's view, 'must be able to accompany all my representations'. He invites us, in the *Science of Knowledge* (*Wissenschaftslehre*, 1794; tr. New York, 1970), to disregard external objects and our mental states and to focus exclusively on the I that apprehends both external objects and mental states. (As a transcendental, rather than a subjective or a psychological, idealist, Fichte cannot presuppose the existence and nature of our mental states.) The I is not a thing or substance; it is simply activity, the activity of 'positing' itself; it exists only in virtue of its own awareness of itself. The I's self-positing is the 'thesis'. But the I's self-positing, though we can be sure that it occurs, has certain conditions and, therefore, implications; if we suppose that the I posits itself, but deny that these conditions are fulfilled, we (and the I itself) fall into a 'contradiction', and it is to resolve such contradictions that the activity of the I (and the *Wissenschaftslehre*) proceeds. To be aware of itself the I must limit itself ('Consciousness works through reflection, and reflection is only through limitation'), and this it can do only by positing something other than itself, a non-I. (Antithesis.) The I is now involved in another contradiction: it both posits and negates itself. This can be resolved only by a synthesis: the I posits a divisible I, limited by, and limiting, a divisible non-I; that is, the non-I, in part, negates the I, and the I, in part, negates the non-I. (Fichte's concepts of thesis, antithesis, and synthesis reappear in Hegel, but Hegel does not use this terminology.)

Of these three principles, the third involves two propositions: (1) The I posits itself as determined by the non-I. (2) The I posits the non-I as determined by the I. These form the basis of, respectively, the theoretical *Wissenschaftslehre* and the practical *Wissenschaftslehre*. The theoretical *Wissenschaftslehre* unfolds the conditions of the determination of the I by the non-I. It does so primarily by the reflection of the I on its own activity and its transcendence of the limit involved in this activity. This reflection involves a new limit, which is in turn transcended by reflection on it. In this way Fichte purports to derive all the conditions required for the determination of the I by the non-I: sensations, space, time, and such categories of the understanding as causality. The *thing-in-itself is replaced, for Fichte, by the 'unconscious self-limitation of the I'—'unconscious', since the products of the I seem to be given to it 'from without'.

The second proposition, that the non-I is determined by the I, gives rise to the practical *Wissenschaftslehre*, and this is, for Fichte, crucial to the I's construction of the world. First, the I's motive for producing a world, and a world of a certain type, is to have a field for its activity, primarily for the performance of its moral duty. Second, it is only with the practical *Wissenschaftslehre* that the world ceases to be merely a network of ideas (*Vorstellungen*) and becomes genuinely objective with respect to the I. The performance of duty requires the existence of other Is on a par with myself and I must regard other people as independent centres of consciousness and activity, not simply as my own ideas. But if the world is perceived by other beings, as well as myself, it is relatively independent of myself and my mental states.

In other works of the period, notably *The Science of Rights* (1796–7; tr. London, 1889) and *The Science of Ethics* (1798; tr. London, 1897), Fichte develops the implications of practical *Wissenschaftslehre*. The latter work attempts to derive the *content* of our duties from the mere fact that we must act morally, arguing, for example, that since moral activity requires the existence of others, we have a duty not to kill others or otherwise impair their capacity for moral activity. *The Science of Rights* applies ethical principles to law, the family, individual rights within the state, and relations between states. The state exists to protect the rights of its citizens and is 'nothing but an abstract conception; only the citizens, as such, are actual persons'. States should form a confederation to secure the freedom of all men, and ultimately all men should belong to a single commonwealth. This did not prevent him from arguing, in *The Closed Commercial State* (1800), that a state should rigidly control the economic activity of its citizens and prohibit international trade.

Fichte's doctrines so far are well summarized in *The Vocation of Man* (1800; tr. New York, 1956), in which he considers three increasingly adequate views of the world: first, naturalistic *determinism, which dissolves man's freedom in the 'rigid necessity of nature'; second, theoretical *idealism, which reduces the world, including oneself and other people, to a 'system of pictures'; and third, practical idealism, in which oneself and others emerge as free, but embodied, moral agents occupying an objective world. The work concludes with the affirmation that God is the moral order of the world and that we exist 'only in God and through God'. But after about 1800 Fichte's thought underwent a change. In the *Wissenschaftslehre* of 1794 he contrasted his own philosophy, idealism, with the 'dogmatism' or realism of such thinkers as Spinoza. (He claimed that which of these philosophies one adopts depends on what kind of man you are, but he also gave reasons, such as dogmatism's inability to explain consciousness and freedom, for preferring idealism.) But now he moves closer to Spinoza, and to Schelling. In *The Way to the Blessed Life or the Doctrine of Religion* (1806) and in various other works of the period—including later reworkings of the *Wissenschaftslehre*—the 'infinite impulse' of the

I is no longer independent and self-sustaining, but emanates from an 'absolute being' (*Sein*) which cannot itself come into being, change, or pass away, and which Fichte also calls God, the Word (*Logos*), and the Absolute. Finite things are still deduced as products of consciousness. But the infinite activity of consciousness is now deduced from the end of 'imitating' God, and our vocation is more the 'blessed life' of contemplating God than moral activity. One of the problems that led Fichte to this conclusion seems to have been the difficulty of maintaining that the I that produces the world and that does not, until a fairly late stage of the *Wissenschaftslehre*, contrast with *other* Is ('you' and 's/he') is in any significant sense an 'I' rather than an 'it'. (Hegel contended that Fichte's absolute I amounts to much the same as pure being.)

Throughout his career Fichte held that the vocation of man is to restore on a higher plain the pure absolute from which the *Wissenschaftslehre* began, whether this be the I or being, and whether the restoration of it consist in philosophical or religious insight, moral perfection, or political harmony. Thus his thought operates on two levels. First, there is a logical development of the relation between the absolute (I, being) and its manifestation; this occurs in his more esoteric works. Second, there is a psychological history of the stages of reflection by which this logical relation is revealed to the finite subject; this tends to appear in his more popular works. In *Characteristics of the Present Age* (1806), he presented a universal history, advancing from the 'Arcadian' stage of 'instinctive reason', by way of the 'complete sinfulness' of the 'state based on needs' (*Nothstaat*), to the 'Elysian' stage of 'artistic reason'. Under the influence of Schiller, the aesthetic is assigned a crucial role in reconciling the antitheses of the *Wissenschaftslehre*. But in other works religion is more prominent than art. According to *The Way to the Blessed Life* absolute being is refracted by consciousness into an endless variety of individual forms. But this world of phenomena and its relation to the absolute is conceived by human reflection in five historically successive stages: (1) empirical phenomena are seen as the sole reality; (2) the ultimate reality is seen as a law-governed community of free, independent persons, with equal rights; (3) the heroic moral life devoted to the realization of the divine will, of the ideas underlying art, science, politics, and religion; (4) the religious withdrawal from heroic conduct into the recognition of all earthly life as a manifestation of the divine; (5) clear philosophical understanding of the plan of existence and of the unity of all men in a community of free intelligences with a common purpose: 'Religion without science is a mere faith, though an immovable faith; science supersedes all faith and converts it into insight.' At this last stage absolute being has in a sense been restored to its original purity.

Fichte's earlier thought had an immense influence on younger philosophers, especially Schelling and Hegel: Hegel's philosophical method, for example, derives largely from Fichte, and his *Phenomenology of Spirit* is the culmination of the tradition represented by Fichte's philosophical histories. Fichte also influenced the literary works of such Romantics as Novalis and their concept of irony: 'The three greatest tendencies of the age are the French revolution, Fichte's *Wissenschaftslehre*, and Goethe's *Wilhelm Meister*' (F. Schlegel).   M.J.I.

*Kantianism.

R. Adamson, *Fichte* (Edinburgh, 1881).

F. Copleston, *A History of Philosophy*, vii: *Modern Philosophy*, pt. 1: *Fichte to Hegel* (Westminster, Md., 1963).

D. Henrich, *Fichte's Original Insight*, in D. E. Christensen (ed.), *Contemporary German Philosophy*, i (University Park, Penn., 1982).

X. Léon, *Fichte et son temps*, 3 vols. (Paris, 1916–28).

E. Tugendhat, *Self-consciousness and Self-determination* (Cambridge, Mass., 1986).

Ficino, Marsilio (1433–99). Italian philosopher who produced Latin translations of all Plato's dialogues, along with a number of Neoplatonic works, making the complete corpus accessible to Western scholars for the first time. He also wrote commentaries on several of the dialogues, most notably the *Symposium* (1469), where he presented his influential theory of Platonic love as an attraction which moves from a physical to a spiritual plane, ultimately leading the lover to God. Shortly after being ordained a priest in 1473, he completed his *Theologia Platonica*, in which he demonstrated that rational confirmation of the Christian belief in the personal immortality of the soul could be found in the doctrines of the Platonists. He argued that *Platonism, unlike *Aristotelianism, was fundamentally compatible with Christianity and claimed for it a central place in the philosophical curriculum.   J.A.K.

*Neoplatonism.

G. C. Garfagnini (ed.), *Marsilio Ficino e il ritorno di Platone: Studi e documenti*, 2 vols. (Florence, 1986).

fiction. Fiction raises puzzles not only about what kind of thing fictional characters are, but also about our attitudes to what is not real. In reading a novel or seeing a drama, people apparently feel emotions towards or about the characters. Aristotle thought that it was essential to tragic drama, for instance, that the depicted course of events should arouse fear and pity in the spectator. However, some philosophers have contended that we cannot feel genuine emotions such as fear and pity, unless we believe a situation to be real. It is a common assumption that fiction is valuable because we are able to learn in a unique way from it, perhaps learning 'how to feel' certain things. How does this happen, if what we feel for fictions is not real *emotion?   C.J.

*fictional names.

C. Radford, 'How can we be Moved by the Fate of Anna Karenina?', *Proceedings of the Aristotelian Society* (1975).

fictional names. Names of fictional (including mythical) characters, places, etc., such as 'Emma Bovary',

'Huckleberry Finn', 'Dotheboys Hall', 'Santa Claus', 'Persephone'. Their use has puzzling features. 'Don Quixote' appears to refer to a fictional character. Yet surely fictional characters do not exist—otherwise they would not be fictional. But how can referring to a non-existent Don Quixote differ from failing to refer to anything? Further, if Austen's Mr Wickham did not exist, how can it be true—as it seems to be—that he eloped with Lydia Bennet? These puzzles have often prompted one or two responses: either fictional characters do somehow exist (but where? e.g. does Sherlock Holmes really live in *London*?) or typical sentences employing fictional names (e.g. 'Maigret smoked') are to be analysed differently from superficially similar sentences employing non-fictional names (e.g. 'Churchill smoked').   P.J.M.

*referring; names; existence.

D. Lewis, 'Truth in Fiction', *American Philosophical Quarterly* (1978).

fideism. Fideists hold that religious belief is based on faith rather than reason. Extreme fideists maintain that it is contrary to reason; moderate fideists argue that what must first be accepted on faith may subsequently find rational support. The maxim *credo quia absurdum est encapsulates the former view; the slogan *credo ut intelligam epitomizes the latter. There being no reason to prefer one absurdity to another, the commitments of extreme fideists are bound to seem arbitrary.   P.L.Q.

T. Penelhum, *God and Skepticism: A Study in Skepticism and Fideism* (Dordrecht, 1983).

Field, Hartry H. (1946–). American philosopher of language and *mathematics. Primarily influential through his fictionalist philosophy of mathematics—the Field programme. Quine and Putnam argue that since mathematics is indispensable in the formulation of scientific theories, any evidence for the truth of a scientific theory is equally evidence for the truth of the mathematical theory which is its essential part. Field's programme aims to undercut this argument in two steps. First, he claims that any scientific theory can be nominalistically rewritten, that is, formulated free from commitment to mathematical entities. Second, he aims to account for the evident usefulness of mathematical formulations of scientific theories by arguing that the mathematical formulations are advantageous because they lead to shorter proofs of nominalistic conclusions, but that those conclusions could be reached more long-windedly from nominalistic premises.   A.D.O.

H. H. Field, *Realism, Mathematics and Modality* (Oxford, 1989).

—— *Science without Numbers* (Oxford, 1980).

—— *Truth and the Absence of Fact* (Oxford, 2001).

field theory. The postulation of fields—regions under the influence of some force—allows the explanation of instantaneous interaction between spatially separated bodies (such as magnetic attraction or repulsion) without requiring *action at a distance. In modern physics, quantum field theory is arguably required in order to reconcile non-relativized *quantum mechanics with *Einstein's special relativity, and it is widely hoped that some version of this theory might provide a 'grand unified theory' or 'theory of everything' in which the four fundamental forces (gravity, electromagnetism, and the strong and weak nuclear forces) are shown to be manifestations of a single field. However, despite success in providing a unified explanation of the latter three forces, quantum field theory has yet to give a satisfactory account of gravity, and thereby remains inconsistent with general relativity, with some suggesting that a radically new physical theory will be needed. Field theory has also generated debate about whether the fundamental ontology of the world is one of fields, rather than individuable, localizable *particles.

S.R.A.

*Bell's theorem; Einstein, Podolsky, and Rosen paradox; energy; identity of indiscernibles; individuation; quantum theory and philosophy.

Marc Lange, *An Introduction to the Philosophy of Physics: Locality, Fields, Energy and Mass* (Oxford, 2002).
Paul Teller, *An Interpretative Introduction to Quantum Field Theory* (Princeton, 1995).

figures of the syllogism: *see* syllogism.

film, philosophy of. Analytic philosophers have written infrequently on the aesthetics of the film though there are some recent signs of increasing interest. It is the question of what is distinctive about the film, what is its essence, that has preoccupied most philosophers. A film is photographic and photographs are of reality or nature, as Cavell puts it. Scruton defines film as photographed dramatic representation. It is the fact that a photograph captures reality which makes film, like photography, unique in the way its creativity is somewhat displaced. It is then an easy move to the proposal that the use of some specific device such as montage is what is essential about film but, in truth, there is no single technique the exploitation of which typifies the major achievements in film, from *Citizen Kane* to *Heimat*. Far more than photography, film has followed traditions of its own making and its debts to painting or architecture are no greater than the influence of drama on opera or on *fiction or film's own influence on the novel. The question of realism has haunted philosophical writing on film in other ways; is the audience under an illusion that the events on the screen are real and present? Does a member of the audience assume the position of the camera? Does he or she identify with the eye of the camera?

R.A.S.

*poetry.

Noel Carroll, *Philosophical Problems of Classical Film Theory* (Princeton, NJ, 1988).
—— *The Philosophy of Mass Art* (Oxford, 1998).
Stanley Cavell, *The World Viewed: Reflections on the Ontology of the Film*, enlarged edn. (Cambridge, Mass., 1979).
V. F. Perkins, *Film as Film* (Harmondsworth, 1972).
Roger Scruton, *The Aesthetic Understanding* (London, 1983).

Filmer, Robert (1588–1653). English political philosopher who defended the divine right of kings. Sir Robert Filmer was an English landowner who wrote a number of Royalist pamphlets. These were not noticed in his lifetime. But after his death his best-known work, *Patriarcha; or, The Natural Power of Kings*, was published in 1680. The book is an attack on what Filmer saw as the two enemies of Royal power, the Jesuits and the Calvinists, and it stated two royalist principles: divine right and the duty of passive obedience. Filmer tried to show that the king's power is derived from the natural authority of parents. In other words, Adam was the first king. John Locke and others attacked the absurdity of this view. Unfortunately this side of Filmer's writings has obscured the fact that (borrowing from Hobbes) he launched a plausible attack on conceptions such as contract and consent as explanations of *political obligation.

R.S.D.

Sir Robert Filmer, *Patriarcha*, ed. with intro. and notes by Peter Laslett (Oxford, 1949).

final causes. One of Aristotle's 'four causes', the final cause is 'that for the sake of which', or the end or goal (Latin *finis*; Greek *telos*; hence *'teleological explanation'). To explain by citing a final cause is to explain something by reference to a goal that it serves. Aristotle invoked final causes throughout his scientific works, including many cases that appear not to involve genuine purpose (as when webbed feet are said to be for swimming). An emphasis on teleological explanation (shared by Plato) characterizes most subsequent Western philosophy of science until the seventeenth century. Whether final-cause explanations are legitimate where no agency is involved, and whether they can ever be fundamental explanations, are regarded as controversial issues by some philosophers.

P.J.M.

*causality.

J. L. Ackrill, *Aristotle the Philosopher* (Oxford, 1981), ch. 4.

Fine, Kit (1946–). Logician, metaphysician, and philosopher of mathematics, known for his contributions to modal logic and the metaphysics of *essence. Since the revival of essentialism in the 1970s through the work of *Saul Kripke in modal logic, it has been widely assumed that the concept of essence is to be explained through the concept of metaphysical *necessity, which is in turn to be explicated in terms of the concept of truth in every *possible world. Fine has argued that the proper direction of explanation is quite the reverse of this. To talk of something's essence is to talk of its very nature or identity. Thus, water is essentially H_2O, because it is in the very nature of any chemical compound to be composed in the way that it is. This is why it is metaphysically necessary that water is H_2O. In the philosophy of mathematics, Fine has developed a general theory of abstraction which provides a foundation for number theory and analysis.

E.J.L.

K. Fine, 'Essence and Modality', in *Philosophical Perspectives*, vol. 8, ed. J. Tomberlin (Atascadero, Calif., 1994).
—— *The Limits of Abstraction* (Oxford, 2002).

fingering slave

> Physician art thou?—one, all eyes,
> Philosopher!—a fingering slave,
> One that would peep and botanize
> Upon his mother's grave?
> (William Wordsworth, 'A Poet's
> Epitaph' (1800), lines 17–20)

Wordsworth's distaste for the philosopher is at least not exclusive, but meted out to the representatives of other professions—statesman, lawyer, soldier, doctor, moralist—whom he imagines approaching an anonymous grave at which he meditates. In fact a philosopher is not among them, but 'philosopher' is an exclamation against the allegedly philosopher-like doctor abhorred for an objectivity which denigrates its human objects. For Wordsworth, it seems, the essence of the philosopher, like that of the moralist for whom he reserves his greatest contempt, is cerebral detachment, a lack of the emotionality he so prized. Perhaps had he been writing today he would have used a word that is not attested till 1840—'scientist'.

J.O'G.

Finnis, John (1940–). Legal philosophy has been influenced by his assault on standard oppositions between *natural law and *legal positivism.

Oxford jurisprudence tutor from 1967, Professor of Law and Legal Philosophy in Oxford University from 1989, his doctoral thesis on the idea of judicial power was supervised by H. L. A. Hart, who commissioned *Natural Law and Natural Rights* (1980) for the Clarendon Law Series. Social theory cannot be value-free, it argues, and Humean ethics, unlike genuine (not neo-scholastic) Thomist ethics, commits a naturalistic fallacy. Finnis bases his radically rearticulated Aristotelian political and legal theory on dialectically defended first principles of practical reason and methodological principles of practical reasonableness (morality). Subsequently he has published *Fundamentals of Ethics* (1983); *Nuclear Deterrence, Morality and Realism* (1987; co-authors include Germain Grisez, on whose philosophical work Finnis openly builds); *Moral Absolutes* (1991); and *Aquinas* (1998).

R.P.G.

*law, philosophy of.

Finnish philosophy. Philosophy has played an important role in the scholarly and cultural life of Finland. Most of the actual philosophical work has, nevertheless, been done in an academic setting—when the University of Helsinki (originally located in Turku) was founded in 1640, philosophy merited two chairs out of eleven.

For a long time, Finnish academic philosophy was little more than a succession of international trends arriving in Finland one after the other, such as neo-Aristotelianism, Cartesianism, Wolffianism, Kantian philosophy, and Hegelianism. However, a unique twist was given to it by Johann Wilhelm Snellman (1805–81), who was not only the most important statesman in the history of the country, but an independent, forceful philosopher in the Hegelian tradition. Partly because of Snellman's impact as an ideologue and statesman, there has ever since been a keener awareness of the public role and general significance of philosophy in Finland than in almost any other country. Even recently, the main impact of some professional Finnish philosophers has been on the general cultural and ideological discussion in the country. Oiva Ketonen (1913–2000) was a distinguished case in point. Some philosophers have become public figures, not to say cult figures, most recently Esa Saarinen (1953–), alias 'Dr Punk' of the popular Press.

Hegelianism did not for very long remain a live force in professional philosophy itself. The main reaction came from a group of young radicals inspired largely by Darwinian ideas. This group included the first Finnish philosophers to have a significant international impact, Edvard Westermarck (1862–1939) in moral philosophy and social anthropology, and Yrjö Him (1870–1952) in aesthetics. Though antiquated, Westermarck's monumental studies *The History of Human Marriage* (1891) and *The Origin and Development of Moral Ideas* (1906–8) are classics in their fields, and his *Ethical Relativity* (1932) was a widely noted contribution to international discussion.

The contemporary philosophical scene in Finland has not been moulded by Westermarckian neo-Darwinism, however, but by a local version of *analytic philosophy, originally inspired largely by Eino Kaila (1890–1958). The label 'analytic' is, nevertheless, both accurate and inaccurate as applied to Kaila. It is historically accurate in that Kaila befriended the Logical Positivists and for a while participated in the discussions of the *Vienna Circle. It is psychologically inaccurate in that Kaila's ultimate stance was that of an old-fashioned philosopher of nature who tried to integrate the insights of contemporary physics, biology, and psychology into a grand philosophical synthesis.

By and large, the best work of subsequent Finnish philosophers has been in the analytic tradition. The philosophers influenced or inspired by Kaila include most notably G. H. von Wright (1916–2003) and Erik Stenius (1922–90). Stenius's early work was in logic and foundations of mathematics. Later he published an excellent book on Wittgenstein's *Tractatus* and a large number of articles known for their critical edge. Among Stenius's former students the best known is Ingmar Pörn (1935–).

Von Wright's early work was on the problem of *induction. He was a friend, later a trustee and a successor, of Ludwig Wittgenstein, and did a lot to bring about Wittgenstein's impact on contemporary philosophy. His own work was not overtly in the Wittgensteinian tradition, however, and included important contributions to modal logic, especially deontic logic, action theory, the problems of explanation and understanding, and ethics. Von Wright was also a most influential, widely respected public figure in Finland.

One of von Wright's former students is Jaakko Hintikka (1929–), who has also been active outside of Finland, mostly in the United States. Several of Finland's most active philosophers are Hintikka's former students or associates. The work of these philosophers and their contemporaries covers most of the field of analytic philosophy, especially philosophy of science, and amounts to a vigorous and extensive contribution to the international discussion in this area. Unlike many other analytic philosophers, the Finns have consistently maintained a strong interest also in the history of philosophy.   K.J.J.H.

*Darwinianism.

Radu J. Bogdan (ed.), *Jaakko Hintikka*, Profiles, viii (Dordrecht, 1987).

Iikka Niiniluoto, 'After Twenty Years: Philosophy of Science in Finland 1970–1990', *Journal for General Philosophy of Science* (1993).

—— et al. (eds.), *Eino Kaila and Logical Empiricism*, Acta Philosophica Fennica, lii (Helsinki, 1992).

P. A. Schilpp and L. E. Hahn (eds.), *The Philosophy of Georg Henrik von Wright*, Library of Living Philosophers, xix (La Salle, Ill., 1989).

Timothy Stroup (ed.), *Edward Westermarck: Essays on his Life and Works*, Acta Philosophica Fennica, xxxiv (Helsinki, 1982).

fire: *see* Bachelard.

first cause argument. This argument for God's existence assumes that each natural thing's existence is caused by something other than itself. It argues there cannot be an infinite series of such causes and concludes there is a first cause of existence whose existence is not caused by something other than itself. Further argument is needed to show there is only one such cause and it has such traditional divine attributes as perfect goodness.   P.L.Q.

*God, arguments against existence; God, arguments for existence; prime mover.

W. L. Craig, *The Cosmological Argument from Plato to Leibniz* (New York, 1980).

first-person perspective: *see* dualism.

five ways. Aquinas's five ways of proving God's existence are based on the necessity of positing (1) a first changer in various observable series of changes; (2) a first efficient cause in various observable causal set-ups; (3) an absolutely necessary being, given the existence of contingent beings; (4) a *maximum* item to ground certain comparatives in particular goodness; and (5) 'some intelligent being . . . by whom all natural things are directed'.   J.J.M.

*God, arguments against existence; God, arguments for existence.

A. Kenny, *The Five Ways* (London, 1969).

flaccid designator. A term designating different objects in different *possible worlds. More precisely, a singular term that would designate different objects if certain circumstances other than its meaning were different. A *definite description like 'the thirty-fifth President of the United States' is a flaccid designator. The term actually designates John F. Kennedy. But if Richard Nixon had won the 1960 election, Nixon would have been the thirty-

fifth President. In that case, 'the thirty-fifth President' would have designated Nixon. Hence 'The thirty-fifth President might not have been the thirty-fifth President' is true on one interpretation. Flaccid designators are opposed to *rigid designators, which designate the same object in all possible cases. A proper *name like 'John F. Kennedy' is rigid. Even if Nixon had won the 1960 election, for example, 'John F. Kennedy' would have designated John F. Kennedy. 'Kennedy might not have been Kennedy' is unequivocally nonsensical.   W.A.D.

Saul Kripke, *Naming and Necessity* (Cambridge, Mass., 1980).

flesh: *see* Merleau-Ponty.

flow of the wind: *see* Korean philosophy.

flux. Everything is in flux according to Heraclitus, who is reputed to have said that 'everything flows', and that 'you cannot step into the same river twice'. The idea, in Plato's interpretation, was that the world consists entirely of perceived items each one of which is relative to the perceiver and time of perception with no place for a stable, objective reality. Plato and Aristotle exposed fatal weaknesses in the view.   O.R.J.

*process.

Myles Burnyeat, *The* Theaetetus *of Plato* (Indianapolis, 1990).

focal meaning. Aristotle's account of the *meanings of grammatically different variations of the same word—'health', 'healthy', and 'healthful', for example—which say different but systematically related things about items of different sorts. Foods and exercises are called healthful because of their connection with health, while organisms are called healthy if they possess health. On Aristotle's account, the words 'healthy' and 'healthful' derive their meanings from what constitutes health, and thus from the meaning of the term 'health'. G. E. L. Owen coined the term 'focal meaning' for this account because it treats the meaning of one member of a family of grammatical variants as the focus toward which explanations of the meanings of the others converge.   J.B.B.

G. E. L. Owen, *Logic, Science, and Dialectic: Collected Papers in Greek Philosophy*, ed. M. Nussbaum (London, 1986), 184 ff.

Fodor, Jerry A. (1935–). American philosopher who has been one of the leading figures in the recent attempt to unify the philosophy of mind with *cognitive science. Against the background of his early influences—Putnam's *functionalism and Chomsky's innatism—Fodor has defended an influential conception of the mind, according to which there are laws of *folk psychology which are underpinned by the computational structure of mental processes. Central to his theory is his bold hypothesis that we think in a *'language of thought': a computational system of symbols, realized in the neural structure of the brain, with semantic and syntactic properties. The nub of the language-of-thought hypothesis is that thinking has a causal structure that mirrors the logical structure of trains of thought. More recently, Fodor has been preoccupied with providing a naturalistic account of the semantics of the sentences of the language of thought.   T.C.

Jerry A. Fodor, *Psychosemantics: The Problem of Meaning in the Philosophy of Mind* (Cambridge, Mass., 1987).
—— *Concepts: Where Cognitive Science Went Wrong* (Oxford, 1998).

Fogelin, Robert J. (1932–). American philosopher who taught at Yale University before moving to Dartmouth College. As his collection *Philosophical Interpretations* (1992) shows, he has worked extensively in the history of philosophy, his work insisting on taking seriously authors' own views of the meaning and importance of their writings. His books reflect his major interests in *Wittgenstein* (1976) and *Hume's Skepticism in the* Treatise of Human Nature (1985). The latter has contributed to reversing a tendency to play down Hume's avowed scepticism. But Fogelin has also written in the area of informal logic and the philosophy of language: his first published book was concerned with meaning and verification, and *Figuratively Speaking* (1988) is an elegant examination of *metaphor and other kinds of non-literal discourse.   C.J.H.

folk psychology. The subject-matter of people's everyday understanding of one another in psychological, or mental, terms; contrasted with scientific, or experimental, psychology.

In recent philosophy, it is sometimes supposed that the basis of our ability to explain and predict what other people will do, using terms like 'believes' and 'desires', is a *theory* which we know implicitly, acquired as we came to gain psychological understanding. The question can be raised how this theory, named folk psychology, relates to others—in the first instance how it relates to scientific psychology, and then how it relates to neuroscientific theories of brains' workings. Traditional questions about the relation between mind and body come to be recast as questions about relations between different theories; and *eliminativism can be stated as the doctrine that folk psychology is a false theory.

Folk psychology may be denied the status of theory. Questions can still be raised about its relations to other subject-matters; but these will not now be questions about intertheoretic relations.   J.HORN.

M. Davies and T. Stone (eds.), *Folk Psychology* (Oxford, 1995).
John D. Greenwood (ed.), *The Future of Folk Psychology* (Cambridge, 1991).

Føllesdal, Dagfinn (1932–). Norwegian philosopher, interpreter of Husserl to analytic philosophers. Føllesdal was educated mainly at the University of Oslo and at Harvard University, where he taught from 1961 to 1964. He is a professor at the University of Oslo (1967–) and at Stanford University (1968–).

In the philosophy of language, Føllesdal emphasized the need of 'genuine singular terms' before Kripke, who renamed them *'rigid designators'. Føllesdal has also discussed the normative element in reference and the reasons for the *indeterminacy of translation in the social nature of language.

Føllesdal has put forward influential interpretations of Husserl's philosophy, which he considers as a generalized meaning theory. For instance, Husserlian noema is a generalization of meaning to the realm of acts. Føllesdal does not consider Husserl as a foundationalist but claims that for Husserl ultimate justification is like Rawls's *'reflective equilibrium'.   K.J.J.H.

Dagfinn Føllesdal, 'Husserl's Notion of Noema', *Journal of Philosophy* (1969).

Foot, Philippa R. (1920–). Best known for her work in moral philosophy, Professor Foot wrote two highly influential articles in the 1950s arguing against *prescriptivism, the analysis of ethical belief and judgement propounded by R. M. Hare. In these papers ('Moral Arguments' (1958), 'Moral Beliefs' (1958)), she argues that moral beliefs must concern traits and behaviour that are demonstrably beneficial or harmful to humans, and that what shall be regarded as beneficial or harmful is not a matter for human decision. Moral beliefs cannot, therefore, be dependent on human decision. For the better part of a decade, the controversy between her brand of naturalistic ethics and Hare's views was at the forefront of Anglo-Saxon moral philosophy. More recently her work has been concentrated on *virtue theory and on the limits of utilitarianism. For many years a Fellow of Somerville College, Oxford, she has also held many posts in America. Many of her best-known articles are collected in Philippa Foot, *Virtues and Vices* (Oxford, 1978).   N.J.H.D.

*conscience; fact–value distinction.

P. R. Foot, *Natural Goodness* (Oxford, 2001).

footnotes to Plato. A. N. Whitehead once wrote that 'the safest general characterization' of Western thought is that 'it consists of a series of footnotes to Plato'. This testy assessment of an entire tradition is often recited by Platonists and has earned for Whitehead the accolades of the aphorism crowd.

The great thinkers of the past certainly did not think that they were adding footnotes to Plato's text. Had Kant thought he was adding one, he would surely have kept the *Critique of Pure Reason* under 500 pages. And should Wittgenstein have suspected that he was producing scholia, he would have spent at least a little time reading the text.

Interestingly, those who say that all subsequent thought is a footnote to Plato or to ancient sages also complain of wholesale and lamentable modern innovations. Aside from the inconsistency, this raises the question what counts as a footnote. Does Descartes, who subverted the starting-point of ancient philosophy, constitute no more than an afterthought to it? Should Hume, who rejected both its premises and its conclusions in favour of his own original views, get no credit beyond having discovered a new wrinkle on wisdom's old face? Can we even think that in his stunning synthesis of everything ancient and modern, Hegel rehearsed only what Plato had always known?

To be sure, sometimes those who wish to write footnotes to Plato manage to establish only a feeble connection with the original text. But this does not imply that philosophical works taking little or no account of anything Plato said are oblique or unsuccessful commentaries on his thought. Supposing that they are makes it impossible to appreciate their novelty and difficult to see their point. It amounts, moreover, to an affront to the integrity of philosophers and a cynical assessment of the significance of their field.

Possibly, however, Whitehead's statement was made in the spirit of rampageous over-generalization one can expect from footnoters to Plato. If so, it must be taken with a grain of salt or greeted by rolling one's eyes. But even then, in one clear respect, the claim he makes is false. For the *safest* way to deal with the history of Western thought is not to characterize it in general terms at all.
                                                              J.LAC.

*philosophy; ancient philosophy; Platonism.

René Descartes, *Meditations on First Philosophy*, in *The Philosophical Works of Descartes* (Cambridge, 1967).
G. W. F. Hegel, *Phenomenology of Spirit* (Oxford, 1977).
David Hume, *A Treatise of Human Nature* (Oxford, 1958).
Immanuel Kant, *Critique of Pure Reason* (London, 1953).
A. E. Taylor, *Plato: The Man and his Work* (London, 1937).
A. N. Whitehead, *Process and Reality* (New York, 1978).

foreknowledge: *see* prediction.

forgery. In art, forgery can mean imitating someone's style, or passing an exact duplicate off as a specific work. The latter raises questions about the nature of artworks. A duplicate painting would be a *distinct* work from the original. But if I write down exactly the notes that make up the 'Moonlight' Sonata, have I not simply copied it out again? If my indistinguishable copy were played to an unsuspecting audience instead of Beethoven's, would they be hearing a forgery? Some would argue that an intentional duplicate of a sonata or novel does not succeed in being a distinct work at all. On the other hand, there are strong arguments for saying that historical context and authorial intentions determine the identity of a work—in which case, my piece and Beethoven's might be distinct though sharing the same notes.   C.J.

*lying; plagiarism.

N. Goodman, *Languages of Art* (Indianapolis, 1968), ch. 3.

forgiveness. To forgive someone is to hold him or her excused from an offence, even in one's thoughts, while still acknowledging his or her *responsibility for the offence. It is, perhaps, only appropriately granted by those affected by the offence. Unlike the granting of a pardon, which may be merely a permitting to go unpunished, the act of forgiveness involves a refusal to blame. However,

the relationship of forgiveness to both contrition and *punishment is imprecise: the possibility of forgiveness appears to make remorse possible and prevents *desert being a sufficient condition of the latter. Though an essential element of all personal relationships, the importance of forgiveness is not much reflected in contemporary ethical theory.   P.W.

*revenge.

J. G. Murphy and J. Hampton, *Forgiveness and Mercy* (Cambridge, 1988).

for-itself and in-itself. The distinction drawn by Sartre between the mode of being of *consciousness ('being for-itself') and that of other things ('being in-itself'). This is not a dualism of substances, since Sartre holds that consciousness is not a substance: it is the view that there are two kinds of truth. But it remains problematic: Sartre's being in-itself is as inaccessible as Kant's *thing-in-itself, and being for-itself relies on a questionable conception of consciousness.   T.R.B.

J.-P. Sartre, *Being and Nothingness*, tr. H. Barnes (London, 1958), intro.

fork, Hume's. Term applied today to Hume's distinction between relations of ideas and matters of fact. Relations of ideas—like the proposition that 'three times five is half of thirty'—are 'discoverable by the mere operation of thought, without dependence on what is anywhere existent in the universe'. Matters of fact—like the proposition that 'the sun will rise tomorrow'—cannot be demonstrated by thought alone, and are contingent, in that their negation is conceivable. Hume's distinction includes elements of the three current distinctions between necessary and *contingent, *a priori and a posteriori, and *analytic and synthetic—and he seems to presume that the three distinctions coincide. This supposition has been challenged in various ways: it leaves no place for the synthetic a priori, which Kant placed at the centre of metaphysics, nor for contingent a priori and necessary a posteriori propositions, of which Kripke has recently proposed examples.

The term has also been applied to Hume's related distinction between 'demonstrative' argument (such as deduction) and 'probable' (or causal) reasoning. Hume uses the dichotomy repeatedly to pose a dilemma for rationalists. If reason tells us, say, that the future resembles the past, then it must be by *demonstrative* arguments or *probable*. But demonstrative arguments cannot prove the uniformity of nature—since non-uniformity is conceivable. And probable arguments cannot prove it either—since probable arguments themselves presuppose the uniformity of nature, hence it would be circular to employ them in support of that uniformity. For another use, see the entry 'reason as slave of the passions'.

Hume's *Enquiry Concerning Human Understanding* ends with a dramatic employment of the fork, beloved of Logical Positivists in the 1930s for making havoc with false metaphysics. 'If we take in our hand any volume; of divinity or school metaphysics, for instance; let us ask, *Does it contain any abstract reasoning concerning quantity or number?* No. *Does it contain any experimental reasoning concerning matter of fact and existence?* No. Commit it then to the flames: for it can contain nothing but sophistry and illusion.'   J.BRO.

*Logical Positivism; verification principle.

David Hume, *Enquiry Concerning Human Understanding*, pt. iii, sect. 4 and 12.
Antony Flew, *Hume's Philosophy of Belief* (London, 1961), ch. 3.

form, logical. The logical form of a sentence—or of the *proposition expressed by the sentence—is a structure assigned to the sentence in order to explain how the sentence can be used in logical arguments, or how the meaning of the sentence is built up from the meanings of its component parts. A translation of a sentence into logical notation is sometimes called its 'logical form'. Views differ on the reality and uniqueness of logical forms, and whether they are in some way prior to the sentences which have them. Analytic philosophers have seen it as a goal of philosophy to uncover the logical forms of propositions. Chomsky and other linguists have argued that a *grammar of a natural language should show how to ascribe logical forms to sentences.   W.A.H.

G. Preyer and G. Peter (eds.), *Logical Form and Language* (Oxford, 2002).

formal and material mode. Influenced by developments in foundations of mathematics, Carnap elaborated on the claim that formal features of a language (L) are clearly distinguishable from semantical features. Formal features of L are given by its syntax, which includes a sorted vocabulary, formation rules for *well-formed formulae, as well as transformation rules for deriving sentences from sentences.

Genuine object sentences of an interpreted language L are not translatable into syntactical sentences about L. It is claimed, however, that there are sentences which seem to be genuine object sentences (characterized as pseudo-object sentences) but which are translatable into sentences about L's syntax. The former are said to be in the material mode, the latter are said to be in the formal mode.

Material mode sentences are often unproblematic. However, some are seen as generating confusions resolvable by translation into the formal mode. Examples adapted from Carnap are the two sentences:

5 and 3 + 2 are the same.
5 and 3 + 2 are equal but not the same.

in the material mode, which are, in the language of arithmetic, both translatable into the single formal mode sentence:

The expressions '5' and '3 + 2' are interchangeable *salva veritate.

The words 'formal' and 'material' were first applied to the distinction in the Middle Ages, but the other way round.
                                                                      R.B.M.
R. Carnap, *Logical Syntax of Language* (London, 1937).

formalism. A number of philosophical views concerning mathematics go by this name. They all seem to focus on the extent to which mathematical proof can be construed or modelled as the following of mechanical rules on sequences of typographic characters. The formulae may as well be meaningless, as far as the philosophies are concerned. One aim is to provide a tractable epistemology for mathematics while avoiding commitment to a presumably dubious ontology.

Opponents of formalism claim that mathematics is inherently informal and perhaps even non-mechanical. Mathematical language has meaning and it is a gross distortion to attempt to ignore this. At best, formalism focuses on a small aspect of mathematics, deliberately leaving aside what is essential to the enterprise.

One version of formalism, which might be called 'game formalism', holds that the essence of mathematics is the following of meaningless rules. Mathematics is likened to the play of a game like chess, where characters written on paper play the role of pieces to be moved. All that matters is that the rules have been followed correctly.

Many formalist programmes are connected to developments in mathematical logic earlier this century. (*Logic, history of.) Formal languages and deductive systems were formulated with mathematical rigour, and the systems themselves became objects of mathematical study. Such efforts became known as *metamathematics*. Presumably, the essence of metamathematics goes beyond the mere following of meaningless rules. Its goal is to shed light on a subject-matter, namely formal languages and deductive systems. Thus, a game formalist would either demur at this point, or else hold that metamathematics is not mathematics—an oxymoron at best. But not all formalists are game-formalists.

David Hilbert and his followers held that the only meaningful, or 'contentful', parts of mathematics consist of finitary assertions about finitary objects, like natural numbers. This includes particular statements like '234 + 123 = 357' and generalizations like '$a + b = b + a$', made with free variables. It does not include statements, like 'for every n there is a p greater than n, such that p and $p + 2$ are both prime', that contain bound variables ranging over an infinite domain. The infinitary, or 'ideal', parts of mathematics, including analysis and set theory, have value only in the role of facilitating the production of finitary, contentful statements. In each case, we need to be assured that the use of ideal mathematics does not yield anything incorrect about the finitary part. (*Instrumentalism.) The Hilbert programme called for each branch of mathematics to be formalized and for the formalisms to be studied metamathematically. Noting that the subject-matter of metamathematics—sequences of characters—is finitary, Hilbert declared that metamathematics be conducted with only finitary means. Then, once the consistency of a formal deductive system is established, the system can confidently be used to produce finitary results. (*Consistency proofs.)

The ensuing metamathematical research culminated with Gödel's incompleteness theorems, which dealt a serious blow to the Hilbert programme. In particular, the 'second' theorem is that if Peano arithmetic is consistent, then its own consistency cannot be established by methods codified in that system, let alone in a finitary fragment. The same goes for classical analysis, set theory, and virtually any other sufficiently rich formal system. If the theory is consistent, its consistency cannot be established in the system itself.

Another formalist philosophy of mathematics was presented by Haskell Curry. The programme depends on a historical thesis that as a branch of mathematics develops, it becomes more and more rigorous in its methodology, the end-result being the codification of the branch in formal deductive systems. Curry claimed that assertions of a mature mathematical theory should be construed not so much as the results of moves *in* a particular formal deductive system (as a game-formalist might say), but rather as assertions *about* a formal system. An assertion at the end of a research paper would be interpreted in the form: 'Such and such is a theorem in this formal system.' For Curry, then, mathematics is an objective science, and it has a subject matter—formal systems. In effect, mathematics is metamathematics. Constructively established results in metamathematics count as legitimate mathematics. (*Constructivism.) Non-constructive results in metamathematics, like most of model theory, are accommodated by producing a formal system for metamathematics, and construing the results in question as theorems about that formal system.   S.S.

*mathematics, problems of the philosophy of; mathematics, history of the philosophy of.

Paul Benacerraf and Hilary Putnam (eds.), *Philosophy of Mathematics*, 2nd edn. (Cambridge, 1983).
Haskell Curry, *Outlines of a Formalist Philosophy of Mathematics* (Amsterdam, 1951).
Michael Detlefsen, *Hilbert's Program* (Dordrecht, 1986).
Michael Resnik, *Frege and the Philosophy of Mathematics* (Ithaca, NY, 1980).

formalism, ethical: *see* ethical formalism.

formalization. To formalize something, such as an argument, is to spell it out in a formal, or perhaps semi-formal, language, such as the *predicate calculus. The purpose may simply be to render perspicuous something that was not so perspicuous in the original. Or it may be to display what is thought to be the *logical form of the original. In either case, certain assumptions will need to be made about the relation of ordinary language to formal languages. One strand in the 'ordinary-language philosophy' of the 1950s and 1960s was an attitude of suspicion towards formalization in philosophy (apart, of course,

from philosophy of logic and maths). Some might think that the pendulum has swung rather too far back now; certainly, the aim of perspicuity is often better served by a lucid vernacular than by symbols.   R.P.L.T.

M. Sainsbury, *Logical Forms* (Oxford, 1991).

formal language. A formal language is a language two of whose features are formally specified: the linguistic symbols of the language and rules for joining together or concatenating these symbols into *well-formed formulae or words which can be assigned precise meanings. In standard first-order logic the formal language consists of variables, constants, logical connectives, function and relational symbols, parentheses, and quantifiers, together with rules for the construction of well-formed formulae. Kurt Gödel discovered a method for assigning natural numbers to the well-formed formulae of standard first-order theory, and this discovery provided the basis for the proof of his famous incompleteness theorem. The development of formal languages for computer programs in the 1950s was inspired by the established formal languages used by logicians.   G.F.M.

R. Wilder, *Introduction to the Foundations of Mathematics* (New York, 1952).

formal logic: *see* logic, formal or symbolic.

formal semantics, the philosophical relevance of. Philosophers and logicians have developed mathematically precise ways to study the relationship between a language and its subject-matter by using methods originally developed for the interpretation of formal systems in logic. The extension of this framework from formal to natural languages is justified by adopting Frege's truth-conditional approach to meaning. The key idea here is that since a declarative sentence can represent the world as being a certain way, the meaning of a sentence can be given by stating the conditions the world has to meet for things to be as the sentence says they are. These are *truth-conditions. To give the meaning of every sentence of the language we must specify the truth-conditions of each declarative sentence, then relate non-declarative to declarative sentences. Formal semantics addresses the former task, the theory of force attempts the latter.

*Semantics studies the relation between language and the world, but the relationship is complicated by the fact that sentences are also inferentially related to one another. For example, by sharing some of the same parts, sentences can be about the same thing, and can even contradict one another. When logical connections obtain between sentences, the truth of one may require or preclude the truth of others. So in relating language to the world these connections must be preserved to ensure the right patterns amongst the truth-values assigned to whole sentences.

Logicians first studied these connections in the context of formal systems: languages in which we construct proofs by applying rules of inference to formulae built up from a fixed set of rules and symbols. To ensure that inferences rules are valid (i.e. that their transitions are truth-preserving) we must interpret the formal language, provide definitions for the truth of its formulae, then discover whether the inferential relations are logical consequences, permitting only the derivation of truths from truths.

Interpretations, or models, of these systems are specified in terms of abstract mathematical structures. First we specify a structure, and then construct an interpretation function by assigning elements of the structure to the basic symbols of the language as their semantic values. The semantic values of complex expressions are then defined inductively in terms of the values of their simpler parts. In this way, the truth-value of a formula is determined by the semantic values of its parts, the syntactic arrangement of the formula, and relations in the structure between those semantic values. Formulae true in all models are *logical truths*; truth links which hold in all models are *logical consequences*.

Model-theoretic and truth-theoretic semantics provide the two leading versions of truth-conditional semantics for natural language. Model theory maps sentences and their parts on to configurations of elements in the domain, or structure, of a model. The mapping reveals meaning-connections between sentences by exhibiting relations between configurations in the domain. Sentences which share parts will have elements of their truth-conditions in common; namely, the entity, or entities, assigned to those expressions. By this mapping we can plot relations between sentences as represented by the patterns amongst the objects, properties, and relations assigned to expressions which figure in those sentences. Each set of assignments, or model, corresponds to a world in which some of those sentences are true and others are false.

The best-worked-out semantics for a fragment of English occurs in Richard Montague's paper 'The Proper Treatment of Quantification in Ordinary English', in which set-theoretical constructs used in specifying the models are not restricted to domains of real entities but include objects existing in other possible worlds and at other times. Thus *possible world semantics* can be carried out model-theoretically to provide truth-conditions for sentences not just in the actual world but in all possible worlds.

Truth theory offers another version of the truth-conditional approach to meaning. Drawing on the work of Tarski in defining truth for formalized languages, a truth theory aims to state the truth-conditions for every declarative sentence of the language *L* by proving every *T*-sentence of the form:

(*T*) *S* is true-in-*L* if and only if *p*,

where the metalanguage 'is true-in-*L*' is appended to a sentence *S* of the object language *L* when and only when certain conditions *p* obtain. Proof of each instance of *T* proceeds from axioms which assign references to the simple parts of the object-language sentence, together with axioms that state the consequences for truth of combining those expressions in sentences. A truth theory for a language is a finite set of such axioms. Davidson has argued that such theories can serve as theories of meaning.

In the early 1980s a new paradigm, called situation semantics, was developed by Barwise and Perry. It treats utterances as containing not only information about the world, as in model-theoretic semantics, but also information about speakers and their relations to the world. Sentence-meanings are not given by truth-conditions, but defined in terms of relations between situations, the utterance being itself a situation which carries information used in interpreting the sentence. Meaning-connections between sentences reflect the relation of one situation-type to another; e.g. kissing involves touching. More work is needed, however, before this serves as a competitor to truth-conditional semantics.   B.C.S.

*snow is white.

J. Barwise and J. Perry, *Situations and Attitudes* (Cambridge, Mass., 1983).

M. Davies, *Meaning, Quantification, Necessity* (London, 1981).

R. Dowty, R. Wall, and S. Peters, *Introduction to Montague Semantics* (Dordrecht, 1981).

G. Evans and J. McDowell (eds.), *Truth and Meaning* (Oxford, 1976).

M. Platts, *Ways of Meaning* (London, 1979).

form and matter. The complementary notions of form and *matter are wholly central to the metaphysical theories of Plato and Aristotle, indeed to all ancient and modern metaphysical inquiry. Most primitively, the matter of any item is the stuff, the material of which it is made, for example clay or iron; the form is the organization, shape, pattern given to that stuff by a craftsman, for example by a potter in making a bowl. From such elementary beginnings the most difficult and exciting metaphysical theses have evolved, such as Plato's theory of Forms (or Ideas), where Forms were conceived of as separate existents which were, somehow, responsible for particulars being of the kind they were. Aristotle, by contrast, believed in immanent forms; the only real existents are already parcels of informed matter or enmattered form. Neither *prime matter (formless and inchoate), nor pure forms, can exist independently. Debates over matter and form merge into debates over *universals; and, although not central to the current agenda of metaphysical debate, these notions are, in some fashion or another, indispensable in thinking about the world and its structure.   N.J.H.D.

*Forms, Platonic.

Jonathan Lear, *Aristotle: The Desire to Understand* (Cambridge, 1988) is useful on this topic.

form of life. An expression which occurs six times in Wittgenstein's published works. Much used by some *Wittgensteinians, it has occasioned exegetical controversy. Wittgenstein employed it to indicate the roots of language and of agreement in application of linguistic rules, in consensual, regular forms of behaviour. This includes natural, species-specific action and response, as well as concept-laden, acculturated activities. Speaking a language is part of a form of life (a culture) and to imagine a language is to imagine a form of life. What has to be accepted, the given, is not the empiricist's mythical sense-data constituting the foundations of knowledge, but forms of life that lie beyond being justified or unjustified.

P.M.S.H.

G. P. Baker and P. M. S. Hacker, *An Analytical Commentary on the Philosophical Investigations*, ii: *Wittgenstein: Rules, Grammar and Necessity* (Oxford, 1985), 238–43.

Forms, Platonic. The word 'Form' is used to translate Plato's Greek word *idea*, which is sometimes transliterated into English as 'Idea'. From an etymological point of view the Greek word means the look of a thing, but it was commonly extended to mean a sort, kind, or type of thing. (Compare the Latin word *species*.) What is called Plato's theory of Forms (or Ideas) is a theory about sorts, kinds, or types, and its main claim is that a type exists independently of whether or not there are things of that type. It appears that Plato was led to the theory in the first place by considering such types as the type of person who is virtuous, but he then extended it to many other types.   D.B.

*Aristotle; cave, analogy of; metaphysics, the history of; phenomena and noumena; Plato; Platonism; third-man argument; transcendentalism.

Almost any book on Plato will say something of his theory of Forms. A classic treatment is W. D. Ross, *Plato's Theory of Ideas* (Oxford, 1951).

formula. The word has no very rigid meaning, but in logic it is customarily applied to written expressions that are strings of symbols containing no words. A formal language consists of a vocabulary of symbols—e.g. 'P', 'x', '$\forall$', '$($'—together with rules determining which strings of them are well formed. The well-formed formulae may then be manipulated mathematically; or they may be 'interpreted' (e.g. as *schemas, or as having meanings); or both.   C.A.K.

Foucault, Michel (1926–84). French intellectual whose politically as well as philosophically motivated examinations of obscure historical materials were aimed at diagnosing the present. He called his early books archaeologies. Although they appear concerned with origins, Foucault insisted that his topic was the implicit knowledge that underlay and made possible specific practices, institutions, and theories: *Madness and Civilization* (1961), on the birth of the asylum, offered an archaeology of how the exchange between madness and reason was silenced; *The Birth of the Clinic* (1963) was 'An Archaeology of the Medical Gaze'; and *The Order of Things* (1966) was 'An Archaeology of the Human Sciences'. In his theoretical manifesto, *The Archaeology of Knowledge* (1969), Foucault redefined archaeology as the set of discourses that constitute 'the archive'.

Foucault's inaugural lecture at the Collège de France, 'The Discourse on Language' (1971), was a transitional text in which he subordinated archaeology to the critical analysis of forms of exclusion and to the genealogical study of the formation of *discourse. Out of concern for prison reform, Foucault returned to the history of practices in *Discipline and Punish* (1975) with a study of the birth of the nineteenth-century prison. He developed its account of the interaction of knowledge and *power further in *The Will to Knowledge* (1976), the first volume of a projected six-volume *History of Sexuality*.

Foucault ultimately came to recognize that what interested him about power was how it produced the subject. The *History of Sexuality* was redesigned to present a genealogy of the desiring subject, conceived on the model of Nietzsche's *Genealogy of Morals; The Use of Pleasure* and *The Care of the Self* studied Greek and Roman texts on the art of living. The theory of historical discontinuity that is still often associated with Foucault's name does not apply to these works and really applies only to *The Order of Things*.   R.L.B.

J. W. Bernauer, *Michel Foucault's Force of Flight* (Atlantic Highlands, NJ, 1990).

G. Deleuze, *Foucault* (Minneapolis, 1988).

foundationalism. The theory that *knowledge of the world rests on a foundation of indubitable beliefs from which further propositions can be inferred to produce a superstructure of known truths. Traditionally, it is beliefs about our sense experience that have formed the foundation, with beliefs about the external world forming the superstructure. However, the assumption that beliefs about sense experience are infallible has come in for heavy criticism, witness Sellars's attack on the 'myth of the *given'.   O.R.J.

*boat, Neurath's.

Jonathan Dancy, *Introduction to Contemporary Epistemology* (Oxford, 1985).

Wilfrid Sellars, *Science, Perception and Reality* (London, 1963), ch. 5, sects. 3–11.

foundationalism in mathematics. Foundationalism is the view that a body of knowledge, such as mathematics (or one of its branches such as arithmetic or analysis), ought to be built on an absolutely secure epistemic foundation. The foundationalist begins with axioms that are self-evident, or, failing that, axioms that are as certain as possible. One might argue, for example, that the truth of the axioms is presupposed by all thought: they cannot be doubted if one is to think at all. The foundationalist derives the truths of the area of knowledge from the axioms using absolutely reliable inferences, a logic which is self-evidently valid. General foundationalism, traced to rationalists like *Descartes, is not widely held any more, but the mathematical version survived well into the twentieth century, if not beyond, motivated in part by the logical and semantic paradoxes. *Gödel's incompleteness theorems dealt a blow to foundationalism concerning mathematics. If a mathematical theory is sufficiently rich, and if the set of axioms and the consequence relation used in the derivations are both effective, then either some truths cannot be derived, or some non-truths can be derived (assuming bivalence). At best, the foundationalist can only claim to have secured the basic truths of mathematics.   S.S.

Stewart Shapiro, *Foundations without Foundationalism: A Case for Second-Order Logic* (Oxford, 1991).

Four Freedoms. Asserted in their canonical form by US President Franklin Delano Roosevelt on 6 January 1941 in his State of the Union address to Congress as the 'four essential human freedoms': freedom of speech and expression, freedom of every person to worship God in his own way, freedom from want, and freedom from fear. They are usually cited in abbreviated form as freedom of speech and of religion, and freedom from want and from fear. Widely regarded during the Second World War as a succinct statement of the Allied war aims, despite notable failures to achieve these 'freedoms' among the Allies. The Four Freedoms are a concise anticipation of what would later become the various 'human rights' declared by the United Nations General Assembly in its 1948 Declaration of Human Rights.   H.A.B.

*freedom; liberty.

Four Noble Truths: *see* Buddhist philosophy.

four-term fallacy. A *syllogism with four, rather than three, terms commits this fallacy. Since the requirement that it must have three terms is generally specified in the definition of a syllogism, it is pointless to regard four terms as a fallacy, and arbitrary to specify four as opposed to any number other than three. This is probably why the four-term fallacy has often been conflated with the 'fallacy of equivocation', i.e. *ambiguity.   C.W.

C. L. Hamblin, *Fallacies* (London, 1970), 44–5, 197–9.

frame problem. An important feature of human intelligence is that people are able to make selective topical use of long-stored background knowledge, and know how to adjust their thinking or behaviour appropriately in the light of new information. They know when to ignore new information as irrelevant, and when and how to take it into account in determining how to proceed. It is difficult to see how exercising these abilities can just be a matter of following a predetermined routine or set of rules, of the sort that might be embodied in a computer programme. For example, although it may be possible to reduce to a set of rules the behaviour typically involved in ordering a meal in a restaurant, people do not slavishly follow such rules, because one's actual behaviour in a restaurant is always sensitive to unforeseen contingencies, such as the unexpected arrival of an old friend or, more alarmingly, the occurrence of an earthquake. The difficulty which this presents for any attempt to replicate or mimic human intelligence by means of a computer programme is known as the frame problem.   E.J.L.

Z. W. Pylyshyn (ed.), *The Robot's Dilemma: The Frame Problem of Artificial Intelligence* (Norwood, NJ, 1987).

Frankena, William K. (1908–94). Influential American philosopher, at the University of Michigan for more than forty years. His first published paper was a telling critique of G. E. Moore's notion of the *naturalistic fallacy. By his own account ('Concluding More or Less Philosophical Postscript') Frankena in his earliest period was 'cognitivistic', combining naturalism about 'good' and intuitionism about 'ought'. Subsequently, he became less satisfied with this position, and took up a greater variety of topics. He absorbed some emotivist ideas, did work on the relation between ethics and religion (sympathetic to religion), and wrote on philosophy of education. Frankena's way of doing conceptual analysis and normative justification has provided a model in some respects for many American philosophers working in ethics.   E.T.S.

William K. Frankena, 'Concluding More or Less Philosophical Postscript', in Kenneth E. Goodpaster (ed.), *Perspectives on Morality: Essays by William K. Frankena* (Notre Dame, Ind., 1976).

Frankfurt, Harry (1929–). Professor of Philosophy at Princeton (1990–), he formerly taught at Yale (1976–89) and Rockefeller University (1965–76). His early work revived the debate over the alleged circularity of Descartes's defence of reason. His essay 'Freedom of the Will and the Concept of a Person' (1971) argued for the special significance of the capacity for reflective self-evaluation apparently unique to human beings that is manifested in the formation of what he labelled 'second-order desires', i.e. the capacity not merely to have desires, preferences, or motives (which capacity human beings share with certain animals) but also to *want to have* (or not to have) certain desires, preferences, or motives.

His recent work develops the implications of his view that volition is more pertinent even than reason to our experience of ourselves. In *The Importance of what we Care About* (Cambridge, 1988), he explores various forms of necessity, our being unable to avoid willing some things, our being unable to will other things. Such facts simultaneously limit our *autonomy and make autonomy possible.   R.P.G.

Frankfurt School. A German philosophical and sociological movement associated with the Institute for Social Research founded within Frankfurt University in 1923. One of its founders, and in 1930 its director, was Max Horkheimer (1895–1973). In the 1930s he expounded the *'critical theory' of the school in its journal, *Zeitschrift für Sozialforschung* (*Critical Theory: Selected Essays*, (1968; tr. New York, 1972)). Only a radical change in theory and practice can cure the ills of modern society, especially unbridled technology. Every one-sided doctrine is to be subjected to criticism, including Marxism: an emancipating proletarian revolution is not inevitable, and thought or theory is relatively, though not wholly, independent of social and economic forces. But since theory and its concepts are a product of social processes, critical theory must trace their origins, and not, like empiricism and positivism, accept them and thereby indirectly endorse the processes themselves. Horkheimer also contributed to the sociological work *Authority and Family* (1936).

In 1934 the institute closed, Horkheimer and other leading members, such as Adorno and Marcuse, emigrated, and it was re-established in New York as the New School for Social Research. Several important works appeared during the period of exile: Marcuse's *Reason and Revolution* (1941), Adorno and Horkheimer's *Dialectic of Enlightenment* (1947; tr. New York, 1972), Adorno's wide-ranging and aphoristic *Minima Moralia* (1951; tr. London, 1974), and the collective work by Adorno and others *The Authoritarian Personality* (New York, 1950). The institute returned to Frankfurt in the early 1950s, and, while Marcuse and others remained in the USA, Horkheimer and Adorno also returned. Adorno was its director from 1958 until his death in 1969.

The leading member of the school in its recent history is Jurgen Habermas (1929–), whose *Theory and Practice* (1963; tr. Boston, 1973) and *Knowledge and Human Interests* (1968; tr. Boston, 1971) argue that the sciences depend on ideological assumptions and interests, and that enlightenment reason has become an instrument of oppression. In contrast to this, he projects the ideal of a communication which involves all rational subjects and is entirely free of domination and error-inducing interest. Like other members of the school, such as Marcuse (*Eros and Civilization* (Boston, 1955)), Habermas is interested in psychoanalysis and other non-Marxian types of liberation.

Since the school in general believes that science and *positivism are riddled with non-theoretical interests and that reason has become repressive, they cannot accept without qualification Weber's view that the sciences should be value-free, avoiding value-judgements about the people and institutions they study. They argue, for example, that science already embodies value-judgements, such as the desirability of the technological domination of nature, which, though in fact questionable, seem so self-evident that they appear not to be value-judgements at all, but simply disinterested devotion to science. The postulate of value-freedom in effect insulates such well-entrenched value-judgements from criticism by disqualifying potential competitors. Adorno and Habermas debated this issue with Popper and his followers in T. W. Adorno *et al.*, *The Positivist Dispute in German Sociology* (1969; tr. London, 1976).   M.J.I.

A. Arato and E. Gebhardt, *The Essential Frankfurt School Reader* (Oxford, 1978).

R. Geuss, *The Idea of a Critical Theory* (Cambridge, 1981).

M. Jay, *The Dialectical Imagination* (London, 1973).

Franklin, Benjamin (1706–90). American statesman and diplomat, scientist and inventor, printer and author. He is honoured as one of the architects of the political independence of the United States and remembered for his experimental and applied science, especially concerning the nature of electricity. In his own lifetime, however, he also secured international recognition and domestic popularity as a political philosopher and moralist. His *Autobiography* and the aphorisms of *Poor Richard's Almanac* described and reflected his distinctive blend of *perfectionism, *utilitarianism, and Aristotelian *virtue theory. He recommended specific rules of conduct and practical aids to the formation of good habits, insisting that an individual's development of these virtuous habits would secure private happiness and prosperity, together with a capacity for and devotion to civic improvement.

K.H.

Charles L. Sanford (ed.), *Benjamin Franklin and the American Character* (Boston, 1955).

fraternity. Relationship between those collectively engaged on a common purpose. The philosophically neglected third child of *revolution, fraternity has been regarded as involving an emotional bond variously relating those who share a common nationalism or, under Marxism, the members of the working class or even, under some *liberalism, all mankind. Fraternity is valued much like *community, and, as with *friendship, for reasons that are not instrumental.   P.G.

*friendship.

R. S. Peters, *Ethics and Education* (London, 1966), ch. 8.

Frede, Michael (1940–). Professor of the History of Philosophy in the University of Oxford. Historian of ancient philosophy who is sensitive to the methodological distinction between writing history of philosophy as history and writing history of philosophy as philosophy. His approach entails locating ancient texts in a causal network of other 'histories': medicine, law, religion, politics, for example, and attempts to exhibit philosophical problems as they were conceived and treated by the ancients themselves. His first book, *Prädikation und Existenzaussage* (1967), initiated a debate over Plato's *Sophist*. *Die Stoische Logik* (1974) provided new ways of understanding Stoic logic. Frede is co-author (with Günther Patzig) of a German translation and commentary on Aristotle's *Metaphysics* Z (1988) and author of many papers. Some of these have been usefully collected in *Essays in Ancient Philosophy* (1987).   S.P.

free, freedom: *see* two groups of entries: (1) freedom and determinism; determinism; scientific determinism; libertarianism; origination; the will; autonomy; voluntariness; embraced and reluctant desires; spontaneity and indifference; compatibilism and incompatibilism; responsibility; fatalism; destiny; (2) political freedom; liberty; liberalism; freedom through reason and goodness; freedom of goodness and reason; self-determination; right to a homeland; hegemony; Four Freedoms; freedom of speech; imperialism.

freedom, academic: *see* academic freedom.

freedom, political. The problem of political freedom can be seen as that of reconciling the value of freedom with the restrictions which seem to be a necessary feature of life in a political society. One natural approach is to view the task as that of effecting a compromise: some degree of freedom must be sacrificed, but it must not be too much. The problem then becomes one of where to draw the line. A popular answer has been to appeal to the idea of basic human *rights (sometimes called *'natural rights') and to suggest that these are the freedoms which ought to be safeguarded in any society. Favourite examples are rights to freedom of speech and freedom of assembly, or to freedom of contract, or the right to ownership and control of one's own body and therefore to the products of one's own labour. Any such list of rights, however, is controversial, and it is difficult to find any objective way of determining *what* basic rights people have.

One philosophical tradition which has tried to provide a way of dealing with this problem is social contract theory. (*Contract, social.) In a *'state of nature', it is supposed, men enjoy what is in one sense an absolute liberty, since there is no government to command them, but each individual's liberty is in practice restricted by every other individual's exercise of liberty. Justifiable restrictions on liberty are therefore those restrictions imposed by the contract which is needed to set up a social order. Thus Hobbes supposes that the state of nature would be one of perpetual war, and that in order to preserve the peace the contract must give the sovereign an absolute power of life and death over every subject. Locke takes a more benign view of the state of nature; it is not, he supposes, a condition of war, but a more settled state of affairs in which men have natural rights to life, liberty, and property, and the power of governments must therefore be limited by respect for those rights and by the consent of the governed. Rousseau's view of the state of nature is more positive still; 'man is born free', and if he is nevertheless 'everywhere in chains' the only thing which can make this authority legitimate is a contract which combines the wills of individuals into a 'general will' in which everyone participates. By such a contract the individual loses his 'natural liberty' but gains a 'civil' and 'moral' liberty which 'makes him truly master of himself'. It is clear, then, that the account of political freedom given by social contract theorists depends on their view of what a state of nature would be like, and since this state of nature is a hypothetical condition which has never actually existed, there are obvious difficulties in using the notion to resolve the problem of freedom.

An alternative approach is the utilitarian idea put forward in John Stuart Mill's essay *On Liberty* that freedom should be limited only by the 'harm' principle: individuals should be free to do anything which does not harm others, but actions which do harm others may properly be restricted by society. Mill especially emphasizes the benefits of freedom of speech. He also maintains that freedom of action should extend to those acts by which individuals might harm themselves, provided they do not thereby harm others. His critics have suggested that this distinction is difficult to sustain, since in harming myself I inevitably make myself a less useful member of society and make demands on shared resources (for example, medical resources), thereby harming others.

A more fundamental criticism of this approach has been that it assumes a purely negative and individualistic view of freedom, as simply the absence of restriction or coercion. In contrast, philosophers such as Hegel and his followers have maintained that individuals are truly free not when they act on this or that arbitrary caprice, but when they have rational control over their lives. They have further suggested that this is possible only through active involvement in the life of a society. Hegel thinks that the duties of political life give an objective rational content to the lives of individuals. Others have suggested that it is through participation in a democratic political system that people can effectively control their lives. A further variant on this approach is the emphasis to be found in Marx and the Marxist tradition on the economic dimension of freedom: to be free, people must be able to employ the material resources which they need to give effect to their choices, and this is possible only through collective control over the productive powers of society. All of these suggestions call into question the idea with which we began, of a compromise between the freedom of the individual and the power of society, since they imply that only as social beings are people capable of exercising freedom in the first place. Underlying these philosophical differences is the continuing debate over whether the concept of *liberty is more properly to be understood in negative or positive terms.   R.J.N.

John Stuart Mill, *On Liberty*, various edns., e.g. in *Utilitarianism*, ed. Mary Warnock (London, 1962).
David Miller (ed.), *Liberty* (Oxford, 1991).
Peter Singer, *Hegel* (Oxford, 1983), ch. 3.

freedom and determinism. The great problem of freedom and determinism is really two problems, one of them metaphysical and empirical in kind, the other ethical and in other ways attitudinal in kind. The first problem is that of whether human choices and actions are causally determined or are in a way free. The second problem is that of the implications of determinism for our moral, personal, and social lives.

*Determinism in the context of these problems, to be more specific, is usually the thesis that all our mental states and acts, including choices and decisions, and all our actions are effects necessitated by preceding causes. Thus our futures are in fact fixed and unalterable in much the same way that the past is. The truth or falsity of the thesis depends upon our natures, including our physical natures, and not at all upon our desires or hopes or other feelings.

What freedom comes to with these problems is much disputed. Different concepts enter into both the factual and the attitudinal problem. Metaphysical freedom or *origination, one of the two main kinds, involves not being completely governed by deterministic causal laws. Those who support it say there are no laws, whether of mind or brain or both, that completely settle what we will choose and do. Metaphysical freedom also involves not just the absence of such laws but also our having a kind of power to choose which path the future will take.

Let us start with the second problem to the fore (they are a little hard to keep apart). In everyday life, we suppose that free actions in some sense or other are the only ones for which we can hold persons morally responsible, or for which we can appropriately feel gratitude or resentment (Strawson). Ordinary morality says that we are excused for doing something that would otherwise be blameworthy if we can establish that in some sense or other we had no choice in the matter, that in some sense or other we could not have done otherwise.

Some philosophers, incompatibilists, believe that determinism if true destroys *moral responsibility, undermines interpersonal relations, and destroys our life-hopes by making all actions unfree. Freedom and determinism are incompatible. Incompatibilists who also believe that determinism is false, and hence that some actions are morally responsible, are often called *libertarians. Incompatibilists who also believe, differently, that determinism is true, and moral responsibility is therefore an illusion, are sometimes called, following William James, hard determinists.

Other philosophers, compatibilists, deny that determinism has any such effect on freedom and moral responsibility. Freedom and determinism are compatible. They are sometimes called soft determinists, but this description has the unfortunate effect of officially conflating the problems of the truth of determinism (the first problem) and our appropriate response to it (the second problem). In fact some of these philosophers do not believe in determinism, and maybe not in the denial of determinism, but only believe that *if* it is true, this does not have the upshot that we are not free and responsible. (Another logically possible position—determinism is false but moral responsibility still fails to exist—has no advocates and no name. Perhaps we should call it libertinism.)

Compatibilists rest their argument on the claim that the sense of 'free' in which actions must be free in order to be morally responsible is *not* the sense that involves origination and is opposed to 'caused' or 'determined'. We only need to be free in the sense in which 'free' is opposed to 'compelled' or 'coerced'. We only need to be voluntary in this sense. All we need is voluntariness. (Think of what men in prison lack, or anyone who is subject to a serious addiction.) In G. E. Moore's famous analysis, I am free in performing an action if *I could have done otherwise*, but this latter proposition is to be understood as *I would have done otherwise if I had chosen*. So I could have done otherwise even if determinism is true.

Moore's analysis seems to capture much of the pretheoretical or everyday-life distinction between excused and unexcused infractions of the moral law. Its essential notion is that some actions result from effective choices by the actor, and hence are free, and some do not result from such choices, and are not free. Moore's analysis, nevertheless, seems beside the point to libertarians, because, as they say, if determinism is true, I could not have *chosen* otherwise in the right sense, and therefore could not have *done* otherwise. I could not have originated anything. Thus, they say, moral responsibility collapses.

Honderich has argued persuasively that the long-running compatibilism–incompatibilism controversy springs from what it overlooks, the systematic ambiguity of talk of freedom. We each have two conceptions of freedom, not one. One involves both origination and voluntariness, while the other involves voluntariness alone. If this is so, compatibilism and incompatibilism are both false—both claim that we have just one conception of freedom or that there is one correct conception of it. For Honderich, *something* of moral responsibility and much else must change if determinism is true, but not everything must change. The problem is more attitudinal than conceptual. Some of our present attitudes and responses, which depend on ideas of origination, are impossible if determinism is true. But other kinds of them *are* possible. Certain kinds of 'life-hopes, personal feelings, knowledge, moral responsibility, the rightness of actions and the moral standing of persons . . . persist, and our lives do not become dark, but remain open to celebration'.

To focus on the factual question, one historical argument against the truth of determinism has to do with our common experiences of choosing and deciding. In a genuine case now of choosing or deciding, according to libertarians, I am directly aware of my freedom to realize either alternative—I know that whatever has happened before now, or whatever is the case now, I can now raise my arm or refrain from raising my arm. This freedom of origination, of which I am indubitably aware, is inconsistent with determinism. Therefore determinism is false. John Stuart Mill responded that this supposed awareness of mine is only a memory of and mistaken inference from past occasions, some occasions on which we took something like the first alternative and some occasions on which we took something like the second alternative. But on all such occasions, Mill argued, we followed our strongest motive, and in the present case we must do so as well. Our supposed awareness of origination may be of a type with awareness of a metaphysical self—universally accepted among philosophers until Hume said, in short, 'I can't find it', and seemed to be right.

It has been argued, in this vein, that *libertarianism does not give us an explanation of human action. It gives us a blank where an explanation should be. And, one might add, it would take a very odd *something* to fill in the blank. The desired entity—whether called mind, soul, self, agent, or originator—must be sufficiently connected to the past to constitute a continuing locus of personal responsibility, but sufficiently disconnected so that its past does not determine its present. It must be sufficiently connected to the causal chain to be able to interrupt it, but sufficiently disconnected not to get trapped. It must be susceptible to being shaped and maybe governed by motives, threats, punishments, and desires, but not totally controlled by them. It resembles very much the river god, who serves as an explanation for what seems to be the free behaviour of the river—the explanation of its surges and whatever else happens—until a better explanation comes along through physical geography, meteorology, and physics. The mind or originator or whatever is, you might think, a lot worse than what Gilbert Ryle disparaged as 'the ghost in the machine'.

If indeterminists seem dated in their description of what fundamental thing is free (Strawson spoke of their 'obscure and panicky metaphysics'), they can be up to date in their arguments that something or other is free. The weight and intellectual respectability of physical science are claimed to be on their side. *Quantum mechanics is said to have rejected causal determinism. But the kind of indeterminism involved in quantum mechanics is randomness, pure chance. If my arm randomly jerks and strikes someone, that is just the kind of thing that *excuses* me from moral responsibility. Indeed, there must be some causal link between my action and my past life for it to make sense to think of it as *my* action. Libertarianism needs to steer a course between the Scylla of randomness and the Charybdis of determinism. Maybe there isn't any such course.   R.C.W.

*agent causation.

J. C. Eccles and K. R. Popper, *The Self and its Brain* (Berlin, 1977).
T. Honderich, *A Theory of Determinism: The Mind, Neuroscience, and Life-Hopes* (Oxford, 1988).
—— *How Free Are You?*, 2nd edn. (Oxford, 2002).
R. Kane (ed.), *The Oxford Handbook of Free Will* (New York, 2001).
G. E. Moore, *Ethics* (London, 1912).
P. F. Strawson, 'Freedom and Resentment', in *Studies in the Philosophy of Thought and Action* (Oxford, 1968).
R. Weatherford, *The Implications of Determinism* (London, 1991).

freedom and liberty. These two words are often used interchangeably, except inasmuch as *'freedom' exists in the form of an adjective ('free') and *'liberty' does not. Thus, we talk of 'free will' and 'free action'. Occasionally, more through stipulation than reflection of ordinary usage, the use of one term rather than the other is appropriate. On these occasions, 'freedom' refers to the *ability* of people to act. Thus in discussions of *freedom and determinism, it is the freedom of the will that is at issue. There are a number of conceptions of 'liberty'. Perhaps the clearest refers to the fact that the relevant political or judicial system gives people *permission* to do something: that is, they have no duty not to do that thing. Thus it is possible that people might have permission to do something they do not have the ability to do (perhaps because of impairment), and the ability to do something they do not have permission to do. In this respect, freedom and liberty can vary independently.   D.M.

J. Feinberg, *Rights, Justice and the Bounds of Liberty* (Princeton, NJ, 1980).

freedom of goodness and reason. The view that a good and reasonable man is free, even though he be a slave, is famously associated with the *Stoics, but it pre-dated them and has long outlived them. Many have thought that to talk of 'freedom' in this way is to part company entirely with established usage, and therefore to render meaningful disagreement impossible. However, if 'freedom' can mean the opposite of 'enslaved', then it is at least meaningful to describe it as threatened by enslavement to bad or unreasonable desires. With the conception of freedom as the capacity to will what is reasonable and good, the problem of *freedom and determinism disappears, since if one is caused to act reasonably and is free in virtue of that, having the capacity to act otherwise, in the indeterminist sense, is otiose.   K.M.

M. J. Adler, *The Idea of Freedom* (New York, 1958).

freedom of speech. Celebrated as first among *civil liberties, freedom of speech (conceived broadly as the expression of verbal as well as non-verbal utterance) is both an instrumental and intrinsic good; instrumental as a necessary condition of inquiry and of intrinsic value as an element in individual well-being and self-fulfilment.

Legitimate grounds for limitations on free speech fall into two categories: procedural, concerning restrictions of time, place, and manner on the form and forums of its exercise; and substantive, involving restrictions on content, such as libel, slander, incitement to riot, etc. Even in the latter cases, however, prior restraints (as distinct from civil or criminal responses after the fact) are rarely justified. Some would argue that speech can offend or annoy but never harm; others would concede that it can harm but that the harms are generally outweighed by the benefits and by avoidance of the harms its suppression would entail. Still others would favour censorship of pornography and obscenity because of the harm they do to vulnerable classes of persons generally.

As with other freedoms, the value of freedom of speech must be contrasted with its *worth*; without opportunities that wealth and power confer, one's freedom of speech even in a liberal society may be worth very little. In any case, it will be distributed unequally even if equality of freedom of speech is otherwise guaranteed by law.   H.A.B.

Frederick Schauer, *Free Speech: A Philosophical Inquiry* (Cambridge, 1982).

Freedoms, Four: *see* Four Freedoms.

free logics. Logical systems in which existential commitment is not assumed, in which names and predicates need not refer to anything, or in which sentences may not be made true or false by what does or does not exist. So, in free predicate logic, $(\exists x)$ (Fx), 'There exists at least one x that is F', does not have to follow from Fa, 'a is F'. Free logic is called 'free logic' because, in contrast with standard predicate calculus, the use of names is free from commitment to the existence of a referent.

Arguably, free logics do justice to the intuitive view that from the fact that the concept of something exists it does not follow that that thing exists: from 'A unicorn has a single horn' it does not follow that there are any unicorns. The intuitive view is not beyond question. Arguably, unicorns do exist but are fictional objects or exist in storybooks or people's imaginations. 'Exists' does not mean the same as 'is a four-dimensional publicly observable object'. Arguably, in a world in which unicorns did not exist, storybooks and people's imaginations would differ from the actual world.

There exists both modal and non-modal free logic. In free modal logic, the use of a name implies commitment to existence in at least one possible world, but this is commitment only to the possible existence of a referent, not to the existence of a referent.   S.P.

Ermanno Bencivenga, 'Free Logics', in Dov A. Gabbay and Franz Guenthner (eds.), *Handbook of Philosophical Logic*, vol. 3 (Dordrecht, 1986).
Graeme Forbes, *Modern Logic* (Oxford, 1994).
Mark Sainsbury, *Logical Forms* (Oxford, 1991).

free riders. Usually unintended beneficiaries of a socially provided public good for which they have made no contribution—a public good being one the consumption or use of which by one individual or group does not diminish or prevent its consumption or use by others, e.g. radio broadcasts and street lights. The 'free rider problem' is that of whether those who benefit in this way do so unjustly and whether, if so, they can rightly be forced to make a contribution.   J.HAL.

*equality; well-being; welfarism.

A. de Jasay, *Social Contract and Free Ride: A Study of the Public Goods Problem* (Oxford, 1989).

free will: *see* freedom and determinism; origination.

Frege, Gottlob (1848–1925). The founder of modern mathematical logic. As a logician and philosopher of logic he ranks with Aristotle; as a philosopher of mathematics he has had no peer throughout the history of the subject. After taking his doctorate in philosophy at Göttingen, he taught at the University of Jena from 1874 until his retirement in 1918; apart from his intellectual activity his life was uneventful and secluded. His work was little read in his lifetime, and for a long time his influence in philosophy was exercised mainly through the writings of others.

Frege had an influence on analytic philosophy through Russell and on continental philosophy through Husserl. He is often thought of as a philosophers' philosopher, but it was his genius that made possible the work of writers who have caught the attention of the general public, such as Wittgenstein and Chomsky; and his invention of mathematical logic was one of the major contributions to the developments in many disciplines which resulted in the invention of computers.

Frege's productive career began in 1879 with the publication of a pamphlet with the title *Begriffsschrift*, which we can render into English as 'Concept Script'. The pamphlet marked an epoch in the history of logic, for within some hundred pages it set forth a new calculus which has a permanent place at the heart of modern logic. The concept script which gave the book its title was a new symbolism designed to bring out with clarity logical relationships which were concealed in ordinary language.

For generations now the curriculum in formal logic has begun with the study of the *propositional calculus. This is the branch of logic that deals with those inferences which depend on the force of negation, conjunction, disjunction, etc. when applied to sentences as wholes. Its fundamental principle is to treat the truth-value (i.e. the truth or falsehood) of sentences which contain connectives such as 'and', 'if', 'or' as being determined solely by the truth-values of the component sentences which are linked by the connectives. Frege's *Begriffsschrift* contains the first systematic formulation of the propositional calculus; it is presented in an axiomatic manner in which all laws of logic are derived, by specified rules of inference, from a number of primitive principles. Frege's symbolism, though elegant, is difficult to print, and is no longer used; but the operations which it expresses continue to be fundamental in mathematical logic.

Frege's greatest contribution to logic was his invention of quantification theory: a method of symbolizing and rigorously displaying those inferences that depend for their validity on expressions such as 'all' or 'some', 'any' or 'every', 'no' or 'none'. Using a novel notation for quantification, he presented a first-order *predicate calculus which laid the basis for all recent developments in logic and formalized the theory of inference in a way more rigorous and more general than the traditional Aristotelian syllogistic which up to the time of Kant was looked on as the be-all and end-all of logic. After Frege, for the first time, formal logic could handle arguments which involved sentences with multiple quantification, such as 'Nobody knows everybody' and 'Any schoolchild can master any language'.

In the course of his work Frege developed other branches of logic, including second-order predicate calculus and a version of naïve *set theory. He did not explore the areas of logic known as modal logic (that part of logic that deals with necessity, possibility, and kindred notions) or tense logic (the logic of temporal or significantly tensed statements). These branches of logic had been studied in the Middle Ages, and have been studied again in the present century in the light of his innovations.

In the *Begriffsschrift* and its sequels Frege was not interested in logic for its own sake. His motive in constructing the new concept script was to assist him in the philosophy of mathematics. (It was his predominantly mathematical agenda which made him comparatively uninterested in the branches of logic which concern inferences about the transient and the changing.) The question which above all he wanted to answer was this: Do proofs in arithmetic rest on pure logic, being based solely upon general laws operative in every sphere of knowledge, or do they need support from empirical facts? To answer this question, Frege set himself the task of seeing 'how far one could get in arithmetic by means of logical deductions alone, supported only by the laws of thought'.

Not only did Frege show how to conduct logic in a mathematical manner: he believed that arithmetic itself could be shown to be a branch of logic in the sense that it could be formalized without the use of any non-logical notions or axioms. It was in the *Grundlagen der Arithmetik* (1884) that Frege first set out to establish this thesis, which is known by the name of *'logicism'.

The *Grundlagen* begins with an attack on the ideas of Frege's predecessors and contemporaries (including Kant and J. S. Mill) on the nature of numbers and of mathematical truth. Kant had maintained that the truths of mathematics were *synthetic a priori, and that our knowledge of them depended on intuition. Mill, on the contrary, saw mathematical truths as a posteriori, empirical generalizations widely applicable and widely confirmed. Frege maintained that the truths of arithmetic were not synthetic at all, neither a priori nor a posteriori. Unlike geometry—which, he agreed with Kant, rested on a priori intuition—arithmetic was analytic, that is to say, it could be defined in purely logical terms and proved from purely logical principles.

The arithmetical notion of number in Frege's system is replaced by the logical notion of *'class': the cardinal numbers can be defined as classes of classes with the same number of members; thus the number two is the class of pairs, and the number three the class of trios. Despite appearances, this definition is not circular, because we can say what is meant by two classes having the same number of members without making use of the notion of number: thus, for instance, a waiter may know that there are as many knives as there are plates on a table without knowing how many of each there are, if he observes that there is just one knife to the right of each plate. Two classes have the same number of members if they can be mapped one-to-one on to each other. We can define the number zero in purely logical terms as the class of all classes with the same number of members as the class of objects which are not identical with themselves.

In order to pass from a definition of zero to the definition of the other natural numbers, Frege has to define the notion of 'successor' in the sense in which the natural numbers succeed each other in the number series. He defines '*n* immediately succeeds *m*' as 'There exists a concept *F*, and an object falling under it *x*, such that the number of *F*s is *n*, and the number of *F*s not identical with *x* is *m*'. With the aid of this definition the other numbers (one, which is the successor of zero, two, which is the successor of one, and so on) can, like zero, be defined without using any notions other than logical ones such as identity, class, and class-equivalence.

In the *Grundlagen* there are two theses to which Frege attaches great importance. One is that each individual number is a self-subsistent object; the other is that the content of a statement assigning a number is an assertion about a concept. At first sight these theses may seem to conflict, but if we understand what Frege meant by 'concept' and 'object' we see that they are complementary. In saying that a number is an object, Frege is not suggesting that a number is something tangible like a tree or a table; rather, he is denying that number is a property belonging to anything, whether an individual or a collection; he is also denying that it is anything subjective, any mental item or any property of a mental item. Concepts are, for Frege, mind-independent, and so there is no contradiction between the thesis that numbers are objective, and the thesis that number-statements are statements about concepts.

Frege illustrates this latter thesis with two examples. 'If I say "Venus has 0 moons", there simply does not exist any moon or agglomeration of moons for anything to be asserted of; but what happens is that a property is assigned to the *concept* "moon of Venus", namely that of including nothing under it. If I say "the King's carriage is drawn by four horses", then I assign the number four to the concept "horse that draws the King's carriage".'

But if number-statements of this kind are statements about concepts, what kind of object is a number itself? Frege's answer is that a number is the extension of a concept. The number which belongs to the concept *F*, he says, is the extension of the concept 'like-numbered to the concept *F*'. This is equivalent to saying that it is the class of all classes which have the same number of members as the class of *F*s, as was explained above. So Frege's theory that numbers are objects depends on the possibility of taking classes as objects.

It will be seen that Frege's philosophy of mathematics is closely linked to his understanding of several key terms of logic and of philosophy; and indeed in the *Begriffsschrift* and the *Grundlagen* Frege not only founded modern logic, but also founded the modern philosophical discipline of philosophy of logic. He did so by making a sharp distinction between the philosophical treatment of logic and, on the one hand, psychology (with which it had often been confused by philosophers in the empiricist tradition) and, on the other hand, epistemology (with which it was sometimes conflated by philosophers in the *Cartesian tradition). In this he was in line with a yet older tradition originating with Aristotle's *De interpretatione*: but in the *Begriffsschrift* and the *Grundlagen* he investigates such notions as *name*, *sentence*, *predicate* with a scope and subtlety greater than Aristotle's.

One of Frege's most fertile devices was the application of the mathematical notions of *function and *argument to replace the analysis of sentences in ordinary language in terms of subject and predicate. Consider a sentence such as 'William defeated Harold'—a laconic description, perhaps, of the battle of Hastings. Traditional grammar will say that 'William' is the subject, and 'defeated Harold' the predicate. To say—as Frege did—that we should look on 'William' as an argument, and 'defeated Harold' as a function, may at first look as if it is simply an alternative terminology—and indeed, for much of his life, Frege was willing to call an expression such as 'defeated Harold' a predicate. But to treat a predicate as a function involves a profound change in the understanding of the construction of sentences.

To see this, suppose that we take the sentence 'William defeated Harold' and put into it, in place of the word 'Harold', the word 'Canute'. Clearly this alters the sense of the sentence, and indeed it turns it from a true one into a false one. We can think of the sentence as in this way consisting of a constant component 'William defeated' and a symbol 'Harold' replaceable by other similar symbols—names naming other people, in the way that 'Harold' names Harold. If we think of a sentence in this way, Frege will call the first component a function, and the second its argument: he is making an extension of the mathematical terminology in accordance with which 6 is the value of the function $x \times 3$ for the argument 2, and 9 is the value of the same function for the argument 3. The sentence 'William defeated Harold' is the result of completing the expression 'William defeated' with the name 'Harold', and the sentence 'William defeated Canute' is the result of completing the same expression with the name 'Canute'. That is to say, in the terminology of Begriffsschrift, 'William defeated Harold' is the value of the function 'William defeated' for the argument 'Harold', and 'William defeated Canute' is the value of the same function for the argument 'Canute'.

The sentence 'William defeated Harold' is, of course, also the value of the function 'defeated Harold' for the argument 'William'. In the same way, 6 is not only the value of the function $x \times 3$ for the argument 2, but also the value of the function $2 \times x$ for the argument 3. Every sentence, for Frege, can be analysed into argument and function in at least one way, but many can be analysed in more than one way.

Corresponding to the distinction in language between functions of this kind and their arguments, Frege maintained, a systematic distinction must be made between concepts and objects, which are their ontological counterparts. Objects are what proper names stand for: they are of many kinds, ranging from human beings to numbers. Concepts are items which have a fundamental incompleteness, corresponding to the gappiness of a predicate as understood by Frege (i.e. a sentence with a proper name removed from it). Where other philosophers talk ambiguously of the *meaning* of an expression, Frege introduced a distinction between the *reference of an expression (the object to which it refers, as the planet Venus is the reference of 'the Morning Star') and the *sense of an expression. ('The Evening Star' differs in sense from 'the Morning Star' though it too, as astronomers discovered, refers to Venus.)

These theories of philosophical logic were worked out by Frege in a series of articles in the early 1890s: 'Funktion und Begriff' (Function and Concept, 1891), 'Begriff und Gegenstand' (Concept and Object, 1892), 'Sinn und Bedeutung' (Sense and Reference, 1892). The most controversial application of Frege's distinction between sense and reference was his theory that the reference of a sentence was its truth-value (i.e. the True, or the False), and the connected theses that in a scientifically respectable language every term must have a reference and every sentence must be either true or false. These theses lead to many difficulties.

In the last years of his life, between 1918 and his death, Frege attempted to write a full treatise of philosophical logic. All that was completed was a series of articles (*Logische Untersuchungen*, 1919–23) in which he returns to the relationship between logic and philosophical psychology or philosophy of mind, and discusses the nature of thought and inference. His work in this area has been largely superseded by the later writings of Wittgenstein, a philosopher much influenced throughout his life, as he himself avowed, by Frege's agenda and Frege's structures of thought.

The climax of Frege's career as a philosopher should have been the publication of the two volumes of *Die Grundgesetze der Arithmetik* (1893–1903), in which he set out to present in formal manner the logicist construction of arithmetic on the basis of pure logic and set theory. This work was to execute the task which had been sketched in the earlier books on the philosophy of mathematics: it was to enunciate a set of axioms which would be recognizably truths of logic, to propound a set of undoubtedly sound rules of inference, and then to present, one by one, derivations by these rules from these axioms of the standard truths of arithmetic.

The magnificent project aborted before it was ever completed. The first volume was published in 1893; the second volume did not appear until 1903 and while it was in the press Frege received a letter from Russell pointing out that the fifth of the initial axioms made the whole system inconsistent. This was the axiom which, in Frege's words, allowed 'the transition from a concept to its extension', the transition which was essential if it was to be established that numbers were logical objects. Frege's system, with this axiom, permitted the formation of the class of all classes that are not members of themselves. But the formation of such a class, Russell pointed out, leads to paradox: if it is a member of itself then it is not a member of itself; if it is not a member of itself, then it is a member of itself. A system which leads to such paradox cannot be logically sound.

With good reason, Frege was utterly downcast by this discovery, though he strove to patch his system by weakening the guilty axiom. We now know that his logicist programme cannot ever be successfully carried out. The path from the axioms of logic to the theorems of arithmetic is barred at two points. First, as Russell's paradox showed, the naïve set theory which was part of Frege's logical basis was inconsistent in itself, and the remedies which Frege proposed for this proved ineffective. Thus, the axioms of arithmetic cannot be derived from purely logical axioms in the way he hoped. Secondly, the notion of 'axioms of arithmetic' was itself later called in question when Gödel showed that it was impossible to give arithmetic a complete and consistent axiomatization. None the less, the concepts and insights developed by Frege in the course of expounding his logicist thesis have a permanent interest which is unimpaired by the defeat of that programme at the hands of Russell and Gödel.

Wittgenstein once described to Geach his final meeting with Frege. 'The last time I saw Frege, as we were waiting at the station for my train, I said to him "Don't you ever find *any* difficulty in your theory that numbers are objects?" He replied "Sometimes I *seem* to see a difficulty—but then again I *don't* see it." '   A.J.P.K.

*logic, history of; logic, modern.

G. E. M. Anscombe and P. Geach, *Three Philosophers* (Oxford, 1961).

M. Dummett, *Frege: Philosophy of Language* (London, 1973).

—— *Frege: Philosophy of Mathematics* (London, 1991).

G. W. Frege, *Collected Papers on Mathematics, Logic and Philosophy*, ed. B. McGuinness (Oxford, 1984).

—— *Conceptual Notation and Related Articles*, ed. T. W. Bynum (Oxford, 1972).

—— *The Foundations of Arithmetic*, tr. J. L. Austin (Oxford, 1950).

—— *The Frege Reader*, ed. M. Beaney (Oxford, 1997).

A. Kenny, *Frege: An Introduction to the Founder of Modern Analytic Philosophy* (Oxford, 2000).

C. Wright, *Frege's Conception of Numbers as Objects* (Aberdeen, 1983).

French philosophy. Although the literary scepticism of François Rabelais (1494–1553) and Michel de Montaigne (1533–92) expresses thought that is in part recognizably philosophical, Descartes is the earliest French philosopher because before him no one systematically attempted to solve philosophical problems and write the results in French. French philosophy since Descartes can be correctly viewed as a series of endorsements and repudiations of *Cartesianism but is still more usefully viewed as essentially oscillating between optimism and pessimism about the powers of reason. Pascal's famous distinction between two mistakes—to deny reason and to allow only reason— arguably applies nowhere more appropriately than to French philosophy over its four centuries.

In the seventeenth century Cartesian optimism about the metaphysical role of reason was subject to two kinds of critique; one metaphysical and theological, the other empiricist. Blaise Pascal maintained that putative metaphysical and theological knowledge acquired by the exercise of the intellect was essentially incomplete and a non-rational leap of faith was required to supplement it. Pierre Gassendi (1592–1655) maintained, against Descartes, the empiricist thesis that the exercise of the senses is the best guide to the nature of reality and that the correct role of reason is confined to drawing inferences from the findings of sense experience.

Although the eighteenth-century *Enlightenment endorsed an empiricist respect for the natural sciences and a burgeoning social anthropology (evident, for example, in the work of Voltaire, Holbach, La Mettrie, Montesquieu, and Condillac), it is a return to optimism about the powers of reason, not this time in any metaphysical employment, but in a naturalistic and human role. The *Encyclopédie* of Diderot and d'Alembert relies on the optimistic principle that no aspect of reality is in principle opaque to human inquiry. The uses of the senses and the intellect are singularly necessary and in principle jointly sufficient for complete knowledge.

No single philosophical thesis is common to all and only those thinkers called the *'philosophes', but most of them combined atheism and anti-clericalism with a respect for science and urged a liberal politics which recommended a constitutional monarchy on the English model (rather than republicanism) against the prevalent absolute monarchy of most European states. Most shared, too, a concern for non-religious education and a synthesis of arts and sciences.

In Rousseau and Maine de Biran the Enlightenment was subject to two kinds of anti-rationalist reaction. Although Rousseau's concept of the general will, which putatively reconciles the freedom of the individual with political society, is consistent with the philosophes' critique of the absolutism of the *ancien régime*, his moral and epistemological attack on the sciences and his postulation of God, freedom, and the immortality of the soul constitute a spiritualist and metaphysical reaction against Enlightenment humanism. In Maine de Biran too, in his emphasis on the spiritual nature of inner experience, there is a pessimism about the power of reason to solve metaphysical problems.

The *positivism of the late nineteenth and early twentieth centuries is essentially anti-metaphysical and anti-theological in its insistence that any problem may, in principle, be solved using the methods of the natural sciences or mathematics (a view endorsed, famously, by Comte). However, the rather empiricist foundations of French positivism are subjected to quasi-Kantian criticism by Poincaré. He argues that science cannot be derived merely from the findings of sense experience, but is also intellectually constructed through the imposition of a set of a priori conventions on those findings.

Although Poincaré suggests a synthesis between rationalism and empiricism, Bergson is the only major French thinker since Descartes who seriously integrates the scientific and the non-rational into his philosophy. Although the living subjective flux of the '*durée réelle*' ('real duration') cannot be explained scientifically, it makes the whole of knowledge (and, *a fortiori*, the whole of science) possible. Bergson's philosophy enjoyed a vogue in France after the First World War comparable to that of Sartre's existentialism after the Second. Bergson is neglected at the time of writing, even though his philosophy has the rare merit of taking seriously both science and the subjective reality of lived experience.

French philosophy since Bergson has been dominated by five philosophical movements: *phenomenology, *existentialism, *Marxism, *structuralism, and *post-structuralism.

JEAN-JACQUES ROUSSEAU, wild man of French literature, harbinger of Romanticism; his polemical demand for popular legitimation of government inspired the revolutionaries of 1789.

AUGUSTE COMTE expounded in the 1830s a positivist theory of knowledge, and put forward sociology as the newest and most complex of the sciences.

HENRI BERGSON distinguished *experienced time* from *measured time*, assigning greater reality to the former; parallel to this was his distinction of the roles of intuition and intellect in acquisition of knowledge.

MAURICE MERLEAU-PONTY argued that a person's apprehension of the outside world is a two-way process: each, in different senses, gives meaning to the other.

Understanding these movements is complicated by three factors: what passes for philosophy in France is distorted by its Anglo-American readership; any 'movement' in philosophy is partly externally constituted by criteria for being a philosopher; and each influential modern French philosopher has been something other than a philosopher too.

Paradigmatically, phenomenology is the presuppositionless description of the contents of experience, without any prior ontological commitment to the objective reality or causal properties of those contents. It has both the quasi-Kantian aim of describing the transcendental conditions for knowledge and the quasi-Cartesian aim of providing an ultimate justification of knowledge in the description of the contents of consciousness or 'phenomena'. By 'knowledge' is meant here 'all knowledge' and so, a fortiori, 'all philosophical and scientific knowledge'.

In the thought of Sartre and Merleau-Ponty this 'pure' or Husserlian phenomenology undergoes a Heideggerian transformation (which is partly anticipated in the later writings of Husserl). Notably, the Husserlian thesis that the world of the natural attitude (roughly, 'common sense') may be 'suspended' to facilitate a phenomenological description of consciousness is rejected and the existential notion 'being-in-the-world' substituted. The Husserlian transcendental ego (as ground of the world) is eliminated as not phenomenologically available and a notion of bodily subjectivity replaces it (notably in Sartre's *L'Être et le néant* and Merleau-Ponty's *Phénoménologie de la perception*). However, arguably the idea of the body-subject is also anticipated in the second book of Husserl's *Ideen zu einer reinen Phänomenologie und phänomenologischen Philosophie*.

Existentialism is an attempt to solve fundamental problems about human existence, notably: what it is to be; the purpose of being; what it is like to face death; the nature of anxiety; the burden of responsibility and freedom; the appropriateness of sexual, political, and religious commitments. Existentialism is a reaction against both metaphysics and the essentialism of 'pure' phenomenology. Its principal thesis is that existence is logically prior to essence and that human essence is not determined a priori but freely created by human actions. Sartre's 'existential' phenomenology is expounded not only in philosophical works but in plays, novels, short stories, and political tracts. The most brilliant existentialist writer was Simone de Beauvoir. Her *Le Deuxième Sexe* (1949) explores the question of the essence of woman: its repressive constitution by men and its possible free constitution by women.

One of the most ambitious projects of post-war French philosophy was Sartre's attempt in *Critique de la raison dialectique* (1960) to synthesize existentialism and Marxism. Marxism and existentialism are prima facie mutually inconsistent philosophies because, while existentialism emphasizes the freedom of the individual, Marxism is a kind of social determinism; existentialism explores the inside of consciousness and the present moment, but Marxism is a materialism which entails a theory of history;

Marxism claims a scientific and objective status for its findings; existentialism deliberately repudiates this for itself. Whether Sartre's putative synthesis is successful or not, in this effort modern French philosophy was engaged in trying to solve genuine metaphysical problems.

Since the 1960s French philosophy has been a part of the broadly neo-Kantian anti-metaphysical orthodoxy within which much European and Anglo-American philosophy operates. The hallmarks of this paradigm are: the impossibility of solving metaphysical problems (but the inevitability of trying to); the linguistic nature of putative philosophical issues; the minimization of the importance of consciousness, subjectivity, and the present; the attempt to 'end' philosophy and replace philosophical problem-solving by something else: political revolution or reform, an examination of language, writing the history of philosophy, literary criticism, the natural sciences. The anthropologist Claude Lévi-Strauss, the psychoanalyst Jacques Lacan, the Marxist structuralist Louis Althusser, and the literary critic Roland Barthes all operate within broadly Kantian assumptions.

The most influential French philosopher at the time of writing is Jacques Derrida. Although Derrida is frequently thought of as making a radical break with previous philosophy, this is in fact far from the case. His strategies may be novel within literary criticism, but they are familiar to anyone who has studied Kant, Hegel, Nietzsche, and Heidegger. All these thinkers are involved, in differing senses and degrees, in a critique of something called 'Western metaphysics', and the permutations of that critique have been the ruling philosophical orthodoxy for the last two centuries.

Modern French philosophy is usually thought to be a part of 'modern continental philosophy', which is contrasted with Anglo-American 'analytical' (or *'analytic') philosophy. This distinction does not stand up to geographical, historical, and philosophical scrutiny and it is an important task of future philosophy to show this. However, while philosophers in the English-speaking countries have usually thought that philosophy (although not a science) should aspire to the rigour and precision of the natural sciences, philosophers in modern France have thought that philosophy should be more like art, more like literature. The conspicuous stylistic divergence this has produced has resulted in the illusion of a bifurcation between two philosophical 'traditions' and the mistaken idea that there is something radical and distinctive called 'modern French philosophy'.   S.P.

*continental philosophy; 'continental' and 'analytic'.

Naguib Balandi, *Les Constantes de la pensée française* (Paris, 1948).

Frederick Copleston, *A History of Philosophy* (London, 1946–75), esp. vol. ix (1975).

Lucien Lévy-Brühl, *A History of Modern Philosophy in France*, tr. G. Coblence (London, 1899).

J. G. Merquior, *From Prague to Paris* (London, 1986).

Herbert Spiegelberg, *The Phenomenological Movement* (The Hague, 1960), ii.

French philosophy today. Recent French philosophy is marked by the decline of the master-thinker. There has been no replacement for the Sartre of the 1950s, the Lévi-Strauss of the 1960s, and the Foucault of the 1970s. Jacques Derrida does continue his immensely productive career and has interestingly expanded his epistemological and metaphysical development of deconstructive readings of texts into ethics and politics. Also, there are important philosophers, such as Jean-Luc Nancy and Philippe Lacoue-Labarthe, who have taken up his dense and nervously involuted philosophical style. But Derrida's impact has from the beginning been much greater in the United States and in literature departments. In so far as there are today 'major figures' of philosophy in France, they are presences from the past such as Emmanuel Levinas and Paul Ricœur, who are of same generation as Sartre, but whose thought was long marginalized, in large part because of its religious roots and implications (Jewish in the case of Levinas, Christian in the case of Ricœur).

As early as the 1930s, Levinas helped introduce Husserl and Heidegger to the French intellectual scene. At first mainly an expositor and critic of their thought, he gradually developed his own distinctive philosophical vision, which appeared with full force in his 1961 book, *Totality and Infinity*. Here Levinas claimed that our concrete experience of other people involves an absolute ethical obligation toward them, a view developed in the larger context of his insistence that almost all of Western philosophy has been contaminated by an effort to reduce the other (including not only other people but difference in general) to unifying categories of sameness. Levinas explicitly relates our absolute ethical obligation to religion, but he is almost obsessively cautious in denying the adequacy of any of our efforts to speak about God.

Ricœur's early work (for example, his influential translation of, and commentary on, Husserl's *Ideas*) was also important for the introduction of phenomenology into France, and his own philosophical views originated from his effort to apply the phenomenological method of carefully describing our immediate experience to the domain of freedom, sin, and evil. His work on these topics developed through several volumes, but increasingly moved beyond phenomenological description to a hermeneutic standpoint, indebted to Heidegger and Gadamer, which emphasized the need not just to describe our experience but to interpret it in a wider literary, cultural, and historical context. Ricœur's hermeneutic philosophy provided the basis for his perceptive critiques of the structuralist and post-structualist philosophies that dominated France during the 1960s and 1970s.

The turn to Levinas and Ricœur has been accompanied by a revival of interest in phenomenology, although the focus has been more on Husserl and Heidegger than on the French existential phenomenologists Sartre and Merleau-Ponty. Here Jean-Luc Marion has done especially important work, which opens new directions of phenomenological reflection and connects them with religious themes (Marion is also a major Catholic theologian). Michel Henry and Jean-François Courtine have also contributed to the return to phenomenology.

The new-found importance of Ricœur and Levinas (and the return to phenomenology) corresponds to a reaction against the philosophical and political radicalism associated with the 1968 student revolution. The same reaction underlies the return to broadly Kantian thinking in the writings of Luc Ferry and Alain Renaut. For example, in their jointly authored *French Philosophy of the Sixties*, Ferry and Renaut agree that Heidegger and his followers have undermined the idea of a 'self-transparent subject that lays claim to mastery of everything that exists'; i.e. the transcendental ego of Kantian idealism. But they go on to argue against the post-structuralist elimination of the subject as a category of theoretical philosophy and for the reality of an ego that is not metaphysically privileged but embedded in historical reality and nevertheless the subject of ethical rights and responsibilities.

Ferry and Renaut also represent an important revival of liberal political theory in France. Whereas earlier thinkers, from Sartre through Lyotard and Deleuze, seemed to allow no alternatives to leftist radicalism or rightist reaction, there is now a striking move to the centre, which has led to a new respect for previously marginalized writers such as Albert Camus and Raymond Aron, and has led important philosophers to see genuine possibilities of co-operation with established governments. (Luc Ferry, for example, is currently Minister of Education.)

The current French scene also includes a lively interest in analytic philosophy. There are roots for this interest in a long and distinguished French tradition of logic and philosophy of mathematics, beginning with Louis Couturat at the turn of the twentieth century and continuing through Jean Nicod, Jacques Herbrand, and Jean Cavaillès. But this group had relatively little impact, partly because none of its members lived beyond the age of fifty. Today, the most prominent French philosopher with a strong commitment to the analytic approach is Jacques Bouveresse, whose earlier work was largely inspired by Wittgenstein, on whom he wrote important commentaries, and whose thought he used as a basis for his own discussions of epistemology and philosophy of mind. More recently, Bouveresse has presented himself as in the line of 'Austrian philosophy', which he sees as beginning with Bolzano's critique of Kant and continuing through Brentano and Meinong to Wittgenstein and the *Vienna Circle. This Austrian line ignored Hegel and his idealistic successors, thereby avoiding the philosophical styles and questions that characterize recent 'continental' philosophy.

More recently, there has emerged a group of younger French analytic philosophers centred on the Centre de Recherche en Epistémologie Appliquée (CREA) at the École Polytechnique, and subsequently at the Institut Nicod. Pascal Engel (who did his doctoral work with Bouveresse), Pierre Jacob, and Daniel Andler are just a few of the French philosophers who have become significant contributors to, for example, analytic philosophy of mind, epistemology, and philosophy of science. There is no doubt that France is quickly taking its place in the increasingly international enterprise of analytic philosophy. The question remaining is whether there will develop a distinctively French school of analytic philosophy or whether French analytic philosophers will remain individual contributors to discussions defined by the dominant interests of American and British philosophy.

A category frequently employed in discussions of recent French philosophy is that of 'French feminist philosophers'. There is no doubt that feminist themes loom large in the work of major French philosophers from Simone de Beauvoir to Luce Irigaray and beyond. But much of the work of many important feminist thinkers in France (e.g. Hélène Cixous, Julia Kristeva) is well beyond the disciplinary boundaries of philosophy, and the work of the major 'feminist philosophers' deserves attention even apart from their contributions to feminist discussions. Luce Irigaray, for example, is best regarded as a 'philosopher of difference', in the general manner of Derrida, Lyotard, and Deleuze. Her focus has been on sexual difference, but in a way that uses feminist issues to overcome what she sees as limitations in traditional thought about the most fundamental issues of human existence. Similarly, Michèle Le Doeuff develops her feminist thought in the context of a historically informed philosophy of science. Her work is particularly interesting because, while originating in the distinctively French tradition of history and philosophy of science (particularly the work of Gaston Bachelard and Georges Canguilhem), it also readily engages with Anglo-American work on science.

Finally, mention should be made of two increasingly influential, if hard to categorize, philosophers: Michel Serres and Alain Badiou. Serres began as a philosopher of science, broadly in the manner of Bachelard, who questioned orthodox distinctions between science and non-science. He later developed, in a series of academic best-sellers, a poetico-philosophical cosmology that presents a metaphysics inspired by chaos theory and fractal geometry. Badiou likewise combines mathematics and ontology in a systematic philosophy that challenges the historicist assumptions of French philosophy of the 1970s and 1980s and rejects the post-structuralist claim that the end of philosophy is near.

Philosophy without master-thinkers has its advantages. Recent French thought lacks the dramatic and disruptive originality of thinkers such as Sartre and Foucault, but it has, in many cases, a stylistic clarity and theoretical openness that were long missing from the philosophical scene. As in the early years of the twentieth century, early twenty-first-century French philosophy is less drastically creative but, perhaps, more able to contribute to the civility and rationality of its age. On the other hand, there is a real danger that this more subdued mode of philosophizing will split into various elements (phenomenology, feminism, analytic philosophy), each merely part of an international discussion, and lose the distinctive flair that has characterized French philosophy for the last sixty years.
G.G.

F. Dosse, *History of Structuralism*, tr. D. Glassman (Minneapolis, 1997).

L. Ferry and A. Renaut, *French Philosophy of the Sixties*, tr. M. Catani (Amherst, Mass., 1990).

A. P. Griffiths (ed.), *Contemporary French Philosophy* (Cambridge, 1987).

G. Gutting, *French Philosophy in the Twentieth Century* (Cambridge, 2001).

M. Lilla (ed.), *New French Political Philosophy* (Princeton, NJ, 1994).

E. Matthews, *Twentieth-Century French Philosophy* (Oxford, 1996).

frequency theory: *see* probability.

Freud, Sigmund (1856–1939). Freud is sometimes said to have discovered the *unconscious, but it is not a claim he made himself. The unconscious which he did *not* discover is the notion that if those everyday explanations which invoke motives, desires, impulses, etc., and normally carry the implication that the subject is authoritative with respect to them, are extended to cases in which this implication is suspended, behaviour otherwise perplexing can be explained. This notion of the unconscious pre-dates Freud. What distinguishes Freud's unconscious is the notion that when the subject's loss of authority with respect to his own mental states is due to a process he called 'repression', these states are subject to transformations which render them unrecognizable by the subject and may have pathological consequences. The conviction that, when the subject came to stand to these contents as to his accessible ones, they were deprived of pathogenic power, yielded a therapeutic method.

Two ingredients were added to produce the characteristic Freudian view of the springs of action—sexuality and infancy. What gave Freud's aetiological speculations their further distinctiveness were the diagnostic procedures on which they were based, in particular the use of interpretation and free association. When these were applied to dreams, errors, and the behaviour of the patient towards the therapist in the analytic setting ('the transference'), they uncovered the repressed pathogenic material. This material was found to display two invariable features—it dated from infancy and pertained to the subject's infantile sexual life.

At first the pathogenic episodes in question were thought to be sexual molestation ('the seduction theory'); these were later replaced by the child's struggle with its own incestuous and perverse wishes ('the Oedipus complex' and 'polymorphous perversity'). The transition from the seduction theory to its successor, the infantile Oedipus complex, was facilitated when, during Freud's self-analysis, an infantile memory of being sexually excited by his mother's nudity was aroused. This helped persuade him that the sexual material which had led him to impute infantile seductions to his patients could have an alternative source in their self-protectively distorted infantile incestuous fantasizing. The anomaly involved in accounting for the neuroses of predominantly female patients by invoking the desires of male infants for their mothers escaped notice for some time, but eventually prompted a suspicion that Freud's aetiological speculations were more remote from clinical experience and dependent on idiosyncratic pre-occupations than the tradition acknowledged.

The major developments in Freud's theorizing after the First World War comprised the replacement of the original division between conscious and unconscious with a tripartite division into id, ego, and superego (with the corollary that portions of the ego were unconscious); the reconstrual of anxiety as the cause rather than the product of repression; the stipulation that the self-preservative instincts were themselves libidinal, with the further extension of the concept of libido to encompass an indeterminate range of phenomena previously excluded, and the introduction of a death instinct. The rationales for these changes are still disputed and their implications for clinical practice unclear. Attempts to clarify Freud's metapsychological speculations or reduce them to consistency have proved vain to date and the suggestion has been often made that they be abandoned.

Freud's postulation of a death instinct, an impulse to return to a pre-organic state of quietude, has in particular provoked much scepticism. It was introduced in 1922, for a combination of reasons which have been found so inadequate that Ernest Jones thought it necessary to impute the innovation to some personal motive which, Max Schur maintained, was the death of a beloved daughter in the influenza epidemic of 1919. The relative contribution of this episode, and of Schopenhauer's view that the goal of life is death, can only be a matter for conjecture. Freud tells us that on his visit to America he was impressed by a sign which read, 'WHY LIVE WHEN YOU CAN BE BURIED FOR TEN DOLLARS?' This suggests a temperamental affinity with the notion of a death instinct which may have led him to overlook its theoretical deficiencies.

Freud's extension of the concept libido to encompass 'love for parents and children, friendship, love for humanity in general, devotion to concrete objects and abstract ideas' also occasioned misgivings in some quarters. It was not clear why such impulses should be repressed, or how, if repressed, they would produce the phenomena of neuroses whose apparently minute articulation with sexual mentation in its previously restricted, carnal sense gave Freud's early libidinal accounts of symptom-formation their persuasive power. Some critics felt entitled to impute the tenacity with which Freud clung to a sexual conception of libido to some deeply personal compulsion and could have cited in support the incoherence between his assertion that the majority of mankind feel degraded by the sexual act and are reluctant to perform it and his contradictory insistence that sexual gratification is 'one of . . . life's

culminations' and that 'apart from a few perverse fanatics all the world knows this and conducts life accordingly'.

During his lifetime Freud was generally regarded as a figure of unquestionable integrity. Several more recent memorialists and commentators have offered a less flattering picture of someone whose pronouncements were too often dominated by the polemical needs of the moment and whose probity deserted him whenever his more profound interests were at stake.   F.C.

*psychoanalysis, philosophical problems of; Reich; unconscious and subconcious mind.

R. Dalbiez, *The Method and Doctrine of Freud* (London, 1940).
Ernest Jones, *Freud: Life and Work* (New York, 1953–7).
M. MacMillan, *Freud Evaluated* (Amsterdam, 1990).
Max Schur, *Freud: Living and Dying* (New York, 1972).

friendship. Attachment characterized by disinterestedness and esteem. Aristotle contrasts friendship proper with relationships entered into for pleasure or advantage, 'because in them the friend is not loved for being what he is in himself'. The philosophical problems of friendship are to explain: (1) how friendship can be worth while if *not* for pleasure or advantage, since, as Aristotle observes, 'no one would choose a friendless existence on condition of having all the other good things in the world'; (2) how friendship, like family relationships, can generate obligations not had towards those who are not my friends; (3) how it can be justifiable to love you as a friend while withholding friendship from others who share the qualities I esteem in you, since to do otherwise is not (for example) to 'love you for yourself alone and not your yellow hair' (Yeats).   P.G.

*loyalty; fraternity; love.

L. Blum, *Friendship, Altruism and Morality* (London, 1980).

function. A function takes objects (*'arguments') and maps them on to objects ('values'). For example, the addition function defined on the set of natural numbers takes pairs of natural numbers as its arguments and maps each pair, say 2 and 3, on to the value, here 5, which is the sum of the pair. Functions are often identified with set-theoretical constructions. So the doubling function, with the set of natural numbers as its domain of arguments, is identified with the set of ordered pairs, $\langle x, y \rangle$, such that y is twice x. Functions need not be numerical; Frege took concepts to be functions which mapped objects on to truth-values. (This has little connection with the non-technical sense of 'function', roughly 'purpose', which is also, of course, widely used by philosophers.)   A.D.O.

P. Suppes, *Introduction to Logic* (Princeton, NJ, 1957), ch. 11.

functional explanation: *see* teleological explanation.

functionalism. The theory that the condition for being in a mental state should be given by the functional role of the state, that is, in terms of its standard causal relationships, rather than by supposed intrinsic features of the state. The role is normally envisaged as being specified in terms of which states (typically) produce it and which other states and behavioural outputs will (typically) be produced by it when the state interacts with further mental states and perceptual inputs. The theory, pioneered by David Armstrong and Hilary Putnam, improves on *behaviourism because it recognizes that behaviour results from clusters of mental states, and allows that the term for the state, e.g. 'S's pain', refers to a real inner condition which has the functional role. In one version the functional analysis was supposed to be a priori, and a ground for affirming a materialist *identity theory. Putnam proposed it as a scientific alternative to identity theories, and analysed function in terms of *Turing machines. Discussion has concerned whether conscious states can be exhaustively analysed in functional terms. A modified version has been suggested in which function is explained in terms of biological (rather than causal) role. P.F.S.

*consciousness; consciousness, its irreducibility; inverted spectrum; mind, syntax, and semantics; dualism; Putnam.

N. Block, 'Troubles With Functionalism', in N. Block (ed.), *Readings in Philosophical Psychology*, i (London, 1980).

future: *see* time.

future contingents. On one definition, a future contingent is a claim about the future, or is the content of a future-tense indicative sentence. On another, it is the possible truth-condition for such a claim: a future state of affairs that might or might not obtain. It may be argued that future contingent claims are neither true nor false until the states of affairs they are used to predict obtain or fail to obtain. S.P.

*sea-battle argument.

Aristotle's Categories and De Interpretatione, ed. J. L. Ackrill (Oxford, 1963): *De Interpretatione*, book IX.
William of Ockham, *Philosophical Writings: A Selection* (Indianapolis, 1990).

future generations. Do we have moral obligations to future generations? Most of us believe that we do. We are obligated, for example, not to harm them in certain ways and also to share the earth's resources with them in a way that is just. Some theorists have argued that we are obligated to ensure that future generations will exist (or at least not to prevent them from existing), while others have claimed that we owe it to them, by controlling population growth, to ensure that there are not too many future people existing at any one time.

Moral theories have, however, had notorious problems in providing an adequate account of the foundations of these obligations. For example, those theories that regard morality as a set of conventions that it is in our interests to obey because they facilitate peace and co-operation cannot ground obligations to future people since the latter cannot benefit or harm us (except perhaps posthumously). And hypothetical contractarianism (*contract, social), to which many theorists have appealed, has been unable to determine who should be included among the contractors who must reach agreement on principles of justice between generations. Some have argued that the contractors should all be members of a single generation; others have said that they should include everyone who has ever lived or ever will live; while others have claimed that they should include all possible people. Each of these proposals has proven unsatisfactory.

Given the problems with approaches of these sorts, many have thought that the best approach is simply to assume that our behaviour must be constrained by a respect for the rights and interests of future people in much the same way that it is constrained by the rights and interests of existing people. There are, of course, problems with predicting how our acts will affect future people, what their needs and interests will be, and so on. And there is a further question whether, because there are presumably so many of them relative to us, we are entitled to apply a discount rate to their interests according to their temporal distance from us. But it has been thought that these problems are in principle manageable.

Views of this sort are, however, all vulnerable to a powerful objection, advanced by Derek Parfit, which is based on the fact that most of the decisions that we make that have a substantial impact on the future quality of life also affect who will exist in the future. For the implementation of a social policy has widespread effects on the details of people's lives—e.g. who meets whom, who marries whom, and when people conceive their children. These effects help to determine who comes to exist. But, if it is true of a future person that he would not have existed had a certain policy not been implemented in the past, then, unless his life is not worth living, it cannot be worse for him that the policy was adopted. Hence even policies that pollute the environment or deplete resources may not be worse for future people, or violate their rights, since those people may owe their existence to the fact that those policies were implemented.

Parfit and others have concluded from this that our obligations with respect to future people must be based, not on facts about how our acts affect individuals for better or worse, but on considerations that are more impersonal in character. But traditional moral theories that take an impersonal form—such as the total and average versions of *consequentialism—have proved to have notoriously implausible implications when applied to questions concerning future and possible people. (*Population.) Hence reflection on our obligations to future generations has resulted in a profound challenge to moral theory itself.

J.McM.

Brian Barry, 'Justice between Generations', in *Liberty and Justice* (Oxford, 1991).
Peter Laslett and James S. Fishkin (eds.), *Justice between Age Groups and Generations* (New Haven, Conn., 1992).
D. Parfit, *Reasons and Persons* (Oxford, 1984).

fuzzy logic. Logical system which allows degrees of truth. For example, where '1' denotes truth, and '0' falsity, p might be true to degree 0.7 and so false to degree 0.3. In general, if p is true to degree n, then p is false to degree $1 - n$. Fuzzy logic is a departure from classical logic, because a proposition may be to some extent both true and false, and a proposition and its negation to some extent both true. Classical logic, in a sense, is a version of fuzzy logic, that version in which the only admissible truth-values in the range from 0 to 1 are 0 and 1.

Arguably, fuzzy logic does justice to the intuitive idea that some indicative sentences are not wholly true and not wholly false. For example, the claim 'He is in the room' seems not wholly true and not wholly false but partly true and partly false if he is leaving the room at the time of utterance.   S.P.

A. Kandel, *Fuzzy Mathematical Techniques with Applications* (Boston, 1986).

L. A. Zadeh, 'Fuzzy Sets', *Information and Control* (1965).

G

Gabirol, Ibn: *see* Ibn Gabirol.

Gadamer, Hans Georg (1900–2002). German philosopher who was a pupil of Heidegger and the leading modern exponent of *hermeneutics.

In *Truth and Method* (1960; tr. London, 1975), he tries to clarify the phenomenon of *understanding. Understanding (*Verstehen*) contrasts with the explanation (*Erklären*) characteristic of the natural sciences. Understanding is performed both by cultural scientists and by non-scientists; even natural scientists understand each other's speech and writing. We understand utterances, texts, people, works of art, and historical events. Earlier hermeneuticists attempted to refine a methodology for the proper interpretation of such entities. But they failed to grasp that their own understanding of an object, and the methodological principles they devised, were historically conditioned. Cultures change over history. The interpreter of a text from a past culture belongs to and is conditioned by his own different culture; he is an 'effective-historical consciousness' who views the past and its remnants from a particular *'horizon', involving a particular 'pre-understanding'. His understanding thus involves an interplay between past and present, a 'fusion of horizons'. Plato, for example, is interpreted differently by Neoplatonists of the sixth century AD, by nineteenth-century Germans, and by twentieth-century English scholars. We cannot decide which of these interpretations is correct, since any verdict we give is historically conditioned and liable to revision by a later age. (We cannot even be sure that our interpretation of past interpretations is correct.) At best our interpretation can be 'authentic', making the best reflective use of the pre-understanding or 'prejudice' from which we inevitably begin. Thus we should explore our own pre-understanding and all the relations to the world and to history that it involves. Our understanding of the past and its remains not only depends on, but also promotes, our 'self-understanding'.

In *Truth and Method* Gadamer begins with the understanding of works of art, and several later essays concern art (*The Relevance of the Beautiful and Other Essays* (Cambridge, 1986)). His central concern is the experience of art, rather than our judgements about art or the intentions and genius of the artist, and he tries to describe it as accurately as possible. The artwork rather than the audience is the pivot of this experience, and thus 'play' is a suitable term to describe it, in the sense of a game that 'tends to master the players'. Truth is not the exclusive preserve of science; thus not only interpretations of art, but the artwork itself, make a claim to truth. Works of art are not isolated from the world, and the experience of art 'does not leave him who has it unchanged'. An authentic experience of it involves not a historical reconstruction of the circumstances of its original production, but a living relationship to it which shows that it still has something to say in our epoch.

Gadamer devoted several works to the interpretation of other philosophers, especially Heidegger, Hegel, and Plato. His interpretations depend on certain principles which are not universally shared. We must take account of the nature of the text, whether it is, for example, a polished dialogue or a set of lecture notes. We must also take account of the context in which a statement is made, its intended audience, and the question which it is designed to answer. For example, an argument in a Platonic dialogue should not be considered and assessed simply as an isolated argument. We should consider its role in the dialogue, its effect on the specific audience to which it is addressed, and the background question to which it is a response. Gadamer thus purports to replace the logic of propositions with 'the logic of question and answer'. (He argues, in *The Idea of the Good in Platonic–Aristotelian Philosophy* (1978; tr. New Haven, Conn., 1986), that if we interpret Plato and Aristotle in this way we shall see that their thought is in essence continuous and that they have far more in common than is usually supposed.) Despite his admiration for Hegel, Gadamer is at odds with him here: for Hegel, unlike Schleiermacher, Plato's use of the dialogue form is an essentially irrelevant adornment for a philosophical system which can be better expressed in continuous prose.   M.J.I.

R. Dostal (ed.), *The Cambridge Companion to Gadamer* (Cambridge, 2002).

H. J. Silverman (ed.), *Gadamer and Hermeneutics* (London, 1991).

G. Warnke, *Gadamer: Hermeneutics, Tradition and Reason* (Oxford, 1987).

J. C. Weinsheimer, *Gadamer's Hermeneutics* (New Haven, Conn., 1985).

Galen (AD 129–c.200). Greek doctor and philosopher from Pergamon, Asia Minor. Although known principally as a doctor, he wrote many books devoted to philosophical topics. He advocated the study of logic and the theory of demonstration as essential for being a good doctor, and wrote several books on logical theory. He also wrote works concerning causation, psychology, moral philosophy, language, and rhetoric, as well as commentaries on Aristotle, Plato, Hippocrates, and Epicurus, and polemical books against the Stoics. Most of these are now lost.

He probably did not invent the fourth figure of Aristotelian syllogistic, but certainly did make one important contribution to logical theory, in his *Introduction to Logic*. He saw that neither Aristotelian nor Stoic logic could account for the validity of the following inference: a = b, b = c, therefore a = c. To account for its validity, and that of other arguments like it, he introduced a third kind of syllogism, 'relational syllogisms'.

Galen thinks that there is a systematic or logical way of discovering the truths of medicine—i.e. the theory of demonstration. But he also concedes that experience plays a role in the acquisition of medical knowledge. It is therefore a matter of some interest what his precise position is concerning how medical knowledge is acquired, and how it relates to the schools of medicine of his time.   B.M.

Jonathan Barnes, ' "A Third Kind of Syllogism"—Galen and the Logic of Relations', in R. Sharples (ed.), *Modern Thinkers and Ancient Thinkers* (London, 1993).

Michael Frede, 'On Galen's Epistemology', in *Essays in Ancient Philosophy* (Oxford, 1987).

R. Walzer and M. Frede (eds.), *Galen: Three Treatises on the Nature of Science* (Indianapolis, 1985).

Galileo Galilei (1564–1642). Galileo was an astronomer and physicist whose influence on the development of scientific and philosophical thought can hardly be overstated. No retiring scholar but a controversialist at home in the leading universities and palaces of Renaissance Italy until condemned by the Roman Inquisition, Galileo opposed by both word and deed the imposition of authority on the study of natural phenomena, and supported freedom of inquiry and expression.

In opposition to *Aristotelianism, Galileo insisted that mathematics was at the heart of physics. He developed his laws of motion by introducing careful measurement into empirical investigations, and combined this with thought experiments and deductive argument to show that he was no narrow inductivist or empiricist. He then demolished the naked-eye astronomy that had existed from prehistoric times by turning his telescope to the sky, discovering evidence that was decisive against the Aristotelian–Ptolemaic cosmos while supporting Copernicus.

The story of Galileo's conflict with the Roman Church is well known—how in 1633 he was condemned for endorsing Copernicanism in his *Dialogue Concerning the Two Chief World Systems* (1632), having been forbidden to do so in 1616. Nevertheless, the standard interpretation of this story has been disputed by Redondi, who, using previously unexplored Vatican archives, claims that Galileo's real crime in the eyes of the Church was not his Copernicanism but his atomist theory of matter, which was incompatible with the doctrine of transubstantiation, and therefore challenged the sacrament of the Eucharist. But a potentially capital accusation of heresy against so well known a figure as Galileo would have been a dangerous scandal, so he faced the lesser, trumped-up charges instead.

Publicly Galileo recanted, but his further scientific work shows that in spite of the real danger he continued to defend the free exercise of human reason and experience and remained a steadfast pioneer of science as a secular vocation, while never wavering in his attachment to religion.   A.BEL.

*persecution of philosophers.

Peter Machamer (ed.), *The Cambridge Companion to Galileo* (Cambridge, 1998).

Pietro Redondi, *Galileo: Heretic* (London, 1988).

gambler's fallacy, or Monte Carlo fallacy. 'Red has come up a lot recently; so probably it won't come up next time.' This is not itself so much a fallacy as just a bad reason. The underlying fallacy is to infer from, say, 'The probability of five reds running is low' to 'Given four reds running, the probability of a fifth is low'. The earlier outcomes do not affect the probability of a red next time; or, if they do, they must make it higher, by being evidence of bias in the wheel.   C.A.K.

game theory. The formalized study of rational action in situations where the welfare of each agent in a group depends on how other group members act. A game is specified by, for each participating agent, a set of permitted strategies and a set of preferences between outcomes. Agents are 'perfectly rational': in particular, they act so as to maximize expected utility, where expected utility is a measure of the likely benefit to them of their actions given their preferences between outcomes. The game specification and each agent's rationality are standardly presumed to be common knowledge: each agent knows these, each agent knows that the other agents know these, and so on. So each agent acts assuming that the other agents are rational and that they will act on the same assumption. Solutions to games standardly prescribe Nash equilibria: each agent's strategy must maximize expected utility given the strategies of the others.   T.P.

*decision theory.

R. Luce and H. Raiffa, *Games and Decisions* (New York, 1957).

Gandhi, Mohandas Karamchand (1869–1948). Hindu political activist with the uncompromising religious–philosophical ideal that non-injury is the only means to truth. In an age ravaged by two world wars, Gandhi successfully practised the method of non-violence in mass *civil-disobedience movements against racism in South Africa and against colonialism and untouchability in India. This method he called *satyāgraha* or 'zest for truth'. In

Gandhi's moral philosophy, *means and ends form a continuum, and no end ever justifies large-scale killing. In any conflict, the antagonist should be looked upon as a fellow searcher for truth. He should be won over through persuasion and self-suffering, not through deceit and brute force. Such unarmed resistance, far from being passive, calls for active love and self-control, which eventually makes individuals fit for political self-government.   A.C.

Joan V. Bondurant, *Conquest of Violence: The Gandhian Philosophy of Conflict* (Princeton, NJ, 1988).

Garden, the: *see* Epicureanism.

Gassendi, Pierre (1592–1655). A Catholic priest too often known to philosophers merely as the author of a set of objections to Descartes's *Meditations*, Gassendi was an important and influential seventeenth-century figure in his own right. Gassendi used the scepticism of Sextus Empiricus against Aristotle and *Aristotelianism, though it is doubtful that he was himself a whole-hearted sceptic. His espousal of Epicurean *atomism, combined with his voluntarism and consequent empiricism, had a profound effect on the subsequent philosophy of the century, strongly influencing both Boyle and Newton. Like them, he was a mechanist, but not a materialist. It was largely as a result of his efforts that atomism was seen as a viable candidate for the vacancy created by the increasing unsatisfactoriness of both the Aristotelian and the Paracelsan pictures of the world.   J.J.M.

Barry Brundell, *Pierre Gassendi: From Aristotelianism to a New Natural Philosophy* (Dordrecht, 1987).

Gauthier, David (1932–). Canadian moral philosopher who has specialized in the study of the relationship between reason and morality. He is a leading contemporary proponent of the view, descending from Hobbes, that morality is based on the long-term self-interest of each individual, rather than on any inherent concern or respect for the interests or moral standing of others. Gauthier has tried to develop this 'contractarian' approach, and its determinate implications, using the tools of rational choice theory, culminating in his influential *Morals by Agreement* (1986). Gauthier has also written a series of intriguing articles that offer radical reinterpretations of Locke, Kant, and Hume, drawing out their contractarian elements. Gauthier is currently the Distinguished Service Professor of Philosophy at the University of Pittsburgh.   W.K.

*contract, social.

David Gauthier, *Morals by Agreement* (Oxford, 1986).

gavagai: *see* translation, indeterminacy of.

Geach, Peter Thomas (1919–). British logician with wide-ranging philosophical interests. An admirer and expositor of McTaggart. *Mental Acts* (1958) attacks abstractionism and dispositionalist accounts of mind, and

interestingly modifies Russell's account of judgement. *Reference and Generality* (1962) demonstrates the inadequacy of medieval and modern theories of *suppositio* or *denotation. Thus in 'Every soldier swears', 'every soldier' does not stand for some entity which is said to swear, but 'every' indicates the way in which the predicate 'swear' latches on to the subject 'soldier'. A vigorous defence of Christian morality and *theodicy is given in *The Virtues* and *Providence and Evil* (both 1977). He holds the controversial view that something could be the same *A*, but not the same *B*, as something (relative identity). Geach's style is combative, jargon-free, and exploits forgotten riches of English vocabulary. Elizabeth Anscombe was his wife.   C.J.F.W.

Harry A. Lewis (ed.), *Peter Geach: Philosophical Encounters* (Dordrecht, 1991).

Geist: *see* spirit.

gender. Term introduced by feminists in order that the social aspect of sexual difference should not be ignored. When the difference between male and female human beings is treated as one of 'sex', it may be thought to be accounted for biologically. Speaking of gender, one acknowledges the socio-cultural determination of the concepts *women* and *men*, and admits a conception of women and men as distinguished primarily by a difference of social position.   J.HORN.

*feminism; sex.

Christine Delphy, *Close to Home* (London, 1984), intro.

generalization. As this term is most commonly used, a generalization is an 'all' statement, to the effect that all objects of a certain general kind possess a certain property—for example, the statement 'All planets move in elliptical orbits'. It is customary to distinguish between 'lawlike' and 'accidental' generalizations, the one just cited being lawlike whereas one such as 'All the coins in my pocket are silver' is accidental. How to analyse this distinction is a disputed issue, but it is widely accepted that only lawlike generalizations support corresponding counterfactual *conditionals. Thus 'All planets move in elliptical orbits' implies 'If Vulcan were a planet, it would move in an elliptical orbit', whereas 'All the coins in my pocket are silver' does not imply 'If this penny were in my pocket, it would be silver'.   E.J.L.

N. Goodman, *Fact, Fiction, and Forecast*, 4th edn. (Cambridge, Mass., 1983).

generalization, rule of. An inference rule of the *predicate or functional calculus. Let α be an individual variable and Φ a *well-formed formula. The rule is:

From Φ infer $(\alpha)\Phi$,

where Φ holds for any arbitrary individual.

The notation '(α)' represents the universal quantifier and is read 'For all α'. Alternative notations are 'Π_α' and '$\forall_\alpha$'.

Where a free variable α occurs in Φ the application of the rule binds the variable. Formalizations specify conditions and syntactic restrictions for application of the rule to ensure that the inferences are valid. An example of a valid application of the rule is the inference of

$$(x)\,(Fx \vee \sim Fx)$$

from

$$(Fy \vee \sim Fy),$$

since the latter holds for any arbitrary individual.   R.B.M.

W. V. Quine, *Methods of Logic*, 4th edn. (Cambridge, Mass., 1982).

general properties: *see* properties, general.

general will. The doctrine of the general will is found in the writings of some theorists in the tradition of contractualist political philosophy. The doctrine has controversial images associated with it, but its central aim is to provide an account of the conditions under which principles and policies for the state are morally acceptable. Citizens are thought of as having 'interests', some of which are 'perceived', and often different from one person to another, and even from one time in a person's life to another, while others are considered 'real' or 'genuine', and hence common to all persons. The doctrine concerns how these common interests may be identified, and how they may gain expression in the policies of the state, and thereby constitute the state just.

Rousseau's version of the doctrine appears to be driven by the figure of society as 'social organism'. The general will is the will of this organism, i.e. the 'collective body' formed by the citizens of a state, and as such is distinguished from the will of any particular individual or group, and even from 'the will of all'. Rousseau's view influenced Kant, but Kant's view leaves aside the notion that society should be thought of as 'organism'. The main idea now is that morality involves principles that are 'valid for all rational beings', and that one may arrive at such principles by setting aside one's 'inclinations' (e.g. particular features of personality or interests associated with social station that differ among real people and tend to ground conflicts among them), and by exercising the 'rational nature' that is the common possession of moral agents. John Rawls's conception of **'justice as fairness' is thought of heuristically as the choice of parties to a hypothetical morally credentialled deliberating-position, one of the main features of which is, again, a setting-aside of those differentiating features of real individuals which are (in Rawls's words) 'arbitrary from the moral point of view'. The principles which are then chosen by agents whose particularity is thereby suspended are construed as providing the normative substance of justice for the basic structure of society, i.e. the standards by which to assess its main economic, legal, political, and educational institutions and practices.

Thus, in different vocabularies, the theories of Rousseau, Kant, and Rawls have in common the claim that the deliverances of reasoning meeting the conditions of impartiality and disinterestedness are morally right. However, interpreting the doctrine in this way makes it attractive but not yet uncontroversial. Recent challenges do not restrict their critiques to the spectre of totalitarianism suggested by the idea of society as 'social organism'. One critique instead cites cases in which particulars about persons, e.g. their special relationships, the meaning-giving projects in their lives, their offices, and roles, are indeed relevant to an understanding of what morality requires, including the substance of justice. This objection suggests that the doctrine does not appropriately recognize the moral relevance of 'partiality', or, more fully, the moral standing of the 'individuality' of persons. This is paradoxical, for the historical and contemporary proponents of the doctrine think of their general theories as endorsing *individualism. Another critique argues not from 'individuality' but from 'community'. Its point is that the doctrine's emphasis on impartiality and disinterestedness ignores the importance of culture, heritage, and tradition to the identity of citizens. This is paradoxical again, for some proponents of the doctrine think of their theories as providing reasonable interpretations of the communitarian ideals of the public interest and the common good.   N.S.C.

*organic society; contract, social.

Brian Barry, 'The Public Interest', *Proceedings of the Aristotelian Society* (1964).
Patrick Riley, *The General Will before Rousseau: The Transformation of the Divine into the Civic* (Princeton, NJ, 1986).
John Rawls, *A Theory of Justice* (Cambridge, Mass., 1971).
Michael Walzer, *Spheres of Justice* (New York, 1983).

generations, justice between. The Brundtland Report, *Our Common Future* (1987), defined sustainable development as 'development that meets the needs of the present without compromising the ability of future generations to meet their own needs'. The responsibility implied in this statement may be regarded as weak or strong. The weak principle of intergenerational justice requires that we pass on natural resources and knowledge to the future in a way that enables future people to meet their basic needs. The strong principle requires us to limit consumption of environmental goods so that future people can be expected to achieve a standard of living, or quality of life, equivalent to that enjoyed by present people. Thomas Schwartz argued that any policy we now undertake will make a difference to who actually exists in future (e.g., by determining who travels where, and who meets whom). Hence, provided future individuals have lives worth living, they cannot be said to be harmed by present policies. Whether Schwartz's argument undermines the strong principle of justice between generations has been very much debated.   A.BRE.

A. de-Shalit, *Why Posterity Matters* (London, 1995).
T. Schwartz, 'Obligations to Posterity', in R. Sikora and B. Barry (eds.), *Obligations to Future Generations* (Philadelphia, 1978).

genetic epistemology: *see* epistemology, genetic.

genetic fallacy. Probably first called such by Morris Cohen and Ernest Nagel, it is the fallacy of confusing the causal origins of a belief with its justification. That this is always a confusion has been queried by reliabilist theories in epistemology, which hold that a belief is justified to the extent that it is the causal output of cognitive devices operating in accordance with their designs, i.e. 'as they should'.

Of particular importance for the analysis of the genetic fallacy is the widespread and indispensable practice of forming one's beliefs, and acting on them, on the basis of the *testimony of others. Assuming the implausibility of declaring fallacious all such cases of belief-formation, it evidently matters whether a believer's testimonial sources satisfy appropriate conditions on reliability. Since the same is true of whether a so-called *ad verecundiam* argument is fallacious, it may be said that *ad verecundiam* arguments are a special case of 'genetic' arguments.   J.W.

*reliabilism.

Morris R. Cohen and Ernest Nagel, *Logic and Scientific Method* (New York, 1934).

genetics and morality. The fast-developing science of genetics, within which the functions of more and more genes, either alone or in conjunction with others, are being discovered, can be seen as providing the latest form of determinism, or reductionism, according to which all human behaviour can be explained by the genes a person has. If genetic determinism were true, no one could be blamed, or indeed praised, for what he or she did, since behaviour would have been programmed from the time a person was an embryo. Though such a theory is wholly implausible, since environment (including education and culture) must be taken into account in the formation of character as much as genetic inheritance, yet, like other forms of determinism, the theory in a less thoroughgoing form may gradually come to have an effect on moral attitudes. If it were shown conclusively that a certain gene or conjunction of genes led to aggressive behaviour, for example, or indifference to the well-being of other people, then there would be less inclination to apportion moral blame to those who exhibited this kind of antisocial behaviour, and less faith in the efficacy of exhortation or example to get people to mend their ways. The language of morals, as well as the practice of punishment, might be subtly changed. It has to be noticed, however, that there have in the past been many forms of determinism, theological, physical, and psychological. None has destroyed the idea of morality, nor the human desire to influence children by education and good upbringing. The fate of genetic determinism may be no different.

A specific way in which our new appreciation of the importance of genes may change our moral attitudes is with regard to children who are born either through an adulterous relationship or by artificial insemination with donor sperm. Hitherto it has been possible to try to justify keeping a child in ignorance of her true paternity (though many have always regarded such deception as morally indefensible). This seems now positively wrong: too much may turn on the knowledge for it to be concealed.

A more dramatic way in which new genetic knowledge may in future impinge on morality is in the matter of genetic intervention. Morality is largely based on the assumption that individual people are unique, each different from one another, to be valued for their own sake and responsible, at least to a large extent, for their own characters. If it became possible for parents to choose not only the sex but the personalities and abilities of their children, according to their own blueprint, the sense of independence and individual responsibility might be gradually eroded. It is difficult to foresee the difference it would make to someone's sense of responsibility and self-image if he had to think that other people, his parents, had decided that this was what he should be. There is something profoundly inimical to our concept of morality in the thought of one person being in a position to dictate in advance the life-chances of another. Though it seems morally right that parents should, by genetic manipulation, see to it that their child does not suffer from serious or life-threatening disease, it seems morally wrong that they should intervene to enhance their child's ability or beauty or talents. This uneasiness may arise partly from the fact that such genetic enhancement, if it were possible, would be extremely expensive. Only the very rich could afford it. The gap between the children of the rich and those of the poor would be widened still further, to the detriment of society. Political considerations apart, however, the thought that we had been manipulated to conform to someone else's blueprint would be profoundly demeaning. The intrinsic value that each individual has, a value that lies at the heart of morality, depends in part on the random and unpredictable mixture of his parents' genes which make up his unique genome. Such moral distinctions may fall to be settled in the future, and are the subject of theoretical discussion even now.   M.WARN.

*bioethics.

John Harris, *Clones, Genes and Immortality: Ethics and the Genetic Revolution* (Oxford, 1998).
Jonathan Glover, *What Sort of People Should there Be?* (Harmondsworth, 1986).
John Habgood, *Being a Person* (London, 1998).
Ellie Lee (ed.), *Designer Babies: Where Should we Draw the Line?* (London, 2002).

genius. Creative ability of an exalted kind. In philosophy creative ability is in the realm of ideas. It would be controversial to attempt either to provide a complete list of those philosophers who would be entitled to the label of genius, or to lay down necessary and sufficient conditions for it. Indeed, some philosophers might regard it as invidious to single out an individual philosopher as a 'genius' on the grounds that this creates a cult of cleverness. But, if one were to allow the term, the following conditions—which are much wider than 'cleverness'—are typically satisfied by the philosophical genius. The genius expresses through his work the main currents of scientific and other thought of his times; he not only synthesizes these but adds the stamp of his own mind to them; the force of the ideas alters the direction of subsequent thought; the ideas embody a vision of the world, they appeal to the imagination as well to the intellect. It will be widely agreed that Plato, Aristotle, Aquinas, Descartes, Hume, Kant, Hegel, and Wittgenstein fit these criteria, and other names can plausibly be added to the category.   R.S.D.

*superman.

R. L. Gregory, 'Genius', in R. L. Gregory (ed.), *The Oxford Companion to the Mind* (Oxford, 1987).

Gentile, Giovanni (1875–1944). Together with Croce, he led the revival of Italian idealist philosophy at the turn of the century. Gentile's 'actualism' represented the subjective extreme of *idealism. He aimed to integrate our consciousness of experience with its creation by uniting thought and will in the self-constitution or *autoctisi* of reality. The 'pure act' of spirit constituted the true synthesis a priori of self and world which made objective knowledge possible. He claimed that his theory explained the phenomenological development of self-consciousness within both the individual and Western thought as a whole. To illustrate the first thesis, he wrote a number of influential books on education. Demonstrating his second claim led him to write a detailed history of modern *Italian philosophy in order to show how the ideas of the German thinkers he admired were adopted or independently conceived by Italian philosophers as part of a single European tradition reflecting the unity of spirit or human consciousness. The embodiment of the individual's self-consciousness was the state, a doctrine that led to his philosophical support of *fascism. He stood by Mussolini to the end, dying at the hands of communist partisans.   R.P.B.

Richard Bellamy, *Modern Italian Social Theory* (Cambridge, 1987), ch. 6.

Gentzen, Gerhard (1909–45). German logician who, in his fundamental paper of 1935, expounded a radically new way of formalizing logic—*natural deduction, which he carried out for both classical and intuitionistic first-order logic. A natural deduction system has rules of inference, but no logical truths assumed axiomatically. A formula may be introduced into a derivation as a hypothesis at any stage. Gentzen divided the rules of his natural deduction system that governed the logical constants into introduction rules and elimination rules. An introduction rule allowed the derivation of a formula with the given logical constant as its main operator from premisses in which it does not occur essentially; thus the introduction rule for '&' allows us to infer $A \& B$ from A and B as separate premisses. An elimination rule allowed an inference from such a formula, perhaps together with additional minor premisses; thus the elimination rule for '→' (if-then) was simply *modus ponens*, whereby B is inferred from $A \rightarrow B$ together with the minor premiss A. In such cases, the conclusion of the inference depends on whatever hypotheses

the premisses depended on. In some inferences, however, it does not depend on all of them. Thus the introduction rule for negation is *reductio ad absurdum*: if from a set Γ of hypotheses, together with the hypothesis A, a contradictory conclusion can be derived, then the negation of A may be inferred as depending on the hypotheses Γ alone. The hypotheses on which the final conclusion of the derivation depends may then be regarded as the premisses of the derivation as a whole.

In order to keep track of the hypotheses on which each line of a natural deduction derivation depends, these lines may be shown as sequents. A sequent is a pair $\Gamma : A$, where A is the formula standing at that line of the derivation, and Γ is the finite set of formulae on which A depends; the introduction of a hypothesis H will be represented by the 'basic sequent' $H : H$. If $\Gamma : A$ occurs as a line of a correct derivation, the formula A will be a logical consequence of the formulae Γ. In the same paper, Gentzen developed another method of formalization, a sequent calculus. For classical, but not intuitionistic, logic, a sequent was now allowed to have finitely many formulae on the right (these formulae being understood disjunctively). The introduction rules remained as before, but the elimination rules were replaced by rules of introduction on the left-hand side of the sequent: e.g. that for & allowed the derivation of $\Gamma, A \& B : \Delta$ from $\Gamma, A : \Delta$ or $\Gamma, B : \Delta$; it is thereby inferred that a conclusion follows from certain premisses from the fact that it follows from other, simpler, premisses. The sequent calculus is easily shown equivalent to the natural deduction system, with the help of the cut rule, allowing the derivation of $\Gamma, \Theta : \Delta, \Lambda$ from $\Gamma : C, \Delta$ and $\Theta, C : \Lambda$, where C is termed the cut formula. Gentzen's cut-elimination theorem (*Hauptsatz*) showed that any derivation using the cut rule could be transformed into one not using it: the introduction of the cut formula had been an unnecessary detour. The cut-free sequent calculus (lacking the cut rule) has the subformula property: any formula occurring within a derivation is a subformula of one occurring in the final sequent. The cut-elimination theorem yielded a decision procedure for intuitionistic sentential logic, and allowed very simple proofs of several theorems hitherto proved by appeal to an algebraic characterization of the set of valid formulae.

Gentzen proceeded to give two proofs of the consistency of formal (Peano) arithmetic (1936 and 1938), using a form of transfinite induction. By Gödel's second *incompleteness theorem, such transfinite induction cannot be so derivable; but in Gentzen's proof, it was applied only to statements with no bound variables.   M.D.

G. Gentzen, *Collected Papers*, ed. M. E. Szabo (Amsterdam, 1969).

genus and species. Terms forming part of a system of classification of entities (most characteristically biological entities); genera constitute a wider class than do species. The terms derive from Aristotle, for whom the principles of classification depend on real relations between things in nature. The Greek word for species is the same as that for *form, and in Aristotle's view species have *essences and are distinguished from other co-ordinate species falling under the same genus by a determinate differentia.   D.W.H.

*determinables and determinates; categories.

Aristotle, *De partibus animalium* I and *De generatione animalium* I, tr. with notes by D. M. Balme (Oxford, 1972).

German philosophy. In Germany, as in other European nations, medieval philosophers (apart from the mystics) wrote in Latin. (The most significant was Albertus Magnus (*c.*1200–80), the learned Aristotelian who taught Aquinas.) But in Germany philosophy continued to be written and taught in Latin later than elsewhere. Leibniz wrote mainly in Latin and French. In 1688 Christian Thomasius (1655–1728) gave, at Leipzig, the first philosophy lectures in German. Christian Wolff (1679–1754) was the first significant philosopher to write mainly in German.

Partly as a result of this, many of the philosophers who wrote in German were very conscious of the fact, and emphasized and exploited the philosophical resources of German. They did not always commend the same features of the language. Leibniz stressed the concrete sensual imagery of German words and their metaphorical potentialities, developed and transmitted by the medieval mystics. Hegel stressed the great variety of abstract, and thus implicitly philosophical, terms in everyday speech. The virtues of German continued to be praised in the twentieth century. Heidegger noted the 'peculiar inner affinity of the German language with the language of the Greeks and their thought. . . . When the French begin to think, they speak German' (*Der Spiegel*, 31 May 1976). Fichte's proposal to extrude foreign loan-words (including 'Philosophie') from the German language found little support, but the belief that German is an ideal philosophical language, whatever its truth, affects the style of much German philosophy.

Owing in part to the nature of the Reformation and to the survival of Catholicism as a potent force, theology was, from the sixteenth to the twentieth century, a flourishing academic discipline with important interconnections with philosophy. Friedrich Schleiermacher (1768–1834), one of the founders of *hermeneutics, was also the greatest Protestant theologian since Luther. Many philosophers were originally trained as theologians: Hegel and Schelling as Protestants, for example, and Heidegger as a Jesuit. In the case of other philosophers too, one cannot ignore their deep religiosity and their theological interests: the pietism of Kant, for example, or the Augustinian Catholicism of Scheler. Even when philosophers initially reject their inherited religious beliefs, they often, though not invariably, return to them later: Fichte's and Schelling's talk about the I or the Absolute eventually becomes talk about God, and Friedrich Schlegel (1772–1829), like many of the Romantic radicals, converted to Catholicism. Conversely, theologians were often decisively influenced by philosophers: Barth by Kierkegaard, Rudolf Bultmann (1884–1976) by his friend Heidegger, and Tillich (1886–1965) by Schelling. The theological

background of many philosophers perhaps accounts for their willingness to transcend, or at least delve beneath, experience in their exploration of the nature of things and to keep the natural sciences in their proper place, if not to ignore them altogether.

Connected with this (since theologians need to interpret ancient texts) is the deeply historical character of much German philosophy and thought in general. Philosophy of history was founded by Vico and baptized by Voltaire, but it came into its own in Germany. Philosophers such as Herder and Hegel became aware that men think differently in different periods and came to ask not (like Hume or Gibbon) 'Given that people think, if they think at all, in a uniformly rational way, how can we explain what they did in the past?', but 'How did it come about that we now think in a certain rational way, when in the past people thought in radically different ways?'

Associated with this historical tendency is the intense study, in the late eighteenth and early nineteenth centuries, of the philosophical and literary works of the past: Homer, Plato, Plotinus, and Shakespeare, etc. were edited, translated, and explored. Dilthey, among many others, continued this tradition into the twentieth century. Nietzsche was a classical philologist as well as a philosopher, but philosophers who were not primarily scholars were often steeped in the works of classical antiquity (Hegel, Schelling, Marx, Heidegger) and occasionally in medieval philosophy (Heidegger). When Hegel speaks of scepticism, for example, he usually has in mind the Greek Sceptics rather than Hume.

In the same period, German philosophers, above all Kant, explored the nature of the self and tended to a form of *idealism. British philosophers did so too, both earlier (Hume) and later (J. S. Mill). But the two approaches differ significantly. Hume and Mill distinguish two realms of entities, the outer objects studied by the natural sciences and the inner objects studied by psychology. Mental events and states are to be studied by the same methods as outer objects; they are to be analysed, classified, and explained by laws of association. Idealism consists in the conclusion that outer objects are reducible to complex patterns of inner events. Kant and his followers, such as Fichte, rejected this procedure. It ignores, they argued, the I or subject that is aware of both inner and outer objects. It omits to ask why the I has experience both of inner and of outer objects, and why its experience takes the form that it does. Hence they abandoned the psychological approach in favour of the transcendental: the I that has experience of both realms is neither physical nor psychical, but transcendental. The rejection of the psychological and the espousal of the transcendental persists into the twentieth century in the work of Husserl. Some philosophers believed they had discovered a 'third realm' distinct from both the physical and the psychological, the realm of the 'ideal'. But this did not go unchallenged. Heidegger rejected this 'banal Platonism' in favour of a radically overhauled psychology that no longer regards man as a compound of 'body', 'soul', and 'spirit', but as *Dasein* or 'being-in-the-world'.

J. G. FICHTE developed Kant's epistemological and ethical ideas at the end of the eighteenth century, and became an apostle of Prussian nationalism.

SØREN KIERKEGAARD gave deliberately anti-academic expression (witness the peculiar forms, titles, and pseudonyms of his works) to a powerful defence of human freedom against systems, rules, and rationalizations.

ARTHUR SCHOPENHAUER'S academic career at the University of Berlin foundered when he opted unwisely to deliver his lectures at the same times as Hegel's; the resulting resentment, and many others, find expression in his writings. In his work Eastern religious traditions first exert a significant influence on Western philosophy.

FRIEDRICH NIETZSCHE'S iconoclastic brilliance brought him international fame too late for him to know it. His unpredictable influence has coursed through modernism and postmodernism.

The transcendental method is connected with several other features of German thought. First, transcendental philosophers regard idealism as entirely compatible with objectivity. While idealists such as Hume and Mill tend to see values and the truths of logic and arithmetic as dependent on our psychological states (or, later, on our language), German idealists often, though not invariably, regard them as wholly objective, albeit transcendentally determined. The transcendental lies deeper than our customary distinction between the subject and the object, the subjective and the objective. Second, since the transcendental I is neither psychological subject nor physical object, and since it is, on some accounts, prior even to the distinction between different people, it tends to be equated with, or to turn into, the Absolute or God; it met with this fate in Fichte and Schelling, if not in Husserl. By contrast, Hume and Mill incline to atheism, since there is little temptation to deify the psychological I. (Berkeley's theology depends on a combination of the psychological and transcendental methods.) Third, psychological or subjective idealism is inimical to a sense of history. If I focus on my own mental states and the laws governing them, I have little reason to suppose that others may have, or have had, mental states of a different type, governed perhaps by different laws. It is even hard to see how the historical past can be more than a dubious inference from my present mental states or a logical construction out of them. *Transcendental idealism, by contrast, presents no such difficulties in the view of its adherents. Indeed, it is plausible to suppose that it favoured historicism: if one pares oneself down to one's bare I, shorn of historically determined physical and psychological contingencies, it is easier to range in imagination over other times and places. What I then find in the past may be as independent of my present mental states as are the laws of logic and mathematics.

The transcendental method is also related to the tendency of German philosophers to reject individualism. Psychological states are decidedly the states of a single individual, and the single individual is, on the whole, what concerns British empiricists. An individual is conceived as a complete person prior to relations with other individuals. The acquisition of concepts and knowledge is regarded as a solitary enterprise, with little attention to the education of children into a shared language and culture. There then arises the problem of other minds: How can I know that there are any other minds or, if there are, what goes on in them? How can there even be psychological states that are not experienced by *me*? (Little attention was paid to this problem before J. S. Mill, however.) Individualism also inspired social contract theories: people are conceived as fully formed individuals, capable of making contracts, etc., prior to relations with others, independently of any shared culture or tradition. The transcendental I, by contrast, is less obviously a complete individual, or even an individual at all. To the questions 'Why can there not be just one person? Why does the I splinter into many individuals?', Fichte and Schelling reply that without others I would not be complete. I would lack moral constraints and thus be unable to display my (Kantian) freedom. Bereft of others and confined to my own perspective on the world, I could hardly extricate the world from myself: it would be *my* world, not an *objective* world. Hegel develops their thought in his concept of *Geist*, a word for 'mind' that expands, more readily than its English counterpart, into a shared mind or 'spirit', into an 'I that is We and a We that is I'. Heidegger too, with his concepts of 'being-with-others' and the They, insists that a shared world and a complete human being require a deep interconnection between individuals, not just a plurality of solitary individuals. Such philosophical anti-individualism converges with the German propensity for cultural history (Herder, Dilthey) and sociology (Weber).

The history of German philosophy is more complex than these generalizations suggest. The first strictly German philosophers, writing in German as often as in Latin, were the mystics, the earliest of whom were nuns, such as Hildegard of Bingen (1098–1173) and Mechthild of Magdeburg (1212–85). These prepared the ground for Meister Eckhart (1260–1337), Heinrich Seuse (1300–66), Johann Tauler (1300–61), and Thomas à Kempis (1379–1471). The mystics were not wholly divorced from scholastic philosophy. Eckhart, for example, made use of *Neoplatonism and of Aquinas, and his thought is essentially scholastic, even if his style and devotion are shaped by earlier mystics. The mystics were much admired by Leibniz, and their influence, especially on the Romantics, but also on, for example, Heidegger, is pervasive. The greatest German philosopher of the Renaissance, Nicholas of Cusa (1401–64), was influenced by Eckhart, as well as by medieval logic, in arguing that the universe flows out of and returns to an unknowable God. Several aspects of his thought, especially his principle of the coincidence of opposites, anticipate Leibniz and Hegel. (Hegel, however, nowhere mentions Nicholas.) Among later mystics, the shoemaker Jakob Böhme (1575–1624) had a large impact on later philosophers, including Hegel and Schelling (who called him a 'miraculous phenomenon in the history of humanity').

Böhme was persecuted by the Protestant orthodoxy established by Martin Luther (1483–1546), who rejected the metaphysical element in German philosophy, attacked Aristotelianism and Thomism, and advocated conceptual and verbal clarity. Philip Melanchthon (1497–1560), who was entrusted by Luther with the task of systematizing the thought of the Reformation, paradoxically returned to Aristotle as the foundation of his system, thus establishing what came to be known as Protestant neo-scholasticism.

The first indisputably great German philosopher is Leibniz, who, although he did not teach philosophy and published relatively little, decisively shaped the future course of philosophy in Germany and was in a sense the founder of German idealism. Christian Wolff, who was a follower of Leibniz, achieved enormous popularity in the late eighteenth century and was largely responsible for establishing a clear, stable philosophical vocabulary in German. Other rationalist philosophers were Mendelssohn and Alexander

Gottlieb Baumgarten (1714–62), who first gave aesthetics its name and established it as a distinct department of philosophy, and whose *Metaphysica* (1739) was used by Kant as the basis for his lectures.

The German *Enlightenment reached its climax with Kant, who initiated the most important period of philosophical activity in modern times. He generated a host of followers, attempting to explain, systematize, and develop his thought: among others, Karl Leonhard Reinhold (1758–1823), Solomon Maimon (1753–1800), J. S. Beck (1761–1840), and Jakob Friedrich Fries (1773–1843). Schiller gave Kantianism a distinctive historical and aesthetic bias that contributed to the growth of post-Kantian idealism. But other forces worked to the same end: for example, Johann Georg Hamann (1730–88), the 'magus of the north', a Protestant mystic who disliked the analytical rationalism of the Enlightenment and saw more creative power in feeling, language, and especially poetry, the 'mother-tongue of the human race'. Friedrich Heinrich Jacobi (1743–1819) argued that our knowledge of mundane and divine matters rests, not on argument, but on feeling and faith. He also initiated the revival of Spinoza, a crucial influence on Herder, Goethe, and the post-Kantian idealists: Fichte, Schelling, and Hegel. The Romantic circle, especially Novalis (1772–1801) and Schlegel, made perverse use of Fichte's doctrines, cultivating the aphoristic style later adopted by Nietzsche. Schelling was seen as their official philosopher. Schleiermacher was another member of the circle. Hegel admired his *On Religion: Speeches to its Cultured Despisers* (1799), but later came to hate him, avowedly because he rejected his view that religion rests on a feeling of 'absolute dependence' (in which case, Hegel said, a dog is the best Christian), but perhaps also because he envied his work on Heraclitus, Plato, and dialectic.

With the death of Hegel in 1831 the period of German idealism, which has no parallel elsewhere, came to end. The growth of the natural sciences cast suspicion on philosophical systems and favoured *naturalism and *materialism. The view of man as essentially rational gave way to the view that he is primarily a biological creature, dominated by will rather than reason. Schopenhauer forms a bridge between idealism and naturalism, shifting freely from the 'I' to the 'brain', and Nietzsche moved further in the direction of naturalism. The best of the Hegelians followed this trend: Feuerbach, Stirner, and Marx. Schelling's late philosophy, essentially an elaboration of idealism, was regarded as an anachronism. Three other developments which began in the nineteenth century contributed to the upsurge of German philosophy in the twentieth. First, the neo-Kantians appealed to Kant both to oppose metaphysical idealism and to supply a more adequate foundation for the sciences. They later included Cassirer and Heidegger's teacher Heinrich Rickert (1863–1936). Second, Dilthey and Georg Simmel (1858–1918) advanced the philosophy of history, making more use of the concept of life than of reason. (History and 'life' are also central in Nietzsche's thought.) Third, Brentano laid the foundations of phenomenology.

The main philosophical trends of the early twentieth century, a period of creativity almost equal to the age of idealism, emerged from these beginnings. Husserl and Scheler developed *phenomenology, though Scheler (as protean as Schelling) moved closer to Nietzsche and Dilthey when he championed philosophical *anthropology. Nicolai Hartmann abandoned neo-Kantianism to establish an empirically grounded ontology. All of these tendencies, along with Kierkegaard, contributed to the *Existenzphilosophie* of Jaspers and Heidegger. Most of these trends continued after the Second World War, but with several additions. Heidegger's thought developed away from, or at least beyond, his pre-war writings. Gadamer elaborated Heidegger's *hermeneutics into a hermeneutical philosophy. The neo-Marxian critical theory of the *Frankfurt School, originated in the 1930s by Adorno and Horkheimer, continued to flourish after their return from exile and has been developed by Habermas. Finally, analytical philosophy prospers in Germany, especially under the influence of the Vienna Circle, Popper, Wittgenstein, and Anglo-American philosophers, but utilizing also the fertile resources of the German heritage.

M.J.I.

*Hegelianism; Kantianism; neo-Kantianism; Schlegel; Schleiermacher; English philosophy; French philosophy.

L. W. Beck, *Early German Philosophy: Kant and his Predecessors* (Cambridge, Mass., 1969).

F. C. Beiser, *German Idealism: The Struggle against Subjectivism, 1781–1801* (Cambridge, Mass., 2002).

R. Bubner, *Modern German Philosophy* (Cambridge, 1981).

J. D. Caputo, *The Mystical Element in Heidegger's Thought* (Athens, Oh., 1978).

A. O'Hear (ed.), *German Philosophy since Kant* (Cambridge, 1999).

H. Schnadelbach, *Philosophy in Germany 1831–1933* (Cambridge, 1984).

German philosophy today. Contemporary philosophizing in the German-speaking realm is characterized by a 'new obscurity' (*neue Unübersichtlichkeit*, Jürgen Habermas). The decline of previous philosophical systems within and after the two World Wars led to a *plurality* of coexisting approaches and directions. They are often in opposition to the idealistic and transcendental traditions which had been dominant for a long time and are still influential (especially the writings of Immanuel Kant and Georg Wilhelm Friedrich Hegel). What appeared in the twentieth century as a revolution or break became established as branches of new traditions, which will likely continue for quite a while. They are of no less importance than the extensive investigations of the history of philosophy and the interpretation of classical texts, the treasures of which are made fruitful for contemporary thinking. Three main currents are characteristic today: (1) the *hermeneutic current*, which evolved out of the plurality of interpretations and deals with them; (2) the *post-modern current*, which is brought about by the plurality of life-forms, partially leading to an extreme relativism, and giving special emphasis to aesthetic points of view; and

(3) the *scientific and science-oriented current*, which reacts to the growth of knowledge and the increase in specialization, and carefully considers the theoretical and practical conditions and consequences of the scientization and mechanization of the world we live in. A shared core of these three main currents is *anthropology* in all its different aspects—a reflection about man as an interpreting, social, and natural being that searches for orientation in an increasingly complex world.

1. *Hermeneutic philosophy* is the only main current today that has persisted relatively intact since before the Second World War, and is the deepest continuation of traditional philosophy in the German-speaking realm. It builds especially upon the analyses of understanding by Wilhelm Dilthey, phenomenology (Edmund Husserl), analyses of being (Martin Heidegger), and subsequent philosophical hermeneutics in a narrower sense (Hans-Georg Gadamer). At the centre of this 'art of understanding' are philosophical, literary, and theological texts and their historical horizon, as well as the methods of the humanities, and everyday life as a whole. This approach is chiefly about interpretations and hence also about the phenomenon of language (which rose—but for different reasons and especially with the aim of a theory of meaning—to be a main subject of analytical philosophy as well). The conditions and features of the communicative society, as well as linguistic practice itself, are analysed (with natural connections to speech-act theory, structuralism, and general semiotics). Not the individual consciousness but, rather, intersubjectivity is regarded as constitutive for reason and the truth of statements. Contrary to the coherence and correspondence theories of truth, which are dominant in scientific philosophy, consensus theories of truth are favoured, and the concept of explanation is confronted with the concept of understanding. The underlying motivations for thought and action are analysed, leading to discourse ethics (Jürgen Habermas, Karl-Otto Apel) and a strong tendency to investigate and criticize social mechanisms (with connections to sociology) and the tradition of philosophical enlightenment. Sometimes social theory has almost demanded the status of a *prima philosophia*. Before the reunification of Germany, Marxist philosophy also had a shaping influence: in West Germany (FRG) as a critical instance within the scope of the Frankfurt School (Theodor W. Adorno, Max Horkheimer, Herbert Marcuse, Jürgen Habermas, etc.), and quite differently in East Germany (GDR) as a state doctrine. Today, the spectrum of the hermeneutic current extends from the attempting of ultimate explanations in ideal-communicative and transcendental-pragmatic contexts, to a 'farewell to principles' (*Abschied vom Prinzipiellen*, Odo Marquard). The search for anthropological and social guide-lines for managing one's own existence took the place of systematizing objective truths in a *philosophia perennis*. This pragmatic turn lead to a self-restriction of philosophy. Ludwig Wittgenstein's later investigations of the philosophy of language gave many impulses for the analysis of everyday

communication and the life-world. In taking very different historical, geographical, but also individual ways of life into consideration, the 'new obscurity' is also reflected in the second contemporary main current:

2. *Post-modern philosophy* which, in the broader sense, separates itself from ways of thinking which are orientated towards strict methods, rationality, linguistic analyses, and the search for objective knowledge. It has been influenced partly by twentieth-century French philosophy. So-called post-modernism (a somewhat misleading term which expresses, quite appropriately, a certain insecurity within this current) tries to interpret the plurality of approaches and perspectives affirmatively and as progress, contrary to sceptical objections. At the same time, earlier philosophical systems and traditions are considered 'grand narratives' among others. Some aspects of the modern are preserved, however, which is why Wolfgang Welsch spoke of 'our postmodern modern age'. Here one continues to emphasize human autonomy; on the other hand, belief in the progress of science and society is questioned or criticized as a form of totalitarianism. The aim is a 'narrative philosophy' similar to Richard Rorty's in the USA.

Questions about forms of life, and how to conduct one's own life, are the focus of interest in this divergent current of thought, which exceeds post-modernism in a narrower sense; traditional philosophizing with its demand for ultimate obligations recedes into the background. Culture and art critics, journalists, artists, movie directors and talk-show hosts now consider themselves competent to answer philosophical questions. The result is a popularization of philosophical topics in philosophical cafés, feature pages, and on television. Aesthetics, philosophy of art, and the search for meaning, happiness, and an art of living become more and more important; occasionally there are even attempts to apply philosophy therapeutically. A philosophy of the media has developed, where virtual reality, simulation, and surrogates acquire paradigmatic status. There is a far-reaching scepticism about metaphysics and rationality, attacking social taboos (e.g. in the evaluation of mental diseases and criminality) and cultural bias. There is an increased exploration of ways of thinking from other cultures, especially Asia. Finally, some post-modern philosophers oppose metaphysical or scientific realism, justifying this with historical investigations of era changes and paradigm shifts, as well as studies of the sociology of science; they argue for diverse forms of anti-realism and relativism. This is in sharp contrast to the third main current:

3. *Scientific and science-oriented philosophy*, which has mostly been influenced by the Anglo-American world, and can be subdivided into a theoretical and a more practical, applied part. The *theoretical side*, with its emphasis of the significance of logic, language analysis, and empiricism, is dominated by analytical philosophy and philosophy of science. It is in the tradition of Cambridge philosophers like G. E. Moore, Bertrand Russell, the early Ludwig Wittgenstein, and especially the Vienna Circle.

Historically its reception did not begin until the emigration of many of its proponents to the USA, and the subsequent radiation of their teachings. Additionally, Karl Popper and his successors had a formative influence on philosophy of science and political philosophy (fallibilism, criticism of totalitarianism). Also initiated by Popper, and in conjunction with biological discoveries, evolutionary epistemology was developed. Here the nature and capacity of our epistemological faculties are viewed objectivistically in the light of the Darwinian theory of selection. Contrary to this, radical constructivism takes a more relativistic and subjectivistic view, culminating in quasi-idealistic epistemological schemes. It is inspired by cybernetics and neurobiology. In the framework of the Erlanger school (Paul Lorenzen), constructivist approaches also exist in philosophy of science (especially of physics) and mathematics. The focus of interest here is the process and methods of gaining knowledge: philosophy of science is transformed into a theory of action, and laws of nature are interpreted as instructions to act. Structuralism (Wolfgang Stegmüller and successors) is another prominent current in philosophy of science; its focal point is, the formal description and reconstruction of scientific theories. Finally, those working within the framework of modern philosophy of nature reflect on scientific knowledge and interpret its implications for an extensive philosophical world-view. Partly this has the character of a counter-movement to post-modern pluralism and splintering, striving for orientation by means of a unification of science and world interpretation. It has, however, by now reached its own high degree of differentiation and, thus, complexity or obscurity. The central issue being dealt with is naturalism (physicalism, materialism). It is both elaborated and stated in rigorous forms, and also criticized. Especially influential upon philosophy of nature and mind are discoveries in physics (cosmology, chaos theory, particle physics) and biology (evolutionary theory, neuroscience). As in the Anglo-American world, the mind–body problem, consciousness, intentionality, personal identity, free will, and artificial intelligence have long been central issues, with interdisciplinary connections to evolutionary and cognitive psychology, linguistics, and computer science. A new topic is evolutionary ethics, which combines sociobiology, ethnology, and behavioural ecology to explore possible biological foundations of morality.

The *applied side* of scientific philosophy is concerned with the decisions required by new results and opportunities of science and technology. There is a political dimension to this, and that is why philosophers participate in advisory boards and parliamentary decision-making. Particularly urgent and controversial are the different domains of bioethics, especially because of the new possibilities in genetics and medicine. Another focus of interest is philosophy of technology. Here, quite pragmatic tendencies are common, which accompany technological developments mainly reflectively and try to evaluate their effects and implications.

The three main currents outlined are not unrelated and separate from each other. There were and are connecting topics, attempts at mediation, and more or less fruitful controversies (e.g. the positivist dispute). Within the philosophy of mind, for instance, phenomenological and analytical approaches are linked to each other, post-modern ideas are discussed ('the end of the subject'), and some aspects of traditional German idealism are maintained (e.g. self-consciousness in the work of Dieter Henrich and Manfred Frank). Philosophers of technology have to deal with the critical hermeneutical tradition since Martin Heidegger. Philosophers of nature derive some inspirations (e.g. for the problem of emergence) from the organismic conceptions of nature which go back to German idealism and romanticism. There is interpollination between hermeneutical and analytical schools, especially in discussions of ethics and ecology. In general pragmatics, there are efforts to integrate hermeneutic, relativistic, and naturalistic perspectives. Whatever its different currents and points of view, philosophy should, after all, always be indispensable as a means for conceptual analysis and reflection, as well as being a critical authority, for science and society.   R.V.
                                                                K.W.

A. Bowie, *Introduction to German Philosophy* (Cambridge, 2003).
P. Gorner, *Twentieth-Century German Philosophy* (Oxford, 2000).
J. Habermas, *Postmetaphysical Thinking*, tr. W. M. Hohengarten (Cambridge, Mass., 1994).
K. Wuchterl, *Bausteine zu einer Geschichte der Philosophie des 20. Jahrhunderts* (Bern, 1995).
—— *Handbuch der analytischen Philosophie und Grundlagenforschung* (Bern, 2002).

Gestalt **theory.** A psychological theory which tried to explain various aspects of psychology in terms of structures (*Gestalten*), particularly in relation to the tendency of forms of *perception to conform to 'good' structures (the so-called law of *Prägnanz*). The movement was initiated by Max Wertheimer (1880–1943), Wolfgang Köhler (1897–1967), and Kurt Koffka (1886–1941) in reaction against earlier sensationalist psychological theories which tried to break down the mental life into atomic sensations and ideas. The Gestaltists emphasized 'wholes' and structures which could not be broken down into elements. Initially the movement was concerned with perception, starting from the phi-phenomenon, the apparent movement of alternating points of light; but gradually other aspects of psychology, including both their physiological and their philosophical backing, were brought within the same principles, especially by Köhler.   D.W.H.

D. W. Hamlyn, *The Psychology of Perception* (London, 1957).
K. Koffka, *Principles of Gestalt Psychology* (London, 1935).

Gettier, Edmund (1927–). Gettier is famous in Anglo-American epistemology for one three-page paper in which he attacks the tripartite definition of *knowledge. This defines '*S* knows that *p*' as:

1. *p* is true.
2. *S* believes that *p*.
3. *S*'s belief that *p* is justified.

Gettier showed by counter-example that this definition is insufficient; there are cases where the three clauses are all true, but *S* does not know. The general idea was that one's true belief might be justified in a way that depends too much on luck, as, for example, when a clock which is normally accurate happens to have stopped, but its hands indicate the very time at which one glances at it. In a case like this, one has a true belief which is justified, but is not knowledge. (Russell made the same point some decades earlier.) Considerable effort has been spent, especially in the USA, on repairing the definition. Counter-examples to suggested repairs are known as Gettier counter-examples.

J.D.

*counter-example, philosophy by.

E. L. Gettier, 'Is Justified True Belief Knowledge?', *Analysis* (1963).

Geulincx, Arnold (1624–69). An occasionalist, a modified Cartesian, and an anti-Aristotelian, Geulincx moved from Louvain to Leiden, and simultaneously from Catholicism to *Calvinism, in 1658. Using the analogy of two synchronized but otherwise unconnected *clocks which strike simultaneously, he pointed out the possibility of there being two law-governed areas with no causal interaction. Applying this to the general case he held that though God acts immediately and in a lawlike manner in the realms of both thought and extension, there is no interaction between the two. Like Descartes, Geulincx was a plenist who held that *body* and *extension* are coextensive. Hence, given his supposition that the universe is infinite, so is matter. Motion, however, may not be. Beyond the universe of events lies infinite space: 'completely solid, completely dark, harder than any adamant'.

J.J.M.

*Cartesianism; occasionalism.

B. Cooney, 'Arnold Geulincx: A Cartesian Idealist', *Journal of the History of Philosophy* (1978).

Gewirth, Alan (1912–2004). Gewirth did important work on Descartes's theory of knowledge and medieval political philosophy, especially Marsilius of Padua, but he is best known for his attempt to develop a stringently rational foundation for morality in *Reason and Morality*. The central argument of this book begins with a claim that every rational agent must accept, which is that he or she must have freedom and well-being. Gewirth claims that when the implications of this claim are fully worked out, it follows that every rational agent must also accept the claim that all prospective purposive agents have a *moral* *right to freedom and well-being. Professor Gewirth spent most of his career at the University of Chicago.

J.P.S.

Alan Gewirth, *Reason and Morality* (Chicago, 1978).
—— *The Community of Rights* (Chicago, 1996).

Ghazālī, al- (1058/9–1111). Persian Abū Ḥāmid Muḥammad Ghazālī (Algazel in Latin texts) was the most influential Ash'arite theologian of his time. His role as head of the state-endowed Niẓāmiyya Madrasa, his monumental work *Revival of Religious Sciences*, and his autobiographical account *Deliverance from Error* (often compared to Augustine's *Confessions*) furthered the triumph of revelation over reason. His specifically anti-philosophical works, *Intentions of the Philosophers* and *Incoherence of the Philosophers*, called on theologians to use philosophical technique to oppose 'heretic' arguments. However, the effects on philosophy proved positive. The study of logic gained widespread theological acceptance. The identification of twenty philosophical problems argued to be false (including eternity, immortality, and rational causality) were brilliantly rebutted by Averroës, thus leading to refinement of Aristotelian arguments, and Sohravardī's philosophy.

H.Z.

W. M. Watt, *The Faith and Practice of al-Ghazālī* (London, 1951).

ghost in the machine. Gilbert Ryle in his book *The Concept of Mind* held that the 'Cartesian' tradition represents the human body as a purely physical thing (the machine), and the human *mind as a purely non-physical thing (the ghost) somehow inhabiting the body and 'operating' it from inside. 'The ghost in the machine' is his derisive title for this—as Ryle argues—fundamentally misleading picture.

G.J.W.

*self; persons; subjectivity; category mistake.

G. Ryle, *The Concept of Mind* (London, 1949), 15 ff.

Gibbard, Allan (1942–). American philosopher, professor at the University of Michigan, who has developed a general theory of normative judgement. According to this expressivist theory, to cite a reason for action or judgement is to accept norms that give it weight in deliberation. Norms serve the biological function of social co-ordination, and Gibbard offers naturalistic accounts of their force and degree of objectivity. Morality concerns the rationality of feelings such as guilt and anger that sanction unco-operative actions. Feelings have rationales stating that the circumstances that elicit them call for the actions they prompt, and moral norms endorse or alter the rationales for these moral feelings that have naturally evolved.

A.H.J.

A. Gibbard, *Wise Choices, Apt Feelings: A Theory of Normative Judgement* (Cambridge, Mass., 1990).
—— *Thinking How to Live* (Cambridge, Mass., 2003).

Giles of Rome (*c.*1247–1316). A member of the Order of the Hermits of St Augustine, rising to become General of the order in 1292. He studied at Paris, possibly under Aquinas, and eventually taught theology there. He produced a number of commentaries on Aristotle's writings, though his most famous treatise *Errors of the Philosophers* was a different sort of work, in which he attacks Aristotle and a number of major Muslim and Jewish thinkers. His aim is, however, not always accurate. For example, although he singles out Maimonides for censure partly on the grounds that the latter taught that some terms predicated affirmatively of *God have to be understood by way of causality, Maimonides did not in fact teach such a doctrine. For example, he did not (*pace* Giles) say that 'God is alive' means 'God is the cause of living things'. For some years Giles was thought theologically unsound, because of his unequivocally stated teaching on the question whether the individual soul has a plurality of forms, but he eventually retracted.   A.BRO.

Giles of Rome, *Errores Philosophorum*, ed. J. Koch, tr. J. O. Riedl (Milwaukee, Wis., 1944).

Gilson, Étienne (1884–1978). French historian of medieval philosophy who was particularly dedicated to rescuing the philosophy of Thomas Aquinas from what he viewed as centuries of distortion foisted on Aquinas by friend and foe alike. He sought to recover an authentic version of Thomism which he understood to focus on the primacy of existence in the account of being. Gilson's first work was a dissertation on Descartes (1913). After the First World War, at the University of Strasbourg and then in 1921 at the University of Paris, Gilson devoted himself to research on the medieval background to modern philosophy. He arrived in North America in 1927 to deliver a course of lectures at Harvard, and in 1929 he founded the Institute of Medieval Studies in Toronto. For nearly a half century after, Gilson divided his teaching between Europe and North America. He produced an extraordinary number of seminal studies on virtually all the major figures and movements in medieval philosophy.   L.P.G.

*neo-Thomism.

Laurence K. Shook, *Étienne Gilson* (Toronto, 1984).

given, the. The epistemological sceptic notes that our faculties of knowledge, in short reason and the senses, are fallible. Fallacious reasoning occurs, just as sensory illusions and hallucinations occur. On account of this fallibility of our faculties of knowledge, the sceptic is disposed to conclude that through reliance on them nothing can be known with certainty. There are many ways in which attempts have been made to answer the epistemological sceptic. Sometimes, the sceptic's claims have been said to be incoherent in the sense that to be true, or even to make sense at all, they require assumptions which make them false. Alternatively, the claims have been said to be unintelligible in the sense that facts about the nature of language and its use preclude them. Also, the sceptic's arguments themselves have been challenged on the score of invalidity—it is denied that they succeed in showing what they purport to show. More and more today, it has been maintained that the sceptic is misdirected about the nature of existence and of knowledge.

There is one other way, different from all of these, in which the sceptic's position has been opposed. This involves a direct challenge to the sceptic's contention that nothing can be known with certainty. Here, an attempt is made to show that there *is* something whose existence cannot be denied and which is such that we can and do know it with certainty. It is commonly referred to as 'the given'. It is what is immediately presented to consciousness. Even in erroneous perception, we are told, *something* is still perceived. Neither illusion nor hallucination is characterized by perceptual vacuity—there always is something given. Berkeley spoke of 'the proper object of the senses', and A. J. Ayer and others of *'sense-data'. When one supposedly sees a penny, according to these philosophers, one sees not the penny itself but an elliptical sense-datum.

This view of sense-data as the incorrigibly given in perception is connected with *foundationalism. Beginning from sense-data, foundationalism seeks to show how, from such elements, we construct objects like the penny. The methods of construction are intended to transfer to our knowledge-claims concerning three-dimensional objects something of the certainty of knowledge associated with sense-data. Rudolf Carnap made strides towards bringing about such a construction, but W. V. Quine's systematic criticisms of the programme and its devices have made it evident to many that it will not be completed. And the assumption of sense-data known incorrigibly has not been without its critics (e.g. the later Wittgenstein and J. L. Austin).   W.E.A.

*boat, Neurath's; scepticism; scepticism, history of; perception.

A. J. Ayer, *The Foundations of Empirical Knowledge* (London, 1964).
Jonathan Dancy, *An Introduction to Contemporary Epistemology* (Oxford, 1986).

globalization, morality, and politics. Although 'globalization' can refer to an increase in international co-operation as represented in organizations such as the United Nations and the European Union, it usually designates the world-wide expansion of market capitalism in the 1990s. This resulted from international agreements reducing barriers to trade and capital flow, the development of information technology, and, with the collapse of the USSR, the seeming elimination of any practical alternative to corporate capitalism. The consequence was a global search for markets, inexpensive labour and production costs, and natural resources, leading to rapid industrialization of Third World countries and the international spread of technology.

Advocates argue that free trade has reduced the cost of living, made available a greater variety of goods to consumers, stimulated economic growth, and increased wealth. Multinational corporations, helped by favourable governmental policies, have been the chief instruments of these changes; the 'invisible hand' has produced world-wide social progress and also immense profits to its corporate owners. Values such as greed and self-interest have come to be seen as promoting social good; corporations are now considered important instruments for international development. Corporate success has given enormous economic and military power to the industrialized West, particularly to the United States.

Yet for non-industrial countries economic globalization has brought imports that undercut prices for locally produced goods; this in turn has forced workers to move to urban centres for jobs. These are often available only for very low pay with long hours and harsh working conditions, and without union representation. While salaries for management and technically trained professionals have greatly increased, pay for untrained labour has declined sharply. These changes have increased the gap between rich and poor.

Although underdeveloped countries can qualify for loans from the International Monetary Fund and the World Bank, usually they must agree to trade deregulation, privatization of state industry, reductions in public welfare, limited government, and fewer environmental restrictions and protections for workers' rights—restricting the authority of borrowing countries in these areas. The World Trade Organization, which oversees economic globalization, can require compensation from member nations, including wealthy ones, for loss of profit due to e.g. laws protecting the environment or health, thus further eroding local democratic control.   C.C.

D. Held and A. McGrew, *Globalization/Anti-Globalization* (Cambridge, 2002).
N. Heertz, *The Silent Takeover: Global Capitalism and the Death of Democracy* (New York, 2001).

Glover, Jonathan (1941–). Professor of Ethics at King's College London, formerly at Oxford, Glover has been a seminal figure in the emergence of 'applied ethics' as an area of vigorous philosophical inquiry. A theorist of broadly utilitarian sympathies, he developed an account of the wrongness of killing that rejects traditional notions of the sanctity of life and instead appeals to the intrinsic value of life that is worth living, respect for autonomy, and side-effects. This account has been influential in its rejection of the moral significance of the distinction between *killing and letting die and in its implication that abortion and infanticide are, except perhaps where side-effects are concerned, morally equivalent to the failure to cause a person to exist. His more recent work on *personal identity argues that the popular conception of the unity of the self is mistaken and that our distinctiveness and value as persons is in part the result of self-creation, which is itself a phenomenon that should be encouraged by social institutions.   J.McM.

Jonathan Glover, *Causing Death and Saving Lives* (Harmondsworth, 1977).
—— *What Sort of People Should There Be?* (London, 1984).
—— *I: The Philosophy and Psychology of Personal Identity* (London, 1988).

gnoseology (or, gnosiology). From the Greek *gnōsis*, a word for 'knowledge'. Any philosophy or branch of philosophy concerned either with solving problems about the nature and possibility of *knowledge, or with delivering knowledge of ultimate reality especially in so far as this is not available to sense-experience. 'Gnoseology' is an archaic term and has been superseded in the former sense by 'epistemology' and in the latter sense by 'metaphysics'.   S.P.

gnosticism. The teachings of a family of sects which flourished from the second to the fourth centuries AD, combining elements of Christianity with *Platonism, drawing in particular from the creation myths of Genesis and of Plato's *Timaeus*. Gnosticism was dualist, distinguishing the spiritual and good world from the evil and material world. Matter was the creation of a wicked demiurge. But a spiritual saviour had come to offer redeeming *gnōsis*, or knowledge, of our true spiritual selves. The gnostic would be released from the material world, the non-gnostic doomed to reincarnation. Gnosticism initially threatened what survived it as orthodox Christianity, stimulating the latter to define its teaching on the nature of authority and revelation. Having been outlawed by the Christian Roman emperors, gnostic teachings survived in Syria and Persia and were absorbed into *Manicheism.   T.P.

E. Pagels, *The Gnostic Gospels* (New York, 1979).

God. The three main Western religions—Christianity, Judaism, and Islam—have all claimed that God is the supreme reality. Sometimes their thinkers have said that God is so great that we cannot say anything in human words about what he is like. All we can say is what he is not—he is not evil, he is not foolish, and so on. This approach known as the *via negativa* was especially prominent in the period AD 500–1000. But if that is all we could say about God, there would be no content to religious doctrines adequate to justify religious practice, such as the worship of God. Hence most philosophical theologians have tried to say something about what God is like. In so doing, they have generally regarded him as a personal being, bodiless, omnipresent, creator and sustainer of any universe there may be, perfectly free, omnipotent, omniscient, perfectly good, and a source of moral obligation; who exists eternally and necessarily, and has essentially the divine properties which I have listed. Many philosophers (influenced by Anselm) have seen these properties as deriving from the property of being the greatest conceivable being. God is the greatest conceivable being and so he has all the great-making properties. Within each of the religions, however, and especially within Christianity, there have been somewhat different ways of understanding some of the divine properties.

God's being omnipresent, present everywhere, is his knowing what is happening everywhere and being able to act everywhere—directly, in the way in which we act on our bodies. To say that God is creator and sustainer of any universe there may be is to say that anything else which exists depends for its existence from moment to moment on God's sustaining action. If the physical universe had a beginning of existence (as Western religions have usually claimed), God caused that beginning; but if not, then God has kept it in being for all past time. God is perfectly free if nothing acts from without to cause or even influence how he chooses to act.

To say that God is omnipotent would seem, literally, to mean that he can do whatever he chooses to do. But how is 'whatever' to be understood? Can God change the rules of logic—can he make $2 + 2 = 5$, or make a thing exist and not exist at the same time, or change the past? Descartes seems to have claimed that he can do all these things; but theists have more usually claimed that it makes no sense to say that God can do the logically impossible, and they have then tried to spell out carefully what that rules out. A chapter (2.25) of Aquinas's *Summa contra Gentiles* is entitled 'How the omnipotent God is said to be incapable of certain things', and goes on to list some twenty such things.

God's being omniscient is (literally) his knowing everything, i.e. every true proposition. But how is that to be understood? It looks as if there are some propositions which can only be known by certain persons or at certain times. Only I can know that I am ill; others can know only that S is ill. So how could God know the true proposition which I know? One response is that what is known by me and others is the same, even if it is differently expressed, and God can know the thing in question. Can God know in advance how free agents will choose to act—if so, how can their choices be free? While some theists have denied that humans have free will, most have affirmed that they do, and they often seem to have affirmed *free will in the libertarian sense in which an action is free if the agent's choice so to act has no total cause, whether brain-state or God. Consider then an agent S at a time t choosing freely whether to do X or not-X. Whatever God or anyone else believed beforehand about what S would do, S has it in his power so to act as to make that belief false. How then can God be essentially omniscient? The answer invariably given by theologians in the Middle Ages was that God's being *eternal is to be understood as his being outside time. It follows that he does not know anything before or after it happens, but knows events only by seeing them happen from his standpoint outside time. But God's seeing us act in no way makes us less free. However, this notion of eternity may not be a coherent one, and in that case God's being eternal is to be understood as his being everlasting, i.e. as existing at each moment. In that case theism needs to construe God's omniscience not as knowledge of every true proposition, but as knowledge of every true proposition which it is logically possible to know. It is not logically possible to know in advance how agents with libertarian free will will act. Hence God by creating us with such free will limits his own knowledge.

God is a source of moral obligation if his commands make actions right or wrong for humans when they would not be otherwise. This suggestion raises immediately the Euthyphro dilemma. Some (e.g. Kant) have claimed that God's commands cannot make any difference to what is right or wrong; others have claimed that nothing would be right or wrong but for God's command. A midway position is that of both Aquinas and Duns Scotus that there are very general first principles of morality which it is not logically possible that even God could change. Among those very general first principles is the duty to please benefactors. God is our supreme benefactor, and hence his commands impose on us obligations to obey. Such a command could not make it obligatory to do anything contrary to any other first principle of morality (e.g. to torture children just for fun); but God's being essentially good would not command us so to act.

God is supposed to exist 'necessarily'. Some have understood this to mean 'of logical necessity', i.e. it would be incoherent to suppose there to be no God. *Atheism does, however, *seem* to be a coherent position, even if false; and so other theists have understood God's being necessary as his being the ultimate brute fact on which all other things depend. In all these ways theists have tried to spell out an internally coherent understanding of God broadly consonant with the tradition of Western religion; while some (but not all) atheists hold that such attempts all fail.   R.G.S.

*creation.

A. Kenny, *The God of the Philosophers* (Oxford, 1979).
T. V. Morris, *Our Idea of God* (Notre Dame, Ind., 1991).
—— (ed.), *The Concept of God* (Oxford, 1987).
R. Swinburne, *The Coherence of Theism* (Oxford, 1977).

God, arguments against the existence of. The most popular line of argument against God's existence involves the problem of *evil. This argument is the inverse analogue of the *teleological argument. Some versions are deductive in form, others are probabilistic.

A rather clear version of the deductive form is given by J. L. Mackie in 'Evil and Omnipotence'. He claims that the propositions *God is omnipotent*, *God is wholly good*, and *Evil exists* form a logically inconsistent triad, and that therefore some important part of theistic belief is false. This seems to be equivalent to an argument which takes *Evil exists* as its main premiss, and the other two propositions as analytic truths expressing (part of) the concept of God. The intended conclusion would be that God does not exist— i.e. that no actual entity satisfies that concept.

Deductive arguments from evil have recently been subjected to very intensive criticism, and enthusiasm for them seems to have waned somewhat. But there has been some increase of interest in probabilistic versions. These acknowledge the logical possibility of God along with evil. But they argue that in view of the amount of evil in the world, its horrific nature, the implausibility of the available theodicies, etc., it is improbable that God exists. Discussion of these attempts, both pro and con, suffer from the comparative obscurity of inductive logic.

Another line of atheological argument claims that the concept of God is *internally* incoherent, rather than incompatible with an obvious fact about the world. This is the inverse analogue of the ontological argument. Some, for example, have argued that being worthy of worship is a necessary condition of divinity, and this requires necessary existence. But nothing, so they say, can exist necessarily. Ergo . . .

Others argue that one or another of the attributes traditionally assigned to God—e.g. omnipotence, omniscience, eternity—cannot be given a coherent sense. There arguments invite responses of two sorts. One may produce even more careful and subtle analyses to show that they are coherent after all. Or one may argue that they are not essential to the concept of God and can be replaced—e.g. God may be everlasting rather than eternal, almighty instead of omnipotent.

A third general line, vigorously proposed by Antony Flew, argues that atheism is the proper 'fall-back' position. In the absence of satisfactory arguments for theism, atheism should be accepted, even without any positive arguments in its favour. This has some similarity to the claim of some theistic philosophers that belief in God is legitimate, even if it is not supported by positive argument.

G.I.M.

Antony Flew, *The Presumption of Atheism* (London, 1976).
R. Le Poidevin, *Arguing for Atheism* (London, 1996).
John L. Mackie, 'Evil and Omnipotence', *Mind* (1955).
Alvin Plantinga, *God and Other Minds* (Ithaca, NY, 1967).
Bertrand Russell, *Why I am not a Christian* (New York, 1957).

God, arguments for the existence of. Most theistic arguments fall into one of two classes—the a priori or purely conceptual arguments, and the world-based arguments. The various versions of the ontological argument constitute the first class. These have a specially 'philosophical' flavour, and give rise to difficult questions in modal logic. They have the advantage of concluding straightforwardly to the *necessary* existence of God, a feature which many take to be essential to the concept of a divine being.

In the other class belong the *cosmological arguments, appealing to general features of the world, and *teleo-logical arguments, based on more special features. These lines of argument are more generally accessible, and have been more widely popular. And there are some even more special arguments (perhaps versions of the teleological family)—arguments based on the demands of morality, the existence of beauty, the normativity of human rationality, religious experience, etc.

Most of these lines of argument have a long history, and they have avid defenders and critics among contemporary philosophers. A crucial question, often ignored in these controversies, is that of the proper standards to be applied to such arguments. Presumably, they should be valid and their premises true. But if God exists, these requirements are trivially easy to satisfy. What else is needed? If, for example, we require that their premises be universally accepted, indubitable, etc., then probably no theistic argument will pass muster. (Probably no interesting argument for anything will measure up to this standard.) If, on the other hand, we require only validity, truth, and that the premises be acceptable to some intended audience, then many of these arguments may be satisfactory. But they will not be universally persuasive. Their effectiveness

will be limited to those for whom their premises are acceptable.

There are other lines of argument which are not really intended to establish the truth of God's existence, but rather the rationality, the intellectual permissibility, etc. of theistic belief. Pascal's wager is an example, and the rather similar 'will to believe' of William James. A different approach to this question of rationality is that of Alvin Plantinga and other contemporary 'Calvinians' (or 'reformed epistemologists') who argue that theistic belief is properly basic, and can be properly adopted and held without any inferential justification, though it may well be grounded in the occurrence of genuine (divinely initiated) religious experience.

G.I.M.

John Hick, *Arguments for The Existence of God* (London, 1970).
William James, *The Will to Believe* (New York, 1897).
George I. Mavrodes, *Belief in God* (New York, 1981).
Alvin Plantinga and Nicholas Wolterstorff (eds.), *Faith and Rationality* (Notre Dame, Ind., 1983).
R. G. Swinburne, *Is There a God?* (Oxford, 1996).

God and the philosophers. The beliefs of most people in the West who have been brought up in the Christian or Jewish religions can be summarized in the following propositions: the natural universe has not always existed, it was created out of nothing by a purely spiritual being; this purely spiritual being known as *God has always existed; this being not only created the universe but has continued to be its ruler ever since the creation, interfering in the course of events from time to time by working miracles; this being, furthermore, has the attributes of omnipotence, omniscience, and perfect goodness. The leading Christian and Jewish philosophers—St Augustine, St Anselm of Canterbury, St Thomas Aquinas, William of Ockham, and Maimonides—supported all these propositions. Ockham did not think that they could be proven, but the other great figures in the Judaeo-Christian tradition maintained that they are backed by decisive evidence.

Plato and Aristotle believed in gods who played a far less central role in the universe than the God of the Christians and Jews. In the *Timaeus* Plato introduces the Demiurge, a kind of cosmic architect or engineer who brings order into a chaotic universe. Aristotle's God is a 'prime mover'—we have to appeal to such a being to explain motion, but the material universe itself is eternal and uncreated. It should be mentioned that although Aquinas believed, on the basis of Scripture, that the universe was created by God out of nothing, he did not think that any of his 'proofs' established this conclusion. They only established God as the *sustaining* cause of the universe, and this conclusion is entirely compatible with the eternity of the world.

We now know that, aside from Ockham, quite a few medieval philosophers were in varying degrees sceptical of the official theology. However, since it was protected by what Voltaire called the 'logic of the sword', heresies were infrequent. In Muslim countries, where there was far greater freedom of thought, several of the leading

AUGUSTINE rose to eminence as the leading churchman in North Africa in the early fifth century; meanwhile he developed his Platonic Christian philosophy in private contemplation.

ABELARD, legendary French lover—but philosophers are more interested in his theory of universals. His teachings on atonement and on the role of intention in human conduct were also influential.

ANSELM, born in Italy, was Archbishop of Canterbury at the end of the eleventh century. He produced rational investigations of the foundations of Christian belief, and is famous for his ontological argument for the existence of God, which holds that it is implicit in the very idea of God that he exists.

BOETHIUS, a Roman politician of noble family, might have made Greek philosophy known in western Europe centuries earlier than its eventual promulgation in Latin, but his translation of Plato and Aristotle was brought to an abrupt end by his execution c.526.

philosophers, most notably Averroës, openly accepted Aristotle's teaching of God as the Prime Mover and of the eternity of the world.

Much of the philosophy of the last 300 years is the story of the attacks on the Judaeo-Christian view and its replacement by a naturalistic outlook which completely dispenses with theological explanations. Some of the great philosophers of the modern period, notably Descartes and Leibniz, offered arguments for traditional theism, but several others were in varying degrees critical of the old scheme. Foremost among the critics were Spinoza, the deists, Hume, and Kant. Spinoza is usually classified as a pantheist who maintained that God and the universe are identical. Voltaire and Frederick the Great regarded him as an atheist who retained theological language, while Goethe, who was himself a pantheist, called Spinoza 'God-intoxicated'. Be this as it may be, Spinoza taught that the natural universe was uncreated, and he was also most emphatic in his rejection of miracles.

*Deism, which began in England in the late seventeenth century, was primarily a rebellion against revealed as distinct from natural religion. The deists did not deny a creator of the universe, but they were highly critical of the Bible, regarding all stories of divine intervention as superstitious and often immoral nonsense. In arguing for the existence of God they preferred the teleological argument to the a priori arguments of earlier believers. Some of them questioned the perfect goodness or indeed any of the moral attributes of the Deity. In his *Poème sur le désastre de Lisbonne* and in *Candide*, Voltaire, the most influential of the eighteenth-century deists, tried to show the absurdity of any cosmic optimism without, however, abandoning belief in a Designer.

Hume has sometimes been called a deist, but in fact he was what we would now call an agnostic. His posthumously published *Dialogues Concerning Natural Religion* contain some of the most incisive criticism of the cosmological and the teleological arguments. In connection with the former he observes that a causal series is nothing over and above the members of the series, so that if we have explained the origin of each member, there is nothing left to explain. As for the teleological argument, we have no reason to suppose that there was a time when order of the kind described in our scientific laws did not characterize the universe. Although not as radical as Hume, Kant had much greater influence on subsequent developments. His *Critique of Pure Reason* contains a devastating examination of the *ontological, *cosmological, and *teleological arguments. Hume's discussion of the latter two arguments was greatly superior, but Kant's refutation of the ontological argument, which Hume barely touched, was masterful.

The work of Hume and Kant no doubt helped to pave the way for agnosticism and *theism, but it also had a significant impact on Christian and Jewish philosophy, resulting in the widespread adoption of a position known as 'fideism'—belief in God (or other religious propositions) on the basis of faith alone. Fideistic believers are ready to concede that the arguments for the existence of God are not valid, but they commonly add that this is not necessarily a cause for concern. Faith, in the words of John Hick, 'stands ultimately upon the ground of religious experience and is not a product of philosophical reasoning'. Kierkegaard, a leading figure in the fideist tradition, went so far as to maintain that those who tried to prove the existence of God are enemies of true faith. Faith, on Kierkegaard's view, involves risk, but there would be no risk if the existence of God or immortality were as solidly established as mathematical theorems and scientific laws.

*Fideism flourished in the nineteenth century and is still widely adopted at the present time, but it goes back at least as far as Blaise Pascal (1623–62), who, in a famous passage in his *Pensées*, asserted that 'the heart has reasons which reason knows not of'. Pascal's heart, needless to say, told him that there is a God, that there is life after death, and that he himself was going to inherit eternal bliss. It did not occur to him that other people's hearts might tell them very different things and that we would then have the problem of whose heart is to be trusted. Rousseau, too, was a champion of faith and the heart. 'I have suffered too much in this life not to expect another', he wrote in a published rebuttal to Voltaire's *Poème sur le désastre de Lisbonne*—'all the subtleties of metaphysics will never make me doubt for a moment the immortality of the soul and a beneficent providence. I feel it, I believe it, I want it, I hope for it, I will defend it to my last breath.' Sceptics have generally not been unduly impressed by such outbursts and have dismissed fideism as nothing but a species of wishful thinking which ought to have no place in serious philosophy.

The open advocacy of atheism effectively began during the middle of the eighteenth century in France. Diderot, Holbach, La Mettrie, and d'Alembert were the most famous defenders of atheism in opposition not only to Christianity but also to deists like Voltaire and Rousseau. All these atheists were also materialists, but atheism is not necessarily connected with any metaphysical system. Fichte and Schopenhauer, for example, were atheists who subscribed to metaphysical idealism. Hegel's views cannot be easily classified, chiefly because they are so obscure. He believed in something called the 'Absolute Idea', and some of his conservative followers, known as the 'Right Hegelians', had no difficulty identifying the Absolute Idea with a personal God. However, almost all his most famous students, known as 'Left Hegelians', were outspoken atheists. They included Marx, Engels, Feuerbach, Bruno Bauer, and D. F. Strauss, the author of the extremely influential *Life of Jesus*. It might be noted that Fichte lost his academic position when his atheism was discovered, and the same was true of Bauer and Strauss. None of the others just mentioned ever had a chance. Even David Hume never obtained an academic appointment.

The most interesting late nineteenth-century atheist was unquestionably Friedrich Nietzsche, whose full influence was not felt until the early decades of the twentieth century. Nietzsche's rejection of God and immortality is combined with a subtle analysis of the emotions which inspire life-denying religions like Christianity. The notion of God, according to Nietzsche, is extremely harmful because it is employed, especially by Christian moralists, to denigrate earthly happiness and other secular values. 'The concept "God"', he wrote, 'was invented as the opposite of the concept "life"—everything detrimental, poisonous and slanderous, and all deadly hostility to life, was bound together in one horrible unit!' Unfortunately, Nietzsche's works, especially those written near the end of his sane period, also contain tirades against compassion and vaguely worded recommendations to exterminate 'the bungled and the botched'.

Nietzsche denied that he was a Social Darwinist, but many passages in his writing show that this is precisely what he was. Along with other Social Darwinists and power-worshippers, Nietzsche was denounced by Bertrand Russell, who was probably the most influential atheist in the Anglo-Saxon world during the present century. Although he disagreed with Nietzsche on certain ethical and political issues, Russell's views were in every other respect quite similar. Like Nietzsche he attacked not only traditional views about God and the soul, but also the harmful influence of Christian moral teachings, especially those relating to sexual morality. Russell also made important contributions of a purely theoretical nature. Following Cantor, he showed that there is nothing contradictory in the notion of an infinite series, an insight that undermines the cosmological argument. Following Frege, he showed that the word 'exists' is a logical constant comparable to such words as 'all' and 'not', and not the name of a characteristic. This insight complements Kant's refutation of the ontological argument.

The two leading French *existentialists, Jean-Paul Sartre and Albert Camus, were outspoken atheists, and in a programmatic essay Sartre also counts Heidegger as an atheist. It is, however, very misleading to describe Heidegger so. He did indeed reject Christian and Jewish theism, but he believed in an ultimate reality called 'Being' which has striking similarities to the traditional deity. Being is in everything and is the source of everything. It is always referred to as 'the Holy' and as something 'transcendent' which cannot be adequately described in language taken from ordinary experience. It can be reached by various mystical techniques, especially one which Heidegger calls *Gelassenheit* and which has been facetiously described as a form of 'creative waiting'. It should be noted that Heidegger felt an affinity with medieval mystics, whom he frequently quoted with approval, and that he was unequivocally opposed to any form of naturalism.

Sartre really was an atheist. He rejected theism because it is incompatible with *free will in the somewhat peculiar sense in which he takes it to be a basic fact about human beings. If there were a God, he would create human beings with a 'nature' or 'essence', and this is incompatible with Sartre's view that in man existence precedes essence. This seems to mean that human beings do not have an essence until they have chosen their initial 'fundamental projects', Sartre's term for character traits. The trouble with such a view is that, regardless of the extent and power of our volitions, *ultimately* we are the result of our heredity and early environment. Like many other philosophers, Sartre manages not to see this disturbing but inescapable fact, which may be compatible with free will in *some* sense, but is incompatible with Sartre's view that our character is self-chosen.

As for free will as an argument against God's existence, it should be observed that even if Sartre's argument is otherwise valid, it would not show that there is no God, but only that God cannot have given human beings their 'essences'.

The twentieth century witnessed perhaps the most lethal of all attacks on traditional belief in God. We may call this the 'semantic' challenge. It consists of questioning the very intelligibility of statements about God. It began in the 1930s with the verificationism of the Logical Positivists, according to which statements about God are meaningless since they are not even in principle verifiable. More recently it has centred on difficulties arising from the view of most sophisticated believers that God does not possess a body. Words like 'good', 'kind', 'compassionate', 'caring', and also of course 'intelligent' and 'powerful', are initially introduced in connection with human beings who possess bodies. Can they retain any meaning when applied to a pure mind?

There is also the problem of how a purely spiritual being could be contacted, and how he (or she or it) could interfere in the universe. Suppose I suffer from an inoperable brain tumour and pray to God for a cure. If God is physical he might hear my prayer and send healing rays, unavailable to earthly physicians, that would break up the tumour. But how could a disembodied mind hear me in the first place, and, if he could, how could he, not being physical, apply the force that would send the rays into my brain? More basically, how could a pure mind create the physical universe, or for that matter how could he create anything at all?   P.E.

*Logical Positivism; religion, scepticism about.

J. B. Bury, *A History of Freedom of Thought* (London, 1913).
J. Hick (ed.), *The Existence of God* (New York, 1964).
A. J. P. Kenny, *The God of the Philosophers* (Oxford, 1979).
Bertrand Russell, *Why I am not a Christian* (New York, 1957).

Gödel, Kurt (1906–78). The greatest mathematical logician and a bold, heterodox philosopher of mathematics. Among his mathematical discoveries are: the completeness of first-order logic, i.e. there is a sound formal system in which every first-order logical truth is deducible; the incompleteness of arithmetic, i.e. there is no sound formal system in which every first-order arithmetical truth is deducible (known as *Gödel's theorem); the internal unprovability of the consistency of any system containing computable arithmetic; the consistency of classical arithmetic relative to intuitionistic arithmetic; the relative consistency of the axiom of *choice and of Cantor's continuum conjecture. (*Continuum problem.) Along the way he invented an arithmetical method of reasoning *about* formal systems and he discovered the hierarchy of constructible sets. As a sideline he showed that general relativity, the theory of his close friend Einstein, allowed the possibility of what may be loosely described as circular time.

Crowning this phenomenal output was a striking view of mathematics, a twentieth-century philosophy akin to Plato's. Its main elements are as follows: the objects of mathematical study, e.g. the structures of numbers and sets, exist independently of thought and language; all clear mathematical statements are true or false, even those which are currently undecidable such as Cantor's continuum conjecture; mathematical concepts such as recursiveness and differentiability exist independently of our formulations; and finally, our mathematical knowledge consists in deductions from axioms which are known by intuition—all against the tide of his time. Though he allowed the possibility of coming to know axioms by the fruitfulness of their consequences, he gave no quarter to the empiricist view that the basis of mathematical knowledge is the evidence of the senses. Aside from Brouwer's view that much of established mathematics is false or nonsense, the only serious alternatives to the empiricist view and Gödel's own were logicism, i.e. the view that mathematics is a body of tautologies deducible from a system of purely logical axioms, and formalism, i.e. the view that mathematics is a purely formal extension of finitary reasoning, an extension which could never lead us into falsehood; but these views, logicism and formalism, had been effectively destroyed by Gödel's mathematical work.

Opinion is sharply divided about the plausibility of Gödel's bold philosophy of mathematics, but its value is unquestionable. It is the product of a deep knowledge of mathematics, a master craftsman's knowledge, combined with great carefulness and clarity of thought.   M.D.G.

K. Gödel, *Collected Works*, ed. S. Feferman *et al.*, 5 vols. (Oxford, 1986–2003).

R. Smullyan, *Forever Undecided: A Puzzle Guide to Gödel* (Oxford, 1988).

Hao Wang, *Reflections on Kurt Gödel* (Cambridge, Mass., 1989).

Gödel's theorem. A formal system is a computable list of axioms stated in a precise language with precise inference rules. The theorem states that for any consistent formal system M containing a certain part of arithmetic, a sentence in the language of M can be constructed which is neither provable not refutable in M. Its discovery amazed those who saw its significance. Assuming that every mathematical proposition is true or false, it entails that there is no consistent formal system in which every mathematical truth is provable, contrary to the view of Frege and Russell. Paired with Gödel's discovery that the consistency of formal systems containing arithmetic is not internally provable, this effectively destroyed attempts to justify classical mathematics by means of formal systems.   M.D.G.

S. Shanker (ed.), *Gödel's Theorem in Focus* (London, 1988).

God is dead. A formula employed by Nietzsche to signify the demise—both cultural and intellectual—of the 'God-hypothesis', the associated 'Christian-moral interpretation' of the world and ourselves, and all kindred notions and interpretations involving the postulation of some sort of ultimate reality and source of meaning and value transcending 'this life' and 'this world'. Nietzsche associated this disillusionment with the advent of nihilism, which while unavoidable must be overcome through the creation of 'new values' in a manner 'faithful to the earth'. (See e.g. *The Gay Science*, sects. 108–9, 125, 343.)   R.S.

Walter Kaufmann, *Nietzsche*, 4th edn. (Princeton, NJ, 1974), ch. 3.

Godmanhood. A theologico-philosophical notion deriving from the Christian doctrine of the Incarnation. According to the latter, Christ was both truly human and truly divine, and thus could be described as a 'God-man'. In scriptural, patristic, and medieval writings a related notion emerges according to which Christ (usually in the resurrected state) represents the perfection of *human nature. Accordingly, human beings possess natures the full and sustained realization of which would bring them to the condition of the transfigured Christ. The term 'Godmanhood' usually refers to a version of this general idea as it was developed in the religious anthropology of the Russian religious philosopher Vladimir Solovyov (1853–1900).   J.HAL.

F. Copleston, *Russian Religious Philosophy* (Tunbridge Wells, 1988).

Godwin, William (1756–1836). British moral and political philosopher, author of numerous political novels, including *Caleb Williams* (1794); husband of Mary Wollstonecraft. *An Enquiry Concerning Political Justice* (1793) was notorious for its extreme *anarchism and *utilitarianism, though Godwin somehow escaped prosecution. His view was grounded in the claim that human beings are naturally equal. Government corrupts governors and people, creating and aggravating inequalities. Only a non-political society will permit unconstrained impartial benevolence. His optimistic faith in reason led him into an equally sanguine view of human moral capacity. Godwin speaks also of rights and natural rights, some of which are in tension with his utilitarianism: we have rights over our present property even if the distribution is not utility-maximizing. His utopian radicalism attracted Romantics such as the young Wordsworth and Shelley, later his son-in-law.   R.CRI.

W. Godwin, *An Enquiry Concerning Political Justice*, ed. I. Kramnick (Harmondsworth, 1976).

—— *Caleb Williams*, ed. D. McCracken (Oxford, 1977).

Goethe, Johann Wolfgang (1749–1832). German poet and thinker who influenced and was influenced by post-Kantian *idealism. 'For philosophy in the strict sense I had no organ': he had no taste for traditional logic and epistemology, but he had a lively appreciation of the works of

Kant and other philosophers, and from his study of Plato, *Neoplatonism, and above all Spinoza he derived an exuberant pantheism that pervades his poetry as well as his prose. Nature is a living unity, in which mind and matter are inextricably linked: 'Where object and subject meet, there is life; when Hegel places himself between subject and object by means of his philosophy of identity, we must do him honour.' Nature reveals her secrets to the discerning eye, but it resists quantitative, mechanistic treatment. Thus Goethe's biological researches, especially on the metamorphosis of plants, were guided by the belief that organisms are constructed on a uniform plan, and he defended the purity of white light against Newton's theory that it consists of the seven prismatic colours.

He had little sympathy for democracy, industrialization, or revolution: 'I see a time coming when God will no longer have any pleasure in mankind; he will once more have to destroy everything to make room for a renewed creation.'   M.J.I.

T. J. Reed, *Goethe* (Oxford, 1984).

Goldbach's conjecture (1742). Christian Goldbach (1690–1764) was born in Königsberg. His conjecture states that every even integer greater than 3 is the sum of two prime numbers; thus $4 = 2 + 2$, $16 = 5 + 11$, etc. The truth of Goldbach's conjecture is still an open question. But curiously, any proof that the conjecture is not refutable would imply that there are no counter-examples, and hence would prove the conjecture!   W.A.H.

Richard K. Guy, *Unsolved Problems in Number Theory* (New York, 1981).

golden mean: *see* mean, doctrine of.

golden mountain: *see* Meinong.

golden rule. This rule designates a guide to conduct which has been thought fundamental in most major religious and moral traditions. It has been formulated either positively as an injunction to 'do unto others as you would have them do unto you' (Matthew 7: 12); or negatively, urging that you not do to others what you would not wish them to do to you, as in the sayings of Confucius or Hillel. The rule's all-encompassing simplicity has invited countless trivializing counter-examples: Should devotees of fried mosquitoes serve them as a special delicacy to their guests? Or masochists inflict their favourite torments on unsuspecting acquaintances? Such questions, however, miss the point of the rule. It was never intended as a guide to practical choice independently of all other principles of conduct. It has nothing to say about specific choices, nor does it endorse particular moral principles, virtues, or ideals.

The golden rule concerns, rather, a perspective thought necessary to the exercise of even the most rudimentary morality: that of trying to put oneself in the place of those affected by one's actions, so as to counter the natural tendency to moral myopia. It enjoins listeners to treat others with the understanding and respect they would themselves wish to encounter, and above all not to inflict misfortunes on others that they would abhor to have inflicted upon themselves.

Precisely because the golden rule has so long been thought fundamental, many moral philosophers have compared it to their own principles concerning moral choice and conduct. Thus Immanuel Kant famously dismissed the rule as trivial and too limited to be a universal law, in a footnote to his *Foundations of the Metaphysics of Morals*, whereas John Stuart Mill claimed, in *Utilitarianism*, that 'In the golden rule of Jesus of Nazareth, we read the complete spirit of the ethics of utility.'   S.B.

*universalizability.

Hans-Ulrich Hoche, 'The Golden Rule: New Aspects of an Old Moral Principle', in D. E. Christiansen *et al.* (eds.), *Contemporary German Philosophy* (University Park, Penn., 1982), i.

Marcus Singer, 'Golden Rule', in Lawrence C. Becker and Charlotte B. Becker (eds.), *Encyclopedia of Ethics* (New York, 1992), i.

Goldman, Alvin I. (1938–). Professor of Philosophy, University of Arizona, best known for a thoroughgoing 'naturalized' approach to epistemology, metaphysics, and the philosophy of mind, an approach that takes philosophical theses to be constrained by our best empirical theories. Goldman envisages 'liaisons' between philosophical domains and their counterparts in the social and behavioural sciences. His theory of *knowledge centres on the notion of a 'reliable belief-forming process', and accords psychology the task of identifying such processes. Goldman's account of mental concepts and ascriptions, including 'simulation theory' (according to which your understanding of my states of mind reflects an ability to put yourself in my shoes), gives a central role to cognitive psychology, and his work on social power and social epistemology exploits findings in political science, social psychology, economics, and the law.   J.HEIL

*justification, epistemic.

A. I. Goldman, *Liaisons: Philosophy Meets the Cognitive and Social Sciences* (Cambridge, Mass., 1991).

—— *Knowledge in a Social World* (Oxford, 1999).

good. G. E. Moore, in *Principia Ethica* (Cambridge, 1903), declared that the term 'good' stood for a simple, non-natural, indefinable quality, known by intuition, and that attempts to define it were inevitably fallacious. (*Naturalistic fallacy.) This somewhat obscure view has not generally prevailed, and philosophical inquiry into good continues. Philosophical concern with good can roughly be subdivided into four sorts. (1) What does the term or word 'good' signify? (2) What things are good, and how do we know them to be so? (3) What is the highest good, the complete good? (4) What sorts of goodness are there, and how, in particular, is moral goodness related to other varieties of goodness? These concerns are plainly interrelated.

With respect to the first, it is natural to think that since 'good' most commonly functions as an adjective it designates some distinctive quality possessed in common by everything that is good. This is implausible. It is doubtful that a good novel possesses any property of significance in common with a good semiconductor, at least no intrinsic property. But the property may not be intrinsic. For something to be good may be for it to meet some human interest, directly or indirectly. This could be a common relational property. Others have argued that the term does not ascribe a property at all. Rather it is used to express approval or commendation of the item dubbed good. Such views are associated with the emotive theory of ethics and with prescriptivism.

Clearly, the issue of how we know what items are good will be much influenced by the view one has of what it is for something to be good. If to hold something to be good is to approve of it, or otherwise feel favourably disposed towards it, then one must consult one's own feelings and dispositions to determine whether some event, object, or outcome is good. If, on the other hand, goodness is a relational property of something concerned with its meeting human interests, then what things are good will be something fairly readily settled by informal inquiry. The rather widespread idea that goodness is 'subjective' usually results from the first of these views, or from a confusion of the question what is good with the question whether some good is preferable to another. The latter can be subjective even when it is a plain matter of fact what is or is not good.

Things that are good may also be viewed from the point of view of how they will contribute to a well-spent or happy human life. The idea of a complete good is that of what will wholly satisfy the complete need and destiny of humans, the *summum bonum*. This may be one thing (e.g. contemplating the face of God); or a combination of many things, as envisaged in Aristotle's account of the 'political' life in the *Nicomachean Ethics*. The notion of the highest good is often obscure. It may signify that one good which is better than any other good; or that one good better than all other goods taken together.

Goods may be taxonomized in other ways also, such as hedonic (goods of or dependent on pleasure); utilitarian (goods derived from usefulness); and so on. Goods may also be distinguished as intrinsic (in and of themselves) or extrinsic (good as a means to an end). Whether the moral goodness of a person, their character, and actions is a distinctive type, or is derived from their goodness in other ways (e.g. in producing happiness for others, as envisaged in utilitarian moral theory) is a vexed matter. The relations between what it is good to do and what it is right to do are also intricate and obscure.   N.J.H.D.

*right action; well-being; obligation.

Discussions of good and goodness are to found in:
R. M. Hare, *The Language of Morals* (Oxford, 1952).
C. L. Stevenson, *Ethics and Language* (New Haven, Conn., 1944).
G. H. von Wright, *The Varieties of Goodness* (London, 1963).

Good, Form of the. In virtue of what, are all beautiful things beautiful? What makes all chairs chairs? For Plato, the answer is their real essence, a Form, in which they somehow partake. There is one Form, it seems, to which every thing that falls under a particular concept is related in this way. Forms, although sometimes called Ideas, are real, rather than being ideas in the ordinary sense. They are unchanging, somehow not in the lower world we know, and, so to speak, are the very perfection of the things in question. The Form of Beauty is ideally beautiful. The supreme Form is the Form of the Good, or just the Good. Its grandeur is beyond description, but it includes its being the foundation and source of all knowledge and all reality, of truth and of all things. It can be no surprise that the Good was identified with God by later philosophers. For Plato, knowledge of it is the ultimate purpose of philosophy in a wide sense, and we are to be ruled only by those who have come to know it. Whatever else, the Form of the Good is an idea of elusive beauty that has endured.   I.C.H.

Plato, *Phaedo*, 73–7.
—— *Republic*, 506 d ff.
G. Santas, 'The Form of the Good in Plato's *Republic*', in J. Anton and A. Preus (eds.), *Essays in Ancient Philosophy*, ii (Albany, NY, 1983).

good, greatest. Goal of human life or *eudaemonia*. The correct conception must include all goods. The view that *eudaemonia* consists in pleasure alone is false, since pleasure fails to include goods such as knowledge. Aristotle held that *eudaemonia* consisted in exercise of the virtues, which itself instantiates all human goods. Cicero and the Stoics spoke of the *summum bonum*. The notion was also used for the collective good of all in *utilitarianism.   R.CRI.

Aristotle, *Nicomachean Ethics*, tr. T. Irwin (Indianapolis, 1985), bk. I.

good-in-itself. A good-in-itself is otherwise referred to as an intrinsic good. Aristotle in the *Nicomachean Ethics* made use of the idea, in attempting to define the *good for man. He distinguished between things pursued for their own sake (such as health) and things pursued for the sake of their consequences (such as money). He concluded that there was a number of different things that were goods-in-themselves. To his list of health, sight, and intelligence, we might now add such values as the continuing existence of diverse species of animals.   M.WARN.

David Wiggins, *Needs, Values, Truth* (Oxford, 1987).

Goodman, Nelson (1906–98). One of the most influential American philosophers of the twentieth century, trained at Harvard and Professor there for thirty years. Goodman's first published book was *The Structure of Appearance* (1951), an attempt to apply techniques of formal logic to 'the analysis of phenomena'. Certain entities are characterized as 'basic individuals'; the objects of ordinary experience are in some sense 'constructions' out of these. Goodman has a partiality (though not a commitment) to *phenomenalism, the view that basic individuals are sensory items rather than physical things. He describes himself as a nominalist and *The Structure of Appearance* as formulated in nominalistic terms. Goodman's *nominalism is sometimes described as a rejection of classes, but may best be summed up in his words: 'the nominalist recognizes no distinction of entities without a distinction of content'. According to Goodman, then, the class whose members are the counties of Utah is not to be distinguished from the class of acres of Utah or from the single individual, the state of Utah. This view has been described as a 'simple materialism' based on the 'crude principle' that the entities supposed unintelligible (classes as distinct from their members) are those things we cannot point at or hold in our hands.

In *Fact, Fiction, and Forecast* Goodman proposed his 'new riddle of induction'. Hume had seen that we make predictions based on regularities in experience, while arguing that there was no rational basis for this. But not all observed regularities form the basis for predictions: though all examined emeralds are *grue we do not imagine that all emeralds are.

Goodman was an art collector, and this interest was also reflected in his philosophical writings. In *Languages of Art* (1968) he discusses such topics as representation, expression, and authenticity from the perspective of what he calls 'a general theory of symbols'.   M.C.

*aesthetics, history of; aesthetics, problems of.

N. Goodman, *Fact, Fiction, and Forecast*, 4th edn. (Cambridge, Mass., 1983).
——— *Ways of Worldmaking* (Indianapolis, 1978).
R. Rudner and I. Scheffler (eds.), *Logic and Art: Essays in Honor of Nelson Goodman* (Indianapolis, 1972).

good will. Moral agents, on a Kantian view, can be held accountable for the orientation of their will, as they can not for their physical and psychological make-up. The will has to be seen as free—initiating action because duty calls for it, or else assenting—also freely—to action out of inclination. Thus, distinctive or 'genuine' moral worth lies not simply in the mere performance of right acts, but in doing them from a motive of duty—that is, from a good will, steadily aligned to whatever duty requires. Such a view is of course compatible with a concern about the consequences of action—but only so long as the supreme value of the good will itself is not lost from sight. Moral theorists dispute whether this account warps and narrows the range of moral appraisal, by undervaluing spontaneous goodness and goodness of character. But it is hard not to agree that my good will is morally appraisable in a distinctive and strong sense. It monitors, endorses, rejects, and modifies the components of my temperament and character for whose existence I am not in the same thoroughgoing way responsible. What I choose to make of these components or do with them is indeed morally appraisable, and is a matter of attention and will.   R.W.H.

*consequentialism.

H. J. Paton, *The Categorical Imperative* (London, 1948).

Gorgias (5th century BC). The most celebrated rhetorician of the century. From Leontini in Sicily, he was a prominent figure in the sophistic movement in Athens in the last quarter of the century. (*Sophists.) He also had philosophical interests, and was reputedly a pupil of Empedocles. The surviving portions of his works not only attest his florid rhetorical style, but also touch on some substantial issues, including responsibility (in his *Defence of Helen*). The curious essay *On What Is Not* is an application (of dubious seriousness) of Eleatic argumentative techniques to establish a variety of sceptical and nihilistic conclusions. He figures prominently in Plato's *Gorgias*.   C.C.W.T.

W. K. C. Guthrie, *A History of Greek Philosophy*, iii (Cambridge, 1969), ch. 11.2.

grace. That which is granted by the will of God. Divine assistance, especially that conducive to sanctification and salvation. It is argued, for example by Augustine, Luther, and Calvin (following Romans 9: 11–26), that the grace of God does not depend on merit. Augustine distinguishes grace necessary for action (*adiutorium sine quo non fit*) from grace sufficient for action (*adiutorium quo fit*). Aquinas calls the inspiring presence of God in the soul 'habitual grace' or 'sanctifying grace', and divine intervention causing a good human act 'actual' grace. The ability to not act sinfully since the Fall, the salvation of the soul, and the possession of Christian faith itself are arguably by the grace of God. The sacraments are symbols or instruments for the reception of grace, but grace may be bestowed without them.   S.P.

Augustine, *De Corruptione et Gratia* xii. 34.
Aquinas, *Summa Theologiae*, Prima Secundae q. 110 a.1.
Martin Luther, *Lectures on Romans* (1515–16).
Jean Calvin, *Institutes* III xxi 1, 5.

grammar. A formal system for describing the structure of natural languages. The term is used, in one sense, to mean traditional grammar, and in another, more theoretical sense, to mean generative grammar. Traditional grammar at best describes ideals of practice offering prescriptive rules that tell us how others would like us to use our language. It is alleged that it can provide philosophical insight into the presuppositions harboured in ordinary language, and that correct attention to it resolves philosophical misunderstanding.

Grammar in the more technical sense, given precision by Chomsky's notion of a generative grammar, is a system of rules or principles from which can be derived all and only the grammatical *sentences of a language. The task in constructing grammars for particular languages is to design a formal system that will account for most of the facts with the fewest number of independent principles and posits. Such a grammar is generative in the formal sense that it makes it explicit how all of the permissible sequences of words follow from a finite set of principles and a finite stock of vocabulary (lexical) items.

The theory of grammar studies linguistic competence, not performance; i.e. it accounts for what speakers know about their language, not all the uses they make of it. This is because performance may be full of slips of the tongue, inattention, false starts, mistakes speakers would like to correct on reflection, etc. A theory of performance would have to include not just a theory of linguistic mastery but also psychological theories of memory, perception, attention, and motor functioning which all contribute to actual language use. This means that the data for theories of grammar will always be indirect. In addition to verbal behaviour, linguists elicit judgements from speakers (misleadingly called intuitions) about which strings of words are grammatical, or belong to their language. For example, 'George drank the wine' and even the semantically anomalous 'The wine drank George' are grammatical; whereas 'George wine drank the' is not. To use it to say what the first sentence says is not to be speaking English. Judgements about what is grammatical, however, are not always reliable; they simply provide the best available evidence of which sentences are well formed (i.e. grammatical) in the speaker's language.

Speakers may find some sentences ungrammatical at first due to parsing problems. Well-known examples are centre-embedded constructions such as 'The girl the cat the dog bit scratched cried' (cf. 'The boy the dog bit cried'), and garden-path sentences such as 'The horse raced past the barn fell'. Difficulties with these are due to processing and memory limitations. Hence even the mentalist hypothesis that grammar is a cognitive state has to distinguish *grammars* as bodies of knowledge, from *parsers* as systems of processing rules for producing and comprehending strings.

A grammar that generates all and only the grammatical sentences of a speaker's language is said to be *observationally adequate*. A grammar is said to be *descriptively adequate* when it also assigns structural descriptions to those strings. Grammar is really the theory of syntactic structures rather than word strings, since it must account for grammatical relations between sentences and explain why certain structures are ruled out. To do this it must postulate real, though hidden, levels of syntactic representation. (*Structure, deep and surface.) For example, the sentences 'John is easy to please' and 'John is eager to please' look on the surface like similar arrangements of words of the same grammatical category. But the first can be transformed into the sentence 'It is easy to please John', whereas the second has no related form 'It is eager to please John'. This is because 'John' is the object of 'to please' in the first structure, but the subject in the second. (Chomsky argues that these subject and object positions should be marked in the syntax by empty categories.) Sentences are hierarchical, not linear, arrangements of constituents, where constituent structures are units of syntax larger than the word and smaller than the sentence. All sentences contain groupings like noun phrase and verb phrase which mark major constituent boundaries. These phrase structures can be represented by tree diagrams, or labelled and bracketed strings; e.g. [$_S$[$_{NP}$ The horse raced past the barn] [$_{VP}$ fell]]. A theory of grammar is said to be *explanatorily adequate* if it is the descriptive grammar

which records the knowledge of language speakers have actually acquired and the structural descriptions they assign to their sentences, i.e. if it is psychologically real.

B.C.S.

N. Chomsky, *Aspects of the Theory of Syntax* (Cambridge, Mass., 1965).

J. Katz (ed.), *The Philosophy of Linguistics* (Oxford, 1985).

P. Sells, *Lectures on Contemporary Syntactic Theories* (Stanford, Calif., 1985).

grammar, autonomy of. In his *Tractatus*, Wittgenstein argued that language is answerable to the essential nature of reality. The logical syntax of simple names (their combinatorial possibilities) must mirror the metaphysical combinatorial possibilities of the simple objects that are their meanings. Names are *connected* with the objects in reality which are their meanings by word–world correlations. Similarly, the use of the negation sign must reflect the essence of the operation of negation, etc.

In *Philosophical Grammar*, chapters II and X, he repudiated this view. He ceased to employ the term 'logical syntax', no longer believing that there is a philosophically significant distinction between syntactical (formation) rules and semantical rules 'connecting language with reality' (e.g. by means of ostensive definitions). Ostensive definitions appear to connect words with objects and properties in reality, but this appearance is deceptive. The object pointed at in an ostensive definition of a colour-word, for example, is being used as a sample, and a sample is part of the means of representation, not an object represented (described) by the ostensive definition. This is evident from the fact that instead of the description '*A* is red' one may say '*A* is *this* ↑ colour [pointing at a sample]', substituting a sample, deictic gesture and indexical for the word 'red'. Here the *ostensive definition is visibly functioning as a substitution rule. So ostensive definition remains within language and does not connect language and reality.

*Grammar, he now suggested, is constituted by *all* the linguistic rules that *determine the sense of an expression*. Here he diverged from the customary use of 'grammar' (which excludes explanations of word-meaning, and admits as grammatical sequences of words that lack sense). But he denied that there are two different kinds of grammar, ordinary grammar and philosophical grammar. Rather there are two different kinds of interest in the rules of language, the grammarian's and the philosopher's. The latter's interest is guided by the purpose of resolving philosophical problems.

Wittgenstein now argued, contrary to his earlier view, that grammar is 'arbitrary' or autonomous, i.e. that it is not answerable to the nature of things. The idea that grammar can be justified by reference to reality in the sense in which an empirical proposition is justified by reference to what makes it true is incoherent. The rules for the use of names, e.g. 'red', do not mirror the metaphysical nature of the colour, but constitute it. Similarly, the rules for the use of the negation sign do not reflect the nature of negation, but determine it. 'Grammatical propositions', e.g. 'Nothing can be red and green all over', are in effect rules, not descriptions of reality. What appear to be metaphysical necessities are in effect no more than the shadows cast upon the world by our methods of representation, our rules for the use of expressions. Concepts are not 'correct', let alone justifiable as true, but only more or less useful for our purposes. Alternative grammars are conceivable. They are constrained, but not made more or less correct, by our nature (e.g. by our perceptual and intellectual capacities) and by the contingencies of the world.   P.M.S.H.

P. M. S. Hacker, *Insight and Illusion: Themes in the Philosophy of Wittgenstein*, rev. edn. (Oxford, 1986), 179–92.

grammatical proposition. Term of art used by the later Wittgenstein to signify a proposition which appears to state truths about the nature of things, but whose actual role is to give a rule for the use of its constituent expressions. 'Red is a colour', 'Nothing can be red and green all over simultaneously', 'Red is darker than pink' look as if they state necessary truths about the nature of colours. Actually they specify rules for the use of colour words, namely that if something is red, it can also be said to be coloured; if something is red all over, it cannot also be said to be green all over; if *A* is red and *B* pink, then the inference that *A* is darker than *B* is licit. Wittgenstein argued that what appear to be necessary metaphysical truths are at best grammatical propositions.   P.M.S.H.

G. P. Baker and P. M. S. Hacker, *An Analytical Commentary on the Philosophical Investigations*, ii: *Wittgenstein: Rules, Grammar and Necessity* (Oxford, 1985), 269–73.

Gramsci, Antonio (1891–1937). Born in Sardinia, Gramsci was a founder-member and the principal ideologist of the Italian Communist Party, which he briefly led prior to his imprisonment by Mussolini. Whilst in jail, where he remained until his death, he wrote the *Prison Notebooks*. These are generally regarded as amongst the founding documents of Western Marxism. Drawing on the writings of Croce, Gramsci modified orthodox historical materialism so as to give an independent role to human consciousness and hence to the superstructure relative to the economic base. He used this insight to develop the concept of hegemony, or ideological power, to explain the resilience of liberal democracy in the advanced industrial nations of the West. He argued that in order to overthrow the state in such countries, revolutionary parties must first overcome the sources of hegemonic power within civil society, such as churches, schools, and the media.   R.P.B.

*dialectical materialism.

Richard Bellamy and Darrow Schecter, *Gramsci and the Italian State* (Manchester, 1993).

greatest happiness principle. This is one name for the leading principle of *utilitarianism, and one which Bentham specifically gave to his central principle towards the

end of his life. The main reason for the change was that he thought that 'happiness' was a clearer designation than *'utility' for the right end of action; the happiness to be considered was of everyone affected by a proposed action or state of affairs.   R.H.

Jeremy Bentham, *Introduction to the Principles of Morals and Legislation*, 2nd edn. (1823), ch.1, sect.1, n.

great man theory of history. An expression used to refer to the claim that the course of the historical process is basically governed by the actions of outstanding individuals, a contention encapsulated in Carlyle's famous dictum that history is 'the biography of great men'. Its nineteenth-century opponents, who included Engels, Tolstoy, and Herbert Spencer, argued instead that history was ultimately determined by such general factors as economic or social relations, the individuals wielding power being themselves the products or instruments of society. Despite the intrinsic interest of problems concerning the role of the individual in history, debates on this score have tended to be vitiated by uncritically monistic conceptions of historical causation, failures to distinguish between the necessary and sufficient conditions of events, and divergences in the criteria employed for estimating the nature and extent of social influence or importance.   P.L.G.

*superman.

S. Hook, *The Hero in History* (New York, 1943).

great-souled man. Greatness of soul (Greek *megalopsukhia*, rendered into Latin as *magnanimitas*) is a self-referential evaluative disposition characteristic of Aristotle's virtuous agent, consisting in a proper sense of his own worth, manifesting itself in the desire to be honoured for his virtues by his equals (coupled with indifference to the opinion of inferiors) and in self-conscious dignity of demeanour (verging on pomposity to the modern eye). Despite the etymological connection, it is nearer to pride than to magnanimity; while the great-souled man appears magnanimous, e.g. in forgiving injuries, he does so not from generosity of spirit, but because nursing grudges is beneath him.   C.C.W.T.

*superman.

W. F. R. Hardie, '"Magnanimity" in Aristotle's Ethics', *Phronesis* (1978).

Greek philosophy: *see* ancient philosophy; Greek philosophy, modern.

Greek philosophy, modern. What point of origin one selects for modern Greek philosophy is to a certain extent an arbitrary matter. For, on the one hand, intellectual phenomena never fall neatly into line with the facts of history, while, on the other, modern Greek philosophy has its roots deep in antiquity, being the prolongation of the classical and Christian spirit during Byzantine rule and the Turkish occupation.

With this caveat, one can usefully think of 'early modern Greek philosophy' as lasting from the year 1453 (the Fall of Constantinople) to the year 1821 (the start of the struggle for national independence). This whole period has certain distinctive features: its attachment to ideals, its Graeco-Christian values, and its unremitting efforts to inform and awaken Hellenic consciousness. 'Later modern Greek philosophy' (and it is with this that the present article is chiefly concerned) emerges from the revolution of 1821. Greece breaks free from the Ottoman Empire, and organizes herself into a nation state. Decisively influenced by the new freedom of thought and action, modern Greek philosophy manifests a number of tendencies.

1. Ancient authors are published, annotated, translated, and interpreted. Thinkers turn to the great philosophers of the past—in particular Plato and Aristotle—for inspiration. A halt is called to the conflict between Platonists and Aristotelians that had prevailed in Byzantium and throughout early modern Greek philosophy. Though a majority of intellectuals opt for *Platonism, they take proper account of Aristotle, a large number of whose doctrines win acceptance. Simultaneously there develops a sort of *scholasticism: the idea that faithfully copying the language of the ancient Greeks is the means whereby to advance spiritual culture.

2. Christian authors are published, and commentaries on them are written. This is because those engaged in philosophy are also theologians, with a lively faith in the power of Christianity to mould the individual, especially from the perspective of the Greek Orthodox religion. (The second tendency is not seldom at loggerheads with the first; but both are in agreement as regards the need for a 'learned' language.)

3. A majority of philosophers attempt a synthesis of Greek and Christian values in the light of the applied sciences now under cultivation in western Europe. The major figure in the nineteenth century is Peter Vraïlas-Armenis (1812–84). Vraïlas-Armenis accepts Plato's theory of *innate ideas. His ontology is based on Aristotle's method in the *Categories*, whereas his argument for a provident deity is derived from the Christian creed. Parallel with this, he endeavours to assimilate the scientific findings of his time and to synthesize them into a unified theory of the cosmos and humankind.

This trend towards synthesis had a new lease of life in the twentieth century, in response to various stimuli: *Kantian ethics, the work of the Baden and Marburg Schools, Hegel's system, and Herbart and Wundt's philosophy. No one school is dominant: instead, an eclectic spirit makes itself felt. The specificity of the cultural sciences is recognized. In the search for a more convincing theory of values, new methodological criteria are adopted. Outstanding figures in this movement include Constantine Tsatsos (1899–1987), President of the Greek Republic, the politician and Prime Minister Panayotis Kanellopoulos (1902–86), Theophilos Voreas (1873–1954), John Theodorakopoulos

(1900–81), Christos Androutsos (1869–1935), and Alexander Tsirintanis (1903–77).

4. From the beginning of the twentieth century onwards, there is a radically different philosophical movement which questions traditional solutions and looks for alternatives to *positivism and in a mechanistic account of life and the universe. A considerable number of its adherents embrace *materialism and follow the *Marxist view of man and society. Three very representative figures in this movement are George Skliros (1877–1919), Demetrios Glinos (1882–1943), and Avrotelis Eleftheropoulos (1869–1964).

5. After the Second World War, a dialogue develops between modern Greek philosophy and contemporary modes of thought such as *analytic philosophy, *existentialism, *philosophy of language, *phenomenology, the *Frankfurt School, *Thomism, personalism. Though the description and analysis of present currents of European thought is carried out by university lecturers and teachers in institutes of philosophy, one cannot make great claims for the existence of any philosophical school. Today's Greek philosopher continues to be an eclectic cherishing a belief in the regenerative powers of humanism.   G.B.

*ancient philosophy.

C. Cavarnos, *Modern Greek Thought* (Belmont, Mass., 1969).
G. E. Voumvlinopoulos, *Bibliographie critique de la philosophie grecque* (Athens, 1966).

Green, Thomas Hill (1836–82). English idealist philosopher and liberal political theorist. His *idealism logically entails that something's being what it is essentially consists in its being related to other things. According to Green, no relations can be detected empirically, but they may be known by the rational self-conscious minds that construct them. Green emphasizes that this idealism is anti-empiricist because it includes the denial that what something is may be known by sense experience. Indeed, Green's contributions to the edition of Hume's works he helped to compile are critical of Hume's empiricism and his naturalism.

Green's *liberalism is the doctrine that a minimal state is justified in so far as it maximizes the freedom of the individual. Hence the state may intervene to prevent the freedom of some citizens being curtailed by others. Green's holistic view of the state owes more to Hegel than to classical English liberalism, despite Green's endorsement of the principle that each individual's freedom should be maximized in so far as this is consistent with a similar freedom for every other individual.   S.P.

T. H. Green, *Prolegomena to Ethics* (Oxford, 1883; new edn. with introduction by D. Brink, Oxford, 2003).

Gregory of Rimini (*c*.1300–58). A member of the Eremite Order of St Augustine, he taught at Paris, Bologna, Padua, and Perugia, and was Prior General of his order from 1357 till his death. He wrote an influential commentary on the *Sentences* of Peter of Lombard, in which he has a good deal to say about our knowledge of the external world. He accepts the common view that perception of the outer world requires species which emanate from outer objects and strike our receptors, and argues that in the absence of those objects we still know them, though 'abstractively', because we have intuitive, that is, immediate knowledge of the species which have lodged in our minds. In the case of our knowledge of outer objects, it is immediate in that though we cannot see such an object without the aid of the species emanating from it, we do not see the species themselves; the causal role they play does not involve their being perceived. To say otherwise would be to deny that we can have intuitive knowledge of external things.   A.BRO.

G. Leff, *Gregory of Rimini: Tradition and Innovation in Fourteenth Century Thought* (Manchester, 1961).

Grelling's paradox. Due to Kurt Grelling (1886–1941), who was killed by the Nazis while trying to escape across the Pyrenees. Grelling defined the adjective 'heterological' to mean the same as 'not self-applicable'. This seems to entail that 'heterological' is heterological if and only if it is not heterological, which is impossible. Now whether 'not self-applicable' is self-applicable depends entirely on what that phrase means in application to itself. If it means 'expresses in itself a property it does not instantiate' then it is not self-applicable (and 'heterological' is heterological) because the phrase (the word), in itself, does not express any property. It expresses different properties depending on its application. If it means 'yields a true sentence when grammatically self-applied', then '"Not self-applicable" is not self-applicable' is a version of the *liar paradox, and similarly with 'heterological'.   J.C.

Kurt Grelling, 'The Logical Paradoxes', *Mind* (1936).
—— and L. Nelson, 'Bemerkungen zu den Paradoxien von Russell und Burali-Forti', *Abhandlungen der Fries'schen Schule* (1907–8).

Grice, H. Paul (1913–88). English philosopher best known for his work on meaning, especially the relation between speaker meaning and linguistic meaning. Grice, who was at Oxford until 1967 and at Berkeley thereafter, introduced several notions commonly employed by philosophers today. These include *conversational implicature*, what a speaker implies as opposed to what he says or what his words imply, and *reflexive intention*, a notion central to the idea of speaker meaning (or *communication). Grice maintained that speaker meaning is prior to linguistic meaning, i.e. that *semantics reduces to *propositional attitude psychology. Taken together, his notions have helped linguists as well as philosophers draw the line between semantics and pragmatics. The distinction between meaning and use has squelched such formerly popular philosophical claims as that looking red precludes being red or that believing something precludes knowing it, claims which were based on the fact that it is misleading to make a weaker statement when a stronger one is justified.   K.B.

Paul Grice, *Studies in the Ways of Words* (Cambridge, Mass., 1989).
—— *Aspects of Reason* (Oxford, 2001).

Griffin, James (1933–). Moral philosopher best known for work on *well-being, interpersonal comparison of well-being, and consequentialism. His first book was *Wittgenstein's Logical Atomism* (Oxford, 1964). In *Well-Being* (Oxford, 1986), Griffin argues for an 'informed-desire theory': well-being consists in the possession of those objects one would desire if rational and informed. These are accomplishment, the components of human existence (autonomy, basic capabilities to act, etc.), understanding, enjoyment, and deep personal relations. The good-making property of these objects is not their fulfilling desires, so Griffin is best interpreted as moving beyond a preference-based theory of well-being to an objective account in the tradition of Aristotle, G. E. Moore, and Rashdall. Though Griffin sees promotion of well-being as the animating aim of morality, he is not clearly utilitarian. He stresses the many levels of moral thinking—personal, political, etc.—and each level has its own characteristic principles.   R.CRI.

*consequentialism.

J. Griffin, *Well-Being* (Oxford, 1986).
—— 'Well-being and its Interpersonal Comparability', in D. Seanor and N. Fotion (eds.), *Hare and Critics* (Oxford, 1988).
—— *Value Judgement: Improving Our Ethical Beliefs* (Oxford, 1996).

Grossmann, Reinhardt (1931–). Born in Berlin; professor at Indiana University, Bloomington, since 1962. Grossmann's work is notable for its openness to both contemporary 'analytical' philosophy and 'modern continental philosophy'. For example, he is the author of not only *Reflections on Frege's Philosophy* (1969) but also *Meinong* (1974) and *Phenomenology and Existentialism* (1984). In his own thinking, Grossmann has developed a neo-Kantian epistemology according to which what passes for reality is determined by an intellectual categorial framework. This is apparent in *The Structure of Mind* (1965) and *The Categorial Structure of the World* (1983).   S.P.

*Meinong.

Grosseteste, Robert (c.1170–1253). A Suffolk man, he became Chancellor of Oxford University c.1221, Archdeacon of Leicester in 1229, and was Bishop of Lincoln from 1235 till his death in 1253. He wrote on a wide range of topics in philosophy and theology from an essentially Augustinian perspective. In line with that perspective, which itself is strongly influenced by Platonic and biblical ideas, he placed the concept of light at the centre of his metaphysics, and also at the centre of his epistemology, where he gives an account of human understanding in terms of natural, and ultimately divine, illumination. Grosseteste also composed numerous scientific treatises, being one of a small but growing band who recognized the importance of experiment in the establishment of scientific truth. He was a pioneer in the Christian West as a translator of Aristotle from Greek into Latin.   A.BRO.

J. McEvoy, *Robert Grosseteste* (Oxford, 2002).

Grotius, Hugo (1583–1645). Lawyer, poet, and theologian, he mediated classical and medieval political and legal theory to the Enlightenment. While Descartes meditated in army winter quarters, Grotius was a political prisoner planning his masterwork, *De Iure Belli ac Pacis* (On the Law [and Rights and Wrongs] of War and Peace, 1625).

The philosophical concepts he elaborated with juridical learning and creative statesmanship were transposed from late medieval theology. Moral requirements would be valid even if one granted (*etiamsi daremus*) God's non-existence. Natural moral law identifies acts as morally necessary or base (and divinely commanded or forbidden) because 'conformable (or disconformable) with rational and social nature'. *Rights are powers or liberties; political society is for safeguarding individual moral rights. Hume's celebrated 'is–ought' paragraph targets his evasive natural law theory, Rousseau's *Social Contract* his social contract theory.   J.M.F.

Richard Tuck, *Natural Rights Theories: Their Origin and Development* (Cambridge, 1979).
—— *Philosophy and Government 1572–1651* (Cambridge, 1993).

grue. Imagine a time *t*—say midnight on 1 January 2020. Define '*x* is grue' to mean '*x* is examined before *t* and is green or *x* is examined after *t* and is blue'. If generalizations are confirmed by their instances, then the fact that all emeralds so far examined are green confirms the generalization that all emeralds are grue as well as the generalization that all emeralds are green: but the consequences of the two generalizations are different and the former seems quite bizarre. This is Goodman's 'new riddle of *induction'. Goodman introduced the idea of the entrenchment of a predicate (or more properly its extension) in an attempt to distinguish those generalizations which are genuinely confirmed by their instances.   M.C.

N. Goodman, *Fact, Fiction, and Forecast*, 4th edn. (Cambridge, Mass., 1983).

Grünbaum, Adolf (1923–). A prolific philosopher of science, he has made many contributions to both philosophy of physics and philosophy of psychiatry. Perhaps the most striking claim argued for in his *Philosophical Problems of Space and Time* (1963; expanded edn. 1973) is the thesis that physical geometry and chronometry are, in part, matters of convention because continuous physical space and time are metrically amorphous. His influential *The Foundations of Psychoanalysis* (1984) contains a critique of the scientific credentials of Freudian psychoanalytic theory; it argues that there are methodological and epistemological reasons to think that some central Freudian doctrines are not well supported by empirical evidence. Grünbaum's more recent studies in the philosophy of psychoanalysis treat in detail such topics as the psychoanalytic theory of transference, the viability of the single-subject case-study method, the placebo concept, and the dream theory.   P.L.Q.

*psychoanalysis, philosophical problems of.

A. Grünbaum, *Validation in the Clinical Theory of Psychoanalysis* (Madison, Conn., 1993).

guilt. The state imputed to a person who has done moral or legal wrong. It is distinguishable from having a sense, or feelings, of guilt, since a guilty person may not experience such feelings, and an innocent person may be burdened by unwarranted feelings of guilt. The crux is the question: Was avoidable wrong done by this responsible moral agent?

Full acceptance and realization of guilt involves remorse and desire to expiate the wrong done. Ill-managed or excessive guilt can be morally crippling: but equally damaging to moral seriousness is the attempt to disown real guilt—as pathological or as never more than the effect of external conditioning. Mature commitment to moral obligations deeply affects a person's conception of his own identity, and entails a strong sense of guilty failure on being disloyal to them. Yet guilt is not simply *self-reproach*: it is inseparable from awareness of the harm, or neglect, brought about to the others affected by one's action or inaction.

The neighbouring concept of shame both overlaps and diverges interestingly from the logical behaviour of guilt. A sense of shame is a sensitivity to the moral criticism of others—especially when one is tempted to fall short of basic standards of decency or integrity. To be ashamed is not only to acknowledge one's objective guilt, but also to be painfully and depressedly aware of moral failure, of lost esteem and self-esteem, prompting withdrawal from others' gaze. To be shameless (compare guiltless!) is to lack such sensitivity: when I am guilty, I ought to be ashamed of myself.   R.W.H.

*forgiveness.

R. Spaemann, *Basic Moral Concepts* (London, 1989), chs. 6 and 7.

guru. The Sanskrit word means 'weighty'. A guru is a preceptor who had the weighty role of preserving the oral wisdom called Veda. Veda is supposed to have been taught originally by God, who is the primordial guru. In ancient times pupils staying at a guru's home for twelve years had to learn Vedic hymns and rituals, along with phonetics, grammar, astronomy, metrics, rhetoric, logic, and metaphysics. A worshipful attitude towards a guru is inherent in Indian culture—whence the perverted Western use of the term for a cult-leader. In the tradition of *Tantra, the word is broken up into *gu* meaning 'darkness' and *ru* meaning 'light', signifying the role of a spiritual eye-opener. Buddhism, which denies the knowledge-yielding capacity of testimony, recommends reliance on one's own reason rather than on a guru.   A.C

*Vedānta; Indian philosophy.

'Guru', in S. Schumacher and G. Woerner (eds.), *Encyclopedia of Eastern Philosophy and Religion*, tr. Michael H. Kohn *et al.* (Boston, 1989).

H

Habermas, Jürgen (1929–). A second-generation member of the *Frankfurt School whose work has ranged widely over issues in epistemology, philosophy of language, political and constitutional theory, ethics, and aesthetics. In the late twentieth century the most eminent (as well as controversial) figure in German socio-cultural debate, chiefly because he engaged with these issues not only at a specialist or academic level but also through regular interventions in the broader public sphere. Indeed, it is among his leading claims that this kind of two-way flow between 'expert' discourses and matters of shared communal concern is vital to preserving the values of an open participant democracy. Hence Habermas's many journalistic writings about the post-war West German constitution, about developments in the wake of unification, about asylum-seekers, global justice, and the issue of national identity *vis-à-vis* the prospects for a federal Europe conceived in terms of a 'cosmopolitical' (post-nationalist) agenda. His earlier contribution to the so-called *Historikerstreit*—the debate about right-wing revisionist accounts of the Holocaust—is one striking instance of Habermas's role as a public intellectual in the wider context of ethico-political discussion. Most recently he has carried this thinking forward to take account of the drastically changed world situation since the events of 11 September 2001 and the emergence of a US foreign policy with thinly veiled global geo-strategic aims.

Perhaps the most impressive feature of Habermas's work is the way that these interests link up with his other, more 'purely' philosophical concerns. Influenced by, but also taking issue with, his teacher, Adorno, Habermas has devoted great energy to defending and reclaiming the values of Enlightenment critique, or what he calls the 'philosophical discourse of modernity'. In early texts, such as *Knowledge and Human Interests* (1968), he adopts a broadly Kantian but also Marxist-inflected approach, one that seeks to reconstruct the genealogy of the modern natural and human sciences by inquiring back into their social, historical, and epistemological conditions of emergence. What this reveals is a process of increasing specialization in the various spheres of knowledge-constitutive interest, leading to a point where there seems little hope of an informed critical dialogue between them. Thus thought gives way to a naïve or unreflecting (positivist) conception of scientific method, on the one hand, and on the other—in philosophy and the humanistic disciplines—to various forms of subjectivist, relativist, or downright irrationalist belief. Habermas's aim is to offer an alternative account of this history that draws out *both* its symptomatic blind spots of prejudice, ideological investment, etc., *and* those critical or emancipatory resources which can yet be recovered through a reading alert to their presence in the texts of that same tradition. Hence his departure from Adorno's mode of 'negative dialectics', a thinking that implacably refused the assurances of system or method, and which held out remorselessly against all ideas of achieved rational consensus. For Habermas, as likewise for Kant, such ideas have an indispensable role in orientating thought toward a regulative notion of truth at the end of inquiry.

In his later (post-1970) work Habermas adopts a very different perspective, an account of 'communicative action' derived largely from speech-act theory, socio-linguistics, and ideas about conversational implicature developed by thinkers like Paul Grice. One reason for this turn toward language (or *discourse) is no doubt the currently widespread rejection of 'foundationalist' arguments in whatever shape or form. Another is Habermas's growing conviction that Enlightenment thinking—or the 'unfinished project' of modernity—had run into precisely such criticism through its over-reliance on a subject-centred epistemological paradigm. His aim is therefore to reformulate that project in terms of a 'transcendental pragmatics', a theory that retains the basic commitment to values of truth, critique, and rational consensus, but which pins its faith on the regulative precept of an 'ideal speech situation', a public sphere of uncoerced participant debate wherein those values might yet achieve their fullest, least impeded, or distorted expression. Only thus can Enlightenment thinking make good its emancipatory claims without falling prey to the objections mounted by wholesale pragmatists (such as Richard Rorty) who carry this linguistic turn to the point of equating truth with whatever is currently and contingently 'good in the way of belief'. During the past decade Habermas has shown a heightened awareness of developments in Anglo-American philosophy. Of particular interest is his lengthy exchange with Robert Brandom with regard to the latter's inferentialist account of epistemic commitment, an account which (as both parties agree) exhibits certain striking points of similarity and contrast with Habermas's theory of communicative action. He has also—in works like *Justification and Application*—explored the consequences of that theory for debates in ethics, jurisprudence, and other normative discourses.

Commentators differ sharply in their views as to how far this project stands up to the objections brought against it from various quarters, e.g. by post-modernists and hermeneutic thinkers in the line of descent from Heidegger and Gadamer. On one point at least there is general agreement: that Habermas has always sought to combine these philosophical interests with an active commitment to promoting informed discussion on issues of urgent socio-political concern. It is an example all the more impressive when compared with the stance adopted by those in the post-modern (counter-Enlightenment) camp who have no time for such old-fashioned ideas as 'the political responsibility of the intellectuals'. C.N.

Jürgen Habermas, *Knowledge and Human Interests*, tr. Jeremy J. Shapiro (London, 1972).
—— *The Theory of Communicative Action*, 2 vols., tr. Thomas McCarthy (Boston, 1984 and 1989).
—— *Justification and Application: Remarks on Discourse Ethics*, tr. Ciaran Cronin (Cambridge, Mass., 1993).
—— *The Habermas Reader*, ed. William Outhwaite (Oxford, 1996).

habit memory: *see* memory.

Hacking, Ian (1936–). Canadian philosopher, long based at the University of Toronto. Insisting upon the importance of the empirical, Hacking argues that philosophers too often over-value theory, and hence he would like to promote a 'back to Bacon' movement. Consistently, he accepts a doctrine of *natural kinds, argues for epistemological differences between the natural and social sciences, and views realism–anti-realism debates which fail to take account of actual scientific practices (both in cosmology and in the microcosm) as empty. He is a noted Leibniz scholar. In *The Emergence of Probability* (1975) and *The Taming of Chance* (1990) he has given us ground-breaking accounts of two important periods in the history of *probability. In philosophy of language he has mustered empirical evidence against claimed radical mistranslation, and similarly has contrasted actual languages without particulars (Wakashan languages such as Nootka and Kwakiutl) to Strawson's theoretical views. J.J.M.

Ian Hacking, *Representing and Intervening* (Cambridge, 1983).
—— *The Social Construction of What?* (Cambridge, Mass., 1999).

haecceity. A *property is something such that some things have or exemplify it; for example, red objects exemplify the property *being red*. A haecceity or individual essence is a property such that exactly one individual thing can have it. Thus, Socrates has the individual property of *being Socrates*. Some philosophers (e.g. Chisholm) argue, however, that there are no individual essences, only the property of *being self-identical* and concrete individuals such as Socrates. M.B.

*qualities; individual property; essence.

A. Plantinga, *The Nature of Necessity* (Oxford, 1974). Cf. R. M. Chisholm, *On Metaphysics* (Minneapolis, 1989).

Halevi, Judah (before 1075–*c*.1141). Hebrew poet and philosopher. Of a cultured family in the early Reconquista, Halevi travelled widely in Muslim and Christian Spain, winning fame for his poems, the finest in Hebrew since the Bible. As the Almoravid invasion devastated his world, Halevi practised medicine and wrote songs of love, wine, friendship, faith, and witness to the destruction around him.

Halevi's philosophic dialogue the *Kuzari* pictures the conversations that led the Khazar king to his historic conversion to Judaism. Having dreamed that his intentions but not his actions are pleasing to God, the king summons advisers. The intellectualism of the philosopher, he finds, critically needs fleshing out by ethical culture. Christian and Muslim doctrines clearly depend on Jewish lore. When a rabbi is finally summoned, he rests his case not on abstract reasoning but on historical experience, urging the primacy of the land, language, and peoplehood of Israel and addressing pure theology only after the Khazar is committed to the historic faith of Israel.

Although widely cited as an anti-philosophical thinker, Halevi is a serious *internal* critic of philosophy. His strikingly modern rejection of the baroque ontology of disembodied intellects between God and nature aids his philosophical task of showing how God's word enspirits the people of Israel, empowering them to achieve their mission to the nations. Like his literary persona, Halevi could not remain exiled in 'the farthest West'. He left Spain for the Land of Israel, where, according to legend, he was ridden down by an Arab and slain. L.E.G.

Judah Halevi, *The Kuzari*, tr. H. Hirschfeld (New York, 1964). The original title is preserved in *The Book of Vindication and Evidence in Behalf of the Despised Faith*. Critical edn. by David Baneth (Jerusalem, 1977).

hallucination. Seeing and hearing things when there is nothing of the sort to be seen or heard. What we observe is usually explained by our surroundings, so theorists readily assume that hallucinations are similarly explained by something image-like and introspectible in our heads. Philosophers who reject this as armchair psychology suggest that hallucinators just form false *beliefs about what they perceive, whatever produces them being unavailable to the victim (if not to brain scientists). This 'belief' description, however, looks too intellectual if interpreted as entertaining thoughts about what you perceive, and too thin if interpreted as a disposition to act as if you perceive it; it is still hard to resist the idea that any false beliefs formed by hallucinators are *based on* what is happening to them, which is something *like* seeing or hearing. So what is the resemblance? J.E.R.S.

*dreams.

P. Smith and O. R. Jones, *The Philosophy of Mind* (Cambridge, 1986), chs. 7 and 8.

Hamilton, William (1788–1856). Educated at Glasgow, Edinburgh, and Oxford, Hamilton first professed civil history at Edinburgh in 1821. He later transferred to logic and metaphysics, achieving eminence as a teacher and editor. His invaluable editions of Dugald Stewart and Reid are scholarly but patronizing. He criticizes Reid effectively, yet misrepresents him as saying that sensation is a subjective feeling of pleasure or pain. He deliberately set out to counterbalance the materialism of natural science which ignores God, freedom, and immortality. Believing *knowledge to be perceptual, he called himself a 'natural or intuitive realist', although he admitted unconscious modifications of mind not accessible to consciousness but revealed through associations of ideas. Mill pointed out his inconsistency in holding that the primary qualities of objects are known while objects in themselves are not.

V.H.

William Hamilton, *Lectures of Metaphysics and Logic*, ed. H. L. Mansell and J. Veitch (Edinburgh, 1869).

Hamlyn, David W. (1924–). Professor of Philosophy at Birkbeck College, London (1964–88), and editor of *Mind* (1972–84). Interests in Aristotle (translation of *De anima* with commentary (Oxford, 1968)) and in Wittgenstein have influenced Hamlyn's approach to questions in epistemology and philosophy of psychology. His central thesis (developed in *Experience and the Growth of Understanding* (London, 1978), *Perception, Learning and the Self* (London, 1983), and *In and Out of the Black Box* (Oxford, 1990)) is that in order to be a knower a being must be active and seek to regulate its beliefs in accord with a norm of truth; this requires membership of a community, interaction with which involves emotional responses. In short, knowers are social, affective agents. The other main area of Hamlyn's writing is history of philosophy.

J.HAL.

*epistemology, history of; epistemology, problems of.

Hampshire, Stuart Newton (1914–2004). English philosopher with special interests in the philosophical theory of freedom and the philosophy of mind.

In the course of a long career in which he was Grote Professor of Philosophy at University College London, a professor at several American universities, and Warden of Wadham College, Oxford, Stuart Hampshire developed a distinctive and influential position. The key to his position is perhaps to be found in his early book *Spinoza* (1951) in which he explores Spinoza's conception of mind and will. These ideas were developed in much more detail in his major work *Thought and Action* (1959). In this book he examines a set of contrasts between that which is unavoidable in human thought and that which is contingent; between knowledge and decision; criticism and

practice; philosophy and experience. These contrasts continued to occupy his thinking in several later works. He was married to Nancy Cartwright.

R.S.D.

*London philosophy.

Hannay, Alastair (1932–). Professor emeritus at the University of Oslo, educated in Edinburgh and London, he continues the Scottish tradition of subjective idealism. In *Mental Images* (1971, reprinted 2003) he argues that visual images, like physical portraits, resemble visible objects. As a kind of sensation a mental image has material properties of its own which allow it to picture. He thus contradicts Ryle and Dennett. Hannay has translated Kierkegaard, and written an intellectual biography and a monograph about his philosophy. Under Hannay's direction (managing editor 1962–71, editor 1971–2002), *Inquiry* grew into a widely read philosophical journal. *Human Consciousness* (1990) reviews contemporary theories of human consciousness while maintaining a characteristic conservatism. Hannay argues that consciousness and the first-person point of view cannot be analysed or displaced by scientific materialism, nor can they be explained functionally, a view close to that of Reid, Hamilton, and Ferrier.

V.H.

*Kierkegaard.

Alastair Hannay, *Kierkegaard* (Arguments of the Philosophers, London, 1982, rev. edn. 1991).
—— *Kierkegaard: A Biography* (London, 2001).
—— *Kierkegaard and Philosophy: Selected Essays* (London, 2003).

Hao Wang: *see* Wang, Hao.

happiness. Philosophical discussion of the concept of 'happiness' has tended to be found mainly within moral philosophy. It is associated especially with the classical *utilitarianism of Jeremy Bentham and John Stuart Mill. The utilitarians assert that happiness is *as a matter of fact* the ultimate aim at which all human actions are directed and that it is therefore the ultimate standard by which to judge the *rightness or wrongness* of actions. 'Actions are right', says Mill, 'in proportion as they tend to promote happiness'—that is to say, 'the general happiness', the happiness of all concerned.

Still following Bentham, Mill goes on to equate happiness with 'pleasure and the absence of pain'. For Bentham the identity of 'happiness' and 'pleasure' is quite straightforward. An action's tendency to promote happiness is determined simply by adding up the amounts of pleasure, and subtracting the amounts of pain, which it will produce. It is a matter solely of quantitative factors such as the intensity and the duration of the pleasurable and painful feelings.

Mill is aware that this is altogether too crude. Happiness, he acknowledges, depends not only on the *quantity* but also on the *quality* of pleasures. Human beings, because of the distinctively human capacities they possess, require more to make them happy than the accumulation of pleasurable sensations. They are made happy not by the 'lower pleasures' but by the 'higher pleasures'—'the pleasures of the intellect, of the feelings and imagination, and of the moral sentiments'.

Mill departs still further from the purely quantitative notion of happiness when he recognizes that it is not just a sum of unrelated experiences but an ordered whole. To say that human beings aim at happiness is not to deny that they pursue more specific goals such as knowledge or artistic and cultural activity or moral goodness, and that they pursue these things for their own sake. These are some of the 'ingredients' which go to make up a life of happiness.

Mill is here attempting, perhaps unsuccessfully, to combine two traditions of thought about 'happiness'. The identification of 'happiness' with 'pleasure' we may call the 'hedonistic' conception of happiness. This we may contrast with what has been called the 'eudaimonistic' conception of happiness. The term comes from the Greek word *'eudaimonia', which is usually translated as 'happiness'. Although one of the Greek philosophical schools, *Epicureanism, did identify eudaimonia with pleasure, the Greek concept lends itself less easily than the English term to this identification. In English one can speak of 'feeling happy', and although the relation between such states of feeling and a life of happiness is not entirely clear, they are undoubtedly connected—one could not be said to have a happy life if one never felt happy. The term eudaimonia refers not so much to a psychological state as to the objective character of a person's life.

The classic account of eudaimonia is given by Aristotle. He emphasizes that it has to do with the quality of one's life as a whole; indeed, he sees some plausibility in the traditional aphorism 'Call no man happy until he is dead' (though he also recognizes that there is little plausibility in calling someone happy after he is dead). For Aristotle happiness is to be identified above all with the fulfilment of one's distinctively human potentialities. These are located in the exercise of reason, in both its practical and its theoretical form. Aristotle is thus the ancestor of one strand in Mill, and of that general conception of 'happiness' which links it with ideas of 'fulfilment' and 'self-realization'.

R.J.N.

*well-being; hedonic calculus.

J. Annas, The Morality of Happiness (New York, 1993).

Aristotle, Nicomachean Ethics, various edns. (e.g. Harmondsworth, 1976).

John Stuart Mill, Utilitarianism, various editions (e.g. London, 1962).

Elizabeth Telfer, Happiness (London, 1980).

hard determinism: see freedom and determinism.

Hare, Richard M. (1919–2002). Probably the most influential moral philosopher of his generation, Hare's ideas very largely shaped Anglo-American moral theory for upwards of twenty years, from the mid-1950s. His best-known works are The Language of Morals (Oxford, 1952) and Freedom and Reason (Oxford, 1963), in which he explores fundamental questions regarding the meaning of value and moral words such as *'good' and *'ought', and regarding the foundations of moral reasoning. Hare argues that moral judgements have 'prescriptive' meaning, and imply universal imperatives. For instance, to declare something wrong is not (or is not principally) to indicate that it has some property of 'wrongness', but is to prescribe or direct its avoidance by anyone relevantly circumstanced. Because prescribing the doing or avoidance of something is logically distinct from giving a factual, descriptive account of the nature of the situation, Hare holds that there is no logical relationship between the facts of any case and the moral judgement we may make about it. But because of the universal (or 'universalizable') side of moral prescriptions, a person may be given cause to change his moral position by pointing out that it will also apply to himself in like circumstances. He will then realize that he is inconsistent if he does not wish to accept the prescription as applied to himself but still wishes to judge others in these terms. He must in consistency withdraw and revise his initial judgement. Hare's full statement of his developed theory of moral judgement and reasoning is in Moral Thinking (Oxford, 1981).

In later years, Hare made extensive application of his theoretical principles to practical questions of morality, the environment, education, and so on. Several collections of his essays in these areas have appeared, including Essays on Political Morality (Oxford, 1989) and Essays on Religion and Education (Oxford, 1992). Hare also wrote a short book on Plato (Oxford, 1982). He was White's Professor of Moral Philosophy at Oxford from 1966 until 1983, and he held many visiting professorships particularly in America and in Australia. A collection of essays debating his work was published in 1988, Hare and Critics (ed. D. Seanor and N. Fotion, Oxford).

N.J.H.D.

*prescriptivism; universalizability.

harm. Important to ethics and political philosophy, the concept is difficult to pin down. One view concentrates on consequences. A person is harmed by another if the actions of the 'harmer' negatively affect the interests of her victim. However, this must be specified further. If my health, say, was going to improve enormously relative to now, and you intervene (lightly poisoning me) so that it improves, but not as much as it would have, you have nevertheless harmed me in spite of my positive increase in health. One could instead say that harm is making me worse off than I would have been. This still faces a problem of overdetermination: what if Jane shoots me a millisecond before a boulder falls on me? She can argue that I am no worse off than I would have been had she not shot me; either way I am dead. But it still seems that she harmed me, even if it made me no worse off. Further, not all negative effects on my interests count as harm. Being fined thousands of pounds for fraud, whilst negatively affecting my interests, or losing my house because of another's contract enforcement, may not count as being harmed. Problems for the view are especially salient in the ethics of creation. Imagine an embryologist who can choose which embryos to implant in women seeking to have children. She knows which embryos would be born with a painful genetic condition and which without. Does choosing embryos with the condition harm the resultant offspring? On the above view, it does not. For the choice with respect to each potential individual is existence with pain versus non-existence. The net gain of existing minus some pain must in most cases be more than not existing. Even if one concedes that comparing existence with non-existence is not to compare like with like, the problem remains. For, then, against what should we compare the offspring's medical state? The offspring's suffering is, nevertheless, due to the embryologist's choice. This perhaps points to some non-consequentialist features of harm, focusing, perhaps, on harmers' intentions, or some other characteristics of their actions.

A further problem is avoiding a collapse of the notion of harm into the related notion of wrong, or being wronged. If harming me is simply the commission of a morally wrongful act against me, then there will be as many notions of harm as there are moral principles of rightful action towards others which can be breached. A key question here is whether there can be a harmful but not wrongful act. Examples of accidental, or unavoidable, harms might bear out this distinction. There are also cases where we can place a person at a (morally) wrongful disadvantage, yet would decline to call this a harm.   s.m.-g.

*consequentialism; ethics.

J. Feinberg, 'Wrongful Life and the Counterfactual Element in Harming', in his *Freedom and Fulfilment* (Princeton, NJ, 1992).
D. Parfit, 'The Non-Identity Problem', in *Reasons and Persons* (Oxford, 1984).

Harman, Gilbert (1938–). Professor of Philosophy at Princeton University, best known for contributions in the philosophy of mind, epistemology, and ethics. Although it is common to equate 'being rational' with 'being logical', Harman distinguishes these sharply. Logic provides a theory of implication relations among sentences. 'If *A* then *B*', coupled with '*A*', logically implies '*B*'. An agent's accepting the first two statements, however, does not thereby rationally oblige him to infer or accept the third. At most, reason demands acceptance of '*B*' or the rejection of either 'If *A* then *B*' or '*A*'. In ethics, Harman advances a robust *moral relativism according to which what agents 'ought' to do depends on socially reinforced principles they come to acquire. Agents imbued with different principles will be differently motivated, hence morally judge and act in different ways.   J.HEIL

G. Harman, *Change in View* (Cambridge, Mass., 1986).
——— *Reasoning, Meaning, and Mind* (Oxford, 1999).
——— *Explaining Value and Other Essays in Moral Philosophy* (Oxford, 2000).

harmony, logical. In a *natural deduction formalization of logic, harmony is a relation between the introduction

and elimination rules governing a logical constant which renders them in accord with one another: it is not possible to infer from a statement of a given form more than is warranted by the way in which that statement was arrived at in the first instance. The condition for this to hold good is precisely the condition that the basic step of normalization can be carried out with respect to a given logical constant, namely that, whenever in a deduction a statement is derived by an introduction rule, only to be used immediately as the major premiss of an elimination rule, a short cut is always possible that makes no use of that statement. This condition is plausible independently of Prawitz's idea for a proof-theoretic justification of the elimination rules: namely as a formulation of the requirement of *harmony* between introduction and elimination rules. For if, with respect to a given logical constant, such harmony does not obtain, the addition of that constant to the language is a non-conservative extension, in that we can derive conclusions not containing that constant from premisses not containing it that we could not have derived in the language lacking the constant.

Disharmony occurs when the elimination rules are stronger than is warranted by the introduction rules, taken collectively. It can also occur that they are weaker. This may also be seen as a defect, though its effects are less serious: the condition that the elimination rules be no weaker than they need be may be termed *stability*.

If we distinguish what justifies the assertion of a form of statement and the consequences that follow from accepting it as two aspects of the linguistic practice governing it, these notions of harmony and of stability may be generalized from logic to the whole of language. They then become conditions, stronger than the requirement of consistency, for the proper functioning of a language, ones not guaranteed satisfaction by the mere existence and use of that language.   m.d.

Nuel D. Belnap, 'Tonk, Plonk and Plink', *Analysis* (1962); repr. in P. F. Strawson (ed.), *Philosophical Logic* (Oxford, 1967).
M. Dummett, *The Logical Basis of Metaphysics* (Cambridge, Mass., 1991).
A. N. Prior, 'The Runabout Inference-Ticket', *Analysis* (1960); repr. in P. F. Strawson (ed.), *Philosophical Logic* (Oxford, 1967).

harmony, pre-established. A theory associated with the philosophy of G. W. Leibniz. It is a basic thesis of Leibniz's philosophy that there are no causal interactions between created *substances, although there appear to be. According to Leibniz the states of a created substance are causal consequences of its own preceding states, except for its initial state, which is brought about by God at its creation. Leibniz held that God so created substances that, although they do not causally interact, they behave just as we would expect them to behave were they to causally interact. Leibniz utilized this theory in order to provide an explanation for the relation of the mind to the body, although that is not its basic motivation.   R.C.SLE.

*occasionalism.

G. W. Leibniz, 'New System of Nature', in *G. W. Leibniz: Philosophical Essays*, ed. and tr. Roger Ariew and Daniel Garber (Indianapolis, 1989).

Hart, H. L. A. (1907–92). Philosopher and lawyer who with J. L. Austin was central to late 1940s Oxford analytical philosophy. His work while Oxford's Professor of Jurisprudence (1952–68) transformed philosophy of law (particularly analytical jurisprudence and *legal positivism) by opening it to social theory mindful of the 'internal point of view' of social actors, and so to normative political and moral theory (conceived by Hart in liberal and Humean fashion). For Hart, our language is a reminder of the complexity and inner dimension of human affairs; philosophically sophisticated attention to it undermines simplifying and sceptical reductivisms, whether about causation (*Causation in the Law* (1959)), punishment and the mental element in crime (*Punishment and Responsibility* (1968)), or the general structure and functions of law (*The Concept of Law* (1961); *Essays on Bentham* (1982)).   J.M.F.

*law, history of the philosophy of; law, problems of the philosophy of.

H. L. A. Hart, *Essays in Jurisprudence and Philosophy* (Oxford, 1983).
Nicola Lacey, *A Life of H. L. A. Hart: The Nightmare and the Noble Dream* (Oxford, 2004).
Neil MacCormick, *H. L. A. Hart* (London, 1981).

Hartley, David (1705–57). Hartley's interest was in the body's role in the production and association of ideas; he found the key in Newton's theory of vibrations. Hartley's major writing in English appeared in 1749. Here he develops the view that vibratory motions in the brain are set up by the nerves receiving impressions of external objects, acting through the ether, and these vibrations typically continue in the brain, as sensations, a short time after the removal of the external objects. Hartley's is a physiological explanation of the short persistence of a feeling after the removal of the stimulus. He also undertakes a 'deduction' of the character of each type of sensation from the theory of vibrations. Ideas of heat, cold, sight, etc. and sexual desires result from the vibratory effect in the 'medullary Particles', specifically from the kind and locality of the vibrations in the brain, and the line of direction of influences from nerves to the brain.

His writings contain a 'natural Assent' argument for a first cause and an account of moral–political matters and their dependence upon 'the Christian Revelation'.   D.G.

*associationism.

David Hartley, *Observations on Man, his Frame, his Duty, and his Expectations: Containing Observations on the Frame of the Human Body and Mind, and on their Mutual Connexions and Influences* (first pub. 1749; Hildesheim, 1967).

Hartmann, Eduard von (1842–1906). German philosopher who tried to reconcile Schopenhauer with Hegel, Schelling, and Leibniz. In *The Philosophy of the Unconscious* (1869; tr. London, 1931) he argued that the unconscious *Absolute is both will and idea, which respectively

account for the existence of the world and its orderly nature. Will appears in suffering, idea in order and consciousness. Thus there are grounds for both *pessimism and optimism, and, since the Absolute is one, these must be reconciled. As the cosmic process advances, idea prevails over will, making possible aesthetic and intellectual pleasures. But intellectual development increases our capacity for pain, and material progress suppresses spiritual values. Hence ultimate happiness is not attainable in this world, in heaven, or by endless progress towards an earthly paradise. These illusions are ruses employed by the absolute to induce mankind to propagate itself. We will eventually shed illusions and commit collective suicide—the final, redeeming triumph of idea over will.   M.J.I.

D. N. K. Darnoi, *The Unconscious and Eduard von Hartmann* (The Hague, 1967).

Hartmann, Nicolai (1882–1950). German philosopher who abandoned his original neo-Kantian belief that objective reality is a mental construct and, in, for example, *New Ways of Ontology* (1942; tr. Chicago, 1953), developed a realist *ontology. There are various levels of being: inorganic, organic, spiritual, etc. A higher level is rooted in a lower, but not wholly determined by it. Some categories are involved at all levels of being: e.g. unity and multiplicity, persistence and change. But each level has its own complex of categories (e.g. matter and causality at the inorganic level) which apply to a higher level (e.g. organic life) only with modifications. As well as general ontology, Hartmann produced a series of 'regional ontologies', exploring the categories of, for example, the human spirit and its objectifications and those of inorganic and organic nature. In *Ethics* (1926; tr. London, from 1932) he developed a non-formal theory of values which, though objective, have only ideal being and affect the world only in so far as men act on them. He denies the existence of a providential God, since it is incompatible with human *freedom. Unlike Heidegger, he was concerned with beings, not *being.   M.J.I.

W. Stegmüller, *Main Currents in German, British, American Philosophy* (Bloomington, Ind., 1969).

Hartshorne, Charles (1897–2000). American process philosopher and theologian at the University of Chicago and the University of Texas who continued to the end of the twentieth century the 'process' tradition in which *becoming is the primary reality. Although strongly influenced by his teacher Alfred North Whitehead, some of his ideas antedate his encounter with Whitehead and others are improvements on him. Like Whitehead, he holds a panexperientialism in which the basic units of reality are creative, experiential events. This doctrine does not imply that the reality of an electron is very similar to the reality of human consciousness, only that both are on a continuous spectrum of processive reality. Hartshorne's chief improvements are in the theory of compound individuals.

Hartshorne and Whitehead, as pantheists, hold that God transcends the world while including it. But, whereas for

Whitehead God is a single, everlasting entity, for Hartshorne God is a temporal society of experiential occasions.

Also an ornithologist, he published notable studies of birdsong.   P.H.H.

*process philosophy.

C. Hartshorne, *Reality as a Social Process* (Boston, 1953).
Robert Kane and Stephen H. Phillips (eds.), *Hartshorne, Process Philosophy and Theology* (Albany, NY, 1989).

Harvard philosophy. Harvard was founded in 1635, a century and a half before the achievement of independence by the United States. There were two distinguished philosophers during the colonial period, but they were both Yale men: Jonathan Edwards, the most rigid of determinists, and the American Samuel Johnson, a follower of Berkeley. The first capable Harvard philosopher was Francis Bowen, an adherent of the Scottish common-sense philosophy of Reid and Dugald Stewart, which dominated American universities from soon after its introduction to the country at the beginning of the nineteenth century. At Harvard it was expounded by Levi Hedge from 1795 to 1832 and then by Bowen from 1835 to 1889. The practical attraction of Scottish common-sense philosophy was that it offered a rational alternative to the fanatical excesses of Calvinist orthodoxy while resisting, on another front, the speculative nebulosities of the amateur philosophers of the Transcendentalist movement. C. S. Peirce, William James, and their early associate Chauncey Wright were all Bowen's pupils.

In the 1870s these three and others, including John Fiske, disciple of Herbert Spencer, formed a Metaphysical Society in which, under the influence of the prevailing Darwinian evolutionism, the ideas were worked out that were to constitute pragmatism, a Harvard invention. Peirce, like Wright, the most positivistic of the group, and Fiske, was associated only informally with Harvard after graduation. But his close relation to the much more immediately influential James gave his ideas, much more sophisticated than those of James, some currency. James was soon joined at Harvard by Josiah Royce, who combined an up-to-date interest in logic with the kind of idealism which holds that only mind is real and that all finite minds are included in an absolute mind.

James's most gifted student, George Santayana, was also his intellectually most disobedient one. Both were naturalists who wanted to find some place for religion in the scheme of things, but they went about the project in very different ways. James adjusted his concepts of truth and reality so as to accommodate his spiritual yearnings; Santayana affirmed the materiality of the real and saw mind as at once its product and decorator. He contributed in 1920 to the collective volume *Critical Realism*. The organizer of the earlier collection *The New Realism* (1912) had been Ralph Barton Perry, another Harvard teacher, loyal to the memory, if not the doctrine, of William James. He went on to write large, soft-centred books about ethics and the theory of value.

James died in 1910, Peirce in 1914, Royce in 1916, and Santayana had departed for Europe in 1912. It seemed that the golden age of Harvard philosophy, and of philosophy in America in general, had come to an end. Whitehead arrived in the mid-1920s to begin, in his sixties, a productive and obscurely brilliant new career as a speculative cosmologist, but he had little effect outside a small circle of devotees and a distantly admiring element in the general reading public. Harvard philosophy turned from James's conversational breeziness, Royce's pulpit eloquence, and Santayana's civilized belletrism to an altogether more rigorous and professional mode of philosophizing. The emblem of this change was C. I. Lewis, intensional logician, analytic theorist of knowledge, and combatively naturalist theorist of value, the best philosopher of the inter-war years in the United States. His abler associates were unproductive, his productive colleagues were not all that able. He was, therefore, somewhat solitary. But his main doctrines had a considerable overlap with those of the analytic philosophers of Britain and the Logical Positivists of Europe.

W. V. Quine arrived for graduate study in Lewis's time. From the start his interest in formal logic was accompanied by a concern for its philosophical underpinnings. He visited the Vienna Circle and was soon discarding some of their most treasured substantive beliefs, although not their methods and aims. As aspects of a comprehensive suspicion of the clarity and usefulness of the idea of *meaning, he rejected the distinction between analytic truths (true in virtue of the meaning of their terms) and synthetic truths, reinstated ontology (condemned by the positivists as meaningless metaphysics), and denied the reducibility of all significant discourse to individually meaningful reports of immediate experience.

Something like a new golden age was clearly under way by the time of his *Word and Object* (1960). Harvard now established itself as the most important philosophical centre in the English-speaking world, reversing a cultural dependence on British philosophy which had been interrupted, but not overturned, by the episode of *pragmatism. Quine's early ally Nelson Goodman joined him there, as, later, did Hilary Putnam and Robert Nozick.
                                                            A.Q.

*American philosophy.

Bruce Kuklick, *The Rise of American Philosophy* (New Haven, Conn., 1977).
—— *A History of Philosophy in America, 1720–2000* (Oxford, 2001).
S. P. Upham (ed.), *Philosophers in Conversation: Interviews from the Harvard Review of Philosophy* (New York, 2002).
Morton G. White, *Science and Sentiment in America* (New York, 1971).

Hayek, Friedrich August von (1899–1992). Although often regarded primarily as an economist (for which he won the Nobel Prize in 1974), Hayek's philosophical work was fundamental to his thinking. His basic insight is epistemological. Human knowledge is limited and reason constrained in many ways. These limitations become particularly acute when attempting to survey and predict the workings of a large society, not just because of its complexity, but also because of general difficulties in knowing human social and economic behaviour in advance of the decision of agents, and because any predicting agency will itself become a player in the game. But the knowledge dispersed among millions of individual agents can be amplified and captured through the workings of the free market, and condenses in spontaneously developing traditions and customs. Hayek's epistemology thus leads to a defence of moral and institutional *conservatism, as against rationalist reformers, and of the free market, as against command economics (which interfere inefficiently with the flow of economic information within a society). The neglect of Hayek's ideas by philosophers is unfortunate because, though at times unclear and incomplete, they are both suggestive and influential.   A.O'H.

F. A. von Hayek, *The Fatal Conceit* (London, 1988).
J. Gray, *Hayek on Liberty* (Oxford, 1986).

heap, paradox of the. Paradox due to vagueness. With a single grain of sand, you cannot make a heap. If you cannot make a heap with the grains you have, you cannot make one with just one more. So even with 10 million grains you cannot make a heap. Despite its antiquity, 'heap' may be badly chosen: arguably, you can make a heap of sand with just four or more grains (enough to make a stable heaping-up without adhesive). But the paradox can be recast, e.g.: 1 is a small number, and any number bigger by 1 than a small number is small; so all numbers are small. Responses include: denying the major premiss, that is, affirming that there is a sharp cut-off (even if we don't know where); and (alternatively) avoiding the conclusion by revamping classical logic and semantics.   R.M.S.

J. C. Beall (ed.), *Liars and Heaps: New Essays on Paradox* (Oxford, 2003).
Mark Sainsbury, *Paradoxes* (New York, 1988), ch. 2.

heaven. The abode of God and the angels. Celestial paradise. The ultimate destination of the redeemed (e.g. in Job 3, Hebrews 12, and Luke 16). Once wholly free of sin, souls or resurrected persons in heaven enjoy the Beatific Vision, the intuition of God's essence. According to Job 3, the wicked no longer trouble those in heaven, the weary are at rest, both 'small' and 'great' are there, and the slave is free from the master. There are graphic descriptions of heaven in Revelation and in Dante's *Divine Comedy*.

Although spatial, heaven is not spatially related to ordinary space-time. Travel to heaven is only by dying and redemption, not by *motion, so the existence of heaven is inconsistent with the Kant's thesis that there is only one space, because putatively distinct spaces will turn out to be spatially related. Heaven exists now (Romans 10: 6, 1 Thessalonians 1: 10, 4: 16) but is concealed by ordinary space-time events and sin. At death, the presence of God is revealed.   S.P.

*hell.

St Augustine, *The City of God* (Harmondsworth, 1972).
St Thomas Aquinas, *Summa Theologiae* (London, 1963–75).
Immanuel Kant's Critique of Pure Reason, tr. Norman Kemp-Smith (London, 1978), esp. 'Transcendental Aesthetic'.
Alister McGrath, *A Brief History of Heaven* (Oxford, 2003).

hedonic calculus. *If* the ultimate object of moral endeavour is to maximize pleasure, satisfaction, happiness; and *if* pleasures, miseries, and pains can be meaningfully represented on a single scale, and summed, *then* it may be thought possible to quantify the overall value or disvalue of particular acts or policies, and the desirability of introducing, or rescinding, laws. Jeremy Bentham (1748–1832) proposed a 'felicific calculus' which would take account of such factors as intensity, duration, the likelihood of an action producing further pleasure or unwanted pain . . . But the project of such a calculus must fail: human good and evil cannot be reduced to homogeneous sensation, positive and negative. Such a scale cannot display the moral urgency of remedying great evils, nor acknowledge that some pleasurable sensations (those of the sadist and rapist, for example) count wholly for the bad.   R.W.H.

*utilitarianism.

J. Bentham, *An Introduction to the Principles of Morals and Legislation* (1789).

hedonism. The doctrine that *pleasure is the *good. It falls into three main types not always distinguished by their proponents:

1. Psychological hedonism: pleasure is the only possible object of desire or pursuit. This may be held on observational grounds, or be thought to be necessitated by what we mean by 'desire'.
2. Evaluative hedonism: pleasure is what we ought to desire or pursue.
3. Rationalizing hedonism: pleasure is the only object that makes a pursuit rational.

(2) and (3), when made explicit, seem to suppose the falsity of (1) in that they suppose it possible, wickedly or irrationally, to pursue something other than pleasure.

Usually the pleasure in question has been thought to be the subject's own pleasure, and so the view has been a form of egoism; but there is no reason in theory why it should not be the pleasure of humans, or even of sentient beings generally. Where psychological hedonism is in question, this has not proved a popular line, but utilitarians have developed altruistic versions of (2).

Utilitarians are committed to comprehensive and long-term calculations of pleasure. Egoists may also consider the subject's long-term pleasure; or they may consider that the immediate option which in itself yields or is thought to yield greater pleasure ought to be or is pursued. Some hedonists seem only or mainly to have so-called physical pleasures in mind; others, like John Stuart Mill, have a penchant for the pleasures of civilized discourse. There are clearly, then, many versions of hedonism, and two apparently identical views may, further, turn out to be very different when one considers the proponents' views of the nature of pleasure.

Arguments for hedonism will vary according to type. Psychological hedonists ought to show either that all pursuits are in fact aimed at what the subject takes to yield pleasure; or that we only count as really wanted what the subject either believes will produce pleasure, or is pleased at the prospect of. There is a risk of retreating into the second kind of position whenever the arguments for the first begin to look a little shaky. There is a further risk of moving without notice from points about what the subject thinks will yield most pleasure to points about what they view with most pleasure in prospect, and in general to do the rounds of a variety of explanations in the pleasure family without inquiring whether there is a legitimate route from one to the other.

Evaluative hedonists may be content to describe their end to us in the hope of winning converts. Sometimes it seems that a supposedly familiar morality is taken as given and desirable, and hedonism is propounded, and so defended, as the rationale of our moral thought and practice. This is particularly likely to happen with utilitarianism, which might, it is hoped, be seen both as making sense of what we do and as enabling us to see how to sort out the muddles we get into morally. Most forms of hedonism are egoistic in form and are seen by opponents, and sometimes by proponents, as hostile to traditional morality and Victorian values.

Rationalizing hedonists will tend to invite us, by consideration of examples, to recognize that our criterion of rationality is the presence of a bedrock justification in terms of pleasure. This is usually a version of psychological hedonism applied not to all our pursuits or desires, but to our practice of reflective evaluation.

All long-term versions of hedonism have to face the problem of how pleasure is to be measured. These problems are aggravated if there have to be cross-personal comparisons, as in utilitarianism.

In classical Greece and Rome (*hedonism, ancient), the doctrine was in various forms popular and much discussed. It underwent a revival in post-Cartesian philosophy, especially among the British Empiricists, although the most unequivocal hedonist, Helvétius, was produced by the continent of Europe. In Britain it tended either to take a utilitarian form, or to be made the basis of a utilitarian development. A combination of partial truth, general cynicism about human motivation, and confusion of a variety of different familiar explanations of behaviour will probably ensure the recurrent attractiveness of some form of the doctrine.   J.C.B.G.

*self-defeating theories; utilitarianism.

Richard B. Brandt, *Ethical Theory* (Englewood Cliffs, NJ, 1959).
Roger Crisp, *Mill on Utilitarianism* (London, 1997).
Fred Feldman, *Pleasure and the Good Life* (Oxford, 2004).
Justin Gosling, *Pleasure and Desire* (Oxford, 1969).
John Plamenatz, *The English Utilitarians* (Oxford, 1958).
John Skorupski, *John Stuart Mill* (London, 1989).
T. Sprigge, *The Rational Foundations of Ethics* (London, 1987).

hedonism, ancient. The central questions of ancient ethical theory concerned the nature of the good life (i.e. the life most worth living) and the conditions of its achievement. (*Eudaimonia*.) Given that focus, the role of *pleasure in the good life was a topic which, throughout antiquity, was rarely far from the central area of debate. In particular, the thesis that pleasure is the good was urged on different grounds by various individuals and schools, and as vigorously disputed by their opponents.

The Pre-Platonic Period. The pre-philosophical beginnings of Greek ethical thought, represented by the didactic poetry of the seventh to the fifth centuries BC, show an ambivalent attitude to pleasure. While a few passages advocate the cultivation of the pleasures of the moment, the prevailing attitude is cautious, stressing the dangers of excessive indulgence. Yet the latter attitude too can tend towards a more enlightened hedonism, as in the *Sophist Prodicus' fable of the choice of Heracles between virtue and vice, in which the hero chooses virtue on the ground that, while vice offers more immediate pleasure, virtue offers a pleasanter life in the long run, taking into account the pleasures of good reputation and friendship, which are forfeited by a life of vice. This contrast between immediate pleasure and the pleasure of one's life, viewed as a whole, comes to the fore in Democritus, who is reported to have held that the supreme good is a state of tranquillity of mind (thereby anticipating Epicurus' doctrine of *ataraxia. But tranquillity must be conceived, not merely negatively, as the absence of disturbance, but as a pleasant state. Democritus seems, then, to have maintained that the choice of particular pleasures and pains must be made on the basis of their contribution to the good life, i.e. to the pleasant life of tranquillity (for which his own term was *euthumia*, whose ordinary sense is cheerfulness). This 'enlightened' hedonism may be contrasted with the view of Aristippus, that the supreme good is the pleasure of the moment.

Plato. Traces of both kinds of hedonism may be discerned in the dialogues. In the *Protagoras* Socrates presents (whether as his own position or as the best available basis for popular morality is disputed) a version of Democritean enlightened hedonism, incorporating the idea of a calculus of pleasures and pains. Callicles in the *Gorgias*, on the other hand, advocates the Aristippean ideal of a life devoted to the satisfaction of short-term bodily appetite, supporting this evaluation by the claim that the goal to which nature prompts every agent (indeed every animal) is the satisfaction of its desires, and by the identification of pleasure with the satisfaction of desire, a conception which is not distinguished from that of the making good of a physiological deficiency. The conception of pleasure as a natural goal is central to most ancient discussions of hedonism. The modern distinction between psychological hedonism (a theory of motivation) and evaluative hedonism (a theory of value) was not drawn. Rather, both proponents and opponents of hedonism agreed that the natural direction of motivation, for humans as well as for other animals, either determined or served as evidence for the good of the organism thus motivated, but differed on whether that direction was towards pleasure. Socrates' response to Callicles is therefore to argue that every agent is naturally motivated to seek his own good, not his immediate pleasure, and that the pursuit of one's good requires that one differentiate good (i.e. good-promoting) pleasures from bad (i.e. harmful) ones. Plato's own views on the topic seem to have undergone some development. While he may at an early stage have espoused Democritean hedonism (*if* the hedonism of the *Protagoras* represents his own view), the position defended in the middle and later dialogues is that, while the good life is indeed pleasant (and in the *Republic* the pleasantest of all lives) its pleasantness is merely an adjunct to its goodness, which consists, not in pleasantness, but in rationality.

Aristotle. Like Plato, Aristotle both provides evidence of ongoing debate on the value of pleasure and contributes to that debate himself. The *Nicomachean Ethics* contains two substantial and independent treatments of pleasure (that in book VII probably belonging originally to the *Eudemian Ethics*), each of which starts from a confrontation of various opposed views, the extreme positions being on the one hand the view of the contemporary philosopher and mathematician Eudoxus that pleasure is the *good, and on the other the thesis, usually attributed to Plato's nephew Speusippus, that pleasure is an evil. Of those two, Aristotle's own position is closer to the former, but it is dubious whether he endorses Eudoxus' view without qualification. He rebuts the attacks on pleasure by arguing that they rely on a mistaken account of its nature, namely the view (see above) that pleasure consists in the process of remedying a natural deficiency in the organism. For Aristotle, pleasure is not any kind of process. Rather it occurs when a natural potentiality (e.g. for thought or perception) is realized in perfect conditions (when, for instance, the mind is working well, free from distractions, thinking about worthwhile objects, etc.). Every kind of actualization has its own specific pleasure, e.g. the pleasures of thought, and the bodily pleasures of sex, food, and drink. Since *eudaimonia* itself consists in excellent realization of the capacities for thought and for rational choice, it follows that the good life is characterized by the greatest degree of pleasure. It is, however, disputed whether Aristotle goes so far as to identify the perfection of perfect realization with its pleasantness. While he appears to endorse that identification in *Nicomachean Ethics* VII, in book x he appears to say (obscurely) that pleasure is not perfection itself, but a feature supervenient on it 'like the bloom on the cheek of youth' ($1174^{b}33$). He gives no hint, however, of what that feature might be, and some commentators argue that it is nothing other than perfection itself, and that what it supervenes upon is not (as normally assumed) perfection, but the simple activity.

The Post-Aristotelian Period. Some of the positions mentioned above continued to have their adherents in this period. Among proponents of hedonism a major dispute

was that between on the one hand the *Cyrenaics, who developed the Calliclean position by maintaining that the supreme good is the pleasure of the moment and that bodily pleasures are of higher value than mental, and on the other Epicurus and his school, who developed the Democritean ideal of the life of pleasant tranquillity as the supreme good. Epicurus took over Eudoxus' argument that the natural impulse of all animals to seek pleasure shows it to be good, and distinguished two types of pleasure, that experienced when the organism is making good a deficiency and that experienced when the organism is in a stable state, free from all pain or disturbance; the latter type was assigned supreme value. His identification of the latter with the absence of pain has been criticized as confused, but seems in fact to have been the unexceptionable doctrine that a painless, trouble-free life is *ipso facto* pleasant.   C.C.W.T.

*hedonism.

D. Bostock, 'Pleasure and Activity in Aristotle's Ethics', *Phronesis* (1988).
J. C. B. Gosling and C. C. W. Taylor, *The Greeks on Pleasure* (Oxford, 1982).
J. M. Rist, 'Pleasure 360–300 BC', *Phoenix* (1974).
J. Tenkku, *The Evaluation of Pleasure in Plato's Ethics* (Helsinki, 1956).

Hegel, Georg Wilhelm Friedrich (1770–1831).

Of all the major Western philosophers, Hegel has gained the reputation of being the most impenetrable. He was a formidable critic of his predecessor Immanuel Kant and a formative influence on Karl Marx. Through his influence on Marx, Hegel's thought has changed the course of nineteenth- and twentieth-century history.

Hegel lived and worked in what we now know as Germany, although in his time the many independent states of the region had not been united into one nation. He came of age at the time of the French Revolution, sharing what he later called 'the jubilation of this epoch'. His career included periods as a private tutor, and nine years as the headmaster of a secondary school, before his growing reputation gained him a university chair. He ended his days as Professor of Philosophy at the University of Berlin, which under the reformed Prussian monarchy was becoming the intellectual centre of the German states.

Hegel wrote several long and dense books, of which the most important are *The Phenomenology of Mind*, *The Science of Logic*, and *The Philosophy of Right*. His *Encyclopedia of the Philosophical Sciences* is a summary version of his philosophical system. A number of other works were delivered as lectures, and in some cases published after his death from his lecture notes. These include his *Lectures on the Philosophy of History*, *Lectures on Aesthetics*, *Lectures on the Philosophy of Religion*, and *Lectures on the History of Philosophy*.

Hegel is a difficult thinker because all his work reflects a systematic view of the world, and he makes few concessions to those not familiar with his way of thinking. In addition his style is anything but 'user-friendly'; at first

G. W. F. HEGEL: the lasting hostility of most Anglophone philosophers to his difficult and ambitious system failed to prevent the diffusion of his influence into most streams of philosophy.

KARL MARX adopted Hegel's theory of the process of historical development, but gave matter rather than spirit the central role in the process. So it was that his philosophy came to be described as dialectical, historical, or scientific materialism; for him, production is the determining material function of humans.

GEORG LUKACS, Hungary's most famous philosopher. The life of a prominent public intellectual was not a tranquil one in the Communist world. Twice briefly a government minister, twice exiled, Lukacs was endlessly attacked by rival ideologues but managed to survive Stalin's Russia and grow old in his native city of Budapest.

BENEDETTO CROCE developed a Hegelian philosophy of spirit, of which his aesthetics was most notable, and put forward a view of philosophy as history. The second great Neapolitan philosopher, 650 years after Aquinas.

glance most readers will find his sentences simply incomprehensible. This has led some to denounce him as a charlatan, hiding an emptiness of thought behind a deliberate obscurity of expression in order to give an air of profundity. Yet the meaning of Hegel's writing does, eventually, become apparent after careful study. Though his philosophical system as a whole finds few adherents today, his writings yield original insights and arguments that illuminate many philosophical, social, and political issues.

The easiest point of entry to Hegel's thought is his *Lectures on the Philosophy of History*. One of Hegel's greatest contributions to our intellectual heritage is—as Marx appreciated—his grasp of the historically conditioned nature of our thinking. One might ask why a philosopher should write a work that is, in one sense, a brief outline of the history of the world, from ancient times to his own day. The answer is that for Hegel the facts of history are raw material to which the philosopher must give some sense. For Hegel thought that history displays a rational process of development, and, by studying it, we can understand our own nature and place in the world. This idea of history having meaning can be interpreted as a reworking of the religious idea that the world was created by a being with some purpose in mind; but it may also be understood in a more limited way, as a claim that history has a direction that we can discern, and is heading to a goal that we can welcome.

Hegel presents his view of the direction of history in a famous sentence from the introduction to *The Philosophy of History*: 'The history of the world is none other than the progress of the consciousness of freedom.' The remainder of the work is a long illustration of this thought. Hegel begins with the ancient empires of China, India, and Persia. Here, he says, only one individual—the ruler—is free. The subjects of these oriental despots, Hegel thought, lacked not merely political freedom, but even the very awareness that they are capable of forming their own judgements about right or wrong. It was only in ancient Greece that the principle of free individual thinking developed, and even then Hegel saw the Greeks as so closely identified with their city-state, and so much ruled by its habits and customs, that they did not see themselves as independent individuals in the modern sense. Though the spark of individuality was lit by the critical thinking of Socrates, individuality did not triumph until the Protestant Reformation recognized that each individual can find his or her own salvation, and gave the right of individual conscience its proper place.

For Hegel the course of history since the Reformation has been governed by the need to transform the world so as to reflect the newly recognized principle of individual freedom. The era of the *Enlightenment, culminating in the French Revolution, was an attempt to abolish every institution that depended on mere custom, and instead ensure that the light of reason, to which every individual can freely assent, guides every aspect of our political and social lives. To Hegel this attempt was based on a 'glorious mental dawn': the understanding that thought ought to

govern reality, instead of the other way around. Yet the French revolutionaries misunderstood reason, taking it in too abstract a way, without considering the nature of existing communities and the way in which these communities have formed their inhabitants. Thus the abstract universalism of the Enlightenment led to the excesses of the guillotine. Yet now that we understand what is needed, Hegel concluded, a fully rational organization of the world—and hence a truly free community—is ready to unfold.

Hegel's conception of freedom is central to his thought, but it often misleads modern readers brought up on a conception of freedom made popular through the writings of such classical liberal thinkers as John Stuart Mill. According to the standard liberal conception, I am free when I am left alone, not interfered with, and able to choose as I please. (*Freedom and determinism; *liberty; political freedom.) This is, for example, the sense of freedom used by economists who picture consumers as free when there are no restrictions on the goods and services they can choose to buy in a free market. Hegel thought this an utterly superficial notion of freedom, because it does not probe beneath the surface and ask *why* individuals make the choices they do. Hegel saw these choices as often determined by external forces which effectively control us. He even anticipates, by more than a century, the modern critique of the consumer society as creating needs in order to satisfy them: he points out that the need for greater 'comfort' does not arise within us, but 'is suggested to you by those who hope to make a profit from its creation'.

Behind such insights lies Hegel's grasp of history as a process that shapes our choices and our very nature. So to be left alone to make our own choices without interference by others is not to be free; it is merely to be subjected to the historical forces of our own times. Real freedom begins with the realization that instead of allowing these forces to control us, we can take control of them. But how can this happen? As long as we see ourselves as independent beings with conflicting wills, we will always regard the existence of other human beings as something alien to ourselves, placing limits on our own freedom. In the classical liberal tradition, that is simply the way the world is, and there is nothing that can be done about it. For Hegel, however, the problem is overcome when we recognize that all human beings share a common ability to reason. Hence if a community can be built on a rational basis, every human being can accept it, not as something alien, but as an expression of his or her own rational will. Our duty and our self-interest will then coincide, for our duty will be rationally based, and our true interest is to realize our nature as a rational being.

In his belief that we are free only when we act in accordance with our reason, Hegel is in agreement with Kant; and so too when he sees our duty as based on our reason; but Hegel criticized Kant's notion of morality, based as it is on a *categorical imperative derived from pure reason, as too abstract, a bare formal framework lacking all content. Moreover, on Kant's view human beings are destined for perpetual conflict between duty and interest. They will always be subject to desires that they must suppress if they are to act as the categorical imperative commands. A purely rational morality like Kant's, Hegel thought, needs to be combined in some way with the ethical customs that are part of our nature as beings of a particular time and place. Thus Hegel sought a synthesis between our concrete ethical nature, formed in a specific community, and the rational aspect of our being. When this synthesis was achieved, we would have a community in which each of us would find our own fulfilment, while contributing to the well-being of the whole. We would be free both in the subjective sense, in that we could do as we wished to do, and in the objective sense, in that we would rationally determine the course of our history, instead of being determined by it. This would then be a truly rational state, reconciling individual freedom with the values of community.

In *The Philosophy of Right*, Hegel describes this rational community in a manner that parallels—though is not identical with—the Prussian monarchy of his own day. For this he was accused by Schopenhauer of selling himself to his employer. After Hegel's death, the Young Hegelians, a group of young radicals that for a time included Marx among its members, thought that in *The Philosophy of Right* Hegel had betrayed the essence of his own philosophy. They determined to develop his ideas in a way that was truer to the core of his thought than Hegel himself had been. From this group arose the criticism of religion developed by Bruno Bauer and Ludwig Feuerbach, Max Stirner's individual anarchism, developed in his *The Ego and its Own*, and such early writings of Marx as *The Economic and Philosophical Manuscripts of 1844* and *The German Ideology*.

More recently Karl Popper has seen Hegel as a precursor of the modern totalitarian state. Popper argues that by exalting the rational state and using the concept of freedom in a way that denies that irrational choices are truly free, Hegel made it possible for later authoritarian rulers to justify their tyranny by saying that they must force their citizens to be free. It may be true that Hegel's philosophy is open to this misreading, but it *is* a misreading. The real Hegel supported constitutional monarchy, the rule of law, trial by jury, and (by the standards of his day) considerable freedom of expression. He would never have regarded the kind of state set up by Hitler or Stalin as a rational state with free citizens.

Yet Popper has touched on a real problem in Hegel's philosophy. Hegel was driven by an extraordinary optimism about the prospects of overcoming conflict between human beings, and hence of bringing about a rational and harmonious community. The roots of this optimistic view lie in his metaphysics, and especially in his concept of *Geist*. This German word can be rendered in English, according to the context, either as *'spirit'* or as *'mind'*. In the former sense it can have religious connotations; in the second it is the normal word used to describe the mental or intellectual side of our being, as distinct from the physical. Because the German term covers both these meanings, Hegel is able to use it in a way that suggests an overarching collective Mind that is an active force throughout history, and of which all individual minds—that is, all human beings, considered in their mental aspect—are a part. Thus Hegel sees the study of history as a way of getting to know the nature of *Geist*, and sees the rational state as *Geist* objectified. Since there is no ideal English translation, I shall henceforth use the capitalized term 'Mind' to express Hegel's concept of *Geist*.

Hegel's greatest work is his *The Phenomenology of Mind* (sometimes referred to in English as *The Phenomenology of Spirit*), described by Marx as 'the true birthplace and secret of Hegel's philosophy'. In it Hegel seeks to show that all human intellectual development up to now is the logically necessary working out of Mind's coming to know itself. The logic of this process is, however, not the traditional logic of the *syllogism, but rather Hegel's own dialectical logic. In dialectical logic, we start from a given position—as an example, we might take the customary ethics of ancient Greece. Then we find that this position contains within itself the seeds of its own destruction, in the form of an internal contradiction. The questioning of a Socrates leads eventually to the downfall of customary ethics, for example, and its replacement during the Reformation by a morality based on individual conscience alone. Yet this too is one-sided and unstable, and so we must move to a third position, the rational community. This third position combines the positive aspects of its two predecessors.

This *dialectic is sometimes referred to as a movement from *thesis* to *antithesis* to *synthesis*. In the example given, the customary morality of ancient Greece is the thesis, the Reformation morality of individual conscience its antithesis, and the rational community is the synthesis of the two. This last is, in Hegel's philosophy of history, the final synthesis, but in other instances, the synthesis of one stage of the dialectic can serve as the thesis for a new dialectical movement. In *The Science of Logic*, Hegel applies the same method to the abstract categories with which we think. Here Hegel starts with the bare notion of existence, or being, and argues that since this bare notion of being has no content at all, it cannot be anything. Thus it must be nothing, the antithesis of being. Being and nothing, however, are opposites, constantly moving in and apart from each other; they require to be brought together under the synthesis, becoming. Then the dialectic moves on, through many more obscure stages, until in the end Hegel claims to be able to demonstrate the necessity of absolute *idealism: that is, that the only thing that is ultimately real is the absolute idea, which is Mind, knowing itself as all reality.

Absolute idealism seems a strange doctrine, but it was by no means unique to Hegel. Kant had already argued that the mind constitutes the known universe because we can only know things within a framework of our own creation, namely, the categories of time, space, and substance.

Yet Kant thought that beyond these categories there must be the *'thing-in-itself', forever unknowable. In doing away with the 'thing-in-itself', and saying that all we know is also all that there is, Hegel was following the line of Kantian criticism developed earlier by Johann Fichte.

Both *The Phenomenology of Mind* and *The Science of Logic*, then, have the same process as their subject, the process of Mind coming to know itself as ultimate reality. In the *Phenomenology* this process is presented by an attempt to show the logical necessity inherent in the historical development of human consciousness. In the *Logic* it is shown as a pure dialectical necessity, as (Hegel tells us) showing 'God as he is in his eternal essence, before the creation of nature and of a finite mind'. The *Logic* is, therefore, by far the more abstract and difficult work. The *Phenomenology* is, by comparison (but only by comparison), a gripping account of how the finite minds of human beings progress to a point at which they can see that the world beyond them is not alien or hostile to them, but a part of themselves. This is so, because Mind alone is all that is real, and each finite mind is a part of Mind.

One curious aspect of the enterprise of the *Phenomenology* is that it seeks to understand a process that is completed by the fact that it is understood. The goal of all history is that mind should come to understand itself as the only ultimate reality. When is that understanding first achieved? By Hegel himself in the *Phenomenology*! If Hegel is to be believed, the closing pages of his masterpiece are no mere description of the culmination of everything that has happened since finite minds were first created: they *are* that culmination.

In the light of Hegel's belief that all finite minds share in a greater underlying reality, we can appreciate why he should have believed in the possibility of a form of society that transcended all conflicts between the individual and the collective, and was truly free while at the same time in no sense anarchic. We can also see why this belief should have made it possible for Hegel's ideas to lead some of his successors, Marx among them, to a similarly misplaced optimism about the possibility of avoiding such conflicts. For while Marx claimed to have rejected the 'mysticism' in which Hegel enveloped his system, Marx never freed himself from the conviction that history is tending toward a final destination in which there will be complete harmony between the interests of the individual and the common interests of the community. That is why he believed that *communism would be a condition in which everyone freely advanced the common interests of all.   P.S.

*Hegelianism.

F. Beiser (ed.), *The Cambridge Companion to Hegel* (Cambridge, 1993).

G. W. F. Hegel, *Hegel's Phenomenology of Spirit*, tr A. V. Miller (Oxford, 1977).

—— *Hegel's Philosophy of Right*, tr. T. M. Knox (Oxford, 1967).

—— *Hegel's Science of Logic*, tr. A. V. Miller (London, 1969).

—— *Lectures on the Philosophy of History*, tr. J. Sibree (New York, 1956).

Michael Inwood, *A Hegel Dictionary* (Oxford, 1992).

—— *Hegel* (London, 1983).

Richard Norman, *Hegel's Phenomenology: A Philosophical Introduction* (Brighton, 1976).

Peter Singer, *Hegel* (Oxford, 1983).

Robert Solomon, *In the Spirit of Hegel* (New York, 1983).

Charles Taylor, *Hegel* (Cambridge, 1979).

Hegelianism. 'Hegelianism' refers not only to the doctrines and methods of Hegel himself, but to those of his followers, especially, but not only, in Germany.

Even in Hegel's lifetime, the obscurity and ambiguity of his teaching gave rise to disagreement over its significance. Does his claim that 'what is rational is actual and what is actual is rational' imply that everything that exists, including for example the Prussian state, is as it should be, or rather that whatever is not as it should be, even though it exists, is not genuinely 'actual'? Do his resounding tributes to the *freedom and self-consciousness attained in the modern world imply that significant history, including the history of philosophy, has come to an end? Does his belief that *God is not *distinct* from the world mean that God does exist or that he does not? Does his claim that religion and philosophy have the same 'content' but present it in different 'forms' (imagination and thought, respectively) imply that religion and the Church are now dispensable? Does his assertion that the spirit is eternal amount to an endorsement of the orthodox belief in immortality?

Hegel himself does not supply unequivocal answers to these questions, and this omission is connected with several important features of his thought:

1. Hegel believed his own philosophy to be not 'one-sided', like most philosophies of the past, but the 'universal' philosophy, embracing and 'sublating' (or cannibalizing) all significant past philosophies, doing justice to realism or materialism as well as idealism, to atheism as well as theism, and so on. (But Hegel is not a dualist, or a monist, or a pluralist. The best numerical account of him is that he is a Three-in-One-ist.)

2. Another reason why Hegel's system refuses to yield 'straight' answers to 'straight' questions is that he attempts to examine the terms in which questions are framed, often pre-empting them for purposes of his own, or assigning them a developing series of interconnected meanings. Does Hegel believe that God exists? It depends on what we mean by 'God', 'believe', and 'exist'.

3. He believes that at their extreme points opposites veer into each other. For example, if we take theism seriously and say that a truly infinite God cannot be distinct from the world, but must be in some sense identical with it, this takes us to the brink of saying that the world is everything and God nothing.

4. In the past, humanity has advanced owing in part to its tendency to reflect on its own condition. In reflecting on a philosophy, we develop new thoughts or categories that are at most implicit in the philosophy on which we reflect, and in reflecting on historical events we acquire new thoughts that were not available to the participants in those events. We cannot learn from history, since in

thinking about past events we change ourselves, so that our situation and the problems it presents are now importantly different from those of the past. It is not the philosopher's or the historian's business to predict, or plan for, the future, in part because significant future events will involve new thoughts or categories which are not yet available to him. But Hegel's reluctance to discuss the future, together with his insistence on the universality and completeness of his own system, left it unclear whether there is any possibility of significant future developments in philosophy or in history. Is his own system 'infinite' in the sense that reflection on it, unlike past philosophies, generates no categories not already contained in it? If so, he seems to exclude the possibility of further interesting philosophical or historical developments. If it is not so, he still gives his followers no firm guidance on what do in the changed historical circumstances following his death.

5. As a philosopher, Hegel inclined to aloof objectivity, to detached observation of the conflicts of the past and the fates of the opposing, but interdependent, parties—factions, states, religions, philosophies, and so on. He also believed, however, that such conflicts and the spiritual advances which they generated would not have been possible if men had not passionately and resolutely championed a one-sided cause, if they had for the most part abstained from a decision in stoical or ironical detachment or dithered in the middle ground. (Conflict, as well as reflection, is required if humanity is to remain alive and awake.) Thus as a *philosopher* he favoured impassioned engagement on the part of the *citizen* in the conflicts of his age. But as a philosopher he can give no clear guidance to the Hegelian citizen as to which side he should choose.

Hence Hegel's followers gave different answers to the above questions, answers which characteristically reflected their *own* prior beliefs, religious and political as well as philosophical, and which tended to fall into coherent clusters. *'Right Hegelians', such as Karl Göschel (1784–1862), interpreted Hegel as a supporter of clerical orthodoxy and of political restorationism, the attempt, under way from 1815, to restore the old order undermined by the French Revolution. By contrast, *'Left Hegelians', such as Feuerbach, Stirner, Bruno Bauer, and David Strauss (1808–74), were religious and political radicals. In the centre stood moderate reformists, such as Karl Rosenkranz (1805–79). (Left and Right Hegelians were also referred to, respectively, as 'Young' and 'Old' Hegelians; but this nomenclature has the defect that it provides no term for the centre and also implies that ideology depends on age.) The Left Hegelians are of more intrinsic interest than the Right or centre. They made significant contributions to theology and biblical criticism (Feuerbach, Strauss) and heavily influenced Marx.

The Hegelian movement disintegrated in Germany in the early 1840s. It remained strong in Denmark long enough to provoke Kierkegaard's continuous polemic against 'the [Hegelian] system'. Hegelianism was established in Britain by James Hutchinson Stirling's *The Secret of Hegel* (1865), and the British idealists (Green, Bradley, Bosanquet, McTaggart) found in Hegel an antidote to empiricism, utilitarianism, and *laissez-faire* economics. (But McTaggart, unlike Hegel, was a staunch individualist and free-trader. This coheres with his intense belief in individual immortality—which he erroneously attributed to Hegel.) In the USA Hegelianism was represented by William Torrey Harris and Josiah Royce, and left its mark on pragmatism. Hegelianism flourished in Italy from the first half of the nineteenth century (Gioberti, Rosmini) until well into the twentieth (Croce, Gentile). In France it was established by Victor Cousin and influenced, among others, Taine and Renan; Hegel was revived in the 1930s by the lectures of Alexandre Kojève, who read him through Marxist and existentialist lenses. (In France in particular, the *Phenomenology of Spirit*, rather than the later system, has been especially influential, along with Marx's early philosophical writings.) In the English-speaking world, Hegel survived the attacks of Russell, Moore, and Popper, and remains popular and influential.

Hegel's influence has outlasted anything resembling a Hegelian 'movement'. It has certain noteworthy features:

1. No one of consequence, with the possible exception of Hegel himself, has been an undiluted Hegelian. The reason for this is not simply that much of his thought is superseded (especially by advances in the natural sciences), but that Hegel's thought is too rich, complex, and ambivalent for any single individual to swallow it whole. But many philosophers, such as Sartre and Derrida, digest parts of his thought and assimilate them to their own constitution. Even Hegel's immediate followers did this, since no single one of them, however Hegelian by profession, could encompass the whole of his thought; his thought is refracted, so that different elements in it are represented by different Hegelians.

2. Hegel's influence has often weighed as heavily on his opponents as on his avowed followers. This influence takes different forms. *Existentialism, for example, arose in conscious antagonism to Hegel: its rejection of systems, its insistence on human finitude, its stress on crucial decisions which cannot be determined by philosophical reason or by historical learning, essentially depend on a contrast with Hegel (or some similar figure, such as Aquinas), who supposedly believed the contrary. But the anti-Hegelian often absorbs Hegel's ideas in the process of combating them. Heidegger, for example, consciously set his own thought in opposition to Hegel's. His view was that Hegel's system deepens our 'forgetfulness of being'. It perpetuates Aristotle's misconception of time. It is a part of the 'tradition' which distorts our view of the genuine philosophers of Greece and which must be 'destroyed' or deconstructed if we are to appropriate the past. For Hegel, the history of philosophy is (circuitously) progressive, later philosophies, especially his own, preserving all that is true in past philosophies. For Heidegger, by contrast, philosophy has declined: crucial questions have been obscured and forgotten, crucial concepts distorted and enfeebled.

The truth can only be recovered by a line-by-line examination of ancient texts (such as Plato's *Sophist*, Hegel's own favourite Platonic dialogue), and also by exploring the history of philosophy in reverse, starting with Kant, for example, and progressively peeling away the accumulated layers of distortion until we arrive at the unblinkered vision of, for example, Parmenides. But the result of Heidegger's quest is a view remarkably similar to Hegel's own: his 'history of being', in which being achieves illumination through man, owes far more to Hegel's 'history of spirit', in which the *Absolute attains self-consciousness in the development of the human spirit, than to Parmenides. (It also owes much to Schelling, whom Heidegger studied intensively in the 1930s and whose portrait, as legend has it, he put up in place of Kant's.)

3. If Hegel saw his own philosophy as complete and definitive, to propose a significant philosophical idea which Hegel did not consider and which he cannot accommodate or sublate is sufficient to refute him. It is, however, less easy than one might suppose to devise a view that Hegel has not already considered. This is due in part to the power of his intelligence and imagination, but in part also to the fact that his work concludes and synthesizes an immensely rich period in the history of human thought, in which he encountered viewpoints similar to those later revived by his critics. Hegel knew of, and rejected, something like Russell's theory of definite descriptions: he, like Russell, found it in Leibniz. He knew of someone rather like Kierkegaard, and described him, under the title of the 'unhappy consciousness', in his *Phenomenology of Spirit*: he found him, perhaps, in Johann Georg Hamann (1730–88) or among the Romantics, for example in Novalis (Friedrich von Hardenberg, 1772–1801). He found a precursor of Sartre's studiedly unsystematic Genet, whom Derrida counterposes to Hegel, again among the Romantics or in Diderot's portrayal of *Rameau's Nephew* (which Hegel read in Goethe's translation of 1805).

Because of this richness Hegel can accommodate a diversity of 'one-sided' interpretations: he has, for example, been variously seen as an existentialist, a Marxist, and a Wittgensteinian. But if the one-sided positions of his successors become tiresome or obsolete, one can always return to Hegel and find in him a new one-sided position or, alternatively, a comprehensive, many-sided objectivity with regard to the multifarious conflicts of the past and the present.   M.J.I.

W. Desmond (ed.), *Hegel and his Critics: Philosophy in the Aftermath of Hegel* (Albany, NY, 1989).

M. Inwood, *A Hegel Dictionary* (Oxford, 1992).

P. Robbins, *The British Hegelians 1875–1925* (New York, 1982).

L. S. Stepelevich (ed.), *The Young Hegelians: An Anthology* (Cambridge, 1983).

J. E. Toews, *Hegelianism: The Path toward Dialectical Humanism 1805–1841* (Cambridge, 1980).

hegemony. From the Greek verb meaning 'to lead', hegemony has sometimes been used as a synonym for domination. In its subtler sense, however, it implies some notion of consent and is particularly associated with the writings of the Italian Marxist Antonio Gramsci. Drawing on writers such as Machiavelli and Pareto, Gramsci argues that a politically dominant class maintains its position not simply by force, or the threat of force, but also by *consent. That is achieved by making compromises with various other social and political forces which are welded together and consent to a certain social order under the intellectual and moral leadership of the dominant class. This hegemony is produced and reproduced through a network of institutions, social relations, and ideas which are outside the directly political sphere. Gramsci especially emphasized the role of intellectuals in the creation of hegemony. The result is one of the most important, if elusive, concepts in contemporary social theory.   D.McL.

*bourgeoisie and proletariat.

Joseph Femia, *Gramsci's Political Thought: Hegemony, Consciousness and the Revolutionary Process* (Oxford, 1981).

Heidegger, Martin (1889–1976). German philosopher usually seen as a founder of Existentialism. He prepared the ground for his major work, *Sein und Zeit* (Being and Time (1927; tr. Oxford, 1962; New York, 1996)), with some lucid and solid, if unremarkable, writings, which anticipated several themes of his mature work. 'The Problem of Reality in Modern Philosophy' (1912) argued against various versions of *idealism, including Kant's critical idealism, and in favour of critical *realism. It criticizes the stress on epistemology characteristic of philosophy since Descartes. 'New Investigations of Logic' (1912) assessed recent work on logic, including that of Frege, Russell, and Whitehead, from the standpoint of Husserl's critique of psychologism. (In conformity with his doctrine of truth as 'unconcealment', the mature Heidegger had little sympathy for the traditional 'logic of assertion'; like the later Wittgenstein, he would be more inclined to found arithmetic on everyday activities such as counting and measurement than on the principles of logic.) *The Doctrine of the Judgement in Psychologism* (1914), his doctoral dissertation, opposed the reduction of logic to psychological facts and processes. His habilitation thesis, *Duns Scotus's Doctrine of Categories and of Meaning* (1916), shows the respect for metaphysics, history, and subjectivity which marks his later work; it examines a treatise, *Grammatica Speculativa*, which has since been attributed to Thomas of Erfurt, but Heidegger's thought has often been seen as akin to Duns Scotus', even as 'secularized Scotism'. His habilitation lecture, 'The Concept of Time in the Discipline of History' (1916), argued that time as seen by historians differs from the quantitative time of physics: it is not uniform, but articulated into qualitatively distinct periods, such as the Victorian era, whose significance depends on more than their temporal duration.

From 1916 to 1927 he published nothing, but studied widely, especially Husserl's *phenomenology, Scheler's philosophical *anthropology, Dilthey's *hermeneutics, and the texts of St Paul, Augustine, and Luther. Christianity supplied examples of momentous, historic decisions, important in his later work, but also an *'ontology' distinct from that of the Greeks. At the same time he lectured, with enthralling brilliance, on these and other themes. (Most of his publications were based on lectures.) He taught at Marburg, 1923–8, and Freiburg, 1928–44. He was elected Rector of Freiburg in 1933, but resigned in 1934. In 1945 he was forbidden to teach, owing to his links with Nazism, until 1951. His initial support for Nazism was rooted not in anti-Semitism, but in distaste for technology and industrialized mass society, which he associated with the USA and the USSR; later he regarded Nazism as an aspect of technological modernity and its 'forgetfulness of being' rather than as an abnormal excrescence. His conduct as Rector, his private beliefs, and the relationship of his thought to Nazi ideology are still matters of controversy.

Being and Time (*Sein und Zeit*, 1927) crystallized his study of virtually the whole of past and contemporary philosophy. Its central concern is the 'question of being'. Since the beginnings of philosophy in Greece, being (*Sein*) has been ill at ease with time. It has been insulated from change by being seen as *presence*, to the exclusion of past and future—not necessarily temporal presence, but also the atemporal, eternal presence of, for example, Plato's Forms. This affects our conception of the world, including man himself. Heidegger proposes to revive the long-forgotten question of the 'sense of being', and to practise 'fundamental ontology', an ontology underpinning the 'regional' ontologies dealing with the being of particular realms of entity, such as nature and history. To examine being as such, we need to consider a particular type of entity: namely, the entity that asks the question 'What is *being?' and whose 'understanding of being' is an essential feature of its own being, i.e. man or *Dasein*. *Dasein*'s being is *Existenz*: it has no fixed nature, but 'its essence lies in its always having its being to be, and having it as its own'. (*Existenz* is used in its root sense of 'stepping forth', as in Walter Bagehot's description of 'those who live during their life, whose essence is existence, whose being is animation'. Heidegger disclaims any similarity to Sartre's doctrine that 'existence precedes essence'.) Why does this mean that being must be approached by way of *Dasein*? In conducting such a large, amorphous inquiry as the question of being, we no doubt need to take our bearings from our ordinary implicit understanding of being, and this will involve a preliminary examination of *Dasein*. But Heidegger also says that 'there is being, only as long as *Dasein* is', suggesting that being, if not entities, depends on our understanding of it. This perhaps gives a stronger reason for approaching being by way of *Dasein*: Heidegger agrees with Kant and Husserl that how things are depends in large measure on what we contribute to them, with the difference that 'we' are concrete, 'existing' human beings, rather than pure consciousness.

Although *Dasein* is essentially 'ontological', that is, has an understanding of being, the philosopher cannot simply adopt *Dasein*'s own understanding of itself and other entities. For *Dasein* tends systematically to misinterpret itself and its world, regarding itself, for example, as a thing on a par with other things. Much of the vocabulary of traditional philosophy—'consciousness', 'subject', 'object', etc.—is infected with such misinterpretation. Thus Heidegger (like 'analytical' philosophers such as Wittgenstein, Ryle, and J. L. Austin) avoids such terminology, preferring non-committal terms such as '*Dasein*' or down-to-earth words (such as *Sorge*, 'care') which carry no burden of philosophical assumptions. (In accordance with Heidegger's view that silence is an 'essential possibility of discourse', his readers need to bear in mind the words he purposely avoids, as well as those he uses.) Like Husserl, he attempts to describe 'the things themselves', without the help of theories and preconceptions; unlike Husserl, he holds that this requires a determined recasting of philosophical language. He uses old words in unusual ways, often appealing (like Austin) to etymology, and sometimes coins new words; but his coinages are invariably in the spirit of the German language. His terminology is marked by an aversion to the static ontology of substance, stemming from Aristotle, and a preference for a more dynamic, verbal ontology: *Dasein*, for example, is not primarily a solid, biological substance that occasionally acts; it is essentially and primarily activity. (*Being and Time* is strangely silent about sleep.) In giving the correct or 'authentic' term for, or account of, a phenomenon (such as man, time, or truth) he does not simply counterpose this to the degenerate term or account; he attempts to explain why the degeneration occurred. It is not enough to show, for example, that Descartes was mistaken to regard man as a *res cogitans*. One must also show, in terms of the correct account of man, how the mistake arose. Misinterpretation is not sheer, unaccountable error, but a 'possibility' to which *Dasein* is essentially prone.

For Heidegger, unlike Descartes, *Dasein* is essentially 'in-the-world' and is inseparable from the world: 'In understanding the world, Being-in is always understood along with it, while understanding of existence as such is always an understanding of the world.' The world is not primarily the world of the sciences, but the everyday world, the *'life-world' (Husserl). It is disclosed to us not by scientific knowledge, but by pre-scientific experiences, by 'care' and by moods. Entities in the world are not primarily objects of theoretical cognition, but tools that are 'ready to hand' (*zuhanden*), such as a hammer, to be used rather than studied and observed. Theoretical cognition, as when I observe a hammer (or a beetle) disinterestedly, is a secondary phenomenon, which occurs especially when a tool fails to give satisfaction, when, for example, the hammer breaks. Tools are not independent of each other, but belong to a 'context of significance', in which items such as hammers, nails, and work-bench 'refer' to each other and ultimately to *Dasein* and its purposes. Tools or equipment form a coherent world, radiating out from *Dasein*, in a way that objects of theoretical cognition (such as Descartes's *res extensae*) do not. This world is correlative to, even 'projected' by, the *Dasein* that 'steps forth' into it.

Just as *Dasein* is in the world, so it is essentially 'with' others of its kind. It does not first exist as an isolated subject and then subsequently acquire knowledge of and relations to others; it is with others from the start. But others threaten its integrity: 'as being together with others, *Dasein* stands in thrall to others. It itself is not; the others have usurped its being'. 'The self of everyday *Dasein* is the they-self, which we distinguish from the authentic self, the self that has itself in its own grip.' 'They' is the German *man*, 'one': the they-self does and believes what *one* does and believes, rather than what it has independently and authentically decided on. Heidegger's theory of the They or One (*das Man*), is influenced by Tolstoy's *The Death of Ivan Ilyich*: Ivan's carefully redecorated house seems quite exceptional to him, but in fact contains 'all the things people of a certain class have in order to resemble other people of that class'; when Ivan's family discuss Sarah Bernhardt's acting, it is 'the sort of conversation that is always repeated and always the same'. The account of everyday life, which Heidegger initially presents as a neutral account of man's bedrock condition, becomes an account of man's 'fallenness' and inauthenticity.

Inauthenticity and the They are not, however, unmitigated evils. Scheler accused Heidegger of a 'solipsism of *Dasein*': each of us inhabits our own world together with our own others. Descartes may be vulnerable to such a charge, but Heidegger is not. For him, the shared, public world is the world as *one* sees it, not the world as *I* see it. Without such a public world, and therefore a dose of inauthenticity, even the most authentic of us would be unable to engage in coherent, purposeful action. Heidegger believed, for example, that to do philosophy properly we must be authentic, somewhat detached, that is, from 'everydayness' and also from the concerns of run-of-the-mill philosophy. We need to rethink the tradition by returning to early philosophers, such as Plato. But Heidegger believes that Plato is an early philosopher because that is what *they* say; he goes to a library to read him because that is where *one* goes to read a book; he is not naked, since *one* wears clothes in a library. If Heidegger had decided all such matters from his own, individual resources, he would hardly have got around to philosophy. On the other hand, we would not expect Heidegger to say about Plato only what *one* says about Plato. Coherent thought and action require a discriminating blend of authenticity and inauthenticity.

The primary form of 'talk' (*Rede*), for Heidegger, is not explicit assertion, such as 'This hammer is heavy', but such utterances as 'Too heavy! Give me a lighter one' made in a context of significance. Explicit assertion arises only with *Gerede*, 'idle talk', which retails talk beyond its original context, and thus gives rise to language. Truth too is not primarily the correspondence between an assertion or proposition and a state of the world, but the disclosure of the world to and by *Dasein*, unmediated by concepts, propositions, or inner mental states; at bottom, truth is '*Dasein*'s disclosedness', a necessary condition for both truth and falsity in the ordinary sense. (He supported this

by appeal to the Greek word for truth, *alētheia*, which, he claimed, means 'unconcealment'.) Meaning, like truth, is extruded from the mind:

Mill's allegedly verbal propositions cannot be completely severed from the beings they intend. Names, words in the broadest sense, have no a priori fixed measure of their significative content. Names, or again their meanings, change with transformations in our knowledge of things, and the meanings of names and words always change according to the predominance of a specific line of vision toward the thing somehow named by the name. All significations, including those that are apparently mere verbal meanings, arise from reference to things. (*The Basic Problems of Phenomenology*, lectures given in 1927 (published 1975; tr. Bloomington, Ind., 1982), 197)

The *representative theory of perception is rejected along with the *correspondence theory of truth: 'What we "first" hear is never noises or complexes of sounds, but the creaking wagon, the motor-cycle . . . It requires a very artificial and complicated state of mind to "hear" a "pure noise".' *Dasein* interprets things all the way down, so that a *Dasein*-independent account of them can hardly be given. Hence the problem of the reality of the *external world, like that of the existence of other minds, is a pseudo-problem: for Kant, the 'scandal of philosophy' is that no proof has yet been given of the 'existence of things outside of us', but for Heidegger the scandal is 'not that this proof has yet to be given, but that *such proofs are expected and attempted again and again*'.

Dasein must be considered as a whole, and this requires an account of *death. *Dasein* can be genuinely authentic only in its 'being towards death', since here it accepts its finitude. *Dasein* is individualized by death: it dies alone, and no one else can die in its place. Death is a criterion of authenticity: I must recognize that *I* will die, not simply that *one* dies. There is a pervasive tendency to conceal the inevitability of one's own death. (Like Kierkegaard and Tolstoy, Heidegger cites the old syllogism 'All men are mortal, Caius is a man, so Caius is mortal': 'That Caius, man in the abstract, was mortal', mused Tolstoy's Ivan, 'was perfectly correct, but he was not Caius, not an abstract man, but a creature quite, quite separate from all the others.') Authentic being towards death is related to 'resoluteness' (*Entschlossenheit*): only if I am aware of my finitude do I have reason to act now, rather than to procrastinate, and it is the crucial decision made with a view to the whole course of my life that gives my life its unity and shape.

Authentic *Dasein*, and even inauthentic *Dasein*, is essentially 'temporal', unfolding in the 'ecstases' of future, past, and present. The future, running ahead to death, is the primary 'ecstasis'. (The root meaning of 'ecstasis', like that of 'existence', is 'stepping forth'.) A decision is also constrained by a situation inherited from the past and the more important it is, the more it will be taken in view of the past. The authentic present is the 'moment' of decision:

To the anticipation which goes with resoluteness, there belongs a present in accordance with which a resolution discloses the situation. In resoluteness, the present is not only brought back from distraction with the objects of one's closest concern, but it gets held in the future and in having been. That present which is held in authentic temporality and which thus is authentic itself, we call the 'moment of vision' [*Augenblick*, 'instant, moment', but literally 'eye-glance'].

Several features of time have been ignored by the Aristotelian tradition. (An Aristotelian view of time inspired Russell's claim that it would make little difference if our present position were reversed, that is, if we barely remembered the past, but foresaw much of the future. This applies to the time of physics, but not to the time of action and decision: in deciding whether to do this or that, I characteristically do not yet know which I shall do.) Time is significant: it is time *to do* such-and-such. Time is datable by events: it is the time *when*, for example, I first went to Marburg. Time is spanned: now is not a durationless instant, but now, *during*, say, the lecture. Time is public: we can all indicate the same time by 'now' or 'then', even if we date it by different events. Time is finite: (my) time does not run on for ever, but is running out. History is to be understood in terms of this account of time and of *Dasein*'s 'historicality'. *Dasein*'s understanding of itself and the world depends on an interpretation inherited from the past. This interpretation regulates and discloses the possibilities open to it. Inauthentic *Dasein* accepts tradition unthinkingly and fulfils the possibilities shaped by it; authentic *Dasein* probes tradition and thereby opens up new and weightier possibilities. Heidegger, for example, does not simply contribute to contemporary philosophical controversy, but by 'repeating' and 'de(con)structing' crucial episodes in the development of our philosophical tradition hopes to change the whole course of philosophical inquiry. It is only because *Dasein* is historical that history in the usual sense is possible: 'Our going back to "the past" does not first get its start from the acquisition, sifting and securing of such material [namely, remains, monuments, and records]; these activities presuppose *historical Being towards* the *Dasein* that has-been-there—that is to say, they presuppose the historicality of the historian's existence.'

Being and Time remained unfinished: the third section of part 1, which was to explicate being in terms of time, and the whole of part 2, which was to examine Kant, Descartes, and Aristotle, never appeared. But shorter works of the same period fill some of the gaps. His Freiburg inaugural lecture, 'What is Metaphysics?' (1929), expands on 'the nothing', which made a brief appearance in *Being and Time*, and which is disclosed in the *Angst* that reveals to *Dasein*, in its freedom and finitude, the ultimate groundlessness of itself, its world, and its projects. *Kant and the Problem of Metaphysics* (1929; tr. Bloomington, Ind., 1962) argues that the first *Critique* is not a theory of knowledge or of the sciences (as such neo-Kantians as Hermann Cohen, Paul Natorp, and Ernst Cassirer held), but lays the foundation for metaphysics. Kant saw that reason, knowledge, and man in general are finite, and thus made the transcendental imagination the basis of the possibility of synthetic a priori knowledge. But since this threatens the

primacy of reason and the foundations of 'Western metaphysics', Kant recoiled from the 'abyss' in the second edition of the *Critique* and made the imagination a 'function of the understanding'. Heidegger's interpretation was attacked by most Kant scholars, including Cassirer; he implicitly retracts some of his views in later essays on Kant.

Heidegger published little in the 1930s, but lectures delivered then and published later suggest that at that time he abandoned many of his earlier views, especially on the centrality of *Dasein*. In 'On the Essence of Truth' (1943), *truth, and by implication being, is no longer located primarily in *Dasein*, but is the 'open region' to which man is exposed. 'Plato's Doctrine of Truth' (1942) argued that in Plato's allegory of the cave truth ceased to be 'unhiddenness' and became, 'under the yoke of the *idea*', mere 'correctness', i.e. *our* ideas' correspondence to things. This initiated the degeneration of thought about being into 'metaphysics': man moved to the centre of things. The history of Western philosophy is a history of decline. This view reached its more or less final form in his 1935 lectures, *An Introduction to Metaphysics* (1953; tr. New York, 1961). The term 'metaphysics' alters its significance. For the early Heidegger it was a favourable term, approximating to '(fundamental) ontology'. In the late 1930s it became unfavourable, implying, among other things, an anthropocentrism of which *Being and Time* is not wholly innocent. However, since the missing third division of *Being and Time* was to examine being independently of *Dasein*, it may be that Heidegger's later works develop ideas he had formed earlier.

Heidegger's late philosophy emerges for the most part in 'conversations' with past thinkers, especially poets such as Hölderlin who offer a way out of 'forgetfulness of being'; and the Pre-Socratic thinkers (Anaximander, Parmenides, and Heraclitus) who preceded it, and the 'most unbridled Platonist in the history of Western metaphysics', Nietzsche (*Nietzsche* (1961; tr. New York, 1979–87). ('Truth', Nietzsche said, 'is the sort of error without which a definite type of living entity could not live. Ultimately, the value for life decides.' This is 'metaphysical', because it locates truth in man's thought; it is 'Platonist', because it assumes a realm of values distinct from the world.) Being becomes ever more elusive in his writings, barely describable except in such tautological terms as 'It gives itself'. The 'ontological difference', the crucial distinction between being and beings, is differently described at different times. Heidegger sometimes supplements this 'twofold' with a 'fourfold' inspired by Plato and Hölderlin: earth, world (or sky), gods, and men. Despite his denials, being resembles God. It is not at man's disposal; it disposes of man. Whatever happens comes from being. Man, the 'shepherd of being', must respond to its directions. It is above history, but since the time of Plato it has been hidden, and the 'history of being' can be reconstructed from the texts of philosophers and poets. Forgetfulness of being, 'nihilism', has culminated in the domination of the world by technology, which is not primarily machines but an event in the history of being, 'the completion of metaphysics': everything, including eventually human beings, is regarded as a disposable resource. Whether or not we can return to genuine thinking of being will determine the future of the planet. He was not wholly pessimistic: 'But where there is danger, the remedy grows too' (Hölderlin). The effects of technology, as Heidegger describes them—homelessness, rootlessness, the flattening out of worldly significance—are similar to the effects he had earlier attributed to *Angst* and boredom, moods especially conducive to philosophy. (Such moods are the counterpart, in Heidegger, of Husserl's *epochē*, supplying what Husserl neglected: a motivation within everydayness for philosophical reflection.) Technology is double-edged. If we succumb to it, it threatens to turn us into the calculating functionaries that Heidegger found in the dystopian works of his friend Ernst Jünger. If we think about it in the right way, it offers an unprecedented prospect of philosophical illumination. How else can Heidegger explain how he, in this benighted age, succeeded in recovering the vision of the early Greeks?

The appropriate response to being is thinking. Thinking is our obedient answer to the call of being: the early Greeks did it, but we have forgotten it. Thinking contrasts with assertion, logic, science ('science does not think'), metaphysics, philosophy itself, and especially technology, which is merely an instrument for the calculation and domination of entities. Language, like thinking, played a subordinate part in *Being and Time*: meaning and language grow out of worldly significance and our understanding of it. Now language becomes central, not language as an instrument of manipulation—into which it has degenerated under the auspices of metaphysics—but language as the 'abode of being': 'Language speaks, not man. Man only speaks, when he fatefully responds to language.' Language no longer emerges from a pre-existing significant world; it opens up a significant world and thus creates speakers and hearers for itself. Art, especially poetry, is critically important for thinking and language. Poetry is not a secondary phenomenon: it has a special relation to being and truth. Poetry is 'founding of truth': it discloses the (or 'a') world and creates a language for its adequate expression. When a painting, such as Van Gogh's peasant shoes, 'opens up' a world, the world of the peasant, when a Greek temple ' sets up' a world, they are essentially 'poetry' (*Dichtung*). Unpoetic thought and language are parasitic on poetry and its vision. Poetry is close to the sacred: 'The thinker says being. The poet names the holy.'

The change from *Being and Time* to Heidegger's later thought is often called 'the turn' (*die Kehre*). Heidegger used this expression (influenced perhaps by the 'turn' of the prisoners in Plato's cave) in his *Letter on Humanism* (1947) for the change of direction involved in his intended, but unfulfilled, continuation of *Being and Time*. (He also used it for the hoped-for change, in the history of being, from forgetfulness of being to thinking.) But he regularly denied any significant difference between his early and his later thought and any similarity of either to Sartre's existentialism. Heidegger's interpretation of his own work, as of much else, is of continuing interest, but open to question.

The ultimate worth of Heidegger's thought is still *sub judice*. Like his great rival Hegel (who also made life difficult for his non-German readers by trying to 'teach philosophy to speak German'), he is alternately worshipped, reviled, or sympathetically assimilated to other, more accessible philosophers, especially Wittgenstein. (Heidegger's relation to Husserl is comparable to the relation of the late to the early Wittgenstein.) But his immense learning, his profound and innovative intelligence, his commitment to philosophical inquiry, and, above all, his intense influence on modern thought, are not in doubt. Philosophers such as Sartre, Gadamer, and Derrida derive many of their basic concepts from him, and his philosophical influence extends to Japan and China. Theologians, Catholic (Karl Rahner) as well as Protestant (Rudolf Bultmann), are in his debt, as are psychologists (Ludwig Binswanger) and literary critics (Emil Staiger). The difficulty of his writings stems partly from the profundity of his questions. Other philosophers asked what it is about a statement or a belief that makes it true rather than false; Heidegger asks what it is that enables us to make any statements or have any beliefs at all, how we get the 'elbowroom' (*Spielraum*) to step back from the world and freely assess it from a distance rather than to remain engrossed in the stimulus of the present moment. Others, such as Husserl, assumed that philosophy was a feasible and respected enterprise; Heidegger tried to explain *Dasein's* transition from everydayness to philosophical reflection, locating it (in division 2 of *Being and Time*) in authenticity, *Angst*, and resoluteness. Others sought the foundations of the sciences; Heidegger asked how the sciences emerge from undifferentiated everydayness. Whether or not Heidegger's answers to such questions are true in the traditional sense, he has disclosed something of the world, and of the possibilities for our 'comportment' to it, that was previously concealed.   M.J.I.

*being-in-the-world.

W. Blattner, *Heidegger's Temporal Idealism* (Cambridge, 1999).

H. L. Dreyfus, *Being-in-the-World: A Commentary on Heidegger's Being and Time, Division I* (Cambridge, Mass., 1991).

C. Guignon (ed.), *The Cambridge Companion to Heidegger* (Cambridge, 1993).

M. Inwood, *A Heidegger Dictionary* (Oxford, 1999).

S. Mulhall, *Heidegger and* Being and Time (London, 1993).

H. Philippse, *Heidegger's Philosophy of Being: A Critical Interpretation* (Princeton, NJ, 1998).

R. Polt, *Heidegger: An Introduction* (London, 1999).

R. Safranski, *Heidegger: Between Good and Evil* (Cambridge, Mass., 1998).

R. Schmitt, *Martin Heidegger on Being Human* (New York, 1969).

Heisenberg, Werner (1901–76). German physicist best known for discovering and articulating the *uncertainty principle in *quantum mechanics. With Schrödinger, he co-founded modern quantum mechanics, improving on the older semi-classical theory of Planck, Einstein, and Bohr. Heisenberg's approach ('matrix mechanics') highlighted the structural features of the physical magnitudes that can be measured on quantum systems, while Schrödinger's ('wave mechanics') focused on their allowed states. But the two approaches were soon shown to be mathematically equivalent ways of expressing the same physical theory. In later years, against the grain of the strict *operationalism that permeated much of his work in physics, Heisenberg regarded the irreducibly statistical predictions of quantum mechanics as representing a system's inherent tendency to react one way or another in response to a measurement (resurrecting Aristotle's idea of intrinsic 'potentiality'): 'In the experiments of atomic physics we have to do with things and facts, with phenomena that are just as real as any phenomena in daily life. But the atoms or the elementary particles themselves are not as real; they form a world of potentialities or possibilities rather than one of things or facts.'   R.CLI.

W. Heisenberg, *Physics and Philosophy* (London, 1958).

hell. Traditionally, Christianity has taught that those who have no faith in Christ (faith typically being manifested by seeking baptism), or, having that faith, commit mortal sin (i.e. obviously bad sin) of which they have not repented, go after death to Hell. There they are punished both with *poena damni* (the punishment of the loss of the vision of God in Heaven) and *poena sensus* (sensory pain) forever. (Islam teaches a similar doctrine.) Not all elements of this doctrine are evident in the New Testament, some later theologians put various qualifications on it, and most modern theologians would deny most aspects of it. Why would a good *God allow anyone to be deprived of him, let alone to suffer forever? Part of the answer may be that it is a generous act to give to humans the ultimate choice of rejecting the *good forever.   R.G.S.

*eschatology; God and the philosophers; heaven.

J. Kvanvig, *The Problem of Hell* (New York, 1993).

Hellenistic philosophy. A rubric invented by scholars to cover the period of Greek philosophy between the death of Alexander the Great in 323 BC and the end of the Roman Republic in 31 BC. More broadly, it applies to the principal philosophical movements of this period—*Stoicism, *Epicureanism, and *scepticism—as well as to their further developments in Imperial Rome and elsewhere. It should be noted that it is wrong simply to identify Hellenistic philosophy with a period of *Greek* philosophy. For there are members of the Hellenistic philosophical schools, e.g. Seneca, and important sources for our knowledge of the schools, e.g. Cicero, who wrote in Latin, not Greek. Further, although the three schools mentioned above certainly dominated during this period, not all the philosophy that was done was under their sponsorship. The successors of Aristotle, especially Theophrastus, should be mentioned in this regard.

Hellenistic philosophy is rooted in the two great philosophical schools of the fourth century BC, Plato's *Academy and Aristotle's Lyceum. A convenient means of orientating oneself to the corpus of Hellenistic philosophical writings is according to the division of philosophy laid down by Xenocrates, the head of Plato's Academy between 339 and 314 BC. Xenocrates divided all philosophy into three wide categories: logic (the study of reasoning and rational discourse); physics (the study of external nature in all its manifestations); and ethics (the study of human nature and how life ought to be lived). This division became standard throughout the Hellenistic period both in the philosophers' own works and in their treatment of their predecessors. For example, the Aristotelian corpus was arranged in the first century BC by Andronicus of Rhodes according to the Xenocratean system.

In physics, Stoics and Epicureans rejected the immaterial entities of Platonism and Aristotelianism—Plato's Forms and the soul and Aristotle's God or unmoved mover. They rejected the claim that the postulation of such entities was required to explain various features of the world. Forms or immaterial gods were unnecessary for explaining the intelligibility of sensible reality or the existence of motion. This view led both Hellenistic schools to new accounts of what things there really are and what they are like. They were inspired by some provocative speculative conclusions of the Pre-Socratic philosophers that Plato and Aristotle had themselves rejected. The Stoics were inspired by Heraclitus. They took Aristotle at his word when he said that if an immaterial god does not exist, then metaphysics is just physics. For the Stoics, theology then becomes a branch of physics, investigating the fundamental immanent materialistic principle of the organic universe. Epicurus recurred to the *atomism of Democritus and Leucippus as a basis for his scientific investigations. Atomism's strength was supposed to lie in its suitability as a framework for unified explanation in areas thought to be widely separate, such as ethics, theology, and epistemology.

The *materialism of both the Stoics and the Epicureans is joined to an empiricist methodology. Careful attention to methodology is a hallmark of the Hellenistic schools. Logic, as understood by these schools, encompasses whatever matters pertain to the methodology of empiricism, including semantics and epistemology as well as formal reasoning. The members of the Old Stoa have left a great deal of impressive work in these areas. Epicurus was particularly conscious of the need to develop a logic suitable to scientific investigation. He gave it the name 'canonic', indicating a study of the proper rules governing the pursuit of knowledge. Sceptics were moved to refine their anti-dogmatic arguments in response to both Stoic and Epicurean innovations. They claimed that *empiricism can provide no basis for claims to knowledge. Within Plato's Academy, however, a sceptical movement arose which was rather more hospitable to empiricism in practice. These Sceptics were prepared to countenance criteria of rational belief, if not of knowledge. The association of scepticism with empiricism is one of the more remarkable developments in the Hellenistic period.

In ethics, Stoics and Epicureans adhered to the *rationalism of Socrates as it is found in the early dialogues of Plato. They believed that the entire human soul was rational and that the road to happiness consisted in using reason correctly. Moral flaws were actually flaws in the functioning of reason. Moral improvement consisted in replacing erroneous beliefs with true beliefs. They rejected Plato's major qualifications of Socrates' position mainly because that involved a dualistic account of the person that conflicted with materialism. They also rejected Aristotle's less extreme approach wherein the affective side of human life and external circumstances contributed to happiness. Stoicism and Epicureanism represent two conflicting types of rationalism in ethics. It is difficult to arrive at a clear idea of what ethics would mean for a Sceptic. No doubt, they would argue that it is not possible to obtain knowledge of universal rules of human behaviour. This would seem to drive them to some form of subjectivism, although the Sceptic would wish to refrain from the dogmatic defence of such a view.

While insisting on the opposition of the Hellenistic philosophical schools to *Platonism and *Aristotelianism, it is well to bear in mind that there is nevertheless a profound continuity of underlying assumptions among them. For instance, apart from the Sceptics, they all believe that philosophy is a serious activity capable of attaining life-enhancing wisdom. In an odd way, this is even true of the Sceptics who believed that destructive argument was after all the key to happiness. There is also a shared assumption about the centrality of the concept of nature in philosophy. The naturalism of the Stoics and Epicureans can be traced back to the Pre-Socratic idea that human nature is illuminated by the study of external nature. This assumption resonates throughout the history of philosophy.

The main Hellenistic schools continued to dominate philosophical work into the period of Imperial Rome. Both Epicureanism and Stoicism appealed to those who were not particularly interested in theoretical issues, but who were eager for guidance on how best to live. Impartial observers of the time looked upon Christianity as just another philosophical school with a relatively new approach to old questions. As Christianity rose in influence, the Hellenistic philosophical schools declined. Important elements of Stoicism and Epicureanism found their way into the writings of Christian theologians.   L.P.G.

B. Inwood and L. P. Gerson (eds.), *Hellenistic Philosophy: Introductory Readings* (Indianapolis, 1988).

A. A. Long, *Hellenistic Philosophy*, 2nd edn. (Berkeley, Calif., 1986).

—— and D. N. Sedley (eds.), *The Hellenistic Philosophers*, 2 vols. (Cambridge, 1987).

Héloïse complex. Diagnosed by Michèle Le Dœuff, this is the tendency of women in philosophy to idolize either a male colleague or teacher (as did Héloïse and de Beauvoir), or a 'great' living or dead philosopher whose banner they carry (as do contemporary women seeking the best male exponent of feminism, and becoming 'Lacanian', 'Foucauldian', even 'Nietzschean' feminists). This situation benefits the man, destroys the woman—removing her intellectual independence and need to create philosophy herself. De Beauvoir, however, escaped the Héloïse complex sufficiently to produce philosophy 'unawares'.

J.O'G.

*women in philosophy.

Michèle Le Dœuff, *Hipparchia's Choice* (Oxford, 1991).

Helvétius, Claude Adrien (1715–71). In *De l'esprit* (1758), Helvétius claimed that all normal humans share the same intellectual potential at birth, so that differences in character and intellectual achievement should be explained as products of environmental difference. To explain differences in intellectual achievement, Helvétius stressed the far-reaching consequences that lucky observations could have for an individual's thinking. He also argued that intellectual development depended on an individual's being motivated to inquiry by stimulation of his passions. Helvétius' doctrine led him to place importance on public education. The goal of social policy was to maximize pleasure and minimize pain. Human action was motivated by a desire for pleasure and this fact should be exploited to encourage virtuous, i.e. socially beneficial, action. Virtue should be encouraged not by moralizing but by reward, including—as Helvétius suggested—sexual gratification.   T.P.

*utilitarianism.

C.-A. Helvétius, *De l'esprit; or, Essays on the Mind and its Several Faculties* (London, 1759).

Hempel, Carl Gustav (1905–97). One of the leaders of the logical empiricist movement in the philosophy of science, which flourished for about three decades after the Second World War, Hempel saw the task of science as that of showing phenomena to be the consequence of unbroken *laws. A major implication was the so-called *covering-law model of scientific understanding, stressing that there is a symmetry between explanation and prediction, where the only difference is temporal—in the case of explanation, that which you are explaining has already occurred, whereas in the case of prediction, that which you are predicting has yet to occur.

With today's move from prescriptive philosophy of science to a more descriptive stance, not to mention the switch from an exclusive concern with the physical sciences to a more general interest in such areas as biology and psychology, Hempel's views now are often contemptuously described as the 'received view' meaning the 'not received by anyone who has read my latest article view'. Whether this will prove to be the end of such an approach to science will presumably be the topic of many future Ph.D. theses.   M.R.

*logical empiricism.

C. G. Hempel, *The Philosophy of Natural Science* (Englewood Cliffs, NJ, 1966).

C. G. Hempel, *The Philosophy of Carl G. Hempel: Studies in Science, Explanation, and Rationality*, ed. J. Fetzer (New York, 2001).

J. Fetzer (ed.), *Science, Explanation, and Rationality: Studies in the Philosophy of Carl G. Hempel* (New York, 2000).

F. Suppe, *The Structure of Scientific Theories* (Urbana, Ill., 1974).

Henry of Ghent (?–1293). He taught in the faculties of arts and theology at the University of Paris, and was also in turn Archdeacon of Bruges and principal Archdeacon of Tournai. His philosophical reputation rests largely upon his *Summa Theologiae* (Summation of Theology) and upon a set of *Quodlibeta*, reports of his response to questions on a wide range of issues, put to him in the context of disputations. His writing is a synthesis of *Aristotelianism and Augustinianism, though important parts of his metaphysical thinking, concerning the nature of being *qua* being, owe a good deal to Avicenna. As regards his Augustinianism, Henry held that knowledge of natural things depends in part upon divine illumination, so that there is no purely natural way of knowing about the natural order.   A.BRO.

J. Paulus, *Henri de Gand: Essai sur les tendances de sa métaphysique* (Paris, 1938).

Heraclitus of Ephesus (*fl. c.*500 BC). Pre-Socratic philosopher. Nothing is known of his life (the ancient 'biographies' are fiction). There is no sign that he ever left his native city, which at that time was part of the empire of the Achaemenid dynasty of Persia. (Iranian influences on his thinking have sometimes been suggested.)

The book of Heraclitus was famous in antiquity for its aphoristic obscurity. About 100 sentences survive. Interpretation of Heraclitus has been a controversial matter since at least the late fifth century BC. Both Plato and Aristotle accepted the view of Cratylus, who attributed to Heraclitus his own version of 'universal *flux'; in consequence they underrated Heraclitus. Later ancient interpreters, e.g. Theophrastus and Cleanthes, also influenced and clouded the later testimony.

Heraclitus' obscurity is a calculated consequence of his style, which is usually compact and often deliberately cryptic. He believed that what he has to say goes beyond the limits of ordinary language. Combined with the fragmentary state of the surviving evidence, his obscurity is a formidable obstacle to understanding. It is clear, though, that Heraclitus' thinking was meant as a comprehensive and systematic whole, covering every aspect of human experience, of which every part was connected with every other. It is clear too that his statements are often intended to be self-applicable: their linguistic form exemplifies the very structure of which they speak.

This observation can serve as the starting-point of an interpretation with some prospect of making sense of the fragments in their totality.

1. The abstract notion of 'structure' is omnipresent, explicitly in the word *harmonia*, but mostly implicitly.

2. There is a parallelism or identity of structure between the operations of the mind, as expressed in thought and language, and those of the reality which it grasps.

3. In general the structure is that of 'unity-in-opposites'. This appears in many examples, static or dynamic, drawn from everyday life: 'People step into the same rivers, and different waters flow on to them'; 'A road, uphill and downhill, one and the same'; 'Sea is water most pure and most polluted: for fish drinkable and life-giving, for human beings undrinkable and deadly'. These remarks and their generalizations are not meant to infringe the law of non-contradiction; rather they trade on it to point out a systematic ambivalence (between polar opposites) in the essential nature of things.

4. The parallelism of structure implies that understanding the world is like grasping the meaning of a statement. The 'meaning of the world', like that of a statement in words, is not obvious, but yet is present in the statement, and can be worked out provided one 'knows the language'. Human reason has the power to know the language, precisely because its own operations are conducted in the very same or an analogous one. The word *logos* (basically 'story', 'account'; then 'calculation, proportion, reason') expresses this analogy or identity.

5. Hence the key to understanding the nature of the world is *introspection: 'I went looking for myself.' The human self ('soul', *psukhē*) is variously occupied: it is combatively active, physically, emotionally, and intellectually; it is reflectively self-discovering and self-extending; and it is constantly self-reversing in the swings of circumstances or passion or thought. Yet it needs firm frameworks (objective truths, fixed rules of conduct) to be at all, or to make sense of its own existence. All this is true of the world too; here also there is no sharp line between what it is and what it means. Behaviour and structure of the world and of the soul run parallel; both are particular cases of the general 'unity-in-opposites'. The image of a child playing both sides of a board game presents the fundamental coexistences: of conflict and law, of freedom and regularity, of intelligence and its lapses, of opposition and unity.

Since he was 'rediscovered' at the end of the eighteenth century, and rescued from crude misunderstandings, Heraclitus' appeal has grown, in spite of his obscurity. Hegel explicitly acknowledged his indebtedness; Heidegger has given lengthy exegesis. Wittgenstein's *Tractatus* is rather similar to Heraclitus in style and perhaps partly in method.
                                    E.L.H.

*Pre-Socratic philosophy.

E. Hussey, 'Epistemology and Meaning in Heraclitus', in M. Schofield and M. Nussbaum (eds.), *Language and Logos: Studies in Ancient Greek Philosophy Presented to G. E. L. Owen* (Cambridge, 1982).

C. H. Kahn, *The Art and Thought of Heraclitus* (Cambridge, 1979).

G. S. Kirk, *Heraclitus: The Cosmic Fragments* (Cambridge, 1962).

Herder, Johann Gottfried (1744–1803). German philosopher who held that thought and *language are inseparable, and that a people's thought and culture are accessible only through its language. All languages descend from a common source, which he mistakenly sought within the short span of recorded history. He studied folk-song, and criticized Kant for neglecting language. His *Understanding and Reason: A Metacritique of the* Critique of Pure Reason (1799) argued that language, which is both sensuous and intellectual, forbids Kant's dissection of the mind into sensibility and understanding, and other ensuing dualisms. History, like language, develops out of nature; it does not begin with a contract or divine intervention. Cultures vary according to a people's natural endowments and circumstances, but they form an organic series which progressively realizes the idea of 'humanity'. In Herder enlightenment became historical.   M.J.I.

F. M. Barnard (ed.), *Herder on Social and Political Culture* (Cambridge, 1969).

I. Berlin, *Vico and Herder: Two Studies in the History of Ideas* (London, 1976).

heredity and environment. The development of human intellect and personality results from a complex interplay of biological and environmental factors. The mind is not wholly the product of nature or nurture. Any 'nurturist' must concede that a creature cannot learn unless it has innate abilities to interact with its environment, process and retain information. Any 'nativist' must admit that the relation between genes and behaviour is so intricate and probabilistic that talk of 'genetic determinism' is rarely appropriate. The exact nature of the interplay between biology and environment remains, however, a matter of profound controversy.

Those who favour nativist explanations argue that findings in cognitive science, behavioural genetics, evolutionary theory, and developmental psychology favour the view that the human mind has significant innate structure, and that the parameters of intellect and personality are genetically defined. We are urged to see the mind as a system of modules each with its own internal developmental trajectory. Chomsky argued half a century ago that we must posit an innate 'language acquisition device' if we are to explain how children acquire natural languages. We now know that children are innately equipped with considerable mental capacities. Immediately after birth, babies are attuned to their mother's voice and can imitate certain facial expressions. In time, they deploy 'folk' theories of the behaviour of physical objects and other people. The emergence of these abilities may require environmental triggers, but they are not learnt. All this makes sound evolutionary sense. In addition, our rapidly expanding knowledge of the human genome suggests that significant genetic factors influence sexual orientation, mental health, moral sensibility, and intelligence.

In response, some critics of nativism have argued that 'connectionist' models of neural architecture are able to explain learning without positing innate structures. But the most compelling arguments are those that invoke culture. Tomasello has argued that natural selection proceeds too slowly to explain the rapid evolution of human cognitive capacities. The latter depends on a process of 'cumulative cultural evolution' whereby each individual inherits the collective achievement of past generations. This distinguishes us from other intelligent primates which lack the means to preserve innovations and transmit them to future generations. Cumulative cultural evolution is a natural process, but one which cannot be understood exclusively in natural-scientific terms.

A more purely philosophical defence of culturalism is found in John McDowell's recent writings. McDowell argues that children become rational agents through enculturation, which equips them with the conceptual capacities that enable them to respond to reasons. But the terms in which we explain the behaviour of rational agents are fundamentally incommensurable with the causal-explanatory framework of the natural sciences. Hence, in so far as we appeal to genetic or neurological factors to explain some action, we do not represent it as the purposive activity of a rational, autonomous being. It follows that our genetic endowment and brain functioning enable, but do not constitute, our mental lives.

The supposed moral and political implications of these various positions often stand as an obstacle to their clear-headed assessment. Hostility to nativism has traditionally inspired egalitarian and democratic political theories, and nativism has been associated with repugnant views of the innate intellectual and/or moral inferiority of women, non-whites, and the labouring masses, and with eugenics. In response, contemporary nativists reply that it is one thing to know the facts about human nature, another to draw moral conclusions from them. They point out that nurturism is itself associated with disastrous visions of social engineering (e.g. the creation of the New Soviet Man) and deplorable environmental explanations of conditions now known to be indifferent to nurture (e.g. the attribution of autism to 'cold' mothering; attempts to condition people out of homosexuality).

The old nature–nurture debate may be dead, but intense controversy about the foundations of human nature promises to continue *ad infinitum*.   D.BAK.

J. McDowell, *Mind and World* (Cambridge, Mass., 1994), lectures V and VI.

S. Pinker, *The Blank Slate* (New York, 2002).

M. Ridley, *Genome* (New York, 2000).

M. Tomasello, *The Cultural Origins of Human Cognition* (Cambridge, Mass., 1999).

hermeneutic circle. Term often used by philosophers in the (mainly continental) tradition running from Schleiermacher and Dilthey to Heidegger, Gadamer, and Ricœur. Has to do with the inherent circularity of all understanding, or the fact that comprehension can only come about through a tacit foreknowledge that alerts us to salient features of the text which would otherwise escape notice. Yet it is also the case that every text (and every reading of it) in some way manages to pass beyond the 'horizon of intelligibility' that makes up this background of foregone interpretative assumptions. The debate is joined between those (like Gadamer) who think of understanding in terms of a dialogue or ongoing cultural conversation, and those—Habermas among them—who wish to maintain a more independent role for the exercise of critical thought.

C.N.

*hermeneutics.

D. C. Hoy, *The Critical Circle: Literature and History in Contemporary Hermeneutics* (Berkeley, Calif., 1978).

hermeneutics. The name of Hermes, the messenger of the Greek gods, gave rise to *hermēneuein*, 'to interpret', and *hermēneutike (technē)* is the 'art of interpretation'. It became important after the Reformation, when Protestants needed to interpret the Bible accurately. Medieval hermeneutics ascribed to the Bible four levels of meaning: literal, allegorical, tropological (moral), and anagogical (eschatological). But the Reformation insisted on literal or 'grammatical' exegesis and on the study of Hebrew and Greek. Modern hermeneutics falls into three phases.

1. Friedrich Schleiermacher (1768–1834), the great Protestant theologian and Plato scholar, gave in lectures, from 1819 on, a systematic theory of the interpretation of texts and speech. (Another Plato scholar, Friedrich Ast (1778–1841), had in 1808 published *Elements of Grammar, Hermeneutics and Criticism*.) The interpreter's aim is to 'understand the text at first as well as and then even better than its author': 'Since we have no direct knowledge of what was in the author's mind, we must try to become aware of many things of which he himself may have been unconscious, except in so far as he reflects on his own work and becomes his own reader.' A text is interpreted from two points of view: 'grammatical', in relation to the language in which it is written, and 'psychological', in relation to the mentality and development of the author. We cannot gain complete understanding of either of these aspects, since we cannot have complete knowledge of a language or a person: we 'move back and forth between the grammatical and the psychological sides, and no rules can stipulate exactly how to do this'. We cannot fully understand a *language, a person, or a text, unless we understand its parts, but we cannot fully understand the parts unless we understand the whole. Thus at each level we are involved in a *hermeneutical circle, a continual reciprocity between whole and parts; a significant 'text can never be understood right away . . . every reading puts us in a better position to understand since it increases our knowledge'. (It is the range of relevant knowledge, not circularity alone, that precludes definitive interpretation. Our understanding of 'Hand me my clubs!' on a golf-course is circular, since only the whole utterance disambiguates 'hand' and 'clubs', but it is definitive and complete.)

2. Schleiermacher's biographer, Dilthey, extended hermeneutics to the understanding of all human behaviour and products. Our understanding of an author, artist, or historical agent is not direct, but by way of analogies to our own experience. We relive past decisions, etc. in imaginative sympathy.

3. Heidegger learned of hermeneutics from his theological training and from Dilthey. Theological hermeneutics considers the interpretation of ancient texts; Dilthey is concerned with understanding in the cultural, in contrast to the natural, sciences, and again mainly, if not exclusively, with the interpretation of the products of past societies. In Heidegger's *Being and Time*, hermeneutics acquires a deeper and wider sense. It is concerned with the interpretation of the being who interprets texts and other artefacts, who may become, but is not essentially, either a natural or a cultural scientist: the human being or *Dasein*. Heidegger's *phenomenology is hermeneutical, rather than, like Husserl's, transcendental. Our approach to *Dasein* must be hermeneutical since the fundamental traits of *Dasein* and its 'world' are not, as Husserl supposed, on open display, but hidden, owing in part to their very familiarity, in part to *Dasein*'s tendency to misinterpret and obscure its own nature and such features of itself as mortality. Understanding *Dasein* is more like interpreting a text overlaid by past misinterpretations (or penetrating the self-rationalizations of a neurotic) than studying mathematics or planetary motions. Hermeneutics no longer presents rules for, or a theory of, interpretation; it is the interpretation of *Dasein*. But hermeneutic phenomenology gives an account of understanding, since a central feature of *Dasein* is to understand itself and its environment, not in the sense of disinterested interpretation or of explicit assertion, but of seeing the 'possibilities' available to it, seeing a hammer, for example, as something with which to mend a chair: 'All pre-predicative simple seeing of the invisible world of the ready-to-hand is in itself already an "understanding-interpreting" seeing.' It is only because *Dasein* has such 'pre-understanding' that it can interpret alien texts and understand itself in an explicit philosophical way. Heidegger's later works rarely mention hermeneutics, but interpret poetic and philosophical texts in a more traditional sense. His hermeneutics differs from Derrida's: for Heidegger, words 'show' something beyond themselves, namely being, and we need to think about this, not simply about the text, in order to understand what is said. *Being and Time* influenced Gadamer, and Rudolf Bultmann's (1884–1976) demythologizing interpretation of the Bible.

M.J.I.

*German philosophy today.

A. Laks and A. Neschke (eds.), *La Naissance du paradigme herméneutique: Schleiermacher, Humboldt, Boeckh, Droysen* (Lille, 1990).

K. Mueller-Vollmer (ed.), *The Hermeneutics Reader* (Oxford, 1986).

R. E. Palmer, *Hermeneutics: Interpretation Theory in Schleiermacher, Dilthey, Heidegger, and Gadamer* (Evanston, Ill., 1969).

P. Ricœur, *Hermeneutics and the Human Sciences* (Cambridge, 1981).

Hermetic corpus. A body of texts composed between AD 100 and 300, but supposed, together with a text advertising ceremonial magic called *Asclepius*, to contain the ancient 'Egyptian' wisdom, from which both Moses and

*Plato borrowed. Translated by *Marsilio Ficino in 1463, they strengthened a growing conviction that human beings could be as gods: through Reason, the child of God, we could be cleansed of 'the twelve madnesses', and come to see the ordered beauty of nature; people have forgotten that they exist to understand and tend the works of God, who is himself beyond our intellectual grasp. Later scholars, beginning with Casaubon in 1614, have discredited the claim to represent an original, pre-Greek theology, but its historical importance is obvious, and its doctrines, however poetically expressed, deserve close consideration.   S.R.L.C.

J. Crowley, *Aegypt* (London, 1987).
G. Fowden, *The Egyptian Hermes* (Cambridge, 1986).

Herzen, Alexandr Ivanovich (1812–70). A leading figure in Russian political thought, Herzen lived according to a youthful vow of hostility to Russian despotism. After periods in exile, he became an influential member of the 'Westernizers' in the 1840s. Though initially influenced by Hegel, whose dialectic he described as 'the algebra of revolution', Herzen developed a 'philosophy of contingency' that stressed the role of chance in history. Though he passionately defended individual *liberty, Herzen saw the peasant commune as a model of an agrarian socialism that might flourish without the prior development of capitalism, a system he abhorred. He emigrated in 1847, settling in London where he published *Kolokol* (The Bell). Smuggled into Russia, the journal became a powerful forum of political debate. Herzen's memoirs, *My Past and Thoughts*, are an outstanding contribution to literature and an engaging chronicle of Russian life.   D.BAK.

A. Herzen, *From the Other Shore*, tr. M. Budberg (London, 1956).
—— *My Past and Thoughts*, tr. C. Garnett, 4 vols. (London, 1968).

heterological and homological. A homological (or autological) word is one that applies to itself, e.g. the word 'polysyllabic', which is polysyllabic. A heterological word is one that does not apply to itself, e.g. the word 'Spanish', which is not Spanish. The heterological, or *Grelling's, paradox, related to the *liar paradox, is an *antinomy: the word 'heterological' is heterological if and only if it is not heterological.   C.A.K.

heteronomy: *see* autonomy and heteronomy.

heuristic. Conducive to *understanding, explanation, or discovery; an item, especially a thesis, that is heuristic. Especially, a heuristic investigation is one conducted by trial and error. In pedagogy, the heuristic method is a type of education through self-learning. In logic, a heuristic is a problem-solving procedure that may fall short of providing a proof.   S.P.

higher-order logic. In each interpretation of a standard logical system, variables range over a single domain of discourse. These are sometimes called 'first-order variables'. In second-order systems, there is also a type of variable

that ranges over sets, properties, functions, or propositional functions on the range of the first-order variables, the domain of discourse. For example, a statement like 'There is a property that holds of all and only the prime numbers' would naturally be interpreted in a second-order system. In third-order systems, there is a type of variable that ranges over properties of properties, or sets of sets, or functions of properties, etc. of whatever is in the range of the first-order variables. For example, according to some philosophical accounts, the number 4 is the property of all properties that apply to exactly four objects. This is a third-order statement. Extensions to fourth-order logic and beyond, even into the transfinite, follow the same pattern. A logical system is higher-order if it is at least second-order.   S.S.

*types, theory of.

Stewart Shapiro, *Foundations without Foundationalism: A Case for Second-Order Logic*, Oxford Logic Guides, xvii (Oxford, 1991).

Hilbert, David (1862–1943). German mathematician of encyclopaedic range. He and his followers pioneered the use of formal *axioms both for logical reasoning and to define classes of mathematical structures. With Ackermann in 1928 he wrote the first textbook to include first-order logic. His work of 1899 on the foundations of geometry was the first to describe a systematic method for proving non-deducibility in logic. 'Hilbert's programme' (sometimes misleadingly called 'formalism', though not by Hilbert himself) aimed to justify the use of infinity in mathematics by producing a finitary (i.e. purely syntactic) *consistency proof for an axiom system of arithmetic. Gödel showed that no such proof can be given. Though Hilbert was philosophically naïve, his controversies with Frege on the foundations of geometry and with Brouwer on formal versus contentful mathematics raised questions worth studying.   W.A.H.

Constance Reid, *Hilbert*, with an appreciation of Hilbert's mathematical work by Hermann Weyl (London, 1970).

Hindu philosophy. The word 'Hindu' comes from a Greek mispronunciation of the name of the River Sindhu, which also gave its name to the 'Indus' Valley civilization that flourished in north-west India between 2500 and 1500 BC. Assimilation of this pre-existent culture by the later Indo-Aryan immigrants resulted in the body of orally preserved literature called *'Veda', divided into hymns, sacrificial texts, and philosophical and mystical musings about ultimate reality and the goal of life. 'Hinduism' is the Western name given to the loosely knit family of diverse religious beliefs and practices which call themselves 'Vaidika' ('Vedic' in English) after these sacred texts.

Unlike Christianity or Islam, Hinduism is a non-proselytizing religion based on the Vedic principle that 'Reality is one, but different religious teachers speak of it differently'. The Vedic belief in universal determinism, coupled with belief in reincarnation of individual souls which are as eternal as God, translates into the law of *karma, which is the principle that no suffering or enjoyment can be undeserved. Unlike fatalism, which takes life as largely accidental and beyond our control, karma-determinism takes it to be nomologically controlled by our own past actions which even God does not condone. *Bhagavadgītā, the Hindu equivalent of the New Testament, says 'The Lord does not create human agency or actions.' Although he has divided society into four castes, God cannot, therefore, be held responsible for a man's birth in a family of priests, soldier-rulers, merchants, or workers. Under the general Vedic tolerance of diversity, Hindu philosophy, as distinguished from *Buddhism, *Jainism, and Indian materialism, divided into the Six Systems called Sāṃkhya, Yoga, Nyāya, Vaiśeṣika, *Vedānta, and Mīmāṃsā.

Sāṃkhya, perhaps the oldest school of independent metaphysical reasoning, is based on a fundamental dualism of many *selves*, which are eternal inactive centres of pure consciousness, and one *nature*, which is a constantly changing fusion of three material principles of illumination, kinesis, and inertia. These three strands of nature are affectively experienced as pleasure, pain, and torpor. The intellect, egoism, sense-organs, and bodies of living beings who suffer in this world are all evolutes of this objective nature with which subjective consciousness mistakenly confuses itself.

Accepting Sāṃkhya ontology for the most part, Yoga suggests an eight-step method of arresting the object-directed modifications of the mind—through which method a self can get back to its pure essence and hence stop suffering. This is the method of liberation through meditative discrimination between the self and nature. Sāṃkhya is atheistic whereas Yoga makes room for a God who does not create the world but is the mot perfect self who can elevate others by teaching.

Differing mostly in their epistemologies, Nyāya and Vaiśeṣika share their atomistic metaphysics of matter, belief in eternal souls, and a general realism in all spheres. The Vaiśeṣika ontology posits seven categories, classifying all knowable and nameable existents into substances, unrepeatable qualities, events, natural universals, the relation of inherence or *being inseparably in*, ultimate individuators of simples, and absences. The Nyāya school is responsible for developing a rigorous theory of sound inference and rules of constructive as well as destructive debate, whence the wider usage of 'Nyāya' to mean logic.

Vedānta, which is exegesis of the original philosophy of the *Upanishad portions of the Veda, branched out into many subschools. Of these, the non-dualism of Saṃkara, which argues for the falsehood of the world of plurality and the identity between the individual and the Absolute Self, is the most well-known.

Mīmāṃsā arose out of the systematic interpretation of apparently conflicting Vedic injunctions. In spite of its obsession with rituals and their karma-theoretic causal powers, Mīmāṃsā developed a sophisticated semantics for 'ought' sentences and a fine-grained taxonomy of hermeneutic devices. Mīmāṃsā authors like Kumarila

(AD 650) offered extremely sophisticated arguments to resist Buddhist anti-realism about the self, the external world, and universals.   A.C.

S. N. Dasgupta, *A History of Indian Philosophy*, i (Cambridge, 1957).
David Zilberman, *The Birth of Meaning in Hindu Thought* (Dordrecht, 1988).

Hintikka, Jaakko (1929–). A leading philosophical logician, Hintikka is known for his development of model set-theoretic *semantics for knowledge and belief. Subsequently Hintikka developed a semantics for perception with two sets of quantifiers, a standard pair which ranges over physically individuated objects, and a second pair which ranges over objects perceptually individuated over model sets (in effect, intensional objects). Later formulations of his epistemic and doxastic systems are similarly equipped with a second set of quantifiers. Through this work Hintikka was able to shed light upon what it means to know who someone is. His work also clarifies what it means to know that one knows. In addition, Hintikka has contributed to the history of philosophy with his original writings on Aristotle, Kant, and Wittgenstein.   G.F.M.

*Finnish philosophy.

J. Hintikka, *Knowledge and Belief* (Ithaca, NY, 1962).

Hippocrates (c.430 BC). A famous physician, head of a medical group or school at Cos. (To be distinguished from his contemporary Hippocrates of Chios, author of the first known geometry textbook.)

The name of Hippocrates became attached to a collection of medical writings (the Hippocratic corpus) of the fifth and fourth centuries BC, a few of which may in fact be by Hippocrates. The more theoretical works in this collection are connected with Ionian cosmology (*Pre-Socratics); some show traces of the philosophical thinking of Xenophanes, Heraclitus, the *Eleatics, or Protagoras; or of the argumentative techniques of the *Sophists. They are evidence for the history of philosophy but not themselves original philosophical works, apart perhaps from the essay entitled 'On Ancient Medicine'. This contains thoughts on the relation between theory and practice which were developed by Plato and influenced Aristotle's discussion of the 'mean' in action.   E.L.H.

G. E. R. Lloyd (ed.), *Hippocratic Writings* (London, 1978).

historical determinism: *see* determinism, historical.

historical materialism. The programme of historical research formulated in the writings of Karl Marx and Friedrich Engels. According to the materialist conception, the fundamental thing in human history is the productive powers of society and their tendency to grow. Productive powers at a given stage of development determine the nature of human labouring activity because labour consists in the exercise of precisely those powers. A given set of productive powers also thereby favours certain 'material relations of production', forms of human co-operation or division of labour which are not directly part of them, but facilitate their employment to a greater degree than rival forms would do. They thereby also favour certain 'social relations of production', systems of social roles relating to the control of the production process and the disposition of its fruits. It is this system of social relations of production which Marx calls the 'economic structure of society', which forms the 'real basis' of social life on the materialist theory, conditioning *'super-structures' such as the political state and the 'ideological' forms of consciousness found in religion, philosophy, morality, and art.

Within the framework of any system of social relations of production, society's productive powers expand at a greater or lesser rate, depending on the historical circumstances, including the social relations themselves. Eventually, however, a given set of social relations of production are outgrown or rendered obsolete by the productive powers. The prevailing relations either make it difficult to employ the existing powers or else fetter the further development of these powers. Powers and relations of production thus come into conflict or 'contradiction'; an 'epoch of social revolution' begins. The outcome of the conflict is the transformation of the relations of production to bring them into line with the productive powers so as to facilitate the further expansion of these powers. Changes in the superstructure of society, including its political and legal institutions, are to be explained by the required changes in the social relations of production. The mechanism by which these adjustments are to be carried out is the *class struggle. At a given stage of history, that class is victorious whose class interests consist in the establishment of that set of production relations which best suits the productive powers at that stage.

The materialist conception of history is a general programme of historical research, an explanatory sketch which is supposed to prove fruitful when applied not only to past changes but also to the historical future. Although Marx occasionally applies it to pre-modern societies, it was obviously suggested to him by the rise of capitalism; Marx envisions the overthrow of capitalism and the rise of socialism as following the same pattern of historical development.

In Marxian theory, historical materialism was closely associated with the thesis that the class rule of the bourgeoisie is incompatible with the continued growth of productive forces, and that capitalism is therefore doomed to be overthrown by the revolutionary proletariat. At the present time, when most people are apt to conclude that this has not happened and is not going to happen, it may be worth pointing out that while Marx may have associated historical materialism with his thesis about the inevitable overthrow of capitalism, the materialist theory of history is quite independent of that thesis, and what are in fact historical materialist explanations are sometimes invoked by people who do not consider themselves Marxists. For example, it is sometimes claimed that Leninist socialism in Eastern Europe survived as long as it did because a command system is compatible with an economy based on heavy industry but incompatible with one based on the high tech of the information age. Whatever may be said for or against such explanations, they should be easily recognized as based on the explanatory framework of Marx's historical materialism.   A.W.W.

*anti-communism; liberalism.

G. A. Cohen, *Karl Marx's Theory of History* (Princeton, NJ, 1978).
Jon Elster, *Making Sense of Marx* (Cambridge, 1985).
Daniel Little, *The Scientific Marx* (Minneapolis, 1986).
Allen Wood, *Karl Marx* (London, 1981).

historicism. A label which has been confusingly applied to distinguishable positions in *social philosophy. It was originally used to refer to a particular conception of the aims of history which emphasized the need to recognize the essential individuality of historical phenomena; these phenomena, being expressive of human thought and feeling, required for their proper understanding an empathetic grasp of the conditions that gave them life and meaning in a social context. A wider interpretation of the term, often held to have relativist implications, involves the claim that the nature of any phenomenon can only be adequately comprehended by considering its place within a process of historical development. Thirdly, it has been employed to designate doctrines which attribute to the social sciences the role of predicting future developments on the basis of discoverable laws of historical change.   P.L.G.

Friedrich Meinecke, *Historism: The Rise of a New Historical Outlook*, tr. J. E. Anderson, foreword by Isaiah Berlin (London, 1972).

histories of moral philosophy. Modern histories of Western moral philosophy generally share a familiar periodic structure: first, the inquiries of the major ancient Greek thinkers and schools and their later Roman followers, whose focus is upon the nature of the human good and the consequent relationships between virtue and knowledge and between virtue and pleasure; next, the writings of medieval Christian, Islamic, and Jewish philosophers, whose moral inquiries have a theological setting; then the moral philosophies of the Renaissance, in which a variety of Greek and scholastic themes are revived, followed by those of the eighteenth and nineteenth centuries, in which the epistemological preoccupations of moral rationalists and moral sense theorists are a prologue to the major constructions of the Utilitarians and of Kant; and finally the range of recent and contemporary standpoints. But what kind of attention is given to each, and how the relationships between them are envisaged, has varied first with whether and if so how far the history of moral philosophy has been embedded within some larger history, and what kind of history that is, secondly with the extent to which views of the present state of the argument in moral philosophy have dictated the perspective in which its history has been understood, and thirdly with how the task of the historian has been defined.

In the eighteenth and early nineteenth centuries episodes in the history of moral philosophy are sometimes treated not primarily in terms of this division into periods, but rather in terms dictated by some philosophical scheme informed by its author's own larger purpose. So it was with Vico, who understood his own account of the morality of natural law as a correction of the errors of his ancient and seventeenth-century predecessors, an achievement which would not have been possible before what he took to be the third and then present stage of a history, through which, on his view, all nations characteristically passed, the stage in which the authority of human reason temporarily displaced older allegiances first to divine authority and later to aristocratic, heroic authority. So too in many of the entries of the *Encyclopédie* of Diderot and d'Alembert a narrative of human *progress is presupposed in which various moral philosophers are taken to have succeeded or failed in so far as they contributed to the emergence of the true and rational account of morality now finally advanced in the *Encyclopédie* and to the defeat of a range of earlier theological superstitions. And so also at various points in the unfolding narrative of Hegel's *Phänomenologie des Geistes* what are recognizably portraits of particular moral philosophies, including *utilitarianism and *Kantianism, are presented under descriptions which represent them as partial and inadequate moments in the rational development of Spirit, a development of which Hegel's own philosophy is so far the most adequate rational articulation. Thus Vico, the Encyclopaedists, and Hegel each made the history of moral philosophy part of a larger philosophical history.

By contrast Adam Smith in part VII of *The Theory of the Moral Sentiments* wrote the history of moral philosophy as a distinct and independent form of inquiry. Having already advanced his own answers to what he had identified as the central questions of moral philosophy, Smith surveyed what he took to be the major systems of the past, testing his conclusions against those of their authors, and arguing that where theirs differ from his, there is good reason to think theirs erroneous. Plato, Aristotle, Stoics, Epicureans, and Eclectics are the ancient authors considered and criticized. Among the moderns most attention is paid to Mandeville and Hutcheson. Medieval moral philosophy merits only two passing references to 'the schoolmen'. As with Vico, the Encyclopaedists, and Hegel, it is the perspective afforded by Smith's own moral philosophy which dictates in key part his treatment of the past. So it was too with Carl Friedrich Staudlin, whose *Geschichte der Moralphilosophie* of 1821, the first history of moral philosophy as such, was written from his own Kantian standpoint.

In the nineteenth and twentieth centuries those who embed the history of moral philosophy or parts of it in some other, larger history include those who understand it as an integral part of the history of philosophy, such as Ueberweg and Windelband in nineteenth-century Germany, and Abbagnano in twentieth-century Italy, those who treat it as one aspect of the history of moral thought

and practice, such as Lecky and Westermarck, and those successors of Vico, the Encyclopaedists, and Hegel for whom it is some overall theory of human history which provides the categories in terms of which the history of moral philosophy is to be understood, the most distinguished of whom were Marx and Nietzsche. Sainte-Beuve as a literary historian contributed to the history of French moral philosophy in some of his essays and in his study of Port Royal. The history of specifically English moral philosophy was presented as an integral part of the history of English literature by such Cambridge teachers as Basil Willey in *The English Moralists* and Dorothea Krook in *Three Traditions of Moral Thought*. Of those who followed Smith in writing the history of moral philosophy as an independent inquiry the single most outstanding figure was Henry Sidgwick, but there were also important histories, of ancient moral philosophy by Jacques Francis Denis in nineteenth-century France, and of the whole history of Western ethics by James Martineau in nineteenth-century England and by Ottmar Dittrich in twentieth-century Germany. From the late nineteenth century onwards the history of moral philosophy has been hospitable to two distinct and contrasting genres: on the one hand large interpretative treatments in which the theses and arguments of particular moral philosophers are construed in terms of their place in some philosophical scheme of progress or regress or both, and on the other scholarly monographs establishing in historical detail what one or more particular moral philosophers said and meant. The ideal history of moral philosophy would therefore have been one which both exhibited the rational superiority of its narrative structure to that of all rival interpretation and also integrated into itself the findings of all the best scholarly monographs. All twentieth-century histories, including my own *A Short History of Ethics*, fall notably short of the standard set by this ideal, but they are to be measured by how far, if at all, they have had a higher degree of success than did Sidgwick's, whose *Outlines of the History of Ethics for English Readers* (1886) remains the major classic in this area of philosophical writing.

On Sidgwick's account ancient Greek ethics was distinctive in aiming at a knowledge of the human good, the achievement of which in a life ordered by reason both required virtue and served the interests of each individual. Christianity by contrast understood *morality as founded upon the knowledge of a divinely authorized code of law and emphasized practical beneficence by exalting love as the root of all the virtues. Medieval scholastic philosophers attempted the impossible task of synthesizing Christianity and Aristotle. Modern moral philosophy differs from its predecessors in two ways. After the Reformation reflective persons began to search for a method in ethics, acceptable independently of one's religious allegiance, appealing only to reason and to common moral experience. And in the early eighteenth century a number of philosophers, but especially Butler, recognized that, while ancient moral philosophers had taken reason to be our practical governing faculty, a reason which treats what is virtuous and what is to our interest as coincident, in fact there are in human beings two independent governing faculties, universal reason, which prescribes impartial benevolence, and egoistic reason, which prescribes the pursuit by each individual of what is to his or her interest. The subsequent history of modern moral philosophy records a number of failures to reconcile these two as well as the achievement of a better understanding of both.

Sidgwick's history is thus a prologue to his own statement of what he took to be the present condition of moral philosophy in *The Methods of Ethics* (1874). Sidgwick's philosophical and historical claims both stand in the sharpest contrast to the claims of Marx and Nietzsche, for both of whom not only the moral beliefs of the past, but also the philosophical theories which provided ostensible justification for those beliefs, were discredited by historical investigation. But on what such investigation has to teach us Marx and Nietzsche were of course at odds.

Marx assigned both past conceptions of what is right and good and past philosophical theorizing about the right and the good to the realm of ideology. Morality and moral philosophy are secondary phenomena, to be explained by class structure and class conflict. Engels in *Anti-Dühring* wrote a history of the idea of equality in what he took to be Marx's terms, showing how it was initially generated and then transformed by the changing relationships between social classes. Lukács, who imputed to Marx a more Hegelian view of things, suggested a more complex way of relating ideas to social and economic development. What *Marxism achieved for the history of moral philosophy was twofold. It made it evident that neglect of the relationships between philosophy and social structure will always be in danger of producing an idealized and distorted history. And it focused attention on the extent to which the history of moral philosophy is a history of conflicts.

Nietzsche's starting-point for his contrasting diagnosis of the failures of moral philosophy was his claim that the teachings of Socrates and Plato were a symptom of the decline of Greek culture. In *Zur Genealogie der Moral* (1887) and elsewhere Nietzsche attempted to explain morality itself as an unrecognized device of the cowardly herd, a self-crippling defence against those who are strong and self-assertive, whose protagonists portray as virtues qualities useful to the weak, while they denigrate the virtues of the strong. Moral philosophy from Socrates onwards is nothing but a series of apologetic rationalizations for morality, and is, like morality and religion, an unacknowledged expression of the will to power. Those modern philosophers who suppose themselves to be emancipated from religious morality are merely victims of a new set of delusions, among them not only those of the moral philosophies of Kant and the Utilitarians, but also belief in the ideal of objectivity prized by academic historians. Nietzsche's perspectivism is designed to undermine appeals to standards of impersonal truth both in understanding morality and in narrating its history.

The issues dividing Sidgwick from Marx and from Nietzsche are of course philosophical as well as historical.

Any attempt to judge which of them is in the right about the history of moral philosophy may be inescapably question-begging, since it seems that whatever methods of evaluation are employed will already presuppose prior commitment on just those philosophical issues on which they are divided. But at least we can inquire how far particular episodes in the history of moral philosophy can be illuminatingly described and explained in Nietzschean or post-Nietzschean terms. Parts of Michel Foucault's history of sexuality and some of the discussions of Greek philosophers in his last lecture series are exemplary post-Nietzschean treatments of the relationship between forms of power and types of moral theorizing. But they do not afford decisive grounds for accepting or rejecting the fundamental Nietzschean claims.

Against both Sidgwick and Nietzsche moral philosophers influenced by the Thomist revival of the late nineteenth and twentieth centuries, most notably Jacques Maritain, have proposed an interpretation of the history of moral philosophy according to which it is the moral philosophy of the high Middle Ages, especially that of Aquinas, which alone provides a standpoint from which ancient and modern moral philosophy can be adequately understood. Their defence of Aquinas's integration of Aristotelian virtue ethics with a biblical conception of a divine law apprehended by natural reason challenged Sidgwick's view of the relationship of ancient to medieval moral philosophy. Their account of the failures of modern moral philosophies to find a due place for both the right and the good is on some matters in agreement with Nietzsche's negative criticisms. But their Aristotelian rejection both of Nietzsche's perspectivism and of his psychology of the will to power puts them fundamentally at odds with Nietzsche. Once again philosophical disagreements are inseparable from disagreements over historical interpretation.

Recent work on the history of moral philosophy has raised more sharply than ever before the question whether it can be adequately narrated in independence of the history of philosophy in general and there is strong evidence to be cited on both sides of the question. T. H. Irwin in *Aristotle's First Principles* (Oxford, 1988) has presented an account of Aristotle's arguments and theses about the good, the virtues, and political association, according to which those arguments and theses are underpinned by and need to be made intelligible in terms of Aristotle's metaphysical and psychological conclusions. Annette Baier in *A Progress of Sentiments* (Cambridge, Mass., 1991) has interpreted the third book of Hume's *A Treatise of Human Nature* on his moral philosophy as related so intimately to the first two books on his epistemology and his philosophical psychology that it cannot be rightly understood in detachment from them. What work such as Irwin's and Baier's strongly suggests is that any attempt to abstract and isolate an account of the moral philosophy from an extended treatment of the larger philosophical intentions and commitments of the greatest moral philosophers is bound to distort and to falsify.

Yet at the same time there have been some equally remarkable achievements in constructing histories specifically devoted to moral philosophy. J. B. Schneewind provided what is for the foreseeable future a definitive account of nineteenth-century British moral philosophy in *Sidgwick's Ethics and Victorian Moral Philosophy*. And on a larger scale it has become clear that what no single author can any longer hope to achieve, because of the large body of scholarly material that needs to be mastered, may none the less be achieved by the co-operative work of a number of authors.

The most impressive co-operative work to date of this kind is the indispensable series of monographs included in the three-volume *Historia de la ética* edited by Victoria Camps. The first volume divides moral philosophy from the Homeric age to Machiavelli between eleven authors. The sixteen contributions to the second volume, including the editor's essay on Locke, and essays both on other individual thinkers and on movements of thought, is to end with Nietzsche. The third volume's fourteen essays on contemporary ethics (Barcelona, 1989) culminate in accounts of Habermas, Rawls, and socio-biology.

Much shorter, but an extraordinary achievement for its length, is *A History of Western Ethics*, edited by Lawrence C. Becker and Charlotte B. Becker (New York, 1992), in which thirteen authors survey the history of Western moral philosophy from the Pre-Socratics to the present. What these two collections jointly ensure is that the need for overall accounts of Western moral philosophy which meet the requisite scholarly standards but avoid any large interpretative commitments has been met for the time being. Indeed they prompt the question whether anything more ambitious is feasible. Is there indeed any possibility, on the basis provided by these and other scholarly monographs, of constructing some narrative of the history of Western moral philosophy, unified by some single, if complex, overall interpretation, superior to those already advanced by Sidgwick, by the Marxists, by Nietzsche's heirs, and by modern Thomists? Or do such books as those by Irwin and Baier warrant the conclusion that we ought not even to attempt to write the history of moral philosophy as a separate history? Should we write the history of moral philosophy only as one strand in the history of philosophy?

Some of the difficulties in answering these particular questions arise from our failure to provide satisfactory answers to another set of questions. Can we write the history of moral philosophy except in the context of writing the history of moral practice? Moral philosophy is after all in significant part theoretical reflection upon certain aspects of a variety of modes of social practice, and Marxists and others have made us aware that changes in those modes have at different times transformed the subject-matter upon which moral philosophers reflect. Moreover, in certain periods moral philosophies have been influential in changing the terms of moral debate and in providing new ways of understanding social practice. Abstract the theories of moral philosophers from the contexts of social practice in which they were at home and you distort the character of those theories. Omit from the histories of social practices those episodes of philosophical reflection in which morality was from time to time reconceived and you distort the history of those practices. But any extended history of moral theory which systematically understands it as embedded in moral practice has yet to be attempted.

There is another limitation on even the best work to date which it is crucial to note. Historians of Western moral philosophy very rarely exhibit any awareness of the history of moral thought in non-Western cultures, so depriving their own narratives of any comparative dimension, and so preventing us from understanding how the history of Western moral philosophy is to be viewed from various non-Western standpoints. Consider, for example, the rival Chinese moral traditions of *Buddhism, *Confucianism, and *Taoism, each with its own modes of philosophizing. In the debates between such traditions, as well as in the discussions internal to each of them, issues and problems instructively similar to those within Western moral philosophy, but with their own distinctive characteristics, continually recur. It is not that the history of these various traditions has yet to be written. Admirable studies by Chinese, Japanese, and Western scholars already exist. But Western comparative historical work remains rare. One seminal inquiry is Lee H. Yearley's *Mencius and Aquinas: Theories of Virtue and Conceptions of Courage* (Albany, NY, 1990). The need for more writing of the same kind about the history of a wide range of non-European moral philosophies is evident.   A.MᴀcI.

*Buddhist philosophy; moral philosophy, history of.

history, history of the philosophy of. Philosophy of history is generally understood as covering two distinct types of inquiry. The first of these—commonly referred to as 'speculative' or 'substantive' philosophy of history—is broadly taken to have as its subject-matter the actual human past, the latter being viewed from a universal or synoptic standpoint and studied with the aim of disclosing the overall workings and significance of the historical process considered as a whole. The second branch of inquiry—usually entitled 'critical' or 'analytical' philosophy of history—is primarily directed towards investigating the manner in which practising historians proceed in the course of eliciting and interpreting the particular events, developments, and so forth of which the human past is composed. Here the focus of attention is upon history regarded as a specific form of knowledge, the philosopher's concern being with such matters as the fundamental concepts or categories historical thinking involves and the presuppositions underlying the historian's cognitive claims and typical modes of inference. Philosophy of history in the speculative sense has enjoyed a long if somewhat variegated career. Critical philosophy of history, on the other hand, is of far more recent origin, only rising to prominence in the twentieth century. As will be seen, however, the two disciplines have not evolved altogether independently of one another, there being discernible points of connection as well as major differences between the two.

Speculative theories. The belief that the course followed by human history ultimately amounts to more than a purposeless sequence or fortuitous flux of happenings and that it should be possible to descry within it some overarching pattern or design which would endow it with a rationally or morally acceptable meaning is very old. So far as Western thought is concerned, a pre-eminent source of speculation along these lines lay in religious conceptions of the destiny of humanity and its place in a divinely governed universe. Thus early in the Christian era certain Church fathers were already to be found reacting against Graeco-Roman cyclical theories of historical development and seeking instead to portray it as conforming to a linear course that reflected the intentions of a supernatural providence. The most influential view of this kind was given sophisticated expression in the fifth century by St Augustine. Augustine's ideas, as presented in the *City of God* and elsewhere, diverged considerably from the cruder notions espoused by some of his predecessors; he drew a crucial distinction between sacred and secular history and displayed a cautious reticence regarding the feasibility of trying to interpret the details of the latter in a providential fashion. It cannot, however, be said that a comparable subtlety and reserve characterized the works of subsequent Christian theorists, who for more than a thousand years after he wrote still looked to him for inspiration in their approach to the past. This was particularly evident in the case of the seventeenth-century French historian and religious thinker J. B. Bossuet, who exhibited a striking confidence in the possibility of plumbing the designs of the 'everlasting mind' as these impinged upon human affairs. In his best-known book, the *Discourse on Universal History* (1681), Bossuet makes no attempt to disguise the theological concerns underlying his enterprise: the interpretation the author provides mirrors his conviction that the direction taken by the historical process was 'contrived by a higher wisdom' and that the fortunes of empires and creeds could be seen to manifest God's purposes in a manner that was as reassuring to the devout as it was—or at least should have been—disturbing to sceptics and infidels.

Although philosophical speculation about history may have been originally prompted and shaped by such preoccupations, this was no longer true of its development in the more secular climate of the eighteenth-century *Enlightenment. The shift in outlook largely derived from the momentous advances that had been achieved in the sphere of the physical sciences, above all from those associated with Newton. For it now appeared that, rather than through relying on the postulates of religious or metaphysical dogma, the search for a meaningful pattern or order in the historical sphere might be more effectively pursued by adopting empirically based methods of inquiry analogous to those that had proved so successful in the scientific investigation of nature. If natural phenomena had been thus shown to be subject to universal laws of immense scope and explanatory power, why should it not be accepted that similarly discoverable uniformities governed the realm of social and historical phenomena?

The project of utilizing past experience in order to construct a universally valid science of man and society found adherents amongst a number of the French *philosophes and was passionately endorsed by Condorcet in his *Sketch for a Historical Picture of the Progress of the Human Mind* (1795). Condorcet held that the principles of such a science would not only serve to explain the course history had so far followed; they would also provide the means of forecasting the outlines of future developments and of facilitating the promotion of social and cultural advances. In so connecting the predictive potential of a 'science of social phenomena' with practical ideals and long-term goals, Condorcet emerges as the forerunner of a line of nineteenth-century theorists who treated knowledge of the fundamental factors governing historical change as lending essential support to radical programmes of institutional reorganization and political or economic reform. Men like Henri de Saint Simon, Auguste Comte, and H. T. Buckle may have differed significantly in what they considered to be the prime determinants of historical progress. Nevertheless, they shared a common commitment to the existence of comprehensive laws, whose operation was invoked in both explanatory and predictive contexts and which tended to be regularly cited as bearing upon the feasibility of reformist policies and aims. Since no serious doubts were entertained regarding the desirability of the ends towards which history was ultimately leading, it seemed clear to such thinkers that the realization of these should be hastened rather than merely awaited, confidence in their eventual fulfilment in the future functioning as a spur to anticipatory exhortation and active planning in the present.

How far, though, was that confidence justified? Those who entertained it were for the most part content to argue that it was warranted on purely inductive grounds. There were contemporary critics, however, who remained unimpressed by current appeals to allegedly scientific modes of reasoning and who questioned both the formal status and the evidential backing of some of the so-called 'laws' to which reference was made; the latter appeared to savour more of what the Swiss historian Jakob Burckhardt termed an 'astrological impatience' to preempt the course of things to come than of an open-minded readiness to formulate and assess empirically testable hypotheses. Furthermore, behind such doubts there often lay a more general uncertainty concerning the theoretical adequacy of the scientific paradigm itself as an appropriate model for the interpretation of the historical process. From the circumstance that the apparently well-regulated realm of natural objects had proved amenable to a particular type of inquiry, it by no means automatically followed that the behaviour of people in societies was comprehensively intelligible along the same lines. On the contrary: the notion that such behaviour could be profitably studied or explained in terms of a methodology approximating that of the physical sciences remained a mere assumption which—at least to some critics—seemed a highly implausible one.

The assumption in question had in fact already been challenged in the previous century by two major speculative theorists who, occupying independent standpoints, shared the conviction that profound differences separate the cognitive resources available to us in our dealings with the world of physical nature from the forms of understanding that are appropriate to the sphere of human beings and their activities. Giambattista Vico's *Scienza nuova* (New Science, 3rd edn. 1744) was a strange and difficult work that attracted little notice on its initial appearance and certainly achieved no immediate recognition for its obscure Neapolitan author. In retrospect, however, it has come to be regarded as a product of genius, introducing conceptions of historical thought and knowledge that were of striking originality and prescience. At the centre of the book is the idea that human societies ('nations') pass through distinct stages of development, each of which manifests a particular type of mentality or outlook that pervades the various institutions, rituals, styles of art, etc. of the time. In the light of this it was a mistake to suppose that human nature and consciousness remained constant and uniform throughout the course of the past, and Vico repeatedly criticized contemporary writers for interpreting the actions or creations of previous generations in inapposite terms that derived from the cultural ethos of their own age. Instead of imposing such 'falsifying pseudo-myths' on what had been produced in other periods, the historian should seek to enter imaginatively into the different beliefs and attitudes that informed it. Vico laid special stress upon the various kinds of evidence—linguistic, archaeological, mythological—which could help him to do so. The task involved might require 'incredible effort' but even so it was in principle practicable. For, as Vico consistently maintained, in order truly to know something it was necessary to have made it. Unlike the world of natural objects, which 'since God made it, he alone knows', the 'world of nations' had been created by human beings and was therefore something they could 'hope to know' in a fashion other than, and superior to, any available mode of comprehending the workings of the material universe.

While there appears to have been no question of direct influence, some of Vico's cardinal themes re-emerged in the writings of the German philosopher J. G. Herder, and especially in the latter's massive panoramic survey of the past, *Ideas for the Philosophy of the History of Mankind* (1784–91). In common with his Italian predecessor, Herder laid stress upon the 'plasticity' of human nature. The human spirit did not conform to the tidy models or formulae within which scientifically minded theorists sought to contain it, but was on the contrary distinguished by the great diversity of forms it manifested in the context of different societies and cultures. Particular human undertakings and achievements must always be interpreted in relation to the cultural milieux to which they essentially belonged, not prized out of these and assessed from some generalizing or abstract standpoint that transcended the limits of time, place, and circumstance. And for Herder, as for Vico, this meant underlining the importance of imaginative understanding as representing an indispensable condition of historical knowledge. What was required was *Einfühlung*, a 'feeling into' the individual significance of actions, characters, periods, each being considered for itself 'without foisting any set pattern upon it'.

A comparable, and perhaps partly derivative, conviction that it was fundamentally misconceived to interpret the historical process in 'naturalistic' or putatively scientific terms underlay what amounted to the most complex and ambitious contribution to speculative philosophy of history in the nineteenth century. G. W. F. Hegel's aims in his famous *Lectures* (1837) on the subject may have been rivalled in scope by those of such near-contemporaries as Comte and Buckle; his own account, however, was rooted in a wholly different tradition of thought. For Hegel combined a rejection of uniformitarian views of human nature with an explicitly teleological approach to the past according to which this involved the unfolding in reality of a certain paramount conception or idea. Thus he maintained that history was essentially concerned with the development of what he termed 'spirit' (*Geist*); the essence of spirit—here contrasted with physical nature or 'matter'—was freedom, and the historical process should consequently be seen as comprising a stage-by-stage realization of that rational notion within a social setting. Hegel did not deny that the societies in which these stages were successively embodied displayed contrasting modes of life, the behaviour of their members being only fully intelligible in the light of whatever distinctive outlook prevailed at a particular epoch; in this sense what he wrote echoed the Herderian contention that human nature was subject to radical variations that set definite limits to the types of interpretation appropriate to distinguishable periods or cultures. He was insistent, on the other hand, that the variations in question occurred in a progressive temporal order; spirit was engaged in an 'ascent to an ever higher concept of itself', overcoming its previous manifestations in a continual process of self-transformation and self-transcendence. In practice this meant that historical advance did not take the form of a smooth or uninterrupted series of changes. Rather, Hegel pictures such transitions in dramatic terms, each new phase involving the 'negation' of a state of society which has lost its original historical role and contains the seeds of its own destruction. History, in other words, is a 'dialectical' process, its forward movement generated by the creative opposition of spiritual principles and its final outcome attributable to a rational purpose 'higher and broader' than any conceived by the innumerable human individuals whose multifarious aims and activities are none the less actually instrumental in bringing it about.

In view of the uncompromisingly anti-naturalistic tenor of Hegel's philosophy of history it may appear somewhat paradoxical that it should have exercised a decisive influence on Karl Marx, the scientific character of whose own theory of social development has been tirelessly emphasized by its proponents. Marx certainly repudiated the idealist or 'mystical' aspects of the Hegelian doctrine, substituting for it one in which the fundamental agents of change were not spiritual but material, the direction of history being ultimately governed by the evolving methods whereby men sought to exploit their natural environment in the course of satisfying their needs. The result was an account that stressed both the role in history played by conflicts between economically determined classes and the extent to which the shape taken by the ideological *'superstructure' of a society was causally dependent on the forces and relations of material production that lay at its foundation. Even so, Marx himself implied that if the basic priorities of Hegel's system were suitably transposed in the manner suggested, the latter's conception of history as proceeding dialectically towards the realization of a rationally ordered community could be seen to yield profound insights into its true meaning. From this point of view the complex origins of Marx's own historical theory may be said to have owed as much to aspects of German post-Kantian metaphysics as they did to the postulates and scientific aspirations of French and British radicalism.

Critical approaches. By contrast with its predecessor the twentieth century witnessed a significant reduction in the popularity and prestige of speculative philosophy of history. Admittedly, it saw the publication of two major contributions to the genre: Oswald Spengler's *The Decline of the West* (1918–22) and Arnold Toynbee's ten-volume comparative study of civilizations, *A Study of History* (1934–54). By the time these works appeared, however, the project of producing general theories which purported to transcend the perspective of ordinary historiography in the name of what Toynbee called 'a scientific approach to human affairs' had been subjected to a variety of wide-ranging critiques. As we have seen, opposition to such an approach had already found expression in the influential methodological contentions which earlier thinkers like Herder and Hegel had advanced within a predominantly speculative setting. But it was only towards the close of the nineteenth century that a systematic reappraisal was initiated by philosophers who were distrustful of the speculative enterprise in any of the protean forms it might assume and who felt that its extravagant ambitions should be eschewed in favour of undertaking a more narrowly focused examination of history's epistemological status. This seemed especially called for in view of the considerable strides historical scholarship and research had made in the previous decades. It was time for philosophy to come to terms with the apparent autonomy of history, investigating the conditions of its possibility and its claims to qualify as an accredited branch of inquiry or discipline.

Foremost amongst the writers who broached these issues were Heinrich Rickert and Wilhelm Dilthey in Germany and Benedetto Croce in Italy. All three underlined features of historical thinking which seemed to them to set it apart from that of natural science. Thus the historian, unlike the scientist, was not concerned with the discovery of laws or theories from which predictions could be derived, his attention being directed instead to delineating things and events in their unique and unrepeatable particularity. And this was connected with further points upon which both Dilthey and Croce laid great emphasis and which were taken up and eloquently developed by their British admirer R. G. Collingwood. Collingwood wrote approvingly of Dilthey's doctrine of *Verstehen* (hermeneutic understanding) and of Croce's characterization of historical thought as the recreation of past experience, going on to elaborate his own conception of what it involved in his posthumously published *The Idea of History* (1946). In that book he claimed that the historian's essential task was to 'rethink' or inwardly re-enact the deliberations of past agents, thereby rendering their behaviour intelligible in a fashion that had no counterpart in the sphere of scientific explanation. Understanding a given occurrence in history was not a matter of subsuming it beneath empirical laws or generalizations but of eliciting its 'inner side', this comprising (for example) considerations that showed what had been done to have constituted a rational, or at least motivationally comprehensible, response to a practical issue or dilemma.

The rapid growth of critical philosophy of history in the English-speaking world after the Second World War owed much to the stimulus provided by the work of these writers. This is not to say that their specific contentions met with general acceptance; a number of analytical philosophers objected to what they felt to be an inappropriately psychological construal of conceptual or epistemic questions, while others maintained that historical and social explanations ultimately conformed to the same logical model as those characteristic of other domains of empirical inquiry. None the less, the original claims made on behalf of the autonomy of the historical studies proved to be a fertile source of subsequent controversies, their traces still being discernible in the fundamental problems that continue to haunt the subject. P.L.G.

R. G. Collingwood, *The Idea of History* (Oxford, 1946).
—— *The Principles of History*, ed. W. H. Dray and W. J. van der Dussen (Oxford, 1999).
P. L. Gardiner (ed.), *Theories of History* (New York, 1959).
F. E. Manuel, *Shapes of Philosophical History* (London, 1965).
L. Pompa, *Human Nature and Historical Knowledge: Hume, Hegel and Vico* (Cambridge, 1990).
K. R. Popper, *The Poverty of Historicism* (London, 1957).
W. H. Walsh, *An Introduction to Philosophy of History* (London, 1951; 3rd rev. edn. 1967).
H. White, *Metahistory: The Historical Imagination in Nineteenth-Century Europe* (Baltimore, Md., 1973).

history, problems of the philosophy of. The distinction that has been drawn between speculative and critical approaches to the philosophy of history may be illustrated by considering the different sorts of problem to which they respectively give rise. Thus speculative theorists have sought to answer substantive questions dealing with such matters as the significance or possible purpose of the historical process and the factors fundamentally responsible for historical development and change. In doing so, they have been inspired by the conviction that history raises issues which transcend the mostly limited concerns of the ordinary working historian and which pertain to perennial demands for an intellectually or morally satisfying overall perspective on the human past. By contrast, the questions that preoccupy critically orientated thinkers are of a radically dissimilar type, these tending instead to be directed to such subjects as the nature of historical understanding, the possibility of objectivity in historical writing, and the kind of truth ascribable to historical interpretations or accounts. So conceived, the problems involved invite comparison with those investigated by contributors to other branches of contemporary philosophy—e.g. philosophy of science—in being essentially second-order ones that here have to do with the distinctive features of history as a particular discipline. It is accordingly to outstanding issues of the latter sort that this article is chiefly addressed. At the same time, however, we should remember that work in this domain has often been influenced—even if only indirectly—by developments in epistemological *hermeneutics that are more readily associated with continental writers than with analytical philosophers representative of the English-speaking world. It is therefore not surprising that tensions due to the impact of divergent traditions of thought should from time to time find expression in some of the discussions which problems in the critical philosophy of history have provoked.

Historical explanation. One topic which has proved to be a persistent source of argument and disagreement concerns the underlying character or structure of explanation in history. Amongst other things, this has thrown into relief the wide gulf separating those philosophers who regard a certain account of scientific *explanation as providing a paradigm to which all explanation should ideally conform and those who on the contrary maintain that the distinctive subject-matter of history is susceptible to, or even requires, a wholly different mode of understanding. We shall begin with the first.

In what has come to be known as the *'covering-law' model or 'deductive-nomological' account, it is implied that any acceptable explanation of events involves showing them to instantiate certain general laws or uniformities. More specifically, an occurrence can only be said to be adequately explained when it is shown to be deducible from premises consisting, on the one hand, of assertions descriptive of given initial or boundary conditions and, on the other, of statements expressive of empirically well-confirmed universal hypotheses. On such a view, the historian who offers a causal explanation of an event is seemingly committed thereby to accepting the existence

of whatever laws or regularities its validity presupposes; for, in the words of a prominent early proponent of the covering-law theory (Carl Hempel), 'to speak of empirical determination independently of any reference to general laws means to use a metaphor without cognitive content'. It might be objected that historical inquiry is primarily directed towards the particular and singular, not to the general or universal. But it is argued that this, though true, does not affect the present issue; the above-mentioned implicit commitment to generality is in no way incompatible with the claim that the historian is occupationally concerned with the detailed delineation and analysis of individual occurrences or states of affairs. It is not even incompatible with the contention that there are respects in which complex historical events may properly be termed 'unique'. All that is requisite for explanatory purposes is that the explananda should be classifiable with other events under *certain* aspects, namely, those relevant to the application of appropriate generalizations or laws to the particular cases in question.

Despite its attractions as apparently combining conceptual economy with a respect for the distinguishing character of the historian's interests and concerns, the covering-law model has encountered various criticisms, of which two may briefly be mentioned. The first relates to the nature of the 'general laws' allegedly presupposed in historical explanation. It has been argued that any attempt to specify them is apt to issue either in formulations too vague and porous to be of use in practice or else in ones so highly particularized as not to qualify as genuine statements of law at all; thus the model has been held at best to require major qualifications or amendments if it is to serve as a plausible representation of how historians actually proceed. Secondly, it has been urged that the proposed analysis fails to do justice to a crucial aspect of the historian's approach to his or her material. History has to do with the activities of human beings, and understanding the latter standardly involves notions like those of desire, belief, and purpose whose explanatory role cannot (it is claimed) be adequately comprehended within the framework of the covering-law theory. Hence it has been maintained by a number of philosophers, of whom William Dray has been one of the most influential, that an alternative model of 'rational explanation' often provides a better guide to the ways in which historians typically seek to render the past intelligible. The happenings of which they commonly treat comprise deliberate actions and their intended consequences, and satisfactorily accounting for these is a matter of reconstructing the reasons that made them appear appropriate or justified in the eyes of the agents concerned rather than of presenting them merely as occurrences that supposedly exemplify inductively attested uniformities. Such a rational model may be regarded as implicitly endorsing the 're-enactment' account of historical thinking propounded earlier by R. G. Collingwood, but without carrying the dubious epistemological implications for which theories embodying appeals to empathetic insight have sometimes been criticized. The question remains, on the other hand, whether it can be validly employed in a manner that altogether dispenses with underlying generalizations concerning the determinants of human behaviour—a question that impinges on some notoriously controversial issues in the philosophy of mind.

Whatever the merits or otherwise of the covering-law and rational models of explanation, it seems clear that neither can be said to do more than offer partial and highly schematic perspectives on a topic which can take a variety of diverse forms and which has tended to prove in consequence resistant to different attempts to encapsulate its essence in a tidy formula or unitary interpretative scheme. Thus explanations in history may range from being ones that purport to demonstrate the inevitability of a particular event to others that are confined to indicating how an unexpected occurrence was possible in a given set of circumstances, and from being ones that focus on the individual motivation attributable to certain historical figures to others whose chief concern is with the influence exerted by such impersonal factors as environmental conditions or advances in technology. Nor is it obvious that explaining something in a historical context is invariably a matter of showing it to be in some sense the causal outcome of other events or states of affairs. Descriptions of an occurrence as being of a certain kind (e.g. as constituting a revolution), or again as being symptomatic of a particular tendency or trend, may perceptibly increase or illuminate our understanding of what took place. They do not, however, appear to do so by providing anything straightforwardly analogous to a causal explanation, whether in the natural sciences or elsewhere.

Objectivity and valuation. What is often referred to as the problem of historical objectivity has been the source of further disputes about the status of history in relation to other branches of study or investigation. Admittedly, it has sometimes been argued that the question whether history is or can be objective is not one that can legitimately be raised in a general or unrestricted way: within the discipline itself there certainly exist accepted criteria according to which the objectivity or otherwise of particular historical accounts may be appraised and relevant comparisons or contrasts drawn; but seeking to identify and critically examine such internal standards is a very different matter from asking whether history as such constitutes an objective form of inquiry. Different it may be; nevertheless, this has not prevented philosophers and historians alike from giving serious consideration to the latter question or from seeing it as touching upon a number of complex and troublesome issues. The notion of objectivity is renowned for being a slippery one. What specific difficulties has it been thought to present here?

One point frequently stressed concerns the fact that history is necessarily selective; a historian whose account aimed to include every conceivable constituent of a particular stretch of the past would be comparable in some respects to Lewis Carroll's imaginary cartographer, whose

ideal map was one that exactly reproduced, both in scale and detail, the piece of country it was meant to chart. Instead it must be recognized that the employment of selective judgements of relevance, together with ones of comparative importance or interest, represents a central and ineliminable feature of historical procedure. And this is held to have significant implications. For such judgements can be said to presuppose a range of preconceptions and attitudes which are in principle contestable and which are liable to vary from person to person, culture to culture, period to period. Individual preferences or contemporary preoccupations, metaphysical or religious beliefs, moral or political convictions—these may all, if at times only unconsciously, influence such things as the presentation of historical findings, the choice of what to put in or omit, the relative weight assigned to different factors or causal conditions, and even the critical assessment of evidence and sources. In consequence, the conclusion has often been drawn that history is infected with a radical 'subjectivity' which casts doubt on its claims to be an indisputably factual discipline with impeccable cognitive credentials.

As with many arguments of a purportedly sceptical character, there is a danger in the present instance of various distinctions being blurred or overlooked. For example, it is an error to suppose that a historian's presentation of material and judgements of inclusion or exclusion must invariably be determined by allegedly subjective or arbitrary considerations. On the contrary, they may be dictated in a quite unexceptionable fashion by the specific nature and parameters of the particular problem that is under discussion. Again, it is one thing to say that a historian's own choice of subject is due to temperamental preference or to matters of current interest, but quite another to suggest that factors of the latter kind will necessarily affect the manner in which the topic is investigated or conclusions about it reached; nor, incidentally, does there seem to be any justification on this score for distinguishing history from other accredited types of inquiry where similar points apply. Furthermore, so far as criteria of historical importance are concerned, it may be contended that these are commonly susceptible to an interpretation involving what has been called 'causal fertility'. Thus the decision over whether some given occurrence was of greater importance than another event may be made on the strength of its having been causally productive of more far-reaching effects or more lasting repercussions. But it is arguable that questions of this type are purely empirical and as such responsive to impartial or detached investigation; they have nothing essentially to do with subjective beliefs or attitudes attributable to the historian and are answerable without any reference to those.

However, the concept of importance cannot invariably be interpreted along such narrowly causal or instrumental lines. It is also frequently used—in history as well as elsewhere—to characterize what is regarded as intrinsically significant or worthy of note on its own account. And it is far from clear that ascriptions of importance, so construed, can be treated as straightforwardly objective in the sense in which scientific statements are often assumed to merit this encomium. For they appear to reflect distinctively evaluative positions or points of view that may be allowed to exercise a definite, though by no means exclusive, influence on the ways in which historians sift and organize the material at their disposal. To maintain that history can to this extent be considered to have an irreducibly evaluative dimension is not, of course, equivalent to suggesting that it is subjective in the pejorative sense of implying personal idiosyncrasy or prejudice. Evaluative outlooks or standpoints can be widely shared and are capable of being understood in a fashion that permits of critical discussion and rational debate; moreover, the logical status of moral judgements in particular continues to be a matter of philosophical dispute. None the less, it cannot be denied that it is on the specific issue of the role and relevance of evaluative considerations that much of the argument about historical objectivity has in fact tended to turn. There are certainly modern historians and philosophers who have felt that moral judgement should be as far as possible excluded from history as strictly conceived, its being—in the words of one of the former—'alien' to history's 'intellectual realm', and similar views have been expressed on other aspects of value. But the problem has also met with quite different types of response, not least on the part of recent analytical writers who have argued that many of the fundamental terms and categories which the historical studies presuppose cannot be fully understood or properly applied without reference to the element of evaluation that pervades the sphere of human life and action. In the eyes of such objectors the conception of a wholly *wertfrei* history is at best unrealizable in practice and at worst perhaps incoherent in principle. Generally, however, they have not seen this as in any way committing them to the opinion that history is not a valid form of inquiry or that there is no such thing as historical truth; despite what has at times been supposed, a suitably circumspect appreciation of the role of value-judgement in historical thinking entails no consequences of a radically sceptical kind.

Narrative and interpretation. The same cannot be said of an aspect of historiography which has increasingly attracted the attention of philosophers and which has undoubtedly come to be viewed by some of them as having revisionary implications for the cognitive status of the subject. This concerns the nature and uses of narrative in the portrayal of the past. In opposition to certain accounts according to which story-telling essentially functions as little more than a convenient device for conveying or writing up the results of independent research, it has been contended that narrative in fact constitutes an autonomous mode of understanding which is distinctive of historical thought. Amongst other things, it involves apprehending historical occurrences in what has been termed a 'synoptic' or 'configurational' fashion that makes it possible to see them as forming part of an intelligible pattern and as contributing to an interrelated whole. When regarded in this light narrative can be said to transcend the presentation of a merely chronological sequence of events; at the same time the kind of interpretation it provides is more comprehensive than what is usually understood by explanation in history, although it may be allowed to overlap with the latter in some of its forms.

Philosophers who have addressed themselves to this topic have often shown insight and subtlety, both in articulating and illustrating the crucial part played in narrative by factors like coherence and followability and in drawing interesting parallels between its uses in history and literature. In invoking such parallels they have been especially concerned to emphasize the role of imagination in historical writing and the extent to which the *stories historians tell are actively constructed rather than 'read off' from the factual or evidential data in a passive or uncritical manner; they should not be thought of as retailing a set of happenings already neatly organized and waiting to be reproduced in linguistic form. But whatever the force of such contentions, it is another thing to suggest—as is sometimes done—that narratives in history must be conceived as artificially 'imposed' or freely 'projected' upon a past which itself lacks a discoverable narrative structure and which may be 'emplotted' (to use a favoured term) in any one of a number of different ways. While it may be salutary to challenge a naïvely mimetic view of their character, it does not follow that historical narratives are not answerable to criteria of truth in a fashion which sharply distinguishes them from works of literary fiction and which practising historians regard as setting recognizable limits to their acceptability. Hence, despite the contributions that writers like Louis Mink and Hayden White have made towards enlarging philosophical perspectives on the place of narrative in history, it is hardly surprising that the strain of epistemological scepticism running through much of their work has provoked lively criticism and is the subject of continuing controversy. Here, as elsewhere in the rich field of philosophy of history, may be found a host of contentious issues with roots often stretching out into adjoining areas of thought and inquiry: it has been possible in this article to touch on only a representative selection of these.   P.L.G.

*historicism.

R. F. Atkinson, *Knowledge and Explanation in History* (London, 1978).

A. C. Danto, *Analytical Philosophy of History* (Cambridge, 1965).

W. H. Dray, *On History and Philosophers of History* (Leiden, 1989).

—— *History as Re-enactment* (Oxford, 1996).

P. L. Gardiner (ed.), *The Philosophy of History* (Oxford, 1974).

L. J. Goldstein, *Historical Knowing* (Austin, Tex., 1976).

M. Mandelbaum, *The Problem of Historical Knowledge* (New York, 1938).

L. Pompa and W. H. Dray (eds.), *Substance and Form in History* (Edinburgh, 1981).

Hobbes, Thomas (1588–1679). Generally regarded as the founder of English moral and political philosophy. He wrote several versions of his moral and political theory, but although he improved many important details, the overall theory remains the same. *Leviathan* (English edition 1651, Latin edition 1668) is generally considered to be his masterpiece, but *De Cive* (1642, new notes and a new preface to the reader added in 1647, English translation 1651) may be the most careful presentation of his moral and political theory. In so far as Hobbes expresses the same view in both *De Cive* and *Leviathan*, this view should be taken as his considered position. *De Cive* was part of a philosophical trilogy in Latin: *De Corpore* (1655), *De Homine* (1658), and *De Cive*. *De Cive*, which was concerned with 'the rights of dominion and the obedience due from subjects', was supposed to be the final book of the trilogy, but Hobbes published it first, saying that the approaching Civil War 'plucked from me this third part'.

Hobbes wrote on a wide variety of philosophical topics: aesthetics, free will and determinism, epistemology, human nature, law, logic, language, and metaphysics, as well as moral and political theory. He also wrote on optics, science, and religion, and is considered by some to be a founder of modern biblical interpretation. He also published translations of Thucydides (1628) and Homer (1674–6) and authored a somewhat biased history of the period of the Civil War. He entered into some unfortunate mathematical controversies by claiming that he had squared the circle. He was a secretary to Francis Bacon, visited Galileo, and engaged in disputes with Descartes.

Hobbes claims that he was born prematurely (5 April 1588) because of his mother's fright over the coming of the Spanish Armada. He seems to have been proud of being fearful, proclaiming that he was the first of all who fled the Civil War; and he did leave England for France in 1640 and remained in Paris for eleven years. However, his writings are very bold. He published views that he knew would be strongly disliked by both parties to the English Civil War. He supported the king over Parliament, which earned him the enmity of those supporting Parliament, but he not only denied the divine right of the king, he said that democracy was an equally legitimate form of government, which earned him the enmity of many royalists, though not of the king. He also put forward views concerning God and religion that he knew would cause those who held traditional religious views to regard him as dangerous. The Roman Catholic Church put his books on the Index, and Oxford University dismissed faculty for being Hobbists. Some people recommended burning not only his books but Hobbes himself. Although he had gained great fame on the continent as well as in England, he remained a controversial person even after his death on 4 December 1679 at the age of 91.

Hobbes not only wanted to discover the truth, he wanted to persuade others that he had discovered it. He believed that if his discoveries were universally accepted, there would be no more civil wars and people would live together in peace and harmony. After praising the work of the geometricians, he says:

If the moral philosophers had as happily discharged their duty, I know not what could have been added by human industry to the completion of that happiness, which is consistent with human life. For were the nature of human actions as distinctly known as the nature of *quantity* in geometrical figures, the strength of *avarice* and *ambition*, which is sustained by the erroneous opinions of the vulgar as touching the nature of *right* and *wrong*, would presently faint and languish; and mankind should enjoy such an immortal peace, that unless it were for habitation, on supposition that the earth should grow too narrow for her inhabitants, there would hardly be left any pretence for war.

Although Hobbes knew that it was extremely unlikely that his moral and political discoveries would be accepted by any significant number of people, let alone universally accepted, he continued to improve his moral and political theory and to present it more forcefully. His interest in other philosophical topics was also practical, although not always quite so directly. He used his philosophical views to argue against and discredit standard religious views. For Hobbes it was a practical necessity to discredit those religious views that were incompatible with his moral and political philosophy. Failure to appreciate how important Hobbes thought it was to make religion compatible with civil peace would make it unintelligible that he explicitly devotes about a third of *De Cive* and about a half of *Leviathan* to the interpretation of Christian scriptures. He knew that belief in some form or another of Christianity was going to be a dominant factor in the political life of England (and of the other European countries). Thus he attempted to provide an interpretation of Christianity that removed it as a threat to civil peace.

Although Hobbes's major interest is in moral and political theory, he is a systematic thinker, and his views about language, reasoning, and science had a significant impact on the presentation of his moral and political theory. His epistemological and metaphysical views were less developed, and he used them primarily as a foundation for his anti-religious views. Although Hobbes explicitly claims to be a materialist, he vacillates between epiphenomenalism and what would now be called 'reductive materialism'. After defining the theoretical concept of endeavour as the invisible beginnings of voluntary motion, he uses endeavour to define the more common psychological terms that are part of his analyses of particular passions. 'This endeavour, when it is toward something that causes it, is called APPETITE or DESIRE ... And when the endeavour is fromward something, it is generally called AVERSION.' He sometimes regards pleasure and pain as epiphenomena, i.e. as appearances of the motions of desire and aversion; but in other places he puts forward a reductive materialist account of pleasure and pain, i.e. pleasure simply is a desire for what one already has. On this account, to take pleasure in something is to desire for it to continue.

All that Hobbes wanted to show was that there is a plausible materialist explanation of all the features of human psychology, e.g. sense, imagination, dreams, appetites, and aversions, in terms of the motions in the body. He did not claim to show how the motions of sense and imagination actually interact with the vital motion, e.g. breathing and blood flow. He simply uses the concept of endeavour to show that his philosophy of motion is compatible with an ordinary understanding of psychological concepts.

Once Hobbes has the concepts of appetite and aversion, pleasure and pain, his account of the individual passions completely ignores the relation between human psychology and his materialist philosophy. He simply proceeds by way of introspection and experience, along with liberal borrowings from Aristotle's account of the passions. Hobbes explicitly maintains that introspection and experience, not a materialist philosophy, provide the key to understanding human psychology. In the introduction to *Leviathan,* he says, 'whosoever looketh into himself, and considereth what he doth, when he does *think, opine, reason, hope, fear,* &c. and upon what grounds, he shall thereby read and know, what are the thoughts and passions of all other men upon the like occasions.' He closes his introduction with the claim that he has provided an account of mankind, and that all that anyone else has to do is 'to consider, if he also find not the same in himself. For this kind of doctrine admitteth no other demonstration.'

Just as Hobbes finds no incompatibility between materialism and human psychology, so he finds no incompatibility between determinism (or God's omniscience and omnipotence) and human freedom. On his view, all that is required for a person to be free is that his action proceeds from his will. Since Hobbes defines the 'will' as 'the last appetite (either of doing or omitting), the one that leads immediately to action or omission', all that is necessary for a person to be free is that he act as he wants. This kind of freedom is compatible with both materialistic determinism and God's omnipotence and omniscience. However, at least since Freud, doing what one wants has not been taken by many philosophers as sufficient for free will. Unlike Hobbes, they do not take free will to mean 'the liberty of the man [to do] what he has the will, desire, or inclination to do'. Rather, they take free will to refer to some power within the person with regard to his desires, e.g. the ability to change one's desires in response to changes in the circumstances. Hobbes thought that people did have that power, which he called reason, and although he does not explicitly relate reason to free will, he may be regarded as the forerunner of contemporary compatibilist views that do so.

Hobbes has a somewhat pessimistic view of human nature, but he did not hold the view that the only motive for human action was self-interest, a view known as 'psychological egoism'. He did hold that children are born concerned only with themselves, but he thought that with appropriate education and training they might come to be concerned with others and with acting in a morally acceptable way. He thought that, unfortunately, most children are not provided with such training. He holds that most people care primarily for themselves and their families, and that very few are strongly motivated by a more general concern for other people. He does not deny

that some people are concerned with others, and in *Leviathan* he includes in his list of the passions the following definitions: '*Desire* of good to another, BENEVOLENCE, GOOD WILL, CHARITY. If to man generally, GOOD NATURE' and '*Love* of persons for society, KINDNESS.' But he does not think that such passions are widespread enough to count on them when constructing a civil society.

Given Hobbes's definition of the will as the appetite that leads to action, it follows that we always act on our desires. Since Hobbes further holds that 'The common name for all things that are desired, in so far as they are desired, is good', it follows that every man seeks what is good to him. This view, which might be called 'tautological egoism', does not provide any limits on the motives of human action. However, it has been confused with psychological egoism, and this confusion has resulted in the claim that Hobbes holds that no one is ever benevolent or desires to act justly. The definitions quoted in the previous paragraph show that Hobbes acknowledges the existence of benevolence and kindness. Similarly, he does not deny that a few are strongly motivated by a desire to act justly. This is shown by the following definitions that he offers: e.g. a just person is one who is 'delighted in just dealings', studies 'how to do righteousness', and endeavours 'in all things to do that which is just'. He also acknowledges that we can be strongly affected by injustice or injury, as is shown by his definition of INDIGNATION as 'Anger for great hurt done to another, when we consider the same to be done by injury'.

Since Hobbes claims that false moral views were one of the main causes of the Civil War, it would be absurd for him to deny that people are motivated by their moral views. As the quote comparing geometers to moral philosophers shows, he thought that the correct account of morality could have significant practical benefits. Further, Hobbes grounds the citizens' obligation to obey the law on their promise of obedience. He explicitly says that a person 'is obliged by his contracts, that is, that he ought to perform for his promise sake'. This is not a claim that would be made by someone who did not think that people were ever motivated by moral concerns. Finally, Hobbes knew that the danger to the stability of the state did not arise from the self-interest of each of its ordinary citizens, but rather from the self-interest of a few powerful persons, who would exploit false moral views. He regarded it as one of the most important duties of the sovereign to combat these false views, and to put forward true views about morality.

Hobbes's account of the relationship between *reason and the *passions is more complex and subtle than it is usually taken to be. Not only is reason not the slave of the passions, as Hume maintains, but the passions do not necessarily oppose reason, as Kant seems to hold. Rather, reason has lifelong, long-term goals, viz. the avoidance of avoidable death, pain, and disability, whereas some passions lead people to act in ways that conflict with reason obtaining its goals, while other passions lead people to act in ways that support the goals of reason. Reason differs from the passions in that its goals are the same for all, whereas the objects of the passions differ from person to person. Reason also differs from the passions in that, since it is concerned with lifelong, long-term goals, it considers not merely immediate consequences but also the long-term consequences of an action. It is also concerned with determining the most effective means of obtaining these goals. By contrast, the passions react to the immediate desirable consequences, without considering the long-term undesirable consequences.

Hobbes's account of rationality and the emotions is a fairly accurate account of the ordinary view. We hold that though people have different passions, rationality is the same in all. Many of us also acknowledge, with Hobbes, that in a conflict between reason and passion, people ought to follow reason, but we realize that they often follow their passions; e.g. many people act on their passions when doing so threatens their life, and this is acting irrationally. That Hobbes's account of reason is so different from the current philosophically dominant Humean view of reason as purely instrumental may explain why it has been so widely misinterpreted.

Hobbes's views about the universality of reason make it possible for him to formulate general rules of reason, the Laws of Nature, that apply to all people. Throughout all of his works Hobbes is completely consistent on the point that the Laws of Nature are the dictates of reason and that, as such, they are concerned with self-preservation. But the dictates of reason that Hobbes discusses as the Laws of Nature are not concerned with the preservation of particular persons, but, as Hobbes puts it, with 'the conservation of men in multitudes'. These are the dictates of reason that concern the threats to life and limb that come from war and civil discord. The goal of these dictates is peace. It is these Laws of Nature that, Hobbes holds, provide an objective basis for morality. 'Reason declaring peace to be good, it follows by the same reason, that all the necessary means to peace be good also; and therefore that modesty, equity, trust, humanity, mercy (which we have demonstrated to be necessary to peace), are good manners or habits, that is, virtues.' Hobbes, following Aristotle, considers morality as applying primarily to manners or traits of character. He regards courage, prudence, and temperance as personal virtues, because they lead to the preservation of the individual person who has them, but he distinguishes them from the moral virtues, which by leading to peace, lead to the preservation of everyone. His account of reason as having the goal of self-preservation provides a justification of both the personal and the moral virtues. The personal virtues directly aid individual self-preservation, and the moral virtues are necessary means to peace and a stable society that are essential for lasting preservation for all. This simple and elegant attempt to reconcile rational self-interest and morality is as successful as it is because of the limited view Hobbes takes of the goal of reason. It may be controversial to maintain that it is always in one's self-interest, widely conceived, to have all of the moral virtues. It is extremely plausible to maintain this, when the goal of reason is limited to self-preservation.

The importance of reason for Hobbes can be seen from the fact that both the Laws of Nature and the Right of Nature are derived from reason. In the State of Nature reason dictates to everyone that they seek peace when they can do so safely, which yields the Laws of Nature; but when they believe themselves to be in danger, even in the distant future, reason allows them to use any means they see fit to best achieve lasting preservation, which yields the Right of Nature. But if each person retains the Right of Nature, the result would be what Hobbes calls the State of Nature, in which the life of man is 'solitary, poor, nasty, brutish, and short'. In order to gain lasting preservation, the goal of reason, people must create a stable society; and this requires them to give up their Right of Nature. This only means giving up the right to decide what is best for your own long-term preservation; it does not mean giving up your right to respond to what is immediately threatening. It would be irrational for a person not to respond to an immediate threat. If he seems to give up the right to respond to such threats, that indicates that either he does not mean what he seems to mean, or that he is irrational and hence not competent to engage in any kind of transfer of rights. That is why Hobbes regards self-defence as an inalienable right; nothing counts as giving it up.

Hobbes provides a powerful argument to show that giving up your right to decide what is best for your long term preservation, and letting that be decided by a designated person or group of persons, called a sovereign, is actually the best way to guarantee your long term preservation, provided that other people also give up their Right of Nature to the sovereign. Since the sovereign makes the laws, this powerful but paradoxical-sounding argument is equivalent to an argument for obeying the law as long as it is generally obeyed; failing to obey the law increases the chances of unrest and civil war, and hence goes against the dictate of reason which commands people to seek self-preservation though peace. By allowing for the exception of self-defence, Hobbes has a strong case for saying that reason always supports obeying the civil law.

Although Hobbes is called a *social contract theorist, he regards the foundation of the state, not as a mutual contract or covenant, but as what he calls a free gift. This free gift may be viewed as the result of people contracting among themselves to make a free gift of their Right of Nature to some sovereign because of their fear of living with each other without a sovereign, i.e. in the State of Nature. However, Hobbes thought that states were naturally formed when people, because of their fear of a person or group who had the power to kill them, made a free gift of their Right of Nature directly to that sovereign. Giving up their Right of Nature to the sovereign was necessary to avoid being killed immediately. In whatever way a state is formed, the subject does not contract with the sovereign, but rather makes a free gift of obedience in the hope of living longer and in greater security.

Making a free gift of one's right to the sovereign obliges the subject to obey the sovereign. It is unjust if he disobeys, for injustice is doing what a person has given up the right to do. Since the sovereign has not conveyed any right to the subjects, he cannot be unjust; however, in accepting the free gift of the subject, he comes under the law of nature prohibiting ingratitude. Thus, he is required to act so 'that the giver shall have no just occasion to repent him of his gift', which is why Hobbes says, 'Now all the duties of the rulers are contained in this one sentence, the safety of the people is the supreme law.' This explains why Hobbes lists the Law of Nature requiring gratitude immediately after the Laws of Nature concerning justice. The former applies to the citizens, the latter to the sovereign.

It is important for Hobbes to show that the sovereign cannot commit injustice, because he regards injustice as the only kind of immorality that can be legitimately punished. He never claims that the sovereign cannot be immoral or that there cannot be immoral or bad laws. However, if immoral behaviour by sovereigns were unjust, any immoral act by the sovereign would serve as a pretext for punishing the sovereign, that is, for civil war. It is to avoid this possibility that Hobbes argues that the sovereign can never be unjust and that there can be no unjust laws. What is moral and immoral is determined by what leads to lasting peace or is contrary to it; what is just and unjust is determined by the laws of the state. Morality exists, even in the State of Nature; justice does not. It is immoral to claim that the sovereign can act unjustly, for to claim this is contrary to the stability of the state and hence incompatible with a lasting peace.

Hobbes took religion very seriously. He believed that if one were forced to choose between what God commands and what the sovereign commands, most people would follow God. Thus, he spends much effort trying to show that Scripture supports his moral and political views. He also tries hard to discredit those religious views that can lead to disobeying the law. Hobbes, like Aquinas, held that God was completely unknowable by human beings. He holds that all rational persons, including atheists and deists, are subject to the laws of nature and to the laws of the civil state, but he explicitly denies that atheists and deists are subject to the commands of God. For Hobbes, reason by itself provides a guide to conduct to be followed by all people, so that even if he regarded God as the source of reason, God plays no independent role in his moral and political theory.

For Hobbes, moral and political philosophy were not merely academic exercises; he believed that they could be of tremendous practical importance. He held that 'questions concerning the rights of dominion, and the obedience due from subjects [were] the true forerunners of an approaching war'. And he explains his writing of De Cive prior to the works that should have preceded it as an attempt to forestall that war. Hobbes's moral and political philosophy is informed by a purpose, the attainment of peace and the avoidance of war, especially civil war. When he errs, it is generally in his attempt to state the cause of peace in the strongest possible form. In this day of nuclear weapons, when whole nations can be destroyed almost as easily as a single person in Hobbes's day, we would do well to pay increased attention to the philosopher for whom the attaining of peace was the primary goal of moral and political philosophy.   B.G.

*Materialism.

D. Boonin-Vail, *Thomas Hobbes and the Science of Moral Virtue* (Cambridge, 1994).
B. Gert (ed.), *Man and Citizen* by Thomas Hobbes (Indianapolis, 1991).
J. Hampton, *Hobbes and the Social Contract Tradition* (Cambridge, 1986).
G. S. Kavka, *Hobbesian Moral and Political Theory* (Princeton, NJ, 1986).
S. A. Lloyd, *Ideals as Interests in Hobbes's Leviathan* (Cambridge, 1992).
N. Malcolm, *Aspects of Hobbes* (Oxford, 2003).
T. Sorell (ed.), *The Cambridge Companion to Hobbes* (Cambridge, 1996).
L. Strauss, *The Political Philosophy of Hobbes* (Oxford, 1936).

Hobhouse, Leonard Trelawney (1864–1929). English social philosopher, sociologist, and political journalist. Hobhouse began his career as a Philosophy Fellow of Corpus Christi College, Oxford. The prevailing outlook in Oxford of British *idealism was uncongenial to him (although his writings on social philosophy reveal its influence), and he joined the staff of the *Manchester Guardian* in 1897. His many newspaper articles express an outlook which might be described as 'liberal or democratic socialist'. For the contemporary philosopher he is instructive for the manner in which he combined interests in animal psychology, sociology, ethics, social philosophy, logic, epistemology, and metaphysics without drawing the contentious demarcation lines between empirical, conceptual, and normative studies which have impoverished philosophy this century. His major contribution to sociology and *social philosophy is in *Principles of Sociology* (1921–4), and the fullest exposition of his philosophical outlook is in *Development and Purpose* (2nd edn. 1927).
                                                            R.S.D.
*liberalism.

Hocking, William Ernest (1873–1966). American idealist at Harvard University who continued the work of his teacher Royce in revising *idealism to incorporate insights of *empiricism, *naturalism, and *pragmatism. Metaphysics must, he held, make inductions from experience. In his 'negative pragmatism', 'That which does not work is not true'. For example, he enjoined us to 'try to get along without God and see what happens', and concluded that we cannot do without God as our associate in facing evil. Liberalism must be superseded by a new form of individualism in which the principle of the state is: 'every man shall be a whole man.' There is only one natural right, the right that 'an individual should develop the powers that are in him'. Consequently, the 'most important freedom' is 'the freedom to perfect one's freedom'. Hocking extensively applied his principles to international problems. Christianity, he urged, should be reconceived to become a powerful agent in the making of world civilization.   P.H.H.

Leroy S. Rouner, *Within Human Experience: The Philosophy of William Ernest Hocking* (Cambridge, 1969).

Hodgson, Shadworth Holloway (1832–1912). British epistemologist and metaphysician who anticipated and/or influenced *phenomenology, *pragmatism, and *process philosophy. He was the founding President of the now well-known Aristotelian Society but taught at no university. His doctrine that things are what they are 'known as' influenced James's radical empiricism and anticipated Husserl's phenomenological reduction. His insistence that the test of truth 'depends upon the future' foreshadowed later forms of empiricism, especially pragmatism. He attached much importance to the relationship between empirical distinguishability and inseparability, a doctrine akin to Husserl's reduction to essences. Before James or Bergson, Hodgson developed a temporalist theory of consciousness as a stream or field, and broadly anticipated process philosophy by treating 'process-contents' as basic to the analysis of experience.   P.H.H.

Andrew J. Reck, 'Hodgson's Metaphysic of Experience', in John Sallis (ed.), *Philosophy and Archaic Experience* (Pittsburgh, 1982).

Høffding, Harald (1843–1931). Danish philosopher who, having first obtained a degree in divinity, was caused by the study of Kierkegaard to break with Christianity. Høffding's positivist and non-metaphysical *Outline of Psychology* (1882; Eng. edn. 1893) and his *History of Modern Philosophy* (1894–5; Eng. edn. 1900) were widely read. In the latter he anticipated Cassirer by stressing the importance of mathematics and the natural sciences for the development of philosophy.

In Høffding's epistemology the fundamental category is that of synthesis, which he considered to be a psychological concept. According to Høffding, synthesis is an act of consciousness studied empirically by psychology, in direct opposition to Kant's critical philosophy in which synthesis is conceived as an epistemological condition for the possibility of human knowledge. Høffding argued in *Den menneskelige Tanke* (Human Thought, 1910 (German and French edns. 1911)) in favour of a theory of *categories in which, in contradistinction to Kant, he maintained that the categories change as human knowledge increases. This implies that it is impossible to provide absolute proofs of their validity. Høffding did not in general differentiate between philosophy and psychology, and his epistemology is in this respect psychologistic.   C.H.K.

F. Brandt, 'Harald Høffding', in P. Edwards (ed.), *The Encyclopedia of Philosophy* (1967), iv.

Holbach, Paul-Henri Thiry, Baron d' (1723–89). A leading Encyclopedist, Holbach was the author of the *Système de la nature* (1770), a systematic defence of an atheistic *materialism. According to Holbach, the universe is a deterministic system, consisting of an eternal and constant totality of matter and motion. Man is an organic machine whose mental life, including the higher faculties, consists in sensation in various forms. The goal of any individual's life is to promote his happiness which, in society, will require the co-operation of others. Ethics is the science of how, through social co-operation, to promote the well-being of the individual. Holbach argued that the function of government is to foster social co-operation, its legitimacy depending on the happiness of its subjects. Holbach opposed absolute monarchy, hereditary privilege, and Christianity as obstacles to happiness.   T.P.

*determinism.

P.-H. d'Holbach, *The System of Nature* (New York, 1970).

holism. Any view according to which properties of individual elements in a complex are taken to be determined by relations they bear to other elements. Holism is less a doctrine than a class of doctrines. One can be a holist about *meaning (the meaning of a sentence turns on its relations to other sentences in the language), without being a holist about justification (a belief's warrant depends on relations it bears to an agent's other beliefs). A holist about theory confirmation (empirical claims face experience, not individually, but all together) need not be a holist about *belief (the content of a belief is fixed by its relations to an agent's other beliefs). It must be admitted, however, that holism tends to induce a frame of mind that finds holistic phenomena widespread.

In this century holism has been particularly associated with the biological and social sciences, and with conceptions of mind and language. Biological holists (e.g. C. Lloyd Morgan) oppose 'mechanists', those who hold biological phenomena to be explicable ultimately in terms of properties of their inorganic constituents. In the social sciences, 'methodological holists' (e.g. Ernest Gellner) deny the contention of 'individualists' that social phenomena are reducible to psychological characteristics of individual agents. In each case, the question is whether 'emergent' properties of a whole can affect the behaviour of its individual constituents in ways that cannot be accounted for solely by reference to properties those constituents possess independently of their membership in the whole.

It is easy to make holism appear trivial. Any collection of individuals exhibits properties its constituents lack. A group of three pebbles could constitute a triangle, though none of the pebbles is triangular. If my attention is attracted by triangles, then the whole has a causal property, the power to attract my attention, not reducible to properties of individuals making it up. An appropriate holist response might focus on particular cases, the putatively holistic character of linguistic meaning, for instance. The meaning of a sentence, it has been argued (e.g. by W. V. Quine and Donald Davidson), depends on its relations with other sentences in a language; thus, understanding a sentence involves understanding a language—

either the language in which the sentence is expressed or one into which it is translatable.

In an attempt to clarify holism about meaning, Jerry Fodor and Ernest Lepore appeal to 'anatomic properties', those possessed by a thing only if they are possessed by at least one other thing. Holistic properties are 'very anatomic', they are 'such that, if anything has them, then lots of other things must have them'. This characterization has the virtue of making more precise something notoriously difficult to make precise, though it is not obvious that it captures what holists have in mind. It is consistent with holism that there be a language, L, with 'very few' sentences. What is crucial, so far as holism is concerned, is that the meanings of these sentences depend on their place in L.

The example brings out an apparently remarkable consequence of holism, however. An element in a holistic system cannot exist apart from that system. Thus, no sentence of L is translatable into English, because no sentence of L bears relations to other sentences of L comparable to those any English sentence bears to every other English sentence. Although it is open to holists to appeal to some principle restricting the scope of the holistic requirement, it is not easy to see how such a restriction could be motivated without tacitly abandoning holism. A further question is whether 'molecular' or 'atomistic' alternatives to holism fare better.   J.HEIL

*methodological holism.

J. Fodor and E. Lepore, *Holism: A Shopper's Guide* (Oxford, 1992).
M. Mandlebaum, 'Societal Laws', *British Journal for the Philosophy of Science* (1957).
C. L. Morgan, *Emergent Evolution* (London, 1923).

holism, methodological: *see* methodological holism.

holy, numinous, and sacred. A spectrum of historical development stretches from the earliest concepts of the holy and sacred as terms marking off the fearful domain of divine power—supernatural, unpredictable, not-to-be-touched, weird. Corresponding to the gradual emergence of concepts of deity as *morally* perfect, the holy also becomes profoundly moralized. Yet it retains also the note of awesome otherness: *God remains the *mysterium tremendum et fascinans*—the One who inspires both dread and exhilaration beyond reason's grasp. That, in phenomenological terms, hints at the felt quality of 'numinous' experience, as Rudolf Otto wrote of it: the distinctive experience of God, at once ineffably transcendent, remote, yet stirring a recognition that here is the primary source of beauty and love.

Although appeal to such experience, by no means uncommon, will hardly amount (on its own) to a 'proof' of the existence of God, philosophy of religion must take heed of it in inquiring how values, moral and non-moral, are related to God's nature, and in attempts to rework cosmological ('contingency') arguments for God's existence as the world's incessantly sustaining uncaused cause. It cannot ignore a striking experiential correlate. Relevant to

aesthetics, also, is the striking parallel between the duality (dread and fascination) of numinous experience and the fearful delight of many accounts of the *sublime.   R.W.H.

*mysticism; religious experience.

R. Otto, *The Idea of the Holy*, tr. J. W. Harvey (London, 1923).
M. Eliade, *The Sacred and the Profane*, tr. W. R. Trask (New York, 1961).
O. R. Jones, *The Concept of Holiness* (London, 1961).

homeland, right to a. The claim that a particular territory belongs to a particular people. The usual basis of the claim is a long history of residence and sentimental attachment, and its usual occasion is some interruption in that history: foreign conquest or colonization of the territory, and/or the exile of the people. Hence the right to a homeland is sometimes asserted from outside the land itself, as in the classic case of early Zionism. More often, though exiles play a part in elaborating the sentimental attachment, the effective political claim is made by a native population, like the Palestinians, describing itself as oppressed, ruled by foreigners, deprived not so much of a home as of the right to rule in its own home—a localized claim for self-determination.

In principle, self-determination can be claimed by any collective self and enacted anywhere in the world. It is possible to leave one's homeland for its sake—especially when the 'self' is religiously or ideologically constituted and focused by its doctrine on a new place, like English Puritans dreaming of America as a 'promised land'. The claim to a homeland, by contrast, is specific with reference to place and people. The place is old and familiar, and the people, as befits men and women at home, commonly think of themselves in familial terms. So homelands are also motherlands and fatherlands, and the people are children of the place, brothers and sisters. Behind the legal or moral right—so they often say—is a bond of blood. (It helps in establishing this bond if blood has actually been spilled in defence of the land—which can then be described as 'sanctified by the blood of our ancestors'.)

It follows from this set of associations that men and women from minority groups, who are not members of the family, are not at home in the land, however many years they or their ancestors have lived there. They are called aliens and may well be persecuted or deported—as if to vindicate the claim that the land belongs to *this* people and no other. So one people's claim to a homeland leads, sometimes, to the homelessness of other people.

Sometimes, again, two groups of people ('nations', usually) claim the same homeland. A serial history in which first one, then the other, was the majority in the land, developed the requisite attachments, governed themselves or aspired to do so, generates two claims of exactly the same sort. It is radically unclear how to adjudicate disputes of this kind. Current possession and dominance do not seem sufficient in themselves to determine the issue, especially not if they were achieved by force. Length of time in residence seems also insufficient so long as both groups include people born in the land (and so not themselves conquerors or colonists). Partition of the land is a solution commonly recommended, but this is more easily justified in principle than it is made effective (or just) on the ground. A 'neutral' regime, with cultural or regional autonomy for the rival groups (*pluralism), is another possible solution, which has worked best, however, where the groups are immigrant communities—that is, where they cannot claim homeland rights.

In recent years, the claims of indigenous peoples have received both moral and political attention. These peoples, originally hunters and gatherers, are currently living in a small part of what was once their homeland, having been 'constrained', as Hobbes wrote in *Leviathan*, 'to inhabit closer together and not range a great deal of ground to snatch what they find'. They now claim territorial rights and some limited version of sovereignty on the land they occupy (including the right to bar 'foreigners' from coming in or from voting in local elections once they are in). And sometimes they also claim reparations for the larger homeland they have lost. States with significant indigenous populations have shown a (perhaps surprising) readiness to grant some portion of these claims, though the extent of the grant is still contested.   M.WALZ.

*international relations, philosophy of; self-determination, political.

Will Kymlicka, *Multicultural Citizenship* (Oxford, 1993).
Conor Cruise O'Brien, *God Land: Reflections on Religion and Nationalism* (Cambridge, Mass., 1988).
James Tully, *Strange Multiplicity: Constitutionalism in an Age of Diversity* (Cambridge, 1995).
Simone Weil, *The Need for Roots*, tr. Arthur Wills (New York, 1951).

homological: *see* heterological and homological.

homosexuality. This phenomenon, erotic interaction between people of the same sex, was condemned by both Christianity and ancient Greek philosophy. Although, supposedly, Plato was himself homosexual, in the *Laws* he argued that since neither animals or birds do it, nor should we humans. Aquinas combined both traditions, concluding that homosexual activity is worse than rape, since the former violates natural law and therefore God, whereas the latter only violates another human being. Uniquely among philosophers, Bentham argued (on utilitarian grounds) for its permissibility, although (as with much that he penned) he left his reflections unpublished.

In the teeth of religion and philosophy, attitudes have changed. In part, this is a function of sex surveys (particularly Kinsey) suggesting that homosexuality is no bizarre minority phenomenon, but a widespread aspect of *human nature. In part, this is a function of advances in biology and psychology (particularly Freud) strongly implying that homosexuality is no freely chosen sin, but an imposed state of nature, whether innately or environmentally caused. Philosophical emphasis today has therefore switched from the moral issue to other questions, primarily the thesis of the French historian-philosopher Michel

Foucault that homosexuality is a 'social construction', invented and forced upon a minority by those seeking power, particularly those in the medical profession who label homosexuality a sickness and thus in need of cure. But while agreeing to the potentially healthy state of the mature homosexual, one suspects that Foucault's thesis might itself be something of a construction, made plausible by a very selective reading of the historical record, and backed by a confusion between the undoubted existence of people whose inclinations are exclusively homosexual and the fact that society picks out such people, labelling them and treating them in distinctive ways.   M.R.

*lesbian feminism.

M. Ruse, *Homosexuality: A Philosophical Analysis* (Oxford, 1988).
E. Stein, *Forms of Desire* (New York, 1992).

homunculus. Literally, 'little man'. The term 'homunculus fallacy' has been applied to theories of mental states and processes that explain the phenomenon in question implicitly in terms of that very phenomenon. For example, suppose seeing objects is explained by postulating a device that 'scans' or 'views' images on an 'inner screen'. This explanation is vacuous, it is claimed, since it appeals to the notion of 'scanning' or 'viewing'—which is precisely what we wanted to explain in the first place. It is as if we said that we see by having a little man in our heads who sees: hence 'homunculus'. However, Daniel Dennett has argued (controversially) that there is nothing wrong with appealing to a hierarchy of homunculi in psychological explanation, as long as they become progressively more 'stupid': that is, the tasks they perform are simpler than the task explained by postulating them.   T.C.

Daniel C. Dennett, *Brainstorms* (Hassocks, 1979).

Honderich, Ted (1933–). British philosopher, Canadian-born. Emeritus Grote Professor of the Philosophy of Mind and Logic, University College London. Advocate of the near-physicalist doctrine of Consciousness as Existence: what it is for you to be perceptually aware of the room you are now in is for an extra-cranial state of affairs to exist in a certain defined way. Thus perceptual consciousness is close to what is identified in other theories with its content. With respect to freedom, Honderich is a determinist opposed to both compatibilism and incompatibilism. In political philosophy, he is a socialist who has authored radical reflections on inhumanity, terrorism, conservatism, and the supposed justifications of punishment. In moral philosophy he is a consequentialist: if we were presented with the power to remove either all the bad consequences or all the bad intentions in the world, we would rightly choose to remove the bad consequences. Honderich has written controversially about the significance of the 11 September 2001 attack on the United States. His autobiography provides a view of philosophy as a profession   S.P.

Ted Honderich, *On Consciousness* (Edinburgh, 2004).
—— *A Theory of Determinism: The Mind, Neuroscience and Life-Hopes* (Oxford, 1988).

Ted Honderich, *Conservatism: Burke to Nozick to Blair?* (London, 2005).
—— *On Political Means and Social Ends* (Edinburgh, 2004).
—— *After the Terror* (Edinburgh, 2003).
—— *Philosopher: A Kind of Life* (London, 2001).

Hook, Sidney (1902–89). American exponent of *pragmatism, *naturalism, and *socialism; a student of Morris R. Cohen and John Dewey. When he was on the faculty of New York University, Hook's writings, often in publications of broad circulation and on social, political, moral, and educational issues, made him widely known to the general public. Early and famously a Marxist activist, he soon became even more celebrated as a critic of communism from the standpoint of democratic socialism, with commitment to freedom and to the method of pragmatic naturalism as the foundation of his thought. Recognizing both the glory and the tragedy of human life, Hook saw 'in men something which is at once . . . more wonderful and more terrible than anything else in the universe—the power to make themselves and the world around them better or worse'.   P.H.H.

Paul Kurtz (ed.), *Sidney Hook and the Contemporary World: Essays on the Pragmatic Intelligence* (New York, 1968).

horizon. The unthematized field of perception or background of understanding accompanying the subject's experience of objects and meaning. The metaphor of the horizon has first proved useful in phenomenological theory of perception (Husserl, Merleau-Ponty). Accordingly, every awareness of a perceptual object is attended by a frame of not directly represented features. While perceiving merely the front of a house, for example, we nevertheless 'see' a complete three-dimensional object. Spatiality, temporality, and a *background of indirectly represented objects thus form the horizon within which we always experience an object as such. In philosophical hermeneutics, the cultural tradition provides the horizon within which the interpreter is capable of making sense of other meaning. Successful *interpretation is conceived as a dialogue between interpreter and text, reaching a new understanding of the subject-matter in a 'fusion of horizons' (Gadamer).   H.H.K.

H. G. Gadamer, *Truth and Method* (New York, 1989), 242–54 and 302–7.

Hornsby, Jennifer (1951–). Professor at Birkbeck College, London, who, in her philosophy of *action, denies that 'actions are bodily movements' and maintains that they all 'occur inside the body'. After distinguishing between causally basic and teleologically basic action, she argues that causally basic actions, like moving an arm, are not bodily movements, but are the 'tryings' which are the inner causes of such movements. Granted, trying to move one's paralysed arm is not an action since it fails to produce movement; but if the trying successfully causes the arm to move in the normal way, via appropriate muscular contractions, then it—the trying—is an action. Thus bodily movements are necessary if the trying is to be an action, but the action itself is to be identified with the trying, which is 'inside the body'.   O.R.J.

*agent; sexism.

Jennifer Hornsby, *Actions* (London, 1980).
—— *Simple Mindedness: In Defence of Naïve Naturalism in the Philosophy of Mind* (Cambridge, Mass., 1996).

horseshoe. The symbol '⊃', used in symbolic logic, signifying *material implication, which is a relation holding between two propositions. Let p and q be symbols for propositions, then '$p \supset q$' is short for 'If p then q', and this is true if and only if (i) both p and q are true, (ii) p is false and q is true, or (iii) both p and q are false. Ruled out is: p true and q false. An alternative symbol for material implication is the arrow, '→'.

Material implication thus defined is different from *implication as informally understood in everyday communication; e.g. one would not normally agree that 'If it's raining then it's blowing' is true just because it isn't raining, though normal intuition would agree with the formal definition that the statement is false if in fact it is raining but isn't blowing.   O.R.J.

Peter Alexander, *An Introduction to Logic* (London, 1969).

Horwich, Paul (1947–). Professor of Philosophy at City University, New York, having previously taught at University College London and at the Massachusetts Institute of Technology. Born in England, he studied physics at Oxford before going to Yale for a year and then to Cornell, from which he received a doctorate in philosophy.

His principal contributions to this subject are in books on scientific methodology, time asymmetry, and the concept of truth. He presented the first broad treatment of the scientific method from a Bayesian point of view, offered a unified theory of the 'directional' aspects of causation, entropy, 'the now', deliberation, explanation, and knowledge, and has recently advanced a deflationary account of truth, examining its implications for debates over realism, vagueness, and the nature of meaning.

His work manifests a strong sense of the interconnectedness of the different areas of philosophy, a belief in the clear distinction between philosophical and scientific problems, and a Wittgensteinian penchant for dissolving questions rather than straightforwardly answering them.   N.B.

Paul Horwich, *Probability and Evidence* (Cambridge, 1982).
—— *Asymmetries in Time* (Cambridge, Mass., 1987).
—— *Truth* (1990; new edn. Oxford 1998).
—— *Meaning* (Oxford, 1998).

Hsün Tzǔ (3rd century BC). Master Hsün was a Chinese Confucian thinker, probably best known for his view that human nature is evil. His full name was Hsün K'uang, and his teachings are recorded in the text *HsünTzǔ*. Like Confucius and Mencius, he sought to defend traditional values and norms associated with established social distinctions. In opposition to Mencius, he held that human nature is evil in the sense that human beings in the natural state are moved primarily by self-regarding desires, and that unregulated pursuit of satisfaction of such desires will lead to strife and disorder. General observance of norms associated with traditional social distinctions serves to transform as well as regulate the pursuit of satisfaction of such desires, thereby making possible order in society and maximal satisfaction of human desires.   K.-L.S.

Hsün Tzŭ: Basic Writings, tr. Burton Watson (New York, 1963).

human, all too human: *see* Nietzsche.

human beings. We humans are animals, classified in the Linnaean system into the genus *Homo* (in which there are now no other living representatives), but with our own distinct species (interbreeding group), *Homo sapiens*. There is some doubt about when we first appeared, and indeed it is all really a matter of definition—certainly not much more than a million years ago and probably not much less than a half million years ago, depending on how much variation you are prepared to allow within a group before you insist on dividing it into two. We fall into various subgroups ('races') which would probably be called 'sub-species' in other organisms; but they are all fully interbreeding and today (thanks to such things as easy travel) there is very considerable breakdown of sharp divisions.

The Greeks, especially that first-class biologist Aristotle, recognized our resemblances with the animals, and traditionally we were always put with them on the same Chain of Being: humans coming at the head of the organic world, but below God and the angels. However, it was not until the coming of evolutionism at the end of the eighteenth century that humans were firmly linked through descent with other organisms. Much time was spent on speculation about who was our immediate ancestor. Many agreed with Lamarck that the orang-utan was the most likely candidate.

It was Darwin, notably in his *Descent of Man*, who moved debate to the modern phase, raising questions about how we evolved and what implication this all has, if any, for *human nature. Yet it was not until the present day that some of the most pressing queries were adequately answered. Thanks to molecular techniques, we now know that, although our ancestors are now extinct, biologically speaking our relationship with today's great apes is very close. Indeed, appearances notwithstanding, we may be more closely related to chimpanzees than they are to gorillas. We know also, thanks to fossil discoveries, that of the two really distinctive human characteristics, the large brain and the upright walk, the second definitely appeared before the former.

However, some of the questions with most obviously philosophical implications remain still unanswered. Notwithstanding massive amounts of individual variation within our species, there are clearly some biological differences between members of different races, as there are clearly some biological differences (and not just those bearing directly on reproduction) between males and females. But what exactly these may be and what implications these might have for fields from education to politics still remain essentially unanswered, despite confident assertions of significance from people of the right and of insignificance from people of the left. Whether it is sensible to inquire into these possible differences is also a question not readily answered.

One biological finding of major philosophical interest is that what really makes us humans successful as a species is our ability to interact socially with our fellows. Notwithstanding the horrendous wars and other human-caused catastrophes of this century, the rate of violence between humans is still significantly below that to be found in the average pride of lions. This is not to deny the reality of evil, but it is to warn against absurd arguments about us and the brutes, claiming that we alone are the killer apes, marked for ever for our misdeeds, as was Cain. This should serve as a cautionary warning for those who would draw instant moral conclusions from our evolved nature.
                                                                          M.R.

*evolution; persons.

J. Dupré, *Humans and Other Animals* (Oxford, 2002).
S. J. Gould, *The Mismeasure of Man* (New York, 1981).
M. Ruse, *Taking Darwin Seriously* (Oxford, 1986).

humanism. The tendency to emphasize man and his status, importance, powers, achievements, interests, or authority. Humanism has many different connotations, which depend largely on what it is being contrasted with. As well as denoting particular claims about man it can also denote the tendency to study man at all. Early Greek thought began by studying the cosmos as a whole and particular phenomena in it, such as the weather, earthquakes, etc., and then turned to questions of logic and metaphysics, but the so-called humanist movement arose in the fifth century BC when the Sophists and Socrates 'called philosophy down from heaven to earth', as Cicero later put it, by introducing social, political, and moral questions.

Humanism is also associated with the *Renaissance, when it denoted a move away from God to man as the centre of interest. God still remained as creator and supreme authority—the Renaissance humanists were far from being atheists—but his activity was seen as less immediate, more as general control than as day-to-day interference, and this enabled a scientific outlook to arise which saw the universe as governed by general laws, albeit these were laid down by God. (A rather similar development had occurred earlier when the Stoics relied on the notion of an impersonal fate to provide the stability needed for a coherent description of the world.) One feature which made this specifically a humanist development was the emphasis it both presupposed and, by its successes, encouraged on the ability of man to find out about the universe by his own efforts, and more and more to control it.

It was when the conflict between science and religion arose in the nineteenth century, largely because of

Darwinism's inconsistency with a fundamentalist reading of the Bible, that humanism acquired its modern association with atheism or agnosticism. Humanism, often called scientific humanism, then becomes associated with *rationalism, not in its main philosophical senses but in that of an appeal to reason in contrast to revelation or religious authority as a means of finding out about the natural world and the nature and destiny of man, and also as giving a grounding for morality; the term 'ethical humanism' is sometimes used in this last context, though the outlook can also be called scientific humanism in so far as it claims that science can provide a basis for morality. However, this appeal to reason in ethics should be distinguished from that common in the seventeenth and eighteenth centuries, and not without echoes in the twentieth, where reason was opposed not to religious authority but to feelings or emotions.

Some humanists in fact demur at the title 'rationalist' or 'scientific humanist' because, though they are quite willing to follow reason rather than authority or revelation (and for that reason are willing to call themselves humanists at all), they do not accept that reason can provide the basis for morality, but may appeal to feelings or emotions instead; in fact throughout their histories the British Humanist Association and the Rationalist Press Association have been independent entities, though allied on most issues. Humanists may also reject the implication in the title 'scientific humanist' that science can at least ultimately answer all questions. (*Naturalism; positivism.) Humanist ethics is also distinguished by placing the end of moral action in the welfare of humanity rather than in fulfilling the will of God.   A.R.L.

W. K. C. Guthrie, *A History of Greek Philosophy*, iii (Cambridge, 1969).

M. Knight (ed.), *Humanist Anthology* (London, 1961). Modern sense, but interpreted rather widely.

A. Rabil Jr. (ed.), *Renaissance Humanism* (Philadelphia, 1988).

human nature. The explication of the notion of human nature, what it is essentially to be a human, is as difficult as it is important to philosophy. A major problem is that it is not immediately obvious what kind of answer would satisfy. Must human nature be defined with respect to the new-born infant, in which case it would seem to be a bundle of potentialities, or is it to be defined with respect to the full-grown adult, in which case does one consider training something crucial to the development of human nature or is it rather something which takes our nature from its true state?

However one answers these questions, or rather in part according to the way in which one answers these questions, there are a number of key issues which have dominated philosophical discussion of human nature: Is there some qualitative difference between humans and other animals, or is it all a question of quantities and balance? Is there one key thing that all humans have, or is there a range of qualities, irregularly dispensed? And, most crucially, is human nature inherently good, bad, or indifferent?

Plato, with his three-part division of the soul, had answers to all of these questions: We are undoubtedly different from other beings in our rational ability to perceive the Forms; all and only humans may have the three key elements, but by nature some have one part more developed and dominant than do others; and as such human nature is neither good nor bad but with appropriate training (or its lack) this nature can be turned to good or ill. In this last claim, Plato differed strongly from the Judaeo-Christian conception of human nature, which through the story of the Fall saw humans as being essentially in a state of sin, from which we can be rescued only by God's grace.

Deeply influential was the thinking of Aquinas, who drew on Aristotelian roots in formulating his doctrine of natural law, thus emphasizing that any adequate account of human nature must not emphasize our spiritual side to the exclusion of the body, although his particular conclusions—for instance, that *homosexuality involves an unnatural and therefore sinful use of bodily parts—remain controversial. As a Christian, nevertheless, he remained committed to our essential uniqueness, a belief which was not really challenged until the eighteenth century, when such writers as David Hume started to stress the continuity between human powers of reason and sentiment and those of animals. Obviously this was a challenge continued by the rise of evolutionary speculations.

Paralleling such developments as these was an increasing turn from the Christian belief in our inherent wickedness. Rousseau and Romanticism pushed the pendulum to the other extreme, suggesting that only the young and undeveloped is the truly good. Based on a totally inadequate grasp of the facts, the belief grew that it is in the 'noble savage' that we find the pure and untainted human nature. Not that all felt this way. John Stuart Mill, and early evolutionists like Thomas Henry Huxley, were convinced of the ape within and of the need to conquer our brute nature. More balanced was Freud, who emphasized both the innate element in human nature and the crucial effects of family environment on its development. In respects, his major contribution lay less in his specific theories and more in his presumption that, inasmuch as we are a product of our past, it is inappropriate to assign guilt or blame to those who do not fit usual patterns.

Extremely influential today, albeit more outside professional philosophy than within, is the view of the 'constructivists' which denies that there is any essential human nature, arguing rather that all such conceptions are merely cultural artefacts, often invented by one part of society to suppress another part. But a spectrum of more traditional positions continues to exist, from those like the sociobiologists, who see human nature as completely determined and thus not appropriately subject to moral evaluation, to those like the existentialists and their successors, who see human nature as entirely a product of human free choice and thus essentially and inherently moral.   M.R.

*evolution; empiricism; rationalism; human beings.

J. Dupré, *Human Nature and the Limits of Science* (Oxford, 2001).

A. MacIntyre, *After Virtue* (Notre Dame, Ind., 1981).

E. O. Wilson, *On Human Nature* (Cambridge, Mass., 1978).

human rights is a more politically correct alternative to the more eloquent 'Rights of Man', designed to stress their possession by Woman (and, for that matter, Boy). They are much the same as the older 'natural rights' which would, however, embrace the rights sometimes claimed for animals. It also serves to detach natural rights from the much criticized doctrine of natural law. The latter is at the centre of the political thought of the Stoics and Cicero and of Christian political theory in the Middle Ages, and so seems antiquated and theological. But it is not obvious that the detachment of right from law is an advantage. Rights without law seem as questionable as law without a lawgiver. Human rights are rights which human beings possess simply in virtue of being human, however widely they differ. Human rights are perhaps more satisfactorily defined as rights which humans possess independently of positive law (*legal positivism). Such rights came into their own through the religious individualism of the Protestant Reformation. That led, in Protestant communities, to a multiplicity of mutually hostile sects, elsewhere to the existence of Protestant subjects under a Catholic sovereign, and vice versa. Protracted wars of religion in France and Germany somewhat muted religious ferocity. The first fully formed, essentially secular theory of human rights was that of Locke's second *Treatise of Government* (1690). His prime instances of life, liberty, and estate (i.e. property) are closely followed by the American Declaration of Independence (1776), in which the pursuit of happiness piously replaces property. In that document Jefferson followed Locke in holding these principles to be self-evident. Such rationally obvious limits to the just sphere of government action were unrecognized by the prevailing absolutism of the early modern period, but were upheld, somewhat patchily, by the medieval Church.

Objections were soon raised, notably by Hume, Burke, and Bentham. The first is that rights, like law, presuppose a sovereign legislator and organized sanctions to enforce them. A second focuses on the variety and continuing proliferation of the rights claimed, including rights to such things as employment, education, and an adequate standard of living. Rights for all to be provided with something are less plausible than rights to non-interference. A third, Burkean, line of criticism takes exception to the universalism of a theory which insists on the same rights for all and ignores historically rooted differences between societies. Part of an answer to the first objection is the emergence of quasi-sovereigns like the United Nations and the European Union which legislate freely enough although their sanctions are ineffective. Despite these objections, it is hard to resist a minimal theory of human rights which maintains that the actions of governments are fit subjects for moral criticism by individuals meditating morally principled disobedience or resistance, most plausibly in matters about which there is some approximation to moral consensus.   A.Q.

Maurice Cranston, *What Are Human Rights?* (London, 1973).

Humboldt, Wilhelm von (1767–1835). German philosopher, linguist, and statesman who was a pioneer of historical-comparative linguistics. He helped to found the University of Berlin in 1811. In *The Limits of State Action* (1791; pub. 1851; tr. Cambridge, 1969), he argued that the sole purpose of the state is to protect the lives and property of its citizens. He supplied an epigraph for J. S. Mill's *On Liberty*: 'The grand, leading principle, towards which every argument unfolded in these pages directly converges, is the absolute and essential importance of human development in its richest diversity.'

His last years were devoted to philology. In *On the Dual* (1828) he argued that older languages, such as Sanskrit, are syntactically more complex than later ones; this ended attempts to find the origin of *language within recorded history. His *magnum opus* on the language of the Kawis of Java remained unfinished. The introduction (1830–5; pub. 1836) argues that the 'inner structure' of a language reflects the 'spirit' of its speakers. Morphology and syntax reveal differences in the 'inner form' of languages and enable us to classify and relate them.   M.J.I.

Wilhelm von Humboldt, *On Language: The Diversity of Human Language-Structure and its Influence on the Mental Development of Mankind*, tr. P. Heath, intro. H. Aarsleff (Cambridge, 1988).

Hume, David (1711–76). Scottish philosopher, essayist, and historian. Perhaps the greatest of British philosophers since Locke, Hume aimed to place 'Logic, Morals, Criticism, and Politics' on a new foundation—the 'science of man' and the theory of human nature. Famous for his *scepticism in metaphysics, Hume also emphasized the limits that human nature places on our capacity for scepticism. In morals, he insisted on the reality of moral distinctions, though our judgements are ultimately founded only in human sentiment. In these and other areas, his concern was to expose the limitations of reason, and to explain how we none the less make the judgements we do, careless of the absence of rational support.

Life. Hume was the second son in a strict Presbyterian family that was a minor branch of the line of the Earls of Home. After two or three years at the University of Edinburgh, Hume began to study for a legal career, but discovered that his interests lay elsewhere. Immersing himself in the classics (with a particular love of Cicero's philosophical works), Hume decided that the existing philosophy contained 'little more than endless disputes', and set out to find 'some medium by which truth might be established'. About the age of 18, there finally seemed to open up to him 'a new scene of thought', which made him 'throw up every other pleasure or business to apply entirely to it'. He decided on the life of 'a scholar and a philosopher'.

After four years of intense study overshadowed by something like a nervous breakdown, Hume left Scotland in 1734. He settled in France, at La Flèche, a town in Anjou at whose Jesuit school Descartes had studied a century before. He conceived his general plan of life: 'to make a very rigid frugality supply my deficiency of fortune, to maintain unimpaired my independency, and to regard every object as contemptible, except the improvement of my talents in literature.'

It was mostly at La Flèche that Hume wrote *A Treatise of Human Nature*, the most widely studied of his works today. He returned to London in 1737, at the age of 26, and the work appeared in 1739 and 1740. It was soon a disappointment to the author. 'Never literary attempt was more unfortunate than my Treatise of Human Nature. It fell *dead-born from the press*, without reaching such distinction, as even to excite a murmur among the zealots.' Hume had hopes for a second edition, but the work was not reprinted in England until 1817.

Hume had some success with two volumes of *Essays: Moral and Political* (1741, 1742). But he failed in an attempt at the Chair of Ethics and Pneumatical Philosophy in Edinburgh, and turned in his mid-thirties to less literary activities. He was tutor for a year to a mad nobleman, and secretary to General St Clair on an abortive attempt to invade France. Hume seems to have appreciated these activities mainly for the contribution they made to his precarious finances.

The neglect of the *Treatise*, Hume believed, arose from going to press too early, 'carried away by the heat of youth and invention'. He reworked book I, and restored a discussion of miracles that he had cut from the earlier work. The result was a slim volume of *Philosophical Essays Concerning Human Understanding* (1748)—known after 1758 as *An Enquiry Concerning Human Understanding*. He developed book III of the *Treatise* into a parallel volume, *An Enquiry Concerning the Principles of Morals* (1751). Hume later asked that his philosophical views should be judged on the basis of the *Enquiries*, rather than the *Treatise*. They are the works that spread his philosophy most widely—and in due course roused Kant from his 'dogmatic slumber'.

A draft of the *Dialogues Concerning Natural Religion* existed by 1751, though for reasons of expediency Hume kept this dangerously sceptical work unpublished. In his forties, Hume's main energies turned from philosophy to politics and history. The *Political Discourses* (1752) contain important essays on money and interest. Having failed again to get an academic post (this time at Glasgow), in 1752 Hume became Librarian to the Faculty of Advocates in Edinburgh. With his own library, he worked fast on a *History of England*, publishing volumes on the Stuarts (1754, 1756), the Tudors (1759), and the period from Julius Caesar to Henry VII (1762). Persuaded at first that he was of 'no party' and 'no bias', he found himself a determined opponent of the Whig interpretation of history. The *History* earned Hume a great following and royalties far larger, he said, than 'anything formerly known in England'.

Hume wrote little of note in his fifties. He lived in Paris for a while (1763–6), where he became the darling of the philosophical salons. He returned to England accompanied by Rousseau, who promptly quarrelled with him, imagining Hume was plotting to ruin his reputation.

Hume served for two years in London as under-secretary in the Northern Department—a position which, ironically, gave him responsibility for ecclesiastical preferment in Scotland. He returned to Edinburgh finally in 1769.

The death of Hume earned him something of the status of a secular saint. Knowing that his disease of the bowel was incurable, he faced death with equanimity, cheerfulness, and resignation. His persistence in irreligion shook the conviction of Boswell, and provoked some strikingly unpleasant comments from Dr Johnson.

Hume died on 25 August 1776. Some months before, he had written a few pages of autobiography under the title 'My Own Life'. Besides his frugality and need for independence, he stresses the 'great moderation' in his passions. 'Even my love of literary fame, my ruling passion, never soured my temper, notwithstanding my frequent disappointments.' Adam Smith commented: 'Upon the whole, I have always considered him, both in his lifetime and since his death, as approaching as nearly to the idea of a perfectly wise and virtuous man, as perhaps the nature of human frailty will permit.'

Logic and Metaphysics. Hume divides the contents of the mind into *impressions and *ideas. Impressions are our 'sensations, passions and emotions'; ideas are 'the faint images of these' in thought, reflection, and imagination. Complex ideas may be formed out of simpler ideas; but simple ideas can enter the mind in only one way, as 'copies of our impressions'.

Causal reasoning. How do we acquire beliefs about things we are not currently experiencing? We see a flame, for example, and conclude that it is hot. Hume notes that we start from a present impression—the sight of the flame—and suppose a causal relation—between flames and heat. But how do we come to believe in that causal relation?

Hume's great claim is that it is not because of reason. *Reason alone* cannot tell us that flames are hot: it is conceivable that a fire might be cold, and therefore possible. *Reason and experience together* cannot produce the belief either. Our experience has been confined to certain tracts of space and time. Within those reaches, we have found flames to be hot. But there is a gap between 'Observed flames have been hot' and 'All flames are hot'. To reach the second, we would need to add the principle that nature is uniform, that the future resembles the past. But how could we ever establish the uniformity principle?

Hume claims that there are only two kinds of reasoning, 'demonstrative' and 'probable' (*see* *fork Hume's), and neither can do the job. Demonstrative reasoning (such as deduction) cannot establish the uniformity of nature—for non-uniformity is conceivable, and therefore possible. 'Probable' reasoning—or causal reasoning from the observed to the unobserved—cannot establish the uniformity either. Probable reasoning itself presupposes the uniformity of nature, so to employ it in support of that principle would be circular. As Russell later explained, even if experience has told us that past futures resembled past pasts, we cannot conclude that future futures will resemble future pasts—unless we already assume that the future resembles the past.

If reason does not give us our beliefs about the unobserved, what does? Simply 'custom or habit', trading on two fundamentally non-rational processes. Repeated experience of the conjunction of flames and heat creates an *association of ideas*—so when we see a flame, by sheer habit an idea of heat will come to mind. A belief differs from a mere conception by being 'lively or vivid'; so when *vivacity* from the impression of the flame is *transferred* to the associated idea of heat, the idea becomes a belief in the presence of heat. Our beliefs are the product not of reason but of these mechanisms of 'the Imagination'.

Does this make Hume a sceptic about *induction? He says that we have 'no reason' to believe that the sun will rise tomorrow. On the other hand, he believes that our inductive reasoning processes are genuinely 'correspondent' to the natural processes in the world; he describes induction as 'essential to the subsistence of human creatures'; and he even says that causal conclusions have their own kind of certainty, 'as satisfactory to the mind . . . as the demonstrative kind'. Perhaps the way to reconcile these claims is to remember that 'reason' is for Hume 'nothing but the comparing of ideas and the discovery of their relations'; so discovering that 'reason', in this sense, is not the source of our inductive beliefs is very different from claiming that induction is, in a more general sense, unreasonable.

Hume's account of causal power builds on his account of causal inference. In accord with the empiricist principle that ideas are derived from impressions, Hume explains that to clarify our idea of necessity we must find and examine the impression that has given rise to it. This proves surprisingly hard. Necessity cannot be found in our experience of *individual* cases of causation. 'We are never able, in a single instance, to discover any power or necessary connexion'; we simply see one event follow another. The idea must therefore come from our experience of a *multiplicity* of similar cases. The *constant conjunction (say, of flames and heat) produces, as we have seen, an association of ideas. Hume now adds that 'this connexion . . . which we feel in the mind' is the true source of our idea of necessity, and therefore all we can be talking about when we talk about power, connection, or necessity.

Hume's view here is not entirely clear. He in fact indicates not one source for the idea of necessity, but a chain of three—conjunction in the objects, association in the mind, and a feeling of connection—and each of these is a candidate referent for our idea of necessity, i.e., a candidate for what necessity *is*. Of the three, the first and second tend to weigh most with Hume, and we find them at the heart of his definitions of cause.

Hume gives two definitions. The notion of cause is made up of the notions of *priority* and *necessary connection*. (The *Treatise* treats *contiguity* as a third constituent.) Taking necessity as constant conjunction, therefore, we may define a cause as '*an object, followed by another, and where all the objects similar to the first are followed by objects similar to the*

second'—the famous account of causation as regular succession. Taking necessity as connection in the mind, we may define a cause as '*an object followed by another, and whose appearance always conveys the thought to that other*'—a rather different account, and one less influential upon Hume's followers.

Does Hume deny the existence of power and necessity? Certainly not—any more than Berkeley denies the existence of tables and trees. 'Necessity, according to the sense in which it is here taken, has never yet been rejected, nor can ever, I think, be rejected by any philosopher.' Far from rejecting necessity, Hume is attempting a reductive explanation of it. There is something, however, that Hume does deny, namely, necessity as misconceived. The mind has a 'propensity to spread itself on external objects': we are apt to treat the feeling of connection, which is really only in the mind, instead as a feature of external objects. This is a mistake—the mistake made by rationalists who believe in an intelligible connection between cause and effect.

External world. The final part of book I of the *Treatise* purports to be a study of 'the sceptical and other systems of philosophy'—as if scepticism were a malady to be studied in other people. In the course of discussion, however, it becomes clear that the malady is one that Hume himself has caught, and only the strongest instincts can save him from succumbing to it. Hume discusses two versions of the belief in external objects, the 'vulgar' and the 'philosophical', and finds both of them unjustified. The vulgar or commonsense belief is, as Hume presents it, a belief in the 'continued and distinct existence' of the 'interrupted images' of sense. (This attributes to common sense a view like that which Berkeley held—and also, surely implausibly, attributed to common sense.) This 'vulgar' view is false. ''Tis a gross illusion to suppose, that our resembling perceptions are numerically the same' after a gap—an illusion due to the *constancy* and *coherence* of our perceptions.

The 'philosophical' or Lockean view does no better, in holding that our impressions are only *representations* of external objects, resembling and caused by them. For 'as no beings are ever present to the mind but perceptions', we can never observe a causal relation (or indeed a similarity) between perceptions and external objects thus conceived.

Hume implies that the 'necessary consequence' is, strictly, that we should altogether reject 'the opinion of a continued existence'—and believe in nothing but interrupted and dependent ideas and impressions. Nature, however, saves us from this fate: 'The sceptic must assent to the principle concerning the existence of body, tho' he cannot pretend by any arguments of philosophy to maintain its veracity. Nature has not left this to his choice.' Hume's arguments may have produced in the reader a moment of philosophical doubt, but an hour hence he will again be 'persuaded there is both an external and internal world'.

Personal identity. Hume rejects the view, apparently shared by philosophers and the vulgar, that we are conscious of a self, simple in itself, and identical from one time to another. We have no impression of a simple, identical *self; so we can have no idea of any such thing. Hume's own view is that mankind 'is nothing but a bundle or collection of different perceptions, which succeed each other with an inconceivable rapidity, and are in a perpetual flux and movement'. The common mistake arises, he thinks, from a tendency to confuse related perceptions with identical.

Hume maintains a more steady scepticism about personal identity than about the external world. In the latter case nature saves us from the hard conclusions of 'intense reflection'; with personal identity, on the other hand, Hume thinks he can live with his own deflationary conclusions. This later proved to be an exaggeration. In an appendix, he admits to feeling confused about his the account of personal identity, though for reasons that few readers find clear.

Scepticism. The concluding section of the *Treatise*, book I, depicts a battle between reason and nature. Hume has exposed the weakness of the human mind—where what passed for reason turns out to be 'imagination', and even the strongest inference can be made to seem uncertain. In the face of this weakness Hume is 'ready to reject all belief and reasoning, and can look upon no opinion even as more probable or likely than another'.

Human nature saves him. 'Most fortunately it happens, that since reason is incapable of dispelling these clouds, nature herself suffices to that purpose.' A few hours of good company and *backgammon make his melancholy and sceptical conclusions seem ridiculous. What is more, 'amusement and company' lead Hume to a third phase—of curiosity and constructive philosophical ambition. Following his own nature, Hume finds a place after all for philosophy and the modest pursuit of science.

Hume here reconciles scepticism and *naturalism. It is not merely that scepticism is a natural attitude. Rather, the best expression of scepticism is one where we follow our nature without pretending we have an independent justification; in doing so we may even contribute to the 'advancement of knowledge'.

Theory of the Passions, Moral Philosophy. Like *Hutcheson before him, Hume models his theory of morality on a theory of aesthetic judgement, linked with an account of the *passions. The picture is roughly this. Finding something beautiful is deriving a certain sort of pleasure from it; and that pleasure is a 'calm passion'. Similarly, approving of someone's character, or finding it virtuous, is simply 'feeling that it pleases' in a certain way; and that feeling is a calm passion, though it is liable to be confused with a 'determination of reason'. Like beauty, morality 'is more properly felt than judged of'.

Hume seems himself to have become less confident of the details of his theory of the passions after the *Treatise*, and he never reworked book II as he did books I and III. He is both acute in analysing the conditions necessary for the various passions and resolute in tracing them to associative mechanisms in the mind.

Hume starts with pride and humility. 'Every thing related to us, which produces pleasure or pain, produces likewise pride or humility.' A beautiful house produces pleasure in anyone who looks at it; but it produces pride only in someone *related* to it, for example, as designer or owner. Hume explains this by two mechanisms. The house is related to the owner, so—by an association of ideas—the idea of the house produces in him the idea of himself. (This contributes to pride, because the self is 'the object of pride'.) At the same time, the house produces pleasure, and—by an association of impressions—pleasure produces pride. By two associative processes, the house produces the feeling of pride.

Hume treats love and hatred in a similar fashion, except that whereas the 'object' of pride and humility is oneself, the object of love and hate is another person. Book II also contains an important argument that determinism is compatible with a form of liberty.

Moral theory. Book III of the *Treatise* begins with a spirited rejection of the view that moral distinctions are derived from reason. 'Morals excite passions, and produce or prevent actions.' By contrast, 'Reason is perfectly inert,' and can never produce or prevent an action. (*Reason as slave of the passions.) The rules of morality are therefore 'not conclusions of our reason'—and the rationalist theories of Clarke and Wollaston must be rejected. Moral distinctions are derived instead from a 'moral sense', not from reason.

Since approval and blame are, respectively, 'agreeable' and 'uneasy', they may be described as varieties of pleasure and pain. By producing pleasure, therefore, a *virtue will tend (in accordance with the theory of the passions) to produce pride in the possessor, and love in other people. (Pride of this kind, therefore, is no sin.) Hume's remaining task is to explain exactly which characteristics produce that variety of love which is the discerning of virtue.

The answer is easy in the case of 'natural' virtues—characteristics which we approve of because of natural instinct. Hume places in this category those features of a person's character that are '*useful* or *agreeable* to the *person himself* or to *others*'; and he invokes *sympathy*, probably the central notion of his whole moral theory, to explain their operation. Qualities that are useful or agreeable to others will directly elicit pleasure and approval in them. Qualities that are useful or agreeable primarily to the possessor—like good sense or a cheerful character—are approved of because of *sympathy*. We have a natural propensity 'to sympathize with others, and to receive by communication their inclinations and sentiments, however different from, or even contrary to our own'. This process—given a complex mechanistic explanation in the *Treatise*, but treated as an ultimate principle in the second *Enquiry*—explains how qualities that give pleasure to one person can inspire pleasure (and hence approval) in others.

The 'artificial' virtues pose a greater problem. An individual act of justice may be approved of, though it benefits no one. Why do we approve of paying back a debt to 'a profligate debauchee, [who] would rather receive harm than benefit from large possessions'? The answer is that we have a conventional or 'artificial' system of rules of property, which as a whole provides security, in an environment where goods are scarce and people are greedy. Even if 'single acts of justice may be contrary, either to public or private interest', the whole scheme is 'absolutely requisite, both to the support of society, and the well-being of every individual'.

Hume's moral theory is in many ways parallel to his general epistemology: he shows the limits of reason, and then explains, in the naturalistic spirit of an empirical student of the mind, how we reach the judgements—or rather, feelings—that we do. But the consequences are less sceptical in the case of morals. To discover that morality is only a matter of feeling, informed by instincts of sympathy, modulated in accord with conventions of justice, and regulated by general rules, is not, it seems, to discover that moral judgement is any less than it could properly be expected to be. On the other hand, to learn that causal judgements are only the effects of habit, to learn that our beliefs in external objects and in the self are false, even if inescapable—all this, Hume seems to think, exposes a tear in the fabric of belief. We may continue to do philosophy, with a kind of confidence that consists in following human nature and being diffident even of our doubts. But Hume does not pretend that to philosophize in that 'careless manner' is to philosophize with no sense of loss.

Philosophy of Religion. The *Dialogues Concerning Natural Religion* appeared in 1779, three years after Hume's death. They present fundamental objections to the ontological and, above all, the cosmological arguments for the existence of God.

It is absurd, Hume suggests, to attempt to demonstrate the existence of God a priori; since the issue is a matter of fact. An a posteriori argument from order in the world to the existence of a designer, however, is also unpersuasive. We can infer only those characteristics which are precisely necessary to produce the features we find in the world; and the only licence we can use in our inference comes from regularities which we have observed. If we agree that order in the world has a cause, the question remains whether 'the cause or causes of order in the universe probably bear some remote analogy to human intelligence'. Even the answer is Yes, the analogy with human intelligence may still be quite remote; and in any case this gives us no licence to attribute to the cause any particular moral qualities.

The first *Enquiry* brought Hume notoriety for its argument against believing in *miracles. On all topics, 'A wise man . . . proportions his belief to the evidence.' Hence: 'No testimony its sufficient to establish a miracle, unless the testimony be of such a kind, that its falsehood would be more miraculous, than the fact, which it endeavours to establish.' Hume adds reasons to suppose that the latter condition has never been met: witnesses have never been of 'unquestioned good-sense' and learning; human nature takes a misleading delight in things that amaze; moreover,

the miracles that supposedly support one religion must in the same way undermine other religions. 'Upon the whole,' Hume concludes, 'the *Christian Religion* not only was at first attended with miracles, but even at this day cannot be believed by any reasonable person without one.'

Having concluded that the source of religion can hardly be reason, Hume gives his own anthropological account of it—in the irreverent essay *The Natural History of Religion*, which appeared in the *Four Dissertations* of 1757.

J.BRO.

Stephen Buckle, *Hume's Enlightenment Tract: The Unity and Purpose of* An Enquiry Concerning Human Understanding (Oxford, 2001).

Don Garrett, *Cognition and Commitment in Hume's Philosophy* (New York, 1996).

J. C. A. Gaskin, *Hume's Philosophy of Religion* (London, 1978, 1988).

N. Kemp Smith, *The Philosophy of David Hume* (London, 1941).

Peter Millican (ed.), *Reading Hume on Human Understanding: Essays on the First* Enquiry (Oxford, 2002).

E. C. Mossner, *The Life of David Hume* (Oxford, 1954, 1970).

David Fate Norton, *David Hume: Common Sense Moralist, Sceptical Metaphysician* (Princeton, NJ, 1982).

—— (ed.), *The Cambridge Companion to Hume* (Cambridge, 1993).

Barry Stroud, *Hume* (London, 1977).

Hume's fork: *see* fork, Hume's.

humour. Although *laughter, like language, is often cited as one of the distinguishing features of human beings, philosophers have spent only a small proportion of their time on it, and on the related topics of amusement and humour. Of the two most widely held theories, the first, that humour expresses a superiority of the individual who is amused over the object of amusement, is the most venerable. The second is that amusement is a response to incongruity. Amongst the topics that have surfaced in recent discussion, three catch the attention. We talk of a sense of humour, and this seems to assume that some are equipped to see what is funny about a situation whilst others cannot. Does it follow that the situation is itself funny antecedent to anybody finding it so? Are we then committed to realism about humour? Secondly, is humour a virtue? How does a sense of humour connect with other virtues, and is its absence a defect in an otherwise good man? Connected with both these issues is the general relevance of moral considerations to humour. Does the fact that a joke is racist or sexist mean that it is not really funny, or that it is merely a fault in us if we laugh at it?   R.A.S.

Ted Cohen, *Jokes: Philosophical Thoughts on Joking Matters* (Chicago, 1999).

J. D. Morreal, *The Philosophy of Laughter and Humour* (Albany, NY, 1987).

Robert C. Roberts, 'Humor and the Virtues', *Inquiry*, 31 (1988).

Hungarian philosophy. In the seventeenth century there were Hungarian Cartesians, mostly Protestant divines in Transylvania. Then at the beginning of the nineteenth century counter-Reformation Jesuit philosophers and Hungarian Kantians created a theoretical vocabulary and so contributed to the inauguration of a national culture without giving the world any great innovation. The 'synthetic philosophy' of the mid-nineteenth century tried to fuse all metaphysical tendencies in a specifically Hungarian world-view. Later, the objectivist theory of values under the influence of Hermann Lotze and Immanuel Hermann Fichte played an important role, along with Hegelian aesthetics.

The first really original Hungarian contribution to philosophy was the *fin-de-siècle* anti-psychologism or *Platonism represented by such thinkers as Akos Pauler (1876–1933), a gifted follower of Bolzano and Brentano, and Georg Lukács (1885–1971). Pauler was a Catholic who tried to reconcile the Aristotelian inclination of the then vigorous *neo-scholasticism with his own strong views on validity. Validity for him is a combination of truth and existence. True assertions and existent objects are both valid, so that the gap between *fact and value is filled; validity is also divine.

Lukács, the best-known Hungarian philosopher, influenced a host of theorists. His work before the First World War was extremely *conservative and romantic. He sought to demonstrate that individual psychic life is nothing but an aberration: any utterance can be meaningful only if it partakes of the objectivity of *forms, created culturally. *Culture, therefore, is more than the sum of individual or group endeavours, it is the primary reality that speaks through people, especially seers, mystics, and poets. The tragedy of life consists in our desire to be ourselves, whereby we demote ourselves from the highest level of objectivity (cultural forms), particularly while experiencing erotic love. The inescapable abdication inherent in every individual life necessitates history, through which second-rate individuality can merge progressively in the impersonality of the meaningful form: civilization. Form is divine: but love turns us away from it, condemning us to superficiality and meaninglessness; love of the 'objective' (religion) seems hopeless. The Sunday Circle, the first Lukácsian group in Hungarian philosophy—of whom only Karl Mannheim (1893–1947) is internationally renowned—took up his views enthusiastically, combining Platonism with Dostoevsky and Kierkegaard, and prophesying a conservative revolution against *individualism and liberal *capitalism.

It is perhaps interesting to note that it was this group rather than the uninspired socialists who were the messianic ideologues of the Hungarian Soviet Republic in 1919, where one young philosopher read excerpts from *The Brothers Karamazov* to capture the minds of right-wing officers.

Between the two world wars Hungarian philosophy was part of the so-called neo-baroque official culture, continuing the Platonist tradition with an added (corporatist) social dimension along the lines of the 'universalism' of Othmar Spann, the theorist of the *Ständestaat*, a sort of modern caste society.

After 1945 the erstwhile messianic revolutionaries returned from Moscow as wizened and dogmatic Marxist-Leninists and built the imposing edifice of institutional philosophy, a vast network of research institutes, university departments, indoctrination schools, periodicals, and popularization courses. For the first time, classic works (particularly, of course, of Spinoza and Hegel) became available in cheap editions. Every dogmatism is beset with heresies and the ritual and public ideological debates were only the visible expression of the fissures within the system: they played a political role rarely associated with philosophy in liberal democracies. The Lukács debates in 1949, 1956, 1957, and the late 1960s gave shape to the so-called revisionism that rejected crude materialist determinism, class theory, and positivist beliefs in progress and science, reconnecting Marxian tradition with its romantic sources in theories of alienation and reification where the ideas of the young, non-Marxist Lukács about objective meaningful forms make a spectacular come-back. Revisionists, through their abstruse disagreements with official doctrine, were the first agents of a *de facto* *pluralism. The condemnation of the revisionists, and their joining forces with other dissidents, quickened the pace of the disintegration of the system. The demand for freedom to philosophize preceded in time-honoured fashion ideological scepticism, which then prompted liberal development. Today in Hungary you can find Heideggerians and Rawlsians, Oakeshottians and Straussians, analytical Marxists and post-moderns, just like everywhere else.   G.M.T.

Béla Tankó, *Hungarian Philosophy* (Szeged, 1934).

Husserl, Edmund (1859–1938). German philosopher who was the founder, and a skilful practitioner, of *phenomenology. His early works, *On the Concept of Number* (1887) and *Philosophy of Arithmetic* (1891), were marked by psychologism, the attempt to base logic and arithmetic on psychology. The concept of plurality, for example, was explained in terms of our mental act of combining different contents of consciousness into one representation, of, for example, seeing distinct people as a single group. Influenced in part by Frege's criticism, Husserl abandoned this view, and in his *Logical Investigations* (1900–1; tr. London, 1970) argued that logic is not reducible to psychology. For example, the statement:

(1) If all men are mortal and all Greeks are men, then all Greeks are mortal

neither entails nor is entailed by:

(2) Anyone who believes that all men are mortal and that all Greeks are men also believes that all Greeks are mortal

or:

(3) No one who believes that all men are mortal and that all Greeks are men believes that not all Greeks are mortal.

(Nor is (1) equivalent to a rule of correct thinking:

(4) Anyone who believes that all men are mortal and that all Greeks are men ought to believe that all Greeks are mortal.

We could argue, with equal justification, that an empirical statement, e.g. 'The earth is not flat', amounts to a rule, 'No one ought to believe that the earth is flat'.) If (1) were equivalent to (2) or (3), (1) would be at most probable and would presuppose the existence of mental phenomena. The claim is also viciously circular in that any attempt to derive (1) from (2) or (3), or, more generally, to derive logic from psychology, must presuppose some rule of logic. (Parallel objections can be raised to the claim that the truth of (1) depends on the meanings of the words used to express it or on 'rules of language', if these are interpreted as empirical generalizations about natural languages.)

We need to distinguish between, on the one hand, what is meant or intended, the objects *of* *consciousness, and, on the other, our psychical acts or experiences, our consciousness of such objects. (The idea of an 'intended' object stems from medieval philosophy by way of Brentano.) Logic deals with what is meant, not with our acts of meaning it. The objects of consciousness appear to us, are 'phenomena', while our psychical acts are merely experienced. (We may in turn reflect on psychical acts and thus convert them into phenomena. They are then no longer real, experienced acts, but the objects of further acts.) Psychical acts, like any other real entity, must be individual entities; but what is meant is an ideal entity and may be universal. If, for example, I am thinking about love, my thinking is a particular act distinct from other acts of thinking; but the love that I think about may be no particular love, simply love in general. Intended objects are thus 'essences', and it is essences and their interrelations that logic describes. Heidegger (like Adorno) was puzzled by the apparent revival of psychologism in the second volume of the *Logical Investigations*: 'But if such a gross error cannot be attributed to Husserl's work, then what is the phenomenological description of the acts of consciousness? Wherein does what is peculiar to phenomenology consist if it is neither logic nor psychology?'

Husserl published little for some years after the *Logical Investigations*, but continued to develop his ideas in lectures. For example, in his 1905 *Lectures on the Phenomenology of Internal Time-Consciousness* (edited for publication by Heidegger in 1928; tr. The Hague, 1964), he wrestled with a problem that had exercised St Augustine and William James: How can I experience a temporally extended object *as such*? Suppose that I am listening to a tune consisting of a succession of notes, 1, 2, 3, 4, ..., each of which occurs at a certain time, $t_1, t_2, t_3, t_4, \ldots$. If at any given time, t_n, I hear only the note that occurs at that time, n, and have no awareness of the notes that occur before and after t_n, then at no time am I conscious of a temporally extended tune, but only of the note that is occurring *now*. (I am not strictly aware even of the occurrence of the note *now*, since the awareness of the present *as such* implies some

awareness of before and after.) If, on the other hand, at t_n I hear with equal force all the earlier notes, then again I hear not an enduring tune, but a deafening cacophony. The basis of Husserl's solution is this: At any given time, say t_9, I have a 'primal impression' of the note that is occurring *now*, note 9. I do not now have a primal impression of note 8, but I 'retain' it, that is I am aware of it as just past. When note 10 occurs, I am aware of 9 as just past and of 8 as further past. As the tune proceeds, note 8 recedes further into the past and 'appears' in ever-changing 'retentional modifications'. Thus I retain not only the individual notes of the tune, but the order in which they occurred. Similarly, at any given point in the tune I 'protain' its future course. If I have not heard the tune before, my protention is less determinate than my retention, but following a tune involves an expectation that its future course will lie within certain limits. (If I were to end this article with the words 'And that concludes my account of the Pyramids', the reader's surprise would indicate *both* that on reading this sentence, he retained (his reading of) earlier sentences *and* that while reading earlier sentences he protained, more or less roughly, the future course of the article.) Ordinary, or 'secondary', memory presupposes, but is distinct from, retention, or 'primary' memory. If I am trying to remember an earlier phase of a tune, this impairs my appreciation of its present phase; retention of earlier phases is, by contrast, essential to my appreciation of the present phase. Expectation similarly presupposes, but is distinct from, protention. Husserl does not (as the example of a tune consisting of notes may suggest) regard time as atomized into a series of discrete instants, or periods: our time-consciousness is a 'continuous flux'.

In his next major work, *Ideas: General Introduction to Pure Phenomenology* (1913; tr. London, 1931), Husserl introduces a range of technical vocabulary. The act of consciousness, for example, is *noēsis*, while its intended object is the *noēma*. Logic and pure mathematics rests on the intuition of *essences (*Wesensschau*) or *eidē*, and 'phenomenology' is the descriptive analysis of essences in general. Not only objects, such as an object of sense-perception, can be analysed in this way, but also acts of consciousness. But the acts must then be 'reduced' to an essence or *eidos* (the 'eidetic reduction'). The phenomenologist is not concerned, for example, with particular acts of sense-perception, but with the essential features common to all such acts. Moral and aesthetic values, and desires and emotions, are also open to phenomenological investigation.

The phenomenologist must, on Husserl's view, perform an *epochē, that is, suspend judgement, with regard to the existence of objects of consciousness. In analysing, for example, the essence of perceived objects, we must not assume that such objects as trees and tables exist and causally engage with our sense-organs, but focus exclusively on the essential structure of perceptual consciousness. We must suspend, or 'bracket', the 'natural attitude' to the world. The reason for this is that Husserl, like Descartes, advocated 'philosophy as rigorous science' (the title of an article of 1911), philosophy as the indubitable basis of our dubitable, if for the most part correct, beliefs about the empirical world.

But Husserl disagreed with Descartes in one crucial respect. Descartes moved swiftly from the proposition that 'I think' to the conclusion that I am a 'thinking thing'. The belief that I am a thinking thing is itself, Husserl claims, to be bracketed. I, who am conscious of objects, am neither a thinking substance, nor an embodied person, nor even the stream of my experiences—for I am conscious of, and in that sense distinct from, my experiences; I am the pure or transcendental ego, what Kant called the 'I think' which 'must be able to accompany all my representations'. The transcendental ego or 'transcendental subjectivity' cannot itself be bracketed, any more than Cartesian doubt can extend to the existence of the doubter. Thus only transcendental subjectivity is 'non-relative . . . while the real world indeed exists, but in respect of essence is relative to transcendental subjectivity, in such a way that it can have its meaning as existing reality only as the intentional meaning-product of transcendental subjectivity'. Husserl here infers an idealist conclusion, namely that objects are constituted by consciousness and could not exist without it, from the the true premiss that nothing can be conceived without being an object of consciousness. The error depends on either or both of two confusions: (1) between an intentional and a real object— in conceiving an object, I make it an object of my consciousness, but I do not thereby make it a real object, e.g. a tree; (2) between making something my intentional object by conceiving it and conceiving it *as* my intentional object—I cannot think of a possible lifeless universe without making it the object of my thought, but I do not thereby think of it *as* an object of my thought and thus suppose myself to be one of its inhabitants. (It is a mistake to suppose that Husserl's *idealism can only be avoided if we reject the methodological use of *epochē*.) In his *Cartesian Meditations* (1931; tr. The Hague, 1960) Husserl tried to relieve phenomenology of the charge that it entails solipsism by explaining how one transcendental ego can experience another transcendental ego on a par with itself.

From the *Ideas* to the *Cartesian Meditations*, Husserl's enterprise is avowedly akin to Descartes's *Meditations* and, unavowedly, to Fichte's *Wissenschaftslehre. But his last great (unfinished) work, *The Crisis of European Sciences and Transcendental Phenomenology* (1936; tr. 1954) is closer to Hegel's *Phenomenology of Spirit*. For it purports to show, 'by way of a teleological–historical reflection on the origins of our critical scientific and philosophical situation, the inescapable necessity of a transcendental–phenomenological reorientation of philosophy'. This is at odds with his earlier approach in at least two respects: (1) a historical or causal account of the genesis of our consciousness was excluded or *'bracketed' in his earlier works; (2) in so far as Husserl is now concerned not so much with particular past events, as with the *eidos* of history, with the essential historicity of consciousness, its burden of preconceptions derived from the traditions of its social milieu, this casts doubt on his own attempt to found a rigorous science, free

of all preconceptions, that goes directly 'to the things themselves'. In part 3 of the *Crisis*, and in other papers intended for incorporation in it (such as 'The Origin of Geometry') he develops the concept of the 'life-world' (*Lebenswelt*), the intersubjective world of our natural, pre-theoretical experience and activity, which, he believes, was neglected by philosophers such as Kant in favour of the world of theoretical science. But the 'theoretical attitude' (exemplified, for Husserl, by Galileo) arose historically, in ancient Greece, against the background of the life-world, and the life-world *essentially* persists even after the development of the theoretical 'spirit'. Even the physicist thinks of the sun as rising and setting, and as marking the phases of his practical life. Husserl's account of the life-world, of its essential priority to theory, and of the emergence of theory from it, owes something to the eidetic method and to *epochē*: to describe the *essential* structures of the life-world involves suspending our scientific presuppositions and our practical engagement with the life-world. Nevertheless, some philosophers, notably Merleau-Ponty, see the *Crisis* as a distinct departure from Husserl's earlier work.

Husserl has had an immense influence in continental Europe. Phenomenological analysis has been applied to psychology (Pfander), law (Reinach), values, aesthetics, and religion (Scheler). Even philosophers who reject Husserl's theoretical doctrines have benefited from his meticulous analyses of particular phenomena. But thinkers such as Heidegger, Sartre, and Merleau-Ponty have used phenomenology in the service of philosophical positions quite different from Husserl's own, and his hope that his rigorous science would put an end to radical philosophical disagreements has remained unfulfilled.   M.J.I.

D. Bell, Husserl (London, 1991).

J. Derrida, *Edmund Husserl's 'Origin of Geometry'* (New York, 1978).

—— *Speech and Phenomena* (Evanston, Ill., 1973).

H. Dreyfus (ed.), *Husserl, Intentionality and Cognitive Science* (Cambridge, Mass., 1982).

F. A. Elliston and P. McCormick (eds.), *Husserl: Expositions and Appraisals* (Notre Dame, Ind., 1977).

E. Levinas, *The Theory of Intuition in Husserl's Phenomenology* (Evanston, Ill., 1973).

Hutcheson, Francis (1694–1746/7). An academic philosopher of Irish origin who taught (and was criticized by) Adam Smith at Glasgow University and strongly influenced Hume, he was the main representative of the *'moral sense' doctrine in ethics, which he inherited from Shaftesbury. The main thrust of his philosophy was to emphasize feeling rather than reason or intuition as the source of what we think of as moral knowledge, though it is unclear whether this feeling detects special moral qualities in actions or situations, as we feel the warmth of fire, or whether we simply have feelings of approval or disapproval towards their non-moral properties. This latter interpretation would place Hutcheson as an ancestor of the twentieth-century *emotive theory of ethics, and similar theories, but the eighteenth century was less sensitive than the twentieth to precise semantic analyses of the meanings of words and phrases.   A.R.L.

M. P. Strasser, *Francis Hutcheson's Moral Theory* (Wakefield, NH, 1990).

hylomorphism. The doctrine that sensible things are composites of matter (Greek *hulē*) and form (*morphē*). Against atomists, who explained big things in terms of varying arrangements of small things, Aristotle found his model in sculptures 'formed' from matter by the artist. Once reified into metaphysical constituents, forms are treated as primitive explanatory entities accounting for both static and dynamic structure of things (e.g. the substantial form of bovinity explains both the organic differentiation of cow bodies and their distinctive digestive processes).   M.M.A.

*atomism.

Marilyn McCord Adams, *William Ockham* (Notre Dame, Ind., 1987), chs. 15–17.

Montgomery Furth, *Substance, Form and Psyche: An Aristotelian Metaphysics* (Cambridge, 1988).

hylozoism: *see* panpsychism.

hypothesis. A hunch, speculation, or conjecture proposed as a possible solution to a problem, and requiring further investigation of its acceptability by argument or observation and *experiment. Hypotheses are indispensable to human thinking, and used by everyone from detectives (Sherlock Holmes) to metaphysicians. They form the basis of an influential account of scientific method (*hypothetico-deductive method), which is closely related to the claim, associated with Popper, that scientific *theories are empirical hypotheses and remain so, however successful they are at withstanding repeated attempts to falsify them.   A.BEL.

*evidence.

Larry Laudan, *Science and Hypothesis* (Dordrecht, 1981).

hypothetical imperative: *see* categorical imperative.

hypothetico-deductive method. A theory in science is a general statement (or *hypothesis) from which particular inferences may be deduced. Thus, from the theory 'All planets have elliptical orbits', given the information that Mars is a planet, we can deduce that Mars has an elliptical orbit. Observations (here, of Mars's orbit) can then be seen as confirming or falsifying the hypothesis.

In the twentieth century Karl Popper and many other philosophers of science before him saw the core of science as the deployment of what is called the hypothetico-deductive method. An unfortunate consequence of this view has been a concentration on the formal relationships between theories and the statements which follow from them. There has been consequent lack of interest in the relationship of theories to the actual practices, evidential and experimental, from which they emerge, despite the fact that even testing a theory is in practice more complex than the hypothetico-deductive model suggests.
                A.O'H.

*Bacon.

E. Nagel, *The Structure of Science* (London, 1961).

I

I and thou. The relation of subject to subject celebrated in Buber's ethical and religious philosophy: I may contemplate a tree 'as a picture: a rigid pillar in a flood of light . . . overcome its uniqueness and form so rigorously that I recognize it only as an expression of the law . . . dissolve it into a number . . . But it can also happen, if will and grace are joined . . . that I am drawn into a relation, and the tree ceases to be an It. The power of exclusiveness has seized me.' Placing relationality (and so, intersubjectivity) ahead of both subject and object, Buber's approach springs from Kant's foregrounding of the subject morally and in constituting experience and from Hegel and Feuerbach's insistence that dialectic constitutes the self. Similar thoughts unfold in Mead, Peirce, and Dewey; they take flight as fully fledged metaphysical themes in Cohen, Rosenzweig, and Buber. L.E.G.

Martin Buber, *I and Thou* (1922), tr. Walter Kaufmann (New York, 1970).

Ibn Gabirol, Solomon (*c.*1022–*c.*1058). Philosopher and poet, author of the *Fons Vitae*, an intricate, highly abstract dialogue on Neoplatonic metaphysics. Since the Arabic original is lost, it was not known until Salomon Munk (1845) recognized Shem Tov ibn Falaquera's Hebrew quotations from it that the Avecebrol of the Latin manuscripts was the well-known Hebrew poet Ibn Gabirol. Born in Malaga and raised in Saragossa, Ibn Gabirol relied on the idea of intellectual or 'universal' matter to explain the emergence of multiplicity from God's unity. Matter here is the passive or receptive aspect of every being but God. Ibn Gabirol's *On the Improvement of the Moral Qualities* (tr. Steven Wise (1902)) offers a physiological treatment of ethics based on the theory of the four humours. 'The Kingly Crown', his Neoplatonic poem on the descent and destiny of the soul, is included in the Sephardic liturgy of the Day of Atonement. L.E.G.

*Neoplatonism.

Solomon Ibn Gabirol, *Fons Vitae ex Arabico in Latinum translatus ab Johanne Hispano et Dominico Gundissalino*, ed. C. Baümker (Munich, 1892–95).

Jacques Schlanger, *La Philosophie de Salomon Ibn Gabirol* (Leiden, 1986).

Ibn Khaldūn (1332–1406). Born in Tunis, he was one of the most creative of Muslim statesmen and political thinkers, widely acclaimed by modern historians as the greatest philosopher-historian. In his major theoretical work, *The Prolegomena*, he introduced the notion of natural causality in history, in contrast to Islamic theology, and called for the definition and study of sociological and political processes (considered to be the principles of historical methodology) with the express investigative intention of recovering historical accuracy. He defined and claimed to be the originator of a 'science of culture' ('*umrān*) that would study cultures in multiple stages in their natural human, social, and political development. His methodology emphasizes the study of environmental impact on social organizations and economic processes that define value, prosperity, and culture. H.Z.

Muhsin Mahdi, *Ibn Khaldūn's Philosophy of History: A Study of the Philosophical Foundation of the Science of Culture* (Chicago, 1964).

Ibn Rushd: *see* Averroës.

Ibn Sīnā: *see* Avicenna.

idealism, British. Movement in nineteenth- and twentieth-century British philosophy according to which ultimate reality is mental or spiritual, or at least not physical. Bradley, Green, and Bosanquet think matter is not real. Physical objects and the subjective points of view of conscious individuals stand in a system of *internal relations called 'the absolute' or 'absolute mind', so British idealism is mostly a kind of quasi-Hegelian *absolute idealism, and *truth is ultimately construed as *coherence. McTaggart, although denying the existence of God and the reality of time and matter, holds that we are essentially immortal souls. His influential argument that time is not real putatively shows that tense is incoherent. Change depends on tense, time depends on change, so time depends on tense, so there is no time. Tense is incoherent because it entails a contradiction to say, for example, that the same (token) event happened last week and will happen the day after tomorrow.

Newton might be an early if unwitting exponent of absolute idealism, depending on the meaning of his claim that absolute space and time are 'the sensoria of God'. Physical objects and events logically depend upon space and time. Space and time logically depend upon the presence of God, so physical objects and events logically depend upon the presence of God.

More recently in Britain, *Timothy Sprigge has argued for a kind of absolute idealism. Non-absolute or individualistic versions of idealism have been defended by John Foster and Howard Robinson. They argue that it is incoherent to maintain that ultimate reality is physical. Foster argues for a quasi-phenomenalist idealism on which physical facts are wholly constituted by experiential facts, even though physical concepts are not analytically reducible to experiential concepts. Foster therefore rejects physical realism and any naïve realist view on which we are directly acquainted with physical objects in sense perception.

Although late twentieth-century British philosophy was dominated by the materialist and positivist ideas common to English language philosophy, it is not impossible that idealism will have a new role once non-reductivist explanations of consciousness come to be taken more seriously. It is now clear, if it was not clear then, that materialism, naturalism, and positivistic science have wholly failed to provide any kind of explanation of the existence and reality of one's own subjective mind.   S.P.

F. H. Bradley, *Ethical Studies* (Oxford, 1876).

—— *Appearance and Reality* (Oxford, 1893).

C. D. Broad, *An Examination of McTaggart's Philosophy*, 2 vols. (Cambridge, 1933, 1938).

John Foster, *The Case for Idealism* (London, 1985).

T. H. Green, *Prolegomena to Ethics* (Oxford, 1883).

J. McT. E. McTaggart, *The Nature of Existence*, 2 vols. (Cambridge, 1921 and 1927, repr. 1968).

Stephen Priest, *Theories of the Mind* (London, 1991).

Howard Robinson (ed.), *Objections to Physicalism* (Oxford, 1993).

Timothy Sprigge, *The Vindication of Absolute Idealism* (Edinburgh, 1983).

idealism, German. Movement in late eighteenth- and early nineteenth-century German philosophy according to which ultimate reality is mental or spiritual, or at least not physical. Kant, Hegel, Fichte, and Schelling are usually classed as German idealists, and Leibniz and Schopenhauer are sometimes included.

Arguably, Kant is not any kind of idealist. He called his critical philosophy 'transcendental idealism', but realized his mistake when readers understood this as a kind of idealism. In the second (B) edition of the *Critique of Pure Reason* he expressly included a new chapter called 'The Refutation of Idealism' (B 274–9). 'Idealism' in 'transcendental idealism' is in fact correctly understood as 'anti-realism'. Kant thinks there are no metaphysical propositions, so transcendental idealism is metaphysical anti-realism. Kant makes many claims consistent with idealism, but they are misunderstood as entailing idealism. Famously, he insists that we have knowledge only of appearances, not of things-in-themselves. This means we can only know things as they appear to us, not as they could not appear to us. There is nothing to suggest that

appearances are mental ('A motor car appeared around the street corner'). 'We can only know possible objects of experience' means: We can only know things as they would appear to us if we were experiencing them. This does not entail that those things are mind-dependent, only that our knowledge has a perspectival nature. Kant makes it clear that the notion of a noumenon is a 'limiting' concept, and 'existence' is a category, so whatever interpretation we give to 'noumena', it had better not imply that there are any. Kant thinks we can know objects only if they are spatio-temporal, Euclidian, Newtonian, countable, could interact causally, and are substances. If this epistemological conservatism carries any ontological implication, it is materialism, not idealism.

There is a huge secondary literature on Kant, most of it, from Hegel to contemporary British, German, and American commentators, mistakenly construing Kant as some sort of idealist. In the hands of Fichte, transcendental idealism does become a kind of idealism. Fichte rejects things-in-themselves, which he misunderstands as in hidden ontological duplication of appearances. Although Kant insists that there is no substantial subject or ego (for example in the *paralogisms), and depicts the transcendental unity of apperception as the purely formal possibility that any thought of mine may be prefaced by 'I think [that] ...' (in the Transcendental Deduction), Fichte nevertheless postulates an inner ego as owner of one's thoughts and experiences, a self-consciousness that 'posits' the external world and, with dubious coherence, itself. Self-consciousness presupposes an 'I–not I' distinction, it arguably making little sense to postulate a portion of what is that I am without positing a distinct portion that I am not.

In the *System of Transcendental Idealism* (1800) Schelling construes consciousness and the unconscious as reciprocally constituting. In the *Exposition of my System of Philosophy* (1801) Schelling advocates an 'identity' or 'indifference' between nature and spirit, object and subject; but 'identity' should not be understood here as 'numerical identity' or 'qualitative identity'. In a partial anticipation of Hegelian dialectic, *a* and *b* are identical if and only if, if not *a* then not *b*, and if not *b* then not *a*, so it is legitimate to regard *a* and *b* as parts or 'moments' of a larger whole. What *a* is a part of is nothing other than what *b* is a part of. Ultimately, nature and mind are aspects of the Absolute. Because nature and spirit are mutually dependent in Schelling's philosophy, it is better construed as *neutral monism than idealism. In *Bruno* (1802) the Absolute is identified with God. In *Of Human Freedom* (1809) God is identified with the source of the universe as pure, infinite free will.

Hegel's philosophy may be understood as the application of Kant's critical philosophy to the totality of what is. The triadic arrangement of Kant's table of categories and the synthetic resolution of the Third Antinomy in which thesis and antithesis are both true, albeit at different levels of explanation, provide Hegel with the immediate model for his dialectic: the exhibiting of philosophical problems as prima-facie contradictions which, on closer inspection, turn out to be mutually consistent depictions of a larger whole. By 'logic' Hegel does not mean logic but, roughly, the exhibiting of semantic, psychological, and ontological relations between universals.

Hegel made two attempts at writing his system: the *Phenomenology of Spirit* (1807) and the *Science of Logic* (1812–14), and, secondly, the so-called *Encyclopaedia of the Philosophical Sciences* (1815–31), including the *Lesser Logic* and *Philosophy of Mind*. In writing two fundamentally different kinds of philosophy book, phenomenology books and dialectic books, Hegel, the greatest synthesizing philosopher, failed to 'overcome' the greatest antithesis of Western philosophy: between empiricism and rationalism. Kant, in his own view, had done this.   s.p.

Henry Allison, *Kant's Transcendental Idealism* (New Haven, Conn., 1983).

Graham Bird, *Kant's Theory of Knowledge* (London, 1961).

Stephen Priest, *Theories of the Mind* (Harmondsworth, 1991).

—— (ed.), *Hegel's Critique of Kant* (Oxford, 1987).

idealism, philosophical. Philosophical idealism is not the same as idealism considered as an attitude to be observed in life; it is not the pursuit of an ideal. It is, rather, a metaphysical theory about the nature of reality, and thus presupposes a distinction between *appearance and reality, drawn in an other than common-sense way. It maintains in general that what is real is in some way confined to or at least related to the contents of our own minds. Plato's theory of Forms is sometimes said to be a species of idealism on the grounds that his Forms are also called Ideas. But those so-called Ideas were not merely contents of our minds; indeed Plato explicitly rejects that supposition in his *Parmenides*. It has been argued by Myles Burnyeat that idealism proper could not appear before Descartes had argued for the epistemological priority of access to our own minds. Although this has been disputed, there is much to be said for the thesis. At all events, whether or not there are to be found any indications of belief in philosophical idealism before Descartes's time, it certainly needed his argument to provide it with any basis. Yet Descartes was not himself an idealist.

What are the reasons, therefore, for thinking that reality is confined to the contents of our minds—*ideas, as they were called by Descartes and others at his time? Berkeley, who was the first idealist proper, generalized Locke's arguments to the effect that where the perception of qualities of things, such as colour, taste, and warmth, is circumstance-dependent (i.e. relative to the context in which perception takes place, e.g. the illumination, the condition of our tongue, or the temperature of our hands) those qualities cannot be real properties of things. Berkeley argued that this applied to all *perception. Since perception is, he thought, a matter of having sensations or ideas, and since to be is to be perceived (Berkeley's cardinal thesis), only sensations or ideas can properly be said to be or to be real. He summed this up towards the end of his *Three Dialogues* by a twofold thesis maintained, he said, both by philosophers and by the 'vulgar': those things they immediately perceive are the real things, and the things immediately perceived are ideas which exist only in the mind. There are many points to question about this thesis, including the whole idea of immediate perception and the claim that, whatever immediate perception is, it is confined to sensations or ideas.

The theory of perception involved, the so-called representative theory of perception, according to which what we perceive is at best mere representations of things, remained part of the apparatus of empiricist thought, and is implicit in Hume's doctrine that what we are given is impressions, of which ideas are in some way copies. In the eighteenth century only Reid challenged the theory, because he thought it led Hume to absurdity. But the theory is still there in the thought of Kant, who held that perception provides us only with representations (*Vorstellungen*), however mediated by concepts. Kant held, however, that a mere subjective, Berkeleian idealism would not do in that it did not make it possible to distinguish properly what is objective from what is subjective in the sense in which flights of fancy are subjective. Kant, followed to this extent by Schopenhauer, thought that idealism must be transcendental, which he tried to define by saying that 'appearances are to be regarded as being, one and all, representations only, not things-in-themselves, and that time and space are therefore only sensible forms of our intuition, not determinations given as existing by themselves, nor conditions of objects viewed as things-in themselves' (*Critique of Pure Reason*, A 369). The main point is that Kant thought that he could distinguish between appearances or representations of perception and *things-in-themselves, but that the conditions for a further distinction within appearances between what is objective and what is merely subjective could also be set out. The spatial–temporal features of objects as given in experience are thus, he said, empirically real but transcendentally ideal. Kant thought that he could, in these terms, show the unacceptability of Berkeleian idealism.

We have, so far, a distinction between two forms of idealism. Post-Kantian philosophy supplied a third, which became known as absolute idealism. Fichte began it (although he called his form of idealism 'critical idealism') by rejecting what Kant had had to say about things-in themselves, seeking to make the distinction between self and non-self purely within what is due to the activities of the self. Hegel took it much further, thinking that he could demonstrate, first, the identity of consciousness with its object and, second, the identity of consciousness with self-consciousness. This led, to simplify his argument grossly, to the idea of a universal self-consciousness, a universal 'notion' (*Begriff*), which is what reality is. This is the *Absolute (a term introduced by Fichte), the one unconditional entity. While both Berkeleian, subjective idealism and Kantian, transcendental idealism, in effect construe reality in terms of the contents of an individual mind, absolute idealism tends to construe it in terms of some interpersonal consciousness. Indeed, in it the distinction between one self and another tends to lapse, leading, as is explicit in F. H. Bradley's *Appearance and Reality*, to a form of *monism, according to which there is only one thing, distinctions within which are simply appearance. This is clearly heady stuff.

All these forms of idealism have in common the view that there is no access to reality apart from what the mind provides us with, and further that the mind can provide and reveal to us only its own contents. This second consideration is supposed to follow from the first, but it does not do so unless one invokes additional considerations, such as those adduced by Berkeley when he claims that the circumstance-dependence of judgements of perception show that the objects of perception are mind-dependent. The effect of the latter is to assimilate perception to *sensation. Something like pain is taken as the paradigm of sensation, and it is then argued that the feeling of warmth can be assimilated to pain, and that other forms of perception can be assimilated to that, in that, perhaps, they are all subject to bodily and other, contextual conditions. Reid reasonably defined sensation in terms of the idea that it has no object other than itself. He did not think that this was true of perception, despite what Hume and other empiricists had said; he thought that perception involves concepts and beliefs, but that these are *of* objects distinct from what takes place in the mind. But, in fact, however correct this last point is, one can *show* that it is so only by meeting the arguments which try to assimilate perception to sensation. G. E. Moore thought that he could refute idealism by drawing attention to the distinction within experience between the experience itself and its object. But one needs to show in addition that that object can be extra-mental.

Recent arguments for what has been called *anti-realism raise difficulties over the idea that there can be forms of understanding reality which are verification-transcendent, so that there are problems about our attaching content to something if there is no way of verifying whether it does or does not hold good. Transcendental idealism can be construed similarly as a form of anti-realism in that Kant argues for limits on what can be understood if it cannot be brought under the conditions of objective judgement. However, anti-realism does not quite entail idealism. Kant depends also, for his transcendental idealism, on a representationalist view of perception, holding that sensible intuitions (i.e. what is given in perception) which are brought under concepts in judgement about the experienced world take the form of representations. Kant inherited that view from his predecessors, and accepted it because it seemed obvious. But it is not obvious (though something approaching it has become the vogue today, particularly among cognitive scientists, who hold that the mind's workings have to do with mental representations). It is not obvious because it is assumed that the stimulation of our sense-organs produces not merely sensations in the ordinary sense, but something that performs the role of representing whatever produces the stimulation, so that it is this which we are directly aware of (or which the mind is directly

concerned with), rather than the object itself. At the same time, without that misconceived view of perception (or something like it) idealism cannot get off the ground.

Idealism has been very pervasive in the history of philosophy since at any rate the eighteenth century. It has been less prevalent in recent times, but tendencies towards representationalism are liable to push adherents of that view in its direction. Consequently, defenders of idealism in some form are still to be found. Indeed, many beginners in philosophy seem to think that it is the most obvious philosophical theory, although nobody before Descartes would have thought just that. It is also noteworthy that Berkeley thought that his idealism amounted to a defence of common sense and that, as indicated earlier, it was what philosophers and the 'vulgar' had in common. Later forms of idealism have been less 'obvious' because they are more sophisticated and more complex. Schopenhauer characterized his form of transcendental idealism by saying that it amounted to the doctrine of 'no object without a subject', and he defended that, partly by appealing to Berkeley and partly by arguing that if we try to imagine a world without a knowing subject, we are bound to realize that we are involved in a contradiction. For what we shall be imagining is something that is indeed dependent on a knowing consciousness—our own. But while it is clear that it is impossible for us to imagine anything without an imaginer existing, namely ourselves, it does not follow that we cannot imagine a scene in which no conscious beings exist. It does not follow, that is, that there cannot be objects the existence of which does not depend on their being *for* a subject. As Hegel might have put it, and despite his arguments to the contrary, what is 'in-itself' need not be 'for another'. In the end, the only positive argument for idealism of any form is to be found in the representative theory of perception, and that theory is false.   D.W.H.

*for-itself and in-itself; idealism, British; idealism, German.

G. Berkeley, *Three Dialogues between Hylas and Philonous* (1713).

D. W. Hamlyn, *Metaphysics* (Cambridge, 1984), ch. 2.

G. Hegel, *The Phenomenology of Spirit*, tr. A. V. Miller (Oxford, 1967).

I. Kant, *Critique of Pure Reason*, tr. N. Kemp Smith (London, 1929).

Godfrey Vesey (ed.), *Idealism, Past and Present* (Cambridge, 1982).

ideal observer theory. A theory of justification in ethics. The theory is that moral judgements can be justified by appeal to what an ideal observer or 'impartial spectator' would do or say in a given situation. The theory has been developed from its origins in the British moralists of the eighteenth century, but it still has a problem in providing a non-circular account of an ideal observer.   R.S.D.

Roderick Firth, 'Ethical Absolutism and the Ideal Observer', *Philosophy and Phenomenological Research* (1952).

ideals, moral. Two levels of moral standards have been distinguished in ethical theory: ordinary moral standards and extraordinary moral standards. The first level is confined to standards in the common morality that apply to everyone—the moral minimum. The second level is a morality of aspiration; here individuals adopt moral standards that do not hold for everyone. These ideals transcend what we appropriately expect of others and thus are aspirational ideals of individual excellence. In so far as a person aspires to *moral* goals that surpass the conventional moral point of view, the person accepts moral ideals. Those who fulfil these ideals can be praised and admired, whereas those who fall short of ideals cannot be rightly blamed or condemned by others.

*Supererogation is a category of moral ideals pertaining principally to *actions*, rather than to *virtues* or *motives*. The etymological root of *supererogation* means paying or performing in addition to what is owed. It has several defining conditions. Supererogatory ideals and acts are those which exceed what is expected or demanded by the common morality; they are intentionally undertaken for the welfare of others (although the actor need not intend to act from an ideal). A supererogatory ideal is optional—neither required nor forbidden by the common morality. Omission of a supererogatory act is not morally wrong and not condemnable by common-morality standards.

Nevertheless, individuals who act from ideals often do not consider their actions to be morally optional. Many heroes and saints describe their actions in the language of *obligation* and even *necessity*: 'I had to do it', 'It was my duty.' The point of this language is to express a *personal* sense of obligation. Some philosophical accounts deny the literal appropriateness of this language, interpreting it as a form of moral modesty designed to deflect merit or praise that might be showered on the person. But a broader and more sympathetic interpretation is that a personal norm is accepted by the person as establishing what ought to be done from a pledge or assignment of personal responsibility.

Supererogatory acts done from moral ideals typically would be required were it not for an abnormal deprivation or risk present in the particular circumstances, but the individual elects not to invoke an exemption from acting based on the abnormal situation. The individual therefore does not make a mistake in regarding the action as personally required and can view failure as grounds for guilt, even though no one else is free to view the act as obligatory.

Not all ideals are exceptionally arduous, costly, or risky. Examples of less demanding ideals include generous gift-giving, volunteering for public service, forgiving another's costly error, devoted and extended kindness, and complying with requests made by other persons when these exceed the requirements of the common morality. Many everyday actions exceed obligation without being at the highest level of ideals.

Aristotelians have held that the ideal of an admirable life of moral achievement is central to the very nature of ethics, not merely a second level beyond ordinary morality. Each individual should aspire to a level as elevated as his or her abilities permit. Some persons are more able

than others, and for this reason they merit more praise, acknowledgement, and admiration. The Aristotelian model does not expect perfection, but rather that one strives toward perfection. Ideals are thus *central* in this model, not merely ornaments to an already commendable life.   T.L.B.

*absolutism, moral.

R. Crisp and M. Slote (eds.), *Virtue Ethics* (Oxford, 1997).

Joel Feinberg, 'Supererogation and Rules', *Ethics*, 71 (1961); repr. in Judith J. Thomson and Gerald Dworkin (eds.), *Ethics* (New York, 1968).

David Heyd, *Supererogation: Its Status in Ethical Theory* (Cambridge, 1982).

J. O. Urmson, 'Saints and Heroes', in A. I. Melden (ed.), *Essays in Moral Philosophy* (Seattle, 1958).

ideas. These are entities that exist only as contents of some mind. Ideas in this sense should be distinguished from Plato's Ideas or *Forms, which are non-physical but exist apart from any conscious beings. The image of a Platonic Form that occurs in a person's mind would be an idea in our sense. Beginning in the seventeenth century all objects of consciousness were held to be ideas. For example, we are conscious of ideas when we imagine, remember, dream, or think about some concept or proposition. Ideas are subjective in that individuals can be aware only of their own ideas. If two individuals are imagining Pegasus or thinking about the Pythagorean theorem each is directly aware of a distinct idea, although these ideas may share many features. This is analogous to the sense in which two reproductions of the Mona Lisa are distinct objects even though most of their properties are identical, but it is impossible for one individual to inspect another's ideas.

Reflection on the nature of our perceptual experience led Descartes and Locke, among others, to argue that even when we are perceiving we are directly aware of ideas, not physical objects. For example, touching a hot object or walking into a wall may cause someone to feel pain. The pain is caused by a physical interaction between the object and the perceiver's body, but the pain exists only as long as the individual is conscious of it. Moreover, pain is subjective: if two people walk into the same wall each experiences a distinct pain that exists only in that individual's experience. Thus to experience pain is to experience an idea. But all perceptual experience arises in the same way as does pain. We feel warmth or solidity, see colour or shape, and so forth, because an object acts causally on our sense-organs. The item we become directly aware of as a result of this interaction is an idea. This thesis receives further support when we consider the way in which the apparent size, shape, and colour of a physical object, such as a distant tower, changes as our distance from the tower and our angle of observation changes. Since the tower presumably remains unchanged it is concluded that we do not directly perceive the tower, but rather ideas that are caused to exist in our minds by the interaction between the tower and our sense-organs.

Once the doctrine that we experience only ideas was accepted, three major philosophical problems immediately arose. First, are the ideas we experience adequate copies of items that exist apart from our experience? In the case of perception it is generally agreed that pain does not exist apart from experience and philosophers argued that other ideas which physical objects cause us to experience may not actually characterize those objects. Thus philosophers sought criteria for assessing which of our perceptual ideas characterize items in the physical world. Second, ideas are mental entities which, according to Descartes's analysis, have nothing in common with physical objects. Thus it is unclear how interactions between a physical object and a human body (also a physical object) can generate ideas. This question is one aspect of the *mind–body problem. Third, if we are directly aware only of our own ideas, it becomes problematic how we know that anything exists other than these ideas. This question also arises for ideas of non-physical objects such as God. After Descartes the doctrine that we are aware only of our own ideas became widely accepted and the three problems just noted became central problems of epistemology and metaphysics.   H.I.B.

*phenomenalism; concepts; content; innate ideas.

G. Berkeley, *The Principles of Human Knowledge*, in *Philosophical Works* (London, 1975).

R. Descartes, *Meditations on First Philosophy*, in *The Philosophical Works of Descartes*, ii, tr. J. Cottingham, R. Stoothoff, and D. Murdoch (Cambridge, 1984).

D. W. Hamlyn, *Sensation and Perception* (London, 1961).

ideas, innate: *see* innate ideas.

ideas of reason. This is Kant's expression for the products of *reason. In the *Critique of Pure Reason* Kant argued that there are three such ideas corresponding to the self, the world, and God; and that human reason is subject to an unavoidable 'transcendental illusion' through which it assumes the existence of non-empirical objects corresponding to these ideas, but that they nevertheless have an important regulative function in the systematic unification of experience.   H.E.A.

Norman Kemp Smith, *A Commentary to Kant's* Critique of Pure Reason, 2nd edn. rev. and enlarged (New York, 1962).

identity. The word 'same' is used sometimes to indicate similarity (*qualitative* sameness), as in 'Rachel is the same age as Tony, and the same height as last year', sometimes to indicate that what is named twice should be counted once (*numerical* sameness), as in 'The morning star and the evening star are the same planet'. The word 'identical' can also have the former sense (identical twins, identical dresses) as well as the latter; hence philosophers are liable to discuss both kinds of sameness under the label 'identity'.

Similarity comes in degrees and ways. Jane may be *exactly* the same *in looks* as she was, or as her sister, but only *roughly* the same *in weight*. Leibniz's thesis of the

identity (i.e. numerical identity) of indiscernibles (i.e. qualitative identicals) states that no two things can be exactly the same in every way, sharing all their qualities. This is disputable, but becomes a tautology if numerical-identity-with-*a* is allowed to count among the qualities of *a*. The converse thesis (often called Leibniz's law), that things differing in quality must be two, is harder to doubt. But it must not be interpreted in such a way as to banish change, since *a* can have some quality that *b* used to lack, and still be numerically the same as *b*: many things persist through change. Hume thought that in the 'proper' sense identity over time requires changelessness. That would be true if the proper sense of identity were exact qualitative identity; but in fact the numerical sense is no less proper, merely different.

Different kinds of thing have different *criteria* of numerical identity. For example, mathematical classes are the same if and only if they have the same members; contrast regiments, clubs, etc., which can survive the addition or withdrawal of members. The criterion of identity of many things is vague, especially over time. For example, even though the plural 'clouds' shows that we sometimes count clouds, as we do not at a single time count fog, nevertheless the question 'How many clouds are there in the sky?' will rarely have even an approximate answer, unless it is 'none'. Sometimes the criterion is purely conventional (one road runs all the way from Edinburgh to London) or stipulated for a particular purpose (you are to count books by titles, not volumes or copies of titles or copies of volumes). Conflicting criteria are even allowed to coexist. For example, someone might count St Mark's and the Palazzo Ducale as different buildings and also as parts of the same building.

Numerical identity is an *equivalence relation, i.e. transitive, symmetric, and strongly reflexive. But philosophers have sometimes proposed criteria, e.g. of personal identity, that fail to respect these properties. For example, it is logically (if not physically) possible that two different persons should both be linked by memory chains with a given later person. But it is not logically possible that two different persons should be numerically the same person as a given person. For the same reason 'is a clone of' lacks the formal properties of numerical identity; and although 'lies on the same, non-branching line of clone-descent with' puts things right formally, it would be odd if, for example, the identity of last year's bulb with its current clone depended on there happening to be no current rivals. Some philosophers have concluded that a criterion of identity need not be logically equivalent to identity, i.e. equivalent in all logically possible situations, whether or not within our experience. Others infer that the search for a precise and helpful criterion cannot always succeed.

Geach and others have used Locke's myth of the prince whose soul comes to 'inform the Body of a Cobler' to argue that numerical identity is relative to sorts, so that it is logically possible, for example, that the prince of today should be the same *person* but not the same *man* as the prince of yesterday, even though both are persons and both are men. (Locke's own conclusion was different, though just as odd.) If this is right, the number you get depends on what sort of things you are counting things *as*. In any case it depends on what sort of things you are counting, as Frege saw: e.g. one atlas is many maps.   C.A.K.

*identity of indiscernibles; of identity criterion.

D. Hume, *A Treatise of Human Nature* (1739), ed. L. A. Selby-Bigge, 3rd edn. (Oxford, 1978), I. iv. 6.

J. Locke, *An Essay Concerning Human Understanding*, 2nd edn. (1694), ed. P. H. Nidditch (Oxford, 1975), II. xxvii.

M. K. Munitz (ed.), *Identity and Individuation* (New York, 1971).

D. R. P. Wiggins, *Sameness and Substance* (Oxford, 1980).

identity, criterion of. A criterion of *identity is a principle specifying, in a non-circular way, the identity-conditions of objects of a given kind. Objects of different kinds can have different identity-conditions. Thus, a criterion of identity for rivers might specify that if x is a river and y is a river, then x and y are the *same* river if and only if x and y have the same source and the same mouth.

So, one common form for a criterion of identity to take is this: if x is a K and y is a K, then x and y are the same K if and only if x and y stand in relation R. But there is another form of identity criterion, commonly associated with Frege, and exemplified by his criterion of identity for the directions of lines: the direction of line x is the same as the direction of line y if and only if line x is parallel with line y.   E.J.L.

E. J. Lowe, 'What is a Criterion of Identity?', *Philosophical Quarterly* (1989).

identity, the paradox of. Wittgenstein says (*Tractatus Logico-Philosophicus*, 5.5303): 'Roughly speaking, to say of *two* things that they are identical is nonsense, and to say of *one* thing that it is identical with itself is to say nothing at all.' If identity is a relation it must hold either between two distinct things or between a thing and itself. To say that *A* is the same as *B*, when *A* and *B* are distinct, is bound to be false; but to say that *A* is the same as *A* is to utter a tautology. Different solutions have been found by different philosophers for this paradox, which is discussed by Plato, Hume, and Frege, amongst others. Frege dealt with the paradox by making a distinction between the *sense and reference of an expression. Wittgenstein's solution is to deny that identity is a relation. Anything useful that is said by means of 'is the same as' can be said by a sentence containing a repeated expression. Thus instead of saying 'The author of the *Iliad* was the same as the author of the *Odyssey*' we can say, repeating the 'x', 'For some person, x, both x wrote the *Iliad* and x wrote the *Odyssey*', and for 'Florence is the same as Firenze' 'For some city, x, both x is called Florence and x is called Firenze'.   C.J.F.W.

C. J. F. Williams, *What is Identity?* (Oxford, 1989).

identity of indiscernibles. The doctrine of the *identity of indiscernibles has various formulations, ranging from a trivially true version to the metaphysically weighty version employed by Leibniz. Here is a trivially true version:

for any individuals x and y, if, for any property f, x has f if and only if y has f, then x is identical with y. Let the property f be the property of being identical with y. Surely y has it. But, then, if x has every property y has, then x has it also. Hence, x is identical with y. Here is Leibniz's version: for any individuals x and y, if for any intrinsic, non-relational property f, x has f if and only if y has f, then x is identical with y. Thus, according to Leibniz's version, if x and y are distinct individuals, they can not differ simply with respect to extrinsic, relational properties; they must differ with respect to some intrinsic, non-relational property as well.

Clearly, the exact content of Leibniz's version of the identity of indiscernibles turns on how we understand the notion of an intrinsic, non-relational property. Subsequent to Leibniz, philosophers have formulated versions of the identity of indiscernibles intermediate in strength between his strong version and the trivial version first mentioned. Others have offered alleged counter-examples to various of the intermediate versions, many having their origin in Kant's examples of *incongruent counterparts. Consider an exactly matching pair of gloves, suppose the entire universe consists in the left glove facing the right glove. There are two distinct gloves. But what is the difference between the two? Consideration of such alleged counter-examples has yielded insights concerning the notion of an intrinsic, non-relational property, as well as the nature of space.   R.C.SLE.

*identity, criterion of.

I. Kant, *Prolegomena to Any Future Metaphysics*, tr. Peter G. Lucas (Manchester, 1953), sect. 13.

G. W. Leibniz, 'On the Principle of Indiscernibles', in *Leibniz: Philosophical Writings*, ed. and tr. G. H. R. Parkinson and M. Morris (London, 1973).

identity theory of mind, the. The contemporary mind–body identity theory, developed in the late 1950s, is that mental events are (that is, are identical with) physical-biological processes in the brain. Pain, for example, is nothing over and above a neural state in the central nervous system, presumably the excitation of certain neurons ('nociceptive neurons') in the brain. Although minds as substantival entities (e.g. Cartesian mental substances) have largely disappeared from philosophy, we can formulate an identity theory for minds as well: minds are brains (of appropriate complexity)—or to have a mind is to have a brain.

The identity theory in this form identifies psychological types (properties, kinds) with physical types (properties, kinds). This is why the theory is sometimes called 'type *physicalism'. When pain is identified with, say, the excitation of c-fibres, it is pain as a *type of event* that is being claimed to be a neural event. The identity can also be put in terms of *properties of events*, as follows: the property of being a pain event is identical with the property of being a c-fibre stimulation event. Of course, if pain is identical with a neural event type, individual occurrences of pain will also be identical with individual events falling under that neural type.

Proponents of the identity theory often invoke considerations of *simplicity (*Ockham's razor) in its support. We observe a regular correlation between pain and a certain neural state, N. Such correlations cry out for an explanation: Why is it that pain is experienced just when N occurs? Why don't we experience, say, an itch when N occurs? But there seems no way to give a more basic explanation of why the pain–N correlation holds, and we seem forced to accept it as a brute, unexplainable relationship whereby a mental state 'dangles' from a physical process. However, by identifying pain with N, and other mental states with their neural substrates, we can, it is argued, be rid of these 'nomological danglers', and simplify both our ontology and our theory.

Mind–body identity is often likened by its advocates to certain identities discovered by empirical science such as 'The temperature of a gas is the mean kinetic energy of its molecules', 'Light is electromagnetic radiation', and 'The gene is the DNA molecule'. Just as scientific research has uncovered these 'theoretical identities', research in neurophysiology has shown, goes the argument, that pain is the excitation of certain neurons, and similarly for other mental states.

Another major argument for the identity theory centres on considerations of mental causation. That mental events are sometimes causes and effects of bodily events is part of deeply entrenched common sense, and it is also a widely shared assumption of philosophers and working psycho-logists. It has been notoriously difficult, however, to explain how *mental causation is possible, as long as mental phenomena are thought to lie outside the physical domain. On the identity theory, however, the problem simply vanishes: there no longer is a special problem about how one's desire for a drink of water can cause one's limbs to move, since to have a desire for water *is* for the brain to be in a certain neural state. On this approach, then, mental causation turns out to be merely a special case of physical causation.

An important objection against the identity theory exploits the *variable realizability (or multiple realizability) of mental states. Consider pain: the neural substrate of pain in humans may be the excitation of c-fibres, but there is ample reason to doubt that the same neural state subserves pain in all pain-capable organisms (think of octopuses). Moreover, there seems no a priori reason to exclude non-biological systems as psychological systems. It appears then that pain as a type cannot be identified with any single physical kind. The best we can do, the objection goes, is the token-identity theory (or 'token physicalism'), which only identifies each instance (or 'token') of pain with an instance of some physical kind, without identifying kinds with kinds. Another major objection to the identity theory is based on the observation that the phenomenological features of the mental (e.g. the hurtfulness of pain, the visual qualities of an after-image), with their characteristic subjectivity and privacy, could not be identical with the neural properties of the brain which are entirely objective and publicly accessible.   J.K.

*materialism; anomalous monism; union theory; dualism.

D. Armstrong, *A Materialist Theory of Mind* (London, 1968).
T. Honderich, *Mind and Brain* (Oxford, 1988).
C. Macdonald, *Mind–Body Identity Theories* (London, 1989).
U. T. Place, *Identifying the Mind: Selected Papers* (New York, 2003).

ideology. In its original use, ideology was to be a general 'science of ideas', of their elements and relations (Destutt de Tracy, 1754–1836). Although interest in ideology in this broad sense has persisted—sometimes with a more a priori character, sometimes more sociological—perhaps the most important usage in contemporary philosophy and politics is narrower and more normative, standing for a collection of beliefs and values held by an individual or group for other than purely epistemic reasons, e.g. bourgeois ideology, nationalist ideology, or gender ideology.

The normative use of the term typically involves two elements.

First, a particular style of *explanation* in which the prevalence of certain beliefs and values is attributed (to some significant degree) to a non-epistemic role that they serve for the individuals who hold them or for society at large. This role can be specified in terms of the satisfaction of the non-epistemic interests of certain groups, or in terms of social–symbolic functions such as stabilization or legitimization of the status quo.

Second, a particular style of *criticism* in which beliefs and values are called into question precisely by giving this sort of interest-based or social–symbolic explanation of their prevalence—an explanation characteristically not known by the believers themselves.

Thus, Karl Marx and Friedrich Engels argued that the dominant ideas in any epoch not only reflect the experience of the dominant class, but also serve its interests. Dominant ideas do this in part by 'inverting' various features of social reality—reifying the historically contingent and class-bound as necessary and universal, or reversing the role of cause and effect in thinking about economic activity or 'human nature'—in ways that make the social order seem natural, inevitable, or just. More recently, members of the *Frankfurt School have developed a conception of ideology as a communicative structure systematically distorted by power relations; Jürgen Habermas in particular developed a notion of 'ideological critique' that stresses the failure of certain beliefs and values to withstand open, uncoerced, but none the less interest-involving, intersubjective discussion. (In more orthodox sociology, Karl Mannheim and others have emphasized the social function of ideologies in opposing change or lessening apparent value conflicts.)

A number of important questions arise. What is the critical force of calling a belief ideological? Perhaps it is an epistemic defect to hold a belief in part for reasons 'hidden' from oneself and that involve interest rather than evidence, but perhaps all belief-forming processes involve unacknowledged causes and (at least some) non-epistemic interests. Moreover, such belief-forming processes might also possess various epistemic virtues, such as reliability. It is an open question whether a given belief, produced by such a process, is true, or reflects available evidence. Would mere failure of a belief to withstand self-awareness about its origins or open social discussion of its content constitute a genuinely *epistemic* defect?

What is the structure of ideological explanations of beliefs and values? Is there a credible theory of the social psychological mechanisms by which social interests or symbolic needs shape individuals' beliefs and values in the unacknowledged ways that are presupposed when ideologies are claimed to have a functional role?

Finally, what does normative use of the concept of ideology presuppose about the existence of contrasting, epi-stemically respectable ways of knowing? In particular, does the normative notion of ideology presuppose the availability of notions of objective inquiry or objective interests of the very sort that attention to the social character of knowledge and valuation renders suspect?   P.R.

*historical materialism; noble lie.

T. Eagleton, *Ideology: An Introduction* (London, 1991).
R. Geuss, *The Idea of a Critical Theory* (Cambridge, 1981).
J. Habermas, *Knowledge and Human Interests* (Boston, 1971).
K. Mannheim, *Ideology and Utopia* (London, 1946).
K. Marx and F. Engels, *The German Ideology* (1846; first pub. 1932).

idiolect. The term 'idiolect' is intended to mark the notion of a *language which is not the language of a community (sociolect) but rather of an individual. Idiolects more than sociolects have been the focus of much philosophical interest in recent years because of the close connection between the language or meanings of an individual and his intentional states. Idiolects are the place where philosophy of language and philosophy of mind meet.

It is possible that one should have a highly social conception of idiolects, but that would still not spoil the idea that when one studies idiolects one's object of study is the individual's linguistic competence and performance rather than the language of a community. There is, in other words, no contradiction in the idea that one should think of idiolects as being socially constituted. In fact Tyler Burge holds precisely such a view of idiolects. This is an important point because it puts us on guard against the widespread and careless use of the term 'idiolect' to talk of a non-social or individualistic conception of the language of an individual. So care must be taken to distinguish between objects of study such as sociolects and idiolects on the one hand (such as Oxford English and Peter Strawson's English respectively) and on the other hand an individualist or social conception of these objects of study (such as those of Chomsky and of Tyler Burge respectively). The term 'idiolect' strictly applies only to a certain object of study (i.e. to an individual's language), not to an individualist conception of an individual's language.   A.B.

Akeel Bilgrami, *Belief and Meaning* (Oxford, 1993), 66–73.
Tyler Burge, 'Wherein is Language Social?', in *Reflections on Chomsky*, ed. A. George (Oxford, 1989).

idols. The danger of allegiance to false gods is a premiss of all orthodoxies which acknowledge nevertheless their powerful appeal to the common people and seek to persuade them that idol-worship is not only futile but also dangerous. For the Christian philosophers Boyle, Malebranche, and Berkeley, idolatry is implied by such common-sense beliefs as the self-sustaining power of nature, the causal efficacy of created things, and the mind-independent existence of the sun, moon, stars, and other objects. The theory of idols is transformed into a general theory of *ideology in the first book of Bacon's *Novum Organum*, which describes the epistemologically pernicious effects of human attachment to the fictions created by language, tradition, custom, and imagination. The accusation of idolatry continues to have philosophical importance in Nietzsche's attacks on Socrates and Kant in his *Twilight of the Idols*, and in the attempts of Marx, Freud, and other social critics to demystify social and economic structures and to assist people in relinquishing their devotion to things which don't actually exist but which have power over them anyway.   CATH.W.

F. Bacon, *Novum Organum*, in *Works*, ed. J. Spedding, R. L. Ellis, and P. D. Heath, 14 vols. (Cambridge, 1857–61; repr. Stuttgart, 1961–3), viii.

if: *see* conditionals.

iff. Abbreviation for the *biconditional connective 'if and only if'. '*P* if and only if *Q*' abbreviates '*P* if *Q*, and *P* only if *Q*'. On the *truth-functional treatment of 'iff', '*P* iff *Q*' is true just when *P* and *Q* are both true or both false; so '*P* iff *Q*' and '*Q* iff *P*' are equivalent. In ordinary contexts, however, reversing the order in a biconditional can make a difference. 'Alicia comes down for lunch if and only if we serve alligator stew', for example, differs in meaning from 'We serve alligator stew if and only if Alicia comes down for lunch'.   D.H.S.

James D. McCawley, *Everything that Linguists have always Wanted to Know about Logic (but were Ashamed to Ask)*, 2nd edn. (Chicago, 1993).
David H. Sanford, *If P, Then Q: Conditionals and the Foundations of Reasoning*, 2nd edn. (London, 2003).

ignoratio elenchi. Literally, ignorance of refutation. A *fallacy of traditional logic, where it was usually taken to mean 'ignorance of what is to be refuted' or, more inclusively, 'of what is to be proved'. *Ignoratio elenchi* is arguing for one thing as if it proved another thing. For example, it is *ignoratio elenchi* to use an argument against euthanasia as if it proved that you shouldn't eat the dead. The 'ignorance' is in the mind of the would-be refuter or prover, and often arises from confusion of similar-seeming conclusions. The rhetorical trick of deliberately infecting an audience with such confusion is not really this fallacy.   C.A.K.

C. L. Hamblin, *Fallacies* (London, 1970).

illocutions: *see* linguistic acts.

illusion, arguments from. The classic example of such an argument appears in the epistemology of *perception; modern versions focus on cases of total hallucination, where one seems to see something when there is nothing there at all, rather than on illusions such as the famous bent-stick case in which there is *something* there (the stick) which looks one way and is another. The argument, which is still called the argument from illusion, starts from the seemingly undeniable fact that it is impossible to distinguish (from the inside, as it were) a hallucination of being faced with an elephant from the state of actually being faced with an elephant. What conclusion can we draw from this?

Suppose we hold that there are two states at issue here, a veridical one which is a relation between perceiver and (external) object, and a hallucinatory one which is a non-relational state of the perceiver. The argument from illusion then maintains that since there is no distinguishable difference between the two states, we must give a broadly similar account of them both. This suggests that the veridical state consists of two elements, one (the common element) which obtains even in hallucination, and the other (the presence of the outer object) which obtains only if we are lucky.

The argument is sometimes supposed to take us beyond this, and to support a particular account of the common element, the 'act-object' theory. The idea here is that since the deluded are not aware of outer things but are still aware of something, they must be aware of an inner thing (an appearance). We then appeal to the indistinguishability of hallucination and genuine perception to argue that in success too we are (primarily) aware of an appearance, sometimes called a *'percept', 'sensum', or *'sense-datum', and only secondarily aware of the outer object. But this move amounts more to an assertion of the act-object theory than an independent argument for it. For it assumes without argument that the content or nature of the hallucination is an inner object, when this was exactly what was in question. The adverbial theory, which denies that assumption, is equally compatible with the argument from illusion.

There is a different, sceptical form of argument from illusion. This is just a special case of Cartesian *scepticism. Descartes argued that we do not know that we are fully clothed, because we cannot distinguish the state of being clothed from that of being naked while dreaming that we are clothed. This is an argument from the general possibility of error; it argues from perceptual error to the conclusion that we never know that things are the way they look.

If that conclusion is intended to be entirely general, the premiss must be that there is no case at all in which we can distinguish our being right from our being wrong; all seemingly veridical states may for all we know be hallucinatory ones. This is a strong claim, and it is one which the first argument from illusion had no need to make. In attempting to support the 'common element' theory, one need only suppose that in a reasonable range of cases we

are unable to distinguish hallucination from genuine perception.

Both of the arguments from illusion that we have considered so far concern perception. But their starting-point is one about indistinguishability. Considered in very general form, the argument from illusion argues from the indistinguishability of two states, one of which is a success and the other a failure, to what we might call the 'conjunctive thesis' that what one gets in success is a conjunction of two independent elements: (1) something which success and failure have in common and (2) something only present in successful cases.

If this is the general nature of arguments from illusion, there will be other examples to be found wherever there is indistinguishability. One such tries to persuade us that knowledge is some form of belief. You cannot tell (from the inside) whether your cognitive state is one of knowing or merely one of believing (truly or falsely, it doesn't matter which). Therefore, knowledge must be defined as belief *plus* something—e.g. as belief *plus* truth and justification, as in the tripartite definition. (*Gettier.) This is a 'conjunctive' theory of knowledge.

In these ways arguments from illusion have been a potent weapon in establishing a broadly Cartesian view of the mind.   J.D.

*oar in water.

A. J. Ayer, *The Foundations of Empirical Knowledge* (London, 1969).
F. Jackson, *Perception* (Cambridge, 1977), 107–11.
J. McDowell, 'Criteria, Defeasibility and Knowledge', in J. Dancy (ed.), *Perceptual Knowledge* (Oxford, 1988).
H. H. Price, *Perception* (Oxford, 1932).

image. The nature of mental imagery and its relation to thought and imagination (as creative thought) are long-standing issues. Aristotle called attention to the mind's ability to present objects for itself (*phantasia*). 'Imagists' take picture-like entities to form the elements of all representational states, and some include here perception. Others claim that no such entities occur even in memory and imagining. The role of imagery in memory and problem-solving is contested in *cognitive science, where Frege's contrast between image as psychological incident and thought is echoed in the view that images are simply arrays on the brain's 'visual buffer', their content fully accountable in general or syntactical terms. 'Pictorialists' argue plausibly that the content has an irreducibly spatial aspect. Some claim that the whole issue, as much in philosophy besides, rests on unexamined imagery in another sense, that is on analogy and figure of speech.   A.H.

*imagination; eidetic imagery.

Alastair Hannay, *Mental Images: A Defence* (London, 1971).
Michael Tye, *The Imagery Debate* (Cambridge, Mass., 1991).
Alan R. White, *The Language of Imagination* (Oxford, 1990).

imagery, eidetic: *see* eidetic imagery.

imagination. Imagination is the power of the mind to consider things which are not present to the senses, and to consider that which is not taken to be real. Just as the imaginary contrasts with the real, so imagination contrasts with both *perception and *cognition. Certain philosophers have nevertheless assigned it to a central role in explaining the mind's ability to represent any reality: thus Hume, despairing of the powers of both the senses and reason, explained the genesis of our idea of body by reference to the imagination; and Kant appealed to the imagination in his explanation of how thought or experience of an objective order was possible. The resources of the imagination have often been thought to be bound by the deliverances of the senses—the power of imagination being the recombination of simple elements presented to the mind through the senses. On accounts of thinking in the tradition of *empiricism, imagination has been implicated through the role of imagery in all thought, the limits of imagination becoming the limits of thought. Berkeley notoriously argued for *idealism by claiming that it was impossible to imagine a tree unperceived, and hence that it was impossible to conceive of objects existing independently of us.

Most heat has been expended debating the nature of mental *images, those exercises of the imagination which correspond to our perceptual modalities. Certain acts of imagination have a distinctive phenomenology which others do not. In complying with the request to imagine that Scotland should be an independent country, one need not perform an act of the former sort, while one would do so in visualizing the destruction of the Houses of Parliament. Correlative to visualizing are other acts of imagination corresponding to the other sense modalities: for example, people are capable of auditory, gustatory, and olfactory imagining. Questions arise concerning both the relation of mental imagery to the corresponding perceptions and the differences between them, for Hume the problem of distinguishing impressions from ideas.

According to the picture theory of imagery, having a mental image consists of being aware of some mental entity before the mind which represents the external scene imagined. Inasmuch as this provides an inner surrogate for the outer object of a mental state, this account parallels the *sense-datum theory of perception. There is now almost universal hostility to both views, not least because of the model of the mind they present: that of the subject surveying the mind's contents as the sole audience within a private theatre.

Those with leanings towards *behaviourism often show the most hostility to the idea of mental imagery. The denial that there is any imagery is likely to be taken as evidence of the sceptic's own lack of imaginative powers while attempts to explain imagination purely in terms of outer performance lack plausibility: for example, Ryle's attempt to explain imagination in terms of pretence.

Mental imagery has become the focus of a debate within psychology since research has suggested that imagery is involved in certain kinds of reasoning. Subjects often report employing imagery in solving certain tasks, such as answering the query 'Do frogs have lips?' Imagery

also seems to be exploited in certain forms of spatial reasoning. This has led to a debate in both psychology and philosophy over the nature of the imagery involved in these cases, in particular whether there are distinct forms of representation within the brain, although it is not clear whether this new debate is continuous with the more traditional debates about imagery and imagination.   M.G.F.M.

G. Currie and I. Ravenscroft, *Recreative Minds: Imagination in Philosophy and Psychology* (Oxford, 2003).

P. F. Strawson, 'Imagination and Perception', in *Freedom and Resentment* (London, 1974).

M. Tye, *The Imagery Debate* (Cambridge, Mass., 1992).

B. Williams, 'Imagination and the Self', in *Problems of the Self* (Cambridge, 1973).

imagination, aesthetic. The *imagination has often been put forward as the mental capacity most essential to the production and appreciation of *art. Fictional representation is an obvious case in point. Instead of believing that we are seeing or reading about real persons and actions, we imagine them. Even if we see a real actor, it is the imagination that converts what we see into the character we are interested in. This form of imagination, which is continuous with a form of childhood play, may also be termed 'make-believe'.

The value of such activity no doubt lies in its broadening of our understanding beyond what we encounter in our own lives. It is a familar fact—which some philosophers, including Plato, have found disconcerting—that emotional identification is to some extent indifferent to the barrier between reality and make-believe: while insulated from the imaginary scene, we can nevertheless 'feel for' the characters. Imaginative involvement with fiction seems to be of value because it allows us to experience vulnerability to a wide range of feelings, whilst not threatening us with the real-life predicament of actually having to do something.

It is arguable that all aesthetic experience brings the imagination into play. To hear a piece of music as expressive of a mood or feeling is not merely to hear sounds of a certain pitch and duration: the mind appears to be active in grouping together what it literally perceives into a form with added significance. Wittgenstein's *duck-rabbit drawing provides a kind of analogy, where what is literally present is neither duck nor rabbit, but where the imagination has freedom to see the drawing as one or the other. Kant's idea that aesthetic experience involves a 'free play of the imagination and the understanding' has been prominent among the influences on this line of thinking.

C.J.

*aesthetic attitude.

R. Scruton, *Art and Imagination* (London, 1974).

K. Walton, *Mimesis as Make-Believe* (Cambridge, Mass., 1990).

immediate inference: *see* inference, immediate.

immortality. According to Christian and other Western theology, God is immortal in the strictest sense that he can never die, either because he is essentially everlasting (i.e. his nature is such that if he exists at one time, he exists at all times) or because he is eternal or timeless (i.e. he exists outside time). Other things—e.g. angels and human souls—have also often been supposed to be immortal in the less strict sense that their nature is such that they will exist everlastingly unless God were to choose to eliminate them.

Plato (*Phaedo* 78b–80c) argued that the *soul, being immaterial and not occupying space, has no parts; that the destruction of a thing consists in separating from each other its parts; and so that the soul can not be destroyed. Many subsequent philosophers—e.g. Berkeley—have repeated Plato's argument. However, it does seem that things can be destroyed (e.g. atoms reduced to energy) without their parts being separated.

Kant argued that the immortality of the soul was a 'postulate of pure practical reason'—that acting morally only made sense if thereby the agent made progress towards being totally holy, something he could attain only in unending life. Others have argued that acting morally only makes sense if there is a life after *death in which the good are rewarded. An obvious response is that acting morally makes no sense unless there is some point in so acting at the time in question. The traditional Christian and Islamic doctrine of an unending life—in heaven or hell—does not, however, require that living for ever is natural for humans. It requires only that they live for ever, and that may happen because God intervenes in the natural order to resurrect the dead—either souls alone or embodied humans. Many modern Christian theologians have held that resurrection rather than natural immortality is what the New Testament and the early Christian Fathers taught; and that revelation, not a priori reasoning, is what provides the grounds for belief in life after death. (A few very radical theologians have interpreted talk of 'immortality' or 'resurrection' in terms of the eternal significance of our present-life choices and attitudes.)

Indian religions teach that the dead are often reincarnated in new bodies, human or animal, on earth, in accordance with the law of karma—i.e. those who have led good lives are reincarnated as superior beings, those who have led bad lives as inferior beings. Those who continue to live good lives eventually reach 'liberation' and escape the round of rebirth. For Hindus *reincarnation is reincarnation of a soul; for Buddhists, some sort of continuity of experience. 'Liberation' is variously interpreted as merging into the one infinite consciousness, or as mere nothingness.

Those who hold that *personal identity is constituted by sameness of body (or brain) can believe it coherent to suppose that humans survive death only if human bodies are reformed with largely the same matter (e.g. around the original bones in the cemetery). That cannot always happen, for bodies may be destroyed beyond the possibility of reassembly. Those who believe in life after death for all (on earth or elsewhere) must hold a non-bodily criterion of personal identity—as consisting in the continued existence of an immaterial soul, or perhaps in mere con-

tinuity of psychological states; even if resurrected persons have bodies (old or new), sameness of body cannot be what constitutes sameness of persons.   R.G.S.

*atheism and agnosticism.

J. Hick, *Death and Eternal Life* (London, 1976).

imperialism. The concept of imperialism is very general, involving the oppression or *exploitation of weak and impoverished countries by powerful ones, though for most of its intellectual career 'imperialism' was a term of approbation. The word goes back to the Roman Empire, recent examples being the British Empire, which saw its heyday at the end of the nineteenth century, the recently deceased Russian Empire, and the contemporary American Empire, known as the New World Order. This latter involves a net transfer of resources from the underdeveloped countries to the developed ones, a process orchestrated by such American-dominated institutions as the International Monetary Fund.

Modern ideas of imperialism owe much to Lenin, who characterized the phenomenon as comprising emphasis on the export of capital, increasingly centralized production and distribution, merging of banking and industrial capital, and division of the world into spheres of influence between capitalist powers who then fight each other over their share of the spoils as, for example, in the First World War. In more recent decades, Lenin's ideas tend to have been replaced by views, going back to Kautsky, which look at imperialism as the relation between developed and underdeveloped countries and argue that conflict between developed countries is disappearing. These views are best exemplified in the trend known as dependency theory, which maintains that exploitation occurs through trade between the centre and the periphery of the world economy which embodies an unequal exchange with a long-run tendency for the terms of trade for Third World countries to worsen.

Explanations of imperialism are as varied as theories of human nature; and several versions of imperialism, including Lenin's and dependency theory, found it difficult to incorporate recent phenomena such as the newly industrializing countries. But it remained the concept around which thinking about international relations in the twentieth century revolved.   D.McL.

*international relations, philosophy of.

Anthony Brewer, *Marxist Theories of Imperialism: A Critical Survey* (London, 1980).
George Lichtheim, *Imperialism* (London, 1971).

implication. Ordinary uses of 'implication' are varied and often equivocal. Two important uses for logic are:

1. Implication understood as a relation between a set of premises and a conclusion deducible from or a logical consequence of those premises.
2. Implication understood as the relation between antecedent and consequent of a true *conditional proposition.

On use (2) the truth of '$(P \supset Q)$' of the propo-sitional calculus is read as 'P materially implies Q' or 'P implies Q'. Given the weak conditions for the truth of $(P \supset Q)$ and the attendant 'paradoxes of material implication', alternative systems have been devised with stronger conditionals. C. I. Lewis's systems of *strict implication introduce the symbol '-3', where the truth of '$(P -3 Q)$' is read as 'P strictly implies Q'. $(P -3 Q)$ is equivalent to $\square (P \supset Q)$, where '$\square$' is a necessity operator. Other systems with stronger conditionals are those of Carnap's system of L-implication, and more recent formal systems of entailment. A motivation for such efforts is to bring the conditional more into line either with (1) or with those uses in (2) which suppose further connections in meaning between antecedent and consequent.   R.B.M.

*truth-function.

A. Anderson and N. Belnap, *Entailment*, i (Princeton, NJ, 1975).
C. Lewis and C. Langford, *Symbolic Logic* (New York, 1959).

implicature. Meaning that is supplementary or contrary to that logically entailed by a sentence. For example, in 'What did you think of his argument?', 'Impeccable scholarship'. The discovery of conversational and conventional implicature by Paul Grice in the 1960s cast doubt on the solution or dissolution of philosophical problems by *linguistic philosophy, because it suggests meaning cannot be wholly and appropriately displayed by *conceptual analysis. If you ask someone, 'Could you direct me to the library?', and they smugly answer only 'Yes', it is appropriate to ask them if they have heard of conversational implicature.   S.P.

Paul Grice, *Studies in the Ways of Words* (Cambridge, Mass., 1989).

impredicative definition. A definition is impredicative if it refers to a collection which contains the object to be defined. For example, the 'least upper bound' of a set is defined to be 'the smallest among the upper bounds' of the set; and the 'Russell set' is the set of all sets that don't contain themselves. The former is a common definition, usually uncontested. The latter leads to Russell's paradox. If one thinks of definitions as somehow creating or constructing the defined objects, then impredicative definitions are circular.   S.S.

*vicious circle; types, theory of; reducibility, axiom of; mathematics, history of the philosophy of.

Allen Hazen, 'Predicative Logics', in D. Gabbay and F. Guenthner (eds.), *Handbook of Philosophical Logic*, i, (Dordrecht, 1983).

incommensurability. Within philosophy of science, theories which, in a radical sense, cannot be compared are often said to be incommensurable, a term first given wide currency by Kuhn. Scientific revolutions, which involve wholesale discarding of one set of theories in favour of another, are thought typically to produce such radical shifts of meaning that the concepts employed in the theories propounded after revolution simply cannot be expressed in terms of the concepts of pre-revolutionary

theory. Commitment to such an incommensurability thesis is liable to lead on to a strong *relativism or antirationalism. But the very intelligibility of this thesis is questionable. Genuinely incommensurable theories cannot be judged incompatible; but then why, and how, do scientific revolutions result in discarding theories—why not just preserve both the earlier theories and the later theories incommensurable with them?   J.L.

T. S. Kuhn, *The Structure of Scientific Revolutions*, 2nd edn. (Chicago, 1970).

incommensurability, moral. The idea of the incommensurability of scientific paradigms has been borrowed by moral philosophers to express the idea that, because there is a plurality of values, moral dilemmas may sometimes be irresolvable. The idea is best illuminated by its converse; *utilitarianism is the classic example of a moral theory which supposes all values to be ultimately reducible to the one value of 'happiness', so that in any situation the various possible courses of action can all be weighed against one another by considering how much happiness each will produce. If, however, there is not just one ultimate value, then in some cases it may be impossible to weigh the competing claims of, say, *'justice' against those of *'friendship', or the claims of 'honesty' against those of *'utility'. If these values are incommensurable, it may then be an illusion to suppose that there is always such a thing as 'the right thing to do'. Indeed, there may be situations of 'moral tragedy' where there is no action open to us which would not be morally wrong.   R.J.N.

R. Chang (ed.), *Incommensurability, Incomparability, and Practical Reason* (Cambridge, Mass., 1997).
Christopher W. Gowans (ed.), *Moral Dilemmas* (Oxford, 1987).

incompatibilism: *see* compatibilism.

incompleteness. A logical system is complete just in case there is no truth of the system that it is incapable of proving. By a theorem of Kurt Gödel in 1931, no formalization of ordinary arithmetic is complete. Either arithmetic is inconsistent or there is at least one of its truths which arithmetic cannot prove. More technically, Gödel demonstrated that any consistent first-order theory of arithmetic, if equipped with an effective procedure for recognizing its own proofs, is incomplete. Alternatively, let T be a first-order formalization of arithmetic and P be the predicate 'is a proof of T'. If the class of objects satisfying P is a decidable class, then T is incomplete.

The incompleteness theorem came as a nasty shock to mathematicians influenced by Hilbert's programme, for whom mathematical truth consisted in demonstrability.   J.W.

*completeness; Gödel's theorem.

Ernest Nagel and James R. Newman, *Gödel's Proof* (New York, 1958).

incomplete symbol. A symbol that is a constituent of meaningful sentences but that has no meaning in isolation. An incomplete symbol is amenable only to a contextual definition, not an explicit one. The idea of incomplete symbol gained prominence primarily through Russell, who used it to express distinctive views in logic and metaphysics. Thus Russell held that the theoretical terms of physics (e.g. 'particle') are incomplete symbols, meaning thereby that these terms do not mean or refer to anything in isolation, but sentences containing theoretical terms can be analysed using only non-theoretical vocabulary. Observe that the notion of incomplete symbol is quite different from Frege's notion of *unsaturated expression. An extended discussion of incomplete symbols and their applications in logic is contained in chapter 3 of A. N. Whitehead and B. Russell, *Principia Mathematica*, i (Cambridge, 1927).   A.GUP.

*descriptions.

incongruent counterparts. Two hands may be identical except that one is left, the other right. An object capable of having an incongruent counterpart (whether or not one actually exists) is called an *enantiomorph*. This phenomenon was thought by Kant to show that space exists independently and is not merely a matter of relations between things. In terms of the spatial relations—distances and angles—between their parts, the two hands are indistinguishable. Since God might have created nothing but a single hand, which would still have been left or right, the spatial relations of the hands to each other or to other things is irrelevant. The difference between the hands must then consist, Kant argued, in a relation to *space itself, though it is not clear how space is supposed to turn the explanatory trick.   M.C.

G. Nerlich, *The Shape of Space* (Cambridge, 1976).

inconsistent triad. A set of three propositions that cannot all be true together. For example, 'She was an orphan; Tim outlived her; Tim was her father'. Often it will be implied that all the subsets of the triad—the units and pairs within it—are consistent. Inconsistent sets can be of any size, and the triads do not deserve special attention.   C.A.K.

incontinence: *see* weakness of will.

incorrigibility. The property of not being open to correction. One philosophical response to epistemological *scepticism is to argue for the existence of a class of propositions which have the property. They would be propositions about which we could not be mistaken. Such incorrigible statements are taken by some philosophers to be a sure basis for our entire knowledge of the world. They are said to include assertions of present sensations and appearances, such as 'I am in pain' and 'It looks green to me'. It can be argued, however, that such statements may be false even if the speaker is sincere, through an error of misidentification or expression.   W.E.A.

*certainty; given, the.

William Alston, *Epistemic Justification* (Ithaca, NY, 1989).

independence, logical. Let *s* be a sentence and let *T* be a set of sentences in a formal language. Informally, *s* is *independent* of *T* if *T* does not determine the truth-value of *s*. In other words, *s* is independent of *T* if *s* is not a logical consequence of *T* and the negation of *s* is not a logical consequence of *T* (some authors omit the last clause). In particular, *s* is *deductively* independent of *T* if neither *s* nor the negation of *s* can be deduced from *T*, and *s* is *semantically* independent of *T* if there is an interpretation of the language in which every member of *T* is true and *s* is true, and also there is an interpretation of the language in which every member of *T* is true and *s* is false. In a logical system consisting of axioms and rules of inference, an axiom is 'independent' if neither it nor its negation can be deduced from the other axioms by the rules.   S.S.

Elliot Mendelson, *Introduction to Mathematical Logic*, 3rd edn. (Princeton, NJ, 1987).

indeterminacy in law. It is a view widely held among legal philosophers that, when competent lawyers dispute about the answer to some difficult question of *law, there is generally no single right answer—the law does not in fact resolve the issue either way, but leaves it open until it is resolved either by new legislation or by the decision of a judge exercising a discretion to make new law.

Such was the view of the advocates of *legal positivism, including John Austin and H. L. A. Hart, who said that there is no right answer in controversial cases because law is only what past authoritative statements or conventions have declared it to be, and in such cases convention or past decisions have not settled the issue either way. It is also the view of more radical legal philosophers, such as the American legal realists and critical legal scholars, who argue that there is never a right answer to a legal question because past legal doctrine is not sufficiently consistent to yield a single result. But judges, at least in Anglo-American law, never refuse to decide a legal dispute on the ground that the law is indeterminate, and rarely claim to be exercising a discretion to create new law and apply it retroactively. Even in very controversial cases they give answers to the questions of law in dispute which they claim to be, at least in their opinion, the right ones. Either the judges are lying to the public, or they are themselves under an illusion, or the no-right-answer thesis, in spite of its popularity, is wrong.

Arguments for the no-right-answer thesis are often corrupted by a failure to distinguish it from other, more plausible, claims. Suppose it is controversial among lawyers, for example, whether someone injured in a particular kind of accident has a legal right to be compensated for his emotional as well as his physical injuries. We must take care to distinguish among the following propositions: (1) The legal case for such a right is, in these circumstances, and all things considered, stronger than the case against it. (2) The case against it is, all things considered, stronger. (3) Competent lawyers disagree about which case is stronger. (4) There are strong arguments on both sides of the issue, and neither view is unreasonable. (5) It is uncertain which is stronger. (6) It is indeterminate which is stronger: the only 'right' answer is that there is no right answer.

Proposition 6—the no-right-answer claim—must of course be distinguished from proposition 3: it does not follow from the fact that lawyers disagree about a controversial case that neither side has the stronger arguments. Nor, obviously, is 6 the same as either 4 or 5: it does not follow from anyone's uncertainty about which case is stronger that neither is. Once these distinctions are made, it is unclear what kind of legal argument could show that proposition 6, rather than one or some combination of the other five choices, is the most accurate description of the law governing recovery for emotional damage. If we define law as the legal positivists did, of course, then proposition 6 might be true in virtue of that definition. But that would be circular reasoning: we should define law to match the practices of lawyers and judges, not redescribe those practices to suit some invented definition of law.

Legal philosophers sometimes make the mistake of thinking that in such a case proposition 6 is true by default: that is, when neither the case for the plaintiff nor for the case for the defendant is obviously much stronger than the other, and reasonable arguments can be made on both sides, it just follows that there is no right answer in the case. But that assumption neglects the difference between 6 on the one hand and 3, 4, and 5 on the other. Proposition 6 makes a very strong legal claim. It claims not just that we have no decisive reason to take one side or the other, and may never have one, but that, no matter how hard we look and think, we will not find any consideration or argument that would make the case on one side even marginally stronger than the case on the other. That is obviously a very ambitious claim, and, given the very wide range of considerations that lawyers regard as pertinent to legal argument, it would seem foolhardy to make it, at least in advance of the most painstaking research and reflection, about any particular legal controversy, let alone about all controversial cases taken together.

In fact, any lawyer or judge or law teacher or law student is likely to form an opinion about which side has the stronger legal argument in any particular case he or she studies, even though in difficult cases that opinion may be hesitant or unstable, and is very likely to be controversial. In practice, that is, almost no one accepts the no-right-answer thesis, even legal philosophers who are most vigorous in its theoretical support. The theoretical popularity of the thesis can be traced, I suggest, to two widespread assumptions. The first is the sound assumption that moral considerations are among the considerations that properly figure in controversies about what the law is. The second is the dubious view that there are often no right answers to moral disputes.   R.D.

*law and morals; moral scepticism.

John Austin, *The Province of Jurisprudence Determined*, ed. and intro. H. L. A. Hart (London, 1954).
Ronald Dworkin, *A Matter of Principle* (Cambridge, Mass., 1985), ch. 10.
H. L. A. Hart, *The Concept of Law* (Oxford, 1961).
John Mackie, 'The Third Theory of Law', *Philosophy and Public Affairs* (1977).

indeterminacy of meaning. A thesis advanced by W. V. Quine on the basis of his famous argument for the indeterminacy of translation. Meaning is what we aim to preserve in translating between languages, and if there is no fact of the matter as to which of two or more incompatible translations of a speaker's words is correct, there is no fact of the matter as to what precisely the words mean. The indeterminacy of meaning is taken to be a consequence of the indeterminacy of translation. Quine's argument for the latter assumes that the only facts that could settle which of two rival translations is correct are facts about the speaker's behaviour and circumstances: facts on show to other speakers. When a speaker of an unknown language utters the word 'gavagai' in the presence of a rabbit, there is nothing to indicate whether his utterance is to be translated as 'rabbit', or perhaps as 'undetached rabbit part'. Since there is no other evidence to decide the issue, there is nothing to chose between the two translations. Quine concludes that translation is indeterminate, and therefore meaning is indeterminate.

Chomsky has criticized Quine's argument for assuming that only behaviourist evidence can settle questions about the nature of linguistic reality. Others have pointed out that while we can deploy Quine's argument from the third-person perspective to a group of speakers we observe, the conclusion makes no sense from the first-person perspective. For how can we understand the two rival hypothesis about the meaning of the word 'rabbit' unless we can mean one thing by 'rabbit' when considering one hypothesis and another thing by 'rabbit' when considering the other hypothesis. And if we can understand each of these hypotheses, how can we accept a conclusion that is supposed to show that we cannot succeed in determinately meaning one thing or another by 'rabbit'?   B.C.S.

W. V. Quine, *Word and Object* (Cambridge, Mass., 1960), ch. 2.

indeterminacy of translation: *see* translation, indeterminacy of.

indeterminism. A view incompatible with *determinism. Since there are several versions of determinism and many kinds of incompatibility, there are many varieties of indeterminism. This article uses a definition of determinism cast in terms of causal sufficiency. (*Causality; *necessary and sufficient conditions.)

When one state or event is causally sufficient for the occurrence or obtaining of another, it determines it. It is causally impossible, when one state of affairs determines another, for the first but not the second to obtain. The thesis of determinism includes the view that everything that happens or obtains is determined by something earlier. By itself, this does not ensure that any particular event is determined by a state of affairs that obtained a week (or day, or hour) earlier. As Łukasiewicz points out, an infinite series of intervals, ordered by temporal priority, may have a finite total temporal extent. Consider, for example, an infinite series of intervals in which the final interval is twenty minutes long, and each interval is twice as long as its predecessor. The thesis of determinism requires some further specification such as that everything is determined by something not merely earlier, but earlier by a certain time increment, such as one second. This does support what determinists generally assume, namely that for any event e at time t and any earlier time $t–1$, some conditions obtaining earlier than time $t–1$ determine the event e. Support for the simpler principle that the conditions determining e are not just earlier than but exactly at time $t–1$ requires principles beyond the scope of this article. According to determinism, the state of the world long before you were born, a world you never made, determines everything that happens.

In one very weak version of indeterminism, its incompatibility with determinism is simple *contradiction. Determinism is false; its negation is true. This view is true so long as somewhere in the universe some occurrence violates the thesis of determinism.

By way of maximum contrast, an extremely strong version of indeterminism is strongly *contrary rather than merely contradictory to determinism. The world at any time and in all its aspects is totally independent of its state at any earlier time. Successive events are never causally related in any way. This form of indeterminism appears to be incompatible with the existence of successive events.

Between these extremely strong and weak versions of indeterminism, views of intermediate strength hold that there are many events, widely scattered in space and time, that violate determinism. These events need not be totally independent of earlier states of the world. Determination and indetermination admit of degrees. The state of the world ten minutes ago may, for example, be causally sufficient for your now being somewhere in the general vicinity without exactly determining your current location. If something determines that a person acts in a certain general way (which thereby precludes acting in many other ways), such as either to walk home on Divinity Avenue or to walk home on Oxford Street, it need not thereby determine which route the person chooses. Intermediate varieties of indeterminism do not imply that our behaviour is 'of an erratic and jerking phantom, without any rhyme or reason at all'. A person with good reason for walking home may have neither good reason nor prior determination for choosing one route over another.

Current science has no deterministic explanations for the emission of alpha particles by radio-active isotopes and some other very small-scale phenomena. One of the philosophical problems of *physics is to examine the claim that deterministic explanations of these phenomena are impossible without a radical revision of physics.

It is hard to know, if the world does manifest a degree of indeterminism, how much actions and occurrences that matter to us are affected by undetermined micro-events that seem insignificant in themselves. It is possible that they are affected a great deal. When sensors, switches, and amplifiers are hooked up in the right way, for example, indeterministic emissions of a few alpha particles can decide the location of the 2008 Olympic Games. Within our brains, perhaps there is often a similar amplification of indeterminacy.   D.H.S.

*chaos theory.

G. E. M. Anscombe, 'Causality and Determination', in E. Sosa (ed.), *Causation and Conditionals* (Oxford, 1975).
C. D. Broad, 'Determinism, Indeterminism, and Libertarianism', in *Ethics and the History of Philosophy* (London, 1952).
John Earman, *A Primer on Determinism* (Dordrecht, 1986).
Ted Honderich, *A Theory of Determinism* (Oxford, 1988).
R. Kane (ed.), *The Oxford Handbook of Free Will* (New York, 2001).
Jan Łukasiewicz, 'On Determinism', in Storrs McCall (ed.), *Polish Logic 1920–1939* (Oxford, 1967).

indexicals. The pronouns 'I', 'here', 'now', 'this', and related expressions like 'today', 'my grandmother', 'your house', etc. are known by philosophers of language as 'indexicals'. The term derives from C. S. Peirce; indexicals are sometimes called 'demonstratives' or 'token-reflexives'. (*Logically proper names.) These expressions seem to fall into the semantic category of *singular terms* or *referring expressions*—i.e. terms whose function in a language is to pick out a particular thing. But where indexicals seem to differ from other apparent singular terms, like names and descriptions, is that they pick out different objects or places or times in different contexts of utterance. So your utterance of 'I'm hungry' picks out you, while my utterance of the same sentence picks out me.

One way of appreciating the philosophical interest of indexicals is to look at them in the light of Frege's influential theory of *sense and reference. For Frege, the sense of a word determines its reference. If two words have the same sense, they have the same reference; if 'oculist' and 'eye-doctor' have the same sense, they have the same reference—they refer to the same entity. Similarly, if two words have different references, they have different senses; if 'the Pope in Rome' and 'the Pope in Avignon' refer to different things, they must have different senses.

How can this theory apply to indexicals? The trouble is that if the sense of 'I' determines its reference, then my utterance of 'I' has a different sense from yours. But surely our uses of these terms have *something* semantic in common, something it is natural to call their common meaning? Likewise with 'here' and 'now'; the common meaning of all tokens of these types is something like 'the place of this utterance' and 'the time of this utterance'. But the common meaning cannot be the sense of these terms, since the meaning determines different references in different contexts.

Non-Fregeans (e.g. David Kaplan and John Perry) have therefore distinguished two components of the meaning of a sentence containing an indexical: (i) The first is the *'proposition' expressed by the sentence. This is thought of in the 'Russellian' style as being composed out of objects and properties. Thus my utterance of 'I'm hungry' expresses a different proposition from yours, but expresses the same proposition as your utterance of 'You're hungry', addressed to me. (ii) The second component is the common meaning of the indexical type-expression, which Perry calls the 'role' of the indexical and Kaplan calls its 'character'. The role of an indexical sentence is standardly thought of as a function taking the context of utterance into the proposition expressed by the utterance. Thus my utterance of 'I'm hungry' has the same role or character as your utterance of that sentence, but has a different role from that of utterances of 'You're hungry'. Neither proposition expressed nor role or character corresponds to Frege's notion of sense, so these philosophers conclude that Frege's theory breaks down at this point.

Fregeans (e.g. Gareth Evans) have responded by claiming that senses can be, as it were, context-sensitive: indexicals express 'ways of thinking' that are tied to particular objects, times, and places (e.g. my uses of 'I' all express the particular way I have of thinking about myself). Essential to Evans's claim is the idea that, in order for an indexical to have sense, this sense does not have to be expressible by a definite description uniquely true of the reference of the indexical.

The issue is important because many philosophers have plausibly argued that indexical thought is essential to our thinking about time, space, the self, and material objects. In particular, indexical thought seems essential to agency: my getting off the bus at Trafalgar Square can only be fully explained by attributing to me the belief that *Trafalgar Square is here*, which is not equivalent in explanatory power to any merely descriptive belief.   T.C.

Gareth Evans, 'Understanding Demonstratives', in Palle Yourgrau (ed.), *Demonstratives* (Oxford, 1990).

Gottlob Frege, 'Thoughts', in *Collected Papers* (Oxford, 1984).

David Kaplan, 'Demonstratives', in J. Almog et al. (eds.), *Themes from Kaplan* (Oxford, 1991).

John Perry, *The Problem of the Essential Indexical and other Essays*, new edn. (Stanford, Calif., 2000).

Indian philosophy. The beginnings of philosophical speculation in India can be traced back to the ancient body of oral literature called Veda. This was compiled and divided into Ṛg-Veda, Sāma-Veda, Yajur-Veda, and Atharva-Veda. Apart from hymns to nature-gods and recipes for rituals each Veda contained cosmological, moral, and mystical reflections which were later collected into *Upanishads.

The eternally existent Vedic wisdom was believed to have been revealed to clear-minded sages who *saw* the truth from different points of view. Hence, the Sanskrit term for philosophy also stands for *seeing*. 'Seers' of the Ṛg-Vedic hymns, at least as early as 1500 BC, raise the question 'What did the universe come from?' and record an intellectual tussle between 'the existent' and 'the non-existent' as answers to it, with the agnostic hint that even gods, being part of the universe, would not know the right answer. Notice, also, the self-referring reflections on thought, life, and language in the opening verse of an ancient Upanishad: 'Propelled by what does a directed mind fall upon its objects? By whom was life first set in motion? Urged by whom are *these* words being spoken? Which God harnesses the eyes and the ears?' The answer given shows that the enterprise was not theology but a phenomenological *ontology of ubiquitous consciousness; no object 'that is worshipped as a *this*' could be the subjective spring of action, thought, and speech, according to these Vedic proponents of transcendental subjectivity.

Systematic philosophies grew up gradually through attempts to understand, rationalize, and react against the Vedic tenets. In spite of mystics and sceptics trying to prove the futility of metaphysical argumentation and the question-begging nature of all 'proofs', many major schools of philosophy—each with its own metaphysics, epistemology, and life-ideal—flourished in India, not in successive waves but side by side until their growth was arrested by colonial education which, however, did promote their preservation as intellectual antiques.

The schools are traditionally classified according to a dichotomy between those who accept the authority of the revealed wisdom of the Vedas and those who do not. Into the class of those who *affirm* the Vedas fall the following six systems: (1) Sāṃkhya (distinctionists), (2) Yoga (mind-stilling theorists), (3) Nyāya (logicians), (4) Vaiśeṣika (atomists), (5) Mīmāṃsā (ritualists), and (6) Vedānta (hermeneutists). Vedānta, in turn, divides into several schools, including (*a*) pure monists, (*b*) qualified monists, and (*c*) dualists. Another Vedic school, the 'panlinguistic monists', was developed by the philosophers of grammar, who identified ultimate reality with the eternal *Verbum* manifesting itself as both words and the world.

Into the class of those who *deny* the Vedas fall (1) the Cārvāka materialists, (2) the *Jaina alternativists, and the four schools of *Buddhist philosophy, namely (3) Vaibhāṣika direct realism, (4) Sautrāntika representative realism, (5) Yogācāra subjective idealism, and (6) Mādhyamika voidism. Besides these there are the earthy but subtle broadly monistic power-and-process philosophies of (7) *Tantrā, and finally (8) Shaivism. The last-named tradition perhaps had pre-Vedic roots in the conception of Shiva as the Lord of fettered animals, that is, *us*. According to Shaivism, we can only be freed and saved by worshipping Lord Shiva with the utmost love.

In ontology these schools came up with competing definitions of reality. In Sautrāntika Buddhism to be real is to be causally efficacious. In non-dualistic Vedānta to be real is never to be negated, spatially, temporally, or otherwise. For the Nyāya–Vaiśeṣika, reality consists in having a determinate nature unique to oneself and hence is being knowable and nameable. These assumptions result in diverse metaphysics. Reality must be changeful and impermanent for the Buddhist, whereas for the non-dualist Vedānta only the changeless and eternal is real. Since all the anti-Vedic schools, and Sāṃkhya and Mīmāṃsā among the Vedic schools, were openly atheistic, the existence of God was a standard topic of rational disputation.

CONFUCIUS was a contemporary of the early Greek philosophers, but the school of philosophy he inspired is still prominent in Chinese thought today.

NISHIDA KITARŌ, the leading figure in twentieth-century Japanese philosophy, developed a systematic philosophy of 'pure experience', drawing together Zen Buddhism and Western thought.

RABINDRANATH TAGORE: poet and philosopher, champion of Bengali culture, humanist and internationalist.

SARVEPALLI RADHAKRISHNAN was a rare example of a philosopher-ruler. President of India and interpreter of the Indian and European philosophical traditions to each other.

Udayana (eleventh century) wrote *Flower-Offerings of Arguments*, detailing five ways of proving the existence of a God. Atheist objectors offered excellent refutations of his cosmological arguments, like this rejoinder: 'If the universe requires a maker because it undergoes change, even God needs a maker because he sometimes creates, sometimes destroys.'

Almost all classical schools had a fully developed account of change and causality. Four major stands here were:

1. The flux theory of the Buddhists: the cause perishes before the effect arises.
2. The emergence theory of Vaiśeṣika: the effect is a new entity emerging as inhering in the material cause even if the cause survives as the stuff.
3. The transformation theory of Sāṃkhya: the effect slumbers in the material cause, with which it is substantially identical.
4. The illusionism of monistic Vedānta: the cause alone is real; the effect is an illusory projection of variety which cannot be unreal or real; change is illusory like magic (*māyā*).

There was fierce discussion over these rival accounts of causation. For example, arguments for commonsensical emergence theory are:

(E1) The perceptibly different lump of clay never does the same work as the pot made out of it.
(E2) If the pot was already there in the clay, the potter's effort must have been in vain, unless it is said to produce something non-pre-existent, namely the pot's structure. If a structure can be added to reality, why not the pot?

Against this, the transformation theorists argue:

(T1) What is unreal, like a rabbit's horn, cannot be made to exist.
(T2) If *a* and *b* are distinct it makes sense to ask 'Bring *a* along with *b*', but 'Bring the coat *along with* the wool with which it was made' is nonsense. So the coat and the wool must be the same in substance.

To T1 the emergence theorist retorts, 'You are confusing absence with non-being. The future sculpture is absent—and not hidden somewhere in the hunk of marble—but it is not a non-entity.' A mere nothing does not qualify as a genuine absentee in the Vaiśeṣika category system. Specifically, this system classifies existents into substances, particular qualities, events, universals, inherence-relation, basic individuators, and absence. The first three have *realness*, which is a universal. Hence, on pain of a vicious regress, universals do not have the universal of realness inhering in them. The first seven classes of existents have positive *being*. But all seven, including absences, are knowable as well as *existent*. Thus, the absence of the effect before its emergence should not be looked upon as a mere nothing.

In epistemology, knowledge is understood by most systems as a doubt-free awareness-episode matching reality and causing pragmatic success. To meet an ancient tradition of tightly argued *scepticism which, by the eleventh century, anticipated Gettier-type counter-examples where truth and justification fell apart, detailed theories of truth and causal routes of knowledge were constructed. Cārvāka materialists had attacked inferential knowledge by asking, 'How do you establish the universal generalization "Whatever has *g* has *f*", without which any inference from *g* to *f* cannot take off? Perception cannot guarantee such a generalization and to base it on inference again would be circular or lead to regress.' In response to this attack Buddhists resorted to admitting an analytically or causally necessary relation between being an elm and being a tree, or between smoke and fire, and Nyāya spoke of intuitive knowledge of the entire class of *g*/*f* through the perceived universals. Apart from questions about perception, inference, and verbal testimony, issues about knowing that one has known, knowing other minds, the knowledge–object relationship, the mechanism of perceptual error, and doubt and ignorance as cognitive states were hotly debated. The seeing of a snake in a rope was understood by some as an unordinary recollective perception of a past real snake; by others as the seeing of a non-existent object; by yet others as mere failure to see the presented rope's distinction from the remembered snake. A fine-grained epistemology of illusion, of course, could well be used by friends and foes of the non-dualists' doctrine that the world is an illusion.

In ethics the *Bhagavadgītā, a central Hindu religious text, synthesized the life of work and the life of wisdom through its ethics of desireless performance of social duties. Buddhism generally prescribed an ethics of selflessness and universal compassion for fellow sufferers in a sorry world. The Mīmāṃsā ritualists developed an elaborate taxonomy of hypothetical and categorical imperatives, sometimes claiming that it is only in the context of an action-prescribing sentence that a word has meaning.

Out of an ancient tradition of defining drama and poetry, a rich philosophical aesthetics of music, poetic enjoyment, and the emotions developed. Disputes about grades of suggestive meaning and analysis of metaphors exercised generations of aesthetes. Except for the Cārvāka naturalists, every classical school believed in *karma and rebirth. Liberation from rebirth was set up as life's highest ideal, but alternative goals of life like pleasure, prosperity, moral rectitude, or piety were also realistically accepted. A methodologically sophisticated philosophy of bodily health was set out by the medical scriptures called *Ayurveda*.

Though we have focused only on ancient and medieval Indian philosophies, rejuvenated Sanskrit learning, especially of neo-Nyāya, with Kantian, Marxian, Wittgensteinian, or Heideggerian reinterpretations of the classical theories, along with original philosophical thinking, keep contemporary Indian philosophy as vibrant as it was a thousand years ago when Nyāya metaphysicians fought with Buddhists about the existence of eternal cowness on top of bovine particulars, and Jaina philosophers tried to reconcile realists and anti-realists with their pluralistic perspective on alternative ways of world-making.   A.C.

J. Ganeri, *Philosophy in Classical India* (London, 2001).
J. N. Mohanty, *Reason and Tradition in Indian Thought* (Oxford, 1992).
Karl Potter, *Presuppositions of India's Philosophies* (Delhi, 1991).
Mark Siderits, *Indian Philosophy of Language* (Deventer, 1991).
Ninian Smart, *Doctrine and Argument in Indian Philosophy* (Leiden, 1992).

indifference: *see* spontaneity and indifference; freedom.

indifference, principle of: *see* probability.

indirect discourse. One paradigm of indirect discourse is reported speech: for example, 'Lambert said that Hume was a great Scottish historian.' Frege argued that in cases like this the term 'Hume' refers to its customary *sense, rather than to Hume: the words after 'said that' do not denote a truth-value, but rather convey the thought (proposition) expressed by Lambert. Frege's account captures the insight that in indirect discourse the sense of a speaker's remarks can be captured in many different ways. Lambert could have said what is reported without using the name 'Hume' at all.   A.BRE.

E. Lepore and H. Cappelen, 'On an Alleged Connection between Indirect Speech and Theory of Meaning', *Mind and Language* (1997).

individualism, moral and political. In ethical theory and political philosophy individualism is a view that gives primary moral value to individual human beings. Different interpretations are possible concerning what it is about individual human beings that justifies their being given primary value, and also concerning how it is that individuals thus valued are to be treated.

In political philosophy, certain forms of libertarian and liberal individualism, for example, are influenced by the Kantian view that individual human beings are *'ends in themselves', and thus agree that persons are owed respect for their *autonomy, which is protected by inviolable rights; but while both these views may be anti-paternalistic, they notoriously differ in other recommendations for the political order; for example, *liberalism will endorse certain welfare practices but *libertarianism will not. Even regarding the shared anti-*paternalism, these forms of individualism may dispute whether the prized feature of the given individual human being is an idealized 'rational nature' or his or her actual capacity for choice, marked as this may be by neurosis, character defects, and self-deception.

Another form of individualism is influenced by classical *utilitarianism, and so prizes the capacity of the individual human being for pleasure and pain; it may also be anti-paternalistic regarding the activities of the state, but tend to regard social practices and institutions generally as instruments for the achievement of the greatest aggregate happiness possible in the society's circumstances, rather than as expressions of or protections for rights, except as the latter might be conducive to the aggregate *well-being.

Within ethics, the valuing of the person characteristic of individualism is especially problematic for the development of a normative theory of individual responsibility. One is oneself an individual, and thus to be prized; but others are individuals, and they too are to be prized. How does one reconcile a principled regard for one's own *rights, self-realization, meaningful relationships, and material well-being with moral respect for these features of the lives and persons of others? The issue may become personally distressing as well as theoretically challenging when the fact is that many millions of people in the world are destitute in one way or other. Does individualism allow one to put oneself first in a world so filled with misery and oppression, or require self-sacrifice in the devotion of time, energy, and talent to the needs of others? Individualism prizes individual human beings, and different forms of individualism offer different accounts of what, morally, is prizeworthy about individual human beings; but what this suggests for the conduct of the responsible agent in a world flawed by destitution and gross disparity in levels of life is not yet settled.

A further issue for individualism in both ethical theory and political philosophy is the question how the basic individual is to be construed. Is the person to be understood as an independent atomic particular whose connections with others are consensual or coerced but not constitutive of the identity of the particular? Or is it instead a being whose make-up includes essentially its relationships, and, indeed, other differentiating factors, such as deep interests, temperament, distinctive activities, or even ethnic or cultural heritage? Construing individuals in these different ways suggests differences in normative content for ethical theory and for political philosophy. 'Respect for persons' may differ among liberal, libertarian, or communitarian philosophies resting on different views of the essential make-up of the person. Similarly, these different views can alter an ethical theory's prescriptions for balancing one's responsibilities regarding others and oneself. An important element in assessing an ethical theory or political philosophy is the adequacy of its basic conception of the individual.   N.S.C.

Steven Lukes, *Individualism* (Oxford, 1973).
Charles Taylor, *Sources of the Self* (Cambridge, Mass., 1989).
Bernard Williams, 'Persons, Character, and Morality', in *Moral Luck* (Cambridge, 1981).

individualism and anti-individualism. Theses in philosophy of mind advocating opposed conceptions of the psychological subject.

The individualist conceives the psychological facts about a person as facts which hold independently of her relation to her physical and social environment. Pressure is put on this conception by the claims (i) that some mental states are world-involving, (ii) that some mental states are linguistic-community-involving. *Twin earth thought experiments are used to argue for (i); thought experiments originating from Burge, in which it is shown that communal standards of correctness prevail where terms are used in ascribing mental states to individuals, are used to argue for (ii). A philosopher who subscribes to a strong anti-individualism takes demonstrations of (i) and (ii) to be symptomatic of the fact that the physical and social environment permeates psychological investigation even where an individual's psychology is in question.

J.HORN.

*externalism.

Tyler Burge, 'Individualism and the Mental', in *Midwest Studies in Philosophy*, iv (1979).

individuation. The determining of what constitutes an individual: that is, *one* of something. Principles of individuation are the principles by which things, normally of a kind, are distinguished into single individuals, most often at some given time. The single principle of *counting which a *sortal term '*F*' supplies is commonly the principle used for distinguishing one *F* (say one table, tree, or person) from another at one time as opposed to doing so over periods of time. Principles of individuation are correspondingly sometimes contrasted to principles of *identity, which concern counting and being the same *F* over periods of time.

Where there is no single principle for determining how many *X*s there are somewhere at some time, it may be said that *X*s cannot be individuated. Thus 'objects' cannot be individuated as such. And while dodos or aardvarks could be, the same is not true for their negative counterparts introduced in some contexts. Supposing there to be not-dodos wherever there are no dodos, not-dodos cannot be individuated, which helps show why these are not entities on a footing with dodos.   s.w.

*things.

P. F. Strawson, *Individuals* (London, 1959).
S. Wolfram, *Philosophical Logic* (London, 1989), ch. 6.2.

indoctrination: *see* teaching and indoctrinating.

induction. Induction has traditionally been defined as the *inference from particular to general. More generally an inductive inference can be characterized as one whose conclusion, while not following deductively from its premisses, is in some way supported by them or rendered plausible in the light of them. Scientific reasoning from observations to theories is often held to be a paradigm of inductive reasoning.

Most philosophers hold that there is a problem about induction: its classic statement is found in Hume's *Enquiry Concerning Human Understanding*. Having observed that all arguments to unobserved matters of fact depend upon the relation of cause and effect, Hume remarks that our knowledge of this relation depends on experience: but, he goes on to argue:

all inferences from experience suppose, as their foundation, that the future will resemble the past . . . If there be any suspicion that the course of nature may change, and that the past may be no rule for the future, all experience becomes useless, and can give rise to no inference or conclusion. It is impossible, therefore, that any arguments from experience can prove this resemblance of the past to the future; since all these arguments are founded on the supposition of that resemblance. (IV. ii. 32)

Hume does not try to counter these arguments by presenting a justification of inductive reasoning; but neither does he suggest that we might eschew inductive reasoning. If we have observed that flame and heat 'have always been conjoined together', our expectation of heat is, he says, 'the necessary result' of seeing the flame. This expectation is 'a species of natural instincts, which no reasoning or process of the thought and understanding is able either to produce or to prevent' (ibid. v. i. 38).

Many philosophers have rejected this disbelief in the rationality of induction. Some have said that, taking deduction as the paradigm of reasoning, Hume has merely noticed that induction is not deduction, arguing against him that it is part of what we mean by rationality to operate in accordance with inductive procedures. Some have suggested that induction is justified inductively by its past successes, and that the circularity here is only apparently vicious. Some have proposed what is known as a pragmatic justification: not that inductive procedures will lead to the truth, but that if there is a truth to be known, inductive procedures are the best way of getting to it. None of these supposed justifications is universally accepted, and some philosophers—notably Popper— argue that scientists proceed not by cheerfully inferring the course of the future from past regularities, but by proposing bold generalizations and then seeking to falsify them.

Some philosophers have assumed the task not of justifying induction, but of setting out principles of inductive inference in a way analogous to that in which the principles of deductive inference have been codified. But there is a major difficulty in any account which seeks to characterize sound inductive argument in an abstract way. The deductive logician tells us that if all *A*s are *B*s and all *B*s are *C*s then all *A*s are *C*s: *A*, *B*, and *C* here might be anything. The trouble with the idea of inductive logic is that whether the fact that all observed *A*s are *B*s gives any support at all to the claim that all *A*s are *B*s depends on what *A* and *B* are. We swallow Hume's examples—like flame and heat— without noticing that we observe all kinds of regularities that we should not dream of expecting to persist. This is the point of Goodman's new riddle of induction.   M.C.

*abduction; deduction.

L. J. Cohen, *An Introduction to the Philosophy of Induction and Probability* (Oxford, 1989).
N. Goodman, *Fact, Fiction, and Forecast* (London, 1983).
R. Swinburne (ed.), *The Justification of Induction* (Oxford, 1974).

inequality. In political and social theory, inequality consists in the differences between individuals or groups in the possession of what is desirable or undesirable. The main categories of inequality embodied in a society are political, legal, social, and economic. The clearest forms of political inequality are aristocracy and the exclusion of certain groups—women, racial or religious minorities, or those without property—from voting or political office. Legal inequality is exemplified by differences in liability to criminal prosecution or civil action, or in freedom of contract. Social inequality involves differences in status, deference, and subordination—systems of racial caste being an extreme example. Class inequalities are both social and economic, marking children with the wealth and professional status of their parents.

Some inequalities are politically enforced; others merely arise unless they are prevented. While most modern political theories are opposed to the enforcement of inequalities between groups, they must all face the question how much should be done to prevent inequalities from developing, between either groups or individuals.

Two factors make it impossible to eliminate inequality entirely: first, the need for hierarchies of power in any political and legal system, and in any economic system except the most primitive; second, the fact that there are natural inequalities—of ability, enterprise, and luck—which affect people's success in life. Left to themselves, some people will accumulate more wealth than others and use it to benefit their children, who will do the same, thus giving rise to a class system. The upper classes will also tend to acquire more legal and political power and a higher social status, even if the system is formally democratic and no groups are legally excluded from these advantages.

The moral question is whether a society should be concerned to narrow gaps of this sort, on the ground that the losers, and more especially their children, do not deserve their disadvantages. The welfare state—provision of social benefits paid for by taxes—is one way of doing this. Moral radical methods, designed to abolish class hierarchy entirely by legal restrictions on the private accumulation of wealth, seem to entail unacceptable general interference by the state with personal as well as economic liberty, and also tend to undermine economic efficiency. Some people believe that so long as there is legal equality of opportunity—so that no one is prohibited from becoming rich and powerful if they can—inequality of results is unobjectionable. But even if it is morally unfortunate, some significant inequality of results probably has to be accepted as a permanent feature of the social world.

T.N.

*equality; justice; well-being; welfarism.

G. A. Cohen, 'Incentives, Inequality, and Community', in *The Tanner Lectures on Human Values* (Cambridge, 1992).

F. A. Hayek, *The Constitution of Liberty* (Chicago, 1960).

R. Nozick, *Anarchy, State, and Utopia* (New York, 1974).

inference. Understood as the upgrading or adjustment of belief in the light of the play of new information upon current beliefs, it is customary to recognize at least three modes of inference: deductive, inductive, and abductive, although abduction is often treated as a special case of induction.

In deductive theories, an inference is justified if it conforms to a principle of logic or to an argument validated by the principles of logic. In some treatments it is also required that the argument be sound. Most deductive theorists since Frege agree that although inference is a psychological process, the principles which make it deductively correct are valid independently of any psychological fact. This raises the question what justifies the laws of logic. The once dominant view that they are true in virtue of the meanings of (certain of) their constituent terms is discouraged by present-day scepticism about meaning as a theoretically fruitful notion in philosophy.

Some critics doubt whether, even if justified, the rules of logic are good rules of deductive *inference*. *Modus ponens* is a case in point. Asserting that it is always permissible to infer B from A and 'If A then B', Harman points out that although B is here *implied*, it would not be correct to accept B for any reasoner who came to notice that B was false.

Inductive inferences are those that project beyond the known data, as in the paradigm of generalizing that all emeralds are green. Since Francis Bacon's day, efforts have been made to formulate an inductive logic which would specify conditions under which such projections are justified. Difficulties lie in wait, chiefly Hume's problem (*induction) or Goodman's variation. That all the emeralds we have so far come upon are green is a fact which no more licenses the proposition that they are all green than it licenses the proposition that they are all green if observed before 1 January 2050, and are blue otherwise. What, then, justifies our making the former projection rather than the latter? A further projection problem arises from a puzzle invented by Hempel. If known instances of emeralds sustain the projection that they are all green, they likewise sustain the *equivalent* proposition that all non-green things are non-emeralds. But any non-green non-emerald will help sustain that generalization and any proposition equivalent to *it*. It would appear, then, that red sunsets, black cats, and all the other non-green non-emeralds sustain the generalization that all emeralds are green, which is strikingly implausible.

Inductive reasoning is also thought to include probabilistic reasoning. It is said that an inference is justified if it conforms to the theorems of the *probability calculus. Against this, it is objected that, if true, a 'computational explosion' would ensue. Even cases of modest evidential complexity are 'too complicated for mere finite beings to make extensive use of probabilities' (Gilbert Harman, *Change in View*). Even so, Harman does seem to concede that the rules of the probability calculus might be thought of as normatively correct, that is, as rules which a human inferrer should use to the extent that he satisfies appropriate assumptions on computationally *ideal* reasons.

*Abduction is recognized in two varieties. In one sense, it is *'inference to the best explanation', which is a means of justifying the postulation of unobservable phenomena on the strength of explanations they afford of observable phenomena. In its other variety, abduction is the process of forming *generic* beliefs from known data. Observations incline us to think that tigers are four-legged, a proposition we hold true even upon discovery of a three-legged tiger. Generic sentences differ from general (i.e. universally quantified) sentences by their accommodation of negative instances, that is, of instances which would falsify general sentences.

Attractive though it is, the idea of inference to the best explanation awaits an adequate generalized specification of what 'best' consists of. And the idea of generic inference requires a satisfactory account of when negative instances do and do not falsify generic claims.   J.W.

*deduction; induction; implication.

Gilbert Harman, *Change in View* (Cambridge, Mass., 1986).
Nelson Goodman, *Fact, Fiction, and Forecast*, 4th edn. (Cambridge, Mass., 1983).

inference, immediate. The name in traditional logic for drawing a conclusion from a single premiss, as opposed to the two premisses of the *syllogism. Thus the move from 'Everything human is corrupt' ('All *S* are *P*') to 'Nothing human is not corrupt' ('No *S* are not *P*') is a valid immediate inference, while that from the regretful 'Only good Indians are dead Indians' ('All *S* are *P*') to the genocidal 'The only good Indian is a dead Indian' ('All *P* are *S*') is an invalid immediate inference.   C.W.

*logic, traditional.

L. S. Stebbing, *A Modern Introduction to Logic* (London, 1930), ch. 5.

inference to the best explanation. Accepting a statement because it is the best available *explanation of one's evidence; deriving the conclusion that best explains one's premisses. According to Gilbert Harman, who uses the phrase in many publications, acceptable inductive inferences are all inferences to the best explanation. One can also use this notion in a response to *scepticism. Do you know you are looking at a reference book right now rather than, say, having your brain intricately stimulated by a mad scientist? The sceptic carefully describes this alternative so that no experiment can refute it. The conclusion that you really are looking at a book, however, explains the aggregate of your experiences better than the mad scientist hypothesis or any other competing view. A sceptic who disagrees with this, instead of telling still more stories in which we cannot distinguish radically different situations, needs to address fresh issues about explanation.   D.H.S.

*explanationism.

Gilbert Harman, 'The Inference to the Best Explanation', *Philosophical Review* (1965).
P. Lipton, *Inference to the Best Explanation*, 2nd edn. (London, 2003).

infima species. Literally, lowest form (sort, species). According to traditional Aristotelianism each individual can be pictured as lying permanently within a finite set of circles of genus, subgenera, and species, whose circumferences do not cross; the outermost circle is the individual's *summum genus*, the innermost its *infima species*. The idea makes some sense in biology, but less obviously elsewhere (e.g. what is the *infima species* of Mount Kenya, or Alpha Centauri, or the Vienna Philharmonic Orchestra?). On the other hand certain scholastics thought that individual angels must each *be* an *infima species*, and some have found the same thing implied in Aristotle's souls and Leibniz's monads.   C.A.K.

*genus and species.

infinite, traversal of the: *see* traversal of the infinite.

infinite regress. Suppose we define a voluntary act as one caused by an act of will: if acts of will are themselves voluntary then the definition requires that they themselves be caused by prior acts of will. But there is no limit to the number of times this train of reasoning can be reiterated: so either the definition is wrong or acts of will are not voluntary. The argument—deployed by Ryle in *The Concept of Mind*—shows that the proposed analysis of what it is for acts to be voluntary involves an infinite regress.   M.C.

infinitesimals. *Numbers greater than 0 but less than ½, ⅓, etc. In mainstream mathematics infinitesimals do not exist, though Leibniz suggested inventing infinitesimals, written dx, dy, etc. as fictions to help in the differential and integral calculus. In 1960 Abraham Robinson used mathematical logic to introduce and justify non-standard analysis, an approach to calculus which allows us to use infinitesimals systematically in proofs and thus recapture Leibniz's intuitions.   W.A.H.

Abraham Robinson, 'The Metaphysics of the Calculus', in Jaakko Hintikka (ed.), *The Philosophy of Mathematics* (Oxford, 1969).

infinity. *Zeno's paradoxes were the first problems of infinity to vex philosophers, provoking Anaxagoras to hold that there was no smallest quantity of anything, and the Greek atomists to the opposite opinion. But the atomists showed no fear of the infinitely large, as they posited an infinite universe with innumerable worlds in it. Aristotle, however, held that there was nothing 'actually' infinite, either infinitely small or infinitely large or infinitely numerous; for him, all infinity was merely 'potential'. Many philosophers since have been wary of infinity. Most famously, Kant argued that it was beyond the reach of reason, and the source of insoluble *antinomies.

In practice the infinitely large (in space or time) has not been troublesome. The change from Aristotle's finite universe to the infinite space of Newton's cosmology, though unsettling in other ways, did not tax the mathematician's understanding. (The real numbers are very naturally correlated with the points of an infinite line, and hence triples of real numbers are naturally correlated with the points of an infinite three-dimensional space.)

The infinitely small proved more difficult. The Greek mathematicians had avoided it, by their elegant method of exhaustion, but when the differential calculus was introduced in the seventeenth century, it did seem to need the puzzling notion of an *infinitesimal, i.e. a quantity smaller than any finite quantity but greater than zero. This puzzle persisted for nearly two centuries, until Cauchy (1789–1857) and then Weierstrass (1815–97) showed how the awkward notion could be eliminated.

The infinitely numerous was first seriously studied by Cantor, whose work led directly to the *paradoxes of logic, and thence to modern *set theory. It is easily seen that two finite sets have the same number of members if and only if there is a relation which correlates their members one to one. Cantor's basic idea was to extend this criterion to infinite sets, introducing infinite cardinal numbers to number their members. It follows from this criterion that an infinite set is not increased by adding to it any finite number of new members, nor decreased by subtracting from it any finite number of members. (For example, we can correlate all the positive integers with integers greater than 100 just by correlating x with $x + 100$.) Thus, where κ is an infinite cardinal and n a finite cardinal, we have $\kappa + n = \kappa - n = \kappa$. Similarly $\kappa \cdot n = \kappa$ and $\kappa^n = \kappa$. But Cantor was able to prove the inequality $2^\kappa > \kappa$, for any cardinal κ whatever, from which it follows that the series of infinite cardinal numbers is itself an infinite series. The set of all finite cardinals is said to have the cardinal number $\aleph_0$ (aleph null), which is the smallest infinite cardinal. The next is $\aleph_1$ (aleph one), and so on. Cantor's *continuum hypothesis states that $\aleph_1$ is the number of the real numbers. It is now known that the hypothesis can be neither proved nor disproved from the currently accepted axioms of set theory.

Cantor also introduced infinite ordinal numbers, which are in fact more important to modern set theory than the infinite cardinals. But there is no space to describe them here.   D.B.

*numbers.

G. Cantor, *Contributions to the Founding of the Theory of Transfinite Numbers*, tr. P. E. B. Jourdain (New York, 1955).

M. Hallett, *Cantorian Set Theory and Limitation of Size* (Oxford, 1984).

A. W. Moore, *The Infinite* (London, 1990).

infinity, axiom of. An axiom of standard set theories. It is required to ensure the existence of a *set which has infinitely many members. A set has infinitely many members just in case there is no natural number n such that the set has exactly n members. An example of such a set is the set S containing the empty set (the set with no members) and the unit sets (sets with just one member) of any sets which S contains; S contains the empty set, the unit set of the empty set, the unit set of the unit set of the empty set, and so on. The axiom of infinity is required for set-theoretical constructions such as the definition of the real numbers as infinite sequences of rational numbers.   A.D.O.

W. V. Quine, *Set Theory and its Logic* (Cambridge, Mass., 1963), sect. 39.

informal logic: *see* logic, informal.

Ingarden, Roman (1893–1970). Polish phenomenologist with a realist leaning. Studied in Lvov, Vienna, and Göttingen, and in Freiburg with Husserl. Professor in Lvov and Cracow. His works, written in Polish and German, deal with various problems of aesthetics (*Das literarische Kunstwerk* (1931) is perhaps the best known of his works outside Poland), and with metaphysics and epistemology (including *Vom formalen Aufbau destindividuellen Gegenstandes* (1935) and *The Controversy about the Existence of the World*, 2 vols., 1947–9, in Polish). He accepted the method of eidetic reduction but utterly rejected the transcendental idealism of the late Husserl; he argued that a realist ontology may be built on a phenomenological basis which provides a method to classify various modalities of being, including specific existence forms of the objects of aesthetic perception. He was a consistent critic of positivism, nominalism, physicalism, and idealism.   L.K.

*phenomenology.

A. T. Tymieniecka, *Essence et existence: Essai sur la philosophie de N. Hartman et R. Ingarden* (1957).

in-itself: *see* for-itself and in-itself.

innate ideas. These are *ideas that exist in the mind without having been derived from previous experience. Plato held that all of our ideas are innate, although we do not clearly grasp them; learning consists of remembering these ideas and we develop a clearer understanding of them through the process of Socratic questioning and dialectic. There is a close relation between a philosopher's views on innate ideas, *a priori knowledge, and *necessary truths. Rationalists typically hold that the mind has a set of innate ideas that provide the source of a priori knowledge of a wide variety of necessary truths. Empiricists deny that there are any innate ideas and limit a priori knowledge and our grasp of necessary truths to *tautologies and propositions derived from arbitrary *definitions of words.

There has been little agreement about the exact nature of innate ideas among either their defenders or their detractors. Descartes allows for a wide variety of innate ideas and principles; sometimes he suggests that virtually all our ideas are innate, at least potentially. He also describes our thinking faculty as an innate idea, and considers the idea of God to be innate, although he also argues that this idea must have been put into our minds by God. Locke held that the mind of an infant is like a blank paper and that all of our ideas are imprinted on the mind by experience. He treated the mind as having a number of inherent powers, such as remembering and imagining, but held that our ideas of these powers are not innate. Locke also denied that there are any innate principles in the mind because (among other reasons) such principles would require innate ideas. Leibniz replied that the mind is more like a block of marble with veins which limit what can be sculpted from the block, rather than like a blank paper. On this view, innate ideas are natural tendencies of the mind and we need not be explicitly conscious of them or of the necessary truths that are based on them; we require experience and thought to determine which of our ideas are innate. Thus Leibniz accepted Locke's claim that much of our learning is from experience, but denied that this shows that the ideas and propositions we learn are not innate. Ultimately Leibniz agreed with Plato that all of our ideas are innate and that all learning is actually the exfoliation of ideas that were always present in our minds.

It can be argued that Kant's *categories are innate ideas on a Leibnizian model. The categories are concepts that are internal to the nature of reason and that provide an a priori framework for all of our experience. Because the categories are imposed on experience by our minds, those aspects of experience that derive from the categories are necessary features of experience and we can know a priori that they will characterize all our experience.

Since innate ideas would provide universal features of human thought and experience, the debate over whether such ideas exist continued to rage in twentieth-century anthropology. Defenders of innate ideas also include Chomsky, who postulates a universal innate *grammar in human beings to account for our ability to learn language and our ability to distinguish an unlimited number of grammatical from ungrammatical expressions in a language we have mastered. The debate over the existence of innate ideas has been superseded by the debate over which aspects of human knowledge (if any) are innate and which are learned; there is no clear resolution of this question at the present time.   H.I.B.

*empiricism; ideas; rationalism.

N. Chomsky, *Aspects of the Theory of Syntax* (Cambridge, Mass., 1965).
G. W. Leibniz, *New Essays on Human Understanding*, tr. and ed. P. Remnant and J. Bennett (Cambridge, 1985).
J. Locke, *An Essay Concerning Human Understanding*, ed. P. Nidditch (Oxford, 1984).

inner sense. Regarded by Locke and Kant as a faculty of the mind whereby it is introspectively aware of its own contents in a manner which is analogous to the perception of external objects. More recent supporters of this notion have argued that the best model for inner sense is bodily perception, that is, one's awareness 'from the inside' of the position and movement of one's own body. One difficulty with this proposal, from a Kantian perspective, is that bodily perception is of something spatial, whereas the objects of Kantian inner sense are supposed to be temporally but not spatially ordered.   Q.C.

*introspection.

D. M. Armstrong, 'Consciousness and Causality', in D. M. Armstrong and Norman Malcolm, *Consciousness and Causality: A Debate on the Nature of the Mind* (Oxford, 1984).
S. Shoemaker, *The First-Person Perspective and Other Essays* (Cambridge, 1996).

instrumentalism. The doctrine that scientific theories are not true descriptions of an unobservable reality, but merely useful instruments which enable us to order and anticipate the observable world. Traditional versions of instrumentalism were influenced by verificationist theories of meaning, and held that theoretical claims about unobservables cannot be regarded as literally meaningful. More recent versions of instrumentalism are motivated by sceptical rather than semantic arguments: they allow that scientists can make meaningful claims about an unobservable world, but deny that we should believe those claims. One motivation for this kind of sceptical instrumentalism is the 'underdetermination of theory by evidence'. However, realist opponents of instrumentalism can respond that the *compatibility* of different theories with the observational evidence does not mean those theories are all equally *well supported* by that evidence. A better argument for sceptical instrumentalism is probably the 'pessimistic meta-induction', which argues that, since past scientific theories have all proved false, we can expect present and future theories to prove false too.   D.P.

*verification principle.

P. Churchland and C. Hooker (eds.), *Images of Science* (Chicago, 1985).
B. van Fraassen, *The Scientific Image* (Oxford, 1980).

instrumental value. Some item has instrumental *value just to the extent that it lends itself (fortuitously or by design) effectively to the achievement of some desired or valued purpose. It is that which is 'good as a means to . . .'. Hammers, chisels, and tools of all kinds are palmary instances of instrumentally valued items. Aristotle described slaves as living tools. In contrast, we think all humans have intrinsic value (or inherent value). Kant's dictum that one should treat all persons 'as ends' expresses this thought. Instrumental and other forms of value are discussed in G. H. von Wright, *The Varieties of Goodness* (London, 1963).   N.J.H.D.

*ends and means.

insufficient reason, principle of. The principle of insufficient reason states that equal probabilities must be assigned to each of competing assertions if there is no positive reason for assigning them different probabilities. Keynes is the chief figure in discussion of this principle, which he preferred to call the principle of indifference. His own definition is 'if there is no known reason for predicating of our subject one rather than another of several alternatives, then relatively to such knowledge the assertions of each of these alternatives have an *equal* probability'. He devoted an entire chapter of his book on *probability to a vehement refutation of the principle.

The principle is of interest in the theory of rational choice. It has been shown to generate paradoxes (e.g. *Bertrand's paradox) and to create difficulties for inductivist theories such as Carnap's, where its employment has to be sharply constrained to prevent the problem that if all a priori probabilities are equal, as Wittgenstein claimed in the *Tractatus*, the possibility of learning from experience is excluded.   A.C.G.

J. M. Keynes, *A Treatise of Probability* (1921), ch. 9.

integrity. The quality of a person who can be counted upon to give precedence to moral considerations, even when there is strong inducement to let self-interest or some clamant desire override them, or where the betrayal of moral principle might pass undetected. To have integrity is to have unconditional and steady commitment to moral values and obligations. For such a person, the fundamental question whether to conduct life on the plane of self-concern or of moral seriousness has been decisively resolved, though particular life situations will doubtless continue to put that commitment to strenuous test. This moral commitment becomes a crucial component in his or her sense of identity as a person: it confers a unity (integration) of *character, and even a simplicity upon the man or woman of integrity. What integrity cannot guarantee is the soundness of the value-judgements themselves, which form the core of that person's commitment.   R.W.H.

  *conscience.

A. Campbell Garnett, 'Conscience and Conscientiousness', in J. Feinberg (ed.), *Moral Concepts* (Oxford, 1969), ch. 7.
J. J. C. Smart and B. Williams, *Utilitarianism, For and Against* (Cambridge, 1973).

intellectual virtues: *see* virtues; virtues, doxastic.

intelligence. A family of intellectual traits, virtues, and abilities occurring in varying degrees and concentrations. An intelligent creature is one capable of coping with the unexpected. An intelligent person is one in whom memory and the capacity to grasp relations and to solve problems with speed and originality are especially pronounced. Despite much study, psychologists have yet to settle on a precise characterization of intelligence. This has not dampened enthusiasm for the design and application of tests purporting to measure intelligence, however, and E. G. Boring's remark that 'intelligence is what the tests test' is apposite. In recent years, debates have raged between those who regard intelligence as genetically fixed, and those who take it to be a product of social, cultural, and educational factors. Undoubtedly, heredity and environment contribute in ways difficult to untangle.   J.HEIL

  *rationality; reason.

R. J. Sternberg, *Metaphors of Mind: Conceptions of the Nature of Intelligence* (Cambridge, 1990).

intension: *see* extension and intension.

intensionality. A context or form of words is intensional if its truth is dependent on the *meanings, and not just the *reference, of its component words, or on the meanings, and not just the truth-value, of any of its subclauses. So, 'He coughed because he smoked' is intensional, since there is no guarantee that truth is preserved if 'he smoked' is replaced by some other true sentence. More problematic are such contexts as 'The sales assistant thought that the customer was wrong', which supposedly may not be true if 'the customer' is replaced by the person's name, or by some other mode of reference, as 'The sales assistant thought that your cousin was wrong'. On the one hand, it has been maintained that we may enlist only referential terms which could have been used by the person whose thought is being *reported*, so that if the sales assistant was unaware that the customer was cousin to the person addressed, this second variant would be false. On the other hand, our ordinary practice would suggest that choice of referential terms is dictated more by what secures reference for those currently *addressed*, a correct mode of reference giving rise at worst to an inapposite form of words, not to a falsehood.   B.B.R.

  *opacity.

B. Rundle, *Grammar in Philosophy* (Oxford, 1979).

intention. Phenomenon, of intending to do something, treated in philosophy of mind and action, and in jurisprudence, and of importance in moral philosophy, e.g. in connection with *akrasia.

Some notion of intention has seemed to be a crucial ingredient in an account of *action: the adverb 'intentionally' may be put to work in marking out a class of actions; and the verb 'intend' introduces a state of mind of a person's intending to do something, which may be present even where the person does not actually do the thing, but which is directed towards action even so. (Whether someone can do something intentionally without having intended to do it is controversial.)

Some philosophers have distinguished between intentions directed at particular pieces of present behaviour, and intentions directed at future action. The former sort, called 'act-related', may be thought to be present wherever something is done intentionally; these are sometimes said to be the things of which we have an experience in acting, so that they may be used to account for the distinctive phenomenology of agency. (*Agent.) It is the latter sort, the 'future-directed', with which accounts of intention are usually primarily concerned.

One aim of an account of intention is to connect the concept with related ones, so as to see how a person's intending to do something features in her practical deliberation and in action. An account may start from the question whether intention can be reduced to desire and belief. (Since the idea of *having a reason for action* can be explicated in terms of desire and belief, these two are often thought of as the two primary psychological attitudes, so that, if a reduction were possible, intentions would not need to be recognized as mental states *sui generis*.) One suggested reduction says that a person intends to do something if and only if she desires to do it and believes that she will do it. But the recent literature contains many arguments against any such reduction. It also contains arguments against the assimilation of intending to either desiring or believing. Like desire, intention moves people to action; but whereas you may desire what you think you cannot achieve, you cannot intend what you think is impossible of attainment. Like belief, intention sets constraints on what is done; but intentions, unlike beliefs, are not straightforwardly evaluable as true or false, and an account of what it is for one intention to be consistent with another is different from an account of what it is for one belief to be consistent with another. Intention, it seems, must be treated neither as an affective state (like desire) nor as a cognitive one (like belief), but as a distinctively practical state, subject to its own 'rationality requirements'.

Michael E. Bratman has developed a planning theory of intention. His approach is initially a functional one: given believing, desiring creatures, who have limited time for deliberation, whose lives are coherent and co-ordinated with others', what would be the features of states of mind that would assist in making them effective agents? Well, those states must carry commitments to practice, and in doing so be such as to control conduct and be available to new episodes of practical reason. Being in such states is what it is for agents to have plans. And plans are typically decomposable into elements, which are intentions.

The idea of 'oblique' intention is sometimes introduced in jurisprudence, following Bentham: roughly, foreseen consequences of actions, although not directly intended, are obliquely so. Recognizing oblique intention introduces a class of things which people may be answerable for doing which is wider than the class of intended things.

J.HORN.

*volition.

Michael E. Bratman, *Intention, Plans, and Practical Reason* (Cambridge, Mass., 1987).
Donald Davidson, 'Intending', in *Essays on Actions and Events* (Oxford, 1980).
J. R. Searle, *Intentionality* (Cambridge, 1983), ch. 3.

intentional fallacy. The alleged mistake of interpreting or evaluating a work of art on the basis of the artist's intentions (or other states of mind), instead of properties 'intrinsic' to the work itself. The idea was favoured by proponents of the post-war 'new criticism', but succumbs to two main objections: historical features of a work's production commonly do affect interpretation, and intentions may be manifest in the work, rather than wholly external to it.

C.J.

W. Wimsatt and M. Beardsley, 'The Intentional Fallacy', in D. Newton de Molina (ed.), *On Literary Intention* (Edinburgh, 1976).

intentionality. Technical term for a distinguishing feature of states of mind: the fact that they are 'about' or represent things. The term derives from the medieval Latin *intentio*, a scholastic term for the ideas or representations of things formed by the mind. The term was revived in 1874 by Franz Brentano for 'the direction of the mind on an object'. Brentano's idea was that intentionality is the mark of the mental: all and only mental states are intentional. This idea, often known as Brentano's thesis, can be expressed by saying that one cannot believe, wish, or hope without believing or wishing something. Beliefs, wishes, desires, hopes, and the like are therefore often called 'intentional states'. (*Propositional attitudes.) Contemporary philosophers sometimes describe the intentionality of mental states as their 'aboutness'.

Used in this way, 'intentionality' does not necessarily involve the idea of intention—in the sense that actions are intentional (though somewhat confusingly, intentions are intentional states in the sense under discussion). The term should also be distinguished from the logical notion of *intensionality. Intensionality is a feature of certain logical and linguistic contexts which exhibit the following features: (i) they are referentially opaque—substitution of co-referring expressions in a sentence may change the truth-value of the sentence; (ii) they do not license existential generalization—from '*Fa*' we cannot infer 'There exists an *x* such that *Fx*'.

Ascriptions of intentional states certainly can exhibit intensionality in this sense. If I believe that Aristotle wrote the *Posterior Analytics*, it doesn't follow that I believe that Alexander's teacher wrote the *Posterior Analytics*, since I might not believe that Aristotle was Alexander's teacher. So ascriptions of intentionality can be opaque. Also, if I want to visit the lost city of Atlantis, it does not follow that something exists which I want to visit. So ascriptions of intentionality do not license existential generalization. But other non-psychological contexts exhibit intensionality too—notably, those contexts involving the ideas of necessity and possibility. (*Modality.) Thus while 'Necessarily Aristotle is Aristotle' is true, 'Necessarily, Aristotle was the teacher of Alexander' is (on the face of it) false.

So treating intensionality as the mark of intentionality will not yield intentionality as the mark of the mental. (In fact, most contemporary philosophers deny that all mental phenomena are intentional in any case, on the grounds that sensations like pains are not 'directed' on anything.) Moreover, it is arguable that there are ascriptions of intentionality (in the sense of 'aboutness') which do not exhibit intensionality. If I see the Pope, and the Pope is a Polish man, then it plausibly follows that I see a Polish man. There is also a sense in which if I see something, there is something that I see. So there seem to be cases of ascriptions of intentionality which are not intensional.

Most contemporary philosophers therefore treat intensional contexts as a general phenomenon of which some of those attributing intentionality are a special case. However, those like Quine who are suspicious of intensionality will use this suspicion as grounds for attacking the psychological notion of intentionality, in the course of attacking intensionality generally.

The intensionality of psychological ascriptions does, however, indicate a number of troublesome features of the idea of intentionality. Intentional states can be about objects that do not exist and they seem to be individuated in many cases not merely by the objects thought about but by the *way* they are thought about. (*Representation; *sense and reference.) How can such a peculiar phenomenon as intentionality be part of the natural order of the world? Contemporary answers to this question—the problem of intentionality—have thus been concerned with 'naturalizing' intentionality. This usually takes the form of giving some account of how intentional states are *causally* related to the things they are about.   T.C.

*belief and desire; mind, syntax, and semantics; intentional relation.

Franz Brentano, *Psychology from an Empirical Standpoint* (London, 1973).
H. Field, 'Mental Representation', *Erkenntnis* (1978).
W. Lyons, *Approaches to Intentionality* (Oxford, 1995).
Roger Scruton, 'Intensional and Intentional Objects', *Proceedings of the Aristotelian Society* (1970–1).
John Searle, *Intentionality* (Cambridge, 1983).

intentional relation. Brentano's thesis of *intentionality, that every mental phenomenon has a direction toward an object, creates the most difficult problem for the philosophy of mind. It leads immediately to the following dilemma. Either a mind is somehow related to what is before it—to what it perceives, desires, fears, asserts, imagines, etc.—or it is not. If one chooses the second horn, then one must give a non-relational account of intentionality. But there is at the present time no plausible non-relational account. If one embraces the first horn, then one is immediately faced with a second dilemma. Since a mind can perceive what does not exist, desire what shall never come to pass, assert what is not the case, etc., either an intentional relation must hold in such cases between a mind that exists and something that does not exist, or else these objects of the mind do exist, contrary to our firm conviction. If we accept the first alternative, then we are forced to hold that there is a relation, totally different from 'ordinary' ones, which connects with what does not exist. If we embrace the second alternative, then we must assume that, say, the golden mountain and the round square do after all exist. We are forced, in other words, to accept either the existence of a 'weird' relation or the existence of non-existent objects. It will not do, one must realize, to try to escape from this dilemma by claiming that the golden mountain and the round square, though they do not exist, have some sort of lesser being, and that the intentional relation can hold between a mind and things with this kind of 'watered-down' being. For, in this case, the fact remains that one has acknowledged the existence of what I just called a 'weird' relation. The intentional relation is still weird in that it is now believed to hold on occasion between an existent mind and

something that does not exist, but has some sort of being. In addition, of course, this attempt to escape from the dilemma has to make sense of the notion of 'watered-down' being.

If the thesis of intentionality in this fashion leads to a dilemma piled on top of a dilemma, it is to be expected that philosophers, in order to avoid the resulting difficulties, will adopt a materialistic (or physicalistic or behaviouristic) attitude. Intentionality disappears, if there are no minds (mental acts). Therefore, the dilemmas disappear, if there are no minds. Perhaps materialistic treatments of philosophical problems are so popular at the present time, because they promise escape from the dilemmas.   R.G.

*behaviourism; materialism; physicalism.

F. Brentano, *Psychology from an Empirical Standpoint* (London, 1973).
K. Twardowski, *On the Content and Object of Representations* (The Hague, 1977).

intentional stance: *see* Dennett.

interactionism. The view that some mental events cause some physical events and some physical events cause mental events, closely related to the commonsense idea that thoughts and desires cause various physical events, such as limb movements, and some physical events cause visual experiences and the like. The view is therefore different from epiphenomenalism, which regards all mental events as causally inefficacious themselves and as effects of physical events. It is also different from and does not entail a philosophically commoner view which takes each mental event to be nomically connected with a neural event. It is also different from identity theories. It is necessarily dualistic in character, but need not involve the view held by many pre-twentieth-century philosophers, most famously Descartes, and wisely regarded as a crucial tenet of theism, that mind and matter are two distinct substances.   N.L.

*dualism; epiphenomenalism; mind–body problem; psychophysical laws.

K. R. Popper and J. C. Eccles, *The Self and its Brain* (Berlin, 1977).

internal and external relations: *see* relations, internal and external.

international law. Term coined in Latin (*ius inter gentes*) in the sixteenth-century renovation of natural law theory after the breakdown of unitary secular-ecclesiastical Christendom, and Englished perhaps by *Bentham. But what it denotes was understood until the mid or late twentieth century as law governing relations between states, rather than nations or peoples. In the absence of standing legislative and judicial institutions, its sources remain largely agreement between states (treaties) and those elements of state practice (custom) that manifest a judgement that, in the relevant domain, general adherence to a common rule of action is desirable (*opinio iuris*).

Plainly a non-central and precarious kind of law and legal system, there seems no reason to doubt either its positivity, as something added by human decision to natural morality, or its obligatoriness in some measure, in a world where no state can plausibly claim to be a fully complete community entitled to constitute the ultimate and unconditional horizon of a just person's allegiance.

Developments in international law in recent decades have responded to a set of interrelated questions: Has an individual person, or a non-state group, the right to move international organs, as a subject of international law with substantive and procedural rights derived from international law? Has an organization such as the United Nations an international personality comparable to that of a state, and are its rights in international law limited to those conceded by the states party to its establishment? Can the same be said of a non-governmental organization such as the International Red Cross? If 'persons' other than states can be subjects of international law rights, can they also be creators of international law rules, as states can? When can individuals, including rulers of states, be tried by internationally authorized tribunals for offences against international law? These questions, like the tentative affirmative answers being given to them, arise from a widespread understanding that new interdependencies, economic, environmental, and cultural, are bringing into being a world-wide human community which might in principle become a fully complete community governmentally equipped to supervise, coercively, the doing of justice everywhere, but that no governmental authority can yet be envisaged such as could be relied upon to act with an effective justice sufficient to merit a general transfer or subordination of state jurisdiction to it. This last proposition, reasonable though it doubtless is, has the practical implication that international law will remain for the foreseeable future a system largely bereft of sanctions and, for that and other reasons, one that is peculiarly open to violation and to change by *fait accompli*, not least by states prominent in shaping and appealing to its rules, principles, and institutions.   J.M.F.

Wilhelm G. Grewe, *The Epochs of International Law* (Berlin, 2000).

Hersch Lauterpacht, 'The Definition and Nature of International Law and its Place in Jurisprudence', in his *Collected Works*, i (Cambridge, 1970).

international relations, the philosophy of. The set of doctrines, ideas, justifications, and excuses that guides the study and, perhaps, the practice of sovereign states in their dealings with one another. Two broadly opposed positions have been articulated, the first mostly by students of politics (and also by politicians), the second mostly by students of law (and by lawyers). Only in very recent years has either one attracted much philosophical attention.

The first position is commonly called 'realist' because its advocates claim to see states as they really are (in the tradition of Thucydides and Machiavelli). On this view, sovereignty is taken as a kind of exemption from the moral restraints that apply to individual men and women. The rulers of states are driven by the 'necessities' of international anarchy, standardly conceived as a Hobbesian *state of nature, to defend the interests of their own people without regard to the rights of anyone else. Thus the Greek generals in Thucydides' Melian dialogue: 'they that have odds of power exact as much as they can, and the weak yield to such conditions as they can get.' Strategic and security studies are the political expression of this realist view.

The second position is best called 'legalist' because it views international society, on analogy with domestic society, as a rule-governed world. In the absence of a global authority that might serve as the source of the required rules, they are derived instead from the tacit or explicit consent of existing states—hence from customs, treaties, and conventions—or from some version of *natural law. *Just war theory is the first moral offspring of this legalist view, though many of its protagonists believe that what the domestic analogy requires is that war should be conceptually, as well as practically, repressed. Unjust wars must be understood as criminal acts, and just wars simply as police actions, aimed at law enforcement.

What is at issue between realists and legalists, above all, is the responsibility of rulers. The realist view is only putatively amoral; its central claim is that rulers are morally bound to their subjects or fellow citizens and must be permitted to do, or be excused for doing, whatever they have to do in order to guarantee the physical security and advance the well-being of those people. The legalist view is that nothing can be done for those people that they could not, as individuals, do for themselves. Since they could not kill innocent people to save their own lives, innocent people cannot be killed on their behalf. As this example suggests, arguments about responsibility have focused mostly on the conduct of war, with realists insisting that *inter arma silent leges* and legalists refusing to be silent even then. But the disagreement extends also to questions of diplomacy and commerce. Here too rulers of states commonly act as if ordinary moral standards were relaxed or lifted entirely in their case: gentlemen do not open each other's mail, but statesmen authorize (and pay for) espionage and think themselves morally justified.

The same issue also arises in discussions of distributive *justice, which is commonly taken to deal with domestic, but not with international, transactions. Of course, trade across borders is governed by the same prohibitions (against fraud, say) as trade within borders. *Markets are international; the old *jus gentium* was first of all market law. Governments, however, are not international, and whatever obligations government officials have to promote justice—to redistribute resources, establish a welfare 'floor', ban discriminatory practices, and so on—are owed to their fellow citizens and not to foreigners. But this view, standard for a very long time, has come increasingly under criticism by writers seeking some way of addressing the radical *inequalities of international society. Perhaps foreign aid is as obligatory as domestic welfare. Perhaps the *difference principle should be applied globally. Legalists are likely to be more sympathetic than realists to such proposals, but even for them these are extensions of law and morality beyond their current reach.

It might be said that international distributive justice would not require the reform of international relations so much as its abolition—in favour of a new global domesticity. The society of sovereign states would be replaced by a new political entity, encompassing all the men and women in the world and treating them with equal respect and concern, as rights-possessing individuals. But it is also possible to imagine states of the world that fall between international anarchy and global rule. Organizations like the United Nations, the International Monetary Fund, and the World Trade Organization have something less than governmental power, but they could still act, if the leading states in the global economy wanted them to do so, in the interests of international distributive justice.

M.WALZ.

Charles R. Beitz, *Political Theory and International Relations* (Princeton, NJ, 1979).

Hedley Bull, *The Anarchical Society: A Study of Order in World Politics* (London, 1977).

Terry Nardin, *Law, Morality, and the Relations of States* (Princeton, NJ, 1983).

Thomas W. Pogge (ed.), *Global Justice* (Oxford, 2001).

John Rawls, *The Law of Peoples* (Cambridge, Mass., 1999).

internet, philosophy on the. The Internet is awash with philosophy. Type 'philosophy' into an Internet search engine, and it returns millions of entries; and EpistemeLinks.com, the leading portal website for philosophy, currently features some 13,000 categorized links to philosophy resources on the Internet. Inevitably, with this quantity of material available, much of it is not of professional standard. In part, this is because the Internet facilitates publication without editorial control or peer review (which itself leads to difficult questions about the reliability of information found on the Internet). Nevertheless, professional philosophers and philosophy publishers are increasingly making use of the opportunities presented by the Internet.

Most significantly, the worldwide web is beginning to change the face of philosophy publishing. Partly, it is doing so because it offers a number of advantages over traditional, non-electronic publishing. (1) A single web publication has a potential audience of millions of people, many of whom, in the case of philosophy, would not otherwise have ready access to such material. (2) The web is a dynamic medium, allowing for published material to be updated frequently. For example, online reference works, such as the *Stanford Encyclopedia of Philosophy* (*http://plato.stanford.edu*), are kept up to date in a way that their paper-based counterparts cannot be. (3) By utilizing embedded hypertext links, web publications allow for sophisticated cross-referencing and facilitate non-linear research strategies. (4) The worldwide web makes it

relatively easy for individuals to embark on their own publishing ventures, something which philosophers such as David Chalmers (at Arizona/ANU), Peter Suber (Earlham), Ted Honderich (UCL), and Stephen Clark (Liverpool) have exploited to excellent effect. (5) It is relatively inexpensive to publish on the worldwide web. Therefore, the option of an exclusively online journal or collection is an attractive one for publishers. Good examples of these are *The Philosophers' Imprint* (*www.philosophersimprint.org*), an online journal with an editorial board the equal of any trad-itional philosophy journal, and the *Marxists Internet Archive* (*www.marxists.org*), a digital library of works by authors sympathetic to Marxism.

The Internet is also transforming the way that philosophers interact with each other. In particular, email and mailing lists such as Philos-L (*www.liv.ac.uk/Philosophy/philos.html*) mean that philosophers around the globe are in constant communication.

J.S.

interpretation. Theoretical or narrative account of facts, texts, persons, or events that renders the subject-matter intelligible. As a genuinely philosophical problem, interpretation became recognized first as a specific feature of the human sciences. Historical interpretation based on lived experience, understanding, and ordinary language is contrasted with scientific explanation based on alien construction, observation, and theoretical concepts. In existential and hermeneutic philosophy, interpretation becomes the most essential moment of human life: The human being is characterized by having an understanding of itself, the world, and others. This understanding, to be sure, does not consist—as in classical ontology or epistemology—in universal features of universe or mind, but in subjective–relative and historically situated interpretations of the social *life-world. Recent trends like *postmodernism or *neo-pragmatism have emphasized the universality of interpretation, arguing that even natural sciences are nothing but interpretations.

H.H.K.

*hermeneutics.

C. Taylor, 'Interpretation and the Sciences of Man', in *Philosophy and the Human Sciences*, ii (Cambridge, 1985).

intersubjective. This term refers to the status of being somehow accessible to at least two (usually all, in principle) minds or 'subjectivities'. It thus implies that there is some sort of communication between those minds; which in turn implies that each communicating mind is aware not only of the existence of the other but also of its intention to convey information to the other. The idea, for theorists, is that if subjective processes can be brought into *agreement*, then perhaps that is as good as the (unattainable?) status of being *objective*—completely independent of subjectivity. The question facing such theorists is whether intersubjectivity is definable without presupposing an objective environment in which communication takes place (the 'wiring' from Subject A to Subject B). At a less fundamental level, however, the need for intersubjective verification of scientific hypotheses has been long recognized.   J.N.

*subjectivism.

D. Davidson, *Subjective, Intersubjective, Objective* (Oxford, 2001).

intrinsic good: *see* good in itself.

introspection. The nature of introspection and sometimes even its existence are a subject of controversy, and so it is difficult to provide a neutral account of it. It is not just the awareness that accompanies some mental states. It is rather a person's internal way of ascertaining what mental state he or she is currently in.

Sometimes introspection is taken to be a type of perception and there is talk of a 'mental eye', or, if minds are thought to be material, brain-scanning. Others deny any similarity with sense-perception and view such talk as misleading. They think it is acceptable to talk of introspection as perception only if a very minimal understanding of perception is brought to bear, in which case it is uninformative. Another alternative is to take introspection to be a form of recollection, or retrospection, in which case we would have to characterize it as a person's internal way of ascertaining his or her mental states just past. The motivation for this approach is that it is thought implausible for one to have a thought simultaneously with having another thought the content of which is the first thought.

Much philosophical discussion has centred around the status of the beliefs we obtain through introspection. 'Are they justified?' and 'How likely are they to be false?' are questions often asked.   P.J.P.N.

*apperception; inner sense.

W. Lyons, *The Disappearance of Introspection* (Cambridge, Mass., 1986).

intuition. Originally an alleged direct relation, analogous to visual seeing, between the mind and something abstract and so not accessible to the senses. What are intuited (which can be derivatively called 'intuitions') may be abstract objects, like numbers or properties, or certain truths regarded as not accessible to investigation through the senses or calculation; the mere short-circuiting of such processes in 'bank manager's intuition' would not count as intuition for philosophy. Kant talks of our intuiting space and time, in a way which is direct and entirely free from any mediation by the intellect—but this must be distinguished from an alleged pure reception of 'raw data' from the senses; the intuiting is presupposed by, and so cannot depend upon, sensory experience.

Intuitions or alleged intuitions have been important in logic, metaphysics, and ethics, as well as in epistemology. Recently, however, the term 'intuition' has been used for pre-philosophical thoughts or feelings, e.g. on morality, which emerge in thought experiments and are then used philosophically.   A.R.L.

*empirical.

D. Pole, *Conditions of Rational Inquiry* (London, 1961), ch. 1.

intuitionism, ethical. Ethical intuitionism is mainly associated with British philosophers; it is sometimes called British intuitionism. But the term 'intuitionist' is used for more than one position. In one sense, intuitionism is the view that basic moral truths are known by intuition—that is, directly, rather than by inference. In this sense, Sidgwick was an intuitionist. More recently, intuitionism has been taken to be a form of pluralism, pluralism in the theory of the right. Monists in the theory of the right say that there is only one way in which an action can get to be right. Kant was a monist, and so was G. E. Moore, who held at one time that for an action to be right is for it to have the best consequences. Against Moore, Ross argued that actions can be made right in any of a number of ways.
                                                              J.D.

W. D. Ross, *The Right and the Good* (Oxford, 1930).

intuitionism, mathematical. A school founded by L. E. J. Brouwer (1881–1966) which construes mathematics as mental constructions, opposing the view that mathematical reality is independent of our thought. (Intuitionism is thus a species of *constructivism about mathematics.) The intuitionist criticizes classical mathematics for its unrestricted use of the law of excluded middle, the claim that '*A* or not-*A*' is always true. Classically, one may prove *A* by refuting not-*A*, or by showing that *A* follows both from *B* and from not-*B*. But for the intuitionist, if a statement is neither provable nor refutable, we cannot assume that either it or its negation is true: there is no mathematical reality, independent of our thought, to settle the truth-value of all mathematical statements. See *intuitionist logic for the framework in terms of which intuitionists investigate how much of mathematics survives their critique. The applicability of intuitionist thought outside mathematics has been explored by Dummett.   D.E.

M. A. Dummett, *Elements of Intuitionism*, 2nd edn. (Oxford, 2000).
A. Heyting, *Intuitionism: An Introduction* (Amsterdam, 1956).

intuitionist logic. A logic in which truth is equated with provability, or warranted assertibility, or something of the kind. Let us use '□' to abbreviate 'We have grounds for asserting' or 'We have a proof' or 'We have a method which, if applied, would yield a proof', and so on. Then the intuitionist connectives answering to 'and', 'or', 'if', and 'not', are explained thus:

$\Box(P \,\&\, Q)$	if and only if	$\Box P$ and $\Box Q$.
$\Box(P \lor Q)$	if and only if	$\Box P$ or $\Box Q$.
$\Box(P \to Q)$	if and only if	$\Box$ (If $\Box P$ then $\Box Q$).
$\Box \neg P$	if and only if	$\Box$ not $\Box P$.

In words, the explanation of '→' would often be given thus: 'We have grounds for asserting that $P \to Q$ if and only if we have a method of transforming any grounds for asserting that *P* into grounds for asserting that *Q*'. And the explanation of '¬' would be: 'We have grounds for asserting that ¬*P* if and only if we have grounds for asserting that we could never have grounds for asserting that *P*'. (An equivalent account defines '¬*P*' as abbreviating '$P \to \bot$', where '→' is understood as above and '⊥' represents an arbitrary contradiction.) As for the quantifiers, where D is the domain of quantification, the explanation is

□∃xFx	if and only if	for some object a, □(a is in D) and □Fa.
□∀xFx	if and only if	□(for every object a, if □(a is in D) then □Fa).

The logic that results from these explanations differs from classical logic primarily where negation is concerned. Notoriously, it lacks the law of *excluded middle '$P ∨ ¬P$', for on the intuitionist account we should have grounds for asserting that $P ∨ ¬P$ only if we have grounds either for asserting that P or for asserting that we could never have grounds for asserting that P. But of course it may be that we do not have grounds for either. Similarly, this logic lacks the law '$¬¬P → P$', and many other classical laws for negation. This has some unexpected consequences. For example, *none* of the connectives and quantifiers listed above can be defined in terms of any combination of the others.

The simplest way of formulating intuitionist logic is in a style suitable for *natural deduction, with one introduction rule and one elimination rule for each sign. The rules are just the same as the classical rules in all cases except for negation, where the introduction rule is *reductio ad absurdum* and the elimination rule is *ex falso quodlibet*. There are several ways of giving a formal semantics for this logic, the most popular being that based on 'Kripke trees', but this topic is too complex to be explained here.

There are also several ways of 'translating' some or all of intuitionist logic into classical logic. The most interesting one, because it seems to be most in accordance with the intended meaning of the intuitionist connectives and quantifiers, is this. In the explanations given earlier, assume that the English expressions used on the right are the classical connectives and quantifiers. Then where $φ$ is any formula of intuitionist logic, the formula □$φ$ will translate, via these explanations, into a formula $φ^*$ containing only classical connectives and quantifiers, interspersed with occurrences of □. It turns out that $φ$ is valid intuitionistically if and only if $φ^*$ is valid in the modal logic S4.

Intuitionist arithmetic is obtained by adding to this logic the same axioms as for classical arithmetic. The two arithmetics differ only on formulae involving quantifiers. The intuitionist theory of the real numbers is a *predicative theory.   D.B.

M. Dummett, *Elements of Intuitionism* (Oxford, 1977).
M. Fitting, *Intuitionistic Logic, Model Theory, and Forcing* (Amsterdam, 1969).
D. Scott *et al.*, *Notes on the Formalization of Logic* (Oxford, 1981), part IV.

inversion. A term introduced by J. N. Keynes to signify inferences in which from a given proposition another proposition is inferred having for its subject the negation of the original subject. One such inference is interesting because it violates a rule of *distribution. A series of *immediate inferences permits us to infer 'Some non-S are not P' from 'All S are P', but P is undistributed in the premiss, distributed in the conclusion.   C.W.

J. N. Keynes, *Formal Logic*, 4th edn. (London, 1906), 137–40.

inverted spectrum. That two people outwardly indistinguishable in their colour discriminating may nevertheless systematically differ in their colour experiences was a possibility raised by Locke (*Essay*, bk. II, ch. xxxii). Under the title 'spectrum inversion' it has entered modern debate via objections to *behaviourist accounts of the mind that at least some conscious mental states have no clear relations to behaviour. Similarly, the causal relations that *functionalists appeal to in accounting for colour discrimination are dogged by the possibility of subjective differences which, being systematic, escape the functional net. Some functionalists argue that spectrum inversion is a metaphysical possibility, but scarcely credible, while, being epiphenomenalists, they may not care anyway. Those who take colour experiences to be states of the brain rely on the possibility of inversion being discounted explanatorily by future neurobiological advances. It is nevertheless difficult to say what precise discoveries would enable science to explain what Locke himself could only describe as God 'annexing' ideas in our minds to certain objects.
                                                                    A.H.

William G. Lycan (ed.), *Mind and Cognition* (Oxford, 1990).
John R. Searle, *The Rediscovery of Mind* (Cambridge, Mass., 1992).

invisible hand. Although in a free transaction the butcher sells me meat to profit himself, and I buy his meat as cheaply as possible, we each benefit the other as well as ourselves. Adam Smith regarded the *market as a whole as a universally beneficent order which comes about spontaneously (as by an invisible hand) from countless such acts, whose agents have no thought of their systemic effects. Any order which arises spontaneously without intention or design can be regarded as an instance of the invisible hand, but Smithian economics was the first study of the phenomenon.   A.O'H.

  *conservatism.

Adam Smith, *The Wealth of Nations* (1776).

inwardness. The inner form or quality of a person's outward-looking engagement, rather than self-scrutiny or silent pondering. A concept associated with existentialism and central in Kierkegaard (*Inderlighed*—drawing on the senses of 'fervent', 'intimate', 'tender', 'sincere', 'with longing', but not of 'directed inward'). Inwardness is measured not by external criteria but by the mental pitch, as it were, of a person's engagement. Kierkegaard's concept is well captured in his ironical reference to 'town criers of inwardness'. It is only when matters of moment are grasped with appropriate inwardness that they can be properly addressed. Noise and show rob human activity of all of the positive characteristics of inwardness. Kierkegaard was especially occupied with those cases in which the noise and show were marketed as expressions of the very matters that call for inwardness.   A.H.

S. Kierkegaard, *Concluding Unscientific Postscript* (Princeton, NJ, 1992).

Iqbāl, Allāmeh Muḥammad (1877–1938). Born in Sialkot (now in Pakistan), Iqbāl was a Muslim thinker and poet. Educated in Berlin, his goal was to revitalize Islamic thought and re-establish its creative role in philosophy. His prose work, *The Development of Metaphysics in Persia*, is one of the first modern non-polemical Muslim texts reflecting Western scholarly methodology. Most of his works are in Persian and Urdu poetry, inspired by classical Persian mystical poetry, especially that of the great Persian mystic Jalāl al-Dīn Rūmī (1207–73). Iqbāl's most accomplished poem, the Persian *The Secrets of the Self*, is a modern reaffirmation of Islamic philosophy's widely held epistemological principle of the primacy of intuition and experience by the self-cognizant 'I', or 'knowledge by presence'.   H.Z.

B. A. Dar, *Iqbāl and Post-Kantian Voluntarism* (Lahore, 1944).

Irigaray, Luce (1932–). French feminist philosopher, linguist, and practising analyst. Her early work focused on psycholinguistics, analysing speech patterns in senile dementia and schizophrenia. She studied with Lacan but was expelled from his Vincennes school for dissenting from his views on women's sexuality. *Speculum of the Other Women* (1974) is a large-scale critical reading of the history of Western philosophy as 'the master discourse', which exposes an exclusion or suppression of the feminine and the maternal and an undue bias towards masculinity, written in her characteristically allusive style. Many of her texts attempt to construct a version of feminine subjectivity ('speaking (as) woman') in the light of the above exclusion, using the strategic and symbolic positioning of Woman as *Other (e.g. *This Sex which is not One* (1979)). Some of her recent work is more explicitly political, some more lyrically poetic.   A.C.A.

*feminism.

Margaret Whitford, *Luce Irigaray: Philosophy in the Feminine* (London, 1991).

Irish philosophy. There has been only one period of continuous, creative philosophy in Ireland—from the 1690s to the 1750s. Before that the only prominent figure is John Scotus Eriugena, whose work has some points of contact with that in the eighteenth century, particularly in its tendency towards *pantheism, negative theology, *idealism, and heterodoxy; although Irish philosophy has been traced back to the so-called Irish Augustine, *c*.sixth century. After the 1750s, the most noteworthy philosophical activity—at least until now—has been derivative and scholarly, either within Catholic scholasticism, or in elucidating and editing the work of Berkeley (A. A. Luce), Kant (T. K. Abbott), and Hegel (H. S. Macran).

The outstanding figure in Ireland's one creative period was George Berkeley, whose principal writings indicate the main concerns of Irish philosophy, i.e. epistemology, theory of perception and language, and philosophy of religion. Also important, however, is the contribution in aesthetics by Francis Hutcheson—who was born and died in Ireland and produced most of his important books while teaching in Dublin in the 1720s—and Edmund Burke, whose chief philosophical work, *Philosophical Enquiry into the Ideas of the Beautiful and the Sublime* (1757), was largely written while he was a student at Trinity College in the late 1740s. While Berkeley, Hutcheson, and Burke are probably the best-known names, there were other able philosophers—among them, John Toland, William Molyneux, William King, Peter Browne, Robert Clayton, and Edward Synge. There were also popular writers, most notably Jonathan Swift, some of whose writings reflect key theories and arguments in Irish philosophy.

The seminal work is Toland's *Christianity not Mysterious* (1696), which, drawing chiefly on Locke's theories of meaning and essence, argues that Christianity either asserts meaningless doctrines—'Blictri'—or is a non-mysterious religion. Toland's rationalist challenge was answered by Browne, then a Fellow of Trinity College, first in his *Letter* (1697) and, more weightily, in his *Procedure, Extents and Limits of the Human Understanding* (1728), which argues for the old negative theology by developing a radical sensationalist account of mind. Browne, like Toland, was influenced by Locke, whose *Essay* is the most important external influence on Irish philosophy.

There are two principal tendencies in Irish philosophy—the left- and right-wing Lockeans. Toland is a left-winger, drawing on Locke's rationalism and enlightened attitude to religion. Browne is in the right-wing, which uses Locke's empiricism and the sceptical and quietistic trends in the *Essay*. Yet neither those on the left nor those on the right were slavish adherents of Locke; instead, they were often his most astute critics, boldly drawing out conclusions from his work which he was either unable or unwilling to accept. Molyneux comes closest to being a follower; yet he is more a collaborator than a disciple. Indeed, the final form of the *Essay* owes more to him than anyone (apart from Locke), as their correspondence, published in 1708, clearly shows. Another creative response to Toland from the right was by Archbishop King, whose *Sermon on Predestination* (1709) defends religious mystery by applying *representationalism and the *primary–secondary quality distinction to theology. King is also remembered for his influential *De Origine Mali* (1702), which is appreciatively discussed by Leibniz in his *Théodicée*.

Toland's challenge also gave rise to Berkeley's precocious emotive theory of meaning, which Berkeley uses in *Alciphron* (1732), dialogue vii, to explain religious mystery. Yet Berkeley was not a clear adherent of the right wing. Thus in *Alciphron*, dialogue iv, he forcefully attacks the Browne–King theological position and in ways remarkably similar to those he had earlier used against matter.

Browne counter-attacked in his *Divine Analogy* (1733), whose scornful and incredulous comments on Berkeley's emotive theory of mystery shows the revolutionary character of the theory, a theory which Burke uses in his *Philosophical Enquiry* along with sensationalism, which he probably derived from Browne. Another topic which shows the inner unity and interest of Irish philosophy is the *Molyneux problem. Not only was it devised by an Irishman, but some of the most interesting responses to it were made by Irishmen—Berkeley, Hutcheson, Synge, as well as (less directly) Swift and Burke.   D.BER.

*English philosophy; Scottish philosophy.

D. Berman, 'Enlightenment and Counter-Enlightenment in Irish Philosophy' and 'The Culmination and Causation of Irish Philosophy', *Archiv für Geschichte der Philosophie* (1982).
—— and P. O'Riordan, *The Irish Enlightenment and Counter-Enlightenment* (Chicago, 2002). (Contains an introduction, chart and bibliographical notes to six volumes of mainly eighteenth-century Irish philosophical writings, from Toland to Burke.)
T. Duddy, *A History of Irish Thought* (London, 2002). (Now the most comprehensive work on Irish thought and philosophy).
R. Kearney (ed.), *The Irish Mind: Exploring Intellectual Traditions* (Dublin, 1985). (The pioneer book on the subject.)
J. Laird, 'Ulster Philosophers', *Proceedings of the Belfast Natural History and Philosophy Society* (1923).

iron block universe: *see* determinism.

irony, Romantic. Notion of irony as an attitude or ethos that calls everything into doubt, from utterer's intentions to our knowledge of the world as given (supposedly) through sensory acquaintance or the concepts and categories of reason. Such 'infinitized' irony—as distinct from its 'stable' or unproblematic varieties—aroused great interest among poet-philosophers in the early-to-mid-nineteenth century, notably Novalis, Hölderlin, and Friedrich Schlegel. These thinkers pursued the various problems bequeathed (as they saw it) by Kant's critical philosophy, e.g. the *antinomies of subject and object, of *freedom and *determinism, and of thought as a perpetual striving for truth in the face of human finitude. Hence their fascination with the giddying depths of uncertainty—the interpretative *mise-en-abîme*—opened up by reflection on this topic. Such thinking was attacked by Hegel and Kierkegaard on account of its sceptical or nihilist implications.   C.N.

David Simpson (ed.), *The Origins of Modern Critical Thought: German Aesthetic and Literary Criticism from Lessing to Hegel* (Cambridge, 1988).

irony, Socratic. Socrates, in the early dialogues of Plato, is depicted as claiming to know nothing, as having no superior doctrine to offer even as he confounds and defeats his interlocutors by his pointed questions. This famous Socratic 'profession of ignorance' is also regarded as an instance of Socratic irony, of his saying less than he thinks or means (as the root of the term in the Greek *eirōn*, a dissembler, suggests). He adopts this affectation, it is said,

simply to avoid being subjected to the same critical treatment himself. It would seem, however that there was no dissembling involved.   N.J.H.D.

S. Kierkegaard, *The Concept of Irony* (1841) is a classic treatment.
G. Vlastos, *Socrates* (Cambridge, 1991) contains a recent discussion.

irrationalism is the opposition to reason on principle as distinct from the mere tendency to lapse into *ad hoc* illogicality or unreason. What this outlook amounts to more specifically depends on the answers to the following questions. What is the *reason* thus opposed? What is counterposed to it? And what is the extent of the opposition?

To start with the last: irrationalism has never involved a total disavowal of *reason. For example, an irrationalist falsely accused of murder can be expected to marshal evidence and argument in proof of his innocence as best he can. Nor is he likely to ignore well-established algorithms in the solution of a computational problem. What he would insist upon is that principles such as those of probable and demonstrative reasoning that are used in the mental activities mentioned are, though appropriate and effective in their own spheres, inapplicable to issues of superior importance like the spiritual self-realization of the ego, the ultimate destiny of humankind, and the transcendent ground of the existence of the world. Within the domain to which these issues belong, he would contend, knowledge can only be attained through some non-logical and non-empirical modes of direct cognition such as are encountered (in purest form) in mystical intuition or in faith induced by some transcendental source.

Faith and *intuition, then, on this reckoning, are and ought to be recognized as the superiors of reason in matters that matter. Although the concept of reason has been variously interpreted, it has an uncontroversial core of reference which includes deductive and inductive inference, to which allusion has already been made, and the logical and semantical analysis of concepts and statements based on clearly ascertainable rules. Given that these procedures of thought are supposed to be incapacitated in the areas of cognition reserved by the irrationalist, it is apparent that any inquiries by the unconverted into the intelligibility, not to talk of the validity, of the deliverances of faith and intuition are irremediably handicapped. And this is, possibly, the most striking thing about irrationalism: it is apt to become a constraint on dialogue.

It is a remarkable fact that some of the greatest thinkers in the history of Western philosophy have had some irrationalist leanings, however peripheral in some cases. Thus so ingenious a dialectician as Plato seems to have credited knowledge of the profoundest truths exclusively to some superior mode of unmediated cognition, exempt from all possibility of error and therefore of debate; and St Thomas Aquinas, for all his demonstrated powers of reasoning, conceded some truths to the sole competence of faith. Even Kant, giant of the Enlightenment, confessedly found it necessary to 'deny *knowledge* in order to make room for *faith*'.

But, of course, reason has not lacked its philosophical celebrants. It is not for nothing, for example, that the seventeenth and eighteenth centuries in European history have been called the Age of Reason. The rational foundations laid in the teachings of seventeenth-century thinkers like Bacon, Locke, Leibniz, Spinoza, reached their denouement in the optimistic rationalism (using this word in the broad sense) of the stalwarts of eighteenth-century Enlightenment such as, to mention only a few, Bentham and Godwin in England and Voltaire, Diderot, and Montesquieu in France. Their shared conviction, which may not at times have been without a touch of hyperbole, was that it was entirely possible to improve the human condition out of all recognition through the expansion of the role of reason in human affairs.

It was in reaction to this enthusiastic trust in reason that Romanticism emerged in art, literature, and philosophy in the nineteenth century as perhaps the most self-consciously irrationalist movement in Western thought. In contemporary culture there are not a few currents of irrationalism—witness, for instance, the 'new age' movement and the even grosser tendencies to demonism in sectarian life—but in serious philosophy familiar animadversions against *Reason*, when duly analysed, are frequently revealed to be in reality more against certain conceits about reason than against reason itself.   K.W.

Henry D. Aiken (ed.), *The Age of Ideology: The Nineteenth Century Philosophers* (New York, 1956).

Peter Gay (ed.), *The Enlightenment: A Comprehensive Reader* (New York, 1973).

W. T. Stace, *Mysticism and Philosophy* (New York, 1960), esp. chs. 5 and 6.

Irwin, Terence H. (1947–). A noted classical philosopher at Cornell University, Irwin has written books on Plato's ethical ideas (*Plato's Moral Theory* (Oxford, 1977)) and on Aristotle's metaphysical and epistemological theses (*Aristotle's First Principles* (Oxford, 1988)). His work is marked by a strong current of active philosophical questioning. Irwin's task has been not only scholarly, but one of understanding and evaluating the theses under examination as significant and living ideas. He has done the bulk of his mature work in America, where he stands alongside a number of other North American classical philosophers in demonstrating the continued power of the intellectual inheritance of Plato and Aristotle.   N.J.H.D.

'is': *see* 'to be'; being; real; subject and predicate.

'is' and 'ought'. Moral philosophy has to give an account of how, if at all, we can legitimately move from *is* to *ought*, from describing how things do in fact stand, to expressing an urgent concern either that they be changed or that they be respected, preserved as they are. If the *is*–*ought* gap is over-dramatized, value is detached altogether from the world and becomes a function of sheer decision. But moral deliberation does not and cannot work in a factual vacuum. To *under*play the gap is to suggest, no less implausibly, that an *ought* can be simply read off from an *is*.

A satisfactory account must start from the idea that *ought* and *is* interpenetrate. We may grasp a situation as demanding action: conversely, reflection on values and obligations powerfully affects our understanding of human nature and its potentialities.

The classical formulation of the 'is'–'ought' issue is David Hume's, in *A Treatise of Human Nature*, III. i. 1.
                                                        R.W.H.
*fact–value distinction.

W. D. Hudson (ed.), *The Is/Ought Question* (London, 1969).

Islamic aesthetics. Much Islamic aesthetics, like Islamic philosophy as a whole, is thoroughly Neoplatonic. This replaced the earlier theories of thinkers like al-Kindī, for whom beauty is taken to be derived from perfection, and since God is the most perfect being in the universe, he is also the most beautiful. He is constantly aware of his beauty, while we are only occasionally able to come close to experiencing it, since it is an essential feature of the deity, but its perception is merely an accidental human attribute. This version of Pythagoreanism was replaced by the argument that we operate on the level of imagination, so our ideas of beauty are limited to what we can experience and abstract from those experiences. On the other hand, we can use our material ideas and experiences to construct more abstract and perfect concepts of beauty, and so come closer to the range of completely pure beauty which exists far from the material world.

The area of aesthetics which came in for much discussion was poetry, and the ways in which poetry works logically. Many of the Islamic philosophers such as al-Fārābī, Avicenna, and Ibn Rushd were convinced that poetry follows a syllogistic pattern of proof, albeit with far weaker premises than most such reasoning processes, and with the conclusion that the audience should be moved to action or emotion. Imagination is again crucial here, blending our ability to be both spiritual and material. Our material ideas reflect our experiences, yet they can be made more abstract, and thereby extend those experiences in novel and exciting ways. Were we to be entirely rational, we would not need imagination, and could be spoken to entirely in terms of what we regard as logical; but since we are emotional creatures, we require to be addressed at least partially through our emotions, and this is where poetry and other art-forms come in. They appeal to us both intellectually and emotionally, and persuade us that we should adopt a certain attitude or share a particular feeling.   O.L.

S. Kemal, 'Aesthetics', in S. Nasr and O. Leaman (eds.), *A History of Islamic Philosophy* (London, 1996).

Islamic ethics. Ethics in Islamic philosophy is a surprisingly uncontroversial area, since most thinkers agreed on the general principles of ethics. There was an early theological dispute as to how objective the principles of ethics are, but this did not really become part of the debate in philosophy. The latter took off when the views of Plato and Aristotle became familiar to Islamic philosophers, especially the notion of the just society in the *Republic* of Plato and virtue as a mean in Aristotle's *Nicomachean Ethics*. One of the issues which the Islamic thinkers had to address was how to discuss happiness in such a way that it would be available to all who were prepared to behave well, as opposed to just those who were intelligent. The Aristotelian debate about how far the moral and social life is important, as compared to the life of the mind, was of particular interest, since the idea that salvation was restricted to those who are intellectually gifted is hardly compatible with Islam. Al-Fārābī and Ibn Sīnā (Avicenna) imply that the masses' route to salvation is through religion and morality, while the philosophers' route is through philosophy.

Ibn Miskawayh (d. 1030) and Naṣīr al-Dīn al-Ṭūsī (d. 1274) produced very elaborate discussions of ethics, and the philosophical psychology which accompanies them displays considerable acuity. God is taken to be the epitome of the religious law which incorporates both spiritual and physical goods. We should obey not only God, but also his representatives on earth, and all those who are superior to us morally. The view of human beings being the representatives of God is particularly attractive to Shī'ite thinkers, who can relate the imam or spiritual leader with the deity in this way.

A particular interesting debate arose in the work of al-Ghazālī (d. 1111) and is his response to an argument produced by Ibn Miskawayh. The latter argues that the religious and moral law is based on what is in our interest, and that we can see what the point of the law is by asking what its point is. Al-Ghazālī replies that the point of the moral and religious law is that it has no point; it is entirely arbitrary and rests on nothing but the will of God. Some people may follow the principles of morality out of some confused idea that they are the right principles, but unless they follow those principles because they believe they are commanded by God to do so, their action is without value. Here al-Ghazālī is using the ideas of an earlier theological debate between the Mu'tazila and the Ash'ariyya on the basis of morality. For the former, morality can be derived from reason, and that is why God establishes it, since he acts in accordance with reason. The Ash'arites argued, by contrast, that morality means nothing more than what God demands of us, and it has no basis apart from that.

It was the Ash'arite view that prevailed in Islamic philosophy. The objectivist account of ethics of the Mu'tazilites was held to suffer from a number of problems. It places huge reliance on the ability of human reason to determine our moral duty. It also implies that religion plays no significant role in determining morality, and that religious law is not an essential part of that morality. Yet the Qur'ān itself points frequently to the significance of guidance for human beings, and although reason is clearly important in assessing what form of guidance is valid, it cannot replace the authority of God as revealed to his representatives on earth. This notion of human beings being divine representatives is often taken to be important morally, and has implications for how we can behave and what our relationships should be with each other and with our environment in general. It is worth pointing out that the starting-point for working out what our duties as God's representatives on earth are is Scripture, and without divine guidance we would have no idea how to behave.   O.L.

O. Leaman, *Brief Introduction to Islamic Philosophy* (Oxford, 1999).
—— *Introduction to Classical Islamic Philosophy* (Cambridge, 2002).

Islamic philosophy. Originally based on Arabic translations of Greek texts, developed as a syncretic yet systematic body of thought in the Islamic world, from Andalusia to India, from the ninth century to the present. Most works were originally written in Arabic, many in Persian. Though marked during its formative period by Mu'tazila theologians, who were influenced by issues of revelation and reason in Christian theology (e.g. Origen, John of Damascus), Islamic philosophy does not constitute a religion; nor was it the 'handmaiden of theology'. Most practitioners were Muslims of various cultural, social, and linguistic backgrounds; some were notable members of other religions.

The Formative Period: The Late Eighth to Mid-Ninth Century. Philosophical activity at this time centred in Baghdad's new Academy ('House of Wisdom'). Supported by the caliphs, notably al-Ma'mūn (reigned 813–33), the school was known for its academic tolerance and freedom of scientific inquiry. Learned representatives of all subject nations participated in the state-endowed centres where a universal world-view was sought to sustain the Empire. Some extremist groups questioned the caliphs' authority, introducing critical political issues (later addressed by theologians such as Bāqillānī and Baghdādī) and theoretical problems (later picked up by Fārābī and Avicenna). Others, drawing upon older traditions (materialist, Manichaean, Jewish, Christian, Zoroastrian, Arabian, and Indian), challenged Islamic philosophy's fundamental doctrine of revealed truths by identifying its supposed contradictions and inconsistencies. The Mu'tazila thus established a set of doctrines regarding anthropomorphism and God's knowledge, creation, prophecy, human free will, and immortality. Greek thought became the most attractive tool for the construction of a defined Islamic theology, providing a rational defence for revealed teachings.

One major thinker of this period was al-Kindī, who was interested in philosophical investigation *per se*. Although upholding the validity of revealed truth, he also proposed its recovery by demonstration. He did not attempt a systematic 'harmonization' of prophecy with philosophy, however, one of the primary goals of the following period. His main contribution was identifying Greek texts and refining their Arabic translations, some of which he commissioned. They include extensive paraphrases of Pre-Socratic authors; Plato's *Laws*, *Timaeus*, and *Republic*, plus paraphrases of *Phaedo*, and other Platonic texts; most of the Aristotelian corpus except the *Politics*; selected Neoplatonic texts, some incorrectly identified (notably parts of Plotinus' *Enneads* IV–VI, thought to be 'Aristotle's theology'), as well as works by Porphyry (especially the *Isagoge*) and Proclus; plus many other texts and fragments, including elements of Stoic logic and physics associated with the late antiquity schools of Alexandria and Athens; and significant Aristotelian commentaries, notably those of Alexander of Aphrodisias, along with their Neoplatonist interpretations.

Al-Kindī's syncretic approach is based on Neoplatonist theories of emanation and the concept of the One, Aristotelian metaphysics of causality and intellectual knowledge, and Platonic doctrines of the soul and dialectic method. Aristotelian logic was used to investigate Hellenic-defined problems as well as the 'new' set of issues fundamental to Islamic revelation. Al-Kindī argued for creation *ex nihilo* as a type of emanation, but not natural causation where the First Being is created simply by God's eternal will. He also argued for immortality of the individual soul as the rational explanation for resurrection. His arguments as well as some of their corollaries were later rejected or revised, but his writings, especially in theoretical philosophy, represent the foundations of Islamic philosophy.

The Creative Period: The Ninth to the Eleventh Century. The rise of anti-rationalist sentiments proclaimed by al-'Ash'arī (912), along with political events and populist movements, curtailed Islam's spirit of scientific discovery, while radical advancements were taking place in areas such as computational mathematics and astronomy. Two notable philosophers of this period, al-Fārābī and Avicenna, met the challenge by harmonizing reason with revelation, introducing innovations, and refining philosophical technique and analysis. There are three seminal innovations of this period:

1. Al-Fārābī's commentaries on Aristotelian texts of the *Organon* define a standard Arabic logical terminology and improve formal techniques. His independent technical works, such as *Utterances Employed in Logic* and the *Book of Letters*, describe a new linguistic structure and examine 'how many ways a thing is said'.

2. Al-Fārābī creates the first works on Islamic political philosophy within the context of Islamic religion. His *Attainment of Happiness* and the *Political Regime* are novel in their technical discussions of prophecy and creation, and the roles of the lawgiver and divine law in the city. Redefined metaphysically as the 'science of politics', these philosophical domains are promoted as the means for attaining happiness and the establishment of just rule, stipulated to be the ultimate purpose of philosophy. Fārābī's most popular work, *The Ideas of the Inhabitants of the Virtuous City*, furthered the doctrine of just rule by encouraging philosophical discourse on prophecy and law, which affected the beliefs and actions of the entire Muslim community. The text describes an epistemology based on Aristotelian theories of intellectual knowledge and active intellect wherein human prophetic knowledge is not restricted by God's will. Thus any person devoted to philosophical inquiry may gain access to unrestricted, objective knowledge, or union with the active intellect. This theory of knowledge, later refined and reformulated by Avicenna into a unified theory of prophecy, is one of the most significant components of Islamic philosophy. It informs the Shī'a political doctrine in the sixteenth century and its later refinements, where the 'Virtuous City' is invoked to describe divinely inspired just rule by the philosopher-ruler, then called 'jurist-guardian'.

3. Avicenna defines Islamic Peripatetic philosophy in the first independent, comprehensive corpus on the subject. Most of his texts were later translated into Latin, and their arguments used by scholastic authors from Bacon to Ockham. Avicenna is distinguished from previous thinkers by his recomposition of the entire range of philosophical subjects, adding fresh arguments and refining earlier ones. He incorporates political theory into a reconstructed metaphysics, describing prophecy as a generalized theory of intellectual knowledge capable of describing mystical experience. His ontological distinction between contingent and necessary being became accepted doctrine. He is the first thinker to state the psychological theory that an individual suspended with no spatial or temporal referents will necessarily affirm his soul as an act of self-identification and that the soul's active imagination is responsible for the feeling of pain or pleasure after separation from the body. These novel concepts were considered by Sohravardī, the founder of Illuminationist philosophy, as essential components in the chain of being. Avicenna's theories of prophetic knowledge, based on notions of 'holy intellect' as well as Koranic exegesis, were accepted by religious scholars, especially in the postmedieval period. Avicenna's students, including Gorgānī and Bahmanyār, become identified as Peripatetics, constituting Islam's first 'school' of philosophy, as such.

The Period of Reconstruction and Reaction: The Twelfth to the Fifteenth Century. Several political and intellectual currents run through this period, which is also marked by the rise of al-Ghazālī's 'Ash'arite theology. After the Abbāsid caliphate was overthrown by Mongol conquests (thirteenth century), Islamic philosophy subsisted in multiple intellectual centres, which had also spread to the West. In the fourteenth century, fundamentalist traditionalism was promulgated through the eclectic polemics of Ibn Taymiyya, who called for believers to rid Islam of all forms of innovation.

Two main types of philosophical writing emerged in Andalusian centres such as Cordoba and Seville in the twelfth century: the philosophical writings of Ibn Bājja (d. 1138), Ibn Ṭufayl (d. 1185), and others extend al-Fārābī's political doctrine; and the Aristotelian commentaries of Averroës, called 'the Commentator' in Latin texts.

Ibn Bājja interprets al-Fārābī's political doctrine in a pessimistic light. Although upholding the virtues of the ideal city, he considers it non-existent, emphasizing the dark aspect of actual cities in which the populace lives in the cave (after Plato) but perceives only shadows. Unlike al-Fārābī, he considers the city incompatible with the philosopher's need for solitude. He supports Avicenna's idea of experiential knowledge, or 'enlightenment', through conjunction with the active intellect (*Directives and Remarks*, IX, X), but considers the value of 'prophetic' knowledge to be individual not collective.

Ibn Ṭufayl also extends al-Fārābī's political doctrine in a pessimistic direction. Inspired by Avicenna's philosophical allegories and mention of an 'Eastern Philosophy' with non-Peripatetic 'wisdom', he created an allegory in which a wise hermit from a deserted island comes to civilization with the gift of theoretical knowledge but fails to save the multitudes (translated in English as *The Improvement of Reason* (London, 1708)).

In the East, the philosophy of illumination, constructed by Sohravardī, represents Islamic philosophy's most successful response to this period's reactionary stance. Commentaries by Mollā Ṣadrā and others extend its political doctrine to other areas. Sohravardī offered a clear and accessible system, calling for the enlightened rule of the divinely inspired, appearing in every age, who manifest signs indicating knowledge and power, and thus become authorities who serve as rulers or 'hidden' guardians of justice. The sixteenth-century Shī'a scholars readily identified with the philosophy of illumination and used it in the formulation of Shī'ite political doctrine. It remains one of the three accepted schools of Islamic philosophy to date.

The philosophy of illumination includes many technical innovations. In logic these include definition of an independent modal operator 'necessarily/it is necessary that' in defining a superiterated modal proposition as the form to which all other propositions are reduced; the impossibility of the 'necessary and always true' validity of the universal proposition because of the necessity of future contingency; and reduction of the figures of syllogism. The principal epistemological innovation was a unified theory of knowledge capable of explaining all types of knowledge—prophetic, inspired, and sensory. In a highly innovative manner, Sohravardī posits a reformulated proposition of the sameness of knowing and being as the foundation for a unified epistemological theory. A most general concept of 'knowing' is assumed, for which the verb 'apprehension' (*idrāk*) is used. It is then stated that any type of 'knowing' is that the 'knower' and the 'known', as the apprehender (*mudrik*) and the apprehended (*mudrak*), the sensing and the sensed, the intellected and intellect, and so on, form a sameness relation. Such a relation is identity preserving one-to-one correspondence among each and every member of the set of all 'knowers' and the set of all 'knowns' in any type of 'know-

ing'. New ideas in ontology and cosmology involved cosmological light essences and time-space continuum, where measured time and Euclidean space apply to the corporeal realm, and time without measure and non-Euclidean space define a separate realm called *mundus imaginalis*. The notion of an intermediary realm of imagination, the *mundus imaginalis*, was a crucial development, especially as elaborated by illuminationist commentators Shahraz'rī (thirteenth century), Ibn Kamm'na (thirteenth century), Davvānī (d. 1501), Dashtakī (d. 1542), and others, whose work contributed to the origins of Islamic religious philosophy.

During the second half of the twelfth century, a new genre of philosophical works by theologians emerged which continue to be taught today. The most significant impetus for these were al-Ghazālī's demands on theologians to defend the faith against rational philosophy by use of philosophical technique and language. Two texts by Athīr al-Dīn Abharī (d. 1264), *Guide on Philosophy* and *Commentary on the* Isagoge, established the range of subjects and language, and elucidated the forbidden aspects of philosophy. These include Avicenna's cosmic motion and Sohravardī's time-space 'will-less' continuum theories of the propagation of lights. The *Guide on Philosophy* is divided into three parts—logic, physics, and metaphysics—consisting of *metaphysica generalis* and *metaphysica specialis*. The most popular commentary on this work, written in 1475 by Mir Husayn Maybudi, is customarily read along with the text. *Commentary on the* Isagoge, a primer in logic, is also read with commentaries, such as that by al-Fanārī (d. 1470), often along with glosses, super-glosses, and versifications.

While numerous works of this genre continue today, most tend to lack the philosophical depth and creativity revived in the sixteenth century by Mollā Ṣadrā and extended by Mollā Hadi Sabzevārī (d. 1878). Exceptions include the treatise *Sun-Radiance* (*Shamsiyya*) by Dabīrān Qazvīnī (d. 1276), presented in Nicholas Rescher's *Temporal Modalities in Arabic Logic* (Dordrecht, 1967), which includes one of the most precise pre-modern definitions and comprehensive listing and discussion of simple and compound modal propositions and modalities, their contradictories, rules for their conversions, as well as an intricate analysis of validating modal syllogisms. Qazvīnī's text, together with its commentary by medieval theologian-philosopher Taftāzānī (d. 1389), author of *Refinements on Logic and Theology*, became a textbook.

The Period of Revival: The Sixteenth to Early Seventeenth Century. This period coincides with Safavid rule in Iran, which established Shī'ism as the state religion, primarily as a defensive measure against conquests by the Ottoman Sunnī Empire. A new world-view with rational but wider appeal was sought to re-establish the ruling Safavid's legitimacy and to defend his position against the better-established theology and judicial doctrine of the Sunnī. Similar to the academies of the formative period, the Safavid's well-endowed centres supported scholarship and scholastic freedom. The results were complex and far-reaching. Major outcomes were the creation of Shī'ite thought based on multiple sources, possessing reason and defining a political–philosophical place for al-Fārābī's 'learned' reformers of law and for the role of a supreme informed source, whose authority was established by unified epistemological theories combining Peripatetic and Illuminationist concepts; and a parallel judicial tradition based on revealed authority. This period of revival led not only to the recovery of nearly the entire range of earlier philosophical works, but also to the third major synthesis and recomposition of philosophy, which proved consistent with theories of revelation and was accepted by most contemporaneous religious scholars. While most problems in earlier syncretic works continued to be debated, many were also added, refined, and redefined to reflect this period's preoccupation with uniform theories.

Foremost thinkers of this period included Mīr Dāmād; his acclaimed pupil Mollā Ṣadrā, and other members of the School of Isfahan; and Mīr Fendereskī and Shaykh Bahā'ī, who excelled in scientific and mathematical discoveries. All contributed to what became a systematic reconstruction defined by Mollā Ṣadrā as 'metaphysical philosophy', which continues to this day as the third independent school of Islamic philosophy. Structurally distinguished from both the Peripatetic and the Illuminationist systems, metaphysical philosophy is principally characterized by a singular emphasis on the question of being. Logic is separated and discussed in independent works which include the subject-matter of the traditional *Isagoge*, exclude the *Categories* and the *Poetics*, and are divided into three parts: semantics, formal techniques, and material logic. Mollā Ṣadrā's own independent *magnum opus* on metaphysical philosophy is the voluminous work *The Four Intellectual Journeys*. This text begins with the study of being, and reduces the traditional subject of physics primarily to the study of time, modality, and motion. A modified theory of five categories is introduced through a unified theory named 'motion-in-category substance' (also called substantial motion).

This further serves to explain a uniform theory of being, further employed to define a unified theory of knowledge, finally explaining creation as a non-natural, non-causal 'substantial motion' away from the One in durationless time, a concept taught by Mīr Dāmād, who is widely known for the theory of creation defined as 'eternal becoming' (*ḥudūth dahrī*). Among the philosophical problems extensively discussed, and reformulated and refined by Mollā Ṣadrā, the following stands out: the reformulated Illuminationist unified epistemological theory of knowledge by presence, where the foundation proposition is stated as the unity of the intellect and the intellected.

The initial creative and innovative phase of this period soon deteriorated, particularly in the areas of science and technology. Philosophical activity, however, continued to take place, mostly among members of the now-defined clergy groups.

The Post-medieval Period: The Early Seventeenth Century to the late Twentieth Century. The final period in Islamic philosophy may be distinguished by a scholastic tradition that continues to the present. One of its main characteristic components is the acceptance of works by religious scholars, especially those of Mollā Ṣadrā. Although a large number of philosophers from this period have not been studied completely, a recent biographical compilation lists some 400 individuals, each with several works on specific philosophical and logical subjects. Most of the authors are identified as members of the clergy class, some of whom also assumed juridical duties. This scholastic tradition marks the final acceptance of philosophy by religion. Mollā Ṣadrā incorporated Fārābī's idea of learned reformers with Sohravardī's 'inspired sources of authority' into a unified theory. Thus, the select religious scholars, possessing knowledge and inspiration, were confirmed as the legitimate 'guardians' of just rule. This unified theory also became the final channel for the continuity of philosophy. Although the study of higher levels of philosophy is still restricted, the scholastic tradition incorporated aspects of philosophy into the school curricula. One of the first 'primers' studied by beginning students includes a section on logic. Some of the Shī'a doctrines that accept the role of independent reason (*ijtihād*) in principles of jurisprudence have been central in the scholastic tradition of Islamic philosophy in Iran from the sixteenth century—which marks the final harmonization of philosophy with religion—to the present. This is exemplified by many prominent contemporary clergy known and revered for their philosophical teachings, such as Abol-Hasan Qazvīnī, Allāmeh Husayn Tabātabā'ī, Mehdi Ashtiyānī, Jalāl Ashtiyānī, and Mehdi Ha'iri Yazdī. The latter also turned to the systematic study of contemporary analytic philosophy, receiving his doctorate in philosophy in Toronto in 1979. His book *The Principles of Epistemology in Islamic Philosophy: Knowledge by Presence* (Albany, NY, 1992) is the first serious work that describes certain key problems of Islamic philosophy within a contemporary analytic frame. This type of scholarship marks the beginning of a new trend in which some Islamic philosophers are studying various Western philosophical systems and methods and making attempts to explain them within the frameworks of one or more of the three Islamic schools of thought. These scholars are also attempting to open a dialogue with Western practitioners, thus reaching beyond the limits of previous historical descriptions and generalizations by Muslims and Orientalists.   H.Z.

Majid Fakhry, *Islamic Philosophy* (New York, 1983).

Ibn Kamm'na, *Refinement and Commentary on Suhrawardī's Intimations: A Thirteenth Century Text on Natural Philosophy and Psychology*, critical edition, with introduction and analysis by Hossein Ziai and Ahmed Alwishah (Costa Mesta, 2003).

O. Leaman and S. H. Nasr (eds.), *The Routledge History of Islamic Philosophy* (London, 1998).

Mohsen Mahdi, *Alfarabi's Philosophy of Plato and Aristotle* (Glencoe, Ill., 1962).

F. Rahman, 'Dream, Imagination and 'Alam al-Mithal', *Islamic Studies*, 3 (1964).

M. M. Sharif, *A History of Muslim Philosophy*, 2 vols. (Wiesbaden, 1963–6).

Sohravardī, *The Book of Radiance*, ed. and tr. Hossein Ziai (Costa Mesa, 1998).

—— *The Philosophy of Illumination*, a new critical edition with English translation, notes, commentary, and introduction by John Walbridge and Hossein Ziai (Provo, Ut., 1999).

Islamic philosophy today. Within modern times a number of themes in Islamic philosophy have become much discussed. One topic is how distinct that philosophy ought to be from other types of world philosophy, in particular systems of thought not based on religion. Another, related issue is what relationship Islamic philosophy should have with Western thought. Further, some thinkers in the Islamic world have taken general philosophical ideas and have applied them to what they see as the leading issues of the day within their cultural environment. Finally, traditional ways of doing philosophy have continued, albeit with some importation of wider theoretical machinery.

An issue which philosophers have dealt with at some length is the relationship that the Islamic world should have with the West. This issue is of course one that has existed for some time, but arose with particular force from the nineteenth century onwards with the success of colonialism, imperialism, and Zionism in apparently gaining supremacy over the Islamic world. In earlier periods the Islamic world had represented a superior cultural and material force in the world, but over the last few centuries it had radically declined, and the reasons for this apparent decadence were, and continue to be, much discussed by philosophers.

Of great significance was the *Nahda*, or Islamic renaissance, which started in the nineteenth century and really took root in Egypt. The idea behind it was to maintain a distinctive Islamic identity within the Islamic world, yet at the same time incorporate modern scientific and cultural values, where these are compatible with Islam. The two leading thinkers were Jamal al-Din al-Afghani and Muhammad 'Abduh, who both argued that Islam is perfectly rational and in no way opposed by Western scientific and cultural ideas. The Egyptian philosopher Mustafa 'Abd al-Raziq extended their ideas and suggested that all the main Islamic schools of thought, even the mystical schools of Sufism which were much suspected by the Nahda thinkers, are inherently rational and in no way opposed to the science and rationality which are such an important feature of Western culture. Some Arab thinkers have been more sceptical of this point. Muhammad 'Abd al-Jabri is critical of much traditional Islamic thought, arguing that we need to analyse clearly the reasons for the decline of the Arab world. He calls for a deconstruction of the clash between those who emphasize the glory of the Islamic past and those who praise Western modernity. What is required is a liberation of the Arab consciousness from its traditional ties with its Islamic heritage, yet also a cautious attitude to the ideas which have come from the West and are part and parcel of foreign domination.

Fu'ad Zakariyya agrees that Arab failure is linked with the failure to criticize tradition, while Fazlur Rahman stresses the links between Islam and social progress. Islamic traditionalism is opposed to Islam itself, since the religion is in favour of economic and social development and change. The attempt to fix a rigid, stultified version of Islam as the ideal is to fail to grasp the ways in which science and technology can improve the life-style and moral welfare of the mass of the community. Zaki Najib Mahmud is not convinced that philosophy has much to contribute to this debate. Hasan Hanafi is one of the many contemporary Arab philosophers who use a novel philosophical technique, in his case phenomenology, to develop a traditional Islamic concept, that of *tawhid*, or unity. He suggests that Islam is dynamic enough to broaden this notion so that it can provide a generally acceptable principle of unity and equality for everyone. He is also critical of the idea of Western progress, suggesting that the West itself is now entering a period of decadence that will require an infusion of ideas from elsewhere, and in particular the East. The idea that Islam is based on fixed rules he finds unacceptable; it is based on a revelation appropriate at its own time and place, but now other interpretations of the message should be adopted to fit present conditions and represent more accurately the dynamism of Islam.

It is often said that philosophy declined in the Islamic world after the death of Ibn Rushd in the twelfth century, but this is far from the truth. Today there is a lively philosophical presence in most of the Islamic world, often with the incorporation into Islamic philosophy of ideas like Logical Positivism, hermeneutics, pragmatism, Hegelianism, and so on. Philosophy continued very vigorously in the Persian cultural world, especially the philosophy of Ibn Sīnā and the Ishraqi (Illuminationist) thinkers developing and commenting on al-Sohravardī and Mollā Ṣadrā. In Iran philosophy has now moved away from the theological school, the *madrasa*, into the university, and a good example is provided by the thought of Mehdi Ha'iri Yazdī. He develops a complex theory of knowledge by presence, a form of knowledge which is incorrigible and which grounds our other knowledge claims using material from both Ishraqi thinkers like al-Sohravardī, and the modern philosopher Wittgenstein. 'Ali Shariati uses the ishraqi school's intermediary position between mysticism and Peripateticism to develop a view of the human being as having God at its essence while maintaining the scope to determine its own form of existence. The notion of unity (*tawhid*) is seen as therapeutic; it is desiged to establish both personal and political justice and harmony. He interprets the main figures of Shī'ite Islam as models for us not only in a personal sense but also to bring about more progressive social ideals; he sees them as fulfilling archetypes which have always been regarded as desirable. Over time the archetypes themselves have not changed essentially, but they have changed in appearance, to make them more suitable to the local audiences for whom they are designed.

This link of the personal and the political is significant in modern Persian thought. It is well represented by Ayatollah Khomeini, who overthrew the Shah and became both the spiritual and the temporal ruler of the Islamic Republic of Iran. He argued that religion does not just apply to private morality but must also be applied to the state as a whole, and the religious authorities should be in charge of the state, since only then will the community be rightly guided. The school of Qom, of which he was a member, contained also Muhammad Hossein Tabataba'i, Murtaza Mutahheri, and Muhammad Taqi Misbah Yazdi, all important religious Shī'ite thinkers who none the less were far from suspicious of intellectual thought coming from the West. They argued that traditional Islamic philosophy can only gain by opening itself to some of the important philosophical achievements created outside the Islamic world. But they uniformly disapproved of the work of Abdul Soroush, who took a rather critical view of religion when he applied what he took to be the arguments of Popper, Moore, and Wittgenstein to them. Soroush was opposed by Sadiq Larijani, the chief representative of the school of Qom, who suggested that Soroush had misapplied the theories of Popper, Stalnaker, Watkins, and Hempel. It is interesting that the debate took the form not of religion as opposed to reason, but of what the correct philosophical view should be, and then how it should be applied to religion. Soroush upset not only the school of Qom, but also the supporters of Heidegger, so he was quite isolated intellectually in Iran.

Perhaps the best-known Iranian thinker outside the country is Seyyed Hossein Nasr. He is highly critical of Western science, praising some of its achievements but pointing to the ecological consequences of a world-view which does not acknowledge the presence of God at the centre of that view. Science without spirituality is without limits, since there is nothing which it holds sacred, and it bases itself entirely on measurements of quantities, not on the quality of existence. More spiritual philosophies are harmonious and integrative; they embed spiritual values in the technological agenda, and so make ecological disasters less likely. For him the question is not what the East should take from the West, but vice versa. Along with this view he has established in some detail the theoretical presuppositions of Sufism, the school of mysticism in Islamic thought, and his historical accounts of this doctrine have played a large role in its increasing domestication outside of the traditional Islamic world.   O.L.

L. Hahn et al. (eds.), The Philosophy of Seyyed Hossein Nasr (Chicago, 2001).

M. Ha'iri Yazdī, The Principles of Epistemology in Islamic Philosophy: Knowledge by Presence (New York, 1992).

S. H. Nasr and O. Leaman (eds.), History of Islamic Philosophy (London, 1996), chs. 61, 63, 64, 65, 69, 71.

F. Rahman, Islam and Modernity: Transformation of an Intellectual Tradition (Chicago, 1982).

Italian philosophy. A self-consciously Italian philosophical tradition only developed in the nineteenth century

with the growth of the movement for national unification. Since that time, Italian philosophy has been dominated by the rival schools of *idealism and *positivism, with the important Italian current of *Marxism drawing on both. However, each of these camps has laid claim to a native inheritance going back to the Renaissance, and their selective interpretations of their intellectual forebears still find an echo in some of the standard histories of Italian philosophy. The idealists traced a lineage from the Platonist *humanism of Ficino and Pico della Mirandola in the fifteenth century, through the rationalist *pantheism of Bruno and the Baconian utopia of Tommaso Campanella (1568–1639), to Vico and Vincenzo Cuoco (1770–1823) in the eighteenth century, which they assimilated to their own reading and critical elaboration of Kant and Hegel. The positivists went back to the more scientifically orientated Paduan followers of Aristotle, such as Pietro Pompanazzi (1462–1525), and found a line of descent that included the mechanistic *materialism and sensationalism of Bernardino Telesio (1509–88), Galileo, Machiavelli, and the social reformers of the Italian Enlightenment, such as Vico (who they also claimed), Antonio Genovesi (1712–69), and Gaetano Filangeri (1752–88) in the south, and the Milanese group of Cesare Beccaria (1738–94), Melchiorre Gioja (1767–1829), and Gian Domenico Romagnosi (1765–1835), who were profoundly influenced in their turn by the *empiricism of Locke and Hume and the associationist and utilitarian doctrines of Helvétius, Condillac, and Bentham. One theme ran through both accounts that persists up to the present: the dialectical tension between the two Romes, between Pope and Emperor, the active and the contemplative life, social emancipation and heavenly contemplation.

The two main figures of the positivist school in the nineteenth century were Carlo Cattaneo (1801–69) and Roberto Ardigo (1828–1920). The first drew on the reformers of the Milanese Enlightenment, Vico and Comte, and urged the need for philosophy to adopt the methods of the natural sciences and develop into a social science. Ardigo, a former priest, became the apostle of a theistic Newtonianism, in which the same mechanistic 'forces' explained all physical and psychical phenomena. In the twentieth century, positivist thinking was continued by the Italian school of criminology, particularly Cesare Lombroso (1835–1909) and Enrico Ferri (1846–1929), historians and social scientists such as Pasquale Villari (1826–1917), some early Marxists, notably Achille Loria (1857–1943), and by the pioneering political sociologists Vilfredo Pareto (1848–1923) and Gaetano Mosca (1858–1941). There were also a number of important philosophers of science within the empiricist tradition, notably Giovanni Vailati (1863–1909) and Mario Calderoni (1879–1914).

Amongst the idealists, Antonio Rosmini-Serbati (1797–1855) and Vincenzo Gioberti (1801–52) mixed the Italian Neoplatonist tradition with *neo-Kantianism, attributing in different ways the activity of the Kantian categories of the understanding to our intuition of the divine being. During the revolutions of 1848 they placed their philosophies at the service of the Catholic-liberal supporters of Pius IX as a rival to the humanistic and democratic nationalism of Giuseppe Mazzini (1804–72), who identified God with the people, but were condemned by conservatives for heresy. Whilst their thinking was eclipsed in the north by the positivist tradition in the latter half of the nineteenth century, it was critically elaborated and secularized by the southern group of Hegelian scholars, particularly Augusto Vera (1813–85), Bertrando Spaventa (1817–82), and Francesco De Sanctis (1817–82). They also sought to integrate the main currents of contemporary European philosophy with the Italian tradition. Spaventa argued that there had been a 'circulation of European thought' in which Italian philosophers had either preempted or independently conceived all the main elements of modern European philosophy, with the Platonists representing the rationalists and the Aristotelians the empiricists, and Campanella and Vico anticipating the resolution of these two schools in Kant and Hegel respectively. This tradition was continued by Croce and Gentile, who both evolved explicitly historicist doctrines and whose ideas dominated Italian philosophy in the early twentieth century. Gentile became the official philosopher of *fascism, and the idealist school also had by far the greatest influence on Italian Marxism, Antonio Labriola (1843–1904) being a pupil of Spaventa's and Gramsci a sympathetic critic of Croce, although an important positivist strand also existed, of which Galvano della Volpe (1895–1968) and Colletti were the main exponents.

Whilst some contemporary philosophers have carried on the positivist tradition, such as Bobbio in law and politics and Ludovico Geymonat (1908–91) in the philosophy of science, most Italian philosophers, such as the existentialists Niccola Abbagnano (1901–90) and Luigi Pareyson (1918–) and the post-modernist Vattimo, remain original reworkers of the German philosophic tradition, although their attention has shifted from Kant and Hegel to Nietszche, Husserl, Jaspers, and Heidegger.   R.P.B.

Richard Bellamy, *Modern Italian Social Theory* (Cambridge, 1987).
J. H. Randall, *The Career of Philosophy* (New York, 1962).
Guido de Ruggiero, *Modern Philosophy* (London, 1921).

J

Jackson, Frank (1943–). Australian philosopher of mind, logic, and metaphysics who is noted for his adherence to a *representative theory of perception and for his work on *conditionals. Jackson is unusual amongst contemporary philosophers in defending the existence of *sense-data, arguing that an adequate account of the truth-conditions of statements about how things 'look' or otherwise 'appear' to us phenomenally requires us to admit reference to such items. In his 1986 essay 'What Mary Didn't Know' he introduced a now-famous thought experiment about knowledge gained through phenomenal experience.

Jackson's work on conditionals builds upon Grice's theory of the indicative conditional as a statement whose truth-condition is that of the so-called material conditional, making 'If *p*, then *q*' true if and only if 'Not both *p* and not-*q*' is true. In order to defuse apparent counter-examples to this in natural language, Jackson gives an account of the assertibility-conditions of conditionals which explains why we do not always assert a conditional whose truth-condition we believe to be satisfied.   E.J.L.

*Mary, black and white.

F. Jackson, *Conditionals* (Oxford, 1987).
—— *From Metaphysics to Ethics: A Defence of Conceptual Analysis* (Oxford, 1997).
—— *Mind, Method, and Conditionals: Selected Essays* (London, 1998).

Jacobi, Friedrich Heinrich (1743–1819), German pietist philosopher of 'faith and feeling'. He was the sharpest of the critics of the intellectualistic German *Enlightenment, represented chiefly by Wolff and Kant. His philosophy and character were important in moving German philosophy and literature to a somewhat mystical and Romantic *Weltanschauung*.

From Hume's scepticism Jacobi inferred the inadequacy of abstract systematic thought and the practical necessity of irrational belief (*David Hume über den Glauben* (1787)). The use of pure reason in philosophy, he held, leads inevitably to Spinozism (then almost universally condemned as pantheism and fatalism). By revealing that Lessing shortly before his death had confessed to being a Spinozist, Jacobi caused a great scandal in making such an injurious charge against the universally admired Lessing, and precipitated the so-called *Pantheismusstreit* between himself and another anti-Spinozist who was Lessing's best friend, Moses Mendelssohn. The *Streit* was carried on in books, articles, and personal correspondence circulated and published without permission. Each participant was egged on by friends and disciples, and the ensuing quarrel was not an edifying spectacle. Mendelssohn's death in 1786 at the height of the dispute prompted allegations that Jacobi had caused it; these slanderous charges exacerbated the quarrel and gave it an emotional depth and a personal drama in which nothing less than the legitimacy of the entire Enlightenment was at stake. Hamann, Herder, Goethe, and Kant were soon involved in the battle.

Jacobi and Mendelssohn agreed that pure reason is not a sufficient instrument for metaphysics and that to avoid the abyss of Spinozism something else is needed: for Jacobi it was an act of faith (*salto mortale*, he called it), for Mendelssohn it was common sense. Each party appealed to the practical (i.e. the moral) aspect of Kant's philosophy. Seeing both participants in the controversy as enemies of reason, 'the touchstone of truth', Kant in *What is Orientation in Thinking?* (1786) rejected both of the opposing views. Jacobi was one of the most effective of Kant's critics, famous even in the twentieth century for his epigram 'Without the *thing-in-itself I cannot enter the Kantian philosophy, and with it I cannot remain'.   L.W.B.

Lewis White Beck, ch. 1 in *The Routledge History of Philosophy*, vol. vi, ed. R. C. Solomon and Kathleen Higgins (London, 1993).
Frederick C. Beiser, *The Faith of Reason: German Philosophy from Kant to Fichte* (Cambridge, Mass., 1988), chs. 2, 3, and 4.
The Spinoza Conversations between Lessing and Jacobi, tr. G. Vallé, J. B. Lawson, and C. G. Chappel (Canham, Md., 1988).

Jainism. Atheistic school of *Indian philosophy much older than Buddhism (dating back to the eighth century BC) and still alive. The ethical principle of non-violence is taken by Jainism to an extreme in both practice and theory. To make peace among the endlessly disputing schools of Indian philosophy, Jaina philosophers made the metatheoretic move of non-exclusivism, which is spelt out as a seven-valued logic, illustrated as follows:

(1) From one perspective, the self is permanent.
(2) From another, it is not.

(3) From a joint perspective, it is and is not so (successively).

(4) From a neutral one, it is indescribable.

Adding the combinations of each of 1, 2, and 3 with 4, you get seven theses, each of which is objectively correct in that it confesses its own conditionality. Jainism accepts the notion of eternal souls which assume the form of a human body and are repeatedly reborn until they are liberated from pleasurable and painful effects of egoistic actions called *karma. Jaina logicians affirmed the existence of the external world, impugning Buddhist idealism.   A.C.

*Buddhist philosophy; atheism and agnosticism.

B. K. Matilal, *The Central Philosophy of Jainism* (Ahmedabad, 1981).

James, William (1842–1910). American philosopher and psychologist, son of Henry James the Swedenborgian religious thinker, brother of Henry James the novelist, and Professor of Psychology and Philosophy at Harvard. Only some of his many concerns can be considered.

1. *The Principles of Psychology* (1890) is officially committed to the scientific study of mind, conceived as the ascertainment of 'the empirical correlation of the various sorts of thought or feeling with definite conditions of the brain'. Although ostensibly avoiding metaphysics, much of it is as philosophical as psychological. Avoiding metaphysics means mainly assuming the existence of a physical world independent of mind, ignoring any philosophical case against this scientifically necessary presupposition. Four themes call for notice here.

(i) For James mind is identified with *consciousness, known primarily through *introspection; scientific psychology explores its physical basis and biological function. This is evidently to assist the organism to cope with its environment more flexibly than can inherited behavioural patterns. The criterion for the presence of mind is, therefore, the occurrence of behaviour which reaches the same goal, as circumstances alter, through differing means.

James thinks it unlikely that such behaviour could ever be explained mechanistically. While consciousness is too obviously a distinct reality in his eyes for anything like the brain–mind *identity theories of today even to be considered, James carefully examines the automaton theory (*epiphenomenalism) but dismisses it (with debatable logic) as failing to explain why consciousness has been picked out for development by natural selection. (James was strongly influenced by Darwinian ideas.) The old-fashioned idea of a distinct soul is better, but James's own view is rather that 'the stream of consciousness' is generated afresh each moment by the current state of the whole brain and reacts back on it, and hence on behaviour, with a modicum of free spontaneity (a view anticipative of the positions of both Whitehead and Roger Sperry).

(ii) This notion of the *stream of consciousness (or thought) is the most famous theme in *The Principles of Psychology*. Among its varied heirs are stream-of-consciousness literature (e.g. Gertrude Stein), aspects of Husserlian phenomenology, and Whiteheadian process thought. Consciousness comes in a continuous flow without sharp breaks or clearly distinguishable components. Thus experience is always of a specious present, a stretch of sensible duration in which the just-past still figures along with the dawning of the future. As against traditional *empiricism, for which a state of consciousness is a complex of individually repeatable impressions and ideas, James contends that no item of consciousness is ever exactly repeated. I may perceive or think of the same thing twice but never by way of numerically or qualitatively identical representations.

(iii) James distinguishes between the I and the Me. The I is the ultimate thinker, the Me is the object of all those concerns we call selfish and which the I and its organism primarily seek to preserve. The Me divides into the material me, my body and my possessions; the social Me (or Mes), the image (or images) I present to the various communities to which I belong; and the spiritual Me, which covers both my mental capacities and achievements, and some supposed inner source thereof. As for the ultimate I, which does the thinking, James, having dismissed a permanent ego, decides that (if there is such a thing at all and not simply each total conscious state in turn) it is the momentary thinker of the total present thought. Personal identity through time consists in the fact that the I of one moment adopts the Mes and Is of earlier times by the peculiarly warm and intimate way in which it recollects them. (James pays particular attention to cases of multiple personality in developing his account.)

(iv) The subject of *free will was of immense emotional significance to James. He was rescued from a phase of serious psychological depression in 1879 partly by discovering Charles Renouvier's defence of free will as 'the sustaining of a thought because I choose to when I might have other thoughts'. This is James's own view. Consciousness cannot determine what ideas are presented to it but, by effortful selective direction of attention, can decide which will affect behaviour. This power can neither be proved nor disproved scientifically, but belief in it is a legitimate exercise of 'the will to believe'.

James's naturalistic approach (and his role at Harvard) contributed significantly to the development of experimental psychology in America (though he had no love of experiment himself); his treatment of the various types of self has had an influence on social psychology; and his introspectionist investigations enormously influenced Husserlian *phenomenology and its offshoots. It should be noted that though James rejects materialism, in any ordinary sense, he does take what might be called a phenomenological materialist view of many mental processes, seeing them as the consciousness of physical states, as in the *James–Lange theory of the emotions or his replacement of the Kantian 'I think' as the constant in experience by the 'I breathe'.

2. The best known of James's purely philosophical works is *Pragmatism* (1908). James takes over from C. S. Peirce the idea that the meaning of a concept lies in its practical bearings but puts it to different (not necessarily worse) uses. Truth, for James's *pragmatism, consists in useful ideas. Their utility may lie in either the power to predict experience they confer or their encouragement of valuable emotion and behaviour. Obvious objections to this appear less strong when it is realized that James's account incorporates what is currently called an external-ist critique of inherent intentionality (sometimes expressed as the rejection of the very idea of consciousness as opposed to experience). Thus an idea (*qua* piece of 'flat' experience) is only about something to the extent that it produces behaviour fitted to deal with it if it exists, and is true only if it does so. (Thus my belief that God exists requires a God it helps me deal with to be true.) This was a response to his colleague Royce, who claimed that only through the mediation of a divine mind can thought be linked to definite external objects and thus enabled James to avoid the absolute idealism to which he had previously felt unwillingly forced. Actually James's pragmatic account of truth is the fulfilment of a variety of strands in his prior thought and takes somewhat different forms according to which is uppermost. Among these are Peirce's operationalism, Royce's account of intentional-ity, and his own doctrine of the will to believe.

3. James's other chief philosophical doctrine is radical empiricism, the view that the ultimate stuff of reality (or at least all knowable reality) is pure experience. When the natures or qualia which compose this occur in one kind of arrangement they constitute minds, when in another, physical things. (The clash with the earlier denial of repeatable components of consciousness is modified in his final pluralistic metaphysics.) This relates to pragmatism because knowledge is conceived as the way in which the experience composing a mind leads it to successful negoti-ation with experience beyond itself (whether in a physical or a mental arrangement). In *Essays in Radical Empiricism* (a posthumous collection of 1904–5 articles) James oscil-lates between various radical empiricist accounts of the physical world, a phenomenalist view for which the phys-ical consists in possible experience, a 'new realist' position for which it consists in sensory vistas only some of them in minds, and the panpsychist view that the physical consists in its own inner experience of itself. Upon the whole he seems to have thought the last the final metaphysical truth and the second the best analysis of our ordinary concep-tion of things.

4. An inherited concern with religious issues was central to James's thought throughout his life. *The Varieties of Religious Experience* (1902) studies the phenomena of mysticism and *religious experience with a view to an eventual empirical assessment of their validity, a concern which also led to James's substantial involvement in psy-chical research, while later works, such as *A Pluralist Uni-verse* (1909), after sharply attacking the metaphysical *monism of absolute idealists like Royce and Bradley,

develop a mystical pluralistic metaphysics in which a 'finite God', or more interestingly a 'mother sea of consciousness', plays some of the roles of an infinite God or Absolute, while leaving us an independence we are refused by monism, and avoiding the apology for evil which it, along with orthodox *theism, imposes. Death prevented the completion of a final working-out of his metaphysics, but *Some Problems of Philosophy* (1911), which particularly focuses on the nature of relations and con-tinuity, taken with other works, sufficiently exhibits its main outlines.

5. In these later works James allied himself with Henri Bergson in arguing that conceptual thought cannot do proper justice to reality. This arises largely from the fact that concepts can only provide a static picture of a world which is essentially dynamic. (It was partly by exploiting this, he argued, that absolute idealists promoted their spe-cious claim that the familiar world of contingency and change is somehow unreal, and that Reality proper con-sists in a static *Absolute.) This is all right so long as that static picture is used to guide our dynamic dealings with things, but it leads to trouble when we expect it to provide a real grasp of the nature of its object. James's treatment of the limitations of conceptual thought is related to his prag-matic conception of truth in a somewhat curious manner. *Truth, he argued, as a pragmatist, is no mere copy of real-ity in another conceptual or verbal medium. There would be little point in it if it were, and we should regard the con-ceptual symbols in which it consists rather as tools for deal-ing with (and perhaps sometimes as a worthwhile addition to) reality than as revelations of its essence. None the less, James did hanker for something which could provide a sense of the real essence of things and, since concepts and truth were precluded from this role, it had to be sought in a metaphysics which turns us towards reality in some more intimate way than they do. And here the standard logic by which we organize our concepts is more an obstacle than an aid. We should not look for a revelation of reality from what are merely tools for dealing with it but must do so by sinking ourselves perceptually in the flux and be prepared to give an account of a world in process which will capture something of its essence even if conceptually it contains some apparent contradictions. The specific upshot of these reflections is, in effect, a process philosophy, incorporating an 'epochal' view of time, not unlike that later developed by Whitehead and Hartshorne (who, however, aimed to put into satisfactory concepts what James thought could not be adequately conceptualized).   T.L.S.S.

A. J. Ayer, *The Origins of Pragmatism: Studies in the Philosophy of Charles Sanders Peirce and William James* (London, 1968). Part 2 on James.

Graham Bird, *William James* (London, 1986).

Marcus Ford, *William James's Philosophy: A New Perspective* (Amherst, Mass., 1982).

Bruce Kuklick, *The Rise of American Philosophy* (New Haven, Conn., 1977), pt. 3.

Gerald Myers, *William James: His Life and Thought* (New Haven, Conn., 1986).

R. A. Putnam (ed.), *The Cambridge Companion to William James* (Cambridge, 1997).

T. L. S. Sprigge, *James and Bradley: American Truth and British Reality* (La Salle, Ill., 1993).

James–Lange theory of the emotions. Independently advanced by Carl G. Lange in 1885 and by William James in 1884, it holds that an emotion is the experience of an appropriate physical response to external stimuli. Sadness and anger don't make us cry and strike, rather they are the feeling of doing so. Typical of a note of 'phenomenological materialism' in James, like his substitution of the 'I breathe', as the accompaniment of all consciousness, for the 'I think'.   T.L.S.S.

Jansenism. This movement in seventeenth-century French Catholic thought is named after the Fleming Cornelius Otto Jansen (1585–1638), whose treatise *Augustinus* inspired it. Jansenists held that it is impossible to do good works without God's grace and that this grace is irresistible. They adopted a rigoristic position in Christian ethics and criticized their Jesuit opponents for moral laxity. Pascal, who was influenced by and sympathetic to Jansenism, satirized the moral reasoning of its opponents in his *Lettres provinciales*.   P.L.Q.

N. Abercrombie, *The Origins of Jansenism* (Oxford, 1936).

Japanese philosophy. The first thing to be said about Japanese philosophy is that it does indeed exist. If philosophy is understood as 'thinking about the fundamental structures and meaning of human existence in the world', it has been practised in Japan for well over a thousand years. But the most striking feature of Japanese philosophy is its distinctly multiple heritage, drawing as it does from a variety of Indian, Chinese, indigenous, and—eventually—Western sources. Also, compared with most European philosophies, East Asian thinking tends to focus on particular, concrete issues, and is correspondingly uninterested in abstract speculation.

A few initial remarks—of necessity quite general—may help to orientate the reader to the very different kind of thinking that one finds in the Japanese tradition. Many of the philosophical categories that seem natural in the West are simply not found in East Asian thought. This is in part a function of the structures of the Chinese and Japanese languages, which are quite different from the subject–predicate structure of languages in the Indo-European family. In Chinese, words that would for us be substantives function more as verbs, corresponding to an experience of the world as dynamic process rather than as substance; and in Japanese, so much emphasis is placed on the predicate that the subject is usually omitted altogether, while there are two verbs for 'is–exists'—neither of which is used for the copula.

There are also considerable differences in philosophical rhetoric and style. In a culture that prizes allusive understatement and subtle indirectness in human intercourse, forcefully to advance arguments in terms of clear and distinct ideas—let alone to attack or defend a philosophical position—would be considered boorish to the point of barbarism. In addition, the ways relative clauses function in Japanese make for even more indeterminacy. But what to the Western student of philosophy might seem impossibly vague may appear to the Japanese reader a pregnant play of multiple meanings that reflects the actual complexities of experience. In general, the line between philosophy and literature is less clearly drawn than in the West.

Most of the dualisms on which Western philosophy tends to be predicated—the intelligible as opposed to the sensible realm, the divine in contrast to the human, culture versus nature, mind (or spirit) in opposition to body (or matter), the logical and rational versus the aesthetic and intuitive—are not prominent in East Asian thinking. And since Japanese philosophy tends to be firmly grounded in *practice*, reading and reflection are best supplemented by engaging in (or at least observing) the relevant practices—going to Japanese theatre, studying Japanese literature, sitting or walking in *Zen meditation, practising Japanese arts (whether martial or fine), watching Japanese films, visiting Japanese gardens, or even eating in traditional Japanese restaurants.

A major reason for the late start of philosophical thinking in Japan was that the indigenous language lacked a system of writing. When the Japanese began 'importing' Chinese culture around the fifth century, one of the first things they took over was the ideographic system of written Chinese. Three major philosophies were embodied in the texts that were brought from China over the next few hundred years: *Confucian, *Taoist, and *Buddhist thought, all of which—together with the indigenous religious world-view of Shinto—shaped the subsequent development of Japanese thought. A major figure in the introduction of Chinese and Indian culture to Japan was Kūkai (774–835), founder of an esoteric school of Buddhism deriving from Indian tantrism. Like many great Japanese thinkers, Kūkai was a man of many talents and a paradigm of the religious thinker who is simultaneously beyond the everyday world and fully engaged in it. He thus exemplifies two general traits of Japanese philosophy: it has a strong religious component, while being inherently embodied in practice.

Several centuries later, two other philosophically fertile schools of Buddhism came to prominence, the first being the 'Pure Land' Buddhism founded by Hōnen (1133–1212) and his disciple Shinran (1173–1262). The other was Zen, which grew out of Chan Buddhism in China. The introducers into Japan of the two major Zen schools were Eisai (1141–1215) for the Rinzai school and Dōgen (1200–53) for the Sōtō school. Of all the philosophies developed in Japan, Zen has had the broadest cultural impact. During the medieval period it profoundly informed the evolution of such arts as poetry and Noh drama, architecture and landscape gardening, calligraphy and painting, the tea ceremony and flower arrangement, as well as swordsmanship, archery, and other martial arts.

Two figures from the Rinzai school deserve mention as exemplifying the fusion of Zen thought with practice. Takuan Sōhō (1573–1645) was a prolific author whose more speculative works attempted a synthesis of Zen thinking with neo-Confucian metaphysics, but who is best known for his writings on the art of the Zen sword. Takuan explicated the Zen doctrine of 'no mind' by showing how, in combat, focusing the mind on any one place, or letting it 'stop' anywhere, leads to disaster; one must rather let one's awareness diffuse through the entire body and beyond, so as to allow immediate response from any part. This schema—in which rigorous psychophysical practice carried out over decades leads to an enlightened spontaneity that is even more rapid and attuned than instinctual responses—is typical of the Zen discipline that underlies practice in meditation and the arts. Two later Zen masters were responsible for a revitalization and efflorescence of the Rinzai school during the Tokugawa period, Bankei Yōtaku (1622–93) and Hakuin Ekaku (1685–1768). Like Takuan, Hakuin was a man of multiple talents and is highly regarded as a poet, a painter and calligrapher, and a thinker of the first rank. For the Rinzai school Zen practice is a matter of 'seeing into one's own true nature', which is basically already enlightened. Hakuin emphasizes that genuine practice consists in 'uninterrupted meditation in the midst of all activities' rather than the 'dead sitting and silent illumination' advocated by the quietistic schools. (There is a remarkable similarity between Hakuin's style of writing and Nietzsche's, as well as between many of their ideas—especially about the role of the emotions in the best human life.)

Towards the end of the Tokugawa period a movement arose in reaction to the dominance of Buddhist and Confucian thinking in Japanese philosophy that came to be known as the Kokugaku ('national learning') school, the primary figures in which were Motoori Norinaga (1730–1801) and Hirata Atsune (1776–1843). While receptive to the neo-Confucian Kogaku thinkers' emphasis on the earliest classical texts, these men called for a return to the study of Japanese antiquity. Through a philosophical reconstruction of Shinto and careful study of the early classics of Japanese myth and literature, they sought to recover the 'true heart' of ancient Japan as a basis for spiritual renewal in the present. While the Kokugaku philosophies are impressive in their philological sophistication, the exclusiveness of their concern with 'pure Japaneseness'—while understandable in view of the multiple heritage of Japanese culture—tends toward a vehement nationalism.

Upon the reopening of the country to the West with the Meiji Restoration of 1868, the Japanese embarked upon a comprehensive programme of 'adopting and adapting' Western philosophies. Around the turn of the century, thorough engagements with the full historical sweep of Western philosophy were complemented by special studies of British *utilitarianism, American *pragmatism, French *positivism, and—above all *German philosophy from Leibniz and Kant, through Hegel and Fichte and Schelling, to Schopenhauer and Nietzsche. The first masterpiece to emerge from the ferment that resulted from this confluence of the Asian and Western philosophical traditions was An Inquiry into the Good (1911) by Nishida Kitarō (1870–1945), an epochal work that sought to articulate an original philosophy rooted in the tradition of East Asian thought by way of concepts derived from Western philosophy. Over the next thirty years Nishida went on to elaborate a vast and complex body of thought ranging over metaphysics and epistemology, ethics and aesthetics, and philosophy of politics and religion.

Nishida influenced a whole generation of younger philosophers, many of whom also taught at Kyoto University and came to be known collectively as the Kyoto School. The thought of these men was often influenced by religious existentialism and always informed by thorough study of the history of Western philosophy. Tanabe Hajime (1885–1962), much influenced by Hegel, wrote extensively in the fields of ethics and phenomenology and philosophy of religion from the perspective of Pure Land Buddhism, while his younger contemporary Nishitani Keiji (1900–90), more influenced by Nietzsche, wrote from a more existential standpoint conditioned by Zen. Watsuji Tetsurō (1889–1960) began his writing career with insightful studies of Schopenhauer, Kierkegaard, and Nietzsche, and went on to publish prolifically on Buddhism, Confucianism, the philosophy of the visual and theatrical arts, and especially ethics.

Several of the major figures in the Kyoto School came in for severe criticism from their Marxist colleagues—among whom the most impressive thinker was Tosaka Jun (1900–45)—for publishing material during the Second World War that was distinctly nationalistic and right-wing in tone. The political writings of these thinkers deserve close attention, since they open some fascinating perspectives on the difficult question concerning the relations between a thinker's politics and his or her philosophy. Unfortunately, much of the recent commentary on these issues in the United States has come from post-Marxist Japanologists so ready to point the accusing finger from positions of ethical superiority that ideological complacency has tended to take the place of responsible scholarship in this area.

Three other thinkers of the period deserve mention. Hatano Seiichi (1877–1950) is distinguished by being a practising Christian and by his broad competence in the history of Western philosophy with special emphasis on the Greeks and philosophy of religion. Miki Kiyoshi (1897–1945) was an existential humanist, strongly influenced by Marxism for a time, who produced important works in the fields of social and political philosophy and philosophical anthropology. Kuki Shūzō (1888–1943) was a cosmopolitan aristocrat who spent the 1920s studying in Europe, where he made a great impression on both Heidegger and Sartre among others. While he is best known for his subtle work on the aesthetics of Japanese taste, Iki no kōzō (The Structure of 'Iki' (1930)), Kuki wrote with great sophistication in the fields of existential philosophy, literary theory, and modern French thought. He was also an accomplished poet who wrote numerous belletristic essays.

At the close of the twentieth century, number of philosophers (such as Abe Masao, Takeuchi Yoshinori, Tsujimura Kōichi, and Ueda Shizuteru) were carrying on the work of the Kyoto School, while their counterparts in Tokyo (Nakamura Hajime and Yuasa Yasuo) were focusing more on historical issues, especially with regard to Buddhism. An exciting feature of current philosophy in Japan is the dialogue being initiated by syntheses of contemporary Western thought with the Japanese philosophical tradition by such thinkers as Sakabe Megumi in Tokyo and Ohashi Ryōsuke in Kyoto.   G.R.P.

*Buddhist philosophy; Chinese philosophy; Indian philosophy.

David A. Dilworth and Valdo H. Viglielmo with Agustin Jacinto Zavala (eds. and tr.), *Sourcebook for Modern Japanese Philosophy: Selected Documents* (London, 1998).

James W. Heisig, *Philosophers of Nothingness: An Essay on the Kyoto School* (Honolulu, 2001).

Thomas P. Kasulis, *Zen Action/Zen Person* (Honolulu, 1981).

Michael Marra (ed. and tr.), *A History of Modern Japanese Aesthetics* (Honolulu, 2001).

Graham Parkes, 'Ways of Japanese Thinking', in Nancy G. Hume (ed.), *Japanese Aesthetics and Culture* (Albany, NY, 1995).

—— 'The Putative Fascism of the Kyoto School and the Political Correctness of the Modern Academy', *Philosophy East and West*, 47/3 (1997).

Jaspers, Karl (1883–1969). German philosopher, who was one of the founders of *existentialism. Originally a psychiatrist, his first book was *General Psychopathology* (1913). *Die Psychologie der Weltanschauungen* (1919) marked his transition to philosophy. It presented a typology of worldviews, and also introduced his philosophy of *Existenz*, which he elaborated in *Philosophy* (1932; tr. Chicago, 1967–71) and other works. The great philosophical systems have collapsed, since men are essentially limited, conditioned and uncertain. We must learn from philosophers, such as Kierkegaard and Nietzsche, who accept and probe human finitude. Only three ways of philosophizing are now open to us: to explore (1) the limits of science (world-orientation), (2) the self, and (3) what transcends world and self. World, soul, and God are the three 'encompassers', within whose 'horizons' we know everything we know: we cannot ascend to the supreme encompasser of these horizons, e.g. to Heidegger's 'being'.

1. Science has only relative, not absolute, truth. It serves for the manipulation of measurable objects, but gives no answers to the crucial questions of life and death. Between the four spheres of reality—matter, life, soul, spirit—there are gaps which science will never succeed in filling.

2. The self is *Existenz*: it has no fixed nature, but is its possibilities, what it can become. It exists only in 'communication' with other existences. It acts not only within the routines and rituals of everyday life, but sometimes 'unconditionally', with a freedom amounting to the 'choice of itself'. Its condition is starkly revealed in 'limit-situations', such as death, suffering, conflict, and guilt, requiring decisions perplexed by uncertainty and antinomy.

3. World and *Existenz* point to the transcendent. This is discernible in the 'ciphers' presented by experience and tradition. One such cipher is the law of the day and the passion of the night, the perennial conflict between orderly reason and destructive unreason. Another is the pervasive defeat of human aspirations. 'Failure is ultimate', but to philosophize is 'to learn to die' and 'to encounter being by means of failure'.   M.J.I.

M. Dufrenne and P. Ricœur, *Karl Jaspers et la Philosophie de l'existence* (Paris, 1947).

H. Ehrlich and R. Wisser (eds.), *Karl Jaspers Today* (Washington DC, 1988).

P. A. Schilpp (ed.), *The Philosophy of Karl Jaspers* (La Salle, Ill., 1957).

jaundice. Favourite philosophical example of how the state of observers can affect their *perception; used from Lucretius and Sextus Empiricus, through Berkeley, and into the twentieth century. 'In the *jaundice*, every one knows that all things seem yellow' (Berkeley, *Three Dialogues*, 1). In sceptics' hands this was used to show that (since there was nothing to choose between the jaundiced eye and the unjaundiced eye) we cannot ascribe to an object a 'true colour'. For other philosophers, the example shows only that, while objects have colours (which in good circumstances are seen by people with good eyesight in good health), a white thing will in particular circumstances look yellow and a person may even mistakenly take it to be that colour.

The example may itself be an instance of mistake. It has been remarked that in jaundice it is the sufferer who looks yellow to the world, not the world that looks yellow to the sufferer.   J.BRO.

*illusion.

J. Annas and J. Barnes, *The Modes of Scepticism* (Cambridge, 1985), ch. 4.

Jefferson, Thomas (1743–1826). Statesman (third President of the United States) and political theorist, author of the Declaration of Independence and the (1779) Act for Establishing Religious Freedom (state of Virginia), among other political and philosophical documents. Jefferson's general philosophical outlook was empiricist and materialist, his religious convictions were deist, and his political opinions were grounded in Lockean social *contract theory. His vision of representative *democracy required an educated and self-sufficient populace, and he insisted that free public education, together with the recognition that no generation's political consent could bind another's, would promote in the new nation the 'natural aristocracy' of 'virtue and talents', eliminating the 'artificial aristocracy' of 'wealth and birth'.   K.H.

Morton White, *The Philosophy of the American Revolution* (New York, 1978).

Jeffrey, Richard (1926–2002). Princeton philosopher. Jeffrey helped develop the subjective interpretation of probability and Bayesian approaches to *decision theory and *confirmation. Using relatively simple mathematical and logical machinery, he developed materials from Thomas Bayes, Frank Ramsey, and others into what amounts to a version of the ancient Sceptic Sextus Empiricus' dream of solving practical and theoretical problems by appeal to one's own desires, preferences, and subjective impressions, without assuming any objective knowledge. Jeffrey's contributions to the epistemology of science include techniques for calculating the probability of a hypothesis from uncertain evidence, and investigations of problems raised for confirmation theories by photographs and other such non-propositional evidence. By popularizing the use of truth trees in teaching introductory logic he saved countless thousands of innocent students from incalculable hours of drudgery.   J.B.B.

Richard Jeffrey, *The Logic of Decision*, 2nd edn. (Chicago, 1983).

---

jen: *see* Confucianism.

Jevons, William Stanley (1835–82). British economist and philosopher who taught in Manchester and London. Much of his work was pioneering and influential, such as his theory of utility in economics, and his inclusive interpretation of the logical connective 'either . . . or'. His logical theory was based on the principle of 'the substitution of similars', the idea that what is true of a thing is true of its like. He recognized that logical deduction is a mechanical process, and invented a machine that could perform inferences. However, his theory of *scientific method, developed in *The Principles of Science* (1874), though more neglected, is equally deserving of respect. He opposed Mill's views on induction, arguing instead for a *hypothetico-deductive account of science, in which theories are not conclusively verified but have a degree of *probability, interpreted as a measure of reasonable belief.   A.BEL.

Margaret Schabas, *A World Ruled by Number: William Stanley Jevons and the Rise of Mathematical Economics* (Princeton, NJ, 1990).

Jewish philosophy. Taking its origin and problematic from the biblical and rabbinic texts, Jewish philosophy, in its critical mode, reflects the rabbinic endeavour to reinterpret and reapply those texts in continually altered circumstances. Its synthetic mode is a creative reappropriation and rediscovery of their core spiritual and moral values.

Judaism is a culture, a nation and ethnicity, and a historical tradition as well as a religion. All these aspects are reflected in Jewish philosophy. They are not always successfully integrated. And not all of Judaism, even conceived intellectually, is philosophical. Mysticism, legal positivism, and certain romantic strains can be actively anti-philosophical, even when they take on philosophical colorations. Fideism and fundamentalism, the most prominent anti-philosophical trends within Christianity, are notably absent in Judaism. Jewish orthodoxy is committed to practice. Piety takes the form of ritual observance rather than credal correctness. The faith of the Hebrew Bible is the moral virtue of faithfulness, conceived as loyalty, which like the biblical ideas of blessing, grace, joy, favour, and love, involves a mutuality between humanity and God, which is echoed in human fellowship. Faith is not in the first instance a cognitive notion. It has nothing to do with 'salvation'. The aim of Jewish life is not the hereafter but fulfilment for individuals and communities, through adherence to the 'laws of life', which reason apprehends in their bare outlines, but which Scripture and tradition richly elaborate in an ongoing historical process. Hence the alienness of fundamentalism. Karaism, the only scripturalist, back-to-basics movement in Judaism, was marginalized precisely because it sought (with notable lack of success) to undermine the intellectual and cultural authority that allowed the continuing thematic elaboration of Jewish law and practice.

The opening lines of the Torah, 'In the beginning God created heaven and earth', typify the oblique biblical method of broaching philosophical issues. God's existence is not 'proved' in the medieval manner, but God's act is offered as the explanation of all the world we know. Similarly, there is no direct polemic against pagan mythology, but the silence of the text about God's motives, ancestry, battles, lineaments, and plans complements its later, practical prohibitions of attempts to represent the divine—speaking volumes, by indirection, about God's sublimity and transcendence, without resort to abstract vocabulary.

The biblical word for transcendence is holiness. Those who would be ruled by God are called upon to share it (Leviticus 19: 2), symbolically and pragmatically, by ritual and moral purity, and by the hygienic purity that links the two. God's love and favour are reciprocated by human love of his creatures and creation. Thus the seeming *non sequitur* 'Thou shalt not hate an Egyptian, for thou wast a stranger in his land' (Deuteronomy 23: 8) generalized in the universal rule 'Love thy fellow as thyself' (Leviticus 19: 18) is transformed into sound reasoning only by the adoption of a Godlike, universal perspective, valuing all persons alike and so capable of adopting their perspectives and acknowledging them as the authors of their own ends. The absoluteness of the source of such moral objectivity, which is not the objectivity of disinterest but that is universal love, is clearly reflected in the biblical tagline 'I am the Lord', repeatedly offered as the reason for God's moral demands, as, for example, in the prohibition of cursing the deaf or putting a stumbling-block before the blind, or otherwise abusing the weak or helpless (Leviticus 19: 4). Thus the central interpersonal commandment to love one's fellows as oneself is a corollary of the commandment to love God. All God's commandments are rabbinically construed as interpretations, that is, applications, of these two.

The prophets, as the rabbis read them, successively refine, order, and sublimate the biblical laws: the barbarism of paganism is condemned, with all its trappings of luxury and cruel pomp, but no merely ritual infraction is ever amongst the sins against which the prophets inveigh. The Talmud writes (*Makkot* 23b–24a): 'Moses was given 613 commandments. David summed these up in eleven (Psalm 15), Isaiah in six (33: 16–17), Micah in three (6: 8), Isaiah in two (56: 1), and finally Habakkuk grounded them all in one principle, fidelity.' The rabbis see themselves as continuing this process. But there is no *reductionism in the reduction. That is, no minimalism. The part does not replace the whole but only voices its intention and thus fosters the interpretative practice that keeps the text alive. Through such continuous sifting the rabbis discover the thematics of Scripture long before Socratic method has taught them the conceptual mode of discourse. They rely on dialogical analysis, the logic of association—puns, hints, and allusions—as their nominal proofs, but never as their grounds. Treating Scripture as a portent, they find significance in the resolution of every seeming redundancy and verbal paradox. But the *nisus* they uncover is never paradox itself, and the objects of their homilies (*midrashim*) are tangential only to the immediate intentions of the contexts that are their springboard, never irrelevant to the core moral and spiritual themes of the canon, which are the real grounds of the argument that is generally left unspoken.

The first explicit philosopher of Judaism is Philo, the learned, highly principled, and highly aesthetic Hellenistic Alexandrian, who reads Scripture through the eyes of Plato, and Plato through the eyes of Scripture, and who solves the problem of God's governance of nature by introducing the Logos as, at once, an attribute and an act of God, transcendent in its wholeness but immanent in its immediacy. The most eloquent is Halevi, the poet and the advocate of the material aspects of the tradition—land, language, culture, and imagination—against a backdrop of intellectualism. Ibn Gabirol, the most abstract Neoplatonist of medieval Jewish philosophy, also spoke for materiality, in the intellectual matter of the divine realm. He too was a major Hebrew poet. The most spiritual of the Jewish philosophers was Bahya ibn Paquda, a profound and cosmopolitan pietist, who spoke compellingly of the need to supplement the 'duties of the limbs' so near to the practice of his contemporaries, with the corresponding Duties of the Heart, including in their number not only spiritual but intellectual and philosophical duties.

The first systematic Jewish philosopher was Saadiah Gaon, the exegete, translator, grammarian, liturgist, jurist, and inductive philologist of biblical thematics, who forged his method from the techniques of his Muslim counterparts, his Greek and rabbinic predecessors, and his Karaite contemporaries, in keeping with the rabbinic maxim that he is wise who learns from every human being. The greatest philosopher committed whole-heartedly to Judaism was the jurist and physician Maimonides, Rabbi Moses ben Maimon, affectionately known by the acronym Rambam, and admired by Muslim contemporaries and Christian successors, including Aquinas, for his brilliant exposition of the theology of transcendence.

The most radically creative Jewish philosopher was the excommunicate Spinoza, whose *Ethics* seems today to be the most popularly appreciated and most professionally misunderstood and neglected major work of philosophy. Too spirited to develop his thoughts in the manner of closet philosophy long practised, for example, in the *Kabbalah, Spinoza was forced as a young man into an open break with the tradition that had nurtured him. That break was aggravated by his need to criticize biblicism systematically, turning the problematics of traditional rabbinic exegesis into a foundation of modern biblical criticism. His hope was to create the intellectual space needed for the philosophical work of the *Ethics* and for its open-minded reception, a reception it would win, but not in his lifetime. The major theses of the *Ethics* respond to the full repertoire of philosophical concerns in the Western tradition from Parmenides to Descartes and beyond. The intellectual resources Spinoza brings to his task are his own. But the detailed strategies he uses are critically informed by the achievements of such Jewish philosophers as Ibn Gabirol, Maimonides, Gersonides, Crescas, Leo Hebraeus, and Abraham Herrera, as Harry Wolfson, Richard Popkin, and others have shown. And the subtle monism of Spinoza's metaphysics, like the perfectionism of his ethics and the calm intuitionism of his epistemology, uniting the correspondence theory of truth with the clear formalism of rationalist coherentism, is as much a fulfilment of the biblical project as it is a response to the problematics of Aristotle and Plato.

All of the thinkers mentioned here use the techniques of their time and place. The biblical writers forge myths and laws, answer authors like those of the epic of Gilgamesh and the code of Hammurabi. The prophets use oracle and symbolic parable. Philo speaks in allegories and homiletic glosses. Saadiah thematizes in the manner of the Arabic *kalām* Muslim dialectical theology. Maimonides devises a hybrid genre, part essay, part commentary, part thematic treatise, allowing philosophy to inform his reading of Scripture, even as Scripture affords him a critical standpoint for examining the underlying assumptions of the prevalent philosophical schools. Spinoza uses the geometrical method of Euclid and Proclus, and of his own reformed Descartes.

Current Jewish philosophy has adopted the mode of the journal article and treatise, although Levinas will revert to the midrashic, homiletic method, as Cohen and Rosenzweig adopted the tones of the lecture hall, and Fackenheim the questioning rhetoric of the synagogue, and as Buber used the Ḥasidic tale and the European novel as vehicles of exposition. Through all the change of style and structure, and all the seeming change of paradigms, the thematic content remains remarkably steady, anchored in tradition and in text: God offers love and demands justice and generosity. Life is a gift; truth, a sacred and unescapable responsibility. L.E.G.

Julius Guttmann, *Philosophies of Judaism: The History of Jewish Philosophy from Biblical Times to Franz Rosenzweig*, tr. D. W. Silverman from the Hebrew 2nd edn. (New York, 1964).

Isaac Husik, *A History of Medieval Jewish Philosophy* (first pub. 1916; New York, 1969).

Norbert Samuelson, *An Introduction to Modern Jewish Philosophy* (Albany, NY, 1989).

Colette Sirat, *A History of Jewish Philosophy in the Middle Ages* (Cambridge, 1986).

Johnson, Samuel (1709–84). As far as his incursions into philosophy are concerned, Samuel Johnson is most often remembered for his choleric rejections of metaphysical claims. When taxed with the arguments of Berkeley he kicked a stone with the words 'I refute it thus'. But Johnson might have been a remarkable philosopher, as is shown by the brilliant and extremely funny review of Soames Jenyn's *Free Inquiry into the Origin and Nature of Evil*, in which Johnson destroys with lacerating logic a facile expression of eighteenth-century *optimism. That Johnson realized this is shown by his proposal to reserve the teaching of logic and metaphysics for himself when he and Boswell, on their Scottish journey, were speculating on the creation of a separate University in St Andrews employing members of 'The Club'. He did, after all, declare metaphysics to be his favourite subject.   R.A.S.

I do not know of any very recommendable account of Johnson on philosophy. As a stopgap, Charles H. Hinnault, *Samuel Johnson: An Analysis* (1988) may be consulted.

Johnson, W. E. (1858–1931). British philosopher who taught first mathematics and then philosophy at Cambridge. Author of *Logic*, and of 'Probability' (*Mind* (1932)), intended as a fourth part. Part I concentrates on informal logic; part II concerns syllogistic logic; and part iii causality. In part I Johnson suggested the *redundancy theory of truth, later attributed to Ramsey, adducing reasons why 'we may say strictly that the adjective *true* is redundant as applied to the proposition *p*' (I. iv. 2). He also explored *determinables (e.g. 'colour') and determinates (e.g. 'red'), drawing contrasts between 'Red is a colour' and 'Plato is a man' and between ways of increasing the intension or *connotation of a term. One can do so by passing from 'coloured' chair to 'red' chair or by adding 'foreign' attributes, like weight or shape, e.g. by going instead to 'coloured and straight-backed chair'.   S.W.

W. E. Johnson, *Logic*, 3 vols. (Cambridge, 1921–4).

joint method: *see* method, joint.

Jørgensen, Jørgen (1894–1969). Danish philosopher, originally a neo-Kantian, later influenced by Russell and Carnap, and a leading member of the group of philosophers called Logical Positivists. He wrote an encyclopaedic work on logic representing an anti-psychologistic point of view (*Treatise of Formal Logic* (1931)). Jørgensen was an ardent supporter of the idea of an encyclopaedia of unified science and became a member of the editorial board of the *Vienna Circle monograph series called *Einheitswissenschaft* (Vienna, 1932–9). He returned later in his *Psykologi paa biologisk Grundlag* (Psychology based on

Biology (1941–5)) to a modified version of *psychologism, and tried to reduce psychology to biology. But he was forced to conclude that this reduction was impossible and developed, instead of biologism, a kind of Spinozism in which consciousness was reduced to its phenomenological, physiological, and behavioural manifestations. According to Jørgensen it is meaningless to ask what consciousness is in contradistinction to its manifestations.   C.H.K.

J. Witt-Hansen, 'Jørgen Jørgensen and the Grammar of Science', in *Danish Yearbook of Philosophy* (1964).

journals of philosophy. The journal is the most recently established of the major institutions of learning. The first, fully developed in ancient Greece, were the academy, or research institute, and the library. The ecclesiastical domination of learning in general, and of philosophy in particular, led to their being pursued in monastic schools and, from the twelfth century on, in universities, on a larger and more productive scale. From the Renaissance to the mid-eighteenth century it was carried on by private individuals or by like-minded groups of men of letters rather than by professors. Printing led to the multiplication of smaller and generally more ephemeral literary forms than the book. The first learned journals, in which a little philosophy was to be found, appeared in the mid-seventeenth century: the *Journal des savants* from 1655 and *Acta eruditorum* (inspired by Leibniz) in 1682. In the 1660s the Royal Society and the French Académie des Sciences were founded and soon began to publish their transactions.

The private individuals whose work made up the unprecedentedly vigorous philosophical life of the seventeenth century were not isolated and out of contact with each other. Their chief medium of communication was correspondence, notable instances being the objections to Descartes's *Meditations* and his replies to them, and the exchanges about the nature of space between Leibniz and Samuel Clarke. With the secularization of philosophy in the universities of Germany and Scotland in the eighteenth century a philosophical profession began to emerge and in Germany some short-lived periodicals were soon brought out.

But philosophical journals proper did not become important until 1876, the year in which both *Mind* and the *Revue philosophique* were started. They had been preceded by the *Archiv für Geschichte der Philosophie* in 1868 and a year before that by the interesting *Journal of Speculative Philosophy* in the USA, which, in its quarter-century of life, published important work by Peirce, James, and Royce. *Mind* has been the main philosophical publication in English from its foundation until comparatively recent times, particularly under the editorships of G. F. Stout (1892–1920) and G. E. Moore (1921–47). F. H. Bradley and William James wrote extensively in it during the early years; Russell and Moore after 1900. The *Revue philosophique*, also still being published, deliberately sought contributors from outside France. From a slightly later period there still survive the American *Monist* (1888) and *Ethics* (1890), the French *Revue de métaphysique et morale* (1893), and the German *Kant-Studien* (1896).

The most interesting products of the 1890s and just afterwards not only still alive, but of the first importance, however, are the *Proceedings of the Aristotelian Society* (1891), more important than the meetings and symposia from which its contents came, the best barometer of the state of British philosophy since its first publication, and the American *Philosophical Review* (1892) and *Journal of Philosophy* (1904) emanating from Cornell and Columbia Universities. The two latter have much increased in distinction and influence since the 1940s with the increasing domination of English-speaking philosophy by the United States. With contributions from C. I. Lewis, Quine, Goodman, and Davidson they became and remain the leading philosophical journals in the English language.

The emergence of Logical Positivism was chronicled, and to a large extent took place, in the pages of *Erkenntnis* between 1930 and 1940, under the editorship of Carnap and Reichenbach, the leaders, respectively, of the Vienna Circle and its Berlin associate. Together with Schlick and Otto Neurath they published copiously in it until it became a casualty of war. It has recently been revived. The slim, pamphlet-like *Analysis* (since 1933) expressed the ideas of British sympathizers with positivism in the 1930s: Ayer, Waismann, Ryle, and Popper contributing in the first twenty years of its history.

The Journal of Symbolic Logic (since 1936) covered its subject at a high level of technical seriousness. Analytic philosophy outside Britain and America was catered for by the *Australasian Journal of Philosophy* (since 1923), admirably combative ever since its early years as the house organ of John Anderson's school, by *Theoria* (since 1935) from Sweden, by the fairly short-lived *Studia logica* and *Studia philosophica* from Poland, and by *Synthese* from Holland (since 1936), which has much improved in quality in recent years. Of more inclusive scope and less narrow doctrinal allegiance are the Belgian *Revue internationale de philosophie* (since 1938), which really is international, the British *Philosophy* (since 1926), and the Scottish *Philosophical Quarterly* (since 1950). Somewhat at odds with the prevailing fashions, but not exclusively so, are the American *Philosophy and Phenomenological Research* (since 1940) and *Review of Metaphysics* (since 1947).

The great age of philosophical journals ran from around 1890 to 1960. Since then they have increasingly come to serve as platforms for budding philosophers, in an expanding and competitive profession, from which to call attention to themselves, rather than as vehicles for the ideas of established leading figures.   A.Q.

*dictionaries and encyclopaedias of philosophy.

William Gerber, 'Philosophical Journals', in Paul Edwards (ed.), *Encyclopedia of Philosophy* (New York, 1967).

Judaism: *see* Jewish philosophy.

judgement. A term meaning *belief* or *decision*. The term has the so-called act–object ambiguity, denoting either the judging that something is true, or that which is judged true. In the object sense, judgements are *propositions: abstract objects that are true or false, stand in logical relationships, and are composed of concepts or other judgements. In the act sense, judgements are *propositional attitudes: introspectible mental states or acts which have a variety of causes and effects, and vary from person to person and time to time. Judgements are commonly distinguished from the *sentences expressing them. 'All men are animals' and 'Every man is an animal' are different English sentences, containing different numbers of words with different grammatical properties. The sentences, nevertheless, express the same judgement, which is not composed of words, and does not belong to any particular language.   W.A.D.

N. Salmon and S. Soames (eds.), *Propositions and Attitudes* (Oxford, 1988).

Jung, Carl (1875–1961). Swiss psychiatrist and psychoanalyst, founder of 'analytical psychology'; from 1906 to 1913 one of Freud's main advocates. They ostensibly separated over Jung's generalization of the concept 'libido' beyond the carnal meaning on which Freud then insisted. Freud was later to adopt a view of libido which many have found impossible to distinguish from Jung's, and which has caused the dispute to be likened to that over transubstantiation in its empirical emptiness. Though Jung complained of Freud's intolerance of dissent, it is noteworthy that during the period of their association he was no less vituperative nor less forward in proposing expulsions and exclusions.

Jung introduced the now familiar notion 'complex' for a constellation of affect-laden ideas which secretly influence behaviour (a term with which he was so closely associated that, after his estrangement from Freud, Ernest Jones proposed its exclusion from the psychoanalytic vocabulary). Other concepts which were distinctive of Jung were those of individuation, the collective unconscious and its archetypes, and the introversion–extroversion typology which has entered into common use and been adapted and operationalized by Hans Eysenck. Jung, though he appears to have been as personally charismatic as Freud, did not have Freud's literary gifts and few of his works make the indelible impression of so many of Freud's.   F.C.

*psychoanalysis, philosophical problems of.

C. Jung, *Memories, Dreams, Reflections* (London, 1963).

jurisprudence: *see* philosophy of law.

justice in one sense is identical with the ethics of who should receive benefits and burdens, good or bad things of many sorts, given that others might receive these things. Although discourse about justice is often influenced by models of law, the ethics of justice is a subject in itself. To 'receive' a benefit or burden is to have any of a large number of more concrete relations to it: not only legal ownership or other entitlement may be relevant, but also non-legal matters. Enjoyment of an experience, having access to many opportunities, getting protection from or exposure to a risk, and so on may be relevant. The 'others' relevant to justice may be those living in a person's community, those in other communities, or even those dead, those yet to live, or perhaps possible persons who will never live. Central cases of justice, however, usually involve persons living at the same time in the same community (although the community may be very narrowly or broadly defined). Here intuitions and arguments seem better grounded.

There are various contexts for talk about justice, including (at least) distributive, retributive, and 'corrective' justice (which apparently overlap to some extent). Distributive justice concerns the ethical appropriateness of which recipients get which benefits and burdens. Retributive justice concerns the ethical appropriateness of *punishment for wrongdoing. Corrective justice concerns the ethical appropriateness of compensating with some good because of a loss or appropriating some good because of a gain. (From Aristotle onward, philosophers have sometimes taken an interest in this.)

A few in philosophy have doubted the rational basis or the desirability of any justice orientation. But many philosophers have advocated some conception of justice, often aligning themselves with some general political tendency: 'liberal democratic capitalism', 'laissez-faire market-oriented capitalism', some variety of 'socialism', etc. Indeed, political and economic power are goods, and to worry about the justice of who has them is familiar, especially for those philosophers who have taken egalitarianism to be basic to justice.

There is indeed a presumption in favour of treating persons equally in distributive matters, unless some relevant difference can be specified to distinguish persons treated unequally. To treat persons unequally with respect to distribution of important benefits and burdens, in the absence of a justification, is a paradigm of injustice. The burden of justification should be regarded as very weighty, strong enough so that a reasonable case might be made (hypothetically, if not actually) to those less favoured by the distribution. Utilitarian arguments, notoriously, seem incapable of discharging this justificatory burden. For one thing, utilitarians arguably are not entitled to a sufficiently strong notion of a moral right to unpack many modern, rights-centred notions of justice. Although considerations of distributive justice might not always trump other sorts of ethical considerations (including utility) in a context, they do properly count a great deal.

Modern accounts of justice tend to be based on ideas about human rationality, human intuitions, human community, or the like (as opposed, say, to 'cosmic justice' or the will of God). John Rawls's very influential A Theory of Justice, and subsequent writings, are instructive in this connection. Rawls argues that his two principles of justice (the first requiring, roughly, an equal right to the most extensive system of equal basic liberties, taking priority over the second, a principle that allows for certain *inequalities subject to various constraints, including the requirement that the inequalities are to the greatest benefit of the least advantaged) would be chosen by autonomous judges behind a veil of ignorance designed to deny them knowledge of their own positions in a social system to which the principles will apply. Increasingly, in post-Theory of Justice writing especially, Rawls stresses the constructivism of his theory, and its roots in a particular community.

A large variety of criteria have been proposed for ethically just distributions. Some think just distributions should be in accordance with contribution, some with effort, some need, some *desert, and so on. Some think that just distributions are a matter of the history of how a certain distribution came about. There seems no finite list of criteria, no definitive decision procedure here.

In light of this, one can see the attractions of 'pluralism' and 'complex equality', as presented by Michael Walzer. People collectively 'create' goods of innumerable sorts and distribute them in accordance with many criteria, the appropriateness of which changes historically and varies with the social sphere concerned, whether we are talking about money, medical care, schooling, political power, love, and so on.   E.T.S.

*economics and morality; equality; fairness; generations, justice, between; well-being; Thrasymachus.

Brian Barry, Theories of Justice (Berkeley, Calif., 1989).
John Rawls, A Theory of Justice (Cambridge, Mass., 1971).
Michael Walzer, Spheres of Justice (New York, 1983).

justice, international. Theories of international relations propose explanatory models for studying relations between states. Theories of international justice, on the other hand, formulate moral principles for judging the legitimacy of non-domestic institutions and policies. Three main schools exist in this respect. First, 'cosmopolitans' hold that the ultimate subject of moral value is the individual person, and consequently institutions, including states, are only legitimate in so far as they advance equal moral treatment of persons, irrespective of their location and affiliation. Claiming a right over a significant resource solely on the basis of territorial ownership, for example, is illegitimate on this view. By contrast, another school identifies an independent value in national affiliation and self-determination which must be taken into account in principles of international justice. Finally, there is a view which, whilst not attributing value to nation-states, nevertheless sees their existence as relevant to questions of principle.

John Rawls explicitly develops principles for the just foreign policy of liberal states, rather than a conception of a just 'world order'. Liberal states should accept other states as legitimate which, whilst not fully liberal, protect basic human rights (not the full liberal complement), and have a well-ordered legal system dispensing a 'common good' conception of justice. No global principle of distributive justice is offered by Rawls. It is not clear why Rawls should require liberal states to accept non-liberal states as legitimate. However, assuming no equivalent coercive structure to the state is present or desirable at a global level, he opts for addressing the external practices of liberal states in a way that maximizes stable external relations, whilst permitting intervention in case of extreme abuses. In doing so he continues the Kantian tradition of international justice as peace and security, rather than principles of justice for a world order.

Cosmopolitan critics of this approach claim that the distinction between just foreign policy and justice for a world order is not sustainable. But it is unclear to which entity standards for global justice could be applied. In circumstances where no global coercive institution exists, any redistributive account will face compliance assurance problems. Furthermore, a principle placing a duty on any state to enforce internationally anything more than a limited number of very important rights would incur such costs as to make it unviable. Consequently, cosmopolitans can either bite the bullet and develop principles which, if acted upon by individuals or states, will lead to a just institutional world order assuring global compliance, or they can simply modify Rawls's principles for foreign policy in a way that will plausibly produce more global justice. Some 'weak' cosmopolitans have adopted the latter course.   S.M.-G.

*international relations, the philosophy of; justice; sovereignty.

S. Caney, 'Cosmopolitans and the Law of Peoples: Survey Article', *Journal of Political Philosophy* (2002).
D. Miller, *Citizenship and National Identity* (Cambridge, 2000).
T. Pogge, *World Poverty and Human Rights* (Cambridge, 2002).
J. Rawls, *The Law of Peoples* (Cambridge, Mass., 1999).

justice and benevolence: *see* benevolence.

justification, epistemic. The property ascribed to a belief in virtue of satisfying certain evaluative norms concerning what a person ought to believe. Such norms measure the 'goodness' of a belief in so far as we are interested in epistemic goals, such as attaining truth and avoiding error.

The classical view conceives of justification as necessary for *knowledge, and sees it as a matter of the adequacy of the reasons or evidence one has for a given belief. This reasons-based view leads to two pressing questions: (1) Is *every* justified belief based upon other beliefs that act as reasons? Is there not some foundation of beliefs whose goodness is not transmitted to them from other beliefs? (2) Under what conditions are a person's reasons for some belief good *enough* that the belief is justified?

*Foundationalism is a theory about the structure of justification that affirms that some beliefs are basic, i.e. justified without being based upon other beliefs. Justified non-basic beliefs are based upon these foundations through good inferences or reasoning. The theory of such reasoning is expected to yield the answer to question 2.

Coherentism denies that any beliefs are foundational, and claims that justification is always a matter of the degree to which a belief 'coheres' with one's other beliefs. Various coherence theories define coherence differently, e.g. as a matter of consistency, explanation, probability, or 'comparative reasonableness'. Some measure of the degree of a belief's coherence is necessary to answer the second question.

*Reliabilism replaces the traditional reasons-based view with the idea that a belief is justified when it is the result of a permissible process or method, where permissibility is a function of that procedure's reliability, and reliability measures the likelihood that the produced belief is true. Delineating the processes or methods that are reliable (an issue to which psychology and cognitive science seem relevant) provides this theory's answer to question 2.   A.I.G.
                                                                J.W.B.

A. Goldman, *Epistemology and Cognition* (Cambridge, Mass., 1986).
K. Lehrer, *Theory of Knowledge* (Boulder, Colo., 1990).
P. Moser, *Empirical Justification* (Dordrecht, 1985).

just war: *see* war, just.

K

Kabbalah. Literally, tradition; specifically, Jewish mysticism as developed by such thinkers as Isaac the Blind, Abraham of Posquieres, Moses ben Naḥman of Gerona (Naḥmanides) (1194–1270), and Isaac Luria of Safed in Galilee (1535–72). Kabbalah invokes an elaborate cosmology based on the theurgic powers of the Hebrew alphabet, conceived in Neoplatonic and neo-Pythagorean terms as the instrument of creation. The letters, whose numerical values figure in esoteric glosses of Scripture, link creation with the supernal *sephirot*, archetypal attributes of the Infinite, whose Self-confinement (*tsimtsum*) gives definition to creation and revelation, but also explains human freedom and the possibility of evil. With the ingathering of divine sparks, confined in shells of darkness since the primal explosion of creation, God will be reunited with his exiled *Shechinah* (Immanence), and the world resolved again into unity. Such repair (*tikkun*) of the broken universe is achieved through spiritual acts of a moral and ritual character, in which man aids in God's self-reconciliation. Kabbalah has been a force in Jewish spirituality since the late twelfth century. Its classic text, the *Zohar*, or Book of Splendour, was written by Moses de León (1240–1305). Modern Ḥasidim (Jewish pietists) and the Renaissance philosopher Pico della Mirandola bear its imprint, as did the tragic pseudo-messiah Shabtai Tzvi (1627–76). Spinoza was influenced by Kabbalah through the work of Abraham Herrera, but forcefully rejected its more fanciful elements.   L.E.G.

*Neoplatonism.

Gershom Scholem, *Major Trends in Jewish Mysticism* (New York, 1971).

Kagan, Shelly (1954–). American philosopher, currently Professor at Yale University. An acute critic and leading consequentialist, Kagan's work offers sustained attacks on the view that morality includes either options or constraints. Options involve permissions to pursue personal goals and interests, even at the cost of maximizing the good; constraints involve prohibitions against performing certain actions, even if they would maximize the good. Kagan's arguments have far-reaching theoretical and practical implications, threatening two pillars of common-sense deontological morality. He challenges standard

methodological assumptions and forms of argument that underlie much of contemporary moral and political philosophy. He has also done work on the structure or geometry of desert, and published articles on the nature of value, addressing such topics as the value of a life, intrinsic value, infinite value, and finitely additive value theory.   L.S.T.

S. Kagan, *The Limits of Morality* (Oxford, 1989).
—— 'The Additive Fallacy', *Ethics* (1988).
—— 'Equality and Desert', in O. McLeod and L. Pojman (eds.), *What Do We Deserve?* (Oxford, 1998).

Kant, Immanuel (1724–1804). Perhaps the most important European philosopher of modern times, Kant was born, spent his entire life, and died in Königsberg in East Prussia. After studying at the University of Königsberg from 1740 to 1746, he worked for a time as a private tutor. In 1755 he returned to the University, received his master's degree, and began lecturing. In 1770 he was appointed professor and he continued to lecture on a wide variety of subjects, including mathematics, physics, anthropology, pedagogy, and physical geography, as well as the central fields in philosophy, until his retirement in 1796. Although he never married or travelled outside of East Prussia and led a highly regimented existence, he was no recluse. On the contrary, he was known as a brilliant lecturer and conversationalist, had a wide circle of friends, and was keenly interested in the intellectual and political issues of the day.

Kant's philosophical career is conventionally divided into three periods. The first, or 'pre-critical period', runs from 1747, the year of his first publication, 'On the True Estimate of Living Forces', to 1770, when he published his inaugural dissertation, *On the Form and Principles of the Sensible and the Intelligible Worlds*. In spite of significant shifting of views, the writings of this period are unified by Kant's abiding concerns with foundational questions in science and the search for the proper method in *metaphysics. The middle period (1771–80) is often called the 'silent decade', because Kant published virtually nothing, devoting himself instead to the reflections that led eventually to the *Critique of Pure Reason*. The third, or 'critical period', dates from the publication of the first edition of the *Critique* in 1781. This was followed by the *Prolegomena to any Future Metaphysic* (1783), the *Groundwork to the*

Metaphysic of Morals (1785), the *Metaphysical Foundations of Natural Science* (1786), a second edition of the *Critique of Pure Reason* (1787), the *Critique of Practical Reason* (1788), the *Critique of Judgement* (1790), *Religion within the Boundaries of Mere Reason* (1793), and the *Metaphysic of Morals* (1797), as well as many important essays on topics in metaphysics, science, morals, legal and political theory, and the philosophy of history. In addition, he published compilations of his lectures on anthropology, logic, and pedagogy. In his last years he devoted himself to a major revision of some of his basic views on metaphysics and the foundations of science. The work remained uncompleted at his death, but has been edited and published under the title *Opus Postumum*. Although earlier dismissed as a product of senility, it has more recently been regarded as providing an important, albeit highly obscure, indication of Kant's late move towards something like a 'post-critical' philosophy.

The central concern of Kant's greatest masterpiece, the *Critique of Pure Reason*, is with the possibility of metaphysics, understood as philosophical knowledge that transcends the bounds of experience. For Kant, such knowledge claims to be both *synthetic and *a priori. In other words, metaphysics purports to provide necessary truths, which, as such, cannot be based on empirical evidence (their apriority), but which also claim more of their referents than can be derived from an analysis of their concepts (their syntheticity). The propositions 'God exists' and 'Every event has a cause' are examples of such claims. By contrast, propositions which merely explicate what is already thought in the concept of a subject, e.g. 'God is omnipotent', are termed *analytic. Since the truth of the latter can be ascertained merely by appealing to accepted meanings and logical considerations, Kant thought that these were non-problematic. Accordingly, the fundamental philosophical task is to account for the possibility of synthetic a priori knowledge; and since Kant also believed that mathematical propositions are of this nature, accounting for their possibility likewise became an integral part of his project.

The second aspect of Kant's concern with metaphysics is with the problem of the *antinomies. As a result of reflection on the concept of a world, he became convinced that reason inevitably falls into contradiction with itself when it endeavours to 'think the whole', that is, when it ventures beyond experience in order to answer such questions as whether the universe has a beginning in time, limit in space, or first cause, or is, rather, infinite in these respects. The contradiction or antinomy arises because it is possible to construct valid proofs for each of the two conflicting positions: the universe has a beginning in time; the universe has existed for an infinite period of time; etc. He also thought that, if unresolved, this problem would lead to a hopeless *scepticism, which he termed 'the euthanasia of pure reason'. Consequently, Kant came to see the 'fate of metaphysics' as crucially dependent on a successful resolution of the antinomies as well as an account of the possibility of synthetic a priori knowledge.

Kant thought that he could deal with both problems at once by means of what is usually called his 'Copernican revolution in philosophy', since he compared his innovation to the 'first thoughts of Copernicus'. This involves reversing the usual way of viewing cognition and instead of thinking of our knowledge as conforming (or failing to conform) to a realm of pre-given objects, we think of objects as conforming to the conditions of our cognition of them. The latter include 'forms of sensibility', through which objects are given in sensory experience, and pure concepts or *categories through which they are thought. Since objects can be cognized only in so far as they are given in accordance with these forms, it follows that we can know them only as they appear, not as they may be in themselves, that is as comprehended from some God's-eye perspective. Accordingly, for Kant human knowledge is limited to *appearances or *phenomena, whereas *things-in-themselves or *noumena are thinkable but not actually knowable. Kant termed this doctrine *transcendental idealism; and juxtaposed it to transcendental realism, which identifies appearances with things-in-themselves. Thus, these two forms of *transcendentalism are effectively viewed by Kant as two all-inclusive and mutually exclusive philosophical standpoints. His central claim is that the former is capable of both accounting for the possibility of synthetic a priori knowledge and avoiding the antinomy, while the latter is not.

This whole project assumes, however, that the human mind is, in fact, endowed with such conditions, and demonstrating this is the main task of the Transcendental Aesthetic and the *Transcendental Analytic in the *Critique of Pure Reason*. In the former, Kant argued that space and time are subjective forms of human sensibility, through which the *manifold of sense is given to the mind, rather than either self-subsisting realities (*Newton) or relations between self-subsisting things (*Leibniz). He also argued that only this conception of space is capable of accounting for the possibility of geometry, which he equated with Euclidean geometry. In the latter, he first tried to establish by means of a 'transcendental deduction' that certain pure concepts or categories, including substance and causality, are universally valid with respect to possible experience, since they are necessary conditions of such experience. On the basis of these results, he then argued for a set of synthetic a priori principles regarding nature, considered as the sum total of objects of possible experience. Prominent among these are the principles that substance remains permanent throughout all change and that every alteration has a cause. The latter is usually viewed as Kant's response to *Hume's scepticism concerning causality.

The immediate consequence of Kant's limitation of knowledge is to rule out virtually all traditional metaphysics, which contains two parts: general metaphysics or *ontology, which is concerned with the universal properties of things (*Aristotle's science of being *qua* being), and special metaphysics, which encompasses the disciplines of rational psychology (the soul), rational cosmology (the world), and rational theology (God). Although the limitation of knowledge to objects of possible experience suffices to rule out both branches of metaphysics, Kant devotes a large portion of the *Critique*, the Transcendental Dialectic, to exposing the 'transcendental illusion' which supposedly underlies the latter. Since this illusion is rooted in the very nature of human reason, it cannot be eliminated; though Kant contends that it is possible to avoid being deceived by it. In fact, the therapeutic function of the *Critique* is to provide the tool (transcendental idealism) for avoiding such deception.

This is best illustrated by Kant's treatment of the antinomies. In each case, the appearance of a contradiction arises from the assumption that there must be some fact of the matter to be determined. This is the illusion, and once it is exposed, it can be seen that the sensible (spatio-temporal) world is neither finite nor infinite in the relevant respects. Similarly, the apparent conflict between the causal determinism presupposed by science and the freedom presupposed by morality, which is the topic of the third antinomy, can be resolved by restricting the former to appearances, thereby leaving room for the latter with respect to things-in-themselves. In other words, though everything in the realm of appearance, including human actions, is causally determined, it remains conceivable that human beings, considered as noumena, are free. Obviously, this does not prove that we are in fact free, but it does supposedly liberate us from the illusion that we must be either one or the other. Thus, for the either/or underlying much of traditional thought regarding the *free-will problem, it opens up the possibility of a both/and. As such, it is a form of *compatibilism; but it differs from the usual forms of compatibilism because the conception of freedom it attempts to reconcile with causal determinism is an *indeterminist one.

Kant's moral theory centres around the *categorical imperative: 'Act only on that maxim which you can at the same time will to be a universal law'. Maxims are the general rules or principles on which rational agents act, and they reflect the end that an agent has in view in choosing actions of a certain type in given circumstances. Thus, maxims are principles of the form: When in an *S*-type situation, act in an *A*-type manner in order to attain end-*E*. For example, I might make it my maxim always to pay my debts as soon as possible so as to avoid incurring unnecessary obligations. The categorical imperative tests maxims by prescribing a thought experiment in which one asks oneself whether one could consistently will one's maxim as a universal law. The idea is to determine not simply whether the imagined universal law is consistent with itself, but whether its universal adoption is consistent with the agent's own ends and, therefore, something that the agent could consistently will. A maxim which passes this test is morally permissible, whereas one which does not is forbidden. Consider the maxim of borrowing money by falsely promising to repay it. This maxim, Kant argues, conflicts with itself when universalized because it assumes a state of affairs in which promises to repay would not be

believed and, therefore, the agent's project of profiting by false promising could not succeed. Consequently, policies such as false promising succeed only in so far as they are not universally adopted, so that in choosing them one makes an exception of oneself to a rule that one wills to hold for others.

The whole issue of the categorical imperative is extremely controversial, however, and there are a large number of interpretations and objections in the literature. The basic problem is that the test seems to yield both false positives such as 'I shall smother infants who keep me awake at night by crying', which is clearly immoral but does not seem to be ruled out by the test, and false negatives such as 'I shall play tennis on Sunday mornings when courts are available since everyone else is in church', which seems both to fail the test and to be morally permissible. Although there have been many attempts to deal with these problems, it is not clear that any has been entirely satisfactory.

A second key notion in Kant's moral theory is that of *autonomy, understood as the capacity of the will to legislate to itself, that is, to choose maxims for itself independently of desires stemming from one's nature as a sensuous being. Since the categorical imperative demands that we select maxims on the basis of their conformity to universal law, which presupposes that we are able to disregard our inclinations and the thought of our own happiness in choosing a course of action, Kant claimed that morality presupposes autonomy. But since he also thought that autonomy, so conceived, itself presupposes freedom in the sense of independence from causal determination by anything in the phenomenal world, he concluded that the possibility of morality rests ultimately on the assumption of such freedom. Thus, the project of grounding or justifying morality for Kant (as opposed to merely analysing its presuppositions) turns crucially on the possibility of establishing our noumenal freedom. Although this poses a problem, since, as we have seen, Kant denies the possibility of any theoretical knowledge of this freedom, he thought that a way out was provided by the fact that its conceivability was assured by the resolution of the third antinomy. In the *Groundwork*, Kant appealed to this result and argued that we must assume the reality of freedom from a 'practical point of view', if we are to regard ourselves as rational agents capable of reasoned choice; and from this he inferred the validity of the categorical imperative or moral law as the 'law of freedom'. He appears to have changed his mind on this point, however, for in the *Critique of Practical Reason* he argues instead that the reality of the categorical imperative is immediately guaranteed as a 'fact of reason', from which the reality of freedom may be inferred.

But morality for Kant involves not only a law (the categorical imperative) and the autonomy of the will but also an object, that is, an ultimate end at which all action is directed. This object is defined as the 'Highest good' or *Summum bonum*, understood as the just apportionment of happiness to virtue. This, in turn, provides the basis for moral arguments for God and immortality as 'postulates of practical reason'. The basic idea is that, since such an apportionment is inconceivable according to the laws of nature, we are constrained to assume the reality of a noumenal ground, that is, God, as its guarantor. This is not an argument for the existence of such a being, however, but rather for the rational necessity of assuming its existence in order to make sense of the demands of morality. Although the latter requires us to strive to be 'worthy of happiness', rather than to be happy, Kant thought that such striving is impossible unless it is combined with the hope for happiness commensurate with one's worthiness of it. Interestingly enough, Kant does not argue for immortality on the grounds that we must assume an after-life in order to account for the reward of the virtuous and the punishment of the wicked, but claims instead that it is necessary in order to conceive of the possibility of the attainment of the moral perfection that is commanded by the categorical imperative yet unattainable in this life.

The Metaphysics of Morals contains the systematic presentation of Kant's practical philosophy broadly construed. It is divided into two parts: a doctrine of *right and a doctrine of *virtue, each of which is concerned with the first principles governing its domain. The universal principle of right is that 'Any action is *right* if it can coexist with everyone's freedom in accordance with a universal law, or if on its maxim the freedom of choice of each can coexist with everyone's freedom in accordance with a universal law'. This principle, which provides the foundation of Kant's political philosophy, concerns the legality of actions. It affirms that an action is right or legal (which is not to be confused with its being morally good), if and only if it does not infringe on the freedom of others to perform their rightful actions. Since anyone who hinders a person's rightful exercise of freedom does that person wrong, this gives rise to a set of negative duties (duties of justice), obedience to which may rightly be compelled. But since in a *state of nature no one is in a position to enforce their rights, there is an obligation to enter into a civil condition in which these rights are protected by a governmental power with the authority to compel obedience to the law. Thus, Kant affirms a version of the *social contract theory, albeit one which treats the latter normatively as an idea of reason rather than as a historical fact.

The second part of *The Metaphysics of Morals* is concerned with moral philosophy more narrowly construed. In it Kant endeavours to establish a set of duties (both to oneself and to others), which, since they must be thought of as self-imposed (through the autonomy of the agent's will), cannot be enforced by an external authority. These are termed 'duties of virtue' and are supposedly grounded in a pair of obligatory ends imposed on us by the categorical imperative: one's own perfection and the happiness of others. This yields both negative or perfect duties not to perform any actions that conflict with these ends, e.g. suicide, and positive or imperfect duties to work towards their furtherance, e.g. beneficence. As open-ended, the latter obligate one to adopt policies (maxims) that promote these ends rather than to specific actions.

The *Critique of Judgement*, or third *Critique*, is an extraordinarily complex work in which Kant attempts to complete his critical programme by finding an a priori principle for judgement. Traditionally, judgement was viewed, together with understanding and reason, as one of the three 'higher' cognitive faculties, and Kant consistently maintained this view. But in the first *Critique*, Kant had regarded judgement as essentially 'determinative', that is, as a capacity to subsume sensibly given particulars under the concepts and principles supplied by the understanding, and from this point of view there is no basis for attributing to judgement (unlike understanding and reason) any 'a priori' principle of its own. In the third *Critique*, however, Kant affirms a distinct function for judgement ('reflection') and argues that with respect to that function it does have a separate a priori principle: namely, the purposiveness of nature. The function of judgement in its reflective capacity is to find concepts and laws in terms of which nature can be cognized in a scientific manner. This requires concepts, such as those of *natural kinds, through which it is possible to represent real connections and distinctions in things rather than merely accidental similarities and differences. Since the first *Critique* argued only that nature necessarily conforms to the universal principles of the understanding, it left open the possibility that the true order of nature might be so complex as to be incapable of discovery by the human mind. Thus, Kant now argues that it is necessary to assume, as a distinct principle, that nature is ordered in such a way as to be intelligible, which means that we are constrained to think of it as if it were designed by a supreme intelligence with our cognitive requirements in view. To think of nature in this way is to regard it as purposive. Naturally, Kant denies that this entitles us to assume that nature really is so designed, but he insists that the necessity of thinking of it in this manner suffices to give to the principle of purposiveness a regulative function.

After discussing this general principle of purposiveness in the introduction, Kant turns in the first part of the *Critique of Judgement* to judgements regarding the beautiful and the sublime, both of which are 'aesthetic' because they are based on feeling rather than concepts of their objects. Confining ourselves to judgements of beauty, with which Kant was primarily concerned, the problem is that, although based on feeling, such judgements claim to be universally valid. In other words, when I claim that an object is beautiful, I am saying not merely that it pleases me but also that it ought to please any other observer who views it in the appropriate manner. The main task, then, is to account for the possibility of such judgements, just as the central task of the first *Critique* was to account for the possibility of synthetic a priori judgements. Not surprisingly, Kant's solution to this problem bears a certain similarity to his solution of the earlier one. The claim is that the peculiar pleasure in the beautiful consists in a feeling of the 'subjective purposiveness' of an object, that is, the accord of its form, which is apprehended in an act of aesthetic reflection, with the general requirements of judgement.

Since these requirements hold for all subjects, the liking for the beautiful may be required of everyone.

The second part of the third *Critique* is concerned with teleological judgement, particularly its role in biology. It also includes a lengthy appendix, however, in which Kant articulates his views on the relationship between teleology, theology, and morality and sketches his philosophy of history, together with his views on culture and its relation to the moral development of the human race. Thus, taken as a whole, the *Critique of Judgement* is an extremely rich and important, if frequently perplexing, work, which exhibits virtually the full range of Kant's interests as a philosopher.   H.E.A.

*Kantianism; neo-Kantianism; transcendental deduction.

H. E. Allison, *Kant's Transcendental Idealism* (New Haven, Conn., 1983).

E. Cassirer, *Kant's Life and Thought* (New Haven, Conn., 1981).

P. Guyer (ed.), *The Cambridge Companion to Kant* (Cambridge, 1992).

O. Höffe, *Immanuel Kant* (Albany, NY, 1994).

S. Körner, *Kant* (Harmondsworth, 1955).

M. Kuehn, *Kant: A Biography* (Cambridge, 2001).

R. C. S. Walker, *Kant* (London, 1978).

Kantian ethics. Ethical theories which have their origins in, or are constructively influenced by, the moral philosophy of Kant.

Kant's outstanding contribution to moral philosophy was to develop with great complexity the thesis that moral judgements are expressions of practical as distinct from theoretical reason. For Kant *practical reason, or the 'rational will', does not derive its principles of action by examples from the senses or from theoretical reason; it somehow finds its principles within its own rational nature. The ability to use practical reason to generate principles of conduct Kant calls 'the *autonomy of the will', and Kant sees it as constituting the dignity of a person. It is this conception of the autonomous will which is the main source of the several sorts of theory which might reasonably be called 'Kantian ethics'.

One sort of Kantian ethics is developed by those who are influenced by Kant's view of the nature of the principles which are generated by the autonomous will. Kant argues that willing is truly autonomous if but only if the principles which we will are capable of being made universal laws. Such principles give rise to *'categorical imperatives', or duties binding unconditionally, as distinct from hypothetical imperatives, or commands of reason binding in certain conditions, such as that we have desires for certain ends. Kant seems to hold that *universalizability is both necessary and sufficient for moral rightness. This thesis has been much criticized, and those espousing Kantian ethics, as distinct from Kant's own position, generally argue more moderately that universalizability is necessary but not sufficient for moral rightness. This is the position of R. M. Hare and the theory of *'prescriptivism' of which he has been the outstanding proponent. The

position is 'Kantian' in that it makes central one version of the universalizability thesis, but it departs from Kant in important ways, such as making room for utilitarian considerations.

Kant argues, as we have seen, that it is in virtue of their autonomous wills that persons have dignity or are 'ends in themselves'. Combining this aspect of the autonomous will with the idea of universalizability, Kant arrives at the ideal of the kingdom of ends in themselves, or of people respecting each other's universalizing wills. This has been an enormously influential idea, and its most distinguished recent exponent has been John Rawls, who accepts the core Kantian idea of mutually respecting autonomous rational wills, but adds to it ideas of his own to constitute the basis of his theory of justice.

It is a nice point in many given cases when a theory is simply influenced by Kantian ethics, as distinct from being an example of Kantian ethics. An Existentialist such as Jean-Paul Sartre would not be happy with the idea that he was offering a version of Kantian ethics, but there is no doubt that he is greatly influenced by Kant. In Sartre (as in Nietzsche before him) Kant's autonomous will, free but constrained by its essentially rational nature, becomes the totally unconstrained will creating its own values in arbitrarily free choice. This is clearly a Kantian idea in origin but developed in a way which Kant would have repudiated.

To stress that these are just a few of the many examples of Kant's influence on ethics is to acknowledge his greatness as a moral philosopher.   R.S.D.

*moral philosophy, the history of; histories of moral philosophy.

R. M. Hare, 'Universal Prescriptivism', in Peter Singer (ed.), *A Companion to Ethics* (Oxford, 1991).

I. Kant, *Groundwork of the Metaphysics of Morals*, tr. H. J. Paton as *The Moral Law* (London, 1953).

Onora O'Neill, 'Kantian Ethics' in Peter Singer (ed.), *A Companion to Ethics* (Oxford, 1991).

John Rawls, *A Theory of Justice* (Oxford, 1972).

Kantianism covers any philosophical view which derives from, or echoes, the central tenets of Kant's critical philosophy. After the publication of the *Critique of Pure Reason* in 1781 that philosophy had an impact that was both immediate and enduring, and few Western philosophers have been able to escape its influence. There is evidently a direct line of descent among German philosophers from Kant through Fichte and Hegel, past Schelling, Schopenhauer, and neo-Kantians such as Hermann Cohen and Natorp, to Husserl and Heidegger. These philosophers mostly incorporated part of Kant's teaching into their own philosophies, though they rarely endorsed everything that Kant said and were often, like Hegel and Heidegger, deeply critical of Kant's own position. Nor, of course, did they all agree in their interpretations of Kant.

Kant's influence in the Anglo-Saxon world has been more variable. In the earliest days De Quincey, in *Blackwood's Magazine*, took the view that Kant's personal life was more interesting than his philosophy—a view that would now be regarded as odd to the point of perversity. Bertrand Russell in his *History of Western Philosophy* quotes James Mill's patronizing judgement 'I see clearly enough what poor Kant would be at', and explicitly dissented from the view that Kant was the greatest of modern philosophers. The American Pragmatists acknowledged the influence that Kant had on them by linking their own term *'Pragmatism' with what Kant had said in the Transcendental Dialectic of 'pragmatic belief' (*Critique of Pure Reason*, B 852). Charles Peirce adopted a strongly Kantian account of categories, but William James rejected what he understood of Kant's *'transcendentalism', and urged that the right way to deal with Kant was to go round him rather than through him. And yet, despite this catalogue of hostility and incomprehension, Kant has constructively influenced many recent analytic philosophers from Wittgenstein to Strawson and Putnam. Nowadays few philosophers in this tradition resist a token reference to Kant, even though their views could not be regarded as Kantian. Davidson's *'anomalous monism', for example, was constructed in part with a conscious reference to Kant's treatment of the conflict between free will and causality.

Two central features of Kant's critical philosophy serve to define Kantianism. First is the fundamental reference to what Kant calls 'transcendental apperception', and especially to that aspect of it which covers personal identity and self-consciousness. Second is the reference to a transcendental method which Kant conceived as a revolutionary way of resolving the endless conflicts in the philosophical tradition from the Greeks to David Hume.

Both aspects are complex, and ramify prolifically through Kant's own writing and that of his Kantian successors. Transcendental apperception, for example, covers for Kant not only the central datum of self-consciousness, but also the a priori network of *categories through which an objective experience is made possible. In its purely personal aspect it defines various conceptions of transcendental idealism, from the extreme subjectivity of Fichte's notion of the 'ego' to Strawson's account of the concept of a 'person' as primitive. It has additionally a vital link through Kant's conception of transcendental freedom to the notions of personal agency, responsibility, and the moral law. Most of the German philosophers influenced by Kant, from Fichte to Husserl and Heidegger, recognized some notion of the self as the hinge about which the critical philosophy revolved. Many of them, like Fichte himself and Schopenhauer, regarded that notion as one with a primary moral significance. In more recent times, through a simple contrast between *Utilitarianism and Kantianism in moral philosophy, this aspect of Kant's view has been associated with a non-consequentialist conception of the intrinsic moral character of acts.

The second feature, Kant's transcendentalism, is also complex and variously interpreted. It covers the ground from a tacit appeal to supernatural, or supersensible, entities which Kant called *'noumena' or *'things-in-themselves', to a purported new form of logic, a transcendental logic, with a claimed revolutionary application to traditional philosophical issues. The former context might be further divided into a positive *acceptance* of such things in themselves, especially in relation to the transcendental self, and a negative *rejection* of any genuine knowledge of such supersensible entities. It was the negative aspect which led Schopenhauer to approve of Kant's rejection of transcendent metaphysics, and the positive aspect which led James to reject a Kantian transcendent self in favour of a modified Humean and empiricist account.

But Kant's transcendental method, and its alleged logic, are less mysterious in Kant than in some of his successors. Husserl's 'transcendental-phenomenological reduction', for example, sought to effect a transition from unreflective common sense to the recognition of a pure consciousness or transcendental ego which was not accessible to empirical observation. But it remains unclear how his phenomenological descriptions could yield a priori knowledge of such items. Peirce took seriously Kant's appeal to an architectonic structure for the critical system in his own account of categories and 'triadicity', but it has more often seemed dubious to attach so much significance to Kant's *architectonic. Moreover, although Kant's references to a transcendental logic as part of his distinctive method may seem to indicate a non-standard version of formal logic, there seems no good reason to think of it in that way.

In fact Kant's transcendental method appeals essentially to two features: first to his novel classification of 'synthetic a priori' judgement, and second to the conception of a 'condition of a possible experience'. The two features coincide naturally with the thought that any proposition which expresses a condition of any possible experience will be bound to have a special status which may be described in terms of the synthetic a priori classification. On one side the conception of a condition of a possible experience places a restriction on what can count as knowledge and licenses it only when it can be brought to bear upon some possible experience. Although such a view is not the same as the Logical Positivists' appeal to verifiability, nevertheless it shares with them and with Hume a tough-minded criterion with which to evaluate speculative philosophy. On the other side the conception offers the prospect of a new and constructive approach to experience, in which the conditions of that experience are identified as a priori and treated as the background framework which makes it possible. It is this aspect which connects so naturally with recent philosophical accounts of *language-games (Wittgenstein), or *conceptual schemes (Strawson), categorial frameworks (Körner), or conceptual relativity (Putnam). It is associated also with Collingwood's account of 'absolute presuppositions' and above all with Strawson's project of 'descriptive metaphysics'.

Wittgenstein's *Tractatus Logico-Philosophicus* is often thought to echo Kantian themes in its account of the inexpressible limits to our experience, and especially in its references to a 'metaphysical' self which marks a limit to the world and is not therefore simply a part of it (5.641). But it is in Wittgenstein's later works, such as *Philosophical Investigations* and *On Certainty*, that a more direct reference to Kantianism is to be found. For Wittgenstein's ideas of a form of life and of a language-game expressing such a form and governed by rules which make that experience possible echo Kant's notion of a condition of possible experience governed by his synthetic a priori principles. Wittgenstein did not classify his rules as synthetic a priori, but he recognized their special status by calling them 'grammatical' rules. Although the notion of a language-game captures the Kantian idea of a systematic experience governed by rules, Wittgenstein's conception, like Körner's account of a categorial framework, is not designed to cover the whole of our experience, but only some differentiable aspect of it. Strawson's account of a conceptual scheme, too, dispensed with the synthetic a priori classification, and so produced a Kantianism with more of an empiricist flavour than Kant would have accepted.

Of all these recent Kantian accounts, however, Strawson's has been the most committed and influential. It brings together the two aspects noted above of a fundamental and irreducible appeal to the notion of the self, and a transcendental method of justifying such fundamental notions. For in Strawson the appeal to conditions of possible experience has been seen as a distinctively Kantian response to traditional scepticism through the notion of a transcendental argument. In a similar way Putnam's 'internal realism' is also a conscious attempt to follow Kant's appeal to a justified objectivity in experience which does not rest on an absolutist 'God's-eye view' of an independent reality.

A doubt, for example, about the feasibility of providing an empiricist analysis of the *self in terms of a closed sequence of sense-impressions might encourage an alternative non-empiricist and Kantian account. If the self, something to which such sequences of impressions belong, is a necessary, a priori, condition of any possible experience, then this may answer, or at least evade, such a traditional scepticism. Strawson's Kantian account of the self as a primitive notion, not to be itself analysed in terms of mental or physical features, echoes such a response. And in his account of a necessary reidentification of objects as a further condition for possible experience the same technique is explicitly used to rebut a traditional scepticism about *identity. The central idea is that if reidentification is a necessary condition for any possible experience, then the sceptic's doubt will be either incoherent or else will embody a revisionary recommendation which is at best optional. The doubt will be incoherent on one side, since without a belief in identity there is no possible experience, and hence no way of making sense of the sceptic's query. It will be an optional revision, on the other side, if the sceptic uses his argument to recommend a change from the standard forms in which such reidentification is realized in our conceptual scheme.

Strawson's appeal to 'primitive' features of our experience such as the concept of a person or of reidentification

provides a modest Kantianism, but there are less modest ways of understanding Kant's own account. With regard to the self, for example, many Kantians have taken the view that for Kant such a reference is unavoidably to noumena or things-in-themselves. Such a view is encouraged by Kant's account of the resolution of the conflict between cause and *freedom in the Third Antinomy, where it is easy to read him as accepting a 'two-worlds' picture of phenomenal causality and noumenal freedom. His remarks on the distinction between empirical and intelligible characters in human agents have sometimes associated Kantianism with an indeterminist doctrine, in which human freedom and responsibility are safeguarded by being exempted from natural causation. Although Kant himself rejects the strategy of exempting humans from causal influence, it remains unclear whether his own resolution of the traditional debate in this context is indeterminist or compatibilist.   G.H.B.

*neo-Kantianism.

H. E. Allison, *Kant's Theory of Freedom* (Cambridge, 1990).
Graham Bird, 'Kant's Transcendental Arguments', in E. Schaper and W. Vossenkuhl (eds.), *Reading Kant* (Oxford, 1989).
D. Davidson, 'Mental Events', in L. Foster and J. W. Swanson (eds.), *Experience and Theory* (London, 1970).
Hilary Putnam, *Realism with a Human Face*, ed. and intro. James Conant (Cambridge, Mass., 1992).
P. F. Strawson, *Individuals* (London, 1959).

Kantianism, neo-: *see* neo-Kantianism.

Kaplan, David B. (1933–). American philosopher at the University of California, known for his work in intensional logic, semantics, pragmatics, and philosophy of language. His initial stance was Fregean as in the influential 'Quantifying In', but his later work evolved into a theory of direct *reference where, for example, expressions such as demonstratives, indexicals, and proper names are held to be unmediated by abstract senses.

In 'Opacity' he addresses problems of substitution, differences between naming and describing, quantifiers, and causal theories of reference. His views are further articulated in studies of demonstratives and *indexicals, at the centre of which is the distinction between the content of an expression and its character. Content is the referent in a given context of use. Character (corresponding roughly to linguistic 'meaning') determines a content for any given context, as in the utterance 'I am here'.

Also influential are papers on *descriptions, and on metaphysical questions raised by modal *semantics.   R.B.M.

J. Almog *et al.*, *Themes from Kaplan* (Oxford, 1989).
L. Hahn (ed.), *The Philosophy of W. V. Quine* (La Salle, Ill., 1986).
Journal of Philosophical Logic, 8 (1979).
L. Linsky (ed.), *Reference and Modality* (Oxford, 1979).
M. Loux (ed.), *The Possible and the Actual* (Cornell, 1979).

karma. Literally action, whether bodily, linguistic, or mental. In most classical Indian traditions, 'karma' can also mean the unseen potentials for future pain and pleasure which we accumulate as the result of good and bad action. Without exhausting these potentials there is no release from rebirth for the soul. Thus karma constitutes bondage in Jaina, Buddhist, and Vedic thought. The law of karma links up the moral quality of past actions with the hedonic quality of present and future life in a deterministic way. Ancient Indian medical and moral philosophers retrodict the birth, life-span, and well-being of an individual in terms of this theory. A slanderer, for example, is allegedly reborn with bad breath. Thanks to this doctrine, the Hindu theist's God is acquitted of responsibility for evil. Buddhists or Jaina atheists take it as a natural law needing no omniscient monitor.   A.C.

*Buddhist philosophy; Indian philosophy; Jainism; Vedānta; reincarnation.

Wendy D. O'Flaherty, *Karma and Rebirth in Classical Indian Traditions* (Berkeley, Calif., 1980).

Kautsky, Karl (1854–1938). The leading Marxist theoretician during the two decades before the First World War, Kautsky expressed the precarious orthodoxy of the time. He defended his view with vigour both against the revisionist tendencies of Bernstein and against the more revolutionary Marxism of Luxemburg and, later, of Lenin. As well as popularizing Marx's economic and philosophical ideas, Kautsky produced pioneering works on such diverse subjects as the agrarian question and the origins of Christianity. He was much influenced by the 'scientific' *materialism of writers such as Haecher and Darwin, and this perspective marked all his writings. Even in his politics Kautsky remained evolutionary, materialist, and essentially passive.   D.McL.

*Marxist philosophy.

Dick Geary, *Karl Kautsky* (Manchester, 1987).
Massimo Salvadori, *Karl Kautsky and the Socialist Revolution 1880–1938* (London, 1979).

Kelsen, Hans (1881–1973). Austrian public lawyer and political theorist, his 'pure theory of law' was central to mid-twentieth-century philosophy of law. Rooted in nineteenth-century German *legal positivism and, later, neo-Kantian concern with the conditions for knowing legal norms *as* norms (neither mere facts nor morally grounded), his sceptically positivist and ethically non-cognitivist work became more Humean after his emigration to America in 1940.

Every legal system's unity and validity derives, he argued, from its basic norm (*Grundnorm*): apply sanctions in accordance with the historically first (after the latest revolution) constitution and norms made thereunder. Juristic thought is possible only on the hypothesis, presupposition, or transcendental-logical postulate of the basic norm, which in late Kelsen is the content of a fictitious act of will and no longer has the role of resolving conflict between norms.   J.M.F.

Hans Kelsen, *General Theory of Norms*, tr. and intro. Michael Hartney (Oxford, 1991).

—— *Introduction to the Problems of Legal Theory*, tr. and intro. B. L. and S. L. Paulson (Oxford, 1992).

Kenny, Anthony John Patrick (1931–). British philosopher who has written on topics in the philosophy of mind, medieval philosophy, ancient philosophy, the philosophy of Wittgenstein, the philosophy of Descartes, moral philosophy, and the philosophy of religion. His output includes over thirty books, beginning with *Action, Emotion and Will*, published in 1963.

Kenny was ordained a Catholic priest in 1955 but returned to the lay state in 1963. He then held various university teaching posts. He has been Master of Balliol College, Oxford. The philosophy of religion has remained one of his major interests and he has produced several volumes in which he has examined arguments for the existence of God.

In the area of philosophy of mind, the greatest influence on him has been Wittgenstein, on whom Kenny has written two volumes, and his influence is also evident in his other writings on the philosophy of mind, on Descartes, and on Aquinas.   H.W.N.

*Frege.

A. J. P. Kenny, *The Metaphysics of Mind* (Oxford, 1992).
—— *A Brief History of Western Philosophy* (Oxford, 1998).

Keynes, John Maynard (1883–1946). Keynes is primarily remembered for his economic works *Treatise on Money* (1930) and *The General Theory of Employment, Interest and Money* (1936), which argued that governments should raise taxes and lower spending during prosperity and lower taxes and increase spending during recessionary periods, and for his practical contributions to developing the international monetary system. Many believe that Keynesian economics was crucial to avoiding the escalating cycle of boom and bust that Marx believed would inevitably contribute to the destruction of capitalism.

Philosophically, Keynes is primarily remembered for his devotion to G. E. Moore's moral philosophy, and admired for his seminal *A Treatise on Probability* (1921), which is one of the most important expressions of the a priori or logical theory of *probability: that probability consists fundamentally of an evidentiary relation between propositions.   R.C.W.

B. W. Bateman and J. B. Davis (eds.), *Keynes and Philosophy: Essays on the Origin of Keynes's Thought* (Cheltenham, 1991).
R. Weatherford, *Philosophical Foundations of Probability Theory* (London, 1982).

Khaldūn: *see* Ibn Khaldūn.

Kierkegaard, Søren Aabye (1813–55). Danish writer and social critic widely credited with setting the stage and providing the conceptual tools for modern *existentialism. Kierkegaard was also one of Hegel's most devastating critics. The formative years in Copenhagen were marked by personal dependence on an oppressively religious father and by the deaths, before he reached the age of 21, of his mother and five of the family of seven of which he was the youngest. Kierkegaard spent ten years at the university before completing his dissertation *On the Concept of Irony with Constant Reference to Socrates* (1841) preliminary to a career in the Church. His second major work *Either/Or* (1843) marked a postponement of that career and was the outcome of the fateful decision to break off an engagement and disappointment at not finding in Schelling's Berlin lectures a philosophical alternative to established *Hegelianism. The work portrays two life-views, one consciously hedonistic, the other ethical in a way which Hegelians would recognize except that the choice of the ethical is a personal one, not the outcome of a philosophical insight. The hedonistic or 'aesthetic' alternative is presented by a gifted essayist, and member of a society called 'companions of the deathbound', who applies it as a consistent principle in his own life, while the ethical perspective is conveyed in two extended admonitory letters addressed to the hedonist by a friend, a state functionary who urges him to admit that his situation is one of *despair so that he can then 'choose himself' in ethical categories, these providing the true fulfilment of the aesthetic values he prizes. Kierkegaard's own intentions are concealed behind an elaborate barrage of *noms de plume* (the work is published by a pseudonymous 'editor' who tells how he has come upon the papers quite by accident).

The impression given by the title that the aesthetic and ethical life-views represent an exhaustive choice is disturbed by a concluding sermon passed on to the hedonist by the functionary on the theme that before God we are always in the wrong. Kierkegaard claimed later that at the time he himself had despaired of finding fulfilment in marriage but said that he had portrayed marriage as a form of fulfilment because it struck him as being 'the deepest form of revelation'. Unable to reveal himself in that way, Kierkegaard embarked on a series of 'edifying' works under his own name. These works, though on the surface in a conventionally religious vein, convey deep moral-psychological insight and it would not be improper to refer to them as philosophical.

The practice of concealment was continued, however, in a parallel series of pseudonymous works which include those more usually regarded as philosophical. These include, already in 1843, two works written largely in Berlin, *Repetition* and *Fear and Trembling*, followed in 1844 by *Philosophical Fragments* and *The Concept of Anxiety*, and in 1845 by *Stages on Life's Way*, in which a religious stage is distinguished from *Either/Or*'s ethical alternative.

The pseudonymous authorship was to have ended with the publication of the *Concluding Unscientific Postscript to Philosophical Fragments* (1846), Kierkegaard having in mind to resume his intention to enter the priesthood. Instead, however, he wrote further non-pseudonymous works on specifically Christian themes motivated in part by the thought that he was better able to serve the truth as a writer. Among them are *Purity of Heart is to Will One Thing* (1847) with its account of *double-mindedness and the

formidable *Works of Love* (1847). But at the same time, virtually ostracized by a feud he had himself provoked with a satiric weekly and which left him a figure of public ridicule, Kierkegaard's plans for at least partial self-revelatory absorption into society had given way to an urge to reveal to society its errors. The popular monarchy and people's Church, newly established in the aftermath of 1848, and which Kierkegaard saw as merely finite institutions catastrophically usurping the true role of religion, provided the political target. Deciding to announce that his intentions as an author had been religious all along, Kierkegaard now planned a second (unrevised) edition of *Either/Or* together with an explanation (*The Point of View of my Work as an Author*) of the relation of that and the subsequent pseudonymous works to the Christian themes of his non-pseudonymous production. For a variety of reasons detailed in his journals the explanation was withheld (but published posthumously by his brother in 1859), and instead Kierkegaard gave out two further works under a new pseudonym.

The first of these, *The Sickness unto Death* (1849), followed hard upon the second edition of *Either/Or*. It typologizes forms of despair as failures to sustain a 'synthesis' which expresses the structure of selfhood. The work introduces a non-substantial but normative concept of the self or 'spirit'. The most common and dangerous form of despair is one which people fail to recognize in themselves and even mistake for its opposite. In a spiritless society whose institutions have taken over spirit's functions also in name, no real basis for spirit, or true selfhood, remains in the established forms of life. Spiritual possibilities then tend to find their outlets outside such forms in madness, religious intoxication, the cult of the aesthetic, or in utopian politics. This, from the individual's perspective, is one way of failing to maintain the synthesis. The other is for the individual to duck below the level of its own spiritual possibilities and lead a spiritually emasculated life of worldliness. The solution which *The Sickness unto Death* prescribes for despair is faith, or willing acceptance of the task of becoming a self 'posited' not by itself but by a transcendent power.

In the final pseudonymous work, *Training in Christianity* (1850), Kierkegaard readdresses themes raised in the earlier *Philosophical Fragments*, in particular the individual's relation to Christ as one not of history but of contemporaneity and of shared human degradation. In the five years remaining until his early death at 42, Kierkegaard lived in increasingly straitened (though never degrading) circumstances, expending the remainder of a considerable inheritance on an explosive broadsheet (*The Instant*), in which, under his own name, he savagely satirized the State Church, its dignitaries, and minions.

According to the withheld explanation the pseudonymous ('aesthetic') works deliberately adopt an aesthetic point of view in order to loosen the grip on their readers of a falsely 'aesthetic' picture of religious fulfilment. They can also be read as mirroring their true author's own struggles as a social outsider playing with the thought that his literary talents and situation might have marked him out for a specifically religious mission. In *Either/Or* human fulfilment, corresponding to the second, 'ethical' stage in the progression from the aesthetic to the religious, meant choice of a self wedded in a conventionally Hegelian way to shared social norms. The subsequent pseudonymous works, beginning with *Repetition* and *Fear and Trembling*, present the radically anti-Hegelian idea that the ethical component in the individual's life is established first in a psychologically unmasked and socially unmediated relation to God. The slim but elegantly crafted *Philosophical Fragments* contrasts an idealist view, identified with Plato's Socrates but clearly to be construed as a progenitor of Hegel, with one where the relationship to truth depends on faith. The massive *Postscript* is described by Kierkegaard as a turning-point in the 'aesthetic' works, since it clearly identifies the latter view with Christianity and raises explicitly the question of what it means to be a Christian. The Christian's proper relation to the 'absolute object of worship' is *inwardness, or a 'passionate' interest in a transcendentally grounded fulfilment, the more passionate because the individual is aware that no empirical or rational inquiry can support acceptance of an assurance based exclusively on the belief that some other existing individual has been the eternal in time (the God-man). This is literally unthinkable and therefore immune to argument or evidence one way or the other. The principal target is Hegel's 'System', which, by treating matters requiring personal choice as topics for a shared rational insight, turns living issues into matters for a generalized curiosity. In fact there are two opposed objections to a scientific approach to the question of personal fulfilment. In Hegelian science the matter is decided already by the truth of being which will emerge as the system of thought develops, but that abstracts from your own existence which 'keeps thought and being apart' and therefore fails to capture the forward movement of the individual's own life. And treating the issue as a scientific matter in a general sense to be decided collaboratively in the light of evidence not all of which is (or ever will be) in, ignores the urgency of the Christian message which stands there, as William James would say, as a 'forced' option that brooks no delay.

Some see in Kierkegaard's philosophical pseudonym (Johannes Climacus) an assassin hired to deal with the Hegelians, so that the absurdity and paradox of Christianity arise only for the misguided 'systematizer'. Wittgensteinians have interpreted the *Postscript* as a demonstration of what happens if you apply the rules of one language-game inappropriately to another, but this inner relativism fits ill with Kierkegaard's emphasis on the 'crucifixion' of reason in faith. In his journals Kierkegaard says that paradox and absurdity are the negative conditions of faith—guarantees, as it were, that the assurance sought in faith is not being treated as though it were achievable through the exercise of some human capacity. That capacity need not be cognitive; the distinction between *Religiousness A and Religiousness B is between, on the one hand, a view which interprets what the pseudonymous author calls 'dying

from immediacy' procedurally, as if a relationship with the object of worship can be established simply by subordinating all 'relative' ends to an 'absolute' end, and on the other hand a non-immanentist view and the 'Christian' view in which human capacities as such extend no further than to history so that a historical event, the Incarnation, offers our only relation to the Absolute. From this point of view the Absolute lies beyond the reach of any kind of natural relationship.

What then is the positive content of faith? The pseudonymous works do not say; their 'dialectic' is, as some have said, merely 'negative'. But the final pseudonymous work, *Training in Christianity*, can be read together with parts of the non-pseudonymous 'religious' corpus as indicating that the saving truth can be grasped in a moral agent's sense, in imitating the example of Christ, of acting out this truth in the form of Christian love. The earlier *Works of Love* presents the Christian ideal of love of one's neighbour in the form of a generalized selflessness. Part of what emerges is that it is only by removing personal preferences that values inherent in other persons, but also in nature, can be truly acknowledged and allowed their fulfilment. This assumes that the value or worth of persons and things is neither, as Hobbes has it, their price nor any degree of natural attachment to them. Values, on this view, reside in possibilities inherent in the persons and things themselves independently of human interests, and indeed these interests stand in the way of those values both in the sense that they do not become visible and in the sense that they fail to be elicited. The inner consistency of the view as a generally applicable ethics depends at least in part on how far the sacrifice of human desires or interests is compatible with the sacrificer's own personal or human fulfilment.

Kierkegaard detects in social forms, and in patterns of human behaviour in general, a pervasive disinclination to face live issues in their appropriately living form. In this respect Hegelianism is not simply a failed attempt to capture the forward movement of life, but part of a general contempt for the individual, evident also in the conflation of the truism that human life is impossible without political groupings with the pernicious idea that the individual's fulfilment can come to expression only in the form of political association or religious community (see *Literary Review: The Two Ages* (1846)). Kierkegaard's writings are profitably grasped in the light of his sense of a prevailing flight from *subjectivity and of society's need to divest itself of protective self-images. The more scandalous views attributed to Kierkegaard, such as the arbitrary defeasibility of shared norms, the subjectivity of truth, and the supposed foundational role assigned to criterionless choice, often vanish on a closer reading of the texts, which in context lend themselves to more readily acceptable readings. Thus the notorious teleological suspension of the ethical in *Fear and Trembling* can be seen as part of Kierkegaard's nowadays uncontroversial insistence that systems of shared social norms are purely historical phenomena set against his championing of the view that a true system of values derives directly from an unconditioned transcendent source, unmediated by contingent and merely finite facts of preference. His target is the common assumption in his time that facts of preference are both historical and expressions of an unfolding Absolute. The claims in the *Postscript* for the subjectivity of truth can be read as the requirement that the relation to the unconditional source of value be one of inwardness and personal devotion both to the source itself and, through it, though distributively rather than collectively, to mankind. As for the rumour of a criterionless choice, in Kierkegaard there is little or no evidence for this idea as distinct from that of the notion of personal commitment and choice. At least the reader of *Either/Or*, the most widely cited source for the rumour, cannot fail to detect signs of dialogue in that work, objections to the ethical life-view implicit in the first part which are then made explicit and countered in the second part, which is also in itself a sustained argument in favour of the ethical alternative. Failure to choose the ethical alternative is presented as more in the nature of a motivated rejection of a form of human fulfilment that the hedonist is already in a position to acknowledge but refuses so to do, than a choice made in a vacuum between two quite independent and equally valid ways of life.

The tendency to ascribe extreme views to Kierkegaard may be due in part to the fanatical anti-humanism of his later rejection of all bourgeois forms of human association, including marriage and the family. Kierkegaard himself remarks on how the original either/or becomes radicalized so that in the end both ethics and institutional religion (castigated as the fraud of 'Christendom') end up on the aesthetic side as merely forms of self-indulgence, while self-abnegation, suffering, and devotion to God now form the saving option. This could be seen as a pattern set from the start; Lukács suggests it is the outcome of Kierkegaard's life-long tendency to spite reality. Or perhaps the extremity was one that Kierkegaard was driven to by circumstances. The radical stance might also, however, at a pinch be interpreted as prescribed by the *Postscript*'s insistence that Religiousness A is a necessary prolegomenon to Religiousness B. The later Kierkegaard may be insisting that the institutions of a spiritless society must be comprehensively vacated before creative alternatives based on true selfhood can replace them. We note that Kierkegaard describes *The Sickness unto Death* as containing a polemic directed at that 'altogether un-Christian conception', Christendom. Regarding the establishment's scorn of sects, he said there was 'infinitely more Christian truth' in the errors of their ways than in 'the mawkishness, torpor, and sloth of the establishment'. The trick is to be rid of the errors of the pagans without losing, as in a spiritless society which shuns true selfhood, their 'primitive' spiritual impetus.

For obvious reasons rationalists and, because of his attitude to shared norms, Hegelians have dismissed Kierkegaard as an *irrationalist*; while what in Kierkegaard's writings repels rationalists and Hegelians alike has drawn sympathy from circles later stigmatized as fascist. Equally, democrats are put off by Kierkegaard's contempt for public opinion, the crowd, and parliamentary institutions, and although Marcuse saw 'traits of a deep-rooted social theory' in Kierkegaard, the Christian framework and the focus on the individual make Kierkegaard an obvious target for the Marxist. Eagerly read in German academic circles at the beginning of the twentieth century, and heralded by theologians as the provider of a radical Christian apologetic, Kierkegaard also influenced agnostic and atheist thinkers of such divergent political sympathies as Heidegger and Lukács. The enormous extent of the former's debt to Kierkegaard is still to be appreciated. The latter in his pre-Marxist days admired what he saw as the tragic heroism with which Kierkegaard, by exalting the notion of choice, vainly defied the necessities of life by seeking, first in his own life, to impose on them a poetic form. The later Lukács blamed Kierkegaard for the 'bourgeois' philosophy of post-war existentialism and even saw in him a source of modern nihilism and decadence. As if in confirmation of this latter charge some post-modern writers, notably Jean Baudrillard, focus on Kierkegaard the 'aesthetic' author and see in this complex man a pre-incarnation of the modern existentialist. Adorno, sympathizing with Kierkegaard's campaign against the tyranny of the universal over the particular though not with the resort to religious concepts, found in Kierkegaard's experimental 'aesthetic' writings the makings of a new style of reasoning which elicits rather than buries the truth of the particular. Many modern philosophers have found in the religious framework of Kierkegaard's writings an impediment to any serious appreciation of his thought. Wittgenstein, however, once referred to Kierkegaard as 'by far the most profound thinker of the last century'.   A.H.

S. N. Dunning, *Kierkegaard's Dialectic of Inwardness: A Structural Analysis of the Theory of Stages* (Princeton, NJ, 1985).

John W. Elrod, *Being and Existence in Kierkegaard's Pseudonymous Works* (Princeton, NJ, 1975).

A. Hannay, *Kierkegaard* (London, 1982; rev. edn. 1991).

Søren Kierkegaard, *Søren Kierkegaards Papirer*, ed. P. A. Heiberg, V. Kuhr, and N. Thulstrup, 16 vols. (Copenhagen, 1909–78).

—— *Søren Kierkegaards Samlede Værker*, ed. A. B. Drachmann, J. L. Heiberg, and H. O. Lange, 20 vols. (Copenhagen, 1961–4).

—— *Kierkegaard's Writings*, ed. H. V. and E. H. Hong *et al.*, 26 vols. (Princeton, NJ, 1978–).

—— *Fear and Trembling*, Eng. tr. (Harmondsworth, 1985).

—— *The Sickness unto Death*, Eng. tr. (Harmondsworth, 1989).

—— *Either/Or*, Eng. tr., abridged (Harmondsworth, 1992).

B. Kirmmse, *Kierkegaard in Golden Age Denmark* (Bloomington, Ind., 1990).

G. Pattison, *Kierkegaard: The Aesthetic and the Religious* (London, 1991).

M. C. Taylor, *Kierkegaard's Pseudonymous Authorship: A Study of Time and the Self* (Princeton, NJ, 1975).

killing. Presumably no society could survive unless it had some restrictions on its members killing each other. But the prohibitions that societies have on killing vary greatly. In Greek and Roman times to be a human—that is, a member of the species *Homo sapiens*—was not sufficient to guarantee that one's life would be protected. Slaves or other 'barbarians' could be killed, under conditions that varied from time to time; and deformed infants were exposed to the elements on a hilltop. The coming of Christianity brought a new insistence on the wrongness of killing all born of human parents, in part because all humans were seen as having an immortal soul, and in part because to kill a human being is to usurp God's right to decide when we shall live and when we shall die. Nonhuman animals, on the other hand, remained unprotected because they were believed to have been placed by God under man's dominion. This doctrine of the sanctity of all (and only) human life remains the orthodox view on the morality of killing.

Some contemporary philosophers, among them Jonathan Glover, James Rachels, and Peter Singer, have challenged this orthodoxy, arguing that membership of a given species—for example, *Homo sapiens*—cannot in itself determine the value of a being's life, or the wrongness of killing that being. Rather, this wrongness must depend on some morally relevant characteristics that the being has. Sentience, or the capacity to feel pleasure or pain, seems to be a minimal characteristic, and so the killing of plants is not wrong in itself. In addition to sentience, however, Glover gives an important place to the being's capacity for *autonomy, for making his or her own decisions (including a decision about whether or not to continue living). Killing an autonomous being against that being's will is the most drastic possible violation of autonomy, and this makes it more seriously wrong than the killing of a sentient being not capable of autonomy.

Rachels focuses on whether the being can live a *biographical*, rather than a merely *biological*, life, which is similar to the emphasis given by Singer to the ability to see oneself as having a past and a future. To kill such a being, unless at the being's request, thwarts the preferences for the future that the being may have, and this makes the killing wrong in a way that is additional to any wrong that may be incurred by the killing of a sentient being unable to form any preferences for the future.

The effect of these arguments is to distinguish a class of beings whom it is especially wrong to kill. The term 'person' is often used to distinguish this class from the class of human beings as a whole, for not all human beings are autonomous, or capable of seeing themselves as having a past and a future. Infants, and the profoundly intellectually disabled, for example, are not. Chimpanzees, on the other hand, appear to be persons in this sense. Hence it is an implication of this view that, other things being equal, it is worse to kill a normal chimpanzee than a profoundly intellectually disabled human being. Of course, to arrive at a final judgement about the wrongness of killing any being, we need to consider also the effect of the killing on relatives and friends, and on the community as a whole.

The *slippery slope argument is often used as an objection to any change in our attitude to killing human beings. We should, however, be equally aware of the possible undesirable effects of, for example, allowing severely disabled infants to die slowly from dehydration or infection because we believe it wrong to kill them.   P.S.

*euthanasia.

Jonathan Glover, *Causing Death and Saving Lives* (Harmondsworth, 1977).
J. McMahan, *The Ethics of Killing* (Oxford, 2002).
James Rachels, *The End of Life* (Oxford, 1986).
Peter Singer, *Practical Ethics*, 2nd edn. (Cambridge, 1993), chs. 4–6.

Kim, Jaegwon (1934–). Author of numerous well-known papers on metaphysics and epistemology, best known for his pioneering work on *events, *supervenience concepts, and psychophysical relations. Kim takes events to be exemplifications of properties (or relations) by an object (or set of objects) at a time. On this view, Oedipus' marrying Jocasta and Oedipus' marrying his mother would be the same event, while Brutus' killing Caesar and Brutus' stabbing Caesar would be different events. Kim has argued for a form of materialism in which mental properties are 'locally reducible' to physical properties by way of species-specific correlating laws. Nonreductive materialism, he argues, collapses either into a position in which mental properties do no causal work (a form of eliminativism) or into one in which mental properties do not depend in any significant way on physical properties (a form of dualism).   N.L.

*mind, problems of the philosophy of.

J. Kim, *Supervenience and Mind: Selected Philosophical Essays* (Cambridge, 1993).
—— *Mind in a Physical World* (Cambridge, Mass., 1998).

kind, natural. It is easier to say what a natural kind *term* is than to say what natural kinds themselves are, ontologically speaking. Natural kind terms constitute a class of general terms and include both mass terms, like 'gold' and 'water', and certain *sortal terms, like 'tiger' and 'apple'. Loosely, they may be said to denote types of naturally occurring stuffs and things. Kripke has argued that natural kind terms are *rigid designators.   E.J.L.

S. P. Schwartz (ed.), *Naming, Necessity, and Natural Kinds* (Ithaca, NY, 1977).

Kindī, Yaaqūb ibn Isḥāq al- (d. after 870). Widely known as the first Arab philosopher, he was instrumental in the spread of Greek philosophy in the state-endowed Academy in Baghdad. He commissioned translations of Greek philosophical texts that served as inspiration for his own Arabic works, which identify the formative, syncretic period of Islamic philosophy. He is the first Islamic philosopher to offer systematic explanations for some of the debated theological issues of his time, such as creation, immortality, God's knowledge, and prophecy. His *On First Philosophy* was the first Arabic work on syncretic metaphysics. Though some of the issues he defined, such as creation *ex nihilo*, were later rejected, many, such as immortality of the individual soul, and the distinction between human and revealed knowledge, helped define lasting problems of Islamic philosophy.   H.Z.

Al-Kindī's Metaphysics, tr. Alfred L. Ivry (Albany, NY, 1974).

kinēsis. Aristotle's distinction between *kinēsis* (motion, change), and *energeia* (activity, actualization) prefigures various contemporary distinctions in the philosophy of agency. Theologically the notion occurs in 'first mover' proofs of God's existence: things changed in a basic quality can only be changed by something which, at the time of change, has that quality. In such a series, argued Aquinas, *infinite regress is impossible; hence there must be a first mover.   J.J.M.

   *prime mover.

T. Penner, 'Verbs and the Identity of Actions: A Philosophical Exercise in the Interpretation of Aristotle', in O. P. Wood and G. Pitcher (eds.), *Ryle: A Collection of Critical Essays* (London, 1970).

Philip Kitcher (1947–). Contemporary philosopher of science, defender of *naturalism* in philosophy, British-born but US-based. Kitcher focused initially on philosophy of biology and mathematics, but is now expansive in his interests. *Vaulting Ambition* (1985) was a harsh critique of sociobiology. But Kitcher has also resisted various arguments alleging conceptual problems with mainstream evolutionary theory. In the 1980s he defended the view that explanation in science is a matter of *unification*. This view, developed partly in reaction to causal theories of explanation, exemplifies his metaphysical outlook—generally realist but attracted to Kantian options in the area of causation. Kitcher presented a total philosophy of science in his weighty *Advancement of Science* (1993). Here and elsewhere, he has engaged in detail with claims that science has been shown to be essentially non-rational when fundamental theoretical choices are made. He defends a moderate conception of scientific progress and rationality, and includes innovative mathematical modelling of science's social organization. Kitcher's recent work has extended into ethics and the political role of science. *The Lives to Come* (1996) was commissioned by the Library of Congress as a philosophical exploration of the human genome project.   P.G.-S.

P. Kitcher, *The Advancement of Science* (Oxford, 1993).
—— *Science, Truth, and Democracy* (Oxford, 2001).
—— *In Mendel's Mirror: Philosophical Reflections on Biology* (Oxford, 2003).

klepsydra. The klepsydra was typically a metal vessel with an aperture at its narrow neck and little holes which could be plugged at its wide end. It is sometimes thought that the ancient Greek philosopher Empedocles used it to prove the reality and substantiality of air, by pointing out that, when inverted in water with the little holes plugged, water was prevented from rising in it, but, with the holes unplugged, water rose unhindered by the air which it expelled. As air was in fact one of the four Greek elements, there was taken to be no need for any proof of its distinct

reality. What Empedocles sought to prove by his remarks was the independent reality of *space, which had just been denied by the Eleatics. The air was expelled, but not its space, which was left behind for water to occupy. The Greeks needed the reality of space to prove the possibility of *motion.   W.E.A.

John Burnet, *Early Greek Philosophy* (London, 1892).

Kneale, William Calvert (1906–90). British philosopher and historian of logic, Fellow of Exeter College, Oxford (1932–60), and White's Professor of Moral Philosophy at Oxford (1960–6). Kneale published in many areas including metaphysics, philosophical logic, philosophy of mind, and moral philosophy. In *Probability and Induction* (1949), he surveys classical theories of induction, argues that probability theory cannot justify induction, and offers his own justification. Here and elsewhere he argues for the importance of natural necessity in understanding law, causation, and subjunctive conditionals. *The Development of Logic*, written with his wife, Martha, is both a history of logic and an introduction to logic and topics connected to it. This thick book devotes about half of its 761 pages to the nineteenth and twentieth centuries, with extended attention to Frege.   D.H.S.

   *necessity, nomic.

William Kneale and Martha Hurst Kneale, *The Development of Logic* (Oxford, 1962).

knowledge. The principal intellectual attainment studied by *epistemology. Virtually all theorists agree that true belief is a necessary condition for knowledge, and it was once thought that justification, when added to true belief, yields a necessary and sufficient condition for knowledge. Its sufficiency, however, was disproved by Gettier as follows. Suppose one justifiably believes *q* although it is false; then one reasonably infers *p*, which is true. The result is a justified true belief in *p*, yet one cannot be said to know that *p*. Can the problem be solved by requiring that no intermediate conclusions like *q* be false? No; other counter-examples remain. Sam believes, through visual appearance, that a lighted candle is before him. There is indeed a candle there but Sam sees only a hologram of a candle, not the real candle, which is blocked from view. Then Sam lacks knowledge, although he has justified true belief that rests on no false intermediate conclusions.

   Other theories of knowledge put less weight on justification. According to the causal theory, knowledge consists in true belief that bears an appropriate causal connection to the fact in question. This handles the candle case because its presence is causally unconnected to Sam's belief. Reliability theories say that someone knows only if his true belief is acquired by a reliable process or method. This may be understood to entail the *counterfactual requirement: *S* would not believe *p* if *p* were false.

   Causal, reliability, and counterfactual theories are generally called 'externalist', because they make it possible to satisfy the conditions for knowledge (e.g. causal-connection conditions) without being aware that one satisfies them. 'Internalist' theories emphasize conditions of which subjects are aware. The demarcation between these types of theory is problematic, however, because paradigmatic internalist theories, such as coherentism, may also make knowledge attainable through subjectively inaccessible conditions. Whether a belief coheres with the rest of one's beliefs, for example, might not be readily accessible to the subject.

Epistemologists often look to theories of knowledge to settle the problem of *scepticism, but how easily this problem can be settled is questionable. One theory says that a person knows p only if he 'discriminates' it from relevant alternatives. This ostensibly favours anti-scepticism because not all logically possible alternatives seem relevant. Suppose Jane sees a barn in the field. Although she cannot discriminate it from a papier-mâché facsimile, such a facsimile is not a relevant alternative (unless facsimiles abound in the neighbourhood). Scepticism might gain a foothold here, however, by claiming that every logically possible alternative is relevant. Who is right in this dispute, and is there a determinate answer?

This raises methodological issues about the theory of knowledge. Is it a theory of some evaluator-independent 'stuff', on the model of the chemical theory of water? Or is it a theory of human concepts and their deployment? On the former approach, there should always be a fact about whether someone knows, but why should our ordinary judgements be reliable guides to such facts? On the latter approach, knowledge may be a very fuzzy concept that has determinate applications only when certain parameters are set, and these parameters can legitimately be set either to the sceptic's or to the anti-sceptic's taste.   A.I.G.

*justification, epistemic; reliabilism; foundationalism; knowledge, limits of; sociology of knowledge; tacit knowledge; virtues, intellectual.

A. Goldman, *Liaisons: Philosophy Meets the Cognitive and Social Sciences* (Cambridge, Mass., 1992).
K. Lehrer, *Theory of Knowledge* (Boulder, Colo., 1990).
R. Nozick, *Philosophical Explanations* (Cambridge, Mass., 1981).
T. Williamson, *Knowledge and its Limits* (Oxford, 2000).

knowledge, the limits of. The issue of the extent and limits of human *knowledge is a perplexing one. There is no way of establishing a proportion between what we know and what we do not. We clearly cannot estimate the amount of knowledge yet to be discovered (both because there is no real measure of what is known and because we have no reliable information regarding new knowledge yet to come). We realize that our knowledge contains errors of omission and commission but do not know just where they lie.

Is human knowledge completable? The incompletability of scientific progress is compatible with the view that every question that can be asked at any particular state of the art is going to be answered—or dissolved—at some future state: it does *not* commit one to the idea that there

are any unanswerable questions placed altogether beyond the limits of possible resolution. No recourse to insolubilia need be made to maintain the incompletability of our scientific knowledge. How could we possibly establish that a question Q will continue to be both *raisable and unanswerable* in every future state of science, seeing that we cannot now circumscribe the changes that science might undergo in the future? If a question belongs to science at all—if it reflects the sort of issue that science might possibly resolve in principle and in theory—then we shall never be in a position to put it beyond the reach of possible future states of science as such.   N.R.

*justification, epistemic.

E. McMullin, 'Limits of Scientific Inquiry', in J. C. Steinhardt (ed.), *Science and the Modern World* (New York, 1966).
N. Rescher, *The Limits of Science* (Berkeley, Calif., 1984).

knowledge, theories of: *see* epistemology, history of; epistemology, problems of.

knowledge and science. Science systematically corrects the errors of *common sense. Thus, from science we learned that, contrary to first appearances, the sun does not go round the earth each day. But what happens when science seems to undermine not particular beliefs, but whole tracts of experience? Can science really tell us that, say, the world is not in itself coloured or that the famous solid, unmoving table of Eddington's physicist is mostly empty space thinly populated with rapidly moving particles? Too radical a correction of common sense by science runs the danger of depriving scientific theories of the ultimately commonsensical evidential basis on which they depend. It would be safer to regard the theories of science as a whole as offering highly generalized and effective abstractions from the richness of what there is, rather than as the only or the whole truth.   A.O'H.

*science, history of the philosophy of; science, problems of the philosophy of.

G. F. Macdonald (ed.), *Perception and Identity* (London, 1979), esp. the essays by M. Dummett and P. F. Strawson and the replies of A. J. Ayer.

knowledge by presence. Distinguished from acquired *knowledge, this technical term is used in Islamic philosophy to designate a non-predicative mode of cognition required prior to the definition and construction of fundamental philosophical principles. Similar in sense to Plato's 'intellectual vision', and in form to Aristotle's 'quick wit' (*ankhinoia*), it was first fully formulated by Sohravardī. This type of knowledge posits priority to the self-conscious subject's immediate grasp of the real, manifest essence of objects. Tantamount to primary intuition, similar to Kant's 'immediate relation to objects', but not reduced to Russell's 'knowledge by *acquaintance', it was given objective validity by later mystics and theologians, who emphasized its mystical and experiential implications, and made rhetorical use of it to 'prove' the primacy and validity of prophetic, inspirational, as well as esoteric and fantastic knowledge.   H.Z.

Mehdi Ha'iri Yazdi, *The Principles of Epistemology in Islamic Philosophy: Knowledge by Presence* (Albany, NY, 1992).

Komenský (Comenius), Jan Amos (1592–1670). Czech philosopher and pedagogue. Bishop and theologian of the Unitas Fratrum (Moravian Brethren), exiled in the period of Counter-Reformation. He found refuge in various parts of Europe, including London, where he wrote the mystically coloured *Via Lucis* (1641). His principal philosophical treatise *De Rerum Humanarum Emendatione Consultatio Catholica* is based on the traditional Neoplatonic scheme of emanations specifically modified and enriched by the humanistic idea of restoration of humans to the divine universal harmony by the way of universal reform (*panorthosia*) and universal education (*pampaedia*). So conceived, his philosophy aimed at a grandiose reform of pedagogy in the spirit of modern didactic realism. In place of scholastic verbalism it turned to demonstrative teaching, conceiving school as play (*schola ludus*) and as a workshop of humanity (*officina humanitatis*). The same principles gave birth to his philosophy of non-violence, peace, and ecumenicity. 'Omnia sponte fluant, absit violentia rebus' became his device.   M.P.
                                                                 V.S.

J. Patočka, *Jan Amos Komenský: Gesammelte Schriften zur Comeniusforschung* (Bochum, 1981).

Korean philosophy. The reigning theme of Korean philosophy is irenic fusionism, as evidenced by the way of the flow of wind (*poong-ryu-do*) that is the substratum of Korean philosophy. The flow of wind is invisible and yet all-pervasive. This is also man's vibrating, unceasing way of communing with nature and fellow beings, thus evincing an 'undifferentiated aesthetic continuum' (to adopt F. S. C. Northrop's phrase) or Nothingness (*mu*).

Poong-ryu-do is the way of overcoming alienation, countenancing solidarity with fellow beings, and helping to achieve harmony of polarities. When *Confucianism, Buddhism, *Taoism, and other 'foreign' strands of thought were introduced to Korea, it was *poong-ryu-do* that helped to bring about their fusion and synthesis. I will illustrate the theme with two notable examples.

Attuned to *poong-ryu-do* was the Buddhist monk Wonhyo (617–86). If Buddhism originated in India and was nurtured in China in Mahāyāna form, it was segmented into various sects when it reached Korea. Wonhyo succeeded in integrating the contentions of these sects by Harmonizing of Contentions (*hwajaeng*): just as all rivers are bound for the sea, so are various sects bound to return to the Buddha mind. For Wonhyo, to attain Nirvana was to attain one heart–mind–body (*ilshimdongchae*) with humanity.

Paradoxically, for Wonhyo, to be exclusively Buddhist was not to be Buddhist. He propounded an all-encompassing cosmic universalism by absorbing elements not only of Buddhism but also of Confucianism and Taoism. Wonhyo was the embodiment of the fusion of the three teachings (*shilnaepohamsamkyo*) and the way of mysterious wondrousness (*hyunmyochido*). He endeavoured to overcome the dichotomies of being and non-being, the true and the false, and the sacred and the secular. For Wonhyo, Nothingness (*mu*) meant integration, fusion, and harmony, and getting away from dogma. His *mu* was the prototype of the Zen Buddhist notion of Absolute Negation and Nothingness.

The theme of harmony, fusion, and synthesis is again manifest in Korean *neo-Confucianism. In dealing with the metaphysical (*i*) and the physical (*ki*), the Chinese philosopher Chu Hsi (1130–1200) was dualistic and said that the Four Beginnings (commiseration, shame, deference, and discernment) of the Four Virtues (humanity, righteousness, propriety, and wisdom) emanate from *i* and the Seven Emotions (joy, anger, sadness, fear, love, hatred, and desire) from *ki*. The Korean philosopher Hwadam (Suh Kyungduk, 1489–1546) moved to integrate *i* and *ki* and spoke of Great Harmony (*taehwa*).

In the Four–Seven Debate with Ki Daesung, Toegye (Yi Hwang, 1501–70), while being still dualistic, broke away from Chu Hsi by espousing the reciprocal emanation (*hobal*) of *i* and *ki*: with the Four, *ki* follows *i* when *i* becomes emanant; with the Seven, when *ki* becomes emanant, *i* 'rides' *ki*. Though he was critical of Toegye's idea that *ki* follows *i* as being dualistic, Yulgok (Yi I, 1536–84) nevertheless embraced his notion that *i* 'rides' *ki*: only *ki* is emanant and *i* moves its emanation; *i* and *ki* are 'neither two things nor one thing', as evidenced by 'wondrous fusion' (*myohap*). For Yulgok, original nature (*i*) and physical nature (*ki*) coalesce into one human nature. Toegye and Yulgok, whose thoughts culminated in an irenic fusionism, constituted the crowning phase of East Asian neo-Confucianism by exhibiting dialectical dexterity in articulating the concepts of *i* and *ki*, left unclarified by the Chinese.

Toegye also developed the neo-Confucianist concept of single-mindedness (*kyung*), which was a manifestation of his unequivocal humanism, as shown by his total rejection of the Mandate of Heaven (*chunmyung*), which still had a hold on the Chinese, including Chu Hsi. Toegye's *kyung* synthesized the primeval Korean sense of supreme-efforts-*cum*-earnest-devotion (*chisung*) with the Confucianist notion of holding fast to mind (*jik-yung*); he advocated self-efforts for creating a meaningful life. In particular, his concept of single-mindedness had a lasting influence on the Japanese neo-Confucianists of the Tokugawa period.

Every major Korean neo-Confucianist shared Toegye's preoccupation with single-mindedness, which signalled new stress on praxis in the development of Korean neo-Confucianism: the fusion of the metaphysical and the physical is better brought about through action than speculation, important as theory might be. That was the point of Yulgok's integration of sincerity (*sung*) with single-mindedness. In this respect Korean neo-Confucianism made a break with the Cheng-Chu school of Chinese neo-Confucianism, which was overly speculative.

It is small wonder that Yulgok's thought flowered into Practical Learning (*shilhak*) in eighteenth- and nineteenth-century Korea. Practical Learning, keener on social issues than idle speculation, once more evinced the way of the flow of wind in striving to achieve the synthesis of theory and praxis. Practical Learning also helped to create an intellectual ambience open and receptive to Western Learning (*suhak*).

K.-S.L.

*Buddhist philosophy.

W. T. de Bary and J. K. Haboush (eds.), *The Rise of New-Confucianism in Korea* (New York, 1985).
International Cultural Foundation (ed.), *Korean Thought* (Seoul, 1982).

Korn, Alejandro (1860–1936). Latin American philosopher born in San Vicente, Argentina. Korn's reading of Kant and Schopenhauer led him to move away from *positivism, the predominant philosophy of Latin America in the late nineteenth century. Like the positivists, however, he maintained that knowledge must be based on experience. But philosophy must not be reduced to a science of empirical facts; it is fundamentally concerned with values. In *La libertad creadora* (1920–2), he proposed a creative concept of *freedom according to which the goal of human actions is to overcome the laws of necessity that govern the objective world. Creative impulse, as manifested in self-control and the technological conquest of nature, enable the subject to accomplish this. In *Axiología* (1930), his most important work, Korn defends a subjectivist position, where value is understood as relative to human evaluation.

E.M.
J.G.

Solomon Lipp, *Three Argentine Thinkers* (New York, 1969).

Korsgaard, Christine (1952–). American philosopher, Professor at Harvard. Korsgaard is one of the leading interpreters of *Kant's moral philosophy and exponents of contemporary Kantian ethics. In her book *The Sources of Normativity* she argues, first, that our reflective nature forces us to look for reasons for our actions, and second, that we find these reasons in our own autonomous nature. The theory is realist, but does not involve metaphysical commitments. Korsgaard argues that in order to act at all we must have a conception of our own practical identity, and that compatibility with this conception is what determines whether a consideration counts a reason. Though Korsgaard admits that we can have many overlapping identities (as a mother, as a philosopher, as a friend), she argues that there is one identity that we must all have—identity simply as a human being among other human beings, and this is the identity that gives rise to traditional Kantian moral reasons.

E.J.M.

*constructivism.

C. Korsgaard, *The Sources of Normativity* (Cambridge, 1996).
—— *Creating the Kingdom of Ends* (Cambridge, 1996).

Kotarbiński, Tadeusz (1886–1981). Polish philosopher and logician, author of a radically nominalist epistemology.

Studied in Darmstadt and Lvov, taught classical languages in high schools, was professor at the Universities of Warsaw, Lodz, and then Warsaw again. He was President of the Polish Academy of Science from 1957 to 1962.

He published a widely used textbook, *Elements of the Theory of Knowledge, Formal Logic and Methodology of Science* (1929, in Polish), a number of works on ethics that are independent of religious and political premises and of the laws of nature (*Meditations on Worthy Life* (1966), in Polish), various historical studies, and studies on praxiology or the general theory of efficient work (*Treatise on Efficient Work* (1955), in Polish). His own metaphysical standpoint he described as reism, a kind of *materialism without matter; it implies that the proper use of the verb 'to exist' is reserved to individual things and that all meaningful propositions (including those related to mathematical objects, literary works, cognitive acts, etc.) can, in principle, be translated into reistic language; without being thus translatable they are meaningless. Both before and after the Second World War Kotarbiński was regarded in Poland as a moral authority, engaged in fighting for tolerance against clericalism and anti-Semitism.

L.K.

H. Skolimowski, *Polish Analytical Philosophy* (London, 1967).

Kraus, Karl (1874–1936). Viennese playwright, poet, and satirist, best known as publisher of *Die Fackel* (The Torch), a fiercely independent journal of social, political, and cultural criticism that created a sensation when it first appeared in 1899. *Die Fackel* was admired by many, including Wittgenstein. An uncompromising opponent of anything he judged to be humbug, Kraus considered *language an important source of truth in its own right, and vigorously attacked any individual or institution, most particularly the Press, that he regarded as corrupting language and thus contributing to the hypocrisy and moral decline of the age. Kraus's scathing satirical attacks on the political and cultural institutions which he took to be responsible for the First World War culminated in an epic drama, *The Last Days of Mankind*, composed largely of quotations he allowed, characteristically, to speak for themselves.

J.HEIL

E. Timms, *Karl Kraus: Apocalyptic Satirist* (New Haven, Conn., 1986).

Kreisel, Georg (1923–). Austrian and cosmopolitan logician. As a mathematician he has chiefly studied proof and computation. Though not the founder of a school, he has had a wide influence in philosophy of mathematics through his many commentaries. Recurring themes in his writings are that 'the data of foundations consist of the mathematical experience of the working mathematician'; that foundational slogans (particularly formalist ones) can usually be proved wrong by careful attention to straightforward facts; that classical and constructivist mathematics each use the appropriate methods to describe different parts of the same world (respectively, mathematical objects and mathematical evidence); that the proof of a theorem may give extra information which is important for understanding the role of the theorem; and that in mathematics one should cultivate a sense of when to be surprised.   W.A.H.

*constructivism; formalism.

Georg Kreisel, 'Mathematical Logic: What has it Done for the Philosophy of Mathematics?', in R. Schoenman (ed.), *Bertrand Russell: Philosopher of the Century* (London, 1967).

Kripke, Saul (1940–). American logician and philosopher of language noted for his work in *modal logic but also for his interpretation of Wittgenstein's views on meaning. Exploiting the terminology of *possible worlds, Kripke argues against descriptivist theories of proper *names, holding instead that proper names are *rigid designators, that is, expressions which (unlike most definite descriptions) retain the same reference in every world in which they refer to anything at all. He repudiates Frege's theory that proper names possess senses determining which objects they refer to, arguing instead that names are initially assigned their references by procedures such as ostension and are then passed on from speaker to speaker in a causal chain, each speaker receiving the name with an intention to use it to refer to the same object as that to which the speaker from which he received it referred.

Kripke appeals to the rigidity of names to defend the metaphysical theses of the necessity of identity and of origin, the latter implying that a composite object could not have been originally composed of parts very different in identity or kind from those from which it was in fact made. His defence of these theses leads him to reject the traditional association between *necessity and the *a priori and to hold that some necessary truths can be a posteriori and some contingent ones a priori. For instance, that water is H_2O is a true identity statement whose truth was discovered only empirically and yet one which is, if Kripke is right, necessary. As a putative example of a contingent a priori truth he cites the statement that the standard metre bar is one metre in length. Kripke's stance on such issues has far-reaching metaphysical implications, as is demonstrated by his appeal to the necessity of identity to challenge the coherence of mind–brain *identity theories.   E.J.L.

C. Hughes, *Kripke: Names, Necessity, and Identity* (Oxford, 2004).
S. Kripke, *Naming and Necessity* (Oxford, 1980).
—— *Wittgenstein on Rules and Private Language* (Oxford, 1982).

Kristeva, Julia (1941–). French theorist, linguist, literary critic, and philosopher, currently a psychoanalyst. Born in Bulgaria but based in Paris since the mid-1960s, she brought Marxist theory and Russian formalism together with *structuralism and *psychoanalysis to produce an eclectic interdisciplinary approach to questions concerning subjectivity. This approach has distinguished all her subsequent work. Initially working with Derrida and others in the intellectual group Tel Quel, her theoretical exploration of literary texts, creativity, and language acquisition has broadened to include relevant political,

sexual, philosophical, and linguistic issues. Some of her work has been in *feminist philosophy, some in aesthetics, cultural studies, and psychoanalysis.   A.C.A.

Toril Moi (ed.), *The Kristeva Reader* (Oxford, 1986).

Kropotkin, Peter (1842–1921). After Bakunin's death in 1876, Kropotkin was the most influential theorist of *anarchism for several decades. Early in his life he rejected his aristocratic background and stubbornly maintained his confidence in the supreme goodness of human nature and attributed any evidence to the contrary to the insidious influence of state authority and exploitative capitalism. For Kropotkin, any external authority was corrupt by definition and thus he never attempted to describe the organizational principles of an anarchist movement or society, believing that it was up to the oppressed masses to arrange the system under which they lived. In his attempt to imbue the whole of society with ethical principles, Kropotkin did produce many practical plans for the improvement of agricultural and industrial communities. And his biting criticisms of the terrible power of the state to disrupt and destroy what he considered natural communities remain impressive.   D.McL.

C. Cahm, *Kropotkin and the Rise of Revolutionary Anarchism 1872–1886* (Cambridge, 1989).
M. Miller, *Kropotkin* (Chicago, 1976).

Kuhn, Thomas (1922–96). In *The Structure of Scientific Revolutions*, the most influential book in modern *philosophy of science, Kuhn argues that scientists work within and against the background of an unquestioned theory or set of beliefs, something he characterizes as a 'paradigm'. Sometimes, however, a paradigm seems to come unstuck, and it is necessary that a new one be provided. What makes Kuhn's position stimulating and controversial is the central claim that there can be no strictly logical reason for the change of a paradigm. As in political revolutions, partisans argue in a circular fashion from within their own camps. Expectedly, this claim was anathema to old-fashioned rationalists like Karl Popper, for whom science is the apotheosis of sound and logical defensible thought. Paradoxically, however, Kuhn and Popper are both evolutionary epistemologists, seeing essential analogies between their (very different) views of scientific change and the evolution of organisms.   M.R.

*evolutionary epistemology; reductionism; revolutions, scientific.

G. Gutting, *Paradigms and Revolutions* (Notre Dame, Ind., 1980).
T. Kuhn, *The Structure of Scientific Revolutions* (Chicago, 1962).

Kūkai (774–835). Posthumous name, Kōbō Daishi. Founder of the Shingon school of esoteric *Buddhism, Kūkai was Japan's first philosophical thinker. He was an accomplished poet and expert calligrapher, an ascetic saint, nature mystic, and influential cultural leader, as well as a prolific writer on religion, philosophy, literature,

THOMAS KUHN'S 1962 monograph on *The Structure of Scientific Revolutions* swiftly established itself as the most important work of the century in the philosophy of science. The influence of its new vision of how theories come and go was felt throughout the academic world.

RICHARD RORTY, who himself once worked in the mainstream of analytic philosophy, became its scourge, and the contemporary philosopher most admired in other disciplines, where his ironic turn seemed a fitting response to doubts about truth and progress.

BERNARD WILLIAMS, impatient with the restricted scope and imagination of academic philosophers, led them to broader conceptions of ethics and the self, and sought to bring philosophy into closer engagement with real life and with the history of Western intellectual culture. Meanwhile his work on government committees helped Britons to address some problems of the self, specifically in connection with sex, drugs, and gambling.

DAVID K. LEWIS granted existence to a plethora of possible worlds in order to answer a wide range of philosophical questions. His systematic worldview was as hard to refute as it was to believe in.

history, art, architecture, linguistics, and education. Kūkai argued that every human being is in principle capable of 'attaining enlightenment in this very existence', on the grounds of a sophisticated synthesis of ideas from the four major schools of Mahāyāna Buddhism that had been transmitted to Japan. He held that through practice of the 'three mysteries' of meditation, mantra (*shingon*, 'true word'), and *mudra* (hand gesture), one can proceed through the 'ten stages' to the ultimate realization of one's identity with Mahāvairocana (Japanese, Dainichi Nyorai), primary embodiment of the cosmic Buddha.   G.R.P.

Kūkai: Major Works, tr. with an account of his life and a study of his thought by Yoshito S. Hakeda (New York, 1972).

L

Lacan, Jacques (1901–81). French psychoanalyst whose riddling style and heterodox (though, as he would have it, scrupulously faithful) reading of Freud have generated numerous controversies and splits within the analytic movement over the past thirty years. Lacan's chief claim—drawing on the linguistics of Saussure and Jakobson—is that the unconscious is literally 'structured like a language', so that Freud's somewhat vague terminology of (e.g.) psychic 'condensation' and 'displacement' can be rendered more precise by translation into the equivalent rhetorical terms, 'metaphor' and 'metonymy'. In which case reason is no longer master in its own house but subject to all the lures and slippages of a language caught up in the toils of desire, or the endless 'defiles of the signifier'. Thus for Descartes's formula *Cogito, ergo sum* Lacan substitutes his own rendition: *'cogito, ergo sum' ubi cogito, ibi non sum*, or 'Where I think "I think, therefore I am", that is where I am not'.   C.N.

J. Lacan, *Écrits*, tr. A. Sheridan (London, 1977).

Lakatos, Imre (1922–74). Born in Hungary. His doctoral study in Cambridge produced *Proofs and Refutations*, a multilogue embodying a fallibilist epistemology for mathematics in which mathematical proofs—and what they prove—are negotiated. After appointment at the London School of Economics, debates with Popper, Feyerabend, and Kuhn helped to forge his Methodology of Scientific Research Programmes (MSRP). According to Lakatos, Popper's naïve falsificationism fails on two counts: the logical Duhem problem, and the mismatch between falsificationist prescription and the history of science. As the chief criterion of scientific success and the neutral judge among competing methodological principles, Lakatos substituted, in the place of truth or truth-likeness, a historically characterized notion of progress.   N.C.
T.CHI.
R.F.H.

*fallibilism; methodology.

I. Lakatos, *Proofs and Refutations* (Cambridge, 1976).
—— *Collected Papers*, i and ii, ed. J. Worrall and G. Currie (Cambridge, 1978).

Lamarck, Jean-Baptiste, chevalier de (1744–1829). French biologist and evolutionary theorist, now principally remembered for his belief that the organs and habits of animals can be altered or newly produced in lawlike ways by pressure from the environment, and that organs and habits thus acquired by individuals are then transmitted to their offspring by hereditary means. The contrary Darwinian belief, that characteristics acquired by environmental pressure cannot be genetically transmitted, is now generally accepted by biologists. Nevertheless, well before Darwin Lamarck had taken the step of seeing the evolution of species as being governed by lawlike processes, even if—again unlike Darwin—he saw the law of *evolution as having a natural drive towards perfection. Nevertheless, human *culture, opposed to biological development, can be seen in broadly Lamarckian terms, as involving the transmission through tradition and education of what has been learned in the experience of earlier generations.   A.O'H.

*determinism; perfectionism.

H. G. Cannon, *Lamarck and Modern Genetics* (New York, 1960).

La Mettrie, Julien Offray de (1709–51). French physician and materialist philosopher, reviled in his own time for his professed *atheism, *determinism, and *hedonism, but an important figure in the history of *materialism. He followed the mechanical approach to medicine of his teacher Boerhaave, and developed a purely naturalistic, empiricist approach to living organisms, including human beings. He regarded his position as an extension of the worthwhile mechanistic aspect of Descartes's philosophy, while abandoning Cartesian *dualism and *rationalism. He first suggested the physiological character of mental processes in *Histoire naturelle de l'âme* (1745) and developed the doctrine in an even more resolutely mechanistic-materialist framework in his most famous work, *L'Homme machine* (Machine Man (1747)). However, he saw matter as essentially active and sensitive, rather than inert. Once neglected, La Mettrie can now be seen as a pioneer of scientific psychology.   A.BEL.

Julien Offray de La Mettrie, *Machine Man and Other Writings* (Cambridge, 1996).
Kathleen Wellman, *La Mettrie: Medicine, Philosophy, and Enlightenment* (Durham, NC, 1992).

language. What do we share when we share a language? Just as we count species by asking whether two candidates for the same species can interbreed, so we count languages by asking whether bringing speakers of them together breeds communication. By such a measure the world contains at least 4,500 natural languages, or languages naturally learned and spoken. Africa contains between 700 and 3,000; New Guinea languages alone number around 1,100, divided into some sixty families (it is the task of anthropological linguistics to bring a theoretical taxonomy into the superficial chaos). The imprecision of counting reflects phonetic, grammatical, and semantic lapses from perfect identity.

It is not surprising that our ability to speak together breaks down when we think of exotic and alien ways of living, perhaps involving different categories and different understanding of what is salient and what is unimportant. But if your experience and your reactions to the world, and your system of beliefs, is different from mine, as it will be, to what extent does superficial sameness of language mask difference of meaning? Exposure to a different generation or gender can be enough to make me ask if you can read my words as I intend them. But is not the way I intend them itself a function of something I already share with you, namely an identical linguistic inheritance? It is not as though my intentions are fixed points for me, independently of the linguistic expression I find it natural to give them. We ought not to think of sharing a language as a kind of accidental coincidence of idiolects (privately owned and defined languages). But how many factors must we take into account before declaring that we know what someone else means—and, for that matter, is it any easier to know what we ourselves mean, or meant a little while ago?

Recoiling from linguistic solipsism we may hope for uniformities: a God's-eye point of view from which all languages are means to one end. It would be nice if one's home tongue—twenty-first-century English, say—contained the resources to say everything that can be said in any language; indeed, some philosophers have argued that if we cannot interpret or translate a candidate back into our own tongue, then we can dismiss its claims to be a language at all. This is best diagnosed as a quaint misuse of the *verification principle (for there is after all the rather less colonial alternative of going out and learning the new language, rather than learning to translate it back into one's home terms).

The conceptual difficulties in thinking about language become vivid when we consider marginal and unusual candidates. Are the signalling systems of animals properly regarded as languages? If a chimpanzee can associate sounds with things, and put sounds together in simple ways, is this acquiring the essence of linguistic behaviour? Is a computer language a kind of language? Does it make sense to posit a *'language of thought' or background language, like the machine code of a computer, whereby human beings process their first natural language? And is there a language of music, or art, or clothes? These questions are not so much troublesome in themselves, since we might just posit a criterion that marginal cases do or do not meet. The problem is that we cannot discern a principle. We are not sure what status any definition or criterion of linguistic behaviour could deserve. And quite apart from difficult cases other problems make themselves felt. Is it an essential aspect of language that it is used to communicate? If so, how do we explain soliloquy and solitary verbal play, and can we rule out a priori the possibility of a Robinson Crusoe from birth, who yet manages to symbolize things to himself? But if not, what other explanation can there be for such a specialized adaptation as linguistic competence?   S.W.B.

*discourse; meaning.

G. Lakoff, *Women, Fire and Dangerous Things: What Categories Reveal about the Mind* (Chicago, 1987).
W. V. Quine, *Word and Object* (Cambridge, Mass., 1960).

language, artificial: *see* artificial language.

language, formal: *see* formal language.

language, history of the philosophy of. The history of philosophical thinking about *language is not easily separated from the history of logic, nor indeed from the entire history of philosophy. There is no division between thought about the major philosophical categories—knowledge, truth, meaning, reason—and thought about the language used to express those categories. Furthermore, many problems can be phrased either metaphysically (Are species real or conventional? Is the number five an object?) or as problems in the philosophy of language (Are words for species controlled by distinctions in nature or by conventions? Does the numeral 'five' function like a name?). There is therefore no major philosopher or school that has not had some doctrine about the relationship between mind and language, and language and the world. In surveying such a history it is possible to concentrate upon the detailed grain and textures separating the problems of one period from those of another, but only at the cost of staying blind to the permanence of the great problems, and the ways in which modern doctrines and approaches are anticipated indefinitely earlier. In this brief survey I concentrate on the continuities rather than the differences.

It is possible that Parmenides attached to his metaphysical *monism the doctrine that nothing false can be said or thought, on the grounds that sentences serve as names of states of affairs; names with no bearers are meaningless; but a false sentence fails to name anything; hence no false sentence has meaning. If the argument raises more astonishment than conviction, it also suggests the problems that prove permanently difficult: What is the relationship between a sentence and the state of affairs that it reports or that would make it true? How is a sentence for which there is no such state of affairs different from a name without a bearer? Are these always meaningless? The *Sophists, who began the process of grammatical categorization, were centrally concerned with 'the correctness of words', or the relationship that words need to bear to things to become instruments of knowledge. They were also concerned with understanding: thus Gorgias is presented as having raised the sceptical trouble that when I give you a word that is *all* that I do: there is no transfer of one and the same idea from my mind to yours and, even if there were, there is a gap between my idea and the features and qualities of things it may seem to represent. Versions of this problem reappear in the twentieth century in concerns of the later work of Wittgenstein, in the problems with translation emphasized by W. V. Quine, and in the general scepticism about determinate *meaning characteristic of *post-modernism.

Plato's dialogue *Cratylus* (*c*.390 BC) is the first general discussion of the role of convention in language. Socrates sees clearly that even if it is arbitrary or conventional whether we use one word or another for horses (one society may call them 'hippos' and another 'equus' with equal propriety) there is something else that it would be possible to be right or wrong about. It is not arbitrary or conventional that this particular animal is a horse, or that it is correct to call it a horse, nor is it conventional that there exists a similarity or form that horses share but cows, for example, do not. The distinction here may be between a word, whose association with anything is a matter of human usage and convention, and a concept or kind, whose application to things is not conventional but a matter of truth or falsity. Plato embodies this in the concept of an 'ideal name', which in more modern terms may be thought of as a correctly framed concept, conforming to the nature of things in the way that classifying substances as liquid or solid does, whereas classifying a substance as phlogiston, or classifying a complex phenomenon as brotherly love or freedom may not. Plato is dealing here with the fact that only an 'adequate' or correctly formed and stocked language can be a vehicle for framing and communicating knowledge. The demand is for a *correspondence* whereby thought reflects the nature of its objects. The ideal this represents surfaces throughout the subsequent history of philosophy, for example in the goal of finding an ideal language, found in Leibniz, Russell, and *Logical Positivism. In Indian philosophy the Mīmāṃsā school celebrates the sacred correctness of Sanskrit, as opposed to the Buddhist emphasis on the conventional and possibly misleading role of language in knowledge. Especially in the *Sophist* Plato also gave extended discussions of the possibility of intelligible talk about the non-existent, and showed some recognition of the difference between stating something and naming something, the crucial distinction overlooked (or perhaps mishandled) in the Parmenidean argument against falsity.

Among the many problems bequeathed by Plato was that of *universals (forms), or unchanging abstractions which make up the proper objects of human knowledge: partly the forms are an answer to the problem that, according to Aristotle, reduced the Sophist Cratylus to wagging his finger, which was that capturing the ever-changing flux in words seemed like attempting to map a cloud. Aristotle saw (as, in some passages, Plato did) that the Forms are at best a stopgap, for it must be a mistake to try to explain what different things have in common by postulating a further *thing* to which they bear some relation. His naturalistic response to Plato's other world of unchanging Forms was to locate the universal in things, or in other words to identify it with the shared common properties lying in particulars. However, the suggestion opens the road to a more thoroughgoing nominalism, according to which everything that exists is particular: the problem is to reconcile this sensible, hard-headed view with the need for general terms if thought is to take place at all. Aristotle's vast contribution to logic and grammar should not conceal another fundamental idea that he brought to the philosophy of language. This is that words work by being symptoms or signs of mental states of the user (he also thought that written words are similarly only symbols of spoken words: the earliest example of the 'phonocentric' tradition railed against in *deconstructionism). Aristotle distinguished names from predicates, and he saw that only a complex sentence was capable of truth and falsity. However, his account of the way in which a sequence of terms comes to be true or false remains unclear, partly because the basis of the difference between names and predicates remains insecure. In the syllogistic logic that descends from Aristotle through medieval philosophy the terms are common nouns (man, horse) that are thought of as *referring* to men or horses, but the idea breaks down when we ask which men or horses are referred to in phrases such as 'some men', or 'no horses', or in sentences such as 'Henry is not a horse'.

It was left to the *Stoics to distinguish clearly the necessary concept of a *lekton* or proposition, as well as that of the sentence (the Stoics also recognized different kinds of *lekta*, corresponding to questions, commands, promises, and so on, so they may be said to have anticipated the theory of *illocutionary force). However, propositions or *lekta* enjoy an uneasy relationship with other things. They are distinguished from the sequences of words, or sentences, that express them, but also from the sensations or images that loom up in conscious life, and from the states of affairs whose existence makes them true and whose non-existence makes them false. Their shadowy nature made them easy targets for both *Epicureans and ancient *Sceptics. Sextus Empiricus, for example, uses the standard modern anti-Platonist argument that abstract entities are not capable of having causal consequences; in which case they can neither 'indicate nor make evident' things, for to do this entails having effects on the person apprehending them; hence they are theoretically useless and should play no part in a naturalistic science of the mind. The argument applies to both Platonic and Aristotelian universals. There are only words and things, or even perhaps only words and sensations. The main problem such sensationalism faces is that in such a world nothing seems to *represent* anything else: meaning is demystified only by being removed altogether. Although both Epicureans and Stoics made moves to fend off the catastrophe, the dilemma that the philosophy of language either makes use of mysterious, abstract, universal objects of thought or descends to the natural and the empirical but loses meaning altogether continues to dominate contemporary approaches to language.

Platonism about universals has an other-worldly flavour congenial to Christian thinkers such as St Augustine, but medieval thought tended either to Aristotelianism (centrally in St Thomas Aquinas) or to the nominalism of fourteenth-century thinkers influenced by William of Ockham. In particular Aquinas's moderate suggestion that a thing might be singular or universal according to different ways of taking it is mercilessly attacked by Ockham: anything whatsoever is one, single thing. But the medieval emphasis on the links between grammar and logic on the one hand and logic and reason on the other make nominalism particularly hard to stomach: utterances considered as physical particulars are not the subject of reason or logic. However, the medieval period saw the first major work in logic since Aristotle, with close attention paid to such problems as those of intensionality and the semantic paradoxes.

The seventeenth-century turn away from scholastic logic saw a surprising unanimity, stretching from Francis Bacon, Thomas Hobbes, and above all John Locke in Britain to Arnauld and the Port Royal Logic in France, that Aristotle was right in supposing that words were the *signs of ideas, and ideas the signs of things. Equally characteristic of the period was the belief that while language was a dangerous medium, apt to distort and obscure ideas as much as to transmit them, it could be refined or reinvented in a form free from these dangers. Partly this was the result of recognizing that the developing sciences needed to find languages and notations adequate to their different tasks. This concern is later echoed in the nineteenth-century recognition of the intimate connection between an apparently notational advance (e.g. finding arabic numerals or Leibniz's notation for the calculus) and a major conceptual advance (learning the importance of the number zero, being able to differentiate). Book III of Locke's *Essay Concerning Human Understanding* is the most thoroughgoing late seventeenth-century attack on the problem. Words become substitutes for ideas, and in order to avoid the danger of being taken in by empty sounds without meaning, we must form the habit of substituting ideas, the real substance of thought, for words whenever possible. Locke's immense influence halted serious philosophy of language, arguably until Kant, although a small rearguard action was fought by Berkeley. For while Berkeley often subscribes to the conventional view that words without ideas give us only 'the husk of science rather than the thing' he does acknowledge 'that there may be another use of words, besides that of marking and suggesting distinct ideas, to wit, the influencing our conduct and actions; which may be done either by forming rules for us to act by, or by raising certain

passions, dispositions, and emotions in our minds' (*Alciphron*, bk. VII). Berkeley had here the ingredients for the later 'use'-based or pragmatist account of meaning, but can scarcely be said to have freed himself from the Lockean or Aristotelian model. A similar struggle to retain the meaning of words whilst realizing that there are no ideas associated with them can be seen in Hume's explorations of causation, identity, and the self. Berkeley's other quarrel with Locke is his rejection of any abstraction in favour of particular ideas standing for other particular things. Here he is later echoed by Bentham, who considered all abstractions as fictions, with meaningful talk confined to reference to concrete situations (too concrete, however, and we end up back with Cratylus, reduced to silence).

It was left to Kant to make the substantial break with the empiricist equation between understanding and the passive possession of mental phantasms. Kant not only repudiated the Lockean theory of ideas, but reintroduced the needed concentration on the nature of judgement, with its own forms and categories, presuppositions, and claims to objectivity. He also provided the terms within which much later philosophy of language became framed: *analytic versus synthetic, *a priori versus a posteriori, *rules versus descriptions. But above all it is Kant's sovereign concern with the question how judgement of such-and-such a sort is possible that marks a reconnection to pre-seventeenth-century priorities, and a heralding of later ones.

Nevertheless, the Kantian judgement might still serve as Aristotle's intermediary, represented by words and itself representing things. Indeed, the other elements in Kant that led to the triumph of German *idealism also provided an historical matrix within which Kantian judgements functioned, rather like the Empiricists' ideas, as fairly self-standing elements of consciousness compared with which everything else was problematic. Nineteenth-century idealism severs any connection between language and the world, at least if the world is conceived of as distinct from thought. Language and thought became entirely self-contained in a kind of solipsistic unity (as they arguably do in the deconstructionist view that nothing lies outside the text, since any attempt to correlate a text with anything else merely produces more text). On such views the main apparent casualty is truth, which stops being a correspondence between language and the world, but becomes either the unity and completeness of the whole structure of judgements (the *coherence theory of truth), or the use words have in directing effective action (the *pragmatic theory of truth).

It was Frege who reconnected language with truth without an intermediary psychology. Frege's revolution in logic is not the issue here (*logic; *quantifier; *variable) but the associated belief that nothing 'psychologistic' gives us anything essential to meaning, which resides rather in the way a term or more fundamentally a sentence is employed in the world: the way it presents things as being. The connection that electrifies sentences is not one between them and ideas or even judgements, but one between them and their 'truth-conditions'. The task of a systematic theory of meaning of a language (a semantic theory) is that of categorizing the expressions it contains, and describing in a systematic fashion the way in which the truth-conditions of sentences are built from the contributions of their components. Frege's description of this goal, and his brilliant application of the ideas to the language of mathematics, was the dominating impulse behind modern analytical philosophy, and the concern with the syntax and semantics of the languages of science that characterized Logical Positivism. However, on the topic of the human user of the language Frege is less forthcoming. He puts in place the idea of sentences as having objective senses, expressing thoughts that are grasped by those using them. But the story is entirely schematic, reminiscent of the Stoic doctrine of *lekta*, and Frege tells us nothing of the nature of this grasp, nor how to answer the old objections to the use of such abstract entities in the theory of language.

It is usually said that twentieth-century philosophy of language began with the eclipse of Hegelian idealism, and the triumph of *realism. This is a half-truth that ignores the large place that both idealism and *pragmatism played throughout the period. Pragmatism in particular promises to circumvent the old opposition between the idealist stasis of ideas-staying-in-the-head and the unargued realist correspondence between elements of language and elements of the world. The ingredient it adds is that of words answering a purpose, or playing a role in a practice or technique (ideas present in Berkeley, as was seen above, and reintroduced in the later work of Wittgenstein). James saw the correspondence between true judgement and reality not in terms of an abstract correspondence but as a dynamic control: true judgements are those that work, truths are what we must take account of if we are to survive. One might see some of James's concern with practice as foreshadowed too by Nietzsche's understanding of the political dimension of language use: by naming and categorizing we do not do something practically neutral, but privilege social attitudes and structures. Dictating thought is also dictating action. In turn there is a connection back to Kant's emphasis on the primacy of practical judgement, and the political turn that this idea is given in Hegel and Marx.

In the twentieth century the political and other practical dimensions of meaning were frequently regarded as a slightly disreputable secondary element, outside the pure theory of representation. For, going entirely the other way, Russell and Wittgenstein looked for an abstract correspondence between language and the world, and developed the application of Frege's logic to problems of language in terms of a structural resemblance between a sentence and that of which it is a picture (the *truth-condition). Their work culminated in Wittgenstein's *Tractatus Logico-Philosophicus*, in which the curiously disembodied atomic constituents of language stand in relations that mirror the structure of the facts that make up the world. Wittgenstein's rejection of any association between

psychology and the philosophy of language went beyond anything to which the more traditional Russell could subscribe. Russell's own version of *logical atomism located the atoms to which basic terms corresponded in an uneasy space between the objective world and the subjective representation of it. Atomism was, however, always a fragile flower, and amongst the hostile winds blowing over it was the work on language done by Ferdinand de Saussure, showing that the phonemes out of which spoken language is made could not be considered as individual, physically definable pulses, but exist only in a system of 'differences'; the same point applied to semantics quickly suggests that no sentence maintains its own private relationship with reality, but that the system as a whole must take priority (as, indeed, the idealists had always maintained). Nevertheless, and in spite of the short-lived adherence of its author, the *Tractatus* in turn gave birth to the fundamental positivist belief that the logic or syntax of language dictates the solution to all other epistemological or metaphysical concerns with it. Either a philosophical problem was solved by essentially Fregean semantics, or it was shown to be a pseudo-problem. Problems in the philosophy of language thus collapse into internal problems about the syntax and semantics of language, thought of as a pre-existent structure. But the foundations of this optimism crumbled on three ancient rocks. Firstly, it went along with no coherent story connecting language with experience. Secondly, it had no description of the status of logic and reason itself: the Fregean advance within logic had not produced a parallel advance in the question of the status of logic. And thirdly, it could produce no theory of the proper domain of the use of reason and experience together, certifying even the simplest movements of scientific thought. The need to reintroduce the excluded issues of experience, understanding, and the place of language use in the context of a set of practical questions was constantly urged against the Frege–Russell tradition by writers such as R. G. Collingwood. Although the possibility of external theory of this kind has been doubted, the authority given to the criticism by the later Wittgenstein means that contemporary works in the philosophy of language may bear as much resemblance to the idealist H. H. Joachim's *The Nature of Truth* (1906) or to the pragmatist William James's *The Meaning of Truth* (1909) as they do to the founding works of analytical philosophy.   s.w.b.

There is no single specialist work on the history of the philosophy of language. But as well as general histories of philosophy, readers may wish to consult:

A. J. P. Kenny, *Medieval Philosophy* (Oxford, 2000), ch. 3.

W. and M. Kneale, *The Development of Logic* (Oxford, 1960).

W. Künne, *Conceptions of Truth* (Oxford, 2003).

B. Mates, *Stoic Logic* (Berkeley, Calif., 1953).

language, knowledge of. Competent use of a language depends on knowing a language, and the nature of this knowledge has been the subject of dispute amongst philosophers. Some conceive knowledge of language as a practical skill, a matter of know-how, like riding a bicycle or swimming. However, competent speakers are in receipt of a vast range of complex knowledge. They can understand indefinitely many sentences they have never heard before: sentences that conform to complex grammatical rules that speakers are unable to articulate. To account for these facts, Noam Chomsky proposes that speakers tacitly know the rules of grammar for their language. Furthermore, he argues that each child's acquisition of language depends on a body of innate knowledge that equips it to develop a language. On this view, each child has a dedicated language faculty configured in accordance with universal grammar, and the grammar of each language is a refinement of it. Knowledge of word meaning is less plausibly a matter of innate endowment, but it can be conceived as knowledge of rules for the correct use of words. Explaining our immediate and effortless knowledge of what our words mean and our ability to follow rules for their use remains a philosophical challenge.   B.C.S.

B. C. Smith, 'Understanding Language', *Proceedings of the Aristotelian Society* (1992).

language, logically perfect: *see* logically perfect language.

language, meta-: *see* metalanguage.

language, object: *see* object language.

language, private: *see* private language problem.

language, problems of the philosophy of. The philosophy of language explores the relationships between ourselves and our *language, and our language and the world. The first kind of exploration asks what it is for us to invest words and sentences with a certain meaning, whilst the second investigates the relationships between words and the things to which they refer, or the facts that they describe. The former topic is sometimes called *pragmatics, and the latter *semantics, although the lines between them can easily blur.

It is given by the nature of a language that some things may be inferred from others. If a shape is square then it is four-sided, and if a person is a bachelor then he is unmarried. It is evident that these relationships are intimately connected to the very meaning of the words involved (either being determined by that meaning, or perhaps themselves playing an important role in fixing it). Logic studies the nature of these inferences, and a common element in the philosophy of language at least since Aristotle has been the desire to codify and lay bare the structure, perhaps hidden on the surface, whereby one thing may be inferred from another. This develops into the formal programme of defining firstly the syntax of a language (the ways in which grammatical strings of elements are generated and separated from ungrammatical ones) and then the logical structures responsible for the inferences which we can and cannot make. One major philosophical problem such inquiries raise is the relationship between the

smooth surface recognition of grammar and of logical relationships, and the extremely complex rules that appear necessary to enable any system to compute the same results. Are we to think of some such system of rules as really implemented at some level of our cognitive systems? Or are they ways of describing what we do that make no claim on how we do it?

To investigate language we might start with a list of platitudes about it. Language consists of *words*, which come in sequences or *sentences*. With our words we express our *ideas*, and we *intend* to *communicate*. Because of our *conventions* the words of a language *refer* to things, or have *meanings. Other languages may, however, have attached the same meanings to their terms, with the result that they can be *translated*. Some words are *synonymous* or mean the same; some are *vague*. Some ('red') seem somehow keyed closely to *experience*, others ('quark') are highly *theoretical*. A whole sentence often expresses a *proposition*, which may be *true* or false (although we also do other things with language, such as issue commands, ask questions, and make promises). The truth or falsity of a sentence will depend on whether the world satisfies some condition, known as the *truth-condition* of the sentence. The philosophy of language is largely a matter of trying to understand these italicized terms, and the revolutions in the subject occur when what seems a satisfactory basis for such understanding to one school or generation seems a very bad place to start to another. To illustrate the scope for dispute it can be recorded that all the terms that have seemed useful starting-points to some (words, language, ideas, convention, meaning, translation, reference, experience, intention, proposition, truth) have not only been denied foundational status by others, but even been violently excommunicated as spurious and unscientific notions.

From the beginnings of philosophy it has been realized that problems of meaning and language are intertwined with those of other areas of inquiry. Our languages are things we understand, so a theory of language must match with a philosophical psychology, or story about the powers of the mind. Furthermore, a theory of what the world is like must conform to the demand that it is describable by language: if, therefore, a linguistically describable world must have some form or another we can infer the structure of the world, at least in so far as we can describe it, from the structure of our representations of the world. The earliest example of this form of reasoning is the argument for the Forms in Plato, where the need for a common feature or form in things is witnessed by the fact that we have a common name (dog, chair) for numbers of them. Again, it is common to deduce that otherwise mysterious entities, such as events or facts or numbers, exist because we have terms for them and these terms function in language in just the way that names of other less suspect entities function. We therefore have no option to deny existence to events or facts or numbers, unless we wish to propose changing or abandoning our language. This latter option indeed shows that we can only infer conclusions about how we *take* the world to be, rather than how it actually is, from facts about the general features of our language, for in principle our language might reflect a misunderstanding and misrepresentation of the real features of things. But in so far as we see no error in our usage, or no prospect of a linguistic reform that would change the feature in question, we will find ourselves committed to the substantive conclusion. And if, as in the *Tractatus Logico-Philosophicus* of Wittgenstein, we can put conditions on the nature of any possible representation of facts, then we have a *transcendental argument that if meaning is possible, then the world must be such as to be representable in those ways.

The philosophical understanding of language must therefore achieve a stable equilibrium with our best philosophy of mind and our best metaphysics. It has been characteristic of twentieth-century philosophy to suppose that it dominates these partners, dictating how we are to think about mind and metaphysics. Thus to analytic philosophers, such as Russell and Moore, and to the Logical Positivists, such as Carnap and Schlick, but above all to Wittgenstein, the best route to a theory of mind is through describing our linguistic powers, since these may claim to be the most characteristic product of our understandings. On most issues, we do not know what to think until we know what to say. And if we cannot mean something, then we cannot understand it either. This suggests that if an investigation into language delivers results about the limits of meaning, then our science and our conception of the world must also conform to those limits. Such a result was claimed by logical atomism, in which the nature of linguistic representation is held to determine the kind of fact that can ever be represented, and most famously by *Logical Positivism with the doctrine that since the meaning of a sentence is its method of verification (the *verification principle), we can attach no meaning to hypotheses that are incapable of verification, and must tailor our concept of the world, and our philosophy of science, accordingly. The same strategy (and, some believe, the same principle) is at work in the *private language argument of Wittgenstein, in which the impossibility of meaningfully describing the recurrence of a private sensation whose nature is independent of any physical or public events, is held to undermine the Cartesian philosophy of mind according to which such sensations exist. 'Linguistic' philosophy or 'Oxford' philosophy of the middle years of the twentieth century, is widely thought to have shown an excessive reliance on the implications of ordinary speech for other matters. More recently deconstructionist emphasis on the fluid contrasts and contingencies that shape an overall linguistic 'field' (pattern of inferences) leads to despair over finding any fixed meaning in our terms, with lurid consequences for the possibility of any objective description of things, or eventually of truth as opposed to falsehood.

The legacy of seventeenth- and eighteenth-century *empiricism was confidence that language would be understood by the way of ideas, or, in other words, by seeing it as a vehicle for making public our ideas, conceived of as the self-standing mental elements whereby we think, but which would otherwise remain private. Ideas and their properties, especially their derivation from experience, were the central topic, with language a mere vehicle for their transmission (although Hobbes, Locke, and others were aware that infirmities or 'abuses' of language affected the task of thinking properly: but this could be remedied by paying closer attention to ideas).

Ideas, however, prove a broken reed, because any inner display of any kind seems inessential to identifying what is thought and understood, and because the power of ideas to represent things other than themselves is just as hard to conceive as the power of words to do so. Competence with a language is not simply competence in packaging already given ideas. This is obvious if we imagine mastering some new area, such as physics, where there is no distinction between mastering the language and mastering the subject. With the work of Frege emphasis came to be placed on objective and public aspects of understanding: when I tell you that the Gulf Stream crosses the Atlantic, I do not excite in you an idea which may or may not be like some subjective idea of my own, but give you a definite and objective piece of information. I transmit a thought or proposition. But Frege remained largely silent on the question what it was to grasp such a thought or proposition. Its content, evidently, concerns the Gulf Stream and the Atlantic, but how my mind is related to such things for me to understand the proposition is left moot.

If we put that question to one side it is possible to sketch further relations between psychological states and meaning. One suggestion is that a term means something if it causes persons hearing it to go into some state. But this fails to distinguish the common consequences of using a term from its meaning: talking about spiders may make most people think of being bitten, but that is no part of the meaning of the term, and indeed only occurs because of its meaning. A better suggestion, although still inadequate, would focus on the intended effect. The most influential development of this line has been that of H. P. Grice, which saw an utterance's meaning in terms of the complex structure of intentions with which it is used. A variant of this approach may locate a public convention of using a type of utterance only with a certain intention, such as intending to induce a certain belief, or intending to signal that one has oneself a certain belief.

Even if such accounts work (and the complexity necessary to protect them from objections has tended to rouse suspicion) they have still put aside the question how it is that my mental state is properly representational, or, in other words, what is involved in my grasping a proposition whose content concerns the Gulf Stream or the Atlantic. The suggestion taking us away from pragmatics and towards semantics would be that this is so if I incline to express the state by using words which refer to those geographical objects. This, of course, requires that we have a separate account of word reference. One suggestion was that of Russell's famous theory of *descriptions, according to which reference is normally accomplished by the subject having in mind (in some sense) a description which the thing referred to satisfies. This in turn raises the demand for an account of what it is to have a description in mind, which in Russell terminates rather disappointingly in an acquaintance with universals, or features that things can share.

But it was also objected by Strawson and others that the account distorts the way in which *reference is normally accomplished and the role that referring terms play in a language. The development of this objection by Kripke and Putnam led to explorations of a causal account, according to which I refer to something when my words are in some favoured causal relationship with that object. This approach is still active. Its chief current competitor is associated with the work of Davidson. This denies that the relationship of reference is a good place to start. Instead we have to consider the overall project of interpreting someone. This will require the simultaneous attribution of beliefs and meanings, done in accordance with the methodological principle that we try to make them appear as rational or sensibly tuned to their environment as possible. The programme this engenders is one of systematically attributing truth-conditions simultaneously to each of the infinite (or indefinitely large) number of possible sentences that a language may contain. The upshot is an *interpretation made not by the piecemeal association of individual words with individual things or features of things, but more 'holistically' or 'top down'. On this approach the reference of a term becomes a mere intervening variable, in the sense that it is simply an aspect of a sentence certified by a procedure that has looked at a quite different thing: the overall pattern of association of truth-conditions with sentences. The approach encounters a notorious problem of determinacy. Unless the constraints are made very severe (possibly incorporating causal requirements) it looks as though arbitrarily different assignments of meaning may be made in conformity with them.

This problem, first identified as the *indeterminacy of radical translation by Quine, has led to scepticism about the very existence of determinate meaning, and to consequent rejection of the idea that sentences ever manage to express single propositions and thoughts. A similar result may be supported (probably not in accordance with its author's intentions) by the 'rule-following considerations' as they appear in the later work of Wittgenstein. These too leave the fact that someone follows a determinate rule in their usage of a term a mysterious 'superlative' fact, and one response is to fear that meaning has disappeared altogether. This nihilism is often thought to accord with a proper appreciation of the contextual and socially rooted nature of meaning, and the genuine difficulties of real-life translation. It is also realistic to remember that, however strict we try to be with words, new situations can easily be envisaged in which we would not know whether a particular term applies or not. But Quine's thesis and a sceptical conclusion to the rule-following considerations go

beyond these proper cautions, for they make no distinction between alien and stressful cases and normal thought and communication. But nihilism about this ultimately self-destructs, since it is only by relying on my own (determinate) understanding of my terms that I can think at all. A dogged resolution to see others just as producers of noise fit to be interpreted in any of a variety of different ways may just about succeed for a time. But a similar resolution with regard to myself is impossible. We may, in the study, be sufficiently baffled by the problem to believe that there is nothing outside the text, and to see linguistic behaviour as a self-contained game of producing and consuming noise and script. But such scepticism is unlivable, and will not survive long when we actually ask directions, give recipes, and tell the time.

There is, then, no agreed solution to the problem what it is determinately to take a term in my language to refer to a particular thing or feature of things. Two recent developments are the extensive links between the philosophy of language and the general field of cognitive science, and the equally promising links between the subject and the biological and evolutionary perspective on the emergence of language. The latter suggests that we can isolate determinate meaning by considering the role of a term in the life of an animal in a determinate environment. That is, if a signal has evolved in order to fulfil some need (which in turn can be analysed in terms of the differential fitness it confers on its users) then it seems a short step to assign to it a determinate semantic role. This is a plausible reconstruction of a meaning for the signalling systems of some animals, for example. Critics respond either that such systems are so simple that they are misleading models for fully fledged language, or more fundamentally that we should not reduce meaning, which is a fact, to evolutionary biological relations, which may remain speculative, or we would be handing ourselves a strange kind of proof that evolutionary theory is true. The computational approach has developed in a different direction. Initially it seems unpromising, since computers respond simply to the syntax of elements of computer languages, without regard to their interpretation. But further thought suggests that by putting a computer in an environment (either 'virtual' or real) with receptors responding to different features of that environment, we get a small-scale version of a causal semantics for the terms in which it computes.

As well as work on these broad and fundamental themes the philosophy of language contains detailed work on the particular forms—*conditionals, *counterfactuals, tensed statements, modal statements—that are indispensable to ordinary *communication. Whilst the classic approach to these has been to try to show that they are disguised versions of the tractable, simple forms of statement dealt with in classical logic, more relaxed and elastic approaches are now equally respectable. Equally important are the discrimination of such things as emotive meaning, derogatory and other attitude-bearing discourse, and the general study of the relation between the vocabulary of a period and the social habits and structures that help to shape it.   s.w.b.

S. Blackburn, *Spreading the Word* (Oxford, 1984).

G. Frege, *Philosophical Writings* (Oxford, 1960).

R. Millikan, *Language, Thought and Other Biological Categories* (Cambridge, Mass., 1984).

W. V. Quine, *Word and Object* (Cambridge, Mass., 1960).

B. Russell, *An Inquiry into Meaning and Truth* (London, 1940).

L. Wittgenstein, *Philosophical Investigations* (Oxford, 1953).

language, religious: *see* religious language.

language, social nature of. We learn language from others in a social setting. But is this enough to show that language is an essentially social phenomenon? Opinions among philosophers are divided. Famously, Wittgenstein argued that the only meanings that speakers could attach to their words were the meanings they had in language of the surrounding community. Meaning, for Wittgenstein, was a matter of publicly sustained patterns of use, not private associations in the minds of individuals. The distinction between using words correctly and incorrectly cannot, he thought, be settled by the judgements of an individual, but depends on agreement among the community of language-users. To use a word correctly is to use it in accordance with a rule, and whether an individual is following a rule on a given occasion is a matter independent of the opinions of that individual. For the sounds speakers utter to have linguistic significance must be independent of the opinions of the individual speaker.

The distinction between the use of a word that *seems* right and a use that *is* right, and something more than the opinion of an individual, is required to set a standard or rule for using a word correctly. For Wittgenstein this is the institution of a social practice, and individuals come to use a language by participating in those practices. Other philosophers have supposed that speakers can communicate successfully only if they attach the same meanings to their words as others do, and this presupposes a shared communal language. However, an objection is that one is only required to know what significance another speaker attaches to the words uttered, not to attach the same significance oneself. Hence, speakers can differ in their use of language, departing from communal practice, and still be understood, so long as they make their meaning publicly available. Those who favour the view that the way language is used by the individual is of primary importance take idiolects rather than communal languages to be primary. An idiolect, or language of an individual, need not be private, and can still be used in a social setting. A further aspect of the social nature of language is what Hilary Putnam has called 'the division of linguistic labour'. This social phenomenon is illustrated by words like 'gold' which have both an ordinary non-technical use and a more precise meaning and application given to them by experts. In this case we may not know everything about the meaning of such words, but we defer to the relevant experts.   b.c.s.

M. Dummett, *The Logical Basis of Metaphysics* (Cambridge, Mass., 1991), ch. 4: 'Meaning, Knowledge and Understanding'.

language-game. Wittgensteinian term of art, introduced in *The Blue and Brown Books* when rejecting the calculus model of language which had dominated his *Tractatus*. It highlights the fact that language use is a form of human rule governed activity, integrated into human transactions and social behaviour, context-dependent and purpose relative. Analogies between games and language, playing games and speaking, justify it. Imaginary language-games are introduced as simplified, readily surveyable objects of comparison to illuminate actual language-games, either by way of contrast or similarity. A description of a language-game may include words and sentences, 'instruments' (gestures, patterns, word–sample correlations), context (which often brings to light the presuppositions of the existence of a language-game as well as the essential background of engaging in it), the characteristic activity of the language-game, the antecedent training and learning in which the rules are imparted, the *use* of components of the language-game, and its *point*. Wittgenstein held the cardinal error of modern philosophy to be the focus on forms of expression rather than on their use in the stream of life.   p.m.s.h.

G. P. Baker and P. M. S. Hacker, *Analytic Commentary on the* Philosophical Investigations, i: *Wittgenstein: Understanding and Meaning* (Oxford, 1980), 89–99.

language of thought. Following Aristotle some have argued that the significance of spoken words derives from intrinsically meaningful interior 'speech'. According to Ockham the *propositio vocalis* is posterior to and dependent upon the *propositio mentalis*. More recently Fodor has argued that thought is a form of symbol manipulation, and that *language-learning involves the correlation of conventional symbols with those of one's innate mental language. Two main considerations are regularly advanced in support of the language of thought hypothesis. First, parallels between the structures of thought and language are brought out in reports of each. Thus, for any proposition *p* one may equally well say 'He thought that *p*' as that 'He said that *p*'—each act seems to involve a relation to a sentence. Second, sounds and marks appear to express meanings without themselves being intrinsically meaningful; this suggests that public language may be a vehicle for the expression of prior mental 'utterances'. It is often argued against the language of thought hypothesis, however, that it is regressive, since if the possibility of linguistic *meaning always requires an explanation, so must that of mental language; on the other hand if the latter is held to be intrinsically significant, then it is false that all linguistic meaning must be derived, in which case why not suppose, after all, that the meaning of speech-acts is non-derivative, i.e. that the significance of spoken words is intrinsic in their use.   j.hal.

J. Fodor, *The Language of Thought* (Cambridge, Mass., 1975).

langue and parole. Distinction drawn by the Swiss founder of linguistics, Ferdinand de Saussure (1857–1913), in his lecture series *Cours de linguistique générale* (1916), between language as a system of formal rules and mutually defining terms and language in its everyday use. (In French, *langue* means 'language', and *parole* means 'speech'.) *Langue* includes linguistic *types or *universals, *parole* linguistic *tokens or *particular inscriptions and utterances. The distinction was influential on *structuralism, in which *langue* is studied as making *parole* possible, in a quasi-Kantian or transcendental fashion.   S.P.

Ferdinand de Saussure, *Course in General Linguistics* (New York, 1959).

David Holdcroft, *Saussure: Signs, System and Arbitrariness* (Cambridge, 1991).

Lao Tzŭ (dates uncertain). An individual whose existence is in doubt, but who is traditionally viewed as the author of the classic of *Taoism *Lao Tzŭ* and as an older contemporary of Confucius (sixth to fifth century BC) in China. Many modern scholars doubt the existence of Lao Tzŭ as a historical figure, and regard the text, also known as the *Tao Te Ching*, as composite and datable to as late as the third century BC. The text highlights how the natural order operates by 'reversion' (anything that has gone far in one direction will inevitably move in the opposite direction), and how the state of 'weakness' enables an object to thrive. Modelling their way of life on the natural order, human beings should avoid striving after worldly goals, which inevitably leads to loss, and should instead be non-assertive and have few desires.   K.-L.S.

Lao Tzu (Tao Te Ching), tr. D. C. Lau (Harmondsworth, 1963).

Laplace, Pierre-Simon, marquis de (1749–1827). French physicist and mathematician who made major contributions to celestial mechanics and *probability theory. In cosmology he was one of the two independent originators of the nebular hypothesis (the other was Kant), according to which the solar system was formed from rotating gas. He showed that Newton's worry that perturbations in the planetary orbits would lead to the long-term instability of the solar system was unfounded. (Newton thought that divine intervention was necessary to ensure stability.) This is the origin of the story that in reply to Napoleon, who complained that he had left God out of his system, Laplace said: 'I have no need of that hypothesis.' Laplacian *determinism is the claim that granted complete knowledge of the state of the universe and the laws of nature, every detail of the future is predictable.   A.BEL.

Charles Coulston Gillispie, Robert Fox, and Ivor Grattan-Guinness, *Pierre-Simon Laplace, 1749–1827: A Life in Exact Science* (Princeton, NJ, 1997).

Latin American philosophy. Latin American philosophy begins with the Spanish and Portuguese discovery and colonization of the New World. Throughout its 500-year history, this philosophy has maintained strong human and social interests, has been consistently affected by scholastic and Catholic thought, and has significantly influenced the social and political institutions in the region. Latin American philosophers tend to be active in the educational, political, and social affairs of their countries and deeply concerned with their own cultural identity.

The history of philosophy in Latin America may be divided into four periods of development: colonial, independentist, positivist, and contemporary. The colonial period (*c*.1550–1750) was dominated by the type of scholasticism officially practised in the Iberian peninsula. The texts studied were those of medieval scholastics and of their Iberian commentators. The philosophical concerns in the colonies were those prevalent in Spain and Portugal and centred on logical and metaphysical issues inherited from the Middle Ages and on political and legal questions raised by the discovery and colonization. The main philosophical centre during the early colonial period, Mexico, was joined in the seventeenth century by Peru. Antonio Rubio's (1548–1615) *Logica mexicana* was the most celebrated scholastic book written in the New World.

Although working within the tradition of *scholasticism, some authors of this period were influenced by *humanism. The most important of these was Bartolomé de las Casas (1484–1566), who became the leading champion of the rights of native Americans at the time. He argued that wars of conquest in the New World were unjustified because they were based on false generalizations and misinformation. He defended the autonomy of native Americans, claiming that neither the Spaniards nor the Catholic Church had rightful authority over them and therefore should not impose European cultural and religious values upon them.

A more complete break with scholasticism was made during the independentist period (*c*.1750–1850). The period began with growing interest in early modern philosophers; among these Descartes was most influential. The intellectual leaders of this period were men of action who used ideas for practical ends. They made reason a measure of legitimacy in social and governmental matters, and found the justification for revolutionary ideas in *natural law. Moreover, they criticized authority, and some of them regarded religion as superstitious and opposed ecclesiastical power. Their ideas paved the way for the later development of *positivism.

Positivism (*c*.1850–1910) was, in part, a response to the social, financial, and political needs of the newly liberated countries of Latin America. Juan Bautista Alberdi (Argentina, 1812–84) and Andrés Bello (Venezuela, 1781–1865) stand out as important figures of the early part of the positivist period. Alberdi argued for the development of a philosophy adequate to the social and economic needs of Latin America, and Bello attempted to reduce metaphysics to psychology; both began trends others were to follow.

Positivists emphasized the explicative value of empirical science and rejected metaphysics. For them, all knowledge is to be based on experience rather than theoretical speculation, and its value rests in its practical applications. The universe is explained mechanistically, leaving little room for freedom and values. Positivism became the official philosophy of some Latin American countries and exerted strong social influence. Testifying to this is the preservation of the positivist inscription 'Order and Progress' on the Brazilian national flag. The most original positivists were the Cuban Enrique José Varona (1849–1933) and the Argentinian José Ingenieros (1877–1925). Ingenieros made some room for metaphysics in his philosophy, claiming that it is concerned with what is 'yet-to-be-experienced'.

Contemporary Latin American philosophy (c.1910–present) begins with the decline of positivism. The first part of the period is taken up by the generation of thinkers who rebelled against positivist ideas. The principal members of this early generation, called 'the Founders' by Francisco Romero, are: Alejandro Korn (Argentina, 1860–1936), Alejandro Octavio Deústua (Peru, 1849–1945), José Vasconcelos (Mexico, 1882–1959), Antonio Caso (Mexico, 1883–1946), Enrique Molina (Chile, 1871–1964), Carlos Vaz Ferreira (Uruguay, 1872–1958), and Raimundo de Farias Brito (Brazil, 1862–1917). Trained as positivists, they became dissatisfied with positivism's dogmatic intransigence, mechanistic determinism, and emphasis on pragmatic values. The arguments against positivism of Deústua, Caso and Vaz Ferreira are characteristic of the period. Deústua attempted to show that the ideas of order and freedom are basic to society but that the second has priority over the first, for order cannot be established without freedom. Caso defended a view of man as capable of altruism and love. And Vaz Ferreira opposed the abstract logic favoured by positivists, developing instead a logic of life based on experience.

Positivism was superseded by the Founders with the help of ideas imported first from France and later from Germany. The process began with the influence of Boutroux and Bergson and of French *vitalism and intuitionism, but it was cemented when Ortega y Gasset introduced into Latin America the thought of Max Scheler, Nicolai Hartmann, and other German philosophers during his first visit to Argentina in 1916.

*Philosophical anthropology developed in response to the desire to move further away from the scientific emphasis of positivism. Samuel Ramos (Mexico, 1897–1959) focused upon what was particular in Mexican culture, thereby inspiring interest in what is culturally unique to Latin American nations. He, like most philosophers of this period, tried to develop a philosophical anthropology based on a spiritual conception of human beings. Francisco Romero (Argentina, 1891–1962) was the most original thinker of the group. In Teoría del hombre (1952) he conceives human nature as involving both intentionality and spirituality.

During the late 1930s and 1940s Latin Americans were exposed to a variety of recent European ideas and methodologies. As a consequence of the political upheaval created by the Spanish Civil War, a substantial group of peninsular philosophers, known as the transterrados, settled in Latin America. Among these, José Gaos (1900–69) had the greatest influence. In particular, he introduced rigorous techniques of textual analysis in Mexico.

With the generation born around 1910, Latin American philosophy reached what Romero later called a 'state of normalcy'. Philosophy established itself as a professional and reputable discipline, and philosophical organizations, research centres, and journals flourished. The core of this eclectic generation was composed of philosophers working in the German tradition who concerned themselves primarily with axiology. Most of them granted some objectivity to values, but a few argued that values were neither objective nor subjective. This position is most clearly presented in Risieri Frondizi's (Argentina, 1910–83) Qué son los valores? (1958), where he proposes a view of value as a Gestalt quality.

Other developments of this period included a renewed interest in scholasticism. There was also a growing interest in the study of the history of ideas and on the question of the identity and possibility of an authentic Latin American philosophy. The latter was raised in the 1940s by Leopoldo Zea (Mexico, 1912–2004) and continues to be a source of interest in the region today.

Until 1960 philosophers working outside the traditions mentioned had limited visibility. This has now changed. *Marxist philosophy and *philosophical analysis have found places in the academy. As a result there has been renewed interest in areas where these philosophical currents are strong, such as social and political philosophy, logic, and the philosophy of science. The theology of liberation prepared the way for the development of the philosophy of liberation, which began in Argentina in the 1970s and combines an emphasis on Latin American intellectual independence with Catholic and Marxist ideas. J.G.
E.M.

William Rex Crawford, A Century of Latin-American Thought, 3rd edn. (New York, 1966).

Harold Eugene Davis, Latin American Thought: A Historical Introduction (New York, 1972).

Jorge J. E. Gracia (ed.), Latin American Philosophy Today, double issue of The Philosophical Forum (1988–9).

—— Eduardo Rabossi et al. (eds.), Philosophical Analysis in Latin America (Dordrecht, 1984).

Leopoldo Zea, The Latin American Mind, tr. J. H. Abbott and L. Dunham (Norman, Okla., 1963).

latitudinarianism. 'Dr Wilkins, my friend, the bishop of Chester . . . is a mighty rising man, as being a Latitudinarian,' said Pepys in 1669, and the 'latitude men', who favoured tolerance in belief and doctrine, were certainly among the late seventeenth century's intellectual élite. Though there is some controversy among historians over the precise application of the term 'latitudinarian', Seth Ward, Ralph Cudworth, Henry More, John Locke, and Robert Boyle provide additional examples of thinkers with latitudinarian tendencies. Of course the latitude was limited. It did not include what Boyle in his Will called 'notorious Infidels (*vizt*) Atheists, Theists [i.e. deists], Pagans, Jews and Mahometans'. None the less latitudinarianism was not without critics. 'There were no such Latitudinarian Principles among the Apostles,' said Thomas Comber, and others found the latitudinarians 'meer moral men, without the power of Godliness'.   J.J.M.

*deism.

R. Kroll, R. Ashcraft, and P. Zagorin (eds.), *Philosophy, Science and Religion in England 1640–1700* (Cambridge, 1992).

laughter. Laughter is a psychophysical phenomenon against which a number of philosophical theories of mental and personal identity can be tested. If laughter is essential to the psychology of *humour, then a creature endowed with humour must be embodied. But since the bodily postures and motions which are characteristic of laughter can occur in the absence of amusement, laughter cannot be a simply physical occurrence. Aristotle uses these considerations to support a theory of *human nature according to which a person is not identical with a body, yet does not exist without a body. More recently John Wisdom has hinted at how humour and its objects can provide helpful pointers to the analysis of the relation between subjective and objective elements in the nature of value. The topic deserves more attention in the philosophy of mind.   J.D.G.E.

For an analytic treatment of the subject, see the symposium 'Laughter' by R. Scruton and P. Jones, *Aristotelian Society Supplementary Volume* (1982).

law, feminist philosophy of. Since the resurgence of the women's movement in the 1960s, scholars have begun to identify and explore distinctively feminist questions of and about law and legal philosophy. The questions which have occupied feminist scholars' attention cover a wide range of jurisprudential questions, encompassing issues identified with analytical, normative, and sociological jurisprudence. Are laws, legal practices, and even the very concept of law implicitly gendered and, if so, is this inevitable? In what ways has woman been constructed within legal discourse and excluded from or incorporated within prevailing notions of legal subjecthood? What role have laws played in constituting or reinforcing ideologies (such as that which assumes and prescribes a division between public and private spheres) which feminist political theorists have identified as influential in maintaining and obscuring women's social and political subordination? At the core of most feminist legal scholarship is a critique of the purported objectivity or gender-neutrality of legal method and legal regulation. The argument is that the purported gender-neutrality of legal concepts and of most legal arrangements in liberal societies in fact disguises the implicit instantiation in laws of a partial viewpoint, and one which generally reflects male rather than female interests and experience of the world. Feminist legal scholars

are therefore much concerned with debates in feminist epistemology and feminist ethics, and particularly with the problem of 'essentialism'—that associated with identifying masculine or feminine viewpoints in a world where both male and female experience is relative not only to gender but also to class, ethnic, and other social structures and axes of subordination. Another feature typical of feminist legal philosophy is scepticism about the idea that law is autonomous in the sense of being both a distinctive and, in significant respects, a discrete practice, insulated from broader political and social influence.

Like all sophisticated intellectual discourses, feminist legal philosophy is characterized by a diversity of both substantive commitment and method. A significant strand of feminist legal scholarship draws on post-modernist ideas and sees the feminist project in this area as a basically critical or deconstructive one. Scholars sympathetic with this position express scepticism about the participation of feminist theory in the enterprise of constructing a 'grand', universal theory of law, which they argue would be likely to reproduce the same kinds of distortion and exclusion which characterize orthodox legal theories. Others envisage the possibility of a feminist jurisprudence which could escape the bias and obfuscation of orthodox legal theories such as positivist or natural law conceptions and which could hold out the promise of conceiving genuinely equal legal subjecthood and gender justice as opposed to gender-neutrality. Similar diversity characterizes feminist approaches to the role of normative or prescriptive thought in legal philosophy. Whilst most feminist scholars are critical of the idea that normative argument can be objectively grounded or proceed 'from nowhere', they vary in terms of what role they see in the feminist enterprise for legal reformism, the reconstruction of normative concepts such as justice, rights, or equality from a feminist perspective, or utopian argument about legal and social change. Thus some feminist legal scholars see immanent critique—the holding-up of legal practices to critical scrutiny in the light of their failure to meet their own professed ideals—as the central task of feminist legal theory, while others see external, more broadly politically or ethically based critique as of equal importance. Like most forms of feminist theory, feminist legal philosophy retains a strong sense of the importance of the link between theory and practice. Much feminist philosophical work in the area of law therefore concerns itself with philosophical critique of concrete legal institutions and practices, notably the regulation of the family, and the structure of constitutional rights and their impact on practices such as abortion and pornography; the regulation of sexuality by and the construction of images of women and men, femininity and masculinity, within a wide range of criminal and civil laws; legal anti-discrimination policies and the ideals of equality and justice which inform them.   N.M.L.

*feminist philosophy.

Drucilla Cornell, *Beyond Accommodation: Ethical Feminism, Deconstruction and the Law* (London, 1991).

Catharine A. MacKinnon, 'Feminism, Marxism, Method and the State: Toward Feminist Jurisprudence', *Signs* (1983).

Susan Moller Okin, *Justice, Gender and the Family* (New York, 1989).

Carole Pateman, *The Sexual Contract* (Oxford, 1988).

Carol Smart, *Feminism and the Power of Law* (London, 1989).

Iris Marion Young, *Justice and the Politics of Difference* (Princeton, NJ, 1990).

law, history of the philosophy of. The philosophical reflections recalled here are about *positive law, in particular the rules and principles authoritatively declared by people who make themselves responsible for (what they claim to be) the good order of their community, an order they specify and promote by proposing obligatory and other authoritative guidance for the actions of their community's members.

Throughout its history, legal philosophy has sought to differentiate positive law (hereafter 'law' or 'the law') from other standards relevant to human deliberation towards choice and action, and from the governing principles and norms of other intelligible orders (the systems of the cosmos or nature, of logic, and arts such as grammar or boat-building). Such differentiation has aimed both to clarify terminology and conceptual boundaries and to inquire whether the analogies or other relations between law and these norms of other orders help explain what is most puzzling about law: that it can 'necessitate' (make obligatory, indeed morally obligatory) actions which, until its enactment, were not so necessitated; that its rules and other 'institutions' somehow 'exist' by virtue of but also long after their positing by enactment or other 'act in the law', or judicial precedent or custom; that many of its rules have a normative form, and a social function, distinct from its obligation imposing rules; that it resorts to punitive and rectificatory coercion to outlaw force (as well as dishonesty and carelessness) in interpersonal relations. (*Law, problems of the philosophy of.)

The surviving fragments of the *Pre-Socratics on these matters suggest a vigorous debate which cannot now be securely reconstructed. The conversation of legal philosophy begins for us with two brief dialogues reflecting the debates in Socratic circles: a witty conversation between Alcibiades and Pericles composed by Xenophon (*Memorabilia* I. 2), and a 'Socratic' dialogue insecurely ascribed to Plato (the *Minos* 314b–315a). Each portrays the embarrassments awaiting philosophers who define law as whatever is decreed by rulers, neglecting or declining to refer to issues of (moral) right such as whether its subjects have in any way consented (Xenophon) or whether what it decrees is good, true, and in conformity with 'what really is' (*Minos*). Both dialogues suggest that, while everyone understands the sense in which a law's (in)justice is irrelevant to its empirical reality as enforced, in a more adequate understanding of law unjust laws are 'more a matter of force than of law' and are 'not without qualification law' (*Minos*).

So by the early fourth century BC two positions emerge, each still defended in the late twentieth century. The one—today called *legal positivism—asserts that to be described with realism and clarity law must be considered without regard to any moral predicates which it attracts in discourse (e.g. moral–political evaluation) outside the philosophy of *law*. The other—usually if confusingly called *natural law theory—asserts that such a description misses the point of law: legal systems get their sense and shape (which a good descriptive account of law will identify) from their point, and a rational evaluation of particular laws or legal systems (or political communities) will use that (perhaps complex) point as a criterion for measuring their conformity to or deviation from the very idea of law. Plato articulates this second position: 'Enactments, to the extent that they are not for the interest of the whole community, are not truly laws' (*Laws* 715b; also 712e–713a; *Statesman* 293d–e). Cicero sums up the philosophical mainstream: 'In the very definition of the term "law" there inheres the idea and principle of choosing what is just and true' (*De legibus* II. 11).

On this issue of definition, Plato had warned that ordinary talk of 'law' is one thing, explanatory definition of law another (*Hippias Major* 284d). Aristotle (*Politics* III. 1275a–b) worked out the appropriate account of definition in social, including legal, theory. In this account, pure description or reportage (these purport to be, and are commonly called, friendships, political communities, constitutions, . . . laws) can coexist with explanatory definition within a theory which treats justification (and, where appropriate, critical delegitimization) as the primary mode of explanation. Thus the humanly good type of friendship, community, constitution, . . . or law is the paradigm, central case picked out by the explanatory definition, and by a corresponding word ('friendship', . . . 'law') in its focal meaning; specimens of this good type are in this sense truly, properly, or unqualifiedly (Greek *haplōs*, Latin *simpliciter*) friendship, law, etc. But instances of a type that is humanly deficient remain within the discipline's philosophical account, precisely as analogous to the central case. The philosophy of human affairs, as it bears on law, reflects on decent laws and legal systems, with due attention to what makes laws bad and how bad laws matter.

Until Bentham (foreshadowed in the seventeenth century by Bacon, Hobbes, and Spinoza), there is little or no legal philosophy which could be called positivist. Yet from Plato to Bentham legal philosophy was substantially a philosophy of positive law, a subject-matter regarded as distinct from the other subjects of moral and political philosophy, but as adequately intelligible only on the basis of the moral principles and political purposes identified, explicated, and defended within moral and political philosophy. Still, legal philosophy's self-interpretation precisely as a philosophy of positive law awaits the *Summa Theologiae* of Thomas Aquinas (*c.*1270). The term 'positive law' emerged *c.*1135, and soon became popular among theoretically minded jurists. But the new terminology did not immediately modify the ancient accounts of the precise subject of philosophical reflection on law(s). Aristotle (*Nicomachean Ethics* v. 1134[b]) had divided political right/just(ice) into the natural and the legal; the latter he also described as conventional and human. Late twelfth- and thirteenth-century jurists divided *jus* (law/right) into natural (the moral law) and positive, subdividing the latter into the Roman-law categories of *jus gentium* (laws common to all peoples) and civil law (peculiar to a given community). Eventually Aquinas (*Summa Theologiae*, 1–2, Q. 95, A. 2) treats the distinction between natural and civil law as a distinction within positive law (i.e. within law humanly laid down). Some parts of positive law are *conclusiones* (entailments) of the principles and norms of natural moral law; for these he appropriates the name *jus gentium*. The other parts are purely positive, though related to moral principles by an intelligible, non deductive relationship which he names *determinatio* (concretization).

Thus human positive law in both its parts is at last differentiated as an integral object of philosophical reflection. It is by analogy with this central analogate that we understand as law (i) the eternal law of God's creative providence (including all the laws investigated by the natural sciences), (ii) the *natural law, or rational principles of good and right human deliberation and action, and (iii) the 'divine law', Aquinas's name for norms of positive law specially promulgated by divine revelation and including, like human positive law (ecclesiastical or secular), elements both of natural law (e.g. most of the Ten Commandments) and of purely positive law (regulating Israel and then the Church).

Aquinas describes human positive law as made by *will* (i.e. by preferring one reasonable scheme to another), but when speaking precisely contends that law is a matter of *reason* rather than will; obligation is a matter of means required for serving and respecting practical reason's ends and principles; the *imperium* by which one directs oneself in executing one's choices belongs to reason rather than will. All this soon met with opposition, and for the next 500 years the philosophy of law is dominated by efforts to explain law's source and obligatoriness by reference to will, whether of superiors or of consenting parties to a social contract.

The polemics launched in 1323 between Pope John XXII (canon lawyer and Thomist) and William of Ockham, concerning the nature of legal (especially property) rights, gave wide currency to Ockham's conceptions: of positive human law as founded on commanding or contracting will and legitimate even when opposed to natural law; of supreme (divine) will as binding to even the most inherently unreasonable act (e.g. hating God); of right as primarily a power or liberty of acting. The second scholasticism of sixteenth- to seventeenth-century Spain sought a balance between Thomist and voluntarist theory. Its monument is Suarez's *De legibus* (On Laws (1612)). Reason's capacity to discern right from wrong is emphasized, but obligation is still a driving force from a superior's will, and Aquinas's conception of *imperium* as reason's directive grasp of an action's intelligent point is rejected as a fiction. Suarez underlines the variety of types of law (eternal,

natural, human, divine) but also the variety of normative types of human law, including laws binding to compliance, laws binding only to payment of the 'penalty' for non-compliance, laws giving juridical acts their form and validity, and laws creating privileges. The principle of Suarez's analyses remains the moralist's interest in issues of conscience (conceived in terms of obligation and liberty).

Grotius, though clearly influenced by Suarez and other philosophical theologians, shifts the focus of inquiry in legal philosophy: the foundations of morality (natural law) and obligation are but lightly and ambiguously sketched. The work of 'philosophy of law' (a term promoted if not invented by Grotius) is conceived as identification of the reasonable scheme of law which will secure justice and rights in a community constituted by social contract. The scheme's content is settled, in effect, by making such adjustments to Roman law's conceptual framework as are suggested to Grotius by an immensely learned survey of classical culture, medieval commentary, and some comparative jurisprudence. Grotian (over)-confidence in reason's ability to identify uniquely appropriate legal solutions to problems of social life persists in the rationalist theories of natural and human law which prevail until Bentham and Kant.

But the seventeenth- to eighteenth-century descendants of Grotian theory had to respond to the radical questioning of their foundations by Hobbes and Spinoza. Paradigmatic is the response of Samuel Pufendorf (*c*.1670). Laws are decrees by which superiors obligate us subjects to conform our acts to their commands. Every law contains both a definition of what we are to do or avoid, and a statement of the punishment awaiting our non-compliance. Obligation is a moral quality created by persons who have not only the power to harm us if we resist them but also just grounds for their claim to limit our freedom by their choice. These just grounds may be the benefits those persons have rendered us, their benevolent ability to provide for us better than we could for ourselves, and/or our agreement to subject ourselves to them. Hobbes's claim that the right to rule is warranted solely from irresistible power must be rejected as failing to account for obligation's significance for conscience. Like the Calvinist Grotius, the Lutheran Pufendorf and the whole mainstream retain the Catholic division of law into natural, divine, and human and the Thomist position that human law is, as such, all positive (though rightly constrained by the natural law, many of whose precepts it should also repromulgate to recalcitrants). Philosophy of law identifies for jurists many details of the law which should obtain within and between states, and for morally upright citizens their duties of conscience in face of legal obligations.

The notion of natural law both limiting and justifying positive law remains in Kant's *Rechtslehre* (Doctrine of Law/Right (1797)), but now the natural law abstracts from all human benefits and reasons for action, other than conformity with the universalizing *form* of reason. Right (and right law) is the coexistence of my freedom (in accordance with universal laws) with everyone else's; wrong is the hindering of such rightful freedom, and is itself rightfully hindered by coercion; strict right or law is a state of universal reciprocal coercibility. Kant seeks to ground the law's primary institutions (property, contract, status, and punishment) in the logical requirements of a self-consistent freedom. The obligation of contracts, as of law, he thinks is entailed by the concept of a (simultaneously) united will. His account thus abstracts from human benefit and empirical realities alike, and rests on fictions (virtually admitted by him in retaining the 'idea of an original contract' of society).

Bentham had taken a very different course. His *A Fragment of Government* (1776), ridiculing late echoes of Pufendorf, proposed a radical distinction between the 'provinces' of expositors, who by attending to facts explain what the law is, and 'censors', who by attending to reasons consider what it ought to be. Bentham's expository jurisprudence included a treatise *Of Laws in General*, not published until 1945 but very like John Austin's less ingenious account, *The Province of Jurisprudence Determined* (1832): all laws properly and strictly so called are commands, expressions of wish (accompanied by threat of sanction) by the sovereign in an independent political community; however influential in courts, rules not made or adopted by sovereign command are not laws properly so called. Having a legal obligation is being the subject of a command and susceptible to its accompanying sanction. Legal rights including powers are all to be explained in terms of commands and more or less complex permissions or negations of obligation.

English-language philosophy of law remained largely within the orbit of Bentham and Austin for more than a hundred years (though historico-comparative jurisprudence ranged widely). American and other legal realists denied that the substance of the law is rules or any other standard posited by commands or any other past acts. But they retained and reinforced the conception of law as an instrument, in itself morally neutral, of 'social control' for the purposes of those in power (most directly courts and other officials).

Hans Kelsen, whose ideas became influential outside German-speaking lands in the 1930s, attempted a union of Kantian with neo-Hobbesian and neo-Humean themes which issued ultimately in a radically will-, indeed command-, centred account of law and legal system. Legal philosophy ('pure theory of legal science') must be free from every value, and from any reference to fact such as might suggest that law's normativity derives from or is reducible to its efficacy or other empirical reality. Kelsen sought in effect a 'third theory', sharing with natural law theory the attempt to reproduce and explain non-reductively law's normativity, and with legal positivism the rejection of every norm or value not posited and made effective by contingent human acts and facts. The quest's failure is manifested in Kelsen's many shifts to and fro between contradictory views about the source and coherence of legal norms, the content of normativity, and the meaning of propositions of legal science, and in his final open reliance upon 'fictitious acts of will'.

That explanations of law and legal obligation must point to commanding or consenting acts of will was denied in H. L. A. Hart's *The Concept of Law* (1961) and *Essays on Bentham* (1982). Legal rules are, rather, content-independent peremptory reasons for actions. Their sources may be commands but may equally be any fact having the normative significance attributed to it by a rule of recognition accepted by judges and officials (for any reason other than fear of immediate sanction). Not all laws are obligation-imposing; many are power conferring and an account which reduces these to conditions or protases of obligation disguises the variety of law's normative functions by overlooking the variety of its social functions. A descriptive legal philosophy can and should be free from moral presuppositions; law is not 'necessarily or conceptually' connected to morality, Hart holds. But legal philosophy should understand and reproduce the viewpoint or 'internal attitude' of those participants in a legal system for whom law is a genuine reason for action and something of (not necessarily moral) value. It therefore cannot maintain that law may have just any content.

Hart's many-sided resistance to reductive accounts of legal realities, and his strategy of understanding law as a type of reason created, maintained, and recognized for distinctive reasons, have encouraged many lines of inquiry into the point and function-related structure not only of law and legal system as a general type of social reality, but also of legal reasoning or judicial deliberation, of the rule of law as a distinctive ideal for politico-legal order, and of the shaping moral point and justification(s) of particular legal institutions such as contract, tort (delict), property, and punishment. Attention to Hart's neo-Aristotelian method of explanation by central and secondary cases has suggested that, despite his insistence on the opposition between the legal positivism he defended and every natural law theory, such opposition is needless unless positivism is taken (like Kelsen's but not Hart's) to deny that valuation and moral judgement have any philosophical warrant or truth.

Many positivist theories before Hart had been modelled on the natural (including mathematical and psychological) sciences. *The Concept of Law* opened legal philosophy to issues of method in descriptive social theory earlier discussed by Dilthey, Weber, and Winch, and showed, as Hart more or less clearly intended, the fruitlessness of seeking a value-free general social science. Interest has since shifted towards integrating legal theory with ethics and/or modelling it on the interpretation of cultural forms such as literature. For example, Ronald Dworkin's critique of positivism seemed at first intended to establish that Hart had misdescribed the types of standard used in judicial deliberation. But Dworkin's real theses were not that legal principles differ from rules, but that there are standards which are *legally* authoritative not because they were created or validated by enactment or usage, but because, given the relevant political community's history, they are morally true (while being irreducibly distinct from utilitarian or other collective-goal-based policies); and that legal theory, as adjudication's prologue, is a practical enterprise of 'creative interpretation', participating in developing a 'liberal' legal system which, without violating integrity by repudiating too many of its 'materials' (constitution, enactments, and precedents), will treat citizens with equality of concern and respect. The debate about these theses asks whether Dworkin's rather unarticulated moral theory is sound, whether the analogy with creative literary interpretation is not a new form of reductive explanation, and whether the claim that the law, even in hard cases, can always be identified by moral reasoning about the legal materials is not, likewise, a reductive oversight of law's dependence on authoritative choice (will) between reasonable alternatives still legally open.   J.M.F.

Guido Fasso, *Storia della filosofia del diritto* (Bologna, 1970).
John Finnis, *Natural Law and Natural Rights* (Oxford, 1980).
Wolfgang Friedmann, *Legal Theory*, 5th edn. (London, 1967).
H. F. Jolowicz, *Lectures on Jurisprudence* (London, 1963).
J. M. Kelly, *A Short History of Western Legal Theory* (Oxford, 1992).
Alfred Verdross, *Abendlaendische Rechtsphilosophie* (Vienna, 1958).
Michel Villey, *Leçons d'histoire de la philosophie du droit* (Paris, 1957).

law, indeterminacy in: *see* indeterminacy in law.

law, moral: *see* moral law.

law, natural: *see* natural law; laws, natural or scientific.

law, positive. A term (*jus positivum*) launched in philosophical commentary (Thierry of Chartres, *c.*1135, then Abelard), and focusing legal theory on to law's sources (*positum*, Latin 'laid down'). As Aquinas noted, earlier terminology confused rules 'human' in *use* with rules human in *origin*, though Plato and Aristotle had in substance distinguished (positive) law from morality. (*Natural law.)

Human positive law includes rules (e.g. against murder) and institutions (e.g. punishment) belonging also to natural law (i.e. morally required willy-nilly). Hart called these the 'minimum content of natural law', but meant the minimum content of positive law. Most laws are 'purely positive'; what they require was not morally required until their positing (though Aristotle, *Nicomachean Ethics* v. 1134[b], exaggerates in saying that they are on 'matters [morally] *indifferent* in themselves').   J.M.F.

*law, history of the philosophy of; feminist philosophy of law; law and continental philosophy.

Karl Olivecrona, *Law as Fact*, 2nd edn. (London, 1971).

law, problems of the philosophy of. How can there be a philosophy of law distinct from ethics, political philosophy, or a general social theory building on social anthropology and comparative history?

If ethics inquires into standards of right judgement in deliberation towards choice and action, philosophy of law investigates the relation of those standards to the directives laid down, by usage or authoritative decision, to guide people's actions in political community and thereby, purportedly, protect basic interests or rights, distribute burdens and advantages fairly, and restore the position of persons wronged. Thus legal philosophy goes beyond but cannot elude the main problems in ethics: whether moral propositions can be known as true; whether moral truths include intrinsic goods and reasons for action richer than Kantian conformity with reason's universalizing abstractness; whether right judgement is by maximizing values consequent on choice; how far choice is free and intention morally decisive.

If political philosophy investigates the grounds on which persons may (and do) claim authority to shape a community's actions by directing individual conduct, legal philosophy investigates reasons for and ways of making such authority and its exercise conditional on criteria of form (source, scope or *vires*, procedure, promulgation and publicity, adjudicative integrity, etc.). Thus legal philosophy adds to but is enmeshed in political philosophy's main issues: e.g. whether authority is justified by consent or by intent to benefit; whether interests are rights and rights secure equality, liberty, or other benefits; whether political action is well understood on the model of decisions in economics or competitive games.

If social theory generalizes from knowledge of particular societies and events in their history, legal philosophy investigates how such societies can be implicit subjects or bearers of legal systems' elements. It thus confronts main problems of general social theory: how to identify a subject-matter which can subsist as regimes and constitutions change and disappear; how to select and justify descriptive and analytical concepts and terms, given the variety of social self-interpretations and competing vocabularies disclosed by ethnography and comparative historical and cross-cultural studies.

Legal philosophy is often (e.g. John Austin, H. L. A. Hart, Joseph Raz) divided into analytical and critical. Analytical jurisprudence is to consider the definition of law, the theory of legal system, the analysis of legal concepts such as duty, transaction, and intention, and the theory of legal reasoning, especially in adjudication. Critical philosophy of law is to evaluate law and legal obligation, the minimum substantive content of legal systems, the interlocking procedural virtues called the rule of law, etc. But against such a division, and the similar recent division between conceptual (or explanatory) and justificatory, it can be said that legal systems are created and maintained for reasons, and these like every reason for action presuppose and/or propose evaluation(s). Any general account of legal systems (or of the concept of law and legal system) must identify those shaping evaluations.

Still, cannot descriptive or conceptual analysis of law's character as means to end(s) proceed without evaluating—and *a fortiori*, or at least, without morally evaluating—the diverse purposes and uses to which the instrument is put? It seems not. For law's characteristic purport as obligatory and authoritative, like its purport as stipulating appropriate procedures and requiring fair trials and judgments based on truth, itself proposes an evaluation and critique—mainly if not exclusively moral—of alternative social conditions (anarchy, arbitrary domination). How, then, could there be an adequately inward understanding or analysis of what characterizes diverse legal systems—an account showing why law deserves a place in any truly general account of human social life—without an understanding of the ways law's characteristic features themselves (even when being unjustly manipulated) manifest a critical evaluation of, and value-affirming constructive response to, the sorts of injustice or other lesion of human good which are inherent in lawlessness? (Analogously, one may understand, describe, and analyse an argument without accepting or approving it; but can one understand, describe, or analyse *argument* unless one accepts some arguments as good and adopts as normative for one's description the criteria by which their soundness is recognizable?)

Law is somehow an institution or product of human deliberative reasoning, and addressed to human deliberative reasoning. Laws and legal systems, like the human persons who are their makers and subjects, somehow belong to all the four sorts of order with which human reason is concerned—roughly, natural, logical, moral, and cultural/technical. Using the conventional symbols and syntax of an ordinary language, and supplementing them with new conventions and techniques, legal rules articulate conceptions of the natural order (which reason does not make but only considers), of logical consistency and implication, and above all of rightness and wrongness in official and unofficial deliberation and action. This articulation is highly reflexive: Kelsen's slogan 'the law regulates its own creation' captures some of this reflexivity. Indeed, even philosophical reflections on law (and nature, logic, morality, and non-legal techniques) are often found among the concepts and terms manipulated in making, interpreting, and using legal rules, institutions, and processes. Legal philosophy is always tempted to resolve the resulting complexity into the relative simplicity of just one paradigm of order, on the basis of just one paradigm of description, analysis, or explanation.

Take causation. Some legal-philosophical accounts, particularly German accounts since Kant, have proposed that causing is by physical movements, and is unaffected by acting persons' purposes or other states of mind (which are relevant only to imputing culpability or legal liability). Such accounts of human causality are modelled on natural-scientific accounts of causality as regularities, or probabilities, or some inherent property of objects or events. Some other legal theories of causation, particularly American theories, have reduced 'cause in fact' to the minimal *conditio sine qua non* ('But for *C*, *E* would not have occurred'), and contended that 'cause in law' is merely a construct of social (i.e. moral and/or cultural) policies

about who is now to take the blame and/or pay. Against these reductions stands an account such as Hart and Honoré's. It accepts that judicial findings that someone's act caused some event and/or loss are justified by considerations substantially independent of moral conclusions or other policies about liability (blame and recompense); it adds, however, that the same is true of judicial findings that the event or loss was caused by someone's omission. It accepts that all such findings are similar to scientific, historical, and common-sense conceptions in distinguishing the causally relevant as a subclass of conditions *sine qua non*. But, on Hart and Honoré's account, the central causal concept, of deviation from normal conditions, itself extends to include conditions culturally established as conventional expectations or legal duties; attributions of causal responsibility are nested in, but are not reducible to, conceptions of role- and liability-responsibility, distributions of burden of proof, criteria and methods of proof, and other, in themselves non-causal considerations. The complexity of such a non-reductive account mirrors the irreducible complexity of the life, deeds, and efficacy of beings who live in the natural world as reasoning and choosing agents, artificers and creators.

Again, take legal personality. Some say: only members of the natural species human being are properly the subject of legal relations; lawyers' talk of other juridical subjects (corporations, unincorporated associations, ships, idols, etc.) is of mere, albeit useful, fictions. Others (e.g. Kelsen) say: the status of legal person is simply a creation of the law, which freely bestows or withholds it; the logic of legal rules leaves no room for attributing to human beings a legally cognizable priority. Another approach denies that human associations are mere fictions, acknowledges the convenience of attributing to associations and even non-human entities the status of subject of legal rules and processes, accepts that in a logical analysis of legal rules and relationships the human subject has no priority, but maintains that since the very point of guiding deliberation by law is to protect and promote the good of human beings, and since, prior to any human decision, subjects of that kind are naturally constituted as persons, in their radical potentiality and/or actuality, laws are radically disordered precisely as laws when they deny to any human being (slaves, embryos, *et al.*) the 'equal protection of the law' (minimally, equality of fundamental legal status and immunity).

As the foregoing makes evident, the vexed problem of *defining* law cannot be resolved by any purely 'analytical' or conceptual technique aspiring to be neutral and conceptually prior to the taking of substantive positions on disputed questions about, for example, the natural and the moral orders. Of course, stipulative definitions and/or lexicographical clarifications assist inquiry and should avoid begging disputed questions. But explanatory definitions summarize the results of, not linguistic data or regulations for, philosophical reflection. In legal philosophy it is particularly easy to see the value of a long-neglected classical technique announced by Aristotle, practised by his medieval followers, and revived, if not fully consistently deployed, by Hart: take as the subject of an explanatory definition the *central case* of the explanandum (and correspondingly the *focal meaning* of the term signifying that reality), and treat as secondary and relatively peripheral, but by no means unimportant or irrelevant, the many realities which instantiate the central case in only a watered-down, immature, or defective way (and correspondingly the secondary uses of the term). Then one can say that a legal system which denies the legal personality and/or fails to protect the fundamental rights of some members of the human community it regulates and serves is not merely unjust and immoral but also a poor specimen of a legal system.

But note: such a thesis depends on the further, widely disputed premiss that what counts as the central case or fine specimen of a subject-matter of social (e.g. legal) philosophy is settled by reference to the evaluative concerns not of 'bad citizens' concerned only to avoid sanctions (as American legal realists proposed), nor of morally unconcerned judges or other officials as such (as Hart proposed), but rather of people who understand, accept, and promote law *as* a morally motivated and justified response to the evils and injustices of legally unregulated human relationships. The premiss is most easily defended when law is being considered in the course of a philosophical reflection which is from beginning to end practical, that is, concerned with the question, What should I (the reflecting person, the philosopher) choose and do?—a question asked not in relation to some particular situation and objective, but in the open horizon of one's whole life. That is the question shaping the whole course of Aristotle's two-volume philosophical reflection on 'human affairs', his *Ethics* and *Politics*, and of philosophical work clear-headedly in the same broad tradition. When this is the question, unjust laws and morally unconcerned or immoral viewpoints, though instructive, are evidently as *non-central* as, analogously, fallacious forms of argument are non-central (though instructive) in a philosophy of argumentation, and doomed strategies, bad recipes, or quack remedies are non-central (though instructive) in the arts of war, cooking, or medicine. Still, the premiss can also be defended even when the legal- or social-philosophical question is not itself practical, but descriptive, seeking merely to understand law, contemplatively, as a kind of reality found in many times and places. The defence will be dialectical: only those who understand, accept, commend, and promote the rule of law as an indispensable means of avoiding the evils and injustices of legally unregulated communities and relationships have sufficient reason not only to maintain and uphold the rule of law when it is in place but also, when it is not in place, to (re)introduce it, with just that complex set of features which legal philosophers of every school agree are its characteristics.

Such issues of definition and explanatory methodology are issues within the order of logic, i.e. of the rational order we introduce into our own thinking. Some of the problems peculiar to legal philosophy arise primarily within this order. How does the propositional character of legal rules differ from that of legal principles or other legal standards? What are the types of logical opposition between rules, and to what extent is contradiction between rules possible in a legal system? Are all rules of, or at least reducible to, one logical type, such as the imposing of obligation on pain of sanction or the hypothetical authorization of sanctions? If so, are the logical types correlated with the social functions or point of different sorts of rules? What are the irreducibly distinct types of right (perhaps claim, liberty, power, immunity)? Are rights mere logical constructs from, or shadows of, a logically or explanatorily prior concept of duty? Is a liberty (permission) the mere absence of a contrary duty, or does it entail a prohibition of some (or all) types of interference by A in the exercise of B's liberty, and if so would it always or ever entail that B has a liberty-right to do what he ought not to?

These and similar issues have an irreducibly logical core. But progress in resolving them requires close attention to the special meaning and use of terms such as 'rule', 'obligation', 'right', and 'liberty' within the specific cultural and technical construct called the law. That construct, in turn, characteristically serves certain human purposes, and does so by guiding deliberation. A truly general account of it cannot be limited to recording the purposes, aims, and techniques of one people, or to reproducing in a 'detached' mode their 'committed' discourse. It must, therefore, engage to some extent in reflection on the moral order (which we bring by reason into our deliberations towards choice and action), by asking when action is intelligently related to basic human purposes and reasons for action. In short, all the questions listed in the preceding paragraph require the taking of some position on the *point* of law. Is law most illuminatingly regarded as an instrument of social control, whatever the controllers' purposes—an instrument which merely *happens* to have the inherent capacity to serve justice, rights, and the common good, as hammers merely happen to have the inherent capacity to serve as murder weapons, paperweights, or wall decorations? Or does such an interpretation render much of the law's vocabulary and logic unintelligible or, at least, radically unexplained? Is law to serve liberty above all, or is the liberty it serves (if it does) only one among many fundamental benefits? Such questions may seem remote from a strictly logical analysis, but answers to them have proved to be necessary (though not sufficient) for analysis of the structure of legal systems as interrelated propositions or quasi-propositional meaning contents.

Efforts to reduce problems of legal philosophy to the logical order have issued in striking failures: e.g. Hobbes's attempt to explain contractual obligation by equating breach with logical absurdity; or Kant's claim that since B's wrong contradicts A's rightful use of freedom, A's (or C's) use of coercion 'to hinder' B's wrong must, 'by virtue of the law of non-contradiction', be compatible with rightful freedom. As such failures powerfully suggest, the normativity of practical reasoning and legal norms is not reducible to logic's normativity, but rests on the necessity of means to or respect for basic ends.

Some have handled law-related moral problems and concepts by declaring them foreign to legal philosophy, or redefining them as cultural/technical, not moral. Does the injustice of a law affect its authority, validity, or authoritativeness? Is equity a matter simply of interpretation, or can it correct the intentions of the law givers? Do laws (and contracts) creating obligations entail no more than an obligation to pay the penalty (or damages) for 'non-fulfilment'? (And if so, is the last-mentioned obligation reducible to an obligation not to assault the bailiffs? And so on . . .) Problems such as these have been said to be matter merely for individual conscience, morality, or ethics. But in the proper (conscientious) performance of their judicial office as such, judges cannot avoid such questions. And there are others even more essentially concerned with the adjudicative role. Is it right for a judge to change the law at the cost of defeating the legitimate expectations of the unsuccessful litigant? Or to override the deliberately adopted policies of a democratic majority? Can judges rely upon their own personal knowledge unsupported or even opposed by the evidence admissibly tendered in the case? And then there are the responsibilities summarized in the ideal of a rule of law (*Rechtsstaat*): to ensure that there is law and that it is clear, coherent, stable, public, practicable, non-retroactive, general, and above all respected in official (including judicial) action. Is this set of purposes and features of legal ordering morally neutral (like the sharpness of a knife for cutting)? Or must the set, taken as a whole, have the moral purpose of securing a relationship of reciprocity between rulers and ruled, in recognition of the dignity and rights of the ruled?

To conclude that such questions are properly part of legal philosophy is not to take sides in the perennial debate whether to define the law as whatever standards are cognizable from social-factual sources (legislation, custom, judicial precedent), or rather as whatever standards judges should take into account in giving judgment.

It remains that laws are manifestly in the cultural/technical order (order which, by reasoning, we bring into matter subject to our power); they are objects created by human decision as an instrument of social co-ordination. This aspect of law's *positivity* seems put in question both by theories (*legal realism) which reduce the law to a prediction of judicial action, and by theories (e.g. Dworkin's 'law as integrity') which locate the law not in any existing rules and standards (considered to be merely 'legal materials') but only in the act of judgment by a judge who, in a 'creative interpretation' subjects the 'legal materials' to ultimately individual moral assessment.

Law's many and varied artefacts include first the rules of law themselves. Even those rules which give legal expression to a moral norm are truly positive laws and usually of an artificial form: the law does not formally forbid murder, but rather specifies that murder is an offence, attaches penalties, disqualifications, and other legal consequences to offences, and posits (usually by implication) that 'offences' are not to be committed. Still, most legal rules are no mere repromulgations of moral norms, but

products of an irreducibly creative social decision. Their authenticity is a matter not immediately of moral truth, but rather of the considerations of form, source, and procedure encapsulated in the characteristically legal concept of validity.

Most other legal artefacts can be classed under another characteristically legal term: institutions. Legal institutions include not only public bodies such as courts and legislatures, but also types of legal arrangement involving clusters of rules (contract, sale, property, corporations, crime, delict, etc.) and specific instances of such types, deliberately instituted for the sake of their legal effect (thus a particular delict or crime). And these artefacts are to be distinguished from any documents used to create or record them. Obviously, then, the description and explanation of such artefacts would be complex even if the cultural/technical order could be sealed off from the orders of nature, logic, and morality. But it cannot, and some of the most intense debates in contemporary legal philosophy concern the moral and other (e.g. causation) foundations of the legal institutions of crime, tort (delict), contract, and property.

Other legal artefacts include definitions, whose purpose is not, as in legal philosophy, to summarize an understanding of central (and non-central) cases and focal (and secondary) meanings, but rather to assign objects and topics of human social life to universal classes for the purposes of a given rule (e.g. taxing or registering 'ships'); and inference rules establishing presumptions for legal judgment on facts. Definitions and inference rules meet in the peculiarly legal practice of *deeming X* to be an instance of *Y*.

Many problems of legal philosophy are displayed in the problems associated with the *interpretation* of constitutions, statutes, judgments, and other legal instruments (documents) and arrangements. Should legal interpreters find and follow the commitments originally made in the morally significant choices and intentions of the makers? Or should they give the language used—a set of conventional objects deployed to make a new and free-standing cultural object (the constitution, the Act of . . ., etc.)—a new meaning and effect in accordance with new conventional understandings of the language? Are not both the act of legislation and the act of judicial interpretation (though immediately and directly exercises of a cultural technique) limited in their plasticity or malleability not only by other conventions but also by the natural givenness of certain necessary pre-conditions for human action, by the requirements of logical coherence, and by the moral significance of every human act?

Reflections on these and other ways in which legal philosophy is distinct from ethics, political philosophy, and general social theory are compatible with expecting (anticipating and requiring) that its concepts and theses be compatible and even harmonious with the concepts and theses of those other disciplines or modes of inquiry. For it is one and the same set of persons and communities of persons that is the subject (subject-matter and agent) of them all.   J.M.F.

*causality.

Jules Coleman, *The Practice of Principle* (Oxford, 2001).
—— and Scott Shapiro (eds.), *The Oxford Handbook of Jurisprudence and Philosophy of Law* (Oxford, 2002).
Ronald Dworkin, *Law's Empire* (Cambridge, Mass., 1986).
Robert George (ed.), *Natural Law Theory* (Oxford, 1992).
—— (ed.), *The Autonomy of Law* (Oxford, 1996).
H. L. A. Hart and Tony Honoré, *Causation in the Law*, 2nd edn. (Oxford, 1985).
Joseph Raz, *The Authority of Law* (Oxford, 1979).

law, rule of: *see* rule of law.

law, scepticism about. Scepticism about law can be understood in at least two senses. In a weaker meaning it is most usually attached to criticisms of the legal profession and refers to scepticism about specific features of legal practice and procedure. In this sense it dates back at least to Plato's castigation of forensic oratory as narrow, constrained, manipulative, and untruthful in the *Gorgias* and *Theaetetus*. In subsequent history criticism of the venality and immorality of legal practice has tended to focus on the obscurity and illogicality of legal argument as well as upon the arbitrariness of legal judgment. From Rabelais to the modern schools of *legal realism, sceptics have argued that legal decision-making is divorced from legal rules and that the power of law-making lies in the unfettered discretion of judges, tribunals, and law enforcement agencies. In contemporary Anglo-American jurisprudence the term 'rule scepticism' thus denotes a scepticism about the necessary relationship between legal rules or the 'law in books' and judicial practice, while 'fact scepticism' asserts that the indeterminacy of fact-finding procedures renders all reference to rules problematic.

In a stronger sense, scepticism about law extends the criticism of the arbitrariness or injustice of legal judgment into arguments for the abolition of law, or predictions of the end of law. In this meaning, criticism of the profession and practice of law are taken cumulatively to condemn the institution of law as an unethical and unnecessary form of human relation. In this sense the earliest radical scepticism about law is to be associated with Sir Thomas More's fictional *Utopia* and subsequently with the various strands of anarchist and socialist political theory. The broad argument of such theories has been that the ideal of human *freedom and specifically of self-determination is antithetical to the demands of legal governance. To the extent that *law is necessarily coercive and repressive of human autonomy it is an evil and can have no part to play in a free society. The authority of law is in this perspective an ideological manipulation and is predicated upon a domination or repression of the ultimate human good which resides in a society of free association. The practice of law was perceived to be violent, irrational, and necessary only for the preservation of private property or the good of an élite minority.

While early anarchistic and utopian-socialist arguments against law tended to be either nostalgic, recalling a primitive age of innocence, or oneiric, specifying utopia in terms of an ideal but unmapped future territory, a more substantive scepticism about law emerged within the *Marxist tradition of political theory. Where Marx had adverted somewhat incidentally and allusively to an end of history, a communist society in which freedom would displace law and in which the state would wither away, subsequent elaborations of a Marxist critique of law developed more specific analyses of legal domination. In its strongest form, Marxist scepticism about law proceeds from an analysis of economic exploitation and argues that the legal order and its substantive rules are a more or less complex reflection of the class relations which constitute the reality of social experience. Within this broadly deterministic view of legal relations scepticism about law takes the form of critique of the ideology of the rule of law. Far from treating all legal subjects as free and equal before the law, legal rules are ideological in the sense of masking the real (economic) conditions of *inequality and constraint which predetermine the content and the effect of law.

In what is arguably its most sophisticated expression in the writings of the post-revolutionary Russian jurist Pashukanis, law was to be understood as a direct expression of the commodity form of production and the legal subject was no more than the fictively free and equal subject who would come to market and buy and sell. The legal relation was thus exemplified by contract and by the unequal economic conditions within which goods were exchanged. For Pashukanis, the legal form was thus a bourgeois species of human relation and law would come to an end with the demise of the economic system upon which it was based. While contemporary scepticism about law derives, both directly and indirectly, from Marxist and *communitarian anarchist critiques of law, it tends to be more partial and less millenarian in its approaches. Contemporary critical legal scholarship is broadly reformist in its goals yet also argues that law exploits and dominates to the benefit of vested economic and political interests. In common with *feminist analyses of law, critical jurisprudence thus proposes an ethical critique law. The doctrinal tradition and its various positivistic justifications are analysed as abstract mystifications of the substantive injustices of legal practice. While such criticisms of law do not predict a foreseeable end to the legal order they are sceptical of the ethical value of law and argue in favour of alternative forms of relation and of social regulation.   P.GOOD.

*indeterminacy in law; law, problems of the philosophy of.

M. Cain and A. Hunt (eds.), *Marx and Engels on Law* (London, 1979).
J. N. Frank, *Law and the Modern Mind* (first pub. 1930; Garden City, NY, 1963).
E. Pashukanis, *Law and Marxism: A General Theory* (London, 1978).
D. Sugarman (ed.), *Legality, Ideology and the State* (London, 1983).
R. M. Unger, *The Critical Legal Studies Movement* (Cambridge, Mass., 1986).

P. Williams, *The Alchemy of Race and Rights* (Cambridge, Mass., 1991).

R. P. Wolff, *In Defence of Anarchism* (New York, 1976).

law and continental philosophy. In its contemporary usage within Anglo-American jurisprudence, continental philosophy refers most broadly to the non-analytic traditions of modern European thought. In this generic sense, *continental philosophy refers initially to Hegelian, Marxian, and Husserlian theories of law and of meaning. In a more recent and particular sense it refers to theoretical and methodological positions associated with or developed from structural linguistics, literary theory, and psychoanalysis. The classic texts are read mainly through their contemporary expositors but the translation and use of continental thought bears an aura of radicalism. Continental philosophy has the connotation of a reaction against the dominant tradition and methodology of common law jurisprudence. Exponents of continental theory, who may generally be termed critical legal scholars, are critical of the *positivism and *empiricism of Anglo-American legal theory and specifically of the belief in the autonomy of law and the determinacy of legal rules. Drawing widely, and often rather loosely, upon a variety of different areas of continental thought, critical legal scholarship seeks to deconstruct the established tradition and legitimizing function of common-law jurisprudence and to elaborate in its place more democratic and ethically based theories of the plurality of laws and of the indeterminacy or socially constructed and contingent character of legal meanings.

The use of continental philosophy as a form or source of critique draws upon too wide a range of thinkers and disciplines for it to be possible to provide a synoptic account of such scholarship. It is possible, however, to point to certain common themes, which include a pronounced comparative dimension to legal study and a concern with the textual character of law and its cultural determinations, an interest which suggests a turn towards historicism. The more distinctive ethical and ontological themes of continental philosophy, the concerns with being and nothingness, identity and difference, similarity and otherness, find a translation and application in a variety of critical theories of legal textuality. While continental influence upon legal scholarship cannot be reduced to radical *hermeneutics, it may not be inaccurate to point to a shared desire to provide political and ethical readings of the legal tradition and of its texts. In this sense the turn to continental philosophy has become synonymous with a pluralistic and interdisciplinary critique of the unity and insularity of the legal tradition. Drawing latterly upon disciplines or movements as distinct as *phenomenology, *feminism, psychoanalysis, literary criticism, and *discourse theory, critical scholarship uses continental philosophy to attack the closure of law and to undermine the doctrinal belief in the law as a discrete system of rules.   P.GOOD.

D. Carlson *et al.* (eds.), *Deconstruction and the Possibility of Justice* (New York, 1992).

D. Cornell, *Beyond Accommodation: Ethical Feminism, Deconstruction and the Law* (New York, 1993).

V. Descombes, *Modern French Philosophy* (Cambridge, 1980).

Costas Douzinas *et al.*, *Postmodern Jurisprudence* (London, 1989).

Peter Goodrich, *Legal Discourse* (London, 1987).

law and morals. Legal philosophers have debated three views about the connection between legal and moral truth—between what the law is and what it should be.

One view—*legal positivism—insists that legal reasoning is entirely factual: what the law is depends only upon what has been declared to be law by whichever officials the public treats as having that authority, or on similar historical facts, and on nothing else. On that view, though moral views that are popular within a community are very likely to influence the laws its legislators adopt, there is no necessary connection between law and moral truth, and abstract moral considerations play no role in deciding what the law is.

According to a second—apparently opposite—view, which is a version of so-called *'natural law' theory, legal reasoning is identical with moral reasoning, so that, at least on fundamental matters, the only real law in force in any community is the moral law, and any laws a legislature might make contrary to that moral law are invalid. On that view, the alleged legal system of a tyranny like Nazi Germany is not law at all.

On the third view, legal reasoning interprets rather than simply describes or judges legal history: it aims to reformulate past legal decisions in the most coherent and morally attractive way consistent with the facts of legal history, that is, with the words past legislators used, the concrete orders past judges actually made, and the political and moral traditions of the community. Understood as interpretative in this sense, legal reasoning is not just historical investigation, nor abstract moral reasoning about what rules or principles would be appropriate to an ideally just world, but combines elements of both.

Neither of the first two positions fits the actual practice of lawyers and judges. Contrary to legal positivism, they often offer moral arguments to support their claims about what the law actually is when the law is controversial or unclear: when the question arises, for example, whether the right to 'due process of law' in the American Constitution includes the right to freedom of choice about abortion, or whether a particular string of past judicial decisions allowing people injured in accidents to recover damages for their pain and suffering does or does not 'embody' a more general principle allowing recovery for any kind of emotional damage. Lawyers and judges divide, in their opinions about such matters, in ways that plainly reflect their moral convictions. They all concede, however, contrary to the natural law theory I described, that there is often a gap between what the law is and what they believe it should be: even lawyers who believe that tax rates are unjustly high or low do not declare them invalid on that ground, and even lawyers who think that the laws of Nazi Germany were so unjust that they should not have been enforced by Nazi judges hesitate to say that they were not law at all.

The third, interpretative, view of law fits the practices of lawyers, judges, and other legal officials naturally and convincingly, however. It explains why, in some cases, they recognize as law even what they believe to be unjust: no 'interpretation' of the tax code which substituted a different tax rate could count as a genuine interpretation of the text. It also explains why, in other kinds of cases, judges do treat moral considerations as relevant. In controversial cases, when a variety of different interpretations would each fit the abstract statutory language or the results of actual past decisions, judges must choose among them by deciding which interpretation—which understanding of the due process clause or of liability for emotional damages, for example—better reflects people's moral and political rights and obligations.

It may be objected that on the interpretative view law is inherently *subjective: that there is no law except what the judge thinks it is. But that presupposes that the morality of rights and obligations is inherently subjective. If it is, then so is law, at least in controversial cases. But though many legal philosophers have endorsed the subjectivity of morals as a philosophical thesis, few actually respect it in practice, and arguments for it are implausible.   R.D.

*moral scepticism.

Ronald Dworkin, *Law's Empire* (Cambridge, Mass., 1986).
Lon Luvois Fuller, *The Morality of Law* (New Haven, Conn., 1964).
H. L. A. Hart, *The Concept of Law* (Oxford, 1961).

laws, natural or scientific. In normal discourse, the term 'law of nature' signifies some basic or fundamental principle of science, such as Newton's law of universal gravitation, or the second law of thermodynamics. Such truths as 'Water always boils at 100° C at standard pressure', or 'Air resistance is proportional to velocity' are normally considered to be too specific to qualify as laws of nature. Within the philosophy of science, however, all these generalizations are counted alike as laws of nature. This is because one of the central problems in the philosophy of science is to explain what distinguishes general truths of all these kinds from accidental patterns.

This problem arises as a corollary of David Hume's analysis of *causality as *constant conjunction*. Philosophers prior to Hume assumed that causation involves some *power* by which causes produce their effects, some *cement*, so to speak, which binds cause and effect together. But Hume argued that there is no such cement. All we observe is first the occurrence of the cause, followed by the occurrence of the effect. There is nothing to bind them together, apart from the fact that they are constantly conjoined, in the sense that events like the causes are always, as it happens, followed by events like the effect.

But if causal laws involve nothing more than constant conjunction, an obvious problem arises. Suppose the following statement is true: 'Whenever I go to Paris, it rains'. Then my going to Paris is constantly conjoined with its raining there. But we wouldn't on this account want to count this as a causal law. It doesn't rain *because* I go to Paris. It just so happens that my visits are invariably followed by rain. However, what then distinguishes real laws of nature from such accidentally true generalizations? For Hume tells us that there isn't anything more than constant conjunction involved in genuine laws either.

Note that genuine laws but not accidents support *counterfactual conditionals. Compare 'If the water in that kettle had been at 100° C, it would have started boiling' (true) with 'If I had gone to Paris last week, it would have started raining' (false). Taken on its own, however, this contrast simply restates the problem. For however we understand counterfactual claims, we will still need some explanation of why laws but not accidents support them, if both are simply statements of constant conjunction.

There are two general lines of solution to the problem of distinguishing laws from accidents. The first remains faithful to the Humean view that law statements assert nothing more than constant conjunction, and then seeks to explain why some statements of constant conjunction—the laws—are more important than others—the accidents. The alternative, non-Humean strategy rejects the Humean presupposition that laws involve nothing more than constant conjunction, and instead postulates a relationship of 'necessitation' or *nomic necessity which obtains between event-types which are related by law, but not between those which are only accidentally conjoined.

At first sight it might seem easy to develop the Humean strategy. Cannot we simply require that laws be truly *general*, and not restricted to such things as what happened to a particular person in a particular city at particular times? However, this does not get to the heart of the matter. For even if we formulate our example in general terms, not mentioning me or Paris, but specifying a certain *kind* of person and city, it may still be that the only instances of these kinds in the universe are still, by accident, constantly conjoined with rain. Conversely, there seem to be examples of laws which are restricted in space and time, such as Kepler's law that the planets move in ellipses, which is specific to our solar system.

A better suggestion is that accidents, unlike laws, are no good for predicting the future. This is not because accidental patterns cannot stretch into the future, but rather because, when they do, we cannot know that they are true. J. L. Mackie has argued that laws differ from accidents in that they are *inductively supported* by their instances, whereas accidents can only be known to be true after all their instances have been exhaustively checked.

However, even if Mackie's criterion is necessary for lawhood, it is not clear whether it is sufficient: couldn't some inductively anticipatable patterns still be accidents? Perhaps a better Humean solution is that proposed by F. P. Ramsey, and later revived by David Lewis: laws are those true generalizations that can be fitted into an ideal systematization of knowledge—or, as Ramsey put it, laws are a 'consequence of those propositions which we should take as axioms if we knew everything and organized it as simply as possible in a deductive system'. Accidents are then those true generalizations which cannot be explained within such an ideal theory.

In recent years a number of philosophers have rejected the Humean tradition, arguing that no account, however sophisticated, which equates laws with constant conjunctions can do justice to the real content of laws. In the late 1970s D. M. Armstrong, Fred Dretske, and Michael Tooley independently developed the thesis that laws express a relationship of 'necessitation' between properties. This relationship holds between properties which are related by law, but not between those which are only accidentally conjoined. So laws involve something more than Humean regularity: necessitation implies constant conjunction, but not conversely. Defenders of this view do not wish to suggest that the relationship of necessitation can be known *a priori; rather, which properties necessitate which others is an empirical matter to be settled by a posteriori investigation.

Critics of the non-Humean approach complain that merely postulating a relationship of necessitation leaves the philosophical issues unsolved. Hume himself rejected necessitation on the grounds that it is not observable. Contemporary critics do not object to unobservability *per se*, but they do object that the non-Humean view gives no real explanation of what necessitation adds to constant conjunction, and of exactly why this extra component should support counterfactual claims about what would happen if things were different.

Despite these objections, some version of the non-Humean approach to laws may prove necessary to deal with probabilistic laws, that is, laws which say that all *A*s have a probability *p* of being *B*s. The natural generalization of the Humean approach would take these laws to state, not that *A* is constantly conjoined with *B*, but rather that 100*p* per cent of *A*s are conjoined with *B*s. Humeans could then seek to explain why some such statements of proportionate conjunction are regarded seriously as laws, while others are merely accidents. The difficulty facing this Humean approach, however, is that the exact proportionate conjunction of 100*p* per cent of *A*s with *B*s is not even a necessary condition for the truth of the probabilistic law—for example, a unique type of coin may have a 0.5 probability of heads, and yet, by chance, come down heads six times in the only ten tosses that are ever made with it. For this reason, it is uncontroversial that probabilistic laws state something other than actual proportions. Non-Humeans conclude that they state quantitative relationships of necessitation—property *A* necessitates property *B* to degree *p*. Whether this is the only way to construe such laws, however, will remain an open question as long as the interpretation of *probability is an area of active philosophical controversy.   D.P.

*ceteris paribus.

D. M. Armstrong, *What is a Law of Nature?* (Cambridge, 1983).
T. Honderich, *A Theory of Determinism* (Oxford, 1988), ch. 1.
D. Papineau, 'Laws and Accidents', in G. Macdonald and C. Wright (eds.), *Fact, Science and Morality* (Oxford, 1986).

laws of thought. Traditionally these are 'What is, is' (confusingly called the law of identity) and 'Nothing both is and is not' (the law of *non-contradiction); and sometimes also the law of *excluded middle. They are certainly not descriptive laws, telling how people think, but rather prescriptive, telling people how to think or, more precisely, to reason. (*Reasoning.) So a better name is 'rules of logic'. There is no good reason to select these laws as special, although the first two of them are not often disputed. Even logicians with the meanest conception of the scope of deductive reasoning, such as the supporters of *Intuitionism, need to add other laws to the first two (besides, non-deductive reasoning might have laws too). And even logicians with the most generous conception of that scope know that all three laws can be presented as 'theorems', derivable from some alternative basis.   C.A.K.

I. M. Copi, *Introduction to Logic* (London, 1978), 306–8.

learning. The acquisition of a form of knowledge or ability through the use of experience. Not all modifications of behaviour as a result of experience involve learning, although behaviourist theories of learning tend to assume otherwise. It is far from clear that changes of behaviour brought about by conditioning should be thought of as involving learning; the same applies to the biological phenomenon of 'imprinting', whereby something that happens at a certain point of an animal's life determines a subsequent form of behaviour. For learning to take place experience has to be *used* in some way, so that what results is in a genuine sense knowledge or is dependent on knowledge. On the other hand, learning need not involve intellectual processes such as those involved in inference, although an inference may produce new knowledge and if it involves experience it may then be a process of learning. It is arguable that all learning itself presupposes knowledge in some way, and this raises problems for *genetic epistemology.   D.W.H.

D. W. Hamlyn, *Perception, Learning and the Self* (London, 1983).

learning paradox. Hegel held that whatever we learn is part of an infinite wealth of knowledge, thoughts, etc. contained in a completely indivisible ego. If we do not remember what is learned we do not possess it and yet it is none the less there within us. It is preserved in us in spite of the fact that it does not exist. This doctrine concerning learning might well be called a paradox.

Other candidates for paradox concerning learning might be found in Plato arising from arguments tending to show that certain things are unlearnable because they must be known before any process of learning could be undertaken.   J.C.

G. W. F. Hegel, *Philosophie des Subjectiven Geistes*, tr. M. J. Petry as *Hegel's Philosophy of Subjective Spirit*, ii (Dordrecht, 1978), sect. 403.

Lebensweisheit: *see* popular philosophy.

Lebenswelt : *see* life and science.

Le Dœuff, Michèle (1948–). French philosopher with a scholarly interest in the philosophy of Francis Bacon, and More's *utopianism. She questions the boundaries of philosophy, while insisting upon philosophy's importance ('Ants and Women'). She is critical of professional philosophers' neglectful attitude to science, and argues that disputes within sciences are often epistemological (that is, properly philosophical). In *Hipparchia's Choice* she questions philosophy's pretensions to being a unique practice which achieves a pure clarity: philosophy is inevitably shaped by language, metaphor, and power relations. According to Le Dœuff feminists make a special contribution. Their critique of gender categories in philosophy, science, and the humanities is empirical, philosophical, political, and interdisciplinary. Feminists see clearly how discourses are elevated to the status of 'philosophical' by a process in which social power is involved.   E.J.F.

*feminism; Héloïse complex.

Michèle Le Dœuff, 'Ants and Women, or Philosophy without Borders', in A. Phillips Griffiths (ed.), *Contemporary French Philosophy* (Cambridge, 1987).
——— *Hipparchia's Choice* (Oxford, 1991).

Left, the. Parties of egalitarian transformation, claiming to speak for the 'people', or the dispossessed and impoverished among them. The term supposedly derives from seating arrangements in the French revolutionary assemblies. But older connotations of left-sidedness, having to do with irregular, spontaneous, free-wheeling, suspicious, or dangerous (*gauche* or *sinister*) attitudes and behaviour, may also play a part. If the designation is attributable to right-minded and respectable people, it is presumably derogatory. But it may also have been willingly embraced as a sign of oppositionist commitments.   M.WALZ.

*equality; well-being.

Leszek Kolakowski and Stuart Hampshire (eds.), *The Socialist Idea* (New York, 1974).

Left and Right Hegelians: *see* Hegelianism.

legal positivism, intending to oppose *natural law theory, denies any 'necessary connexion between law and morality'. Central theses among a loose cluster: (1) law is definable and explainable without evaluative predicates or presuppositions; (2) the law (e.g. of England now) is identifiable from exclusively factual sources (e.g. legislation, judicial precedents). Some versions deny that there is knowable moral truth. Most understand positive law as products of will, some as imperatives.   J.M.F.

*law, positive.

Gerald J. Postema, *Bentham and the Common Law Tradition* (Oxford, 1986).

legal realism maintains that positive law's normativity is reducible to social facts. American legal realists (e.g. Holmes, Llewellyn), influenced by *pragmatism, suggested that law is not really rules as directives but official

(particularly judicial) behaviour which legal propositions predict. Scandinavian legal realists (e.g. Olivecrona, Ross), more anti-metaphysical and nearer Comte's *positivism, typically hold that law's reality consists in experiences of being bound that are induced ('mystically' or 'psychologically') by legal directives.   J.M.F.

*law, positive.

Karl Olivecrona, *Law as Fact*, 2nd edn. (London, 1971).

legitimacy. Theories of legitimization attempt to offer reasons why a given state deserves the allegiance of its members. In a famous analysis, Max Weber identified three sources of legitimacy—traditions and customs, legal–rational procedures (e.g. voting), and individual charisma—some combination of which can be found in most political systems. Many philosophers have felt unhappy with this scheme, however, which leaves out substantive questions about the justice of the state and the protection it offers the individuals who belong to it. These theories have generally argued that a state's legitimacy depends upon its upholding certain human *rights, a thesis that is often expressed in terms of its ability to meet the criteria one would expect to emerge from some form of social contract between autonomous agents. This position was classically expressed by Hobbes, Locke, and Rousseau, and in more recent times by Rawls, although with important differences.   R.P.B.

D. Beetham, *The Legitimation of Power* (Basingstoke, 1991).
M. Weber, *Economy and Society*, ed. G. Roth and C. Wittich (Berkeley, Calif., 1978), pt. 1, ch. 3.

Lehrer, Keith (1936–). Arizona-based philosopher, best known for work in epistemology and philosophy of mind. Lehrer has steadfastly defended 'coherence' theories of *knowledge. The human mind, he argues, is essentially self-reflective: minds are 'metaminds'. Knowledge, justified belief, and freedom stem from the capacity to reflect on one's beliefs and desires and to evaluate these in the light of one's intellectual and practical values. A positive evaluation of a belief leads to its 'acceptance'; a positive evaluation of a desire to a preference for its satisfaction. When such evaluations are 'trustworthy' they yield, respectively, knowledge (providing the accepted belief is true) and freedom. In the social domain, one's positive evaluation of the beliefs and desires of others produces 'consensus'.   J.HEIL

*justification, epistemic.

K. Lehrer, *Metamind* (Oxford, 1990).

Leibniz, Gottfried Wilhelm (1646–1716), eminent rationalist philosopher who was born in Leipzig and died in Hanover. Leibniz was acquainted with all the major scientific developments of the second half of the seventeenth century. He made important contributions in geology, linguistics, historiography, mathematics, and physics, as well as philosophy. His professional training was in the law; he earned his living in the Court of Hanover by combining the roles of councillor, diplomat, librarian, and historian. He did his philosophy (as well as his physics and mathematics) in his spare time. Although the vast bulk of Leibniz's writings remained unpublished at his death, and a considerable amount is still unpublished, his contributions in the law, mathematics, physics, and philosophy were known and appreciated by his educated European contemporaries in virtue of what he did publish and in virtue of his vast correspondence with intellectuals in a variety of fields. He was best known in his lifetime for his contributions to mathematics, especially to the development of the *calculus. The debate concerning to whom priority of discovery should be assigned—Newton or Leibniz—captured the attention of their contemporaries. Current scholarly opinion seems to have reached the conclusion that each discovered the basic foundations of the calculus independently, that Newton's discovery preceded that of Leibniz's, but Leibniz's publication of the basic theory of the calculus preceded that of Newton.

Although Leibniz published only one book on philosophy in his lifetime—*The Theodicy* (1710)—he did publish considerable philosophical work in the leading learned European journals of the time; for example, 'Meditations on Knowledge, Truth, and Ideas' (1684), 'Brief Demonstration of a Notable Error of Descartes' (1686), 'Whether the Essence of Body Consists in Extension' (1691), 'New System of Nature' (1695), and 'On Nature Itself' (1698). He also wrote a book-length study of John Locke's *empiricism, *New Essays on Human Understanding*, but decided not to publish it when he learned of Locke's death.

Leibniz's philosophical thinking underwent significant development; the mature metaphysics, presented in barebones form in the *Monadology* (1714), is strikingly different from his early work on the nature of bodies. None the less, certain themes persist—the requirement that the basic individuals of an acceptable *ontology (the individual *substances) satisfy the most rigorous standards of substantial unity, and the requirement that individual substances be endowed with causal powers and, hence, be centres of genuine activity. In the *Monadology* Leibniz presented the main outlines of his mature metaphysical system unaccompanied by much in the way of argumentation in favour of the conclusions therein presented. Consider, for example, the first two paragraphs of the *Monadology*:

1. The Monad, which we shall discuss here, is nothing but a simple substance that enters into composites—simple, i.e. without parts.

2. And there must be simple substances, since there are composites; for the composite is nothing more than a collection, or aggregate, of simples.

These are striking doctrines. If true, the consequence would seem to be that there are no spatially extended substances. But surely the argument of paragraph 2 is in need of considerable support. Perhaps the most complete formulation of the relevant doctrines, and Leibniz's reasons for accepting these doctrines, occurs in his correspondence (1698–1706) with Burcher de Volder, a professor of philosophy at the University of Leiden. In this correspondence Leibniz formulated his basic ontological thesis in the following passage:

considering matters accurately, it must be said that there is nothing in things except simple substances, and, in them, nothing but perception and appetite. Moreover, matter and motion are not so much substances or things as they are the phenomena of percipient beings, the reality of which is located in the harmony of each percipient with itself (with respect to different times) and with other percipients.

In this passage Leibniz claimed that the basic individuals are immaterial entities lacking spatial parts whose properties are a function of their perceptions and appetites. In the correspondence with de Volder, as in the *Monadology*, Leibniz presented his major metaphysical theses concerning these simple immaterial substances. With respect to *causality he held the following theses. God creates, conserves, and concurs in the actions of each created substance. Each state of a created monad is a causal consequence of its preceding state, except for its initial state at creation and any other states that result from miraculous divine intervention. While intrasubstantial causality is the rule among created substances, according to Leibniz, he denied the possibility of intersubstantial causal relations among created substances. In what he denied, he agreed with Malebranche, but in affirming spontaneity, i.e. that each individual substance is the cause of its own states, he separated himself from Malebranche's occasionalism. The doctrine of the spontaneity of substance ensured for Leibniz that created individual substances were centres of activity, a feature he took to be a necessary condition of genuine individuality.

Leibniz was sensitive to the idea that this scheme is at odds with common sense—that there appear to be material entities that are spatially extended, existing in space, causally interacting with each other and with us. More than some of his rationalist contemporaries, Leibniz took the claims of common-sense seriously. In the second sentence of the passage quoted above Leibniz outlined his way of 'saving the appearances' that are sufficiently well-founded to deserve saving. Two theses are at the heart of his effort: (1) the thesis that each created monad perceives every other monad with varying levels of distinctness; (2) the thesis that God so programmed the monads at creation that, although none causally interacts with any other, each has the perceptions we would expect it to have, were they to interact, and each has the perceptions we would expect it to have, were there extended material objects that are perceived. The first is the thesis of universal expression; the second, the thesis of the *preestablished harmony. In the case of material objects, Leibniz formulated the rudiments of a version of phenomenalism, based on the pre-established harmony among the perceptions of the monads. In the case of apparent causal interactions among monads, Leibniz proposed an analysis according to which the underlying reality is an increase in the clarity of the relevant perceptions of the apparent causal agent, accompanied by a corresponding decrease in the clarity of the relevant perceptions of the entity apparently acted upon.

Leibniz's mature metaphysics includes a threefold classification of entities that must be accorded some degree of reality: ideal entities, well-founded phenomena, and actual existents, i.e. monads with their perceptions and appetites. Material objects are examples of well-founded phenomena, according to Leibniz, while space and time are ideal entities. In the following passage from another letter to de Volder, Leibniz formulated the distinction between actual and ideal entities:

in actual entities there is nothing but discrete quantity, namely, the multitude of monads, i.e. simple substances . . . But continuous quantity is something ideal, which pertains to possibles, and to actuals, insofar as they are possible. Indeed, a continuum involves indeterminate parts, whereas, by contrast, there is nothing indefinite in actual entities, in which every division that can be made, is made. Actual things are composed in the manner that a number is composed of unities, ideal things are composed in the manner that a number is composed of fractions. The parts are actual in the real whole, but not in the ideal. By confusing ideal things with real substances when we seek actual parts in the order of possibles and indeterminate parts in the aggregate of actual things, we entangle ourselves in the labyrinth of the continuum and in inexplicable contradictions.

Leibniz's consideration of the labyrinth of the continuum was one source of his monadology. Ultimately, he reached the conclusion that whatever can be infinitely divided without reaching entities that can not be further divided is not a basic individual in an acceptable ontology. In part, Leibniz's reasoning here turns on his beliefs that divisible entities of the sort noted can not satisfy the standards for substantial unity required of basic individuals. The originality and complexity of Leibniz's reasoning concerning these topics is on display in his correspondence with de Volder, and in his correspondence with Arnauld. In the process of refining the metaphysical considerations that shaped the monadology, Leibniz formulated and defended the following doctrines: the *identity of indiscernibles—the thesis that individual substances differ with respect to their intrinsic, non-relational properties; the theory of minute perceptions—that each created monad has some perceptions of which it lacks awareness; as well as the theses of universal expression, the pre-established harmony, and spontaneity, previously mentioned.

An important element in Leibniz's treatment of entities he regarded as ideal is his treatment of *space and *time, which is formulated in his correspondence with Samuel Clarke. Leibniz set out to explicate the notion of place and space in terms of the spatial relations among material objects, thereby avoiding commitment to space as an independent entity.

Another route to Leibniz's monadology may be traced beginning from some of his conclusions concerning certain of the well-founded phenomena, in particular, material objects. He argued that a correct application of Galileo's

discoveries concerning the acceleration of freely falling bodies to the phenomena of impact established that force is not to be identified with quantity of motion, i.e. mass times velocity, as Descartes had held, but is to be measured by mass times the velocity squared. From these physical results, Leibniz drew important metaphysical conclusions—that force, unlike quantity of motion, cannot be identified with some mode of extension and that, therefore, Descartes was mistaken in identifying matter with extension and its modifications. He concluded that each material substance must have an immaterial component, a substantial form, which accounts for its active force.

The labyrinth of the continuum, previously noted, is one of two labyrinths that, according to Leibniz, vex the human mind. The second concerns the possibility of free choice. The nub of this problem for Leibniz is to explain how things might have been otherwise than they are. Leibniz was committed to the concept-containment account of truth, i.e. that a proposition is true just in case the concept of its predicate is contained in the concept of its subject. But that seems to imply that all true propositions are conceptually true, and, hence, necessarily true, and that, therefore, things could not have been otherwise than they are. Leibniz denied that all conceptually true propositions are necessarily true, employing the doctrine of infinite analysis, affirming that in the case of contingent truths, the subject concept contains the predicate concept, but there is no finite analysis of the relevant concepts that establishes that fact. By contrast, Leibniz argued that in the case of necessary truths there is always a finite analysis of the relevant concepts that constitutes a proof of the proposition in question.

Leibniz made important contributions to philosophical theology. The *Theodicy* contains his solution to the problem of *evil, i.e. to the question how the facts concerning evil in this world can be consistent with the conception of God as omnipotent, morally perfect, and creator—a conception to which Leibniz was committed. One basic element in his answer to this question is his thesis that this is the best possible world. In outline, Leibniz reached this conclusion in the following manner. He was totally committed to the *principle of sufficient reason, i.e. the thesis that for every state of affairs that obtains there must be a sufficient reason why it obtains. Applied to God's choice of a possible world to create, the principle of sufficient reason implies that God must have a sufficient reason for creating just this world, according to Leibniz. But, given God's moral perfection, this reason must have to do with the value of the world selected. Hence, the world selected must be the best possible.

Leibniz also made what he took to be a significant contribution to the formulation of the *ontological argument for the existence of God. He claimed that the ontological argument, as formulated by Descartes, for example, proved that a perfect being exists, with one crucial proviso, namely, the premiss that a perfect being is possible. Leibniz believed that none of his predecessors had shown this premiss to be true, and so he set out to do so. The basic idea of his purported proof is this. A perfect being is a being with every perfection. A perfection is a simple, positive property. Therefore, there can be no demonstration that there is a formal contradiction involved in supposing that one and the same entity has all the perfections. Since there can be no demonstration of a formal contradiction, it must be possible for one and the same being to have them all. Such a being would be a perfect being. Hence, a perfect being is possible.

Although Leibniz was not as taken with epistemological problems as Descartes or the British Empiricists, none the less he made significant contributions to the theory of knowledge. In his commentary on John Locke, the *New Essays on Human Understanding*, Leibniz argued forcefully for the thesis that the mind is furnished with innate ideas. Leibniz summarized his debate with Locke on this point as follows:

Our differences are on matters of some importance. It is a matter of knowing if the soul in itself is entirely empty like a writing tablet on which nothing has as yet been written (tabula rasa) . . . and if everything inscribed there comes solely from the senses and experience, or if the soul contains originally the sources of various concepts and doctrines that external objects merely reveal on occasion.

The claim that some concepts and doctrines are innate to the mind is important for Leibniz's metaphysics as well as his theory of knowledge, because he held that some of the central concepts of metaphysics, e.g. the concepts of self, substance, and causation, are innate.

Throughout his career, Leibniz developed various systems of formal logic, most based on the concept containment account of truth, previously mentioned. Some of those systems provide the elements of an approach to formal logic that is a genuine alternative to Aristotelian logic and contemporary quantification theory.   R.C.SLE.

The definitive edn. of Leibniz's work, still a long way from completion, will be *G. W. Leibniz: Sämtliche Schriften und Briefe* (Darmstadt, 1923–). Series 2 and 6 are, respectively, the philosophical correspondence and writings. Currently, the most useful edn. is *G. W. Leibniz: Die philosophischen Schriften*, ed. C. J. Gerhardt, 7 vols. (Berlin, 1875–90).

The best source of bibliographical information concerning Leibniz's work is Émile Ravier, *Bibliographie des Œuvres de Leibniz* (Paris, 1937), as supplemented by Paul Schrecker, 'Une bibliographie de Leibniz', *Revue philosophique de la France et de l'Étranger* (1938).

The best source of bibliographical information concerning the secondary literature on Leibniz's work is Kurt Muller and Albert Heinekamp (eds.), *Leibniz-Bibliographie: Die Literatur uber Leibniz bis 1980* (Frankfurt am Main, 1984).

The most complete edn. of Leibniz's philosophical work in English is Leroy E. Loemker, *Gottfried Wilhelm Leibniz: Philosophical Papers and Letters* (Dordrecht, 1969). Also available are the *New Essays on Human Understanding*, tr. Peter Remnant and Jonathan Bennett (Cambridge, 1981), and the *Theodicy*, ed. Austin Farrer, tr. E. M. Huggard (New Haven, Conn., 1952). A useful selection with introduction and notes is *Leibniz: Philosophical Texts*, tr. and ed. R. Woolhouse and R. Francks (Oxford, 1998).

As a sample of the vast secondary literature on Leibniz, the following may be recommended: C. D. Broad, *Leibniz: An Introduction* (Cambridge, 1975); Benson Mates, *The Philosophy of Leibniz* (Oxford, 1986); Nicholas Rescher, *Leibniz: An Introduction to his Philosophy* (Totowa, NJ, 1979); Catherine Wilson, *Leibniz's Metaphysics* (Manchester, 1989); N. Jolley (ed.), *The Cambridge Companion to Leibniz* (Cambridge, 1994).

Leibniz's law: *see* identity of indiscernibles.

lemma. A lemma is a proposition put forward in the course of an *argument, often accompanied by its own proof. It thus differs from a premiss in that it need not occur at the start of the argument. In discussions of knowledge, the 'No false lemmas' principle is sometimes mentioned: this is the principle that a belief will not count as knowledge if the chain of reasoning that leads to it contains a false lemma.   R.P.L.T.

W. Hodges, *Logic*, sect. 11 (Harmondsworth, 1977).

Lenin, Vladimir Ilyich Ulyanov (1870–1924). Lenin was the leader of the Bolshevik faction in Russian politics and architect of the 1917 Revolution. Although thus not primarily interested in philosophy, his two major contributions in this field were of considerable influence.

The first of these, *Materialism and Empirio-Criticism* (1909) was an extended polemic against his fellow Bolshevik Bogdanov's espousal of Mach's view that the world consisted entirely of sensations. Lenin's account was largely a simplified version of the philosophy found in Engels's later writings. It consisted in a fairly crude materialism whose central themes were the two doctrines of the external reality of the world and the 'copy' theory of knowledge. Lenin was not so much interested here in the philosophical arguments as in maintaining his view that, under the circumstances, this was the only philosophy that would benefit the proletariat.

After the 1914 débâcle, however, Lenin took a much less instrumental view of philosophy. In order to reorientate his perspective in face of the catastrophe that had overtaken European socialism, Lenin spent an amazing amount of time studying Hegel in great detail. The contrast between *materialism and *idealism characteristic of his earlier work was now replaced by a contrast between dialectical and non-dialectical thinking. Lenin emphasized the influence of Hegel's *Logic* on Marx and even went so far as to claim that human consciousness not only reflected the objective world but created it. Although only published posthumously in 1929, the *Philosophical Notebooks* in which this study was recorded did much to renew interest in the Hegelian roots of Marxism.   D.McL.

*empirio-criticism.

L. Althusser, *Lenin and Philosophy* (London, 1972).
V. Lenin, *Materialism and Empirio-Criticism* (Moscow, 1964).
—— *Collected Works*, xxxviii: *Philosophical Notebooks* (Moscow, 1967).

lesbian feminism. Lesbian feminists are largely concerned with issues at the intersection of female identity and sexual–affectional orientation. Issues which arise at this intersection are distinct from those that arise around sex–gender and sexual–affectional orientation in general. Most lesbian feminists hold that self-conscious lesbianism threatens dominant political and social systems in a way that other identities (e.g. as woman or as gay man) do not. The reasoning is this: Patriarchal systems are founded on valuing men above women. Both heterosexuality and male *homosexuality preserves this valuing of men above women. Only lesbian *feminism which explicitly values women and is largely unconcerned with men really challenges this valuing. For a woman to love another woman is thus a political and revolutionary act. Other philosophical issues associated with lesbian feminism include: whether lesbian identity is essential or socially constructed, whether there is a distinctly lesbian ethics, whether lesbian feminists should be separatists (withdraw as far as possible from patriarchal political and social systems).   C.McK.

Marilyn Frye, *The Politics of Reality* (Trumansbrug, NY, 1983).
Adrienne Rich, *On Lies, Secrets and Silences* (New York, 1979).

Leśniewski, Stanisław (1886–1939). Polish logician. He reacted to the logical *paradoxes by demanding extreme rigour in logic. For example, he maintained that a system of logic should involve no assumptions about the world, except what is involved in identifying a written formula. This led him to develop three unorthodox axiomatic systems of logic: protothetic, ontology, and mereology. Protothetic is a system of propositional logic based on the notion of equivalence, mereology axiomatizes the part–whole relation, and ontology involves a controversial attempt to interpret *quantifiers without assuming that anything exists beyond written expressions. Leśniewski also proposed an unusually sophisticated theory of *definitions. His influence has largely been indirect, through his students (notably Tarski, whose definition of truth owes much to him). This may change if his writings become available in English.   W.A.H.

Peter M. Simons, 'Leśniewski's Logic and its Relation to Classical and Free Logics', in Georg Dorn and P. Weingartner (eds.), *Foundations of Logic and Linguistics: Problems and their Solutions* (New York, 1985).

Lessing, Gotthold Ephraim (1729–81). German philosopher and dramatist, who upheld the *Enlightenment ideals of freedom and tolerance, but in aesthetics anticipated Romanticism. In *Laocoon: On the Limits of Painting and Poetry* (1766) he tried to distinguish the laws governing the literary and the pictorial arts, and opposed Winckelmann's classical aesthetics, in favour of expressive art free of formal constraints. In a series of papers, the *Hamburg Dramaturgy* (1767–9), he discussed the true nature of Aristotelian catharsis and the superiority of Shakespeare to French tragedy. His theological works, especially *The Education of the Human Race* (1780), attacked religious dogmatism in the name of true religion. 'What education is to the individual man, revelation is to the whole human race': an age in which men will fulfil their duty for its

own sake will follow the present age of pleasure and ambition. His avowal of Spinozism, just before his death, stimulated the revival of Spinoza, previously treated as a 'dead dog'.   M.J.I.

A. Ugrinsky (ed.), *Lessing and the Enlightenment* (London, 1986).

Leucippus (5th century BC). The founder of *atomism. Virtually nothing is known of his life, and his very existence was disputed in antiquity, but his role as the originator of atomism is firmly attested by Aristotle and Theophrastus, though the evidence does not allow any distinction between his doctrines and those of his more celebrated successor Democritus. He wrote a comprehensive account of the universe, the *Great World-System*. The single surviving quotation from his work (from a work entitled *On Mind*, which may have been a part of the *Great World-System*) asserts universal *determinism: 'Nothing happens at random, but everything from a rational principle and of necessity.'   C.C.W.T.

D. Furley, *The Greek Cosmologists* (Cambridge, 1987), ch. 9.

Leviathan. LEVIATHAN *or the Matter, Form, and Power of A* COMMONWEALTH *Ecclesiastical and Civil*, Hobbes's masterpiece on moral and political philosophy, was published in 1651 (Latin version 1668). The title comes from chapter 41 of the book of Job. The leviathan is a sea monster who 'is a king over all the children of pride' (verse 34). That Hobbes chose *Leviathan* as the title of his book shows that he regarded pride, in particular the view that the individual citizen knows enough to challenge the laws of the sovereign, as providing an explanation of why an artificial leviathan, the state, needs to have absolute power. The book is divided into four parts: the first provides an account of persons prior to the state; the second shows how the state must be constructed to serve its purpose, lasting peace; the third shows how this is compatible with Christian Scripture; and the fourth is an attack on Roman Catholicism. The importance of religion is shown by the fact that the third and fourth parts comprise half of the book.   B.G.

Levinas, Emmanuel (1906–1995). French philosopher influenced by *phenomenology and *Jewish philosophy. Born in Lithuania, Levinas introduced phenomenology into France in the 1930s after studying with Husserl and Heidegger, thinkers to whom he owes a clear debt. His lectures (*Time and the Other* (1948)) introduced themes such as time, death, and relations with others which are expanded in his major work, *Totality and Infinity* (1961). His main concern is to delineate an ethical 'face-to-face' relation with the Other, which, while immediate and singular, is none the less transcendent. Seeking such a possibility takes him to the 'limits of phenomenology', and to criticize many previous philosophers for their preoccupations with ontology. In *Otherwise than Being* (1974) he seeks language forms which might circumvent such preoccupations, and enable an ethical exchange with the *Other. Levinas also published religious Talmudic readings.   A.C.A.

*French philosophy, today.

Sean Hand (ed.), *The Levinas Reader* (Oxford, 1989).

Lévi-Strauss, Claude (1908–). Anthropologist and ethnographer; leading exponent of the method of *structuralism as applied to myth, ritual, oral narrative, kinship systems, and modes of symbolic representation. His aim is not so much to interpret particular instances, but rather to reveal the underlying structure—the deep grammar of mythical thought—which unites the otherwise endless multiplicity of culture-specific meanings and forms. Thus an ancient Greek and a modern Amerindian or Eskimo myth may well turn out, despite all their surface differences, to derive from the same generative matrix of conflicts posed and resolved. For Lévi-Strauss, mythical thought is a kind of 'bricolage', a logic that makes do with all manner of found or improvised cultural material, but which cannot be regarded as in any sense more 'primitive' than our own. His work thus combines a rigorous formalism with an immense range of sources—drawing upon cultures past and present—and a style that on occasion seeks to orchestrate these themes in a quasi-Wagnerian polyphony of themes.   C.N.

Claude Lévi-Strauss, *The Raw and the Cooked*, tr. J. and D. Weightman (New York, 1969).
—— *The View from Afar*, tr. J. Neugroschel and P. Hoss (New York, 1985).

Lévy-Bruhl, Lucien (1857–1939). Largely remembered for his studies *Primitive Mentality* and *How Natives Think*. Lévy-Bruhl argued that the mentality of so-called primitive peoples was radically different from that of Western rationality. He characterized primitive experience as 'mystical' in the sense of being dominated by affectivity, whereas scientific experience is largely cognitive. Furthermore, the 'pre-logical thought' of primitive peoples is bound, not so much by the law of non-contradiction, as by participation, as when members of a totemic group understand themselves to be identical with their totem. However, in the *Notebooks* written during his last two years, Lévy-Bruhl conceded that the isolation of a general primitive mentality had misdirected him: mystical participation is more easily observable among primitive peoples, but is present in every mind.   R.L.B.

J. Cazeneuve, *Lucien Lévy-Bruhl* (New York, 1972).

Lewis, Clarence Irving (1883–1964). American philosopher whose early work focused on symbolic and modal logic and who then went on to work in epistemology, general value theory, social philosophy, and ethics. He argued that empirical knowledge depends upon both a sensuous or subjective *'given' and an *a priori set of principles and categories through which we interpret the given. According to his 'conceptualistic pragmatism', however, the a priori 'has alternatives'; it is not a set of eternal or self-evident truths or necessary structures of the mind, but a set of conceptual schemes whose organization of our experience

is subject to modification on pragmatic grounds, subject to change, that is, when it does not conduce to the 'long-run satisfaction' of our human needs.   K.H.

P. A. Schilpp, *The Philosophy of C. I. Lewis* (La Salle, Ill., 1966).

Lewis, David K. (1941–2001). One of the most important and influential figures in American philosophy in the late twentieth century. Lewis studied at Harvard with Quine, and spent four years at UCLA (in the company of Montague and Carnap) before moving to Princeton, where he taught for thirty years. He was also a regular visitor to Australia, where he found, and helped to shape, a lively philosophical scene. He contributed significantly to the philosophies of mind, language, and logic, but he is best known for his systematic metaphysical system dominated by two ideas. One is the thesis he calls 'Humean supervenience': the claim that the world entirely consists of local physical matters of fact, and all other facts supervene on these facts. (*Supervenience.) This thesis is Humean in its denial of necessary connections between matters of fact. The other is his modal realism: other possible worlds and their inhabitants exist. (*Possible worlds.) Lewis argues for his modal realism by appealing to its philosophical utility: real possible worlds are invoked to explain such diverse phenomena as causation, conditionals, the contents of propositional attitudes, and the nature of properties. As Lewis says, his modal realism has met with many 'incredulous stares' but few convincing counter-arguments.   T.C.

*modal realism.

D. K. Lewis, *Philosophical Papers*, 2 vols. (Oxford, 1986).

Lexicon, the Philosophical. Originally compiled by Daniel Dennett and Joe Lambert, and later by Dennett alone, this collection of definitions converts proper names of (mostly twentieth-century) philosophers into common nouns, verbs, adverbs, and adjectives. Entry examples follow. *braithwaite*, n. The interval of time between two books. 'His second book followed his first after a long braithwaite.' *carnap*, n. A formally defined symbol, operator, special bit of notation. *grice*, n. Conceptual intricacy. 'His examination of Hume is distinguished by erudition and grice.' Hence, *griceful*, adj., and *griceless*, adj., 'An obvious and griceless polemic'. *hintikka*, n. A measure of belief, the smallest logically discernible difference between beliefs; 'He argued with me all night, but did not alter my beliefs one hintikka.' *quine*, v. To deny resolutely the existence or importance of something real or significant. 'Some philosophers have quined classes, and some have even quined physical objects.' Occasionally used intr., e.g., 'You think I quine, sir. I assure you I do not!' The eighth edition of the Lexicon is available from the American Philosophical Association.   D.H.S.

lex talionis. The law of retaliation, according to which deserved *punishment is neither more nor less than the harm done in a crime, and ideally mirrors the crime. It appears in the Code of Hammurabi (*c*.1700 BC) but is best known in the biblical statement 'life for life, eye for eye, tooth for tooth . . . wound for wound . . . ' (Exodus 21: 22–5). Commentators agree that the biblical *lex talionis* was introduced as a moral upper bound on permissible *revenge, i.e. take in retaliation *no more than* an eye for an eye, etc.

Lex talionis, also referred to as *jus talionis* (the right of retaliation), e.g. by Kant, is most plausibly confined to crimes against the person. Yet even here adjustments must be made; thus, the Code of Hammurabi provided that the son who strikes his father is not to be struck in return; he is to lose his hand. As Blackstone pointed out in his *Commentaries on the Laws of England* (1765–70), 'there are very many crimes, that will in no shape admit of these penalties, without manifest absurdity and wickedness'.

H.A.B.

Marvin Henberg, *Retribution: Evil for Evil in Ethics Law, and Literature* (Philadelphia, 1990).

li : *see* Confucianism.

liar paradox. Semantic paradox, known in antiquity, focus of much recent work. Jack says 'I am now speaking falsely', referring to the words he is then uttering. If Jack speaks truly when he says he is speaking falsely, he is speaking falsely. If he is speaking falsely when this is what he says is going on, he is speaking truly. So what he says is true if, and only if, it is false; which seems absurd. One response claims that Jack says nothing true and nothing false. But a variant makes trouble: Jill says 'I am now not speaking truly'. If Jill is not speaking truly when this is what she says she is up to, she is speaking truly. If she is speaking truly, then she must be doing what she says, that is, not speakingly truly. So, it seems, what she says is true if, and only if, it is not true.

R.M.S.

*paradoxes.

Mark Sainsbury, *Paradoxes* (New York, 1988), ch. 5.

liberalism. One of the major political ideologies of the modern world, liberalism is distinguished by the importance it attaches to the civil and political *rights of individuals. Liberals demand a substantial realm of personal *freedom—including freedom of conscience, speech, association, occupation, and, more recently, sexuality—which the state should not intrude upon, except to protect others from harm. Major philosophical exponents of liberalism include Locke, Kant, Constant, Humboldt, J. S. Mill, Green, Hobhouse, and, in the post-war era, Berlin, Hart, Rawls, and Dworkin.

Liberalism first emerged as an important movement in Europe in the sixteenth century. Today, particularly after the decline of *communism, it is the dominant ideology in many parts of the world. There are two familiar ways of explaining the rise of liberalism. On one view, liberalism grew out of the recognition that *toleration was the only alternative to the Wars of Religion. After innumerable wars, both Protestants and Catholics accepted that the

state could not impose a common faith, and that the only stable basis for a political regime was to separate Church and State. Liberalism has simply extended this principle from the sphere of religion to other areas of social life where citizens have conflicting beliefs about the meaning of life. A liberal state does not seek to resolve these conflicts, but rather provides a 'neutral' framework within which citizens can pursue their diverse conceptions of the good life. Liberalism, on this view, is the only humane response to the inevitable pluralism and diversity of modern societies.

Liberalism's critics, however, argue that liberalism emerged as the ideological justification for the rise of *capitalism, and that its image of the autonomous individual is simply a glorification of the pursuit of self-interest in the market. Liberalism replaced the web of mutual obligations which bound people together in ethnic, religious, or other communities with a society predicated on competition and atomistic *individualism.

There is perhaps some truth in both of these explanations. Liberalism was historically associated with capitalism, although most liberals today accept that *justice requires regulating the market to ensure equality of opportunity. Those who continue to defend free markets and absolute property rights, such as Hayek and Nozick, are now called classical liberals or *libertarians, as opposed to welfare liberals or liberal egalitarians, such as Rawls and Dworkin. (In Europe, the term 'liberal' is more likely to refer to a defender of the free market; in North America, to a defender of the welfare state.)

A major challenge for liberal philosophers has been to explain why individual freedom should have priority over competing values such as community or *perfectionism. Why should the state allow individuals to criticize and abandon the traditional customs of the community, or engage in degrading or worthless life styles?

It is often assumed that the defence of liberalism must ultimately rest on some form of *subjectivism or *scepticism about values. If people's values are merely subjective preferences, lacking any rational or objective basis, then there is no justification for the state to prefer some ways of life over others.

Few liberals have endorsed this subjectivist argument, although it is commonly attributed to them by critics. Subjectivism provides a weak defence of individual freedom. For one thing, it conflicts with the way most people understand the value of their own lives, since we typically assume that some ways of leading our lives are intrinsically better than others. Moreover, if subjectivism were true, it would leave liberal values equally without rational foundation. When liberals argue that a state which upholds individual rights and equality of opportunity is better than a totalitarian or caste society, they view this as a rationally defensible moral belief, not simply as their subjective preference. But if claims about rights and justice are rationally defensible, then so presumably are claims about the value of different conceptions of the good. As a result, most liberals have sought to defend freedom of choice without denying that the worth of different conceptions of the good life can be rationally evaluated.

There are a variety of non-sceptical arguments for freedom of choice within the liberal tradition. *Utilitarian and *pragmatist liberals offer various reasons why state coercion and paternalism are counter-productive over the long-term. For example, they argue that truth emerges from free debate with falsehood, and that valuable ways of life emerge from initially unsuccessful experiments in living. Moreover, giving the state the power to decide which ways of life are valuable and which are not increases the potential for the abuse of state power, arbitrary discrimination, tyranny, and civil strife. The advocates of different ways of life will end up fighting over which conceptions of the good should be promoted by the state, and which should be discouraged. Given that the merits of different ways of life are controversial, liberalism's neutrality provides the only way for the proponents of conflicting ways of life to live together.

These considerations are not insignificant, but they provide only contingent and indirect support for freedom. They point to various undesirable social consequences that might accompany the restriction on individual liberty, but they do not yet provide any reason for thinking that individuals have an inherent *right* to a certain sphere of liberty, or that there is any intrinsic *injustice* in limiting people's freedom.

Many liberals have sought to find a more principled argument for individual freedom. Kantian liberals, for example, argue that the capacity for rational *autonomy is the highest capacity humans possess, and so is worthy of inherent respect. To restrict someone's freedom of choice, on this Kantian view, is to treat them as less than a fully mature and responsible human being, and this is wrong regardless of the desirable or undesirable social consequences that might follow. To respect someone entails respecting her capacity to judge for herself which customs, practices and traditions are worth maintaining.

This Kantian view has been very influential in the liberal tradition. However, it rests on a controversial claim about the nature of moral value and moral respect. The Kantian view is disputed by many cultural and religious traditions that emphasize instead the value of piety, deference to authority, and respect for tradition. Indeed, many critics argue that using the state to promote the Kantian ideal of rational autonomy is as 'sectarian' as using the state to promote Protestantism, and as likely to lead to civil strife. Some groups, particularly conservative religious groups, will view the state promotion of Kantian autonomy as a direct attack on their own way of life.

Critics of the Kantian approach argue that liberals should therefore avoid appealing to the value of autonomy, and instead defend liberalism simply as the only viable basis for peaceful coexistence in culturally and religiously plural societies. These 'modus vivendi' liberals argue that liberalism should be defended as guaranteeing tolerance between different ways of life, not as promoting the autonomy of individuals.

Kantian liberals respond, however, that without appealing to the value of individual autonomy, there is no reason why coexistence *between groups* should take the form of guaranteeing the rights *of individuals*. Why not just allow each group in society to organize itself as it sees fit, even if this involves restricting the rights of its individual members? Enforcing individual rights sometimes means interfering with, rather than tolerating, various group practices, and this can only be justified (or so Kantians claim) by invoking the value of individual autonomy.

This internecine disagreement between Kantian autonomy-based liberals and *modus vivendi*, tolerance-based liberals remains unresolved. (The two sides are also sometimes described as 'comprehensive' versus 'political' liberals, or as 'Enlightenment' versus 'Reformation' liberals.)

Even if one accepts the liberal commitment to individual freedom, there are questions about its social and cultural pre-conditions. The capacity to make choices in a rational and informed manner is not innate—it must be developed in the course of one's upbringing and education. Moreover, freedom of choice is only meaningful if individuals have an adequate range of options to choose from—that is, if diverse life-styles and customs exist in society. Some *communitarian critics argue that liberalism has not attended to these wider social pre-conditions of *liberty. Indeed, critics argue that the unfettered exercise of individual freedom of choice will undermine the forms of family and community life which help develop people's capacity for choice and provide people with meaningful options. On this view, liberalism is self-defeating—liberals privilege individual rights, even when this undermines the social conditions which make individual freedom valuable.

Liberals respond to this criticism by arguing that individual rights, far from dissolving valuable social groups and associations, provide the best protection for them. Those groups which are truly worthy of people's allegiance will survive through the free assent and voluntary participation of their members. Those groups which need state support to survive, because they cannot maintain or recruit members, are often not worthy of allegiance or support. The example of religious toleration suggests that there is some merit to this liberal response. Legal guarantees of individual freedom of conscience have provided ample protection for a wide range of religious groups, while preventing the dangers that often accompany state-sponsored religion. Whether this example can be generalized is open to debate.

A similar question has been raised about the long-term political stability of a liberal society. Non-liberal societies are typically held together by shared conceptions of the good, such as a common religion, or by common ethnicity. Members of these societies are willing to make sacrifices for each other because of their commonalities. But what holds a society together when its members come from different ethnic and racial backgrounds and do not share a common conception of the good life?

Some liberals suggest that the tie that binds the citizens of a liberal society is simply a shared commitment to liberal principles of freedom and *equality. It is debatable whether this is a 'thick' enough bond to keep a *multicultural society together. After all, a liberal society makes many demands of its members: they must be willing to accept considerable sacrifices (e.g. military service), to take an interest in public affairs, and to exercise self-restraint in their personal actions and political demands. Liberals have tended to focus on the rights of *citizenship, but a liberal society would stop functioning if its citizens did not also accept certain duties and exercise certain virtues. It seems likely that a sense of commonality is needed for individuals to accept these sorts of duties.

*Conservative critics have argued that the stability of liberal societies is based on a pre-liberal sense of shared identity. Citizens of England, for example, do not see each other primarily as individual rights-holders, but as fellow members of the English *nation, with a shared history and culture. This gives rise to a sense of solidarity which is prior to, and deeper than, a shared commitment to liberalism. It is this national solidarity which explains why the English work together, and make sacrifices for each other. Conservatives worry that this sense of being members of the same 'people' or culture or community is gradually being eroded by the individualism of liberal rights, which treats people in abstraction from their communal ties and responsibilities.

Interestingly, many nineteenth-century liberals, agreed that liberalism is viable only in countries with a sense of common nationhood, a new shared by some recent theorists of 'liberal nationalism'. Most post-war liberal theorists, however, have rejected the idea that liberalism should ally itself with nationalism, and have instead asserted that a common commitment to liberal principles is a sufficient basis for social unity even in multicultural countries. Habermas's idea of 'constitutional patriotism' is one example of this view, explicitly offered as an alternative to nationalist theories of social cohesion.

One difficulty with this view is that it provides no guidance on how the boundaries of distinct political communities should be drawn. Indeed, it provides no explanation for why there should be distinct political communities at all. Why shouldn't all societies that share liberal values merge into a single state, aiming ultimately to create a single world state? If we reject the nationalist belief that states have the right and responsibility to express particular national identities, languages, and cultures, why shouldn't liberals favour abolishing existing nation-states and replacing them with a thoroughgoing *cosmopolitanism of open borders within a single global state?

Few liberal theorists are willing to take this step towards an unqualified liberal cosmopolitanism, and most believe that nation-states remain the only viable forum for the implementation of liberal-democratic values. Yet equally few liberals are willing to acknowledge that these liberal nation-states depend for their viability not only on adherence to liberal values, but also on the inculcation of deeper feelings of national identity.

Whether the cohesion of a liberal society depends on some prior sense of identity remains an important topic for debate. Whatever the explanation, national liberal societies have in fact proven remarkably stable. Dire warnings about liberalism's inability to contain the centrifugal tendencies of individual freedom can be found in every generation for the last three centuries, yet it appears that liberal societies have managed to endure while various forms of monarchy, theocracy, authoritarianism, and communism have come and gone.

Despite these disagreements about its philosophical foundations and sociological feasibility, the basic language of liberalism—individual rights, liberty, equality of opportunity—has become the dominant language of public discourse in most modern democracies.   w.k.

*anti-communism; civil society; liberty and equality; utilitarianism; well-being.

Ronald Dworkin, 'Liberalism', in *A Matter of Principle* (Cambridge, Mass., 1985).
L. T. Hobhouse, *Liberalism* (Oxford, 1964).
J. S. Mill, *Utilitarianism, On Liberty, Considerations on Representative Government*, ed. H. B. Acton (London, 1972).
John Rawls, *Political Liberalism* (New York, 1993).
Michael Sandel (ed.), *Liberalism and its Critics* (New York, 1984).
Yael Tamir, *Liberal Nationalism* (Princeton, NJ, 1993).

libertarianism. The theory about freedom that despite what has happened in the past, and given the present state of affairs and ourselves just as they are, we can choose or decide differently than we do—act so as to make the future different. Libertarianism asserts the freedom of the *will or *origination, and is contrasted with *determinism. Contemporary libertarians may cite quantum mechanics as evidence that determinism is false. Even if this is so, the random behaviour of atoms certainly does not by itself make for the freedom and moral responsibility asserted by libertarians.   r.c.w.

*freedom and determinism; determinism, scientific.

C. A. Campbell, 'Is "Freewill" a Pseudo-Problem?', *Mind* (1951).
J. C. Eccles and K. R. Popper, *The Self and its Brain* (Berlin, 1977).

libertarianism, left-. 'Left-libertarianism' is a new term for an old conception of *justice, dating back to Grotius. It combines the *libertarian assumption that each person possesses a natural right of self-ownership over his person with the *egalitarian premiss that natural resources should be shared equally. Right-wing libertarians argue that the right of self-ownership entails the right to appropriate unequal parts of the external world, such as unequal amounts of land. According to left-libertarians, however, the world's natural resources were initially unowned, or belonged equally to all, and it is illegitimate for anyone to claim exclusive private ownership of these resources to the detriment of others. Such private appropriation is legitimate only if everyone can appropriate an equal amount, or if those who appropriate more are taxed to compensate those who are thereby excluded from what was once common property. Historic proponents of this view include Thomas Paine, Herbert Spencer, and Henry George. Recent exponents include Philippe Van Parijs and Hillel Steiner.   w.k.

*libertarianism, political.

P. Vallentyne and H. Steiner (eds.), *Left-Libertarianism and its Critics* (Basingstoke, 2000).

libertarianism, political. A theory grounded in the right of free choice. Libertarianism comes in at least two varieties, both with roots in the writings of John Locke. One variety starts from the stipulation of particular *rights, often by direct intuition. The other grounds individual rights in causal assumptions about what leads to *freedom and productivity. Some libertarians mix these elements, arguing from intuition but hedging their discussions with references to the effects of a system of rights. Two issues, one conceptual and one practical, drive much of the discussion of libertarianism. Conceptually, there is a conflict between individual interest and its collective provision—it is odd that libertarian rights may work against our interests. Practically, it seems virtually impossible that a state could arise and survive by strictly libertarian principles in a competitive world.   R.C.W.

*libertarianism, left-.

Robert Nozick, *Anarchy, State, and Utopia* (New York, 1974).

libertinism. A sixteenth- and seventeenth-century, mainly French and Italian, current which rejected Christian revelation and set up reason and nature alone as the criteria of morality, law, and politics. The term *libertin* was first used by Calvin against religious dissenters who wanted freedom of conscience in matters of faith and morals. Libertinism was then applied more widely to the following positions: the rejection as invalid of theology and metaphysics anchored to 'divine' revelation (especially the immortality of the soul, punishments and rewards in the afterlife, teleology in nature, and a providential ordering of history); pluralism in matters of religion and ethics; a sceptical defence of doubt in philosophical and religious matters; assertion of the historical origin and consequent human fabrication of religions, creeds, and dogmas; *atheism or at least *deism; and Epicureanism. Major French figures include Pierre Charron, Montaigne, François de La Mothe le Vayer, and Pierre Gassendi. In Italy, libertine thinkers like Pietro Pomponazzi, Giulio Cesare Vanini, Bruno, and Campanella follow a naturalistic interpretation of Aristotelian psychology and physics. A popular image of the allegedly depraved libertine is preserved in the character of Don Juan–Don Giovanni: sexually promiscuous, atheist, mocker of human and divine law.   L.P.

R. Pintard, *Le Libertinage érudit dans la première moitié du XVIIᵉ siècle* (Geneva, 1983).
G. Spini, *Ricerca dei libertini* (Florence, 1983).

liberty. What is political liberty? In the ancient world, particularly among the Greeks, to be free was to be able to participate in the government of one's city. The laws were valid only if one had had the right to take part in making and unmaking them. To be free was not to be forced to obey laws made by others *for* one but not *by* one. This kind of *democracy entailed that government and laws could penetrate into every province of life. Man was not free, nor did he claim freedom, from such supervision. All democrats claimed was that every man was equally liable to criticism, investigation, and if need be arraignment before the laws, or other arrangements, in the establishing and maintaining of which all the citizens had the right to participate.

In the modern world, a new idea—most clearly formulated by Benjamin Constant—makes itself felt, namely that there is a province of life—private life—with which it is thought undesirable, save in exceptional circumstances, for public authority to interfere. The central question posed by the ancient world is 'Who shall govern me?' Some said a monarch, some said the best, or the richest, or the bravest, or the majority, or the law courts, or the unanimous vote of all. In the modern world, an equally important question is 'How much government should there be?' The ancient world assumed that life was one, and that laws and the government covered the whole of it—there was no reason to protect any corner of it from such supervision. In the modern world, whether historically because of struggles of the Churches against intervention by the secular State, or of the State against the Church, or as a result of the growth of private enterprise, industry, commerce, and its desire for protection against State interference, or for whatever reason, we proceed on the assumption that there is a frontier between public and private life; and that, however small the private sphere may be, within it I can do as I please—live as I like, believe what I want, say what I please—provided this does not interfere with the similar rights of others, or undermine the order which makes this kind of arrangement possible. This is the classical liberal view, in whole or part expressed in various declarations of the rights of man in America and France, and in the writings of men like Locke, Voltaire, Tom Paine, Constant, and John Stuart Mill. When we speak of civil liberties or civilized values, this is part of what is meant.

The assumption that men need protection against each other and against the government is something which has never been fully accepted in any part of the world, and what I have called the ancient Greek or classical point of view comes back in the form of arguments such as this: 'You say that an individual has the right to choose the kind of life he or she prefers. But does this apply to everyone? If the individual is ignorant, immature, uneducated, mentally crippled, denied adequate opportunities of health and development, he or she will not know how to choose. Such a person will never truly know what it is he or she really wants. If there are others who understand what human nature is and what it craves, and if they do for people, perhaps by some measure of control, what they would be doing for themselves if they were wiser, better informed, maturer, more developed, are they curtailing the freedom of these others? They are interfering with people as they are, but only in order to enable them to do what they would do if they knew enough, or were always at their best, instead of yielding to irrational motives, or behaving childishly, or allowing the animal side of their nature the upper hand. Is this then interference at all? If parents or teachers compel unwilling children to go to school or to work hard, in the name of what those children must really want, even though they may not know it, since that is what all men and women as such must want because they are human, then are they curtailing the liberty of the children? Surely not. Teachers and parents are bringing out their submerged or real selves, and catering to their needs, as against the transient demands of the more superficial self which greater maturity will slough off like a skin.'

If you substitute for parents a church or a party or a state, you get a theory on which much modern authority is based. We are told that to obey these institutions is but to obey ourselves, and therefore no slavery, for these institutions embody ourselves at our best and wisest, and self-restraint is not restraint, self-control is not slavery.

The battle between these two views, in all kinds of versions, has been one of the cardinal political issues of modern times. One side says that to put the bottle beyond the dipsomaniac's reach is not to curtail his liberties; if he is prevented from drinking, even by force, he will be healthier and therefore better capable of playing his part as man and citizen, will be more himself, and therefore freer, than if he reaches the bottle and destroys his health and sanity. The fact that he does not know this is merely a symptom of his disease, or ignorance of his own true wishes. The other side denies not that anti-social behaviour must be restrained, or that there is a case for preventing men from harming themselves or from harming the welfare of their children or of others, but that such a restraint, though justified, is liberty. Liberty may have to be curtailed to make room for other good things, security or peace or health; or liberty today may have to be curtailed to make possible wider liberty tomorrow; but to curtail freedom is not to provide it, and compulsion, no matter how well justified, is compulsion and not liberty. Freedom, such people say, is only one value among many, and if it is an obstacle to the securing of other equally important ends, or interferes with other people's opportunities of reaching these ends, it must make way.

To this the other side replies that this presupposes a division of life into private and public—it assumes that men may wish in their private lives to do what others may not like, and therefore need protection from these others—but that this view of human nature rests on a fundamental mistake. The human being is one, and in the ideal society, when everyone's faculties are developed, nobody will ever want to do anything that others may resent or wish to stop. The proper purpose of reformers and revolutionaries is to knock down walls between men, bring everything into the open, make men and women live together without partitions, so that what one wants all want. The desire to be left alone, to be allowed to do what one wishes without needing to account for it to some tribunal—one's family, or one's employers, or one's party,

or one's government, or indeed the whole of one's society—this desire is a symptom of maladjustment. To ask for freedom from society is to ask for freedom from oneself. This must be cured by altering property relations as socialists desire to do, or by eliminating critical reason as some religious sects and, for that matter, communist and fascist regimes seek to do.

In one view—which might be called organic—all separateness is bad, and the notion of human rights which must not be trampled on is that of dams—walls demanded by human beings to separate them from one another, needed perhaps in a bad society, but with no place in a justly organized world in which all human streams flow into one undivided human river. On the second or liberal view, human rights, and the idea of a private sphere in which I am free from scrutiny, is indispensable to that minimum of independence which everyone needs if he is to develop, each on his own lines; for variety is of the essence of the human race, not a passing condition. Proponents of this view think that destruction of such rights in order to build one universal self-directing human society—of everyone marching towards the same rational ends—destroys that area for individual choice, however small, without which life does not seem worth living.

In a crude and, some have maintained, a distorted form, totalitarian and authoritarian regimes have stood for one of these views: while liberal democracies incline to the other. And, of course, varieties and combinations of these views, and compromises between them, are possible. They are the two cardinal ideas that have faced one another and dominated the world since, say, the Renaissance.   I.B.

*freedom through goodness and reason; political freedom.

Isaiah Berlin, *Four Essays on Liberty* (London, 1969), esp. 'Two Concepts of Liberty'.
—— 'Herzen and Bakunin on Individual Liberty', in *Russian Thinkers* (London, 1978).
John Gray, *Liberalism* (Milton Keynes, 1986).
J. S. Mill, *On Liberty* (London, 1859).
David Miller (ed.), *Liberty* (Oxford, 1991).
John Rawls, *Political Liberalism* (New York, 1993).

liberty and equality. Some philosophers have argued that these two values are bound to conflict with one another. Given the differences in people's abilities, they say, there will be an inevitable tendency for some to be more successful than others. Inequalities can therefore be prevented only by the strict exercise of authority to limit the prosperity of the more successful. To this others have replied that all members of society need to share equally in the material wealth and political power which are the pre-conditions of effective freedom; liberty and equality are therefore not conflicting but complementary values.   R.J.N.

*liberty; equality; political freedom; well-being.

Richard Norman, *Free and Equal* (Oxford, 1987).

Lichtenberg, Georg Christoph (1742–99). German physicist whose fame rests, apart from an experiment in electricity, on aphorisms. He was a man of the Enlightenment: 'All the mischief in the world may be put down to the general, indiscriminate veneration of old laws, old customs and old religion.' He straddles *Kantianism and *scepticism: 'If an angel were to tell us his philosophy, I think many of his statements might sound like "2 × 2 = 13".' He doubted even Descartes's *cogito: 'It thinks, we really ought to say, just as we say, it thunders. To say cogito is too much, if we translate this as "I think" '; 'I and myself. I feel myself—these are two distinct things. Our false philosophy is incorporated in our whole language; we cannot reason without, so to speak, reasoning wrongly. We overlook the fact that speaking, no matter of what, is itself a philosophy.' Schopenhauer often quotes him, and Hegel, in his *Phenomenology of Spirit*, cites his satirical critique of Lavater's theory of physiognomy (*On Physiognomy* (1778)). What he said of others applies to himself: 'Earth has greater need of their kind than Heaven.'   M.J.I.

J. P. Stern, *Lichtenberg: A Doctrine of Scattered Occasions* (Bloomington, Ind., 1959).

lie, noble: *see* noble lie.

Lieh Tzu. Daoist philosopher (440?–360 BC?). The *Lieh Tzu* text (*c.*third century AD?) is polysemic in style: a collection of narratives having multiple application—cosmological, linguistic, personal, socio-political. Developing the philosophies of Lao Tzu and Chuang Tzu, it interprets the processes of life and death with a yin-yang cosmology. Investigation of the way (*tao*) is not a theoretical enterprise, but a psycho-physical discipline resulting in an embodied understanding of processes of transformation, and in an exceptional skill in negotiating our life activities.   S.C.

The Book of Lieh-tzu: A Classic of Tao, tr. A. C. Graham (New York, 1990).

life. This, the distinguishing feature of organisms, is best thought of as involving some kind of complex organization, giving an ability to use energy sources for self-maintenance and reproduction. Efforts to find some distinctive substance characterizing life have proven as futile as they have been heroic. The one thing which is clear is that any analysis of life must accept and appreciate that there will be many borderline instances, like viruses. Inconvenient as this may be for the lexicographer, this is precisely what *evolution theory would lead us to expect.   M.R.

  *vitalism.

J. B. S. Haldane, 'What is Life?'; repr. in M. Ruse, *Philosophy of Biology* (New York, 1989).

life, form of: *see* form of life.

life, the good. Perhaps the most fundamental question in ethics is that posed by Socrates: How should one live? But this question covers not just the 'moral' aspects of our conduct, such as the observance of duties, or our contribution to the general welfare, but also those other more personal and individual aspects of a life which may make it worthwhile, or give it meaning. Aristotle's theory of virtue aimed to lay down the ingredients of *eudaimonia* (or human fulfilment), and though this included many elements of what we would now call morality, it was also concerned with the good life for humans in the sense of a flourishing or successful life. Later *Stoic and *Christian systems of ethics continued this tradition, though often in a more 'inner-oriented' way: they gave particular prominence to what we might now call 'spiritual' practices, the cultivation of disciplines aimed at deepening our self-awareness, and enabling us to live harmonious and ordered lives.

Several modern philosophers have been interested in these more personal and individual aspects of what makes a life worthwhile, and have begun to reconsider notions that were prominent in the ethical writings of earlier ages—the importance of character, self-reflection, the nature of the self , and the relationship between the intellect and the emotions. The stress on the 'interior' dimension connects up with the ancient theme of self-awareness as basic to the good life, as in the Delphic motto, 'Know thyself'; the 'descent into the inner self' was also a fundamental theme of St Augustine's famous ethical and religious work, the *Confessions*. More recently, psychoanalytic writers have underlined the importance of uncovering the hidden drives and projections that may distort our perceptions and choices, and this has influenced philosophical work on self-integration as fundamental to the good life. There are also important philosophical questions to be asked about the relationship between these broadly ethical concerns and other quite distinct ingredients of good human lives, such as creativity and artistic achievement, the pursuit of which may often appear to conflict with personal equilibrium or commitments to others. Finally, a good human life is often supposed to be one that has *meaning*; it may be asked whether this simply refers to the fact that a life contains various individually worthwhile ingredients, or whether it implies some overarching purpose or goal.   J.COT.

John Cottingham, *Philosophy and the Good Life* (Cambridge, 1998).
Charles Guignon (ed.), *The Good Life* (Indianapolis, 1999).
Pierre Hadot, *Philosophy as a Way of Life* (Oxford, 1995).
John Kekes, *Moral Wisdom and Good Lives* (Ithaca, NY, 1995).
Alexander Nehamas, *The Art of Living* (Berkeley, Calif., 1998).
Charles Taylor, *Sources of the Self* (Cambridge, Mass., 1989).

life, the meaning of. 'What is the meaning of life?' is one of those Big Questions about Ultimate Things that recent philosophers have so often been accused of neglecting. It may invite the retort that the meaning of our lives is what we care to give them; we cannot expect meanings to be handed to us on a plate, and even if they were, what use would they be to us? God may have his purposes in creating me, but why should I adopt them? First I must be convinced that they are good purposes (we can ignore the effects of the threat of hell-fire on non-conformists), and if they are, why should I not adopt them anyway, without bothering whether they are God's?

Another version of the question focuses not on our individual lives but on the whole scheme of things: what is the point of it all? An implication of this, in the spirit if not in the letter, seems to be that without some overall purpose in things all our own projects are somehow worthless or doomed to frustration. But why should that be so? Often the underlying thought seems to be that real values can only exist if they are permanent. But why should something in itself valueless acquire value by being permanent, or belonging to a set of things which is permanent? The value of my having just passed my exam and the disvalue of having painfully stubbed my toe are surely not affected if the sun will explode in eight billion years and I myself face annihilation somewhat sooner? Perhaps the thought is that our projects will fail unless ultimately 'God is on our side'. But our short-term projects often succeed. Sometimes events may later make us wish they had not done so, but this is relatively rare, and often success is definite and there are no hidden snags.

But now perhaps the question broadens into something else: what *are* the conditions for our lives to reach ultimate success? Many philosophers have held, with Sidgwick, that ultimately nothing can be of value but certain conscious states, for how could values exist without conscious beings to appreciate them? But recently this inference has been attacked. No doubt a lifeless desert would lack value (*pace* G. E. Moore, who thought that if it was beautiful it would not), but perhaps the value of at least many conscious states presupposes that their owners value other things; how, for instance, could one see any value in the state of mind consequent on fulfilling one's ambition to climb Everest if one saw no value in having climbed Everest (which is not itself a state of mind)? The question then becomes: how should we assess these further values? Can any rational grounds be given for pursuing some of them rather than others; or one life plan rather than another?

A further, and age-old, question which arises out of this concerns the value to us of things that happen after our *deaths, so that we cannot know about them. 'Call no man happy until he is dead' said the Greek sage Solon; but how can he be happy then? Suppose someone dies after an apparently happy and successful life, but his achievements are then shown to be nugatory, for reasons he could not have anticipated, and his children all come to grief: would we still call him a happy man, who lived a happy life? If not, happiness cannot be a state of mind, and even if the meaning of life is to acquire happiness, it cannot be simply to acquire a state of mind.   A.R.L.

John Cottingham, *On the Meaning of Life* (London, 2002).

E. D. Klemke (ed.), *The Meaning of Life*, 2nd edn. (Oxford, 2000).

R. Nozick, *The Examined Life* (New York, 1989), ch. 10. Like Wiggins (cited below), criticizes Sidgwick's outlook, though without mentioning him.

H. Sidgwick, *The Methods of Ethics*, 7th edn. (London, 1907), IV. xiv.

D. Wiggins, *Needs, Values, Truth* (London, 1987), essay III, esp. sects. 1–6, 10–15.

life, philosophy of: *see* abandonment; absurd; Arendt; Aristippus; Buddhist philosophy; Chinese philosophy; existentialism; freedom and determinism; Hindu philosophy; Indian philosophy; Kierkegaard; life, meaning of; Marcel; Marxist philosophy; moral philosophy, history of; moral philosophy, problems of; nirvana; pessimism and optimism; Plato; religion, history of philosophy of; religion, problems of the philosophy of; Schopenhauer; Spinoza.

life, quality of: *see* quality of life.

life and death. Biological life is best understood as a *family resemblance concept, because there is no one property common to all and only animate things. To be alive is to have some of: an organic chemistry, a digestive and excretive system, a reproductive capacity, a genetic make-up. Being alive is a property distinct from being sentient, conscious, or intelligent. For example, grass is alive but lacks those three properties. If there is artificial intelligence, then some computer is intelligent but not alive. Death is at least the cessation of life, but it is philosophically controversial what death consists in. Biologically and medically, death is brain death, or brain-stem death.

Should we fear death? Parfit has suggested that it is not personal identity that should matter to us, and one's own death is not the destruction of a unique Cartesian self but the ending of a certain series of connected experiences and actions. Nagel has argued that there is a fundamental problem about *being someone*: the unique fact of someone's being oneself resists *reductionism in psychological theories of personal identity. Should we fear death less if there is life after death? Bernard Williams argued that immortality is not desirable, because everlasting life would become tedious. Perhaps this is not right. Perhaps the afterlife would be infinitely interesting and fulfilling.

Immortality requires that the person who lives after death be numerically identical with the person who lives the earthly life. For example, any resurrected person has to be oneself rather than some being qualitatively similar but numerically distinct from oneself. Arguably, this requires that each of us is a soul that could remain unchanged by such profound physical and psychological changes. Arguably, Nagel's problem of being someone can be solved only if we are souls.

Why are the living the living? Why are the dead the dead? These are hard philosophical questions to answer once it is realized that *any* life has some duration ending in death. To be one of the living is to be living now, or to be actual. To be one of the dead is not to be actual but to have been actual. It is an unsolved philosophical problem what actuality is. We do not have an answer to 'Why is it now now?', which means, 'Why is this particular time the present?'   S.P.

Thomas Nagel, *Mortal Questions* (Cambridge, 1979).

—— *The View from Nowhere* (Oxford, 1986), esp. 223–31.

Derek Parfit, *Reasons and Persons* (Oxford, 1984).

Sogyal Rinpoche, *The Tibetan Book of Living and Dying* (San Francisco, 1992).

Bernard Williams, *Problems of the Self* (Cambridge, 1973) esp. ch. 6: 'The Makropulos Case'.

Palle Yourgrau, 'The Dead', *Journal of Philosophy*, 84 (1987).

life and science. Science describes and explains the world in terms of causal regularities. Effects simply follow causes because that is the way the world is ordered, not because it is better that one thing happens rather than another. The theories of science are mathematically based abstractions, prescinding, as far as possible, from much that is important in the world as lived and experienced by human beings (the *Lebenswelt* of the phenomenologists). In the *Lebenswelt* descriptions and explanations are irreducibly normative, coloured by values, feelings, and emotions. To describe a person as temperate or handsome, or a landscape as beautiful, is to praise them, implying that they are better than if they had turned out some other way. Reconciling the value-free theories of science with what we say and think in the *Lebensvelt* has troubled philosophers since the time of Kant. The best hope seems to be to regard neither scientific nor everyday accounts as exhaustive of the whole of reality, but both as valid within their own spheres.   A.O'H.

*phenomenology; science, history of the philosophy of; science, problems of the philosophy of.

A. O'Hear, *The Element of Fire: Science, Art and the Human World* (London, 1988).

life-world. The universally structured realm of beliefs, assumptions, feelings, values, and cultural practices that constitute meaning in everyday life. In criticism of the classical theory of knowledge (Descartes to Kant), the concept of the life-world is first introduced as the insurmountable basis for scientific experience. Scientific theories are seen as 'idealized constructions' (Husserl), dependent on immediate sense-perception which itself, however, is part of the human everyday world that is taken for granted. Accordingly, the life-world as such is understood as the unproblematic and pre-scientific presupposition of any understanding and meaning, providing an implicit *background of once explicitly held or intended and now 'sedimented' beliefs, assumptions, and practices. Whereas the life-world has first been conceptualized as the world of the subject (Husserl, Schütz), more recently its genuinely social character has been emphasized (Gadamer, Habermas).   H.-H.K.

*Frankfurt School.

J. Habermas, 'The Concept of the Lifeworld and the Hermeneutic Idealism of Interpretive Sociology', in *Theory of Communicative Action*, ii (Boston, 1987).

light of nature. In Cartesian philosophy, the faculty of the soul by which knowledge, especially a priori knowledge, is discerned. Descartes's 'principles of natural light' are put forward as fundamental metaphysical truths; for example; an (efficient) cause must contain as much reality as an effect; what can exist from its own power always exists; if I doubt, then I exist; deception is caused by some defect; if something happens, it cannot then not have happened; nothing can cause nothing. If *p* is a principle of natural light, then *p* is self-evident, *p* is indubitable, and *p* is a necessary truth. According to Descartes, there is no faculty more authoritative than the light of nature which could be deployed to call its findings into question.   s.p.

Philosophical Works of Descartes, tr. E. S. Haldane and G. R. T. Ross, 2 vols. (Cambridge, 1967).

Anthony Kenny, *Descartes: A Study of his Philosophy* (New York, 1968).

linguistic acts. Things done with words, an account of which may cast light on human language and its use.

J. L. Austin believed that the study of *language had been too much focused on words, and the study of action too much focused on 'ordinary physical actions'. His stated overall project in *How to Do Things with Words* was to characterize performatives—utterances on the occasion of which something is *done* rather than stated. He wanted to draw a line between performatives and another sort of utterance which he thought had received all the attention and at whose expense performatives had previously been ignored. (*Constatives.) But Austin's attempt to draw the line undermined the assumption that there was a line to be drawn in the first place, and this made way for the idea that *all* utterances have a performative dimension. Thus Austin's work led to 'speech-act theory', a branch of language studies premissed originally in the thought that speech is a species of action.

In any use of language—any occasion of someone's speaking, that is—there are many things the speaker does—many linguistic acts she performs. (For example, an action might be someone's doing at least these four things: *uttering the words 'It's 10 o'clock', saying what time it is, reminding Jane that it's time to go to the lecture, alarming Ted.*) Each linguistic act corresponds to a type of action; and a principled way of organizing linguistic acts provides a framework into which the particularities of occasions on which one or another is done can potentially be fitted so as to provide for illuminating accounts of speech-actions. The classification of linguistic acts which Austin got started may be thought of as a means of imposing system on to the actual data of linguistic communication.

Austin's own primary classification was into locutionary (which incorporates phonetic, phatic, and rhetic), illocutionary, and perlocutionary. Each of these categories subsumes some range of acts; and an action of speaking is typically a speaker's performing some act within each range. Locutionary acts are of saying something; illocutionary acts are acts done *in* saying something; and perlocutionary acts are acts done *by* saying something. (In the example, *uttering the words* . . . is a phonetic act, *saying that* . . . a locutionary one, *reminding* . . . (arguably) an illocutionary one, and *alarming* . . . (arguably) a perlocutionary one ('arguably', because Austin in fact had difficulty in making the illocutionary–perlocutionary distinction clearly).

The idea that speaking a language is engaging in behaviour of a rule-governed kind was developed by John Searle in *Speech Acts*. He attempted to account for a variety of phenomena in the setting of an institutional theory of communication, and to clarify particular speech-acts, e.g. referring (sometimes called a subsentential speech-act, because it is done using a word or two rather than a whole sentence) and promising.

Subsequent work in speech-act theory has been confined to the area that comes under Austin's illocutionary head, so that what is usually meant by 'a speech-act' is in the category that Austin called illocutionary. Speech-act theory may then be thought of as a branch of pragmatics. It can be divided into two types, depending on the attitude taken to that which determines a speech-action to be of the illocutionary act it is of. In the work of such linguists as John Ross and Jerrold Katz, illocutionary force is absorbed into a more or less formalized account of locution. In the work of Searle and others, illocutionary force is a function of unformalized circumstances. The latter kind of speech-act theory is more in keeping with its Austinian beginnings.   J.HORN.

J. L. Austin, *How to Do Things with Words* (Oxford, 1961).

John Searle, *Speech Acts* (Cambridge, 1969).

S. L. Tsohatzidis (ed.), *Foundations of Speech Act Theory: Philosophical and Linguistic Perspectives* (London, 1994).

linguistic philosophy. Linguistic philosophy may be regarded either as a variant form, or as a competitor, of *analytic philosophy. The latter arose from the early collaboration of Wittgenstein and Russell. Linguistic philosophy was more particularly Wittgenstein's creation, although it had some elements of affinity with the philosophical practice of G. E. Moore, and, in its later development at Oxford with Ryle and Austin, showed some dependence on the thought of their Oxford predecessors Cook Wilson and H. A. Prichard.

The central principle of linguistic philosophy is that the traditional problems of philosophy (or metaphysics) are not genuine problems at all but confusions generated by misunderstandings about language or by the misuse of it. The apparent problems cannot be solved; but they can be dissolved, confusion can be dispelled. A philosophical puzzle is created by an inclination to assert something absurdly at variance with common sense for what seem convincing reasons (that we have no knowledge of, or that there are, no material things, people other than ourselves, past events, laws of nature).

Moore's defence of *common sense was direct and primitive. It rested on Thomas Reid's assumption that the beliefs of common sense 'are older and of more authority than the arguments of philosophy'. Holding out his hand, he said that he knew for certain that this was a hand and, since a hand is unquestionably a material thing, it followed that he knew for certain that there was at least one material thing. This was more a rhetorical device for showing that philosophers commonly do not mean what they say than a way of getting to grips with what it is that concerns them.

Wittgenstein's technique was much more elaborate. He himself compared it to psychotherapy, in which a kind of intellectual neurosis is relieved by a long-drawn-out process of reminding the puzzled philosopher of the way in which the crucial terms in the expression of his puzzlement are ordinarily used. Wittgenstein's treatment resembled psychotherapy not only in its apparently interminable duration but also in its failure to bring about lasting cures. But some successes should be acknowledged. No one will ever now suppose that understanding is a matter of inward illumination. We tell whether someone has understood a lesson in long division or French pronunciation by his capacity to do some sums or make the correct sounds, and so does he, whatever flashes of inward illumination he may, or may not, have had.

Devotional commentators on Wittgenstein have argued that there are not two Wittgensteins, but one, developing a single line of thought. There are, indeed, common elements in the thinking of the earlier and the later Wittgenstein. Both are centrally concerned with language, both insist that philosophy is not only quite distinct from science, but that it is an activity rather than a theory of any kind whatever. But what was formerly seen as 'the logical clarification of thoughts', the revelation by analysis of the formal structure which is hidden by ordinary language, is explicitly rejected by the later Wittgenstein and replaced by an absolutely opposed conception of the matter.

*Language, on this new view, has no logical essence. It is an accumulation of a great number of different *'language-games', of which the reporting or description of facts is just one. Each of these has its own way of working and they are no more identical in essential form than ordinary games are, being related to one another, as ordinary games are, only by 'family resemblance', an idea on which Wittgenstein laid much stress. Just as it is not the universal function of sentences to describe, so it is not the universal task of the words making up those sentences to name or refer to objects, concrete or abstract, or to ideas or images in the minds of their users. The meaning of a word or sentence lies in the rules for its actual use in real life, not philosophical reflection; these rules are best discerned in the activity of learning how to use the expressions involved; they are the result of decisions which can be altered; but these conventions must be public and shared, a *private language is impossible. That last point is argued for with something very like a traditional philosophical argument, and has not been found universally convincing. In the same spirit, Wittgenstein argues that the elemental truths Moore thought he could prove in his blunt way are really background assumptions without whose acceptance nothing we could recognize as doubt or its settlement could take place.

It is impossible not to see Wittgenstein's loosely affirmed principle that 'inner processes stand in need of outward criteria', in which he claimed some kind of necessary connection between mental states and their behavioural manifestations, as lying behind the less cautious view of Ryle on the same topic. Ryle proposes something like a generally applicable pattern of analysis of categorical statements about mental events and processes into collections of hypothetical statements about what those referred to would do if certain conditions were satisfied. Ryle held that the familiar dualist conception of *mind and body as distinct worlds with proprietary kinds of event going on in them was a large-scale 'category mistake', in which the matters under discussion were treated as belonging to the wrong logical class, as happens more obviously in wondering what colour a number is or what is the weight of a shadow.

Ryle's preoccupation with thinking paralleled Wittgenstein's with meaning. To think what one is doing is not to carry out some sequence of bodily movements while consciously rehearsing some appropriate sequence of inner thoughts. It is to make the bodily movements in an intelligent way, reacting quickly and adequately to obstructions and difficulties.

The most exquisite of linguistic philosophers was J. L. Austin, who from 1945 until his death in 1960 exercised a powerful influence in Oxford, which rapidly faded away after that. Austin's acute sensitivity to nuances of meaning led him to stress that the language we actually use is the evolutionary by-product of its long and various application. Philosophers, he held, persistently over-simplify, running together words which, although similar, are by no means identical in meaning: 'look' with 'appear' and 'seem', 'inadvertently' with 'accidentally' and 'unintentionally'. Admiration for the refinement and, indeed, correctness of these distinctions is compatible with doubt about whether they cut any philosophical ice.

Large claims were made for his identification and naming of *'performative' utterances, such as 'I promise to pay you back' and 'I name this ship *Gladys*', which rather constitute than describe the performance of promising or naming. His suggestion that 'I know that so-and-so' is also performative as a kind of guarantee of the speaker's claim did not survive inspection. Something of the flavour of this detection of performativeness is present in the account of truth given by Sir Peter Strawson, ironically enough in a powerful criticism of Austin's own attempt to attempt to rehabilitate the *correspondence theory of truth. To say '*p* is true', Strawson held, is not to say something about '*p*', such as that it corresponds to the facts, but is at once to assert it and to confirm its assertion or suggestion by someone else. In his later work, from *Individuals* (1959), he moved on from linguistic philosophy to a sophisticated kind of Kantianism, reinforced by the analytic philosophy of the twentieth century, which aimed to set out the general presuppositions of the possibility of articulate discourse about our experience. In his earlier phase he had produced a powerful criticism of the account of reference embodied in Russell's theory of *descriptions and he went on to point out the lavishly Procrustean distortions of the logical rules of ordinary, natural language made by modern, mathematically inspired formal logic.   A.Q.

K. T. Fann (ed.), *A Symposium on J. L. Austin* (London, 1959).
Anthony Kenny, *Wittgenstein* (Harmondsworth, 1975).
C. W. K. Mundle, *Critique of Linguistic Philosophy* (Oxford, 1970).
J. A. Passmore, *A Hundred Years of Philosophy* (London, 1957), ch. 18.
O. P. Wood and G. Pitcher (eds.), *Ryle: A Collection of Critical Essays* (London, 1970).

linguistics, formal. An empirical discipline which provides a mathematical framework for characterizing properties of possible human languages, with different branches characterizing phenomena at different though related levels in the speech chain from sound to meaning. Each branch of linguistics provides a theory that isolates a unit of linguistic significance, such as property of sound, form, or meaning, which it analyses and relates to notions analysed at the levels above and below. The minimal units of analysis are abstract notions used to segment the continuous sound signal of human speech into phonemes, then syllables, then words and morphemes, constituents and phrases, sentences and discourse structures. Corresponding to these levels we have the theories of phonetics, phonology, morphology, syntax, semantics, and discourse representation theory. The general theory of language comprising these subtheories will also contain a formal treatment of the learnability of languages.   B.C.S.

M. Atkinson, D. Kilby, and I. Roca, *Foundations of General Linguistics*, 2nd edn. (London, 1988).

linguistics, philosophical relevance of. Linguistics bears on certain issues in *epistemology and in *philosophy of mind and, of course, is directly relevant to philosophy of language. For example, Chomsky has forcefully argued that the exigencies of language learning strongly favour *rationalism over *empiricism in the traditional debate on *innate ideas. The facility with which children learn their native languages, despite the severely limited quantity and variety of data available to them, indicates that language acquisition is hardly a matter of stimulus generalization. Rather, Chomsky proposes, we possess a language faculty specially equipped for acquiring languages with just those features that distinguish natural human languages. Characterizing these features is the task of what he calls universal grammar. Also, he draws a distinction between competence and performance. Though applied to knowledge of language, it is relevant to philosophy of psychology in general, for it points to the distinction, crucial to *cognitive science, between explaining abilities and explaining behaviour. Chomsky's account of knowledge of language suggests that Ryle's distinction between knowing-that and knowing-how is not exhaustive, and it provides an antidote to Wittgenstein's and Kripke's scepticism about *rules and rule-following.

Underlying these issues is the question of how grammatical information is represented and utilized in language production and comprehension. The findings of psycholinguistics strongly support the claim that grammatical information is not an artefact of theory but is psychologically real. Although the categories and principles of modern linguistic theory generally do not correspond to those of school grammar, and are not otherwise intuitively accessible to language-users, people's linguistic behaviour and grammatical judgements seem sensitive to such principles. Accordingly, it is plausible to suppose that knowledge of language is not conscious but tacit, and that this knowledge includes representations of sentential structure corresponding to the categories of linguistic theory (not that there is any consensus on the best such theory). Otherwise, there would seem to be no explanation for a multitude of linguistic regularities or for the robustness of people's linguistic intuitions.

Various branches of linguistic theory are relevant to the philosophy of language. Syntactic theory sheds light on such concepts as argument structure, binding, scope, and *logical form. Also, because some semantic information is encoded structurally rather than lexically, the theory of meaning (*semantics) in philosophy cannot ignore syntactic theory in linguistics. Linguistic semantics illuminates such concepts as *ambiguity, *vagueness, and *synonymy, and offers a framework for explicating the distinction between *analytic and synthetic statements. Linguistic *pragmatics overlaps with the philosophical theory of *speech acts, and, as Grice showed, the distinction between pragmatic and semantic questions has important consequences for a variety of philosophical issues.

From a linguistic standpoint, the logical form of a sentence is not the form of a logical formula used to represent the proposition expressed by the sentence, but a level of syntactic structure. It is often construed as the input to semantic interpretation, the stage of a grammar at which information about the semantic contents of lexical items is applied to yield, as a function of this level of syntactic structure, the semantic content of the entire sentence. Logical form helps explain scope relations among quantified noun phrases, connectives, and other operators, and binding and anaphoric relations between noun phrases and pronouns. Also, there is often reason to impute hidden variables to the logical forms of sentences containing expressions of certain sorts, such as relational terms like 'local' and 'alien', and temporal adverbs and connectives, like 'usually' and 'whenever'. These latter terms, as they occur in such sentences as 'Usually Abe drinks wine with dinner' and 'Whenever Bob is late for work, he skips breakfast', function as quantifiers, and, plausibly, these sentences contain event variables bound by those quantifiers.

Lexical semanticists distinguish polysemy from lexical ambiguity. The ambiguity of nouns such as 'club', 'joint', and 'trunk', each with several unrelated meanings, is a linguistic coincidence, evident from their translation into other languages. However, polysemous words, such as the verbs 'call', 'go', and 'play', have closely related meanings that need to be explained systematically. From a philosophical standpoint, the phenomenon of polysemy challenges the simplistic view that for a word to have several literal uses is just a matter of its having several senses. This is clear from the case of adjectival modification, as illustrated by the different relations between adjective and noun in 'fast runner', 'fast track', and 'fast race', or between the nouns in 'child abuse' and in 'drug abuse'. K.B.

L. Antony and N. Hornstein (eds.), *Chomsky and his Critics* (Oxford, 2003).

N. Chomsky, *Knowledge of Language* (New York, 1986).

A. George (ed.), *Reflections on Chomsky* (Oxford, 1989).

T. Parsons, *Events in the Semantics of English* (Cambridge, Mass., 1990).

G. Preyer and G. Peter (eds.), *Logical Form and Language* (Oxford, 2002).

Y. Ravin and C. Leacock, *Polysemy: Theoretical and Computational Approaches* (Oxford, 2000).

linguistic turn. Collective designation for a range of otherwise quite disparate trends in twentieth-century thought. What they all have in common is an appeal to language, to *discourse, or forms of linguistic representation as the furthest point that philosophy can reach in its quest for knowledge and truth. There are no 'facts' outside language, and no 'reality' other than that which presents itself under some linguistic description. Thus philosophers can only be deluded if they seek to render language more accurate or perspicuous by removing its various natural imperfections—ambiguity, metaphor, opaque reference, etc.—and achieving a crystalline transparency of logical form. Rather they should follow Wittgenstein's example and acknowledge the open multiplicity of *'language-games' (or cultural *'forms of life'), each with its own criteria for what counts as a valid or meaningful utterance. In short, the proper business of philosophy in this therapeutic mode is to cure language of its abstract cravings and (in the words of Stanley Cavell) to 'lead it back, via the community, home'.

The project thus described was pursued most zealously by J. L. Austin and the proponents of so-called 'ordinary language' philosophy. 'Our common stock of words', Austin wrote, 'embodies all the distinctions men have found worth drawing . . . in the lifetimes of many generations: these are surely likely to be more numerous, more sound, and more subtle . . . than any that you or I are likely to think up in our arm-chairs of an afternoon—the most favoured alternative method'. But the trouble with this approach, as many have felt, is its tendency to consecrate the nuances of received ('common-sense') wisdom while failing to address more substantive philosophical issues. Thus it can easily give rise to an outlook of *laissez-faire* relativism or an inert consensus based recommendation that philosophy should cease asking awkward questions and be content—in Wittgenstein's phrase—to 'leave everything as it is'. C.N.

J. L. Austin, 'A Plea for Excuses', in *Philosophical Papers* (London, 1961).

Richard Rorty (ed.), *The Linguistic Turn: Recent Essays in Philosophical Method* (Chicago, 1967).

—— *Philosophy and the Mirror of Nature* (Oxford, 1980).

Ludwig Wittgenstein, *Philosophical Investigations*, tr. G. E. M. Anscombe (Oxford, 1953).

literature and philosophy. Some philosophical writing, though not very much, it has to be said, displays literary merit. Plato was a great writer and the British Empiricists are admired for the vivacity of their prose. However, imaginative literature—poetry, drama, and the novel—has presented problems to philosophers. Plato's hostility to art in general is well known. For him, art was a rival in the pursuit of truth, and liable to corrupt. Plato's antagonism, though shared to an extent by Tolstoy, finds few modern supporters. But, as usual, Plato raises, albeit obliquely, profound questions about literature.

There are two major issues. Firstly, there is what is sometimes described as the problem of belief. If a work of literature asserts or assumes propositions which I know or believe to be false, what difference does that make? If I do not share Milton's metaphysics, am I debarred to that extent from an appreciation of *Paradise Lost*? If I do not share his beliefs, can I nevertheless empathize with the poet by 'suspending my disbelief' or 'making believe' that these beliefs are true? Certainly I can be moved by *poetry or prose which proceeds on assumptions which I do not share. An atheist may find the poetry of George Herbert moving. Yet there are limits. I may bridle at the anti-Semitism in Pound's cantos. I do not suspend my disbelief in order to enter sympathetically into the world of a racist. And we certainly will resist literature which tries to suborn us. We cannot take seriously and may even resent fiction which, as we say, verges on propaganda. So although we can learn from literature we certainly do not commonly learn by absorbing maxims; it exemplifies and displays truths rather than argues for them. Indeed it is not part of a proper reaction to literature qua literature to assess the validity of the arguments it contains. Its 'truth-fulness' is, *pari passu*, not a matter of the truth of the claims it makes. The famous generalizations about marriage and the family which begin *Pride and Prejudice* and *Anna Karenina* are not exceptionless; it would be easy to find counter-examples. The truth of literature is generally a matter of the convincingness of the characters it portrays. Seen in this context, Plato's reservations about the arts seem less strange. If we believe that philosophy can increase our knowledge by its criticism of superstition and speculation, then philosophy teaches in a way which literature does not.

What literature does do is to offer us imaginary scenes, concentrated and complex settings, in which imaginary beings act. It is sometimes described as inductive. From literature I may learn about individual human propensities and peculiarities. In order that it can do this in its own peculiar fashion, it is necessary that literature move and involve us, and this raises the second of the two problems to which I alluded at the beginning. Not only am I moved by Hamlet's conversation with the ghost of his father, even though I do not believe in ghosts, I can be deeply moved by the death of Anna Karenina, even though I know that she has no existence outside these pages. But how can I be moved by the fate of somebody who does not exist? Is it that she is 'really dead' but only in the 'possible world' of Tolstoy's novel? Am I being irrational? It cannot be that I am moved by the general truth that there are real women who escape from a boring life into an ultimately unsatisfactory affair. I know there are such women but it is the fate of Anna which moves me and not theirs. *Imagination is crucial here for I can moved by what I can imagine and the fact that I can be so moved is an important factor in planning the course of my life. Literature, we could say, is important because it nurtures the imagination in ways which moral maxims or philosophical discourse cannot.   R.A.S.

*fiction.

David Caute, *The Illusion* (London, 1971).

John Hospers, 'Implied Truth in Literature', *Journal of Aesthetics and Art Criticism* (1960).

Peter Lamarque and Stein Haugom Olsen, *Truth, Fiction and Literature* (Oxford, 1994).

Colin Radford, 'How can we be Moved by the Fate of Anna Karenina?', *Proceedings of the Aristotelian Society*, supp. vol. (1975).

Morris Weitz, 'Truth in Literature', *Revue Internationale de Philosophie* (1955).

Locke, John (1632–1704). The foremost English philosopher of the early period of modern post-Cartesian philosophy was educated at Westminster School and Christ Church, Oxford. Besides studying, and then teaching, subjects such as logic, moral philosophy, rhetoric, and Greek, he had a deep and abiding interest in medicine. Through the Earl of Shaftesbury, he became involved in Protestant politics; this resulted in exile in Holland from 1683 to 1689, when, after the 'Glorious Revolution' which put William of Orange on the throne, he returned to England and a life of private study and public service.

He wrote widely—on various branches of philosophy, on education, economics, religion, and medicine. He is best known for his *Treatises of Government* (1690), *Letter Concerning Toleration* (1689), and his *Essay Concerning Human Understanding* (1690).

The *Treatises*, which contain Locke's political philosophy, were composed in the years of the Exclusion Crisis, during which Locke's patron, Shaftesbury, and others, sought to exclude James, then Duke of York, from the succession to the throne, and argued for government by consent and for the right to religious dissent.

The *First Treatise*, contains criticism of Robert Filmer's theory (*Patriarcha* (1680)) of absolute monarchy and the divine right of kings. Locke found this account of political *authority, according to which God granted Adam absolute and total political authority, unworkable. It could not be used to justify any actual political authority; we cannot show of any particular ruler that he is one of Adam's heirs. In an alternative account the *Second Treatise* argues that though subjects do have a duty to God to obey their ruler, their ruler's power is not God given or absolute, and it goes along with duties to his subjects.

Locke's account begins with the idea of a *state of nature, in which people live, free from external authority, in families and loose groups. In this state people have a duty to God not to 'harm another in his life . . . liberty, or . . . goods' (sect. 6), and so have a corresponding right to defend against such attack. But these rights and duties may not actually be respected and obeyed; we may lack the power to defend our rights, or may go too far in our own defence. For such reasons people agree to 'enter into society to make . . . one body politic, under one supreme government' (sect. 89). Leaving the state of nature, they 'set up a judge . . . with authority to determine all . . . controversies and redress . . . injuries' (sect. 89). But this authority is not absolute; they are answerable to 'the will and determination of the majority' (sect. 96). Popular consent not only creates, but also produces, the continued existence of a Lockean political society.

A distinction between tacit and explicit *consent provides Locke's answer to the objection that there is no historical evidence for his account of the creation of political authority, and that people are simply born into civil societies and come under their laws and authority without choice. By remaining in society, one gives one's tacit consent to it. Locke's suggestion that a person is always 'at liberty to . . . incorporate himself into any other community, or . . . to begin a new one' (sect. 121) is even less plausible now than then. But his account can be seen as a picturesque way of analysing the structure of legitimate political authority, and of revealing it to be essentially based on the consent of the governed. The notion of tacit consent is given further substance by Locke's allowing the possibility of legitimate resistance or *revolution. 'The community perpetually retains a supreme power of saving themselves from . . . their legislators, whenever they shall be so foolish or so wicked, as to . . . carry on designs against the[ir] liberties and properties' (sect. 149).

Locke's *Letter Concerning Toleration*, written during exile in Holland, considers how far the state can legitimately concern itself with religious practices. Convinced that Christianity as such requires toleration, Locke is scathing about states which persecute religious dissidents 'with a pretence of care of the public weal', and of national churches which persecute them 'under pretence of religion' (17). He then argues further against religious intolerance by the state by differentiating 'the business of civil government from that of religion' (17). States are constituted 'only for the procuring, preserving, and advancing their [subjects] civil interests': 'life, liberty, health . . . money, land, houses' (17); so a ruler's duty is never 'to be extended to the salvation of souls' (18). This conclusion is based on three considerations. First, the 'civil magistrate' has no more duty than anyone else has to concern himself with 'the care of souls': God has given him no authority 'to compel any one to his religion' (18); nor have his subjects left it to him to 'prescribe . . . what faith or worship [they] shall embrace' (18). Second, the means used by a ruler cannot bring about convictions in his subjects' minds. Civil power consists in outward force and earthly penalties, and these are unable to bring about 'inward persuasion' (18): 'the understanding . . . cannot be compelled to the belief of any thing by outward force . . . [which has no] efficacy as to make men change the inward judgement that they have framed of things' (18). We cannot simply believe what we are told to believe. Thirdly, even if it were possible, imposition of a religion by the state would in many cases not help to save souls. While there is, Locke believed, 'but one truth, one way to heaven', there nevertheless is a 'variety and contradiction of opinions in religion, wherein the princes of the world are . . . divided' (19); so state interference in religious matters would mean that 'men would owe their eternal happiness or misery to the places of their nativity' (19).

But though the state's sole concern is to protect the civil interests of its subjects, laws might still properly be enacted which have consequences for some sects or churches. Things prejudicial to the state and its members 'ought not to be permitted to the churches in their sacred rites' (37); nor are 'opinions contrary to human society, or to those moral rules which are necessary to the preservation of civil society' (45) to be tolerated. Equally, a church should not be tolerated by the state if membership involves allegiance to another earthly power. It is Roman Catholics whom Locke has in mind in this case, but they are not the only group to whom toleration is not to be extended: atheists are similarly untrustworthy. 'Those are not at all to be tolerated who deny the being of God. Promises, covenants, and oaths, which are the bonds of human society, can have no hold upon an atheist. The taking away of God . . . dissolves all' (47).

Locke resists the suggestion that toleration should be denied to certain dissenting, non-conformist sects, even though these had sometimes been 'nurseries of factions and seditions' (47). Their civil unruliness was not rooted in their very nature, he thought, but had developed precisely through lack of toleration. 'If men enter into seditious conspiracies, it is not religion inspires them to it . . . but their suffering and oppressions' (48–9).

Locke also concerned himself with interdenominational toleration. What he says turns on his account of the nature of a church as a society of people who have voluntarily come together 'in order to the public worshipping of God, in such manner as they judge acceptable to him, and effectual to the salvation of their souls' (20). Societies need rules and regulations, and in the case of a church the authority to make and apply them resides in members. Locke explicitly denied that a church requires 'a bishop, or presbyter with ruling authority derived from the very apostles' (20–1). Christ did not say that churches should have governments of these kinds; he promised to be present simply 'wheresoever two or three are gathered together in his name' (21).

In short, then, 'the care . . . of every man's soul . . . is to be left unto himself' (28). But Locke is not allowing that someone might enter into private and solitary communion with God: God should be publicly worshipped, and people should 'meet together . . . to own to the world that they worship God' (32). He is not allowing, either, that there are many, equally good ways to eternal happiness: there is 'one only narrow way which leads to heaven' (30). But it is not for the state or some national church to prescribe what it is. 'Those things . . . every man ought sincerely to inquire into himself' (29). Even though there is only one narrow way to heaven I cannot be on it unless I am thoroughly persuaded in my own mind: 'I cannot be saved by a religion that I distrust, and by a worship that I abhor' (32).

Locke is best known for his *Essay Concerning Human Understanding*, which contains his theory of knowledge. Believing we have been put here by God with some expectation of an afterlife, Locke's aim is to discover what kind of things God has fitted us to know, and so how we should direct and use our intellect and understanding. His purpose is 'to enquire into the original, certainty, and extent of human knowledge' (II. i. 2).

He maintains from the outset that none of our ideas or knowledge (whether theoretical or ethical) is innate: the mind at birth is like 'white paper' (II. i. 2), and all our ideas are derived from experience. But such experience-based ideas are only 'the materials' of reason and knowledge (II. i. 2). Knowledge itself is *not* 'made out to us by our senses' (Draft A, 157). It is a product of reason working out the connections between those ideas. Locke's *empiricism about ideas is combined with a *rationalism about knowledge: without reason all we have is belief, not knowledge.

His claim that all our *ideas, the materials of knowledge, come from experience is facilitated by a distinction between simple and complex ideas—the former being unanalysable and indefinable, the latter being mentally constructible out of simples. Complex ideas are of various sorts: substances (e.g. gold, lead, horses), which represent things in the material world; modes (e.g. triangle, gratitude), which are 'dependences on, or affections of substances' (II. xii. 4); and relations (e.g. parent, whiter). He defends his view that all our ideas derive from experience by consideration of such cases as 'space, time, and infinity, and some few others' (II. xii. 8) such as perception, solidity, memory, number, volition, pure substance in general, cause and effect, identity. Besides offering these as difficult test cases, Locke obviously finds them philosophically interesting too.

Locke's discussion of 'pure *substance in general' (II. xxiii. 2) became notorious, and there are different accounts of what he means. Often he is taken to be rejecting the kind of view which was later held by Bertrand Russell, according to which a material thing is no more than 'a bundle of properties'. He is often, that is, supposed to hold that, in addition to properties, things have a 'substratum' which 'supports' their properties. According to another interpretation, Locke's 'substratum' should not be seen in the context of abstract logical questions about the difference between 'things' and 'properties'. It should be identified simply with matter as understood by the 'corpuscularians' of his century, who revived classical Greek atomism, or, more specifically, with particular arrangements of corpuscles of that matter, arrangements which Locke calls the real essences of material things.

His discussion of identity has been of lasting interest. There is, he points out, a relativity about identity. 'Is this what was here before?' It depends what kind of thing *this* is meant to be. If a mass of matter, it is the same if it consists of the same particles; if a living body, this need not be so: 'a colt grown up to a horse . . . is all the while the same . . . though there may be a manifest change of the parts' (II. xxvii. 3). Identity consists here in matter's being continuously arranged in a similar way so that it 'partakes of the same life' (II. xxvii. 4). The point is important for his distinction, made in connection with *personal identity, between the idea of 'man' and that of 'person'. A man's identity is basically no different from that of any other animal. But a person is not simply a living body. Identity here is that of 'a thinking intelligent being, that has reason, and reflection, and can consider itself as itself, the same thinking thing in different times and places' (II. xxvii. 9). Locke's description of a person as 'a thinking intelligent being' does not mean that the continuity of self-consciousness which constitutes personal identity is the continuity of some immaterial substance, which is self-conscious, for he is clearly unhappy with this view of Descartes's.

In fact the *Essay* contains a fair amount of criticism of Descartes: the identification of extension as the whole essence of material substance, and the claim that the mind is always thinking, are further things to which he objects. Nevertheless, it was that 'justly-admired gentleman' Descartes who rescued Locke from the obscurantism (as it seemed) of the then-prevailing Aristotelian scholasticism to which he had been exposed as a student (*Works*, iv. 48). From Descartes too Locke takes his central and hard-worked notion of an 'idea' ('whatsoever is the object of the understanding when a man thinks' (*Essay*, I. i. 8)) as an essentially mind-dependent thing, rather than a Platonic entity with a reality of its own quite independent of any relation it might have to our minds.

Locke refers to the 'vague and insignificant forms of speech' of the scholastics in his 'Epistle to the Reader'. They come in for criticism in book III, 'On Words', where he rejects the idea that classificatory words stand for 'real essences', understood, not as Locke prefers (as corpuscular constitutions), but as so-called substantial forms which, by being embodied in things, make them to be of one sort or another. Instead, he argues that classification is a matter of human interests and convenience, and that general words stand for 'nominal essences', abstract ideas which we ourselves construct. Generality and universality, he says, 'belong not to the real existence of things; but are the inventions and creatures of the understanding, made by it for its own use' (III. iii. 11).

In book IV, *knowledge is defined as 'the perception of the connection and agreement, or disagreement . . . of any of our ideas' (IV. i. 2). Some propositions are true because the relevant ideas are connected and related in such a way as to make them true. Any number is even or odd by virtue of there being a connection between the idea of 'number' and those of 'evenness' and 'oddness'. It is by 'perceiving' these relations by the light of our reason that we come to have knowledge. Where either intellectual incapacity or lack of any actual connection, means we can perceive no connection, then, 'though we may fancy, guess, or believe, yet we always come short of knowledge' (IV. i. 2).

The definition of knowledge as the perception of connections *between ideas* is ill suited to a third degree of knowledge, our 'sensitive knowledge' of the existence of *things* 'without us' (IV. ii. 14) *which correspond to our ideas*. Moreover, though the certainty of sensitive knowledge is not so great as that of the other two degrees, it still, Locke says, deserves the name of knowledge; and he is dismissive of those who might be sceptical about the existence of an external world. Because of his talk of a correspondence between external things and our ideas, Locke has usually been taken to be a representational realist about perception; but in recent years, and despite his saying that the mind 'perceives nothing but its own ideas' (IV. iv. 3), some have interpreted him as a direct realist.

Locke's definition of knowledge seems perfect for our a priori knowledge in a subject such as geometry, which deals with modes such as 'triangle'. But what of our knowledge in the area of what was known as 'natural philosophy', for example, the knowledge that the substance gold is malleable and graphite not? This is surely based on observation and experience and not on intellectual perception of any connection between ideas. Locke recognizes such cases where, because there is 'a want of a discoverable connection between those ideas which we have . . . we are . . . left only to observation and experiment' (IV. iii. 28) and explicitly says that they do not constitute 'knowledge', but what he calls belief or opinion.

The contrast between knowledge proper and belief or opinion is inherited from the scholastics. But, unlike them, Locke does not think that 'opinion' or 'belief' about the properties and behaviour of substances in the material world is not worth having. He clearly supports the idea of a systematic observationally and experimentally based study of nature, a study of the kind being pursued by his colleague and friend, the chemist Robert Boyle, whom he refers to as one of the 'master builders' of the 'commonwealth of learning'.

The reason why 'natural philosophy is not capable of being made a science' (IV. xii. 10), i.e. into a systematic body of *knowledge* as Locke defines it, is that we do not know the real essences, the corpuscular constitutions, of the substances with which it is concerned. The fact that *we* can perceive no connection between being gold and being malleable does not mean that there is not one. The properties of gold depend on or result from its corpuscular constitution, and if we knew just how its corpuscles are structured and arranged, we would be able to see just why it has those properties. If, that is to say, our idea of gold were an idea of its real essence, we might see a connection between being gold and being malleable.

But this limitation on our knowledge is no cause for pessimistic concern. The 'belief' and 'opinion' we have about the properties of substances in the world are sufficient for daily practicalities. 'Men have reason to be well satisfied with what God hath thought fit for them, since he has given them . . . whatsoever is necessary for the conveniences of life' (I. i. 5).

Unlike 'natural philosophy', geometry is a science and falls on this side of the horizon of our knowledge. This is because it deals not with substances (e.g. gold, lead) but with modes (e.g. the triangle), whose real essences we know. As with a substance such as gold, it is because a mode such as a triangle is what it is that it has the properties it has; but whereas in the first case we do not know the real essence, in the second, Locke says, we do. It is because it is a figure of three lines enclosing a space that a triangle's external angle equals its internal opposites; and because our idea of a triangle is an idea of that real essence we can see a connection between being a triangle and having angles like that.

Our knowledge is bounded by our ideas, and, in general, extends only so far as they are ideas of real essences. But geometrical figures are not the only things whose real essences we might know. The ideas of morality are modes too, and Locke thinks that, with proper application, a systematic science of ethics similar to that of geometry could be developed.

Yet though moral principles are neither innate nor easy to acquire by reason, no one need remain ignorant of his duties and obligations; for the Bible teaches us them too. This need not mean taking things on authority and abandoning all thought of moral knowledge. We can in hindsight find rationally justifying arguments for what the Bible first suggests. Nevertheless, some people, 'perplexed in the necessary affairs of life' (I. iii. 25) may have no time for this, and their morality must be a matter of 'faith' or 'belief'.

Locke's general conclusion concerning the extent of our knowledge is, then, that not only has God 'put within the reach of [our] discovery [beliefs sufficient for] the comfortable provision for [this] life' (I. i. 5), he has also put within our grasp knowledge of 'the way that leads to a better'. He has given us the means to acquire knowledge of 'whatsoever is necessary for . . . the information of virtue' (I. i. 5).

Many of the early reactions to the *Essay* were critical. Locke was sometimes supposed to be a sceptic; but though he does put limits on our ability to know and understand, he is hardly pessimistic about the human situation. He explicitly aimed to defeat the despairing idea 'that either there is no such thing as truth at all; or that mankind hath no sufficient means to attain a certain knowledge of it' (I. i. 2). Nevertheless, his polemic against innate ideas was taken to imply an impersonal deism, and his suggestion that matter might think (despite stressing that 'all the great ends of morality, and religion, are well enough secured, without philosophical proofs of the soul's immateriality' (IV. iii. 6)) was pointed to with horror. Berkeley, the first great British philosopher after Locke, reacted against what he saw as the sceptical and atheistical consequences of Locke's philosophy.

The framework of Locke's approach to the human mind influenced psychology and epistemology for a long time. David Hartley (1705–57), Joseph Priestley (1733–1804), Francis Hutcheson (1694–1747), James Mill (1733–1836), and Étienne Condillac (1715–80) all approached this problem by analysing experience, after the manner of Locke, into elements and their combinations and associations.

Many of the ideas in the *Essay* (the stress on observation and the corpuscular theory of matter, the attack on the scholastics, the place of reason in religion) can be found in Locke's lesser contemporaries too. But he was a powerful and vigorous spokesman for them. Along with Isaac Newton, he became one of the figureheads of the Age of *Enlightenment. Both then, and in our own time, he is valued for a judicious, sober reasonableness, and an individualistic insistence that opinions are to be weighed carefully on their merits by each of us, independently of what others, particularly those in majority or authority, say. 'Trial and examination must give [truth] price.'   R.S.W.

Richard Ashcraft, *Locke's* Two Treatises of Government (London, 1987).

Michael Ayers, *Locke*, 2 vols. (London, 1992).

John Dunn, *John Locke* (Oxford, 1984).

Nicholas Jolley, *Locke: His Philosophical Thought* (Oxford, 1999).

John Locke, *Draft A of Locke's* Essay Concerning Human Understanding (1671), in *Drafts for the* Essay Concerning Human Understanding, *and other Philosophical Writings*, vol. 1, ed. P. H. Nidditch and G. A. J. Rogers (Oxford, 1990).

—— *Two Treatises of Government* (London, 1690). The partially modernized quotations are from Peter Laslett's critical edn. (Cambridge, 1960).

—— *Essay Concerning Human Understanding* (London, 1690). The partially modernized quotations are from P. H. Nidditch's authoritative edn. (Oxford, 1975).

—— *Works* (London, 1823).

—— *A Letter Concerning Toleration* (London, 1689). References are to the edn. by John Horton and Susan Mendus (London, 1991).

R. S. Woolhouse, *Locke* (Brighton, 1983).

locutions: *see* linguistic acts.

logic, deontic: *see* deontic logic.

logic, formal or symbolic: *see* modern logic; traditional logic; history of logic; logical theory; calculus; propositional calculus; propositional logic; sentential calculus; predicate calculus; modal logic; deontic logic; many-valued logics; relvance logic; tense logic; higher-order logic; intuitionist logic; logicism; logical harmony; metalogic; logical paradoxes; logical notations; Appendix on logical symbols.

logic, higher-order: *see* higher-order logic.

logic, history of. Aristotle was the first thinker to devise a logical system. He drew upon the emphasis on universal definition found in Socrates, the use of *reductio ad absurdum* in Zeno of Elea, claims about propositional structure and *negation in Parmenides and Plato, and the body of argumentative techniques found in legal reasoning and geometrical proof. Yet the theory presented in Aristotle's five treatises known as the *Organon*—the *Categories*, the *De interpretatione*, the *Prior Analytics*, the *Posterior Analytics*, and the *De sophisticis elenchis*—goes far beyond any of these.

Aristotle holds that a proposition is a complex involving two terms, a *subject and a predicate, each of which is represented grammatically with a noun. The logical *form of a proposition is determined by its quantity (universal or particular) and by its quality (affirmative or negative). Aristotle investigates the relations between two propositions containing the same terms in his theories of opposition (*square of opposition) and conversion. The former describes relations of *contradictoriness and *contrariety, the latter *equipollences and *entailments.

The analysis of logical form, opposition, and conversion are combined in syllogistic, Aristotle's greatest invention in logic. A *syllogism consists of three propositions. The first two, the premisses, share exactly one term, and they logically entail the third proposition, the conclusion, which contains the two non-shared terms of the premisses. The term common to the two premisses may occur as subject in one and predicate in the other (called the 'first figure'), predicate in both ('second figure'), or subject in both ('third figure'). A given configuration of premisses and conclusions is called a 'mood'.

In the scholastic period, mnemonic names for the valid moods canvassed in the *Prior Analytics* were devised. Two first-figure valid moods were considered perfect and not in need of any further validation: *Barbara (consisting entirely in universal affirmatives) and *Celarent (consisting in a universal negative and a universal affirmative, concluding in a universal negative). For the validation of the rest, Aristotle used three techniques: reduction, where a given mood is transformed through conversions into Barbara or Celarent; *reductio ad absurdum*; and *ekthesis*, which proceeds by selection of an arbitrary individual. He regularly describes moods by using variables in place of terms. To reject a proposed inference he typically gives a list of terms that, when substituted as values of the term-variables, produce true premisses and false conclusion. This is similar to the modern technique of constructing 'counter-arguments' to establish invalidity.

Aristotle may also be credited with the formulation of several metalogical theses, most notably the law of *non-contradiction, the principle of *excluded middle, and the law of *bivalence. These are important in his discussions of *modal logic and tense logic. Aristotle referred to certain principles of propositional logic and to reasoning involving hypothetical propositions. He also created two non-formal logical theories: techniques and strategies for devising arguments (in the *Topics*), and a theory of fallacies (in the *De sophisticis elenchis*). Aristotle's pupils Eudemus and Theophrastus modified and developed Aristotelian logic in several ways.

The next major innovations in logic are due to the Megarian–Stoic School. They developed an alternative account of the syllogism, and, in the course of so doing, elaborated a full *propositional logic which complements Aristotelian term logic. There are fragmentary records of debates over the *truth-conditions for various propositional connectives, which include accounts of *material implication, *strict implication, and relevant implication. The Megarians and the Stoics also investigated various logical *antinomies, including the *liar paradox. The leading logician of this school was Chrysippus, credited with over 100 works in logic.

There were few developments in logic in succeeding periods, other than a number of handbooks, summaries, translations, and commentaries, usually in a simplified and combined form. The more influential authors include Cicero, Porphyry, and Boethius in the later Roman Empire; the Byzantine scholiast Philoponus; and al-Fārābī, Avicenna, and Averroës in the Arab world.

The next major logician known to us is an innovator of the first rank: Peter Abelard, who worked in the early twelfth century. He composed an independent treatise on logic, the *Dialectica*, and wrote extensive commentaries. There are discussions of conversion, opposition, quantity, quality, tense logic, a reduction of *de dicto* to *de re* modality, and much else. Abelard also clearly formulates several semantic principles, including the Tarski biconditional for the theory of truth, which he rejects. Perhaps most important, Abelard is responsible for the clear formulation of a pair of relevance criteria for logical consequences. (*Relevance logic.) The failure of his criteria led later logicians to reject relevance implication and to endorse material implication.

Spurred by Abelard's teachings and problems he proposed, and by further translations, other logicians began to grasp the details of Aristotle's texts. The result, coming to fruition in the middle of the thirteenth century, was the first phase of *supposition theory, an elaborate doctrine about the reference of terms in various propositional contexts. Its development is preserved in handbooks by Peter of Spain, Lambert of Auxerre, and William of Sherwood. The theory of *obligationes*, a part of non-formal logic, was also invented at this time. Other topics, such as the relation between time and modality, the conventionality of semantics, and the theory of *truth, were investigated.

The fourteenth century is the apex of medieval logical theory, containing an explosion of creative work. Supposition theory is developed extensively in its second phase by logicians such as William of Ockham, Jean Buridan, Gregory of Rimini, and Albert of Saxony. Buridan also elaborates a full theory of consequences, a cross between entailments and inference rules. From explicit semantic principles, Buridan constructs a detailed and extensive investigation of syllogistic, and offers completeness proofs. Nor is Buridan an isolated figure. Three new literary genres emerged: treatises on syncategoremata (logical particles), which attempted to codify their behaviour and the inferences they license; treatises on sentences, called 'sophisms', that are puzzling or challenging given background assumptions about logic and language; and treatises on insolubles, such as the liar paradox.

The creative energy that drove the logical inquiries of the fourteenth century was not sustained. By the middle of the fifteenth century little if any new work was being done. There were instead many simplified handbooks and manuals of logic. The descendants of these textbooks came to be used in the universities, and the great innovations of medieval logicians were forgotten. Probably the best of these works is the *Port Royal Logic*, by Antoine Arnauld and Pierre Nicole, which was published in 1662. When writers refer to 'traditional logic', they usually have this degenerate textbook tradition in mind. (*Logic, traditional.)

Since the beginning of the modern era most of the contributions to logic have been made by mathematicians. Leibniz envisioned the development of a universal language to be specified with mathematical precision. The syntax of the words is to correspond to the metaphysical make-up of the designated entities. The goal, in effect, was to reduce scientific and philosophical speculation to computation. Although this grandiose project was not developed very far, and it did not enjoy much direct influence, the Universal Characteristic is a precursor to much of the subsequent work in mathematical logic.

In the early nineteenth century Bolzano developed a number of notions central to logic. Some of these, like analyticity and logical consequence, are seen to be relative to a collection of 'variable' concepts. For example, a proposition C is a consequence of a collection P of propositions relative to a group G of variable items, if every appropriate uniform substitution for the members of G that makes every member of P true also makes C true. This may be the first attempt to characterize consequence in non-modal terms, and it is the start of a long tradition of characterizing logical notions in semantic terms, using a distinction between logical and non-logical terminology.

Toward the end of the nineteenth century one can distinguish three overlapping traditions in the development of logic. One of them originates with Boole and includes, among others, Peirce, Jevons, Schröder, and Venn. This 'algebraic school' focused on the relationship between regularities in correct reasoning and operations like addition and multiplication. A primary aim was to develop calculi common to the reasoning in different areas, such as propositions, classes, and probabilities. The orientation is that of abstract algebra. One begins with one or more systems of related operations and articulates a common, abstract structure. A set of axioms is then formulated which is satisfied by each of the system. The system that Boole developed is quite similar to what is now called Boolean algebra. Other members of the school developed rudimentary *quantifiers, which were sometimes taken to be extended, even infinitary, conjunctions and disjunctions.

The aim of the second tradition, the 'logicist school', was to codify the underlying logic of all rational, scientific discourse into a single system. For them, logic is not the result of abstractions from the reasoning in particular disciplines and contexts. Rather, logic concerns the most general features of actual precise discourse, features independent of subject-matter.

The major logicists were Russell, the early Wittgenstein perhaps, and the greatest logician since Aristotle,

Gottlob Frege. In his *Begriffsschrift* (translated in van Heijenoort (ed.), *From Frege to Gödel*), Frege developed a rich formal language with full mathematical rigour. Despite the two-dimensional notation, it is easily recognized as a contemporary *Higher-order logic. Quantifiers are understood as they are in current logic textbooks, not as extended conjunctions and disjunctions. Unlike the algebraists, Frege did not envision various domains of discourse, each of which can serve as an interpretation of the language. Rather, each (first-order) variable is to range over all objects whatsoever. Moreover, in contemporary terms, the systems of the logicists had no non-logical terminology.

Frege made brilliant use of his logical insights when developing his philosophical programmes concerning mathematics and language. He held that arithmetic and analysis are parts of logic (*logicism; mathematics, history of the philosophy of), and made great strides in casting number theory within the system of the *Begriffsschrift*. To capture mathematical induction, minimal closures, and a host of other mathematical notions, he developed and exploited the *ancestral relation, in purely logical terms.

Unfortunately, the system Frege eventually developed was shown to be inconsistent. It entails the existence of a concept R which holds of all and only those extensions that do not contain themselves. A contradiction, known as *Russell's paradox, follows.

A major response was the multi-volume *Principia Mathematica*, by Russell and Whitehead, which attempts to recapture the logicist programme by developing an elaborate theory of *types. (*Higher-order logic.) Antinomies are avoided by enforcing a *'vicious-circle principle' that no item may be defined by reference to a totality that contains the item to be defined. Despite its complexity, *Principia Mathematica* enjoyed a wide influence among logicians and philosophers. An elegant version of the theory, called simple type theory, was introduced by Ramsey. It violates the vicious-circle principle, but still avoids formal paradox.

The third tradition dates back to at least Euclid and, in this period, includes Dedekind, Peano, Hilbert, Pasch, Veblen, Huntington, Heyting, and Zermelo. The aim of this 'mathematical school' is the axiomatization of particular branches of mathematics, like geometry, arithmetic, analysis, and set theory. Zermelo, for example, produced an axiomatization of set theory in 1908, drawing on insights of Cantor and others. The theory now known as Zermelo–Fraenkel set theory is the result of some modifications and clarifications, due to Skolem, Fraenkel, and von Neumann, among others.

Unlike Euclid, some members of the mathematical school thought it important to include an explicit formulation of the rules of inference—the logic—in the axiomatic development. In some cases, such as Hilbert and his followers, this was part of a formalist philosophical agenda, sometimes called the Hilbert programme. (*Formalism.) Others, like Heyting, produced axiomatic versions of the logic of *intuitionism and intuitionistic

mathematics, in order to contrast and highlight their revisionist programmes (see Brouwer).

A variation on the mathematical theme took place in Poland under Łukasiewicz and others. Logic itself became the branch of mathematics to be brought within axiomatic methodology. Systems of propositional logic, modal logic, tense logic, Boolean algebra, and *mereology were designed and analysed.

A crucial development occurred when attention was focused on the languages and the axiomatizations themselves as objects for direct mathematical study. Drawing on the advent of non-Euclidean geometry, mathematicians in this school considered alternative interpretations of their languages and, at the same time, began to consider metalogical questions about their systems, including issues of *independence, *consistency, *categoricity, and *completeness. Both the Polish school and those pursuing the Hilbert programme developed an extensive programme for such 'metamathematical' investigation. (*Metalanguage; *metalogic.) Eventually, notions about syntax and proof, such as consistency and derivability, were carefully distinguished from semantic, or model-theoretic counterparts, such as satisfiability and logical consequence.

This metamathematical perspective is foreign to the logicist school. For them, the relevant languages were already fully interpreted, and were not to be limited to any particular subject-matter. Because the languages are completely general, there is no interesting perspective 'outside' the system from which to study it. The orientation of the logicists has been called 'logic as language', and that of the mathematicians and algebraists 'logic as calculus'. Despite problems of communication, there was significant interaction between the schools. Contemporary logic is a blending of them.

In 1915 Löwenheim carefully delineated what would later be recognized as the first-order part of a logical system, and showed that if a first-order formula is satisfiable at all, then it is satisfiable in a countable (or finite) domain. He was firmly rooted in the algebraic school, using techniques developed there. Skolem went on to generalize that result in several ways, and to produce more enlightening proofs of them. The results are known as the Löwenheim–Skolem theorems. (*Skolem's paradox.)

The intensive work on metamathematical problems culminated in the achievements of Kurt Gödel, a logician whose significance ranks with Aristotle and Frege. In his 1929 doctoral dissertation, Gödel showed that a given first-order sentence is deducible in common deductive systems for logic if and only if it is logically true in the sense that it is satisfied by all interpretations. This is known as Gödel's completeness theorem. A year later, he proved that for common axiomatizations of a sufficiently rich version of arithmetic, there is a sentence which is neither provable nor refutable therein. This is called Gödel's incompleteness theorem, or simply *Gödel's theorem.

The techniques of Gödel's theorem appear to be general, applying to any reasonable axiomatization that includes a sufficient amount of arithmetic. But what is 'reasonable'? Intuitively, an axiomatization should be effective: there should be an *algorithm to determine whether a given string is a formula, an axiom, etc. But what is an 'algorithm'? Questions like this were part of the motivation for logicians to turn their attention to the notions of computability and effectiveness in the middle of the 1930s. There were a number of characterizations of computability, developed more or less independently, by logicians like Gödel (recursiveness), Post, Church (lambda-definability), Kleene, Turing (the *Turing machine), and Markov (the Markov algorithm). Many of these were by-products of other research in mathematical logic. It was shown that all of the characterizations are coextensive, indicating that an important class had been identified. Today, it is widely held that an arithmetic function is computable if and only if it is recursive, Turing machine computable, etc. This is known as *Church's thesis.

Later in the decade Gödel developed the notion of set theoretic constructibility, as part of his proof that the axiom of *choice and Cantor's *continuum hypothesis are consistent with Zermelo–Fraenkel set theory (formulated without the axiom of choice). In 1963 Paul Cohen showed that these statements are independent of Zermelo–Fraenkel set theory, introducing the powerful technique of forcing. (*Independence.) There was (and is) a spirited inquiry among set theorists, logicians, and philosophers, including Gödel himself, into whether assertions like the continuum hypothesis have determinate truth-values. (*Continuum problem; *mathematics, problems of the philosophy of.)

Alfred Tarski, a pupil of Łukasiewicz, was one of the most creative and productive logicians of this, or any other, period. His influence spreads among a wide range of philosophical and mathematical schools and locations. Among philosophers, he is best known for his definitions of *truth and logical consequence, which introduce the fruitful semantic notion of *satisfaction. This, however, is but a small fraction of his work, which illuminates the methodology of deductive systems, and such central notions as completeness, decidability, consistency, satisfiability, and definability. His results are the foundation of several ongoing research programmes.

Alonzo Church was another major influence in both mathematical and philosophical logic. He and students such as Kleene and Henkin have developed a wide range of areas in philosophical and mathematical logic, including completeness, definability, computability, and a number of Fregean themes, such as second-order logic and sense and reference. Church's theorem is that the collection of first-order logical truths is not recursive. It follows from this and Church's thesis that there is no algorithm for determining whether a given first-order formula is a logical truth. Church was a founder of the Association for Symbolic Logic and long-time guiding editor of the *Journal of Symbolic Logic*, which began publication in 1936. Volumes 1 and 3 contain an extensive bibliography of work in symbolic logic since antiquity.

The development of logic in the first few decades of this century is one of the most remarkable events in intellectual history, bringing together many brilliant minds working on closely related concepts.

Mathematical logic has come to be a central tool of contemporary analytic philosophy, forming the backbone of the work of major figures like Quine, Kripke, Davidson, and Dummett. Since about the 1950s special topics of interest to contemporary philosophers, such as modal logic, tense logic, *many-valued logic (used in the study of *vagueness), *deontic logic, relevance logic, and nonstandard logic, have been vigorously studied. The field still attracts talented mathematicians and philosophers, and there is no sign of abatement.   P.K.
                                                          S.S.

*logic, traditional; logical laws.

I. M. Bocheński, *A History of Formal Logic*, tr. and ed. Ivo Thomas (New York, 1956).

Alonzo Church, *Introduction to Mathematical Logic* (Princeton, NJ, 1956).

Martin Davis (ed.), *The Undecidable* (New York, 1965).

Jean van Heijenoort (ed.), *From Frege to Gödel* (Cambridge, Mass., 1967).

William Kneale and Martha Kneale, *The Development of Logic* (Oxford, 1962).

Alfred Tarski, *Logic, Semantics and Metamathematics*, 2nd edn., tr. J. H. Woodger, ed. John Corcoran (Indianapolis, 1983).

logic, informal. Informal logic examines the nature and function of arguments in natural language, stressing the craft rather than the formal theory of reasoning. It supplements the account of simple and compound statements offered by *formal logic and, reflecting the character of arguments in natural language, widens the scope to include inductive as well as deductive patterns of inference.

Informal logic's own account of arguments begins with assertions—the premisses and conclusions—whose rich meaning in natural language is largely ignored by formal logic. Assertions have meaning as statements as well as actions and often reveal something about the person who makes them. Not least, they are the main ingredient in patterns of inference. Apart from the crucial action of claiming statements to be true, the assertions found in an argument may play other performative roles, such as warranting a statement's truth (on one's own authority or that of another), conceding its truth, contesting it, or—instead of asserting it at all—assuming the statement as a hypothesis. Assertions also have an epistemic dimension. It is a convention of natural language (though hardly a universal truth) that speakers believe what they assert. Appraising the full meaning of a premiss or conclusion therefore involves gauging whether the statement was asserted merely as a belief or, in addition, as an objective fact or even as an item of knowledge. Finally, assertions have an emotive side. Few arguments of natural language are utterly impersonal. Attitudes and feelings seep from the language of argument and can easily influence what direction a sequence of reasoning may take. Because informal logic sees assertions and arguments as woven into the fabric of discourse, the threads it traces are extremely varied: embedded but possibly incomplete patterns of deductive and non-deductive inference, hidden assumptions, conversational implications, vagueness, rhetorical techniques of persuasion, and, of course, fallacies. Such topics, though important for understanding arguments in natural language, lead it far from the concerns of formal logic. That informal logic lacks the precision and elegance of a formal theory is hardly surprising, therefore, but it probably comes as close as any enterprise ever will to being a science of argumentation.   R.E.T.

I. Copi, *Informal Logic* (New York, 1986).

F. W. Dauer, *Critical Thinking: An Introduction to Reasoning* (Oxford, 1989).

logic, intuitionist: *see* intuitionist logic.

logic, many-valued: *see* many-valued logic.

logic, modal: *see* modal logic.

logic, modern. Logic, whether modern or traditional, is about sound reasoning and the rules which govern it. In the mid-nineteenth century (say from 1847, the date of Boole's book *The Mathematical Analysis of Logic*), logic began to be developed as a rigorous mathematical system. Its development was soon speeded along by controversies about the foundations of mathematics. The resulting discoveries are now used constantly by mathematicians, philosophers, linguists, computer scientists, electronic engineers, and less regularly by many others (for example, music composers and psychologists). Gödel's incompleteness theorem of 1931 was a high point not only for logic but also for twentieth-century culture. Gödel's argument showed that there are absolute limits to what we can achieve by reasoning within a formal system; but it also showed how powerful mechanical calculation can be, and so it led almost directly to the invention of digital computers.

Many arguments are valid because of their *form*; any other argument of the same form would be valid too. For example:

> Fifty-pence pieces are large seven-sided coins.
> This machine won't take large coins.
> Therefore this machine won't take fifty-pence pieces.
>
> An auk is a short-necked diving bird.
> What Smith saw was not a short-necked bird.
> Therefore what Smith saw was not an auk.

Both of these arguments can be paraphrased into the form:

> (1) Every X is a Y and a Z.
> No Y is a W.
> Therefore no X is a W.

(Thus for the first, X = fifty-pence piece, Y = large coin, Z = seven-sided object, W = thing that this machine will take.) This form (1) is an *argument schema*; it has schematic letters in it, and it becomes an argument when we translate the letters into phrases. Moreover, every argument got from the schema in this way is valid: the conclusion (after 'Therefore') does follow from the premisses (the sentences before 'Therefore'). So we call (1) a *valid argument schema*.

Likewise some statements are true purely by virtue of their form and hence are *logically valid*. We can write down a statement schema to show the form, for example:

> If p and q then p.

Here the schematic letters p, q have to be translated into clauses; but whatever clauses we use, the resulting sentence must be true. Such a schema is logically valid; we can regard it as a valid argument schema with no premisses.

What does it mean to say that a particular argument, expressed in English, has a particular argument schema as its form? Unfortunately this question has no exact answer. As we saw in the examples above, the words in an argument can be rearranged or paraphrased to bring out the form. Words can be replaced by synonyms too; an argument doesn't become invalid because it says 'gramophone' at one point and 'record-player' at another. For the last 100 years or more, it has been usual to split logic into an exact part which deals with precisely defined argument schemas, and a looser part which has to do with translating arguments into their logical *form.

This looser part has been very influential in philosophy. One doctrine—we may call it the *logical form doctrine*—states that every proposition or sentence has a logical form, and the logical forms of arguments consist of the logical forms of the sentences occurring in them. In the early years of the century Russell and Wittgenstein put forward this doctrine in a way which led to the programme of *analytic philosophy: analysing a proposition was regarded as uncovering its logical form. Chomsky has argued that each sentence of a natural language has a structure which can be analysed at several levels, and one of these levels is called *LF* for logical form—roughly speaking, this level carries the meaning of the sentence. However, Chomsky's reasons for this linguistic analysis have nothing to do with the forms of valid arguments, though his analysis does use devices from logic, such as quantifiers and variables. One can hope for a general linguistic theory which gives each natural-language sentence a logical form that explains its meaning and also satisfies the logical form doctrine; logicians such as Montague and his student Kamp have made important suggestions in this direction, but the goal is still a long way off.

Let us turn to the more exact part of logic. Experience shows that in valid argument schemas we constantly meet words such as 'and', 'or', 'if'; moreover, the sentences can be paraphrased so that these words are used to connect clauses, not single words. For example, the sentence

Fifty-pence pieces are large seven-sided coins can be paraphrased as

Fifty-pence pieces are large coins AND fifty-pence pieces are seven-sided.

We can introduce symbols to replace these words, for example ∧ for 'and', ∨ for 'or', ¬ for 'it is not true that . . . ' and → for 'if . . . then'. Unlike the schematic letters, these new symbols have a fixed meaning and they can be translated into English. They are known as *logical constants.

Round about 1880 Frege and Peirce independently suggested another kind of expression for use in argument schemas. We write

∀ x ...x...

to mean that '...x...' is true however x is interpreted. The expression ∀ x can be read as 'For all x'. For example, the sentence

Fifty-pence pieces are large seven-sided coins can be rewritten as

∀ x (if x is a fifty-pence piece then x is a large seven-sided coin),

or, using the logical constants,

(2) ∀x (x is a fifty-pence piece → (x is a large coin ∧ x is seven-sided)).

This last sentence says that whatever thing we consider (as an interpretation for x), if it's a fifty-pence piece then it's a large coin and it's seven-sided. The symbol x is not a schematic letter in (2), because the expression ∀x becomes nonsense if we give x an interpretation. Instead it is a new kind of symbol which we call a *bound variable*. The expression ∀x has a twin, ∃x, which is read as 'For some x'. These two expressions are the main examples of logical *quantifiers.

Quantifiers are somewhere between logical constants and schematic letters. Like logical constants, they do have a fixed meaning. But this meaning needs to be filled out by the context, because we need to known what range of interpretations of the bound variable is allowed. This range is called the *domain of quantification*. (Frege assumed that the domain of quantification is always the class of all objects. But in practice when we say 'everybody' we usually mean everybody in the room, or all adults of sound mind, or some other restricted class of people.)

With the help of the symbols described above, we can translate English sentences into a *formal language. For example we can translate (2) into

∀x (A(x) → (B(x) ∧ C(x))).

Here A, B, and C are schematic letters which need to be interpreted as clauses containing x, such as 'x is a fifty-pence piece'; this is what the (x) in A(x) indicates. The grammar of this formal language can be written down in a mathematical form. By choosing a particular set of symbols and saying exactly what range of interpretations is allowed for the schematic letters and the quantifiers, we single out a precise formal language, and we can start to ask mathematical questions about the valid argument schemas which are expressible in that language.

For example a *first-order language* is a formal language built up from the symbols described above, where all quantifiers are interpreted as having the same domain of quantification but this domain can be any non-empty set. *First-order logic* is logic based on argument schemas written in a first-order language.

What is the dividing-line between valid and invalid argument schemas? There are two main approaches to this question. In the first approach, which we may call the *rule-based* or *syntactic* one, we suppose that we can intuitively tell when a simple argument is valid, just by looking at it; we count a complicated argument as valid if it can be broken down into simple steps which we immediately recognize as valid. This approach naturally leads us to write down a set of simple valid argument schemas and some rules for fitting them together. The result will be a *logical *calculus*, i.e. a mathematical device for generating valid argument schemas. The array of symbols written down in the course of generating an argument schema by the rules is called a *formal proof* of the schema.

Once we have a logical calculus up and running, the mathematicians may suggest ways of revamping it to make it easier to teach to undergraduates, or faster to run on a computer. There is a great variety of logical calculuses for first-order logic, all of them giving the same class of valid argument schemas. Two well-known examples are the *natural deduction calculus (Gentzen, 1934), which breaks down complex arguments into intuitively 'natural' pieces, and the tableau or truth-tree calculus (Beth, 1955) which is very easy to learn and can be thought of as a systematic search for counter-examples (see the next paragraph).

There is another approach to defining validity, the *semantic* approach. In this approach we count an argument schema as valid precisely if every interpretation which makes the premisses true makes the conclusion true too. To phrase this a little differently, a *counter-example* to an argument schema is an interpretation which turns the premisses into true sentences and the conclusion into a false sentence; the semantic definition says that an argument schema is valid if and only if it has no counter-examples.

At first sight this is a very paradoxical definition; it makes the following highly implausible argument schema valid just because the conclusion is true whatever we put for X:

The Emperor Caligula's favourite colour was X.

Therefore Omsk today is a town in Siberia with a population of over a million and a large petroleum industry, and X = X.

Nevertheless, one can argue that the semantic approach works if the language of our logic doesn't contain any words (such as 'Omsk' or 'today') that tie us down to specific features of our world. This is an untidy view, because the notion of a specific feature of our world is not sharp;

should it include the physical laws of the universe, or the mathematical properties of sets? One has to answer questions like these in order to draw a line between logical necessity and other kinds of necessity (physical or mathematical), and probably there will always be philosophical debate about how best to do this.

For first-order logic the problem happily doesn't arise. One can prove that every first-order argument schema which is justified by any of the standard logical calculuses is valid in the semantic sense. This is a mathematical theorem, the *soundness theorem* for first-order logic. Conversely if an argument schema is *not* proved valid by the logical calculuses, then we can show that there is an interpretation of the schema which makes the premises true and the conclusion false. This again is a mathematical theorem, the *completeness theorem* for first-order logic (Gödel, 1930; this is quite different from his incompleteness theorem of 1931). The completeness theorem justifies both the rule-based approach and the semantic one, in the following way. The chief danger with the rule-based approach was that we might have overlooked some rule that was needed. The completeness theorem assures us that any schema not justified by our logical calculus would have a counter-example, so it certainly wouldn't be valid. And conversely the chief danger with the semantic approach was that it might make some argument schema valid for spurious reasons (like the example with Omsk above). The completeness theorem shows that if an argument has no counter-example, then it is justified by the logical calculus. In this way the valid first-order argument schemas are trapped securely on both sides, so we can be very confident that we have the dividing-line in the right place.

For other logics the position is less clear. For example, in *monadic second-order logic* we have some quantifiers whose domain of quantification is required to be the family of subsets of a particular set. Because of this restriction, some truths of set theory can be expressed as valid schemas in this logic, and one consequence is that the logic doesn't admit a completeness theorem. In *temporal logics* there are logical constants such as 'until' or 'it will sometime be true that . . .'; to define validity in these logics, we need to decide what background assumptions we can make about time, for example whether it is continuous or discrete. For these and other logics, the normal practice today is to give a precise mathematical definition of the allowed interpretations, and then use the semantic definition of validity. The result is an exact notion, even if some people are unhappy to call it logical validity.

This is the place to mention a muddle in some recent psychological literature. The question at issue is how human beings carry out logical reasoning. One often reads that there are two possible answers: (1) by rules as in a logical calculus, or (2) by models (which are interpretations stripped down to the relevant essentials) as in the semantic approach. This is a confusion. There is no distinction between rule-based and semantic ways of reasoning. The rule-based and semantic approaches are different explanations of what we achieve when we do perform a proof: on the rule-based view, we correctly follow the rules, whereas on the semantic view we eliminate counter-examples.

Can we mechanically test whether a given argument schema is logically valid, and if so, how? For first-order logic, half of the answer is positive. Given any standard logical calculus, we can use it to list in a mechanical way all possible valid argument schemas; so if an argument schema is valid, we can prove this by waiting until it appears in the list. In fact most logical calculi do much better than this; we can use them to test the schema systematically, and if it is valid they will eventually say 'Yes'.

The bad news is that there is no possible computer program which will tell us when a given first-order argument schema is invalid. This was proved by Church in 1936, adapting Gödel's incompleteness theorem. (Strictly it also needs Turing's 1936 analysis of what can be done in principle by a computer.) This does *not* mean that there are some first-order argument schemas which are undecidable, in the sense that it's impossible for us to tell whether they are valid or not—that might be true, but it would need further arguments about the nature of human creativity. Church's theorem does mean that there is no purely mechanical test which will give the right answer in all cases.

A similar argument, again based on Gödel's incompleteness theorem, shows that for many other logics including monadic second-order logic, it is not even possible to list mechanically the valid argument schemas. On the other hand there are many less adventurous logics—for example, the logic of Aristotle's *syllogisms—for which we have a decision procedure, meaning that we can mechanically test any argument schema for validity.

A final question: Is there a particular logical calculus which can be used to justify all valid reasoning (say, in science or mathematics)? For the intuitionist school of Brouwer, it is an article of faith that the answer is 'No'. On the other side, Frege believed that he had given a logical calculus which was adequate at least for arithmetic; but *Russell's paradox showed that Frege's system was inconsistent.

For the moment, the heat has gone out of this question. In modern mathematics we assume that every argument can be translated into the first-order language appropriate for set theory, and that the steps in the argument can all be justified using a first-order logical calculus together with the axioms of Zermelo–Fraenkel *set theory. This has become a criterion of sound mathematical reasoning, though nobody ever carries out the translation in practice (it would be horrendously tedious). Versions of this translation are used to check the correctness of computer software, for example where lives may depend on it.

There is a more radical reading of our question. In many situations we carry out reasoning along quite different lines from the logical calculuses mentioned above. For example, when someone pays us money, we normally take for granted that it is legal tender and not a forgery, and so when it adds up correctly we infer that we have been given the correct change. Strictly this is not logical reasoning, because even when the premises are true, the conclusion could be false (and occasionally is). But it is reasoning of a kind, and it does follow some rules. Logicians generally disregarded this kind of reasoning until they found they needed it to guide intelligent databases. For this purpose a number of *non-monotonic* logics have been proposed; the name refers to the fact that in this kind of reasoning a valid conclusion may cease to be valid when a new premiss is added (for example, that the five pound note has no metal strip).

Several other alternative logics have been suggested, each for its own purposes. *Linear logic* tries to formalize the idea that there is a cost incurred each time we use a premiss, and perhaps we can only afford to use it once. An older example is *intuitionist logic* (Heyting, 1930), which incorporates a *verifiability principle: we can't claim to have proved that there is an *A* until we can show how to produce an example of an *A*. Each of these logics must be justified on its own terms. There is no reason to think that the list of useful logics is complete yet.   W.A.H.

*logic, traditional; quantification.

J. C. Beall and Bas C. von Fraassen, *Possibilities and Paradox: An Introduction to Modal and Many-Valued Logic* (Oxford, 2003).

H. D. Ebbinghaus, J. Flum, and W. Thomas, *Mathematical Logic*, 2nd edn. (New York, 1996).

D. Gabbay, *Elementary Logics: A Procedural Perspective* (London, 1998).

——and F. Guenthner (eds.), *Handbook of Philosophical Logic*, 2nd edn. in 18 vols. (Dordrecht, 2001–).

Wilfrid Hodges, *Logic*, 2nd edn. (London, 2001).

W. H. Newton-Smith, *Logic: An Introductory Course* (London, 1985).

W. V. Quine, *Philosophy of Logic*, 2nd edn. (Cambridge, Mass., 1986).

A Tarski, *Introduction to Logic and to the Methodology of Deductive Sciences*, 4th edn. (New York, 1994).

logic, paraconsistent. A logical system is paraconsistent if it does not sanction the principle that anything follows from a contradiction. The rejected inference is called *ex falso quodlibet*, and is expressed in symbols thus: $p, \neg p \vdash q$. Paraconsistent logics have application to the logic of belief, and other propositional attitudes, especially if one wants to develop something analogous to *possible worlds semantics. A person who has contradictory beliefs is not thereby committed to every proposition whatsoever. A 'world' that is 'compatible' with one's beliefs need not be consistent, but it should not trivially make every proposition true. Other applications of paraconsistent logic concern reasoning with faulty data and *dialetheism, the view that some contradictions are true. Dialetheism is one attempt to deal with paradoxes like the Liar. Most systems of *relevance logic are paraconsistent.
                                                                    S.S.

Graham Priest, 'Paraconsistent Logic', in Dov M. Gabbay and F. Guenthner (eds.), *Handbook of Philosophical Logic*, vi, 2nd edn. (Dordrecht, 2002).

logic, philosophical: *see* philosophical logic.

logic, relevance: *see* relevance logic.

logic, second-order. Consider 'Socrates is wise'. In a first-order logic the name 'Socrates' may be replaced by a bound variable to yield 'something is wise'. It is a further question whether the predicate in this sentence may also be replaced by a bound variable. A formal logic that permits this replacement is called 'second-order'. In the standard semantics for second-order logic, first-order variables range over a domain of individuals, whereas second-order variables range over sets, properties, relations, or functions on the range of the first-order variables. So understood, second-order logic is extremely powerful. It is *incomplete (there can be no finite deductive system in which every second-order logical truth is deducible), *categorical (any two models that satisfy a set S of sentences are isomorphic), and not compact (even if every finite subset of S has a model, S itself may lack a model). In a nonstandard (Henkin) semantics the second-order variables range over a separate domain of individuals. So understood, second-order logic is complete, categorical, and compact.   F.MacB.

*higher-order logic; categoricity; incompleteness.

Stewart Shapiro, *Foundations without Foundationalism: A Case for Second-Order Logic* (Oxford, 1991).

logic, traditional. The rough-and-ready title given by later logicians to the methods and doctrines which once dominated the universities, but which were supplanted in the twentieth century by the 'modern' or 'mathematical' logic with which the names of Frege and Russell are especially associated. Sometimes called 'Aristotelian'—or 'syllogistic', or the 'logic of terms'—it originated with Aristotle in the fourth century BC, though it acquired a great many accretions in the intervening 2,000 years.

The older logic was limited, it is customary to say, by the uncritical assumption that propositions are of the subject–predicate form. This contention, however, is misleading; not least because the subject–predicate distinction is actually quite at odds with the formal system which is supposed to be based on it.

Most traditional logicians certainly accepted that non-compound propositions invariably contain *subjects and predicates. At its vaguest, the idea was perhaps that to make any judgement at all is to say something about something. It is easy to drift from this to the more specific doctrine that every proposition contains two distinct elements: an element which names or refers to something (a 'subject-term'), and an element (the 'predicate-term') which expresses what is said about it. Thus, in 'Socrates is bald', the name 'Socrates' refers to a person, and the expression 'is bald' says something about this person.

The subject of a proposition in this sense—what it is about—is not part of the proposition but something to which part of it refers, not the name 'Socrates' but the person who bears it. If some traditional logicians failed to stress the difference, this may have reflected uncertainty about the status of the predicate. The difference between 'Socrates' and Socrates is perfectly clear; not quite so clear is the difference between 'is bald' and is bald.

This asymmetry is one aspect of what is really a very considerable difference: subjects and predicates belong to quite distinct categories. Granted that an expression like '. . . is bald' plays a predicative role, a subject is anything of which this may be said. A subject-term is therefore a word or expression which fulfils two conditions: it constitutes a grammatical answer to a question like 'You said that something (someone) is bald: of what (whom) did you say this?' and it must produce good English when it is substituted for x in 'x is bald'. Proper names, referring expressions like 'Plato's teacher', and a variety of other items, satisfy these conditions; but it is obvious that predicative expressions cannot themselves be subject-terms, because 'is bald is bald' makes no sense at all.

The subject–predicate distinction, then, revolves around the difference between naming or referring to something and saying something about it. But no such distinction can sensibly be applied to the traditional system. The crowning glory of that system, it is agreed on all sides, is the doctrine of the syllogism. But this doctrine, as we shall see, requires—as indeed does the rest of the system— that what is the predicate of one proposition can be the subject of another.

Traditional logic was for the most part concerned with the logical properties of four forms of proposition. More often than not these were said to be

> All S is P.
> No S is P.
> Some S is P.
> Some S is not P.

'All S is P' was called the 'universal affirmative' or 'A' form, 'No S is P' the 'universal negative' or 'E' form, 'Some S is P' the 'particular affirmative' or 'I' form, and 'Some S is not P' the 'particular negative' or 'O' form. That a proposition is universal or particular was called its quantity, and that it is affirmative or negative was called its quality.

A moment's reflection shows that 'All S is P' cannot properly belong in the same list as the rest, because 'No Greek is bald' is good English, while 'All Greek is bald' is merely good gibberish. This drawback, though, could be remedied simply by taking 'Every S is P' to be the correct form. A more serious problem concerns the innuendo in the symbolism, which is in any case frankly espoused by those who use it, that S and P stand for subjects and predicates. If 'is bald' is a predicative expression, P clearly cannot be a predicate in 'No S is P', since 'No Greek is bald' looks like a mere typing error.

The stuttering 'is' could be removed in one of at least two ways. One would be to give up the idea that the predicate is 'is bald' in favour of saying that it is merely 'bald'. This is no doubt the ulterior motive behind the half-baked suggestion that pro-positions contain a third element, over and above the subject and the predicate, namely the copula (i.e. 'is'). Another way would be to give up the practice of writing, for example, 'No S is P' in favour of 'No $S P$'.

But the difficulties do not end there. We have seen that a subject-term is anything that takes the place of x in an expression like 'x is bald'. According to this criterion, 'Every man', 'No man', and 'Some man' are perfectly good subject-terms. But substituting them in the standard forms again produces meaningless repetition: 'Every every man is bald', and so on. Again there are two ways of coping: one is to say that not 'Every S is P' but the simple S P is the correct form, the other that not 'Every man' but merely 'man' is the subject-term.

These different ways of coping led our symbolism in quite different directions. One leaves us with only two elements (subject and predicate); the other first with three elements (subject, predicate, copula), then with four (subject, predicate, copula, and a sign of quantity). All these distinct, and mutually inconsistent, ways of analysing propositions are at least hinted at in the traditional textbooks.

As we saw at the outset, the subject–predicate distinction arises in the context of singular propositions like 'Socrates is bald'. In the traditional textbooks, singulars are treated as universals, on the feeble pretext that in 'Socrates is bald' the name 'Socrates' refers to everything it can. This notion was generally expressed in technical terminology: the name was said to be 'distributed' or to 'refer to its whole extension'. These obscurities presumably reflect a disinclination to say something that is obviously absurd (that one is talking about the whole of Socrates), something that is obviously false (that only one person can be called Socrates), or something that is obviously vacuous (that the name is here meant to name everyone it is here meant to name). Be that as it may, it is worth noticing that the singular propositions which are paradigmatic in the exposition of the subject–predicate distinction become quite peripheral in the exposition of the syllogism. What this indicates is that the subject–predicate distinction is merely a nuisance so far as the formal system of traditional logic is concerned.

How then should the propositions discussed in traditional logic be symbolized? The only analysis which is truly consistent with the traditional system is one in which propositions are treated as containing two distinct sorts of elements, but these are not subjects and predicates; they are logical *constants and *terms. The constants, four in number, are:

'All . . . are . . . '	(A)
'No . . . are . . . '	(E)
'Some . . . are . . . '	(I)
'Some . . . are not . . . '	(O)

These are two-place term-operators, which is to say, expressions which operate on any two terms to generate propositions.

What are terms? Given our operators and the requirement that a term must be capable of filling either place in them, this question answers itself. A term is typically a plural noun—like 'baldies'—or any expression—like 'persons challenged in the hair department'—that does the work of an actual or possible plural noun ('possible' because any particular language may or may not have a single word with the same meaning as a complex expression). Small letters from the beginning of the alphabet will be used to stand for terms, i.e. as term-variables, and these will be written after the term-operator. Thus 'Anyone who disagrees with me is a complete fool' is of the form A*ab*, where *a* = 'persons who disagree with me' and *b* = ' complete fools'.

The traditional system relied upon two kinds of *negation. The distinction between 'Not everything which glisters is gold' (negating a proposition) and 'Everything which glisters is not gold' (negating a term) is worth fighting for, despite the common practice of using the second to mean the first. Propositional-negation will be represented by *N* (meaning 'It is not that . . . '); term-negation by *n* (meaning 'non-'). Term-negation may preface either or both terms. Thus 'Everything which doesn't glister is gold' is A*nab*, 'Everything which glisters isn't gold') is A*anb*, and 'Everything which doesn't glister isn't gold' is A*nanb*.

We need in our symbolism also ways of representing connections between propositions. A*ab* & A*bc* will signify the conjunction of these two propositions. A*ab* → A*nbna* will signify the (in this case true) assertion that the second proposition follows from the first, and A*ab* ≡ A*ba* the (in this case false) assertion that these two propositions are equivalent, i.e. that each follows from the other.

The laws of the traditional system may be classified under two headings: those which apply to only two propositions, and those which apply to three or more. The square of opposition and immediate inference fall under the first heading, syllogisms and polysyllogisms under the second.

The *square of opposition depicts various kinds of 'opposition' between the four propositional forms. A and E are contraries, meaning that, if *a* and *b* stand for the same terms in A*ab* and E*ab*, these two propositions cannot both be true but may both be false; hence A*ab* → NE*ab* and E*ab* → NA*ab*. I and O are subcontraries, meaning that they cannot both be false but may both be true; hence N*Iab* → O*ab* and NO*ab* → I*ab*. A and O are contradictories, as are E and I, meaning that one of each pair must be true, the other false; hence A*ab* ≡ NO*ab* and E*ab* ≡ N*Iab*. I is subaltern to A, as O is to E, meaning that in each instance the second implies the first; hence A*ab* → I*ab* and E*ab* → O*ab*.

*Immediate inference, which consists in drawing a conclusion from a single premiss, encompasses conversion, obversion, contraposition, and inversion. Conversion consists in reversing the order of terms. It is valid for E and I, invalid for A and O; hence E*ab* → E*ba* and I*ab* → I*ba*. The valid inferences E*ab* → O*ba* and A*ab* → I*ba* are called conversion *per accidens*. Obversion consists in negating the second term of a proposition and changing its quality. It is valid for all four forms; hence E*ab* → A*anb*, A*ab* → E*anb*, O*ab* → I*anb*, and I*ab* → O*anb*. Contraposition consists in

negating both terms and reversing their order. It is valid for A and O; hence A*ab* → A*nbna* and O*ab* → O*nbna*. Inversion consists in inferring from a given proposition another having for its subject the negation of the original subject. It is valid in the following cases: E*ab* → I*nab*, E*ab* → O*nanb*, A*ab* → O*nab*, and A*ab* → I*nanb*.

*Syllogisms draw a conclusion from two premisses. They contain three terms: one (the middle term) is common to the premisses, another is common to the conclusion and one of the premisses, and the third is common to the conclusion and the other premiss. We will use *b* to signify the middle term, *a* and *c* to signify what are called the extreme terms. Perhaps the best-known syllogism (it was called Barbara) may be illustrated by the following simple example:

> Any workers who voted for that party were voting for their own unemployment.
> Those who vote for their own unemployment are fools to themselves.
> Any workers who voted for that party are fools to themselves.

Traditionally syllogisms were set out this way, with the conclusion under the premisses like the lines of a sum. In our symbolism, this example is of the form (A*ab* & A*bc*) → A*ac*.

Polysyllogisms have more than two premisses but may be reduced to a series of conventional syllogisms:

> Some university teachers profess to believe in academic freedom but do nothing to defend it.
> Those who profess such a thing but do nothing about it are not practising what they preach.
> Teachers who fail to practise what they preach are a disgrace to their profession.
> Some university teachers are a disgrace to their profession.

This has the form (I*ab* & A*bc* & A*cd*) → I*ad*, but it may be regarded as the summation of two conventional syllogisms, namely (I*ab* & A*bc*) → I*ac* and (I*ac* & A*cd*) → I*ad*.

It is customary to say that there are 256 forms of syllogism. This number results from a convention concerning how syllogisms are depicted: the order of terms in the conclusion is fixed, but that in the premisses is reversable. The conclusion is thus restricted to taking one of four forms: E*ac*, A*ac*, O*ac*, or I*ac*. Each premiss, however, may take any one of eight forms: one is E*ab*, E*ba*, A*ab*, A*ba*, I*ab*, I*ba*, O*ab*, or O*ba*, and the other is E*bc*, E*cb*, A*bc*, A*cb*, I*bc*, I*cb*, O*bc*, or O*cb*. The number 256 is simply 4 × 8 × 8.

Syllogisms were classified in the traditional textbooks according to their mood and figure. The mood of a syllogism is essentially the sequence of term-operators it contains. The mood of Barbara, for example, is AAA (hence the name). The various moods, 64 in all, are therefore EEE, EEA, EEO, EEI, and so on. The figure of a syllogism is determined by the arrangement of terms in its premisses. Aristotle distinguished three figures; later logicians, whose conception of figure differed significantly from his, decreed that there are four:

(1) *ab, bc.*
(2) *ab, cb.*
(3) *ba, bc.*
(4) *ba, cb.*

The identity of a syllogism is completely specified by its mood and figure, so the number 256 is the product of 4 (figures) and 64 (moods). Of these 256, 24 are said to be valid (some authors, for reasons that will be indicated in a moment, say 19, or even 15). Omitting brackets, the 24, arranged in their figures, are:

(1)
Aab & Abc → Aac   Aab & Abc → Iac   Iab & Abc → Iac
Aab & Ebc → Eac   Aab & Ebc → Oac   Iab & Ebc → Oac

(2)
Aab & Ecb → Eac   Aab & Ecb → Oac   Eab & Acb → Eac
Eab & Acb → Oac   Iab & Ecb → Oac   Oab & Acb → Oac

(3)
Aba & Abc → Iac   Aba & Ibc → Iac   Iba & Abc → Iac
Aba & Ebc → Oac   Aba & Obc → Oac   Iba & Ebc → Oac

(4)
Aba & Acb → Iac   Eba & Acb → Eac   Eba & Acb → Oac
Aba & Ecb → Oac   Aba & Icb → Iac   Iba & Ecb → Oac

Of these, five are 'weakened', meaning that they draw particular conclusions from premises that merit a universal one. If these are omitted, the number of valid forms is 19. Among these 19, 15 either draw a universal conclusion from universal premises or a particular conclusion from one universal and one particular premise: these were sometimes called 'fundamental'.

But the convention behind the numbers given in the traditional textbooks is wholly improper. The effect of reversing the order of terms in E and I propositions is to produce mere equivalents, while in A and O non-equivalents are produced. The textbook account therefore includes duplication. It excludes from the syllogism, moreover, the varieties of negation that are permitted in immediate inferences, and is as a consequence incomplete.

The traditional system encompassed what were really eight logically distinct propositional forms:

Eab	(Eba, etc.).
Enab	(Aba, etc.).
Eanb	(Aab, etc.).
Enanb	(Anab, etc.).
NEab	(Iab, etc.).
NEnab	(Oba, etc.).
NEanb	(Oab, etc.).
NEnanb	(Onab, etc.).

Any one of these eight forms is expressible in eight ways. Eab, for example, is equivalent to Eba, Aanb, Abna, NIab, NIba, NOanb and NObna. A proper account of the syllogism, then, would cover 64 forms of proposition:

the correct number of syllogisms is therefore 262,144 (i.e. 64 × 64 × 64).   c.w.

P. T. Geach, 'History of the Corruptions of Logic', in *Logic Matters* (Oxford, 1972).

J. N. Keynes, *Formal Logic*, 4th edn. (London, 1906).

J. Łukasiewicz, *Aristotle's Syllogistic*, 2nd edn. (Oxford, 1957).

A. N. Prior, *Formal Logic*, 2nd edn. (Oxford, 1962), pt. 2, ch. 6.

C. Williamson, 'Traditional Logic as a Logic of Distribution-Values', *Logique et analyse* (1971).

—— 'How Many Syllogisms Are There?', *History and Philosophy of Logic* (1988).

logic of discovery. *Deduction in the testing of scientific theories. For example, the exhibiting of logical relations between the sentences of a theory (such as equivalence, derivability, consistency, inconsistency) or between a theory and established theories; the logical inferring of predictions from a theory. *Popper argues against the view that scientific theories are conclusively inductively verifiable but argues for their deductive and empirical falsifiability. A claim of the form $(\forall a)\,(Fa)$, 'Every a is F', cannot be confirmed by any finite number of observations of a's that are F, because there could always in principle exist an undiscovered a that is not F, but $(\forall a)(Fa)$ can be refused by the discovery of just one a that is not F.

*Popper has an evolutionary epistemology of scientific discovery. The formulation of theories is analogous to genetic mutation in evolutionary theory. Theories and mutations arise randomly as putative solutions to environmental problems, and only those conducive to the survival of the species in that environment themselves survive through trial and error. Popper adopts a Platonist view of logic, on the grounds that proofs are (sometimes surprising) discoveries not unsurprising inventions.   s.p.

Karl R. Popper, *The Logic of Scientific Discovery* (London, 1980), ch. 1, sect. 3.

logical atomism: *see* atomism, logical.

logical constants. An argument's logical form is shown by analysing its constituent propositions into constant and variable parts, constants representing what is common to proportions, variables their differing content. The constants peculiar to syllogistic logic are 'All … are …', 'No … are …', 'Some … are …', Some … are not …'; those of propositional calculus are truth-functional connectives like implication, conjunction, and disjunction; those of predicate calculus add the quantifiers 'For all x …' and 'There is an x such that …'. Constants concerning identity, tense, modality, etc. may be introduced in more complex systems.   c.w.

logical determinism: *see* determinism, logical.

logical empiricism: *see* empiricism, logical.

logical form: *see* form, logical.

logical laws. Propositions true on logical grounds alone; logical truths. For example, the laws of non-contradiction, identity, excluded middle, and double negation. In propositional calculus the law of non-contradiction is:

$-(p \,\&\, -p)$, 'It is not the case that both p and not p'

in predicate calculus:

$(\forall x) -(Fx \,.\, -Fx)$ 'For any x, it is not the case that x is F and x is not F'

In propositional calculus the law of identity is:

$(p \rightarrow p)$, 'If p then p'

in predicate calculus:

$(\forall x) (Fx \rightarrow Fx)$, 'For any x, if x is F then x is F'

in predicate calculus with identity:

$(\forall x) (x = x)$, 'For any x, x is x'

in modal predicate calculus with identity:

$\square (\forall x) (x = x)$, 'Necessarily, for any x, x is x'

In propositional calculus the law of excluded middle is:

$p \vee -p$, 'Either p or not p'

in predicate calculus:

$(\forall x) (Fx \vee -Fx)$, 'For any x, either x is F or x is not F'

In propositional calculus the laws of double negation are:

$--p \rightarrow p$, 'If not not p then p', and
$p \rightarrow --p$, 'If p then not not p'

and in predicate calculus:

$(\forall x) (--Fx \rightarrow Fx)$ 'For any x, if x is not not F then x is F' and

$(\forall x) (Fx \rightarrow --Fx)$, 'For any x, if x is F then x is not not F'.

Aristotle does not distinguish sharply between logical laws, laws of thought, and laws of being, so the consistent, the *conceivable, and what could exist coincide, and the inconsistent, the inconceivable, and what could not exist coincide. Aristotle's informal statements of the law of non-contradiction include: '*For the same thing to hold good and not to hold good simultaneously of the same thing and in the same respect is impossible*' (*Metaphysics* Γ 1005^b): $(\forall x)$ $-(Fx \,.\, -Fx)$ or arguably: $(\forall x) -\lozenge (Fx \,.\, -Fx)$, and '*Nor* [. . .] *is it possible that there should be anything in the middle of a contradiction*' (1011^b): $-\lozenge (p \,.\, -p)$. His statement of the law of excluded middle is '*but it is necessary either to assert or deny any one thing of one thing*' (1011^b), $(\forall x)$ $(Fx \vee -Fx)$ or arguably; $\square (\forall x) (Fx \vee -Fx)$. Aristotle says it shows a lack of education to demand a proof of logical laws. He does, however, bring a self-refutation argument against their putative denial by his Pre-Socratic predecessors, Protagoras, who thinks that every claim is true but there is no truth over and above belief by or appearance to persons, and Heraclitus, who thinks that everything is changing in every respect so there is no truth. Aristotle points out that saying anything meaningful or true—for example, making Protagorean or Heraclitean claims—presupposes logical laws.

Mill maintains that logical laws are not a priori or necessary, but empirical generalizations confirmed by all experience but, so far, refuted by none. He thinks all deduction is really induction.

Quine has suggested revision of the law of excluded middle to simplify quantum mechanics. Plantinga has commented that this is rather like revising a law of arithmetic to simplify the doctrine of the Holy Trinity.

It is widely taken as axiomatic that if the description of a putative phenomenon entails a violation of a logical law, then that phenomenon cannot exist. However, if we are persuaded, for example, that Zeno has found contradictions in the concept of motion (for example: If x moves, then x is at a place at a time and x is not at that place at that time), we do not thereby conclude that nothing moves; 'Foolish, foolish us! We thought things *moved*. But no. That philosopher Zeno has shown that the concept of motion entails a contradiction. Clearly we should give up this widespread, perceptually compelling but incoherent assumption! Motion is *logically impossible.*' Rather, we retain the view that things move and look for a consistent theory of motion. The implications for philosophy, science, and theology are wide. Perhaps time-travel is not logically impossible, it is just that we so far lack a consistent theory of it. Arguably, something is possible if and only if there is at least one consistent description of it.

Perhaps nothing is logically impossible, because contradictions do not pick out any putative states of affairs. If not, they do not pick out any impossible putative states of affairs. 'Ah yes, "Both $(p \,.\, -p)$", it is the putative state of affairs picked out by *that* sentence that could not come about!' But what state of affairs could not come about?

S.P.

Aristotle's Metaphysics, Book Γ, tr. with notes by Christopher Kirwan (Oxford, 1971).

E. J. Lemmon, *Beginning Logic* (London, 1967).

John Stuart Mill, *A System of Logic*, 2 vols. (London, 1879).

Alvin Plantinga, *The Nature of Necessity* (Oxford, 1974).

W. V. O. Quine, 'Two Dogmas of Empiricism', in his *From a Logical Point of View* (Cambridge, Mass., 1953), 20–46.

logically perfect language. Natural *languages may be thought in various ways to be 'logically imperfect'. Certain grammatical forms may mislead us about logical form; thus, 'It is raining' *looks* as if it refers to something ('it'). More radically, certain concepts may even involve us in contradiction or incoherence. For example, Tarski argued that the ordinary concept 'true' did this, since it generated such paradoxes as the *liar. A logically perfect language would be one lacking these faults, as well, perhaps, as some other 'defects', such as ambiguity and redundancy. Frege attempted to create such a language (the *Begriffsschrift*), in which to couch the truths of logic and mathematics. Rather later, the *Logical Positivists were interested in the idea of a logically perfect language with which to express the whole of natural science. R.P.L.T.

G. Frege, *Begriffsschrift*, in *Translations from the Philosophical Writings of Gottlob Frege*, tr. P. T. Geach and M. Black, 2nd edn. (Oxford, 1960), ch. 1.

logically proper names. The term Bertrand Russell uses for names that are logically guaranteed to have a bearer. For Russell the meaning of a logically proper name is the object it stands for. If there is no object that the name stands for, it is literally meaningless. To know the meaning of a logically proper name is to know the object it stands for, where this is a matter of being directly acquainted with the object. Since Russell supposed that the only objects we were directly acquainted with were private items of sensory experience or memory, only these items could be picked out by logically proper names. Conversely, if a name could be used in a sentence meaningfully even if it did not stand for an existing entity, for example 'Santa Claus', then that name could not be a logically proper name, but was instead an abbreviation of a definite description. For Russell ordinary proper names did not count as logically proper names. The only genuine examples of logically proper names in English were expressions such 'this', 'that', and 'I', standing for items with which the thinker was immediately acquainted. Wittgenstein thought Russell had matters the wrong way round. Instead of starting with a logical test of a genuine name, only to discover that hardly any of the expressions we ordinarily called names passed the test, a proper account of names should start by characterizing the expressions we called names. Others maintain that Russell is right about names, but wrong to restrict the entities we can name and know to items in sensory experience. To mean something by a name, we must know who, or what, we are referring to, but such knowledge can take many forms, and is not limited to direct acquaintance with the object itself.   B.C.S.

B. Russell, 'The Philosophy of Logical Atomism', in R. C. Marsh (ed.), *Logic and Knowledge* (London, 1984).

logical notations: *see* notations, logical.

Logical Positivism. This twentieth-century movement is sometimes also called logical (or linguistic) empiricism. In a narrower sense it also carries the name of the *Vienna Circle since such thinkers in this tradition as Rudolph Carnap, Herbert Feigl, Otto Neurath, Moritz Schlick, and Friedrich Waismann formed an influential study group in Vienna in the early 1920s to articulate and propagate the group's positivist ideas. In the broader sense, however, Logical Positivism includes such non-Viennese thinkers as A. J. Ayer, C. W. Morris, Arne Naess, and Ernest Nagel.

Central to the movement's doctrines is the principle of verifiability, often called the *verification principle, the notion that individual sentences gain their meaning by some specification of the actual steps we take for determining their truth or falsity. As expressed by Ayer, sentences (statements, propositions) are meaningful if they can be assessed either by an appeal directly (or indirectly) to some foundational form of sense-experience or by an appeal to the meaning of the words and the grammatical structure that constitute them. In the former case, sentences are said to be synthetically true or false; in the latter,

analytically true or false. If the sentences under examination fail to meet the verifiability test, they are labelled meaningless. Such sentences are said to be neither true nor false. Famously, some say infamously, many positivists classed metaphysical, religious, aesthetic, and ethical claims as meaningless. For them, as an example, an ethical claim would have meaning only in so far as it purported to say something empirical. If part of what was meant by 'x is good' is roughly 'I like it', then 'x is good' is meaningful because it makes a claim that could be verified by studying the behaviour of the speaker. If the speaker always avoided x, we could verify that 'x is good' is false. But the positivists typically deny that 'x is good' and similar claims can be assessed as true or false beyond this sort of report. Instead, they claim that the primary 'meaning' of such sentences is *emotive or evocative. Thus, 'x is good' (as a meaningless utterance) is comparable to 'Hooray!' In effect, this sort of analysis shows the positivists' commitment to the fact–value distinction.

Given the role that the verifiability principle plays in their thinking, it is not surprising that the Logical Positivists were admirers of science. One might say they were science-intoxicated. For them it was almost as if philosophy were synonymous with the philosophy of science, which in turn was synonymous with the study of the logic (language) of science. Typically, their philosophy of science treated sense-experience (or sense-data) as foundational and thus tended to be 'bottom up' in nature. That is, it tended to consider the foundational claims of science as being more directly verifiable (and thus more trustworthy) than the more abstract law and theoretic claims that science issues. Their philosophy of science also tended to be 'atomistic' rather than holistic in nature. Each foundational claim was thought to have its own truth-value in isolation from other claims. After the Second World War these doctrines of positivism, as well as the verifiability principle, atomism, and the fact–value distinction, were put under attack by such thinkers as Nelson Goodman, W. V. Quine, J. L. Austin, Peter Strawson, and, later, by Hilary Putnam and Richard Rorty. By the late 1960s it became obvious that the movement had pretty much run its course.   N.F.

*verificationism.

A. J. Ayer, *Language, Truth and Logic* (New York, 1946).
Herbert Feigl and May Brodbeck (eds.), *Readings in the Philosophy of Science* (New York, 1953).
Jørgen Jørgensen, *The Development of Logical Positivism* (Chicago, 1951).

logical symbols: *see* Appendix on Logical Symbols; notations, logical.

logical theory. Like all parts of philosophy, logical theory is best seen as a vaguely delimited and shifting group of *problems*. A rough characterization would be that they concern (1) how to understand the activities of logicians and the nature of the systems that logicians construct (philosophy of logic), and (2) how to apply the systems to what has always been logic's primary purpose, the appraisal of *arguments. In its heyday, the twentieth century, the subject has also had important ramifications (3)

1. It is possible to see a logical system as something abstract, formal, and uninterpreted (unexplicated). The logician takes a vocabulary of words or symbols (elements), and devises rules of two kinds: rules for concatenating the elements into strings (well-formed formulae), and rules for selecting and manipulating formulae or sequences of them so as to produce other formulae or sequences (derivation rules). Doing logic consists in following these rules; logical results, or theorems, are to the effect 'Such-and-such an output can be got by the rules'. So conceived, the activity has no *use* at all: it is part of pure mathematics.

It is no surprise that, historically, the pure-mathematical approach came late: in its origins, logic was supposed to serve a purpose. If it is to do so, the rules must be designed to detect some property or relation, and if the purpose is to count as logical in the currently accepted sense, that property or relation must be defined in terms of *truth* (or of some allied notion such as satisfaction, or warranted assertibility). The way this works out is as follows: first we define 'Formula ϕ is valid' (a kind of *logical truth) to mean 'ϕ is true on all interpretations', and 'Formula ϕ is a consequence of the set of formulae Γ' to mean 'ϕ is true on all interpretations on which all the members of Γ are true'; and then we understand 'Such-and-such an output can be got by the rules' as asserting that the output is a valid formula or a consequence-related sequence of formulae, provided that the input is (or unconditionally, if there is no input to a particular rule).

This procedure interprets (explicates) the originally abstract claim that some result comes out by the rules; it gives us interpreted logic. But at once it imposes two new obligations on the logician: he must tell us what *he* means by 'interpretation' in his definitions of 'valid' and 'consequence', and he must show us that the rules do establish what we are now to understand their users as asserting. The first of these obligations can, in fact, be discharged in more than one way, but roughly speaking an 'interpretation' (or instance) of a formula is a sentence that results from it by replacing all its schematic letters uniformly by ordinary words. The second obligation requires the logician to prove that his system of rules is *sound*, i.e. does what he (now) says it does.

Proof of soundness depends on ways of telling when an 'interpretation' of a formula is true—or rather, what turns out to be enough, on ways of telling when it's bound to be the case that *every* 'interpretation' of a given formula is true (or of a given sequence of formulae is 'truth-preserving'). That means that we need truth-conditions for the constant elements in each formula, the elements which are unchanged through all its various 'interpretations'. So soundness depends on truth-conditions of constants. This is something that has come to consciousness in twentieth-century logical theory, but was implicit all along.

Besides soundness, logical theory is concerned with other properties of logical systems, among them completeness, which is the ability of a system to generate *everything* that is, according to a given set of truth-conditions, valid or a consequence.

2. If you want to apply logic to appraising an argument, two steps are needed: fitting the argument's premises and conclusion to a sequence of logical formulae, and evaluating the sequence. Evaluation goes by the rules of the logical system, provided they are sound, and is sometimes wholly mechanical. Logical theory must then argue (or assume) that only valid arguments fit the favourably evaluated sequences—the ones for which the consequence relation holds.

Fitting is a quite different kind of operation, not mechanical and often difficult: it is symbolizing or formalizing or 'translating from' ordinary words into a 'logical language'. Pitfalls have long been known: for example, why is this not a valid argument?

> Man is a species. Socrates is a man. So Socrates is species.

The twentieth century saw a strong revival of interest in these pitfalls, whose existence is a large part of the reason why in the first half of the century logic seemed to analytic philosophers to lie at the centre of their subject. Here are a few more examples.

> The President of New York is or is not black.

Is that true, given that there is no such person? If not, does it falsify the law of *excluded middle? If not true, is it false? If it is false, is that because the definite *description 'the President of New York' is, as Russell thought, not its logical subject but an *incomplete symbol like 'some president'?

> If you swallow an aspirin, you will feel better. So if you dip an aspirin in cyanide and swallow it, you will feel better.

If 'if' worked in the same way as its surrogate ' $\rightarrow$ ' in propositional logic, the argument would be valid. If the argument is invalid, as it certainly appears to be, how does 'if' work?

> Some things don't exist (Gandalf, for example).

According to Kant 'existence is not a predicate', and this developed into Frege's doctrine that 'exist' 'really' has the syntactic role of a *quantifier equivalent to 'some existing thing', making a sentence when attached not to a subject but to a predicate. If so, the last proposition above is nonsense, mere bad grammar. Even if we readmit 'exists' as a genuine predicate and symbolize the last proposition in the way of predicate logic as '$\exists x \neg (x$ exists)', that has the unintended feature of being false, or even self-contradictory. One solution is to rejig the truth-conditions of predicate logic so that '$\exists x \phi(x)$' means 'Something is ϕ', where that is to be distinguished from 'Some existing thing is ϕ' (free logic).

> Everyone who voted could have been a teller. So there could have been voting tellers.

One trouble is that the premiss is three-ways ambiguous. Does it mean 'There's a possible situation in which all those who would then have voted would then have been tellers' or 'There is a possible situation in which all those who actually voted would have been tellers', or 'For any one of those who actually voted, there is a possible situation in which that one would have been a teller'? Only the first meaning licenses the inference, and then only if its 'all' implies 'some'. A second difficulty is that classical predicate logic rejects that implication: 'all', 'every', etc. do not always work in the same way as their logical surrogate '∀'. Examples of similar problems could be multiplied.

3. During the twentieth century logical theory infiltrated three other disciplines: linguistics, mathematics, and metaphysics. The influence on *linguistics* came partly from logicians' interest in well-formedness—what were called above the rules of concatenation. In linguistic study such rules are a part of syntax, which is a part of grammar, and although the grammar of real languages is immensely more complex, and never stable, some linguists have found the logicians' model a helpful one. Also, as logicians came to see that the logical powers of sentences, their interrelations of *entailment and consistency and the like, depend on truth-conditions, so the thought naturally arose that truth-conditions determine meaning. Frege's distinction of sense and tone had already moderated that enthusiasm, but the theory of meaning (semantics) has remained beholden to logicians' ideas, and philosophy of *language is still not quite an independent domain.

Logic was assured of an influence on *mathematics* by the circumstance that its nineteenth-century revival was due to mathematicians. At first they wanted foundations for arithmetic and geometry (Frege, Russell). By the 1930s conceptions (e.g. ω-consistency) and theorems (e.g. Gödel's *incompleteness theorems) had emerged which belong to pure logic but which only a mathematical mind could compass.

The infiltration into *metaphysics* was due mainly to Wittgenstein and Russell, and proved short-lived. In 1919 both those philosophers thought that the outline of the way things are is to be discovered by attention to how one must speak if one's speech is to be formalizable into predicate, or even propositional, logic. 'Practically all traditional metaphysics', said Russell, 'is filled with mistakes due to bad grammar' ('The Philosophy of Logical Atomism', 269). Kant's idea that metaphysics explores the bounds of sense came, at the hands of Ryle and also of the *Logical Positivists, to be combined briefly with the hope that logic could chart those bounds. A bright afterglow remains in the work of Strawson, Quine, D. K. Lewis, Davidson, and very many others.   C.A.K.

*logic, modern; logic, traditional; metalogic.

Aristotle, *De interpretatione*, tr. J. L. Ackrill, in *Aristotle's Categories and* De interpretatione (Oxford, 1963).

G. Frege, 'Über Sinn und Bedeutung', *Zeitschrift für Philosophie und philosophische Kritik* (1892), tr. as 'On Sense and Reference', in *Translations from the Philosophical Writings of Gottlob Frege*, ed. P. T. Geach and M. Black (Oxford, 1952).

C. A. Kirwan, *Logic and Argument* (London, 1978).

B. A. W. Russell, 'On Denoting', *Mind* (1905), repr. in *Logic and Knowledge*, ed. R. C. Marsh (London, 1956), and elsewhere.

—— 'The Philosophy of Logical Atomism', in *Logic and Knowledge*, ed. R. C. Marsh (London, 1956).

P. F. Strawson, *Individuals* (London, 1959).

logical truth. The expression has various meanings, all connected to the idea of a logical system.

Logical systems have always shared two features: they are at least partly symbolic, using letters or similar devices, and they assert, or preferably prove, results about their symbolic expressions (in the modern jargon, the 'formulae' of their 'logical language'), results such as: any argument of the form 'No Bs are Cs, some As are Bs, so some As are not Cs' is valid; '¬P' is a consequence of '(P → ¬P)'.

1. One current meaning of 'logical truth' is 'result in some sound logical system' ('sound' is not redundant here: it excludes faulty logical systems in which not all the results are true). A true result will usually be a proved result, therefore a theorem, for example (as above):

'¬P' is a consequence of '(P → ¬P)'.

2. Sometimes certain symbolic expressions are themselves described as logical truths, for example:

If some As are Bs, then some Bs are As.
((P → ¬P) → ¬P).

Here explanation is needed, since strictly speaking these expressions are not truths at all (they do not say anything). What is meant is that all their instances are true, where an instance is what you can express by uniformly replacing certain schematic or—in a loose sense—'variable' symbols (the letters A and B in the first example, the letter P in the second) by syntactically permissible words from an adequately rich vocabulary; or, alternatively, that they are true under all interpretations, where an interpretation assigns meanings uniformly to those same 'variables' from a syntactically limited but adequately rich range of meanings. In this usage, truth and falsity do not exhaust the field: in between logical truths, all of whose instances are true, and logical falsehoods, all of whose instances are false, are symbolic expressions such as 'P or not Q', having some true and some false instances.

3. Finally, and perhaps most commonly, 'logical truth' may mean 'truth that is true in virtue of some result in a sound logical system'. The basic kind of case is a truth that *is* an instance (or interpretation) of a symbolic expression *all* of whose instances (or interpretations) are true, i.e. an instance of a type 2 logical truth, for example:

If some men are Greeks, then some Greeks are men.
If a condition for your believing erroneously that you exist is that the belief is not erroneous, then it is not erroneous.

The range of type 3 logical truths is indeterminate, since it depends on which sorts of system you are willing to count as logical. Propositional logic, predicate logic, and syllogistic are accredited systems, but not all philosophers are so happy about, say, *modal logic, epistemic logic, *tense logic, *deontic logic, *set theory, *mereology. On the other hand it is disputable whether any boundary conditions can rationally be set; certainly none are agreed.

Type 3 logical truths can be defined in other roughly equivalent ways: 'true in virtue of its (logical) form', that is, in virtue of being an instance of some type 2 logical truth; 'true in virtue of the meanings of its logical words', that is, of the words in it that can be represented by constants in some logical system; or 'true under all reinterpretations of its non-logical words', similarly.

Basic type 3 logical truths are often described as 'logically necessary', as if their origin in logic guarantees their necessity. Part (only part) of the guarantee comes from using intuitively satisfying methods to prove the logical results, the type 1 truths, methods which may be *semantic*, resting on the truth-conditions of the system's constants, or *logistic*, resting on self-commending manipulation of ('derivation from') self-commending primitive expressions ('axioms').

Other truths can be deduced from the basic logical truths by means of definitions; for example, 'A mastax is a pharynx' from 'The pharynx of a rotifer is a pharynx' by the definition of 'mastax'. But usually these aren't counted as logical truths, though they are counted as logically necessary.

There's a warning in all the above: it would be mistake to suppose that you can always tell at a glance whether some proposition is a type 3 logical truth. You must know your type 1 truths, the theorems of sound systems, many of which are far from obvious; you must judge whether the systems they belong to deserve to be called logical; you must take care over the notions of 'instance' and 'interpretation' (for example, 'If she's wrong, she's wrong' will not be an instance of the type 2 logical truth 'If P, P', unless the 'she's' refer to the same person); and definitions—if the use of them is allowed—are often hazy (for example, is water liquid by definition?).   C.A.K.

W. V. Quine, 'Carnap and Logical Truth', in B. H. Kazemier and D. Vuysje (eds.), *Logic and Language* (Dordrecht, 1962); repr. in P. A. Schilpp (ed.), *The Philosophy of Rudolf Carnap* (La Salle, Ill., 1963), and in *The Ways of Paradox* (New York, 1966).

—— *Philosophy of Logic* (Englewood Cliffs, NJ, 1970), ch. 4.

P. F. Strawson, 'Propositions, Concepts, and Logical Truths', *Philosophical Quarterly* (1957); repr. in *Logico-linguistic Papers* (London, 1971).

logicism. The slogan of the programme is 'Mathematics is logic'. The goal is to provide solutions to problems in the philosophy of *mathematics, by reducing mathematics, or some of its branches, to logic. There are several aspects of, and variations on, this theme. On the semantic front, logicism can be a thesis about the meaning of some mathematical statements, in which case mathematical truth would be a species of logical truth and mathematical knowledge would be logical knowledge. Mathematics, or some of its branches, might be seen as either having no ontology at all or else having only the ontology of logic (whatever that might be). In any case, the value of the enterprise depends on what logic is.

The traditional logicist programme consists of systematic translations of statements of mathematics into a language of pure logic. For Frege, statements about natural numbers are statements about the extensions of certain concepts. The number three, for example, is the extension of the concept that applies to all and only those concepts that apply to exactly three objects. Frege was not out to eliminate mathematical ontology, since he held that logic itself has an ontology, containing concepts and their extensions. Frege's complete theory of extensions was shown to be inconsistent, due to the original *Russell's paradox. For Russell, statements of arithmetic are statements of ramified *type theory, or *higher-order logic. Here, too, logic has an ontology, consisting of properties, propositional functions, and, possibly, classes. To complete the reduction of arithmetic, however, Russell had to postulate an axiom of *infinity; and he conceded that this is not known on logical grounds alone. So statements of mathematics are statements of logic, but mathematical knowledge goes beyond logical knowledge. On the other hand, a principle of infinity is a consequence of the (consistent) arithmetic fragment of Frege's system. Apparently, there was no consensus on the contents and boundaries of logic, a situation that remains with us today.

There are a number of views in the philosophy of mathematics which resemble parts of logicism. It was held by some positivists that mathematical statements are *analytic, true or false in virtue of the meanings of the terms. Some contemporary philosophers hold that the essence of mathematics is the determination of logical consequences of more or less arbitrary sets of axioms or postulates. As far as mathematics is concerned, the axioms might as well be meaningless. To know a theorem of arithmetic, for example, is to know that the statement is a consequence of the axioms of arithmetic. On such views, mathematical knowledge is logical knowledge.

Today, a number of philosophers think of logic as the study of first-order languages, and it is widely held that logic should have no ontology. Higher-order systems are either regarded as too obscure to merit attention or are consigned to set theory, part of mathematics proper. From this perspective, logicism is an absurd undertaking. Nothing that merits the title of 'logic' is rich enough to do complete justice to mathematics. It is often said that the logicists accomplished (only) a reduction of some branches of mathematics to set theory. On the other hand, a number of logicians do regard higher-order logic, and the like, as part of logic, and there is extensive mathematical study of such logical systems. It is not much of an exaggeration to state that logic is now part of mathematics, rather than the other way round.   S.S.

*Logical Positivism.

Paul Benacerraf and Hilary Putnam (eds.), *Philosophy of Mathematics*, 2nd edn. (Cambridge, 1983).

Gottlob Frege, *Die Grundlagen der Arithmetik* (Breslau, 1884).

Alfred North Whitehead and Bertrand Russell, *Principia Mathematica* (Cambridge, 1910).

logistic method. A postulational method of constructing *formalized* logical systems by specifying one's symbols, recursively defining the well-formed formulae, and laying down an economical set of axioms and inference rules for proving theorems. Such a procedure is axiomatic, which historically was the norm. The currently more popular variant, *natural deduction, uses only rules of inference, for proving theorems as well as the validity of derivations. Generally, the notion of proof or of valid derivation is given a strict formal definition. This approach is motivated by a desire for rigour and interpretative versatility.

K.W.

Alonzo Church, *Introduction to Mathematical Logic* (Princeton, NJ, 1956), i, Intro., sect. 7.

logocentrism. Term deployed most frequently by Jacques Derrida and the proponents of *deconstruction in philosophy and literary theory. In this usage a logocentric discourse is one that subscribes to the traditional order of priorities as regards language, meaning, and truth. Thus it is taken for granted first that language (spoken language) is a more or less adequate expression of ideas already in the mind, and second that writing inhabits a realm of derivative, supplementary signs, a realm twice removed from the 'living presence' of the *logos* whose truth can only be revealed through the medium of authentic (self-present) speech.

C.N.

*différance.

Jacques Derrida, *Of Grammatology*, tr. G. C. Spivak (Baltimore, 1976).

logos. A Greek word, of great breadth of meaning, primarily signifying in the context of philosophical discussion the rational, intelligible principle, structure, or order which pervades something, or the source of that order, or giving an account of that order. The cognate verb *legein* means 'say', 'tell', 'count'. Hence the 'word' which was 'in the beginning' as recounted at the start of St John's Gospel is also *logos*. The root occurs in many English compounds such as biology, epistemology, and so on. Aristotle, in his *Nicomachean Ethics*, makes use of a distinction between the part of the soul which originates a *logos* (our *reason) and the part which obeys or is guided by a *logos* (our *emotions). The idea of a generative intelligence (*logos spermatikos*) is a profound metaphysical notion in Neoplatonic and Christian discussion.

N.J.H.D.

As good a place as any to see the notion of *logos* at work in general is in Stoic metaphysics; see J. M. Rist, *Stoic Philosophy* (Cambridge, 1969).

London philosophy. For a long time after the foundation of University College London in 1828 the main centres of philosophy in Britain were still Oxford, Cambridge, and the universities of Scotland. There was nothing in London like the circle of philosophers round Mersenne in seventeenth-century Paris or the salons where the *philosophes met in the eighteenth century until the philosophical radicals came together in the early nineteenth century, presided over by Bentham and united, for a time, by the *Westminster Review*. The first element of what was to become the University of London was brought into existence by this group of Benthamites. Their firmly secular intentions were at first frustrated in philosophy by the appointment of a clerical nonentity as the first professor of the subject.

The official exponents of philosophy in London University, although often worthy and competent, did not have much impact. Croom Robertson, the first editor of *Mind*, James Sully, principally a psychologist, Carveth Read, a follower of Mill who attached evolutionary speculations to his empiricist inheritance, H. Wildon Carr, a businessman who dabbled in Bergson and Croce, and the more professional and durable (he was professor at University College from 1904 to 1928) George Dawes Hicks, a critical realist hostile to the prevailing sense-datum theory, can have set no one's pulses racing. Between the wars there were some more colourful figures in various parts of the university. At Bedford was L. Susan Stebbing, aggressive critic of the metaphysical speculations of such scientists as Jeans and Eddington; at Birkbeck C. E. M. Joad, ardent and useful popularizer after his initial investment in Bergson had proved unrewarding; at University College, John Macmurray, a gifted lecturer and writer, an exponent of British *idealism in its Scottish and more religious form. But they were intellectually lightweight.

There was, however, an altogether more interesting set of thinkers, concerned with philosophy and of high philosophical capacity, teaching mathematics and science in London: the logician Augustus de Morgan (who impressed his pupil Walter Bagehot), the brilliant, short-lived W. K. Clifford (whose severe ethics of belief was rejected by William James), and his follower, Karl Pearson. Clifford and Pearson, both admirable writers, elaborated a phenomenalistic *positivism closely similar to that of Mach. (London, it may be noted, was the centre of the increasingly sectarian and eccentric English branch of Comtian positivism, a different and philosophically more questionable undertaking.)

Other London professors of philosophical interest whose chairs were not in philosophy were L. T. Hobhouse, the sociologist, and Edward Westermarck, the anthropologist, theorists, respectively, of the evolution and of the relativity of morals. The great reviews of the Victorian age were hospitable to such gifted metropolitan philosophical amateurs as G. H. Lewes, Leslie Stephen, Samuel Butler, and Fredric Harrison.

Philosophy in London came into its own after 1945 and the arrival of K. R. Popper and A. J. Ayer, in their different ways continuing the tradition of Clifford and Pearson, Popper as a philosopher of science, Ayer as a scientistic philosopher. With their respective circles of active followers they greatly enhanced the philosophical vitality of the capital. It came to be a third force, opposed to the amorphous Wittgensteinianism of Cambridge and the minute lexicography of Austin's Oxford. Ayer's seminars of the post-war years were notable for their hard-hitting argumentativeness. His readiness to appear in public, on television and in the press, and the liveliness with which he did so, made him the exemplar of a philosopher for the general public. He conveyed his argumentative energy to a number of influential philosophers, just as Popper passed on his commitment to clarity to others.

Ayer was succeeded by the very different Stuart Hampshire, shortly after the latter's *Thought and Action* came out in 1959, a book whose systematic aim and fine mandarin prose were both unusual for an Oxford philosopher of the time. Also in London throughout the 1950s and 1960s was Michael Oakeshott, the even more stylish reanimator of conservative political theory. Through much the same period J. N. Findlay was at King's College, a former Wittgensteinian who proclaimed to a surprised philosophical community in 1955 the merits of Hegelianism. But these imaginative, rather literary philosophers did not succeed in undermining the science-favouring tendency of London philosophy. A.Q.

*Cambridge philosophy; Oxford philosophy.

lore, social: *see* social science, philosophy of.

lottery paradox. Suppose I buy one ticket in a lottery with a million tickets and one prize. It would be irrational to believe my ticket will win. Some philosophers have thought that because we are so prone to error, we are bound to believe what is no more than highly probable, hence, as here, to believe that my ticket won't win. But the same holds for each ticket, so we are bound to believe that no ticket will win. But one ticket is, *ex hypothesi*, certain to win: hence the paradox. What the paradox shows is that there is a difference between believing that something is—to however great a degree—probable and believing it. M.C.

L. J. Cohen, *The Probable and the Provable* (Oxford, 1977).

Lotze, Rudolf Hermann (1817–81). German physiologist and philosopher, who tried to reconcile the idealist tradition, running from Leibniz to Fichte and Hegel, with natural science. He argued, especially in *Mikrokosmos* (1856–64), that nature, including life, can be explained mechanistically, but the unity of consciousness (our ability to compare two presentations and judge them (un)like) resists mechanical explanation. The causal interactions of nature presuppose that it is an organic unity of relatively permanent entities. Such entities can only be understood as finite spirits, analogues of our consciousness, and their unity is grounded in an infinite spirit or (personal) God. Natural laws are the mode of God's activity, which aims at the realization of moral value and is to be understood by analysis of the concept of the good. 'His work is characteristic of the woolly and emotional nebulosities which in Germany followed the collapse of the idealist school' (Collingwood). M.J.I.

H. Schnädelbach, *Philosophy in Germany 1831–1933* (Cambridge, 1984).

love. Affection or attachment, especially sexual, and in this sense studied by philosophers since Plato, who viewed love as a desire for beauty, which should transcend the physical and even the personal, culminating in *philosophy—the love of wisdom itself. In reaction to such lofty views, love has been thought of as reducible either to the sex drive (e.g. Schopenhauer) or to a struggle for power—'in its means, war: at bottom, the deadly hatred of the sexes' (Nietzsche). The latter view is close to that of much *feminist philosophy, which regards love as part of a male ideology for securing the subordination of women. Yet reductionism of these sorts encounters the objection that *true* love must be something over and above these things in virtue of the high value we set on it (as on *friendship). P.G.

Irving Singer, *The Nature of Love* (Chicago, 1989).

love-feast: see *agapē*.

Lovejoy, Arthur O. (1873–1962). American philosopher and historian of ideas at Johns Hopkins University who advocated *Critical Realism, temporalistic realism, and a method of tracing ideas through history. A dualist in epistemology, he held that there are 'changes in certain physical structures which generate existents that are not physical . . . and these non-physical particulars are indispensable means to any knowledge of physical realities'. '[T]emporalism', he said, 'is the metaphysical theory which maintains . . . the essentially transitive and unfinished and self-augmentative character of reality'. In his conception of intellectual history unit-ideas are assumptions or habits which become 'dialectical motives' when, vague and general as they are, they 'influence the course of men's reflections on almost any subject'. The historian traces each unit-idea 'through . . . the provinces of history in which it figures in any important degree, whether those provinces are called philosophy, science, literature, art, religion or politics'. Lovejoy was also an influential and courageous advocate of academic freedom. P.H.H.

Daniel J. Wilson, *Arthur O. Lovejoy and the Quest for Intelligibility* (Chapel Hill, NC, 1980).

loyalty. A disposition, normally regarded as admirable, by which a person remains faithful and committed to a person or cause, despite danger and difficulty attendant on that allegiance, and often despite evidences that that person or cause may not be quite as meritorious or creditable as they seem. The fact that loyalty can be blind to or unmoved by such evidences gives rise to problems about its value, as the phrases misguided, misplaced, or unquestioning loyalty suggest. None the less, we are apt to see the capacity for selfless commitment contained in loyalty as presumptively good (if it does not become fanaticism). Loyalty need not be to universal or impartial causes; it is often very limited and exclusive in its scope. In this way, too, it can give rise to injustice. Only rarely has it been seen as a cardinal *virtue. N.J.H.D.

*trust.

J. Royce, *The Philosophy of Loyalty* (New York, 1908) contains an exhaustive discussion.

Lucretius (*c*.95–52 BC). He was a Roman poet whose work *De rerum natura* (On the Nature of Things) is both a major source for Epicurean philosophy and one of the masterpieces of Latin literature. He wrote the poem to transmit into Latin culture the message from Greek *Epicureanism that nothing infringes our autonomy in securing happiness. The centre-piece of the poem is an extended argument that human beings are purely material things and so they cannot survive the destruction of their physical bodies; religion which seeks to teach otherwise, is damaging superstition. To support his case he had to mount extensive investigations of physical and psychological phenomena, which are described with great literary power. His attempt to prove that people are irrational to be worried about their future non-existence is often cited in contemporary moral philosophy. J.D.G.E.

C. Bailey, *Titi Lucreti Cari: De rerum natura* (Oxford, 1947), i. 1–171.
D. Sedley, *Lucretius and the Transformation of Greek Wisdom* (Cambridge, 1998).

Lukács, Georg (1885–1971). The most prominent Marxist philosopher in the Hegelian tradition, Lukács is best known for his book *History and Class Consciousness* (1923), which attempts a philosophical justification of the Bolshevik enterprise. He stressed the distinction between actual class consciousness and 'ascribed' class consciousness—the attitudes that the proletariat would have if they were aware of all the facts. Lukács here emphasized *dialectics over *materialism, and made concepts such as *alienation and reification central to his theory well before the publication of some of Marx's key earlier writings vindicated this interpretation. Later in his long life, which he divided between his native Hungary and the Soviet Union, Lukács became the leading Marxist theoretician of literature, before producing a monumental work on social ontology in his last decade. D.McL.

*Marxist philosophy.

G. Parkinson (ed.), *Georg Lukács: The Man, his Work, and his Ideas* (London, 1970).

Łukasiewicz, Jan (1878–1956). Logician who is the author of many innovative ideas in logic, including *many-valued logic, bracketless or *'Polish' notation, a formal axiomatization of *syllogisms including modal syllogistic, and the historical recognition of Stoic logic as the original form of modern propositional logic. Łukasiewicz intended three-valued logic to reflect Aristotle's ideas about future contingent propositions in *De interpretatione*. If 'There will be a sea battle tomorrow' is true today then the sea battle's occurrence seems predetermined or inevitable; if false then its non-occurrence seems inevitable. But by the principle of bivalence every proposition is either true or false. To ensure the contingency of future events Łukasiewicz proposed that future-tense propositions be considered neither true nor false, but instead take a third truth-value 'indefinite' or 'possible'. Where 1 is 'true', 0 'false', and ½ 'indefinite', Łukasiewicz's three-valued logic is defined by the following matrices:

$\supset$	1	½	0	~
1	1	½	0	0
½	1	1	½	½
0	1	1	1	1

S.McC.

*modal logic; many-valued logic.

J. Łukasiewicz, *Aristotle's Syllogistic from The Standpoint of Modern Formal Logic* (Oxford, 1957).
—— *Selected Works* (Amsterdam, 1970).

Lumber of the Schools.

'Tis you must put us in the Way;
Let us (for shame) no more be fed
With antique Reliques of the Dead,
The Gleanings of Philosophy,
Philosophy! the Lumber of the Schools . . .
(Jonathan Swift, 'Ode to Sir William Temple', line 20)

Virtue, says Swift in this over-long ode, was broken at the Fall, and ancient wisdom will never reconstitute it. To 'dig the leaden Mines of deep Philosophy' only produces lifeless leavings—a perverse confirmation, apparently, of Plato's theory of recollection. The poem's almost existentialist excoriation of academia is perhaps connected with Swift's having obtained his degree only by 'special grace' three years before writing it. Its dedicatee, Sir William Temple, who was kind enough to employ him, is declared to be the one person fit to discover 'Virtue's Terra Incognita'. J.O'G.

Luther, Martin (1483–1546). German theologian, Professor of Philosophy and then of Theology at Wittenberg, leader of the Protestant Reformation. Luther is notorious among philosophers for speaking of *reason as 'the Devil's Whore', which must be sacrificed as the enemy of God. He sees reason as having being corrupted by original sin, and therefore incapable of coming to a true estimate of the relation between God and man. The Mosaic law, which crushes men but which would at the same time bind God to a human contract, is the fruit of reason. Salvation can only come through the divine gift of grace and revelation. While in human affairs reason ought to be followed, in the theological realm it must stand aside for the rebirth afforded by grace, confining its efforts to the elucidation of what God reveals through Scripture. Historically and theologically Luther is a pivotal point in the tradition leading from Paul's doctrine of justification through faith and Augustine's two cities through to the anti-rationalism of Karl Barth.   A.O'H.

B. A. Gerrish, *Grace and Reason: A Study in the Theology of Luther* (Oxford, 1962).

Lycan, William G. (1945–). Lycan develops a *truth-conditions theory of sentence-meaning in *Logical Form and Natural Language*, and assays the standard kinds of objections to truth-conditions semantics. These arise from facts about vagueness, indexicality, tense, and other features of language in use, e.g. presupposition and conversational implications of what one says. Lycan's truth-theoretic semantic theory is applied to fundamental questions in psycholinguistics and in an account of linguistic and cognitive abilities.

In *Consciousness* he develops a functionalist theory of the nature of mind, 'homuncular functionalism'. This view emphasizes the levels at which psychological and cognitive accounts of thought and action find application, from the surface level of common sense to the level at which representations are attributed to cognitive systems housed in the brain and thence to subcognitive systems which carry out semi-intelligent roles the execution of which constitute our psychological lives. *Judgement and Justification* contains an application of this form of *functionalism to the nature and role of belief. Here and elsewhere Lycan defends the representational theory of mind.   D.G.

William G. Lycan, *Consciousness* (Cambridge, Mass., 1987).
—— *Judgement and Justification* (Cambridge, 1988).

lying. Some church fathers held that lying, almost always prohibited, is occasionally right, as when only thus can the community be protected from invasive inquiries by persecutors. Augustine argued that lying is always prohibited and Aquinas agreed. Later moral philosophers divide similarly. Kant judged that a lie violates a duty to oneself and to others, because rational beings owe each other truthfulness in communication. Mill severely condemned almost all lying as injurious to human trust and therefore to the social fabric, but judged it right on rare occasions, as when only thus can some great and unmerited evil be averted. An adequate treatment of lying would have to consider whether and how it violates the norms governing speech-acts of assertion and what kind of injury it involves to the trust which constitutes central human relationships.   A.MacI.

*absolutism, moral; self-deception; noble lie.

Sissela Bok, *Lying* (New York, 1978).

Lyotard, Jean-François (1924–). An exponent of so-called *'post-modernism', lately much in vogue among cultural and literary theorists. His arguments may be summarized briefly as follows. Our epoch has witnessed the collapse of all those grand 'metanarrative' schemas (Kantian, Hegelian, Marxist, or whatever) that once promised truth or justice at the end of inquiry. What we are left with is an open multiplicity of 'heterogeneous' or strictly incommensurable *language-games, each disposing of its own immanent criteria. This requires that we should not presume to judge any one such discourse according to the standards, values, or truth-conditions of any other, but should instead seek to maximize the current range of 'first-order natural pragmatic' narratives. Moreover, anyone who rejects these premises—who seeks (like Jürgen Habermas) to uphold the values of enlightenment, critique, and rational consensus as against Lyotard's ill-defined notion of 'dissensus' as the touchstone of democratic freedom—must *ipso facto* be arguing from a 'totalitarian' or rigidly doctrinaire standpoint. What this amounts to, in short, is a *mélange* of Wittgensteinian, post-structuralist, and kindred ideas presented in an oracular style that raises bafflement to a high point of principle.   C.N.

Jean-François Lyotard, *The Postmodern Condition: A Report on Knowledge*, tr. Geoff Bennington and Brian Massumi (Minneapolis, 1983).

M

Mach, Ernst (1838–1916). Austrian scientist, several times nominated for the Nobel Prize. He made important contributions to optics (Doppler effect), acoustics (shock waves), physiology (Mach bands), and the history and philosophy of *science. Writing in a vivid style he recommended the 'bold intellectual move', emphasized that sensations and physical objects were 'as . . . preliminary as the elements of alchemy', and criticized the scientists of his time (the defenders of the theory of relativity included) for neglecting this aspect. Making physics a measure of reality, they blocked the unification of physical, biological, and psychological phenomena. Most of Mach's demands have by now become commonplace (*evolutionary epistemology, *constructivism, *complementarity), though not always in a way Mach would have enjoyed.   P.K.F.

Bibliography, literature, and evaluations in R. S. Cohen and R. J. Seeger (eds.), *Ernst Mach, Physicist and Philosopher* (Dordrecht, 1970); P. K. Feyerabend, *Studies in the History of the Philosophy of Science* (1984); J. T. Blackmore, *Ernst Mach* (Los Angeles, 1972).

Machiavelli, Niccolò (1469–1527). Italian statesman and political theorist who turned political thought in a new direction. Whereas traditional political theorists were concerned with morally evaluating the state in terms of fulfilling its function of promoting the common good and preserving justice, Machiavelli was more interested in empirically investigating how the state could most effectively use its *power to maintain law and order (political science). His famous claim that the end justifies the means also seems to advocate the use of immoral means to acquire and maintain political power. However, what he seems to mean by this is that sometimes in order to maintain law and order it is necessary for a ruler to do things that, considered in themselves, are not right, but which, considered in their context, are right because necessary to prevent great evils.   R.D.M.

*ends and means; dirty hands.

N. Machiavelli, *The Discourses* (1513).
—— *The Prince* (1513).

MacIntyre, Alasdair C. (1929–). MacIntyre is best known for the work he has produced since 1980, although there was significant output before then. His work is primarily concerned with morality, especially with the historical changes which have shaped moral belief and practice, and also shaped theorizing about morality. Starting with his early *A Short History of Ethics* (London, 1966), MacIntyre has eschewed the close, often narrow, analytical and linguistic work which characterized much academic moral philosophy, preferring to explore the significance of moral ideas (and shifts in moral vocabulary) against the wider background of historical, cultural, sociological, religious, and other influences forming society and the individual. This has given his work an unusual breadth of reference, and has made it more accessible to non-professional persons interested in understanding our moral predicament.

It is central to MacIntyre's more recent work, as set out in three substantial books *After Virtue* (London, 1981), *Whose Justice? Which Rationality?* (London, 1988), and *Three Rival Versions of Moral Enquiry* (London, 1990, the Gifford Lectures given at the University of Edinburgh in 1988), that what many recent moral philosophers have presented as timeless truths about the nature of moral discourse or the foundations of moral judgement are nothing of the kind. The representation of the individual as a sovereign chooser who by his or her own decision determines the values to live by is, in fact, the obscure manifestation of massive dislocations in society, and the dissolution of social ties and modes of life which alone can give dignity and meaning to human activity. MacIntyre has argued for an attempt to recover an Aristotelian way of viewing the purposes and activities central to human realization and fulfilment.

Born in Scotland and largely educated in England, MacIntyre has worked in America since 1970.   N.J.H.D.

*narrative; histories of moral philosophy.

Mackie, John L. (1917–81). Born in Australia, lived and taught in Australia and New Zealand before moving to England, teaching finally at Oxford University. He was the author of six books and numerous papers on a wide range of topics, especially in metaphysics, ethics, philosophy of religion, and the history of philosophy. Mackie was influential for his 'error theory' of moral values—the view that there are no objective moral values, yet ordinary moral judgements include an implicit claim to objectivity, and hence are all false. The objectivity-claim is at least partly prescriptive in pointing to reasons for performing certain actions regardless of one's wants. He thinks it possible and desirable to jettison this objectively prescriptive element in moral discourse and to continue using the same moral terms, not necessarily accepting previously held moral views, but (re)inventing morality as a device for counteracting limited sympathies, and giving it whatever content we think best serves this purpose.

In his comprehensive study of *causality, which draws extensively on historical sources, Mackie distinguishes an analysis of causation 'as it is in the objects' from an analysis of our ordinary concept of causation, offering a regularity analysis for the former, and a *counterfactual analysis for the latter, supplementing each with an account of the direction of causation. The regularity analysis is his memorable development from Mill, that a cause is an 'inus' condition of an effect—an insufficient but necessary part of an unnecessary but sufficient condition. His counterfactual analysis is that a cause is necessary in the circumstances for an effect, such counterfactual claims being, according to him, strictly speaking neither true nor false.   N.L.

J. L. Mackie, *The Cement of the Universe* (Oxford, 1974), chs. 2 and 3.
—— *Ethics: Inventing Right and Wrong* (Harmondsworth, 1977), ch. 1.

Macmurray, John (1891–1976). British philosopher who held chairs in London and Edinburgh. He maintained that the error of traditional philosophy consisted in making its starting-point the self as subject—'I think'. Macmurray proposed as the starting-point the self as agent—'I do.' He argued that thought is derivative from action, and that the identity of the self as agent is constituted by its relationships with other agents in communities. His belief that we are members not just of the human community but of the natural world gives his thinking a contemporary flavour reminiscent of much 'applied philosophy'. He held that religion is distinctive of personal life, in that it celebrates and expresses the unity of persons in fellowship. He had a large following among the general public through his many broadcasts in the 1930s and 1940s which illustrated his desire, expressed in his Gifford Lectures, to 'transfer the centre of gravity in philosophy from thought to action'.   R.S.D.

David Fergusson and Nigel Dower (eds.), *John Macmurray: Critical Perspectives* (New York, 2002).
John Macmurray, *The Form of the Personal* (London, 1991).

macrocosm and microcosm. This pair of terms encapsulates the idea that a systematic analogy can be drawn between larger- and smaller-scale phenomena, particularly between the cosmic and the human. Thus it may be supposed that astronomical bodies bear the same mutual relations as do the parts of an individual animal body, or that the universe is ordered in the way that a human society is. The terminology may have been introduced in the fifth century BC by Democritus; but such analogies are also characteristic of Pythagorean, Platonic, and Stoic

philosophy. They are not justified by argument, but they may have heuristic value as facilitating exploration of what would otherwise be hard to access for investigation. Plato certainly supposed natural science could be prosecuted effectively only by one who appreciated the element of value which was implicit in the designation of the universe as *kosmos*, 'order'.   J.D.G.E.

A recent discussion of *Pre-Socratic philosophy which takes the analogy very seriously is A. Capizzi, *The Cosmic Republic* (Amsterdam, 1990).

Madhva (13th century AD). Dualist commentator on *Vedānta, part of the revealed scriptures of the Hindus. Madhva defends the reality of the external world, including infinitely divisible space, time, souls, bodies, and their unique particularities. Warning that you cannot adore God if you think that you are identical with him, he also celebrates all five differences denied by the idealist monists, namely, God ≠ the world, God ≠ I, I ≠ you, I ≠ the table, the table ≠ the chair. Such pluralism provoked astute rebuttals from the monists and counter-replies from the dualists for centuries. Distinctions, according to Madhva, are objective negative facts witnessed *directly* by the self rather than perceived through outer or inner sense. His rich epistemology tackles issues such as 'If knowledge is self-validating, how can one tell its claim from an error's claim to knowledge?' Liberation, attainable only through devoted worship of the personal God, brings blissful proximity to, but never equality with, God, though some sinners (non-dualists?) remain eternally damned!   A.C.

*Indian philosophy.

S. S. Raghavachar, *Dvaita Vedanta* (Madras, 1977).

magnitude. The particular amount, degree, or extent of a quantitative property. Thus 1 metre and 10 metres are different magnitudes of length. Magnitudes are represented mathematically by scales of *measurement, which assign a unique numerical value to each magnitude of the quantitative property. Scales are typically (but not exclusively) defined by selecting a standard whose magnitude becomes the unit, 1. The *number assigned to any other magnitude is determined by how many times greater it is than that of the standard. Thus a length ten times greater than that of the standard metre is represented by 10 on the metric scale. Magnitudes are measured by empirically comparing objects directly or indirectly to the standard.   W.A.D.

B. Ellis, *Basic Concepts of Measurement* (Cambridge, 1966).

Maimonides, Moses (1135–1204). Jewish philosopher, jurist, physician. Exiled from his native Cordoba by the Almohad conquest (1148), Moses ben Maimon (also known as Rambam) settled finally in Egypt, where he became physician to Saladin's wazir. His Arabic *Commentary on the Mishnah*, his *Book of the Commandments*, and his fourteen-volume Code of Jewish Law, the *Mishneh Torah*, written in Mishnaic Hebrew, established his unparalleled authority in Jewish law. His *Guide to the Perplexed* (written in Arabic), addressed to a philosophically minded disciple, deconstructs the seeming anthropomorphisms of prophetic language to reveal the underlying logic of God's absolute perfection. Neither biblical creationism nor Aristotelian eternalism is demonstrable, it argues. But creation is more probable, and preferable theologically, since it can explain the difference God's act makes in the world and can rely on God's freedom to explain how multiplicity emerges from sheer divine simplicity. Revelation accommodates its recipients intellectually and culturally. Its fundamental demand is that we pursue the human likeness to God by perfecting humanity in ourselves—minimally, by living in peace with one another, as we might have known without revelation. What distinguishes God's law is its further expectation that we perfect ourselves morally and intellectually, improving our character through such exercises as reloading our enemy's fallen ass (Exodus 23: 5); and improving our minds by seeking contact with God through study of nature, mathematics, and human and divine institutions, and contemplating God's perfection. Prophets are (as al-Fārābī claimed) philosophers whose imaginative gifts afford the rhetoric, symbol, and story that transform abstract ideas and values into laws, rituals, and beliefs, allowing non-philosophers access to the moral and intellectual fruits of philosophic insight. Philosophy is universal; but the moral prerequisites of intellectual receptivity and the material perquisites of prophetic creativity (confidence, contentment, a fertile and wholesome imagination, fostered by appropriate linguistic and cultural traditions) make true prophecy rare. Pagan religions are primitive, superstitious, or perverse; but Islam and Christianity, which have spread monotheism through the world, preparing for the Messianic age, are derivative from Israelite prophecy.   L.E.G.

L. E. Goodman (ed.), *Rambam* (New York, 1976).

Maine de Biran, François-Pierre (1766–1824). French philosopher and politician. Maine de Biran is an empiricist philosopher because he holds that all knowledge is acquired through experience. However, while the classical British Empiricists tend to the view that inner experience is made possible by outer experience, Maine de Biran reverses this picture. For example, while Locke holds that acquaintance with sensations is a necessary condition for the operations of reflection, Maine de Biran holds that unless we were acquainted with the contents of our own minds we could not have knowledge of the external world. He claims that there is a *sens intime* (inner sense) or *lumière intérieure* (inner light) through which each person is aware of his own mental states, especially states of 'croyance' (belief), and aware of his own 'effort voulu' (voluntary physical action).

It is not clear that acquaintance with one's own mental states is a sufficient condition for knowledge of anything else, but it could be argued that Maine de Biran has isolated a necessary condition for knowledge if, for example,

a person's knowing that they know that *P* is a condition for their knowing that *P*. This claim is, however, contentious.
                                                S.P.

*empiricism.

Œuvres philosophiques de Maine de Biran, 4 vols. (Paris, 1841).

Mair, John (or John Major) (1467–1550). Leader of a group of philosopher-logicians, many of them Scots, active in Paris and Scotland in the decades before the Reformation. Educated at Paris, where he rose to become Professor of Theology, he was subsequently Principal of Glasgow University. During his last years, while Provost of St Salvator's College, St Andrews, he was the theology teacher of John Knox. He wrote numerous treatises on formal logic, presenting in great detail a system in direct line of descent from the logic of William Ockham. Many things he had to say on *supposition and *quantification, particularly on sentences containing several quantifiers, repay study.   A.BRO.

A. Broadie, *The Circle of John Mair: Logic and Logicians in Pre-Reformation Scotland* (Oxford, 1985).

Maistre, Joseph Marie de: *see* de Maistre.

Malcolm, Norman Adrian (1911–90). One of the most distinguished of Wittgenstein's pupils and the main conveyor of his ideas to the USA, where Malcolm taught for many years at Cornell. His writings were primarily in epistemology and philosophy of mind. They are distinguished not only by force of argument, but also by lucidity and simplicity of expression. His book *Memory and Mind* is the finest on that subject, submitting both classical empiricist and modern neurological representationalist theories of memory to devastating criticism. In *Consciousness and Causality*, he developed Wittgenstein's ideas on that theme, undermining introspectionist and materialist theories of *consciousness alike. His *Ludwig Wittgenstein: A Memoir* has rightly been called 'a classic of biographical literature', and his last book, *Nothing is Hidden*, is a valuable study of Wittgenstein's later philosophical criticisms of his own earlier work.   P.M.S.H.

*Wittgensteinians.

G. H. von Wright, 'Norman Malcolm', *Philosophical Investigations* (1992).

Malebranche, Nicolas (1638–1715). Highly regarded in his own day, and long regarded in the francophone world as a philosopher of major importance, the author of *The Search After Truth* (*De la recherche de la verité* (1674–5)) and the *Dialogues on Metaphysics and Religion* (1688) has only quite recently been brought in from the cold by English-speaking philosophers. The doctrine for which he is chiefly remembered, the theory of *occasionalism, seems bizarre to many modern readers who tend (following the damning verdict of Leibniz) to see it as a blundering piece of adhocery: an attempt to plug a logical gap in Cartesian *dualism (its inability to explain how mind and body, being incompatible substances, can interact causally) by dumping on to the Deity the task of obligingly ensuring that my jaw moves for me when I want to eat a meal. But in fact Malebranche invokes the efficacious will of God for all causal transactions, not just psychophysical ones. 'A true cause, as I understand it', he wrote in the *Recherche*, 'is one such that the mind perceives a necessary connection between it and its effect'; and if causation implies necessary connection, then the divine will must be involved in all causality, since true necessity applies only to events willed by God (it being a contradiction that anything willed by an omnipotent being should not come about).

In the Malebranchian universe individual objects and events are thus stripped of their causal powers. Talk of causal 'influence' or 'transfer of force' is only a *façon de parler*. In reality, what we call the cause is merely the *occasion* for God to exercise his efficacious will. Malebranche thus radically rejects the scholastic conception whereby each kind of object behaved the way it did in virtue of its specific nature or essence, with properties being 'transmitted' from cause to effect. In the new Cartesian conception of physics (which Malebranche strongly supports), the idea of some kind of essential connection or similarity between causes and effects is ultimately redundant; all that is needed is a specification of initial conditions, and a set of mathematical equations describing the (divinely decreed) regularities that in fact obtain. Seen in this light, Malebranchian occasionalism can be viewed as a bridge theory between Cartesian and the later Humean account of *causality.

Malebranche subscribed to what is commonly called a *'representative' theory of perception, arguing that 'we do not perceive objects external to us by themselves' since 'it is not likely that the soul should leave the body to stroll about the heavens to behold the sun and the stars'; when we perceive the sun, what we see is 'not the sun but something intimately joined to our soul, which I call an "idea"'. In developing his account of the direct objects of perception, Malebranche went on to advance a distinctive theory of *ideas, summed up in the slogan that 'we see all things in God'. Condemned by Locke as 'an opinion that spreads not, and is like to die of itself', Malebranche's theory at least tidies up some of the ambiguities in Descartes's broad use of the term 'idea'. Malebranche is careful to distinguish the mental phenomena he calls 'sentiments' (feelings or sensations) which are purely subjective and lack any intentionality (do not have representational content), from what he calls ideas in the strict sense; the latter are abstract objects of cognition whose presence 'in God' may be viewed as a graphic way of conveying their independence from any subjective mode of consciousness. The resulting theory has the merit of making a firm distinction between the province of psychology and that of logic.

A further important subject on which Malebranche takes issue with *Cartesianism concerns the alleged transparency of the mind—its supposed perfect internal awareness of its own nature as a 'thinking thing'. Descartes has achieved this result by the dubious move of subsuming a large number of different operations (understanding, willing, imagining, sensing) under the single label 'thought'. Malebranche argues persuasively that the various possible modifications of consciousness are not clearly and distinctly deducible from a known essence (in the way in which the modifications of matter are deducible from the nature of extension); further, introspection can reveal only the presence of conscious activity, not the essential nature of the thinking self: 'to myself, I am but darkness, and my own substance seems something which is beyond my understanding' (*Christian Metaphysical Meditations* (1683)).   J.COT.

S. Brown (ed.), *Nicolas Malebranche: His Philosophical Critics and Successors* (Maastricht, 1991).

N. Jolley, *The Light of the Soul* (Oxford, 1990).

C. McCracken, *Malebranche and British Philosophy* (Oxford, 1983).

S. Nadler (ed.), *The Cambridge Companion to Malebranche* (Cambridge, 2000).

malin génie. Descartes hypothesized a *malin génie* (evil spirit) in the course of his search for a truth that was absolutely immune from doubt. He found that even the truths of mathematics were not thus immune, for an evil spirit might be causing him to give his assent to mathematical propositions which are in fact false.   A.BRO.

*brain in a vat; scepticism.

R. Descartes, *Meditations on First Philosophy*, Meditation 1.

Mandeville, Bernard (*c.*1670–1733) was trained in medicine in his native Holland, and settled in England in the early 1690s. He was a polemical writer, and the principal target of his polemics was hypocrisy. For Mandeville, behind the mask of respectability and virtue lay a Hobbesian egoism, which had to be faced up to in any throughgoing moral, political, and economic theory, and he was prepared to follow the consequences for all three of these areas. His most important work, *The Fable of the Bees*, began as a 433-line poem in 1705, but by the sixth edition of 1729 it had turned into a substantial treatise. It is an extremely witty and provocative book, if somewhat chaotic. Mandeville imagines a hive of bees each going about their own business in their own way and argues that their success is due as much to vice and fraud as it is to industry and virtue: all these are necessary for a flourishing market society, and indeed they mirror the egoistic qualities of the individuals who make up this society.

                                              S.GAU.

B. Mandeville, *The Fable of the Bees*, 2 vols., with commentary by F. B. Kaye (Oxford, 1924).

E. G. Hundert, *The Enlightenment's Fable* (Cambridge, 1994).

Manichaeism. This widely influential gnostic religion of late antiquity, founded and spread by the Persian Mani (216–77), taught a radical dualism of good and evil that is metaphysically grounded in coeternal and independent cosmic powers of Light and Darkness. This world was regarded as a mixture of good and evil in which spirit represents Light and matter represents Darkness.

Manichaean morality was severely ascetic. Before his conversion to Christianity, Augustine was an adherent of Manichaeism.   P.L.Q.

*Gnosticism.

H. Jonas, *The Gnostic Religion* (Boston, 1958).

manifold of sense. This is the expression Kant uses to refer to the data supplied to the mind through *sensation. In the *Critique of Pure Reason*, he argues that these data are given in accordance with the mind's forms of sensibility, space and time, and that their unification, which is necessary for experience, is brought about through the synthetic activity of the imagination guided by the understanding.   H.E.A.

H. J. Paton, *Kant's Metaphysic of Experience* (New York, 1936).

Mannheim, Karl (1893–1947). Hungarian-German-British philosopher, father of the sociology of knowledge. He was originally a member of the Sunday Circle in Budapest, led by Georg Lukács, which opposed *Kantianism, *positivism, and individualist liberal *capitalism, was nostalgic for the Middle Ages, and held a strongly Platonic view of psychic life and art. After his emigration to Germany in 1919 Mannheim tried to initiate a theoretical social science that could replace political philosophy. Social thought expresses rather than explains human life. Implicitly, this relegates political philosophy to the rank of a half-conscious projection of social aspirations. The task of theory is therefore to understand what people think about society rather than propose hypotheses about it. This did not prevent Mannheim from expressing his own political preferences in favour of an *étatiste* (statist–welfarist) democracy led by rational planners and scientists.   G.M.T.

His main works are:
Ideology and Utopia (London, 1929).
Man and Society in an Age of Reconstruction (London, 1940).

mantra. Literally, words which if meditated upon can save us. A subsection of the ritualistic part of the orally preserved sacred texts called Veda was also called 'Mantra' because it consisted of revealed holy words, often addressed to nature-gods, chanted during sacrificial acts. Subsequently, the term signified any mystic syllable or strings thereof which were to be repeated, aloud or subvocally or mentally, often while keeping count on rosary beads. 'Om' is such a syllable, often identified with the word-God which became the world. Elaborate metaphysical and semantic theories developed to support the putative identity between the name and the named which went hand in hand with the worship of sound.   A.C.

*Vedānta; Indian philosophy.

'Mantra', in Mircea Eliade (ed.), *Encyclopedia of Religion*, ix (London, 1987).

many questions fallacy. Illustrated by 'Have you stopped beating your wife?', the fallacy was first noticed by Aristotle. It lies not in the question but in what is inferred from the answer. Putting *B* for 'I have been a wife-beater' and *S* for 'I have stopped', then a negative answer is equivalent to '(*B* and not-*S*) or (not-*B* and not-*S*) or (not-*B* and *S*)'. If the questioner infers that he may disregard one or more of these alternatives, his inference is transparently invalid.

                                                J.WOO.

John Woods and Douglas Walton, *Fallacies: Selected Papers 1972–1982* (Dordrecht, 1989).

many-valued logic. Logical systems in which formulae may be assigned truth-values other than merely 'true' and 'false'. The term is often used more narrowly to refer to many-valued *tabular* logics, in which the truth-value of a formula is determined by the truth-values of its subformulae. (This characteristic distinguishes many-valued logics from standard *modal logics.)

The idea that logic ought to countenance more than two truth-values arose naturally in ancient and medieval discussions of *determinism and was re-examined by C. S. Peirce, Hugh MacColl, and Nikolai Vasiliev in the first decade of this century. Explicit formulation and systematic investigation of many-valued logics began with writings of Jan Łukasiewicz and Emil Post in the 1920s and D. Bochvar, Jerzy Stupecki, and Stephen Kleene in the late 1930s. There has been some renewed interest in the subject recently, because of perceived connections with programming languages and artificial intelligence.

Łukasiewicz's work is inspired by a view of 'future contingents' often attributed to Aristotle. There is a sense in which whatever happens in the present or past is now unalterable. This idea sometimes finds expression in the doctrine that sentences now true are unalterably true and those now false are unalterably false. But, although it seems that 'There will be a sea battle tomorrow' is now either true or false, it does not seem *unalterably* true or *unalterably* false. Considerations like this led Łukasiewicz to adopt the view that future contingent sentences are not either true or false, but have an *intermediate* truth-value, 'the possible'. He constructed a formal language, taking the conditional ($\rightarrow$) and negation ($\neg$) as primitive connectives and false (0), possible (½), and true (1) as truth-values. Truth-values of compound formulae are determined by the tables below.

A	¬A		A	B	A→B
1	0		1	1	1
½	½		1	½	½
0	1		1	0	0
			½	1	1
			½	½	1
			½	0	½
			0	1	1
			0	½	1
			0	0	1

To obtain a many-valued logic from a table like this, one specifies certain truth-values as designated. The argument from set Γ to formula A is logically valid if A gets a designated truth-value under any assignment in which all the members of Γ do. A is logically true if it gets a designated value under any assignment. For example, if figure 1 and fi are both designated, then $(P \rightarrow \neg P) \rightarrow \neg P$ is a logical truth by these tables; if (as Łukasiewicz intended) only figure 1 is designated, then it is not. With Łukasiewicz's understanding that $P \vee Q$ abbreviates $(P \rightarrow Q) \rightarrow Q$, the formula in question expresses the law of excluded middle.

It is doubtful that these (or any) truth-tables capture precisely the kind of possibility exhibited by future contingents. Why, for example, should 'If there won't be a sea battle there will be one' be considered true, while 'If $2 + 2 = 4$ then there will be a sea battle' is merely possible? Nevertheless, Łukasiewicz's original system has been generalized, axiomatized, reinterpreted, modified, and otherwise studied.

Łukasiewicz himself considered generalizations permitting more than one intermediate truth-value: $\neg A$ gets truth-value 1 minus the truth-value of A; $A \vee B$ gets the greater of the truth-values of A and B. Other many-valued systems have been motivated by the idea that additional truth-values might express the notion of a proposition's being paradoxical (its truth implying its falsity and its falsity implying its truth), of its having uncomputable truth-value, of its being approximately true, and of its having failed presuppositions of various sorts. Most of the systems considered generalize classical logic in the sense that, if truth-values other than 0 and 1 are dropped, classical logic is obtained.

Post formulated a technically advantageous system in which Łukasiewicz's negation is replaced by a 'cyclic' negation—the truth-values are 0, 1, . . ., m and the truth-value of $\neg A$ is 0 if the truth-value of A is m and it is $1 + the truth-value of A otherwise. Post's negation and disjunction are truth-functionally complete: any connective in a finite-valued logic (including the conditional and negation of Łukasiewicz's three-valued logic discussed above) can be defined from them. This result has practical significance, for just as the formulae of classical propositional logic correspond to logic circuits, the formulae of m-valued logics correspond to switching-circuits in which inputs and outputs can assume m states. More recent investigations have examined the model theory and proof theory of general many-valued logic and of continuous logic, in which the truth-values are assumed to have a topological structure. It is enlightening to see certain results of classical logic proved in a more general setting. S.T.K.

The works cited below are a small sample of the large and varied literature on the subject, but they do contain references to much of the rest.

N. Rescher, *Many-Valued Logic* (New York, 1969).

A. Urquhart, 'Many-Valued Logic', in D. Gabbay and F. Guenthner (eds.), *Handbook of Philosophical Logic*, iii (Dordrecht, 1986).

R. Wójcicki, *Theory of Logical Calculi: Basic Theory of Consequence Operations* (Dordrecht, 1988).

R. Wolf, 'A Survey of Many-Valued Logic 1966–1974', in J. M. Dunn and G. Epstein (eds.), *Modern Uses of Multiple-Valued Logic* (Dordrecht, 1975).

Marcel, Gabriel (1889–1973). French philosopher, playwright, and literary and music critic who converted to Roman Catholicism in 1929. Marcel (despite, in common with the other Existentialists, repudiating the title 'Existentialist') provides Christian solutions to existentialist problems.

In *Être et avoir* (Being and Having (1935)) Marcel draws a distinction between one's being and one's life. 'I am' is existentially prior to 'I live' (meaning, approximately, that being is a necessary condition for living but not vice versa). Marcel takes this as a ground for believing that my life was 'given to me', a fact which is sufficiently impressive to suggest the existence of God.

In a fashion analogous to Heidegger's use of 'being-toward-death' Marcel notes that one's being is at every moment 'in jeopardy' and concludes that the only way to understand the 'ordeal' of living is to have faith in one's being 'beyond' one's life, that is, surviving one's death.

Marcel's existentialist metaphysics faces the difficulty that from the fact that I am not numerically identical with the life that I lead it does not logically follow that I pre-date or post-date that life. Similarly, from the fact that life is a senseless ordeal without God it does not logically follow that God exists. However, neither of these objections is strong enough to show that the central tenets of Marcel's theological *existentialism are false.

In 'Existence and Freedom' (1946) Marcel criticizes Heidegger, Jaspers, but especially Sartre for their 'dogmatic negativism' (their *pessimism about human prospects), a charge Sartre attempts to repudiate in his maligned but brilliant 1946 speech 'L'Existentialisme est un humanisme'. S.P.

K. T. Gallagher, *The Philosophy of Gabriel Marcel*, foreword by Gabriel Marcel (New York, 1962).

G. Marcel, *The Mystery of Being*, tr. René Hague (London, 1950–1).

Marcus, Ruth (1921–). Ruth Marcus is known as an early pioneer of *modal logic, the logic which formalizes the philosophical notions of possibility and necessity. Marcus, originally Ruth Barcan, was instrumental in exploring modal logics with quantifiers and assessing the philosophical implications of mixing modality and quantification. A well-known formula in quantified modal logic, the *Barcan formula, bears her name; in one version it states that if everything necessarily bears a certain property, then it is a necessary truth that everything bears it. Marcus has also done a great deal of work in other areas of logic, most notably on the substitutional interpretation of quantifiers, an approach which takes quantifiers to range not over ordinary objects but over linguistic symbols (in a prescribed formal language) which produce true substitution instances. G.F.M.

R. Marcus, *Modalities: Philosophical Essays* (Oxford, 1993).

Marcuse, Herbert (1898–1979). One of the most original and provocative non-Soviet Marxists of the century, Marcuse received a doctorate in literature (1922) but soon became attracted to Heidegger's philosophy with its focus on the individual as thrown into a world of objects and populated with others. But the writings of the young Marx convinced Marcuse that a genuine theory of individuality must take into account prevailing socio-economic structures. Joining the *Frankfurt School in 1933, he contributed to the development of the dialectical criticism characteristic of the school: major concepts were analysed and traced to their material origins, and then reconstructed to show their altered political functions.

His post-Second World War writings, however, present his most characteristic proposals and social critique. Freudian psychology provided a theory of human instincts, which are repressed under capitalism but which, when liberated, can be the basis for a life of sensousness, playfulness, peace, and beauty. This liberation requires a total transformation of present society: technology would be utilized to abolish poverty and provide for abundance; there would be a different relation to nature in which art and production are unified; the sexes and generations would overcome artificial constraints, and a new kind of person with advanced sensibilities would appear.

Marcuse's optimism for the actual achievement of these transformations was at its lowest in *One Dimensional Man* (1964); the student rebellions of the 1960s gave him renewed hope (e.g. *Essay on Liberation* (1969)). *Counter-revolution and Revolt* (1972) retreats from advocating revolutionary violence and confrontation and recommends working for change within the system. *The Aesthetic Dimension* (1978) argues that the sensuous appearance of beauty in the artwork preserves the memory of a liberated way of living and so escapes the domination of the present, repressive order.

Marcuse's revised Marxism provides both a broad critique of advanced capitalist society and utopian proposals for a post-capitalist world.   C.C.

*Marxist philosophy.

Barry Katz, *Herbert Marcuse and the Art of Liberation: An Intellectual Biography* (London, 1982).
Douglas Kellner, *Herbert Marcuse and the Crisis of Marxism* (Berkeley, Calif., 1984).

Maritain, Jacques (1882–1973). The best-known neo-Thomist of the twentieth century. Having become dissatisfied with secularism and scientism, at the age of 24 Maritain converted to Roman Catholicism and spent the following sixty or so years elaborating a comprehensive philosophical system based on the writings of Thomas Aquinas and of his scholastic followers, most especially John of St Thomas (1589–1644). His major contributions are to epistemology (*The Degrees of Knowledge* (1932)), social philosophy (*The Person and the Common Good* (1947)), and aesthetics (*Art and Scholasticism* (1920)). Maritain is a staunch realist in metaphysics and epistemology: he advocates ontological pluralism, claiming that there are various non-reducible levels of existence, e.g. the physical, the biological, the psychological, the social, and the spiritual; and similarly he insists upon the diversity of our ways of knowing reality, emphasizing the role of

rational and creative intuition and thereby linking metaphysics and aesthetics.   J.HAL.

*neo-Thomism.

R. McInerny, *Art and Prudence: Studies in the Thought of Jacques Maritain* (Notre Dame, Ind., 1988).

markets. Originally, places at which independent sellers, who were usually also the producers, made their goods available to consumers coming there specifically to shop for them; terms of exchange (prices) were characteristically established for each individual transaction by haggling. The term 'market' is currently used to refer not only to particular local places but to the entirety of *free exchanges of goods and services within a society, by contrast with the sphere in which exchanges are enforced by an authority external to the transfer of goods or services. The term 'market' is thus usually used interchangeably with 'free market', the implication being that prices are set by agreement between buyers and sellers. In this more abstract sense, the idea of the market is defined by the set of socially understood or enforced rights of participants: an arena of transfers is a market in so far as the disposition of the goods and services in question is at the will of voluntarily acting individuals or co-operating sets of individuals, terms of exchange (prices) being freely negotiated. Prices are then determined by effective supply and demand on the part of participants.

Constraints imposed by governments, requiring that goods or services transfer on certain terms even though one or both parties would not freely exchange on those terms, is called 'intervention in the market'. *Socialism involves collective, political control, rather than market determination, of much economic activity, especially of capital (productive) goods; *capitalism leaves the allocation of capital as well as all consumer goods to private control (ownership). There is extensive political and moral discussion about the proper role of markets in society, ranging from those who think that the allocation of *all* goods and services should be determined by free market mechanisms (*'libertarianism') to those who think that *none* of them should ('collectivism'). The latter, which Stalinism approximated, is defended by no one. The former, or close approximations, has many advocates, due in part to its theoretical elegance and in part to the enormous empirical success of markets. The chief problem for the unlimited advocacy of market methods is what to do about externalities—involuntary effects (especially negative ones) on persons outside the transaction, as with, say, an assassination contract; and especially about public goods, which are roughly externalities, such as pollution, whose involuntary costs are imposed on miscellaneous others rather than some few specific others, making it very difficult to allocate costs and benefits precisely.

                                                          J.N.

*anti-communism.

For a fascinating radically pro-market book, see David Friedman, *The Machinery of Freedom*, 2nd ed. (La Salle, Ill., 1989). For a good, brief discussion of many basics, see Allen Buchanan, *Ethics, Efficiency, and the Market* (Totowa, NJ, 1985).

markets and the public good. Markets are places or networks where buyers and sellers exchange goods or services for money. Capitalism is the economic system whereby the mass production of goods to be sold in markets is financed by private capital for individual or corporate profit. According to the 'law' of supply and demand, market price rises with the scarcity of items for sale and falls with their abundance; current price thus provides sellers with information enabling them to distribute their resources for maximum profit. This allows for an efficient allocation of resources based entirely on decisions of purchasers and without government or other intervention. A market economy also encourages innovation and individual initiative as incentives for profit. Mass production makes technologically advanced, inexpensive goods widely available, gradually improving the general welfare.

Yet a market economy benefits most those sufficiently well-off to buy its products; those with few financial resources are seriously disadvantaged. Those born into poverty are likely to continue to suffer from economic deprivation. Secondly, unavoidably, there are long periods of unemployment after a period of economic contraction; and market solutions to issues such as inflation, environmental destruction, and pollution are also problematic. Finally, capitalism distributes wealth very unevenly, with investors and management highly rewarded by profits from sales, while workers are limited to labour for wages often lowered by competition among labourers for jobs. This tends to create a small wealthy class with great economic power in contrast to a large number of relatively impoverished, powerless workers.

Liberals try to retain the advantages of capitalism by advocating that government protect basic civil rights but also provide medical services, education, transportation, access to positions of power, and a clean, sustainable environment. Guaranteeing broad rights and also a just distribution of wealth and services is to counterbalance market inequities.

Socialists contend that even under liberal democracy the wealthy will inevitably have disproportionate economic and political power. Their solution is to eliminate or reduce the market system, either gradually through general education and democratic means or quickly through revolution. An economy with state control of production and distribution of goods for the benefit of all will retain the advantages of industrialism without the injustices of the market.   C.C.

M. Kelly, *The Divine Right of Capital: Dethroning the Corporate Aristocracy* (San Francisco, 2001).

J. A. Schumpeter, *Capitalism, Socialism and Democracy*, 3 edn. (New York, 1983).

marriage. Contractual union for the purpose of raising a family, or, derivatively, for the sex, domestic security, etc.

associated with this. By contrast with the biological phenomenon of mating, marriage is, to taste, 'made in heaven' or instituted by human societies. The former view offers a theological justification for some particular conception of marriage, e.g. as an indissoluble union constituting the only permissible locus of sexual activity. The latter view emphasizes the variety of forms of marriage, e.g. polygamy and polyandry, and typically offers justifications of these in terms of their social function. Forms of marriage may thus be criticized as dysfunctional: so Plato regards monogamous marriage carrying parental responsibilities as a threat to social solidarity, and he recommends instead that wives and children should be shared in common. Other criticisms of marriage complain of the restrictions it imposes on individual liberty. These may be met by noting its voluntary *contractual* character. This reply appears to require that divorce be readily available to terminate the contract and also, perhaps, that different types of marital contract should be possible. Yet an exclusive emphasis upon contracts seems unromantic in the face of the contemporary Western insistence that marriage is only justified by *love. But in view of the notorious mutability of romantic love, we can either reply that marriage makes possible a commitment that gives conjugal love its value (e.g. Kierkegaard), or conclude that marriage is indefensible, creating 'that moral centaur, man and wife' (Byron).   P.G.

*sex; Augustine; friendship; sexual conduct.

B. T. Trainor, 'The State, Marriage and Divorce', *Journal of Applied Philosophy* (1992).

Marsilius (Marsiglio) of Padua (*c.*1280–1342). Italian medieval political theorist who contested the dominant view of hereditary kingship as the best form of government. Drawing on Aristotle's *Politics*, Cicero (as the defender of republican liberty), and his experience of vibrant Italian city states ruled *de facto* by assemblies, Marsilius elaborately argued a theory of popular sovereignty, opposed to Dante, in *Defender of the Peace* (1324). Legislative power most appropriately resides within the lay citizen body, which may delegate executive power to an aristocracy or even to a monarch, but which does not thereby lose it. Of the three forms of government discussed by Aristotle, monarchy, aristocracy, and the city state or 'polity', only the last for Marsilius fully guarantees political *liberty, and the flourishing of justice and peace. The two main threats to peace are (1) factionalism and, more serious, (2) the papacy's demands for supreme sovereignty in the secular sphere. Marsilius' arguments were known to fifteenth-century Italian humanist defenders of republicanism.   L.P.

A. Gewirth, *Marsilius of Padua: The Defender of Peace*, 2 vols. (New York, 1957).

Q. Skinner, *The Foundations of Modern Political Thought*, 2 vols. (Cambridge, 1980).

Martin, Charles B. (1924–). Professor of Philosophy, University of Calgary, formerly Chair of Philosophy,

University of Sydney, past President of the Australasian Philosophical Association, noted for work in metaphysics and the philosophy of mind. Citing Locke as his inspiration, he was an early proponent of causal theories of perception, knowledge, and memory, and a principal architect of Australian metaphysical *realism. Martin advocates an uncompromising materialist conception of minds as complex neurologically based propensities for the manipulation of sensory materials. The 'ofness' and 'aboutness' of thoughts and images arises from their dispositional realizations in the nervous system. More generally, Martin holds that property instances invariably possess both dispositional and non-dispositional aspects, and that causal transactions are best regarded, not as relations between distinct events, but as the 'mutual manifestations of reciprocal dispositional property partners'.

J.HEIL

*Australian philosophy.

D. M. Armstrong, C. B. Martin, and U.T. Place, *Dispositions: A Debate* (London, 1996).

C. B. Martin, 'Protolanguage', *Australasian Journal of Philosophy* (1987).

Martineau, James (1805–1900). Leader of the Unitarians in Victorian England and brother of social critic Harriet Martineau, Martineau taught at Manchester New College, where he eventually served as Principal. He was an intuitionist about morality, and a chapter of Sidgwick's *Methods of Ethics* is devoted to criticism of his views. Today he is best remembered for his advocacy of an agent-based form of *virtue ethics according to which motives are the fundamental objects of moral evaluation (with reverence ranking highest, followed by compassion) and all actions are to be evaluated derivatively in terms of their relation to such motives. Martineau's theory is perhaps the purest example of agent-basing in the entire history of philosophy.

M.S.

*agent-relative moralities.

J. B. Schneewind, *Sidgwick's Ethics and Victorian Moral Philosophy* (Oxford, 1977), esp. ch. 7.

Marx, Karl Heinrich (1818–83). Radical social theorist and organizer of the working class, whose thought is widely regarded as the chief inspiration for all forms of modern social radicalism. Born 5 May 1818 in the Rhenish city of Trier, Marx was son of a successful Jewish lawyer of conservative political views who converted to Christianity in 1824. He studied law at the University of Bonn in 1835 and at the University of Berlin in 1836, changing his course of study in that year to philosophy, under the influence of Ludwig Feuerbach, Bruno Bauer, and the Young Hegelian movement. Marx completed his doctorate in philosophy in 1841. With the accession of Friedrich Wilhelm IV in 1840, however, the Young Hegelians came under attack from the government, and Marx lost all chance of an academic career in philosophy. Between 1842 and 1848 he edited radical publications in the Rhineland, France, and Belgium. He married his childhood sweetheart, Jenny von Westphalen, in 1843; despite their exceedingly hard life after 1850, the marriage was a happy one, and lasted until her death in 1881. (While in London the Marxes' family servant, Helene Demuth, gave birth to an illegitimate child; during the present century it was believed for a time that Marx was the father, but it is now widely held that he was not.)

In 1844, while in Paris, Marx was introduced both to the working-class movement and to the study of political economy by his former fellow student at Berlin, Friedrich Engels, with whom he began a lifetime of collaboration. While in Brussels, he formulated the programme of historical materialism, first expounded in the unpublished manuscript *The German Ideology*. Marx returned from Belgium to Paris in 1848 after the revolution, and then went back to the Rhineland where he worked as a publicist on behalf of the insurrection there. In the same year Marx and Engels played a key role in founding the Communist League (which lasted until 1850); the *Communist Manifesto* was part of their activity in the League. After successfully defending himself and his associates in a Cologne court on charges of inciting to revolt, Marx was expelled from Prussian territories in 1848. After a brief stay in Paris, he took up residence in London. The first years in England were a time of bitter, brutal poverty for the Marx family: three of their six children died of want and Marx's health suffered a collapse from which it never fully recovered. For much of the 1850s his only regular income was from Horace Greeley's *New York Tribune*, for which he served as European correspondent, receiving a fee of £1 per article. Throughout the 1850s and 1860s, when not confined to bed by illness, Marx regularly spent ten hours of every day in the library of the British Museum studying and writing. His first scientific work on political economy, *Contribution to a Critique of Political Economy*, was published in 1859; the Preface to this work contains a succinct statement of the materialist conception of history, usually regarded as the definitive formulation of that doctrine. This was only a prelude to Marx's definitive theory of *capitalism. Volume i of *Capital* was published in 1867, but two more volumes were left uncompleted at his death. Engels edited and published them in 1884 and 1893 respectively. Marx was instrumental in founding the International Working Men's Association in 1864, and guided it through six congresses in nine years. The demise of the First International in 1876 was brought about by a combination of factors, notably the organization's support for the Paris Commune (see Marx's *The Civil War in France*) and internal intrigues by Mikhail Bakunin (expelled in 1872). Marx died of long-standing respiratory ailments on 13 March 1883, and is buried next to his wife in Highgate Cemetery, London.

Marx's interest in philosophical *materialism is evident as early as his doctoral dissertation on the philosophy of nature in Democritus and Epicurus. But the dissertation's focus on Epicurus' philosophy of self-consciousness and its historical significance equally displays Marx's education in German idealist philosophy and his preoccupation with its themes. As a philosopher Marx self-consciously sought to marry the tradition of German *idealism, especially the philosophy of Hegel, with the scientific materialism of the radical French Enlightenment. This was to some extent the tendency of the Young Hegelian movement generally, but Marx's emphatic admiration for English and French materialism in contrast to the Young Hegelians' depreciation of it is displayed in a well-known passage from *The Holy Family* (1844).

Of greater significance for Marx's later thought is the way in which his famous Paris manuscripts of 1844 address to the 'materialistic' science of political economy a set of issues which Hegel and his followers had treated as questions of religious subjectivity. German idealism was concerned with problems of human selfhood, the nature of a fulfilling human life, and people's sense of meaning, self-worth, and relatedness to their natural and social environment. They saw modern culture as both a scene of *'alienation' for human beings from themselves, their lives, and others, and also as holding out the promise of the conquest or overcoming of alienation. Hegel, however, saw the task of self-fulfilment and reconciliation as a philosophical–religious one. It was Marx in the Paris manuscripts who first attempted to see it as fundamentally a matter of the social and economic conditions in which people live, of the kind of labouring activities they perform and the practical relationships in which they stand to one another. Marx's concern for the plight of the working class was from the beginning a concern not merely with the satisfaction of 'material needs' in the usual sense, but fundamentally with the conditions under which human beings can develop their 'essential human powers' and attain 'free self-activity'.

The Paris manuscripts view human beings in modern society, human beings as they are understood by the science of political economy, as alienated from themselves because their life-activity takes an alien, inhuman form. Truly human and fulfilling life activity is an activity of free social self-expression. It is free because it is self-determined by human beings themselves; it develops and expresses their humanity because, as Hegel had realized, it is the nature of a spiritual being to create itself by objectifying itself in a world and then comprehending that world as its adequate expression, as the 'affirmation', 'objectification', and 'confirmation' of its nature; and it is social because it is the nature of human beings to produce both with others and for others, and to understand themselves in the light of their mutual recognition of one another and their common work. The social relationships depicted by political economy, however, are relationships in which the life-activity of the majority, the working class, is increasingly stunted, reduced to meaningless physical activity which, far from developing and exercising their humanity, reduces them to abstract organs of a lifeless mechanism. They do not experience the products of their labour as their expression, or indeed as theirs in any sense. For these products belong to a non-worker, the capitalist,

to whom they must sell their activity for a wage which suffices only to keep them alive so that they may sustain the whole absurd cycle of their lives. Political economy, moreover, depicts human beings whose social life and relationships are at the mercy not of their collective choice but of an alien, inhuman mechanism, the market-place, which purports to be a sphere of individual freedom, but is in fact a sphere of collective slavery to inhuman and destructive forces.

Hegel had earlier conceived of alienation in the form of the 'unhappy consciousness' (a misunderstood Christian religiosity which experiences the human self as empty and worthless, and places everything valuable in a supernatural 'beyond'). The cure for alienation in Hegel's view is the recognition that finite nature is not the absence of infinite spirit but its expression. Feuerbach brought to light the latent *humanism in Hegel's view and attacked all forms of religion (and even Hegel's speculative metaphysics) as forms of alienation. The true being of human individuals, he maintained, is in the enjoyment of sensuous nature and of loving harmony with other human beings. What both Hegel and Feuerbach had in common is the perception of alienation as fundamentally a form of false consciousness, whose cure was a correct perception or interpretation of the world. Alienated consciousness contains both a lament that our natural human life is unsatisfying and worthless, and also the hope of consolation in the beyond. Hegel and Feuerbach agree that the illusion of alienated consciousness consists in its negative attitude toward earthly life; the comforting assurances of religion, according to both philosophers, contain the truth, if only we know how to put the right philosophical interpretation on them. To Marx, however, alienation becomes intelligible as soon as we adopt just the reverse supposition: that the alienated consciousness tells the truth in its laments, not in its consolations. Religion, according to Marx, gives expression to a mode of life which is really empty, unfulfilled, degraded, devoid of dignity. Religious illusions have hold on us because they provide a false semblance of meaning and fulfilment for a mode of life which without this illusion would be seen for the unredeemed meaninglessness that it is. For Marx religious misery is both an expression of actual misery and an attempt to flee from it into a world of imagination: it is the 'opium of the people'. The way out of alienation is not, as Hegel and Feuerbach thought, a new philosophical interpretation of life, but a new form of earthly existence, a new society in which the material conditions for a fulfilling human life would no longer be lacking. 'The philosophers have only *interpreted* the world in different ways; the point is to *change* it.'

For Marx the ultimate tendency of history is the Promethean drive of the human species to develop its 'essential human powers', its powers of production. Under capitalism these powers, and the complex network of human co-operation through which they are exercised, have for the first time grown far enough to put within the reach of human beings themselves the collective, rational control of the social form of their own production. This self-conscious self-determination is the true meaning of human freedom. But human beings under capitalism are alienated because capitalist social relations, by dispossessing the vast majority of producers and subjecting the form of social production to the market mechanism, frustrate this collective self-determination. The historic mission of the proletariat is to actualize the capacities for human freedom which the capitalist mode of production has put within our reach, by abolishing class society. In this way, historical materialism gives the working class a full conscious understanding of its historic mission, so that unlike previous ruling classes it may fulfil this mission consciously, and thus truly enable the human species to master itself and its destiny. The materialist conception of history thus serves as the link between Marx's concern with the conditions for human fulfilment, his theoretical enterprise as economist and historian, and his practical activity as a working-class organizer and revolutionary.

According to Marx's materialist conception of history, the goals of a class movement are determined by the set of production relations the class is in a position to establish and defend. This implies that historically conscious revolutionaries should not proceed by setting utopian goals for themselves and then looking around for means to achieve them. Revolutionary practice is rather a matter of participating in an already developing class movement, helping to define its own goals and to actualize them through the use of the weapons inherent in the class's historical situation. The definition of these goals, moreover, is an ongoing process; thus it is pointless to speculate about the precise system of distribution which a revolutionary movement will institute after its victory when the movement itself is still in its infancy.

Marx believed that future society would see the abolition of classes, of private ownership of means of production, and even of commodity production (production of goods and services for exchange or sale). He believed communist society would eventually eliminate all systematic social causes of alienation and human unfulfilment. Yet he never thought of future society as an unchanging state of perfection. On the contrary, he thought of the end of class society as the true beginning of *human* history, of the historical development of human society directed consciously by human beings. Above all, Marx never attempted to 'write recipes for the cookshops of the future' or to say in any detail what distribution relations in future socialist or communist society would be like. He equally scorned those who concerned themselves with formulating principles of distributive justice and condemning capitalism in their name. Marx conceives the justice of economic transactions as their correspondence to or functionality for the prevailing mode of production. Given this conception of justice, Marx very consistently (if rather surprisingly) concluded that the inhuman exploitation practised by capitalism against the workers is not unjust, and does not violate the workers' rights; this conclusion constitutes no defence of capitalism, only an attack on the use of moral conceptions within the proletarian movement. Marx saw the task of the proletarian movement in his time as one of self-definition and growth through organization, discipline, and self-criticism based on scientific self-understanding. He left for later stages of the movement the task of planning the future society which it is the historic mission of the movement to bring to birth. A.W.W.

*anti-communism; Marxist philosophy.

Isaiah Berlin, *Karl Marx: His Life and Environment*, 4th edn. (Oxford, 1978).

Hal Draper, *Karl Marx's Theory of Revolution*, 2 vols. (New York, 1977–8).

David McLellan, *The Thought of Karl Marx*, 2nd edn. (London, 1980).

Richard Miller, *Analyzing Marx* (Princeton, NJ, 1984).

Paul Walton and Andrew Gamble, *From Alienation to Surplus Value*, 2nd edn. (Cambridge, 1972).

Allen Wood, *Karl Marx* (London, 1981).

Marxism after communism. Eastern European and Soviet communism as a political system collapsed after the fall of the Berlin Wall in 1989. Marxism understood as the philosophical basis of this system collapsed at the same time. Whether or not a philosophy can be taken as refuted by a political system's defeat in a kind of war, something like this has been accepted. Leninist Marxism (one-party rule in the name of the working class) and Stalinist Marxism (the 'planned economy' and 'socialism in one country') have all but vanished. Elements of this conjuncture of theory with practice were preserved in Cuba, Vietnam, North Korea, and China. Elsewhere Marxism survives as a politically engaged philosophy.

Marxism after communism is grounded in concepts of human social activity. In particular it is concerned with historical stages of technological development and criticisms of contemporary capitalism. Marxism thus presents many political issues as philosophical problems, and embraces many concepts that belong to history and economics. In Marxism many traditional problems in moral philosophy, metaphysics, and philosophy of mind, for instance, get little attention. The problems addressed by Marxism as a social philosophy are economic exploitation, distributive inequalities, social class, and political change. This makes it a form of 'critical theory'.

Marxism offers philosophically based criticisms of the capitalist economic system, and of the linkage between liberal democracy and commercial interests. It currently presents very little in the way of utopian thinking about communism, even as a philosophical ideal. Instead it has broadened Marx's central notion of class struggle to include a wider variety of human differences and broader movements in identity politics. This gives an economic slant to nationalist and gender conflict, for example, particularly when conceptualized with respect to international capitalism.

For some philosophers Marxism is still a 'grand theory' searching for directionality in human history, and for mechanisms that determine social change. For other philosophers it represents a science of society, based on a well-grounded ontology (human activities and social consciousness are the basis of existence) and a well-defended 'realist' epistemology (knowledge is derived empirically from social interactions with the material world). More radically, post-modern Marxists have reconceptualized Marxism as grounded in a democratic and egalitarian civil society. This cuts Marxism loose from historical teleology and philosophical determinism, while retaining its critical engagement with politics.   T.CAR.

R. Bhaskar, *Scientific Realism and Human Emancipation* (London, 1986).

G. A. Cohen, *Karl Marx's Theory of History: A Defence*, expanded. edn. (Oxford, 2000).

E. Laclau and C. Mouffe, *Hegemony and Socialist Strategy: Towards a Radical Democratic Politics*, 2nd edn. (London, 2001).

L. Sargent (ed.), *Women and Revolution: A Discussion of the Unhappy Marriage of Marxism and Feminism* (London, 1981).

Marxist philosophy. The idea of a Marxist philosophy is, at first sight, paradoxical. Marx himself was originally a student of philosophy but soon came to talk of abolishing philosophy: the coming of a socialist society would render philosophy (like religion) redundant. It is, nevertheless, clear that Marx and his followers appropriated much of the philosophy of (at least) Aristotle, the *materialism of the *Enlightenment, and Hegelian dialectics. It is equally clear that when Marx talked of the abolition of philosophy, he meant that, in so far as philosophy posed ideal principles or essences, it would lose its function after a socialist revolution which embodied these essences in socio-economic reality. It is far from clear that Marx's *historical materialism contradicts or supersedes philosophy as such. The century and more that has elapsed since Marx's death has been a largely fruitless search by his followers to establish a distinctively Marxist philosophy. Since the authoritarian Communist regimes established in Marx's name did not encourage philosophical enterprise, their demise is unlikely to have much effect on the future of Marxist philosophy.

Although Marx himself had apparently disparaged philosophy, after his death and with the revolution still a long way off, the 'footnotes to Plato' had to be dealt with and the growing membership of Marxist parties required a 'philosophy' in the sense of a coherent system of principles giving a total explanation of the universe. Given the cultural climate of the late nineteenth century, this had to be couched in scientific—and even positivist—terms. Although the later Marx certainly had traces of such attitudes in his work, it was given systematic form by Engels and culminated in the philosophy of dialectical materialism propagated by Communist orthodoxy.

Engels proclaimed the Marxian *dialectic to be 'the science of the general laws of motion and development of nature, human society, and thought'. More specifically, the most important of these were the laws of the transformation of quantity into quality, of the interpretation of

opposites, and of the negation of the negation. Engels thought these laws to be operative in a nature that was objectively given and independent of the human mind. Thus the world of nature and the world of human history were two separate fields of study—whereas for Marx one of the central aspects of his dialectic had consisted precisely in the interaction of human beings and their surroundings, a view stemming from Hegel. Engels did indeed claim to be simply applying Hegel's dialectic, and, in a sense, Hegel also saw a dialectic in nature but it was still subject to the universal mediation of human consciousness. The concept of matter as some kind of *materia prima* is entirely foreign to Marx.

For many interpreters of Marx's thought, however, the publication of his early writings around 1930 marked a decisive turning-point. These writings, particularly the *Economic and Philosophical Manuscripts*, revealed a very different Marx from both the rather arid economist of Kautsky and the dialectical materialist of Soviet dogma. Marx appeared to be a philosopher, a humanist not only with a devastating account of the alienation of man in capitalist society but with a rich and varied account of the potential latent in every individual waiting to be realized under communism. This enthusiasm for the early Marx was helped by the pioneering writings of Georg Lukács, who rediscovered in full Marx's debt to Hegel and put concepts such as alienation and reification at the centre of his interpretation. This tradition has been embodied most systematically in the work of the *Frankfurt School, where 'critical' theorists such as Adorno, Marcuse, and Habermas have aimed to restore a philosophical dimension to Marxism. Retaining an enviable confidence in the power of human rationality, these theorists have developed a series of concepts intended to go beyond Marx in interpreting the changes that have taken place in the world since his death. These consist mainly in adding the dimension of social psychology to Marx's work, and emphasizing the basic proposition that if society is increasingly under the control of technocrats, then any purely empirical approach to social reality must end up as a defence of that control.

In sharp contrast to the evidently Hegelian and humanist elements present in the Marxism of the Frankfurt School, the Marxist philosophy evolved by Althusser and his disciples in the early 1960s attempted to purge Marxism of any such elements. Taking advantage of the current prestige of structuralist linguistics, psychology, and anthropology, it was the aim of Althusser to 'rehabilitate' Marx as a structuralist before his time. Thus Althusser continued the Stalinist division of an early pre-Marxist Marx and a later scientific Marx—though with a conceptual sophistication quite foreign to the previous versions of this view. Roughly speaking, *structuralism is the view that the key to the understanding of a social system is the structural relationship of its parts—the way these parts are related by the regulative principle of the system. And Althusser's search for a timeless rationality reminiscent of Comte (for whom Marx himself had no time) involved the banishment of both history and philosophy. When applied to Marx, this involved cutting his work into two separate conceptual structures with the dividing-point around 1845. Any reading of Marx as a humanist, a Hegelian, or a historicist must (since these ideas are clearly contained in his early works) be rejected. Since it has become increasingly implausible to claim (particularly after the publication of the *Grundrisse*) that there are no humanist or Hegelian elements in the later Marx, a 'real' Marx has been uncovered who employs a methodology— never clearly defined—almost totally at variance with concepts that he actually employs.

More recently, there have been attempts to rethink many aspects of Marxism through the medium of rational choice theory. This approach, exemplified in the writings of such authors as Elster and Roehmer, has come to be known as analytical Marxism. Central to it is a *method-ological individualism which borrows concepts and tech-niques from game theory and contemporary economics. Particularly when combined with *analytical philosophy, this can yield a highly rigorous discussion. But the concep-tual framework is so much at variance with the Marxist tradition that it is not surprising that the theses of the ana-lytical Marxist school are highly revisionary. And the same is true of Marxist attempts to come to terms with the rise of new social movements, particularly those inspired with an ecological or feminist perspective.

The most striking fact about the relation between Marxism and philosophy, in the West at least, is how eclectic Marxists have been in their attitude to philosophy. Marxists have usually tried to articulate their ideas through whatever happened to be the current dominant philosophy. The revival of interest in Hegel between the wars, coupled with the influence of Freud, was decisive for the formulations of the Frankfurt School; the post-war vogue for existentialism led to all sorts of New Left vari-ations on Marxism with a human face, of which Sartre's later work is only the most prominent example; the subse-quent prestige of structuralism in the 1960s and 1970s led to the arcanely theoretical Marxism of Althusser and his disciples; while the rational choice Marxism of more recent years is evidently an effort to come to terms with some of the dominant concepts of the Reagan–Thatcher years.

The inevitable tension in all the above approaches lies in the fact that all the philosophies they invoke are the product of bourgeois societies—the very societies that Marxism is dedicated to superseding. This tension is only exacerbated by the tendency of western Marxists to become more theoretical and more philosophical with the decreasing prospect of success for Marxist practical activ-ity. The migration of Marxism into the universities has necessarily undercut the unity of theory and practice so central to the outlook of Marx himself. For him, all philosophy (like all religion) is ultimately idealist and mystificatory. Holding that 'the dispute over the reality or non-reality of thinking that is isolated from practice is a purely scholastic question', Marx looked forward to a

society which would abolish the division between mental and manual work—which he saw as the root cause of all philosophical mystification. Such a society would be intel-ligible to its members, since the social relationships in it would be transparent, and would not require philosoph-ical mediation.

The history of Marxist thought has thus been charac-terized by a strong ambivalence towards the viability of the philosophical enterprise. The result has been the invisibility of a distinctively Marxist philosophy: Marxism has been eclectic in its borrowings from 'bourgeois' phil-osophy. These borrowings have been extremely fruitful, particularly in the realm of social theory. Indeed here, as elsewhere, Marxism has proved at its strongest as a cri-tique of philosophy rather than in adumbrating a plausible alternative.   D.McL.

*socialism; communism; anti-communism.

P. Anderson, *Considerations on Western Marxism* (London, 1976).
R. Bhaskar, *A Realist Theory of Science* (Brighton, 1978).
K. Korsch, *Marxism and Philosophy* (London, 1970).
J. Mepham and D.-H. Ruben (eds.), *Issues in Marxist Philosophy* (Brighton, 1979).
New Left Review, *Western Marxism: A Critical Reader* (London, 1977).

Mary, black and white. Omni-competent in the neuro-physiology of vision, Mary is confined to a black-and-white environment. However omniscient she becomes in the neurophysics of the experience of ripe tomatoes, the blue sky, etc., she will find, if released into the chromatic world, that she still has something to discover: namely, what the relevant visual experiences are like. The thought experiment was designed to show that physicalism is false, and discussion has turned, among other things, on whether the kind of knowledge Mary lacks is propos-itional at all, let alone knowledge of a non-physical fact.

                                                                  A.H.

Frank Jackson, 'Epiphenomenal Qualia', *Philosophical Quarterly* (1982).

Masaryk, Tomáš Garrigue (1850–1937). Czech philoso-pher, sociologist, and politician who influenced gener-ations of Czech and Slovak thinkers. From 1882 to 1914 he was Professor at Charles University in Prague, from 1918 to 1935 President of the fledgeling Czechoslovakia. He was an opponent of clericalism, monarchism, anti-Semitism, and Bolshevism.

He sought to explain the crisis in Czech and European society at the end of the nineteenth century, a significant feature of which was an increase in suicide (*The Suicide . . .* (1881)). In *The Principles of Concrete Logic* (1885) he follows Comte's classification of sciences, adding logic and psy-chology, as understood in J. S. Mill's terms. He also dealt with Czech history, and the struggle of every human being and society to attain the human ideal of active love. This religious humanity was more emotional than the political and rational humanity of the French Revolution. In *The Social Question* (1898) he rejects Marxism as objectivism, positivistic amoralism, and materialistic fatalism, although he admits its temporary political and ideological sense. In *The Spirit of Russia* (1913) he analyses Russian culture in the nineteenth century, emphasizing the thinking of Dostoevsky.   M.P.

Jan Patočka, *Three Studies about Masaryk* (Prague, 1991).

masculism. Defining 'masculism' is made difficult by the fact that the term has been used by very few people, and by hardly any philosophers. In its most general meaning, the word *'feminism' refers to promotion of the interests or rights of women, and a reasonable definition of 'masculism' would have it refer to promoting the interests or rights of men. (This is very different, it must be noted, from promoting attributes of womanliness or manliness, as they might be construed, which could be labelled femininism and masculinism.) Thus defined, the two parallel terms are too vague to be very useful. A more precise definition of both would be something on this order: 'the belief that women/men have been systematically discriminated against, and that that discrimination should be eliminated'. Evidently, such a definition for 'feminism' is commonly understood, and among the few who apply the term 'masculist' to themselves, such is also their intent. Of course, under these meanings there is no necessary conflict between them, and in fact some are happy to call themselves both feminists and masculists. Much more often, the belief that one sex currently faces a much greater threat from discrimination would lead to accepting one label and rejecting the other.

However one understands these particular terms, there is today a small movement of 'men's rights' activists. Their fundamental claim is that very serious discrimination is currently being committed against individual males on account of their sex. These activists fall roughly into two categories, traditionalist and liberal–progressive. The traditionalists hold that inherited gender roles, though 'discriminatory' in the neutral sense of treating the sexes differently, have been more or less fair and just to both, because, they believe, the disadvantages faced by males and females have been comparable (at least in this culture, in this century) and because the traditional sex roles represent more or less the optimal division of benefits and burdens, the best arrangement for children and for society as a whole. What sets 'men's rights' traditionalists apart from traditionalists in general is their belief that contemporary feminism is not only bad for society but seriously unjust to men as well.

In sharp contrast—and in spite of attempts by many to label all talk of men's rights as reactionary, a 'backlash'—progressive men's rights activists regard the traditional differential treatment as seriously unfair to members of both sexes. Inherited *gender roles and stereotypes are not just burdensome to both men and women, they say, but unjust to both, and must be eliminated. (Unlike traditionalists, they have no need to pronounce the roles equally burdensome, and tend to treat the two sets of injustices as incommensurable.) Progressive masculists

have thus welcomed many feminist efforts toward societal change, adding, however, that feminism addresses only half the problem. Furthermore, they maintain that many feminist efforts ostensibly aimed at ending sexism are actually increasing sexism against men. This has been especially true, they say, in the 1980s and 1990s, as mainstream feminism has left its inclusivist roots in favour of separatist efforts based on an extreme oppressor–oppressed picture of relationships between the sexes.

Thus, both forms of contemporary masculism promote equality between men and women as its adherents envision it. Of course, whether they are mistaken about what moral equality would consist in, or even at some level dishonest about that being their goal, is another matter—as it also is for feminists. This leads us to the extremist versions of masculism and feminism, those that promote some degree of male or female supremacy, and are generally based on belief in the inferiority of the other sex. Many contemporary feminists consider men to be morally and even intellectually inferior, by virtue of being raised in an oppressor class, or even by nature. And of course the long history of male domination since hunter-gatherer times has generally included doctrines of the intellectual inferiority, and, although the record is mixed, sometimes moral inferiority of women. Nicholas Davidson discusses an extreme brand of masculism and masculinism which he dubs 'virism'. In its world-view, he says,

What ails society is 'effeminacy'. The improvement of society requires that the influence of female values be decreased and the influence of male values increased. . . . Contemporary virists perceive themselves to be fighting a last-ditch action against a neutered or feminized society, of which feminism is merely one recent expression. . . . [In movies such as] *Rambo* and *Commando*, the world has gone soft. The protagonists struggle to avert dangers caused by society's loss of the masculine principle.

Davidson sees precise similarities between extremist masculism and extremist feminism, remarking that 'the parallel association of Hellenic virism with a cult of [male] homosexuality and modern feminism with a cult of lesbianism is not accidental'.

However that may be, most men's and women's rights activists profess belief in *equality, different though their visions of it may be. Indeed, they do not divide strictly along gender lines. Besides feminist (or 'pro-feminist') men, there are many women—some embracing the label 'feminist', some rejecting it, and many ambivalent about it—who actively advocate men's rights. Such groups as the Women's Freedom Network (mostly libertarians) and the Women's International Network (liberal) in the USA have been established largely to oppose the harms they see contemporary mainstream feminism as doing to both sexes. Traditionalist women's groups such as Eagle Forum (USA) and REAL Women (Canada) also often speak out against discrimination toward men, or at least against the recent varieties promoted by feminists.

Space is not available here to describe adequately (much less to argue for and against) the standard men's rights issues. They include discrimination against fathers in child custody cases (in terms of numbers of activists, this is the largest issue); discrimination against men in the criminal law, military conscription, and various other societal institutions; contemporary discrimination against men in employment, insurance and pensions, and other economic matters; and many others. (See Farrell, *The Myth of Male Power*, and Thomas, *Not Guilty*, for representative treatments of men's rights issues.)

The above discussion describes masculism as a set of political beliefs, not as philosophy in any abstract sense. Apart from advocacy (genuine, not just alleged) of male supremacy, however, there arguably *is* no masculist philosophy. Consider the traditionalist belief that if nature were allowed to take its course, men would fill most of the leaderships roles (see Goldberg, *Why Men Rule*) and women fill the nurturing roles. The belief is better described as a general philosophy of human nature than as one centred on males and maleness. And liberal advocates for men's rights typically describe their philosophy as egalitarian rather than as either male- or female-orientated. By the same reasoning, however, apart from brands of feminism embracing genetic female superiority, there is no *genuine* *feminist philosophy, or at least none with unique relevance to females or femaleness. The perfectly justified desire to open up to women the opportunities, which only men (a small minority of men) have had in the past, to engage in formal philosophy, had led, this writer would judge, to the wishful beliefs that (*a*) past philosophy, in virtue of having been written by individual males, is somehow specifically male or masculist in its nature, and that (*b*) there is a distinct type of philosophy that is specifically female in its nature. All the post-Gilligan talk about women's 'special ways of seeing' notwithstanding, as this liberal masculist–feminist writer views the evidence, *'feminist epistemology' and its like is a grand illusion.

F.CHR.

Nicholas Davidson, *The Failure of Feminism* (Buffalo, NY, 1988).
Warren Farrell, *The Myth of Male Power* (New York, 1993).
Steven Goldberg, *Why Men Rule* (Chicago, 1993).
David Thomas, *Not Guilty: The Case in Defence of Men* (London, 1993).

masked man fallacy. One of a group of puzzles (the *liar paradox is another) due to Eubulides (third century BC), the masked man, extensively discussed by medieval logicians, is concerned with referentially opaque contexts: 'You say you know your brother, but that masked man is your brother, and you did not know him'. By contrast, normal (extensional) contexts are transparent: if you touched the masked man you thereby touched your brother.

J.J.M.

W. V. Quine, *Word and Object* (Cambridge, Mass., 1960), ch. 4.

master and slave. The master and slave metaphor has occurred in philosophy since ancient times. Aesop admonished that reason should be the master and passion the slave. (Hume was to say otherwise.) Politically, of course, the duality of master and slave and later lord and

serf were quite literal social realities for Aristotle and most feudal thinkers. The master and slave imagery enters into modern philosophy in Rousseau, Fichte, and most famously in Hegel, who made the master–slave interaction the centrepiece of the most famous section of his *Phenomenology*. According to Hegel, the master–slave relationship is the result of an uncompleted fight to the death for 'recognition' or status, and it is marked by a topsy-turvy logic (or *'dialectic') such that the master, through increasing dependence on the slave, and the slave, who develops independence through labour, switch roles. Hegel is at pains to point out that such roles, dependent on competition and power, are unsatisfactory as a basis for social relationships.

Toward the end of the nineteenth century, Nietzsche picked up the opposition as a metaphor for two distinct modes of morality. Master morality prizes independence, creativity, and excellence. *Slave morality, by contrast, is servile, fearful, and, above all, resentful. In a Hegelian-type turn-about, Nietzsche traces ethics through history as 'the slave revolt in morals'. Slave morality is victorious, and, according to Nietzsche, servile obedience and mediocrity replace the masterly Greek ideals of virtue and excellence.

R.C.SOL.

G. W. F. Hegel, *The Phenomenology of Spirit* (Oxford, 1977).
F. Nietzsche, *On the Genealogy of Morals* (New York, 1967).

Master Argument. The Master Argument was highly influential on Hellenistic debates about *freedom and determinism. Diodorus Cronus (Greek, d. *c*.284 BC) devised it to support his definition of the possible as that which either is or will be true. Diodorus relied on two premisses: 'Every past truth is necessary' and 'The impossible does not follow from the possible'. He concluded: 'Nothing is possible which neither is nor will be true'. One guess, less fanciful than most, is that Diodorus reasoned: suppose some proposition is and always will be untrue; then at some time in the past, it was going to be untrue at all later times; from that past truth, it follows that our proposition is untrue; but that past truth is necessary; and so is what follows from it; hence our proposition is necessarily untrue.

N.C.D.

*fatalism.

Nicholas Denyer, 'Time and Modality in Diodorus Cronus', *Theoria* (1981).

master of those who know: *see* Aristotelianism.

material constitution. That which something is composed of. For example, the statue is not identical with the bronze it is made of, but the bronze is the material constitution of the statue. Nevertheless, there is a constitutive sense of 'is'. Arguably, something is not identical with what it is made of because the two have different persistence conditions. If *a* is composed of constituents, they might continue to exist even if *a* ceases to exist. Also, if *a* is composed of constituents, and if *a* ceases to exist, and then *b* is made out of those same constituents, it seems wrong to say *a* is therefore *b*. On some quasi-materialist views, if I am not identical with my body, my body is my material constitution. s.p.

John Locke, *An Essay Concerning Human Understanding*, book II.
D. Wiggins, *Sameness and Substance* (Oxford, 1980).

material contradiction. The idea that *contradictions exist not only in thought but in material reality has been a distinctively philosophical preoccupation within *Marxism. It refers to activities within organisms and systems that generate opposing forces (thus, 'capitalism creates its own grave-diggers'), and also the claim, adapted from Hegel, that adequate descriptions of material reality necessarily involve contradictions. It need not, therefore, imply a metaphysical realist conception of contradictions as having an extra-linguistic existence. k.m.

R. Norman and S. Sayers, *Hegel, Marx and Dialectic: A Debate* (Brighton, 1980).

material implication. A connection between statements which has sometimes seemed to be supposed by logicians to represent statements of the form 'If . . . then . . .'. A statement *p* materially implies another, *q*, when the propositional calculus conditional $p \rightarrow q$ is true, i.e. if and only if it is not the case that *p* is true and *q* false. One 'paradox' of material implication is that this relation holds between statements wholly unrelated in subject-matter: 'If Oxford is a city, then Italy is sunny'. Another 'paradox' is that the relation holds merely if *p* is false ('If pigs can fly, then . . . ') or merely if *q* is true ('If . . . then Plato was a philosopher'). These are all ways in which material implication diverges from 'if . . . then . . . ' as ordinarily used. s.w.

*Implication; conditionals; relevance logic

P. F. Strawson, *Introduction to Logical Theory* (London, 1952), chs. 2 and 3.

materialism. Basically the view that everything is made of matter. But what is *matter? Probably the most innocent and cheerful acceptance of it comes right at the start of materialism with Democritus of Abdera (in northern Greece) in the fifth century BC, for whom the world consisted entirely of 'atoms', tiny, absolutely hard, impenetrable, incompressible, indivisible, and unalterable bits of 'stuff', which had shape and size but no other properties and scurried around in the void, forming the world as we know it by jostling each other and either rebounding (despite being incompressible) or getting entangled with each other because of their shapes. They and the void alone were real, the colours and flavours and temperatures that surround us being merely subjective (see fragment 9). This model has lasted, with various modifications and sophistications, right down until modern times, though the notion of solidity was causing qualms at least as early as Locke. But in the last century all has been thrown into confusion by Einstein's famous $E = mc^2$ and also by general relativity. Mass, the sophisticated notion

that has replaced crude matter, is interchangeable in certain circumstances with *energy, and in any case is only a sort of distortion of the *space in which it was supposed to be floating. Photons and neutrons have little or no mass, and neither do fields, while particles pop out of the void, destroy each other, and pop back in again.

All this, however, has had remarkably little overt effect on the various philosophical views that can be dubbed 'materialism', though one might think it shows at least that materialism is not the simple no-nonsense, tough-minded alternative it might once have seemed to be. What actually seems to have happened is that the various materialist philosophies have tended to substitute for 'matter' some notion like 'whatever it is that can be studied by the methods of natural science', thus turning materialism into *naturalism, though it would be an exaggeration to say the two outlooks have simply coincided. Materialism concerns the composition of things, while naturalism, though concerned with what exists, ranges more widely, covering properties as well as substances, and its concern with methods of studying things is more direct and central.

So far, however, we have only considered apparent exceptions to naïve materialism like photons and fields; but common sense might regard these as on the material side of the fence, since they are linked to what is unambiguously material in established and fruitful scientific theories. In any case they are of little interest to common sense. Philosophers too, outside philosophy of science perhaps, often take as their starting-point the concerns of common sense, and perhaps it is for these reasons that materialism in philosophy has also been relatively unaffected by these complications.

By far the most important contrast in this area, for philosophy as for common-sense, has been between matter and mind or spirit or consciousness, or the contents of these entities (ideas etc.). Common-sense for all the time and philosophers for much of it (i.e. when they are not being idealists or phenomenalists) accept the reality of the body as relatively unproblematic. But mind or consciousness manifestly exists too in some form, at least in our own case. Does it then exist as a separate entity? This question forms a major part of the *mind–body problem, and the materialist will answer 'No'. He might hard-headedly deny that mind exists at all, thereby raising a question that has its roots in Protagoras of Abdera (a contemporary of Democritus) and Descartes: what then is the status of the illusion that it does? Don't even illusions need minds to have them? But he is more likely to appeal to some form of non-eliminative materialism and say that minds do exist but not as something separate from matter. Either they belong to a different category, as Ryle would say, so that talk about them is a sort of abbreviation for talk about kinds of behaviour (*behaviourism), or they are simply identical with brains—or, to put it less crudely, what we call mental phenomena, like pains or thoughts, are identical with phenomena going on in the brain (the *identity theory of mind): in principle this can leave open whether there are any substantive minds to have these pains etc., but if there are they must be identical with something material. Although the material item will be identical with the mind or the pain as much as vice versa, the theory counts as materialist because the material items are integrated into a whole set of such items, only a few of which are involved with minds, while the mental items are not (on the theory) similarly integrated into a set of mental items most of which are independent of matter.

There is, however, a mistake to be avoided in this area which goes back at least to Plato. In his relatively early dialogue the *Phaedo* he opposes the soul (to adopt the usual translation of the Greek word *psukhē*) and the body. The soul is a single thing (unlike the tripartite soul of his slightly later dialogue the *Republic*), but it is represented as in conflict with the body, and pulled by bodily desires and passions. These desires and passions are opposed to the soul as such, and are clearly regarded as bodily phenomena, which they are surely not, at least on the sort of view Plato is holding; human bodies no more have desires than tables do. It is true, of course, that the identity theory we have just been discussing would treat these desires as identical with events in the brain or nervous system, but only as part of a doctrine treating all desires as such in this way, including the most spiritual; it would not single out certain desires for such treatment merely because what the desires were *for* involved states of the body, or what caused them were such states. In his later dialogue the *Philebus* Plato revised his view on this point.

Sometimes a distinction is made, as it has been in different ways by Frege and Popper, between three kinds of real things (three 'realms' or 'worlds'). The first contains material things, including the things like photons that are associated with centrally material things and might be called quasi-material. The second contains psychological things like thoughts, feelings, pains, desires, including the substantive minds that have these, if there are any; if there are, then the thoughts etc. that they have will not be independent substantive entities, but will still count as denizens of the second realm. The third contains abstract things like numbers, properties, classes, truths (and perhaps falsehoods), values, or some selection of these, all those selected being treated as substantive entities, though not material nor properly speaking spiritual either. Philosophers have tended to treat these three realms not so much as lying in a straight line, with one in the middle between the other two, as lying in a triangle, so that the rejection of one was compatible with accepting either or both of the other two. Materialists strictly speaking say that only matter exists, but in modern times they have tended to direct their fire primarily against believers in the second realm, and some of them (e.g. Armstrong) accept at least a moderate realism in connection with the third realm. But this was not always so. Plato, with whom so much of philosophy began, was primarily concerned to assert the existence of the third realm (indeed he is commonly taken to have introduced it, and belief in it is often called *Platonism), and in his dialogue the *Sophist* he contrasts materialists with certain defenders of that realm. Although he devoted another dialogue, the *Phaedo*, to defending the immortality of the soul, a member of the second realm, its existence he tended to take for granted, leaving its status *vis-à-vis* the other two realms rather uncertain. However, despite all this it is perhaps true that most materialists are thoroughgoing and reject both the other two realms, even if directing their fire primarily at one of them.

We started our discussion by asking 'What is matter?' and finding that our notion of matter was getting a bit frayed at the edges. There is a further difficulty with it, which appears to be what led Berkeley to his version of *idealism, which he called 'immaterialism'. Aristotle contrasted matter with form, and treated it as a *substratum for form and thus ultimately for attributes. This led him, at least as traditionally interpreted, to a notion of 'prime matter', which was the ultimate subject for all attributes and therefore had no attributes of its own. Locke, again as traditionally interpreted, took over this notion of prime matter and made it the underlying but unknowable *substance of all things—unknowable because it had no attributes by which we could know it. Actually Locke's position on this question is open to dispute, but Berkeley rejected the notion as simply ridiculous and a source of scepticism because of the bewilderment it led to. Evidently the materialist, and indeed everyone who accepts matter at all, must give some account of the nature of matter which will rescue it from these strictures. That this task will not be easy is suggested by the growing revival of idealism in current philosophy.

So far we have considered materialism as a metaphysical doctrine. But in ordinary thinking it often refers to a doctrine about values. Here again it is often contrasted with idealism, which now refers to the pursuit of ideals that may be high-flown but are likely to be impossible to achieve in practice. The materialist by contrast pursues ends connected with the bodily pleasures, or the possession of material goods, or else with such things as money, thought of as a means to such pleasures or goods. One might ask, however, just what count as bodily pleasures. If they are those involving states of the body, what happens to the aesthetic pleasures of music and visual art? We should be hard put to it to enjoy these without ears or eyes, and these are not being used simply to give us information as when we hear or read poetry (or philosophy for that matter); to enjoy a piece of music is not simply to know what it sounds like, but to hear it sounding like that, even if only in the 'mind's ear'. It is also possible that the term 'materialist' involves some confusion due to the sort of considerations we discussed concerning Plato above. But in any case we should not confuse two distinctions: that between pleasures that involve the body more closely and those that involve it less closely or not at all, and that between values that are in some sense 'lower' and less worthy of pursuit and those that are 'higher'. The contrast between materialism and idealism in this context suggests such a confusion, but the pleasures, or values, of the materialist are not necessarily any 'lower', presumably, than those of the pursuit of, say, malice.   A.R.L.

*atomism; physicalism; phenomenalism; Quinton; central-state materialism; behaviourism; eliminativism.

S. E. Toulmin and J. Goodfield, *The Architecture of Matter* (London, 1962). Historical.

G. Amaldi, *The Nature of Matter* (first pub. in Italian, 1961; London, 1966). Scientific.

D. M. Armstrong, *Universals: An Opinionated Introduction* (Boulder, Colo., 1989).

A. Melnyk, *A Physicalist Manifesto* (Cambridge, 2003).

materialism, central-state: *see* central-state materialism.

materialism, dialectical: *see* dialectical materialism.

materialism, eliminative: *see* eliminativism.

materialism, historical: *see* historical materialism.

material mode: *see* formal and material modes.

mathematical intuitionism: *see* intuitionism, mathematical.

mathematical logic: *see* formal logic.

mathematics, history of the philosophy of. Many areas of philosophy owe their beginning to Plato, and the philosophy of mathematics is a star example. It was he who first reflected on the fact that the geometers speak of *perfect* squares, *perfect* circles, and so on, though no examples are to be found in this world. He thought that the same applied to arithmetic too, on the ground that in arithmetic we study numbers that are composed of units perfectly equal to one another in every way, whereas again there are no such units to be found in this world. So he concluded that mathematics was not about the objects to be found in this world, but about some different 'purely intelligible' objects, which he was apt to think of as inhabiting 'another world'. Moreover, since the objects were not of this world, our knowledge of them must also be independent of our experience of this world, i.e. it must be *a priori. Initially he attempted to explain this a priori knowledge as a recollection of our past experiences of the other world, before birth. Later he appears to have abandoned this explanation, but he never ceased to insist that the knowledge is a priori. Mathematics, then, has both a special ontology and a special epistemology.

Aristotle challenged both of these claims. In his philosophy there was no place for a distinctive kind of knowledge that could be called a priori, and he equally could not accept Plato's ontological extravagance. So he was the first to propose a consciously 'reductive' account of the objects of mathematics. In his view the geometer is speaking of ordinary and perceptible squares and circles, but considered generally, and in abstraction from the ordinary and perceptible matter that they are made of. Similarly,

the arithmetical thesis that $2 + 3 = 5$ is to be construed simply as a generalization over such ordinary facts as that if there are 2 horses in this field, and 3 in that, then there are 5 horses altogether. But unfortunately he never did set out a full argument for these claims, so the rival positions were outlined, but battle was never properly joined.

Space does not permit an account of the skirmishes between what were broadly speaking Platonic and Aristotelian positions in the centuries that followed, and we may pick up the tale again with the quite different outlook of the 'modern' period. There we find a dispute between *rationalism on the one side and *empiricism on the other, but it is a dispute in which there is actually a large measure of agreement. The ontology is shared, for on both sides the objects of mathematics are taken to be our ideas. And the epistemology is at least partly shared. The difference is that the rationalists suppose (as Plato once did) that the relevant ideas are innate, whereas the empiricists think that our idea of three, or of a triangle, owes its existence to our perceptions of three-membered groups and triangular objects. But both are agreed that, once the relevant ideas are obtained, the further pursuit of mathematical knowledge is independent of any further experience. Yet despite all this agreement there is nevertheless an important opposition: rationalists such as Descartes stress the *importance* of mathematics for our understanding of the world, whereas Empiricists such as Locke and Berkeley and Hume belittle it.

Descartes first extends the sphere of mathematics, so that it includes time, and hence motion, as well as space. Then, just as he supposes that the basic principles of (Euclidean) geometry are known a priori, so he presumes that the same will apply to the laws of motion, and he offers an a priori derivation of them. (Descartes's supposed laws use only spatio-temporal concepts, such as size and velocity.) With this as a basis he professes to be able to deduce, without any aid from observation, the organization of the solar system as a whole (i.e. as a system of 'vortices'). He also promises us that these same basic laws can in principle explain all further phenomena, from the behaviour of light to the action of the heart. The whole of science, then, in its completed form, will be just an application of a priori reasoning from innate principles. This is perhaps the boldest view that there has ever been of the scope and power of pure mathematics. Of course, parts of Descartes's system were soon found to be wrong, and it needed Newton to produce a much better system, which apparently did square with observation. Moreover, Newton himself did not suppose that either his laws of motion or his law of gravitation could claim any a priori status. Instead, he made a point of citing experiment and observation in their support. But, even after Newton's 'corrections', Descartes's vision of a wholly a priori science remained a temptation to many (including Kant).

It did not tempt Locke, or Berkeley, or Hume. Locke, indeed, was drawn to think that science proper *should* be a priori (for only so could it provide genuine explanations), but for that very reason he thought that we should never attain it. For all three Empiricists were well aware that in practice science must be based upon observation and experiment (and they all failed to see the importance of theorizing). But Berkeley and Hume actually attacked mathematics itself, claiming that it was based upon assumptions about infinite divisibility which had no basis in experience, and which in fact led to intolerable paradoxes. In so far as these charges concerned the notion of the *infinitesimal, there was indeed some truth in them, and they were not properly answered until Weierstrass (see below). But in any case, Hume's general attitude should be noted: our knowledge of mathematics (so far as it is genuine) is knowledge of 'relations between ideas', and this is to be *contrasted* with knowledge of 'matters of fact and existence'. Hume was interested in the latter. But Kant returned to the former, asking what kinds of 'relations between ideas' these were, and how they were discovered.

Kant thought of an *analytic truth as one which can be established simply by an analysis of the concepts involved. Since he supposed that conceptual analysis was the mental analogue of taking something to bits, he framed his criterion in terms of concepts and their parts: an analytic truth is one in which the concept of the predicate is contained within the concept of the subject. His point was that it is not surprising that such truths can be known a priori. But he also supposed that some synthetic truths can be known a priori, his chief example being the truths of mathematics, and his main problem was to explain how this could be so. He seems to have thought that, once we are clear about the distinction between the analytic and the synthetic, we will readily agree that the truths of geometry and arithmetic are indeed synthetic. At any rate, his arguments on this point are very superficial. But with hindsight we can now say that he was certainly right about geometry. When this is understood, with Kant, as a theory about the space in which we find ourselves, then certainly its basic assumptions are not analytic. But the difficulty here is with the other claim, that they are known a priori. Kant's argument is just that we cannot imagine things otherwise, and that is why we feel that the knowledge is independent of experience, and could not be falsified by experience. He adds a 'justification' for this last point, namely that the spatial arrangement of what we perceive is *our* contribution to the interpretation of the data of sense. So it is due to our own nature, and not to the nature of the data, that we cannot perceive in any other way.

This account of geometry was forcibly challenged by J. S. Mill. He admitted that we could not imagine things otherwise, but explained that this was due simply to the weakness of our imaginations, which were in practice limited by what we had experienced and how we had understood it. To back this up, he pointed to several instances, from the history of science, of other propositions which once could not be imagined otherwise, but were later rejected (e.g. Aristotle's laws of motion). And he inferred from this that what can be imagined may change as scientific theories change, and is no safe guide to necessary truth. His application of this line of thought to geometry is nicely done, and we can now say that on this topic he was definitely right. The mathematical development of *non-Euclidean geometries has provided strong support for his view that if Euclidean geometry does have any special status then that can only be because of its fit with experience; and the fact that modern physical theory actually prefers a non-Euclidean geometry clearly vindicates his refusal to draw any conclusion from the limits to what can be imagined. Mill's views on geometry are now orthodox.

Both Kant and Mill attempted to treat arithmetic in the same way as they had treated geometry, Kant claiming that it was both synthetic and a priori, Mill that it was (synthetic and) empirical. But in this case the arguments on both sides were quite unconvincing, and were well criticized by Frege (see below).

The second half of the nineteenth century saw two important developments in mathematics which together provoked a surge of philosophical thinking amongst the mathematicians themselves, and gave rise to three philosophies of mathematics which are influential even today. The one development began with what is known as 'the arithmetization of analysis'. First Weierstrass (1815–97), building upon work by Canchy (1789–1857), succeeded in reducing to good order the differential and integral calculus introduced long ago by Newton and Leibniz. For two centuries it had been clear that this method led to many extremely useful results, but its basis had remained mysterious, apparently relying on the incomprehensible notion of the infinitesimal. Weierstrass showed how this notion could simply be eliminated. This work on the 'foundations' of a branch of mathematics was soon carried further. Both Dedekind and Cantor offered foundations for the theory of real numbers, by which it was freed from reliance on geometrical intuition, and derived instead from the theory of rational numbers. (Some *set theory was also employed in the derivation; this point received little attention at the time.) The theory of rational *numbers in turn could easily be derived from the theory of the natural numbers, and Dedekind went on to produce a foundation for this latter, i.e. a proper axiomatization of elementary arithmetic. So apparently Dedekind had now provided a foundation for 'all' of traditional mathematics. But the second development was in a different direction: Cantor created an entirely new branch of mathematics, i.e. the theory of *infinite numbers, which certainly could not be derived from these same foundations. Yet it cried out for foundations of its own, for it appeared to spawn contradictions (e.g. Cantor's paradox) no better than those that had once characterized the differential calculus. So on the one hand there was, for the first time since Greek mathematics, a new emphasis on foundational thinking; and on the other there was a new branch of mathematics, standing outside the area covered by existing foundations, and evidently controversial. This led to three new philosophies of mathematics, namely *logicism, a special variety of *formalism due to Hilbert, and *intuitionism.

The founder of logicism was Frege. Though he was sympathetic to Cantor's theory of the infinite, in his main work he concentrated just upon elementary arithmetic. In opposition to both Kant and Mill, he redefined an analytic truth as one that can be proved just from general logical laws and definitions, and set out to show that arithmetic is in this sense analytic. That is, it needs only logic for its foundation. At the same time he rejected the prevailing *'psychologism', i.e. the assumption that arithmetic is about our ideas, and reinstated the Platonic conception of numbers as abstract objects, existing quite independently of us. Putting these points together, he held that numbers were 'logical objects', and in effect he took them to be sets. This was the cause of his disaster, for it led him to adopt a very general ('logical') principle for the existence of sets, which Russell showed to be inconsistent. (*Russell's paradox.) Moreover, the inconsistency was clearly very similar to that affecting Cantor's theory of the infinite, and so subsequent developments in the logicist tradition have generally attempted to deal with both problems at once, providing a single foundation both for finite and for infinite numbers. One important example is Russell's theory of *types, which at the same time abandons Frege's Platonism about numbers. But in practice, mathematicians have preferred an explicit set theory as a foundation, and this strongly suggests the Platonist interpretation. In any case, logicism can in principle be combined with either the Platonic or the Aristotelian view of what numbers are. It is also compatible with either view on epistemology. For if we say that the main claim of logicism is that there is no firm boundary to be drawn between logic on the one side and mathematics on the other, then one can accept this claim while holding either that both have an a priori status (as Frege and Russell desired), or that both are empirical (as Quine once claimed).

Hilbert is often counted as a formalist, but he differs from most others who are so-called because he wishes to apply the formalist approach, not to all mathematics, but only to some of it. He begins with the thought that Cantor's theory of the infinite should certainly be retained, but must be protected from contradiction in some way. At present it is vulnerable, because we do not really understand the notion of infinity, and so do not attach a clear 'content' to our reasoning. Then he generalizes this thought to all other areas of mathematics that involve infinite totalities, taking this to include not only the theory of the real numbers (since they may be construed as infinite sets, or infinite sequences, of rational numbers), but even the use of quantifiers in elementary arithmetic, since these quantifiers range over all the infinitely many natural numbers. The most basic part of mathematics, then, is limited to what can be done in elementary arithmetic without quantifiers, using only free variables and recursive functions. This part has genuine content, is well understood, and can safely be assumed to be free from error. But in other areas we have no such guarantee. So his programme is first to formalize these other areas, proposing a formal theory that is adequate to represent all ordinary mathematical reasoning in that area, and then to argue in the metalanguage that this formal theory is free from contradiction. The metalinguistic argument, of course, must be confined to methods of proof that are guaranteed, i.e. to those already available in quantifier-free arithmetic. (This is one of several proposals on what may be counted as a 'constructive' method of proof. *Constructivism.)

*Gödel's incompleteness theorems destroyed this programme. The more far-reaching result was the first theorem, which implies that, for any sufficiently rich formal system, there are methods of reasoning about that system which evidently do establish the truth of a formula of the system, but which go beyond what can be proved within the system. So one cannot even carry out Hilbert's first step, of formalizing the area of mathematics to be proved consistent. But the second theorem shows that in any case the consistency of the system cannot be proved even by the methods available in that system itself, let alone by methods that Hilbert permitted as constructive. So Hilbert may perhaps be right in saying that, in some areas, all that the mathematician needs as a basis for his investigations is a consistent formal system, and that he need not attach any 'content' to that system. But we now know that we cannot use this idea to guarantee the safety of mathematical reasoning.

Brouwer, who founded intuitionism, shared Hilbert's distrust of the infinite and his commitment to constructive reasoning. But whereas Hilbert had aimed to rescue the non-constructive parts of mathematics, Brouwer simply abandons them. Against formalism, then, he sees no merit in formal systems without true 'content', and against logicism he believes that mathematics is prior to logic, and does not need it. However, in 1930 his pupil Arend Heyting did elaborate a logic suitable for intuitionistic reasoning, which Brouwer then endorsed. It is quite different from classical logic, mainly because its leading idea is that truth cannot be distinguished from provability. (*Logic, intuitionist.) In Brouwer's own thought one can find two bases for this idea. One is that mathematical objects have a special status: they are 'mental constructions'. (This is a Kantian thought; it reverts to the 'psychologism' that Frege had attacked.) Since the objects do not exist independently of human thinking, it may seem to follow that we cannot adopt for them the same theory of truth as we use in other cases, namely a correspondence theory. In their case, then, there is nothing else for truth to be but provability. The other line of thought relies not on the alleged special status of the numbers, but just on the point that there are infinitely many of them. This means that, on the classical conception of truth, there could be some truth about all numbers which we could never verify, even in principle. But the intuitionist rejects this conception of truth as no less 'metaphysical' than the Platonic conception of numbers as independently existing objects.

Intuitionism is a revisionist theory in the philosophy of mathematics, for it involves abandoning much of classical mathematics. A more extreme form of this revisionism is 'strict finitism', which will not allow truth to go beyond what we can *in practice* verify. It is disputed whether Wittgenstein should be counted as a strict finitist.   D.B.

*formalism.

P. Benacerraf and H. Putnam (eds.), *Philosophy of Mathematics: Selected Readings*, 2nd edn. (Cambridge, 1983).

W. Ewald (ed.), *From Kant to Hilbert: A Source Book in the Foundations of Mathematics* (Oxford, 2000).

M. Giaquinto, *The Search for Certainty: A Philosophical Account of Foundations of Mathematics* (Oxford, 2002).

I. Grattan-Guinness (ed.), *From the Calculus to Set Theory 1630–1910* (London, 1980).

M. Kline, *Mathematical Thought from Ancient to Modern Times* (New York, 1972).

W. and M. Kneale, *The Development of Logic* (Oxford, 1962).

M. Potter, *Reason's Nearest Kin: Philosophies of Arithmetic from Kant to Carnap* (Oxford, 2000).

J. van Heijenoort (ed.), *From Frege to Gödel* (Cambridge, 1967).

mathematics, knowledge of. Interpreted at face value, mathematics appears to be a science concerned with an extraordinary array of objects and structures that are abstract, necessary, and infinite (geometrical shapes and patterns, the natural numbers, the real numbers, the set-theoretic hierarchy, and so on). It is, however, deeply mysterious how knowledge of such objects and structures could ever be acquired by us, mundane and finite creatures that we appear to be. Of course, mathematicians employ proofs to confirm their assertions. But proofs only tell us what follow from the axioms of a mathematical theory; they cannot inform us that the axioms are true. A variety of different epistemological strategies have been proposed to overcome this difficulty. According to one popular strategy, mathematical axioms are confirmed by the indispensable (auxiliary) role they perform in scientific practice. But this ties the practice of mathematics to the empirical fortunes of science. To avoid this consequence, *logicism claims that mathematical axioms are truths of higher-order logic.   S.S.

*logicism; mathematics, problems of the philosophy of.

Stewart Shapiro, *Thinking about Mathematics* (Oxford, 2000).

mathematics, philosophy of, problems of. The aim of the philosophy of mathematics is to provide an account of the nature and methodology of mathematics and to illuminate the place of mathematics in our overall intellectual lives. The problems fall into categories familiar to contemporary philosophers. There are ontological problems concerning the subject-matter of mathematics. What is mathematics about? There are epistemological problems. How do we know mathematics? What is the methodology of mathematics, and to what extent is this methodology reliable? There are problems of logic and semantics. How are the languages of mathematics understood, learned, communicated, etc.? What do mathematical assertions mean? Are unambiguous mathematical statements objectively true or false? What is the proper logic for mathematics? And there are problems concerning the relationship between mathematics and the rest of the intellectual enterprise. What is the relationship, if any, between the philosophy of mathematics and the practice of mathematics? (See the text by Shapiro and the collection edited by Benacerraf and Putnam, listed in the selected bibliography.)

Many of the problems and issues in mathematics are counterparts of central items on the agenda of general epistemology and metaphysics. Mathematics provides a good case-study for many of the issues concerning existence, semantics, and knowledge that occur throughout philosophy. Nevertheless, mathematics at least appears to be different in kind from other types of investigation. Its basic assertions enjoy an extremely high degree of certainty. Indeed, theorems of at least elementary mathematics, like '2 + 2 = 4' or 'There are infinitely many prime numbers', are often taken to be paradigms of *necessary truths and *a priori and infallible knowledge. How can such things be false, and how can any rational being doubt them? Thus, it is incumbent on any complete philosophy of mathematics to account for the necessity and apriority of mathematics, or else to show why mathematics appears that way.

Mathematics also plays an important role in virtually every scientific effort aimed at understanding the natural world. Consider, for example, the prerequisites of just about any natural or social science. It is thus incumbent on any complete philosophy of mathematics to show how mathematics is applied to the material world or, in other words, to show how the subject-matter of mathematics is related to the subject-matter of the sciences, and how the methodology of mathematics fits into the methodology of the sciences.

There are two distinct types of *realism in the philosophy of mathematics. Realism-in-ontology is the view that the subject-matter of mathematics is a realm of objects that exist independent of the mind, conventions, and language of the mathematician. Most advocates of this view hold that mathematical objects—numbers, functions, points, sets, etc.—are abstract, eternal, and do not enter into causal relationships with material objects. Because of this, realism-in-ontology is sometimes called *'Platonism', noting the resemblance between mathematical objects and Platonic Forms. This label can be misleading, however. Realism-in-ontology does not, by itself, presuppose anything like a Platonic epistemology, and there are realists-in-ontology who hold that at least some mathematical objects are not eternal and not outside the causal nexus.

Realism-in-truth-value is the view that unambiguous assertions of mathematics are non-vacuously true or false, independent of the mind, language, and conventions of the mathematician. This view is sometimes called *realism.

There is a natural connection between the two varieties of realism. Consider the following statement:

There is a prime number greater than 1,000,000.

The realist-in-truth-value holds that this is an objective truth. But what does it mean? Prima facie, '1,000,000' is a singular term, and 'prime number' is a common noun. If the surface grammar of this sentence reflects its *logical form, and if 'there is' means 'there exists', then the sentence entails that both the number 1,000,000 and a greater prime number exist. For the realist-in-truth-value, this existence is objective, and so we are led to realism-in-ontology. In sum, if one is a realist-in-truth-value, then realism-in-ontology is the result of taking mathematical assertions at face value.

Conversely, realist-in-ontology at least suggests a straightforward, Tarskian semantics. If mathematical objects exist independently of the mathematician, then there is no impediment to a straightforward model-theoretic semantics, which would presumably render assertions true or false objectively.

Despite these natural alliances, the literature reveals no consensus on logical relationships between the two varieties of realism. Each of the four possible positions is articulated and defended by established and influential philosophers of mathematics. Kurt Gödel and Penelope Maddy adopt both forms of realism; Hartry Field and the traditional intuitionists L. E. J. Brouwer and Arend Heyting reject both forms; Geoffrey Hellman and Charles Chihara defend realism-in-truth-value, anti-realism-in-ontology; and Neil Tennant adopts the reverse, realism-in-ontology, anti-realism-in-truth-value (see the selected bibliography, especially the Benacerraf and Putnam anthology).

Typical forms of realism-in-ontology nicely account for the necessity of mathematics and give impetus to the traditional view that mathematical knowledge is a priori. If mathematics is about a realm of eternal, abstract objects, then mathematical truth is surely independent of any contingencies of the material world around us, and mathematics is not known through sensory experience. Of course, this alone does not *account* for the a priori nature of mathematics, until the realist provides an epistemology. It is not clear what these two varieties of realism have to say about the application of mathematics to science. Presumably, there is some sort of connection between the realm of abstract objects and the material world. The problem is to articulate it.

For the most part, alternatives to realism-in-ontology fall into two groups. First, there are those who agree that mathematics has a distinctive subject-matter, but hold that mathematical objects are not independent of the mind, conventions, or language of the mathematician. The most common views in this camp take mathematical objects to be mental constructions, and so are varieties of *idealism (or applications of idealism to mathematics). Within this group, one unlikely possibility is to hold that mathematics is subjective, and so, presumably, each person has his own mathematics. A problem with this subjective idealism is to account for the fact that for the overwhelming most part, mathematicians agree with each other. It is more common for the idealist to hold that mathematics is both mind-dependent and objective or at least intersubjective in a principled way, perhaps by

following *Kant in asserting that mathematics deals with structures common to human minds. The Kantian view accounts for the necessity of mathematics by holding that mathematics represents ways we *must* think, perceive, and apprehend, if we are to think, perceive, and apprehend at all. Mathematical knowledge is a priori to the extent that we have a priori access to the structures common to our minds. A Kantian might attempt to account for the application of mathematics to science by relating mathematics to the forms of sense perception. The writings of traditional *intuitionists, such as Brouwer, have both subjective and Kantian themes, mostly the latter (see also *constructivism).

The other alternative to realism-in-ontology is to simply deny that mathematics has a subject-matter: there are no numbers, functions, sets, etc. If this view is not to lapse into a general scepticism, denying the truth of ordinary or scientific assertions, the burden is to give an account of mathematics, and its role in the intellectual enterprise, that does not involve a mathematical ontology. One common manœuvre in this direction is to reconstrue mathematical assertions in modal terms. For example, instead of asserting that there is a natural number with a given property, one asserts that it is possible to construct a certain item with the given property. If the modal assertions have objective truth-values, then the result would be a realism-in-truth value, anti-realism-in-ontology (see the items by Hellman and Chihara in the selected bibliography).

Another irrealist programme construes mathematics as fiction, much like what we read in novels. Statements about prime numbers are akin to statements about Miss Marple. At least prima facie, fictional discourse does not have ontological commitments. We do not believe that Miss Marple exists. On this view, mathematical assertions, taken literally, are vacuous. 'There are at least a million prime numbers' is false, for the simple reason that there are no numbers, and so no prime numbers. 'All numbers are prime' is vacuously true. With fiction, we distinguish literal truth from truth-in-the-story. 'Miss Marple is a nosy busybody' is false, but true in the relevant stories (or most of them). In this sense, mathematical assertions get their usual truth-values 'in the story'. To account for the applications of mathematics, a fictionalist might then try to give an account of the role of fictional mathematics in presumably non-fictional discourses, like science. (See the items by Field and Burgess and Rosen in the selected bibliography.)

Another view, developed by *logicism and adopted by *Logical Positivism, is to construe mathematical truths as *analytic, true in virtue of the meanings of its terms. The necessity of mathematics is semantic, or linguistic. Mathematical knowledge is knowledge of meaning, which is presumably a priori. The problem, however, is to square this view with mathematics as practised. One needs to give an explication of the meanings of mathematical terminology according to which every mathematical truth is analytic.

The logicist Gottlob Frege showed how to derive the usual principles of arithmetic from what has come to be known as Hume's principle:

The number of *F*'s is identical to the number of *G*'s if and only if the *F*'s are equinumerous with the *G*'s.

This result has considerable mathematical interest. Who would have thought that so much mathematics can be derived from a simple fact about the application of arithmetic to counting? Contemporary neo-logicists, such as Crispin Wright, propose to make this derivation the foundation of arithmetic. Hume's principle, and *second-order logic, provide an epistemological *foundation of mathematics. Neo-logicism accounts for the a priori nature of arithmetic, to the extent that we know Hume's principle a priori, and that second-order derivation preserves a priori knowledge. The neo-logicists are realists-in-ontology, holding that the existence of numbers follows from Hume's principle (together with some uncontroversial logical truths).

Structuralism is a philosophy of mathematics that turns attention away from individual mathematical objects. The subject-matter of arithmetic, for example, is the natural number structure, the form common to any infinite system of objects that has a distinguished initial object, which plays the role of zero, and a successor relation or operation that satisfies the induction principle. The natural number structure is exemplified by the arabic numerals, sequences of characters on an alphabet in lexical order, an infinite sequence of distinct moments of time, etc. Similarly, real analysis is about the real number structure; topology is about topological structures; etc. According to the structuralist, the application of mathematics to science occurs, in part, by discovering or postulating that certain structures are exemplified in the material world. Mathematics is to material reality as pattern is to patterned (see the items by Hellman, Resnik, and Shapiro in the selected bibliography).

Most structuralists are realists-in-truth-value, but they differ among themselves on the question of ontology. *Ante rem* structuralism is a version of realism-in-ontology, taking structures, and their places, to be bona fide objects that exist independently of the mathematician. On this view, mathematical assertions are understood at face value. Against this, eliminative, or modal, structuralism takes statements about structures, and assertions within mathematics generally, to be generalizations over all systems, or possible systems, that exemplify the structure. It is a structuralism without structures.

There is a relatively recent tradition, traced to the later Wittgenstein, that attempts to accommodate mathematics in terms of the normative social practice inherent in a linguistic community. This denies that mathematics is necessary and a priori, but it does account for the perceived necessity of mathematics. We have to accept the basic principles because we cannot imagine living any other way: they are fundamental to our 'form of life'.

To a large extent, epistemology depends on ontology and semantics. How we know mathematics is surely related to what mathematics is about and what its assertions mean. The most difficult problem with realism-in-ontology lies in this area. How can we know anything about a realm of eternal, acausal objects? Indeed, how can we have any confidence that what we say about these objects is true? To produce an adequate epistemology, a realist-in-ontology must tell us something about ourselves, the knowers, and something about mathematical objects, the known. A tall order.

One route is to postulate a special faculty of mathematical intuition, something that gives the mathematician direct or indirect access to the abstract, eternal, acausal mathematical universe. Supposedly, this mathematical *intuition* is analogous to sense perception, which gives us access to material objects. Plato and Gödel proposed epistemologies like this. Despite the eminence of these thinkers, this view is rejected, almost out of hand, by those who put constraints of *naturalism on epistemology. The idea is that humans must be understood as organisms in the natural world, and, as such, all faculties must be amenable to ordinary scientific scrutiny. For example, many philosophers hold that a person cannot have knowledge about a certain type of object unless he or she has causal contact with at least samples of the objects. This rules out the sort of mathematical intuition envisioned above, assuming that mathematical objects are acausal.

The few varieties of realism-in-ontology that deny that mathematical objects are abstract and eternal do not automatically run afoul of the naturalistic constraint. Presumably, if mathematical objects are material, then knowledge of them is no more problematic than knowledge of any other material objects. Of course, this view gives up realism's prima-facie account of the necessity and apriority of mathematics, but for some, this is a welcome loss. The problem is to square this view with mathematics as practised, and its apparent massively infinite ontology.

W. V. O. Quine and Hilary Putnam, among others, have proposed a hypothetico-deductive account of mathematical epistemology. The view begins with the observation that virtually all of science is formulated in mathematical terms. Moreover, as far as we know, this is the only way to formulate scientific theories. So mathematics is 'confirmed' to the extent that scientific theories are. The argument is that because mathematics is indispensable for science, and science is well-confirmed and (approximately) true, mathematics is well-confirmed and true as well. On this view, mathematical objects, like numbers and functions, are theoretical posits. They are the same kind of thing as electrons, and we know about them the same way we know about electrons—via their role in mature, well-confirmed scientific theories. Articulations of this view should (but usually do not) provide a careful analysis of the role of mathematics in science, rather than just noting the existence of this role. Such an account would shed some light on the 'abstract' nature of mathematical objects and the relationships between mathematical objects and scientific or ordinary material objects. Typically, an advocate of the Quine–Putnam indispensability argument denies the necessity and apriority of mathematics. Mathematics is *only* known through its role in science, which is clearly a contingent, a posteriori affair. Because mathematics plays a central role in virtually every science, its disconfirmation is unlikely, but still possible in principle. Against such accounts, it does not seem that assertions like '2 + 3 = 5' are really of a piece with assertions about small molecules. Indeed, it would seem to follow from the view in question that the mathematical assertions are *less* firmly established than assertions about molecules, since mathematics is more theoretical—it lies further from sensory experience. Moreover, the view in question does not account for branches of mathematics, like higher set theory, that have not found application in science. In general, mathematicians usually do not look for confirmation in science before publishing their results, or otherwise claiming to know them.

A typical strategy among both realists and anti-realists (of any stripe) is to relate mathematics to some other area of knowledge. This allows the philosopher to appropriate epistemological gains from the other area or, more often, to claim that mathematical knowledge is no more problematic than knowledge in the other area (while conceding that the latter has its own epistemological problems).

For example, according to *ante rem* structuralism, a mathematical structure and a pattern are the same kind of thing. Patterns are at least prima facie abstract, and yet we manage to have knowledge of them. Thus, some structuralists attempt to account for some mathematical knowledge via the psychological mechanism of pattern recognition. Patterns themselves are abstract, but we know about them, in part, by ordinary perceptual contact with systems of physical objects that exemplify them. At best, however, this suggestion accounts for knowledge of small, finite structures. One still needs to accommodate knowledge about the infinite structures studied in live mathematics.

Along similar lines, modal structuralists and some fictionalists assimilate mathematical knowledge to knowledge of modal assertions. There is no consensus concerning knowledge of what is necessary and possible, but it is generally agreed that we have such knowledge.

In relatively recent history, there have been disputes concerning some principles and inferences within mathematics. These include the law of *excluded middle, the axiom of *choice, the *extensionality of mathematical functions and properties, and *impredicative definitions, linguistic entities that define an item by reference to a class that contains the object being defined (e.g. 'the least upper bound'). Such principles have been criticized (and defended) on philosophical grounds. For example, if mathematical objects are mental constructions or creations, as the traditional intuitionists contend, then impredicative definitions are circular. One cannot create or construct an object by referring to a class of objects that

(already) contains the item being created or constructed. On the other hand, for a realist-in-ontology, a definition does not represent a recipe for creating or constructing a mathematical object. Rather, a definition is a characterization or description of an object that already exists. From this point of view, there is nothing illicit in definitions that refer to classes containing the item in question. Characterizing 'the least upper bound' of a set is no different from defining the 'elder jurist' as 'the oldest member of the Supreme Court'.

The meaning of mathematical locutions like 'There is a number such that . . .' is related to one's philosophy of mathematics. Intuitionists, for example, take this locution to mean 'One can construct a number such that . . .', while realists-in-ontology take existence to be independent of construction, or any human abilities for that matter. It follows that the proper logic of mathematics is also tied to philosophical considerations. No doubt, how mathematics is done, or should be done, has something to do with what mathematical discourse means. Typically, intuitionists propose revisions in mathematical practice, based on philosophical considerations. The arguments concern the nature of mathematics and mathematical objects, with Brouwer, or the learnability of mathematical language and the ability of mathematicians to communicate with each other, with Michael Dummett. There is a substantial technical question of whether mathematics could serve the needs of science if the intuitionistic revisions were adopted. That is, if mathematics were changed to conform to intuitionism, would the rest of the scientific enterprise suffer?

As far as contemporary mathematics is concerned, the aforementioned disputes are substantially over. The law of excluded middle, impredicative definitions, and the like are central parts of the enterprise nowadays. But this battle was not fought on philosophical grounds. Mathematicians did not temporarily don philosophical hats and decide that numbers, say, really do exist independent of the mathematician and, for that reason, that it is correct to engage in the erstwhile disputed methodologies. Rather, the practices in question were found to be conducive to the practice of mathematics.

This raises a meta-question concerning the relationship between mathematics and the philosophy of mathematics. It is a central tenet of the naturalistically minded philosopher that there is no first philosophy that stands prior to science, ready to criticize it. Science should guide philosophy, not the other way around. I presume that the same goes for mathematics. If so, then one must either reject intuitionism or else find some mathematical or scientific reasons to revise mathematics, reasons that mathematicians have overlooked to date, but which they would accept as compelling on mathematical grounds alone. That sort of quest does not seem to be under way—intuitionists are not naturalists, or else they do not extend naturalism to mathematics.   S.S.

*foundationalism in mathematics; intuitionism.

Paul Benacerraf and Hilary Putnam (eds.), *Philosophy of Math-ematics* (Englewood Cliffs, NJ, 1964) (comprehensive anthol-ogy).

John Burgess and Gideon Rosen, *A Subject with No Object: Strat-egies for Nominalistic Interpretation of Mathematics* (Oxford, 1997).

Charles Chihara, *Constructibility and Mathematical Existence* (Oxford, 1990).

Hartry Field, *Science without Numbers* (Princeton, NJ, 1980).

Gottlob Frege, *Die Grundlagen der Arithmetik* (Breslau, 1884), tr. J. L. Austin as *The Foundations of Arithmetic*, 2nd edn. (New York, 1960).

Geoffrey Hellman, *Mathematics without Numbers* (Oxford, 1989).

Penelope Maddy, *Realism in Mathematics* (Oxford, 1990).

—— *Naturalism in Mathematics* (Oxford, 1997).

Michael Resnik, *Mathematics as the Science of Patterns* (Oxford, 1997).

Stewart Shapiro, *Philosophy of Mathematics: Structure and Ontology* (Oxford, 1997).

—— *Thinking about Mathematics: The Philosophy of Mathematics* (Oxford, 2000) (general text).

Neil Tennant, *The Taming of the True* (Oxford, 1997).

Crispin Wright, *Frege's Conception of Numbers as Objects* (Aberdeen, 1983).

matter. 'What is matter?—Never mind. What is mind?—No matter'. This Victorian joke has some substance to it, in that it draws attention to the fact that it is easier to dis-tinguish matter by contrasting it with something else than to say what it is. The joke also shows that if **substance* is the ultimate ontological category, the fundamental stuff of *being or *existence, then matter is not the only candi-date for substantial status: common-sense *ontology holds that there are two substances, matter and some-thing else, *mind, *soul, or *spirit, the main characteristic of which is that it is non-material! Thus 'contrast' accounts of matter, though in some ways illuminating, are also frustrating.

Alternative, non-contrasting accounts of matter tend merely to substitute something equally puzzling. Does it help to say that matter is *physical* substance, the basic raw material from which everything physical is composed? But some help is at hand through the suggestion (or the-ory) that matter is what is *preserved* during any process of physical change. The search by the *Pre-Socratics for what would later be called matter arose from their adherence to a generalized conservation principle: something cannot be created out of nothing and something cannot disappear into nothing. Thus whatever exists fundamentally can be neither created nor destroyed but persists and is con-served throughout all changes in nature. This doctrine was clearest among the *atomists, who claimed that what exists fundamentally is material atoms and the void, and all change or alteration, such as motion, combustion, or the growth and decay of living things, is merely the rearrangement of atoms in the void. But it was left to Aris-totle to establish matter as a category, by contrasting it with *form.

The contrast between matter and mind also has Greek origins, but it was Descartes who elevated it into the metaphysical dualism that has proved so compelling to common sense, in spite of obvious difficulties (how do matter and mind interact?). Descartes equated matter and extension, adhering to the ancient principle that empty space is an impossibility, but his seventeenth-century rivals were reviving Greek atomism, or the 'corpuscular philosophy'. Thus in Locke, for example, is found the idea that matter consists of microscopic particles, though this idea coexists uneasily with an influential alternative the-ory, that matter is the underlying *substratum that sup-ports the observable properties of things.

Another contrast is that between matter and life. If mat-ter is simply inert substance, how can it produce the phe-nomena of *life and *consciousness? It cannot, according to *vitalism: something non-material must be added for living organisms to exist, a vital spark, a soul or spirit. But other theories of matter deny this contrast, and claim that life and consciousness are *emergent properties of matter, exhibited at a sufficiently complex level of organization. A variation is *panpsychism, according to which matter itself has non-physical properties of life and consciousness, in addition to the usual physical properties.

What then *is* matter? From the point of view of science, it is matter as what-is-conserved that matters. But hasn't modern physics 'dematerialized' matter, replacing it with energy or something even more abstract, like variations in the *space-time curvature? It is true that conservation principles—of mass, of momentum, of energy, etc.—are susceptible to the progress of science. Still, matter can be thought of as both what is fundamental in existence and what is conserved in change, granted that ideas about this are dependent on changing scientific theory. So matter persists. But conceptions of it change, sometimes rad-ically, but only for good theoretical reasons.   A.BEL.

*prime matter; materialism; change.

Rom Harré (ed.), *The Physical Sciences since Antiquity* (London, 1986).

Thomas A. Holden, *The Architecture of Matter: Galileo to Kant* (Oxford, 2004).

Ernan McMullin (ed.), *The Concept of Matter in Modern Philosophy* (Notre Dame, Ind., 1978).

Stephen Toulmin and June Goodfield, *The Architecture of Matter* (London, 1962).

matter, prime: *see* prime matter.

maximin and minimax. Game- and decision-theoretical strategies which require one to make one's worst possible outcome as good as possible (that is, to maximize the min-imum). Maximin grounds Rawls's *'difference principle', that political institutions should make the position of the worst-off group as good as possible. 'Minimax' is occasion-ally used as a synonym for 'maximin'. Used more precisely, it refers to maximin in zero-sum games, where the gain to one equals the loss to another. Maximin rationality is criti-cized for its extreme risk-aversion, and maximin justice for its insensitivity to the aggregation of welfare.   R.CRI.

*game theory; decision theory.

J. Rawls, *A Theory of Justice* (Cambridge, Mass., 1971), sect. 26.

Maxwell's Demon. A *thought experiment created by James Clerk Maxwell in which the second law of thermodynamics—that *entropy always increases—is apparently violated. The demon operates a trap-door in a partition which separates two compartments, A and B, of randomly moving particles of gas, letting those of above average velocity pass into A and those of below average velocity into B. The result will be greater temperature and pressure in A than B, a differential which can be exploited to run a perpetual motion engine. This conclusion is disputed on the grounds that entropy does increase within the whole system of gas plus the demon.   S.R.A.

*energy; time.

Harvey S. Leff and Andrew F. Rex (eds.), *Maxwell's Demon 2: Entropy, Classical and Quantum Information, Computing* (Bristol, 2002).

McDowell, John (1942–). Oxford philosopher, subsequently professor at the University of Pittsburgh. McDowell has developed a conception of mind, language, and morality that derives its main inspiration from the later work of Wittgenstein. McDowell argues that most contemporary philosophy of mind is committed to the Cartesian picture of the subjective realm as something private, essentially detachable from its relations to the world. This picture leads to an intolerable scepticism about the *external world, or to the 'darkness within': the inability to explain genuine *intentionality. Much of McDowell's work is an attempt to free the philosophy of mind from this picture; to this end he has articulated a radically externalist theory of the mind, in which certain thoughts are not thinkable in the absence of the objects they are about ('Russellian Singular Thoughts'; *Evans).   T.C.

*externalism; anti-individualism; heredity and environment.

J. McDowell, *Mind and World* (Cambridge, Mass., 1994).
—— *Mind, Value, and Reality* (Cambridge, Mass., 1998).
—— *Meaning, Knowledge, and Reality* (Cambridge, Mass., 1998).

McGinn, Colin (1950–). First studied psychology at Manchester University and then philosophy at Oxford. He won the John Locke Prize at Oxford in 1973, going on to teach at University College London from 1974 to 1985, whereupon he became Wilde Reader in Mental Philosophy at Oxford until 1990, at which time he joined Rutgers University. His early work was mainly in philosophy of language, this giving way to an interest in philosophy of mind and metaphysics. He has written on subjectivity and objectivity, on the content of propositional attitudes, on the later Wittgenstein, and on metaphilosophy. His most recent work is concerned with the solubility or otherwise of philosophical problems, particularly the mind–body problem. He maintains that the deepest metaphysical problems—such as the nature of the self, meaning, free will—have solutions that lie outside the contingent bounds of human cognitive power.   N.B.

Colin McGinn, *The Problem of Consciousness* (Oxford, 1991).

—— *Problems in Philosophy: The Limits of Inquiry* (Oxford, 1993).
—— *Knowledge and Reality: Selected Papers* (Oxford, 1998).

McTaggart, John McTaggart Ellis (1866–1925). Cambridge atheistic idealist now best known for his argument (in *Mind* (1908)) that *time is unreal. McTaggart distinguished *'A-series' terms like 'past', 'present', 'future', and 'B-series' terms like 'precede', 'simultaneous', 'follow'. He argued first that the B-series presupposes the A-series (e.g. if X precedes Y, there must be a time at which X is past and Y present), and then that the A-series is incoherent, since any event must have all three A-properties ('past', 'present', 'future'), yet these are inconsistent. Saying it has them at different times, the apparently obvious way out, leads to an infinite regress, he claimed, since then we must raise the same question about these different times themselves. The coherence of the A-series is still disputed, but so too is the alleged need for it.   A.R.L.

C. D. Broad, *An Examination of McTaggart's Philosophy*, 2 vols. (Cambridge, 1933, 1938).
J. M. E. McTaggart, *Philosophical Studies*, ed. S. V. Keeling (London, 1934).

Mead, George Herbert (1863–1931). American philosopher of social *pragmatism and pioneer of sociology who taught at the University of Chicago as a prominent member of the Chicago School. The self, for Mead, 'arises in the process of social experience and activity'. Essential to this process is the role of language as the form of reflexive communication. 'It is in addressing himself in the role of an other that his self arises in experience.' The social in humans generalized as fundamental to all nature is 'sociality', 'the capacity of being several things at once'. '[T]he emergent object belongs to different systems in its passage from the old to the new because of its systematic relationship with other structures, and possesses the characters it has because of its membership in these different systems.' Human minds capable of occupying other systems as well as their own are, Mead said, 'only the culmination of that sociality which is found throughout the universe'   P.H.H.

David L. Miller, *George Herbert Mead: Self, Language and the World* (Austin, Tex., 1973).

mean, doctrine of the. A central doctrine in Aristotle's account of excellence of *character. Aristotle describes that excellence as concerned with *pathē*, i.e. motivational impulses, chiefly emotions, and with actions (sc. which issue from those motivations), and defines it as 'a settled state issuing in choice, in a mean determined by a rational principle, viz. the one by which the agent of practical wisdom would determine it'. This settled state is in a mean in the sense that the virtuous agent is neither excessively given to the various motivations prompting to action (e.g. excessively irascible) nor insufficiently sensitive to them, but responsive to the right extent, so at to choose to act on each motivation to the right degree, on the right occasions, for the right reasons, with reference to the right people, etc. The determination of what is right in all these particular respects cannot be captured in any formula, but has to be the task of the educated judgement of the practically wise agent, responding to the indefinitely variable range of circumstances in which action is required.

C.C.W.T.

J. O. Urmson, 'Aristotle's Doctrine of the Mean', *American Philosophical Quarterly* (1973); repr. in A. Rorty (ed.), *Essays on Aristotle's Ethics* (Berkeley, Calif., 1980).

meaning. Twentieth-century philosophy, in both the 'analytic' and 'contintental' traditions, was preoccupied with questions about linguistic meaning and the way language relates to reality. In the analytic tradition, this was largely as a consequence of the revolutions in logic initiated by Frege and Russell. Indeed, Michael Dummett has argued that the distinctive feature of *analytic philosophy is its assumption that 'the philosophy of language is the foundation of the rest of the subject'. Even if one does not accept this claim, it is undeniable that the phenomena of meaning present some of the most intractable problems of philosophy.

The meaning of a word looks, as it were, both 'outwards' into the world, and 'inwards' to other words. The meaning of the word 'tiger', for example, is related both to those things in the world—tigers—to which it applies, and to other words with which it combines to make sentences which can be used to make assertions, ask questions, give warnings, and so on: 'Tigers are animals', 'Is that a tiger?', 'Look out! A tiger!' Whatever else is involved in meaning, it is clear that these two roles are clearly essential: for if one knows the meaning of the word 'tiger', one must have some grasp of how it applies to things in the world, and one must also be able to employ the word in an indefinite number of sentences. A theory of meaning—a 'semantic theory'—is therefore obliged to explain how words can perform this dual function.

In the seminal semantic theory of Gottlob Frege these two roles are explained together. Frege associated with each meaningful part of a *language something he called its 'Bedeutung', normally translated as 'reference'. The reference of an expression is, intuitively, what it 'stands for': the reference of 'George Orwell', for example, is a particular man. Frege's insight was to see that the references of the parts of a sentence contribute in a systematic way to the truth or falsehood of sentences in which those parts occur. Thus the truth or falsehood of the sentence 'George Orwell wrote *1984*' is determined by the references of the individual words and the way they are put together. The overall significance of the sentence—for Frege, its truth or falsehood—is fixed by what the parts of the sentence 'stand for' in the world, and the relations between those parts.

It follows from this claim that if you replace a word in a sentence *S* with a word having the same reference, the truth or falsehood of *S* will not change. But this gives rise to a notorious problem. Suppose that Alf believes that George Orwell wrote *1984*, but does not know that Orwell is Blair. Then while the sentence 'Alf believes that George Orwell wrote *1984*' will be true, the sentence 'Alf believes that Eric Blair wrote *1984*' will be false. So if meaning is what determines the truth or falsehood of a sentence, there must be more to the meaning of a sentence than the references of its parts.

Frege accounted for this by introducing another notion into the theory of meaning, which he called 'Sinn', usually translated 'sense'. The sense of an expression is, intuitively, not what is referred to by an expression, but the *way* it is referred to. Each sense determines one reference, but to one reference there may correspond many senses. (*Sense and reference; *intension and extension.) Central to Frege's view is that senses are abstract objects, not ideas in people's minds. (*Psychologism.)

Frege's basic idea is very appealing. However, one natural question arises that Frege's own work (deliberately) doesn't address: given that words do refer to things, how do we *explain* this relation of reference? What makes it the case that any word refers to any object at all? A natural if vague answer is in terms of the psychological capacities of users of a language: words mean what they do because of what speakers of the language do with them. An example of this approach is *Logical Positivism, which held that the meaning of a sentence is given by an account of what it would take to verify the sentence. Here meaning is explained in terms of the psychological and other abilities of speakers to tell whether a sentence is true.

The demise of Logical Positivism's account of meaning was followed by an outbreak of scepticism about the notion of meaning, most influentially expressed in the work of W. V. Quine. Quine followed the positivists in linking meaning to experience, but argued that experience does not relate to individual sentences but to whole theories. Since he thinks that meaning must be empirically available, Quine frames the question thus: What evidence determines that someone means something by making certain sounds? Quine thinks that the only acceptable evidence is behavioural, and therefore shuns any appeal to introspection or Frege's senses (the latter are 'creatures of darkness' whose criteria of identity are utterly obscure). But no amount of behavioural evidence can *determine* that a person's words mean one thing rather another—it is always possible to construct alternative and incompatible 'translations' of the evidence. From here Quine moves to his famous claim that *translation is indeterminate, and reference is inscrutable: strictly speaking, there are no facts about what words and sentences mean. This is not an epistemic claim: reference is inscrutable because 'there is nothing to scrute'. (We also find a very different scepticism about philosophical accounts of meaning in the later writings of Wittgenstein.)

A significant attempt to explain meaning, with one eye towards Quine's scepticism, was propounded by Donald Davidson in the 1960s and 1970s. Sharing Quine's sympathies with *extensionality, Davidson attempted to account for meaning in terms of truth, which for some time had seemed more logically tractable than meaning. In particular, the Polish logician Alfred Tarski had defined truth for the sentences of certain *formal languages in terms of the relation of *satisfaction holding between the parts of sentences and sequences of objects. A sentence's truth is determined systematically by the satisfaction of its parts; thus Tarski could show how to formally derive, from the axioms and rules of the theory, sentences (so-called 'T-sentences') which state what might intuitively be regarded as the conditions under which any sentence of the language is true. (The apparently banal T-sentence '"Snow is white" is true if and only if snow is white' is a favourite example.)

As we saw, the idea of the parts of a sentence making a systematic contribution to the meaning of the whole sentence was a key idea in Frege's work. But Davidson explains meaning without using the troublesome idea of sense. Instead he proposes using a theory of truth in Tarski's style to 'serve' as a theory of meaning. In outline, the idea is this: a theory of meaning for a language should at least entail, for any sentence of the language, a sentence that 'gives its meaning'. The most obvious sort of case would be the 'homophonic' case: to give the meaning of a sentence would just be to give the sentence itself. For example, we recognize immediately that the sentence '"Snow is white" means that snow is white' gives the meaning of 'Snow is white'. This looks trivial, of course, but that is only because we already know what 'Snow is white' means. (The sentence '"La neve è bianca" means that snow is white' does not look so trivial.) The theory must also show how the individual parts make a systematic contribution to the sentences in which they occur. So now we know what the consequences of a theory of meaning must be—but how can we construct a theory that does actually have these consequences? Davidson's insight was to see that if we replace 'means that' in the above sentence with 'is true if and only if', we will get the T-sentences that Tarski showed how to prove. And Tarski did this by showing how the truth of sentences was systematically determined by the semantic properties of their parts. By employing Tarski's theory of truth as a theory of meaning, Davidson put flesh on the skeletal idea that to give the meaning of a sentence is to give the conditions under which it is true. (*Truth-conditions.)

But how does Davidson's theory account for the phenomena Frege explained by employing the notion of sense? Giving truth-conditions alone will not do this—since 'Orwell wrote 1984' and 'Blair wrote 1984' have the same truth-conditions. Davidson replies that it is one thing to construct a formal theory that shows how the semantic properties of whole sentences are systematically formed from the semantic properties of their parts; it is another thing to establish how such a theory applies to individual speakers. The latter task is to provide an *interpretative* Tarskian truth-theory. In applying a truth-theory to a speaker, we must apply the constraints of a theory of radical interpretation, notably the 'principle of charity': assume that on the whole speakers are speaking the truth. Interpretation then proceeds as follows: collect the sentences that a speaker 'holds true', and devise a

truth-theory that has these sentences as a formal consequence. To respect the intensionality of meaning, we need a theory that proves sentences like '"Orwell wrote 1984" is true if and only if Orwell wrote 1984', and not '"Orwell wrote 1984" is true if and only if Blair wrote 1984'. But the *theory* that proves the interpretative T-sentences will be purely extensional.

For Davidson, belief and meaning are interdependent—one of the lessons he draws is that nothing can genuinely have beliefs unless it also has a public language. Many philosophers have recoiled from this, both because they think that it is undeniable that certain non-linguistic creatures—such as dogs and apes—do have beliefs, and because they hope that meaning may yet be explained in terms of, or ultimately reduced to, the contents of mental states. One influential proposal is that of H. P. Grice, who suggested that the meanings of sentences can be reduced to a speaker's intention to induce a belief in the hearer by means of their recognition of that intention.

Although Grice's programme is not as popular as it once was, the general idea of reducing meaning to the psychological states of speakers is now widely accepted (*pace* Davidson, Wittgenstein, and their followers). This is illustrated by the fact that, at the time of writing, the philosophy of language has to some extent yielded the centre stage to the philosophy of mind—and the problem of meaning has become the problem of intentionality.   T.C.

*cognitive meaning; communication; emotive and descriptive meaning; focal meaning; implicature; indeterminacy of meaning; linguistic acts; phrastic and neustic; picture theory of meaning; language, problems of the philosophy of; use and meaning.

Donald Davidson, *Inquiries into Truth and Interpretation* (Oxford, 1984).
Gottlob Frege, *Collected Papers* (Oxford, 1984).
H. P. Grice, 'Meaning', *Philosophical Review* (1957).
A. W. Moore (ed.), *Meaning and Reference* (Oxford, 1993).
W. V. Quine, *Word and Object* (Cambridge, Mass., 1960).
Ludwig Wittgenstein, *Philosophical Investigations* (Oxford, 1953).

meaning, cognitive: *see* cognitive meaning.

meaning, emotive and descriptive: *see* emotive and descriptive meaning.

meaning, focal: *see* focal meaning.

meaning, picture theory of: *see* picture theory of meaning.

meaning of life: *see* life, meaning of.

means: *see* ends and means; instrumental value.

measurement. An empirical procedure for ascertaining the *magnitude of a given quantitative property possessed by an object. Objects are measured on a scale, which assigns a unique numerical value to each magnitude of the quantitative property. The same quantitative property may be measured on different scales, and by different procedures. Thus length can be measured in either feet or metres, with a ruler or by triangulation. Scales are typically (but not always) defined by selecting a standard whose magnitude becomes the unit, 1. Other objects are then measured by determining how many times greater their magnitude is than that of the standard. An object found to be five times longer than the standard metre measures five metres. Sometimes scales are defined in terms of other scales, as with the cubic metre scale of volume. In that case, the quantitative property is measured by measuring the quantities in terms of which the scale was defined and then calculating. The metre and cubic metre scales are called ratio scales, since numerical ratios among the scale values represent quantitative ratios among the magnitudes represented by those values. If the numerical value assigned to A is twice the numerical value assigned to B, then A is twice as long or twice as large as B. Many important scales of measurement lack this property, such as the Fahrenheit and Celsius scales of temperature, and the Mohs scale of hardness. A 60° day is not twice as hot as a 30° day. Measurement in general has been crucial to scientific and technological progress, which in turn has increased phenomenally the precision and range of measurement. W.A.D.

*number.

N. R. Campbell, *An Account of the Principles of Measurement and Calculations* (London, 1938).

B. Ellis, *Basic Concepts of Measurement* (Cambridge, 1966).

mechanism. In the philosophy of mind, the doctrine that we are machines. Descartes held that other animals are machines, but only to emphasize his own view that human beings are not machines because they have *minds, which he supposed to be non-physical. The idea that human beings are machines was later urged by La Mettrie. Some form of this idea is widely accepted today. But decisions must be made about how to understand it, and there is resistance to it for other reasons than a commitment to *dualism.

Leibniz argued in a famous passage that 'perception, and what depends on it, cannot be explained mechanically'. For 'if we imagine a machine whose construction ensures that it has thoughts, feelings, and perceptions, we can conceive it to be so enlarged . . . that we could enter it like a mill. On that supposition, when visiting it we shall find inside only components pushing one another, and never anything that could explain perception' (*Monadologie*, sect. 17). Such reasoning can seem very persuasive, but it begs the question. Leibniz just *assumes* that 'components pushing one another' could not amount to the machine's thinking, feeling, or perceiving. Of course the assumption is easily made. Even mechanists concede that it is difficult to acquire even a faint idea of how a machine might have thoughts and feelings. The difficulty is all the greater if our conception of machinery is restricted to

hydraulic and clockwork systems. However, if Leibniz had known about *computers he would at least have wanted to supplement his argument.

The mathematical and logical thinking which contributed to the design and construction of computers also produced the basis for a definition of mechanism. According to the 'Church–Turing thesis' any mechanical process can be modelled by means of a certain kind of abstract system known as a *Turing machine, and therefore by any equivalent system, such as a computer program. So we might define mechanism as the view that the workings of human beings exemplify computer programs. It is now clear that decisions have to be made. We are, after all, very complex systems, whose 'workings' may be considered from different points of view and at different levels of description and explanation. Assuming we are purely physical systems, we are composed of swarms of elementary particles. But these particles are organized into atoms, and these into molecules. The molecules in their turn make up the organs and other components of our bodies. You might assume that if our workings exemplify computer programs at some level of description and explanation, they must do so at the other levels as well. But conceivably the behaviour of the elementary particles does not exemplify a program (as in effect we learn from *quantum mechanics) while the behaviour of the bodily organs does. If so, our workings—like those of computers themselves—are in the relevant sense mechanical at some levels of description but not at others. It seems that any variety of mechanism needs to be relativized to a level of description and explanation.

An extreme variety might claim that we instantiate computer programs whose basic data represent the beliefs and desires of everyday psychology. That used to be the claim of some *artificial intelligence enthusiasts. The practical difficulties of that approach are now fairly well known. One interesting theoretical objection, tenaciously developed by J. R. Lucas but widely attacked, has been that *Gödel's theorem implies that human logicians can do things which would be impossible if we instantiated such programs. R.K.

*determinism; determinism, scientific; freedom and determinism; mental reductionism.

M. A. Boden (ed.), *The Philosophy of Artificial Intelligence* (Oxford, 1990).

D. R. Hofstadter, *Gödel, Escher, Bach* (New York, 1979).

J. R. Lucas, 'Minds, Machines, and Gödel', repr. in R. Anderson (ed.), *Minds and Machines* (Englewood Cliffs, NJ, 1964).

A. M. Turing, 'Computing Machinery and Intelligence', repr. in R. Anderson (ed.), *Minds and Machines* (Englewood Cliffs, NJ, 1964).

medical ethics. The study of ethical problems in medicine using the concepts, theories, literature, and techniques of moral philosophy. The phrase is used also to refer to the ethical beliefs or habits of behaviour of doctors and nurses, or to explicit codes governing professional behaviour, such as the International Code of the World Medical

Association. The subject has burgeoned since the 1960s into what amounts to an independent discipline, with its own specialists, centres, and journals. Many medical students are now exposed to at least some medical ethics education.

Much medical ethics involves the deployment of philosophical moral theories in an attempt to solve medical ethical problems. This is useful not only in promoting understanding of the problem and possible solutions, but in elucidating and developing the theories themselves. For example, consider one of the many life-and-death issues which have come to dominate medical ethics: paternalism. A utilitarian philosopher who believes that welfare should be maximized might be tempted to suggest that a doctor should do whatever she believes to be in her patient's best interests. But when she realizes that her theory may allow the doctor completely to ignore the patient's wishes, she may attempt to incorporate the value of autonomy into her theory, perhaps as part of welfare.

Over recent years, antipathy towards ethical theory in an abstract and systematic form (so-called anti-theory) has come to influence some writers in medical ethics, who tend to place weight less on the application of principles than on careful and sensitive appreciation of the particular case. It is worth noting also that pluralistic positions are available, combining, say, a utilitarian principle requiring medical personnel to do the greatest good for their patients with a Kantian principle setting various constraints on maximization. For example, transplant surgeons might be required to do the greatest good, but not at the price of forcibly violating the bodily integrity of involuntary 'donors'. These issues are discussed in great depth in the work of Frances Kamm and Jeff McMahan.

The teaching of medical ethics, especially in the USA, has been dominated by a pluralistic position: the four principles of Beauchamp and Childress—autonomy, non-maleficence, beneficence, and justice. One standard objection to the Beauchamp and Childress position applies to pluralistic views more generally: in cases of conflict, unless we are to advocate some kind of *incommensurability, we must make some decision, and can that decision not itself be seen as an articulation of a higher-order principle? And, if so, is there not a highest-order principle? Further, while it is true that the four principles are useful in alerting medical students to the various values at stake in ethical dilemmas, it is equally important that emphasis in teaching be placed on the character or virtues involved in everyday 'good practice'.

Other life-and-death issues commonly discussed include *abortion and *euthanasia. Utilitarians have found it difficult to show why infanticide, on their view, can be any worse than abortion. The abortion debate has revolved around the partly Kantian question whether the foetus is a *person with *rights. Some have argued that the status of the foetus as a *potential* person is important here. At the other end of life, similar theoretical issues arise. If I have a right to life, can I waive it voluntarily, enabling a doctor to administer a lethal dose if I am in the terminal stages of some illness? Should we administer such doses to decrease overall suffering? These questions have become more urgent as medical life-preserving technology has advanced.

Advances in reproductive technology have also raised several significant issues. Many people have seen techniques such as *in vitro* fertilization for infertility as the first step on a slippery slope to a Brave New World. The nature of the family has also been thrown into doubt: why should a homosexual couple or a single person not bring up a child created using reproductive technology? Is it acceptable that a child might have three 'mothers' (genetic, birth, nurturing)? Genetics too has thrown up many problems, concerning, for example, genetic screening or the genetic modification of non-human animals for xenotransplantation.

Other topics concern the everyday practice of health care personnel more directly. Positions taken on confidentiality, for example, again arise from differences at the level of ethical theory. A Kantian may argue that the promise implied in the contract between doctor and patient forbids any breach of confidentiality for the benefit of others or the patient herself. Or a utilitarian may point to the harm which might occur if people were no longer able to trust doctors, thus supplying a welfare-based ground for the practice of respecting confidentiality. Finally, a philosopher attracted to the *virtues might stress the importance of confidentiality in the relationship of trust between the patient and the doctor.

The main political issue discussed in medical ethics is the allocation of resources. A popular notion here is the QALY (quality-adjusted life-year), which represents an attempt to make length or quantity of life commensurate with its quality. Thus a year of healthy life is said to be worth 1, while a year of rather poor health might be worth only 0.5. The QALY theory most often used is essentially a health-maximizing version of *utilitarianism. It therefore runs into the same problems as most versions of utilitarianism: its conception of what is to be maximized, and how, is dubious, and it ignores fairness.   R.CRI.

*Applied ethics; bioethics.

T. Beauchamp and J. Childress, *Principles of Biomedical Ethics*, 5th edn. (New York, 2001).

H. T. Engelhardt, *The Foundations of Bioethics* (Oxford, 1986).

K. W. M. Fulford, Donna L. Dickenson, and T. H. Murray (eds.), *Healthcare Ethics and Human Values: An Introductory Text with Readings and Case Studies* (Oxford, 2002).

J. Glover, *Causing Death and Saving Lives* (Harmondsworth, 1977).

F. Kamm, *Morality, Mortality*, vol. 2: *Death and Whom to Save from It* (New York, 1993).

J. McMahan, *The Ethics of Killing: Problems at the Margins of Life* (New York, 2002).

P. Singer, *Rethinking Life and Death: The Collapse of our Traditional Ethics* (New York, 1994).

medicine, philosophy of. The philosophical, as distinct from the ethical and historical, problems in and around medicine are not largely discussed. There are fragments in

Greek and Arabic writings, but in recent years there have been surprisingly few philosophical, as distinct from ethical, writings on medicine. Yet the philosophical problems of medicine are of great interest, because they include most of those discussed within the philosophy of science and the philosophy of social science, with the added twist that they occur in a distinctive context. Without claiming to cover every area of philosophical interest, I shall briefly mention four problems.

First, there are problems of a kind familiar in the philosophy of science. For example, 'evidence-based medicine' has become a slogan in medical circles. But what is the nature of the evidence? The evidence often cited as the 'gold standard' is that of randomized control trials. Yet such trials are largely statistical correlations of treatments with percentage success rates using volunteer patients who may not be at all typical. Again, the evidence in diagnosis, in identifying the patient's medical problem, is quite different from that in control trials, being more like that used by a detective. And of course familiar problems of realism versus anti-realism arise if we ask 'What is disease?' Secondly, much medical research is qualitative, involving questionnaire-based inquiries into concepts such as 'quality of life'. The problem which arises here is over the attempt to quantify and produce measurement scales for such inquiries. These are problems in the philosophy of social science. Thirdly, there are problems of personal identity thrown up by genetics. How far are my personal traits determined by my genotype? Finally, there are problems of the acceptable limits of medicine. It used to be a set of techniques for repairing the human body when it broke down, but there are some who hold that it has the potential to make us immortal. The charm of the philosophy of medicine is that its problems are at the cutting edge of science, but these problems must be discussed from a humanistic perspective which prevents them from becoming dry abstractions. R.S.D.

R. S. Downie and Jane Macnaughton, *Clinical Judgement: Evidence in Practice* (Oxford, 2001).

Carl Elliott, *A Philosophical Disease: Culture, Identity and Bioethics* (New York, 1998).

medieval philosophy. Histories of medieval philosophy tend to start with St Augustine (354–430), if not earlier; but Augustine was of the late Roman Empire, centuries before the Middle Ages, and is included in such books not because he was a medieval thinker but because he cast such a long shadow across medieval philosophy. He provided a role model in that he thought deeply, systematically, and in a philosophical way about Christianity. He was familiar with the writings of the philosophers of Greece and Rome, particularly the Stoics and the Neoplatonic schools, and put that knowledge to work in the elucidation of fundamental concepts such as those of God, eternity, time, good and evil, and creation. The first great philosopher of the Middle Ages, St Anselm of Canterbury (1033–1109), was deeply influenced by him, and St Thomas Aquinas (1224/5–74) cited him

far more often than he cited any other of the Church Fathers.

Like St Augustine the medieval thinkers philosophized because they wished to understand Christianity. Indeed Anselm's famous phrase *fides quaerens intellectum* (faith seeking understanding) is a perfect description of the philosophy written in the Christian West throughout the Middle Ages. A major part of their task of clarification involved demonstrating that Christianity is not incompatible with what can be demonstrated by reason. The doctrine of *double truth, particularly associated with Averroës, which declares that a truth of faith can be incompatible with truths sanctioned by reason, made very little impact upon thinkers in the Christian West. For them it was crucially important to establish that Christianity was not incompatible with any proposition demonstrated by philosophy. For a proposition thus demonstrated must be true and anything incompatible with the truth is false.

At the start of the period Aristotle's works had been unknown except for a few treatises (fewer than was realized at the time since two treatises attributed to him were spurious, the *Theology of Aristotle*, which is really part of Plotinus' *Enneads*, and the *Book of Causes*, which is an Arabic epitome of Proclus). As time passed more of Aristotle's writings became available, reaching the Christian West from the Muslim world, often accompanied by detailed and profound commentaries by Muslim thinkers such as al-Fārābī (died *c*.950), Avicenna (980–1037), and Averroës (1126–98). These texts with their Arabic commentaries were promptly translated into Latin. Averroës' interpretation of Aristotle was so influential that philosophers of the Christian West referred to him simply as 'the Commentator'. And since Aristotle's was the system to which every philosopher and theologian had to react (indeed he was referred to almost universally simply as *philosophus*—the Philosopher), the crucial question tackled was not whether Christianity and philosophy were compatible, but whether Christianity and Aristotelian philosophy were compatible. For the most part the answer given was affirmative. When, as rarely happened, it was not, then of course Aristotle's position had to be rejected.

Much the most important point of conflict concerned Aristotle's analysis of motion in the *Physics* and *Metaphysics*, which led him to conclude that the world was eternal. Many medieval philosophers, believing that the world had a beginning in time, found it necessary to argue against Aristotle's arguments. It should be noted that most did not attempt to prove that the world did have a beginning in time. A consensus formed round the opinion that the question whether it was eternal or had a temporal beginning was not philosophically demonstrable, and that the doctrine was to be accepted on faith, being the plain meaning of the first sentence of Genesis. Some indeed held that Aristotle did not think that he had demonstrated the eternity of the world but had merely presented the doctrine as a probable opinion. On that interpretation the standard interpretation of Genesis 1:1 was compatible with Aristotle's teaching. Aquinas was one major figure

AVICENNA is the Latinized name by which the Persian Ibn Sina is known in the West; he was the most brilliant of the Islamic Aristotelians and a leading figure in the vigorous debate which accompanied the development of Islamic philosophy and theology in the fifth century after Muhammad.

THOMAS AQUINAS, born and educated in southern Italy, became the greatest teacher of the Dominican monastic order. In the mid-thirteenth century he developed Aristotle's legacy into an exhaustive, rigorously argued philosophical and theological system.

ROGER BACON was the first great Oxford philosopher; he enlisted scientific method in philosophical and theological enquiry.

DUNS SCOTUS was called Doctor Subtilis for his subtle reconciliation of Aristotelian philosophy with the doctrines of the Franciscan monastic tradition.

who held that the eternity of the world was neither provable nor disprovable. His teacher, Albert the Great, held, to the contrary, that Aristotle's position on this matter was false, and that the doctrine that the world had a beginning in time could be demonstrated.

There is a common belief that the problem of *universals is *the* philosophical problem of the Middle Ages. It should be said that that belief, in any case exaggerated, does not address the fact that the problem of universals is not one problem but a large cluster of problems. And indeed problems about universals have always been centre-stage in the history of philosophy; and universals are as much an issue now as they have ever been. Nevertheless, the fact remains that a philosopher's position on whether certain entities were mind-independent (in which case they had real existence, the solution of 'realists') or were mind-dependent (in which case they had nominal existence, the solution of 'nominalists') entered into the interstices of many debates.

One problem concerning universals was this: granted that several individual things have a common nature as a result of which they are members of the same species, what is the mode of existence of this common nature? Does it exist in the individuals that have the nature? Those, for example Wyclif, who replied affirmatively are realists. But there are difficulties associated with this position. For example, if the universal doghood, which must be in an animal if the animal is a dog, is in fact in a given animal, then how can it also be in another animal? Must the universal be divided in two for it to be in a second animal? If so then it surely follows that since each of these animals has only half the universal in it, each must be only half a dog—which is an absurd conclusion. Realists had a problem explaining how a universal can really be in many things at once. Yet they must say that a universal can be in many things at once, for if it cannot, then it cannot be universal. The chief alternative proposal to realism is this, that a universal is the concept that we form under which we can bring all the things in that species, as the nominalists (or conceptualists) such as Ockham thought. On this account the universality of a universal lies in the fact that the concept thus formed is equally predicable of many things. There is a direct line of descent to Ockham's position from that of Abelard, who argued famously that common natures are really utterances (*voces*) or mental entities. For both Abelard and Ockham the doctrine of universals had a central role in the theory of predication.

A version of the debate between realists and nominalists was conducted in the Middle Ages in connection with the existence of values. Does God command us to perform acts of a given kind because they are in any case good, or is their goodness caused by the fact of God's commanding them? (*Euthyphro problem.) An affirmative answer to the first question implies a realist position, namely that values have a real existence independently of God's will, whereas an affirmative reply to the second question implies a nominalist position, namely that values owe their existence to an act of divine will. This latter doctrine, known as voluntarism, was associated, though inaccurately, with Duns Scotus. Secular versions of not only this, but also many other medieval debates, constitute a large part of the philosophical scene today.   A.BRO.

*Aristotelianism.

A. J. P. Kenny, *Medieval Philosophy* (Oxford, 2005).
D. Knowles, *The Evolution of Medieval Thought*, 2nd edn. (London, 1988).
N. Kretzmann et al. (eds.), *The Cambridge History of Later Medieval Philosophy* (Cambridge, 1998).
A. S. McGrade (ed.), *The Cambridge Companion to Medieval Philosophy* (Cambridge, 2003).

Megarics (4th century BC). The Megarics scorned analogical reasoning ('If it's from like to like, one should consider the things themselves, rather than those like them; if it's from unlike to unlike, the comparison is pointless'), modalities ('Only the actual is possible; e.g. someone who isn't building cannot build'), and predication ('If we predicate to run of a horse, subject and predicate differ. Since they differ, it's wrong to say that a horse runs'; 'What I'm pointing to isn't cabbage. For cabbage existed ages ago. So this isn't cabbage'). So how could wisdom, God, and intellect all be, as the Megarics insisted, good? Simple: they were 'one thing, with many names'.

In ancient times, 'Megaric' was applied only to the school founded by Euclides of Megara in Greece. Much modern scholarship perversely applies the term to others too.   N.C.D.

Gabriele Giannantoni (ed.), *Socratis et Socraticorum Reliquiae* (Naples, 1990), i. 375–483 (= *Elenchos*, vol. XVIII*).

Meinong, Alexius (1853–1920) is one of the most misunderstood and reviled philosophers of recent times. According to a prevalent view, he was a spendthrift metaphysician who delighted in multiplying entities continuously and needlessly. Gilbert Ryle, for example, speaks of him as the 'supreme entity-multiplier in the history of philosophy'. Meinong's fatal mistake allegedly consisted in mistaking the meanings of words for objects. With this distorted perspective, his importance derives entirely from the fact that he forced Russell, Wittgenstein, Ryle, and later English philosophers to realize that *meanings are not objects. But this conception of Meinong's philosophical importance is quite mistaken.

Meinong attended the University of Vienna in the fall of 1870 and graduated in the summer of 1874 with history as his major. In the fall of the same year, he entered the law school of the University of Vienna. Soon afterwards, under the guidance of Franz Brentano, he turned to philosophy. In his autobiographical notes, Meinong states that he may have jealously guarded his independence of the forceful personality of Brentano, and that this may have caused misunderstandings between him and his teacher. 'But what in life could not be laid to rest', he concludes, 'in death has been reconciled; and before the inner eye of my memory, there stands once again, as a treasure I shall never lose, my admired teacher, a figure of spiritual beauty, bathed in the golden sunshine of the summer of his own and my youth.' From 1878 until 1882, Meinong was Privatdozent at the University of Vienna. Then he was appointed Extraordinarius of philosophy at the University of Graz, and, later, Ordinarius. He lived and worked for the rest of his life in Graz. The following story, I think, is characteristic of his way of life. When he was repeatedly urged to take a vacation, he finally and very reluctantly consented. He packed a suitcase and moved from his house in Graz to a hotel a few blocks away, where he stayed for two weeks and undoubtedly worked on his philosophy, before he returned to his home!

To understand Meinong's philosophy, it is necessary to see how it develops step by step over many years from an idealistic (Berkeleian) and most austere beginning into a realistic and ample philosophical system. In his earliest publications, the *Hume Studien I* (1877) and *II* (1882), Meinong deals with two thoroughly traditional philosophical problems, the problem of *universals and the problem of *relations. In *Hume Studien I*, Meinong adopts a Berkeleian ontology. An ordinary perceptual object, like Berkeley's apple, is conceived of as a complex of property instances: a certain colour instance, associated with a certain shape instance, associated with a certain taste instance, etc. These *property instances (*individual properties, *abstract individuals), in turn, are associated with a place and a moment. A complex is individuated, according to Meinong, by these places and moments. The property instances themselves are both particular and universal: if they are viewed, through acts of abstraction, in isolation from the places and moments, they are universal; if viewed as associated with places and moments, they are particular. This is Meinong's early solution of the nominalism–realism problem. Finally, all of these complexes of property instances are identified, in Berkeley's fashion, with complex presentations, that is with mental entities.

This view calls for a closer inspection of the relations required by an ontology of complexes. This is the topic of *Hume Studien II*. Here Meinong discusses the three relations involved in complexes. Firstly, there is the relation of equality among instances which guarantees that property instances can be grouped in the required way. Where a realist speaks of two things as sharing the same property, Meinong speaks of two numerically different but equal property instances. Secondly, there is the relation of association which binds the various instances together into a complex. And thirdly, there is the part–whole relation between an instance and the complex to which it belongs. This relation corresponds in Meinong's scheme of things to predication. The great achievement of the *Hume Studien II* consists in Meinong's eventual recognition that there are mind-independent relations. Like Frege and Russell, he thus breaks with a long philosophical tradition, according to which relations are merely the creations of mental acts of comparison.

But even in the *Hume Studien II*, we find the pervasive idealistic confusion between presentations (*ideas) and their objects. However, this confusion does not last long.

Meinong, just like another student of Brentano's, Edmund Husserl, realizes that one must distinguish between the *content of a mental act, on the one hand, and the intention or object of the act, on the other. And just as it does for Husserl, who discovers *phenomenology, this distinction eventually opens up for Meinong a new field of philosophical inquiry, namely, his so-called theory of objects.

In 1894 there appeared a rather slim book by Kasimir Twardowski, another student of Brentano's, which greatly influenced the course of philosophy: *On the Content and Object of Presentations* (tr. R. Grossmann (The Hague, 1977)). In this book, Twardowski argued that the object of a mental act is not 'immanent' in the act, that is, is not a part of the act. He therefore distinguished between the individual mental act, its content, and its object. Even more importantly, Twardowski argued that the question whether or not an act has an object must be sharply distinguished from the question whether or not the object exists. And he held that even though every mental act has an object or intention, many of these objects do not exist at all. Meinong adopts Twardowski's distinction as well as his contention that there are many objects (of acts) which do not exist. By adopting Twardowski's view, Meinong breaks out of the idealistic prison: a presentation, as a mental act with a content, can now be clearly separated from the object which it intends.

At about the same time, 1899, Meinong also realizes that his implicit *ontology is much richer than the explicit one consisting of nothing but property instances combined with places and moments. It comprises also complexes of property instances (or properties) and relations. With this realization, Meinong's eyes are opened to his own and other philosopher's ontological commitments. From now on, Meinong's philosophical inquiries are primarily ontological inquiries.

Meinong's most famous book is called *On Assumptions* (*Über Annahmen*). The first edition appeared in 1902; the second and more important one in 1910. The topic indicated by its title hardly warrants its fame. The discovery of one more kind of mental act is not the most exciting thing in philosophy. But the title is misleading. What Meinong really discovers, and finally fully appreciates in the second edition, is the *category of states of affairs, what he calls 'Objektives'. With the discovery of the category of states of affairs as the intentions of judgements and assumptions, Meinong, just like Husserl, breaks decisively with Brentano's philosophy, according to which only individual things exist.

But Meinong's fame, unfortunately, does not rest on this epochal ontological discovery—think of Wittgenstein's later pronouncement that the world is a collection of facts, not of things—but on Meinong's view about intentional objects and their properties.

Like many recent philosophers, Meinong distinguished between two modes of *being. Let us call them existence and subsistence. Things that are located in space and/or time are said to exist. Things which are not in space and time subsist. For example, individual things exist; the relation of equality between property instances, on the other hand, subsists. Now, it is clear that there are intentional objects before a mind which neither exist nor subsist, for example, the golden mountain of which someone may be thinking. And this raises the important question whether this intentional object has perhaps a third mode of being. The most important argument that speaks for such a further mode of being starts from the fact that there subsists, according to Meinong, the fact (objective) that the golden mountain does not exist. If one assumes that something can only be a constituent of a fact if it has some sort of being, then it follows immediately that the golden mountain must have being of some sort. Or else, it seems, one must reject this principle and assume that something can be a constituent of a fact even if it has no being at all. Meinong discusses this issue extensively and arrives at the conclusion that the principle must be rejected. Of course, one can escape from the apparent dilemma in Russell's way, namely, by showing that the golden mountain is not a constituent of the fact that the golden mountain does not exist. Meinong does not take this way out. But, contrary to a common misunderstanding, he does not hold that the golden mountain has some kind of being.

However, Meinong does hold a view that is highly suspect, namely the view that the golden mountain, even though it has no being, is nevertheless golden and a mountain. Things without being, in short, are held to have certain quite ordinary properties. I think that it is this view which is most characteristic of Meinong's metaphysics. And it is this view which leads him to claim that there is a whole field of inquiry which has been neglected by philosophy, namely, the so-called theory of objects. The golden mountain, for example, is an intentional object of the mind. Now, if it has no properties, as one is apt to assume, then there can be no theory about it, no informative truths would be forthcoming. Only if one assumes, as Meinong does, that such intentional objects have a number of properties, can there be knowledge about them.

In a review (*Mind* (1905)) of one of Meinong's works, Bertrand Russell raises two objections against Meinong's claim that non-existent objects have common properties. Firstly, Russell objects that if impossible objects, like the round square, really had the properties Meinong attributes to them, like being both round and square, then such objects would violate the law of contradiction. Meinong, in reply, readily admits that this is the case, but points out that nobody has ever tried to apply this law to anything but the actual or possible (*Über die Stellung der Gegenstandstheorie im System der Wissenschaften* (Leipzig, 1907)). Contradictory things, in other words, quite obviously must violate the law of contradiction or they would not be what they are. Perhaps Russell thought that his objection had some force because he thought of logic, at that time, not just as applying to what there is, but as encompassing everything.

Russell's second objection, however, is to the point, and Meinong devotes several paragraphs to it. If the round square is really round and square, then the existing round square, according to Russell, must also exist. But this is absurd. The round square does not exist. Meinong tries to escape from this objection by distinguishing between ordinary existence and the 'existential determination' to be existing. The latter, he claims, behaves like an ordinary property in that just as the golden mountain is golden, so the existing golden mountain has the existential determination of being existing. It follows that the existing golden mountain is existing, but it does not exist. In a letter to Meinong, Russell replies that he cannot see how one can distinguish between 'to exist' and 'to be existing'.

It may be thought that Meinong could have avoided Russell's objection without the dubious distinction between existence and to be existing by claiming that existence is not a property like being made from gold or being a mountain. While it is true that the golden mountain is golden and the round square is round, it is not the case that the existing golden mountain exists, since existence is not a property. In a way, Meinong makes this move. He holds that while the golden mountain is golden, the existing golden mountain does not exist. But then he adds the so-called existential determination to be existing, and this addition seems merely to cloud the issue. Why does Meinong think that there is a property which somehow corresponds to existence without being existence? An answer follows from Meinong's acceptance of the so-called principle of unlimited freedom of assumption, according to which one can think not only of a round square, but even of an existing round square. Clearly, to think of an existing round square is not the same as to think of a round square. Therefore, the objects before the mind must be different in these two cases. Meinong has to introduce the existential determination in order to distinguish the one intentional object from the other.

In view of these and other difficulties, why is Meinong so convinced that the golden mountain is made from gold and that the round square is both round and square? Surely, this view is rather implausible, to say the least. I think that he may have been misled by his conception of individual objects as complexes of property instances (or of properties). The complex object which is the golden mountain must obviously consist, among other things, of the property of being golden. Now, if inclusion in a complex is conceived of as predication, then it follows immediately that the complex which is the golden mountain, since it contains the property of being golden, must be golden. Hence one arrives at the view that every complex, no matter what its ontological status may be, must have the properties which constitute it.   R.G.

Meinong's works have been collected in a *Gesamtausgabe*, 7 vols. (Graz, 1968–78). Some of them have been translated into English, e.g. 'Über Gegenstandstheorie', tr. I. Levi as 'The Theory of Objects', in R. M. Chisholm (ed.), *Realism and the Background of Phenomenology* (New York, 1960); also *Über Annahmen*, 2nd edn., tr. J. Heanue as *On Assumptions* (Berkeley, Calif., 1983). Books about Meinong's philosophy:

J. N. Findlay, *Meinong's Theory of Objects and Values* (Oxford, 1963).

R. Grossmann, *Meinong* (London, 1974).

Richard Routley, *Exploring Meinong's Jungle and Beyond* (Canberra, 1980).

Melissus (*fl. c.*440 BC). Metaphysician of the Eleatic group (he also had success as a naval commander). While the ground-plan of his philosophical treatise seems to have followed that of Parmenides, he diverged in significant ways. He freely applied spatial and temporal predicates to his reality, suggesting that it stood closer to the world of ordinary experience. Yet his criticism of sense-perception was much more radical than that of Parmenides: he argued not merely that it is not a means to knowledge, but that it is necessarily illusory.   E.L.H.

*Eleatics.

G. S. Kirk, J. E. Raven, and M. Schofield, *The Presocratic Philosophers*, 2nd edn. (Cambridge, 1983), 390–401.

Mellor, D. H. (1938–). British metaphysician and philosopher of science, noted for his work on chance and probability, dispositional properties and laws of nature, the problem of induction, and the philosophy of *time.

Mellor rejects the dynamic view of time which regards temporal becoming as an objectively real phenomenon. He denies that there are any tensed facts (that is, facts involving pastness or futurity), while conceding that tensed beliefs are not translatable into tenseless beliefs and are indispensable for practical reason and action. According to Mellor it is tenseless facts which make tensed beliefs true, the key to this possibility being the indexical character of tensed expressions like 'now' and 'yesterday'. He endorses McTaggart's argument that tensed language, construed purely realistically, leads to contradiction. Unusually for an adherent of the tenseless view of time, Mellor rejects the doctrine of temporal parts, which holds that persisting objects consist of spatio-temporally continuous and causally connected stages or time-slices. Mellor extends his approach to indexical language to first-person expressions like 'I', as part of an overall metaphysical view which is naturalistic and scientifically informed and yet sceptical of physicalist and reductionist dogmas.

Mellor's approach to issues concerning belief and action, probability and induction, and causality and natural law follows recognizably in the Cambridge tradition of F. P. Ramsey and Richard Braithwaite, whose work he has done much to promote. His Cambridge inaugural lecture, 'The Warrant of Induction' (1988), provides new insight into the solution of an old problem by setting it within the context of an externalist approach to knowledge and warranted belief. This, along with his defence of dispositions and of objective chance in terms of *propensities, marks him off as a metaphysical realist well able to counter the subjectivist and relativist leanings of many other leading philosophers of science.   E.J.L.

D. H. Mellor, *Real Time* (Cambridge, 1981).

—— *Matters of Metaphysics* (Cambridge, 1991).

memory. To have a good memory is to be able to remember many things, accurately and easily. But what is it to remember anything at all? Evidently the past comes in somehow. A creature with no past, assuming such a creature is possible, would have no memories, even if it had some innate knowledge of facts about the past, or vivid and unexplainably accurate images of past events; this follows simply from the logic of the words 'memory' and 'remember'. What one remembers may refer to, though it cannot be in, the future: one can remember that one will die, but not one's own death. But perhaps one can only remember what one previously knew? Certainly this will not be sufficient; a teacher who forgets the things he taught and relearns them later from his pupils is not remembering, even though he not only previously knew what he now knows but only knows it now *because* he knew it previously. A pure causal theory of remembering, then, whereby to remember something is to have known it in the past and to be caused by this to know it now, is not enough. Perhaps one cannot remember a fact without having previously known it, but if I remember to turn the gas out I need only have previously intended to turn it out—I need not have known something; but the previous intention must not be completely irrelevant to my present condition. Some link then is needed, and though causation may not be enough, if we abandon it what can replace it? But if we keep it what form can it take? Perhaps that of some trace in the brain (but see Bursen, *Dismantling the Memory Machine*)?

Memory, especially of past events which we not only previously knew about but experienced, often seems to involve images: in trying to remember something we think we succeed if we can form an *image of it. But how can we distinguish remembering it from imagining it? No property intrinsic to the image itself will do, even if we could find one that belonged to all and only memories (of the relevant kind), for how could such a property tell us that something outside the image (the event in question) was real and not imaginary? It is true that a memory may suddenly come upon us in the form of an image, but it is not the image's vividness that makes it a memory, and when we try to remember something we are not looking for an image to tell us about the past, for how would we know what to look for? Rather we must already know what happened in order to create the image, or vet those images that come before us. To remember an event (as opposed to remembering the fact that it occurred) we must have experienced it, and so perhaps remembering it involves remembering our experiencing of it, which involves somehow reproducing, and how could we reproduce it except by an image? This may be where images are important for memory, but the image still need not constitute the memory. It will probably be both inaccurate and incomplete, and I may know this. The most we can say seems to be that remembering an experience must include having some sort of an image which can be regarded as corresponding to it to some degree.

As the above illustrates, memory is of various kinds. As well as facts, events, people, places, and experiences, one can remember how things looked, where to find them, what to do with them, to do something, and also how to do it; this last (remembering how) has sometimes been singled out for special contrast with another kind involving images (Bergson, Russell), but without much justification, one might think (see Holland, 'The Empiricist Theory of Memory').   A.R.L.

*quasi-memory; mnemic causation.

H. A. Bursen, *Dismantling the Memory Machine* (Dordrecht, 1978).
R. F. Holland, 'The Empiricist Theory of Memory', *Mind* (1954); repr. in S. Hampshire (ed.), *Philosophy of Mind* (New York, 1966). Includes discussion of images.
E. F. Zemach, 'A Definition of Memory', *Mind* (1968) (the misprinted reference to Urmson on p. 535 should be to *Mind* (1967); Urmson replies in *Mind* (1971)).

Mencius (4th century BC). Confucian thinker in China probably best known for his view that human nature is good. His full name was Meng K'o and he was also known as Meng Tzŭ (Master Meng), latinized as Mencius. He defended the ethical and political ideal of Confucius against challenges from rival schools of thought, and his teachings are recorded in the *Meng Tzŭ*, a collection of his sayings and conversations with disciples, friends, rulers, and philosophical adversaries. According to him, all human beings share certain ethical predispositions such as an affective concern for others, a sense of shame, love for parents, and respect for elders. The Confucian ideal is a full realization of such predispositions, and self-cultivation involves nurturing them to make possible their full development.   K.-L.S.

Mencius, tr. D. C. Lau (Harmondsworth, 1970).

Mendelssohn, Moses (1729–86). Jewish *Enlightenment philosopher, a Leibnizian who admired Spinoza and Maimonides, and was the model for Nathan the Wise in Lessing's play of that name. Supplementing his Hebrew education by learning High German, Latin, Greek, French, and English, Mendelssohn won the Berlin competition (1764) in which Kant took honourable mention. His defence of immortality (*Phaedon* (1776)) won him fame. His *Jerusalem* (1783) brilliantly exposes as incoherent the idea of spiritual authority. His German Pentateuch anchored the Jewish Enlightenment (*Haskalah*). His vision of humanity's vocation to unending progress profoundly influenced Kant, who became his lifelong friend. Mendelssohn is credited with distinguishing beauty from metaphysical perfection, arguing that the latter is unity in multiplicity, known in its purity only to God; the former is a human substitute based on our introducing an artificial uniformity into those objects we perceive as wholes. Managing a silk firm and forced by Christian controversialists into extended defences of his loyalty to Judaism, Mendelssohn lost his health, but campaigned heroically against the civil disabilities imposed on Jews, especially the invidious requirements regarding oaths. His son, a banker, raised *his* son Felix as a Christian, composer of the Reformation Symphony.   L.E.G.

Alexander Altmann, *Moses Mendelssohn* (Philadelphia, 1973).

Meno's puzzle: *see* learning paradox.

men's rights: *see* masculism.

mental acts: *see* acts, mental.

mental causation. It is a prevalent view that mental events or states, e.g. desires and beliefs, contribute causally to the bodily movements involved in action. Descartes, holding that mental states are non-material, thought the point of interaction was the pineal gland.

As against this, it is often held nowadays that the notion of non-physical interference is incoherent, since the physical world is a closed system. So Davidson, working with this assumption, has argued that in order for mental states to produce their physical effects they must themselves be physical.

However, dissatisfaction with Davidson's theory arises from three points: (i) Davidson denies the existence of strict *psychophysical laws, (ii) mental states, even if physical, have mental properties, and (iii) mental states explain action in virtue of their mental properties, which should therefore be assigned a causal role. The objection is that Davidson cannot do justice to this last requirement because of (i), and much current debate has turned on the task of trying to resolve this issue.

Some reject (i), holding that there are psychophysical laws, albeit with *ceteris paribus* clauses attached (Fodor)—a view that is challenged by Schiffer. Crane and Mellor reject the physicalist closed-system assumption, arguing that psycho-physical laws are every bit as genuine as the laws of physics. An alternative position (Honderich) holds a *union theory according to which mental and neural states operate together as a pair in causal transactions.

Dretske has a structural-cause theory: he fixes on the mental as a representational property of beliefs and holds that it operates, not as the neural event which triggers an appropriate bodily movement, but as the structuring cause which contributes to the setting-up of appropriate neural-event → bodily-movement connections. Mental causation remains very much a subject of live debate.

                                    O.R.J.

*volition; will.

Donald Davidson, *Essays on Actions and Events* (Oxford, 1980).
John Heil and Alfred Mele (eds.), *Mental Causation* (Oxford, 1993).

mental events. Deciding what counts as a mental event is not easy. The efficacy of tests like the event's being immaterial, subjective, private, or incorrigibly known have been hotly disputed. A *privileged-access criterion seems best for sensations, but not for acquiring intentions, beliefs, or desires. Brentano's criterion of intentionality fares better here. This test requires that certain implications of existence or identity do not follow from attribution of mental events. Falling into Lake Wobegone implies that it exists, but *forming an intention* to find Lake Wobegone does not (nor that it doesn't). Again, hitting Ali implies that I hit Clay (Clay and Ali are identical), not so if I acquire a desire to hit Ali (I might be unaware of the identity). Thus falling and hitting are not mental events; acquiring intentions and desires are.

Having an intention (contrast forming one), or having a belief (contrast acquiring one) are reckoned to be *mental states rather than events, but if the above-mentioned criteria are good for mental events they are good equally for mental states.   O.R.J.

*dualism; functionalism; materialism; physicalism.

Donald Davidson, *Essays on Actions and Events* (Oxford, 1980).

mental indispensability. The claim of mental indispensability or mental efficacy is that reference to mental events is an essential part of any correct full explanation of behaviour and of the occurrence of other mental events. It has seemed plausible to take the contribution of mental events to be causal. In which case, the claim that the mental is indispensable is a recognition of its causal efficacy and is a denial of *epiphenomenalism.   P.J.P.N.

*mental causation.

T. Honderich, *A Theory of Determinism* (Oxford, 1988), ch. 2.

mentality. The attribute of having a mind, but what are minds? As many use the word, the *mind is the *apparatus or mechanism or inner works* which explains how humans are capable of such things as action, rationality, emotion, perception, and imagination. In that sense it has been discovered to be (roughly) the brain or central nervous system, and the remarkable properties of this mind–brain have become the target for the most exciting research projects of our time. Others use the word as a shorthand way of talking of *those capacities and features which qualify us as distinctively human.* Thus there are conceptual debates about the nature and relative importance of rationality, agency, free will, consciousness, social awareness, capacity for abstract thought, and so on. These are elucidations of and suggestions about everyday notions which developed from social interactions in response to practical needs and interests. If listing these qualities gives what makes us human, thereby revealing our mentality, it is *not* the sense in which brain researchers investigate the mental, for they are interested in what makes us human in a causal or theoretical way. Our everyday minds are what they seek to explain by their interesting discoveries about the scientific mind.

In the theoretical or scientific sense, most of us know very little about minds. But in the descriptive or everyday sense, we all know a great deal about them, including and especially our own. Philosophy sometimes just articulates an unwarranted fear of drowning when it seeks to put limits on what brain research could show, but some of its warnings may be salutary. Successive and transient internal models of the scientific mind have been based on available technology, such as clocks, hydraulic robots, telephone exchanges, *computers, and *programs. It is fair criticism to point out when these fall short of simulating human powers. Homing rockets do not exhibit purposes as we do, pocket calculators do not show mathematical intelligence, and so on. Also, by comparing the performance of machines with human performance, we can sharpen our everyday acquaintance with what is involved in the latter. Delineation of everyday mentality is both essential to and aided by the attempt to model how it works.

It is tempting to help the mechanical models out with internal directors or subagents in order to get them to work as explanations of what people do. This is harmless as a linguistic place-holding device, indicating just where more work on the mechanism needs to be done. But it is damaging if the internal operators are transformed into Cartesian *egos, the kind of invisible metaphysical controller which Ryle caricatured as the *ghost in the machine. The trouble is that such things are inaccessible (at least in practice), their form or location being unspecified, and there is a danger of endowing them with the kind of powers the mechanism was introduced to explain, thereby duplicating the explanatory project.

What locks the myth of Cartesian egos into place is that we suppose that our knowledge of our own unscientific minds is yielded by a species of continuous inner perception. Our being conscious, it is easy to think, consists in introspecting what goes on in our thinking, feeling, and willing parts. Then it looks as is if we all have a hot-line either to the Cartesian ego or to the machinery which the brain researchers posit in their latest models. The everyday and the scientific concepts of mind seem to converge, though it will usually be said that we have access only to a small part of our minds, the bit of the electronic iceberg above the surface. As if someone who tells you what is in her mind and the brain researcher who tells you how her mind works are reporting on the same subject-matter (observed, no doubt, from a different 'aspect').

In my view, this perceptual view of consciousness as *introspection is a mistake. When we give our motives, state our beliefs, express how we feel, announce the course of our deliberations, or reveal our imaginings, we are not at all describing our scientific minds 'from a subjective point of view', but providing more evidence about how our everyday minds work. The sense in which everyday thoughts may be revealed or hidden is not the sense in which brain mechanisms may be revealed or hidden, and our interpretation of puzzling behaviour by our friends is not in competition with the explanations of brain researchers. On any view, adjudicating skirmishes at the boundaries between the everyday and the scientific concepts of mentality remains important philosophical work.

                                                              J.E.R.S.

*mind, syntax, and semantics; mind–body problem; mind, problems of the philosophy of; mind, history of the philosophy of; inner sense.

D. C. Dennett, *Brainstorms* (Brighton, 1979).
R. Descartes, *Meditations on First Philosophy* (1642), in many edns. and translations, e.g. E. Anscombe and P. T. Geach, *Descartes: Philosophical Writings* (London, 1954).
G. Ryle, *The Concept of Mind* (London, 1949).

mental reductionism. Reductionism about a given subject-matter *X* is the claim that facts about *X* can be 'reduced' to—that is, can be shown or construed to be—facts about another subject-matter *Y* ('the reduction base'). Reductionism in philosophy of mind is the claim that facts about mentality are reducible to physical facts, i.e. facts about matter and material processes.

What is required to implement mind–body reduction? According to the *dualism of Descartes, minds exist as 'mental substances', objects wholly outside the physical domain. On this view, facts about mentality would be physically irreducible since they would be facts about these immaterial entities. The first requirement for mind–body reduction, therefore, is the renouncement of minds as non-physical objects. This can be done either by identifying minds with brains or other appropriate physical structures, or by refusing to countenance minds as substantival entities and attributing mental properties to organisms and other physical systems. In either case, it is physical systems that have psychological properties.

The remaining step in mind–body reduction concerns mental properties, e.g. being in pain, sensing a green patch, believing that snow is cold, and their analogues in systematic psychology. Let *M* be a mental property: the physical reduction of *M* is usually thought to require a 'physical correlate' of *M*, i.e. a physical property with which *M* is necessarily coextensive. When a pervasive system of physical correlates is found for mental properties, mental properties could, it is thought, be identified with their physical correlates.

*Logical behaviourism sought to reduce mental properties by defining them in terms of behaviours and behavioural dispositions. Although mentality seems intimately tied to behaviour, it is now widely agreed that mental terms resist behavioural definitions. The demise of behaviouristic reductionism has led to the hope that the mental might be physically reduced through empirical laws connecting mental and physical properties. Nomological reduction of mental properties would proceed by providing for each mental property *M* a nomologically coextensive physical property *P*—that is, where '*M* occurs if and only if *P* occurs' holds as a matter of empirical law. According to the *identity theory of mind, every mental property has a neural correlate with which it is to be identified; if pain is uniformly correlated as a matter of law with, say, the activation of c-fibres, pain may be reductively identified with c-fibre activation, and similarly for other mental properties and kinds.

The significance of mind–body reduction is claimed to be twofold: ontological economy and unity of theory. By dispensing with minds as substances of a special sort and their irreducibly psychic features, we simplify our ontology. By construing mental properties as complex neural properties and taking physical organisms as their bearers, psychology can be integrated with the underlying biological and physical sciences.

Two lines of consideration have been responsible for the decline of reductionism. One is psychophysical anomalism, the claim that there are no laws connecting mental and physical phenomena, and hence no laws of the sort required for the nomological reduction of the former to the latter. The other is the *variable (or multiple) realizability of mental properties. If a mental property is multiply realized by a variety of physical properties in diverse species and structures, it could not, the argument goes, be identified with any single physical property. These considerations have led many philosophers to favour non-reductive physicalism (*mind–body problem; *physicalism; *functionalism), the doctrine that although all the individuals of this world are physical, certain properties of these individuals, in particular their psychological properties, are not reducible to physical properties.   J.K.

D. Davidson, 'Mental Events', in *Essays on Actions and Events* (Oxford, 1980).
J. Fodor, 'Special Sciences, or the Disunity of Science as a Working Hypothesis', *Synthese* (1974).
J. Kim, 'The Myth of Nonreductive Materialism', in *Supervenience and Mind* (Cambridge, 1993).
T. Nagel, 'What Is It Like to Be a Bat?', *Philosophical Review* (1974).

mental states. A disputed notion. Many philosophers have held that beliefs, desires, intentions, etc. are real states, but have disagreed profoundly on their nature, some maintaining that they are non-material states (Descartes) and others that they must be physical states if interactions with sense-organs and bodily movements are to be possible. Tough materialists (Churchland) hold that talk of such states will become dispensable in favour of neural descriptions, while others (Dennett) concede the non-reality of mental states but hold that use of psychological terms is indispensable. Ryle held that belief-claims are really claims about *dispositions to behaviour, but Arthur Collins has recently argued they are epistemic risk claims—'I believe that *p*' means '*p* and I am right, or not-*p* and I am wrong'—with no reference to a state involved.

For questions about criteria for mental states, see the entry on mental events. The above disputes extend to the notion of mental events, since most mental events are reckoned to be the arrival or cessation of mental states.

                                                                O.R.J.

*dualism; functionalism; materialism; physicalism.

Arthur Collins, *The Nature of Mental Things* (Notre Dame, Ind., 1987).
Peter Smith and O. R. Jones, *The Philosophy of Mind* (Cambridge, 1986).

mereology. Mereology is the formal theory of part–whole relations, whose early developers included Leśniewski, Tarski, and Goodman. The standard theory regards any whole as identical with the sum of its parts and consequently identifies any two objects containing all and only the same parts. This makes it difficult to accommodate the case of organic wholes, such as living organisms, which can survive the replacement of some of their parts and consequently cannot be identified at any one time with the sum of their concurrently existing parts. However, modal and temporal extensions of the standard theory promise solutions to such difficulties.

The relationship of a whole to its proper parts is importantly different from that of a set to its members, though David Lewis has recently argued that a set may be regarded as the mereological sum of its unit subsets.

E.J.L.

*thing.

D. K. Lewis, *Parts of Classes* (Oxford, 1991).
P. M. Simons, *Parts: A Study in Ontology* (Oxford, 1987).

meritocracy. Any society that creates an élite by suitable rewards based on accomplishments that distinguish some from others is a meritocracy. Thus it has been described as a society characterized by 'careers open to talents' (John Rawls). The aristocracy of merit is thought to be natural, since it is grounded on the exercise of esteem-worthy personal traits. Merit is definable as the superior productivity or performance that results when intelligence is joined with effort, popularized in the formula $I + E = M$ (Michael Young). A meritocracy requires equality of opportunity and some form of central planning; it must prohibit egalitarian levelling as well as any form of nepotism or hereditary aristocracy.

H.A.B.

*aristocracy, natural; conservatism; élites; élitism.

Michael Young, *The Rise of the Meritocracy 1870–2033* (London, 1958).

Merleau-Ponty, Maurice (1907–61). French phenomenologist and co-founder with Sartre of existential philosophy. Merleau-Ponty's constant target was the subject–object *dualism of *Cartesianism, which arguably still continued to dominate Sartre's existentialism. Drawing on Husserl's notion of a pre-predicative *intentionality and on Heidegger's exposition of human existence as being-in-the-world, Merleau-Ponty developed a description of the world as the field of experience in which I find myself. Descartes's Cogito was transformed to read 'I belong to myself while belonging to the world'. Any attempt to constitute the world as an object of knowledge is always derivative in relation to that primary access to the world that Merleau-Ponty located in the body.

Phenomenology of Perception (1945) established Merleau-Ponty as the pre-eminent philosopher of the body. The body is neither subject, nor object, but an ambiguous mode of existence that infects all knowledge. Merleau-Ponty drew on the critical examination of contemporary psychology and physiology presented in his first book, *The Structure of Behaviour* (1942), to argue the primacy of perception. Merleau-Ponty questioned the attempt of traditional philosophy to look to *perception to provide some

guarantees that mark its difference from hallucination. What is given in perception is ambiguous. However, this does not lead to scepticism, any more than does the experience of disillusionment. The discovery that one was the victim of an illusion does not challenge faith in perception altogether. It is only in the name of a new perception that a previous perception is doubted.

Merleau-Ponty distinguished what reflection reveals from what is given in unreflective experience. This led him to the idea of a radical reflection. Radical reflection was Merleau-Ponty's alternative to *analysis, which he consistently criticized. Analytic thought on his view breaks up experience into constituents, for example sensations and qualities, and is thus obliged to invent a power of synthesis in an attempt to rebuild the world of experience. In spite of this, his work has found a more receptive audience among analytic philosophers than other phenomenologists have managed to receive.

Throughout his writings Merleau-Ponty sought ways to explore the body's primordial contact with the world prior to the impact of analysis. In doing so, he was resisting a tendency of contemporary scientific and philosophic thought to valorize autonomous knowledge arrived at under experimental conditions. In the late essay 'Eye and Mind' (1961) Merleau-Ponty turned to painting for evidence of the character of the body's relation to the world, evidence that provides no consolation for those in search of definitive conclusions. A similar conclusion arose from his studies on language that introduced Saussurean linguistics into phenomenology. In the abandoned manuscript 'The Prose of the World' and in the collection of essays *Signs* (1960) Merleau-Ponty challenged the ideal of an algorithmic language.

In *The Visible and the Invisible* Merleau-Ponty introduced the notion of flesh in a new attempt to explore the sense in which the seer is caught up in what he or she sees. Merleau-Ponty had come to recognize his earlier conception of the body as still tied to the dualistic metaphysics he was committed to challenging. For that reason flesh was not presented in opposition either to the mind or to the world, but as an element, much as air and water are elements. Unfortunately, the book was still incomplete at the time of his death. Scholars have had to rely heavily on his working notes in order to assess the extent to which the emphasis on ontology in *The Visible and the Invisible* represents a departure from his earlier phenomenological studies and not just their fulfilment.

R.L.B.

M. Langer, *Merleau-Ponty's Phenomenology of Perception* (Tallahassee, Fla., 1989).
G. B. Madison, *The Phenomenology of Merleau-Ponty* (Athens, Oh., 1981).
E. Matthews, *The Philosophy of Merleau-Ponty* (London, 2002).
M. Merleau-Ponty, *Basic Writings* (London, 2003).

meta-ethics is the philosophical study of the nature of moral judgement. So, instead of being concerned with questions of what actually is right or wrong (or good or bad), it is concerned with the meaning or significance of calling something right or wrong (or good or bad). Since both of these kinds of inquiry can properly be called ethics, the term *meta-ethics* may be used more precisely to denote the latter kind. Meta-ethics includes both the meaning of moral terms and also such questions as whether moral judgements are objective or subjective. It also includes others of the *problems of moral philosophy.   R.H.

> *moral philosophy, history of; emotivism; prescriptivism; moral realism.

metalanguage. The one in which the properties of a language under study, the object language, are stated. The metalanguage may be identical to the object language, as when the grammatical properties of English are stated in English, but it is often distinct from the object language. According to an influential view of Tarski, some semantic properties of a language *L* can be expressed only in a distinct metalanguage, not in *L* itself.   A.GUP.

A. Tarski, 'The Semantic Conception of Truth', *Philosophy and Phenomenological Research* (1944).

metalogic. The mathematical and philosophical study of the components of systems of logic. Examples include rigorous analyses of notions like logical consequence, *deduction, *logical form, *satisfaction, and *denotation. A typical result of metalogic is a *completeness theorem establishing that a model-theoretic notion of consequence is captured by the arguments derivable in a given deductive system.   S.S.

> *logical theory.

Stephen Kleene, *Introduction to Metamathematics* (Amsterdam, 1952).

metaphilosophy. The philosophy of philosophy. Philosophy is the attempt to solve philosophical problems. 'What is philosophy?' is itself a philosophical problem, so metaphilosophy is essentially the attempt to solve that problem.

On metaphysical conceptions of philosophy, philosophy is the attempt to describe reality as opposed to appearance. For example, Plato draws a distinction between the world of *doxa* (belief, opinion) and the world of *epistēmē* (knowledge). The perfect, unchanging *eidea* (Forms, essences) which exist independently of minds and spatio-temporal objects are the true objects of philosophical study. By this picture, Plato reconciled the competing views of his Pre-Socratic predecessors Parmenides, according to whom there is only unchanging being, and Heraclitus, according to whom there is only becoming, or the transition between being and nothingness. Arguably, Augustine's distinction between the city of God and the earthly city, Descartes's distinction between mental and physical substances, Leibniz's postulation of monads, Spinoza's one substance, Schopenhauer's *Wille* and (partly *malgré eux*) Hegel's *Geist* (Spirit) and Heidegger's *Sein* (Being) are metaphysical doctrines in this broad sense.

On anti-metaphysical conceptions of philosophy, knowledge of reality is impossible, either because of the constraints of the senses or because it leads to contradictions or because it deploys terminology beyond the limits of significance. Hobbes, Locke, Berkeley, and Hume, in very different ways, regard knowledge as constrained by possible sense perception. Kant thinks the attempt to do metaphysics generates seemingly valid pairs of arguments with mutually exclusive conclusions called 'antinomies'.

Since Kant, philosophy has operated within a Kantian anti-metaphysical paradigm. Because metaphysical philosophy is allegedly impossible, attempts have been made to replace it by something else: the overthrow of capitalist society (*Marxism), the description of appearances (*phenomenology), natural science (*Logical Positivism), the description of conceptual schemes (*structuralism), the analysis of the meanings of ordinary language (*linguistic philosophy), literary criticism (*post-structuralism).

In medieval Christian, Jewish, and Islamic philosophy the true object of study is *God. However, faith and *revelation are needed because the powers of the finite human intellect are inadequate tools of theological understanding.

Non-Western philosophy exhibits the same tension between metaphysics and anti-metaphysics. The inconsistencies between, say, Taoism and Confucianism, or Tibetan Buddhism and Indian materialism, are at least as difficult to reconcile as those between, say, Plato and Aristotle, Descartes and Hume or Hegel and the Logical Positivists. It is not true that all and only Western philosophy is naturalist and anti-metaphysical and all and only Eastern philosophy is spiritualist and metaphysical.

Whitehead famously said that Western philosophy could be understood as a series of *footnotes to Plato. It is certainly not misconstrued as an oscillation between Platonic metaphysics and Aristotelian naturalism. In philosophy, the twentieth century was an Aristotelian age.   S.P.

A. J. Ayer, *Language, Truth and Logic*, 2nd edn. (Harmondsworth, 1976).

Charles J. Bontempo and S. Jack Odell (eds.), *The Owl of Minerva* (New York, 1975).

Martin Heidegger, *What is Philosophy?*, tr. W. Kluback and J. T. Wilde (New York, 1958).

John Hospers, *An Introduction to Philosophical Analysis* (London, 1997).

Anthony Kenny, *A Brief History of Western Philosophy* (Oxford, 1998).

metaphor. The starting-point for philosophical discussion of metaphor is whether or not metaphors are paraphrasable in literal terms. On what has been called the 'substitution theory' a metaphor is assumed to stand in for a literal equivalent. The metaphor 'Achilles is a lion' can be teased out to give 'Achilles is like a lion in respect of the following features . . .'. However, after Max Black's influential paper in which he proposed what he called an 'interaction' theory, philosophers have become acutely aware of the way in which different hearers or readers pick out different common features between the terms of a metaphor. Metaphors are interpreted and they are interpreted differently by different readers and hearers. Consequently, the idea that there can be a literal paraphrase of a metaphor which preserves its sense is no longer widely held, for such a literal paraphrase would have to command common agreement as expressing what the metaphor means. A powerful metaphor like Macbeth's 'sleep that knits up the ravell'd sleave of care' invites us to join in an exploration of points of similarity and difference. Black, in a later paper, speaks of metaphors as 'inciting the hearer' and likens the process to game-playing. Since this also characterizes the understanding of similes, few writers would now make a sharp distinction between metaphor and simile.

Black argued that when we read a metaphor like 'Achilles is a lion', we read it armed with a number of commonplace beliefs about 'lion'; these, metaphorically applied to Achilles, we draw on as we construe it. In Claudius' line in Shakespeare's *Hamlet*, 'When sorrows come, they come not single spies, but in battalions', we may reflect that spies threaten and undermine, carrying the fear of worse to follow; battalions, on the other hand, embody open aggression.

One interesting recent contribution in a philosophical debate that goes back to Aristotle is Donald Davidson's rejection of the idea that there is a special sort of *meaning which metaphors have, over and above the literal meaning. Taken literally metaphors seem nonsensical or false or only trivially true. For Davidson, it is the use of metaphor which is crucial, in making us aware of some likeness, often surprising, between apparently disparate things but without asserting that likeness.

Metaphors are the growing-points of *language. A cursory glance shows just how much of the language of mind is metaphorical in origin. These metaphors die, of course, and lose their metaphorical force though their origins may be still visible. In recent decades, philosophers have, as well, become more aware of the role played by metaphor in science and religion.   R.A.S.

D. E. Cooper, *Metaphor* (Oxford, 1986).

Andrew Ortony (ed.), *Metaphor and Thought*, 2nd edn. (Cambridge, 1993).

metaphysics, history of. Metaphysics is the most abstract and in some views 'high-falutin' part of philosophy, having to do with the features of ultimate reality, what really exists and what it is that distinguishes that and makes it possible. Nevertheless, the exact nature of the subject has been constantly disputed, as indeed has its validity and usefulness.

Philosophy at its very beginnings with the Pre-Socratics was metaphysical in character, although it was initially presented in a dress which made it sound more like physics, as witness Thales' claim that everything is made of water. Subsequent Pre-Socratics were concerned with other attempts to understand nature and the possibility of change within it, although Parmenides argued (for the

first time by means of a formal argument, even if that was given a poetical dress) that coming to be, ceasing to be, and change in general were impossible, so that his successors had to counter his claim, even if they did not fully understand his arguments. By the time of Plato, with his theory that the true realities were Forms (or Ideas), abstract exemplars or paradigms, of which sensible things were only imperfect copies, the distinction of metaphysics from physics became clear, since these realities were quite distinct from the world with which physics has its concern. Since the Forms were also universal in character his theory also initiated metaphysical arguments concerning the status of *universals, something that has gone on ever since.

The *term* 'metaphysics' originated, however, as a title given to some of Aristotle's works in the catalogue of the edition of them produced by Andronicus of Rhodes in the second half of the first century BC (although it may have come from an earlier library classification). It meant simply the works which followed those on physics in the catalogue. But those works, which were concerned with being, both as such and in respect of various *categories of it, especially *substance, contain discussions concerning matters which have an obvious continuity with later metaphysical theories. Hence it is reasonable to see Aristotle's *Metaphysics*, untidy though it is in the form in which it has come down to us, as the first systematic treatise in metaphysics, containing not only discussions of the notion of being and what has the best claim to that title but also criticisms of earlier thought on the subject, particularly Plato's Theory of Forms. Those Forms are soundly rejected. Aristotle believes in universals, certainly, but they are features of the world itself, which is made up of things with *essences, belonging to a system organized in terms of genera and species. The notion of species corresponds to that of *form as Aristotle construes that, but material things have not only form but *matter too. Among beings, which Aristotle thought were classifiable in terms of a system of categories, things in the category of substance have the greatest claim to that title, and among them those which are nearest to being pure form. God, whose nature is, in Aristotle's view, pure form, is the highest kind of substance, and thus the highest kind of being, so that what it is for something to be is best seen in God, who comprises the end or goal to which other things tend, and who, as the *prime mover, is also the so-called *final cause of the movements of the heavenly bodies.

Post-Aristotelian philosophy saw the world as organized under different principles, though the influence of Aristotle was strong. Epicurus thought that everything, including ourselves, was composed of atoms moving in a void, and was to be explained in those terms. The Stoics, by contrast, thought of matter as forming a continuum, but subject to rational or so-called 'seminal' principles due to *pneuma* (breath or spirit), which gives everything life. Platonism went though many vicissitudes, and at the end of the period of Greek philosophy took a somewhat mystical form in Neoplatonism, led by Plotinus, according to which the Forms are organized under a unitary principle, the One. At the opposite extreme from this is the world of matter, responsible by its negativity for evil. The mystical goal is an identification with the One, but it is a goal to be reached through philosophy, not by any religious process. Nevertheless, Neoplatonic ideas had a considerable influence on religious thinking, including that of Augustine. Plotinus' main disciple, Porphyry, wrote on, amongst other things, the Aristotelian doctrine of categories, saying that the ontological status of species and genera was uncertain, and Boethius, commenting on that, thereby transmitted to later medieval thought the problem of the status of universals, which loomed large throughout that period.

There was considerable argument between schools of thinking about universals in the early Middle Ages, between realists (e.g. William of Champeaux), nominalists (e.g. Roscelin of Compiègne), and conceptualists (e.g. perhaps Abelard, although his position on the issue is not entirely clear), who respectively claimed that what was general was to be found in nature, words only, or thoughts only. With the rediscovery of Aristotle in the thirteenth century, after a period of ignorance of his philosophy in the West, realism about universals became the accepted view, until a revival of nominalism, particularly with William of Ockham, in the fourteenth century. There was, however, a connection between the issues over universals and theological issues, particularly the doctrine of the Trinity. The other main metaphysical concerns of medieval philosophers were similarly theologically orientated—particularly the existence of God and the nature of the soul. Anselm in the eleventh century became famous or notorious for his so-called *ontological proof of the existence of God, maintaining that God's existence followed from the fact that God is that than which no greater can be conceived. The great Thomas Aquinas in the thirteenth century took a more Aristotelian line on the arguments for God's existence, relying in the main on considerations (which owe much to Aristotle) concerning the supposed nature of the world which point to the need to assume the existence of a deity. Aquinas also took, with modifications, an Aristotelian line on the nature of the soul as the form of the body, provoking questions, not easily answered, about how this view was to be reconciled with belief in immortality.

After the Renaissance, during which there was a revival of Platonism, often in other forms of mystical dress, Descartes initiated a change in the approach to philosophy, although preoccupation with scholastic notions such as that of substance remained. Descartes's orientation in philosophy was mainly epistemological in character; it might indeed be said that his metaphysics was founded on epistemological considerations. For the thesis for which he has become known—the radical dualism between mind and body as distinct substances—was founded on the claim that we have a more direct access to (and thereby a clearer and more distinct idea of) our minds than to our bodies. His rationalist successors Spinoza and Leibniz were also very concerned with the *mind–body problem. Spinoza maintained that mind and body were to be construed simply as different aspects of one substance, but that was in a context of argument which was directed to the conclusion that there can be only one substance, God or nature, and that what we are and what happens to us is strictly determined because we are modifications of that one substance. Spinoza thought, nevertheless, that there was a sense to speaking of freedom which lies in an acceptance of the necessity that the determinism entails. Leibniz, by contrast, thought that there was an infinite number of substances, which were simple, though capable of reflecting an infinite number of points of view. He came to think that these substances could only be what he called *'monads', which were simple, like the ego in ourselves. Monads were organized in such a way as to fall under a dominant monad, which was God. Leibniz also held that everything that happened to a substance was necessary to it, but that God created the world of substances according to the principle of *sufficient reason, which made this world the best of all possible worlds. Despite the Spinozistic necessity that this seemed to entail as far as human-beings are concerned, Leibniz thought, but did not convince others, that a form of freedom was still possible.

One might think that the British Empiricists, Locke, Berkeley, and Hume, were, because of the empiricism, mainly epistemologically orientated. This is superficially true of Locke, whose Essay tries to set out the structure and limits of human understanding, but he is concerned with substance, for example, although in a way that owes much to Boyle and contemporary physicists. He also presents a theory of *persons and *personal identity, which has provoked considerable recent interest, and, in his theory of abstract ideas, he sets out once again a conceptualist theory of universals. Berkeley was more nominalistically inclined, and attacked that theory because he thought that it let in a doctrine of material substance to which he was also opposed. In place of the latter Berkeley put forward the view that 'to be is to be perceived', so that the only things that properly exist are ideas (the objects of perception, as he thought) and spirits (which include ourselves and particularly God). Berkeley's theory is thus the first instance of full-blooded *idealism. Of the three British Empiricists, Hume was the most anti-metaphysical, but his doctrine of impressions and ideas in a way continues Berkeley's thinking, and Hume admits at one point that his impressions are in one sense what deserve the title of substances. Ontologically, therefore, Hume regards reality as consisting merely of impressions and corresponding ideas, and he expresses a form of scepticism about both material bodies and self. In both cases we have bundles of impressions and ideas which have a certain constancy and coherence, and it is these characteristics which make us believe, but do not justify such belief, in bodies and the self. It has to be said, however, that Hume thought, with some reason, the resulting position over the self particularly worrying.

It is Kant who stands at the culmination of this, being opposed to what he regarded as the speculative metaphysics handed down by the rationalists, but concerned, as the Empiricists were, with the limits of the human understanding in such a way as to allow more than they had done. Kant accepts a form of idealism, which he called *'transcendental', saying that space and time were merely forms of experience and had no application to what he called *'things-in-themselves', the unknowable reality which he thought must be assumed to underlie and in some way be responsible for experience. Kant's idealism was not, however, merely subjective, as Berkeley's was, in that he sees the *understanding as bringing to bear in judgement certain principles, derived from the *categories or formal concepts which it supplies, in such a way that the forms of objective judgement can be distinguished from merely subjective ones. In particular, Kant thought, objective experience can be seen to involve causality and principles of necessary connection, despite Hume's scepticism on this. All this, a sort of metaphysics of experience, can be regarded as a substitute for traditional metaphysics, which Kant thought of as concerned with God, freedom, and immortality, but as involving an attempt to use reason beyond the boundaries to which it was properly limited. Part of his *Critique of Pure Reason* involves an attempt to show that such improper uses of reason lead to contradictions and the like.

Kant's account of what is necessary about human understanding and the limitations, by comparison, of reason presented a kind of watershed for metaphysics, but philosophers were soon to try to circumvent his conclusions in a variety of ways. Fichte objected to the whole idea of things-in-themselves, arguing that the ego or self actively posits a non-self opposed to it, so that in effect that non-self exists only for the self, while constituting something necessary, an absolute. His idealism is thus the first instance of so-called absolute *idealism. Schopenhauer, on the other hand, thought he could produce good reason for believing that there was only one thing-in-itself and that this was to be identified with will. Both philosophers, however, accepted a form of idealism. The most radical development in that respect was the philosophy of Hegel, who thought that reason could certainly do what Kant thought impossible, leading to the idea of an identification of self and object. This form of absolute idealism was worked out in terms of a system of developing categories, culminating in what Hegel called the absolute notion in which 'Spirit knows itself as Spirit'. Hegel's metaphysical system is both monumental and encyclopaedic in character, claiming to bring all phenomena within its terms of reference. It has been seen as either marvellous or repulsive by different commentators.

There were, of course, reactions to it. *Existentialists, beginning with Kierkegaard, objected that existence precedes essence, and that Hegel's thought left out individuality. This was an objection to the idea that reality could be seen as such only in terms of an all-comprehensive system. Marx, using, at any rate initially, somewhat Hegelian terms, tried to turn the system on its head by insisting on the materialist and social basis of all thought and thereby of reality. Hegelian thought had a late influence in England towards the end of the nineteenth century, particularly in F. H. Bradley, although he objected to the more systematic aspects of Hegel's thought. To his *monism (the belief that reality was one) there was in turn a reaction in the *logical atomism of Russell and perhaps the early Wittgenstein, according to which reality involves a plurality of *sense-data, which, like Leibniz's monads, constituted absolute simples. Subsequently, the anti-metaphysical theory of the Logical Positivists, such as Ayer, who, on the basis of the principle that the meaning of a statement is to be found in its method of verification, argued that metaphysical statements were nonsensical, put metaphysics out of fashion, where on many popular views it remains.

In fact, however, it continues, and Strawson's so-called 'descriptive metaphysics', according to which ontological distinctions between individuals or objects of identification are made relative to speaker–hearer discourse, is something of a return to Kant, though without the idealism. Elsewhere in Europe there has been, for example, Heidegger's anti-scientific concern with the nature of being and with *Dasein* or presence in the world. This presence is of a kind that only human individuals have, and Heidegger saw it as having an intimate connection with time, on a view of time which sees it as having fundamentally to do with the ideas of past, present, and future, and not simply temporal relations between events. These alternative conceptions of time have been a central issue in Anglo-Saxon metaphysics too, ever since the Cambridge Hegelian McTaggart argued, early in the twentieth century, that time must, essentially, have to do with past, present, and future (or, as it is sometimes put, 'tense') and that, because every event is all three and thus in possession of incompatible attributes, time is unreal. To the objection that events have all three attributes at different times, McTaggart argued that this only produced an infinite regress. Different philosophers have drawn different morals from these claims, including the moral that time must fundamentally have nothing to do with 'tense'. It is equally arguable that the correct conclusion is that the 'tensed' point of view is indispensable to an account of reality and that it is the attempt to do without it in characterizing reality that causes the trouble. Heidegger has his own and different reasons for emphasizing a 'tensed' conception of time, in that he is concerned to bring out what presence in the world, in his sense, entails—in particular that it must have its end in death, when time ends for us.

In other quarters again, particularly in the USA and Australia, an emphasis on science has produced its own scientistic metaphysics, according to which only supposedly scientific characterizations of reality will do. Such views not only reject the kind of 'tensed' conceptions of time which I have noted above, but also underplay the kinds of point of view that are arguably involved in selfhood and thereby in any reality which involves selves.

Such a metaphysics tends inevitably to be materialist, though not necessarily in the kind of way in which Marxian thought is materialist. It is simply assumed that all that exists in the end is particular incidences of matter in motion and that what seems at first not to be that is in fact identical with some form of it. Nevertheless, although Cartesian *dualism is widely rejected as a great mistake as well as a great obstacle to the successful development of philosophy, the pressures deriving from what led to that dualism in the first place—the first-person point of view—remain, and are emphasized by some philosophers, e.g. Thomas Nagel. And so it goes on.   D.W.H.

*descriptive metaphysics; materialism; modality and metaphysics; opposition to metaphysics; revisionary metaphysics.

D. W. Hamlyn, *Metaphysics* (Cambridge, 1984).
—— *The Penguin History of Western Philosophy* (London, 1987).
A. J. P. Kenny, *Ancient Philosophy* (Oxford, 2004), ch. 6.
——*Medieval Philosophy* (Oxford, 2005), ch. 6.
Jonathan Lear, *Aristotle: The Desire to Understand* (Cambridge, 1988).
T. L. S. Sprigge, *Theories of Existence* (Harmondsworth, 1984).
Ralph C. S. Walker, *Kant* (London, 1978).
Margaret D. Wilson, *Descartes* (London, 1978).

metaphysics, opposition to. Opposition to metaphysics has come from both within philosophy and outside it. *Logical Positivism, though now defunct, was particularly hostile to what its adherents saw as the meaningless, because unverifiable, claims of metaphysics. These objections foundered on the impossibility of providing an acceptable criterion of *verifiability. But the deference to empirical science displayed by the Logical Positivists is still a feature of much Anglo-American analytic philosophy, creating an intellectual climate inimical to the pursuit of speculative metaphysics. This hostility is paralleled in the popular writings of many scientists, who seem to think that any legitimate issues once embraced by metaphysics now belong exclusively to the province of empirical science—issues such as the nature of *space and *time, and the mind–body problem. Such writers are often blithely unaware of the uncritical metaphysical assumptions pervading their works and the philosophical naïvety of many of their arguments. But it is ironic that the deference shown by many philosophers to the latest scientific theories is not reciprocated by the popularizing scientists, who do not conceal their contempt for philosophy in general as well as metaphysics in particular.

More recent hostility to metaphysics comes from the post-modernists and deconstructionists, who wish to proclaim that philosophy—and certainly metaphysics—is dead. These writers represent metaphysics as a temporary aberration of the Western intellect, denying the notion that it is a pursuit of perennial questions for which timeless answers may legitimately be sought. Of course, these critics of metaphysics, in repudiating any objective conception of truth in favour of a fashionable cultural relativism, can make no common cause with the scientific critics, whose quite contrary assumption is that science provides the royal road to objective truth and ultimately to a final 'Theory of Everything'. With enemies so divided amongst themselves, metaphysics may comfort itself with the thought that so many people can't be right. The very fact of such widespread disagreement over fundamentals demonstrates the need for critical and reflective metaphysical inquiry, pursued not dogmatically but in the spirit of Kant.

Despite all this hostility, metaphysics and *ontology are currently enjoying a modest revival amongst professional philosophers, who are no longer embarrassed to discuss such issues as the nature of substance and to advance realist theories of *universals. But much of this work is highly technical, involving sophisticated applications of *modal logic, and consequently it is difficult to convey its results to a lay public. There is thus a danger that such work will be dismissed as a revival of scholasticism without relevance to everyday concerns. That would be a pity, and so it is not only the duty but also in the interest of metaphysicians to make their work more accessible, with a view to countering the relativistic and scientistic dogmas of our time.

Perhaps the most serious intellectual threat to metaphysics as traditionally conceived comes from the movement towards *naturalism in contemporary philosophy, taking its lead from W. V. Quine's advocacy of 'naturalized epistemology'. With the theory of knowledge reconceived as, in effect, a branch of empirical psychology and the concomitant rejection of the traditional distinction between *a priori and a posteriori truth, the claim of metaphysics to have a distinctive subject-matter and method has been put under some pressure. However, just as the cruder scientistic and relativistic enemies of metaphysics may be accused of promoting a particular metaphysical dogma under the guise of an onslaught on metaphysics in general, so too may this charge be levelled at its naturalistic critics. The normative categories of reason and truth transcend naturalistic reduction and cannot, without pragmatic incoherence, be argued out of existence.   E.J.L.

H. Kornblith (ed.), *Naturalizing Epistemology* (Cambridge, Mass., 1985).
R. Rorty, *Philosophy and the Mirror of Nature* (Oxford, 1980).
S. Stich, *The Fragmentation of Reason* (Cambridge, Mass., 1990).

metaphysics, problems of. In contemporary philosophy, problems of metaphysics often take the form of a trilemma concerning some large and important feature of our lives or discourse, a trilemma whose terms are: illusion, well-founded appearance, and fundamental reality. In recent decades these problems most often tend to arise against the backdrop of a broad *naturalism and, often, scientific *realism. The problems themselves may be viewed as demands for possibility explanations: How are values and norms possible in a world of facts? How are minds and mental phenomena possible in a world of matter in motion? How is freedom of action or will possible in a world of scientific law? How can there be abstract entities in a world of events and other contingent particulars? In each case the same troublesome trilemma presents itself.

Concerning any of these realms or dimensions—e.g. values, the mental, freedom, and abstract—there is the view that it is all a big illusion, that there is really nothing in that realm or dimension. Alternatively, it may be held that there are real denizens of the realm in question, with a reality as fundamental as that of any particle or field postulated by our physics. And according to a third, irenic view, though there are real enough entities or phenomena in the target realm, none is fundamental, all deriving rather from more basic entities or phenomena. All indeed are said to resemble ordinary bodies—tables, quantities of water, cats and dogs, etc.—in being real enough, though derived from the existence and organization of more basic entities: from cells or molecules, etc.

For example, it might be held that values and the normative are a complete illusion. Thus, for the non-cognitivist, normative and evaluative concepts do not represent any mind- or language-independent constituent or aspect of reality. Rather, their significance is only functional: like that of the imperative mood or the exclamation mark. It is an illusion to suppose that the goodness of a juicy, sweet apple attaches to it just as do its redness and its roundness. For others, however, the goodness of an apple is just as objective a property of it as its roundness, or, certainly, its redness: just as objective a property, and just as real, and fundamental. But there is a third, irenic, option, according to which the goodness of the apple and the rightness of biting into it are real and objective enough, but 'well founded' on more fundamental properties: e.g. on the apple's disposition to cause, or on the biting into it actually causing, a sufficient balance of pleasure over pain (especially when compared with the alternatives open to the agent at the time). This third option comes with two interesting suboptions: first, adding further that the evaluative and normative phenomena in question are not only well founded (*bene fundata*) but also actually reducible by definition or analysis to the underlying realities that give rise to them; and, alternatively, remaining deliberately non-committal on that issue, claiming only that the phenomena in question do supervene on underlying realities, whether or not they are reducible to them or definable or analysable in their terms.

Similar issues arise with regard to the realm of *minds and the mental. Let us assume that reality is constituted of particulars (whether substances or events) with the properties that characterize them and the relations that interrelate them. Just what is included among these particulars, properties, and relations has been a matter of considerable controversy in the history of Western philosophy.

Idealists view reality as ultimately spiritual or mental. For them the basic particulars are subjects of thought or experience, souls or spirits or monads, the world of matter in motion being nothing more than a stable appearance to our minds. If we say there are snowballs, for the idealist we are right at best in the sense that in certain circumstances our minds are disposed systematically to experience combinations of whiteness, roundness, and coldness. The *foundation* of the existence of such supposed objects therefore lies in the contents of our minds. For the idealist, physical bodies are rather like images in a rich and stable dream. And we are essentially minds, subjects of thought and consciousness. Leibniz and Berkeley were idealists.

Materialists and physicalists view material or physical objects or events as more fundamental than minds or egos or their modes of thought or experience. Accordingly, they would reduce mind to matter rather than matter to mind. For the materialist there are no fundamental subjects of consciousness, no souls or spirits. We have minds simply because we think, sense, feel, etc., and we do all this as rational animals with properly functioning brains and nervous systems. Hobbes was a materialist, as have been most contemporary philosophers who write in the analytic tradition. The token physicalism (and *anomalous monism) of Donald Davidson is also a kind of physicalism of particulars, since it accepts events as basic particulars and regards these as without exception physical.

Finally, dualists admit both souls and bodies as fundamental entities. Neither mind nor matter is reducible to the other and there is no problem of reducing either to the other. For the dualist the problem lies rather in understanding how mind and matter can possibly interact. Descartes was a dualist.

So far we have considered metaphysical options on the nature of basic particulars. There are also similar options on the nature of fundamental *properties or states of affairs. Thus one can be a property phenomenalist, for whom the only fundamental states are mental, e.g. sensory experiences, all other states being 'reducible' to or at least derivative from these.

For a physicalist with regard to states or properties, on the other hand, only physical properties are fundamental; hence any state constituted by a particular having a property, or by a number of particulars related by a certain relation, is a fundamental state only if the particulars are all physical and the properties and relations are all physical. The type–type identity theory is an option open to such a physicalist, and believers in type–type identity might hold the identity to be necessary, as did logical behaviourists, and as do functionalists. Alternatively, a believer in type–type identity might opt for 'contingent identity', as with the functional-specification view of David Lewis.

Finally, property dualists admit both physical properties irreducible to the mental, and mental properties irreducible to the physical. Recent debates over qualia, over the existence of irreducibly qualitative and experiential aspects of one's experience, have divided mentalists on the affirmative (e.g. Ned Block and Jerry Fodor with their 'absent qualia' argument, and Thomas Nagel with his appeal to subjectivity), from physicalists, especially functionalists, on the negative (such as David Armstrong and Daniel Dennett, with their attempt to reduce consciousness in general to propositional attitudes). Some (e.g. Sydney Shoemaker) have tried to reconcile *functionalism with acceptance of qualia, but for our purposes the acceptance of qualia is the important move, if such qualitative aspects of experience are supposed a fundamental sort of mental property not reducible to the physical, nor supervenient upon it.

With regard to *freedom of action or of the will, one faces the same set of options. One might hold freedom to be a complete illusion, since we are natural beings caught in the web of physical law from cradle to grave. Or one might alternatively hold that freedom is a basic fact of life: one might rather deny that a human life could ever be wholly caught within a web of natural laws. A third, more irenic, position is possible, moreover, according to which we do enjoy freedom, but a freedom that is after all compatible with the sway of physical law over every detail of human life. There is important support for this alternative, quite apart from the implausibility of any metaphysics that tries to set a priori limits to how much science might achieve in understanding human behaviour. For consider the postulation of libertarian action not produced by antecedent conditions in accordance with physical law. This is what the libertarian believer in fundamental freedom accepts. But it is puzzling how that can help secure the kind of freedom desired: namely, the kind that would support the attribution of responsibility to the agent, and the assignment of praise or blame, reward or punishment. The reconcilist—or compatibilist—camp for its part still owes a large and challenging debt: reconcilists must still explain how such freedom can be reconciled with the fact that, on the assumption of *determinism, every physical detail of one's life is already determined prior to one's birth. They must introduce, in the teeth of that impressive fact, some crucial distinction among one's actions, between those that are nevertheless not 'compelled' in some appropriate sense, and for which we can remain responsible, and those that *are* thus compelled, which relieves the agent of responsibility.

Metaphysical world-views have derived from epistemological constraints. Thus one might be impressed by the difference between one's own consciousness, to which one enjoys introspective access, on one side, and, on the other, the supposed world of physical fact beyond. Philosophers have long puzzled over how such a fundamental chasm could ever be bridged by reason. How could one ever know about the reality beyond on the basis of what one knows immediately about one's own consciousness? One cannot deduce how it is beyond one's consciousness simply from how it is within it: illusions, hallucinations, dreams, sceptical scenarios like that of the *brain in a vat and the Cartesian evil demon, establish that impossibility clearly enough. (*Malin génie.*) So it would seem that at best one must argue one's way to the external world through some inductive form of reasoning. But to many this has seemed hopeless if the world beyond is constituted by phenomena of a wholly different order and inaccessible to our experience. For how could one so much as understand such 'phenomena'? And, besides,

even if one could somehow understand them, how could one know about them? Presumably one would have to establish inductive correlations from which one could then generalize and on the basis of which one could argue from the character of one's experience to what lies outside. Considerations such as these, deriving from the needs of epistemology, have led philosophers in the empiricist tradition to one or another form of idealist *phenomenalism, to the view that reality is through and through constituted by experience, in the form of impressions and ideas (and, for some, subjects of such experience).

Rationalists for their part have equally reasoned from assumptions concerning knowledge and understanding to metaphysical conclusions of great scope. For the rationalist mind, reality must be comprehensible through and through. It must be *possible* for a mind powerful enough and well enough stocked with information to attain a complete understanding of the universe. Here the following assumptions are in play: (*a*) the universe is the totality of facts; (*b*) to understand a fact is to understand why it is a fact, why it obtains; (*c*) if a fact cannot be understood in its own terms, if it is not self-explanatory, then in order to understand why it obtains one needs an explanation of it, an explanation of why it obtains; (*d*) a complete understanding of the universe would be an understanding of *all* facts; (*e*) X is an explanation of the fact that *p* (of why it is the case that *p*) only if X is a set of true assumptions (facts) that jointly logically imply the fact that *p* via some principle of lawful regularity.

Fundamental *laws would be (by definition) unexplained, there being no more fundamental laws to explain them. But that would be an obstacle to complete understanding only if the laws in question would *require* explanation in order to be understood. Could any laws or facts be (in a sense) self-explaining? Consider the fact (*F*) that nothing is diverse from itself. What could possibly explain such a fact? It is not easy to think of anything else which might explain anything so fundamental. Even if it turns out that in fact there is nothing external that can supply such explanation, would that show a lack in our understanding of F? Don't we understand F as well as we ever understand anything, even without need of external explanation? If so, we have then in F a fundamental fact that requires no (external) explanation in order to be understood. The two relevant features of F are evidently, first, its *necessity*, i.e. the fact that things could not possibly have been otherwise than F says they are, and, second, the *obviousness* of that necessity, it being obvious that things could not possibly have been otherwise than F says they are. Any such fact will be perfectly well understood in its own terms and will need no further, external explanation.

Suppose the natural order to consist of material particles in various configurations, moving and reconfiguring in accordance with physical law. Even if we assume that the series never had a beginning in time, why is there such a series when there might have been a different one or even a changeless void instead? In answer to this it would not do to spin an infinite series of explanations of particular contingencies within the series by appeal in each case to other antecedent contingencies in that same series, and expect to have answered thus the legitimate question why there is such a series at all.

Leibniz understands our predicament in roughly these terms and takes it as his own. Here is a very brief sketch of his resolution: (a) the best possible world is necessarily best; (b) *God, being necessarily omniscient, necessarily sees it to be best; (c) God, being necessarily infinitely good, necessarily wills that world to be; (d) since God is necessarily omnipotent, that world necessarily comes to be, and it is hence, of course, our world.

If a world (or universe) is a totality of facts, then if a world W differs from a world W' in any detail no matter how small, then W and W' must be two different worlds. Hence if by Leibniz's account our world necessarily comes to be, then every detail in it, no matter how small, necessarily comes to be. Not one grain of sand could have been different in its qualities or location. But this conclusion is not idiosyncratic to Leibniz's particular proposal for how it might be possible to attain a complete understanding of the universe. For, as we have seen already, however we fill in assumptions and laws in order to explain fully the existence and character of the natural order of events (e.g. of matter in motion from eternity to eternity), the resulting assumptions and laws had better be necessary facts if we are not just to extend the problem to another series of contingencies in the vertical direction. Suppose we lump all the assumptions into one big assumption A and all the laws into one big law L. If such necessary A and L are to explain the existence and character of the natural order (at least to an infinite being who could grasp it all), then by our account of explanation, A and L must jointly entail that the natural order does exist and has exactly the character it does have. But anything thus entailed by what is necessary must itself be necessary. It follows that if we have such explanation, then the natural order must necessarily exist and must necessarily have exactly the character that it does have. So, again, no grain of sand could possibly have been different in its qualities or location. And this result is thus seen to derive not just from anything special in Leibniz's particular explanation, but from the very nature of what a complete explanation would have to be. What is made plausible by our reasoning is that if a complete understanding of the universe is to be attainable to anyone, even to a being with access to all information and with no limit to his faculty of reason, then the universe must be necessary in every detail. (As an alternative to Leibniz's, compare Spinoza's very different but equally rationalistic and equally necessitarian worldview.)

Once again we see how an epistemic commitment drives powerful thinkers to a metaphysical view about broad and fundamental features of reality. One can, of course, deny the commitment, denying that there is anything deeper than the natural order of contingent events. Unless there is some mistake in our reasoning, however,

this would commit one to the view that there is inevitable opacity to reason, inevitable absurdity built into the universe, something that even an omniscient being with infinite reason could not wholly eliminate. And this consequence contributes to a powerful intellectual movement alternative to both the broad empiricism and the broad rationalism already sketched, a movement that culminates in works such as the *Nausea* of Jean-Paul Sartre, obsessed with the contingency of the world, and deriving its existentialist consequences about human life and society.

In the twentieth century linguistic philosophy rejected traditional metaphysics as a pseudo-inquiry whose real point is or should be linguistic. This has taken the form of a linguistic *relativism (LR) according to which: When we say 'There are three objects here, not eight' we are really saying 'The following is assertible as true in our language L: "There are three objects here, not eight".' This is, for example, in the spirit of Carnap's *Logical Syntax of Language*, where Carnap defends the following theses: (i) Philosophy, when cognitive at all, amounts to the logical syntax of scientific language. (ii) But there can be alternative such languages and we are to choose between them on grounds of convenience. (iii) A language is completely characterized by its formation and transformation rules. In that same book Carnap also distinguishes between:

(s1) object sentences: e.g. 'Five is a prime number', 'Babylon was a big town';
(s2) pseudo-object sentences: e.g. 'Five is not a thing but a number', 'Babylon was treated in yesterday's lecture';
(s3) syntactical sentences: e.g. '"Five" is not a thing-word but a number-word', '"Babylon" occurred in yesterday's lecture'.

And he defends the thesis that although s2 sentences seem deceptively like s1 sentences, actually they are really s3 sentences in 'material mode' disguise. Quine agrees that a kind of 'semantic ascent' is possible, as when we shift from talk of miles to talk of 'mile', but he thinks this kind of semantic ascent is *always* trivially available, not just in philosophy but in science generally and even beyond. Thus we can paraphrase 'There are wombats in Tasmania' as '"Wombat" is true of some creatures in Tasmania'. Quine does grant that semantic ascent tends to be especially useful in philosophy. But he explains why as follows (*Word and Object*, 272):

The strategy of semantic ascent is that it carries the discussion into a domain where both parties are better agreed on the objects (viz., words) and on the main terms concerning them. Words, or their inscriptions, unlike points, miles, classes, and the rest, are tangible objects of the size so popular in the marketplace, where men of unlike conceptual schemes communicate at their best . . . No wonder it helps in philosophy.

However, the use of that strategy is clearly limited to discourse about recondite entities of controversial status. No relevant gain is to be expected from semantic ascent when the subject-matter is the inventory of the market-place itself. Tables and chairs, headaches and beliefs, and even good apples are no more controversial than words: in fact, some at least of these seem less so, by a good margin. No general conceptual or linguistic relativity, no avoidance of metaphysical discourse, can be plausibly supported by the semantic-ascent strategy offered by Quine. In addition, questions of coherence arise concerning LR. When we say something of the form 'The following is assertible in our language L: . . .' can we rest with a literal interpretation that does not require ascent and relativization? If not, where does ascent stop? Are we then *really* saying 'The following is assertible in our language L: "The following is assertible in our language L: . . ."'. This way lies vicious regress. But if we *can* stop the regress with metalinguistic reference to our sentences of L (and to ourselves), why can we not stop it with our references to headaches and good apples, and to tables and chairs and other medium-sized dry goods? Other ways of attacking the problems of metaphysics as mere pseudo-problems have also gained prominence and a wide following in recent decades, but this linguistic turn will have to serve as our example, and, as revealed with this example, metaphysics is neither destroyed nor even silenced by such attacks.

This article has focused on the following general facts about metaphysical problems: (*a*) that many take the form of a trilemma among illusion, well-founded appearance, and fundamental reality, and arise in recent decades against a backdrop of naturalism; (*b*) that interrelated solutions to them—i.e. broad metaphysical positions—sometimes derive from epistemological assumptions concerning what is comprehensible or knowable, and the ways in which this might be so; and (*c*) that in contemporary philosophy metaphysical problems have been denigrated by positivist and linguistic philosophers as pseudo-problems or as linguistic issues with a mask of profundity. I have discussed particular metaphysical problems mainly as examples, and there are many that I have not so much as mentioned: problems, for example, about *space and *time, about *substance and attribute, about *events and states, about *universals and particulars, and about *change and *identity through time. Discussion of these and other metaphysical problems may be found in this Companion under specific headings.   E.S.

> *causation; descriptive metaphysics; idealism; materialism; opposition to metaphysics; pseudo-philosophy; revisionary metaphysics.

R. M. Chisholm, *On Metaphysics* (Minneapolis, 1989).
M. Dummett, *The Logical Basis of Metaphysics* (Cambridge, Mass., 1991).
T. Honderich, *A Theory of Determinism: The Mind, Neuroscience, and Life-Hopes* (Oxford, 1988).
J. Kim, *Supervenience and Mind* (Cambridge, 1993).
S. Kripke, *Naming and Necessity* (Cambridge, Mass., 1980).
T. Kuhn, *The Structure of Scientific Revolutions*, 2nd edn. (1st edn. 1962) (Chicago, 1970).
D. Lewis, *Philosophical Papers*, i and ii (Oxford, 1983).
T. Nagel, *The View from Nowhere* (Oxford, 1986).
R. Nozick, *Philosophical Explanations* (Cambridge, Mass., 1981).
H. Putnam, *Reason, Truth, and History* (Cambridge, 1981).
W. V. Quine, *Word and Object* (Cambridge, Mass., 1960).

N. Rescher, *A System of Pragmatic Idealism*, i–iii (Princeton, NJ, 1992–3).

metaphysics, revisionary: *see* revisionary metaphysics.

metempsychosis: *see* reincarnation.

method, joint. J. S. Mill proposed to unify two of his five canons of experimental inquiry, the *method of agreement and the *method of difference, in a third, the 'joint method': namely, 'If two or more instances in which the phenomenon occurs have only one circumstance in common, while two or more instances in which it does not occur have nothing in common save the absence of that circumstance, the circumstance in which alone the two instances differ is the effect or the cause or an indispensable part of the cause of the phenomenon'. However, this canon allows the possibility that a type of phenomenon under investigation may have more than one type of cause or that it may have a single underlying cause that is not revealed. Nor does Mill's method show how the strength of a causal hypothesis may be only a matter of degree, though he accepts this elsewhere.   L.J.C.

> *method of concomitant variations; method of residues.

method, scientific: *see* scientific method.

methodic doubt: *see* doubt.

method in philosophy: *see* philosophical inquiry: first premisses and principles.

method of agreement. J. S. Mill's *A System of Logic* (1843) proposed the 'method of agreement' as the first of five canons of experimental inquiry. It determines that 'If two or more instances of the phenomenon under investigation have only one circumstance in common, the circumstance in which alone all the instances agree is the cause (or effect) of the given phenomenon'. For example, if an alkaline substance is combined with an oil in several otherwise different varieties of circumstance, and in each case a soap results, then the combination of an oil and an alkali causes the production of a soap. It is thus not an observed regularity of co-occurrence that evidences the causation but an observed elimination of all but one hypothesis. However, to secure this elimination we need to test, and may not in fact know, all the eligible hypotheses.   L.J.C.

> *method, joint; method of concomitant variations; method of difference; method of residues.

method of concomitant variations. The fifth of J. S. Mill's five canons of experimental inquiry (*A System of Logic* (1843)). Phenomena which vary concomitantly can be assumed to be causally related, whether one causes the other, or they are effects of a common cause. The method is useful, Mill thinks, for cases where the methods of agreement and difference cannot be applied because we are facing phenomena which can be neither excluded (to see what happens in their absence) nor isolated (to exclude irrelevant factors); but it has limitations, he adds, because we often cannot tell whether *all* of one phenomenon relates causally to the other, and it cannot tell us what happens outside the limits of the observed variations. Like the other canons it assumes that there are causes to be found within the sphere of our present knowledge.

A.R.L.

J. S. Mill, *A System of Logic*, bk. 3, ch. 8 (London, 1843).

method of difference. J. S. Mill proposed the 'method of difference' as the second of five canons of experimental inquiry. It determines that 'If an instance in which the phenomenon under investigation occurs, and an instance in which it does not occur, have every circumstance in common save one, that one occurring only in the former; the circumstance in which alone the two instances differ is the effect, or the cause, or an indispensable part of the cause of the phenomenon'. For example, when a man is shot through the heart, it is by this method we know that it was the gunshot which killed him: for he was in the fullness of life immediately before, all circumstances being the same except the wound. But in some cases it may be difficult to establish that two instances have every circumstance in common save one.

L.J.C.

*method, joint; method of agreement; method of concomitant variations; method of residues.

method of residues. J. S. Mill's fourth canon of experimental inquiry was entitled the 'method of residues': namely, 'Subduct from any phenomenon such part as is known to be the effect of certain antecedents, and the residue of the phenomenon is the effect of the remaining antecedents'. For example, said Mill, if the movements of a comet cannot be wholly accounted for by its gravitation towards the sun and the planets, the residual feature must be explained by the resistance of the medium through which it moves. But Mill recognized that in practice we may not be able to be certain that one particular factor is the only antecedent to which the residual phenomenon may be referred. So any induction by the method of residues needs to be confirmed by obtaining the residual phenomenon artificially and trying it separately, or by deriving its operation from otherwise known laws.

L.J.C.

*method, joint; method of agreement; method of concomitant variations; method of difference.

methodological holism and individualism. There are two large debates in *social philosophy or social ontology, both with methodological ramifications for the *philosophy of social science (Pettit, *The Common Mind*). One is concerned with how far human beings (non-causally) depend on their social relationships for the possession of the ability to think, or for the possession of some such

characteristic human capacity. The atomist denies any such dependence while the non-atomist asserts that it obtains. The other debate is concerned with whether the existence of aggregate social entities—in particular, the obtaining of aggregate-level regularities—means that human beings do not conform in full to our commonplace psychological image of them as more or less autonomous, more or less rational creatures. The individualist denies that aggregate entities entail any compromise of such commonplace psychology while the non-individualist maintains that there is some more or less significant compromise involved.

There are also many other methodologically relevant debates that are loosely associated with these divisions. Some examples are the debates over whether aggregate-level social theory is reducible to psychological theory; whether individual-level explanation is preferable to aggregate-level explanation in social science; whether social scientific discovery is likely to force any revisions on our commonplace psychology; whether individual subjects are reciprocally influenced by the aggregate entities they constitute, as they form the concepts of such entities; whether individual agents are so constrained by the circumstances of their social setting that we need only attend to those circumstances—we can ignore psychological matters of belief and desire—in predicting what they will do; and whether historically significant individual actions are generally dispensable, in the sense that had the individuals involved not done what they did, there would have been others to take their place.

The term 'methodological individualism' is usually employed with a variety of connotations across the range of positions identified here. The self-described methodological individualist will certainly be an individualist in the sense defined above; he will probably be an atomist; and he will tend to go for the position that is thought most flattering to the status of the individual in each of the other debates. The term 'methodological holism' is less commonly employed and its connotations will vary in the same way.

P.P.

Philip Pettit, *The Common Mind: An Essay on Psychology, Society and Politics* (New York, 1993).

methodology. The philosophical study of *scientific method. The central question arising from this study is how to interpret methodological statements. There are three alternatives: description, convention, prescription.

Under the first option, methodological statements are either interpreted as descriptions of scientific practice, or methodology is seen as a 'science of science' which establishes correlations between practice and results. Just as science has methods which allow the successful study of electrons, so too philosophers could apply the scientific methods of, say, *cognitive science or *biology to the study of science itself. Objectors to such an approach point to the lack of a non-contentious stock of results and methods in the human sciences. Therefore, the human sciences would not be able to provide a consensus on what the methods of science in fact *are*. An obvious reply would be to advocate the application of the methods of physical science itself. Of course, if we do not know what these methods are, we cannot apply them. Thus it seems descriptivism is either question-begging or viciously circular. A common reply to be found in the writings of the *Vienna Circle and Quine is that a virtuous spiral is a better geometrical analogue than a vicious circle. Under this account, the application of a method to questions of method provides a sharpening of both the method and the questions asked.

If, as Popper has argued, scientific method constitutes the rules which govern scientific behaviour, these rules may be as conventional as the rules which govern the game of chess. A problem arises if two mutually contradictory rule books are proposed: Which game of science should be chosen? The obvious answer is to decide which set of rules is more 'useful' or 'suitable'. This assumes, of course, that we have non-conventional criteria of 'usefulness' and 'suitability'. We could appeal to the intuitions of practitioners about their activity. There are two possible sources of these intuitions. In the first case they result from the practitioner's previous experiences of similar activities, and their association—or lack of association—with some desired outcome. This answer seems to require knowledge about what methods are correlated with what outcomes, which is the central problem of descriptivism. In the second case there *is* a correct answer to the question what sort of rationality motivates the rules of science. This leads us to our third position.

According to normativists, methodological imperatives are true or false much as ethical norms are under an objectivist account. In its pure form, this view is not widely held, with the exception of decision theorists like Keynes and the later Carnap. A problem arises if we ask whether a transgression of such norms could make an observable difference to the life of the transgressor. On the one hand, if it makes *no* difference, one might question the subject-matter: are judgements of rationality really so much hot air? On the other hand, if transgression does make a difference, the desirability of following the norms of rationality would depend on the factual differences in outcomes that result. Thus this position is also in danger of collapse into descriptivism.

N.C.
T.CHI.
R.F.H.

*Mill's methods; science, problems of the philosophy of.

Rudolf Carnap, 'Inductive Logic and Rational Decisions', in R. Carnap and R. Jeffrey, *Studies in Inductive Logic and Probability* (Berkeley, Calif., 1971).
K. R. Popper, *The Logic of Scientific Discovery* (London, 1980), ch. 2.
W. V. Quine, *The Pursuit of Truth* (Cambridge, Mass., 1992), ch. 1, sect. 8.

Meyerson, Émile (1859–1933). Born in Lublin, became a naturalized Frenchman, and worked for Jewish agencies after a brief spell as an industrial chemist. Meyerson wrote on philosophy of science and general epistemology, his main interest being the nature of thought as exemplified in its successful products.

An anti-positivist, he argued, for example in *Identity and Reality* (1908), that scientific knowledge attempts to reach beyond mere descriptive and predictive laws to an understanding of the nature of the reality beyond appearances. The human mind seeks the permanent behind phenomenal change, the identity within diversity as exemplified in conservation laws, such as the law of inertia and the law of conservation of energy. And yet this identity which our reason apprehends (or perhaps constructs) cannot embrace the totality of reality, for there is also change.

A.J.L.

*positivism; thinking.

Émile Meyerson, *Identity and Reality*, tr. Kate Loewenberg (London, 1930).

microcosm: *see* macrocosm and microcosm.

Mill, James (1773–1836). Scottish thinker who, after being educated at Edinburgh University, came to London and worked for a considerable time as assistant and publicist for Bentham. Most famous for the strenuously intellectual education to which he subjected his more famous son, John Stuart Mill, he wrote influential pamphlets on education and government from a utilitarian point of view, as well as a thoroughgoing associationist psychology, *The Analysis of the Phenomena of the Human Mind* of 1829 (which was later republished with extensive notes by his son). His most discussed philosophical work is the short pamphlet *On Government*, which is a rigorous a priori argument for majoritarian *democracy: since everyone acts in their own interest, only the greatest number can be relied on to protect the greatest happiness of the greatest number.

R.H.

*utilitarianism.

Jack Lively and John Rees, *Utilitarian Logic and Politics* (Oxford, 1978).

Mill, John Stuart (1806–73), son of James Mill. He was the greatest British philosopher of the nineteenth century, bringing Britain's traditions of *empiricism and *liberalism to their Victorian apogee.

The *System of Logic*, a product of his thirties, published in 1843, made his reputation as a philosopher. The *Principles of Political Economy*, of 1848, was a synthesis of classical economics which defined liberal orthodoxy for at least a quarter of a century. His two best-known works of moral philosophy, *On Liberty* and *Utilitarianism*, appeared later—in 1859 and 1861. In the 1860s he was briefly a Member of Parliament, and throughout his life was involved in many radical causes. Among them was his enduring support for women's rights—see *The Subjection of Women* of 1869.

The leading element in Mill's thought is his lifelong effort to weave together the insights of enlightenment and romanticism. He subscribed unwaveringly to what he called the 'school of experience and association'. He denied that there is knowledge independent of experience and held that attitudes and beliefs are the products of psychological laws of association. His view of human beings is *naturalistic and his ethics is utilitarian. But he redesigned the liberal edifice built on these foundations to the romantic patterns of the nineteenth century. For these he was himself one of the great spokesmen. He learned much of the historical sociology which was so important to his liberalism from Frenchmen; but it was to German romanticism, via his Coleridgean friends, that he owes his deepest ethical theme—that of human nature as the seat of individuality and autonomy, capable of being brought to fruition through the culture of the whole man.

The controversy over Mill's achievement has always centred on whether the synthesis he sought, of enlightenment and romantic-idealist themes, is a possible one. Kant had argued that the naturalism of the *Enlightenment subverted reason, and idealist philosophers of the nineteenth century followed him in that. Kant and Mill do in fact agree on a vital aspect of this question. They agree that if the mind is only a part of nature, no knowledge of the natural world can be *a priori. Either all knowledge is a posteriori, grounded in experience, or there is no knowledge. Any grounds for asserting a proposition that has real content must be empirical grounds. However, much more important is the difference between them: whereas Kant thought knowledge could not be grounded on such a basis, and thus rejected naturalism, Mill thought it could. This radically empiricist doctrine is the thesis of the *System of Logic*.

There Mill draws a distinction between 'verbal' and 'real' propositions, and between 'merely apparent' and 'real' inferences. The distinction corresponds, as Mill himself notes, to that which Kant makes between analytic and synthetic judgements. But Mill applies it with greater strictness than anyone had done before, insisting with greater resolution that merely apparent inferences have no genuine cognitive content. He points out that pure mathematics, and logic itself, contain real propositions and inferences with genuine cognitive content. This clear assertion is central to the *System of Logic*, and the basis of its continuing importance in the empiricist tradition. For if Mill is also right in holding that naturalism entails that no real proposition is a priori, he has shown the implications of naturalism to be radical indeed. Not only mathematics but logic itself will be empirical.

His strategy is a pincer movement. One pincer is an indirect argument. If logic did not contain real inferences, all deductive reasoning would be a *petitio principii*, a begging of the question—it could produce no new knowledge. Yet clearly it does produce new knowledge. So logic must contain real inferences. The other pincer is a direct semantic analysis of basic logical laws. It shows them to be real and not merely verbal. The same strategy is applied to mathematics. If it was merely verbal, mathematical reasoning would be a *petitio principii*. But a detailed semantic analysis shows that it does contain real propositions.

Why do we think these real propositions in logic and mathematics to be a priori? Because we find their negations inconceivable, or derive them, by principles whose unsoundness we find inconceivable, from premisses whose negation we find inconceivable. Mill thought he could explain these facts about unthinkability, or imaginative unrepresentability, in associationist terms. His explanations are none too convincing, but his philosophical point still stands: the step from our inability to represent to ourselves the negation of a proposition to acceptance of its truth calls for justification. Moreover, the justification *itself* must be a priori if it is to show that the proposition is known a priori. (Thus Mill is prepared, for example, to concede the reliability of geometrical intuition: but he stresses that its reliability is an empirical fact, itself known inductively.)

All reasoning is empirical. What then is the basis of reasoning? Epistemologically, historically, and psychologically, Mill holds, it is *enumerative induction*, simple generalization from experience. We spontaneously agree in reasoning that way, and in holding that way of reasoning to be sound. The proposition 'Enumerative induction is a valid mode of reasoning' is not a verbal proposition. But nor is it grounded in an a priori intuition. All that Mill will say for it is that people in general, and the reader in particular, in fact agree on reflection in accepting it. It is on that basis alone that he rests his claim.

He does not take seriously Hume's sceptical problem of *induction; his concern in the *System of Logic* is rather to find ways of improving the reliability of inductive reasoning:

if induction by simple enumeration were an invalid process, no process grounded on it would be valid; just as no reliance could be placed on telescopes, if we could not trust our eyes. But though a valid process, it is a fallible one, and fallible in very different degrees: if therefore we can substitute for the more fallible forms of the process, an operation grounded on the same process in a less fallible form, we shall have effected a very material improvement. And this is what scientific induction does.

So Mill's question is not a sceptical but an internal one—why is it that some inductions are more trustworthy than others? He answers by means of a natural history of induction, which traces how enumerative induction is internally vindicated by its actual success in establishing regularities, and how it eventually gives rise to more searching methods of investigation.

The origins are 'spontaneous' and 'unscientific' inductions about particular unconnected natural phenomena. They accumulate, interweave, and are not disconfirmed by further experience. As they accumulate and interweave, they justify the second-order inductive conclusion that *all* phenomena are subject to uniformity, and, more specifically, that all have discoverable sufficient conditions. In this less vague form, the principle of general uniformity becomes, given Mill's analysis of causation, the law of universal causation. This conclusion in turn provides (Mill believes) the grounding assumption for a new style of reasoning about nature—*eliminative induction*.

Here the assumption that a type of phenomenon has uniform causes, together with a (revisable) assumption about what its possible causes are, initiates a comparative inquiry in which the actual cause is identified by elimination. Mill formulates the logic of this eliminative reasoning in his 'methods of empirical inquiry'. The improved scientific induction which results spills back on to the principle of universal causation on which it rests, and raises its certainty to a new level. That in turn raises our confidence in the totality of particular enumerative inductions from which the principle is derived. This analysis of the 'inductive process' is one of Mill's most elegant achievements.

Mill and Hume then are both naturalistic radicals, but in quite different ways—Hume by virtue of his scepticism, Mill by virtue of his empiricist analysis of deduction. The only cognitive dispositions which Mill recognizes as primitively legitimate are the disposition to rely on memory and the habit of enumerative induction. The whole of science, he thinks, is built from the materials of experience and memory by disciplined employment of this habit.

This is Mill's *inductivism*—the view that enumerative induction is the only *ultimate* method of inference which puts us in possession of new truths. Is he right in thinking it to be so? In his own time the question produced an important, if confused, controversy between him and William Whewell. Whewell argued that fundamental to scientific inquiry was the hypothetical method, in which one argues to the truth of a hypothesis from the fact that it would explain observed phenomena. Mill, on the other hand, could not accept that the mere fact that a hypothesis accounted for the data in itself provided a reason for thinking it true. The point he appealed to is a powerful one: it is always possible that a body of data may be explained equally well by more than one hypothesis.

What he does not see, and this is one of the points of weakness in his philosophy, is how much must be torn from the fabric of our belief if inductivism is applied strictly. Thus, for example, while his case for empiricism about logic and mathematics is very strong, it is his methodology of science which then forces him to hold that we know basic logical and mathematical principles only by an enumerative induction. That is desperately implausible; accepting the hypothetical method would be one, though only one, possible remedy.

Inductivism also plays a key role in Mill's metaphysics. He sets this out in his *Examination of Sir William Hamilton's Philosophy* (1865)—a detailed criticism of the Scottish philosopher who had attempted to bring together the views of Reid and Kant. Here Mill endorses a doctrine which was then accepted, as he says, on all sides (though it would now be treated with greater mistrust). The doctrine is that our knowledge and conception of objects external to consciousness consists entirely in the conscious states they excite in us, or that we can imagine them exciting in us.

This leaves open the question whether objects exist independently of consciousness. It may be held that there are such objects, although we can only know them by hypothesis from their effects on us. Mill rejects this view—as, given his inductivism, he must. Instead he argues that external objects amount to nothing more than 'permanent possibilities of sensation'. The possibilities are 'permanent' in the sense that they obtain whether or not realized; they would occur if an antecedent condition obtained. (As well as 'permanent' Mill uses other terms, such as 'certified' or 'guaranteed'.)

Our knowledge of mind, like our knowledge of matter, Mill thinks to be 'entirely relative'. But he baulks at resolving it into a series of feelings and possibilities of feeling. For 'the thread of consciousness' contains memories and expectations as well as sensations. To remember or expect a feeling is not simply to believe that it has existed or will exist; it is to believe that *I* have experienced or will experience that feeling. Thus if the mind is to be a series of feelings, we would, he thinks, be forced to conclude that it is a series that can be aware of itself as a series. This drives him to recognize in mind, or self, a reality greater than the existence as a permanent possibility which is the only reality he concedes to matter. He fails to note that the doctrine that mind resolves into a series of feelings need not literally *identify* selves with series: it paraphrases talk of selves in terms of talk of series.

Discounting this uncertainty about what to say of the self, all that ultimately exists in Mill's view is experience in a temporal order. But he claims this to be consistent with *common-sense realism, and he continues to see minds as proper parts of a natural order. The difficulties of this begin to emerge when we ask whether the experiences referred to in Mill's metaphysics are the very same as those referred to by common sense—and explained by physical antecedents. The same difficulties emerge for later *phenomenalists, but Mill never addresses them.

To the succeeding generation of philosophers, who took Kant's philosophy seriously, Mill's naturalism seemed thoroughly incoherent. He fails to see the need for a synthetic a priori to render any knowledge possible, even though he gives an account of real propositions and inferences which agrees in essentials with Kant. On top of that, in accepting phenomenalism he accepts a doctrine which must lead to a transcendental view of consciousness, yet he remains determinedly naturalistic in his view of the mind. Perhaps present-day naturalism is finding ways of avoiding this second impasse, by being more rigorously naturalistic about experience than Mill was. But it has yet to cope clearly with the first.

In ethics and politics Mill's premises remain those of enlightenment *humanism. Value resides in the well-being achieved within individual lives; the interests of all make an equal claim on the consideration of all. Happiness is most effectively attained when society leaves people free to pursue their own ends subject to rules established for the general good. A science of man will ground rational policies for social improvement.

His reason for thinking that *happiness is the only ultimate human end is just like his reason for thinking enumerative induction is the only ultimate principle of reasoning. He appeals to reflective agreement, in this case of desires rather than reasoning dispositions: 'the sole evidence it is possible to produce that anything is desirable, is that people do actually desire it. If the end which the utilitarian doctrine proposes to itself were not, in theory and in practice, acknowledged to be an end, nothing could ever convince any person that it was so.'

But do we not, in theory and in practice, desire things under ends other than the end of happiness, for example under the idea of duty? Mill's response to this question has strength and subtlety. He acknowledges that we can will against inclination: 'instead of willing the thing because we desire it, we often desire it only because we will it'. There are, he agrees, conscientious actions, flowing not from any unmotivated desire but solely from acceptance of duty. But his point is that when we *un*motivatedly desire a thing we desire it under the idea of it as pleasant. He further distinguishes between desiring a thing as 'part' of our happiness and desiring it as a means to our happiness. Virtuous ends can be a part of happiness: consider, for example, the difference between a spontaneously generous man and a conscientious giver. The first wants to give because he takes pleasure in giving. The second gives from a 'confirmed will to do right'. The benefit of another is for the first, but not the second, a 'part' of his own happiness.

The *virtues can become a part of our happiness, and for Mill they ideally should be so. That ideal state is not an unrealistic one, for the virtues have a natural basis and a moral education can build on it by association. More generally, people can come to a deeper understanding of happiness through education and experience. Mill holds that some forms of happiness are inherently preferred as finer by those able to experience them fully—but these valuations are still in his view made from within the perspective of happiness, not from outside it.

So Mill deepened the Benthamite understanding of happiness; however, he never adequately examined the principle of utility itself. It was a philosopher of the generation after Mill's, Henry Sidgwick, who probed its groundings most deeply. But when we turn to Mill's conception of the relationship between the utility principle and the texture of norms by which day-to-day social life proceeds, we find him at his most impressive. His ability to combine abstract moral theory with the human understanding of a great political and social thinker here comes into its own. Benthamite radicalism lacks historical and sociological sense. The philosophes of the eighteenth century, 'attempting to new-model society without the binding forces which hold society together, met with such success as might have been expected'.

The utilitarian, he says, need not and cannot require that 'the test of conduct should also be the exclusive motive of it'. This historical and concrete aspect of Mill's *utilitarianism is the key to his view of the institutions of justice and liberty; though his analysis of rights follows Bentham. A person has a right to a thing, he holds, if there is an obligation on society to protect him in his possession of that thing. But the obligation itself must be grounded in general utility.

The rights of *justice reflect a class of exceptionally stringent obligations on society. They are obligations to provide to each person 'the essentials of human well-being'. The claim of justice is the 'claim we have on our fellow-creatures to join in making safe for us the very groundwork of our existence'. Because justice-rights protect those utilities which touch that groundwork they take priority over the direct pursuit of general utility as well as over the private pursuit of personal ends.

With *liberty we find again that Mill's liberalism is grounded on a utilitarian base. He appeals to 'utility in the largest sense, grounded on the permanent interests of man as a progressive being'. In that respect, his liberalism stands opposed to the classical natural-rights liberalism of Locke. The famous principle which Mill enunciates in his *On Liberty* is intended to safeguard the individual's freedom to pursue his goals in his private domain: 'the only purpose for which power can be rightfully exercised over any member of a civilised community, against his will, is to prevent harm to others. His own good, either physical or moral, is not a sufficient warrant.'

Mill magnificently defends this principle of liberty on two grounds: it enables individuals to realize their individual potential in their own way, and, by liberating talents, creativity, and dynamism, it sets up the essential precondition for moral and intellectual progress. Yet the limitations of his Benthamite inheritance, despite the major enlargements he made to it, residually constrain him. His defence of the principle would have been still stronger if he had weakened (or liberalized) its foundation—by acknowledging the irreducible plurality of human ends and substituting for aggregate utility the generic concept of general good.   J.M.S.

Fred R. Berger, *Happiness, Justice and Freedom: The Moral and Political Philosophy of John Stuart Mill* (London, 1984).

Wendy Donner, *The Liberal Self: John Stuart Mill's Moral and Political Philosophy* (Ithaca, NY, 1991).

Alan Ryan, *J. S. Mill* (London, 1974).

Geoffrey Scarre, *Logic and Reality in the Philosophy of John Stuart Mill* (Dordrecht, 1989).

John Skorupski, *John Stuart Mill* (London, 1989).

—— (ed.), *The Cambridge Companion to Mill* (Cambridge, 1998).

C. L. Ten, *Mill on Liberty* (Oxford, 1980).

Millikan, Ruth (1933–). In her work *Language, Thought and Other Biological Categories* (Cambridge, Mass., 1984), and in subsequent articles, Ruth Millikan has presented arguably the most detailed application of evolutionary theory to certain philosophical problems. She develops a notion of a thing's function in terms of things of that type, in the past, having being selected to play a particular causal role, so capturing the intuition that a thing can have a function that, in fact, it does not now carry out. She applies this notion to thought and language, claiming that, in each case, representation is the biological function of the medium of thought and of language. This impels her to espouse a type of realism, and deny what she calls 'meaning rationalism', the view that language-users and thinkers have privileged access to the meanings they have conveyed by their language use, or which constitute their thought.   P.J.P.N.

*evolution.

Mill's methods: *see* method of agreement; method of difference; method, joint; method of residues; method of concomitant variations.

mimesis. Imitation, representation. Plato's well-known attack on the poets begins with the assertion that poetry is a kind of 'mimesis'. The word is evidently used in two senses. (1) Playing a dramatic role or reciting a speech from Homer is *imitating* (or impersonating) someone. Such mimesis can harm the actor if the character imitated is bad. (2) Narrative *poetry *represents* people's behaviour. Mimesis in this sense is also exemplified by reflections in mirrors and representational painting. To produce such representations, Plato says, one does not need knowledge of the thing represented, but only of how it appears. His complaint is that poets achieve with their skills a dangerous reputation as authorities on matters, such as good conduct, of which they are ignorant. 'Children and fools' are similarly taken in by *trompe-l'œil* paintings.

                                                    R.J.H.

Plato, *Republic* x. Various translations available, e.g. that by G. M. A. Grube and C. D. C. Reeve (Indianapolis, 1992).

mind. You have a mind if you think, perceive, or feel. Your mind is like your life or your weight, an abstract version of an unproblematic property. When minds are thought of as objects in their own right, with parts as if they were spatially extended and with continuity through time as if they were physical objects, then they become much more thought-provoking. They become like souls or selves. We don't have to take minds as objects. They can be features of other objects, such as persons (persons typically have heights and weights and minds) or features of person's lives. Still, we can study minds inasmuch as we can study thinking, perceiving, and feeling. This is psychology.

The concepts of thinking, perceiving, and feeling are among a large family of concepts, including, for example, remembering, loving, and wishing, which every person picks up in childhood when they acquire their culture's conception of mind. Developmental psychologists have differing opinions about whether this conception is a fairly arbitrary theory which could vary in essential respects from one culture to another, or whether there is a core way of thinking about mind to which humans inevitably gravitate. Such a core conception would correspond to what functionalist thinkers in the philosophy of mind, such as Putnam and Fodor, have postulated as the set of essential connections between beliefs, desires, memories, and other states, which characterize mind: a mind is

anything, be it human, animal, or extraterrestrial, which has states connected in the way the core conception describes.

Even if there were a core concept of mind, it could be wrong. That is, the underlying neurological facts about why we act in the ways that we describe as thinking, perceiving, and feeling may be so different from our characterizations of them in everyday or 'folk psychological' terms that to think of people as being or having minds is positively misleading. This is the position of eliminative materialism, associated with Feyerabend, Rorty, and Patricia and Paul Churchland. It is not at all obviously right. There is a lot of philosophical and scientific work to do before we can see where the answer lies.

If minds are real features of people then there may be aspects of these features which are not easily described in terms of everyday concepts such as thinking, perceiving, and feeling. For example, there might be subconscious processes which are best described in the language of psychoanalysis. Psychology, psychoanalysis, and other disciplines might tell us things about what we call mind which are unavailable to common-sense or to introspection. Certainly one conclusion that seems to be emerging from cognitive psychology, for example in the work of Nisbett and Ross, is that the explanations people give of the reasons for their actions are much more often wrong than they imagine. Whatever our limitations in knowing what we are thinking or feeling, our limitations in knowing *why* we think or feel seem to be very much greater. In one way this might not be surprising, for the reasons why we think or feel surely include many physical causes of which a person is completely unaware. And in fact one of the sources of the impression of free will may be the blindness of consciousness to the causes of thought and feeling.   A.M.

*cognitive architecture; consciousness, its irreducibility; mind, syntax, and semantics; psyche; dualism; mind–body problem; eliminative materialism; freedom; functionalism; self.

Paul Churchland, *Matter and Consciousness* (Cambridge, Mass., 1988).

D. C. Dennett and R. Hofstadter, *The Mind's I* (New York, 1981; Harmondsworth, 1982).

Henry Wellman, *The Child's Theory of Mind* (Cambridge, Mass., 1990).

mind, history of the philosophy of. Philosophizing about the mind is as old as philosophy itself, whereas philosophy of mind, proper—a distinctive subfield of philosophy—is of relatively recent advent. Both Plato and Aristotle present mature theories of the nature, structure, and types of psyche, theories that clearly depended on prior theorizing. And every great philosopher of the modern period, most notably Descartes, but also Hobbes, Locke, Berkeley, Hume, and Kant, propose theories of mind. In general, this theorizing takes place within metaphysics, epistemology, or moral theory and not in the service of developing a theory of mind for its own sake. Plato's tripartite division of psyche into rational, appetitive, and temperamental parts occurs in the *Republic* as part of the rationale for structuring political life in a certain way. Aristotle's distinction among the types of psyche in nature are part of his biological metaphysic; and his vision of the distinctive features of the human psyche as involving the capacity for reason and virtue serves his ethical theory. *Mind–body dualism emerges as a fundamental truth within Descartes's epistemological project. Hobbes's mechanistic psychology in the first part of *Leviathan* prepares the way for the famous claims about human nature in chapter 13. The laws of association of the Empiricists were attempts to answer distinctively philosophical questions about the nature and limits of human knowledge. And, of course, Kant's Copernican turn in philosophy, the proposal that mind lays down certain a priori conditions for experience, was meant to answer the deep scepticism about causation, *self, and transcendental matters such as the existence of God generated by Hume's epistemology.

The philosophy of mind now exists as a distinctive subfield of philosophy. There are journals devoted to work in it; job applicants claim to specialize in it; and so on. But its emergence cannot be precisely dated. It is best to think of the philosophy of mind as emerging during the late nineteenth century and first half of the twentieth century. Professional recognition of it as a distinct and important subfield comes only after 1950, despite the fact that one finds 'philosophical anthropology' and 'philosophy of mind' on medieval lists under the entry 'Metaphysics', and works like that of the Scottish philosopher Thomas Brown's *Lectures on the Philosophy of the Mind* appear as early as 1820.

The following developments were seminal in the early stages. First, the founding of scientific psychology as an offshoot from philosophy is, in the lore, dated to Wilhelm Wundt's founding of a psychological laboratory in Leipzig in 1879. Here master introspectors were trained and memory and reaction-time experiments were set up and carried out. All the founding documents of scientific psychology attest to acute self-concern on the part of the founders in making clear and defensible philosophical assumptions and in developing empirically secure methods that would be immune from the scorn the new science brought against a priori theorizing about mind. So psychology was born in the late 1800s as a philosophically self-conscious discipline.

Second, in 1874 Franz Brentano published his *Psychology from an Empirical Standpoint*. It is here that Brentano resurrected Aristotle's and Aquinas's notion of *intentionality — from the Latin, *intendo*, meaning 'to aim at or point toward'. The idea was that paradigm-case mental states, beliefs, desires, hopes, expectations, and the like, have intentional objects. Beliefs, desires, wishes, expectations, and so on, are of or about something: I believe that [Thatcher was Prime Minister]; I wish that [Reagan had not been President]. What a belief or wish is *about*— Thatcher or Reagan—is its 'object', whereas the propositional thought expressed—that Thatcher was Prime Minister or that Reagan had not been elected—is its 'content'.

Brentano's thesis is that *intentionality is the ineliminable mark of the mental. Psychology will need to be intentional, that is, the explanation of human thought and action will require us to make an inventory of all the types of mental state (beliefs, desires, and so on) that human minds are capable of going into, and it will also need to focus on the intentional objects and contents of these states (it remains a possibility that not all mental states are intentional; perhaps pains and moods have no objects or propositional contents and thus are not of or about anything at all). To explain why an individual reaches for that cool drink, we will need to posit not only belief and desire states, but belief and desire states with a particular intentional object, a cool drink, and content, that this is a cool drink.

A lively contemporary debate concerns the issue of whether only conscious mental states can be intentional, and whether other states involved in belief or desire formation are purely computational, not 'mental' at all in any interesting sense. It is noteworthy that Sigmund Freud took three and a half years of elective courses with Franz Brentano while he was in medical school. Indeed, one fruitful way of thinking of psychoanalysis is as involving an extension of Brentano's basic insight. Not only are conscious intentional states causally efficacious, but so too are unconscious intentional states. So just as my desire for a cool drink and my belief that this is a water-fountain in front of me explains my taking a drink, so too my unconscious desire to kill the boss explains my hostile verbal edge towards him.

Third, in 1890 William James published his monumental *Principles of Psychology*. Not only was this great work a compendium of all known psychological knowledge, culled mostly from the new scientific psychologists but also from more traditional philosophical sources, it was also a troubled testimony to James's own recognition that a scientific theory of mind was in deep tension with traditional philosophical ways of thinking about mind. This comes out clearly in the book when James discusses the deterministic assumption made by psychologists and the assumptions about human freedom made in ethics. James indicates that for purposes of living, but not for doing psychology, the assumption of *free will is the stronger. This same ambivalence carried over to James's ambivalence about what field he himself worked in. Over a brief period in the late 1880s and 1990s, James switched his Harvard appointment several times between medicine, psychology, and philosophy, before finally settling into philosophy for the remainder of his career.

James's *Psychology* treats all the great metaphysical and epistemological problems in the philosophy of mind. In addition to the problem of *free will and free action, he discusses the status of introspection, the problem of other minds, the nature of the emotions, the mind–body problem. And he takes not only Cartesian dualism, but Malebranche's occasionalism, Leibniz's parallelism, and Huxley's epiphenomenalism, as live options.

Wundt, Brentano, and James together represent some of the most important foundational work in the science of the mind. But it is, at the same time, important work in the philosophy of mind, work filled with philosophical assumptions about the nature of mind, analyses of competing models, and recommendations about the proper methods for studying mind and conceiving its nature. In their hands, mind becomes an important topic in its own right, worthy of attention in a science of its own, the fledgling psychology, and in need of a general philosophical analysis of such questions as: What is this thing called 'mind'? What is its place in nature? How is mind to be known?

The next phase in the development of the philosophy of mind, a phase which leads to its finding a distinctive niche, and to its professional recognition as a subfield, occurs between 1900 and 1950. Roughly, what happens is this: scientific psychology emerges not as a unified theory but as a bundle of theories with radically different methodological approaches. There were introspectionists, and anti-introspectionists, behaviourists, and functionalists, depth psychologists, and their opponents. In 1933 Edna Heidbreder wrote her important *Seven Psychologies*, still an excellent survey of the theory diffusion affecting psychology at its birth. This theoretical diffusion forced debate about the proper methods and assumptions of psychology, both among leading psychologists like Wundt, Titchener, John B. Watson (whose manifesto 'Psychology as a Behaviorist Views It' was published in 1913), and eventually B. F. Skinner—who left a poet's life in Greenwich Village for the halls of psychology (in what is today William James Hall, the philosophy department at Harvard being housed in Emerson Hall) after reading a popular magazine article by Bertrand Russell about *Logical Positivism—and also among philosophers as diverse as James and Russell, and John Dewey and Rudolf Carnap. Indeed, so close were the relations between *psychology and philosophy even after the new science had declared its independence that three philosophers, William James, Mary Calkins, James's student and a professor of philosophy and psychology at Wellesley College, and John Dewey, held the presidencies of both the American Philosophical Association and the American Psychological Association during the early years of psychology's development. And it was only in 1974 that *Mind* dropped the fifth and sixth words from its subtitle, 'A Quarterly Review of Psychology and Philosophy'.

Dewey and Carnap can be thought of as representatives of what were to become the two sides of the philosophy of mind, one side concerned primarily with the metaphysics of mind, the other with the methodological foundations of psychology and the epistemic status of first- and third-person psychological reports. In a series of papers published at the turn of the century, Dewey began to defend a picture of mind that was naturalistic without being mechanistic. He rejected the picture of mental action as consisting of simple reflexes or complexes of reflexes, as well as the Cartesian picture of the mind as an incorporeal sub-stance. Dewey proposed instead a picture of mind inspired by Darwin and James. The human mind is the result of selective forces building the most powerful and adaptive organism ever known. If Dewey was concerned primarily with developing a naturalistic metaphysic of mind consonant with evolutionary theory, Carnap was concerned primarily with the epistemological status of first- and third-person psychological reports. In part this concern was motivated by the appeal the positivists made to observation reports as the rock-bottom foundation for all science. Statements such as 'Water is H_2O' or 'The atomic number of gold is 79' depend on grounding theory in observation, often observations mediated by instrumentation. Perceptual reports ground all science—even chemistry and physics. How trustworthy are such reports? The positivists were quick to defend intersubjective observation reports, reports made by several independent observers, as reliable enough for the physical sciences. But what about the status of intrasubjective, first-person psychological sentences, such as 'I'm in a good mood' or 'I'm visualizing my mother's face'? What about the whole idea that expertise in introspection could be developed? How could such expertise be measured or verified? In his 1931 paper 'Psychology in a Physical Language', Carnap asserted that first-person psychological reports were 'intertranslatable with some sentence of physical language, namely, with a sentence about the physical state of the person in question'. Such reports refer (inadvertently, we might say) 'to physical processes in the body of the person in question. On any other interpretation' such reports 'become untestable in principle, and thus meaningless'.

The two strands, concern with the metaphysics of mind and with the logical status of sentences about mind, come together in Gilbert Ryle's *The Concept of Mind* (1949). If there is a founding document in the contemporary philosophy of mind proper, Ryle's book is it. First, there is a spirited attack on the Cartesian picture of mind as a *'ghost in the machine'. Second, there is a relentless attack on the doctrine of *privileged access, the view that the mind is transparent to its owner, and that we each have unmediated and incorrigible access to our own mental states. Third, there is the proposal that *'mind', the Cartesian conception of mind, at any rate, is simply a mystifying way of speaking about certain behavioural dispositions of the organism. According to Ryle's logical behaviourism, just as 'solubility' is nothing mysterious, referring simply to the disposition of a substance to dissolve in liquid, likewise talk of mental states, talk of 'belief' and 'desire', is, in so far as it is meaningful, talk of dispositions of the organism to behave in certain ways. It is ironic that the *locus classicus* of contemporary philosophy of mind argued in a sense that there really was no such thing as 'mind' as traditionally understood.

The work after Ryle constitutes the recent history of the philosophy of mind, a period characterized by two somewhat distinct sorts of work. First, there was work of analysis—work devoted to the analysis of *sensation and *perception (Chisholm, Armstrong, Sellars), intentionality, free action, the *emotions (Kenny), the debate about *reasons and causes, the possibility of *private language, and of knowledge of one's own and *other minds.

Ryle while claiming to be no behaviourist emphasized the centrality, indeed the indispensability, of behaviour in the ascription of mental terms. Wittgenstein did much the same thing in his *Philosophical Investigations* (Eng. tr. 1953). Wittgenstein's specific argument against the development of a private language was developed, clarified, and defended by Norman Malcolm in his review of the *Philosophical Investigations* in the *Philosophical Review* in 1954. Malcolm pointed out the relevance of the private language argument for the problem of other minds in his 'Knowledge of Other Minds' (1958). Other important work on other minds includes A. J. Ayer's, *The Concept of a Person* (1956) and *The Problem of Knowledge* (1963).

Important works on free action and the question whether reasons can be causes include: G. E. M. Anscombe's *Intention* (2nd edn. 1963), Hart and Honoré's *Causation in the Law* (1959), A. I. Melden's *Free Action* (1961), J. L. Austin's 'Ifs and Cans' (1961), and Donald Davidson's 'Actions, Reasons, and Causes' (1963).

It was P. F. Strawson's *Individuals* (1959), an essay in 'descriptive metaphysics', that made the radical but extremely helpful proposal that the traditional mind–body problem be reconceived along the following lines: the concept of a person is primitive and both mental and physical predicates are ascribable to persons, that is, to one and the same thing.

In addition to the latter work of philosophical analysis of mental concepts and attempts to state more clearly and helpfully traditional philosophical problems, there was a spate of work specifically devoted to developing distinctive materialistic alternatives to Cartesian *dualism and to each other, and by debates among the proponents of these different theories about the nature of psychological explanation. The three main materialistic theories are *identity theory, *eliminative materialism, and *functionalism.

Type-identity theory (reductive materialism). J. J. C. Smart, U. T. Place, and David Armstrong proposed this simple and compelling solution to the mind–body problem: each type of mental state is identical to some type of yet-to-be-discovered neural state. Just as water is H_2O and common salt is NaCl and the temperature of a gas is mean molecular kinetic energy, mental terms like 'believing', 'desiring', and 'loving' will be shown to be synonymous with terms that refer to types of neural events, so that some day we shall be able to say 'Love is such-and-such activity in sector 1704'.

Eliminativism. Paul Feyerabend and Richard Rorty issued this objection to identity theory: identity theory assumes that our ordinary mentalistic ways of taxonomizing psychological events, in terms of beliefs, desires, and the like, are not only good ways to taxonomize things for ordinary purposes, but in fact map perfectly on to (yet-to-be-discovered) underlying neural kinds. But why think that the case of belief and its kin is more like the case of

water, where the mapping to H_2O in fact works out, than like the case of our ordinary concept of fish, or, even worse, like the concepts of witch or phlogiston? In the case of fish, whales and dolphins were picked out by the concept for millennia, but are now known not to be fish at all, but mammals. The concepts witch and phlogiston both had great importance in their day, but both are now known to refer to nothing at all. Type identity theory assumes precise mappings from the mental to the neural which warrant a reduction or replacement of the mentalistic vocabulary with the neural vocabulary, and at the same time legitimizes the mentalistic vocabulary by showing that it always (inadvertently) referred to the underlying types of neural events. But Feyerabend and Rorty contend that mental talk was not intended to refer to neural events, nor did it inadvertently succeed in so doing. *'Folk psychology', with its strong Cartesian roots, was intended as, and succeeded in being, a theory that rivals scientific ways of conceiving of mind. The eliminativist position has been developed further and championed in recent years by Patricia S. Churchland and Paul M. Churchland and is a challenge to 'mental realism', our ordinary way(s) of conceiving of the mental.

Functionalism challenges both type-identity theory and eliminativism. An important but iconoclastic paper in this genre is Donald Davidson's 'Mental Events' (1970), in which he proposed the view he called *anomalous monism. According to this doctrine mental events are physical events but they are not reducible by definition or natural law, nor are they in any other straightforward way intertranslatable with physical terms. Against type-identity theory, the functionalist thinks it implausible that every person's belief that 'snow is white' is or must be realized in the same type of neural state. Functionalists think that all beliefs in the whiteness of snow are physical but allow for multiple physical *realizations of the belief. Just as 'capital' comes in many different forms, any form of cash or property will do, so too my belief that snow is white, and yours, and a Martian's, could be realized in different ways. The idea of multiple realizations has made functionalism a favourite doctrine among believers in strong artificial intelligence, the view that there is no reason in principle why computers shouldn't have bona fide mental states—indeed even be conscious. Different realization would be consistent with physicalism (token-physicalism), but would dash hopes for smooth type–type reductions since there would be no bridge law translating predicates such as 'believes snow is white', 'is in love', 'wants a drink' into single predicates in physical language (to be fair to identity theory, it can accommodate this idea up to a point by allowing for species-specific type-identities, so that cat-thoughts that 'there is water' and human ones are realized in different ways). Against the eliminativist, the functionalist holds out hope for folk psychology or, better, sees it as a starting-place, subject to refinement and rigour, for the development of an autonomous science of the mind. We start with a conception of mind as roughed out by folk psychology but with a commitment to physicalism. We then do experiments, draw inferences about how different cognitive subsystems work to produce the phenomenon being studied, e.g. language comprehension, memory, etc., and in so doing arrive at an abstract conception of how the mind works—without ever mentioning how these workings are realized physically.

As identity theory, functionalism, and eliminativism bumped up against each other throughout the 1960s, 1970s, and 1980s, they also began to bump up against the emerging amalgam of disciplines known today as *cognitive science. Cognitive science was rooted in work of logicians, psychologists, computer scientists, and neuro-scientists, great thinkers such as Alan Turing, Kenneth Craik, Claude Shannon, Norbert Wiener, Warren McCulloch, Walter Pitts, Karl Lashley, and John von Neumann (Howard Gardner dates the birth of cognitive science from the Hixon Conference at Caltech in 1948), who were thrilled by the prospect of blending insights from their different disciplines in order to understand the mind.

The interdisciplinary attitude and the wait-and-see-we-are-early-in-the-game attitude that pervade cognitive science made philosophers of mind aware that we could not know a priori how the relations among folk psychology, more refined cognitive models, and neuroscience would work out. It could be that identity theory is true in certain domains and in species-specific ways, e.g. chimpanzee vision might map neatly in chimps' brains and human vision in human brains. And it might be that neuroscience will spell doom for certain ways of thinking about mind, while certain abstract functional modes of explanation retain their value. The view favoured by most contemporary philosophers of mind is the co-evolutionary idea. P. S. Churchland, cooling recently towards eliminativism, expresses the basic idea in terms of constraining and developing each type of explanation by what is known at other levels of explanation, especially at adjacent levels.

The co-evolutionary strategy has important implications for the very idea of philosophy of mind as traditionally conceived, for it suggests that there is no subfield of philosophy proper that can deepen our understanding of mind. Mind will be understood, if it is understood, by our best science. Philosophers who study work in the relevant sciences will be welcomed in the interdisciplinary quest to understand mind. Quine proposed that philosophy was continuous with science; philosophy of mind as practised today has taken Quine to heart. At the same time it has become somewhat less clear what if anything the distinctively philosophical, as opposed to the scientific, issues are. In what sense, one might ask, is the question of the nature of mind a philosophical question rather than a foundational question within the science of the mind? O.F.

*consciousness; consciousness, its irreducibility; mental events; mental states; identity theory; eliminativism; functionalism.

Patricia Smith Churchland, *Neurophilosophy* (Cambridge, Mass., 1986).

Owen Flanagan, *The Science of the Mind*, 2nd edn. (Cambridge, Mass., 1991).

Jerry Fodor, 'Special Sciences', in *Representations: Philosophical Essays on the Foundations of Cognitive Science* (Cambridge, Mass., 1981).

Howard Gardner, *The Mind's New Science: A History of the Cognitive Revolution* (New York, 1985).

John Heil and Alfred Mele (eds.), *Mental Causation* (Oxford, 1993).

A. J. P. Kenny, *Ancient Philosophy* (Oxford, 2004), ch.7.

—— *Medieval Philosophy* (Oxford, 2005), ch.7.

David Rosenthal (ed.), *Materialism and the Mind–Body Problem* (Indianapolis, 1987).

Gilbert Ryle, *The Concept of Mind* (first pub. 1949; Chicago, 1984).

mind, problems of the philosophy of. Philosophical problems about the mind are among the enduring problems of philosophy; arguably, they are among the most deeply puzzling and challenging issues that philosophy has had to face.

1. Characterizing the mental. We come face to face with one of these issues when we try to give an initial delineation of the sphere of the mental. Mental events or states seem to fall under two broad kinds. One is comprised of those involving sensory qualities, or *'qualia', such as pains and itches, seeing colours and hearing sounds, experiencing pangs of hunger, and having after-images, and the like. As it is often put, there is 'something it is like' to be in one of these states—it is like something to see a yellow field of sunflowers, and that is different from what it is like to see the blue sky above it. These may be called 'qualitative mental states' or, more simply, 'experiences'. The second class of mental states, called 'propositional attitudes' or 'intentional states', includes states that have *content*, such as believing that Mt. Everest is the tallest mountain, being pleased that the home team has won the football match, and remembering one's telephone number. (Some mental states, such as emotions and perceptions, appear to possess both content and sensory aspects; e.g. feeling annoyed that your flight has been cancelled, noticing that the traffic-lights have just turned red.) But it has not been easy to answer the following question: What common property, or properties, do phenomena of these two kinds share in virtue of which they are all mental? What do itches and beliefs have in common that makes both mental?

One might say, following Descartes, that your knowledge that you are in one of these states is in some sense 'immediate' or 'direct' and carries a special sort of first-person authority. However, people often have beliefs and desires of which they are not aware, much less 'immediately aware'; and research in cognitive psychology has shown that much of our perceptual information-processing is not at all accessible to the subject. Moreover, it has been argued that there can be sensations, such as pains, of which the subjects, in the heat of combat or intense absorption in another activity, are unaware. Can we say then, following *Brentano, that the *mentality of mental phenomena consists in their *'intentionality'— their 'aboutness' or 'being directed upon' an object? Thus, your belief that Mt. Everest is the tallest mountain is about Mt. Everest, and is directed upon it. Or, as we may say, your thought has Mt. Everest as its 'intentional object'. However, it is difficult, if not incoherent, to conceive of a pain, or a tickle, to be 'about', or 'directed upon', anything. There are perhaps other possible approaches to this issue, but the problem of formulating an adequate 'criterion of the mental' has resisted solution. It may be that all mental states are characterized by a certain kind of subjectivity, a 'point of view' or 'perspectivalness'; however, precisely what this subjectivity amounts to is still an open question.

2. *The mind–body problem.* In a broad sense, the problem of accounting for the place of mind in a world that is fundamentally physical is coextensive with philosophy of mind. In a narrower sense, the problem is that of explaining the relationship between mentality and the physical nature of our being. Substance dualism, which posits immaterial souls or minds as bearers of mental states, has largely disappeared from contemporary discussion, and the focus of discussion in the mind–body debate has shifted to the status of mental states, processes, and properties *vis-à-vis* physical states, processes, and properties. We know, from familiar daily experience as well as scientific and clinical observations, that mental phenomena are correlated in lawlike ways with various specific physical processes going on in the body, and neurophysiological research has amassed huge amounts of information on the details of how specific mental capacities, functions, and processes depend on the structure and functioning of our central nervous system. But is it possible that the mental depends on and yet remains distinct from the physical? If so, what is the nature of this dependency? Or is the mental in fact a subspecies of the physical?

The mind–body identity theory, also known as central-state materialism, brain-state theory, and type *physicalism, holds that mental properties, or kinds, are reducible to, or can be reductively identified with, physical (presumably, neurobiological) properties and kinds. Just as scientific research has shown that light is a form of electromagnetic radiation and that genes are DNA molecules, argues the reductionist, neurophysiological research will show (perhaps, it has already shown) that pain is just the excitation of a certain group of neurons in the hypothalamus, that consciousness is 40 Herz synchronized neuronal oscillation, and, in general, that mental states are just neural processes in the brain. Physical reductionism of this form, however, has not been popular, since the 1970s. *Functionalism, which has been influential since the late 1960s, maintains that mental kinds are not physical kinds, but rather 'functional kinds', defined by their causal role in relation to sensory inputs, behaviour outputs, and other mental states. On this approach, pain, for example, would be an internal state of an organism that is typically caused by tissue damage and that in turn causes such effects as winces, groans, and a sense of distress. However, the ontological status of functional properties, in particular their status as causal powers, has

remained elusive; and serious doubts have been raised as to whether the sensory or qualitative character of mentality can be captured on the functionalist approach. Moreover, it is not clear exactly how functionalism differs from the identity theory, and it remains an open question whether functionalism is a form of reductionism. Others maintain that the mind–body relation is adequately characterized as one of *'supervenience'—that is, in the claim that there could not be two entities, or worlds, that are exactly alike in all physical respects but differ in some mental respect. But it is arguable that supervenience in this sense lacks sufficient content to qualify as a full theory of the mind–body relation; this is perhaps evident in the apparent fact that the reductionist, the functionalist, and even the epiphenomenalist are all committed to mind–body supervenience. There is also the *eliminativist alternative: mentality, like the posits of discarded scientific theories such as phlogiston and magnetic effluvia, will be expunged from our ontology as the neuroscientific understanding of human nature makes its inexorable advance.

3. *How can my mind move my limbs?* Impingements on our sensory surfaces cause sensations and perceptions, which in turn cause us to form beliefs about our surroundings. Our desires and wants, in concert with the beliefs we hold about the world, cause us to act, by moving our limbs or making our vocal cords vibrate in appropriate ways. Mental causation—that is, causality involving mental events as causes or effects—seems an undeniable fact of daily experience. Evidently, moreover, it is essential to our conception of ourselves as cognizers and agents: the acquisition of knowledge about our surroundings requires our perceptions and beliefs to be appropriately caused by ambient events, and genuine agency requires that the agent's intentions and decisions have the power to cause his limbs to move and thereby alter the arrangements of objects around him.

A fundamental difficulty with Descartes's interactionist dualism of mental and material substances was its perceived inability to explain how mental causation was possible. How could some wholly immaterial substance, entirely outside physical space, affect the motion of even a single molecule? By what mechanism is this miraculous transmission of causal influence accomplished? Moreover, there is reason to believe that the physical domain is *causally closed*; that is, tracing back a causal chain starting with a physical event should not take us out of the physical domain. To deny this would be tantamount to denying the completability of a physical theory of the physical world; it would be to assert that only by importing nonphysical causal agents or forces could physics hope to be a complete explanatory theory of physical phenomena. For these reasons, some have found *epiphenomenalism attractive: mental phenomena are caused by physical (presumably, neural) phenomena, but they are themselves mere 'epiphenomena' with no causal powers of their own. They are like shadows or afterglows cast by neural processes.

DONALD DAVIDSON addressed in seminal articles a variety of the most prominent questions in late twentieth-century philosophy of mind and language; their prominence is largely attributable to his treatment of them.

HILARY PUTNAM has deployed mathematical and scientific expertise to establish a clearer view of the status of scientific and philosophical knowledge and truth.

JOHN SEARLE first came to prominence in the 1960s with his work on the philosophy of language; now he is a leading critic of cognitive science, specifically of the aim of giving a materialist account of the mind.

THOMAS NAGEL has not shrunk from the big questions: What does it all mean? What is it like to be a bat? (The second is about the nature of consciousness.)

Photographs by Steve Pyke

Epiphenomenalism, however, has difficulties of its own. For one thing, it isn't clear that physical-to-mental causation is any easier to understand than mental-to-physical causation. Second, and far more importantly, depriving the mental of causal powers simply goes against almost all of what we believe about mentality—that is, about us. To most of us it is just not believable to say that our desires and intentions have nothing to do with what we do, or that the same human civilization would have developed even if no humans had ever had a thought, an idea, or a hope.

Mental causation is a simple matter for physical reductionism, for it identifies mentality with physical processes, and this means that mental causation is simply a species of physical causation. But reductionism has not been a popular option for some time. Non-reductive physicalism, which arguably is the current orthodoxy on the mind–body problem, encounters serious difficulties with the causal closure of the physical: if the physical domain is 'causally closed', as all serious physicalists believe, how can mental states, states that are irreducibly distinct from the physical, inject their causal influence into the physical domain? The problem of mental causation remains a central issue in the continuing debate over the nature of mind.

4. *Intentionality*. Wittgenstein asked: 'What makes my image of him into an image of *him*?' Many mental states, including thoughts, beliefs, and desires, are 'intentional' in Brentano's sense—that is, they are 'about' or 'directed upon' an object. My thought that Boston is to the north of New York is *about*, and is *directed upon* or *refers to*, Boston and New York. As earlier noted, Brentano claimed that intentionality is the defining characteristic of mentality. Earlier debates on intentionality during the twentieth century (notably, R. M. Chisholm's work) focused on the project of validating Brentano's thesis by providing a precise definition of intentionality. Mentality, however, is not the only phenomenon with intentionality; our words and sentences, too, have meanings and can refer to, or be about, things. This gives rise to a profound question: Is the intentionality of mind more basic than, or prior to, the intentionality of language, or is it rather the reverse? Perhaps, neither is prior to the other, both being interdependent. Moreover, we seem to be able to have thoughts about things that do not exist, like Pegasus and the fountain of youth (surely Ponce de León had thoughts about the latter). But how is it possible for our minds to direct themselves upon things that do not exist? We are apt to think that our thoughts about Pegasus and our thoughts about Cerberus are about different things. But how can that be? Given that neither exists, why aren't the thoughts about the same thing, namely nothing?

Lately, however, the focus of discussion has shifted to the project of 'naturalizing' intentionality. It is useful to distinguish two problems here: the problem of 'referential intentionality' (or the problem of reference, for short) and that of 'content intentionality' (the problem of content).

The first is the problem just reviewed, namely that of giving an account of the conditions under which a thought, or an expression, is about, or refers to, an object. The second is the problem of specifying the conditions under which a mental state has the specific 'content' or 'meaning' it has; that is, what it is about your belief that *snow is white* that makes it the case that its content is that *snow is white*, or that it represents the state of affairs of *snow being white*. The naturalization constraint in this context is usually taken to mean that any acceptable account of intentionality of either type must be formulated without the use of any unanalysed intentional or other overtly mentalistic concepts (for example, Frege's notion of 'grasping' a thought or proposition and Chisholm's notion of 'conceiving' a property). The causal approach has been the most popular in developing naturalistic accounts of intentionality. A causal theory of reference would attempt to explain 'expression x refers to object y' in terms of an appropriate causal relation holding between the uses of term x and object y; a causal theory of content would try to analyse 'Person S has the belief that p' in terms of a causal, or lawful, relationship between S's belief that p and the state of affairs represented by p. Some philosophers have stressed the importance of the inferential relations into which a thought enters in fixing its content; others have focused on the constraints of rationality and coherence as central to the determination of a speaker-thinker's mental contents. As this very brief survey shows, many different approaches and perspectives are in play in this area, and the situation is still very fluid.

One problem about content that has received much attention recently is *content externalism*. This is the view, first advanced by Hilary Putnam and Tyler Burge, that physical and social factors external to the subject play a crucial role in determining the contents of that subject's beliefs and other intentional states. This means that what goes on 'within' you—your mind or your body—does not wholly determine the meanings of your thoughts or words (as it is put sometimes, meanings are not in your head). For example, you have the belief that *water is wet*, whereas your exact twin on 'Twin Earth', where water (that is, H_2O) is replaced everywhere by a different but observationally indistinguishable substance, XYZ, has the belief that *XYZ is wet*, rather than the belief that *water is wet*. Or take a simpler example: you are looking at an apple, and your twin is also looking at an apple, which, as it happens, is qualitatively exactly similar to the one you are looking at. Your perceptual experience, let us say, is exactly similar to your twin's. However, your thought that *here is a red apple* and your twin's thought that *here is a red apple* have different contents—they are about different objects and their truth-conditions are different. This difference in thought content seems to stem not from any internal physical or mental differences between you and your twin, but from differences in the external environment. Just what the implications of content externalism are in regard to such questions as the truth of materialism, the causal powers of mental states, first-person epistemic authority on one's own mental states, and the nature of psychology as a science, are open questions.

5. *Consciousness*. Thanks largely to the influence of behaviourism and positivism early in the twentieth century, consciousness was studiously avoided, or at least ignored, by both psychologists and philosophers as a topic for serious investigation for much of that century, a fact that may strike one as deeply paradoxical. For one might wonder how mentality could be discussed or studied without examining consciousness. The common-sense conception of mentality gives consciousness the pride of place. In 1904, Ivan Pavlov, in his Nobel Prize acceptance speech said: 'In point of fact, only one thing in life is of actual interest for us—our psychic experience.' But by the 1940s and 1950s, behaviourism was firmly established as the reigning orthodoxy in psychology and social science, and a well-known and influential psychology textbook defined psychology as 'the science that studies the behavior of man and other animals' (Ernest Hilgard, *Introduction to Psychology*, 3rd edn. (1953)). As it turned out, however, the reign of behaviourism was short-lived, and since the 1960s there has been a sea change in the philosophical and scientific perspectives on consciousness. With the loosening of behaviourist and hyper-empiricist constraints, consciousness has made a strong come-back, both in systematic psychology and in philosophy, and serious philosophical works on consciousness have been appearing again, in large numbers.

The ill repute of consciousness was due in part to certain questionable characteristics attributed to it by both friend and foe, such as absolute ineffability, immediate and infallible accessibility to the subject combined with a total inaccessibility to the third person, and its interpersonal incomparability. It seemed to many that given these characteristics, consciousness could not be scientifically studied and explained, and, worse, that such essentially private experiences couldn't even be talked about in public language. In so far as we are able to learn and use expressions like 'pain', 'thought', and 'anger' for interpersonal communication, their meanings could not, it was argued, be fixed by some private episodes in an inner theatre accessible only to a single privileged subject. And surely we can, and do, use 'pain' and other mental expressions to communicate public meaning; how else could we explain a simple exchange like this: 'Does this give you pain?' (asks the dentist); 'Yes, it does' (the patient replies). Consciousness conceived as something essentially private and subjective thus seems to drop out of the picture, with no role to play in our public discourse, whether it is the language of science or the common language of everyday life.

Much recent work in cognitive psychology, however, appears to assume all but explicitly that subjects of certain psychological experiments are having specific sorts of conscious experience, such as mentally rotating an image. But the methodological assumptions that govern such references to consciousness are usually left vague and inexplicit, and the issue of their justification is seldom openly addressed. There are two broad issues concerning consciousness in psychology: first, how useful consciousness is as an explanatory concept, a concept in terms of which psychological theories can be formulated to explain the data in their domain, and second, whether it is possible to explain consciousness itself scientifically. Views are divided on both questions. There still are those (eliminativists and epiphenomenalists) who either outright reject, or are dubious about, the explanatory utility of consciousness. Some argue, as the classic epiphenomenalist did, that any intelligent behaviour for whose explanation we are apt to invoke conscious states can be explained perfectly well in terms of the underlying neural processes, and that this shows the dispensability of consciousness in psychology and cognitive science. Others have stressed the differences that consciousness supposedly makes to behaviour—e.g. performance levels of activities that require monitoring and control. There is also the metaphysical issue of whether or not it is ever necessary to invoke conscious states over and above their underlying neural substrates in the causal explanation of behaviour.

Can consciousness be explained scientifically? There are those who accept consciousness as a natural phenomenon arising out of physiological processes but despair of ever fully understanding it. Some have argued that the essential subjectivity of consciousness (i.e. the purported fact that all experiences involve a 'point of view' and are accessible only from the subject's point of view) precludes scientific understanding, which, being entirely objective, is unable to accommodate subjectivity. More optimistic are those who pin their hopes on the concerted efforts of neuroscience and cognitive psychology for an eventual naturalistic understanding of consciousness. What isn't clear in this debate is what exactly is required of a 'scientific understanding' of consciousness—that is, what specific factual or theoretical information we need to obtain if we are to gain a scientific understanding of consciousness. Some who think that consciousness can be neurobiologically explained appear to think that all that is needed for the success of their project is to identify a neural substrate for every type of conscious experience and for consciousness itself. Many will challenge this assumption, however, holding that these correlations are exactly what is in need of explanation. Suppose we discover that pains and itches are correlated respectively with neural states M and N. Why is it that pains, not itches, occur when M occurs? Why is it that pains occur only when M occurs and not when N occurs? (Can neurobiology explain why pains, not itches, mediate between tissue damage and wincing, and why itches, not pains, come between mosquito bites and scratching?) Why does consciousness emerge *at all* when M or N occurs? Even the noted biologist-neuroscientist Francis Crick has observed: 'we may be able to say that you perceive red if and only if certain neurons (and/or molecules) in your head behave in a certain way. This may, or may not, suggest *why* you experience the vivid sensation of color and why one sort of neural behavior necessarily makes you see red while another makes you see blue, rather than vice versa' (*The Astonishing Hypothesis* (New York, 1994), 10). Perhaps, these questions have no answers, and these correlations have to be taken as 'brute facts' of the world that resist further explanation—facts which Samuel Alexander, a leading emergentist, once claimed we must accept with 'natural piety'. This of course would be to admit that consciousness could not be fully understood on a neurobiological or any other kind of physical basis.

It is not an exaggeration to say that the 'mystery of the mind' is by and large the mystery of consciousness, and this mystery consists in our seeming inability to understand the phenomenon of consciousness as part of a world that is essentially physical, and, what is worse, not knowing just what it is that we need to know if we are to achieve such an understanding.

6. *Persons.* The nature of personhood has been a topic of perennial philosophical interest; it is one where philosophy of mind and moral philosophy come together, since a person is also an agent, someone who is able to deliberate, form intentions, and perform actions, and hence is evaluable from the moral point of view. The question 'What is a person?' can be approached in two ways, synchronically and diachronically.

Synchronically, the question concerns the properties and powers something must possess at a time to be a person at that time. It will generally be agreed that a person must have a rich mental life and be endowed with certain psychological capacities and functions. But what exactly is required? Evidently, a person must be capable of having intentional states such as beliefs, desires, and the rest if he, as an agent, is to be able to form intentions and decisions. Should a person also be conscious? Should she also be self-conscious in the sense of having a sense of self-identity and being aware of her distinctiveness as an individual person among others? Should a person be rational in some clear and determinate sense? There is also the following metaphysical question: Must a person be embodied or could there in principle be persons who are immaterial? A traditionalist, especially one who is religiously inclined, might answer that not only can a person be wholly immaterial but she must be possessed of an immaterial soul, an answer that will be rejected by most naturalistically inclined philosophers. At any rate, these are some of the questions that arise with respect to being a person at a time.

The diachronic question, however, has received far more attention historically, and this continues to be true today. This is the so-called problem of 'personal identity': what makes a person existing at a given time (say, the retired general) *the same person as* one that existed at an earlier time (the little boy in the photograph). Persons, like anything else, change over time; both your mental and bodily characteristics change, sometimes rather strikingly, over a period of time, without your ceasing to be the same person. Changes could of course be so huge and

drastic that it would be correct to say that you have ceased to exist, or that another person has come into being. But what general principles govern our judgements about such cases? There are two important approaches to this issue, both commanding the allegiance of many philosophers. One is the bodily continuity theory; it says that for you to be the same person as a person existing at another time, your body, or an appropriate part of your body, must be continuous, in some appropriate sense, with the body of that person—namely, that the continuity of embodiment is what underlies the identity of a person over time. The second is the psychological continuity theory, according to which the continuity of mental life— that is, the continuity of character, personality, and, in particular, memory—rather than bodily continuity, is what is constitutive of the sameness of a person. Many details need to be supplied: e.g. precisely what the supposed 'continuity' is supposed to consist in, and just when the required continuity must be considered broken. There is also the question whether psychological continuity can be considered independent, conceptually or nomologically, of bodily continuity. In any case, each of the two approaches appears vulnerable to persuasive counter-examples, and plausible arguments have been presented in recent years for the position that personal survival is a matter of degree, not an all-or-nothing affair, and that there are situations in which no clear-cut answer exists to the question 'Has the same person survived?' Although our understanding of these problems has been deepened in many ways in recent years, the concept of personhood continues to test our philosophical ingenuity and imagination.   J.K.

*theory theory of mind; mind–body problem.

D. Armstrong, *A Materialist Theory of the Mind* (London, 1968).
N. Block, O. Flanagan, and G. Güzeldere (eds.), *The Nature of Consciousness* (Cambridge, Mass., 1997).
T. Burge, 'Individualism and the Mental', *Midwest Studies in Philosophy*, v (1979).
D. J. Chalmers, *The Conscious Mind* (New York, 1996).
—— (ed.), *Philosophy of Mind: Classical and Contemporary Readings* (New York, 2002).
R. M. Chisholm, *The First Person* (Minneapolis, 1981).
P. M. Churchland, *Matter and Consciousness*, rev. edn. (Cambridge, Mass., 1988).
P. S. Churchland, *Neurophilosophy* (Cambridge, Mass., 1986).
D. Davidson, *Essays on Actions and Events* (Oxford, 1980).
D. C. Dennett, *Consciousness Explained* (Boston, 1991).
J. Fodor, *Psychosemantics* (Cambridge, Mass., 1989).
T. Honderich, *Mind and Brain* (Oxford, 1988).
J. Kim, *Mind in a Physical World* (Cambridge, Mass., 1998).
J. Levine, *Purple Haze* (New York, 2000).
Colin McGinn, *The Problem of Consciousness* (Oxford, 1991).
D. Papineau, *Thinking about Consciousness* (Oxford, 2002).
D. Parfit, *Reasons and Persons* (Oxford, 1984).
H. Putnam, *Mind, Language, and Reality* (Cambridge, 1975).
G. Ryle, *The Concept of Mind* (London, 1949).
J. Searle, *The Rediscovery of the Mind* (Cambridge, 1992).
S. Shoemaker, *Identity, Cause, and Mind*, 2nd edn. (Oxford, 2003).
J. J. C. Smart, *Philosophy and Scientific Realism* (London, 1963).
L. Wittgenstein, *Philosophical Investigations* (New York, 1953).

mind–body problem. The mind–body problem is the problem of giving an account of how minds are related to bodies, or how mental states and processes are related to bodily states and processes. That they are intimately related seems beyond doubt, and has not been seriously disputed. Evidently, our perceptual experiences depend on the way external physical stimuli impinge on our sensory surfaces, and, ultimately, on the processes going on in the brain; your desire for a drink of water somehow causes your body to move in the direction of the water-cooler; a bruised elbow causes you pain when it is touched, and the pain in turn causes you to groan and wince; and so on. But how do conscious experiences emerge out of the electrochemical processes in a grey mass of neural fibres? How do our beliefs and desires manage to get the appropriate neurons to fire and thereby cause the right muscles to contract? Schopenhauer called the mind–body problem 'the world knot', a puzzle that is beyond our capacity to solve.

The mind–body problem as it is now debated, like much else in contemporary philosophy of mind, has been inherited from Descartes. Descartes conceived of the mind as an entity in its own right, a 'mental substance', the essential nature of which is *'thinking', or *consciousness. In contrast, the defining nature of material bodies, or material substances, was claimed to be spatial extendedness—that is, having a bulk in physical space. Thus, Descartes envisaged two disjoint domains of entities, one consisting of immaterial minds with their mental properties (e.g. thinking, willing, feeling) and the other of material bodies with their physical properties (e.g. size, shape, mass, motion). For Descartes, not only did minds lack spatial extension; they were not in physical space at all. However, the two domains are not to be entirely unconnected: a mind and a body can form a 'union', resulting in a human being. Although the nature of this 'union' relationship was never made completely clear, (Descartes claimed it to be a primitive notion that is intelligible in its own right), it evidently involved the idea that a mind and a body joined in such a union are involved in intimate and direct causal interaction with each other.

Thus, Descartes's mind–body doctrine combines *substance dualism*, i.e. a dualism of mind and body, each conceived as an independent substance, with the idea that there is causal interaction between the two. Many of his contemporaries, like Leibniz and Malebranche, were substance dualists, but they rejected the idea of mind–body causal interaction. They found it difficult to make sense of the idea that immaterial minds with neither extension nor mass, and not even in physical space, could somehow move material bodies with mass and inertia. Substance dualism, however, has largely dropped out of contemporary discussions, although it has by no means disappeared; few philosophers now find the idea of minds as immaterial substances coherent or fruitful. There has been a near consensus, one that has held over almost a century, that the world is essentially physical, at least in the following sense: all that exists in the space-time world are bits of matter and complex structures aggregated out of bits of

matter, and the space-time world is the whole world. If all matter were to be removed from this world, nothing would remain—no minds, no 'entelechies', no 'vital forces', and not even an empty space-time. According to this physical monism (or 'ontological physicalism'), mental states and processes are to be understood as states and processes occurring in certain complex physical systems, such as advanced biological organisms, not as states of some ghostly immaterial beings. This means that the principal remaining project for contemporary discussions of the mind–body problem is that of explaining how the mental character of an organism or system is related to its physical nature.

The heart of contemporary *physicalism is the primacy and priority of physical properties and the laws that govern them. The following *'supervenience thesis' is one way of expressing this idea: once all the physical facts about your body are fixed, that fixes all the facts about your mental life. That is to say, what mental properties you instantiate is wholly determined by the features and characteristics of your bodily processes. In fact, the physical facts of a world determine what mental facts will hold in that world; that is, if God were to make an exact physical duplicate of this world, it would necessarily be a mental duplicate as well. This thesis, often called 'supervenience physicalism', can be given different formulations of varying degrees of strength. But there is a sense in which emergentism, a form of non-physicalist dualism, is committed to mind–body supervenience; the emergentist will surely accept the claim that if two systems are physically identical, they must be identical in respect of the non-physical (e.g. mental) properties that emerge in them. Many physicalists, therefore, want something stronger than mind–body supervenience. Granted that mental properties are supervenient on physical ones, they may yet be distinct from them, just as aesthetic properties of works of art, in spite of their supervenience on the works' physical properties, seem to remain distinct from them. We know that mentality is subserved and determined by neural processes. But are mental properties 'over and above' their neural correlates?

A negative response to this question constitutes the *identity theory of mind, or 'type physicalism', which identifies mental properties with their neural–physical correlates. So pain is identified with the excitation of C-fibres (assuming this to be its neural correlate); pain isn't some shadowy epiphenomenon of a brain process—it *is* a brain process. And similarly for all other mental states and properties. This is a classic form of mind–body reductionism: mentality is not renounced or eliminated, but conserved as a neural process, and thereby becomes a legitimate subject of scientific inquiry. Among the arguments for this view of the mind–body relation are the following: the argument that this gives us the simplest overall picture of the world in which physical science can explain all the phenomena; the argument that the identification of a mental property (pain) with its neural correlate (C-fibre stimulation) gives the simplest and best explanation of the observed correlation between them; and the argument that only by identifying mentality with a neural-physical process is it possible to explain how mentality can have a causal influence in the physical world.

Like *behaviourism, an earlier form of reductionism which attempted to identify mentality with facts about observable behaviour, type physicalism has failed to win enduring support. The most influential objection has been the variable (or multiple) realizability of mental kinds. Consider pain: there is no reason to expect that the same neural process underlies pain for all the different actual and possible pain-capable organisms (the neural substrate of pain is probably very different in humans and in octopuses). Moreover, there seems no a priori reason to deny the capacity for pain to all inorganic, or non-biological, systems. There seems then no single physical kind with which pain, as a mental kind, can be identified. Note, however, that supervenience physicalism as such is perfectly consistent with the variable realizability of mental properties.

These considerations have led to the formulation of *functionalism, arguably the most influential position on the mind–body relation during the past four decades. Functionalism conceives of mental kinds as 'functional kinds', not physical kinds. Pain, for example, is to be understood in terms of its function as a causal intermediary between sensory input (e.g. tissue damage), behaviour output (e.g. wincing, groaning, and escape behaviour), and other mental states (e.g. desire to be rid of it). An internal state of an organism that serves this function, which can vary from species to species (and perhaps from individual to individual), is said to be a 'realizer' of pain. Most functionalists are physicalists in that they hold that only appropriate physical states could serve as realizers of mental states functionally conceived. But they differ from type-physicalists in holding that, on account of their variable realizability, mental states cannot be identified with physical–biological states. Functionalism construes psychology as an autonomous science of these functional properties and kinds, specified in terms of their causal roles and abstracted from their specific physical-biological realizations. This view of psychology has been influential; it can be considered the received view of the nature of cognitive science. The question whether or not functionalism is a non-reductive form of physicalism depends crucially on exactly what physical reduction requires, and it must be considered an open question.

*Eliminativism urges that our commitment to mentality is nothing more than an outdated folklore, and that it is certain to be superseded by a more scientific understanding of our nature. Thus, the standard eliminativist argument begins with the premiss that vernacular ('folk') psychology—in particular, the psychology of beliefs, desires, and other 'propositional attitudes'—is infested with massive and irremediable systemic errors and gaps, and concludes that it will be made obsolete as the scientific—in particular, neuroscientific—understanding of our behaviour continues to advance. Beliefs and desires will ultimately meet the fate that befell phlogiston and magnetic effluvia, the forgotten posits of discarded theories. This eliminativist argument is sometimes advanced against intentional psychology countenancing cognitive states that are analogous to propositional attitudes of vernacular psychology.

Recently, the Schopenhauerian *pessimism has been resurrected by some philosophers, who argue that the mind–body problem is insoluble, and that we will never be able to understand how consciousness, subjectivity, and intentionality can arise from material processes. In any case, one thing that is certain is that the mind–body problem is one of the deepest puzzles in philosophy, and that it will continue to test our philosophical intelligence and imagination.   J.K.

*eliminativism; emergence.

D. Chalmers (ed.), *Contemporary Philosophy of Mind* (New York, 2002).
P. M. Churchland, *Matter and Consciousness*, rev. edn. (Cambridge, Mass., 1988).
J. Kim, *Philosophy of Mind* (Boulder, Colo., 1996).
C. McGinn, *The Problem of Consciousness* (Oxford, 1991).
T. Honderich, *Mind and Brain* (Oxford, 1988).
D. Rosenthal (ed.), *The Nature of Mind* (Oxford, 1991).

mind, syntax, and semantics. Mental phenomena such as beliefs, desires, hopes, fears, love, hate, perception, and intention are said to be *'intentional' in the sense that they are directed at or about or of objects and states of affairs in the world. These phenomena may be conscious or unconscious. All of these intentional mental phenomena have mental contents. Thus, for example, a belief is always a belief that such and such is the case, where the 'that' clause specifies the content of the belief.

Some efforts have been made to analyse intentional mental states as computational states, but such efforts suffer from the following objection: The computational states could not be identical with the mental states because computational states are defined solely in terms of their syntax. That is, computation is a matter of the manipulation of symbols, for example, 0s and 1s, and these are defined purely in terms of their formal or syntactical features. But these could not be equivalent to mental states, because though mental states often have a syntax, they also have a semantics—a thought content or an experiential content. Thus, a person who thinks that the earth is round has not only the appropriate symbols going through his mind, but he attaches a *meaning, interpretation, or understanding to these symbols. It is this meaning, interpretation, or understanding which constitutes semantics. The argument against the view that intentionality can be reduced to computation is simply that syntax is not equivalent to nor sufficient for semantics.   J.R.S.

*chinese room; functionalism.

J. R. Searle, 'Intrinsic Intentionality', *Behavioral and Brain Sciences* (1980).
—— 'Minds, Brains, and Programs', *Behavioral and Brain Sciences* (1980).
—— *Minds, Brains and Science* (Cambridge, Mass., 1984).

minimax: *see* maximin.

minimalism. The term describes philosophical positions that draw on few conceptual or ontological resources. One example would be Noam Chomsky's use of the term to describe his recent attempt to rationally reconstruct our grasp of grammar; another would be the *redundancy theory of truth—the view that '*p* is true' says no more than '*p*'. 'Minimalism' also describes a movement in the arts, which featured highly undifferentiated objects. This was philosophically problematic, but arguably rested on confusing the different roles played by some property of an object when considered as a work of art and when considered as a mere real thing.   D.M.

Richard Wollheim, 'The Work of Art as Object', in *On Art and the Mind* (London, 1973).

miracles. Usually defined as violations of a *law of nature by a supernatural being. Questions have been raised about how to articulate a notion of law of nature which is not exceptionless by definition, and how and whether such a definition applies to indeterministic laws of nature. Any argument that a miraculous event has occurred faces the tough challenge of showing both that the event in question did occur and that it was miraculous. A famous argument from Hume's chapter 'Of Miracles' shows how difficult a challenge this is to meet: to suppose that a miracle has occurred is to suppose that something has happened contrary to the entire weight of inductive evidence supporting the law of nature. In Hume's words 'no testimony is sufficient to establish a miracle, unless the testimony be of such a kind, that its falsehood would be more miraculous, than the fact, which it endeavours to establish'.   N.L.

David Hume, *An Enquiry Concerning Human Understanding*, sect. x.

mixture of labour. According to John Locke, if an individual has laboured upon a previously unowned resource and left enough for others, then he has acquired private property rights in it irrespective of their consent. Thus, '*Labour* being the unquestionable Property of the Labourer, no Man but he can have right to what is once joyned to, at least where there is enough and as good left in common for others' (II. v. 27). Locke's belief that God gave the world 'to the use of the Industrious and Rational, (and *Labour* was to be *his* Title to it)' (II. v. 34) suggests a religious basis for his view. The foremost modern Lockean advocate of private property, Robert Nozick, notes that pouring a can of tomato juice into the sea can be regarded as *losing* rather than *acquiring* rights, and consequently stresses not the mixture of owned with unowned resources but the alleged non-detrimental effects of appropriation.   A.D.W.

*property.

John Locke, *Two Treatises of Government* (Cambridge, 1988).

mnemic causation. According to Russell (*The Analysis of Mind* (London, 1921)), a 'kind of causation . . . in which the proximate cause consists not merely of a present event, but of this together with a past event'. The term originated with psychologist Richard Semon, who held that 'mnemic phenomena' like remembering necessitate the postulation of intervening 'engrams' or 'traces', because 'what is past cannot operate now', a suggestion Russell, undeterred by the prospect of action at a distance, thought unduly 'metaphysical'.   J.HEIL

*causality; memory.

J. Heil, 'Traces of Things Past', *Philosophy of Science* (1978).

Mochus. 'Learned men', said Robert Boyle, attribute 'the devising of the atomical hypothesis . . . to one Moschus a Phenician.' The learned men were relying chiefly on Sextus Empiricus and Strabo, who somewhat sceptically report Posidonius' belief that 'the ancient doctrine about atoms originated with Mochus, a Sidonian, born before the Trojan times'. Boyle's contemporary Cudworth reports without dissent the bizarre suggestion that 'this *Moschus* was no other than the Celebrated *Moses* of the *Jews*'.   J.J.M.

*atomism.

I. G. Kidd, *Posidonius: The Commentary* (on L. Edelstein and I. G. Kidd (eds.), *Posidonius: The Fragments*), 2 vols. (Cambridge, 1988), ii.2.

modality. The modal *value* of a statement is the way, or 'mode', in which it is true or false: e.g. certainly so (epistemic modality), currently so (temporal modality), necessarily so (logical modality). In logic, 'modality' usually means 'logical modality', that is, the logical *necessity or possibility of a statement's truth or falsity. A modal *statement is one in which some (usually logical) modality is actually claimed: e.g. 'It is not impossible that pigs should fly', 'Necessarily not everyone is below average intelligence'. On a simple view these features interconnect: e.g. the modal statement 'Necessarily *P*' is true just when '*P*' has the modal value necessarily true. *Modal *logic* studies the logical relations of modal statements.   S.W.

de re and *de dicto*.

A. N. Prior, *Formal Logic* (Oxford, 1962), pt. III, ch. 1.
W. V. Quine, 'Three Grades of Modal Involvement', in *The Ways of Paradox* (New York, 1966).

modality and metaphysics. There is an intimate relation between modality and metaphysics, because not only are the nature and ground of modal truth fundamental issues for metaphysics, but the primary task of metaphysics itself may be seen as that of charting the realm of possibilities. Empirical sciences such as physics may tell us, on the basis of observation and experiment, what kinds of objects, events, and processes actually do exist, but they cannot tell us what *must* exist, nor what *could* (but actually does not) exist. A priori sciences such as mathematics may disclose a limited range of necessary truths to us, such as the truths of arithmetic, but appear to be limited in their scope of inquiry to certain domains of abstract entities, such as the numbers. Moreover, even the empirical sciences cannot tell us what actually does exist, in the absence of a principled account of what could and could not exist, of the sort that metaphysics alone is equipped to provide. For empirical evidence can only be evidence for the actual existence of something if the existence of that thing is at least possible.   E.J.L.

E. J. Lowe, *The Possibility of Metaphysics* (Oxford, 1998).

modal logic. In classical *propositional logic all the operators are truth-functional. That is to say, the truth or falsity of a complex formula depends only on the truth or falsity of its simpler propositional constituents. Modal logic is concerned to understand propositions about what *must* or about what *might* be the case, and it is not difficult to see how you might have two propositions alike in truth-value, both true say, where one is true and could not possibly be false while the other is true but might easily have been false. For instance, it *must* be that $2 + 2 = 4$, but while it is true that I am writing this entry it might easily not have been. Modal logic extends the well-formed formulae (wffs) of classical logic by the addition of a one-place sentential operator L (or $\Box$) interpreted as meaning 'it is necessary that'. Using this operator a one-place operator M (or $\Diamond$) meaning 'it is possible that' may be defined as $\sim L \sim$, where $\sim$ is a (classical) negation operator, and a two-place operator -3 may be defined as $\alpha -3 \beta =_{df} L(\alpha \supset \beta)$, where $\supset$ is classical material implication. In fact any one of $L, M,$ or -3 can be taken as primitive and the others defined in terms of it.

In the early days of modal logic disputes centred round the question whether a given principle of modal logic was correct or not. Typically these disputes involved formulae in which one modal operator occurs within the scope of another—formulae like $Lp \supset LLp$. Is a necessary proposition necessarily necessary? A number of different modal systems were produced which reflected different views about which principles were correct. Until the early 1960s, however, modal logics were discussed almost exclusively as axiomatic systems without access to a notion of validity of the kind used, for example in the truth-table method, for determining the validity of wffs of the classical propositional calculus. The semantical breakthrough came by using the idea that a necessary proposition is one true in all *possible worlds. But whether another world counts as possible may be held to be relative to the world of origin. So an interpretation or *model* for a modal system would consist of a set W of possible worlds and a relation R of *accessibility* between them. For any wff α and world w, $L\alpha$ will be true at if and only if α itself is true at every w' such that wRw'. It can then happen that whether a principle of modal logic holds or not can depend on properties of the accessibility relation. Suppose that R is required to be transitive, i.e. suppose that for any worlds w_1, w_2, and w_3, if w_1Rw_2 and w_2Rw_3 then w_1Rw_3. If so then $Lp \supset LLp$ will be valid, but if non-transitive models are permitted it need

not be. If R is reflexive, i.e. if wRw for every world w, then $Lp \supset p$ is valid. So different systems of modal logic can represent different ways of restricting necessity.

First-order predicate logic can also be extended by the addition of modal operators. The most interesting consequences of such extensions are those which affect 'mixed' principles, principles which relate quantifiers and modal operators and which cannot be stated at the level of modal propositional logic or non-modal predicate logic. Thus $\exists x L\alpha \supset L\exists x\alpha$ is valid but $L\exists x\alpha \supset \exists x L\alpha$ is not. (Even if a game must have a winner there need be no one who must win.) In some cases the principles of the extended system will depend on the propositional logic on which it is based. An example is the formula $\forall x L\alpha \supset L\forall x\alpha$, which is provable in some modal systems but not in others. If both directions are assumed, so that we have $\forall x L\alpha \equiv L\forall x\alpha$, then this formula expresses the principle that the domain of individuals is held constant over all possible worlds.

When identity is added even more questions arise. The usual axioms for identity easily allow the derivation of $(x = y) \supset L(x = y)$, but should we really say that all identities are necessary? Questions like this bring us to the boundary between modal logic and metaphysics and remind us of the rich potential that the theory of possible worlds has for illuminating such issues. The possible-worlds semantics can be generalized to deal with any operators whose meanings are operations on propositions as sets of possible worlds and form a congenial tool for those who think that the meaning of a sentence is its truth-conditions, and that these should be taken literally as a set of possible worlds—the worlds in which the sentence is true.

M.J.C.

B. F. Chellas, *Modal Logic: An Introduction* (Cambridge, 1980).
G. E. Hughes and M. J. Cresswell, *An Introduction to Modal Logic* (London, 1968; repr. corr. 1972).
—— —— *A Companion to Modal Logic* (London, 1984).

modal realism. Rightly or wrongly, modal realism has come to be identified with David Lewis's seemingly extravagant view of the ontological status of *possible worlds, according to which each possible world is an aggregate of spatio-temporally and causally interrelated concrete objects, and all such worlds equally exist. On this view, the world that we inhabit—what *we* call the actual world—is in no way ontologically privileged, since every world is 'actual' to its own inhabitants. Modal realism, thus understood, involves a commitment to *counterpart theory, which denies that objects existing in different possible worlds can ever be identical, allowing each object only to have 'counterparts' in other worlds. For Lewis, modal realism is to be contrasted with *ersatzism*, which takes possible worlds to be linguistic or abstract entities, such as maximal consistent sets of sentences or propositions. Arguably, however, the term 'modal realism' might better have been employed to denote the more sober view that modal truths simply have an objective and mind-independent status.   E.J.L.

D. Lewis, *On the Plurality of Worlds* (Oxford, 1986).

mode. 'Mode' is a term of traditional metaphysics used correlatively with *'substance' and 'attribute'. An example would be the square shape of a particular piece of wood. Here the wood is the substance possessing the mode, and spatial extension is the attribute of which the mode is an instance. Another example would be a particular thought or experience enjoyed by someone. Here the person (or *self) qualifies as the 'substance' possessing the mode, and consciousness is the attribute.

A crucial logical feature of modes is that they depend for their identity upon the identity of the particular substances which possess them. Thus, that a thought is the particular thought it is is partly determined by *whose* thought it is. For two different people cannot share numerically the same thought. The modern term closest in sense to 'mode' is 'particular quality' or *'individual property'.   E.J.L.

E. J. Lowe, 'Real Selves: Persons as a Substantial Kind', in D. Cockburn (ed.), *Human Beings* (Cambridge, 1991).

model theory. When a set of sentences contain symbols that need interpreting, an interpretation that makes the sentences true is called a 'model' of the set. In 1954 Alfred Tarski introduced the name 'model theory' for the study of this notion when the sentences are mathematical axioms and the interpretations are mathematical structures in which the axioms are true or false. A structure *M* is said to be a model of a set *S* of formal sentences if the sentences in *S*, when their formal symbols are interpreted as being about *M*, are all true. An early result of model theory says that if *T* is a set of sentences in a first-order language and every finite subset of *T* has a model, then *T* itself has a model. Within mathematics, model theory became a vehicle for studying definability, with applications in algebra and geometry; an offshoot was non-standard analysis, which justified the use of infinitesimals in calculus. Within philosophy and linguistics, an approach is called model-theoretic if it involves set-theoretical criteria for the truth of sentences, as for example in *Montague semantics.   W.A.H.

K. Doets, *Basic Model Theory* (Stanford, Calif., 1996).

models. These are used extensively by scientists, coming in different forms and guises. All types involve some kind of analogy between the model and either reality or some other scientific claim. Most familiar are physical models, usually small- or large-scale material constructions—a famous example being the metal macro-model of the double helix, built by Watson and Crick. As or even more important are theoretical models, where scientists try to map limited aspects of reality, introducing simplifying assumptions, which are adjusted or removed in the light of the models' predictive successes. There is a school of thought which argues that scientific *theories are best understood semantically, in the sense of being families of theoretical models—interpreted according to specific empirical circumstances—rather than as general systems attempting to explain selected chunks of reality at one fell swoop. Even if one protests that such families could never capture completely what one aims for in a theory, it is hard to deny that sets of interrelated models are what face scientists most of their working lives.   M.R.

P. Achinstein, *Concepts of Science* (Baltimore, 1968).
R. Giere, *Explaining Science* (Chicago, 1988).

modernism. On the longest view, modernism in philosophy starts out with Descartes's quest for a knowledge self-evident to reason and secured from all the demons of sceptical doubt. It is also invoked—with a firmer sense of historical perspective—to signify those currents of thought that emerged from Kant's critical 'revolution' in the spheres of epistemology, ethics, and aesthetic judgement. Thus 'modernity' and 'enlightenment' tend to be used interchangeably, whether by thinkers (like Habermas) who seek to sustain that project, or by those—the post-modernist company—who consider it a closed chapter in the history of ideas.   C.N.

*post-modernism.

Jürgen Habermas, *The Philosophical Discourse of Modernity*, tr. Frederick Lawrence (Cambridge, 1987).

modus ponens. The 'affirming mode'. In *propositional calculus, any inference of the form 'If *p* then *q*, and *p*; therefore *q*' is an instance of *modus ponens*. In the *traditional logic of terms, inferences like 'If *A* is *B*, it is *C*; *A* is *B*; therefore *A* is *C*' were said to be in the *modus ponens*. Not really *syllogisms at all, such inferences were often called 'hypothetical syllogisms'.   C.W.

*affirming the antecedent.

J. N. Keynes, *Formal Logic*, 4th edn. (London, 1906), 352.

modus tollens. The 'denying mode'. In *propositional calculus, any inference of the form 'If *p* then *q*, and not *q*; therefore not *p*' is an instance of *modus tollens*. In the *traditional logic of terms, inferences like 'If *A* is *B*, it is *C*; *A* is not *C*; therefore *A* is not *B*' were said to be in the *modus tollens*. Like *modus ponens* inferences, not really *syllogisms at all. These inferences too were often called 'hypothetical syllogisms'.   C.W.

*denying the consequent.

J. N. Keynes, *Formal Logic*, 4th edn. (London, 1906), 352.

Molina, Luis de (1535–1600). Jesuit theologian and philosopher, born in Cuenca, Spain. He studied and taught at various leading Iberian universities. Molina is best known for his doctrine of middle knowledge (*scientia media*), expounded in *Concordia liberi arbitrii cum gratiae donis* (1588). This doctrine's aim was to preserve human *free will while maintaining the Christian doctrine of the efficacy of divine grace. For Molina, although God has foreknowledge of what human beings will choose to do, neither that knowledge nor God's grace determine human will. Middle knowledge, God's knowledge of what persons would do under any set of circumstances, enables

God to arrange for certain human acts to occur by pre-arranging the circumstances surrounding a choice without determining the human will. God's grace is concurrent with the act of the will and does not predetermine it, rendering the Thomistic distinction between sufficient and efficacious grace superfluous.   J.G.

E.M.

Alfred J. Freddoso, *On Divine Foreknowledge: Part IV of the Concordia. With an Introduction and Notes* (Ithaca, NY, 1988).

Mollā Ṣadrā (?–1641). Persian philosopher Ṣadr al-Dīn Shīrāzī is widely considered to be one of the most original thinkers in post-classical Islamic philosophy. His most widely quoted philosophical problem (one of twelve considered original contributions) is 'substantial *motion', the unifying principle underlying all of philosophy and capable of describing existence, time, motion, and change pertaining to all physical, psychological, and non-corporeal things. This problem, encountered in every domain from semantics to eschatology, consists of: essential motion initially observed in external reality, never ceasing, and covering all physical and ontological distinctions, resulting in the continual 'evolution' of higher beings, transformation of material existence, intensely moving from one level to another into the unchanging *mundus imaginalis* beyond ordinary time and space where individual 'evolved' essences with 'formal', or 'imaginalis' bodies will then permanently exist.   H.Z.

Fazlur Rahman, *The Philosophy of Mullā Ṣadrā* (Albany, NY, 1975).

Molyneux problem. A problem about correlating visual and tactual *perception, one of several that William Molyneux of Dublin posed in letters to John Locke. (Molyneux was also interested in the visual perception of distance.) Suppose that a blind person who can distinguish spheres from cubes by touch suddenly becomes able to see. Will this person be able to distinguish these shapes visually before correlating sight and touch? Locke (*Essay Concerning Human Understanding*, II. ix. 8) and Berkeley (*Essay Towards a New Theory of Vision*, sects. 121–46) answer negatively. Berkeley went on to deny that sight and touch ever perceive the same property, strictly speaking. Leibniz (*New Essays Concerning Human Understanding*, sections that correspond to Locke) answers positively on the basis of structural properties in common to tactual and visible shapes. Careful observations of patients who acquired vision by surgery, such as cataract removal, have not resolved the Molyneux problem.   D.H.S.

Gareth Evans, 'Molyneux's Question', in *Collected Papers*, (Oxford, 1985).

Michael J. Morgan, *Molyneux's Question* (Cambridge, 1977).

monadology. A philosophical system usually associated with the mature metaphysics of Leibniz, as outlined in the *Monadology* (1714).

The fundamental thesis of Leibniz's monadology is that the basic individual *substances that make up the universe are soul-like entities, the monads, which are

non-extended, hence immaterial, entities. The properties of the monads may all be reduced to perceptions and appetites. Whatever other entities we may wish to recognize must be reduced to this base. Thus Leibniz treated material objects as appearances of collections of monads.

R.C.SLE.

monism, anomalous: *see* anomalous monism.

monism, neutral: *see* neutral monism.

monism and pluralism. These are doctrines concerning how many *substances exist, and may relate either to kinds of substances or to their individual instances. Monism regarding the kinds of substance holds that only one such kind exists, whereas pluralism admits a multiplicity of kinds. Monism regarding the instances of a given substantial kind holds that only one such individual does or can exist, pluralism that many do or may. Thus a materialist who is also an atomist is a monist as regards the kinds of substance that exist but a pluralist with regard to how many individual substances of that kind there are. By contrast, Descartes was a pluralist as regards the kinds of substance that exist and also a pluralist regarding the number of individual mental substances—but, rejecting *atomism, he was a monist regarding the number of individual material substances.   E.J.L.

D. W. Hamlyn, *Metaphysics* (Cambridge, 1984).

Montague, Richard (1930–71). American philosophical logician. During the 1960s he developed a mathematical formalism to define what it is for a sentence of a precisely defined fragment of English to be true at a time and place in a possible world. Under the name of 'Montague semantics' his proposals soon became accepted among linguists as a paradigm for formalizing the semantics of natural languages. Two characteristic points were his treatment of the meaning of a sentence as a homomorphic copy of its syntax (following Tarski's truth definitions for formalized languages) and his proposal to treat proper names like 'John' as a special case of quantifier phrases such as 'every man' or 'a fish'. Montague's other contributions include work on the metamathematics of set theory, a study with David Kaplan of the paradox of the unexpected examination, a logical analysis of determinism, and unsurpassed standards of rigour and accuracy in philosophical logic.

W.A.H.

R. Montague, *Formal Philosophy*, ed. R. H. Thomason (New Haven, Conn., 1974).

Montaigne, Michel Eyquem de (1533–92). A fluent essayist who mistrusted the pretensions of systematic philosophy, Montaigne's writings are richer in allusion and anecdote than in formal argumentation, but none the less sparkle with philosophical insights. His *Apology for Raymond Sebond* (1580) is an entertaining and discursive essay, steeped in the classical learning which typifies the humanist movement of which he was a notable exemplar. The book examines some of the sceptical theses of Sextus Empiricus (whose writings had recently been translated into Latin), and maintains the need for faith and divine revelation to overcome the inherent limitations of human reason. It also suggests that the supposed superiority of human reason over the natural instincts of animals is largely illusory. Montaigne's writings set the scene for the attempts of rationalists such as Descartes to establish a new a system of knowledge whose foundations would be independent of the deliverance of the senses.   J.COT.

*rationalism.

R. A. Sayce, *The Essays of Montaigne: A Critical Exploration* (London, 1972).

Monte Carlo fallacy: *see* gambler's fallacy.

Montesquieu, Charles-Louis de Secondat, Baron de (1689–1755). French philosopher and jurist, who contributed to political sociology and to philosophy of history. *Persian Letters* (1711, tr. New York, 1973) initiated the fashion of criticizing European culture by comparing it with the Orient. *Considerations on the Causes of the Greatness of the Romans and their Decline* (1734, tr. New York, 1965) and *The Spirit of the Laws* (1748, tr. Cambridge, 1989) distinguish three forms of government, each with its special structure and each animated by its own 'principle'. Republics are animated by virtue (patriotism and egalitarian fraternity rather than moral virtue), monarchies by honour, and despotisms by fear. Forms of government depend in part on physical, especially climatic, factors. But wise legislators can counteract physical disadvantages by intellectual and moral forces, especially once they know the laws governing the social world. Montesquieu's advocacy of a division of powers (legislative, executive, and judicial), which he saw in the English constitution, greatly influenced the American founding fathers.   M.J.I.

M. Richter (ed.), *The Political Theory of Montesquieu* (Cambridge, 1977).

Monty Hall problem. Game show host Monty Hall conceals a prize behind one of three curtains, *A*, *B*, or *C*. Asked to guess where the prize is, you choose *A*. Before disclosing the prize's location, Monty opens *B*, revealing that it is not there, and offers you the option of sticking with *A* or switching to *C*. You reason as follows: once Monty opens curtain *B*, the *probability that the prize is behind *A* or *C* is the same: ½; so switching affords no advantage. But is this right? Assuming that Monty opens a curtain only if the prize is not behind it, the relevant probability is the *conditional* probability that the prize is behind *A given* that Monty has revealed that it is not behind *B*. Bayes's theorem shows that this probability is ⅓, so the probability that the prize is behind *C* is ⅔. You should switch! For those not steeped in probability theory, there is a simple way to see the point. Once Monty opens a curtain, you will win by switching just in case your original choice was wrong. Assuming your original choice is wrong

two-thirds of the time, you will win by switching two-thirds of the time, so you should switch.   J.HEIL

Martin Gardner, 'Probability Paradoxes', *Skeptical Inquirer* (1992).

mood. States of mind of an emotional cast which are temporary, yet which colour a person's responses and reactions quite generally, qualify as *moods*, as when someone is said to be in a sombre, sullen, or sunny mood. The focus is on a pattern of behaviour manifesting a current state of mind, and not, as with motives, on the intended consequences of the behaviour.

'Mood' also enjoys a use with respect to language. Commonly misconstrued in this connection, mood is properly a feature of verbal phrases—indicative, imperative, subjunctive, optative. As embodying the different speech-acts of asserting and asking a question, utterances of, say, 'He is out' and 'Is he out?' are said to differ in *force*. However, they agree in mood, the verb in either receiving the same description, 'third-person singular present indicative'.   B.B.R.

*emotion and feeling.

J. Lyons, *Semantics*, ii (Cambridge, 1977).
G. Ryle, *The Concept of Mind* (London, 1948).

moods of the syllogism: *see* syllogism.

Moore, George Edward (1873–1958). Moore was a philosopher of immense, even revolutionary, influence by reason—most unusually—of the extreme simplicity and directness, even seeming naïvety, of his approach to philosophy. He was moved in his early days, as he recorded in 1942, not by any perplexities about 'the world or the sciences', but by the baffling things said about the world and the sciences by other philosophers. In the tradition prevailing at that time he found it usually taken for granted that ordinary language was probably defective, that commonly held beliefs were probably false or at any rate inadequate, and that the task of philosophy was to work its way towards deeper, perhaps odd-looking truths set out in purer, probably novel and unfamiliar terms. Moore was sincerely amazed by this. Why was it thought necessary? He insisted ('A Defence of Common Sense' (1925)) that there is actually a vast body of shared convictions about 'the world', expressible in quite ordinary propositions whose meanings are perfectly clear, and which are known for certain to be true—even by those philosophers who appear to deny them. Take, say, 'There exist conscious beings other than oneself'—everyone knows what that means; or take, say, 'There exist material objects, such as shoes and inkstands'—everyone knows that that is certainly true. But if so, Moore concluded, philosophers must have been radically confused as to the nature, or perhaps the purpose, of their own activities. They cannot really have been confronting problems about meaning, since typically there were, he held, simply no such problems; nor can they really have been denying, or even doubting, that certain propositions were true, since typically we all—themselves included—knew that they *were* true. What then was seriously, genuinely problematic? Moore's answer—hugely influential for most of the twentieth century—was: the *analysis* of propositions. Among English-language philosophers, at any rate, this seemed radically to transform the philosophical agenda. We know what a given proposition means, and we know it to be true; the question, then, is not 'Is it true?' or even 'Do we know it to be true?', but 'What is its correct analysis?'

The notion of *analysis was itself always controversial, but Moore's own most persistent pursuit of analyses dealt with very ordinary propositions about familiar objects, for example 'This is a hand'. He held that the analysis of these must always bring in the very puzzling items he called *'sense-data'—the proposition is really about a sense-datum that one has, and the problem is how in the analysis the relation between sense-datum and object should be spelled out. He never believed that he had worked this out quite satisfactorily.

Also vastly influential was Moore's work in ethics, notably in *Principia Ethica* (1903). Here his insistence on the indefinability of 'good' and his exposition of the so-called *'naturalistic fallacy' were long regarded by many as path-breaking advances in moral philosophy. In historical perspective, however, this work looks a good deal less impressive and durable than his contributions in other fields. See also his *Ethics* (1912).

Moore's working life was spent mainly in Cambridge, though he taught for some years in America during the Second World War. He was a university lecturer from 1911, and Professor of Philosophy and Fellow of Trinity College from 1925 to 1939. He was editor of the periodical *Mind* from 1921 to 1947, and was appointed to the Order of Merit in 1951.   G.J.W.

*common-sense; paradox of analysis.

A. Ambrose and M. Lazerowitz (eds.), *G. E. Moore: Essays in Retrospect* (London, 1970).
Thomas Baldwin, *G. E. Moore* (London, 1990).
G. E. Moore, *Philosophical Studies* (London, 1922).
—— *Some Main Problems of Philosophy* (London, 1953).
P. A. Schilpp (ed.), *The Philosophy of G. E. Moore* (Chicago, 1942).

Moore's paradox. '[S]uch a thing as "I went to the pictures last Tuesday, but I don't believe that I did" is a perfectly absurd thing to say, although what is asserted is something perfectly possible logically' (Moore 1959). Perhaps I have my dates mixed up, and someone else says, 'You went to the pictures last Tuesday, but you don't believe that you did'. If what is asserted here is true, why is it an absurd thing for *me* to say about *myself*? The task is to give an account of the absurdity. Moore's attempt turns on the notion of implied belief—saying or asserting *p* implies believing *p*—and in the case above the belief implied by the first clause conflicts with the belief asserted in the second. Hence the absurdity. But what should we make of a philosophically inclined scientist, who sincerely says, 'Although I believe our current theories are true, I

have good inductive grounds based on the dramatic failures of past science for my belief that some of our current theories are false'? Some expressions, at least akin to Moore Paradoxical ones, are not perfectly absurd things to say, and debates about the nature of such claims continue.
                                                            J.GAR.

G. E. Moore, *Philosophical Papers* (London, 1959).
—— 'A Reply to My Critics', in P. A. Schilpp (ed.), *The Philosophy of G. E. Moore* (Chicago, 1942).

moral ideals: *see* ideals.

moralities, agent-relative: *see* agent-relative moralities.

morality, public: *see* enforcement of morals; public morality; public–private distinction.

morality, sexual: *see* sexual morality.

morality, slave: *see* slave morality.

morality and art: *see* art and morality.

morality and religion: *see* religion and morality.

morality in political philosophy. Whether morality has a role to play in political philosophy is controversial. Political economists of the eighteenth century argued that the good of the collective was best achieved by encouraging agents to act in their self-interest, not by rousing their moral sentiments or their pity for the unfortunate. Marx maintained that morality is a figment of the imagination, though his political theory is arguably influenced by moral values. Gauthier's conception of the ideal market as a 'morally free zone' that is a model of social justice reflects the conviction that at least some sectors of political philosophy can be given non-moral foundations and that the notions of virtue and self-sacrifice that are central to the concept of morality can be expunged from the theory of just distributions. Yet the claim that agents are entitled to retain or exchange all resources they have extracted from the human or non-human environment through the market and need not bestow them *gratis* on other claimants is itself morally controversial.

Many pressing issues in political philosophy, including socio-economic inequality, racism and sexism, conscription and war, punishment, rights of self-determination, and free speech appear to have an ineliminable moral dimension. They raise the question how much security, utility, or liberty *A* should be called upon sacrifice in order to improve *B*'s lot, when *A* and *B* are differently situated, and what motives should induce *A* to make any sacrifice whatsoever. Socio-economic inequality is implausibly treated as requiring a bargaining solution in the form of a deal struck between wealthy *A* and poor *B*. For *B*'s best option from amongst those *A* is prepared to offer or threaten may be an improvement relative to his current level, but not just, and all *B*'s offers except the *status quo* may be unacceptable to *A*. The postulate that *A* should be prepared to accept his own offer, were he *B*, changes nothing. Justice is a feature of the offer or threat *we* observers will judge that *A* ought to make and *B* to accept, given the respective positions of *A* and *B*.   CATH.W.

David Gauthier, *Morals by Agreement* (Oxford, 1986).

moral judgement. Is *'judgement' the most appropriate word for what properly terminates moral deliberation? Or are we seeking, when we reflect on a morally perplexing situation, rather to elicit and stabilize some response of feeling, whether of attraction or repulsion? Or again, do we (more accurately) decide on our moral stance—in a personally inventive or even creative way, much as a painter decides after thought to add a highlight here or to deepen a shadow there, where there is no pre-existing reality to guide or constrict him?

Against the ultimacy of feelings and *emotions, it may be argued that our feelings themselves are properly subject to moral judgement: even love needs to be monitored, as it may take selfish and corrupt forms.

There may well be room for creativity in the moral life, but with basic moral values and principles, the agent's characteristic experience is: 'Here I have no option: my will and judgement are constrained'. I cannot decide that a life dedicated, say, to the expression of sadistic impulses is a morally fine life. It is not up to me. Even my rebellion against a particular moral code or principle or practice will be fuelled by a commitment to values to which there seem to be no alternatives—I grasp these as (judge them to be) basic or ultimate. Early and immature anticipations of moral judgement may be nothing more than unreflective responses of feeling learned in early childhood. Somewhat later, the pressures of peer group and 'society' may modify these—but still as external pressures to conform. Crucial for moral maturity, however, is the possibility of distancing oneself from all pressures from without, reflectively and critically sifting the evaluations of others, endorsing some and rejecting others, forming a ranking of one's own. Not, however, wilfully and idiosyncratically; rather with the sense of clarifying, 'tuning', or 'focusing' more accurately on moral values, principles, goals that are not of one's own contriving. For all this activity of discrimination—without which there can be no moral growth, moral reform, necessary dissidence—the vocabulary of 'judgement', with its cognitive and rational connotations, is more appropriate by far than its rivals.

What are the proper objects of moral judgement?—the particular acts of responsible agents, their general policies, their traits of character: but these considered in a special (moral) context or from a special point of view. Understanding these is a major task of normative ethical theory. However humanly complex and specific the situation in which I have to act, to reach a distinctively moral judgement on how I *ought to act is to introduce an impersonal note. It is to ask what universal rules or principles bear upon my situation, and what are their relative urgencies? Does a strong requirement of *justice or fairness take precedence, for instance, over all other, even benevolent, actions? Am I considering the interests of everyone involved, not self-deceivingly masking, giving privilege to, my personal inclinations?

For a serious and convincing moral judgement, there are both formal and substantive requirements to be met. The readiness to universalize, the impersonal note: but also deference to basic human values that alone can make these procedures and attitudes intelligible, and a concern with the regulation of life that furthers their realization and enjoyment.

In some moral contexts, 'judgement' refers not to an epistemological act, but rather to the quality possessed by someone with a particular sensitivity to complex moral situations, where no rule of thumb, no simple appeal to a single principle, can ensure a rational outcome. A case in which none of the conflicting factors loses its serious claim to compliant action calls upon, not arbitrary decision, but fine or 'nice' moral judgement.   R.W.H.

*good; right; right action; moral philosophy, histories of; moral philosophy, problems of.

J. Finnis, *Fundamentals of Ethics* (Oxford, 1983).
J. McDowell, 'Are Moral Requirements Hypothetical Imperatives?', *Proceedings of the Aristotelian Society*, supp. vol. (1978) and later articles on moral philosophy.

moral knowledge presupposes that there are moral truths accessible to us. It is often said that the opposing view that moral judgements are devoid of truth-value does not do justice to our conviction that having true moral beliefs matters in a way that having certain, e.g. aesthetic, preferences does not.

It is not easy, however, to make sense of the hypothesis that there are reliable methods for acquiring moral knowledge. Clear and distinct perception of wrong-making features in actions by a competent moral observer might be proposed as the criterion of their truth. Thus I might be supposed to know that torturing cats is morally wrong on the grounds that when I observe or merely think about the action of torturing cats I perceive immediately its wrongness. However, my claim to be a competent observer is established by my delivering judgements taken by others to be correct. If moral perception is as uniform across the species as colour perception, and if incompetent observers can be identified by ingenious tests, we might accept this account of moral knowledge. If there are no such convenient tests, it will be impossible to obtain moral knowledge in controversial matters, since claims to perceive wrong-making features in e.g. wearing leather shoes leave the competence of the perceiver an open question.

Another approach to the problem of moral knowledge, more appropriate to the settling of controversial moral questions, involves supposing that the provision of new evidence and argument has the effect of reinforcing or transforming beliefs about how morally good and bad agents behave. If the evidence supplied consists of true propositions, and if the arguments employed are valid, the resulting moral beliefs should count as moral knowledge, provided they are sufficient to decide the question. This account lends itself to an interpretation of how we came to know that slavery was wrong when this was formerly a controversial proposition. However, it is unclear that apprehension of this allegedly previously unknown fact can be distinguished from the formation of a new preference, formally analogous to an aesthetic preference, for abolishing slavery. Whether widely shared preferences acquired in this manner should be termed 'knowledge' remains controversial.   CATH.W.

John McDowell, *Mind, Value and Reality* (Cambridge, Mass., 1998).

moral law. Most generally, the idea of the moral law is the idea of that set of standards or principles, cast in the form of 'Thou shalts' or 'Thou shalt nots', which set down how one should behave morally. The Ten Commandments provide the classic model for what moral laws will be like. More specifically, the notion of the moral law is central to Kant's moral philosophy. He argues that moral requirements have the form of *categorical imperatives which prescribe what is to be done regardless of what one may want. He then proposes that the (singular) moral law is a test by which to determine whether or not we should do what we intend. It states that we should act only on those maxims (rules of action) which we can will to be a universal law for all agents. Both Hume and Schopenhauer think it is a fundamental mistake to conceive of morality as a form of law.   N.J.H.D.

*right action.

I. Kant's *The Groundwork of the Metaphysic of Morals* should be read on this topic.

moral luck. Phenomenon that, supposedly, challenges traditional ideas about moral assessment. For Kant and others, moral judgement ought not (unfairly) to depend on factors not under the agent's control. Reflection on our actual judgements, however, reveals their widespread determination by various kind of luck. A driver who neglects to check his brakes is guilty, if no harm ensues, of mere negligence. But if (through bad luck) the driver kills a child in his path, he is judged (and judges himself) more harshly, even though his input is the same.   S.D.R.

Thomas Nagel, 'Moral Luck', reprinted in his *Mortal Questions* (Cambridge, 1979).

Bernard Williams, 'Moral Luck' reprinted in his *Moral Luck* (Cambridge, 1981).

moral motivation. Motivation to do what one (believes one) morally ought to do or what one (believes one) has moral reasons to do. A central topic of debate is whether moral motivation differs from other kinds of motivation only in its subject-matter or in a deeper way. Some philosophers maintain that, necessarily, anyone who believes that she herself morally ought to help Joe has motivation to help him, even though they would deny that the same is true of people who believe that they legally ought to help Joe. Other philosophers argue that

the former claim is true of rational agents, even though they would reject a parallel claim about rational agents who believe that they legally ought to help Joe. There are also philosophers who reject both claims about moral motivation and argue that such motivation is on a par with non-moral motivation.   A.R.M.

M. Smith, *The Moral Problem* (Oxford, 1994).

moral particularism. The particularist holds that the possibility of moral thought and judgement in no way depends on an adequate supply of moral principles or general rules. Moral judgement is primarily concerned with the particular case. Experience can help us discover moral generalities, such as that it is normally or standardly wrong to lie. Such generalities are as important in morality as elsewhere. But they can serve only as rules of thumb; the moral aspects of a particular situation are not constructed out of relations between its non-moral features and relevant principles. Particularists tend to base their view on the claim that what is a moral reason in one case may be an opposite reason, or no reason at all, in another—a sort of moral reasons-holism. They argue for this either by appeal to examples, or by trying to show that this sort of holism is true of all reasons, and *a fortiori* of moral ones.   J.D.

B. W. Hooker and M. Little (eds.), *Moral Particularism* (Oxford, 2000).

moral philosophy, histories of: *see* histories of moral philosophy.

moral philosophy, history of.

Greek Ethics. Ethical thought, in the sense of the attempt to formulate codes and principles of moral behaviour, has always been a necessary feature of human cultures, but moral philosophy in the more precise sense can be said to begin with the *Sophists of the Greek world in the fifth century BC. They were the first thinkers we know to have raised critical questions about the very idea of moral conduct, about what morality is and why it should exist. Their teaching of rhetoric and of techniques of persuasion invited the charge that such techniques could be used to make wrong more persuasive than right, and would enable people to flout moral standards with impunity. The more conservative Sophists such as Protagoras defended the idea of moral codes as useful human creations, sets of customs and conventions which make social life possible, and were thus committed to a form of ethical relativism and to the denial of any universal code of morality or any absolute moral truth. The more radical of their followers, such as the perhaps fictional Callicles and Thrasymachus portrayed in Plato's dialogues, concluded that, since traditional moral standards are mere conventions, they have no binding force, and the rational way to live is therefore to pursue one's own interests and power, acting unjustly if one can get away with it. These challenges to traditional moral codes thus raised the fundamental question 'Why be moral?' The moral philosophies of Plato and Aristotle can be seen as systematic attempts to answer that question.

Plato's early dialogues, which probably reflect the activity of the historical Socrates, portray him searching for definitions of the traditional *virtues—temperance, courage, justice, piety. The theme which emerges is that if these are good qualities, this must be because they make for a good life for those who possess them, and underlying all the virtues must therefore be the ability to know what constitutes the human good. Plato's own positive attempt to answer that question obtains its classic formulation in the *Republic*. There Plato argues that the good life consists in the harmony of the soul, with each part of the soul—reason, spirit, and appetite—performing its proper function. The traditional virtues can then all be defined as aspects of this underlying condition of psychic harmony. Since such a condition is one in which the person is happy and flourishing, the morally good life lived in accordance with the virtues is thereby shown to be the best life for human beings. This is Plato's answer to the question 'Why should I be moral?'

Although there are important differences between the moral philosophies of Plato and Aristotle, the latter employs the same broad framework. In the *Nicomachean Ethics* (generally regarded as the definitive version of his lectures on ethics), Aristotle asserts that the ultimate end of all human action is *happiness (*eudaimonia). To know what this happiness or flourishing consists in, Aristotle suggests that we must identify the distinctive function of human beings, and this he takes to be activity in accordance with reason. This then provides the basis for a general account of the moral virtues; they are dispositions in which our feelings and emotions are guided by reason so that our behaviour is appropriate to the situation. In particular the guidance of reason requires the avoidance of excess or deficiency, and therefore each virtue is, in Aristotle's famous phrase, a *'mean' between these extremes.

The later Greek schools shared this same broad ethical framework, the concern with the relation between the virtues and happiness, but we should note two ideas introduced by the *Epicureans and the *Stoics which were to play important roles in the philosophical tradition. Epicurean ethics was a form of *hedonism, identifying the good with *pleasure. Plato appears, at least in his *Protagoras*, to have given hedonism serious consideration, though later decisively rejecting it, and some of Plato's pupils explicitly defended hedonism, but the doctrine finds its classic formulation with the Epicureans. For this reason the word 'epicurean' has become a label for the pursuit of sensuous pleasures, but unjustly so, for the pleasure which they advocated was principally that of mental tranquillity, to be achieved by banishing superstitious fears of the gods and the afterlife. The influential concept introduced by the Stoics was that of the good life as one lived 'in accordance with nature' or 'the natural law'. Such an idea had been to some extent implicit in the ethics of Plato and Aristotle, and the Stoics followed them in equating the

idea of living 'according to nature' with that of acting in accordance with reason. Since for the Stoics this meant especially rendering oneself immune to the disturbances of the emotions, their ideal was in practice akin to the mental tranquillity of the Epicureans. The concept of *'natural law' can, however, lend itself to a variety of interpretations, and was subsequently to do so.

Christian Ethics. Popular conceptions of morality often assume some kind of link between morality and religion, equating moral precepts with divine commands. Although both Plato and Aristotle were theists, their ethics is not a religious ethics and their god is not a divine lawgiver; at most he is an exemplar of the ideal life. The moral philosophy of medieval Christendom, however, involved an attempt to marry Christian morality to Greek philosophy, and the most influential version of this enterprise was that of Thomas Aquinas. Aristotle had talked of a human 'function', but had made no use of the idea that this function might be seen as a purpose with which human beings are endowed by a divine creator. Such was the idea which enabled Aquinas to effect the synthesis he needed. From an understanding of human nature we can identify the natural purposes proper to human beings, and to fulfil these purposes is to follow 'natural law'. Since this natural law reflects our participation in the eternal law by which the universe is governed, it is exhibited also in the divine law laid down for us by the divine creator, and the moral precepts of natural law will therefore coincide with the moral rules revealed by the Christian religion.

It is doubtful whether this synthesis can be a stable one. Any attempt to identify moral principles with divine commands must run up against a dilemma first formulated in Plato's *Euthyphro*. Is the good good because God commands it, or does God command it because it is good? If the former, then morality is the product of arbitrary will, and obedience to morality is mere obedience to authority. If the latter, then morality is independent of God's will, and knowledge of the divine will is at best redundant. Aquinas's synthesis is therefore liable to collapse in one of two directions. If we maintain that morality is to be found in the commands of God revealed in a particular organized religion, these commands will have to be taken on trust and moral philosophy will have no role to play. Alternatively, if philosophical understanding can lead to the formulation of moral theory, religious belief will play no distinctive part in this process. The second alternative is the one adopted by moral philosophy in the modern epoch; the mainstream tradition has been essentially a secular one.

Ethical Naturalism. A moral philosophy which looks to 'nature' as the foundation for moral beliefs, independently of any religious framework, is most likely to appeal to the facts of human psychology. The tradition often referred to as that of the 'British Moralists' in the seventeenth and eighteenth centuries is a prime example of this way of doing moral philosophy. Two questions dominate the tradition: the question whether morality is ultimately grounded in *'self-love' or *'benevolence', and the question whether moral judgements are the product of *'reason' or 'sentiment'.

The first question is posed sharply by Hobbes, whose egoistic view of human nature and morality is the controversial stimulus for the work of his successors in much the same way as the Sophists were for Plato and Aristotle. Hobbes is usually thought of as a political philosopher rather than a moral philosopher, and that is essentially the point: morality, for him, can have no authority over our behaviour unless backed by political authority. All human passions are manifestations of the desire for good for oneself. In a *state of nature, men's desire for happiness brings them into conflict with one another, their lives are governed by a 'perpetual and restless desire of power after power', and their condition is therefore one of 'a war of every man against every man'. It is in everyone's interest to escape from this condition of war. Hobbes uses the vocabulary of natural law to express this requirement of self-interest; it is the fundamental law of nature 'that every man ought to endeavour peace'. This law of nature is not yet, however, a moral law, since in a state of nature the ideas of right and wrong, justice and injustice, have no meaning. A law of nature is merely a rule of reason directing one to the effective means of self-preservation. This law dictates that men should contract with one another to restrict their liberty for the sake of peace, provided others do likewise. Hobbes's egoistic theory entails, however, that in a state of nature there can be no moral obligation to abide by such a *contract. Men therefore have to establish a sovereign who will enforce the contract, for 'covenants without the sword are but words'. Thus the constraints of morality, though they are in everyone's interests, are binding only in so far as they are backed by political authority.

Attempts to answer Hobbes took two forms. One was the 'rationalist' response: that our reason acquaints us with moral duties which are, in some sense, part of the natural order of the universe, and which are independent both of the divine will and of any social contract or political authority. Samuel Clarke, for instance, claims it to be a requirement of reason that we should 'deal with every man as in like circumstances we could reasonably expect he should deal with us', and that we should 'endeavour, by an universal benevolence, to promote the welfare and happiness of all men'. This 'rule of righteousness' is part of our knowledge of the natural relations and 'fitnesses' of things. Our certainty of its truth is comparable to our certainty of the truths of mathematics. Similar claims about the capacity of reason to apprehend moral truths were made by Ralph Cudworth, John Balguy, and Richard Price.

The other response to Hobbes was to question his view of human nature and of human passions and affections. Shaftesbury asserts that human beings have not only an 'affection towards private good' but also a natural 'affection towards public good', though these are not in opposition to one another since virtue, grounded in the social affections, is to the advantage of everyone. Hutcheson claims that the moral virtues all flow from our feelings of benevolence towards others, and that there is no need to trace them back to self-love. Butler argues that the egoistic view of *human nature is in any case incoherent. Self-love is the desire for our own happiness, but this, he says, we can experience only through the satisfaction of our 'particular passions' for external things. Therefore self-love cannot possibly be the only passion. It presupposes and is consistent with the 'particular passions', and there is no reason why these should not include also benevolence, an affection to the good of our fellow creatures.

With such anti-Hobbesian views of human nature goes also a view of the basis of moral judgements. If human beings are naturally benevolent, then it can be similarly supposed that they have a natural liking for virtue, which Shaftesbury calls a 'sense of right and wrong' akin to our natural sense of the sublime and beautiful, and which Hutcheson calls a 'moral sense'. Though they regard this capacity to perceive moral qualities of good and evil as unique to rational beings, their description of it as a 'sense' implies something different from the rationalists' apprehension of moral truths, and more akin to sense-perception.

The high point in the tradition of the British Moralists is generally acknowledged to be the moral philosophy of Hume. A key concept for Hume is that of *'sympathy', which he also calls 'humanity' and 'fellow-feeling'. By this he means our capacity to share other people's feelings of happiness and misery. Hume rejects the 'self-love' hypothesis; though sympathy may often lack the strength to have a decisive influence on our conduct, all human beings are to some extent moved by it. It is through the operation of sympathy that we regard as 'virtues' those qualities which are useful or agreeable to their possessor (such as 'courage' and 'industry') and those qualities which are useful or agreeable to others (such as 'benevolence', 'justice', and 'fidelity'). In the last analysis, therefore, our moral judgements stem from this sentiment rather than from reason. Reason is necessary to instruct us in the consequences of actions, but when all such facts are known, some feeling or sentiment is necessary to lead us to a judgement of approbation or disapprobation. Reason by itself, says Hume, is no motive to action, but it is in the nature of our moral principles that they should guide our actions. Hence, though reason has a part to play, sentiment must be decisive in the forming of moral conclusions.

Utilitarianism. Hume stressed the *utility* of the virtues. Hutcheson suggested that, since benevolence is the foundation of all moral virtue, 'that action is best which procures the greatest happiness for the greatest numbers'. These phrases went to the making of the moral theory which was the most important successor to the work of the British Moralists—the theory of *utilitarianism. Though it builds on much previous thought, the first classic formulation of modern utilitarianism is the work of

Jeremy Bentham. The 'principle of utility' is, according to Bentham, the test of all morals and legislation. Actions are right or wrong to the extent that they tend to increase or diminish the general happiness.

The attraction of utilitarianism is its apparent simplicity. It purports to provide a succinct criterion to settle all moral disputes. Its weakness is that it seems over-simple. Bentham's version is certainly pretty crude. He suggests (as Hutcheson had done) that one can quantify the amounts of pleasure or pain to be produced by any action, and by a process of addition and subtraction one can then determine which action ought to be performed. The general happiness is thus envisaged as a sum of *pleasures, minus the pains, and these pleasures and pains differ from one another only in quantitative respects such as their duration and intensity. Critics of utilitarianism were not slow to point out how limited a view of the good life this appeared to be. The most influential attempt to produce a more plausible version of the theory was that of John Stuart Mill. He allowed that pleasures may differ from one another not only in quantity but also in quality. The pleasures of the intellect, of the feelings, and the imagination are what Mill calls the 'higher pleasures', and a good human life is one in which such pleasures are predominant. It is debatable whether Mill can consistently maintain this within a utilitarian context, for if pleasure is itself the only criterion of value, it is not clear how one pleasure can be better than another, other than by being greater in quantity. Nevertheless, utilitarianism as refined by Mill and by others such as Henry Sidgwick has occupied a dominant place in the moral philosophy of the nineteenth and twentieth centuries.

Kant and Post-Kantian Ethics. In stark contrast to utilitarian ethics is the moral philosophy of Kant. The only thing which is good without qualification is, according to Kant, 'the good will', which is good not because of the effects which it produces in the world, not because of its utility, but simply in its character as will. It is the motivation to perform one's *duty simply for its own sake. Since duty gets its distinctive character from its contrast with our natural inclinations, including both our desire for our own happiness and our benevolent inclinations towards others, no understanding of these natural inclinations can contribute to our understanding of morality, and Kant's ethics therefore stands opposed not only to utilitarianism but to ethical naturalism in general. Kant nevertheless thinks that reason, without any reference to the inclinations, can determine the form of our moral duty. Since the requirement of duty is that of acting in accordance with the *moral law, and since this moral law cannot get its content from any consideration of desirable consequences, there remains simply the formal requirement that one's actions should conform to the idea of moral law as such. One must therefore act in such a way that one can will the maxim of one's action to be a universal law. This requirement is what Kant calls the *'categorical imperative'. From such exiguous resources Kant nevertheless

thinks that we can arrive at concrete judgements about the morality of particular actions. It would, for instance, be wrong to make a false promise, one which I do not intend to keep, for if it were a universal law that people made false promises, promises would themselves become impossible, and this is therefore not something which I can consistently will.

Kant offers also a second formulation of the categorical imperative. This uses in a different way the idea of the universality of reason which is shared by all moral agents. Morality requires that I should respect this capacity for rational agency, and therefore that I should treat all persons never merely as means to an end but always also as ends in themselves. This idea of 'respect for persons' may again conflict with utilitarian morality. Utilitarianism can set no absolute limit to the evils which I might, in certain circumstances, be justified in inflicting on others, provided that the overall sum of human happiness is maximized by my so doing. In contrast, 'respect for persons' implies that I may not use others simply as instruments for however worthy an aim. It thus reflects the common idea that morality imposes certain constraints on the permissible treatment of others, that all human beings have certain basic moral rights which may not be overridden, and it is this dimension of Kantian ethics which has perhaps been the most influential.

Within this section we may notice briefly three nineteenth-century philosophers who have in common only their reaction against Kantian ethics. Schopenhauer rejects Kant's separation of morality from natural human feelings of compassion. This can be seen as a reversion to the British Moralists' emphasis on natural benevolence, but in Schopenhauer's case it is linked with an ambitious metaphysical thesis: that the 'principle of individuation' is an illusion, that the essential being of all persons is literally one and the same, and that our moral concern for the suffering of others is a recognition of this.

Hegel reacts against what he sees as the empty formalism of Kant's categorical imperative, particularly in its first version. Any maxim can in itself, according to Hegel, be willed as a universal law. If our willing it generates a contradiction, this must be because it contradicts some moral content which is already presupposed. Where does this content come from? According to Hegel, from the institutions and practices of society. What prevents us from willing the making of false promises as a universal law, for instance, is the social institution of promising which is already presupposed by the moral dilemma. More generally, the substantial content of our moral lives is drawn from 'ethical life', from the ethical institutions of the family, civil society, and the state. Ethics is essentially a social phenomenon.

That conclusion is one with which Nietzsche could agree. Where Hegel, however, sees different historical societies as stages in the evolving self-consciousness of reason, Nietzsche has no such unifying conception. For him, therefore, there is no such thing as morality, there are only different moralities. He is particularly preoccupied with the opposition between two types of morality, 'master morality' (in which ideas of nobility, courage, and honesty have a central place) and *'slave morality' (which he tends to identify with Christian morality and ideas of duty and self-sacrifice). Nietzsche appears to oscillate between seeing any distinctive morality as an achievement of human creativity, and denigrating slave morality as the psychological veneer of concealed resentment and vindictiveness.

Twentieth-Century Ethics. For much of the century, philosophers within the English-language tradition have been preoccupied with questions of *meta-ethics. The tone was set by G. E. Moore's book *Principia Ethica* of 1903. Moore espoused a normative theory akin to utilitarianism, but much more influential was his criticism of what he called the *'naturalistic fallacy'—the fallacy of identifying the simple and unanalysable property 'good' with some 'natural' property. According to Moore, no argument can be offered to show that something is good as an end in itself. We cannot, for instance, argue, as Moore thinks that the classical Utilitarians were guilty of arguing, that pleasure is good because that is part of the meaning of the word 'good'. It may be true that pleasure is good, but it is not true by definition, and this we can see, Moore thinks, when we recognize that any question of the form 'Is pleasure good?' is always an *open question. Moore's rejection of naturalism as fallacious seems to rule out any attempt to base ethics on an understanding of human nature or human psychology. No facts about features of human existence, nor indeed any metaphysical facts about the nature of reality, can entail any conclusion about what is good. Moore himself thinks that, once the question is properly understood, people can recognize that the most important things which are good in themselves are the pleasures of human intercourse and the enjoyment of beautiful objects. No argument, however, can be provided in support of these truths. They are simply self-evident.

Other philosophers, however, took issue with the very idea of moral truths which are 'self-evident' or can be known 'intuitively'. If such supposed truths cannot be supported by any argument, then, it was suggested, they cannot be called 'truths' at all, they are merely expressions of personal feeling. Bertrand Russell, for instance, who had at one time accepted Moore's theory, subsequently came to reject it and to maintain instead that if two people disagree over whether, say, the enjoyment of beautiful objects is good in itself, and if neither can offer any argument, then they are not disagreeing about facts which can be true or false, but simply expressing their differing feelings and desires.

The suggestion that, strictly speaking, there are no moral facts was developed further within the context of *Logical Positivism. If, as philosophers such as A. J. Ayer maintained, the only meaningful statements are either empirically verifiable propositions or analytic truths, value-judgements do not fall into either category and are therefore not meaningful statements at all; they are merely expressions of feelings and emotions. A more accommodating version of this *emotive theory of ethics was formulated by Charles Stevenson, who maintained not that moral utterances are meaningless but that they have a distinctive kind of meaning, *'emotive meaning', to be distinguished from descriptive meaning. The emotive meaning of ethical terms consists in their lending themselves to use, not only to express the speaker's own feelings, but also to arouse or affect the feelings and attitudes of others. Moral discourse is thus seen by Stevenson as a kind of behaviour modification.

Critics retorted that this account of moral discourse made it indistinguishable from emotionally manipulative practices such as advertising and propaganda. What many philosophers retained, however, was the idea that there is a distinction between 'prescriptive' and 'descriptive' meaning, and that the distinctive feature of moral terms is their prescriptive meaning, their use to guide actions and tell people what to do. 'Values', it was suggested, must not be confused with 'facts'. Much writing of the 1950s and 1960s was concerned with meta-ethical questions about the validity of the *'fact–value distinction', the relation between *'is' and 'ought', and whether 'is' statements can ever logically entail an 'ought' conclusion.

More recently there has been a revival of interest in substantive moral theory. Utilitarianism was the first of the traditional normative theories to be resurrected. R. M. Hare, for instance, argued that moral terms are not only 'prescriptive' but also 'universalizable', and that when properly understood the *universalizability of moral language commits us to some form of utilitarianism. The revival of utilitarian thinking has been particularly apparent in work on *applied ethics.

Other normative theories which were current in the 1970s and 1980s can usefully be seen as responses to the perceived shortcomings of utilitarianism. One principal criticism of it has been that it is an aggregative theory. It allows the interests of some to be outweighed by the interests of others, and can therefore justify the infliction of terrible atrocities on some persons for the sake of the greater good. What this shows, it has been said, is that utilitarianism, by aggregating interests into a single 'general good', fails to recognize the separateness of individuals. Two forms of ethical theory which have aspired to incorporate that recognition have been 'contractarian' theories and 'rights-based' theories. Contractarianism came to the fore in political philosophy with John Rawls's theory of *justice. The idea of basing principles of justice on a hypothetical *contract is that, if they are principles which everyone can agree to, then no one's basic interests will be sacrificed to anyone else's. Contractarian attempts to develop a general moral theory include those of Russell Grice and David Gauthier. Gauthier's theory is very much in the spirit of Hobbes as an attempt to show how morality can be generated by agreement between self-interested individuals. Basing morality on rights has likewise been seen as a way of building in the requirement that no one's basic interests should be sacrificed. The focus on rights, like contractarianism, first emerged in political philosophy, and the work of Robert Nozick and that of Ronald Dworkin have, in contrasting ways, emphasized the importance of *rights as a counter to utilitarian social theory. Alan Gewirth and John Mackie are among those who have proposed a comprehensive moral theory based on the concept of rights.

Other critics of utilitarianism have argued that by focusing exclusively on outcomes it gives insufficient importance to the significance of moral agency. A more 'agent-centred' approach can be found, for instance, in the work of Bernard Williams. He suggests that a person's moral identity is constituted by his or her 'ground projects' and 'commitments' and that utilitarianism, in so far as it would require one to abandon these whenever the actions of others so order the consequences as to make it necessary, can give no adequate account of concepts such as 'moral integrity'. Another approach which can be called 'agent-centred' is the work of Philippa Foot and others which refocuses attention on the *virtues. Whereas utilitarianism assesses actions by their production of good consequences, virtue ethics aims rather to identify those ways of acting which go to make up a good human life. Foot, indeed, has argued that the idea of 'the best state of affairs', which is supposed to serve as the utilitarian criterion of right action, does not as it stands have any clear sense.

Contemporary virtue ethics traces its ancestry to Aristotle, and rights-based theories look to Kant. Considering also the continuing vitality of utilitarianism, and of contractarian ethics in the Hobbesian mode, we may fairly conclude that the main ethical traditions of previous centuries are still, in one incarnation or another, alive and well.   R.J.N.

*histories of moral philosophy; moral philosophy, problems of; consequentialism; deontological ethics; applied ethics; intuitionism, ethical.

W. D. Hudson (ed.), New Studies in Ethics, 2 vols. (London, 1974).
Alasdair MacIntyre, A Short History of Ethics (London, 1967).
J. B. Schneewind, The Invention of Autonomy: A History of Modern Moral Philosophy (Cambridge, 1998).
—— (ed.), Moral Philosophy from Montaigne to Kant: An Anthology (Cambridge, 1990).
Henry Sidgwick, Outlines of the History of Ethics (first pub. 1886; 6th edn. 1931).

moral philosophy, problems of. If we include in moral philosophy the entire history of ethics going back all the way (at least) to Socrates, the topic of right and wrong action is perhaps the most important single issue in the discipline. Although in the present century scepticism about the possibility of moral truth or objectivity has led philosophers to pay attention to semantical issues in ethics, to questions about the meaning of terms like 'right', 'wrong', and 'obligatory', most ethicists have been and still are interested in offering, debating, and criticizing substantive conceptions of moral rightness and wrongness. Perhaps the major problem of current and traditional moral

philosophy, then, is coming up with a rationally defensible theory of right and wrong action. Such a theory would presumably ground or defend certain principles of right action (or, as with Aristotle, show us why rightness cannot be captured by general principles and must be perceived situationally).

The current scene in moral philosophy is dominated by five basic views or theories of right and wrong action. (Here I exclude approaches that are principally concerned with the political sphere.) Utilitarians (or at least 'act-utilitarians', who represent, I think, a current majority among all utilitarians) hold that *right action must be understood in terms of human good or well-being. The latter is conceived hedonistically in terms of pleasure, desire-satisfaction, or, more broadly, happiness, and right action is then said to be action that leads, or is likely to lead, to the greatest balance of human (or sentient) pleasure or happiness over pain or unhappiness. (This is one version of the so-called *principle of utility.) Such a purely instrumental or consequentialistic conception of morality and also virtue—in effect, any means can be justified by a good enough end—has always been controversial, but in fact one of the biggest problems now facing *utilitarianism is to defend itself against less monolithic forms of *consequentialism that are willing to accommodate intrinsic human goods other than pleasure or desire-satisfaction and to acknowledge considerations of equality and fairness and even of natural beauty and diversity that go considerably beyond the purely quantitative utilitarian approach. A consequentialist can say, for example, that (a fair degree of) equality in happiness or income is itself a good that should be taken into account in seeking to act for the best, and on such a view and contrary to act-utilitarianism an act might produce more pleasure on balance than any alternative but be wrong because of how unequally it caused the pleasure to be distributed.

By contrast with the utilitarian emphasis on human desire-satisfaction, *Kantianism argues that morality must be understood independently of all empirical or sensuous motives. For Kant and many contemporary Kantians, moral rightness in behaviour is a matter of acting consistently and rationally, and a major challenge and burden of Kantianism has been to show how ordinary immoralities like promise-breaking, stealing, and indifference to the welfare of others can be fundamentally understood as forms of conative or practical inconsistency. Formulations of the *'categorical imperative' in terms of one or another form of inconsistency (or in terms of the idea that people should never be used simply as means) have typically ruled out too little or too much as morally wrong. Or else they have been unacceptably vague in their implications. However, present-day Kantians are actively engaged in trying to make good on these deficiencies.

A third approach to right and wrong, intuitionism or common-sensism, insists, against both Kant and utilitarianism, that there can be no unified or unifying account of our moral obligations; these, it claims, are irreducibly plural, and the only general moral principles it is willing to

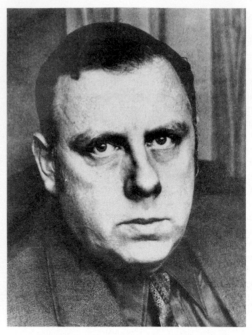

JOHN RAWLS's *A Theory of Justice* galvanized political philosophy in the early 1970s: it was a careful elaboration of an original approach to the eternal problem of accommodating egalitarianism and liberalism.

ALASDAIR MACINTYRE's distinctive and often polemical approach to moral enquiry insists on the historical dimension of ethics.

SAUL A. KRIPKE published innovations in logic in his teens, but later became reluctant to commit his ideas to print. In his published lectures on *Naming and Necessity* he examined standard theories of reference and pulled back the curtain to reveal a metaphysics of modality and necessity.

DANIEL C. DENNETT has been one of the leading figures in the project of fertilizing the philosophy of mind with the findings of the sciences of the mind. After arguing for a scientific explanation of consciousness, he looked to evolution, 'Darwin's dangerous idea', for the explanation of humanity's place in the natural universe.

recognize are prima-facie principles (it is prima-facie wrong to harm another person, it is prima-facie wrong to break a promise, etc.) that are individually defeasible and cannot be ranked in any absolute order of precedence. But, unlike Kantianism, intuitionism doesn't even attempt to explain why it is wrong, e.g., to kill an innocent person in order to prevent a greater number of deaths. The latter claim is typical of *deontological theories like intuitionism and Kantian ethics, and definitely runs counter to act-utilitarianism. But the intuitionist can only insist on the intuitive implausibility of the implications of act-utilitarianism for such cases and has no (further) philosophical argument against it.

A fourth way of dealing with substantive issues of right and wrong action can be found in Thomas Scanlon's 'contractualist' view of the morality of obligation (of what we 'owe to each other'). This new approach in part derives from *John Rawls's contract theory of social justice, but, unlike the latter, its principal focus is on issues of personal morality. It holds, roughly, that an act is wrong if it would be disallowed by any principle that no one seeking an agreement on moral principles for the general regulation of behaviour could reasonably reject. This form of contractualism has encountered the criticism that it builds too much of morality into its claims about reasonableness; but others worry that the approach isn't strong enough to justify all the claims that are plausible within the sphere of moral obligation.

The final (major contemporary) way of dealing theoretically with right and wrong can be found in virtue ethics, a kind of moral theory with origins in the schools of ancient philosophy. Virtue ethicists think right and wrong cannot be captured by independently or basically valid moral rules or principles, but are a matter rather of situational sensitivity (Aristotle) or of the expression or maintenance of fundamentally good or admirable inner motives or states (Plato, Hume). Among the chief problems for such views are explaining how agents can perceive what is right to do in given situations without the help of general principles and/or showing how evaluations based *in* the moral agent can sufficiently constrain what the agent does *outside, in the world, to other people*.

However, ethics or moral philosophy in the broadest sense includes much more than attempts to describe or explain the nature of moral right and wrong. As I indicated just above, the utilitarians attempt to ground our understanding of right and wrong in an independent understanding of human good. But all systematic theories of ethics seek to understand human good, or the good life, and not just the issue of right and wrong action. What is good for a person is not necessarily morally good (there is nothing morally good about enjoying a sauna bath), and the distinction, therefore, between moral good and obligation, on the one hand, and non-moral personal, human, or life goods, on the other, raises two further important problems for ethics.

First, the nature of human good and the good life is not self-evident. Utilitarians think of human or personal good

in hedonistic terms, but it is not necessary to do so, and some self-realization theorists and *virtue ethicists have, for example, held that (some of) the greatest human, personal, or life goods are things like knowledge, autonomy, achievement, honour, and virtue itself. One of the main problems of ethics, then, is to determine what things are (basic) personal goods in addition to such obvious goods as pleasure and desire-satisfaction. But this problem raises a second interesting issue. The utilitarians understand right and wrong derivatively from human good: the moral is what is instrumental to the greatest abundance of personal good(s). But it is possible to reverse the order, in the manner of the Stoics, and claim that human well-being or good is confined to and understandable in terms of human virtue: to be well-off is simply to be virtuous. (This means pain is no evil, is not a bad thing in one's life, unless it undermines one's virtue.) But there is also the possibility that neither well-being nor virtue is ethically prior to the other, so that ethics is faced with a dualism of fundamental concepts (this is Kant's and Ross's view). And so ethics faces a general issue about its basic values that goes beyond the confines of morality proper: the question how to connect moral values with personal well-being and the question whether either of these notions or notion-types is the basis for the other.

I mentioned earlier that recent moral philosophy has been greatly concerned with issues about the meaning of moral terms. In fact, *'meta-ethics', which deals not only with semantic issues but also with questions about the objectivity and verifiability of moral judgements, practically dominated English-speaking philosophy during the first half of the twentieth century. The reason has something to do with the emergence of *Logical Positivism during the early part of that period. The positivists questioned whether moral, religious, or metaphysical discourse was cognitively meaningful; and the force of their sceptical views, and of questions raised by G. E. Moore about whether goodness was a natural or non-natural property, led many or even most ethicists to abandon substantive issues of right and wrong and good for a consideration of questions about the meaning and rational or epistemic status of moral and other value-claims.

In the heyday of meta-ethics, certain schools of thought dominated the scene and their disagreements constituted the main substance of moral-philosophical discussion. Non-naturalists like Moore held that goodness and rightness were not understandable in terms of purely natural phenomena or properties, but were metaphysically real and rationally intuitable ethical properties none the less. Their targets, the naturalists, argued that ethical terms or concepts were analysable in terms of such natural notions as pleasure, evolutionary fitness, or (more complexly) what would be chosen by a totally informed and dispassionate human(-like) observer. Against such anti-sceptical 'cognitivist' views, another school of meta-ethics, the emotivists, held that there is no property of goodness or rightness and that moral discourse simply expresses the emotions or preferences of speakers rather than making any claim about the world. Subjectivists, by contrast, deflated ethics by treating moral and evaluative claims as mere *descriptions of* the emotions or preferences of speakers—'this is good' being equivalent in meaning to 'I like (or prefer) this'. Finally, prescriptivists likened moral and indeed all evaluative claims to imperatives—'this is good (or right)' being regarded as meaning the same as 'choose this (sort of thing)!'—and sought to induce a certain rationality into moral discourse via a logic of imperatives.

More recently, meta-ethicists have focused more directly on the question whether moral and other value-claims correspond to reality or are in any sense objective, and there have been a wide variety of different and opposing responses to that question. Given the apparent widespread disagreement about ethical (and other) values that has existed between different societies and different epochs of the same society, there is reason to wonder whether there really are any facts or truths for ethics to discover, and although most ethicists ever since Socrates have tended to believe in one or another form of moral objectivity, the problem remains of justifying such objectivity in the face of continually different forms of scepticism about its possibility.

However, in addition to meta-ethical questions, ethics naturally leads to certain substantive (non-semantical) metaphysical issues, and perhaps most important among these is the question of *free will. If human beings lack free will, then, it has traditionally been argued, they cannot be held responsible for their actions and cannot be bound by moral obligations any more than animals or small children are. So those who have systematically elaborated one or another view of moral right and wrong and of human good have also usually thought it necessary to defend (or at least explicitly assume) the existence of human freedom, and that defence, in the first instance, has usually involved saying something about freedom in relation to causal *determinism. If the universe is universally governed by causal laws, then human freedom would seem to be very much in jeopardy. So defenders of morality typically feel called upon either to deny determinism and argue that human beings are in important ways not subject to causal determination or else to show that causal determinism does not in fact deprive us of free agency.

Another metaphysical or quasi-metaphysical issue that moral philosophers have devoted attention to concerns the human capacity for morality. Most moral codes and moral philosophies require, for example, that people occasionally put aside self-interest in the name of honour, fairness, decency, loyalty, or the general good, but if one is a *psychological* egoist, one will hold that people lack the capacity for these forms of self-sacrifice, and it then becomes problematic whether human beings really have the obligations that various ethically non-egoistic theories or views claim they do. As a result, psychological egoism, most notably at the hands of Bishop Butler, has been the target of philosophical criticisms on the part of philosophers wishing to defend one or another substantive, ethically non-egoistic morality.

But even if one rejects both forms of egoism, there are questions about how much morality validly or fairly can demand of people, and some of these issues arise in connection with utilitarianism and Kantianism. Utilitarianism is usually stated in a 'maximizing' form that treats it as a necessary and sufficient condition of right action that one do the best one circumstantially can for humankind as a whole (or for all sentient beings). But such a doctrine seems to entail that if one is in a position to relieve the suffering, hunger, or disease of others, one is morally obligated to do so, even if that means giving up one's life plans and most of what one really cares about in life. Unless one's current life does as much good on the whole for people, one must give up one's life plans to the extent necessary to confer greater benefits on (prevent greater harm to) other people. The utilitarian moral standard is thus very demanding, and some philosophers have questioned whether morality can properly, or, one might say, fairly, require so much of people. In particular, it may be wondered whether people, most people, have the capacity to live up to such a stringent morality as maximizing utilitarianism presents. Utilitarianism requires that one always do the most good one can for people and in effect leaves no room for what are called supererogatory degrees of morality, for going *beyond* the call of duty. And this seems too demanding because it means, in effect, that if one fails always to do the most for humankind that one can, if one isn't like Schweitzer or Mother Teresa, one acts wrongly and fails to fulfil one's moral obligations. Thus if ethical egoism is too undemanding, morally speaking, so too, on the other side, does utilitarianism seem too demanding upon human nature.

Kantianism can likewise be seen as grating against our human nature or capacities, not by demanding too much sacrifice of self-interest, but by insisting that only moral conscientiousness is a proper and laudable moral motive. If one gives out of fellow-feeling or friendship to another human being, one's act lacks all moral worth, according to Kant, because one's action was not performed out of a sense of duty and respect for the moral law. Many philosophers have thought such a view of moral virtue to be too narrow and out of keeping with human psychology, and feminists like Carol Gilligan and Nel Noddings have argued, contrary to Kant, that a morally good person will directly focus on other people and their welfare, rather than be guided by a sense of duty. In fact, there has been and remains a great deal of disagreement over what kinds of motive really are morally praiseworthy and worthy of encouragement.

Today moral philosophers are very much engaged in all the kinds of issue we have discussed here. There may be no generally accepted solutions to (most of) these problems, but there is also no doubt that moral philosophers have been developing a better critical understanding of their nature and of what solutions to them might look like.

M.S.

*moral knowledge; moral particularism; pornography.

F. Feldman, *An Introduction to Ethics* (Englewood Cliffs, NJ, 1978).

P. Foot, *Virtues and Vices* (Berkeley, Calif., 1978).

T. Hill, *Dignity and Practical Reason in Kant's Moral Theory* (Ithaca, NY, 1992).

L. Pojman, *Ethics: Discovering Right and Wrong* (Belmont, Calif., 1990).

T. M. Scanlon, *What We Owe to Each Other* (Cambridge, Mass., 1998).

S. Scheffler, *The Rejection of Consequentialism* (Oxford, 1982).

M. Slote, *Morals from Motives* (Oxford, 2001).

J. J. C. Smart and B. A. O. Williams, *Utilitarianism: For and Against* (Cambridge, 1973).

B. A. O. Williams, *Morality: An Introduction to Ethics* (New York, 1972).

moral pluralism holds that the foundational level of morality consists of a plurality of values or duties. For example, *equality and aggregate *well-being are often claimed to be values that serve as the foundation for the rest of morality. According to other pluralistic theories, the foundational level of morality is instead composed of duties not to physically harm others, not to harm or take others' possessions, not to break one's promises, not to tell lies, plus general duties to do good for others, and duties of extra concern for those with whom one has special connections. Different versions of moral pluralism add to or subtract from such lists of foundational duties or values.

Most moral pluralists hold that we do not have strict principles of priority that will resolve all conflicts among the foundational values or duties. These moral pluralists hold that we thus to need to exercise judgement in order to resolve some conflicts among these values or duties. Giving judgement such a large role, however, strikes critics of moral pluralism as failing to provide a defensible decision procedure for moral deliberation.   B.H.

W. D. Ross, *The Right and the Good* (Oxford, 1930, 2002).

P. Stratton-Lake (ed.), *Ethical Intuitionism* (Oxford, 2002).

moral psychology. A part of moral theory devoted to the analysis of concepts used to describe the psychological make-up of persons as moral *agents, and the examination of normative issues involving those concepts. Some of these concepts may be explored for their own sake, e.g. the ideas of fear, anxiety, despair, or *love, and here the aim is to understand emotional states, motivations, or relationships of major importance in the lives of human beings.

Moral psychology also explores moral-emotional aspects of important moral practices. When the actions of responsible persons are morally wrong, those who hold them to account typically expect the wrongdoers to experience such negative moral *emotions as guilt, shame, remorse, or regret. Moral psychology attempts to understand the cognitive and phenomenological structures of such emotions, the differences among them, and the conditions under which they are justified or not. These emotions are usually thought of as painful, and as reflecting a change in a person's standing in the moral community.

Ordinarily, pain is construed as a condition from which a person is entitled to seek immediate relief. In the case of the negative moral emotions, then, how long must a person suffer them? And how may a person suffering them gain release from them, and perhaps restoration to good standing in the moral community? Here the notions of forgiveness, mercy, excuse, and repentance become important, and the practices of making amends and of moral or legal punishment need investigation. Accordingly, moral-psychological inquiry may lead on to the theory of punishment and the philosophy of law.

There are positive moral-emotional states to be understood, too, such as the satisfaction, contentment, or pride one may take in doing right, and the humility that may be recommended when such positive states turn toward arrogance. Approaches to these issues concerning the negative and positive moral emotions may be influenced by prior inquiries into the ideas of freedom and intentionality, and into the logic of moral deliberation and practical reasoning. Under a wide interpretation, moral psychology may be considered to include these latter inquiries as well.

N.S.C.

*moral judgement; expressivism in ethics.

S. W. Blackburn, *Ruling Passions* (Oxford, 1999).

Owen Flanagan and Amelie Oksenberg Rorty (eds.), *Identity, Character, and Morality* (Cambridge, Mass., 1990).

Herbert Morris, *On Guilt and Innocence* (Berkeley, Calif., 1976).

moral realism. The view that moral beliefs and judgements can be true or false, that there exist moral properties to which moral agents are attentive or inattentive, sensitive or insensitive, that moral values are discovered, not willed into existence nor constituted by emotional reactions. Far from being a function of wishes, wants, and desires, moral demands furnish reasons for acting, reasons that take precedence over any other reasons. Debate centres on the nature and credentials of moral properties as the moral realist understands them. In what sense are they 'real'? Real, as irreducible to discrete affective experiences of individuals. In this and other respects they share characteristics of the *'secondary qualities' of our life-world: filtered by our mentality, but not on that account illusory. They can be well-founded, making a real difference to situations and individuals that possess (or lack) them.

Moral realists are arguably justified in displaying the inadequacies of subjectivist moral theories; but less successful so far in developing a convincing positive account of the 'reality' of values.   R.W.H.

*truth; realism and anti-realism; emotive theory; prescriptivism; moral scepticism; quasi-realism.

D. McNaughton, *Moral Vision* (Oxford, 1988).

I. Murdoch, *The Sovereignty of Good* (London, 1970).

—— *Metaphysics as a Guide to Morals* (London, 1992).

G. Sayre-McCord, *Essays on Moral Realism* (Ithaca, NY, 1988).

morals and law: *see* law and morals.

morals, enforcement of: *see* enforcement of morals.

moral scepticism. We must distinguish two kinds of *scepticism about the possibility of objectively valid moral judgements. *Internal* scepticism argues that it is a mistake in moral judgement to make certain kinds of moral evaluation or criticism or (in the case of global internal scepticism) to make any such judgements at all. Examples of the latter, global scepticism, include the argument that morality is ridiculous because there is no God, that it is misconceived because all human decisions and acts are predetermined, and that it is barren because there is no point or purpose in human life anyway. Such scepticism is internal to morality because it is based on normative, ethical assumptions about the true or adequate ground of moral claims: it assumes that a basis for morality would exist if there were a God, or if human acts were genuinely free, or if the universe including human life could be understood as planned and purposeful. Each of these assumptions represents an abstract normative judgement—an assumption about the true grounds of moral commitment—even though each claims to generate sceptical conclusions. Internal scepticism is powerful and threatening, for those who find its underlying assumptions persuasive, because it is practical: it must change the behaviour of anyone who is converted to it. People who sincerely believe that morality is bunk because free will is an illusion must reject moral restraints for themselves, and refuse to criticize others for behaving dishonestly or in ways other people find morally wicked.

External scepticism, on the other hand, is supposedly based not on abstract or general normative assumptions about the adequate grounds of moral commitment or responsibility, but rather on wholly non-moral, philosophical assumptions about the possibility of any kind of objective *truth or *knowledge. Contemporary examples include Gilbert Harman's argument that moral judgements cannot count as objective knowledge because moral beliefs are not caused by anything in the world, and John Mackie's argument that there cannot be moral facts because moral properties would be such 'queer' entities. External scepticism is widely thought to have only theoretical rather than practical consequences—someone who is converted to the philosophical opinion that morality is a matter not of objective truth or falsity but rather of subjective reaction need not, on this view, change his first-order moral convictions—he may still think that dishonesty is detestable or that genocide is wicked—though he will now recognize that these are not ordinary beliefs about some objective reality, but are only expressions of his own subjective state of mind.

It is very difficult, however, to make any real sense of the idea of external moral scepticism. Consider the statements that supposedly express this kind of scepticism: that genocide is not 'really' or 'objectively' immoral, or that its immorality is not 'out there, in the universe', or that its immorality is not 'part of the fabric of the universe', for example. It is, in fact, impossible to assign any sceptical sense to such philosophically loaded or metaphorical statements that does not make them equivalent in mean-ing to the simple internally sceptical statement (which is, of course, full of practical consequences) that genocide is not immoral. Since the latter is plainly a moral judgement, and could be supported, if at all, only through internally sceptical abstract moral claims of the kind I mentioned, there is no such thing as external scepticism. The only intelligible moral scepticism is internal to morality.

That is an important conclusion, among other reasons because many philosophers have assumed that *subjectivism, *relativism, and other forms of moral scepticism can be established by default; that is, that since we cannot prove that abortion or taxation or racial discrimination are or are not morally wicked to those who think the contrary, it follows that there is no objective truth in moral matters. But if we understand the denial of objective moral truth as a piece of internal rather than supposedly external scepticism, we see that it is as much in need of a positive moral argument as any other moral position, and its supporters can no more win by default than can their non-sceptical opponents. Whether you accept some general sceptical position about morality—for example, the subjectivist position that moral obligations only hold for those who accept them, or the relativist position that moral obligations hold only within a community whose conventional morality endorses that obligation—must depend on whether you accept whatever moral arguments can be made for these particular forms of scepticism—that it is wrong to condemn people morally unless they act in a way they themselves believe to be wrong, for instance. In fact, very few people (including those philosophers who claim to be external sceptics) find that they can actually accept those arguments or embrace and act on the internally sceptical conclusions they recommend.

R.D.

*ethical objectivism; ethical relativism; moral realism.

Ronald Dworkin, *Law's Empire* (Cambridge, Mass., 1986).
Gilbert Harman, *The Nature of Morality* (Oxford, 1977).
R. Joyce, *The Myth of Morality* (Cambridge, 2002).
John Mackie, *Ethics: Inventing Right and Wrong* (Harmondsworth, 1977).

moral sense. 'Moral sense' is the name given by, for example, Francis Hutcheson and David Hume to the capacity we have to distinguish virtue from vice. Such moral philosophers are referred to as sentimentalists, because we are supposed by them to feel things to be good or bad rather than to reason that they are so. However, in Hume's philosophy such feelings are not divorced from judgement. A feeling of admiration for virtuous action is properly called 'moral sense' only if it arises from disinterested reflection on the good tendencies of such actions in general. Moral sense, like aesthetic taste, may be ill-founded or well-founded. This view was taken for granted by, for example, Jane Austen, who thought it a fault if someone did not 'feel as he ought'. Since the moral theories of Kant, however, it has generally been held that moral judgements are matters either of reason or of purely personal preference.
M.WARN.

*conscience; moral realism.

J. L. Mackie, *Hume's Moral Theory* (London, 1980).

moral sentiments. States of mind associated with moral character and response, including guilt, anger, shame, pride, sympathy, hatred, resentment, and other feelings and emotions connected with approval and disapproval. According to the eighteenth-century sentimentalists, moral distinctions are explicable in terms of non-rational sentiments experienced by agents in response to states of the world, including states of character. Thus to be virtuous is to be such as to elicit approval or sympathy in others. On some views, including that of Hume, moral judgements of approval and disapproval are themselves a kind of experienced sentiment. The distinction between sentimentalists and their opponents is undermined by cognitivist theories of the *emotions, according to which propositionally articulated emotions are partly constituted by beliefs with their own conditions of correctness. If moral sentiments have distinctive conditions of correctness as given by the nature of their objects, then the eighteenth-century distinction between reason and sentiment is put into question.   H.L.

*Hume.

J. Schneewind (ed.), *Moral Philosophy from Montaigne to Kant* (Cambridge, 2003).

moral virtues: *see* virtues.

more things in heaven and earth

> There are more things in heaven and earth, Horatio,
> Than are dreamt of in your philosophy.
>   (Shakespeare, *Hamlet*)

What Hamlet says to his friend Horatio could be an indictment of *philosophy in general or specifically of Horatio's philosophy. Or if, as some Shakespearian scholars contend, the correct reading is 'our', the philosophy referred to could be that of Horatio and Hamlet, whose undergraduate faith in rationality Hamlet may be mocking, or of all humans. No amount of scholarship, however, will dislodge people's tendency to counter scepticism about the supernatural, or philosophical stringency, with this quotation. The quoter usually purports to ally him or herself to 'the Bard', and flourishes Hamlet's rhetoric as if it were Shakespeare's own assertion—and decisive proof of the existence of God, the paranormal, or anything else that it is thought desirable to believe in.   J.O'G.

mortalism. The mortalist heresy (that human *souls are mortal—punishable by *death in the 1648 Blasphemy Ordination) was connected with a burning mid-seventeenth-century controversy: sentience requires a soul; all animals perceive; so do 'brutes' have immortal souls? or do we have mortal ones? Both alternatives were championed; neither was generally accepted. The mortalist Richard Overton offered a surprising compromise: body and soul both die, but both are resurrected.   J.J.M.

*immortality.

N. T. Burns, *Christian Mortalism from Tyndale to Milton* (Cambridge, Mass., 1972).

motion. x moves if and only if x is at some place, P_1, at some time, t_1, and x is at some numerically distinct place, P_2, at some later time, t_2, and x exists at some juxtaposed set of places between P_1 and P_2 and at all times between t_1 and t_2.

Philosophical problems about motion include: What is it to begin to move? How long does starting to move last? as well as the proof or refutation of both the materialist thesis that all change is motion and the Parmenidean thesis that change (and, *a fortiori*, motion) does not exist. Four of *Zeno's paradoxes are philosophical problems about motion: Achilles and the tortoise, the dichotomy, the flying arrow, and the stadium.   S.P.

Aristotle, *Physics*, bks. I and II, tr. with intro. and notes by William Charlton (Oxford, 1970); bks. III and IV, tr. with intro. and notes by Edward Hussey (Oxford, 1983).

George Berkeley, *De Motu*, in *The Works of George Berkeley, Bishop of Cloyne*, ed. A. A. Luce and T. E. Jessop (London, 1948–57).

motives and motivation. Explanations of behaviour may be in terms of reasons—someone waves because he wants to attract our attention and thinks he may do so thereby—or in terms of causes—a person shivers as a result of the cold. But may not reasons themselves be causes? There are indeed contexts in which 'cause' and 'reason' may interchange, as in the phrases 'give cause' and 'give reason', and we may use 'because' with reference to either. However, there is a use of 'cause' in which experimentation is in principle required to verify that C caused E, as with cold and shivering, whereas it requires no more than the agent's honest word for his reason for acting for this to be so. Motives have their place among the latter.

Or so it would seem in the simpler cases. But 'motive' is often invoked precisely when there is a departure from normal reasons. A person goes into a shop to buy a newspaper. That, he says, is his reason. We wonder about his motive if we suspect that there is more than meets the eye, something beyond the declared reason for acting thus. Might he not be unaware of his true motive?

We may wish to speak of an *unconscious* motive in such a case, but it is questionable whether we should sever all connection with the agent's awareness. The explanation why the agent acted can still count as a motive explanation provided we leave open the possibility that he should come round to acknowledging that he did indeed act for the reason suggested. Rule out any such possibility and, while we may be able to speak in terms of a cause of the behaviour, we rule out any justification for speaking in terms of desire, intention, trying, and the like. But, despite his sincere protestations to the contrary, might it not be true that a person is acting out of such motives as greed, vanity, or ambition? That could be so, but in a way that does not undermine the agent's honestly avowed reason. Rather, in the circumstances, we may say, acting as he did *counts* as acting out of vanity; or, whatever the protester may say, 'greedy' is just the word for that sort of behaviour. So long as this is the point of dispute, it is not one on which the agent's authority is final. But nor is it a question of identifying a cause.

While motive explanations are not causal, an appeal to causes may explain why such-and-such counts as a reason for the agent; why, for instance, reasons for acting which would show a person to be vain carry so much weight with that person. Relatedly, the cause–reason division provides a way of finding room for considerations of self-interest while allowing the possibility of disinterested motives. Why did *A* come to *B*'s assistance? His sincerely avowed reason: He thought he must, that it was the proper thing to do. No suggestion that there was anything in it for *A*; indeed, the thought that he might in some way benefit from his act, or at least avoid the guilt which would come with inaction, did not even enter his head. On the other hand, there is also the question why *A* is disposed to respond altruistically to those in need, and the answer to this may well lie not with *A*'s reasons for acting, but with his upbringing. Perhaps it has taken rewards and punishments to bring him to a state where such other-regarding considerations weigh with him. Similarly, abuse suffered by a person as a child may explain how he comes to have the motives he has, but as a cause, not as something which figures among his reasons.　B.B.R.

> *choosing and deciding; egoism and altruism; mental causation; reasons and causes; volition.

A. Kenny, *Action, Emotion and Will* (London, 1963).
A. I. Melden, *Free Action* (London, 1961).
G. Ryle, *The Concept of Mind* (London, 1948).

Mo Tzu (579–438 BC?). Born in the year of Confucius' death, Mo Tzu was his major philosophical rival. He criticized Confucians for what he perceived to be their élitism, partiality, nepotism, fatalism, extravagance, and wastefulness. He founded an extraordinary guild of religious, pacifist, itinerant, artisan soldiers, who practised their idealistic philosophy of impartial concern *jianai* ('universal love') by defending weak states against aggressors. According to Mo Tzu, social values (*yi*) must be imposed with laws and punishments, to prevent reversion to state of individualist antagonism. Mo Tzu proclaimed three standards for the evaluation of social doctrines: success of historical precedent, observations of the people, projected utility. The later Mohists developed theories of optics, and a logical system of dichotomous distinctions, both linguistic and evaluative: *shi* affirmation, *fei* denial / rejection.　S.C.

Later Mohist Logic, Ethics, and Science, ed. A. C. Graham (London, 1978).
Mo Tzu: Basic Writings, tr. Burton Watson (New York, 1963).

moving rows paradox: *see* stadium paradox.

multiculturalism. Most countries today are 'multi-cultural' in the sense that they contain many distinct ethno-cultural groups, as a result of the historic incorporation of minority groups or the admission of new immigrants. Multiculturalism, understood as a normative claim or political *ideology, argues that this ethno-cultural diversity should be accommodated, not suppressed, and celebrated, not feared. In this sense, multiculturalism stands opposed to traditional models of nation building and *nationalism that sought to create homogeneous national societies within each state. Multiculturalism is a widespread movement in both Western political theory and Western political practice, but its defenders face two key challenges. First, what are the limits to the legitimate accommodation of diversity? In particular, should traditional cultural practices that violate liberal-democratic norms be tolerated? Second, what holds multicultural societies together? In particular, can the celebration of multicultural differences be reconciled with the promotion of common national identities and loyalties? These issues remain a matter of lively ongoing debate.　W.K.

W. Kymlicka, *Multicultural Citizenship: A Liberal Theory of Minority Rights* (Oxford, 1995).

mundus imaginalis ('*ālam al-khayal*). The term was used first by Sohravardī to define a 'boundary' realm that connects the sensory and the abstract intellectual segments of the whole continuum of being, and is the distinguishing component of non-Aristotelian *cosmology in *Islamic philosophy. It is constructed as the locus of visions, prophecy, and sorcery, and also defines *eschatology. This wonderland is described by negating Aristotelian logical principles and laws of physics, and is employed to explain non-standard experiences such as 'true dreams' and 'miraculous powers'. As the individual subject moves away from the centre of the sensory segment of the continuum nearing the boundary realm, qualitative change takes place. Material bodies change to *imaginalis* ones; time changes, no longer confined to measure of linear space; and space is no longer limited by the Euclidean.　H.Z.

> *possible worlds.

Fazlur Rahman, 'Dream, Imagination and '*Ālam al-Mithāl*', *Islamic Studies* (1964).

Murdoch, Iris (1919–99). Iris Murdoch DBE, better known as a novelist than as a philosopher, taught philosophy in Oxford for fifteen years. In 1954 she wrote the first book in English on Jean-Paul Sartre, relating his early philosophy to his plays and novels. The crossing of boundaries between literature and philosophy marks all her work. Her main philosophical interest is in ethics, and she held that goodness has a real, though abstract, existence in the world. This thesis was expounded at length in *Metaphysics as a Guide to Morals* (1993). She could be called a modern Platonist, and wrote perceptively on Plato (e.g. *The Fire and the Sun* (1977)). She also wrote about education and religion. The actual existence of goodness is, in her view, the way it is now possible to understand the idea of God.   M.WARN.

*Platonism; novel, the philosophical.

music. Although we can find philosophical writing on music as early as Plato and Aristotle, and discussion of it by philosophers outside the analytic tradition such as Schopenhauer, Adorno, and Nietzsche, the philosophical problems which we now identify as comprising the aesthetics of music received their first classic treatment by the Viennese critic Eduard Hanslick. Although his treatment is not always lucid, and debate continues as to what Hanslick meant, it seems fairly clear that his prime target was a Romantic conception of music which subsequently became known as the expressionist theory of art, that beauty in music depends upon the accurate representation or expression of the feelings of the composer. (Expressionist theories characteristically maintain that a psychological state of the artist is communicated via the work to the listener.) Of most philosophical significance in his objections are the claim that there is a cognitive element in the feelings of hope, anger, etc. A judgement is involved that may be a necessary component in individuating the particular feeling. Such an element of judgement is absent in music. The English writer Edmund Gurney, in a large and rambling book, *The Power of Sound*, developed, apparently independently, a parallel line of criticism. Both emphasize the looseness of fit between music and the expressive descriptions we make of it. Both are, not unfairly, viewed as formalists who believe that the worth of music lies in the beauty of its patterns rather than in its expressive power.

The aesthetics of music has flowered since the 1980s. The debate as to how music can be properly described as 'sad' or 'exuberant' has continued apace. The most widely held view is probably the view that it is the music itself which is sad, and not the composer, listener, or performer, and that we describe the music in this way because of the way the music moves, because of its pace or the angularity or otherwise of its lines. However, this orthodoxy has been challenged by a number of writers, who have argued that sad music does have a tendency to make the listener sad, a position which has become known as 'arousalism'.

There has been much recent philosophical discussion of what it is for something to be a work of music. The debate has largely been between Platonists, such as Peter Kivy, and others. Platonists have tended to argue that the work of music is an abstract sound pattern which is discovered, rather than created, by its composer. It is fair to say that the centre of controversy here is how we should understand the creativity of the composer: Does he create *ex nihilo*, or is he more in the position of the great and innovative scientist whose genius enables him to see what others have missed? A more moderate Platonism, such as that of Jerrold Levinson, allows that the work of music is a pattern or a type of which performances or interpretations are tokens, but that it is a type which is created by a composer. Recently, there has been a greater realization of the extent to which the concept of a work of music is itself a historical phenomenon which developed as the concert-hall became the sonic equivalent of the art gallery or museum, a place where works can be displayed through performance. Through this, a deep distinction between work and performance became the norm, with the notion of fidelity to the work coming progressively to the fore.

Consequent on this, philosophers have become increasingly interested in a concept which has been central to musical performance over the last half-century, the notion of 'authentic performance' or, as it is now sometimes called, the 'historically informed performance'. The debate is very involved. Should we attempt to re-create the sound the composer would have heard or the effect his music had on the first audiences? Do we have a moral duty to the composer to present his work as he wished? Should we give precedence to the tradition of playing the work, incorporating the insights of generations of interpreters?

There is also a growing interest in the ontology of music outside the Western classical tradition, such as jazz, rock, and world music. All in all the aesthetics of music is currently the liveliest branch of the philosophy of the arts.

R.A.S.

Stephen Davies, *Musical Meaning and Expression* (Ithaca, NY, 1994).
—— *Musical Works and Performances* (Oxford, 2001).
Lydia Goehr, *The Imaginary Museum of Musical Works* (Oxford, 1992).
Peter Kivy, *Authenticities* (Ithaca, NY, 1995).
—— *The Fine Art of Repetition* (Cambridge, 1993).
—— *Sound Sentiment* (Philadelphia, 1989).
Jerrold Levinson, *Music, Art and Metaphysics* (Ithaca, NY, 1990).
R. A. Sharpe, *Music and Humanism* (Oxford, 2000).

my station and its duties: *see* Bradley.

mysticism. The concept of mysticism is closely related to that of religious experience, but probably they should not be thought to be identical. It seems useful to distinguish mystical experience from numinous experience of the sort described by Rudolf Otto, and from the more 'ordinary' sort of experience of the presence and activity of *God, which is well illustrated by John Baillie. William James characterized mystical experience by four marks: transiency, passivity, noetic quality, and ineffability. Perhaps we should add a fifth, that mystical experiences often, perhaps characteristically, involve what is now called an 'altered state of consciousness'—trance, visions, suppression of cognitive contact with the ordinary world, loss of the usual distinction between subject and object, weakening or loss of the sense of the self, etc. These features constitute an interesting 'syndrome'. Not all *religious experience is mystical and not every mystical experience includes all of the features of this syndrome, but there is a large body of individual testimonies and descriptions derived from all the major religious traditions (and perhaps from minor traditions also) which involve many of these features.

Much of this mystical experience is taken to be religiously significant by the subject, but there is an interesting and difficult question about whether all mysticism is inherently religious, with some (e.g. William Stace) suggesting that it need not be. Some mystical experience is overtly theistic, having an ostensible reference to God, roughly as he is conceived in the theistic religions. And it is dualistic, in the sense of retaining the distinction between the mystic and the God who is ostensibly experienced. St Teresa of Avila, a Spanish Catholic of the sixteenth century, is a good example of such a mystic. Other mystics, however, even within the Catholic tradition, tend towards monism, emphasizing the unity of all things and the lack of real distinctions, even between the mystic and the divine reality. Mysticism of the theistic, dualistic sort seems to generate no particular difficulty for Christian metaphysics, and indeed often includes specifically Christian elements, such as visions of Christ. Strongly monistic mysticism, however, is harder to square with a Christian view, and when such mystics have themselves been Christians they have often been suspected of heresy. This sort of mysticism is likely to find a more comfortable religious home in the great non-theistic religions.

There are two principal ways of trying to derive some religious significance from mysticism. The first way is indirect and inferential, and it is accessible to non-mystics. It takes the prevalence of reported mystical experience as a premiss, and derives some conclusion from it in conjunction with some auxiliary principles. Often an analogy is drawn with sense-experience. C. D. Broad, for example, holds that a widely shared sort of experience, tending towards a similar interpretation, is plausibly taken to be the result of contact with some corresponding objective reality (unless we have some special reason to think otherwise). This, he says, is the way we treat sense-experience, and mystical experience should be treated likewise.

The other way is especially attractive for the subjects of mystical experiences which have a strong noetic element. For in those experiences the subject is strongly convinced that he or she is acquiring a piece of knowledge, a sort of revelation, in the course of the experience itself. Such subjects may well take that element of their experience at face value. Indeed, they may find that the convictions which are thus generated are among the very strongest in their entire intellectual life (for example, St Teresa). This way of assessing the significance of mysticism is, however, not readily accessible to non-mystics. Normally these powerful convictions are generated by the experience itself, in those who have had that experience, and not in others who have only the reports of such experiences. In James's terminology, mystical experience is 'authoritative' for those who have it, but not for others. G.I.M.

*holy, numinous, and sacred.

John Baillie, *Our Knowledge of God* (New York, 1959).

William James, *The Varieties of Religious Experience* (Cambridge, Mass., 1985).

George I. Mavrodes, *Belief in God* (New York, 1981).

Rodolf Otto, *The Idea of The Holy*, tr. John W. Harvey (New York, 1970).

St Teresa of Avila, *The Life of the Holy Mother Teresa of Jesus* (London, 1979).

Evelyn Underhill, *Mysticism* (first pub. 1911; New York, 1961).

myth of the given. Expression introduced by *Wilfred Sellars to suggest there is no uninterpreted content of experience that is foundational in epistemology: e.g. Locke's ideas, Hume's impressions, the sense-data of the Logical Positivists. The myth of the given implies that facts can in principle be known non-inferentially. No non-inferentially known fact presupposes knowledge of any other fact or general truth. Such non-inferentially known facts are ultimately authoritative. The attack on the given is arguably anticipated by Vico and Kant. S.P.

Wilfred Sellars, *Science, Perception and Reality* (London, 1963), ch. 5, sects. 3–11.

N

Nāgārjuna (*fl.* 150 AD). Greatest sceptic-mystic dialectician of the Voidist school of Mahāyāna Buddhism. Nāgārjuna interpreted Buddha's 'middle way' as emptiness of all things. This emptiness, best shown through silence, is realized when assent is withheld from all four logically possible answers to a metaphysical question (yes, no, both, neither). For example: 'Entities do not originate from themselves, from a wholly other entity, or from both, and nor do they originate without a cause'. This relegates Buddha's own teachings about dependent origination, suffering, selflessness, and *nirvana to the level of relative rather than absolute truth. These levels of truth are distinguished to meet the charge of self-refutation which Nāgārjuna anticipates: 'Isn't the Voidist yelling "Don't yell"?' Somewhat like the sentences of Wittgenstein's *Tractatus*, the Voidist's own utterances count as therapeutically useful nonsense.   A.C.

*Buddhist philosophy.

M. Sprung, *Lucid Exposition of the Middle Way* (London, 1979).

Nagel, Ernest (1901–85). A leading figure in the logical empiricist movement, Nagel was perhaps somewhat unfortunate in that he published his definitive work, *The Structure of Science*, just one year before Thomas Kuhn published his *The Structure of Scientific Revolutions*. This latter effectively spelt the end for the ahistorical, prescriptive approach to the philosophy of science that Nagel epitomized. Nevertheless, by virtue of his clear, comprehensive, and unemotional approach to the problems of science, Nagel did continue to have much influence, particularly in his standard account of 'reduction', the process where one science or theory is absorbed into another.

Seeing this relationship as essentially one of deductive consequence, the older of the newer, and everything of physics, Nagel came to consider in some detail the prima facie distinctive nature of the biological sciences, especially inasmuch as they use 'teleological' or 'functional' language. Unexpectedly, inasmuch as he thought this language significant, he thought it eliminable, and inasmuch as it is uneliminable, it is insignificant. Forty subsequent years of discussion of this subject suggests that this was a mistaken judgement.   M.R.

*logical empiricism; reductionism; teleological explanation.

E. Nagel, *The Structure of Science* (New York, 1961).
M. Ruse, *The Philosophy of Biology Today* (Albany, NY, 1988).

Nagel, Thomas (1937–). American philosopher, Professor at New York University. Nagel's philosophical work has been dominated by concern over how to reconcile the personal, subjective, first-person view we have of events, the world, of what is valuable and important, and the impersonal, objective, impartial view we have of these things, a view which is ordinarily thought of as more likely to be true just because impartial, untainted by local or personal concerns and horizons. His first book, *The Possibility of Altruism* (Oxford, 1970), considered issues of this character in connection with reasons for action of a personal or impersonal kind, but he has pursued related themes into questions in the philosophy of mind, epistemology, free will, and general metaphysics. Possibly his most influential piece is his journal paper 'What Is It Like to Be a Bat?', published in 1974, where he contends that all materialist and functionalist theories of mind and consciousness omit the central fact of *mentality—that there is something it feels like to be in a certain material or functional state. In this case, we see a tension between the lived experience intimate to the individual subject and the generalizing theoretical accounts which seem to provide the best overall explanations. This paper is in his collection *Mortal Questions* (Cambridge, 1979). He has explored this cluster of issues most fully in *The View from Nowhere* (Oxford, 1986).

Nagel's writing is characterized by a lightness which makes it accessible to a very wide range of readers. He has written a brief and witty introduction to philosophy, *What Does It All Mean?* (Oxford, 1987).   N.J.H.D.

*dualism; inequality; functionalism.

naïve realism. A theory of *perception that holds that our ordinary perception of physical objects is direct, unmediated by awareness of subjective entities, and that, in normal perceptual conditions, these objects have the properties they appear to have. If a pickle tastes sour, the sun looks orange, and the water feels hot, then, if conditions are normal, the pickle is sour, the sun orange, and the water hot. Tastes, sounds, and colours are not in the heads of perceivers; they are qualities of the external objects that are perceived. Seeing an object is not (as *representative theorists maintain) seeing it, so to speak, on mental television where the properties of a subjective *sense-datum or *percept (e.g. colour) represent or 'stand in for' the objective, scientific properties of the external object (wavelength of reflected light). Although this theory bears the name 'naïve', and is often said to be the view of the person on the street, it need not deny or conflict with scientific accounts of perception. It need only deny that one's perceptual awareness of objective properties involves an awareness of the properties of subjective (mental) intermediaries.   F.D.

H. H. Price, *Perception* (London, 1932).

names. In the broadest sense of the term 'name', names divide into two classes—proper names and common names, these being species of singular and general terms respectively. Proper names are names of individuals, such as 'London', 'Mars', and 'Napoleon', whereas common names are names of kinds of individuals, such as 'city', 'planet', and 'man'. Not all singular terms are proper names; for instance, pronouns like 'I' and 'he' are not, nor are demonstrative noun phrases like 'this city' and 'that man'. Definite descriptions, such as 'the capital city of England', are also commonly contrasted with proper names (though Frege treated them as belonging to the same semantic category). Similarly, not all general terms are common names; for instance, adjectival or characterizing general terms like 'red' are not, nor are abstract nouns like 'redness' and 'bravery' (if indeed the latter are deemed to be general terms).

Recently, philosophical debate has focused on proper names much more than on common names (apart from the special case of natural-kind terms). A prominent issue has been whether such names have both sense and reference, as Frege believed, or whether they are purely referential devices, as J. S. Mill held and as Kripke now contends. (An implication of the latter position is that proper names do not have linguistic meanings specifiable by way of *definition.) Frege's claim draws sustenance from the fact that an identity statement involving two different proper names—for instance, 'George Orwell is Eric Blair'—can be informative, which seems to imply that it expresses a different proposition from that expressed when one of those names is merely repeated, as in 'George Orwell is George Orwell'. On the other hand, Kripke plausibly argues that speakers can use proper names to refer to individuals about whom they possess no uniquely identifying information, as when a speaker affirms that Kurt Gödel proved the *incompleteness theorem even though she cannot clearly differentiate in thought between Gödel and many other eminent logicians. (A Fregean *'sense' is supposed to provide just such identifying information about, or a 'mode of presentation' of, its reference.)

For Kripke, proper names are *rigid designators—in which respect they differ from (most) definite descriptions—and their reference is secured not by some 'sense' which a speaker attaches to them, but rather by an external causal chain linking the speaker's use of a name to an original 'baptism' in which the name was first assigned to a certain individual. As the name is passed on from speaker to speaker, all that is required for a later recipient of the name to use it successfully to refer to the individual originally named by it is that each speaker in the chain should use it with the intention to refer to the *same* individual as it was used to refer to by the speaker from whom he received the name. However, this so-called causal theory of reference is not without its difficulties; for instance, Gareth Evans has argued that it cannot accommodate some of the ways in which names *change* their reference over time.

The Kripkean account of proper names (and natural-kind terms) as rigid designators is linked to certain metaphysical doctrines of an essentialist character—such as the theses of the necessity of identity and of origin—because of the ways in which such names are thought to behave in modal contexts. For instance, it is held that, given that George Orwell *is* Eric Blair, George Orwell *could not* have been different from Eric Blair—though this impossibility is a posteriori rather than a priori. Similarly, given that George Orwell was in fact born of certain parents, it is held to be an a posteriori *metaphysical necessity that he was born of just those parents.   E.J.L.

S. A. Kripke, *Naming and Necessity* (Oxford, 1980).
A. W. Moore (ed.), *Meaning and Reference* (Oxford, 1993).
N. Salmon, *Reference and Essence* (Princeton, NJ, 1982).

names, fictional: *see* fictional names.

names, logically proper: *see* logically proper names.

narrative. A narrative in its widest sense is a representation of a sequence of events between which there is some connection. In this wide sense, a film, for example, can count as a narrative, even in the absence of an explicit narrator. Not every representation counts as a narrative, however. A minimal criterion is that the represented events exhibit some temporal order. The sentence 'Lucy is wearing pink today' thus fails on this criterion to be a narrative. But mere temporal structure is not sufficient. Consider the following: '833: Two comets appeared. 834: In this year Bishop Wulfstan passed away. 835: There were great floods.' This is simply a chronicle of events. In a true narrative, the represented events should exhibit some causal connectedness, making each event more intelligible than it would be if reported in isolation, or as part of a mere chronicle. Within this broad category we can go on to distinguish historical from fictional narrative.

The concept of narrative has of course great interest and importance for literary theorists, but it has also been of interest to philosophers. It has, for example, been used by Alasdair MacIntyre to express the way in which a human life is a structured, unified whole, and not simply a series of discrete events. Human actions are made intelligible though being part of a narrative. (This is in marked contrast to the view expressed in Sartre's *Nausea*, that any narrative misrepresents human life, which in reality is unstructured and has no *denouement*.) Philosophies of action that attempt to isolate what are sometimes called 'basic actions' that are considered simply as behaviour that is the outcome of an intention, and then analyse agency in terms of such actions, thus run the risk of providing an unduly artificial and idealized picture of what intentional action consists in. The point can be put in ethical terms: in so far as we construct our ethical theory from consideration of actions, choices, and situations that are abstracted from any wider narrative that would give them meaning, that theory will be correspondingly impoverished.

The link between narrative and our understanding of *time has been explored within the continental tradition by Paul Ricœur.   R.LE P.

*action; basic action; fiction; history, problems of the philosophy of.

Alasdair MacIntyre, *After Virtue*, 2nd edn. (London, 1985).
Paul Ricœur, *Time and Narrative*, tr. K. Blamey, K. McLaughlin, and D. Pellauer, 3 vols. (Chicago, 1984–8).
Jean-Paul Sartre, *Nausea*, tr. R. Baldick (Harmondsworth, 1965).

nasty, brutish, and short. '. . . and which is worst of all, continual fear, and danger of violent death; and the life of man, solitary, poor, nasty, brutish, and short' (*Leviathan*, I. xiii. 9). This is one of Hobbes's most memorable phrases and comes at the end of his description of what life is like in the *state of nature when 'men live without a common power to keep them all in awe'. This powerful description, like everything Hobbes writes on moral and political matters, has as its goal the attempt to persuade people to obey the law and thereby to avoid civil war. For civil war leads to the state of nature with all of the horrors mentioned in the above quote.   B.G.

national and regional philosophies: *see* African; American; Australian; Canadian; Chinese; continental; Croatian; Czech; Danish; English; Finnish; French; German; Greek philosophy, modern; Indian; Irish; Islamic; Italian; Japanese; Korean; Latin American; Netherlands; New Zealand; Norwegian; Polish; Russian; Scottish; Serbian; Slovene; Spanish; Swedish.

national character. From the time of Vico, it has been widely held that *human nature develops through history, with pervasive patterns of thought and behaviour in any one group of people distinguishing it from others. What, then, gives the language, culture, and collective experience of a group its particular identity? For Herder, to whom the very term *'nationalism' is attributed, it was the soul of the nation to which the group belonged. He argued, against liberal universalism, that an individual could develop spiritually only within a national community, though, unlike Fichte, he did not think any one nation favoured over the rest. Recognizing the cultural significance of national character and history need not be militaristic or supremacist or based on race. But, if not tempered by a substratum of timeless and universal values, it can, as demonstrated in Herder himself, lead to the relativistic conclusion that the values of different nations are incommensurable, and criticizable only from within.   A.O'H.

*conservatism; people, the.

Isaiah Berlin, *Vico and Herder* (London, 1976).

nationalism. A doctrine which holds that national identity ought to be accorded political recognition, that nations have rights (to autonomy, *self-determination, and/or sovereignty), and that the members of the nation ought to band together in defence of those rights. Nationalism can be distinguished from, though it is often in practice indistinct from, chauvinism, which makes one's own national identity the overriding moral–political consideration. The theoretical distinction here runs parallel to the distinction between individualism and egoism, and it can be elucidated in the following way: national rights (like individual *rights) are properly reiterated for each newly arriving nation (individual). Hence, the limits of these rights are necessarily fixed by the rights of the nation that comes next. Chauvinism, by contrast, acknowledges no limits except those dictated by national interest. It is entirely possible, then, to be a liberal nationalist, defending the rights of nations other than one's own and seeking negotiated settlements, compromises, even in disputes involving one's own. But this position is relatively rare in political life or, better, it is a position that seems to erode rapidly whenever the disputed issues touch upon (what are taken to be) vital national interests.

As an *ideology of identity, attaching political significance to the history and culture of an *ethnos* or *people, nationalism is a modern phenomenon, though it is not without precedents and parallels in the ancient world. Similarly, nations, conceived as groups whose members are prospective nationalists, are modern creations, politically fashioned out of diverse social materials. Citizenship, religious faith, common language, some defining historical experience: all these in some cases, any one of them in others, have played a formative part (or, in another version of the story, have been exploited by publicists and politicians) in shaping national identity. The resulting nationalisms differ among themselves—more political and open, more ethnic and exclusive—depending on the achieved shape. But it does not appear that national rights are dependent in a similar way. They must be (like individual rights again) the same for all nations that are prepared to recognize their limits.   M.WALZ.

*national character; international relations, philosophy of; homeland, right to a.

Benedict Anderson, *Imagined Communities: Reflections on the Origin and Spread of Nationalism* (London, 1983).
Hans Kohn, *The Idea of Nationalism* (New York, 1946).
R. McKim and J. McMahan (eds.), *The Morality of Nationalism* (New York, 1997).
K. R. Minogue, *Nationalism* (New York, 1968).

natural. Belonging to or concerned with the world of *nature, and so accessible to investigation by the natural sciences. 'Natural' may be contrasted with various terms, such as 'artificial', 'unnatural', 'supernatural', 'non-natural'. The first three of these occur in ordinary language, though 'unnatural' in particular leads to problems about its real meaning. But 'non-natural' is a philosopher's term, and (with 'non-naturalistic') is the usual contrast term to 'natural' or 'naturalistic' in philosophy. Roughly it refers to what cannot be studied by the methods of the natural sciences, or defined in terms appropriate to them, and is applied to subject-matters that are essentially abstract, or outside space and time. A famous use of it was made by G. E. Moore, who applied it to the term *good*, which he regarded as indefinable.   A.R.L.

*naturalistic fallacy; naturalism.

G. E. Moore, *Principia Ethica* (Cambridge, 1903), sects. 5–14, 'Natural' and 'Non-natural'.

natural aristocracy: *see* aristocracy, natural.

natural deduction. A method of formalizing logic, introduced independently by S. Jaśkowski in 1934 and Gerhard Gentzen in 1935. All previous mathematical logicians—including Frege, Russell and Whitehead, Hilbert, and Heyting (*intuitionism, mathematical)—had formalized logic axiomatically, their method being modelled on the misleading analogy of formal *theories. In these formalizations, certain logically valid formulae were assumed as axioms, from which a minimum of rules of derivation preserving logical validity yielded the rest. This older method required ad hoc definitions of derivability from a set of premisses (since not all rules of derivation preserved truth under a given interpretation of the schematic letters); it often demanded much ingenuity to obtain the formal *theorems. Worse, it concentrated philosophical and logical attention on the notion of *logical *truth* in place of that of logical *consequence*.

By contrast, a natural *deduction system has no *axioms, but only rules of *inference, thus placing the emphasis where it belongs, on the relation of logical consequence from premisses to conclusion, and making a formalized deduction resemble far more closely the reasoning used in ordinary life. A formula representing one of the premisses of a deduction can be introduced at any stage; its introduction requires no justification. The price of dispensing with logical truths assumed axiomatically is that the rules must include some that 'discharge' hypotheses. One such rule is *reductio ad absurdum: under this, not-A can be asserted as following from a set Γ of premisses if a contradiction has been derived from Γ together with A as hypothesis; a hypothesis, like a premiss, may be introduced at any stage. The use of such rules makes it necessary to keep track of the hypotheses on which each line of a deduction depends. In order to do this, these lines may be shown as *sequents*—pairs Γ : A consisting of a finite set Γ of formulae and another formula A; the introduction

of a premiss or a hypothesis is then displayed as a *basic sequent* of the form A : A. No formal distinction between premisses and hypotheses is needed: a premiss of the whole deduction is simply a hypothesis that is never discharged, but is among those on which the final conclusion depends.

In a natural deduction system, the rules governing the logical *constants are divided into *introduction rules* and *elimination rules*. An introduction rule allows the derivation of a formula with the given constant as principal operator from premisses in which it does not occur essentially; an elimination rule allows an inference from such a formula, perhaps together with additional minor premisses. Thus the introduction rule for & allows the derivation of Γ : A & B from Γ : A and Γ : B and the elimination rules allow the derivation of Γ : A or of Γ : B from Γ : A & B. As this example shows, the rules are very natural and simple, and it is usually very straightforward to devise a deduction of a given conclusion from premisses from which it follows. Logically valid formulae fall out as a by-product, being those formulae deducible from, or as depending on, no premisses at all.   M.D.

*normalization.

Dag Prawitz, *Natural Deduction* (Stockholm, 1965).

naturalism. In general the view that everything is *natural, i.e. that everything there is belongs to the world of *nature, and so can be studied by the methods appropriate for studying that world, and the apparent exceptions can be somehow explained away. In central philosophy the term has been applied in two main ways, both stemming from the above definition, one more general and the other more particular.

The more particular one is *ethical naturalism, which is concerned with rejecting *non-natural properties in that sphere and rejecting the idea that ethics is a *sui generis* subject which involves special methods of argument.

The more general application is to philosophy as a whole, and again involves both the objects studied and the methods used in studying them, i.e. both metaphysics and epistemology. In metaphysics naturalism is perhaps most obviously akin to *materialism, but it does not have to be materialistic. What it insists on is that the world of nature should form a single sphere without incursions from outside by souls or spirits, divine or human, and without having to accommodate strange entities like non-natural values or substantive abstract *universals. But it need not reject the phenomena of consciousness, nor even identify them somehow with material phenomena, as the materialist must, provided they can be studied via the science of psychology, which can itself be integrated into the other sciences. One naturalist in fact, Hume, was rather ambivalent about whether there was really a material world at all, except in so far as it was constructed out of our experiences, or impressions and ideas, as he called them. The important thing for the naturalist in the metaphysical sphere is that the world should be a unity in the sense of being amenable to a unified study which can be called the study of nature, though it may not always be easy to say what counts as a sufficient degree of unification. Obviously there are different sciences, which to some extent employ different methods as well as studying different subject-matters. What seems to be needed is that they should form a continuous chain, and all be subject to certain general requirements regarded as necessary for a science as such, like producing results which are amenable to empirical testing. Whatever entities such sciences come up with must then be allowed into the naturalistic framework, and these will include 'theoretical' entities which cannot be directly observed, but whose existence is postulated to explain various phenomena, such as the electrons of physics, whether this existence is taken to be real or only 'logically constructed' in the way in which the average man is logically constructed out of ordinary men.

But the main thrust of naturalism is probably best taken to be epistemological. Throughout most of the twentieth century, in particular, and for at least part of the nineteenth, epistemology was taken to be the study of how we can properly come to have knowledge of the world around us, or indeed of anything else for that matter, the emphasis being on the 'properly'. How people do think has been taken to be the subject of empirical psychology, and no doubt most of us think in atrocious ways at times, but that seems irrelevant to how we ought to think if we are going to find out about the world effectively. A stock question for philosophers is 'How do you know?', and on the face of it it can be given two kinds of answers. We might simply offer a historical or biographical account of how we came by the belief in question, or, if the 'we' is not an individual but a, or the, scientific community, then an account of the relevant part of the history of science up to the time in question. But this may seem an irrelevance. The question was not 'Why do you believe?' but 'How do you know?', and the questioner probably has in mind the further question 'Why should I believe?' But if so, he wants a justification for believing, and how could a mere history of somebody else's belief give him that? Similarly, in ethics, if I ask for a justification for thinking some things to be morally wrong I shall not be very impressed if I am simply told how our moral sense grows out of childhood fears of parental authority. If anything, I might take that to undermine the belief and show it to be illusory (though it would not in fact do the latter, since there is nothing to stop us holding the right beliefs for the wrong, or even no, reasons). For this sort of reason a vigorous reaction occurred towards the end of the nineteenth century against naturalism, especially in its epistemological form, often called *psychologism, though to some extent in its metaphysical form too, notably in Moore's rejection of the *'naturalistic fallacy' in ethics, which involved him in denying that values, and *good* in particular, formed a *sui generis* class of entities, whose presence could not be empirically observed or inferred but could only be detected by some special intuition. Logic in particular was to be purified from any contamination by psychology, and the epistemological writings of

philosophers like Locke, Hume, and J. S. Mill were often regarded as asking the wrong questions. (Though it should be added that Hume himself was responsible for what has become in the twentieth century a famous attack on one form of the naturalistic fallacy, albeit a form more on the metaphysical side of the fence, since it consisted in connecting certain ethical and metaphysical notions; Hume wanted to disconnect the ethical ones—though, some might say, only to reconnect them in a different way with certain psychological ones.)

However, this purist attitude, though dominant for much of the twentieth century, has also sparked off a certain reaction to itself, largely through despair. *Empiricism tends to move towards extremism in its attempts to beat off the ever-present challenge of the sceptic, the extremism appearing because of the concessions it is forced to make. How can we really know anything except perhaps a few things we are immediately confronted with? In particular, how can we justify the belief we all have in the ordinary world of common sense outside us? Here we return to Hume again, who in what might seem a final capitulation to the sceptic decided that we could not. What we could do, he thought, was to show that it was impossible—psychologically impossible—to take the sceptic seriously once we leave the philosopher's study. In order to do this, starting from his extreme empiricist base, he elaborated an account of how we (or he himself—but for convenience of exposition he takes the existence of other people for granted at this point) do in fact come to think in terms of an external world. No one would complain at this as a programme in its own right. What is controversial, and is rejected by anti-naturalists, is the claim that this is all that can be done in the face of the sceptic, or, even worse, the claim that this somehow *is* a justification of our knowledge. The twentieth-century reaction in favour of naturalism really took the form of a repeat performance of Hume's enterprise, though put in the terms of a later framework of thought.

Following the title of a famous article by Quine this programme is now known as *'naturalized epistemology'. It can take a moderate or an extreme form. The extreme, and less common, form abandons all hope of justification and in effect amounts to a philosophy of 'anything goes': whatever the scientists, or the astrologers, do, we must simply describe or analyse it, and leave it at that—a policy with echoes outside philosophy of science in the mid-twentieth century *linguistic philosophy ushered in by Wittgenstein.

The moderate form does not abandon all hopes of justification, but claims that the history of a scientific theory is not irrelevant to its justification. (Twentieth-century naturalism in both its forms tended to concentrate on science as the most disciplined and self-conscious area of human reasoning.) The main reason for this appeal to history is that we cannot break free from the context in which our thought arises. We must start from where we are. We may pass judgements on a theory or procedure, it is thought, but to ignore its content—what *could* have been known at the time in question etc.—and demand some exercise in pure thought starting from nothing is to cry for the moon. The issue remains open. To what extent is it worth trying to construct a pure logic of inquiry if it could only be applied in ideal circumstances to which we can never attain? But there is in any case some connection of thought with *reliabilism, since on that view in order to decide whether a certain belief amounts to knowledge we must ask not about the reasons that the belief's holder can produce for it but about the method by which the belief was reached, and whether that method has in fact proved to be a reliable method in other cases—in other words we must ask about the actual history of the method and about its success-rate.

In aesthetics 'naturalism' refers not so much to an aesthetic theory but to a movement in art associated particularly with the nineteenth century and related to that called realism; it claimed that art or literature should aim to represent the world as it is in itself, in ways that will appeal to our aesthetic feelings or draw our attention to aspects that we might have overlooked, but without distorting it in order to produce special effects, as Turner tried to do in the case of light, or appealing to certain standard conventions concerning the representation of attributes, as in medieval iconography, or introducing conventions of the artist's own, as in symbolist poetry, or in general deliberately representing the world otherwise than as one would normally take it to be. Naturalism in this sense is also of course to be contrasted with abstract art, as represented by, say, Mondrian.   A.R.L.

P. Kitcher, 'The Naturalists Return', *Philosophical Review* (1992). Fully referenced survey of current revival.
T. S. Kuhn, *The Structure of Scientific Revolutions* (Chicago, 1962; rev. edn. 1970). Naturalistic approach.
G. E. Moore, *Principia Ethica* (Cambridge, 1903), sects. 5–14. Challenges ethical naturalism.
L. Nochlin, *Realism* (Harmondsworth, 1971). Naturalism in art.
W. V. Quine, 'Epistemology Naturalised', in *Ontological Relativity and Other Essays* (New York, 1969).

naturalism, biological: *see* biological naturalism.

naturalism, ethical. The views that (i) ethical terms are definable in non-ethical, natural terms, (ii) ethical conclusions are derivable from non-ethical premisses, (iii) ethical properties are natural properties. A 'natural' term or property is one that can be employed or referred to in natural scientific explanations. Version (i) was attacked by G. E. Moore for committing the *naturalistic fallacy. 'Good' could not *mean*, say, 'pleasurable', since it is an open question whether what is pleasurable is good. Emotivists and prescriptivists object that ethical terms have non-reducible 'attitudinal' content. (*Descriptivism.) Version (ii) is open to Hume's 'is' and 'ought' objection: valid 'ought' conclusions require an 'ought' in at least one premiss. (*Fact–value distinction.) Version (iii) is criticized by non-naturalists such as Wiggins for *scientism—the claim that genuine properties must be scientific.   R.CRI.

*emotivism; prescriptivism.

G. Harman, *The Nature of Morality* (Oxford, 1977), ch. 2.
G. E. Moore, *Principia Ethica* (Cambridge, 1903), chs. 2–3.

naturalistic fallacy. G. E. Moore (*Principia Ethica* (1903)) argued that no matter what definition of 'good' is proposed (e.g. as what satisfies desire, maximizes happiness, or furthers evolution), it can always be asked, 'But *is* that good?' The question always remains open, and never becomes trivial. 'Good' resists definition or analysis: and the attempt to pin it down to an invariable, specific content is, in Moore's phrase, the 'naturalistic fallacy'.

Moore was concerned to retain an objectivist position over judgements about *good. If these could not refer to natural properties (he argued), they must refer to *'non-natural' ones. It is questionable, however, whether objectivism needs such a concept, and whether 'non-natural' can be defended from emptiness.   R.W.H.

*open question argument.

Bernard Williams, *Ethics and the Limits of Philosophy* (London, 1985), ch. 7.

naturalized epistemology. Whereas traditional epistemology is concerned with analysing the concepts of knowledge, justification, etc., and with explaining what should count as good reasons for forming and retaining beliefs, proponents of naturalized epistemology think that the theory of knowledge is a branch of the scientific enterprise. Such theorists deny that we can find a fixed point outside science from which to scrutinize the credentials of our beliefs and the tenability of our practices of acquiring knowledge. Naturalized epistemology sees itself as concerned primarily with exploring the mechanisms by which perceptual information about the world is transformed into the complex edifice of scientific and everyday knowledge. The naturalized approach to epistemology goes hand in hand with a rejection of the traditional distinction between *analytic and synthetic statements. Naturalized epistemologists tend to be externalists about justification, holding that what makes a belief justified is the overall reliability of the mechanisms that generated it.   J.BER.

*naturalism.

H. Kornblith (ed.), *Naturalizing Epistemology* (Cambridge, Mass., 1985).

natural kind: *see* kind, natural.

natural law. Moral standards which, on a long-dominant but now disfavoured type of account of morality, political philosophy, and *law, can justify and guide political authority, make legal rules rationally binding, and shape concept-formation in even descriptive social theory.

The sounder versions (e.g. of Plato, Aristotle, and Aquinas) consider morality 'natural' precisely because reasonable (in an understanding neither consequentialist nor Kantian). Likewise, contemporary versions plead not guilty of the 'is–ought' fallacy: natural law's first (not yet specifically moral) principles identify basic reasons for action, basic human goods which are-to-be (ought to be) instantiated through choice. Practical knowledge of these presupposes, but is not deduced from, an 'is' knowledge of possibilities; full 'is' knowledge of human nature is partly dependent on, not premiss for, practical ('is-to-be') understanding of the flourishing (including moral reasonableness) of human individuals and communities.   J.M.F.

*good; well-being; 'is' and 'ought' Pufendorf.

John Finnis (ed.), *Natural Law* (New York, 1993).

natural or scientific laws: *see* natural or scientific.

natural rights. Human rights, as articulated in a moral or political theory of *natural law. Of high philosophical and historical interest is the still inadequately understood linguistic and conceptual transformation of the Roman term *ius* from its primary sense (roughly, what is right, just, lawful) to its late-medieval and modern sense: a power, liberty, immunity, or claim—i.e. a right (in justice or law) relationship between persons articulated precisely from the standpoint of the relationship's *beneficiary*. This terminological specialization facilitates understanding of the wrong in abuse of one person by another: its unreasonableness (e.g. violation of the *golden rule, or choice precisely to damage a basic human good) not only deforms the agent, but also offends the victim's fundamental equality of human dignity, in a respect specified in the natural right thus violated.   J.M.F.

John Finnis, *Natural Law and Natural Rights* (Oxford, 1980).

natural theology. The acquisition of truths about God through the natural human capacity to know, rather than by *revelation. The study of God through the exercise of human reason, especially as legitimated by Romans 1: 18 ff. Natural theology includes the study of God through his works and the drawing of conclusions about God from premisses about creation. All putative proofs of the existence and nature of God belong to natural theology.

Kant and the Logical Positivists think natural theology impossible, Kant on the ground that the transcendent misuse of the categories generates contradictions, the Logical Positivists partly on the Humean ground that there is no valid inference from empirical premisses to transcendent conclusions, but also on the ground that the sentences of theology are without meaning because in principle unverifiable. Aquinas takes the view that human reason provides only a limited perspective on reality, which needs to be supplemented by faith. Faith is by *grace.   s.p.

Aquinas, *Summa Theologiae* (London, 1963–75).
David Hume, *Dialogues Concerning Natural Religion*, ed. Norman Kemp Smith (Indianapolis, 1962).
Immanuel Kant's Critique of Pure Reason, tr. Norman Kemp Smith (London, 1978).

nature. As with a very large number of concepts important to philosophers, 'nature' is a term with various meanings. Three seem especially worthy of note.

First, by 'nature' we mean everything that there is in the physical world of experience, very broadly construed. The universe and its contents, in short. To be natural is to be part of this world, and its distinguishing feature is usually taken to be the universal action of *laws, meaning unbroken regularities. For philosophers like Plato, as well as for those standing in the Christian tradition, the Creator necessarily exists outside his creation, although able to intervene miraculously in it. A matter of some dispute has been the question whether nature, as God's creation, is thereby necessarily good. If this be so, how then do we account for the apparent existence of evil in the world? Well known are such saving explanations as that based on the effects of human *freedom.

It is not altogether easy to maintain a reasoned belief in a dimension of existence beyond nature considered in this broad sense. Almost by definition, such a supernatural world has to be unknowable, and if (as in the Thomistic tradition) one attempts to achieve understanding through analogy, the temptation is to slide into a description of a state which seems remarkably like our own. For instance, even though God may be outside our law, does this mean that he is outside law altogether? Many have thought not, and this has proven a slippery slope, as was the case for the *Naturphilosophen, who started by seeing God's patterns being repeated through the world, inorganic and organic, and who ended with something close to pantheism, identifying God with his creation. Thomas Carlyle's 'natural supernaturalism', taking the change of ice into water to be miraculous, speaks to the confusion.

The second sense of 'nature' identifies with the living world (past and present) as opposed to the non-living. It is such a distinction that one intends when one speaks of a museum of *natural* history. The burning philosophical problem here is chiefly that of definition and demarcation. Today we think that the world of organisms is the product of *evolution, beginning (on our earth) almost four million years ago. Does this then mean that we can distinguish a mammal from a lump of rock only in terms of their respective histories, or will there be essential defining characteristics of the living which set the two aside?

From Aristotle on it has been argued that organisms are distinguishable from the inert world by virtue of the fact that they possess some sort of life force—most recently called the *'entelechy' by the vitalist Driesch. However, although it is true that organisms manage to do some remarkable things—for instance, sustaining themselves by taking in energy from the outside—it is not easy to see how an explanation of such facts as these is aided by reference to unseen vital powers. Modern opinion therefore inclines to the belief that the distinguishing mark of the organic lies in its high degree of organization rather than anything physical as such.

To the Darwinian, as to the natural theologian, the mark of such organization is that it sustains 'adaptation', whereby the features of organisms promote the survival and reproduction of their possessors. It should be noted that, although this may all be of value to the individual organism, in a world which has produced the AIDS virus it is not immediately obvious that because something is living it thereby inherently possesses absolute value. Many—from Plato to the socio-biologist Edward O. Wilson —believe nevertheless that value does emerge from the living world, because organic organization permits an ordering according to some scale of progress. However, especially inasmuch as this progress is linked to evolution, there are as many who are adamant in their opposition.

The third sense of 'nature' is that which sees everything, especially the organic world, set off against humans and the consequences of their labours. It is this sense which is being invoked when breakfast cereals are described as 'natural', and the real point of philosophical controversy arises over whether one should argue that it is nature in its raw pristine state which is truly good and worth while, or if one should argue that it is only inasmuch as nature has been altered and cultivated by humans that true worth appears. Although the organic-food industry thrives on the first disjunct, there have been many ready to endorse the second. To John Stuart Mill, for instance, it was clear that 'the very aim and object of action is to alter and improve Nature'.

Perhaps the best way out of this seemingly insoluble dilemma is to recognize that, as with those who have tried to characterize *human nature, the very attempt to draw the distinction is to invite sterile disputes. Although the science of ecology is still at a relatively primitive state, it is very clear that interference in one part of nature (in the present sense) is liable to have unexpected and unwelcome consequences elsewhere. But not to interfere is no less liable to be disastrous, especially if the animal side of *human beings is included in this conception of nature and only our intellectual abilities are excluded and barred from taking action.   M.R.

L. Gruen and D. Jamieson (eds.), *Reflecting on Nature: Readings in Environmental Philosophy* (New York, 1994).
J. S. Mill, *Three Essays on Religion* (London, 1874).
J. Passmore, *Man's Responsibility for Nature* (London, 1974).

nature, human: *see* human nature.

nature, state of: *see* state of nature.

nature, uniformity of: *see* uniformity of nature.

Naturphilosophie. Generally associated with the philosopher Schelling, *Naturphilosophie* was a widely supported although much derided general view of *nature, popular in Romantic German circles at the beginning of the last century. Owing much to Kantian *idealism, with a generous dash of *Platonism, the *Naturphilosoph* saw the whole of reality underpinned by certain basic archetypes, which have ever more perfect manifestations as one moves up the chain of being. Significant in such areas as the newly developing theory of electricity, *Naturphilosophie* made its greatest impact in the biological sciences, especially through such notions as the vertebrate theory of the skull,

where one sees all the bones of the mammalian body as variations on one theme, namely that of a typical piece of the backbone. Even in today's biology, there are whispers of *Naturphilosophie*, especially through such claims as that of the American evolutionist Stephen Jay Gould that the key to understanding animal form is the repetition and modification of certain shared blueprints or *Baupläne*.
                                                                M.R.

*evolution; naturalism.

A. Cunningham and N. Jardine (eds.), *Romanticism and the Sciences* (Cambridge, 1990).

necessary and contingent existence. Entities are held to exist necessarily if *natural processes will not lead to their cessation, contingently if such processes will lead to their cessation. The distinction stems from Plato, who, concentrating on the contrast with mathematical and other abstract entities, emphasized the corruptibility of ordinary spatio-temporal objects. Aristotle provided a physics which accounts for and indeed requires such (sublunary) corruptibility, and the distinction was famously utilized by Aquinas in the third of his five ways. By the later Middle Ages a number of such necessarily existing entities were known, such as human souls, angels, demons, the 'heavenly luminaries', and God, who, unlike the others, does not have his 'necessity from another'. In this sense of 'necessary' there is no entailment from 'X has necessary existence' to 'Necessarily, x exists'.   J.J.M.

Patterson Brown, 'St Thomas' Doctrine of Necessary Being', *Philosophical Review* (1964); repr. in A. Kenny (ed.), *Aquinas: A Collection of Critical Essays* (London, 1969).

necessary and sufficient conditions. If a *conditional of the form 'If *p*, then *q*' is true, then the state of affairs expressed by *p* is said to be a sufficient condition of the state of affairs expressed by *q* and, correlatively, the state of affairs expressed by *q* is said to be a necessary condition of the state of affairs expressed by *p*. If the conditional in question is true of logical necessity, as in the case of 'If this table is round, then it is not square', then we may speak of *logically* necessary and sufficient conditions. Weaker conditionship relations are expressed by correspondingly weaker conditionals—for instance, the conditional 'If this match is struck, it will light' implies that striking this match is, in the circumstances in which the conditional is asserted, a *causally* sufficient condition of the match's lighting.   E.J.L.

*causality; necessity, logical.

E. Sosa and M. Tooley (eds.), *Causation* (Oxford, 1993).

necessary statements: *see* contingent and necessary statements.

necessitarianism: *see* determinism.

necessity: *see* causality; contingent and necessary statements; natural or scientific laws; necessary and contingent existence; necessary and sufficient conditions; necessity, epistemic; necessity, logical; necessity, metaphysical; necessity, nomic.

necessity, epistemic. Sometimes the modal auxiliaries 'must' and 'may' appear to be used in an epistemic sense to express, respectively, what is entailed by and what is consistent with what a thinker knows. Thus, someone who knows that a train is due but has not yet arrived may assert 'It must be late', and one who knows that it is due but does not know whether it has yet arrived may assert 'It may be late'. Epistemic necessity is often expressed in terms of *certainty, as in 'The train is certainly late'. E.J.L.

*knowledge.

A. R. White, *Modal Thinking* (Oxford, 1975).

necessity, logical. In the narrowest sense, what is logically necessary is what follows from the laws of logic alone (though there is some debate over what those laws are). Thus, a statement like 'Either it will rain or it will not rain' expresses a logically necessary truth, because it is an instance of the law of excluded middle. Again, 'If all men are mortal and Socrates is a man, then Socrates is mortal' expresses a logically necessary truth, because in standard logic if we may deduce the consequent of a *conditional from its antecedent, then the truth of the conditional follows from the laws of logic alone.

A sentence expressing a logically necessary truth, in this narrow sense, is true solely in virtue of its logical form: the meanings of any non-logical terms which it contains are irrelevant to its status as expressing a logical necessity. Thus 'Either it will rain or it will not rain' expresses a logically necessary truth because it has the logical form 'Either *p* or not *p*'. However, in a wider sense a sentence may be said to express a logical necessity if, although not itself a sentence true solely in virtue of its logical form, it may be transformed into such a sentence by replacing certain terms in it by other, definitionally equivalent terms. For example, 'All bachelors are unmarried' does, in this wider sense, express a logically necessary truth, because 'bachelor' may be defined as 'unmarried man', and 'All unmarried men are unmarried' is true solely in virtue of its logical form. In this wider sense, logically necessary truths are often identified with *analytic truths.

In a still broader sense, a logical necessity may be characterized as a proposition which is true in every *possible world, without restriction—that is to say, in every *logically* possible world, the assumption being that every such world is at least a world in which the laws of logic hold. This is sometimes called 'broadly' logical necessity and is assumed to conform to the principles of a system of modal logic known as S5, first formulated by C. I. Lewis. In that system—to give a simple example—if it is possible that *p*, then it is *necessarily* possible that *p* (because if proposition *p* is true in *some* possible world, then in *every* possible world it is true that *p* is true in some possible world. If the ontological argument is valid, then 'God exists' expresses a logically necessary truth in this broad sense, because the argument can be construed as concluding that that sentence is true in every possible world.

It does not appear that 'God exists' could be said to express a logical necessity in either of the *narrower* senses previously mentioned, for at least two reasons. First, it is clear that 'God exists' is not a sentence which is true solely in virtue of its logical form—and it is doubtful whether the term 'God' could be replaced by a definitionally equivalent term, since 'God' appears to be a proper *name. Secondly, it is very arguable, in any case, that no *existential proposition follows from the laws of logic alone. Broadly logical necessity seems to be closely akin to *metaphysical necessity, though the latter is, in general, assumed not to be knowable *a priori. E.J.L.

*modal logic.

G. E. Hughes and M. J. Cresswell, *An Introduction to Modal Logic* (London, 1968).
A. Plantinga, *The Nature of Necessity* (Oxford, 1974).
W. V. Quine, *From a Logical Point of View*, 2nd edn. (Cambridge, Mass., 1961).

necessity, metaphysical. The notion that there is a kind of objective necessity which is at once stronger than physical necessity and yet not simply identifiable with *logical necessity owes much to the work of Kripke. Logically necessary truths are, it seems, knowable a priori, but Kripke argues that metaphysical necessity is, typically, only discoverable a posteriori—that is, on the basis of empirical evidence. For instance, Kripke holds that if an identity statement like 'Water is H_2O' is true, then it is *necessarily* true—in the sense that it is true in every *possible world in which water exists. However, plainly, we can only know that water *is* H_2O on empirical grounds, through scientific investigation—and we *might* be mistaken about this. It is vital, then, not to confuse metaphysical necessity with epistemic necessity. E.J.L.

S. A. Kripke, *Naming and Necessity* (Oxford, 1980).

necessity, nomic. The world of experience seems to be understandable and user-friendly primarily because it is reliable, in the sense that it is regular. This is not to say that everything happens in the same way on every occasion. Some people die of lung cancer, some do not. But underlying the contingent happenstances of existence there seems to be order and regularity. The world runs according to rules or laws. Moreover, for all that these laws lead to different effects, it seems to us that in themselves they are *necessary*. It is not mere chance that water boils when it is heated, any more than it is chance that blue-eyed parents tend to have blue-eyed children or that spring follows winter as winter follows autumn.

Wherein lies the source of this necessity? For Plato it lay in the relations between the Forms, and thus had at least the status of mathematical and logical necessity. For Christian philosophers, down to and beyond Descartes, it was a consequence of God's power and goodness, and our ability to recognize it (given the right precautions and training) lay in the powers he had conferred on us. God could break this necessity at will, as he did whenever he decided to intervene miraculously in his Creation.

But sceptics, most notoriously David Hume, have challenged this presumption. They argue that there seems to be no logic to the necessity of experience. We may expect the sun to rise tomorrow, but (as Bertrand Russell pointed out) logically we are in no different position from the turkey who expects his lunch on Christmas Eve on the reasonable grounds that he has had such a lunch on every day previously. Things could go wrong at any time.

Yet this is not to deny such necessity—generally called 'nomic' (meaning 'lawlike') to distinguish it from other sorts of necessity, like 'logical'. Nor that it does seem to be marked by its ability to bear counter-factual conditionals. Suppose someone asks if a particular sample of a metal is copper. You heat it and find that it melts at 1,000 degrees centigrade. Thus you reply: 'This cannot be copper, because if it were, it would melt at 1083.4 degrees'. If there is no such necessity, there can be no such counter-factual.

Obviously, none of this explains nomic necessity or, perhaps more importantly, why we believe some claims about the world are thus necessary. With the coming of scepticism it has generally been realized that there does not seem to be something 'out there' guaranteeing that the world must run in a regular manner, and that even if God is maintaining his Creation, this in itself does not account for our feeling of necessity.

Famously, Kant tried to explain things in terms of our psychology, namely that it is we ourselves who put the necessity into our perceptions, thus ensuring that it ends up in our understanding. Trying to regain some of the old security, he argued also that, as rational beings, this is the way that we must think. The imputation of nomic necessity therefore becomes a condition of rational thought. But although many would agree with Kant about the psychology, fewer would go on to agree about the additional claim. In a world which has challenged the necessity of traditional mathematics as well as traditional concepts of causation, it seems rash to suggest that we must think in the ways that we have always thought.

One might argue that there can be no proof of nomic necessity and that therefore we should abandon it. This seems to be the position of Karl Popper, but most of us are not that convinced that one should throw out what seems to be a generally good guide to life. In any case, such advice is more easily given than followed. Can one or should one go through life pretending that every move into the future is a leap into the dark?

One seems therefore to be thrown back just on psychology, which was essentially the position of Hume. Frankly, you cannot justify your belief in necessity, but fortunately your nature makes you believe in it, and that is quite enough for human living. The one point where some today think that they can go beyond Hume is in showing that our conviction about necessity is surely linked to our evolutionary origins, and that those would

be ancestors who assumed necessity tended to outsurvive and outbreed those that did not. We may all be turkeys fast approaching Christmas Eve, but at least we are the descendants of those who had the biology to get through the summer.   M.R.

*laws, natural or scientific; necessity, logical; induction.

N. Goodman, *Fact, Fiction and Forecast* (Cambridge, Mass., 1983).
T. Honderich, *A Theory of Determinism* (Oxford, 1988), ch. 1.
E. Nagel, *The Structure of Science* (New York, 1961).

needs. An organism's (basic, fundamental) needs are what it requires to live the normal life of its kind—flourishing rather than merely surviving—and if a need is unmet, the organism will suffer harm. Applying this analysis to human needs raises three related questions. Are human needs objective? Are they distinguishable from wants? Are they universal or culturally relative? It seems indisputable that human beings objectively and universally need air, water, food, and shelter, whatever cultural wants, desires, or preferences they happen to have. Objective human needs can plausibly be defined more abstractly as the necessary conditions for flourishing through the exercise of essential human capacities; in brief, physical and psychological health, and freedom. This account links needs to *human nature and naturalistic ethics. Needs are also the basis for an influential explication of distributive justice.   A.BEL.

*ethical naturalism.

Len Doyal and Ian Gough, *A Theory of Human Need* (Basingstoke, 1991).

negation and double negation. Negation is denial. When a person denies something, (1) her *act*, and (2) her *assertion* (i.e. what she asserts in so acting), are negations. (3) A *proposition*, even if not being used to assert anything, is the negation of another when it would, if asserted, deny—i.e. be the negation of—what the other would, if asserted, affirm. A negative particle or other expression, e.g. 'not', is one which can (amongst other things, and when suitably placed) take a sentence suitable for affirming something and transform it into a sentence suitable for denying the same thing. (4) The resulting negative *sentence* is also called a negation.

Is the negation of the negation of *A* equivalent to *A*? That depends on what denial is, and hence what negative particles mean. In logic the classical answer is 'yes', and accordingly operations of eliminating and introducing double negatives are permitted. Intuitionist logic disallows the elimination.   C.A.K.

*logic, intuitionist.

G. Frege, 'Die Verneinung', *Beiträge zur Philosophie des deutschen Idealismus* (1919), tr. P. T. Geach as 'Negation', *Translations from the Philosophical Writings of Gottlob Frege*, ed. P. T. Geach and M. Black (Oxford, 1952).
H. Price, 'Why "Not"?', *Mind* (1990).
A. N. Prior, 'Negation', in P. Edwards (ed.), *The Encyclopedia of Philosophy* (New York, 1967).

negative and positive freedom: *see* liberty.

negative proposition: *see* affirmative proposition.

negritude. A black consciousness movement originating in the 1940s in the prose and poetry of Aimé Césaire of Martinique. It received its specifically philosophical dimension from the varied publications of Senghor, past President of Senegal, who argued, among other things, that African cognition is marked, principally, by an emotional rationality which knows through embrace rather than through the dissection characteristic of Western analytical rationality. This doctrine has had a mixed reception among African intellectuals.   K.W.

*black philosophy.

Senghor: *Prose and Poetry*, ed. and tr. John Reed and Clive Wake (London, 1965).

neo-Confucianism. A revival of Confucian philosophy in Sung dynasty China, distinguished by an interest in ontology prompted by influences from Taoism and Buddhism, and with a later efflorescence in Japan. The major figure was Chu Hsi (1130–1200), who developed a sophisticated philosophy according to which a dynamic universe results from the interplay of a supreme ordering principle (*t'ai ch'i*, or *li*) with a medium of matter–energy (*ch'i*). Chu Hsi's thought was developed with greater emphasis on ethical issues by Wang Yang-ming (1472–1529), who made the idea of the human heart–mind (*hsin*) foundational. Schools based on their teachings came to flourish in Japan, together with a movement known as the Kogaku ('ancient learning') school, whose primary representatives were Itō Jinsai (1627–1705) and Ogyū Sorai (1666–1728). Placing unprecedented emphasis on philological concerns, these thinkers led a return to the careful study of the earliest texts of the classical Chinese canon.   G.R.P.

*Confucianism; Buddhist philosophy.

Wing-tsit Chan (ed.), *Chu Hsi and Neo-Confucianism* (Honolulu, 1986).

neo-Kantianism. Neo-Kantianism was a family of schools in *German philosophy from about 1870 to about 1920. It was marked by repudiation of *irrationalisms, speculative *naturalisms, and *positivisms. It was motivated by the conviction that philosophy can become a science (and not just a world-view) only if it goes back to the spirit of Kant, in whom epistemology was seen as propaedeutic to metaphysics and all other philosophical disciplines. There were, of course, many ways to understand and follow so complex a thinker as Kant, and the historian of philosophy Windelband was correct in saying that 'To understand Kant means to go beyond Kant.' So numerous were the philosophers who sought Kantian foundations for their diverse systems that historians cannot agree on how many neo-Kantian schools there were (two? seven?) or on which school to assign many philosophers to. In spite of (or, perhaps, because of) this diversity, neo-Kantianism was the dominant philosophy in the Wilhelmine universities and it maintained this hegemony until phenomenology, positivism, and philosophy of life began capturing the best minds in the early twentieth century.

After the death of Hegel in 1831 Germany entered a period of philosophical sterility during which the flourishing natural sciences and their reflection in materialism and positivism reigned in the universities. Especially after the Revolution of 1848 the position of philosophy in the universities had become politically compromised. A few philosophers who attempted to maintain some traditional philosophical position (e.g. theism) or to develop their own philosophical system (e.g. Eduard von Hartmann) bowed in the direction of Königsberg. Outstanding among these proto-neo-Kantians was Hermann von Helmholtz (1821–94), the great scientist who gave a genetic, physiological account of sense-perception with empirical analogies to Kant's transcendental psychology. But there was no concerted effort to rehabilitate Kant; perhaps there were neo-Kantians, but no neo-Kantianism.

Marburg neo-Kantianism. In 1865 Otto Liebmann (1840–1912) published his *Kant and the Epigoni*, in which all the epigoni were accused of a common fault, the acceptance, sometimes disguised, of unknowable *things-in-themselves. Each chapter of this manifesto closed with the epigraph: 'We therefore must go back to Kant!' This book was followed a year later by Friedrich Albert Lange's classic *History of Materialism*, in which Lange showed that there were Kantian epistemological foundations for materialistic science, but rejected the metaphysics of Kant's Dialectic and regarded all talk of unknowable supersensible things as mere fantasy. Lange became *ordinarius* in Marburg in 1872, and one year later he was joined by a student of Adolf Trendelenburg in Berlin, Hermann Cohen (1842–1918), who succeeded Lange upon his death in 1876. Thus was established the Marburg School.

Cohen began his career writing commentaries on Kant's three *Critiques*, and he expounded his own philosophy in three volumes corresponding to the three volumes of commentary. All six volumes tried to replace Kant's psychologistic theories (intuitions as passively received; thought as organizing intuitions; the creation of images, etc.) with Cohen's own understanding of the transcendental method. This method begins not with the facts of perception or self-observation, but with the fact (*Facta*) that science, ethics, and law exist as cultural products. Only that which the mind has conceptually established can be known a priori. Science is not the study of *given facts*—nothing is *given (gegeben), says Cohen; 'all is assigned (aufgegeben) as a task' of producing categorially constituted scientific facts. Cohen interprets this production on the model of integration in mathematical knowledge. There is no thing-in-itself; but the *concept* of the thing-in-itself is essential as a limiting concept of the goal of knowledge approached asymptotically.

Paul Natorp (1854–1924), Cohen's disciple and successor, carried through investigations in the foundations of post-Einstein physics; then he applied Cohen's transcendental method to psychology itself. In his *Platons Ideenlehre* (1902) he gave a Platonistic account of Kant's categories and transcendental ideas (or, alternatively, he Kantianized Plato's theory of Ideas). After Cohen's retirement Natorp became a more independent thinker, and the distance between Heidelberg and Marburg became noticeably less.

The last important representative of Marburg neo-Kantianism was Ernst Cassirer (1874–1945), who replaced the cognitive categories with a series of 'symbolic forms' which generate a priori structures not only in science but also in mythology, language, and politics.

The Heidelberg School. The Heidelberg School does not show the simple pattern (*Gestalt*) of the Marburg. In fact it is sometimes called the Baden or the South-West German School, since its masters were sometimes in the Universities of Zurich, Freiburg, and Strasbourg; the founding father of the school, Kuno Fischer, was for a time banished from Heidelberg. The long (1865–72), vituperative, and scurrilous controversy between him and Adolf Trendelenburg (Cohen's teacher in Berlin) over whether Kant had shown that space and time were only forms of intuition or also forms of things-in-themselves divided German philosophers into two camps, with adherents of both sides publishing more than fifty polemical papers on the quarrel. Köhnke wittily says: 'Just as in Charlottenburg, in Berlin, two parallel streets, a Kuno Fischer Strasse and a Trendelenburg Strasse lead to the Neue Kant Strasse, so the road to Neo-Kantianism led either through the school of Fischer or that of Trendelenburg' (*The Rise of Neo-Kantianism*, 170).

Kuno Fischer was pre-eminent as a historian of philosophy, and his influence was felt in the second and third generation of the Heidelberg School. Wilhelm Windelband (1848–1915), as a historian of philosophy, was the natural heir to Fischer, and Heinrich Rickert (1863–1936) was at his best in providing a philosophy of historiography. Windelband produced only one large work—his *The History of Philosophy* (still a classic)—and one must gather his systematic thoughts from scattered papers, or by reading Rickert, who had a more systematic mind than his master.

The basic fact with which Heidelberg neo-Kantianism begins is that there is a cognitive as well as an ethical imperative; logic is the ethics of thinking. The world is not as we perceive it, but as we *must* perceive it, where this *must* has the modality of ethical or more generally of a *Geltungs*-imperative (*Geltung* = validity). There is an absolute *ought* and *must* whose categorial structure we establish, and this is specified into truth, goodness, beauty, and holiness. Philosophy is the study of the validity (*Geltung*) of norms, universal rational necessities, and a priori forms of all culture.

Windelband's successor, Heinrich Rickert, likewise extended Kant's primacy of practical reason to theoretical philosophy. He interpreted valid norms as anchored in the a priori structure of a value-world (*Wertwelt*). Perhaps

Rickert's most important contribution was developing Windelband's distinction between the nomothetic sciences, which generalize (e.g. the natural sciences), and the ideographic sciences, which individuate (the historical and human sciences). Each has its own a priori categorial structure.

This hasty review of neo-Kantianism has had to omit many German philosophers who did not found, or did not belong in, any school, but whose contribution to an understanding and use of Kant in later philosophy was perhaps as great as that of the philosophers reported on here. We can only mention the most prominent names: Hans Vaihinger, Friedrich Paulsen, Aloys Riehl, Leonard Nelson, and Georg Simmel.   L.W.B.

*Kantianism.

Ernst Cassirer, 'Neo-Kantianism', in *Encyclopaedia Britannica*, 14th edn.
Klaus Christian Köhnke, *The Rise of Neo-Kantianism: German Academic Philosophy between Idealism and Positivism* (Cambridge, 1991).
Thomas E. Willey, *Back to Kant: The Revival of Kantianism in German Social Thought 1860–1914* (Detroit, 1978).

Neoplatonism. A later form of Platonic philosophy that had its primary development as a school of thought in the Roman Empire from the third to the fifth century AD. Countering dualistic interpretations of Plato's thought, it is a highly monistic version, namely, one that posits a superexistent Source of all being that extends itself into various lower levels of being, with each lower level being a weaker extended expression of the level just above it. Its founder was Plotinus (204–70), a Hellenized Egyptian who at the age of 40 established an academy of philosophy in Rome and taught in it for the next twenty-five years. Some of its basic tenets, however, likely came from his teacher, Ammonius Saccas (185–250), with whom he had studied philosophy in Alexandria for eleven years when he was a young man. The term 'Neoplatonism' itself is of fairly recent origin, going back only to the mid-nineteenth century when German scholars first used it to distinguish the views of the later Greek and Roman Platonists from those of Plato.

Plotinus saw himself as a latter-day disciple of Plato, and urged his Roman contemporaries to return to Plato's teachings. He wrote only one book, a series of fifty-four carefully reasoned philosophical essays composed over a period of fourteen years late in his life. His disciple, fellow teacher, biographer, and critic Porphyry (c.232–304) later edited and arranged them into a book with six divisions of nine essays each, called the *Enneads* (the Nines).

Although in the *Enneads* he always defers to Plato, Plotinus is very much aware of the teachings of Aristotle, and mentions Aristotle more times than he does Plato. More specifically, he is aware of Aristotle's objections to Plato and seeks to overcome them through his own revised version of *Platonism, a version in which he endeavours to retain the basic teachings of Plato, but to reshape them in a new rational metaphysical system similar in type to the metaphysical system of Aristotle. In this sense, he can be considered to be an Aristotelian Platonist, or even, as one scholar has suggested, a neo-Aristotelian. He also shows his knowledge of both Gnosticism and *Stoicism and integrates some elements of the latter into parts of his own system. He was familiar with some of the purely mystical philosophies that flourished in the Roman Empire at the time, and presents his own philosophy as a strong form of rationalism in reaction to them.

In the *Enneads*, he affirms the same themes common to the general Platonic tradition, namely, (1) the non-materiality of the highest form of reality, (2) belief that there must be a higher level of reality than visible and sensible things, (3) preference for intellectual intuition over empirical forms of knowing, (4) belief in some form of immortality, and (5) belief that the universe is essentially good. The difference, however, is that Plotinus affirms all of these as a monist interested in asserting a real identity between the natural and the supernatural both in man and throughout all of nature.

In his metaphysics Plotinus sets forth his vision of the logical structure of all being and sees two movements running throughout the whole of nature, namely, the coming-out of all things from their original unitary source, and their subsequent return back to that source. He attempts to answer the primary question of Greek metaphysics 'How does the one become many?', by positing an Ultimate Being, the One, as supernatural, incorporeal, self-caused, absolutely free, and absolutely good. Since it is absolutely good it necessarily extends its goodness and power into all lower beings. Without any loss of any of its own essence, it projects itself into lower stages of itself to form lower and weaker beings. The first stage of this projection is *Nous, or Mind, and the second is *Psykhē*, or Soul, which in turn is a projection of *Nous*. All things in nature, namely, all life-forms and all corporeal beings, including man, are souls. As such they are both in a state of becoming and dependent upon *Nous* for the fixed orders of their being. Thus the one becomes many by the necessary extension (*proödos*) of the One into lower, progressively weaker multiple phases of itself as the principles (*Nous*) and life-forms (*Bios*) of all natural things. The many, in turn, always seek to return to the one, for all natural things seek to return (*epistrophē*) to some higher unity as their source.

Most of the credit for the survival of Neoplatonism must go to Porphyry, Plotinus' successor in his academy. Porphyry differed from Plotinus on some points; and by denying some of the categories that Plotinus affirmed, and substituting for them some of Aristotle's categories, he created another type of Neoplatonism. As a matter of fact, his version of Neoplatonism later had a greater impact on the development of early European philosophy than did the Neoplatonism of Plotinus.

Other versions of early Neoplatonism also emerged in later centuries. One of Porphyry's students, Iamblichus (*c*.250–326), returned to his native Syria and founded the Syrian School around 300. The Pergamum School was founded around 330 by Aedesius, a former student of Iamblichus. Its most famous member was the Roman Emperor Julian, called Julian the Apostate, who died in 363. The School of Athens was founded by Plutarch of Athens, at the end of the fourth century. Its most famous proponent was Proclus (410–85). Proclus is now regarded as the third most important Neoplatonist after Plotinus and Porphyry. His ploy was to use the concept of triads, or evolutionary development by triadic extensions, both vertically and horizontally to explain the interconnectedness of all things. This school continued in Athens until 529 when it was closed by decree of the Emperor Justinian.

One of Proclus' pupils, Ammonius, was instrumental in establishing the Alexandrian School in the fifth century, a school which lasted until the end of the sixth century. Among its members were Simplicius, Olympiodorus, and Hypatia, the famous female philosopher and mathematician who was pulled from her carriage and killed by a mob of Christians.

Both Plotinus and Porphyry rejected Christianity because of its personalistic brand of supernaturalism and doctrine of salvation by grace through faith. Porphyry even wrote a book entitled *Against the Christians*. But their rejection of Christianity did not prevent some later Christian philosophers from importing large elements of Neoplatonism into their own philosophies. Notable among these were: some of the Greek Church fathers, such as the Cappadocians, Basil and the two Gregories, the great Latin Church father St Augustine (354–430), Boethius (470–525), Eriugena (*c*.820–70), and St Thomas Aquinas (1225–74).

Marsilio Ficino's translation of the *Enneads* into Latin in 1492 introduced Plotinian Neoplatonism with its broader humanism into Italy and later into some other European countries. It was taken to England in the late 1490s by John Colet, who paved the way for the emergence in the seventeenth century of a group of English Christian Neoplatonists known as the *Cambridge Platonists.

Certain medieval Jewish thinkers also imported elements of Neoplatonism into their philosophies. Notable among these were Isaac ben Solomon Israeli (850–950), Avecebrol (1020–70), and Abraham Ibn Ezra (*c*.1092–1167). Some Islamic philosophers did the same. Notable among them were al-Kindī (d. *c*.866), al-Fārābī (*c*.870–950), Avicenna (980–1037), and Averroës (1126–98). Neoplatonic themes may also be found in Meister Eckhart (1260–1327), in Nicholas of Cusa (1401–64), in most of the German idealist philosophers, in a few French philosophers, especially in Bergson, and in some British poets (Blake, Shelley, Keats). They also occur in Jonathan Edwards and Emerson and the *New England Transcendentalists in America.

Neoplatonism emphasizes the necessity of both reason and experience in philosophy and sanctions the idea that human experience may even go beyond metaphysics on rare occasions. As a holistic form of thinking it can serve as a prototype for the production of some greatly needed forms of holistic philosophy for our own age.   R.B.H.

A. H. Armstrong (ed.), *The Cambridge History of Later Greek and Early Medieval Philosophy* (London, 1967).

R. B. Harris (ed.), *The Structure of Being* (Norfolk, Va., 1982).

G. Reale, *The Schools of the Imperial Age*, tr. J. R. Catan (Albany, NY, 1992).

R. T. Wallis, *Neoplatonism* (London, 1972).

neo-pragmatism. Recent philosophical movement embracing a radical form of social and practical contextualism that denies the possibility of universal conceptions of truth or reality. Neo-pragmatism emerged as a critical reaction to traditional and *analytic philosophy. Building mainly on Dewey, Wittgenstein, Quine, and Sellars, Richard Rorty's *Philosophy and the Mirror of Nature* (1979) initiated a return to a *pragmatism. Because all philosophical attempts to distinguish in principle between analytical and empirical, necessary and contingent, universal and historical, reality and fiction are taken to have failed, truth and meaning are taken to be nothing but moments of specific social practices. Philosophical questions, however, remain: How can the social pragmatist avoid self-refuting relativism? Is all social practice just 'coping with entities', regardless of whether these are objects or persons? And how about the ethical and political consequences of a 'frank ethnocentrism' (Rorty) that privileges one's own interpretative perspective without constraint?   H.-H.K.

Richard Rorty, 'The World Well Lost', in *Consequences of Pragmatism (Essays: 1972–1980)* (Minneapolis, 1982).

neo-realism: *see* New Realism.

neo-Thomism. 'Neo-Thomism' is an imprecise term applied since the nineteenth century to diverse authors, doctrines, procedures, and topics that have or claim to have some relation to the thought of Thomas Aquinas. Its origin is usually located in Pope Leo XIII's letter *Æterni Patris* (1879). The letter urges Catholic philosophers to demonstrate the existence and attributes of *God and to combat the speculative and practical errors of modern philosophy by reappropriating the teachings of the major Christian writers from the European Middle Ages. Leo picks out as chief among these writers Thomas Aquinas, who is supposed to have unified in his teaching the best of patristic and medieval theology. While *Æterni Patris* did mobilize large-scale ecclesiastical support for a new *Thomism, its programme had been worked out in Catholic educational circles during the previous four decades. For example, a number of thinkers in or about the Jesuits' Roman and German Colleges began in the 1840s and 1850s to advocate a systematic Thomism as the only philosophically adequate alternative to various modern *empiricisms and *idealisms. Among these thinkers were Matteo Liberatore and Joseph Kleutgen. If Liberatore represents the Italian side of the new movement, with its combative sense of philosophical system, Kleutgen brought to Rome from Münster and Fribourg an attention to the historical context for medieval thought. *Æterni Patris* ratified and institutionalized the labour of these and similar teachers.

Of course, by the date of *Æterni Patris* neo-Thomism was already beginning to break up into camps. These camps were partly determined by institutional arrangement and partly by avowed task or purpose. So, for example, the different religious orders maintained separate educational systems and tended to teach rather different versions of Thomism. Some orders were also concerned to promote their own medieval authors as alternatives to Thomas. The Franciscans regularly espoused Bonaventure or Scotus, while a few Jesuits taught from Suarez. Again, neo-Thomism from its inception was both exegetical and constructive or polemical. If it wanted to be considered Thomism, it had to ground itself in a historically sensitive reading of Thomas. If it wanted to be a neo-Thomism, it had to extract from Thomas principles or arguments useful in dispute with modern philosophies. By the early decades of this century there were neo-Thomists who were principally known as able interpreters of medieval thought and neo-Thomists who were principally known as builders of 'Thomistic' systems and debaters of modern doctrines. The interpreters would include Martin Grabmann, Pierre Mandonnet, and Maurice De Wulf; the builders and debaters, Réginald Garrigou-Lagrange and Désiré Mercier. Some neo-Thomists, most famously Étienne Gilson, were able to do both.

The principal neo-Thomists tend to be classified by their attachment to some particular theme or preoccupation. One persistent theme has been the engagement with epistemological questions raised by Kant and the neo-Kantians. This kind of neo-Thomism, called 'transcendental Thomism', is associated with Joseph Maréchal and Karl Rahner. A different kind of transcendental analysis, more driven by the concerns of experimental science, is offered in the Thomist writings of Bernard J. F. Lonergan. Another class of neo-Thomists is associated with questions in metaphysics and chiefly with expounding the Thomist doctrine about being (*esse*). Writers put into this class include Gilson and Jacques Maritain. But these classifications are at best a preliminary guide to complex authors, each of whom wrote on a wide range of philosophical topics.

The Roman Catholic Church's institutional support for neo-Thomism was much weakend during and after the second Vatican Council (1961–5). Since then, neo-Thomism has tended to become largely historical and to be submerged in the study of the history of medieval philosophy.   M.D.J.

*neo-Kantianism.

Gerard A. McCool, *Nineteenth-Century Scholasticism: The Search for a Unitary Method* (New York, 1989).

Anton C. Pegis (ed.), *A Gilson Reader* (New York, 1957).

Netherlands philosophy. As one would expect of a philosophy within a culture which has always been so open to foreign influences, the Dutch philosophical tradition has given rise to many interesting variations on well-known international movements. It is in many respects an ideal microcosm of Western European philosophical developments from the thirteenth century onwards.

Siger of Brabant (1240–81), as Dante realized when he placed him in the Fourth Heaven, and allowed Aquinas to characterize him as one of the noblest champions of Christian philosophy, left works which take us to the very heart of the thirteenth-century confrontation between Augustinianism and *Aristotelianism. Arnout Geulincx (1624–69) provides us with a unique insight into the transition from Descartes to Spinoza.

If Dutch philosophy has been very open to foreign influence, it is also true that many Dutch thinkers have had at least a considerable influence upon European intellectual history. Spinoza is of course the outstanding case. (His influence on philosophy within the Netherlands, however, by contrast with that of Descartes, was minimal prior to the second half of the nineteenth century. Even then, it consisted of very little more than free-wheeling speculative interpretations of the first book of the *Ethics*.) Spinoza was by no means the only Dutch philosopher who affected the history of philosophy. Rudolf Agricola (1444–85), now known mainly on account of the ways in which his *humanism foreshadows that of Erasmus, did in fact write the first work to break decisively with the medieval logical tradition. Hugo Grotius (1583–1645) laid the philosophical foundations of international law. Those concerned with the roots of German Romanticism are aware of the enthusiasm with which the dialogues of Frans Hemsterhuis (1721–90) were read by Kant, Jacobi, Goethe, and Novalis.

Prior to the founding of the Universities of Louvain (1425) and Leiden (1575), nearly all the most distinguished thinkers were obliged of necessity to pursue their careers abroad—Siger of Brabant in Italy, Buridan in Paris, Marsilius of Inghen in Heidelberg, Agricola in Italy, Erasmus in Europe at large.

Philosophy was for long only a propaedeutic subject in the universities, leading on to the study of theology, law, and medicine. A Royal Decree of 1815 and an Act of Parliament of 1876 left it with one professor in each university, with no assistants. However, things have looked up. Faculties of philosophy, with philosophy regarded mainly as an interdisciplinary activity, were made obligatory for university status in 1960. The interdisciplinary policy came to be seen as a failure, and in 1985 truer faculties of philosophy came into being. M.J.P.

Documentatieblad van de Werkgroep Sassen (Rotterdam, 1989–), journal ed. M. R. Wielema, Faculty of Philosophy, Erasmus University, Rotterdam.

Geschiedenis van de wijsbegeerte in Nederland, ed. H. A. Krop and M. J. Petry, 21 vols. (Baarn, 1986–93). Contains anthologies of the work of the thinkers mentioned above.

J. J. Poortman, *Repertorium der Nederlandse Wijsbegeerte* (Amsterdam, 1948); supplements 1958, 1968, 1983.

F. Sassen, *Geschiedenis van de Wijsbegeerte in Nederland tot het einde der negentiende eeuw* (Amsterdam, 1959).

—— *Wijsgerig Leven in Nederland in de Twintigste Eeuw* (Amsterdam, 1960).

Neumann, John von (1903–57). American mathematician born in Budapest. His genius ranged from logic to atomic energy. He introduced the Foundation Axiom of *set theory, which excludes 'paradoxical' sets such as those which are members of themselves. Building on Alan Turing's idea that a program is a form of data, his blueprint for the first electronic digital computers was the influential 'von Neumann architecture', now criticized because it does not allow parallelism. The theory of *games is largely his creation. With Oskar Morgenstern he laid the foundations of econometrics. He gave the first mathematically rigorous treatment of *quantum theory, including a proof that the theory cannot be made deterministic by assuming that there are hidden parameters. In philosophy he confined himself to advertising the programme of Hilbert. W.A.H.

Norman Macrae, *John von Neumann* (Providence, RI, 1999).

Neurath, Otto (1882–1945). Born in Vienna. Died in Oxford a refugee from the Nazis. Member of the 'left wing' of the *Vienna Circle, famous for his anti-foundationalist *boat metaphor. In the protocol-sentence debate with Carnap, Neurath insisted that knowledge is intersubjective and historically conditioned. Neurath rejected both metaphysics and epistemology, admitting only positive knowledge about happenings in space and time. He argued against all fictional idealizations, such as *reductionism or completed science, and opposed foundations and fixed methods, urging instead judgement, technique, negotiation, and, finally, decision and action. Marxism was for Neurath a science and science was a tool for change. He headed Bavaria's programme for full socialization in 1919, invented easily readable 'picture statistics', founded the Vienna Social and Economic Museum, was active in adult education, and spearheaded the Unity of Science Movement—to unite the separate sciences locally 'at the point of action'. N.C.
T.U.

*foundationalism.

Otto Neurath, *Philosophical Papers 1913–1946*, ed. R. S. Cohen and M. Neurath (Dordrecht, 1973).

T. Uebel (ed.), *Rediscovering the Forgotten Vienna Circle* (Dordrecht, 1991).

Neurath's boat: *see* boat, Neurath's.

neuroscience, the philosophical relevance of. Neuroscience has philosophical relevance even if minds are distinct from brains or, as it is better to say, mental properties are distinct from neural properties. We would still need to look to neuroscience to determine whether mental events and properties had a causal influence upon neural events and thereby on the human body and behaviour. If neuroscientists were unable to find signs of causal influence, some form of *epiphenomenalism would appear to be true. In the eyes of many, the implausibility of epiphenomenalism implies that either the neuroscientists should carry on looking for signs of influence, or that it is wrong to think of mental properties as distinct from neural properties.

Neuroscience may also show that we are not free if, as seems plausible, there is a sense of freedom which is incompatible with determinism. (*Freedom and determinism.) Its investigations have given some support to the claim that there is an intimate relationship between mental and neural events. (*Psychoneural intimacy.) If relations between neural events, and between neural events and behaviour, are shown by neuroscience to be governed by deterministic laws, then we are not free in the sense of freedom mentioned. Unfortunately, it is debatable whether neural indeterminism makes us any freer. In this respect, neuroscience may only have the capacity to disappoint.

If minds are not distinct from but identical with brains, neuroscience will be potentially relevant to other philosophical issues. At first, it may look as if you will merely discover more about things which have philosophical currency, such as beliefs, desires and their role in the explanation of action, the nature of reasoning and mental representation, and the means by which we arrive at justified beliefs and learn concepts. In this anodyne light, it is possible that the study of neuroscience is relevant to philosophy, but the upshot may just be that neuroscience in a way fills in the story for which philosophy has given us some headlines. It will tell us more about what these things are, but not unsettle, to any great extent, the distinctions upon which philosophy has already alighted.

However, certain philosophers have boldly suggested that the influence of neuroscience is likely to be altogether different. Neuroscience will be no lackey. It will be in the driving-seat. Philosophy will be seen to have appealed to distinctions or categories that neuroscience provides us with reasons to replace. For instance, according to this view, there may be no such things as beliefs as we have understood them—no things which fall under concepts of our *folk psychology. Naturally, this would alter our approach to a number of the issues identified above and more than likely radically alter our conception of ourselves. (*Eliminativism.)

Is this likely to happen? Here is an analogy. Zoology is the relevant discipline for the study of zebras. It is possible that zoologists will come to the conclusion that there are no zebras because we should categorize those stripy animals in a different way. But it is reasonable to think that any such changes will not radically alter our familiar appreciation of these animals. If neuroscience is the relevant discipline by which we may understand minds and their contents, one might expect, at worst, a like degree of reform of our mental categories. A philosopher who is non-committal at the appropriate points, and who speaks at a suitable level of abstraction, is only likely to blanch at something different, a veritable revolution. It is not clear why we should expect one unless the analogy breaks down, and it is not obvious that it will. To think otherwise, we would need to be told a thoroughly convincing story of why we grossly misconceive our minds.

Finally, the extent to which neuroscience makes good its initial promise to provide us with some scientific understanding of much of what we understand by our talk of minds may have a more general philosophical relevance. It would be a further vindication of what may be loosely called 'the scientific picture of the world' and thereby the philosophy that underpins it. Some spiritual and religious concerns may look very different as a consequence. It would probably be more difficult to believe reasonably in certain doctrines such as the *immortality of the human soul.   P.J.P.N.

*mind–body problem.

W. Bechtel et al. (eds.), Philosophy and the Neurosciences: A Reader (Oxford, 2001).
M. R. Bennett and P. M. S. Hacker, Philosophical Foundations of Neuroscience (Oxford, 2003).
P. M. Churchland, A Neurocomputational Perspective (Cambridge, Mass., 1989).
P. S. Churchland, Neurophilosophy (Cambridge, Mass., 1986).
A. Clark, Microcognition (Cambridge, Mass., 1989).
T. Honderich, A Theory of Determinism (Oxford, 1989).

neustic and phrastic. This pair of terms was coined by R. M. Hare in 1952 to distinguish the content (phrastic) from the mood or force (neustic) of a sentence. Thus commands and statements could agree phrastically, while differing neustically. Hare concludes from this analysis that the same logical principles can apply in ethical as in non-ethical language. There is an inconsistency between posting a letter and burning it; and that logical point affects commands, wishes, etc. which may arise in this connection.   J.D.G.E.

*prescriptivism.

R. M. Hare, The Language of Morals (Oxford, 1952).

neutral monism. The theory, associated with William James and Bertrand Russell, that the world is composed of one sort of entity, or stuff, the fundamental nature of which is neither mental nor physical. The mind consists of these entities under one aspect, and matter consists of them under another. The theory was intended to preserve the advantages of *monism, in particular ontological parsimony, while avoiding the problems of reduction present in both pure *idealism and *materialism. It never became popular both because no proper characterization of the basic neutral stuff could be given, and because it had some tendency to appear as a notational variant on idealism. Something like it is occasionally revived, for example by T. Nagel in The View from Nowhere (1986).   P.F.S.

Mark Sainsbury, Russell (London, 1979), 261–8.

Newcomb's paradox. Paradox about prediction and choice. There are two boxes before you, A and B, and you are allowed to choose either just box A or alternatively both boxes. You may keep anything you find in any box you choose. You know that a very powerful Being, with an untarnished record of successfully predicting human behaviour, has acted in the following way: he has put

£1,000 in box *B*; and he has put £1,000,000 in box *A* if and only if he predicts that you will choose just box *A*. What should you do?

1. You should choose just box *A*. For the Being will have predicted this, and so filled it with £1,000,000, so you will be rich; whereas if you choose both boxes, he would have predicted *that*, and you would only get £1,000.

2. You should choose both boxes. For either the Being has predicted this or he hasn't. If he hasn't (but has instead predicted you will choose just box *A*), you will end up with £1,001,000 as opposed to £1,000,000 had you chosen just *A*. If he has, then you will at least get £1,000, as opposed to nothing had you chosen just *A*. Either way, you'll be better off choosing both boxes.

The paradox consists in the incompatibility between these apparently well-argued recommendations.   R.M.S.

Mark Sainsbury, *Paradoxes* (New York, 1988), ch. 3.

New England Transcendentalism. A religious, philosophical, literary, and social movement that flourished in the 1830s and 1840s and whose leaders tended to live around Concord or Boston, Massachusetts. Transcendentalism reacted against 'corpse-cold' Unitarianism, which limited itself to the 'understanding', the faculty employed in practical affairs and scientific theorizing. As German and British *philosophical romanticism had discovered, there is also 'reason', a faculty able to range beyond sensation and intuit spiritual and metaphysical truths. Reason allows one to dispense with religious texts and institutions, philosophical argumentation, and social and ethical traditions. In *Nature* (1836) Ralph Waldo Emerson claimed that reason reveals that we are one with nature, which has a spiritual source beyond definitive comprehension. Henry David Thoreau in *Civil Disobedience* (1849) appealed to higher law in rejecting immoral civil laws, and in *Walden* (1854) provided a sweeping critique of American society. Transcendentalists also initiated influential reforms in education and developed model communities intended to unify the practical with the ideal.   C.C.

*transcendentalism.

Paul F. Boller Jr., *American Transcendentalism 1830–1860: An Intellectual Inquiry* (New York, 1974).
B. Kuklick, *A History of Philosophy in America 1720–2000* (Oxford, 2002).

new philosophy calls all in doubt.

And new philosophy calls all in doubt,
And element of fire is quite put out;
The sun is lost, and th' earth, and no man's wit
Can well direct him where to look for it.'
                    (John Donne, 'An Anatomy of the World:
                    The First Anniversary', lines 205–8)

Donne published the 'Anatomy' in 1611, the year after Galileo published the first accounts of his observations with the telescope, and when Descartes was 15. It balances on the brink between medievalism and the Renaissance—regret about the Fall and original sin and assumptions that the world is running down like a clock come together with references to Copernicus, Brahe, and Kepler and debate over whether the fire round the world really exists. The 'new philosophy' seemed to threaten disruption and chaos.

Twelve years later Galileo under threat of torture disavowed belief in a revolving earth (muttering 'yet it does move'), and Descartes, hearing of this, suppressed publication of his *Le Monde*, which also taught the Copernican system.   J.O'G.

New Realism (also called neo-Realism). An American philosophical movement against Royce's idealism, led by his former students and young colleagues at Harvard (Ralph Barton Perry, William P. Montague, and E. B. Holt). It was a co-operative movement involving a common manifesto and joint publications, and as such was a significant factor in the professionalization of American philosophy. Its members had allegiances to other compatible intellectual movements (e.g. *behaviourism and *pragmatism), but all held a theory of direct acquaintance with physical objects. They were unable to work out a common theory of *illusion, and gave way to attacks from *Critical Realism.   L.W.B.

new riddle of induction: *see* grue.

New Right, political: *see* Right, the political New.

Newton, Isaac (1642–1727). Strongly interested in both theology and alchemy, to each of which he devoted a great deal more time and intellectual energy than he did to his more orthodox scientific pursuits, Newton none the less found time to be an outstanding mathematician and theoretical and experimental physicist. He invented the *calculus earlier than, and independently of, its first publisher, Leibniz. Side-stepping Aristotle's question 'What keeps moving things moving?', Newton took inertial laws as axiomatic. Deducing Kepler's empirical laws of planetary motion from the inverse square principle, Newton held that gravity was not an *occult* force, nor an *essential* quality of bodies, but, perhaps influenced by the *Stoics, tacitly accepted mechanically inexplicable forces. In religious terms Newton was an Arian, believing that the Church had taken a wrong turning when it opted for the Athanasian doctrine of the Trinity.   J.J.M.

R. S. Westfall, *Never at Rest: A Biography of Isaac Newton* (Cambridge, 1980).

New Zealand philosophy. Academic philosophy in New Zealand belongs to the British side of the bicultural partnership established by the Treaty of Waitangi between Maori and the Crown in 1840. Accordingly, it has developed in tandem with the prevailing Anglo-American traditions in philosophy, and in strong mutual relationship with *Australian philosophy. New Zealand's professional philosophical association continues to count as a 'division' of the Australasian Association of Philosophy, which is responsible for the editorship of the *Australasian Journal of Philosophy*.

New Zealand philosophers have not been, however, merely consumers and transmitters of Northern philosophical culture. They have been active contributors to the discipline, and in many cases innovators influencing its direction internationally. Karl Popper wrote *The Poverty of Historicism* (not published in book form until 1957) and the two volumes of *The Open Society and its Enemies* (1945) while holding a lectureship at Canterbury College of the University of New Zealand from 1937 to 1945. It was there that Popper met the neurophysiologist (and Nobel Prize winner) John Eccles, with whom he later collaborated in *The Self and its Brain* (1977). Canterbury, too, was home to the New Zealander Arthur Prior, as lecturer from 1945, and then as Professor from 1952 to 1959. While there, Prior published his *Formal Logic* (1955) and *Time and Modality*, the John Locke lectures for 1955/6, providing a systematic presentation of modern tense logic. John Passmore's *Hume's Intentions* (1952) appeared while he held the Chair at Otago: his successor was J. L. Mackie, whose publications at that time include 'Evil and Omnipotence', *Mind* (1955).

Since 1960 some areas of special concentration can be discerned. Prior's influence set a focus on logic that became the most distinctive feature of New Zealand philosophy for three or more decades after he left for a chair at Manchester and eventually a fellowship at Balliol (from 1966). This focus is exemplified by the work of George Hughes and Max Cresswell at Victoria University of Wellington (*An Introduction to Modal Logic* (1968) and Cresswell's *Logics and Languages* (1973)), Pavel Tichy's work in type theory, logic, and the philosophy of logic at Otago (*The Foundations of Frege's Logic* (1988)), and Krister Segerberg's development of dynamic logic at Auckland.

Work in the philosophy of the arts has been prominent in New Zealand, with the main contributors being Greg Currie (previously at Otago), Stephen Davies at Auckland, and David Novitz and Denis Dutton, editor of the journal *Philosophy and Literature*, at Canterbury. New Zealand has participated in an international trend towards greater emphasis on applied ethics, with a Bioethics Centre established at Otago in 1988, and a Diploma in Professional Ethics at Auckland in 1992. Old divisions between 'continental' and 'analytic' philosophy have become less relevant—consider, for example, Julian Young's work on Nietzsche and Heidegger at Auckland—and New Zealanders are well represented in many areas of emerging importance, such as the philosophy of biology (Kim Sterelny at Victoria University of Wellington edits *Biology and Philosophy*), the philosophy of artificial intelligence (Jack Copeland, of Canterbury, is director of the Turing Archive for the History of Computing), and virtue ethics (Rosalind Hursthouse and Christine Swanton at Auckland).

The sixty or so members of the community of academic professional philosophers in New Zealand (as in 2003) contribute across all main areas of philosophy, however: note, for example, Alan Musgrave's contributions in epistemology and the philosophy of science since his appointment to the Otago chair in 1970. Yet the question does arise whether New Zealanders should take opportunities to develop distinctively regional philosophies. The challenge to achieve this has been presented by the New Zealander Richard Sylvan—whose work on non-classical logics has been influential in Australasia and beyond—in his 'Prospects for Regional Philosophies in Australasia' (*Australasian Journal of Philosophy* (1985)). An interest in philosophical engagement with Maori culture has emerged with the work of John Patterson at Massey (*Exploring Maori Values* (Dunmore Press, 1992)), and the prospect of philosophical work on the Maori side of the bicultural partnership is held out by the development of whare wananga (Maori universities). Issues in social and political philosophy of special reference to the New Zealand context have also received attention: see e.g. Graham Oddie and Roy Perrett (eds.), *Justice, Ethics and New Zealand Society* (Oxford, 1992). Perhaps the most distinctive feature of contemporary New Zealand philosophy, however, is something widely remarked by visitors: the congeniality and friendliness which seem to be a function both of the small size of the academic community and of the national ethos of Aotearoa-New Zealand.   J.BISH.

Nicholas of Autrecourt (*c*.1300–?). A student at Paris, he later taught there, delivering a series of lectures on the *Sentences* of Peter Lombard. Certain of his theological views caused offence in the Church and under pressure from the Church he burned his writings and retracted his offensive views. He is in some respects a forerunner of David Hume, placing emphasis on the principle that if two things are really different from each other then it is not possible to argue with certainty from one to the other. On this basis he presents an account of *causality very similar to the account that Hume was later to present. Nicholas's account of the relation between *substance and accident also anticipates Hume.   A.BRO.

J. Weinberg, *Nicholas of Autrecourt* (Princeton, NJ, 1948).

Nicholas of Cusa (1401–64). A student at Heidelberg and Padua, he subsequently became active in Church politics, making an impact at the Council of Basle (1432), and seeing some of his ecumenical work bearing fruit some years later at the Council of Florence. He became a cardinal in 1448. Nicholas is famous for his teaching on *docta ignorantia* (educated ignorance), in which he focuses upon the ineffability of *God, and the implication that those who think they have affirmative knowledge of God are truly ignorant, the knowledgeable ones being those who are aware that they are ignorant of him. The unknowability of God follows from Nicholas's doctrine of the 'coincidence of opposites', that in God there exist as identities what are utterly distinct in us. For example, the existence of a created thing is distinct from its *essence, for it is not of the essence of any created thing that it exists. But in God his essence and existence are identical. Also God is the maximum, the greatest possible being, and is also the minimum, the least, for he does not occupy any part of space, however small.   A.BRO.

J. Hopkins, *A Concise Introduction to the Philosophy of Nicholas of Cusa* (Minneapolis, 1978).

Nietzsche, Friedrich Wilhelm (1844–1900). German philosopher and critic *par excellence*. A classical philologist by training and academic profession, Nietzsche's philosophical efforts—deriving chiefly from the last dozen years of his short productive life—were little heeded until long after his physical and mental collapse in 1889 (at the age of only 44). He subsequently emerged as one of the most controversial, unconventional, and important figures in the history of modern philosophy. His influence upon European philosophy in the twentieth century has been profound; and he has belatedly come to receive considerable attention in the English-speaking world as well, as the shadow cast by the travesty of his appropriation by the Nazis and Fascists has receded, along with the sway of philosophical fashions inhospitable to his kind of thinking and writing. He gave his *Beyond Good and Evil* the subtitle *Prelude to a Philosophy of the Future*; and in this he may well have been prophetic.

Nietzsche's philosophical enterprise grew out of his background as a philologist schooled in the study of classical languages and literatures, his deep concern with issues relating to the quality of life in the culture and society of his time, his conviction that the interpretative and evaluative underpinnings of Western civilization are fundamentally flawed, and his determination to come to grips with the profound crisis he believed to be impending as this comes to be recognized. He sought both to comprehend this situation and to help provide humanity with a new lease on life, beyond what he called 'the death of God' and 'the advent of nihilism' following in its wake. He deemed traditional forms of religious and philosophical thought to be inadequate to the task, and indeed to be part of the problem; and so he attempted to develop a radical alternative to them that might point the way to a solution.

Nietzsche had no formal philosophical training. His introduction to philosophy came through his discovery of Schopenhauer's *The World as Will and Representation* while studying philology at the university at Leipzig. This encounter with Schopenhauer's thought profoundly influenced him, as can be seen in his first book *The Birth of Tragedy* (1872), which he published soon after being appointed to a professorship of philology at Basle University (at the astonishingly early age of 24, before he had even been awarded his doctorate). He was convinced of the soundness of Schopenhauer's basic conception of the world as a godless and irrational affair of ceaseless striving and suffering; but he was repelled by Schopenhauer's starkly pessimistic verdict with respect to the worth of existence in such a world, and sought some way of arriving at a different conclusion. In *The Birth of Tragedy* he made his first attempt to do so, looking to the Greeks and their art for guidance, and to Wagner (with whom he had become acquainted and enthralled) for contemporary inspiration. His attachment to Wagner subsequently gave way to disenchantment and then to scathing criticism (culminating in his late polemic *The Case of Wagner*), and he gradually emancipated himself from Schopenhauer as well; but the fundamental problem of how *nihilism might be overcome and life affirmed without illusions remained at the centre of his concern throughout his life.

Nietzsche's brief academic career ended in 1879, owing to the drastic deterioration of his health. His only significant publications after *The Birth of Tragedy* prior to its final year were the four essays he subsequently gathered together under the title *Untimely Meditations*, of which 'The Uses and Disadvantages of History for Life' and 'Schopenhauer as Educator' (both 1874) are of the greatest interest. Then in 1878 he published the first of a series of volumes of aphorisms and reflections under the title *Human, All Too Human*. It was followed during the next few years by two supplements which became a second volume under the same title, by *Daybreak* in 1881, and then by the initial four-part version of *The Gay Science* in 1882. In these works, which he described as 'a series of writings . . . whose common goal is to erect *a new image and ideal of the free spirit*', Nietzsche found his way to his kind of philosophy.

It was only in 1886, however, with the publication of *Beyond Good and Evil*, that he pursued it further in something like the same manner. In the interval (1883–5) he published only the four parts of his great literary-philosophical experiment *Thus Spoke Zarathustra*. A mere three more years remained to him prior to his collapse in January of 1889, from which he never recovered. During this brief but phenomenally productive period he wrote prefaces to new editions of most of his pre-*Zarathustra* writings, added a fifth part to a new edition of *The Gay Science* (1887), published *On the Genealogy of Morals* in the same year, and then in the final year of his active life (1888) wrote *Twilight of the Idols*, *The Case of Wagner*, *The Antichrist*, and his autobiographical *Ecce Homo*—all the while filling many notebooks with reflections and thought experiments. (The significance of this 'Nachlass' material is much debated. After his collapse and death, selections from it were gathered into a volume published under the title *The Will to Power*.)

From his early essays to these last works, Nietzsche showed himself to be an astute, severe, and provocative critic on many fronts. Cultural, social, political, artistic, religious, moral, scientific, and philosophical developments and phenomena of many kinds drew his polemical attention. Everywhere he looked he saw much that was lamentably 'human, all too human', even among those things and thinkers generally held in the highest regard. This has given rise to the common impression that the basic thrust and upshot of his thought is radically negative, contributing greatly to the advent of nihilism that he announced (and of worse things as well).

This impression, however, is deeply mistaken. Nietzsche actually was a profoundly positive thinker, concerned above all to discover a way beyond the nihilistic reaction he believed to be the inevitable consequence of the impending collapse of traditional values and modes of interpretation, to a new 'affirmation' and 'enhancement' of life. His critical fire was only a means to this end, preliminary to the twin philosophical tasks of *reinterpretation* and *revaluation* he advocated and pursued with growing explicitness and determination from *The Gay Science* onward.

As a further means to this end, and likewise preliminary to these tasks, Nietzsche developed and undertook a variety of forms of analysis, of which the kind of 'genealogical' inquiry exemplified by his investigations in *On the Genealogy of Morals* is one notable and important example. His analytical acumen was as extraordinary as his critical astuteness; and his writings both before and after *Zarathustra* contain a wealth of cultural, social, psychological, linguistic, and conceptual analyses from many different perspectives, upon which he drew not only in his critiques but also in his reinterpretative and revaluative efforts. His recognition of the importance of engaging in and drawing upon a multiplicity of such analyses in philosophical inquiry is reflected in his insistence that such inquiry is inescapably perspectival—and that this circumstance is by no means fatal to it, if one can learn to capitalize upon the possibility of bringing a variety of perspectives to bear upon many of the matters with which it may concern itself. This is his practice as well as his prescription, in his explorations of issues ranging from moral and religious phenomena to aspects of our human nature and to knowing and reasoning themselves.

The form of Nietzsche's philosophical writings both before and after *Zarathustra*, which for the most part consist of collections of relatively brief aphorisms and reflections on such issues rather than sustained systematic lines of argument, is well suited to this multiply perspectival tactic. It greatly complicates the task of understanding him; but it also makes his thinking far more subtle and complex than is commonly supposed. He returned to problems repeatedly, in one work after another, approaching them from many different angles; and it is only if account is taken of his many diverse reflections on them that anything approaching justice to his thinking about any of them can be done. Even then he can be—and has been, and no doubt will continue to be—interpreted in quite different ways. Precisely for this reason, however, and because he has so much of interest to say (on almost any such interpretation) about so many things, he is certain to continue to attract, deserve, and reward philosophical attention.

Nietzsche was greatly concerned with basic problems he discerned in contemporary Western culture and society, which he believed were becoming increasingly acute, and for which he considered it imperative to try to find new solutions. Chief among them were questions of meaning and value, and of our understanding of ourselves and our place in the world, which can no longer be answered in traditional religious and philosophical ways. He prophesied the advent of a period of nihilism, with the death of God and the demise of metaphysics, and the discovery of the inability of science to yield anything like absolute knowledge; but this prospect deeply worried him. He was firmly convinced of the untenability of the *'God-hypothesis' and associated religious interpretations of the world and our existence, and likewise of their metaphysical variants. Having also become persuaded of the fundamentally non-rational character of the world, life, and history, Nietzsche took the basic challenge of philosophy to be that of overcoming both these ways of thinking and the nihilism resulting from their abandonment. This led him to undertake to reinterpret ourselves and the world along lines which would be more tenable, and would also be more conducive to the flourishing and enhancement of life. The 'de-deification of nature', the tracing of the 'genealogy of morals' and their critique, and the elaboration of 'naturalistic' accounts of knowledge, value, morality, and our entire 'spiritual' nature thus came to be among the main tasks with which he took himself and the 'new philosophers' he called for be confronted.

Unlike most philosophers of importance before him, Nietzsche was openly and profoundly hostile to most forms of *morality and religious thought. He declared 'war' upon them, on the grounds that they not only are indefensible and untenable, but moreover feed upon and foster weakness, life-weariness, and *ressentiment*, poisoning the wellsprings of human vitality in the process by 'devaluing' all 'naturalistic' values. He further rejected not only the God-hypothesis (as a notion utterly without warrant, owing its acceptance only to naïvety, error, need, or ulterior motivation), but also any metaphysical postulation of a 'true world of "being"' transcending the world of life and experience, and with them the related 'soul-' and 'thing-hypotheses', taking these notions to be ontological fictions reflecting our artificial (though convenient) conceptual shorthand for products and processes. In place of this cluster of traditional ontological categories and interpretations, he conceived of the world in terms of an interplay of forces without any inherent structure or final end, ceaselessly organizing and reorganizing themselves as the fundamental disposition he called *'will to power' gives rise to successive arrays of power relationships among them. It is debatable whether his thoughts along these lines amount to a kind of philosophical cosmology; but if so, it is a very minimalistic one, because for him there is little more to the general character of life and the world than this, and so there is little more about it to be said, other than to give perspectival accounts of contingently obtaining states of affairs accessible in one way or another to us.

There is a good deal about our own human reality that is accessible to us in various ways, however; and so, even if there is nothing immutable (let alone divine) about it, its comprehension is a task to which Nietzsche thought it would be well for philosophers to turn their attention, learning what they can from the human sciences, but supplementing what these sciences can tell us about ourselves by way of other attainable perspectives upon human life as well. So he construed our human nature and existence naturalistically, insisting upon the necessity of 'translating man back into nature', in origin and fundamental character, as one form of animal life among others. 'The soul is only a word for something about the body,' he has Zarathustra say; and the body is fundamentally an arrangement of natural forces and processes. At the same time, however, he insisted upon the importance of social arrangements and interactions in the development of human forms of awareness and activity, and moreover upon the possibility of the emergence of exceptional human beings capable of an independence and creativity elevating them beyond the level of the general human rule.

So Nietzsche stressed the difference between 'higher types' and 'the herd', and through Zarathustra proclaimed the 'over-man' (*Übermensch*) to be 'the meaning of the earth', representing the overcoming of the 'all too human' and the attainment of the fullest possible 'enhancement of life'. Far from seeking to diminish our humanity by stressing our animality, he sought to direct our attention and efforts to the emergence of a 'higher humanity' capable of endowing existence with a human redemption and justification. Nietzsche has long been associated with such existential philosophers as Kierkegaard, Heidegger, and Sartre; but his general approach to the reinterpretation of human reality actually differs markedly from theirs, and is better conceived as an important naturalistic alternative and rival to theirs, inaugurating the project of a kind of human—scientifically, psychologically, historically, and culturally sensitive—philosophical anthropology as one of the tasks of his 'philosophy of the future'.

Nietzsche proposed that life and the world be interpreted in terms of his conception of 'will to power'; and he framed his 'Dionysian value-standard', and the 'revaluation of values' that he called for, in terms of this interpretation as well. The only positive and tenable value-scheme possible, he maintained, must be based upon a recognition and affirmation of the world's fundamental character, and so must posit as a general standard the attainment of a kind of life in which the assertive–transformative 'will to power' is present in its highest intensity and quality. This in turn led him to take the 'enhancement of life' and creativity to be the guiding ideas of his revaluation of values and development of a naturalistic value-theory; for he thought that naturalistic sense can be made of both of these ideas, and that they can also be utilized to breathe new life into the idea of value, making possible a constructive 'revaluation' rather than a bleakly nihilistic devaluation of all received values and human possibilities.

This way of thinking carried over into Nietzsche's thinking with respect to morality as well. Insisting that moralities as well as other traditional modes of valuation ought to be understood and assessed 'in the perspective of life', he argued that most of them are contrary rather than conducive to the enhancement of life, reflecting the all-too-human needs and weaknesses and fears of less-favoured human groups and types. Distinguishing between 'master' and *'slave' moralities, he found the latter increasingly to have eclipsed the former in human

history, and to have become the dominant type of morality at the present time, in the form of a 'herd-animal' morality well suited to the requirements and vulnerabilities of the mediocre who are the human rule, but stultifying and detrimental to the development of potential exceptions to that rule. He further suggested the possibility and desirability of a 'higher' type of morality for the exceptions, in which the content and contrast of the basic 'slave–herd-morality' categories of 'good and evil' would be replaced by categories more akin to the 'good and bad' contrast characteristic of master morality, with a revised (and variable) content.

Nietzsche's naturalistic approach to normativity, however, allows for the conception of differing sorts of moralities attuned and conducive to the flourishing and development of different forms of individual, social, institutional, and cultural life, and so appropriate to them and to whoever might participate in them to the extent that they do so, rather than for their conception as the moralities of distinct types of human beings. So he did not advocate the abolition of 'herd-animal' morality, but rather its restriction to 'herd-animal' human types and human situations; and so he likewise did not advocate a general human reversion to the 'master morality' he supposes to have prevailed among barbaric 'beasts of prey', but rather a shift of some human beings in areas of their lives in which they have exceptional ability to norms better suited to the cultivation and expression of that ability.

The strongly creative flavour of Nietzsche's notions of such a higher humanity and associated higher morality reflects his linkage of both to his conception of *art, to which he attached great importance. Art, as the creative transformation of the world as we find it (and of ourselves thereby) on a small scale and in particular media, affords us a glimpse of the possibility of a kind of life that would be lived more fully in this manner, and constitutes a step in the direction of its emergence. In this way, Nietzsche's mature thought expanded upon the idea of the basic connection between art and the justification of life which was his general theme in his first major work, *The Birth of Tragedy*.

Nietzsche was highly critical of traditional and commonplace ways of thinking about truth and knowledge, maintaining that as they are usually construed there is and can be nothing of the kind (except in highly artificial contexts), that all thinking is 'perspectival', and that 'there are no facts, only interpretations'. This has led some to suppose that he rejected the idea of truth and knowledge altogether, and so was a radical epistemological nihilist. Yet he manifested a passionate commitment to 'truthfulness', and pursued philosophical tasks which he quite clearly supposed to have something like knowledge as their aim. (So, for example, this is the avowed objective of his 'genealogical' investigations in *On the Genealogy of Morals*, as well as in many of the lines of inquiry he pursues in *The Gay Science*.) He did reject various *absolutist* conceptions and criteria of truth and knowledge (or, alternatively, contended that, *on* such conceptions and *by* such criteria, there is no 'truth' and can be no 'knowledge'). But he also sought to replace traditional ways of thinking about truth and knowledge with viable alternatives that make important sense of them, and to give a significant array of forms of cognitive inquiry—including various forms of natural- and human-scientific inquiry—new post-absolutist, anti-nihilist credentials and legitimacy.

Both in principle and in practice Nietzsche's thinking was avowedly interpretive, multiply perspectival, experimental, and tentative, and made free use of language that is highly metaphorical and figurative. He preferred to offer suggestions, hazard guesses, and propose hypotheses rather than attempt to construct rigorous lines of reasoning. He further acknowledged that the upshot of what he (or anyone else) has to say on any substantive issue neither is nor can ever be beyond all dispute. Yet he repeatedly insisted upon the distinction between the plausibility and soundness of various ideas on the one hand, and their 'value for life' on the other (between their 'truth-value' and their 'life-value', as it were). Although some of his unguarded remarks may seem to suggest otherwise, he inveighed explicitly against the conflation of the two—even while also arguing that the *value* of all knowledge and truthfulness ultimately must be referred to their 'value for life' for human beings with differing constitutions and conditions of preservation, flourishing, and growth, and judged before that tribunal.

Philosophy for Nietzsche involves the *making of cases* for and against various proposed interpretations and evaluations. For the most part he did not present arguments of the sort that one usually finds in the writings of philosophers and expects of them. He attempted to make his criticisms stick and his own ideas stand in other ways. On the attack, he typically sought to make cases against ways of thinking he found wanting by presenting an array of considerations intended collectively first to make us suspicious of them and aware of just how problematical they are, and then to deprive them of their credibility. He generally did not claim that the considerations he marshals actually *refute* the targets of his criticism. Rather he typically aimed to *dispose* of them by undermining them sufficiently to lay them to rest, exposed as unworthy of being taken seriously any longer.

When advancing alternatives to them Nietzsche proceeded in a somewhat similar manner, presenting various supporting considerations—both general and specific—none of which by themselves may be decisive, but which taken together are intended to be compelling. They are purported to establish his 'right' to the ideas he puts forward, notwithstanding the novelty they may have, and the reluctance many may feel to entertain and embrace them. And he conceived this 'right' as a cognitive one. Here, too, he was generally prepared to acknowledge that the cases he makes do not actually *prove* his points, and couched his hypotheses and conclusions in tentative and provisional language. He also not only admitted but insisted that they leave open the possibility of other interpretations as well as of subsequent modifications, as further considerations are hit upon and introduced. But it is

clear that he supposed it to be possible to make cases for his interpretations and evaluations, the positive upshot of which is strong and clear enough to warrant confidence that he is at least on the right track, and has got hold of something important. He often did say things to the effect that these are '*his* truths', to which others may not easily be entitled. But this way of speaking may be understood as a challenge to others to *earn their right* to lay like claim to understand what he has grasped, rather than as an admission that they are nothing more than figments of his own creative imagination.

A consequence of the perspectival approach Nietzsche favoured is that one must employ models and metaphors drawn from whatever resources are available to one in conceptualizing and articulating what may be discerned from the perspectives adopted—and, indeed, that these perspectives themselves are to no little extent framed by means of such resources. He himself took his models and metaphors from literature and the various arts, from the natural sciences, and also from the social and behavioural sciences, from economics to psychology. He further availed himself of conceptual resources and images drawn from a multitude of other domains of discourse, including law, medicine, linguistics, and even theology. In this way he was able to take advantage of the different ways of thinking associated with and suggested by them, and to play them off against each other, thereby avoiding becoming locked into any one or particular cluster of them. They afforded him the means of discovering and devising an expanding repertoire of perspectives upon the matters with which he was concerned, and so of developing and sharpening what he called the many and different 'eyes' needed to contribute to a growing and deepening comprehension of them. This has an important bearing upon the question of how his perspectivism is to be understood, and how it works in practice.

Nietzsche clearly held that neither this sort of inquiry nor any other that is humanly possible will suffice to enable one to attain the sort of knowledge to which metaphysicians have traditionally aspired. It by no means follows, however, that for him there is nothing of any significance to be comprehended. He considered the forms of morality that have arisen in the course of human events to admit of better-than-ordinary comprehension if approached in this manner and spirit, for example; and he clearly supposed that the same applies to a broad range of other such phenomena that are to be encountered within the compass of human life, history, and experience—and indeed to our attained and varying human reality itself, down to its basic character and general conditions. Rather like a latter-day Vico, he seized upon the idea that it is humanly possible to comprehend at least something of whatever has been humanly constituted. He came to take this idea quite seriously, concluding that it has important implications for the possibility of knowledge, and that its scope is very wide indeed. For what he called 'the world that concerns us'—which includes ourselves—consists in phenomena that are in various and very real respects 'our doing'.

Nietzsche thus in effect proposed to replace the Holy Grail of an ultimate reality conceived along the lines of a transcendent deity or 'true world' of 'being', and the quest for it conceived as the proper mission and picture of true knowledge, with a different paradigm of reality and associated conception of comprehension. Suppose we take as our paradigm the sort of reality in which human life and the world of our activities and experience consist, and conceive of knowledge in terms of the kind of comprehension of them of which they admit and we are capable. Making them our point of departure, we then can consider how far it is possible to go by expanding the scope of their application into the world with which we find ourselves confronted—while devoting our main efforts to the exploration of those things that are to be encountered *within* the realm of the human, and to the devising of the strategies of inquiry that will be most appropriate to their comprehension. If in this way we manage to achieve some measure of understanding of the kind of world in which our human reality has emerged and taken the various forms and associated expressions it has, so much the better. But even if we cannot do much more than comprehend ourselves and things human, this will at least be something—and something quite significant and well worth achieving at that.

We can, however, do something more than this—and something that is, for Nietzsche, in the end, a good deal more important: we can come to understand what meaning and value amount to, and how it is possible to endow life with forms of meaning and value that it may not have in the first place, but is capable of attaining. Nietzsche's reinterpretative efforts are not pursued for their own sake, but rather for what they can contribute to the revaluative part of his philosophical agenda. If humanity is to outgrow its childish need for absolutes without despairing at their absence and winding up nihilistically willing either nothing or nothingness, we must find a new and more viable way to the affirmation of life than those that have been based on fictions, illusions, impossible dreams, and leaps of faith. We must rethink meaning and value, and find ways to attune ourselves sufficiently to attainable forms of them that this 'disillusioned' affirmation becomes not only humanly possible, but humanly compelling. Nietzsche's kind of philosophy is not itself intended to be the answer, meeting this need out of its very own resources and accomplishments; for that requires more than thought. It requires life, lived in ways that creatively enhance its quality. What Nietzsche's kind of philosophy is intended to be here is rather like what Nietzsche's *Thus Spoke Zarathustra* is intended to be: a reflection on meaning and value that can open our eyes to what they are or can be all about, and a call to make them come true. R.S.

*God is dead; superman.

Maudemarie Clark, *Nietzsche on Truth and Philosophy* (Cambridge, 1990).
Arthur Danto, *Nietzsche as Philospher* (New York, 1965).
Ronald Hayman, *Nietzsche: A Critical Life* (Oxford, 1980).
Walter Kaufmann, *Nietzsche: Philosopher, Psychologist, Antichrist*, 4th edn. (Princeton, NJ, 1974).
Bernd Magnus and Kathleen M. Higgins (eds.), *The Cambridge Companion to Nietzsche* (Cambridge, 1996).
Alexander Nehmas, *Nietzsche: Life as Literature* (Cambridge, Mass., 1985).
John Richardson, *Nietzsche's System* (New York, 1996).
Rüdiger Safranski, *Nietzsche: A Philosophical Biography*, tr. Shelley Frisch (New York, 2002).
Richard Schacht, *Making Sense of Nietzsche* (Urbana, Ill., 1995).
——*Nietzsche* (London, 1983).

nihilism. The extreme view that there is no justification for values and, in particular, no justification for morality. It is sometimes used to mean the active rejection of and attack on such values. The word was invented by the Russian novelist Turgenev to describe young rebels in Tsarist Russia. Ever since, the word has been used to condemn those who refuse to accept certain preferred prevailing values. Philosophically, 'nihilism' is often employed as an ominous alternative characterization of *relativism and other views that deny the existence of 'absolute' moral standards. Friedrich Nietzsche, for example, is often called a nihilist. His case is instructive. Nietzsche is said to be a nihilist because he questions the value of such ideals as truth and morality, but he does so because they eclipse other, more important values. He thus accuses the Judaeo-Christian tradition of nihilistic tendencies by emphasizing the 'other-worldly' and rejecting 'naturalistic' values. By definition, the nihilist believes in nothing and disdains all values. But it is worth asking, along with Nietzsche, whether any such stance is possible, in theory or in practice. R.C.SOL.

F. Nietzsche, *The Will to Power* (New York, 1968).

nirvana. In *Buddhist philosophy, the blowing out of the flame of the self. Hence the end of all suffering—by living without craving or by dying never to be reborn. Commonly understood as pure extinction, it is described by some Buddhist scriptures as a positive state of perpetual peace. 'Since the self, strictly speaking, does not exist anyway, *who* enjoys this permanent painlessness?' 'Is it *real*—since nothing real can be permanent?' These remain questions to be answered by silence. A.C.

T. Stcherbatsky, *The Conception of Buddhist Nirvāna* (Benares, 1989).

Nishida Kitarō (1870–1945). Foremost Japanese philosopher of the twentieth century and founding father of the Kyoto School, Nishida is best known for his path-breaking work of 1911, *An Inquiry into the Good* (*Zen no kenkyū*). With this book he began to articulate a system of thought based on the *Zen Buddhist experience in terms borrowed from French, German, and Anglo-American philosophy, psychology, and natural science. Drawing on William James and Henri Bergson, Nishida developed a philosophy based on 'pure experience' as that which underlies the subject–object relation. A thinker of great erudition and learning, he developed and refined his system over several decades to encompass the social and historical worlds as well as the world of religion. Central to Nishida's thinking are the ideas of the *'topos* of nothingness' and of the world as the 'self-identity of absolute contradictories'.   G.R.P.

*nothingness, absolute.

Nishitani Keiji, *Nishida Kitarō*, tr. Yamamoto Seisaku and James Heisig (Berkeley, Calif., 1991).

Nishitani Keiji (1900–90). Deeply influenced by such Western figures as Meister Eckhart, Dostoevsky, Nietzsche, and Heidegger, and yet firmly rooted in the Chinese and Japanese *Zen traditions, Nishitani was the major figure of the 'second generation' Kyoto School and a consummately existential religious philosopher. More prepared than his mentor Nishida to engage the Western philosophical tradition on its own terms, Nishitani was a pioneer in the field of East–West philosophical dialogue. Concerned throughout his career with the problem of nihilism, he developed an existential philosophy in which, if the self is plumbed to sufficient depth, the *nihilum* or void at its base may be realized as the absolute *nothingness (*mu*) or fertile emptiness (*kū*) of Mahāyāna Buddhist philosophy. The philosophical synthesis effected in his masterwork, *Religion and Nothingness* (1962), matches the achievements of Kierkegaard, Nietzsche, and Heidegger in depth of insight.   G.R.P.

The Religious Philosophy of Nishitani Keiji ed. Taitetsu Unno (Berkeley, Calif., 1989).

Nkrumah, Kwame (1909–72). African statesman and philosopher, who was educated in the United States and Great Britain, Kwame Nkrumah spearheaded the movement that led Ghana to independence from colonialism in 1957, and became Prime Minister and subsequently President of Ghana. He expounded a comprehensive, physicalist theory of nature and society, which he applied to his vision of a political economy for the whole of Africa in a Pan-African Union.   W.E.A.

*philosopher-king.

Basil Davidson, *A View of the Life and Times of Kwame Nkrumah* (London, 1973).

noble lie. A myth proposed in Plato's *Republic* according to which when human beings were formed in the earth, those who should rule had gold mixed with them, the soldiers silver, and farmers and craftsmen iron. The aim of the myth is to keep individuals happy with their designated roles, but would anyone believe it, even after generations of indoctrination? The speakers in the dialogue are doubtful, while insisting firmly, scandalously, and possibly defensibly that rulers may legitimately lie for reasons of state.   A.O'H.

*ideology; teaching and indoctrinating.

Plato, *The Republic*, 414–15, 459–60.

nocturnal council: *see* Plato.

no false lemmas principle: *see* lemma.

nomic. A term meaning *scientifically* lawlike, thus distinguishing a claim both from the merely contingent (as 'John is very happy') and the moral or legal (as 'You ought to keep promises'). Nomic statements, like 'All bodies attract each other with a force inversely proportional to the square of the distance between them', are generally thought both *universal* and *necessary*. The analysis of the exact nature of the latter, especially as it has been thought to be causal, has provided a good living for a good many philosophers for a good many years.   M.R.

*causation; necessity, nomic.

E. Nagel, *The Structure of Science* (New York, 1961).

nominalism. Nominalism, traditionally understood, is a doctrine which denies the real existence of *universals, conceived as the supposed referents of general terms like 'red' and 'table'. In order to explain how and why we classify different individual things alike as being red or as being tables, nominalists appeal to particular resemblances between those things. Realists object that such an account involves tacit reliance on universals because resemblance is always similarity *in some general respect*, pointing out that different things resemble each other in many different ways. But nominalists reply that such objections are misconceived and question-begging.

In more recent usage, 'nominalism' is often employed as a label for any repudiation of *abstract entities, whether universals or particulars, and thus embraces the rejection of such things as propositions, sets, and numbers.   E.J.L.

*realism.

D. M. Armstrong, *Nominalism and Realism* (Cambridge, 1978).

nomological: *see* nomic.

nomological danglers: *see* identity theory of mind.

non-being and nothing. Negative events, which seem to be needed as the worldly correspondents of true *negative propositions, are troublesome because we lack criteria of identity for them, there being no non-arbitrary answer to 'How many forest fires did not occur yesterday?' To avoid commitment to them attempts have been made to analyse negative into positive propositions. That Theaetetus does not fly is analysed either as that every property of Theaetetus is other than being in flight or that there is some positive property of Theaetetus that is incompatible with being in flight, such as being planted on the ground. It is objected that these analyses are viciously circular, since otherness and incompatibility are themselves negative relations. To settle this dispute an adequate criterion for distinguishing between negative and positive properties must be formulated, the most promising of which is based on a difference in their degree of specificity or entailment relations. Positive properties, unlike negative ones, entail properties of both the same and different qualities than themselves; for example, non-red entails only non-crimson and other properties of the same quality, while red entails both coloured and non-green, the former being of the same and the latter of a different quality than itself.

In contrast with absences within the world, Nothing is the absence of the world itself—a total absence of every positive contingent reality. Bergson utilized the above incompatibility analysis to show that the concept of Nothing is contradictory, since every absence requires an existent positive reality that logically excludes it. The application of this analysis to 'No contingent beings exist' results in 'Every existent being has some positive property that is incompatible with being existent', but it is unclear what this positive property of existent being could be.

R.M.G.

R. M. Gale, *Negation and Non-Being* (Oxford, 1976).
A. N. Prior, 'Negation', in P. Edwards (ed.), *Encyclopedia of Philosophy* (New York, 1967).

non-cognitivism. The name of a position in ethics. Like many such names it is used more by its opponents than by its supporters. This one is used to designate that family of ethical positions in which it is supposed that moral judgements do not possess truth-value and hence can not be known. An example of a non-cognitivist position is *emotivism; that is, the claim that moral judgements are merely expressions of emotion. R.H.

*moral realism; quasi-realism; prescriptivism.

non-contradiction, law of. The conjunction of a proposition and its negation is a *contradiction and is necessarily false. In *traditional logic the principle was sometimes taken to be a law of thought, along with the principles of *identity and *excluded middle. In the *propositional calculus the principle is reflected in the theorem $\sim (P \cdot \sim P)$, which is a *tautology.

A theory in which this law fails, where a proposition P and its contradictory not-P are deducible, is an inconsistent theory. R.B.M.

B. Mates, *Elementary Logic* (Oxford, 1972).
W. Kneale and M. Kneale, *The Development of Logic* (Oxford, 1962).
G. Priest *et al.* (eds.), *The Law of Non-Contradiction: New Essays* (Oxford, 2004).

non-Euclidean geometry. Any geometry some of whose axioms and theorems contradict Euclid's. Euclid's axiomatization was often thought to provide the paradigm of *knowledge, by making deductive steps from necessary and self-evident truths. But as the parallel axiom, in particular, seemed less obvious than the others, many attempts were made to derive it from them. If it were derivable, then by adding its negation to the others a contradiction would be deducible from the new axiom set.

Over several centuries many propositions were deduced from the new set which appeared self-contradictory, so the work then petered out; but no plain contradiction of the form 'P and not-P' was produced. In the nineteenth century Bolyai, Lobachevsky, and Riemann deduced more theorems, and proposed these systems as independent 'non-Euclidean' geometries. It has since been shown that if Euclid's geometry is consistent then so are the others, so presumably all are. Most physicists now believe that *space is non-Euclidean. At least it is not necessarily Euclidean, as many philosophers had argued or assumed.

A.J.L.

*space-time.

Morris Kline, *Mathematics in Western Culture* (London, 1954), ch. 26.

non-natural properties. To ethical naturalists, moral terms refer to 'natural' properties, properties most often confirmable by sensory experience. Other philosophers have argued that the distinctiveness of moral properties is lost in such an analysis (*naturalistic fallacy), and have claimed that moral terms refer to 'non-natural' properties, detectable by 'intuition' alone. This was how G. E. Moore understood *'good'. Others again have challenged the credentials of intuition as a mode of knowledge and questioned how appeal to such properties could, intelligibly, guide the action of moral agents. R.W.H.

*ethical naturalism.

G. E. Moore, *Principia Ethica* (Cambridge, 1903).

nonsense. A favoured term of condemnation in philosophy, 'nonsense' tends to enjoy here a different range of application from that found in everyday usage. In the latter, statements are often pronounced nonsense on the grounds that they are outrageously improbable or patently false, whereas nonsense is commonly taken by philosophers to be such a fundamental defect as to exclude even falsity. The everyday usage may be hard to avoid. Suppose that a proposition, P, is declared to be nonsense because unverifiable. If, by reflecting on P, we come to see that it must indeed elude all attempts at verification, this realization is one which would in all likelihood depend on our grasp of the meaning of P, in which case falsity rather than unintelligibility would appear the most that could coherently be claimed. B.B.R.

*verification principle.

A. J. Ayer, *Language, Truth and Logic* (London, 1946).

nonsense upon stilts. How Bentham described the claim of the French Revolutionary Declaration of the Rights of Man and the Citizen that there were 'natural and imprescriptible' rights. The claim that there were *natural rights was, to him, 'simple nonsense'; it was the claim that these rights were imprescriptible (that is, unrevisable) which made it into 'nonsense upon stilts'. R.H.

Jeremy Bentham, *Anarchical Fallacies* (Edinburgh, 1843), article II.

no-ownership theory. The theory that experiences do not require a real *subject to whom they must belong. Mental occurrences are treated as independent events, and our normal language for describing them, with its apparent reference, using personal pronouns, to subjects who have them, is viewed either as not designating anything, as with the first person, or as designating the body to which the experiences are causally linked, in the third person. The theory was attributed by P. F. Strawson to middle-period Wittgenstein and to Schlick. Its point is to avoid non-physical selves, but independent, unowned, experiences are counter-intuitive, and, although Strawson's charge of incoherence may be unfounded, there are less extreme alternatives to *cartesianism.   P.F.S.

*mind–body problem; mind, problems of the philosophy of; persons; other minds.

P. F. Strawson, *Individuals* (London, 1959), ch. 3.

normalization. Dag Prawitz proved (1965) an analogue for *natural deduction systems of Gentzen's cut-elimination theorem: every derivation could be transformed into a normalized one. The concept of a normalized proof is more complicated to explain than that of a cut-free proof in the sequent calculus, but the essential idea is the same, the basic step being that of removing any part of the formal *proof in which a formula is first derived by means of an introduction rule and thereupon eliminated as the major premiss of an elimination rule: an unnecessary detour. Suppose, for instance, that $A \& B$ is inferred from separate premisses A and B, and that A is then immediately inferred from it. Plainly, the detour through $A \& B$ was redundant; the two lines on which stood, first, $A \& B$ and then A can be excised, together with the entire part of the derivation leading to the premiss B. This is the basic step in a normalization. If the application of the elimination rule was delayed, the derivation must first be rearranged to make it follow immediately upon the application of the introduction rule.

Building on a remark of Gentzen's that a logical *constant is *defined* by the introduction rules, of which the elimination rules are consequences, Prawitz has explored means of justifying elimination rules by appeal to the introduction rules. The strategy is to show that canonical proofs of the premisses of an elimination rule can be transformed into a canonical proof of its conclusion, a canonical proof being one whose last line is inferred by means of an introduction rule: this is a justification only under the assumption that, if a logically complex statement is known to be true, its truth could be known by a canonical proof of it. The condition that an elimination rule can be so justified is precisely that the basic step of normalization can be carried out.   M.D.

D. Prawitz, *Natural Deduction* (Stockholm, 1965).
—— 'Towards a Foundation of a General Proof Theory', in P. Suppes *et al.* (eds.), *Logic, Methodology and Philosophy of Science*, iv (Amsterdam, 1973).
—— 'On the Idea of a General Proof Theory', *Synthese* (1974).

normative. 'Normative' is the adjective derived from the noun 'norm', which signifies *either* the average or usual level of attainment or performance for an individual or group; *or*, and more usually in philosophical discussion, a standard, rule, principle used to judge or direct human conduct as something to be complied with. The phrase 'moral norm' is used generically to mean anything which proffers moral guidance, instruction, or a basis for appraisive judgement. It is a term of fairly recent coinage, but having the same root as the more familiar 'normal' in the Latin word *norma*, a carpenter's rule or square. 'Normal' and 'normative' are importantly distinct, however, since it is not plainly the case that what is normal represents a standard to be complied with. The same issues arise over what is *'natural' or 'unnatural' being used as a standard.   N.J.H.D.

See G. H. von Wright, *Norm and Action* (London, 1963) for a treatment of issues in this area.

norms, epistemic. Epistemic norms are the rules or standards by which we epistemically evaluate beliefs. For example, we often criticize beliefs that are formed in ways that are not appropriately sensitive to the available evidence, and this has led some commentators to suggest that the rule *proportion one's belief to the evidence that one has in favour of that belief* is an epistemic norm, although this is controversial. Epistemological theories which analyse the key epistemic concepts like *justification entirely in terms of whether the agent in question adheres to (or at least does not flout) the epistemic norms are known as deontological theories, though such accounts have fallen out of favour in contemporary epistemology. Instead, the currently dominant view of epistemic norms is that they should play only a peripheral role in one's epistemological theory. Indeed, the view that a deontological conception of justification is not an essential component of *knowledge is often thought to be a defining thesis of epistemological externalism, a subspecies of which is *naturalised epistemology.   D.PRI.

R. W. Miller, 'The Norms of Reason', *Philosophical Review*, 104 (1995).
J. Pollock, 'Epistemic Norms', in his *Contemporary Theories of Knowledge* (Lanham, Md., 1986), ch. 5.

Norwegian philosophy. Norway enjoys a varied and vigorous philosophical life. Yet by European and even Scandinavian standards her academic institutions are of quite recent origin. The 400-year Dano-Norwegian union meant that between the founding of the universities of Uppsala in Sweden and Copenhagen in the 1470s and that in 1811 of Norway's first, the King Frederick University in Christiania (now, as the University of Oslo, Scandinavia's largest) Copenhagen was the centre of Norwegian academic life. In 1802 a Norwegian-born philosopher, scientist, and writer, Henrich (Henrik) Steffens (1773–1845), first set in motion the Romantic movement in Denmark, and when the new university opened in 1813 (a year before the dissolution) it was a Norwegian philosopher with ten years of tenure in Copenhagen who became Norway's first Professor of Philosophy. Niels Treschow (1751–1833) was a Spinozistically inclined critic of Kant and the first notable Scandinavian proponent of determinism. He propounded a dual-aspect theory of mind and body and argued for the primacy of particulars over universals. Treschow's thought is summed up in a late three-volume work *Om Gud, Idee- og Sandseverdenen* (On God and the Worlds of Idea and Sensation) (Christiania, 1831–3). Anticipating later evolutionary theories, Treschow surmised that the human ability to react inwardly to outward stimuli has its origins in some animal species. The ability to react to a diverse environment interacts dynamically with a formative impulse to unity and generates the idea of the One, combining the idea of God's immanence in all things with that of God's transcendence and bringing with it a teleological notion of the unity of mankind.

It was the Danish philosopher, aphorist, and novelist Poul Martin Møller (1794–1838), later Kierkegaard's mentor, who introduced Norway to Hegel, in 1827–31. The Hegelian tradition was consolidated by Marcus Jacob Monrad (1816–97), the first major thinker to succeed Treschow (in 1851). An orthodox Hegelian, Monrad was critical of most post-Hegelian thought including that of Schelling, Feuerbach, and Kierkegaard. His opposition to these, as well as to Millian politics, Comptean positivism, and Darwinism ('purposefulness without purpose'), put him at odds with the spirit of the age, but Monrad's objections—these views and movements were one-sided and therefore latently dualistic—were acute and even prescient. He saw a paradigmatic case in point in what he called the Englishman's predilection for 'facts' at the expense of the 'universal idea'.

What followed may seem to confirm Monrad's diagnosis. The early twentieth century saw a turn towards empirical psychology (facts) and psychoanalysis, the universal idea being entrusted to historians of ideas (among them notably A. H. Winsnes (1889–1972)). In 1928 one of two philosophy chairs was converted during its incumbency by Harald K. Schjelderup (1895-1974) into a chair in psychology. Until after the Second World War the remaining chair, to which Arne Naess (b. 1912) was appointed in 1939, was Norway's single tenured position in philosophy. Philosophy's present place in Norwegian academic life, as in the society at large, is due in large measure to Naess. In the 1930s he had participated in Moritz Schlick's seminar and retained regular contact with the *Vienna Circle despite disagreement with some of its tenets. Opposed to the views that traditional philosophical puzzles are pseudo-problems and that empirical investigation plays no part in philosophical discussion, Naess claimed that empirical investigations can play an evidential role in philosophical discussions. In a seminal work written in the 1930s (*Erkenntnis und wissenschaftliches Verhalten* (Cognition and Scientific Behaviour (Oslo, 1936)), Naess anticipated many themes familiar in postwar *analytic philosophy. His ideas had a marked influence on social research in Norway, the promise of collaboration between philosophers and social scientists giving rise to the journal *Inquiry*, which Naess founded in 1958. Philosophers themselves were divided. Some exploited the methodology of Naess's 'empirical semantics'

(e.g. Harald Ofstad (1920–93)) or reconstructed it (Ingemund Gullvåg (1925–98)). Others, provoked by a residual *positivism and *behaviourism in Naess's programme, followed a path marked out by Hans Skjervheim (1926–99) in *Objectivism and the Study of Man* (1959), a work which had an early influence on *Jürgen Habermas. These philosophers—among them Audun Øfsti (b. 1938) and Gunnar Skirbekk (b. 1937)—pursued inquiries into what Karl Otto Apel has labelled 'transcendental pragmatics', stressing discontinuities between explanation in natural science and understanding in social science. Meanwhile Naess himself, after a period of concern with systemic aspects of his combined empirical and philosophical enterprise, resigned his chair in 1970 to concentrate on ecological issues.

In Norway mathematical logic is famously represented by Thoralf Skolem (1887–1963), Professor of Mathematics in Oslo from 1938 to 1957. A classical tradition is maintained by E. A. Wyller (b. 1923). The Wittgenstein Archives are located in Bergen, where a Wittgensteinian tradition in aesthetics has also taken root. From the late 1980s, several philosophers, notably Knut Erik Tranøy (b. 1918), have co-operated in the work of new centres for research into ethical and normative aspects of science, medicine and politics. Today's Norwegian philosophy departments house many non-Norwegians and many Norwegians have pursued their graduate studies abroad. This accounts for a degree of cross-fertilization between the 'analytic' and 'continental' traditions (Jon Elster (b. 1940) (Marx), Dagfinn Føllesdal (b. 1932) (Husserl), and Alastair Hannay (b. 1932) (Kierkegaard)).

A long-established introductory course (*examen philosophicum*) required of all university students, together with the founding of universities in Bergen, Trondheim, and Tromsø in the post-war years, has meant that a rapidly increasing university-trained population is conversant with philosophical traditions and thought, while the University of Oslo's Institute of Philosophy has become one of Europe's largest.   A.H.

*Danish philosophy; Swedish philosophy.

M. J. Monrad, *Den menneskelige Viljefrihed og det Onde* (Human Freedom and Evil) (Christiania, 1897).

A. Naess, *Truth as Conceived by Those who are not Professional Philosophers* (Oslo, 1939).

—— *Interpretation and Preciseness: A Contribution to the Theory of Communication* (Oslo, 1953).

H. Ofstad, *An Inquiry into the Freedom of Decision* (Oslo, 1961).

N. Treschow, *Gives der noget Begreb eller nogen Idee om eenslige ting?* (Is there any Concept or Idea of Particular Things?) (Copenhagen, 1804).

notations, logical. We still have not emerged from the symbolic turmoil of the early history of modern logic. A wide variety of notations are currently employed even for the simplest of logical calculi, the variety stemming from a number of competing interests ranging from typographical economy to the ease with which the logical structure of formulae can be determined and proofs devised. There are two dimensions of variation: the system of punctuation and the symbols of the logical and non-logical vocabulary. There are three main systems of punctuation used to prevent syntactic ambiguity: the use of brackets, the dot notation of *Principia Mathematica*, and the bracket-free Polish notation of Łukasiewicz. Differences of non-logical vocabulary are usually trivial differences in the choice of letters and their case. Below is a table, admittedly selective, of variations in logical vocabulary, the more common symbols beginning each row, Polish notation at the end.

Negation	$-P, \sim P, \neg P, P', \bar{P}, Np$
Disjunction	$P \vee Q, Apq$
Conjunction	$P \& Q, P \wedge Q, P \cdot Q, PQ, Kpq$
Material conditional	$P \rightarrow Q, P \supset Q, Cpq$
Material biconditional	$P \leftrightarrow Q, P \equiv Q, P \sim Q, Epq$
Universal quantifier	$(x)Fx, (\forall x)Fx, \forall xFx, \Pi xFx$
Existential quantifier	$(\exists x)Fx, \exists xFx, (Ex)Fx, ExFx, \Sigma xFx$
Necessity operator	$\square, L$
Possibility operator	$\lozenge, M$ A.D.O.

*Appendix on Logical Symbols.

R. Feys and F. B. Fitch, *Dictionary of Symbols of Mathematical Logic* (Amsterdam, 1969).

nothing: *see* non-being and nothing; nothingness; nothingness, absolute.

nothingness. Philosophers have often seen nothingness as an ontological, not simply a logical, category. Plato and Plotinus regarded matter, in contrast to form, as non-being. Heidegger claimed in *Being and Time* and *What is Metaphysics?* (1929; 5th edn. 1949, tr. in *Basic Writings*, ed. D. Krell (London, 1967)) that the nothing, which becomes apparent in objectless *Angst*, is crucial to our experience; it is prior to, and forms the basis of, logical negation. Human *Existenz* has no ground; it arises from the abyss of nothing. It culminates in the nothingness of death, and its meaning consists in the anticipation of death. The natural interpretation of this (though one rejected by Heidegger) is that *Dasein confers meaning, i.e. being, on non-human beings and on itself, and thus draws them out of meaningless chaos, i.e. nothing. To avoid saying that the nothing *is*, he says 'The nothing nihilates' (*Das Nichts selbst nichtet*), which Carnap regarded as a paradigm of metaphysical *nonsense. For Sartre, specifically human being consists in nothing or self-negation; this is why we can discern 'negative realities', such as the absence of a guest. For both philosophers, man's radical *freedom is rooted in nothingness.   M.J.I.

H. Kühn, *Encounter with Nothingness* (Hinsdale, Ill., 1949).

M. Murray (ed.), *Heidegger and Modern Philosophy: Critical Essays* (New Haven, Conn., 1978).

nothingness, absolute. In modern Japanese philosophy, this idea is central for many of the Kyoto School philosophers. It stems from the Mahāyāna Buddhist notion of 'emptiness', according to which nothing is what it is in isolation, but arises and perishes only within a network of relationships with everything else. In Buddhist practice,

however, one must avoid cleaving to the experience of emptiness: the nothingness that, as non-being, is the negation of beings, must itself be negated before one can arrive at *absolute* nothingness. For Nishida the 'locus of nothingness' is the basis of all experience; for Tanabe absolute nothingness is mediation through absolute 'Other-power' (of Amida Buddha); in Watsuji's ethics the individual self has to undergo absolute negation to be fully integrated into society; and for Nishitani nothingness is above all to be *experienced*—since it loses its absolute character if it is merely 'thought'. There are thought-provoking parallels with *das Nichts* in Heidegger's philosophy.   G.R.P.

*non-being and nothing; nothingness.

Robert E. Carter, *The Nothingness beyond God: An Introduction to the Philosophy of Nishida Kitarō* (New York, 1989).

nothing so absurd.

Pythagoras and Plato, who are most respectable authorities, bid us, if we would have trustworthy dreams, to prepare for sleep by following a prescribed course in conduct and in eating. The Pythagoreans make a point of prohibiting the use of beans, as if thereby the soul and not the belly was filled with wind! There is nothing so absurd but some philosopher has said it.

(Cicero, *De divinatione* II. lxviii. 120)

Cicero's dialogue *De divinatione* attacks divination. Its apologist Quintus cites the important philosophers who have believed in it, but Marcus, his opponent, argues that 'those superstitious and half-cracked philosophers of yours would rather appear absurd than anything else in the world'. The Stoics, for instance, regarded current disbelief in the Delphic oracle not as a sign of superstition's abatement but as abatement of the 'virtue' of local subterranean exhalations, which, if it had really ever existed, would obviously have been eternal. Yet Cicero himself practised augury, and defended it on other occasions in the belief that it promoted law-abiding behaviour.   J.O'G.

*Stoicism.

nothing so extravagant and irrational.

Those unhappy people were proposing schemes for persuading monarchs to choose favourites upon the score of their wisdom, capacity and virtue; of teaching ministers to consult the public good; of rewarding merit, great abilities and eminent services; of instructing princes to know their true interest by placing it on the same foundation with that of their people; of choosing for employments persons qualified to exercise them; with many other wild and impossible chimeras, that never entered before into the heart of man to conceive, and confirmed in me the old observation, that there is nothing so extravagant and irrational which some philosophers have not maintained for truth.

(Jonathan Swift, *Gulliver's Travels*, ch. 6)

Like their scientific colleagues trying to cure flatulence by applying bellows to the rectum, philosophers at the imagined Academy of Lagado reach absurd conclusions, presuming that the world conforms to their principles.

Swift was a Tory from the age of 43, and regarded the human as not 'animal rationale', only 'animal rationis capax', and wickedness as 'all according to the due course of things'. Yet the aim of his satires was in fact social improvement, and, even if Tory pessimism pillories these as chimeras, it is after all the unworkable utopian measures that are *really* *common-sense. Swift's reactionary thrust is double-edged, for it ridicules the engrained human folly that engenders and necessitates it. J.O'G.

noumena: *see* phenomena and noumena.

nous. In Greek philosophy, the highest form of rationality which is capable of grasping the fundamental principles of reality. In contrast to perception, which delivers awareness of the changing, accidental properties of things, *nous* consists in understanding their essential, immutable nature. Moreover, it supersedes belief, which may attain truth but falls short of explaining the why and wherefore of things. For Aristotle, the unmoved mover of the universe was a cosmic *Nous*. O.R.J.

*prime mover.

F. E. Peters, *Greek Philosophical Terms* (New York, 1967).

novel, the philosophical. The philosophical novel is usually understood as that subspecies of *fiction which endeavours to present a specific philosophical viewpoint, sometimes metaphysical, sometimes ethical, and sometimes aesthetic. Thus it is perhaps closer to the allegory or *roman-à-clef* than to fiction proper. For whereas it is usually a defect in a work of fiction that it ally itself closely with a particular viewpoint, for a philosophical novel, a grasp of the fact that a particular world-view is embodied is a pre-condition of understanding the novel.

Henry Fielding's *Tom Jones*, for example, embodies a particular moral philosophy, one in which the virtues of an unpremeditated warmth and responsiveness are valued above an alternative morality which is essentially conceived as rule-governed, though Fielding's *Bildungsroman* also charts the dangers and limitations of a morality which is so reactive and spontaneous. Other examples which leap to mind are the novels of George Eliot or Proust's analysis of memory and identity in *A la recherche du temps perdu*. Characteristically, such philosophical ideas are illustrated rather than asserted, as in *Middlemarch*, where George Eliot shows us various forms of egoism. In the twentieth century the novels of Sartre presented existential themes more memorably and vividly than his philosophical writing, and Camus's *The Outsider* is a paradigm of the philosophical novel.

The free exploration of literary space in interpretation is thereby placed within bounds set by the philosophical presuppositions of the novelist. *Interpretation is not only limited by the text but also by the recognition that a certain philosophical standpoint is involved. The decision to place a novel within this genre is consequently as much a critical act as a matter of pre-critical classification. R.A.S.

*literature and philosophy; poetry.

Peter Jones, *Philosophy and the Novel* (Oxford, 1975).
Stephen D. Ross, *Literature and Philosophy* (New York, 1969).

Nozick, Robert (1938–2002). A philosopher of remarkably varied interests, whose most influential work presented an articulate defence of a bare-bones *libertarianism. Nozick argued that the state cannot have a very large role in the economy and society if the libertarian rights of individuals are to prevail. In general, he argued against end-state theories, such as *utilitarianism or John Rawls's theory of *justice, and in favour of process theories that focus on the rightness of piecemeal actions independently of their contribution to a final state of affairs. Nozick had a gift for finding memorable cases to represent his problems and an energetic style that pulls readers into debate. He also worked on decision theory, epistemology, theory of value, and the good life. R.HAR.

*conservatism.

Robert Nozick, *Anarchy, State and Utopia* (Oxford, 1974).
——— *Philosophical Explanations* (Cambridge, Mass., 1981).
——— *The Nature of Rationality* (Princeton, NJ, 1993).

n-tuple: *see* ordered set.

number. There are several kinds. Ordinal numbers provide the structure to order collections of distinct objects (first, second, third, etc.); cardinal numbers are used to indicate the sizes of collections of distinct objects (zero, one, two). Natural numbers are finite cardinal numbers. Integers are whole numbers, including negative numbers. Rational numbers are ratios of integers, sometimes called 'fractions'. Real numbers are used to measure (potentially) continuous quantities in terms of a unit, such as length in meters and mass in grams. Complex numbers include so-called 'imaginary numbers', which are square roots of negative real numbers. Arithmetic, number theory, and real and complex analysis study the structures of the various number systems. There are philosophical problems concerning the ontological status of the various numbers—do they exist, are they mental, etc.—and there are epistemological problems concerning how we know anything about numbers.

There are theories of infinitely large numbers. Contemporary *set theory, derived from the work of Georg Cantor and Ernst Zermelo, studies both infinite cardinals and infinite ordinals. It can be shown that there are just as many integers and rational numbers as there are natural numbers, in that there is a one-to-one correspondence between the sets. Nevertheless, Cantor showed that there are distinct infinite cardinal numbers and, in particular, that for any set S, the set of all subsets of S is larger than S. A set is said to be 'countable' or 'denumerable' if it is the same size as or smaller than the natural numbers, the smallest infinite set. (*Continuum problem.)

There are also theories of 'infinitesimals', which are like real numbers, but are infinitely small. Infinitesimals came up in the study of continuous change, such as motion, both in the medieval period and in the original development of the calculus. The theory of infinitesimals saw a rebirth in the twentieth century, through certain results in mathematical *logic.   s.s.

*infinity; magnitude; mathematics, problems of the philosophy of; measurement.

Paul Benacerraf and Hilary Putnam (eds.), *Philosophy of Mathematics*, 2nd edn. (Cambridge, 1983).

numinous: *see* holy, numinous, and sacred.

Nussbaum, Martha C. (1947–). Nussbaum first came to prominence as a scholar of classical philosophy: her substantial book *The Fragility of Goodness* was the culmination of her work on questions to do with the meaning of life and sources of value as these are treated in Plato and Aris-
totle and also in Greek tragedy. The scope of her work subsequently broadened greatly. She has sought to illuminate issues of moral inquiry and insight by examining how philosophy and literature overlap and show cognate concerns; she has examined questions of social justice and the ethics of development with particular reference to women's place in society; and she has presented an ambitious theory of the emotions. She holds a joint chair in philosophy and law at the University of Chicago, with associate appointments in classics, political science, and even the divinity school.   N.J.H.D.

Martha C. Nussbaum, *The Fragility of Goodness* (Cambridge, 1986).
—— *The Therapy of Desire: Theory and Practice in Hellenistic Ethics* (Princeton, 1994).
—— *Sex and Social Justice* (Oxford, 1998).
—— *Upheavals of Thought: The Intelligence of Emotions* (Cambridge, 2001).

O

Oakeshott, Michael (1901–92). British philosopher, who read history at Cambridge and taught it there for many years before taking the chair of political science at the London School of Economics in 1950. Oakeshott's basic philosophical orientation was idealist. He believed that reality is mediated to us only in a number of distinct human practices, such as history, morality, politics, science, philosophy, and poetry. Each practice is a specifically human achievement, each reveals only part of the whole, and none is superior to the rest. In becoming apprised of a practice, we enter something which must be lived and which cannot be reduced to formulae or analysed in terms of extrinsic goals. The rationalist, Oakeshott's great bugbear, thinks it can. Particularly in politics, he attempts to turn what should be a conversation between friends, a mode of living together, into an enterprise or set of enterprises. The enterprise state will be deformed by ideology, by managerial techniques and abstractions, and by ceaseless legislation and litigation. Oakeshott's work has obvious affinities with Wittgenstein's and some of the same difficulties. Oakeshott's practices, like Wittgenstein's *language-games, are elusive, and while Oakeshott's targets are clear enough, his alternative to the modern managerial state is fastidiously underdefined. None the less, all politicians and most philosophers would benefit from a closer acquaintance with Oakeshott than they generally manifest. A.O'H.

*conservatism; idealism, philosophical.

Robert Grant, *Oakeshott* (London, 1990).
Michael Oakeshott, *Rationalism in Politics* (London, 1962).
—— *On Human Conduct* (Oxford, 1975).

oar in water. Favourite example of how circumstances can affect the *perception of an object, and make it seem other than it is. 'The same object seems to us bent or straight, according to whether we see it in water or out of water' (Plato, *Republic* x. 602c). Familiar in philosophy after Aristotle, the example divided sceptics (like Sextus Empiricus), who thought it showed that the senses give us no knowledge of an objective world, from Epicureans, who insisted that if there is mistake or ignorance in such cases, it must be attributed to the judgement, and not the senses (Lucretius, *De rerum natura* IV. 439 ff). Employed later by Descartes and Berkeley, the example was hackneyed enough by the time of Hume to count as one of the 'trite topics, employed by sceptics in all ages, against the evidence of sense'. It continued to feature in twentieth-century discussion, used, for example, by Ayer in support of a *sense-datum theory of perception.

J. L. Austin's dry comment was: 'What is wrong, what is even faintly surprising, in the idea of a stick's being straight but looking bent sometimes? Does anyone suppose that if something is straight, then it jolly well has to *look* straight at all times and in all circumstances? Obviously no one [does] . . . So . . . what is the difficulty?'

J.BRO.

*representative theory of perception.

J. Annas and J. Barnes, *The Modes of Scepticism* (Cambridge, 1985), ch. 8.
J. L. Austin, *Sense and Sensibilia* (Oxford, 1962), iii.

objectivism and subjectivism. Theories that various kinds of judgement are, respectively, objective, i.e. pertain to objects, or subjective, i.e. pertain to subjects (people). (1) 'Fish have fins' is an objective claim: its truth or falsity is independent of what anyone thinks or feels about the matter. (2) 'Raw fish is delicious' is a subjective claim: its truth or falsity is not thus independent, and indeed arguably it is neither true nor false, even though taste can be sophisticated, discriminating, insensitive, etc. The statement (3) 'Most Japanese find raw fish delicious (while most Britons do not)' is an *objective* truth or falsehood *about* subjects. It is therefore perhaps surprising that one theory labelled 'subjectivism' about morality, aesthetics, etc. is the view that evaluative claims within these fields are of kind (3), while another theory asserts they are of kind (2).

It is counter-productive to use a different term, 'relativism', to mean the same as 'subjectivism'. If by 'relativism' we mean the theory that what is valuable (or even true) depends on changing circumstances, then it does not entail subjectivism. A.J.L.

Richard Lindley, 'The Nature of Moral Philosophy', in G. H. R. Parkinson (ed.), *An Encyclopaedia of Philosophy* (London, 1988).

objectivism and subjectivism, ethical. There is a range of views about moral judgements. At the subjectivist pole, they are taken to be discrete feeling-responses of individuals to situations actual or imagined. To move towards the objectivist pole is to argue that moral judgements can be rationally defensible, true or false, that there are rational procedural tests for identifying morally impermissible actions, or that moral values exist independently of the feeling-states of individuals at particular times. To dismiss 'objective moral values' as illusions or fictions—claims the objectivist—violates our experience of the pressure they put on our will and on our emotions and interests. Only if they are misconceived as mysterious entities, lacking perceptual qualities, can they be deemed too 'queer' or fanciful to be taken seriously.

That there can be protracted disagreement over moral issues does not rebut the objectivist: equally persistent disagreement in other fields—e.g. historical study—hardly calls in question the objective occurrence of historical events.

Subjectivism too has more and less plausible forms. If it sees moral judgements as simply individual avowals of feeling, then certainly no adequate account, in these terms, can be given of moral disagreement—or of deliberation either. To understand them as the expression and evocation of emotions and attitudes still does no justice to the logic of moral discourse. A distinctively moral point of view must be acknowledged, and the moral requirement to 'be objective'—in the minimal but crucial sense of discounting selfish bias. If such a view still rests upon contingently common human 'sentiments', as for Hume it did, we have a mid-position—intersubjectivism. That has obvious attractions, but it is no less open to the objectivists' complaint, that this account still badly underestimates the resources of practical reasoning.   R.W.H.

J. L. Mackie, *Ethics: Inventing Right and Wrong* (Harmondsworth, 1977).

D. M. McNaughton, *Moral Vision: An Introduction to Ethics* (Oxford, 1988).

T. Nagel, *The View from Nowhere* (Oxford, 1986).

objectivity, historical: *see* history, problems of the philosophy of.

object language. When a second language is introduced to talk about a given language it is called the metalanguage; the given language is the object language. These are relational terms: one language is an object language, another a metalanguage only in relation to one another. Thus, the metalanguage can, in turn, be an object language in relation to another language. The necessity for the object language–metalanguage distinction in semantic theory is revealed by the semantic paradoxes.   H.W.N.

John L. Pollock, *Technical Methods in Philosophy* (Boulder, Colo., 1990).

obligation. To be under an obligation signifies being tied, required, or constrained to do (or from doing) something by virtue of a moral rule, a duty, or some other binding demand. There are also familial or parental obligations deriving from a role or relationship. Obligations are nor-

mally understood to form a subset of the moral factors which impinge on a person; there are other moral concerns such as to be kindly or generous which are not usually thought of as obligations. Kant, however, called these latter 'broad' obligations, allowing some latitude in their execution, in contrast to, for example, the strict obligation (as he saw it) always to tell the truth. Kant thought all moral requirements were 'categorical' obligations. Obligations oblige one to do something in a way analogous to the way, for example, a closed road obliges one to find another route: they force or demand a course of action. Obligation is sometimes contrasted with *value, as being what is peremptory and demanding rather than enticing and attractive. The topic of moral obligation is challengingly discussed by G. E. M. Anscombe in her 'Modern Moral Philosophy' (1958), reprinted in her collected philosophical papers, *Ethics, Religion and Politics*, iii (Oxford, 1981).   N.J.H.D.

*categorical imperative; ought; ethics and aesthetics.

obligationes. A late-medieval disputation-form involving two parties, the 'opponent' and the 'respondent'. After laying down some proposition as the initial case, the opponent proposes other propositions to the respondent, who must reply to each in turn by either conceding, denying, or doubting it. The respondent must do this according to rules describing the relation of the proposition at hand to the initial case and to what has gone before. Medieval philosophers argued about the proper rules to adopt for *obligationes*; one common set of rules has features of constructive *counterfactual reasoning. The terminology and methods of *obligationes* appear in theological, metaphysical, and scientific investigations.   P.K.

*logic, history of.

Paul Vincent Spade, 'Three Theories of Obligationes: Burley, Kilvington, and Swyneshed on Counterfactual Reasoning', *History and Philosophy of Logic* (1982).

observation and theory. Provide different points of access to the world—observation from the bottom up, theory from the top down. Empiricists favour observations as a secure and objective basis for knowledge; we and the Babylonians would have seen eye to eye. Theory, in contrast, is prone to error and prejudice; too many theories have turned out to be false and require speculative conjectures. Advocates of theory find observationally based epistemologies too pinched in their scope; attempts by the logical empiricists and others to construct theory on the basis of observations failed dramatically. Yet there is great danger in speculative theory, especially in the social sciences where data is scarce, and a judicious balance between theory and data is the hallmark of good practice. What is observed is generally agreed to exist, but *realists, in contrast to *empiricists, allow that some non-observational terms in well-confirmed theories genuinely refer.   P.H.

Robert Klee, *Introduction to the Philosophy of Science* (Oxford, 1997), ch. 3.

obversion. A proposition is obverted by negating its second term and changing its *quality from affirmative to negative or vice versa. Thus 'All rabbits are herbivores' (All *S* are *P*) becomes 'No rabbit is a non-herbivore' (No *S* are non-*P*). All the four forms of proposition considered by traditional logic may be validly obverted.   c.w.

   *logic, traditional.

J. N. Keynes, *Formal Logic*, 4th edn. (London, 1906), ch. 4.

occasionalism. A theory about the nature of much of what we take to be causation. It asserts that all relations between physical things, or between human minds and physical things, which we intuitively suppose to be causal, are in fact not causal. Instead, the relations are a consequence of God's will in the sense that particular events, the 'causes', are constantly conjoined with other events, their 'effects', because when a cause occurs God wills the effect to occur. One reason it was put forward was as the only conceivable explanation of causal necessity.   P.J.P.N.

   *causality; parallelism, psychological; pre-established harmony.

N. Malebranche, *The Search after Truth* (1674–5), tr. T. M. Lennon and Paul J. Olscamp (Columbus, Oh., 1980), vi. II. 3.

Ockham, William (1285–1347). An English Franciscan dubbed the 'More than Subtle Doctor', Ockham defended *nominalism, condemning the doctrine that universals are real things other than names or concepts as 'the worst error of philosophy'. Rejecting *atomism in favour of *hylomorphism, he practised poverty in metaphysics by refusing to posit distinct kinds of entities for each of Aristotle's ten categories and restricting his philosophical diet to really distinct substances and qualities with certain relations thrown in for good theological measure. Yet, he defended the Franciscan school's recognition of a plurality of substantial forms in living things (in humans, really distinct forms of corporeity, of sensory and intellectual soul).

   By contrast with Hume and Malebranche, Ockham maintains the Aristotelian distinction between efficient *causality properly speaking and *sine qua non* causality, based on whether the correlation between *A*s and *B*s is produced by *A*'s power or by the will of another. Against Henry of Ghent, he denies that there is any *sine qua non* causality in nature, and finds it metaphysically impossible that regularities in nature be drastically rearranged, although natural functioning can be obstructed by God and creatures alike. Like other Aristotelians, Ockham deems physics and biology possible because the uniformity of nature principle is true. Even for a nominalist, natures are powers; co-specific individuals, maximally similar powers that operate in maximally similar ways.

   An Aristotelian reliabilist in epistemology, Ockham takes for granted that human cognitive faculties work 'always or for the most part'—indeed, that we have *certain* knowledge of material things and of our own mental acts.

Ockham draws no sceptical conclusions from the logical, metaphysical, or natural *possibility* of their obstruction, because he defines certainty in terms of freedom from *actual* error.

   Notoriously enthusiastic about logic, Ockham's distinctive treatment of the logic of terms ('supposition theory') reflects his metaphysical disagreements with other notables (e.g. William of Sherwood, Peter of Spain, and Walter Burleigh). His *Summa Logicae* rearranges the traditional syllabus somewhat by subsuming the 'topics' under the theory of inference; and contains his brilliant and extensive development of modal syllogistic.

   In action theory, Ockham defends the liberty of indifference or contingency for divine and created rational beings. Not only is the will a self-determining power for opposites (as Scotus insisted), its options include willing evil under the aspect of evil and willing against good under the aspect of good! So far as non-positive morality or ethics is concerned, Ockham endorses a 'modified right reason theory', according to which virtuous action requires the agent's free co-ordination of choice with right reason (the primary norm). Because suitably informed right reason dictates that God, the infinite good, should be loved above all and for his own sake and hence obeyed, *divine commands become a secondary norm. Priorities are reversed in the soteriological category of merit and demerit, where free and contingent divine statutes make following the dictates of right reason a necessary condition of merit and eternal blessedness.

   Excommunicated for his defiant defence of Franciscan poverty against Pope John XXII, Ockham spent the rest of his career under the protection of Louis of Bavaria, energetically promoting a 'separation of Church and State' according to which the authority of neither is *regulariter* subordinate to that of the other, although each might interfere with the other *casualiter* in a grave crisis.   M.M.A.

   *reliabilism.

Marilyn McCord Adams, *William Ockham*, 2 vols. (Notre Dame, Ind., 1987).

Philotheus Boehner, *Collected Articles on Ockham*, ed. Eligius M. Buytaert, OFM (St Bonaventure, NY, 1958).

Guillelmi de Ockham: Opera Philosophica et Theologica (St Bonaventure, NY, 1967), i–vi, i–x.

Arthur Stephen McGrade, *The Political Thought of William of Ockham: Personal and Institutional Principles* (London, 1974).

P. V. Spade (ed.), *The Cambridge Companion to Ockham* (Cambridge, 2000).

Ockham's razor, or the principle of parsimony. A methodological principle dictating a bias towards *simplicity in theory construction, where the parameters of simplicity vary from kinds of entity to the number of presupposed axioms to characteristics of curves drawn between data points. Although found in Aristotle, it became associated with William Ockham because it captures the spirit of his philosophical conclusions.   M.M.A.

Marilyn McCord Adams, *William Ockham* (Notre Dame, Ind., 1987), ch. 5, pp. 143–67.

O'Neill, Onora (1941–). British moral and political philosopher. She has written on Kant's moral philosophy and employs a Kantian approach in considering ethical and political issues, including such traditionally neglected issues as the position of children and the role of parenting, gender, and questions of international justice. She criticizes much political and moral philosophy which is commonly called Kantian by both its proponents and detractors. Such work often emphasizes moral imperatives and duties; but is not really true to Kant's emphasis on principles that *can* be universally adopted. In recent (mainly US) liberal political philosophy *'Kantianism' is understood to be rights-based and therefore to de-emphasize such categories as virtue, need, and obligation. O'Neill argues that a properly Kantian approach encompasses these categories.   E.J.F.

Onora O'Neill, *Faces of Hunger* (London, 1986).
—— *Constructions of Reason* (Cambridge, 1989).
—— *Towards Justice and Virtue* (Cambridge, 1996).
—— *Autonomy and Trust in Bioethics* (Cambridge, 2002).

one-over-many problem. How can many things, e.g. Frances, Sarah, and Geoffrey, all *be* one thing, e.g. left-handed? Age-old solutions postulate a 'universal', e.g. the idea of left-handedness, related to these particulars and standing 'over' them. Doubtless various kinds of such *universals exist. But we can still ask: How can many things all *be* related-to-one-universal? Explanation of 'being so-and-so'—predication—seems inevitably to presuppose the very thing it seeks to explain.   C.A.K.

D. F. Pears, 'Universals', in A. Flew (ed.), *Logic and Language*, 2nd series (Oxford, 1955).

ontological argument for the existence of God. A line of argument which appears to appeal to no contingent fact at all, but only to an analysis of the concept of God. The argument is that this concept (unlike many others) is *necessarily* instantiated. Sometimes an intermediate step is the argument that if it is possible for this concept to be instantiated then it is instantiated, and this concept is obviously possible.

Anselm gives the classical formulation, and the classical critique is Immanuel Kant's. The argument has recently been subtly reformulated and defended by (among others) Charles Hartshorne, Norman Malcolm, and Alvin Plantinga.   G.I.M.

Anselm, *Proslogion*, tr. S. N. Deane (La Salle, Ill., 1991).
Alvin Plantinga, *The Ontological Argument: From St Anselm to Contemporary Philosophers* (Garden City, NY, 1965).

ontology. Ontology, understood as a branch of metaphysics, is the science of *being in general, embracing such issues as the nature of *existence and the categorial structure of reality. That existing *things belong to different categories is an idea traceable at least back to Aristotle. Different systems of ontology propose alternative categorial schemes. A categorial scheme typically exhibits a hierarchical structure, with 'being' or 'entity' as the topmost category, embracing everything that exists. Some schemes take the division between *universals and particulars as the next step in the hierarchy, others the division between abstract and concrete entities. These divisions do not necessarily coincide, since some philosophers believe in the existence of *concrete universals and some in the existence of abstract particulars. Universals may be further subdivided into properties, kinds, and relations. While many metaphysicians hold universals to be abstract entities, they disagree over whether universals exist separately from the particulars which instantiate them (the 'Platonic' view) or only exist 'within' those particulars (the 'Aristotelian' view). There is also disagreement over what distinguishes abstract from concrete entities, the most common view being that abstract entities do not exist in physical space and *time, and so lack physical extension and do not undergo change. As a corollary it is often held that abstract entities lack causal powers and so are incapable of entering into causal relations with other entities, though this threatens to make our knowledge of abstract entities problematic. Many philosophers, for this and related reasons, deny the existence of abstract entities, holding that only concrete particulars exist.

Concrete particulars are commonly further divided into *substances and non-substances, the hallmark of the former being that they are logically capable of independent existence, whereas non-substances depend logically for their existence upon that of other things, and ultimately upon the existence of substances. Material bodies provide the most obvious example of particular substances, but Cartesian egos or souls, if they existed, would also belong to this category. The concrete non-substances traditionally include such entities as particular events, particular qualities, and particular places and times. However, some revisionist metaphysicians hold that some or all of these categories are in fact more basic than the category of material objects, attempting to construct the latter from 'bundles' of particular events or qualities located at particular places and times.

Traditional ontological concerns, such as those just described, are currently enjoying a modest revival after a period of neglect prompted by widespread opposition to metaphysics. It is now better appreciated that the natural sciences embody implicit ontological schemes which cannot be wholly justified on purely empirical grounds and which can on occasion engender theoretical perplexities, as in the quantum-mechanical disputes over wave–particle duality. Only metaphysical reflection can ultimately dispel such perplexities.

The term 'ontology' has some additional special uses in philosophy. In a derivative sense, it is used to refer to the set of things whose existence is acknowledged by a particular theory or system of thought: it is in this sense that one speaks of 'the' ontology of a theory, or of a metaphysical system as having such-and-such an ontology (for example, an ontology of events, or of material substances). In a separate, technical sense the term 'ontology' is the official name of a logistical system created by the Polish logician

Stanisław Leśniewski—a system similar in scope to modern predicate logic and developed by him in conjunction with *mereology, the formal theory of part–whole relations. Leśniewski's system differs in important respects from the now orthodox formal logic of Frege and Russell, especially in the more general role it assigns to names.   E.J.L.

K. Campbell, *Abstract Particulars* (Oxford, 1990).
R. Grossmann, *The Existence of the World: An Introduction to Ontology* (London, 1992).
M. Loux and D. Zimmerman (eds.), *The Oxford Handbook of Metaphysics* (Oxford, 2003).
S. McCall, *Polish Logic 1920–1939* (Oxford, 1967).

opacity and transparency: *see* referential opacity.

opacity, opaque contexts: *see* referential opacity.

open and closed thought. Modern theories of knowledge focus on change of *belief. They ask what, given a background of beliefs and expectations, is the best way to change one's beliefs in the face of new evidence. A fertile and flexible system of beliefs will be able to change in response to unexpected evidence. This gives it a chance of containing truths. Similar points hold for desires and for emotions. Some systems of belief, desire, and emotion are such that they can evolve. Others are traps from which it is hard to escape, as they have ways of reinterpreting or neutralizing the impact of contrary evidence, unwelcome example, or unorthodox art. One function of philosophical *scepticism is to combat the tendency to closure in human ways of thinking. Yet total openness is probably impossible: a more reasonable ideal is that of a flexible cage, which can slowly change its shape. Indeed, the claim to have a completely open mind is usually a sign of some deep and inflexible self-deception.   A.M.

Karl Popper, *The Open Society and its Enemies* (London, 1961).
W. V. Quine and J. Ullian, *The Web of Belief* (New York, 1970).

open question argument. Argument used by G. E. Moore against ethical naturalists, especially J. S. Mill. Influenced by Hume on 'is' and 'ought', the argument runs thus: Naturalists claim that ethical words—e.g. 'good'—can be defined in natural terms—e.g. 'pleasure-maximizing'. But, since it is an open question whether what maximizes pleasure is good, the definition fails, committing the *naturalistic fallacy. It is not an open question whether, say, bachelors are unmarried men, so a definition of 'bachelor' as 'unmarried man' would succeed. Since Mill was trying not to define ethical words, but to tell us what *is* good (something Moore himself does), the argument fails *ad hominem*. It was taken over by emotivist and prescriptivist anti-naturalists, though Moore himself used it to support non-naturalism.   R.C.

  *fact–value distinction; non-natural properties.

T. Baldwin, *G. E. Moore* (London, 1990), ch. 3.
G. E. Moore, *Principia Ethica* (Cambridge, 1903).

open texture. This term has been used for an apparently unavoidable feature of empirical *concepts, namely that there is always the possibility of some unforeseen kind of case in which it is not clear whether, or how, the concept should be applied. Wittgenstein's discussion of *rules strongly supports this. Open texture is not *vagueness, but more like the possibility of vagueness; not all concepts are actually vague. For example, until the advent of test-tube fertilization, biological motherhood was a precise concept, but now 'mother' is ambiguous between 'she who was the source of genes' and 'she who gave birth'. The concept was always open-textured, because it could not provide in advance for all such possible new situations.   L.F.S.

F. Waismann, 'Verifiability', in G. H. R. Parkinson (ed.), *The Theory of Meaning* (Oxford, 1968).

operation. An expression E_1 operates on another expression (or expressions), E_2, when a further expression, E_3, results, and where E_2 is (or are) said to fall within the scope of E_1. E_1 might be 'Tom thinks that'; E_2, 'Mike is a vegetarian'; E_3 will be 'Tom thinks that Mike is a vegetarian'. The operators most commonly discussed by logicians are operators on sentences (like 'Tom thinks that'), particularly *truth-functional ones, where the truth-value of the sentence E_3 would be a function of the truth-value of the sentence(s) E_2. Examples of truth-functional operators are 'It's not the case that' (or 'not') and 'or'.   R.P.L.T.

W. Hodges, *Logic* (Harmondsworth, 1977), sects. 12–14.

operationalism. A grass-roots movement in philosophy of science, articulated and defended by P. W. Bridgman, which grew out of what was perceived to be the actual practice and views of physicists around the time that the theories of relativity and *quantum mechanics were first developed. Like *Logical Positivism, operationalism emphasizes close contact with experiment as necessary to objective discourse, but focuses on concepts rather than statements, seeking to safeguard them against meaninglessness by defining them solely with reference to precisely defined experimental operations. For example, 'the length of a table' may be said to be the number of times a measuring-rod needs to be laid end to end on the table, going from one end of it to the other. If there is more than one way to measure length, such as recording the time taken for light to travel out and back along the table, then there is more than one concept of 'length' involved. Furthermore, questions which cannot be decisively answered with reference to operations are banned from science, such as 'Did everything in the universe double in size overnight?' Given the radical departure of modern *physics from previously sacrosanct ideas such as Euclidean geometry, it is not difficult to see why Bridgman sought to purify scientific concepts operationally so as to avoid any further impediments to progress.   R.CLI.

P. W. Bridgman, *The Logic of Modern Physics* (New York, 1927).

optimism: *see* pessimism and optimism.

or: *see* conjunction and disjunction.

ordered pair: *see* ordered set.

ordered set, or *n*-tuple. Set (of any size, e.g. ordered pair or 2-tuple) in which order and repetition matter. For example, since Russell knew Leibniz's work but not conversely, and each knew his own work, the relation *knew the work of* holds of the ordered pairs ⟨Russell, Leibniz⟩, ⟨Russell, Russell⟩ and ⟨Leibniz, Leibniz⟩, but not of ⟨Leibniz, Russell⟩. By contrast the (unordered) pair {Russell, Leibniz} is the same as {Leibniz, Russell}, and {Russell, Russell} is just {Russell}.   C.A.K.

G. J. Massey, *Understanding Symbolic Logic* (New York, 1970), app. A.

ordinary language and philosophy. If proof were needed that philosophy cannot be reduced to or conducted wholly in ordinary language, some is provided by the fact that the two are in conflict. Ordinary language has largely succeeded in obscuring or obliterating vital linguistic differences, and thus in subverting distinctions that are essential to philosophical discourse. Consider the word 'valid', which has a clear meaning in logic but an unclear (though popular) use in ordinary language. Even more, consider the following pairs: begs the question–raises the question; reform–change; refute–reject; infer–imply; disinterested–uninterested. In everyday language the first term of each pair has largely replaced the second, thus making the distinction unintelligible in most contexts, and impoverishing conceptual and analytical resources. However, whereas close attention to language is essential in philosophy, the ideas that all philosophical problems are problems in language, or that they can be settled by grammatical analysis, or attention to everyday usage, are quite different and quite absurd. Philosophy can and should concern itself with genuine, substantive problems, and like any other problem-solving discourse is fully entitled to its own necessary technical terms.   A.BEL.

*analytic philosophy; philosophical inquiry: first premises and principles; Wittgenstein; linguistic philosophy.

Oswald Hanfling, *Ordinary Language and Philosophy* (London, 1999).

ordinary-language philosophy: *see* linguistic philosophy; J. L. Austin.

organic society. A view of society as a unitary natural growth, as opposed to views which depict it as an aggregate of individuals pursuing self-interest or as a planned or constructed entity.

If society is seen in terms of the biological metaphor of a living organism, certain features are typically attributed to it. It is thought to persist through time, and consequently the importance of maintaining tradition is stressed. Since it has grown rather than been constructed,

it ought not to be subjected to sudden and drastic changes, for drastic change may weaken or destroy it. The parts of an organism are mutually dependent, and indeed their identity depends on there being members of one organism rather than another. This implication is characteristically extended not just to the institutions of society but to the individual persons who have their being in it. In some political philosophies, notably that of Hegel, the organic view passes from metaphor to metaphysics and society as the *Volkgeist* is thought literally to have a life of its own. In that direction lies totalitarianism and racism. But the metaphor need not be twisted in that direction and in the moderate position of Burke the organic view of society offers a persuasive rival to the metaphors of building, construction, and planning.   R.S.D.

*conservatism.

E. Burke, *Reflections on the Revolution in France* (1790), ed. Conor Cruise O'Brien (Harmondsworth, 1968).
Ted Honderich, *Conservatism* (London, 1990).

original position. In Rawls's theory, the imaginary situation in which principles of *justice are to be chosen. We are asked to agree in advance on principles for evaluating social institutions under a *veil of ignorance—as if we didn't know what place we would occupy in the society. It is a hypothetical social contract designed to ensure that the principles chosen will be fair to all, because if you don't know who you are, you have to be equally concerned for the interests of everyone—though it may be just as difficult to decide what you should choose in this situation as it is to decide what is just.   T.N.

J. Rawls, *A Theory of Justice* (Cambridge, Mass., 1971).

original sin. According to this Christian doctrine, the *sin of early humans, represented in the Hebrew Bible by Adam and Eve disobeying a divine command not to eat the fruit of the tree of knowledge, had disastrous consequences for their progeny. An influential tradition founded by Augustine claims that the descendants of Adam inherit by causal transmission from him both an innate propensity to sin and innate *guilt. This view is problematic because it seems that guilt can be neither inherited nor innate.   P.L.Q.

*shame.

N. P. Williams, *The Ideas of the Fall and of Original Sin* (London, 1927).

origination. The creation of new causal chains by free human choices. The traditional doctrine of free will or *libertarianism asserts that there are such genuine creations. Not everything is a link in a deterministic causal chain. Random atomic variations are, of course, not sufficient for origination, which requires a kind of control by the *will, a self, a soul, or a mind—this being required for *responsibility. Determinists argue that origination does not exist, or that it is an essentially vacuous and unintelligible notion filling the space where a genuine cause should be.   R.C.W.

*freedom and determinism; determinism.

J. C. Eccles and K. R. Popper, *The Self and its Brain* (Berlin, 1977).

T. Honderich, *A Theory of Determinism: The Mind, Neuroscience, and Life-Hopes* (Oxford, 1988).

Ortega y Gasset, José (1883–1955). Philosopher and essayist, born in Madrid. Among his most influential books are *El tema de nuestro tiempo* (1923) and *La rebelión de las masas* (1932). Ortega's two most distinctive contributions to philosophy are a metaphysics of vital reason and a perspectival epistemology. For Ortega, reality and truth are defined with respect to my life, a combination of myself and my circumstances ('yo soy yo y mi circunstancia'). Something is real only in so far as it is rooted and appears in my life. The *self is not an entity separate from what surrounds it; there is a dynamic interaction and interdependence of self and things which together constitute reality. Because every life is the result of an interaction between self and circumstances, every self has a unique perspective and truth is perspectival.　　　J.G.

E.M.

Andrew Dobson, *An Introduction to the Politics and Philosophy of José Ortega y Gasset* (New York, 1989).

ostensive definition. Explaining the meaning of a word by ostension, by pointing to something to which the word applies, has been variously thought to constitute (i) a form of explanation which provides language with a foundation, (ii) an explanation which, in presupposing a general grasp of language, is only secondary, and (iii) a procedure which does not qualify as a *definition or explanation at all. While ostension may serve to point the learner in the right general direction, there is certainly a question as to how much eventual understanding may owe to any such procedure, and how much it requires exposure to word usage over a period of time.　　　B.B.R.

B. Rundle, *Wittgenstein and Contemporary Philosophy of Language* (Oxford, 1990).

Other. Primarily understood as the other human being in his or her differences. The problem of *other minds was first formulated clearly by John Stuart Mill in *An Examination of Sir William Hamilton's Philosophy*, although there are clear antecedents in Descartes. It was taken up by Husserl in the Fifth of his *Cartesian Meditations* where the other is constituted as an *alter ego*. However, it is only with Levinas that the philosophy of the Other was freed from the epistemological problematic. In *Totality and Infinity* Levinas charged previous philosophy, including that of Husserl, with reducing the Other to an object of consciousness and thereby failing to maintain its absolute alterity: the radically Other transcends me and the totality into whose network I seek to place it. According to Levinas, by challenging my self-assurance the Other opens the question of ethics. The priority of the Other becomes equivalent to the primacy of ethics over ontology.

Questions have been raised about this conception of the Other. Derrida asked whether the absolute alterity of the Other is not inevitably compromised by the fact that the Other is *other than* what is given initially. The logical problem has especially devastating consequences in the political realm, particularly if the Other is not accorded the ethical priority Levinas gives it. In this way the now widespread use of the language of otherness in anthropological discourse to describe the West's encounter with non-Western cultures tends to keep the dominant discourse intact, just as the reference to the feminine as Other reasserts male privilege.

The notion of the Other is also used by other European thinkers in a broader sense. Death, madness, the unconscious are all said to be Other. In each case the challenge of the Other is the same: that in some way the Other cannot be encapsulated within the thought-forms of Western philosophy without reducing the alterity of the Other.　　　R.L.B.

J. Derrida, 'Violence and Metaphysics', in *Writing and Difference* (Chicago, 1978).

M. Theunissen, *The Other* (Cambridge, Mass., 1984).

other minds. A problem in the theory of knowledge about whether—and if so, how—one can know, or be justified in believing, that other individuals (humans and animals) have thoughts and feelings. Also sometimes taken to include a related question: How do we know that plants and rocks (not to mention machines) do not have minds? Also, more specifically, a problem about the character of another's thoughts and feelings: How do I know strawberries taste the same to you as they do to me?

Assuming that one has some kind of *introspective access to one's own thoughts and feelings (so that there is no problem about one's *own* mind), the problem of other minds is usually taken to be a question about what our judgements about other people's minds are based on. Are they based solely on observable behaviour? If so, what reason do we have to think that such behaviour is a reliable symptom (expression) of mental activity? If people can act one way and feel another, if they can believe something without ever showing it, why not suppose a daffodil does the same—thinks and feels without *ever* showing it? If a machine can beat us at chess without (according to some) having a mental life, why suppose our neighbour is any different?

*Behaviourism is a view that identifies mental activity with behavioural tendencies and dispositions. If someone acts jealous and is disposed, in a wide variety of circumstances, to behave jealously, then that person *is* jealous. There is no further fact about this mental state that is hidden from our view. Behaviourism provides a convenient solution to the problem of other minds since, according to it, 'other minds' are as accessible as 'other behaviour'. This solution to the problem does not, today, enjoy much support. Although some aspects of our mental life may consist of behavioural tendencies (vanity and shyness, for example), others do not. An itch isn't just a tendency to scratch.

For those who (unlike behaviourists) take the mental life of another person or animal to consist of inner, unobservable (by others), events and states, the argument from analogy has always been an attractive answer to the problem of other minds. Just as I am entitled to infer that X will do A because it resembles in a variety of significant ways (is analogous to) Y, and Y generally does A, so we know (or at least are reasonable in believing) X feels pain because X resembles me—acts in many of the same ways I do—when I feel pain. Arguments from analogy have been criticized as a very feeble sort of argument for other minds—much too feeble to support the knowledge claims we typically advance about such matters. It is true that I tend to yell and suck my finger when I burn it. I do so because it hurts. But is this a reason to conclude, by analogy, that it must also hurt my neighbour because he behaves that way when he burns his finger? Perhaps it is, but the inference is from a single case (one's own case), and analogies from a single case are notoriously weak. Is the fact that *one* chocolate in the box, the one you ate first, was caramel-filled a reason to think that every (any?) other similar-looking chocolate will be filled with caramel? Is it a good enough reason to say you *know* it is?

The argument from analogy can be strengthened by looking not at a single piece of behaviour but at the full range of behaviour exhibited by other organisms. Many philosophers have thought that verbal behaviour is particularly relevant. People *say* it hurts. At least they make noises similar to those I make when I say it hurts. We can, of course, make machines that will produce the same noises when they are poked, but will they (can they?) exhibit the full range of dispositions—verbal and otherwise—that human beings do? There is also the fact that other human beings (and some animals) have nervous systems remarkably like one's own—something daffodils, rocks, and computers lack. In so far as there is reason to think mental activity *supervenes on the neural substrate (something that many materialistic theories of the mind maintain), then this similarity of hardware is an even stronger analogical basis for inferring similarity of mental life in biologically and behaviourally similar organisms.

F.D.

*introspection; Other; persons; supervenience.

C. D. Broad, *The Mind and its Place in Nature* (London, 1925).

N. Malcolm, 'Knowledge of Other Minds', *Journal of Philosophy*, 23 (1958).

H. H. Price, 'Our Evidence for the Existence of Other Minds', *Philosophy*, 13 (1938).

G. Ryle, *The Concept of Mind* (London, 1949).

other-regarding actions: *see* self-regarding and other-regarding actions.

ought. 'Ought' can express purely personal counsel—'I ought to move my Queen, or I'll lose it next move'. It can also express an impersonal or 'transpersonal' moral imperative. I may be urging myself (or another similarly placed) towards morally desirable or necessary action, or away from the morally deplorable. The context of its use may be the small scale of an individual act, or the grandest

scale of a vision of what human life 'ought to be like'. Essential to the moral 'ought' is the sense of a strong constraint laid upon the will: it contrasts with the operating of a moral ideal which, rather, beckons and attracts the moral agent.

'*Why* ought I?' is a legitimate question, inviting answer in terms of intelligible moral rules or practices, until one reaches such an ultimate limit as, for example, respect for persons or right to life. It may be argued that 'ought implies can', in the strenuous sense that to recognize an unconditional moral 'ought' itself supplies the motivation to respond.

R.W.H.

*'is' and 'ought'; obligation; ideals, moral.

J. N. Findlay, *Values and Intentions* (London, 1961).

'ought' and 'is': *see* 'is' and 'ought'.

overdetermination and underdetermination. The *problem of overdetermination* is a problem for our understanding of *causality. An effect is overdetermined when it has two independent causes, each sufficient on its own for its effect. The problem is that in such cases neither cause satisfies our ordinary criteria for causal efficacy: neither cause, for example, is necessary in the circumstance for the effect. So we either have to deny that causal overdetermination occurs, or show that our preferred account is not incompatible with it, or modify that account. The *problem of underdetermination* concerns the relationship between *theory (scientific theory, or any generalization) and the *empirical data. For any given theory, the evidence will never determine the choice between that theory and some rival theory. The problem then is to show how theory choice can ever be rational.

R.LE P.

*induction; translation, indeterminacy of.

J. L. Mackie, *The Cement of the Universe: A Study of Causation* (Oxford, 1974).

overman: *see* superman.

Owen, G. E. L. (1922–82). Gwil Owen greatly influenced the study of ancient philosophy world-wide. He was professor successively in Oxford, Harvard, and Cambridge. He published a few very influential articles, notably on the place of the *Timaeus* in Plato's philosophy and on the role of dialectic in Aristotle's philosophical method; and he was a protagonist in the group of European scholars which produced the series of Symposia Aristotelica. A recurring theme in his work was the importance of method and argument, as against thesis and doctrine, in the practice and history of philosophy. He applied this insight to challenge a number of orthodoxies in the interpretation of Plato and Aristotle. Owen was active in the recruitment and motivation of graduate students and junior faculty members. His medium was the cut-and-thrust of dialectic, through which he showed that the study of ancient philosophy demands philosophical acuity combined with philological rigour. A seminal article, which illustrates many features of his thought and style, is 'The Platonism of Aristotle', reprinted in his *Logic, Science and Dialectic* (London, 1986).   J.D.G.E.

owl of Minerva. Minerva, the Roman goddess of *wisdom, was the equivalent of the Greek goddess Athena. She was associated with the owl, traditionally regarded as wise, and hence a metaphor for philosophy. Hegel wrote, in the preface to his *Philosophy of Right*: 'The owl of Minerva spreads its wings only with the falling of the dusk.' He meant that philosophy understands reality only after the event. It cannot prescribe how the world ought to be.   P.S.

G. W. F. Hegel, *Hegel's Philosophy of Right*, tr. T. M. Knox (Oxford, 1967).

Oxford Calculators. In the 1320s and 1330s, a group of natural philosophers based at Oxford—principally Thomas Bradwardine, William Heytesbury, Richard Swineshead—produced a series of path-breaking treatises on the analysis of motion. Distinguishing between the study of motion with regard to its causes and its study with regard to its effects, they developed a quasi-mathematical account of the latter in which motions are characterized in terms of 'intensive' magnitudes which cannot be measured directly, but must be assessed according to their spatio-temporal effects.   S.GAU.

N. Kretzmann *et al.* (eds.), *The Cambridge History of Later Medieval Philosophy* (Cambridge, 1982).

Oxford philosophy. The study and teaching of philosophy in Oxford go back at least to the early thirteenth-century Augustinian, or Neoplatonist, Robert Grosseteste, one of the few medieval philosophers to know Greek. In the early fourteenth century Duns Scotus and William of Ockham were the most important of a large number of Franciscan scholars who opposed the rationalism of the Dominican St Thomas Aquinas. They held that reason is not competent to establish any but the most general elements of religious faith. In their epoch Oxford superseded Paris as the centre of philosophical study. After the Black Death of 1348 and, even more, after the heresies of Wyclif had led, later in that century, to the imposition of ecclesiastical control over religious speculation, Oxford remained, for the most part, philosophically infertile for some 500 years. Hobbes and Locke studied there, unprofitably in their opinion, and Locke taught in Oxford for some years, but neither became a philosopher until a considerable time after they had left it.

Two distinguished philosophers taught in Oxford around the middle of the nineteenth century in an isolated and, philosophically, uninfluential way: J. H. Newman, drawing on Aristotle, the British Empiricists, and Bishop Butler, and H. L. Mansel, chief disciple of the last important Scottish philosopher, Sir William Hamilton. Newman's theory of belief and Mansel's theory of the limits of religious thought remotely echo the resistance of Scotus and Ockham to the pretensions of reason in the domain of religious belief.

In the last quarter of the nineteenth century a major new school emerged: the anglicized *Hegelianism that was initiated by T. H. Green and had as its most distinguished exponent F. H. Bradley. They rejected the claim of the common view of the world, and of its scientific extension, to be genuine knowledge, seeing it as a practical makeshift, riddled with internal contradictions. True knowledge can be achieved, not by the analytic understanding, but only by that philosophic reason which recognizes that nature is a product of mind or, at any rate, is formed and articulated by it.

Russell and Moore in Cambridge drove this idealistic orthodoxy from the field, even if its adherents long continued to dominate the philosophical professoriate of the British Isles. Its last notable exponent was the brilliant but intellectually wayward R. G. Collingwood. *Idealism was less impressively criticized on its home ground by J. Cook Wilson and H. A. Prichard, in and after the Edwardian decade. They set about it with something of the relentless literalism of G. E. Moore, but with a numbing rather than inspiring effect.

In the 1930s Oxford philosophy came to life again. The new Cambridge ideas had been imported with style, rigour, and authority by H. H. Price and were given a more radical turn by Gilbert Ryle. He took philosophy to be concerned not so much with genuine problems as with puzzles or muddles. 'The whole and sole task of philosophy', he wrote, 'is . . . the detection of the sources in linguistic idiom of recurrent misconstructions and absurd theories'. That conviction culminated in his chief work, *The Concept of Mind* (1949) in which mind–body *dualism is attributed to a mistaken assimilation of statements about minds to statements about physical things. The former, he contends, do not report private inner episodes of thought and feeling but refer to the dispositions of human bodies to act, and talk, in certain ways in given circumstances.

The Oxford philosophy of ordinary language, as it came to be called, received its most exquisite expression in the highly entertaining work of J. L. Austin, who shared Moore's power to dominate a generation of philosophers by the force of his personality and exceeded Moore in the refinement of his linguistic discrimination. After Austin's death in 1960, the return of A. J. Ayer to Oxford after a twenty-year absence, and a focusing of interest on the work of W. V. Quine and other American analytic philosophers, the ordinary-language school disintegrated and nothing specifically Oxonian has replaced it.   A.Q.

A. J. AYER brought logical positivism from Vienna to Oxford, presenting it as continuous with the British empiricist tradition. For fifty years he was a figurehead of philosophy in Britain, addressing epistemological questions in a distinctively skilful and forceful style.

P. F. STRAWSON planted the seed of his Kantian metaphysics in the fertile Wittgensteinian soil of 1950s Oxford. He moved from an early critique of Russell's philosophical logic to foundational metaphysical questions; this shift in focus offered a model response to the decline of 'ordinary language' philosophy in Britain.

GILBERT RYLE, leading light of Oxford philosophy in the middle decades of the twentieth century, hunter of conceptual confusion and category-error.

KARL POPPER urged that the mark of a scientific theory is that it is open to falsification, and that the mark of a good society or government or social institution is that it is open to change by the people.

P

pain. A feeling of pain can be either 'physical', a *sensation (e.g. toothache), or 'mental', an emotion (e.g. the pain of a bereavement). There are two main kinds of philosophical theory of sensations of pain. According to one of them, a sensation is painful in virtue of having a special, intrinsic quality, a quality which happens to be universally disliked for its own sake. According to the other, there is no such intrinsic quality shared by all sensations of pain; what they have in common is simply that they are all disliked for their own sake. Which of these theories is true is of consequence for the status of a claim of *hedonism, namely that pain and only pain is or should be shunned for its own sake.   I.S.P.

*pleasure; happiness.

R. Trigg, *Pain and Emotion* (Oxford, 1970).

Paine, Thomas (1737–1809). Born in Thetford, Norfolk, the son of a Quaker farmer, he died in New York after an adventurous career on both sides of the Atlantic. Arriving on American shores in 1774, he put his talents as a pamphleteer at the service of the rebellious colonists, notably in his *Common Sense* (1776). Back in England when the French Revolution broke out, he immediately came to its defence in his most influential work, *The Rights of Man* (1791–2), penned as a reply to the conservative attack on the ideology of the Revolution by Edmund Burke. In part II of that book, Paine defended a then novel view: among the *natural rights governments must respect are welfare rights of all citizens to education, old-age pensions, and the like. In *The Age of Reason* (1794–95), enormously popular in its day, he gave a spirited defence of deistic anticlericalism unmarked, however, by any novel philosophical arguments. His radical ideas for social, political, and economic reform were most fully developed in his last major work, *Agrarian Justice* (1797).   H.A.B.

*deism; justice.

A. J. Ayer, *Thomas Paine* (Chicago, 1988).

panpsychism. A doctrine about the nature of spatiotemporal reality. It asserts that each spatio-temporal thing has a mental or 'inner' aspect. Few panpsychists would be happy with a characterization of their view as that all things have minds, even sticks and stones. Instead, they

want to say that there may be varying degrees in which things have inner *subjective or quasi-conscious aspects, some very unlike what we experience as consciousness. A full-blown mind would only be possessed by things approaching the complexity of human beings. On the other hand, it is difficult to characterize precisely to what extent all spatio-temporal things are supposed to have an inner 'mental' aspect. Most of those who espouse this doctrine feel impelled to do so because they do not see how the mental can be caused by, or composed from, nonmental things.   P.J.P.N.

*pantheism.

T. Nagel, *Mortal Questions* (Cambridge, 1978), ch. 13.

B. Spinoza, *Ethics*, in *The Collected Works of Spinoza*, i, ed. and tr. E. Curley (Princeton, NJ, 1988).

pantheism. First used by John Toland in 1705, the term 'pantheist' designates one who holds both that everything there is constitutes a unity and that this unity is divine. Pantheists thus deny the radical distinction between God and creatures drawn in monotheistic religions. A familiar philosophical example of pantheism is Spinoza's doctrine that there is only one *substance and it is divine; he describes this substance as *Deus sive natura* (God or nature). Pantheism is distinguished from *panpsychism by the fact that panpsychists, who maintain that everything is psychic in nature, need not also hold that everything is divine.   P.L.Q.

O. L. Reiser, *Nature, Man and God: A Synthesis of Pantheism and Scientific Humanism* (Pittsburgh, 1951).

Papineau, David (1947–). English philosopher, currently Professor of Philosophy of Science at King's College London. Papineau has worked in metaphysics, epistemology, and the philosophies of science, mind, and mathematics. His overall stance is vigorously realist and physicalist in metaphysics, and reliabilist in epistemology. He is one of the originators of the teleological theory of mental *representation, a solution to the problem of *intentionality which derives the intentional content of our beliefs from the conditions under which actions based on these beliefs and certain desires will succeed in satisfying those desires. Since 'satisfying' desires amounts to making their contents true, the theory needs to explain how desires get their contents. Papineau explains the contents of basic desires in terms of the biological functions with which natural selection has endowed them.   T.C.

*science, problems of the philosophy of.

D. Papineau, *Philosophical Naturalism* (Oxford, 1993).
—— *Thinking about Consciousness* (Oxford, 2002).

paradigm, scientific: *see* Kuhn.

paradigm case argument. A type of argument common in the heyday of *linguistic philosophy, with its emphasis on actual linguistic usage. Philosophers have long disputed over whether there are such things as, say, free will or a good inductive argument. The paradigm case argument claims that if the expressions 'free will' and 'good inductive argument' are standardly applied in some situations and rejected in others, then the former must represent genuine cases of free will etc., or the expressions could not have the meanings they do have. It can, however, be doubted whether this proves the existence of free will etc. in any but a trivial sense. The argument is akin to, but weaker than, *transcendental arguments, which appeal not to how we actually do speak but to how we must if we are to speak at all, either in general or on some given subject-matter.   A.R.L.

R. J. Richman, 'On the Argument of the Paradigm Case', *Australasian Journal of Philosophy* (1961), discussed by C. J. F. Williams (ibid.) and Richman (ibid. 1962).

paradox of analysis. An ambition of much twentieth-century analytic philosophy was to give the correct analysis of certain terms, concepts, or propositions. Yet, as G. E. Moore pointed out, if an analysis is correct, the *analysans* must state no more or less than the *analysandum*. Hence analysis, if successful, is trivial, and if unsuccessful, is false. Moore's paradox recalls a question tackled by Plato (in *Meno*) and Aristotle (in the *Posterior Analytics*): whether—and by what means—we can ever know new things. Paul Feyerabend argued that the paradox of analysis showed that philosophy cannot be analytic and scientific at the same time.   A.BRE.

J. King, 'What is Philosophical Analysis?', *Philosophical Studies*, 90 (1998).

paradoxes. There are many separate entries in this work for this or that 'paradox'. Is there a common feature marked by this term? Part of any such feature would be the idea of conflict.

One interpretation of 'paradox' is 'statement conflicting with received opinion'. Thus one of the Socratic paradoxes is the remark that no one ever knowingly does wrong, which is inconsistent with the popular opinion that people often do things they know they shouldn't. Here the 'paradox' represents a philosophically serious challenge to the received opinion.

A different use of 'paradox' is also marked by *'antinomy', which applies not to a statement which conflicts, but to the conflict itself, when it is a conflict between what are (or have been) regarded as fundamental truths. For example, Kant maintains that an antinomy arises between basic principles involved in reasoning about space and time. From these principles, a good argument can be given for the conclusion that the world must be finite in space and time, but the principles also allow an equally good argument that the world cannot be finite, but must be infinite.

'Antinomy' marks a different feature of a case from the first use of 'paradox', but 'paradox' is often given this latter use as well. It is common to find one philosopher calling a case a paradox and another calling the same case an antinomy. In so far as it is a received opinion that given principles do not conflict, then the report that they do conflict will be contrary to that opinion and paradoxical in the first sense. But that does not reduce this second use to the first. They mark different features.

A third use of 'paradox' is to mark conflict in criteria for classification. A phenomenon may be called paradoxical when it resists classification not because there is insufficient information about it, but because the information brings out conflicts in the criteria for classification which may have been previously unnoticed. Thus 'paradoxical sleep' (REM sleep) has features once thought distinctive of a waking state and other features supposed distinctive of a sleeping state. The paradoxes of quantum physics involve light phenomena exhibiting both wave characteristics and particle characteristics. If criteria are regarded as fundamental principles, this interpretation might be reduced to the 'antinomy' reading. But the feature of involving a classification problem is worth keeping track of.

Use of the term 'paradox' may leave unclear just what is being called paradoxical and what is meant by so calling it. This is not merely because of unclarity about which of the three foregoing meanings of the term is intended. There may be disagreement about what is in conflict. For example, it is sometimes said that Kant's antinomy calls for a rejection of the law of excluded middle: the world is neither finite nor not-finite (infinite). Others will argue that it is quite unnecessary to answer in this way. Kant's idea was that there is no world as a completed whole. This could be expressed by saying that both the claim that the complete world is finite and the claim that the complete world is non-finite are false because there is no such world. That is perfectly compatible with the law that for every proposition whatever, either it or its negation must be true. The negation of 'The world as a complete whole is finite' is not 'The world as a complete whole is not finite', but rather, 'Either there is no such thing as the world as a complete whole or there is but it is not finite'. Another alternative would be to question the quality of either or both of Kant's arguments for the two sides of his antinomy, without questioning general logical principles.

Here we have a disagreement over just which fundamental laws are in conflict in the sense of constituting an inconsistent group. Of course, whenever any group of claims is in conflict, adding any additional claims will give a larger group which is still in conflict. 'P and not-P' is a group in conflict, and adding any other claim, Q, gives us 'P and not-P and Q', which is also in conflict. But it may be that Q is not to blame for the conflict—not a genuine party to the conflict belonging under the heading of conflictant. A logical-revisionist side wants to put in the law of excluded middle as a conflictant in Kant's antinomy and thereby consider its rejection as a way out of the conflict. A logical-traditionist side will refuse to consider that a possibility and identify other conflictants which may have been unnoticed. They will hold that in any case of logical conflict, it is confused to blame logical laws, since they are essential to the idea of *logical* conflict. Without at least an intuitive grasp of logical laws it would be impossible to recognize the existence of any logical conflict. They are necessary truths indispensable in good reasoning which are above the conflicts they enable us to identify.

The logical revisionists may respond that it is possible to make some changes in logic while retaining the basis for classifying some groups of claims as logically consistent or inconsistent. They can point to many honourable candidates for 'alternative logics'. It is important to ask, however, whether these candidates are presented as universally applicable criteria of conflict which are themselves beyond conflict. This is not to suggest that it is acceptable to presume that there are such criteria and ignore the view that every claim whatever is revisable, that no claim is beyond conflict. But the significance of attributions of 'paradox' or 'antinomy' often depends on how the idea of 'conflict' implicit in these terms is itself understood.

This may be illustrated by considering one of the most famous philosophical paradoxes, the *liar paradox. What might be called a 'version' involves the sentence A: The sentence A is not true. A good candidate for a fundamental principle about truth is the principle that a sentence is true if and only if what it says to be the case is in fact the case. (And that means 'all of what it says'. '2 + 2 = 4 & 2 + 2 = 5' does not qualify as true just because it says correctly that 2 + 2 = 4.) Suppose then, that we assume that what the sentence A says to be the case, all of what it says, is correctly reported as the claim that A is not true. This claim is true if A is not true, and not true if A is true. That entails that A is true if and only if A is not true, which is a contradiction.

Now, what is the paradox? What should be identified as conflictants in this case? The logical traditionist will treat classical logical principles as immune from blame for the trouble. So just what are the conflictants? One answer compatible with the traditionist approach is as follows: It is natural and common to assume that what the sentence A says can be correctly reported simply by quoting the sentence, either directly or indirectly. The claim that this assumption is false thus conflicts with a received opinion and is in that sense paradoxical—but it happens to be the truth of the matter none the less. The assumption to the contrary, that all of what A says is just that the sentence A is not true, leads to a contradiction by traditional logical rules.

This has not been the most popular response to the 'paradox'. It is far commoner to respond in a revisionist

way. But then it is appropriate to ask: What is to be identified as the paradox?

An early propounder of the liar paradox, Eubulides of Megara, did actually present his version as an assertion—'I am lying'. But was that a statement contrary to received opinion? His intention was to discredit rationalism by showing that its basic standards of reasoning themselves lead to what they reject—inconsistency. The derived contradiction may be contrary to reason, but it is also derived according to reason.

It is not Eubulides' assertion, or the sentence A, which conflicts with respectable opinion. Rather, it is attempts to determine the truth-value of these sentences which provoke conflicting claims. In so far as we can derive a contradiction from an 'unquestionable recognition' of what A says along with classical logical rules we have a conflict which is a candidate for 'antinomy'. The commonest contemporary responses to this problem take it in this way, as an antinomy calling for restrictions on classical logical principles.

The most popular restriction holds that there is no such thing as truth *simpliciter*—only truth at a level, where to say that a claim is not true-level-n is to make a claim of level n +1 to which 'true-level-n' cannot be meaningfully applied. This cannot be formulated in unrestricted natural language without undoing its purpose. B: 'The sentence B is not true at any level' will raise trouble unless some restriction is placed on what we are allowed to say. So it is denied that we can talk meaningfully about 'truth-at-some-level-or-other'. These denials of meaning are quite implausible. If 'truth *simpliciter*' is meaningless then 'There is no such thing as truth *simpliciter*' should also be meaningless, just as 'There is no blah-blah-blah' is meaningless. The fact that the former is not meaningless suggests that it is not true. The 'levels' response requires denying that there even were general principles about truth that led to inconsistency. The 'universal laws' would not be false or conflicting but rather 'blah-blah'—and 'blah-blah' is not a candidate for logical conflict.

This criticism could be parried by taking a nominalistic approach and saying not that there is no truth *simpliciter* but rather that the traditional use of the word 'true' without implicit or explicit levels tended to lead its users into inconsistencies. The 'universal laws' would then be certain sentences of a sort found to be no longer useful, but still easily distinguishable from 'blah-blah'.

However, this does not satisfactorily explain why the alleged inconsistencies of plain 'true' ought to be avoided. The traditional answer would be that it is absolutely impossible, universally impossible, in all possible languages, for inconsistencies to be true. This can't be allowed on this 'nominalist' line any more than it could on the previous one. The universality of the logical criteria are given up on this approach, and that deprives the 'inconsistencies' of their problematic significance.

A more recent approach to the liar paradox treats criteria for truth or falsity as sequential. The ruling that the paradox is true satisfies a criterion for ruling it false; that finding satisfies a criterion for finding it true; and so on, *ad infinitum*. Where other sentences get a permanent truth assignment, some self-referential sentences (the liar paradox is one) oscillate indefinitely. Various interpretations may be placed on such data, including assigning 'values' other than the true–false pair. The patterns of 'valuation' produced by various rules may make an interesting object of mathematical study. It is rather like a psychiatrist classifying 'paradoxical' personality types, love–hate relationships, double or multiple binding personal interactions, manic-depressives, etc., from a detached perspective.

Classical logical laws cannot be treated as applicable sequentially without ignoring the universality which is essential to their identity. If a claim is found true, then found false, then true, and so on indefinitely, then either half of these 'findings' are mistaken or else it was not the same claim from one 'finding' to the next.

However, the anti-traditionalist may not be concerned with how classical laws need to be applied. He may have been led by his exposure to paradoxes and antinomies to have given up the belief that there is in matters of theory any mandatory received opinion or any fundamental principles to get into conflict of a privileged logical kind which it is essential to proper thinking to resolve. He can agree with the classicist that without the absolutely universal and necessary logical principles there is no fixed basis for determining the correct response to a paradox or antinomy, but draw a very different moral. His response to those troubled by paradox may be like that of the psychiatrist easing a patient's distress not by answering his questions, but by changing his attitude towards them.

This conflict over the very identity and nature of the conflict illustrates how, in a paradox case, we may encounter considerable difficulty in achieving agreement about the correct description of the problem. Whether an opinion has a status that would make its rejection significant, or a 'law' is really fundamental, may be unclear. And even the significance of rejection or conflict may be a matter of disagreement. It is perfectly compatible with classical logic to regard difference of opinion as healthy or even desirable. But those who wish further not to be constrained by the idea that one side in a contradiction must be wrong will not settle for that. Paradox cases raise general questions about method and principle, which is one reason the topic has been of such interest in philosophy.   J.C.

*Moore's paradox; two-envelope paradox.

J. C. Beall (ed.), *Liars and Heaps: New Essays on Paradox* (Oxford, 2003).

John Buridan, *Sophisms on Meaning and Truth*, tr. Theodore Kermit Scott (New York, 1966).

James Cargile, *Paradoxes* (Cambridge, 1979).

Robert L. Martin (ed.), *Recent Essays on Truth and the Liar Paradox* (Oxford, 1984).

W. V. Quine, 'The Ways of Paradox', in *The Ways of Paradox* (New York, 1966).

Bertrand Russell, 'Mathematical Logic as Based on the Theory of Types', in *Logic and Knowledge* (London, 1956).

R. Sorensen, *A Brief History of the Paradox* (Oxford, 2003).

paradoxes, logical. F. P. Ramsey held that 'the well known contradictions of the theory of aggregates . . . fall into two fundamentally distinct groups'. The first group 'involve only logical and mathematical terms' and have come to be called (by many) 'logical paradoxes'. The second group 'cannot be stated in logical terms alone' and 'contain some reference to thought, language, or symbolism, which are not formal, but empirical terms'. Ramsey held that the *paradoxes of the second group 'may be due not to faulty logic or mathematics, but to faulty ideas concerning thought and language', and in that case, 'they would not be relevant to mathematics or logic, if by "logic" we mean a symbolic system, though of course they would be relevant to logic in the sense of the analysis of thought'. Those who follow Ramsey's suggestion call the second group 'semantic paradoxes'.

All but one of Ramsey's examples come from *Principia Mathematica*, where they are listed under the common heading of 'Contradictions which have Beset Mathematical Logic'. The ones he calls 'logical' are Russell's paradox, Burali-Forti's paradox, and the paradox of the relation which holds 'between two relations when one does not have itself to the other'. The ones now called 'semantic' (by those who accept this distinction) are the liar paradox, Berry's paradox, Konig's paradox of the least indefinable ordinal, Richard's paradox, and Grelling's paradox. (The last is the one paradox not in the *Principia* list.)

Ramsey's distinction should be regarded as controversial. His two alternative meanings for 'logic'—'a symbolic system' and 'the analysis of thought' do not rule out non-logical symbolic systems or psychology, and are, anyway, not mutually exclusive. The notions of reference, definition, or truth have as much claim to belong to logic as does the notion of a class. This was clearly the intention of the authors of *Principia* since they attempted to allow these terms to occur in their ideal language while at the same time laying down rules which would prevent contradictions formulated in such terms from being derivable in their system.

A pragmatic motive for Ramsey's distinction arises from the fact that, in order to both allow the 'semantic' terms and avoid contradictions, *Principia* presents what is known as 'the ramified' (as opposed to 'the simple') theory of types. On the simple theory, both the propositional functions 'x is a general' and 'x has all the qualities of a great general' would be of type 1, one type above that of the things (individuals) to which they apply. But the latter function is built up by quantifying the function 'x is a quality of a great general', which, in the simple theory, would be of type 2. And this fact about its derivation is important to the *Principia* treatment of 'semantic' paradoxes. Functions are not ordered simply by the order of their arguments but by the order of the arguments to the 'matrices' from which the functions are derived. (Matrices, roughly, are what is left when quantifiers are deleted from a formula.) The ramified hierarchy of orders is the basis for a rule requiring that a proposition of the nth order can only be allowed apparent variables of order $n - 1$. This is much

more restrictive than the simple type rule that a propositional function of type *n* determines a class whose members are of type *n* −1. The simple rule would have 'a
property of individual *a*' represent a property of type 2
whose instances would be type 1 properties of *a*. But the
ramified rule would make that phrase illegitimate and give
us instead an infinite hierarchy of properties: 'a first-order
property of *a*', 'a second-order property of *a*', etc. This was
so restrictive as to rule out the definition of the least upper
bound of a class of real numbers. The *Principia* response
was 'the axiom of reducibility', which guarantees that for
every such function of *a* in the infinite hierarchy, there is
an extensionally equivalent first-order function.

Ramsey argued that the axiom of reducibility is implausible, and unnecessary if *Principia* is restricted to terms of
set theory, which would be all that is required for its primary mission of being a foundation for mathematics. This
has been a popular idea, and today it is the simple theory
of types that would be most likely to be discussed by set
theorists. There is nothing wrong in that, but it would be
unfortunate if the success of a simplification of one theory
of sets were mistaken for a conclusive basis for a distinction between 'logical' and 'semantic'.   J.C.

F. P. Ramsey, 'The Foundations of Mathematics', in *The Foundations of Mathematics and Other Logical Essays*, ed. R. B. Braithwaite (London, 1945).

Bertrand Russell and Alfred North Whitehead, 'Introduction
 to the Second Edition', in *Principia Mathematica* (Cambridge,
 1962).

parallel distributed processing. A form of computation
in which items are represented not by symbols but by patterns of activity distributed over a network of simple processing units. Particular patterns result from massively
parallel computations of the levels of activation in individual units. Connections between the units excite or inhibit
the spread of activation. As a model of human *cognition
it is proposed as a rival to the *language of thought
hypothesis, one that offers a closer approximation to brain
processing.   B.C.S.

*connectionism.

P. Smolensky, 'The Proper Treatment of Connectionism', in
 Behavioural and Brain Sciences (1988).

parallelism, psychophysical. The thesis that mind and
body never influence one another, but nevertheless
progress along parallel paths, as though they interacted.
This response to the *mind–body problem is partially
motivated by the view that two distinct kinds of being or
substance exist, immaterial and material, and by the difficulty of understanding how substances of either kind can
act upon substances of the other. Leibniz held that God
arranged things in advance so that our minds and bodies
would be in harmony with one another and with what
happens to all other substances: the doctrine of *pre-
established harmony. In the absence of some such explanation, parallelism would be a remarkable coincidence; but
one suspects that a being capable of instituting pre-

established harmony could also find a way to allow mind
and body to interact.   A.R.M.

*occasionalism.

G. W. Leibniz, *Philosophical Papers and Letters*, ed. L. E. Loemker
 (Chicago, 1956), chs. 35–6, 47, 52, 54–5, 58, 60–1, 63, 67, 71.

paralogisms. In Kant's critical philosophy, a fallacious
argument. In the *Critique of Pure Reason* Kant identifies
three paralogisms in the first edition and a fourth in the
second edition. They are invalid inferences to conclusions
expressing the simplicity of the soul, the personality of the
soul, the immortality of the soul, and the existence of the
external world. In each case, the mistake is to try to derive
a tenet of transcendental realism from premisses expressing only transcendental idealism—that is, conclusions
about a putative non-spatio-temporal reality from premisses only about possible appearances.   S.P.

Kant, *Critique of Pure Reason*, tr. Norman Kemp Smith (London,
 1978).

paraphrasis: *see* Bentham; contextual definition.

Pareto optimality. Pareto optimality, developed by
Vilfredo Pareto, is the most widely accepted criterion of
economic efficiency. A state of a given system (e.g. a
distribution of a given quantity of goods) is Pareto optimal, and thus efficient, if and only if there is no feasible
alternative state of that system (e.g. no feasible alternative
distribution of those goods) in which at least one person is
better off and no one is worse off. And, for purposes of this
criterion, a person is 'better off' with some alternative *A*
rather than *B* if and only if this person *prefers A to B*. An
advantage of this criterion is that it provides a way of evaluating alternative social states that does not require interpersonal utility comparisons.   D.W.HAS.

Allen Buchanan, *Ethics, Efficiency, and the Market* (Totowa, NJ,
 1985).

Parfit, Derek (1942–). Best known for his innovative
ideas about the nature of *personal identity, where he
contends that, in a significant sense, 'identity' is not what
matters in the continuity and persistence of persons
throughout their lives. This view was outlined in a number of articles in the 1970s but was fully expounded in his
Reasons and Persons (Oxford, 1984). In that book, he draws
out some of the consequences of his views for moral theory, arguing that certain traditional conceptions of prudence and self-interest must be questioned once the
conception of the nature of the self on which they depend
is criticized. His theories have excited considerable comment. Since 1967 a Fellow of All Souls, Oxford, he is also a
keen architectural photographer.   N.J.H.D.

Parmenides (*fl. c.*480 BC). Citizen of Elea and leading figure of the *Eleatics. His philosophical work was
expounded in his poem, of which more than a hundred
lines survive. The poem begins with a first-person narrative of an allegorical journey, at the end of which the

narrator meets a goddess. The goddess tells him: 'you are to find out everything: both the steadfast heart of well-rounded Reality, and the opinions of mortals, which contain no genuine proof'. In the rest of the poem, in a long speech, the goddess fulfils the double promise.

The section on 'Reality' (or 'Truth': the translation is controversial), of which much survives, expounded and claimed to prove the truths Parmenides took to be demonstrable.

An indubitable foundation for knowledge is found, as by Descartes, in the mind and its relation to its objects. (1) One cannot coherently doubt that thinking is possible and actually occurs. (2) Thinking must have an object which exists. On these two principles all positive knowledge rests. It follows that (3) something exists; and (4) 'what is not' is not a possible object of speech or thought, so that any attempted theory must be incoherent if it involves apparent reference to anything as non-existent.

The next step, since it must be that something exists, is to consider the aggregate of all that exists, 'that which is' or 'whatever is'. Arguments relying heavily on (4) above are deployed to show that this must have certain properties. (1) It cannot come to be nor cease to be. (2) It has no gaps but is a coherent whole. (3) It is 'not deficient', hence complete and bounded, hence cannot be changed or moved, 'but remaining the same in the same and on its own it lies, and so remains steadily there'. (4) It is 'perfect from every direction, like the mass of a well-rounded ball, in equipoise every way from the middle'. Another thesis, announced but not explicitly proved, states: 'nor was it ever nor will it be, since it all is now together, one, coherent'.

There is continuing controversy about the meaning of these conclusions and about the arguments by which they are supported. The arguments are presented as compelling demonstrations of necessary truths, but they indisputably contain gaps and ambiguities. They often seem to appeal to intuitions drawn from common experience of a spatially and temporally extended world; and the words used to express the conclusions are drawn from everyday vocabulary and have spatial and temporal connotations.

The problems in the theory of Reality therefore raise the central question of Parmenides' view of ordinary experience. This is perhaps to be found in the last part of the poem, the account of 'the opinions of mortals' (of which not much survives), and in occasional asides earlier. The 'opinions', as expounded by Parmenides, constitute a systematic cosmological theory (dualistic, showing interest in astronomy and biology, and traces of the ideas and interests of Pythagoras and his sect). This theory, however, is said to be undemonstrable, 'deceptive', and based on a mistake. Yet it is also described as 'likely' and 'reliable', and as the best of its kind. The 'mistake' or 'deception' therefore is not that of taking the false for the true but of taking the unprovable for the true; and it is a purely theoretical mistake, with no practical consequences.

On this reading, Parmenides does not deny the reality of the ordinary world, but denies only the possibility of knowledge about it. It must therefore be identified, not

with Reality, but with some non-essential aspect of it. The logical exploration of Reality reveals, then, its essential and ascertainable structure. This structure can hardly be spatio-temporal, if that implies some real connection with the spatial and temporal relationships of ordinary experience. For Parmenides denies the applicability of the past and future tenses to Reality, so that temporal succession must be an illusion. Likewise, ordinary spatial perspectives, and therefore all ordinary spatial intuitions, are presumably no certain guides. If Reality is 'bounded' and 'spherically symmetrical', the words must be understood in transferred senses, indicating that Reality is essentially complete, definite, and without differences of aspect.

If Reality is known by human thought, it would seem that that thought too cannot be purely superficial but must find a place within the essential structure of Reality. Cryptically, Parmenides says that 'you will not find thinking apart from what is, in which it [thinking] is made manifest'. This may indicate an idealist conclusion: that Reality is itself a thinking thing, and the object of its own thought.

E.L.H.

A. H. Coxon, *The Fragments of Parmenides* (Assen, 1986).

A. P. D. Mourelatos, *The Route of Parmenides* (New Haven, Conn., 1970).

G. E. L. Owen, 'Eleatic Questions', *Classical Quarterly* (1960).

parsimony, law of: *see* Ockham's razor.

partiality and impartiality. Moral philosophers with widely different outlooks, including Kantians and utilitarians, have argued that impartiality is an important, or even constitutive, element in moral thinking. Some dissidents, however, suggest that this ideal is defective, and that partiality, in some cases, is morally permissible, or even desirable. But disagreement about what impartiality requires threatens this debate with collapse.

Impartiality enjoins us, at the least, to give equal consideration to all persons in our moral thinking. Nepotism, which favours one's relatives, violates the requirement. But does impartiality demand that we *treat* everyone equally? Partialists often insist that relational facts can sometimes justify different treatment: we invite friends rather than strangers to parties, and we take our own children, excluding others, on holiday. In response, impartialists claim that their requirement comes into play at a more fundamental level. Relational facts may be granted relevance, so long as the principles we adopt can *themselves* be impartially endorsed (I must allow, in caring especially for my children, that others may care for theirs).　S.D.R.

*equality; justice.

Ethics, 101, no. 4 (July 1991), contains a symposium on Impartiality and Ethical Theory.

particular proposition. In *traditional logic propositions construed as having the form 'Some S are P' or 'Some S are not P' were called particular and contrasted with the universal forms 'All S are P' and 'No S are P'. In *predicate calculus, propositions like 'Some men are mortal' are regarded as having existential import and represented as 'There is an *x* such that *x* is *S* and *x* is *P*', which may be symbolized as '∃*x*(*Sx* & *Px*)'. c.w.

P. F. Strawson, *Introduction to Logical Theory* (London, 1952), chs. 6, 7.

particulars and non-particulars. Particulars are normally contrasted with *universals, the former being instances of the latter—as a particular apple is an instance of the universal, or kind, *apple*. Particulars (in this broad sense) may be concrete, existing in space and time—as does a particular apple—or they may be abstract, as in the case of mathematical particulars like sets. (Sometimes, however, the term 'abstract particular' is used to denote what is otherwise known as a particularized quality or individual property, such as the redness of this apple.)

Some philosophers, notably P. F. Strawson, draw a distinction between particulars and *individuals*. On this view, some but not all individuals are particulars, though all particulars are individuals—particulars being spatio-temporally existing individuals governed by determinate criteria of *identity. Amongst 'non-particulars' Strawson lists such items as properties, numbers, propositions, and facts. E.J.L.

P. F. Strawson, *Individuals: An Essay in Descriptive Metaphysics* (London, 1959).

Pascal, Blaise (1623–62). A near contemporary of *Descartes, Pascal played a considerable role in the scientific revolution of the early modern period, and his achievements included inventing the first mathematical calculator, and establishing the possibility of a vacuum. He is best known for his religious writings, which began after his *nuit de feu* ('night of fire') on 23 November 1654, when he had a powerful conversion experience. Pascal rejected conventional philosophical 'proofs' of God's existence, maintaining that the nature and existence of God were beyond the power of human reason to establish; instead, God was the 'God of Abraham, Isaac and Jacob, not the God of the philosophers', and had to be approached via a living tradition of faith.

Pascal is famous for his 'wager' argument, which is not a demonstration of God's existence, but a 'pragmatic argument'—an attempt to show it is rational to set about becoming a religious believer; for if there is a God, the believer can look forward to an 'infinity of happy life', while if there is no God, nothing of significant value will have been lost. In order to acquire belief, Pascal recommends that we embark on a course of praxis, such as regularly going to church, which 'in the natural course of events will make you believe'. J.COT.

Blaise Pascal, *Pensées* [*c.*1660], ed. L. Lafuma (Paris, 1962); English tr. A. J. Krailsheimer (Harmondsworth, 1966).

A. J. Krailsheimer, *Pascal* (Oxford, 1980).

Ward E. Jones, 'Religious Conversion, Self-Deception and Pascal's Wager', *Journal of the History of Philosophy*, 36 no. 2 (April 1998).

Pascal's wager. An argument for the rationality of believing in God, assuming that no satisfactory evidence is available. Pascal argues that the expected value of theistic belief is vastly greater than that of unbelief, since if one believes, and commits oneself to a life of faith in God etc., and it turns out to be true, then one wins an enormous good (Heaven etc.). But if one believes, and it turns out to be false, then one has lost little, if anything. Therefore (unless the probability of God's existence is infinitesimal), it is rational to adopt theistic belief and the corresponding mode of life. G.I.M.

William James, *The Will to Believe* (New York, 1897).
Blaise Pascal, *Pensées*, tr. H. F. Stewart (London, 1950).

passion and emotion in the history of philosophy. The term 'passion' has a long and convoluted history, both in and out of philosophy. Aristotle used the term *pathé* (plural) to refer to such things as 'anger, fear, pity, and the like' which lead to 'one's condition becoming so transformed that his judgment is affected, accompanied by pleasure and pain' (*Rhetoric*). Aristotle's analysis of anger included a distinctive cognitive component, a specified social context, a behavioural tendency, and physical arousal. (He had little to say of 'feeling'.) He insisted that having the right passions was essential to the virtuous life.

The Stoics, too, took an interest in emotion on the way to forming their ethics. But whereas Aristotle took emotion to be essential to the good life, the Stoics analysed emotions as conceptual errors, conducive only to misery. Passions are mistaken judgements about the world and one's place in it. In the Middle Ages, passions remained central to concerns in religion and ethics, especially matters of faith and sinfulness. Aquinas distinguished between the higher and the lower passions, faith and love among the former, greed, lust, anger, envy, and pride among the latter. So, too, in Buddhism, there were important distinctions between desirable aesthetic *rasas* (e.g. the erotic) and ordinary agitating *klesas* (e.g. lust).

Descartes summarized a good deal of his philosophy in his treatise *The Passions of the Soul*, where he insisted that the passions involve the interaction of mind and body in an undeniable way. A passion is both physiology (the agitation of the 'animal spirits'), a 'perception which we relate to our soul', and an attitude toward the world. Hatred, for example, 'arises from the perception of an object's potential harmfulness and involves a desire to avoid it'. But Descartes also uses the term 'emotion', as did Spinoza and Hume after him, to refer to the move unruly passions. That term, which has all but replaced 'passion' as the general term for the various phenomena grouped together by Aristotle, did not receive its current broad meaning until the mid-nineteenth century with the psychologizing of the field. Today, 'emotion' is the category term, and 'passion' is reserved for an overwhelming and all-absorbing emotion or desire.

The psychological maturity of the concept of emotion is marked Charles Darwin's 1872 treatise *On the Expression of Emotion in Animals and Men*, and William James' seminal essay 'What is an Emotion?', of 1884. Darwin pointed out the continuity between humans and their near kin in the mammalian world, and James urged a somewhat reductive understanding of emotion as the sensations that accompany physiological disturbances caused by upsetting perceptions. The recent history of interest in emotion has been largely framed by reactions to James and a renewed defence of physiology-based (or neurology-based) theories of emotion. Jean-Paul Sartre is one of those who reacted to James. In a 'phenomenological' analysis of emotion, he argued that emotions are 'magical transformations of the world'—strategies for coping with a difficult world.   R.C.SOL.

Thomas Dixon, *From Passions to Emotions* (Cambridge, 2003).
Susan James, *Passion and Action* (Oxford, 1997).
Robert C. Solomon, *Not Passion's Slave* (Oxford, 2003).

passions, reason as the slave of the: *see* reason as the slave of the passions.

past: *see* time.

paternalism. The power and authority one person or institution exercises over another to confer benefits or prevent harm for the latter regardless of the latter's informed consent. Paternalism is thus a threat to autonomy as well as to liberty and privacy. On any normative theory, however, paternalism is desirable toward young children, the mentally ill, and others similarly situated. Liberals invariably seek to limit paternalism to the minimum; their criterion is whether a fully rational person informed of all the relevant facts would consent to the intervention—as might be presumed of an unconscious accident victim whose life is at risk—on the ground that the current paternalism would protect or augment freedom at later stages. Under such a criterion, legal paternalism in the form of legislation that creates 'crimes without victims' (e.g. gambling, homosexuality) would be unjustified state interference with consensual private conduct among adults.   H.A.B.

*liberalism; liberty.

Joel Feinberg, *Harm to Self* (New York, 1986).
Rolf Sartorius (ed.), *Paternalism* (Minneapolis, Minn., 1983).

patriotism. Patriotism, is, unlike nationalism, a sentiment, not a doctrine. It involves love of and support for one's country, which, while etymologically one's 'fatherland', i.e. native land, may be an adoptive homeland, though not, perhaps, as the Latin motto *ubi bene ibi patria* has it, simply the place where one is well off. Yet, in classical *republicanism, by contrast with most sorts of nationalism, there is a connection between the fact that one's country benefits one and one's supposed special *obligation to love and support it. Enemies of such special obligations, like *cosmopolitans (e.g. Martha Nussbaum), thus tend to be suspicious of patriotism, while *communitarians (e.g. Alasdair MacIntyre) are more favourably disposed to it. Its bad press—'the last refuge of a scoundrel'

(Samuel Johnson), 'no patriot yet but was a fool' (Dryden)—is referable to the fact either that it may, as a sentiment, be unreasonably immoderate, or that, as Hume argued, it involves pride in what relates to oneself, which, while natural, cannot be justified to those with other attachments.   P.S.

*nationalism.

M. C. Nussbaum *et al.*, *For Love of Country* (Boston, 1996).
I. Primoratz (ed.), *Patriotism* (New York, 2002).
M. Viroli, *For Love of Country* (Oxford, 1995).

Peacocke, Christopher (1950–). Professor at New York University, formerly at Oxford, Peacocke has worked in the philosophy of mind, language, and logic, and more recently at the intersection of metaphysics and epistemology, where he has argued for a new *rationalism. In *Sense and Content* (1983) he argued that experiences have 'sensational properties': properties which are not simply a matter of how the experience represents the world to be. Subsequently he developed an account in which experiences have *non-conceptual* contents: the representational content of the perceiver's experience is not wholly determined by the concepts the perceiver possesses. Whether this claim is defensible depends on what the concepts are—and this naturally became a focus of Peacocke's work. He argues that there is no more to a concept than what is specified by an account of what it takes for a thinker to possess that concept. The theory of any given concept, then, is the theory of the possession conditions for that concept.   T.C.

C. Peacocke, *A Study of Concepts* (Cambridge, Mass., 1992).
—— *Being Known* (Oxford, 1999).
—— *The Realm of Reason* (Oxford, 2004).

Peano, Giuseppe (1858–1932). Italian mathematician, now mainly remembered for what are called 'Peano's postulates', characterizing the natural numbers. They state that 0 is a number which is not the successor of any number, that every number has just one successor which is a number, and that no two numbers have the same successor. In addition, there is the crucial postulate of mathematical induction, which ensures that the natural numbers are the *least* class containing 0 and closed under the successor function. In fact Peano took the postulates (with acknowledgement) from Dedekind, who should be counted as their author.

Peano was an important influence on Russell, and gave him the idea of deriving mathematics from logic. Much of the notation of *Principia Mathematica* is in fact based on that of Peano and his school.   D.B.

*logic, history of.

H. Wang, 'The Axiomatisation of Arithmetic', *Journal of Symbolic Logic* (1957).

Pears, David (1921–). British philosopher who has written extensively on topics in the philosophy of language and the philosophy of mind, on Wittgenstein, on Russell, and on

Hume. He was a Student of Christ Church, Oxford and has taught at the University of California, Los Angeles.

Pears is the translator, with Brian McGuinness, of Wittgenstein's *Tractatus*, and his major interest is, perhaps, in the work of Wittgenstein, both early and late. The culmination, to date, of this work, is his two-volume study of the development of Wittgenstein's philosophy, *The False Prison*. In this study Pears stresses the continuity of Wittgenstein's philosophy and emphasizes the importance of his post-*Tractatus* discussions of *solipsism and *phenomenalism to the philosophy of the *Philosophical Investigations*. The second volume also contains a lengthy discussion of the rule-following considerations and the *private language argument and an assessment of Kripke's interpretation of Wittgenstein's argument.   H.W.N.

D. Pears, *The False Prison* (Oxford, 1988).

Peirce, Charles Sanders (1839–1914). American philosopher who is perhaps best known as the originator of *pragmatism. He was educated at Harvard, where his father was a mathematics professor. His greatest philosophical influence was Kant, and he saw himself as constructing the philosophical system that Kant might have developed had he not been so ignorant of logic. But the influence of Thomas Reid and other common-sense philosophers became increasingly important: in late writings, the two influences were combined in his 'critical common-sensism'. Describing himself as a logician, Peirce made major contributions to formal logic (independently of Frege he and his students developed a logic of quantifiers and relations after 1880) and to the study of the logic of science. Indeed, he lectured on these topics at Harvard in the late 1860s and held a lectureship in logic at Johns Hopkins University from 1879 until 1884. But he also served as an experimental scientist, working at the Harvard laboratory after he had graduated in chemistry, and being employed for over twenty years by the United States Coastal Survey.

Peirce was a difficult man, widely perceived as an immoral libertine, prone to paranoia and wild mood swings, and possessing an assessment of his own intellectual powers which may have been accurate but which was sometimes accompanied by contempt for the capacities of those of lesser talents. In 1884, when confident of obtaining tenure at Johns Hopkins, information about his irregular life-style, together with suspicion of his unorthodox religious beliefs, led to his being removed from his post. From then until his death, it was understood that he could expect no orthodox academic employment: he lived precariously with his second wife in north-eastern Pennsylvania, writing extensively and giving a few important series of lectures arranged by his friend William James. He never completed the canonical statement of his philosophical position that he sought, but he published extensively and left hundreds of thousands of manuscripts; his work is gradually becoming more readily available.

Theory of Inquiry and Pragmatism. In a late paper, Peirce described himself as a 'laboratory philosopher', claiming that years of laboratory experience encouraged him, like any experimentalist, to approach all issues in the distinctive manner which comprises his pragmatism. This is clearest in the approach to epistemological matters which emerges in his earliest published work, from the 1860s and 1870s—most clearly in a series of papers in the *Popular Science Monthly* (1877–8).

His epistemological work begins from a rejection of Cartesian strategies in philosophy. They do not, he pointed out, accord with our ordinary practice of carrying out investigations: the latter is a co-operative venture, while Descartes suggests that a responsible investigator should carry out a solitary investigation of his or her cognitive standing. Ordinary inquiry takes for granted all the propositions we find certain as we begin the inquiry, while Descartes's sceptical arguments prompt philosophical doubt about what occasions no real doubt. And ordinary inquiry is impressed by the number and variety of the arguments supporting a conclusion, while the Cartesian requires a single indubitable train of reasoning to ground any belief. Peirce proposes to begin from our everyday and scientific experience of inquiry, and to investigate the norms which govern cognition on that basis.

The first paper of the series suggests that inquiry begins only when one of our previously settled beliefs is disturbed, and it is ended as soon as we have a new answer to the question that concerns us: the aim of inquiry is to replace doubt by settled belief. What methods should we use if we are to carry out our inquiries well? He considers four, the first three being devised to bring to light the key features of the fourth. (1) The method of tenacity requires us to choose any answer, and to take all means necessary to maintain it; (2) the method of authority requires us to defer to an authority and accept whatever the authority requires (it may be no accident that Peirce wrote soon after the bull of papal infallibility had been promulgated); and (3) the a priori method requires us to go by what seems agreeable to reason. It will be no surprise that these methods fail: the second has the advantage over the first that our beliefs will escape the constant buffeting of disputes from those who have decided differently, but we are still likely to meet those who accept a different authority, and our own authority will not be able to settle matters about everything. So fixation of belief must be independent of will or human choice. The third method secures that, but it is likely to make belief a matter of fashion: selection of belief still has a subjective basis. Hence we should adopt (4) the 'method of science', which holds that 'there are Real things, whose characters are entirely independent of our opinions about them; those realities affect our senses according to regular laws, and, though our sensations are as different as our relations to the objects, yet, by taking advantage of the laws of perception, we can ascertain by reasoning how things really are'.

Peirce probably believed that this claim was a presupposition of inquiry and that we should adopt only such methods as were in accord with it. The remainder of the series of papers offers a more detailed account of what this method involves: Peirce was one of the first philosophers to arrive at a satisfactory understanding of statistical reasoning, and this is central to his account of science. He is a 'contrite fallibilist': any of our current certainties might turn out to be mistaken, but relying upon them will not prevent our making cognitive progress; any errors will emerge with time.

The 'pragmatist principle' forms part of this theory of inquiry, and was elaborated in the second paper of the series, 'How to Make Our Ideas Clear'. When William James won notoriety for pragmatism, crediting it to Peirce, the latter renamed his principle *'pragmaticism'. It is a rule for clarifying the content of concepts and hypotheses, and is supposed to reveal all features of the meaning of concepts and hypotheses that are relevant to scientific investigations. Suppose I wish to test whether a sample before me is sodium. In the light of my knowledge of sodium, I can predict that if it is sodium then, if I were to drop it into hot water, it would ignite: I make predictions about the consequences of actions if the hypothesis is true. Peirce expresses his principle: 'Consider what effects, which might conceivably have practical bearings, we conceive the object of our conception to have. Then our conception of those effects is the whole of our conception of the object.' When I have listed *all* the predictions I would make about the consequences of my actions if the substance were sodium, I have a complete clarification of my understanding of the hypothesis: nothing which could be relevant to testing it scientifically has been omitted.

As well as showing its value in clarifying hypotheses, and arguing that it can be used to dismiss some metaphysical 'hypotheses' as empty, Peirce illustrates the value of his pragmatism by clarifying our conception of truth and reality. If a proposition is true, then anyone who investigated the matter long enough and well enough would eventually acknowledge its truth: truth is a matter of long-term convergence of opinion. 'The opinion which is fated to be ultimately agreed upon by all who investigate, is what we mean by the truth, and the object represented in this opinion is the real.' Although the principle bears a superficial resemblance to the *verification principle of the later Logical Positivists, there are important differences. First, there is no suggestion that, in clarifying our conception, we list only those conditional expectations that are analytic or true by definition: Peirce expects the content of a conception or hypothesis to develop as our scientific knowledge advances. And, second, as he developed his philosophical position, he insisted that the principle could only be taken seriously by someone who shared his realism about natural necessity: the conceptual clarifications are expressed as subjunctive *conditionals ('would-bes'); and such conditionals report real facts about the world.

System. Peirce's logic is a theory of cognitive norms: methods of inquiry, standards of inference, rules for identifying plausible hypotheses, principles for clarifying meanings, and so on. He was unsatisfied with the kind of grounding he provided for cognitive norms in the papers just discussed, and his attempts to correct the Kantian framework were directed at remedying this. His sophisticated *architectonic approach to philosophy rested upon a classification of the sciences. Logic was the least fundamental of three normative sciences, being a special application a system of norms initially developed in ethics and aesthetics. All of these investigations made use of a system of *categories, a correction of Kant's system, which was defended through a kind of phenomenological investigation. And these philosophical and phenomenological inquiries used mathematical methods to study experience and reality, mathematics being the only discipline which had, and needed, no foundations. So Peirce's later work developed a highly sophisticated account of how we can have knowledge of cognitive or logical norms.

His system of categories is most easily understood from the perspective of his logic of relations. Properties and relations can be classified according to the number of relata they have: ' . . . is blue' is a *one*-place predicate, ' . . . respects . . . ' is a dyadic, *two*-place relation, and ' . . . gives . . . to . . . ' is a triadic, *three*-place relation. Peirce argued that a language adequate for scientific or descriptive purposes must contain terms of all these three kinds, but that there are no phenomena which can only be described in a language which contains expressions for four-place relations. Thus he classified phenomena and elements of reality numerically: according to whether they are forms of *firstness*, *secondness*, or (like giving) *thirdness*. The irreducibility of thirdness is, he thinks, a distinctive part of his philosophical outlook, something which allies him with realist philosophers in opposition to nominalism. In early work, his defence of his categories was largely found in his work on formal logic, but later he turned to phenomenology: reflection on experience of all kinds was to convince us that triadicity was ineliminable but that no more complex phenomena were involved in experience.

Thus we are aware that our experiences have raw qualitative characters which do not directly involve relations with other things: they exhibit firstness. They also stand in relations to each other, interacting against one another and so on: this involves secondness, as when fire immediately follows our dropping the sodium in hot water. But we are aware that this interaction is intelligible, it is 'mediated': we can bring it down into a continuous spread of small changes which go together to make up the big one; and we are aware that it conforms to a law. Finding it intelligible introduces thirdness: we understand the two elements of the interaction by reference to a third mediating fact. The aim of inquiry, for Peirce, is to find the thirdness (law and pattern) in the manifold of sensory experiences that we undergo. The norms employed by the scientific method are to be vindicated by showing how they provide means for finding more and more pattern and mediation (more and more thirdness) in the world of our experience.

Signs. According to Peirce, the most important forms of thirdness involve *meaning and representation, and all of his work is underpinned by a sophisticated theory of meaning: his semiotics. He probably believed that every-thing was a sign, but the signs of most interest to him were thoughts and 'the assertions of a scientific intelligence'. This theory of meaning ('speculative grammar') was to provide foundations for his writings in logic.

The key to the thirdness involved in signs was Peirce's notion of *interpretation*. A *sign denotes an object only by being understood or interpreted as standing for an object: and this interpretation will always be another sign with the same object. Semiotics is thus primarily a theory of understanding, an account of how we are guided and constrained in arriving at interpretations of signs. Interpretation often involves inference, developing our understanding of the object in question. Thus my under-standing of your assertion that you are tired may be manifested in my thinking that you want me to believe you are tired, in my believing you are tired, in my expect-ing you to fall asleep, in my offering you a cup of coffee, and so on. The interpreting thought mediates between the sign and its object.

Peirce was famous for his classifications of signs, and some of his terminology has acquired wide currency. For example, signs can be distinguished according to the fea-tures of them exploited in arriving at an interpretation. A symbol denotes a particular object because there exists a practice of interpreting it as denoting that object; an index denotes an object to which it stands in a direct existential relation; the conventions governing the use of ordinary indexical expressions such as 'this' do not fix the reference unaided but rather guide us in interpreting it as an index. And iconic signs share some feature with their object which each could possess if the other did not exist: maps are straightforward examples, the conventions governing their use fixing how we are to interpret them as icons. Mathematical and logical symbolisms are iconic represen-tations, and it was important for Peirce that sentences of natural languages have iconic elements too: formal infer-ence exploits the fact that sentences exhibit a form which is shared with their subject-matter. Much of Peirce's later work attempted to use this systematic theory of meaning to provide a proof of the pragmatist principle.

Science itself is a process of sign interpretation. And Peirce's account of scientific reasoning has some import-ant elements. As mentioned above, Peirce models all inductive reasoning on statistical sampling: quantitative induction involves attempting to estimate the chance of a member of a population having a particular property; and qualitative induction tests hypotheses by sampling their consequences. He denies that induction ever establishes that a conclusion is true or even probable. Rather, the practice of inductive testing is justified because continued use of it will eventually lead us to converge on the correct value for the chance of a member of the population having the property in question. The pragmatist principle teaches that *probability is a *propensity: if the chance of a coin coming up heads is 0.43, then, if we were to continue to toss it fairly, the proportion of times on which it comes up heads *would* converge on 0.43.

The logic of *abduction is a logic of discovery: it studies how we are guided in constructing new hypotheses from the ruins of defeated ones; and it examines the norms guid-ing us in deciding which hypotheses are worth testing. All scientific activity is grounded in the hope that the universe is intelligible, and intelligible to us. And we are to take ser-iously no hypothesis that 'blocks the road of inquiry', forc-ing us to accept regularities as brute or inexplicable. It is connected to this that Peirce espouses 'synechism', the doctrine that we are to expect the universe to display con-tinuities rather than discontinuities. Peirce contributed to the mathematical analysis of continuity, exploiting his ideas about the logic of relations and trying to use it as the basis of his realism about natural necessity: continuity is 'ultimate mediation'. The logic of abduction advises us to favour theories that posit continuities over those that allow for brute unmediated discontinuities.

Metaphysics. Although Peirce envisaged that pragmatism would eliminate 'ontological metaphyics', he claimed that scientific progress demanded that we construct a 'scien-tific metaphysics'. Supposedly this was an empirical discip-line, differing from the special sciences in using no sophisticated techniques of experiment and observation: it was 'coenoscopic', relying only on familiar everyday observations which are surprising only because their familiarity prevents our noticing them. In part, it was an attempt to describe how the world must be if science was to be possible—if there were to be no inexplicable phe-nomena, if 'realism' was to be true, if the three categories were to be as Peirce suggested. And in part it was an exer-cise in 'descriptive metaphysics': drawing out features of our everyday conception of mind or matter (for example) can be a valuable corrective to unthinking theoretical prejudices, especially in psychology.

Two elements of this metaphysics are especially inter-esting. Peirce defended an evolutionary *cosmology, explaining how the world of existing things and law-governed behaviour evolved from pure possibility. Offer-ing an evolutionary explanation of law, he argued, was the only alternative to asserting that fundamental laws are simply true, with no explanation of why they obtain being available. If every regularity must have an explanation, we avoid a regress of ever more general and abstract laws by invoking a historical explanation. And Peirce's account of how this evolutionary process works leads to a form of objective idealism according to which matter is 'effete mind', and physical phenomena are modelled on thought and sign interpretation rather than the mental being reduced to the physical. This is because a 'realist' account of law involves finding 'mediation' in the natural world, and sign interpretation is our best model of mediation.

Secondly, it may accord with the importance he attached to statistical reasoning in science that he accepted *tychism*, the thesis that there is absolute chance, that the universe is not wholly governed by determinist laws. This partly reflects his understanding of the importance of statistical laws in science, and his understanding that observation could never establish that laws were so exact as never to permit slight deviations. He also supposed it was required to explain the evolutionary process discussed in his cosmology: without appeal to such 'chance spontaneity', he doubted that we could make sense of growth and increasing complexity.   c.j.h.

*fallibilism.

J. Brent, *Charles Sanders Peirce: A Life* (Bloomington, Ind., 1993).

M. Fisch, *Peirce, Semeiotic and Pragmatism* (Bloomington, Ind., 1986).

N. Hauser and C. Kloesel (eds.), *The Essential Peirce* (Bloomington, Ind., 1992).

C. J. Hookway, *Peirce* (London, 1985).

C. Kloesel *et al.* (eds.), *Writings of Charles S. Peirce: A Chronological Edition* (Bloomington, Ind., 1982–).

C. Misak (ed.), *The Cambridge Companion to Peirce* (Cambridge, 2004).

C. S. Peirce, *Reasoning and the Logic of Things* (Cambridge, Mass., 1992).

Pelagius (*fl.* 400). British theologian. Settled at Rome, he enjoyed a following of high-born Christian rigorists, to whom he taught that perfection is possible. When he fled to Palestine via Africa before the impending sack of Rome by the Visi-goths in 410, Augustine, apprised of his teachings, accused him of denying *original sin and the need for grace. Pelagianism is the doctrine that without God's aid men are 'able to fulfil the divine commands', or at least (semi-Pelagianism) to 'believe, will, desire, try'. Both versions are ambiguous between denying that the powers of good acting or willing must be granted by God and denying that the exercise of those powers must be helped or caused by God. The doctrines were anathematized in the fifth and sixth centuries, and again by the Council of Trent (1545–63), agreeing in this with Luther and Calvin.   c.a.k.

B. R. Rees, *Pelagius: A Reluctant Heretic* (Woodbridge, 1988).

Penelope's wooers.

> Aristippus said that those that studied particular sciences, and neglected philosophy, were like Penelope's wooers, that made love to the waiting women.
>
>   Francis Bacon, *Apophthegmes*
>   *New and Old* (London, 1625).

This aphorism could mean either that any study other than philosophy is only indulged in because of inability to succeed at philosophy, or that those frustrated in reaching satisfactory philosophical conclusions scientize the subject. The tendency of Logical Positivists to do the latter led Wittgenstein to accuse them of not really doing philosophy, and he would probably say the same of today's *cognitive-science philosophers. Despite his dogmatic-sounding strictures, however, he himself produced a new way of philosophizing.   j.o'g.

*Logical Positivism.

people. The whole body of enfranchised or qualified citizens, generally linked by a common language and history,

considered in democratic theory as the ultimate source of political *authority. The general slogan that political authority derives from the people is compatible with a large number of modes in which the will or consent of the people is made known to the political authority, and it is compatible with despotic as well as liberal forms of government. For example, according to Hobbes, individuals covenant with each other to submit their wills to the will of one who is thereby authorized to act on their behalf. The authority of this Leviathan therefore derives from the people, but it is an absolute and potentially despotic authority. Locke, on the other hand, grants the people power to alter the legislature when it acts contrary to the trust they have placed in it. Burke recommends yet another form of representation of the people—one in which there is a communion of interests and a sympathy in feelings and desires. This 'virtual representation' of a *'natural aristocracy' does not attach importance to a universal franchise. In the nineteenth century the idea of 'the people' became identified in philosophers such as Hegel with 'the nation'. The spirit of the people became a mystical entity, or *Volkgeist*, which identified and unified a nation.   r.s.d.

*democracy.

G. H. Sabine, *A History of Political Theory* (London, 1937).

perception. The extraction and use of information about one's environment (exteroception) and one's own body (proprioception). The external senses—sight, hearing, touch, smell, and taste—though overlapping to some extent, are distinguished primarily by the kind of information they convey (e.g. about light, pressure, sound, and temperature). Proprioception concerns stimuli arising within, and carrying information about, one's own body: acceleration, position and orientation of limbs, and so on.

Perception is of either things or facts. Seeing an object or an event (both count as things for this classification), a cat on the sofa, a man on the street, an eclipse, or a robbery, does not require that the object or event be identified or recognized in any particular way (perhaps, though this is controversial, in any way whatsoever). One can see a cat on the sofa and mistake it for a rumpled sweater; see a man (in camouflage or at a distance, for instance) and take him for a tree. People have believed all manner of superstitious things about the eclipses they observed. Seeing objects and events is, in this sense, non-epistemic: one can see O without knowing or believing that it is O. Perceiving facts, on the other hand, is epistemic: one cannot see that there is a cat on the sofa without, thereby, coming to know that there is a cat on the sofa. Seeing a fact is coming to know (that this is a fact) in some visual way. Smelling a fact (e.g. that the toast is burning) is coming to know this fact in an olfactory way. In this way, then, thing-perception is cognitively less demanding than fact-perception. Both the dog and the cook can smell the burning toast (a thing), but unless it is a very smart dog (or a very dumb cook), only the cook will be able to smell, thereby coming to know (the fact), that the toast is burning.

Other ways of describing what we perceive are variations on these two themes. In seeing *where* he went, *when* he left, *who* went with him, and *how* he was dressed we are describing the perception of some fact without revealing exactly what fact it is. One cannot see where he went unless one sees some fact about where he went—that (for instance) he went to the attic. We often describe what facts we have observed (e.g. that Judy was at the ball-game) by mentioning only the thing we observed (Judy) and where we observed it (at the ball-game). What we end up explicitly saying (that we saw Judy at the game) is non-epistemic (we could see Judy at the game without ever recognizing her, without ever knowing that she was at the game) although what we normally succeed in communicating by this form of words (this is called a conversational implication) is something epistemic: that we saw (i.e. came to know by seeing) *that* Judy was at the game.

A great deal of perception (of both things and facts) is indirect. We perceive things on television, in the movies, and on records. One sees that the gas tank is empty by seeing not the gas tank, but the gas gauge and the fact that it reads 'empty'. This gives rise to questions about whether there are objects, and facts about those objects, that are seen directly. Direct realists believe that physical objects (some of them anyway) and certain facts (though not all facts) about these objects are seen in some direct, unmediated fashion. One does not see the cup (nor the fact that it is a cup) by perceiving, in some more direct manner, an internal object (a cup-ish *sense-datum) and certain facts about this datum (e.g. that it resembles a coffee-cup). A *representative theory of perception denies this—taking sense-data as the primary objects, and facts about sense-data as the basic facts, of perception. F.D.

*body; content, non-conceptual; Honderich.

R. Chisholm, *Perceiving: A Philosophical Study* (Ithaca, NY, 1957).
F. Dretske, *Seeing and Knowing* (Chicago, 1969).
T. Gendler and J. Hawthorne (eds.), *Perceptual Experience* (Oxford, 2005).
H. H. Price, *Perception* (London, 1932).

perception, representative theory of: *see* representative theory of perception.

perception, veil of: *see* veil of perception.

percepts. The subjective *experience accompanying *perception of objects and events. Percepts are ordinarily distinguished from *sensations or *sense-data in being cognitively enriched by past experience and memory and by the constancy mechanisms (for shape, size, colour, etc.) that make our experience correspond more closely to the objective state of affairs (the distal stimulus) than to conditions at the sensory surfaces (proximal stimulus). Sense-data of round pennies (seen at an oblique angle) may be elliptical, but in normal viewing conditions the percept is supposed to correspond to the known shape (round) of the penny. F.D.

R. Firth, 'Sense-Data and the Percept Theory', *Mind* (1949–50).

perfectionism. The view that promotion of human excellence is one of the factors that should be weighed in judging the political and social worth of a society. Much recent discussion is keyed to the treatment in John Rawls's *A Theory of Justice*. Rawls lumped together thinkers as different as Aristotle and Nietzsche as perfectionists. The rejection of perfectionism follows from Rawls's stipulation that in the *'original position' designers of the political and social order do not have a 'conception of the good'. Any case for perfectionism must contain two elements. One is an argument that some forms of human activity or experience have special value. The other is that a policy of furthering this special value should play a part in some aspects of our conduct toward others, including some social and political decisions. An extreme perfectionism could be used to justify élitist social attitudes, but a moderate perfectionism might merely argue that governments should spend modest amounts of tax money on support for the arts and for the kinds of scientific research that are most unlikely to have practical applications.

J.J.K.

A representative modern perfectionism is to be found in Hastings Rashdall, *The Theory of Good and Evil* (Oxford, 1907).

performative utterances: *see* linguistic acts.

performing arts. The performing arts include music, theatre, opera, dance, mime, and so on. What distinguishes them as a group is the fact of human performance being involved in the end-stage products of the art. In such art-forms, what we appreciate directly and what we importantly critically attend to are concrete performances; and in so far as there are works in such art-forms, they are conceived as works *for* performance. Performing arts thus contrast with arts such as painting, sculpture, etching, and the novel, where the primary product is an object that does not stand in need of performance in order to be experienced directly by a public. Performing arts are all temporal arts, in the sense that performances and experiences of them are necessarily extended in time, but not all temporal arts are performing arts. The art of film provides an obvious exception: films are screened, over a period *of* time, but they are not performed. The genres of tape music, computer music, and electro-acoustic music are additional examples of temporal yet non-performing arts, since their presentation does not involve human performance.

Within the performing arts an important distinction is between art-forms that involve the creation of repeatable *works*, defined by scripts, scores, or other notational artefacts, and ones not involving works, but instead performances devised on the spot, or improvised, on every occasion. In the former case it is common to think of the work defined by a notation as a kind of abstract object—a *type*—whose performances are thus instances—or *tokens*—of that type. Again, though most performing arts involve instantiable types, it is not true that all arts involving instantiable types are performing arts; witness the arts of poetry, photography, and cinema.

One important issue about the performing arts concerns the matter of the *authenticity* of performances, usually construed as something more than mere correctness, and covering matters such as conformity to the intentions of artists, to antecedent performing traditions, or to the historical contexts of creation of works. A second important issue concerns the role of *interpretation* in performance, and what the relationship is between such performative interpretation and the more straightforward sort of interpretation—critical interpretation—involved in criticism.   J.LEV.

Stephen Davies, *Musical Works and Performances* (Oxford, 2001).

Peter Kivy, *Authenticities: Philosophical Reflections on Musical Performance* (Ithaca, NY, 1995).

Paul Thom, *For an Audience: A Philosophy of the Performing Arts* (Philadelphia, 1993).

Peripatetics. This is the name given, first, to philosophers who worked in the school founded by Aristotle (the Lyceum or Peripatos), and, secondly, to later philosophers who commented on and interpreted his writings. Notable members of the first group are Theophrastus (371–287) and Strato (c.335–270), as well as Eudemus and Aristoxenus; of the second, Aristocles of Messene, Aspasius (second century AD), and above all Alexander of Aphrodisias (early third century AD). Peripatetics were characteristically scientists or scholars, rather than philosophers. That stance reflects Aristotle's division of inquiry into autonomous specialisms for which he claims to have completed, in main outline, the philosophical foundations. But it ignores the tentative and dialectical character of the philosophical originator of the Peripatos.   J.D.G.E.

There is no satisfactory study of the Peripatetics in English; but for Theophrastus, see W. W. Fortenbaugh *et al.*, *Theophrastus of Eresus*, 2 vols. (Leiden, 1992).

perlocutions: *see* linguistic acts.

Perry, Ralph Barton (1876–1957), a leading figure in the movement of American *New Realism and the editor of its manifesto (1912). Perry occupied the most extreme position among his fellow realists—he was purest of the pure. He agreed with James' neutral monism and negative answer to the question 'Does consciousness exist?', and tried to explain perception without duplicating objects, some of whose configurations were 'physical' and others were what we ordinarily take to be 'psychical'. In *General Theory of Value* (1926), written after the steam had gone out of New Realism, he gave a naturalistic account of values, defining value as 'any object of any interest'. By virtue of his long tenure at Harvard, along with his colleague C. I. Lewis, he did much to professionalize philosophical teaching and research. His biography of William James won the Pulitzer Prize in 1936.   L.W.B.

Bruce Kuklick, *The Rise of American Philosophy* (New Haven, Conn., 1977), pts. 3 and 4.

R. B. Perry, *Present Philosophical Tendencies* (New York, 1912).

persecution of philosophers. Even the most unworldly of intellectual disciplines has never been able to divorce itself entirely from the worldly conflict which determines the course of human history. Philosophy was born into a society dominated by revolution and counter-revolution, and the earliest of its great exponents, Socrates, was executed because his teachings, it was said, corrupted the young. Modern philosophy originated in an era no less revolutionary, and some of its leading exponents were exposed to similar dangers.

Unused to having their own ideas taken seriously, philosophers today may be surprised to learn that the Parliament of the time regarded the doctrines of Thomas Hobbes (1588–1679) as a probable cause of the Great Fire of 1666. Safely dead, Hobbes is the greatest of British philosophers; alive and kicking, he was dangerous to know, and those in charge of the universities were not distracted by the notion of academic freedom from persecuting anyone who sympathized with his 'lewd, scandalous and immoral doctrine'. In 1668 Daniel Scargill was deprived of a fellowship at Corpus Christi College and expelled from Cambridge for being 'an Hobbist and an Atheist'. Scargill was promised in 1669 that he could return if he delivered a public recantation: two drafts of this were rejected; in the third, the unfortunate Scargill confessed to having been an agent of the Devil, but he was never restored to his fellowship and was obliged to live in extreme poverty.

The hostility of more orthodox thinkers was aroused above all by the intellectual ruthlessness with which Hobbes insisted that all divine authority must reflect earthly power. Nothing is more binding than the word of God: this Hobbes would be the first to allow. But, he argued, the word of God, like all words, may be interpreted in rival ways. What counts as an authoritative interpretation must therefore depend on the power of those capable of enforcing it.

Benedict de Spinoza (1634–77) shared with Hobbes the honour of being regarded by all respectable persons with the horror of 'atheism' which is matched by the horror of 'communism' in the twentieth century. Educated in the rabbinical tradition, Spinoza broke with Judaism: he was formally anathematized in 1656, and it is reliably reported that an attempt was made on his life. Like Socrates, he took no payment from his pupils: 'mischief', said one of his biographers, 'could be had from him for nothing'. Like Hobbes, he repudiated the conventional conception of God and subjected the authority of Scripture to critical scrutiny. His *Tractatus Theologico-Politicus* (1670) was prohibited by the authorities and placed on the Index of the Catholic Church.

Bertrand Russell (1872–1970) challenged conventional wisdom throughout his long life. His opposition to the First World War led to imprisonment and his being deprived of his lectureship at Trinity College, Cambridge. A decisive influence on the campaign against nuclear weapons in the 1960s, and an advocate of civil disobedience, he was also—with Jean-Paul Sartre (1905–80)—a leading light in the International War Crimes Tribunal investigating American atrocities in Vietnam. His book *Marriage and Morals* (1929) was cited as evidence of his depravity when he was deprived of the professorship he had been offered at the City College of New York in 1940. La Guardia, the Mayor of New York, described Russell as 'an ape of genius, the devil's minister of men'. An application was made to the State Supreme Court to compel the Board of Education to rescind the appointment. Russell, the Court was told, should be regarded 'not a philosopher in the accepted meaning of the word' but as someone who 'by cunning contrivances, tricks and devices and by mere quibbling . . . puts forth fallacious arguments and arguments that are not supported by sound reasoning', an advocate of everything 'lecherous, libidinous, lustful, venerous, erotomaniac, aphrodisiac, irreverent, narrow-minded, untruthful, and bereft of moral fibre'. Russell, it was added, also 'winks at homosexuality'.

It would honour the profession if it could be said only that philosophers have been persecuted; but the truth is that, if philosophers have been among the hunted, they have also been among the hunters. Hobbes's contemporary Ralph Cudworth was a philosopher too, but he was also Master of Corpus Christi: when Scargill was expelled, Cudworth's name was on the expulsion order. Spinoza's contemporary Leibniz, a great philosopher in his own right, must surely have recognized Spinoza's greatness; but he pretended otherwise. Russell's contemporary J. M. E. McTaggart thought that 'academic freedom is very precious and fragile', but he also argued for Russell's removal from Trinity: 'it is quite different', McTaggart said, 'when he had done something the law pronounced to be a crime'.

M.C.
C.W.

R. W. Clark, *The Life of Bertrand Russell* (London, 1975).
S. I. Mintz, *The Hunting of Leviathan* (Cambridge, 1962).

persistence through time. That something continues to exist from one moment to the next has been seen by some philosophers as requiring explanation. Each point in *time, they say, is 'logically independent': from the fact that anything exists at a particular time, it does not follow that it must exist at some later time. Hence, if an object persists through time, this must have some cause. Descartes and Spinoza both hold, though in significantly different ways, that God is the cause, the former presenting this as a proof of God's existence. Leibniz relies on the same considerations to argue that all true propositions are analytic: if you are the same individual you used to be, he says, this can only be because your existence then and now are both essential to your nature. Hume, by contrast, argues that the very notion of an object persisting through time is a 'fiction' derived from our propensity to run into one a sequence of experiences that are essentially distinct.

C.W.

Descartes, *Third Meditation*.
Spinoza, *Ethics*, First Part, prop. XXIV.
Leibniz, *Philosophical Writings*, ed. Parkinson (London, 1973).
Hume, *A Treatise of Human Nature*, book I, sect. II.

person-affecting principles. Some moral principles evaluate choices in what Parfit calls 'person-affecting terms', which appeal to a choice's effects upon the interests of particular individuals. One choice is morally worse than another in these terms only if it is *worse for* at least some specific individual, who would have fared better given the other choice. According to Parfit, person-affecting principles at best are only part of a plausible moral theory since they fail to explain why certain choices which affect the membership, as well as interests, of *future generations are wrong. For example, if a choice between risky and safe energy policies determines both whether a catastrophe occurs and which distinct set of individuals (all with lives worth living) exists, in the distant future, then the former cannot be criticized in person-affecting terms, since there is no affected individual who would have fared better had the latter been chosen.

A.D.W.

*population.

D. Parfit, *Reasons and Persons* (Oxford, 1984), pt. 4.

personal identity. The way philosophers refer to facts about *persons which are expressed in identity judgements such as 'The person over there now is identical to the person who was there yesterday', the truth of which is a consequence of the fact that persons remain in existence over time. The problem is to say in an informative way what the necessary and sufficient conditions are for this kind of fact. These conditions are called criteria of identity for persons. A second related problem, raised by Parfit, is what importance facts about such identities should have in our evaluative thought.

No consensus on the first problem has emerged. What has proved difficult is finding a balance between the intuitions that are generated by imaginary cases, for example, brain transplants, which indicate that psychological continuities are crucial, and, by contrast, our actual practices of tracing people plus a sense of our identity as concrete substances, which seem to link us to something substantial.

Theories can be classified in various ways; one division is between those which state the criteria in psychological terms and those which do not; another, regarded as important by Parfit, is between theories which view personal identity as reducible to other continuities and those which do not; a third division is between theories which tie the person to a continuing substance, say the body, brain, or soul, and those which do not.

Locke's influential theory is of the latter sort. He proposed that persons are essentially capable of self-consciousness. Their identity should be analysed in terms of *consciousness, which is standardly interpreted as the proposal that a person is identical with whoever's exploits they remember as their own—the memory criterion. His negative thesis is that this consciousness is not necessarily tied to a body or soul.

The neo-Lockean research strategy defends a modified Lockean view. To avoid possible circularities in the use of the concept of memory they have constructed psychological concepts, which are explicitly defined without using the concept of personal identity. The psychological continuities required are weakened. The structure of the theory is more complex to deal with problems of fission.

The major alternative approach to this tradition requires the persistence of some substantial item for the person to survive. A Cartesian view is that we have non-material souls and survive so long as the particular soul does. More popular, though, are accounts according to which the continuant required must be physical. One suggestion, defended by Williams, is that the person is tied to the body. This fits our treatment of actual cases, but generates a counter-intuitive verdict when we consider imaginary ones. A related theory, developed by Wiggins, is that it is a mistake to allow, as Lockeans do, any distinction between the person and the animal. Personal identity is, on this view, a case of animal identity.

An alternative physicalist account claims that a person is tied to that (physical) item which sustains the person's basic psychological capacities, supposedly the brain. This fits certain intuitions better than bodily theories, but has difficulty explaining exactly why psychological continuities grounded in more radically non-standard ways are not also enough for the person to survive.

The difficulty of constructing a defensible theory has led to a reconsideration of the methods philosophers have employed, which has been encouraged as well by Parfit's discussion of whether personal identity matters. He argues, in various ways, that it does not, one being that brain-splitting plus transplants would give what matters to us but, because it generates two candidates, does not preserve the original person. So, he concludes, identity does not matter. Many are unhappy with Parfit's conclusion, and also wish to reconsider the method employed to reach it.

These methodological inquiries have led to no agreement, and all of the described theories are under active development.   P.F.S.

*animalism; reductionism, psychological, in personal identity.

R. Martin and J. Barresi (eds.), *Personal Identity* (Oxford, 2002).

H. Noonan, *Personal Identity* (London, 1989).

D. Parfit, *Reasons and Persons* (Oxford, 1984), esp. pt. 3.

J. Perry, *Identity, Personal Identity, and the Self* (Indianapolis, 2002).

S. Shoemaker and R. Swinburne, *Personal Identity* (London, 1984).

P. F. Snowdon, 'Persons, Animals, and Ourselves', in C. Gill (ed.), *The Person and the Human Mind* (Oxford, 1990).

personalism. As a label applied primarily to the philosophy of the French thinker Emmanuel Mounier (1905–50), a Christian version of existentialism stressing communion on the basis of shared values, with the person, as distinct from the political individual, as the locus of a 'unique vocation' directed towards fellowship. Other philosophers who have made personhood a fundamental concept include the German philosopher Rudolf Hermann Lotze (1817–81), the American idealists Josiah Royce (1855–1916) and Edgar Sheffield Brightman (1884–1953),

and the Scottish humanist, John Macmurray (1891–1976). Common to these thinkers is the view that the finite individual is somehow grounded in and seeks its fulfilment in an infinite spirit, or God, understood as personal, though Macmurray opposed idealism and considered 'God' mainly a negative concept given positive content only in actual relations among persons. Personalism in these wider senses has affinities with the process theism of Alfred North Whitehead (1861–1947) and Charles Hartshorne (1897–2000). An early exponent was the Norwegian philosopher Niels Treschow (1751–1833).   A.H.

E. S. Brightman, *Person and Reality* (New York, 1958).

J. Macmurray, *Persons in Relation* (London, 1961; repr. Amherst, NY, 1999).

E. Mounier, *Le Personnalisme* (Paris, 1949).

persons. On a purely functional view, possession of a range of specific psychological capacities is both necessary and sufficient for being a person. The characteristics in question are determinable *a priori by reference to our concept of a person. Locke's definition of a person as 'a thinking intelligent Being, that has reason and reflection, and can consider it self as it self, the same thinking thing in different times and places' is an example of a functional definition. Given this approach, there is no reason in principle why an artefact or immaterial soul should not count as a person, as long as the functional conditions are met. On the other hand, a brain-damaged human being who lacks the relevant capacities will fail to count as a person.

Descartes claimed that a person is a compound of body and soul. It has been objected that talk of immaterial souls is illegitimate because of difficulties in specifying singularity and identity conditions for them. Instead, P. F. Strawson proposes that the concept of a person is 'primitive', that is to say, it is of a type of entity such that both predicates ascribing states of consciousness and those ascribing corporeal characteristics are equally applicable to a single individual of that single type.

The most familiar examples of persons in the Strawsonian sense are human beings. Some have claimed that only human beings can be persons, or, more modestly, that persons must at least be animals of some sort. According to what David Wiggins calls the animal attribute view of persons, a person is any animal that is such by its kind as to have the biological capacity to enjoy fully an open-ended list of psychological attributes. The list of attributes is to be filled in by reference to the class of actual persons.

The animal attribute theory is, in some respects, more restrictive than a purely functional approach. It rules out non-animal persons, and does not even allow that possession of the enumerated psychological attributes is sufficient for an individual animal to count as a person; the animal must also be a *typical* member of its kind. On the other hand, the animal attribute theory is more permissive than the purely functional approach to the extent that it does not exclude from the class of persons a brain-damaged human being who has lost the psychological capacities included in the functional definition.

The most serious challenge facing the animal attribute view results from reflection about what the identity of a person consists in. If, as Locke argued, the persistence of the animal with which a person shares her matter is neither necessary nor sufficient for the persistence of the person, the person and the animal cannot be identical. For writers influenced by Locke, *personal identity is to be understood as consisting in the obtaining of various forms of psychological continuity or connectedness. This approach may be motivated both by ethical considerations and by reflection on puzzle cases. From the fact that the continuities in question are not all or nothing, some have drawn the conclusion that persons have an ontological status akin to that of clubs or nations. Another view would be that a person is what underlies her psychological capacities, namely, her brain.

In defence of his position, the 'animalist' may argue that thought experiment and conceptual analysis are not the best way of theorizing about persons and personal identity. The most reliable point of reference for an understanding of the nature of persons is what is known about the nature of *human beings, even if such an approach lays itself open to accusations of parochialism. If some of our intuitions about puzzle cases conflict with our best overall theory of persons then we may be entitled to reject those intuitions as deviant.   Q.C.

*animalism.

J. Locke, *An Essay Concerning Human Understanding* (Oxford, 1975), II. xxvii.

E. Olson, *The Human Animal: Personal Identity without Psychology* (Oxford, 1997).

D. Parfit, *Reasons and Persons* (Oxford, 1984), pt. 3.

P. F. Snowdon, 'Persons, Animals, and Ourselves', in C. Gill (ed.), *The Person and the Human Mind* (Oxford, 1990).

P. F. Strawson, *Individuals* (London, 1959), ch. 3.

D. Wiggins, *Sameness and Substance Renewed* (Cambridge, 2001), ch. 7.

perspectivism: *see* Nietzsche.

persuasive definition: *see* definition.

pessimism and optimism. The metaphysical theories that this world is, respectively, the worst and the best of all that are possible. Taken in this literal, cosmic sense—worstism and best-ism—the theories are of relatively recent date, at least in Western thought, optimism going back to the eighteenth century, pessimism to the nineteenth century. The history of the terms themselves reflect the recent growth of the theories. 'Optimisme' came into currency in France towards the middle of the eighteenth century, with the English word 'optimism' following somewhat later in the century. From the outset, the term was used to describe Leibniz's position, particularly as developed in his *Théodicée* (1710). The first recorded use of the antithetical term 'pessimism' is in a 1794 letter of Coleridge. By the 1880s it had also generally established itself as the name of a metaphysical system—that in Schopenhauer's *Die Welt als Wille und Vorstellung* (1819).

Hence there are good historical and etymological grounds for regarding—as I shall here—the metaphysical theories as embodying the primary meanings of the two terms, even though current usage is much vaguer, largely indicating a negative or positive attitude towards things. The two terms are also used more precisely and narrowly to refer to the value of human existence. In this anthropological sense, the Platonic and Aristotelian ideas of human perfectibility are taken to be optimistic; whereas statements of pessimism are to be found in the books of Ecclesiastes and Job as well as in *Oedipus at Colonus*, where Sophocles writes that 'Not to be born is the most to be desired; but having seen the light, the next best is to die as soon as possible'.

Leibniz's metaphysical optimism is based on his rationalistic theology. From the ontological argument, he knows that God, the most perfect being, exists; and such a being must have created the best of all possible worlds; hence this must be that world. Imperfections are explained as necessary for this richest compossible whole—just as shadows are required by a picture to give form to the light and colour.

For Schopenhauer, on the other hand, this world is so bad that if it were to become even slightly worse it would collapse into chaos. Any goods and pleasures are required for this compossibly worst whole. Schopenhauer's position is based on his metaphysics, although this is often overlooked by those more familiar with his popular essays than his main philosophical work. Whereas Leibniz's metaphysics is rationalistic, Schopenhauer's is empirical, based on an inner, immediate experience of our living bodies as will or desire. Hence the real, underlying nature of the world is not a most perfect being; rather it is will, feeding and preying upon itself. Desire is positive, satisfaction is the negation or suspension of desire. Hence the world is wrong, both morally and in the preponderance of pain over pleasure. Nor is there any hope that it can be rectified, since the fault lies in the substance rather than any accident or form of the world. Schopenhauer develops this thesis by drawing on Kant: the apparent orderliness, goodness, satisfaction in the world derive not from what the world is in itself, but from the structuring required to make it into a perceivable, livable world at all. Schopenhauer also draws inspiration from Buddhism and Hinduism, which he regards as essentially pessimistic religions—as opposed to Judaism and Islam, which he takes to be optimistic. Yet at times he seems to recognize that, like Christianity, most major religions contain both optimistic and pessimistic elements: they are more or less pessimistic about this world and more or less optimistic about the next or real world.

While pessimism and optimism have never been central issues in philosophy, pessimism did have some vogue in Germany towards the end of the nineteenth century, chiefly from Eduard von Hartmann's elaborate *Philosophy of the Unconscious* (Eng. tr. 1884), which develops Schopenhauer's pessimism, while trying to combine it with Hegelian elements. Anglo-American philosophers have shown little interest in the debate, apart from Sully's work (see below) and occasional witty criticism—as, for example, in William James's 'German Pessimism' (1875).

What is probably most memorable about Leibnizian optimism is its satirical rebuttal in Voltaire's *Candide* (1759). While Schopenhauer's pessimism has produced no similar satire—which is itself, perhaps, notable—it has inspired the influential reactions of Nietzsche, beginning with his *Birth of Tragedy* (1872), which largely accepts Schopenhauer's pessimism, although sublimating it through the ideal of tragic life. Yet in his later writings, Nietzsche is hostile; for while he agrees in general with Schopenhauer's description of the will, he forcefully opposes his negative, ascetic attitude towards it with a joyous affirmation.

Nietzsche's provocative views on truth can also be seen as a reaction to Schopenhauer. For while Schopenhauer was a pessimist about the world, he was an optimist about knowledge and truth; for it is through knowledge, he holds, that any good is achieved—either in transitory, will-less aesthetic contemplation, or in the insight leading to ascetic renunciation and nirvana, the highest and most lasting good. Nietzsche, in short, reverses this: he is a metaphysical optimist, but an epistemological pessimist, warning of the dangers for life of knowledge or truthfulness.   D.BER.

*life, the meaning of.

A. O. Lovejoy, *The Great Chain of Being* (Cambridge, Mass., 1936).
P. Siwek, 'Pessimism in Philosophy' and 'Optimism in Philosophy', in *The New Scholasticism* (1948).
J. Sully, *Pessimism: A History and a Criticism* (London, 1877).

Peter of Spain (*c*.1205–77). Born in Lisbon he studied at Paris (*c*.1220–9), taught medicine for several years at Siena, and was later Court physician of Gregory X at Viterbo. He was appointed Archbishop of Braga (1273), Cardinal-Archbishop of Frascati (1273), and was elected Pope John XXI in 1276. His writings cover a wide range of subjects, but he is most famous for the treatise *Summule Logicales*. It covers practically all the topics then taught under the heading of logic and became one of the great logic textbooks of the Middle Ages. During the two and a half centuries after its publication it was the subject of numerous commentaries.   A.BRO.

Peter of Spain: Tractatus called afterwards Summule Logicales, ed. L. M. de Rijk (Assen, 1972).

petitio principii: see begging the question.

Petrarch (Francesco Petrarca) (1304–74). Italian medieval poet and moral philosopher who revived practical ethics with its emphasis on introspection and experience for the Renaissance, taking as his models the classical Latin essayists and letter-writers Cicero and Seneca, as well as the early Christian Augustine. In *On his Own Ignorance*, Petrarch elaborated a mature critique of contemporary *scholasticism, such as was found especially at the University of Padua with its concentration on logical sophisms

and philosophy of nature, and its scorn for moral issues. Petrarch preferred a rhetorical approach to ethics, realizing the importance of appealing to the imagination and the emotions in discourse aimed at moving the will. His major moral philosopical work, *On Remedies for Fortune, Fair and Foul*, a manual of Stoic psychotherapy, aims at tempering and healing disturbed passions. Reason dialogues with Elation and Hope in one book, and with Pain and Dread (linked to *melancholia*) in another in order that an inner equilibrium can be attained, the Stoic 'peace of soul'.   L.P.

N. Mann, *Petrarch* (Oxford, 1984).
L. Panizza, 'Petrarch's *De Remediis* and Stoic Psychotherapy', in M. Osler (ed.), *Atoms, Pneuma and Tranquillity* (Cambridge, 1991).

phenomena and noumena. These terms mean literally 'things that appear' and 'things that are thought'. Platonic Ideas and Forms are noumena, and phenomena are things displaying themselves to the senses. In Plato's metaphor of the divided line (*Republic*, bk. 6), whatever lies above the dividing-line is noumenal, that which is below it is phenomenal. In *Republic* 517b the distinction is between that which is revealed to sight and that which is intelligible; at 524c the contrast is between terms cognate with noumena and phenomena. This dichotomy is the most characteristic feature of Plato's dualism; that noumena and the noumenal world are objects of the highest knowledge, truths, and values is Plato's principal legacy to philosophy.

Kant deals with this duality in his Inaugural Dissertation (1770), *On the Form and Principles of the Sensible and the Intelligible World*. The intelligible world of noumena is known by pure reason, which gives us knowledge of things as they are. Things in the sensible world (phenomena) are known through our senses and known only as they appear. To know noumena we must abstract from and exclude sensible concepts such as space and time.

Kant called the determination of noumena and phenomena the 'noblest enterprise of antiquity', but in the *Critique of Pure Reason* he denied that noumena as objects of pure reason are objects of knowledge, since reason gives knowledge only of objects of sensible intuition (phenomena). Noumena 'in the negative sense' are objects of which we have no sensible intuition and hence no knowledge at all; these are things-in-themselves. Noumena 'in the positive sense' (e.g. the soul and God) are conceived of as objects of intellectual intuition, a mode of knowledge which man does not possess. In neither sense, therefore, can noumena be known. For both Plato and Kant, nevertheless, conceptions of noumena and the intelligible world are foundational for ethical theory.   L.W.B.

I. Kant, *On the Forms and Principles of the Intelligible and Sensible World* (1770), in *Kant's Latin Writings*, ed. L. W. Beck, 2nd edn. (New York, 1992).
—— *Critique of Pure Reason*, 2nd edn. (1787), A 236/B 295–A 260/B 315.

phenomenalism. The doctrine that physical objects are reducible to sensory experiences, or that physical object statements can be analysed in terms of phenomenal statements describing sensory experience. The main twentieth-century defenders of the view, A. J. Ayer and C. I. Lewis, tried, each in his own way, to show how the content of a physical-object statement involves appeal to nothing more than sense-*contents or *sense-data, or anyhow sensory *experience. Consider: (1) This snowball is white. (2) There is a white sense-content. Does 1 have an analysis in terms of 2? If so, 1 must entail 2, but it does not. Nor does it help to assume that one is looking at the snowball and only at the snowball, or to ignore the experience of everyone else, etc. This last is especially problematic if we wish to construct selves from sense-contents. Let us waive that, however, and consider further the following: (3) The light shining on this is red. The conjunction of 1 and 3 together with assumptions of the sort indicated will actually entail not-2, and hence cannot entail 2. And it is then hard to conceive of *any* sense-contents whose existence would be *entailed* by a particular physical fact, even one as simple and observational as that reported by 1, even when combined with assumptions like those above (exclusive of 3). (See R. M. Chisholm, 'The Problem of Empiricism'.)

Moreover, phenomenalists must invoke not only actual but also merely possible phenomena, possible experiences. For a particular grain of sand may never be associated with any *actual* phenomena, since no one may ever perceive it. There is of course no hope of isolating the single fact of *there being a snowball before me* by means of the one *conditional that if I were to open my eyes I would have a visual experience of whiteness and roundness. There are ever so many different conditions that in the absence of snow still give rise to the truth of that conditional. But perhaps the idea is rather this: if we consider the possible courses of action open to me at the moment and the experiential outcomes conditional upon those courses of action, some such infinite set of conditionals would capture the single fact of there being a snowball before me. If so, we could perhaps say that there being a snowball before me was necessarily equivalent to the joint truth of that set of conditionals.

However, the introduction of such possible phenomena imports a complication, for the possibilities in question must be in some sense 'real' and not just logical. But real possibility is grounded in actual conditions. And what could function as the 'base' or 'ground' for the phenomenalist's actual conditions relative to which his possible phenomena are to be defined? What can ground such conditionals as: I would experience a sense-content of something white if I acted in a certain way? Presumably it would be just me and my properties (whether or not I myself am also to be reduced, as in *neutral monism, or to be left standing as in Berkeley's subjective *idealism). If so, then the fact that there is a white piece of paper before me has a status relative to me similar to the status of the elasticity of a rubber band relative to the rubber band.

A major problem for such phenomenalism stems from perceptual relativity: white paper looks white under white light, red under red, etc. Any possible course of experience resulting from a possible course of action will apparently underdetermine our surroundings: it will determine, for example, that there is *either* white paper under red light *or* red paper under white light, or the like. For this reason among others, phenomenalism now has few defenders.

E.S.

*perception; representative theory of perception.

A. J. Ayer, *Language, Truth, and Logic* (New York, 1952).
R. M. Chisholm, 'The Problem of Empiricism', *Journal of Philosophy* (1948).
R. Firth, 'Radical Empiricism and Perceptual Relativity', *Philosophical Review* (1950).
R. Fumerton, *Metaphysical and Epistemological Problems of Perception* (Lincoln, Nebr., 1985).
C. I. Lewis, *An Analysis of Knowledge and Valuation* (La Salle, Ill., 1946).

phenomenology. One of the most important philosophical movements of the twentieth century. It was founded by Edmund Husserl at the beginning of this century and has had many followers, for example, Moritz Geiger, Alexander Pfaender, Max Scheler, Oscar Becker, up to the present. Quite naturally, it has undergone many changes, refinements, shifts of emphasis, etc. Originally, it was primarily a theory of *knowledge. Later on, in the years after 1913, phenomenology developed into a form of *idealism.

Phenomenology distinguishes sharply between perceptual properties on the one hand, and abstract properties on the other. Consider two white billiard balls, called A and B. The white colour of A, which one can see with one's eyes, is said to be located in space where A is. The white colour of B, similarly, is taken to be located where B is. Furthermore, it is maintained that the colour of A is not identical with the colour of B, since they are located at two different places. The same shade of colour, according to this analysis, divides into as many 'colour instances' of that shade as there are individual things with this colour shade.

However, all of these instances are instances of the same colour shade. There exists, therefore, according to phenomenology, also the abstract colour shade of which the instances are instances. Let us call this abstract colour the 'universal whiteness'. Phenomenology asserts that there is not only a direct perception of instances of whiteness, but also a sort of direct perception of the universal whiteness. This perception is called 'eidetic intuition'. By means of eidetic intuition we have knowledge of the essential features of the world. Phenomenologists call such universals *essences.

An essence can be presented to the mind in its totality in one mental act of intuition. Perceptual objects, however, can never be so presented. According to phenomenologists, we can only perceive aspects of them. This is one of the fundamental differences between essences and certain individual things. What does it mean to perceive merely aspects of, say, one of our billiard-balls? There seem to be two notions of an aspect at work. Firstly, we must distinguish between the colour instance of billiard-ball *A*, which is a part of *A*, and the differently coloured sensations which we experience when we look at *A*. Assume, for example, that *A* is illuminated from one side, so that half of it lies in the shadow. Even though that billiard-ball is uniformly coloured, our colour sensation of it is not uniformly white: one part of it is much darker than the other. And if we were to put on coloured glasses, our colour sensation would not be white at all. Now, what phenomenologists sometimes seem to have in mind when they speak of perception through aspects is that the property instances of a perceptual object, its colour, its shape, appear to us only through the perspective variations of our colour sensation and the variations of our shape sensations.

Secondly, and much more obviously, spatial perceptual objects can only be perceived from a point of view. For example, when we look at billiard-ball *A*, only one side is turned towards us and we cannot see its back. In this sense, therefore, we can only perceive, from a given point of view, a spatial 'aspect' of it. It is clear that this notion of an aspect is quite different from the one mentioned in the last paragraph.

According to phenomenology, therefore, our knowledge of things divides into direct and indirect knowledge, that is, into direct knowledge and knowledge through aspects. Essences (universal properties) are known directly, but perceptual objects are only known through their aspects. However, in addition to perceptual things, there are also mental things and selves. How are they known? *Consciousness, according to phenomenology, is known, like essences, directly. The mental act of seeing a billiard-ball, a desire to be once again in Venice, a remembrance of strolling down the beach in Manly, all of these so-called mental acts are presented to us without aspects. There is thus a fundamental difference between the objects of the outside perceptual world and the objects of the world of consciousness: the former are never given to us wholly and completely in single mental acts of perception, the latter are fully given to us when we attend to them. But the self, the mental individual from which all mental acts issue, is only presented to us indirectly, like a perceptual object. The realm of individual things thus divides into an 'immanent' part, consciousness, and two 'transcendent' parts, perceptual objects and the self. This makes consciousness special, because what we truly and directly know is only consciousness. But some phenomenologists go even further and claim that consciousness has a kind of being quite different from all other things. This claim plays an essential role in *existentialism.

So far we have appraised phenomenology as a theory of knowledge. But it is often viewed not as a new philosophical view about old epistemological problems, but as a new method of doing philosophy, and one speaks then of the phenomenological method. Sometimes, one even talks of the science of phenomenology, which is claimed to have its own method and subject-matter.

So-called eidetic reflection, reflection on essences and their connections, is of course the heart of phenomenology. This reflection requires eidetic reduction. By means of eidetic reduction, we shift our attention from a particular instance of a property to the abstract property (essence) itself. After the shift has taken place, one will 'see' the essence directly and in its totality. Furthermore, after eidetic reduction, one also intuits connections among essences. One may intuit, for example, that the essences of ego and of spatial being reveal that the former can perceive the latter only in spatial perspective. Phenomenology, from this point of view, inquires into the structures formed by essences.

The knowledge gained by a study of the relationships among essences, according to most phenomenologists, is non-empirical. For example, the insight just mentioned that an ego can perceive a spatial being only in perspective is gleaned from a connection between the essence of an ego and the essence of something spatial; it is not inferred by induction from individual cases. Such an inference, for example, would be involved if one concluded from repeated observations of particular whales that all whales are mammals. But phenomenological truths are thought to be not only non-empirical in this sense, but also necessary. The inductive law about whales may be proven false, for example, by the discovery of a whale that is not a mammal but a fish. No such possibility exists, however, for the phenomenological truth about the connection between the essence of being an ego and the essence of observing spatial things. Since phenomenological truths are thought to be both non-empirical and necessary, they are said to be true a priori.

But this is not all there is to the phenomenological method. There is also phenomenological reduction. It seems that there are two sides to phenomenological reduction. Firstly, there is a general prescription to look at things without prejudice, to go to the things themselves, to leave theoretical speculation behind, etc. Secondly, however, there is also a more specific side to phenomenological reduction. It consists, as a first step, in the *'bracketing of the objective world'. Phenomenologists rely at this point on a thesis which was defended by the Polish philosopher Twardowski, who, like Husserl, was a student of Brentano's. Twardowski distinguished between an individual act of presentation, the content of this act, and the object of the act. Assume that one is presented with the billiard-ball *A*. Then there occurs a particular mental act of presentation. This act has a unique content which is a property of the mental act, and it has, as its object, the billiard-ball *A*. Twardowski's thesis is that every act has an object, even those acts which intend things which do not exist. If one hallucinates a big polka-dotted bat, one's act of seeing has an object, even though this object does not exist. In general, Twardowski insisted (for example, against Bolzano) that we must distinguish between the question whether a mental act has an object and the question whether its object exists. Some mental acts have objects which do not exist. Phenomenological reduction is then a method of revealing the essences of the objects of our mental acts, irrespective of whether these objects exist in reality, even irrespective of whether there really is a non-mental reality.

Phenomenological reduction enjoins us to study the objects of our mental acts precisely as they are, and irrespective of their existence. But for some phenomenologists this is only the first step. They adhere to the much more radical prescription that we must eventually turn away from the 'outside world' and concentrate exclusively on consciousness. In one of Husserl's later versions of the nature of phenomenology, this exclusive concentration on consciousness sets phenomenology apart from the natural sciences. Phenomenology thus has its own method, reflection on the essences of mental acts, and it has its own subject-matter, consciousness. Phenomenology, according to this conception, is the study of the essence of consciousness. The idealistic tenor of this position is obvious.   R.G.

For Husserl's development of phenomenology see his *Ideas: General Introduction to Pure Phenomenology*, tr. W. R. Boyce Gibson (London, 1931); also his 'Phenomenology', tr. C. V. Solomon, in *Encyclopaedia Britannica*, 14th edn. (Chicago, 1927), and *Cartesian Meditations*, tr. Dorian Cairns (The Hague, 1960). For a description of the phenomenological movement see Herbert Spiegelberg, *The Phenomenological Movement: A Historical Introduction*, 2 vols. (The Hague, 1960). For a general introduction, see D. Moran, *Introduction to Phenomenology* (London, 2000), and accompanying anthology: D. Moran and T. Mooney (eds.), *The Phenomenology Reader* (London, 2002).

Philo (*c*.20 BC–*c*.AD 50). Called Philo Judaeus or Philo of Alexandria. Foremost Jewish philosopher of the Hellenistic age, a leader of Alexandrian Jewry, who defended his co-religionists in an embassy to Caligula and in sophisticated apologetics. Philo's thoughtful, cosmopolitan, often allegorical Greek commentaries on the Septuagint Bible synthesize Platonic, Stoic, and Jewish values and ideas, laying a foundation for Christian, and later Muslim and Jewish, rational theologians—although the impact on Jews and Muslims was largely indirect. Philo's idea that the *Logos*, the word or wisdom of God, mediates God's absoluteness to creation by articulating divine wisdom in nature and in human intelligence, and his conception of philosophy as the handmaid (*ancilla*) of theology, were vital to the medieval synthesis. Cast, seemingly, in a subordinate role, philosophy would shape all three monotheistic cultures.   L.E.G.

Philo, *Works*, ed. and tr. F. H. Colson, 10 vols., Loeb Classical Library (Cambridge, Mass., 1929–53), with 2 suppl. vols. of Ralph Marcus's Eng. renderings of works preserved in Armonian translation.

H. A. Wolfson, *Philo: Foundations of Religious Philosophy in Judaism, Christianity and Islam* (Cambridge, Mass., 1962).

Philo (the Dialectician) (Greek, 4th–3rd century BC). By contrast to the *Master Argument, Philo maintained that a predicate's 'bare suitability to a subject' was enough to make something capable of happening. This, he pointed out, would mean that things were capable of happening,

even though they were 'necessarily prevented by external circumstances'; thus a log, he held, would still be capable of burning, even though it was in mid-Atlantic. Philo also invented *material implication: one proposition implies another, he held, when and only when either the first proposition is false or the second proposition is true; in particular, he held that the *conditional 'If it is day, it is night' is true, and that the argument 'It is day; so it is night' is valid, throughout the night but never in daytime.

N.C.D.

Gabriele Giannantoni (ed.), *Socratis et Socraticorum Reliquiae* (Naples, 1990), i. 414–37 (= *Elenchos*, vol. XVIII*).

Philoponus, John (*c*.490–570s). From Alexandria, Philoponus opposed Aristotle's science, defending the Christian doctrine that the universe had a beginning. He argued thus: without a beginning, the universe must already have endured an infinite number of years; but then how could it be true that, by the end of next year, the universe would have endured a greater number of years? For how could infinity be added to? Philoponus also attacked Aristotle's dynamics, denying (as later did Galileo) that velocity in a vacuum need be infinite. He also denied that a thrown javelin continued to move because propelled onwards by the air behind it—if so why not propel javelins by bellows?—suggesting instead that a force or impetus was imparted to the javelin by its thrower.   T.P.

R. Sorabji (ed.), *Philoponus and the Rejection of Aristotelian Science* (London, 1987).

philosophe. A French word now domesticated into English, denoting any member of a very diverse though loosely associated group of scientists, writers, statesmen, and practical 'men of affairs' whose works and activities constituted the eighteenth-century *Enlightenment movement in Europe and America (e.g. Voltaire, Hume, Franklin, Buffon, and Diderot). The philosophes were bound together as a group by their vigorous support of the developing natural sciences, by their insistent (and frequently courageous) challenges to the pervasive influence of outdated traditions, superstition, and prejudice, and by their common desire to facilitate the growth and spread of more liberal and humane political institutions. All of these concerns, in the philosophes' view, were only different sides of a single intellectual mission: to advance the cause of human reason, to perfect its methods, and extend their application across an ever widening range of pursuits.   P.F.J.

Peter Gay, *The Enlightenment: An Interpretation*, i: *The Rise of Modern Paganism* (New York, 1977).

philosopher-king. One of the rulers of the ideal state in Plato's *Republic*. (Plato himself does not use the term, referring to the rulers as 'Guards' (*phulakes*).) The basic principle of the organization of the ideal state is that government should be in the hands of those who, in virtue of their knowledge of the Good, are uniquely able to order the state for the good of its citizens. The central books of the *Republic* are devoted to an account of the educational system (largely mathematical, but culminating in metaphysics) which is to lead to knowledge of the Good.

C.C.W.T.

C. D. C. Reeve, *Philosopher-Kings* (Princeton, NJ, 1988).

philosopher may preach.

> The satirist may laugh, the philosopher may preach, but Reason herself will respect the prejudices and habits which have been consecrated by the experience of mankind.
>
> (Edward Gibbon, *Memoirs of My Life*, ch.1)

The historian Gibbon was perhaps influenced by Hume, who professed himself unable, despite his scepticism, to avoid the 'current of nature' ineluctably sweeping him into belief in the very things he professed to doubt, such as the *external world. But Hume gave this thought an additional twist. It is not just that habit and experience 'conspire' to make us see everything in certain ways, but that reason itself is 'nothing but a wonderful and unintelligible instinct' arising from them.

J.O'G.

philosophers, persecution of: *see* persecution of philosophers.

philosophers and God: *see* God and the philosophers.

philosopher's stone. A conjectural and, in fact, imaginary substance capable of transmuting base metals into gold. Its discovery and preparation was the fruitless task of alchemists from early China and India, by way of medieval Arabs, down to various Faust-like figures of the Renaissance such as Paracelsus. It was a solid variant of the liquid elixir of life. The alchemists' pursuit of it led to the acquisition of much genuine chemical knowledge and, indeed, to the foundation of chemistry as a science.

A.Q.

philosophical anthropology: *see* anthropology, philosophical.

philosophical dictionaries and encyclopaedias: *see* dictionaries and encyclopaedias of philosophy.

philosophical inquiry: premises and first principles.
There is an aspect of philosophy that is pervasive enough to be sometimes used to define it: the criticism of assumptions. Considering various ways of arriving at or approximating to knowledge, Plato places at the top 'dialectic'. It seems to be what *philosophy essentially consists of, and its nature is explained by contrasting it with mathematics, in which unargued and unexamined assumptions are taken for granted. Rational thinking without assumptions is, however, an inconsistent notion. *Reasoning is movement from an accepted or assumed belief to some other belief. Even if the premiss is merely assumed and not accepted, supposed, as the saying is, for the sake of argument, some rules of inference (and very often some suppressed premisses as well) are required to provide the conclusion drawn.

A certain amount of philosophy has been presented in an explicitly deductive form, with axiomatic premisses set out at the start as in the fascinating model of Euclid's geometry. Spinoza gave his great work *Ethics* the subtitle *Demonstrated in a Geometrical Manner*. His axioms turn out to be quite numerous; there are seven for the first book, five for the second, and comparable handfuls for the other three, supported in each case by definitions. Spinoza did not think that any philosophy set out in this way, even if all the inferences in it were valid, was on that account correct. He produced a version of Descartes's system in this rigorous form but thought it in many respects mistaken. The axioms had to be true, and that meant, since they could not be inferred, that they had to be self-evident.

It is a general characteristic of rationalist philosophers to argue in this way, for example of Descartes and Leibniz and, in our century, of McTaggart. Descartes presents 'I think, therefore I exist' as a kind of ultimate premiss, but does argue for it, assuming that 'I think' entails 'I exist' and asserting that the denial of 'I think' is self-refuting. He then goes on to conclude that, since his premiss has the self-certifying property of being 'clear and distinct', any other belief with that certifying property is also known for certain to be true, a principle used to authorize a number of substantial propositions. McTaggart claims to deduce his entire philosophy from the axioms that something exists and an obscure 'principle of determining correspondence'.

Rationalist philosophers commonly proceed, at least in the first stages of their work, by way of indirect proof or *reductio ad absurdum*, in which a proposition is established by inferring a contradiction from its negation. If that is to work it must be assumed that the inference involved is validated by a true logical law and that a contradiction is necessarily false. The thesis about contradictions is not and the relevant logical laws need not be things anyone would be likely to question.

But full-blooded deductive metaphysicians of this kind are rare; a rationalist need not be a rationalist through and through. On the other hand, the minimization of assumptions is also to be found among empiricists, particularly if they are mathematically trained and inspired. Russell proposed, and sketched, the achievement of a 'minimum vocabulary' for the description of the world by definitional reduction, and that project was realized in Carnap's *Logical Structure of the World*, in which the main elements of the whole apparatus of description are defined in terms of items of sense-experience and the relation of recollected similarity. But most empiricists follow a less arduous path.

The absolute first principle of *rationalism would seem to be: whatever it would be a contradiction to deny is necessarily true. Empiricists would not deny that, but would maintain that while it determines the form of our representation of the world, it implies nothing about what the world is in fact like. Yet they too have, and give prominence to, large basic principles.

Locke, Hume, and Mill hold that all, or most, substantial items of knowledge (or justified belief) derive their title to acceptance from sense-experience (or introspection). That seems broadly correct, but is it really self-evident? The claims of alleged moral, aesthetic, and religious experience have to be dealt with as do those of such substantial, but apparently unempirical, generalities as that every quality inheres in a substance, every event is part of the history of an object, and every event has a cause.

The classical Empiricists were, in fact, committed by their conception of the nature of philosophy as an empirical study of the cognitive aspects of human nature to the view that the empiricist principle was itself empirical. The problem came to the surface in connection with the principle of verifiability, the twentieth-century version of the empiricist principle. Critics asked what sort of truth it itself was: empirical or, the only alternative its proponents acknowledged, analytic, true in virtue of the meaning of the words expressing it? Neither option was very attractive. To admit it was empirical left it weak and refutable. To claim it was analytic seemed to conflict with the facts of our use of the word 'meaning'. Popper frankly admitted that his roughly similar criterion of falsifiablity, as a means of demarcating not sense from nonsense, but science from metaphysics, was a proposal or convention, recommended on the grounds of its intellectual advantages.

That undogmatic, persuasive conclusion is supported by the widespread recognition that the theory of knowledge is a normative discipline, an 'ethics of belief', setting out rules for the right acceptance of beliefs. That would make it nonsense on the strict letter of the verifiability principle, but, one might say, so much the worse for the verifiability principle. Many present-day philosophers, however, following Quine, have gone back to the position of the classical empiricists by taking the theory of knowledge to be the cognitive part of empirical psychology.

Many unexamined assumptions are more embedded in philosophical writing than those mentioned so far. One, which had a long and significant career, is that the greater cannot emerge from or be produced by the less. It is stated, as something too obvious to require discussion, by Descartes, and drawn on by Locke to prove the existence of God. It was mobilized again in the nineteenth century to dismiss Darwin's doctrine of evolution, but Darwin's view emerged victorious from the collision. Another is that sturdy support of mind–body dualism which denies the identity of a mental event with any corresponding brain event on the ground that it is conceivable or logically possible for either to occur without the other occurring. J. J. C. Smart pointed out that there is such a thing as contingent identity as of a lightning-flash and an electrical discharge, or, one might add, of a billiard-ball that is seen and one that is touched.

A philosophical treatise may be presented in a systematic order which does not correspond at all to the way in which the ideas it contains were arrived at. Premises and first principles are, therefore, more part of the expository rhetoric of philosophy than of its real substance. But orderly exposition nevertheless contributes valuably to making philosophy accessible to the kind of rational criticism on which it thrives. A.Q.

*empiricism; verification principle.

W. W. Bartley, *Retreat to Commitment* (London, 1964).

E. J. Craig, *The Mind of God and the Works of Man* (Oxford, 1987).

J. A. Passmore, *Philosophical Reasoning* (London, 1961).

K. R. Popper, *The Open Society and its Enemies* (London, 1945), ch. 24.

philosophical journals: *see* journals of philosophy.

philosophical logic. Despite its name, philosophical logic is neither a kind of logic nor simply to be identified with the philosophy of logic(s)—the latter being the philosophical examination of systems of logic and their applications. Though the subject of philosophical logic is hard to define precisely, it may loosely be described as the philosophical elucidation of those notions that are indispensable for the proper characterization of rational thought and its contents—notions like those of reference, predication, truth, negation, necessity, definition, and entailment. These and related notions are needed in order to give adequate accounts of the structure of thoughts—particularly as expressed in language—and of the relationships in which thoughts stand both to one another and to objects and states of affairs in the world. But it must be emphasized that philosophical logic is not concerned with thought inasmuch as the latter is a psychological process, but only in so far as thoughts have contents which are assessable as true or false. To conflate these concerns is to fall into the error of *psychologism, much decried by Frege.

No single way of dividing up the subject-matter of philosophical logic would be agreed upon by all of its practitioners, but one convenient division would be this: theories of reference, theories of truth, the analysis of complex propositions, theories of modality (that is, of necessity, possibility, and related notions), and theories of argument or rational inference. These topics inevitably overlap, but it is roughly true to say that later topics in the list presuppose earlier ones to a greater degree than earlier ones presuppose later ones. The order of topics in the list reflects a general progression from the study of parts of *propositions, through the study of whole and compound propositions, to the study of relations between propositions. (Here we use the term 'proposition' to denote a thought content assessable as true or false—something expressible by a complete sentence.)

Theories of *reference are concerned with the relationships between subpropositional or subsentential parts of thought or speech and their extra-mental or extra-linguistic objects—for instance, with the relationship between *names and things named, and with the relationship between predicates and the items to which they apply. According to some theories, a name refers to a particular thing by virtue of its being associated with some description which applies uniquely to that thing. Other theories hold that the link between name and thing named is causal in nature. (Theories of either sort are intimately bound up with questions concerning *identity and *individuation.) As for predicates—where a predicate may be thought of as what remains when one or more names are deleted from a sentence—these are variously held to carry reference to *universals, *concepts, or *classes. Thus the predicate ' . . . is red', formed by deleting the name from a sentence like 'Mars is red', is held by some philosophical logicians to stand for the property of redness, by others to express our concept of redness, and by yet others to denote the class of red things. Monolithic theories of reference are unpromising, however. Even if some names refer by way of description, other names and namelike parts of speech—such as demonstratives and personal pronouns—plausibly do not. And even if some predicates stand for universals, others—such as negative and disjunctive predicates—can scarcely be held to do so.

*Truth and falsehood—if indeed they are properties at all—are properties of whole sentences or propositions, rather than of their subsentential or subpropositional components. Theories of truth are many and various, ranging from the robust and intuitively appealing *correspondence theory—which holds that the truth of a sentence or proposition consists in its correspondence to extra-linguistic or extra-mental *fact—to the *redundancy theory at the other extreme, according to which all talk of truth and falsehood is, at least in principle, eliminable without loss of expressive power. These two theories are examples, respectively, of substantive and *deflationary accounts of truth, other substantive theories being the *coherence theory, the *pragmatic theory, and the *semantic theory, while other deflationary theories include the prosentential theory and the performative theory (which sees the truth-predicate ' . . . is true' as a device for the expression of agreement between speakers). As with the theory of reference, a monolithic approach to truth, despite its attractive simplicity, may not be capable of doing justice to all applications of the notion. Thus the correspondence theory, though plausible as regards a posteriori or empirical truths, is apparently not equipped to deal with *a priori or *analytic truths, since there is no very obvious 'fact' to which a truth like 'Everything is either red or not red' can be seen to 'correspond'. Again, the performative theory, while attractive as an account of the use of a sentence like 'That's true!' uttered in response to another's assertion, has trouble in accounting for the use of the truth-predicate in the antecedent of a conditional, where no assertion is made or implied.

Whichever theory or theories of truth a philosophical logician favours, he or she will need at some stage to address questions concerning the *value* of truth—for instance, why should we aim at truth rather than falsehood?—and the *paradoxes to which the notion of truth can give rise (such as the paradox of the *liar). In the course of those inquiries, fundamental principles thought to govern the notion of truth will inevitably come under scrutiny—such as the principle of *bivalence (the principle that every assertoric sentence is either true or false). A rejection of that principle in some area of discourse is widely supposed to signify an *anti-realist conception of its subject-matter.

*Propositions and *sentences can be either simple or complex (atomic or compound). A simple sentence typically concatenates a single name with unitary predicate, as, for example, in 'Mars is red'. (Relational sentences involve more names, as in 'Mars is smaller than Venus', but a sentence like this is still regarded as simple.) One way in which complex sentences can be formed is by modifying or connecting simple ones; for instance, by negating 'Mars is red' to form the *negation 'Mars is not red', or by conjoining it with 'Venus is white' to form 'Mars is red and Venus is white'. Sentential operators and *connectives, like 'not', 'and', 'or', and 'if', are extensively studied by philosophical logicians. In many cases, these operators and connectives can plausibly be held to be *truth-functional—meaning that the truth-value of complex sentences formed with their aid is determined entirely by the truth-values of the component sentences involved (as, for example, 'Mars is not red' is true just in case 'Mars is red' is not true). But in other cases—and notably with the conditional connective 'if'—a claim of truth-functionality is less compelling. The analysis of *conditional sentences has accordingly become a major topic in philosophical logic, with some theorists seeing them as involving modal notions while others favour probabilistic analyses.

There are other ways of forming complex sentences than by connecting simpler ones, the most important being through the use of *quantifiers—expressions like 'something', 'nobody', 'every planet', and 'most dogs'. The analysis and interpretation of such expressions forms another major area of philosophical logic. An example of an important issue which arises under this heading is the question how *existential propositions should be understood—propositions like 'Mars exists' or 'Planets exist'. According to one approach, the latter may be analysed as meaning 'Something is a planet' and the former as 'Something is identical with Mars' (both of which involve a quantifier), but this is not universally accepted as correct. Another issue connected with the role of quantifiers is the question how definite *descriptions—expressions of the form 'the so-and-so'—should be interpreted, whether as referential (or namelike) or alternatively as implicitly quantificational in force, as Russell held.

The fourth topic in our list is theories of *modality, that is, accounts of such notions as *necessity, possibility, and contingency, along with associated concepts such as that of analyticity. One broad distinction that is commonly drawn is that between *de re* and *de dicto* necessity and possibility, the former concerning objects and their properties and the latter concerning propositions or sentences. Thus, a supposedly *analytic truth such as 'All bachelors are unmarried' is widely regarded as constituting a *de dicto* necessity, in that, given its meaning, what it says could not be false. But notice that this does not imply that any man who happens to be a bachelor is incapable of being married—though should he become so, it will, of course, no longer be correct to describe him as a 'bachelor'. Thus there is no *de re* necessity for any man to be unmarried, even if he should happen to be a bachelor. By contrast, there arguably *is* a *de re* necessity for any man to have a body consisting of flesh and bones, since the property of having such a body is apparently essential to being human.

As for the question how, if at all, we can analyse modal propositions, opinions vary between those who regard modal notions as fundamental and irreducible and those who regard them as being explicable in other terms—for instance, in terms of *possible worlds, conceived as 'ways the world might have been'. (Although this appears circular, in that 'possible' and 'might' are themselves modal expressions, with care the appearance is arguably removable.) For instance, the claim that every man necessarily has a body made of flesh and bones might be construed as equivalent to saying, of each man, that he has a body made of flesh and bones in every possible world in which he exists. However, we should always be on guard against ambiguity when talking of necessity, because it comes in many different varieties—*logical necessity, *metaphysical necessity, *epistemic necessity, and *nomic necessity being just four.

Modal expressions give rise to special problems in so far as they often appear to create contexts which are non-extensional or 'opaque' (*extensionality)—such a context being one in which one term cannot always be substituted for another having the same reference without affecting the truth-value of the modal sentence as a whole in which the term appears. For example, substituting 'the number of the planets' for 'nine' in the sentence 'Necessarily, nine is greater than seven', appears to change its truth-value from truth to falsehood, even though those terms have the same reference. (No such change occurs if the modal expression 'necessarily' is dropped from the sentence.) How to handle such phenomena—which also arise in connection with the so-called *propositional attitudes, such as belief—is another widely studied area of philosophical logic.

Finally, we come to questions concerning relations *between* propositions or sentences—relations such as those of *entailment, presupposition, and *confirmation (or probabilistic support). Such relations are the subject-matter of the general theory of rational *argument or *inference, whether *deductive or *inductive. Some theorists regard entailment as analysable in terms of the modal notion of logical necessity—holding that a proposition p entails a proposition q just in case the conjunction of p and the negation of q is logically impossible. This view, however, has the queer consequence that a contradiction entails any proposition whatever, whence it is rejected by philosophers who insist that there must be a 'relevant connection' between a proposition and any proposition which it can be said to entail. (*Relevance logic.) The notion of presupposition, though widely appealed to by philosophers, is difficult to distinguish precisely from that of entailment, but according to one line of thought a statement S presupposes a statement T just in case S fails to be either true or false unless T is true. For instance, the statement that the present King of France is bald might be said to presuppose, in this sense, that France currently has

a male monarch. (Such an approach obviously requires some restriction to be placed on the principle of bivalence.) As for the notion of confirmation, understood as a relation between propositions licensing some form of non-demonstrative inference (such as an inference to the truth of an empirical *generalization from the truth of observation statements in agreement with it), this is widely supposed to be explicable in terms of the theory of *probability—though precisely how the notion of probability should itself be interpreted is still a matter of widespread controversy.

No general theory of argument or inference would be complete without an account of the various *fallacies and *paradoxes which beset our attempts to reason from premiss to conclusion. A 'good' argument should at least be truth-preserving, that is, should not carry us from true premisses to a false conclusion. A fallacy is an argument, or form of argument, which is capable of failing in this respect, such as the argument from 'If Jones is poor, he is honest' and 'Jones is honest' to 'Jones is poor' (the fallacy of *affirming the consequent), since these premisses could be true and yet the conclusion false. (Strictly, this only serves to characterize a fallacy of deductive reasoning.) A paradox arises when apparently true premisses appear to lead, by what seems to be a good argument, to a conclusion which is manifestly false—a situation which requires us either to reject some of the premisses or to find fault with the method of inference employed. An example would be the paradox of the *heap (the Sorites paradox): one stone does not make a heap, nor does adding one stone to a number of stones which do not make a heap turn them into a heap—from which it appears to follow that no number of stones, however large, can make a heap. This paradox is typical of many which are connected with the *vagueness of many of our concepts and expressions, a topic which has received much attention from philosophical logicians in recent years. This is again an area in which the principle of bivalence has come under some pressure.

Although philosophical logic should not be confused with the philosophy of logic(s), the latter must ultimately be responsive to considerations addressed by the former. In assessing the adequacy and applicability of any system of formal logic, one must ask whether the *axioms or *rules it employs can, when suitably interpreted, properly serve to articulate the structure of rational thought concerning some chosen domain—and this implies that what constitutes *'rationality' cannot be laid down by logicians, but is rather something which the formulators of logical systems must endeavour to reflect in the principles of inference which they enunciate.   E.J.L.

A. C. Grayling, *An Introduction to Philosophical Logic* (London, 1990).

L. Linsky (ed.), *Reference and Modality* (Oxford, 1971).

J. L. Mackie, *Truth, Probability and Paradox* (Oxford, 1973).

A. W. Moore (ed.), *Meaning and Reference* (Oxford, 1993).

W. V. Quine, *Philosophy of Logic* (Englewood Cliffs, NJ, 1970).

P. F. Strawson (ed.), *Philosophical Logic* (Oxford, 1967).

philosophical novel, the: *see* novel, the philosophical.

philosophical practice, the ethics of. Philosophical practice makes strenuous moral demands: honesty and fairness to opponents in argument; an ability to tolerate prolonged uncertainty over serious issues; the strength of character to change one's mind on basic beliefs, and to follow the argument rather than one's emotional leanings; independence of mind rather than readiness to follow philosophical fashion.

Moral respect for readers and hearers requires that a philosopher avoid non-rational persuasion, cajoling, deriding, or otherwise manipulating them into agreement. Philosophy should demonstrate that we can disagree profoundly over fundamentals without lapsing from a common reasonableness. That same respect requires a philosopher to expose the structure of his argument as perspicuously as possible, so as to encourage, not impede, its criticism.

Clarity and simplicity of style, the minimizing of technical expressions, abstaining from formal apparatus when ordinary language can be adequate, also express concern to be understood and to let argument and evidence alone carry the persuasive weight. A turgid and obscure style may veil real gaps in argument. A pretentious style may covertly work to disarm critical appraisal, replacing the authority of good argument with the would-be personal authority of the philosopher as sage.

Philosophy has a serious responsibility for language. It is one of its most important custodians—obliged to oppose terminologies that arrest or confuse thinking. Slipshod and imprecise language loses sensitivity to distinctions between reasonable and unreasonable, between good and bad argument—in any field, including the fields of personal and political morality. To impoverish the resources of language risks also impoverishing human experience, denying us the words we need to articulate its varieties.

Does a stress on style and the stewardship of language imply that philosophy is a branch of literature? In some important ways it *is* literature. But the *rapprochement* is carried too far when a philosopher lets the imaginatively vivid presentation of a slant on the world give it an appearance of self-evidence, and deflects critical alertness from the fact that categories have not been deduced and reasoned justification has been subordinated to expressing the quasi-poetic 'vision'.

Philosophers, then, need a wholesome sense of their fallibility. It is unwise for a philosopher to aspire to the role of expert or authority; for that works towards weakening the critical attentiveness constantly needed from readers and hearers.   R.W.H.

*pseudo-philosophy.

Max Black (ed.), *The Morality of Scholarship* (Ithaca, NY, 1967).

philosophy. Most definitions of philosophy are fairly controversial, particularly if they aim to be at all interesting or profound. That is partly because what has been called philosophy has changed radically in scope in the course of history, with many inquiries that were originally part of it having detached themselves from it. The shortest definition, and it is quite a good one, is that philosophy is thinking about thinking. That brings out the generally second-order character of the subject, as reflective thought about particular kinds of thinking—formation of beliefs, claims to knowledge—about the world or large parts of it.

A more detailed, but still uncontroversially comprehensive, definition is that philosophy is rationally critical thinking, of a more or less systematic kind about the general nature of the world (metaphysics or theory of existence), the justification of belief (epistemology or theory of knowledge), and the conduct of life (ethics or theory of value). Each of the three elements in this list has a non-philosophical counterpart, from which it is distinguished by its explicitly rational and critical way of proceeding and by its systematic nature. Everyone has some general conception of the nature of the world in which they live and of their place in it. *Metaphysics replaces the unargued assumptions embodied in such a conception with a rational and organized body of beliefs about the world as a whole. Everyone has occasion to doubt and question beliefs, their own or those of others, with more or less success and without any theory of what they are doing. *Epistemology seeks by argument to make explicit the rules of correct belief-formation. Everyone governs their conduct by directing it to desired or valued ends. Ethics, or *moral philosophy, in its most inclusive sense, seeks to articulate, in rationally systematic form, the rules or principles involved. (In practice ethics has generally been confined to conduct in its moral aspect and has largely ignored the large part of our actions that we guide by considerations of prudence or efficiency, as if these were too base to deserve rational examination.)

The three main parts of philosophy are related in various ways. For us to guide our conduct rationally we need a general conception of the world in which it is carried out and of ourselves as acting in it. Metaphysics presupposes epistemology, both to authenticate the special forms of reasoning on which it relies and to assure the correctness of the large assumptions which, in some of its varieties, it makes about the nature of things, such as that nothing comes out of nothing, that there are recurrences in the world and our experience of it, that the mental is not in space.

The earliest recognized philosophers, the Pre-Socratics, were primarily metaphysicians, concerned to establish the essential character of nature as a whole, from the first cryptic utterance of Thales: 'All is water.' Parmenides is the first metaphysician whose arguments have come down to us. For the reasons given by the famous paradoxes of Zeno, he concluded that the world did not move and occupied all space. The Sophists, by sceptically challenging conventional moral assumptions, brought ethics into existence, notably in Socrates. Plato and Aristotle wrote comprehensively on metaphysics and ethics; Plato on knowledge; Aristotle on (deductive) logic, the most rigorous technique for the justification of belief, setting out its rules in a systematic form which retained their intellectual authority for over 2,000 years.

In the Middle Ages philosophy, in service to Christianity, drew first on the metaphysics of Plato, then on Aristotle's, to defend religious beliefs. In the Renaissance free metaphysical speculation revived and, in its later phase, with Bacon and, more influentially, Descartes and Locke, turned to epistemology to ratify and, as far as possible to accommodate to religion, the new developments in natural science. Hume argued that such an accommodation is impossible, as indeed is metaphysics generally. In continental Europe Spinoza and Leibniz practised deductive metaphysics in the style of Parmenides and with comparably astonishing results. Kant, brought up in that tradition, was shaken out of it by reading Hume, rejected metaphysics in its traditional varieties, and ascribed the order of the public world to the formative work of the mind on its experiences. His German successors, taking advantage of some inconsistencies in Kant, revived metaphysics in the grand manner. In Britain the empiricism of Locke and Hume prevailed, and epistemology remained the central philosophical discipline up to the middle of the present century.

Metaphysics has various ways of setting about its none too clearly formulated topic: the general nature of the world. The first is that of purely rational demonstration. In this, large and striking conclusions are arrived at by showing that their denials involve self-contradiction. A prime example is the ontological proof of the existence of God. God is defined as perfect. A God that exists is more perfect than something, otherwise identical, that does not. Therefore God necessarily exists. In the same style Leibniz proves that reality is, in its ultimate constitution, mental, and Bradley finds contradictions lurking in the whole repertoire of fundamental notions of common belief and science (relation, plurality, time, space, the self, and so on) to arrive at the conclusion that reality is a single, indisseverable tissue of experience, a spiritual unity in which nature and personal individuality are absorbed.

A second metaphysical procedure is to derive conclusions about what lies behind 'appearance', the perceptible surface of the world, about the true or ultimate reality that transcends appearance. Prime examples here are the arguments for God's existence from the world's need of a first cause and from the marks of intelligent design in the order of the perceived world. Even more important for the history of philosophy is Plato's theory of Forms or objective universals, not in space and time but in a world of their own, invoked to explain our recognition of recurrent properties in the flux of appearance and to serve as the objects of eternally true items of mathematical knowledge.

Hume attacked demonstrative metaphysics on epistemological grounds. Purely rational argument can establish only the formal truths of logic and mathematics. The denial of a self-contradictory statement is not a substantial truth of fact, it is merely verbal, reflecting conventions for the use of words. Kant attacked transcendent metaphysics, arguing that the notions of substance and cause which it applies beyond the bounds of experience can yield knowledge only when applied to the raw material supplied by the senses. The Logical Positivists attacked transcendent metaphysics more vehemently with their verifiability principle, contending that its affirmations are devoid of meaning since uncheckable by experience.

Kant also opposed a kind of metaphysics which does not so much go behind the scenes of appearance as sideways from them by extrapolating indefinitely from them, as in the theses that the world is infinitely large, has existed from eternity, is composed of infinitesimal parts, and so on. He paired off assertions of these kinds with their denials and argued, in apparent defiance of logic, that both members of each pair were self-contradictory. This kind of metaphysics, dealing with the quantitatively (rather than, as transcendent metaphysics does, with the qualitatively) inaccessible, would seem open to the same objections, if they are correct.

Survivors of the long conflict between metaphysics and its detractors are theories of what has been called 'categories of being'. Dualism of the mental and physical, most sharply focused in Descartes, but pervasive long before and after him, is the most familiar of these. It has epistemological roots. One is the distinction between two kinds of experience: sensation and introspection. Another is the alleged infallibility of beliefs about one's own mind as contrasted with the fallibility of all beliefs about the objective material world. Materialists such as Hobbes argue that mental activity is bodily, if on a very small scale. Idealists such as Berkeley (and, in a way, phenomenalists such as Mill) argue that material bodies are complexes of sensations, both actual and either in the mind of God or hypothetical.

The Platonic realm of ideas houses a third alleged category, that of abstractions, such as properties, relations, classes, numbers, propositions. Values have been installed as a category so as to provide something for judgements of value to be true of.

Monism may be neither materialistic nor idealistic, but neutral. Russell, William James, Mach, even Hume up to a point, regarded both bodies and minds as composed of the same kinds of sensation, actual and possible, and the images that copy them. The two kinds of sensation combine to constitute bodies; sensations and images constitute minds.

Beside the kind of large-scale metaphysics considered hitherto, which aims at a conception of the world as a whole, there is a kind of small-scale metaphysics which examines the detailed structure of the world: individuals, their properties, and their relations to one another; the events in their history, and thus change, and also the states which are the dull, and the processes which are the more eventful, parts of that history; the facts which are the having of properties by individuals; and so on. Aristotle's doctrine of categories set this going as an organized inquiry (his categories being quite different from the categories of being mentioned earlier). It has now been to some extent absorbed into philosophical logic, since its pervasive features of the structure of the world correspond to the formal characteristics of discourse (of thought and speech) which are assumed as the basic distinctions of formal logic.

The fundamental, but not most interesting, question of epistemology is that of the definition of knowledge. Plato addressed it in his *Theaetetus* and came up with the crucial result that it is something more than true belief, although it includes it. The idea that justification is the missing element runs into difficulties unless, as many hold, the infinite regress it seems to generate is stopped by maintaining that some beliefs are not justified by others, but by experience. For many philosophers, however, the problem is in itself of little interest since knowledge is of little interest. What matters is rational or justified true belief. However, it has been persuasively suggested that the missing third element in the definition is that the true belief should be non-accidental or that it should be caused by the fact that makes it true.

Nearly all epistemology involves two large distinctions: the first between what Leibniz called truths of reason and truths of fact, the second between what is acquired directly or immediately and what is acquired by inference. Truths of reason are necessarily true and discoverable a priori, that is to say without reliance on the senses and purely by thinking. Truths of fact are contingent and rest on experience for their justification. The two distinctions overlap. Some truths of reason must be immediate if any are to be inferred. These, primarily, are taken to be the axioms or first principles of logic and mathematics. The conventional view about non-immediate truths of fact is that they are indeed inferred, but not by deductive logic. For them, it is held, induction, the derivation of unrestricted generalizations from a limited number of their singular instances, is required. Whewell, Peirce, and, most vehemently, Popper have denied, or, at any rate, marginalized, induction. As they see it, general statements are first proposed as hypotheses worthy of examination, then their singular deductive consequences are examined; they are rejected if these turn out to be false, but preserved, with increasing confidence, the larger the number of tests they survive. This corresponds more closely to scientific practice than does the conventional theory of induction, but has the appearance of letting induction in by the back door.

Leibniz thought that all truths of reason rested on the law of contradiction but did not go on to conclude, as Hume and most subsequent empiricists have, that they are therefore analytic, in the sense that they are verbal, simply reiterating in what they assert something they have already assumed. Kant took the central problem of philosophy to be that of whether and how any beliefs are both synthetic, really substantial in content, and also a priori, discoverable by reason alone. He concluded that there were such beliefs: those of arithmetic and geometry and such 'presuppositions of natural science' as that there is fixed, permanent quantity of matter in nature and that

every event has a cause. He went on to ascribe the necessary truth of these substantial beliefs to the mind's imposition of order on the chaos of experience to which it is subjected. Few have followed him this far. Mill held that mathematical truths are really empirical; Herbert Spencer that what seem to be necessary truths are the well-confirmed empirical beliefs we inherit from our ancestors. More recently Quine has argued that there is no difference in kind between truths of reason and truths of fact at all, only in the degree of our determination to hold on to them in the face of discouraging evidence.

The distinction between the direct and the inferred has also been challenged at various times, the present included, by philosophers who cannot see a way out of the maze of beliefs. Current coherence theorists of knowledge follow in the steps of Hegelian idealists and the Viennese positivists (until Tarski led them out of the maze). Part of the hold of the distinction comes from the ancient principle that our perception of objective, material things is not direct, since it is always fallible, as shown by our liability to illusion, and so must be inferred from the supposedly infallible knowledge we do have of our private, subjective sense-impressions. Is this inference valid, or, at least, defensible? If not, must we sceptically suspend belief in the material world? If it is, what sort of inference is it: to more things of the same kind, actual and possible impressions, or to something of a different, experience-transcending kind, namely unexperienceable matter? The pattern of this problem, and the form of its possible solutions, has been seen to be repeated in a number of other cases. The evidence for our beliefs about the past is all present, our recollections and traces; how do we cross the gap, if we can? Our beliefs about other minds are based on what we observe their bodies to do and say. A solution not mentioned so far is that of denying the assumption that we are confined to the evidence specified. That seems more attractive in the case of perception, where it would imply that we perceive material objects directly, although not infallibly, and in the case of our beliefs about the past, where our recollections simply *are* our straightforward beliefs about the past, not evidence for them, than in the case of other minds, where some sort of telepathy would seem needed. The importance and centrality of these three kinds of belief hardly need to be stressed, not just for science, history, and psychology, but for our entire cognitive life.

A curious feature about epistemology is the very slight attention it has given to the source of by far the greater part of our beliefs, namely the testimony of others: parents, teachers, textbooks, encyclopaedias. There is an interesting problem here. If we depend on them for the principles by which we check the reliability of what we are told, how do we ever achieve cognitive autonomy?

*Logic, which, as was said earlier, is the most powerful or coercive instrument for the justification of belief, is never taken to be part of epistemology. It was systematically organized before epistemology had established itself as an identifiable discipline. It began as, and still partly remains, as orderly arrangement of rules of inference which apply to all kinds of thought and speech. From Aristotle to the mid-nineteenth century it largely slumbered. Since then it has been greatly enlarged, with Aristotle's logic included in a mildly modified way, and has become from one point of view a branch of mathematics. Its elements have always been seen as an essential preamble to the study of philosophy, and still are today. It is not exactly a part of philosophy, although critical reflection on its assumptions, philosophical logic, unquestionably is.

There are a large, and indeed indeterminate, number of specialized philosophical disciplines, philosophies of this and that—mind, language, mathematics, science (natural and social), history, religion, law, education, even sport and sex. Where the special field is, as in the cases of science and history, a form of the pursuit of knowledge, the corresponding philosophy is primarily epistemological. The metaphysics of nature is an idea calculated to put scientists off, although the problem of the reality of theoretical entities such as fundamental particles could well be remitted to it. Speculative or metaphysical philosophy of history, the elaboration of general schemes or patterns (cyclical or progressive) of the totality of historical events, is also regarded with suspicion. The rational basis for that suspicion is a topic for the critical, epistemological philosophy of history.

The *philosophy of mind, as currently pursued, began from the epistemological problem of how we can know what is going on in another's mind. But it has come to be metaphysical. The old problem of personal identity can be posed either as 'How do we know that someone existing now is the same person as someone who existed at some previous time?' or as 'What is it for a person existing now to be identical with a person who existed before?' If personal identity, our own as well as that of others, is not to be inaccessible and unknowable, the two questions should receive much the same answer.

The *philosophy of science is often taken to embrace topics which are important for pre-scientific thinking. One of these is that of the nature of causation and the associated issue of how a lawful connection is to be distinguished from a merely accidental concomitance. Another is that of the justification of induction and of the interpretation of the probability, or kinds of probability, it confers on its conclusions. Causal relations, general beliefs, and beliefs held to be no more than probable are all indispensable features of ordinary common-sense thinking.

The third and final main division of philosophy is ethics, or theory of value, the rationally critical examination of our thinking about the conduct of life. Action, as contrasted with mere behaviour, is the result of choice, the comparison of alternatives, undertaken in the light of the desirability or otherwise of their consequences and of the possibility or easiness of doing them. Two kinds of belief, then, are involved in action: ordinary, straightforward factual beliefs about what is involved in doing something and what its results will be, and beliefs about the value of those results and, perhaps, the disvalue of what we must do to secure them.

In fact, in post-Greek ethics, the kind of action that has monopolized attention is *moral* action, fairly narrowly conceived. That is probably the result of religious enthusiasm. Christianity began as a millennialist religion, indifferent to worldly concerns and preoccupied with salvation, partly out of conviction of the worthlessness of the world and the flesh, even more from a belief that the world was about to end anyway. Whatever the cause of this narrow vision it has had a distorting effect. In principle ethics should consider all kinds of deliberate, thoughtful conduct: prudent conduct and self-interested conduct, which aim, respectively, at minimum loss and maximum gain for the agent, technically efficient conduct, economical conduct, healthy conduct, and so on. Moral goodness and rightness are only one kind of rightness. Logic and epistemology, indeed, since they are concerned to distinguish right from wrong in reasoning and belief, can be described as the ethics of inference and belief without metaphorical licence.

Religious influence on morality caused it to be seen as God's commands to mankind. Since this led to problems of authentication and interpretation, God's voice was internalized, either as a kind of moral sense, perceiving the moral quality of actions and the characters of agents, or as a kind of moral reason, apprehending the self-evident necessity of moral principles. Two questionable assumptions are involved in these two kinds of moral intuitionism. The first is that moral characteristics are *sui generis*, quite unrelated logically to any natural, perceivable characteristics of agents and their actions. The second is that actions, or kinds of action, are intrinsically right or wrong, whatever consequences they may have or be expected to have. Both features, if really distinctive of morality, would make it wholly different from other modes of action.

Utilitarians reject both the distinguishing assumptions. They derive the rightness or wrongness of actions from the goodness or badness of their consequences, most plausibly from the consequences it would have been reasonable for the agent to have expected rather than from the actual consequences. Secondly, they take goodness to be pleasure or happiness, more exactly the general happiness, the greatest happiness of the greatest number. The doctrine would have been in closer accord with unreflective moral sentiment if it had been formulated negatively: an action is wrong if it causes harm to another, is permissible if it does not, and is morally creditable if it prevents or alleviates the suffering of another.

For all their differences intuitionists and utilitarians agree that there are objective moral truths and falsehoods. The bulk and intensity of moral disagreement lend colour to the claims of moral sceptics, who claim that moral judgements are no more than expressions of our likes and dislikes and that disagreements about moral issues are collisions of feeling that cannot be settled by rational means. The fundamental question for ethics, conceived simply as moral philosophy, is whether our moral convictions have any objective validity and, if so, of what kind. Are they, as intuitionists suppose, convictions of a unique and special kind, or can they be brought into logical connection with the rest of our beliefs? Are the moral properties of actions intrinsic to them or are they dependent on the consequences of action? In what does virtue or moral goodness consist? Is it the disposition to do right actions or, more narrowly, the disposition to do right actions just because they are right? Under what conditions do agents deserve blame (or praise) for their actions? Does moral responsibilty presuppose freedom of the will in the sense of freedom from any causal influence on choice?

Two other established forms of the theory of value are *political philosophy and *aesthetics. Political philosophy is an extension of ethics into the domain of organized social institutions and, like ethics generally, is perhaps over-moralized. Its fundamental problem is the basis of the moral obligation of the citizen to obey the state and its laws, which, viewed from the other end, is that of the state to compel the citizen to obey it. (It might be more interesting to inquire what it is that makes it generally reasonable for citizens to obey.) Does the obligation to obey depend on the content of the laws or on the way the state was set up and is maintained? Do men have rights that limit the morally legitimate sphere of action of the state?

Aesthetic value is recognized as distinct from moral value despite the appearance of moral elements in criticism—sometimes relevantly, sometimes intrusively. It is not very satisfactorily indicated by the word 'beauty'. Other languages do better. 'Beau' and 'schön' mean *fine*, the property of objects of art or nature deserving attentive contemplation for their own sake, independently of any further use we may put them to or any information we may get from studying them.

The more established parts of philosophy have all been mentioned here, but there is no evident limit to its field of application. Wherever there is a large idea whose meaning is in some way indeterminate or controversial, so that large statements in which it occurs are hard to support or undermine and stand in unclear logical relations to other beliefs we are comparatively clear about, there is opportunity and point for philosophical reflection.   A.Q.

*Appendix: Maps of Philosophy; Appendix: Chronological Table of Philosophy; philosophy, the influence of; philosophy, value and use of; philosophy, world and underworld; metaphilosophy; pseudo-philosophy; publishing philosophy; world philosophy.

A. J. Ayer, *The Central Questions of Philosophy* (London, 1973).
Keith Campbell, *Metaphysics* (Encino, Calif., 1976).
Anthony O'Hear, *What Philosophy Is* (Harmondsworth, 1985).
W. V. Quine and J. Ullian, *The Web of Belief* (New York, 1970).
Bertrand Russell, *The Problems of Philosophy* (Oxford, 1980).

philosophy, chronology of: *see* Appendix.

philosophy, history of centres and departments of.
*Philosophy is a collaborative pursuit, unlike the meditative activity of sages which is commonly conceived to flourish best in isolated or even hermetic conditions. The form of collaboration involved, however, is not co-operative, like that of a surgical team, but competitive, a business of critical argument. Argument is meant to persuade, and to succeed must overcome counter-argument. Sages merely issue pronouncements to those who visit their retreats. Philosophers, therefore, are to a large extent found in groups, as is suggested by the large number of philosophical works composed in dialogue form: most of Plato's, for example, Scotus Eriugena's *De Divisione Naturae*, some of Berkeley's and Hume's *Dialogues on Natural Religion*.

The first three universally recognized philosophers—Thales, Anaximander, and Anaximenes—all came from Miletus, a prosperous Greek city in Ionia, on the western coast of what is now Turkey. It was overwhelmed by the Persians in 494 BC. Pythagoras was born in the neighbouring island of Samos, but removed himself—perhaps from dislike of the tyrant Polycrates, perhaps from fear of the Persians—to Croton in southern Italy, where he set up a tightly knit and disciplined school. Parmenides and his followers came from Elea on the lower shin, rather than, as with Croton, the fall of the foot of Italy. Anaxagoras, another Ionian, first brought philosophy to Athens, where he lived for some thirty years around the middle of the fifth century BC. From that date until the emperor Justinian closed the Athenian philosophical schools in AD 529, Athens remained the centre of philosophy, drawing people from other parts of the Greek, and later Roman, world to it, such as the Macedonian Aristotle, as well as producing philosophers of its own, of whom the greatest was Plato. The Sceptics Arcesilaus and Carneades were, at different times, heads of Plato's *Academy. Zeno, from Citium in Cyprus, and Epicurus, from Samos, the founders of Stoicism and Epicureanism, both settled in Athens.

After the political collapse of Athens at the end of the fifth century BC two other great culturally significant cities developed, and philosophy was pursued there. In Alexandria, more notable for science and mathematics than for philosophy, there were Aenesidemus, Philo Judaeus, and the great systematizers of Christian doctrine Clement and Origen. Plotinus was educated there, but settled in Rome. The native Roman philosophers were of a popular, literary character: Lucretius, Cicero, Seneca, Epictetus, and the emperor Marcus Aurelius. Tertullian lived in, and St Augustine near to, Carthage but 200 years apart, which hardly makes Carthage a philosophical centre. But since Augustine did not leave it until he was 28 it must have had some philosophical culture. Boethius, the last ancient philosopher, or the first medieval one, was of an ancient Roman family and lived in Italy until his execution by the Ostrogoth king Theodric.

Between Boethius' death in 525 and the active career of St Anselm in the latter half of the eleventh century, philosophy outside the Arab world is almost a blank, probably as much in fact as in our knowledge of it. The solitary figure of substance in these 500 years is the Irish Neoplatonist John Scotus Eriugena. He was called to the Frankish Court of Charles the Bald in the late ninth century because of a reputation the Christian civilization of Ireland had been able to retain until the Vikings destroyed it. The complexity and professional sophistication of his work and his knowledge of Greek throw a favourable, if not very informative, light on the state of Irish culture in his time.

Learning gradually revived, first in monastic schools such as those of York, Fulda, and St Gall. Of particular philosophical interest is that of Bec, in Normandy, where Lanfranc taught Anselm. Both were Italians and both became Archbishop of Canterbury. By the beginning of the twelfth century, around the time of Anselm's death, Paris emerged as the major philosophical centre. William of Champeaux, of the cathedral school there, is the first notable figure. More important was the brilliant and charismatic Abelard, who drew great numbers of students to the city. He was followed by Peter Lombard, compiler of the *Sentences* on which many medieval philosophers felt bound to produce a commentary, and by the Victorines. By 1215 the cathedral schools of Paris were sufficiently unified to be recognized as a university. There had been universities before, most notably at Salerno and Bologna, but they specialized in medicine and law respectively and were governed by their students.

Rashdall descried signs of a university in Paris around 1170. By the thirteenth century it was fully fledged and philosophically dominant. The Englishman Alexander of Hales, his pupil St Bonaventure, the German Albertus Magnus, St Thomas Aquinas, Roger Bacon, Duns Scotus, and William of Ockham, even the fourteenth-century German mystic Meister Eckhart, all studied or taught there, often both. Oxford, where Franciscans secured a dominance like that of the Dominicans in Paris, started soon after Paris, but did not displace it until the fourteenth century. The Augustinian Robert Grosseteste, the first important Oxford philosopher and first Chancellor of the university, had Roger Bacon for a pupil, and from his time until the Black Death in 1348 Oxford was the home of a host of productive philosophers. The first of these to be of major significance was Duns Scotus, who shared with the largely very different William of Ockham a conviction of the impotence of reason in the supernatural domain. That marked Oxford off from the Paris of Aquinas, who held and copiously expressed the opposite view.

Oxford declined as a philosophical centre after the middle of the fourteenth century. The persistent heresies of Wyclif, its ablest late fourteenth-century philosopher, bringing down ecclesiastical repression, completed the work done by the Black Death. The Ockhamist tradition survived in Paris with John Buridan, Albert of Saxony, Nicole d'Oresme, and the combatively sceptical Nicholas of Autrecourt. With Gerson, who died in 1429, who used Ockham's nominalism to support mystical conclusions, the first great age of Parisian philosophy came to an end.

The first centre of the new Platonic humanism of the Renaissance was the Academy in Florence, founded in the mid-fifteenth century by Cosimo dei Medici, under the inspiration of the Byzantine Gemistus Pletho and his pupil Cardinal Bessarion and with Ficino and Pico della Mirandola as its most gifted members. The Florentine Academy had more influence on literature and culture generally than on philosophy proper. Much more philosophically important was the University of Padua, site of a protracted controversy between two schools of interpreters of Aristotle: the Alexandrists (Pomponazzi, Zabarella, Cremonini) and the Averroists. Padua had been taken over by Venice in 1403; its thinkers benefited from the firm resistance of the parent city to papal interference. Galileo was Professor of Mathematics at Padua from 1592 to 1610.

There was some philosophical vitality in Spain in the sixteenth century, notably at Salamanca, the chief figures being Vittoria and the great, last-ditch systematizer of scholasticism: Suarez. But in France and England there was little going on in the religious turmoil of the sixteenth century as Protestantism was suppressed in the former and Catholicism in the latter. There was an active group of young English humanists at Oxford early in the sixteenth century, assembled around the visiting Erasmus, Colet, Thomas More, and Grocyn. Its interests were largely theological and after ten years its members went off in different directions. For most of the sixteenth century there was no philosophical centre of note.

From this time until the mid-eighteenth century in Germany and Scotland and the mid-nineteenth century in France and England the universities were largely torpid. Interesting philosophers were all independent men of letters. But there were some significant informal groupings. The most eminent of these was the circle of the abbé Mersenne, who served as a link between Descartes, Pascal, Gassendi, Arnauld, and Hobbes, recruiting the last three to write critical comments on Descartes's *Meditations*. Locke's *Essay Concerning Human Understanding* was the outcome of a discussion group considering questions of morality and revealed religion, which proved to need a philosophical foundation. But, for the most part, Locke worked alone, as did Spinoza and Leibniz, Berkeley and Hume. In Cambridge, a little earlier, there had been the circle of Platonists led by Cudworth and Henry More.

Holland was not exactly a philosophical centre in the seventeenth century, but major philosophers flourished there, despite a measure of persecution: Spinoza above all and Hugo Grotius. Equally important, Holland, because of its comparative tolerance of unorthodox religious opinions, was much favoured as a place of refuge for philosophers from France and England who were, or reasonably thought they would become, objects of oppression: Descartes early in the century, Locke and Bayle later.

Hume at least had the beneficent social setting of eighteenth-century Edinburgh and the friendship of Adam Smith. During his lifetime the Scottish universities came to life intellectually, keeping him out but taking in to the professoriate Hutcheson, Ferguson, Adam Smith, Reid and Dugald Stewart. So did the universities of Germany. There were a great many of them, none, after the brief initial glory of Halle, particularly predominating. That may be the cause, if it is not the effect, of the characteristically dogmatic and authoritarian character of German professorial behaviour, which does not invite, or even allow for, critical exchange.

The most attractive philosophical centre of the eighteenth century was the world of the *philosophes in Paris, agreeably anchored to the material world by the salons of Mme d'Holbach and Mme Helvétius. D'Holbach and Diderot were the philosophically most substantial of the group; Voltaire and Rousseau were, in different degrees, spiritually and, for the most part, physically remote. The contemporary drinking-clubs of Edinburgh performed a similar service in an even more philosophically marginal way. In England the circle around Bentham, animated by James Mill and culminating in J. S. Mill, was a more austere kind of salon.

Kant, notoriously, spent his entire life in the spiritual Siberia of Königsberg. Fichte and Hegel were at Jena and Berlin (Schelling was also briefly at Berlin, as Schopenhauer had been even more briefly). Schleiermacher was active in Berlin through the whole Hegelian period. After the middle of the nineteenth century German philosophers seemed to be spread broadly over the universities of the whole country. Lotze was at Göttingen, where Herbart had finished his career. Cohen and Natorp were at Marburg, Windelband and Rickert at Heidelberg, leading the two neo-Kantian schools. Dilthey and Cassirer both wound up in Berlin after various wanderings. Wundt was at Leipzig, Brentano at Vienna. This monadic organization of philosophy continued into the present century, with Husserl at Göttingen and then Freiburg im Breisgau, where his pupil Heidegger supplanted him.

By the middle of the nineteenth century, when German philosophy was fully professionalized, it was just taking the first steps in that direction in Britain and France. The concentration of the French university system on Paris has persisted to the present day, with nearly every philosopher of note winding up there sooner or later. In Britain, as Scottish philosophy petered out with the death of Hamilton in 1856, its doctrines were kept going with style and professionalism in Oxford by H. L. Mansel. Soon after his death in 1871 the idealist school of T. H. Green, Bradley, and Bosanquet quickly expanded and penetrated the rest of the country with the partial exception of Cambridge (for there were idealists there too, McTaggart, Ward, and Sorley, for example). But the latter soon gave way to the realists Russell and Moore after 1903, and they, in turn, in the 1930s, to Wittgenstein. (*Oxford philosophy; *Cambridge philosophy.)

Cambridge had made little contribution to philosophy in the Middle Ages, although it had come into existence very soon after Oxford. However, under the Tudor monarchs its former Protestantism had secured royal favour and, while Oxford slept, it produced Bacon and, later in the sixteenth century, the Cambridge Platonists with their massively learned reaction to Hobbes. In more recent times Cambridge, where philosophy has been studied as a full-time specialized subject, has always had many fewer students of philosophy than Oxford, where it has always been studied in conjunction with other subjects. Never-

theless the two universities achieved philosophical professionalism at much the same time, in Cambridge with Whewell, John Grote, and finally Sidgwick. Then, from about 1900, there was an extraordinary efflorescence. Four philosophers of outstanding gifts—Russell, Moore, Wittgenstein, and Ramsey—enabled Cambridge to dominate English philosophy until after the Second World War, despite the overwhelming numbers of their less inspiring Oxford colleagues. When Oxford philosophy revived, it was through the work of Cambridge-influenced Oxford philosophers: Price, Ryle, and Ayer. With these three, together with Austin and Strawson, Oxford took the lead and attracted visiting American philosophers in the first few post-war decades to such an extent that one of them reasonably described it as 'a philosophical boom town'. But since about 1970 the direction of movement has been reversed.

The universities of America were not much more than high schools or seminaries until well into the nineteenth century. Before that the only centre had been the Boston area, where Emerson and the Transcendentalists were to be found. (*Transcendentalism.) There was a great period or golden age at Harvard from about 1890 up to the First World War, in the epoch of James, Santayana, and Royce, and with Peirce in the background. Another, still in progress, began at the end of the Second World War. (*Harvard philosophy.) Dewey presided over an active department at Columbia, in the inter-war years the official headquarters of pragmatism. Berkeley, Princeton, and Michigan have been important departments since the 1940s. This period has been one in which a Germanic system of scattered local heroes has been largely overcome by the dominance of a few major centres, above all Harvard. Recently, after a period in which it either produced or drew to itself a very large proportion of the most highly regarded American philosophers, Harvard has suffered by the departure from the scene, either by death or retirement, of most of these leading figures: Quine, Goodman, Putnam, Nozick, and Rawls, who have not been replaced by quite such magnetic people. A new centre appears to be developing in the New York metropolitan area, embracing Columbia and New York University in the city itself and Princeton and Rutgers in neighbouring New Jersey.

A.Q.

*pragmatism.

Randall Collins, *The Sociology of Philosophers* (Cambridge, Mass., 1998).

B. Kuklick, *A History of Philosophy in America, 1720–2000* (Oxford, 2001).

J. H. Newman, *Rise and Progress of Universities in Historical Sketches* (London, 1873), i.

philosophy, literary genres of. Philosophers have often been reluctant to admit that what they write is, in a sense, literature. Plato, a great poet, had the poets expelled from his Republic. Nevertheless, philosophy has been written through the centuries with regard to literary form and in accordance with various literary genres.

The dialogue was more or less invented by Plato and was used by him with unsurpassed mastery. But it has been used by other philosophers as well. Cicero in his philosophical dialogues imitated Plato. Berkeley, Hume, and Schelling (among others) used the form in more recent times. The dialogue serves to make clear that philosophy essentially is debate, controversy, dialectical argument.

The commentary is also a venerable genre. It was used in antiquity by e.g. Proclus in his influential commentaries on Plato. Among Arabic philosophers it was a favourite genre. Al-Farabi and Averroës became famous for their commentaries on Plato and Aristotle, and through them influenced later Latin medieval philosophy. But the commentary did not lose its importance with the waning of scholasticism. Even in modern times commentaries on Kant (Cohen, Cassirer, Bennett), on Hegel (McTaggart, Kojève, Hippolyte) or on Marx (Lukács, Althusser) have had an important impact. Philosophy feeds on philosophy. New interpretations of major thinkers open up new vistas.

The intellectual autobiography is useful for showing why a certain line of argument has seemed plausible or even necessary to the author and for bringing out the interplay between ideas and personalities. Plato's *Seventh Letter*, Augustine's *Confessions*, Descartes's *Discourse on the Method*, Mill's *Autobiography*, and Popper's *Unended Quest* could be mentioned here.

The short article is a genre adapted to the specialized philosophical journal of modern times. Within analytical philosophy the short article has suited the idea that the aim of philosophy is piecemeal problem-solving rather than building of systems.   S.N.

Berel Lang, *The Anatomy of Philosophical Style* (Oxford, 1990).

philosophy, the influence of. The most direct influence of philosophy has been the speculative initiation, and incubation within itself, of other intellectual disciplines: physics and mathematics from the early Greeks, Christian theology from Plato, Plotinus, and Aristotle, law from Hobbes and Bentham, economics and psychology from Locke, Hume, and the Utilitarians, criticism from Aristotle and Kant. This is really too intimate a relation to be described as influence and is, accordingly, a little more fully discussed in this Companion under the heading *philosophy, the value and use of.*

The main influence, properly speaking, of philosophy has been to underlie and, to a considerable extent, to inspire a great number of significant movements of thought embodying attitudes to man and society and, as bearing on them, nature and the universe at large. The first of these is *Stoicism, whose ideals of fortitude, cosmopolitanism, and public service suited the traditional outlook of the Romans and served them well as the working ideology of their world empire.

More profound and lasting was the influence of the philosophies of Plato, and, even more, Plotinus, on the elaborate and sophisticated system of Christian theology with which the Fathers of the Church transformed an intellectually rudimentary kind of dissident Judaism into the operative faith of the Western world for a millennium and a half. With the recovery of Aristotle for the West in the twelfth century, Augustine's Neoplatonic theology was greatly modified by Thomist *scholasticism, but was revived by the Protestant Reformation, which was to a large extent anti-philosophical, despite the part played in its emergence by men trained in philosophy: Wyclif, Luther, Calvin, and Melanchthon.

The rejection of Thomist rationalism by Ockham, and his confinement of rational knowledge to the empirically intuitable natural world, led his followers, notably Buridan and Oresme, to anticipate the great scientific flowering of the seventeenth century with theories of inertia and a mechanical conception of nature. A renewed study of Plato was at the centre of the preoccupation of the leading figures of the Renaissance with the human soul. Descartes, although finally overwhelmed by Newton, for some time took a dominant place in the seventeenth-century scientific revolution, in which, like Leibniz, he directly participated.

The application of 'the experimental method of reasoning to moral subjects' practised by Hobbes and Hume (and so described by the latter) was too scandalous in its first appearance to have much immediate influence. Locke, in whom empiricism and Gassendi's materialism were mitigated by borrowings from Descartes, in effect invented *liberalism. He exerted a major influence on the *philosophes of eighteenth-century France by way of Voltaire. They cleared the ground for the French Revolution by their criticisms of absolute monarchy and its ideological instrument, the Church. But it was Rousseau who was to inspire the extreme, Jacobin phase of the Revolution. In the United States Locke was taken over wholesale and was honourably plagiarized in the Declaration of Independence. As the ideologist of the Glorious Revolution of 1688, he was not without honour at home. His principles were invoked by the Whig governments which were dominant through most of the eighteenth-century in Britain; wholly until the accession of George III in 1760 and from time to time until the start of a long period of Tory rule in 1784.

*Romanticism was heavily dependent on philosophy. Its emphasis on emotion and liberation (especially of creative spirits) derived from Rousseau. Its notion of a higher, non-analytic kind of reason was taken from the post-Kantians, Fichte, and Schelling, most directly by Coleridge. Of romantic affiliation was Herder's notion of the unique individuality of particular peoples. The nationalism this implied was more aggressively affirmed by Fichte and bureaucratized by Hegel, with some marginal borrowings from Rousseau and Burke. The way was prepared for the rampant nationalism of the nineteenth century and the erosion of dynastic absolutism.

In Britain, where national identity had been assured, with some help from geography, for 400 years, the emphasis was on reform, intensified by the effects of urbanization and the growth of industry. The *utilitarianism of Bentham and the Mills discarded the natural-rights liberalism of Locke and reached back to the starker doctrines of Hobbes and Hume. Marx depended on Hegel, even if he turned him upside-down, basing history on man's material and economic life rather than on the progress of Spirit. Schopenhauer and Nietzsche rejected the rational optimism of the Enlightenment, respectively accepting and glorifying the will and preparing the way for all kinds of anti-rational excess in belief and practice.

In the wasteland of modernity a host of belief systems largely untouched by philosophy sprang up, like the oriental religions of imperial Rome: *fascism, nudism, *vegetarianism, parapsychology, environmentalism. *Feminism broke away from its demure nineteenth-century liberal form, along with parallel movements for the emancipation of homosexuals and animals. Psychiatry turned from Freud's sombre recognition of the dependence of civilization on the control of instinct to ecstatic doctrines of the total liberation of impulse. If not inspired, all this was at least abetted by philosophies such as *existentialism and *post-structuralism which proclaimed the inescapable arbitrariness of choice, the death of man, and the inherent self-deceivingness of any kind of rationalism. English-speaking analytic philosophers, notably Russell and Popper, both widely read by non-philosophers, sustained the battered programme of the Enlightenment, arguing for the continuing liberalization of constraining institutions: education, marriage, property, and the state.   A.Q.

> *philosopher may preach; pseudo-philosophy; Marxist philosophy; Platonism; Thomism.

philosophy, maps of: *see* Appendix.

philosophy, popular: *see* popular philosophy.

philosophy, pseudo-: *see* pseudo-philosophy.

philosophy, radical: *see* radical philosophy.

philosophy, teaching: *see* teaching philosophy.

philosophy, the value and use of. The direct value and use of philosophy is either intrinsic or educational. Intrinsically it satisfies, or seeks to satisfy, the intellectual desire for comprehensive knowledge or understanding. We approach the world and the management of our lives within it with a miscellany of more or less unconnected beliefs, preferences, and habits of action, largely acquired from or imposed by others. There is a natural, if by no means universal, desire to order this material systematically, to find out how all the bits and pieces fit together, and to achieve theoretical and practical autonomy by a critical sifting and purification of the beliefs and preferences with which we find ourselves equipped. To be philosophically inclined is to want to make one's convictions systematic and authorized by ourselves by way of critical reflection on what we might otherwise take for

granted. It is to pursue a rationally founded conception of the world and system of values and, as a pre-condition of that, an understanding of what we really know or have good reason to believe. That is an idealized picture, no doubt, but it defines the intrinsic value and use of philosophy in terms of its aims, if not altogether in terms of what is achieved.

Educationally the direct value and use of philosophy is its emphasis on *argument or *reasoning. These are to be found, of course, in the study of any intellectual discipline, pretty much by definition. But the proportion of argument to data argued from is much higher than in any other study, apart from mathematics. And the data of philosophy are much more concrete and various in kind than those of mathematics. Philosophy starts from the commonest and most elemental items of common knowledge: that there are material things, past events, and other people, and that we have, or seem to have, knowledge of them. It goes on to ask whether that is so and what is required if our supposed knowledge is to be possible. Philosophy can claim, on this account, to be a good training in self-critical rationality and a valuable accompaniment to any study in which reasoning plays an important part, but is not explicitly reflected on. In so far as the study of philosophy includes the study of its history it can provide some acquaintance with the overall shape of the large movements of the mind in history. It often does this badly by disconnecting past philosophers from each other and from their intellectual environment.

Philosophy also has indirect uses. The most important of these has been that of first nurturing and then setting free other disciplines (often with a familiar kind of parental reluctance and retentiveness). Physics and mathematics proper (as distinct from mere reckoning in trade or surveying) derived from early Greek cosmology. Christian theology, in successive phases, was the child of the philosophies of Plato and Aristotle. Scientific psychology and economics developed from associationist and utilitarian philosophies of mind and action. Jurisprudence emerged from various kinds of political philosophy (from the Stoics, Bacon, and Hobbes), as did political science. Philosophy at least played some part in the transformation of history from mere chronicle into explanatory narrative and has tempted it at times into metahistorical systematization of history as a whole. In the present epoch linguistics has largely extricated itself from the maternal embrace of philosophy.

Finally, philosophy, in a popular sense of the word, has aimed to satisfy a widespread popular need, typically by way of guidance in the conduct of life (from Socrates, the Stoics, and the Epicureans onward) or, where there is no scope for guidance, as with the inevitability of death and other blows of misfortune, by way of consolation, for the most part more austerely than religion does. (*Popular philosophy.)   A.Q.

> *Lumber of the Schools; bladders of philosophy; divine philosophy; fingering slave; clip an angel's wings.

philosophy, women in: *see* women in philosophy.

philosophy and literature: *see* literature and philosophy.

philosophy and ordinary language: *see* ordinary language and philosophy.

philosophy and psychology: *see* psychology and philosophy.

philosophy and real life. Claims by one philosophical tradition to capture real life better than another presuppose further claims concerning what it is about reality that philosophy should aim to capture. Traditional metaphysics bears the mark of *Parmenides' conclusion that there is no real change in the world. In the light of the One, the life that does change is lost to view or dismissed as illusory. The complaint that philosophy has treated its questions at too abstract a level is often laid at the door of *Plato's appropriation of *Socrates, for whom philosophy was an activity designed educatively to recast questions rather than provide any answers. When *Kierkegaard asked his philosophy teacher what relation philosophy had to actual life, it was with the thought that this long-standing trend should be reversed. That philosophical questioning begins with the 'existing' individual is the view of existentialists, whose reaction to the tradition culminating in *Hegel was led by Kierkegaard himself. Whereas he focused on philosophers' attempts to capture within a closed system something that is essentially open-ended, later critics were concerned to replace the traditional vocabulary with one that better maps the contours of life as it is lived. *Existentialism thus re-situated philosophy by replacing its impersonal viewpoint with a subjective one, and the methods of philosophical reasoning with a descriptive approach claiming to do better justice to life itself. Some *linguistic philosophy may be said to be informed by a similar aim. This shift of viewpoint contrasts with *Marxist philosophy's quasi-scientific socio-economic focus and with the generalizing tendencies of philosophical *anthropology, but also with the approach of 'applied' philosophy which focuses on the ethical dilemmas of professional and political life. Employing traditional methods of reasoning, this draws on an armoury established by philosophy's recent analytic past and on standard versions of the more enduring moral theories. Apart from generating large and specialized literatures, *bioethics and *business ethics have contributed to a public image of the philosopher as a professional among others, and of philosophy itself as a service industry of use in formulating guide-lines for ethically acceptable behaviour. In this endeavour what counts is less any special philosophical insight than an ability inherited from analytic philosophy to give debates a manageable and surveyable form.   A.H.

J. Cottingham, *On the Meaning of Life* (London, 2003).

A. Hannay, 'What Can Philosophers Contribute to Social Ethics?', *Topoi* (1998).

D. Moran and T. Mooney (eds.), *The Phenomenology Reader* (London, 2002).

philosophy and science. How are *philosophy and science related to one another?

I. It has often been claimed that the method of reasoning adopted by modern science is the method of reasoning that philosophy should also adopt in dealing with at least some of its problems. Thus Hume subtitled his *Treatise of Human Nature* 'An Attempt to Introduce the Experimental Method of Reasoning into Moral Subjects'. It was as if he took his sceptical philosophy to be a pioneering contribution to what we should now call experimental psychology. Similarly on Quine's view, in *Ontological Relativity and Other Essays* (New York, 1969), 82–3, epistemology should be regarded 'as a chapter of psychology and hence of natural science' because it studies 'a natural phenomenon'. Specifically, according to Quine, it studies a physical human subject that receives as input a sequence of patterns of irradiation in assorted frequencies and delivers as output a description of the three-dimensional external world and its history.

We need to ask the following question, however: how much of the procedures adopted by physicists, chemists, biologists, etc., since AD 1600 or thereabouts is to count here as a part of the method of natural science? Kant described himself, in the preface to the second edition of his *Kritik der reinen Vernunft* (tr. N. Kemp Smith (London, 1929)), 21–3, as seeking to put metaphysics 'on the sure path of a science'. He thought that via his critical method metaphysics could achieve the same level of consensual certainty as that which was supposed to belong to the mathematics and physics of his time. In the reformed metaphysics it would no longer be possible to construct pairs of arguments that were both apparently sound yet had mutually opposed conclusions. But this would not make metaphysics a branch of mathematics or physics. Similarly Russell held, in his *History of Western Philosophy* (London, 1946), 862–4, that in the practice of philosophical analysis (as, for example, in his own philosophy of mathematics) a method of procedure is used that resembles scientific reasoning in respect of its ability to achieve definite, consensually acceptable answers for certain problems and therewith successive approximations to the understanding of a whole field of inquiry. But Russell's claim was not as bold as that of Hume and Quine. In particular he did not share their view that the extent of the resemblance between philosophical and scientific method included a shared use of controlled experiment and observation. Popper too has theorized, in his *Conjectures and Refutations* (London, 1963), 198–200, that like any science philosophy must first proceed by the isolation of a problem and then by the proposal and criticism of a hypothesis for the problem's solution. But he does not expect an epistemological theory of this nature to be empirically refutable. How *could* he expect it to be empirically refutable if the subject-matter that might refute it does not belong either to the mental or to the physical world but to what, in *Objective Knowledge: An Evolutionary Approach* (Oxford, 1972), 107–9, he calls 'the third world . . . of problems, theories and arguments'? Again Comte, in his *Cours de philosophie positive* (Paris, 1830), i. 2–56, held it to be a fundamental law of mental development that both communities and individuals pass from a 'theological or fictitious state' into a 'metaphysical or abstract state' and from the latter into a 'scientific or positive' one. And it is from Comte's use of the term 'positive' in this connection that *'positivism' has come to be the name given to any philosophical theory that assigns a dominant intellectual role to empirical science. But Comte's view was that metaphysical thinking should be replaced by scientific thinking, not that metaphysical thinking should consist in a kind of scientific thinking.

Many philosophers have implicitly or explicitly rejected any such scientistic paradigm. Certainly the sceptical tradition cannot easily be reconciled with this conception of philosophy. If you deny that knowledge is possible, then *a fortiori* you deny that any paradigm of knowledge exists. If genuine science is beyond human capacity, it is pointless to urge philosophers to imitate it. Indeed, when Socrates claimed to know nothing but his own ignorance, he was scorning those of his contemporaries who claimed to know more than this. Nor can philosophy stand in unbiased judgement over the principles and assumptions of the sciences if it is itself one of them: for example, in Plato's *Republic*, book 7, the author's conception of philosophy—under the name of *'dialectic'—as an architectonic discipline left no room for it to take geometry, arithmetic, or one of the other sciences as its paradigm. Moreover, against Russell's thesis that philosophy should proceed like a science, there stands the emphasis placed by some other analytical philosophers, like Ayer in his *Language, Truth and Logic* (London, 1946), 33–70, on the importance of the difference between *analytic and synthetic propositions, with the conclusions of philosophical inquiry being said to be characteristically analytic while the conclusions of physical, chemical, or biological inquiry are said to be characteristically synthetic. The former articulate the implications of a word's or phrase's meaning; the latter describe features of objects. And, whereas scientific conclusions need always to be based on valid reasoning from appropriate premises, there are philosophers, like Samuel Alexander and Derrida, who purport to spurn all attempts at philosophical reasoning. Alexander claimed, in his 'Some Explanations', *Mind* (1931), 423, to 'dislike argument'. And Derrida has said, in 'Limited Inc abc', *Glyph* (1977), supplement, 56, that he detests discussion, subtleties, and ratiocinations.

II. In the face of so much disagreement the best way forward is to seek out those features in which philosophy does seem to resemble a natural or social science and those in which it does not.

For example, it is scarcely to be denied, even if it verges on platitude to assert, that both types of inquiry involve the solution of intellectual problems. In particular cases they may involve the solution of practical problems also, but this is not a necessary feature. On the one side, for a scientist, to know what causes a given process is very often also to know how to produce it. But practical knowledge does not accompany theoretical if the process caused is the explosion of a supernova. On the other side, if as a philosopher one accepts an appropriate type of analysis of *personal identity, one may have acquired thereby the ability to reconcile oneself to a loved one's apparent death. Perhaps people are really immortal, so that reflection on the relevant philosophical analysis provides a technology of consolation. But others who accept the same analysis may nevertheless be inconsolable. A well-constructed analysis of logical entailment may assist the task of persuading someone to acknowledge the validity of a long and subtle argument. But others may still be unable to grasp it.

Again, the results of scientific inquiry are always expected to be consistent with one another overall, and so too are the results of philosophical inquiry. In either case any inconsistency is regarded as a fault or inadequacy, and functions as a sign of where more work needs to be done.

More interestingly, perhaps, it is worth noting that, as in science, so too in philosophy both deductive and inductive patterns of argument are to be found. Thus on the one hand Descartes, in his *Discours de la méthode* (Leiden, 1637), part v, sought to *deduce* the existence of God from certain self-evident first principles, and Ryle, in *The Concept of Mind* (London, 1949), 8, claimed to be mainly using *reductio ad absurdum* arguments. On the other hand the movement of philosophical thought is often inductive rather than deductive. This occurs when the validity of some general principle is supported by an appeal to involuntary intuition in a particular kind of case. For example, Bernard Williams, in his 'Moral Luck', *Proceedings of the Aristotelian Society* (1976), 117 ff., declares that his 'procedure in general will be to invite reflection about how to think and feel about some rather less usual situation, in the light of an appeal to how we—many people—tend to think about other more usual situations'. Again Quine, for example in his *Word and Object* (Cambridge, Mass., 1960), 157–61, defends his hostility to logical modalities, intentional objects, and subjunctive conditionals by appeals to the logical intuitions that this or that utterance may provoke. And Putnam, in his 'Mind, Language and Reality', in *Philosophical Papers* (Cambridge, 1975), ii. 224, tells a science-fiction story to evoke an intuition about the use of the term 'water' on a look-alike planet earth in order to support the thesis that the meaning of a scientific term is never just a function of the speaker's psychological state.

Important features of dissimilarity, however, are also to be found.

In science the data that support inductive conclusions are data that emerge, albeit involuntarily, from experiment or observation, not from intuition or intellectual conscience. Correspondingly, whatever the field of their research, scientists are expected to achieve consensus, and the history of modern science is full of such achievement.

Moreover, this expectation is embodied in accepted patterns of institutional endorsement, i.e. in the publication of universally respected textbooks, in elections to official academies, and so on. Nor could science progress through teamwork, as it often does, unless consensus were the norm.

But, where two philosophical theories oppose one another, that opposition is not necessarily seen as showing that one or both of the theories must be faulty. In this way philosophy is perhaps more like art than like science. An art gallery is the richer for the fact that it possesses paintings in the realist style as well as in the impressionist one. Our culture also profits analogously from the opposition between philosophical realism and philosophical idealism, albeit philosophical theories are constructed with the help of language and argument, not of canvas and paint, and convey an outlook on intellectual or social issues, not on visual ones.

Moreover, philosophy often has a normative aspect, which science lacks. Thus scientists set out to describe some aspect of how the world is, or of why it is so, or of what can be done to change it. But philosophers often set up ideals of how intellectual inquiry should proceed, or of what rationality requires, or of which socio-economic objectives should animate legislation. Roughly, while science can often supply knowledge of means, it is for philosophy to discuss the choice of fundamental ends.

III. Despite the important differences that exist between science and philosophy, each has had an important influence on the other. For example, the readiness of philosophers to question any customary assumption, or to explore any interesting speculation, has sometimes helped to open up new avenues of scientific inquiry or to provoke major revolutions in scientific theory. Empiricist theories of meaning, like Hume's, when mediated through the work of Mach, had a part in creating the climate of ideas in which it was possible for Einstein to regard the concept of absolute simultaneity as meaningless. Truth-functional analyses of implication, like the Stoics', are ancestors, via Boole's mathematical logic, of the systems of logic-gates that are essential to digital computers. But there is also the possibility that interest in methodological or epistemological problems may sometimes divert a scientist—especially a young and inexperienced one—from working on substantive scientific issues.

Conversely, major new developments in science tend to pose new problems for philosophers. Thus the triumph of quantum theory in physics sets new puzzles for those who investigate the structure of scientific explanation, since familiar deterministic assumptions seem no longer tenable. And new medical technology has generated many new problems in medical ethics with regard to the use of life-support mechanisms, organ transplants, experimentation on patients, choice of an infant's sex, etc.

Moreover, in addition to such interconnections between particular scientific developments and particular philosophical ones, the general notion of scientific progress has also been linked—sometimes positively and sometimes negatively—with philosophical attitudes.

Thus Utilitarians like John Stuart Mill have looked to science for a technology of happiness and have therefore been especially keen that the social sciences should emulate, wherever possible, the style and method of the natural sciences and attain a comparable level of success at prediction and explanation. And even though a *deontological ethics does not normally require assistance from science in order to achieve the realization of what it values, it does not repudiate such assistance either.

Some philosophers, on the other hand, have actually adopted a negative attitude to science, or part of science, as normally conceived. Sometimes this attitude rests on the claim that a superior science is relevant, such as a philosophically argued metaphysics or a creationist alternative to Darwinian *biology. Sometimes it rests instead on the claim that modern science is itself to be blamed for all the environmental pollution that its users have generated. But neither claim is well founded. Not a single consequence of an alternative epistemology has ever been generally accepted by all those who repudiate or despise modern experimental science. And the sources of environmental pollution are all to be traced to the activities of those who misuse scientific knowledge, not to the activities of those who discover it.

IV. Even if philosophy is not a kind of science, nor a rival of science, and even if it has had differences from science that are crucial to its nature, it may nevertheless be conveniently thought of, like science, as a species of knowledge—the self-knowledge of reason. At least three kinds of knowledge are then recognized. Science gives us systematic, institutionally warranted, and technologically exploitable knowledge of the uniformities and probabilities in our natural and social environments. Everyday knowledge informs us about the immediately obvious features of the facts that confront us. And philosophy provides knowledge of the fundamental principles and assumptions in accordance with which we reason. It is that kind of knowledge which is provided when a paradox is discovered, discussed, and resolved; when some form of *scepticism is proposed or refuted; when the body–mind interconnection is investigated; when the nature of mathematical proof is clarified; when foundations of moral or aesthetic value are established; when the possibility of the world's being subject to the control of an omniscient, omnipotent, and benevolent deity is examined; and so on.

Against this view of the relationship between science and philosophy a number of objections may be urged.

One possible objection is that belief is about matters of fact, as in science or everyday awareness, whereas philosophy is often concerned with rules, norms, values, or ideals. But again the premiss is false. Beliefs are not always about matters of fact. For example, one can claim to believe that a *modus ponens type of argument is necessarily valid or that children should be taught to read and write by the age of 7.

A second possible objection is that if philosophy does not, like science, aim at consensus it cannot be a species of knowledge. But there is a confusion here. Certainly it would be self-contradictory to say of one person that he knows that *p* and of another that he knows that not-*p*. But it is quite admissible to say of one person (whether in science, in everyday experience, or in philosophy) that he thinks that he knows that *p* and of another that he thinks that he knows that not-*p*—just as one painter or art critic may think that he knows the superiority of realism and another may think that he knows the superiority of impressionism. In other words to seek philosophical knowledge is to seek consensus, in that philosophers use argument in order to persuade one another of the correctness of their view. But a wise philosopher does not expect that philosophical consensus will ever be achieved, except locally and in the short run. So he does not expect that his arguments on a philosophical issue will be as cogent as those of a competent scientist on a scientific issue.

Thirdly, it might be said that philosophy cannot be a species of knowledge that ought to be classified co-ordinately with scientific knowledge since a sufficiently advanced neuroscience, matching software to hardware, could itself provide consensual knowledge about the fundamental principles and assumptions in accordance with which we reason. In other words, it will be said, a sufficiently detailed knowledge of the human brain's genetically controlled architecture will reveal the structure of our thinking ability. So philosophy is just a variety of scientific knowledge.

But that is to suppose the existence of a fully determinate, genetically programmed system of principles and assumptions, with no room for major variation in accordance with cultural inheritance or individual choice. *Evolution would instead have given the human species a survivally more valuable endowment if the genetically programmed system constituted only a loose framework within which a variety of alternative patterns of reasoning were possible, with the choice or construction of a particular pattern being settled in accordance with the perceived needs of the situation. Thus it may be tempting to suppose, for example, that people have an innate ability, which a well-developed neurology could explain, to learn to calculate arithmetically in the scale of 10. But in fact the ancient Greeks and Romans, and early medieval Europeans, had no such ability because their arithmetic lacked the number 0.

How are these vast areas of conceptual space, left neurologically indeterminate by genetic programmes, to be filled and used? Much of this great task is achieved by the unreflective endeavour of scientists or of intelligent people building on the inherited achievements of their forebears. But there is also room for philosophers to contribute through the critical and reflective exploration of alternative options. And neuroscience cannot take on this task because, even if a neuroscientist were able to detect the patterns of reasoning preferred by particular philosophers, he would still be left with the task of criticizing and

evaluating those patterns. That is, he would still need, in important respects, to operate as a philosopher.   L.J.C.

*science, history of the philosophy of; science, problems of the philosophy of.

J. Burnet, *Greek Philosophy: Thales to Plato* (London, 1914).
E. A. Burtt, *The Metaphysical Foundations of Modern Physical Science* (London, 1932).
L. J. Cohen, *The Dialogue of Reason* (Oxford, 1986).
R. G. Collingwood, *An Essay on Metaphysics* (Oxford, 1940).
T. Nagel, *The View from Nowhere* (Oxford, 1986).
M. Schlick, *The Problems of Philosophy in their Interconnection* (Dordrecht, 1987).

philosophy and theology: *see* theology and philosophy.

philosophy and the public. In an old Monty Python sketch on television, two teams of philosophers play a football match. The German idealists are competing against a squad of ancient Greeks for an undisclosed honour. But the game is a disaster because all the players waddle around scratching their beards rather than engaging with the ball. Such is philosophy's public image in Britain—philosophers are comic, their concerns inscrutable, and their capacity for recommending courses of action even to themselves terribly limited. To some members of the public, at least, philosophers remain as socially useless as Cratylus, the Hericlitean who found the world so perplexing that he was reduced to silently wagging a finger.

Behind the satire, though, there is a real disappointment that broadly empiricist philosophers seem temperamentally unable to answer purportedly profound and profoundly romantic philosophical questions that press themselves on the public—about the meaning of life, the nature of time, how to lead the good life. Even Stephen Hawking has rebuked philosophers for allegedly abandoning the great tradition of philosophy from Aristotle to Kant in favour of the mere analysis of meaning.

Julian Baggini suggests that the public's disappointment in philosophers now stems from a misconception. 'Carrying around some weird image of philosophers as New Age gurus or spiritual leaders, they don't seem to realise that the vast majority of modern philosophy is technical, specialised and about as relevant to the concerns of everyday life as theoretical physics.'

No wonder, then, that anxious members of the public, seeking happiness or the meaning of life, take succour in glib answers to questions that some professional philosophers might regard as strictly senseless. The extent to which the public buys books by non-philosophers purporting to be philosophy, such as *Sophie's World* by Jostein Gaarder or *Consolations of Philosophy* by Alain de Botton, is perhaps a good measure of the need for such succour. Worse yet, traditionally philosophical problems have been appropriated in considerable measure by charismatic academics from other disciplines who have have achieved much public success with popular books. Thus the nature of time has been tackled by physicists, and consciousness by evolutionary biologists and quantum theorists. Often such appropriations have been regarded as disastrous over-simplifications by professional philosophers. But when pitted against the showmanship of the evolutionary biologist Steven Pinker or the gusto of the zoologist Richard Dawkins, the compunctions of philosophers, and their concern that scientists' answers sometimes elide what makes a particular problem fascinating or at least difficult, are likely to be about as compelling to the public as an all-philosophers' football match.

In part, philosophy's public-relations problem is to do with the current dearth of philosophers who are good public performers. This is hardly a purely British problem, if it is a problem at all: the late John Rawls, for instance, was an impeccably reticent American academic, but in the age of the mass media this dignified reticence may well be taken as intolerable. Perhaps one thing that philosophy needs to improve its public image is a few charismatic monsters of egotism—a latter-day Russell, for instance— but monsters who are good on telly.

This PR problem applies primarily to anglophone philosophy. In France, to take one example, deference to philosophers is such that Pythonesque satire is all but inconceivable. One might well ask why. An answer might well take in the following points. In France, there is a tradition of the *philosophe engagé*, one who gets rather noisily involved in public affairs and who can perform his or her thoughts compellingly in newspapers or on TV. One need only think of Sartre or Bernard-Henri Lévy to get the idea. Across the Channel, too, philosophical work, such as it is, often has a romantic tenor that is publicly compelling. It may well be seductive to the public that Heidegger dealt with the question of being, a matter of great pomp and mystique; rather less sexy is an anglophone analytical philosophy that deals with questions of meaning. And yet, even when a continental philosopher such as Jacques Derrida engages with what are primarily linguistic matters, his tilting at the windmills of meaning has a romantic flourish that makes what he does publicly appealing and superficially comprehensible. Everyone thinks they know what he means by 'deconstruction', and many suppose it to be a grand philosophical project of the kind that anglophone empiricists seem incapable of pursuing.

What future for anglophone philosophers seeking a public role? One suggestion is that they can serve as intellectual firefighters, called in to quell blazing rows that are the result of muddled thinking or sloppy arguments over such issues as abortion, euthanasia, cloning, and war. Whether there is a public demand for them to perform this role is questionable. s.j.

Julian Baggini, *Making Sense: Philosophy behind the Headlines* (London, 2002).

Alain de Botton, *Consolations of Philosophy* (London, 2002).

Vincent Descombes, *Modern French Philosophy* (Cambridge, 1981).

Jostein Gaarder, *Sophie's World*, tr. Paulette Moller (London, 1996).

Stephen Hawking, *A Brief History of Time* (London, 1988).

Bertrand Russell, *History of Western Philosophy* (London, 1946).

philosophy and war: *see* war and philosophy.

philosophy of education: *see* education, history of the philosophy of; education, problems of the philosophy of.

philosophy of history: *see* history, history of the philosophy of; history, problems of the philosophy of.

philosophy of language: *see* language, history of the philosophy of; language, problems of the philosophy of.

philosophy of law: *see* law, history of the philosophy of; law, problems of the philosophy of.

philosophy of life: *see* life, philosophy of.

philosophy of mathematics: *see* mathematics, history of the philosophy of; mathematics, problems of the philosophy of.

philosophy of mind: *see* mind, history of the philosophy of; mind, problems of the philosophy of.

philosophy of religion: *see* religion, history of the philosophy of; religion, problems of the philosophy of.

philosophy of science: *see* science, history of the philosophy of; science, problems of the philosophy of.

philosophy of social science: *see* social science, philosophy of.

philosophy: world and underworld. Ideas which either violate important canons of reasoning or which are simply far out and unfamiliar are frowned upon by some philosophers and are assigned by them to a philosophical underworld. Examples are concerns about black and white magic, revivals of alchemical and occult systems, offshoots of psychoanalysis and of C. G. Jung's psychology, large parts of New Age thinking, certain versions of feminism, general views surrounding astrology, unclear ideas proposed by scientists (Bohr's idea of complementarity or Kuhn's idea of incommensurability), and so on.

However, speaking of an *under*world of *philosophy assumes that there is a *world* of philosophy, i.e. a well-defined and more or less uniform domain of discourse and/or activity. Such *worlds* do indeed exist. Every school of philosophy that has not yet started falling apart has the unity required by the assumption. But it seems doubtful that the collection of all schools, at all times and in all places, or even the sum total of today's philosophy departments at Western universities shares ideas and standards that are sufficiently substantial to define a world and a corresponding underworld.

We have no comprehensive studies of the matter; however, there exists strong anecdotal evidence undermining any sort of uniformity. No self-respecting British philosopher would try to revive the idea, found in Augustine, that the harmonious musical intervals represent truth in a way inaccessible to human reason. The Herder of the *Ideen* was beyond the pale for Kant, Kant for the Nietzsche of the *Antichrist*, Hegel for Schopenhauer, the Wittgenstein of the *Investigations* for Russell, Tarski for the Wittgenstein of the *Investigations*, and all of traditional philosophy for the founders of the Vienna Circle and the practitioners of deconstruction. All these ideas are now held (by Anglo-American philosophers) to belong to philosophy proper and are deposited in its history. Making them measures of philosophical excellence we obtain an 'underworld' devoid of content.

And this is exactly as it ought to be. Both in the West and elsewhere philosophy started out as a universal criticism of earlier views (in Greece the earlier views were those of the Homeric epics). The gradual subdivision of research and its professionalization left philosophers with two options: to become specialists themselves or to continue dealing with and being nourished by *all* human ideas, efforts, procedures. In the first case we do get underworlds—but there will be different underworlds for different schools (in the sciences the situation is the same; molecular biologists have an underworld that differs from that of, say, cosmologists and certainly from the underworld of some sociological schools). An honest professional philosopher would therefore say: 'Being a positivist [for example] I reject Jung's idea of a collective unconscious' and not: 'Jung is *philosophically* absurd'. In the second case we move beyond the domain of academic philosophy into a form of life that excludes nothing though it does not hesitate to make definite suggestions for definite occasions.　　　　　P.K.F.

*pseudo-philosophy.

phrastic: *see* neustic and phrastic.

phronēsis. Practical *wisdom. In ancient Greek the term (frequently interchangeable with *sophia*) has connotations of intelligence and soundness of judgement, especially in practical contexts. In Aristotle's ethics it is the complete excellence of the practical intellect, the counterpart of *sophia* in the theoretical sphere, comprising a true conception of the good life and the deliberative excellence necessary to realize that conception in practice via choice (*prohairesis*).　　　　　C.C.W.T.

R. Sorabji, 'Aristotle on the Rôle of the Intellect in Virtue', *Proceedings of the Aristotelian Society* (1973–4); repr. in A. Rorty (ed.), *Essays on Aristotle's Ethics* (Berkeley, Calif., 1980).

physicalism. The doctrine that everything is physical. Also called *materialism, the view is associated with Democritus, Epicurus, Lucretius, Hobbes, Holbach, T. H. Huxley, J. B. Watson, Carnap, Quine, and Smart. Physicalists hold that the real world contains nothing but matter and energy, and that objects have only physical properties, such as spatio-temporal position, mass, size, shape, motion, hardness, electrical charge, magnetism, and gravity. Exceptions are sometimes made for *abstract entities such as numbers, sets, and propositions.

The principal argument for physicalism is the success of physics. Physicists have been able to explain a large and diverse range of phenomena in terms of a few fundamental physical laws. The principle that the properties of larger objects are determined by those of their physical parts is confirmed daily. The physical basis of celestial phenomena was recognized in the seventeenth century, that of chemistry in the eighteenth, and of biology in the nineteenth. The neurophysiological basis of psychology has become increasingly apparent in the twentieth century.

The principal objections to physicalism have come from theology, epistemology, and psychology. Theological objections stem from the widespread belief in supernatural, immaterial gods, and in special creation and life after death. Epistemological objections come from idealist or phenomenalist philosophers such as Berkeley, Hume, Kant, Hegel, and Mill, who hold that our ideas or sense-data are the only objects of direct perception, from which they conclude that everything must reduce to the mental. Psychological objections have been especially acute since Descartes, whose *dualism still has many vigorous adherents. The basic objection is that thinking, emotions, and sensations seem utterly unlike length, mass, and gravity. And physiologists are far from specifying neural states perfectly correlated with even one mental state. Physicalists respond either by denying the existence of the allegedly non-physical phenomena (*eliminative materialism), or by arguing that it must really be physical (reductive materialism; also *identity theory; *behaviourism; *central-state materialism).　　　　　W.A.D.

C. Gillett and B. Loewer (eds.), *Physicalism and its Discontents* (Cambridge, 2001).

D. Hull, *Philosophy of Biological Science* (Englewood Cliffs, NJ, 1974).

D. M. Rosenthal (ed.), *The Nature of Mind* (Oxford, 1991).

physicalism in the philosophy of mind. Physicalism in the philosophy of mind is an application of the general metaphysical thesis of physicalism, namely the claim that everything in the space-time world is physical. Concerning the sphere of the mental, then, physicalism claims that all the facts about minds and mentality are physical facts. This claim is usefully divided into two parts: *ontological physicalism*, which holds that there are no mental particulars, all the individuals of this world being physical particulars and their aggregates, and *property physicalism*, which holds that all properties of these individuals are physical properties.

Ontological physicalism excludes such putative entities as immaterial souls, Cartesian mental substances, 'entelechies', and 'vital forces'. If all physical entities (e.g. all physical particles) were taken away from this world, nothing would remain—not even an empty space-time framework. This contrasts with Cartesian substance dualism according to which minds are substances of a special kind and could in principle exist even if nothing material existed. Many ontological physicalists, however, reject the reductionist view that all properties had by physical systems are exclusively physical properties; they hold the dualist thesis that complex physical structures, like biological organisms, can have irreducibly non-physical properties, such as *consciousness and *intentionality, two properties often taken to be constitutive of mentality. This is what is known as non-reductive physicalism, a position that combines physical monism with property dualism. In contrast, property physicalism, or reductive physicalism, holds that all properties of physical systems are either physical properties or reducible to them; that is, in so far as mental properties are genuine properties of physical systems, they must be reducible to physical properties.

A general characterization of 'physical property' is a difficult, and controversial, matter; for the present purposes, we may skirt this general issue by taking as our paradigmatic physical properties the fundamental properties and magnitudes of theoretical physics (e.g. mass, energy, charge) and properties definable or reducible in terms of them.

*Emergentism is a form of non-reductive physicalism. On this view, when a physical structure reaches a certain level of structural complexity, it comes to exhibit novel, *emergent properties, most notably life and consciousness, whose occurrences are unpredictable and inexplicable on the basis of its physical constituents and the laws that govern them. A majority of those who hold a functionalist view about mentality, too, think of themselves as non-reductive physicalists; for, according to them, mental properties and kinds are functional—perhaps computational—properties and kinds defined in terms of input and output, not physico-chemical ones or biological ones. Non-reductive physicalism has been the most influential position on the *mind–body problem since the 1970s. However, it has recently come under attack by reductive physicalists on the ground that it is not able to account for mental causation, and that it supports an incorrect view of the interlevel relationships of the sciences.

Most non-reductive physicalists acknowledge the priority of physical properties and physical laws, at least in the following sense ('the *supervenience thesis'): the physical character of a thing determines its whole character, including its mental character. That is, there could not be two objects, or events, exactly alike in all physical respects and yet differing in some mental respect.

The principal argument against reductive physicalism has been the *variable (or multiple) realizability of mental, and other higher-level, properties. Pain, for example, may be 'realized' in humans by the activation of C-fibres (let us say), but in different animal species (perhaps also in electro-mechanical systems) we must expect different physical mechanisms to subserve pain. In fact, there may be no upper bound to the possible realizers of pain in all actual and possible systems. If this is true, pain cannot be identified with any single physical kind. This point holds generally, it has been argued, for all higher-level properties, including biological properties in relation to physico-chemical properties. (See *functionalism; reductionism.)

However, those who reject reductive physicalism for this reason, hold the thesis that mental and other higher-level properties can be realized only by physical properties. This view can be called 'realization physicalism', and it can explain why mind–body supervenience obtains; it entails that physically identical systems realize the same higher-level properties, including mental properties. Realization physicalism, even if it may fall short of full reductive physicalism, is a strong physicalism position.

Another objection to reductive physicalism is based on the frankly dualist claim that, given their distinctively mental character, mental properties simply could not be physical properties. Even if, say, pain should turn out to have a single neural-physical correlate across all organisms and other possible pain-capable systems, how could the painfulness of pain be a neurobiological property? In moving from the mental to the physical, we lose, it has been argued, what is mental about mental properties, such as their qualitative character and their subjectivity. In this vein, it has been argued that for physicalism to be true, conscious events and processes must be shown not to be 'over and above' physical-biological processes, and that showing this requires showing that physical-biological facts of this world must logically entail facts about consciousness. But this cannot be shown, it has been argued in a manner reminiscent of the dualist arguments of Descartes, since we can perfectly well conceive of a world just like the actual world but one in which no consciousness exists and human-like creatures in it are mindless *'zombies', and hence such a world is a logically possible world. This argument remains highly controversial, however.   J.K.

*Mary, black and white.

D. Chalmers, *The Conscious Mind* (New York, 1996).

J. Fodor, 'Special Sciences, or the Disunity of Science as a Working Hypothesis', *Synthese*, 28 (1974).

C. Gillett and B. Loewer (eds.), *Physicalism and its Discontents* (Cambridge, 2001).

S. Kripke, *Naming and Necessity* (Cambridge, Mass., 1980).

D. Papineau, *Thinking about Consciousness* (Oxford, 2002).

J. J. C. Smart, *Philosophy and Scientific Realism* (London, 1963).

physics, philosophical problems of. Most of these are distinctly *metaphysical*, and arise from attempting to take seriously the picture of the world provided by modern physics. Typically what philosophers of physics do is to employ recent thinking in metaphysics, about the *identity of indiscernibles, *dispositions, *causality, *time, etc., to inform our understanding of modern physics—though they frequently argue for revising current metaphysical thought as well. However, philosophers of physics are also concerned with the more general *epistemological* problems of philosophy of science, like the underdetermination of theory by empirical data or the status of unobservable entities. For such problems come into sharp focus when posed in the context of particular physical theories (e.g. string theory) or particular theoretical entities (e.g. quarks), bringing the hope that these problems may be better understood—perhaps even resolved.

The involvement of philosophy in physics is not new. Newton, Leibniz, Descartes, Mach, and Poincaré, to name but a few classical physicists, all couched their ideas about the physical world in philosophical, as well as quantitative, terms. But the intermingling of philosophy with physics has become even more apparent with the emergence of the kind of abstract theories that have come to dominate physics in this century.

For example, as a prelude to establishing in his special theory of relativity that simultaneity is not an objective concept independent of an observer's state of motion, Einstein needed to 'clear the way' by giving an epistemological critique of the methods observers can use to establish whether spatially separated events are simultaneous. And Einstein cleared the way for his general theory of relativity by arguing (from the way that gravity affects objects independently of their size or make-up) that an object's motion under gravity is indistinguishable from the motion it would be seen to have, in the absence of gravity, from the perspective of an observer accelerating past it (Einstein's celebrated 'principle of equivalence'). Similar epistemological critiques, for example of the procedures by which we can determine both the position and momentum of a particle (the *uncertainty principle), were formative in the early development of *quantum mechanics.

In light of this, it is unfortunate that many physicists today regard philosophers as having little to contribute to the advance of physics; either because the problems that capture their attention are too mundane or idiosyncratic to be relevant, or because philosophers are perceived to lack the necessary mathematical training for settling fundamental issues.

Nevertheless, the twentieth century has given rise to a 'new breed' of physically trained philosophers in close contact with the technical side of physics and how it affects philosophical issues: like how to reconcile the tendency of macroscopic systems to approach equilibrium over time with the underlying time-reversal invariance of physical laws; how to make sense of removing the infinities predicted by quantum field theory by 'renormalizing'; and whether a plausible formulation of the 'cosmic censorship' hypothesis holds true in general relativity so that *determinism can be safeguarded against naked singularities. Reichenbach was probably the first of this new breed, though since then the philosophers that immediately spring to mind are Earman, Fine, Grünbaum, Malament, Redhead, Shimony, Torretti, and van Fraassen.

Two examples will serve to indicate the capacity modern physics has to impinge on both metaphysics and epistemology. Both examples will again be drawn from the special and general theories of *relativity (but *quantum mechanics is also relevant).

The relativity of simultaneity in special relativity affects traditional metaphysical views about the nature of time; in particular, the view that only events occurring in the present (or past) are real, while events in the future are not yet 'fixed', or have yet to come into being. At the moment two observers in relative motion pass, their differing standards of simultaneity will force them to disagree on what

events are in the 'future' and what are in the 'past'. So, on the traditional view, they would have to disagree on which events are real, even when they (momentarily) occupy the same point in space! The obvious way to reinstate agreement is for the observers to say that only those events which can causally influence the event of the observers' coincidence are real, since relativity predicts that both observers will necessarily agree on events those are. (*Space-time.) But this will now make what events are real dependent upon the particular spatial location of the observers' coincidence! Hence some (e.g. Putnam) have argued that any objective, ontological distinction between 'present' (or 'past') and 'future' events must be abandoned.

General relativity's prediction that space can fail to obey the axioms of Euclidean geometry naturally leads to the epistemological question how we can know which geometry is applicable to our universe. Imagine a world of two-dimensional creatures confined to a flat disk of finite radius who are using measuring-rods to try and determine the geometry of their world. Suppose there is a temperature gradient on the disk which makes all measuring-rods expand or contract equally, with the gradient suitably arranged so that rods shrink to zero length as they approach the disk's periphery. Then from their measurements the creatures will get the distinct impression that they live on a plane of infinite extent with a 'Lobachevskian' geometry. Of course, if they knew how the temperature of the disk was affecting their rods, the creatures could redescribe their situation as Euclidean. But since they are forever confined to the disk, there is no way of checking. So apparently they can either *assume* their instruments behave in a straight-forward way and adopt a more complicated geometry, or *assume* that the geometry is simply Euclidean and adopt a more complicated physical story about their expanding–contracting rods. Hence some (e.g. Poincaré and Reichenbach) have argued, using this disk parable, that which geometry is appropriate to *our* universe can only be a matter of convenience.   R.CLI.

R. Boyd, P. Gasper, and J. D. Trout (eds.), *The Philosophy of Science* (Cambridge, Mass., 1992), pt. II, sect. 1: 'The Philosophy of Physics'.

M. Redhead, *Physics for Pedestrians*, Cambridge University Inaugural Lecture (Cambridge, 1988).

—— *From Physics to Metaphysics* (Cambridge, 1993).

L. Sklar, *Philosophy of Physics* (Boulder, Colo., 1992).

Pico della Mirandola, Giovanni (1463–94). Italian philosopher who developed a form of syncretism according to which all systems of thought and belief could be reconciled on the basis of their shared truths. Although no philosophy or religion was entirely bereft of such truths, Christianity held a privileged position, acting as the standard by which all other truths were judged. At the age of 23 he challenged all comers to debate 900 *Conclusiones* embodying his attempts to reconcile such apparently incompatible trends of thought as Scotism and *Thomism, *Kabbalah and Christianity. The alleged heterodoxy of some theses led to a papal condemnation and a brief period of imprisonment. His project to produce a full-scale harmonization of *Platonism and *Aristotelianism was cut short by his early death, with only *De Ente et Uno* (1491), dealing with metaphysics, reaching completion. J.A.K.

F. Roulier, *Jean Pic de la Mirandole (1463–1494): Humaniste, philosophe et théologien* (Geneva, 1989).

picture theory of meaning. An account of the nature of *meaning central to Wittgenstein's early philosophy, but which he later largely or entirely rejected. In attempting to understand the relation between language and world, Wittgenstein was struck by the analogy with picturing or modelling. Different coloured counters, variously arranged, might be used in a courtroom to model a motoring accident, for instance. Superficially, the counters may not resemble the physical objects they model, any more than propositions resemble the world; but propositions may still depict states of affairs, provided there are as many distinguishable elements within the proposition as within the situation it represents, so that the proposition possesses the appropriate pictorial form to be isomorphic to the state of affairs. Pictorial form may not be evident on the surface, but will always be revealable by deep analysis. J.L.

L. Wittgenstein, *Tractatus Logico-Philosophicus*, with Eng. tr. D. F. Pears and B. F. McGuinness (London, 1961).

pictures. In aesthetics, following classical writers, a picture has been taken to be a mimesis, a *representation of reality. But the word 'representation' here at once suggests the question which has absorbed recent writers. Do pictures denote as sentences or words denote? If they do, they must do so through conventions. Or do pictures resemble their objects? Either view faces problems. Why do artists accept with alacrity a new way of painting a wheel in motion if the new device is merely conventional? If pictures represent because they resemble their objects, how can a picture represent a mythological being? Flint Schier proposed a theory which he describes as 'generative'. Once you grasp that a picture represents the President then you can recognize the objects of any other pictures which use the same style of depiction. Thus we can then acquire a grasp of the method of representation from a single example; in this way learning to understand pictorial representation is quite unlike language-learning. R.A.S.

E. H. Gombrich, *Art and Illusion* (London, 1963).
Nelson Goodman, *Languages of Art* (Indianapolis, 1985).
Flint Schier, *Deeper into Pictures* (Cambridge, 1986).
Richard Wollheim, *Painting as an Art* (Washington, DC, 1987).

piecemeal engineering. Popper thought that politics should proceed by piecemeal social engineering rather than by large-scale reform or revolution. Because any policy will have unforeseen and often unintended consequences, we should only change institutions bit by bit and monitor carefully the effects of so doing. This is doubtless sensible advice, but regarding political activity purely in terms of piecemeal engineering presupposes a consensus on aims and goals not characteristic of pluralist societies. A.O'H.

*conservatism; pluralism.

K. R. Popper, *The Open Society and its Enemies* (London, 1945).

pietism. Pietism, the religion of Immanuel Kant, springing from Lutheranism, influencing Wesley, and itself influenced by *Calvinism and the Mennonites, emphasized conversion, salvation, and personal morality. In *Pia Desiderata* (1675) Philipp Jakob Spener (1635–1705) castigated corrupt conditions in the Church, and proposed various reforms. He and his followers were mocked as 'pietists', Spener said, by 'those who feared through such holiness to have their own deeds put to shame'. J.J.M.

D. Brown, *Understanding Pietism* (Grand Rapids, Mich., 1978).

pineal gland. This small protrusion in the centre of the brain is, in Descartes's notorious theory of mind–body interaction, singled out as the 'principal seat of the soul'. When the gland is stimulated by the *animal spirits flowing through the nerves and brain, the soul residing in the gland will have a certain kind of sensation; conversely, when the soul wills a movement, it is able to transmit instructions to the body via the gland (*Treatise on Man* (1633)). Critics have standardly objected that positing a *location* for these supposed psychophysical transactions hardly removes the difficulty in seeing how an entirely immaterial substance can initiate, and respond to, physical thrusts. J.COT.

Virgil Aldrich, 'The Pineal Gland Updated', *Journal of Philosophy* (1970); repr. in G. Moyal (ed.), *René Descartes: Critical Assessments* (London, 1991), iv.

placebo. A pharmacologically inert substance administered blind to a control group as a way of testing the active substance as a treatment for illness. Allegedly, the patient's belief in the effectiveness of a drug or treatment often brings about a cure or improvement in itself—the 'placebo effect'. This creates a bind which calls out for philosophical therapy. There may be certain conditions (warts, say) where no treatments are effective unless the patient has faith in them. How can someone who recognizes this fact be cured? Suppose I am a warty sceptic who is realist enough to realize that if I firmly believe the warts will go, then they will. How can I cultivate that belief without selling my critical soul? So far my consultants assure me I cannot avail myself of what may be the only known cure unless I surrender to irrationality. Know yourself and die! Whoever said rationality had survival value? J.E.R.S.

plagiarism is not just a problem for university professors. It is the conceptual brother of *forgery: both are defined in terms of an artefact (e.g. a poem) not being genuine, but being represented as genuine, and so represented with the intention to deceive. Genuineness has to do with authorship, or source of issue, and, roughly speaking, the difference between plagiarism and forgery is that a person plagiarizes when he tries to pass off another's work as his own, but he forges when he tries to pass off his own work as another's. Both are prima facie morally wrong, but the more difficult question is the aesthetic one: Is there anything prima facie aesthetically wrong with either (or both)? Some have argued for a Yes answer on the basis of the role that knowledge of authorship plays in aesthetic perception and discrimination, while others have argued for a No answer on the basis of the irrelevance of plagiarism and forgery to aesthetic judgements respecting such things as cheques and articles in reference works, such as this one. Now I wonder who the author of this article really is?   M.W.

There is very little philosophical literature on plagiarism, but Denis Dutton (ed.), *The Forger's Art: Forgery and the Philosophy of Art* (Berkeley, Calif., 1983) contains a number of good papers on forgery.

Planck, Max (1858–1947). German physicist who discovered the formula for black-body radiation. Taking his cue from Boltzmann's statistical reformulation of the second law of thermodynamics, he found that radiant energy may be treated statistically as if it exchanged only in discrete amounts involving a new constant h, subsequently known as Planck's constant. This prepared the way for Einstein's discovery that light could be treated as both wave and particle, the two aspects being related through Planck's constant. This constant took on a universal significance when physicists later extended the theory from light to matter generally, proposing that energy possessed by matter can be changed into radiant energy only in integral multiples of quanta. This set the foundation for *quantum mechanics, which inaugurated a revolutionary break with classical physics. Planck was awarded a Nobel Prize for his contribution to physics in 1918.

The arrival of quantum mechanics gave rise to a variety of philosophical problems; it presented difficulties for *traditional logic, constituted a challenge to scientific *realism, and undermined deterministic views of the universe, with further repercussions in epistemology.   O.R.J.

*determinism; determinism, scientific.

Thomas Kuhn, *Black-Body Theory and the Quantum Discontinuity 1894–1912* (Oxford, 1978).
Hilary Putnam, *Mathematics, Matter and Method: Philosophical Papers*, i (Cambridge, 1975).

Plantinga, Alvin (1932–). American philosopher known for the way in which he applies results of his work in other areas of analytic philosophy to traditional issues in philosophy of religion. In *God and Other Minds* (1967), he defended the view that belief in *other minds and belief in *God are, epistemically speaking, on a par: if the former is rational, so is the latter. In *The Nature of Necessity* (1974), he used contemporary modal logic and metaphysics to formulate a valid *ontological argument for the existence of God and a rigorous freewill defence of the logical consistency of the existence of God and the existence of *evil. In

more recent work in epistemology, Plantinga has argued for the view that belief in God can, in certain circumstances, be rational and warranted even if it is not based on propositional evidence.   P.L.Q.

*philosophy of religion, problems of.

A. Plantinga, *Warrant and Proper Function* (New York, 1993).
J. E. Tomberlin and P. van Inwagen (eds.), *Alvin Plantinga* (Dordrecht, 1985).

Plato (*c*.428–347 BC). The best known and most widely studied of all the ancient Greek philosophers. He was an Athenian, born into a noble family, and might have been expected to play a part in the politics of that city. But in fact he came under the influence of Socrates, who fired him with an enthusiasm for philosophy. When Socrates was condemned to death and executed in 399, Plato gave up all thought of a political career, and left Athens in disgust. It is said that he then travelled to various places, including Egypt, but we have no trustworthy information on this part of his life, until we come to his first visit to Italy and Sicily in 387. From that visit he returned to Athens, and soon after founded his *Academy, just outside the city. This may be regarded as the first 'university'. Apart from two further visits to Sicily, in 367 and 361, he remained at the Academy until his death in 347.

It is often assumed that his first philosophical work was the *Apology*; this purports to be a record of the speeches that Socrates delivered at his trial. Apart from this one example, all Plato's philosophical works are dialogues. They are standardly divided into three periods: early, middle, and late. On the usual chronology, the early period includes *Crito, Ion, Hippias minor, Euthyphro, Lysis, Laches, Charmides, Hippias major, Meno, Euthydemus, Protagoras, Gorgias*. Many of these dialogues are short. They are listed here in order of length, from the *Crito* at 9 pages, to the *Euthydemus* at 36, the *Protagoras* at 53, and the *Gorgias* at 80. No one is confident of their order of composition. The usual chronology for the middle period includes *Phaedo, Symposium, Republic, Phaedrus*, in that order. The *Republic* is very long, and is divided into ten books. Some count the *Cratylus* as belonging to this period (placed after the *Republic*); some count it as an early dialogue. Finally, on the usual chronology for the late period, it begins with *Parmenides* and *Theaetetus*, and then (after a break) it contains *Sophist, Statesman, Timaeus* (and *Critias*), *Philebus, Laws*. Again there is one work which is very long, namely the *Laws*, which is divided into twelve books. The orthodox view is that this may be counted as Plato's last work, though in fact the evidence for this claim is very insecure. Another important dispute concerns the date of the *Timaeus*, which some would classify as a middle dialogue (after the *Republic*). A great deal of work has been done, and is still being done, towards establishing the order of the dialogues, but one cannot say that a consensus has been reached. (The above list simply omits all works whose authenticity may be considered doubtful.)

I. The early dialogues are our only worthwhile source for the philosophy of Socrates. They illustrate his preoccupation with ethics, and his insistence that it is vitally important to find correct definitions for ethically significant concepts, since otherwise we will not know how to live. No doubt Plato himself shared these views at the time. But he shows a more independent attitude to the Socratic claim that virtue (*aretē*) is knowledge, and to its associated paradoxes, e.g. that all wrongdoing must be due to ignorance (so that no one does wrong on purpose), and that all *virtues must somehow be the same (so that one cannot have one but lack another). The dialogues show Plato to be very *interested* in these claims, but he is not clearly *endorsing* them. On the contrary, he seems rather to be exploring them, and recognizing the problems they involve. He can achieve this neutral stance partly because he is writing dialogues, between Socrates and other speakers, and we need not suppose that Plato believes whatever he makes his character Socrates say; and partly because most of the dialogues are anyway inconclusive. They will begin by propounding some problem for discussion, and during the discussion several answers will be proposed, but all will be rejected, so that officially no conclusion is reached. (Often one is tempted to read between the lines, to find an answer that Plato is recommending, despite its official rejection; but even so one should suppose that he is recommending it for further consideration, not for acceptance.) In these early dialogues, then, Plato is mainly concerned with Socrates' philosophy, but he is trying out lines of thought, and objections to them, and he is not confident that he has found answers. In a few cases (notably the *Meno* and the *Gorgias*) one can see that his confidence is growing, and that he has something to say which he very much wants his audience to believe. But that is because the middle period is dawning.

II. In the middle period Plato's interests broaden very considerably, and we find the metaphysical and epistemological doctrines for which he is best known. They now form the background against which he works out his new thoughts on how one ought to live, and on a number of other topics, ranging from the true role of *love (Symposium, Phaedrus)* to the structure of the physical world (*Timaeus*—assuming that to be a middle dialogue). There is space here only for a brief account of some of the better-known doctrines. Although Socrates remains the chief speaker of these dialogues (except for the *Timaeus*), still one can now be quite confident that the views put into his mouth are Plato's own views, and often they owe very little to the historical Socrates.

Knowledge and the Forms. Socrates had insisted that we must be able to answer the question 'What is *X*?' before we can say anything else about *X*. He understood this question as asking for the one thing common to all the many instances or examples of *X*, and he continued to stress its importance for ethical inquiry, even though he never found any answers that satisfied him. One may conjecture that this led Plato to ask *why* the search was yielding no

results, and that he came to the conclusion that it was because even the supposed instances and examples of *X* were unreliable. At any rate, he certainly did come to hold that, in interesting cases such as *justice and goodness and *beauty, every instance of *X* will *also* be an instance of the opposite to *X*. But this provokes a problem, for instances and examples seem to be crucial for language-learning. That is, one could not come to understand the word 'red' if there were no examples of red things, nor if every example of something red were at the same time an example of something non-red. How, then, do we manage to attach any meaning at all to words such as 'just', 'good', and 'beautiful'? This problem led Plato to suppose that there must *be* an unambiguous example of justice, not in this world but in some other, and that we must once have been acquainted with it. This is what he calls the 'Form' of justice. So his theory is that we are born into this world with a dim recollection of this Form, and that is why we do have *some* conception of what justice is, though it is only an imperfect conception, which explains why we cannot now answer the Socratic question 'What is justice?'

This is the theory of *Phaedo* 73–7. It significantly extends a line of thought introduced earlier in the *Meno*, which had noted that there is such a thing as *a priori knowledge (since mathematics is an example), and had offered to explain this as really recollection of what we had once known in an earlier existence. The *Meno* had *hoped* that philosophical inquiry could yield similar knowledge of justice and the like, obtained by examination of what was already latent within us, but had offered no ground for such a hope. The *Phaedo* provides a ground, at the same time adding a new conception of what it is that must be known (or recalled), namely a paradigm example of *X*, a reliable and unambiguous guide to what *X* is, which the perceptible things of this world 'imitate', but always 'fall short of'. These are the Forms. Yet at the same time, and inconsistently, the Forms are thought of as themselves *being* the answers to the question 'What is *X*?', i.e. as being the one thing common to all the many instances of *X*, that in which they all 'participate'. In other words, the Forms are *both* perfect paradigms *and* universals. This ambivalent conception is found in all the middle dialogues (including the *Timaeus*). The associated theory of recollection (*anamnēsis*) is not so constantly mentioned; in fact it is restated only once after the *Phaedo*, i.e. at *Phaedrus* 249.

The Soul (psukhē or psyche) and Morality. In the *Apology* Socrates had been portrayed as agnostic on the immortality of the soul. In the *Phaedo* he is convinced of it, and the dialogue is as a whole a sustained argument for that claim. We find further arguments for the immortality of the soul in *Republic* x and in the *Phaedrus*, but in those dialogues there is also a more complex view of what the soul is. Whereas the *Phaedo*, like the early dialogues, had been content with a simple opposition between soul and body, in *Republic* iv the soul itself is divided into three 'parts', which roughly correspond to reason, emotion, and desire. (But in *Republic* VIII–IX the 'reasoning' part is associated with the desire for knowledge, the so-called 'spirited' part with the desire for honour and prestige, and the 'desiring' part—itself recognized to be 'many-headed'—is clearly confined to bodily desires.) An explicit motive for this division is to allow for conflict within the soul, and one consequence of this is that Plato is no longer tempted by the Socratic claim that all virtue is knowledge, and its associated paradoxes. He does retain the early view that virtue is a condition of the soul, but wisdom is now viewed as a virtue of the reasoning part, whereas courage is a virtue of the spirited part, and justice is explained as a suitable 'harmony' between all three parts. Another consequence of the threefold division of the soul is that Plato seems to have become uncertain how much of the soul is immortal. (*Republic* x. 611–12 is deliberately evasive; *Phaedrus* 245–9 clearly claims that the team of all three parts is immortal; *Timaeus* 69–72 is equally clear in its claim that only the reasoning part is immortal.) Plato thinks of the immortal soul as subject to reincarnation from one life to another. Those who live virtuous lives will be somehow rewarded, but the detail differs from one treatment to another.

Political Theory. In the *Republic* Plato sets out his 'ideal state'. It is very decidedly authoritarian. He begins from the premiss that only those who know what the good is are fit to rule, and he prescribes a long and rigorous period of intellectual training, which he thinks will yield this knowledge. In a famous analogy, it will loose the bonds that keep most men confined in a *cave underground, and allow us to ascend to the 'real' world outside, which is a world of Forms, available to the intellect but not to the senses. This is to be accomplished by a full study of mathematics, which will turn one's attention towards the Forms, since it is an a priori study and does not concern itself with what is perceptible; and after that a study in *'dialectic', i.e. in philosophical debate. Those who complete this training successfully, and so know what the good is, will form the ruling élite. From time to time they will be required to give up their intellectual delights and go back into the cave to govern it. They will govern with a view to maximizing the happiness of the state as a whole, but Plato thinks that the way to achieve this is to impose a strict censorship to prevent wrong ideas being expressed, to ensure that each person sticks to his own allotted job, so that he does not meddle with affairs that are not his concern, and so on. Plato was firmly against democracy, and seems to have seen no connection between happiness and individual liberty.

III. The late dialogues open with two criticisms of the theories of the middle period, in the *Parmenides* and the *Theaetetus*. The *Parmenides* is concerned with metaphysics, and its first part raises a series of objections to the middle period's theory of Forms. The most famous of these is the so-called *third man argument, which evidently exploits the fact that Forms are supposed to be *both* universals *and* perfect paradigms. Scholars differ in their

view of how Plato himself reacted to these objections. Provided that the *Timaeus* is regarded as a middle dialogue, one can hold that Plato saw that the objections depend upon Forms being both universals and paradigms, and thereupon ceased to think of them as paradigms. But if the *Timaeus* is later than the *Parmenides*, as stylometric studies appear to indicate, then one is forced to conclude that Plato made no such modification to his theory. The second part of the *Parmenides* is a riddle. It draws a bewildering array of contradictory conclusions, first from the hypothesis 'The One is' and then from its negation 'The One is not', and then it just ends without further comment. There have been many attempts to extract a serious moral that Plato may have intended, but none have won general approval.

As the *Parmenides* attacks the metaphysics of the middle dialogues, so the *Theaetetus* attacks their epistemology, but again the attack has its puzzling features. The middle dialogues (and in particular the *Timaeus*) claim that perceptible things are not stable, and for that reason there can be no knowledge of them; rather, only Forms can be known. The first part of the *Theaetetus*, however, argues that it is self-refuting to ascribe such radical instability to perceptible things, and it proceeds to assume that we do know about them. But it nevertheless insists upon distinguishing this knowledge from perception, on the ground that knowledge requires belief (or judgement) while mere perception does not. The second part of the dialogue then professes to be exploring the claims that knowledge is to be identified with true belief, or with true belief plus an 'account'. But what is puzzling about this discussion is that it appears to focus not upon knowledge of facts (*savoir*) but upon knowledge of objects (*connaître*), and on the face of it the latter does not involve belief or judgement at all. Again, the solution to this puzzle is a matter of controversy.

Although the late dialogues begin with two enigmatic and self-critical pieces, in which Plato's own position is once more unclear, in subsequent writings he has evidently recovered the confidence of his middle period. In the *Sophist* he gives us a new metaphysics and a more sophisticated investigation of language, in the course of a long investigation of 'not being'. This includes the important point that even in the simplest sentences one may distinguish two expressions, *subject and predicate, that have different roles to play. In the *Statesman* he reaffirms his view that ruling is a task for experts, and argues that the expert should not be bound either by law or by the wishes of the people. But it is admitted that law is a second best, where no expert is available. Of constitutions bound by law he considers that monarchy is best, oligarchy in the middle, and democracy worst. But in the absence of law this order is reversed. In the *Philebus* he once more weighs the claims of knowledge and of pleasure to be the good, and at the same time undertakes a full examination of what pleasure is. He does not award victory to either contestant, arguing instead for the mixed life, but knowledge is ranked higher.

In all three of these dialogues Plato pays much attention to what he calls the method of 'collection and division'. At an earlier stage he had recommended the different method of 'hypothesis'. This is introduced in the *Meno*, apparently as a device which allows us to make progress with philosophical problems without first having to answer the awkward question 'What is *X*?' Then in the *Phaedo* and the *Republic* it receives a much fuller exposition, and becomes Plato's account of how a priori knowledge is possible. This method makes its final appearance in the *Parmenides,* and one way of reading the second part of that dialogue is as a prolonged demonstration of its inadequacy. Meanwhile, the new method of 'collection and division' has been introduced in the *Phaedrus*, and it is then both preached and practised at some length in the *Sophist* and the *Statesman*. It is presented as a method of finding definitions, though it is clear from what those dialogues say about it that it must be handled very carefully if it is not to lead us astray. The version in the *Philebus* introduces some new, and very puzzling, considerations concerning 'the indefinite'. This appears to connect with what Aristotle tells us about Plato's so-called 'unwritten doctrines', but that topic is too obscure to be pursued here.

Finally, in the *Laws* we find Plato again building an ideal state, but now in a very different mood from that of the *Republic* and the *Statesman*. He is now much more ready to compromise with principle in order to find something that will work in practice, and he puts a very high value on the law. In fact the work is remarkable for proposing a great deal of extremely detailed legislation. But Plato's general attitude remains very authoritarian, and he still pays no attention to individual *liberty. It is justly said that the 'Nocturnal Council', which turns out to be the supreme authority in this state, would certainly not have tolerated the subversive ideas of Socrates, from which Plato began.   D.B.

*Platonism; Good, Form of the; knowledge; psyche.

GREEK TEXT
Platonis Opera, ed. J. Burnet (5 vols., Oxford Classical Texts 1900–7).

TRANSLATION
E. Hamilton and H. Cairns (eds.), *The Collected Dialogues of Plato* (New York, 1961).

COMMENTARY
I. M. Crombie, *An Examination of Plato's Doctrines*, 2 vols. (London, 1962–3).
G. M. A. Grube, *Plato's Thought*, 2nd edn. (London, 1980).
T. Irwin, *Plato's Moral Theory* (Oxford, 1977).
R. Krant (ed.), *The Cambridge Companion to Plato* (Cambridge, 1993).
R. Robinson, *Plato's Earlier Dialectic*, 2nd edn. (Oxford, 1953).
W. D. Ross, *Plato's Theory of Ideas* (Oxford, 1951).
N. P. White, *Plato on Knowledge and Reality* (Indianapolis, 1976).

Platonism. 'Platonism' refers to (1) the doctrines held by Plato; (2) some central doctrine of Plato, especially the theory of Forms, or Ideas, or a doctrine relevantly similar to it, such as the view (contrasting with 'constructivism') that logical and/or mathematical entities subsist independently both of the empirical world and of human thought (Frege); (3) the tradition of thinkers claiming allegiance to Plato, whether or not their doctrines were in fact held by him.

Plato's literary career spanned fifty years, and, apart from some letters of doubtful authenticity, he wrote only dialogues in which he himself never appears, but is, at best, represented by a leading participant, usually, but not invariably, Socrates. The dialogues are commonly placed in three groups: (1) The early dialogues consider a question such as how we are to define virtue or whether it is teachable, and examine various answers to it, but do not usually endorse a positive conclusion; these dialogues and their characteristic procedures are commonly known as 'Socratic' rather than 'Platonic'. (2) The middle dialogues, such as the *Republic*, expound metaphysical, political, and psychological doctrines. It is these doctrines which are most usually associated with Plato and known as 'Platonic'. (3) The late dialogues, such as the *Sophist*, reassess and modify the doctrines of the middle period.

Even within each of the two latter periods, dialogues differ significantly in method and doctrine. Thus it is not easy to extract from Plato's works a single consistent set of doctrines. (The Neoplatonist Olympiodorus reports that Plato dreamt that he had become a swan which flew from tree to tree, eluding the arrows of its hunters. This means that Plato eludes his interpreters, and his works must be 'understood in many senses, both physically, and ethically, and theologically, and literally'.) But it is tempting to suppose that Plato had a coherent view on the questions asked and the doctrines expounded by his characters, or at least more tempting than it is to suppose that Shakespeare had a coherent doctrine that can be extracted from the utterances of *his* characters. Many interpreters have attempted to elicit a system from Plato, among them Hegel, who, regarding (unlike Schleiermacher) the dialogue form as inessential, attributed to him a tripartite system consisting of *dialectics, philosophy of nature, and philosophy of spirit. Most 'Platonists' have seen themselves as such by reason of their adherence to supposedly Platonic doctrines rather than to Plato's methods or his dialogue form. But different thinkers stress different aspects of his legacy.

Platonism as a tradition falls into six broad periods: (1) the Old Academy; (2) the Hellenistic ('Middle' and 'New') Academy; (3) ancient *Neo-platonism; (4) medieval Platonism; (5) the Renaissance; (6) the modern period.

1. After Plato's death, his nephew Speusippus (405–335 BC) became head of the *Academy, and he was succeeded in 339 by Xenocrates (396–314 BC). (The reason why Plato's most distinguished pupil, Aristotle, did not succeed him is probably that, as a non-citizen, he was unable to own property in Athens, rather than, as Anscombe suggests, his heterosexuality.) They continued to work, in the manner of Plato's later work, on metaphysics, logic, and mathematics.

2. Under its sixth head, Arcesilaus, the Academy espoused *scepticism and deployed it especially against

Stoicism. Carneades continued and extended this approach. Academic scepticism stressed its continuity with the early aporetic dialogues, and persisted for two centuries. Augustine's *Contra Academicos* (AD 386) is directed against the scepticism that he knew from Cicero's *Academica*, but he attempted to reconcile this with the Neoplatonism he had learned from Plotinus by arguing that the Academy had a secret doctrine which they did not reveal to outsiders. Under Antiochus of Ascalon (*c.*130–68 BC) the Academy abandoned scepticism and adopted a synthesis of Platonism, *Stoicism, and *Aristotelianism.

3. Antiochus prepared the ground for so-called 'Middle Platonism', represented by, among others, the anti-Christian Celsus (late second century AD). In the second century Numenius of Apamea attempted to purge Platonism of later accretions and regarded the result as identical to *Pythagoreanism. But the greatest Middle Platonists were in Alexandria: Philo (*c.*25 BC–AD 50), who combined Platonism with Judaism, Clement (*c.*AD 150–215) and, later, Origen (185–254), who, like Plotinus, was a pupil of Ammonius Saccas (*c.*175–242), generally regarded as the founder of Neoplatonism. (The distinction between Middle Platonism and Neoplatonism is not, however, sharp: from the first century BC Platonism was transformed into a metaphysical or theological system, involving, for example, ideas as thoughts in God's mind, the ideal of assimilation to God, and demonic intermediaries between men and God; the aporetic element in Plato was ignored.) The Alexandrians became Christian, and were less inclined to theurgy than the pagan Athenians. Plotinus, the greatest of the Neoplatonists, was not a member of the Academy, nor was his follower Porphyry (*c.*232–304), the author of an introduction (*Isagoge*) to Aristotle's *Categories*, which in Boethius' Latin translation, became a standard medieval work, nor Iamblichus (d. *c.*330). Iamblichus was responsible for many of the concepts, especially the triads, that appear in Proclus. The Academy was closed by Justinian in AD 529 (whereas the Alexandrian school survived the Arab conquest of 641), but through the works of Augustine (Plotinus) and pseudo-Dionysius the Areopagite (Proclus) Neoplatonism entered medieval Christianity.

4. Platonism persisted in the three main spheres of the medieval world: Islam, Byzantium, and the Latin West. Its impact on the Arabs, with their predominantly scientific interests, was less than that of Aristotle. But al-Fārābī was influenced not only by the ideal state of Plato's *Republic*, but also by the entirely apolitical Plotinus. His follower Avicenna developed Neoplatonism further. In Byzantium, Plato's dialogues continued to be read, and the revival of Platonism by Michael Psellos (1018–78/96) prepared the way for the later champions of Plato against Aristotle, Basilius Bessarion (1403–72) and Georgios Gemistos Pletho (*c.*1355–1450). They propagated Platonism in Italy, and Pletho inspired Cosimo dei Medici to found a new Platonic Academy in Florence in 1459. It was headed by Marsilio Ficino (1433–99) and attracted Greek refugees from Constantinople, who brought with them hitherto unknown Platonic texts. It lasted until 1521. In the West, the philosophical works originally available were Platonic: Plato's *Timaeus*, Boethius, Apuleius (the author of works on Socrates and Plato, as well as of *The Golden Ass*), and Augustine. Later John Scotus Eriugena (*c.*810–77) translated Dionysius. (That *The Divine Names* etc. were not the work of the Athenian converted by St Paul was suspected by Lorenzo Valla (1405–57) and finally established by Erasmus. Earlier it was widely believed that Platonists such as Proclus had stolen his ideas.) But by the thirteenth century, despite more translations of Plato and Proclus, Aristotle eclipsed Platonism.

5. In the Renaissance, Plato became a focus of rebellion against scholasticism, and the need was felt for direct acquaintance with his texts. Eventually, though not immediately, this tended to undermine the so-far-unquestioned Neoplatonic interpretation of Plato. Petrarch (1304–74), though he had 'no Greek', championed Plato, 'the prince of philosophy', against Aristotle. Ficino translated Plato, Plotinus, and Hermes Trismegistus (the supposed author of a body of early post-Christian writings, which Ficino believed to be the work of an ancient Egyptian priest and one of the sources of Platonism). He produced a sustained defence of Plato's doctrine of the immortality of the soul, and regarded him as a forerunner of Christianity, in a tradition of 'pious philosophy' extending from Zoroaster to Nicholas of Cusa. Pico della Mirandola was also influenced by, among others, Plato, and was associated with Ficino's Academy. Platonism migrated to England through Erasmus, Thomas More (1478–1535), and others, giving rise to the *Cambridge Platonists, who, as Coleridge observed, could as well be called the 'Cambridge Plotinists', since they revered Plotinus and did not doubt his interpretation of Plato.

6. In Ficino's day the only rival to the Neoplatonist interpretation of Plato was the persistent, if sometimes muted, tradition that Plato was a New Academic sceptic. This view, backed by the authority of Cicero, revived in the late fifteenth century: among its adherents were the Lutheran reformer Philip Melanchthon (1497–1560) and the French sceptic Michel de Montaigne (1533–92). But a third view now began to form, namely that Plato had a positive doctrine, distinct from Neoplatonism, and that this could be discerned from his original texts. This view appealed to Protestants, who deplored the Neoplatonic influence on Christianity but often found Plato himself more tolerable. One of its pioneers was Jean de Serres (Ioannes Serranus) (1540–98), a Calvinist Huguenot, who contributed a Latin translation and an introduction to Henricus Stephanus' famous 1578 edition of Plato. Its most distinguished adherent was Leibniz, who on several occasions bemoaned the tendency to read not Plato but his commentators: we can recover such valuable doctrines as the theory of Ideas and recollection only if we remove the Neoplatonic covering. This view was confirmed by the history of philosophy, which emerged, especially in Germany, as a distinct discipline, alongside theology and philosophy itself: Jakob Brucker (1696–1770), Dietrich Tiedemann (1748–1803), Wilhelm

Tennemann (1761–1819), and Hegel, whatever the faults of their own attempts to reconstruct Plato's doctrines, finally demolished the Neoplatonic interpretation. (Like Friedrich Schleiermacher (1768–1834), Hegel dismisses Tennemann's view—which still finds supporters—that Plato had an *'esoteric' system which he did not commit to writing.) The discovery of the 'real' Plato also put an end to Platonism as a distinct and credible large-scale doctrine, partly because the dialogues cannot be plausibly read as advocating a definitive creed, and partly because they are usually interpreted as presenting a primitive version of some more developed modern philosophy, such as Kantianism (Tennemann) or Hegelianism (Hegel), which the interpreter believes in preference to Plato himself.

However, Plato provides an ingredient, often an essential ingredient, in much of subsequent Western philosophy. Galileo, for example, was a Platonist, not in the sense that he endorsed the mathematical theories of the *Timaeus*, but because he distinguished between the appearances of nature and its true mathematical structure, the latter being the object of true knowledge. Quasi-Platonic ideas play an important role in Kant and Schelling. In Schopenhauer ideas are what art, apart from music, portrays, and (contrary to Plato's own intentions) Plato has often been of service both to artists and to philosophers of art. Moreover, even in modern times Plato is often seen as containing in embryo the whole of Western philosophy; thus any serious philosopher must come to terms with him, whether as an ally or as an opponent. J. F. Ferrier (1808–64) claimed that 'all philosophic truth is Plato rightly divined; all philosophic error is Plato misunderstood', and Whitehead saw later philosophy as a series of *footnotes to Plato. Nietzsche regarded Plato in this light (e.g. 'Christianity is Platonism for the people'), but since he rejected Plato's claim to a non-perspectival insight into true being, he saw his own thought as 'inverted Platonism'. For Heidegger, Plato initiated the decline of truth from 'unhiddenness' to 'correctness', and thus gave rise to the metaphysics and humanism that afflicted all later philosophy, including Nietzsche's. He also lectured, in 1924–5, on Plato's *Sophist*, in preparation for his revival of the 'question of *being'. Jaspers interpreted Plato in terms of his own thought, and saw him as the 'representative of philosophy in general', an open-ended thinker more concerned with philosophizing as a way of life than with the advocacy of specific doctrines. (Sartre's *Being and Nothingness*, by contrast, refers only fleetingly to Plato's *Sophist*; but his early story *Er the Armenian* was inspired by the Myth of Er in the *Republic*.) While Platonism as a full-scale doctrine is no longer a live option, modern philosophers, including analytical philosophers such as Ryle, have often developed their own ideas, and their powers of argumentation and interpretation, in interaction with Plato.   M.J.I.

M. J. B. Allen, *The Platonism of Marsilio Ficino* (Berkeley, Calif., 1984).

V. Goldschmidt, *Platonisme et pensée contemporaine* (Paris, 1970).

E. N. Tigerstedt, *The Decline and Fall of the Neoplatonic Interpretation of Plato: An Outline and Some Observations* (Helsinki, 1974).

J.-L. Vieillard-Baron, *Platon et l'idéalisme allemand (1770– 1830)* (Paris, 1979).

C. M. Woodhouse, *Gemistos Plethon: The Last of the Hellenes* (Oxford, 1986).

Platonism, Neo-: *see* Neoplatonism.

plausibility. A weaker counterpart to *truth. It turns on a claim's credibility via the acceptance-justifying backing that a duly weighty source (human, instrumental, or methodological) can provide. Thus if we think of informative sources as being graded by reliability, then the plausibility of a contention is determined by the best authority that speaks for it. A proposition's plausibility accordingly depends on its probative status rather than on its specific content in relation to alternatives. In this regard it differs crucially from *probability. The plausibility status of a group of conjoined propositions (unlike its probability status) is that of the least plausible of its members: plausibility is a chain that is as exactly strong as its weakest link.   N.R.

George Polya, *Patterns of Plausible Inference* (Princeton, NJ, 1954).

Nicholas Rescher, *Plausible Reasoning* (Amsterdam, 1976).

pleasure. Philosophers have discussed the nature of pleasure from an interest either in *hedonism, or in *philosophy of mind. The former was the main interest up to the mid-twentieth century.

Ancient Greece. A popular early view was to see pleasure as the replenishment of a natural lack; for instance, quenching thirst. This was modified by adding that the replenishment must be noticed. It was then realized that some pleasures involved no replenishment, as those of anticipation, or enjoying the exercise of abilities. Aristotle came to see pleasure as the perfect actualization of a sentient being's natural capacities, operating on their proper objects. This, however, is the account of 'real' pleasure, and other pleasures are approximations to this on the part of beings not in perfect condition. With humans, Aristotle holds that those who enjoy something are aware of that fact. This makes it natural to suppose that those who experience pleasure believe that they are actualizing in good condition—correctly in the case of those who are, falsely in other cases. The Stoics, taking familiar pleasures as their model, thought of pleasure as such a belief, and as false.

Later. These views set the parameters for later discussions up to the time of Descartes. The latter's sceptical arguments led the Empiricists in particular to concentrate on the inner data of the mind as what we really know. Since it seems that subjects know what they enjoy, it seemed natural to class pleasure as one of the inner givens of the mind. To English-speakers this seemed the more natural because pleasure would be classified as a feeling. Pleasure now becomes the experience of a feeling from some source or other. Then either all these feelings feel alike, or they share some hedonic tone, or they have the characteristic of being wanted for their own sake, or preferred.

Early to Modern. In the early period there is no sharp distinction made between an interest in the concept of pleasure and in what it is that occurs when pleasure occurs. The latter, however, seems to predominate. By the time of Hume matters are muddier. In the twentieth century, interest shifted to philosophy of mind, to whether attributions of pleasure are attributions of publicly accessible facts or of inner events. Given that the attributions are in a public language, philosophers have turned to consider the meanings of various pleasure-expressions, with the assumption that criteria for their application will be publicly accessible. Attributing pleasure has been variously thought to be attributing a manner of indulging or a relation of the indulgence to a subject's desire or preference.

The discussion has been complicated by distinctions between enjoyment and pleasure, and the variety of pleasure-expressions. There are methodological problems: how do we determine that the expressions cover the same concept? or that different uses of the same expressions are genuine examples of the concept?

None of the above questions have won agreed answers, but the answers clearly affect one's attitude to hedonism. Different answers on the nature of pleasure give hedonism a different air; different selections of pleasure-expression give arguments for different forms of hedonism. None of them work. J.C.B.G.

*pain; pushpin and poetry; happiness; well-being.

Roger Crisp, *Mill on Utilitarianism* (London, 1997).
Fred Feldman, *Pleasure and the Good Life* (Oxford, 2004).
J. C. B. Gosling, *Pleasure and Desire* (Oxford, 1969).
—— and C. C. W. Taylor, *The Greeks on Pleasure* (Oxford, 1982).
Gilbert Ryle, *The Concept of Mind* (London, 1949).
John Skorupski, *John Stuart Mill* (London, 1989).

Plekhanov, Georgii Valentinovich (1856–1918). The leading Russian Marxist theoretician in the two decades before 1914, Plekhanov is chiefly known as the teacher of Lenin and the first to have given serious formulation to the doctrine of *dialectical materialism. In his major work *The Development of the Monist View of History*, he gave an account of modern social and philosophical thought as culminating in Hegel and Marx and seen through the materialism of Feuerbach, for whom Plekhanov had a high regard. He consistently applied this dialectical materialist method to all branches of human knowledge, thus helping to create the subsequent philosophical orthodoxy of the Soviet Union. D.McL.

S. Baron, *Plekhanov: The Father of Russian Marxism* (London, 1963).

plenitude, principle of. 'If a proposition *P* is possible then at some time *P* is true.' The principle, accepted by Aristotle, clashes with a common intuition that the non-realization of a *possibility does not imply that the possibility did not exist. The question how to interpret Aristotle's principle in such a way that it squares with the common intuition has proved a fertile debating-ground. A.BRO.

Arthur O. Lovejoy, *The Great Chain of Being* (Cambridge, Mass., 1936).

Plotinus (204/5–270). Platonist philosopher, initiator of what we call *Neoplatonism. We do not know his origins. He studied for over eleven years at Alexandria. Then he joined a Roman military expedition to the East, in order to learn from Persian and Indian philosophers (so says his editor and biographer Porphyry). But the expedition was aborted, and he came to Rome, aged 40. There he earned court patronage and spent the rest of his life teaching. From the age of 50 he wrote in Greek a series of essays and shorter articles, chatty in style but at the same time difficult and earnest, and enriched with superb similes. After his death Porphyry chopped them up and gathered them into six groups of nine, the *Enneads*.

Plotinus was a contemplative, who sought contact with a supreme principle, the Good, or One. He tells us that he often achieved momentary success. Religious rites were useless for the purpose; what was needed was an ascent of the soul, away from bodily things. It demanded personal goodness—and Plotinus appears to have been conscientious and competent in his help and advice to friends, though he deprecated involvement in public affairs. It also demanded hard philosophical inquiry.

His teaching defended the metaphysics that made this ascent desirable, and to the defence he brought a good scholar's knowledge of the state of his subject and also a good teacher's willingness to share and examine his pupils' difficulties on a footing of equality. Even his deference to Plato, whom he used only selectively but revered as faultless, does not really imprison Plotinus' thought, though it sometimes strains the ingenuity of his interpretations. He takes no notice of Christianity.

The essence of his metaphysics is: It is only possible to make things by thinking them, and to think things as a maker by being them. (It is backwards to regard thinking as *imagining*; it is *realizing* what the manufacturer then makes an image of.) Bodies are phantoms (*'idols'), present in matter as an image is in a mirror, and the realities behind them are Forms. But even a thinker will produce only an idol unless the Forms he thinks are in him, and thus collectively are him. Original thought, which does not reason from previous thoughts, Plotinus calls Intellect. So Intellect is a maker. But there is no process in its making, only the timeless activity of thinking the intelligible Forms that it is.

Everything that has power must exercise it, by what he calls emanating (or 'beaming') something less powerful. Such 'procession' (as it is also called) accounts for the existence of the perceptible 'here' (our world), beamed from the intelligible 'there'. 'Here' contains *souls as well as bodies, because many bodies—including the perceptible universe itself—are alive (i.e. ensouled), and their souls have spontaneously descended from, and can return to, 'there'. Human souls have parts, and the highest part is still linked with Intellect 'there'. We humans choose which part our souls shall 'incline' to, and thereby we gain different future lives as plants or animals or demons (in no bad sense) or gods. These future lives will reward and punish us, so keeping the moral balance in our necessarily imperfect but providentially ordered 'here'.

Soul is the lowest of Plotinus' three universal principles, or 'hypostases'. It depends on Intellect, which in turn depends on the One, or Good. The One himself is 'beyond being', because attribution of being or any other predicate would make him more than One. The other hypostases are multiple (for example, the thoughts that Intellect is are composite), and therefore could not exist independently of this Unity. Desire to touch him is the pang of being smitten by 'beauty above beauty'. C.A.K.

A. H. Armstrong (ed.), *The Cambridge History of Later Greek and Early Medieval Philosophy* (Cambridge, 1967), chs. 12–16.
L. Gerson (ed.), *The Cambridge Companion to Plotinus* (Cambridge, 1996).
D. J. O'Meara, *Plotinus* (Oxford, 1993).
J. M. Rist, *Plotinus: The Road to Reality* (Cambridge, 1967).

pluralism: *see* monism and pluralism.

pluralism, political. A condition marked by the multiplicity of religions, ethnic groups, auto-nomous regions, or functional units within a single state; or a doctrine that holds such a multiplicity to be a good thing. The alternative is a unitary state where one religion or ethnicity is dominant and the central government rules everywhere. Pluralism can be an adaptation to an existing and unavoidable multiplicity for the sake of peace (*toleration) or it can be a programme aimed at sustaining cultural difference, conceived as a good in itself or as the legitimate product of communal *self-determination. A considerable variety of institutional arrangements are consistent with pluralism in either of these senses, including decentralized government (federalism), functional autonomy (particularly with regard to education and family law), and voluntary association.

The hard questions posed by political pluralism mostly have to do with its limits. It isn't only a multiplication of groups but also of loyalties that pluralism legitimizes. And in the case of individual men and women, multiplication is also division. Attachment and obligation are both divided: what then is the individual to do when their various versions come into conflict? At what point is division incompatible with a common citizenship? States committed to pluralism will set this point fairly far along the continuum that extends from unity to disintegration. None the less, they are likely to defend some significant commonalities: a single public language or a civic education for all children or a 'civil religion' with its own holidays and ceremonies.

Political pluralism also refers to the existence of legal opposition parties or competing interest groups in a unitary state, where what is pluralized is not culture or religion but political opinions and conceptions of material interest. The ruling group, whatever its character, concedes that its ideas about how to govern are not the only legitimate ideas and that its understanding of the common good must incorporate some subset of more particular understandings. M.WALZ.

*liberalism.

Arthur Bentley, *The Process of Government* (Chicago, 1908).
W. Kymlicka (ed.), *The Rights of Minority Cultures* (Oxford, 1995).
Arend Lijphart, *Democracy in Plural Societies* (New Haven, Conn., 1977).
D. Miller and M. Walzer (eds.), *Pluralism, Justice, and Equality* (Oxford, 1995).
David Nichols, *The Pluralist State* (New York, 1975).

plurality of causes. A term sometimes used where more than one cause is required for a particular effect, e.g. ignition plus oxygen for an explosion, or (more frequently) where alternative causes can produce the same (type of) effect, e.g. poisoning or decapitation cause death. Arguably, such cases are only apparent, and further analysis would indicate the 'true' causal relationship, which is claimed to be always one–one. The latter view—not required by counterfactual analyses of *causality—encourages, for example, monetarism in economics. A.J.L.

J. L. Mackie, *The Cement of the Universe* (Oxford, 1974).

pneuma. Breath, sometimes equated by the Greeks with air, the breath of the cosmos. Aristotle thought that heat in the *pneuma* enables the transmission of sensitive soul to the embryo, and that it is located near the heart in the mature organism, serving to mediate movement and perception. The Stoics thought of it as a fine, subtle body forming the *soul of the cosmos, and explaining growth, behaviour, and rationality. Descartes used the Latin equivalent, *spiritus*, from which come 'spirit' and 'sprite' in English. O.R.J.

*psyche.

Martha Craven Nussbaum, *Aristotle's* De Motu Animalium (Princeton, NJ, 1978).

poetry. No satisfactory single-concept theory of poetry has been produced: a poem is not essentially a representation, or essentially expression, or essentially a formal or 'organic' unity. Not because none of these functions is relevant to poetry, but because no one of them does justice to its complexity and many-levelled nature.

Poetry can indeed represent or describe: but it may also celebrate, praise, mourn, present alternative worlds. It certainly expresses, but it can also transform, the emotions of ordinary life, and display emotions with more than usual precision, not least because of the discipline and constraints of poetic *form*.

Distinctive of poetry at its best is an 'all-in', maximally dense, simultaneous deployment of linguistic resources—sound and rhythm as well as sense, the bringing-together of numerous strands of meaning, through metaphor and other figures, through ambiguities (often unresolved), controlled associations and resonances, allusions: all of these contributing to a well-integrated, unified effect.

The reference a poem makes to the world is often given a heightened, pregnant character through symbolical or allegorical or mythical language—in some cases the personal mythology of the poet. (William Blake and W. B. Yeats are notable examples.)

Given the total dependence of the poem's meaning and effect on the precise words in their order, any attempt at paraphrase must become 'heresy'. A poem is not a disposable wrapping for a detachable and re-expressible message.

Now, this emphasis on the thinglike integrity of a poem makes for suggestive analogies between poems and non-linguistic artefacts (a vase, sculpture, or melody): hence a claim like 'A poem should not mean but be' (MacLeish). But this exaggerates: meaning is indispensable—as is reference to the world beyond the poem—if poetry is not to be impoverished: and, in any case, the sound of words can hardly work in sustained disregard of their sense.

The subject-matter of poetry is limitlessly varied. Often enough a poem presents some vividly imagined concrete particular, a momentary, fugitive sensory impression or a recollected emotion, but also—and no less legitimately—its concern may be with abstract ideas and relationships, or with a wide-ranging religious or metaphysical perspective. Crucial here is the absence of any hierarchy of poetic subject-matter: 'ontological parity', in Justus Buchler's phrase: 'All appearances are realities for the poet.'

The relevance to philosophy of the study of the language of poetry is already obvious enough. But there is more to note. Poetry is forever fighting against the pressures and seductive power of ordinary language to falsify experience in easy, slack cliché. Poetry feels itself often up against the 'limits of language', and forced to modify, maybe do violence to, normal syntax. Theory of knowledge and philosophy of religion cannot ignore poets' claims to 'timeless (visionary) moments'—'epiphanies'.

That is easy to say: but to distinguish veridical from illusory in this area is notoriously hard.   R.W.H.

*expression; music; representation.

Justus Buchler, *The Main of Light* (New York, 1974).

Poincaré, Jules Henri (1854–1912). A leading contributor to the brilliant French tradition of applied mathematics and physics, Poincaré also wrote extensively on *methodology and the philosophy of science, in which he is usually classified as a conventionalist. He regarded scientific structures as containing conventional elements which either are principles held to be true by definition or are selected from competing alternatives on pragmatic grounds of *simplicity and convenience. But science must also be empirically adequate, and so Poincaré could also be called a metaphysical realist, since science is based on a belief in the unity and simplicity of nature, and it is the (endless) task of science to discover the most general order. But like Duhem, Poincaré distinguished sharply between scientific and metaphysical claims. Although never fully

developed, Poincaré's ideas were influential on scientists like Einstein and on later positivist and pragmatist philosophers of science.   A.BEL.

*conventionalism; pragmatism; Duhem.

Peter Alexander, 'The Philosophy of Science 1850–1910', in D. J. O'Connor (ed.), *A Critical History of Western Philosophy* (New York, 1964).

polar concepts. When a pair of *concepts opposite in meaning is such that neither of the pair can be understood unless the other is understood also, as with 'genuine–counterfeit', 'straight–crooked', 'up–down', they are said to form a 'conceptual polarity'. Ryle used the notion in an attempt to refute scepticism by arguing that if, as the sceptic's argument requires, we understand the concept of error, we must also understand that of being right; which Ryle thought proved that we must sometimes be so.

Ryle misses the sceptical point, however. The sceptic can grant that we might have to understand the conceptual polarity 'error–correctness' in order to understand the concept of error, but simply demands how we know on any given occasion that we are not in error. And the sceptic need not even grant so much: he can point to apparent polarities which are such that one of the poles has no clear application, as in 'mortal–immortal', 'perfect–imperfect', 'finite–infinite', where we can only be said properly to understand one of the poles, the other being merely its indefinite negation, possessed of no unequivocal sense or use.   A.C.G.

*scepticism.

Gilbert Ryle, *Dilemmas* (Cambridge, 1954), 94 ff.

Polish notation. Logical symbolism devised by Łukasiewicz. Propositional constants represented by capital letters: K*pq* is '*p* and *q*', A*pq* is '*p* or *q*', C*pq* is 'If *p*, *q*', and so on. Similar devices are used for quantifiers and modalities. Because *constants are written before their *arguments, the ambiguity of expressions like '*p* and *q* or *r*' is removed without using brackets: '(*p* and *q*) or *r*' is AK*pqr*, while '*p* and (*q* or *r*)' is K*p*A*qr*.   C.W.

A. N. Prior, *Formal Logic*, 2nd edn. (Oxford, 1962).

Polish philosophy. Political philosophy, especially concerning nationhood, and formal logic—these have been two areas of distinction for Polish philosophy. Although philosophy in Poland goes back to the thirteenth century and Witelo, famous for his works on optics and the metaphysics of light, its real academic life began at the University of Cracow (established in 1364) in the fifteenth century. Subsequently all the controversies of medieval philosophy were addressed in Poland. Jan of Głogów, Michał of Wrocław, Jan of Stobnica, and Benedykt Hesse were among the most important Polish schoolmen. Conciliarism became a dominant position among writers working on political matters. Paweł Włodkowic (Paulus Wladimirus) was perhaps the most famous Polish thinker of that time. He developed the concept of just war, which influenced the development of international law. According to Paweł, it is prohibited by natural law to convert pagans to Christianity by war.

During the *Renaissance (the golden period of Polish culture), Copernicus was the nation's most remarkable thinker. Although he was not particularly interested in typical philosophical questions, his astronomical work had obvious philosophical sources. His mathematical approach to astronomy had its roots in Padua in Italy, where he studied and became influenced by Platonism. He combined this view with the Aristotelian empiricism of his Cracow teachers. A famous controversy as to whether he was an instrumentalist or realist in his approach to heliocentric astronomy influenced many subsequent scientific discussions. The Polish Renaissance was also a period of intensive development in political and social philosophy. Andrzej Frycz-Modrzewski wrote a treatise *De republica emendanda* (1551) in which he proposed a deep programme of reforms of the state, church, and society. Similarly, as in Western European countries, the Renaissance brought a revival of *Stoicism in Poland (*Dialectica Ciceronis* by Adam Burski is a particularly valuable work in this tradition).

The Reformation brought into being another important stream of philosophical thought, namely Socinianism, a movement established by Faustus Socius, who came to Poland (then the most tolerant country in Europe) from Italy, and developed by the Polish Brethren. Joachim Stegmann, Samuel Przypkowski, and Andrzej Wiszowaty contributed to Socinian philosophy: they focused on ethics and social philosophy, basing their doctrines on the ideals of non-violence, justice, and tolerance. The Counter-Reformation policy forced the Socinians to emigrate from Poland. They moved to the Netherlands and England, and influenced several great European philosophers, including Grotius and Locke. The early post-Renaissance period in Poland was marked by the return of *Aristotelianism with Sebastian Petrycy of Pilzno, the first translator of Aristotle into Polish.

The period of 1650–1750 witnessed a deep political and cultural crisis in Poland. The *Enlightenment brought a major change. It happened in close connection with attempts to save Polish independence, which was imperilled by Russia, Prussia, and Austria. Stanisław Staszic and Hugo Kołłątaj were the most important political thinkers in Poland in the eighteenth century. Their ideas considerably influenced the content of the 3 May Constitution (1791), the second constitution in nation's history. A type of *positivism (Jan Śniadecki) was the most popular philosophy of the Polish Enlightenment, but *Kantianism and *Scottish philosophy were also fairly influential.

Poland finally lost its independence in 1795. Subsequent philosophy was largely a response to the national tragedy, deepened by the defeat of the national uprising in 1830–1. The philosophy of this period (approximately until 1863) is called the Polish national philosophy. This philosophy was related to *Romanticism and to German *idealism. Polish Messianism, which originated with Józef Hoene-Wroński (also a famous mathematician) and was represented by great Polish national poets (notably Adam Mickiwicz and Juliusz Słowacki), attributed to Poland a special historical role as the Christ of nations and promised a new era. Józef Gołuchowski, Józef Kremer, Karol Libelt, Bronisław Trentowski, and August Cieszkowski (he invented the term 'Historiosophie') developed other kinds of the Polish national thought, more akin to academic philosophy. The defeat of the national uprising (1863–4) led to a strong criticism of the national philosophy in Poland. It was accused of unrealistic and irresponsible political claims, harmful to nation and individuals. The group of Warsaw positivists, influenced by the ideas of *Comte, *Mill, and *Spencer, demanded that Polish thought be sober and strongly rooted in reality. Polish positivism recommended a programme of foundational work in all domains important for society.

Philosophical life in Poland intensified at the turn of nineteenth century, and this continued in independent Poland after 1918. Kazimierz Twardowski, a student of Brentano, established an analytic movement at the University of Lvov, and between 1918 and 1939 the Lvov group grew into the Lvov–Warsaw School, in which the main figures were Jan Łukasiewicz, Stanisław Leśniewski, and *Alfred Tarski. Polish mathematical logic developed partly as a result of Twardowski's programme of *analytic philosophy, partly out of the interests of Polish mathematicians in set theory and topology. Its innovations included many-valued logic, general metamathematics, the *semantic definition of truth, Leśniewski's systems, and Chwistek's systems. The Lvov–Warsaw School had affinities with the *Vienna Circle, but eschewed its anti-metaphysical radicalism and was more sympathetic toward the philosophical tradition. *Kazimierz Ajdukiewicz and *Tadeusz Kotarbiński were other distinguished exponents of Polish analytic philosophy. *Phenomenology flourished in Poland—it was *Roman Ingarden who introduced Husserl's ideas and developed a realistic version of phenomenology. Neo-Thomism was also influential.

Afyer 1945 Poland became part of the Communist bloc. While Marxism was dominant, other currents persisted in Polish philosophical life, and this phenomenon, unique in Eastern Europe, contributed to the anti-Communist revolt in 1989. At present, analytic philosophy, phenomenology, and Catholic philosophy are the main features of the philosophical map. But pluralism, respect for logic, and sensitivity to the essential problems of national life remain characteristic of Polish philosophy. In spite of honouring idealistic Messianism as the glorious past, most Polish philosophers are inclined to realistic and anti-speculative thinking.   J.WOL.

J. Czerkawski, A. B. Stępień, and S. Wielgus, 'Philosophy in Poland', in E. Craig (ed.), *Routledge Encyclopedia of Philosophy* (London, 1998).

G. Krzywicki-Herburt, 'Polish Philosophy', in P. Edwards (ed.), *The Encyclopedia of Philosophy* (New York, 1967).

H. Skolimowski, *Polish Analytical Philosophy* (London, 1967).

J. Woleński, *Logic and Philosophy in the Lvov–Warsaw School* (Dordrecht, 1989).

political obligation. The sense or fact of being bound to obey the laws of a political community and the commands of its legally constituted officers and/or to act consistently in ways that serve the common good. Principled refusals of obligation can take the form of treason, rebellion, passive resistance or disobedience, and conscientious objection (the last of these is sometimes legally recognized in specific cases; military service is the most common example). How an individual, originally free of all bonds, comes to be obligated is perhaps the central question of liberal political theory. It is usually answered by pointing to some intentional act or presumed show of intention, taken as the political equivalent of a promise. (*Consent.) Just as unreasonable promises (to live as a slave or to commit suicide) or promises made under duress or without full understanding are not binding, so with acts of consent: free individuals cannot obligate themselves to obey a dictator or a totalitarian regime (the political equivalent of accepting slavery); even more obviously, unfree individuals cannot do so: their declarations of commitment have no moral effect at all.

Political theorists from other traditions (conservatives, communitarians, rationalists of various sorts) who doubt the liberal starting-point, the reality of original freedom, commonly regard individuals as bound whether they consent or not—born bound or objectively constrained. But they too must address the limits of this obligation, arguing either that only regimes of a certain sort (which maintain just social arrangements or support the good life or are, at least, very old) can bind their subjects or that individuals are released from pre-existing obligations by specific acts of tyranny or oppression.

It is entirely possible, however, to deny the existence of anything like political obligation. On this view, there are only moral duties, which sometimes require individuals to obey, sometimes to disobey, the laws of the state, sometimes to serve, sometimes to refuse to serve, the interests of the community. Since political communities are always morally imperfect, no general obligation is possible; judgement is necessary at every moment. If this is right, then citizenship loses much of its specific moral character. For a citizen, as the term is usually understood, is a person with a particular set of political obligations—to these other people (fellow citizens) and to the community they constitute. Some of the actions that follow from such obligations would still be morally required, but they would now be required of all capable persons. The particularist reference, however, might well be immoral, since it deprives non-citizens of equal attention and regard, and hence is required of no one at all.

Assuming that there is such a thing as political obligation, it is an interesting question whether it is singular in character: are all obligated persons bound in the same way or to the same degree? Other particularist obligations (to friends or relatives, say) vary in their intensity and reach depending on the nature of the relationship and of the commitments actually made. The test case here is perhaps the resident alien, who is commonly conceived to have some, though not all, of the obligations of a citizen. But what about citizens variously disadvantaged or disengaged or committed elsewhere? Can all citizens be equally bound to vote, pay taxes, serve on juries, and so on, even though they are not equally benefited by these activities and by the acts of state they make possible, and even though they are not equally committed to or equally approving of this political regime and its characteristic works?   M.WALZ.

*civil disobedience; equality; political violence.

Carole Pateman, *The Problem of Political Obligation: A Critique of Liberal Theory* (Chichester, 1979).

A. John Simmons, *Moral Principles and Political Obligations* (Princeton, NJ, 1979).

Michael Walzer, *Obligations: Essays on Disobedience, War, and Citizenship* (Cambridge, Mass., 1970).

political philosophy, history of. Political philosophy evaluates social organization, especially government, from an ethical viewpoint, but also studies the facts about social organization. There are thus two not sharply distinguishable aspects of political philosophy, and how they ought to be related is a good question: the ethically normative aspect ('ethics'), and the descriptive-explanatory. Arguably, some close connection between these aspects is necessary for political philosophy to flourish, and the history of political philosophy can be interpreted in this light. Among ethical concepts, *autonomy, or *freedom as rational self-determination, is central, but other concepts, including *justice, *democracy, *rights, and *political obligation, are also fundamental. The important concepts of a political philosophy must be combined coherently into an account of a properly structured and functioning community. In the history of political philosophy, the term 'community', or its synonyms or translations, is sometimes prominent, sometimes not, and when used it may have very varying meaning. Political philosophy as such, however, arguably tends to aspire to an account of a appropriately structured and functioning community, with its main constitutive institutions and values. Which institutions are emphasized is one of the interesting variables in the history of political philosophy. Institutional detail, for example, provides an essential framework for interpreting what is meant by autonomy, if that notion plays a role in a political philosophy.

Plato's *Republic* is the beginning. This colossal work, whose main subject is justice in the individual and the state, contains conceptual analysis crucial for both ethics and descriptive-explanatory inquiry. Plato attempts to define what justice is, first as a matter of individual just action, and eventually as a characteristic of the just individual and the just society. Plato wishes to show how, for the individual, being just can be a good in itself. In the just individual, the three parts of the psyche are so ordered that reason rules, the 'spirited' part of the psyche responds to reason, and the appetites obey. In the just state, there is a supposedly corresponding clear division of classes among the rulers (qualified as such chiefly by personal capacity, eugenics, careful and lengthy education, life conditions including absence of personal property and of family, and ultimately a knowledge of the Form of the Good), the soldier auxiliaries, and the bulk of the population. We should value justice not only for its extrinsic advantages, but also for its own sake, because only when just are we really happy or flourishing. Arguably Plato has a concept of autonomy (and may well be an important contributor to the theory of autonomy) but thinks it is a realistic goal only for the few who are fit to rule, in contrast to some later authors who expand the group whose autonomy ought to be expressed or promoted through politics. Arguably, also, Plato's approach to political philosophy is weakened by his utopianism and his anti-empirical theory of knowledge, dominated by a certain picture of mathematical knowledge. Plato's attack on the arts is another notable feature of his views. It suggests to some modern readers that Plato's notion of reason ruling in the individual and community downgrades much emotion, especially sympathetic identification across class lines. The arts as institutions in Plato's community are to be subject to strict state controls. Plato's political philosophy, although anxious about arts institutions, thus at least pays them the tribute of close attention.

Aristotle, Plato's student, like him insists that the city state (*polis*) is higher than the individual. In this sense, community matters more than the individual for Aristotle, as it did for Plato. Aristotle is often said to be more empirically minded than Plato. His aversion to *utopianism, his classification of different sorts of constitutions and states, and other points are often adduced to show that Aristotle emphasizes more than his teacher the descriptive-explanatory component of political philosophy. Although this is true, Aristotle's work in ethics and his politics cannot be understood apart from one another. The point of ethical theory is the improvement of moral education, carried on especially though not exclusively by the *polis*. The statesman should apply ethical theory to promote happiness (*eudaimonia*), an activity of the soul in accordance with virtue. The promotion of happiness requires morally educating persons into the appropriate virtues. Arguably Aristotle is a 'perfectionist' in politics (who thinks a social system is justified by producing some persons of excellence, rather than by taking account of the flourishing of all). He has been criticized for toleration of slavery and the subordinate status of women, cultural chauvinism (including his low estimation of non-Greek 'barbarians'), and his acceptance of class divisions. As to autonomy, some think Aristotle lacks the notion. It might be argued, however, that Aristotle's virtue of practical wisdom (*phronēsis*) comes close to doing some of the work that autonomy does in some later philosophers. The person educated into *phronēsis* has a capacity to recognize the relevant principles or reasons in deciding what to do, in relation to happiness or flourishing. Like any virtue or

vice, *phronēsis* is in some sense allegedly voluntary, and one deserves praise for it, although this is in some ways puzzling. The virtues and vices in general require a good *polis* for their development, which suggests that it is not entirely up to the individual whether to become virtuous or vicious. Aristotle never resolves this apparent conflict between ethical assessment and his explanation of how virtue develops.

Little will be said about the period between Aristotle and the rise of modernity. This is not for lack of important political philosophy, such as Augustine's *City of God* or Aquinas's extension of Aristotelianism. Perhaps the major issue bequeathed to Western modernity by Augustine and by Aquinas and others from the medieval part of that period is the question of the proper relation between religious authority and political authority. (One way to express this question is to ask for an account of human community that appropriately combines religious and political institutions.) Aquinas in particular expounds views which give human government the role of providing the conditions for attainment of ultimately religious goals. His views allow human government some authority, which may, however, be resisted under certain circumstances, when it deviates from its proper function. The question of the proper role of religious and political institutions in a community is still very much alive.

Thomas Hobbes's political philosophy might be viewed as an attempt to lay the foundation for what was developing as the modern secular nation state. Hobbes none the less and very logically also discusses various nongovernmental institutions supportive of government and fitting into a larger picture of community. The Hobbesian community, however, with its tendency towards individualist egoism, is very far from what some have meant by the notion of community. In his *Leviathan* Hobbes insists on the importance of avoiding by means of a strong sovereign the war of all against all of the *state of nature. Given men's desires, it is rational for them to agree to abide by the laws of a sovereign who provides them with security. Despite Hobbes's authoritarianism, his work also leads to the thought that if the sovereign does not provide appropriate protections, the point of abiding by the law is lost. Hobbes is much influenced by materialism and geometric method, as well as by hostility to Catholicism and to individualistic Puritanism.

Some scholars argue that John Locke must not be read as replying directly to Hobbes's political philosophy, though a more complex Lockean reaction to Hobbes can be acknowledged. In the *First Treatise of Government* Locke's target is the patriarchal religious traditionalism of Sir Robert Filmer. Here, and to a lesser extent in the more widely read *Second Treatise*, religion plays a significant role in Locke's politics, along with rationality and empiricism. In the *Second Treatise* Locke holds that 'Civil Government is the proper Remedy for the Inconveniences of the State of Nature.' Above all, government is necessary for the protection of a right to property. Locke founds legitimate government on the *consent of the governed, and affirms constitutionalism and the right of revolution. Locke might plausibly be read as an expositor of a form of positive freedom, a freedom requiring government and law in order to be realized. A comparison with Rousseau on this point will be instructive.

Jean-Jacques Rousseau's *Social Contract* has been plausibly interpreted as an attempt to define a form of political organization in which autonomy and political *authority can be reconciled, a state in which there is a moral obligation to obey the law. Rousseau's work is very much an attempt to picture an appropriately arranged community, with an emphasis on the authoritative state but also with some attention to subordinate institutions such as religion and the family. Rousseau seems to recognize two stages of the social *contract. Presumably in the first stage there is unanimity about the binding authority of majority votes. For this unanimity to be more than a mere contingency, presumably Rousseau thinks that reasons could be given appealing to our capacity for rational self-determination to show why majoritarianism is a decision-making rule to be embraced. On one way of reading Rousseau, he may think a theorem by Condorcet supplies an argument why (under the circumstances Rousseau assumes) we should subsequently prefer majority judgements over individual judgements about the common good. This arguably makes it seem autonomous for an individual to accept the majority's judgement who subsequently votes on what the law should be (under the circumstances Rousseau describes) and finds himself in a minority. All citizens (males: a very regrettable expression of Rousseau's sexism) vote on whether a law should be passed, sincerely aiming at the common good, with approximate equality of influence on the outcome (presumably one reason for absence of discussion). The effort is to determine the *general will, which aims at the common good. The general will itself 'cannot err'. It aims at a law of general form which also furthers the general interest, not mere particular interests. If anyone shows partiality, if factions develop, if economic inequality allows some to buy others or requires some to sell themselves, or other failures occur, the social contract is nullified. Otherwise, the law passed by the majority is morally binding on the citizen who has participated in making it. Direct participation is vital; representation will not do. Many interpreters have doubted, on numerous grounds, whether Rousseau's scheme really preserves autonomy. Rousseau is actually pessimistic himself about the prospects for real-world instances of reconciliation of autonomy and authority. In general, Rousseau (although a great psychologist) is not very helpful on the descriptive and explanatory side of political theory, and not very helpful about telling us what to do to promote the main goals of his politics under the refractory circumstances of actual history. He tends toward scorn of corrupt realities and a sometimes wistful utopianism. For all that, in Rousseau a version of autonomy is at work which has been enormously influential. One sign of this, ironically, is in the seriousness with which influential political leaders (e.g. Robespierre, Bolivar) have taken Rousseau, even

when they should have found it difficult to justify their acts on the basis of Rousseau's ideas. Rousseau's community has seemed to some so all-encompassing as not to allow adequately for individual conscience, private life, freedom of religion, and political dissidence. Some liberals, in particular, have found the Rousseauian community stifling of individual freedom.

A classical expression of *liberalism attempting to find space for individual freedom in a broader community context is to be found in John Stuart Mill. Mill combines normative ethics and factual inquiry in his political philosophy and related work. His most frequently read work of explicit political philosophy is probably *On Liberty*, in which he attempts to distinguish when society has legitimate authority over the individual and when not. Mill argues that a necessary condition of society's controlling the individual (through either governmental penalties or the coercive influence of public opinion, which has its own penalties) should be that such control is needed to prevent one individual from harming another or others. This is often called 'the harm principle'. Mill acknowledges some exceptions in applying this doctrine, which only applies to those in 'the maturity of their faculties' (a notion which seems to exclude not only the young, but also, alarmingly, those societies in which 'the race itself may be considered as in its nonage'). One justification for social control which is mostly ruled out by Mill under normal circumstances is what others often call *'paternalism', control of a person for that person's own good. For society to proceed with the exercise of control, prevention of harm is not sufficient but there must also be violation by one individual of another's right, or violation of an obligation of the first to the second. *On Liberty* also includes a defence of liberty of thought and discussion, a plea for individuality, a rejection of religious authority in political matters, and discussion of many specific applications of Mill's views, in which Mill's anti-statism emerges. The ultimate moral basis here, as in all of Mill, is the *greatest happiness principle or principle of utility, most clearly defined and defended in *Utilitarianism*. On Mill's version of the principle, quality as well as quantity of pleasure counts morally, a doctrine that has interesting and probably élitist political implications. Mill's *Considerations on Representative Government* deserves close study in conjunction with his other major works. In it, Mill defends the importance of some popular participation in government, but also argues that society needs to choose exceptional political representatives of superior intelligence and morality, and then allow them to choose what is best, voting them out if necessary. Mill's fears about the tyranny of the majority, so evident in *On Liberty*, also show up in *Considerations* in other ways, for example in his argument for special voting procedures to allow for the representation of minorities, and in his argument that extra votes ought to be given to those of superior intelligence. It should be added that Mill appears in other works to have become more sympathetic to socialism in his later years, although the exact nature of his commitments is somewhat controversial. Whether compatible with *socialism or not, Mill's emphasis on individual *liberty is only possible in the context of a broader community structure and set of traditions, however open to change Mill wants these to be. Some critics claim that liberal *individualism (with its commitments to such institutions as the *market) tends to subvert community, but there is also a sense of community in which the liberal individualist (such as Mill) is simply offering still another sort of account (to be evaluated on its merits) of the properly functioning community.

Marx and Engels give a very different, historically dynamic account of society, critical of liberal individualism among other rival visions of community. An adequate understanding of Marx requires some acquaintance with Hegel, but we shall not comment on Hegel here except to note that Marx thought of his own work as standing Hegel upon his head. By this, Marx seems to have meant that the Hegelian interpretation of history as primarily a study of leading ideas and their dialectical changes, which explain other institutional changes, needed to be radically revised. For Marx, *historical materialism distinguishes between economic base or infrastructure and superstructure, including non-economic institutions and ideological aspects of the society. Historical materialism depicts changes in the former as, for the most part, the causes of changes in superstructure, including ideological *superstructure. Marx and Engels argue that after the ancient world and feudalism, the economic structures of capitalism, including its two main antagonistic classes, the bourgeoisie and the proletariat, have come to the fore in world history. Class conflict is a main characteristic of all history, but conflicts between owners of the means of production and wage-earners within the capitalist system are seen as central in this period. Sharpening class conflict and accompanying contradictions will eventually force a coming to consciousness of class analysis, and eventually (first, they predict, in the more advanced countries) a revolution in which *capitalism is overthrown. They argue that capitalism is a global system which will exhaust all possibilities by its own logic before falling, a view later elaborated by Lenin. During the transitional 'dictatorship of the proletariat', it is to be expected that there will be greater centralization of economic and political power in the state, but eventually a 'withering away of the state' is to be expected (Engels's phrase). These changes are meant to occur in some sense in accordance with historical–economic laws, though the exact nature and status of such laws is a matter of dispute. Marx and Engels want to combine description and prediction in various ways that generate interpretative puzzles, but that are a consequence of the desire both to avoid utopianism and to stay consistent with leading historical trends, but also to contribute actively to historical change that the authors consider desirable. Marx and Engels do not necessarily rule out normative ethical and political theory, but given their historical materialism, the study of history and economics generally seems to them more important. It has been left to some subsequent Marxists (including some of the Praxis

group from what was formerly Yugoslavia) to stress the importance of what Marx and Engels did not entirely overlook, but de-emphasized. Arguably Marx and Engels have a concept of collective autonomy or self-determination which requires for its realization as freedom growth in understanding of historical laws and an ending of the exploitation and domination of some classes by others.

In the twentieth century a plethora of political and intellectual developments shaped political philosophy. For a long time, after the Russian Revolution and before recent changes, including the dissolution of the Soviet Union, the main political positions thought by many to be in contention were one or another variety of liberalism (including under this broad category the sort of *'conservativism' which argues for a limited state, 'free markets', private property, and certain other traditional values) and Marxism. This sort of opposition was always over-simplified. Two counter-examples can be mentioned. In the USA John Dewey's avowedly democratic pragmatism was indebted both to Hegelianism and at times even to aspects of Marxism, but also preserved many features of the legacy of liberalism. Dewey's respect for scientific method, although tempered in later years, was combined with an interest in normative 'democratically' orientated thought of a non-utopian variety. Dewey asserted the importance of a critique of capitalist economic relations even as he tended to remain critical of Marxism. The concept of democratic community, used in a eulogistic way, is very prominent in Dewey. Within the quite distinct, broad and diverse tradition of anarchism, there had developed (over a long period, but especially from William Godwin and Pierre-Joseph Proudhon on) a critique of centralized state power along with a critique of capitalism. Anarcho-syndicalism is a notable example. In more recent academic philosophy in the English-speaking world, these bodies of work have had some but rather limited influence. Recent academic political philosophy in English has been mostly a quarrel among liberalisms (well exemplified by the contrast between John Rawls's *Theory of Justice*, with its two principles of justice constructed by an autonomous choice by rational beings in the 'original position' behind a 'veil of ignorance', and Robert Nozick's 'conservative' (old-liberal), rights-centred (though selectively so), pro-capitalist, minimal-state *Anarchy, State, and Utopia*) the practical relevance of which may have been diminished by recent economic and political changes. Since the widely proclaimed 'end of the Cold War' between capitalism and *communism, with the collapse of Soviet communism and a decline in living-standards in parts of the capitalist world, including some dependent regions, both Marxism and militant free-market capitalism have come to seem to some observers (rightly or wrongly) no longer as straightforwardly relevant as was once the case. Also, in recent political philosophy, *'communitarianism' has come to be a label applied to a variety of views stressing ideas about community and critical of individualist liberalism. Communitarians (including Charles Taylor, Michael Sandel, Alasdair MacIntyre, and perhaps Michael Walzer) are sometimes critical of liberalism, but sometimes are themselves types of liberals.

There may perhaps at other times have been a more assured consensus on which great authors should be included in the canon of 'Western' political philosophy, and less suspicion of the very idea of a canon. Feminists, certain minorities in the 'developed world', and persons from the 'underdeveloped world', among others, have made a compelling case for reassessment of the traditional canon. Then, too, the growth of descriptive and explanatory studies relevant to political philosophy (not a sudden development, but a tendency with a long history of its own) as well as normative work in other disciplines has complicated study of the history of political philosophy. Subjects such as political science, anthropology, sociology, history, jurisprudence, literary studies, and the like sometimes generate work which deserves inclusion in the category of political philosophy. Some of the most interesting discussions in political philosophy over the last few decades in the English-speaking world, for example, have involved philosophers who are also legal scholars (say, H. L. A. Hart, Ronald Dworkin, Joseph Raz, and proponents of critical legal studies such as Roberto Unger).

The idea of autonomy (requiring for its intelligibility some value-laden picture of a community with its main constitutive institutions) has been central in much important Western political philosophy, especially for modernity. Autonomy has been considered a crucial part of human welfare, a focus for describing favoured political institutions such as democratic government, and a notion useful in supporting other notions such as political obligation, rights, justice, and the like. Whether the idea of autonomy should survive critique (especially critique from the descriptive-explanatory side of the subject) remains to be seen, but the idea's defeat would require a radical shift in political perspective. Isaiah Berlin distinguishes negative and positive freedom in politics and opts to support the former as a primary value. (For Benjamin Constant in the nineteenth century, similarly, the liberties of the ancients and the moderns are fundamentally different, and the ancient emphasis on political participation and public life is no longer appropriate in the modern world.) For Berlin, positive freedom (often denominated autonomy) is recognizable in many great philosophers, including Plato, Rousseau, and Marx, but allegedly easily leads to totalitarian excesses. Arguably, Berlin's view is exaggerated, and has been effectively criticized by Charles Taylor in his paper 'What's Wrong with Negative Liberty'. This family of concepts of freedom as autonomy, combined with an institutionally detailed account of community, still has an important potential use for any political philosophy critical of arbitrary political and economic power.   E.T.S.

*equality; inequality; republicanism; socialism.

Isaiah Berlin, 'Two Concepts of Liberty' (1958), in *Four Essays on Liberty* (Oxford, 1969).

D. Boucher and P. Kelly (eds.), *Political Thinkers: From Socrates to the Present* (Oxford, 2003).

Benjamin Constant, 'The Liberty of the Ancients compared with that of the Moderns' (1820), in *Benjamin Constant: Political Writings*, ed. Biancamaria Fontana (Cambridge, 1988).

Alasdair MacIntyre, *After Virtue*, 2nd edn. (Notre Dame, Ind., 1984).

D. D. Raphael, *Concepts of Justice* (Oxford, 2001).

George Sabine, *A History of Political Theory*, 3rd edn. (New York, 1961).

political philosophy, problems of. Political philosophy in Western civilization began as the philosophy of the ancient Greek *polis* (the Greek word from which 'political' is derived). Accordingly, political philosophy in its inception took as its subject how best to govern and to live in a city-state of that day. Its goal was the creation and preservation of an ideal society. Although Plato devoted several dialogues to issues of political philosophy, it is his *Republic* (*c*.380 BC) that is arguably the most memorable, widely read, and pioneering contribution to the subject. Apart from the question of its actual influence on statecraft, it provided both theorists and practitioners with a model of a political philosophy in which the author undertook to identify a range of problems concerning governance and social order, and then tried to ground their solution on appropriate metaphysical, epistemological, and anthropological principles. These solutions in their turn raised questions of educational philosophy, both moral and cognitive, because in the absence of the right sort of educational regimen there is (or so Plato argued) no hope of at least creating (let alone preserving) the ideal society that was the intended purpose or aim of political philosophy.

In the centuries after Plato, the problems of political philosophy ceased to focus on the governance of face-to-face societies on the scale of the ancient city-state. Today, especially, it is much larger political units, typically nation-states (with their increasingly global scope) that are the political entities whose structure is under discussion. What might be called the apparent Platonic prejudice in favour of identifying the ideal, possibly even an ideal beyond reach, has been generally subordinated by political philosophers to what might be called the Kantian prejudice in favour of exploring the presuppositions of the actual as well as the ideal political possibilities.

From this perspective, and despite the importance of the *Republic*, it is Aristotle rather than Plato who provided philosophy with its first genuine political treatise. In his *Politics* (*c*.330 BC) Aristotle made no attempt to imitate his teacher's style of presentation, which was to use imaginary dialogues between Socrates and his companions to sketch a portrait of the ideal society, its origin, and the obstacles to its preservation. Instead, Aristotle's treatise concentrates on stating, defending, and applying the principles that governments actually as well as ideally rely on. Yet it was not only in style that Aristotle deviated from Plato. On the most fundamental question—what is the nature and structure of the ideal society—they differed radically. Plato argued in the *Republic* that there is exactly one form of ideal state, its class structure is based on the fixed differential capacities of its citizenry, rigidly orchestrated so that each class of persons performs the tasks for which the natural talents of its members best fits them. Aristotle in his *Politics* is far more tolerant of diverse forms of government and social structure. He saw advantages under the right conditions for allocating governing authority in any of three main ways: monarchy, aristocracy, and 'polity'. (The latter is roughly what we would call constitutional democracy. Plato in the *Republic* insisted on rule by philosopher-kings.)

The problems of political philosophy (in the material mode) that have preoccupied thinkers for the past several centuries are essentially the questions (in the formal mode) concerning political life and institutions. These are what the authors of the great treatises in political philosophy since the Reformation and Renaissance have endeavoured to answer, plus an array of issues and questions to which those answers in their turn have given rise. Thus to identify these problems and some of the major proposed solutions to them, one must quarry in works as diverse as Thomas Hobbes's *Leviathan* (1651), John Locke's *Second Treatise* (1690), Jean-Jacques Rousseau's *Social Contract* (1762), William Godwin's *Enquiry Concerning Political Justice* (1793), G. F. W. Hegel's *Philosophy of Right* (1830), J. S. Mill's *On Liberty* (1859), T. H. Green's *Lectures on the Principles of Political Obligation* (1895), Friedrich Hayek's *Constitution of Liberty* (1960), John Rawls's *Theory of Justice* (1972), and Jürgen Habermas's *Theory of Communicative Action* (1984, 1987). This is to name but a representative few of the best-known. The problems of political philosophy that these philosophers undertake to solve would appear to be divisible, at least provisionally, into three distinct sets differentiated from each other in various ways and subject to solution by different methods. Given the range and complexity of matters that can legitimately be considered relevant to the goals of political philosophy, it is hardly surprising that a vast library exists of attempts to deal with those problems in both abstract theoretical and relatively practical terms.

First and foremost, there are problems of political philosophy that are essentially *conceptual*. Thus, Plato opens book 1 of the *Republic* by asking, What is justice?, and Aristotle opens book 3 of the *Politics* by asking, What is a state? Political philosophies will differ from one another as they vary in their starting places, as they provide different conceptions of certain central ideas, and as they allot greater or lesser centrality to the values represented by a given concept in their theory. These concepts play a double role: first, they are proper topics of philosophical inquiry in their own right; second, they serve as the building-blocks of any possible political theory. Although there is no canonical set of such concepts, virtually every comprehensive political philosophy will find it necessary to explain, in order to use effectively, many if not all of the following three dozen concepts: *authority, *autonomy, *citizenship, *coercion, *collective responsibility, *community, *consent, *desert, devolution, *duty, *equality, *fairness, *justice, *law, *liberty, *loyalty, majority rule,

*obligation, order, ownership, *power, *property, public interest, *punishment, representation, *rights, slavery, social class, *society, sovereignty, *State, *terrorism, *toleration, *violence, welfare, *well-being. The variety and complexity of these concepts, and the interconnections among them, show that the problems of political philosophy overlap, intersect, and merge with the problems of legal, social, economic, ethical, and educational philosophy. In so far as the task of political philosophy is thought to be one primarily of analysis and clarification, conceptual questions will be regarded as fundamental.

Some philosophers have gone so far as virtually to identify the problems of political philosophy with all and only the problems that can be settled by conceptual analysis. Notable examples can be found in T. D. Weldon's *Vocabulary of Politics* (1953), Anthony Quinton's *Political Philosophy* (1967), and Felix E. Oppenheim's *Political Concepts: A Reconstruction* (1981). The self-denying approach manifest in these volumes was mainly a product of the positivistic and linguistic phases of general philosophy in the mid-twentieth century, when all philosophical problems were held to be 'conceptual', and the only method of philosophical discussion was 'analytic'. By the end of the century this approach had few if any adherents. There is no doubt that conceptual questions are central to any possible political philosophy, as they are (or at least have been) to the nature of philosophical problems generally. But as politics itself is a matter of eminently practical importance, its philosophical problems must reflect this fact. The discussion of nothing but conceptual questions—even questions about political concepts—cannot suffice for the task.

This brings us to the second category of problems, the *normative*, in which a philosopher undertakes to state and defend substantive principles that can serve to answer normative questions. Among them are these: What principles ought to be adopted and enforced such that compliance with them will achieve social justice? What principles are used and presupposed in defending a given political practice or institution? Just as there is no established canon of the conceptual issues in political philosophy, so there is no fixed set of normative principles in the workshop of political philosophy. Yet some questions are so central and typical that they arise again and again across the centuries for anyone who reflects on social order and disorder and the lessons they teach about human frailty and aspirations. A partial list looks like this: What is the proper scope and role of law in providing conditions for social stability? What forms of coercion to secure compliance with just laws are permissible? Under what conditions, if any, may the citizen violate the law and even forcibly resist its enforcement? What conditions must be satisfied if nonviolent resistance to lawful orders are to be justified? Is there any legitimate role for violence against persons or property in a constitutional democracy? Can political terrorism be justified, at least as a last resort? What rights, if any, apart from those provided by the laws of the land, do individuals or groups have? What obligations do individuals have to obey the laws and governments set over them, and what is the source of these obligations? How can political authority best be reconciled with individual autonomy? To what extent ought individuals to be left free to bargain with others in acquiring and transferring property, including even property in their own bodies and lives? How should conflicts between social utility (efficiency) and distributive justice (equity) be resolved? Under what conditions, if any, should claims based on the equal worth of all persons prevail over considerations of efficiency? Is a strict meritocracy a threat to equality? How free are persons when the options among which they must choose are not all of their own making? What normative principles in general ought to be seen as presupposed by preferred political practices and policies, and how are these principles to be justified? Again, in this more practical arena there are many questions that political philosophy needs to deal with.

Standard political philosophies or ideologies, such as anarchism, fascism, totalitarianism, socialism, communism, liberalism (whether in its contractarian, utilitarian, or libertarian versions), and communitarianism are constituted by their different answers to these and related questions. In so far as the task of political philosophy is thought to involve justifying a set of political institutions of one sort rather than of another—or, at a minimum, evaluating them—it is the answers to these normative questions that form the core of political philosophy. But how philosophers ought to answer the normative questions of political philosophy admits of no simple answer. This question is itself one of the perennial higher-order problems of political philosophy.

In addition to conceptual and normative problems, systematic and comprehensive political thinking also involves various *empirical* problems. By way of illustration, consider these questions: Which institutions and practices are appropriate to implement the principles of distributive justice? How can the self-interest of governors and other officials be harnessed to serve the interest of the general public? What constitutional mechanisms will provide effective checks on executive power without causing governmental paralysis? Does equality of opportunity require inequality of liberty? Which forms of punishment—corporal, incarcerative, pecuniary, etc.—provide the most effective deterrence to crime? What constraints do the best political principles impose on the recourse to punishment? Is a capitalist economy causally related to liberal-democratic political institutions? How plastic is human nature?

In raising questions such as these—questions that are at least in part answerable only by empirical inquiry and data from history and the social sciences—we not only approach but actually cross the boundary that divides political philosophy from political science. (We might think of political *theory* as a third point, along with political *science* and political *philosophy*, the three of which triangulate a space subdivided by somewhat vague and elastic boundaries.) Although every classic political

philosophy contains views on some empirical questions (they are prominent in Aristotle, rarer in Plato), most philosophers today would argue that to the extent that such questions can be answered only by experiential data, systematic observation, the investigation of practices, statistical methods, and the answers then devoted to describing, predicting, or explaining individual or group behaviour, to precisely that extent the questions are not philosophical at all. For practical political purposes it is constantly necessary to ask and answer such questions, but philosophy has little or nothing to contribute to the answers.

Such a convenient and familiar sorting of the problems of political philosophy into conceptual, normative, and empirical categories, however, eventually runs afoul of two difficulties. The lesser is that as the boundaries between concepts, norms, and empirical generalizations are themselves somewhat blurred and uncertain, particular cases will arise—often these are among the most interesting cases—where the attempt to keep the problems and their methods of solution precise and distinct from each other will fail. Consider a question such as this, brought to prominence in John Rawls's *Theory of Justice*: Would a rational and self-interested person situated behind a veil of ignorance choose some version of the principle of utility as the fundamental principle for the society in which he expects to live? Is this question primarily conceptual or normative? or is it partly empirical? or perhaps a mixture of two or even all three of these?

The graver difficulty arises from (in the phrase of W. B. Gallie) the 'essentially contested' nature of political concepts. Their analysis and interpretation typically is shaped by implicit practical concerns. Or, to put the point another way, the central political concepts are not—and so cannot be used as if they were—merely descriptive and unblemished by the ideological concerns of the philosopher who employs them. As a result, what may begin by seeming to be the wholly neutral task of defining or analysing a political concept will probably end by merging subtly (and perhaps tacitly) with normative considerations. Thus, the image—(and for some, the ideal)—of unbiased, ideologically neutral answers to the problems of political philosophy is likely to be elusive at best. It is considerations of this sort that are the first step toward a post-modernist perspective on political theory.

Cutting orthogonally across the distinctions among the conceptual, the normative, and the empirical problems of political philosophy is the contrast between pure and applied philosophy and the issues properly belonging to each. For every great treatise in political philosophy, from Hobbes to Rawls, in which conceptual and normative problems in their pure form are addressed to the relative exclusion of empirical and applied issues, there are as many and more essays and books by thinkers hardly less eminent that focus on making first-order political judgements, evaluating the prevailing political order, and proposing revisionary (even revolutionary) practices and policies—as evidenced by such classic tracts as Thoman

Paine's *Rights of Man* (1791–2), Karl Marx and Friedrich Engels' *Communist Manifesto* (1848), J. S. Mill's *The Subjection of Women* (1862), Georges Sorel's *Reflections on Violence* (1906), and R. H. Tawney's *Equality* (1931). More recent works written in this vein include F. A. Hayek's *Road to Serfdom* (1944), Karl Popper's *Open Society and its Enemies* (1945), Jean-Paul Sartre's *On Genocide* (1968), Peter Singer's *Animal Liberation* (1975), Michel Foucault's *Discipline and Punish* (1975), Michael Walzer's *Just and Unjust Wars* (1975), Onora O'Neill's *Faces of Hunger* (1986), Amartya Sen's *Inequality Reexamined* (1992), and Ted Honderich's *After the Terror* (2002). In books such as these, philosophers have displayed their interest in evaluating and criticizing substantive political, social, and economic practices and institutions, and they have done so by relying on and invoking principles and ideals not themselves the primary focus of the author's argumentative or analytic attention. The problems thus addressed are more plausibly viewed, many would argue, as mainly or wholly political rather than philosophical. Yet it would be a mistake to press this distinction too hard; to do so would be to ignore some of the most interesting and influential contributions philosophers have made to some of the problems that fall on the boundary between political advocacy and applied political philosophy.

As the history of political philosophy shows, what interests philosophers is shaped in part by the great issues of the day. These typically provide the fuel not only for political organization and agitation but for political reflection as well. And as these issues change over tine, with the changing material circumstances of life, so do the paramount problems of political philosophy.

Thus, ancient writers were concerned to explain how the state emerged from family and tribal units, a problem that political philosophers today are happy to leave to cultural and historical anthropology. Late medieval and early modern philosophers focused on the proper division of authority between church and state, the sacred and the secular, another set of issues largely ignored by philosophers in recent decades (though there is some possibility that they may return to the agenda because of the increased number of sectarian fundamentalist religious movements world-wide). The explorations, conquests, and colonizations by Europeans of African, Indian, American, and Asian peoples four centuries ago provoked philosophers to reflect on the nature of property, freedom, and rights as these issues became focused in the twin practices of enslaving native peoples and colonizing their territories. With the struggle to promote liberal democratic ideas in Western Europe since the Protestant Reformation, problems of political equality versus inequality, of tradition and stability versus liberation and progressive change, or collective versus centralized political decision-making, and of individual autonomy versus communal solidarity came to dominate the concerns of political philosophy just as they dominated political debate and political struggle during the same period. The Industrial Revolution, factory labour, and imperialism of the nine-

teenth century forced new sets of problems and new ways of conceptualizing human relations on to the agenda of political philosophy. Such vexed matters as racism, sexism, ageism, human population growth, maldistribution of the world's material resources, and the unremitting assault on the natural environment, are all issues that bedevil governments and provoke partisan disagreement and, accordingly, have begun to find a place on the agenda of political philosophy as well.   H.A.B.

*morality in political philosophy; social philosophy.

Brian Barry, *Political Argument* (London, 1965).

S. I. Benn and R. S. Peters, *The Principles of Political Thought* (New York, 1965).

Adam Finlayson (ed.), *Contemporary Political Thought: A Reader and Guide* (Edinburgh, 2003).

Robert E. Goodin and Philip Pettit (eds.), *A Companion to Contemporary Political Philosophy* (Oxford, 1993).

Virginia Held, Kai Nielsen, and Charles Parsons (eds.), *Philosophy and Political Action* (Oxford, 1972).

Will Kymlicka, *Contemporary Political Philosophy* (Oxford, 1990).

Peter Laslett *et al.* (eds.), *Philosophy, Politics, and Society* (Oxford, 1956–).

Nomos (New York, 1958–), various eds., yearbook of the American Society of Political and Legal Philosophy.

Michael Rosen and Jonathan Wolff (eds.), *Political Thought* (Oxford, 1999).

Leo Strauss, *What is Political Philosophy?* (Glencoe, Ill., 1959).

political scepticism. V. S. Naipaul observed that in the late twentieth century the opium of the people was not religion but politics. Naipaul is certainly expressing a widespread and justifiable suspicion after high hopes had been raised about just what politicians and politics can achieve, but this need not amount to political scepticism in any systematic sense. Such scepticism derives from two sources. First, there is the sociological observation, enshrined in public choice theory, that bureaucrats and politicians tend to serve themselves and the interest of their bureaucracies before those of their clients. This would explain recent phenomenal increases of state power, even where governments are ostensibly committed to reducing it. Then, secondly, there are doubts, particularly associated with Hayek and Oakeshott, about whether centrally planned political attempts to achieve results are ever well directed or based on enough information to make them truly rational. The moral of both these points would seem to be to reduce government as much and as quickly as possible, but with the paradoxical proviso that in most countries it would need a massive political initiative to do so.   A.O'H.

*conservatism.

John Gray, *Limited Government* (London, 1989).

political violence: *see* violence, political.

politics and determinism. Setting aside the special cases of economic and historical determinism, the clearest consequences of *determinism in politics are for a cluster of ideas about punishment and reward, in which the concept of *desert is central. Conservative advocates of tougher sentencing are apt to stress the mischievousness and evil of criminals, just as they discount the circumstances and aetiology of criminal behaviour. Tougher punishment, they argue, is what evil men and women *deserve*. Philosophers disagree about the implications of determinism for responsibility and punishment (*compatibilism and incompatibilism), but there is at least one understanding of desert that takes it to follow from actions that are wholly within the power of the agent, and which is therefore incompatible with determinism. Indeterminism is thus a natural accompaniment to beliefs that some criminals are evil out of their own choosing and deserve to be punished for it.

The argument about the compatibility of determinism with responsibility and punishment can be viewed, therefore, as a theoretical counterpart to the political debate about how much weight should be given to social deprivation in combating crime.

The idea that unequal possession of wealth is more or less deserved is also a recognizable (though not universal) feature of conservative thought. It is argued that since left-wing thought about distribution can be said to be founded on a principle of equality rather than desert, *conservatism, by contrast, is especially vulnerable to determinism. Desert is less fundamental to conservative thinking about distribution, however, than it is to conservative ideas about crime and punishment: conservatives will more readily acknowledge the role of circumstance and luck in the distribution of property than in the causes of crime.   K.M.

*historical determinism.

D. Hume, *An Enquiry Concerning the Principles of Morals*, ed. L. A. Selby-Bigge (Oxford, 1975), iii. ii.

K. Joseph and J. Sumption, *Equality* (London, 1979).

T. Honderich, *A Theory of Determinism* (Oxford, 1988).

politics and the philosophers. Before the professionalization of the universities in the eighteenth and nineteenth centuries, political service of one kind or another was the main alternative to the Church as a source of steady income for a good many philosophers. As a result, many have had cause to dabble in politics. From ancient times onwards, however, philosophers have debated whether they should seek to guide their political masters according to their philosophical ideals or whether instead they should adapt their skills to the political requirements of the moment. Plato offered the model for the first view, and attempted unsuccessfully to persuade Dionysius I and his successor Dionysius II of Syracuse in Sicily to adopt a code of laws modelled on his political ideas. *Enlightenment thinkers also followed this approach, hoping to turn the monarchs of their time into philosopher-kings. Voltaire briefly sought to serve Frederick the Great in this capacity, for example, and Diderot was taken up by Catherine the Great. Bentham's numerous attempts to get governments to take up his various constitutional schemes and reforms, such as his proposal for an ideal

prison based on his Panopticon design, also fits into this line of thinking. In the twentieth century Gentile believed he had persuaded Mussolini that Fascism was the embodiment of his actualist philosophy, whilst Heidegger tried with rather less success to make similar claims about Nazism, and Lukács and Sartre even more disastrously about Stalinism. However, all these philosophers generally discovered that even when politicians invite their advice they rarely take it, or only do so for as long as it proves convenient, leaving the philosopher looking politically naïve.

Machiavelli offers the model for the second view. Superficially this tack seems less honourable, requiring the philosopher to adapt his or her ideals to the prevailing political wind. However, as we have seen, it has generally been the first view that has involved philosophers in being the dupes of tyrants, whereas the second has proved both more democratic and more successful. Locke, for example, acted as medical adviser and ideologist in residence for the Earl of Shaftesbury, and although the initial failure of his patron's political activities briefly forced him into exile, his services to the Whig cause were ultimately rewarded with a number of government offices. Tom Paine was perhaps the democratic philosopher *par excellence*, contributing theoretical support to both the American and the French Revolutions, and causing the British government to prosecute and outlaw him for seditious libel in the process. Modern examples include the Italian Marxist Antonio Gramsci, whose philosophy was intimately connected to his activity as one of the founders of the Italian Communist Party, and Bertrand Russell, who played a major role in the pacifist movement during the First World War and was one of the leading lights of the Campaign for Nuclear Disarmament during the 1950s.

In general, however, philosophers have found themselves wavering between these two positions. They have been deeply ambivalent about politics and rarely successful at it, perhaps because whilst compromise is a political virtue it is rarely regarded as a philosophical one. Burke's end-of-poll address to the voters of Bristol, in which he stressed that the duty of the MP was representation rather than delegation, epitomizes the resulting ambivalence of philosophers towards politics. Unsurprisingly, the electorate rejected him at the next election, and he sat for the rest of his parliamentary career for a rotten borough in the gift of his patron, Lord Rockingham. J. S. Mill's parliamentary career was not dissimilar. MP for Westminster from 1865 to 1868, he confined his electioneering to telling his electorate that it was unnecessary for him to consult them directly since he undoubtedly knew their own interests better than they themselves. In recent times John Hospers is one of the few philosophers to enter the electoral lists, standing in 1972 as the first Presidential candidate for the Libertarian Party in the United States—he polled 5,000 votes.   R.P.B.

M. Cranston, *Philosophers and Pamphleteers* (Oxford, 1986).

J. Hamburger, *Intellectuals in Politics* (New Haven, Conn., 1965).

M. Walzer, *The Company of Critics* (London, 1989).

Pomponazzi, Pietro (1462–1525). Italian Aristotelian philosopher who provoked a controversy in 1516 with his treatise *De Immortalitate Animae*. Defying a decree of the Fifth Lateran Council (1513) which enjoined philosophers to teach that the personal immortality of the soul was demonstrable on rational grounds, he maintained that neither Aristotelian philosophy nor reason provided support for Christian dogma. He claimed to accept the authority of the Church as a matter of faith, but refused to allow such considerations to influence his judgement in the realm of philosophy, whose autonomy he staunchly defended. Despite attempts to convict him of heresy, he was able to hold on to his chair at the University of Bologna. Fearing another uproar, he forbore to publish a treatise in which he explained miracles in terms of astrological influences and other forms of occult causation.   J.A.K.

M. Pine, *Pietro Pomponazzi: Radical Philosopher of the Italian Renaissance* (Padua, 1986).

pons asinorum (Latin: asses' bridge). Proof given of theorem 5 in book 1 of Euclid's *Elements* (concerning the angles of isosceles triangles): inability to follow the proof is supposed to demonstrate stupidity. In medieval times the theorem was described as *elefuga*, the flight of the miserable (from geometry). The term is sometimes applied to Pythagoras' theorem, sometimes to a medieval logic teaching aid, and sometimes to any argument supposed to separate intellectual sheep from goats.   M.C.

Popper, Karl (1902–94). British (originally Austrian) philosopher, whose considerable reputation rests on his philosophy of science and his political philosophy. In his early work he was associated with the positivists of the *Vienna Circle, and shared their interest in distinguishing between science and other activities. However, Popper did not think that it was possible to approach that (or any other philosophical problem) by an analysis of language or meaning, nor did he see the success of science in terms of its being more verifiable than, say, ethics or metaphysics. For Popper always took a sceptical Humean stand on *induction, as a result of which he claimed it is impossible to verify or even to confirm a universal scientific theory with any positive degree of probability. What we can do, though, is to disprove a universal theory. While no number of observations in conformity with the hypothesis that, say, all planets have elliptical orbits can show that the hypothesis is true or even that tomorrow's planet will have an elliptical orbit, only one observation of a non-elliptical planetary orbit will refute the hypothesis. Falsification can get a grip where positive proof is ever beyond us; the demarcation between science and non-science lies in the manner in which scientific theories make testable predictions and are given up when they fail their tests.

Popper, in contrast to the Logical Positivists, never held that non-scientific activities were meaningless or even intellectually disreputable. What is disreputable is *pseudo-science, which arises when holders of an empirical theory refuse to be deflected by observational disproof or where a supposedly scientific theory never makes any empirical predictions. Popper convicts Marxists of the first sin and psychoanalysts of the second, contrasting them with a true scientist like Einstein.

Questions, though, remain. Is it true that scientists always reject their theories when faced with counter-evidence, as Popper says they should? And if the most we can ever do in science is to disprove theories, how do we know which theories to believe and act on? Popper says that we ought to act on those theories which have survived severe testing. His critics, though, find this hard to distinguish from the induction he officially rejects.

The themes of human ignorance and the need for critical scrutiny of ideas are also prominent in Popper's political philosophy. This is an advocacy of so-called open societies against the pretensions of planners and politicians who claim the right to impose their blueprints on the rest of us by virtue of supposed knowledge of the course of history. There can be no such knowledge. History is affected by discoveries we will make in the future, and do not know now. Moreover, any policy, however well-intentioned, has unforeseeable and unintended consequences. The only way to overcome our ignorance is to allow those affected by policies to voice their criticisms and for people in a society to be able peacefully and regularly to change their rulers. This last right, rather than formal democracy, is the mark of the open society, a concept taken for granted in the western Europe, but of increasing interest currently in eastern Europe and South America.

In his later years, Popper placed his theory of scientific and political error-seeking within a generalized theory of evolution. He also defended versions of scientific realism, *indeterminism, and *dualism with commendable valour, if not always with great subtlety of argument.   A.O'H.

*hypothetics-deductive method; Logical Positivism; London philosophy.

A. O'Hear, *Karl Popper* (London, 1980).
K. R. Popper, *The Logic of Scientific Discovery* (London, 1959); tr. of *Logik der Forschung* (Vienna, 1935).
—— *The Open Society and its Enemies*, 2 vols. (London, 1945).
—— *Conjectures and Refutations* (London, 1963).
—— *Objective Knowledge* (Oxford, 1972).

popular philosophy. There are three main kinds of popular philosophy: first, general guidance about the conduct of life; secondly, amateur consideration of the standard, technical problems of philosophy; thirdly, philosophical popularization.

At the start some recognition should be given to a movement explicitly called 'popular philosophy' in mid- and late eighteenth-century Germany. Its leader was Moses Mendelssohn, and it set itself against obscure technicalities and systematic elaboration, in the interests of closeness to experience and usefulness for life. The acquisition of imperial authority by Kant soon put an end to this project, and installed a style of German philosophy from which even Christian Wolff would have shrunk.

General guidance about the conduct of life is what is colloquially meant by the word 'philosophy' and is what most people expect from philosophers and are, for the most part, disappointed not to receive from them. Dispensing such guidance soon became an important aspect of Greek philosophy. It began with Socrates' attacks, through the mouth of Plato, on the calculating amorality of his Sophist contemporaries, permeated Aristotle's *Ethics*, and became the main substance of philosophy in the long epoch from the reign of Alexander the Great to the fall of the Roman Empire. The Stoics and Epicureans did not wholly ignore logic and 'physics', which Aristotle saw as making up philosophy, together with ethics. But, especially in the Roman period, in Epictetus, Seneca, and others, the ethical element was overwhelming.

In the Middle Ages, only the clergy were literate and educated, and guidance for the conduct of life became professionalized and legalistic. The moral life, directed as it was towards the eternal, disdained man's earthly existence and took little account of personal individuality. Philosophy, in so far as it touched non-philosophers, was official and authoritative. The humanism of the Renaissance reversed all that. The diversity of human beings was celebrated, as in the *Colloquies* of Erasmus. The rational, if unsystematic, exposition of *Leben-sweisheit* emerged in the form of the essay, in Montaigne and, then, by imitation, in Bacon (whose essays were, in fact, congelations of aphorisms). In the seventeenth and eighteenth centuries the *moralistes* of France, such as the rather laboriously cynical La Rochefoucauld, had an earnest British associate in Samuel Johnson, a lively American one in Benjamin Franklin, and a brilliant German one in Lichtenberg. Chamfort, who died in 1794, is a latter-day *moraliste*; the rough and hearty William Cobbett of *Advice to Young Men* is a more likeable Franklin. Addison's *Spectator* essays are a bland English version of the same sort of thing. By the end of the eighteenth century, prudence, and the idea of rational management of life, had been obscured by the clouds of romanticism.

One major philosopher of the nineteenth century applied himself with supreme wit and penetration to *Lebensweisheit*: Schopenhauer, mainly in the non-technical parts of his *Parerga und Paralipomena*. Nietzsche may be seen as carrying on the same task, for which he was marvellously equipped as a writer but hopelessly unfitted as a human being. Earlier in the century Emerson had addressed himself to the subject; towards its end Shaw, particularly in his prefaces, dispensed a great deal of advice, in the style of Samuel Butler, whom he much admired. Together they dismantled Victorian respectability for the English-speaking world.

Perhaps the most distinguished popular philosopher of the present century was Alain (Émile Chartier), who published his thoughts in several thousand 600-word pieces in a daily paper. Havelock Ellis, John Cowper Powys, and Aldous Huxley were less copious but comparably influential. On a more modest level is the American Sydney Harris, a syndicated columnist, raised above such writers as

Ann Landers and Abby by the generality of his concerns. G. K. Chesterton contributed marginally to the tradition, as did such aphorists as Logan Pearsall Smith and Gerald Brenan. In the last three decades professional philosophers, after a long period of abstention from anything but the most abstract and uncommitted attention to problems of conduct and practice, have resumed a measure of direct involvement, mainly at the political or collective level, but to some extent more personally, as in Richard Robinson's *An Atheist's Values* and Robert Nozick's unkindly treated *The Examined Life*.

The second kind of popular philosophy, namely amateur philosophy, presupposes the existence of professional *philosophy to define itself against. That, in effect, is much the same thing as institutionalized philosophy, which was to be found in ancient Greece with Plato's Academy, Aristotle's Lyceum, and the other Athenian schools; emerged again, by way of cathedral schools, in the medieval efflorescence of universities from the twelfth century onwards; but subsided, with the Renaissance, until the slow revival of universities in the eighteenth and nineteenth centuries. In that last gap all notable philosophers, from Descartes to Hume, were, formally, amateurs. Amateur philosophy as a genre is really a creation of the nineteenth century with its mass literacy and self-education.

Coleridge, for all his plagiarism and incoherence, is too substantial to count as an amateur. Carlyle was a prophet rather than any sort of philosopher, as was Ruskin. Herbert Spencer achieved a sort of professionality by the sheer bulk of his output. The historian of philosophy J. D. Morrel was a school inspector like Arnold. J. H. Stirling, the enraptured expositor of Hegel, was a doctor. Shadworth Hodgson was a gentleman-philosopher with private means. More perfect cases are the eighth duke of Argyll, Secretary of State for India among other things, and James Hinton, author of *The Mystery of Pain*. A. J. Balfour was about as grand as, and a better philosopher than, the duke of Argyll.

In the twentieth century amateur systems increasingly failed to find their way into print; most of them languished in typescript and photocopy. One arresting exception is *The Social Contract of the Universe* by C. G. Stone, a most ambitious piece of deduction. There are also the works of L. L. Whyte and George Melhuish and, in the United States, Ayn Rand, stren-uous exponent of objectivism and self-interest.

Philosophical popularization, the third of the kinds mentioned earlier, was made necessary by the conjunction of ever greater professional obscurity and difficulty with a public demand for enlightenment. G. H. Lewes's *Biographical History of Philosophy* is the first important book in English to respond to this opportunity. The introductions to philosophy by Paulsen and by Windelband were fairly soon translated from German after their late nineteenth-century publication. A. W. Benn wrote excellent little histories of ancient and modern philosophy. But the best piece of philosophical popularization remains Russell's *Problems of Philosophy*. In the years between the wars there were Olaf Stapledon, the stylish John MacMurray, pioneer of philosophy on the radio, and the irrepressible and in every sense fluent C. E. M. Joad. Since 1945 what was a modest cottage industry has become a large productive field as university populations have increased. Hospers's *Introduction to Philosophical Analysis* and *Human Conduct* may be singled out for their scope, reliability, and well-deserved circulation, although the former, at any rate, first published in 1956, is, understandably, showing signs of age. The most convincing successor to Hospers's *Introduction* (which has been badly watered down in later editions) is Roger Scruton's *Modern Philosophy* (London, 1994), which covers a great deal of ground, is replete with historical references, and mitigates its passages of comparative toughness with plenty of wit. Only the most austere of professionals nowadays seem able to resist enticements to explain themselves to a wider public. There are two recent new developments in the field of popularization by professionals. The first is the appearance of very short books covering most, or at any rate a large part, of the subject, such as Thomas Nagel's *What Does It All Mean?* (Oxford, 1987) and Simon Blackburn's *Think* (Oxford, 1999) and *Being Good* (Oxford, 2000). The second is the publication of books by professional philosophers on subjects of direct general human interest that are the topics of current public controversy: for instance, Mary Midgley's *Beast and Man* (Hassocks, Sussex, 1978), Jonathan Glover's *Causing Death and Saving Lives* (London, 1977) and *What Sort of People Should There Be?* (London, 1984), and Peter Singer's *Practical Ethics* (Cambridge, 1979). There was a period after the deprivations of war had driven people back to almost Victorian levels of reading and thinking in which there was much philosophical popularization on the British radio and television, and even in the colour magazines of Sunday papers. The profit motive and dumbing-down egalitarianism have since turned television into a mirror in which Caliban can contemplate himself and the Sunday magazines into vehicles for fashion advertising. A.Q.

*philosophy of life; pseudo-philosophy.

W. E. H. Lecky, *The Map of Life* (London, 1899).
W. Tatarkiewicz, *Analysis of Happiness* (The Hague, 1976).

population. How many people ought there to be? According to traditional *consequentialism, which holds that we ought to do what maximizes value, it is good to increase the population provided that the increase in value derived from causing people to exist with lives worth living is greater than any decrease that this might also cause in the value of pre-existing lives; and we ought to increase the population provided that there is no alternative that offers a greater increase in overall value. Most moral theorists reject this view, since it seems to make procreation often obligatory and, in particular, implies that it can be obligatory to cause more and more people to exist, even if this continually lowers the overall quality of life, provided that the total amount of good in the world continues to increase. Some consequentialists contend, alternatively,

that we ought to maximize average value per life lived. On this view, it is obligatory to increase the population only if each new life would contain more value than the average life. But this view also implies, implausibly, that it is wrong to cause a person to exist if his life would contain less than the average value, even if his life would be well worth living.

Faced with these problems, many moral theorists embrace the commonsensical view that the optimum population size must be determined solely by reference to the interests of existing people. There is no reason to increase the population for the sake of those who would thereby be brought into existence. This view, however, ignores what is surely relevant—namely, that our present action can affect the welfare of people who will later exist. (For complications, see the entry on future generations.) Thus many theorists have revised their view to hold that the interests of only present and future people count. The possible interests of possible people do not count.

While initially this view seems compelling, it has proved untenable. If future people are those who definitely will exist, while possible people are those who might or might not exist, then the two categories overlap, since some of those who might or might not exist will in fact exist. But, if some people are both future people and possible people, then we cannot discriminate in the way suggested between future and possible people. Alternatively, we might define a future person as someone who will exist independently of one's present choice and a possible person as someone who might or might not exist depending on the outcome of one's choice. Given this distinction, the claim that the interests of possible people do not count supports the desired conclusion that the expectation that a person would have a life worth living does not itself provide a moral reason to cause him to exist. The problem is that it also implies that the expectation that a person would have a life that would be worse than no life at all provides no reason not to cause him to exist, since the person's existence depends on the outcome of one's choice.

What most of us believe is that, while there is no moral reason to cause people to exist just because they would have lives worth living, there is a reason not to cause people to exist if their lives would not be worth living. Moral theorists have tried to defend this view in many ways; for example, by appealing to the claim that wrongs require victims, to the asymmetry between harming and failing to benefit, or to the distinction between doing and not doing. The current consensus is that an adequate defence has yet to be found. J.McM.

*person-affecting principles.

David Heyd, *Genethics: Moral Issues in the Creation of People* (Berkeley, Calif., 1992).
Thomas Hurka, 'Value and Population Size', *Ethics* (1983).
Derek Parfit, *Reasons and Persons* (Oxford, 1984), pt. 4 and app. G.

pornography. In everyday use, 'pornography' refers to an array of images and texts, now including ones on the Internet, that are meant to produce sexual arousal in those who see or read them and that are, standardly, sexually explicit—offering direct representations of sexual acts or sexualized body parts. Etymologically, 'pornography' derives from the Greek roots 'porne', which means 'sexual slave' or 'harlot', and 'graphos', which means 'depiction of', thus connoting a depiction of sexual slavery or prostitution. And indeed, much actual pornography, even when it takes children, men, or animals as its objects, is modelled on a male–female, master–slave paradigm. Pornography comes in many genres, including heterosexual, homosexual, transsexual, and sado-masochistic; it can be more or less explicit and is sometimes frankly violent. Some distinguish 'pornography' from 'erotica', reserving the latter label for sexualized depictions conveying mutuality, love, and respect or for those that, at a minimum, do not sexualize coercion and violence. Others challenge the viability of the distinction or criticize its role in privileging culturally favoured over more marginalized and idiosyncratic sexual tropes and tastes.

Traditionally, objections to pornography have condemned it as obscenity. Recent feminist critics eschew this tactic as hostile to sexuality. Their objections to pornography, instead, are based on claims of its harms—harms taken to be located in its effects, but for some, found also in the very speech acts that constitute pornography. The harms claimed include the coercion and abuse of those used as subjects in pornography's production, an increase in acts of sexual violence throughout society, and a diffuse but powerful tendency to eroticize the degradation of women. 'Pornography makes sexism sexy' (MacKinnon). In contrast, 'pro-sex' feminists defend and at times celebrate the practice of pornography. Praising free sexual experimentation, they argue that pornographic speech, if is to be countered at all, should be countered with more speech, including more sexual speech. Civil libertarians defend the legal protection of pornographers, claiming that there are fundamental liberty rights at stake in sexual expression. Navigating the challenges that pornography presents is difficult. In terms of social policy, toleration of pornography is in many ways perilous to women's safety and freedom, yet constraints on free expression often have serious costs. In personal morality, subtle questions arise in determining when graphic sexual depictions are expansive, and when degrading, of the erotic life. The sophistication of the current debate about pornography's moral and legal status evinces an acknowledgement of the peculiar power of sexual speech and the complex connections between viewing and doing, fantasy and reality.   A.CAR.
M.L.

S. E. Keller, 'Viewing and Doing: Complicating Pornography's Meaning', *Georgetown Law Journal* (1993).

R. Langton, 'Speech Acts and Unspeakable Acts', *Philosophy and Public Affairs* (1991).

C. MacKinnon, *Only Words* (Cambridge, Mass., 1993).

Porphyry (*c*.232–*c*.305), Porphyrius Malchus. Greek philosopher, editor of Plotinus. Brought up in Tyre, he studied at Athens and from 263 under Plotinus at Rome.

Around a score of his numerous works survive in whole or part, including *Against the Christians* (fragments), *Lives* of Pythagoras and Plotinus, commentaries on Homer, Plato's *Timaeus* (fragments), Aristotle's *Categories*, and Ptolemy's *Harmonica*, and a short Introduction (*Eisagogē*) to Aristotle's *Categories* that quickly became and long remained a standard textbook. The so-called Tree of Porphyry traces a species (commonly man) from its *summum genus* (substance) through differentiae (e.g. corporeal) that yield successive subgenera (e.g. body).   C.A.K.

*Neoplatonism; genus and species.

Porphyry, *Introduction*, tr. and ed. J. Barnes (Oxford, 2003).

A. Smith, *Porphyry's Place in the Neoplatonic Tradition* (The Hague, 1974).

Port-Royalists. Port-Royal was a monastery near Paris committed to the teachings of Bishop Cornelius Jansen (*Jansenism). Antoine Arnauld, Blaise Pascal, and Pierre Nicole wrote influential Jansenist theological treatises at Port-Royal, and Arnauld and Nicole co-authored *La Logique; ou, L'Art de penser* (Logic; or, The Art of Thinking (1662)), generally known as the Port-Royal Logic. This work was a manual on method in logic and semantics, with overtones of epistemology. It built on the foundations of the Cartesian doctrine of clear and distinct ideas and attacked *Pyrrhonism and medieval theories of logic. It heavily influenced subsequent manuals in logic for over two centuries. This work was also a key source for reflections on controversies about miracles, including how to weigh apparently reliable human testimony in favour of miracles against the improbability of the miracle's occurrence.   T.L.B.

*Cartesianism.

A. Arnauld and P. Nicole, *Logic or the Art of Thinking*, ed. and tr. Jill Vance Buroker (Cambridge, 1996).

Jean Racine, *Abrégé de l'histoire de Port-Royal* (Brief History of Port-Royal), 1st edn. (Cologne, 1742, in part; 1747, in whole).

posit. In Quine's terminology a 'posit' is anything we say exists. So if we say there are rabbits, rabbits are among our posits. Does this commit him to *relativism? He claims not: 'To call a posit a posit is not to patronise it.' His idea seems to be that although *positing* depends on us, we treat our posits as real, hence cannot regard *them* as dependent on us.   R.K.

W. V. Quine, *Word and Object* (Cambridge, Mass., 1960), ch. 1.

positive and negative freedom: *see* liberty.

positivism. A movement akin to *empiricism and *naturalism introduced towards the middle of the nineteenth century by Comte, the French sociol-ogist (to use a term he himself invented), with the social reformer Saint-Simon as a forerunner, whom he served as secretary in his youth. What is distinctive about positivism in its original form is its attempt to describe the history of human thought as evolving through certain definite stages, which

Comte called the religious, the metaphysical, and the scientific. Of these the last was the most productive and valuable, though the earlier ones had their value too and were not to be simply dismissed as primitive and useless; indeed Comte himself, towards the end of his life, thought it necessary to introduce a sort of 'religion of humanity'. Positivism fitted in well with the evolutionary tendencies of the age. It was both descriptive and normative, describing how human thought had in fact evolved and prescribing norms for how our thinking, including thinking about human thought itself, should proceed. In this respect it could be said to link the eighteenth-century doctrines of inevitable progress to the evolutionary ethics of later in the nineteenth century, which saw our duty as that of furthering a process that was going on anyway, though positivism was more concerned with prescribing methods of thought than ethical norms. This emphasis on furthering the inevitable, if perhaps little else, it shared with Marxism, though a later version of positivism (that of Mach) was to be the subject of a vigorous attack in Lenin's *Materialism and Empirio-Criticism* (Moscow, 1908).

In the form Comte gave it, positivism was rather fond of categories and hierarchies, though these were seen not as static and cut off from each other, but as dynamic and developing along a certain path, so that positivism emphasized the unity of the sciences. Not only did human thought itself develop through the three stages mentioned above, but the sciences form a natural hierarchy in terms of method and subject-matter, ranging from astronomy through physics and the biological sciences to the human science of sociology. They also developed historically in this order, though of course without the earlier ones being superseded by the later ones so that they disappeared. (Mathematics stood rather outside this scheme, being presupposed by it.) It is not surprising then that the emphasis fell on the newest stage, the science of humanity, with the growing realization that human beings, at least in the mass, were suitable objects for scientific study, a realization which led to the study of them as institutionalized in societies which were themselves developing, i.e. to sociology. Psychology, however, which at that time was amenable only to study through the subjective method of introspection, Comte ignored, presumably because introspection did not seem subject to proper scientific control.

Many philosophers have been labelled 'positivist', especially those of an evolutionary persuasion, but after Comte there was less emphasis on categorizing and on the historical development of thought, and also perhaps less on the social-reformist and somewhat authoritarian zeal that had a lot to do with the personality of Comte himself. The emphasis on the value and all-embracing capability of science remained, and indeed was intensified in so far as theology and metaphysics tended to get short shrift. But there was a more critical approach to science itself, to what it was and what it could do; the point was not to limit its scope, which became ever wider, but to examine its presuppositions and proper procedures. Science became more self-conscious, and more concerned to extrude metaphysical elements from science itself. It is based on observation, and so should not, it was thought, appeal to what cannot be observed, on pain of reintroducing metaphysics. This means that things like atoms and electrons should not be treated as real but unobservable entities, but as devices which help the scientist to give the simplest unifying description of phenomena and make accurate predictions, rather as the square root of minus one is usually treated by mathematicians and physicists as a convenient device which does not correspond to anything real, even in the sense in which numbers might be real, but is distinguished from the 'real' numbers by being called 'imaginary'. This approach (*instrumentalism) was especially pursued by Mach, who used it also in denying a place in proper scientific descriptions to physical objects, which cannot strictly be observed, he thought. Positivism here has obvious affinities with the empiricism of earlier philosophers, especially, so far as philosophy of science goes, with Berkeley, who also anticipated Mach in rejecting Newton's attempt to prove the existence of absolute space by observing the behaviour of the surface of the water in a bucket as it started and stopped rotating. Berkeley (in his *De Motu*, or *Of Motion*) and Mach argued that the deformation of the surface might occur because the rotation was relative to the framework provided by the fixed stars rather than to that provided by an absolute space; Mach in fact thought that it was not just relative to, but caused by, this relation to the fixed stars.

Mach, with other philosophers of science of an anti-metaphysical bent, notably Duhem and, a little later, Poincaré, was writing towards the end of the nineteenth century. The trend continued, but in the twentieth century the emphasis shifted very much towards logic and language, resulting in *Logical Positivism, the form usually referred to when the word 'positivism' is used by itself in a twentieth-century context, at any rate when that context is philosophical rather than scientific. Concerning science, the emphasis was then on the unity of the sciences, especially their reducibility to physics. (*Reductionism.) In science today 'positivism' refers especially to the unity of the natural and social sciences, but in philosophy is less used. Logical Positivism has been sublimated into anti-realism, and reductionism in the sense of the attempt to reduce all sciences to physics has been largely abandoned. (*Realism and anti-realism.) But the appeal to science in matters concerning the mind remains vigorous, and both here and in anti-realism the spirit of positivism still flourishes in philosophy, though it is far from being unchallenged, and it is open to dispute how far it can be called dominant.

*Legal positivism shares something of the spirit and motivation of positivism in the general sense, and originated at about the same time, but in fact has developed rather independently.   A.R.L.

E. Mach, *Popular Scientific Lectures* (first pub. in German, 1894; La Salle, Ill., 1943).

R. Carnap, *The Unity of Science* (first pub. in German, 1932; London, 1934).

L. Kolakowski, *Positivist Philosophy* (first pub. in Polish, 1966; Harmondsworth, 1972).

positivism, legal: *see* legal positivism.

Positivism, Logical: *see* Logical Positivism.

possibility. Possibility, *actuality, *necessity are interdependent modalities. On most accounts, and in some sense of 'entail', necessity entails actuality and actuality entails possibility, but the converses are not valid.

To characterize ϕ as a possibility is generally to claim for some appropriate ϕ, ϕ is possible.

Where ϕ is a proposition, it can be understood as:

(1) ϕ is logically possible; its negation entails a contradiction.
(2) ϕ is metaphysically possible; consistent with metaphysical necessities. Kant's necessary synthetic truths are examples of the latter.
(3) ϕ is nomologically possible; consistent with scientific laws.
(4) ϕ is epistemologically possible; consistent with what is known.
(5) ϕ is temporally possible; consistent with truths about the past.
(6) ϕ is conceivable to a rational agent.

A distinction has been drawn between *de re* and *de dicto* modalities, as, for example, where there is a mix of quantifiers and modal operators. Consider the propositions (i) It is possible that something has the property *P* and (ii) There is something that possibly has the property *P*. (i) is characterized as a *de dicto* use, attributing possibility to a proposition. (ii) is characterized as *de re*, attributing to a particular object the property of possibly having the property *P*. On such a *de re* use what follows the modal operator is not a complete sentence. (ii) can be represented as 'There is a particular *x* such that it is possible that *x* has *P*'.

The clarity or usefulness of the distinction has sometimes been questioned. For example, the *Barcan formula endorses equating (i) and (ii). Also, a determination of *de re* versus *de dicto* use is often unclear, as, for example, where sentences with proper names follow the modal operator, as in 'It is possible that Napoleon was assassinated'.   R.B.M.

*conceivability.

T. Gendler and J. Hawthorne (eds.), *Conceivability and Possibility* (Oxford, 2002).
G. E. Hughes and M. J. Cresswell, *An Introduction to Modal Logic* (London, 1968).
M. Loux (ed.), *The Possible and the Actual* (Ithaca, NY, 1979).
A. Prior, *Time and Modality* (London, 1957).

possible worlds. We often talk about what might have been the case, about what is possible. I might have been a vicar—that is, although I am not actually a vicar, my being a vicar is possible. Philosophers have become accustomed to talking of such possibilities in terms of the idea of a possible world: to say that I might have been a vicar is to say that there is a possible world in which I am a vicar. A possible world is a world which differs in some possible way from our 'actual' world: e.g. a world in which tigers have no stripes, or in which no people existed.

The idea of a possible world in something like the contemporary sense is normally credited to Leibniz, who thought that God chose this world, from an infinity of possible worlds, to be the actual world. Since God must choose the best, this world is therefore the best of all possible worlds—the doctrine famously satirized by Voltaire in *Candide*.

Possible worlds became a focus for philosophical interest in this century with the development, by Saul Kripke and others, of a semantic interpretation for *modal logic. Modal logic adds two symbols to the basic vocabulary of logic: ◊, read as 'possibly' or 'it is possible that', and □, read as 'necessarily' or 'it is necessary that'. (There are different systems of modal logic, which differ in which modal formulae are taken as *axioms.) Thus we can construct formulae such as □(p & q), ◊p, ◊□p, and so on. Intuitively, these formulae should be interpretable as saying something about what is necessarily or possibly true. But how should we understand their *truth-conditions? Possible worlds provide the answer. The modal sentence '□(p & q)' is true if and only if '(p & q)' is true at all possible worlds. (*Formal semantics.) The essential idea is fairly intuitive. A necessary truth, such as '2 + 2 = 4', is one that is true in all possible worlds: there is no possible situation in which it is false. Something that is merely possibly true, such as 'I am a vicar', is true in some possible situation. There is no impossibility in the idea of a situation in which I am a vicar.

This suggests a way of *reducing* problematic modal claims into claims that do not contain any modal notions. If we take the idea of a *world* as primitive, we can understand the modal operators 'possibly' and 'necessarily' as quantifiers over worlds: 'Possibly *p*' is thus rendered 'There is a world in which *p*', and 'Necessarily *p*' becomes 'At all worlds, *p*'. Modality is explained away!

However, it could be objected that we cannot really take the idea of a world as basic, since hidden within it is the idea of possibility: a 'world' here is being tacitly understood as a *possible* world. If we are to reduce modality, we must have an independent account of what these possible worlds are. So what are these possible worlds? The most striking answer is David Lewis's idea that other possible worlds are real: they exist in just the same sense as the actual world exists. What makes worlds distinct is the fact that they are spatio-temporally separated from one another. And what makes the actual world actual is simply the fact that we inhabit it—other speakers in other worlds who utter the words 'the actual world' will be referring to their world. 'Actual' therefore becomes an indexical.

The idea of a possible world can be put to use in other areas of philosophy. Two examples: first, Lewis and Robert Stalnaker have explicated the idea of a proposition as a *set of possible worlds*. The proposition expressed by the sentence 'Pigs fly' is that set of worlds in which 'Pigs fly' is true. Second, Lewis has argued that we understand the idea of a property, such as redness, not as a universal, but as a *set of possible individuals*: all those individuals, in this world and others, to which the predicate 'is red' truly applies. Lewis argues forcefully that we cannot make adequate sense of the applications of the notion of a possible world unless we accept worlds as real. This idea has met with much resistance. Others think that we should rather explain possible worlds in terms of sets of sentences, or as constructions out of the inhabitants of the actual world, or think with Kripke that possible worlds are stipulated rather than 'discovered'.   T.C.

mundus imaginalis.

D. M. Armstrong, *A Combinatorial Theory of Possibility* (Cambridge, 1989).

David Lewis, *On the Plurality of Worlds* (Oxford, 1986).

R. Stalnaker, *Ways a World Might Be: Metaphysical and Anti-Metaphysical Essays* (Oxford, 2003).

possible-worlds semantics: *see* formal semantics, the philosophical relevance of.

post hoc, ergo propter hoc. 'After this, therefore because of this.' Strictly, the *fallacy of inferring that one event is caused by another merely because it comes after it. More loosely, the fallacy (characteristic of superstitious beliefs) of assuming too readily that an event that follows another is caused by it without considering factors such as counter-evidence or the possibility of a common cause. (*Causality.) The name appears to derive from Aristotle's *Rhetoric* (1401^b29–34).   P.J.M.

H. W. B. Joseph, *An Introduction to Logic*, 2nd edn. (Oxford, 1916), ch. 27.

post-analytic philosophy. A somewhat amorphous tendency (hardly 'school') of thought which defines itself mainly in opposition to the mainstream 'analytic' line of descent. This reactive movement may be dated back to Quine's essay 'Two Dogmas of Empiricism' (1953) which launched a root-and-branch attack on the logical empiricist programme and thereby did much to promote the turn toward a radically holistic conception of meaning, knowledge, and truth. Other sources include late Wittgenstein on 'language-games' and cultural 'forms of life' as the furthest we can get by way of epistemic justification, and Richard Rorty's neo-pragmatist view of truth as what's currently and contingently 'good in the way of belief'. These ideas have found additional support in Thomas Kuhn's paradigm-relativist conception of scientific theory change—itself much influenced by Quine—and in the 'strong' sociology of knowledge where priority is accorded to the socio-cultural determinants of whatever passes for 'truth' at any given time.

Feminist philosophers have likewise argued for a more holistic and context-sensitive approach, one that would emphasize those factors in the process of knowledge acquisition that are standardly treated—by 'malestream'

analytic philosophers—as belonging to the background 'context of discovery' rather than the scientific 'context of justification'. Ideas have also come from farther afield, e.g. from hermeneutic approaches (Dilthey, Heidegger, Gadamer); from Michel Foucault's Nietzsche-inspired sceptical genealogies of knowledge; and from post-structuralist ideas about 'reality' as a linguistic or discursive construct. Meanwhile, some thinkers in the broadly post-analytic camp would reject these more extreme versions of the case against 'old-style' analytic philosophy. Very often this involves an attempt to reformulate its scope and limits in response to such sceptical relativist arguments. Thus the prefix 'post-' sometimes betokens 'farewell to all that', while sometimes it announces 'business continued under different management'.   C.N.

J. Rajchman and Cornel West (eds.), *Post-Analytic Philosophy* (New York, 1985).

post-modernism. In its broad usage, this is a 'family resemblance' term deployed in a variety of contexts (architecture, painting, music, poetry, fiction, etc.) for things which seem to be related—if at all—by a laid-back pluralism of styles and a vague desire to have done with the pretensions of high-modernist culture. In philosophical terms post-modernism shares something with the critique of Enlightenment values and truth-claims mounted by thinkers of a liberal-communitarian persuasion; also with neo-pragmatists like Richard Rorty who welcome the end of philosophy's presumptive role as a privileged, truth-telling discourse. There is another point of contact with post-modern fiction and art in the current preoccupation, among some philosophers, with themes of 'self-reflexivity', or the puzzles induced by allowing language to become the object of its own scrutiny in a kind of dizzying rhetorical regress. To this extent post-modernism might be seen as a ludic development of the so-called *'linguistic turn' that has characterized much philosophical thinking of late.   C.N.

*modernism; German philosophy today.

Thomas Docherty (ed.), *Postmodernism: A Reader* (Hemel Hempstead, 1993).

post-structuralism. School of thought which emerged in the late 1970s, claiming to supersede—or at any rate to 'problematize'—the earlier *structuralism. Best understood as a French-inspired variant of the so-called *'linguistic turn', it is the idea that all perceptions, concepts, and truth-claims are constructed in language, along with the corresponding 'subject-positions' which are likewise (so it is argued) nothing more than transient epiphenomena of this or that cultural *discourse. From Saussure post-structuralism takes the notion of language as a system of immanent relationships and differences 'without positive terms'; from Nietzsche, its outlook of extreme epistemological and ethico-evaluative relativism; and from Foucault, its counter-Enlightenment rhetoric of 'power/knowledge' as the motivating force behind talk of reason or truth. Such thinking is vulnerable to all the familiar criticisms—including forms of transcendental refutation—rehearsed against thoroughgoing sceptics and relativists down through the ages.   C.N.

J. Sturrock (ed.), *Structuralism and Since* (Oxford, 1979).

potentiality. A potentiality, or latent ability, is a second-order *capacity of an object or person, a capacity to acquire, develop, or regain another (first-order) capacity. Thus a normal new-born human infant has a potentiality to speak English, meaning that it has the capacity (absent, for instance, in infant chimpanzees) to acquire the ability to speak English. The realization of such a potentiality—that is, the acquisition of the relevant first-order capacity—may involve both natural processes of maturation and the presence of suitable environmental conditions.

In a more general sense, potentiality is traditionally contrasted with actuality, a distinction intimately related in Aristotelian metaphysics to the distinction between matter and form, and one which more or less coincides with the modern distinction between the dispositional and the occurrent.   E.J.L.

*disposition; propensity.

R. Tuomela (ed.), *Dispositions* (Dordrecht, 1978).

pour soi: *see* for-itself and in-itself.

power. A central concept in political philosophy and, often metaphorically, in other inquiries as well. Discussions of power in politics typically refer to one of two sources of power, or to an amalgam of both. These are the physical and organizational resources produced by an economy, and the simpler but less tangible resource of co-ordinated individuals. We may call these exchange power and co-ordination power. They enable different things. For example, the power of a charismatic leader backed by large numbers may readily bring down a regime but may not have much value in creating a new one in its place or in maintaining one. Exchange-power may be especially valuable in maintaining a regime.

Power is typically a causal notion: its application produces results. A presumption of much power talk is that it is somehow additive: put enough little bits together and you have a big chunk of power. There may often be truth in this view, as in a military engagement. But it is also often conspicuously wrong and misleading. It is wrong directly in that bits of power need not add any better than other things do. Addition can fail when power is all of one type or when the two types are mixed. For a transparent example of the former, note that the charismatic leaders of two groups with different goals or values could dissipate all their power by attempting to add it together. For an example of the latter, note that a regime might amass greater and greater exchange power only to find itself now destitute of co-ordination power, as did the military junta in Argentina in the 1980s. That regime destroyed almost all of the opposition to its general policies and its dictator-

ship only to create opposition to its destruction of those people.

Among the greatest political power theorists have been Thomas Hobbes and Karl Marx. Hobbes supposed that an all-powerful sovereign would produce such order as to make life better for all. In his fiction of the contractual creation of a sovereign out of the conditions of the state of nature, Hobbes recognized but largely ignored the difficulty of creating power merely by willing it. But without power, the sovereign would be of no value to those who want order. For Marx the power of a ruling class is to be explained by relations of production. There are subjective elements at play because a class must come to have class consciousness before its members are likely to co-ordinate properly for their class interests. Marx grasped the role of the co-ordination of large numbers of individuals in his schematic accounts of failed and potential revolutions. But he may finally have underestimated the potential role of power from exchange as the technology of weapons and of policing benefited from the evolving capitalist mode of production. That mode, while it created a proletariat, also created a state apparatus that, while it has remained intact, has been impervious to threats from Marx's revolutionary class.

Historically, power has been invoked most by conflict theorists. In the view of these theorists, there is usually someone or some group who are thought to have power and to use it for some purpose. In contemporary debates, especially those centring on the work of Michel Foucault, this assumption is sometimes not made. There is somehow power in the system or in the culture we have inherited, and that power controls us, sometimes in deleterious ways. Hence, despite the language of power and exploitation, there is relatively little connection to the long tradition from Thrasymachus into the present. In Western academic life, the older tradition seems to fit the increasingly bitter conflict between these two power schools.   R.HAR.

*authority.

Russell Hardin, 'The Social Evolution of Cooperation', in Karen Schweers Cook and Margaret Levi (eds.), *The Limits of Rationality* (Chicago, 1990).
Steven Lukes, *Power: A Radical View* (London, 1974).
Dennis Wrong, *Power: Its Forms, Bases, and Uses* (Oxford, 1979).

power, will to: *see* will to power.

practical reason. Argument, intelligence, insight, directed to a practical and especially a moral outcome. Historically, a contrast has often been made between theoretical and practical employments of *reason. Aristotle's 'practical syllogism' concludes in an *action* rather than in a proposition or a new belief: and *phronēsis* (see book VI of *Nicomachean Ethics*) is the ability to use intellect practically. In discussions of motivation, furthermore, appeals to practical reason may seek to counter claims that only desire or inclination can ultimately prompt to action. A measure of disengagement from personal wish and want, a readiness to appraise one's acts by criteria which (rising above individual contingent desire) can be every rational moral agent's criteria, marks a crucial point of insertion of reason into practice. To Kant, the bare notion of being subject to a moral law suffices to indicate how practical reason can operate. Considering any moral policy, ask: Could it consistently function as universal law? The scope of practical reason, however, is much wider than this: practical reasoning must (for example) include the critical comparison and sifting of alleged human goods and ends, and the reflective establishing of their ranking and place in a life plan.   R.W.H.

E. Millgram (ed.), *Varieties of Practical Reasoning* (Cambridge, Mass., 2001).
O. O'Neill, *Constructions of Reason* (Cambridge, 1989).

practical syllogism. A kind of inference whose function is to produce action. Aristotle says that the premisses of practical syllogisms move agents to act (*De Anima* 434^{a}16–21). On one interpretation, these premisses express desires and beliefs (e.g. a desire for warmth and a belief that making a fire would do) that, via inference, issue in actions. It is debated whether the conclusion of an Aristotelian practical syllogism is a mental item (e.g. a desire to make a fire now) or an overt action. Whether the action-producing function claimed for practical syllogisms is instead performed by non-inferential causal processes is an open question.   A.R.M.

D. Charles, *Aristotle's Philosophy of Action* (Ithaca, NY, 1984).

pragmaticism. A rule for clarifying the meaning of concepts and hypotheses defended by Charles S. Peirce: we should list the experiential consequences our actions would have were the hypo-theses true. The name was introduced in 1905 to distinguish Peirce's *pragmatism from rival versions: he hoped it was 'ugly enough to be safe from kidnappers'. Pragmaticism differed from other versions in its commitment to realism and in the claim that a strict proof of it could be given.   C.J.H.

C. S. Peirce, 'What Pragmatism Is', in *Collected Papers*, v (Cambridge, Mass., 1934).

pragmatics. The study of language which focuses attention on the users and the context of language use rather than on *reference, *truth, or *grammar. Thus, pragmatic analysis of a command notes that the speaker must be a superior and that the hearer has the ability to carry out the command. On the discourse level, pragmatic analysis tells us how participants in a conversation interact with one another as when a speaker signals the hearer that he or she is telling a story or is engaged in prayer. Also on the discourse level, pragmatic analysis shows us how conversational settings disambiguate what is being said. At a party attended by Bill Adams, we understand that the speaker is referring to that Bill and not Bill Baker when he says 'Bill is stupid'. In like fashion, this sort of analysis shows us how the conversational setting implicates. Bill Adams is applying for a job, and you are asked about his application. If all you say is that he is a nice fellow, you imply conversationally that there is not much more to be said on his behalf.
                                                         N.F.

*semantics; syntactics.

Paul Grice, *Studies in the Way of Words* (Cambridge, Mass., 1989).
Z. Szabo (ed.), *Semantics versus Pragmatics* (Oxford, 2005).

pragmatic theory of truth. For pragmatists, *truth, like other concepts, is to be understood in terms of practice. The notion of truth as a relation of correspondence between belief and reality is not rejected but clarified by reference to actions, future experiences, etc. Each of the pragmatists has a distinctive way of carrying out this practical clarification.

Peirce defines truth as the ultimate outcome of inquiry by a 'community of investigators', an outcome of 'settled' 'habits of action'. James clarifies truth in terms of 'leading'. True beliefs, he says, 'lead to consistency, stability and flowing human intercourse'. Dewey identifies truth ('warranted assertibility') with the solution of a problem. Inquiry, he holds, starts from a 'problematic situation' and, if successful, ends with a situation that is so 'determinate' and 'unified' that hesitancy to act has been eliminated.

Although classical pragmatists repeatedly affirm their allegiance to *realism, today the debate still rages over whether the relativity to practice in this theory of truth entails a type of *idealism or *scepticism.   P.H.H.

C. J. Misak, *Truth and the End of Inquiry: A Peircean Account of Truth* (Oxford, 1991).

pragmatism. The characteristic idea of philosophical pragmatism is that efficacy in practical application— 'What works out most effectively in practice'—somehow provides a standard for the determination of truth in the case of statements, rightness in the case of actions, and value in the case of appraisals. However, it is the first of these contexts, the epistemic concern for meaning and truth, that has historically been the most prominent. With Immanuel Kant, pragmatism insists that since our limitedly human efforts at inquiry can never achieve *totality*, we must settle for *sufficiency*, which is ultimately a practical rather than a theoretical matter, so that prioritizing practical over theoretical reason is an inescapable part of the human condition.

In matters of cognition and inquiry, pragmatism calls for a steadfast refusal to allow us to view the very best that we can possibly do as not being good enough. Its operative injunctions are: Approach the issue of the cognitive accessibility of truth by asking the classical pragmatic question: If that is indeed how realities stand, then what would be the best sort of evidence for it that we could expect to achieve? The operative injunctions are: 'Realize that we have no access to matters of fact save through the mediation of evidence that is often incomplete and imperfect. And realize too that to say that the best evidence is not good enough is to violate Peirce's cardinal pragmatic imperative never to bar the path of inquiry.'

In line with this perspective, a realistic cognitive pragmatism insists upon pressing the question: 'If *A* were indeed the answer to a question *Q* of ours, what sort of evidence could we possibly obtain for this?' And when we obtain such evidence—as much as we can reasonably be expected to achieve—then pragmatism sees this as good enough. ('Be prepared to regard the best that can be done as good enough' is one of pragmatism's fundamental axioms.) If it looks like a duck, waddles like a duck, quacks like a duck (and so on), then—so pragmatism insists, we are perfectly entitled to stable the personal claim that it is a duck—at any rate until such time as clear indications to the contrary come to light. Once the question 'Well, what more could you reasonably will ask for?' meets with no more than hesitant mumbling, pragmatism says: 'Feel free to go ahead and make the claim.'

It is not that true *means* warranted assertibility, or that warranted assertibility *entails* truth. What is the case, rather, is that evidence here means 'evidence *for truth*', and (methodologically) warranted assertibility means 'warrantedly assertible *as true*'. After all, evidentiation is here a matter of truth estimation, and where the conditions for rational estimation are satisfied—*ipso facto*—there is rational warrant for letting those estimates stand surrogate for the truth. The very idea that the best we can do is not good enough for all relevant reasonable purposes is—so pragmatism and common sense alike insist—something that is simply absurd, a thing of unreasonable hyperbole.

Although pragmatism is largely epistemic in orientation, it has a metaphysical component as well. This pivots on the idea that human concepts and distinctions are generally dichotomous and on-off, while nature herself is not hard-edged. In consequence, we think in black and white about a reality that admits various shades of grey, or—to put it into more contemporary terms—we think by digital concepts about an analogue reality. The subtlety and complexity of nature are such that what we see as differences in kind are in fact differences in degree, with thought imposing discontuities upon a continuously standard reality. It is the purposes at hand that determine the *modus operandi* of our conceptualizations even as the line between childhood and maturity may be set at 18 for consent in marriage, at 16 for purchasing alcoholic beverages, and at 21 for voting. But pragmatism also holds that our distinctions—though partly conventional—are never totally so but will inevitably hinge on purposive efficiencies inherent in the inexorable rulings of a non-negotiable reality.

Pragmatism as a philosophical doctrine traces back to the Academic *Sceptics in classical antiquity. Denying the possibility of achieving authentic knowledge (*epistēmē*) regarding the real truth, they taught that we must make do with plausible information (*to pithanon*) adequate to the needs of practice. Kant's stipulation 'contingent belief, which yet forms the ground for the effective employment of means to certain actions, I entitle *pragmatic belief*' (*Critique of Pure Reason*, A 824/B 852) was also influential for the development of the doctrine. Another formative step was Schopenhauer's insistence that the intellect is universally subordinate to the will, a line of thought that was elaborated by several German neo-Kantian thinkers, including Hans Vaihinger and Georg Simmel, who stressed the controlling dominance of practical over theoretical reason. Moral *utilitarianism, with its tests of the rightness of modes of action in terms of their capacity to provide the greatest good of the greatest number was yet another step in the development of pragmatic thought. For it too invokes much the same utility-maximization model, and there is a deep structural analogy between the (act-utilitarian) contention that an action is right if its consequences redound to 'the greatest good of the greatest number', and the thesis-orientated version of a pragmatic theory of truth, holding that an empirical claim is correct if its acceptance is maximally benefit-producing.

However, pragmatism as a determinate philosophical doctrine descends from the work of Charles Sanders Peirce. For him, pragmatism was primarily a theory of meaning, with the meaning of any concept that has application in the real world inhering in the relations that link experiential conditions of application with observable results. But by the 'practical consequences' of the acceptance of an idea or a contention, Peirce meant the consequences for *experimental* practice—'experimental effects' or 'observational results'—so that for him the meaning of a proposition is determined by the essentially positivist criterion of its observable consequences. And, moving beyond this, Peirce also taught that pragmatic effectiveness constitutes a quality-control monitor of human cognition—though here again the issue is that of *scientific* praxis and the standard of efficacy pivoting on the issue of specifically *predictive* success. Peirce developed his pragmatism in opposition to idealism, seeing that the test of applicative success can lead mere theorizing to stub its toe on the hard rock of reality. But his successors softened up the doctrine, until with present-day 'pragmatists' the efficacy of ideas consists in their mere *adoption* by the community rather than in the success that the community may (or may not!) encounter as it puts those ideas into practice.

Although Peirce developed pragmatism into a substantial philosophical theory, it was William James who put it on the intellectual map in his enormously influential *Pragmatism: A New Name for Some Old Ways of Thinking* (New York, 1907). However, James changed (and—as Peirce himself saw it—ruined) Peircean pragmatism. For where Peirce saw in pragmatism a road to impersonal and objective standards, James gave it a personalized and subjectivized twist. With James, it was the personal (and potentially idiosyncratic) idea of efficacy and success held by particular people that provided the pragmatic crux, and not an abstracted community of ideally rational agents. For him, pragmatic efficacy and applicative success did not relate to an impersonalized community of scientists but to a diversified plurality of flesh-and-blood individuals. Truth for James is accordingly what reality impels and compels human individuals to believe; it is a matter of 'what pays by way of belief' in the course of human activity within the surrounding environment; and its acquisition is an

JONATHAN EDWARDS's Puritan faith runs throughout his philosophy, where all explanation ends in God.

C. S. PEIRCE, perhaps the greatest American philosopher, inventor of pragmatism, published no books and found little recognition in his lifetime.

WILLIAM JAMES, in philosophy as in psychology, sought to understand any thing by asking what difference it makes in practice or in experience—by seeking to discover its function.

GEORGE SANTAYANA's writings proclaim him a truly American philosopher in their rejection of European idealism in favour of a naturalistic view of the world and the place of humankind in it.

invention rather than a revelation. With James, the tenability of a thesis is determined in terms of its experiential consequences in a far wider than merely *observational* sense—a sense that embraces the affective sector as well.

John Dewey, like Peirce before him, saw inquiry as a self-corrective process whose procedures and norms must be evaluated and revised in the light of subsequent experience. But Dewey regarded this reworking as a social and communal process proceeding in the light of values that are not (as with Peirce) connected specifically to science (viz. prediction and experimental control), but rather values that are more broadly rooted in the psychic disposition of ordinary people at large—the moral and aesthetic dimension now being specifically included. Peirce's pragmatism is scientifically élitist, James's is psychologically personalistic, Dewey's is democratically populist.

Pragmatism had a mixed reception in Europe. In Italy Giovanni Papini and Giovanni Vailati espoused the doctrine and turned it into a party platform for Italian philosophers of science. In Britain, F. C. S. Schiller was an enthusiastic follower of William James, while F. P. Ramsey and A. J. Ayer endorsed pivotal aspects of Peirce's thought. Among continental participants, Rudolf Carnap also put pragmatic ideas to work on issues of logic and philosophy of language, and Hans Reichenbach reinforced Peirce's statistical and probabilistic approach to the methodology of induction. However, the reception of pragmatism by other philosophers was by no means universally favourable. F. H. Bradley objected to the subordination of cognition to practice because of the inherent incompleteness of all merely practical interests. G. E. Moore criticized William James's identification of true beliefs with useful ones—among other reasons because utility is changeable over time. Bertrand Russell objected that beliefs can be useful but yet plainly false. And various continental philosophers have disapprovingly seen in pragmatism's concern for practical efficacy—for 'success' and 'paying off'—the expression of characteristically American social attitudes: crass materialism and naïve democratism. Pragmatism was thus looked down upon as a quintessentially American philosophy—a philosophical expression of the American go-getter spirit with its success-orientated ideology.

However, Americans have had no monopoly on practice-orientated philosophizing. Karl Marx's ideas regarding the role of practice and its relation to theory have had a vast subsequent influence (some of it upon otherwise emphatically non-Marxist thinkers such as Max Scheler). Important recent developments of praxis-orientated philosophy within a neo-Marxist frame of reference are represented by Tadeusz Kotarbiński in Poland and Jürgen Habermas in Germany. Kotarbiński has endeavoured to put the theory of *praxis on a systematic basis within a special discipline he designates as praxiology. Habermas has pursued the concept of praxis deeply into the domain of the sociological implications of technology.

Be this as it may, pragmatism has found its most favourable reception in the USA, and has never since Peirce's day lacked dedicated advocates there. At Harvard in the next generation after James, C. I. Lewis was concerned to apply pragmatism to the validation of logical systems. He focused upon (and in his own work sought to develop) the idea of alternative systems of logic among which one must draw on guides of pragmatic utility. And for all his differences with Lewis, W. V. Quine continued this thinker's emphasis on the pragmatic dimension of choice among alternative theoretical systems. Richard Rorty has endeavoured to renovate John Dewey's rejection of abstract logical and conceptual rigidities for the flexibilities of expediency in practice. In a cognate spirit, Joseph Margolis has re-emphasized pragmatism's anti-absolutism based on the transiencies of historical change. And Nicholas Rescher's 'meth-odological pragmatism' sought to return pragmatism to its Peircian roots by giving the doctrine a specifically methodological turn, seeing that anything methodological—a tool, procedure, instrumentality, programme, or policy of action, etc.—is best validated in terms of its ability to achieve the purposes at issue, its success at accomplishing its appropriate task. It follows that even the factual domain can be viewed in such a light that practical reason becomes basic to the theoretical.

One overarching and ironic fact pervades the development of pragmatism, namely that the doctrine can be seen either as a validation of objectively cogent standards or as a subverter of them. There is a Peircian or objective pragmatism of 'What works *impersonally*'—though proving efficient and effective for the realization of some appropriate purpose in an altogether person-indifferent way ('successful prediction', 'control over nature', 'efficacy in need fulfillment'). And there is a Jamesian or subjective pragmatism of 'What works for *X*' in proving efficient and effective for the realization of a particular person's (or group's) wishes and desires. The objective pragmatists stand in the tradition of Peirce and include F. P. Ramsey, C. I. Lewis, Rudolf Carnap; the subjective pragmatists stand in the tradition of William James and include F. C. S. Schiller and Richard Rorty. (John Dewey straddles the fence by going to an social interpersonalism that stops short of impersonalism.) Looking at James, Peirce saw subjective pragmatism as a corruption and degradation of the pragmatic enterprise, since its approach is a venture not in validating objective standards but in *deconstructing* them to dissolve standards as such into the variegated vagaries of idiosyncratic positions and individual inclinations. And this is how objective pragmatists view the matter down to the present day—this writer included.   N.R.

*American philosophy.

D. S. Clarke, Jr., *Rational Acceptance and Purposes* (Totowa, NJ, 1989).

Elizabeth Flower and Murray G. Murphy, *A History of Philosophy in America*, ii (New York, 1977).

Bruce Kuklick, *A History of Philosophy in America: 1720–2000* (Oxford, 2001).

John P. Murphy, *Pragmatism from Peirce to Davidson* (Boulder, Colo., 1990).

Nicholas Rescher, *Methodological Pragmatism* (Oxford, 1977).

—— *Cognitive Pragmatism* (Pittsburgh, 2001).

Richard Rorty, *Consequences of Pragmatism* (Minneapolis, 1982).

John E. Smith, *Purpose and Thought: The Meaning of Pragmatism* (New Haven, Conn., 1978).

Henry S. Thayer, *Meaning and Action: A Critical History of American Pragmatism* (Indianapolis, 1968).

pragmatism, neo-: *see* neo-pragmatism.

praxis. The Greek word for 'action'. It enters the philosophical literature as a quasi-technical term with Aristotle (meaning 'doing' rather than 'making [something]'), is developed by some of the Left Hegelians, and is now primarily associated with Marx and Marxism. In the 1960s and 1970s the term characterized the approach of east European (especially Yugoslav) Marxists (known as the Praxis Group), whose central concern was to study and influence the role of free creative activity in changing and shaping ethical, social, political, and economic life along humanistic socialist lines.   R.DE G.

Nicholas Lobkowicz, *Theory and Practice: History of a Concept from Aristotle to Marx* (Notre Dame, Ind., 1967).

predicate: *see* subject and predicate.

predicate calculus. A device (also called the functional calculus, or calculus of relations) for formalizing and systematizing the logical relations between propositions when these are considered not (as for the *propositional calculus) as unanalysed, but as analysed to bring out their structures, so that two different propositions, instead of being identical or totally different, may be partially different, having something in common, like 'All cats are black' and 'Some cats are black'. This *calculus, like the propositional calculus, can be presented either as an axiom system or as a natural deduction system for the relevant area. Unlike the old Aristotelian logic it takes account of relational predicates (which can be dyadic like 'greater than', triadic like 'between', or in general *n*-adic), as well as of non-relational predicates like 'black' (which yield the monadic predicate calculus, to which certain special theorems apply). The predicate calculus is called *extended* or *second-order* if its variables range over what its predicates, as well as what its subjects, stand for; otherwise it is called *restricted* or *first-order*. (*Higher-order logic.)   A.R.L.

D. Hilbert and W. Ackerman, *Principles of Mathematical Logic* (first pub. in German, 1928–38; New York, 1950).

predicative theories. Theories which aim to obey the principle that an abstract object exists only if it has a predicative definition. (*Vicious-circle principle.) Russell's *type theory is not one, since it contains an axiom of reducibility which nullifies that principle. The axiom was needed to obtain the classical theory of real numbers, which a predicative theory cannot do. For on the classical theory there are uncountably many real numbers, whereas the predicative universe must be countable, since it cannot outrun the available definitions.

H. Weyl produced the first predicative theory of real numbers in *Das Kontinuum* (1918). His results have since been extended, and it turns out that a surprisingly large amount of the classical theory can be reconstructed. Accordingly, some philosophers have claimed that predicative mathematics includes all the mathematics that is actually needed in the sciences, and therefore all that is empirically justified.

The intuitionist theory of real numbers is also a predicative theory, but further constrained by being restricted to *intuitionist logic.   D.B.

*impredicative definition.

C. S. Chihara, *Ontology and the Vicious Circle Principle* (Ithaca, NY, 1973).

S. Feferman, 'Systems of Predicative Analysis', *Journal of Symbolic Logic* (1964).

H. Wang, *A Survey of Mathematical Logic* (Amsterdam, 1962), esp. chs. 23–5.

prediction. The key role of prediction in human affairs inheres in our stake in the future. After all, we are all going to have to spend the rest of our lives there. And from the outset, the existence of *Homo sapiens* has hinged on predictive knowledge: 'What will happen when I enter that cave? Will I find shelter or fierce animals?' 'What will happen when I eat those mushrooms? Will they nourish or poison me?' Without some degree of cognitive control over the future, we humans could not exist as the intelligent creatures we are.

Prediction is literally *foretelling*, specifying occurrences in advance of the fact. A correct forecast can, of course, be the result of pure accident, of lucky guesswork and pure chance. But only *rational* prediction that is based on grounds whose merits are discernible prior to the event is of epistemological interest: predictions whose merits are discernible only after the fact are useless. It can be questioned as a matter of principle whether such cogent predictions can be made at all. Every rational prediction is an *induction—a projection of some sort from past experience, though it need not, of course, be a simple linear projection that is at issue. Thus only in the setting of lawful regularity—where occurrences fall into discernible patterns—will rational prediction be possible at all. The extent to which *this* world is such an orderly cosmos is a discussable question. But the course of wisdom is clearly to hope for the best. Two extremes can be contemplated: (1) that of *determinism, of a 'Laplacian' cosmos in which literally everything that happens can in principle be precalculated, and (2) that of a chaotic world where nothing can be securely predicted because all apparent patterns are at best transitory stabilities. Since classical antiquity, most philosophers have taken an intermediate position, holding that the real world admits of rational prediction in many cases, but with many important exceptions, preeminently relating to chance ('stochastic') events in physical nature—such as quantum phenomena or the 'swerve' of Epicurus—and to the spontaneous decisions that manifest the *free will of human beings.

Some cogent predictions can be equipped with an explicit explanatory rationale. Others may have no further backing than the unarticulated judgement of an informed expert. But even here rational control is possible through establishing a 'track record'.

The ability to underwrite successful predictions is our best quality-control test of the adequacy of scientific theorizing. To be truly satisfactory, our scientific explanations must have a rationale that also engenders adequate predictions. (In this regard the linkage of cosmology to quantum theory becomes crucial.)

The most important feature of a good prediction, rational cogency apart, is its specificity or detail. It is safe (and uninteresting) to predict that Henry will die some time, but far more risky (and interesting) to predict that he will die exactly 756 days hence. It is a consequence of *Bayes's theorem that the more daring a prediction—the lower its a priori likelihood—the more informative it is, other things being equal. To be sure, other things are not in general equal. For example, a great deal more turns on predicting the outcome of a war or the course of a nation's economy than on the result of a boxing-match. This factor of inherent significance of the matter at issue is the third principal consideration in assessing the merit of a prediction.

There are many obstacles to predictability. In nature we have volatility and *chance (stochastic phenomena); in human affairs innovation and chance (free will). *Chaos is a phenomenon that straddles both domains. Processes are chaotic whenever minute differences in conditions (so small as to fall beneath the threshold of detectability) can produce large-scale differences in result. (Lightning bolts and smoke swirls are an example in nature, political assassinations and battlefield fatalities in human affairs.) Chaos is to all appearances a more important source of impredictability than any putative indeterminism in physics.

Would we want the predictive project to be perfectible? Our psychological and emotional condition is clearly such that we would not want to live in a pre-programmed world where the rest of our fate and future is fully discernible in the realities of the present. The human yearning for novelty—for new experiences and prospects and possibilities—is surely a characteristic aspect of what makes us into the sorts of creatures we are. The feeling of open horizons—of new developments that make for suspense and surprises—is integral to our human nature. Without some exposure to chance and uncertainty we cannot function as the creatures we are—the sort of creatures we have become under the pressure of evolutionary development. We thrive in the interstices of chance that pervade a world of predominantly lawful order.   N.R.

John L. Casti, *Searching for Certainty: What Scientists can Know about the Future* (New York, 1990).

Paul Horwich, *Asymmetries in Time: Problems in the Philosophy of Science* (Cambridge, Mass., 1989).

J. R. Lucas, *The Future* (Oxford, 1989).

Nicholas Rescher, *The Limits of Science* (Berkeley, Calif., 1989).

Stephen Toulmin, *Foresight and Understanding* (New York, 1980).

prediction paradox. A variety of distinct puzzles have come to be associated with this name. (1) involves the sentence *A*: 'Event *E* will happen tomorrow and it cannot be proven by a sound argument using *A* as a premiss that *E* will happen tomorrow'. *A* begins with a prediction but goes on to deny that *A* could be a true premiss leading to the prediction. This could only happen if *A* were not true. So *A* involves a denial of its own truth, making it a relative of the *liar paradox. (2) A notoriously unreliable speaker can say *B*: '*E* will happen but you don't know it will' and tease his audience by making a prediction which can turn out true even though his audience, being unable to trust him, will not *know E* is going to happen.

In both these cases, the 'prediction' can be replaced by a non-prediction *P* and still leave the same essential problem. So the title 'prediction paradox' is not well-deserved. A somewhat better candidate for the title is (3): *X* needs to stage event *E* on just one of the next *n* days without *Y* (who knows that *X* is committed to staging *Y* on these terms) being able to predict in advance which day it will be. The last day looks like a bad choice for *X*. This tends to make the next-to-last day also look bad, and then the next-to-next, leading to a paradoxical argument ruling out the whole series of days. The contest between *X* and *Y* raises interesting problems in game theory. Unlike (1) and (2), which crucially involve statements (*A* and *B*), no statements need be made for the contest to arise between *X* and *Y*.   J.C.

*exam paradox.

James Cargile, 'The Surprise Test Paradox', *Journal of Philosophy* (1967).

pre-established harmony: *see* harmony, pre-established.

preface paradox. Paradox about belief and rationality. Recognizing his own fallibility, the author writes in the preface, with all sincerity, 'Though I believe everything I've written, no doubt this book contains mistakes (for which I apologize)'. He believes each of the statements in the book, yet also believes that at least one of them is false, which is close to believing a contradiction; yet his position seems both modest and rational. The paradox stems from the fact that it cannot be rational to believe a contradiction.   R.M.S.

A. N. Prior, *Objects of Thought*, ed. P. T. Geach and A. Kenny (Oxford, 1971), 84 ff.

prejudice, Burkian: *see* Burke.

prescriptivism. A theory about the meaning of moral terms such as *'good', *'right', and *'ought'. Its principal advocate has been R. M. Hare. The theory draws a contrast between descriptive meaning, whereby language is used for stating facts, and the 'prescriptive' meaning which is characteristic of moral language. Moral terms are used primarily for *guiding action*, for telling people what to do. As such they are similar to imperatives, which also have prescriptive meaning. Moral discourse is not, as the *emotive theory of ethics had seemed to suggest, a manipulative process of playing on people's feelings. It is a rational activity, addressed to others as rational agents. It is, however, logically distinct from the activity of descriptive discourse, and hence no statements of fact can entail any conclusion about what one 'ought' to do.   R.J.N.

R. M. Hare, *The Language of Morals* (Oxford, 1952).

present: *see* time.

presentism. The presentist maintains that only presently existing objects and presently occurring events are real, thereby excluding from reality past and future objects and events. Indeed, for the presentist, only the present *time is real, so that our talk about past and future times must be interpreted very differently from our talk about the present. He will be perfectly happy to allow that certain objects *did* exist or *will* exist, which do not presently exist and so are not real. What he wants to avoid saying is that *there really are* past and future times, ontologically on a par with the present time, at which these presently nonexistent objects exist. His position may be likened to that of the opponent of *modal realism, who contends that non-actual *possible worlds are not ontologically on a par with the actual world, but are merely maximal consistent sets of propositions representing ways the world could have been.   E.J.L.

M. J. Loux, *Metaphysics: A Contemporary Introduction*, 2nd edn. (London, 2001).

Pre-Socratic philosophy. The term includes all early Greek theorists, with cosmological or philosophical interests, active before the end of the fifth century BC, except for the *Sophists. This convenient though arbitrary usage recognizes that philosophy began in Greece from, or in conjunction with, abstract cosmological theorizing, and was not generally recognized as a separate discipline in this period.

Abstract cosmology was founded by the sixth-century Milesians: Thales, Anaximander, and Anaximenes. They aimed to construct probable theories about the universe as a whole. They sought economical explanations in well-defined terms, and used the principle of *sufficient reason as a guide to these. Lacking the means of experimental verification, they tied their theories to the observable world by the concept of *phusis* (nature), which implied a basic uniformity of behaviour in the natural world. There was an overall teleology (guidance by a supreme intelligence identified with the fundamental component of the physical world). This style of 'natural philosophy' (*phusiologia*) was continued in the fifth century by Anaxagoras and Democritus among others.

Like every ambitious scientific programme, natural philosophy generated philosophical problems. The most pressing was the epistemological one, particularly since the project required the rejection of all traditional authorities. It is likely that the Milesians were not explicit about their epistemology; but Xenophanes rejected all human claims to knowledge outside the area of immediate experi-

ence. Instead he envisaged the construction (and cumulative refinement) of 'better opinion', the criterion for which was 'resemblance to truths', i.e. the truths of immediate experience. His own cosmology systematically makes parsimonious extrapolations from ordinary experience. This strain of empiricism, revived in the later fifth century, can be traced in Anaxagoras, some of the medical writings attributed to Hippocrates, and perhaps Socrates.

A different type of approach appears in the theology of Xenophanes, which deduced the properties of God from a priori principles of what is 'fitting' for a divinity. The outstanding theorists of the late sixth and early fifth centuries claimed to discover truths of which the denial would be in some way unreasonable or unthinkable. Pythagoras possibly appealed to occult or mystical experience. But Heraclitus and Parmenides (leader of the Eleatics) in their different ways focused on the workings of human reason itself, thereby founding logic and metaphysics. Heraclitus' *logos*, to which he appealed for confirmation, reflects or embodies reason. Parmenides, in the first surviving attempt at consciously rigorous argument, claimed to start from a premiss which cannot coherently be denied, and to deduce step by step the properties of any possible object of knowledge.

Both Heraclitus and Parmenides were concerned with another systematic legacy of the 'natural philosophers': the problem of unity and diversity in the universe, and (arising from that) the problem of appearance and reality. Heraclitus detected a general pattern of 'unity-in-opposites', exemplified in the identity of the river which survives the change of its waters. He did not (as some have thought) deny the principle of *non-contradiction, but rather saw ambiguities in the very essence of things. Parmenides, by contrast, argued that anything knowable must be fully determinate and absolutely unified. This led him to a strong form of monism about underlying reality.

Parmenides' ideas, particularly his arguments against 'coming-to-be' and 'ceasing-to-be', and his insistence on absolutely definite objects of knowledge, were widely influential. His immediate follower Zeno of Elea turned his style of argumentation to destructive ends, exposing the logical inadequacy of certain natural assumptions about the physical world. Another near-contemporary, Empedocles, idiosyncratically blended Parmenidean metaphysics and Pythagorean doctrines of the soul with a cosmology, which, in parallel to the medical theory of Alcmaeon of Croton (*fl. c.*450?), explained the diversity of appearances by a finite but plural number of basic 'roots' (the first appearance as such of the 'four elements') with clearly defined properties.

The later part of the fifth century was dominated, in the western Greek world (southern Italy and Sicily), by (real or self-styled) Pythagoreans. Pure mathematics was taken as the paradigm, perhaps the only possible kind, of knowledge. (A reduction of all sciences to arithmetic seems to have been seriously attempted.) Philolaus (*fl. c.*450?) argued for finite units and quantities as the only possible objects of knowledge.

PYTHAGORAS, one of the earliest known Greek thinkers: the mythology that attached itself to him in antiquity has made it difficult to affirm much more than that he was a charismatic founder of a religious sect with strong ethical ordinances.

HERACLITUS, was to be a model for various modern European philosophers in point of the oracular obscurity of his style, his supposed disregard for his fellow humans, the ambition of his philosophy, and the importace in it of opposition and flux.

SOCRATES: Plato paid homage to his mentor by his literary representation and continuation of the Socratic enterprise in a series of philosophical dialogues, in which Socrates seldom meets his match.

DEMOCRITUS, perhaps a younger contemporary of Socrates, was one of the earliest proponents of an atomic theory of the universe, and seems to have been a forerunner of Epicurus in ethics.

In mainland Greece and the Aegean islands, the later fifth century was the age of the Sophists (of whom one, Protagoras, was an original philosopher); and of Socrates. Of those others denominated 'Pre-Socratics', most revived the original programme of natural philosophy, taking account of the new situation created above all by the Eleatics and by the new attention to biological theory and psychology. (An isolated figure, Melissus, belongs with the *Eleatics, and is most notable for his radical critique of sense-perception.) The leading figures were Anaxagoras and the early proponent of *atomism, Democritus. Anaxagoras and Democritus represent opposite, repeatedly recurring tendencies in physics: Anaxagoras is a 'field theorist', assuming the continuity and ubiquity of physical forces, while Democritus is a 'particle theorist', claiming that they are localized and particulate. Anaxagoras was closer in spirit and style to the original Milesian enterprise, identifying the cosmic intelligence as 'Mind' (*nous) and attributing to it an overall teleological control. The Atomists made a fundamental break in creating reductive *materialism: there are only (lifeless and mindless) atoms and void with their essential properties. They aimed to derive, from these foundations, not only living and sentient beings of familiar kinds, but 'gods' (large, long-lived beings inhabiting intercosmic void) and moral values.

Pre-Socratic philosophy never entirely broke free, except with the Eleatics, from its origins in the problems of a scientific programme. Democritus is the first and only Pre-Socratic known to have elaborated an ethical theory, though in Heraclitus and Empedocles ethical values are given a place in the natural world. The scepticism about moral and religious systems associated with the antithesis between *nomos* ('custom') and *phusis* ('nature' or 'reality'), which figured in the discussions of the Sophists, has its roots in Xenophanes' attacks on traditional religion and values. Even in the limited sources, an increasing philosophical sophistication in ontology and epistemology, and an increasing command of the techniques of argument, can be traced.

The interpretation of the Pre-Socratics has been controversial at least since the late fifth century BC. (*Cratylus.) Many of their works were already lost or scarce in late antiquity, and the rest perished thereafter, apart from quotations in surviving writers. In the scarcity of primary sources Aristotle's remarks on them were generally taken as authoritative from medieval times until recently. Only in the nineteenth century did a new climate of thought, and advances in scholarship, allow some Pre-Socratics to emerge as important philosophers in their own right. Understanding has been both furthered and impeded by the imperialism of those modern philosophers who, like Aristotle, have sought to force the history of philosophy into a preconceived mould. In default of substantial new primary materials, scholarship can advance only by gradually reaching a better (philosophically informed, but not prejudiced) understanding of (*a*) the nature and aims of the sources; (*b*) the language and concepts used by the Pre-Socratics and their contemporaries; (*c*) their philosophical intentions, as shown by the totality of the evidence.   E.L.H.

J. Barnes, *Early Greek Philosophy* (London, 1987).
H. Fränkel, *Early Greek Poetry and Philosophy*, tr. M. Hadas and J. Willis (Oxford, 1975).
E. Hussey, *The Presocratics* (London, 1972).
G. S. Kirk, J. E. Raven, and M. Schofield, *The Presocratic Philosophers*, 2nd edn. (Cambridge, 1983).
A. A. Long (ed.), *The Cambridge Companion to Early Greek Philosophy* (Cambridge, 1999).

presumption. A concept borrowed by epistemology from law that represents a way of filling in—at least *pro tem*—certain gaps in our otherwise available information. The 'presumption of innocence' is a paradigm case here; a presumption is a matter not of secured facts, of *given* information, but rather of answers that are *taken* in the absence of counter-indications. Presumptions are accordingly defeasible, vulnerable to being overturned—but only by some duly established conflicting considerations. A presumption accordingly has a favourable burden of proof on its side: counter-evidence is needed to effect its undoing.

A specific presumption is always grounded in a principle of presumption. Such principles operate in various domains. For example, a cognitive presumption operates in favour of the data of sight ('Accept what you see to be so'). In communicative contexts we have a presumption to the effect that people are truthful ('Accept what your interlocutors maintain'); in everyday enquiry we have the presumption that our sources are reliable ('Accept what encyclopedias and authorities maintain'); in science we have the presumption of evidential sufficiency ('Accept what the most strongly established theory or explanation maintains'). However, the result of applying such principles of presumption is always tentative and provisional: the rider 'until such time as indications to the contrary come to view' is attached to all presumptive principles.

The validations of the principle of presumption can be of two sorts. Some are justified a priori and proceed by showing that they are *sine qua non* prerequisites of a certain cognitive practice. Others are a posteriori and experiential, grounded in the *ex post facto* consideration of a track record showing that operating on this basis yields better results for the enterprise at issue than would otherwise be available. Practical efficacy is the crux for presumption.

Presumptions play a key role in the cyclic justifications at issue in an epistemological coherentism that dispenses with the self-evident certainties of an epistemic foundationalism.   N.R.

N. Rescher, *Methodological Pragmatism* (Oxford, 1977).
E. Ullman-Margalit, 'On Presumption', *Journal of Philosophy* (1983).

Price, Henry Habberley (1899–1984). Wykeham Professor of Logic and Fellow of New College, Oxford, 1935–59; a shy, reclusive figure, belonging to no school or group and seeking no disciples. His major work is *Perception*, in which, adopting from Russell and Moore the term *'sense-datum' for the basic object of perception, he seeks to clarify the sense in which sense-data 'belong to' material objects, rejecting, on the one hand, the causal theories of Locke and Russell and, on the other hand, the *phenomenalism of, for example, J. S. Mill. He pursues these issues further in *Hume's Theory of the External World* (Oxford, 1940). In *Thinking and Experience* (London, 1953) he explores the nature of thinking, playing down the then fashionable emphasis on the use of 'symbols', and arguing that concepts should be seen as 'recognitional capacities'. G.J.W.

H. H. Price, *Perception* (London, 1932).

Price, Richard (1723–91). Welsh dissenting minister noted for his defence of a non-naturalist moral philosophy. His argument for the non-definability of goodness anticipates G. E. Moore, and elements of his intuitionism have reappeared in the work of H. A. Prichard and W. D. Ross. Price's defence of individual freedom and national independence figured prominently in his criticism of the British declaration of war against the American colonies, and his advice to the Americans after the war helped to shape their new Constitution. He edited Bayes's essay on the doctrine of chances, pioneered actuarial theory, and became a Fellow of the Royal Society. His enthusiasm for the cause of the French Revolution provoked Edmund Burke to write his famous and severely critical *Reflections on the Revolution in France*. O.R.J.

*Bayesian confirmation theory.

D. O. Thomas, *The Honest Mind: The Thought and Work of Richard Price* (Oxford, 1977).

Prichard, Harold Arthur (1871–1947). Oxford philosopher who emphasized the unanalysability of certain epistemological and ethical concepts, notably knowledge and moral obligation (see his *Knowledge and Perception* (London, 1950) and *Moral Obligation* (London, 1949)). Knowledge, or being certain, was an infallible state of mind, which its possessor could *know* that he possessed, though it had to be distinguished from merely feeling certain, or thinking without question. Moral philosophy, he suggested, rested on a mistake in that it tried to justify moral obligation by reducing it to something else, such as interest, but any such analysis could only succeed by destroying what was supposed to be analysed; like knowledge, moral *obligation presented itself directly to our intuitions. Prichard's moral philosophy therefore contains obvious analogues both to Moore's view of good as unanalysable and to Kant's view of duty as entirely independent of interest. A.R.L.

H. A. Prichard, *Moral Writings*, ed. J. MacAdam (Oxford, 2002).

Priestley, Joseph (1733–1804). English Utilitarian philosopher, scientist, and unorthodox theologian. Priestley's main political work is his *Essay on the First Principles of Government* (1768). This work is of interest because it is here that Bentham may have discovered the formula of the *greatest happiness of the greatest number. Priestley, again before Bentham, attempts to bring about the fusion of the principle of utility with democratic ideas. The problem of government is therefore that of finding a way to identify the interest of the governors with the interests of the governed. Priestley's solution is that identity of interests can be achieved by making it necessary for the rulers to court the favour of the people. 'It is nothing but the continued fear of a revolt in favour of some rival, that could keep such princes within bounds.' Priestley is important for many discoveries in chemistry and physics. R.S.D.

Elie Halevy, *The Growth of Philosophical Radicalism*, tr. Mary Morris (London, 1928).

prima-facie duties: *see* duty.

primary and secondary qualities. Deriving from the Greek Atomists and common in the seventeenth century (Galileo, Descartes, Boyle) the distinction between these is famously found in Locke's *Essay Concerning Human Understanding*, where primary *qualities (e.g. shape) are 'utterly inseparable from . . . [a] body', however small (II. viii. 9) and secondary qualities (e.g. colour) 'in truth are nothing in . . . objects themselves, but powers to produce various sensations in us' (II. viii. 10). It is often supposed to be an epistemological doctrine concerning perceptual error and illusion, and so to depend on some idea that while we often err about the colours of objects we do not do so about their shapes, or that our perception of colour can vary with our position or with our mental and physical states. In fact, however, it is really a corollary of the corpuscular theory of matter, or, more generally, of the 'mechanical philosophy'.

Primary qualities belong not only to observable things such as an almond, but also to the insensible minute corpuscles which were supposed to make it up. An almond has solidity, extension, shape, mobility, and number, and according to the corpuscular theory the almond's corpuscles have these qualities too. Secondary qualities, such as colour and taste, belong to the almond but not to its corpuscles. They arise from the arrangement of the solid, shaped, and mobile corpuscles themselves. Of course, like its colour, the almond's primary qualities of solidity and extension also result from its consisting of solid, extended corpuscles. What distinguishes them from secondary qualities is that these are those features which corpuscles need to have in order to account for *all* the qualities (primary and secondary) of the things they make up.

Because material things consist of arrangements of insensible corpuscles, they act on our sense-organs in certain ways. Interaction between an almond's corpuscles and those of our taste-buds results in the production, in our minds, of a certain idea, that of sweetness; though quite how such causation between the physical and the mental takes place is, Locke says, a mystery. Similarly, via the intermediary of reflected light, interaction between an almond's corpuscles and those of our eyes produces in us the idea of its colour. Secondary qualities of objects are those arrangements of its corpuscles which cause certain ideas *in us*.

Fire causes pain in us, and snow causes ideas of coldness and whiteness. However, while we think of pain simply as something caused in us by the interaction between fire and our bodies, we think of snow as being, in itself, white and cold. Locke suggests that the corpuscular account of objects, and our perception of them, gives us no reason to think of snow's coldness and whiteness like this. We do perceive snow as being cold and white in itself; but since our doing so is a result of the arrangement of primary-qualitied corpuscles, there is no need to suppose snow really is as we perceive it. Snow does have a certain corpuscular arrangement, which fits it to produce ideas of coldness and of whiteness in us; but just as there is nothing in fire resembling pain, so there need be nothing in snow resembling the whiteness and coldness it appears to have. The case is otherwise with primary qualities. In order to explain how we perceive objects as having shape, and being solid, we need to suppose that objects have those properties in the way they appear to have.   R.S.W.

*representative theory of perception.

Peter Alexander, *Ideas, Qualities and Corpuscles* (Cambridge, 1985).
Margaret D. Wilson, 'History of Philosophy in Philosophy Today; and the Case of the Sensible Qualities', *Philosophical Review* (1992).
R. S. Woolhouse, *John Locke* (Brighton, 1983), ch. 4.

prime matter. (Latin *materia prima*; Greek *prōtē hulē*; 'first' or 'primary' matter.) Traditionally, *matter which 'in itself' has no determinate positive qualities, but the potential to have such qualities. Prime matter is posited as what persists through a *change in which one Aristotelian element (e.g. water) turns into another (e.g. air). This conception of prime matter is traditionally ascribed to Aristotle, although the attribution has been challenged (as has the notion's intelligibility).   P.J.M.

*substratum; *apeiron*.

Aristotle, *De generatione et corruptione*, tr. and ed. C. J. F. Williams (Oxford, 1982), app.

prime mover. This is a label given to an ultimate cause of motion or change in the universe; it is an idea of fundamental importance in rational *cosmology. In ancient philosophy the topic is most fully developed by Plato and Aristotle. Both maintain that the original cause of motion must possess mind. But Aristotle argues against Plato that the prime mover must be itself unmoved. Although criticized by Kant, it re-emerges in current big bang theory. The idea has never been more succinctly expressed than in its earliest presentation in Plato's *Phaedrus* 245c–e.   J.D.G.E.

principle. The history of philosophy abounds in principles: the principle of *sufficient reason, Hume's principle ('No ought from an is'), the principle of *double

effect . . . A principle will often be put forward as an allegedly obvious truth from which to derive further truths. The principle or principles may be thought so basic and general that all or most of knowledge, or anyway of philosophical knowledge, can be derived: we then have philosophical *foundationalism, as typified in the work of Spinoza. But Descartes's 'I think therefore I am' is not of the general form required of a principle. Using it, or something like it, as a starting-point would amount to a different, epistemological, form of foundationalism.

A moral principle is less a starting-point for reasoning than a guide for deliberation and action. In moral philosophy, you may find a hybrid of the two—for example, the 'utility principle'.   R.P.L.T.

arkhē; utilitarianism; regulative principles; rules.

B. de Spinoza, *Ethics*, in *The Chief Works of Benedict de Spinoza*, ed. R. H. M. Elwes (New York, 1955).

principle of sufficient reason: *see* sufficient reason, principle of.

principles, regulative: *see* regulative principles.

Prior, Arthur Norman (1914–69). New Zealand-born philosopher who taught at the University of Canterbury in New Zealand and the University of Manchester before becoming a Fellow of Balliol College, Oxford. He first gained his reputation in ethics, and then went on to do fundamental work in logic and metaphysics. Prior was a leading figure in the movement to apply modal logic to the formalization of a wide variety of linguistic phenomena. In 1953 he invented tense logic, introducing two new modal operators 'It will be the case that' and 'It has been the case that'. Prior used his tense logic to articulate theories about the structure and metaphysics of time, and to mount a robust defence of free will and indeterminism. Tense logic is also employed for the manipulation of time-dependent data and has numerous applications in computing. In 1956 Prior and Carew Meredith were the first to give a possible-worlds semantics employing the 'accessibility' relation between worlds. Their idea, now standard in modal semantics, was that 'Necessarily *p*' is true in a world *w* iff *p* is true in every possible world accessible from *w*. An iconoclast and a resourceful innovator, Prior inspired many to undertake work in tense and modal logic.   B.J.C.

B. J. Copeland (ed.), *Logic and Reality: Essays on the Legacy of Arthur Prior* (Oxford, 1996).
A. N. Prior, *Papers on Time and Tense*, new edn. ed. T. Braüner, B. J. Copeland, P. Hasle, and P. Ohrstrom (Oxford, 2003).

prioritarianism is the view that gains in the well-being of the worse-off are morally more important than the same size gains for the better-off. This view contrasts with *utilitarianism, which counts a gain in the well-being of one individual the same as it counts the same size gain for anyone else. Pure *equality in the distribution of well-being is often accused of favouring reducing the well-being of the better-off even when this will not benefit the worse off. Prioritarianism rejects such 'levelling down'.   B.H.

M. Clayton and A. Williams (eds.), *The Ideal of Equality* (London, 2002).

prisoner's dilemma. The prisoner's dilemma describes a possible situation in which prisoners are offered various deals and prospects of punishment. The options and outcomes are so constructed that it is rational for each person, when deciding in isolation, to pursue a course which each finds to be against his interest and therefore irrational. For example, if I am an employer and you a worker, it may be to my advantage not to pay you (rather than pay you) whether or not you do the work, and for you not to do the work (rather than do it) whether or not I pay you; but it is to the advantage of neither of us that I should not pay and you should not work. Such a scenario postulates a lack of enforced co-operation; and to avoid the undesirable outcome, the actors in the drama need to be forced into co-operation by a system of rules. So it has been argued that we can find in this dilemma a basis for the generation of the institutions of morality—or, at least, of prudent co-operation. But that conclusion is challenged by others who point out that the same choice-theoretic problems also arise with ends that are immoral or prudentially harmful.   J.D.G.E.

From an immense literature on this topic, I select the collection of essays, classic and modern, edited by David P. Gauthier, *Morality and Rational Self-Interest* (Englewood Cliffs, NJ, 1970).

privacy. In US legal philosophy the area of individual rights. In philosophy of mind the characteristic of each person's experiences and thoughts that they are known immediately only to that person. Epistemological *foundationalists took such supposedly infallible and self-intimating knowledge to be the firm basis they sought. The alleged privacy of each person's thoughts and experiences gives rise to the *'other minds' problem as well as to general *scepticism regarding knowledge. Attempts to avert such consequences include appeals to the public nature of language, the medium in which thoughts have in any case to be formed. More general attacks on the notion of the mind as an inner realm uniquely accessible to each individual are found in *Heidegger's *Dasein from the 1920s and *Ryle's behavioural analysis of mind from the 1940s. Latterly, *Dennett and *Churchland, respectively, see in the flow of subjective experience but a scrambled version of, and a poor way of accessing, what really happens at more basic 'sub-personal' levels.   A.H.

A. J. Ayer, 'Basic Propositions', in *Philosophical Essays* (London, 1954).

G. Ryle, *The Concept of Mind* (London, 1949).

private language problem. Sections 243–315 of Wittgenstein's *Philosophical Investigations* criticize the idea, presupposed by Cartesianism and empiricism, of a language whose primitive terms signify the speaker's 'private' sensations and perceptions, allegedly inalienably owned and truly known only by their bearer. 'Ownership' of experi-ence is misconstrued, since different people can have the very same sensation. Private knowledge of experience is misconceived, since neither knowing nor being ignorant of one's current experience make sense. That the mutual intelligibility of a putative 'private' language is problem-atic is obvious. The originality of Wittgenstein's argu-ment is to show that it must be unintelligible even to its speaker. For it presupposes the possibility of private ostensive definition, of a private (mental) *sample func-tioning as a standard for the correct application of a word, and of a rule which cannot logically be followed by another person, all of which are shown to be incoherent. The consequences of the argument, if it is correct, ramify throughout metaphysics, epistemology, and philosophy of mind. Unsurprisingly, it was heatedly debated in the fol-lowing decades and controverted both by traditional empiricists and by contemporary materialists and func-tionalists.   P.M.S.H.

P. M. S. Hacker, *An Analytical Commentary on the* Philosophical Investigations, iii: *Wittgenstein: Meaning and Mind* (Oxford, 1990), 1–287.

privatization is the granting of individual property rights over previously communally owned or unowned resources. Efficiency-based arguments and justice-based arguments are given in its favour. The least plausible just-ice-based argument is from the right to property, since many theorists today agree that distribution of property rights should be derived from principles of justice, rather than vice versa. Justice-based arguments for privatizing communal resources, such as service-providing institu-tions, focus on personal responsibility and increases in freedom of choice which come with competition by providers on a market. It is not clear, however, that all goods allocation should be responsive to individual prefer-ences. Informed choices about education and health care are limited by lack of expertise of precisely the kind sought. Furthermore, even if markets hold individuals responsible for their market choices, those choices are themselves limited by the market advantages and disadvantages that individuals start with. It is also not clear that individuals should be held accountable for all their choices. A moral duty of assistance requires helping those not in a position to help themselves, even if they once were.

Arguments from efficiency highlight the state's moral duty not to waste communal resources. Market competi-tion reduces waste, whilst publicly run services are notori-ously wasteful. So, it is argued, why not improve efficiency through privatizing, whilst giving credits to less advantaged citizens to purchase services? This, however, reduces benefits to market preferences, and efficiency to market efficiency. Market efficiency modifies the goods supplied. For efficient exchange on a market, benefits need clear boundaries, which, for example, are lacked by a 'good state of public health'. Consequently, privatization encourages 'commodification': changes to goods making them more market-friendly, such as turning them into dis-tinctly priced units or solely developing their revenue-yielding properties. This has negative side-effects. Elephant populations in Zimbabwe increased after elephants were privatized. Yet, the value inherent in having 'free-roaming creatures in their natural habitat' is lost when individuals have control-conferring property rights over these creatures. In the social sphere, it can be argued, all aspects of the provision of goods representing a society's assistance to its disadvantaged members should be subject to democratic, communal control. S.M.-G.

*economics and morality; socialism.

Bo Rothstein, *Just Institutions Matter: The Moral and Political Logic of the Universal Welfare State* (Cambridge, 1998).

privileged access. The supposed special authority possessed by a subject's beliefs about his or her current mental states, as compared with others' beliefs about those states. Attacked as a myth by Ryle, the idea is still debated. Accounts of first-personal authority vary, ranging from, at one extreme, *incorrigibility, that the subject cannot be wrong, to the subject's merely being better placed in some respects than others. Recent debate has focused on reconciling it with *externalism. P.F.S.

*introspection; inner sense.

W. Alston, 'Varieties of Privileged Access', *American Philosophical Quarterly* (1971).
B. Gertler (ed.), *Privileged Access: Philosophical Theories of Self-Knowledge* (Aldershot, 2003).

probabilistic causality. If classical *determinism is true, every event has a sufficient cause which necessitates its occurrence. However, since the advent of quantum physics, we may have to acknowledge that some events, such as the spontaneous decay of a radium atom, lack any such determining cause. Even setting aside such considerations, we are frequently confronted with situations—most obviously in games of chance—in which the outcome of a process cannot be predicted with certainty, but in which some possible outcomes appear to be more probable than others. For these reasons, some philosophers of causation have argued that we need to generalize any account of *causality to accommodate the possibility of probabilistic causation. According to one widely adopted approach, to say that an event *c* was a probabilistic cause of another event *e* is to say that, in the circumstances in which *c* occurred, the occurrence of *c* raised the chance of *e* occurring—although spelling out what precisely may be meant by this and dealing with various apparent counter-examples is no easy matter, quite apart from the fact that it is difficult to dissociate the notion of causation from that of some kind of necessitation. E.J.L.

D. H. Mellor, *The Facts of Causation* (London, 1995).

probability. Although there is a well-established mathematical calculus of probability, the nature of its subject-matter is still in dispute. Someone who asserts that it will probably rain is not asserting outright that it will: the question is how such guarded assertions relate to the facts.

The modern mathematical treatment of probability owes its origins to Pascal's treatment of games of chance, and the classical equipossibility theory arises most naturally in this context. To say that the probability of a fair die landing six uppermost is one-sixth is to say that among the six equally likely outcomes, the ratio of favourable to unfavourable cases is one to five. But paradoxes arise where there are different, equally possible candidates for the set of equally possible outcomes. And in defining probability in terms of equal possibility the theory runs into circularity.

The possibility of deriving probabilities from statistical data has often been thought to require a 'relative frequency' interpretation. The probability of a 50-year-old man who smokes forty cigarettes a day dying within ten years is, on this view, simply the number of deaths in that period among such men. The attraction of this interpretation is that it appears to make the probability of an event as objectively ascertainable as the height of a house. But a given individual will generally belong to various classes with differing life expectancies. In such cases we can no longer speak of *the* probability of a given individual's dying: but this may be just what concerns us.

Much discussion of the frequency theory has concentrated on games of chance, where prior assumptions about frequencies rather than actual frequencies take the lead. What happens in the 'long run' in 'roughly' a given proportion of cases is introduced to bring these into line with each other. But this account owes explanations of what 'roughly' means, and of how long a long run is, and these seem to depend on the notion of probability. (It is improbable, not impossible, that a fair coin never shows heads in however long a run.) More sophisticated versions involve the idea of a limit to which actual frequencies tend as the number of events increases; but no data guarantee the existence of this limit.

The frequency interpretation has no obvious application to a statement like that made by John Dalton in 1803 that 'the most probable opinion' about the nature of heat was that it was 'an elastic fluid of great subtilty'. This has led some philosophers to attempt to analyse probability in terms of so-called 'degrees of belief'. This account has often been thought of not as an alternative to the frequency interpretation, but as the analysis of a different concept, the word 'probability' being ambiguous. Personalist theories take probability judgements to be expressions of the willingness to make certain bets: to believe that the probability of the coin showing heads is one-tenth is to be willing to stake a pound to win nine if heads show. To avoid this arbitrariness by substituting 'degree of *reasonable* belief' is to invite an explanation of reasonable belief. It is difficult to see how this might be given without reference to probability, hence without circularity.

'Logical relation' theories attempt to avoid arbitrariness by building evidence into the probability judgement. On this view a probability judgement concerns a logical relation between a statement and the evidence: 'It will probably rain tomorrow' is really in shorthand, the statements of supporting evidence being suppressed. On this view we have no dispute with Dalton, since he was speaking (presumably correctly) about the relation of a theory to the evidence available to him. M.C.

L. J. Cohen, *An Introduction to the Philosophy of Induction and Probability* (Oxford, 1989).
D. Gillies, *Philosophical Theories of Probability* (London, 2000).
I. Hacking, *An Introduction to Probability and Deductive Logic* (Cambridge, 2000).
J. R. Lucas, *The Concept of Probability* (Oxford, 1970).
S. E. Toulmin, *The Uses of Argument* (Cambridge, 1958).
R. von Mises, *Probability, Statistics and Truth* (New York, 1957).

probability, conditional: *see* conditional probability.

problematic. (1) Perplexing, questionable. (2) In traditional logic, problematic propositions are those that are marked with a sign of *possibility, especially in connection with Aristotle's modal syllogistic; e.g. 'It is *possible* for all eggs not to be speckled', 'Some people *can* touch their toes'. The possibility might be logical, physical, epistemic, etc. Its *scope is often ambiguous. (3) The word is sometimes used in the German manner as a noun, for a set of problems or a way of seeing problems. C.A.K.

H. W. B. Joseph, *An Introduction to Logic*, 2nd edn. (Oxford, 1916).

process. A process is a series of *changes with some sort of unity, or unifying principle, to it. Hence 'process' is to 'change', or 'event', rather as 'syndrome' is to 'symptom'. What sort of *unity* might a given process have? Perhaps just this: that the process is found to recur sufficiently often in nature—it seems to belong to a 'natural kind'. In this case, lumping the constituent changes together is as natural as lumping the different features of a cow together as a unity. But with both cows and processes, some philosophers have thought there must be some *underlying* principle of unity that binds the constituent features, or changes, together.

Whitehead made much use of the notion of a process, and 'process theology' grew out of his work. On the whole, however, modern metaphysics has rather dropped the notion of a process in favour of the notion of an event, the influence of Einstein perhaps supplanting that of Whitehead, Bergson, *et al.* R.P.L.T.

*event; process philosophy.

A. N. Whitehead, *Process and Reality* (New York, 1929).

process philosophy. The doctrine that either what is is becoming, or that what is ultimately consists in *change, or both. A *process is a sequence of changes.

Strong and weak process philosophy may be usefully distinguished. On the weak version, x changes if and only if either x is F at a time, t_1, and x is not F at a later time, t_2, or x is not F at t_1 and x is F at t_2; so something's changing consists in its gaining or losing at least one property. It is sometimes maintained (with dubious coherence) that each thing is always changing in every respect.

On the strong version, there are only changes or, at least, the existence of enduring items logically depends upon changes such that it is ontologically misleading to speak of what is or things that are. One *locus classicus* of strong process philosophy is Plato's *Theaetetus*, where the thesis is ascribed by Socrates to Protagoras, Heraclitus, and Empedocles; another is Heraclitus' *Cosmic Fragments*.

More recently, 'process philosophy' has been used as a name for the *event ontologies of James, Bergson, and Whitehead (notably, in his *Process and Reality*). It should also be extended to Russell's neutral monist doctrine that minds and physical objects are logical constructions out of events.

The existence of change, which is logically entailed by the existence of process, has been denied by Parmenides in his poem, by F. H. Bradley in *Appearance and Reality*, and by J. M. E. McTaggart in *The Nature of Existence*. If some of the arguments of these philosophers are sound then there really is no change and *a fortiori* no true process philosophy. However, at least prima facie, change is a pervasive feature of what is, and many things that are may be described without contradiction as processes. S.P.

*neutral monism.

Aristotle, *Physics*, books 1 and 2, tr. William Charlton (Oxford, 1970).
Aristotle, *Physics*, books 3 and 4, tr. Edward Hussey (Oxford, 1983).
Jonathan Barnes (ed.), *Early Greek Philosophy* (London, 1987).
Plato, *Theaetetus*, tr. John McDowell (Oxford, 1973).
Alfred North Whitehead, *Process and Reality* (New York, 1929).

process theology: *see* theology and philosophy.

Proclus (*c*.AD 410–485). Pagan philosopher of *Neoplatonism who became head of the Academy at Athens and was the last great systematizer of Greek philosophy. His works, which survive in bulk, include: *The Elements of Theology* (tr. E. R. Dodds, 2nd edn. (Oxford, 1963)), *Platonic Theology*, and commentaries on several Platonic dialogues and on Euclid. His thought abounds in triads: Plotinus' procession (emanation) and return is replaced by abiding–procession–return. He is theurgical, magical, and often fanciful, as when he derives the Greek *khronos*, 'time', from *khoros* and *nous*, arguing that time is the (circular) 'dance' of the 'mind'. By way of Dionysius the Areopagite (*c*.AD 500) he influenced medieval thought and especially the Renaissance revival of Platonism. Hegel admired him: he was compared to Proclus and Schelling to Plotinus. M.J.I.

A. H. Armstrong (ed.), *The Cambridge History of Later Greek and Early Medieval Philosophy* (Cambridge, 1967).

professional ethics. The codes and guide-lines which govern the conduct of professions. Such codes can be seen as the application of general morality to the specific contexts of professional relationships. The oldest and most familiar of these is the Hippocratic oath, which in a modified form still applies to the doctor–patient relationship. In the contemporary world many occupations consider themselves professions, and the governing bodies of these occupations issue codes of professional ethics. They have a status in between that of morality and that of law, in the sense that while their content is like that of morality, any breach of their prohibitions can result in serious disciplinary sanctions by the relevant governing body. The content of professional codes always contains provisions that the professional will work for the best interests of the patient / client. For this reason professional ethics can be in conflict with *consumerist ethics, which approaches the professional relationship from the point of view of client demand and rights rather than professional perceptions of need and duty.   R.S.D.

*business ethics.

R. S. Downie, 'Professional Ethics and Business Ethics', in S. A. M. McLean (ed.), *Contemporary Issues in Law, Medicine and Ethics* (Aldershot, 1996).

programs of computers. A formally specified set of instructions which guide the operations of a symbol-manipulating device. A program written in a particular programming language is executed in a given computer when a processor carries out the sequence of instructions in the program, or converts them into instructions corresponding more closely to the basic operations of the machine. The resulting process, which consists in the manipulation of symbols, or data structures, determines the subsequent behaviour of the machine. By programming computers we enable them to produce certain behaviours in response to certain inputs. Psychologists use programs to model the structure of human psychological processes; e.g. reasoning (*cognition); and philosophers dispute whether mind is a program implemented in neural hardware (*computers) or whether a correctly programmed computer can replicate as well as simulate mentality (*artificial intelligence). Constructivist logic offers another application of programming where a proof can be treated as a class of programs for verifying a formula.
                                                                    B.C.S.

J. Haugeland, *Artificial Intelligence: The Very Idea* (Cambridge, Mass., 1985).
P. Martin-Lof, 'Constructive Mathematics and Computer Programming', in *Logic, Methodology and Philosophy of Science*, vi (1982).

progress. Improvement over time, especially the gradual perfection of humanity. A robust sense of confidence in human progress is characteristic of the philosophers of the eighteenth-century *Enlightenment. The French philosopher Condorcet enthusiastically expressed this view of 'the human race, emancipated from its shackles, released from the empire of fate and from that of the enemies of its progress, advancing with a firm and sure step along the path of truth, virtue and happiness'. But philosophers have not always been so sanguine about the future. Some historians (e.g. J. B. Bury) have argued that the idea of progress is a peculiarly modern concept, although a few (e.g. Robert Nisbet) have argued that it is an idea which

has its origins in the medieval Christian conception of providence, if not even earlier. In its most straightforward version, the belief in progress acknowledges a single, temporal progression of all peoples from the most 'primitive' to the most advanced, usually one's own society. The epitome of this sort of teleological thinking is to be found in G. W. F. Hegel, who argued that not only in philosophy and the arts, but in human history and religion too, rational progress is demonstrable, if only we turn a 'rational eye' to look for it.

It is important to distinguish between progress in the realm of science and technology, where improvements in medical cures, modes of transport, and various scientific theories are easily established, and moral or spiritual progress, which raises profound philosophical problems about the nature of happiness and morals. It is by no means obvious that we are happier, more moral or compassionate, less dogmatic or belligerent, than our more 'primitive' peers and ancestors. Jean-Jacques Rousseau, for example, argued (during the Enlightenment) that advances in the arts and sciences had corrupted rather than improved humanity.

At the end of the twentieth century, after two world wars and fifty years of potential nuclear conflict, the concept of progress had come into ill repute. The conservative philosopher Friedrich von Hayek bemoaned the fact that confidence in progress had become a mark of 'a shallow mind'. But even those who see history as 'just one damn thing after another' (in the eloquent phrase of poet John Masefield) tend to insist that we can nevertheless learn from history, improve ourselves, and progress beyond it.   R.C.SOL.

*pessimism and optimism.

J. B. Bury, *The Idea of Progress* (London, 1920).
R. Nisbet, *History of the Idea of Progress* (New York, 1980).

projectivism. The thesis that some apparent properties of the external world really belong to the mind that perceives it. For example, the world appears coloured, auditory, olfactory, gustatory. Actions seem good or evil, and objects ugly or beautiful, events necessary or contingent, but, according to projectivist views, these characteristics are at least partly due to our mental constitution and are not, or are not wholly or really, in the object. If *Hume is right about causation, we do not perceive objective causal necessities but mistake our own psychological expectation that one event will follow another for such mind-independent inevitability. This is projectivism about causation. Projectivism is *idealism about a restricted class of properties.   S.P.

*quasi-realism; primary and secondary qualities.

Simon Blackburn, *Essays in Quasi-Realism* (Oxford, 1993).
John McDowell, 'Values and Secondary Qualities', in Ted Honderich (ed.), *Morality and Objectivity: Essays in Honour of J. L. Mackie* (London, 1985).

proletariat: *see* bourgeoisie and proletariat.

proletariat, dictatorship of the: *see* dictatorship of the proletariat.

proof theory. The study of formal proofs in logic. As a discipline in its own right, proof theory is usually reckoned to begin in 1934, when Gerhard Gentzen introduced *natural deduction and the sequent calculus for classical first-order logic. He showed that any proof in either of these systems can be converted to a proof in the other. His cut elimination theorem—still undoubtedly the best theorem in proof theory—showed that any sequent calculus proof can be converted into a tableau (or truth-tree) in which formulae are steadily broken down, not built up. He adapted this theorem to give a *consistency proof for arithmetic. Gentzen's intuitionist versions of the natural deduction and sequent calculuses are an essential tool for studying intuitionist logic.   W.A.H.

S. R. Buss (ed.), *Handbook of Proof Theory* (Amsterdam, 1998).

propensity. A propensity is a probabilistic *disposition of an object or person to behave in a certain way—for example, the disposition of a radium atom to undergo radioactive decay in a given time-period with a certain degree of chance. Propensities are more firmly linked to behaviour than mere tendencies are, because the mere tendencies of an object may be counteracted by the contrary tendencies of other objects.   E.J.L.

*capacity; power; potential.

R. Tuomela (ed.), *Dispositions* (Dordrecht, 1978).

proper names: *see* names.

properties. Things may be said to own in some sense the attributes that they are acknowledged to have; hence the term 'property'. In traditional logic, deriving from Aristotle, however, the term has a more restricted use. According to the so-called doctrine of the predicables, which is concerned with the different things that can be predicated of a species (i.e. whether or not they are essential to the species and whether or not all and only members of the species can have these things predicated of them), a property or *proprium* is something that is not essential to the species but is such that all and only members of the species have it. Thus, arguably, the ability to laugh might be a *proprium* of man.

However that may be, a property has come to be regarded as the same as an attribute, and anything that is picked out by a predicate which can be applied to a thing in such a way as to characterize it is thus a property of that thing. Likewise, 'property' and 'quality' are sometimes used synonymously, although according to Aristotle's doctrine of the categories a *quality is simply one category of things that can be predicated of a subject, and thus just one kind of property.

There has been much discussion among philosophers about the exact ontological relation which holds between a thing (and more specifically a *substance) and its properties. Leibniz, for example, argued that substances were nothing but collections, though infinite collections, of properties. Other philosophers have argued, in a similar spirit, that statements about substances can be analysed into statements about the location of properties at given places and times. But the notion of a predicate, of which that of a property is a counterpart, depends on the idea that there is a subject for predicates to be *of*, and there seems to be no good reason for supposing that properties have any ontological priority among the kinds of entity that exist.

Like predicates, properties are general and can in principle belong to many things, whether or not they do so in fact. There is nothing in the generality of a property that prevents its belonging in fact to one thing only; but it must be logically possible for it to be attributed to more than one thing. Whether there are, despite this, such things as individual properties is a disputed matter.   D.W.H.

*essentialism; properties, individual.

D. W. Hamlyn, *Metaphysics* (Cambridge, 1984).
H. W. B. Joseph, *An Introduction to Logic*, 2nd edn. (Oxford, 1916).
D. H. Mellor and A. D. Oliver (eds.), *Properties* (Oxford, 1997).
P. F. Strawson, *Individuals* (London, 1959).

properties, individual. Consider a red tomato. Some philosophers (e.g. Stout) argue that there exists a particular redness of the tomato. This redness is an individual property, or 'abstract particular'. Other objects may be the same shade of red; those *rednesses* resemble, but are not identical to, the redness of the tomato. It is sometimes claimed, further, that individual properties are constitutive of events and physical objects and they play a key role in causal relations. In contrast, others (e.g. Armstrong) argue that ontological economy speaks to eliminating individual properties in favour of ordinary particulars, which exist in any case, and universal properties, which can be exemplified in indefinitely many ordinary particulars.   M.B.

*haecceity; properties; tropes.

D. M. Armstrong, *Universals and Scientific Realism*, i (Cambridge, 1978).
G. F. Stout, *Studies in Philosophy and Psychology* (New York, 1930).

properties, non-natural: *see* non-natural properties.

property. What is owned. Property in general is defined by a system of rules that assigns to persons rights over things, where the things capable of being owned can range from a person and his or her labour to land, natural resources, and what is produced by labour from land and natural resources. The rules of property defining rights of owners and duties owed to owners may be moral, legal, or both. Specific forms of property differ from each other depending on the rights and duties which the rules confer, how the rights or duties are acquired, and the kinds of things which are capable of being owned. Thus, all specific forms of property rules must perform two essential functions: to assign rights to persons (natural or artificial), and to prescribe mechanisms for the acquisition, transfer, and alienation of those rights.

One specific form of property is private property. This form, associated with John Locke's political philosophy and with *capitalism, assigns to owners the rights to use what they own in any way they choose so long as they respect the moral or natural rights of others. In private property persons acquire rights over things that are not owned by being the first to appropriate them or labour upon them, and they acquire rights to own things from others by gift, bequest, or exchange. First appropriation and labour, according to private property, justifies persons owning and profiting from land, natural resources, and material goods they produce from what they own. Not everyone will be able to have private property in land if all land is already owned; however, land may be purchased or leased from owners by those who have sufficient money or goods to exchange. In private ownership each person owns himself or herself; that is, each person has the right to decide how he or she is to labour, and has the right to exchange his or her labour for goods or money with whoever will pay.

Communal property, a specific form associated with Karl Marx and with *socialism, assigns rights over land and the means of production to the workers or the community as a whole, rather than to individual persons. As communal property, land and the means of production may not be privately appropriated. Rather, decisions concerning the use of land or the means of production are made collectively by the workers involved or, depending on the specific form of communal ownership, by all the members of the community or their elected representatives. Any surplus or profits realized from land and resources may be distributed to the workers or community members equally, in proportion to their labour and contribution, or according to their needs.

Corporate property, public property, and joint property are forms which combine elements of the private and communal forms. Corporate ownership resembles private ownership in the rights of owners to use what they own as they, alone, choose; but it resembles communal ownership in that there may be many persons who share the ownership rights.

Great interest lies in discovering which specific form of property is morally or politically justifiable. While private ownership has often been considered superior because it supposedly stimulates efficient production of great wealth and preserves the freedom of owners, it is also criticized because it perpetuates unjust distributions of income, creates unnatural desires for material goods, and lacks respect for the quality of the environment. Communal ownership is supposed to create insufficient incentives for economic growth, be wasteful of labour and energy, and inadequately satisfy consumer demand. But communal ownership is believed to create more just distributions of wealth, less *exploitation and *alienation among workers, and greater control by the community as a whole over its environment and economy.   J.O.G.

*libertarianism, left; markets; conservatism; Proudhon.

James O. Grunebaum, *Private Ownership* (London, 1987).
Stephen R. Munzer, *A Theory of Property* (Cambridge, 1990).
Jeremy Waldron, *The Right to Private Property* (Oxford, 1988).

proposition. The precise formulation varies, but a proposition, or propositional content, is customarily defined in modern logic as 'what is asserted' when a sentence (an indicative, or declarative, sentence) is used to say something true or false, or as 'what is expressed by' such a sentence. The term is also applied to what is expressed by the subordinate clauses of complex sentences, to forms of words which, if separated from the complex sentences of which they are part, can stand alone as indicative sentences in their own right. Accordingly, such sentences and clauses are often called 'propositional signs'.

In medieval logic, by contrast, a *propositio* was what would now be called a propositional sign. It was with this sense in mind that some of the 'traditional logicians' of the nineteenth century held that we should not be concerned with the proposition, a mere linguistic entity, but with the *judgement*, the (possibly mental) act of affirming or denying a predicate of a subject. Some modern logicians have argued what would appear, were it not for this shift in meaning, to be the opposite view: that we should not be concerned with the *sentence*, a mere linguistic entity, but with the proposition, an abstract entity designated by declarative sentences in particular languages. It is, though, an obvious mistake to suppose that, because different sentences say the same thing, there must be a same thing they say. Probably the most sensible view is that a proposition is neither a sentence 'in itself' nor some entity other than a sentence, but merely a certain sort of sentence used in a certain sort of way.   C.W.

*statements and sentences.

A. N. Prior, 'Propositions and Sentences', in *The Doctrine of Propositions and Terms* (London, 1976).
C. Williamson, 'Propositions and Abstract Propositions', in N. Rescher (ed.), *Studies in Logical Theory* (Oxford, 1968).

propositional attitude. A kind of state of mind, the term for which was introduced by Russell and has gained currency in recent philosophy of language and mind.

Predications of some mental states (e.g. of belief in 'Ted believes that *p*') appear to express a relation between a person (here Ted) and a proposition (here the proposition that-*p*); these states are the propositional attitudes. Want and desire, though not usually ordinarily attributed using 'that' clauses, are often included.

The class is singled out by philosophers for two reasons: (i) a set of questions pertains to the sentences used in ascribing attitudes; (ii) the attitudes feature in a distinctive mode of explanation—of rational beings; one species of such explanation is of action, considered usually to require ascriptions of the attitudes belief and desire.   J.HORN.

*content; intentionality; referential opacity.

Jerry A. Fodor, 'Propositional Attitudes', *Monist* (1978).

propositional calculus. A systematization of that part of logic concerned with operators corresponding to some uses of 'not', 'or', 'and', 'If . . . then', and 'If and only if', some of which are interdefinable. They are represented in the *propositional calculus (PC) in one standard notation as '~', 'ᵥ', '·', '⊃', and '≡', respectively. A class of *well-formed formulae is defined for PC and a definition of *proof which generates the set of *theorems of PC. A desideratum is a system where the set of well-formed formulae of PC which are logical truths are derivable as theorems. This can be shown for PC quasi-syntactically by a method of normal forms. Alternatively, on the semantics of the connectives given by *truth-tables, it can be shown that a formula is a theorem if and only if it is a *tautology. (*Completeness; *consistency; *decision procedure; *decidability.)

There are alternative axiomatizations of PC which generate the same set of theorems. In an axiomatization a theorem is defined as an axiom or derivable from axioms in accordance with the specified rules.

An alternative to axiomatization of PC is to dispense with axioms and to use only rules of inference. (*Natural deduction.) Here a theorem will be a formula derivable from the empty set of premisses.   R.B.M.

B. Mates, *Elementary Logic* (Oxford, 1972).

propositional function. A function from individuals to propositions with a common structure about those individuals, or a formula representing such a function. Thus $C(x)$ might assign *Bach was a composer* to Bach, *Chopin was a composer* to Chopin, and so on. When a *quantifier is prefixed, propositional functions are used to represent general propositions. Thus $\forall x C(x)$ asserts that all $C(x)$ is true for all x, and so represents the false proposition *Everything was a composer.*   W.A.D.

*propositional calculus.

I. M. Copi, *An Introduction to Logic*, 6th edn. (New York, 1982), ch. 10.

proprioception: *see* perception.

Protagoras (c.490–420 BC). The most celebrated of the *Sophists of the fifth century BC, he came from Abdera on the north coast of the Aegean, also the birthplace of Democritus. He travelled widely throughout the Greek world, including several visits to Athens, where he was associated with Pericles, who invited him to write the constitution for the Athenian colony of Thurii. The ancient tradition of his condemnation for impiety and flight from Athens is refuted by Plato's evidence (*Meno* 91e) that he enjoyed a universally high reputation till his death and afterwards. He was famous in antiquity for agnosticism concerning the existence and nature of the gods, and for the doctrine that 'Man is the measure of all things', i.e. the thesis that all

sensory appearances and all beliefs are true for the person whose appearance or belief they are; on the most plausible construal that doctrine attempts to eliminate objectivity and truth altogether. It was attacked by Democritus and Plato (in the *Theaetetus*) on the ground that it is self-refuting; if all beliefs are true, then the belief that it is not the case that all beliefs are true is itself true. While that charge of self-refutation fails because it ignores the relativization of truth in the theory, it may be reinstated as follows: either the theory undermines itself by asserting as an objective truth that there is no objective truth or it merely asserts as a subjective truth that there is no objective truth. But to assert a subjective truth is to make no assertion. So either the theory refutes itself, or it asserts nothing. In the *Protagoras* Plato represents him as maintaining a fairly conservative form of social morality, based on a version of social contract theory; humans need to develop social institutions to survive in a hostile world, and the basic social virtues, justice and self-control, must be generally observed if those institutions are to flourish.   c.c.w.t.

G. B. Kerferd, *The Sophistic Movement* (Cambridge, 1981).

protasis. In a conditional proposition, the 'if' clause, i.e. 'P' in such forms as 'If P, Q', 'Q, if P', '$(P \rightarrow Q)$' or '$(P \dashv 3\, Q)$', is called the protasis, or antecedent, and the main clause 'Q' is called the apodosis, or consequent.   c.a.k.

protocol sentences. According to *Logical Positivism, 'protocol sentences' provide a record of scientific experience which is to be used in assessing theories and hypotheses. In accordance with his *empiricism, Carnap insisted that they should record experience directly, contain nothing which resulted from induction. Whether protocol sentences described *sense-data or were like ordinary observation reports was a matter of controversy which, Carnap eventually held, was to be settled by a decision.   c.j.h.

O. Neurath, 'Protocol Sentences', in A. J. Ayer (ed.), *Logical Positivism* (London, 1959).

Proudhon, Pierre-Joseph (1809–1865). French philosopher and social critic whose book *What is Property?* influenced many nineteenth-century socialists, anarchists, and communists. His famous answer to the question posed by the title of his book is that *'property is theft'. Man, Proudhon believed, is born a social being who seeks justice and equality in all his relations, but large landed estates that create rent for the owner of private property make these impossible. He did not oppose all forms of property. Rather, he believed that small producers and farmers bound together by free contracts were the best safeguards of liberty, justice, and equality. Many of his ideas were adopted by the syndicalist trade union movement. Both Bakunin and Sorel recognized their debt to Proudhon, while Marx attacked many of his ideas as too utopian.

                      J.O.G.

*syndicalism.

George Woodcock, *Pierre-Joseph Proudhon* (London, 1956).

pseudonyms, philosophical. Søren Kierke-gaard's elaborate use of pseudonyms inspires scholarly attention. His motives apparently included the desire to attack under one name his own writings under another. Posterity thereby knows his disdain for the construction of unified systems. Research on the motives of other philosophers who use pseudonyms awaits further identifications of these writers. Here are a few examples. Several anthologies include 'Free Will as Involving Determinism and Inconceivable without It', by 'R. E. Hobart', without mentioning that the author's real name is Dickinson S. Miller. In collections she edits herself, Amélie Oksenberg Rorty sometimes includes essays of her own signed by 'Leila Tov-Ruach'. The author of this entry does not know the real name of the entrant to the *Analysis* Competition 'Problem' No. 10, *Analysis* 17/3 (January 1957), who uses the pseudonym 'Al. Tajtelbaum'. The name is interesting because it belonged originally to the philosopher-logician-mathematician better known as Alfred Tarski.   D.H.S.

pseudo-philosophy consists in deliberations that masquerade as philosophical but are inept, incompetent, deficient in intellectual seriousness, and reflective of an insufficient commitment to the pursuit of truth. In particular, this encompasses discussions that deploy the rational instrumentalities of philosophical reflection in the interests of aims other than serious inquiry—the fostering of power interests or ideological influence or literary éclat or some such. (To be sure, philosophers in general incline to pin this charge of insufficient intellectual seriousness and cogency on those who adhere to rival schools of thought that differ from their own position in matters of fundamental principle.)

Such ineptitude is seldom professed by exponents on their own account but emerges in the objections of opponents. Some key examples are the no-truth theory attributed by the Platonic Socrates to the Sophists of classical antiquity, the conflicting-truth theory attributed to the so-called Averroists by the medieval schoolmen, the radical nihilism sometimes attributed to Renaissance sceptics, and the irrationalism and relativism imputed to existentialists and post-modernists by the more orthodox philosophers of our own day. The more extreme enthusiasts of Derrida-inspired deconstruction afford a graphic case in point. For there is little point in spinning elaborate textual webs to demonstrate that texts never bear any stable interpretative construction. If texts are unable to convey any fixed message, there is clearly no point to any endeavour to convey this lesson by textual means.

The 'pseudo-' label is particularly apt in application to those who use the resources of reason to substantiate the claim that rationality is unachievable in matters of inquiry. For their practice patently belies their teaching. About that which cannot be treated with philosophical cogency, philosophers must needs remain silent.   N.R.

*ideology; pseudo-science; philosophy: world and underworld.

Avner Cohen and Marcelo Dascal (eds.), *The Institution of Philosophy: A Discipline in Crisis* (La Salle, Ill., 1989).
Hugh J. Silverman and Gary E. Aylesworth (eds.), *The Textual Sublime: Deconstruction and its Differences* (Albany, NY, 1990).

pseudo-science. A term of epistemic abuse of variable and disputed content. The most general feature of the situation is one in which one segment of the epistemic community attempts to alert another that certain theses have had conferred on them an epistemic status they do not deserve. Important features of these discussions are at variance with the common philosophical assumption of the centrality of testability. But testability appears not to exonerate, nor its lack to inculpate. If we consult the grounds implicit in adverse appraisals we find that objections are commonly to spurious claims as to the warrantability of a thesis rather than its untestability. Someone who maintains that Cassius was wrong, and that the fault was in our stars but that he could not say which stars, is advancing an untestable thesis, but ought not to be conflated on that account with someone who casts horoscopes.

Another ostensibly pertinent ground is failure to capitulate to repeated falsification reports. But it is conceded both that there are no rules for determining when a thesis should be abandoned and that there have been occasions when those who clung to their theories did well to do so. Moreover, non-capitulation is often a misleading description of a more pernicious practice—that of implying that a thesis has been repeatedly confirmed when the most that has been shown is that it can be reconciled with its apparent falsifiers. Popper's Adler anecdote, in which Adler explains away an apparent refutation on the score of his 'thousandfold experience' and is met with the sarcastic rejoinder, 'And now I suppose your experience is a thousand-and-one fold', illustrates a distinct and more pertinent malpractice than wanton tenacity—that Adler will henceforth illicitly treat his ability to turn the force of a falsifier as further confirmation of the theory.

Neither can capitulation to falsification reports serve as a rebuttal of the charge, for it is not uncommon for exceptions to a general thesis to be generously conceded while the putatively verified instances on which the prestige of the theory depends are without rational justification. Freud's concession that not all dreams are wish-fulfilments in the light of the recurring traumatic dreams of war neurotics does not absolve his dream theory of suspicion if there is reason to think that his reports of confirming instances were the outcome of Procrustean methods of interpretation.

Popper introduced the relevance of the investigator's sincerity. Once it is recognized that the charge of pseudo-science involves not just methodological inadequacy but imponderable judgements about its tendentious motivation, the intractability and longevity of the disputes is less surprising. Those who characterize an epistemic doctrine or practice as pseudo-scientific are normally responding to a *Gestalt* which they may then confusedly rationalize according to whatever view of the nature of science prevails. In the end we may be compelled to say of pseudoscience what Duke Ellington said about jazz—that it is impossible to define because it is a matter of how it sounds.   F.C.

*pseudo-philosophy.

Ernest Gellner, *The Psychoanalytic Movement* (London, 1985).
Terence Hines, *Pseudo-Science and the Paranormal* (Buffalo, NY, 1988).

psyche ('soul'). In ancient philosophy the psyche is the animator of each animated (living) or 'ensouled' thing (*empsukhon*). Plato uses the idea that the psyche is the principle of *life in a famous argument for the immortality of the psyche (*Phaedo* 105c–e). Aristotle, in his *De anima*, counts self-nutrition, reproduction, movement, and perception as 'psychical' powers, as well as thinking, and then speculates that the rational part of the psyche may be separable from the body.   G.B.M.

*soul.

M. Nussbaum and A. Rorty (eds.), *Essays on Aristotle's* De Anima (Oxford, 1992).

psychic research: *see* ESP phenomena, philosophical implications of.

psychoanalysis, philosophical problems of. Philosophers have long debated whether psychoanalysis is a *science, a *pseudo-science, or something *sui generis*. There are many reasons for the longevity of the controversy which are of little philosophic interest. These include a lack of consensus on whether what is in question is a therapeutic or an explanatory enterprise and, if explanatory, which theses are to be considered definitive of it. There is also a general ambiguity. Is substantive or methodological psychoanalysis under discussion? Is the subject such statements as 'the main sources of human character are, for example, the incestuous and sexual conflicts of infancy', or such statements as 'the main formative influences and pathogenic occasions in a person's life can be discovered by the use of a method devised by Freud deploying *dream interpretation, free association, and analysis of the behaviour of the subject in the analytic situation'?

A great deal of discussion has been devoted to testability and kindred notions such as the willingness to capitulate to falsification reports. The lack of consensus on the testability of psychoanalytic theory is due not merely to differing conceptions of psychoanalytic theory but to differing conceptions of testability. Those who hold the theory untestable are often said to have confused the obstinacy of its adherents with the formal properties of 'the theory in itself'. This meets the objection that it is inappropriate to speak of the 'in-itself' of a theory much of which is so neologistic that we can only discover what falsifies it by taking note of what is permitted to count against it, and is so equivocal that almost a century later radically divergent accounts are still given of its commitments. The testability

of psychoanalytic theses is sometimes confused with the testability of statements about the consequences of crediting them. Catholic theology does not become testable because the consequences of pilgrimages to Lourdes are.

The testability of the therapeutic claims themselves is also in dispute because it has been argued that, although a thesis may seem to be indisputably testable where its advocates have in fact modified it in the light of falsifying reports, this does not show the theory to be testable unless the advocates had no discretion in the matter.

In view of these considerations it is understandable that even when precautions are taken to restrict discussion to the same substantive theses, or at least the same verbal formulas, disagreement persists. Some analysts think that Freud's claims about infantile life could be validated by a movie camera (Robert Waelder); others have denied this (Joan Riviere). Some think that Freud's aetiological claims are as epidemiologically testable as those linking smoking to lung cancer (Grunbaum); others do not. The relevance of the outcome of controlled inquiry is in any case bypassed by those who hold that psychoanalytic discourse ought not to be subjected to the same modes of assessment as are conventionally held to characterize sciences such as medical epidemiology. An alternative criterion often invoked, and to which Freud himself frequently appealed, is that of narrative comprehensiveness. Freud holds his infantile sexual aetiology up like the missing piece of a jigsaw puzzle and defies his critics to give an adequate account of the neuroses without it. A disabling assumption of much discussion is that it is the legitimacy of this narrative rationale which divides critics from supporters of psychoanalytic theses; but just as divisive is the conviction that psychoanalytic narratives tend to be unpersuasive or tendentious.

Another mode of validation whose merits have been debated is that of therapeutic efficacy. Therapeutic efficacy is incapable by its nature of warranting the historicity of a reconstruction or the veridicality of an interpretation; these may be false and the therapy based on them nevertheless efficacious, just as they may be true but therapeutically unhelpful. A further, though philosophically redundant, difficulty is that the appeal to therapeutic results played a nugatory role in the controversies. Freud himself seemed to have little confidence in it since he normally met the suggestibility objection by denying that he had any prior conviction which might have influenced his patients' responses, and by invoking data such as the fantasies of psychotics, or the anonymous productions of culture in which contamination was presumed not to operate. Where it was the generality of his conclusions about infantile life that were disputed, it was maintained that these had been confirmed (and the method thus vindicated) by the direct observation of children.

Another much discussed issue is whether unconscious wishes are *reasons or causes. The substantive question 'Are unconscious wishes like reasons?' must be distinguished from 'Are even rationalizing wishes deterministically related to the behaviour they rationalize?' Put otherwise, the first question is whether the hysteric, say, stands in relation to his symptoms as a malingerer to his deceptive performances, except that he is not consciously monitoring them, or whether repressed wishes act, rather, like psychic splinters and the symptoms they produce are thus conceptually analogous to inflammations. Whether the assimilation of causes to reasons is justifiable has no bearing on this question, which can only be resolved by an inspection of the grounds proffered for believing an unconscious wish operative, and these vary.

The pertinent question is thus: What makes an explanatory narrative credible? This in turn resolves into two distinct problems: the degree of circumstantiality required to support a causal narrative, or to warrant a choice between narratives, and the degree to which the subject's epistemic authority (belated in the case of analytic accounts) allows us to dispense with both laws and circumstantiality.

The first problem is one of devising rules of thumb for judging the goodness of a case for a causal connection when all we have to go on is the circumstantial density of a narrative (and perhaps its analogy to better-attested, less questionable ones).

The second problem is that of deciding, in cases where narrative coherence is insufficiently probative, whether its probative value can be enhanced, or even replaced, by the endorsement of the subject. Is not Shylock the arbiter of the sources of his resentment of Antonio? Why then can we not allow that someone who is initially ignorant of the sources of his attitudes, propensities, vulnerabilities, etc. might not ultimately come to stand in relation to them as Shylock continuously did to his murderous resentment? The assessment of this argument requires delicate taxonomizing not often in evidence. Apologists have often claimed for Freud's narratives virtues which he did not consistently claim for them himself, appealing rather to unreproducible nuances of the psychoanalytic interaction. This raises a distinct issue: What makes a narrator credible? This absolves those who insist on discussing the credibility of psychoanalytic narrators of gratuitously personalizing the issue.

Beyond the dispute over whether the knowledge psychoanalysis aims to provide is to be judged by natural science or humanistic standards looms another: whether epistemic criteria of either kind are in order. It is held that, however matters may stand with respect to vulgar notions of correspondence truth, psychoanalysis has provided vistas whose poetic truth is beyond reproach. F.C.

*stories and explanation; unconscious and subconscious mind.

Behaviour and Brain Research (1986). Précis and peer group review of Grunbaum's Foundations of Psychoanalysis.

F. Cioffi, 'Wollheim on Freud', Inquiry (1972).

Peter Clark and Crispin Wright (eds.), Mind, Psychoanalysis and Science (London, 1988).

R. Wollheim, Freud, 2nd edn. (London, 1990).

psychologism. Acceptance of some or all of the following commitments jointly define a psychologistic outlook: a belief that logical laws are 'laws of thought', i.e. psychological laws; a conflation of truth with verification; a belief that the private data of consciousness provide the correct starting-point for epistemology; and belief that the meanings of words are ideas. Gottlob Frege rejected all these theses, and therefore much of prevailing nineteenth-century germanophone philosophy. His criticisms converted Edmund Husserl to anti-psychologism. They have been profoundly influential in anglophone *analytic philosophy. A.C.G.

M. A. E. Dummett, Frege: Philosophy of Language, 2nd edn. (London, 1981), ch. 5.

psychology and philosophy. Psychology, for most of its history, coincided with the philosophy of mind. Everyday reflections on one's own thoughts and deeds and on the behaviour—bodily motions, verbal and otherwise—of others lead naturally to speculations concerning the springs of action. Such speculations, refined and systematized, are prominent in the writings of Plato and Aristotle, and in the philosophical tradition that runs from them through Descartes, Hobbes, Hume, Kant, and James, to our own day. Along the way, psychology as a self-standing discipline gradually condensed from the philosophical fog. Recent years have seen a partial reversal of this process as philosophers, anxious to attain scientific respectability, have sought to psychologize philosophy under the banner of *'cognitive science'.

While it is convenient to date the onset of psychology's emancipation from philosophy from 1879, the year Wilhelm Wundt established the first psychological laboratory at the University of Leipzig, it was well into the twentieth century before psychology became generally recognized as a distinguishable academic speciality. Even today, however, it is easy to find parallels in empirical psychology to virtually any philosophical view of the mind. This is scarcely surprising. Our conception of the mental as comprising a distinctive subject-matter, one that includes perceiving, knowing, imagining, planning, and the initiating of action, is a philosophical staple. Psychology emerged as a science once questions about such things began to be formulated in a way that demanded empirical investigation. Thus Hume, impressed by Newton, advanced associative principles designed to account for familiar mental operations and to set the study of *'human nature' on an appropriately scientific footing. Hume holds that ideas—mentalistic counterparts of material particles—attract one another in accordance with three simple associative principles: resemblance, contiguity, cause and effect.

Hume was not the first associationist, nor was he the last. Clark Hull's conception of stimulus–response bonds and B. F. Skinner's notion of reinforcement put a behaviourist spin on *associationism. More recently, advocates of 'connectionist' or 'neural network' accounts of the mind, abjuring *behaviourism, have advanced mathematically sophisticated associationist models of cognitive and perceptual processes. These compete with computational approaches traceable to Hobbes.

Early psychologists wore their philosophical commitments on their sleeves. William James's *Principles of Psychology* (1890) mingles chapters on the brain, instinct, and hypnotism with chapters advancing views on the *mind–body problem, and E. B. Titchener's debt to the atomistic, sensationalistic doctrines of the British Empiricists in *Lectures on the Experimental Psychology of the Thought Processes* (1904) is explicit. Nowadays psychologists are less aware of, or at any rate less willing to acknowledge, their philosophical roots.

The ongoing influence of philosophical theses might be thought to provide a partial explanation of the fitful, two-steps-forward, one-step-back quality of theoretical advance in psychology, but it would be naïve to imagine that the discipline might be streamlined simply by writing out the philosophers. The exclusion of philosophers does not amount to the exclusion of philosophical presuppositions, and wholesale elimination of these presuppositions, in eliminating as well everything that depends on them, would amount to changing the subject. Still, it is widely believed that philosophy, *qua* philosophy, has little to offer physics, biology, or medicine. Why, then, should anyone imagine that philosophers *are* in a position to offer advice about the nature of *mind? Perhaps minds are distinctive, different from hearts, or livers, or the amino acids. But why should anyone presume this to be so?

The question is not whether imaginary disciplinary boundaries between philosophy and the empirical sciences are to be enforced, but whether the relation between philosophy and psychology is, or has been, or must be, special. According to one influential view, emanating from the work of Wittgenstein and aggressively promoted by D. C. Dennett, psychology presupposes a discredited Cartesian conception of mind according to which mental states and processes occur in private. Our access to mental items is asymmetrical: you observe the contents of your own mind directly, I can only infer those contents from what you say and do. Such a picture frustrates both philosophers, bent on resolving epistemological and metaphysical puzzles, and psychologists, who seek scientific legitimacy for their inquiries.

Skinner, following John B. Watson in turning *empiricism on its head, declared that, because we observe only behaviour, reference to inferred mental causes of behaviour must be eliminated. Psychological explanation, then, amounts to the correlation of environmental contingencies and subsequent behavioural responses. On the philosophical front, Gilbert Ryle in *The Concept of Mind* (1949) attacked the 'Cartesian Myth' on very different grounds. Ryle held that descriptions of mental goings-on are descriptions of what agents say and do (or are apt to say and do), not descriptions of hidden occurrences causally responsible for sayings and doings. Although Ryle is often called a behaviourist, the arguments he deploys have little in common with those used in support of the psychological doctrine of the same name.

The 'functionalist' conception of mind, traceable to Aristotle, fine-tuned by Hilary Putnam, D. M. Armstrong,

and Jerry Fodor, and now beloved of philosophers and psychologists alike, can be seen as a direct descendant of Ryle's anti-Cartesianism. *Functionalism, as a replacement for psychological *behaviourism, however, has proved attractive in part owing to the increasing prominence of the digital computing machine. Perhaps the brain resembles such a device. Were that so, we could assume that minds are 'realized' in brains just as programs are 'realized' in computing machines. To engage in psychology, on such a view, is to seek to discover by empirical means the brain's program. A view of this sort promises simultaneously to liberate psychology from traditional metaphysical worries about the mind and its relation to the body, and to provide it with a subject-matter distinct from neurophysiology and biology.

Although psychologists have been on the whole happy with these results, functionalism is under fire in philosophy. In characterizing mental items exclusively by reference to actual and possible inputs and outputs, functionalism evidently ignores their qualitative dimension. In the earliest accounts of the doctrine, this was touted as a virtue, a way of factoring out spooky mental *qualia and allowing for the 'multiple realizability' of mental characteristics. (A characteristic is multiply realizable if it is capable of being embodied in very different sorts of physical system: human brains, computing machines, possible alien silicon-based 'brains'.) Recently, however, Thomas Nagel, Frank Jackson, David Chalmers and others have argued that any account of the mind must accommodate non-material mental qualities, exhibited in *consciousness. Some of these arguments are intended to encourage us to return to a fundamentally Cartesian conception of mind, a conception not unlike that embraced by Wundt and Titchener in the earliest days of experimental psychology. Does this portend the reintroduction into psychology of non-physical entities? Perhaps not. Perhaps it is simply a reflection of a powerful conviction that, as C. B. Martin puts it, 'every quantity stands in need of a quality'. The subjectivity of consciousness poses additional problems. Conscious awareness incorporates a point of view inaccessible to objective scientific investigation. Some, like Colin McGinn, have despaired at finding a home for points of view in the natural world; others—Ted Honderich, for instance—locate subjectivity in perfectly natural relations which perceivers bear to their environments.

Such considerations make it clear that the historical break between philosophy and psychology was never a clean one. Psychologists continue to look over their shoulders at philosophers, and philosophers continue to offer advice to psychologists. There is no reason to think that it should always be this way, but there is no reason to suppose that things are destined to change much in the foreseeable future.   J.HEIL

*consciousness;   epistemology   and   psychology; dualism; qualia.

D. J. Chalmers, *The Conscious Mind* (New York, 1996).

D. C. Dennett, *Consciousness Explained* (Boston, 1991).

B. A. Farrell, 'Experience', *Mind*, 59 (1950).

R. J. Herrnstein and E. G. Boring (eds.), *A Source Book in the History of Psychology* (Cambridge, Mass., 1965).

T. Honderich, 'Consciousness as Existence', in A. O'Hear (ed.), *Current Issues in the Philosophy of Mind* (Cambridge, 1998).

F. Jackson, 'Epiphenomenal Qualia', *Philosophical Quarterly* (1982).

T. H. Leahey, *A History of Psychology*, 6th edn. (Upper Saddle River, NJ, 2003).

C. B. Martin, 'The Need for Ontology: Some Choices', *Philosophy*, 68 (1993).

C. McGinn, 'Can We Solve the Mind–Body Problem?', *Mind* (1989).

T. Nagel, 'What Is it Like to Be a Bat?', *Philosophical Review* (1974).

Hilary Putnam, 'The Nature of Mental States', in *Mind, Language, and Reality* (Cambridge, 1975).

psychoneural intimacy. The term is used to describe what is generally recognized to be the close tie between neural events and mental events. It is held that there is a necessary co-occurrence of some sort between types of mental events and types of neural events. The thesis of psychoneural intimacy is compatible with most of the doctrines put forward in the literature concerning the relationship between mental events and physical events—but not some that radically separate mind and brain, perhaps to safeguard free will. Most doctrines of the psychoneural relation can be read as different proposals about the nature of the necessity involved.   P.J.P.N.

*mind–body problem.

T. Honderich, *A Theory of Determinism: The Mind, Neuroscience and Life-Hopes* (Oxford, 1988), ch. 2.

psychophysical laws. Putative natural *laws reporting regular or necessary relationships between mental events and physical events. For example, if, as Honderich maintains, the occurrence of some neurological event is a sufficient condition for the occurrence of some psychological event (and, as is entailed by this, the occurrence of that psychological event is a necessary condition for the occurrence of that neurological event), then arguably some psychophysical law could be discovered which would facilitate the prediction of psychological events from knowledge of neurological events, because true neurological sentences would logically entail the occurrence of psychological events.

Not only Honderich's physicalistic *determinism but certain versions of the mind–brain *identity theory logically imply the existence of psychophysical laws. Some philosophers have maintained that types of mental event may be identified with types of physical process in the brain (or central nervous system) and that there is no a priori reason why predictive inferences about mental event-types should not be drawn from premisses about physical event-types. Unfortunately such type identifications have proved most difficult to establish empirically.

On a token version of the mind–brain identity theory it is less plausible that there should exist psychophysical laws. Although, on this theory, any token mental event is numerically identical with some token neurological event, it does not follow that qualitatively similar mental events are numerically identical with qualitatively similar neurological events. From the fact, then, that an event of some specifiable neurological type had occurred it would not follow that an event of some specifiable psychological type had occurred (even though it would still follow that a psychological event of some psychological type had occurred). Donald Davidson, for example, argues that, although every mental event is numerically identical with some physical event and although every event (including every mental event) may be subsumed under some natural law, nevertheless there are no psychophysical laws. This is because it is *qua* physical events, not *qua* mental events, that mental events are law-governed, and even a complete knowledge of physical events would not facilitate predictions of (specifiable) types of mental event.

All the philosophical problems accruing to natural laws accrue *a fortiori* to psychophysical laws. For example, whether natural laws are causal laws, Humean regularities, relations between *universals, essentially predictive, or descriptive of necessities are all also questions about psychophysical laws. Deciding whether there are psychophysical laws and if so what they are like requires specifying correctly the ontology of the psychophysical relation. However, their existence is consistent with most traditional solutions to the *mind–body problem.   S.P.

*anomalous monism.

Donald Davidson, 'Mental Events', in *Essays on Actions and Events* (Oxford, 1980).

Ted Honderich, *A Theory of Determinism: The Mind, Neuroscience and Life-Hopes* (Oxford, 1988).

Stephen Priest, *Theories of the Mind* (London, 1991).

public morality. As traditionally understood, the 'police powers' of government extend to the protection of public health, safety, *and morals*. Legislation to protect public morals prohibits or restricts acts and practices judged to be damaging to the character and moral well-being of persons who engage in them or who may be induced to engage in them by the bad example of others. Typical forms of 'morals legislation' prohibit or restrict prostitution, pornography, and other forms of sexual vice, as well as gambling, cruelty to animals, and the recreational use of drugs.

In recent times, the legitimacy of such legislation has come under severe attack from certain forms of liberal political thought. Under pressure from 'law reform' movements inspired by the philosophy of J. S. Mill and others, many jurisdictions have decriminalized a variety of putatively 'victimless' offences.

In the early 1960s the legitimacy of morals laws, particularly the legal prohibition of consensual homosexual sodomy, was the subject of a celebrated debate between two eminent British jurists: Patrick Devlin defended 'legal moralism' on the ground that a society is constituted in significant measure by the sharing of moral beliefs by its members and that the legal toleration of acts condemned by a society's constitutive morality puts that society at risk of disintegration. Therefore, Devlin argued, a society has the right to enforce the morality prevailing within it, irrespective of the critical soundness of that morality, for the sake of preserving social cohesion. H. L. A. Hart countered that Devlin's 'social disintegration thesis' was either an empty 'conceptual' thesis which trivially identifies society with whatever moral views happen at the moment to be dominant in a community, or else it was an 'empirical' thesis which historical evidence fails to vindicate.

Contemporary defenders of morals legislation typically eschew Devlin's approach in favour of the traditional justification of morals legislation under which its primary purpose is not social cohesion *per se*, but, rather, the protection of morally good character against the corrupting influences of vice. Thus, they reject Devlin's *relativism and understand the critical soundness of a moral judgement to be a necessary condition of its justified legal enforcement.   R.P.G.

*liberalism; liberty; toleration; public–private distinction; enforcement of morals.

Patrick Devlin, *The Enforcement of Morals* (London, 1965).
Robert P. George, *Making Men Moral: Civil Liberties and Public Morality* (Oxford, 1993).
H. L. A. Hart, *Law, Liberty, and Morality* (Stanford, Calif., 1963).
D. A. J. Richards, *Sex, Drugs, Death, and the Law* (Totowa, NJ, 1982).

public–private distinction. Privacy is an important, though a recent and by no means a universal, value. Analyses of it are dominated by liberal conceptions of a 'private sphere' which sets normative and empirical limits to state and social power over the individual. In his private life the individual is not and should not be regulated by laws or subject to social pressure; in public life he shares, assents to, or anyway obeys, norms and laws governing his relations with others, and accepts social and political authority.

Conceptions of the boundary between public and private have altered. Economic relations have been understood to be private, and their legal regulation resisted. Now 'the family' epitomizes the private sphere. However, the implication that family relations are not and should not be regulated by the state or subject to shared, publicly accepted standards of morality is contested.   E.J.F.

*liberalism; liberty; public morality.

Carole Pateman, 'Feminist Critiques of the Public/Private Dichotomy', in S. Benn and G. Gaus (eds.), *Public and Private in Social Life* (London, 1983); repr. in Carole Pateman, *The Disorder of Women* (Cambridge, 1989).

publishing philosophy. The Greek word for bookseller dates from the time of Plato, who foreshadowed the alliance between philosophers and publishers when he prescribed his own work the *Laws* as the set text for study in the ideal city it describes. Cicero's friend Atticus was one of those who made a business of the copying and distribution of books in the ancient world. In the early Roman Empire some books were priced as low as six sesterces; Cicero had claimed that a feeble slave could earn

three sesterces a day at Rome. Nor did mass production await the age of printing: the emperor Constantine ordered multiple copies of works by Christian writers for dissemination through his empire.

At some medieval universities students were required to own copies of their teacher's lectures, and they might pay someone to supply them with a copy. In 1304, thirty years after Aquinas's death, his *Quaestiones disputatae de veritate* could be rented from a Paris bookseller for four shillings. But, since the work runs to more than a thousand pages, a substantial burden of labour remained. Aquinas's output of eight million words in thirty years is equivalent, in today's terms, to two substantial monographs per annum and a few journal articles too.

Descartes moved to Leiden in 1636 specifically to be at the centre of publishing. The liberal Dutch laws had allowed the Elseviers to become the leading publishers of the time; they numbered Galileo among their authors, and had expressed interest in Descartes's work. But they 'made difficulties' for him, and so it was their neighbour Jan Maire who became known to posterity as the publisher of the *Discours*. The print run was 3,000, out of which Descartes received 200 free copies.

The late seventeenth century saw the flourishing of learned journals. Until 1710, that was where one had to look to find Leibniz's work: he first published his 'New System' in 1695 in the *Journal des savants* (the official organ of the French Academy of Sciences, founded in 1666); he also wrote in Latin for such journals as the Leipzig-based *Acta eruditorum*.

Spinoza dared not let his greatest work, the *Ethics*, be published while he was alive, and sought refuge in pseudonymy for his *Tractatus Theologico-Politicus* of 1670; just as well, since it was generally considered blasphemous. More surprising, perhaps, that Kant too was the author of a banned book: in 1794 King Frederick William II's Spiritual Affairs Commission issued an order forbidding professors to lecture on his *Religion within the Bounds of Mere Reason*. Kant had published it under the imprint of the Königsberg philosophy faculty in order to avoid censorship.

The three greatest works of English-language philosophy were published in London. Thomas Hobbes entrusted his *Leviathan* to Andrew Crooke, who was to be found at the sign of the Green Dragon in the precinct of St Paul's cathedral. The controversy over the book both aroused demand and made the publisher nervous about satisfying it, with the result that the price rose from eight and a half shillings in 1651 to thirty in 1668, before settling at seventeen in 1692. The notoriety of *Leviathan* made publishing difficult for Hobbes: after 1662 he was obliged to seek a licence from the Archbishop of Canterbury for the publication of any work on politics or society; and in the case of *Behemoth* this was refused, even though the work was a favourite of the king.

Thirty-eight years after *Leviathan*, Locke's *Essay* was first printed by Elizabeth Holt in 1689 for the publisher Thomas Bassett, at the George in Fleet Street, just down the road from St Paul's. Locke had signed a contract with Bassett in May 1689; printing began immediately, and copies were on sale by the end of the year. By 1700 the book was in its fifth edition, with another publisher, the rights having been sold on twice before the second edition.

The first two books of Hume's *Treatise* were published by John Noon in 1739, at the White Hart in Cheapside, on the other side of the cathedral. Noon specialized in philosophy and religion, and paid Hume £50 for the right to print an edition of no more than 1,000 copies. By the time the third book appeared in the following year, Thomas Longman had already supplanted Noon as publisher. Some were more loyal: the Paris publisher Rey was one of the few people whom Rousseau did not suspect of scheming against him, and voluntarily settled an annuity of 300 francs on Rousseau's 'womenfolk' in grateful acknowledgement that the publisher owed his prosperity to the philosopher.

Up to the middle of the twentieth century, much philosophy publishing in English was undertaken by general commercial presses, British and American. But as philosophy books have become more specialist, they have mainly been handled by specialist publishers. Large commercial presses like Penguin and Harper Collins occasionally show interest in the subject, but most philosophy books are published either by specialists in academic publishing or by specialists in textbook publishing. One or two of the European giants of science publishing, such as Kluwer of Dordrecht, dabble in philosophy, usually at the technical end of the subject where it is most like a science.

At the start of the twenty-first century there are two large commercial presses with a strength in philosophy. Blackwell built on its prestige as publisher of Wittgenstein and disciples to head the field for a period in the 1980s, but in the 1990s decided to concentrate mainly on textbook, reference, and journal publishing. Routledge now publishes a broader range of philosophy than any other press, having inherited a legacy of works by such as Russell, Popper, and Wittgenstein from companies that it swallowed. In 1922 Kegan Paul had offered Wittgenstein no fee and no royalties for the English publication of his *Tractatus*; when the author tried to negotiate some money at the time of a reprint in 1933, he received no reply, and so that was the end of his dealings with the company. In 1998 Routledge was itself taken over by an ancient publishing company, long moribund, now growing fast: Taylor and Francis, then still auspiciously located just off Fleet Street. One of the parent company's founders, Richard Taylor, had established a pioneering independent academic journal, the *Philosophical Magazine*, in 1798.

Most publishers of academic philosophy today are university presses, helped or hindered in their business by their relationships with their parent institutions. The university presses of Oxford and Cambridge are the largest and most international of academic philosophy publishers. CUP claims to be the oldest university press in the world, having published its first book in 1584, just in time for the birth of modern philosophy. Their leading American counterparts are Harvard and Princeton; others have

strengths in specific areas—for instance, MIT in cognitive science, Chicago in social and political theory, Cornell in aesthetics and philosophy of religion. In 2002 the University of California Press withdrew from philosophy publishing, despite the university's continuing prominence in the subject: increasing difficulties in the academic book market were cited.

Charges frequently made against academic publishers are that they encourage the proliferation of books beyond what the readership can cope with, and that they sell back to universities books that the universities have paid their members to write. But it was the universities that built publication into the career structure for academics. And any profiteer would be scared off by the margins in philosophy publishing.

The electronic revolution in publishing is proceeding more slowly than predicted by zealots and Jeremiahs. Paper will continue to be the principal commercial medium for philosophy publishing for a while yet, even though informal electronic dissemination has become a staple of philosophical intercourse.

Most philosophers who publish several books do not stick with one publisher for all of them; they optimistically hope that the next one will be free of the shortcomings of the last. But monogamy is less meaningful when it can only be one-way. And a good publishing relationship may even be refreshed by the author's straying into an unsuitable dalliance. To complicate matters, philosophy editors often turn out to be consorts of philosophers; which of those blessed estates leads to the other varies from case to case.   P.N.M.

Pufendorf, Samuel von (1632–94). German legal and political philosopher. A follower, at some distance, of Grotius and Hobbes, he carried on their project of secularizing natural law. Other, less direct, influences were Descartes and Spinoza, from whom he derived a mathematical ideal of philosophical exposition. A Protestant, in his first book he attacked the (Catholic) Holy Roman Empire. He served as court librarian to the king of Sweden, during twenty years in that country, and then to the elector of Brandenburg. Nevertheless he entertained the idea of a European federation. While in Sweden he wrote a history of the country which was exemplary in its reliance on archival materials. His chief work, *The Law of Nature and Nations* (1672), firmly distinguishes natural law from divine law. He consistently concluded that in terrestrial matters the church should be subordinate to the state. Like Althusius, he argues for two contracts: one to form a community out of mere individuals, the other between the community so formed and a ruler. Where Hobbes derived the law of nature from our fear of violent death at each others' hands, Pufendorf more cheerfully deduced it from man's sociable instinct.   A.Q.

Leonard Krieger, *The Politics of Discretion* (Chicago, 1965).

punishment. Since punishment involves intentionally inflicting deprivations on persons by someone with authority to do so, and since the deprivations themselves are typically not unlike the harms that crimes cause (fines are like theft, imprisonment like kidnapping, etc.), punishment has generally been thought to need justification, especially in a constitutional democracy committed in theory to the protection of human rights and the values of individual liberty, privacy, and autonomy. Justification may be undertaken either by reference to extrinsic (consequentialist) considerations, or by reference to intrinsic (retributive) factors.

In an effort to accommodate both retributive and consequentialist norms, some recent theories justify punishment by dividing the issue in a manner reflecting the different competencies of an ideal legislature and judge. Thus, the primary concern amounts to answering a legislative question: Why is *anyone* punished, or made liable to punishment, in the first place? The secondary issue is in effect the judicial question: Why is *this* person being punished, and in why in *this* manner?

The former can be answered best by citing the benefits conferred on a society (family, organization, civil polity) by the institution of punishment as a permanent, public threat-system that provides an indispensable incentive to obey the law. In so far as the justification of punishment is conceived in this manner, it is inescapably forward-looking, purposive, and consequentialist in nature (though not necessarily utilitarian).

Assuming such a system to be in place, with its various offices (judges, prosecutors) and rules (crimes and punishments defined by statute, due process of law), then the punishment of a given individual is justified to the extent that the rules of the system incorporate appropriate constraints on trials and sentencing and are correctly applied to the individual case. Central to such rules is the procedure by which the accused is found guilty of a crime on the basis of suitable evidence weighed in an unbiased manner. If the actual infliction of punishment is understood in this fashion, it is always backward-looking (resting on the conviction and sentencing of a guilty offender) and thus plausibly viewed as retributive.

Retribution accommodated in this narrow manner falls far short of its role in a full-blown retributive theory of punishment, such as Kant's or Hegel's. They appeal to retributive notions not only to determine who ought to be punished, but also to determine what punishment the guilty person deserves and the very rationale for a system of punishment in the first place. Deserved punishment for the retributivist is equivalent (as in *lex talionis*) or at least proportional in its severity to the harm done in the crime and the culpability of the offender. The retributive rationale of a system of punishment is that justice requires inflicting harm on wrongdoers. Whether such an a priori principle as this can be defended against alternative (typically consequentialist) principles continues to be debated.

The goals or purposes of any system of punishment are likely to be several and diverse, including vindicating the law, crime prevention, and offender rehabilitation. Philosophical disputes over punishment typically focus on

which goal is to take priority over others and why. As Friedrich Nietzsche shrewdly observed, 'punishment is overdetermined by utilities of every kind' (*Genealogy of Morals*, II. 14). He failed to note that the penalty schedule—the actual ordering of crimes ranked in their gravity with punishments ranked in their severity—is underdetermined by every theory of punishment. The two-tiered theory described above can reasonably claim to offer the most hospitable accommodation to the diverse relevant principles, but it provides no solution to this problem.   H.A.B.

*capital punishment; desert.

R. A. Duff, *Trials and Punishments* (Cambridge, 1986).
—— and D. Garland (eds.), *A Reader on Punishment* (Oxford, 1995).
David Garland, *Punishment and Modern Society: A Study in Social Theory* (Chicago, 1990).
Ted Honderich, *Punishment: The Supposed Justifications* (Cambridge, 1989).
C. L. Ten, *Crime, Guilt, and Punishment* (Oxford, 1987).

punishment, capital: *see* capital punishment.

pushpin and poetry is a critical slogan popularized by J. S. Mill in criticism of the work of Bentham. (Pushpin was a primitive game which involved shoving pins.) Mill cites Bentham as holding that *poetry is no more valuable than pushpin, if they give the same amount of *pleasure. This is in accord with the principle of *utility. However, Bentham's point when he made the remark was not about private value but that the two activities should be equally worthy of governmental subsidy if they give the same amount of pleasure.   R.H.

J. Bentham, *The Rationale of Reward* (London, 1825), 206.
J. S. Mill, 'Bentham', in *Works*, x. 113.

Putnam, Hilary (1926–). Harvard philosopher, trained originally in the tradition of *Logical Positivism, especially by Rudolph Carnap. Putnam later came under the influence of such philosophers as W. V. Quine, Ludwig Wittgenstein, and Nelson Goodman. In the process, he strayed from the fold, and eventually became a severe critic of that movement. Against positivism, he argues that there is no privileged foundation (e.g. *sense-data) to our knowledge, no fixed principle of verifiability, no *fact–value distinction as the positivists characterized it, and that sentences (our beliefs) cannot be assessed as true or false individually (i.e. *holism rather than atomism is correct).

Putnam is also a critic of another foundationalist position, which he calls metaphysical realism. All God's eye points of view that claim to give us *the* account of the Furniture of the World are wrong-headed whether they come from a relativist–positivist or a realist–materialist perspective. His own 'middle' position he characterizes as 'internal realism'. It is a kind of latter-day *Kantianism that talks about the (real) world, but does so always within the framework of our mind (concepts, sets of beliefs, commitments). His position, Putnam claims, characterizes the objectivity of both science and ethics better than do the extreme positions he opposes. If anything, these extreme views undermine rather than support objectivity.

Of late, Putnam has rejected *functionalism, the theory that mental states are computational states—a theory he himself founded earlier in his career. Of late he has also written about matters of ethics and politics. Like his views in metaphysics and epistemology, he tends to want to hold a middle, yet somewhat liberal, position between two extremes—although he confesses there were times (e.g. during the Vietnam War) when he flirted with Marxism, a position he now finds extreme.   N.F.

*verification principle.

Hilary Putnam, *Representation and Reality* (Cambridge, Mass., 1988).
—— *Realism with a Human Face* (Cambridge, Mass., 1990).
—— *Renewing Philosophy* (Cambridge, Mass., 1992).

Pyrrho (4th–3rd century BC). A citizen, and priest, of Elis, identified (through the writings of Timon of Phlius) as the first representative of 'Pyrrhonian *scepticism', the refusal to commit oneself to any positive belief. Anecdotes were told of his indifference to disaster (and his friends' saving him from accidental falls). He was said to have accompanied Alexander to the borders of India and learned this detachment from the 'gymnosophists', or naked philosophers. Like Diogenes the *Cynic he pointed to animals as living undisturbed, and enviable, lives: a pig on board ship during a severe storm continued to eat while people (except Pyrrho) panicked. Mocked for being alarmed by a fierce dog, he conceded that it was hard to strip off human nature, but attempted to maintain tranquillity by balancing any plausible-sounding thesis with its plausible opposite, and binding himself to nature, custom, impulse, and craft-discipline without affirming any thesis to be true.   S.R.L.C.

Myles Burnyeat and Michael Frede (eds.), *The Original Sceptics: A Controversy* (New York, 1997).
Diogenes Laertius, *Lives of the Philosophers*, tr. R. D. Hicks (London, 1925).

Pyrrhonism. A sceptical tradition whose leading figure was Pyrrho of Elis (c.365–270 BC), but handed down to us in the works of Sextus Empiricus. Pyrrho argued that the reasons in favour of a belief are never better than those against (*isostheneia*—a situation of equal strength), and that the only possible response to this is to stop worrying (*ataraxia*) and to live by the appearances. He suggested that this life would have a lot to recommend it; critics maintained that it would be very uncomfortable, at best. The question who was right depends on what is meant by 'live by the appearances'.

Sextus' work was rediscovered in the mid-sixteenth century; the sceptical concerns of Montaigne and Descartes are a direct response, though Cartesian scepticism seems to be directed more against the possibility of knowledge than against the possibility of having better reasons in favour of some belief than against it.   J.D.

*scepticism, history of; scepticism.

J. Annas and J. Barnes (eds.), *The Modes of Scepticism: Ancient Texts and Modern Interpretations* (Cambridge, 1985).

Pythagoras (c.550–c.500 BC). An elusive figure who may have been an intellectual catalyst. Little is known of his life; authentic detail has been drowned in the many legends and tendentious later 'reconstructions' of his activities. A polymath and a charismatic figure, he emigrated from his native Samos to southern Italy, where he founded a sect characterized by common beliefs and observances. These included prescriptive rules (such as a ban on the eating of beans and certain meats), the preservation and pursuit of esoteric knowledge, and reverence for the founder himself.

Modern scepticism about the alleged political, philosophical, mathematical, and scientific achievements of Pythagoras is mostly justifiable. The earliest sources present him primarily as a magician claiming 'occult' or mystical experiences like those of a Siberian shaman. On this basis he asserted 'metempsychosis', a doctrine of repeated incarnations of souls, with punishments and rewards for behaviour in previous lives.

Apart from this, no definite meaning attaches to the term '(early) Pythagorean'. The original society did not last long, but throughout the fifth century BC (and even after) various theorists in the western Greek world were called 'Pythagoreans'. Many of these were interested in mathematics and astronomy, and their cosmic or occult significance; the interest may go back to Pythagoras himself. Some apparently attempted to reduce all knowledge to mathematics (using such identifications as 'Justice is the number 4'). Systematic dualism of associated polarities (right = male = good, left = female = bad, etc.) is also attested. Pythagorean influence, in this wider sense, appears in Parmenides and Empedocles, and later in Plato and the Neoplatonists.   E.L.H.

*Pythagoreanism.

W. Burkert, *Lore and Science in Early Pythagoreanism*, tr. E. L. Minar (Cambridge, Mass., 1972).

Pythagoreanism. Way of life and doctrines attributed to Pythagoras. There were proponents of Pythagoreanism for at least eight centuries from Pythagoras' day, but there was no persisting core of Pythagorean doctrines. From the fourth century BC onwards, teachings from other schools were borrowed and regularly attributed to Pythagoras himself. This, together with our lack of early writings, makes it hard to discover the original nature of the school.

There was, reportedly, an early split between those for whom Pythagoreanism was a way of life, something like a religion, and those for whom it was a body of scientific, mathematical, and philosophical teaching. The ethical and religious teachings were broadly puritanical, often bizarre, and of little philosophical interest. Pythagorean contributions to geometry were reputedly great, but their extent is uncertain. Aristotle records some of the philosophical doctrines, notably that numbers are 'the first things in the whole of nature', and that 'the elements of numbers are the elements of all things'. Pythagoreans knew that concordant musical intervals (octave, fourth, and fifth) could be expressed by arithmetical ratios. This may have led them to believe that the universe as a whole could be explained and understood in mathematical terms—an idea that has since proved remarkably fruitful. But Aristotle understood their theory as confused: they represented things as *composed* of numbers, and failed to 'separate' the numbers from the things numbered. Aristotle may be right about the crudeness of early Pythagorean thought. But there is earlier evidence of some subtlety of argument.

Philolaus (born *c.*470 BC) was the first to write down Pythagorean doctrines, and a few fragments of his work survive. Among his conclusions are that the 'being' of things is eternal, and 'admits of divine, but not human, knowledge'; and that 'all the things that are known have number'. Evidently he held that *human* knowledge was possible only of things that can be numbered. His reasoning seems to be this. Anything that can be known must have limits (spatial or temporal) to distinguish it from everything else. But things thus distinguishable from one another may be counted. The universe *as we know it*, then, must consist of things that can be counted. He also argued that the universe must contain 'limiting things' and 'unlimited things', united by 'harmony'. Perhaps he thought that only if things of one sort had imposed limits on things of the other could there be 'things with limits' (and hence knowable things). But his words are obscure and their interpretation disputed.

Some early Pythagoreans believed that the soul was an 'attunement', like that of a lyre. This suggests that to have a soul is to have one's bodily components related to one another in a certain (mathematically expressible) way. This, however, seems inconsistent with the well-attested Pythagorean belief in reincarnation.

Plato's successors attributed much of his thought to Pythagoras. No doubt Plato *was* influenced by Pythagoreans, for example, in his views on immortality in the *Phaedo* and his exercise in mathematical cosmology in *Timaeus*, but his philosophical debt was probably small. After Plato, 'Pythagoreanism' became in effect a brand of Platonism, with emphasis on number theory and the more mystical aspects of his thought.

In the first century BC there was a revival of the school (often called neo-Pythagoreanism), from which many writings survive. These contain a medley of teachings from various schools. What marks them as Pythagorean is their religious rather than their philosophical content: miracle stories, a reverence for numbers and concern with an ascetic way of living.

Pythagoreanism influenced the development of *Neoplatonism, and in writers such as Iamblichus (*c.* AD 300) the two schools became indistinguishable.   R.J.H.

W. Burkert, *Lore and Science in Ancient Pythagoreanism* (Cambridge, Mass., 1972).

W. K. C. Guthrie, *A History of Greek Philosophy*, i (Cambridge, 1967), 146–340.

H. Thesleff, *An Introduction to Pythagorean Writings of the Hellenistic Period* (Åbo, 1965).

Q

qualia. The subjective qualities of conscious experience (plural of the Latin singular *quale*, 'of what kind'). Examples are the way sugar tastes, the way vermilion looks, the way coffee smells, the way a cat's purr sounds, the way it feels to stub your toe. Accounting for these features of mental states has been one of the biggest obstacles to materialist solutions to the mind–body problem, because it seems impossible to analyse the subjective character of these phenomena, which are comprehensible only from the point of view of certain types of conscious being, in objective physical terms which are comprehensible to any rational individual independently of his particular sensory faculties.   T.N.

*subjectivity; consciousness, its irreducibility.

T. Nagel, 'What Is It Like to Be a Bat?', *Philosophical Review* (1974).

qualities. In 'Napoleon had all the qualities of a great general' we could, in everyday usage, substitute 'features', 'properties', 'traits', 'characteristics', 'attributes', and some other terms, for 'qualities'. Aristotle included 'quality' in his list of 'categories' of the various possible kinds of objects of thought. He said 'By "quality" I mean that in virtue of which people are said to be such and such.' However, he goes on to discuss qualities of things other than people, such as the sweetness of honey.

A quality is something which can be possessed, as, for example, Napoleon possessed the quality of courage. Qualities can also be attributed, as the quality of courage was just attributed to Napoleon. Furthermore, the same quality may be possessed by more than one thing, as, for example, Alexander possessed courage just as Napoleon did, and in a very different way from the common possession of a yacht by joint owners or of a spouse by polygamists. And a quality can be attributed to a number of things, truly or falsely.

These qualities of qualities, their possessability by, and attributability to, numbers of things, have made them puzzling to many philosophers, who find it peculiar that there should be things with those qualities. One source of puzzlement seems to arise from finding it incredible that one and the same thing could be understood and attributed by several different minds and also possessed by or 'in' several different things. Locke says 'a snowball having the power to produce in us the ideas of white cold and round,—the power to produce those ideas in us, as they are in the snowball, I call qualities; and as they are sensations or perceptions in our understandings, I call them ideas'. Jonathan Bennett points out that the interpretation of the pronoun 'they' in this passage, as referring back either (ungrammatically) to 'power' or to 'ideas' raises problems. The quality, say round, is both identified with the idea round, and distinguished from it.

Locke then goes on to speak of a subclass of 'qualities which . . . are nothing in the objects themselves, but powers to produce sensations in us' as 'secondary qualities'. Secondary qualities, then, are qualities which are 'nothing but' qualities. 'Primary' qualities of a body, by contrast, have further qualities such as being 'utterly inseparable from the body'. It was held further that the idea of a *primary quality *resembles* the quality, while the idea of a secondary quality does not.

These distinctions, or attempts at them, make verificationism about qualities hard to resist, since the notion of an undetectable quality is hard to square with the quality of being a power to produce an idea. If we say that the idea produced needn't convey any idea of the quality, then Locke's project of explaining how we understand qualities in order to attribute them is undermined. This problem as to how the idea points to the quality also arises in connection with what Locke calls a 'third sort' of qualities, which are powers in one object to produce powers in another which then reach us. For example, a quality in the sun causes the mercury to rise in a thermometer. A primitive man may get from the thermometer the idea of a red column rising, but with no idea at all of the sun's role.

The view that it is an essential quality of a quality that it produce some distinctive sort of idea in us ought to be given up. It may be true of *sensory* qualities, such as red, or cold have been held to be, though even that is interestingly controversial.   J.C.

*properties; properties, individual; universal.

Aristotle, *Categories*.
Jonathan Bennett, *Locke, Berkeley, Hume: Central Themes* (Oxford, 1971), 27–8.
John Locke, *An Essay Concerning Human Understanding*, II. viii.

quality of life (QOL) in a population is often defined in terms of social indicators such as nutrition, air quality, incidence of disease, crime rates, health care, educational services, divorce rates, etc. The difficulty is in knowing how to weigh these factors. Is clean drinking-water more or less important than good schools? Should a high divorce rate be counted negatively? One way of achieving a unified index would be to define QOL as a subjective measure of perceived satisfaction or dissatisfaction, summed over a members of the population. But it is possible to conceive of circumstances in which perceived satisfaction could vary quite independently of what we regard as QOL. Even Ivan Denisovitch, in his Siberian labour camp, went to bed a 'satisfied' man. A third alternative is to define QOL in terms not of perceived happiness but of the availability of happiness requirements: what human beings need in order to be happy. If requirements such as Maslow's need hierarchy can be found which are universal rather than idiosyncratic, an objective definition of QOL is possible.   S.McC.

*well-being.

S. McCall, 'Quality of Life', *Social Indicators Research* (1975).
A. H. Maslow, *Motivation and Personality* (New York, 1954).
M. Nussbaum and A. Sen (eds.), *The Quality of Life* (Oxford, 1993).

quantification. The application of quantifiers (for example: 'all', 'some', 'a few', 'more than half'). In predicate logic, the prefacing of a sentence by either the universal quantifier ($\forall x$), 'For any x', or the existential quantifier ($\exists x$), 'There exists at least one x such that'. Quantification turns a sentence with free variables into a sentence with bound variables, for example: Fx, 'Something is F', into ($\exists x$) Fx, 'There exists at least one x that is F'. The propriety of the universal and existential quantifiers is not beyond philosophical question. The use of the universal quantifier assimilates 'all', 'any', and 'every', which are arguably distinct concepts. The use of the existential quantifier enshrines formally the doctrine that 'exists' is not a first-order predicate, but 'exists' might be some kind of first-order predicate.   S.P.

Martin Davies, *Meaning, Quantification, Necessity: Themes in Philosophical Logic* (London, 1981).
Mark Sainsbury, *Logical Forms* (Oxford, 1991), ch. 4.

quantifier. A logical symbol used to do roughly the same work as 'every' or 'some'. The word 'quantifier', which stems from the logicians' sense of *'quantity'*, was first used by Peirce in 1883, but the idea is present in Frege's *Begriffsschrift* (1879). Combined with *variables, quantifiers provide an adequate symbolism for representing relational propositions involving both the universal ($\forall$, read 'for every'), and the existential ($\exists$, read 'for some'), quantifier: 'Someone is loved by everybody', can mean either ' $\forall x \exists y(y$ is loved by $x)$' or '$\exists x \forall y(x$ is loved by $y)$'. *Ambiguity is thus avoided by quantifier notation. Quine christened two interpretations of the quantifiers 'objectual' and 'substitutional', respectively. The first gives the *truth-condition for, for example, '$\exists x(x$ is heavy)' as ' "x is heavy" is satisfied by some object', the second as 'Some sentence of the form "x is heavy" is true'.   C.J.F.W.

C. J. F. Williams, *What is Existence?* (Oxford, 1981), chs. 6–8.

quantity and quality. From at least the thirteenth century onwards, that a proposition is *universal ('All S are P' and 'No S are P') or *particular ('Some S are P' and 'Some S are not P') was called its quantity; and that it is affirmative ('All S are P' and 'Some S are P') or negative ('No S are P' and 'Some S are not P') was traditionally called its quality.

C.W.

*logic, traditional.

I. M. Bochenski, *A History of Formal Logic*, tr. and ed. I. Thomas (Indiana, 1961), 210–11.

quantum logic. Originating with von Neumann and Birkhoff in the mid-1930s, the name 'quantum logic' denotes an intepretation of quantum experimental results by means of a non-Boolean lattice. According to some critics, the name is misleading. They see von Neumann and Birkhoff as having shown that the mathematics, not the logic, of the quantum realm has this non-classical character. More generally, the idea of a quantum logic has both a negative and a positive part. Negatively, it is the thesis that classical, e.g. first-order, formalization of quantum physics is one in which certain principles of logic cease to be valid. More particularly, classical laws of logic, such as distributivity, fail under any formalization in which atomic formulae of quantum physics are formalized as truth-functionally atomic formulae of classical logic and, likewise, if the quantum 'connectives' of *meet* and *join* are construed truth-functionally. Further factors that impede classical formalization include the apparent failure of quantum objects to be well individuated and the inherently probabilistic character of quantum claims. The positive part of the quantum logic thesis requires the specification of a suitably non-classical logic to fit the quantum realm. There is as yet no settled consensus among those who favour the idea. For those who don't, a purpose-built logic for quantum physics has no more rationale than a purpose-built logic for household economics. This scepticism may be influenced by the thought that, from the fact that quantum mechanics lacks an adequate formalization in classical logic, it hardly follows that there must be some other non-classical logic in which the formalization succeeds.   J.WOO.

M. Dalla Chiaro and Roberto Giuntini, 'Quantum Logics' in D. M. Gabbay and F. Guenthner (eds.), vol. 6 of *Handbook of Philosophical Logic*, 2nd edn. (Dordrecht, 2000).

quantum mechanics, philosophical problems of. These concern how best to interpret the theory, and are still being pursued, as in the famous Bohr–Einstein debates in the 1930s, through the use of various 'thought' experiments designed to play off one interpretation against another. The problems still receiving most attention, first raised in classic 1935 papers by Einstein and Schrödinger, are the question whether quantum mechanics is a complete theory—does it 'say all there is to say' about physical reality?—and the measurement problem, or the paradox of Schrödinger's *cat.

Both problems arise in response to the superposition principle in quantum mechanics, which is what distinguishes the theory most from Newtonian mechanics. This principle says that if a physical magnitude M is assigned a definite value m_1 when a quantum system is in state ψ_1, and similarly if the (distinct) value m_2 is assigned by the state ψ_2 to the system, then there are also states of the system achieved by combining ψ_1 and ψ_2 in which M has no definite value whatsoever! To see the peculiarity of the situation, just let M be position and m_1 be 'the particle is *here*' while m_2 is 'the particle is *over there*'. The way in which ψ_1 and ψ_2 are combined, or superposed, determines the respective probabilities that a *measurement of M will be found to yield m_1 or m_2. And this superposition of states extends to composite systems: two particles can be in limbo between, say, both having value m_1 and both m_2, with equal probabilities of finding them with either combination.

The completeness problem starts from the worry that superpositions might not really indicate that magnitudes fail to have definite values, but just that quantum mechanics is not able to tell us what the true values are and so resorts to predicting only what values we would probably find if we looked. In fact Einstein (with his collaborators Podolsky and Rosen) argued that quantum predictions themselves give reasons for thinking this. Consider a pair of widely separated particles emitted from a source in opposite directions in a superposed state like the one mentioned at the end of the last paragraph. Since there are only two possibilities—that both particles will be found to have value m_1 or both m_2—and they have equal probability, once we have measured the M-value of one of the particles, say particle A, we can predict with certainty the M-value of particle B (since it must be the same). Now surely such a prediction gives us good reason to attribute a definite M-value to B (whether it turns out to be m_1 or m_2). And surely the A measurement could not bring that value into existence, since it would be performed at great distance from particle B, and so could not affect it without influences travelling faster than light. Thus B must actually have had a definite M-value all along, despite the fact that it started out locked in a superposition with A!

Tantalizing though this argument is, it is not sound. For in 1964 Bell cleverly showed that, even if we accept its conclusion of incompleteness, we must *still* invoke some sort of faster-than-light influence to reproduce the quantum predictions—so, in this context, the completeness issue turns out to be a red herring! But this pushes us to still other problems, such as whether the required faster-than-light influences are truly *causal* influences, and whether they can be tolerated by relativity theory (even given that we know they cannot be exploited to transmit a signal faster than light). The debate continues to rage.

The other main problem raised by superpositions pertains to measurement. We may be happy with indefiniteness of values as long as it is consigned to the micro-realm; but there is as yet no principled way in quantum mechanics to prevent it from infecting the everyday world of macroscopic objects, like tables and chairs. Suppose we set

up a device whereby if a radioactive atom decays it sets off a chain reaction terminating in the death of a cat, whereas if it does not decay the cat lives—so the cat's state of being functions as our device for measuring the state of the atom. The law governing the time evolution of quantum states then requires that when the atom evolves into a superposition of 'decayed' and 'not decayed' it drags the cat's state with it, and together they end up in limbo between 'decayed–dead' and 'not decayed–alive'. Not only do we not get an answer from our (now admittedly perverse) measurement of whether the atom has in fact decayed, but we are left saying that much-cherished properties of everyday macroscopic beings do not exist!

There is of course no problem here if quantum mechanics is incomplete. But those who think otherwise have been hard pressed to resolve the problem. Some say quantum evolution somehow gets temporarily suspended so that any unwanted superposition between macroscopically distinguishable states 'collapses' into one or the other of its components ψ_1 and ψ_2; others search for a precise mechanism for this collapse, which only operates when systems are sufficiently macroscopic; and still others refuse to acknowledge the problem by arguing that the difference between the collapsed and uncollapsed state of a macroscopic object is so difficult to detect experimentally that 'for all practical purposes' we can live with the superpositions the theory predicts. This list in no way exhausts the avenues that have been pursued, and none has yet come out on top.

The two problems outlined above are far from being the only ones; perhaps they are not even the most interesting. But others peculiar to relativistic quantum mechanics and quantum field theory (like problems to do with particle localization and identity), though increasingly being addressed by philosophers, would involve too much mathematics to elaborate here.   R.CLI.

*determinism, scientific.

D. Z. Albert, *Quantum Mechanics and Experience* (Cambridge, Mass., 1992).

J. S. Bell, *Speakable and Unspeakable in Quantum Mechanics* (Cambridge, 1987).

J. T. Cushing and E. McMullin (eds.), *Philosophical Consequences of Quantum Theory* (Notre Dame, Ind., 1989).

quantum theory and philosophy. The philosophical issues raised by quantum theory are largely dependent upon how *quantum mechanics is interpreted in order to minimize the philosophical problems that arise within the theory, which is a matter of ongoing controversy.

1. The fact that there are mutually incompatible quantum theories, each with a claim to being empirically adequate, presents difficulties for realist interpretations of quantum mechanics which maintain that theoretical terms refer to objectively existing features of the world. Which theory is the correct one? Since empirical adequacy rules out an experimental basis for this choice, it has been suggested that *anti-realism or *instrumentalism about

quantum entities or laws should be adopted, a view which may find application in other areas of science.

2. Quantum theory is often presumed to provide a strong counter-example to the truth of *determinism. The location of an electron (say) can best be described in terms of the probability of its being found at a particular location, the shape and evolution of such probabilities, known as wave-functions, being governed by the Schrödinger equation. However, if a measurement of location is made, we do not observe the electron to be in a superposition of possible states: the electron will be found at a particular location, and it is no longer possible for it to be anywhere else. Thus, von Neumann postulated that Schrödinger evolution is interrupted and the wave-function 'collapses', it is discontinuously and indeterministically reduced to a particle-like state.

The postulated collapse of the wave-function is more problematic for determinism than Schrödinger evolution, since according to the latter, the state of a system is uniquely determined by any earlier state. But, even if indeterministic collapse can be avoided, this provides little comfort to a strong determinist, since construing Schrödinger evolution realistically involves accepting that the fundamental *ontology of the world is irreducibly probabilistic. The determinist has two main options: to regard the statistical element of quantum mechanics as epistemic, a sign that the theory is incomplete, in the hope that probability will be eliminated on discovery of a hitherto hidden variable; or to adopt an instrumentalist or anti-realist stance towards the entities and processes the theory describes. According to one such approach, the 'Copenhagen interpretation', which is perhaps the current orthodoxy in physics, we need not understand the superposition of probable states that the Schrödinger equation describes as assigning mutually incompatible properties to the same entity, if observables, such as location or momentum, exist *only when a measurement is being taken*. Thus, the determinist might argue, the wave-function and its collapse are not objective features of causal reality, and so are not genuine instances of 'effects' which lack deterministic causal antecedents.

3. Quantum theory conflicts with intuitions about *causality. The *Einstein, Podolsky, and Rosen paradox presents a dilemma for quantum theory: either it is incomplete, or the presumption of the spatio-temporal *locality* of physical interactions—the impossibility of *action at a distance—fails. However *Bell's theorem, in so far as his inequalities have been empirically shown to be false, shows that any hidden variable theory would *also* violate locality (or another of Bell's assumptions).

4. Supporters of 'many-worlds' interpretations of quantum mechanics avoid both the indeterministic collapse of the wave-function and action at a distance by maintaining that each time a quantum experiment is performed with different outcomes of non-zero probability, *all* outcomes obtain, each in a *different* world. Hence the universe (everything that exists) incorporates many worlds, where

a world is understood as a totality of classically defined macroscopic objects which are perceived by a conscious observer as being in a definite state—a *cat is never both alive *and* dead—and excludes microscopic entities which might be in superposition, which explains why we do not experience superpositions. The postulation of the existence of many worlds has been compared to *Lewis's modal realism—the metaphysical claim that *possible worlds exist in the same sense as the actual one—and has sometimes been taken to offer empirical support for it. However, the many-worlds hypothesis currently lacks empirical confirmation, and there is doubt whether such confirmation is possible in principle. It also postulates far fewer worlds than Lewis, who maintains that every logically possible world exists.

5. The peculiarities of quantum theory, or some extension of it, are also invoked to provide accounts of *mind, specifically to explain *consciousness, because quantum events are causally relevant to the working of the brain, or cognitive processes can be modelled in terms of quantum computation. Such approaches are hindered, however, both by the lack of consensus about the interpretation of quantum theory and by the absence of empirical evidence that quantum-theoretic phenomena are relevant to the explanation of the mind.   S.R.A.

*Bell's theorem; field theory; quantum logic.

John Gribbin, *Schrödinger's Kittens and the Search for Reality* (London, 1995).

Michael Lockwood, *Mind, Brain and Quantum: The Compound 'I'* (Oxford, 1989).

Christopher Norris, *Quantum Theory and the Flight from Realism: Philosophical Responses to Quantum Mechanics* (London, 2002).

Henry P. Stapp, *Mind, Matter and Quantum Mechanics* (New York, 1993).

quasi-memory. An artificial *memory concept, so defined that the quasi-rememberer need not have been the person involved in the original event. X quasi-remembers E if and only if E occurred, X apparently recalls something E-like, and the apparent recalling causally depends on the occurrence E in an appropriate way. This does *not* require that X witnessed E. The point is to avoid circularity objections to psychological analyses of *personal identity.   P.F.S.

S. Shoemaker, 'Persons and their Pasts', *American Philosophical Quarterly* (1970).

quasi-realism is a modern label for a position similar to Hume's in which, although judgements have in fact no independent object, they nevertheless behave from the perspective of the judger as if they did. More specifically, it is the name of a research programme in which, without supposing an independent reality for a set of judgements to be about, an attempt is made to explain and capture the same inferential relations between these judgements as they would have if they did have such independent truth-values.   R.H.

*moral realism.

Simon Blackburn, *Essays in Quasi-Realism* (Oxford, 1993).

quasi-virtue: *see* shame.

quiddity. Historically meaning 'essence', 'quiddity' has come to denote the unique nature, or 'whatness', of a property. According to 'quidditism' each property has its own quiddity that distinguishes it from every other property. So two properties may be indiscernible (have the same individuals falling under them and the same higher-order properties holding over them) but nevertheless distinct (fail to be identical) because their quiddities differ. The rejection of quidditism is therefore equivalent to the acceptance of the *identity of indiscernibles applied to the case of properties.   F.MacB.

*identity of indiscernibles; haecceity.

Robert Black, 'Against Quidditism', *Australasian Journal of Philosophy*, 78 (2000).

quietism, philosophical. The view, associated with the later Wittgenstein, that philosophy should not aspire to produce substantive theories (e.g. of the nature of meaning, the foundations of knowledge, or of the mind's place in the world), adjudicate disputes in science or mathematics, make discoveries, or dictate how language should be used. Philosophy's proper role is therapeutic rather than constructive: the philosopher diagnoses conceptual confusions. Although the results of such therapy can be profoundly liberating, philosophy does not itself advance human knowledge, but 'leaves everything as it is'.   D.BAK.

P. M. S. Hacker, 'Philosophy', in Hans-Johann Glock (ed.), *Wittgenstein: A Critical Reader* (Oxford, 2001).

Quine, Willard Van Orman (1908–2000). Probably the most important American philosopher since the war, Quine spent his career at Harvard University. His extensive writings have shaped the development of recent philosophy, particularly in logic, the philosophy of language, epistemology, and metaphysics. After completing his doctorate, he visited the Vienna Circle, coming under the influence of Rudolf Carnap. Although critical of its fundamental doctrines, Quine remained true to the underlying spirit of *Logical Positivism. He shared its commitment to *empiricism and to the belief that philosophy should be pursued as part of science.

The papers published in *From a Logical Point of View* (1953) defended views about language and ontology, challenging the assumptions of the prevailing orthodoxy. After 1960, with the publication of *Word and Object*, Quine emphasized his *naturalism, the doctrine that philosophy should be pursued as part of natural science. *Pursuit of Truth* (1990) is a clear, concise formulation of his philosophical position.

Most modern empiricists had held that the meanings of everyday and scientific propositions determine which experiences count as evidence for or against them:

there are *analytic truths (truths which hold by virtue of meanings) which record these links with experience and guide us in forming our opinions. 'Two Dogmas of Empiricism' (1953) rejected this picture: experience counts for or against our entire body of beliefs in a holistic manner, and little that is systematic can be said about the meanings of particular sentences. The analytic–synthetic distinction is to be abandoned, and with it the idea that mathematics and logic have a status radically distinct from that of empirical science: 'Any statement can be held true come what may, if we make drastic enough adjustments elsewhere in the system.' We can even retain an ordinary belief about our surroundings in the face of contrary experience 'by pleading hallucination or by amending certain statements of the kind called logical laws' (p. 43).

In *Word and Object*, this denial that anything systematic can be said about the meanings of particular sentences leads to Quine's most famous doctrine, the *indeterminacy of translation. We undertake 'radical translation' when we attempt to translate a previously unknown language, relying only on information about the evidence that native speakers take to be relevant to the truth or falsity of their utterances. Quine argued that many alternative translation manuals will always fit the evidence, there being no fact of the matter which is correct. There are no objective facts about which words and sentences have the same *meanings.

Among the consequences of these views about meaning is a deep scepticism about the possibility of *modal logic, and the doctrine of ontological relativity. The ontology of a theory is the range of objects that must exist if the theory is true; Quine holds that we can state the ontology of a theory only relative to a translation manual and a background language. There is no non-relative fact of the matter what the ontology of a theory is; or indeed what the ontology of any theorist is.

Quine's own ontological taste is for *physicalism: the physical facts are all the facts, all changes in the world involving physical changes. And this helps to support his philosophical naturalism. The philosophical study of knowledge, for example, is a branch of natural science, drawing on psychology to explain how sensory stimulation gives rise to scientific beliefs. Controversy has surrounded the claim of naturalized epistemology that our philosophical needs are met by such a study: some have objected that it changes the subject by failing to address *scepticism directly, or by focusing on how we *do* form our opinions rather than on normative questions of how we *ought* to assess them.   C.J.H.

*contextual definition; indeterminacy of meaning; American philosophy, today.

W. V. Quine, *From a Logical Point of View* (Cambridge, Mass., 1953).
—— *Word and Object* (Cambridge, Mass., 1960).
—— *Pursuit of Truth* (Cambridge, Mass., 1990).
R. Gibson (ed.), *The Cambridge Companion to Quine* (Cambridge, 2004).

Quinton, Anthony (1925–). British philosopher, based in Oxford and member of the House of Lords, who has written on political philosophy, ethics and metaphysics, the philosophy of mind, and a variety of historical figures. His lengthiest work is his treatise on *The Nature of Things*, which takes as its central notion the concept of *substance. By exploring the questions associated with this concept Quinton develops, in three parts, his views on a wide-ranging set of traditional philosophical problems. In part I, problems of identity and individualism, the relation between matter and extension, and personal identity and the soul are discussed; in part II knowledge, scepticism, and the concept of perception are the topics; in part III the notion of essence, the distinction between theory and observation, mind–body dualism, and fact and value are discussed. The general position defended is a form of materialism.   H.W.N.

*philosophy; English philosophy; philosophical inquiry; philosophy, value and use of.

Anthony Quinton, *The Nature of Things* (London, 1973).

R

race. Higher-level organisms form species, that is groups of organisms that breed among themselves but that are reproductively isolated from all other organisms. We humans belong to the species *Homo sapiens*. Although species are the fundamental units of biological classification, they can often be subdivided into groups that are distinguishable by special features. Early biologists of the modern era, notably the French naturalist Buffon, assumed that this is true of humans, and they spent much time and effort trying to decide what constitute the true divisions, generally known as races. In his *Descent of Man* (1871), Charles Darwin argued that many human differences are due to sexual selection, where differing standards of beauty are the chief causal factors tearing human populations apart.

Notoriously, the German Nazis were keen race theorists, believing that distinctions can be drawn between Aryans and others, especially Jews. Naturally, in the post-Second World War years, the very idea of race fell from favour, and it was argued that not only is it a socially pernicious notion but that it has little or no scientific validity. The major defining mark of the human species is how little difference there is between peoples, not how much.

In recent years, the pendulum has swung back a little. Anthropologists now recognize that there are several distinctive human forms, and medical geneticists are keenly aware that there are distinctive diseases much more commonly associated with certain groups than with others. For instance, Ashkenazi Jews (those from Eastern Europe) are more prone to carry a gene for Tay-Sachs diseases than are other peoples. M.R.

*anti-Semitism.

T. Dobzhansky, *Mankind Evolving* (New Haven, Conn., 1962).
C. P. Groves, *The Biology of Race* (Berkeley, Calif., 1989).

racism. Although the roots of theoretical racism can be traced back at least to the fifteenth century, the term did not come to prominence until the 1930s when it was used to describe the pseudo-scientific theory that 'race', as a decisive biological determinant, established a hierarchy among different ethnic groups. Racist theories were largely developed after the fact to justify practical racism, which can exist independently of them. Polygenesis, the attempt to explain the differences among kinds by positing diverse origins, provided a basis for maintaining permanent inequalities between peoples; by contrast, the philosophies of history that imposed a single goal on history could be used to justify colonialism, as well as the destruction of indigenous cultures and peoples. Most potently, the two tendencies are combined to demand an assimilation that is still withheld on the basis of blood purity or skin colour. R.L.B.

*fascism.

B. Boxhill (ed.) *Race and Racism* (Oxford, 2001).
R. H. Popkin, 'The Philosophical Bases of Modern Racism', in *The High Road to Pyrrhonism* (San Diego, 1980).

Radcliffe Richards, Janet (1944–). English philosopher whose book *The Sceptical Feminist* was published in 1980 and provides a vigorous defence of liberal feminism against both anti-feminists and radical feminists. According to Radcliffe Richards, *feminism should not be concerned with benefiting a particular group of people (women), but with removing a particular kind of injustice. The central task of the book is to expose the faulty thinking which grounds that injustice. Although influential, it has been said to be too unworldly in its understanding of women's oppression, and insufficiently radical in the remedies it proposes. There is not much discussion of the inequalities of power which perpetuate injustice, and an acceptance that 'women's work' is less fulfilling and valuable than work outside the home. Richards's feminism is logical rather than ideological, cerebral rather than celebratory. S.M.

*justice.

Radhakrishnan, Sarvepalli (1888–1975). Idealist philosopher who taught at Oxford and was the President of India during 1962–7. Best known for his elegant exegesis of *Indian philosophy and Hinduism in English, this prolific statesman broadly adhered to monistic *Vedānta, trying to reinterpret it as a kind of universal religion. Rejecting both Berkeleian and Hegelian idealisms, he upheld a teleological and openly religious view of matter, life, and mind as all evolving with a divine purpose or *idea* which gives meaning to existence. Interpreting classical Indian and modern Western philosophies in a syncretic manner, Radhakrishnan argued that ultimate reality is a changing but 'ordered' whole which science can only understand incompletely. It is directly accessible to a blissful intuitive experience that mystics of all religions describe in strikingly similar ways as ineffable.   A.C.

*science, art, and religion.

S. Radhakrishnan, *The Idealist View of Life* (London, 1988).

radical feminism: *see* feminism, radical.

radical interpretation and translation: *see* translation, indeterminacy of.

radical philosophy. Movement formed in 1971, in opposition to narrowness and insularity of professional philosophy in Britain, particularly Oxford. The Radical Philosophy Group has organized various national conferences, but its main influence has been through the magazine *Radical Philosophy*. This has persistently forsworn allegiance to any particular doctrine, but describes itself as a journal of socialist and feminist philosophy. Additionally, although it is not a Marxist journal, many of those involved with it have seen themselves as continuing a Marxist philosophical tradition. Other preoccupations include a commitment to interdisciplinary work, widening interest in continental philosophy, and reforming bad practices in academic philosophy.

Since some of its defining concerns are now shared by many distinguished philosophers, it is to be wondered whether its self-image of opposition to the narrowness of the professional discipline is any longer appropriate (although the attempt by Cambridge philosophers to deny an honorary degree to Derrida might suggest that this is premature).   K.M.

*Oxford philosophy.

R. Edgley and R. Osborne, *A Radical Philosophy Reader* (London, 1985).

Rāmānuja (1017–1137). South Indian consolidator of devotional theistic interpretation of Vedic philosophy called qualified non-dualism. Unlike the unqualified monists, Rāmānuja postulates three realities—God, matter, and individual souls—the last two being parasitic on the first. God, a person with infinite excellent attributes, is the self of selves, and the universe is his inseparable body. Highest liberation consists not in identification with God (as in non-dualism), but in enjoying a God-*like* state of joy at knowing one's eternal dependence upon the Lord. With a distinctively realistic epistemology of error, Rāmānuja opposes the idealism of *Śaṅkara, who deemed the world an illusion that is 'neither real nor unreal'. Rāmānuja bombards this illusionism with charges of inconsistency, asking tough questions: 'Whose illusion is it? It could not be *God's* because he never errs, and could not be *ours* because we are its effects according to non-dualism!'   A.C.

*Indian philosophy; Vedānta.

Julius Lipner, *The Face of Truth: A Study of Meaning and Metaphysics in Rāmānuja* (Albany, NY, 1986).

Ramsey, Frank P. (1903–30). Cambridge mathematician, logician, and philosopher whose short career included important, though brief, contributions to a wide range of subjects, including probability theory, economics, and the foundations of mathematics. He was amongst the first to understand and recognize the importance of Wittgenstein's *Tractatus*, and one of the few contemporary philosophers whose opinion Wittgenstein respected. But he was not uncritical of Wittgenstein's ideas at the time.

Ramsey did pioneering work in the theory of subjective *probability, arguing that degrees of rational belief should conform to the axioms of the probability calculus. He developed a method for eliminating reference to theoretical entities in science by framing what are now called 'Ramsey sentences'. His analysis of generalizations was to treat them as expressing rules for the anticipation of experience rather than propositions to which truth-values could be assigned. He was also a proponent of the *redundancy theory of truth.   E.J.L.

F. P. Ramsey, *The Foundations of Mathematics and Other Logical Essays* (London, 1931).
——*Philosophical Papers*, ed. D. H. Mellor (Cambridge, 1990).

Rashdall, Hastings (1858–1924). English philosopher who expounded a theory known as 'ideal utilitarianism'. Rashdall was a Fellow of New College, Oxford, and dedicated his main work, *The Theory of Good and Evil*, to the memory of his teachers T. H. Green and Henry Sidgwick. The dedication is appropriate, for the particular version of *utilitarianism put forward by Rashdall owes elements to both Green and Sidgwick. Whereas he holds that the concepts of *good and *value are logically prior to that of *right, he gives right a more than instrumental significance. His idea of good owes more to T. H. Green than to the hedonistic utilitarians. 'The ideal of human life is not the mere juxtaposition of distinct goods, but a whole in which each good is made different by the presence of others.' Rashdall has been unfairly eclipsed as a moral philosopher by G. E. Moore.   R.S.D.

H. Sidgwick (with additional ch. by A. G. Widgery), *Outlines of the History of Ethics* (London, 1946).

ratiocination. Reasoning. St Thomas Aquinas distinguished ratiocination (*ratiocinatio*) from the direct, non-inferential apprehension of truth possessed by God and angels. Human beings, he claimed, arrive at 'the knowledge of intelligible truth by advancing from one thing to another'—i.e. by an inferential process, ratiocination. Ratiocination, understood simply as *reasoning, sometimes misses its mark; and, plausibly, some human knowledge is acquired non-inferentially.   A.R.M.

*inference; argument.

St Thomas Aquinas, *Summa Theologiae*, pt. 1, Q. 79, Art. 8.

rational choice theory explores the extent to which complex social and economic phenomena can be regarded as the outcome of calculative, self-interested individual action. The advent of game theory (during the Second World War) showed that the outcomes of action can often be understood as the joint result of individual choice in combination with the choices of other actors ('players'), all of whom aim at maximizing (or at least satisficing) individual preference-satisfaction. Where two or more actors have regular interactions on the same matter, a strategy that reliably provides utility to all of them may emerge, and become enshrined in a convention. Rational choice theory has been claimed to explain many social institutions, from marriage to morality, though sceptics doubt its usefulness in the face of limits to obtainable information and to the time available for weighing indefinitely many alternative possible outcomes.   A.BRE.

K. S. Cook and M. Levi (eds.), *The Limits of Rationality* (Chicago, 1990).

rationalism. Any of a variety of views emphasizing the role or importance of reason, usually including *intuition, in contrast to sensory experience (including introspection), the feelings, or authority. Just as an extreme empiricist tries to base all our knowledge on experience, so an extreme rationalist tries to base it on reason. But whereas *empiricism appears in the eighteenth century and again in the first half of the twentieth century, extreme rationalism has been considerably less popular. In fact it reached its peak in the brash days when philosophy itself was beginning, back in the ancient Greek world. Parmenides maintained that, whatever the senses might say, the very notion of change involved a contradiction, and so reason demanded that reality be entirely devoid of change. As usually interpreted he said the same about plurality too. His fellow citizen and near-contemporary Zeno of Elea supported him with a set of paradoxes, including the famous Achilles and the tortoise. (*Zeno's paradoxes.) These two, together with a handful of followers (including to a certain extent, but only to a certain extent, Plato), represent the acme of extreme rationalism, and later rationalists have seldom been willing to dismiss the senses quite so single-mindedly. They perhaps have in mind the words the slightly later philosopher Democritus, by no means an extreme empiricist, gives to the senses to defend themselves against pure reason (fragment 125): 'Wretched mind, do you take your evidence from us and then overthrow us? Our overthrow is your own downfall!'

It is indeed hard to see how a being entirely devoid of any contact with the world through the senses could ever amass the materials needed to exercise its reason at all. How, for instance, could it acquire a language to express its thoughts in, and what sort of thoughts could it have if it had no language at all?

Rationalism, however, does not have to take an extreme form. It can content itself with claiming simply that some of our knowledge, though not all of it, can come to us otherwise than through the senses. This is quite compatible with saying that without some use of the senses we would not have any knowledge at all. Rationalism in fact can take two main forms, according as it claims that some of our propositional knowledge, i.e. knowledge of the truth of certain propositions, comes to us without coming through the senses, or claims that some of the materials from which our knowledge is constructed are present in the mind without coming through the senses. This latter will be the case if some of our concepts are *a priori, where this just means 'prior to experience'. It might be, for instance, that concepts such as those of substance or causation are present with us from the beginning in the sense that, as Kant thought, we do not *find out* that the world contains substances and causes, but cannot help but see the world as composed of substances which have attributes and of events which are caused by other events. Having the concepts in this way, however, must be distinguished from having them explicitly, in the sense of having words for them or consciously thinking about them, as we are doing now. On the theory in question, small children and possibly even animals can do the former without its following that they can do the latter.

It is not surprising that, contrary to the claims of the extreme empiricist, we must bring some equipment with us if we want to know something about the world. If we could really start as blank tablets, then why don't ordinary blackboards, or at any rate photoreceptive camera plates, know things about the world? On the other hand, it is only in a backhanded sense that we can be said to 'know' that the world contains substances and causes if the truth of the matter is that we can only know the world at all by treating it as though it did. A more substantive rationalism is that which says that we can know certain propositions to be true without deriving this knowledge from our senses, even if in some or all cases we must use our senses to get the concepts that are involved in the propositions: I may know without looking that whatever has a size has a shape, but only if I already have the concepts of size and shape, i.e. if I know what size and shape are.

Kant made, or at least brought into clear and explicit focus, a distinction between *analytic and synthetic statements (or judgements in his case, as he was more concerned with the workings of the mind than with linguistic analysis). Even empiricists usually allow that we know analytic statements a priori, but they defuse this concession by adding that such knowledge hardly counts as knowledge in any meaty sense, since such statements do not say anything substantive about the world. Synthetic statements, however, do, and rationalism in its stronger versions is concerned to claim that some of them can be known a priori. The one about everything with size having shape would be a standard example, and others would be mathematical propositions, which empiricists usually try to treat as analytic, though without much success in the opinion of rationalists. In fact around the start of the twentieth century a sustained attempt was made by Frege and Russell to reduce mathematics to pure logic in their

RENÉ DESCARTES: 'had he kept himself to geometry,' said Hobbes in tribute, 'he had been the best geometer in the world'. But Descartes's vision of the unity of mathematics and the natural sciences inspired his philosophical project.

GOTTFRIED WILHELM LEIBNIZ left such voluminous writings on philosophy, mathematics, and physics that a complete edition is still not in sight; one scholar estimated it would be twenty years' full-time work just to read his manuscripts.

IMMANUEL KANT was the fountainhead from which the main stream of continental European philosophy flowed in the nineteenth and twentieth centuries; his influence has steadily spread through English language philosophy too, especially in metaphysics and ethics.

BARUCH SPINOZA's greatest work, his *Ethics*, is in fact a systematic metaphysical treatise which builds theorems upon axioms upon definitions. His intellectual adventurousness led to his ejection from the orthodox Jewish community in Amsterdam.

theory known as logicism; but it is now generally agreed, especially since Gödel's first incompleteness theorem in 1931, that this cannot be done.

However, even what I have called this 'more substantive' rationalism, which claims that we can know certain interesting truths a priori, does not escape a certain tension in its relations with the weaker rationalism which says that we have to treat the world in certain ways if we are to make sense of it. For when it comes to justifying these claims to know the world without looking at it, the rationalist is in danger of being driven to say simply that we cannot think coherently without accepting these propositions—which is rather weaker than claiming some special insight which definitely tells us that they are true. Would not such an insight be a sort of magic?

Be that as it may, the main form that rationalism has taken in the last few decades has been of the weaker kind, and connected, like so much of philosophy during that period, with language. It stems from Chomsky, who holds that certain grammatical structures are innate in our minds, so that all human languages share certain common features which make it possible for children to learn them. Other sorts of language may be spoken by, say, Martians, but our children could not learn them, nor their children ours.

An interesting recent development concerning the a priori is the claim by Kripke and Putnam that the a priori–empirical distinction does not coincide, as it has usually been thought to do, with the necessary–contingent distinction. Kripke claims that some propositions that are true only contingently can be known a priori (an example might be that the knower himself exists), while some propositions that are necessarily true can only be known empirically (an example here might be the chemical composition of some substance). This latter might sound rather strange: might not water, say, have turned out to have some structure different from H_2O? Kripke and Putnam would agree that we might have found ourselves faced with a liquid that was wet and colourless, filled the oceans, and was good for making coffee with, i.e. had all the ordinary and easily observable properties of water, but which had a structure quite different from H_2O. But such a liquid would not be water, because the word 'water' gets its meaning from its use to name the liquid we actually have around us, which is H_2O. Of course we might have called the other stuff water had we come across it, but then the word 'water' would have had a different meaning from the one it actually has, because it would have acquired its meaning in a different way, i.e. by its relations to a different stuff. This doctrine, incidentally, that water is essentially H_2O, i.e. would not be what it is unless it had the structure H_2O, illustrates the essentialism whose recent revival has been pioneered by Kripke and Putnam among others, and which is itself in the spirit of rationalism rather than empiricism, even though our finding out that water is H_2O relies on observation: the fact that things have essences at all is not something that observation can tell us.

Finally, rationalism, like empiricism, can refer either to the psychological genesis or to the philosophical justification of our knowledge; i.e. it can say either that we do in fact get some or all of our knowledge, or all of our knowledge in a certain sphere, from reason, or else that only to the extent that we do so can we properly claim to have knowledge. Again, as in the case of empiricism, we are bordering on *naturalism, but rationalism has perhaps more usually been concerned with the genetic questions. When justification is at issue rationalism is usually concerned (as with Plato and to a lesser extent Aristotle) with distinguishing real or proper knowledge from lesser grades of cognition like true opinion, which are unstable and cannot be relied upon.

When contrasted with feeling or sentiment, especially in the eighteenth-century opponents of the *'moral sense' school, rationalism, often then called intuitionism, takes the form of an ethical doctrine claiming that we have a priori intuitions of moral truths. Ethical intuitionists vary in whether they treat such intuitions as isolated or as linked together in a rational system.

In the latter case logical reasoning is involved, and though no one would deny that ethical conclusions can be logically derived from premises which include ethical premises, the rationalist, defying one form of the *naturalistic fallacy, will claim that they can be so derived sometimes from purely non-ethical premises. It is in this sort of case that the ethical intuitions involved have the air of arising from reason, in parallel with logical intuitions, and so are thought to belong most appropriately under rationalism.

Rationalism can also oppose reason to authority, in particular to religious revelation, and the name has been used in this sense, especially since the end of the nineteenth century, though not usually in philosophy.   A.R.L.

*clear and distinct ideas; humanism.

G. Ryle, 'Epistemology', in J. O. Urmson (ed.), *The Concise Encyclopaedia of Western Philosophy and Philosophers* (London, 1960). Shows how rationalism and empiricism shade into each other.

S. P. Stich (ed.), *Innate Ideas* (Berkeley, Calif., 1975). Includes discussions of Chomsky as well as of earlier ideas.

S. Kripke, *Naming and Necessity* (Oxford, 1980).

C. Peacocke, *The Realm of Reason* (Oxford, 2003).

L. A. Selby-Bigge (ed.), *British Moralists* (London, 1897). Selections from moral sense theorists and their intuitionist opponents.

rationality. This is a feature of cognitive agents that they exhibit when they adopt beliefs on the basis of appropriate reasons. Aristotle maintained that rationality is the key feature that distinguishes human beings from other animals. The adjective 'rational' is used to characterize both agents and specific beliefs. In both cases rationality can be contrasted with either non-rationality or irrationality. A stone or tree is non-rational because it is not capable of carrying out rational assessments. A being who is capable of being rational but who regularly violates the principles of rational assessment is irrational. Among rational beings some beliefs are non-rational since they are matters of taste and no reasons are required. Beliefs that are contrary to the dictates of reason are irrational. Rational beliefs have also been contrasted with beliefs arrived at through *emotion, faith, authority, or by an arbitrary choice. The point of each contrast is to capture a sense in which we believe a proposition either without carrying out an appropriate assessment or in spite of the results of such an assessment. For example, we determine the balance in a cheque-book rationally when we enter the correct credits and debits and do the arithmetic. Irrational ways of determining a balance include picking a number at random or choosing a number because we find it pleasant. When dealing with empirical matters, rational beliefs are arrived at by accumulating relevant evidence; a rational individual will suspend belief until an adequate body of evidence has been accumulated and evaluated. Rational belief is established in mathematics by providing a formal proof. There has been an intense debate throughout the history of philosophy on the question whether matters of value are subject to rational assessment.

It has long been held that rational assessment requires rigorous rules for deciding whether a proposition should be believed. Formal logic and mathematics provide the clearest examples of such rules. Science has also been considered a model of rationality because it was held to proceed in accordance with the *scientific method which provides the rules for gathering evidence and evaluating hypotheses on the basis of this evidence. In this view, rational assessment yields results that are universal and necessary; if two individuals who have access to the same evidence arrive at incompatible conclusions, at least one of them must be behaving irrationally.

More recent discussions have proposed accounts of bounded rationality that pay closer attention to human cognitive limitations and recognize considerable scope for rational disagreement. The central role attributed to rules in rational evaluations has also been challenged. Following rules is not always required, since one task of rational assessment is to determine which rules should be followed in a particular situation. To insist that this decision must be made by following other rules can create an *infinite regress that would make it impossible to arrive at rational results in many situations that serve as paradigms of reason, such as constructing mathematical proofs or evaluating scientific hypotheses. Nor is following rules—even correct rules of logic—automatically rational. Consider again an individual who is constructing a logical proof: this individual must decide which rules to apply at each stage of the proof. Mindlessly applying rules just because they are logically correct is foolish. In addition, Kuhn and others have argued that there are no fixed rules of scientific method. Rather, we must learn what the correct rules of method are as science develops. These considerations suggest that our ability to be rational depends on a basic ability to exercise intelligent judgement that cannot be completely captured in systems of rules.

H.I.B.

*reasoning; maximin and minimax.

H. Brown, *Rationality* (London, 1988).
C. Cherniak, *Minimal Rationality* (Cambridge, Mass., 1986).
A. R. Mele and P. Rawling (eds.), *The Oxford Handbook of Rationality* (New York, 2003).
N. Rescher, *Rationality* (Oxford, 1988).

ravens, paradox of the. A problem in *confirmation theory to which attention was first drawn by Hempel. Prima facie, a generalization such as 'All ravens are black' is confirmed by—gains strength from—each new observed instance of a black raven. But this generalization is logically equivalent to 'Anything which is not black is not a raven'. And this latter generalization is confirmed by each new instance of a non-black non-raven, such as white handkerchiefs and pale pine writing-desks. So, if we accept the seemingly innocent principle that whatever confirms a hypothesis *h* also confirms any hypothesis logically equivalent to *h*, we must conclude that observations of white handkerchiefs will confirm that all ravens are black—which would render ornithology paradoxically easy. Yet it is not obvious which of the premises of this argument could be rejected.   J.L.

C. G. Hempel, 'Studies in the Logic of Confirmation', in *Aspects of Scientific Explanation and Other Essays in the Philosophy of Science* (New York, 1965).

Rawls, John (1921–2002). Major social and political philosopher. Educated at Princeton, he taught at Cornell and Harvard, and in 1971 published *A Theory of Justice*, whose leading idea is that of *justice as fairness—the hope for social institutions that do not confer morally arbitrary lifelong advantages on some persons at the expense of others. This condemns as unjust not only racial, sexual, and religious discrimination, but also many forms of social and economic inequality; the view is a strongly egalitarian form of *liberalism. It is based on a new form of social *contract theory—not an actual social contract but a hypothetical one.

We are to imagine ourselves in an *original position of equality, in which we do not know most of the socially significant facts about ourselves—race, sex, religion, economic class, social standing, natural abilities, even our conception of the good life. Under this *veil of ignorance, we are to decide what principles we could agree to on the basis of a desire to further our own aims and interests, whatever they may be. Not knowing our position in society or our conception of the good, we are driven by this fiction to an equal concern for the fate of everyone, and Rawls maintains that we would give priority in choice of principles to avoiding the worst possible life prospects, with emphasis first on the preservation of personal and political liberty and second on the amelioration of socio-economic inequality.

The principles he defends are: (1) each individual is to have a right to the greatest equal liberty compatible with a like liberty for all; (2) (*a*) social and economic inequalities are to be attached to offices and positions open to all under conditions of fair equality of opportunity; and (b) such inequalities are justified only if they benefit the worst-off (the *difference principle). The first principle has priority over the second, and both principles are to govern not detailed political choices but the basic structures—political, economic, and social—which determine people's chances in life. Equal *liberty rules out persecution, discrimination, and political oppression. Equal *opportunity ensures that those with equal ability and motivation have equal chances of success, whatever class they are born into. The difference principle allows unequal abilities to produce differential rewards only to the extent that this is instrumentally necessary for the good of all, especially the least fortunate (for example, by providing the incentives which fuel productivity).

Rawls opposes *utilitarianism, holding that the maximum total good may not be pursued by means which impose unfair disadvantages on minorities, including the unskilled. More generally, he claims that the right is prior to and independent of the good, and cannot be defined as that which will promote or maximize the good. Certain conditions on the social relations between people and the way they may be treated take precedence over the production of desirable results. This is opposed to the idea that rights are just human conventions justified instrumentally by their usefulness in promoting the general welfare.

In numerous essays after the book, some collected in *Political Liberalism* (New York, 1993), Rawls further develops the theory of *justice and its relation to general moral theory and moral epistemology. He employs what he calls the method of 'reflective equilibrium', by which coherence in our moral views is achieved through mutual adjustment between particular moral judgements, general principles, and theoretical constructions like the social contract which model the ideas of morality.   T.N.

*equality; inequality; contractarianism.

B. Barry, *Theories of Justice* (Berkeley, Calif., 1989).
N. Daniels (ed.), *Reading Rawls* (New York, 1975).
Thomas Pogge, *Realizing Rawls* (Ithaca, NY, 1989).
J. Rawls, *A Theory of Justice* (Cambridge, Mass., 1971; new edn. 1999).
—— *Political Liberalism* (Cambridge, Mass., 1993).
—— *The Law of Peoples* (Cambridge, Mass., 1999).
—— *Lectures on the History of Moral Philosophy* (Cambridge, Mass., 2000).

Raz, Joseph (1941–). Legal, moral, and political philosopher, based in Oxford since 1970. Principally known for three theories. First, a conception of *authority invoking second-order practical reasons, reasons in favour of or against acting on an existing reason one might have to act (or not to act). Authority requires second-order reasons not to consider the independent merits of performing actions commanded, and these reasons must not themselves be based on those merits. The theory is used to develop a qualified form of *legal positivism. Secondly, his interest theory of *rights sees rights as successful

justifications for imposing duties on others, based on the recognition of the fundamental interests of creatures capable of possessing rights (persons). Thirdly, he is the best-known contemporary proponent of the political theory of *perfectionism, which holds that liberal states should not be neutral across the values and practices of their citizens, but should in fact promote individual life-styles which most advance personal *autonomy.

S.M.-G.

*law and morals.

J. Raz, *The Authority of Law* (Oxford, 1979).
—— *The Morality of Freedom* (Oxford, 1986).
—— *Practical Reason and Norms* (Oxford, 1990).

real. 'Real' is often used with some opposite term in mind, such as 'ideal', or 'fake'. In these cases, one can infer from '*A* is not a real *F*' that *A* is not an *F* at all (one of the things that tempts philosophers to equate 'real' with 'existent'). Hence to contrast 'real' with a term like 'relational' may mislead: from '*A* was a relational change' one *can* infer that *A* was a change.

If 'reality' is taken to be the sum total of all that is real, then for 'real' we do have to read something like 'existent'. Talk of such a sum total may itself be problematic, of course: it can smack of treating 'everything' as a name for an enormous entity.   R.P.L.T.

*appearance and reality; existence; 'to be', the verb; being; transcendence.

J. L. Austin, *Sense and Sensibilia* (Oxford, 1963), 70.

Realism, Critical: *see* Critical Realism.

realism, direct: *see* naïve realism.

realism, legal: *see* legal realism.

realism, mathematical: *see* mathematics, history of the philosophy of; mathematics, problems of the philosophy of; Platonism.

realism, moral: *see* moral realism.

realism, naïve: *see* naïve realism.

Realism, New: *see* New Realism.

realism, quasi-: *see* quasi-realism.

realism and anti-realism. Primarily directions, not positions. To assert that something is somehow mind-independent is to move in the realist direction; to deny it is to move in the opposite direction. No sane position is reached at either extreme. Not everything is in every way independent of minds; if there were no minds, there would be no pain. Not everything depends in every way on minds; if I forget that Halley's comet exists, it does not cease to exist. Many philosophical questions have the general form: Is such-and-such mind-independent in so-and-so way? Given specifications of such-and-such and so-and-so, one may call someone who answers 'Yes' a realist. Since different philosophers take different specifications for granted, the word 'realism' is used in a bewildering variety of senses.

In medieval scholastic philosophy, realism was a theory of predication opposed to *nominalism* and *conceptualism*. On a realist analysis, the sentence 'Snow is white' is true if and only if the substance snow has the property of whiteness; whiteness exists independently of our thought and talk, just as snow does. Unlike substances, properties are predicative: their nature is to be properties of something. In contrast, conceptualists deny that any thing predicative exists independently of thought; the truth of 'Snow is white' requires only our concept of white to apply to snow. Nominalists go further, holding the only predicative item required for the truth of 'Snow is white' to be the word 'white' itself, whose existence depends on a particular language, not just on a kind of thought.

Kant opposed realism to *idealism*, distinguishing transcendental and empirical versions of each. The empirical realist holds (like Kant) that we can have knowledge of the existence and nature of material objects in space and time. The transcendental realist holds (unlike Kant) that the existence and nature of the objects so known is wholly independent of our knowledge of them. Kant argued that the two kinds of realism make an untenable combination, because perception yields knowledge only of appearances. Thus the empirical realist should be a transcendental idealist, for whom material objects are nothing beyond their appearances to us; the transcendental realist should be an empirical idealist, a sceptic. However, the argument relies on the dubious premiss that *perception yields knowledge only of appearances. Realists may deny that the nature and existence of what we perceive (e.g. a tree) depends on our perception of it. Perhaps the dependence is the other way round: my perception of the tree depends essentially on the tree, because I could not have had *that* perception without perceiving *that* tree. If so, the combination of transcendental and empirical realism may be defensible.

After Kant, 'realism' meant above all the view that we perceive objects whose existence and nature are independent of our perceptions. The issue has subsequently been generalized. For any linguistic or psychological act (e.g. a judgement, a perception), one can ask whether it involves a relation to something independent of it. That something (e.g. a property, a material object) would constitute an independent standard of correctness for the act. The standard makes the act correct only if they are related. Realists see anti-realists as sacrificing the independence to the relation; anti-realists see realists as sacrificing the relation to the independence.

An independent standard of correctness need not be a particular *thing*. To discuss whether the judgement 'Rape is wrong' is correct independently of being judged is to discuss the objectivity of moral truth, not the existence of

moral objects (to adapt Kreisel's remark that what matters is the objectivity of mathematical truth, not the existence of mathematical objects). The existence of objects is relevant only when it is required for a judgement to be true. The truth of a perceptual judgement may depend on the existence of trees, that of a scientific theory on the existence of electrons.

Realism is still accused of leading to *scepticism by disconnecting our beliefs from their standard of correctness. To know something is to believe it because it is true, but to assume that a belief is true in the realist sense is not to explain why it is believed. The problem is particularly acute where the realist cannot postulate a causal connection between the facts and our beliefs. How, for example, could our belief that $5 + 7 = 12$ be caused by a fact about abstract objects? Even where a causal connection is postulated, e.g. between the existence of electrons and our belief that electrons exist, the question is whether it is of a kind to help the realist. If the observational evidence can be explained by many mutually inconsistent theories, how except by luck can we choose the true one?

Many anti-realists take the argument further, giving it a linguistic turn. They infer that we cannot even understand what realist *truth is; the epistemologically inaccessible is also semantically inaccessible. If we could never know the realist *facts, how could we even think about them? Realism is held to make nonsense of our thought and talk by attributing to it an unintelligible standard of correctness.

Anti-realist alternatives take many forms. It may be global or restricted to a local practice (anti-realist accounts of morality and realist accounts of natural science often reflect the same confidence in a scientific world-picture). The anti-realist may hold (1) the practice does not involve judgements at all, or (2) the judgements it involves are incorrect, or (3) they are correct only in some mind-dependent sense.

1. *Emotivists* treat moral principles as expressions of approval or disapproval. *Formalists* treat mathematical proofs as series of moves in a formal game like chess. *Instrumentalists* treat scientific theories as calculating-instruments used to predict future experience. In each case, apparent judgements are treated as not really candidates for truth. Emotivists say 'Rape is wrong' while denying that 'Rape is wrong' is genuinely true. This risks inconsistency: given the usual practice in speaking of truth, if rape is wrong then 'Rape is wrong' is true.

2. *Error theorists* treat morality as a vast illusion; moral judgements are untrue because no values exist to make them true. *Eliminativists* believe that neuroscience has refuted everyday psychology by showing that beliefs and desires do not exist. Even the truth of arithmetic has been denied on the grounds that numbers do not exist. On such views, we are mistaken in judging 'Rape is wrong', 'I want a drink', or '$5 + 7 = 12$'; although what we say may be useful, it is not literally true.

3. The truth of ordinary judgements may be admitted, but treated as mind-dependent, in order to allow us access

to it. Mind-dependence comes in many varieties. Stipulation provides an extreme case. By stipulating that my fish is named 'Mary', I make it true that my fish is named 'Mary'; my knowledge of that truth is correspondingly unproblematic. Both fictional and mathematical truth have been assimilated to the stipulative model. A story is created by being told; anti-realists have called mathematics the free creation of the human mind. The model is more complex than it appears. Stipulating something does not automatically make it true. Some stipulations are inconsistent, others made without due authority.

In most practices, no single act of stipulation is authoritative. A river is named 'Thames' by long-standing agreement. Anyone can mistake the name, but the mistake lies only in deviation from social consensus (the people cannot all be fooled). However, this is still an extreme model of mind-dependence. Many practices would be radically changed if their participants came to regard the truth of their judgements as constituted by present consensus. As we now think of morality, we allow that everyone in our society may share a false moral belief, all being blind to some morally relevant consideration.

A more subtly mind-dependent standard of truth is consensus in the long run. By refining our current morality we might eventually overcome our present blindness. Such a standard has been suggested for science as well as morality. Of course, we must not achieve the long-run consensus by lapsing into barbarism. What counts is an imaginary long run in which rational inquiry is pursued, unhindered by the contingent limitations of finite humans in constricting environments. Mind-dependent truth becomes something like idealized rational acceptability, in Putnam's phrase. The mind on which truth depends is not the human mind, as described by empirical psychology, or groups of human minds, as described by empirical sociology; it is an ideal mind, as prescribed by normative rules embodied in our thought and talk. Hegel's *objective idealism* prefigured this view.

Rational inquiry is not guaranteed to stabilize in consensus. We cannot assume that each moral disagreement will be resolved, or that historians will discover who killed the Princes in the Tower, or that mathematicians will either prove or refute Goldbach's conjecture ('Every even number greater than 2 is the sum of two primes'). If truth implies consensus, we cannot assume that either a proposition is true or its negation is. This jeopardizes *bivalence, the principle that every proposition is either true or false. Anti-realism may, as Dummett has argued, require revisions of logic.

For realists, a proposition is true or false even if we can never know which. Anti-realists ask how we can grasp such a standard of truth, if not by magic. How can we refer to conditions whose obtaining we cannot recognize? Many reject the challenge, arguing that such notions cannot be reduced to more basic terms. Others accept it. Some argue that reference is a causal relation; our use of, for example, the word 'rain' is causally related to a

condition that also obtained in the inaccessible past. The idea that the world contains mind-independent conditions, properties, and relations is central to such an account; scholastic realism supports modern realism.

When we have a thought, its truth or falsity is not a fact about us, unless we are thinking about ourselves. But it is a fact about us that we are having that thought. In having it, we refer to what it is about. *Reference to something requires at least indirect acquaintance with it, and therefore with states of affairs involving it. Such acquaintance constitutes knowledge. Thus a pre-condition of thinking about something is possession of at least some knowledge about it. Realists and anti-realists may agree that such a pre-condition exists. For anti-realists, it is substantial. Reflection on it uncovers surprising incoherences in our thought of things as independent of us. For realists, the pre-condition is minimal. It permits us no end of ignorance and error.   T.W.

*coherence theory of truth; correspondence theory of truth.

M. Devitt, *Realism and Truth*, 2nd edn. (Oxford, 1991).
M. Dummett, *Truth and Other Enigmas* (London, 1978).
T. Nagel, *The View from Nowhere* (Oxford, 1986).
H. Putnam, *Realism and Reason* (Cambridge, 1983).

realism in metaphysics. A problem of metaphysics much discussed in recent decades is that of realism. But the first problem here is *how to formulate* the problem. Here is one way:

Realism: Tokens of most common-sense, and scientific, physical types exist objectively, independently of the mental.

This, however, can be variously interpreted; here is just one possibility:

Realism 1: Most physical types commonly postulated by humanity have tokens that exist as such independently of the mental: i.e. these tokens might have existed and might have been of their respective types even had there been nothing mental.

One problem with this is that the truth of realism would require that there be humanity, and that it postulate types, indeed physical types. Surely the philosophical doctrine or realism is not specifically about humanity and what humanity does or does not postulate. So we try again.

Realism 2: Consider the physical types commonly postulated by humanity, and the statements, about each of these, that its tokens exist independently of the mental. Realism is the doctrine that most of these statements are true.

This is a realist doctrine all right. But so is the doctrine about the first physical type mentioned in the Bible and the statement that its tokens exist independently of the mental. And there are indefinitely many 'realist' doctrines of a similar cast, all of which seem inappropriately tied to the vagaries of human postulation. Why should realism be restricted to *these* statements, or, worse, to *most* of them?

For a doctrine less tied thus to humanity, consider this:

Realism 3: There are tokens independent of the mental in that they might have existed and have been of their respective types even had there been nothing mental.

This is indeed a kind of realism, but it is compatible with a Kantian doctrine of a noumenal reality beyond our ability to know or even to comprehend, and with the view that ordinary common-sense reality is dependent on human construction through conceptualization. So realism 3 is a rather weak doctrine. According to a stronger version:

Realism 4: The world of common-sense reality exists as it is thought to exist by at least the main lines of common sense, and this it does largely independently of the mental, in that it might have existed propertied and interrelated much as it is in fact propertied and interrelated even in the absence of anything mental.

Here 'common-sense reality' is the world as we commonsensically believe it to be, composed of things large and small, along with the medium-sized dry goods of daily commerce. For Kant such common-sense reality has only 'phenomenal' reality, constituted by human construction. Beyond this there is the 'noumenal' in-itself reality independent of human construction. But this is inaccessible to human cognition. Unlike Kant, more recent constructivists appeal to conceptual schemes distinctive of a particular culture. (Here Wittgenstein may be an exception, but his views are elusive: Is there a human form of life, unlike that of the lion, or is there more than one human form of life?)

Note how brief reflection has led us back to the aspect of realism 1 that we found initially off-putting. The problem is that if we abstract from humanity and its postulations, then we are left with too thin a notion of realism, one compatible with a Kantian view: an inaccessible noumenal reality along with a constructivist account of our ordinary world. A more interesting realism does after all apparently require reference to ourselves and our common-sense postulations.

Many and varied are the constructivist heirs of Kant in more recent times. For Nelson Goodman we make stars through our 'versions'. According to Hilary Putnam's 'internal realism', the world is somehow internal to our conceptual scheme. As Benjamin Whorf would have it, language is itself our main world-making tool. For Thomas Kuhn different thinkers live in different worlds, each defined by its own theoretical ontology. And many other varieties of anti-realism and relativism are now on the market.   E.S.

N. Goodman, *Ways of Worldmaking* (Indianapolis, 1978).
R. Rorty, *Philosophy and the Mirror of Nature* (Princeton, NJ, 1979).
B. Whorf, *Language, Thought, and Reality*, ed. and intro. John B. Carroll (Cambridge, Mass., 1956).

reality, levels of. The old conception of reality as hierarchical, embodied in the Great Chain of Being, re-emerged, secularized and purged of supernatural elements, in the late twentieth century. The world comprises not merely levels of complexity and levels of description, but levels of *being*: higher-level items depend on, but remain distinct from, items at lower levels. At the most basic level (if there is a most basic level) is the world described by physics. Arrangements of entities at this level 'realize' higher-level entities, and arrangements of these realize entities at still higher levels. The economy of Saskatchewan—a very high-level entity—is realized by the inhabitants of Saskatchewan, relations they bear to one another and to persons and institutions elsewhere. Persons and institutions are themselves realized by complex arrangements of psychological, biological, and inorganic entities. These in turn have still lower-level realizers.

Proponents of levels point to the 'irreducibility' of descriptions of and laws governing higher-level items. This encourages a picture of these higher-level items as 'floating above' their lower-level supports. Higher-level goings-on are thought to be governed by higher-level laws discoverable by the special sciences.

The nature of the realizing relation remains something of a mystery. *Supervenience* is occasionally invoked, but this is to re-label the relation, not to explain it. Some have doubted the coherence of levels: if higher-level entities depend on, but are distinct from, entities at lower levels, how could something at a higher level have a higher-level effect except by bringing about a lower-level change? Such 'downward' causation threatens the idea that the fundamental physical level constitutes a closed system governed by inviolable laws.

One possibility is that philosophers have conflated the innocuous idea that ways of describing and explaining the world exhibit a hierarchical structure with the much less innocuous idea that corresponding to each of these ways is a level of being. Moves of this kind have a chequered philosophical pedigree. They express the remarkable idea that we can 'read off' the structure of reality from the structure of the language we use to describe reality. Perhaps we can get by with one complex world capable of being described in endless ways depending on our interests and the level of detail we hope to comprehend.   J.HEIL

J. Heil, *From an Ontological Point of View* (Oxford, 2003).
J. Kim, 'The Layered Model: Metaphysical Considerations', *Philosophical Explorations*, 5 (2001).

realization. This is a term commonly used in contemporary metaphysics and philosophy of mind to denote a relationship between properties at different levels which is supposedly at once weaker than identity and stronger than mere causal connection. Thus, it is often held that mental properties are 'realized' by physical properties of the brain and nervous system, but that one and the same mental property—such as a certain quality of pain—may be realized by different neural properties in different sentient creatures. This is known as the 'multiple realization thesis'.   E.J.L.

*variable realization.

J. Heil, *The Nature of True Minds* (Cambridge, 1992).

reason. The general human 'faculty' or capacity for truth-seeking and problem-solving, differentiated from instinct, imagination, or faith in that its results are intellectually trustworthy—even to the extent, according to *rationalism, that reason is both necessary and sufficient for arriving at *knowledge. Although the reason–emotion and reason–experience distinctions are overworked, the claim that reason is the defining characteristic of human beings (the human essence) remains powerful.   A.BEL.

*reasoning; rationality; ratiocination; bladders of philosophy.

Nicholas Rescher, *Rationality: A Philosophical Inquiry into the Nature and the Rationale of Reason* (Oxford, 1988).

reason, practical: *see* practical reason.

reason as slave of the passions. A fundamental claim of Hume's moral psychology, used in his rebuttal of the rationalist pretence that reason can oppose the passions and teach us moral truths. 'Reason is, and ought only to be the slave of the passions, and can never pretend to any other office than to serve and obey them' (*Treatise*, II. iii. 3). In an employment of *Hume's fork, Hume insists that *demonstrative* reasoning (for example, in mathematics) plainly has no effect in itself on the passions; and *probable* reasoning is of significance to the passions only by 'directing' our aversion to pain, or our propensity to pleasure, to those things that we take to be causally related to them.

Hume may have inherited the expression from the article on Ovid in Bayle's *Dictionnaire*, one of the favourite works of Hume's early adulthood: 'Reason has become the slave of the passions'.   J.BRO.

J. L. Mackie, *Hume's Moral Theory* (London, 1980), ch. 3.

reasoning. Suppose you have (in mind) *reasons for believing you have been lied to, or reasons against visiting the dentist, or reasons to be proud of your children. These are mental states, states of holding reasons for, or against, believing something or doing (or choosing or aiming at) something or feeling somehow. The word 'reasoning' describes two associated *processes*: searching for such reasons (often co-operatively), and giving them when you or somebody else has found them. A third process, gaining understanding of reasons that somebody else has given, is similar.

Searching for reasons involves cogitation (thinking things through) and commonly also—though this is not reasoning—research. If you are confronted by a practical problem ('What should I do on this matter?') or a theoretical problem ('What is the truth on this matter?') or a response problem ('How should I feel on this matter?'), solving it is bound to involve some cogitation, however perfunctory: you must bring to mind further questions that seem relevant to solving the problem, you must ponder ('weigh') their relevance, and, if you have answers to them, you must finally derive (work out, calculate) a solution 'in the light of' the answers. Any answers you lack may be worth trying to discover, either by further cogitation (e.g. proving a lemma in mathematics) or by gathering information. The latter is where research comes in: ask someone, go and look, devise an experiment, etc. Since both parts of this composite activity contribute to finding reasons, both parts might with justice have been counted as reasoning, but in fact the research part is not—which is why philosophers who play down the role of research in theoretical inquiry can be called rationalists (Latin *ratio*, reason) and philosophers who emphasize it empiricists (Greek *empeiria*, experience).

Giving reasons is setting them out, to oneself or someone else. This too is a process, though a quite different one from searching for reasons. Since it can be rehearsed and repeated, it is likely to be more orderly than the search was. And since it is useful for persuading people, and necessary for transmitting knowledge (at the least, for displaying your *authority* as a purveyor of correct solutions), there is a motive for making it as orderly and lucid as possible. Even if you are not going public, reason-giving is a way of checking for yourself that a search has been conducted properly—that you have reasoned well.

You reason well when the reasons that you find, or give, *favour* (and not just seem to you to favour) the belief or action or response they are presented as reasons for; that is, they make it more likely that the belief is true or the action right or the response appropriate. So standards are required for judging whether, and preferably also for measuring how strongly, such-and-such reasons favour (or, as we often say, support) such-and-such a solution. Logic has sometimes been seen as the science of determining these standards, although nowadays its pretensions are narrower. The full-blown science would do two things: first represent each process of reasoning as the statement or production of an abstract entity called an argument, and then propose rules and principles that good arguments must observe (the rules license progressions through an argument, the principles are unspoken premisses we are allowed to add to any argument). Deductive logic achieves a bit of this brilliantly, but attempts to go beyond it have had little success. For example: what would be the *inductive* rule that specifies rightly when and to what degree observations (e.g. 'All your known ancestors were male') support generalizations (e.g. 'All your ancestors were male')? and what would be the *moral* principle that specifies rightly when and to what degree somebody's wanting a service from you is a good reason for your providing it? If such questions cannot be answered, good reasoning is an art that has no science.   C.A.K.

*ratiocination; rationality.

R. Descartes, *Rules for the Direction of the Mind* and *Discourse on the Method*, in *The Philosophical Writings of Descartes*, tr., J. G. Cottingham *et al.*, i (Cambridge, 1985).

G. Harman, *Change in View* (Cambridge, Mass., 1986).

S. E. Toulmin, *The Uses of Argument* (Cambridge, 1958).

reasoning, psychology of. Logicians are concerned to formulate normative principles of deductive and inductive reasoning, which instruct us how to reason correctly. Psychologists, on the other hand, seek to discover by empirical means what sorts of inferences human beings typically do make when confronted by reasoning tasks and what kinds of psychological processes underlie our reasoning activity. Some of their empirical evidence suggests that we are subject to deep-seated reasoning biases which often lead us to draw incorrect conclusions from the premises or data presented to us. For example, performance on the Wason selection task suggests that people make systematic errors of deductive reasoning with conditional sentences, sometimes failing to see that 'If p, then q' can be falsified by finding p to be true when q is false. Other studies indicate that people are subject to fundamental biases in their probabilistic reasoning, such as so-called base rate neglect. However, how do we know what constitutes *correct* reasoning if we really are so subject to reasoning bias? A paradox looms here.   E.J.L.

J. St B. T. Evans and D. E. Over, *Rationality and Reasoning* (Hove, 1996).

reasons, internal and external. This distinction between two sorts of practical reasons is owed to Bernard Williams. An agent S has an internal reason R to act only if R would motivate him to act if he were fully informed and deliberated correctly, starting from what he is presently motivated to do. Any reason that does not satisfy this condition is called 'external', but Williams claims that there are no external reasons. The thrust of Williams's *internalism* is, then, that each agent's reasons are constrained by what he is actually motivated to to, i.e. by his actual desires. One can have a reason to do something that one does not want to do, but only if one's actual desires would be changed by the provision of full information or by correct deliberation in such a way that one ends up wanting to do what one initially did not want to do. One's actual desires constitute the starting-point for this process, and so are bound to affect the result. Since people differ in their actual desires, the internalist claims that there can be no considerations that are reasons for everyone, irrespective of their own aims and purposes. Universal moral reasons thus become potentially suspect.   J.D.

reasons and causes. Phenomena the relation between which bears on the status of rational, or free, beings in the natural world.

Much common-sense psychological and historical explanation of people's beliefs and actions proceeds by saying what their *reasons* were. There are questions whether such explanations (i) are *causal*, (ii) mention items which are *causes* of what is explained. A negative answer to (i) is given by philosophers who place the study of human beings outside the causal sphere (often assumed to be coextensive with the objective sphere of science). An affirmative answer to (ii) ensures that accounts given from an internal human perspective and from a more external, causal perspective are concerned with the same items. Intermediate positions are possible.

When *action explanation is in question, the central question is often put, perhaps misleadingly, by asking 'Are reasons causes?'   J.HORN.

*mental causation.

Donald Davidson, 'Actions, Reasons and Causes', in *Essays on Actions and Events* (Oxford, 1980).

recurrence: *see* eternal recurrence.

recursion, definition by. A recursive *definition of an expression proceeds by first specifying a special subclass of the items it applies to and then specifying the remaining items it applies to in terms of a relation which any such item bears to an item to which the expression already applies. Thus the term 'ancestor' may be defined recursively as follows: (1) both of a person's parents are ancestors of that person; (2) any parent of an ancestor of a person is also an ancestor of that person; (3) nothing else is an ancestor of a person.   E.J.L.

B. C. van Fraassen, *Formal Semantics and Logic* (New York, 1971).

reducibility, axiom of. An axiom scheme of Russell's ramified theory of *types. This theory was constructed to avoid vicious-circle fallacies, which at one time Russell held to be the root error behind a wide variety of paradoxes including the *liar paradox and his own *Russell's paradox.

The ramified theory imposes a twofold classification on propositional (sentential) functions. First, such functions are arranged in a hierarchy according to the type of argument they take. So, for example, there are functions of individuals, functions of functions of individuals, etc. Second, the theory stratifies the functions which take a particular type of argument into orders according to the kind of expression that picks out the function (this is the ramification).

Russell prohibited unrestricted quantification over *all* the functions taking a particular type of argument. But this prohibition restricts the expressive power of the theory. So, to achieve the effect of the unrestricted quantification, Russell proposed the axiom of reducibility. Included in the lowest order of propositional functions are the predicative functions, which are picked out by expressions free from bound variables. The axiom of reducibility guarantees that the legitimate quantification over all predicative functions achieves the effect of the prohibited quantification over all functions regardless of order. The axiom applying to functions of individuals says that for any such function there is a predicative function that is formally equivalent (i.e. agrees in its mapping of arguments onto values).

A.D.O.

B. Russell and A. N. Whitehead, *Principia Mathematica* (Cambridge, 1910), i, ch. 2 of the Introduction and *12.

reducibility of consciousness: *see* consciousness, its irreducibility.

reductio ad absurdum. One of the following proof strategies:

1. A proposition P is proved by taking as a premiss the negation of P and demonstrating that, in conjunction with previously established premisses or axioms, a contradiction follows. Also known as indirect proof.

2. The negation of a proposition P is proved by taking P as a premiss and demonstrating that, in conjunction with previously established premisses or axioms, a contradiction follows.

In the notation of the *propositional calculus, if $((\sim P \cdot Q) \supset R)$ and $((\sim P \cdot Q) \supset \sim R)$ are provable and Q is a conjunction of established premisses, then a contradiction $(R \cdot \sim R)$ follows, which suffices for a *reductio* proof of P.

R.B.M.

reductio ad impossibile.

B. Mates, *Elementary Logic* (Oxford, 1972).

reductio ad impossibile. Proof of a proposition which involves demonstrating that its negation entails a contradiction; since a contradiction cannot be true, whatever entails it cannot be true. Proofs that $\sqrt{2}$ is irrational and that there are infinitely many primes are classic examples. Sometimes called indirect proof, and commonly called *reductio ad absurdum*, though this term is sometimes applied to arguments where what is entailed is merely an obvious falsehood rather than a contradiction.

M.C.

reductionism. One of the most used and abused terms in the philosophical lexicon, it is convenient to make a (three-part) division.

Ontological reductionism refers to the belief that the whole of reality consists of a minimal number of entities or *substances. One could be referring simply to entities of a particular kind (as in 'All organisms are reducible ultimately to molecules'), but often the claim is meant in the more metaphysical sense that there is but one substance or 'world stuff' and that this is material. Hence, ontological reductionism is equivalent to some kind of *monism, denying the existence of unseen life forces and such things, claiming that organisms are no more (nor less) than complex functioning machines. However, one might well be trying to reduce material things to some other substance, like *consciousness. Alternatively, one might even think that there are two or more irreducible substances. The aim would then be to reduce all other substances to these fundamental few.

Methodological reductionism claims that, in science, 'small is beautiful'. Thus the best scientific strategy is always to attempt explanation in terms of ever more minute entities. It has undoubtedly been the mark of some of science's greatest successes, and not just in physics. The major methodological reductive triumph of recent years has been the demonstration that the unit of classical heredity, the gene, is a macro-molecule, deoxyribonucleic acid (DNA). One should, however, keep in mind that 'small' in this context is a relative term, and one should be wary of making a straight identification between methodological reductionism and the commonly used 'micro-reductionism', especially if the latter implies that explanation is to be done in terms of micro-entities. The psychologist may try to reduce major sociological movements to the feelings and behaviours of individual humans; but may yet (with reason) think it would be silly to attempt a further reduction to molecules or below.

Despite its successes, methodological reductionism has been highly controversial, for it denies the claims of those (especially Marxists) who argue that the world is ordered hierarchically, and that entities at upper levels can never be analysed entirely in terms of entities at lower levels. Especially contentious has been so-called 'biological reductionism', generally associated with the socio-biological movement, where human nature is supposedly fully understandable in terms of genetics. It may be doubted whether anybody has ever truly argued that we humans are mere marionettes manipulated by the double helix; but it cannot be denied that some senior biologists have been much given to silly (and socially dangerous) flights of fancy about the control exerted on our lives by our biology.

Theory reductionism raises the question of the relation between successive theories in a field, as between Newton's theory and that of Einstein. Is it always one of replacement, where the new entirely expels the old, or is it sometimes one of absorption, or 'theoretical reduction', where the older is shown to be a deductive consequence of the new? Many have argued that, as in the Newton–Einstein case and also the classical–molecular genetics episode, one gets reduction rather than replacement. In the 1930s this kind of thinking was taken to the extreme, with the 'Unity of Science' movement committed to the belief that eventually all the sciences will (and should) be reduced to one super-theory (inevitably taken to be something in physics).

This kind of thinking has been strongly challenge by such thinkers as the philosopher-historian Thomas Kuhn, who believes that because the terms between theories are always 'incommensurable', theory reduction is never possible. Since this view of reduction is tied strongly to the picture of scientific theories as hypothetico-deductive systems, and since this latter picture has now fallen very much out of favour, many philosophers today would agree with their scientist colleagues that what matters is less the relationship between old and new than the relative merits of successive theories through time. This meshes also with the conviction of those who have turned their philosophical gaze from the physical sciences to other fields such as biology and psychology. Although few would deny the ontological claim that organisms, including humans, are made from the same materials as the rest of the physical world, it does not necessarily follow that the modes of explanation are the same throughout the scientific world or that a theoretical reduction is always possible or indeed fruitful.

M.R.

*reductionism, mental; methodology; scientific method; simplicity.

E. Nagel, *The Structure of Science* (New York, 1961).

M. Ruse, *Philosophy of Biology Today* (Albany, NY, 1988).

reductionism, mental. Reductionism about a given subject-matter *X* is the claim that facts about *X* can be 'reduced' to—that is, can be construed to *be*—facts about an apparently different subject-matter *Y* ('the reduction base'). Reductionism in philosophy of mind is the claim that facts about mentality are reducible to physical facts, i.e. facts about matter and material processes.

What is required to implement mind–body reduction? According to the *dualism of Descartes, minds exist as 'mental substances', objects wholly outside the physical domain. On this view, facts about mentality would be physically irreducible since they would be facts about these immaterial entities. The first requirement for mind–body reduction, therefore, is the renouncement of minds as non-physical objects. This can be done either by identifying minds with brains or other appropriate physical structures, or by attributing mental properties to organisms and possibly other types of physical systems, rather than to immaterial minds. In either case, it is physical systems that have psychological properties.

The remaining step in mind–body reduction concerns mental properties (e.g. being in pain, sensing a green patch, believing that snow is cold) and their analogues in systematic psychology. Let *M* be a mental property: the physical reduction of *M* is usually thought to require a 'physical correlate' of *M*, i.e. a physical property with which *M* is necessarily coextensive. When a pervasive system of physical correlates is found for mental properties, mental properties could, it is thought, be identified with their physical correlates.

Logical *behaviourism sought to reduce mental properties by defining them in terms of behaviours and behavioural dispositions. Although mentality seems intimately tied to behaviour, it is now widely agreed that psychological concepts in principle resist behavioural definitions. The demise of behaviouristic reductionism has led to the hope that the mental might be physically reduced through empirical laws connecting mental and physical properties. Nomological reduction of mental properties would proceed by providing for each mental property *M* a nomologically coextensive physical correlate *P*; that is, where '*M* occurs at time *t* if and only if *P* occurs at *t*' holds as a matter of law. According to the *identity theory of mind, every mental property has a neural correlate with which it is to be identified; if pain is uniformly correlated as a matter of law with, say, the activation of c-fibres, pain may be reductively identified with c-fibre activation, and similarly for other mental properties and kinds.

The significance of mind–body reduction is claimed to be twofold: ontological economy and unity of theory. By dispensing with minds as substances of a special sort and their irreducible psychic features, we simplify our ontology. By construing mental properties as complex neural properties and taking physical organisms as their bearers, psychology can be integrated with the underlying biological and physical sciences.

Two lines of consideration have been responsible for the decline of reductionism. One is psychophysical anomalism, the claim that there are no laws connecting mental and physical phenomena, and hence no laws of the sort required for the nomological reduction of the former to the latter. The other is the variable (or multiple) realizability of mental properties. If a mental property is multiply realized by a variety of physical properties in diverse species and structures, it could not, the argument goes, be identified with any single physical property. These considerations have led many philosophers to favour non-reductive physicalism, the doctrine that although all the individuals of this world are physical, certain properties of these individuals, in particular their psychological properties, are not reducible to the physical properties. (*Mind–body problem; *physicalism; *functionalism.) However, it remains a controversial question whether the variable realizability of the mental should be considered an obstacle to mental reductionism; it might be argued that the variable realizability in fact entails reducibility, that is, the possibility of *variable reductions* (or 'local reductions') relative to the species of organism or type of physical system involved.   J.K.

*simplicity.

D. Davidson, 'Mental Events', in *Essays on Actions and Events* (Oxford, 1980).

H. Feigl, *The 'Mental' and the 'Physical'* (Minneapolis, 1967).

J. Fodor, 'Special Sciences, or the Disunity of Science as a Working Hypothesis', *Synthese* (1974).

J. Kim, 'The Myth of Nonreductive Materialism', in *Supervenience and Mind* (Cambridge, 1993).

reductionism, psychological, in personal identity. The thesis, advocated by *Parfit, that our identity over time should be understood as psychological connectedness or psychological continuity with its normal cause, or with any other cause so long as there exists no other person psychologically connected with or continuous with us as we were. Parfit calls such connectedness or continuity 'Relation R'. Psychological connectedness is realized by, for example, direct memories, the relation between an intention and its later implementation in action, the persistence of beliefs or desires. Psychological continuity is the holding of overlapping chains of strong connectedness. For example, a person remembers some of their experiences the previous day, and on that day they remembered some of their experiences on the day before that, and so on.

The thesis is reductionist in avoiding the postulation of a Cartesian soul or substantial ego. Parfit argues that personal identity is not necessarily determinate. It need not be true or false that a later person is numerically identical with an earlier person, so answers to the questions 'Will it be me who suffers?' or 'Will it be me who dies?' need not be true or false.

As Parfit recognizes, there are interesting affinities between his view and some Buddhist views. The Buddha taught that it in a sense is and in a sense is not the same person who is reborn. Locke is also a psychological reductionist about personal identity, because he thinks sameness of person over time extends as far and only as far as may be established by memory, because being the same person presupposes the possibility of considering oneself the same person. Although Locke insists that the soul is redundant to the explanation of personal identity, he nevertheless claims it likely that the soul is that which is consciousness. S.P.

John Locke, *An Essay Concerning Human Understanding*, book II, ch. 27: 'Of Identity and Diversity'.

Derek Parfit, *Reasons and Persons* (Oxford, 1984), esp. part 3: 'Personal Identity'.

Walpola Rahula, *What the Buddha Taught* (Bedford, 1967), esp. ch. 6: 'The Doctrine of No-Soul: Anatta'.

redundancy theory of truth. This theory of *truth, pioneered by F. P. Ramsey, draws on the apparent equivalence between asserting a proposition *p* and asserting that *p* is true to claim that the truth-predicate 'is true' is redundant, in the sense that it is, in principle, always eliminable without loss of expressive power.

Difficulties appear to arise for the theory from cases in which propositions are said to be true even though the speaker may not know which propositions they are, and so cannot assert them himself, or when there are too many such propositions for each to be asserted individually, for example when someone claims 'Something that John said yesterday is true' or 'Everything asserted by a Cretan is true'. If the latter sentence is paraphrased as 'For any proposition *p*, if a Cretan asserts that *p*, then *p* is true', it is arguable that deleting the concluding words 'is true' renders the sentence ungrammatical and so senseless.
E.J.L.

*deflationary theories of truth; disquotation.

S. Haack, *Philosophy of Logics* (Cambridge, 1978).

Rée, Paul (1849–1901). German philosopher, noted for his radical *empiricism and uncompromising rejection of metaphysics and religion. The son of a wealthy Prussian landowner, Rée fought in the Franco-Prussian war of 1870. On his return he devoted himself to the study of philosophy, receiving a doctorate from the University of Halle.

In 1875 he published *Psychologische Beobachtungen* (Psychological Observations), a slim volume of aphorisms. In 1877 he published the much more substantial *Ursprung der moralischen Empfindungen* (The Origin of the Moral Sentiments). Strongly influenced by the British Empiricists and the work of Darwin, Rée argued that there are no universal moral principles whose truth is given a priori. What is regarded as right or wrong in any given society reflects the needs and cultural conditions of that society. Nietzsche, with whom Rée was on terms of close friendship from 1875 until 1882, commended this work as a 'decisive turn-ing-point in the history of moral philosophy'. Rée was Jewish, and his influence on Nietzsche was resented by several of Nietzsche's anti-Semitic friends. Rée had no contact with Nietzsche after 1882 and in his last years he expressed a low opinion of Nietzsche's achievements. Granting that Nietzsche was often very clever and that he could write superbly, Rée dismissed Nietzsche's *transvaluation of values as a 'mixture of insanity and nonsense'.

In 1885 Rée published *Die Illusion der Willensfreiheit* (The Illusion of Free Will) in which he maintained that it was entirely possible to abandon the belief in freedom and moral responsibility *in practice* and not only in one's philosophical theorizing.

Rée fell to his death from a Swiss mountain, and *Philosophie*, which was intended as a summation of his most basic convictions, was published posthumously in 1903. Here he offers a forthright defence of *atheism. Metaphysical systems Rée dismisses as 'fairy-tales' and 'lies'. Religions, he concludes, 'are true neither in the literal nor in an allegorical sense—they are untrue in every sense. Religion issues from a marriage of error and fear.' P.E.

Paul Rée, *Die Illusion der Willensfreiheit* (Berlin, 1885). Eng. tr. of key passages of this book contained in P. Edwards and A. Pap (eds.), *A Modern Introduction to Philosophy*, 3rd edn. (New York, 1973).

——*Basic Writings*, tr. and ed. R. Small (Champaign, Ill., 2003).

reference: *see* sense and reference.

referential opacity. Truth about a given object is not usually affected by the manner of referring to it, so that you could switch between, say, 'James', 'he', 'the fat one', 'Angela's ex'. But some (linguistic) contexts—i.e. verbal surroundings—do limit this freedom. For example, 'She knows who . . . is' may be true with 'that novelist' in its blank, but false when the novelist is referred to as 'the owner of the footprint' (this is the ancient *masked man fallacy). Such contexts are called referentially opaque, as opposed to referentially transparent. Possible explanations are: the expression does not really refer (Russell), or refers to something else (Frege, perhaps Aristotle), or does more than refer (Quine). C.A.K.

W. V. Quine, 'Reference and Modality', in *From a Logical Point of View*, 2nd edn. (Cambridge, Mass., 1964).

referring. Both expressions and their users can refer, and it is a matter of controversy which kind of referring is more fundamental. Intuitively, for an expression to refer is for it to stand for or pick out something, but what this involves has been long debated. According to Frege the reference of an expression is determined by its *sense, but lately Kaplan and Kripke have argued that some terms, such as demonstratives, proper names, and natural-kind terms, refer directly. A speaker refers if, in the course of expressing a *propositional attitude (e.g. the belief expressed in uttering 'Magritte was a philosophical painter'), he uses an expression ('Magritte') with the communicative intention of indicating to his audience the individual this attitude is about (Magritte).   K.B.

*communication.

Kent Bach, *Thought and Reference* (Oxford, 1987).

reflective equilibrium. Philosophers often attempt to justify general *principles on the grounds that they accord with our intuitive judgements concerning particular cases. It must be conceded that our unreflective intuitions may be confused or inconsistent. However, by successively advancing principles which seem to accord with most of our intuitions and re-examining any conflicting intuitions in the light of those principles, we may hope to move step by step towards a position of 'reflective equilibrium', in which our considered intuitions are fully in harmony with our considered principles. Whether the principles thus emerging would thereby be justified is a disputed issue.   E.J.L.

*Rawls.

reflexivity. A reflexive *relation is a binary, i.e. two-term, relation which everything has to itself (in symbols, *R* is reflexive if and only if ∀*xRxx*). 'Reflexive' may be understood relatively to what one is talking about (the domain of discourse); for example, *being the same age as* and *being no older than* are both reflexive relative to the domain of animals. Or one can distinguish 'strongly reflexive' (everything has it to itself) from 'weakly reflexive' (everything has it to itself that has it to anything). 'Irreflexive' means: nothing has it to itself. 'Non-reflexive' may mean either 'not reflexive' or 'neither reflexive nor irreflexive'.   C.A.K.

W. Hodges, *Logic* (Harmondsworth, 1977).

reform. The attempt to improve social, political, or legal institutions or policies without altering what is fundamental to them. The distinction between reform, as described above, and change (which does attempt to alter what is fundamental) was introduced by Burke and made by him central to *conservatism. The distinction can be used to defend the politics of modifying tradition against those of revolution. Yet the distinction between reform and change can be hard to defend in many political contexts, partly because it is not always clear what is of the essence and what is simply an accident, and partly because of uncertainty about how long a change has to be in existence before it ceases to be a change and becomes a new tradition. Moreover, even if the distinction can be clarified, it cannot be used to characterize all forms of conservatism because some are in favour of certain kinds of revolutionary change.   R.S.D.

E. Burke, *Letter to a Noble Lord* (1796).

A. Quinton, *The Politics of Imperfection: The Religious and Secular Traditions of Conservative Thought in England from Hooker to Oakeshott* (London, 1978).

regress, infinite: *see* infinite regress.

regulative principles guide our conduct although we have no assurance that they are actually true. Thus Kant claimed that it was rational to look for (and hope for) a system of knowledge which was complete and coherent in certain ways although we had no a priori guarantee that it could be found. A later Kantian philosopher, Peirce, held that all logical principles were hopes or regulative *principles.   C.J.H.

*rules.

I. Kant, *Critique of Pure Reason*, tr. N. Kemp Smith (London, 1968), app. to the Transcendental Dialectic.

Reich, Wilhelm (1897–1957). Austrian psychiatrist and social theorist whose notoriety for the orgone theory (an energy that is supposed to permeate the cosmos and possess healing powers) has obscured his earlier ideas, some of which are of philosophical interest.

Undoubtedly Reich's philosophically most interesting idea is that of the 'muscular armour' which grew out of his earlier notion of the 'character armour', Reich's term for the set of chronic defensive attitudes a person adopts to protect himself against external injury (such as being hurt or rejected by other human beings) and against his own repressed emotions, especially rage and anxiety. Even in his earlier psychological studies, which were brought together in *Character Analysis* (1933), Reich repeatedly pointed to the chronic tensions he noted in the faces and movements of many of his patients. While teaching at Oslo University in the 1930s he undertook a systematic study of the anchoring of neurotic attitudes in the body, e.g. anxiety in the hunching of the shoulders and in veiled eyes, rage in a tight chin, disgust in a certain expression of the mouth, etc. Reich from then on rejected the purely verbal approach of Freudian and other analytic techniques. In retrospect he observed that, prior to the discovery of the muscular armour and methods of dissolving it, analytic treatment could not achieve more than a very limited measure of success. He now abandoned the dualistic theories about body and mind tacitly or explicitly accepted by many psychologists and most psychoanalysts. In the place of *dualism he advocated an *identity theory: the muscular armour and the character armour are 'functionally' identical in the sense of serving the same function, namely that of blinding emotions such as anger and anxiety. It is a mistake to regard the muscular rigidity as a mere accompaniment or an effect of the corresponding character attitude: it is 'its somatic side and the basis for its continued existence'.

Reich developed social theories during the 1930s when he was attempting to fashion a synthesis of *Marxism and *psychoanalysis. Opposing what he described as the 'feudal individualistic psychology' of Freud, Reich denied that a given society is the result of a certain psychic structure. The reverse is true: 'character structure is the result of a certain society'. The ideology of a society can anchor itself only in a certain character structure, and the institutions of that society serve the function of producing this character structure. These ideas were presented in 'Character and Society' (1936) and in two books, *The Mass Psychology of Fascism* (1933) and *The Sexual Revolution* (1936).   P.E.

Paul Edwards, 'Wilhelm Reich', in Paul Edwards (ed.), *Encyclopedia of Philosophy* (New York, 1967), contains biographical information and discussions of all of Reich's major theories.

Reichenbach, Hans (1891–1953). Although closely identified with the Logical Positivist movement, Reichenbach was critical of the narrow scope of its verificationism, and preferred to speak of himself as a *'logical empiricist'. Most significant and influential was his thinking on probability and *induction. He was one of the most powerful advocates of a frequency interpretation of induction, believing the assignment of probabilities to be an empirical matter rather than something for a priori determination. Thus the estimation of the probability of throwing a six on a die is to be understood as the converging limit of a long series of throws rather than the simple result of an evenly distributed apportioning of the total possible number of outcomes. Probability thus understood, induction in turn is to be analysed empirically. This means that there can be no ultimate proof of induction; but, through discovered frequencies one can calculate which strategies or options are most reliable, given that induction does work.

Reichenbach was also much interested in problems of *space and *time, feeling that the physics of his day pointed him towards conventionalism. Notions like equality and simultaneity depend as much upon convention and definition as they do on empirical necessity. To talk, for instance, of the *equality* of successive time sequences requires a definition rather than empirical determination, for the result can only be understood relative to some particular system. Likewise, in dealing with *quantum mechanics, Reichenbach felt that he must break from the strict traditions of earlier thinkers, for issues such as the supposed wave and particle nature of electrons demand more than classical logic. Therefore, although the answers of physics may be meaningful, with respect to the real world they must be considered as in some sense indeterminate in truth-status.   M.R.

H. Reichenbach, *The Rise of Scientific Philosophy* (Berkeley, Calif., 1951).

W. Salmon, 'Should we Attempt to Justify Induction?', *Philosophical Studies* (1957).

Reid, Thomas (1710–96). Deservedly remembered as Hume's most famous critic, Reid, a clergyman's son, attended Aberdeen Grammar School and Marischal College. His first job was as a presbytery clerk. During his next, as Librarian to Marischal, he was active in philosophical circles. His subsequent appointment as a parish minister was achieved through the patronage of King's College, Aberdeen, causing the congregation to protest and some even to assault him. At this time he was a keen astronomer. He presented a paper on quantity to the Royal Society of London. He then became Regent in Philosophy at King's College. There he published *An Inquiry into the Human Mind, on the Principles of Common Sense* (1764), his most remarkable work, which combines philosophy and science. In the same year, as recognition of his talent grew, he replaced Adam Smith as Professor of Moral Philosophy in Glasgow. His *Essays on the Intellectual Powers of Man* (1785) and *Essays on the Active Powers of the Human Mind* (1788) appeared after his retirement at the age of 70. They were widely used as textbooks, especially in America. He then helped to found Glasgow Infirmary. Having himself always relied on patronage, he supported the French Revolution, but was disappointed by its excesses. His work became an official part of the French university curriculum.

He writes plainly but with authority. His aim is to expose the faults of 'the ideal system' and to replace it with 'the principles of *common sense', a form of *realism. The mind works according to innate principles of conception and belief which are challenged by the ideal system, whose proponents include Descartes, Locke, Berkeley, and Hume. Concerning belief in the external world, according to Reid the mind is so constituted that *sensation automatically causes belief in external objects. A sensation of smell, for example, causes the belief that there is an external cause of the sensation. The belief is neither inferred nor rational but is caused by the occurrence of the sensation. Reid thus analysed *perception into sensation and belief in what causes sensation. To Descartes and Locke, who say that there is an external physical world which we perceive by means of sensory representations, Reid replies that sensations cannot represent physical objects, since they do not resemble them in any way. To Berkeley and Hume, who argue that we take our perceptions for external objects, he replies that sensations cannot be taken for objects, since their difference from external objects is intuitively obvious to common-sense. In short the ideal system does not acknowledge the obvious qualitative differences between sensations and objects. The role of sensation is not representational but significational. How sensation can signify its external cause is inexplicable and certainly non-rational. Because sensations are unlike objects they give no content to belief in external objects, except in the case of secondary qualities like smell, taste, and colour, which are conceived as external causes of the corresponding sensations, but causes of indeterminate character. Sensations of primary qualities, unlike sensations of secondary, occasion clear conceptions of the external qualities causing them. This is an interesting departure from Locke's primary–secondary distinction.

Reid was an ethical intuitionist who argued that we naturally develop a power to judge what is due to a person as a right. Hume failed to see that approval is a power of judgement rather than feeling. What we judge, unlike what we feel, is true or false and can be contradicted. Reid stressed the importance of *free will as a condition of deserving praise or blame, when the agent has the power to determine what he wills by conceptions of good and ill.

Free will is inconsistent with necessity but not with fore-knowledge, any more than with memory.

Reid's criticism is frequently sound, and his positive theory occasionally inspired, as when, in discussing visible figure, he tries to marry optical fact with philosophical fancy. Here he departs from his original theory of perception when he says that we directly perceive what he calls 'visible figure', which is a real figure projected on to the retina, a figure representing the spatial relations of the parts of an external object. We have no sensation of visible figure. Reid thus preserves his fundamental principle that sensation is unlike anything external, while asserting that we are directly aware of something—visible figure—which does represent something external. Reid hoped that Hume would reply to his criticisms, but Hume's disdainful response was to recommend him to avoid Scotticisms and improve his English.   v.h.

T. Cuneo and R. van Woudenberg (eds.), *The Cambridge Companion to Thomas Reid* (Cambridge, 2004).

Keith Lehrer, *Thomas Reid* (London, 1989).

Thomas Reid: Inquiry and Essays, intro. R. E. Beanblossom, ed. R. E. Beanblossom and Keith Lehrer (Indianapolis, 1983).

D. Schulthess, *Philosophie et sens commun chez Thomas Reid* (Berne, 1983).

P. B. Wood, *Thomas Reid and the Scottish Enlightenment* (Toronto, 1985).

reincarnation. A distinct new bodily life, generally with a new identity and usually as a rebirth, of someone who has died. Beliefs in reincarnation can be found both in ancient Greece and in ancient India, and the Greek idea that the soul about to be reincarnated drinks from the river Lethe (forgetfulness) is typical of the assumption that those who are reincarnated remember little or nothing. The interesting philosophical question is: In what sense does the reincarnation count as the same person as the deceased? The Buddhist critique of Hindu metaphysics centred on this, and *The Questions of King Milinda* argues that any determination of sameness is essentially arbitrary. Even if psychic drives of the deceased in some way led to the new life, the relation between the two lives could be compared to that of a new flame to the pre-existing flame from which it is lit. 'Are these two different flames or the same flame?', the Buddhist philosopher asks; and the implication is that there is no basis for an answer.   j.j.k.

*Buddhist philosophy; death; immortality.

Wendy O'Flaherty (ed.), *Karma and Rebirth in Classical Indian Traditions* (Berkeley, Calif., 1980).

relations. Ways in which things can stand with regard to one another (for example, some things are *older* than others), or to themselves (for example, each thing is *identical* to itself).

If one thing, *x*, stands in some relation, *R*, to any thing, *y*, then only if *y* stands in the same relation to *x* is *R* a *symmetrical* relation. Thus 'as old as' is symmetrical; if *x* is as old as *y*, *y* is as old as *x*. Other relations are *asymmetrical*; Bud can't be heavier than Thelonius if Thelonius is

heavier than Bud. If *x* is larger than *y*, and *y* is larger than *z*, then *x* is larger than *z*. Such relations are *transitive*. By contrast fatherhood is *intransitive*: your father's father is no father of yours. Relations which hold only between numerically distinct objects are *irreflexive*. But not all relations are irreflexive; each thing is as old as itself.

Logicians treat both relations and non-relational properties as sets. Non-relational properties are identified with sets of single objects; for example, 'red' is the set which includes such things as ripe tomatoes, drops of fresh blood, etc. Two-term relations (e.g. 'double') are sets of ordered pairs (e.g. $\langle 2,1 \rangle$, $\langle 4,2 \rangle$, etc.) Three-term relations, like 'between', are sets of ordered triples. And so on. The identity of a relation, so conceived, depends upon the membership of the set with which it is identified. The truth of a relational claim will depend upon whether the objects it says are related belong to ordered pairs (triples etc.) in the relevant set.

Relations might seem to be special sorts of object which can connect other things, but which are numerically distinct and ontologically independent from items they connect. But then, by an argument best known from F. H. Bradley, 3 is not the successor of 2 unless in addition to 'successor', there is a second relation—'connector', say—which links the numbers to 'successor', a third relation to connect 'connector' to 'successor', and so on. Frege avoids this sort of regress by treating relations as structurally incomplete partial objects which cannot occur without relata to complete them. So conceived, relations no more require additional relations to connect them to their relata than bricks require additional bricks to connect them to their shapes. Relations are not objects which can occur all by themselves until something connects them to relata.

An alternative solution from Wittgenstein's *Tractatus* banishes relations from the ranks of ontologically basic items: basic objects hang together without connectors like links in a chain, and facts which seem to involve relations between non-basic objects reduce to chainlike concatenations of basic objects.   j.b.b.

*relations, the nature of.

F. H. Bradley, *Appearance and Reality*, 2nd edn. (Oxford, 1930), 27 ff.

Michael Dummett, *Frege: Philosophy of Language*, 2nd edn. (Cambridge, Mass., 1981), 173–9.

Benson Mates, *Elementary Logic* (New York, 1965), 32 ff.

Ludwig Wittgenstein, *Tractatus Logico-Philosophicus* (London, 1961).

relations, internal and external. A distinction important to arguments between turn-of-the-century idealists and their opponents. If one item, *x*, stands in some relation, *R*, to another item, *y*, but neither its identity nor its nature depends upon this being the case, *x* is *externally* related to *y*. If *x* could not be the same item, or an item of the same kind, without standing in relation *R* to *y*, the relation is *internal*. You would think relations come in both flavours. Since no number can be identical to 2 unless it is greater than than 1, 2 is *internally* related to 1. But presumably your copy of the *Oxford Companion* would be exactly the same individual of exactly the same kind even if you did not own it, and even if it were lying on your floor instead of your table. If so, it is *externally* related to you and your table.

But F. H. Bradley and other idealists tried to show that either there are no relations at all, or else all relations must be internal. Like Parmenides and Zeno before them, they held that without relations nothing could be larger or smaller, nearer or farther, older or younger, or in any other way different from anything else, and the universe would be a completely undifferentiated whole. But since everything is related (e.g. temporally or spatially) to everything else, if all relations are internal, the nature and identity of each thing depends upon its relation to everything else. This dilemma was invoked to support extravagantly holist claims. The attempts of Bertrand Russell, G. E. Moore, and their followers to understand relations in such a way as to avoid holisms thus generated were decisive to the development of British *analytic philosophy.   J.B.B.

*idealism; relations, the nature of.

Peter Hylton, *Russell, Idealism, and the Emergence of Analytic Philosophy* (Oxford, 1992), 54 ff., 121 ff., 184, 225 ff., 281, 327.
G. E. Moore, 'External and Internal Relations', in *Philosophical Studies* (Paterson, NJ, 1959).

relations, the nature of. The nature of *relations first became an important metaphysical issue in modern philosophy with Leibniz. He regarded it as a problem where the relation R which links individuals *a* and *b* is located. It cannot just be in one of them, for it would not then link them, nor can it be in some kind of void between them. Such reflections on relations were one main source for his monadistic metaphysics of windowless *monads. For he had to interpret '*a* is R to *b*' as ascribing a separate predicate to each of *a* and *b*. 'Adam is the father of Cain' thus means that Adam has a certain property (being father of such-and-such a person) and Cain has a certain property (being child of such-and-such a father). These two individuals thus have properties which in a manner reflect each other but which do not bring them really together except in an 'ideal' or 'conceptual' way. A rather similar puzzle about the location of relations figures in the rationale of some forms of metaphysical monism (or absolute *idealism) for which there is only one ultimate subject of predication. For since relations cannot be in either (or any) of the related terms separately it seems that they must really be a property of the whole the terms make up together, so that, if every item in the world is related to every other, then, according to a fairly obvious line of argument, the relations between them collapse into *gestalt* properties of that all inclusive whole to which they all belong, i.e. the Universe, the One, or the Absolute.

This account of the metaphysical significance of theories of relations is that of Bertrand Russell (especially in *The Principles of Mathematics*), and it certainly throws some light on Leibnizian monadism and Bradleian monism, though Russell is less than just to them in detail. For Rus-

sell a pluralistic metaphysics, stopping short of the extreme pluralism of monadism, becomes defensible once we realize that propositions of a relational form ('*Rab*') cannot and need not be reduced to ones of (single) subject–predicate form ('*Fa*' or '*Fa · Gb*'). William James also developed a (phenomenologically rather richer) account of relations than Russell's, similarly designed to resist the lure of monism; Husserl, Whitehead, and Hartshorne are all important in this context too.

Closely connected with such debates is the issue of the externality or internality of relations. A relation between two (or more) terms is said to be 'internal' if its holding is either necessitated by or necessitates the so-called 'natures' of these terms; otherwise it is external. (Their natures are best understood as what they are within their own bounds.) Russell claimed that all relations are external; absolute idealists, so far as they countenance relations at all, incline to think them all internal. Other philosophers affirm relations of both types, and some (e.g. Hartshorne) hold that the most important two-term relations are internal to one term, external to the other.

Discussion is often complicated by confusion between two different types of putative internal relation. Sometimes internal relations are those which Hume described as depending entirely on a comparison between ideas and external relations are those which may vary though the ideas remain the same (*Treatise*, I. iii. 1 and 2). A similar more modern classification (by Meinong and others) of relations is into *ideal* relations whose holding follows from what each term is 'like' (what one-place universals it exemplifies) within its own bounds (a colour contrast, for example) and *real* relations not thus settled by facts about what each term is 'like' considered on its own (juxtaposition in space or time and causality are typically thus conceived). (This classification concerns relations between particulars; relations between *universals in abstraction from any exemplification may be called ideal in an obviously related sense.) It is a mistake, however, to take monists who claim that all relations are internal as claiming that they are all simply ideal in this sense; that way lies monadism rather than monism. They mean rather that their holding is a matter of their terms belonging together within a whole the character of which modifies that of each of them (rather than that they hold in virtue of the character of each term as that can be discovered separately). In short, for them it is as much the relation which determines the characters of the terms as the converse.

The fact that modern formal logic takes relational propositions easily on board, as Aristotelian and scholastic logic did not, tends to blind people to the fact that there are real metaphysical problems about relations essential to dealing with what William James described as 'the most central of all philosophical problems', the problem of the one and the many.   T.L.S.S.

*relations, internal and external.

F. H. Bradley, *Appearance and Reality* (1897), 2nd edn. (Oxford, 1930), chs. 2 and 3, app. B.

William James, *A Pluralistic Universe* (New York, 1909).

B. Russell, *The Principles of Mathematics* (1903), 2nd edn. (London, 1937), ch. 26.

—— *Philosophical Essays* (London, 1910), ch. 6.

T. L. S. Sprigge, *The Vindication of Absolute Idealism* (Edinburgh, 1983), ch. 5.

relativism, epistemological. Relativist theories of *knowledge are as old as Methuselah, or at least Protagoras, and as fashionable as Foucault or Rorty, but their exact import remains elusive. Protagoras put it pithily, and provoked Socrates to question what he meant, and how it could possibly be true, by saying: 'Man is the measure of all things; of what is that it is, and of what is not that it is not.'

This *bon mot* is striking but susceptible of many interpretations. Protagoras was principally concerned with perceptual knowledge and individual human variations. He seems to have thought that whatever any given individual believed was true (for him or her). Socrates has little trouble showing the absurdities of this, since the individual has to understand what it is to make perceptual mistakes, whether detected by himself or others. Indeed, global *relativism at the level of 'true for me' has so little to recommend it that its popularity with ordinary people is truly astonishing. We need only ask whether the claim that 'X is true for me' is itself merely true for me (and so on) to realize that what merit there may have been in the original relativization attached not to the truth-predicate, but to something in the content of the belief. One can indeed make a case for certain local relativisms, such as the relativities supposed to be involved in judgements of taste. But if such judgements do amount to no more than affirmations of personal or group likings, then these affirmations themselves seem to stand beyond relativization.

Sometimes the rhetoric of relativism merely draws our attention to the need for a conceptual framework to interpret reality without denying that there is a reality to be thus understood, but full-blooded relativism eschews the very idea of an uninterpreted reality that is as it is independently of us or of some scheme of understanding. Here the issues merge with those of metaphysics and semantics and the relativism debate moves confusingly between such issues as *idealism and *realism, *coherence versus *correspondence theories of truth, *pragmatism and (again) realism. One persistent argument for radical relativism is that which points to the impossibility of saying, understanding, or communicating any truth without employing a language or conceptual scheme. It is then urged that the truth so conveyed is radically dependent upon the scheme in which it is set. If the relativist denies that truths expressed in one language or culture are capable of expression in others, there is room for argument about this thesis. But in fact the argument itself must be couched in a scheme or a language, and that would apparently prejudge the issue. The idea of a *conceptual scheme here staggers under the weight that relativism puts upon it, since, understood in an everyday fashion, the topic is

perfectly discussable (e.g. the question 'Can the concept of ennui be expressed in English?' can be discussed in English), whereas the relativist will always insist that there is a philosophical sense in which no vantage-point is available from which to gain a purchase upon the conceptual scheme itself. The scheme seems to be at once in the world and beyond it. This is simply one aspect of the problem posed by the status of relativism itself as a truth. Is it true relative only to some culture or language or individual, or does its truth transcend such restrictions? If the former, then there are perhaps contexts in which it counts (relatively) as false; if the latter, then the thesis seems to be abandoned.

The range of the relativist relation is important. Perhaps we should take Protagoras seriously when he offers mankind as the relativization, and see this as an alternative to individual, cultural, or linguistic relativization. But what then of Martians?   C.A.J.C.

D. Davidson, 'On the Very Idea of a Conceptual Scheme', in *Inquiries into Truth and Interpretation* (Oxford, 1984).

Plato, *Theaetetus*.

Richard Rorty, *Philosophy and the Mirror of Nature* (Princeton, NJ, 1979).

relativism, ethical. The view that moral appraisals are essentially dependent upon the standards that define a particular moral code, the practices and norms accepted by a social group at a specific place and time. Given that there is in fact a plurality of social groups, with differing mores, the relativist argues that there exists no point of view from which these codes can themselves be appraised, no 'absolute' criteria by which they can be criticized.

In support of his claims, the relativist refers to anthropological evidence of cultural diversity, historical and geographical, now known to be enormously greater than could have been suspected by moralists like Hume or Kant. The relativist theory also draws on notions extensively deployed elsewhere in recent philosophy, such as 'alternative *conceptual schemes' and *'language-games'. On some accounts cultural divergence can amount to 'incommensurability', the complete absence of common concepts and perspectives.

Accepting the prima-facie divergences of moral outlook, a critic can none the less argue that the relativist tends to exaggerate their implications. Some common basic human values *can* be discerned over a great range of cultures, communities, social groups: e.g. moral condemnation of the leader who uses his power to exploit and oppress his people; and the agreement, among radically different groups, about the need for impartial determination of disputes by an authorized individual or body. Some writers, John Finnis for one, propose several 'basic forms of good' including knowledge, life, sociability, 'practical reasonableness', that underlie and give a rationale to moral rule-making, and provide significant common ground between groups and their codes. That suffices to give access to reasonable dialogue and makes possible criticism both of one's own moral outlook and of the outlooks of others.

It has sometimes been thought that moral relativism gives a special support to toleration as a moral attitude to codes which diverge from one's own. Paradoxically, however, if that were accepted as a universal (and universally morally approvable) attitude, it would contradict the relativism which disallows any universally authoritative principles!   R.W.H.

J. Finnis, *Natural Law and Natural Rights* (Oxford, 1980).
D. McNaughton, *Moral Vision: An Introduction to Ethics* (Oxford, 1988).
B. Williams, *Morality* (London, 1973).
—— *Ethics and the Limits of Philosophy* (London 1985).

relativism, linguistic: *see* metaphysics, problems of.

relativity theory, the philosophical relevance of. In Einstein's special relativity temporal relations are not absolute; events happening simultaneously at different places in one frame of reference will not be simultaneous in all frames of reference. Minkowski's geometrical interpretation of the theory, which treats time as a fourth dimension, has been widely regarded as profoundly affecting our conceptions of *space and *time: but his often quoted remark that space and time will 'sink into mere shadows, and only a kind of union of them shall survive' is the sort of purple pronouncement which should be treated with scepticism.

General relativity raises questions about the relation between physics and geometry, denying the latter its traditional role as an *a priori discipline; and it bears on the traditionally metaphysical dispute whether all motion is relative and whether space and time are relations among things or exist independently.   M.C.

J. R. Lucas and P. E. Hodgson, *Spacetime and Electromagnetism* (Oxford, 1990).

relevance logic. A system of logic in which premisses and conclusion are relevant to one another. It was born out of a paper by Wilhelm Ackermann, 'Begründung einer strengen Implikation', in the *Journal of Symbolic Logic* for 1956. In that paper Ackermann developed a formal theory of implication which was free of both the paradoxes of *material implication (which C. I. Lewis had avoided in his calculus of *strict implication) and those of strict implication (to which Lewis had succumbed). Ackermann's idea was of an implication in which the antecedent 'has a logical connection' with the consequent. Anderson and Belnap transmuted this, and gave two explications of 'logical connection' or 'relevance': one was 'variable-sharing', meaning at the propositional level sharing of content (in a valid entailment, premisses and conclusion must share a variable); the other was of dependency, that when an entailment is valid there is a way of deducing the conclusion from the premisses with no funny business, that is, in which the premisses really are used to obtain the conclusion. In satisfying these criteria, relevance logic distances

itself from classical logic, in which a contradiction entails any proposition whatever (so premisses and conclusion need share no variable) and any logically true proposition is derivable from any other propositions whatever (so the latter are not 'used' in deriving the former).

Several decades after its conception, relevance logic is now an accepted logic. What is not accepted, however, is—as was intended—that it is the one true logic to displace classical logic. It is part of a panoply of logics—classical, modal, intuitionist, linear, substructural, and so on—each one of which benefits from being elaborated in the context of others. Relevance logics are essentially those which reject weakening or dilution in its full classical form, as being a source of irrelevance. (Weakening says that if one proposition follows from another, it also follows from it in conjunction with any other proposition.) Linear logics do so too, and reject contraction as well (that repeated uses of an assumption can be replaced by a single use), emphasizing for constructive purposes the need to track uses of assumptions; they reintroduce irrelevance through the so-called 'exponentials', or modal connectives.

Relevance logics have axiomatic, natural deduction, and sequent (or 'consecution') proof theories; algebraic and possible-worlds semantics; and have been used as the basis for arithmetic and set theory. They should be distinguished from dialetheic or paraconsistent logics, in which true contradictions are admitted. The idea of relevance simply has the consequence that contradictory assumptions do not spread or permeate to force triviality—as in classical theories—because of the rejection of the idea that a contradiction entails everything. As a consequence of this rejection, these logics also reject detachment for material implication (or disjunctive syllogism), basing valid detachment instead on the relevant conditional (or entailment).   S.L.R.

J. M. Dunn, 'Relevance Logic and Entailment', in D. Gabbay and F. Guenthner (eds.), *Handbook of Philosophical Logic*, iii (Dordrecht, 1986).
S. Read, *Relevant Logic* (Oxford, 1988).

reliabilism. In traditional epistemology what makes a belief justified, being a matter of the believer's rationality and responsibility, must lie within his 'cognitive grasp'. That is, for a belief to be justified the believer must be aware of what makes it justified. This restrictive, internalist conception of justification has the sceptical effect of disqualifying far too many beliefs that intuitively seem justified. Reliabilism, a form of externalism, holds that a belief can be justified if formed as the result of a reliable process, even if the believer is unaware of what makes it justified. Different versions of reliabilism impose various constraints designed to meet certain internalist objections, such as that reliabilism cannot disallow irrational and irresponsible epistemic behaviour without lapsing into internalism, and they spell out in different ways the operative standard of reliability, which may involve explanatory as well as statistical factors.   K.B.

*justification, epistemic; knowledge; epistemology, problems of.

The Monist, 68/1–2: *Knowledge, Justification, and Reliability* (1985).

religion, history of the philosophy of. Since the terms English-speakers translate as 'philosophy' and 'religion' have taken dozens of meanings in the European languages from antiquity on, it is impossible to speak of 'philosophy of religion' as if it were one subject-matter stretched across Western intellectual history. The term is ambiguous even in contemporary usage, and its historical application provokes any number of problems. But the term has taken on a fairly specific technical sense in recent English-language philosophy. 'Philosophy of religion' comprises philosophical analyses of certain concepts or tenets central to the monotheistic Western religions and especially to Christianity. These concepts or tenets typically include the rationality of belief in *God, the demonstrability of God's existence, the logical character of religious language, and apparent contradictions between divine attributes and features of the world—say, between omnipotence and evil, miraculous interventions and natural law, omniscience and free will. The field has also reached out to include topics concerning the incarnation of God, the inspiration of Scripture, religious rituals or sacraments, the forgiveness of sin, mystical experience, and personal immortality.

'Philosophy of religion' and its equivalents in other European languages are fairly new, as philosophical terms go. They were coined towards the end of the eighteenth century as replacements or specifications of the earlier term 'natural theology'. Hence in texts of the 1780s and 1790s the content of 'philosophy of religion' is a set of rationally discoverable truths helpful to religion and accessible to philosophy. This Enlightened philosophy of religion is the means of accommodating a newly critical philosophy with a somewhat sanitized Christianity. But the term had already changed its meaning by the early decades of the nineteenth century. For readers of Schleiermacher on religion, 'philosophy of religion' comes to refer to a moralized and aesthetic teaching about cosmic purposes. For Hegel, it is at least a study of the ways in which God is represented in religious consciousness. Hence it is one of the last stepping-stones on the way towards a properly philosophic understanding of the divine. 'Philosophy of religion' has something very much like the Hegelian sense in John Caird's *An Introduction to the Philosophy of Religion* (1880), which is one of the texts by which the term was popularized in English. Indeed the Hegelian sense of the phrase remained so strong for English-speakers into the 1950s that some analytic philosophers preferred to speak of 'philosophical theology' rather than 'philosophy of religion'. These terms are now used for the most part as if they were interchangeable.

Whatever the terms used, it is important to see that contemporary English-speaking 'philosophy of religion' treats topics and arguments that were earlier conceived as belonging to very different studies. The topics and arguments fell under what certain Greek philosophers called simply 'philosophy' or 'metaphysics', what patristic and medieval Christians called 'wisdom' or 'holy teaching' or 'theology', and what philosophic writers in the modern period called 'natural theology' or 'preambles of faith' or 'natural religion'. These different titles indicate very different views on the principles and procedures to be used in addressing such topics and arguments. The remainder of this entry will point to a few of the more interesting or influential of those views.

Greek philosophers before Socrates took up what we call religious matters in at least three ways. First, some of them criticized and even mocked implausible or contradictory features of ordinary religious conceptions. So Xenophanes attacks both the immorality and the anthropomorphism of the poets' depictions of the gods. Second, some Pre-Socratics proposed mechanical or physical causes for events earlier attributed more directly to divine intention or design. Third, many of them wanted to understand the divine itself in ways at odds with conceptions drawn from ordinary experience. Their efforts in both directions were caricatured by the public imagination as a badly concealed impiety. So Aristophanes could in *Clouds* depict all philosophizers as irreligious, and Socrates could plausibly be accused in court of inventing new gods.

With Plato and Aristotle, these three relations to religion are transformed in ways that fix much of the later philosophical discussion. Plato's Socrates defends traditional mythology and participates in civic rituals. He recounts to Phaedrus details of the myth about Boreas and Orithyia, for example, and he dismisses those who would explain it more naturalistically (*Phaedrus* 229b–230a). He makes a point of going to religious festivals (*Republic* 327a) and frequently alludes to the Mysteries. His last words are a command to carry out a ritual sacrifice on his behalf (*Phaedo* 118a). More formally, Plato's dialogues often turn on a rejection of doubts about the divine. The Eleatic Stranger extracts from Theaetetus a heartfelt rejection of *scepticism and a profession that all of nature issues from the divine (*Sophist* 265c–e). The Athenian in the *Laws* provides numerous sample arguments against those who would deny the existence, nature, or providence of the gods (book 10). At the same time, Plato advocates and performs extensive revaluations of the poetic accounts of the Olympian gods, and he composes his own myths to teach how different the divine is from ordinary conceptions of it. His constant teaching is that human beings in the present life know little enough of their own souls and less of the divine. The work of philosophy is thus to lead souls out the snares of sensory and especially political illusion so that they may begin to participate in the divine. The Platonic representations of this journey include references to various kinds of divine agency, including revelation and judgement. But Plato's most enduring representation of divine action comes in the *Timaeus*, which tells the story, however ironically or allegorically, of a divine artisan who makes the cosmos.

It is impossible to say how much of the language and images of civic religion and of initiation into the mystery cults there may have been in Aristotle's public works. Only the private or school writings survive intact. In them there are certainly both criticisms of popular misconceptions and moments of piety. More important for the later traditions are Aristotle's arguments for the existence of a divine first mover of the cosmos and his characterization of that entity. At the end of *Physics* (book 8) and then summarily at the high point of *Metaphysics* (book 12), Aristotle argues that the impossibility of infinite regress in motion requires that there be a fully actualized being who causes all other motions by being the universal object of desire. In the same passage of *Metaphysics*, Aristotle describes the life of this being as an endless thinking on itself, a thinking that produces uninterrupted blessedness. Beyond this passage, and a few tantalizing allusions elsewhere, the Aristotelian writings give no sense of a divine agent and certainly none of a cosmic artificer.

The Platonic and Aristotelian doctrines were elaborated in many different directions during antiquity. Both entered into complex relations with the teachings of Stoicism, which was at some times and in some places the philosophy preferred by the Roman ruling classes. The Stoic reinterpretation of pain and misfortune was made possible by an absolute doctrine of divine providence. The Stoics were quite interested in physical doctrine, and they confected a number of theories about cosmic origin. But the physical processes were held to be under the control of a divine mind, a mind that could perfectly well be associated with the traditional civic gods. These three schools—the Platonists, the Aristotelians, and the Stoics—contended at length with the gentle irreligion of the Epicureans, for whom the gods' interventions in human affairs were hurtful fictions. What 'gods' the Epicureans allowed were fully physical and natural, subject to the same laws of pleasure and tranquillity that bound human life. A very fine illustration of the contest among these views, and of the general disdain for the Epicurean doctrines, is given by Cicero in *On the Nature of the Gods*.

The course of philosophical speculation about the divine was altered from as early as the first century AD by contact with Judaism and then Christianity. So too were the courses of those religions. In pagan philosophy, the contact produces renewed interest in describing and pursuing the divine. In Judaism and Christianity, there is a energetic and perhaps surprising effort to present the claims of revelation in philosophically articulate ways. The renewal among pagans is most evident in the extraordinary flowering of Neoplatonism, which includes such figures as Plotinus, Porphyry, and Iamblichus. It led not only to mystagogical rereadings of Plato, but also to philosophical defences of the documents and practices of paganism. The new effort of philosophical expression can be seen among Jewish thinkers in Philo, among Christians in Clement of Alexandria and Origen. It led not only to philosophical explorations of Scripture, but also to a claim that the best philosophy is found in Scripture—indeed, that philosophy had passed to the Greeks from Israel.

Beginning with the fourth or fifth century AD, it becomes increasingly difficult to speak in any sense of 'philosophy of religion', because it becomes difficult to talk of philosophy apart from religion. After about 500 AD, philosophy is subsumed within the three monotheistic religions—Judaism, Christianity, Islam. It is subsumed, not abolished. The most important thinkers of the three religions carried on teaching and wrote works that engaged the legacy of ancient philosophy powerfully and creatively. But they understood their teaching and their writing not as philosophy, but as the study of divine law, as interpretation of divine revelation, as the codification and clarification of religious traditions. It is irresponsible to call this simply 'philosophy' or even 'philosophy of religion'. Medieval religious thinkers knew what 'philosophy' meant to the ancients, who had invented the word and the thing. They admired and appropriated the ancient legacy, but they also held that the aims of ancient philosophy had been met and decisively superseded in divine revelation. To apply the name 'philosophy' to the writings of those medieval thinkers is thus to ignore or undo what they made clear with such emphasis. Most medieval writing about God, nature, human knowledge, and human living is both philosophical and deeply religious, but it is self-consciously not a philosophy of religion.

During the thousand years from the fifth to the fifteenth century, the largest part of speculative talent in the West was devoted to considering questions about God. The body of writings is correspondingly enormous. A first survey of philosophically articulated doctrines in those writings is best found in a history of Jewish, Byzantine, Islamic, or 'medieval' philosophy. What can be said here is that hardly one of these writings neglects the issues raised by the confrontation of ancient philosophy with the monotheistic religions. In many of them the conversion or ascent from philosophy to faith is the central theme—as in Augustine's *Confessions* and Bonaventure's *The Mind's Way to God*. For other medieval texts, philosophy serves as a propaedeutic to faith grasped and expressed as theology. In Boethius' *Consolation of Philosophy*, the figure of Philosophy reminds him of truths without which his faith cannot be restored. Though Christ never appears, Christ is the end of the whole teaching. Again, in Martianus Capella and Bernard Silvestris and Alan of Lille, philosophical doctrines are presented allegorically as exterior symbols of the Christian doctrine represented within. Other authors insist that philosophy must be studied thoroughly before proceeding to higher reaches of theology. Maimonides begins the *Guide of the Perplexed* by rebuking his student for wanting to jump over philosophical physics in order to reach higher. Roger Bacon argues that nothing can be known of God without the prior study of languages, mathematics, optics, experiential science, and moral philosophy. In other authors, and certainly the 'scholastic' authors writing in Latin after 1200, the terms, topics, and arguments of Aristotelian philosophy are so fully appropriated that academic theology could not proceed well without them.

Any list of the most influential 'scholastics' would include Thomas Aquinas, John Duns Scotus, and William of Ockham. These three can illustrate both the range and the diversity of engagements between Christian theology and the Aristotelian inheritance. For Aquinas, theology uses, corrects, and completes the best of ancient philosophy. Aquinas pays respectful attention to pagan philosophers and chiefly to Aristotle, whose works he expounds in detail. But whenever he writes in his own voice, as an ordained teacher of theology, Aquinas systematically transforms every Aristotelian doctrine he touches, often in a direction quite opposed to Aristotle's own intention. Duns Scotus begins by refusing frankly to accommodate Aristotle, but what is called his 'Augustianism' is in fact a dialectical juxtaposition of doctrinal inspirations from Augustine, Islamic Neoplatonism, his immediate predecessors, and Aristotle read through Averroës. Scotus typically deploys these sources to address questions that are explicitly theological and to analyse examples at the boundary between the present dispensation and the dispensation of heaven, between the mundane and the miraculous. Finally, in Ockham, one has an immensely learned critique of Aristotle fuelling an assault on the linguistic and epistemic presuppositions of any theology that employs Aristotelian models or demonstrations. But Ockham hardly intends to undo Christianity. His whole hope is to keep in view the unbounded and yet saving power of God.

Many of the medieval dispositions of faith towards philosophy carry forward into what we call the Renaissance and the early modern period, but they are complicated in at least three ways. First, the Christian reform movements that culminated in the Reformation were often sharply critical of the use of philosophy in theology or, indeed, of philosophical approaches to the divine. This criticism varied in intensity from one reforming group to another, and often coexisted with much philosophical erudition. Petrarch mocks Aristotle in favour of experience, then subordinates both to the Gospel. Erasmus criticizes the scholastic uses of ancient philosophy as bad theology and bad philology. But more commonly the criticisms of philosophy arose from claims about the opposition of philosophy and the Gospel, or from a vivid conviction of the impotence of sinful human reason, or from a confidence that God would teach what was needed by inspiration— and would do so often to the least lettered.

The second complication in the relations of philosophy to theological topics arose from fierce disputes over the conclusions of the new sciences. The condemnation of Galileo is the most famous example in these quarrels, though also the most misunderstood. Religious opposition to the philosophical implications of new science made philosophic authors cautious in expressing their views. It thus becomes difficult to know how to construe their writings. On the surface of Descartes's texts, for example, there is a scrupulous Catholic orthodoxy and

protestations of obedience. But Descartes is also coy about some of his cosmological views and he conceals them in various ways before publishing. Spinoza builds into his *Theologico-Political Treatise* a series of miscues and misdirections in order to make it unlikely that a casual or dull reader will discover his views on the truthfulness of Scripture. A similar caution in writing about religious matters can be felt well into the nineteenth century.

The third complication comes from a hardening and indeed impoverishment of the conceptions of philosophical reason and of religious knowing. One can see this in the Catholic writers in and after the Counter-Reformation. The threat of the Reformation was met within the Catholic Church by legislating on innumerable points of doctrine. This not only shrank the scope for religious speculation, but also reduced much of theology to law. Religious argument was consequently reduced to the forms of forensic argument—to aggressive demonstrations, to the collection of proof-texts, to extended attacks upon opposing positions.

These complications could by no means undo the ancient engagement of philosophy with religious topics or the ancient dependence of religious thought on philosophical lessons. While the rediscovery of certain ancient texts led to a flourishing of scepticism in some sixteenth-century authors, the overwhelming majority of modern philosophers up to the first half of the nineteenth century affirmed the existence and activity of God, and most of them counted themselves Christians or Jews of one sort or another. In retrospect it is possible to suggest that some of their notions about God or religion and some of their ways of dividing religion from science hastened the demise of the intellectual engagement with questions of religion. But one cannot hold that most philosophers in modernity were uninterested in religion or that they considered questions about God defectively rational. If many of the propagandists of Enlightenment were trenchant critics of religion, they often enough professed views about a divine origin or governance of nature. The only major philosophical figure who is often cited as obviously anti-theistic is David Hume. His *Dialogues Concerning Natural Religion* are typically regarded as the charter for modern philosophy of religion. But it is exceptionally difficult to argue that atheism is the conclusion of the *Dialogues*, and such evidence as there is for Hume's own atheism is biographical rather than philosophical.

The relations of religion and philosophy at the end of the eighteenth century and beginning of the nineteenth were mentioned above in narrating something of the origin of the term 'philosophy of religion'. What needs to be added is that the two main philosophers of these decades, Kant and Hegel, by no means exclude religious topics or even religious sentiments. If neither seems quite an orthodox Christian, both labour to save religious conclusions and to open a space for religious experience. Now it may be that their notions are so opposed to those of ordinary religion as to encourage anti-theistic scepticism. If Kant wants his reader to pass through a 'critique of all theology based on speculative principles' in order to reach what seems a positive moral theology (*Critique of Pure Reason*, 2. 3. 7), many of his readers took only the negative lesson. If Hegel accredits Christian theology as a necessary misapprehension of higher truths, he condemns it as a misapprehension. So, after Kant and Hegel, one encounters resolutely anti-religious and anti-theistic philosophers. The best known are Marx, Schopenhauer, and Nietzsche. For Nietzsche in particular the falsity and, indeed, the iniquity of Christian doctrine need no demonstration and little reflection. What does interest him is the 'natural history' of religions and religious persons, that is, the cultural and individual pathologies produced by religious practice. 'God is dead' not because a divine entity has perished, but because human beings, who once confected God, have now murdered God by acting out their as yet unuttered disbelief (*Gay Science*, sect. 125). Yet Nietzsche's thought, as he well knew, remains so thoroughly conditioned by his quarrel with religion that he still stands within the theocentric traditions of Western philosophy.

Indeed it was only in the twentieth century that it became common for Western philosophers to write philosophy without so much as raising questions about God. The very existence of 'philosophy of religion' as a subfield within philosophy is good evidence for this. The subfield was created in the twentieth century as an academic speciality because philosophy as a whole was no longer engaged with questions about God or about religious beliefs about God. Of course, the relegation of these questions to a speciality has hardly meant their demise. English-speaking philosophers have returned to questions about God, sometimes along unexpected paths, and have addressed them convincingly with philosophic methods or presuppositions that might have seemed little suited to religion. In recent decades, indeed, there has been a remarkable if still specialized resurgence of philosophic concern with a whole range of religious issues, including some of the most technical aspects of Christian theology.

M.D.J.

*God and the philosophers; God, arguments against; God, arguments for; Bonhoeffer.

For reasons already made clear, it is not sensible to write a unitary history of 'philosophy of religion'. No such history has in fact been written, nor has anyone attempted to compile the corresponding bibliography. There are historical anthologies of texts selected according to one or another notion of 'philosophy of religion', but these are necessarily both partial and anachronistic in their selections. One representative recent anthology in English is Louis P. Pojman, *Philosophy of Religion: An Anthology* (New York, 1987); a somewhat older and well-established one is Max J. Charlesworth, *Philosophy of Religion: The Historic Approaches* (London, 1972). To pursue these topics before the 20th cent., one would better begin with some of the individual works mentioned above or with the bibliographies in the entries for pertinent periods in the history of philosophy.

For a more extended narrative, see now the first two volumes of Anthony Kenny's *New History of Western Philosophy*: *Ancient Philosophy* (Oxford, 2004) and *Medieval Philosophy* (Oxford, 2005).

religion, problems of the philosophy of. The philosophy of religion is an examination of the meaning and justification of religious claims. Claims about how the world is, often embodied in creeds, are more typical of Western religions—Christianity, Judaism, and Islam—than of Eastern religions such as Buddhism, Hinduism, and Confucianism. These latter tend to concentrate much more on the practice of a way of life than on a theoretical system by means of which (among other things) to justify that practice. Hence Western religions have proved a more natural target for the philosophy of religion. The central claim of Western religions is the existence of *God; and the two major problems here are: Can a coherent account be given of what it means to say that there is a God; and, if it can, are there good reasons to show that there is or that there is not such a God?

In order to explain what it means to say that there is a God and to make other religious claims, theists use ordinary words such as 'personal', 'creator', 'free', 'good', etc., which we first learn to use from seeing them applied to mundane objects and states; or technical terms such as 'omnipotent', defined ultimately in terms of ordinary words. The question then arises: Do these ordinary words have different senses when used for talking about God from the senses they have when used for talking about mundane things, or the same senses? To use the technical terms: Are they used equivocally or univocally with their mundane senses? If the former, how could we understand what the new, religious senses are? If the latter, how could God be the inexpressible mysterious other which he is supposed to be, when he can be described by the same words having the same senses as can mundane things? The answer given by *Aquinas was that religion often uses words in somewhat the same and somewhat different senses from their mundane senses, i.e. in analogical senses. We learn the meanings of the relevant words from their application to mundane things—e.g. learn the meaning of 'wise' from seeing it applied to wise men, such as Socrates—and then, when they are applied to God, suppose them to be attributing to him the nearest thing to the mundane property which could belong to the cause of all things. This answer presupposes that at least some words—e.g. 'cause'—are used univocally in religious and mundane discourse; and it has the consequence that the other words are not used in senses very different from their mundane senses.

God is said to be 'personal', 'bodiless', 'omnipresent', 'creator and sustainer of any universe there may be', 'perfectly free', 'omnipotent', 'omniscient', 'perfectly good', and 'a source of moral obligation', and to have these properties 'eternally' and 'necessarily'. It has been a major concern of the philosophy of religion to investigate whether a coherent account can be given of the meaning of these expressions (bearing in mind the possibility that some of them have senses analogical with their normal senses), and whether they can be combined in a logically consistent way, so that the claim that there is a God can be expressed in an intelligible and coherent way. For example, is God's being eternal to be understood as his being everlasting (existing at each moment of unending time), or as his being timeless (outside time). (*Eternity.) There are serious difficulties in making sense of the idea of a personal being existing timelessly—that is, at no moment of time. How could he cause events, except by acting as or before they happen; or know about events, except by those events causing his knowledge as or after they occur? Yet if we think of him as everlasting, does his omniscience mean that he knows what we will do before we do it; and in that case how can our actions be free? Does God's being a source of moral obligation mean that he could command us to torture children, and that it would become our duty to do so if he commanded it?

Given that a coherent account can be offered of what it is for there to be a God in more or less the traditional sense, we come to the question of whether there is any good reason to believe that such a God exists. Some have claimed that if one finds oneself believing that there is a God, then it is rational to believe this without looking for arguments in support of the claim—just as it is rational for me to believe that I ate toast for breakfast or am now listening to a car passing the window, if I find myself believing these things. I do not need further evidence in order rationally to believe such a thing—unless, that is, I acquire evidence to suppose that the belief is false, and in that case I may need evidence confirming the belief in order to outweigh the former evidence and so to continue rationally to hold the belief. The view that the belief that there is a God needs no prior support from other evidence in order to be held rationally is the view of 'reformed epistemology', advocated by Alvin Plantinga and developed in a 1984 collection on *Faith and Rationality* which he co-edited. Basic beliefs are ones which the subject believes, but not for the reason that they are supported by any other beliefs which he holds. Beliefs are 'properly basic if the subject is justified in holding them even if not supported by other beliefs'. What Plantinga calls 'classical foundationalism' is the view that the only properly basic beliefs are self-evident beliefs (beliefs in obvious *logical truths, such as that $2 + 2 = 4$), incorrigible beliefs (beliefs about our current mental states), and beliefs evident to the senses (beliefs about what we are now perceiving via the five senses). It would seem to follow from classical foundationalism that belief that there is a God cannot be properly basic, and so requires to be based on other beliefs, i.e. to be justified by argument from other beliefs. Plantinga argues (for reasons quite apart from those concerned with religious beliefs) that classical foundationalism has too narrow a class of properly basic beliefs (it should, for example, include memory beliefs). And further, he argues, it is self-defeating, because belief in classical foundationalism itself is neither (by its own standards) a properly basic belief nor, apparently, supportable by properly basic beliefs. Yet once we abandon classical foundationalism, he claims, we have no good reason for denying that belief that there is a God may be properly basic.

There is much to be said for the principle that it is rational to hold any belief with which one finds oneself, in the absence of counter-evidence—a principle sometimes called 'the principle of credulity'. But Plantinga is not advocating this as a general principle; rather, he holds that 'there is a God' may be held without further justification, even if 'I am now aware of the Great Pumpkin' may not; and he has recently developed a theory of epistemology which has this consequence. (See his *Warranted Christian Belief*.) This theory concerns what makes a belief 'warranted'. Warrant is the characteristic which turns true belief into knowledge. If my belief that the Second World War ended in 1945 is warranted, then if it is also true, I know that the Second World War ended in 1945. (A belief being 'warranted' is very similar to its being justified or rational—that is, the believer being justified or rational in holding the belief.) Plantinga's account of warrant is a complicated one, but its central component is that to be warranted a belief must be produced in the right way—that is, by a 'properly functioning process'. Thus perception, memory, and induction are all processes which lead us to acquire beliefs; and plausibly we are functioning properly when we acquire beliefs by means of them (in the absence of counter-evidence). So, any belief of mine acquired by perception will be warranted (in the absence of counter-evidence—for example, my memory that I have just ingested a hallucinatory drug). So too will any belief acquired by induction from my perceptual beliefs. Plantinga suggests that we all have a sense additional to the normal five, a 'sense of divinity' which produces in many of us the belief that there is a God; and that, since there is a God (Plantinga claims), our cognitive faculties are functioning properly when the 'sense of divinity' does produce that belief. If he is right about this, then (unless—improbably—the belief is acquired by some other process) whenever we find ourselves with the belief that there is a God, we are warranted in continuing to hold it (so long as we do not find evidence or arguments tending to show that there is no God). But if we do not find ourselves with the belief that there is a God to start with, or our belief is only a weak one outweighed by counter-evidence (for example, the evidence of suffering suggesting that there cannot be a perfectly good being in charge of the universe), Plantinga does not give any positive reason to hold that belief or hold it in a stronger form so that it is not outweighed. He is concerned only to show that a simple religious believer who can give no arguments for his belief *may* still be warranted in holding it.

If atheists and weak believers are to be given a strong belief that there is a God, they need to be shown that other things which are more evident to them make it probable that there is a God by public standards of what is evidence for what. There has been a long history in Western philosophy of positive *arguments for the existence of God. Anselm, Aquinas, Duns Scotus, Descartes, and Leibniz and innumerable other philosophers have given such arguments. Most of these arguments are arguments from observable phenomena to a God who, it is claimed, provides the explanation of their occurrence. (One exception is the *ontological argument, which has as its premisses pure conceptual truths.) The *cosmological argument argues from the universe to a God who creates it; the *teleological argument argues from the orderliness of the universe (either in respect of conforming to laws of nature, or in containing animals and humans in an appropriate environment) to a God who makes it thus. The argument from consciousness argues from the existence of conscious embodied agents (humans and animals) to a God who endows them with consciousness. The argument from religious experience argues from the occurrence of religious experiences, in the sense of experiences in which it seems to the subject that he is aware of God, to millions of people of different centuries and cultures, to a God of whom they really are aware.

It is crucial for assessing the worth of such arguments whether they are to be regarded as deductive or inductive (or probabilistic) arguments, and whether they are to be taken separately or together. A deductively valid argument is one in which if you assert the premiss or premisses from which it starts, but deny the conclusion, you contradict yourself. So, for example, the cosmological argument will be a valid deductive argument if and only if 'there is a universe, but no God' involves a contradiction—if it is like 'he is less than 5 feet tall and more than 6 feet tall at the same time'. It does not at first sight look as if 'there is a universe, but no God' is self-contradictory. If, however, the arguments are taken as inductive arguments, then they will be like the scientist's arguments from observable data to his hypothesis of unobservable entities which cause the observable data—like the physicist's observations of lines on photographic plates to his conclusion that they are caused by electrons or positrons; the arguments do not guarantee the truth of the scientist's hypothesis, but they can make it very probable. Arguments for the existence of God have to be weighed against *arguments against the existence of God. The most important of these is provided by the *problem of evil: that an omnipotent and perfectly good God would not allow the occurrence of pain and suffering.

The arguments for the existence of God are more plausible if regarded as inductive, and taken together. Arguments from observable data to an explanatory hypothesis in science, history, or any other area, in the opinion of this writer, make the hypothesis probable in so far as (1) the hypothesis makes probable the occurrence of the data, (2) the occurrence of the data is not otherwise probable, and (3) the hypothesis is simple. (*Simplicity.) Thus the hypothesis that Jones committed some crime is probable in so far as the clues are (1) such as you would expect to find if Jones committed the crime, and (2) not otherwise to be expected, and (3) the hypothesis is simple. The simplicity of this hypothesis consists in it being a hypothesis that one person did some act, which caused each of the many clues. A hypothesis that many different individuals, not in collusion with each other, did quite separate acts which caused the clues, would be much more complicated, and

so would satisfy criterion (3) far less well. If arguments for the existence of God are regarded as arguments to an explanatory hypothesis, they must be judged by these criteria. Consider the teleological argument from the almost total conformity of all material objects to laws of nature, i.e. from the fact that all material objects throughout endless space and time have exactly the same powers and liabilities to act as each other (e.g. attracting each other in accordance with Newton's laws, or with whatever are the fundamental laws of nature; and the regularities of chemistry and biology which follow from the fundamental laws). Since God, by hypothesis, is omnipotent, he will be able to bring about this order; and if it is a good thing that such order should exist, then in virtue of his perfect goodness he will have reason for bringing it about. So the argument tries to show that (1) this order is a good state, which in consequence a God would probably bring about, but which (2) otherwise would be a vast improbable coincidence, and (3) that a God is a simple being. It argues for (1) by pointing out that the existence of finite beings (such as humans) with the ability to make differences to themselves, each other, and the world is a good thing. In order for humans to be able to make these differences, there have to be simple regularities in the world which humans can discover and utilize—for example, if there is a regularity that watered seeds grow into plants, humans can develop an agriculture; but otherwise they cannot do this. It argues for (3) that the hypothesis postulates one being who is the simplest kind of person that there can be, having infinite degrees of (i.e. zero limits to) the characteristics of knowledge, power, and freedom which are involved in being a person.

The main argument against the existence of God has always been the 'argument from evil'—that is, from pain and malevolence. Theists sometimes claim that since by hypothesis God is so much greater than us, we cannot expect to understand why he allows all the things that happen to happen; there are bound to be puzzling phenomena such that we cannot understand why God allows them to occur, and so we should not count evil as evidence against the existence of God. However, almost all atheists and many theists have felt that the claim that God is perfectly good would be empty of meaning unless some explanation could be given of why, being perfectly good, he allows the enormous amount of pain and malevolence that there is in the world. An explanation of this is called a 'theodicy'. Evils are traditionally divided into moral evils (ones knowingly caused or allowed to occur by humans) and natural evils (the ones for which humans are not responsible, such as the effects of disease and earthquake). A central plank of most theodicies is the 'free will defence' to moral evil: the claim that if God is to give humans the great good of a free choice between good and evil, it is inevitable that there will be some moral evil. (There would be, it is claimed, a contradiction in supposing that God could cause us freely to choose the good—for to choose 'freely' is to choose without being caused how to choose.) Theodicy needs more complicated arguments to attempt to deal with the problem of natural evil. (*Evil, the problem of.)

All religions have set a high value on faith. But how is 'faith' to be understood? (*Faith and reason.) If it is understood as forcing yourself to believe what seems probably false, there would seem to be little merit in it. But if it is seen as giving oneself totally to attain a great good (e.g. the vision of God for oneself and others), when it is no more than probable that this goal is attainable, it would seem more plausibly a virtue.

Other claims, common to all Western religions, include the claims that God hears prayers and answers them, sometimes by miracles; that God has revealed certain truths; and that there is a life after death in which the good will enjoy the vision of God and the bad will be deprived of it for ever. A miracle has often been understood as a violation of a law of nature, by God intervening in the world. But then, how can something be a law of nature if it can be violated, and so there can be exceptions to its operation; is not a purported law of nature which does not always predict accurately not really a law of nature? One answer to this is to regard exceptions to the operation of a purported law of nature as showing it to be no true law of nature only if they are repeatable exceptions; you only show 'all metals expand when heated' not to be a law of nature if you show that regularly when a certain metal is heated under certain conditions, it expands. The occasional non-repeatable exception is a violation; and, if brought about by God, a *miracle. Hume (*Enquiry Concerning Human Understanding*, sect. 10) has a famous argument purporting to show that there could never be a balance of evidence in favour of the occurrence of a miracle thus understood. To show a miraculous event E to have occurred at time t, we need to show first that there is some law of nature which its occurrence would violate. We need a lot of evidence from what has happened on many other occasions to show some purported law L to be a law of nature (e.g. evidence of observers to show that on many other occasions, objects have behaved in the way predicted by L). But then that evidence will tend to show that L will be obeyed at other times also, including at t. The evidence in favour of the occurrence of E will consist only of the testimony of a small number of observers; and so the force of their evidence will always be outweighed by the force of the testimony of many observers who testify to the operation of L on many other occasions. An obvious response is that the sums are not quite so simple—evidence of observers as to what happened on other occasions is only indirect evidence about what happened at t, whereas the evidence of the observers at t is direct evidence, and so has much more force.

Why does God not make nature perfect to begin with? Why does he need to intervene in the natural order? One reason that he might have is—in order to answer prayer. He wishes to bring about good in response to human request; and, to make that possible, he leaves nature capable of improvement. Another reason for performing a miracle would be to give his authority to some prophet who had publicly prayed for the miracle to occur or whose teaching was forwarded by the miracle, and so thereby publicly to authenticate the prophet's teaching as a revelation from God. Philosophy of religion has a concern with whether God would be expected to provide a revelation, and what are the tests that he has done so (e.g. whether the Koran, or the Christian Bible and Creeds record such a revelation). Joseph Butler's *The Analogy of Religion* is a famous discussion of these issues.

Whether it is coherent to suppose that human beings can survive their death depends on the correct account of *personal identity (see also *immortality). If there can be such life, the issue arises whether what Christianity, Islam, and some other religions have claimed as the character of the afterlife is compatible with the goodness of God. Such religions claim that the good (judged so to be in virtue of their faith or works—Protestants have emphasized one, Catholics the other) will enjoy the vision of God for ever, whereas the bad will be permanently deprived of it, possibly in a *Hell of endless sensory pain. Could a good God act thus? One answer is that in their life on Earth human beings freely form their character; and only a person with a good character would want to have, and so be capable of enjoying, a vision of God—it is humans who make the ultimate choice of their fate.

In recent years the philosophical techniques and results of the Anglo-American tradition of philosophy have been applied not merely to the most general claims of Western religions, but also to specifically Christian doctrines (as well as occasionally to the specific doctrines of other religions). The Christian doctrines include the three central Christian doctrines of the Trinity (that God is three persons of one substance), the Incarnation (that God became incarnate as a human being, Jesus Christ), and the Atonement (that Christ's life and death atoned for the sins of humans). The initial philosophical task is to see how far a clear meaning can be given to these doctrines; and the next task is to consider if there are any grounds for believing them true. It is normally supposed that revelation will provide the main grounds, but there may also be a priori arguments for or against their truth. This interest in specifically Christian doctrines has gone along with investigation of how far it is possible to compare religions in respect of their truth-claims and their ability to provide 'salvation', and to whether one can say with justification that one religion is 'the true religion' or at least better than other religions.

R.G.S.

*religion, scepticism about; God, arguments for the existence of; God, arguments against the existence of; religion and epistemology; creation; revelation.

R. M. Adams, *The Virtue of Faith* (Oxford, 1987).

W. L. Craig (ed.), *Philosophy of Religion* (Edinburgh, 2002).

P. Helm (ed.), *Faith and Reason* (Oxford, 1999).

J. L. Mackie, *The Miracle of Theism* (Oxford, 1982).

M. Peterson *et al.* (eds.), *Reason and Religious Belief*, 2nd edn. (Oxford, 1997).

A. Plantinga, *Warranted Christian Belief* (Oxford, 2000).

R. Swinburne, *Is There a God?* (Oxford, 1996).

religion, scepticism about. There has been an undeniably powerful current of anti-religious thought in the history of modern philosophy. Among its several quite distinct sources, the following are noteworthy.

In his *Dialogues Concerning Natural Religion*, Hume's 'Philo' showed how, in cosmological speculation, imagination outruns our ability to confirm or rebut. We might (with 'Cleanthes') argue to a finite, anthropomorphic cause of the world; or (with 'Demea') do more justice to divine transcendence and mystery—but at the cost of virtual (if religiously toned) agnosticism. Neither route would lead to the *God of Christian theism.

For Kant, the traditional arguments to God were all dependent on the *ontological argument, which in turn treated existence, invalidly, as a predicate and a perfection. To argue from the world to God involved, also, illicit extension of categorial concepts ('cause', notably), which functioned reliably and necessarily within the phenomenal world, and there alone.

Both Schopenhauer and Nietzsche saw the case for theistic belief as quite destroyed: theism was no longer a live option—God could be pronounced 'dead'. The task was now to accept and develop the implications of a nontheistic view of the world.

Critics of teleological arguments deemed them too weak to reach beyond the world's orderer to its creator; they also were seen as decisively damaged by naturalistic, evolutionary explanations of the development of living forms. It was no longer necessary to claim that the cause must manifest a higher level of being than its effect, e.g. that the causal origin of mind and intelligence must itself be intelligent; and an increasingly detailed and desentimentalized understanding of the life-world, e.g. the mutual predatoriness of species, made it correspondingly harder to superimpose a benign teleology upon nature or to see the working there of a 'divine hand'.

Some theologians welcome the demise of natural religion, arguing that it is wholly in revelation that Christian belief is founded. An appeal to revealed doctrine, however, referring back essentially to scriptural documents, was, for many, less readily seen as a path to renewed belief than to anxieties of another kind—over the radical historical uncertainties uncovered by scholarly biblical criticism. Besides, the 'revealed' component could not furnish the *entire* grounding of Christian belief. Philosophical sense still needs to be made of the connecting of revealed content with the alleged divine Source: a rational-theological component is indispensable.

A further set of difficulties for Christian belief has centred upon issues in the philosophy of mind. Science and philosophy again converge in the setting of the problem. The more detailed understanding is available of the embodiedness of conscious and personal life, the stronger the pressures towards forms of materialism and physicalism, and the less plausible become religious beliefs that involve bodiless mental or 'spiritual' life—whether God's life or that of the human 'soul'. If the believer responds with a doctrine of resurrection rather than survival of disembodied spirits, there remains a serious philosophical problem over personal identity: is the resurrected individual the 'same' person who died, or a new, though qualitatively identical, person?

Problems in that area continue into the field of *religious experience. All direct encounters of person with person involve bodily presence and behaviour, visible and audible. An already well-founded religious belief is not daunted by, for example, the idea of prayer to an invisible and inaudible deity; and a believer may experience a powerful, vivid sense of the reality of God. It has become much less convincing, however, to use such religious experience as an argument to God's reality. Naturalistic forms of explanation, Freudian and other, have been proposed for religious experience; and analogies are often drawn between religious or mystical experiences and drug-induced or pathologically abnormal states of consciousness. These cannot displace the theist's explanation, but they certainly challenge the use of such experiences in theistic apologetic.

Some religious philosophers have looked to moral experience for an alternative to the traditional theoretical arguments for God. To mount a plausible moral argument to God, however, would seem to require as a starting-point a cognitivist, 'realist' or rationalist type of moral theory. No account of moral judgement in emotivist, expressivist terms could ground an inference to a divine source of the world's being. Even today's advocates of *moral realism most often insist that they are dealing with human insights into a human reality, not with disclosures of a transcendent realm of values.

Perhaps the area in which the difficulties facing theism are most formidable—even intractable—is the *'problem of evil'. Once it is claimed that the being upon whom the universe depends is personal, that theistic explanation is personal explanation, then, given also that the deity is the unique, unrivalled, omnipotent ground of the world, what are we to make of the vast extent of suffering in that created world? If in nature's fundamental laws of operation we find intelligibility, simplicity, elegance, beauty, how to explain the absence of any analogous beauty in the pattern (or absence of pattern) in the distribution of satisfaction, fulfilment, and suffering in the lives of sentient individuals? Stories about the world as a 'vale of soul-making' are of very limited applicability: unhelpful *vis-à-vis* the suffering of non-human animals, or with the congenitally mentally handicapped. Nor has sense been made of the 'allowing' of human suffering of such undeserved intensity that no promised beatitude hereafter seems a morally tolerable compensation.

It would be, however, absurdly one-sided to leave the matter there. It can be claimed that significant philosophical work goes on in all of these problem areas, work of relevance to the religious questions, and that in some at least of these the sceptical case is seriously challenged. Hume and Kant failed in fact to demolish the theistic 'proofs'. Debate has rekindled on every one of these arguments. Impressive reworkings of the *cosmological argument have recently appeared (Grisez, Miller); *teleological arguments are defended in new forms (Swinburne); and the 'fine tuning' witnessed to by recent cosmology has initiated a new phase in the dialogue between science and religion.

Finally, the theories of *meaning on which philosophical scepticism in the mid-twentieth century heavily relied have been displaced by more complex accounts. If a philosophy of language and meaningfulness is complex enough to cope with contemporary scientific theorizing (e.g. with the thought models and paradoxes of quantum theory), it will not also be able to be sharply dismissive of all religious and theological language. The thought models, the metaphors, the paradoxes that arise in that context, will continue to deserve patient and attentive analysis.   R.W.H.

*God and the philosophers; atheism and agnosticism; religion, history of the philosophy of; religion, problems of the philosophy of.

C. F. Delaney (ed.), *Rationality and Religious Belief* (Notre Dame, Ind., 1979).

G. Grisez, *Beyond the New Theism* (Notre Dame, Ind., 1975).

J. L. Mackie, *The Miracle of Theism* (Oxford, 1982).

B. Miller, *From Existence to God* (London, 1992).

R. Swinburne, *The Existence of God* (Oxford, 1979).

religion and epistemology. The epistemology of religion is the attempt to solve philosophical problems about *knowledge which arise from religion. For example: Is there mystical knowledge? Is there knowledge by *revelation or *natural theology? Can *God be known to exist, for example, if there is a sound proof of God's existence? Is it possible to have knowledge of the properties of God: omnipotence, omniscience, benevolence, simplicity, and eternity? (Omniscience is arguably a part of omnipotence, if omnipotence is the ability to do anything, and knowing is something that can be done.)

Arguably, religion yields ways of experiencing and understanding that exceed the secular powers of the senses and the intellect. Augustine's claim *creo ut scio*, 'I believe in order to know', rather than a dogmatic reversal of ordinary intellectual priorities, is a principle conducive to non-reductivist explanation. Aquinas maintains that reason needs to be supplemented by faith in order to obtain a fuller understanding of reality, even if this falls far short of adequate knowledge of God, because we are finite and imperfect beings. Pascal famously said there are two mistakes: to deny reason and to allow only reason.

Hume and Kant have argued that in a sense there is no epistemology of religion if this implies knowledge of God. Hume criticizes arguments from design in *Dialogues Concerning Natural Religion* and the likelihood of miracles in the *First Enquiry*. In the *Critique of Pure Reason* Kant argues that there is no persuasive a priori or a posteriori argument for the existence of God. Nevertheless, in his moral philosophy he allows God, freedom, and immortality as postulates of pure practical reason.

All the problems of epistemology are problems for the epistemology of religion. For example, knowing what belief is, is necessary for knowing what belief in God is. Knowing whether there is knowledge is necessary for knowing whether there is mystical knowledge.

It could be that once metaphysical problems about ultimate reality and one's own existence are grasped with clarity, it is seen that their answers have to be theological. For example, 'Why is a particular person you?', 'Why is it now, now?', 'Why is there a universe?', 'Where is there metaphysical room for what ought to be as well as what is?' only admit of answers if theism is true. Nevertheless, a God whose existence and nature could be established by human beings with logical certainty would arguably not be the God of Judaism, Christianity, or Islam, the God of faith.   S.P.

Brian Davies (ed.), *Philosophy of Religion* (Oxford, 2000).

Anthony Kenny, *The God of the Philosophers* (Oxford, 1979).

Thomas V. Morris (ed.), *The Concept of God* (Oxford, 1987).

religion and morality. Ethical requirements can readily be thought of as commands—with authority behind them. Whose authority? Could it be that the sole ground for moral judgements is their being willed or forbidden by *God? Could his will, alone, constitute moral rightness? That would imply that we can understand moral requirements *only* if we believe in God and can know his command.

On such a view, to speak of morality is no more than to speak of what, as a matter of fact, God wills or commands: a disquieting view, because it follows that if God were to will a set of imperatives totally at variance with those of morality as we know it, that set would at once have unconditional moral authority, whatever its content.

A religious person wants to say (meaningfully, seriously) that *what God commands is right and good*. But if all we mean by 'morally right and good' is 'what God commands', then the statement 'What God commands is right and good', means no more than 'What God commands is ... what God commands': no longer news, but only a trivially true statement. We must, then, see moral obligatoriness and goodness not as constituted by divine command, but as having a distinct and irreducible character of their own, a character that we ourselves have the moral competence to recognize, and which requires no further authentication.

Perhaps, however, we have not acknowledged with full seriousness what a *divine command is: the command of a being with total power over his universe. How can we speak of appraising the command of such a being? Natural though this response is, it would reduce morality to mere passivity under divine power. The worship of God (in the Judaeo-Christian tradition) has been very different indeed from the worship of sheer power.

Supposing, however, that there is no God, no life after the death of the body, and no final vindication of good and defeat of evil, can the moral life still be lived seriously, and altruistic concern sustained?

A secular moralist will argue that far from morality losing its viability and seriousness in the absence of a God and a future life, the opposite is at least as reasonable: individual moral agents are more thoroughly responsible for one another. Why should people matter less, on a secular, agnostic view? With their limited life-span, it becomes more urgent and important that they have just and fair treatment in their one life here and now. Removal of promised reward or compensation does not undermine the genuinely moral, though it does undermine the merely prudential; and the prudential often masquerades (even within 'moral education') as the moral.

But it must be acknowledged, nevertheless, that the religions have played an important role in moral learning. To have (some) moral competence or capability does not mean we are morally omnicompetent, with nothing to learn. Any number of central moral notions, attitudes, qualities of character, have in fact come to general awareness only or chiefly through religious teachers.   R.W.H.

> *categorical imperative; moral philosophy, problems of; religion, problems of the philosophy of; slave morality.

P. Helm (ed.), *Divine Commands and Morality* (Oxford, 1981).
Plato, *Euthyphro*.
J. Rachels, *The Elements of Moral Philosophy* (New York, 1993), ch. 4.

religion, art, and science: *see* science, art, and religion.

religious belief and cosmology: *see* cosmology and religious belief.

religious experience, argument for the existence of God from. This can be considered a special version of the teleological argument, claiming that the widespread occurrence of religious experience, with a common phenomenological core and giving rise to a common core of interpretation, requires explanation. And it is argued (e.g. by C. D. Broad and Richard Swinburne) that the most plausible explanation involves the existence and activity of *God.

Alternatively, religious experience can be construed as a *non-inferential* mode of cognition, analogous to sense, which grounds a knowledge of God in a more direct way than argumentation. It is especially important not to treat this sort of appeal to religious experience as if it were an appeal to argument, since that would invite inappropriate sorts of citicism and defence.   G.I.M.

> *holy, numinous, and sacred.

W. Alston, *Perceiving God* (Ithaca, NY, 1991).
John Baillie, *Our Knowledge of God* (New York, 1959).
C. D. Broad, *Religion, Philosophy, and Psychical Research* (London, 1953).
George I. Mavrodes, *Belief in God* (New York, 1981).
—— *Revelation in Religious Belief* (Philadelphia, 1988).
Richard Swinburne, *The Existence of God* (Oxford, 1979).

religious language. What is religious language? It is cosmogony, historical narrative, myth, moral discourse, as well as blessing and cursing, confessing, adoring. It crucially involves metaphor, symbol, analogy, parable, paradox. It is, typically, language avowing the inexpressible, unconceptualizable nature of its object, or the indescribability of mystical experiences which nevertheless it strives to express! Given the diversity of religious language, there can be no single way of confirming or rebutting its many and complex claims.

It should not surprise one that the language we use to describe temporal events, material objects, and our dealings with them will not suffice also to describe the *God of Judaeo-Christian theism and our supposed encounters with him. Unlike finite objects, God is thought of as without limits: not a constituent of the universe, not the effect of any cause.

Obliqueness is uneliminable from discourse about deity. The language of revelation is oblique through and through: likewise the metalanguage in which revelation is affirmed to have occurred. (But then so too is some of our discourse about the life of the mind.) Even attempts to ground all the 'revealed' talk and all accounts of religious experience in a cosmologically argued 'uncaused cause' requires an analogical extension of that basic category of cause, beyond its home in everyday and scientific explanation.

A decision about accepting or rejecting the claims of theistic language to have a real object must be based on a holistic judgement. Do we do more damage to our overall experience of the world if we reject the theistic paradoxes and the perilously stretched analogies than if we retain them? And this is a test we can carry out only roughly, since what we think of as our 'experience' cannot be more than partially extricated from the 'interpreted'—religious or agnostic or atheistic—views of the world, between which we are attempting to make a reasoned decision.
>   R.W.H.

> *religion, problems of the philosophy of; Logical Positivism.

B. Davies, *An Introduction to the Philosophy of Religion* (Oxford, 1993), ch. 2.
W. D. Hudson, *Wittgenstein and Religious Belief* (London, 1975).
A. O'Hear, *Experience, Explanation and Faith* (London, 1984), ch. 1 and index.

Religiousness A and B. Kierkegaard's distinction between two 'stages' or 'spheres' of existence, the former said to be a necessary preliminary to the latter. As in Kierkegaard's ethical stage, Religiousness A retains the idealist assumption that the eternal truth is humanly accessible, except that, where in the case of ethics self-revelatory social and familial duties provide the access, in this case the relation to truth is established by self-abnegation and is expressed in categories of *inwardness (resignation, suffering, and guilt). Religiousness A conceives the truth as something to be recollected. By confining human knowledge to history Religiousness B makes truth practical, future-orientated, and dependent on the eternal having entered time in human form as an ethical example. This is Christianity, and, by having to face the paradox of the Incarnation, Christian faith achieves the highest pitch of inwardness.

A.H.

S. Kierkegaard, *Concluding Unscientific Postscript* (Princeton, NJ, 1990).

remembering: *see* memory.

Renaissance philosophy. That of the West during the fifteenth and sixteenth centuries. The principal concerns of Renaissance writers were philosophy of nature (embracing science, occultism, and metaphysics), psychology (including theory of knowledge), and moral and political philosophy—one of the main contributions to which was the employment of fables of golden ages, past and future, in order to retrieve and refashion personal and social virtues associated with antiquity.

Arguably the first major Renaissance philosopher was Nicholas of Cusa (1401–64) and the last was Francisco Suarez (1548–1617). Other important figures include Marsilio Ficino (1433–99), Pietro Pomponazzi (1462–1525), Giovanni Pico della Mirandola (1463–94), Thomas de Vio Cajetan (1468–1534), Francesco de Vitoria (1480–1546), Giordano Bruno (1548–1600), and Tommaso Campanella (1568–1639). During the same period lived several important writers, such as Desiderius Erasmus (1466–1536), Niccolò Machiavelli (1469–1527), and Thomas More (1478–1535), who though not philosophers were influential humanist thinkers.

The Renaissance cannot match the medieval and modern periods for the originality and influence of its philosophical ideas. For the most part it was concerned with the elaboration of systems of thought originating in the classical period. The main sources of philosophical inspiration were Plato and Aristotle, and although the tradition of *scholasticism was maintained by figures such as Cajetan, de Vitoria, and Suarez, most Renaissance writers regarded the medievals as idle sophisters writing a Latin that appeared barbaric by comparison with the courtly version contrived by Cicero. Throughout the Renaissance, works by classical philosophers were retranslated and new commentaries were produced. This led to the establishment of revivalist schools, the most important of which was the Neoplatonic academy in Florence founded by Ficino under the patronage of Cosimo de' Medici.

J.HAL.

*Aristotelianism; Platonism.

B. P. Copenhaver and C. B. Schmitt, *Renaissance Philosophy* (Oxford, 1992).

J. Haldane, 'Medieval and Renaissance Ethics', in P. Singer (ed.), *A Companion to Ethics* (Oxford, 1990).

Renouvier, Charles Bernard (1815–1903). French personalist who used the critical method of Kant to develop a pluralism in which chance, time, novelty, and freedom are irreducible realities while absolutes and infinites do not exist. Although he never held an academic position, he was one of the most prolific philosophers in French history.

Renouvier's *empiricism strongly influenced William James's 'radical empiricism'. A fideism in which Renouvier held that belief is voluntary (a radical form of what today is called *doxastic voluntarism) helped James out of a suicidal depression in 1870, a crisis from which James's doctrine of 'the Will to Believe' emerged.

Renouvier's stress on freedom in belief was buttressed by an indeterminism in which chance is an irreducible aspect of nature, a rejection of determinism James endorsed too. The notion of infinity was also attacked by Renouvier, and James at his death was still struggling with his friend's claim that infinity is a self-contradictory notion.

P.H.H.

Ralph Barton Perry, *The Thought and Character of William James* (Boston, 1936), i. 654–710.

representation. It is a truism that a representation is anything that represents something. Thus words, sentences, thoughts, and pictures may all be considered representations, though the manner in which they represent things is very different. Representation is a philosophically puzzling relation. To take one simple example, '*x* represents *y*' seems to express a relation between two things. But while the existence of a relation between two things trivially entails that they exist, this is not true for the relation of representation: a picture, thought, or sentence can represent the Judgement of Paris even if there was in fact no such event. Yet who can deny that all representations do in fact represent something?

Pictorial representation seems initially to be the most straightforward form of representation, since the relation between a picture and what it represents seems so natural and obvious to us. Surely a picture represents something simply by resembling it? And isn't resemblance a perfectly natural relation? The apparent simplicity of pictorial representation might suggest that it is the most basic form of representation. A caricature of this position would be: a sentence represents something because it is associated in its user's mind with a mental picture which represents in virtue of resembling the thing represented.

But explaining pictorial representation in terms of resemblance raises many problems. While resemblance is reflexive (everything resembles itself) and symmetric (I resemble my identical twin, and he resembles me), representation is neither. Even near perfect resemblance between two things doesn't guarantee representation: my copy of today's newspaper does not represent any of the million others. These sorts of considerations have led philosophers like Nelson Goodman to deny that resemblance has anything to do with representation at all. (However, Malcolm Budd has recently come to the defence of the resemblance theory of pictorial representation.)

Resemblance is, of course, not necessary for representation; words, for example, do not resemble the things they represent. But our caricature theory explains linguistic representation in terms of associating words with mental pictures, which then represent in virtue of resemblance.

The trouble with this is that even pictures do not represent intrinsically. To take an example of Wittgenstein's, a picture of a man walking uphill could also be a picture of a man sliding backwards downhill. There is nothing intrinsic to the picture that determines that it is a picture of the first kind rather than the second. We therefore have three choices: either the picture represents what it does by being interpreted, in which case the explanation of representation is borne by the idea of interpretation, not resemblance. Or some pictures are 'self-interpreting': mental pictures or images, perhaps, determine their own interpretation. But this amounts to taking the idea of representation as fundamental and unanalysed, and leaves us without any explanation of representation at all. Finally, we could say that the picture represents everything it resembles—each picture has an indefinite number of representational 'contents'. But this too seems to leave the idea of representation entirely unexplained.

Even without this difficulty, the idea that representation is based on resemblance is untenable. For many words ('prime number', 'because') could not have mental pictures associated with them that explain their representational powers; and much thought is not pictorial or imagistic in any case. Pictures too cannot explain the logical structure of thoughts or sentences: how could a purely pictorial representation represent the thought that 'If it isn't raining next Saturday, we'll go to the sea'?

So whether or not we can explain pictorial representation in terms of resemblance, we certainly cannot explain all forms of representation in terms of pictorial representation. The various kinds of representation have distinctive features which need their own explanation. An account of linguistic representation, for instance, has to explain how the meanings of words systematically combine to produce the meanings of sentences. (*Meaning.) In recent philosophy of mind and psychology, the notion of mental representation has become central, and many hope to explain linguistic representation in terms of it. Moreover, the hope that representation can be revealed to be a natural relation has been fuelled by the use of the notion of mental representation in *cognitive science and psychology.   T.C.

*pictures.

H. Clapin (ed.), *Philosophy of Mental Representation* (Oxford, 2002).
Robert Cummins, *Meaning and Mental Representation* (Cambridge, Mass., 1989).
Nelson Goodman, *Languages of Art* (Indianapolis, 1976).

representation in art. Visual *art is markedly suited to representing things, and the way in which it does it seems irreducible to any other form of representation. In music, by contrast, representation seems peripheral, while the ability of linguistic artforms such as poetry or novels to represent is inevitably taken up with the larger question of how language itself has meaning.

Two conceptual distinctions should be borne in mind. Firstly, some representations refer to particular things, and some refer to no particular thing. For example, a portrait has to relate to some actual person, but another picture can be a picture of a woman reading a book, without there being any particular woman or book which it is about. Secondly, there is a difference between a picture's standing for something as a symbol and its depicting something. In a painting, a lamb may *stand for* or symbolize Christ, but what is *depicted* in the painting is a lamb.

Depiction is an utterly familiar practice which proves hard to analyse. The apparently common-sense idea that the surface of a picture resembles what it depicts is usually rejected by philosophers. They try instead to specify the state of mind of someone who both sees the surface of a picture and understands what it depicts. Different accounts invoke the notions of 'seeing a woman in' the painted surface, or making believe that our seeing the picture is our seeing a woman, or experiencing a resemblance between the picture's appearance and the two-dimensional appearance which a woman would have if we saw her literally. This is a challenging area of philosophy, which has to negotiate the sophistications of contemporary philosophy of mind, while remaining alive to the history of representation in the arts and the interest which pictures actually have for their audience.   c.j.

N. Goodman, *Languages of Art* (Indianapolis, 1968), ch. 1.
R. Wollheim, *Art and its Objects*, 2nd edn. (Cambridge, 1980), suppl. essay v.

representative theory of perception. A theory maintaining that in ordinary perception one is directly, and most immediately, aware of subjective representations (*sense-data, *percepts, *sensations) of the external world. Our knowledge of objective (mind-independent) reality is, thus, derived from (based on) knowledge of facts about one's own subjective experience. Typically this view is contrasted with *naïve realism.

A representative theorist need not (and typically does not) maintain that our knowledge of objective conditions is reached by a conscious inference from premises describing the effects on us of this external reality. In seeing that there are cookies in the jar (an objective state of affairs), I do not arrive at my belief that there are cookies in the jar by a conscious inference from premises describing my experience of the cookies. None the less, the belief about the cookies is based on a knowledge of a subjective condition (the sensation the cookies cause in me), in the same way that one's knowledge of a distant football game (being watched on television) is based on knowledge of what is happening on the nearby TV screen. Even if there is no conscious inference, there is a dependency of one piece of knowledge on another.

Arguments for a representative theory of perception typically appeal to hallucinations and illusions. Seeing a white rabbit is (or can be) the same from a subjective standpoint as hallucinating or dreaming of a white rabbit. The causes may be different, but the experiences are the same. Since (it is argued) one is aware of a mental representation or image in the case of hallucinations and dreams, it is reasonable to infer that in ordinary perception one is also aware of something subjective. The only difference between seeing a white rabbit (veridical perception) and hallucinating one is the cause of the sensation. In veridical perception, the effect (the internal image of which one is directly aware) represents the cause—the white rabbit—in some more or less accurate way. In the case of hallucination the cause—drugs in the bloodstream, maybe—is misrepresented.

Arguments appealing to the fallibility of one's knowledge of the external world have also been used to support a representative theory of perception: our knowledge of reality is based on a more certain (infallible?) knowledge of the appearances (the internal representation) of reality. Even if this is, in some sense, true, it does not support a representative theory unless it is combined with the questionable premiss that knowledge of the appearances—that something looks red, for instance—requires an awareness of something that is red. This questionable premiss has been called the 'sense-datum fallacy'. If it is not assumed, the fact that our knowledge of the world's objects is based on their appearance does not imply that we are aware of anything other than the external objects themselves.

Representative theorists typically distinguish between *primary and secondary qualities. Primary qualities are supposed to be the ones that are shared by the mental representation and the physical object it represents. The shape of an object, for instance, is represented (sometimes misrepresented) by the shape of the visual image that results from our seeing that object. Colours and sounds, on the other hand, are secondary qualities: these are properties of the sensory experience that do not resemble the objective powers in objects that cause us to experience these qualities. The greenness of grass is in the perceiver, not in the grass.   F.D.

J. Locke, *An Essay Concerning Human Understanding* (1690), bks. II and IV.

M. Perkins, *Sensing the World* (Indianapolis, 1983).

republicanism. To contemporary political and historical understanding, it is the doctrine of opposition to monarchy or any other form of one-person rule. In practice it first emerged in the Greek city-states after the overthrow of the tyrants. Its first fully developed expression was in the form of government of Rome, before Augustus and his imperial successors. As a theory, it is most elaborately set out in James Harrington's *Oceana* (1656). It was suppressed by Oliver Cromwell, who had by that time become an autocrat. Republicanism, following Roman practice, tends to favour a balancing of separated powers, with a ruling oligarchy mitigating institutions as safety-valves for popular discontent and swift rotation in the higher offices, The US Constitution—the work of enlightened English country gentlemen—established a scheme close in spirit to that of the Roman Republic. In Britain, since the overthrow of Stuart absolutism—in the 1640s and then again in 1689—there has prevailed what H. G. Wells called 'a crowned republic'. The chief objection to

one-person rule is the frequent descents of autocrats into megalomania, to which is added, when the post is hereditary, incompetent heirs.   A.Q.

James Harrington, *Oceana* (1656 and later editions).

Rescher, Nicholas (1928–). An amazingly prolific contemporary American philosopher who has written over 100 books in the process of constructing a synoptic system: pragmatic idealism. The system aims at knowledge of reality. Its approach is (*a*) idealistic because it regards the constructive contribution of the inquiring mind as essential to knowledge, and because it regards systematic *coherence as the criterion of truth; (*b*) fallibilistic because it denies that knowledge can provide more than an imperfect approximation of reality; and (*c*) pragmatic because it maintains that the validity of knowledge-claims depends on their utility in furthering human purposes. The epistemological part of the system aims at improving human knowledge, while its axiological part aims at deriving values from human needs and purposes and evaluating knowledge-claims in the light of them. As a whole, Rescher's development of pragmatic *idealism is characterized by an unusually wide range of sympathy and information.   J.KEK.

*American philosophy; pragmatism; pseudo-philosophy.

Rescher encapsulates his overall position in the trilogy *A System of Pragmatic Idealism* (Princeton, NJ, 1992–3). The coherentist aspect of his position is presented more fully in *The Coherence Theory of Truth* (Oxford, 1973). For biographical information, see his *Ongoing Journey* (Lanham, Md., 1986). Rescher founded and edited the scholarly journals *American Philosophical Quarterly*, *History of Philosophy Quarterly*, and *Public Affairs Quarterly*.

res cogitans. Literally, 'thinking thing'. In the Second Meditation, Descartes uses a process of systematic doubt to reach the conclusion that he is 'in the strict sense only a thing that thinks, that is, a *mind or intelligence or intellect or reason'. In the Sixth Meditation, Descartes contrasts *res cogitans*, or mind, with *res extensa* ('extended thing', or body), and argues that the mind is 'really distinct from the body and could exist without it'.   J.COT.

*self; dualism.

N. Malcolm, 'Descartes' Proof that his Essence is Thinking', in W. Doney (ed.), *Descartes* (London, 1967).

resentment. A bitter emotion based on a sense of injury, inferiority, oppression, or frustrated vindictiveness. It plays a central role in the ethics and philosophical psychology of Nietzsche as an 'act of most spiritual revenge'. The German word *Empfindlichkeit*, like the French *ressentiment* (preferred by Nietzsche), suggests an extreme sensitivity. Resentment is a 'reactionary' emotion, a bitter but frustrated response to slights, humiliation or oppression, 'submerged hatred, the vengefulness of the impotent'. In Nietzsche's view, resentment is the mark of *'slave morality', a rejection of what is noble and exceptional. As such, it originated with and still defines the Judaeo-Christian tradition. According to Nietzsche: 'the noble man lives in trust and openness with himself, the man of *ressentiment* is neither upright nor naïve nor honest and straightforward with himself. His soul squints' (*On the Genealogy of Morals*).

Early in the twentieth century, the phenomenologist Max Scheler took on Nietzsche's psychological attack and denied that resentment was essential to Christianity or Judaeo-Christian morality. He did not, however, question the degrading status of resentment. He only shifted its locus, to the bourgeoisie. More recently still, and in a very different vein, P. F. Strawson has intricately examined the extent to which resentment presupposes free will, and John Rawls, in his *Theory of Justice*, suggests that resentment (as opposed to envy) carries with it a presupposition of *equality and, as such, is related to our sense of *justice.

                                                                R.C.SOL.

F. Nietzsche, *On the Genealogy of Morals* (New York, 1967).

M. Scheler, *Ressentiment* (London, 1961).

P. F. Strawson, *Freedom and Resentment and Other Essays* (London, 1974).

residues, method of: *see* method of residues.

respect. 'Respect' is a term which has become central to the Western moral outlook since the Enlightenment. It is basically an attitude or a special kind of feeling. If we consider the deference which might be thought appropriately directed to someone of great creative ability or perhaps to a great statesman, we can say that it was the moral insight of the Enlightenment, perhaps especially that of Kant, to suggest that such deference should be accorded to persons as such. In other words, respect is an attitude of deference, or reverence, directed at persons not just for their individual gifts or status, but for being the kind of creatures they are. Kant is often rightly criticized for taking an unduly narrow view of the nature of persons by restricting it to the rational side of human beings. But he also used a more appropriate term for the object of respect—'human dignity'. Respect is not simply a transitory feeling, but, in Kant's obscure phrase, it is a feeling 'self-wrought by a rational concept'. In other words, it has both the stability of reason and the motivating force of feeling. As such, respect can plausibly be depicted as expressing the moral attitude which is basic to liberal democracy.

Nevertheless, there are two problems with the term 'respect'. First, the object of respect easily slips from human dignity to human decisions. Yet what is it to 'respect a decision'? Many writers, e.g. on bioethics, take 'respecting an autonomous decision' to mean that they must agree to it or follow it, otherwise they are violating the autonomy or human dignity of the person. More plausibly, other writers take 'respecting a decision' to mean 'taking that decision into account, or taking it seriously'. This ambiguity can have unfortunate consequences. The second problem which arises over the word 'respect' is that it tends to make morality a human-centred affair; only human beings are thought to possess the 'moral status' of

dignity. But there is no reason why the attitude of respect or reverence should not also be accorded to animals and indeed the environment. Just as respecting persons means treating them appropriately in terms of the kind of creatures they are—namely, creatures with an essential dignity—so treating animals or the environment with respect means treating them according to their essential nature. Perhaps this is all too abstract to generate moral policies but it does identify a basic moral attitude.   R.S.D.

Jonathan Glover, *Humanity: A Moral History of the Twentieth Century* (London, 2001).

I. Kant, *Groundwork of the Metaphysic of Morals*, tr. H. J. Paton (London, 1948).

P. Taylor, *Respect for Nature* (Princeton, NJ, 1986).

responsibility. A term which covers a number of distinct but related notions, among the most important of which are causal responsibility, legal responsibility, and moral responsibility. To be causally responsible for a state of affairs is to bring it about either directly or indirectly, e.g. by ordering someone else to bring it about. To be legally responsible is to fulfil the requirements for accountability under the law: either the requirements for having a legal obligation, or the requirements for liability to the penalties for a particular offence (which may, but need not, consist in failing to fulfil a legal obligation). The term 'moral responsibility' covers (i) the having of a moral obligation and (ii) the fulfilment of the criteria for deserving blame or praise (punishment or reward) for a morally significant act or omission. These two notions of moral responsibility are linked, in that one can be deemed blameworthy for failing to fulfil a moral obligation. (In what follows, 'moral responsibility' will be used in its blame-deserving sense, and 'legal responsibility' in its penalty-warranting sense.)

Although there are connections between the three main kinds of responsibility, they are not necessary ones. Thus while causal responsibility is usually a criterion for legal responsibility, there are 'vicarious liability' offences with which someone can be charged without having either caused or foreseen the event in question. (For example, a tavern-keeper can be charged if, without his knowledge, an employee sells alcoholic drinks after hours.) And although causal responsibility is usually considered an essential criterion for moral responsibility, a person can be held morally responsible for deliberately *failing* to act. Since not all legal offences are moral wrongs and not all moral wrongs are legal offences, a person who is morally responsible may not be legally responsible and vice versa. On the other hand, one essential requirement for moral responsibility, that the wrong-doer should have known what he was doing and been willing to do it, is, apart from 'strict liability' offences, also essential for legal responsibility. (Bigamy and dangerous driving are examples of strict liability offences.)

The belief that, in order to be liable for *punishment or deserving of blame, the legal or moral offender needs to have been in the state of mind described above is connected with the belief that such offenders need to be 'responsible' in yet another sense, namely that of possessing the general ability to understand what they are doing and to control their behaviour. The term 'diminished responsibility' is linked with this sense of 'responsible'.

Finally, there is one more commonly used notion of responsibility which, following H. L. A. Hart, can be called that of 'role responsibility' (see his book *Punishment and Responsibility*). This refers to the duties (often culturally determined) which are attached to particular professional or societal or (as in the case of parents) biological roles. Failure to fulfil such duties can expose the role-holder to censure which may—depending on what the roles and duties are—be of a moral or legal kind.

It is in connection with moral responsibility that the *free will–determinism debate has traditionally arisen between compatibilists, who believe that such responsibility is compatible with the truth of *determinism, and incompatibilists, who deny this. Incompatibilists hold that if determinism is true, then no one can be morally responsible, although they acknowledge that people may be treated as if they were, perhaps for consequentialist reasons, such as the need to deter, or to protect others.   M.K.

*compatibilism and incompatibilism; desert.

H. L. A. Hart, *Punishment and Responsibility* (Oxford, 1973).
—— and A. M. Honoré, *Causation in the Law* (Oxford, 1959).
F. Schoeman (ed.), *Responsibility, Character and the Emotions* (Cambridge, 1987).

responsibility, collective: *see* collective responsibility.

retribution: *see* desert.

revaluation of values: *see* transvaluation of values.

revelation. The self-disclosure of God to humanity. The body of theological fact which God allows human beings to know unnaturally, especially through his 'mighty acts' (*magnalia Dei*) Acts 2: 11. Revealed theology is distinguished from *natural theology. Aquinas distinguishes sharply between 'truths of reason' and 'truths of revelation' in knowledge of God. Karl Barth thinks that revelation is a necessary condition for any human knowing of God.

Revelation is the last book of the New Testament, authored by St John the Divine (who is almost certainly not St John the Apostle). A series of vivid visions is related, culminating in the pouring out of the wrath of God from seven bowls (14–16) and the defeat of Satan (19 ff.), followed by the general resurrection of the dead and the judgement of souls. Revelation raises difficult metaphysical issues: How can a benevolent God be wrathful? What has to exist if good and evil exist? What makes some resurrection my resurrection? What is *heaven? Do angels exist?   S.P.

Aquinas, *Summa Theologica* (London, 1963–75).
Karl Barth, *Church Dogmatics*, 1/1 (Edinburgh, 1975), esp. 191, 193–4.

revenge. The intentional infliction of *punishment or injury in return for a wrong to oneself or one's family or close friends. (Compare 'vengeance', which is the satisfaction of such an intention, and 'avenge', which is to take revenge on behalf of someone else who cannot do so for him- or herself.) Revenge and vengeance have a long and controversial history in the development of retributive justice. In Homeric Greece, 'revenge' and 'justice' were more or less equivalent, but Plato's Socrates taught that 'the return of evil for evil' is always unjust. The Hebrew Bible describes a 'vengeful God' and prescribes 'an eye for an eye' (a limitation of vengeance, not an exhortation), while the New Testament encourages forgiveness, and reserves vengeance for a loving God. Modern social philosophy generally rejects the very idea of revenge as irrational and always unjustified. But among those philosophers who still defend the idea of *retribution (as opposed to deterrence and rehabilitation), the line between revenge and retribution is not obvious. Immanuel Kant declares the latter justified and required by reason, but he dismisses the former entirely. Robert Nozick similarly suggests that revenge is emotional and merely personal, while retribution is justifiable and impersonal. In fact, revenge is sometimes justified and often deliberative, and it is a much debated question to what extent revenge should be part of the purpose of punishment in the criminal law. Nor should revenge be viewed as simply a raw, unreasonable emotion. Revenge is a dish, says one ancient proverb, which is 'best served cold'.
          R.C.SOL.

M. Henberg, *Retribution* (Philadelphia, 1989).
S. Jacoby, *Wild Justice* (New York, 1986).
J. Murphy and J. Hampton, *Mercy and Forgiveness* (Cambridge, 1988).

revisionary metaphysics. A term coined by P. F. Strawson to describe the philosophical efforts of Descartes, Leibniz, and Berkeley, who are contrasted with the practitioners of *descriptive metaphysics. Revisionary *metaphysics is said to substitute for the actual structure of the world a picture of one which is aesthetically, morally, emotionally, or intellectually preferable. The charge that philosophical systems are so many well-organized and pleasing fictions is anticipated in numerous earlier accusations of the visionary character and distance from experience of all metaphysics. Each is nevertheless deserving of study, Strawson maintained, on account of the 'intensity of its partial vision' and its utility as a source of philosophical puzzles.

The existence of revisionary metaphysics depends upon a metaphilosophical confusion between 'is, really' and 'ought to be', and between logical and existential concerns. Yet the satisfactions it supplies ensure that revisionary metaphysics remains a permanent temptation of philosophy, not simply a useful term for historical analysis.   CATH.W.

S. Haack, 'Descriptive and Revisionary Metaphysics', *Philosophical Studies* (1979).

P. F. Strawson, *Individuals: An Essay in Descriptive Metaphysics* (London, 1959), pp. xiii–xvi.

revolution. A radical political upheaval or transformation. Originally understood through an astronomical metaphor, revolutions were cyclical processes moving through four stages: tyranny, resistance, civil war, and restoration. In modern times, the term has shed that reference and come to designate a change in constitution, regime, and social order. The change is intentional and programmatic, undertaken on the basis of an ideological argument painting the old regime as tyrannical, corrupt, or oppressive, promising a new age, and justifying the (usually high) costs involved.

Revolution should be distinguished from *coup d'état*, where only the rulers are changed, not the system as a whole ('palace revolution' is a *coup* in a monarchist or autocratic *état*), and also from secession and national liberation, where the goal is independence from foreign rule, not or not necessarily a radically new state and society. Hence, the justifications for revolutionary politics, once the cyclical metaphor is dropped, must extend beyond a catalogue of the crimes of a particular ruler or set of rulers, domestic or foreign. If they are to justify what needs justifying, they will have to include a detailed defence of the proposed new regime and a description of the transformations this regime will effect in society as a whole. A struggle for independence can be called revolutionary only when its protagonists defend their enterprise in this large way, aiming, like eighteenth-century Americans, at a 'new order for the ages'.

Given the scope of the changes promised, the newness of the 'new order', revolutionary politics is sometimes described as a form of secular messianism, a reproduction in political terms of Jewish and Christian visions of the end of days. Certainly, revolutionaries sometimes adapt and use religious rhetoric, but their programme, while necessarily radical in relation to the old regime, is not necessarily radical in relation to the whole of human history. It can and often does describe a particular system of oppression, not a fallen humanity, and a particular set of transformations, not a singular and universal redemption.

Nor is it the case that the transformations must be given a redemptive form in order to justify the costs of overthrowing the old regime and building the new. The standard defence of revolutionary violence probably has more to do with the supposed entrenchment of established ideologies and practices and the strength and stubbornness of the established rulers than with the glories to come. Unhappily, this defence often finds continuing uses after the overthrow of the old regime, when ideologies and practices persist and are sometimes upheld with a new stubbornness by ordinary men and women. The subsequent course of revolutionary politics is largely determined by the relation of the programmatically committed leaders (the 'vanguard') to their own increasingly reluctant followers. The hardest question for the leaders (it probably is not hard for anyone else) is whether rule by violence is morally permitted or politically prudent during this period. How much can revolutionary aspiration justify?

A modest answer to this last question ('not much') points toward a reformist rather than a revolutionary politics. Or, perhaps, it points toward what has been called a 'long revolution', where the radical programme is maintained but a systematic effort is made to hold down the costs of achieving it. But most revolutionaries would probably argue that the changes they intend require a historical break—the total defeat of the old regime and the seizure of power by people like themselves—and in fact justify the attendant costs.   M.WALZ.

*Marx; Marxism; conservatism; liberalism.

Crane Brinton, *The Anatomy of Revolution*, rev. edn. (New York, 1952).
John Dunn, *Modern Revolutions* (Cambridge, 1972).
Ted Honderich, *Violence for Equality* (Harmondsworth, 1980).
J. L. Talmon, *The Origins of Totalitarian Democracy* (New York, 1960).

revolutions, scientific. An idea most closely associated with Thomas Kuhn, scientific revolutions are shifts from one scientific paradigm to another, where a paradigm is a fundamental research framework that provides common methods, theories, and shared interpretations. Revolutions happen because problems arise that resist solution by methods of the existing paradigm. If the failure is perceived as serious, a crisis can arise, an alternative paradigm will be constructed, and a large-scale transition to a new paradigm may occur. Well-known examples are the change from classical mechanics to relativistic mechanics, and rule-based artificial intelligence to neural nets. Kuhn held that revolutions were discontinuities in science—paradigms are *incommensurable, the shift is not based on rational inference from data, and cumulative progress towards the truth is destroyed. Historically, the thesis is contentious; Kuhn's historical sketches suggest less continuity than was actually present. Philosophically, the issue is arguable; one's theories of reference and meaning play a crucial role in whether the necessary semantic discontinuities exist.   P.H.

Thomas S. Kuhn, *The Structure of Scientific Revolutions*, 3rd edn. (Chicago, 1996).

rhetoric. The art of making speeches. Learning rhetoric was prized in the Greek democracies as a means to success in public life, but criticized by Plato for being concerned with the means of persuasion, not with the ends. Aristotle's *Rhetoric* contains a fairly systematic discussion of forms of rhetorical argument (notably the *enthymeme). For the Stoics, rhetoric became a branch of logic, and a proper study for philosophers.   R.J.H.

G. A. Kennedy, *The Art of Persuasion in Greece* (London, 1963).

Richard's paradox, due to Jules Richard, arises from the assumption that expressions of (say) English which denote numbers can be enumerated in an alphabetical (infinite) list *L*. If so, then a diagonal number—one differing from the *n*th number in *L* at its *n*th decimal place—can be defined (as in Cantor's proof that the reals are non-denumerable) in a finite number of English words. But then this phrase must be in list *L* as, say, entry *k* and thus must define a number differing from the one it does define, at the *k*th place. This contradiction shows there is no such list *L*. There is an enumeration of all finite strings of English letters. But whether such a string defines a number cannot be specified recursively.   J.C.

Jules Richard, 'Les Principes des mathématiques et le problème des ensembles', *Revue générale des sciences pures et appliquées* (1905); tr. in J. van Heijenoort (ed.), *Source Book in Mathematical Logic 1879–1931* (Cambridge, Mass., 1964).

Ricœur, Paul (1913–). French philosopher and theorist of symbolic forms. Ricœur's project since the 1950s has been to mediate in the 'conflict of interpretations' that has grown up among the various schools of linguistic, hermeneutic, and literary-critical theory. His earliest writings were mainly concerned with the debate between *phenomenology and *structuralism, the one aimed towards interpreting language in its creative (i.e. symbolic, metaphorical, or artistic) manifestations, the other premissed on a formal methodology that took for granted, following Saussure, the priority of code and system over expressive content. This work often had a markedly theological cast, most evident in books (like *The Symbolism of Evil*) where Ricœur sought to establish links between presentday schools of thought and their various precursory movements in the history of Jewish and Christian exegetical tradition. If there is one major theme that has preoccupied his thinking since then, it is the idea that all interpretation partakes of a double ('negative' and 'positive') hermeneutic. Such is the argument of his book *Freud and Philosophy*. On the one hand psychoanalysis involves an 'archaeology' of meanings, motives, and desires, an attempt to delve back into the unconscious layers of repressed or sublimated memory. On the other—on its forward-looking or redemptive side—Freud's project points a way *through and beyond* that condition by offering the patient renewed possibilities of self-knowledge and creative fulfilment.

Ricœur finds a kindred dialectic at work within Marxist and other politically orientated theories of interpretation. Here also there is a negative (demystifying) moment of *Ideologiekritik*, joined to a positive—implicitly utopian— hermeneutics of transcendence. Given this approach, it is understandable that Ricœur should avoid the kinds of polarized thinking and attendant polemics that have characterized so much recent debate. But he does take issue with structuralism and *post-structuralism for what he sees as their relentlessly negative stance with regard to questions of meaning, subjectivity, and truth. His recent works on metaphor and narrative again show Ricœur treating these issues through a dialogue that patiently engages all sides to the dispute while seeking a perspective atop their (often sterile) antinomies.   C.N.

*French philosophy today.

Paul Ricœur, *The Conflict of Interpretations: Essays in Hermeneutics*, tr. Don Ihde *et al.* (Evanston, Ill., 1974).
—— *Time and Narrative*, 3 vols. (Chicago, 1984–7).

right. What it is right to do, as distinct from what it is good to do. One of the traditional problems of moral philosophy is that of relating the right and the good. For the utilitarian, or more generally the consequentialist, the right is instrumental in bringing about good in the form of the best possible consequences. Other philosophers, deontologists, have held that at least some actions are right for reasons intrinsic to their own natures, and independently of 'the good'. Yet it seems hard to accept that the right has no relation to 'the good'. One solution is to suggest that the right is indeed a means to 'the good' though not an external, instrumental means as the utilitarian suggests, but an internal, component means: the very performance of the right or of duties is itself an expression of 'the good'.   R.S.D.

*deontology; moral philosophy, problems of; right action; utilitarianism.

W. D. Ross, *The Right and the Good* (Oxford, 1930).

right, the political: *see* conservatism.

Right, the political New. Vague label for cluster of political doctrines emerging from *conservatism and contrasting with it in their demand for radical change. New Right thinkers believe that political decline can be arrested only by encouraging individual initiatives and competition. This requires a reduction in the welfare provision and redistributive taxation which characterize the state influenced by *socialism. The resulting emphasis on a minimal state distinguishes the New Right from Fascism and pushes some thinkers (e.g. Nozick) towards *libertarianism. However, the New Right embraces *nationalism, sometimes based, like its *individualism, on a form of *social Darwinism.   P.GIL.

*liberalism.

Norman Barry, *The New Right* (London, 1987).
Ted Honderich, *Conservatism* (Harmondsworth, 1990).

right action. No subject is more central to moral philosophy or ethics than that of right and wrong action. Although the correlative terms 'right' and 'wrong' have important non-moral uses—as, for example, when we speak of the right or wrong way to fix a car—ethicists are primarily interested in moral right and wrong, and they typically regard a theory of right and wrong in this sense as the most important element in any overall conception or view of ethics.

To be sure, there are related notions like *'ought' and 'moral *obligation' that play a role in any complete or overall moral theory. But it is usually assumed that such notions can be defined in terms of rightness and/or wrongness (though the definitions could also proceed in the reverse direction). Roughly speaking, an act is (morally) obligatory or ought (morally speaking), to be done if it would be wrong not to perform it, and so a theory of right and wrong is tantamount to a theory of obligation and of what morally ought to be done. (The question whether moral goodness and praiseworthiness can also be understood in terms of rightness and wrongness is much more difficult, and some philosophers would hold that explanation should work in the opposite direction, with so-called 'deontic' notions like obligation, right, and wrong being understood as derivative from 'aretaic' notions like goodness, badness, and admirability. (*Aretē.))

Of course, one in any event needs to distinguish theories or conceptions of right and wrong (or of moral goodness) from analyses or definitions of the terms 'right' and 'wrong' (or 'morally good'). During the heyday of Anglo-American meta-ethics, philosophers were often on principle more interested in defining ethical notions than in offering a substantive view of what actions are right and what actions are wrong. And one can, therefore, be an emotivist, or prescriptivist, or naturalist about the meaning of (sentences or assertions involving) the terms 'right' and 'wrong', without taking sides on various issues having to do with what actually is right or wrong. But over the longer history of philosophy and certainly nowadays as well, a greater interest has been taken in giving a substantive account of rightness, as opposed to simply defining the term, and there currently are and always have been a great many opposing views about what rightness, i.e. the moral rightness of actions, substantively amounts to. (One can also talk about right attitudes and right desires, but moral philosophers have paid much, much more attention to what makes actions right.)

To a large extent, philosophers' views about right action(s) have depended on what they wanted to say about moral rules and principles. It is natural to think of morality as some kind of code containing action-guiding rules or principles and thus to think of valid morality or the true morality philosophers are seeking to formulate or describe as consisting in an appropriately ordered set of such rules or principles. Then different theories of right action would be based in differences about what were the ultimately valid principles or rules of morality. Act-utilitarianism in one standard form holds, for example, that there is one basic principle of morality, the principle of utility, which treats actions as right or wrong depending on whether they maximize the utility or welfare of the people (or sentient creatures) they affect. By contrast, Rossian intuitionism accepts a small set of basic moral principles no one of which always takes precedence over any other and regards (our knowledge of) the rightness or wrongness of particular acts (I don't think we need here distinguish actions from acts) as often a matter of delicate balancing among the different ultimate principles that apply in a given situation.

However, such a picture, though it covers most cases, is somewhat misleading as a general account of what is at stake in theories of right action, because there are some theories, notably Aristotle's, according to which knowledge of right and wrong is not a matter of applying or weighing or balancing general moral rules or principles. The virtuous individual, for Aristotle, is capable of knowing what is right in particular circumstances by delicate perception unaided by general (even primafacie) principles. It is also worth pointing out that some principles of right or permissible action are not rules for the guidance of individuals *in situ*. If it is morally permissible or one has the moral right to defend oneself against deadly force, that is a right one has even and especially in situations where one is too threatened to be paying any attention to moral issues or principles. A theory of right and wrong action is not necessarily a theory of what principles should guide one in daily life, and utilitarians, for example, are fond of saying that the principle of utility is a valid *standard* of right action, but not a reasonable or useful moral guide for people to use in the course of daily life. People may be more likely to do what maximizes utility, and thus to live up to the principle of utility as a standard of moral evaluation, if they don't try to maximize utility, but instead, for example, try to help those they love or those whose distress or need immediately assails them.

Having mentioned Aristotelian, intuitionist, and utilitarian views of right action, we should complete the overview of the main competing contemporary conceptions of right action by saying something very briefly about Kantian, contractarian, and agent-based virtue-ethical theories of moral rightness. The last of these treats the rightness of actions as a matter of the motives or inner states of character they express or sustain, acts counting as right if and only if, for example, they come from sympathy or compassion or inner health or strength. Contractarians treat right action as a matter of conformity to the principles or rules that people would agree upon in some hypothetical or ideal bargaining situation. Finally, Kantians regard the rightness of an action as a matter of whether the maxim or underlying purpose of the action is one which could be consistently willed (or imagined) to govern *everyone's* behaviour—though some Kantians may prefer to say, instead, that acts are right if they don't involve treating anyone merely as a means, which idea has seemed promising to many, but is quite obviously in need of expansion. All the above-named theories have sizable or at the very least vocal followings among contemporary philosophers.   M.S.

*utilitarianism; deontology.

F. Feldman, *Introductory Ethics* (Englewood Cliffs, NJ, 1978).

T. Hill, *Dignity and Practical Reason in Kant's Moral Theory* (Ithaca, NY, 1992).

W. D. Ross, *The Foundations of Ethics* (Oxford, 1939).

S. Scheffler, *The Rejection of Consequentialism* (Oxford, 1982).

J. J. C. Smart and B. A. O. Williams, *Utilitarianism: For and Against* (Cambridge, 1973).

rights. In their strongest sense, rights are justified claims to the protection of persons' important interests. When the rights are effective, this protection is provided as something that is owed to persons for their own sakes. The upholding of rights is thus essential for human dignity.

Although Wesley N. Hohfeld distinguished four different meanings of 'a right'—claims, liberties, powers, and immunities—claim-rights are the most important kind of rights because they entail correlative necessary duties to forbear from interfering with persons' having the objects of their rights or, in some situations, to help persons to have these objects. The general structure of a claim-right is given by this formula: A has a right to X against B by virtue of Y. There are five main elements here: first, the subject (A) of the right, the right-holder; second, the nature of the right; third, the object (X) of the right; fourth, the respondent (B) of the right, the duty-bearer; fifth, the justifying ground (Y) of the right.

Two problems about 'redundancy' are answered by reference to this formula. First, although rights are correlative with duties, rights are not redundant because their objects are benefits to the right-holder, while duties are burdens of the respondent. Second, rights cannot be dispensed with in favour of benefits or interests, because having a right adds that there is strong justification for being protected in one's benefit or interest, such that the right-holder is personally entitled to have the benefit as his due and for his own sake (as against utilitarian justifications).

The 'benefit theory' of the nature of rights emphasizes the relation between the subject and the object of rights: to have a right is to be the directly intended beneficiary of someone else's performance of a good-providing duty. The 'choice theory' emphasizes the relation between the subject and the respondent: to have a right is to be in a justified position to determine by one's choice how other persons shall act. There are arguments for and against each theory; the most acceptable account involves some combination of the two theories.

Legal rights, to be justified, must ultimately have moral justification. Because of the normative necessity involved in claim-rights, their primary justification must be found in their having as objects the goods that are necessary for human action or for having general chances of success in achieving one's purposes by action. The two main such goods are *freedom and *well-being, which are, respectively, the procedural and the substantive necessary conditions of action and of generally successful action. Well-being, which consists in having the general abilities and conditions needed for achieving one's purposes by action, falls into a hierarchy from life and physical integrity to education and opportunities for earning wealth and income. All actual or prospective agents have equal moral rights, positive as well as negative, to freedom and well-being; a cogent argument can be given for the moral principle that grounds this thesis. (*Liberty.) The argument shows that every actual or prospective agent logically must accept that he and all other agents have these rights because of their enduring needs for the necessary conditions of their action and generally successful action.

Conflicts of rights can be resolved by consideration of the degrees of their objects' needfulness for action. Although *utilitarianism can 'accommodate' rights, in that it can require that special protection be provided for persons' interests and needs, this protection would be only contingent because it would be owed to persons not for their own sakes but rather as means to the maximization of utility, so that the rights could be overridden whenever such maximization required this. On the other hand, the universality of human rights requires that each person act with due regard for other persons' freedom and well-being as well as her own.   A.GEW.

*nonsense upon stilts.

Ronald Dworkin, *Taking Rights Seriously* (Cambridge, Mass., 1977).

Alan Gewirth, *Reason and Morality* (Chicago, Ill., 1978).

Wesley N. Hohfeld, *Fundamental Legal Conceptions as Applied in Judicial Reasoning* (New Haven, Conn., 1964).

J. Waldron (ed.), *Theories of Rights* (Oxford, 1985).

rights, natural: *see* natural rights.

rigid designator. This is a term introduced by Kripke to characterize an expression which has the same *reference in every *possible world in which it has any reference at all. Kripke holds that proper names and natural-kind terms are rigid designators, unlike most definite descriptions. Thus, whereas 'the inventor of bifocals' is non-rigid, designating Benjamin Franklin in the actual world but other people in other possible worlds, 'Benjamin Franklin' designates Benjamin Franklin in every world in which it designates anything at all.   E.J.L.

*flaccid designator.

S. A. Kripke, *Naming and Necessity* (Oxford, 1980).

risus sophisticus. Philosophical counter-ploy identified by Gorgias of Leontini (*c*.483–376 BC) as 'destroying one's adversaries' seriousness by laughter and their laughter by seriousness'. Characteristically employed by aged philosopher commenting upon a paper of unfollowable complexity by young post-doctoral Fellow. For instantiation see *Professional Foul* etc. by Tom Stoppard.   J.C.A.G.

*ad hominem argument.

Roman philosophy. The distinction between ancient Roman philosophy and the Greek tradition from which it sprang and which continued alongside it can only be partial; the same is true of many other aspects of ancient Graeco-Roman culture. The term Roman philosophy will here be taken to apply (i) to philosophical writing in Latin from the beginnings to the sixth century AD, and (ii) to works which, whether in Greek or in Latin, reflect distinctive developments in the Stoic school after the Roman conquest of Greece. Here the label 'Roman' is partly a chronological one, but it also reflects distinctive emphases characteristic of Roman philosophy more generally.

Greek philosophy was initially seen as subversive of Roman customs; philosophers were expelled from Rome in 173 and 161 BC, and the *scepticism of Carneades, who visited Rome in 155 BC, angered the elder Cato, as did other Greek cultural imports. Later in the century the Stoic Panaetius was an associate of Scipio the Younger. Philosophical writing in Latin began in the next century, with Epicurean prose writings (now lost, and scorned by Cicero), Lucretius' Epicurean poem, and Cicero's own philosophical works. The popularity of *Epicureanism prompted Cicero to attack its recommendation of withdrawal from public life as the antithesis of Roman civic duty. In the politically unsettled times of the late Republic and early Empire there was interest in the astrological and numerological aspects of neo-*Pythagoreanism.

Panaetius' concern with those progressing towards virtue rather than having arrived at it, with the importance of positive action, and with the relevance to ethics of individual personality have been seen as an adaptation of *Stoicism to practical Roman interests. The extent of his divergence from earlier Stoicism has sometimes been exaggerated. Once Roman philosophy proper developed, there was an emphasis on ethics and on man's relation to the gods. Cicero himself inclined not to the Stoa but to the *Academy—whether the epistemological scepticism of the New Academy or the more dogmatic ethics of Antiochus—but he developed the Stoic theme of the universe as common home of gods and men, and made it the basis for a theory of *natural law. He also applied Academic suspension of judgement to theology and divination; here it should be remembered that, for ancient *Sceptics, denial of certainty about religion, or anything else, was neither a dogmatic assertion of disbelief nor inconsistent with continuing traditional observances.

In the first century AD Stoicism became identified with the senatorial opposition to the emperors; by the second century AD there had been such a change that one of the emperors, Marcus Aurelius, is himself counted as a leading Stoic writer. Marcus, like his fellow Stoic the former slave Epictetus, wrote in Greek; Seneca, the Stoic tutor of Nero, had written in Latin. Their writings are alike characterized by concern with the practical aspects of ethics and psychology, including the notion of the *will as distinct from the *understanding—a specifically Roman contribution later given its fullest development in antiquity by Augustine. There is also a new stress on the divine element in each individual as the true self.

Roman philosophy was, however, still only the junior partner in the Graeco-Roman philosophical enterprise. Platonists such as Plutarch, *Peripatetics, and Sceptics continued and developed their traditions in the first two centuries of the Empire, but, unlike the Roman Stoics, hardly count as 'Roman philosophers'; nor in the third century AD does Plotinus, the founder of *Neoplatonism, even though Rome was where he taught. In the later Empire 'Roman philosophy' most naturally indicates that minority of philosophers who wrote in Latin; above all Augustine, and, after the western Empire had already fallen, Boethius. Boethius began by translating and interpreting Aristotle's logic in the Neoplatonic tradition; but in the Consolation of Philosophy he not only gave moving literary expression, drawing on Platonic and Stoic ideas, to belief in divine providential concern and the powerlessness of wicked rulers to harm good men, but also developed a solution to the problem of reconciling divine foreknowledge and human freedom (to God all time is as the present: so his foreknowing what I will do no more removes my freedom than your seeing what I am doing now) which improved on its Greek Neoplatonist origins and was taken over by Aquinas seven centuries later.

The question why Roman philosophy has in general been less significant than Greek can be approached in more than one way, like the definition of Roman philosophy itself. On one level there was simply less Roman than Greek philosophical activity, even in the period of the Roman Empire; on another, both Greek and Roman philosophy in that period were characterized—as was much else in the culture of the time—by looking back to earlier thinkers as models, the commentary and the scholastic compendium being the characteristic forms of writing. But the contribution of Roman philosophy as here defined to the European tradition should not be underestimated.

R.W.S.

A. H. Armstrong (ed.), *Cambridge History of Later Greek and Early Medieval Philosophy* (Cambridge, 1967), chs. 21–7 (Augustine), 35 (Boethius).

M. Griffin and J. Barnes (eds.), *Philosophia Togata*, 2 vols. (Oxford, 1989 and 1997).

D. Sedley (ed.), *The Cambridge Companion to Greek and Roman Philosophy* (Cambridge, 2003).

romantic irony: *see* irony, Romantic.

romanticism, philosophical. The idea of Romanticism is at once indispensable and embarrassing to cultural historians. They cannot do without it; something is needed to distinguish Pope from Wordsworth, David from Delacroix, Handel from Beethoven. But they are acutely worried by the problem of defining it, which they create for themselves. Like most interesting general terms applying to human affairs, and unlike 'prime number' or 'nitrous oxide', it is not definable in a short formula made up of precisely demarcated terms. That is not necessarily a fault. Romanticism is a cluster of attitudes and preferences each of which is usually to be found with a good number of the others and, in extreme cases, with most, or even all, of them.

The Romantic favours the concrete over the abstract, variety over uniformity, the infinite over the finite, nature over culture, convention, and artifice, the organic over the mechanical, freedom over constraint, rules, and limitations. In human terms it prefers the unique individual to the average man, the free creative genius to the prudent man of good sense, the particular community or nation to humanity at large. Mentally the Romantic prefers feeling to thought, more specifically, emotion to calculation, *imagination to literal common-sense, intuition to intellect. This fairly coherent array of preferences is fleshed out in all sorts of specific ways: in literature, art, and music, in moral conduct and moral convictions, in religion, in politics, in the writing of history and, not least, in philosophy.

Kant created philosophical romanticism, although he was himself only very marginally and partially a Romantic. His most important contribution was inadvertent: the idiosyncratically expressed distinction he drew between *reason and *understanding. Kant was critical of the pretensions of what he called reason, partly for the more or less Romantic purpose of 'making room for faith', but also in the interests of the understanding, to which, in conjunction with the senses, is due, he held, all our substantial knowledge of the world. That does not make him an anti-rationalist in any ordinary sense of the word, and his ethics are even more narrowly rationalistic, since for him the supreme principle of morality is an a priori necessary truth. In the same spirit, the only kind of intuition he allows for is sense-perception. The direct apprehension of what transcends sense-experience is merely the 'dreams of a ghost-seer'.

The German Idealists who came after Kant, notably Fichte, Schelling, and Hegel, accepted his distinction between reason and understanding, but reversed the value he had ascribed to them. They saw understanding, the intellect as it works in science and everyday life, as an inferior faculty supplying useful, but distortedly abstract, opinion about fragments torn from reality for practical purposes. Reason, on the other hand, was for them intellect in its highest form as an apprehension of the totality of things in their essential interconnectedness. Coleridge, who studied Kant, Fichte, and Schelling, and lavishly borrowed from the last of them, applied their way of distinguishing reason from understanding in his own distinction between imagination, the 'esemplastic' or unifying power which fuses things together, and fancy, which merely juxtaposes 'fixities and definites'.

Non-philosophical Romanticism disdains ordinary *rationality as a practical makeshift for the earth-bound, yielding only a truncated, superficial, and distorted picture of the world as it really is. The directly intuitive, even mystical, apprehension of the world which we owe to poets and other such creative geniuses does not stand in need of any reasoned support or articulation. A philosophical Romantic cannot be so easygoing. He has to provide the conception of the world as some kind of spiritual unity with rational credentials. These are supplied by Fichte's notion of the *dialectic, conceived as a progressive surmounting of oppositions or contradictions and which is best known as the organizing principle of the philosophy of Hegel.

The essentially Enlightenment character of Kant's thought is shown in his rigoristic, petty bourgeois moral outlook, in his liberal, pacific, and internationalist politics, and in his religion, unencumbered with Gothic detail or liturgical tradition. The *nationalism of Fichte and Hegel,

taking off from the more moderate celebration of cultural nationality by Herder, is another and altogether more Romantic matter. Kant was much affected by Rousseau, whose distinction between the organic general will and the mechanical will of all can properly be seen, as it was by Hegel, as another application of the reason–understanding distinction.   A.Q.

F. Copleston, *History of Philosophy*, vii (London, 1963), pt. I.

A. O. Lovejoy, *The Reason, the Understanding and Time* (Baltimore, 1961).

Jacques Barzun, *Classic, Romantic and Modern* (Garden City, NY, 1961).

Romanticism and conservatism: *see* conservatism and Romanticism.

Romero, Francisco (1891–1962). Argentinian philosopher, born in Seville, Spain. He began his career in the military, but taught philosophy from 1930 until his death in 1962. Romero's *Teoría del hombre* (1952) displays the influence of Max Scheler and Nicolai Hartmann. In it he develops a systematic *philosophical anthropology within the context of a metaphysics of *transcendence. According to Romero, reality includes physical, organic, intentional, and spiritual levels and is arranged hierarchically by degrees of transcendence. Physical objects are devoid of psychic life, whereas animals are characterized by a pre-intentional psychism but lack self-consciousness. *Self-consciousness appears at the level of *intentionality with man; he alone is able to view the world in terms of himself. Man reaches the level of the spiritual when he achieves absolute objectivity. The duality resulting from the merging of the intentional and spiritual levels of reality is what characterizes man.   J.G.
                                                                                E.M.

Marjorie Silliman Harris, *Francisco Romero on Problems of Philosophy* (New York, 1960).

Rorty, Richard (1931–). American philosopher of mind and, subsequently, notable critic of the pretensions of traditional epistemology. Rorty did his first degree at Chicago, got a doctorate at Yale, and taught at Princeton between 1961 and 1982, in which year he moved to the University of Virginia, significantly as Professor of Humanities. He began as an able, but fairly conventionally analytic, philosopher, until the publication in 1979 of his *Philosophy and the Mirror of Nature*, whose vigorous repudiation of the idea that it is possible to pass judgement on our beliefs from some objective, transcendental standpoint excited wide attention.

Rorty's central idea, in its main outlines, repeats the objection of nineteenth-century idealists to the *correspondence theory of truth; that there is no access, except through other beliefs, to the facts in correspondence to which the truth of our beliefs is supposed to consist. Rorty found support for this rejection of any secure touchstone or foundation for knowledge partly in the pragmatist tradition and partly in recent developments tending in the same direction: Sellars's attack on the 'myth of the given' and Quine's attack on analyticity.

He pushed his critique of the idea that there are firm foundations from which epistemology can authoritatively pass judgement on beliefs in general to something like the extreme point of Derrida's rejection of the 'metaphysics of presence', which holds not only that there are no absolute foundations, but that no belief is more fundamental than any other. The implication he draws is that philosophy cannot establish anything and that it should be understood as a, possibly edifying, conversation, with the same sort of claim to finality as the conversations of cultural and literary critics. Heidegger, Wittgenstein, and Dewey are invoked as a kind of pantheon for this undermining of the conception philosophers have ordinarily held of their philosophical activity.   A.Q.

*idealism; neo-pragmatism.

Richard Rorty, *Philosophy and the Mirror of Nature* (London, 1979).
—— *Consequences of Pragmatism* (London, 1982).
—— *Contigency, Irony, and Solidarity* (Cambridge, 1989).
Alan R. Malachowski (ed.), *Reading Rorty* (Oxford, 1990).

Rosenzweig, Franz (1886–1929). Jewish philosopher. On the point of following his cousin Rosenstock-Huessy into Christianity, Rosenzweig found that he could turn Christian only 'as a Jew'. He attended the Day of Atonement service (1913) at a traditional Berlin synagogue, discovering, to his wonder, the spirituality of his ancestral faith. Sustained study of the Jewish sources and of Hermann Cohen's work led him to the philosophical Judaism of *The Star of Redemption*, begun on postcards mailed from the Front in 1915–16. There he argues that God, world, and man cannot be explained from (or reduced to) one another but are linked in a dialogue of *I and thou (a phrase derived from Feuerbach's critique of Hegel), by 'paths' of creation, revelation, and redemption, as if forming a shield of David, the six-pointed star of his title. Creation gives being, but also transitoriness. It is complemented by revelation, which brings man to his true self. Man responds to God's love with a love of God, which he translates into love of his neighbour, helping to lead the world to redemption. Rosenzweig's two-volume study of Hegel's political thought (1920) and his translations of Halevi's poetry and (with Martin Buber) of the Hebrew Bible show the poles that orientate him. Of the story of Balaam's ass, he said that through the year it is a fairy-tale, but when read from the scroll on the appointed Sabbath it contains the word of God speaking directly to him.   L.E.G.

Franz Rosenzweig, *The Star of Redemption* (1921), tr. from the 1930 2nd edn. by William Hallo (Boston, 1974).

Ross, William David (1877–1971). Oxford philosopher and scholar. An outstanding Aristotelian and Platonic scholar, his main original, and still influential, contribution to philosophy was in ethics. Ross accepted G. E. Moore's argument that any equation of intrinsic good with a natural property commits the *'naturalistic fallacy'.

However, Ross argues that Moore committed a similar fallacy in equating the rightness of an action with its maximization of good. That we ought always to maximize good is a synthetic and, in fact, false proposition. We have a number of distinct prima-facie *obligations, of which this is only one and not always the most stringent. An act may be prima facie obligatory for a number of different reasons, and is *absolutely* right if the prima-facie obligation to do it is the weightiest. His attack on *consequentialism and notion of a *prima-facie* moral obligation has had an enduring influence.   T.L.S.S.

W. D. Ross, *The Right and the Good* (Oxford, 1930; new edn. 2003).
—— *Foundations of Ethics* (Oxford, 1939).

Rousseau, Jean-Jacques (1712–78). Rousseau is best known for his contributions to political philosophy, with his *Social Contract* (1762) being generally regarded as his masterpiece. In that he argues for a version of sovereignty of the whole citizen body over itself, expressing its legislative intent through the *general will, which is supposed to apply to all equally because it comes from all alike. The general will tends to promote *liberty and *equality, in Rousseau's view, and it both arises from and promotes a spirit of *fraternity. Rousseau is standardly seen as one of the presiding geniuses of the French Revolution, and attracts admiration or detestation accordingly. In fact, it would seem that his ideas were merely exploited opportunistically, particularly by Robespierre. One of Rousseau's most memorable epigrams, 'Man is born free; and everywhere he is in chains' comes from the *Social Contract* and has been a rallying-cry for revolutionaries and reformers ever since.

Another central thought in Rousseau's work is that man is by nature good, but he is corrupted and depraved by society. The idea of oneself as an ill-used victim, which this seems to suggest, was certainly prominent in Rousseau's personal psychology; he suffered an acute paranoiac breakdown in the late 1760s. It is doubtful, however, that this is how he wished this thought to be taken. The sources of corruption lie in the individual's own makeup, but tend to be deepened and consolidated by social processes or envious competition and desire for precedence. It is possible, none the less, to envisage a different basis for human society and hence a different destiny for men. This is most completely explained by Rousseau in his educational treatise *Émile* (1762).

Rousseau was born in Geneva, but spent twenty years of his adult life in Paris. When he first arrived there in 1742, he hoped to find fame and fortune as a musical theorist, teacher, and composer. One delightful opera, *Le Devin du village*, performed before Louis XVI at Versailles in 1745, has survived. Rousseau had, in the mean time, made friends with members of the young Paris intelligentsia, particularly Diderot. Through this relationship, he was drawn into considering social and political issues, his other major work in this area before the *Social Contract* being his *Discourse on the Origin of Inequality* (1755). After the publication of the *Social Contract* and *Émile* in 1762, Rousseau was persecuted for his blasphemous views about natural religion, and fled Paris. He also renounced his citizenship of Geneva, where too his books were burned. After some extremely unsettled years, he was eventually permitted to resettle in France, on sufferance, and he returned to Paris in 1770. Most of the writing of his last decade is autobiographical, including his outstanding *Confessions* but also the prolix and uneven exercise in self-justification *Dialogues de Rousseau juge de Jean-Jacques*. His body was transferred to the Panthéon in 1796.

As well as his work in social and political theory, education, and music, Rousseau wrote extensively on botany (for which he had a passion), on language, on religion, and he wrote some indifferent plays and poems. He also wrote a novel, *Julie, ou la Nouvelle Héloïse*. He continues to excite great controversy as both a theoretician and a person: as a theoretician because it is possible to see him both as a great liberator of the individual or as the apologist for populist totalitarianism; as a person because it is possible to see him as an ill-starred genius or as a self-righteous bully.

N.J.H.D.

*human nature.

Rousseau's life is recounted by M. Cranston in a 3-vol. biography (i: *Jean-Jacques* (London, 1983); ii: *The Noble Savage* (London, 1991); iii, *The Solitary Self* (London, 1996). For a general introduction, R. Grimsley, *The Philosophy of Rousseau* (Oxford, 1973) is useful. More specialist works are J. Shklar, *Men and Citizens* (Cambridge, 1969); N. J. H. Dent, *Rousseau* (Oxford, 1988); and *The Cambridge Companion to Rousseau*, ed. P. Riley (Cambridge, 2001).

Royce, Josiah (1855–1916). American absolute idealist philosopher, Harvard professor. *The Religious Aspect of Philosophy* (1885) is the first, and remains one of the finest, of his many major works. Royce argues for the existence of an *absolute mind including all finite minds as the only explanation of how thought targets objects other than by description, as it must do if there is to be such a thing as error (as there must be, on pain of pragmatic contradiction). William James's pragmatism was in part an attempt to reply by showing how thought could pick out its objects purely behaviourally. This same work also contains one of the best ever statements of the basic problem of ethics, how moral thought can have the motivating force of will and still be factual, solving it by regarding facts about will itself as peculiarly motivating. Royce was important in the development of formal logic in the USA.

T.L.S.S.

*idealism.

Bruce Kuklick, *Josiah Royce* (Indianapolis, 1972).
John E. Smith, *Royce's Social Infinite* (New York, 1950).

rule, golden: *see* golden rule.

rule of law. A system of governmental behaviour and authority that is constrained by law and the respect for law, in contrast to despotic rule. States respecting the rule of law typically divide the powers of government among separate branches; entrench *civil liberties (notably, due process of law and equal protection of the law) behind constitutional walls; and provide for the orderly transfer of political power through fair elections. All versions of political *liberalism stress the importance of the rule of law. Elements of the idea are at least as old as Pericles' Funeral Oration (431 BC). As a modern technical term, 'rule of law' was brought to prominence by A. V. Dicey in *An Introduction to the Study of the Law of the Constitution* (London, 1885).

H.A.B.

rules. In general, norms which either guide or constrain behaviour or thought.

Ever since Wittgenstein, philosophers have focused their interest on the notion of rule or norm which is relevant to linguistic behaviour, in particular whether our concepts or the meanings of our words are governed by rules. Kripke's commentary on Wittgenstein has done much to revive interest in this topic.

One question that has been the focus of interest is about the source of the normativity which attaches to meaning. Some, such as Kripke and Wright, have argued that meaning has a *normative force which it gains from the linguistic practice of the community, and others, such as Blackburn, have tried to characterize the rules of meaning in terms of the dispositions of the individual. The latter view has been criticized (by Kripke himself) for leaving out the normative element in meaning. And others have applauded Kripke for stressing the normative, but criticized him in turn for eventually abandoning it for the dispositions of the individuals who comprise the community. Every one of these philosophers has sought authority for their views in Wittgenstein.

Whatever stand philosophers have taken on this dispute, there seems to be agreement among all of them that a minimal commitment to norm and rule issues from the notion of intention that goes into *meaning. That notion is normative in that any intention divides all behaviour into correct or incorrect in the sense that any action is either a case of fulfilling that intention or failing to fulfil it. Applied to the question of meaning, this insight, it is said, amounts to the claim that if I intend in my behaviour to apply the word or concept 'stick' to sticks, then if I ever were to apply it to a rope, say (if, for instance, I were to say 'That is a stick' pointing to a rope), then I would be doing something incorrect. Only if I applied it to sticks would I be following the rule for 'stick'.

It may be questioned whether this notion of norm is relevant to the meanings of words in this way. This is not to question whether the notion of intention is a normative one in the sense just mentioned. Rather it is questionable whether the intentions involved in meaning are properly described above. The right way to describe the intention involved in meaning is to say that I intend to use the words 'That is a stick' to say something which has certain truth-conditions or assertibility-conditions or whatever we take the meaning-giving conditions to be. In other words by 'That's a stick' I intend to say something which is true (taking *truth-conditions to be the meaning-giving conditions) if and only if that is a stick. But this intention *is* fulfilled even if I say 'That is a stick' when pointing to a rope. What is not fulfilled is my intention to say something true, but that intention is not the intention relevant to the *meaning* of words.

It is even doubtful whether this notion of norm is relevant to *concepts in thoughts quite apart from words in communication. Even if I were to think the thought that that is a stick and not utter any words, it would be doubtful that I am failing to fulfil an intention that I apply my concept 'stick' to sticks only. When I think that that is a stick I do not have any intention at all to apply a concept. I intend various things with my words (however tacitly) when I speak and communicate, but it seems to misdescribe things to say that I intend to apply my concept 'stick' to sticks when I *think* that that is a stick, or even that I intend to think something with certain truth- or assertibility-conditions. I have said that something like the latter intention, but not the former, is relevant to *saying* 'That is a stick' but *neither* is operative in *thinking* that that is a stick.

If the intention involved in meaning is the intention to use words with a certain meaning, it is not clear how we could fail to fulfil this intention without failing to know what we are thinking. No doubt we sometimes fail to know what we are thinking, but that is due to self-deception and other such psychological phenomena, not due to some philosophical doctrine about the normativity of meaning. So if I cannot fail to fulfil the intention involved in meaning, it is not clear whether there is even this minimal notion of correctness and incorrectness applying to meaning. The only sense in which I seem to have done something incorrect in thinking that that is a stick in the presence of a rope is simply to have thought something false (in this case due to misperception).

But if that is the only notion of incorrectness and correctness relevant to concepts and meaning, it is doubtful that there is the philosophical significance in the notion of norms or rules that these philosophers have seen in it. A standard and widely agreed upon starting-point in all of the contemporary discussion of rules and meaning thus seems to be off base.   A.B.

*principles.

A. Bilgrami, *Belief and Meaning* (Oxford, 1992), ch. 3.
D. Davidson, 'A Nice Derangement of Epitaphs', in E. Lepore (ed.), *Truth and Interpretation* (Oxford, 1986).
S. Kripke, *Wittgenstein on Rules and Private Language* (Oxford, 1982).
A. Miller and C. Wright (eds.), *Rule-Following and Meaning* (Chesham, 2002).
L. Wittgenstein, *Philosophical Investigations*, tr. G. E. M. Anscombe (Oxford, 1953).
C. Wright (ed.), *Synthese: Special Issue on Rules* (1984).

Russell, Bertrand (1872–1970). Third Earl Russell, British philosopher, mathematician, Nobel Prize-winner (Literature, 1950), civil-rights activist, and public figure. His most important philosophical works date from the first two decades of the century, and include the magisterial *Principia Mathematica* (1910–13), written jointly with Alfred North Whitehead. In the period between the world wars, he came to public notice through some influential books about morals and mores, which he claimed were written for money. After the Second World War, he was a prominent member of the Campaign for Nuclear Disarmament (and was arrested for participating in one of their protest demonstrations), and helped initiate the Pugwash conferences, international gatherings of distinguished intellectuals, mainly scientists, devoted to discussing ways to achieve and maintain world peace. His *Autobiography* caused a stir by its selective frankness, and by the rather unattractive picture it conveyed of the great man's tardy yet intense emotional development.

Russell was a marvellously wide-ranging philosopher, and it is hard to think of an area of philosophy to which he did not contribute. His best-known philosophical work, the *History of Western Philosophy*, exemplifies this breadth of interest and understanding, and shows that no two areas of philosophy can be guaranteed to be mutually irrelevant.

His own work can be presented under three headings: first, *philosophical logic, not so much an area of philosophy as a method which influenced most of his work; second, the foundations of mathematics; third, epistemology and metaphysics. His interest in mathematics is one of his earliest, and his main idea, which came to him towards the end of the last century and was first presented in *Principles of Mathematics* (1903), was that mathematics is simply logic. Developing this line of thought led him to fundamental questions in logic, and to the approach he was to call *'philosophical logic', which came to colour most of his work in philosophy.

Philosophical Logic. A good route to philosophical fame is to found a method, for then even philosophers who disagree entirely with one's results may honour one's name by working within the method. Around 1914 Russell invented the phrase 'philosophical logic' to describe the approach to philosophy which he had already been employing for some years: recasting problematic propositions in their 'logical *form', using a language with the formal structure of *Principia Mathematica*. His motivations were various, and not very clearly articulated. He felt that ordinary language enshrines the 'savage superstitions of cannibals' ('Mind and Matter', 143) and other errors, confusions, and vagueness, and makes it impossible to give correct expression to some fundamental philosophical truths. For example, it confuses, in the word 'is', existential quantification (as in 'Serendipity *is*', to be formalized using '∃'), identity (as in 'Hesperus *is* Phosphorus', to be formalized using '='), and predication (as in 'Socrates *is* human', whose 'is' vanishes into the concatenation of the predicate for humanity and the name of Socrates in the formalization '$F\alpha$'); and it is very hard to say in ordinary language that existence is not a property of individuals. An example of the way ordinary language embodies cannibalistic superstitions is that expressions like 'Socrates' incline us to think of people and other things as simple metaphysical substances, when they are really complexes.

The best-known application of Russell's philosophical logic is to the problem of denoting phrases. The result is a general account of quantification, including the 'theory of *descriptions' presented, in a rather clumsy form, in the famous article 'On Denoting' (1905). The problem is how to understand such phrases as 'a man', 'every man', 'no man', and 'the man'. In his *Principles of Mathematics* (1903), Russell assumed that they should be viewed in the same way as he then thought names like 'Socrates' and predicates like 'red' should be: as standing for some entity in the world. However, it is impossible to discover an appropriate entity, and the 1903 work clearly does not succeed in doing so. The 1905 theory is that these phrases should not be regarded as having any theoretical unity. They contain a quantifier, 'some', 'every', 'no', and, on Russell's view, a quantifier attaches to a 'propositional function', like ' . . . is happy' to make a sentence (e.g. 'Someone is happy'). A quantifier attached to a predicate like 'man' (as opposed to a propositional function) in the phrase 'some man' is not an intelligible unit of language: it is essentially 'incomplete' and 'has no meaning in isolation'. A sentence like 'I met a man' is analysed as follows: 'There is some x such that x is human and I met x'. The analysis shows that what corresponds to 'a' has become 'there is some x such that' and it attaches to the propositional function 'x is human and I met x'. In the analysis there is no unit corresponding to 'a man'. (See the entry 'descriptions, theory of' for the application of the approach to phrases like 'the man'.)

To feel the full impact of Russell's work on quantification, one must recall his background assumption that the fundamental way in which a word has meaning is by standing for something. Russell held to this model for many words, simple singular and general terms, like 'this' and 'red', and it led him to a corresponding view of the world: the basic constituents, the logical atoms, are the things corresponding to such words. Quantifiers, and, if Russell is right, phrases like 'the King of France', function very differently, not standing for anything in the way that the basic words do.

The logic Russell brought to bear in his philosophical logic included the apparatus of classes, originally developed in his philosophy of mathematics, and he used this to provide logical forms within which to analyse various empirical things, like material bodies. (See the section below, 'Epistemology and Metaphysics'.)

The method of philosophical logic, though it was of great significance in the twentieth century, is now, I suspect, on the wane. Russell himself took an impish and aristocratic delight in claiming that logical forms are very different from surface forms, and that the untrained cannot be expected to appreciate the real complexity of their thoughts. More recently, concern with providing explanations of how the mind actually works has made many philosophers think that one should focus closely on the detailed workings of natural language, rather than treating it as the confused manifestation of some more orderly underlying language of logical forms.

Mathematics. Russell's *logicism in the philosophy of mathematics involves two theses: (1) Mathematical truths can be *translated* into truths of pure logic; thus mathematics has no distinctive subject-matter (e.g. numbers). (2) Mathematical truths, once presented in their proper logical form, can be *proved* by logic alone. The first claim concerns the sort of meaning mathematical statements have; the second concerns how they can be established.

The key idea behind the translation is that a *number can be treated as a class of classes, and operations on numbers can be regarded as class-theoretic ones, definable in terms of intersection, union, difference, and so on. Thus the number one can be thought of as the class of all one-membered classes, the number two as the class of all two-membered classes, and so on. In these stipulations, number-words like 'one' and 'two' figure as adjectives, and such occurrences can be treated within pure logic by means of quantification and identity. (Thus 'There are two dogs' means 'Something, x, is a dog, and something, y, is a dog, and x is distinct from y, and nothing distinct from either x or y is a dog'.) The addition of one and two (to take an example) is thought of as the class of classes each of which is the union of a member of one with a member of two (cases in which the member of one has a member in common with the member of two to be ignored): in other words, the class of three-membered classes.

The translation assumes that logic includes the theory of classes. In general, this can be disputed; and the dispute gained special prominence from the fact, to which Russell drew attention close to the turn of the century, that the theory of classes, at least as it was understood at that time, is inconsistent. This made it unsuitable for any serious purpose, and, *a fortiori*, unsuitable for serving as a foundation in logic or mathematics.

The inconsistency arises upon the intuitively correct supposition (called, in formal dress, the comprehension axiom) that every coherent condition determines a class. Thus it seems right to say that the condition *being a man* determines the class of men, *not being a man* determines the class of non-men, *being round and square* determines the class of things which are round and square, that is, the class with no members (the empty class). On this supposition, there should be a class, R, satisfying the condition *not being a member of itself*, a class, that is, consisting of just those things, including classes, which are not members of themselves. Is R a member of itself? If it is, then it meets the condition *not being a member of itself*, and so it is not a member of itself; if it is not, then, because it meets this condition, it is a member of itself. So there is no such thing as R; the problem is how to reconcile this with the intuition underlying the comprehension axiom, an intuition apparently forcing us to accept that there is such a class as R.

After exploring many other roads in the early years of the century, Russell finally (1908) arrived at the view that classes are entirely dispensable: the 'no-class' theory of classes, as he called it. The idea is that although his theory has expressions which seem to stand for classes, they do not really. This is not, in itself, enough to ensure that the kind of *paradox illustrated by the Russell class will not arise, for a similar paradox can be formulated without mentioning classes (e.g. on the basis of the property of not being self-applicable). However, the no-class theory of classes enabled Russell to bypass the intuition underlying the comprehension axiom. In his theory of *types, things like 'x is a man', which he called 'propositional functions', cannot be applied to themselves. The grounding intuition was that self-application involves a kind of *'vicious circle', and so can justifiably be banned, with the result that the old paradoxes could not be formulated.

In 1931 Gödel published a proof that no consistent theory like Russell's in *Principia Mathematica* (one whose axioms are recursively enumerable) has every mathematical truth as a theorem. This seems to have made Russell think that his logicism had failed. In reality, however, only one component fails, the claim that every mathematical truth can be proved by logical means. It remains open whether every mathematical truth can be expressed in purely logical terms, and whether, thus expressed, it constitutes a truth of logic; for perhaps not every logical truth is provable.

Epistemology and Metaphysics. Russell's most important position in this area is his logical atomism, best elaborated in his lectures of that title (1918). The basic idea is that the world is composed of things like little patches of colour, their properties, and the (atomic) facts they compose. His approach is guided by the following considerations: (1) We can non-inferentially know only what is proof against Descartes's demon. (2) A view about the nature of things which vindicates our intuition that we know the things is to be preferred to one which does not. (3) Logical constructions are to be substituted for inferred entities.

The problem of 'knowledge of the external world' presented itself to him in an entirely traditional way: 'I think on the whole the sort of method adopted by Descartes is right: that you should set to work to doubt things and retain only what you cannot doubt because of its clearness and distinctness' ('Lectures', 182). This led him to the view that enduring material objects like mountains, thought of in the ordinary way as 'substances', could not be 'retained': no adequate account of how we know about such things, thus regarded, could be provided. The first two guiding considerations thus led him to favour an alternative view of the nature of mountains, one upon which we can account for our apparent knowledge of them, and this is supplied by applying the third consideration: they are to be thought of as logical constructions out of non-inferentially known entities; more specifically, as classes whose only individuals are 'sensibilia', things which, like *sense-data, can be known in an immediate and demon-proof way.

It is open to dispute whether this view of mountains gives a better explanation of how we have knowledge about them than the ordinary view. A mountain is construed as a very large class of sensibilia, and no one subject's experience contains them all. Thus no subject can know any proposition of the form 'This mountain is thus-and-so' merely by knowing what sense-data he has. New principles of knowledge are involved, and these principles are no more plausible when they involve extrapolation to the existence of sensibilia with which one will never be acquainted than when they involve extrapolation to material continuants which will never themselves be directly accessible to experience.

Logical atomism involves not only an account of all individuals in terms of the atomic ones, but also an account of all facts in terms of atomic ones. An atomic fact consists of a universal combined with an appropriate number of individuals. The contrast is with a molecular fact, which is expressed by means of such logical expressions as 'and' and 'not'. Russell wanted to believe that at bottom there are only atomic facts: once these are fixed, everything is fixed. Hence there is no *sui generis* fact that 'p or q', since this obtains in virtue of the existence of the fact that p or the existence of the fact that q. However, Russell argued that general facts, though not atomic, have to be added. Suppose that there are just three cats, c_1, c_2, c_3, and that each is hungry. This does not guarantee that there is such a fact as that all cats are hungry. To guarantee this general fact we have to add to the fact that c_1 is hungry and the fact that c_2 is hungry and the fact that c_3 is hungry the fact that c_1, c_2, and c_3 are all the cats there are, and this is itself a general fact. Russell was also worried that one might have to add negative facts. The fact that Socrates is not alive is guaranteed by the fact that he is dead, and perhaps this is atomic. To generalize this we would have to say something like: the existence of any negative fact is guaranteed by the existence of some incompatible fact, but 'this makes incompatibility fundamental and an objective fact, which is not so very much simpler than allowing negative facts'. However, Russell's reasoning at this point is confused. Russell is happy to use disjunction when explaining what makes disjunctions true, so he should find it legitimate to use negation, or incompatibility, when explaining what makes negations true. The original aim was not to provide an explanation of the meaning of the logical constants, but to expose certain metaphysical relations.

Russell's logical atomism, in particular the technique of logical construction, is in some ways similar to *phenomenalism, except that he did not take the atoms (sensibilia) to be mental. At other points in his development, he adopted different views. Thus in *The Problems of Philosophy*, and again in *The Analysis of Matter*, he tries to identify a kind of knowledge (merely structural) of physical continuants which could be acquired even if they are metaphysically very different from the things of which we can have non-inferential knowledge. He laid down the basic postulate that experiences are caused by something other than experiences—call the causes material events.

Implicitly assuming some principle of like cause, like effect, he says that one can infer that properties of or relations among experiences mirror properties of or relations among material events. Material continuants are constructed out of material events. The upshot is that we know the structure of matter, but not its intrinsic nature. The strategy leaves room for scepticism about the real nature of material continuants, but is supposed to capture enough for an interpretation of science upon which most scientific beliefs are true.

Yet another approach is provided in *Human Knowledge: Its Scope and Limits* (1948). Here he argues that the alternative approaches do not do justice to all our cognitive capacities. Unless we have a priori knowledge of certain substantive contingent facts, which he called 'postulates of scientific inference', then 'science is moonshine' (p. 524). One postulate is: 'Given any event *A*, it happens very frequently that, at any neighbouring time, there is at some neighbouring place an event very similar to *A*' (p. 506). Russell implies that we do indeed have a priori knowledge of such facts, of a kind which he explains in terms of 'animal expectation'. This kind of knowledge is available to non-language-users and is arguably non-propositional. This is a cognitive faculty often ignored in attempts to show how scepticism can be avoided. In this late work, Russell shows signs of breaking out of the Cartesian problematic in favour of naturalizing epistemology.

The most influential themes in Russell's work have proved those relating to *meaning and quantification. It is hard to imagine any new work in this area not confronting Russell's idea that basic words have meaning by standing for a corresponding entity, and that quantifiers and quantifier phrases function quite differently.　R.M.S.

*atomism, logical.

N. Griffin (ed.), *The Cambridge Companion to Bertrand Russell* (Cambridge, 2003).

B. Russell, 'On Denoting', *Mind* (1905); repr. in *Bertrand Russell: Logic and Knowledge. Essays 1901–1950*, ed. R. C. Marsh (London, 1965).

—— 'Mathematical Logic as Based upon the Theory of Types', *American Journal of Mathematics* (1908); repr. in *Bertrand Russell: Logic and Knowledge. Essays 1901–1950*, ed. R. C. Marsh (London, 1965).

—— *The Problems of Philosophy* (London, 1912).

—— 'Lectures on the Philosophy of Logical Atomism', *Monist* (1918, 1919); repr. in *Bertrand Russell: Logic and Knowledge. Essays 1901–1950*, ed. R. C. Marsh (London, 1965).

—— 'Mind and Matter', *Nation and Athenaeum* (1925); repr. in *Portraits from Memory* (London, 1958).

—— *The Analysis of Matter* (London, 1927).

R. M. Sainsbury, *Russell* (London, 1979).

Russell's paradox. Central paradox in the theory of classes. Most classes are not members of themselves, but some are; for example, the class of non-men, being itself not a man, is a member of itself. Let *R* be the class of all classes which are not members of themselves. If it exists, it is a member of itself if and only if it is not a member of itself: a contradiction. So it does not exist. This is paradoxical, because it conflicts with the seemingly inescapable view that any coherent condition determines a class. (Even a contradictory condition, like being round and square, determines a class: the class with no members.) Standard responses, like Russell's theory of *types, aim to find some limitation on what classes there are which is (*a*) intuitively satisfactory, (*b*) excludes *R*, and (*c*) includes all classes needed by mathematicians.　R.M.S.

B. Russell, 'Mathematical Logic as Based upon the Theory of Types', *American Journal of Mathematics* (1908); repr. in *Bertrand Russell: Logic and Knowledge. Essays 1901–1950*, ed. R. C. Marsh (London, 1965).

R. M. Sainsbury, *Paradoxes* (Cambridge, 1988), ch. 5.

Russian philosophy. Though a significant force in Russian history, Russian philosophy did not begin until the reign of Catherine the Great (1762–96), when Enlightenment ideas began to filter into Russia. Thereafter philosophy flourished not as an academic discipline, but in the intelligentsia's passionate debates about the liberation of humanity and the destiny of Russia, conducted in political and religious writings and most famously in the literature of Dostoevsky, Tolstoy, and others. The theories of Karl Marx gripped the radical intelligentsia in the late nineteenth and early twentieth centuries, and inspired the Bolshevik Revolution in 1917. Thereafter, Marxism-Leninism, conceived as an all-embracing world-view, was propagated by the Soviet state as its official philosophy until its collapse in 1991, while Russian religious philosophy was preserved by philosophers in exile abroad.

A defining moment in Russian philosophy was the publication of Pyotr Chaadaev's first *Philosophical Letter* in 1836. Chaadaev (1794–1856) portrayed Russia as a spiritual desert populated by nomadic souls bereft of traditions and community, who had contributed nothing to the progress of humanity. This damning vision provoked contrasting responses. The 'Slavophiles', led by Ivan Kireevsky (1806–56) and Aleksei Khomyakov (1804–60), held that Chaadaev's criticisms applied only to the 'superfluous men' of the intelligentsia. He had ignored Russia's indigenous traditions of Orthodox Christianity and the peasant commune, which jointly made possible a form of community exemplifying *sobornost'*, the free and integral unity of human beings in the love of God. Only such a genuine community promised to save world civilization from the ruinous effects of Western rationalism and individualism. In contrast, the 'Westernizers' urged the modernization of economic and political institutions and the appropriation of Western ideas of scientific progress and political liberty. The movement, originally Left Hegelian in inspiration, included literary critic Vissarion Belinsky (1811–48), Mikhail Bakunin (1814–76), and Alexandr Herzen. Though anxious for Russia to take its place among Western nations, the Westernizers were perceptive critics of capitalism.

The Westernizers' heirs in the 1860s were the Russian nihilists, so called for their denunciation of religion and traditional morality in favour of a positivistic reverence for natural science and utilitarian ethics. (Nihilism is evocatively portrayed in Turgenev's novel *Fathers and Sons*.) Prominent was Nikolai Chernyshevsky (1828–89), whose Feuerbachian materialism and realist aesthetics influenced an entire generation of Russian radicals. Chernyshevsky believed that collective ownership would soon replace capitalism in the West and that the communal traditions of the peasantry might facilitate the immediate transition to socialism in Russia. More utopian views of the peasantry found expression in the 1870s in various forms of populism which argued that Russia must find its own way to socialism. These were in turn eclipsed by *Marxism, with its recognition of the historical necessity of capitalism and its focus on the urban proletariat. Intriguing revisionist versions of Marxism developed, such as the neo-Kantian 'legal Marxists' and Bogdanov's empiriomonism. It was, however, Lenin's theory of revolution and Plekhanov's *dialectical materialism that prevailed to form the core of *Soviet state philosophy, wherein the atheism and scientific optimism of the Russian radical tradition mingled with a Slavophile belief in Russia's pre-eminent role in human emancipation.

Slavophile ideas were more faithfully pursued in the philosophy of Vladimir Solovyov in the late nineteenth century. His concern with the reintegration of humanity in the Kingdom of God on earth inspired a generation of idealist philosophers, like Nikolai Berdiaev and Lev Shestov (1866–1938), who became leading figures in the 'Russian Religious-Philosophical Renaissance'. These thinkers were also influenced by Dostoevsky (1821–81), whose novels, especially *The Devils* and *The Brothers Karamazov*, contained a prophetic critique of Russian radicalism and a profound exploration of Russian religious consciousness. In 1909, Berdiaev and a number of other former legal-Marxists participated in the *Vekhi* (Signposts) symposium, which attacked the intelligentsia's traditional allegiance to materialism as morally and intellectually bankrupt. This provoked passionate debate, interrupted only when prominent idealist philosophers were expelled from Russia in 1922 in a purge of non-Marxist intellectuals. Many became leading lights of the Russian émigré philosophical communities in Paris and Berlin.

With the idealists vanquished, Soviet Marxists energetically debated philosophy's role in the new order. Soviet 'mechanists' argued that science can in principle provide a complete account of reality. Philosophy's task is not to guide science, but to elucidate concepts and laws by generalization from scientific practice. In contrast, the 'dialecticians', led by A. M. Deborin (1881–1963), maintained that science is explained and enhanced by the correct philosophical world-view, which they identified with dialectical materialism. A philosophical stalemate, the debate was eventually resolved politically. In 1929 mechanism was officially condemned for *'positivism' and 'revisionism'. This pattern was repeated one year later, when Deborin and his colleagues were attacked as 'Menshevizing idealists' (a heresy named after the Bolsheviks' former political rivals), whose 'formalist'

preoccupation with dialectics betrayed a lack of 'Party spirit'. The Party endorsed these charges, and the dialecticians were finished. Only Deborin himself and a handful of others survived the purges.

The 1930s saw the codification of dialectical materialism into rigid dogma. The *History of the CPSU (Bolsheviks): Short Course* (Moscow, 1938) inveighs against 'idealism' and 'metaphysics', and declares that matter is primary and spirit secondary; the phenomena of reality are interconnected; nature undergoes changes which occur, not gradually, but by 'qualitative leaps'. Historical materialism is portrayed as the application of these principles to the phenomena of social life. Striking here is not the content of the doctrine (essentially a simplification of Plekhanov's and Lenin's views), but its presentation as unquestionable truth. Stalinist Russia was deemed to be living proof of *Marxism; hence no significant philosophical questions needed to be debated. Philosophy's role was reduced to 'a weapon in the class war'.

The brief 'thaw' after Stalin's death brought a new generation of Soviet philosophers eager to return to the critical study of Hegel and Marx. Some, such as M. K. Marmadashvilli (1930–90) and E.V. Ilyenkov (1924–79), sought to develop Marx's method and his idea of social phenomena as 'objectified' activity. Ilyenkov, for example, argues that our forms of thought are objectified in our mode of interaction with nature and in the form our activity lends the world. Children acquire consciousness and selfhood through their inculturation into this externalized 'spiritual culture'. Here his views complement the 'socio-historical psychology' developed by L. S. Vygotsky in the 1920s and 1930s. Ilyenkov's critical Marxism brought him into frequent clashes with the establishment, which continued to propagate 'textbook' dialectical materialism until the *glasnost* era.

Though Marxism in some way influenced almost all Soviet thinkers, the period also produced a number of independent figures. Three such are Mikhail Bakhtin, whose 'dialogism' has enjoyed considerable influence in the West, A. F. Losev (1893–1988), author of important studies on aesthetics, myth, and ancient Greek thought, and the philosopher of culture, V. S. Bibler (1918–2000). Interestingly, the significant figures of the Soviet era, for all their diversity, can be seen as parts of a single philosophical culture unified by certain prominent themes, such as the reality of the cultural, the social nature of personhood, and the world-constituting power of human activity. Unfortunately, this culture is poorly understood, as political circumstances made it impossible for Soviet philosophers to write the history of their own tradition. It survives, however, in the imaginative philosophy of F. T. Mikhailov (b. 1930) and others.

The collapse of the USSR in 1991 stimulated numerous reflections on the fate of Marxism, followed by the emergence of a panoply of new approaches and schools. Over the following decade, notable trends include the appearance of political philosophy as an independent discipline, renewed interest in Russian religious philosophy and the work of the émigrés, the emergence of Russian post-modernism, and attempts to blend analytic philosophy with phenomenology and hermeneutics. Many new journals have sprung into existence, but *Voprosy filosofii* (Questions of Philosophy), founded in the 1940s, remains the leading philosophy publication in Russia. Under the editorship of V. A. Lektorsky (b. 1930), the journal negotiated the collapse of the old order to become a forum for many new developments and for the introduction of hitherto neglected fields, such as bioethics and philosophy of ecology. As well as spotlighting the work of formerly forbidden thinkers, the journal has sought to preserve the best of the Soviet era.

The overarching concern of Russian philosophy is the quest for an all-embracing vision to facilitate the revitalization, even divination, of humanity, so that human beings should be at one with each other and the world. Though the Communist version is no more, the aspiration for such a vision will no doubt continue to define the Russian tradition, which promises to remain as fascinating as it is distinct from the traditional concerns of English-speaking philosophy.   D.BAK.

David Bakhurst, *Consciousness and Revolution in Soviet Philosophy* (Cambridge, 1991).

James M. Edie, James P. Scanlan, and Mary-Barbara Zeldin, *Russian Philosophy*, 3 vols. (Chicago, 1965).

Leszek Kolakowski, *Main Currents of Marxism* (Oxford, 1978), ii and iii.

E. Lampert, *Studies in Rebellion* (London, 1957).

—— *Sons against Fathers* (Oxford, 1965).

James P. Scanlan, *Marxism in the USSR* (Ithaca, NY, 1985).

A. Walicki, *A History of Russian Thought* (Oxford, 1980).

Ryle, Gilbert (1900–76). Waynflete Professor of Metaphysical Philosophy and Fellow of Magdalen College, Oxford (1945–68), editor of the periodical *Mind* (1948–71). Probably the most conspicuous, fertile, and influential figure in a notably flourishing period of British philosophy, and in earlier years the chief instigator of the reanimation, particularly in Oxford, of the philosophical scene.

His first efforts, in the 1920s, to 'break the mould' led him into the study of continental phenomenology; but by about 1930 he came to be preoccupied chiefly with the question what philosophy itself is. If it was, as he felt and found it to be, a live subject and not merely the scholarly study of classical texts, what were its problems? What was it about? What would be distinctively philosophical methods?

His first thought was that philosophy investigates the meaning of expressions—a thought close to the idea (compare G. E. Moore and *Logical Positivism) that philosophy's proper business is *'analysis'. But philosophy surely is not mere lexicography; and, further, in what cases is 'analysis' philosophically called for? Ryle came to the conclusion, substantially never abandoned, that the

philosopher's business is not directly with meanings but rather with a certain kind of meaninglessness—not with what expressions mean, but with why certain combinations of expressions make no sense. Characteristic of his early work is the paper 'Systematically Misleading Expressions' (1932), which argues that some quite ordinary forms of expression are 'improper' to the states of affairs they record, invite thereby misassimilation to other forms of expression, and so tend to generate perplexity, even flat nonsense, from which it is the business of philosophical argument to rescue us.

Soon thereafter, notably in his paper 'Categories' (1938), Ryle abandoned the rather obscure notion of an expression's being 'improper' to a state of affairs in favour of the thesis that expressions can be grouped into 'types' or 'categories', and that philosophical trouble arises from attempting to handle an expression of one *category as if it belonged to another. On this view the source of trouble is a 'category mistake'; the curative work of philosophy is to exhibit and correct categorial misassignments, it being distinctive of such misassignment that it results in a 'certain kind' of meaninglessness or, as Ryle also often put it, of 'absurdity'.

This programmatic notion is famously and extensively pursued in his major work *The Concept of Mind* (1949), an impressive but perhaps not wholly coherent book. Its milder thesis is that the many and various ways we speak about 'the *mind' are potentially misleading; that philosophers, particularly those Ryle calls 'the Cartesians', have been misled; and that they have been misled in particular into picturing the mind as a ghostly counterpart of the body, a non-physical 'thing' mysteriously 'in' the physical body, and the scene or agent of non-physical states, happenings, and acts. There constantly obtrudes, however, a more extreme, apparently ontological thesis, that, contrary to what ordinary ways of speaking suggest, there *really are* only physical objects and physical happenings, and that all talk seemingly 'about' minds is really no more than a certain way of talking about bodies. Ryle often denied, and critics often asserted, that his book preached *behaviourism. The fact is that it both did and did not, in different passages.

Ryle was sometimes regarded as a man of this one book, *The Concept of Mind*; but that dismissive suggestion could not survive the publication of his two-volume *Collected Papers* (1971)—fifty-seven articles (to which he later added a few more) over a period of fifty years, which leave few areas of philosophy untouched and unenlivened. *Dilemmas* (1954) and *Plato's Progress* (1966) should also be mentioned.   G.J.W.

*ghost in the machine.

W. Lyons, *Gilbert Ryle: An Introduction to his Philosophy* (Brighton, 1980).

O. P. Wood and G. W. Pitcher (eds.), *Ryle: A Collection of Critical Essays* (New York, 1970).

S

Saadiah Gaon (882–942). Philosopher, exegete, Hebrew grammarian and lexicographer, liturgist, translator of much of the Hebrew Bible into Arabic. Born in Egypt, Saadiah became head (Gaon, lit. 'eminence') of the ancient Talmudic Academy located by his time in Baghdad. The first systematic work of Jewish philosophy, his *Book of Critically Chosen Beliefs and Convictions*, the book commonly known as *The Book of Beliefs and Opinions* or *Sefer Emunot ve-De'ol*, more properly, *Sefer ha-Nivhar ba-Emunot ve-De'ol*, defends creation, revelation, and a carefully balanced ethical pluralism, explains providence and the afterlife, and refutes *scepticism, *relativism, and dogmatism. Saadiah works inductively from Scripture, using philological techniques developed after the translation of Greek works into Arabic. He favours the familiar sense of biblical expressions, except where reason, experience, authentic tradition, or another scriptural text preclude it. Then a figurative usage must be found and warranted by tight textual parallels. An intuitive psychologist, Saadiah rejects asceticism for the morbid and misanthropic mood it engenders. His aesthetics celebrates contrast and diversity, arguing (as against the monism of Plotinus' account of beauty) that God is one, but we humans are multifold and diverse.   L.E.G.

Saadiah, *The Book of Beliefs and Opinions*, tr. S. Rosenblatt (New Haven, Conn., 1948).
—— *The Book of Theodicy* (Commentary on the Book of Job), tr. L. E. Goodman (New Haven, Conn., 1988).

sacred: *see* holy, numinous, and sacred.

Sainsbury, Mark (1943–). English philosopher, at London and Austin, Texas, specializing in philosophical logic and the history of analytic philosophy. In particular he has developed the view that truth has degrees and that objects can be inherently vague: the border between a mountain and its plain is fuzzy, but so is the border between the mountain and that fuzzy region, and the border between the mountain and this new fuzzy region, and so on. The statement that a certain point is on the mountain may therefore be true to a certain degree, where this does *not* mean it has some true parts and some false parts. (Paradox of the *heap.) However, this still implies a sharp trichotomy between definitely true, intermediate (of whatever degree), and

definitely false. He has therefore developed more recently a revised view whereby concepts, including those of truth and falsity, no longer have boundaries.   A.R.L.

*Russell.

R. M. Sainsbury, *Paradoxes* (Cambridge, 1988).
—— *Departing from Frege* (London, 2002).

Saint-Simon, Claude-Henri de Rouvroy, comte de (1760–1825). The father of French *socialism, Saint-Simon was an ardent enthusiast for the philosophy of *progress, providing the (French) link between the *philosophes of the eighteenth century and the science and technology progressionists of the nineteenth, especially Comte, his sometime disciple and collaborator. Saint-Simon worked out his position essentially on the basis of one case, namely the rise of modern society from the feudal system of the Middle Ages. In common with many who had lived through the French Revolution, Saint-Simon did not want to deny absolutely the virtues and stability of traditional Christianity; but he saw all such societies as having the seeds of their own decay, as they fail to speak to the needs of the economic and socially dominant classes. Post-medieval Europe was a tale of the rise of independent producers and merchants, conflict with the established powers, and uneasy resolution of the struggle. That these ideas sound familiar is a direct result of their influence on Marx.   M.R.

F. E. Manuel, *The New World of Saint-Simon* (Cambridge, Mass., 1956).
C.-H. Saint-Simon, *Selected Writings*, tr. F. M. H. Markam (Oxford, 1952).

Salmon, Wesley (1925–2001). US philosopher of science, who devoted most of his attention to scientific explanation and the epistemology of science. Salmon rejected the Logical Positivist doctrine that the adequacy of an *explanation depends upon whether what is to be explained can be deduced (the 'deductive-nomological' account) or is inductively inferrable (the 'inductive-statistical' account) from the explanation. He first proposed that explaining an occurrence is a matter of finding factors which are statistically relevant to it (the 'statistical relevance' account), and later required in addition that the explanation must show the place of the occurrence in a system of real-world causal processes and interactions (the 'causal– Mechanical' account). His epistemological studies apply Bayesian probability to traditional problems in confirmation. Salmon also worked on issues connected with space, time, and motion, as well as a variety of historical topics.   J.B.B.

*Bayesian confirmation theory.

Wesley C. Salmon, *Scientific Explanation and the Causal Structure of the World* (Princeton, NJ, 1984).
—— *Causality and Explanation* (New York, 1998).

salva veritate. Literally, 'without loss of truth'. A rule of *inference must be truth-preserving: it must take one from truths to truths. (*Validity.)

Questions arise concerning a rule of the predicate calculus with identity which reflects a principle attributed to Leibniz, who asserted that if *a* and *b* are the same, what is true of *a* is true of *b*. The rule of the calculus is:

> From $(a = b)$ and Φ infer Ψ, where 'Ψ' is like 'Φ' except that 'a' and 'b' have been exchanged at one or more places.

The rule seems to support substitutions that cannot be made *salva veritate* in some contexts, such as those involving *propositional attitudes. Such contexts have been designated as indirect or *referentially opaque.   R.B.M.

R. Barcan Marcus, 'Does the Principle of Substitutivity Rest on a Mistake?', in *Modalities* (Oxford, 1993).
W. V. Quine, *From a Logical Point of View* (Cambridge, Mass., 1953, 1961, 1980).

Śaṅkara (788–820 AD). Philosopher-monk, founder of non-dualist *Vedānta. In his fiercely polemical commentaries on the *Upanishads and *Brahma Sūtras*, Śaṅkara rejects both pluralistic realism and subjective idealism. Using *'third-man'-type regress arguments against causal, mereological, intentional, or any other kind of relation or difference, he seeks to show the manifold world of change to be neither real nor unreal. It is a dream *like* superimposition of contents projected by the veil of ignorance on pure unobjectified consciousness. This consciousness is the one reality behind both God (Brahman), who became the world, and the individual (Ātman). Unlike a dream-world which is nullified by 'practically true' wakeful experience, the world-appearance is dispelled only by a direct mystical dawning of the 'transcendentally true' oneness indicated by such scriptural sentences as 'You are that' and 'All this is Brahman'.   A.C.

Kari Potter (ed.), *Encyclopedia of Indian Philosophies*, iii: *Advaita Vedanta* (Princeton, NJ, 1982).

samples, explanation by. According to Wittgenstein, a subcategory of ostensive explanations of word-meaning involves explanation by reference to a paradigmatic sample. Names of perceptual properties (e.g. colour-words), lengths (e.g. 'metre'), or weights (e.g. 'kilogram'), are (or were) introduced thus. The sample is not the property pointed at, but the *object* (the patch on the colour chart, or the metal rod) that fulfils the canonical role in the practice

of using the word. Whether something is a sample is not an intrinsic property of an object, but a matter of its *use* as a standard for the correct application of the definiendum. Hence something can be a sample only if it satisfies the conditions for such use, e.g. relative permanence or reproducibility, reidentifiability, comparability with objects that can truly or falsely be said to instantiate the feature defined.

Associated with each defining sample is a method of comparison involved in the practice of its use. Hence subjective sensations, e.g. pain, cannot fulfil the role of defining samples in a 'private ostensive definition'. What were sometimes thought to be synthetic a priori truths, e.g. that black is darker than white, or that nothing can be red and green all over simultaneously, are explained by Wittgenstein as grammatical propositions associated with the constituent expressions which are defined by reference to samples. Thus any ordered pair of samples of black and white is also used to give an ostensive definition of the relation 'darker than', and the grammatical proposition that black is darker than white is no more than a consequent rule that if *A* is black and *B* white, the inference that *A* is darker than *B* is licit. Colour exclusion is similarly explained, not as a metaphysical necessity lying in the nature of things, but as a rule that if something is rightly said to be *this* colour (pointing at a sample of red) all over, then it may not also be said to be *that* colour (pointing at a green sample), since *this* defines a different colour from *that*.   P.M.S.H.

*ostensive definition; private language argument.

G. P. Baker and P. M. S. Hacker, *An Analytical Commentary on the Philosophical Investigations*, i: *Wittgenstein: Understanding and Meaning* (Oxford, 1980), 168–205.

Santayana, George (1863–1952). Born in Madrid of Spanish parents, complicated family circumstances took him to Boston at the age of 9 and an American career, though he always remained a Spanish citizen. In January 1912 he resigned his Harvard professorship and lived subsequently in Europe, mostly in hotels in Rome. All his many books were written in English, and he himself said that it was as an American philosopher that he must be counted, if he was to be counted at all. Very different from his older colleague William James, he stands with him as a major figure in 'the golden age of American philosophy'. Santayana is distinguished not only as a philosopher, but as a poet, novelist, and literary and cultural critic, famous for his characterization of what he called 'the genteel tradition' in American culture.

The Sense of Beauty (1896) argues that *beauty is the pleasure of contemplating an object conceived as a quality of the object itself. Santayana did not wish to disparage beauty by thus analysing it. Indeed, he urged that the experience of beauty was the highest value in human life. (In his later treatment of art in *Reason in Art* the somewhat shifted emphasis was on the undesirability of separating the aesthetic and the practical; in the good life all human activity is both.) It was the high valuation of aesthetic experience combined with a thoroughly naturalistic account of its basis that made an especial impression. It is perhaps (rather unfortunately) this work which has received most attention of all Santayana's work. Described as a 'pot-boiler' by Santayana, it still sounds a theme basic to his thought that the roots of good lie in man's animal nature but that its value transcends this.

The Life of Reason; or, The Phases of Human Progress, in five volumes, (1905–6) sketches the extent to which the main branches of human thought and activity, common-sense concepts, social organization, religious beliefs and institutions, art, and science have served the life of reason. Every impulse of a conscious being carries a sense of the goodness of its object, a goodness which, if that impulse stood alone, would be as absolute a good as there could be. *Reason is simply a higher-order impulse whose good is the harmonization of other more particular ones and the life of reason is an ideal for all those in whom it is strong enough, but since value is relative it is not the only respectable human option. The work was an important influence on the development of American *naturalism, and praised by Dewey.

In the next phase of his philosophy Santayana developed a form of *Critical Realism (in fact, somewhat Thomist in character) and as such was still working in a distinctively American debate. Thus he contributed to an American philosophical manifesto called *Essays in Critical Realism* (1920) (a riposte to *The New Realism: Comparative Studies in Philosophy* (1912), the manifesto of a very sophisticated sort of naïve realism partly inspired by James). Whereas naïve realism holds that a perceived (or perhaps otherwise known) physical object is directly present to our consciousness, and indirect realism that what is directly present is particular sense-impressions from which we infer the existence of physical things, Critical Realism holds that what is directly present is an essence which characterizes the known object. Thus there is nothing from whose presented character we infer the existence of an object; rather, we are presented with a character which rightly or wrongly we take to be the character of something upon which we are intent. This intentness upon an object, considered as a purely mental phenomenon, is simply a kind of primitive preconceptual directedness on something beyond one's own mental state. What settles the object I am intent on is that I am actually physically affected by and physically adapting to it. Thus physical relations pick out the object and the essence intuited characterizes it for me (thus 'externalism' about subjects, 'internalism' about predicates).

If I am perceiving something correctly, then the essence intuited somehow applies to the physical thing on which my behavioural response is directed. If it is ever part of the very essence of the thing, then I know that thing literally (though the essence is still exemplified twice over, once for my mind, once in the object); if, as is more usual, it is simply a suitable symbol of it for human purposes, our knowledge is symbolic.

This point of view is developed most fully in *Scepticism and Animal Faith* (1923) and *Realms of Being* (1927–40) as part of an element in an elaborate and carefully worked-out ontological system. Many admirers of *The Life of Reason* were dismayed by these works, misunderstanding them as a retreat from naturalism.

Although *Scepticism and Animal Faith* is primarily a work in epistemology, Santayana was far from thinking epistemology the core of philosophy; he is simply concerned to clear away the objections of epistemologists before presenting his ontology.

If knowledge is required, in Cartesian fashion, to be inherently certain, then knowledge, as opposed to the mere intuition of presented 'essences', is indeed impossible. But we should not pretend to a scepticism we cannot really hold, and should admit to a system of beliefs which, its truth once granted, can be seen as inevitable in a conscious animal. We rightly call this 'knowledge' because we believe it true and generated in a manner which is, in fact, reliable. This naturalistic epistemology differs from some later views, which it anticipates, by stressing that most of our knowledge is symbolic rather than literal. It provides us with a sense of how things are, adequate for practical purposes, but not revealing the real essence of the facts it registers. Such knowledge consists of 'faith mediated by symbols', the symbols being the essences, sensory and value-laden in ordinary thought, more purely structural in science, which present themselves to human perception and thought as we grapple with the world.

The four volumes of *Realms of Being* deal in turn with the four realms of being or categories of reality which Santayana distinguishes.

The character of any part of the physical world at any moment is an essence. *The realm of essence* also includes all characters which *might* have been possessed by some part of the physical world, or which *might* present themselves as possible characters of things to spirit (any mind); it is, in short, the realm of pure possibilities. There is one peculiarly basic essence, the essence of pure being. Every other essence is some determinate form of this, standing to it as all more specific colours stand to the essence of pure colour. It is a common something present in each specific essence, from which it can be abstracted and contemplated apart in one kind of mystical experience. Pure being should be distinguished from existence; it is equally present in the essence unicorn, and the essence horse, but only the latter occurs existentially.

The realm of matter consists of material or physical substance spread out in space and changing from moment to moment according to temporal patterns called the laws of nature. It allows essences to stand in external relations not determined by their own inherent nature as are their internal relations one to another; such standing in external relations distinguishes existence from mere being.

Certain processes in matter generate spirit. This is primarily the consciousness which some part of the physical world has of its environment, but the spirit or consciousness generated within an organism also contains much fantastic imagination, sometimes recognized and rightly enjoyed merely as such, sometimes serving as spirit's only vaguely true grasp of the world it inhabits. The totality of spirit in the world constitutes *the realm of spirit*.

Santayana subscribes to what he calls materialism: not the doctrine that all reality is physical, but that only the physical has causal power. For spirit is simply an emanation from certain processes in the physical world, in particular the 'psyches' of animals, from which it should be sharply distinguished. Psyches consist in the genetically determined patterns of life-sustaining behaviour of organisms, adapted to changing circumstances in higher animals by physical representations of the environment in their brains, representations which should be distinguished from the non-efficacious thinking pertaining to the realm of spirit which they sustain, whose pragmatic truth therefore strictly consists not in its own usefulness but in that of the physical processes which give rise to it. But though spirit is non-efficacious, it alone brings value into the world. The tension between Santayana's *epiphenomenalism and the pragmatic element in his account of knowledge stops short of inconsistency and is important for his value theory.

There remains *the realm of truth*. This 'is the total history and destiny of matter and spirit, or the enormously complex essence which they exemplify by existing'. *Truth, for Santayana, is supertemporal; it is the unwritten record of all events through all times, and our truths are simply such fragments of this one total truth as we humans happen to grasp, mostly only in symbolic form. (The truth about the future is as determinate as that about the past, not because of determinism, but because the distinction between past and future has no standing for absolute truth.) His stress on the reality of such an absolutely objective truth about the world, which far surpasses any possible knowledge, represents his strongest divergence from the idealists and pragmatists who dominated philosophy in his earlier student and professorial days (and whose central claims are still very much with us in various transformations). There is, however, a strong pragmatist element in his treatment of the symbolic truth through which we deal effectively with our environment (or at least which expresses our dealing with it), which constitutes most human knowledge. This partly justifies the tendency to classify him as a pragmatist.

In *The Realm of Spirit* (1940) and other such later works as *The Idea of Christ in the Gospels* (1946) Santayana develops a somewhat Platonic account of 'the spiritual life'; one dedicated to a kind of mystical intuition of essences for their own sake, rather than as a guide to practical action; in particular those essences which can be contemplated under the form of the good. This, however, represents just one possible human option, and Santayana still declares his preference for the life of reason, in which spirituality is just one ingredient in a wider human harmony. Moreover, because Plato makes his forms efficacious agencies in the natural world, operating on it from another realm, he regards himself as finally closer to Aristotle and Spinoza. What particularly evoked Santayana's hostility was any idea that the world, and the truth about it, are somehow a human construction. He deplored such human egotism, which he saw as the besetting sin of modern idealism and pragmatism, as expressing a dangerous resentment of our dependence on a greater non-human cosmos and unrealistic glorification of human power. In opposition to all such 'cosmic impiety' Santayana called himself a naturalist, regarding Spinoza as one of the chief teachers of this viewpoint.   T.L.S.S.

Noel O'Sullivan, *Santayana* (St Albans, 1993).

John Lachs, *George Santayana* (Boston, 1988).

H. S. Levinson, *Santayana, Pragmatism and the Spiritual Life* (Chapel Hill, NC, 1992).

T. L. S. Sprigge, *Santayana: An Examination of his Philosophy* (London, 1974).

Sapir–Whorf hypothesis. A relativistic doctrine. According to Sapir, 'We see and hear . . . very largely as we do because the *language habits of our community predispose certain choices of interpretation' ('The Status of Linguistics as a Science' (1929)). Whorf developed the idea, attempting to illustrate it from American Indian languages. The doctrine risks collapse into the truism that some things can be said more easily in some languages than in others.   R.K.

B. L. Whorf, *Language, Thought, and Reality: Selected Writings of Benjamin Lee Whorf*, ed. J. B. Carroll (Cambridge, Mass., 1956).

Sartre, Jean-Paul (1905–80). Sartre's œuvre is a unique phenomenon. No other major philosopher has also been a major playright, novelist, political theorist, and literary critic. It is still too early to judge which facet of Sartre's extraordinary genius posterity will regard as the most important, but since his philosophy permeates his other works, its enduring interest is assured.

After a provincial childhood spent, if we can trust Sartre's captivating autobiographical essay *Words*, in his grandfather's library, Sartre studied philosophy at the École Normale in Paris. In 1931 he became a teacher of philosophy in Le Havre, which he hated (Le Havre is 'Bouville' in *Nausea*). In 1937 he moved to Paris, and the next year his brilliant philosophical novel *Nausea* was published. Many of the themes of this book recur in his first major philosophical book *L'Imaginaire* (1940) (whose botched English translation bears the title *The Psychology of Imagination*). But then the war intervened: Sartre was mobilized in 1939, and served as a meteorologist in the French Army. He later described the war as the turning-point in his life, one which changed him from an academic philosopher and avant-garde writer into an intellectual deeply committed to the fate of the 'Wretched of the Earth' (the title of the famous work by Fanon for which Sartre wrote an eloquent preface). Military service did not, however, stem the flow of words: he wrote voluminous diaries (excellently translated as his *War Diaries*), which contain early drafts of his philosophical work, mixed in with marvellous descriptions of his experiences and colleagues. In 1940 Sartre was captured and imprisoned: in prison he continued his study of Heidegger's philosophy and wrote his first play. Released a year later, he returned to occupied Paris and to his post as a teacher of philosophy. His desire to work with the Resistance was complicated by his unwillingness to commit himself to either the Communists or the Gaullists, and in the end he devoted most of this time to writing his most important philosophical work, *Being and Nothingness* (1943).

With the liberation came instant fame, as dramatist (thanks to *Flies* and *No Exit*) and philosopher: his optimistic 1945 lecture *Existentialism and Humanism* seized the imagination of a generation. Sartre could have continued his academic career, but he chose to refuse all academic positions and to make his living as a writer, an occupation which he combined with an active concern for the political and social affairs of the day. The nature of Sartre's engagements was at first largely shaped by his complex relationships with the Communist Party, which he joined at the time of the Korean War and then left, never to return, after the Russian suppression of the Hungarian Revolution in 1956. Not surprisingly, his reflections on *Marxism date from this period, and over the next decade he developed the 'existentialist Marxism' first expounded in his 1957 essay *Search for a Method*, and then further developed in his second large-scale philosophical treatise, *Critique of Dialectical Reason* (1960). Towards the end of this period he committed himself whole-heartedly to the struggle for liberation in Algeria (a cause which nearly cost him his life in 1961). A few years later the same passions stirred him to lead the French opposition to the American involvement in Vietnam, and these commitments are reflected in several long essays on behalf of the Third World. In 1964 he was offered the Nobel Prize for Literature, but chose to decline the offer. The student uprising of May 1968 seemed to show that Sartre's writings were still as influential as ever, as he addressed thousands in the Sorbonne; but in truth, his intellectual reputation was now eclipsed by structuralists (such as Lévi-Strauss and Althusser), and post-structuralists (such as Derrida and Deleuze). Sensing this loss of intellectual sympathy, and combating increasing blindness and other illnesses, Sartre largely withdrew from public affairs and turned his attention to the completion of his final *magnum opus*, his vast study of Flaubert, *L'Idiot de la famille*; sadly, his eyesight gave out in 1973, when only three out of five projected volumes had been completed. Yet his funeral showed that he retained an extraordinary hold on the public imagination: over 50,000 people turned up in a spontaneous demonstration of respect.

In his early philosophical writings from the 1930s Sartre was primarily concerned to develop Husserl's phenomenological methods and apply them to the study of the *imagination. He argues that the traditional conception of mental imagery derived from the theory of *ideas is incoherent, and needs to be replaced by a recognition that imagination, like perception, is a distinctive mode of intentional consciousness whose contents should not be treated as if they were inner objects. Sartre's special interest in the imagination derives partly from its connections with aesthetics and the use of the imagination in creating ideal worlds which contrast with the perceived actual world (this is a prominent theme of *Nausea*); but also from the fact that he regards the exercise of the imagination as the paradigmatic exercise of freedom. He argues that, because the content of the imagination, 'the imaginary', characteristically goes beyond the actual world, there simply cannot be an adequate causal theory of the imagination, since the effects of actual causes cannot be anything but actual. This argument is unsatisfactory, for Sartre confuses the fact that what is imagined is characteristically not actual with the claim that the act of imagination itself is not actual; but we can agree with him that the imagination is a primary manifestation of human freedom without accepting his argument.

*Freedom is not just a phenomenon of the imagination, however: according to Sartre, all consciousness is in some way free (so that the imagination is a privileged manifestation of consciousness in general). In order to understand Sartre's conception of the essential freedom of consciousness we need now to turn to *Being and Nothingness*. Sartre begins this work by arguing that consciousness belongs to a different ontological category from that of the physical world. The key premiss for this ontological distinction is an obscure thesis that consciousness is always constituted by a tacit *self-consciousness. Sartre argues that the conception of a conscious mental state which does not include this self-conscious dimension is incoherent, since it would be an unconscious conscious state; but this argument is plainly fallacious, although there may be other reasons for thinking that consciousness implies the possibility of self-consciousness. What is distinctive about the Sartrean conception, however, is not just the association between consciousness and self-consciousness, but the claim that the self-conscious dimension is constitutive. It is not easy to see why Sartre holds this, but it seems to rest on a presumption, similar to that employed in his discussion of the imagination, that the *intentional content of consciousness is in principle inexplicable in causal terms. If that presumption is granted, then it follows that consciousness cannot get its essential intentional content from the physical world; in which case, if there is to be an explanation of any kind for it, it is tempting to have recourse to a constitutive self-consciousness, though this requires the dubious assumption that the content of this self-consciousness is itself unproblematic.

This constitutive role for self-consciousness, however exactly it is understood, explains why Sartre now proceeds to call those aspects of human life which involve consciousness the 'for-itself' (*pour-soi*). This contrasts with all physical facts, which are independent of consciousness and comprise the 'in itself' (*en-soi*). This distinction is not, however, one between substances of two different kinds; for Sartre denies that consciousness is a substance at all. Instead, the distinction is one between types of fact. Physical facts satisfy ordinary classical logic: 'they are what they are'. But, according to Sartre, the same logic does not hold of consciousness: here things 'are what they are not and are not what they are'. This thesis connects with the feature of Sartre's philosophy which is most difficult to come to terms with—his treatment of negation. Like other opponents of negative facts, Sartre argues that negation does not reside 'in things themselves'; instead, he holds, it is introduced into our conception of the world as a quasi-Kantian category whose transcendental justification lies in the fact that the self-conscious structure of consciousness involves negation—'the being by which Nothingness comes to the world must be its own Nothingness' (*Being and Nothingness*, 23). This baffling doctrine implies that the constitutive role of self-consciousness is at the same time self-nihilating. One would like to set this doctrine aside as a rhetorical extravagance; but this is impossible, since, according to Sartre, this capacity for reflexive self-negation is the core of human freedom and, indeed, human life. The best one can do to grasp Sartre's intention is to point to the phenomena he uses to illustrate our self-directed 'nothingness'—such facts as that we can always detach ourselves from the roles we find ourselves occupying (as in Sartre's famous example of the waiter in a café), and that in cases of self-deception we convince ourselves of something precisely because we already believe the opposite.

This theory of consciousness so far lacks any reference to the *self, or subject of consciousness. This omission is deliberate, for in one of his first essays (*The Transcendence of the Ego*) Sartre took issue with Husserl's doctrine of the transcendental subject and argued that consciousness is fundamentally impersonal. In *Being and Nothingness* this thesis is significantly modified in the light of that of the constitutive role of self-consciousness: Sartre argues here that this self-consciousness characteristically includes a set of commitments and aspirations that gives a projective unity to the acts of consciousness that they inform, and, in doing so, strings them together as the acts of a single person—'consciousness by the pure nihilating movement of reflection makes itself *personal*' (*Being and Nothingness*, 103). In the last part of the book Sartre develops this theme in a rich and detailed elucidation of the purposive structures of psychological explanations. Two aspects of this account are specially worthy of notice. The first concerns Sartre's attitude to Freud. In an early section of the book Sartre launches a well-known critique of Freud's theory of the unconscious which is motivated by Sartre's claim that consciousness is essentially self-conscious. Sartre also argues here that Freud's theory of repression is internally flawed, but this argument is based on a misunderstanding of Freud. What is of more interest, however, is Sartre's attempt, towards the end of the book, to adapt some of Freud's ideas to his own account of human life, and thereby to develop an 'existential psychoanalysis' in which Freud's causal categories are replaced by Sartre's own teleological ones. The theme of consciousness is not so dominant here, and the method of psychological inquiry Sartre began here is one that he was to employ fruitfully in several biographical works (including *Baudelaire* (1946), *Saint Genet—Actor and Martyr* (1952), and *The Idiot of the Family* (1971–2)).

One feature of these studies is the emphasis Sartre comes to place upon the formation during childhood of a 'fundamental project' which gives unity to the person's subsequent life, and this brings me to the second notable aspect of Sartre's psychological theory. In *Being and Nothingness* Sartre writes of the formation of this fundamental project as a 'choice', and it is easy to see why he says this in the light of his emphasis on freedom—he calls this choice 'the fundamental act of freedom' (*Being and Nothingness*, 461). Sartre is here reviving a doctrine central to Kant's conception of freedom, but, like Kant, Sartre faces insoluble problems in explaining how such an act can be a choice at all, since all the subject's reasons for choice are referred back to their fundamental project. Hence it is not surprising that when Sartre attempted to apply this conception in his biographical studies, a causal mode of explanation concerning the formation in childhood of one's fundamental project appears to replace the abstract schemata of *Being and Nothingness*.

We have seen how subjectivity is achieved through the reference of acts of consciousness, through their tacit self-conscious structure, to a single project. Sartre makes it clear in *Nausea* that Roquentin's abandonment of his project brings with it the end of his subjectivity—'suddenly the I pales, pales and goes out' (*Nausea*, 241). One can ask whether subjectivity does not also involve reference to other persons, perhaps, as Hegel supposed, to their recognition of one's status as a subject. In *Being and Nothingness*, however, Sartre argues that although, for each of us, there is an aspect of ourselves that is dependent on recognition by others (our 'being-for-others'), this is an alienated conception of ourselves that we cannot integrate into our own self-consciousness; in relation to ourselves as we are for ourselves we are not dependent upon others. Sartre's discussion of this thesis includes a sustained analysis of a variety of situations in which we become aware of each other (most famously, that of the peeping Tom who hears someone behind him), and in my judgement these analyses provide the finest example of the application of phenomenological methods of analysis, not only by Sartre, but by any philosopher. Yet their conclusion is paradoxical—that we are always '*de trop* in relation to others' (*Being and Nothingness*, 410).

The ethical implication of this is that 'respect for the Other's freedom is an empty word' (*Being and Nothingness*, 409). Yet how can this be combined with the thesis which he proclaims in his 1945 lecture *Existentialism and Humanism*, that 'I am obliged to will the liberty of others at the same time as mine' (p. 52)? One part of the explanation is that *Being and Nothingness* is incomplete, and was always intended primarily as an exploration of human life as guided by illusions such as a belief in determinism and in the independent reality of ethical values. It was supposed to be balanced by a further book in which a life freed from these illusions was explored. This book was never completed, though *Existentialism and Humanism* and Sartre's 1947 notebooks *Cahiers pour une morale* (now published) reveal his broad intentions. The crucial point that emerges from them is that Sartre maintains that although our meta-physical freedom does not depend upon others, there is another kind of freedom, moral freedom, which does depend upon others; as he puts it in the 1947 notebooks, 'morality is only possible if everyone is moral'.

Sartre's acceptance of this thesis coincides with his growing awareness of the need to fill out the rather abstract account of consciousness he had offered with an account of the relationships between an individual and their society. His approach to these relationships is, of course, deeply influenced by his study of Marx, and he likes to portray himself as a historical materialist ('I have said—and I repeat—that the only valid interpretation of human History is historical materialism' (*Critique of Dialectical Reason*, 39–40)). But in *Search for a Method* he is a brilliant critic of the reductive historical materialism familiar from orthodox Marxist theory; he offers instead a version which incorporates parts of the account of human life presented in *Being and Nothingness*. But the theme of human freedom is now given little direct emphasis: in a striking passage in the *Critique of Dialectical Reason* (pp. 233–4) he describes how workers who have some monotonous task are prone to engage in sexual fantasies—thereby contradicting his youthful insistence that the imagination is a citadel of absolute freedom. Indeed in a 1972 essay ('The Itinerary of a Thought') Sartre describes his earlier views about freedom as 'scandalous' and 'incredible'. Yet he remains as strongly committed as ever to the distinctiveness of human affairs: 'dialectical reason' is the mode of rationality characteristic of social and psychological explanations, and contrasts with 'analytical reason', which is the rationality appropriate to the physical sciences.

A central mark of 'dialectical reason' is the involvement of holistic explanations. This was already a feature of the account of psychological explanation given in *Being and Nothingness*, and to some extent the account of social explanation in Sartre's later works is an extrapolation into a broader historical and interpersonal field of the earlier account. In this case, however, the holistic theme is underpinned by an assumption basic to all Sartre's later work, that all human affairs are conducted under conditions of relative scarcity. For this implies that humans always confront each other as potential competitors, and, according to Sartre, it is this threat which both motivates all social and economic structures, and, in the end, unifies human history. This assumption of scarcity also provides one basis for the *alienation which Sartre, like Marx, regards as an endemic feature of human history up to the present. But Sartre differs significantly from Marx in holding that alienation also arises from the fact that the realization of human purposes creates material structures (houses, machines, etc.—the 'practico-inert') that are inherently liable themselves to place further demands on people and, in some cases, to subvert the very purposes they were intended to promote. A central theme of Sartre's *Critique of Dialectical Reason* is, indeed, one of the attempt to overcome the constraints of the practico-inert through social institutions, and then of the failure of this attempt as social institutions

themselves ossify and join the practicoinert. In the *Critique of Dialectical Reason* as published, this theme is developed with particular reference to the French Revolution; in the projected second volume of the *Critique* (which was published posthumously) the same theme is discussed with reference to the Russian Revolution.

The *Critique* bears witness to Sartre's disillusionment with the fate of communist states (though not with Marxism), and in it he returns to the pessimism of *Being and Nothingness*. The kind of moral freedom that he had envisaged in *Existentialism and Humanism* is now presented as entirely utopian. Yet it was the themes of that lecture which once captivated the post-war generation, and, I suspect, it will be as protagonist of the value of existential freedom that he will be remembered.   T.R.B.

*existentialism; continental philosophy.

P. Caws, *Sartre* (London, 1979).
P. Chiodi, *Sartre and Marxism* (New York, 1976).
A. Cohen-Solal, *Sartre* (London, 1987).
C. Howells (ed.), *The Cambridge Companion to Sartre* (Cambridge, 1992).
F. Jeanson, *Sartre and the Problem of Morality* (Indiana, 1980).
G. McCulloch, *Using Sartre* (London, 1994).
J.-P. Sartre, *La Nausée* (Paris, 1938); tr. Robert Baldick as *Nausea* (Harmondsworth, 1965).
—— *L'Être et le néant* (Paris, 1943); tr. Hazel Barnes as *Being and Nothingness* (London, 1969).
—— *L'Existentialisme et un humanisme* (Paris, 1946); tr. Philip Mairet as *Existentialism and Humanism* (London, 1948).
—— *Critique de la raison dialectique* (Paris, 1960); tr. Alan Sheridan-Smith as *Critique of Dialectical Reason* (London, 1976).

satisfaction. The relation of satisfaction was introduced into logical investigations by Alfred Tarski. A *formula like '$x < 7$', for example, is satisfied by some values (in this case, those less than 7) of its 'free' number-variable x, and not by others. Tarski extended such an account to formulae of any degree of logical complexity, as a preliminary to defining truth for those formulae whose variables, if any, are bound by a *quantifier.   C.H.

E. Mendelson, *Introduction to Mathematical Logic*, 3rd edn. (Monterey, Calif., 1987).

satisficing. 'Satisficing' means 'seeking or achieving a satisfactory, but less than a maximum or optimum, result for the agent or for some group'. The term was originally introduced by economists, and satisficing models in *economics, biology, and other sciences explain phenomena without assuming that nature or people are maximally efficient or rational. In ethics and rational-choice theory, the term refers to choices and actions that seek or achieve enough, but not maximal or optimal, well-being or desire-satisfaction, given other situational possibilities. Satisficing choice is sometimes rationally or morally recommended for cases where the calculations necessary to maximizing purposes are too difficult or costly to perform. But although such justifications are clearly *instrumental*, some ethicists hold that satisficing choices or actions can also be *inherently* admirable or rational as an expression of moderation in one's desires and thus of admirable self-sufficiency.   M.S.

*utilitarianism.

M. Slote, *Beyond Optimizing* (Cambridge, Mass., 1989).

saturated expression: *see* unsaturated expression.

saying and showing. For the early Wittgenstein, the logical form of a proposition, and of the reality mirrored by it, 'showed itself' in that proposition; it was not something that could be stated. At paragraph 4.1212 of the *Tractatus*, Wittgenstein wrote: 'What *can* be shown, *cannot* be said'. It is from this thought that the 'mystical' strain in the *Tractatus* really springs; Wittgenstein's remarks towards the book's end, on ethics, death, and the 'sense of the world', are all to the effect that what is at issue is something which cannot be put into words, but which makes itself manifest. That the idea expressed at 4.1212 should there relate to the logical properties of propositions thus indicates how far the author thought that the whole of philosophy (ethics etc.) could be dealt with—and to a large extent dismissed—by consideration of the nature of logic.   R.P.L.T.

L. Wittgenstein, *Tractatus Logico-Philosophicus*, tr. D. F. Pears and B. F. McGuinness (London, 1961).

Scanlon, T. M. (1940–). Moral and political philosopher best known for his work on contractualist moral theory. Scanlon published influential papers in the 1970s (e.g. 'Preference and Urgency', *Journal of Philosophy*, 1975, and 'Rights, Goals, and Fairness', in S. Hampshire (ed.), *Public and Private Morality*, 1978), but what established him as a leading moral philosopher was his 'Contractualism and Utilitarianism', published in A. Sen and B. Williams (eds.), *Utilitarianism and Beyond* (1982). Scanlon's contractualism held that an act is wrong if it is forbidden by any system of rules that no one could reasonably reject as the basis for informed, unforced general agreement. Books by Thomas Nagel (1991), Peter Carruthers (1992), Richard Miller (1992), and Brian Barry (1995) and a wide array of journal articles drew on Scanlon's theory. Scanlon's book *What We Owe to Each Other* (1998) not only develops his contractualism but also advances important arguments concerning normative reasons, well-being, moral motivation, responsibility, honesty, and relativism.   B.H.

Social Theory and Practice, special issue on Scanlon's book, April 2002.
Ratio, special issue on Scanlon's book, December 2003.

scepticism. Philosophical scepticism questions our cognitive achievements, challenging our ability to obtain reliable knowledge. Global scepticism casts *doubt upon all our attempts to seek the truth; more restricted forms of scepticism may question our knowledge of ethical matters, of the past, of other minds, of the underlying structure of matter, and so on. Since Descartes, the defence of our knowledge against scepticism has seemed to be the first task of epistemology. (*Scepticism, history of.)

To say that sceptics deny the possibility of *knowledge* may distort the discussion: we might not feel threatened if we were capable of justified belief but not of knowledge (properly so called). Some recent writers pose the issues in terms of claims: when I put something forward as true, I present myself as making a *legitimate* claim and as able to resist intelligible challenges that may be made to it. If sceptical writings present ways of offering intelligible challenges to our claims which we cannot deal with, it seems that we cannot take responsibility for the legitimacy of any of our claims. We cannot carry out our inquiries in a responsible, self-controlled manner. It is only through tunnel vision or self-deception, closing our eyes to challenges we ought to take account of, that we are able to hold on to our opinions about the world.

The most discussed challenge in recent writing is a variant on Descartes's evil demon (*malin génie). Our ordinary practice of defending opinions requires us to reject explanations of our beliefs which are compatible with their falsity: if I cannot discriminate house sparrows from tree sparrows, my claim to have seen a tree sparrow should be withdrawn unless I can explain why no confusion was possible on this occasion. It is alleged that my experience may have been just as it is now had my brain been removed from my body, placed in a vat of nutrients, and wired up to a computer which was providing me with a coherent sequence of (misleading) experiences. This presents me with an analogous challenge which cannot be defeated: anything I might appeal to in order to show that I am not a *brain in a vat could have been planted in my mind by the computer. It seems that my everyday claims are legitimate only if I can answer this sceptical challenge; and there seems no possibility of my doing this. An alternative structure of sceptical argument points out that, whenever I make a claim, I can be asked for its ground or justification. When I offer a ground, this involves making yet another claim, which can in turn be questioned. Since it is question-begging to use a circular argument to justify a claim to knowledge, my first claim is only legitimately made if I am prepared to enter an infinite regress of justifications.

Of course, such challenges have no role in our ordinary practice of making and defending views: if we were to invoke them, we would appear silly or mad. But the significance of this is unclear: it might be a sign that these sceptical doubts are unnatural or improper that the legitimacy of our beliefs is not affected by our ignoring them. If that is correct, then we could safely avoid any engagement with arguments in the sceptical canon. If, on the other hand, it simply reflects the ways in which we cope practically with the fact that scepticism is unanswerable (by ignoring it), then it would be evasion of responsibility to ignore sceptical arguments when, as philosophers, we seek an overall assessment of our cognitive position. Several contemporary philosophers, notably Barry Stroud, suspect that scepticism may be unavoidable.

In the background of much recent discussion is G. E. Moore's 'proof of the *external world': holding his hand before him, he affirmed his knowledge that he had two hands, and, since hands were objects in the external world, he concluded that there was an external world. Many philosophers are attracted by the robust insistence that these beliefs need no defence, but also have a strong sense that Moore missed an important point. One reaction, associated with Stroud, is that although my certainty that I have two hands needs no defence in our everyday practices, the same is not the case when we attempt a distinctively *philosophical* assessment of our position. The sense that Moore's argument settles nothing gains support from Wittgenstein's suggestion, in *On Certainty*, that talk of 'knowledge' is appropriate only when doubt is intelligible and grounds are available: if Moore claims 'knowledge', challenge and criticism is appropriate. If we are to resist the suggestion that sceptical challenges are relevant to the evaluation of our beliefs, the attractive element of the view needs a more sophisticated formulation than it received from Moore.

An influential argument that standard sceptical possibilities are irrelevant to our practice of epistemic evaluation was contained in Robert Nozick's *Philosophical Explanations*. He proposed an analysis of knowledge as belief that 'tracked the truth': simplifying slightly, my belief that Wittgenstein was Austrian counts as knowledge if it is true and if, had Wittgenstein not been Austrian, I would not have believed he was. Since, if I had been a brain in a vat, I would still have believed that I was not one, I do not know that I am not a brain in a vat. But this is irrelevant to the evaluation of more commonplace beliefs: it remains true that if my computer was not switched on, I would not believe that it was; so I do know that it is switched on. Sceptical challenges are thus of no epistemological importance.

Some are unhappy about the 'externalist' character of Nozick's approach: whether my beliefs count as knowledge may not be something I am well placed to judge. Reflection on my ways of monitoring my beliefs suggests that I cannot do this responsibly unless I can be confident of which of my beliefs are justified; or I must be able to identify which of my opinions are knowledge. Even if one of my beliefs tracks the truth, I may be in no position to tell whether it is. Nozick's claims about 'knows' need supplementing by an account of how such confidence is possible; and it is not yet obvious that sceptical challenges cannot threaten this sort of confidence in our ability to monitor our cognitive achievements.

Since Logical Positivists attempted to deny the meaningfulness of dream or demon possibilities on the grounds that we do not know what experience would be relevant to assessing their truth-value, philosophers have appealed to the theory of meaning. It is part of Donald Davidson's theory of interpretation that, when we assign meanings to someone's utterances or contents to their beliefs, we are guided by a demand that we make their beliefs largely truthful and their inferences largely sound. If that is correct, then it is impossible that someone's beliefs should be overwhelmingly false or unwarranted: that they seemed to be so would show simply that we had misinterpreted

them. If we encountered a brain in a vat, then, *if* we ascribed beliefs to it at all, they would be predominantly true beliefs about the 'world' created by the computer rather than predominantly false beliefs about our familiar external world. Whether or not we can conceive of the possibility that we are the victims of demons or wicked scientists, we can make no sense of our claims being both meaningful and substantially false. In that case, we can be confident of our ability to acquire information about the world, and revise our opinions in rational and defensible ways. But again, this does not satisfy those who are uneasy about the details of Davidson's account of *interpretation: extrapolating from the ways we interpret our fellows to our ways of interpreting the poor brain is not easy to do; and since the 'experiences' undergone by the brain in a vat are supposedly indistinguishable from ours, we find it hard to escape the conclusion that it is indeed grossly deceived.

In an influential and controversial discussion, Hilary Putnam has argued that sceptical possibilities are self-refuting: a brain in a vat could not formulate the thought that it is one (*Reason, Truth and History*, ch. 1). Even if the brain in a vat could utter the words 'I might be a brain in a vat', they could not have the meaning they have in our speech. The argument depends (like Davidson's) on views about how words acquire reference: roughly, the sceptical use of these possibilities requires the agent to use a word 'vat' which 'refers' to a kind of thing (a real vat in the external world) which has no role in the brain's experience. Putnam rejects the claim that this rests upon a kind of 'intrinsic' or magical connection: we can make no sense of our referring to objects which have no role in the causation of our beliefs and concepts. If we understand the reference of our words and concepts in terms of their role in making sense of experience and classifying things in ways which answer to our needs, then we find that the brain in a vat uses 'vat' to refer to the 'vats' in the world of its experience rather than to these objects which are wholly independent of it. He is an internal realist rather than a metaphysical realist.

In our ordinary practice, we make 'local' challenges to particular beliefs and particular methods of inquiry against a background view of the world that stands firm and can be relied upon in meeting the challenge. Global challenges, like the 'brain in a vat' possibility, threaten this background view of the world along with more controversial claims. If Davidson's argument works, then we can legitimately refuse to take global challenges seriously: we can always trust our background view of the world in meeting any challenges that arise; and global challenges are importantly different from local ones: they are unnatural and we do not act irresponsibly in ignoring them. Many would agree that our best hope for avoiding scepticism rests on finding a way to treat global challenges as not analogous to local ones: we cannot be forced to take them into account by thinking through the consequences of our ordinary practice of challenging and defending claims and beliefs.

A major influence upon this line of thought has been Wittgenstein's *On Certainty*. Having criticized Moore's claims to 'knowledge', he continued: 'I should like to say that Moore does not *know* what he says he knows, but it stands fast for him, as also for me; regarding it as absolutely solid is part of our *method* of inquiry' (para.151). My certainty that I have a hand is proof against sceptical arguments; and it is one of a heterogeneous group of certainties that form the background to all my ways of forming hypotheses, challenging claims, and conducting inquiries. Describing them as 'known' blinds us to the distinctive role occupied by these certainties which provide the 'scaffolding' for our inquiries. When the giving of grounds comes to an end, he urges, it is not in 'a kind of *seeing* on our part; it is our *acting*, which lies at the bottom of the language game' (para. 204). These certainties are manifested in the ways in which we react to evidence and to hypotheses, in our activities and our instinctive responses to the world. They are not expressed in conscious assent to propositions or in the search for evidence to support them. Local challenges are met by relying upon this scaffolding to guide our responses; since the scaffolding is not presented as 'knowledge', challenges to it cannot be posed or understood.

Whether this provides a perspective from which we can resist the traditional philosophical obsession with scepticism may still be an open question. Our best hope for doing so may well be to argue, with Wittgenstein, that the 'scaffolding' which guides us in forming and questioning beliefs cannot itself be questioned. But whether this suggestion will carry conviction for those who feel vividly the force of traditional sceptical arguments must remain uncertain.   C.J.H.

*knowledge, limits of; fallibilism; Pyrrhonism; foundationalism.

D. Davidson, 'A Coherence Theory of Truth and Knowledge', in E. Lepore (ed.), *Truth and Interpretation* (Oxford, 1986).

K. DeRose and T. Warfield (eds.), *Skepticism: A Contemporary Reader* (New York, 1999).

C. J. Hookway, *Scepticism* (London, 1990).

M. McGinn, *Sense and Certainty* (Oxford, 1989).

R. Nozick, *Philosophical Explanations* (Cambridge, Mass., 1981).

H. Putnam, *Reason, Truth and History* (Cambridge, 1981).

B. Stroud, *The Significance of Philosophical Scepticism* (Oxford, 1985).

L. Wittgenstein, *On Certainty* (Oxford, 1977).

scepticism, history of. The sceptical tradition questions our ability to obtain knowledge: if we are to seek the truth in a responsible manner, we need to meet challenges and difficulties to which no defensible answer is available. When we examine the history of this tradition, we study both the developments in the kinds of challenges used to unsettle our confidence, and changing views of the philosophical importance that these challenges have.

The history falls into two main periods. During the Hellenistic age, sceptical schools emerged in Greek philosophy, challenging the claims of scientists and philosophers to plumb the nature of reality. And, in the fifteenth and sixteenth centuries, new vigour was given to the question of

philosophical *scepticism by the intellectual ferment resulting from battles between different theological positions and from the challenge posed by the new sciences to our everyday view of the world. Many date the birth of 'modern philosophy' from the time when Descartes identified the defeat of scepticism as the first task of philosophy.

Plato's philosophy bequeathed an ambiguous legacy. Socrates appeared to possess the ability to question and undermine any dogmatic assertion that was put to him, insisting that wisdom consisted in awareness of the extent of one's own ignorance. But having emphasized the importance of knowledge that was properly grounded or tethered, he explained how such knowledge was possible, suggesting that it was necessary for the exercise of virtue. During the centuries following Plato's death, his *Academy became associated with a subtle form of scepticism, which focused more on the first part of this legacy than the second. And a breakaway sect took the name of *'Pyrrhonism', after Pyrrho of Elis, a post-Socratic philosopher whose life exhibited extreme scepticism. Our best source of Pyrrhonist thought is the writings of Sextus Empiricus, a late member of the school, whose *Outlines of Pyrrhonism* is a handbook of the position.

The Pyrrhonist 'modes' were used to challenge the beliefs of 'dogmatists': their use could supposedly force anyone to suspend judgement on any matter. Exposure to such techniques could produce a 'life without belief': a general suspension of judgement. A common objection was that without belief one cannot act, supported by the story that Pyrrho required constant support from friends to save him from natural dangers which he did not believe in. But, according to Sextus, Pyrrhonists could expect a quiet, conservative life: they passively acquiesced in 'appearances', going by perceptual information and by what appeared right and wrong; they conformed to local religious and ethical customs; and they acquired a trade. What they lacked was information about non-evident properties of things; and they accepted appearances passively, avoiding active endorsement of positions and taking no responsibility for their truth. This 'life without belief' turned out to yield the tranquillity and fulfilment (ataraxia) that others had sought through actively seeking knowledge.

Pyrrhonists challenged 'beliefs' by proposing contrasting 'appearances': when you assert that the tower is round, I point out that it does not appear round from a distance. To sustain your belief, you must propose a criterion that shows why it is correct. Since these criteria, in turn, can be challenged, your attempt to defend your view can only lead to a regress of criteria or go round in a circle, unless you stubbornly insist upon a criterion that you cannot support. If this picture of the structure of challenging beliefs is correct, it seems that you will not be able to avoid admitting that the matter is not settled.

During the sixteenth century, the writings of Sextus Empiricus and other Sceptics become more widely known, and questions about the criterion of religious truth and issues about the foundations of the new science became pressing. Montaigne, in *Apology for Raimond Sebond*, made sceptical arguments available in the vernacular, and encouraged a more general scepticism concerning whether any system of ideas could resist doubt. An early user of sceptical themes was Erasmus, who defended the Catholic Church against Reformation ideas: he used sceptical arguments to attack Luther's doctrines and proposed (like Sextus) that we should passively conform to existing practices since no defensible criterion of truth was available which could be trusted when we try to criticize them. But at a time of intellectual and religious ferment, Pyrrhonist prescriptions about how to live yielded conflicting recommendations; and many, like Luther, insisted that conformity to prevailing customs is too tepid a style of religious observance to meet the demands of Christianity. It is no accident that epistemological scepticism came increasingly to be associated with the religious variety. And, of course, once the force of sceptical arguments is acknowledged, they cannot easily be prevented from spreading doubt to all areas of life, including the new sciences.

Descartes set out to provide secure foundations for science, metaphysics, and religion by defeating scepticism. This required him to formulate and overcome the strongest possible sceptical arguments. Rather than appealing to particular challenges, particular contrasting appearances, to question each opinion he considered, he needed systematic doubts which put all our beliefs into question. The possibility that I might be dreaming challenged all perceptual beliefs; and the possibility that I was wholly under the influence of an evil demon (*malin génie*) threatened logical and metaphysical principles as well. Unless Descartes could legitimately appeal to a criterion enabling him to reject those possibilities, none of our knowledge would be secure. In his *Meditations* (1641), he attempted to provide such a criterion. Since few of his contemporaries considered his attempt successful, he bequeathed to later philosophers only a more powerful battery of sceptical challenges and a greater awareness of the importance and difficulty of defeating them. His 'refutation' of scepticism left it in better shape than before, encouraging a sense of the power of scepticism which culminated in Pierre Bayle's *Historical and Critical Dictionary* (1697–1702).

Descartes transformed thought about scepticism in another way, by introducing the idea that our knowledge of the contents of our own minds is more certain than our knowledge of things outside the mind. The problem of the external world, of showing how our subjective data provide us with reason for believing that there are external things, has seemed for many modern philosophers to be the fundamental issue of scepticism, although it was unknown to ancient Sceptics. This may have distorted our understanding of the force and importance of philosophical scepticism.

Sceptical considerations had a role in the development of a new *empirical* approach to science in the sixteenth and seventeenth centuries. Many of those involved in the development of the new science, for example Mersenne and Gassendi in France and John Locke and John Wilkins in England, would have agreed that sceptical arguments undermine the pretensions of dogmatic metaphysics and also of any scientific claim to reveal the real underlying essence of matter. Locke claimed that the study of nature yields *opinion* rather that *knowledge*, and Gassendi presented a version of the atomic theory which claimed only to accord with the patterns found in appearances. A growing modesty in the claims made for hypotheses followed sceptical awareness of the limitations of the human understanding.

This emerges clearly in the work of David Hume. Agreeing with those who reject Descartes's demand that our methods of inquiry be subjected to trial through scepticism in order to achieve certainty, Hume sought to emulate Newton and study cognition by constructing a scientific account of the mind. But he concluded that our beliefs extend beyond our own impressions and ideas only by exploiting causal inferences which have no legitimate basis. He arrives at the sceptical conclusion that the faculties giving rise to our view of the world are wholly unfitted to the task. The despair that this threatens to induce is avoided only because, when we turn aside from philosophy and science, we are psychologically incapable of taking their discoveries seriously. We are naturally drawn to philosophical investigations, but we find their results absurd and incredible.

But Hume believed that to be 'convinced of the force of the Pyrrhonian doubt, and of the impossibility that anything, but the strong power of the natural instinct, could free us from it' has a beneficial effect upon us. Inducing a sense of modesty, it discourages us from attaching too much importance to theory; we become aware of our cognitive limitations. Although we can benefit from scientific results (while sceptical that they promise the last word about things), we shall not allow them to undermine otherwise valuable beliefs and ideas. When philosophy encourages scepticism about the reliability of our knowledge, it is reasonable to extend that scepticism to philosophy: it turns into a useful activity, but not one which can provide dogmatic knowledge.

There have always been those who respond to sceptical challenges by impatiently denouncing them as absurd stratagems which no one takes seriously, and which can thus be ignored. From the time of Hume, two rationales have emerged for arguing that this response is legitimate. Since these sceptical doubts seem to be introduced in a natural way, resembling challenges we use all the time, we need to understand why they are different. We must explain how they do not show that our inquiries are governed by cognitive aims which we are incapable of achieving. The need, then, is to show that Pyrrhonist and Cartesian sceptical arguments are 'unnatural' or improper.

*'Common-sense' philosophers, from the sixteenth century on, have insisted that demanding reasons and challenging their adequacy can distort the structure of justification. Thomas Reid is an important figure in a

tradition that also includes twentieth-century thinkers such as G. E. Moore. The belief that there is an external world, for example, is not the sort of thing which is supported by particular arguments or reasons: it has stood the test of time, and 'everything counts for it, nothing counts against it'. Sceptics force us to treat it as one hypothesis among others, thus needing the kind of defence appropriate to controversial hypotheses. But such certainties work differently from ordinary hypotheses. Indeed, anything we might introduce as an argument in their support is less certain than they are themselves: I cannot offer evidence in favour of my belief that Rome exists, because any evidence suggesting otherwise would automatically be discredited for conflicting with such an obvious truth.

Kant, by contrast, argued that sceptics posed the wrong question: we unquestionably do possess knowledge, and the philosophical task is only to explain how this is possible. He concluded that our knowledge concerns the empirical world, whose character is determined by the structuring properties of our minds. Sceptical arguments may challenge our ability to know about the noumenal world, about things as they are in themselves. But since our aim in inquiry is to develop knowledge of a world which is shaped by our cognitive constitution, these arguments do not touch the only kind of knowledge which really matters to us.   c.j.h.

*Sceptics, ancient.

J. Annas and J. Barnes (eds.), *The Modes of Scepticism: Ancient Texts and Modern Interpretations* (Cambridge, 1985).

M. Burnyeat (ed.), *The Skeptical Tradition* (Berkeley, Calif., 1983).

C. J. Hookway, *Scepticism* (London, 1990).

R. H. Popkin, *The History of Scepticism* (1960; new edn. New York, 2003).

scepticism, moral: *see* moral scepticism.

scepticism about law: *see* law, scepticism about.

scepticism about religion: *see* religion, scepticism about.

Sceptics, ancient. The Greek word *skeptikoi* refers to those philosophers who refused to take dogmatic positions, but rather claimed to be always engaged in 'investigation' or 'consideration' (*skepsis*) of questions. Pyrrho of Elis (*c.*360–*c.*270 BC) is generally regarded as the founder of this school. Nevertheless, later sceptics and historians of *scepticism have often noted that a disposition to reject various claims to knowledge can be found throughout early Greek philosophy. For example, Xenophanes, Parmenides, and Democritus evince scepticism to a greater or less degree regarding claims to know reality. Thus, a denial of knowledge in one or more areas of investigation does not strictly speaking distinguish the Sceptics. Rather, they are distinguished by their adherence to certain generalized arguments against dogmatic claims and by their view of the salutary effects of a sceptical stance.

Pyrrho is said to have been a painter by training. He was probably not the author of the technical arguments that later came to characterize the thinking of his disciples. He is reputed to have been a man of remarkable calmness and humility, and it was evidently thought by his admirers that these qualities arose from his refusal to commit himself to dogmatic claims.

The basic Sceptical strategy is to argue that the sorts of assertion dogmatists make are supposed to be inferred from elementary data such as sense-perceptions. But, the Sceptics argue, these claims are only warranted if the data entail them. Various arguments—the so-called 'Sceptical tropes'—can be employed to show that the supposed entailment is illusory. In effect, the only evidence a Sceptic will allow is entailing evidence. On this basis, one is no more justified in accepting the dogmatists' claims than their opposite. So, the only rational response is to say 'I no more accept *p* than its opposite', whatever claim *p* might express. What is the supposed result of being thus disposed to the dogmatists' claims? Tranquillity of mind and an absence of anxious attention to putatively life-enhancing knowledge.

It is not surprising that no ordinary philosophical school would be founded on the exiguous negativism of Scepticism. Pyrrho did, however, have one disciple, Timon of Phlius (*c.*320–*c.*230), who travelled to Elis as a young man and later arrived in Athens to challenge the prevailing dogmatisms in the spirit of his master. Timon crafted his attacks on dogmatists in the form of *silloi*, or satirical poems, some fragments of which survive.

The principal development within Scepticism in the third century was its introduction into Plato's *Academy by Arcesilaus. Since the prevailing dogmatism of the day was *Stoicism, Arcesilaus and the Academic Sceptics directed their increasingly refined destructive arguments against Stoic claims in theology and ethics. We do not know to what extent Arcesilaus was influenced by Pyrrho or whether he was in contact with Timon, but the inspiration for these Sceptical attacks was not Pyrrho so much as it was Socrates, understood by the Sceptics as one of their own. He was for them, in word and deed, a model of how one ought to respond to dogmatic assertions and of the results of such a response.

The most famous of the Academic Sceptics after Arcesilaus was Carneades. The historical evidence suggests that Carneades developed an epistemological theory of probabilism which apparently aimed to mitigate the extreme alternatives—certain knowledge or ignorance—of Pyrrhonian Scepticism.

A reversion to dogmatism within the Academy, that is, to Platonism, in the first century BC ended with a revival of Pyrrhonism by Aenesidemus, whose version of Scepticism is partially preserved by the great chronicler of Scepticism, Sextus Empiricus.

Scepticism can be either global or local. That is, one can be a sceptic regarding knowledge in general or only regarding a particular area of knowledge. The later history of scepticism is replete with attempts to combine a local scepticism, say regarding religious knowledge, with vigorous knowledge-claims in other areas, such as science.

Such an approach has even been embraced by *defenders* of religion, who want to claim that religious faith is beyond the reach of that which is scientifically knowable.   L.P.G.

J. Annas and J. Barnes (eds.), *The Modes of Scepticism: Ancient Texts and Modern Interpretations* (Cambridge, 1985).

J. Barnes, *The Toils of Scepticism* (Cambridge, 1990).

M. Burnyeat (ed.), *The Skeptical Tradition* (Berkeley, Calif., 1983).

L. Groarke, *Greek Scepticism* (Montreal, 1990).

Schacht, Richard (1941–). American philosopher; Professor of Philosophy, Criticism and Interpretive Theory at the University of Illinois at Urbana-Champaign. Schacht's writings make room for some understanding between philosophers writing in the 'analytical' tradition and so-called 'modern continental philosophy'. Notably, *Nietzsche* (1983) presents arguments for and against that philosopher's perspectivism and repudiation of Western morality in an idiom that is not Nietzschean but which preserves many of Nietzsche's insights. In *Alienation* (1971), *Hegel and After: Studies in Continental Philosophy between Kant and Sartre* (1975), and *Classical Modern Philosophers: Descartes to Kant* (1984), Schacht has made Anglo-American philosophers more aware of the need to read modern European philosophers.   S.P.

*Nietzsche.

Scheler, Max (1874–1928). German philosopher called 'the Catholic Nietzsche'. He applied Husserl's phenomenology to ethics, culture, and religion. He was a founder of philosophical *anthropology and of sociology of knowledge (*Problems of a Sociology of Knowledge* (1926); tr. London, 1980). In *Formalism in Ethics and the Non-Formal Ethics of Values* (1913–16; tr. Evanston, Ill., 1973), he argued (against Kant etc.) that values are objective, unchanging, a priori, non-formal, and objects of emotions and feelings rather than reason. Values form a hierarchy: (1) pleasure–pain (values of sensible feeling), (2) noble–vulgar (values of vital feeling), (3) beautiful–ugly, just–unjust, pure knowledge of truth (spiritual values), and (4) holy–unholy (religious values). Moral values consist in the realization of other values. Our feeling for values and their social embodiment, but not values themselves, vary in sociologically explicable ways. A person is not a substance nor an object, but the concrete unity of acts. He is essentially both individual and a member of a community. Most persons lack feeling for higher values, and cannot participate in the types of community devoted to them; but all should have adequate, and perhaps equal, access to what they do value. Values are better promoted by aristocracy than by liberal democracy.   M.J.I.

M. S. Frings, *Max Scheler: A Concise Introduction into the World of a Great Thinker* (Pittsburgh, 1965).

R. Perrin, *Max Scheler's Concept of the Person: An Ethics of Humanism* (Basingstoke, 1991).

Schelling, Friedrich Wilhelm Joseph von (1775–1854). German philosopher, who was the Proteus of post-Kantian *idealism and the main philosopher of the Romantic circle. His earliest works, from 1793 on, were variations on Fichte's *Wissenschaftslehre*, though he contrasted idealism and 'dogmatism' less sharply than Fichte. From 1797 he produced several works on philosophy of nature, which attempt to 'construct' or 'deduce' nature as the 'objective system of reason'. For Fichte and Kant, nature, though objective in relation to the finite ego, is a product of 'consciousness in general'. Thus, as a book bears the mark of its author, *nature will be an organic whole tending to the realization of *reason. Fichte initially believed that Schelling was trying to establish this, as a supplement to *Wissenschaftslehre*. Nature begins in the emergence of matter from the forces of attraction and repulsion and ends in the human organism, the embodiment of practical reason: nature is the I, or mind, in the process of becoming. Every natural phenomenon has its place in a logically ordered system of development. Schelling, like Goethe, rejects quantitative, mechanical science, and stresses life, the organic, purpose, and polarity (especially electricity and magnetism).

Schelling's next (un-Fichtean) step was to view philosophy of nature and *Wissenschaftslehre* as two *parallel* sciences, respectively deriving mind from nature and nature from mind. The *System of Transcendental Idealism* (1800; tr. Charlottesville, Va., 1978) develops theoretical and practical *Wissenschaftslehre*, in which, respectively, the conscious is determined by the unconscious and the unconscious by the conscious. The theoretical self surveys the productivity of unconscious reason in feeling, perception, and thought; the practical self freely transforms this unconscious reality in individual morality, political life, and history. But both these series are endless; reason is here realized only at infinity. It is fully realized only in the unconscious, yet conscious, activity of the artistic genius: art is the true 'organ' of philosophy. He expanded this view in lectures on *Philosophy of Art* (1802–5, pub. 1859; tr. Minneapolis, 1989).

Schelling next sought a common basis for nature and the self, for philosophy of nature and transcendental idealism, i.e. a system of 'identity'. In *Exposition of my System of Philosophy* (1801), this basis is 'absolute reason', the 'indifference of nature and spirit, of object and subject'. He acknowledges its affinity to Spinoza's substance. The Absolute is the quantitative indifference of reality and ideality. Reality or objectivity predominates over ideality or subjectivity in the real series: it runs from matter, via light, electricity, and chemistry, to the organism, the most spiritual phase (or 'potency') of nature. Subjectivity predominates in the ideal series, running from morality and science to art, the most natural phase of spirit. The full manifestation of the Absolute, the universe, is a perfect organism and work of art. In *Bruno* (1802; tr. Albany, NY, 1984) the Absolute is called 'God' or the 'infinite', and the potencies are seen as (Neo)-platonic 'ideas', God's eternal vision of himself, the intermediary between the Absolute and the empirical world.

In 1804 Schelling came to believe that though the world can be shown to be rational in its content, no rational account can be given of its *existence*, of why there is anything rather than nothing. The finite world originates from God not by a rational, comprehensible process but by a *leap*, a free (timeless) fall of the ideas from God into finite actuality. The content of reality is rational, embodying God's ideas; its being actual (nature) is apostasy, sin, unreason. Nature's essence strives to return to God, and this return is history: its goal is to reunite the ideas to God. Man's development is parallel to God's: he freely breaks loose from God and is redeemed by returning to him.

Of Human Freedom (1809; tr. Chicago, 1937) postulates a 'primordial ground' or 'abyss' in God, which is indeterminate, unconscious striving or *will; all reality is ultimately will. This self-directed will creates as its self-image or self-revelation the ideas, reason. The world proceeds from the interaction between the ground and ideas. Nature reveals the conflict between irrational striving and rational purpose. History displays the triumph of man's rational universal will over his irrational particular will. Reality develops from primordial will to rational self-knowledge and self-determination.

Religion, not art, is now the organ of philosophy. God develops in the successive ideas that men have of him. In lectures on mythology (1842) and revelation (1842–3), Schelling seeks knowledge of God from the history of *all* religions: God's self-revelation and -development advances from primordial will to reason and love. Schelling's and Hegel's earlier 'negative philosophy' showed only that *if* God reveals himself, he does so in certain rationally comprehensible forms. The new 'positive philosophy' is needed to show *that* he reveals himself in man's religious history.

Schelling had a mind of great depth and range, capable of original insights as well as of fusing those of others (the Neoplatonists, Spinoza, Kant, Fichte, Hegel, etc.). Many of his ideas re-emerge in Schopenhauer, Tillich, and Existentialism: Schelling's God is both the will to power and existentialist man.   M.J.I.

*romanticism, philosophical.

A. Bowie, *Schelling and Modern European Philosophy: An Introduction* (London, 1993).
F. Copleston, *A History of Philosophy*, vii: *Modern Philosophy*, pt. 1: *Fichte to Hegel* (Westminster, Md., 1963).
M. Heidegger, *Schelling's Treatise on the Essence of Human Freedom* (Athens, Oh., 1985).

schema. Literally shape, pattern, form; plural, schemata or schemas. In logic a schema is an expression, often a sentence, from which certain word-groups have been removed and replaced by blanks or more commonly by 'schematic letters', the role of these being to mark places where any word-group of the type removed can be inserted: e.g. '*P*', '*F*', '*G*' in 'If not *P*, *P*; therefore *P*', '*G* belongs to some *F*', '$\exists x(Fx \wedge Gx)$' ('Something is *F* and *G*'). Some schemata are *formulae, i.e. contain no words. But there are also formulae with meanings, e.g. the true sentence '$\forall x(x = x)$' ('Everything is the same as itself') or the functional expression 'π^2'; whereas schemata mean nothing—and so cannot, for example, be true or false—until their letters are replaced or (as some say) interpreted. The role of a schematic letter is different from that of a quantifiable *variable, although the same letter might be assigned both roles at once.   C.A.K.

W. V. Quine, *Methods of Logic*, 3rd edn. (London, 1974).

Schiffer, Stephen (1940–). American philosopher (D.Phil., Oxford) currently at New York University, best known for his three books on meaning and for his quest for rigour and clarity. In *Meaning* he defended the view that *semantics reduces to propositional-attitude psychology, by presenting an intricate version of *Grice's intention-based semantics. He later repudiated this view in *Remnants of Meaning*, where he argued against the very possibility of a theory of *meaning or *propositional attitude content. He subsequently found a new possibility for such a theory, based on a distinctively deflationary but anti-reductionist, or 'pleonastic', conception of meanings and propositions. This theory is developed in *The Things We Mean*. Schiffer is also known for having introduced and later debunked the 'hidden-indexical theory' of propositional attitude ascriptions. Other papers treat such topics as the nature of desire, Descartes on his essence, rigid designation, singular thought, 'Kripkenstein' (Kripke's rendition of Wittgenstein on rules and private language), epistemic contextualism, and vagueness.   K.B.

Stephen Schiffer, *Meaning* (Oxford, 1972).
—— *Remnants of Meaning* (Cambridge, Mass., 1987).
—— *The Things We Mean* (Oxford, 2003).

Schiller, Johann Christoph Friedrich von (1759–1805). German philosopher, poet, and dramatist, who developed Kant's ethics and aesthetics towards post-Kantian *idealism. His main concern was the role of art and beauty in man's rational life and its history. (He became Professor of History at Jena in 1789, and wrote several historical works, besides his inaugural lecture: *What is, and to what End does one Study, Universal History?*) On the basis of Kant's *Critique of Judgement* (1790) he argued that *beauty is 'freedom in phenomenal appearance'. Aesthetic contemplation of an object does not involve cognitively understanding it: we do not apply concepts to it or investigate its causal conditions, but view it as if it were free. The beautiful, again, is not an object of desire or moral will. In aesthetic contemplation the 'play impulse' prevails.

*Aesthetics, rather than (as Kant supposed) religion, plays the central part in educating the sensuous nature of man to morality. Art and beauty refine man's feelings, so that he is more inclined to act *legally*, and thus prepare him for morality. In *On the Aesthetic Education of Man* (1795; tr. Oxford, 1967) he envisaged an advance, both in the life of the individual and in the history of man, from the physical state in which man is ruled by needs and nature, by way of the aesthetic state, in which he frees himself from nature by the elimination of his sensuous will, to the moral state, in which man controls nature by his moral will. But aesthetics also perfects man's moral condition. By ennobling his sensuous nature, beauty reconciles the conflict between it and his rational will. Thus man becomes a 'beautiful soul' (*schöne Seele*), who fulfils the moral law from inclination.

In *Naïve and Sentimental Poetry* (1796; tr. New York, 1966) he argues that different ages and types of poetry depend on different relations between nature and freedom. In the 'Arcadian' stage (Greece) nature and freedom are in primitive harmony: men act morally by unconscious instinct and poetry is naïve. Modern poetry feels a conflict between nature and freedom, the real and the ideal, and strives to reconcile it: sentimental poetry. In the 'Elysian' age to come, when harmony is reflectively restored, poetry will be at once naïve and sentimental.

M.J.I.

R. D. Miller, *Schiller and the Ideal of Freedom* (Oxford, 1970).

T. J. Reed, *Schiller* (Oxford, 1991).

A. Ugrinsky (ed.), *Friedrich von Schiller and the Drama of Human Existence* (London, 1988).

Schlegel, Friedrich von (1772–1829). Central in the German Romantic movement and responsible for converting the classical notion of irony, as a mere figure of speech, into an entire literary or quasi-philosophical perspective that named *Socrates among its antecedents. Early influenced by Kant and Fichte, Schlegel criticized the former for failing to bring ideas into touch with reality and the latter's world-creating ego for leaving out nature and history. Schlegel's views on irony nevertheless draw upon Fichte's view of philosophy as animated by the thoughts and counter-thoughts generated by reflection. Philosophy is a reflective art, as with Socrates, and its goal is to bring the real and the ideal into touch with each other on a broad front (poetry, art, society, politics, literary communication). Irony as reflective freedom raises the thinker to a sense of transcendence and of the divinely creative spirit. A convert to Roman Catholicism, Schlegel saw history as a process in which irreducibly single individuals, nations, and languages found their universal nature in the knowledge of God. He founded *The Athenaeum*, a periodical of the early Romantics, and was for a time a politician.   A.H.

F. Schlegel, *Dialogue on Poetry and Literary Aphorisms*, tr. E. Behler and R. Stone (University Park, Pa., 1968).

—— *Lucinde and the Fragments*, tr. P. Firchow (Minneapolis, 1971).

Schleiermacher, Friedrich Ernst-Daniel (1768–1834). German Protestant theologian and philosopher of religion. Translator of Plato. Inventor of *hermeneutics in its modern form. Religion is properly understood by intuition and feeling (*Anschauung und Gefühl*) and 'a sense and taste for the infinite', rather than through reason or doctrine. In his philosophy of the person Schleiermacher emphasizes the dependence of each of cognition, feeling, and action on the other two. In his theology, God is the highest and only unity of what is. All particular things are disclosed only through God. The deepest awe at the existence of the universe as a whole is possible only through a feeling of devotion. The profound experience of union with the infinite implies the existence of God. Christianity is not the only true religion, but the most complete.

Schleiermacher accepted Kant's critique of arguments for the existence of God, took seriously his construal of God, freedom, and the immortality of the soul as 'postulates', and was positively influenced by the Romantic movement, especially by *Schlegel. Until the renewed emphasis placed upon Scripture by Karl Barth, Schleiermacher's influence on Protestant theology was immense.

S.P.

Wilhelm Dilthey, *Leben Schleiermachers*, 2nd edn. (Berlin, 1920).

Friedrich Schleiermacher, *On Religion: Speeches to its Cultured Despisers*, tr. John Oman with an introduction by Rudolf Otto (New York, 1958).

—— *Werke* [selections], ed. O. Braun (Leipzig, 1910–13).

Kurt Mueller-Vollmer (ed.), *The Hermeneutics Reader* (Oxford, 1986), esp. 72–97.

Schlick, Friedrich Albert Moritz (1882–1936). In 1922 Schlick, a physicist turned philosopher, became Professor of the Philosophy of the Inductive Sciences in Vienna (a predecessor had been Mach), where he became the centre of a group of like-minded advocates of logical and scientific rigour in philosophy, the Vienna Circle. Out of their discussions grew *Logical Positivism, the most profound and creative (though ultimately mistaken) school of philosophy in the twentieth century. But Schlick was not altogether typical of the Circle. Of course, he shared the view that science had a unique status, but he also included ethics in science by analysing value-judgements as desires, and therefore as psychological facts. But further development of his ideas was tragically denied to him, when in mid-career he was murdered on his way to a lecture by an insane student.   A.BEL.

Oswald Hanfling, *Logical Positivism* (Oxford, 1981).

—— (ed.), *Essential Reading in Logical Positivism* (Oxford, 1981).

scholasticism. The philosophy of the 'schools', i.e. the tradition which arose in the medieval universities and is associated with the methods and theses of the major philosophers of the thirteenth and fourteenth centuries, namely, Aquinas, Scotus, and Ockham. Scholasticism remained the dominant European philosophy until the fifteenth century, when it gave way to, in turn, Renaissance humanism, rationalism, and empiricism. There have, however, been several revivals, and *neo-scholasticism remains a feature of the philosophical landscape.   J.HAL.

*medieval philosophy.

N. Kretzmann, A. Kenny, and J. Pinborg (eds.), *The Cambridge History of Later Medieval Philosophy* (Cambridge, 1982).

Schopenhauer, Arthur (1788–1860). German philosopher of inherited independent means, who gained distinction only towards the end of his life as a result, partly, of the notice taken of him in the British utilitarian journal the *Westminster Review*. His mother, who thoroughly disliked her son for his gloomy outlook, ran a literary salon in Weimar, frequented by Goethe, and this led to a short period of intellectual friendship during Schopenhauer's youth, as Goethe initially thought Schopenhauer's philosophy relevant for his own theory of colours. Schopenhauer arrived at his general philosophical position very early and all his works are developments of the same basic initial ideas. His chief inspirations were Plato, Kant, and the *Upanishads. He is, in fact, the first (and remains among the few) Western philosophers to have related his thought to Hindu and Buddhist ideas. However, his most distinctive contribution to philosophy is in his insistence that *Will is more basic than thought in both man and nature.

1. Schopenhauer's starting-point for his solution to 'the riddle of the world' is a form of transcendental *idealism which he owes to Kant, though he seeks to establish it in a less contorted way. The physical world is phenomenal and exists only for 'the subject of knowledge'. Only by recognizing this can we explain how we know certain necessary *synthetic a priori truths about it. Our cognitive faculties construct the world on the basis of four versions of the 'principle of *sufficient reason', to which all phenomena must conform. (This is elaborated most fully in the book of his early youth, On the Fourfold Root of the Principle of Sufficient Reason (1813).) Our sensibility operates with the principle that everything is situated in a space of which the parts are mutually determining according to Euclidean geometry, and a time the mutual conditioning of whose moments is the topic of arithmetic (via the temporal nature of counting); our understanding works with the law of causality, and yields perception of a physical world which it pictures as the cause of our sensations. Our reason—whose conceptual representations (Vorstellungen) are quite secondary to the representations which understanding produces in perception and from which they are abstracted (Schopenhauer particularly scorns the many philosophers who confuse these or, like Hegel, treat concepts as primary)—works on the principle that every judgement must have its justification. A fourth principle bids us conceive of human action as necessarily determined by motive. The world constructed on these principles can only exist for the subject of knowledge to whose faculties they correspond.

2. Matters are taken further in Schopenhauer's magnum opus The World as Will and Representation (Die Welt als Wille und Vorstellung (1818)). Kant's greatest merit, for Schopenhauer, was the distinction of the phenomenon from the *thing-in-itself. He was also right (though not consistently) that the thing-in-itself is not the cause of our sensations or of phenomena, since causation applies only within the phenomenal world and cannot relate it to something else. But that, for Schopenhauer, does not mean that we can form no idea of the nature of the thing-in-itself. For our perceptual experience of the phenomenal world of things in space and time is not our only experience. We are aware of ourselves, both in the perceptual fashion by which we know external things, and, quite differently, 'from within' as Will, more specifically as Will to Live. So our behaviour presents itself to us not only as the

movements of a physical object but more intimately as the phases of a Will. The latter is not, and is not felt to be, the cause of the behaviour; rather, these are the same thing known outwardly and inwardly.

From knowledge of my own nature as thing-in-itself I can infer something of the nature of the physical world in general. For while I cannot prove that the rest of nature is more than mere appearance, namely the appearance of something in itself, to deny this would be a form of *solipsism, something which belongs only to the madhouse. If we are to look upon the world sanely, we must suppose that everything in it is the appearance of what in itself is Will in basically the same sense as is my body and its behaviour. This argument is treated by some commentators with less respect than it deserves. If it is true that my body is Will in its real inner being, then, since the physical world outwardly seems homogeneous with it, and belongs to the same unitary interacting system, it is reasonable to suppose that the same is true of physical nature, not only in other humans and animals, as is quite easily granted, but throughout. The reasonable doubt is whether Schopenhauer has shown that Will is the inner being of my organism and behaviour, rather than the justification of extending this conclusion to the world at large.

3. The natural world, then, is the appearance of Will to itself, when this generates the subject of knowledge as an affection of itself. But is it one Will or many which appears to itself as the organic and inorganic world? Schopenhauer takes the former view (as Nietzsche was later to take the latter). For, so he argues, number, as an operation of the human intellect, only applies to the world of representation and cannot be relevant to reality as it is in itself. This cannot, then, be many, but must be one, not, indeed, in the sense that this would be the upshot of a count, but in the sense that number is inapplicable. (Whether this gives him the oneness he requires is doubtful.) He could have argued more effectively, however, that since causality cannot apply to reality in itself, it cannot figure there as 'the cement of the universe' (in Mackie's phrase) and that the unity of the cosmos must not depend upon such external relations between its parts.

But if what each of us experiences as his own inner being is Will at all, surely it is Will as a series of acts of willing, something both temporal and plural? Schopenhauer, more especially in the greatly enlarged second edition (1844) of his great work, is alert to this problem. It only shows, he says, that the thing-in-itself is still revealing itself incompletely, and has divested itself only of the more external garments in which it is dressed by consciousness. In fact, there seems some oscillation between the claim (characteristic later of Nietzsche) that introspectible processes of desire, pleasure and pain, and so forth are what I find as the inner being of myself and the claim that I can detect at the core of my being a dim unvarying drive to satisfaction. No reading of the text makes him altogether consistent on such matters. But the general upshot, that the universe is a single, 'vast', cosmic Will to

Exist which experiences itself through an apparent diversity of conscious beings in a spatio-temporal and deterministic world, is clear enough and strongly argued. This Will is said to be unconscious in inanimate nature, but it is hard to see how one can understand Schopenhauer unless it is supposed that it has some sort of dumb feeling of itself, even if there is not the contrast between subject and object required for consciousness in any full sense.

4. More than anything else, Schopenhauer is famous as the philosopher of *pessimism. The wretchedness of the world (with whose horrors he became obsessed early in life) and the nastiness of human nature, he contends, with many striking examples, is evident enough empirically. But it is also a necessary truth, following from the very nature of its underlying reality, the Will. Will seeks constantly for a quietus which from its very nature as striving it could only reach by forfeiting its main goal, existence; indeed pleasure has really only a negative character as the relief from the suffering which is its normal state. Moreover, in its apparent pluralization, each part of the phenomenal world is powered by a drive to survive at the expense of others, so that there is a universal and appalling war of all against all. This is no time to consider the psychological sources of Schopenhauer's extreme pessimism, nor weigh its pros and cons empirically; we remark only that, central as it was to his philosophy as he conceived it, it does not seem entailed by his most interesting metaphysical conclusions. It is not so obvious as he thought that a world of Will *must* have been one of misery, while some have found it possible to delight in a world thus conceived even with the miseries actually pertaining to it.

5. Glum as his view of the world is, Schopenhauer offers two ways of escape from its horrors, one temporary, the other in principle permanent.

First, there is aesthetic experience, Schopenhauer's detailed and brilliant account of which has had considerable influence. Here our faculty of knowledge, in particular perception, normally only an instrument to the Will's satisfaction, gains a certain independence as pure will-less contemplation for its own sake, freeing us briefly from our misery, while the veil which hides the true nature of reality from us is partially rent. We no longer experience ourselves as one individual standing in contrast to others, but rather as the impersonal and universal pure subject of knowledge. And with this change in our experience of ourselves goes a change in the character of the object presented to us. It is no longer particular things in space and time which present themselves, but rather the basic types and principles by which the Will manifests itself, types and principles which Schopenhauer identifies with the Platonic Ideas, believing that he is uncovering the true significance of Plato's doctrine. There is a distinct law, or system of laws, of nature which is the phenomenal manifestation of each of these (the laws of physics, of chemistry, of biology, etc., and of each animal species, a partially distinct one also for every human being constituting his innate character). The artist produces a perceptual representation which yields us awareness of these Ideas (*Ideen*) rather than of the particular thing before us. (Music alone depicts the Will in its various grades as it is in itself rather than as manifested in the phenomenal world.)

Aspects of this account are puzzling. Why are aesthetic contemplation, and its peaceful objects, so free of the travails essential to Will, if they really bring us closer to the reality underlying phenomena? And in what sense does the Will objectify itself in these different grades? Schopenhauer often writes as though this objectification was a kind of real entry into all the variety of the world's phenomena, but he should be referring not to a real pouring of itself into an external world, but to the way in which the one Will manifests itself to itself, *qua* subject of knowledge.

The only lasting solution, however, to our misery comes when people become so aware of the necessary wretchedness of life, of the misery of existing as futile manifestations of the cosmic Will to Live, that they lose all wish for existence and gratification. This is what happens in the case of the genuine saint, an ascetic who has no concern with living and prospering. In him the Will to Live has denied itself. Or rather, there is only a faint twinkling of it left, hardly enough to sustain the picture of a world of things in space and time. When he dies this twinkling will utterly cease, and with it the world of which he was conscious, since this consisted in nothing but his picture of it. For Will and its picture of the world cannot continue to be when it no longer desires, and the world cannot be when the Will ceases, since it is only the Will's own delusive picture of itself.

But surely the Will as personalized in me, and the world for me, end equally, when I die, whether I have reached will-denying sainthood or not, while in both cases the Will continues its life in others and in nature? The answer seems to be that, when the saint dies, his particular grade or type of Will is at an end, whereas when the ordinary man dies, though he is at an end, his type is not. (Thus suicide is self-defeating, a mere complaint over current conditions on the part of one particular grade of Will.) Moreover, universal sainthood would somehow bring everything to an end (though the real truth here must be somehow non-temporal). Will anything be left at all? Yes, Schopenhauer darkly hints, something inconceivable by us but experienced by the saint in mystic contemplation. For what is *nothing* from one point of view must always be *something* from another. The analysis of *nothing* here is similar to Bergson's.

Schopenhauer's ethics (*On the Freedom of the Will* and *On the Basis of Morality*, published together in 1841) is closely related to his metaphysics. It is prefaced by a critique of Kant's account of morality. For Schopenhauer the very idea of a categorical, as opposed to a hypothetical, imperative, is an absurdity. An intelligible imperative is normally an order given by someone who can impose sanctions on those who do not conform to it, and has the form of 'Do this . . . or else'. Schopenhauer believed that the *categorical imperative only seemed to make sense to

Kant because unconsciously he took it as the command of God. Moreover, in spite of himself Kant comes too near to giving ethics an egoistic foundation, effectively basing it, claims Schopenhauer, on our concern with how it would affect us personally if everyone acted according to our example.

In contrast, moral goodness is identified by Schopenhauer with unselfish compassion for others. The good man is one who, not making the usual distinction between himself and others, is filled with universal compassion. Thus he acts on the principle 'Injure no one; on the contrary, help everyone as much as you can'. In doing so, he is concretely aware of what metaphysics teaches in the abstract, the oneness of the Will in all its manifestations. Thus this principle is not really an imperative but rather a description of how the good man acts. As an instruction it would really be useless, because each man acts according to his innate character anyway. So-called moral education may make men more tolerable by pointing out the advantages of co-operation with others, but our behaviour can only possess true moral worth if it stems from a moral goodness which cannot be taught. That moral worth consists in this capacity for compassion has hardly been recognized by most official moralists, but all over the world nothing is really admired in a morally relevant way except genuine concern with the welfare of others.

The compassion which constitutes moral worth manifests itself in its lesser form in justice based on the principle of non-interference with anyone's obtaining by their activity what they would otherwise legitimately achieve by it. By an illegitimate achievement is meant one made at the expense of someone else's achieving what they would otherwise—judged by the same criterion—legitimately achieve by their action. It manifests itself in a fuller form, as the loving kindness which inspires an active concern to help others in their need. It should be noted that for Schopenhauer the goal of compassion is the relief of misery and does not include the creation of positive happiness. This is partly because his pessimistic view of life implies that positive happiness, as opposed to relief from the worst sort of unhappiness, is impossible, and partly because he thinks that the kind of identification with others which constitutes compassion can only occur when one becomes aware of another as a fellow sufferer.

Schopenhauer's treatment of the freedom of the will is a brilliant (if ultimately implausible) development of Kant's. For Schopenhauer universal *determinism holds necessarily for the phenomenal world. This follows from the fact that consciousness constructs the world on the principle of sufficient reason, in particular in its causal form. However, the thing-in-itself has freely chosen to manifest itself as a phenomenal individual answering to the particular Platonic Idea which constitutes each human being's character. This character (just like one of the laws of nature) settles just what he will do in every possible empirical circumstance. Each action is causally determined in that it flows necessarily from the combination of the agent's character and his beliefs about the conse-

quences of acting in one way rather than another. The beliefs are the cause of the action, but, like all other causes, they operate because they affect something with a determinate nature. At the level of causation specific to physics it is only the determinate nature of matter in general that is involved, while chemistry and biology explore the type of causation which arises in matter which has reached a higher level of complexity. The causation of human activity is just as inevitable, but there is no one single set of causal laws, because each single human has a quite unique determinate nature. This is his moral character, the special quality of his will. It is this which is the ultimate possessor or otherwise of moral worth. A man is blamed not so much for what he does, but for what his action shows that he is. This cannot change, because all change in a man's outward behaviour arises from causes which can only operate on him in consequence of his unchanging basic character. Causes only affect him as they do in virtue of his character and therefore cannot act on it. Nevertheless, *qua* the thing-in-itself or Will which has chosen to manifest itself in an individual with my particular character, I am to blame for what I am and do, and deserve whatever fate this brings me. The only behaviour which does not thus follow deterministically from an individual's innate character, operating in particular conditions, occurs in those rare cases when a saint reaches liberation; while his character and its consequences manifested the Will's futile but free assertion of itself, his liberation manifests the Will's wiser and equally free return to the mysterious Nothingness whence it emerged thereby.   T.L.S.S.

TRANSLATIONS

On the Basis of Morality (1841), tr. E. F. J. Payne (Indianapolis, 1965).
On the Freedom of the Will (1841), tr. K. Kolenda (Indianapolis, 1960).
The World as Will and Representation (1818), tr. E. F. J. Payne, 2 vols. (New York, 1966).

COMMENTARIES

Michael Fox (ed.), *Schopenhauer: His Philosophical Achievement* (Brighton, 1980).
Patrick Gardiner, *Schopenhauer* (Harmondsworth, 1963).
D. W. Hamlyn, *Schopenhauer* (London, 1980).
Christopher Janaway, *Self and World in Schopenhauer's Philosophy* (Oxford, 1989).
—— *Schopenhauer: A Very Short Introduction* (Oxford, 2002).
—— (ed.), *The Cambridge Companion to Schopenhauer* (Cambridge, 2000).
B. Magee, *The Philosophy of Schopenhauer*, expanded edn. (Oxford, 1997).
T. L. S. Sprigge, *Theories of Existence* (Harmondsworth, 1985), ch. 4.

Schrödinger: *see* cat, Schrödinger's.

Schutz, Alfred (1899–1959). German philosopher, who emigrated to the USA, a pupil of the phenomenologist Husserl. In the philosophy of *social science, he is taken to be a key critic of the positivist tradition (although he saw himself as building bridges between *positivism and the *hermeneutic and *phenomenological traditions). In

The Phenomenology of the Social World (first German edn. 1932; Evanston, Ill., 1967), Schutz analysed the process by which we typify the basic stream of meaningless sense-experience into 'stocks of knowledge', which are shared. Together all stocks of knowledge constitute the 'life-world' (our reality and our knowledge of it are one and the same). Social scientists produce 'second-order typifications'. Schutz's analysis was developed by phenomenological sociologists into a social scientific methodology which takes 'scientific knowledge' to have only the same status as the common-sense knowledge of the life-world possessed by us all.   E.J.F.

M. Natanson, 'Phenomenology and Typification: A Study in the Philosophy of Alfred Schutz', *Social Research* (1970).

science, diversity of. The tentative view that science is a network of theories that mutually support and partially explain each other and do not have a privileged foundational level—say, physics. Opposed to kinds of *foundationalism and *unity of science, which arrange science hierarchically, with theories at the higher levels dependent on and to be explained by those below. The view of science as diverse is thus also opposed to kinds of *reductionism. It may, further, also resist the physicalism that reduces all science to physical science. As a full account of science, the view needs to develop generalizations about kinds of evidential relations, etc. between theories, but it remains pessimistic that true bridging laws between sciences will be established.   V.SUCH.

John Dupré, *The Disorder of Things* (Cambridge, Mass., 1993).
Margaret Morrison, *Unifying Scientific Theories: Physical Concepts and Mathematical Structures* (Cambridge, 2000).

science, feminist philosophy of. Would scientists with distinctively feminist commitments do science differently? If the answer to this question is 'yes', does this mean that our conception of 'scientificity' must be adjusted?

Feminists are not the only philosophers to have questioned the demarcation of science from the ordinary run of knowledge, and therefore the philosophy of science from epistemology more generally. However, they have made a particularly significant contribution to the body of sceptical literature which asks whether conventional scientific methods and methodology are as successful at tracking or converging on truth and validity as they have claimed to be.

Feminist philosophers have also engaged with the problem of establishing what methodologies, if any, might be guarantors of good science. They have considered a number of candidates, including an adapted *historical materialism (Nancy Hartsock), *phenomenology (Dorothy E. Smith), and interactive observation processes (Evelyn Fox Keller). A principled rejection of a model of objectivity which relies on detachment is common to these various possibilities. Feminist philosophers do not suggest that only women could be successful scientists using such methodologies—methodology may be systematically connected with gender, but not with sex.   E.J.F.

*knowledge and science; feminism; feminist philosophy.

Sandra Harding, *The Science Question in Feminism* (Milton Keynes, 1986).
Evelyn Fox Keller, *A Feeling for the Organism: The Life and Work of Barbara McClintock* (New York, 1983).
——and Helen E. Longino (eds.), *Feminism and Science* (Oxford, 1996).
Nancy Tuana (ed.), *Feminism and Science* (Bloomington, Ind., 1989).

science, history of the philosophy of. Ancient Greek artisans, including navigators, farmers, architects, merchants, blacksmiths, shipbuilders, physicians, and chroniclers, were familiar with a great variety of materials, plants, animals, people, events. They dug tunnels, found ways to transport and to store perishable goods, and could identify and alleviate bodily and mental afflictions. They travelled across national boundaries and assimilated foreign ideas and techniques. Archaeological discoveries show how much was known, for example, about the properties of metals, their compounds and alloys, and how skilfully this knowledge was used. An enormous amount of information resided in the customs, the industries, and the common sense of the time.

Most Greeks took this abundance for granted. Not all of them were impressed by it. Aiming at something more profound, some early thinkers started the work of knowledge all over again, this time without details but with increased explicitness and rigour. They were *philosophers* because they preferred words to things, speculation to experience, principles to rules of thumb, and they did not mind when their ideas conflicted with traditions and phenomena of the most obvious kind. They were also religious and social reformers; they derided popular customs and beliefs, heaped scorn on the gods of tradition and replaced them by monsters (example: the God of Xenophanes, who is all thought and power, but lacks compassion). They were even scientists of sorts. They did not just pontificate, they argued for their views, and some of their ideas have survived until today.

Thus Parmenides claimed that the world was one, that change and subdivision did not exist, and that the lives of human beings which contained both were a chimera. The proof (which he presents as being revealed by a goddess) rests on three assumptions said to be self-evident: that *being is (*estin*), that not-Being is not (*ouk estin*), and that nothing is more fundamental than Being. The argument then proceeds as follows: if change and difference exist, then there exists a transition from Being to not-Being (which is the only alternative); not-Being is not, hence change and difference are not either. We have here an early example of a *reductio ad absurdum*—a type of reasoning that extended the domain of demonstrable truths and separated it from intuition. The premiss, *estin*, is the first explicit conservation law—it asserts the conservation of Being. Used in the form that nothing comes from nothing, it suggested more special conservation laws such as the conservation of matter (Antoine Lavoisier) or the conservation of energy (Robert von Mayer, who started a decisive paper with this very principle). The uniformity of Being survived as the idea that basic laws must be independent of space, time, and circumstance. 'For us physicists', wrote Einstein, almost repeating Parmenides, 'the distinction between past, present and future has no other meaning than that of an illusion, though a tenacious one.'

A third group that affected Western science and its philosophy were the early *scientists* themselves. They differed from philosophers by favouring specifics and from artisans by their theoretical bias. With the exception of physicians like Alcmaeon of Croton, who wrote a medical textbook and who lived, probably, in the early fifth century BC, they became professionals only at the time of the Sophists. Towards the middle of the fifth century BC arithmetic, geometry, astronomy, and harmonics were already dreaded subjects of instruction (Plato, *Protagoras* 318d–f). They were also centres of intellectual activity and popular interest; even Aristophanes made fun of mathematicians. The arguments between scientists, philosophers, and those artisans who explained and defended their enterprise in writing, as well as the more specific arguments between scientific, philosophical, and practical schools, form an early, rather heterogeneous, and not always fully documented, philosophy of science.

Thus we may conjecture that the transition from a geometry and *number theory whose propositions could be confirmed, one by one, by intuitively evident arrangements (pebble figures, drawings) to systems of statements based on principles and proofs was accompanied by a vigorous debate—but it is difficult to identify stages and individuals. In many subjects 'scientific' assumptions were closely intertwined with magical and religious ideas. This bothers historians, who want to describe the past exactly as it was but without conferring honour on what they regard as superstitious nonsense. It did not bother the author of *On the Sacred Disease*, who ridiculed temple medicine and regarded health and illness as purely natural phenomena, or the author of *On Ancient Medicine*, who rejected philosophy as being too remote for medical practice. Galen's essays on the nature of science illustrate the debate between empiricists and theoreticians in the second century AD.

In contrast with these local quarrels, Plato tried to build a philosophy that combined technical excellence with religion and an orderly politics. Outstanding scientists assisted him. Starting from the divine properties of judgement, foresight, and wisdom (*Laws* 892b2 ff.), Plato postulated that the basic *laws of the universe must be simple and timeless. Observed regularities, he said, do not reveal basic laws. They depend on matter, which is an agent of change. Even the best-established astronomical facts do not last for ever (*Republic* 530a8 ff.). To find the principles, say, of planetary motion, it is therefore necessary to develop mathematical models 'and to leave the phenomena of the heavens aside' (*Republic* 530b7 ff.). Strangely enough, this passage was reviled by scientists, who, being

aware of the many disturbances that conceal the 'pure case' (perturbations, the effects of tidal friction, precession, atmospheric refraction, instrumental failure, subjective errors, etc., in the case of planetary motion), often started with theories and considered observations only later. It is theory that teaches us what observations are and what they mean, said Einstein. Important discoveries (the stability of the planetary system, the details of Brownian motion, the particle character of light, the *uncertainty relations) were made by proceeding accordingly.

This was not the procedure favoured by Aristotle, however. Taking experience at face value, he tried to reconcile observations, common-sense, and abstract thought. He was the first systematic philosopher of science of the West. He raised many of the issues that constitute the subject today and suggested solutions that are still influential. He described how facts turn into concepts and, further, into principles (*Analytica posteriora* 99^{b}35 ff.) and how things give rise to perceptions (*De anima* 418^{a}4 ff., 424^{a}17 ff.). For Aristotle these were natural processes which obeyed his general laws of motion and guaranteed the consistency of his empiricism. The deductive structure he proposed for *explanations served the exposition, not the discovery, of knowledge: Aristotle had no explicit theory of research. However, he left us examples which show what he did.

He began with 'phenomena'. These could be observations, common opinions, traditional beliefs, conceptual relations, or the views of earlier thinkers. Aristotle used special teams to collect them; he established a natural history museum and a library of maps and manuscripts, and laid the foundation of all histories of Greek philosophy, mathematics, astronomy, medicine, and forms of government. Next he analysed the phenomena in a particular area; he extrapolated and removed contradictions, staying close to observation when the area was empirical, or to linguistic usage when it was abstract. His notion of place, for example, retains the idea that place is a container of sorts, but with the meaning of 'being in' freed from *paradoxes. Finally, he formulated definitions to summarize what he had obtained. A general theory of change and interaction, the conceptual possibilities discussed, for example, in his *Metaphysics*, and a theory of mathematics which explained how mathematical concepts functioned in his largely qualitative universe served as a framework. Aristotle also started and considerably advanced the study of social, biological, and psychological phenomena. 'No one prior to Darwin has made a greater contribution to our understanding of the living world than Aristotle', wrote E. Mayr, a leading modern biologist.

The rise of modern science undermined important parts of the Aristotelian enterprise. It was a complex process which is still not fully understood. Some earlier historians and philosophers have described it in a simple and tendentious way. This is not surprising. The participants themselves misled them.

Thus Newton asserted that natural laws could be made manifest by collecting 'phenomena' (which for him were either particular experimental findings or observable regularities like Kepler's laws), inferring conclusions, generalizing them 'by induction', and checking the result by comparing it with further facts. He thought that gravitation, the laws of motion, and the basic properties of light had been discovered and established in precisely this fashion. He added that known laws might be explained by 'hypotheses' and proposed a variety of models to make sense of the properties of light and matter.

This account suggests a hierarchy reaching from observations, measurements, low-level generalizations, and theories to entire sciences and overarching theoretical schemes. Indeed, such a hierarchy for a long time formed the background of discussions about the support, the implications, the explanatory (reductive) power, and the meaning of scientific statements. Scientists like Herschel and Whewell, and philosophers like Mill, Carnap, Hempel, Ernest Nagel, Popper, inductivists and deductivists alike, used the scheme, packing whatever fissures they perceived into 'evidence', 'initial conditions', 'auxiliary hypotheses', 'approximations', 'correspondence rules', and 'ceteris paribus clauses'. In a purely formal way they preserved the coherence of the knowledge 'on top' and its continuity with what went on 'below'.

Kant's codification of Newtonian science, the attempt of *logical empiricists to 'reconstruct' or 'explicate' science by translating it into a uniform language, and the idea of a uniform *scientific method centred in physics further increased the impression of compactness. Remaining cracks were concealed by distinguishing, after Herschel, between a context of discovery and a context of justification: discovering new laws, facts, theories, may be a wildly irrational process—but establishing and presenting what has been found is subjected to strict and rational rules. This wonderfully harmonious and rather overwhelming fiction was gradually dismantled by a series of developments in the philosophy, the history, and the sociology of science as well as in the natural and social sciences themselves.

Problems occur already in Newton. Discussing the derivation of his law of gravitation, he admits that Kepler's laws are not strictly true, but decides to neglect 'those small and inconsiderable errors' (*Principia*, tr. Andrew Motte (1729), 401), which means that his empirical premisses are idealizations. Starting from here, Duhem argued that *all* experimental reports and low-level laws are idealizations and that the corresponding theories do not describe anything, while Cartwright showed that such theories are almost always false.

Newton also gave different weight to different phenomena. Being confronted with facts that contradicted his views (on light), he declared that his own results had already decided the matter. Again he admitted in practice what he had denied in philosophy, namely that the selection of data involves personal judgements. More recent research (Pickering, Galison, Rudwick, and others) has added that scientific facts are constituted by debate and compromise, that they harden with the distance from their origin, that they are manufactured rather than read

off nature, and that the activities that produce and/or identify them form complex and, with respect to theory, relatively self-contained cultures. Even laws and theories belonging to the same general field may split into separate domains with separate criteria. There are many breaks in the alleged hierarchy from fact to theory.

In the mean time historians and sociologists are taking a new look at power centres, institutions, and social groups; they point out that scientists often depend on patronage and choose their problems and their methods accordingly; they inquire how instruments like the telescope, the microscope, the air pump, or Millikan's oil-drop experiments could produce results and change views long before they were theoretically understood; they trace the changing relations between philosophers (who had defined reality), mathematicians (who had ordered events in it), and artisans (who were granted skills but denied understanding). On a more theoretical level they explore the role of terms not directly related to observation and describe how even relatively simple acts of perception (such as seeing a fly) were gradually broken up into processes (propagation of physical light; physiological reaction of eye and brain; 'mental' phenomena) whose mutual coherence is still a problem.

The role of experience turns out to be vastly more complex than empiricists up to and including the members of the *Vienna Circle had assumed. Common-sense and sciences such as biology, meteorology, geology, medicine, provide ample evidence for regularities *and* exceptions. Nature is what happens always, or almost always, said Aristotle (*De partibus animalium* 663^{b}27 ff.). Thus the belief in inexorable laws of nature which inspired Galileo, Descartes, and their followers, which gave rise to important theoretical developments and became a decisive ingredient of modern physics, not only was not based on experience, but clashed with it in many areas. This further widened the gap between common-sense, qualitative knowledge, and the gradually emerging edifice of modern science.

The edifice started falling apart in the twentieth century. *Mathematics, apparently the most secure and well-founded science, divided into schools with different philosophies and different conditions for acceptable results. Logicists argued that mathematics was part of logic and therefore as unambiguous and compelling as that discipline. Intuitionists interpreted mathematics as a human enterprise and inferred, for example, that some of Cantor's theorems and methods could not be accepted. Trying to save these and other parts of classical mathematics, Hilbert and his collaborators formalized the relevant proofs and examined the resulting structures in a way that satisfied the intuitionists' criteria. The programme collapsed when Gödel showed that the idea of mathematics as a comprehensive and provably consistent system was incoherent. Following Einstein, Reich-enbach, Grün-baum, and Michael Friedmann developed new philosophies of *space, *time, and *confirmation, while quantum mechanics opened a gulf between space-time and matter and closed the traditional gulf between observer and reality in ways that keep troubling scientists and have philosophers in a tizzy. Wittgenstein and Quine revealed the wishful thinking implicit in logical empiricism; biologists, chemists, historians, social scientists, aided by philosophers, reasserted an independence they had possessed in the nineteenth century, while the 'New History' reached levels of concreteness unimagined before. Surrounded by the ruins of once well-established patterns of knowledge, Kuhn, in 1962, proposed a new and, to most philosophers, rather upsetting account of scientific change. Like Aristotle, Kuhn emphasized the collaborative character of science and the role of shared facts, concepts, procedures. But he also asserted that change ('progress' in the older philosophical versions) might sever all logical connections with the past. Adopting his views, one could no longer assume that science accumulates facts, or that theories can be reduced, by approximation, to their more precise and more comprehensive successors.

Kuhn's book, *The Structure of Scientific Revolutions*, was the last major attempt so far to subject a complex practice, science, to abstract thought. It clashed with important ingredients of *rationalism. After 1962 philosophers tried either to reinforce these ingredients or to show that they were not in danger, or they introduced less binding rules, or else they concentrated on problems apparently untouched by Kuhn. Older approaches are still producing interesting results (example: Achinstein's Bayesian reconstruction of nineteenth-century debates about light and matter, which seemed to call for a less orderly account). The issue between *realism and *empiricism, which changed with the arrival of *quantum mechanics and was sharpened by the interventions of G. Maxwell, Richard Boyd, Ernan McMullin, Putnam, van Fraassen, Cartwright, and others, is as alive as ever. Already before Kuhn some writers had opted for cognitive models of scientific knowledge which are naturalistic—they do not distinguish between logical and empirical *'laws of thought'—and based on only partly rational patterns of adaptation. Others had emphasized details and objected to premature generalizations. These researchers appreciate what Kuhn did, but think that his approach is still far too abstract. They study particular events, conduct interviews, invade laboratories, challenge scientists, examine their technologies, images, conceptions, and explore the often glaring antagonisms between disciplines, schools, and individual research groups. Summarizing their results, we can say that the problem is no longer how to articulate the monolith SCIENCE, but what to do with the scattered collection of efforts that has replaced it.

A topic that was often neglected or dealt with in a dogmatic way is *the authority of science*. Is science the best type of knowledge we possess, or is it just the most influential? This way of putting the question has by now become obsolete. Science is not one thing, it is many; it is not closed, but open to new approaches. Objections to novelty and to alternatives come from particular groups with vested interests, not from science as a whole. It is therefore possible to gain understanding and to solve problems by combining bits and pieces of 'science' with prima facie 'unscientific' opinions and procedures. Architecture, technology, work in *artificial intelligence, management science, ecology, public health, and community development are examples. Purely theoretical subjects have profited from foreign invasions. One can even succeed by altogether staying outside 'science'. Numerous non-scientific cultures supported their members materially and spiritually. True, they ran into difficulties—but so did our science-based Western civilization. The old antagonism between practice and theory and the related antagonism between 'scientific' and 'unscientific' approaches may still survive in practice, or in some archaic slogans; however, it has lost much of its philosophical bite.   P.K.F.

*medicine, philosophy of; revolutions, scientific.

The many aspects and schools of ancient science are discussed, with ample literature, in the books and articles of G. E. R. Lloyd. Ernan McMullin, *The Inference that Makes Science* (Milwaukee, 1992) is a concise account that includes the medieval period. For the changing ways of dealing with scientific practice see A. Pickering (ed.), *Science as a Practice and Culture* (Chicago, 1992). I. Hacking, *Representing and Intervening* (Cambridge, 1983) describes the fruitful confusion of post-Kuhnian thought, to which Hacking himself has made important contributions.

science, problems of the philosophy of. The philosophy of science can be divided into two broad areas: the epistemology of science and the metaphysics of science. The epistemology of science discusses the justification and objectivity of scientific knowledge. The metaphysics of science discusses philosophically puzzling aspects of the reality uncovered by science.

Questions about the epistemology of science overlap with questions about knowledge in general. A central issue is the problem of induction. *Induction is the process which leads us from observations of particular cases to such universal conclusions as that 'All bodies fall with constant acceleration'. The problem is that such arguments are not logically valid. The truth of the particular premisses does not guarantee the truth of the universal conclusion. That all bodies observed so far have fallen with constant acceleration does not guarantee that all future ones will do so too.

One popular response to the problem of induction is due to Karl Popper. In Popper's view, science does not rely on induction in the first place. Rather it puts forward hypotheses in a conjectural spirit, and then strives to refute them. Popper argues that as long as such hypotheses are falsifiable, in the sense that there are possible observations that would disprove them, then the objectivity of science is assured.

Critics of Popper's 'falsificationism' complain that it offers no account of our entitlement to believe in the truth of scientific theories, rather than their falsity. Popper only accounts for negative scientific knowledge, as opposed to positive knowledge. He rightly points out that a single counter-example can show us that a scientific theory is wrong. But he says nothing about what can show us that a scientific theory is right. Yet it is positive knowledge of this latter kind that is supposed to follow from inductive inferences. What is more, it is this kind of positive knowledge that makes induction so important. We can cure diseases and send people to the moon because we know that certain causes do always have certain results, not because we know that they don't. If Popper cannot explain how we sometimes know that 'All A's are B's', rather than just 'It's false that all A's are B's', then he has surely failed to deal properly with the problem of induction.

An alternative response to the problem of induction is offered by *Bayesian confirmation theory. Bayesians argue that our beliefs come in degrees, and that such degrees of belief, when rational, conform to the probability calculus. In itself, this does not imply that any particular degree of belief in universal scientific theories is mandated—only that an individual's degrees of belief must respect the axioms of probability. However, Bayesians also argue that *Bayes's theorem implies a rational strategy for updating our degrees of belief in response to new evidence, and in particular that it implies we should increase our degree of belief in a scientific theory when its predictions are confirmed. On this basis they argue that everybody ought to come to attach a high credence to any universal generalization that is repeatedly borne out by experience. The idea is thus that, given enough evidence, everybody will eventually end up believing true universal generalizations, even if they attach different degrees of belief to them to start with. However, this doesn't work for all possible initial degrees of belief. Some eccentric initial degrees of belief are consistent with the axioms of probability, but will not lead to eventual convergence. So, for example, Bayesians don't explain what is wrong with people who never end up believing universal generalizations because they always think it is probable that the course of nature is going to change tomorrow. This shows that Bayesianism provides at best a partial solution to the problem of induction. Bayesianism may show us how our initial degrees of belief constrain the way we should respond in response to new evidence. But it needs to be supplemented by some further account of why some initial degrees of belief are objectively superior to others.

Another central problem in the epistemology of science is the possibility of knowledge of unobservables like viruses and electrons. Instrumentalists deny that scientific theories about unobservables can be accepted as true descriptions of an unobservable world. Rather they hold that such theories are at best useful instruments for generating observational predictions. They are opposed by those who take the realist view that science can and does discover truths about unobservables.

Some instrumentalists defend their view by appeal to the underdetermination of theory by data. According to this claim, any given body of observational data will always be compatible with a number of mutually incompatible theories about unobservables, and so cannot compel the choice of any particular such theory. This claim can be defended in turn by appeal to the 'Duhem–Quine thesis', which says that you can always retain any particular theoretical proposition in the face of apparently contrary evidence, by making adjustments to other auxiliary hypotheses in your overall theory. An alternative route to the underdetermination of theory by data is to observe that, given any successful theory that explains the observational data, we can always 'cook up' an alternative theory which explains the same observational facts. For example, Darwinism may successfully explain the fossil record, but so does Philip Henry Gosse's hypothesis that God put the fossils there in order to test our faith.

The doctrine of *instrumentalism rests on a distinction between what is observable and what is not. This distinction is not unproblematic. Some philosophers of science, most notably T. S. Kuhn and Paul Feyerabend, argue that observation is 'theory-laden', by which they mean that our prior theories influence what observations we make and what significance we attach to them. They infer from this that different scientific theories are often 'incommensurable', in the sense that there is no theory-neutral body of observational judgements to adjudicate between them. Kuhn argues that the history of science displays a succession of 'paradigms', sets of assumptions and exemplars which condition the way scientists solve problems and understand data, and which are only overthrown in occasional 'scientific revolutions' when scientists switch from one theoretical faith to another.

Kuhn and Feyerabend thus in effect generalize the instrumentalists' doubts about scientific truth. Whereas instrumentalists hold that claims about scientific unobservables cannot be accepted as true descriptions of reality, Kuhn and Feyerabend say the same about observational claims too. Not all epistemologists of science accept Kuhn's and Feyerabend's *epistemological relativism. On the issue of observational claims, most would maintain that, even if the line between observables and unobservables is neither sharp nor immutable, basic observational judgements can still provide an impartial test of a theory's predictions. And, on the issue of theories about unobservables, many would maintain that, even if theories are always underdetermined in the sense that a number of different theories will always be *compatible* with any given body of data, it does not necessarily follow that we cannot rationally choose between such theories, for some of those theories may be better *supported* than others by that body of data.

There is, however, another powerful argument against the realist view that scientific theories are true descriptions of an independent reality. This is the poor past form of such theories. Many past scientific theories, from Ptolemaic astronomy to the phlogiston theory of combustion, have turned out to be false. So it seems we should infer, by a 'pessimistic meta-induction', that since past scientific theories have normally been false, present and future scientific theories are likely to be false too.

In response, it can be argued that even false past theories contained a large element of truth, and therefore that present and future theories can be expected to *approximate* to the truth. Moreover, some philosophers detect a pattern of convergence, and argue that the succeeding scientific theories are moving *closer and closer* to the truth. These views, however, presuppose a notion of 'likeness to truth', or *verisimilitude. It has proved surprisingly difficult to give a clear meaning to this notion. The earliest attempts to define this notion, due to Popper and others, have proved incoherent, and it is not clear whether a satisfactory clarification of this notion is possible.

During the 1980s a number of philosophers adopted a *naturalized* approach to the epistemology of science. Rather than seeking to identify *a priori rules of scientific method, they look to the history of science and other *a posteriori disciplines to show which methodological strategies are in fact effective means to the achievement of scientific goals. It is possible to combine this naturalized approach with the realist view that the goal of scientific theorizing is to uncover the truth. However, in the light of the arguments mentioned above, most naturalized epistemologists of science reject truth as a sensible goal for science, and instead investigate strategies for achieving such theoretical goals as simplicity, predictive success, and *heuristic fertility.

Turning now to the metaphysics of science, a central issue is the analysis of *causality. According to *David Hume, causation, as an objective relation, is simply a matter of constant conjunction: one event causes another just in case events of the first type are constantly conjoined with events like the second. This analysis, however, generates a number of problems. First, there is the question of distinguishing genuine causal *laws of nature from accidentally true constant conjunctions: being a screw in my desk could well be constantly conjoined with being made of copper, without its being true that those screws are made of copper *because* they are in my desk. Second, there is a problem about the direction of causation: how do we tell causes from effects, given that a constant conjunction of A-type events with B-type events immediately implies a constant conjunction of B-type events with A-type events? And, third, there is the issue of probabilistic causation: do causes have to determine their effects, or is it enough that they are probably (rather than 'constantly') conjoined with them?

Many philosophers of science this century have preferred to talk about *explanation rather than causation. According to the popular *covering-law model of explanation, developed by Carl Hempel, a particular event is explained if its occurrence can be deduced from the occurrence of other particular events, with the help of one or more laws. But this is little different from Hume's account of causation, and not surprisingly faces essentially the same problems. How do we tell laws from accidents? Can't we sometimes deduce 'backwards', from causes to effects—as when we infer the height of the flagpole from the length of the shadow—even though we don't want to

say that the length of the shadow explains the height of the flagpole? And aren't there cases where we can explain one event—Mr X contracting cancer, say—by another—his smoking sixty cigarettes a day—even though we can't deduce the former from the latter, since their connection is only probabilistic?

On the question of distinguishing laws from accidents, there are two possible strategies. The first remains faithful to the Humean view that law statements assert nothing more than constant conjunction, and then seeks to explain why some statements of constant conjunction—the laws—are more important than others—the accidents. The best-known version of this Humean strategy, originally proposed by F. P. Ramsey and later revived by David Lewis, argues that laws are those true generalizations that can be fitted into an ideal systematization of knowledge—or, as Ramsey put it, laws are a 'consequence of those propositions which we should take as axioms if we knew everything and organized it as simply as possible in a deductive system'. The alternative, non-Humean strategy, whose most prominent defender is D. M. Armstrong, rejects the presupposition that laws involve nothing more than constant conjunctions, and instead postulates a relationship of 'necessitation' which obtains between event-types which are related by law, but not between those which are only accidentally conjoined.

On the question of the direction of causation, Hume himself simply said that the *earlier* of two constantly conjoined events is the cause, and the *later* the effect. But there are a number of objections to using the earlier–later asymmetry of time to analyse the cause–effect asymmetry. For a start, it seems to be at least conceivable that there should be causes that are simultaneous with their effects, or even causes that come after their effects. In addition, there seem to be good reasons for wanting to run the analysis in the opposite direction, and use the direction of causation to analyse the direction of time. If we do this, then we will want some time-independent account of the direction of causation. A number of such accounts have been proposed. David Lewis argues that the asymmetry of causation derives from the 'asymmetry of overdetermination': while the *overdetermination of effects by causes is very rare, it is absolutely normal for causes to be 'overdetermined' by a large number of chains of independent effects, each of which suffices for the earlier cause. Other writers have appealed to a related probabilistic asymmetry to explain causal asymmetry, pointing out that the different causes of any given common effect are normally probabilistically independent of each other, but the different effects of a common cause are normally probabilistically correlated.

The rise of *quantum mechanics, and in particular the experimental disproof of Bell's inequality, has persuaded many philosophers of science of the falsity of *determinism. In line with this, they have sought to develop models of causation in which causes only probabilify, rather than determine, their effects. The earliest such models, influenced by Carl Hempel's account of 'inductive-statistical' explanation, required that causes should give their effects a *high* probability. However, while smoking unequivocally causes cancer, it never makes it highly probable. So more recent models simply require that causes *increase* the probability of their effects, even if this is merely from a low figure to a slightly less low figure. Models of probabilistic causation need to guard against the possibility that probabilistic associations between events may be *spurious* rather than genuinely causal, like the association between barometers falling and subsequent rain. It is an open question whether such spurious associations can be ruled out by purely probabilistic means, or whether further non-probabilistic criteria need to be introduced.

The notion of *probability is of philosophical interest independently of its connection with causation. There are a number of different ways of interpreting the mathematical calculus of probability. *Subjective* theories of probability, which developed out of J. M. Keynes's logical theory of probability, understand probabilities as subjective degrees of belief. This is the interpretation assumed by Bayesian confirmation theorists. However, most philosophers of probability argue that we need an *objective* interpretation of probability in addition to this subjective account. According to the *frequency* theory of Richard von Mises, the probability of any given type of result is the limit of the relative frequency with which it occurs in longer and longer sequences drawn from some infinite 'reference class'. One difficulty facing the frequency theory is that it will ascribe a different probability to a given single-case result when that result is considered as a member of different reference classes. To rule this out, Karl Popper proposed that probabilities should be regarded as *propensities* of specific experimental set-ups, in the sense that only frequencies in reference classes generated by repetitions of the same experimental set-up should count as genuine probabilities. Later versions of this *propensity* theory dispense with the reliance on infinite reference classes, and simply take probability to be a quantitative feature of particular set-ups, which is evidenced by frequencies in repetitions of those set-ups, but cannot be defined in terms of frequencies.

The philosophical interpretation of objective probability is tied up with our understanding of modern quantum mechanics. The interpretation of quantum mechanics, however, is still an open problem in the *philosophy of physics. Taken at face value, quantum mechanics says that when physical systems are measured, they suddenly acquire definite values of observable parameters which they did not have before. The theory specifies the probabilities of different such values, but cannot predict with certainty which will be observed. Albert Einstein's response was that quantum mechanics must therefore be incomplete, and that a future theory would identify the 'hidden variables' which do determine observed results. However, since Einstein's time new evidence against such hidden-variable theories has emerged. John Bell showed that any version of such a hidden-variable theory that respected the principles of special relativity would contra-

dict the observational predictions of quantum mechanics; moreover, experiments have now confirmed that these quantum-mechanical predictions are correct. True, this does leave the possibility of hidden-variable theories that do not respect special relativity and allow faster-than-light causal influences, like David Bohm's version of quantum mechanics, but these now have only minority support. If hidden variables are rejected, quantum mechanics then faces the problem of making sense of quantum *measurement as a process in which a previously indeterminate reality somehow 'collapses' into some definite observable state. It is not obvious that it can answer this challenge. Even though measurements are themselves physical processes, orthodox quantum mechanics offers no theory of why measurements precipitate definite observable values, but instead simply assumes this. It thus seems likely that a satisfactory understanding of quantum measurement will depend on some radically new interpretation of the theory. According to one increasingly popular view, it is an illusion that prior indeterminacies 'collapse' into a definite state when measured; rather, reality 'branches' into a plurality of distinct non-interacting futures, one for each possible result of the measurement.

A further metaphysical aspect of the philosophy of science is the issue of *teleology. This is mainly a topic in the philosophy of *biology, since it is in the biological realm that we find the paradigm examples of teleological explanation, as when we say, for example, that chlorophyll is present in plants *in order to* facilitate photosynthesis. Explanations like these are of philosophical interest because they explain causes by effects, and so seem to run counter to the normal pattern of explaining effects by causes. Carl Hempel argued that such explanations are simply a species of covering-law explanation in which the fact used to explain—the photosynthesis—happens to come later in time than the fact which gets explained—the chlorophyll. However, there are counter-examples to this proposal, and attempts to tighten it up by requiring that the items involved be parts of some self-regulating system have proved problematic. The majority of philosophers of science would probably now favour a different approach, according to which teleological explanations in biology are a form of disguised causal explanation, in which implicit reference is made to a hypothesized history of natural selection during which the trait in question—chlorophyll—was favoured because it produced the relevant effect—photosynthesis. Some philosophers would question whether such 'backward-looking' explanations really deserve to be called 'teleological', since they do not in fact explain the present by the future, but by past histories of selection; this issue, however, is essentially a terminological matter.

'Special sciences' like biology, chemistry, geology, meteorology, and so on raise the question of *reductionism. One science is said to be 'reduced' by another if its categories can be defined in terms of the categories of the latter, and its laws explained by the laws of the latter. *Reductionists* argue that the sciences form a hierarchy in which the higher can be reduced by the lower: thus biology might be reduced by physiology, physiology by chemistry, and eventually chemistry by physics.

The issue of reductionism can be viewed either historically or metaphysically. The historical question is whether science characteristically progresses by later theories reducing earlier ones. The metaphysical question is whether the different areas of science describe different realities, or just the one physical reality described at different levels of detail. Though often run together, these are different questions. Taken as a general thesis, historical reductionism is false, for reasons relating to the 'pessimistic meta-induction' discussed above: while there are some historical episodes where new scientific theories have reduced old ones, there are as many where new theories have shown old theories to be false, and so eliminated rather than reduced them. This does not mean, however, that metaphysical reductionism is false. Even if science proceeds towards the overall truth by fits and starts, there may be general reasons for expecting that this overall truth, when eventually reached, will reduce to physical truth.

One possible such argument stems from the *causal interaction* between the phenomena discussed in the special sciences and physical phenomena. Thus biological, geological, and meteorological events all unquestionably have physical effects; this might seem to require that they be made of physical components. It is doubtful, however, whether this suffices to establish full-scale reductionism, as opposed to the thesis of supervenience, which holds that special properties are determined by physical properties, even though they are not identical with them as types. For example, whether or not some being is adding 2 and 2 is arguably determined by its physical make-up; yet the property of adding 2 plus 2 cannot be identified with any specific physical property, for many different beings, with different physical constitutions, are in principle capable of adding 2 plus 2. If we accept supervenience, and reject the stronger claim of 'type identity' between special and physical properties, then we will also reject the reductionist thesis that all special laws can be explained by physical laws. Instead we will hold that there are *sui generis* special laws, patterns which cover special types which vary in their physical make-up, and which therefore cannot be explained in terms of physical law alone.   D.P.

*science, history of the philosophy of; scientific method; hypothetico-deductive method; nomic necessity; natural law.

I. Hacking, *Representing and Intervening* (Oxford, 1983).
C. Hempel, *Aspects of Scientific Explanation* (New York, 1965).
T. S. Kuhn, *The Structure of Scientific Revolutions* (Chicago, 1962).
E. Nagel, *The Structure of Science* (New York, 1961).
K. Popper, *The Logic of Scientific Discovery* (London, 1959).
B. van Fraassen, *The Scientific Image* (Oxford, 1980).

science, pseudo: *see* pseudo-science.

science, social philosophy of. General term for the investigation of moral and political issues in the practice of science. These issues are very varied, ranging from the morality of animal experimentation to the accusation that science promotes a reductive, disenchanting world outlook. There are two overall questions: whether scientists should subscribe to an ethical code (like the Hippocratic Oath); and whether there is a clear distinction between cognitive ('purely scientific') and ethical values in science.

A.BEL.

David B. Resnik, *The Ethics of Science: An Introduction* (London, 1998).

science, the unity of: *see* unity of science.

science and knowledge: *see* knowledge and science.

science and life: *see* life and science.

science and philosophy: *see* philosophy and science.

science, art, and religion. The theories of science aim at accounts of the world which depend on no particular perspective on the world and no particular type of observer. Though in practice they never completely abstract from idiosyncratically human perceptions and forms of thought, their success, or otherwise, depends on how they fare against a nature which is impervious to our feelings and perceptions. *Art, by contrast, works with visions of the world expressed in concrete form, adapted precisely to human sensory faculties and emotional sensibilities. Works of art are judged by their success over time in evoking responses to human perceivers.

Religion shares the scientific aim of giving an account of the world as it is in itself, not as it is for us. But, unlike science, and closer to a work of art, it reveals the world as informed by purpose, will, and personality, as expressing the intentions of a transcendent being. In presupposing a transcendent being, religion avoids the possibility of direct refutation by empirical or scientific evidence. Even the facts of evil and suffering are normally, and from his point of view not unreasonably, taken by the religious believer to be consistent with a divine purpose which, being transcendent, we cannot fully fathom. But equally, although religion provides an answer to the questions of the meaning and ultimate genesis of the world's totality, which science raises but cannot answer, at least while staying within a strictly empirical framework, religion's appeal to transcendence deprives it of any direct empirical support. Religion, properly conceived, is based on the experiences of meaning and value which it is the province of art rather than science to express and explore. In seeing value and personality written into the very fabric of the world, in a way which does not depend on our wishes or desires, is the religious believer indulging in mere projection or wish-fulfilment? In considering this question, we should remember that science as such cannot pronounce on the questions relating to the world as a whole, and also reflect on how hard it is to live as if our values were just projections of human feeling, individual or collective.   A.O'H.

T. Nagel, *The View from Nowhere* (New York, 1986).

A. O'Hear, 'Science and Religion', *British Journal for the Philosophy of Science* (1993).

scientific determinism: *see* determinism, scientific.

scientific method. Although the question of scientific method is generally thought to resolve itself into two parts—the problem of discovery and the problem of justification—it seems fair to say that philosophers have felt significantly more comfortable with the latter than the former. Indeed there are those (like Karl Popper) who have argued that philosophy can say nothing of value about discovery and that the whole topic is best left to the historian or psychologist.

Certainly it seems the case that the problem of justification lays itself more readily open to the forming of rules and criteria for identifying and producing the best kind of science. Traditionally, the discussion has been located against the ideal of an *axiom system, a powerful model set by the successes of Greek geometry. Transcending mere common-sense knowledge, science shares with mathematics some elements of its necessity and universality, although what distinguishes science from pure thought is its mandate to understand the world of empirical experience.

How does one establish the truths of science? Francis Bacon argued that scientific knowledge is gained and confirmed by a process of *induction. Precisely how this should be understood and performed has been a matter of ongoing debate. Many, although not Bacon himself, have argued that the process of induction is merely one of simple enumeration, where essentially what one does is count the cases favourable to a particular hypothesis. But this suggestion can be faulted on at least two grounds. First, it is simply false of the way in which real science proceeds. No one just goes out and counts instances, without a prior theory for inspiration. Second, no matter how much one counts, the result will always be in doubt, because of the ever-present possibility of counter-examples.

Seizing on this second point, a number of philosophers have made a virtue out of necessity, arguing that the aim of science is never to achieve certain knowledge. Rather, in the light of intuitions and previous understanding, one proposes hypotheses which one then judges against experience. Inasmuch as they stand the test of time, understanding advances; but since all scientific claims are by their very nature falsifiable (to use Popper's term), there is always the possibility of disconfirmation and the need for replacement by a more powerful hypothesis.

An important body of scientific claims are causal, meaning that in some sense they tell us why things work. Newton set the modern agenda for discussion about *cause, arguing that the best causes are *verae causae*. This claim has been variously interpreted. The English empiricist philosopher John Herschel argued that one must aim always for analogical support, based on everyday easily understood and encountered examples. The English

rationalist philosopher William Whewell argued that one should aim to locate one's causes at the focus of a 'concilience of inductions', where many different pieces of evidence combine to point to one true explanation. To use a detective-story analogy, whereas Herschel argues that to pin the guilt on a suspect one must have eyewitness testimony, Whewell preferred circumstantial evidence, where the clues all pointed to the guilty party.

This century's advances in the understanding of the micro-world beyond the senses have led to refinements in discussions of method, as have the successes of the non-physical sciences. Much effort has been given to the question of whether there is one method uniquely for all science. Although Bacon argued strongly against teleology in science, many biologists would still claim that their material demands an understanding in terms of purpose or final cause. This is neither something theological nor something demanding causes acting out of the future and on to the present. It is something which recognizes the distinctively adapted nature of organic beings. One has a metaphor of design—a metaphor because the work of organic organization is being done by Darwin's mechanism of natural selection rather than a conscious being—which yet forces one to think of the ends that features serve, rather than merely their material causes.

Although discovery may be problematic, there are always those who try to approach it philosophically. Many have thought that Mill's so-called methods are a good start, for here one has a number of recipes for working out the existence and nature of causes. (For example, the *method of agreement claims that if one has a number of different cases of the production of an effect and only one antecedent phenomenon in common, then it is the cause.) However, as Whewell pointed out, although Mill's methods may be valuable in the discerning of causes, they are not very helpful in deciding initially what phenomena are worth explaining and what different circumstances lead to these phenomena. In other words, their virtue lies truly in the context of discovery.

In recent years, there have been renewed attempts to crack the discovery problem. Working from insights of the *pragmatists, Norwood Russell Hanson argued that one needs a kind of logic of *abduction, which throws up plausible hypotheses. Some have been attracted to the nature of analogy in their quest for insight. And yet others have turned to the newly developed power of computers for clues to a logic and method of discovery. But although certainly much has been learned thereby about the nature of human creative reasoning, it seems fair to say that, in the search for formal rules of method, we are little further ahead than we were when we began. Perhaps there are some things which simply do not yield to philosophical analysis, and Popper's conclusion is less one of despair than of realism. Or perhaps the very distinction itself is ill-taken, and (as various historians and sociologists would argue) the very act of scientific creativity can take place only within a certain culture and against a background of already held belief. Hence, there never can be a claim which is epistemically neutral nor can there be a discovery except some commitments have already been made.   M.R.

*methodology; scientism.

J. Losee, *The History of the Philosophy of Science* (Oxford, 1972).
K. Popper, *The Logic of Scientific Discovery*, Eng. tr. (London, 1959).

scientism. 'Scientism' is a term of abuse. Therefore, perhaps inevitably, there is no one simple characterization of the views of those who are thought to be identified as prone to it. In philosophy, a commitment to one or more of the following lays one open to the charge of scientism.

(a) The sciences are more important than the arts for an understanding of the world in which we live, or, even, all we need to understand it.

(b) Only a scientific methodology is intellectually acceptable. Therefore, if the arts are to be a genuine part of human knowledge they must adopt it.

(c) Philosophical problems are scientific problems and should only be dealt with as such.

A successful accusation of scientism usually relies upon a restrictive conception of the sciences and an optimistic conception of the arts as hitherto practised. Nobody espouses scientism; it is just detected in the writings of others. Among the accused are P. M. and P. S. Churchland, W. V. Quine, and *Logical Positivism.   P.J.P.N.

T. Sorell, *Scientism* (London, 1991).

scope. Many words have the syntactic role of building one or more expressions of some type into another expression of some type, as 'but' can build the sentences 'Bill is rich' and 'Jill is stinking rich' into the sentence 'Bill is rich but Jill is stinking rich'. The scope of such a word is the immediate outcome of this process. For example, the scope of 'fashion' in 'He kept his house Bristol fashion' is the adverbial phrase 'Bristol fashion', but in 'The Bristol fashion experts were wrong' it is the noun phrase 'fashion experts'. Some structural ambiguities are ambiguities of scope, for example 'superfluous' in 'Try our superfluous hair remover'. A virtue of the *artificial languages of logic is to represent many structural ambiguities of English, e.g. 'Some professors get drunk every night', as demanding a decision on the scope of some logical *constant.   C.A.K.

R. M. Sainsbury, *Logical Forms: An Introduction to Philosophical Logic* (Oxford, 1991).

scope fallacies. Scope fallacies are endemic in philosophy and in ordinary language. 'If it snows the crops will inevitably fail' suggests misleadingly that the scope of 'inevitably' is the consequent rather than the whole conditional. A standard example is to be found in proofs of God's existence which move from 'For every contingent being there is a time when it does not exist' to 'There is a time when every contingent being does not exist'. Subtler is 'Statements of identity are, when true, necessarily true. Therefore since Elizabeth is the Queen of England, neces-

sarily Elizabeth is the Queen of England'. It is true, of the person who is, contingently, the Queen of England that, necessarily, she is identical with Elizabeth, but it is not true of that person that, necessarily, she is Queen of England.

J.J.M.

de re and *de dicto*; scope.

S. Kripke, 'Speaker's Reference and Semantic Reference', in P. A. French, T. E. Uehling Jr., and H. K. Wettstein (eds.), *Contemporary Perspectives in the Philosophy of Language* (Minneapolis, 1979).

Scottish philosophy. Scottish universities had, until recently, a traditional reverence for philosophy, which was compulsory for every degree. The tradition began in the University of St Andrews, founded in the fifteenth century. Initially the universities relied on their seniors in England and France to train their teachers. But by the end of the sixteenth century they were ready to provide their own. The subject was divided into logic, pneumatology (psychology), moral philosophy, and natural philosophy (physical science). There was no idea of exclusive specialization, let alone that the best results require it. The policy of non-specialization allowed Hume, Smith, and Reid, at the tradition's high point, to variously combine psychology, moral philosophy, optics, mechanics, economics, history, and jurisprudence. Philosophy and science were taken to be one. But, as physical science advanced and the mind–body distinction took a firmer grip, philosophers in Scotland, as elsewhere, increasingly doubted the philosophical competence of science and instead concentrated on developing metaphysical *idealism.

The earliest Scottish philosophers of note came from the south-east. They were Duns Scotus (*c.*1266–1308), the 'subtle doctor', and John Mair (or Major) (*c.*1467–1550). The former was a Franciscan academic who lectured in Cambridge, Oxford, and Paris. Primarily a theologian, he had a distinctive doctrine of *free will, emphasizing the possibility of genuine altruism, a view subsequently resumed by Hutcheson and his followers. John Mair, educated in Cambridge, also lectured in Paris, before returning to take up teaching and administrative posts in his native land. His approach seems to have been logico-linguistic.

Lacking a conception of intellectual progress, Scottish philosophy of this period assumed that anything worth knowing had already been divinely imparted to the ancient Jews or discovered by the ancient Greeks. The Reformation did not dispel this prejudice, but, if anything, reinforced it, favouring classical writers, like Plato and Cicero. The prevailing practice was to comment on whatever texts could be retrieved from ancient times, whether in Latin, Greek, or Hebrew. Thus the seventeenth century produced no original philosopher in the universities educating the professional classes. Scottish academics, by no means insular, were conscious of continental and English genius, like that of the Dutch lawyer Grotius, the French mathematician and natural philosopher Descartes, and the English natural philosophers Newton and Boyle. They also admired John Locke, who based his epistemology on physical science.

The time was ripe to earn the benefit of an educational system which was non-specialist yet capable of imparting the latest discoveries in mental and natural philosophy. The results were impressive. In mental philosophy emphasis on feeling and sensation as sources of belief produced the great works of Hutcheson, Hume, Smith, and Reid. Hutcheson showed that moral approval is a kind of pleasure, and therefore is not purely rational. Hume accepted this and went on to extend anti-rationalism in a unique claim that important beliefs, in causes, in the *external world, and in *personal identity, are instinctive and non-rational. He showed that a cause can never be completely proved and that belief in a cause is a conditioned reflex, not a logical deduction. Belief in the external world, and in personal identity, is also the result of conditioning and cannot be proved; so is belief in God. His views were widely misunderstood as being sceptical about any kind of unperceived existence, whereas he was only pointing out that beliefs about the world, causes, and personal identity go beyond any evidence. Reid, using contemporary science to develop indirect realism, and seeing Hume as a sceptic, blamed him for saying that we mistake sensations for external objects and that beliefs are images of sensations. Though critical of Hume, he agreed that the mind generates beliefs from materials which are logically inadequate—and a good thing too, he thought. Whereas Hume and Reid were not sceptical about the mind's irrational usefulness, they were sceptical about philosophy's power to do any better. It was felt by some that they had downgraded reason and the nobility of their subject. Kant disparaged them, while thanking them for waking him from his dogmatic slumber, and argued that philosophy can justify belief in the external world, in causality, and in personal identity, as necessary presuppositions for objective understanding. Hume and Reid had never doubted the need for such presuppositions, but thought it obvious, as indeed it is, that such need is no evidence of truth.

Reid's philosophy had critics, beginning with Dugald Stewart who made minor refinements. William Hamilton went further, declaring that the cause of sensation cannot be known. James Frederick Ferrier, an idiosyncratic idealist, proposed that sensations have a dual nature as occurring in perceptible sense-organs, while at the same time presenting themselves to consciousness as external objects, a view not unlike Hume's. Later, Andrew Seth, the first non-professorial lecturer appointed in Scotland (thanks to A. J. Balfour), attacked Hamiltonian agnosticism. He proudly defended what he called 'the Natural Realism of the Scottish philosophy', arguing that substance and quality are not distinct: sensation of qualities must be of substance, revealing what it is. Henry Langueville Mansel, an English theologian and pupil of Hamilton's, used his philosophical agnosticism to defend revealed religion, as Hume's agnosticism had been used for the same purpose in Germany. Anti-Hamiltonianism flared up in Glasgow, led by Edward Caird, Professor of

Moral Philosophy, who had imbibed German idealism at Balliol, to whose Mastership he gratefully returned.

In the twentieth century England escaped into empiricism, and the canny Scots concentrated on the history of philosophy. The early tradition of combining philosophy and science, weakened by idealism, had ended, though there was still a strong connection between philosophy and psychology, felt of all the sciences to be closest to spiritual reality. This may explain the subsequent appearance in Hume's university of a chair of paranormal psychology.

V.H.

*English philosophy; Irish philosophy.

A. Broadie, *The Tradition of Scottish Philosophy* (Edinburgh, 1990).
G. E. Davie, *The Scotch Metaphysics* (London, 2001).
James M'Cosh, *The Scottish Philosophy* (London, 1875).
Rudolf Metz, *A Hundred Years of British Philosophy* (London, 1938).
Andrew Seth, *Scottish Philosophy* (Edinburgh, 1890).

Scotus, John Duns: *see* Duns Scotus, John.

Scotus Eriugena, John: *see* Eriugena, John Scotus.

sea battle: *see* Łukasiewicz; many-valued logic.

sea-battle argument. Argument criticized by *Aristotle in *De Interpretatione*, book IX. Either there will be a sea battle tomorrow or there will not. These possibilities are mutually exclusive and jointly exhaustive. It seems, therefore, to be a necessary truth that there will be a sea battle tomorrow or there will be no sea battle. The future is inevitable now, it is just that we are presently ignorant of which future events will happen. The argument putatively establishes the fatalistic conclusions that everything that happens happens necessarily, and that it was always true that those events that do happen would happen.

In criticism, Aristotle argues that from the necessity of the disjunction $(p \lor -p)$ it does not follow that the disjunct p is necessary nor that the disjunct $-p$ is necessary. Although it is necessary that either a sea battle take place tomorrow or not, it is not necessary that it should take place tomorrow, and is it not necessary that it should not take place tomorrow. Therefore the argument does not validly establish that future events are inevitable. This is consistent with its being a necessary truth that either there will or will not be a sea battle tomorrow.

S.P.

*future contingents.

Aristotle's Categories and De Interpretatione, tr. J. L. Ackrill (Oxford, 1963).

Searle, John R. (1932–). Philosopher of mind and language at the University of California at Berkeley. The mind, for Searle, is *intentional (*à la* Brentano) in that perceptions, memories, imaginings, desires, and many other mental states take objects (e.g. I see *the car* and I remember *Aunt Fanny*). Language, seen by Searle mainly from the *speech-act tradition of J. L. Austin, is also intentional, but derivatively so. His intentional theory, and the emphasis he places on *consciousness as an intrinsic feature of the mind, put him at odds with behaviouristic, functional, and other materialistic theories of mind. For Searle, although the mind emerges from the body, it possesses an ineliminable subjective character with which materialistic accounts cannot adequately deal. In relation to this claim, he uses his famous *Chinese room argument to show that even though a 'system' (a computer and a person) inside a room can manipulate Chinese symbols, it does not necessarily operate on the level of meaning. To do that, mental (intentional) concepts need to be introduced into the system.   N.F.

J. R. Searle, *Speech Acts* (Cambridge, 1969).
—— *The Rediscovery of the Mind* (Cambridge, Mass., 1992).

secondary qualities: *see* primary and secondary qualities.

seeing as. In his later writings, Wittgenstein showed an interest in the phenomenon to which the *Gestalt* psychologists had drawn attention, of seeing (or hearing, or, . . .) something *as* something. The *duck-rabbit is an example: a picture that can be seen either as a duck or as a rabbit. Part of Wittgenstein's interest in this phenomenon had to do with his rejection of a naïve account of *perception; he took the interpretation of what is seen to be less separable from seeing itself than empiricist philosophers had been wont to think. But perception was not his only concern. We see one continuation of a number-series as 'more natural' or 'simpler' than another; see one grouping of objects in a class as 'cutting Nature at the joints', another not; and so on. Our use of concepts depends on 'seeing as'.   R.P.L.T.

*illusion, arguments from.

L. Wittgenstein, *Philosophical Investigations*, tr. G. E. M. Anscombe, 3rd edn. (Oxford, 1967).

self. The term 'self' is often used interchangeably with *'person', though usually with more emphasis on the 'inner', or psychological, dimension of personality than on outward bodily form. Thus a self is conceived to be a subject of consciousness, a being capable of thought and experience and able to engage in deliberative action. More crucially, a self must have a capacity for *self-consciousness, which partly explains the aptness of the term 'self'. Thus a self is a being that is able to entertain first-person thoughts.

A first-person thought is one whose apt expression in language requires the use of the first-person pronoun 'I', or some equivalent *indexical expression. However, it may not be right to insist that a self be capable of expressing its thoughts in language—even its first-person thoughts. Happily, we possess locutions for ascribing first-person thoughts to others without implying that they are capable of articulating those thoughts. One such locution is the 'he himself' construction. Thus if I ascribe to Fred the thought that *he himself* is fat, I ascribe to him a thought whose apt expression in English by Fred would be 'I am fat', though I do not imply that Fred is capable of so expressing that thought. Note that we must distinguish

this thought from a similar *third*-person thought that Fred might have about himself, whose apt expression in English by Fred might be 'Fred is fat' or 'That person is fat' (the latter said by Fred in reference to a person he sees reflected in a mirror, not realizing that it is himself that he sees).

It is plausible to require of a self not only a capacity to entertain first-person thoughts but also the possession of certain kinds of first-person knowledge. For example, it seems right to insist that a self must know, of any of its present, conscious thoughts, experiences, and actions, that they are *its own*. This is why the response of Mrs Gradgrind (in Charles Dickens's *Hard Times*), when asked on her sick-bed whether she was in pain, strikes us as so bizarre: 'I think there's a pain somewhere in the room, but I couldn't positively say that I have got it.' Our possession of such self-knowledge is connected with the phenomenon of 'immunity to error through misidentification' (Sydney Shoemaker). An example involving memory is provided by the apparent absurdity of supposing that I might accurately remember (as it were, 'from the inside') a meal in a restaurant attended by a number of people, and yet be in some doubt about whether *I* was one of those people. (As against this, however, Derek Parfit has argued that we could in principle inherit 'quasi-memories' from other people, including first-person 'memories' of what they, but not we, had done.)

So far we have largely been concerned with the *meaning* of the term 'self', that is, with the essential characteristics of selfhood. But metaphysicians are also interested in exploring the *nature* of the self, that is, what sort of *thing the self is, if indeed it is a 'thing' at all. In traditional terms, a distinction may be drawn between substantival and non-substantival theories of the self, the former contending that the self is a *substance, either physical or non-physical, the latter that it is a mode of substance. Philosophers like Hume, who regarded the self as 'nothing but a bundle of different perceptions', effectively treat the self as belonging to the category of modes. A problem with the Humean approach is that perceptions—that is, thoughts and experiences—seem to depend for their identity upon the identity of the selves who possess them, which implies that perceptions are modes *of selves* and hence that the latter have the status of substances *vis-à-vis* their thoughts and experiences, rather than being reducible to them.   E.J.L.

*homunculus.

D. Parfit, *Reasons and Persons* (Oxford, 1984).
S. Shoemaker, *Self-Knowledge and Self-Identity* (Ithaca, NY, 1963).
B. Williams, *Problems of the Self* (Cambridge, 1973).

self, bundle theory of the: *see* bundle theory of the self.

self-consciousness. One view of self-consciousness would be that it is the *consciousness of a special kind of object, 'the *self'. In reply, it has been claimed that just as the eye cannot see itself, so the self, understood as a subject of awareness, cannot be aware of itself as an object. According to Schopenhauer, for example, the suggestion that a subject can be an object to itself would be 'the most monstrous contradiction ever thought of'. More cautiously, it might be argued that the core of the intuitive notion of self-consciousness is what might be called *introspective* self-awareness, and that one cannot be introspectively aware of oneself as an object. Sydney Shoemaker's defence of this view of introspective self-awareness is to point out that in those cases in which one might be said to be conscious of oneself as an object—seeing oneself in a mirror, for example—one always has to identify the presented object as oneself. Since identification always carries with it the possibility of misidentification, first-person statements based on such awareness are not 'immune to error through misidentification' relative to the first-person pronoun. Yet, it seems to be a requirement on introspective self-awareness that it is capable of grounding first-person statements that are immune to this kind of error.

To say that a statement of the form 'I am *F*' is immune to error through misidentification relative to the first-person pronoun is to say that the following is not possible: one knows that someone is *F*, but one's statement is mistaken because, and only because, the person one knows to be *F* is not oneself. For example, if one were to judge 'I am in pain' on the basis of feeling pain, it could not happen that the person one knows to be in pain is not oneself. If self-ascriptions of mental states are immune to error through misidentification, then the awareness on which they are based may be introspective, but could not be awareness of oneself as an object.

Kant expressed this point by saying that the self as it is in itself cannot be 'intuited' or perceived by means of *inner sense. Since, for Kant, knowledge of an object requires both a concept and an intuition of it, he concluded that knowledge of the self as it is in itself is impossible. Kant did not, however, accept the Humean idea that there is no more to self-consciousness than consciousness of subjectless mental occurrences. Instead, he argued that consciousness of self consists in an ability to ascribe one's thoughts and experiences to oneself. The self-ascription of experiences was in turn claimed to require experience and knowledge of objects other than oneself. A variation on this suggestion is the idea, associated with P. F. Strawson, that for one to be able to ascribe experiences to oneself, one must also be able to ascribe them to subjects other than oneself.

A somewhat different approach would be to claim that self-consciousness necessarily involves awareness of one's own body. Since bodily self-ascriptions such as 'My legs are crossed' appear to be immune to error through misidentification when based on awareness of one's own body 'from the inside', this makes it plausible that such awareness is a genuine form of self-consciousness. If bodily awareness is also awareness of oneself as an object, then Shoemaker's argument may not, after all, be decisive. On the other hand, some have argued that the peculiarities of bodily awareness are such as to cast doubt on the idea that it is awareness of oneself as an object. The suggestion that self-consciousness requires bodily awareness is also controversial.   Q.C.

*introspection.

J. L. Bermúdez, *The Paradox of Self-Consciousness* (Cambridge, Mass., 1998).

Q. Cassam (ed.), *Self-Knowledge* (Oxford, 1994).

G. Ryle, *The Concept of Mind* (London, 1949).

S. Shoemaker, *Identity, Cause, and Mind*, expanded edn. (Oxford, 2003).

—— *The First-Person Perspective and Other Essays* (Cambridge, 1996).

P. F. Strawson, *Individuals* (London, 1959).

L. Wittgenstein, *The Blue and Brown Books* (Oxford, 1958).

self-control. Traditionally, a capacity to conduct oneself as one judges best when tempted to do otherwise. Self-control is the contrary of weakness of will or *akrasia*. Aristotle distinguishes self-control (*enkrateia*) from temperance (*sōphrosunē*). The latter, a moral virtue, is possessed only by individuals who have no improper or excessive desires regarding bodily pleasures and pains; self-controlled individuals have such desires, but they characteristically resist them, acting as they judge best. On more recent views, self-control may be exhibited in any sphere in which motivational states compete with a person's values, principles, or practical judgements, including practical and theoretical reasoning and the gathering and assessment of evidence for motivationally attractive or unattractive hypotheses (e.g. the hypothesis that one is popular or that one's spouse has been unfaithful).   A.R.M.

A. R. Mele, *Autonomous Agents: From Self-Control to Autonomy* (Oxford, 1995).

self-deception. Everything about the concept of 'self-deception' is controversial among philosophers, beginning with its definition. That human beings play a large and often wilful role in perpetuating their own ignorance and befuddlement is beyond dispute; but how legitimate is the traditional characterization of the activities subsumed under this role as 'self-deception'?

Dictionaries define the term unilluminatingly as the act of deceiving oneself or the state of being deceived by oneself. Since deception involves intentional misleading, such a definition invites the question precisely how one can both intend to be misled by oneself and succeed in such an endeavour. Can the *self perhaps be divided into a deceiving and a deceived part, as in Freud's view of the unconscious keeping information from the conscious self? Or must one adopt Sartre's paradoxical view, in *Being and Nothingness*, that 'I must know, as deceiver, the truth that is masked from me as deceived'?

Many reject such views as logically or psychologically impossible. Some claim that 'self-deception' refers to one or more of four restrictions on perception, none of which need involve the paradox of simultaneously deceiving and being deceived: first, the ignorance resulting from our necessarily limited capacity to respond to incoming information; second, the 'psychic numbing' that constitutes a reflex response to prolonged exposure to facts which would, if truly confronted each time, be difficult to bear—as when children shield themselves from fully responding to the violence they witness within the family or on television; third, mechanisms of denial whereby we may end up deceived about information that would otherwise be too painful to confront, even though we are not consciously deceiving ourselves; and, fourth, processes of more conscious avoidance such as procrastination, rationalization, and compartmentalization.

Advocates of political and religious doctrines have further disputed the nature of what we hide from ourselves. The greater their zeal in promoting particular truths, the more tempting it becomes for them to assume that non-believers are not merely in error but actually engaged in blocking truths they would otherwise have to acknowledge as utterly self-evident. In practice, this assumption easily leads to indoctrination and worse, as witch-hunts ancient and modern make clear.

A final controversy about self-deception, however defined, has to do with its desirability. The injunction of the Delphic Oracle—'Know thyself'—that underlies much philosophy has long been pitted against dismal suspicions of what we would find if we took the Oracle seriously. The drive for attaining greater understanding about ourselves and our role in the world has clashed with the fear of inviting revulsion or misfortune by probing too deeply. Some have further claimed that judicious self-deception is conducive to better mental and physical well-being, as if to underline Jonathan Swift's (ironical) remark, in *A Tale of a Tub*, defining happiness as 'the perpetual Possession of being well Deceived'.

The continuing debate over the desirability of self-deception reveals two incompatible views of optimal human functioning. These views, in turn, generate incompatible conceptions of the role of all involved in therapy: to what extent and by what means should they encourage fuller self-understanding, or on the contrary promote in patients what they take to be life-enhancing false beliefs? If therapists choose the latter path, they run up, once more, against one of the paradoxes of self-deception: for how can they be honest with patients about their intent and about any illusory belief they wish to encourage? But if they cannot, why should their patients trust them?   S.B.

*lying.

Sissela Bok, 'Secrecy and Self-Deception', in *Secrets: On the Ethics of Concealment and Revelation* (New York, 1992).
Herbert Fingarette, *Self-Deception* (London, 1969).
Mike Martin (ed.), *Self-Deception and Self-Understanding: New Essays in Philosophy and Psychology* (Lawrence, Kan., 1985).
Alfred R. Mele, *Self-Deception Unmasked* (Princeton, NJ, 2001).

self-defeating theories. In the simplest sense, a theory is self-defeating if the truth of the theory would imply the falsity of the theory. However, the expression is usually applied to theories that purport to guide action in some sense—particularly normative ethical theories. A theory is self-defeating if attempting to achieve what the theory says ought to be achieved is bound to fail because of that attempt. The best-known example is sometimes referred to as the paradox of hedonism. Hedonism tells us that hap-

piness is the ultimate goal, but clearly if we spend our lives single-mindedly seeking happiness, we are unlikely to achieve it. *Parfit introduces distinctions between individually self-defeating theories (self-defeating when one person acts according to the theory) and collectively self-defeating theories (self-defeating when a group of people act according to the theory), and between indirectly self-defeating theories (self-defeating when the aims of the theory are consciously adopted by the agent) and directly self-defeating theories (self-defeating when the aims of the theory are successfully achieved by the agent). Some forms of consequentialism seem to be indirectly self-defeating in the same way that hedonism is indirectly self-defeating.   E.J.M.

D. Parfit, *Reasons and Persons* (Oxford, 1984).

self-determination, political. The rule of a particular group of people—nation or religious community or, more simply, the residents of a place— over their own affairs. Self-determination is not the same as self-government, which usually implies some version of *democracy. A group of people, freed, say, from imperial rule, might choose the government of a king, an oligarchy, or a clerical élite and, assuming that the choice is not coerced from outside, this would still be called self-determination. A right to self-determination is a right to make choices of that sort. In recent times, this right is most often claimed on behalf of a nation. (*Nationalism.) But the character and standing of the 'self' in 'self-determination' is often a matter of dispute. In principle, the right was invented for the sake of existing collective selves, but it may also happen that collectivities are invented in order to exercise the right.   M.WALZ.

*homeland, right to a.

Alfred Cobban, *The Nation State and National Self-Determination* (New York, 1970).
Dov Ronen, *The Quest for Self-Determination* (New Haven, Conn., 1979).

self-interest: *see* egoism, psychological.

self-love: *see* Butler.

self-regarding and other-regarding actions. A distinction among actions which becomes important if one attempts to formulate *liberalism by defining an area of conduct in which society has no business to interfere; as does J. S. Mill, when he says that 'the only part of the conduct of any one, for which he is amenable to society' is that which concerns the interests of others. Critics claim the distinction cannot be made.   J.M.S.

*liberty; state intervention; public and private.

J. S. Mill, *On Liberty*.

Sellars, Roy Wood (1880–1973). American critical realist, evolutionary naturalist, materialist, and socialist who taught at the University of Michigan. Knowing, for Sellars, is an activity which, in disclosing objects by means of ideas, is about external things and consequently transcends the cognitive organism. 'The sensory complex arises in the brain under patterned stimulation of the sense organs and has the role of guidance of response. Such guidance is a transcending role . . . we do not need to get mystical about transcendence.' Evolutionary *naturalism is not reductive, since nature undergoes cumulative change in which new patterns emerge. 'Matter is . . . existent in its own right. And I shall think it in terms of the category of substance', not process. For Sellars, *'socialism is a democratic movement whose purpose is in securing of an economic organization of society which will give the maximum possible at any one time of justice and liberty.' His son, Wilfrid Sellars, acknowledged close philosophical affinity with his father, though he wrote in the idiom of a different generation.   P.H.H.

*Critical Realism; materialism.

R. W. Sellars, *Critical Realism* (Chicago, 1916).
Symposium in Honor of Roy Wood Sellars (*Philosophy and Phenomenological Research*, 15; 1954).

Sellars, Wilfrid (1912–89). American philosopher notable for his thoroughgoing investigations in metaphysics and the philosophy of mind. He distinguishes between the manifest image of man as a being with beliefs, desires, and intentions, and the scientific image of him as an embodied being subject to study by physicists, biochemists, and physiologists. The task of reconciling those two images is a major problem in the philosophy of mind. Typical of Sellars's own approach to the problem is his verbal behaviourist account of thought and meaning in terms of the functional role of linguistic items. (*Functionalism.) Thought is inner speech which is modelled on overt speech, and overt speech is the exercise of a capacity to use words and sentences appropriately in relation to the world and to each other. Thus nothing repugnant to the scientific image is invoked.   O.R.J.

*myth of the given.

W. Sellars, *Essays in Philosophy and its History* (Dordrecht, 1974).
—— *Empiricism and the Philosophy of Mind*, with intro. by R. Rorty and study guide by R. Brandom (Cambridge, Mass., 1997).

semantic ascent. The move from talk about the world to talk about the semantic properties of a language (e.g. the move from 'Snow is white' to ' "Snow is white" is true'). This is said to involve *ascent* because of the doctrine that the semantic properties of a language *L* cannot, in general, be expressed in *L* itself, but only in a higher *metalanguage. The move is useful because ascent to a semantic level enables one to express certain kinds of generalizations that are otherwise inexpressible. Thus, the sentence 'Every axiom of Peano arithmetic is true' makes, it is argued, a claim about numbers. But, since Peano arithmetic contains infinitely many axioms, the claim cannot be expressed, without resorting to semantic ascent, by any finite sentence.   A.GUP.

W. V. Quine, *Philosophy of Logic* (Englewood Cliffs, NJ, 1970).

semantics. In *Foundations of the Theory of Signs* (1938) C. W. Morris divided the general study of signs (*semiotics) into three branches. These are *syntactics, or the study of the relation of signs to other signs; semantics, or the study of the relation of signs to the things they represent; and *pragmatics, or the study of the relation of signs to their users. Semantics is thus the general study of the interpretation of *signs, and in particular the interpretation of the sentences and words of languages. Following Carnap, it is commonly divided into pure semantics, or the study of artificial and formally specified languages in the abstract, and applied semantics, or the study of natural, empirically given languages such as English or French. The language studied is called the *object language, and the language in which interpretations are given, the *metalanguage. A semantic statement typically mentions a sentence or other term of the object language, and says what it means, or refers to, or what otherwise provides its interpretation using the metalanguage. An object language can function as its own metalanguage, at least to an extent circumscribed by the need to avoid semantic *paradoxes. A *formal semantics is a fully systematic description of the way in which an object language is to be interpreted, standardly given by a recursive account of the way in which larger meanings or truth-conditions for entire and progressively more complex sentences depend upon the interpretations assigned to their elements.

The fundamental problems for semantics are first to discover what linguistic categories we need to distinguish, and then the *kind* of description of the function of terms that is appropriate. The great advances in the subject came with realizing, for instance, that 'Some men are mortal' is semantically quite different from 'Aristotle is mortal': the phrase 'some men' does not function as a name or 'term' interpreted as referring to some men. The difference in function is clearly seen when we look at the different kinds of inference such expressions create. The theory of this difference (quantification theory) is well understood, but other semantic problems have proved less tractable. Are we content to say of a *name, for example, that it refers to its bearer? In that case we see no difference between two names that have the same bearer. Or is some more fine-grained description needed, separating what is said about each of two such names? The former option makes for a more simple and logically more tractable system (extensional semantics) while the latter initiates a search for principles governing the more fine-grained (intensional) features that separate terms with the same extension, but which mean different things. Controversies in semantics frequently centre on the use of various devices, such as possible worlds, to provide the necessary interpretations. But it is generally accepted that the more fine-grained the discriminations or contexts that a language permits, the richer are the categories and descriptions that a semantics must adopt in representing its structure.

Even when these problems are solved, others remain for a full philosophical semantics. For any semantics is apt to deal in terms such as *reference, predication, and *truth, and perhaps in addition the richer intensional concepts of *meaning, *sense, and *synonymy. And even if we are quite happy using such terms, the question remains *in virtue of what* they apply (for instance, do predicates mean what they do in virtue of shared universals, and what are *universals and how do we apprehend them?). If we consider a pure or formal specification of a language as an abstract structure, then the equivalent problem will be the question what is necessary for it to be correctly attributed to a population. Divisions rapidly arise over whether the appropriate empirical grounding is given by one kind of fact or another. These problems separate semantics in a narrow sense from the wider concerns of the philosophy of language.   s.w.b.

*semiotics; language, problems of the philosophy of; Montague.

R. Carnap, *Introduction to Semantics* (Cambridge, Mass., 1947).
P. Ludlow (ed.), *Readings in the Philosophy of Language* (Cambridge, Mass., 1997).

semantics, formal: *see* formal semantics.

semantic theory of truth. This theory was developed by Tarski, who was particularly concerned to overcome the semantic *paradoxes to which talk of *truth gives rise in natural languages, such as the *liar paradox. He held that truth could only be adequately defined for a language which did not contain its own truth-predicate. Calling such a language, L, the object language, Tarski undertook to provide a definition by *recursion of truth-in-L, the definition being formulated in an appropriate *metalanguage. For such a definition to be satisfactory, Tarski held, it would have to enable one to prove all true equivalences of the form '*S* is true-in-L if and only if *p*', where '*S*' is a structural specification of a sentence of L and *p* constitutes the correct translation of that sentence into the metalanguage. He showed how this task could indeed be carried out for certain artificial, formalized languages, but believed that the method could not be extended to provide a definition of truth for any natural language, such as English.   E.J.L.

*snow is white.

S. Haack, *Philosophy of Logics* (Cambridge, 1978).

semiotics. General theory of *signs. Peirce distinguished three kinds of sign: icons, which are like the objects signified (e.g. naturalistic paintings); natural signs (e.g. clouds signify rain); and conventional signs (e.g. red for danger, and at least the majority of words). Semiotics is usually divided into three fields: *semantics, the study of meaning; *syntactics, the study of (surface 'grammatical' and also 'deep') structure; and *pragmatics, which deals with the extra-linguistic purposes and effects of communications.   A.J.L.

C. W. Morris, *Signification and Significance* (Cambridge, Mass., 1968).

Sen, Amartya K. (1933–). Indian economist and philosopher at Harvard, winner of the Nobel Prize for Economics in 1998. Working on the foundations of welfare and development economics, Sen is a leading theorist of social choice. In the debate following *Arrow's paradox, Sen has been a critic of *welfarism, which appraises the value of outcomes wholly in terms of individuals' preferences between them. Sen has argued for a consequentialist ethics that incorporates respect for rights in its doctrine of the good. He raised the 'paradox of the Paretian liberal'—an inconsistency, given plausible background assumptions, between the welfarist claim that if everyone prefers an A to a B, then A must rank above B in a social ordering, and a condition of minimal liberty that each agent possess a personal sphere where her preferences dictate the social ordering. Sen has worked on the nature of personal *well-being and the measurement of poverty.   T.P.

A. K. Sen, *Choice, Welfare and Measurement* (Oxford, 1982).
—— *On Economic Inequality*, new edn. (Oxford, 1997).

Seneca, Lucius Annaeus (*c*.2 BC–AD 65). Stoic, tutor to Nero, chief administrator of the Roman Empire with Burrus AD 54–62, and author of ten *Moral Discourses*, 124 *Moral Epistles*, a satire on Claudius, nine tragedies, and a work on natural philosophy. At worst Seneca is an unoriginal philosopher and a contrived stylist. At best, in the *Epistles* and *Discourses* (note particularly 'De providentia', a Stoic dissertation on suffering, and 'Ad Marciam de consolatione', addressed to a mother on the death of her sons), he writes with a vividness of illustration and a persuasive brilliance unrivalled in philosophy: philosophy is practical goodness; excessive passion is evil; external goods are ultimately valueless; life is infinitely worth while; tragedy can be overcome or endured. Driven to suicide by Nero, his reputation and his life alike were blighted by his infamous pupil.   J.C.A.G.

*Stoicism.

V. Sørensen, *Seneca: The Humanist at the Court of Nero* (Edinburgh, 1984).

sensation. The subjective aspect of *perception—usually taken to denote the sensory (as opposed to conceptual) phase of a perceptual process. In hearing a concert, for instance, the sensation is the conscious auditory event preceding whatever thoughts and beliefs (if any) the sensation arouses in the perceiver. One might hear—thus have a sensation caused by—a French horn without coming to know or believe that it is a French horn. One might misidentify it as a trombone or not have any thoughts at all about it. This, presumably, is what happens with animals and young children. They can hear French horns. They can, therefore, have sensations—perhaps even sensations similar to ours—without these sensations necessarily producing beliefs similar to ours. Perhaps (though this is controversial and depends on just what is meant by having a *belief) they can have sensations (be sentient) without having any beliefs at all.

Aside from the sensations (visual, auditory, olfactory, and so on) associated with the various sense modalities, there is also a wide variety of other sensory-like phenomena that are ordinarily classified as sensations: twinges, tickles, pains, itches, thirst, hunger, feelings of sexual arousal, and so on. If there is any feature that distinguishes this odd assortment of mental entities, it is, perhaps, their introspectively salient quality. The sound of a French horn is utterly unlike the look or feel of a French horn. If the sensation is identified, as it typically is in the case of perceptual awareness, with the way things sound, look, and feel, then these sensations, though they are all of the same thing (a French horn), have an intrinsic, an introspectively obvious, quality that distinguishes them from one another. This is quite unlike such *propositional attitudes as thought, belief, judgement, and knowledge. Beliefs differ only with respect to their content—the proposition believed—not in their intrinsic quality or 'feel' to the person having them. Sensations, on the other hand, can be of, about, or directed upon the same thing (a French horn)—thus having, in this sense, the same content—and yet remain entirely different. As a result, thoughts are classified in terms of their *intentionality, what they are of or about, while sensations are specified in terms of their intrinsic character, what they feel or seem like to the person having them, quite apart from what, if anything, they are of or about.

A second feature of sensations that sets them apart from such discursive events as reasoning, thinking, knowing, and remembering is that sensations are, in the first instance at least, independent of the conceptual or intellectual assets (if any) of the subject. One cannot want chocolate, believe that there are chocolates in the box, or remember that one ate chocolate without understanding what chocolate is. One can, however, taste chocolate, smell it, and see it—and in this sense have chocolate sensations—while remaining completely ignorant of what chocolate is. In this way sensations constitute a primitive level of mental existence. They occur at a level—presumably in certain animals—at which discursive thought and reason are, if possible at all, not well developed. One does not need the concept of an itch or a pain, the capacity to have itch-thoughts and pain-beliefs, in order to *feel* itches and pains.

Though sensations, unlike thoughts, differ from one another in some intrinsic way, their epistemological status remains moot. Is one directly aware of (say) a visual sensation when one perceives, in a perfectly normal way, an external object? If so, is one aware of two things in normal perception—the external object (we say we perceive) and the internal sensation which it (the object) arouses in us? Or is one directly aware of only one thing, the sensation, while the external object is reached (known? perceived?) by some inferential or constructive mental process (thus being known or perceived indirectly) as the *representative theory maintains? Or is one only aware of the external object, the internal sensation being known only by inference, as *naïve realism asserts? If so, how is one's

knowledge—which seems direct—of the character of sensations to be understood?   F.D.

A. Clark, *A Theory of Sentience* (Oxford, 2000).
F. Dretske, *Knowledge and the Flow of Information* (Cambridge, Mass., 1981).
C. Peacocke, *Sense and Content* (Oxford, 1983).
B. Russell, *The Analysis of Mind* (London, 1921).

sense, manifold of: *see* manifold of sense.

sense and reference. Standard translations of Frege's terms *Sinn* and *Bedeutung*, originating in his 1892 paper 'Über Sinn und Bedeutung'. The reference of an expression is the entity it stands for: referring expressions stand for objects, predicates stand for *functions (in the mathematical sense, which Frege called 'concepts'), and sentences stand for truth-values. Referring expressions and predicates combine to form whole sentences, whose references are a function of the references of their parts. Senses are 'modes of presentation' of *references: the terms 'Cicero' and 'Tully' have the same reference but different senses. Sense was initially introduced by Frege to solve the puzzle of identity: if 'Cicero' has the same reference as 'Tully', then how can 'Cicero is Tully' be informative when 'Cicero is Cicero' is not? The senses of the parts of sentences combine to form the senses of sentences, which Frege called 'thoughts'.   T.C.

*connotation and denotation; meaning.

Gottlob Frege, 'On Sense and Meaning', in *Translations from the Philosophical Writings of Gottlob Frege*, ed. P. T. Geach and Max Black (Oxford, 1980).

sense awareness: *see* awareness, sense.

sense-data. Subjective entities (allegedly) having the properties the perceived external object (if there is one) appears to have. In seeing a white circle under red light and at an oblique angle, the sense-datum would be red and elliptical (the way the white circle looks). According to sense-data theorists, one perceives an external object, a white circle, but what one senses (is acquainted with, directly apprehends) is a red ellipse: the subjective sense-datum. Then, if one is clever (and knows about the funny lighting), one infers, on the basis of the sense-data one directly apprehends, that there is (probably) a white circle causing the red, elliptical sense-datum. In this way our knowledge of sense-data is supposed to provide a foundation for all empirical knowledge.   F.D.

*perception; phenomenalism; representative theory of perception.

B. Russell, *The Problems of Philosophy* (New York, 1959), ch. 1.
C. D. Broad, *Scientific Thought* (London, 1923), chs. 7 and 8.

sensibility. In one sense this can mean a set of individual or collective dispositions to emotions, attitudes, and feelings. As such, sensibility is relevant especially to value theory, including ethics, aesthetics, and politics. Arguably, there are at least three important interrelated types of judgement one can make about a sensibility: that some constitutive emotions can be criticized or justified against criticism in various ways (e.g. are 'irrational', 'exaggerated', 'well-founded', etc.); that some constitutive emotions ought to be regulated in certain ways, in light of criticism; and that individual or collective responsibility is appropriate for some of the emotions, in light of the possibility of regulation.   E.T.S.

*aesthetic attitude; taste.

Ronald B. De Sousa, *The Rationality of Emotion* (Cambridge, Mass., 1987).

sentences: *see* statements and sentences.

sentential calculus. Where a *proposition is understood to be a completely interpreted indicative sentence of a language, 'sentential calculus' and *'propositional calculus' may be used interchangeably.

Where, as in Frege, a proposition is an abstract entity which is the sense or content of a sentence, those objects are *represented* by sentences. Different sentences in a given or a different language may express the same proposition. Given the elusiveness of such entities, the logic of interpreted sentences remains the vehicle for presenting the logic of propositions as in the propositional calculus.

R.B.M.

B. Mates, *Elementary Logic* (Oxford, 1972).

sentential function. An expression which can be joined to another expression or expressions to form a sentence. Sentential functions include *connectives, such as 'and', which form a complex sentence from a sentence or sentences. Predicates are also counted as sentential functions since, for example, the predicate ' . . . is wise' when joined with the singular term 'Socrates' forms the sentence 'Socrates is wise'.   A.D.O.

sentimentalism: *see* moral sense.

sentiments. A sentiment is an attitude, in favour of or against people and their actions, which may involve both *judgement and *emotion. The term 'sentiment' has also been used, as by Hume and Smith, to refer to a possible basis for our moral attitudes. In this use sentiment is a feeling which the objects of moral appraisal evoke in us; as a possible basis for our moral attitudes, sentiment is opposed to reason.   T.P.

A. Smith, *The Theory of Moral Sentiments* (London, 1759).

Serbian philosophy.

1863–1945. Emerging after the foundation of Belgrade University in 1863, Serbian philosophy gained a reputation through the work of Branislav Petronijević, whose articles were later cited as authoritative in such works as Lee's *Zeno of Elea* (Cambridge, 1936) and Boyer's *The Concepts of the Calculus* (New York, 1939).

1940s–1960s. The philosophical tradition was dismantled in post-war Yugoslavia by the communist regime. The official establishment of 'humanist Marxism' followed the 1953 ideological cleansing of 'dogmatists'. The critical attitude of members of the 'Praxis Group' such as Svetozar Stojanović to the governing regime led to their dismissal from Belgrade University in 1975. The international reputation of 'Praxis Marxism' partly rests on non-philosophical grounds. Non-Marxist approaches were not tolerated and Alexandar Kron's work in formal logic represents the only such achievement of that time.

1970s and since. Although both politicians and Marxist academics became more tolerant in the early 1970s, it is hard to understand how a critical mass of analytically orientated, practically self-taught non-Marxist students was reached so quickly. The 'September Meetings' in Dubrovnik, established in the early 1980s by David Charles, Timothy Williamson, and their Belgrade colleagues, resulted in what was later called the 'England–Belgrade axis'. The distinctively analytic character of Serbian philosophy is underlined in that fourteen of the sixteen Yugoslav contributors to the collection cited below are, or have been, active at Belgrade University. Hopefully, though now either spread throughout the world or still working at home under unfriendly conditions, some will make important contributions to metaphysics, logic, epistemology, philosophical psychology, ethics, philosophy of action, and philosophy of science. Very well trained in philosophical analysis and symbolic logic, they are particularly successful in using thought experiments and the *reductio ad absurdum* method.   M.A.

*Croatian philosophy; Slovene philosophy.

A. Pavković (ed.), *Contemporary Yugoslav Philosophy: The Analytic Approach* (Dordrecht, 1988).

set theory. The property of being human is said to 'pick out' or 'determine' the *set* of all human beings. This has *subsets*—the sets of Scots, English, etc.—and *members*—e.g. David Hume and Jane Austen. At least normally, if not always, a set is not a member of itself: thus the set of City University philosophers is not itself, alas, another philosopher, who could help increasing numbers of students. It is an abstract object.

Our basic logical thoughts often embody relations between sets, subsets, and members, for example in syllogistic argument. Thus 'All robots are musical' says 'The set of robots is a subset of the set of musical things'; or, every member of the first set is a member of the second. Between 1874 and 1897 Cantor developed an astonishingly rich theory of infinite sets, including ones whose members are ordered, and sets having even more members than the so-called 'denumerably' infinite set of all integers—thus proving the existence of 'higher' infinities. Later, Russell and Whitehead tried to show that pure mathematics is a branch of the logic of sets, and is thus *analytic. Set theory has applications within many areas of mathematics.

It is therefore extremely embarrassing that our simplest intuitive thoughts about sets very quickly lead to contradiction. For if *every* property determines a set, then the set

(R) of all 'normal' sets, namely, 'those which are not members of themselves' is, if a member of itself, then not, and vice versa (*Russell's paradox). Alternative set theories are formal, symbolic expressions of relationships between sets which attempt to avoid contradictions with minimal loss of intuitive acceptability. The Russellian approach rejects as malformed symbolic expressions of both 'S is a member of itself' and its denial. Sets are put in hierarchies, and one can only meaningfully express membership relations between sets of immediately neighbouring levels. Such an axiomatization may be consistent, but only through inordinate loss of expressive power. Zermelo–Fraenkel–Skolem set theory only allows the *construction* of sets from properties when certain other conditions obtain: these entail the non-existence of R. Von Neumann–Bernays– Gödel set theory is more comprehensive but even more complex. It allows the existence of R, but it is not a member of any other set (it is then called a 'class'). This seems counter-intuitive: for if R exists, then why should there not be a merely two-membered set containing, say, R plus the set of all philosophers?. A.J.L.

Abraham Fraenkel, 'Set Theory', in Paul Edwards (ed.), *The Encyclopedia of Philosophy* (New York, 1967).
Paul Halmos, *Naïve Set Theory* (Princeton, NJ, 1960).
Michael Potter, *Set Theory and its Philosophy* (Oxford, 2004).

sex. Biological feature distinguishing males and females in respect of their reproductive roles (contrast *gender). Thus, by extension, sex is thought of as a biological drive which gives rise to activity that typically results in reproduction, or as that activity itself. This suggests that the kind of explanation required for such activity is a biological one, occasioning such protestations as 'My sex life is not my fault: I'm programmed by my genes'. As well as presupposing a crude determinism, this underplays the role of *culture in giving rise to multifarious forms of sexual activity (e.g. *homosexuality). Yet sexual desire has usually been viewed as a *blind* desire, i.e. one the desirability of whose object is not apparent to reason. It is perhaps for this reason that the character of Freudian explanations of behaviour in terms of sexual desire (and their scope) remains mysterious. P.G.

*sexual morality.

Roger Scruton, *Sexual Desire* (London, 1986).

sex, philosophy of. The theoretical examination of human sexuality, desire, and pleasure. Analysis has focused on the attempt to establish non-moral standards to rank sexual behaviours as 'natural' or good, as opposed to perverse or bad. Central to this examination is determining whether sexual desire is localized simultaneously within the phantasmatic as well as the sensory boundaries of the skin. Thomas Nagel reworks Sartre's notion of 'a double reciprocal incarnation' into an account of sexual desire as a serial unfolding of nested desirings of two reflective persons. On this view, the category of perverted sex would extend to include any solitary sexual practice.

This analysis of sexual desire in terms of reciprocating psychic structurings has ramifications for justifications of sado-masochism. Patrick Hopkins argues that rape simulations are logically distinct from rapes, since certain sexual behaviours cannot be properly individuated except by their links with a shared sexual imaginary. Robert Solomon not only continues this mentalist reading of sexual desire, but refigures bodily gestures as having semantic content: an intimate behaviour is a 'natural expression' that can be perverse if untruthful or feigned. Alan Goldman, on the other hand, rejects any account of sexual desire that is not straightforwardly 'bodily'. For Goldman, sexual desire is directed toward the physicality of another person and involves only a minimal, short-lived psychological component. On this account, the deliberate delay of coitus and bestiality each count as perverse. Other issues involve Kant's claim that objectification is necessarily involved in any sexual relation between persons. Martha Nussbaum separates 'benign' objectification from the malignant sorts marked by one or more of the following: viewing the desired other as essentially replaceable, lacking 'boundary-integrity', and failing to be the possessor and owner of a unique personal narrative.

Michel Foucault challenges this entire analytic schema by running a genealogy of sex. On his view, sex for modern subjects in the West is discursive: subjectivities, bodies, and pleasures are produced by the operations of a particular regime of knowledge/power/pleasure. Foucault delineates 'a *scientia sexualis*' that naturalizes the phenomena it extracts and organizes through medicalizing the confession, replacing the priest with the psychoanalyst. He claims that any natural/unnatural schematic is a mythic construction, since there is no non-linguistic access to any pre-social human nature. B.T.

*sex; sexual morality.

Michel Foucault, *The History of Sexuality*, vol. i: *An Introduction*, tr. Robert Hurley (New York, 1978).
Alan Soble (ed.), *The Philosophy of Sex: Contemporary Readings*, 3rd edn. (Lanham, Md., 1997).

sexism. Thought or practice which may permeate language and which assumes women's inferiority to men. The existence of sexism is acknowledged from a variety of ideological perspectives, and sexism may be conceived either as something one encounters instances of, or as a pervasive phenomenon endemic to society. Thus 'sexist' is applied pejoratively to individuals and to institutions both by liberal feminists and by feminists who advocate a radical transformation of existing *gender relations. J.HORN.

*feminism.

Mary Vetterling-Braggin, Frederick A. Elliston, and Jane English (eds.), *Feminism and Philosophy* (Totowa, NJ, 1977).

Sextus Empiricus (AD *c.*200). Sceptic and physician. Sextus, about whose life we know practically nothing, wrote a number of works on the complex history of the Sceptical movement. The surviving works are: *Outlines of Pyrrhonism*;

Against the Dogmatists; and *Against the Professors*. The second two are usually coupled together and titled *Against the Mathematicians*, that is, all those who profess any sort of technical knowledge. *Outlines of Pyrrhonism* provides an account of the philosophy of Pyrrho, including a comparison of *Pyrrhonism with versions of Academic *scepticism. The other works examine at considerable length various dogmatic claims in the arts and sciences and sceptical strategies that may be employed to undermine confidence in them. These works are therefore a mine of information on many ancient philosophical schools. Sextus argues for the superiority of Pyrrho's Scepticism to that of the *Academy, although the difference between these are disputed in the scholarship. Although Sextus is unrelentingly critical of all other philosophical positions, he believes that Scepticism has a positive practical purpose, namely, the tranquillity of soul arising from abandoning the quest for knowledge of any sort.   L.P.G.

Julia Annas and Jonathan Barnes (eds.), *The Modes of Scepticism* (Cambridge, 1985).

Jonathan Barnes, *The Toils of Scepticism* (Cambridge, 1990).

Sextus Empiricus, *Outlines of Scepticism*, ed. and tr. J. Annas and J. Barnes, 2nd edn. (Cambridge, 2000).

Philip P. Hallie (ed.), *Sextus Empiricus* (Indianapolis, 1985).

sexual morality. Principles of right conduct in matters of *sex, or their observance. Two questions arise: *What* sexual acts are morally permissible? *With whom* are they permissible?

The view that some kinds of sexual act are morally wrong can spring from several sources. The most obvious employs the *consequentialist test of whether they cause harm. Thus some sexually sadistic acts may, by this criterion, be condemned, though de Sade himself would reply that they cause less harm than the acts resulting from their repression. In the absence of reliable empirical evidence on the effects of sexual behaviour (e.g. of reading pornography), non-consequentialist criteria may be turned to. One employs the notion that some kinds of sexual acts are unnatural and therefore wrong. Two problems arise. First, the mere fact that many sexual acts are not conducive to reproduction (or to other biological purposes) does nothing to show that they are unnatural, in the sense of tending, or intended, to frustrate what, if anything, is *natural to human beings. Second, even if they were, they would not thereby be shown to be immoral without further premises such as the Roman Catholic belief that what is contrary to created nature's purposes is wrong because contrary to its Creator's will.

A more widely acceptable criterion condemns some kinds of sexual acts as failing to treat those with whom they are performed, or oneself, as *persons rather than as objects. Kant seems to have treated all sex like this, holding that 'sexual love makes of the loved person an object of appetite; as soon as that appetite has been stilled, the person is cast aside as one casts away a lemon which has been sucked dry'. Sartre thinks of ordinary sexual desire as aiming to avoid this, but failing, so that either one makes

the other an object, as in sadism, or one becomes an object for the other, as in masochism. With Sartre's pessimism discarded, this has provided an influential criterion, particularly for *feminism. It does, however, require additional argument to conclude that depersonalized sex is morally impermissible.

The view that a sexual partner should be treated as a person offers one in a series of answers to the question *with whom* one may, morally, have sexual relations. The most stringent answer restricts sex to *marriage partners, ruling out, *inter alia*, *homosexuality; the next to those in a relationship of *love, ruling out casual sex; then to those desired and respected as persons, excluding, perhaps, prostitution; and uncontroversially, to consenting adults, ruling out sex with children and animals, who are incapable of informed consent. The first three answers correspond roughly to three general approaches in moral philosophy. The ban on extramarital sex goes with an ethics of *duty. The restriction of sex to love implies an ethics of *care. And the person-centred approach emphasizes an ethics of *virtue, of self-creation rather than spontaneity. It may not be fanciful to suggest that the application of each approach here is a reaction to viewing sex as a potentially disruptive force—disruptive, respectively, to society at large, so that exceptionless formal restrictions need to be imposed; to personal relationships, so that sex must be tied to concern for another's welfare; and to the individuals themselves, whose integrity as persons is put at risk by it.

Few philosophers have, by contrast, developed an ethics of sexuality as something other than an appetite requiring regulation. They have, however, attacked the first two moral restrictions—on consequentialist grounds, like Plato, as socially dysfunctional; on the grounds that they inhibit individual *autonomy in relationships; and on feminist grounds that they impose a pattern of relationships which actually benefits men at the expense of women. As to the third restriction, Nagel bravely maintains that 'bad sex is generally better than none at all'.

Yet such *essentialist assumptions about sexuality run counter to currently popular views, deriving from feminism and *post-structuralism, which see different sexualities as constitutive of people's identities as e.g. a lesbian woman or a straight man. These identities, like those of any cultural minority, are regarded as prior to and formative of the particular moralities which apply to them. Thus the attempt to formulate general principles of sexual conduct is viewed (as in a wider *ethical relativism) as the imposition of the morality of one identity group—typically that of straight men—at the expense of members of others. There are, however, many difficulties with this approach: how fine-grained are the relevant sexual identities? Are *all* identities (e.g. paedophile) to be tolerated, and, if not, why not? Is the implied *libertarianism compatible with social organization? Can the objections to a general ethical relativism be evaded? The absence of a middle way between universalizing and relativizing approaches to sexual morality is sympathetic to contemporary practical, as well as philosophical, uncertainties in this area of life.   P.G.

R. Baker and F. Elliston (eds.), *Philosophy of Sex* (Buffalo, 1984).

T. Nagel, 'Sexual Perversion', in *Mortal Questions* (Cambridge, 1979).

I. Primoratz, *Ethics and Sex* (London, 1999).

A. Soble (ed.), *The Philosophy of Sex: Contemporary Readings*, 3rd edn. (Lanham, Md., 1997).

J. Weeks, *Invented Moralities* (Cambridge, 1995).

Shaftesbury, third Earl of (1671–1713). Named Anthony Ashley Cooper, like his descendant, the nineteenth-century philanthropist, he is normally known simply as Shaftesbury. Partly educated under the politically radical Locke (though he later criticized Locke on both ethics and epistemology), he was an early, if not always consistent, representative, in his *Characteristics of Men, Manners, Opinions, Times* (1711), of the **'moral sense' doctrine in ethics, inventing that phrase. For much of the time, though not all of it, he emphasized feeling rather than reason as the source of morality: we approve of, or take pleasure in the contemplation of, virtue, and this is because we are by nature altruistic and not just selfish. Morality with him becomes human-orientated rather than God-orientated, though religion can motivate us further towards it. He also foreshadowed to some extent *utilitarianism, which came to prominence later in the eighteenth century. A.R.L.

S. Grean, *Shaftesbury's Philosophy of Religion and Ethics* (Athens, Oh., 1967).

shame. An emotion that serves as the focal point of ethics in many ancient and non-Western philosophies, but its comparative neglect in many ethical theories is illustrative. The Judaeo-Christian tradition and many modern theories place considerable emphasis on *guilt, but the difference between shame and guilt is profound and symptomatic of a larger omission in ethics. Guilt (not causal or legal guilt, but the feeling of guilt) is a highly individualistic emotion, a matter of self-scrutiny and self-condemnation. Shame, by contrast, is a highly social *emotion, and it has to do with violating a common trust, 'letting the others down'. Like guilt, it is self-accusatory, but it is so through the eyes of others, as an inextricable member of a group or a community. The capacity to feel shame has thus been cited as a pre-condition of all the virtues, as in the Ethiopian proverb 'Where there is no shame, there is no honour'. Thus Aristotle, in his *Ethics*, takes shame to be a 'quasi-virtue'. It is not good to feel shame, because it is not good to have done something about which to be ashamed, but to do something wrong and not feel shame is the ultimate proof of a wicked character. R.C.SOL.

Aristotle, *Nicomachean Ethics* (Indianapolis, 1985).

Shoemaker, Sydney (1931–). American philosopher at Cornell, known principally for his work in metaphysics and the philosophy of mind. In the former he has argued for the possibility of time without change. He has defended a causal theory of properties, which has as a consequence that the laws of nature are a posteriori necessary rather than contingent; and a causal theory of identity over time.

In the philosophy of mind he is a vocal proponent of ana-lytic *functionalism, in defence of which he offers a subtle discussion of *qualia: he denies the possibility of absent qualia, that someone might be functionally identical to us, yet lack qualitative mental states; but accepts the possibility of inverted qualia, that two people may be be functionally alike but differ in their qualitative mental states. In addition, his work has covered personal identity, memory, self-consciousness, and dualism. M.G.F.M.

S. Shoemaker, *The First-Person Perspective and other Essays* (Cambridge, 1996).

—— *Identity, Cause, and Mind: Philosophical Essays*, expanded edn. (Oxford, 2003).

side constraints: *see* ends and means.

Sidgwick, Henry (1838–1900). British moral philosopher, who developed the most sensitive, sophisticated (and complicated) account of *utilitarianism in the nineteenth century. Sidgwick was educated as a classical scholar at Cambridge, resigned his college position because of religious doubts in 1869, but later became the first secular Professor of Philosophy at Cambridge (1883). He was the professor when McTaggart, Russell, and Moore were philosophy students. Sidgwick wrote on many areas, but his only great work is *The Methods of Ethics* (1874; and then five other editions in his lifetime). This is not intended as a defence of utilitarianism so much as an account of the ways in which it is possible to reach a rational basis for action. Starting with common sense, Sidgwick identifies three such methods: *intuitionism, universal hedonism (i.e. utilitarianism), and individual *hedonism (i.e. *egoism). He finds that the particular maxims of common-sense morality do not meet the criteria he lays down for something being an intuitively self-evident principle; but that these are met by certain 'absolute practical principles' of a more abstract nature, such as that future good is as important as present good, or 'that the good of any one individual is of no more importance, from the point of view (if I may say so) of the Universe, than the good of any other'. With such principles he manages to reconcile intuitionism and utilitarianism. However, he thinks that egoism is also an intuitive principle of action, which would only be made compatible with utilitarianism by the work of God. Being reluctant to introduce God for this purpose, Sidgwick had no solution for what he called the 'dualism of *practical reason', and hence ended the first edition with the sombre words that 'the prolonged effort of the human intellect to frame a perfect ideal of rational conduct is seen to have been foredoomed to inevitable failure'. R.H.

J. B. Schneewind, *Sidgwick's Ethics and Victorian Moral Philosophy* (Oxford, 1977).

Bart Schultz (ed.), *Essays on Henry Sidgwick* (Cambridge, 1992).

sign and symbol. A distinction first explored in these terms by C. S. Peirce. Signs are a highly general category, including natural indications of things. Spots are a sign of measles, clouds a sign of rain to come. A sign of a state of affairs or event may be any indication, evidence, manifestation, portent, trace (which seems to be what Peirce called an 'index'), or mark that is regularly correlated with it, and hence can be used to infer its presence. In that case, to take something as a sign of something else is to use it to infer the presence of the other thing. This is the use of natural signs, but we can of course invent signs or signals: in heraldry specified emblems indicate the identity of the person wearing them; or a picture of a man with a shovel on the roadside indicates the presence of roadworks; or the picture of beans on the can indicates beans within. In Peirce's view the latter signs work as *icons*, by bearing a natural resemblance to what is depicted. Icons are signs that work in virtue of sharing properties with what is signalled. But most such signals work by *convention, and it requires a process of being inducted into the convention to learn to interpret them.

Peirce may have supposed that a symbol was a manufactured sign. He defines a symbol as a 'sign which is constituted a sign merely or mainly by the fact that it is used and understood as such' (*Collected Papers*, ii. 307). But this is quickly seen to be inadequate. With symbols we enter a different domain from that of the sign, since the role of a symbol is not that of correlating with the presence of the thing signified. There is no regular correlation of this kind in question. A portrait is not a signal that the sitter is near, but a representation of her. A symbol is not used as a mark that something else is present, but in place of the something else, to bring it to mind, or to identify it as a topic (or, of course, to elicit the emotions and reactions that are supposed appropriate to that other thing, as when a flag is a symbol of a country). Certainly, if we are to think of words as symbols, it is hopeless to see them as kinds of signal or sign of whatever it is they represent. The presence of the word 'giraffe' on a page is no sign that there are giraffes about. A symbol is not something that is used as a sign of things, given the function of signs that we have sketched.

The alternative position is that words and symbols do function as signs, but of states of their producers rather than the states of the world that they signify. Thus Locke took it that words are external signs, in the signalling sense, of ideas in the mind of the person producing them. But this can only be one part of an overall theory, since it requires a supplementary story about the way in which ideas serve as symbols or representations of whatever it is that we end up talking about. Peirce himself was driven to the regressive suggestion that as well as a sign and its object we need to postulate a 'more developed sign' or *interpretant* in the mind of the user. The problem of how such things represent substitutes for the problem about how words represent. A more modern view is that they may be signs of the beliefs or intentions of the person, but the question arises how the presence of belief or other intentional states can consist in the presence of something invested with representative power.   S.W.B.

*representation; semantics; meaning.

C. S. Peirce, *Collected Papers* (Cambridge, Mass., 1932–5), ii.

simplicity. Sometimes thought to provide a criterion for choice among scientific theories, with varying accounts of how simplicity might be measured. If simple theories are easier to use, their adoption might be on pragmatic grounds. Poincaré, in contrast, identified mathematical simplicity as a marker for *truth*, which makes sense only if one believes that nature *is* simple, and will appear so through the filter of theory and language.   N.C.
R.F.H.

*Ockham's razor.

Henri Poincaré, *The Foundations of Science*, tr. G. B. Halstead (Washington, DC, 1982).

Hans Reichenbach, *The Philosophy of Space and Time*, tr. M. Reichenbach (New York, 1957).

simulation. How best to understand the nature and basis of folk-psychological predictions, explanations, and descriptions of human behaviour and mentality couched in terms of belief, desire and the like? Theory theorists maintain that in such activities folk psychological ascriptions are underwritten by the tacit grasp of a theory specifying the use of notions such as belief and desire—informally much like theoretical explanation in the sciences. Simulation theorists claim that we understand one another by using our own minds in a process of simulation, generating processes in ourselves similar to those in other people, informing ourselves of the mental states of others by running our own cognitive machinery 'off line'. This is in contrast to the positing by theory theorists of a system of laws and logical relations which connect beliefs, desires, and the like with behaviour. But if we can use our own minds to simulate the minds of others without invoking such laws, parsimony counsels against theory theory. Much is made of the pretend play of young children, and the importance of simulation in ethical evaluation, empathy, fictional narrative, and aesthetics. Whether this amounts to new interpretations of phenomena or genuine arguments for the view remains unclear.   J.GAR.

*theory theory of mind.

M. Davies and T. Stone (eds.), *Folk Psychology: The Theory of Mind Debate* (Oxford, 1995).

—— (eds.), *Mental Simulation* (Oxford, 1995).

sin is moral wrongdoing, or in some cases the omission of what one ought to do. It is usually thought of as the violation of natural law or the commands of a deity. A person's sins are ordinarily characterized in terms of actions or omissions, but in some cases sin can be more meaningfully construed in terms of faults of character or in terms of states, such as a state of rebellion against God or estrangement from God. From medieval times the Church has distinguished mortal sins from venial, or less serious, sins. More controversial is the notion of *original sin, or guilt inherited from Adam, the first man. Those who take seriously the notion of original sin place great emphasis upon the effects of sin in the world. Some religious traditions allow for the possibility of the forgiveness of sin.   G.F.M.

L. Berkhof, *Systematic Theology* (Grand Rapids, Mich., 1939).

H. Davis, *Moral and Pastoral Theology*, 4th edn. (London, 1945), vol i, treatise 4.

sin, original: *see* original sin.

sincerity. In his *History of England* Hume described men as given to 'feigning'. Sincerity implies by contrast that we have given a full and frank account of ourselves and have not added anything extra. So philosophers have debated whether true morality requires sincerity, or simply appropriate conduct and the 'external' performance of one's duties, and how sincere anyone can be morally required to be. Kant's discussion, 'Concerning Lying', in the *Groundwork of the Metaphysic of Morals* concludes that insincerity with oneself 'deserves the greatest censure, for . . . from such a rotten spot . . . the evil of untruthfulness spreads itself also into one's relationships with other men'.

The special problem of philosophical insincerity arises because of the dual role of the philosopher as custodian of the virtues and critic of orthodoxies. Thus Descartes has been accused of hypocrisy in disguising his hostility to religion and pandering to the Sorbonne, and Hume's *Treatise of Human Nature* invites us to reflect on whether a philosopher can be a sincere and believing sceptic.

CATH.W.

*lying.

I. Kant, *Groundwork of the Metaphysic of Morals*, tr. J. W. Ellington (Indianapolis, 1983), pt. II: 'The Metaphysical Principles of Virtue'.

Singer, Peter A. (1946–). Best known for his writing in areas of *applied ethics, starting with his best-selling *Animal Liberation* (London, 1976), in which he argues that most treatment meted out to animals is morally intolerable. He has continued to write about such issues, but has also put the ideas and theories of moral philosophy to work to provide assessments of the morality of euthanasia, *in vitro* fertilization, the distribution of world resources, and many allied topics (see especially his *Practical Ethics* (Cambridge, 1979)). His work is marked by a strong commitment to *utilitarianism and by a wish to displace the morality of what he has referred to as the 'Judaeo-Christian inheritance'. He lived and worked for many years in Australia, along the way serving on government committees and running a Centre for Human Bioethics, but in 1999 took a professorship at Princeton. N.J.H.D.

*animals; Hegel.

P. A. Singer, *How Are We to Live?* (Melbourne, 1993).
—— *Rethinking Life and Death* (Melbourne, 1994).

Sinn: *see* sense and reference.

Skolem paradox. A collection is *countable* if it is either finite or has the same size as the natural numbers, the smallest infinite set. It is a theorem of standard *set theory, due to Cantor, that the set of real *numbers is not countable—there are more real numbers than natural numbers. However, the Löwenheim–Skolem theorem states that if a countable set of (first-order) sentences has a model at all, then it has a model whose domain is at most countable. The 'paradox' is that if real analysis is consistent, it has a countable model. Similarly, if set theory is consistent, it has a countable model that satisfies an assertion that one of its members is not countable. Such models are called 'non-standard'. The fact that a model of set theory satisfies an assertion that a set is uncountable only entails that there is no function in the model that maps the natural numbers on to the 'members' of the set. It does not rule out the existence of such a function—outside the model. The 'paradox' has been thought to raise doubts concerning the referents of expressions like 'natural number' and 'finite'. In what sense can we say that the aforementioned non-standard models are 'unintended'? S.S.

*satisfaction.

Thoralf Skolem, 'Einige Bemerkungen zur axiomatischen Begründung der Mengenlehre'; tr. as 'Some Remarks on Axiomatized Set Theory', in Jean van Heijenoort (ed.), *From Frege to Gödel* (Cambridge, Mass., 1967).

slave morality. Nietzsche's designation of one basic type of morality which he contrasts with another he calls 'master morality'. Whereas 'master morality' is fundamentally a morality of self-affirmation on the part of the powerful, 'slave morality' is a reactive morality originating in resentment of the powerful on the part of the powerless. The qualities of the powerful which they affirm as 'good' are deemed 'evil' by the powerless, for whom 'good' is derivatively conceived in terms of the absence or repudiation of those qualities. Nietzsche contends that this reactive, fearful, and resentful type of morality (and its 'good versus evil') has triumphed over its ancient rival (and its contrasting opposition of 'good versus bad', i.e. superior versus inferior) in the modern world, to the detriment of the quality of human life. (See *Beyond Good and Evil*, sects. 260–8; *Genealogy of Morals*, First Essay.) R.S.

Richard Schacht, *Nietzsche* (London, 1983), ch. 7.

slave of the passions: *see* reason as slave of the passions.

slime. Sartre invokes *le visqueux* (slime, stickiness, the viscous) in discussing how feelings, acts, character traits, are 'charged with something material', while, equally, material substance is engrained with 'affective meaning'. The disgustingness of slime seems to have an objective quality, neither physical nor psychic but transcending both. Slime's connotations cannot be derived from slime as brute fact, but they cannot be a projection of our feelings either, since to establish the connection between literal physical sliminess and the slimy quality of a person requires us to recognize baseness *already* in sliminess, and sliminess in a type of baseness: there is 'pre-ontological comprehension'. However experienced, slime is compromising, duplicitous, 'leechlike', the potential 'revenge of the in-itself' on the *for-itself it seeks to engulf. J.O'G.

slingshot arguments. Such arguments purport to show that distinct true sentences *p* and *q* (or nominalizations of them, such as 'the fact that *p*' and 'the fact that *q*') can never have different references. Assuming, as seems plausible, that any sentence logically equivalent to *p* has the same reference, and that the reference of a sentence is not altered by replacing any term in it by another term with the same reference, it appears to follow that the reference of *p* is the same as the reference of any other true sentence *q*. This seems to spell trouble for the *correspondence theory of truth and for an *ontology of *facts, but it is thought by many that the fault lies more with slingshot arguments than with their targets.   E.J.L.

S. Neale, *Facing Facts* (Oxford, 2001).

slippery slope. The 'slippery slope' is the name of an argument based on a certain view of human nature, not on logic, and commonly used in non-philosophical discussions of moral issues. The reasoning is that, though a practice may be unobjectionable in one type of case, if it is once permitted, its use will inevitably be extended to other more morally dubious cases. Thus it is argued that, though research using human embryos immediately after fertilization may be morally defensible, the period for research will inevitably be extended, until we shall find ourselves using children and adults for research, without their consent. The inevitability here supposed is not logical inevitability, but is thought to result from people's always wanting more than they have. In fact legislation or other forms of regulation can usually control an undesirable slide down the slippery slope.   M.WARN.

Michael Lockwood (ed.), *Dilemmas in Modern Medicine* (Oxford, 1985).
Mary Warnock, *The Uses of Philosophy* (Oxford, 1992).

Slovene philosophy. Its main areas of activity have been ethics, natural philosophy, and philosophical psychology, while the Aristotelian and Thomistic traditions have been the principal influences.

Medieval disputes in ontology and logic were chiefly concerned with the meaning, interpretation, and definition of terms; in the twelfth century, Hermanus de Carinthia wrote a treatise on essences.

At the time of the Slovene Cultural Revival (the late eighteenth century) the most prominent philosopher was Franc Samuel Karpe (1747–1806), whose central philosophy was associative psychology in the tradition of Locke. His empirical psychology distinguished between the lower epistemic capabilities, such as sensations and presentations, and the higher epistemic powers including the ability to form concepts, conceptual association, memory, speech, and prediction. Others followed a psychological approach to epistemic certainty.

Ethics was empirically and psychologically based, taking as its starting-point the needs of human beings and their desire for survival as the spur to cultural development. Morality was felt to be required where life does not follow the exigencies of nature. For Karpe, moral philoso-

phy was an extension of thought and imagination by the introduction of the emotive element. Reflexes determine personal behaviour, but human beings also possess the power of decision and free will. Whereas the pure qualities of mind are measurable, a particular soul may only be compared to them. Also in the period of the Cultural Revival mathematical metaphysics aimed to replace verbal argumentation by a system of mathematically based pictorial argumentation.

Starting from Meinongian theory of objects, France Veber developed his idea of knowledge of reality with the help of basic sensory experience. Recently the Veberian tradition has seen a revival with meetings of the Slovene–Austrian Philosophical Society (Ljubljana and Graz), and with *Acta Analytica*, an international journal dedicated mostly to the philosophy of psychology, edited by the Ljubljana-based Slovene Society for Analytical Philosophy, one of several active Slovene philosophical societies. Important work is also being done in the philosophy of science.   M.POT.

*Croatian philosophy; Serbian philosophy.

F. Jerman, 'The History of Philosophy in Slovenia', *Slovene Studies*, i (Indiana, 1991).
M. Stock and W. G. Stock, *International Bibliography of Austrian Philosophy*, i: *Psychologie und Philosophie der Grazer Schule* (Amsterdam, 1990).

Smart, J. J. C. (1920–). Emeritus Professor of the Australian National University and the University of Adelaide, Companion of the Order of Australia, Cambridge-born, educated at Glasgow and Oxford, and since the early 1950s a leading Australian philosopher, widely recognized for contributions in the philosophy of mind, philosophy of science, metaphysics, and ethics. Smart was an original architect of the brand of tough-minded *realism nowadays associated with philosophy in Australia. His realism, like his uncompromising *materialism, is the product of a conviction that philosophical theories are constrained by their scientific plausibility. This conviction underlies Smart's defence of a 'non-cognitivist' account of the basis of moral judgement and an advocacy of utilitarian normative principles, which are recommended by their simplicity and generality, features they share with an appropriately modest scientific perspective on the world.   J.HEIL

J. J. C. Smart, *Philosophy and Scientific Realism* (London, 1963).

Smith, Adam (1723–90). The famous economist was born in Kirkcaldy and educated at Glasgow and Oxford. Between 1751 and 1763 he was Professor of Logic and then of Moral Philosophy in Glasgow. He became tutor to a Scottish nobleman, whom he accompanied to Europe, returning to Kirkcaldy in 1767 where he lived with his mother. Latterly he was a Customs Commissioner in Edinburgh. He was intimate with Hume, whose views on morals and economics he shared. A Stoic rather than an Epicurean, he inherited the spectator theory of virtue from his teacher Francis Hutcheson. The theory is a form of psychological *naturalism, explaining moral good as a particular kind of pleasure, that of a spectator watching virtue at work. Smith suggested that the reason for the pleasure is the similarity between the virtue of the agent and that of the spectator himself. What makes the spectator's pleasure moral is its object, the agent's motive of consciously conforming with agreed standards of not harming the innocent, benefiting oneself, one's family and friends, and the societies to which one belongs, and being grateful to one's benefactors.   V.H.

*hidden hand.

Adam Smith, *The Theory of Moral Sentiments*, ed. D. D. Raphael and A. L. Macfie (Oxford, 1976).

snow is white. ' "Snow is white" is true if and only if snow is white' was Tarski's celebrated example of what he called an equivalence of the form *T*. He showed how truth, for sentences of a formalized language *L*, could be defined in such a way that an equivalence of the form *T* for each sentence of *L* is a consequence, and yet without generating the notorious *liar paradox. Some, notably Davidson, have attempted to exploit Tarski's ideas to provide an analysis of the *semantics of natural language. The interpretation of Tarski's results in the context of natural languages, as a theory of meaning, or as a diagnosis and solution of the liar paradox, has attracted criticism, however, largely because of what are seen as strong disanalogies between the structures of formalized and natural languages.   C.H.

*semantic theory of truth.

A. Tarski, *Logic, Semantics, Metamathematics*, 2nd edn. (Indianapolis, 1983).

social change, means of. In a democracy, ideally speaking, citizens produce social change by bringing problems to the attention of a government, which then gathers evidence and expert opinion. All important social issues are addressed, evidence is publicly discussed, and decisions are made by the people as a whole. Transparency and maximum citizen participation characterize all stages. Reasoned, just, and non-violent social change is the result.

Since this ideal process is realizable only in democracies, and achieved only rarely there, activists have used extra-governmental means to try to bring about change. Social movements, which may include demonstrations, heroic or self-sacrificial acts, advocacy and organizational groups, spokespeople, promotional writings, and artistic expressions, have brought important reform. Such movements—e.g. those for women's rights and for civil rights—typically go through many stages over long periods of time. They may be limited to civil disobedience and other non-violent tactics to appeal to conscience and generate sympathy, or they may employ violence to retaliate for perceived wrongs or to weaken opposing forces and compel negotiations. More extreme are revolutions attempting to alter basic social institutions and not work within them; proponents justify them as the only means of eliminating pervasive and destructive conditions (e.g. a repressive regime, an exploitative economic system).

One country may try to produce social change in another by diplomatic means, by imposing economic sanctions, or by supporting revolutionary movements or terrorist activities within it. Even more direct is the invasion and subjugation of another country, defended as alone effective in eliminating great evils within that country or in preventing it from causing enormous harm to others. These methods are increasingly controversial, as they appear to violate moral standards, international law, or the United Nations Charter.

Attempts at reform always face the conservatism of the public media, controlled by the state in authoritarian regimes and strongly constrained by financial pressures in liberal ones. The media are usually part of the very power structure being challenged. Recognizing that media have a central role in shaping public opinion, activists use mass demonstrations, art, sympathetic publishers, and 'alternative' media developed by the activist community itself to gain a public voice.   C.C.

Edward S. Herman and Noam Chomsky, *Manufacturing Consent: The Political Economy of the Mass Media* (New York, 2002).
J. L. Holzerefe and Robert O. Keohane (eds.), *Humanitarian Intervention: Ethical, Legal and Political Dilemmas* (Cambridge, 2003).
S. Tarrow, *Power in Movement: Social Movements and Contentious Politics*, 2nd edn. (Cambridge, 1998).

social constructionism. Analysis of 'knowledge' or 'reality' or both as contingent upon social relations, and as made out of continuing human practices, by processes such as reification, sedimentation, habitualization. Schutz's *phenomenology—the analysis of the structure of the common-sense world of everyday life—is an important influence, although current exponents draw on a variety of sources including *hermeneutics, the later Wittgenstein's intersubjective theory of meaning, and the Marxist conception of *praxis (which emphasizes how knowledge and politics are contingent upon work and economic relations). Social constructionists do not believe in the possibility of value-free foundations or sources of knowledge, nor do they conceptualize a clear objective–subjective distinction, or a clear distinction between 'knowledge' and 'reality'. The position, therefore, has profound implications for the practice and philosophy of science, and for political philosophy.   E.J.F.

*social facts; communitarianism.

Peter Berger and Thomas Luckmann, *The Social Construction of Reality: A Treatise in the Sociology of Knowledge* (Harmondsworth, 1967).

social contract: *see* contract, social.

Social Darwinism. Social Darwinism is a diverse collection of nineteenth- and early twentieth-century doctrines that enjoyed considerable popularity and that interpreted various human social phenomena in the light of (what was taken to be) Darwinian evolutionary theory. Perhaps the most influential form of Social Darwinism viewed society and the economy as a competitive arena in which the 'fittest' would rise to the top. With this doctrine went the worry that various cultural practices and social reforms meant to provide for the least well-off in fact lessen this 'natural selection' and promote instead a 'degeneration' of the species. From a contemporary perspective, Social Darwinists conflated social success with reproductive fitness (wealth and education in fact tend to be inversely correlated with birth-rate) and questions of moral rightness with matters of a supposed 'natural order'.   P.R.

*evolution.

R. C. Bannister, *Social Darwinism: Science and Myth in Anglo-American Social Thought* (Philadelphia, 1979).

social engineering. Concept popularized by Karl Popper's critique in his *Open Society and its Enemies* (Princeton, NJ, 1950), it takes two forms. *Utopian* social engineering, associated with Plato, Hegel, Marx, and their totalitarian heirs, is committed to the wholesale transformation of society through central planning according to a comprehensive ideal plan and unlimited by any constraints from competing social institutions (e.g. the church). *Piecemeal* social engineering involves only 'searching for, and fighting against, the greatest and most urgent evils of society'. Popper's distinction aside, social engineering as a legitimate activity of government is essential to the welfare state and to all versions of *socialism and *communism. It is anathema to *libertarianism but endorsed under constraints by modern *liberalism.   H.A.B.

Friedrich A. Hayek, *The Road to Serfdom* (Chicago, 1944).
Barbara Wootton, *Freedom under Planning* (Chapel Hill, NC, 1945).

social epistemology. Two distinct, but not unrelated, fields of study compete for this label. The first is a version of the theory of knowledge which fully acknowledges our dependence on other people in this matter, and does not relegate it to the marginal or supplementary status of 'testimony'. All but the most elemental knowledge—of the sort possessed by infants and animals—presupposes the mastery of the indisputably social institution of language. The second, and less philosophical, is a concern with the social determinants of belief. It has obvious relevance to moral and political convictions. Attempts to apply it to the findings of natural science—let alone those of mathematics—are less persuasive.   A.Q.

*sociology of knowledge.

Alvin Goldman, *Knowledge in a Social World* (Oxford, 1999).

social facts. A *fact is a social fact when it is a statement concerning the forms of organization present in a society or it ascribes an irreducibly social property to an entity. According to Durkheim, social facts result from treating social phenomena, including ourselves, as *things*; they can therefore be approached, it is claimed, in the same objective way as the facts with which the natural sciences deal.

Social facts, such as 'George W. Bush is President of the United States' and 'France is a charter member of the United Nations', are the concern of sociologists, whose task it is to attain a body of knowledge on the basis of which the actions of human beings as members of society can be understood. The main question in this area concerns the relationship of such facts to facts about individuals: are social facts reducible to, or explained solely by, facts such as the beliefs and desires of individuals, i.e. non-social facts? Methodological individualists have answered in the affirmative, insisting that there are not both societies and their members, and that everything that happens can be explained without recourse to social entities and social properties. Methodological holists, on the other hand, claim that understanding some types of behaviour necessarily depends upon understanding the holistic phenomena of social structures.

The debate about social facts has thus centred on ambiguities in the important but unclear concept of 'reduction' and is bound up with the question of the merits and demerits of functionalist explanations in sociology. Clearly, it is also a debate about the purposes of social science.   P.W.

*methodological holism and individualism.

E. Durkheim, *The Rules of Sociological Method* (New York, 1964).
M. Gilbert, *On Social Facts* (London, 1989).
D. Ruben, *The Metaphysics of the Social World* (London, 1985).

socialism. It is difficult to subsume all the various socio-economic beliefs that have been referred to as 'socialism' under one definition. In its broadest sense, socialism refers to the views of those who: (1) claim that *capitalism has grave moral flaws and (2) advocate some revolutionary socio-economic reform to remedy these flaws.

Certain elements of what is typically thought of as socialist thought appear throughout the entire history of philosophy, such as in Thomas More's *Utopia* and even Plato's *Republic*. But the term 'socialism' was first used in connection with the views of early nineteenth-century social critics, such as Robert Owen, Saint-Simon, Charles Fourier, and Pierre Proudhon. These social critics were reacting to the excesses and injustices of early capitalism, and advocated reforms such as the transformation of society into small communities in which private *property was to be abolished and the radical redistribution of wealth. Socialism is also an important part of the philosophy of Karl Marx and *Marxism. For Marxists, socialism is viewed as a stage in history characterized, in part, by state ownership of all capital goods and central planning of the economy. This stage in history they see as transitional between capitalism and the final stage of history, *communism, which will be characterized by the absence of differing social classes and thus the end of class warfare.

Among the grave moral flaws that socialists typically claim to be inherent in capitalism are vast, unjust inequalities in wealth, income, opportunities, and power. Other moral flaws seen in capitalism include excessive individualism, competition and materialism, and the *exploitation of ordinary working people. Perhaps more than anything else, however, socialists oppose the unjust oppression of one group by another, whether through class domination, discrimination, or an unequal distribution of power. In short, socialism, in the broad sense, champions the 'underdogs' of society. The revolutionary socio-economic reforms that have been proposed by socialists for remedying the declared moral flaws of capitalism are so diverse as to defy any precise characterization. Typically, these reforms involve radical changes in the ownership or distribution of property throughout society. It is questionable, however, whether 'socialism' in this broad sense is a specific enough term to be very useful. Moreover, not all those who see grave moral flaws in capitalism and call for major reforms, or who have joined the fight against oppression, consider themselves to be socialists; to call them 'socialists' anyway invites confusing their views with socialism in the narrower sense to be considered next.

The narrower, and thus perhaps more useful, sense in which the term 'socialism' is often used is to refer to an economic system which features: (1) state ownership of the means of production and control over investment throughout the economy; (2) a more equal distribution of income and wealth than typically found in capitalism; and (3) democratic election of government officials responsible for economic decisions. Those who advocate a system with the above three features have, in the past, often advocated a fourth feature as well: government planning of not just investment, but the entire economy; that is, government planning of what goods and services are to be produced, how they are to be produced, in what quantities, and at what prices they are to be sold, rather then simply allowing these matters to be determined by the market through supply and demand. If the economic system includes this fourth feature, it is referred to as 'central-planning socialism'.

The most significant of these features for defining socialism in the narrow sense is state ownership of the means of production and control over investment; this is, arguably, the only feature that qualifies as being both a necessary and a sufficient defining characteristic. The second feature, that of income and wealth under socialism being distributed more equally than under capitalism, is something about which socialists generally agree, although there is much disagreement about what principle, exactly, should govern this distribution. A number of alternatives that have been advocated, including, for example, 'To each equally', 'To each according to his or her effort', and 'To each according to his or her need'. The third feature, democratic elections, is one that most socialist theorists insist upon, although whenever socialism of the central-planning variety has been put into effect in a country, *democracy has not flourished. The fourth feature—namely, government planning of the entire economy—has been, perhaps, the most controversial feature. Advocates of this feature argue that central-planning remedies well-known flaws of capitalism, such as monop-

olies, business cycles, unemployment, vast inequalities in the distribution of wealth, and the mistreatment of workers. On the other hand, conservative economists, such as Ludwig von Mises and Friedrich Hayek, argue that central-planning can never come close to matching the efficiency of the *market, because central-planners can never match the overall information inherent in the decision-making throughout a market economy, nor can business managers in a centrally planned economy ever match the motivation of entrepreneurs in a market economy, who are driven by private profit.

The arguments of these conservative economists, as well as the relatively poor performance of economies that, for the most part, have been centrally planned, have led many socialists to abandon feature four, and to propose instead a reliance upon the market for almost everything other than investment. State control over investment, combined with a reliance upon the market for almost everything other than investment, will, these new socialists argue, remedy the main flaws inherent in capitalism while, at the same time, retaining the productivity advantages of the market. The economists Oskar Lange and Fred M. Taylor were early proponents of such an approach, which is referred to as 'market socialism'. Recent proponents of a similar approach, such as the philosopher David Schweickart, have added the feature of *worker control to the general idea of market socialism to form a system often referred to as 'worker-control socialism'. With worker control, the workers of each business enterprise are to manage it themselves through direct democracy or, as will more often be the case, are to elect, periodically, a team of managers who then manage the enterprise for them. An advantage of worker control is claimed to be that managers who must face workers in periodic elections will therefore be motivated, above all else, to do what is *beneficial* for workers, rather than exploiting them. Still other reformers propose an economic system featuring worker control, but without state ownership of the means of production and control over investment; rather, the workers of each business enterprise are themselves to own its means of production, and investment is to be left to the market. But since, with such an economic system, all the means of production are privately owned and the market prevails throughout the entire economy, this system is more appropriately referred to as 'worker-control capitalism', not socialism.

D.W.HAS.

*conservatism; liberalism; anti-communism; markets and the public good; privatization.

N. Scott Arnold, *Marx's Radical Critique of Capitalist Society: A Reconstruction and Critical Evaluation* (Oxford, 1990).

G. D. H. Cole, *History of Socialist Thought*, 7 vols. (London, 1953–60).

D. W. Haslett, *Capitalism with Morality* (Oxford, 1994).

Kai Nielsen, *Equality and Liberty: A Defense of Radical Egalitarianism* (Totowa, NJ, 1985).

David Schweickart, *Capitalism or Worker Control?* (New York, 1980).

social philosophy. The term 'social philosophy' does not have a fixed meaning in current philosophical circles. Sometimes it is used as more or less equivalent to *'political philosophy': that is, to the normative discussion—analytical or substantive—of questions about how society should be organized. But usually it is taken to be the non-normative discussion—again, analytical or substantive—of what is involved in having social organization: the non-normative discussion of what sorts of entity appear with the onset of society and of how they relate to individual human subjects. I shall take social philosophy in this latter sense, as a sort of social ontology: as an account of what there is in the social world.

Social philosophy in the ontological sense takes as granted that there is no society without individual intentional agents: without subjects who apparently act, other things being equal, on the basis of their beliefs and desires, and who are capable of exhibiting rationality—and of seeking to exhibit rationality—in the formation and maintenance of those beliefs and desires (Pettit, *The Common Mind*, pt. 1). The question which it raises bears on what more we should include in our ontological stock-taking of society; and of how the more we should include, if there is any, relates to individual intentional subjects.

This question may be raised on the basis simply of our everyday experience and understanding of social life: on the basis of our commonplace sociology, as we might call it. But it is usually raised not just on this basis, but equally on the basis of what the best social science—whatever that is taken to be—tells us about the social world. Social philosophy becomes in good part an ontology of social science. (*Social science, philosophy of.) Consider an analogy. The philosophy of mind seeks to tell us what is involved in a creature's being a psychological subject, as social philosophy tries to say what is involved in an arrangement's being a social form of organization. In raising the psychological question, the philosopher will take account of all that we know, in our experience of ourselves and others, of human psychology. But if he is serious, he will also take account of what the best psychology and neuroscience, as he sees it, says about psychological subjects. Similarly, the social philosopher who is anxious to provide an ontological inventory of the social realm will take account not just of the sociological commonplaces, but also of the scientific verities—as he sees them—about the social realm.

We should note, in passing, that the stock of commonplaces that a social philosopher recognizes may vary, depending on the scientific verities that he recognizes. Someone who takes a radical Marxist view of social science, for example, is likely to be less impressed than someone of a more conservative bent about the alleged commonplace status of the claim that people generally know the reasons why they do things: that they are not generally ignorant or deceived about their motivations. The situation here is again parallel to the situation in psychology. As there are rival theories in social science, so there are competing stories in psychology and neuro-science; and as the social-scientific variation impacts on what sociological commonplaces are recognized, so the psychological and neuroscientific diversity correlates with a variation in what are taken to be commonplaces about psychological subjects.

What we have been saying bears on the *dialectic whereby a particular social philosophy, a particular ontology of society, will be defended. The dialectic will involve arguing for a particular trade-off of apparent commonplaces for alleged social-scientific verities and investigating what the preferred package of commonplaces and verities suggests about the ontology of the social world. But what are the different social philosophies between which we are to judge? What are the main lines of division in the area?

There are two aspects to social life. There is the social *interaction* between individuals in virtue of which various relationships get formed: relationships involving communication, affection, collaboration, exchange, recognition, esteem, or whatever. And there is the social *aggregation* of individual attitudes and actions in virtue of which various institutions get established: these institutions will include common instrumentalities such as languages, cultures, and markets; groups, like the club or union or party, whose essence it is to have a mode of collective behaviour; groups that may have only a non-behavioural collective identity like genders, races, and classes; and shared resources of the kind illustrated by museums, libraries, and states.

Social philosophy concerns itself both with issues raised by interaction and with questions associated with aggregation. I will look at the interaction area first and then at that of aggregation. But before going on, one preliminary comment. Interaction need not involve people's intentional attitudes: after all, my breathing the oxygen that you would otherwise consume is a form of interaction. And, equally, aggregation need not involve such attitudes either: aggregation accounts for the fact, for example, that together you and I weigh twenty stone. When I speak of social interaction and social aggregation, I assume that these are forms of interaction and aggregation that require the people involved to have certain intentional attitudes; I ignore interaction and aggregation of the purely physical, and certainly non-social, sort.

On the side of interaction, the main issue in social philosophy is that which divides so-called atomists from non-atomists (Taylor, *Philosophy and the Human Sciences*). The atomist holds that individual human beings do not depend on social relationships for the appearance of any distinctive human capacities. The non-atomist holds that they do. The atomist defends an image of human beings under which they come to society with all the characteristic properties that they will ever display; social life does not transform them in any essential manner. The non-atomist denies this, believing that it is only in the experience of social relationships that the human being comes properly into his own.

This formulation of the issue is crucially vague, in at least two respects. First, it is not clear what sort of social dependence is in question; and second, it is not obvious what are to count as distinctive human capacities. The traditional resolution of the second vagueness is to nominate the relevant capacity as the ability—the actualized, concrete ability—to reason and think. And this resolution prompts a resolution of the first vagueness. It suggests that the question cannot be whether human beings depend causally on their relationships with one another for having the capacity to think. If that were the question, then the atomist's position would be extraordinarily weak; all the evidence of children raised in isolation, as well as our sense of what we learn from our parents and teachers, argues against it. Thus the issue must be whether individual human beings depend on their relationships with one another in a non-causal way for having the ability to reason and think (Pettit, *The Common Mind*, ch. 4).

It is plausible that individuals depend on social relationships in a non-causal way for having the ability—the actualized, concrete ability—to speak the local language; without other individuals, or without social relationships to such individuals, it is unclear how a person could count as speaking a language shared with them. The non-atomist holds that the same sort of social dependence governs the ability of an individual to reason and think: the ability, as we may take it, not just to have beliefs and desires, but to act with a view to having rational beliefs and desires. The atomist denies this, sticking by the view that all that is involved in reason and thought, all that is non-causally required for their appearance, is available to the individual outside society.

The debate between atomists and non-atomists has centred around the connection between thought and language. Atomists have taken their lead from Hobbes, who argues that, however useful language is for mnemonic, taxonomic, and communicative purposes, thinking is possible without speech, even without any inchoate form of speech. Non-atomists have tended to follow Rousseau and the Romantic tradition with which he is associated—a tradition also encompassing Herder and Hegel—in arguing, first, that language is social and, second, that thought requires language.

The atomist tradition has been dominant in English-speaking philosophy, while the non-atomist has had a considerable presence in France and Germany. One source of non-atomism in the English-speaking world has been the work of the later Wittgenstein, in which it is suggested that following a rule—and, therefore, thinking—is possible only in the context of social practices and relationships. This very strong non-atomist thesis may also be weakened, so that the claim is that following a rule of a characteristic kind—say, a suitably scrutable kind—requires such a social context (Pettit, *The Common Mind*, ch. 4). Another source of non-atomism in recent English-speaking philosophy has been the argument that the content of a person's thoughts is fixed not just by what goes on in his head, but by the linguistic community to which he belongs and to which he aspires to remain faithful (Hurley, *Natural Reasons*).

So much for the main question raised in social philosophy by the interactive side of social life. What now of the issues generated by the aggregative aspect of society? There are a number of interesting questions raised by the aggregative structure of society (*methodological holism and individualism), but one issue is of striking importance. This is whether the entities that appear with the social aggregation of individual attitudes and actions give the lie to our ordinary sense of intentional agency: whether their presence means that our commonplace psychological sense of one another—our sense of one another as, most of the time, more or less rational creatures—is unsound; whether it means that, contrary to appearances, we are in some way the dupes of higher-level patterns or forces (Pettit, *The Common Mind*, ch. 3). The individualist, to use a name that also bears further connotations, denies that aggregate entities have this effect; the non-individualist insists that they do.

One extreme sort of individualism would say that intentional agency is not compromised by any aggregate, social entities, because in strict truth no such entities exist; they have the status of logical fictions, as it is sometimes put, or something of the kind. This doctrine is not very plausible, for who can sensibly deny, at least for reasons specific to the social domain, that there are languages and organizations and collectivities and the like? The more appealing form of individualism would say that while there are indeed a variety of aggregate entities, there is nothing about those entities that suggests that our received, commonplace psychology is mistaken. True, there are aggregate regularities associated with such entities: for example, a rise in unemployment tends to be followed by a rise in crime; the fact that something is in an organization's interest generally means that agents of the organization will pursue it; and the optimality of a certain procedure in certain contexts—say, an economic decision-making procedure—often ensures its stability. But the individualist will argue that the obtaining of those regularities does not signal the presence of forces unrecognized in commonplace psychology, nor the operation of any mechanism—say, any selection mechanism—that belies the assumptions of that psychology. That the regularities obtain can be explained within that psychology, given the context in which the relevant agents find themselves and given their understanding—perhaps involving relevant aggregate-level concepts—of that context.

The issue between individualism and non-individualism, as this should make clear, ties up closely with questions of social explanation: questions in the philosophy of social science about the resources required in order to make sense of social happenings and regularities (James, *The Content of Social Explanation*; Ruben, *The Metaphysics of the Social World*). The individualist may admit that social explanation can happily invoke structural or aggregate factors, but he must be able to argue that the causal relevance ascribed to those factors is not inconsistent with the assumptions of commonplace psychology. The non-individualist will maintain that, on the contrary, aggregate factors have causal relevance in such a predetermining way, or on the basis of such a predestining form of selection, that our commonplace psychology has to be seen as deeply misleading (Pettit, *The Common Mind*, ch. 3).   P.P.

*social facts.

Susan Hurley, *Natural Reasons* (New York, 1989).
Susan James, *The Content of Social Explanation* (Cambridge, 1984).
Philip Pettit, *The Common Mind: An Essay on Psychology, Society and Politics* (New York, 1993).
David-Hillel Ruben, *The Metaphysics of the Social World* (London, 1985).
Charles Taylor, *Philosophy and the Human Sciences* (Cambridge, 1985).

social science, philosophy of. The philosophy of any science comes in two varieties, as the methodology or as the ontology of the discipline. The methodology looks at questions to do with the nature of observations, laws and theories, the logic of induction and confirmation, the requirements of understanding and explanation, and so on. The ontology looks at questions to do with what the discipline posits—what it says there is—and with whether those posits are consistent with more or less commonplace beliefs.

The philosophy of social science, as this distinction would lead us to expect, has both a methodological and an ontological aspect; we might do better, indeed, to regard it as two disciplines, one methodological, the other ontological. The methodology of social science concerns itself with the implicit claim of social science to be able to generate knowledge, especially knowledge otherwise unavailable, of the social world; in particular, it has tended in recent years to focus on the claim of social science to be able to provide distinctive explanations (James, *The Content of Social Explanation*; Ruben, *The Metaphysics of the Social World*). The ontology of social science concerns itself with the sorts of entity that the discipline posits— entities like aggregate regularities and structural constraints—and at how far those entities are consistent with our more or less commonplace view of human beings and their relationships. I will discuss only the methodology of social science here, as the ontology of social science is covered under the heading of *social philosophy. (See Ryan, *The Philosophy of the Social Sciences*, for an overview.)

The methodology of social science may be motivated in one of two ways: internally or externally. The externally motivated methodology of social science sees its job as the replication, in the social area, of the methodological discussion of natural science. Every methodology of natural science will offer an account of observation, induction, explanation, and related topics. The externally motivated methodology of social science looks at social science with a view to seeing how far that account is borne out there, and with what nuances. In principle, the possibility is open that the account will be revised in the light of reflection on social science. In practice, the lessons from the area of natural science are often taken as more or less canonical.

The upshot of this approach to the methodology of social science may be conservative or critical. The conservative methodologist holds that, in general, social science conforms to the canonical methods and that it deserves to be treated as seriously as natural science (Papineau, *For Science in Social Science*). The critical methodologist, on the other hand, argues that at least in some cases social science deviates from the standards fixed by the natural sciences and to that extent should be regarded as something less than science: as pseudo-science, for example, or common sense. The dominant methodology of natural science in this century has been associated with the positivist movement and with post-positivist variations such as that developed by Karl Popper and his school. It is striking that such positivists and post-positivists have sometimes been conservative in their methodological reflections on the social sciences, sometimes critical. Among the critical trends, we find a tendency to see history and ethnographic anthropology as exercises in common sense rather than science, and a disposition to dismiss speculative theories influenced by the work of Marx and Freud as pseudo-scientific.

So much for the externally motivated methodology of social science. What now of the internally motivated variety? This alternative approach, unparalleled in the methodology of natural science, has its source in a peculiar feature of the social sciences. The social sciences were conceived and pursued, from the very beginning, under the influence of ideals, particularly ideals of scientific objectivity and progress, deriving from the eighteenth-century *Enlightenment movement. The first social scientists were economists and sociologists, as we would call them today, and they were self-consciously concerned about producing something that would count not as philosophy, not as literature, not as common sense, but as science: as a project faithful to the image forged by natural science.

The scientific intention—the intention to make science—has remained characteristic of work in the social sciences. It puts social scientists, paradoxically, under an obligation of a philosophical kind: the obligation to show that the sort of analysis they pursue is of a properly scientific kind. And in this way it gives rise to the internally motivated approach to the philosophy—strictly, the methodology—of social science. Under this approach, the task for the methodology of social science is not primarily to map the practices of the social sciences, as if they were on a par with the natural sciences, but rather to interrogate and assess the philosophies or ideologies whereby the social sciences try to legitimize what they do: that is, try to show that what they do is genuinely scientific in character.

It is not usual to present things in this way, but, broadly speaking, there are three main ideologies that have been invoked—individually or in various combinations—by social scientists, in the scientific legitimization of their enterprise. These each mark a feature that putatively distinguishes social science from mere common sense, mere social lore. The first ideology hails social science as an explanatory enterprise of culturally universal validity; the second as an enterprise that is interpretatively neutral, not being warped by people's self-understanding; and the third as an enterprise that enjoys evaluative independence: value-freedom. The universality, neutrality, and independence claimed are each meant to establish social science as objective, and therefore scientifically respectable, in a way in which social lore is not; each notion offers an explication of what scientific objectivity involves.

Social lore is always lore about a particular social milieu and culture, and an aspiration to cultural universality, if it can be vindicated, would certainly give social science a distinctive status. Such an aspiration is supported in a variety of traditions: among anthropologists and sociologists of a Durkheimian cast, among many Marxist scholars, and among those economists who think that all human behaviour, and the patterns to which it gives rise, can be explained by reference to *Homo economicus*. But methodologists of social science have claimed many reasons to question the possibility of any universalist, or at least any straightforwardly universalist, theory. The hermeneutic tradition that has long been dominant in Germany and the analytical tradition sponsored by the work of the later Wittgenstein both suggest that any explanation of human behaviour has to start with the culturally specific concepts in which people understand their environment and cannot aspire, therefore, to a substantive universality. The debate on these questions ranges widely, encompassing issues to do with cultural and other forms of relativism (Winch, *The Idea of a Social Science and its Relation to Philosophy*; Hollis and Lukes, *Rationality and Relativism*).

Social lore is not only particularistic, it is also designed to represent people as subjectively understandable or interpretable. We, the local consumers of such lore, know what it is like to be creatures of the kind represented and know how we would go about communicating with them. The second, and perhaps least persuasive, ideology of social science suggests that this disposition to represent people as subjectively understandable comes of a limited perspective which social science transcends. It suggests that social science can aspire to an objective explanation of people's behaviour without worrying about whether the explanation fits with their self-understanding: without being anxious to ensure that it makes native sense of them and facilitates interpersonal communication. The ideology suggests that social science, in the received phrases, can aspire to a form of *Erklären*, or explanation, that need not service the needs of interpersonal *Verstehen*, or understanding. Methodologists of social science have claimed many reasons to question this aspiration to *Verstehen*-free explanation. The hermeneutic and Wittgensteinian thinkers mentioned earlier both reject the idea that people can be properly understood without facilitating communication (Winch, *The Idea of a Social Science*). And the many philosophers who follow the lead of Donald Davidson on interpretation argue that there is no interpreting human subjects without representing them as more or less rational and more or less interpersonally scrutable (Macdonald and Pettit, *Semantics and Social Science*).

Social lore is often evaluatively committed, as well as being particularistic and orientated to subjective understanding. It takes a form which is premissed on an evaluative characterization of the status quo. Thus it may characterize the beliefs, and explain the behaviour, of rulers on the assumption that the regime they sustain is unjust. The third and most common legitimizing ideology of social science, one associated in particular with the German sociologist Max Weber, holds that in this respect—and perhaps in this respect only—social science can do scientifically better than social lore. It can acknowledge that the agents in the society have evaluative beliefs, and it can take account of these in its explanation of what they do, without itself endorsing any such beliefs; it can be objective, in the familiar sense of remaining uncommitted on evaluative questions. Methodologists of social science have also sought reasons to doubt this claim, but the debate has been confused by differences over what sorts of evaluative commitment would really be damaging to the pretensions of social science (Macdonald and Pettit, *Semantics and Social Science*, ch. 4).   P.P.

*social facts.

Martin Hollis and Steven Lukes (eds.), *Rationality and Relativism* (Oxford, 1982).

Susan James, *The Content of Social Explanation* (Cambridge, 1984).

Graham Macdonald and Philip Pettit, *Semantics and Social Science* (London, 1971).

David Papineau, *For Science in Social Science* (London, 1978).

David-Hillel Ruben, *The Metaphysics of the Social World* (London, 1985).

Alan Ryan, *The Philosophy of the Social Sciences* (London, 1970).

Peter Winch, *The Idea of a Social Science and its Relation to Philosophy* (London, 1958).

society. A set of individuals and/or institutions in relations governed by practical interdependence, convention, and perhaps law—which relations may vary from the local to the international. The modern concept emerged in later eighteenth-century Europe (in arguments against absolutism and civic republicanism) to denote a supposed sphere of causal and moral self-sufficiency lying between the political and the personal. The concept was the ground for the new 'science' of 'sociology'. It later came to be used more loosely to include the political and the personal. Many *liberalisms have resisted the idea of 'the social', preferring to see individuals as self-sufficient. Some philosophers, however, including Williams and Rawls, as well as some critics of liberalism, like MacIntyre, have recently reasserted conceptions of the social as the ground of moral possibility and moral judgement.   G.P.H.

*communitarianism; organic society; social philosophy; social science, philosophy of.

'Democracy', 'Equality', 'Feudal System', 'Liberty', 'Nation', 'Sovereignty', 'Burke', 'Constant', 'Hegel', 'Marx', 'Montesquieu', 'Rousseau', 'Sieyès', 'Tocqueville', in F. Furet and M. Ozouf (eds.), *A Critical Dictionary of the French Revolution* (Cambridge, Mass., 1989).

society, organic: *see* organic society.

sociobiology. Sociobiologists attempt to explain patterns of interaction in group-living organisms ranging from ants to human beings within the categories established by Darwin's theory of natural selection and the mathematical theory of genetics. Of particular interest is the behaviour involved in herding, co-operation, aggression, altruism, mate selection, and sexual exclusivity or non-exclusivity. Sociobiology is often criticized on the grounds that its explanatory hypotheses are not easily verified, or that they reflect conventional, unexamined, or impossible assumptions, especially about natural patterns of behaviour for human beings.   CATH.W.

  *biology, philosophical problems of; evolutionary ethics.

Richard Dawkins, *The Selfish Gene* (London, 1978).
E. O. Wilson, *Sociobiology: The New Synthesis* (Cambridge, Mass., 1975).

sociolect: *see* idiolect.

sociology: *see* Adorno, Comte; Durkheim; Mead; Spencer; Weber.

sociology of knowledge. This explores the social causes of the formation and diffusion of beliefs. Forerunners include Bacon, Comte, Nietzsche, Marx, and Engels. It was established as an independent discipline by Scheler and Mannheim, and also by anthropologists, such as Durkheim and Lévy-Bruhl, studying the social causes of religions and ideologies. Natural science was generally credited with privileged access to reality and thus immunity to sociological explanation. This discrimination is unwarranted. If sociology gives sufficient conditions for beliefs without reference to their truth-value, it undermines their claim to truth, leading to scepticism or relativism. But this consequence is avoided if it gives only necessary conditions for the formation and spread of beliefs, conditions which need not determine the content of beliefs in detail, or if it explains the emergence and acceptance of a theory despite its being underdetermined by the evidence. In these cases, the truth of beliefs and/or evidence for it remains an essential part of their explanation, supplemented, but not excluded, by social factors.
                                        M.J.I.

J. E. Curtis and J. W. Petras (eds.), *The Sociology of Knowledge: A Reader* (New York, 1970).
Karl Mannheim, *Ideology and Utopia: An Introduction to the Sociology of Knowledge* (1929, tr. London, 1960).
Max Scheler, *Problems of a Sociology of Knowledge* (1924, tr. London, 1980).

Socrates (470–399 BC). Athenian philosopher, teacher of Plato. Socrates is one of the most significant yet most enigmatic figures in the history of philosophy: significant because his relation to Plato was crucial to the development of the latter, and thus indirectly to the development of much later philosophy; enigmatic because he wrote nothing himself, and therefore presents the challenge of reconstructing him from the evidence of others. It is therefore necessary to start with a brief account of that evidence.

Sources. Assuming the truth of the generally (though not universally) accepted view that all Plato's dialogues were written after Socrates' death, the only evidence from his own lifetime consists of references to him in Athenian comedy from the last quarter of the fifth century BC. While most of these are very brief, a sentence or so mentioning some singular trait such as Socrates' loquacity, or his going barefoot, we have a full-scale portrayal in Aristophanes' *Clouds*, first produced in 423, in which Socrates is a central character. Though this portrayal does preserve some traits of the actual Socrates as recorded elsewhere, such as his peculiar gait, it is recognized that the Socrates of the play is not a realistic portrait but a caricature of a representative 'Sophist' combining features of various individuals (e.g. the theory of the divinity of the air propounded by the contemporary natural philosopher Diogenes of Apollonia) and of stock comic types, such as the half-starved Pythagorean ascetic. The fact that Aristophanes chose Socrates as a peg on which to hang this caricature shows that he was by then a comparatively well-known figure, and the dramatic circumstances of his condemnation and death (see below) gave rise to a considerable Socratic literature, comprising both imaginative reproductions of his conversations and controversial works (some hostile, some favourable) focusing on his trial. Apart from fragmentary remains of some other authors (e.g. Aeschines of Sphettus), the only substantial survivors of this literature are the dialogues of Plato and the Socratic writings of Xenophon, which include a version of his speech at his trial and purported 'memoirs' of various conversations. While these are in broad agreement with Plato in attributing to Socrates certain modes of argument (e.g. inductive arguments) and certain specific doctrines (e.g. that virtue is knowledge), their tone is much less speculative and their picture of Socrates much more conventional and practically orientated than Plato's, reflecting the different characters and interests of the respective authors. While Plato's dialogues present a consistent and compelling portrait of Socrates' highly individual personality, his primary purpose in writing them was not that of a biographer (at least on the modern conception as a chronicler one of whose primary aims is historical accuracy). Rather, he writes as a philosophical apologist, who seeks to present Socrates as the ideal embodiment of philosophy, unjustly traduced by confusion with bogus practitioners (*Sophists) and unjustly condemned for his dedication to the philosophical life. It is, therefore, quite natural that he should in some places put into the mouth of Socrates doctrines of his own which the historical Socrates did not hold (see below). In what are standardly regarded as his later dialogues the importance of the figure of Socrates diminishes, and his role as a figure of philosophical authority is taken over by others, in some cases by impersonal figures such as the Eleatic Visitor of the *Sophist* and *Statesman* and the Athenian of the *Laws* (traditionally regarded as Plato's last dialogue, and the only one in which Socrates does not figure at all). It is reasonable to explain this progressive disappearance of Socrates as a reflection of the development of Plato's views and methods in directions independent of the elder philosopher. Aristotle, who was born in 384 and came to Athens to study in the Academy in 367, must have derived his knowledge of Socrates primarily (though doubtless not exclusively) from Platonic sources. That is not, of course, to say that his only information was Plato's dialogues; though some of his references to Socrates are clearly, and others possibly, to passages in the dialogues, there is ground for thinking that some are independent (see below).

Life. Socrates spent all his life in Athens, apart from military service abroad. The sources represent him as spending his time in philosophical discussion, and how he made his living is unclear; while there is a tradition that he followed (at least for a time) his father's trade as a stonemason, he may have depended largely on support from friends. Plato is emphatic that he never took money for philosophizing, and makes that a central point of differentiation between him and the (professional) Sophists. He was married to Xanthippe, whose bad temper (together with Socrates' equanimity in putting up with it) became a stock element in a comic tradition which endured from antiquity to at least the nineteenth century. (For instance, Chaucer's Wife of Bath tells how Socrates sat quietly when Xanthippe 'caste pisse upon his heed', merely remarking mildly, 'Before the thunder stops the rain starts.') If there is any factual basis to this legend it is worth noting that Xanthippe, who, as Plato recounts in the *Phaedo*, had two infant children at the time of Socrates' death, must have been least thirty years younger than her husband, and also that Socrates' life-style can hardly have made him a reliable bread-winner. Some ancient sources mention a second wife, or perhaps concubine, named Myrto; the comic tradition represents Socrates as living bigamously with her and Xanthippe (doubtless another source of irritation to the latter), but the historical basis is very dubious.

The 'intellectual autobiography' which Plato puts into Socrates's mouth in the *Phaedo* represents him as having been at one time keenly interested in natural philosophy, but as having become disillusioned by the neglect of teleological explanation by its leading theorists. Assuming the historical accuracy of that account, his interests seem to have shifted to questions of conduct and especially of its fundamental principles, while the magnetism of his personality attracted to him a circle of mainly younger men, some of whom, including Plato and some of his relatives, were opposed to the Athenian democratic system. It is impossible to determine how far Socrates himself shared such views; however critical he may have been of democracy in theory, he was in practice a loyal citizen, serving with distinction on the battlefield and adhering strictly to his ideals of legality and justice under severe pressure, once under the democracy, when he was alone in opposing an unconstitutional proposal in the Assembly, and once under the tyrannical regime which briefly ousted the democracy at the end of the Peloponnesian War, when he refused an order to participate in the arrest (and subsequent death) of an innocent man. None the less, his association with notorious anti-democrats, especially Alcibiades and Plato's relatives Critias and Charmides, probably contributed, after the restoration of the democracy, to his indictment on vague charges of neglect of the state religion and corruption of the young, and to his condemnation to death. In addition to Xenophon's account of his trial (mentioned above) the events of his trial and its aftermath are immortalized in three of Plato's works, the *Apology* (Defence) an idealized version of Socrates' defence at his trial, *Crito*, which gives his reasons for refusing to take the opportunity (which was apparently available) of escape from prison, and *Phaedo*, a moving re-creation of his final hours, containing first a Platonic treatise on the philosophy of life, death, and immortality and then a depiction of the ideal philosophic death.

Philosophy. It cannot be doubted that Socrates was a major, perhaps the most significant, influence on Plato's philosophical development, but the nature of this influence is not altogether easy to determine. Because our main access to Socrates is via the works of Plato, we have the problem of determining what, if any, doctrines Socrates himself held (see above). One extreme position is that we can know nothing whatever about the views of the historical Socrates, another that whatever views Plato ascribes to Socrates in any dialogue were actually held by him. Neither seems to me tenable. Aristotle distinguishes the views of Plato from those of Socrates (*Metaphysics* 1078^{b}27–32) by attributing to the former the theory of separate *Forms, which, he says, Socrates did not hold. Since Socrates is represented as expounding that theory in the *Phaedo* and other dialogues, it is clear that Aristotle does not derive that information from the dialogues, and it is therefore plausible that he learned either from Plato himself or from other sources in the Academy that the theory was Plato's own. So not everything in the dialogues is Socratic. But is anything Socratic? In the same passage Aristotle ascribes to Socrates an interest in general definitions and the practice of inductive arguments, both of which we find attributed to Socrates by both Plato and Xenophon. Both the latter also attribute to Socrates the 'Socratic paradoxes' that virtue is wisdom or knowledge and that no one does wrong willingly. Though it is likely that Xenophon's portrayal of Socrates is not totally independent of Plato's, it is at least plausible that those methods of argument were employed, and those doctrines held, by the historical Socrates.

Though Socrates is represented as maintaining these doctrines by Plato, he figures in the dialogues, especially those generally regarded as early, not primarily as a dogmatic philosopher (indeed he was famous for claiming that he was not wise in any respect), but as a critic, eliciting opinions from his interlocutors and subjecting them to critical scrutiny, usually producing a refutation by showing the doctrine in question to be inconsistent with other propositions agreed by both parties to be true. This 'method of *elenchus' (a Greek word meaning 'examination') has obvious affinities with the argumentative strategies employed and taught by the Sophists, and Plato is concerned to stress that in Socrates' hands it was intended not to produce victory in a debating contest, but to lead to genuine understanding by purging the person subjected to it of false beliefs. Philosophical inquiry conducted by this method is supposed to be not a contest between opponents (eristic), but a co-operative search for truth and understanding (*dialectic). Though Plato's conception of the methods of dialectic clearly developed considerably in the course of his life (see above) the ideal of a co-operative critical inquiry, conducted by the spoken word, remained his paradigm of philosophy, and we have every reason to think that it was his memory of the power of Socratic conversations which gave that ideal its perennial attractiveness for him.

Later influence. The influence of the figure of Socrates did not cease with Plato. In the Hellenistic and Roman periods the various schools (with the exception of the Epicureans) each sought to appropriate him as a patron saint, the Cynics appealing to his ascetic mode of life, the Sceptics and sceptical Academics to his profession of ignorance (see above), and the Stoics, notably Epictetus, to his alleged claim that virtue is the only intrinsic good. The Christian apologist Justin (second century AD) claimed him as a forerunner of Christ, a characterization which was revived in the fifteenth century by Neoplatonists such as Marsilio Ficino. In medieval Islam he was revered (though not well understood) as a sage and upholder of monotheism against idolatry. In the later Renaissance and in the eighteenth-century Enlightenment he came to be seen as a paradigm of human virtue and a martyr to rationalism at the hands of superstition. In different ways Hegel, Kierkegaard, and Nietzsche saw him as a pivotal figure in the development of human thought and constructed central aspects of their own thought in reaction to him, and in our own day he has been an important influence on the later work of Foucault. It is no exaggeration to claim that as long as personal and intellectual integrity remain compelling ideals, Socrates will be a suitable embodiment of them.   C.C.W.T.

T. C. Brickhouse and N. D. Smith, *The Philosophy of Socrates* (Boulder, Colo., 2000).

B. S. Gower and M. C. Stokes (eds.), *Socratic Questions* (London, 1992).

W. K. C. Guthrie, *A History of Greek Philosophy*, iii (Cambridge, 1969), pt. 2.

G. B. Matthews, *Socratic Perplexity and the Nature of Philosophy* (Oxford, 1999).

A. Nehamas, *The Art of Living: Socratic Reflections from Plato to Foucault* (Berkeley, Calif., 1998).

C. C. W. Taylor, *Socrates: A Very Short Introduction* (Oxford, 2000).

P. A. Vander Waerdt (ed.), *The Socratic Movement* (Ithaca, NY, 1994).

G. Vlastos (ed.), *The Philosophy of Socrates* (Garden City, NY, 1971).

—— *Socrates: Ironist and Moral Philosopher* (Cambridge, 1991).

Socratic method. The question-and-answer method of philosophizing (dialectic) used by Socrates in Plato's early dialogues (e.g. *Euthyphro*), often in conjunction with pretended ignorance (Socratic irony), whereby a self-professed expert's over-confident claim to knowledge is subverted. Sometimes the idea is to clear the mind for the subsequent development of more adequate views. More generally, Socratic method is any philosophical or pedagogical method that disinterestedly pursues truth through analytical discussion.   A.BEL.

*philosophical inquiry.

Leonard Nelson, *Socratic Method and Critical Philosophy* (New York, 1965).

Socratic paradox. Several claims put by Plato in the mouth of Socrates have been called 'Socratic paradoxes', but the one which the description fits best is the dictum 'No one does wrong voluntarily'. This is more plausible in its Greek original, where the word translated 'does wrong' can also mean 'misses the mark'. It implies that all wrong-doing is due to lack of knowledge, so that another version of the paradox is 'Virtue is knowledge'.   C.J.F.W.

H. H. Benson, *Essays on the Philosophy of Socrates* (Oxford, 1992).

soft determinism: *see* freedom and determinism.

Sohravardī, Shihāb al-Dīn Yaḥyā (?–1191). Persian thinker whose Philosophy of Illumination was the first attempt to construct a consistent non-Aristotelian system in *Islamic philosophy. His intention was to improve upon the Avicennan system by avoiding its logical gaps; to uphold the rational validity of revealed knowledge; and to construct a unified epistemological system that would include 'scientific' explanations of inspirational as well as sense-perceived knowledge.

The Philosophy of Illumination employs a specifically defined symbolic 'language of Illumination'. Objects, depicted as lights, are inherently knowable because, as part of the propagated whole as continuum, they include essential light that may be 'seen' by subjects who, recovering their own essential lightness, become self-cognizant and capable of 'seeing' the object's manifest light-essence.

Sohravardī redefined and refined problems pertaining to every domain of philosophical investigation. In logic, he defines the modal 'necessary' as an independent operator to construct a superiterated modal proposition to which all other propositions are reduced. Most critically, he argues that Avicenna's complete essentialist definition, deemed the first step in science, cannot be constructed, thus refuting the basis of Peripatetic scientific method. Similar to the impossibility of definition by extension through exhaustive enumeration of elements, he argues that the thing's essentials may not all be known when constructing the formula. Further, he criticizes the universal proposition on the grounds that universal validity must be necessary and always true; but because of necessary future contingency (possible worlds), the formal validity of a 'law' deduced 'now' may be invalidated at some future time by the recovery of exceptions. The most prior, necessary, and always true knowledge thus cannot be predicative. Rather, it is *'knowledge by presence' when the 'illuminationist' relation between the subject and the object is actualized in durationless time. However, foundations must be renewed in all future time, or in other possible worlds, based on future or other knowing subjects' 'observations', thus according a principal role for the enlightened 'observer'.   H.Z.

John Walbridge, The Science of Mystic Lights: Quṭb al-Dīn Shīrāzī and the Illuminationist Tradition in Islamic Philosophy (Cambridge, Mass., 1992).
Hossein Ziai, Knowledge and Illumination: A Study of Suhrawardī's Ḥikmat al-Ishrāq (Atlanta, 1990).

solipsism. The view that only oneself exists. 'Is anybody there?' asks the visitor trapped in the waxworks museum after closing time, 'Or is there only me?' Philosophers raise eyebrows by discussing similar-sounding questions when there are no special circumstances. One debate is whether other creatures have an inner life (thoughts, wants, feelings) of the kind which makes the subject a person. Even if they do, is the inquirer in a position to know or reasonably believe that? This 'problem of *other minds' presents solipsism as an apparently inescapable conclusion from certain (Cartesian) assumptions, whereby access to others' mental states is indirect, involving a dodgy inference from behaviour.

A more radical version is that one's own immediate experience has a fundamental, self-certifying reality and that comparable knowledge of 'physical' or 'public' items is unobtainable. This is sometimes anchored in the thought that, when a person loses consciousness, his whole world crashes. Arguments that cast doubt on the existence or accessibility of a mind-independent world leave us with no lifeline to the presence of others, no defence against the threat of solipsism.

Characteristically, these sceptical arguments take a yet more radical turn when the link between grasping the meaning of words and being presented with examples is remembered. If I am never acquainted with your experience and can gain no knowledge about it, how can I understand the words that allegedly refer to it? It seems to a solipsist that I have to learn what words refer to by connecting them with items of my own experience. How can I even get the idea that there are things outside that experience? The world has to be my world.

Counter-attacks often focus on what the sceptic keeps. In stating his view he may use 'I' or 'my', thus assuming a distinction between himself and others. But, if there are no other takers, what is meant by claiming that experience is *mine*? Where there is no possibility of others, the idea of

signalling one person rather than another, presupposed in the normal use of 'I', seems to fail. For this reason, Lichtenberg's famous suggestion that we should do better to say 'It thinks' rather than 'I think' finds favour with solipsists. (Also, presumably, 'It hurts', 'It chooses', and so on.)

In *Philosophical Investigations*, §§243 ff., Wittgenstein seeks to undermine this further position by questioning the possibility that anyone could acquire a *private language. The need to observe a distinction between correct and incorrect judgement finally forces us to admit that language itself is essentially social. This seems to allow a return to the common-sense position that if the solipsist *says anything*, this ought to be an intelligible communication; but that the thesis should be understood seems to be a possibility which it itself rules out.

But if solipsism is absurd, discussing it is not. Solipsistic conclusions may be used as powerful *reductio ad absurdum* arguments against some common assumptions, and the interesting mistakes that generate solipsism also embody real insights into our language and thought. It leads us to reconsider how the words 'I' and 'mine' work, what the relation is between the relatively permanent objects around us and the testimony of our senses, and how we learn to speak about sensations. It also leads us to question common ideas about the primacy of private experience in fixing the meaning of words in general. There is method in the madness of losing your head when all about you are keeping theirs.   J.E.R.S.

*scepticism.

A. J. Ayer, The Foundations of Empirical Knowledge (London, 1940), ch. 3.
P. M. S. Hacker, Insight and Illusion, rev. edn. (Oxford, 1986), chs. 8–10.
P. F. Strawson, Individuals (London, 1959), ch. 3.
L. Wittgenstein, The Blue and Brown Books (Oxford, 1958), 44 ff.

Solovyov, Vladimir Sergeevich (1853–1900). Idealist philosopher and poet. Solovyov's lectures on *'Godmanhood' at St Petersburg University in 1878 established him as Russia's first significant academic philosopher (though he was forced out of academe after appealing for clemency for Alexander II's assassins). Influenced by German idealism, Solovyov saw development as a progression from primitive unity through differentiation to a higher reintegration. The world of spatio-temporal objects was created when Sophia, or the world-soul, separated from God. Reintegration requires the establishment of 'all-unity': the reuniting of the world with God in a kingdom of heaven on earth. For a time, Solovyov envisioned a theocratic utopia with all Churches and nations united under the Pope and the Russian Tsar. His later philosophy is more contemplative and less dogmatic, though prey to pessimism. Solovyov inspired a significant revival in Russian religious philosophy and influenced the Russian symbolist poets.   D.BAK.

*Russian philosophy.

V. S. Solovyov, A Solovyov Anthology, tr. N. Duddington (London, 1950).

Song of God: see *Bhagavadgītā*.

sophism. A sophism is a type of *fallacy that is not just an error of reasoning, or an invalid argument, but a kind of tactic of argumentation used unfairly to try to get the best of a speech partner. Aristotle called these kinds of tactics *sophistici elenchi*, or sophistical refutations. For an example of a sophism, see the entry 'straw man fallacy'.   D.N.W.

*fallacy.

Douglas Walton, *The Place of Emotion in Argument* (University Park, Penn., 1992).

Sophists. Itinerant professors of higher education. From its original senses of 'sage' and 'expert' (lit. 'one who is wise', from *sophizesthai*, cognate with *sophos*) the word came to be applied in the fifth century BC in the technical sense given above to a number of individuals who travelled widely through the Greek world, giving popular lectures and specialized instruction in a wide range of topics. They were in no sense a school, or even a single movement. They had neither a common set of doctrines nor any shared organization, and while our evidence indicates that some of them knew one another, their attitude to one another was rather that of professional rivals than colleagues.

Their intellectual activities included the popularization of the Ionian tradition of inquiry into nature (which was concurrently being developed by more original thinkers such as Anaxagoras and the *Atomists) and mathematics. The polymath Hippias included both in his range of expertise, and Protagoras is reported to have written a work on mathematics, which may have included criticism of mathematics from the standpoint of his subjectivist epistemology. The fifth century saw the development of what might broadly be called the 'social sciences' of history, geography, and speculative anthropology, as represented, for example, by the works of Hecataeus, Herodotus, and Thucydides; Hippias and probably Protagoras were also active in these fields. Another significant development in this period was the systematic study of techniques of persuasion and argument, which included the beginnings of the study of language in various forms, including grammar, literary criticism, and semantics. In all these areas Protagoras seems to have been a pioneer; he was reputedly the first person to write a treatise on techniques of argument, and was notorious for his claim, reported by Aristotle, to be able to 'make the weaker argument the stronger', a claim apparently based on the view that to every thesis there was opposed an equipollent contrary thesis. If all these have equal evidential support (a thesis logically independent of, but doubtless psychologically connected with, the famous doctrine that 'Man is the measure of all things' (cf. Protagoras)), then it is an appropriate task for the technique of persuasion to devise arguments on either side sufficient for their political or forensic function.

This side of their activities brought the Sophists into the public arena, where it is clear that they aroused strong reactions, both positive and negative. On the positive side, the long and financially highly successful careers of the most celebrated testify to a considerable demand for their services, both in satisfying the educational aspirations of the well-off, especially in Athens, then at the height of its prosperity and political and cultural influence, and in providing rhetorical and forensic training for aspiring politicians. On the negative side, they were regarded as socially and morally subversive, especially by those of conservative views. Suspicion focused both on their naturalistic outlook, especially in its application to morality and theology, and on their teaching of techniques of argument, which could be seen as encouraging those who acquired them, especially the young, to subvert sound morality and hallowed tradition by clever cavilling. The caricature of sophistic education given by Aristophanes in his *Clouds* brings the two points together; Socrates, who is presented as the representative of sophistry, first replaces the traditional gods by naturalistic processes such as 'Swirl', and then provides his pupils with arguments, including arguments from the non-existence of the gods, to the conclusion that they can welsh on their debts. Criticisms of traditional theology were not, indeed, introduced by or restricted to the Sophists. In the previous century Xenophanes had ridiculed anthropomorphism and maintained the existence of a single cosmic deity, and Heraclitus had castigated certain rituals as absurd and obscene, and that tradition was continued by Plato's demand for the suppression of all mythical accounts of divine wrongdoings. In the fifth century we see the rise of a climate of thought which casts doubt on religion itself, either on epistemological grounds, as in Protagoras' agnostic writings, or by providing naturalistic explanations of the celestial phenomena traditionally regarded as divine, and of the origins of religion itself. Anaxagoras famously taught that the sun was a molten rock, while Prodicus (otherwise chiefly known for his technique of distinguishing near-synonyms, parodied in Plato's *Protagoras*) is said to have maintained that the gods were either personifications of natural objects of special importance in human life, e.g. the sun, or benefactors of earlier generations deified after death.

In this climate of thought, morality was no more immune from critical scrutiny than was religion. Various positions may be distinguished. Protagoras maintained (apparently inconsistently with his universal subjectivism) a form of *moral relativism, in which moral beliefs are true for those communities in which they are maintained. Plato's dialogues provide evidence of more radical challenges to morality associated with Sophists. In the *Republic* the Sophist Thrasymachus (a historical person) argues that, since it is contrary to self-interest to accept the constraints of morality, immorality is a virtue and morality a defect (*aretē*; *eudaimonia*), while in the *Gorgias* Callicles, a pupil of Gorgias, maintains yet more radically that conventional morality is in fact a form of injustice, since it attempts to deprive the strong of their natural right to exploit the weak. It is, however, over-simplified to regard the Sophists collectively as having had a common doctrine, or even as having shared a generally sceptical or radical outlook on morality. Xenophon, for instance, reports Hippias as maintaining the traditional doctrine that there exist certain natural laws, e.g. that one should worship the gods and honour one's parents, which are common to all societies, while Protagoras, in Plato's dialogue of that name, holds that the educational function of the Sophist is continuous with that of the traditional educational institutions of the community, namely, to impart the basic social virtues of justice and self-control.

The writings of the Sophists, which were in some cases voluminous, are lost, with the sole exception of a substantial papyrus fragment from a work by Antiphon, critical of conventional morality on the grounds of its conflict with self-interest. The principal source of our information is Plato, who is a hostile witness, partly on the grounds that he believed the Sophists to have claimed an educational role to which they were not entitled, perhaps even more because he believed, very probably truly, that the suspicion which certain Sophists had attracted had contributed to the unpopularity and ultimately to the condemnation of Socrates, whose critical stance and destructive methods of argument were no doubt hard to distinguish from typically Sophistic tactics. Plato is therefore at pains to depict the Sophists as bogus practitioners of philosophy, in contrast to Socrates, the paradigm of true philosophy. The gravamen of his charge is not that they were subversive (though, as pointed out above, he does reflect that aspect), but that they pretended to knowledge that they did not possess, and that they sought popularity and success by dressing up popular prejudices with a specious appearance of novelty. At the same time his portrayal of Protagoras in the *Protagoras* and his detailed critique of his subjectivism in the *Theaetetus* show that he regarded him as a figure of major intellectual stature (his portrayals of some other Sophists are decidedly less friendly). The complexity of Plato's attitudes should remind us of the complexity of the subject, and put us on our guard against uncritical acceptance of an over-simplified stereotype.   C.C.W.T.

R. Bett, 'The Sophists and Relativism', *Phronesis* (1989).
W. K. C. Guthrie, *A History of Greek Philosophy*, iii (Cambridge, 1969).
G. B. Kerferd, *The Sophistic Movement* (Cambridge, 1981).
—— (ed.), *The Sophists and their Legacy*, *Hermes* Einzelschriften xliv (Wiesbaden, 1981).

Sorabji, Richard Ruston Kharsedji (1934–). Based in London and Oxford, Sorabji has written widely on all periods of ancient Greek philosophy, linking it with contemporary issues, especially in metaphysics, philosophy of mind, and ethics, and contributing substantially to the current revival of post-Aristotelian philosophy. In this last respect he has aimed to take the story beyond the Stoics and Epicureans, where it usually stops, to the end of Greek philosophy around AD 600, thereby showing its continuity with the succeeding philosophies of the Arabs, the Middle Ages, and the Renaissance. In particular he has used ancient writers to support the claims that causation is more closely linked to explanation than to necessitation,

and that time could in principle be circular, so that any given event may lie both in the past and in the future. He is the originator and general editor of a major edition, in English translation, of the ancient commentators on Aristotle. He is also concerned with the rationality of animals, both in ancient thinkers and in fact.   A.R.L.

Richard Sorabji, *Time, Creation and the Continuum* (London, 1983).

Sorel, Georges (1847–1922). It was only after his retirement from working for the French government as an engineer that Sorel began to publish the idiosyncratic views on politics which have earned him a permanent, if minor, place in the annals of revolutionary theory. Drawn initially to an ethical interpretation of Marxism and the reformist ideas of Bernstein, he became disillusioned following the Dreyfus affair and emerged as the leading exponent of revolutionary *syndicalism. In his most famous work, *Reflections on Violence* (1906), Sorel argued that the main doctrines of Marxism, and in particular the general strike, should be seen as myths capable of inspiring the working class to violent acts of revolution that alone would be capable of effecting a fundamental transformation of society. Towards the end of his life Sorel became an admirer of Lenin and, to a lesser extent, of Mussolini.   D.McL.

*violence, political.

Isaiah Berlin, 'Georges Sorel', in *Against the Current* (Oxford, 1979).
Jeremy Jennings, *George Sorel: The Development and Character of his Thought* (London, 1985).

sorites paradox: *see* heap, paradox of the.

sortal. A type of term, usually a noun, e.g. 'cat' or 'person', that supplies a single principle of individuating and counting the instances it applies to. A sortal contrasts with characterizing terms, e.g. 'red', with material names, e.g. 'butter', and with terms like 'thing', 'action', 'place', none of which, unless variously completed (as in 'red *chair*' '*pat* of butter', the place we are in), supply such a principle.   s.w.

*individuation.

P. F. Strawson, *Individuals* (London, 1959), esp. 168.
S. Wolfram, *Philosophical Logic* (London, 1989), ch. 6.2.2.

Sosa, Ernest (1940–). Romeo Elton Professor of Natural Theology at Brown University, recognized for contributions in epistemology, metaphysics, and the philosophy of mind. Sosa is best known for 'virtue perspectivism', an attempt to reconcile traditional 'coherentist' and 'foundationalist' epistemological concerns. On this view, whether a belief constitutes knowledge depends both on how it was produced and on the believer's perspective on his own situation as knower. To be candidates for knowledge, beliefs must be products of truth-conducive intellectual virtues. Elsewhere, Sosa argues that belief (*de re*) about a referent is a kind of propositional belief that picks out its object from the believer's perspective, some propositions being 'indexical' and perspective-dependent. Sosa has also defended a broad Aristotelianism against the charge that it implies that one's survival cannot matter rationally even to oneself.   J.HEIL

*metaphysics, problems of.

E. Sosa, *Knowledge in Perspective* (Cambridge, 1991).

soul. The human soul is that which gives life to the human being. For Aristotle, the soul was simply the form of the body, i.e. the way the body behaved, and thus not capable of existing separately from it; plants and animals also had souls of their own kinds. For Plato, most Christian theologians of the first millennium AD, Descartes, and many others, the soul was the essential immaterial part of a human, temporarily united with its body. Aquinas also held this, while emphasizing that union with a body was the natural state for a soul. Most modern philosophers deny the existence of an immaterial soul. (*Mind–body problem.) One strong argument for the existence of such a soul given in essence by Descartes is this. I am now conscious. But it is logically possible that my body should suddenly be destroyed and yet I continue to be conscious and so to exist. But a thing such as I am can only continue to exist if some part of the thing continues to exist. So I must now already have an essential non-bodily part, i.e. a soul, if my continued existence is to be logically possible.   R.G.S.

pneuma; self; bundle theory of self.

R. Swinburne, *The Evolution of the Soul* (Oxford, 1986).

soul, world-: *see* world-soul.

South American philosophy: *see* Latin American philosophy.

sovereignty. The right, by a governing power, held against other powers, to rule a designated territory, people, and their resources—a jurisdiction—and defend these from incursion. It requires, first, criteria for according the right, and secondly, correlative duties on the part of other states. Until the Treaty of Westphalia (1648), after the Thirty Years War, the accepted sources of the right were principally religious. Post-Westphalia a secular basis for the right became established, granting sovereignty to *de facto* independent political entities. The corresponding duties developed to include equal treatment and respect in international relations, and non-interference by other states in affairs internal to the jurisdiction, save for extreme circumstances. Recently, 'liberal internationalists' have argued that justice demands that sovereignty be conditional on democratic self-governance and respect for basic rights. Thus, whilst a degree of self-determination is accepted, powers failing to uphold citizens' basic rights and democracy are said to be illegitimate whatever their *de facto* status. Westphalia sovereignty is, on this argument, wrong, and one extreme version adds that liberal states should act on illiberal states to export rights and democracy.   S.M.-G.

*international relations, philosophy of; justice, international; State; war, just.

R. Jackson (ed.), *Sovereignty at the Millennium* (Oxford, 2000).

F. Teson, *A Philosophy of International Law* (Oxford, 1998).

M. Walzer, *Just and Unjust Wars* (New York, 1977).

space. We all ask where things are, how big they are, and what room there is for them or in them. Classifying these enquiries generates the concepts of extension in one or more dimensions, distance, direction, and emptiness; and discussions of these more sophisticated concepts may be grouped together as philosophizings about space.

The first Greek Atomists conceived the void through which their atoms moved as having positive reality, and called it 'the empty' or 'that which is not'. The latter phrase may have been intended to provoke the Eleatics, who wished to impose a veto on saying 'That that which is not, is'. A term closer to our 'space' is introduced by Plato. In the *Timaeus* he applies '*khōra*' to a confessedly weird medium in which simple numerical ratios are represented by tiny polyhedra whose fluctuations constitute the fabric of the perceived world. To modern readers he may seem to have grasped the notion of space dominant in our thinking. But Aristotle interprets him as proposing a (bad) theory of matter, drops the technical use of '*khōra*', and discusses place instead of space. Influenced, perhaps, by Plato's *Parmenides* (138a–b etc.), he analyses this in terms not of distance and direction but of containment. Later Greek writers take '*khōra*' to signify a special kind of place or extension (*diastēma*) and speak chiefly of those. Neglect of space persists through the Middle Ages. Perhaps interest in it goes with the belief, which Aristotle's authority opposed, that mathematics is the paradigm for all knowledge and illuminates the heart of reality. If reality consists of geometrical solids or, as modern physics suggests, of punctiform events fixed by four spatio-temporal coordinates, space is just about all there is.

Anyhow it makes a joint comeback with mathematics in the seventeenth century. Newton's description of it (*Principia*, definition 8, scholium) as an eternal, infinite, isotropic continuum (like air, only thinner) captivates philosophers like the Sirens' song. He held that spatial relations are mind-independent and that objects stand in them not just to one another but to subregions of this continuum. Most people wonder about the second contention: he wants space to be a physical reality that can neither affect other things nor be affected by them, and that sounds like a contradiction in terms. Leibniz rejected both claims about spatial relations, and Kant only the first. We conceive objects, Kant argues, as products of a perceiver's imagination; what makes them non-identical is occupying non-identical chunks of space; space is unique in that there could not be two unrelated systems of spatial relations; but our idea of it is an idea, not of an individual we experience, but of how we experience other things as individuals.

Philosophers still debate Kant's and Newton's claims, and have developed a literature of metaphysical fiction in which people visit spaces with unconventional numbers of dimensions or pass from one spatial system to another by means that defy physical laws. But they also study the conceptual demands of modern physics. Until 1900 people assumed that space and time are measurable independently. According to the special theory of *relativity, if two events are distant from each other in space, their distance apart in time will vary with the frame of reference we select; relatively to one frame they might be simultaneous and relatively to another, an hour apart; and these differences in temporal separation are not independent of differences in spatial separation. It also used to be assumed that things in space satisfy Euclid's theorems—that if three events are connected by straight lines, the triangle enclosed will be Euclidean. The general theory of relativity makes the geometry of space dependent on the distribution in it of matter, and thereby forces us to reconsider the status of Euclid's theorems. w.c.

*space-time.

E. Abbott, *Flatland* (Oxford, 1926).

R. Le Poidevin, *Travels in Four Dimensions: The Enigmas of Space and Time* (Oxford, 2003).

G. Nerlich, *The Shape of Space* (Cambridge, 1976).

Richard Sorabji, *Matter, Space, Motion* (Ithaca, NY, 1988).

space-time. The set of all events occurring in *space and *time, like the explosion of a fire-cracker or the snapping of one's fingers. Space-time is four-dimensional, in that each event can be located by four numbers, three for its position and one for its time of occurrence. In the space-time underlying Newtonian physics, spatial separations and temporal durations between events are independent of an observer's state of motion. But in Einstein's *relativity theory, these measures cease to be absolute—the length of a rigid rod will be judged shorter when moving than if stationary, and similarly a moving clock runs slower. Nevertheless, there is still an absolute measure in the form of the space-time interval between events, which moved the mathematician Minkowski to remark: 'Henceforth space by itself, and time by itself, are doomed to fade away into mere shadows, and only a kind of union between the two will preserve an independent reality.' The space-time interval not only determines by how much a rod will be seen to contract, or clock run slow, but whether or not a pair of events can be causally connected, that is, whether a signal not exceeding the speed of light can be sent from the (space-time) location of one event to the other—an 'invariant' fact independent of one's state of motion. R.CLI.

R. Geroch, *General Relativity from A to B* (Chicago, 1978).

Spanish philosophy. Although notable Roman and medieval philosophers, such as Seneca, Averroës, Ramon Llull, and Maimonides, were born in the territories of Spain long before it appeared as a unified state in 1492, it is more appropriate to think of Spanish philosophy as the philosophy produced in Spain after its political constitution. As a matter of fact, 1492 is also the year of the discovery of America, and the starting-point of its domination and colonization, which turned Spain into a worldly empire. It marked as well an extraordinary flourishing of Spanish culture, which made the sixteenth century the Golden Age of Spanish culture.

Philosophy was not alien to this flourishing. Most philosophical trends of this epoch are well represented. *Scholasticism received a strong impulse at the University of Salamanca. Vitoria, Suárez, and Molina developed a metaphysics separate from theology. Their main contribution, though, was their argument for a right of peoples, a *ius gentium*, which later became the basis for our current international law. Challenged by the problems of legitimacy that the conquest and domination of 'The New World' raised, Vitoria and Suárez argued against the legitimacy of war to impose a faith, and contended that native American peoples, as humans, had rights to property and self-government.

*Humanism and *Neoplatonism were also well represented at that time. The humanist J. L. Vives (1492–1540), a close friend of Erasmus, defended the importance of human subjectivity as the ground of human dignity and religious life. Moreover, during turbulent years of wars of religion in Europe, he argued in favour of peace and concord, as higher standards of human dignity. On the other hand, the philosopher-physician Francisco Sánchez (1550–1623), in his work *That Nothing is Known*, developed the humanist themes of distrusting authority and tradition as foundations of knowledge, and proposed a principle of 'methodical doubt' as the right way of inquiry, which was later to influence Descartes.

Spanish Neoplatonism of the time finds perfect expression in the Jewish writer Leo Hebraeus, whose *Dialogues on Love* continue the themes of Marsilio Ficino, and culminates in the poetry of the great Spanish *mystics, Teresa de Jesús (1515–82) and Juan de la Cruz (1542–91), whose central idea was that of love as the path to an intimate knowledge of God.

The commitment of Spain to the defence of orthodox Roman Catholicism against the Reformation, and the converted Jews and Muslims, brought about a long period of persecution of free thought, exercised by the infamous and powerful Inquisition. By the beginning of the seventeenth century, even study abroad was forbidden. It took 300 years for philosophy to become invigorated again, at the end of the nineteenth century, when it started a new period of cultural flourishing; a period that was to be dramatically interrupted by the Spanish Civil War (1936–9).

Since academic philosophy at that time was in the hands of the Church, this new philosophical movement found expression in a literary genre, the novel. Unamuno (1865–1936) is the most notable writer of this philosophical bent, whose works depict characters deeply influenced by the sort of existential worries first formulated by Kierkegaard. But a powerful character was to appear in the next generation, Ortega y Gasset (1883–1955), called to renew academic philosophy in Spain. Under German influence he opted for the essay genre. His philosophy is called ratio-vitalism, a variety of Husserlian phenomenalism, according to which the self is conceived not in the abstract, but in the context of the circumstances of the individual life. Accordingly, truth is perspectival.

The defeat of Spanish democracy in 1939 forced into exile most of the intellectuals and scientists of the time (Ferrater-Mora can be considered the best representative of Spanish philosophy in exile). By the end of the Sixties, though, some academic philosophers played an important role in introducing current European philosophical styles and ideas, as a form of dissidence. In large part, the task was one of translation, but some names deserve mention as much for their intellectual contribution in renewing Spanish philosophy as for their ethical attitude of vindication of intellectual, and political, freedom: J. M. Valverde and J. L. López Aranguren. Since the restoration of democracy, in 1978, this pluralist reception of philosophical traditions has continued, but it is on the analytical side that contributions of international significance can be found. Philosophy of mind and of language, and logic, are the more active areas.   A.GOM.

J. L. Abellán, *Historia crítica del pensamiento español* (Madrid, 1979–90).

J. E. Corbí and J. L. Prades, *Minds, Causes and Mechanisms* (Oxford, 2000).

M. Menéndez-Pelayo, *Historia de los heterodoxos españoles* (Madrid, 1978).

Moya, C., *The Philosophy of Action* (Cambridge, 1990).

species: *see* genus and species.

specious present. The specious present is the finite interval of *time embracing experiences of which the mind is conscious as happening 'now', and constitutes the boundary between the remembered past and the anticipated future. That it exceeds a mere instant is demonstrated by our capacity to perceive continuous movement. Although the concept of the specious present is subjective, 'dynamic' theories of time regard it as having an objective counterpart.   E.J.L.

R. M. Gale (ed.), *The Philosophy of Time* (New York, 1967).

speech-acts: *see* linguistic acts.

Spencer, Herbert (1820–1903). English evolutionist, father of sociology, and self-appointed philosopher, Spencer enjoyed immense popularity in his own time, especially in America. His huge output, the 'Synthetic Philosophy', was made possible by the fact that he troubled himself little with the writings of others, claiming indeed that the reading of books with which he disagreed gave him headaches. Sinking in esteem by the century's end to hitherto unfathomed depths, Spencer is today remembered primarily as the enthusiast for extreme *laissez-faire* or *Social Darwinism, and the classic exemplar of the *naturalistic fallacy as he attempted to derive the force of morality from the fact and course of *evolution. In his day, however, he was far more popular as the prophet of progress, claiming that nature tends always towards equi-

librium and that this sparks an upward evolutionary move from homogeneity to heterogeneity. One suspects that, even to this day, the unsung figure of Spencer rides on, paradoxically among both right-wing politicians decrying the dangers of state interference and left-wing ecologists hymning the virtues of balance.   M.R.

R. Richards, *Darwin and the Emergence of Evolutionary Theories of Mind and Behavior* (Chicago, 1987).

H. Spencer, *First Principles* (London, 1862).

Speusippus (*c*.410–337 BC). An Athenian philosopher who was Plato's nephew and successor as head of the *Academy. He wrote extensively on topics in metaphysics, the philosophy of logic and language, philosophy of nature, and ethics; but his thoughts have reached us only in tantalizingly incomplete and obscure form. There is some evidence for attributing to him a nominalist, anti-essentialist tendency in his theorizing on semantics, mathematics, and natural kinds. Thus he is reported by Aristotle as denying independent, substantive existence to numbers, and as maintaining that things should be defined not by their own intrinsic characters but rather in terms of their relations of similarity and dissimilarity to other things. If more were known about these ideas, it might illuminate many aspects of Aristotle's theorizing about essence.   J.D.G.E.

Speusippus' writings have been collected and discussed by P. Lang, *De Speusippi Academici Fragmenta* (Bonn, 1911) and more recently by L. Tarán, *Speusippus of Athens* (Leiden, 1981).

Spinoza, Baruch (or Benedictus) (1632–77). Dutch Jewish philosopher. Spinoza's family were Portuguese Judaizing Marranos (forced converts to Christianity living secretly as Jews). His father had emigrated to Amsterdam to avoid persecution, where he built up a successful merchant business. Spinoza's mother died when he was 6 and his father when he was 22. Spinoza continued for a time as a respected member of his synagogue, running the family business with his brother. However, a crisis arose when he would not renounce the heterodox opinions he had been heard to voice, and, after unsuccessful efforts to buy his silence, he was cursed and excommunicated from the Jewish community. Opinions differ over why such strong action was taken against him. One view is that the peculiar religious position of the Marranos had encouraged scepticism and laxity in Jewish practice and that the rabbis felt that they must affirm the religious unity of their community (there were some other similar instances of *herem*). Others emphasize the need to reassure the city fathers that the Jewish community was committed to the same basic theism as Christianity.

A few years after the ban Spinoza (with the family business wound up) left Amsterdam and lived for some years in Rijnsburg, near Leiden, lodging with a member of the Collegiant sect, with which he was developing an association. After four years he moved to Voorburg and then to The Hague, living in modest lodgings. (The houses at Rijnsburg and The Hague now contain the library and offices of the Dutch Spinoza society, the *Vereniging het*

Spinozahuis.) He was a skilled optical lens grinder and some of his income came from this, though he also accepted some small financial support from his followers. He acquired international fame, and, with the publication of the *Tractatus Theologico-Politicus* in 1670, notoriety. Among his friends and frequent correspondents was Henry Oldenburg, Secretary of the Royal Society in London. Oldenburg and some other Christians may have hoped that Spinoza would lead that mass conversion of the Jews to Christianity which their millenarian beliefs led them to expect. However, Spinoza conceived Jesus as at most the last of the great Jewish prophets.

Spinoza only published two books in his lifetime: *The Principles of Descartes's Philosophy* (written initially for a young man he was informally tutoring, published 1663) and the *Tractatus Theologico-Politicus*. The latter was published anonymously at Amsterdam, though for reasons of prudence with a falsely titled frontispiece and binding. It soon became explosively infamous and Spinoza, once he became known as the author, much reviled for it.

It is part biblical study, part political treatise. Its overriding goal is to recommend full freedom of thought and religious practice, subject to behavioural conformity with the laws of the land. As virtually the first examination of the Scriptures (primarily the Pentateuch) as historical documents, reflecting the intellectual limitations of their time, and of problematic authorship, it opened the so-called higher criticism. What is important, claims Spinoza, is the Bible's moral message; its implied science and metaphysics can stand only as imaginative adjuncts for teaching ethics to the multitude. Though Spinoza unobtrusively identifies *God and *nature, one of the opinions leading to his excommunication (as he was already doing in his work in progress on the *Ethics*), he writes in a seemingly more orthodox vein, even while denying the genuinely supernatural character of reported miracles. It is much debated whether this shows that those who now read the *Ethics* in too secular a way are misunderstanding it, or whether Spinoza was adapting his presentation not indeed to the masses, but to conventionally religious intellectuals of his time, among whom he wished to promote tolerant liberal ideals. The study of the Bible is designed to show that there is nothing in it which should sanction intolerance within Judaism or Christianity, or between them, and to illustrate certain political facts by reflections on Jewish history, such as the desirable relations between Church and State. Spinoza's political theory owes a good deal to Hobbes, utilizing similarly the idea of a *social contract, but deriving a more liberal and democratic lesson from it. Spinoza was personally committed to the republican policies of the De Witt brothers in Amsterdam, was outraged at their murder, and was against the royalist ambitions of the House of Orange.

Shortly after his death *Opera Postuma* was published by his friends, containing the *Ethics*, one of the major and most influential works of Western philosophy, the unfinished *Tractatus Politicus*, some lesser works, and some important correspondence. So notorious had Spinoza's opinions become that they still only gave the name of the author as B.D.S. (Two other works have come to light since.)

Spinoza has been more variously interpreted than most philosophers. Perhaps this only shows his system's resemblance to the universe it mirrors. A less contentious explanation is that, depending on the reader's starting-point, it may come either as a call to abandon traditional Jewish or Christian religious belief and practice, or as a revitalization of the conception of a God who seemed to be dying. In the seventeenth and eighteenth centuries he was widely regarded with horror as a scarcely covert atheist, in the nineteenth as a precursor of absolute *idealism. Some twentieth-century thinkers interpreted him, rather one-sidedly, as a precursor of a *'cognitive science' interpretation of mind, others almost as a logical atomist, while others again hailed his *pantheism as providing a metaphysical foundation for 'deep ecology'. Among the many very different thinkers who have either regarded themselves as, in a broad sense, Spinozists, or as strongly influenced by him, are Goethe, Lessing, Heine, Nietzsche, George Eliot, Einstein, Freud, Bertrand Russell, and George Santayana, while Hegel saw Spinoza's philosophy as a particularly important dialectical stage on the road to his own absolute idea. Historically, Spinoza was strongly influenced by Descartes, though the upshot of his thought is markedly different, and, to a debatable degree, by various Jewish thinkers.

Spinoza's great work, the *Ethics*, is presented as a deductive system in the manner of Euclid. Each of its five parts ('Concerning God'; 'On the Nature and Origin of the Mind'; 'Concerning the Origin and Nature of the Emotions'; 'Of Human Bondage, or the Strength of the Emotions'; 'Of the Power of the Intellect, or of Human Freedom') opens with a set of definitions and axioms and is followed by a series of theorems proved upon the basis of what precedes them, with more informal remarks in scholia and appendices.

In part 1 Spinoza proves (understand henceforth: or intends to prove) that there is only one substance (in the sense of genuinely individual thing with an intelligibility not derivative from that of other things), and this answers both to the traditional meanings of 'God' (for example, its existence follows from its essence) and of 'nature' (that of which the laws of nature are the operations). (Thus God did not create but *is* nature.) Spinoza derives this claim by pushing the traditional notion of an individual substance to its limit in a complex argument roughly as follows.

1. First we must note some of his opening definitions: 'By *substance I understand what is in itself and is conceived through itself, i.e. that whose concept does not require the concept of another thing, from which it must be formed.' 'By *attribute I understand what the intellect perceives of a substance, as constituting its essence.' 'By *mode I understand the affections of a substance or that which is in another thing through which it is also conceived.' 'By God I understand a being absolutely infinite,

i.e. a substance consisting of an infinity of attributes, of which each one expresses an eternal and infinite essence.'

2. After certain initial moves Spinoza proves proposition 5, 'In the universe there cannot be two or more substances of the same nature or attribute', by considering what could possibly distinguish two such substances. It could not be their affections or modes, because they must be different in order to have different affections (just as two men could not be distinguished by the fact that one was angry and the other not, for this possibility rests upon their being different men—compare some recent arguments for bare particulars). However, on the only alternative, that they are distinguished by their natures or attributes, they would not be instances of what is denied. Why Spinoza did not consider the apparently obvious objection (noted by Leibniz) that they might share one but not all their attributes has been debated. The solution recommended here is that, since an attribute is simply a way of conceiving the essence or nature of a substance, any shared attribute implies a shared essence which in turn implies the same set of attributes as ways of conceiving it.

3. The next crucial proposition (part 1, proposition 11) affirms the necessary existence of God as we have seen him (or it—to say 'her' would be wildly anachronistic) defined. Spinoza's *ontological argument for this is derived with peculiar abruptness from proposition 7, according to which existence appertains to the nature of substance (and so must pertain to the divine substance), this being derived in turn from the impossibility, established in previous propositions, of one substance producing another (because such causation requires a community of nature that is impossible granted that two substances cannot share their nature).

One might think that this only shows that if a substance exists at all, then it must exist of its own nature, and does not tell us which if any substances do exist. However, the underlying thought seems to be that any coherently conceivable substance (with a possibly actualizable essence) must exist, since the conception of it cannot be derived from anything but its own existing self. In the case of that which could only exist as the modification of something else, the case is different, for the conception of it may be derived from the conception of that of which it is a possible modification. Thus (my examples) the conception of Horatio's bravery in some non-actual situation may be derived from a proper conception of Horatio himself, and the conception of a unicorn may be derived from the conception of the universal space within which it could figure as a possible form. But in the case of a coherently conceivable substance, such as God, there can be no such derivation, and its coherent conceivability must derive from its own actual being. (Leibniz's claim that the ontological argument should first establish the coherent conceivability of God is apt here. In fact in the course of the first of two further proofs Spinoza does try to show this.)

4. Since a perfect substance exists possessing all attributes, and since there cannot be more than one substance possessing the same attribute, it follows that this perfect substance is the only substance, since there are no attributes left for any other substance. Thus (part 1, proposition 14) 'Except God, no substance can be or be conceived.'

We must continue in even less detail. All ordinary finite things are modes of this one substance, that is, stand to it as, say, an emotion pertains to a person or a movement to a moving thing. Thus the existence of a person consists in the one substance being in a certain state, just as the existence of my anger consists in my being in a certain state. (This traditional reading of Spinoza is sometimes challenged.) In effect, my anger is the mode (Spinoza says 'affection') of a mode.

Some commentators resist the usual idea that for Spinoza God simply is the universe, insisting that he is rather the one substance in which all natural phenomena inhere. But though we should distinguish between the essence-and-attributes-of-God and his modes, that still leaves all natural phenomena as his states just as my moods are mine. However, certainly God is not merely the physical universe for Spinoza. (Though that God was, among other things, physical, was, indeed, one of his most shocking claims.) For the essence of God is expressed in an infinite number of attributes of which physical extension is just one. Thus the physical world is God's body, God in his physical aspect, rather than the totality of what God is. Humans, as it happens, only know of one other of these attributes, namely thought. God or the universe is thus both an infinite physical thing and an infinite thinking thing (as well as an infinite number of other infinite things the nature of which is hidden from us).

The one substance and its modes exhaust the things which are. But where does that leave the essence and attributes of the one substance and the essences-of-its-modes (of which Spinoza also makes much)? On the face of it, these seem additional sorts of entity. However, this is not really so.

(i) The essence of a finite thing (that is, a finite mode) is simply the thing itself (or rather that core thereof which must endure so long as the thing exists at all) *qua* possibility whose actualization constitutes it an existent or whose non-actualization leaves it merely as something which might exist (so far at least as the general character of the universe goes). The essence of the one substance is similarly one with the substance itself, that core of the universe which must endure so long as anything does and of which all finite things are passing states. However, there is no question of its ever having or having had status as a mere possibility and it is a necessarily actualized essence. That something is possible but non-existent must be a fact about something which does exist. The non-existence of unicorns is the fact that nature has no place for them, but there is nothing which could have no place for Nature, that is, the one divine substance. There is an implied further proof of God's existence here.

(ii) Much discussion has centred on how Spinoza conceived the relation between the essence of the one substance and its attributes. The 'subjective' interpretation regards them as the subjective appearances to a mind of some unknown ultimate noumenal essence. Modern commentators mostly prefer the objective interpretation according to which they are genuine constituents of the essence rather than a veil behind which it hides. There are difficulties in both accounts, both as interpretation and as philosophy. This writer holds the intermediate position that each attribute is one of various alternative ways of conceiving the essence correctly. (Among other reasons for this are the justification we have seen that it provides of part 1, proposition 5.) Thus the world can be truly seen either as a physical system (the attribute of extension) or as a mental system, that is, a system of ideas (the attribute of thought) while there are other in principle possible ways of seeing it (the unknown attributes) beyond human mental capacity.

In short, neither the essence of substance nor its attributes are items in addition to substance itself.

Qua system of thought God, or Nature, is the idea of itself *qua* physical system, and every finite thing, as mode of the one substance, is both a physical thing and the idea of that physical thing, that is, that component of God's mind which is his awareness of it. Thus every genuine unit in physical nature, animal, plant, or ultimate particle, has its mental counterpart, that is, may be conceived not as a physical thing but as the idea of a physical thing. The human mind is the idea of the human body (of how it functions as a whole, rather than of its every detail). Here again commentators interpret Spinoza somewhat divergently, but most agree that this implies that every physical thing has some kind of sentience. However, it is only in so far as a physical thing has a certain wholeness to it that its mental counterpart constitutes a mind with much distinctness from the rest of cosmic mentality.

Every finite thing has a built in *conatus* (striving or endeavour) to persist in its own being, that is, to keep its own essence actualized (in fact, the *conatus* simply is the essence with its own tendency to persist) until it is defeated in so doing by external causes. This produces self-preserving behaviour suited, to the extent that it can internally register them, to current circumstances. The human mind–body is especially apt in such registration, which constitutes its own ideas of its current environment. (Its ideas of its environment are part of God's current idea of it as affected by this.) Pleasure and pain are the mental analogues of an increase or decrease in the effectiveness of its *conatus*, differing in character with the thing's essence. Spinoza defines all the emotions in terms of pleasure, pain, and the basic *conatus* they manifest. He aims to study human psychology dispassionately 'just as if it were an investigation into lines, planes, or bodies', in contrast to those 'who prefer to abuse or deride the emotions and actions of men rather than to understand them'. For only by understanding ourselves can we win freedom in Spinoza's sense.

Spinoza is an uncompromising determinist. Everything that happens is determined by two factors, in the manner of Hempel's account of scientific explanation, the standing nature of God, that is, the laws of nature, and previous conditions likewise determined back through infinite time. There is no human 'freedom of indifference' but there are various degrees of human freedom in a more worthy sense. The physical and mental behaviour of a human being (or, in principle, of any other finite thing) may be active or passive to various degrees. The more it stems distinctively (or creatively) from its own *conatus*, the more active it is; the more it is merely acted on by external things, the more passive it is. The active behaviour of the mind consists in what Spinoza calls adequate ideas, the passive behaviour in inadequate ideas; adequate ideas necessarily constitute more genuine knowledge. Knowledge has three main grades, in order of its adequacy: (1) knowledge by hearsay and vague experience; (2) knowledge by general reasoning; (3) intuitive rational insight. The first type of knowledge yields emotion and activity of an essentially enslaved sort; human liberation consists in movement through the second to the third type of knowledge. Only at that level do we cease to be victims of emotions which we do not properly understand and cannot control. The third type of knowledge ultimately yields the 'intellectual love of God', Spinoza's version of salvation.

More informally put, Spinoza regards us in bondage so far as we are under the control of external things (in a sense which includes especially mental processes of our own which we do not properly understand) and as free to the extent that we meet life with creative understanding of what will best serve the purposes that adequate ideas will determine in us.

One may still wonder how far Spinoza is really committed to what one might call a religious view of the world.

Well, he was certainly against all forms of religion which he regarded as life-denying and which view the present life as a mere preparation for a life to come; rather, our primary aim should be joyous living in the here and now. This, however, should ideally culminate in that quasi-mystical grasp of our eternal place in the scheme of things, and oneness with God, or nature, which he calls the intellectual love of God. Love of God, in this sense, should be the focal aim of the wise man's life.

So far as religion, as most people conceive it, goes, he clearly thought that a good deal of it was mere superstition, fomenting intolerance and in many ways unhelpful as a basis for a genuinely good life. But he also thought that for the mass of people, who are incapable of the philosopher's intellectual love of God, a good popular religion could act as a morally worthy substitute, providing a less complete form of salvation available to all who live morally and love God, as they conceive him, appropriately, provided only that their love of God is of a type which promotes obedience to the basic commands of morality.

Spinoza is arguably the only really great 'modern' Western philosopher who develops what can be properly called a personal *philosophy of life.   T.L.S.S.

*determinism; freedom.

TRANSLATIONS

Baruch Spinoza: The Ethics and Selected Letters, tr. Samuel Shirley (Indianapolis, 1982).

The Collected Works of Spinoza, ed. and tr. Edwin Curley (Princeton, NJ, 1985).

Spinoza: Ethics, ed. G. H. R. Parkinson (London, 1989).

Tractatus Theologico-Politicus, tr. Samuel Shirley (Leiden, 1991).

COMMENTARIES

Jonathan Bennett, *A Study of Spinoza's Ethics* (Cambridge, 1984).

Edwin Curley, *Behind the Geometrical Method: A Reading of Spinoza's Ethics* (Princeton, NJ, 1988).

—— *Spinoza's Metaphysics: A Study in Interpretation* (Cambridge, Mass., 1969).

Alan Donagan, *Spinoza* (Brighton, 1988).

D. Garrett (ed.), *The Cambridge Companion to Spinoza* (Cambridge, 1996).

Stuart Hampshire, *Spinoza* (Harmondsworth, 1951).

Errol Harris, *Salvation from Despair: A Reappraisal of Spinoza's Philosophy* (The Hague, 1973).

S. Nadler, *Spinoza: A Life* (Cambridge, 1999).

G. H. R. Parkinson, *Spinoza's Theory of Knowledge* (Oxford, 1953).

T. L. S. Sprigge, *Theories of Existence* (Harmondsworth, 1984), ch. 8.

COLLECTIONS

E. Freeman and M. Mandelbaum, *Spinoza: Essays in Interpretation* (La Salle, Ill., 1975).

Marjorie Grene (ed.), *Spinoza: A Collection of Critical Essays* (New York, 1985).

S. P. Kashap (ed.), *Studies in Spinoza: Critical and Interpretive Essays* (Berkeley, Calif., 1972).

spirit. Spirits hover between *minds, *souls, and vapours. The original idea of a spirit is of a disembodied agent, as an immaterial soul or a non-material intelligent power. In the seventeenth century and earlier there was a belief in spirits as gaslike substances intermediate between matter and mind. For all his dualism Descartes in *Les Passions de l'âme* uses the idea. When we talk now of the spiritual we refer to neither of these but typically to the kind of emotion one might have towards God or some other factor beyond one's material life. An image common to all three of these seems to be one of distillation, of a more refined product of a crude original.   A.M.

*pneuma.

Richard Burton, *The Anatomy of Melancholy* (1621).

spontaneity and indifference. These medieval terms are used for two kinds of liberty or freedom. The two kinds continue to be discussed, under the names 'voluntariness' and 'origination', the first sometimes being denied to be real liberty or freedom. To have liberty of spontaneity is to be able to do as you choose. That is, unlike a man in jail, or a man with a gun at his head, you are unconstrained or uncompelled to act as you do. To have liberty of indifference is to be able, given things exactly as they are, to choose or originate another action different from the one you actually choose. If determinism is true, we still often enjoy liberty of spontaneity, because our actions still result from our own choices, but not liberty of indifference, because the choices themselves are caused or deter-

mined. According to the doctrine of *compatibilism, spontaneity is the freedom that is important, and is sufficient for moral responsibility. According to incompatibilism, the only true freedom is indifference, and it is necessary for moral responsibility.   R.C.W.

*freedom and determinism; origination; embraced and reluctant desires.

A. Kenny, 'Freedom, Spontaneity, and Indifference', in T. Honderich (ed.), *Essays on Freedom of Action* (London, 1973).

sport. Despite Plato's reputation as a wrestler, the worlds of philosophy and sport have rarely collided. Unlike other social practices such as art, education, or medicine, sport's characteristic conceptualization as 'non-serious' reinforces scepticism as to the possibility of genuine philosophical interest therein. As a professional field of some thirty years, philosophy of sport has analysed key concepts such as 'competition', 'game', 'play', and 'sport', and explored more generally their nature and significance. As a field of applied philosophy, it has often drawn from work in other fields such as aesthetics, epistemology, and the philosophy of rules. Only in ethics does sport give rise to issues of substantial and original interest, where research might contribute to new thinking in the parent discipline. Sports ethics is certainly the most vibrant dimension of the philosophy of sport, where analytical and normative issues surrounding practices such as doping, cheating, gamesmanship, and genetic manipulation are widely disputed, though largely from within a deontological framework.   D.McN.

M. McNamee and S. J. Parry (eds.), *Ethics and Sport* (London, 1998).

W. P. Morgan, *Leftist Theories of Sport: A Critique and Reconstruction* (Chicago, 1994).

Sprigge, Timothy L. S. (1932–). British idealist philosopher, formerly at the University of Edinburgh. In *The Vindication of Absolute Idealism* (1983) he argues that the reality which appears to us as the physical world of daily life, and of which physical science specifies the abstract structure, is 'in itself' (or 'noumenally') a system of mutually interacting centres of experience. Thus he defends a form of *panpsychism. This conclusion is supported by an argument that a totally unexperienced reality is impossible. Reflections on relations and on temporality suggest that the system must have its own overall consciousness, as an eternal changeless unity within which temporal processes occur. This position is Spinozistic in that the universe is held to be both a mental and a physical totality, though on Sprigge's view the mental is its inner essence and the physical only its structure.

In his moral philosophy Sprigge defends a qualified moral realism and utilitarianism which is not only consistent with his metaphysics but depends upon it for premisses. It is entailed by his moral philosophy that non-human animals have rights, and Sprigge is known as a defender of *animal rights through both publications and active campaigning.   S.P.

*idealism; Spinoza; Santayana.

T. L. S. Sprigge, *The Vindication of Absolute Idealism* (Edinburgh, 1983).
—— *The Rational Foundations of Ethics* (London, 1988).
—— *James and Bradley: American Truth and British Reality* (London, 1993).

square of opposition. Traditionally 'All men are mortal' and 'No men are mortal' are *contraries, meaning that they cannot both be true but may both be false; and 'Some men are mortal' and 'Some men are not mortal' are *subcontraries, meaning that they cannot both be false but may both be true. 'All men are mortal' and 'Some men are not mortal' (like 'No men are mortal' and 'Some men are mortal') are *contradictories, meaning that one must be true, the other false. The square is a traditional diagram summarizing these 'oppositions':

All men are mortal   Some men are mortal

contraries   contradictories   subcontraries

No men are mortal   Some men are not mortal

In traditional logic 'Some men are mortal' is entailed by 'All men are mortal', and 'Some men are not mortal' is entailed by 'No men are mortal'. Though it is implausible to regard this subalternation as a variety of opposition, it was sometimes included in the diagram too.   c.w.

*traditional logic; subaltern.

C. Williamson, 'Squares of Opposition', *Notre Dame Journal of Formal Logic* (1972).

stadium or moving rows paradox. The most mysterious of *Zeno of Elea's paradoxes of motion. The rows are like trains of coaches; the train of *A*-coaches is stationary, those of *B*-coaches and *C*-coaches are moving past it at equal speeds in opposite directions. Zeno seems to infer that a *B* takes as long, and also half as long, to pass a moving *C* as to pass a stationary *A*; hence that a time is equal to its half. One suggestion is that he is attacking the idea of a minimum time-stretch: a *B*'s *A*-passing time is supposed for argument's sake to be such a minimum; but if so, even though two *C*-passing times evidently equal that minimum, one *C*-passing time cannot be less. Another suggestion has him ignore the relativity of motion: since the coaches are equal in length, it *must* take the same time for a *B* to pass one *A* as to pass one *C*.   c.a.k.

W. C. Salmon (ed.), *Zeno's Paradoxes* (Indianapolis, 1970).

Stalnaker, Robert C. (1940–). American philosopher who is especially noted for his work on *conditionals. Like David Lewis, but independently of him, Stalnaker has devised an analysis of conditionals in terms of *possible worlds. Loosely, Stalnaker regards a conditional of the form 'If *p*, then *q*' as being true in the actual world if and only if *q* is true in the closest possible world in which *p* is true. There are important differences between Stalnaker's and Lewis's systems of conditional logic, the most notable being that only Stalnaker's supports the principle of conditional *excluded middle, that is, the principle that 'Either if *p*, then *q*, or if *p*, then not *q*' is true of *logical necessity. Apparent counter-examples can be deflected by denying that the principle of bivalence holds for conditionals.

Stalnaker has also done influential work on the ontological status of possible worlds, the theory of mental content, the nature of belief, and the problem of how beliefs undergo rational revision.   e.j.l.

R. C. Stalnaker, *Inquiry* (Cambridge, Mass., 1984).
—— *Context and Content: Essays on Intentionality in Speech and Thought* (Oxford, 1999).
—— *Ways a World Might Be: Metaphysical and Anti-Metaphysical Essays* (Oxford, 2003).

State, the. The political organization of a body of people for the maintenance of order within its territory by coercion, or, more loosely, the body of people so organized or its territory. There have been *stateless* societies, characterized by lack of a definite territory or, perhaps, by the absence of a form of government with coercive powers for securing obedience. The State, however, is taken to have the *power to regulate the behaviour of all individuals and of any other organizations within its boundaries. For this purpose the State has, or at least claims, a monopoly on the use of force.

Among several theories of the nature of the State the simplest holds that it is simply an organization for subordinating the many to the will of a dominant few. But even on this account a distinction has to be drawn between the *private* acts of individuals and their *public* acts as agents of the State. This is done through marking out the latter as the exercise of power through the administration of the law and the maintenance of security for a territory within which the law can be administered. But is the State more than simply 'a conspiracy of the rich who call their intrigues laws' (Sir Thomas More)?

*Anarchism denies that it is, holding that the State lacks any necessary or desirable function in regulating society. Other theories characterize the State in terms of one. According to Hobbes it prevents a 'warre of every man against every man', and is legitimized by a *social contract between citizens to submit to it in order to secure this benefit. This leads naturally to a view of the State as a voluntary association for mutual protection. Under the theory of *democracy such an association will be governed legitimately only if in accordance with the electorally expressed wishes of its members.

In democracies decisions may be made which apparently involve the State in going beyond its role of maintaining social order. Is this admissible? Under *conservatism, the State's provision of welfare or even its redistribution of wealth can be viewed as simply averting strife, or otherwise as inadmissible. This reflects the doctrine of the 'minimal' State. The State's prevention of discord may, however, be viewed as only an example of its general provision of public benefits. Thus according to *socialism the task of the State is the creation of a good life for all, towards which radical social policies are permissible.

All the above theories view the State as conducing to the satisfaction of *individual* wishes, which are logically prior to it. Under some forms of *communitarianism, however, the State is itself the condition of any rational choice. Thus 'the Fascist conception of the State is all-embracing: outside it no human or spiritual values can exist, much less have value' (Mussolini). *Fascism legitimizes the State by according it the role of supreme moral arbiter.

The theory of the State as an association and some theories of nationalism have different approaches to the question which territory should make up the State. For example, the former should be sympathetic to well-supported secessionist movements, while the latter may regard them as a threat to national unity. However, although the rights of a State to self-preservation against internal threats are unclear, their right and duty to defend themselves against external ones is readily conceded. Indeed, in the absence of international government, Hobbes viewed the relation between States as one of perpetual war.   P.G.

Kenneth Dyson, *The State Tradition in Western Europe* (Oxford, 1980).

Robert Nozick, *Anarchy, State and Utopia* (Oxford, 1974).

statements, basic: *see* basic statements.

statements and sentences. Most modern logicians maintain that statements are distinct from sentences, citing the fact that not all sentences are used to make statements or arguing that the same statement may be expressed by different sentences. Some use 'statement' and *'proposition' interchangeably, regarding them as alternative names for what is 'expressed' by an indicative sentence or 'asserted' when such a sentence is used. Others distinguish between the two, so that a proposition is what is asserted when such a sentence is used to make a statement. Some—Strawson, for example—have held that statements must be distinguished from sentences because mere sentences cannot contradict one another. We imagine that 'I am under six foot tall' and 'I am over six foot tall' are inconsistent, the argument runs, only because we think of them being uttered by the same person in the same breath, i.e. being used to make contradictory statements. What this argument really shows, however, is the importance of taking context into account. Adding the sentence–statement distinction is arbitrary, but it reflects a deep-seated tendency to incorporate in a separate entity what properly belongs to the way that a sentence is used in some particular setting.   C.W.

P. F. Strawson, *Introduction to Logical Theory* (London, 1952), 3–4, 9–12, 174–6.

state of nature. This notion was employed by *social contract theorists to indicate the condition of human beings prior to or without government. By showing what was lacking in this natural condition, or state of nature, they hoped to demonstrate the benefits of politically organized society and the rationality of accepting governmental authority. The state of nature was characterized by certain deficiencies for which government was said to be the proper remedy. It is therefore rational for individuals to pull themselves out of this condition by agreeing among themselves to accept some form of political authority. However, social contract theorists differed sharply with one another about what kind of government provides the best remedy, and this disagreement stems largely from how each characterizes the state of nature. Hobbes, for example, characterized it as an utterly lawless state of affairs in which 'the notions of right and wrong, justice and injustice . . . have no place', and where each man has the right (or liberty) to do whatever he deems necessary to preserve himself. Such a condition, he says, is 'called war; and such a war as is of every man against every man'. He observes that under such circumstances 'the life of man [is] solitary, poor, nasty, brutish, and short'. Thus, Hobbes concludes that the only kind of political authority strong and stable enough to safeguard us from ever falling into such a horrible condition again is unlimited political authority, preferably an absolute monarchy. The authority of such a sovereign must be unconditional and indissoluble; the right to rule conferred on the sovereign must be such that 'whatsoever he doth, it can be no injury to any of his subjects, nor ought he to be by any of them accused of injustice'. Locke, on the other hand, characterized the state of nature as a pre-political state, but insists that 'the state of nature has a law of nature to govern it, which obliges everyone; and reason, which is that law, teaches all mankind who will but consult it that, being all equal and independent, no one ought to harm another in his life, health, liberty, or possessions'. Because of this he views the state of nature as merely involving certain inconveniences. These inconveniences consist in (1) the lack of an established, known law that gives an authoritative interpretation of the law of nature, (2) the absence of an impartial judge to determine violations of the law and their proper punishment, and (3) the want of a power sufficient to ensure enforcement of the law. Thus, while granting that 'civil government is the proper remedy for the inconveniences of the state of nature', Locke also admonishes us 'to remember that absolute monarchs are but men' and asks, 'if government is to be the remedy of those evils which necessarily follow from men's being judges in their own cases, and the state of nature is therefore not to be endured, I desire to know what kind of government that is, and how much better it is than the state of nature, where one man commanding a multitude, has the liberty to be judge in his own case, and may do to all his subjects whatever he pleases . . . and in whatsoever he does, whether led by reason, mistake, or passion, must be submitted to'. Locke concludes that the proper remedy for the state of nature must place ultimate political authority in the will of the majority, who will then entrust political power to governmental officials only under the condition that the latter promote the common good, reserving the right to remove them if they violate this trust.   R.D.M.

Thomas Hobbes, *Leviathan* (1651).
John Locke, *Two Treatises of Government* (1690), Second Treatise.
Jean-Jacques Rousseau, *The Social Contract* (1762).

Stevenson, Charles L. (1908–79). Stevenson is the best known, and arguably the most compelling, exponent of what is known as the *emotive theory of ethics. In two papers written in the 1930s ('The Emotive Meaning of Ethical Terms' (1937), 'Persuasive Definitions' (1938), collected in his *Facts and Values* (New Haven, Conn., 1963)) Stevenson presented this theory, that moral judgements do not describe properties of people or actions but express approval or disapproval and seek also to influence the feelings of approval and disapproval of others. He worked out his ideas in detail in *Ethics and Language* (New Haven, Conn., 1944), a substantial work of considerable depth and originality. The emotive theory of ethics is sometimes taken to encourage, or to imply, immorality, and because of this (wholly unwarranted) idea Stevenson was discharged from a university post in 1945. However, he subsequently worked at the University of Michigan until his retirement in 1977. He is certainly one of the most influential ethical theorists of this century, for all that the emotive theory continues to be widely criticized.   N.J.H.D.

Stewart, Dugald (1735–1828). Son of a professor of mathematics in Edinburgh, for whom he deputized, and pupil of Ferguson, he heard Reid lecturing in Glasgow and was persuaded that mind can be studied scientifically. Clarifying Reid's principles of common sense, he saw the difference between the axiomatic deduction of mathematics and natural generation of belief about the world. Such existential belief had to be governed by laws, not operating as deductive premisses but as constituents of human reason. As Ferguson's successor to the Chair of Moral Philosophy, Stewart argued, as had Reid, that moral qualities really exist independently of perception. He proclaimed his philosophy in extensive writings, promoting Adam Smith's science of legislation, or political economy, which he believed to presuppose moral philosophy. He foresaw that British liberty would develop among 'the oppressed and benighted nations around us'. Although James Mill was one of his students, M'Cosh applauded him for saving England from 'low sensational, materialistic, and utilitarian views'.   V.H.

*Scottish philosophy.

K. Haakonssen, 'From Moral Philosophy to Political Economy: The Contribution of Dugald Stewart', in V. Hope (ed.), *Philosophers of the Scottish Enlightenment* (Edinburgh, 1984).
D. Stewart, *Elements of the Philosophy of the Human Mind* (London, 1843).
—— *Outlines of Moral Philosophy*, with a memoir by J. M'Cosh (London, 1864).

Stich, Stephen (1944–). American philosopher. Stich's work in philosophy of psychology and theory of know-

ledge uses results from cognitive psychology to question the view—called *'folk psychology'—that intentional behaviour is to be explained by appeal to the agent's beliefs and desires (where beliefs and desires are construed as attitudes toward propositions) along with traditional accounts of what it is for a method of inquiry to be rational. Cognitive psychological evidence has suggested to Stich that people often do not act in ways that fit what they sincerely claim they believe or desire, and therefore that there may be no such things as beliefs or desires whose contents can be determined as required by folk psychology explanations of behaviour. Further evidence that people often make up their minds in violation of standards of rationality derived from elementary logic and probability theory has led Stich to a radical critique of the notion of rational belief and the goals of inquiry.   J.B.B.

Stephen Stich, *The Fragmentation of Reason* (Cambridge, Mass., 1990).
—— *Deconstructing the Mind* (New York, 1996).

Stirner, Max (1806–56), pseudonym of Johann Kaspar Schmidt. German philosopher who heard Hegel lecture and became a Left Hegelian. In his major work, *The Ego and his Own* (1845), he attacks the 'new radicalism' of Bauer, Feuerbach, and Marx as much as the 'old orthodoxy'. The only reality, he argues, is the individual ego, and things have value only in so far as they serve the ego. The individual must become conscious of his power over his own ideas. Once ideas escape the ego's control, they become 'ideals' and dominate the ego that produced them. This is true not only of the old ideas of Church and State, but of the new ideas of humanism and socialism. This, like Bauer's, exaltation of individual self-consciousness is a reversion to pre-Hegelian romanticism. Marx and Engels attacked 'Saint Max' (Stirner) in *The German Ideology*.   M.J.I.

*romanticism, philosophical.

R. W. K. Paterson, *The Nihilistic Egoist: Max Stirner* (Oxford, 1971).

stochastic process. Any sequence of trials the outcomes of which are only probabilistically determined. The term is usually applied to sequences of trials ordered in time. As an example consider a time-ordered sequence of tosses of a fair die with specified probabilities for any given face coming up in a given toss. Two fundamentally important kinds of stochastic processes are Bernoulli sequences, in which the trials are all probabilistically independent of one another, and Markov processes. In a Markov process the probabilities for the outcome of a trial may depend conditionally on the outcome of the previous trial, but they are probabilistically independent of the outcomes of any trials before the one immediately preceding the trial in question.   L.S.

*chance; probability.

W. Feller, *An Introduction to Probability Theory and its Applications* (New York, 1950), vol. i, ch. 15.

Stoicism. Philosophical tradition founded by Zeno of Citium, developed by Cleanthes and Chrysippus, and named from the *Stoa poikilē* or 'Painted Porch' in Athens where they taught. The last major figure in antiquity to have Stoicism as his primary allegiance was the emperor Marcus Aurelius in the second century AD, but the influence of the school's ideas lived on, and 'stoical' has become a common expression to indicate acceptance of misfortune without complaint.

Stoicism placed ethics in the context of an understanding of the world as a whole, with reason being paramount both in human behaviour and in the divinely ordered cosmos. The Stoic view of divinity and its relation to the world has been historically influential, contributing to the context in which *Neoplatonic and Christian thought developed, and especially to *theodicy; but it is perhaps Stoic ethical views that are of most immediate philosophical interest to us today, and it is these that have been given most prominence in what follows. The systematic nature of Stoic philosophy indeed reflected the school's view of the systematic nature of the world itself, which it sought to explain without recourse to a Platonic other-worldliness. Some of the paradoxes for which Stoicism was notorious were deliberately adopted for the sake of a striking exposition; but the system was ultimately unable to succeed in explaining everything without internal incoherences.

Stoic ethics indicated that if a perfectly wise, i.e. virtuous, man saw his child in danger of drowning (say), he would try to save it; but that if he failed he would accept this without feeling distress or pity, and without his happiness being diminished. Since everything that happens is governed by divine providence, his failure must have been for the best, even if he could not understand why. Moreover, moral virtue is the only good, and wickedness the only evil; so the child's death was not itself an evil. Furthermore, since moral virtue *is* the only good, and being perfectly virtuous the wise man will by definition have done the best he could, there is nothing for him to regret. (This example is adapted from Long, *Hellenistic Philosophy*, 197–8; it is not based on any single ancient text, but brings out the implications.)

Such a view may seem repellent, even incomprehensible, especially as the Stoics made 'following *nature' the centre of their ethics, explaining the development of moral awareness by the individual's progressive realization of what was naturally appropriate for him (*oikeiōsis*). But context and motivation are important. Ancient Greek society placed considerable emphasis on material achievement, and in spite of Socrates' insistence on the importance of moral goodness, Aristotle had maintained the relevance of bodily and material goods, as well as virtue, to human happiness (*eudaimonia*); indeed some Aristotelian virtues require considerable resources and social standing. The Stoics reacted against such views, still within a eudaemonistic framework, by insisting that all that matters is our attempts to do what is right; health and wealth are naturally *preferable* to sickness and poverty, and we should *pursue* them if we do not wrong others thereby, but *achieving* them is beyond our control. A slave, as Epictetus had been, can be as virtuous as a free man.

Stoicism did not teach withdrawal and inaction (the Stoic school, unlike others, was in the Athenian city centre); but the wise man, while doing the best he can in the circumstances as he sees them, is prepared to accept the eventual outcome as the will of providence, and thus he alone is free. He is like an archer who cares less about actually hitting the target than about doing the best he can to hit it, and his wisdom includes understanding the difference between what is in his power and what is not. (That Chrysippus was a thoroughgoing compatibilist, holding that our actions are predetermined but still our responsibility, is a separate issue; what is important—from his point of view—is that the actions are still ours.)

Only the perfectly wise man is good—and he is as rare as the phoenix; all others are both mad and bad, and all crimes are equal. Like the insistence that virtue alone is good, this can be seen as straining language to make a serious point; all imperfection *is* imperfection, and one can drown an arm's length from the surface as well as 500 fathoms down. The paradox was lessened by recognition of a class of those not yet virtuous but 'making progress'. The actions which such people should perform are 'proper' (*kathēkonta*, often rendered 'duties'); it is only when such actions are performed by the wise man that they count as virtuous. *Emotions are interpreted in intellectual terms; those such as distress, pity (which is a species of distress), and fear, which reflect a false judgement about what is evil, are to be avoided (as also are those which reflect a false judgement about what is good, such as love of honours or riches). It is for such emotions as these that the Stoics reserved the usual Greek term *pathē*. They did, however, allow the wise man such 'good feelings' as 'watchfulness' or kindness, the difference being that these are based on sound (Stoic) reasoning concerning what matters and what does not. The wise man will thus be *apathēs*, 'without *pathē*', but not in our terms 'apathetic'. The experience of internal conflict which Plato had interpreted as a struggle between rational and irrational parts of our psyche was for the early Stoa rather a rapid wavering between conflicting judgements.

By taking nature as a moral guide (like their Cynic predecessors, for whom, however, 'following nature' meant little more than rejecting the institutions of the city state), the Stoics founded the tradition of *natural law. In the Roman period Stoicism became linked with the senatorial opposition to the autocratic rule of emperors like Nero and Domitian. The Stoics were pantheists; *God not only orders everything for the best, but is present in everything as *'spirit', conceived in corporeal terms (as fiery air), because only what is corporeal exists, and determining the character of each thing by its degree of physical 'tension'. In animate beings spirit is present as psyche, in plants as 'nature', and in inanimate things as their 'state' (*hexis*). But God exists in a special way in the fiery heavens, and at fixed periods the whole world becomes fire (an apotheosis, rather than a destruction) before again repeating its predetermined history.

The Stoics developed *propositional logic; they engaged in epistemological debate with the sceptical

*Academy, and partly anticipated Frege's distinction between *sense and reference. In spite of their influential attempts to reconcile providence and *evil, they could not adequately explain why, when virtue was the only good, divine providence should bring it about that almost everyone is bad. Theism eventually proved more congenial than pantheism, and a psychology of conflict than the unity of the psyche; Stoicism declined as Neoplatonism developed.   R.W.S.

B. Inwood (ed.), *The Cambridge Companion to the Stoics* (Cambridge, 2003).
A. A. Long, *Hellenistic Philosophy* (London, 1974).
—— and D. N. Sedley (eds.), *The Hellenistic Philosophers* (Cambridge, 1987). Texts and commentary.

stories and explanation. Narrative understanding is our most primitive form of explanation. We make sense of things by fitting them into stories. When events fall into a pattern which we can describe in a way that is satisfying as narrative then we think that we have some grasp of why they occurred. It is not obvious what makes a satisfying story, but at the very least a story requires purposes fitting into a time-frame. Religions sometimes make sense of the whole world and of individual lives by fitting them together as connected stories. Nations tell stories of their past in terms of which they try to shape their futures. (Such a story is based on a chronicle of real or imagined facts, but adds to it national aims, and the idea of victory and defeat.) Scientific understanding is different. It finds patterns that are not narratives, and forces us to see the stories of our lives as patterns that we make for ourselves, which do not fit into any bigger story.   A.M.

*history, philosophy of; narrative.

David Carr, *Time, Narrative, and History* (Indiana, 1986).
Daniel C. Dennett, *Consciousness Explained* (New York, 1991).
Adam Morton, *Disasters and Dilemmas* (Oxford, 1991).

Stout, George Frederick (1860–1944). Taught philosophy and psychology at Cambridge, Aberdeen, Oxford, and finally St Andrews, where he established an experimental laboratory. His central work, however, was in 'armchair' philosophy of psychology. He held that *every* experience embraces a 'thought reference' to a real object, for even in illusions and hallucinations there is reference to *something* other than the experiencing subject. We do not need to impose Kantian categorical conceptions of space, time, causality, etc. on to our experiences, for we have a natural disposition to experience things in these ways.

The subject of mental attributes—cognition, feeling, and 'conation' (*intention)—is not a Cartesian ego or a mere material object, but a unitary 'embodied *mind' which has both physical and mental attributes occurring in parallel.   A.J.L.

G. F. Stout, *Mind and Matter* (Cambridge, 1931).

straw man fallacy. The straw man fallacy is the tactic in argument of misrepresenting an opponent's position, making it appear more implausible, so that it can more easily be refuted, then going ahead and arguing against the imputed position as though it were really that of your opponent. For example, against an opponent who has taken a 'green' position, an arguer might reply that she wants to make the earth into a natural place like it was hundreds of years ago, and that therefore her argument would require the elimination of industrial production.

                                                                    D.N.W.

Douglas N. Walton, *Informal Logic* (Cambridge, 1989).

Strawson, Peter F. (1919–). British philosopher of logic and metaphysician, noted also for his exposition of Kant. Many of the themes which run through his work are to be found in his most influential book, *Individuals* (1959). Those themes include: the problem of *individuation, the distinction between *subject and predicate, the ontological status of *persons, and the possibility of objective knowledge—all of which Strawson handles in a way which is coloured by his respect for Kant's approach to metaphysics. Strawson characterizes his own approach to metaphysics as *'descriptive' rather than *'revisionary', aspiring to articulate the fundamental structure of our common-sense conceptual scheme rather than to reject it in favour of a radically new vision of reality.

In an early but highly influential paper, 'On Referring' (1950), Strawson attacks Russell's theory of definite *descriptions as unnecessarily revisionary of our ordinary modes of speech. On Russell's account, a sentence of the form 'The *F* is *G*' (for instance, 'The present Prime Minister of the UK is grey-haired') is not really of subject–predicate form, but is equivalent rather to an existentially quantified sentence of the form 'There is one and only one *F* and it is *G*'. Thus, for Russell, 'the *F*' is never a referring expression, having as its *reference a particular object. Strawson complains that Russell fails to distinguish between *sentences* and the *statements* made by speakers in uttering them, arguing that whenever a speaker makes a statement by uttering a sentence of the form 'The *F* is *G*', he uses 'the *F*' to make reference to a specific object which has the property of being *F*. That there *is* such an object is, according to Strawson, a *presupposition* of the speaker's statement rather than, as Russell implied, part of what is being stated.

In *Individuals*, Strawson explores the Kantian claim that our ability to reidentify *things over time presupposes the locatability in space of at least some of those things as objects existing independently of our subjective experiences of them. Although he suggests that this claim is in some respects too strong, he is broadly sympathetic to its thrust. He contends that certain privileged kinds of objects—namely, material bodies and persons possessing such bodies—constitute 'basic' *particulars in our common-sense conceptual scheme. It is ultimately by reference to particulars of these kinds that we are able, in general, to individuate and identify items of other kinds, such as events.

It is noteworthy that Strawson assigns equal weight to both material bodies and persons, rather than regarding the latter as merely a species of the former. For Strawson, persons constitute a fundamental and irreducible category of being, distinctive in having both physical and psychological characteristics predicable of them. A person is not simply a physical thing, nor yet a combination of a physical body and a mind: rather, the notion of a whole person, as a psychophysical being, is conceptually prior both to the notion of a person's body and to the notion of a mind.

In his contributions to epistemology, Strawson argues for *direct realism in perception but concedes that scepticism concerning the external world is not conclusively refutable. At the same time, he contends that such scepticism is literally unbelievable, endorsing a view which he describes as 'naturalism'. His book on Kant, *The Bounds of Sense*, though widely admired, is seen by some as being unduly dismissive of Kant's doctrine of transcendental idealism and over-optimistic in its suggestion that many of the central arguments of Kant's critical philosophy can survive the repudiation of that doctrine. Strawson has also written influentially on the problem of *freedom and determinism, notably in a paper entitled 'Freedom and Resentment' (1962).   E.J.L.

P. F. Strawson, *Individuals: An Essay in Descriptive Metaphysics* (London, 1959).
—— *The Bounds of Sense* (London, 1966).
—— *Logico-Linguistic Papers* (London, 1971).
—— *Freedom and Resentment and other Essays* (London, 1974).
—— *Skepticism and Naturalism: Some Varieties* (London, 1985).

stream of consciousness. William James's famous metaphor for the way *consciousness seems. In *The Principles of Psychology* (1890) the metaphor is introduced in a chapter entitled 'The Stream of Thought'. Two years later, in *Psychology: The Briefer Course*, the corresponding chapter is entitled 'The Stream of Consciousness'. It may be that James, who devotes much of his psychology to unconscious processes, changed the title, and thus the metaphor, in order to emphasize that the metaphor is a purely phenomenological one—consciousness *seems* streamlike. Since only part of thinking, the conscious part, *seems* any way at all, the metaphor is restricted to this part, to consciousness. The conscious stream, according to James, is personal, feels continuous, forward-moving, and in constant change. We tend to speak and focus on particular contentful states. But the metaphor is designed to draw our attention to the deep and wide currents that surround, and render meaningful in particular ways, these thoughts. The 'halo of relations' surrounding and constituting each image or thought, James called the 'penumbra' or 'fringe of consciousness'.   O.F.

William James, *The Principles of Psychology* (1890), 2 vols. (New York, 1950).
—— *Psychology: The Briefer Course* (1892), ed. G. Allport (New York, 1961).

strict implication: *see* implication.

Stroud, Barry (1935–). A Canadian by birth and citizenship, Stroud has lived in the United States since studying at Harvard in the early 1960s. He has been a Professor of Philosophy at the University of California at Berkeley since 1974. Stroud's philosophical interests range widely, but he has been particularly concerned with epistemology, certain aspects of the philosophy of language, and with the thought of Hume and Wittgenstein. His philosophy is more exploratory than system-building, and his outlook is broadly Humean, in that he has little sympathy for rationalistic approaches to philosophy. He has written influentially on transcendental arguments, and his early article 'Wittgenstein and Logical Necessity' has been extensively anthologized.   C.A.J.C.

Barry Stroud, *The Significance of Philosophical Scepticism* (Oxford, 1984).
—— *Hume* (London, 1977).

structuralism. An interdisciplinary movement of thought which enjoyed a high vogue through the 1960s and early 1970s—when it acquired a certain radical cachet—but which has left its most durable mark in the fields of linguistics, anthropology, and literary theory. What unites structuralists in these different fields is the principle, derived from Ferdinand de Saussure, that cultural forms, belief systems, and *'discourses' of every kind can best be understood by analogy with language, or with the properties manifest in language when treated from a strictly synchronic standpoint that seeks to analyse its immanent structures of sound and sense.

In literary criticism, theorists now rejected mere interpretation as a fruitless endeavour subject to all the vagaries of *ad hoc*, intuitive response. Only by examining the structural features of texts—poetic devices, narrative functions, techniques of linguistic 'defamiliarization'— could criticism place itself on a firm (inductive and adequately theorized) methodological footing. In this sense the movement is a part of that wider formalist enterprise which started out with Aristotle's *Poetics* and has since then enjoyed periodic revivals, mostly—as now—in response to new ideas about language, rhetoric, or the function of criticism *vis-à-vis* other disciplines. Where structuralism can claim to represent a real advance is in its highly sophisticated treatment of rhetorical figures like metaphor and metonymy, figures which (according to Roman Jakobson) are the structural axes of all linguistic communication, and which are raised to their highest expressive power in poetry and other art-forms.   C.N.

*post-structuralism.

Michael Lane (ed.), *Structuralism: A Reader* (London, 1970).

structural violence. Popularized by the Norwegian sociologist Johan Galtung, the idea of structural violence involves a wide construal of violence aimed at showing that its menace is present in institutional ways even where no literal or 'narrow' *violence occurs. Structural violence does not involve agents inflicting damage by force, but is equivalent to social injustice. Apart from its potentiality for confusion, a key problem with the concept is its dubious suggestion that a variety of apparently quite different social problems are all essentially the same and will therefore yield to the one approach.   C.A.J.C.

J. Galtung, 'Violence, Peace and Peace Research', *Journal of Peace Research* (1969).

structure, deep and surface. Originally used by Chomsky as part of a theory of *grammar that would generate all and only the grammatical sentences of a speaker's language. The deep structures of sentences (e.g. 'Bill saw whom') were akin to their *logical forms: the level of semantic interpretation. Surface structures (e.g. 'Whom did Bill see?') were derived by transformation rules which moved constituents to new positions, sometimes adding structure, sometimes deleting it. In Chomsky's current theory, mappings from deep to surface level preserve structure. Moved items (like 'whom') leave traces at S-structure to mark their original positions (e.g. direct object) at D-structure. The presence of traces indicate that S-structures are not surface forms: they are shallow structures occurring just below the level of perceived speech. S-structures or logical forms replace D-structures to become the levels where semantic interpretation occurs.   B.C.S.

N. Chomsky, *Knowledge of Language: Its Nature, Origin, and Use* (New York, 1986).

Suárez, Francisco (1548–1617). Jesuit philosopher and theologian, born in Granada, Spain. He taught primarily at Salamanca and Coimbra. Suárez's metaphysics, epistemology, and philosophy of law, though influenced by Aristotle and Aquinas, challenged traditional scholastic views. His *Disputationes Metaphysicae* (1597) was the first systematic and comprehensive work of metaphysics written in the West that was not a commentary on Aristotle's *Metaphysics*. For Suárez, metaphysics is the science of 'being in so far as it is real being' (*ens in quantum ens reale*) and its proper object of study is 'the objective concept of being'. This doctrine is regarded by some as having contributed to the development of mentalism in early modern philosophy. Suárez's theory of individuation reveals the influence of Ockham. The principle of individuation is 'entity', which Suárez identifies with 'essence as it exists'. Existing reality is composed exclusively of individuals.   J.G.
    E.M.

*Spanish philosophy.

Jorge J. E. Gracia, *Suárez on Individuation* (Milwaukee, Wis., 1982).

subaltern. 'Some *S* are *P*' was traditionally said to be the subaltern of 'All *S* are *P*', 'Some *S* are not *P*' the subaltern of 'No *S* are *P*', meaning that the first proposition is in each case entailed by the second. The second was sometimes called the 'superimplicant' of the first, the first the 'subimplicant' of the second. A *syllogism which draws a conclusion about *some* things from premisses which merit a conclusion about *all* of them was said to be in the 'subaltern mode'.   C.W.

J. N. Keynes, *Formal Logic*, 4th edn. (London, 1906), ch. 3.

subconscious mind: *see* unconscious and sub-conscious mind.

subcontraries. Two propositions *p* and *q* are subcontraries when, as with 'There are fewer than 5 million unemployed' and 'There are more than 3 million unemployed', they cannot both be false (so the falsity of one entails the truth of the other) but the truth of one does not entail the falsity of the other, i.e. when 'Either *p* or *q*' is true. Traditionally 'Some *S* are *P*' and 'Some *S* are not *P*' were called subcontraries.   C.W.

*square of opposition.

J. N. Keynes, *Formal Logic*, 4th edn. (London, 1906), ch. 3.

subject: *see* self.

subject and predicate. Grammatically, a subject–predicate sentence consists of any noun phrase and verb phrase in combination, the constraints on the combination being syntactic rather than semantic. Of greater interest to philosophers has been the narrower notion of a 'logical' subject–predicate sentence, where the eligible noun phrases are restricted to those having a certain semantic function, namely, that of *referring to something or someone. Thus, whereas 'Nothing dies' and 'Nero fiddled' would both satisfy the grammatical description, only the latter would be reckoned a logical subject–predicate sentence. More precisely, the predicate in such a sentence is described as a 'first-order' predicate, whereas a predicate which attaches not to a name but to a first-order predicate is known as a 'second-order' predicate. The logical variety is in question when it is said that 'exists' is not a predicate. In saying, for example, 'The Loch Ness monster does not exist' we can hardly be referring to a monster in the loch, so the grammatical subject is not a logical subject, and the predicate accordingly not a logical predicate. The hierarchy of predicates indicated is also thought important to an understanding of related terms, as 'there is' and 'something'. Starting with 'atomic' sentences, as 'Rome burned' and 'Vesuvius is a dormant volcano', we can derive the forms 'Something burned' and 'There is a dormant volcano'. 'Something' and 'there is' are not logical subjects, but are predicates of a predicate, or second-order predicates. This whole mode of classification calls for scrutiny.

    Consider 'Here is a key'. This provides a good contrast to a subject–predicate sentence in that we are not saying of something named 'here' that it is a key, but the adverb simply demarcates the locality where the description ostensibly applies. Similarly with 'There is a key', and not merely when this features 'there' as an adverb of place. In the existential reading what we have is a variation on this pattern, even though 'there' now lacks demonstrative force, approximating more to 'somewhere': provided a key is somewhere to be found, the form is in order. At all events, so long as the behaviour of 'is a key' can be reckoned the same whether it follows 'here' or 'there', we have reason not to think of 'There is a key' as in some way deriving from particular predications, as 'This is a key'. Since we do not then have a predicative use of 'a key' in 'There is a key', nothing which can be attached to the former phrase can be described as a predicate of a predicate.

It can also be queried whether 'Something is a key' features a second-order predicate, but now because 'is a key' may be said to function in just the same way as in 'This is a key', despite the absence of any namelike term. More generally, there is good reason for broadening the category of subject to include a greater range of noun phrases than is customary, even those that are negative, as 'nothing' or 'no one'. So we might include here 'Every dog has its day', 'Gentlemen prefer blondes', and 'Nothing surprises him any more'. In 'Every dog has its day' the phrase 'every dog' is a genuine unit, relevantly on a par with 'Fido', though of course not a name. It is relevantly on a par in so far as we can say: 'has its day' is true of every dog. Similarly, 'prefer blondes' is true of gentlemen and 'surprises him any more' is true of nothing. The contrast here continues to be with 'Here is an *F*', where we cannot say: 'is an *F*' is true of here.

B.B.R.

P. T. Geach, 'Subject and Predicate', *Mind* (1950).

B. Rundle, *Grammar in Philosophy* (Oxford, 1979).

P. F. Strawson, *Subject and Predicate in Logic and Grammar* (London, 1974).

subjective truth. This self-consciously paradoxical description was employed by the Danish philosopher Søren Kierkegaard to describe the force of passionate conviction and commitment, particularly with reference to religion. The intended contrast, obviously, is objective truth, scientific truth, matters which can be verified or established by proof. But 'subjective truth', although conscientiously 'unscientific', is not therefore meaningless or irrational, as some later positivists would argue (and as Kierkegaard sometimes suggests himself). Subjective truth is a commitment to believe, in the face of 'objective uncertainty', in matters which cannot be demonstrated or verified, such as the existence of God. The defence of such convictions, in so far as there can be such, are strictly personal, a matter of personal passion (not mere 'preference'), and refer to an outlook on life, a way of 'existing', rather than a set of cognitive or ontological commitments.

R.C.SOL.

*double truth.

S. Kierkegaard, *Concluding Unscientific Postscript* (1846; Princeton, NJ, 1944).

subjectivism: *see* objectivism and subjectivism.

subjectivity. Pertaining to the subject and his or her particular perspective, feelings, beliefs, and desires. The term pervades modern philosophy, usually contrasted with 'objectivity', but it plays various and sometimes ambiguous roles in epistemology, in contemporary Continental philosophy, and in cognitive science. In casual philosophical and other conversation, the term often refers to unargued or unjustified personal feelings and opinions as opposed to knowledge and justified belief. In epistemology, especially since Descartes, the term is often used to refer to the realm of experience, however circumscribed and defined, and is typically defined with reference to the first-person standpoint. The project of much of modern epistemology, accordingly, has been the attempt to argue from this admittedly limited standpoint to objective knowledge, whether by ingenious deduction (Descartes), causal inference (Locke), transcendental argument (Kant), dialectical development (Hegel), or phenomenological analysis (Husserl). In recent Continental philosophy, the subject of subjectivity has been under severe scrutiny, and the very idea has been rejected by more radical recent opinion. Revolting against Jean-Paul Sartre, who followed Descartes in insisting that free subjectivity (as *'consciousness') was the ontological essence of being human, such thinkers as Michel Foucault and Jacques Derrida have rejected the notion of 'the subject' altogether and insisted that what is mistakenly identified by that name is a 'construction' of politics, language, and culture. In cognitive science, subjectivity has been argued, e.g. by Thomas Nagel, to be the ultimate obstacle to any reduction of the mental to the physiological. Subjectivity, on this account, is phenomenological experience, or 'what it's like to be' a certain conscious being (for example, a man, a woman, or a bat), the tendency to project (and take one's own attitudes as properties of the world). The notion of subjectivity is also used, particularly in multicultural contexts, to underscore the importance of perspective, the fact that everyone sees the world from his or her (or its) individual vantage-point, defined in part by nature, by culture, and by individual experience. Philosophers have often asked, Can we 'escape' our subjectivity? But what would it mean to do so? What would it mean *not* to do so?

R.C.SOL.

D. Dennett, *Consciousness Explained* (London, 1993).

J. Derrida, *Speech and Phenomena* (Evanston, Ill., 1973).

E. Husserl, *Cartesian Meditations* (The Hague, 1960).

T. Nagel, *The View from Nowhere* (New York, 1986).

J.-P. Sartre, *Being and Nothingness* (New York, 1956); tr. from *L'Être et le néant* (Paris, 1943).

J. Searle, *The Rediscovery of Mind* (Cambridge, 1992).

sublime. The concept of sublimity is seen by some aesthetic theorists as of only historical interest, but by others as a lastingly important mode of response to basic items of human experience. From the later seventeenth century there developed accounts of experience of objects that exceeded our perceptual and imaginative grasp, and defied neoclassical conceptions of form and *beauty. Although these objects were daunting and dreadful, they were nevertheless exhilarating to contemplate: Alpine crags and ravines, storms at sea, the sky at night . . . Given this duality, writers differed over the source of our resilience *vis-à-vis* such intimidating phenomena. For Kant, for example, despite the failure of imagination's synthesizing powers (we cannot *realize* the interstellar distances), our reason and our status as free moral beings allow us to cope with the sheer magnitudes and energies of phenomenal nature and to be aware of a personal value that these do not threaten. A religious note was, and is, never very far from many accounts of sublimity: its dual quality can be analogous to experience of the divine—a *mysterium tremendum et fascinans*, as Rudolf Otto famously described it in *The Holy*.   R.W.H.

*holy, numinous, and sacred.

P. Crowther, *The Kantian Sublime: From Morality to Art* (Oxford, 1989).

R. W. Hepburn, 'The Concept of the Sublime: Has it Any Relevance for Philosophy Today?', *Dialectics and Humanism* (1988).

S. Monk, *The Sublime* (first pub. 1935; Ann Arbor, Mich., 1960) is the classic historical account.

substance and attribute. The idea of substance has been widely and differently used throughout the history of philosophy from the time of Greeks onward—by Plato, Aristotle, Locke, Descartes, Spinoza, Kant, and many other philosophers. What is perhaps the main distinction between substance and attribute originally gave support to the feeling that reality is independent and objective, robust and solid, that there is something out there which is abiding and remains the same in spite of varieties and changes encountered in the world. Substance was taken as the abiding and constant, while attributes and properties changed. However, if changing, the attributes and properties were objective as a result of their association with and dependence on the substance. Without an underpinning substance or substratum to which to belong, could they have reality? Originally, the distinction between substance and attribute was taken literally, but subsequent revisionism has often made it almost grammatical or functional (e.g. Leibniz, Hume).

There is indeed reason to believe that the substance–attribute distinction, like the object–property distinction, is parasitic on some other distinction. One reason is that when we see an apple, for instance, we grasp it at once as a whole object. We do not see it, as it were, compositionally, first seeing its red shape, then conjoining with this a taste, a texture, etc., and finally proceeding to unify these elements into a single apple. We do not perceptually grasp an apple through the distinction between substance and attribute. Perception seems not to be the source of the distinction.

With the imposition of the substance–attribute distinction, objects which initially were perceived as wholes now come to be analysed or restructured. The need to do so seems to be pressed upon us by various considerations. But the manner of the restructuring appears to be suggested not by reality, so to speak, but by the linguistic distinction between subject and predicate, this being the very means available to us for describing objects in their varieties and alterations. Whereas the perception of objects is as wholes, speech, on the other hand, is almost always construed from parts, and is in this sense compositional. Conceiving the unitary apple in terms of the distinction between substance and attribute or object and property seems to be parasitic on, and a suggestion from, the linguistic distinction between subject and predicate.

Three considerations or aims have moved philosophers to engage in the restructuring of things in terms of substance and attribute. The first aim is to secure the ability to speak of similar objects whose features are nevertheless being contrasted (e.g. a green banana and a yellow banana). This aim encourages the idea of the object as comprising a thoroughly denuded substance (often called the ultimate subject of properties) on to which the attributes which it shoulders, and with respect to which object and object can be compared, are grafted. This view of things was held by John Locke, who made famous the phrase 'substance or something-I-know-not-what'. It was also formulated by Aristotle in terms of 'primary substance'. It was accepted by philosophers for centuries.

While the first aim addresses static and compositional aspects of the existence of objects, the second addresses dynamic aspects of the existence of objects, thereby involving a reference to time, as Kant noted. It secures the ability to speak of an object remaining the same yet different, invoking the idea of *change. In this context, substance is proclaimed to be the perdurant in change, the absolutely unchanging core, the ground which enables an object to be the same in spite of the newness of its features. The third aim also involves a reference to time, and addresses intra-active and interactive aspects of the existence of objects. It imbues an object with the active power to initiate change in itself (Leibniz) or in another object (Locke and Kant) and the passive power to allow change to be initiated in it (Locke and Kant). In this sense, substance is seen as the ultimate centre of force used in grounding change-producing actions and causalities.

It is customary to think of substance and attribute in terms of ordinary things. But it needs to be noted that two sorts of primary substance have been discussed historically: material substances for the extended physical world, and spiritual substances for the non-physical, unextended world (Descartes). Spiritual or mental substances enter into the attempted solution of the mind–body problem in terms of substance *dualism.

All of this still leaves disagreement possible over the necessity of a conception of substance. There is also the question of the precise nature of its supposed relations with the properties of an object. Why do the properties of an object hang together? How should one think of the relation between an object and its properties so that properties do not simply fall off and scatter, but are instead collected in the object? Think of the difference between a fruit with a pit (where the flesh corresponds to the properties of an object and the pit corresponds to the primary substance) and a vegetable like an onion whose layers aggregate without a supporting pit. This difference between the two is over a sort of metaphysical arithmetic: would subtracting just its properties from an object leave anything behind, the substance or something-I-know-not-what of John Locke, or would it leave absolutely nothing behind?   W.E.A.

William R. Carter, *The Elements of Metaphysics* (New York, 1990).

D. W. Hamlyn, *Metaphysics* (Cambridge, 1984).

Richard Taylor, *Metaphysics* (Englewood Cliffs, NJ, 1963).

substratum: *see* substance and attribute.

sufficient condition: *see* necessary and sufficient condition.

sufficient reason, principle of. Leibniz held that the principle of sufficient reason is fundamental to all reasoning. It states, in his own words, that 'there can be found no fact that is true or existent, or any true proposition, without there being a sufficient reason for its being so and not otherwise, although we cannot know these reasons in most cases'. In short, the principle is that nothing is without a reason for its being, and for being as it is: *nihil fit sine ratione*.

Schopenhauer devoted his earliest philosophical work to discussion of the principle, which he characterized as what 'authorizes us everywhere to search for the *why*'. He rightly criticized his predecessors, Leibniz included, for misunderstanding it, chiefly by confusing the notions of *reason* and *cause*. Schopenhauer himself distinguished four distinct explanatory applications of the principle: the physical (in explaining change in the natural world), the logical (in deriving truths a priori), the mathematical (in giving geometrical demonstrations), and the moral (in explaining actions in terms of motives). This classification might be unsatisfactory, but the principle itself captures something intuitively compelling, in having it that whatever is or happens must from some point of view be finally explicable.   A.C.G.

G. W. Leibniz, *The Monadology* (1714), sects. 31, 32.

A. Schopenhauer, *The Fourfold Root of the Principle of Sufficient Reason* (1813).

Sufism. A variety of Muslim *mysticism characterized by the concept of a union of the human being with God through the power of love. The union was thought by many to be of the will and it was held that suffering, as well as love, was a necessary condition of the union. Its days as a major force in Islam are long since past.   A.BRO.

A. J. Arberry, *Sufism* (London, 1950).

suicide. The most conventional definition of 'suicide' is intentionally caused self-destruction. However, several problems for this simple definition arise from sacrificial death, martyrdom that could have been avoided, actions that risk near-certain death or mutilation, refusals of medical treatment with foreknowledge of death, addiction-induced overdosing, coercion to self-caused death, and the like. Some definitions of 'suicide' have tried to take account of these cases by not requiring suicidal intent, but only foreknowledge of death or the acceptance of a risk of death. These different definitions have led to disagreements over cases—for example, whether Socrates and Samson committed suicide.

Starkly different views about the moral justifiability of suicide have also been defended in the history of philosophy. Debates traditionally centred on whether suicide violates one or more of three types of obligation: to oneself, to others, or to God. St Thomas Aquinas's arguments are typical (*Summa Theologiae* II. ii, q. 64, Art. 5):

It is altogether unlawful to kill oneself, for three reasons: [1] everything naturally keeps itself in being . . . . Wherefore suicide is . . . contrary to the natural law and to charity. [2] Because . . . every man is part of the community, and . . . by killing himself he injures the community. [3] Because life is God's gift to man, and is subject to His power . . . . Hence whoever takes his own life, sins against God.

In a famous rebuttal of such traditional views, David Hume identified with a handful of pre-Christian classical writers who considered suicide an honourable and sometimes praiseworthy act. An autonomous suicide, from Hume's perspective, is permissible (and on occasion laudable) if, on balance, more value is produced for the individual or more value is produced for society than would be produced by not performing the act of taking one's life ('Of Suicide', posthumous, although suppressed by Hume in 1757).

Sir William Blackstone (1723–80), codified English law by using arguments similar to Aquinas's to explain the state's right to prevent and punish suicide. Blackstone categorized suicide as 'self-murder' and a grave felony (*Blackstone's Commentaries*, ch. 14). But when laws against suicide progressively fell, Hume's theses came to prevail, both in Britain and in North America.

Philosophical controversy has recently centred on (1) *paternalism in suicide intervention and (2) the justification of assisted suicide. Regarding (2), see the entry on euthanasia. Regarding (1), if individuals have a *right* to commit suicide, then others appear to have a correlative obligation not to intervene to prevent the suicide. Yet we often do intervene, either by reporting a suicide threat or preventing a suicide attempt. Many believe that we are justified in intervening in these ways and possibly are *obligated* to do so or at least to report suicide threats. But if there is a *right* to commit suicide, are we as justified in intervening as we commonly think? In the case of almost any similarly intrusive, liberty-limiting action, the person impeded could successfully sue those who intervene.

No one doubts that we should intervene to prevent suicide by incompetent persons. But if we accept an unrestricted, free-choice principle, the imprudent but competent suicide who would want to live under more favourable circumstances could not legitimately be prevented from committing suicide. Both law and philosophy continue to struggle with issues about the extent to which paternalism is justified in such cases, if it is.   T.L.B.

M. P. Battin, R. Rhodes, and A. Silvers (eds.), *Physician Assisted Suicide: Expanding the Debate* (New York, 1998).

Tom L. Beauchamp, 'Suicide', in Tom Regan (ed.), *Matters of Life and Death*, 3rd edn. (New York, 1992).

John Donnelly (ed.), *Suicide: Right or Wrong?* (Buffalo, 1991).

summum bonum: *see* good, greatest.

supererogation occurs when one's action goes beyond the demands of duty. Supererogatory acts are praiseworthy to perform but not blameworthy to omit. Saintly or heroic acts are generally considered to be paradigm examples. However, some philosophers (for example, strict act-utilitarians) and theologians (for example, those who emphasize that God demands our best at every moment) hold that there is no possibility of performing good or praiseworthy actions which exceed the demands of duty, and on their view acts of supererogation are not possible.   G.F.M.

*ideals, moral.

D. Heyd, *Supererogation* (Cambridge, 1982).

superman (or overman). Nietzsche's image conveying the idea of human life enhanced and transformed in a manner sufficient to render it worthy of affirmation, in contrast to all that is 'all too human' about it, dispensing with all other-worldly hopes and illusions, and overcoming all disillusionment. The apotheosis of human vitality and creativity, this image functions as a guiding idea by reference to which 'higher' and 'lower' human types can be distinguished, and as the locus of meaning ('the meaning of earth') in Nietzsche's naturalistic reassessment of this life in this world. It has élitist rather than racist overtones and implications for Nietzsche, emphasizing the importance of the respects in which human beings individually differ in their abilities, and of the manner in which their differing abilities are cultivated and employed. This reflects his fundamental conviction that what matters most, and so what is decisive with respect to human worth and 'rank' alike, is 'the enhancement of life', which he conceives above all in terms of the flourishing of cultural life. (See e.g. *Thus Spoke Zarathustra*, prologue; *The Antichrist*, sect. 4; *The Will to Power*, sect. 866.)   R.S.

*slave morality; great-souled man.

Arthur Danto, *Nietzsche* (New York, 1965), ch. 7.

superstructure: *see* base and superstructure.

supervaluation. A method of valuation that supervenes on several different lower-order valuations. A statement is super-true (or super-false) if it is true (or false) on all admissible valuations. Otherwise it is neither super-true nor super-false. Statements in which the components have no determinate truth-value can thus themselves be super-true or super-false. 'This is a really big book, or it's not', for example, is super-true because it is true on all admissible valuations, even if 'This is a really big book' is too vague to have a single admissible precise valuation.   D.H.S.

James D. McCawley, *Everything that Linguists have always Wanted to Know about Logic (but were Ashamed to Ask)* (Chicago, 1993).

supervenience. A kind of dependency relation. One set of properties is supervenient on a second set when they are so related that there could not be a difference in the first without there being a difference in the second, though there could be a difference in the second with no difference in the first. It has been argued that mental properties are supervenient upon, rather than nomically identical with or related to, physical properties.   O.R.J.

*psychophysical laws.

David Charles and Kathleen Lennon (eds.), *Reduction, Explanation and Realism* (Oxford, 1992).

supposition theory. Medieval philosophers developed supposition theory in the late twelfth century to specify the *reference of a term in various propositional contexts. A term has personal supposition when it is used to talk about what it signifies, for example 'lion' in 'She is feeding the lion now'. A term has material supposition when it is used autonymously to talk about its inscription or utterance, as in 'Lion has four letters'. A term has formal supposition when it stands for a concept or a *universal, as in 'Lion is a species'. The modes of personal supposition specify how many objects a term is used to talk about: either exactly one (discrete supposition) or at least one (determinate supposition); if the latter, either all instances (distributive supposition) or several (non-distributive confused supposition). Supposition theory was used to codify and explain the inferential relations among sentences. It was an important part of medieval theories of *truth, *quantification, *entailment, and *fallacy.   P.K.

*logic, history of.

Peter King, *Jean Buridan's Logic: The Treatise on Supposition and the Treatise on Consequences*, Synthese Historical Library, xxvii (Dordrecht, 1985).

survival: *see* immortality.

Swedish philosophy. The history of Swedish philosophy contains few really original or pioneering achievements. To a large extent it has mirrored the general philosophical development of Europe, though in a way that has been marked by national prejudices and national concerns.

It was Christianity that first brought Sweden into contact with the higher European culture. In the later Middle Ages we find Swedish scholars who had studied at Italian or French universities and were familiar with the best contemporary culture. Perhaps the most important figure was Matthias Ovidi (d. 1350). He was the confessor of St Bridget but also a learned philosopher and theologian. His commentary on the Book of Revelation (*Expositio super Apocalypsin*) was studied all over Europe.

When Sweden became a great power in the seventeenth century it became more interesting to the philosophers of Europe. René Descartes went to Stockholm to give lessons to Queen Christina—and to die. Samuel Pufendorf became professor at the newly founded university of Lund (1668). And Swedes began to take a keener

interest in philosophy. The heavy hand of Lutheran orthodoxy lay over all intellectual life in Sweden, so out of
necessity philosophical questions also became theological
ones. The adherents of Aristotle fought a bitter battle with
the adherents of Peter Ramus. The main question was
which philosophy would best serve the purposes of theology. When the new philosophy of Descartes reached
the Swedish universities it was at once suspected of theological heresy. Indeed *Cartesianism was officially condemned by Charles XI in a decree of 1689. Perhaps the
suspected role of Descartes in converting Queen Christina
to Catholicism had some part in the prejudice against
Cartesianism.

The most original philosopher and one of the most fascinating personages of the Swedish seventeenth century
was George Stiernhielm (1598–1672). His unfinished
work *Monile Minervae* (The Necklace of Minerva) contained the fragments of his philosophy, where hermetic
*mysticism was mingled with Neoplatonic *humanism.
His theory of language stressed the non-arbitrary nature
of words. According to Stiernhielm etymology is the key
to deep insights into the essence of things.

At the end of Sweden's period as a great power there
appeared another mystic and philosopher who was destined to fame. Emanuel Swedenborg (1688–1772) began
his career as a natural scientist, but was later captivated by
theology and religious speculation. Swedenborg's visions
from the world of the spirits were scornfully dismissed by
Kant as *Träume eines Geistersehers* ('dreams of a spirit-seer').
But to the philosophers of the Romanticism Swedenborg
was an inspired genius. He was not typical of Swedish
eighteenth-century philosophy, however. The philosophy taught at the universities was sterner and drier. The
arid rationalism of Christian Wolff for a long time held
academic philosophy in its thrall. Later the empiricism of
Locke and Hume found some adherents.

The era of Romantic idealism was pioneered by the
Uppsala philosopher Benjamin Höijer (1767–1812).
Höijer was influenced by Kant and Fichte, but developed
their ideas in an original way. His *Afhandling om den
philosophiska construktionen* (Dissertation on Philosophical
Construction, 1799), anticipated some of Schelling's theories. It was also favourably reviewed by the German
philosopher. At the same time its emphasis on the liberty
of the thought and the activity of the spirit was regarded
with suspicion by the authorities. Höijer's academic
career was for a long time held in suspense. His importance to the Swedish philosophy of the next century was
nevertheless immense. The transcendental idealism that
Höijer had introduced held the stage for more than a
hundred years.

The dominant Swedish philosopher of the nineteenth
century was Christoffer Jacob Boström (1797–1866), who
was professor at the university of Uppsala. Boström has
been described variously as 'the Plato of the North' and as
'the Swedish Hegel'. His sternly rational *idealism made
no concessions to empirical reality—material things
didn't exist. According to Boström true reality was

identical with God and his ideas. Boström worked out his
metaphysical system in great detail. It proved to have
important implications for every sphere of human life,
not least the political one, where Boström's conclusions
were strictly conservative. Boström had many clever
disciples. In fact 'Boströmianism' dominated Swedish
academic philosophy until the turn of the century.

During the first part of the twentieth century Swedish
philosophy was torn between rival schools. Particularly
important was the feud fought between the Uppsala philosophy of Axel Hägerström (1868–1939) and the Lund
philosophy of Hans Larsson (1862–1944). Hägerström
was famous for his *emotive theory of ethics. He denied
the possibility of practical knowledge and the existence of
objective values. According to him values were just projections of emotional attitudes. Ethical propositions were
said to be neither true nor false, being in fact just noises
indicative of certain emotional states.

Larsson, on the other hand, upheld the *objectivity of
values. But his most important contribution to philosophy lay in the field of aesthetics. His book *Poesiens logik*
(The Logic of Poetry, 1899), was intended to show that
logical reasoning and poetic intuition are compatible and
indeed complementary.

After 1945 the strong German influence on Swedish
philosophy was broken and was replaced by an Anglo-
Saxon one. Swedish philosophers began to call themselves
'analytical philosophers'. Among the most influential
philosophers of the first post-war generation were
Ingemar Hedenius and Anders Wedberg.

Ingemar Hedenius (1908–82) became the best-known
philosopher of his generation through his book *Tro och
vetande* (Belief and Knowledge, 1949). The book contained
a savage attack on Christian dogma and on contemporary
Swedish theology. Hedenius formulated a 'maxim for
intellectual morality' (to some extent inspired by Russell),
saying that you should only believe what there are rational
grounds for believing. As Christian belief is muddled,
contradictory, and incompatible with modern science, it
has to be rejected. Some theologians argued that religious
faith is atheoretical and does not aspire to say something
that is true or false. Hedenius rejected this view and tried
to show that Christianity is indeed making statements
about reality and is thus open to philosophical or scientific
refutation.

Anders Wedberg (1913–78) is best known for his work
on the history of philosophy. His *Plato's Philosophy of
Mathematics* (1955) is still useful. But his most ambitious
work in the field was his *Filosofins historia*, i–iii (1958–66),
translated into English as *A History of Philosophy* (1982–4)).
Wedberg's aim was to write the history of philosophy in a
new way. He carefully distinguished the philosophical
way of writing history of philosophy (which he chose)
from the historical way (which he left to others). The
philosophical way of doing history of philosophy was to
treat the philosophers of the past as contemporaries, to
look out for what might still be interesting in their theories
from a philosophical point of view, and to interpret them

in a way that would make their arguments as coherent and as plausible as possible, as seen by a modern analytical philosopher. This should be done, Wedberg argued, even at the price of the occasional anachronism.

Nowadays Swedish philosophers to a large extent publish their results in English. Logic, decision theory, and applied ethics are among the areas where Swedish philosophers have been particularly successful in recent decades.   S.N.

*Danish philosophy; Norwegian philosophy.

R. E. Olson, and A. M. Paul, *Contemporary Philosophy in Scandinavia* (Baltimore, 1972).

Swinburne, Richard (1934–). Nolloth Professor of the Philosophy of the Christian Religion at Oxford from 1985 to 2002. His chief contribution has been to philosophical theology. Perhaps his most interesting achievement is a rigorous formulation of a cumulative case for *God's existence. In *The Existence of God* (1979), he used Bayesian reasoning to argue that the probability of theism is raised by such things as the existence of the universe, its order, the existence of consciousness, human opportunities to do good, the pattern of history, evidence of miracles, and religious experience. He also argues that the existence of *evil does not count against the existence of God. His conclusion is that on our total evidence theism is more probable than not. Swinburne's more recent investigations have focused on distinctively Christian doctrines such as sin and atonement, sanctification, and revelation. He has also contributed to philosophy of science through work on confirmation and on space and time.   P.L.Q.

*religion, problems of the philosophy of.

R. Swinburne, *The Existence of God*, 2nd edn. (Oxford, 2004).
—— *The Christian God* (Oxford, 1994).
—— *Providence and the Problem of Evil* (Oxford, 1998).

syllogism. Originally defined by Aristotle as 'discourse in which, certain things being posited, something else necessarily follows', it came to have the narrower meaning typified by 'All men are mortal; Greeks are men; therefore Greeks are mortal'. Until the revolution in logic in the late nineteenth and early twentieth centuries, most logicians regarded four types of 'categorical' proposition as lying at the heart of proper reasoning: 'All *S* are *P*', 'No *S* are *P*', 'Some *S* are *P*', and 'Some *S* are not *P*'. A syllogism is an inference made up of three propositions of these types. Propositions not obviously of these forms (e.g. singulars like 'Socrates is a man') were generally regarded as mere variants on them, just as apparently non-syllogistic inferences were analysed, and sometimes distorted, to fit the orthodox structure. A syllogism may be defined as a piece of reasoning analysable into:

1. three categorical propositions such that the third (the *conclusion*) is presented as following from the first two (the *premisses*), and
2. three terms such that one of them (the *middle term*) is common to the premisses, the second is common to

the conclusion and one of the premisses, and the third is common to the conclusion and the other premiss.

The first term (the *subject*) of the conclusion is called the *minor term*, the premiss containing it the *minor premiss*; and the second term (the *predicate*) of the conclusion is called the *major term*, the premiss containing it the *major premiss*.

Inferences like 'All men are mortal; all Greeks are men; all Athenians are Greeks; therefore all Athenians are mortal' were called *polysyllogisms*. Polysyllogisms contain more than two premisses but are analysable into a sequence of two or more conventional syllogisms.

Syllogisms were classified according to their *figure* and *mood*, and various rules were invoked to distinguish between valid and invalid forms.   C.W.

*logic, traditional.

I. M. Bochenski, *Ancient Formal Logic* (Amsterdam, 1951), 36–54.
W. D. Ross (ed.), *Aristotle's Prior and Posterior Analytics* (Oxford, 1949).

symbol: *see* sign and symbol.

symbolic logic: *see* logic, formal or symbolic.

symbols, logical: *see* Appendix on logical symbols; notations, logical.

symmetric relation. A binary, i.e. two-term, *relation is symmetric, or symmetrical, when it holds both ways if at all, i.e. if it holds from x to y, it holds from y to x (in symbols, R is symmetric if and only if $\forall x \forall y (Rxy \rightarrow Ryx)$); for example, *living with*. 'Asymmetric' means: if it holds from x to y, it does not hold from y to x; for example, *being half of*. 'Non-symmetric' may mean either 'not symmetric' or 'neither symmetric nor asymmetric'.   C.A.K.

W. Hodges, *Logic* (Harmondsworth, 1977).

sympathy. (*a*) Emotional affinity between two or more persons similarly affected by a given circumstance or (*b*) disorder occasioned in one living entity by the disorder of another. In moral philosophy, (*b*) is developed by Hume to provide a quasi-mechanical psychological explanation of why the well-being or misery of one person is of concern to others. Adam Smith takes Hume's ideas further in his *Theory of Moral Sentiments* (1759), in which sympathy is the analogous feeling that is experienced by the impartial observer at the *thought* of the situation of the other person.
                                               J.C.A.G.

Philip Mercer, *Sympathy and Ethics* (Oxford, 1972).

syncategorematic. Literally, what is predicated together with (sc. some other predicate). So traditional logic defined as syncategorematic a word that converts one or more simple predicates into what was thought to be a complex predicate, as in '*no* man', 'white *and* shiny'. The word now has no technical utility, but is sometimes applied to logical *constants or other *topic-neutral expressions, such as 'not', 'every', 'if', 'is', 'was', 'must', 'the'.   C.A.K.

N. Kretzmann and E. Stump (eds.), *The Cambridge Translations of Medieval Philosophical Texts* (Cambridge, 1988), i. 163–215.
——— A. J. P. Kenny, and J. Pinborg (eds.), *The Cambridge History of Later Medieval Philosophy* (Cambridge, 1982), ch. 11.

syndicalism. Late nineteenth- and twentieth-century revolutionary movement among industrial workers aiming at transferring ownership and control of the means of production and distribution from the capitalist class to unions of workers (*syndicats*) by means of strikes. Syndicalism traditionally marched with *anarchism to produce anarcho-syndicalism. *Sorel misappropriated this term for his quasi-fascist theory of action through irrational *violence, but mainstream syndicalism continued as a radical-left workers' movement.   A.BEL.

*worker control.

Rudolf Rocker, *Anarcho-Syndicalism* (London, 1938).

synonymy. Identity of *meaning. Different occurrences of the same expression (e.g. word, phrase, sentence) are all synonymous unless the expression has more than one meaning. Occurrences of different expressions, in the same or different languages, may also be synonymous: e.g. 'bucket' with 'pail', 'j'ai froid' with 'I am cold', 'gift' with some occurrences of 'present'. Expressions that *apply* in some situation to the same thing or things need not be synonymous: e.g. 'I' and 'you' when the former is said by, and the latter to, someone, or 'boiled water' and 'pure water' when boiling and nothing else purifies. Conversely, in some situations synonymous expressions are forced to apply to different things: e.g. 'I' said by different speakers. The view sometimes held that synonymy of expressions is the same as necessary identity of application seems incorrect.   S.W.

B. Mates, *Synonymity*, University of California Publications in Philosophy (Berkeley, Calif., 1950), repr. in L. Linsky (ed.), *Semantics and the Philosophy of Language* (Urbana, Ill., 1952).

syntactics. The study of syntax, i.e. of the kinds of expression in a language, and the rules which govern how they combine together. In developing modern logic, Frege suggested a theory of syntactic categories which is also applicable to natural languages. In Ajdukiewicz's notation, the two basic categories are sentences (S), and singular terms (N); from any categories *A* and *B* we can form the new category *A*/*B*, containing all those expressions which can be combined with *B*s to form *A*s.   L.F.S.

*pragmatics; semantics.

K. Ajdukiewicz, 'On Syntactical Coherence', *Review of Metaphysics* (1966–7).

synthetic a priori judgements. The classification 'synthetic a priori' applied to judgements, or to true judgements, owes its origin to Kant's *Critique of Pure Reason* (Introduction, B 1–19). It is a hybrid form constructed from the separate distinctions between analytic–synthetic and a posteriori–a priori truth. Kant held that we were able to know some truths a priori rather than a posteriori, independently of sense-experience, such as mathematical truths, and that there was a separate contrast to be drawn between analytic and synthetic truths. Analytic truths involved judgements in which the predicate was semantically contained in the subject-term or alternatively those whose denial yielded a contradiction. With these separate classifications four hybrid forms can be theoretically constructed, although Kant believed that one (analytic a posteriori) was impossible and two others (synthetic a posteriori and analytic a priori) were uninteresting standard cases. The remaining hybrid, synthetic a priori truth, was an important innovation, but both controversial and variously understood. For the Logical Positivists the classification was contradictory, since they treated the two basic classifications as equivalent; for Quineans the classification was flawed since the analytic–synthetic distinction was ambiguous and rested on an unelucidated notion of 'semantic containment'. More recently Kripke's separate classifications of necessary–contingent and a priori–a posteriori truth, and the resulting hybrids necessary a posteriori and contingent a priori truth, have been thought to parallel Kant's innovation. Kripke shares with Kant the idea that one of the basic classifications (analytic–synthetic) is semantic, or logical, while the other (a posteriori–a priori) is epistemic, but their conception of the resulting hybrids is not the same. Kant's case for the existence of synthetic a priori truth rests essentially on the idea that not all a priori truths owe their status to their analytic character. If it is allowed that a priori truth is not necessarily analytic, then some room is available for synthetic a priori truth.   G.H.B.

*analytic and synthetic statements; a priori and a posteriori.

I. Kant, *Critique of Pure Reason*, tr. Norman Kemp Smith (London, 1929).
S. Kripke, *Naming and Necessity* (Oxford, 1980).
W. V. Quine, 'Two Dogmas of Empiricism', in *From a Logical Point of View* (Cambridge, Mass., 1953).

synthetic statements: *see* analytic and synthetic statements.

T

tabula rasa. A phrase (meaning blank writing-tablet) from the Latin translation of Aristotle's *De anima* (430ᵃ). It does *not* occur in Locke's *Essay* (1690), though it is present in Pierre Coste's French translation (1700). The *Essay*, in its statement of the empiricist thesis that there is nothing in the mind that was not previously in the senses, speaks rather of the mind at birth as 'white paper' (II. i. 2), awaiting ideas from experience.   R.S.W.

*empiricism.

R. I. Aaron, *John Locke*, 3rd edn. (Oxford, 1971), 32, 35, 114.

tacit knowledge. Thinkers often perform complex rule-governed tasks even though they have no conscious or explicit knowledge of the rules involved. To explain these capacities, philosophers and psychologists have supposed that thinkers have unconscious or tacit knowledge of the rules for executing the tasks. A prominent example is speakers' ability to produce and understand indefinitely many grammatical sentences of their language even though they cannot state the rules of grammar they conform to. To credit speakers with tacit knowledge of grammar is to suppose they have information-bearing states of mind—inaccessible to consciousness—that encode the rules of their language and enable speakers to produce and comprehend grammatical speech. To say that thinkers are able to perform tasks described by a theory because they tacitly know the theory is to say that they encode the information recorded by the theory but not necessarily in the form in which the theory represents it.   B.C.S.

M. Davies, 'Tacit Knowledge and Subdoxastic States', in A. George (ed.), *Reflections on Chomsky* (Oxford, 1989).

Tagore, Rabindranath (1861–1941). Poet, novelist, playwright, literary critic, painter, composer, and educationist. He won the Nobel Prize for literature, and refused a knighthood. Although he deeply influenced the Indian nationalist movement, he himself embraced a humanist inter-nationalism. This *humanism also coloured his metaphysics, in which the universal I of the human enjoyer bestows beauty and hence truth on an otherwise valueless universe. The Absolute Person who craves for the love of a human other remains unknown like the protagonist of *King of the Dark Chamber* (Tagore's play which Wittgenstein retranslated). Apart from love of nature and humanity, the highest religion of man, according to Tagore, is to try to enhance our creativity, which is 'the surplus in man' allowing us an occasional glimpse of the deeper truth that 'each of us is King, in our King's Kingdom'. Thus, we can communicate with God, the cosmic artist, only through our individual artistic freedom.   A.C.

*Indian philosophy.

Rabindranath Tagore, *The Religion of Man* (London, 1988).

Tanabe Hajime (1885–1962). Widely regarded as Japan's next greatest thinker after Nishida, Tanabe is remarkable for the immense compass of his thought, which ranges from the philosophy of science and mathematics, through the philosophy of history, to major works dealing with ideas from Shin Buddhism and Christianity. Having studied with Husserl and Heidegger in the mid-1920s, Tanabe became increasingly influenced by Hegel and Kant; and during the 1930s he developed a 'logic of species' (*shu no ronri*), which emphasized the role of the nation (as species) as mediating between humankind (as genus) and the historical individual. Increasingly concerned with philosophy of religion, Tanabe wrote towards the end of the Second World War his major work, *Philosophy as Metanoetics*, in which he presented a 'philosophy without philosophy' based on the phenomenon of 'repentance' (*zange*) and a way of thinking purged of the nationalistic elements that he felt had vitiated the logic of species.   G.R.P.

Taitetsu Unno and James Heisig (ed.), *The Religious Philosophy of Tanabe Hajime: The Metanoetic Imperative* (Berkeley, Calif., 1990).

Tantra. Ancient and medieval Sanskrit texts containing somewhat unorthodox guidelines, followed by Hindus, Buddhists, and Jainas, for rituals, meditation, and life-orientation. The Tantras are deeply monistic and idealistic in spite of positing numerous female and male deities as immediate objects of worship. Some celebrate the body, esoteric geometric patterns, and sexuality as instrumental to spiritual transcendence. Elaborating a transformationist account of *causality, Tantrism identifies the cosmic knowing–wishing–acting power which has become the universe with the energy that lies latent in the human body. This feminine power is represented as a coiled snake at the base of the spinal cord—waiting, as it were, to be woken up and eventually united with the Supreme Male Spirit in the cortex. The task is to *recognize* oneself as identical with this pulsating all-pervasive World-spirit. This recognition-philosophy was developed into a full-fledged metaphysics and epistemology by the great aesthete of Kashmir Abhinavagupta (AD 980).   A.C.

*Indian philosophy; Buddhist philosophy.

Arthur Avalon, *Shakti and Shakta* (New York, 1978).

tao: *see* Confucianism.

Taoism. Major school of thought in China which has been influential on various aspects of Chinese culture, such as art, literature, and religion. The two best-known Taoist texts are the *Chuang Tzŭ* and the *Lao Tzŭ*, both probably composite and compiled in the fourth and third century BC. Other texts traditionally regarded as Taoist include the syncretic *Huai Nan Tzŭ*, composed in the second century BC, and the *Lieh Tzŭ*, compiled in the second or third century AD. Taoist thought further developed in the third and fourth century AD, such development being often referred to as neo-Taoism. Better-known texts of the period include Wang Pi's (226–49) commentary on the *Lao Tzŭ*, and Kuo Hsiang's (d. 312) commentary on the *Chuang Tzŭ*, which either borrowed from or built on a commentary by Hsiang Hsiu (*fl.* 250). Development of Taoist ideas in this period subsequently exerted influence on the Chinese interpretation of Buddhism as well as on the later development of Confucian thought.

A basic tenet of Taoist thought is that the operation of the human world should ideally be continuous with that of the natural order, and that one should restore the continuity by freeing the self from the restrictive influence of social norms, moral precepts, and worldly goals. The Taoist ideal is often characterized in terms of *wu wei* (non-action, not-doing); the *Chuang Tzŭ* presents it as involving one's responding spontaneously to situations with no preconceived goals or preconceptions of what is proper, while the *Lao Tzŭ* presents it as involving few desires and absence of striving after worldly goals. The actual way of life involved is subject to different interpretations. For example, some scholars interpret the *Chuang Tzŭ* as advocating a withdrawal from social life, while others interpret it as advocating a relaxation of concern which is compatible with ordinary social activities. Subsequent developments of Taoist thought likewise took different directions. For example, while some Taoist thinkers of the third century AD advocated a life of disregard for established social conventions and values, others such as Wang Pi and Kuo Hsiang regarded the Taoist ideal as compatible with ordinary ways of life, including social and political participation. For Kuo Hsiang, the Taoist ideal is, for certain individuals, even compatible with their being sages in some more ordinary sense, such as that advocated by the Confucians—it is in the nature of some (but not all) to become such sages.

Taoist thought also has implications for politics. *Wu wei* can characterize the ideal form of government, which does not teach or impose on the people standards of behaviour, including those of conventional morality, and which provides conditions making possible their functioning in a way continuous with the natural order. With regard to the relation between states, the *Lao Tzŭ* regards non-contention as enabling a state to outlast competitors. There is also a metaphysical dimension to Taoist thought. For example, the *Lao Tzŭ* portrays *tao* (the Way) as a metaphysical entity which is the source of all things and which is characterized by *wu* (non-being, vacuity), an idea further developed in Wang Pi's commentary. According to Wang Pi, *tao* is the ultimate reality which transcends all distinctions and conceptualizations. Its substance is *wu* and its function *wu-wei*; that is, it does not create or do anything, but just lets things follow their natural course. Similarly, the sage has *wu* as substance and *wu-wei* as function in that he has eliminated all attachments of the self and just lets everything follow its natural course, without devising and imposing a way of life on himself or others.

K.-L.S.

*Chinese philosophy; Confucianism.

Chuang Tzŭ: The Inner Chapters, tr. A. C. Graham (London, 1981).
Commentary on the Lao Tzŭ *by Wang Pi*, tr. Ariane Rump and Wing-tsit Chan (Honolulu, 1979).
Lao Tzŭ (Tao Te Ching), tr. D. C. Lau (Harmondsworth, 1963).

Tarot. The Tarot pack, in its original form, was invented in the early fifteenth century, at the Court either of Milan or of Ferrara. It consists of seventy-eight cards, being essentially an ordinary pack of cards (save for having four instead of three court-cards in each suit) to which twenty-two additional picture-cards, not belonging to any of the four suits, have been added; the suit-signs are those then ordinarily used in Italy, and still used in many parts of it, for ordinary playing-cards. The only use for these cards recorded before the eighteenth century was to play a particular type of card-game, still played in numerous versions in many parts of Europe: one of the picture-cards, the Fool, or Matto, is a kind of wild card, and the remaining ones, which form a sequence and depict standard subjects such as Love, the Devil, the Star, and so forth, are permanent trumps. In 1781 Antoine Court de Gébelin propounded the theory that the cards had been invented by ancient Egyptian priests as a symbolic expression of their beliefs; the theory was rapidly exploited by professional fortune-tellers. In the mid-nineteenth century the French writer Éliphas Lévi incorporated 'the Tarot' into his cloudy brand of occultist doctrine, principally by entwining its images with the Kabbalah, with which they had in origin nothing to do. In the last twelve years of the nineteenth century these ideas were taken up in Britain, and in the early years of the twentieth century spread throughout the world.   M.D.

T. Depaulis, *Tarot: Jeu et magie* (Paris, 1984).
M. Dummett, *The Game of Tarot* (London, 1980).

Tarski, Alfred (1902–83). Tarski was born in Poland, and taught mathematics at the University of Warsaw until he emigrated to the United States in 1939. Appointed Professor of Mathematics at the University of California at Berkeley in 1946, he made important contributions to the subject. It is for his work in logic that he is best known to philosophers, for it established the foundations of modern logical theory.

The seminal ideas appear in an early paper (tr. as 'The Concept of Truth in Formalized Languages' (1935), repr. in *Logic, Semantics, and Metamathematics*), whose goal was a definition of truth for sentences, in a way that both ensures satisfaction of the schema of type T (*'snow is white') and avoids the *liar paradox. In this paper Tarski distinguishes between a formalized language L, on the one hand, whose sentences meet a purely syntactical criterion of well-formedness, and an *interpretation* $\mathfrak{I}$ of L, a structure consisting of domains of individuals and predicates and relations defined in these domains, on the other. The domains supply the values of variables of appropriate type in the language, and the predicates and relations of $\mathfrak{I}$ are correlated with predicate and relation symbols of L. A general characterization of *truth* in $\mathfrak{I}$ for sentences of L can then be specified in terms of the inductively defined relation of *satisfaction*. Tarski showed also that this definition could not be carried out in L itself, but required the resources of a richer metalanguage (Tarski's theorem).

If each of a set Q of sentences of L is true in $\mathfrak{I}$, $\mathfrak{I}$ is said to be a *model* of Q. In his 1936 paper 'On the Concept of Logical Consequence' (reprinted in *Logic, Semantics, and Metamathematics*), Tarski founded what quickly became the accepted theory of logical consequence on the model concept: a sentence s is a consequence of a set P of premisses just in case, when both are formalized, every model of P is a model of $\{s\}$. Such has been the comprehensiveness of the Tarskian revolution in logic that only recently have dissenting voices been raised (for example, Etchemendy, *The Concept of Logical Consequence*). C.H.

*semantic theory of truth.

J. Etchemendy, *The Concept of Logical Consequence* (Cambridge, Mass., 1990).

A. Tarski, *Logic, Semantics, and Metamathematics*, 2nd edn. (Indianapolis, 1983).

tar-water. Made by stirring together tar and cold water, and drawing off the impregnated water after the solid residues have settled. Advocated by Berkeley in his strange work *Siris: A Chain of Philosophical Reflexions and Inquiries* (1744) for its 'extraordinary virtues' as an all-purpose medicine. His enthusiasm, though excessive, was widely shared in the later eighteenth century and, as a mild antiseptic, tar-water was probably not entirely useless. G.J.W.

A. A. Luce, *The Life of George Berkeley* (London, 1949), 196–206.

taste. The appreciative *sensibility of observers who experience delight when disinterestedly contemplating certain natural and artefactual objects ranging from meteoroid showers over Death Valley to performances of *Der Rosenkavalier*. This concept evolved from Dominique Bouhours's use of 'la délicatesse' in 1687 to mark the importance of emotion in aesthetic appreciation and the ultimacy of individual response over classical canons of correctness. In England, taste was first modelled as a quasi-perceptual inner sense of beauty not involving judgement (Hutcheson). Hume expected standards to be established by isolating features which pleased most serene, experienced observers. Kant argued that taste judgements were subjective and universally valid. In the twentieth century taste was redefined by some as a discriminatory sensitivity to aesthetic qualities of artworks by insightful percipients. The correct perception is triggered by knowledge of history, biography, intention (Croce), or boosted by use of simile and metaphor like 'His canvasses are fires, they crackle, burn, and blaze' (Frank Sibley). B.T.

Harold Osborne, *Aesthetics and Art Theory* (New York, 1970).

tautology. A *well-formed formula ϕ of the *propositional calculus is a tautology if the formula is true whatever truth-values are assigned to its basic (atomic) propositional components. This can be determined by *truth-tables. (*Decision procedure.) Tautologies in the predicate calculus can be determined by treating quantified formulae as if they were basic components of well-formed formulae and testing for tautologousness. For example,

$$((x)Fx \lor \sim(x)Fx)$$

is a tautology, corresponding as it does to $(P \lor \sim P)$, whereas

$$((x)Fx \lor (x)\sim Fx)$$

is not a tautology.

In an earlier use, the entire set of logically valid propositions or analytic truths were sometimes designated as tautologies.

On still another use, the theorems of the propositional calculus

$$\phi \equiv (\phi \lor \phi)$$
$$\phi \equiv (\phi \cdot \phi)$$

are sometimes described as principles of tautology. R.B.M.

B. Mates, *Elementary Logic* (Oxford, 1972).

E. L. Post, 'Introduction to a General Theory of Propositions', *American Journal of Mathematics* (1921).

Taylor, Charles (1931–). Canadian philosopher and political theorist (primarily at Oxford and McGill) whose writing includes a critique of behaviourism in psychology (*The Explanation of Behaviour* (1964)), work in and about political science, and support for the general view that the methodology of natural science and that of *social science (the latter centring on interpretation) differ fundamentally. He has defended positive freedom, contributed to theory of responsibility, and written on Hegel. Though not reducible to one theme, Taylor's work often criticizes *'naturalism'. His active as well as scholarly engagement with politics is evident in his life and writings. Most recently, he has produced a major volume on modernity (*Sources of the Self*), in which the self is conceived as constituted by a relation to the good; an essay on 'multiculturalism'; and *The Ethics of Authenticity*, readily accessible but also of scholarly interest.   E.T.S.

Charles Taylor, *Sources of the Self* (Cambridge, Mass., 1989).
——*The Ethics of Authenticity* (Cambridge, Mass., 1992).

Taylor, Richard (1919–2003). Taylor, an American philosopher who held professorships at Brown and Columbia, was among those who saw common sense as the basis for reasoning. He was particularly known for his well-written prose, shrewd dialectics, iconoclasm and, especially in his later writings, advocacy of *wisdom over mere learnedness. Among his main works are *Action and Purpose* (Englewood Cliffs, NJ, 1966), *Metaphysics* (4th edn., Englewood Cliffs, NJ, 1992), *Good and Evil* (Buffalo, NY, 1970), and *With Heart and Mind* (New York, 1973).

To illustrate Taylor's approach, common-sense yields that it is up to us what we do *and* that every event is caused. These apparently conflicting claims are reconciled by saying that a person is an agent, a substantial self, and not a bundle of events (as Hume thought); and agency is outside the scope of the claim that all events are caused. This approach to the conundrum of *free will, however, faces serious challenges in specifying the nature of an agent and in explaining how an agent can be influenced by external events without being caused to act.   M.B.

P. van Inwagen (ed.), *Time and Cause: Essays Presented to Richard Taylor* (Dordrecht, 1980).

te : *see* Confucianism.

teaching and indoctrinating. Indoctrination is the teaching of what is known to be false as true, or more widely the teaching of what is believed true in such a way as to preclude critical inquiry on the part of learners.

Teachers are thus in a strong position to indoctrinate, as their pupils are usually in no position to judge the truth or reasonableness of what they are being taught. While in the *Republic* Plato advised the guardians to teach the people a *'noble lie' to get them to accept their station in life, few teachers actually teach things they believe untrue or unfounded. Although non-believers often accuse Catholic teachers of indoctrinating because they teach Catholic dogma as true, they are not guilty of Platonic insincerity. They might, though, be teaching in such a way as to preclude inquiry on the part of pupils. To avoid indoctrinating, teachers must ensure that at some stage in a course of study pupils will hear competing points of view on disputed questions. Judgement, though, will still be required as to just which questions are really disputed, which points of view are worth considering, and when young pupils are ready to consider alternatives without becoming utterly confused.   A.O'H.

I. A. Snook (ed.), *Concepts of Indoctrination* (London, 1972).

teaching philosophy. Teachers teach two things: what the results of inquiry are, and how to get more of them. Teachers of *philosophy want to find and pass on philosophical truths and, more importantly, the knack of both getting them and distinguishing them from competitors such as nonsense and falsehood. Two near-paradoxes result.

Philosophical results are important, and philosophers typically have firm and, they hope, well-thought-out views on philosophical issues. But they want students to acquire the ability to form justified beliefs for themselves, even if the cost is occasionally going astray. So good philosophers typically do not mind students rejecting their beliefs; indeed they positively welcome it, as long as the disagreement is well supported. As all good teachers know, this feature of the pedagogical process makes certain students very nervous. Actually, as all good students know, it also makes certain teachers very nervous.

The second semi-paradox concerns the tension between what is taught and the way it is taught. Philosophers emphasize *rational persuasion, *rational* discourse, and *rational* examination. As Robert Boyle said, 'Philosophy, when it deserves that name, is but Reason, improv'd by Study, Learning, and the use of things.' However, the *way* in which the importance of rational persuasion is instilled may have very little to do with rational persuasion. Humour, irony, analogy, intonation, sentence structure, allusion, arguments *ad hominem* and from authority, the perceived enthusiasm and confidence of the speaker, the amount of self-motivation required of the student, and a host of other factors, including even the very order in which opposing views are presented, all affect the likelihood of students' accepting or even comprehending the points presented. Even intellectually extraneous factors such as the room's light or the presence of moving air affect uptake and acceptance. Preaching the primacy of reason involves a host of non-rational methods.

Plato believed that philosophy could only be taught soul to soul, and encounters in small groups provide the best way to convey both the excitement involved in, and the abilities required for, the practice of philosophy. In such settings, the student can try out ideas *en route* to truth which will then be subjected to detailed constructive scrutiny by herself, her teachers, and her peers.

However, the realities of teaching often make this wildly utopian. It is difficult for soul to speak to soul when the souls are clustered in groups of up to 300. What one politician has called 'negative increases' in educational funding, and the consequent deterioration in the educational process, ensure that the Platonic ideal is seldom realized before the graduate stage. (Detailed discussions concerning real-world teaching are offered quarterly in *Teaching Philosophy*. Also of interest is *Thinking*, a journal concerned with philosophy for children.)

Plato also believed that students need a rigorous educational background for philosophy: something contemporary educational systems find difficulty in providing. Many first-year university students do not know so much as the *names* of Archimedes or Newton. However, such gaps can be filled, and many universities offer general introductory courses to attempt just that. More pernicious is the deliberate inculcation of irrationality. Unsure of how to cope with multiculturalism, many teachers and too many academics retreat into the relativism they confuse with tolerance. Schools now turn out a host of contemporary Averroists, prepared to say straightfacedly, 'Well, it's true for you, but not for me.' Thus, in addition to the more or less standard familially inspired religious, political, and moral prejudices, contemporary education adds another, moral and epistemological relativism, impressed in the schools, and reinforced by a number of non-philosophical disciplines, which the working philosopher is called upon to remove before the real business of education can begin.   J.J.M.

*teaching and indoctrinating; American philosophy.

H. P. Grice, 'Reply to Richards', in Richard E. Grandy and Richard Warner (eds.), *Philosophical Grounds of Rationality* (Oxford, 1986).
David Stove, *The Plato Cult and Other Philosophical Follies* (Oxford, 1991).

technology: *see* Frankfurt School.

teleological argument for the existence of God. A world-based line of argument appealing to special features, those aspects of the world which appear to be designed and purposive, analogous to cases of human design. It is usually put probabilistically, arguing that the most plausible explanation is that of a world designer and creator, with intelligence, purposes, etc.

The theory of *evolution, suggesting an alternative explanation for some kinds of order, has sapped some of the persuasiveness of older versions, and has incited the formulation of more broadly based versions of this argument, such as those of F. R. Tennant and Richard Swinburne.   G.I.M.

David Hume, *Dialogues Concerning Natural Religion* (1777).
Richard Swinburne, *The Existence of God* (Oxford, 1979).
F. R. Tennant, *Philosophical Theology* (Cambridge, 1968).

teleological explanation. From the Greek word for goal, task, completion, or perfection. Teleological explanations attempt to account for things and features by appeal to their contribution to optimal states, or the normal functioning, or the attainment of goals, of wholes or systems they belong to. Socrates' story (in Plato's *Phaedo*) of how he wanted to understand things in terms of what is best is an early discussion of teleology. Another is Aristotle's discussion of 'final cause' explanations in terms of that for the sake of which something is, acts, or is acted upon. Such explanations are parodied in Voltaire's *Candide*.

There are many cases in which an item's contribution to a desirable result does not explain its occurrence. For example, what spring rain does for crops does not explain why it rains in the spring. But suppose we discovered that some object's features were designed and maintained by an intelligent creator to enable it to accomplish some purpose. Then an understanding of a feature's contribution to that purpose could help us explain its presence without mistakenly assuming that everything is as it is because of the effects it causes. There are many things (e.g. well-designed clocks in good working order) known to have been produced by intelligent manufacturers for well-understood purposes, whose features can, therefore, be explained in this way. But if all teleological explanation presupposes intelligent design, only creationists could accept teleological explanations of natural things, and only conspiracy theorists could accept teleological explanations of economic and social phenomena.

Teleological explanations which do not presuppose that what is to be explained is the work of an intelligent agent are to be found in biology, economics, and elsewhere. Their justification typically involves two components: an analysis of the function of the item to be explained and an aetiological account.

Functional analysis seeks to determine what contribution the item to be explained makes to some main activity, to the proper functioning, or to the well-being or preservation, of the organism, object, or system it belongs to. For example, given what is known about the contribution of normal blood circulation to the main activities and the well-being of animals with hearts, the structure and behaviour of the heart lead physiologists to identify its function with its contribution to circulation. Given the function of part of an organism, the function of a subpart (e.g. some nerve-ending in the heart) can be identified with its contribution—if any—to the function of the part (e.g. stimulating heart contractions). Important empirical problems in biology and the *social sciences and equally important conceptual problems in the philosophy of science arise from questions about the evaluation of ascriptions of purposes and functions.

Functional analysis cannot explain a feature's presence without an aetiological account which explains how the feature came to be where we find it. In natural-selection explanations, aetiological accounts typically appeal to (*a*) genetic transmission mechanisms by which features are passed from one generation to the next and (*b*) selection mechanisms (e.g. environmental pressures) because of which organisms with the feature to be explained have a better chance to reproduce than organisms which lack it. The justification of teleological explanations in sociobiology, anthropology, economics, and elsewhere typically assumes the possibility of finding accounts of transmission and selection mechanisms roughly analogous to (*a*) and (*b*).   J.B.B.

*causality; biology, philosophical problems of; Nagel, Ernest.

A. Ariew, R. Cummins, and M. Perlman (eds.), *Functions* (Oxford, 2002).
Morton O. Beckner, *Biological Ways of Thought* (Berkeley, Calif., 1968), chs. 6–8.
Larry Wright, 'Functions', Christopher Bourse, 'Wright on Functions', Robert Cummins, 'Functional Analysis' (along with

further references to standard literature), in Elliott Sober (ed.), *Conceptual Issues in Evolutionary Biology* (Cambridge, Mass., 1984).

teleology: *see* teleological explanation; Aristotle; causality; biology, philosophical problems of; Nagel, Ernest.

temperance: *see* self-control.

temporal properties and relations: *see* A-series and B-series.

tender- and tough-minded. 'The history of philosophy is to a great extent that of a certain clash of human temperaments', said William James in *Pragmatism* (1907), listing typifying characteristics of each as below. An almost perfect example of the second is A. J. Ayer; pure forms of the first are scarcer.

The tender-minded	The tough-minded
Rationalistic	Empiricist
(going by 'principles')	(going by 'facts')
Intellectualistic	Sensationalistic
Idealistic	Materialistic
Optimistic	Pessimistic
Religious	Irreligious
Free-willist	Fatalistic
Monistic	Pluralistic
Dogmatical	Sceptical

T.L.S.S.

T. L. S. Sprigge, 'A. J. Ayer: An Appreciation of his Philosophy', *Utilitas* (1990).

tense. Grammatically, tense is a feature of verbs, exemplified by the past, present, and future forms 'he went', 'he is going', and 'he will go'. Philosophers think of tense in broader terms, to include any kind of temporal expression whose reference is dependent on its time of utterance, such as 'yesterday', 'now', or 'next week'. Thus, 'yesterday' refers to the day before the one on which it is uttered. The truth-values of tensed sentences can change over time: on one day it may be true to say 'Yesterday it rained', while on the next day it may be false to say this. Adherents of tensed theories of *time hold that tensed sentences are made true by tensed *facts, and that facts change as time passes, whereas adherents of tenseless theories of time hold that tensed sentences are made true by unchanging, tenseless facts. For the tenseless theorist, tense is merely a feature of our language or thought about the world, not a feature of temporal reality itself.   E.J.L.

D. H. Mellor, *Real Time*, 2nd edn. (London, 1998).

term. A word or phrase denoting an individual or class, or the propositional component it expresses. Thus 'John is a man' contains two terms, 'John' and 'man' (or 'is a man'), denoting John and the set of men respectively. More generally, any word or phrase that determines the proposition expressed. In this sense, the above sentence contains the *syncategorematic term 'is', which does not denote an individual or class.   W.A.D.

H. W. B. Joseph, *An Introduction to Logic* (Oxford, 1916), ch. 2.

terrorism. 'Terrorism' is a highly emotive, pejorative label, originally applied to the Reign of Terror following the French Revolution, but now most commonly used of *political violence as employed by insurgents against a *state, unless specifically qualified as 'state terrorism'. Its definition has proved philosophically elusive, depending, as it does, on whether, and, if so, how, the pejorative force is to be captured definitionally; or, in other words, on whether terrorism is to be viewed as *ipso facto* unjustifiable, and, if so, why, which evidently raises substantive philosophical issues.

Broadly speaking, there are two approaches to characterizing terrorism in a way that views it as, *ceteris paribus*, morally wrong. One regards it as not just any tactic which induces terror by the use of violence, for such terror is routinely employed in wartime by the use of military force, which is not thereby terroristic. Rather, it is the use of force of a military character in contravention of the rules of war as adumbrated in the theory of the just *war. Thus, on the one hand, terrorism may be seen as the use of such force without a *jus ad bellum because its perpetrators—as non-state actors—lack proper authority. To this criticism those dubbed terrorists typically reply that the states they oppose have forfeited authority over them by their unjust behaviour, which furnishes them with a just cause (an argument advanced by John Locke). It is this line of thought that commonly leads so-called terrorists to view themselves as 'freedom fighters'.

On the other hand, however, what may be attributed to terrorists is a failure of *jus in bello, resulting from breaches of the principle of non-combatant immunity by the targeting of civilians. One response to this charge (adopted by Sartre in his defence of FLN violence in Algeria) is that the civilians targeted are not innocent of the injustices combated. Another is that the exposure of civilians to injury through terrorism is no greater, and perhaps less, than that routinely accepted in conventional wars.

The major drawback of this unjust war model of terrorism is that, in regarding terrorism as prima facie wrong because contrary to the rules of war, it concedes that terrorism is indeed a form of war; albeit often one in which terrorist tactics are employed precisely because the resources for a conventional war are lacking, and therefore, since military victory is impossible, success can be achieved only by terrorizing a people and its government into submitting to demands. Yet, though terrorists usually claim to be fighting a war, this is exactly what governments are loath to allow, since this would give terrorists the same protections as soldiers against the operation of the ordinary criminal law.

A second approach to terrorism is, therefore, to view it as wrong for the same sort of reason as any violent crime is wrong, and distinguished from other such crimes only by having a political motive. The usual anti-terrorist strategy is thus to employ a criminal justice rather than a military approach, though this can prove problematic in the case of international terrorists operating from beyond the attacked state's jurisdiction. So-called terrorists will deny that their violence is morally wrong just because contrary to the laws of a possibly unjust government, however, and will go on to repudiate the pejorative label. It may still be applied to them, Michael Walzer argues, if they contravene a 'political code' of anti-state violence by targeting civilians rather than, on this account, only politicians and the like.

These definitional problems may, perhaps, be overcome by using the word 'terrorism' without pejorative force and viewing it as a species of political violence not accorded the legitimacy of war. Then the substantive question comes to the fore of when such violence (including the violence of the state) is justified.   P.G.

*political violence; war, just.

P. Gilbert, *New Terror, New Wars* (Edinburgh, 2003).
—— *Terrorism, Security and Nationality* (London, 1994).
T. Honderich, *After the Terror* (Edinburgh, 2003).
M. Walzer, *Just and Unjust Wars* (New York, 1992).
M. Warner and R. Crisp (eds.), *Terrorism, Protest and Power* (Aldershot, 1990).
B. T. Wilkins, *Terrorism and Collective Responsibility* (London, 1992).

tertium non datur : *see* excluded middle, law of.

testimony. The role of testimony in getting and spreading reliable belief or *knowledge has been a relatively neglected epistemological issue. Traditional epistemology has had a marked individualist flavour in its stress upon the status and vindication of information gleaned from individual perception, memory, or inference. But it is clear that most of what any given individual knows comes from others: palpably with knowledge of history, geography, or science, more subtly with knowledge about everyday facts such as when one was born. Recently, more attention has been paid to this topic, and amongst the problems discussed are the scope of the dependency each of us has on the word of others, the difficulty of validating the dependency via inferences from an individual's experience of witness reliability, and the problems of expert evidence.   C.A.J.C.

C. A. J. Coady, *Testimony: A Philosophical Study* (Oxford, 1992).

test of time. For a work or idea of any sort to evoke admiration or agreement over many generations implies that it transcends fashion and can be appreciated from different standpoints. In the aesthetic realm, where what is at issue is particular objects for which there can be no universally applicable standard of taste, the test of time may be the best, if not the only, determinant of ultimate quality. In politics, too, where knowledge of the effects of institutions and policies may be hard to gauge directly, the test of time becomes a strong criterion of value, particularly for *conservative thinkers.   A.O'H.

*tradition.

A. Savile, *The Test of Time* (Oxford, 1982).

Thales of Miletus (6th century BC). By tradition he was the first philosopher and the founder of the Ionian School.

According to Herodotus, Thales predicted (within a year) the solar eclipse of 585 BC. Aristotle attributes to him the conjecture that (1) water is the material principle of all things and that (2) a soul (*psyche) is a sort of 'motor' (*kinētikon*), for he said that a magnet has a soul because it moves iron.   G.B.M.

G. S. Kirk, J. E. Raven, and M. Schofield, *The Presocratic Philosophers*, 2nd edn. (Cambridge, 1990).

theism: *see* God.

theodicy. A justifying explanation of why God permits *evil, responding to the problem of evil. The theodicist puts forward what he or she takes to be the *actual* purposes, rationales, etc. that explain and justify the divine actions, and inactions, with respect to evil. It contrasts with a defence, which has a more modest project, that of refuting atheistic arguments from evil without committing to a positive claim about the divine reasons. John Hick, for example, proposes a theodicy, while Alvin Plantinga formulates a defence. The idea of human *free will often appears in a both of these strategies, but in different ways.

John Hick, *Evil and the God of Love* (London, 1968).
Alvin Plantinga, *God and Other Minds* (Ithaca, NY, 1967).

theology and philosophy. That the two have important overlapping concerns seems beyond question. A systematic philosophy that fails to give any thought to the question of *God's existence could be judged seriously incomplete: likewise a theology that fails to enter into discussion with opposed views of the world, or to explore whatever philosophical support is available for its principal claims.

Other and related topics that have clearly both philosophical and theological relevance include questions, for example, of personal identity—in relation to life beyond the death of the body, metaphysical questions about time and eternity (God's relation to time), and moral questions about the Christian doctrine of *Atonement.

Theologians sometimes claim that philosophical appraisal has no legitimacy in relation to what they see as a 'revealed' system of belief. But surely this cannot be right. First: to preface a statement of doctrine with such words as 'It is divinely revealed that . . . 'cannot confer coherence on what is logically incoherent or make a contradiction come out as true. There is therefore legitimate work for logic and philosophy of language in the analysis of such doctrinal claims. Second: however much of his religious beliefs a theologian regards as revealed, that cannot constitute a complete theistic system. The revealed totality has to be intelligibly related to the deity who allegedly revealed it, imparted it to mankind; and its authority needs to be more convincingly established than that of rival claimants. What is taken to be the essential nature of that deity, *qua* revealer, cannot itself be derived from revelation. It is a proper topic for philosophical (metaphysical) inquiry. A philosophical component—an epistemology of belief—is thus vitally necessary to a revealed theology.

There is, of course, one route of escape from that model of 'revealed package plus metaphysical account of its divine origin': namely, to see the 'revealed' package as a set of 'pictures', stories, parables, by which to regulate human life, and for which no further grounding is possible or appropriate. The religious authority and the efficacy of these pictures, however, when taken in that way, become enigmatic—and questionable.   R.W.H.

*God and the philosophers; religion, history of the philosophy of; Bonhoeffer.

C. F. Delaney, *Rationality and Religious Belief* (Notre Dame, Ind., 1979).

J. C. A. Gaskin, *The Quest for Eternity* (1984), esp. ch. 1.

R. W. Hepburn, 'The Philosophy of Religion', in G. H. R. Parkinson (ed.), *An Encyclopaedia of Philosophy* (London, 1988).

John Hick, *An Interpretation of Religion* (New Haven, Conn., 1989).

Richard Swinburne, *Faith and Reason* (Oxford, 1981).

Theophrastus (*c*.371–*c*.287 BC). Younger colleague of Aristotle, his partner in his researches and his successor as head of the Lyceum, the school Aristotle founded. Theophrastus wrote on everything from *modal logic (where he introduced the rule that the conclusion cannot be stronger than the weakest premiss) to penalties for gazumping. His surviving writings include sketches of (faulty) human character-types, fundamental works on botany, and shorter pieces, including a *Metaphysics* which contains more questions than solutions. He has been seen as rejecting Aristotelian positions for increased *mechanism and *materialism; but the differences can be exaggerated, and he is best regarded not as deliberately rejecting Aristotelian positions but as continuing Aristotle's own procedure of questioning and criticism, influenced by his own preferences and inclinations.   R.W.S.

W. W. Fortenbaugh *et al.* (eds.), *Rutgers University Studies in Classical Humanities*, ii, iii, v, vii (New Brunswick, NJ, 1985, 1988, 1992, 1995).

theorem. In an *axiomatic system a theorem is the last of a sequence of formulae or propositions each of which is an axiom or follows from preceding steps in accordance with specified rules. Such a sequence is a proof or a derivation. A proof is clearly formal where the entire process is syntactical and can be employed without further attention to meanings, as in a computer computation.

In some formal systems of logic using *natural deduction, theorems of logic can be generated without recourse to axioms. In such cases a theorem of logic is one which is derivable from the empty set of premisses.   R.B.M.

B. Mates, *Elementary Logic* (Oxford, 1972).

theory. A scientific theory is an attempt to bind together in a systematic fashion the knowledge that one has of some particular aspect of the world of experience. The aim is to achieve some form of understanding, where this is usually cashed out as explanatory power and predictive

fertility. The traditional analysis, going back to the Greeks and most recently championed by such logical empiricists as Carl Hempel and Ernest Nagel, sees theories as 'hypothetico-deductive systems', meaning that one has sets of laws bound together through the fact that, from a few high-powered axioms or hypotheses, everything else can be shown to follow as a deductive consequence. Explanation therefore is a matter of showing how things happened because of the laws of the theory. Prediction is a matter of showing how things will happen in accordance with the laws of the theory. Most significant is the fact that really successful theories bind together information from many hitherto disparate areas of experience, thus exhibiting what the philosopher William Whewell characterized as a *'consilience of inductions'.

In recent years, this picture of theories has come under some considerable attack. Although it may apply fairly well to such a theory as Newton's theory of gravitational attraction, something like Darwin's theory of *evolution through natural selection seems not to be as tightly integrated (deductively) as is supposed. Moreover, while such a theory as Darwin's certainly has some predictive power, it can hardly be said that this is a compelling attraction. Hence, rather than relying on the traditional excuses ('biology is immature' and so forth), an increasing number of thinkers have started to promote a view of theories which (they claim) pays far greater attention to the actual practice of science. Supporters of this 'semantic view' of theories argue that theories should not be seen as overall systems trying to cover, at one move, major areas of experience. Rather, more informally, they should be considered as sets of theoretical *models which are given empirical meaning only inasmuch as they can be applied directly (semantically) to certain limited areas of empirical reality. The virtues of the theory (like explanation and prediction) are not prescribed beforehand, but are very much a function of the particular model in use at the time.

Debate continues, but undoubtedly at least part of the divide is between an older philosophy of science which sees the task to be that of *prescription* of the ideal form of science, and a newer philosophy of science which rests content with a *description* of the way in which science is actually performed.   M.R.

*observation and theory.

R. B. Braithwaite, *Scientific Explanation* (Cambridge, 1953).

R. Giere, *Explaining Science* (Chicago, 1988).

theory-ladenness. The idea that all observations are interpreted through the medium of theories. The position has three versions. The first insists that when observations are described, the description inescapably involves some theoretical perspective. Thus, observations will report the ant species *Solenopsis invicta* engaged in foraging rather than as red objects moving along linear paths. More dramatic is the claim that what is sensed is affected by one's theory—that our conceptual frameworks affect the sensory inputs. With the appropriate knowledge base, we see the Old Bailey as a criminal court rather than as a building inhabited by oddly garbed humans engaged in hectoring and wheedling. A contemporary version of theory-ladenness asserts that 'observations' are constructed—one counts certain observations as being of psi particles rather than as blips on a cathode-ray tube because there is general agreement in the relevant social community on the former interpretation. Theory-ladenness has been widely used as a reason to question the objectivity of observational data.   P.H.

Ian Hacking, *Representing and Intervening* (Cambridge, 1983), ch. 10.

theory theory of mind. Humans have a natural ability to attribute mental states to one another in order to explain and predict behaviour. This common-sense psychological reasoning enables us to make sense of what others do and say. To the extent that this reasoning consists in a body of knowledge about the workings of people's minds and their connection with their acts and utterances, we can call such reasoning a theory; although the term 'theory of mind' is often used just to refer to the ability to attribute mental states to others. To explain this ability, many philosophers and psychologists have supposed that humans are equipped, perhaps innately, with a theory of mind which they deploy to makes sense of others as rational agents. Such a theory is not consciously or explicitly known, but it is said to be tacitly known. This is the theory theory of mind. The rival view of how we attribute mental states to others is *simulation theory. According to this view, we work out what others think and feel, or might do and say, by using ourselves to simulate their predicament and discovering what we would think or feel, do or say, were we in their predicament, subject to the same factors. Simulation theory privileges the first-person point of view in our understanding of others, whereas 'theory' theory privileges the third-personal observation of others.   B.C.S.

M. Davies and T. Stone, *Folk Psychology: The Theory of Mind Debate* (Oxford, 1995).

theosophy. In a broad sense, theosophy is the mystical doctrine of various German thinkers of the later *Renaissance period, most notably Jakob Boehme. It holds that man can have knowledge of God only by some kind of mystical acquaintance. More narrowly, and comically, it is the name of a movement led by Madame Blavatsky and Mrs Annie Besant in the late nineteenth century which sought to bring enlightenment to the Western world from Eastern religion and metaphysics.   A.Q.

thing-in-itself. This is Kant's expression for the object considered as it is independently of its cognitive relation to the human mind. It is contrasted with the object as it appears, or phenomenon, which is the object *qua* given to the mind in accordance with its sensible forms. Although Kant denies that we can know the thing-in-itself, he maintains that we must think of it as the ground of appearance.   H.E.A.

*phenomena and noumena.

H. E. Allison, *Kant's Transcendental Idealism* (New Haven, Conn., 1983).

things. 'Thing', in its most general sense, is interchangeable with 'entity' or *'being' and is applicable to any item whose *existence is acknowledged by a system of ontology, whether that item be particular, universal, abstract, or concrete. In this sense, not only material bodies but also properties, relations, events, numbers, sets, and propositions are—if they are acknowledged as existing—to be accounted 'things'. In this sense, then, the statement 'Everything is a thing' amounts to an analytic triviality. However, it is more common for philosophers to use 'thing' in a more restricted sense, in which it is interchangeable with 'object' and stands in opposition to such terms as *'property', *'relation', and *'event'. In the restricted sense, things are items which possess properties, stand in relations to one another, and undergo the changes which constitute events. Thus understood, the notion of a thing is closely linked to the traditional notion of a *'substance'. As such, it is a notion also linked to the grammatical and logical notion of a *subject (as opposed to a predicate). Indeed, Frege's well-known distinction between 'objects' and 'concepts' precisely mirrors the subject–predicate distinction (at least as it is employed in logic).

What, then, is the hallmark of thinghood in this restricted sense? Two competing answers to this question dominate current debate. One, the linguistic answer, espoused by Frege but also by more recent philosophers such as Quine, holds that an object is whatever may be referred to by a proper *name or can be made the value of a variable of quantification. But a problem with this answer is to specify without circularity what constitutes a genuine proper name (or, more generally, a genuine singular term) or variable of quantification. For instance, when a soldier is described as having died for the sake of his country, should the noun phrase 'the sake of his country' be regarded as genuine singular term naming some object or thing? Surely not: but it is arguably only because we already believe, on independent grounds, that there are no such things as 'sakes' that we refuse to regard this noun phrase as a genuine singular term. Here an adherent of the linguistic answer may follow the lead of Frege and Quine by insisting that the application of genuine names or variables of quantification demands the provision of criteria of identity for the things named or quantified over: in Quine's words, 'No entity without identity'. But this suggests that in fact metaphysical rather than linguistic considerations lie at the root of our concept of thinghood, and more particularly that the hallmark of thinghood consists in the possession of determinate and objective identity conditions. This is the contention of the alternative, metaphysical answer to the question 'What is a thing?' By this account, a thing is any item falling under a sortal concept supplying a criterion of identity for its instances. Thus shoes and ships and sealing-wax are things, but certainly not sakes and probably not propositions.

There is a special sense of the term 'thing' or 'object' in which it is used to draw a contrast with the term 'subject', in the sense of the latter in which it is used to denote a subject of consciousness or experience, that is, a person or *self. Of course, in a broader sense subjects or persons are themselves 'things', and indeed apparently things with determinate identity conditions, however difficult it may be to specify those conditions satisfactorily. What chiefly motivates the subject–object or person–thing distinction is the fact that objects or things in this sense are thought *about* rather than thinking, that is, are passive rather than active relata of consciousness. This fact is mirrored in the grammatical structure of statements of cognition, which typically feature transitive verbs taking a grammatical object—statements like 'I see a tree' or 'You are reading this book'. Indeed, the terminology of 'subject' and 'object' clearly draws on these grammatical categories.

E.J.L.

*vague objects; real.

M. Dummett, *Frege: Philosophy of Language*, 2nd edn. (London, 1981).

E. J. Lowe, *Kinds of Being* (Oxford, 1989).

A. Quinton, *The Nature of Things* (London, 1973).

thinking. In its diverse forms—as *reasoning, believing, reflecting, calculating, deliberating—thinking appears to enjoy an intimate connection with speech, but just what that connection might be is difficult to establish. It is seldom, as Plato would have it, a matter of an inward dialogue carried on by the mind with itself. Not only is wordless thought possible, as when we think how a room would look with the furniture rearranged; it does not even require attention to the matter in question for us to have thought that something was so, as when, tripping on a stair, we say we thought there was one fewer stair than there in fact was.

Is thinking that *p* a matter of being disposed to say that *p*? This is tempting through making reliance on the spoken word basic, but it does not get us far as it stands. First, while thinking that *p* we need have no inclination whatsoever to say that *p*; at best, the disposition must be restricted by an appropriate condition, as 'if asked to give our opinion'. Even then there is a supposition that we are speaking truthfully, and this would seem to be a matter of saying what we really think. A more satisfactory characterization might run: to think that *p* is to be in a state of mind expressible by saying that *p* with an intention to speak the truth. The latter condition is not 'intending to speak truthfully', which would again reintroduce thinking, but 'intending to say something that is in fact true'.

This characterization allows for a suitably loose connection between thought and speech in several respects: those who cannot in fact speak are not being denied the capacity to think, and indeed it is possible that someone should suggest a form of words which better expresses another's thought than the words originally used. It is also allowed that there should be a range of quite different propositions to which one might assent as expressing one's thought. You ask whether I thought the window was dirty. Yes indeed, I reply, but I could also have agreed if you had asked whether I thought there was a smudge on the window-pane, this being equally adequate to conveying how things struck me at the time. It is not as if the formulation ventured has to match unspoken words. I did not think in words. On the other hand, the characterization is also congenial to the idea that there are limits to the range of thoughts possible without language. Lacking the relevant vocabulary, a person could hardly be in a state of mind expressible by saying, with the relevant intention, that Sofia is the capital of Bulgaria.

Can animals think? We might say of a monkey which takes refuge from a snake by going up a tree that it knows that it is safe there. We might say this, because the monkey no longer behaves as if in imminent danger, but observes the snake in a detached fashion. However, while we may be prepared to say that it knows, we may be less happy to say that the monkey *thinks* that it is safe. That threatens to demand more of the monkey's mental capacities than we are willing to concede. On the other hand, we need a description for the case where there would be knowledge that *p* but for the fact that *p* is false, and while 'thinks that *p*' has the disadvantage of suggesting a mastery of concepts, an inner mental response, which it would be fanciful to attribute to the animal, so long as 'knows that *p*' can be affirmed solely on the strength of observed behaviour, the same status can be extended to the ascription of thought.

B.B.R.

*belief; cognition; deliberation; understanding; language of thought.

P. M. S. Hacker, *Wittgenstein: Meaning and Mind* (Oxford, 1990).

H. H. Price, *Thinking and Experience* (London, 1953).

G. Ryle, *On Thinking* (Oxford, 1979).

thinking, critical: *see* critical thinking.

thinking causes are causally efficacious *propositional attitudes. Conflict arises over what is required for thinking causes to be causally efficacious. For instance, Donald Davidson only requires that the event be causally related to another event, and that the correct application of mental predicates ascribing propositional attitudes supervenes on the correct application of physical predicates. Others argue that something can only be a thinking cause if the event in question is causally efficacious in virtue of its *intentional properties and believe that Davidson's approach does not capture this requirement.

P.J.P.N.

*mental causation.

D. Davidson, 'Thinking Causes', in J. Heil and A. Mele (eds.), *Mental Causation* (Oxford, 1993).

third man argument. Aristotle coined the expression 'third man' (which refers to an extra entity beyond the individual man, such as Socrates or Plato, and the general kind man) to designate a notorious ontological-regress argument which first appears in Plato's *Parmenides* and has impressed philosophers ever since. Apparently directed against Plato's own earlier theory of *Forms, the argument shows that the premisses which are needed to entail the existence of a Form can then be reapplied to entail the existence of further Forms in infinite regress. The nerve of the argument is whether a Platonic Form (or other similar entity) is or is not to be counted in with the other objects which are related to it. There has been vigorous debate about the effectiveness of the argument; a majority maintain that it exploits genuine deficiencies in Plato's earlier thought, while a minority argue that he would reject its premisses or reasoning.   J.D.G.E.

A judicious article from the heyday of modern interest in this argument is Colin Strang, 'Plato and the Third Man', *Proceedings of the Aristotelian Society*, supp. vol. (1963).

Thomism. A philosophical–theological movement based upon leading ideas of St Thomas Aquinas. Successive generations have taken his philosophy as a starting-point for their own speculations and have developed his ideas in many directions. Thomism, an ongoing enterprise with its own schools and disputes, is particularly associated with the Catholic Church, although much of his theology has proved acceptable to Christians of a wide variety of denominations and his theological teachings are by no means peculiar to the Catholic Church. Indeed philosophical parts of Thomism, for example on predication, on being, on the nature of mind, and on the relations between law and human nature, do not depend logically upon Christian *dogma and can appeal to people of any religion or none. It should be added that Aquinas's philosophy was never universally accepted by his own Church, and a number of his propositions were denounced in Paris and Oxford in 1277 shortly after his death.

In due course while Thomism was establishing itself its proponents, such as John Capreolus, whose title was *Princeps Thomistarum* (chief of Thomists), had to defend themselves against other movements, especially those based on the ideas of Duns Scotus and of Ockham. In the sixteenth century, in the face of the Protestant Reformation, Thomism, represented by men such as Domingo de Soto, held a prominent place in the armoury of the Counter-Reformation, and in the nineteenth century, after a period of decline, it gained renewed vigour as a result of a papal bull commending the study of Aquinas. *Neo-Thomism, which was in part a result of that bull, is still with us. Among its exponents are Jacques Maritain and Étienne Gilson. We shall consider here three topics which at different times have been high on the agenda of Thomists, namely, the doctrine of analogy, the relation between free will and grace, and probabilism.

Thomas de Vio (1468–1534), Cardinal Cajetan, was perhaps the greatest of the Thomists during the earlier stages of the Reformation. His finest work was his commentary on the *Summa Theologiae* of Aquinas, but in many other books also, such as his *De nominum analogia* (The Analogy of Names) he attended directly to Aquinas's doctrines. In that latter work he developed Aquinas's doctrine of anal-

ogy far beyond anything to be found in Aquinas's writings. The question at issue was the meaning of terms predicated affirmatively of *God, terms such as 'good', 'wise', and 'powerful'. Aquinas had said that they should be understood neither literally nor negatively but analogically, and though deploying widely the concept of analogy he did not expound it systematically or in detail. Cajetan filled that gap.

The crucial move in his systematization was to identify a jointly exhaustive set of three heads of division for analogy. Any instance of analogy was an analogy either of inequality, or of attribution, or of proportionality. The first two, however, turn out to be analogies by an improper use of the term 'analogy'. Only analogy of proportionality is analogy properly speaking. Two things are analogous by proportionality if they have a common name and the notion expressed by this name is proportionally the same. For example, to see by corporeal vision and to see by intellectual vision are instances of seeing, for just as corporeal seeing presents something to the living body so also the faculty of intellect presents something to the mind. Thus there is a kind of act which is related to the intellect as seeing is related to the living body, and that kind of act is therefore a seeing, analogically speaking, where the analogy is that of proportionality. This kind of analogy is commonly deployed in metaphor, as when we speak of a smiling meadow, on the analogy of a smiling face, for in general people look most attractive when smiling, and a meadow, when looking its best, can therefore be described, by analogy of proportionality, as smiling. But it was upon the non-metaphorical uses of analogical terms that Cajetan concentrated, and in so doing he shed a good deal of light on Aquinas's problem of how we are to make sense of affirmative terms predicated of God in the Bible. God's goodness, wisdom, and so on are to be understood on an analogy of creaturely goodness and wisdom: as our goodness and wisdom are proportional to us so are God's proportional to him. There is considerable dispute among Thomists over whether Cajetan's teaching on analogy faithfully reflects, as he intended, the mind of Aquinas, but there is no doubt that his *De nominum analogia* is a major Thomist document.

A second major area of Thomist thought concerns the relation between human *free will, divine foreknowledge of human acts, and God's grace. Aquinas had seen the need to refute the argument that God's foreknowledge of human acts implies that we humans cannot do otherwise than we do. He had no doubt that God knows human acts that lie in the future in relation to us now. This doctrine does not, however, imply that God determines those human acts. He knows them not because he has determined them but because he sees them happening as present to him, though future in relation to us. Aquinas had also seen the need to deal with the closely related question of whether God's grace by which a person is saved is something that the recipient freely accepts, or whether his acceptance is determined by God. If his grace is not freely accepted, then a question arises of the contribution if any that a person can make towards his own salvation or damnation. In the latter part of the sixteenth century a major dispute arose in this area, particularly between Dominican thinkers, whose chief spokesman in this matter was Domingo Báñez, and Jesuits, whose chief spokesman was Luis de Molina. As part of his rejection of Aquinas's teaching Molina developed the doctrine of *scientia media* (middle knowledge) and the associated concept of a 'free futurable', which is an act with a conditional existence, not an act that will be performed or one that might be but in fact will not be, but instead one that would be freely chosen if certain conditions were satisfied. God, as omniscient, must know eternally not only all events (including all free human acts) past, present, or future in relation to us, but also all events which would happen given the satisfaction of certain conditions. God's middle knowledge of human acts is his knowledge of acts which have this metaphysical status of a 'would-be'. These acts are the 'free futurables'. Amongst them are the acceptance by human beings of God's saving grace. According to Molina God, in an absolutely free act, gives grace in the light of his middle knowledge that the recipient would accept it, and the recipient accepts that grace with an entirely free consent. Thus the doctrine of 'determinism by grace' is totally rejected by Molina. Against this teaching Domingo Báñez and his fellow Dominicans deployed the concept of *praemotio physica* (physical pre-motion) and argued, in the spirit of Aquinas, that a person cannot freely accept the grace that God offers unless moved by God to do so. This is a difficult doctrine to maintain, in its own way as difficult as the doctrine of middle knowledge, and the consequent dispute between Dominican Thomists and Jesuit anti-Thomists rumbled on for decades. There is some point to the claim that the Jesuits were standing dangerously close to the Pelagian heresy, and that the Dominicans were standing dangerously close to Calvinist teaching on predestination.

In the course of his commentary (1577) on a part of the *Summa Theologiae* of Aquinas, Bartholomew Medina presents a doctrine which he thought of as according to the mind of Aquinas and which has been disputed by Thomists ever since. The doctrine is probabilism. If a person wishes to perform a given act and is in doubt over whether the moral law forbids that act, then he is morally at liberty to perform it on condition that the opinion that he is at liberty to perform it is supported by a probable argument, that is, by an argument whose conclusion has some degree of probability, and even if the argument supporting the claim that the moral law forbids the act is more probable. There is an evident danger of probabilism leading the unwary into the vice of laxity, when a barely probable opinion on the side of liberty will be followed in preference to a highly probable opinion on the side of the moral law. It was because of this danger that some insisted that the opinion on the side of liberty had first to be shown to be soundly based; shaky grounds for acting on the side of liberty are never sufficient. At the other extreme is the vice of rigorism, associated especially with the Jansenists,

who argued that in the face of a probable argument on the side of the moral law and another probable argument on the side of liberty, there was always a presumption on the side of the law. Given that probabilism occupies an intermediate position between the two extremes of laxity and rigour, there was room for dispute, which duly took place, over how nearly a probabilist may approach one extreme or the other without straying into moral error. There is no doubt that probabilism has its roots in Aquinas's writings, and the fact that the doctrine is still a matter for dispute is due in part to the very fact that the protagonists in the dispute see themselves as enjoying the support of Aquinas. It is precisely this that makes them Thomists.   A.BRO.

*Thomism, analytical.

Good accessible material is hard to come by. The following are relevant:

É. Gilson, *The Spirit of Thomism* (New York, 1964).

B. Hamilton, *Political Thought in Sixteenth Century Spain* (Oxford, 1963).

Thomas de Vio (Cardinal Cajetan), *The Analogy of Names* (Louvain, 1959).

Thomism, analytical. A broad philosophical approach that brings into mutual relationship the styles and preoccupations of recent English-speaking philosophy and the concepts and concerns shared by Aquinas and his followers. This approach bears some relation to that of those post-war Oxford philosophers, e.g. Austin and Ryle, who sought to reintroduce certain concepts into the analysis of thought and action, such as those of capacities and dispositions, which are prominent within Aristotelian philosophy. In the case of analytical Thomists the primary areas of interest have been intentionality, action, virtue theory, philosophical anthropology, causation, and essentialism. The expression 'analytical *Thomism' is rarely employed, but it usefully identifies aspects of the writings of philosophers such as Anscombe, Donagan, Geach, Grisez, Kenny, and MacIntyre.   J.HAL.

P. T. Geach, 'Form and Existence', in *God and the Soul* (London, 1969).

A. MacIntyre, *First Principles, Final Ends and Contemporary Philosophical Issues* (Milwaukee, 1990).

Thomism, neo-: *see* neo-Thomism.

Thomson, Judith Jarvis (1929–). American philosopher best known for her use of hypothetical examples to elicit intuitions that help to reveal the structure of common-sense morality. The most influential of her arguments of this sort grants the assumption that the foetus is a person but defends the permissibility of *abortion by appealing to an analogous case in which a person can stop providing life support for another innocent person, to whom she has been involuntarily connected, only by killing that person. Thomson believes that rights, which she analyses as non-absolute constraints on the behaviour of those against whom they hold, are the central components of morality. So, for example, she argues that self-defence is permissible if and only if the person one defends oneself against would otherwise violate one's rights; for such a person cannot have a right not to be prevented from violating one's rights. J.McM.

J. J. Thomson, *Rights, Restitution, and Risk*, ed. William Parent (Cambridge, Mass., 1986).

Thoreau, Henry David (1817–62). *New England Transcendentalist, natural historian, and social critic, Thoreau proclaimed, in *Walden*, that most people spend their lives superficially, by pursuing wealth and following custom. Genuinely encountering reality is to be found only by separating oneself from the artificialities of city, economic, and family life and communing directly with nature, where one could 'front only the essential facts of life'. Nature preserves a spontaneity and wildness that civilization suppresses; the civil liberties democracy provides are far less important than the spiritual freedom nature embodies and inspires: 'all good things are wild and free'. *'Civil disobedience' is the classic defence of conscience above unjust law. One must not support an immoral law and can protest by, for example, not paying taxes that implement it, or refusing to obey it and accepting a jail term. This appeals to the conscience of others and so begins a social movement. C.C.

Leo Stoller, *After Walden: Thoreau's Changing Views on Economic Man* (Stanford, Calif., 1957).

thought: *see* thinking; cognition; language of thought.

thought, language of: *see* language of thought.

thought, laws of: *see* laws of thought.

thought experiments are employed both by philosophers and by theoretical scientists to examine the implications of theories and to explore the boundaries of concepts. They are controlled exercises of the imagination in which test cases are envisaged with a view to establishing their conceptual coherence or their compatibility with some proposed theory. For example, in assessing the merits of rival theories of *personal identity, philosophers commonly propose thought experiments envisaging the consequences of procedures which would apparently result in the fission or fusion of persons—for instance, brain bisection followed by transplantation of the two cerebral hemispheres into separate bodies.

Some philosophers object vehemently to the philosophical use of thought experiments as substituting fantasy for reality, but since philosophical argument is often concerned to establish precisely what is *possible*, it is hard to see how philosophy could do without them altogether. E.J.L.

R. A. Sorensen, *Thought Experiments* (New York, 1992).

Thrasymachus. Notable figure in Plato's *Republic*. Having had enough of the preceding high-minded, convivial but thin discussion of justice, Thrasymachus falls on Socrates and his interlocutors like a beast, arguing that justice is nothing else than the advantage of the stronger. Some interpret Thrasymachus as claiming that justice is nothing deeper than the bare fact that those in power enact laws which protect their interests—justice is nothing more than the weak obeying the will of the strong. Some see Thrasymachus as arguing for more: it is just that the strong ought to rule the weak, and justice consists in the strong holding sway. Might makes right. Thrasymachus is claimed as spokesman by nihilists, ethical egoists, relativists, and realists. J.GAR.

Plato, *Republic* 336b–354c.

threats and offers. Threats express intentions to inflict injury or damage. They are menacing proposals, paradigmatically expressed in 'Your money or your life'. Offers, by contrast, are proposals that expand opportunities: 'I'll pay you $10 to weed the garden.' Threats can masquerade as offers. Since they present pairs of options, their surface grammar can suggest expansion of opportunity. Such proposals none the less are threats just in case either option would leave one worse off than one would otherwise have been. In standard cases, such a set-back is measured relative to the welfare one would have enjoyed had one not encountered the robber in the first place. In other cases, the set-back is measured against a morally defined baseline, which includes the welfare one should enjoy as one's due: a proposal to stop beating you if you weed the garden constitutes a threat. Thus threats, in contrast to offers, are coercive, which is not to say that all offers are morally innocent—they may be disrespectful, exploitative, or exert undue influence. A.CAR.
M.L.

*coercion.

A. Wertheimer, *Coercion* (Princeton, NJ, 1987).

time. The dimension of *change, a fact which distinguishes it from the three dimensions of *space. But how does genuine temporal change differ from mere variation as exhibited in space? When a road is said to change in breadth along its length, 'change' is being used only metaphorically, in contrast to its literal use when a child is said to change in height as it becomes older. Some theories of time and change do not really accommodate this distinction, and as such are sometimes accused of 'spatializing' time or denying the reality of temporal 'becoming'. Some philosophers believe, indeed, that developments in physics connected with the theory of *relativity necessitate this denial, because they seem to demonstrate that the notion of an absolute 'now' must be abandoned along with the Newtonian notion of the absoluteness of simultaneity. Events deemed 'past' in one frame of reference must be deemed 'future' in other frames, apparently indicating that the distinction between past and future is only a subjective, experientially based one rather than reflecting a genuine ontological divide. Philosophers of this persuasion adopt what is commonly called a 'static' view of time, thus partaking in a tradition stretching back to Parmenides and Zeno, who held the appearance of temporal change to be an illusion.

In opposition to the 'static' view stands the 'dynamic' view of time, traceable back to Aristotle and before him to Heraclitus. By this account the future lacks the reality of the past and present, and indeed reality is continually being added to as time passes. The objection mentioned earlier is not difficult to overcome, since even the theory of relativity acknowledges that some events are past and others future, no matter which frame of reference is selected, and these may be said to lie in the absolute past or future. The relativity of simultaneity only requires us to revise our conception of the present, allowing it to embrace all events not causally connectable to us by a physical signal. A more serious challenge to the dynamic view of time comes from an argument of J. M. E. McTaggart, who claimed that the notion of temporal becoming (bound up with the *A-series of past, present, and future) leads to contradiction. But it seems fair to protest that McTaggart's argument demonstrates not so much the absurdity of the notion of temporal becoming as the incoherence of his representation of that phenomenon. According to McTaggart, the phenomenon supposedly consists in future events 'becoming present' and then 'receding into the past', whence it apparently follows, absurdly, that all events are past, present, and future. But the lesson is just that we should not think of 'the present' as somehow 'moving' along the sequence of events from past to future. In denying the reality of the future, we may appeal to the fact that not all future-tensed statements appear to be determinately true or false.

The asymmetry of time is perhaps its most striking feature and the most difficult to explain. The fundamental laws of physics are time-reversible, and yet complex macroscopic processes like the growth of a tree or the breaking of a glass could not happen in reverse save by a miracle. This is often supposed to be explicable by reference to the second law of thermodynamics, which implies that closed systems tend to evolve from conditions of less to greater disorder, or 'entropy'. But why should the universe have been created in a particularly low state of entropy—or was this just an accident without which time might have been isotropic? And how does the asymmetry of time as we know it relate to the apparent non-existence of phenomena involving *'backwards' causation, such as *time-travel? These are problems which are still very little understood by either metaphysicians or physicists.   E.J.L.

*endurance and perdurance; persistence through time; presentism; space-time; specious present; tense.

P. Horwich, *Asymmetries in Time* (Cambridge, Mass., 1987).
J. R. Lucas, *The Future* (Oxford, 1989).
R. Le Poidevin and M. MacBeath (eds.), *The Philosophy of Time* (Oxford, 1993).

time preference. We are often prepared to opt for a good thing now even if we know that a better thing can be obtained later with at least as much probability. This sort of attitude is known by decision theorists as time prefer-

ence, and the question of its rationality is much debated. Some suggest that time preference is a biologically evolved strategy to discount future goods—a sensible enough one for creatures for whom the calculation of future probabilities would be too difficult or a waste of cognitive resources.   E.J.L.

*decision theory.

R. Nozick, *The Nature of Rationality* (Princeton, NJ, 1993).

time's arrow. Time has, it seems, both a 'forward' and a 'backward' direction, unlike any of the dimensions of space. But is this a feature internal to *time itself? Is it related to *causal asymmetry? If an event *e* is earlier than another event *d*, then, unless time is circular, *d* is not also earlier than *e*. But in virtue of what is one event or moment of time earlier, rather than later, than another? Some philosophers attribute time's 'arrow' or directionality to the Second Law of Thermodynamics, which says, in effect, that complex systems become increasingly disordered over time: glass vases frequently break into fragments, but fragments of glass never reassemble themselves into intact glass vases. However, the fundamental laws of physics appear to be time-symmetric, which makes the Second Law appear to be a contingent consequence of the fact that the physical universe came into existence at the Big Bang in a highly ordered state. Why, though, should we say that the Big Bang was at the *beginning*, as opposed to the *end*, of time?   E.J.L.

S. F. Savitt (ed.), *Time's Arrow Today* (Cambridge, 1995).

time-travel. The philosophy of time-travel is a serious subject with a burgeoning literature. Early objections to the logical possibility of time-travel have now been answered. For instance, there is no contradiction is saying that the time-traveller has gone back 100 years in time but become a day older in the process, provided we distinguish between 'external' or 'historical' time and the 'personal' time of the traveller. Again, it is no objection to say that if time-travel were possible the time-traveller could murder his own grandparents and thus prevent his own birth: for time-travel is not a licence to *change* the past, but at most to *affect* it—and, given that the time-traveller *was* born, no effect he has on the past can alter that.

The philosophical value of imagining cases of timetravel lies in what such *thought experiments reveal about our concepts of time, *causality, *personal identity, and the like.   E.J.L.

P. Horwich, *Asymmetries in Time* (Cambridge, Mass., 1987).

'to be', the verb. Russell declared that it was 'a disgrace to the human race' that it used the same word in such different contexts as the following: 'John *is* bald', 'There *is* a robin on the lawn', 'A dolphin *is* a mammal' and 'The square of three *is* nine'. These uses of 'be' have been called respectively the copulative, the existential, the class-inclusion, and the identity use of 'be'. Aristotle too had affirmed that the Greek equivalent of 'be' was used in more than one way (*Metaphysics* v. 7), although his list of the different ways is not the same as Russell's. Medieval philosophers were divided on the matter, Aquinas following Aristotle and maintaining that being was 'analogical', i.e. had different though connected senses, and others such as Duns Scotus insisting on the univocity of being, i.e. that 'be' had only one sense. Arguably all these senses can be reduced to two, the copulative and the existential sense. In its existential sense 'be' seems to be doing work otherwise done by 'some': 'There are blue buttercups' means 'Some buttercups are blue'. In its copulative sense 'be' seems to have the purely syntactic function of converting a non-verbal expression into the equivalent of a verb: 'is a smoker' is an alternative to 'smokes'. These two uses seem to have little to do with each other, and it is tempting to regard the verb as used in these two ways as purely equivocal, i.e. as having two unconnected senses. But this plurality of senses is a phenomenon which occurs in practically all languages (see John M. W. Verhaar (ed.), *The Verb 'Be' and its Synonyms* (Dordrecht, 1967–72)), so it is difficult to regard it as accidental. For one attempt to explain it, see C. J. F. Williams, *What is Existence?* (Oxford, 1981), chapters 1 and 12. C.J.F.W.

*being; existence.

token. Contrasted with 'type', originally in semiotics, and nowadays in the formulation of identity theses in philosophy of mind.

A 'token' was said by Peirce to be a 'replica of a symbol'. Tokens, then, are particular meaningful items, which belong to the same type (or replicate the same symbol) if and only if (very roughly) they have the same significance. Following Peirce it can be said, for example, that there are three tokens of the word 'the' (that type) in the previous sentence, and that the actual book you're now reading is a token of the type *Oxford Companion to Philosophy*.

In recent philosophical usage of 'type' and 'token', different kinds of abstraction from that which concerned Peirce are thought to relate tokens (particulars) to types (abstract things). It is said, for instance, that the event which is your now reading is a token of the type *reading*, and that the event which is Jane's believing that *p* is a token of the type *belief that p*. J.HORN.

Colin McGinn, 'Anomalous Monism and Kripke's Cartesian Intuitions', *Analysis* (1977).

C. S. Peirce, 'On the Algebra of Logic', in *Collected Works of Charles Sanders Peirce*, ed. C. Hartshorne and P. Weiss (Cambridge, Mass., 1931–5), iii.

Toland, John (1670–1722). A radical thinker, born a Roman Catholic in the north of Ireland, who, after abandoning Catholicism at 15—by 'his own reason and such as made use of theirs'—moved from latitudinarianism, to *deism, and finally to a materialistic form of *pantheism, coining the word 'pantheist' in 1705. Toland's deism is most evident in his *Christianity not Mysterious* (1696), a seminal work in both free thought and Irish philosophy.

His pantheism is developed esoterically in *Letters to Serena* (1704)—which contains an acute attack on Spinoza's theory of matter—and more openly in *Pantheisticon* (1720). He was a prolific controversialist and scholar. His *Tetradymus* (1720) contains the first published essay on the esoteric–exoteric distinction, a distinction important for understanding his own views as well as those of his fellow free thinkers, such as Anthony Collins. D.BER.

R. E. Sullivan, *John Toland and the Deist Controversy* (Cambridge, Mass., 1982).

tolerance, principle of: *see* Carnap.

toleration. Requires people to coexist peacefully with others who have fundamentally different beliefs or values. Within Western political philosophy, toleration was first discussed during the Wars of Religion between Catholics and Protestants. When the attempt to impose a single religion failed, the assumption that political stability required a common religion was replaced by the principle of toleration. This principle has now been extended to other areas of moral disagreement, including sexual orientation and political belief. Why should we tolerate those whom we see as mistaken, or as heretics? Arguments for toleration include the fallibility of our beliefs, the impossibility of coercing genuine religious belief, respect for autonomy, the danger of civil strife, and the value of diversity. These parallel the arguments for liberalism. Theorists of toleration include Spinoza, Locke, Voltaire, and Mill; critics include Rousseau and Comte. W.K.

Susan Mendus, *Toleration and the Limits of Liberalism* (New York, 1989).

tone. Used by philosophers to translate Frege's *Beleuchtung* and *Farbung*. Followers of Frege and J. L. Austin distinguish three ways in which a word or construction can have *meaning: by determining what the speaker says; by indicating whether the utterance is a statement, order, promise, or what not; and (thanks, perhaps, to its sound or associations) by making the utterance more or less apt to affect the state of mind of someone who understands what is said—to illuminate or confuse, to arouse or quiet a feeling. This last is its contribution to tone. W.C.

W. Charlton, 'Beyond the Literal Meaning', *British Journal of Aesthetics* (1985).

M. Dummett, *Frege: Philosophy of Language* (London, 1973), ch. 5.

topic-neutral. The term was introduced by Ryle for expressions that indicate nothing about the subject-matter, for example, 'inside' indicates place, and so is not topic-neutral, but 'of' is topic-neutral. Smart introduced a much more specific sense in which a topic-neutral analysis of a property term entails neither that the property is physical nor that it is non-physical. He gave topic-neutral analyses of mental terms which were the first functionalist identity-claims. Further, he argued that anyone who accepts an empirical physicalist or functionalist identity thesis (e.g. pain = c-fibre stimulation, or pain = such-and-such a computational state) should also accept a topic-neutral (functionalist) conceptual analysis of mental-state terms. Suppose S_{17} is a brain state or a functional state and that the claim that pain = S_{17} is offered as an empirical identity-claim. Then the terms flanking the '=' must pick out the common referent via different modes of presentation. The mode of presentation of 'pain', however, presumably will be something mental, even something phenomenal, requiring the empirical identity theorist to claim that the mode of presentation is also a physical–functional state, say, S_{18}. A regress can be avoided only by accepting an a priori identity, and the only candidate is a topic-neutral analysis of mental-state terms in terms of the states' normal causes and effects. (Only in an a priori identity will the terms flanking the '=' refer via the same mode of presentation.) Thus, according to Smart's argument, empirical identity-claims engender topic-neutral analyses.

N.B.

*identity theory; functionalism.

Stephen White, 'Curse of the Qualia', *Synthese* (1986).

tradition. Customary sets of belief, or ways of behaving of uncertain origin, which are accepted by those belonging to the tradition as persuasive or even authoritative and which are transmitted by unreflective example and imitation.

It is a conceptual joke for a school to announce that as from June it will be a tradition that . . . The nature of traditions is such that they cannot (logically) be willed; rather they have grown up. Traditions exist in all areas of life—literature, religion, legal institutions, and so on—but the term is of particular interest in political philosophy. For those political philosophers hostile to the idea of tradition it is perceived as representing entrenched privileges holding back political and social progress, and it is to be contrasted with a vision of human beings controlling their own destinies with rational decisions and asserting rationally based rights. This latter was the position of revolutionary political thinkers such as Rousseau, Tom Paine, and Richard Price. Their position was opposed by thinkers such as Edmund Burke, who had less faith in reason. For traditionalists like Burke social life is kept going not mainly by rational decision-making but by feeling, habit, emotional attachments, and conventions.

R.S.D.

*conservatism; revolution; reform.

Charles Parkin, *The Moral Basis of Burke's Thought* (Cambridge, 1956).

tragedy. Philosophical reflection on tragic drama is as old as tragedy itself. Plato found tragedy antithetical to philosophy, claiming that it nourishes an irrational part of the soul which takes pleasure in empathizing with fierce emotions. Indeed, only by opposing tragedy's pre-eminence, and its claim to provide a comprehensive ethical education, could Plato establish philosophy's claim to be uniquely concerned with truth and the good'. Aristotle, in response,

saw tragedy as a representation of universal truths which engages our pity and fear in a beneficial way. Of later views, Nietzsche's is the most well known. For him, tragedy unites a terrifying insight into the destructibility of the individual (associated with Dionysus) with the beautiful dream-image (associated with Apollo), producing a uniquely powerful form of art. Tragedy continues to fascinate philosophers interested in aesthetics and moral psychology.

C.J.

Aristotle, *Poetics*.

transcendence. Existence beyond; independent existence. For example, God, numbers, and universals are sometimes held to exist beyond space, time, the physical world, or experience (in some non-spatial sense of 'beyond'). In theology, the transcendence of God is contrasted with his immanence or pervasion of the world. In medieval philosophy, the transcendentals are notions that are too fundamental to be accommodated in Aristotle's ten categories: for example, unity, truth, goodness, and being. In Kant's critical philosophy, 'transcendent' knowledge of non-spatio-temporal reality that cannot be subsumed under the *categories is impossible; 'transcendental' knowledge, *a priori knowledge of how knowledge is possible, is possible and is the content of the critical philosophy.

One of the most fundamental and persistent divisions within philosophy is between philosophers who think there is a transcendental reality and those who do not. Indeed, the history of philosophy can be understood as the recurrent advocacy and repudiation of transcendence. A clue to understanding belief in metaphysical reality lies in taking the world with which we are acquainted as only part of a greater whole. The known arguably depends upon the unknown, because metaphysical questions can be raised within and about the empirical world but cannot be answered by any further empirical inspection: Why is there a universe? Why is a particular person oneself? Why is it now, now? What is being? Is there life after death?

S.P.

Aquinas, *Selected Philosophical Writings*, tr. Timothy McDermott (Oxford, 1993), 51 ff.

Immanuel Kant's Critique of Pure Reason, tr. Norman Kemp Smith (London, 1978).

transcendental analytic. This is Kant's title for the portion of the *Critique of Pure Reason* dealing with the nature and function of the understanding. Kant argues that the understanding is equipped with a set of *a priori concepts or *categories, including substance and causality, which are required for the knowledge of an object or an objective realm. From this he concludes that all objects of possible experience must conform to these categories.

H.E.A.

H. J. Paton, *Kant's Metaphysic of Experience* (New York, 1936).

transcendental arguments. Anti-sceptical arguments of the form: There is experience; the truth of some proposition p is a conceptually necessary condition of the possibility of experience; therefore p. Kant, with whom transcendental arguments are mainly associated, regarded them as only capable of providing *synthetic a priori knowledge of the world as it appears rather than as it is in itself. Q.C.

I. Kant, 'The Discipline of Pure Reason in Regard to its Proofs', in *Critique of Pure Reason*, tr. N. Kemp Smith (London, 1929).

R. Stern (ed.), *Transcendental Arguments: Problems and Prospects* (Oxford, 1999).

transcendental deduction. Kant's name in the *Critique of Pure Reason* for the reasoning which simultaneously justifies both the applicability of the pure concepts of the understanding (*categories) to objects of experience and the objectivity of experience itself. The term 'deduction' here is borrowed from contemporary jurisprudence regarding the need to address matters of right as well as of fact. Starting from the fact that all my representations are grasped together in one consciousness (the unity of apperception), the argument asserts that such unity is possible only because synthesized according to the rules contained in the pure concepts. A.H.

H. E. Allison, *Kant's Transcendental Idealism: An Interpretation and Defense* (New Haven, Conn., 1983), ch. 7.

transcendental idealism is Kant's name for his overarching metaphysical doctrine. Some commentators confine the name to Kant's own version of the doctrine, while some extend it to other self-proclaimed versions, notably Schopenhauer's, and even to positions, like Śaṅkara's, that anticipated Kant's. Transcendental idealism maintains, in Kant's version, that the world as known to creatures like ourselves, who rely on perceptual experience and conceptual understanding, is not the world of *things-in-themselves—of things as they are independently of cognition— but of 'appearances'. We have knowledge only of *phenomena (things in the sensible realm), and not of the *noumena which are knowable only by a being, like God, capable of a non-sensory 'intellectual intuition'. For example, we experience the world as spatio-temporal, even though space and time are 'forms of (our) sensibility', not features of reality-in-itself. Kant favourably contrasts his transcendental idealism with transcendental realism and empirical idealism, which respectively hold that our knowledge extends to things-in-themselves, and that objects of experience are not grounded in extra-mental reality. Schopenhauer criticized Kant for overlooking a non-representational mode of knowledge whereby we are acquainted, albeit imperfectly, with reality-in-itself as *will. D.E.C.

H. E. Allison, *Kant's Transcendental Idealism: An Interpretation and Defense* (New Haven, Conn., 1983).

A. C. Ewing, *Idealism: A Critical Survey*, 3rd edn. (London, 1974).

transcendentalism. The word 'transcendentalism' can be applied either to something large, shapeless, and generic or, more straightforwardly, to something historically and geographically distinctive, which willingly accepted the name. In the larger sense transcendentalism is belief in the existence of things that transcend sense-experience or, more reflectively, belief in the possibility of transcendent metaphysics, that is to say, philosophical reasoning which aims to establish beliefs about transcendent entities. *God might seem an obvious example of a transcendent, but those who accept religious or mystical experience as a source of knowledge might resist that. The *Forms or Ideas of Plato, which are not in space and time and not encountered in the world of the senses, are more incontestably transcendent. Some have said, or, like Berkeley, implied, that Locke and representationalists generally, who take our beliefs in the existence of material things to be causal inferences from our sense-experiences, are transcendent metaphysicians. Many philosophers of science, along similar lines, have said the same about belief in the literal existence of such theoretical entities as atoms and subatomic particles.

Transcendent metaphysics has been attacked in two main ways. In the first place it can be argued that there can be no rational warrant for the inferences that transcendental metaphysicians make from experience to what transcends it. Secondly, it has been argued by positivists of various kinds that since the terms that figure in the utterances of transcendent metaphysicians have no criteria of empirical application, those utterances are devoid of meaning. The philosophy of Kant contains elements of both approaches. He does not deny meaning to the theses that the world is infinite in size or has a first cause (and their opposites), but he holds them to be undecidable or unknowable for the reason that the concepts employed in them are being used outside the sphere of their legitimate application, which is within experience. To make things more complicated he also holds that there are transcendent things-in-themselves, noumenal objects or selves, indeed, perhaps, that these are the only truly real things that there are. With a final turn of the screw he describes his own inquiries and their results as transcendental, meaning by this not that they are concerned with the transcendent, but that they are concerned with the possibility of knowledge.

More definite in outline, if not in content, is *New England Transcendentalism. This was the body of ideas elaborated by Emerson and a group of associates—among them Thoreau, George Riley, Orestes Brownson, and Bronson Alcott—who lived in or met at Concord, Massachusetts between about 1830 and 1860. It was a very diluted variety of philosophical thought. Plato and Plotinus, Coleridge and Carlyle, Eastern scriptures, German mystics like Boehme and the Romantic German idealists, all contributed to a doctrine which stressed the spiritual unity of the world (thus interpreting God in an untranscendentally pantheistic way) and the superiority of intuition as a source of knowledge as opposed to logical reasoning and sense-experience. They relied heavily on the distinction of true reason from the merely analytic understanding, the doctrinal cornerstone of *philosophical Romanticism. It supplied a foundation for the 'spiritual religion' they upheld against the natural religion of the Enlightenment and the revealed religion of Calvinism.

As important deliverances of intuition they affirmed the natural goodness of man and his freedom, in opposition to the emphasis of *Calvinism on original sin and predestination. Many of the Transcendentalists had started out as Unitarians. Rejecting the Calvinist orthodoxy of their time and place, they were equally hostile to scientific materialism, the conception of the world formed by the mere understanding.

New England Transcendentalism was more a social movement than a philosophical school. It expressed itself in the formation of ideal communities such as Brook Farm—the inspiration of Hawthorne's *Blithedale Romance*. Its adherents took progressive positions on the emancipation of women and the abolition of slavery.   A.Q.

O. B. Frothingham, *Transcendentalism in New England* (New York, 1876).
Perry Miller (ed.), *The Transcendentalists* (Cambridge, Mass., 1950).
P. F. Strawson, *The Bounds of Sense* (London, 1966).
W. H. Walsh, *Metaphysics* (London, 1963), ch. 3.

transcendental unity of apperception: *see* apperception.

transitive relation. A binary, i.e. two-term, *relation is transitive when if anything x has it to anything y, and y to anything z, then x has it to z (in symbols, R is transitive if and only if $\forall x \forall y \forall z((Rxy \wedge Ryz) \rightarrow Rxz)$); for example, *being older than*. 'Intransitive' means: if anything x has it to anything y, and y to anything z, then x does not have it to z; for example, *being twice as old as*. 'Non-transitive' may mean either 'not transitive' or 'neither transitive nor intransitive'.   C.A.K.

W. Hodges, *Logic* (Harmondsworth, 1977).

translation, indeterminacy of. W. V. Quine argued that there are no uniquely correct translations between languages. This is not the banal point that languages contain words with no precise equivalents in others, but the extraordinary claim that there is *no such thing, ever, as a uniquely correct translation of a word*. It forms part of Quine's argument that 'there is no objective matter to be right or wrong about' where the *meaning of words is concerned (*Word and Object*, 73), and it has implications in the philosophy of mind: if words have no meaning, then beliefs and other *propositional attitudes do not exist. Quine sees this as an acceptable result of behaviourist psychology; the apparatus of stimulus and response will not vindicate common-sense views about meaning, and 'the very question of conditions for identity of propositions presents not so much an unsolved problem as a mistaken ideal' (*Word and Object*, 206).

The doctrine arises from Quine's dissatisfaction with the Logical Positivists' version of the distinction between *analytic and synthetic statements, which requires the meanings of words to be explained in terms of the experiences appropriate or inappropriate to their use. Quine

retorts that single words cannot be paired with experiences, since they confront experience in clusters. His celebrated illustration involves an imaginary community who say 'gavagai' when confronted by a rabbit. Other things being equal, it is natural to translate the word as 'rabbit'. But why not translate it as, say, 'undetached rabbit-part'? For any experience which makes the use of 'rabbit' appropriate would also make that of 'undetached rabbit-part' appropriate.

One reply is that we should discover what their word for 'same' is (let us say 'emas') and then point to different parts of a rabbit and see if the community's members keep agreeing that this is the 'emas gavagai'. One would expect them to dissent at some point if this phrase translates 'same undetached rabbit-part'. However, how are we to obtain the translation of 'emas'? It seems that this awaits translation of words like 'gavagai'. For if this translates as 'rabbit', then their failure to dissent from 'emas gavagai' indicates that the latter may translate as 'same rabbit'. But if 'gavagai' translates as 'undetached rabbit-part', then their failure to dissent indicates that 'emas gavagai' should translate as, say, 'part of the same group of undetached rabbit-parts'. We are trapped in a circle, and Quine contends that this always happens if we try to translate 'gavagai' by translating other words first. Since experience is not enough to tie down individual words, there is no initial point on which to base a uniquely correct translation.

A different reply is that finding out more about the brains and nervous systems of the members of the community would indicate which translation is correct. But Quine argues that the indeterminacy thesis holds even given all facts about the world (past, present, and future) that could be stated in terms of physics. The situation here is delicate: on the one hand, Quine's critics accuse him of unfairly restricting the range of facts relevant to translation, while he on the other replies that such critics beg the question by smuggling in assumptions about meaning and translation.

The imaginary community is only a metaphor. If there is nothing to choose between linguist A's translation of 'gavagai' as 'rabbit', and linguist B's translation of it as 'undetached rabbit-part', then why should not B translate A's uses of 'rabbit' as 'undetached rabbit-part'? Hence, if the argument works, it works within a single language.

Responses tend to involve attacks on Quine's *behaviourism. But this is not the best approach to his nihilism about meaning, given the currency of nihilism in philosophy of mind (and critical theory). The root of the trouble lies in attempts to give 'scientific' accounts of language and thought, and Quine's outlook is more typical of its time than some treatments indicate.   G.W.McC.

C. Hookway, *Quine* (Cambridge, 1988), pt. III.
R. Kirk, *Translation Determined* (Oxford, 1986).
W. V. Quine, *Word and Object* (Cambridge, Mass., 1960), ch. 2.

transparency: *see* opacity and transparency.

transposition (also known as *contraposition). The rule in classical logic whereby we derive 'If not-*q* then not-*p*' from 'If *p* then *q*'. While admitting its occasional acceptability, many find transposition ('an antiquated notion': Dudman) deeply suspect. Difficult cases include 'There's cake if you want it', and Prior's 'If God exists, go to church'. Transposition is the sentential-logic analogue of the argument form *modus tollens*, and of traditional logic's contraposition (whereby from a given sentence we infer another whose subject is the contradictory of the original's predicate).   J.J.M.

V. H. Dudman, 'Parsing "If"-Sentences', *Analysis* (1984).

transvaluation of values (or **revaluation of values**). Nietzsche's project of reassessing the worth of things commonly valued positively or negatively. He proposed and undertook to revalue them in terms of their 'value for life', i.e. the extent to which they are conducive or detrimental to the preservation and enhancement of various types of human beings and of human life more generally. This is neither to devalue nor to reverse all prevailing *value-determinations, but rather to revise them in a naturalistic manner sensitive to the varying requirements of human flourishing. (See e.g. *Beyond Good and Evil*, sect. 4; *Genealogy of Morals*, preface; *The Antichrist*, sects. 1–7.)

R.S.

George Morgan, *What Nietzsche Means* (New York, 1965), ch. 5.

traversal of the infinite. An argument for the finitude of the world's past which originated with Philoponus (490?–575?). An infinite series cannot be completed (the infinite cannot be traversed). But if the world were infinite in past time, then 'up to every given moment an eternity has elapsed' (Kant) and thus an infinite sequence would have been completed. Therefore the world is finite in past time. This argument has been offered by, among others, al-Ghazālī, St Bonaventure, and Kant. It was, however, decisively refuted by Aquinas and, somewhat more subtly, by Ockham. Aquinas pointed out that traversal requires *two* termini: a beginning and an end. But any past time which could count as a beginning is only a finite time ago. Consequently we do not, in the required sense, have a traversed infinity.   J.J.M.

*infinity.

Norman Kretzmann, 'Ockham and the Creation of the Beginningless World', *Franciscan Studies* (1985).

triangulation. Davidson invokes this puzzling notion while arguing that thought is an essentially social phenomenon. The content of our thoughts, he contends, is determined by their causes. Yet, when you see, and think, there is a table before you, many causal factors contribute to your having this thought. What makes it a thought about the *table* as opposed to some other link in the causal chain (e.g. your retinal image)? Davidson maintains that this question cannot be answered if we consider you in isolation. Once we introduce another person, it becomes evident that communication is possible only on the assumption that your respective thoughts converge on public objects of a shared world. The 'triangle' <person-person-object> is essential to the determination of the mental content and thus, as Davidson puts it, there can be no first person without a second person.   D.BAK.

Donald Davidson, *Subjective, Intersubjective, Objective* (Oxford, 2001).

trolley problem. Suppose you are driving a trolley whose brakes have failed. Ahead of you five people are standing on the track. But here the track forks, and on the alternative path one person stands. Is it morally permissible, or even required, to divert the trolley to save the five from death, at the cost of one? Most people's intuition is that this is at least morally permissible. Why, then, do we not think it permissible for a surgeon, in urgent need of five different organs to save five patients, to kill a healthy patient to procure them?   S.D.R.

*acts and omissions.

Philippa Foot, 'The Problem of Abortion and the Doctrine of Double Effect', reprinted in her *Virtues and Vices* (Oxford, 1978, 2002).
Judith Jarvis Thomson, 'The Trolley Problem', reprinted in her *Rights, Restitution and Risk* (Cambridge, Mass., 1986).

trope. The term 'trope' was introduced into philosophy by D. C. Williams to mean a particular unrepeatable property, like the particular blueness of a blue patch that cannot be shared by any other patch, not even a patch that *exactly* matches the blue patch in colour. Other patches may nevertheless share the same shade of blue by virtue of the fact that their particular bluenesses resemble one another. Tropes are to be contrasted with *universals, which are repeatable properties, like a specific shade of blue that can be shared by many different patches. A particular property may be thought to be a complex of a particular (a patch) and a universal (a shade of blue). By contrast, trope theory claims, a trope is not complex but simple.   F.MacB.

*properties, individual; universals.

Donald C. Williams, 'On the Elements of Being: I', in D. H. Mellor and A. D. Oliver (eds.), *Properties* (Oxford, 1997).

Trotsky, Leon (1879–1940), real name Lev Davidovich Bronstein. The most famous of the Bolshevik leaders after Lenin, Trotsky played a prominent role in the 1917 Revolution and its aftermath, only to be subsequently exiled and murdered by Stalin. Although less interested in philosophy than most of his fellow Bolsheviks, Trotsky did address himself to these matters on two occasions. First in the 1920s he became interested in the philosophy of science. He defended the heterogeneity of the sciences, argued against those who assimilated the method of social science to that of natural science, and refused to claim that dialectical materialism was integral to the creativeness of science. Trotsky displayed the same approach in psychology through his continued preference for the imagination and enterprise of Freud over the plodding behaviouralism of Pavlov.

Towards the very end of his life, however, Trotsky dealt more systematically with philosophical questions—but with regrettable results. Prompted by the attack on Marxist philosophy by his hitherto loyal lieutenants Burnham and Shachtman, Trotsky wrote *In Defence of Marxism* which consisted in a dogmatic insistence on the essentiality of *dialectical materialism to Marxism. For Trotsky here, the politics and economics of Marxism had to be ensconced within the framework of a consistent and well-defined philosophical outlook. Anyone who divorced sociology from dialectical materialism and politics from sociology would, in the end, lose any capacity for political activity.   D.McL.

B. Knei-Paz, *The Social and Political Thought of Leon Trotsky* (Oxford, 1978).

true for me: *see* relativism, epistemological.

trust. Whether one trusts a specific other commonly depends on whether one thinks the other is trustworthy in the relevant circumstances. This depends on what knowledge one has of the other's future commitments to behave as one trusts. Some writers treat trust as a matter of rational assessment and rational choice on the parts of both the truster and the trusted. Perhaps because of its relation to trustworthiness, some theorists treat trust as inherently normative—even to the point of assigning an obligation of trustworthiness to one who is trusted. John Locke thought trust central to consensual government. Contrary to the purely rational-choice vision, many theorists suppose that only a normative commitment to some degree of trustworthiness can explain the success of many institutions and organizations in serving their clienteles.   R.HAR.

*consent; testimony; loyalty.

Diego Gambetta, *Trust: Making and Breaking Cooperative Relations* (New York, 1988).

truth. The term 'truth' seems to denote a property, one which is also expressed by the truth-predicate 'is true'. But if so, of *what* is truth a property? What are the primary 'bearers' of truth, and of its counterpart, falsity? (Whether truth and falsity are indeed polar opposites, as the principle of *bivalence implies, is itself a disputed issue.) At least three candidates can be put forward: sentences, *statements, and *propositions. Loosely, a *sentence* is a linguistic token or type, such as the string of written words 'This is red'. A *statement* is the assertoric use of a sentence by a speaker on a particular occasion. A *proposition* is what is asserted when a statement is made—its 'content'. Thus two different speakers, or the same speaker on two different occasions, may assert the same proposition by making two different statements, perhaps using sentences of two different languages. And the same sentence (conceived of as a linguistic type) may be used in two different statements to assert two different propositions.

In addition to speaking of sentences, statements, and propositions being true or false, we also speak of *beliefs* (and other *propositional attitudes) being true or false. So is the notion of truth ambiguous, or is there a primary notion which attaches to just one of these classes of items? Opinions differ, but a broad division can be drawn amongst theories of truth between those that regard truth as being a property of *linguistic or mental representations* of some sort—such as primarily sentences, statements, and beliefs—and those that regard truth as primarily a property of *propositions*, conceived as items that are *represented* or *expressed* in thought or speech, but exist independently of mind and language. Disputes between theorists of truth are sometimes confused by a failure to discern this division.

The best-known theory of truth is the *correspondence theory. On this view, a candidate for truth is true if and only if it 'corresponds to a fact'. Some objectors complain that the notion of a *fact is itself only to be explained in terms of truth (for instance, as being the worldly correlate of a true sentence or proposition), so that the theory is vitiated by circularity. Others complain that the notion of 'correspondence' is either vacuous or unintelligible. It is hard to say which philosophers have really held this theory. Aristotle is sometimes said to intimate allegiance to it in his remark that 'to say of what is that it is, and of what is not that it is not, is true'. Wittgenstein's 'picture' theory of the *Tractatus* is often cited as exemplifying it. Even Tarski's *semantic theory of truth has been described as a version of it. But in modern times its clearest advocate has perhaps been J. L. Austin. The theory is often thought to be vulnerable to devastating criticism in the form of the so-called *slingshot argument. This argument seems to show that, given any two truths p and q, the expressions 'the fact that p' and 'the fact that q' must have the same reference, the implication being that there cannot be more than one fact—sometimes ironically called 'the Great Fact'. The problem is that correspondence theorists typically maintain that distinct truths correspond to *different* facts, but it now appears that these supposed differences between facts inevitably collapse. Very arguably, however, the proper lesson to draw is not that there is something wrong with the correspondence conception of truth as such, but rather that not just its enemies but even some of its friends have unnecessarily embroiled it in bad metaphysics.

Almost equally well known is the *coherence theory, whose proponents are usually led to it by the perceived difficulties of the correspondence theory. Accepting that truth cannot consist in a relation between truth-bearers and items which are not themselves truth-bearers (such as 'facts'), these theorists propose instead that it consists in a relation which truth-bearers have to one another—such as a relation of mutual support amongst the beliefs of an individual or a community. Opponents object that this leads to an unacceptable *relativism about truth, since many different and mutually incompatible systems of belief could be internally consistent and self-supporting. They also sometimes complain that advocates of the theory are guilty of a confusion between stating a *criterion* of truth—that is, a rule for the evaluation of a belief as being true—and stating what truth *consists* in.

In order to overcome the objection of relativism, some advocates of the coherence theory suggest that the notion of truth is a regulative ideal, which could only be fully realized in a unified and completed science far in advance of the fragmented and partial belief systems of any human community that actually exists or is ever likely to. In this guise, the theory overlaps with some versions of the so-called *pragmatic theory of truth, associated with the American philosophers Peirce, James, and Dewey. The latter theory—particularly in the hands of James—urges a connection between what is true and what is useful, pointing out, for instance, that one mark of a successful scientific theory is that it enables us, through associated developments in technology, to manipulate nature to our advantage in ways hitherto unavailable to us. Detractors protest that this (alleged) conflation of truth with utility is pernicious, because the ethics of belief require us to pursue the truth with honesty even if its consequences should prove detrimental to our material well-being.

All the theories of truth so far mentioned may be called *substantive* or *robust*, as opposed to *deflationary*, in the sense that they all take truth to be a real and important property of the items—whatever they are—that the theories take to be the primary bearers of truth. But in recent times deflationary theories of truth have become quite popular, the earliest example being the *redundancy theory (a later variant of this being the so-called prosentential theory of truth). This theory, building on the apparent equivalence between asserting a proposition *p* and asserting that *p* is true, holds that the truth-predicate 'is true' exists only in order to enable economy of expression, and that what is said with its aid could in principle be said without it. A closely related view is that the truth-predicate plays a performative role, enabling speakers to express their approval or endorsement of the assertions of other speakers. Serious-minded philosophers will deplore such views for taking truth to be so flimsy.

Some theorists in the pragmatic tradition, such as Stephen Stich, now urge that truth as such has no cognitive value—that we literally should not care whether our beliefs are true or false, but only whether they enable us to achieve more substantive goals such as happiness and well-being. However, *Sophists were urging much the same in the time of Plato and—fortunately!—it seems unlikely that philosophers will ever entirely give up asking 'What is truth?' and assuming that the answer is something of importance. Quite apart from anything else, giving up the question of truth would deprive them of the endless enjoyment to be derived from attempting to solve the various paradoxes, such as the *liar paradox, which the notion of truth throws up.

In recent years, metaphysicians have been emphasizing again the connection between *realism and truth that seems to have inspired many advocates of the correspondence theory. This attitude often finds expression in some version of the so-called truth-maker principle—the principle that every truth (or, at least, every contingent truth) must be *made* true by the existence of something in reality. Some advocates of the principle, such as David Armstrong, maintain that truth-makers are *states of affairs*, others that they are particularized *properties, or *tropes*. So, for example, on the former view it is *Mars's being red* that makes true the proposition that Mars is red, while on the latter it is *Mars's redness* that makes this true. Both approaches contend that the world contains a multiplicity of truth-makers, but neither insists, as some versions of the correspondence theory do, that there is a one-to-one correlation between truths and truth-makers. Indeed, truth-maker realism is not committed to the claim that truth *consists* in, or is definable in terms of, any independently specifiable relation between truth-bearers and other entities of any specific kind. For this reason, it is not vulnerable to many of the objections traditionally raised against the correspondence theory of truth, while at the same time inheriting the attractive realist and anti-relativist implications of that view.   E.J.L.

*true for me; art and truth.

D. M. Armstrong, *A World of States of Affairs* (Cambridge, 1997).

S. Blackburn and K. Simmons (eds.), *Truth* (Oxford, 1999).

S. Haack, *Philosophy of Logics* (Cambridge, 1978).

P. Horwich, *Truth*, 2nd edn. (Oxford, 1998).

R. L. Kirkham, *Theories of Truth* (Cambridge, Mass., 1992).

R. L. Martin (ed.), *Recent Essays on Truth and the Liar Paradox* (Oxford, 1984).

S. P. Stich, *The Fragmentation of Reason* (Cambridge, Mass., 1990).

truth, coherence theory of: *see* coherence theory of truth.

truth, correspondence theory of: *see* correspondence theory of truth.

truth, deflationary theories of: *see* deflationary theories of truth.

truth, double: *see* double truth.

truth, logical: *see* logical truth.

truth, pragmatic theory of: *see* pragmatic theory of truth.

truth, redundancy theory of: *see* redundancy theory of truth.

truth, semantic theory of: *see* semantic theory of truth.

truth, subjective: *see* subjective truth.

truth and truthfulness. The assumptions that one is truthful when speaking truly, and that truthfulness is a virtue, because truth is valuable, are both questionable. True statements can be intentionally misleading (e.g. 'Someone stole your book', said by the culprit), and a would-be liar may, through ignorance, inadvertently say something true. In neither case would we describe the speaker as being truthful. In *The Gay Science* (§344), Nietzsche denies that truthfulness is admired because it helps disseminate truth, for 'truth at any price' may be 'inimical to life'. Rather, we admire truthfulness, irrespective of practical benefits, on the *'moral ground'* that 'I will not deceive, even myself'. The virtue of truthfulness is therefore relatively independent of the value of truth.   D.E.C.

B. Williams, *Truth and Truthfulness: An Essay in Genealogy* (Princeton, NJ, 2002).

truth-conditions. Usually short for 'truth- and falsity-conditions'. The truth-conditions of an indicative *sentence* are the conditions under which it would be true, or false: e.g. 'I'm exheredated' is true if the speaker is at the time of speaking exheredated, and false otherwise. The truth-conditions of a *word* or *phrase* are its contribution to the conditions under which an indicative sentence containing it would be true, or false: e.g. (for the word 'exheredated') any sentence *'a is exheredated'* is true if *'a'* in it refers to something exheredated, and false otherwise. (These are very simple examples; even so, it is not implied that they are necessarily accurate, especially over falsity.)
    C.A.K.

D. K. Lewis, 'General Semantics', in *Philosophical Papers*, i (New York, 1983).

truth-function. A proposition is a truth-function if its truth-value is determined by the truth-value of its components (or arguments). In the standard *propositional calculus (PC), propositions have truth-values True or False exclusively. The logical constants ∼, ∨, ·, ⊃, ≡ (in one standard notation), which approximate to the English 'not', 'or (inclusive)', 'and', a use of 'if', and 'if and only if', respectively, are so defined that a *well-formed formula of PC which is a proposition is a truth-function.

For example, where ϕ and ψ are propositions,

∼ϕ is true if and only if ϕ is false,
(ϕ ∨ ψ) is true if and only if ϕ is true or ψ is true or both are true,

and so on as given in the *truth-tables for the logical constants.

There is therefore an effective procedure for determining the truth-value of any PC proposition given the truth-value of its basic (atomic) propositional components.
    R.B.M.

B. Mates, *Elementary Logic* (Oxford, 1972).

truth-table. In the *propositional calculus, if ϕ and ψ are propositions, then the truth-value True or False of the truth-functions ∼ϕ , (ϕ ∨ ψ), (ϕ · ψ), (ϕ ⊃ ψ), (ϕ ≡ ψ) may be determined from the following matrices:

ϕ	∼ϕ
T	F
F	T

ϕ	ψ	(ϕ ∨ ψ)	(ϕ · ψ)	(ϕ ⊃ ψ)	(ϕ ≡ ψ)
T	T	T	T	T	T
T	F	T	F	F	F
F	T	T	F	T	F
F	F	F	F	T	T

where '∼', '∨', '·', '⊃', '≡' may be translated as 'not', 'or', 'and', 'if . . . then – – –', and ' . . . if and only if – – –' respectively.

The truth-value of truth-functions constructed out of n basic (atomic) propositions can be determined from a truth-table of 2^n lines by systematic application of the matrices.

For example, if p and q are basic or atomic propositions, then the truth-table for ((p · q) ⊃ p) may be given as follows.

p	q	((p · q) ⊃ p)	
T	T	T	T
T	F	F	T
F	T	F	T
F	F	F	T

and translated as: If p and q, then p.   R.B.M.

B. Mates, *Elementary Logic* (Oxford, 1972).
E. L. Post, 'Introduction to the Theory of Elementary Propositions', *American Journal of Mathematics* (1921).

truth-value. The truth (T or 1) or falsity (F or 0) of a proposition is its truth-value. In *propositional calculus, propositions are regarded primarily as the bearers of these two values: the *truth-table method is used to calculate the value of compound expressions. Systems using more than two such values have been developed by some modern logicians, e.g. Łukasiewicz.   c.w.

A. N. Prior, *Formal Logic*, 2nd edn. (Oxford, 1962), pt. III, sect. 2.

trying, or attempting; phenomenon whose relation to *belief, *desire, *intention, is investigated in philosophy of action.

Some philosophers accord trying a prominent role in *action*'s elucidation, believing both that someone who does something intentionally tries to do it, and that trying marks a point where *mental* and *physical* concepts meet in their application. A person's trying to do something is naturally thought of as 'mental'; but an event of a person's trying to do something is, arguably, usually the same as a 'physical' action of hers.   J.HORN.

*volition.

Jennifer Hornsby, *Actions* (London, 1980), ch. 3.

Tugendhat, Ernst (1930–). One of the most important contributors to the re-establishment of *analytic philosophy in Germany after the Nazi period, in which almost all analytic philosophers had to leave the country. Tugendhat, born in Brno as a Jew, emigrated to Venezuela, received his BA at Stanford 1949, his Ph.D. in Freiburg 1956, and his Habilitation in Tübingen 1966. He has held professorships in Heidelberg, Starnberg, and Berlin.

Trained by Heidegger in the Aristotelian and phenomenological tradition, he argues in an original way that analytic philosophy of language is the culmination of Aristotle's ontological project. Throughout Tugendhat's work the central characteristic of philosophy is 'the idea of organizing life as a whole in accordance with truth, i.e. the idea of a life of critical responsibility'. Along the same lines, he argues that Wittgenstein's view of self-knowledge and Heidegger's account of practical self-understanding are intrinsically connected because consciousness of the self arises only when I ask the question what kind of human being I aspire to be. This question also plays a central role in ethics as Tugendhat conceives it: morality can only be justified relative to conceptions of good personhood.   S.G.

E. Tugendhat, *Traditional and Analytical Philosophy: Lectures on the Philosophy of Language*, tr. P. A. Gorner (New York, 1982).

Turing, Alan (1912–54). English mathematician best known for the *Turing machine and the Turing test, both concerned with the relation between computation and mind. Turing's work in mathematical logic in the late 1930s systematized ideas of Gödel and Church in the form of an abstract description of what an idealized finite agent could compute. During the Second World War Turing worked on deciphering German codes, and in particular on the computational machinery required. After the war he worked on early digital computers and in 1950 published 'Computing Machinery and Intelligence' in *Mind*. In this article he proposes a test for thought: a machine can think if its replies to questions are indistinguishable from those of a human.   A.M.

*computers.

Andrew Hodges, *Alan Turing* (London, 1985).
The Essential Turing, ed. B. J. Copeland (Oxford, 2004).

Turing machine. A Turing machine is an idealization of an ideal finite calculating agent. It is usually described as if it were a mechanism, but a description as an ideal clerk would also be possible. So a Turing machine has an infinite tape (or notepad), a head which reads or writes symbols from a finite list to it (or pen), and a finite number of states. A machine-table specifies what, given a state and a symbol, will be overwritten at that point, and the next state. It can calculate anything any digital computer can. Three fundamental facts are (*a*) the characterization does not depend on details of how many symbols etc. there are; (*b*) there is a 'universal' Turing machine which can mimic the output of any other machine; (*c*) there is no Turing machine which, given a specification of any arbitrary Turing machine and an input, will halt when that machine halts, given that input. The last, (*c*), is closely related to

Gödel's theorem. Turing machines can give substance to *functionalism in the philosophy of mind.   A.M.

*computer; Gödel's theorem.

George Boolos and Richard Jeffrey, *Computability and Logic*, 3rd edn. (Cambridge, 1990).
The Essential Turing, ed. B. J. Copeland (Oxford, 2004).

Twardowski, Kazimierz (1866–1938). Polish philosopher who became the father of Polish *analytic philosophy. Twardowski studied in Vienna with Brentano (Ph.D. 1891, Habilitation 1894). In 1895 he was appointed a professor of philosophy at the University of Lvov. Twardowski was a distinguished teacher who trained many Polish philosophers and logicians, including Ajdukiewicz, Kotarbiński, Leśniewski, and Łukasiewicz. In his essay *Zur Lehre vom Inhalt und Gegenstand der Vorstellungen* (1894) Twardowski introduced a distinction between the content and the object of presentations which completed Brentano's earlier analysis of psychic phenomena in terms of acts and objects. Twardowski also argues for the thesis that there are no objectless presentations and develops a theory of objects. His *Habilitationsschrift* considerably influenced Meinong's ontology and Husserl's preparatory studies to *Logische Untersuchungen*. The actions–products distinction is another of Twardowski's conceptual clarifications which deserves to be mentioned.   J.WOL.

K. Twardowski, *On the Content and Object of Presentation*, tr. H. Grossmann (The Hague, 1976).

twin earth. Imaginary counterpart to earth introduced in thought experiments in philosophy of mind and language.

In Putnam's famous example, on twin earth the stuff which falls from the sky, comes out of taps, and constitutes oceans, etc. is XYZ, not H_2O. Putnam argued that a person's meaning what she does cannot be 'in her head', since twin earth's inhabitants' heads are not relevantly different from earth's, but what they mean by 'water' is different from what earth's inhabitants mean.   J.HORN.

John Heil, *The Nature of True Minds* (Cambridge, 1993), ch. 2.

two-envelope paradox. Imagine that you are offered a choice between two envelopes, each containing money. One has twice as much money as the other, but you are not told which. Once you have selected an envelope, *A*, you are offered a further choice. You can either open the envelope or swap it for the other, *B*. You reason as follows.

Let the amount of money in *A* be *x*. The other envelope, *B*, contains either $2x$ or $x/2$. The two possible outcomes are equally probable. Therefore, the expected value of swapping *A* for *B* is $(0.5 \times 2x) + (0.5 \times x/2) = 5/4x$. Since the expected value of hanging on to *A* is *x* (given that it is certain that *A* contains *x*), if I want to maximize expected value, I ought to swap *A* for *B*.

This is paradoxical because, once I have swapped *A* for *B*, a similar line of reasoning will show that I ought to swap back—and so on indefinitely.   J.BER.

*decision theory; paradoxes.

Timothy J. McGrew, David Shier, and Harry S. Silverstein, 'The Two-envelope Paradox Resolved', *Analysis* (1995).

tychism: *see* Peirce.

type: *see* token.

types, theory of. Let r be the set of all sets that are not members of themselves: $\{x \mid x \notin x\}$. It follows that $r \in r$ if and only if $r \notin r$, a contradiction. This is known as *Russell's paradox. A similar result can be obtained from the property of those properties that do not hold of themselves (i.e. $R(P)$ if and only if $\neg P(P)$). Type theory avoids these consequences by segregating properties, relations, and sets into 'types'. Type 0 items are ordinary objects, which are not properties. Type 1 items are properties of ordinary objects; type 2 items are properties of type 1 properties, etc. 'Personhood' is type 1, and 'holding of exactly six objects' is type 2. Things get more complex when relations are considered. There is, for example, a type of relations between type 1 properties and ordinary objects. In 'ramified type theory', types are further segregated into levels. Type 1, level 0 properties are those that can be defined with reference to type 0 items (ordinary objects) alone. Type 1, level 1 properties are those that can be defined with reference to type 0 items and type 1, level 0 properties, etc. In general, each property must be defined with reference to only properties of lower type and properties of its type but lower level. 'Simple type theory' does not employ levels, and allows unrestricted, or impredicative, definitions.   S.S.

*higher-order logic; vicious circle; reducibility, axiom of; logic, history of.

Allen Hazen, 'Predicative Logics', in D. Gabbay and F. Guenthner (eds.), *Handbook of Philosophical Logic*, i (Dordrecht, 1983).

U

ugliness. The property of having aesthetic disvalue, eliciting not indifference but discomfort or misery. Modes of ugliness in art correspond to the various modes of beauty or aesthetic value. If the mode is formal, ugliness is the ill-formed or deformed, misshapen, ill-placed. If the mode is expressive, the ugly may be the sentimental, the mawkish, clichéd, sickening: or it may arise from uncontrolled emotion—bombastic, ranting, or hysterical. If considered from a representational point of view, the objects represented may be judged unrelievedly disagreeable or painful to contemplate. Nevertheless, art can make use of the ugly; and the question must always be asked: Does this prima facie ugly work possess any justifying, compensating features—perhaps social or moral point? Or has this ugly component been transformed—by the medium—by the context—to be an ingredient in a new whole with positive aesthetic value?

R.W.H.

*beauty.

There is a dearth of recent substantial discussions. One *locus classicus* is Plotinus, *Enneads*, I. 6. See also Bernard Bosanquet, *Three Lectures on Aesthetics* (London, 1915).

Unamuno, Miguel de (1865–1936). Multi-faceted Spanish writer (novelist, poet, essayist) and professor (philologist). Deeply concerned about the meaning of life and death, which inspired all his writings, and dissatisfied by the sceptical answers of science and reason as regards eternal life, Unamuno argued for an existential attitude—the 'tragic sense of life'—consisting in acting as if human life has in fact a transcendent significance, even given our uncertainty that it has.

Unamuno found this attitude exemplified in lonely heroes such as Don Quixote and Jesus: men who, despite their respective folly and doubts (or maybe because of them), carried out their missions, thus redeeming themselves and others. This attitude has a clear religious dimension, closer to Protestant spirituality than to Spanish orthodox Catholicism. In fact, some of Unamuno's works were included in the Index, until the Second Vatican Council.

A.GOM.

R. R. Ellis, *The Tragic Pursuit of Being: Unamuno and Sartre* (Tuscaloosa, Ala., 1988).

uncertainty principle. Also called the indeterminacy principle, it is based on the orthodox ('Copenhagen') interpretation of a set of mathematical inequalities entailed by *quantum mechanics, called uncertainty relations. Roughly, these put a fundamental limit on the accuracy with which one can simultaneously predict the values of certain pairs of physical magnitudes (termed 'incompatible'), such as the position and momentum of a particle. More precisely, if one can predict that a particle's position will (most probably) be found on measurement to fall within some narrow range of values, then accuracy in predicting its momentum to fall within a similarly narrow range must be sacrificed, and vice versa. Orthodoxy interprets this as more than just a limitation on the statistical spread of measurement results, but as a principle governing what can be said about a single particle. Heisenberg mainly argued that the limitation is epistemic, preventing the simultaneous determination of a particle's position and momentum (and so forever blocking the possibility of predicting its future behaviour); while Bohr argued that the limitation is also ontic, rendering inapplicable the classical concepts of 'position' and 'momentum' to a particle.

R.CLI.

M. Jammer, 'The Indeterminacy Relations', in *The Philosophy of Quantum Mechanics: The Interpretations of Quantum Mechanics in Historical Perspective* (New York, 1974).

unconscious and subconscious mind. Although Freud claimed to have discovered the unconscious mind, there is little doubt that the view that there are aspects of our mental life to which we are not privy was widely available throughout the nineteenth century. Anticipations are to be found in Leibniz, Schelling, and Nietzsche. Freud's own preference was for the term 'unconscious' rather than 'subconscious', which was also widely used, on the grounds that the latter term encourages the equation of the psychical with the conscious. His conception of the unconscious allows that we may possess wishes which may be inaccessible to us. Freud believed that we need assistance from *psychoanalysis to recover them.

R.A.S.

H. F. Ellenberger, *The Discovery of the Unconscious* (New York, 1970).

undecidability. Term not only used in the philosophy of mathematics but also deployed by Jacques Derrida and those who have adopted his heterodox procedures in the deconstructive reading of philosophical and literary texts. Here it signals the impossibility of deciding between discrepant (often contradictory) orders of meaning, as for instance between the constative and performative, the literal and metaphoric, or the overt and the latent orders of sense.   C.N.

*deconstruction; *différance*; logocentrism; decidability.

Jacques Derrida, *Margins of Philosophy*, tr. Alan Bass (Chicago, 1982).

underdetermination. The *problem of underdetermination* concerns the relationship between *theory (scientific theory, or any generalization) and the *empirical data. For any given theory, the evidence will never determine the choice between that theory and some rival theory. The problem then is to show how theory choice can ever be rational.   R.Le P.

*induction; translation, indeterminacy of.

W. H. Newton-Smith, *The Rationality of Science* (London, 1981).

understanding. What it is about humans, uniquely so far as is known, that enables us to understand other minds, do mathematics and science, cheat evolution by manipulating our environment, and speculate about itself in philosophy. Philosophers debate about the limits of understanding—for instance, how could we know either that there are or that there are not things for ever beyond our grasp? But it is easier to be amazed at its scope. Why should an average mammal on a peripheral planet be able to fathom the nature of preceding creatures millions of years back, the interior of stars, the laws of nature, the early moments of the whole universe? That is far in excess of what we need in order to get by, as the other animals (who do not reciprocate our interest in them) get by. The most astounding thing in the world, it may seem, is that we can understand it and the creatures within it. So much understood so recently. Yet the brains of Stone Age people were as capacious as ours. I wonder if they felt the same awe.   J.E.R.S.

*thinking; belief; cognition; wisdom.

John Leslie, *Universes* (London, 1989), e.g. ch. 5.
L. Wittgenstein, *Philosophical Investigations* (Oxford, 1953), sects. 143–242.

underworld of philosophy: *see* philosophy, world and underworld.

undistributed middle. It was a rule of traditional logic that the middle term of a valid *syllogism (the term common to the premises) must be distributed in at least one of its occurrences: not meeting this requirement was the fallacy of undistributed middle. (*Distribution of terms.) On this view

All who train regularly are fit
All Olympic athletes are fit
Therefore, all who train regularly are Olympic athletes

is invalid because the middle term ('those who are fit') is in both instances the predicate of a universal affirmative (*logic, traditional) and therefore undistributed. The uneasy wording of the rule, which permits the middle term to be distributed either once or twice, reflects weaknesses in the standard doctrine of distribution.   c.w.

J. N. Keynes, *Formal Logic*, 4th edn. (London, 1906), 288–94.

unhappy consciousness: *see* alienation; Feuerbach.

uniformity of nature. Newton stated that certain qualities (such as inertia and impenetrability) 'which are found to belong to all bodies within the reach of our experience, are to be esteemed the universal qualities of all bodies whatsoever'. Such an inference must be based, Mill said, on the 'ultimate major premise' that 'the course of nature is uniform'. Taking that to mean that 'whatever is true in any one case, is true in all cases of a certain description', Mill thought that 'the only difficulty is, to find what description'. But any doubts about the truth of such generalizations are not settled by invoking as an assumption the alleged 'uniformity of nature': without the relevant descriptions the principle is empty, while with them it says no more than the generalizations themselves.   M.C.

*grue; induction.

E. Nagel, *The Structure of Science* (London, 1961).

union theory. The union theory concerns the relation between mental events and neural events, and their combined causal efficacy. It holds that all types of mental event are nomically correlated with types of neural event, that the correlation is most likely to be that of one type of mental event with one of many types of neural event, and that these 'psychoneural' correlates are pairs. The last idea is the most distinctive and original component of the theory. Psychoneural pairs are thought to function as a causal unit, in other words as a single cause and effect of things, rather than being separable into individual causes and effects. The principal recommendation of the theory is that it allows for the irreducibility of the mental while avoiding *epiphenomenalism.   P.J.P.N.

*consciousness, its irreducibility.

T. Honderich, *A Theory of Determinism* (Oxford, 1988), chs. 2 and 3.

unity of science. The unity of science, in its traditional positivistic formulation, is the view that all science is reducible to physics, in that lawful relations for any science can be derived in an appropriate way from the laws of physics. Alternatively, the unity of science might be understood as a methodological constraint on scientific-theory formation, where reduction to physics plays a regulatory role in scientific practice. Many philosophers (e.g. Fodor) argue that the special sciences, such as psychology, are legitimate even though they cannot in principle be so reduced.   M.B.

*reductionism.

A classical statement is R. Carnap, *The Unity of Science*, tr. Max Black (London, 1934). Cf. J. Fodor, *The Language of Thought* (Cambridge, Mass., 1979), ch. 1.

universal grammar. A set of principles true of all human languages and thought to be mentally represented in the minds of language-users. The principles characterize the genetically determined initial state of the language faculty—a biological endowment, specific to the human species, which provides the innate conditions for the growth of linguistic knowledge in the individual. Grammars for particular languages result from the exposure of the language faculty to the available linguistic data.   B.C.S.

*grammar.

N. Chomsky, 'On Cognitive Structures and their Development', in M. Piattelli-Palmarini (ed.), *Language and Learning: The Debate between Jean Piaget and Noam Chomsky* (London, 1980). V. Cook, *Chomsky's Universal Grammar* (Oxford, 1988).

universalizability. A judgement about an individual instance of a certain kind is universalizable if it applies also to every relevantly similar instance of that kind. An assumption of universalizability underlies appeals to the *golden rule (in ethics), the uniformity of nature (in science), equality before the law (in jurisprudence), logical form (in deductive proof), reasonableness (in commonsense inference), etc. In sum, all arguments about individual things ought to be universalizable.   L.J.C.

R. M. Hare, *Moral Thinking: Its Levels, Method and Point* (Oxford, 1981), 107–29.

universalizability, moral. The concept of *universalizability has been thought by some philosophers to provide a rational basis for moral principles of impartiality and justice. It is suggested that, if I maintain that I ought to act in a certain way towards others, the universalizability of 'ought' requires me to accept that others ought to act in the same way towards me. This then commits me, it is said, to accepting only those 'ought' judgements which give the same consideration to others' interests as to my own.

Critics have retorted that this is an attempt to build too much on the purely formal requirement of consistency. I can be a consistent egoist; if I think that I ought to pursue my own interests, universalizability commits me only to accepting that others ought also to pursue their own interests. And why should I not accept this?   R.J.N.

R. M. Hare, *Freedom and Reason* (Oxford, 1963).

universal proposition. In traditional logic propositions construed as having the form 'All S are P' or 'No S are P' (which implies 'All S are not P') were called universal and

contrasted with the particular forms 'Some S are P' and 'Some S are not P'. In *predicate calculus, propositions like 'All men are mortal' are represented as having the form 'For all x: if x is S, x is P', which may be symbolized as $\forall x\,(Sx \rightarrow Px)$.   C.W.

P. F. Strawson, *Introduction to Logical Theory* (London, 1952), chs. 6 and 7.

universal quantifier: *see* quantifier.

universals. Universals are the supposed referents of general terms like 'red', 'table', and 'tree', understood as entities distinct from any of the particular *things describable by those terms. But why should we suppose that such entities exist, and what must be their nature if they do? One traditional argument for their existence, traceable to Plato, is that they are needed to explain why all and only the particular things correctly describable as red, say, are indeed correctly describable as such. Surely all these distinct particular things must have something identifiable in common in order to be legitimately classified alike?—and that which is common to all and only red things is precisely the universal red. Red things are all red by virtue of their relationship to this one universal, according to traditional 'realism'. As to the nature of this relationship and the nature of universals themselves, however, realists are divided. 'Platonists' hold that the universal red has a non-spatio-temporal existence distinct and separable from all particular red things, which need not even exist in order for that universal to exist. 'Aristotelians' hold, conversely, that the universal red only exists inseparably from the existence of particular red things. But the Platonic view creates difficulties concerning the relationship between particular red things and the universal red, while the Aristotelian view seems to render the sense in which universals are 'real' somewhat tenuous. Furthermore, the argument just mentioned for the existence of universals is not entirely convincing. 'Conceptualism' holds that our classification of particulars under general terms is a product of our selective human interests rather than a reflection of metaphysical truth, while *'nominalism' holds that resemblances between particulars are sufficient to justify our application of the same general term to them without appeal to any additional entity.

However, the failure of one traditional argument for realism and internal difficulties in certain realist positions do not suffice to undermine the realist case. In recent years new arguments for realism have emerged which invoke universals to explain the status of natural laws and causal generalizations. Philosophers like D. M. Armstrong urge that natural necessity is to be explained as a relationship between universals, and that only by appeal to this notion can the logical distinction between lawlike and accidental generalizations be captured. On this view, it is not necessary to suppose that every meaningful general term refers to a real universal, since only those universals need be admitted that play a role in scientific laws. Hence this view need not be embarrassed by Wittgenstein's observation that there are general terms like 'game' for which it seems impossible to isolate any single feature common to all and only the particulars to which it applies.

Another reason why a realist need not be totally undiscriminating about general terms is that such terms clearly fall into a number of distinct semantic categories, not all of which equally invite a realist treatment. Thus, of the three general terms mentioned at the outset—'red', 'table', and 'tree'—only the latter two are *sortals, and of these only the last is a natural-kind term. Sortals differ from general terms like 'red' in that they convey not only a criterion of application but also a criterion of identity for the particular things to which they apply. Since particulars cannot be individuated at all save relative to an appropriate sortal classification, it is arguable that realism with regard to particulars demands realism with regard to at least some universals, namely, those that are the putative referents of *bona fide* natural kind terms.   E.J.L.

*qualities; properties; properties, individual.

D. M. Armstrong, *Universals and Scientific Realism* (Cambridge, 1978).
M. J. Loux (ed.), *Universals and Particulars* (New York, 1970).
E. J. Lowe, *Kinds of Being* (Oxford, 1989).

universals, concrete: *see* concrete universals.

unlikely philosophical propositions. Perhaps most philosophers are ready enough to make a list of these. Certainly in their talk they give evidence of having the materials ready to hand. Philosopher-editors, being accessories to the publication of much that by their lights is unlikely to be true, maybe even a thing or two that are just confused, are readier to make a list. It may be a *cri de cœur*. Here is mine.

1. *Philosophy is one subject in which formal logic is fundamental.* This book is a proof that philosophy is a family of subjects, indeed an unruly one. In that family, as the book also demonstrates, formal logic is neither father nor even elder brother. (Maybe philosophical logic has more claim to such a position, but still not a large claim.) How many large philosophical problems have been solved or made more tractable by formal logic? Have any? Why is there no formal logic to speak of in the greatest works of philosophy?

2. *A service is done to students or other innocents, or to logic, by those logicians who allow it to be thought that the ordinary 'If . . . then . . . ' thoughts that we depend on in life and science somehow come down to a thing, fundamental to a basic part of logic and called a material implication, which by definition is true except when its first part is true and its second part false.* If you are tempted to go along with the idea, reflect on 'If Hollywood is in California, then Edinburgh is in Scotland.' Do not neglect, either, 'If Edinburgh is in California, then Aristotle was a photographer'.

3. *Our own conscious thoughts and feelings are not different from electrochemical events in our brains. They are nothing but electrochemical events which are causally or logically related to* certain other things, notably what is called input and output. This is the root proposition of functionalism, cognitive science, and much psychologized and computerized philosophy of mind in so far as it applies to us rather than computers, Martians, or whatever else. If it is true, then what we are most sure about does not exist.

4. *If you and I both see the same copy of this book, there are two objects of awareness in question—each of us is just aware of a subjective thing, a 'sense-datum' or whatever.* Great philosophers have thought so. They have thought in this way about the external world in general. If so, as far as perception goes, each of us is in a kind of perpetual solitary confinement. No books, either. There's got to be something wrong with *that*, doesn't there, even if perceptual consciousness like the rest of consciousness somehow has a subjective side?

5. *The truth of a statement about the world, say about the weight of this book, does not consist in the statement's corresponding to actual things, but in some quite different relation, maybe one of coherence with other statements.* If so, whatever the attractions of anti-realism for mathematics and logical systems, the world is as incidental to truth as it is to consistent imagining. Nor, by the way, can difficulties in getting clear about the general relation between language and the world, or the mistake of talking about facts rather than things, reduce us to the deflationary policy of saying ' "Snow is white" is true if and only if snow is white', and a like thing about any other proposition—and saying no more than that.

6. *'In the possible world where I'm wearing brown shoes and a hat . . . ' can mean something other than and grander than 'In this world, if I were wearing brown shoes and a hat . . . '.* Some who want to give a helping hand to modal logic think so, and some others, a lot more, mystify the impressionable by joining into the talk. Conditional statements, and notably the counterfactual ones, aren't easy to explain, but we can get somewhere without the science fiction.

7. *An effect is not something that had to happen or was necessitated, but just an event which was preceded by something necessary to it, something without which the event wouldn't have happened.* If so, we can say our choices and decisions are effects without getting worried about whether we have free will. But effects aren't what we thought they were, which is things that actually have explanations.

8. *An effect by itself, as distinct from a thought of it in advance or earlier similar effects or anything else, sometimes explains why its cause happened.* This, the ancient and wonderful idea of teleological or functional explanation, is sometimes veiled by technicalities, sometimes turns up in Marxist reflections on base and superstructure, and is sometimes discerned in biology. The idea is aided by the example, about which it is a good idea to think again, that birds have hollow bones because that enables them to fly better.

9. *Moral judgements, say the judgement 'Socialism is morally right', are not a matter of our disputable attitudes or inclinations, but are like 'That rose is red', which, although it is somehow dependent on our perceptual apparatus, is definitely true or*

false in the plain sense. This, too good to be true, has stolen the name of moral realism. Maybe moral judgements can be rooted in real truths of human nature. That is a different realism, less dramatic but more reassuring.

10. *There are moral reasons for actions that do not rest on consequences of those actions. So consequentialism as it is called is a mistake, a low one.* The idea is edifying but surely it can't be right. A moral reason, like any reason, is a kind of desire that an action is to satisfy. How could there be such a desire without reference to consequences of or in the action? How could the reason 'He's my son' be such? Supposedly non-consequentialist reasons are about somehow self-serving consequences, aren't they?

11. *To argue for punishment by saying, in one way or another, that it is deserved or is a retribution is to give some reason for it other than the disagreeable one that it satisfies grievances—desires for the distress of offenders.* What is offered instead in analysis or explanation of arguments of desert or retribution is usually high-minded, but not such as to provide an actual reason.

12. *There is some principle of justice or equality or well-being, or some other principle of political morality, that should have priority over this: that we must seek by rational means to make well-off those who are badly off, one of our means being the reducing of demands for rewards by larger contributors to society.* I don't think we'll find anything closer to true than the Principle of Humanity. In liberalism or anything else.

13. *Philosophy, to come back to that whole subject, has less to contribute to the understanding of realities of one kind and another than science, literature, economics, history, or narrower specialities.* You can think instead that there is a division of labour in thinking about consciousness, the world of which Quantum Theory as interpreted is a theory, time, free will, genes, terrorism, and more. There are scientific and other disasters in those neighbourhoods. Decent philosophy's contribution, as essential as any, is a general logic—a clarity, consistency and completeness. We can't get along without it. There should be a book, too, on why science regularly gets philosophical subjects so wrong.

Why are philosophers not detained by the certainty that their published or unpublished lists of unlikely philosophical propositions have no chance of being widely accepted as unlikely? (There is *some* philosopher, decent enough and paid for his work, whose list contains exactly the contradictories of the propositions above.) Does this show that philosophy is the particular line of life whose questions are hardest, and that surviving in its resulting climate of uncertainty brings out bumptiousness?   T.H.

*Honderich.

unsaturated expression. An expression that needs supplementation before it has what Frege calls a complete sense; an expression that refers to functions, not objects. Frege views an expression such as 'Caesar conquered Gaul' as analysable into two sorts of constituents, one complete in itself and the other unsaturated. 'Caesar' and 'Gaul' are of the first sort; these refer to objects. '—— conquered ——' is of the second sort; it must have its blanks 'saturated' before it can express a complete sense. Other examples of unsaturated expressions are 'the father of——' and 'either—— or——'. Observe that the notion of unsaturated expression is quite different from Russell's notion of *incomplete symbol. Frege explains the notion in, among other places, 'Function and Concept', in *Collected Papers on Mathematics, Logic, and Philosophy* (Oxford, 1984).   A.GUP.

Upanishads. Theoretical sections of the orally transmitted corpus of sacred Sanskrit literature called 'Veda' and traditionally believed to have no beginning in time. The Upanishads were compiled in India 400 to 500 years before Socrates. These parts of the Vedic corpus were so named because pupils had to sit (*ṣad*) down (*ni*) close (*upa*) to their teacher to learn them. There are nearly 100 of them, many of which are apocryphal. The twelve principal ones include texts called 'The Lord', 'By Whom?', 'Questions', 'The Big Forest', etc. Commenting upon these major Upanishads was essential for a philosopher starting a new school of *Vedānta. The Upanishads use the forms of dialogue, anecdote, parable, and allegory to make their point.

For example, we find a dialogue in the court of philosopher-king Janaka between Yājñavalkya and a woman philosopher Gārgī about the phenomenology of dreams and deep sleep; the anecdotes of the candid son of a prostitute who was treated as belonging to the highest caste of priests because of his love of truth, and of the young lad Nachiketas walking up to the palace of Death to ask about the afterlife; a parable of ten people who could never find the tenth because no one counted himself; the allegory of transcendental and empirical selves as two birds on a branch, one watching the other nibble at objects of experience. There are also pieces of straightforward reasoning like 'Fear and constraint come from a second, therefore to realize that the self alone is real without a second, is to be fearless and free'.

By distinguishing pleasure from the good, the Upanishads claim self-knowledge to be the ultimate good. The notion of the Self or Ātman is analysed in much detail, with accounts like that of the 'five sheaths' of food, breath, mind, intellect, and bliss being the progressively subtler individuators of consciousness yielding progressively deeper notions of a person. True self-knowledge is attained by philosophical reflection supported by greedless performance of social duties. A virtue ethics enjoining truthfulness, universal love, self-control, and inwardization of the senses is developed with a liberating union of the self with the world-spirit Brahman, as the final goal of life.

The notion of a world-spirit is arrived at by ignoring structural and functional differences and reducing effects to their material causes. The appeal here is to intuitions like 'What is the nail-clipper except the steel?' Such reductive logic is then applied to resolve all objects into intentional transformations of the knowing consciousness.

This witnessing consciousness, like the watching bird mentioned in the allegory above, can never really be made an object. Since the real is that which stays the same through change and cannot be thought away, the undifferentiated unlimited pure Consciousness is arrived at as the stuff of which both we and the world are made.

This Supreme Reality is also pure Being and pure Bliss. It is essentially formless and indescribable in words, but when personalized it is called God or the Lord. At its monistic height, meditation on this first philosophy shows that I am Brahman, which is all there is. Wittgenstein's remark that 'the spirit of the snake . . . is *your* spirit for it is only from yourself that you are acquainted with spirit at all' (*Notebooks*, 85e) reveals the impact of the Upanishads, which trickled down to him through Schopenhauer, who admits to being deeply influenced by them.   A.C.

*Indian philosophy.

Paul Deussen, *Philosophy of the Upanishads* (New York, 1966).

use and meaning. What gives words their *meaning? According to Wittgenstein, in his later writings, what breathes life into dead signs is their use. His thesis that meaning is use replaces views of word meaning as ideas in the minds of speakers, or as the things words stand for. But what is the relationship between meaning and use? Not every way of using a word is part of its meaning. There are correct and incorrect uses of words. Wittgenstein saw the correct use of a word as governed by a rule, and supposed that it was the existence of common rules of use for words that guaranteed them a meaning among a linguistic community. On this account, meaning does not precede use but is constituted by rule-governed use of a word. Equally, meaning cannot transcend use: there can be no more to the meaning of an expression than can be discerned by observing the use that speakers make of it. Thus Wittgenstein treats meaning as a public not a private matter. However, problems remain. Rules extend beyond any instance we reach, but how can their indefinite application be extrapolated from current use? Furthermore, rules suggest a normative dimension to meaning, but which features of use reveal these linguistic norms? These problems remain matters of intense philosophical scrutiny.   B.C.S.

P. Horwich, *Meaning* (Oxford, 2001).

use and mention. A distinction between talk about the world by means of a word and talk about that word. For example, in 'Numbers are abstract objects' the word 'number' is used, but in ' "Number" has six letters' the word 'number' is mentioned. To mark the distinction, it is customary to place a word in quotation marks in cases where it is being mentioned. As a test for the distinction, translate the sentence embedding the word into another language. If the word is mentioned, it is appropriate to leave it untranslated; if used, inappropriate.

It is important to observe the distinction to avoid confusion between ascribing properties to language and ascribing properties to non-linguistic reality.   S.P.

*formal and material mode.

utilitarianism is an approach to morality that treats pleasure or desire-satisfaction as the sole element in human good and that regards the morality of actions as entirely dependent on consequences or results for human (or sentient) well-being. Utilitarianism has its origins in late seventeenth-century Britain, received its 'classical' formulations in the work of Bentham, Mill, and Sidgwick, and has continued to have a prominent place in the English-speaking philosophical world up to the present day. Bentham and most subsequent utilitarians discard religious traditions and social conventions in favour of treating human *well-being or *happiness as the touchstone for all moral evaluation; and in the nineteenth century, in Britain and elsewhere, the doctrine played an important role in democratic and humane political reforms.

Present-day utilitarianism is best understood by breaking it down into its separable elements, by focusing on certain formal and controversial aspects of utilitarian thought, and by indicating important variations and disagreements within utilitarianism itself. In its earliest and best-known examples, utilitarianism is a *hedonistic* doctrine: it treats pleasure and pain as the sole good and bad things in human lives. This *ethical hedonism was originally tied to *psychological hedonism about human motivation. Bentham assumed that all humans are basically and exclusively motivated by the desire to gain *pleasure and avoid *pain, but it is possible to maintain ethical hedonism while rejecting, as most present utilitarians are inclined to do, psychological hedonism. However, certain later and contemporary versions of utilitarianism broaden the notion of ethical hedonism so that human or personal good is understood to be constituted by whatever satisfies people's desires or preferences or makes people *happy*.

Utilitarians nowadays also typically accept some form of *outcome utilitarianism* (Amartya Sen's term), according to which, roughly, the goodness of any state of affairs is solely a matter of how much overall (or average) well-being people (or sentient beings generally) are enjoying in that state of affairs. But the major ethical element in most contemporary utilitarianism is *direct *consequentialism*, the view that the rightness and goodness of any action, motive, or political institution depends solely on the goodness of the overall state of affairs consequent upon it (this state of affairs includes the act or motive itself). Combining these elements (and adding the assumption that morality requires us to *do our best*), most current direct (or act-) utilitarians want to say that an act is morally obligatory if and only if it produces a greater balance of pleasure over pain, or of desire satisfaction, than any alternative action available to the agent. An act is then morally right, or not wrong, if it produces as great a balance of pleasure over pain as any alternative action open to the agent. (An act may be right but not obligatory if it is tied for first place with one or more alternatives.) These general claims about rightness and obligation are often referred to as (forms of) the principle of *utility.

JEREMY BENTHAM did not invent the principle of utility, but he devised the first comprehensive theory of utilitarianism and urged its practical application.

JOHN STUART MILL, famous first for his system of logic, then for his moral philosophy, devoted himself largely to political reform after the death of his wife Harriet, who had shared his work and influenced him greatly.

MARY WOLLSTONECRAFT was one of the 'English Jacobins'; social reformers of the revolutionary era at the end of the eighteenth century. She envisioned a new social order which would free every person to develop her or his own capabilities.

EDMUND BURKE, aesthetician, parliamentarian, Conservative icon, scourge of the French Revolutionaries, advocate of independence for Britain's overseas territories.

On a direct utilitarian view, moral evaluation is a form of instrumental evaluation: acts are not right or obligatory because of their inherent character, their underlying motives, or their relation to divine or social dictates, but because of how much overall human or sentient well-being they *produce*. Moreover, if one thinks one should produce the best state of affairs one can, but believes, for example, that equality (rather than sheer quantity) of well-being or (unobserved) natural beauty makes a fundamental difference to the goodness of states of affairs or situations, then one may be a consequentialist but one is not a utilitarian. (According to an older, now discarded usage, such a position would be characterized as 'ideal utilitarianism'.)

Some utilitarians reject direct consequentialism in favour of 'rule-consequentialism', according to which the rightness of an action depends on the consequences not of the action itself, but of various sets of rules. Such indirect consequentialism says, for example, that an act is right if it accords with a set of rules whose being accepted, or followed, would have consequences as good as those that would result from any other set of rules' being accepted, or followed. Act-consequentialism, by contrast, evaluates actions directly in terms of *their own* consequences. The chief advantage of rule-consequentialism is that its evaluations of actions accord better with ordinary moral beliefs and intuitions than familiar forms of act-consequentialism do. For direct (or act-) consequentialism, any means can be justified by a good-enough end, and if framing an innocent person will almost certainly prevent race riots and many consequent fatalities, act-utilitarianism and most other forms of direct consequentialism tell us it is (or may well be) our obligation to frame the innocent person. But this seems morally unacceptable to most people, and rule-consequentialism can avoid such a result by claiming that any accepted set of social rules that permitted framing innocent people would be more destructive of social harmony and well-being than could possibly be made up for by the occasional prevention of a race riot, and then saying that the act of framing an innocent person is wrong because it fails to accord with that set of social rules that would best produce overall social harmony and well-being. However, rule-consequentialism has been criticized on the theoretical grounds that it offers no adequate or consistent reason why rules should be evaluated by *their* consequences but acts should *not* be, and most present-day utilitarians accept direct consequentialism, while at the same time in one way or another attempting to reduce or play down the importance of the divergence between utilitarian moral views and common-sense moral thinking.

By contrast with ordinary or common-sense morality, utilitarianism is an *impartial* or *impersonal* moral view. Ordinarily, we think a person is morally entitled to favour herself or her family (to some extent) over other people, but direct (or act-) utilitarianism claims that our obligations depend on an impersonal assessment of the consequences of our actions, and if we have a choice between doing more for strangers or less for ourselves and/or our friends and relations, then we must give preference to the strangers. Ordinary morality is 'agent-relative' and allows each person to favour those near and dear to him, but for utilitarianism each person is fundamentally morally equal to every other, and any favouritism must be justified by overall good consequences for people generally. This ends up making direct (or act-) utilitarianism a rather demanding moral doctrine, and opponents of such utilitarianism often criticize it for being too demanding. But this charge can be evaded or rendered less damaging if one adopts a form of direct utilitarianism that doesn't require the production of as much good/pleasure as possible as a condition of right action. Utilitarians must hold that producing more good is always *better*, but Bentham (in his earlier years), Karl Popper, and (more recently) Judith Lichtenberg, Michael Slote, and Michael Stocker have all formulated versions of act-utilitarianism allowing for an act to count as morally (all) right if it produces *enough* on-balance good/pleasure, even if the agent could have produced *more* on-balance good/pleasure. Such *'satisficing' utilitarianism allows for moral *supererogation and is therefore less demanding than more standard optimizing/maximizing versions of act-utilitarianism. But recent theorists such as Peter Railton, Samuel Scheffler, and Shelly Kagan have questioned whether the charge of overdemandingness really can be made to stick against standard forms of act-utilitarianism (and act-consequentialism).

Ordinary morality is also agent-relative in a way not mentioned above: it allows us to do to and against ourselves what we are not morally permitted to do to and against others. We are allowed to throw away our own possessions, but not those of others, and negligent self-damage is not criticized the way the negligent damaging of others is. Utilitarianism allows of no such moral distinctions. And, furthermore, in keeping with the justification of means by ends, act-utilitarianism treats it as morally permissible and even obligatory to kill or injure people in order to prevent other people from killing or injuring some greater number of people (or in order simply to prevent a greater number of deaths overall). Common sense, again, balks at such an instrumental view of morality, but although utilitarians have been much criticized for this aspect of their doctrine, defenders of common-sense (or of Kantian prohibitions on using people as means) have not found it easy to pinpoint what is morally indefensible in utilitarian instrumentalism. The utilitarian can say, for example, that although she sometimes recommends using people as means to the general or overall (greatest) welfare of human beings, such 'using' is not morally objectionable because (unlike most ways people use other people) it acknowledges the value of each individual human and her happiness. The topic is a subject of continuing philosophical debate.

The great strength of utilitarianism as an ethical theory lies in its ability to replace the hodgepodge (and, arguably, inconsistency) of our common-sense moral intuitions with a unified system of thought that treats all moral questions in uniform fashion and in relation to an ideal, human happiness or desire-satisfaction, that is both less obscure and more attractive than most alternatives.   M.S.

J. Bentham, *An Introduction to the Principles of Morals and Legislation* (London, 1982).

S. Kagan, *The Limits of Morality* (Oxford, 1989).

J. S. Mill, *Utilitarianism* (1863).

H. Sidgwick, *The Methods of Ethics*, 7th edn. (Chicago, 1962).

J. J. C. Smart and B. A. O. Williams, *Utilitarianism: For and Against* (Cambridge, 1973).

utility refers in philosophy to what is of use to human beings (or sometimes, more generally, to all sentient creatures). It therefore denotes what is good for humans, most frequently welfare. Argued to be of fundamental importance for ethics by Cicero and Hume, it was promoted by Bentham as the sole end of right action; hence the doctrine known as *utilitarianism. For Bentham utility meant *happiness or *pleasure; a more particular sense which has sometimes been preserved by later philosophers.

                                                            R.H.

R. D. Collison Black, 'Utility', in John Eatwell *et al.* (eds.), *The New Palgrave*, iv (London, 1987).

utility, principle of: *see* greatest happiness principle; utilitarianism.

utopianism. Critical and creative thinking projecting alternative social worlds that would realize the best possible way of being, based on rational and moral principles, accounts of human nature and history, or imagined technological possibilities. Utopian thinking invariably contains criticism of the status quo. It aims to overcome social *inequality, economic *exploitation, sexual repression, and other possible forms of domination that make well-being and happiness in this life impossible; death is thus often seen as its critical limit. Utopian thought like Plato's *Republic*, Thomas More's classic *Utopia* (1515–16), Tommaso Campanella's *La Città del Sole* (1623), and the social utopianism of Saint-Simon, Fourier, and Owen, concentrates on conceptions of an ideal commonwealth.

While both criticizing social life and aiming at new forms of it, utopianism nevertheless attempts to transcend the boundaries of so-called realistic and pragmatic considerations. The tension thereby created between utopian thought and social reality has led to harsh criticisms of its fantastic character. The derivation of 'utopia' is Greek words meaning 'not-place', and utopianism is generally identified with unrealistic speculation, providing the adjective 'utopian' with its everyday pejorative meaning. While Marx and Engels, for example, emphasized utopianism's positive function of relativizing existing social reality, they nevertheless criticized its lack of a thorough comprehension and analysis of current society that alone would make concrete political action possible. Thus utopianism is rejected by Marxism not because of its potential in alternative imaginative thinking but rather because of its theoretical unconnectedness with the social status quo.

Thinkers like Bloch and Marcuse, however, distinguish between 'abstract' and 'concrete' utopias. The former are mere dreams and fantasies, while the latter are based on insights derived from critical social theory. Utopian thought is seen as springing from the unconscious, whose imaginative capacity confronts, challenges, surpasses, and overrides conscious reality by means of projected counter-pictures containing hopes, desires, and wishful thinking. This utopian faculty, however, is only critical if disconnected from existing *ideologies, and based on an understanding of social totality and the means of realizing better conditions of existence. As Mannheim points out, utopian thought is directed toward change of existing social structures while the function of ideologies is the preservation of the status quo. Of course, utopias as private or unrealizable fantasies may take on an ideological function of preserving what is, while religious or 'bourgeois' ideologies contain a utopian core by confronting existing suffering and injustice with the ideal of paradisaic or just forms of being.

Accordingly, utopianism is limited neither to a literary genre nor to specific conceptions of the good life. It rather plays a genuine role in relation to possible or intended change in existing social conditions. To be sure, the identification of utopian thinking with socialism has often led to an over-hasty dismissal of utopianism as such. Today, for instance, post-Marxist social theory tries to use 'the utopia of an ideal communication community' (Habermas) merely as a 'counterfactual' standard to judge existing reality, while post-structuralist philosophers like Foucault criticize even this ideal as 'utopian', describing modern society as a dystopia of all-pervasive power relations. Social movements like *feminism, the civil rights movement, and multiculturalism, however, seem to require—and allow!—more concrete alternatives to the existing state of affairs.

Concrete and responsible utopian thinking may thus be an indispensable part of social criticism. First, the projection of alternative worlds helps to relativize the present; it creates distance and estrangement from the realm of assumed necessities of social life. Second, it explores concrete alternatives and realizable possibilities that could lead to practicable changes and improvements. And third, utopias seem indispensable for motivation. The sense of a better, realizable state of affairs not only gives meaning and significance to critical engagement, but also encourages interest in and hope of achieving real change in political action.   H.H.K.

E. Bloch, *The Principle of Hope* (Oxford, 1986).

R. Levitas, *The Concept of Utopia* (Syracuse, NY, 1990).

K. Mannheim, *Ideology and Utopia* (London, 1979).

V

vagueness. Words like 'smart', 'tall', and 'fat' are vague, since in most contexts of use there is no clear line separating them from 'not smart', 'not tall', and 'not fat' respectively. Vagueness needs to be distinguished from *ambiguity, which is a property of a word with two distinct meanings. Whereas 'is drunk' is vague; 'is at the bank' (river? commercial?) is ambiguous. Vague terms are said to be tolerant, in that they are used in settings where small changes (e.g. in colour) often make no difference to us. How we react to vagueness can vary. We can tolerate or even approve of vagueness, as when we engage in diplomatic negotiations. Or we can react less tolerantly by viewing vagueness as a kind of language failure ('I can't tell where your land ends and mine begins').   N.F.

Rosanna Keefe and Peter Smith (eds.), *Vagueness: A Reader* (Cambridge, 1997).

vague objects. If they exist, they challenge the common idea that reality itself is not vague, only our representations of it being so. If, for example, Mount Everest is a vague object, it has vague boundaries; some rocks are neither clearly part of it nor clearly not part of it. Thus the vagueness is not blamed on the name 'Everest', which is allowed to refer determinately to a unique, vague mountain. Vagueness may also infect temporal boundaries (e.g. the moment of death). Vague objects are identical only if they have the same clear parts and the same clear non-parts; it is controversial whether this relation too can be vague. One can suppose an object vague without supposing it indeterminate, if one (controversially) regards its vagueness as the impossibility of finding its sharp boundaries.   T.W.

T. Williamson, *Vagueness* (London, 1994).

Vaihinger, Hans (1852–1933). German philosopher, who from his study of Kant and Nietzsche derived the *Philosophy of As If* (*Die Philosophie des Als Ob* (1911; tr. London, 1924)). Sensations and feelings are real, but the rest of human knowledge consists of pragmatically justified 'fictions'. The laws of logic are fictions that have proved their indispensable worth in experience and are thus held to be undeniably true. Of a religious or metaphysical doctrine, we should ask not whether it is true in some non-pragmatist sense (we cannot discover this), but whether it is useful to act *as if* it were true. (The concepts of fiction and as-if vary, Vaihinger concedes, according to different types of truth, e.g. logical, scientific, religious.)

The theory involves familiar, though not necessarily insurmountable, difficulties. In saying that we should act as if a doctrine were 'true', it presupposes a perhaps ineliminable non-pragmatist notion of truth. (If we explicate this occurrence of 'true' in pragmatist terms, we fall into an infinite regress: 'We should act as if we should act as if, etc.') According to the theory, claims about the utility of holding doctrines, and indeed the theory itself, will themselves be no more than useful fictions.   M.J.I.

*pragmatism.

A. Seidel (ed.), *Die Philosophie des Als Ob und das Leben: Festschrift zu Hans Vaihingers 80 Geburtst* (Berlin, 1932).

validity. In logic, validity is most commonly attributed to either:

1. Deductive arguments, which are such that if the premisses are true the conclusion must be true. Traditional logic studies the validity of syllogistic arguments. Modern logic, more generally, identifies as valid those arguments which accord with truth-preserving rules. (*Salva veritate*.) Any argument is valid if and only if the set consisting of its premisses and the negation of its conclusion is inconsistent.

2. Propositions which are semantically valid, i.e. are true under any alternative interpretation of the non-logical words.

In a formal uninterpreted system of logic a derivation is (syntactically) valid where it is in accordance with specified axioms or rules.   R.B.M.

*completeness; theorem; logic, traditional.

B. Mates, *Elementary Logic* (Oxford, 1972).

Valla, Lorenzo (*c*.1407–57). Italian humanist who promoted rhetoric, grammar, and philology at the expense of scholastic logic and metaphysics. He reduced logic to a tool of rhetoric and held that most metaphysical terminology was nothing more than ungrammatical jargon which should be replaced by a philosophical discourse based on the accepted usage of the best ancient Latin authors. Highly critical of the philosophical theology of medieval thinkers such as Aquinas, he wanted to return to the rhetorical theology of the Church Fathers. For Valla certain issues, such as the compatibility of divine predestination and human *free will, had to be accepted as matters of faith and were not open to rational investigation. In ethics, he championed a Christianized version of *Epicureanism, which saw the highest good in the pleasure which the soul attains in the afterlife.   J.A.K.

O. Besomi and M. Regoliosi (eds.), *Lorenzo Valla e l'umanesimo italiano* (Padua, 1986).

value. Philosophical concern with value has focused on three connected issues: first, on what sort of property or characteristic of something its 'having value' or 'being of value' is; second, on whether having value is an objective or subjective matter, whether value reposes in the object or is a matter of how we feel towards it; third, on trying to say what things have value, are valuable. These concerns closely parallel concerns with the nature of good, from which value is seldom carefully distinguished in philosophical discussion, though the terms are clearly not synonymous.

In regard to the first concern, the value something has is clearly not a property of it which can be discerned by the senses or by scientific measuring instruments. This may be because it is a *sui generis* property, requiring a special sort of awareness or thought process to detect it. Or it could be a relational property of things, such as their meeting human needs; or not a property of things at all but rather a matter of the loving regard we pay to things. Something would thus be called 'valuable' in so far as we cherish it, though common-sense might well say that this gets matters the wrong way round: we cherish it because it is valuable.

Plainly, the view reached about what sort of characteristic having value is will strongly influence any view about whether it is an objective or subjective matter. Presumably if having value is a *sui generis* property, then whether or not something has value cannot depend on human opinion, but is a matter of fact. On the other hand if to bear a cherishing regard towards something is what thinking it valuable consists in, then it would seem that whether something has value is a subjective issue. It can be argued that such regard could be appropriate or inappropriate, and thus some standard of correctness of attitude could be introduced, giving some measure of objectivity.

On the third matter, of what things have value, clearly the list is endless. Many things have value to people because of a special role they play in their lives. This is not to be confused with a subjective theory of the nature of value. It could be an objective truth that something which holds special significance in the life of a person will have value for that person. Other things, such as human life, are sometimes said to have absolute value. Value may be inherent or intrinsic or relational, extrinsic.

The task of a 'valuer' of jewellery or property is an interesting one. Does he, like Oscar Wilde's cynic, 'know the price of everything and the value of nothing'? Or does he have more discerning judgement than the rest of us? Or perhaps indeed his approval helps to *set* the value of the thing he is looking at.   N.J.H.D.

*good; axiological ethics; ethics and aesthetics; supervaluation.

Notable discussions of these, and, many related topics are:
J. N. Findlay, *Values and Intentions* (London, 1966).
N. Hartmann, *Ethics* (London, 1932).
J. Laird, *The Idea of Value* (Cambridge, 1929).
C. I. Lewis, *An Analysis of Knowledge and Valuation* (La Salle, Ill., 1946).

value, aesthetic. We say that the performance of an opera was good, that one painting is a finer example of a certain style than another, or that a combination of colours looks just right. The 'good', 'fine', and 'right', in these cases appear to concern a kind of value which is neither moral value, nor utility value, nor the rightness of being true. We have to acknowledge that there is a peculiarly aesthetic way of being 'good' or 'right', or at least that people talk as if there is. The traditional way of marking out aesthetic value from truth, goodness, or utility is to provide an account of *beauty.

With all *value, philosophers will sooner or later ask whether it is objective or subjective, whether it is really in the objects of which we appear to predicate it, or only a product of the mind of the judging subject. If the former, it is arguable that what is 'in' the object will be a power to affect the mind in a certain way, so that a thing may have a real value in a way parallel to its having a real colour, as some would see it. In the history of aesthetics, views range from the notion that beauty resides as an objective property in objects, through to ideas more akin to the popular saying 'Beauty is in the eye of the beholder'. Philosophers should be wary of subscribing to this slogan. For there is public discourse about aesthetic standards, and *aesthetic judgements are usually put forward as true, not merely as reports of one person's subjective response. The central problem concerning aesthetic value is that it is not merely in the eye of the beholder, while yet it seems to require the eye of the beholder in order to exist.   C.J.

I. Kant, *Critique of Judgement*, tr. J. C. Meredith (Oxford, 1969).
E. Schaper (ed.), *Pleasure, Preference and Value: Studies in Philosophical Aesthetics* (Cambridge, 1983).

value, error theory of: *see* error theory of value.

value, instrumental: *see* instrumental value.

values, transvaluation of: *see* transvaluation of values.

values and facts: *see* fact–value distinction.

van Fraassen, Bas C. (1941–). Princeton logician and philosopher of science who, in *The Scientific Image* (1980), develops a well-reasoned anti-realist empiricist alternative to both the *Logical Positivism of

Rudolf Carnap and the scientific realism of Wilfrid Sellars and Hilary Putnam. For the realist, the point of constructing scientific theories is to 'aim to give us a literally true story of what the world is like'. So accepting any scientific theory is supposed to involve, automatically, belief that terms describing postulated structures and processes have existential import. Van Fraassen attacks this position and defends an alternative: empirical adequacy is the only aim of scientific theorizing. The belief that the theory fits the observable phenomena is the only belief involved in accepting a scientific theory; explanatory power is not grounds for believing that all theoretical terms refer. In *Laws and Symmetry* (1989), van Fraassen argues against a realist construal of *laws of nature and natural necessities.

B.T.

*realism and anti-realism.

Paul M. Churchland and Clifford A. Hooker (eds.), *Images of Science: Essays on Realism and Empiricism, with a Reply from Bas C. van Fraassen* (Chicago, 1985).

B. C. van Fraassen, *The Empirical Stance* (New Haven, Conn., 2002).

variable. A letter substituted for one or more occurrences of an expression in a wider expression, as in '*x* admires *x*'. When a *quantifier is prefixed to this, the variable is 'bound'. Only if repeated variables or two or more quantifiers are involved is this apparatus necessary, the letter attached to each prefixed quantifier indicating which variable it binds in the remaining sentence. See the example given in the entry 'quantifier'.

C.J.F.W.

W. V. Quine, 'Variables Explained Away', in *Selected Logic Papers* (New York, 1966).

variable realization. An argument of Hilary Putnam's against the type-*identity theory of mind: the theory that mental properties are physical properties. On this view, every instance of a mental property is an instance of the physical property with which that mental property is identical. But it seems very unlikely that every instance of pain is an instance of the same brain property. A creature could have a very different physical nature from us, yet still be in pain: this possibility renders the type-identity theory empirically implausible.

T.C.

*realization.

Hilary Putnam, 'The Mental Life of Some Machines', in *Mind, Language and Reality: Philosophical Papers*, ii (Cambridge, 1975).

Vattimo, Gianni (1936–). A scholar of nineteenth- and twentieth-century German philosophy, which he teaches at the University of Turin, he is the leading Italian theorist of *post-modernism. Vattimo believes that the modern, *Enlightenment project of human emancipation as the unfolding of reason through the self-conscious appropriation of nature and the rational organization of society, has been undermined by the effects of new technology and the mass media upon contemporary societies. These developments have produced a complex and fragmented world, in which the continual elaboration of numerous heterogeneous interpretative schemata has removed the possibility of any privileged or 'objective' point of view upon which to build a unitary or progressive conception of human history. He argues that this situation produces a 'weak ontology' that demands a corresponding weakening of philosophy's traditional metaphysical aspirations in the direction of 'weak thought' (*pensiero debole*), an approach he associates with the notions of *nihilism and difference elaborated by Nietzsche and Heidegger.

R.P.B.

Richard Bellamy, 'Post-Modernism and the End of History', *Theory, Culture and Society* (1987).

Vedānta. End or cream of the revealed scriptures of the Hindus (collectively called 'Veda'), which traditionally includes the more philosophical *Upanishads, a root-text called *Brahma Sūtras*, and the ethico-religious text *Bhagavadgītā*. The philosophy contained in the Upanishads is polemically distilled in the *Brahma Sūtras*, which are aphorisms regarding the Supreme Reality. These aphorisms, ascribed to Bādarāyaṇa (second or first century BC) controvert heterodox views like atheism, and respond to the problem of evil, naturalism, no-self theories, etc. They seek to establish God as the material and efficient cause of the cosmos, they analyse dreaming, deep sleep, life after death, re-embodiment, and the state of liberation, and they prescribe techniques of meditation leading to that state. Competing commentaries on the *Brahma Sūtras* engendered schools of Vedānta such as the non-dualism of *Śaṇkara, the qualified monism of *Rāmānuja, the dualism of *Madhva, the identity-in-difference of Nīmbarka, etc.

Non-dualist Vedānta upholds absolute subjective consciousness as the only reality, regards the external world of plurality as false appearance, and establishes that the individual self is strictly identical with that absolute consciousness. This eventually enables each of us to realize the Vedic truth 'I am all that exists'. Qualified monists and dualists reject the above monistic views and interpret the *Brahma Sūtras* differently.

In the late nineteenth century Śrī Ramakrishna, an unlettered mystic saint, rejuvenated Vedantic Hinduism, winning over Christian missionaries and Unitarian-influenced reformers by reaffirming the catholic Vedic truth that the same spiritual goal of God-realization can be attained through many alternative routes adopted by different religions of the world. His disciple Swami Vivekānanda stole the show at the 1893 Parliament of Religions in Chicago by his eloquent opposition to sectarian exclusivism and advocacy of what he later called 'practical Vedānta', i.e. an active recognition of the divinity in every living being to be achieved by serving each living being like God. This is more than altruism or social service because it has to be based on contemplative faith in the spiritual oneness of all.

Among professional philosophers the influence of Kant and Hegel mingled with the resurrection of Vedānta to produce neo-Vedāntists like K. C. Bhattacharya, whose strikingly original phenomenology of bodily, introspective, and spiritual subjectivity yields a very subtle but ill-understood theory of the 'unmeant' self as freedom from all objectification.   A.C.

K. C. Bhattacharya, *Search for the Absolute in Neo-Vedānta* (Honolulu, 1976).
Eliot Deutsch, *Advaita Vedānta: A Philosophical Reconstruction* (Honolulu, 1969).

Veda, Vedic: *see* Indian philosophy; Vedānta.

vegetarianism. The view that we should avoid eating meat or fish has ancient philosophical roots. In the Hindu *Upanishads (about 1000 BC) the doctrine of reincarnation leads to opposition to eating meat. Buddha taught compassion for all sentient creatures. Buddhist monks were not to kill *animals, nor to eat meat, unless they knew that the animal had not been killed for their sake. Jains hold to *ahimsa*, or non-violence toward any living creature, and accordingly do not eat meat.

In the Western tradition, Genesis suggests that the first diet of human beings was vegetarian, and permission to eat meat was given only after the Flood. After that, vegetarianism gains little support from either the Jewish or Christian scriptures, or from Islam. Philosophical vegetarianism was stronger in ancient Greece and Rome: it was supported by Pythagoras, Empedocles, Plutarch, Plotinus, Porphyry, and, in some passages, Plato. Pythagoreans abstained from eating animals partly because of their belief that humans and animals share a common soul, and partly because they appear to have considered the diet a healthier one. Plato shared both these views to some extent. Plutarch's essay *On Eating Flesh*, written in the late first or early second century of the Christian era, is a detailed argument for vegetarianism on grounds of justice and humane treatment of animals.

Interest in vegetarianism revived in the nineteenth century, on grounds of health and humanity towards animals. Notable vegetarian thinkers included the poet Percy Bysshe Shelley, Henry Salt (who wrote a pioneering volume entitled *Animals' Rights*), and George Bernard Shaw, who said that he put into his plays the ideas that he learned from Salt. In Germany Arthur Schopenhauer urged that ethically we should become vegetarian, were it not for the fact that the human race cannot exist without animal food 'in the north'!

Since the 1970s vegetarianism has gained strength from three major lines of argument: health, ecology, and concern for animals. The first of these grounds rests on a scientific, rather than philosophical, claim and will not be discussed further here. Ecological concerns about eating meat arise from the well-documented inefficiency of much animal-raising. This applies especially to intensive farming, in which grain is grown on good agricultural land and fed to animals confined indoors, or in the case of cattle, in crowded feed-lots. Much of the nutritional value of the grain is lost in the process, and this form of animal production is also energy-intensive. Hence concern for world hunger, for the land, and for energy conservation provide an ethical basis for a vegetarian diet, or at least one in which meat consumption is minimized.

Arguments for a reassessment of the moral status of animals have also given support to vegetarianism. If animals have rights, or are entitled to have their interests given equal consideration with the similar interests of human beings, it is easy to see that there are difficulties in claiming that we are entitled to eat non-human animals (but not, presumably, human beings, even if through some accident they are at a similar mental level to the animals we do eat). These ethical arguments for vegetarianism may be based on the view that we violate the rights of animals when we kill them for our food, or on the more utilitarian grounds that, in raising them for our food, we cause them more suffering than we gain by eating their flesh.   P.S.

Keith Akers, *A Vegetarian Sourcebook*, 2nd edn. (Denver, 1989).
Francis Moore Lappé, *Diet for a Small Planet*, 2nd edn. (New York, 1985).
Tom Regan and Peter Singer (eds.), *Animal Rights and Human Obligations*, 2nd edn. (Englewood Cliffs, NJ, 1989).

veil of ignorance. The setting-aside of all information about your distinguishing social characteristics, to ensure a fair choice of principles of justice. In Rawls's theory, it is a feature of the *original position, an imaginary situation in which you are supposed to make a blind choice of principles, as if not knowing what position you occupy in society—not knowing your race, sex, religion, wealth, talents, or ultimate values and aims in life. The idea is that this will force you to choose as if you might be in any social position, so that you must take into account the interests of everyone equally, thus ensuring fairness to all.   T.N.

J. Rawls, *A Theory of Justice* (Cambridge, Mass., 1971).

veil of perception. This is a sceptical problem that arises for a certain analysis of perception. If our senses only reveal knowledge about how things *seem*, how can we hope to use them to find out how things really *are*? The appearances are in danger of obstructing rather than helping us in our attempts to discern the nature of reality.

The obvious way to escape this difficulty is to hold that in perception we are directly aware of material things, not just of appearances; the name for such a position is *naïve or direct realism. Something still needs to be said about appearances. One promising line is the adverbial theory, which holds that appearances themselves are not the primary objects for the mind, but the way in which our primary objects are presented.   J.D.

F. Jackson, *Perception* (Cambridge, 1977).

vengeance: *see* revenge.

verifiability: *see* verification principle.

verification principle. This, also called the Verifiability Principle, has two forms: (1) The meaning of a statement is the method of its verification. (2) A statement is meaningful if and only if it is in principle verifiable. (1) implies (2) but not all recognize the converse implication. Verification may cover only observational procedures, in which case the principle is applied only to 'factual' statements, allegedly analytic statements (including pure mathematics), somehow true by definition, receiving a separate treatment. Alternatively, verification may cover calculations for establishing these. The verification principle was a main tenet of the original Logical Positivists, inspired by remarks of Wittgenstein. Prominent supporters have included Moritz Schlick and A. J. Ayer. Problems have been its judgement on itself and the fact that any statement will have verifiable implications if conjoined with suitably chosen others. None the less the general idea that genuinely factual knowledge must increase our powers of empirical prediction has influenced many.   T.L.S.S

*Logical Positivism; verificationism; nonsense.

verificationism. Any view which embraces some version of the *verification principle. Verificationists characterize the meaning of a proposition, or the conditions required for a proposition to have meaning, in terms of the difference its truth makes to the senses, the conditions under which it is verified (or falsified) by empirical test. Variations on both the principle itself and its implications are possible. Perhaps the most influential thinkers in this neighbourhood are gathered together under the banner of *Logical Positivism—A. J. Ayer, Rudolph Carnap, Herbert Feigle, Ernest Nagel, Otto Neurath, Moritz Schlick and others—all offering articulations of both the verification principle and its implications for metaphysics, aesthetics, and ethics. Some phenomenalist philosophers have derived from verificationism the view that statements about physical objects are reducible to talk of sense-data, actual and possible sense experiences. The difficulty, which most take as decisive, is that the list of conditional observation statements for any reduction would be very long and worryingly vague. Abandoning reduction, Carnap was led to conclude that the best one can hope for is a specification of the observation statements implied by particular non-observation statements. Quine, holding that theories are underdetermined by evidence and following Duhem's claim that non-observation sentences cannot be verified individually, did not on those grounds reject verificationism, but instead concluded that a non-observation sentence has no meaning in isolation, has no empirical consequences of its own, makes no difference to our senses individually. Individual sentences mean what they do only against the backdrop of the theory in which they are embedded.   J.GAR.

A. J. Ayer, *Language, Truth and Logic* (London, 1946).
R. Carnap, *The Logical Structure of the World* (London, 1967).
W. V. O. Quine, *From a Logical Point of View* (Cambridge, Mass., 1953).

verisimilitude. A concept of central importance within Popper's anti-inductivist philosophy of science, but also of independent interest. Given a view of science as a paradigm of rational activity, it seems natural to take its goal to be the production of true theories. But all past *theories have turned out to be false, and only wild immodesty could let us suppose that currently accepted theories will escape such an ultimate fate. How can it be rational to pursue an unattainable goal? How can there be scientific progress in these circumstances? One answer is to suggest that science has the more limited goal of developing theories which approximate more closely to the *truth, i.e. possess increasing verisimilitude. However, there are severe problems involved both in defining and in developing a measure or ranking-mechanism of, verisimilitude.   J.L.

W. H. Newton-Smith, *The Rationality of Science* (London, 1981).

Veritatis Splendor. The title, taken from its opening words, 'The Splendour of Truth', of the most widely discussed of recent papal encyclicals. In it Pope John Paul II responds to *subjectivism, *relativism, and *consequentialism, and reaffirms traditional Catholic teaching that there is an objective universal moral order (*natural law) involving intrinsic goods and evils. The philosophical exposition and argument draw primarily upon Thomist and neo-Kantian moral theories. The main philosophical discussion is in a section called 'The Moral Act', where it is argued that 'The rational ordering of the human act to the good in its truth and the voluntary pursuit of that good, known by reason, constitute morality. Hence human activity cannot be judged as morally good merely because it is a means for attaining one or another of its goals, or simply because the subject's intention is good.'   J.HAL.

Veritatis Splendor: Encyclical Letter Regarding Certain Fundamental Questions of the Church's Moral Teaching (London, 1993).

Verstehen. Although this is the ordinary German word for understanding, philosophers have often invested it with special senses. For Kant, understanding is the faculty, distinguished from sensibility and reason, whereby sensory items are brought under concepts. Within *hermeneutics (the study of interpretation) and the *social sciences, however, it usually has the sense given it by Wilhelm Dilthey: an interpretative understanding sharply distinguished from the explanatory understanding, in terms of natural laws, sought in the natural sciences. *Verstehen* is therefore confined to the humane sciences (*Geisteswissenschaften*). While, for Dilthey, *Verstehen* requires an empathetic 're-living' of the 'mental life' of those whose 'expressions'—texts, actions, etc.—we seek to interpret, his main emphasis is upon identifying the expressions' meanings by locating them in larger cultural wholes. 'Meaning means nothing except belonging to a whole' (1968, p. 233). An expression is only fully understood when referred back to the total cultural 'life-form' (*form of life) that it manifests. The distinctive character of *Verstehen* informs the writings of such social theorists as Alfred Schutz and Peter Winch. D.E.C.

W. Dilthey, *Dilthey: Selected Writings*, tr. H. P. Rickman (Cambridge, 1968).

A. O'Hear (ed.), Verstehen *and Humane Understanding* (Cambridge, 1996).

vices. States of bad or undesirable character, definable partly in contrast to *virtues. The favoured list of vices varies across time and place, depending on differences in corresponding conceptions of virtue. Thus, the change from classical pagan to medieval Christian morality brought with it a change of emphasis from the virtues of courage and temperance to the virtues of love and charity, with corresponding vices being defined in contrast to these virtues. On the classical Aristotelian view, a paradigmatic vice consists in the possession of some character trait out of proportion to the nature of its associated object. Thus, a coward is someone who fears what is not dangerous. On this view, vice is understood negatively in terms of a failure to possess virtuous character traits. One limitation of this view is that it fails to fully account for such bad character traits as cruelty, maliciousness, and spite, which consist partly in an agent consciously aiming for the bad. H.L.

*virtue.

M. Midgley, *Wickedness* (London, 1984).

vicious circle. An argument assuming its conclusion as a premiss (*begging the question), or a definition of an expression in terms of itself. Russell argued that paradoxes in the foundations of mathematics—for example, his paradox of the class of all classes that are not members of themselves—depend on a kind of vicious circularity, violating the maxim 'Whatever involves all of a collection must not be one of the collection'. M.C.

*vicious-circle principle.

vicious-circle principle. First propounded by Poincaré in 1906 as a diagnosis of the contradictions then besetting logicism. The basic idea is that a vicious circle is involved if, in the definition of an object of some kind, we quantify over all objects of the same kind. Definitions with this feature are called 'impredicative', others 'predicative'. (For example, the set of all natural numbers is commonly defined as the *least* set containing 0 and containing the successor of everything it contains. But this definition is impredicative, since the 'least' such set means the one that is a subset of *all* such sets.) Russell claimed to base his theory of *types upon this principle, but that claim can hardly be upheld. Gödel observed that from a Platonist standpoint there need be nothing wrong with impredicative definitions, though they should be suspected by the conceptualist, who holds that abstract objects exist only as a result of our constructions. D.B.

*predicative theories; constructivism; impredicative definition.

K. Gödel, 'Russell's Mathematical Logic', in P. A. Schilpp (ed.), *The Philosophy of Bertrand Russell* (Evanston, Ill., 1944).

B. Russell, 'Mathematical Logic as Based on the Theory of Types', in R. C. Marsh (ed.), *Logic and Knowledge* (London, 1956).

Vico, Giambattista (1668–1744). Arguably the most significant Italian philosopher, he was Professor of Rhetoric at the university of his native Naples from 1699. Underlying Vico's thought is the principle that 'the true (*verum*) and the made (*factum*) are convertible', so that we can only know for certain that which we have created. The natural sciences can only yield approximate truths based on our attempts to imitate nature in experiments, whereas the human sciences can offer exact knowledge because societies are our own creations. Vico used this thesis in his *The New Science* of 1725 to develop a whole philosophy of history that anticipated many of the central tenets of nineteenth-century *historicism. He argued that historical change parallels the passage of the individual from birth to maturity and ultimately death, so that history follows a cyclical pattern of *corsi* and *ricorsi* in which linguistic, cultural, intellectual, political, and economic development are all interrelated. Past societies had to be understood in their own terms, and social change was to be seen as the unintended and providential product of the evolving needs, reason, and interests of essentially egoistic individuals. R.P.B.

L. Pompa, *Vico* (Cambridge, 1975).

Vienna Circle (Wiener Kreis). A group whose work was central to the development of *Logical Positivism. The Circle emerged from discussions, beginning in 1907, between Otto Neurath, a sociologist, Hans Hahn, a mathematician, and Philip Frank, a physicist. Like its founders, most Circle members, including its philosophers, had considerable scientific and mathematical training. The Circle flourished under the leadership of Moritz Schlick, who filled Ernst Mach's chair at the University of Vienna in 1922. But the rise of Nazism in the 1930s led to a diaspora of the Circle's members, many of whom were Jewish, Marxist, or both. Herbert Feigl left in 1931, arriving eventually at the University of Minnesota, where he helped build an influential philosophy of science programme. Rudolf Carnap, who came to Vienna in 1926, left in 1931. He was installed at the University of Chicago in 1936, the year Schlick was assassinated in Vienna on the university steps. In 1938 the Circle's last Vienna organization was officially dissolved, Neurath and Friedrich Waismann went to Oxford, and Kurt Gödel went to Princeton.

Tarski's work on the semantics of formal languages and Popper's attempts to explain the difference between real and spurious science were important influences on the Circle. Another was the work of Wittgenstein. His *Tractatus* was read aloud and studied line by line by Vienna Circle members, a few of whom were allowed to meet him—in diminishing numbers, and varying configurations and degrees of discomfort—from 1927 into the early 1930s. From these discussions emerged a strong version of the *'verification principle' according to which the significance of non-analytic sentences depends upon whether they can be tested, and utterances which are neither analytic nor empirically testable are meaningless. Different versions of this principle are distinguished by the strengths of their testability requirements.

Vienna Circle philosophizing utilized logical machinery invented by Frege, Russell, and Whitehead (long before its general acceptance) and formal techniques in semantics and inductive reasoning, many of which were invented or enriched by its members. These tools were applied to classical philosophical issues concerning the nature and possibility of knowledge. The main examples of knowledge the Circle urged philosophers to study came from the exact sciences, which it supposed were models of properly conducted inquiry whose epistemic standards should be extended to the social sciences. This, along with its demanding formalisms, helped make Vienna Circle philosophy unpopular among academics who considered their work more humane. So did the Circle's crusade against 'metaphysics', its derogatory term for discourse which purports to make substantive claims but which is susceptible neither to rigorous empirical testing nor to formally rigorous explication. It offended intellectuals to have words they lived by (and made a living from) condemned as metaphysics.

Others were unhappy for political reasons which should be taken seriously by anyone interested in the history of analytic philosophy. A host of German philosophers—Heidegger, for one—were promoting the idea that only pure Germans could understand, and should be allowed to teach, subjects bearing on German history and culture. Hitler, supported by no less than Nobel Laureate physicist Philipp Lenard, vowed to save German youth from un-German science, including relativity and quantum physics. The discourse used to justify such positions included some targets of the Circle's war against metaphysics. 'The tear is running . . . It'd be to throw up, if one didn't have to laugh . . . . behind it all stands Hitler . . . Here come God, and Religion . . . and ancestral truths, and the German *Volk*, and what you need to stab a Jewish socialist . . . between the ribs . . . Oh Carnap! Oh World!' That was Neurath in 1932 (quoted in Gallison, 'Aufbau/Bauhaus', 742), describing the situation the Vienna Circle and other positivists faced as they developed and promulgated formal methods in philosophy, set the agenda for twentieth-century philosophy of science, and helped to invent *analytical philosophy.   J.B.B.

T. R. Baldwin (ed.), *The Cambridge History of Philosophy 1870–1945* (Cambridge, 2003).

Rudolf Carnap, 'Intellectual Autobiography', in Paul Arthur Schilpp (ed.), *The Philosophy of Rudolf Carnap* (La Salle, Ill., 1963).

J. Alberto Coffa, *The Semantic Tradition from Kant to Carnap: To the Vienna Station* (Cambridge, 1991).

Peter Gallison, 'Aufbau/Bauhaus: Logical Positivism and Architectural Modernism', *Critical Inquiry* (1990).

violence, democratic: *see* democratic violence.

violence, political. Resort to force for political ends, outside its normal use in international warfare or in the internal administration of justice. Political violence covers a wide spectrum from stone-throwing at demonstrations to *revolution and civil war. Violence is conventionally distinguished from force in general as unlawful; thus political violence oversteps the limits placed upon the lawful pursuit of political purposes. Indeed the breaking of laws is sometimes part of the point of violent protest, as it is in *civil disobedience; for political violence is characteristically expressive of its political purposes (e.g. by challenging the authority of the *state to enforce its laws) rather than simply instrumental in achieving them (e.g. by undermining the power of the state).

*Terrorism is the paradigm of political violence, but it eludes easy definition. One type of analysis views it as political killing rendered illegitimate, in contrast to tyrannicide, either by the availability of peaceful alternatives or by its targeting of innocent citizens rather than responsible politicians. Another type regards terrorism as low-level warfare directed, contrary to the principles of the *just war, against harmless civilians, often owing to the terrorists' lack of adequate resources to defeat a military force. Neither analysis seems adequate to cover what is regularly referred to as terrorism, namely, activity which is regarded by its protagonists as part of a war and by its opponents as common crime (or, perhaps, as a crime against humanity but not, strictly speaking, as a war crime).

Characterizing terrorism in these terms we can sensibly ask: When, if ever, is terrorism justified? On some theories of deontological ethics it is never justified, either because it inevitably involves the death of innocents, or because it is in breach of political obligations. Under *utilitarianism, however, it may be justified if it is likely to avert a greater evil. Typically terrorists not only appeal to utilitarian considerations but also answer deontologists by arguing either that innocents are unintended victims who suffer no more, and perhaps less, than in conventional war, or that the citizens who are targeted have collective responsibility as members of an oppressor group. Terrorists also deny the existence of political obligations to a state which is oppressive or which they refuse to recognize, e.g. when they are actuated by *nationalism. In neither case, they argue, are there adequate alternatives to the adoption of military means for pursuing their political goals. As a result, terrorists, under the influence of one or other of the analyses mentioned above, deny that they *are* terrorists, rather than freedom fighters etc., since on these analyses terrorism is always unjustified.

Political violence includes not only the use of force against the state, but also some of its uses by, or on behalf of, the state, e.g. state terrorism, as directed against minority groups under Fascism. Though the law may be changed to accommodate it, it still has the criminal character of terrorism, since 'unjust law is not law', while it is intended as part of a war against those to whom the state recognizes no obligation of care. The distinction between political violence and the ostensibly legitimate use of force may itself be called into question if the actions of some, or all, states are thought of as aimed at terrorizing their subjects into submission. Such *'structural violence' is, in a loose sense, criminal, through infringing natural rights, and warlike, since 'government is begotten of aggression and by aggression' (Herbert Spencer). It may be held to justify a response comprising more overt political violence.   P.G.

Ted Honderich, *Terrorism for Humanity* (London, 2004).
Burleigh Taylor Williams, *Terrorism and Collective Responsibility* (London, 1992).

violence, structural: *see* structural violence.

virtue, unity of. This doctrine is advanced by Plato, Aristotle, and other ancient philosophers, although its correct interpretation has been the subject of much scholarly debate. Understood as the claim that having one virtue entails having them all, it is defended in many recent formulations of virtue ethics.

The following line of thought seems to support the doctrine: the proper scope of each virtue is determined collectively by the others. We would not describe someone's action, motivated by the desire to spare *x*'s feelings, as 'kind' if it involved his knowingly being unfair to *y*. Against this, opponents claim that one can, without contradiction, describe a villain as brave. And do we not observe, in different individuals, that people may excel in some virtues while lacking others?

While the doctrine appears to require empirical confirmation, its defenders typically appeal to conceptual constraints, such as the claim that virtue must issue in right conduct.   S.D.R.

Philippa Foot, 'Virtues and Vices', reprinted in her *Virtues and Vices* (Oxford, 1978, 2002).
John McDowell, 'Virtue and Reason', reprinted in his *Mind, Value and Reality* (Cambridge, Mass., 1998).

virtue epistemology. Virtue epistemologists attempt to apply to epistemology the insights of virtue ethics. Virtue epistemologists do not say that a justified belief is one suitably related to something foundational, or one that is a member of a coherent set; they say that it is one that a virtuous cognizer, someone with the cognitive virtues, would have. They tend then to give a complex picture of cognitive virtues; the virtues of the rational enquirer need not be restricted to (say) the ability to discover truths and avoid errors, but are many and various, perhaps including such traits as imaginativeness, a sense of the absurd, and some blend of epistemic stubbornness and modesty.   J.D.

G. Axtell (ed.), *Knowledge, Belief and Character: Readings in Virtue Epistemology* (Oxford, 2000).

virtues. Almost all systematic approaches to ethics have something to say about what traits count as virtues and about the character of virtue as a whole. A distinction is typically made between intellectual and moral/ethical virtues, but there is an important difference also between those traditions of moral theory that highlight and focus on virtue—which can be classed together under the title 'virtue ethics'—and approaches to ethics that make room for an account of virtue(s) only alongside, and by way of supplementing, the main business of formulating the ultimate principles or rules of morality. For the latter, virtues and virtue are effectively the internal analogue of (a set of) moral principles—they amount to dispositions to obey or follow what the rules prescribe (as, mainly, with *Kantianism) or else (as with direct *utilitarianism) to dispositions whose existence furthers the same goals as are specified in principles of right action.

By contrast, various forms of virtue ethics play down the importance or even deny the existence of generally valid moral rules or principles, and claim that morality is most fundamentally to be understood in terms of inner traits, virtues, that cannot be cashed out in terms of rules or goals. Aristotelian virtue ethics regards matters of right and wrong as unencapsulable in rules, and describes the virtuous individual as someone who perceives and fairly effortlessly acts upon situationally unique moral requirements. And philosophers such as Elizabeth Anscombe, Philippa Foot, Rosalind Hursthouse, John McDowell, Martha Nussbaum, Amélie Rorty, Michael Stocker, and Michael Slote have sought to develop versions or aspects of *Aristotelianism that are sensitive to the current situation in ethical theory. Other forms of virtue ethics— arguably those defended, for example, by Plato and James Martineau (a nineteenth-century British ethicist)—think of the virtuous agent not as perceiving what is independently right or noble to do, but as having independently admirable motives or other inner states whose very expression in her actions serves to *make* those actions right or admirable. For Plato, virtue is an inner state, is the harmony, health, beauty, or strength of a soul made up of interacting parts or aspects, and right or just action is action that sustains or enhances inner virtue. Such a view treats the morality of actions as derivative from the morality or ethics of agents' inner states (in a way that Aristotle's theory of situationally perceived right or noble actions arguably does not), and one also finds such 'agent-basing' in Martineau's view, according to which there is an intuitive hierarchy of moral motives (reverence, followed by compassion, being at the top) and the rightness of actions depends on which of possibly conflicting motives determines one's actions. More recently, Michael Slote and Jorge Gracia have, respectively, begun to explore updated versions of Plato's inner-strength approach and Martineau's intuitive hierarchy.

Let us turn now to the discussion of particular virtues, which has varied over the centuries in a number of important ways. Ancient (virtue) ethics recognized four cardinal ethical virtues: temperance, justice, courage, and (practical) wisdom, but in the Middle Ages Christian philosophers tended to add three theological virtues: faith, hope, and charity or love, to the list of major virtues. In the ethics of Socrates, Plato, and Aristotle, a thesis of the *unity of the virtues* emerged as a pivotal doctrine, the idea being (very roughly) that each virtue requires that one be sensitive to potentially inconsistent claims deriving from the other virtues, so that in the end one cannot really possess one virtue without possessing them all. However, this doctrine is not widely accepted by those who have treated the virtues during the modern period. What *is* accepted and goes back to ancient times is the idea of virtues as dispositions, rather than skills or capacities. Someone who is *able* to control his appetites but in fact does not cannot be regarded as having the virtue of temperance or moderation. But there has, over the millennia, been strong disagreement about whether it is more virtuous and admirable to overcome strong temptations or to lack such temptations altogether. And in discussions of virtue(s) there has also been much disagreement over whether conscientious adherence to duty is morally preferable to 'natural' motivations like compassion or love as a basis for actions (Kant gives preference to the motive of conscientiousness and even says that other motives have no moral value, but in recent years a whole host of philosophers, including Philippa Foot, Michael Stocker, Lawrence Blum, and Bernard Williams, have opposed this view).

In recent years, the whole topic of virtue and the virtues has been of increasing interest to moral philosophers, and there are more and more philosophers who think a focus on virtue can form the basis for an entire free-standing account of morality and ethics.   M.S.

R. Crisp (ed.), *How Should One Live? Essays on the Virtues* (Oxford, 1996).
—— and M. Slote (eds.), *Virtue Ethics* (Oxford, 1997).
P. Foot, *Virtues and Vices* (Berkeley, Calif., 1978).
R. Hursthouse, *On Virtue Ethics* (Oxford, 2000).
A. Rorty (ed.), *Essays on Aristotle's Ethics* (Berkeley, Calif., 1980).
M. Slote, *From Morality to Virtue* (Oxford, 1992).

virtues, doxastic. Breaking down traditional barriers between epistemology and ethics, some philosophers stress the central roles of virtue and character in the evaluation of our doxastic life (believing, doubting, etc.). An assumption is made that doxastic states are voluntary in at least a weak sense. A person of virtuous doxastic character habitually avoids the vices of *scepticism and dogmatism while exhibiting such virtues as intellectual impartiality and courage. The doxastic states (e.g. beliefs) of such a balanced personality come about through a process that is responsible in a sense of 'responsible' similar to its sense when we speak of a father's parenting as responsible.

P.H.H.

*voluntarism, doxastic.

Jonathan L. Kvanvig, *The Intellectual Virtues and the Life of the Mind: On the Place of the Virtues in Contemporary Epistemology* (Savage, Md., 1992).

virtues, intellectual. The intellectual, or epistemic,

*virtues are those character traits of an agent that are conducive to the agent forming true beliefs and, thereby, gaining *knowledge. The character traits of being open-minded or conscientious could thus be regarded as intellectual virtues (though perhaps not exclusively: they may also be thought to be moral virtues). Although discussion of the intellectual virtues has always been a part of epistemology, in recent years it has come to the fore with the development of so-called virtue epistemologies, where the intellectual virtues take centre stage. For example, Linda Zagzebski offers a broadly Aristotelian account of the intellectual virtues which presents an integrated account of the moral and intellectual virtues in terms of the kind of character that an agent needs if she is to lead the good life. This is in contrast to the type of *reliabilism proposed by Ernest Sosa, who argues that an intellectual virtue might merely be a reliable cognitive faculty of the agent, such as the faculty of sight, and thus need not be part of the agent's intellectual character at all.

D.PRI.

E. Sosa, 'Knowledge and Intellectual Virtue', *Monist*, 68 (1985).
L. Zagzebski, *Virtues of the Mind: An Inquiry into the Nature of Virtue and the Ethical Foundations of Knowledge* (Cambridge, 1996).

virtuous circle. Particular deductions must conform to general logical principles; but such principles must conform to accepted deductive practice. For Goodman, this circularity is virtuous and means only that our principles and practices should be brought into agreement. But if this involves the amendment of both principle and practice, it is not clear that what we have here is properly speaking a circle at all.   M.C.

*vicious circle.

N. Goodman, *Fact, Fiction, and Forecast* (London, 1957).

viscous: *see* slime.

vitalism. The idea that life cannot be explained in material terms stems from Aristotle, but life as a potent explanatory and evaluative concept rose to importance in the late nineteenth century in reaction to scientific *materialism and Kantian *idealism. It appealed, among others, to Bergson, Nietzsche, and Dilthey. While vitalists differ in detail, they share some general beliefs: Life, and reality in so far as it is living, consists in movement and becoming, rather than in static being. Reality is organic, not mechanical: biology, and often history, are more central than physics. Life is known empirically or by intuition, rather than by concepts and logical inference. Life is objective and transcends the knowing subject. Vitalism stresses the diversity of life and tends towards pluralism, and occasionally relativism, rather than monism. It is not sharply distinct from philosophical *anthropology.   M.J.I.

H. Schnädelbach, *Philosophy in Germany 1831–1933* (Cambridge, 1984).

Vitoria, Francisco de (1480–1546). A member of the Dominican Order, he was a student at Paris, and later lectured at Salamanca. He wrote lengthy commentaries on theological writings of Thomas Aquinas but is most famous for his political and legal writings, and especially for his contribution to international law. He believed in *jus gentium*, a 'law of nations' established on the basis of natural law and universally valid. Living at the time of the conquest of the Americas, Vitoria developed his teaching partly in the context of his discussions on the appropriate treatment of the native peoples of the New World.

A.BRO.

B. Hamilton, *Political Thought in Sixteenth Century Spain* (Oxford, 1963).

Vlastos, Gregory (1907–91). Professor of Philosophy at Princeton and at Berkeley. Vlastos brought to the understanding of Greek philosophers, above all Socrates and Plato, an unsurpassed combination of flair and rigour, both philosophical and philological. He also propounded a radical doctrine of *equality: people vary in 'merit', but each has the same 'individual human worth' and *justice requires that people be treated in accordance with their identical human worth, not in accordance with their various merits. This egalitarianism has been more admired than followed.

N.C.D.

Gregory Vlastos, 'Justice and Equality', in Richard Brandt (ed.), *Social Justice* (Englewood Cliffs, NJ, 1962).
——*Platonic Studies* (Princeton, NJ, 1981).
——*Socrates: Ironist and Moral Philosopher* (Cambridge, 1991).

void. This word (Greek *kenon*, Latin *vacuum*) was a term of art in ancient philosophy of nature, used to designate utterly empty space or extension. Some philosophers (notably Aristotle, perhaps also Plato) rejected the notion as incoherent. Others (the Stoics) gave it a marginal role in ontology; it enabled them to posit a limited universe, for which the external void supplied a defining condition. But for the fifth-century Atomists and the Epicureans it was a key component in ontology. They used the idea to underpin the possibility of a universe which contains many objects undergoing change: void effected the separation of one object from another, and the distinctness of an actual state of affairs from its non-existent successor. The explanatory adequacy of this ontology was also used, particularly by the Epicureans, to bring out the ethical implications of their materialism. Since the only alternative to an existing object was empty space, the option of survival in the form of an incorporeal *soul was excluded.

J.D.G.E.

*atomism; Epicureanism.

For a thorough and penetrating survey of the void and related notions in ancient philosophy of nature, see R. R. K. Sorabji, *Time, Creation and the Continuum* (London, 1983).

Voidism: *see* Buddhist philosophy; Nāgārjuna.

volition. The faculty of the *will; or an item (sometimes alternatively called an act of will) conceived as the product of such a faculty.

In many dualist and empiricist accounts of *action, volitions are mental items that cause bodily motions on occasions of human agency. Ryle criticized such accounts. In recent philosophy, volitions are introduced in various roles, sometimes as a species of *intention. It remains controversial exactly what Ryle's arguments rule out, and whether volitions can or ought to play any role in explicating *agency.

J.HORN.

*trying.

Jennifer Hornsby, *Actions* (London, 1980), ch. 4.
R. Kane (ed.), *The Oxford Handbook of Free Will* (Oxford, 2001).

Voltaire, François-Marie Arouet de (1694–1778). Though not an original thinker, Voltaire was in his time a major playwright and novelist, and a brilliant scientific and philosophical popularizer. After exile in England, Voltaire communicated Locke's philosophy and Newton's science through his *Lettres philosophiques* (1734). With strong and lifelong social concerns, Voltaire used the letters to praise what he portrayed as English constitutionalism and freedom of thought, and so criticize their lack in France. Voltaire controversially shared Locke's agnosticism about the immateriality of mind. He believed that God's existence could be proved by the *cosmological and *design arguments. However, he was hostile to Leibniz's theodicy, and denied any particular providence. A believer in natural religion, Voltaire condemned the social effects of revealed religion as pernicious. He campaigned energetically for freedom of religion and judicial reform.

T.P.

F.-M. de Voltaire, *Philosophical Letters on the English Nation* (Indianapolis, 1961).

voluntariness: *see* compatibilism and incompatibilism; embraced and reluctant desires; freedom; spontaneity and indifference; voluntarism, doxastic.

voluntarism, doxastic. The question whether doxastic states (e.g. beliefs) are voluntary is important because such voluntariness seems to be assumed by any ethics of belief or theory of doxastic virtue. Doxastic voluntarists from René Descartes to Roderick M. Chisholm have held that believing is a voluntary act. Opponents from David Hume to Bernard Williams have argued that it makes no sense to speak of deciding to believe—the concept of voluntary belief is simply incoherent. A plausible form of doxastic voluntarism is developed by conceding that *beliefs cannot be voluntary acts because they are not acts at all, while insisting that genuine acts of assent and other of the myriad acts involved in acquiring, sustaining, and removing doxastic states are often voluntary in a sense robust enough to justify holding a person responsible for being in such states.

P.H.H.

*virtues, doxastic.

Peter Kauber, 'Does James' Ethics of Belief Rest on a Mistake?', *Southern Journal of Philosophy* (1974).

voluntarism, ethical. Voluntarism can be characterized as any philosophical view in which prominence is given to the *will over against one's other mental faculties. Ethical voluntarism is the view that whether an act qualifies as right or wrong depends primarily upon how the act is willed and that the consequences of one's act are judged good or bad primarily in accord with the goodness or badness of the will which produces the act. In general, Kantian ethics is quite hospitable to ethical voluntarism. Ethical voluntarists are inclined to doubt that there is such a thing as moral luck, since fortuitous circumstances are unrelated to whether one's will is good and hence to whether one can be judged as having done right or wrong.

G.F.M.

D. Statman, *Moral Luck* (New York, 1993).

von Hartmann, Eduard: *see* Hartmann, Eduard von.

von Neumann, John: *see* Neumann, John von.

von Wright, Georg Henrik (1916–2003). In 1939, G. H. von Wright, a member of Finland's Swedish-speaking minority, went from Helsinki to Cambridge to pursue his interest in induction and probability. He met Ludwig Wittgenstein, who influenced him greatly, and in 1948, at the age of 33, von Wright succeeded Wittgenstein as Professor of Philosophy at Cambridge University. He resigned the chair in 1951 to return to Finland. From 1961 to 1986 he was Research Professor at the Academy of Finland. Besides editing many of Wittgenstein's works, he produced biographical, expository, and critical writings about Wittgenstein. A survey of the three volumes of his *Philosophical Papers* indicates the scope of his interests: *Practical Reason* (vol. i, 1983) continues themes from *The Varieties of Goodness* (1963), *Norm and Action* (1963), *An Essay in Deontic Logic* (1968), and *Explanation and Understanding* (1971). *Philosophical Logic* (vol. ii, 1983) continues themes from *A Treatise on Induction and Probability* (1951) and *Logical Studies* (1957) and includes essays on paradoxes, preference, and tense logic. *Truth, Knowledge, and Modality* (vol. iii, 1984) continues themes from *Causality and Determinism* (1974) and *Freedom and Determination* (1980) and includes essays on propositions, causal knowledge, and modality.

D.H.S.

P. A. Schilpp and L. E. Hahn (eds.), *The Philosophy of Georg Henrik von Wright*, The Library of Living Philosophers, xix (La Salle, Ill., 1989).

Vorstellung. German for 'putting forward', hence 'representation' or 'idea' as used by British Empiricists. Like 'idea', *Vorstellung* has a narrow and a wide sense. (1) It is a mental *image, picture, or conception produced by prior perception of an object or objects. It contrasts with 'sensation', 'intuition', and 'perception', since these require the actual presence of an object, and also with 'thought', 'concept', and 'idea (*Idee*)', since these need no pictorial component and are more objective than *Vorstellungen*. (One speaks of *my Vorstellung* (*ideal, conception) of God, but *the

*concept (*Begriff*) of God.) *Vorstellungen* are involved in memory, imagination, etc., and are, in the view of older psychologists, subject to laws of 'association'. (2) In a wide sense, a *Vorstellung* is any mental item that refers to an intentional object. Hence a thought, a concept, or a perception is also a *Vorstellung*.

Some idealists argued that we cannot know objects in themselves, but only 'the *Vorstellungen* that they produce in us when they affect our senses' (Kant), or that 'the world is my *Vorstellung*' (Schopenhauer). Hegel's *idealism depends on thought, the 'concept', and the *Idee*, rather than *Vorstellungen*. In his view, religion presents in *Vorstellungen* (in the narrow sense of 'pictorial imagery') the 'content' that art presents in sensory intuitions (*Anschauungen*) and philosophy in thoughts.

M.J.I.

M. Clark, *Logic and System: A Study of the Transition from 'Vorstellung' to Thought in the Philosophy of Hegel* (The Hague, 1971).

W. A. de Vries, *Hegel's Theory of Mental Activity: An Introduction to Theoretical Spirit* (Ithaca, NY, 1988).

C. Knüfer, *Grundzüge der Geschichte des Begriffs 'Vorstellung' von Wolff bis Kant* (Halle, 1911).

voting paradox. Suppose that three people, Alice, Brian, and Cait, are choosing between three candidates, Primus, Secunda, and Tertius, for a job. Alice prefers Primus to Secunda to Tertius. Brian prefers Secunda to Tertius to Primus. Cait prefers Tertius to Primus to Secunda. So a majority prefer Primus to Secunda, and a majority prefer Secunda to Tertius, and, paradoxically, a majority prefer Tertius to Primus. So preferences obtained by majority voting between pairs do not give a coherent ranking. Or, to put it differently, the outcome depends on the order in which the options are presented. If the first choice is between Primus and Secunda then Secunda will be eliminated and Primus will win when compared with Tertius. But if the first choice is between Primus and Tertius then Primus will be eliminated and then Secundus will win when compared with Tertius. These facts are special cases of Arrow's theorem, which shows that there can be no perfect voting system.

A.M.

*democracy; Arrow's paradox.

Kenneth Arrow, *Social Choice and Individual Values*, 2nd edn. (1963).

Michael Dummett, *Voting Procedures* (Oxford, 1984).

Vygotsky, Lev Semenovich (1896–1934). Innovative Russian psychologist and philosopher who argued that only by understanding the role of culture in psychological development can we attain an account of consciousness that overcomes the shortcomings of *behaviourism and *reductionism without embracing *dualism. While human beings are endowed with elementary mental functions that can be explained naturalistically, the higher mental functions are mediated by psychological tools, such as language and other externalized systems of representation, which the individual acquires, not naturally, but through the internalization of social activity. Each child therefore attains consciousness as she is inaugurated into human culture. Shortly after Vygotsky's death from tuberculosis in 1934, the Stalin regime blacklisted his works for many years, but his ideas were preserved by his collaborators, especially A. R. Luria and A. N. Leontiev, and formed the foundation of Soviet 'socio-historical psychology'. His thought has also been influential in the West, particularly among educationalists.   D.BAK.

David Bakhurst, *Consciousness and Revolution in Soviet Philosophy* (Cambridge, 1991), ch. 3.

L. S. Vygotsky, *Thought and Language* (Cambridge, Mass., 1986).

W

Walton, Kendall (1939–). American philosopher. Walton's work in philosophical aesthetics makes him one of the most influential thinkers in that field since Monroe Beardsley and Nelson Goodman. One of Walton's early contributions (1970) was to show that the aesthetic properties of works of art were not intrinsic to them, but were instead relative to the medium, style, and genre categories in which those works were correctly perceived, and thus that, as a consequence, strong versions of formalism and anti-intentionalism regarding works of art must be mistaken. Walton's major contribution to aesthetics, however (1990), consists in his elaboration of a general theory of representations or fictions, which are treated as equivalent, in terms of an activity of prop-guided imagination, or 'make-believe'. In subsequent important papers Walton has addressed issues concerning the aesthetics of photography, the aesthetics of music, the embedding of moral perspectives in literature, and the role of simulation in aesthetic appreciation.   J.LEV.

Kendall Walton, 'Categories of Art', *Philosophical Review* (1970).
—— *Mimesis as Make-Believe* (Cambridge, Mass., 1990).

Walzer, Michael (1935–). American political philosopher who has specialized in the study of democracy, justice, and ethical relativism. He is particularly interested in the processes through which each community arrives at its own shared understanding of justice and the good society. Walzer believes that these processes and understandings are necessarily community-specific, and hence a certain degree of cultural relativism must be respected. However, Walzer also recognizes a non-relativist 'minimal code', prohibiting slavery, genocide, and gross cruelty in any community. His most important works include *Just and Unjust Wars* (1977), *Spheres of Justice* (1983), and *Interpretation and Social Criticism* (1987). Walzer has been variously described as a liberal, a communitarian, and a radical democrat, but the originality of his thought makes him difficult to label. Walzer is currently a professor at the Institute for Advanced Studies in Princeton.   W.K.

Michael Walzer, *Spheres of Justice: A Defence of Pluralism and Equality* (Oxford, 1983).

Wang, Hao (1921–95). American mathematical logician and philosopher of mathematics, born and educated in China. He supplied the axioms of membership for Quine's *set theory in *Mathematical Logic*, replacing an earlier inconsistent version. He extended Russell's ramified type hierarchy to infinite levels. He was the first to write (in 1959) a computer program which efficiently proved all the first-order theorems of Whitehead and Russell's *Principia Mathematica*. His contributions to mathematical philosophy often took the form of historical analyses of major figures; his reports of his discussions with Gödel in the 1970s are a main source for Gödel's unpublished philosophical views on truth and the nature of mathematics. Wang argued that philosophers of mathematics should take mathematical knowledge and intuition as given, and seek to describe their structure and their place in life.   W.A.H.

Hao Wang, *Beyond Analytic Philosophy: Doing Justice to what we Know* (Cambridge, Mass., 1986).
—— *A Logical Journey: From Gödel to Philosophy* (Cambridge, Mass., 1996).

Wang Yang-ming (1472–1529). Confucian thinker in China, also known as Wang Shou-jen. His thinking partly drew inspiration from that of Lu Hsiang-shan (1139–93), and scholars speak of a Lu–Wang school which competed for influence with the Ch'eng–Chu school of Ch'eng I (1033–1107) and Chu Hsi (1130–1200). Wang's fundamental ideas are contained in the work *Ch'uan-hsi-lu* (*Instructions for Practical Living*). Though sharing Chu Hsi's view that human beings already have a fully virtuous disposition which has been obscured by distortive desires and thoughts, he opposed Chu on various issues. For example, for Wang, self-cultivation should involve one's directing attention to the mind, constantly watching out for and eliminating distortive desires and thoughts, rather than engaging in such inquiries as the study of classics and historical records.   K.-L.S.

*Confucianism.

Instructions for Practical Living and Other Neo-Confucian Writings by Wang Yang-ming, tr. Wing-tsit Chan (New York, 1963).

war, just. The tradition of 'just war' theory has aimed at identifying those conditions which make it morally legitimate to wage war. It was developed originally by the Christian Church, and more recently has been expressed in the conventions of international law. The early

Christian attitude of abstention from involvement in war was difficult to sustain when Christianity became the established religion of the Roman Empire, and thinkers such as Augustine turned to the idea that the waging of war was a legitimate exercise of the authority of rulers. As the ruler may justly punish wrongdoing on the part of his subjects, so likewise war could be 'just' if it was waged to punish external wrongdoers.

Over the centuries this position was elaborated in detail, and divided into the theory of *jus ad bellum*—what makes it right to go to war—and the theory of *jus in bello*—what it is right to do *in* war. Typical conditions laid down for *jus ad bellum* were that war may be undertaken only by a legitimate authority, it may be waged only for a just cause, it must be a last resort, there must be a formal declaration of war, and there must be a reasonable hope of success. The two most important conditions for *jus in bello* were that the means employed should be 'proportional' to the end aimed at (that is, the war should not be fought in such a way as to constitute a greater evil than the evil it was intended to remedy), and that it was not permissible to kill 'the innocent' (understood to mean non-combatants, civilians).

More recent versions of 'just war' theory have focused especially on two ideas: (i) that war can be justified only as a response to aggression (this is presented as the principal condition for *jus ad bellum*); and (ii) the idea of non-combatant immunity as the principal condition for *jus in bello*. The difficulty with both ideas is their dependence on an analogy between individuals and communities. The right to resist aggression is standardly compared to individuals' right of self-defence. However, even if it is permissible for an individual to kill his attacker in order to defend his own life, is it equally justifiable to kill thousands of people in order to defend the borders of a nation? It can be argued that individuals have a right of self-defence because the attacker has forfeited his own right to life by threatening someone else's life. It does not follow, however, that the inhabitants of a country, or even its military personnel, have forfeited their right to life because their country's rulers have decided upon aggression against another country.

The application of the principle of non-combatant immunity raises similar problems. Even if a nation waging war is not 'innocent', most of the individual combatants would seem to be, in any morally relevant sense, just as 'innocent' as non-combatants. They are not responsible for the war. They may have been compelled to fight, and if civilians are in an appropriate sense 'innocent', then most individual combatants would seem to be no less so. Moreover, the nature of modern societies and the immensely destructive power of modern weapons makes it very difficult in practice to discriminate between combatants and non-combatants. In most modern wars it is virtually impossible to target a country's military forces and military installations without attacking centres of population and killing large numbers of civilians. In that case no modern war can be waged without killing the innocent. Perhaps we should conclude that no war can be 'just'.

R.J.N.

*international relations, philosophy of; violence, political.

Robert L. Holmes, *On War and Morality* (Princeton, NJ, 1989).
David Rodin, *War and Self-Defence* (Oxford, 2003).
Jenny Teichman, *Pacifism and the Just War* (Oxford, 1986).
Michael Walzer, *Just and Unjust Wars* (Harmondsworth, 1977).

war and philosophy. Philosophers of every era have tried to understand the nature and problems of war—from Heraclitus' conception of war as the father of all things to Kant's treatise on eternal peace. Philosophers have debated the value of war as a school for virtue, the misery of war, the causes of war, the *just war, and the possibility of creating peace and universal brotherhood. But war has been important to philosophy in other ways too. The disastrous Peloponnesian War certainly influenced Plato's bad opinion of Athenian democracy. The capture of Rome by Alaric made St Augustine write *Civitas Dei*. Montaigne's scepticism was strengthened by the religious wars of the sixteenth century. The Civil War of seventeenth-century England gave Hobbes the problematic of *Leviathan*.

In modern times too, war has influenced philosophy, sometimes in unexpected ways. Some illustrations of this can be drawn from the First World War. In quite a new way the First World War made scholars and scientists participate in the war of propaganda. The role of the philosophers was important. They contributed grand metaphysical interpretations of the war aims of their own nations. In Germany philosophers like Paul Natorp, Max Scheler, and George Simmel, to name a few, did their bit for the Vaterland. The war was depicted as a struggle between profound German 'culture' and shallow Anglo-French 'civilization'. The value of war as existential experience was stressed. All the German philosophical heritage was mobilized for the fight. 'Send Fichte to the trenches!' became a catchword. The French philosophers were not to be outdone. In his *La Signification de la guerre* (1915; tr. into English the same year) Henri Bergson explained that the war was one between 'life and matter'. It takes no deep knowledge of the philosophy of Bergson to guess which among the combatants in the war represented 'life' and which represented 'matter'. Those French historians of philosophy who had taken Fichte or Hegel as their subject had an unpleasant choice before them. Should they sacrifice thinkers, whom formerly they had venerated, on the altar of patriotism? Or should they try to make a distinction between the old good Germany and the new bad one?

Nor did the philosophical struggle in Great Britain escape the bitterness of war. Until its outbreak *Hegelianism had been firmly entrenched in the universities of England and Scotland. Now everything emanating from the enemy was seen as highly suspect. One victim of this wave of hatred against all things German was the philosopher-statesman R. B. Haldane. Haldane was a Hegelian philosopher and a follower of T. H. Green. He was also a liberal politician. When the war broke out Haldane was Lord Chancellor in Asquith's Cabinet. In 1916 he was forced to resign. A hue and cry had been raised against this states-man who had once said that Germany was his 'spiritual home'. Wartime animosity against German philosophy is exemplified in another way by L. T. Hobhouse in his *The Metaphysical Theory of the State* (1918). The book is a critique of Bernard Bosanquet's Hegelian political philos-ophy. In his preface Hobhouse dedicated it to his son, who was fighting in the trenches against the very enemy whom his father tried to overcome with philosophical argu-ments—the German spirit.

Of course there were other, more subtle ways in which the war influenced philosophy. One of the most import-ant works of twentieth-century philosophy, Ludwig Wittgenstein's *Tractatus Logico-Philosophicus*, was pre-pared and written while its author was an active combat-ant or a prisoner of war. Does not the agonized tone of this strange and remarkable work bear some relation to that biographical background?

The First World War had the effect of making philoso-phy more national and the differences between national traditions in philosophy more important. The Second World War and the ensuing Cold War had similar conse-quences, national and ideological cleavages parting philosophers and other scholars from each other. Philo-sophical arguments had their share in the wars of propa-ganda. World congresses of philosophy were held and other efforts made to bring philosophers together in amic-able discussions. But there was great difficulty in finding a way back even to the climate of discussion of the nineteenth century. The Stoic utopia of a peaceful world state of philosophers seems very distant.   S.N.

Modris Eksteins, *Rites of Spring: The Great War and the Birth of the Modern Age* (Boston, Mass., 1989).

Robert Wohl, *The Generation of 1914* (Cambridge, Mass., 1979).

Warnock, Geoffrey J. (1923–96). Warnock's first major publication was a monograph on Berkeley (*Berkeley* (Har-mondsworth, 1953)) in which he brought some of the tools of modern 'linguistic philosophy' to bear on Berkeley's ideas, to considerable effect. The bulk of his subsequent work concentrated on moral philosophy, including an inci-sive critique of developments in that subject this century (*Contemporary Moral Philosophy* (London, 1967)), and an exposition of his own developed theory (*The Object of Moral-ity* (London, 1971)). Warnock takes a broadly naturalistic approach to the phenomenon of morality, arguing that it exists to help regulate conflict and promote social stability. He was the husband of Mary Warnock, and spent his work-ing life in Oxford, where he was Vice-Chancellor from 1981 to 1985. He was knighted in 1986.   N.J.H.D.

*Berkeley.

Warnock, Mary (1924–). Baroness Warnock has done notable work in at least four fields: academic philosophy (narrowly conceived); the theory and practice of educa-

tion; the morality and legality of new methods of embryo fertilization; public service associated with these concerns. In academic philosophy, she has written extensively on ethics, and particularly existentialist ethics. Other work has been in the philosophy of mind, with monographs entitled *Imagination* (London, 1976) and *Memory* (London, 1987). She chaired a government inquiry into special educational needs, in the mid-1970s, and has written widely on educa-tional issues, at both school and university level. She add-itionally chaired the Committee of Inquiry into Human Fertilisation in the early 1980s. Much of her working life was spent in Oxford, as college tutor but also Headmistress of Oxford High School. She was Mistress of Girton Col-lege, Cambridge, 1985–91. She was created a life peer in 1985 and was married to Geoffrey Warnock.   N.J.H.D.

*bioethics; moral sense.

M. Warnock, *Making Babies: Is There a Right to Have Children?* (Oxford, 2003).

war of all against all: *see* state of nature.

Watson, John Broadus (1878–1958). An American psy-chologist, Watson was the father of *behaviourism, the dominant theory of psychology through most of the early and middle decades of the twentieth century. For Watson, if psychology is to be scientific, its data must consist of external (public) stimuli and external (behavioural) responses; and not introspective (private mental) reports. Introspective reports give psychologists only indirect access to whatever data they need to develop their sci-ence. In contrast, behavioural reports give psychologists access to data that are as direct as those found in the phys-ical sciences. As a method for how the science of psych-ology should proceed, Watson's (as well as Clark Hull's and B. F. Skinner's) behaviourism should be distinguished from logical or conceptual behaviourism, which argues that the meaning of mental terms is wholly or primarily analysable behaviourally and/or dispositionally.   N.F.

John Broadus Watson, *Behaviourism* (London, 1925).

Watsuji Tetsurō (1889–1960). A prominent philosopher associated with the Kyoto School, Watsuji proposed the East Asian idea of *ningen*—'human-beings-in-relationship'—as the basis for a philosophical anthropology. Torn in his youth between attractions to philosophy and literature, Watsuji produced early works on Schopen-hauer, Nietzsche, and Kierkegaard, before turning to a study of Asian traditions of thought. A polymath like many of his colleagues, he continued to write on such top-ics as Homer, Greek politics, and early Christianity, but devoted most of his energies to writings on Buddhism and the cultural history of Japan, with special emphasis on eth-ical thought. In his works on cultural anthropology—of which *Climate* (1935) has been translated into English— Watsuji criticized Heidegger for neglecting human spa-tiality in *Being and Time* and for making his notion of *Dasein* overly individualistic.   G.R.P.

*Japanese philosophy.

Watsuji Tetsurō, *Climate: A Philosophical Study*, tr. Geoffrey Bownas (Tokyo, 1961).

weakness of will: *see akrasia.*

Weber, Karl Emil Maximilian (Max) (1864–1920). German sociologist, whose polymathy defied his characterization of our age as one of specialization and bureaucracy. Men attach meanings to their actions and these become embodied in social norms. Hence sociology involves 'understanding' (*Verstehen*). But it can causally explain social phenomena by the comparative method and by 'ideal types'. Ideal types include the three types of authority: traditional, charismatic, and legal-rational or bureaucratic (which prevails in both *capitalism and *socialism). Social phenomena, e.g. the rise of capitalism, depend not only on economic factors but on ideas, e.g. Calvinism's 'Protestant ethic'. Status groups are as important as Marx's economic classes. In response to the political upheavals of 1919 he distinguished the 'ethic of responsibility' from the 'ethic of conscience' and quoted Goethe's *Faust*: 'The devil is old; you must become old to understand him'.   M.J.I.

R. Bendix, *Max Weber: An Intellectual Portrait* (London, 1960).

Weil, Simone (1909–43). A pupil of the radical individualist philosopher Alain, Simone Weil evolved a Platonic interpretation of the world with strong mystical leanings. Her ideals, which first lay in the direction of anarcho-syndicalism, she pursued with a consistent eccentricity. After her conversion to Christianity, she combined her strong commitment to many of its Catholic forms with a thoroughgoing interpretation of its main themes—God, creation, redemption—through the concepts of ancient Greek philosophy. This involved an emphasis on the impersonal and the contemplative. Always a political activist, she also attempted to sketch the politics of a society equal to these aspirations. As such she represents the most striking example of twentieth-century Christian *Platonism.   D.McL.

D. McLellan, *Simone Weil: Utopian Pessimist* (London, 1990).

welfarism. A view which assigns to the state the function of looking after the well-being or welfare of the people.

In the seventeenth and eighteenth centuries liberal-democratic theorists (such as Adam Smith) held that the state had a largely negative function of protecting security from outside or inside and only a minimal welfare function, such as the provision of large works which individuals could not manage on their own or the ensuring of minimum standards of education. Welfarism became a large function of the state in Britain after the Beveridge Report (1942), which propounded state responsibility for individual welfare 'from the cradle to the grave'. Other European states adopted the idea of welfarism to a greater or lesser extent. Indeed, Germany pioneered both modern social insurance in the 1880s and the concept of *Wohfahrstaat* in the 1920s. The USA has been much less influenced by these ideas. At the moment there seems to be a move away from welfarism in the UK and other parts of Europe, partly on the grounds that it is difficult to sustain the expenditure involved in such welfare concerns as the National Health Service, and partly on broader moral grounds, that welfarism saps the moral fibre of the people and is really massive state paternalism or, as it is often described by its opponents, that it constitutes the 'nanny state'.   R.S.D.

*conservatism.

R. Hattersley, *Choose Freedom: The Future for Democratic Socialism* (Harmondsworth, 1987).

R. Nozick, *Anarchy, State and Utopia* (Oxford, 1974).

well-being. Variously interpreted as 'living and faring well' or 'flourishing', the notion of well-being is intricately bound up with our ideas about what constitutes human *happiness and the sort of life it is good to lead. Well-being is said to be both a condition of the good life *and* what the good life achieves.

However, the phrase 'the good life' is ambiguous between the morally good life and the sort of life most people aspire to, a life in which comfort and enjoyment have a large part. Indeed we may even suspect that the two sorts of life are mutually exclusive—and that well-being belongs firmly in the latter, or would be a surprising *central* feature of the former. It seems that the ambiguity can at least be taken as an indication of how unclear we find the connection between being morally good and possessing health, wealth, and happiness, and the other components of well-being.

Some philosophers have, nevertheless, objected to the suggested dichotomy between what is morally good and what is enjoyable. Aristotle, for example, insists in his discussion of *eudaemonia* that the morally good life is essential to human flourishing and, conversely, that being good is possible only for a person who has well-being. Thus, according to this view, well-being is a notion which spans both the moral and non-moral aspects of life. It follows that any adequate conception of a good life *cannot* be limited to either a narrowly moral, or a non-moral, account. It will be a highly complex account, akin to the answer a parent might give when asked 'What sort of life do you wish for your children?', with all the intricacies such an answer would involve.

Furthermore, because a good person cannot enjoy well-being in conditions of poverty or oppression, it is clear that well-being is also a political notion. It must therefore be explicated in both moral and political terms, with the focus of interest placed firmly on the interdependence of these. While common sense accords with this view of the matter, the notion of well-being has tended to be the subject of much dispute, and prey to the conflicting conceptions of what enables human beings to flourish which are provided by different moral and political philosophies.

Nevertheless, it seems possible to specify, as Rawls and Honderich do, the primary goods which are necessary, if not sufficient, conditions of well-being, and the political arrangements which will therefore facilitate it. The question of the distribution of well-being will then be essentially a matter of social justice. Since it is hard to justify inequalities of well-being even when it seems possible to justify inequalities of socio-economic goods, the question will be best answered, perhaps, by some principle of equality which gives priority to policies whose end is to make well-off those who are badly off in terms of well-being.   P.W.

Aristotle, *Nicomachean Ethics*.
J. Griffin, *Well-Being* (Oxford, 1986).
T. Honderich, 'The Question of Well-Being and the Principle of Equality', *Mind* (1981).
J. Rawls, *A Theory of Justice* (Cambridge, Mass., 1971).
W. Sumner, *Welfare, Happiness, and Ethics* (Oxford, 1996).

well-formed formula. A formal calculus has a basic vocabulary and rules for forming acceptable sequences (well-formed formulae or wffs) of that vocabulary. Well-formed formulae are analogues of grammatical sentences in natural language. The rules for well-formedness are analogues of rules of grammar. For example, for a version of the *propositional calculus where

(1) $\sim$ and $\vee$ are basic logical constants ('not', 'or'),
(2) $A_1, A_2, \ldots, A_n$, are atomic propositional expressions,

the set of wffs is defined as follows:

(3) wffs are either atomic propositional expressions or molecular, i.e. of the form $\sim \phi$ or $(\phi \vee \psi)$, where
(4) $\sim \phi$ is a wff if and only if ϕ is a wff,
(5) $(\phi \vee \psi)$ is a wff if and only if ϕ and ψ are wffs. ('(' and ')' are analogues of punctuation.)
(1)–(5) provide a *decision procedure for well-formedness.   R.B.M.

B. Mates, *Elementary Logic* (Oxford, 1972).

Weltanschauung. German for 'world-view', a general view of the universe and man's place in it which affects one's conduct. For Dilthey philosophies are world-views, and fall into three types: *materialism, pantheistic *vitalism, *idealism. Husserl contrasted culturally and historically relative world-views with 'scientific' philosophy. Scheler argued that we cannot avoid a world-view; but we should choose it reflectively and by a valid method. Jaspers investigated the roots of world-views in our subjective experience.   M.J.I.

M. Heidegger, 'Anmerkungen zu Karl Jaspers *Psychologie der Weltanschauungen*', in *Wegmarken*, 2nd edn. (Frankfurt, 1978).
E. Husserl, *Philosophy as a Rigorous Science* (1910–11), in *Phenomenology and the Crisis of Science*, tr. Q. Lauer (New York, 1965).

Weyl's paradox is a name that has been used for the paradox concerning the term 'heterological', which is supposed to apply to all and only terms which do not apply truly to themselves. The problem is that it then seems that 'heterological' is heterological if and only if it is not. This paradox was originally presented in 1908 in a paper by Kurt Grelling and Leonard Nelson, so that the term 'Weyl's paradox' is incorrect. Herman Weyl (1885–1955) was a German-American mathematician, physicist, and philosopher of science.   J.C.

*Grelling's paradox.

wff: *see* well-formed formula.

Whewell, William (1794–1866). Influential Cambridge philosopher, mineralogist, and educational reformer. Son of a Lancaster carpenter, Whewell became Master of Trinity College in 1841. In his *The Philosophy of the Inductive Sciences Founded upon their History* (London, 1840) he sought to update the methodology advocated programmatically in Francis Bacon's *Novum Organum*, and to base this updating on consideration of how science had actually progressed—a consideration made possible by his own *History of the Inductive Sciences from the Earliest to the Present Time* (London, 1837). He asserted a fundamental antithesis between the facts studied by a scientist and the concepts that a scientist invents in order to colligate the facts, and owed to Kant the idea that certain very general laws are presuppositions of empirical inquiry. Correspondingly he opposed J. S. Mill's views about the epistemology of such general laws.   L.J.C.

*natural law.

M. Fisch, *William Whewell: Philosopher of Science* (Oxford, 1991).

Whitehead, Alfred North (1861–1947). British mathematician and philosopher who spent his later and philosophically most productive years in the United States at Harvard University, where he and his wife hosted legendary Sunday teas. *Principia Mathematica* (1910–13), his three-volume attempt in collaboration with his former student Bertrand Russell to show that mathematics can be reduced to logic (i.e. to establish *logicism), is considered by many to be one of the great intellectual achievements of all time. *Process and Reality* (1929), a metaphysical system in which substance (as traditionally conceived in Western philosophy) is rejected in favour of process, is regarded as having importance in the history of metaphysics comparable to the significance of his earlier work for logic and the foundations of mathematics.

Whitehead's work is usually divided into three periods: before 1914, mathematics and logic; 1914–24, philosophy of physical science; and 1924–47, metaphysics and the historical role of metaphysical ideas in civilization. Although during most of his life he considered himself and was considered by others to be a mathematician, study of his intellectual development reveals it to be unified by philosophical concerns (e.g. 'modes of togetherness').

In *Science and the Modern World* (1925), his first metaphysical work, Whitehead rejected the idea of 'simple location' presupposed by scientific materialism. Everything, he said, is a field spread out temporally and spatially; every object, from a human body to an electron, is composed of events or processes. In *Process and Reality* he systematically elaborated this metaphysics, in which the basic unit is an experiential event called an 'actual entity'. An actual entity is a unifying of its relations to the other actual entities of the world it appropriates. These appropriating relations are 'prehensions', vectors which transform everything experienced into that entity's distinctive actuality.

God plays a central role in this appropriating process. In his 'Primordial Nature' God orders possibilities ('eternal objects') to make them relevant to the becoming of an entity. In his 'Consequent Nature' God preserves the immediacies of all past actual entities and unites them with his envisionment of the primordial unity of all eternal objects. God is not only necessary to every becoming: becomings are necessary to the development of God as Consequent. Like any actual entity, God is a process of becoming.

Whitehead's books after *Process and Reality* avoid technicalities in exploring imaginatively the significance of his metaphysical ideas. *Religion in the Making* (1926) is a richly suggestive discussion of the nature of religion; *Adventures of Ideas* (1933) presents, for example, his conception of experience in luminous prose; and *Modes of Thought* (1938) is intended as 'a free examination of some ultimate notions, as they occur naturally in daily life'.

P.H.H.

*process philosophy.

George A. Lucas, 'Outside the Camp: Recent Work on Whitehead's Philosophy', *Transactions of the C. S. Peirce Society* (1985).
Paul Arthur Schilpp (ed.), *The Philosophy of Alfred North Whitehead* (New York, 1941).

why. The question 'Why . . . ?' is answered by explaining why, which is stating a reason why (explaining-what is different). Often such reasons are causes, but even when 'cause' is not the natural description, 'Because – – –' is the natural formula for answering 'why' questions. Other idioms do exist, as in: 'Why did she flood the bathroom?'—'Out of mischief'; 'Why do animals have hearts?'—'For pumping the blood'; 'Why walk?'—'To save money'. But such answers can always be expanded into 'Because – – –' answers, usually becoming more informative in the process (the expansion will often indicate that the thing to be explained does some good, or—differently—aims at some good, these being two kinds of *teleological explanation).

A 'why' explanation must, first, state a *reason for thinking* that the matter to be explained is true: for example, 'Bangkok is hot because it is in the tropics'. This may, secondly, need amplification—different things go without saying in different contexts of 'why' inquiry. The amplification may fill the reason out, for example by adding that most tropical cities are hot, or strengthen it, for example by substituting 'Because it is at sea-level in the tropics, and *all* sea-level tropical cities are hot', or extend it, for example by explaining why sea-level tropical cities are hot (this last

process is potentially endless). But thirdly, some 'why' questions do not need, or even cannot get, answers—for example, 'Why is Bangkok a sea-level tropical city?' Finally and crucially, many reasons for thinking fail to be *reasons why* even after these amplifications. For example—an example of Aristotle's—'Because they do not twinkle' does not begin to explain why the planets are near us (here the explanation goes the other way round). The question what extra is required connects with the mysterious question what *causality is.

C.A.K.

*explanation; reasons and causes.

P. T. Geach, *Reason and Argument* (Oxford, 1976), ch. 17.
D.-H. Ruben, *Explaining Explanation* (London, 1990).

Why be moral? *see* moral philosophy, history of.

Wiggins, David (1933–). Oxford philosopher specializing in metaphysics, philosophical logic, and ethics, noted for his work on *identity. He challenges P. T. Geach's doctrine of the relativity of identity, advancing instead an 'absolute' conception whereby if particulars are identical under one *sortal concept, then they are identical under any other that applies to them. Geach's supposed counter-examples are dismissed as turning on equivocation. Thus Geach suggests that *x* and *y* might be the same *river*, but different *bodies of water*. Wiggins's response is that rivers are not identical with bodies of water, but rather *constituted* by them.

One consequence of Wiggins's position is that two different *things—for instance, a river and the body of water currently constituting it—may exist in the same place at the same time. This may seem odd, but is unobjectionable provided, as here, the things in question are of different kinds.

E.J.L.

D. Wiggins, *Needs, Values, Truth*, 3rd edn. (Oxford, 1998).
—— *Sameness and Substance Renewed* (Cambridge, 2003).

will. Traditionally the will was taken to be a mental faculty responsible for acts of volition such as choosing, deciding, and initiating motion. This faculty of the soul or mind was taken as one of the characteristics, the most important, separating us from animals and inanimate objects. Usually the will was explicitly taken to be capable of *origination—the creation of a new beginning and escape from the past. Kant stressed the moral importance of acts of will, as opposed to practical consequences of actions, but the will reached its philosophical apotheosis in Schopenhauer's *The World as Will and Idea* (1818, 1844). Contemporary philosophy of mind is less accepting of ontologically real mental faculties, although the will has continued to have attention paid to it. The traditional problem of the freedom of the will concerns itself partly with (*a*) the possible incompatibility between free will and determinism, and (*b*) the alleged dependency of moral responsibility upon free will.

R.C.W.

*freedom and determinism.

A. Kenny, *Will, Freedom, and Power* (Oxford, 1975).

Brian O'Shaughnessy, *The Will* (Cambridge, 1980).
Gilbert Ryle, *The Concept of Mind* (London, 1949).

William of Ockham: *see* Ockham.

Williams, Bernard A. O. (1929–2003). Bernard Williams was one of the leading British intellectuals of the late twentieth century. Among philosophers he is best known for his work in moral philosophy and on the metaphysics of mind, especially in connection with issues of personal identity. He also made contributions to classical philosophy, notably *Shame and Necessity* (Berkeley, 1993), and wrote an important book on Descartes (*Descartes* (Harmondsworth, 1978)), in which he gives prominence to the idea of there being an 'absolute conception of reality' inherent in Descartes's philosophical project.

Williams's work on *personal identity resists easy summary. In general, though, it is marked by a particular inventiveness in devising examples or possible cases to refute or to develop theses about the physical or mental bases of personal identity, and by great fertility and incisiveness in seeing new ways of approaching issues. This freshness in tackling problems is a notable feature of much of Williams's work, which is widely influential. His papers on this topic are collected in *Problems of the Self* (Cambridge, 1973).

In moral philosophy, Williams argued against both Kantian and utilitarian approaches. In both cases, he objects that these views require agents to view themselves unrealistically as simply one person among others, which neglects to acknowledge the special significance that a person's own projects must have for them. In particular, he gives emphasis to the role of emotions in moral responsiveness. Williams is also sceptical that many of the claims morality makes for itself (that it is universal, absolutely binding, and so on) can cogently be justified. Many of these themes are prominent in his *Ethics and the Limits of Philosophy* (London, 1985).

Williams chaired the government Committee on Obscenity and Film Censorship in the late 1970s. He held professorships in London, Oxford, and Berkeley, California, and was Provost of King's College Cambridge from 1979 to 1987. Not long before his death he completed a long-awaited book on *Truth and Truthfulness* (Princeton, NJ, 2002). N.J.H.D.

*moral luck; reasons, internal and external.

Williamson, Timothy (1955–). British logician and epistemologist, currently Wykeham Professor of Logic at the University of Oxford.

Williamson defends the epistemic theory of *vagueness. Vague terms have borderline cases. Most philosophers assume that there is no fact of the matter about whether a vague term can truly be applied in a borderline case. Williamson, however, maintains that vague terms have sharp boundaries, which are in principle inaccessible, even though they are determined by the ways in which language is used. Since Williamson understands knowledge in terms of margin of error principles, which require that *p* must be true in all cases sufficiently similar to cases in which *p* is known, it remains possible to apply vague terms knowledgeably. In more recent work Williamson has developed a broader epistemological perspective. Taking knowledge to be conceptually prior to belief, he offers new perspectives on the plausibility of scepticism, the nature of evidence, the accessibility of our own mental states, and the limits of knowledge. J.BER.

T. Williamson, *Knowledge and its Limits* (Oxford, 2000).

will to believe. In his 1897 article entitled 'The Will to Believe', William James said that, under certain specified conditions, we have a right to let our passional nature decide which of two alternative hypotheses to adopt. These are that the matter cannot be settled on intellectual grounds, and that the choice between them is *living* (we find each credible), *forced* (we must act in the light of one or the other), and *momentous* (really important). Examples are the choice between theism and atheism or free will and determinism. T.L.S.S.

*voluntarism, doxastic.

William James, 'The Will to Believe', in *The Will to Believe and Other Essays in Popular Philosophy* (New York, 1897).

will to live: *see* Schopenhauer.

will to power. Nietzsche's formula for what he took to be the basic disposition manifested in all that transpires in human life, and in all other phenomena as well. Everything that happens in our lives and in the world of which we are a part, for Nietzsche, may be interpreted in terms of *power-relationships within and among configurations of forces the basic tendency of which is to assert themselves towards others in an expanding or expending and transforming manner. (See e.g. *Beyond Good and Evil*, sect. 36; and *The Will to Power*, sect. 1067.) R.S.

Richard Schacht, *Nietzsche* (London, 1983), ch. 4.

Wilt Chamberlain argument. In what is his best-known argument from *Anarchy, State and Utopia* (New York, 1974), Robert Nozick asks us to imagine that we are in a society that has just distributed income according to some ideal pattern, possibly a pattern of *equality. We are to further imagine that in such a society someone with the talents of Wilt Chamberlain offers to play basketball for us provided that he or she receives a small fraction of the proceeds from every home game ticket that is sold. Suppose we agree to these terms, and a large number of people attend the home games to watch this super-talented player, thereby securing for him or her a sizeable income. Since such an income would surely upset the initial pattern of income distribution whatever that happened to be, Nozick contends that this illustrates how an ideal of *liberty upsets the patterns required by other political ideals, and hence calls for their rejection. J.P.S.

*libertarianism; conservatism.

Winch, P. G. (1926–97). A prominent Wittgensteinian, whose writings explore the implications of the claim that to understand a language is to understand a *form of life. His most influential work, *The Idea of a Social Science*, was highly critical of received empiricist anthropological and sociological conceptions of understanding human action. It stimulated extensive debate about the methodology of the social sciences. Subsequent writings on the understanding of primitive societies were equally influential. Winch's ethical writings are distinguished not only by their seriousness, but also by the concreteness of examples and the attention to the context of moral predicaments, as well as the texture of life in which they are embedded.

P.M.S.H.

*social science, philosophy of.

P. G. Winch, *The Idea of a Social Science* (London, 1958).
—— *Ethics and Action* (London, 1972).
——*Trying to Make Sense* (Oxford, 1987).

wisdom. A form of understanding that unites a reflective attitude and a practical concern. The aim of the attitude is to understand the fundamental nature of reality and its significance for living a good life. The object of the practical concern is to form a reasonable conception of a good life, given the agents' character and circumstances, and to evaluate the situations in which they have to make decisions and act from its point of view. These evaluations are often difficult because many situations are complex, conceptions of a good life are incompletely formed, and the variability of individual character and circumstances render general principles insufficiently specific. Wisdom may be identified then with good judgement about the evaluation of complex situations and conceptions of a good life in the light of a reflective understanding of the human condition.

Although wisdom is what *philosophy is meant to be a love of, little attention has been paid to this essential component of good lives in post-classical Western philosophy. It is perhaps for this reason that those in search of it often turn to the obscurities of oriental religions for enlightenment.

J.KEK.

*understanding.

B. Blanshard, *Reason and Goodness* (London, 1961).
J. Kekes, *Wisdom and Good Lives: The Virtue of Reflection* (Ithaca, NY, 1995).

Wisdom, John (1904–93). Professor of Philosophy at Cambridge 1952–68, and at Virginia and Oregon. Wisdom was enormously appreciative and yet critical of the anti-metaphysical arguments of both G. E. Moore, with his emphasis on common sense, and the later Wittgenstein, who claimed that metaphysical theories are basically misconceptions caused by our failure to appreciate the variety of functions of ordinary language. Wisdom argued on the contrary that the extraordinary, paradoxical-sounding claims of poets and scientists, theologians, and metaphysicians can be illuminating as well as misleading, and are often both. Plain thought can conceal what extravagant

metaphor reveals—but also vice versa. Thus insight can often be obtained only by appreciating the dialectical argument between the apparently obvious and the flamboyantly surreal, each of which may have something to be said for it.

In *Other Minds* (1952) Wisdom particularly applied these insights to *scepticism and the philosophy of mind.

A.J.L.

John Wisdom, *Philosophy and Psycho-analysis* (Oxford, 1953).

Wissenschaftslehre. German for the 'theory of science or knowledge'. For Fichte, it is simply philosophy, since no opponent of the enterprise is a philosopher; it derives all knowledge and science from a self-evident axiom: 'All other propositions will have only a mediate certainty, derived from it, while it must be immediately certain.' Bolzano's *Wissenschaftslehre* (1837) argues (and helped to convince Husserl) that logic has nothing to do with psychology; it studies non-temporal, non-spatial, ideal objects: proofs, propositions, concepts.

M.J.I.

B. Bolzano, *Theory of Science* (Dordrecht, 1973).
J. G. Fichte, *Science of Knowledge (Wissenschaftslehre)* (New York, 1970).

Wittgenstein, Ludwig Josef Johann (1889–1951). The leading analytical philosopher of the twentieth century, whose two major works altered the course of the subject. Whether by agreement or by disagreement, whether through understanding or misunderstanding, his influence has moulded the evolution of philosophy from the 1920s.

Born in Vienna, he studied engineering, first in Berlin, then in Manchester. Gravitating towards philosophy, he went to Cambridge in 1912 to work with Russell. He served in the Austrian army in the First World War, and while on active duty completed his first masterpiece (and only book published in his lifetime) the *Tractatus Logico-Philosophicus* (1921). From 1920 to 1926 he worked as a schoolteacher. The next two years were occupied with designing and building a mansion in Vienna for his sister. During this period he came into contact with the *Vienna Circle, a group of philosophers much influenced by his early ideas, which, sometimes through misunderstanding, were the mainspring of their Logical Positivism. In 1929 he returned to philosophical work at Cambridge, where he spent the rest of his teaching life. Between 1929 and 1932 his ideas underwent dramatic change, which he consolidated over the next fifteen years. Reacting against his own early philosophy, he developed a quite different viewpoint. Initially communicated only through pupils, these ideas revolutionized philosophy in mid-century. They were given definitive expression in his second masterpiece, the *Philosophical Investigations* (1953), published two years after his death. Over subsequent decades, a further dozen unfinished books and four volumes of lecture notes taken by pupils were published.

Wittgenstein's greatest contributions to philosophy can be classified under five headings: philosophy of language, philosophy of logic, philosophical psychology, philosophy of mathematics, and the clarification of the nature and limits of philosophy itself. In each of these his views are revolutionary and virtually without precedent. On every subject he tackled, he eschewed received positions and rejected traditional alternatives, believing that where philosophy was caught between apparently unavoidable poles, e.g. realism and idealism, Cartesianism and behaviourism, Platonism and formalism, it was the common presuppositions of both that need to be rejected.

The *Tractatus* is a mere seventy-five pages long, written in sybilline, marmoreal sentences. It ranges over metaphysics, logic, and logical truth, the nature of representation in general and of propositional representation in particular, the status of mathematics and of scientific theory, solipsism and the self, ethics and the mystical.

According to the *Tractatus*, the world is the totality of *facts, not *things. The substance of all possible worlds consists of the totality of sempiternal simple objects (e.g. spatio-temporal points, unanalysable properties, and relations). The form of a simple object consists in its combinatorial possibilities with other objects. The possible concatenation of objects constitutes a state of affairs. The obtaining of a state of affairs is a fact. A representation of a state of affairs is a model or picture. It must possess the same logical multiplicity as, and be isomorphic with, what it represents. Propositions are logical pictures. They are essentially bipolar, i.e. capable of being true and also capable of being false. In this their nature reflects the nature of what they represent, since it is of the essence of a state of affairs that it either obtains or does not obtain. An elementary proposition depicts an (atomic) state of affairs. Its constituent names (unanalysable, logically simple names) go proxy for the objects in reality which are what they mean. The logico-syntactical form of a simple name must mirror the metaphysical form of the object that is its meaning. Hence the combinatorial possibilities of names mirror the combinatorial possibilities of objects. It is the fact that the names in a proposition are arranged as they are, in accord with the rules of logical syntax, that says that things are thus-and-so in reality. The sense of a proposition is a function of the meanings of its constituent names. Sense must be absolutely determinate; so any vagueness betokens analysability, and will disappear on analysis. The essence of the proposition is given by the general propositional form, which is: 'This is how things are', i.e. the general form of a description of how things stand in reality. A proposition is true if things in reality are as it depicts them as being.

The logical analysis of propositions must yield propositions which are logically independent of each other, i.e. elementary propositions whose truth depends only on the existence or non-existence of (atomic) states of affairs. Elementary propositions can be combined to form molecular propositions by means of truth-functional operators—the logical connectives. These, contrary to Frege and Russell, are not names of anything (logical objects, functions).

They are merely truth-functional combinatorial devices, which generate truth-dependencies between propositions. All possible forms of truth-functional combination can be generated by the operation of joint-negation on a set of elementary propositions. All logical relations between propositions turn on the inner complexity (the truth-functional combination) of molecular propositions. The only (expressible) form of necessity is *logical necessity. Two limiting cases of combination are senseless (not nonsense): tautologies, which are unconditionally true, and contradictions, which are unconditionally false. In an ideal notation their truth-value would be perspicuous from mere inspection of the symbolism. The necessary truths of logic are not, as Russell thought, descriptions of the most general features of the world; nor are they descriptions of relations between logical objects, as Frege thought. They are *tautologies, molecular propositions which are so combined that bipolarity, and hence all content, cancels out; they all say the same thing, namely nothing. They are 'degenerate' propositions in the sense in which a point is a degenerate conic section. So the truths of logic are not a domain for pure reason alone to attain knowledge about reality, since to know a tautology is to know nothing.

Metaphysical utterances, by contrast, are nonsense—violations of the bounds of sense. For the apparent categorial concepts that occur in them, e.g. 'proposition', 'fact', 'object', 'colour', are not genuine concepts at all, but unbound variables that cannot occur in a well-formed proposition. But what one tries to say by means of the pseudo-propositions of metaphysics (e.g. that red is a colour) is *shown* by features (forms) of genuine propositions containing substitution-instances of these formal concepts (e.g. '*A* is red'). What is shown by a notation cannot be said. Truths of metaphysics are ineffable; and so too are truths of ethics, aesthetics, and religion.

Hence there are no philosophical propositions, i.e. propositions describing the essential natures of things or the metaphysical structure of the world. So the very propositions of the *Tractatus* itself are finally condemned as nonsense—attempts to say what can only be shown. The task of the *Tractatus* was to lead one to a correct logical point of view. Once that is achieved, one can throw away the ladder up which one has climbed. Philosophy is not a science; nor is it in competition with the sciences. It is not the accumulation of knowledge about a subject-matter. Its sole function is to monitor the bounds of sense, to elucidate philosophically problematic sentences, and to show that attempts to traverse the bounds of sense are futile.

The achievement of the *Tractatus* is manifold. (*a*) It brought to full fruition the atomist and foundationalist traditions, the conception of philosophy as analysis of hidden logical structures, the venerable quest for an ideal language or notation, the logico-metaphysical picture of language and logical form as a mirror of the logical structure of the world. Thenceforth these were ripe for demolition—a task that was carried out in the *Investigations*. (*b*)

Its numerous criticisms of Frege and Russell were definitive. (c) The radical conception of philosophy it propounded initiated the so-called *'linguistic turn' characteristic of modern analytical philosophy, and paved the way for the similar, but immeasurably richer, conception of philosophy delineated in the *Investigations*. (d) Its elucidation of the nature of logical necessity and logical truth, though still to be modified and elaborated in the later *Remarks on the Foundations of Mathematics*, was its crowning achievement.

Although the *Philosophical Investigations* was meant to be seen against the backcloth of the *Tractatus*, it is the whole tradition of which the *Tractatus* was the culmination that is being criticized. The criticisms are often indirect, confronting not doctrines and theses, but the presuppositions that inform them.

In his philosophy of language, Wittgenstein now rejected the assumption that the meaning of a word is the thing it stands for. That involves a misuse of the word 'meaning'. There is no such thing as *the* name-relation, and it is confused to suppose that words are connected with reality by semantic links. That supposition rests on a misconstrual of ostensive definition. Not all words are or need to be sharply defined, analysable by specification of necessary and sufficient conditions of application. The demand for determinacy of sense was incoherent. Vagueness is not always a defect, and there is no absolute standard of exactness. The very ideal of analysis (inherited from the Cartesians and Empiricists, and developed afresh by Moore and Russell) was misconceived. The terms 'simple' and 'complex', which are relative, were misused. Many concepts, in particular philosophically crucial ones such as 'proposition', 'language', 'number', are united by family resemblance rather than by common characteristic marks. The thought that all propositions share a common essence, a general propositional form, was misguided. Not all propositions are descriptions, and, even among those that are, there are many different logical kinds of description. It was an error to suppose that the fundamental role of the proposition is to describe a state of affairs. It was a mistake to think that the meaning of a sentence is composed of the meanings of its constituents, and confused to think that truth consists in correspondence between proposition and fact. The institution of language can only be elucidated by attending to the use of words and sentences in the stream of life.

In opposition to the conception that makes truth pivotal to the elucidation of meaning, letting understanding take care of itself, Wittgenstein argued that *meaning is what is given by explanations of meaning, which are rules for the use of words. It is what is understood when one understands what an utterance means. Understanding is an ability, the mastery of the technique of using an expression. It is exhibited in using an expression correctly, in explaining what it means, and in responding appropriately to its use—which are severally criteria of understanding. Forms of explanation are diverse, formal definition being

only one among many, e.g. ostension, paraphrase, contrastive paraphrase, exemplification, explanation by examples, etc. Ostensive definition, which looks as if it links word and world, in fact introduces a sample providing a standard for the correct application of the definiendum. The sample belongs to the method of representation, not to what is represented; hence no link with reality, i.e. with what is represented, is thereby forged.

Consequently the central thought of the *Tractatus*, that any form of *representation is answerable to reality, that it must, in its formal structure, mirror the metaphysical form of the world, is misconceived. Concepts are not correct or incorrect, only more or less useful. Rules for the use of words are not true or false. They are not answerable to reality, nor to antecedently given meanings. Rather they determine the meanings of words, are constitutive of their meanings. Grammar is autonomous. Hence what appear to be necessary metaphysical truths (e.g. that red is a colour), which the *Tractatus* held to be ineffably shown by any symbolism (e.g. any language for the description of coloured things), are actually no more than rules for the use of words in the guise of descriptions (e.g. that if anything can be said to be red, it can also be said to be coloured). What seemed to be a metaphysical co-ordination between language and reality, e.g. between the proposition that p and the fact that p which makes it true, is merely an intragrammatical articulation, namely that 'the proposition that p' = 'the proposition which is true if it is a fact that p'. The apparent harmony between language and reality is merely the shadow cast upon the world by grammar. Hence too, puzzles about the intentionality of thought and language are not to be resolved by means of relations between word and world, or thought and reality, but by clarifying intragrammatical connections within language.

Running through the mainstream tradition of European philosophy is the thought that what is given is subjective experience, that a person knows how things are with him (that he is in pain, is experiencing this or that), but must problematically infer how things are 'outside' him. So the private is better known than the public, mind is better known than matter. Subjective experience was conceived not only as the foundations of empirical knowledge, but also as the foundations of language, i.e. that the meanings of words are fixed by naming subjective impressions (e.g. 'pain' means *this*, which I now have). Wittgenstein's *'private language arguments' mount a comprehensive assault on the presuppositions of this conception.

Conceiving of one's current experience as an object of subjective knowledge is misleading, since the ability, for example, to avow one's pain does not rest on evidence, and one does not find out or verify that one is in pain. Being ignorant of or doubting one's own pain makes no sense, nor therefore does knowing or being certain that one is in pain. To say 'I know I'm in pain' is either an emphatic avowal of pain or a philosopher's nonsense. The thought that no one else can have what I have when I am in pain, hence that I enjoy an epistemically privileged position, is confused. For it rests on the assumption that the pains of different people are at best qualitatively, but not numerically, identical. But that is a distinction applicable to substances, not to impressions. Two people have the same pain if their pains tally in intensity, phenomenological features, and occur in corresponding locations of their bodies. The whole traditional picture is a distortion of the 'inner', under the pressure of misleading pictures embedded in our language and of misconstruals of grammatical asymmetries between first- and third-person psychological sentences. Hence we misconstrue the 'outer' likewise. We do often know that others are in pain on the basis of their behaviour, but this is not inductive or analogical evidence. It is a logical criterion for their pain. Although such criteria are defeasible, in the absence of defeating conditions, it is senseless to doubt whether the sufferer is in pain. The behavioural criteria for the application of a psychological predicate are partly constitutive of its meaning. For expressions signifying the 'inner' are not given their meaning by a private ostensive definition in which a subjective impression functions as a sample. There can be no such thing as a logically private sample, and a sensation cannot fulfil the role of a sample. The elaborate argument to establish this negative conclusion undermines the conception of the 'inner' as a private domain to which its subject enjoys privileged access by means of a faculty of introspection construed on the model of perception.

Contrary to the dominant tradition, Wittgenstein argued that *language is misrepresented as a vehicle for the communication of language-independent thoughts. Speaking is not a matter of translating wordless thoughts into language, and understanding is not a matter of interpreting—transforming dead signs into living thoughts. The limits of thought are determined by the limits of the expression of thoughts. The possession of a language not only expands the intellect, but also extends the will. A dog can want a bone, but only a language-user can now want something next week. It is not thought that breathes life into the signs of a language, but the use of signs in the stream of human life.

Wittgenstein also worked extensively on the philosophy of mathematics. His *Remarks on the Foundations of Mathematics* is as original and revolutionary as everything else he wrote. He developed further his earlier account of logical truth, cutting it free from the metaphysical apparatus of the *Tractatus*. He rejected *logicism, *formalism, and *intuitionism alike. In their place he delineated a normative conception of mathematics. Arithmetic is a system of rules (in the form of descriptions) for the transformation of empirical propositions about the numbers or quantities of things. The propositions of geometry are not descriptions of the properties of space, but are rather constitutive rules for the description of spatial relations. A mathematical proof is misconceived as a demonstration of *truths* about the nature of numbers or geometrical forms. It determines

concepts and so too forms of inference. It is a matter of invention (concept-formation), rather than discovery. To truth in mathematics corresponds sense in inferences among empirical propositions about numbers and magnitudes of things. Wittgenstein's views here, however, have proved to be too radical and difficult for the age, and have met largely with incomprehension and misinterpretation.

The revolutionary conception of philosophy propounded in the *Tractatus* finds its counterpart in Wittgenstein's later philosophy. Philosophy, he continued to argue, is not a cognitive discipline. There are no philosophical propositions and no philosophical knowledge. If there were theses in philosophy, everyone would agree with them, for they would be mere grammatical truisms (e.g. that we know that someone is in pain by his behaviour). The task of philosophy is to clear away the conceptual confusions that stand in the way of accepting these rule-governed articulations in our language. There is no room for theories in philosophy, for in philosophy we are moving around within our own grammar, dissolving philosophical questions by examining the rules for the use of words with which we are familiar. For there are no such things as hidden rules which are followed, or discoveries about the real meanings of expressions in use which are unknown to all users. Philosophical problems stem from entanglement in linguistic rules, e.g. projecting the *grammar of one kind of expression upon another (the grammar of 'pin' on to 'pain'), or projecting norms of representation on to reality and thinking that we are confronting metaphysical necessities in the world (e.g. 'Nothing can be red and green all over'), or placing demands upon certain concepts, e.g. that they lend themselves to certain kinds of explanation, which are only appropriate for concepts of a different category. The methods of philosophy are purely descriptive. The task of philosophy is conceptual clarification and the dissolution of philosophical problems. The goal of philosophy is not knowledge but understanding. P.M.S.H.

*quietism, philosophical; Wittgenstein, the new; Wittgensteinians.

L. Wittgenstein, *Tractatus Logico-Philosophicus* (first pub. 1921; London, 1961).
——*Philosophical Investigations* (first pub. 1953; Oxford, 1958).
INTRODUCTIONS AND COMMENTARIES
G. P. Baker and P. M. S. Hacker, *An Analytical Commentary on the* Philosophical Investigations, i: *Wittgenstein: Understanding and Meaning*, 2nd rev. edn., (Oxford, 2005); ii: *Wittgenstein: Rules, Grammar and Necessity* (Oxford, 1985). P. M. S. Hacker, *An Analytical Commentary on the* Philosophical Investigations, iii: *Wittgenstein: Meaning and Mind* (Oxford, 1990); iv: *Wittgenstein: Mind and Will* (Oxford, 1995).
M. Black, *A Companion to Wittgenstein's* Tractatus (Cambridge, 1964).
P. M. S. Hacker, *Insight and Illusion: Themes in the Philosophy of Wittgenstein*, rev. edn. (Oxford, 1986).
A. J. P. Kenny, *Wittgenstein* (London, 1973).
M. McGinn, *Wittgenstein and the* Philosophical Investigations (London, 1997).

H. Sluga and D. Stern (eds.), *The Cambridge Companion to Wittgenstein* (Cambridge, 1996).

Wittgenstein, the new.

In recent years a revisionary view of Wittgenstein's thought has emerged, championed by Cora Diamond, Stanley Cavell, Hilary Putnam, and others. Its two central tenets are that the early and late work of Wittgenstein (respectively and chiefly the *Tractatus* and the *Philosophical Investigations*) are continuous with each other, and share a fundamental purpose in common, which is a 'therapeutic' one, aimed at curing the philosophical disease of creating problems where none exist by misunderstandings about the way language works.

The standard view repudiated by proponents of the 'new Wittgenstein' is a familiar one. It says that in the *Tractatus* Wittgenstein set out a view of the relation between language and the world in which the structure of each mirrors the other, as a result of a denoting relation between the simplest elements of language ('names') and the world ('objects'). His later philosophy is premised on an emphatic rejection of this view in favour of the idea that meaning is a function of use within 'language-games' embedded in 'forms of life'. In the earlier philosophy, accordingly, his account can be described as truth-conditional and realist, while in the latter it is closer to an assertibility-conditions account, and is anti-realist.

The 'new Wittgenstein' advocates reject this story completely. They argue instead that Wittgenstein's aims were the same throughout his earlier and later work, and that its basis is the rejection of the idea that language can be understood from an external point of view. Grasping this cures one (hence the invocation of the idea of 'therapy') of the temptation to undertake traditional philosophical inquiry. The principal concerns of the *Investigations* are thus to be found in the *Tractatus*, and vice versa, and this—so these advocates urge—requires a radical new view of Wittgenstein's philosophy.   A.C.G.

Cora Diamond, *The Realistic Spirit* (Cambridge, Mass., 1991).

Wittgensteinians.

Wittgenstein's impact upon analytical philosophy is second to none. Although he did not, nor indeed did he wish to, found a philosophical school of thinkers, the evolution of twentieth-century philosophy would be as unintelligible without his work as would that of twentieth-century art without Picasso's. His influence is marked by two waves and their aftermath. The *Tractatus* (1921) was the leading text of *logical atomism and the main inspiration of the *Vienna Circle (and acknowledged as such in their Manifesto). The positivists' conception of philosophy as analysis, of logical truths as vacuous tautologies, and of metaphysical assertions as nonsense, was derived from the *Tractatus*. The *principle of verification was derived from discussions with Wittgenstein, and so too, with considerable misunderstanding, was their conventionalism in logic and mathematics. Although Carnap could not be called 'a Wittgensteinian', he acknowledged Wittgenstein's formative influence, and his *Logical Syntax of Language* is heavily indebted to the *Tractatus*. Logical

Positivism developed its own momentum in the 1930s, and, through A. J. Ayer in Britain and Carnap in the USA, became extremely influential. M. Schlick and F. Waismann, however, were more influenced by the second phase of Wittgenstein's thought, and their work, from the early 1930s onwards, bears its hallmark.

While the Circle was developing their *Wissenschaftliches Weltauffassung*, a research programme for a 'scientific world-outlook', Wittgenstein, then teaching in Cambridge, was moving off in fresh directions, which led to the *Philosophical Investigations*. He repudiated much of his earlier philosophy, replacing it with a very different viewpoint. His main work in this second phase of his career focused upon philosophy of language and logic, philosophy of mind, and philosophy of mathematics. In each of these he adopted revolutionary and wholly original positions. His primary influence was exerted through his teaching. Among his pupils in the 1930s were A. Ambrose, M. Black, D. A. T. Gasking, M. MacDonald, N. Malcolm, G. A. Paul, R. Rhees, C. L. Stevenson, G. H. von Wright, and J. Wisdom. During the post-war years, G. E. M. Anscombe, P. Geach, N. Malcolm, I. Murdoch, and S. Toulmin attended his classes. Through these and others, and through the circulation of unpublished dictations, the influence of Wittgenstein's later philosophy spread.

The scene was transformed by the publication of the *Investigations* (1953), which was followed by further unfinished works and lectures. This made his thought available to a wider philosophical public. From the 1960s a fresh generation of philosophers followed Wittgenstein's footsteps. They, together with Wittgenstein's pupils, contributed to the elucidation and extension of Wittgenstein's ideas. The clarification and interpretation of his thought has been a major task occupying numerous writers. More than 7,000 books and articles have been published on his work. The extension and further application of his ideas has borne a rich harvest. Important work was done in the philosophy of mind, repudiating empiricist conceptions of the mental as well as behaviourist and materialist ones, and developing teleological, anti-causalist, accounts of action and its explanation: on intention, action, and the will, Anscombe, A. J. P. Kenny, F. Stoutland, and von Wright; on consciousness and memory, Malcolm; on psychoanalysis, F. Cioffi, I. Dilman, and Wisdom; on sensation and perception, P. M. S. Hacker and B. Rundle; on aspect-perception, S. Mulhall; on personal identity and the first-person pronoun, Anscombe, Kenny, S. Shoemaker, and P. F. Strawson. Noteworthy applications of Wittgenstein's ideas to anthropology and the social sciences were made by Cioffi and P. Winch, to philosophy of religion by D. Z. Phillips. In philosophy of language, Wittgenstein's views were very influential during the 1950s and 1960s, emphasis being placed upon use rather than on logical form, on description rather than on theory-construction. Anscombe's and Geach's work here was broadly Wittgensteinian (though also Fregean). Other extensions of his philosophy of language were made by J. Hunter and Rundle. It was applied in criticism of contemporary linguistic theory and philosophical theories of meaning by G. P. Baker and Hacker. Wittgenstein's philosophy of mathematics received least attention, but important attempts to come to grips with it were made by Waismann, Ambrose, and S. Shanker, who has also applied Wittgenstein's ideas in criticism of cognitive science and artificial intelligence. Although Wittgenstein wrote little on ethics, attempts to elaborate his ideas were made by P. Johnston, and to apply them by Winch. A highly original application of Wittgensteinian methodology to general value-theory was made by von Wright.

Disagreements among Wittgensteinians, over both the interpretation and application of his ideas, has been almost as extensive as the disagreements between Wittgensteinians and other philosophers. Some main areas of controversy among his followers have been: (*a*) the interpretation of the private-language arguments, in particular whether they commit one to the view that the concept of a language and hence of a language-user is internally related to that of a linguistic community; (*b*) the interpretation of his discussion of following a rule, in particular whether his purpose was to resolve a paradox about rule-following by reference to community agreement in acting on a given rule, or to show that the paradox itself rests on a philosophical confusion; (*c*) the elucidation of his concept of a *criterion, which has been variously interpreted as a necessary condition, necessary and sufficient condition, or as necessarily, but defeasible, good evidence for that for which it is a criterion; (*d*) whether his discussion of ostensive definition is intended to show that it is a defective form of explanation of word-meaning, or rather to show that it is not a privileged form of explanation which links language to reality; (*e*) how much continuity there is between his early and later philosophy; (*f*) whether his later philosophy consists of systematic argument which purports to demonstrate the incoherence of opposing positions, or whether it consists of unsystematic *aperçus* designed to effect a *Gestalt*-switch.

Critics of Wittgenstein's later philosophy have argued that he must, in the private language arguments, rely on a principle of verification, that he is a crypto-behaviourist, that he is committed to a form of linguistic idealism or anti-realism, that his philosophy of mathematics involves a 'full-blooded' or 'existentialist' form of conventionalism, or that he is propounding a use-theory of meaning. These criticisms demonstrably rest on misunderstandings and misinterpretations. More serious criticisms, still currently debated, turn on whether his general conception of philosophy justifiably excludes theory-construction in philosophy, whether his philosophy of mathematics does not neglect the extent to which mathematical proof is predetermined by antecedent commitments of axioms and proven theorems, and whether his animadversion to the construction of a theory of meaning and his elucidations of meaning in terms of use are defensible.

P.M.S.H.

A more comprehensive delineation of his impact can be found in P. M. S. Hacker, *Wittgenstein's Position in Twentieth-Century Analytic Philosophy* (Oxford, 1996), the fifth and final vol. of his *Analytical Commentary on the* Philosophical Investigations.

Wolff, Christian (1679–1750). German philosopher who presented much of Leibniz's philosophy in the format of Protestant scholasticism. The dominant doctrine and ideology of the German Enlightenment before Kant was the so-called Leibniz–Wolffian philosophy; but both Leibniz and Wolff objected to this name, rightly, because Wolff was ignorant of, or rejected, some of Leibniz's main teachings, and besides was closer to Descartes than to Leibniz. Wolff was banished from the University of Halle (1723) for denying the necessity of a Christian foundation for ethics and for allegedly teaching a fatalistic ethics. He then had a successful career at Marburg until recalled to Prussia by Frederick the Great (1740). He was a prolific and verbose (and ruthlessly boring) writer in both Latin and German, and his most lasting contribution was in establishing German as a language for philosophy. His many disciples were among Kant's foremost critics. L.W.B.

L. W. Beck, *Early German Philosophy* (Cambridge, Mass., 1969), ch. xi.
——'From Leibniz to Kant', in *Routledge History of Philosophy* (London, 1993), vol. vi, ch. 1.

Wollheim, Richard (1923–2003). English philosopher (at University College London and at Berkeley) who wrote on philosophy of mind, ethics, aesthetics, political philosophy, and history of philosophy. Wollheim worked on, *inter alia*, the ontology of art and the nature of painting. He was a sympathetic interpreter of Freudian ideas, especially as developed by Melanie Klein. Wollheim's interest in *psychoanalysis is basic to much of his philosophy, including his ethics. He described his attraction to 'moral philosophy . . . pursued as moral psychology', both 'the study of those mental processes which are involved in moral deliberation, moral decision, and moral action . . . moral reasoning, its nature and the defects to which it is susceptible', and especially the study of 'the growth of the moral sense'. E.T.S.

Richard Wollheim, *Art and its Objectives* (1968; 2nd edn. Cambridge, 1980).
—— *On the Emotions* (New Haven, Conn., 1999).

Wollstonecraft, Mary (1759–97). Political writer and novelist, sometimes (inaccurately) called the first feminist. *A Vindication of the Rights of Woman* (1792) expresses the liberal longing for, and belief in the possibility of, a social order in which every individual is free from the shackles of superstition and false authority. Wollstonecraft believed that the moral and intellectual capacities essential to such an order are latent in humanity, their actual presence thwarted by male power. Reason has been involved in error, having been confined to partial, male experience; the truth of which men pretend to judge in relation to women has been shaped to their convenience. Women, deprived of education, taught to defer to men, and appraised according to the double standard of morality, have been prevented from exercising genuine judgement or attaining genuine virtue.   J.HORN.

*feminism.

Claire Tomalin, *The Life and Death of Mary Wollstonecraft* (Harmondsworth, 1985).

women in philosophy. Women philosophers seem to be largely absent from the history of philosophy, according to many philosophy department syllabuses. In fact, women have been practising philosophers for many centuries, but a great deal of research has had to be dedicated to recovering their work in order to be able to evaluate it; see e.g. Mary Ellen Waithe (ed.), *A History of Women Philosophers*, 4 vols. (Dordrecht, 1984).

The apparent invisibility of women in philosophy or lack of 'great' women philosophers has been attributed to many causes. One reason is the selection process which has been used to construct the canon of philosophy, a framework which has used certain criteria to determine which topics, individuals, or texts can be defined as philosophical and included in the canon. Women have tended to fare badly in this selection process in the past because social perceptions of their basic abilities have affected assessment of their philosophical achievements.

Such perceptions of women's abilities are also to be found within philosophy. Many philosophers have written *about* women; much of what has been said has been largely derogatory or dismissive. For example, Plato, Aristotle, Kant, Rousseau, Schopenhauer, and Nietzsche all discuss the topic of women, often with regard to women's capacity for philosophical rationality, and frequently find them inferior in this respect.

Although it is easy to document examples of misogynistic remarks, it is only comparatively recently that their implications have been considered, in the context of feminist reappraisals of philosophy and attempts to explain women's invisibility in philosophical history. Because such remarks may be seen as embarrassing, irrelevant, or outdated historical prejudice, they have often been disregarded in the overall assessment of a philosopher's work. Such remarks may have been discounted because it is assumed that liberal intellectuals no longer hold such views. Or it may be that such passages are seen as irrelevant to real philosophical matter and can be easily discarded. But this position assumes (i) that we can clearly identify first-order philosophical problems and (ii) that such passages are independent of what the philosopher says elsewhere (for example, about human nature in general), and can be removed without affecting the overall framework.

If the exclusion of women from philosophy is merely a social–historical accident and due to lack of opportunity, then it may be corrected with time. But the problem may run much deeper. The association of philosophy with a professional, public practice of rationality may mean women have tended to avoid such a 'masculine' role and have chosen more characteristically 'feminine' interests.

Within philosophy, the identification of certain dominant topics or interests with 'masculine' values may have implicitly or explicitly excluded women: ways of looking at knowledge, the self, reason, and ethics which seem to reinforce 'masculine' values may discourage or exclude women, either by implying that they are less able practitioners, or by valuing their work on alternative topics as 'less' philosophical.

But despite such discouragement, and as a result of social and economic changes, many more women were professional philosophers in the last century than in previous centuries. Well-known examples of recent women philosophers include Philippa Foot, Iris Murdoch, Elizabeth Anscombe, and Luce Irigaray, and earlier thinkers include Hannah Arendt, Simone Weil, Simone de Beauvoir, and Mary Wollstonecraft. Not all of these philosophers would necessarily describe themselves as feminists, but it may be as a result of feminist arguments in favour of their worth that they are given more prominence. Debates are continuing over whether there are specifically female, feminine, or feminist viewpoints within philosophy, what characteristics they might display, and whether they help or hinder women philosophers in their work.   A.C.A.

*feminism; feminist philosophy.

Ellen Kennedy and Susan Mendus (eds.), *Women in Western Political Philosophy: Kant to Nietzsche* (Brighton, 1987).
Michèle Le Dœuff, *Hipparchia's Choice: An Essay Concerning Women, Philosophy, etc.* (Oxford, 1991).
Susan Moller Okin, *Women in Western Political Thought* (Princeton, NJ, 1981).

worker control. An economic system that is characterized by (1) each individual business enterprise being managed democratically by its workers, and (2) the economy as a whole relying upon the market—that is, upon supply and demand rather than central planning—for determining the prices of all goods and services and the incomes people get for producing them. Democratic management by the workers may take the form of direct democracy, but, for larger enterprises, it will usually take the form of representative democracy where the workers, periodically, elect a management team, and the management team will then control the everyday affairs of the enterprise. Worker-control systems can be classified as either *worker-control* *socialism* or *worker-control* *capitalism*. Worker-control socialism (sometimes referred to as *market socialism*) is characterized by public ownership of the means of production and government planning of most new investment throughout the economy. Worker-control capitalism is characterized by the means of production for each business enterprise being owned privately by the workers of that enterprise themselves, and by the absence of any government planning of investment, which is to be left to the market.

Among the advantages that advocates of worker control claim for this system are greater worker autonomy and a more equal distribution of income. With worker control, income, being market-determined, will not be distributed equally. Since, however, investment income will no longer be concentrated largely in the hands of just a relatively few wealthy individuals, and since control of each business enterprise will be in the hands of its workers, incomes will, so it is argued, be distributed more equally than in traditional capitalism. But perhaps the greatest alleged advantage is that worker-controlled enterprises are structured so that management, having to face workers in periodic elections, will thus be motivated primarily to please *them*, which will lead to safer, more pleasant working conditions, less tedious, more challenging work, a more favourable balance between work and leisure, and any number of other benefits for workers.　　D.W.HAS.

David Miller, *Market, State and Community* (Oxford, 1989).
David Schweickart, *Capitalism or Worker Control?* (New York, 1980).

world philosophy. The first important European philosopher seriously to consider the philosophical traditions of other civilizations, Hegel, viewed them as episodes in a development that culminated in his own metaphysics. While some recent books on world philosophy share Hegel's comparative concerns, their authors eschew his teleological predilections and reject his disdainful attitude to non-Western traditions. Instead, they write from the conviction that these traditions, especially *Chinese, *Japanese, and *Indian, are sophisticated ones that have been wrongly ignored by Western philosophers. (Sometimes the expression 'world philosophy' is confined to non-Western thought.) At a minimum, examination of these traditions acquaints us with thinkers of genius and challenging ideas, and may, in addition, contribute fruitful perspectives on live philosophical issues that know no geographical or cultural boundaries. A matter which divides advocates of world philosophy is whether the belief systems of non-literate civilizations, such as some African ones, should be included in its purview.　　D.E.C.

D. E. Cooper, *World Philosophies: An Historical Introduction*, 2nd rev. edn. (Oxford, 2002).
E. Deutsch and R. Bontekoe (eds.), *A Companion to World Philosophies* (Oxford, 1997).

world-soul. Hegel was living in Jena in 1806 when Napoleon crushed the Prussian army at the battle named after that city. He wrote in a letter: 'The Emperor—this world-soul—I saw riding through the city to review his troops. It is indeed a wonderful feeling to see such an individual who, here concentrated into a single point, reaches out over the world and dominates it'. Since history has, for Hegel, a goal, the world-soul is the instrument of a larger destiny.　　P.S.

G. W. F. Hegel, *Lectures on the Philosophy of History*, tr. J. Sibree (New York, 1956).

Wright, Chauncey (1830–75). American pragmatist and enthusiast for *evolution, Wright so impressed Darwin that the Englishman had his writings on the subject

reprinted and published in book form as a refutation of critics. Wright was nevertheless a stern critic of Spencer, especially the way in which the latter was trying to make a world philosophy from an amalgam of progressivist evolution, Lamarckian inheritance of acquired characters, and a misunderstanding of the second law of thermodynamics. Never a prolific writer, and better in tutorial than lecture theatre, Wright nevertheless influenced many of the better-known pragmatists, especially James. His own most original contribution was in an analysis of *causality, distinguishing between those causes which entirely explain their effects and those where something new appears. In this second category, Wright was clearly hinting at doctrines of *emergence (like that of Alexander) that were to become so popular fifty years after his death. Whether so clear-headed a thinker would have welcomed so fuzzy a philosophy is another matter.　　M.R.

E. H. Madden, *Chauncy Wright* (New York, 1964).
C. Wright, *Philosophical Discussions* (New York, 1877).

Wright, Crispin (1942–). British philosopher who has written extensively on the work of the later Wittgenstein, Frege, the debate between realists and anti-realists, vagueness, and scepticism.

The most notable aspect of Wright's work has been his attempt to develop and defend his anti-realist position, according to which whatever is true must be in some sense knowable. In this area Wright is deeply influenced by Dummett, who has been engaged in the same enterprise. However, the views of the two philosophers are not identical, and there are definite disagreements concerning, for example, the revisionary consequences of an anti-realist theory of meaning for logic.

In his work on Wittgenstein, Wright has been centrally concerned with the rule-following considerations and has developed a sophisticated interpretation not identical with, but in many ways similar to, that of Kripke.　　H.W.N.

*realism and anti-realism.

Crispin Wright, *Realism, Meaning and Truth*, 2nd edn. (Oxford, 1993).

Wyclif, John (before 1330–after 1380). A student at Oxford, and Master of Balliol (1360), he wrote widely on philosophy and theology, and made a major contribution to the first English translation of the Bible. His writings contain strong criticisms of Church teachings and practice, and those criticisms plus his contribution to the translation of the Bible led to his being termed, with some justice, 'the Morning Star of the Reformation'. His chief philosophical work, the *Summa de Ente*, contains a treatise on the problem of *universals, in which he presents and defends a strongly realist position, maintaining that the common nature in virtue of which something is a member of its species must have an existence entirely independent of any mind.　　A.BRO.

A. Kenny (ed.), *Wyclif in his Times* (Oxford, 1986).

X

Xenocrates (396–314 BC). Successor to Speusippus as head of Plato's *Academy. Xenocrates wrote treatises in which he attempted to systematize Platonism. These treatises are lost, but the range of his work may be guessed at from a list of titles contained in the brief biography by Diogenes Laertius. Xenocrates was the first of the school of Plato to attempt to respond to Aristotle's criticisms. His formulation of *Platonism was to become highly influential in the later tradition. In particular, Xenocrates' division of philosophy into three branches, physics, ethics, and logic, helped shape *Hellenistic philosophy and its understanding of its fourth-century predecessors.   L.P.G.

John Dillon, *The Middle Platonists 80 BC to AD 220* (Ithaca, NY, 1977).

Xenophanes of Colophon (c.560–c.470 BC). Pre-Socratic philosopher, cosmologist, and theologian; author of the first known discussion of epistemology. He made the fundamental point that, to claim knowledge, it is not suffi-cient to 'speak what is completely true', and seems have to have thought that there was no possibility of *knowledge outside the realm of direct experience. In its place he proposed to put 'opinions resembling the things which are true', which must mean that they are straightforwardly extrapolated from the world of direct experience. What is known of his cosmology seems to show that he practised what he preached.

In theology he satirized traditional anthropomorph-ism, remarking that each race represented its gods in its own image, and concluding that, if horses could draw, they would draw their gods looking like horses. He also attacked the traditional stories about the Greek gods as immoral. In its place he proposed a transcendent monotheism. He seems to have deduced the properties of his god from an overall principle of what is 'fitting'; the first known attempt at philosophical theology.   E.L.H.

J. H. Lesher, *Xenophanes of Colophon* (Toronto, 1992).

Y

yin and yang: *see* Chinese philosophy.

Yoga: *see* Aurobindo; Hindu philosophy.

Yugoslav philosophy: *see* Croat philosophy; Serbian philosophy; Slovene philosophy.

Z

Zeitgeist. In retrospect, ages seem to have spirits, which historians identify. But is it possible to identify the spirit of a present age, and, if so, what if anything should we do as a result? Talk of the spirit of the age in the twentieth century was often used by tyrants and bureaucrats to suppress criticism from those who objected to their vision of the age. We should remember that individuals create their ages, and that individuals of *genius transform them.   A.O'H.

K. R. Popper, *The Poverty of Historicism* (London, 1957).

Zen. A form of Buddhism that developed in China and spread to Japan which gives central importance to meditation and to the idea that the world, seen through eyes unclouded by desire, is beautiful. It is like a philosophical iceberg: almost all of the philosophy is beneath the surface. Buddhism in general is dedicated to the proposition that desires (i.e. strong preferences that involve attachment) are the primary cause of suffering, and that liberation will be the result of shedding the illusion of a substantial self and losing one's desires; this is generally implicit rather than explicit in Zen texts. They also take from the Mādhyamika school of Buddhist philosophy the anti-realist claim that there is no objectively correct and definitive perspective on anything. This is dramatized in the Zen literature, rather than argued for, by use of puzzles (*Koans*) for which there could be no literally correct solution and by amusing exchanges intended to undercut any tendency to believe in, or take seriously, the literal truth of anything.   J.J.K.

*Buddhist philosophy.

An examination of Zen that is more philosophically probing than most is to be found in D. T. Suzuki, *The Zen Doctrine of No-Mind* (York Beach, Me., 1972).

Zeno of Citium. This Zeno (334–262 BC) must be distinguished from the earlier (fifth century) Pre-Socratic Zeno of Elea. Zeno of Citium was the founder of the Hellenistic school of Stoic philosophy. The main features of early Stoic thought were a corporealist and dynamic philosophy of nature, an empiricist epistemology, an absolutist conception of moral duty, and an internationalist theory of social organization. Zeno's writings are all lost; but his contribution to this complex system seems to have been

particularly in the areas of epistemology and political philosophy. He wrote a widely admired *Republic*, which expounded such key Stoic themes as the importance of the rule of law and the universality of human political institutions. In epistemology and ethics he is explicitly associated with the absolutist view, according to which a person either completely attains or totally misses scientific knowledge and virtue.   J.D.G.E.

*Stoicism.

For a judicious assessment of the distinctly Zenonian features of early Stoicism, see A. A. Long and D. N. Sedley, *The Hellenistic Philosophers*, 2 vols. (Cambridge, 1987).

Zeno of Elea (*c*.470 BC). Fellow citizen and associate of Parmenides; admired by Plato as 'the Eleatic Palamedes' and by Aristotle as the inventor of philosophical dialectic. Zeno is not known to have advanced any positive views. He devised an arsenal of destructive arguments, directed against opponents of Parmenides. (Some seem to be *ad hominem*.) These exploit properties of the infinite, and use (perhaps for the first time) *infinite regress as an argumentative device. Those for which there is evidence may be grouped as: (1) arguments against plurality (against the thesis 'There are many things'); (2) arguments against the possibility of motion; (3) others.

1. The arguments against plurality systematically deduced contradictions from the premiss that 'There are many things'. Three survive in whole or in part. (*a*) 'If there are many things, they must be both great and small: so small as to have no size, so great as to be infinite.' The second limb of the argument employs the 'dichotomy' principle: anything with size can be divided into two things each with size; hence there is a process which never terminates. (*b*) If there is plurality, the total of things must be both finite and infinite in *number*: finite because a plurality implies a definite and therefore a finite number; infinite because two or more things require boundaries or more generally distinguishing marks, and here again a progression to infinity sets in. (*c*) 'If there are many things they must be both like and unlike.' The supporting arguments are not recorded.

(2). The famous *'paradoxes of motion', recorded by Aristotle, use assumptions about the spatial and temporal properties of change to demonstrate that change is impossible. (*a*) The 'race-course' (also known as the 'stadium' or 'dichotomy'). A runner has to run a given length. Before running the whole length, he must have run half of it. Then, before running the second half, he must have run half of that half. And so on. Since the division again never terminates, the whole stretch is composed of infinitely many successive pieces, each of some length. But the runner cannot finish the task of traversing infinitely many substretches in succession. (*b*) The 'Achilles'. A slow runner is given a start by a fast runner. The fast one can never catch up: again he has to traverse infinitely many successive stretches, first to the slower runner's starting-point, then to the point the slow runner has reached by then, and so on. (*c*) The 'arrow'. In any indivisible instant of its flight, is a flying arrow moving or at rest? If the former, how can it move in an instant? If the latter, it is never moving, and therefore is at rest. (*d*) The 'moving rows' (also known as the 'stadium') A paradox involving relative motion; the details are unclear.

(3). Other arguments recorded are: (*a*) one about 'place', again constructing an infinite progression (if everything that is in a place, and place is, then a place is in a place, and so *ad infinitum*); (*b*) possibly the first sorites argument (about the smallest *heap of grain to make an audible noise when dropped; details unreliable).   E.L.H.

G. E. L. Owen, 'Zeno and the Mathematicians', *Proceedings of the Aristotelian Society* (1957–8).

W. C. Salmon (ed.), *Zeno's Paradoxes* (Indianapolis, 1970).

G. Vlastos, 'Zeno of Elea', in P. Edwards (ed.), *The Encyclopedia of Philosophy* (New York, 1967).

zombies. The zombies of Haitian voodoo lore and horror movies are the 'living dead', but the philosopher's zombies are merely the stuff of *thought experiments. A zombie, if there could be such a thing, would be a living creature that was indistinguishable in its physical constitution and in terms of its outward appearance and behaviour from a normal human being, but in whom the light of *consciousness was completely absent: a being with no inner, conscious mental life, no first-person point of view, no *qualia—in short, a being such that there would be *nothing it was like* to be that being. But could there be such a being? It is not enough to point out that we can *imagine* there being zombies, because not everything that we can imagine is really possible (*time-travel may be an example). It may be difficult to determine whether zombies really are possible, but the issue undoubtedly has far-reaching implications for the metaphysics of mind.

E.J.L.

D. J. Chalmers, *The Conscious Mind* (Oxford, 1996).

Zoroastrianism. An ancient Persian religion, most likely to be known to philosophers either in connection with Nietzsche's naming the central character of *Thus Spoke Zarathustra* after its founder or because Pierre Bayle in his *Dictionary* (1697) presented it as a key to the problem of evil. Zarathustra is now thought to have flourished in the middle of the second millennium BC. In an audacious transvaluation, he proclaimed the gods (*daevas*) worshipped by the very ancient Persians to be evil. The leader of the *daevas* is the eternal opponent of the one good God, Ahura Mazda. The feature of Zoroastrianism that attracted Bayle is that the forces of good and evil are about equally matched. At the end of time Ahura Mazda will score a final victory, but until then he often fails to control events. Consequently Zoroastrianism, unlike Christianity, Judaism, and Islam, escapes the paradox of an all-powerful God who is responsible for what many people take to be unnecessary *evil.   J.J.K.

Mary Boyce, *Zoroastrians: Their Religious Beliefs and Practices* (London, 1979).

Logical Symbols

A book like this cannot define the logical symbols precisely, both because they may have somewhat different definitions in different logical systems, and because the methods of definition used by logicians cannot be explained in a few words. The following list merely offers rough equivalents in English for symbols and letters that are used in the *Companion*, with a few comments. For a more generous list of some of the alternatives see the entry 'notations, logical'. And do note that any explanation given within a particular article overrides what is said here.

~ or ¬ or – or N	not
· or & or ∧	and
∨	or
⊃ or →	if (i.e. '$P \supset Q$' and '$P \rightarrow Q$' mean 'If P, Q'; signs for material implication)
⥽	if (similarly; a sign for strict implication)
≡ or ↔	if and only if (material equivalence)
=	is the same as, *or* if and only if (strict equivalence)
∀	all ('∀x' etc. are sometimes written '(x)' etc.)
∃	some, at least one, there exists, i.e. not ∀ not
□ or L	necessarily
◊ or M	possibly, i.e. not □ not
∈	is a member of (a set or class)
∉	negates ∈
≠	negates =
∩	indicates intersection
∪	indicates union

Letters are very variously employed, and the following is no more than a guide to usage in the *Companion*. What are here called schematic letters (*schema) are sometimes brought under the general label *'variables'.

P, Q or p, q, etc.	schematic letters for replacement by indicative sentences, or by names of such sentences
F, G, etc.	schematic letters for replacement by predicates (e.g. 'is a swan', 'laughs', 'is to the left of'), *or* by terms (e.g. 'swans', 'black things')

R	schematic letter for replacement by two-place predicates (e.g. 'is to the left of'), *or* by indicative sentences
S, P	schematic letters for replacement by terms
a, b, etc. or X, Y	schematic letters for replacement by singular names or referring expressions (in predicate logic these are written after predicate letters, e.g. '*Fa*', '*Rba*'), *or* by terms
x, y, z, etc.	individual variables
α, Γ, Δ, etc.	variables used informally, i.e. not as parts of a logical language, for talking about—usually generalizing over—expressions of a logical language, or sets of them
n, m	the same for talking about numbers
t, t_1, etc.	the same for time instants
w, w_1, etc.	the same for possible worlds
E, F	the same for events
ϕ, ψ	like α, Γ, Δ etc. *or* general like x, y, z, etc.
A, B, etc.	very general—used *either* like S, P, etc. *or* like α, Γ, etc. *or* like a, b, etc. *or* even like P, Q, etc.

Other letters are explained in their places in the book, or are self-explanatory.

C.A.K.

Maps of Philosophy

Mapping philosophy is as difficult as mapping the world. Asia and Alaska are likely to be a whole map-width apart, despite the mere 56 miles that really separates them. On one projection Africa will look like a squashed-up kidney bean, on another like a woebegone banana. On one the world itself will appear as an ellipse, on another as two circles. The world has two hemispheres (east and west) but also two other hemispheres (north and south). Equal-area and equal-population maps (where equal areas on the page represent equal areas on the ground, or equal populations, respectively) may be almost unrecognizable as

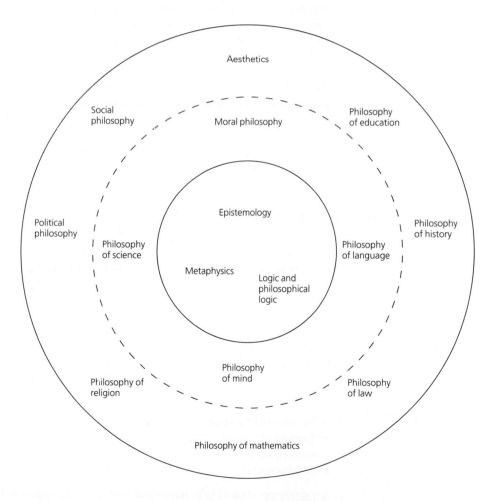

Inner and outer circles of philosophy

referring to the same planet. Yet maps are made and are useful. Most normal maps (though not all possible ones) will show London as between Cambridge and Brighton. The situation is the same in philosophy. There is no one way of mapping it. Different, perhaps overlapping, perhaps inconsistent, maps may be used for different purposes, and will all be horribly misleading unless used merely as over-simplified rough guides. It is essential that the reader remember these points when looking at the following pages.

Inner and Outer Circles of Philosophy

Philosophy can be thought of as concerning what in the most general sense there is, what we can know and how, and the most general conditions that must be satisfied by any coherent thought. This gives us the three items in the central circle. The items in the outer circles are less general and concern limited areas. They also tend to depend on the central items in ways that those do not depend on them in return. For instance, moral philosophy often depends on theories of implication, which belong in logic and philosophical logic, but logic and philosophical logic do not themselves depend for their tools on moral philosophy. The relation between the two outer circles is somewhat similar, though less markedly so. Political philosophy, for instance, seems to presuppose moral philosophy without being presupposed by it. No doubt for these reasons philosophers have given more attention to the more central items, so that the diagram also to some extent maps popularity. However, both the circles themselves and the regions within them should be thought of as only rather vaguely delimited. There are multiple overlaps, and in particular no attempt has been made to order the items within each ring, which are arranged alphabetically, reading clockwise from the top; no significance attaches to co-radiality.

Groups of Parts of Philosophy

I

Epistemology
Philosophy of science

II

Metaphysics
Philosophy of mind
Philosophy of religion

III

Aesthetics
Moral philosophy
Political philosophy

IV

Logic
Philosophical logic
Philosophy of language
Philosophy of mathematics

V

Philosophy of education
Philosophy of history
Philosophy of law
Social philosophy

Any grouping is bound to be somewhat arbitrary and roughshod, but the reader may find it helpful for certain similarities to be pointed out, bearing in mind always that the grouping presented here, though it has the rationale explained below, is certainly not unique.

Group I has in common a concern with the conditions under which we can know something, the justifications that we can offer for claims to know it, and the methods that may help us to come to know it.

Group II asks primarily about what there is, either completely generally or in certain obviously important spheres such as that of beings as developed as ourselves or that of the ultimate power, if any, behind the universe. It then asks about the nature of these various things.

Group III combines various questions concerned in one way or another with value: what sorts of value there are, what things are valuable in these various ways, and what connection there is between value and a duty to produce it, as well as the question what alternatives, if any, to value can be offered as a foundation for our duties.

Group IV mainly concerns abstract structures, and in particular the structure of any coherent thinking and the tools that are essential for such thinking—since presumably we could not think in any effective way without language.

Group V, finally, is a bit of a ragbag since it consists of philosophical problems directed at various particular subject areas. The list could be extended almost indefinitely, since there are usually at least some philosophical problems attached specifically to each of the special sciences or other major areas of human activity. Those mentioned have achieved a certain entrenchment, presumably because, although each of them has connections with various items in the other four groups, they are thought to raise more problems of their own than the philosophies of, say, physics or economics. One special case deserving mention is the subject often called philosophy of action: its subject is quite general and not a *particular* sphere of human activity; but in fact it is usually regarded as a branch of philosophy of mind.

Parts of Philosophy and Philosophical Positions and Doctrines

In what follows, those diagrams headed 'Epistemology', 'Metaphysics', 'Logic and philosophical logic', 'Philosophy of mind', 'Moral philosophy', 'Political philosophy', 'Philosophy of language', and 'Philosophy of science' represent the parts of philosophy, or questions that can be asked, while the others represent philosophical positions and doctrines, or answers that might be given. Solid lines represent relations in a tree diagram. Dotted lines represent connections, as when in the former group the 'main related subjects' are listed, or else emphasize that the items they connect share a greater than usual degree of overlap, or merge into each other and cannot be sharply distinguished. For instance, in 'Theories on mind and body' property dualism, though presumably to be classified under dualism, is closely bound up with certain monist views. The lists of 'main related subjects', and items linked only by dotted lines to the main subject, are not always limited to subjects within philosophy itself. The few attributions of views to named figures should be regarded as approximate, sometimes controversial, and of course not exhaustive. There are more philosophers who might be mentioned in connection with each view.

A.R.L.

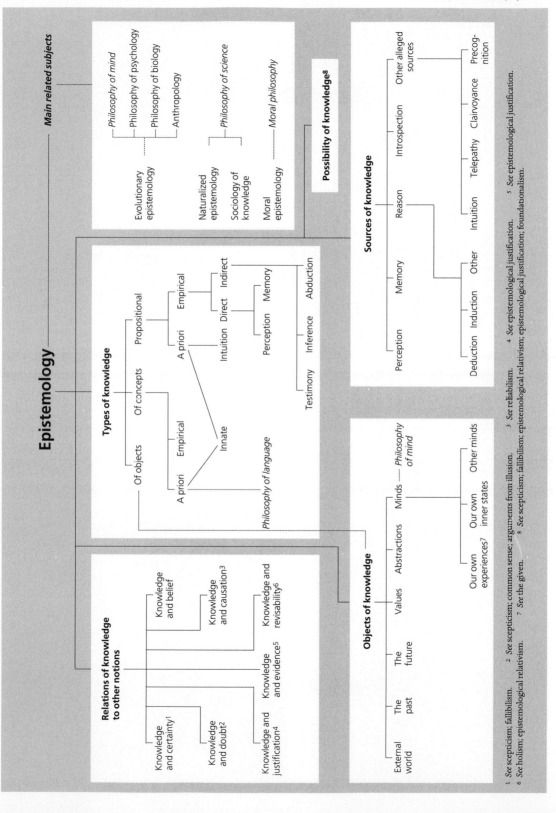

Epistemology

Main related subjects

Philosophy of mind
Philosophy of psychology
Philosophy of biology
Anthropology

Philosophy of science

Moral philosophy

Evolutionary epistemology

Naturalized epistemology

Sociology of knowledge

Moral epistemology

Possibility of knowledge[8]

Types of knowledge

Propositional

Of concepts

Of objects

A priori — Empirical

A priori — Empirical

Innate

Direct — Indirect

Intuition

Perception — Memory

Testimony

Inference

Abduction

Philosophy of language

Sources of knowledge

Perception   Memory   Reason   Introspection   Other alleged sources

Deduction   Induction   Other   Intuition   Telepathy   Clairvoyance   Precognition

Relations of knowledge to other notions

Knowledge and belief

Knowledge and causation[3]

Knowledge and revisability[6]

Knowledge and certainty[1]

Knowledge and doubt[2]

Knowledge and justification[4]

Knowledge and evidence[5]

Objects of knowledge

External world   The past   The future   Values   Abstractions   Minds —— *Philosophy of mind*

Our own experiences[7]   Our own inner states   Other minds

[1] *See* scepticism; fallibilism.   [2] *See* scepticism; common sense; arguments from illusion.   [3] *See* reliabilism.   [4] *See* epistemological justification.   [5] *See* epistemological justification.
[6] *See* holism; epistemological relativism.   [7] *See* the given.   [8] *See* scepticism; fallibilism; epistemological relativism; epistemological justification; foundationalism.

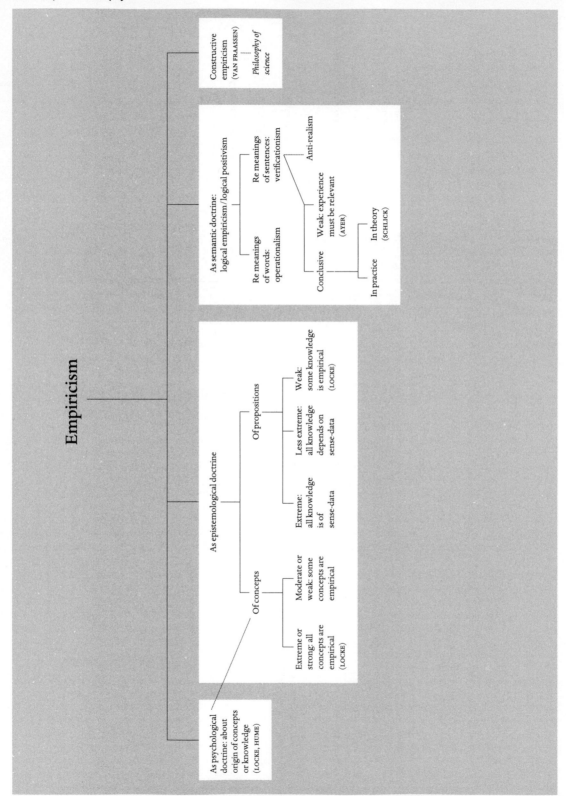

Empiricism

As psychological doctrine: about origin of concepts or knowledge
(LOCKE, HUME)

As epistemological doctrine

Of concepts

Extreme or strong: all concepts are empirical
(LOCKE)

Moderate or weak: some concepts are empirical

Of propositions

Extreme: all knowledge is of sense-data

Less extreme: all knowledge depends on sense-data

Weak: some knowledge is empirical
(LOCKE)

As semantic doctrine: logical empiricism / logical positivism

Re meanings of words: operationalism

Re meanings of sentences: verificationism

Anti-realism

Conclusive

Weak: experience must be relevant
(AYER)

In practice

In theory
(SCHLICK)

Constructive empiricism
(VAN FRAASSEN)

Philosophy of science

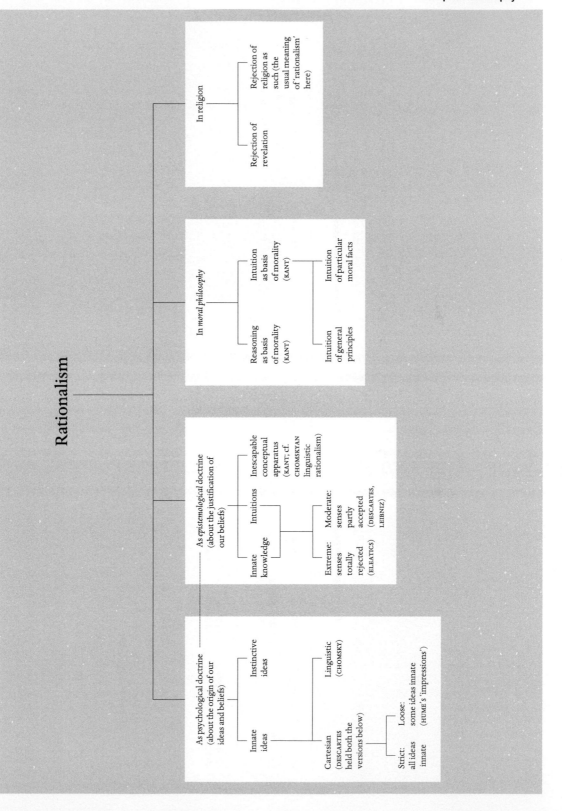

Rationalism

As psychological doctrine (about the origin of our ideas and beliefs)

- Innate ideas
  - Instinctive ideas
  - Cartesian (DESCARTES held both the versions below)
    - Linguistic (CHOMSKY)
    - Strict: all ideas innate
    - Loose: some ideas innate (HUME's 'impressions')

As epistemological doctrine (about the justification of our beliefs)

- Innate knowledge
- Intuitions
  - Extreme: senses totally rejected (ELEATICS)
  - Moderate: senses partly accepted (DESCARTES, LEIBNIZ)
- Inescapable conceptual apparatus (KANT; cf. CHOMSKYAN linguistic rationalism)

In moral philosophy

- Reasoning as basis of morality (KANT)
- Intuition as basis of morality (KANT)
  - Intuition of general principles
  - Intuition of particular moral facts

In religion

- Rejection of revelation
- Rejection of religion as such (the usual meaning of 'rationalism' here)

Metaphysics

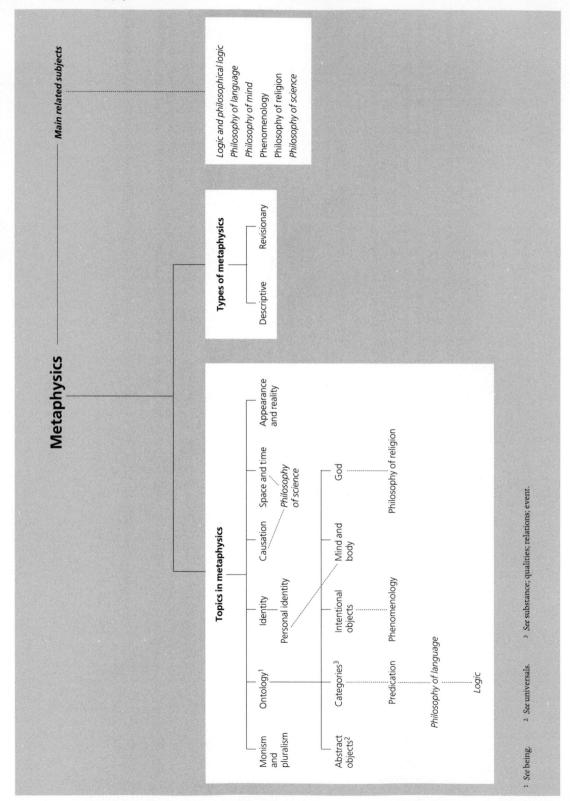

Main related subjects

Logic and philosophical logic
Philosophy of language
Philosophy of mind
Phenomenology
Philosophy of religion
Philosophy of science

Types of metaphysics

Descriptive   Revisionary

Topics in metaphysics

Monism and pluralism

Ontology[1]   Identity   Causation   Space and time   Appearance and reality

Personal identity   *Philosophy of science*

Abstract objects[2]   Categories[3]   Mind and body   God

Predication   Intentional objects   Philosophy of religion

Phenomenology

Philosophy of language

Logic

[1] *See being.*   [2] *See universals.*   [3] *See substance; qualities; relations; event.*

Realism

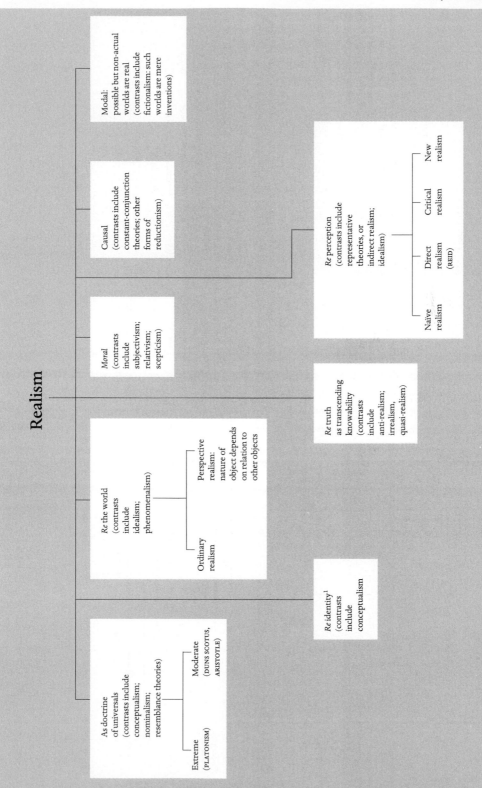

Modal:
possible but non-actual
worlds are real
(contrasts include
fictionalism: such
worlds are mere
inventions)

Causal
(contrasts include
constant-conjunction
theories; other
forms of
reductionism)

Moral
(contrasts
include
subjectivism;
relativism;
scepticism)

Re the world
(contrasts
include
idealism;
phenomenalism)

    Ordinary
    realism

    Perspective
    realism:
    nature of
    object depends
    on relation to
    other objects

As doctrine
of universals
(contrasts include
conceptualism;
nominalism;
resemblance theories)

    Extreme
    (PLATONISM)

    Moderate
    (DUNS SCOTUS,
    ARISTOTLE)

Re identity[1]
(contrasts
include
conceptualism

Re perception
(contrasts include
representative
theories, or
indirect realism;
idealism)

    Naïve
    realism

    Direct
    realism
    (REID)

    Critical
    realism

    New
    realism

Re truth
as transcending
knowability
(contrasts
include
anti-realism,
irrealism,
quasi-realism)

1 The view that one can say 'A is the same as B' without specifying 'A is the same so-and-so as B'.

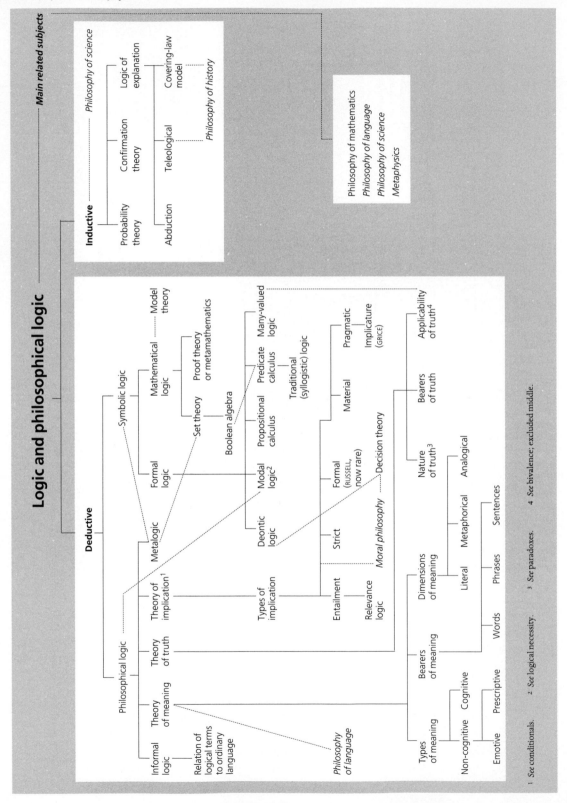

Logic and philosophical logic

Main related subjects

Philosophy of science

Inductive

Probability theory

Confirmation theory

Logic of explanation

Abduction

Teleological

Covering-law model

Philosophy of history

Philosophy of mathematics
Philosophy of language
Philosophy of science
Metaphysics

Deductive

Philosophical logic

Theory of meaning

Theory of truth

Theory of implication[1]

Metalogic

Symbolic logic

Formal logic

Mathematical logic

Model theory

Set theory

Proof theory or metamathematics

Boolean algebra

Propositional calculus

Predicate calculus

Many-valued logic

Modal logic[2]

Deontic logic

Traditional (syllogistic) logic

Material

Pragmatic

Implicature (GRICE)

Bearers of truth

Applicability of truth[4]

Nature of truth[3]

Analogical

Strict

Formal (RUSSELL, now rare)

Decision theory

Moral philosophy

Types of implication

Entailment

Relevance logic

Dimensions of meaning

Literal

Metaphorical

Phrases

Sentences

Informal logic

Relation of logical terms to ordinary language

Philosophy of language

Bearers of meaning

Words

Types of meaning

Non-cognitive

Cognitive

Emotive

Prescriptive

1 *See conditionals.*   2 *See logical necessity.*   3 *See paradoxes.*   4 *See bivalence; excluded middle.*

Philosophy of language

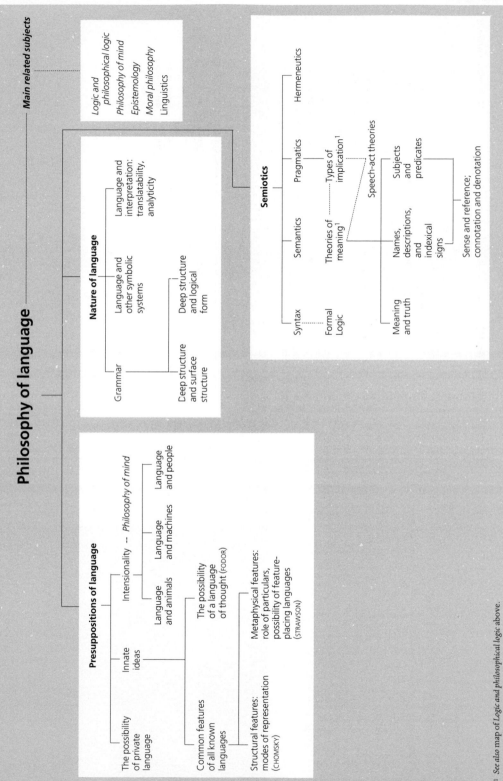

Main related subjects

Logic and
philosophical logic
Philosophy of mind
Epistemology
Moral philosophy
Linguistics

Nature of language

Grammar
- Deep structure and surface structure
- Deep structure and logical form

Language and other symbolic systems

Language and interpretation: translatability, analyticity

Presuppositions of language

The possibility of private language

Innate ideas
- Common features of all known languages
- Structural features: modes of representation (CHOMSKY)

Intensionality -- Philosophy of mind
- Language and animals
- Language and machines
- Language and people
- The possibility of a language of thought (FODOR)
- Metaphysical features: role of particulars, possibility of feature-placing languages (STRAWSON)

Semiotics

Syntax
- Formal Logic

Semantics
- Theories of meaning[1]
- Meaning and truth

Pragmatics
- Types of implication[1]
- Speech-act theories
- Names, descriptions, and indexical signs
- Subjects and predicates
- Sense and reference; connotation and denotation

Hermeneutics

1 *See also map of Logic and philosophical logic above.*

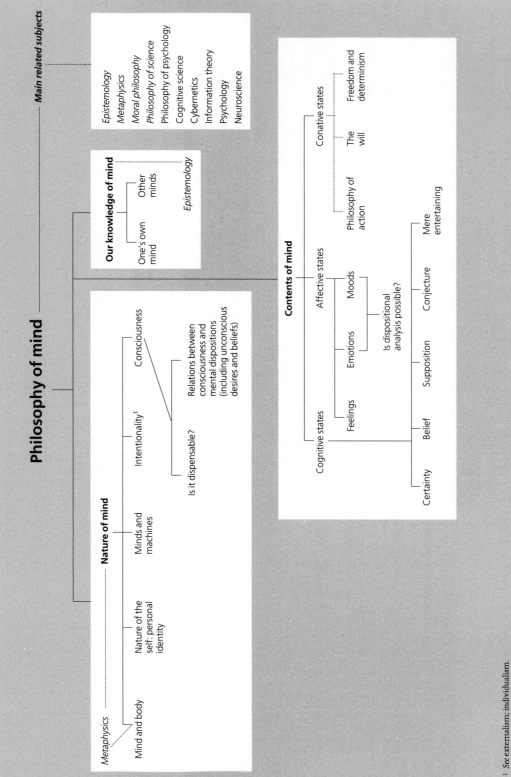

Philosophy of mind

Main related subjects

Epistemology
Metaphysics
Moral philosophy
Philosophy of science
Philosophy of psychology
Cognitive science
Cybernetics
Information theory
Psychology
Neuroscience

Our knowledge of mind

One's own mind — Other minds

Epistemology

Nature of mind

Metaphysics

Mind and body — Nature of the self: personal identity — Minds and machines — Intentionality[1] — Consciousness

Is it dispensable?

Relations between consciousness and mental dispositions (including unconscious desires and beliefs)

Contents of mind

Cognitive states — Affective states — Philosophy of action — Conative states

Feelings — Emotions — Moods

Is dispositional analysis possible?

The will — Freedom and determinism

Certainty — Belief — Supposition — Conjecture — Mere entertaining

1 *See* externalism; individualism.

Theories of mind and body

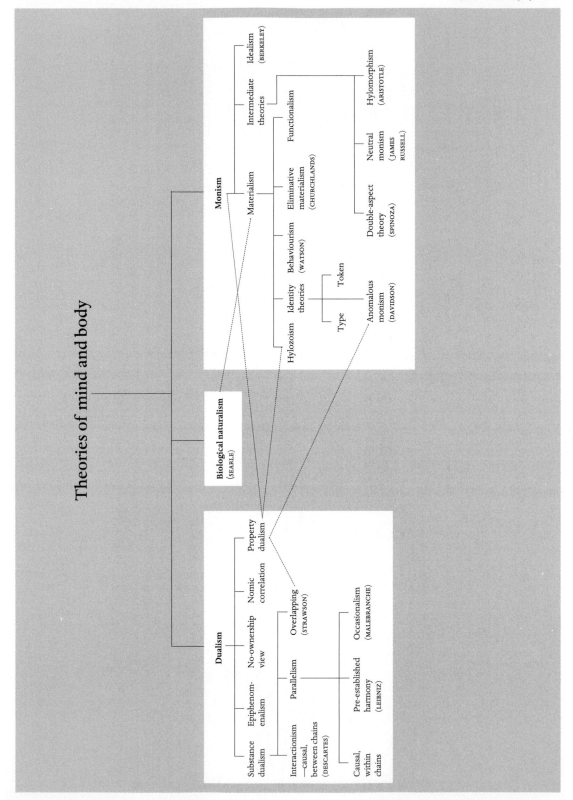

Monism

Intermediate theories
- Idealism (BERKELEY)
- Hylomorphism (ARISTOTLE)

Materialism
- Functionalism
- Eliminative materialism (CHURCHLANDS)
- Neutral monism (JAMES RUSSELL)
- Double-aspect theory (SPINOZA)

Behaviourism (WATSON)

Identity theories
- Type
- Token
- Anomalous monism (DAVIDSON)

Hylozoism

Biological naturalism (SEARLE)

Dualism

Property dualism

Nomic correlation
- Overlapping (STRAWSON)

No-ownership view

Epiphenom-enalism

Parallelism
- Pre-established harmony (LEIBNIZ)
- Occasionalism (MALEBRANCHE)

Substance dualism

Interactionism
—causal, between chains (DESCARTES)

Causal, within chains

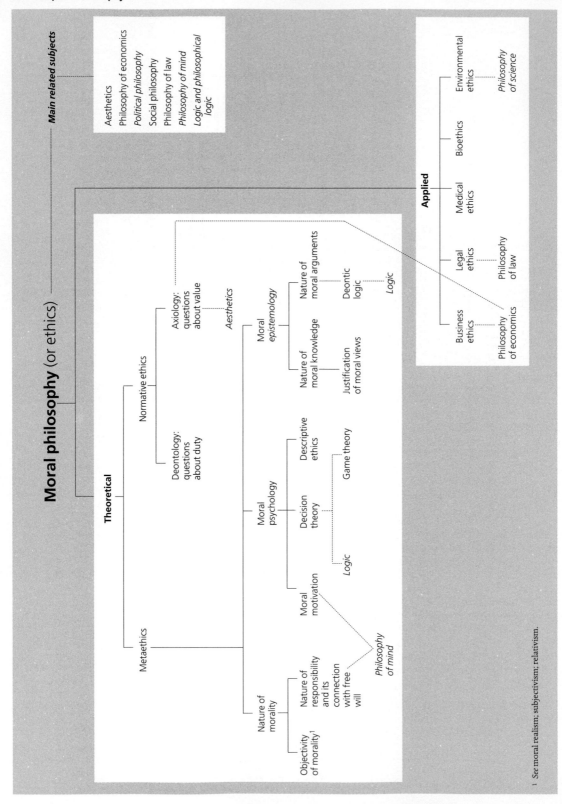

Moral philosophy (or ethics)

Main related subjects

- Aesthetics
- Philosophy of economics
- *Political philosophy*
- Social philosophy
- Philosophy of law
- *Philosophy of mind*
- *Logic and philosophical logic*

Theoretical

Metaethics

- Nature of morality
  - Objectivity of morality[1]
  - Nature of responsibility and its connection with free will
  - *Philosophy of mind*

- Moral motivation
  - Moral psychology
    - Decision theory
      - Game theory
    - Descriptive ethics
    - *Logic*

Normative ethics

- Deontology: questions about duty
- Axiology: questions about value
  - *Aesthetics*

- Moral *epistemology*
  - Nature of moral knowledge
  - Justification of moral views
  - Nature of moral arguments
    - Deontic logic
    - *Logic*

Applied

- Business ethics
  - Philosophy of economics
- Legal ethics
  - Philosophy of law
- Medical ethics
- Bioethics
- Environmental ethics
  - *Philosophy of science*

1 *See moral realism; subjectivism; relativism.*

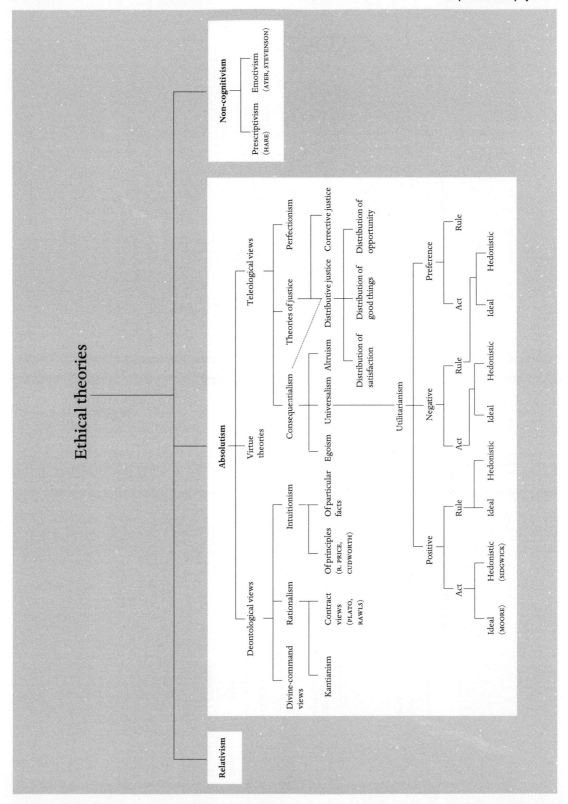

Ethical theories

Non-cognitivism
- Prescriptivism (HARE)
- Emotivism (AYER, STEVENSON)

Relativism

Absolutism

Deontological views

Divine-command views

Rationalism
- Kantianism
- Contract views (PLATO, RAWLS)

Intuitionism
- Of principles (R. PRICE, CUDWORTH)
- Of particular facts

Virtue theories

Teleological views

Consequentialism
- Egoism
- Universalism
- Altruism

Perfectionism

Theories of justice
- Distributive justice
  - Distribution of satisfaction
  - Distribution of good things
  - Distribution of opportunity
- Corrective justice

Utilitarianism

Positive
- Act
  - Ideal (MOORE)
  - Hedonistic (SIDGWICK)
- Rule
  - Ideal
  - Hedonistic

Negative
- Act
  - Ideal
  - Hedonistic
- Rule
  - Ideal
  - Hedonistic

Preference
- Act
  - Ideal
  - Hedonistic
- Rule

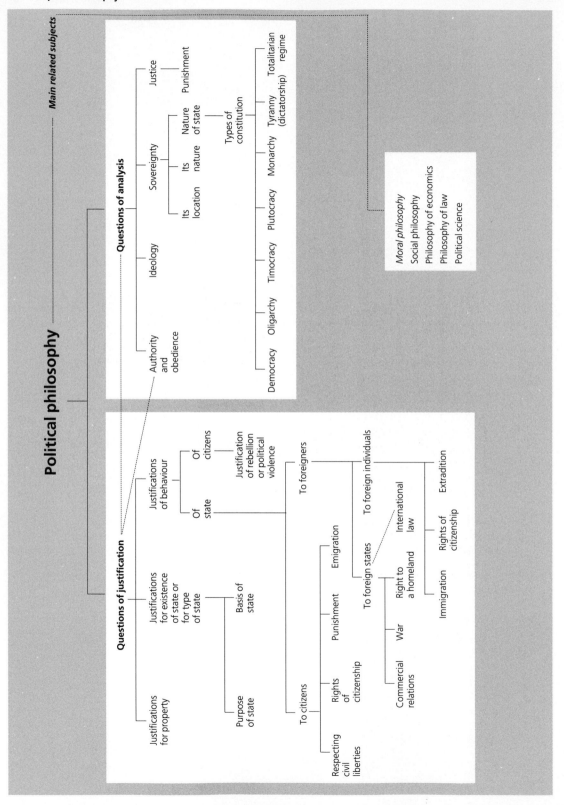

Political philosophy

Questions of analysis

Authority and obedience

Ideology

Sovereignty
- Its location
- Its nature

Nature of state
- Justice
  - Punishment

Types of constitution
- Democracy
- Oligarchy
- Timocracy
- Plutocracy
- Monarchy
- Tyranny (dictatorship)
- Totalitarian regime

Main related subjects

Moral philosophy
Social philosophy
Philosophy of economics
Philosophy of law
Political science

Questions of justification

Justifications for property

Justifications for existence of state or for type of state
- Purpose of state
- Basis of state

Justifications of behaviour
- Of state
- Of citizens

Justification of rebellion or political violence

To citizens
- Respecting civil liberties
- Rights of citizenship
- Punishment
- Emigration

To foreigners
- Commercial relations
- War
- Right to a homeland
- To foreign states
- To foreign individuals
  - International law
  - Immigration
  - Rights of citizenship
  - Extradition

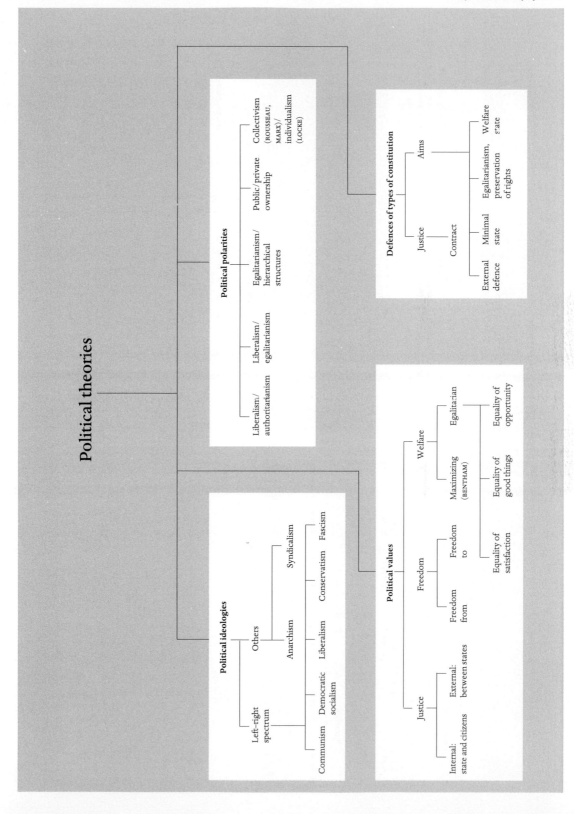

Political theories

Political ideologies

Left–right spectrum
- Others
  - Anarchism
  - Syndicalism
- Communism
- Democratic socialism
- Liberalism
- Conservatism
- Fascism

Political values

Justice
- Internal: state and citizens
- External: between states

Freedom
- Freedom from
- Freedom to
  - Equality of satisfaction

Welfare
- Maximizing (BENTHAM)
  - Equality of good things
- Egalitarian
  - Equality of opportunity

Political polarities

- Liberalism / authoritarianism
- Liberalism / egalitarianism
- Egalitarianism / hierarchical structures
- Public / private ownership
- Collectivism (ROUSSEAU, MARX) / individualism (LOCKE)

Defences of types of constitution

Justice
- Contract
  - External defence
  - Minimal state
  - Egalitarianism, preservation of rights

Aims
- Welfare state

Philosophy of science

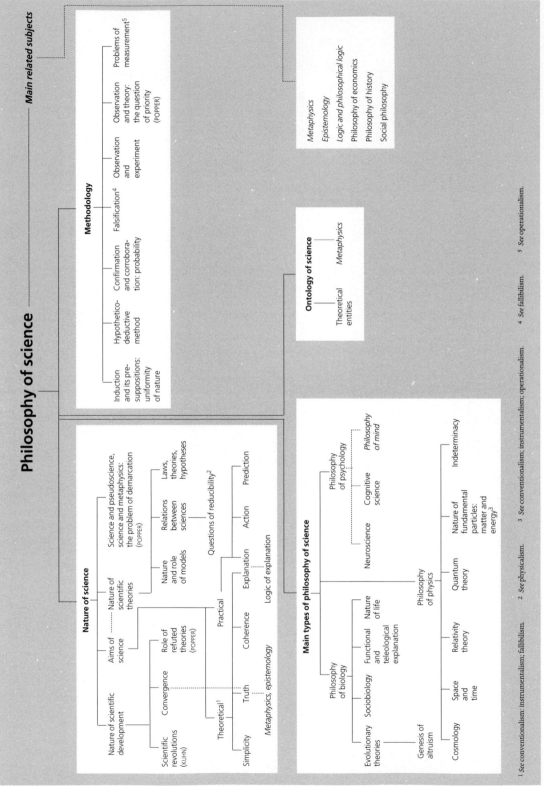

—— *Main related subjects*

Nature of science

Nature of scientific development

Scientific revolutions (KUHN)

Convergence

Theoretical[1]

Simplicity   Truth   Coherence   Practical

Metaphysics, epistemology

Aims of science ········ Nature of scientific theories

Role of refuted theories (POPPER)

Science and pseudoscience, science and metaphysics: the problem of demarcation (POPPER)

Nature and role of models

Relations between sciences

Laws, theories, hypotheses

Questions of reducibility[2]

Logic of explanation

Explanation   Action   Prediction

Methodology

Induction and its pre-suppositions: uniformity of nature

Hypothetico-deductive method

Confirmation and corrobora-tion: probability

Falsification[4]

Observation and experiment

Observation and theory: the question of priority (POPPER)

Problems of measurement[5]

Metaphysics
Epistemology
Logic and philosophical logic
Philosophy of economics
Philosophy of history
Social philosophy

Ontology of science

Theoretical entities   *Metaphysics*

Main types of philosophy of science

Evolutionary theories

Genesis of altruism

Cosmology

Philosophy of biology

Sociobiology   Functional and teleological explanation   Nature of life

Space and time   Relativity theory   Quantum theory   Nature of fundamental particles: matter and energy[3]

Philosophy of physics

Neuroscience   Cognitive science

Philosophy of psychology

Philosophy of mind

Indeterminacy

Maps of philosophy by A. R. Lacey

[1] *See conventionalism: instrumentalism; fallibilism.*   [2] *See physicalism.*   [3] *See conventionalism; instrumentalism; operationalism.*   [4] *See fallibilism.*   [5] *See operationalism.*

A Chronological Table of Philosophy

Any table of this nature must reflect a certain arbitrariness. The left column represents philosophers or events of philosophical importance. Some attempt has been made to list philosophers in the order in which they produced their main work or had their main influence; normally each philosopher is listed once only, at the time when he was most active or most influential. Titles are given in the language in which they are most familiar. Similar considerations in general apply to the right column, which lists, with considerably greater arbitrariness, public events or people, partly to give a general temporal framework and partly to pick out items that might be thought to have some relevance to the development of philosophy. The correlation between the columns, however, cannot be anything but very rough and approximate.

600 BC			
	First flourishing of Greek philosophy (Thales, Anaximander, Anaximenes) through the sixth century in the town of Miletus in Asia Minor	Zoroaster c.630–c.553	THE ARCHAIC PERIOD IN GREECE
		Solar eclipse, allegedly predicted by Thales, 585	
		Beginnings of Greek mathematics, attributed to Thales	
	Pythagoras and his followers found religious movement in southern Italy	Buddha c.563–?	
		First systematic edition of *Iliad* and *Odyssey* (probably composed two or three centuries earlier)	
	Xenophanes criticizes anthropomorphic religion		
	Heraclitus propounds a bold metaphysics in Ephesus	Cleisthenes expels tyrants from Athens 510, and introduces democracy 508	
500 BC			EASTERN CHOU ERA IN CHINA
	Confucius c.557–479	Ionian revolt against Persia 499–494	
		Persian wars unite Greece, temporarily; Persia effectively defeated in 479	
	Parmenides discusses philosophical method in verse		
		Persian-war veteran Aeschylus becomes first great European dramatist	THE CLASSICAL PERIOD IN GREECE
		Athens founds Delian League as bulwark against Persia, but uses it for imperialist purposes (and to finance building of Parthenon, completed 438)	
	Lao Tsŭ founds Taoism		
	Zeno of Elea develops Parmenides' ideas	Periclean age c.460–429, ending with plague which killed Pericles	
	Empedocles in Sicily; Anaxagoras in Athens; Melissus in Samos	Sophocles writes prize-winning tragedies from 468 until his death in 406	
	Protagoras, the leading Sophist, visits Athens		

	Philosophy	Events	Period
		Abortive attempt to found Panhellenic colony at Thurii in Italy 444, with Protagoras invited to write its laws	
		Herodotus presents a panorama of the world known to the Greeks in his *Histories*	
	Democritus develops early atomism	Peloponnesian War between Sparta and Athens, 431–404, ends in defeat of Athens, which quickly revives	
		Earliest of many medical treatises attributed to Hippocrates (*c.*450–*c.*370)	
	Socrates (469–399)	Euripides' tragedies show Sophists' influence	
		Aristophanes mocks Socrates in his comedy *Clouds*	THE CLASSICAL PERIOD IN GREECE
		Thucydides examines political behaviour and motivation in his history	EASTERN CHOU ERA IN CHINA
400 BC	Death of Socrates, 399, has profound effect on Plato and others	Pentateuch of Old Testament receives definitive form	
	'Socratic schools' (Megarians, Cynics, Cyrenaics) form	Xenophon (*c.*428–*c.*354), historian and one source for our knowledge of Socrates	
	Plato (427–347) founds Academy *c.*380	Greek mathematics flourishes under Theodorus and Theaetetus	
	Plato's *Republic c.*380–370	Greek oratory and rhetoric flourish under Isocrates, Demosthenes, Aeschines	
	Diogenes the Cynic *c.*400–*c.*325		
	Aristotle (384–322) enters Academy 367, tutors Alexander *c.*343–339, founds Lyceum *c.*336, writes main works *c.*350–323	Aristoxenus, theorist of Greek music	
	Headship of Academy falls to Speusippus 347, and then Xenocrates	Second battle of Chaeronea 338 ends independence of Greek city states, thereafter under Macedonian rule	
	Theophrastus (Aristotle's successor in Lyceum) 370–*c.*288	Greek comedy turns, especially with Menander, from political and social to domestic satire	
	Pyrrho the Sceptic *c.*365–*c.*275	Alexander succeeds Philip of Macedon 336	
	Epicurus (341–270) founds Epicurean school	Death of Alexander 323	
	Zeno of Citium (335–263) founds Stoic school	Euclid the geometer active	
300 BC	Mencius (*c.*372–289) and Chuang Tzŭ active	Aristarchus presents heliocentric hypothesis	
	Arcesilaus (*c.*316–*c.*242) founds 'Middle Academy', representing Sceptical rival to Stoics	Septuagint (Greek version of Old Testament) written	THE HELLENISTIC PERIOD
	Cleanthes and Chrysippus (*c.*280–207) second and third heads of Stoic school	Scientist-engineer Archimedes *c.*287–212 (killed at fall of Syracuse)	
		Asoka emperor and law-giver in India	
		Eratosthenes (*c.*276–194) makes good estimate of earth's circumference	
		Hannibal in Italy; finally defeated at Zama (near Carthage) 202	HAN DYNASTY IN CHINA
200 BC		Plautus and Terence develop Roman comic theatre	
	Carneades (*c.*214–*c.*129) founds 'New Academy', continuing Sceptical tradition	Sack of Corinth by Rome finally ends Greek independence of Rome 146	

100 BC	Panaetius the Stoic c.185–109	Political reforms attempted by the Gracchi in Rome
	Posidonius the Stoic c.135–c.51	Aristotle's works brought to Rome by Sulla 84, and subsequently edited by Andronicus
		Rebellion of slaves under Spartacus defeated 71
	Cicero 106–43	Caesar crosses Rubicon and starts civil war 49
		Julian calendar adopted 46
	Lucretius (98–c.51) publishes poetic version of Epicureanism c.60	Library of Alexandria wholly or partially destroyed 47
		Battle of Actium ends Roman republic and independence of Egypt (where defeated parties, Antony and Cleopatra, were based), thereby closing the Hellenistic or Alexandrian period, 31
		Augustan or Golden Age of Roman literature: Virgil, Livy, Horace, Ovid, et al.
AD BC		Jesus Christ 4 BC–AD c.29
		Augustus dies 14; succeeded by Tiberius
	Seneca c.1 BC–AD 65	Nero (emperor 54–68) orders suicide of Seneca and persecutes Christians
	Beginning of Nyāya philosophy (Hindu logical school) in India	
		Naturalist Pliny the Elder dies while investigating eruption of Vesuvius which destroyed Pompeii 79
		Silver Age of Roman literature begins: Tacitus, Suetonius, Pliny the Younger, Martial, Juvenal, Quintilian, et al.
		Greek historian Plutarch of Chaeronea
100		Trajan (emperor 98–117) extends Roman Empire to its greatest size
	Epictetus c.55–135	
	Marcus Aurelius 121–80	Encyclopaedic medical writer Galen 129–99
200	Mahāyāna Buddhism inaugurated by Nāgārjuna	Origen (c.185–254) tries to reconcile Christianity with Platonic philosophy by interpreting the Bible
	Alexander of Aphrodisias lecturing in Athens	
		Diogenes Laertius, important source for history of philosophy, writing
	Sextus Empiricus active	Diophantus the mathematician active c.250
		Manichean religion founded by Mani
	Plotinus (205–c.269) introduces Neoplatonism	Roman Empire begins to be invaded from the north-east
	Porphyry c.232–c.305	Roman Empire first divided into east and west by Diocletian 285
300		Constantinople founded 324, becoming seat of Roman Empire 331
		First Council of Nicaea condemns Arians (who stressed God's unity and so gave Christ subordinate status) in favour of Athanasius 325

THE HELLENISTIC PERIOD

HAN DYNASTY IN CHINA

ROMAN EMPIRE

		Books start to replace scrolls c.360	BREAK-UP OF OLD ROMAN EMPIRE
		Roman Empire finally divided into east and west after death of Theodosius 395	
400	Augustine (354–430) composes his major philosophical works		
	Proclus c.410–85	Western Roman Empire falls to Germans under Odoacer 476	
		First schism between Eastern and Western Churches 484	OLD MAYAN EMPIRE IN CENTRAL AMERICA
500		John Stobaeus' literary anthology, of some importance as source for history of philosophy	
	Boethius c.480–524	Closing of Athenian schools by Justinian 529	
	Philoponus (c.490–570) and Simplicius active, Simplicius being the last main Neoplatonist, and Philoponus helping to replace Neoplatonism with Christianity in Alexandria	Simplicius temporarily migrates to Persia	
		Justinian promulgates legal code	
600		Hegira: flight of Muhammad (570–632) from Mecca to Medina, 622; start of Muslim Calendar	
		Islam replaces Zoroastrianism in Persia 641	
	Nestorians translate ancient Greek philosophers into Syriac		
700		Muslim Empire reaches its height, with capital first at Damascus and then at Baghdad	
		Beginning of Arabic science and philosophy at Baghdad	BYZANTINE ERA
		'Arabic' (in fact Indian) numerals known in Baghdad 760	
800		Charlemagne crowned at Aix (Aachen) as first Holy Roman Emperor 800	
	Al-Kindī c.801–66	Revival of classical learning at Aix	ARABIC INTELLECTUAL FLOWERING
	John Scotus Eriugena active		
900		Buddhist influence in India starts to decline	
		Start of Christian reconquest of Spain	
	Al-Fārābī 870–950	Cordoba becomes centre of Arabic culture in Spain, with university founded 968	
1000	Avicenna (Ibn Sīnā) 980–1037		
	Avecebrol (Ibn Gabirol) 1020–c.1070	Norman Conquest of England 1066	
	Anselm 1033–1109	Greek medicine brought to West by Constantine the African 1071	
	Al-Ghazālī 1058/9–1111		
	Arabic philosophers start to be translated into Latin	First Crusade launched by Pope Urban II 1095	
1100		First modern European university founded at Bologna 1113	
	Abelard 1079–1142	Arabs in Spain manufacture paper 1150	

		University of Paris founded 1150
		University of Oxford founded 1167
Averroës 1126–98		Thomas à Becket murdered at Canterbury 1170
Maimonides 1125–1204		
		Francis of Assisi 1182–1226
		MagnaCarta 1215
		Genghis Khan (c.1162–1227) establishes Mongol Empire
Albert the Great c.1200–80		Fourth Crusade captures Constantinople 1204, giving West access to Greek writings
Roger Bacon c.1214–c.1292		
Bonaventure 1221–74		
Thomas Aquinas c.1224–74		Cordoba falls to Spain 1236
Duns Scotus c.1266–1308		
William of Ockham c.1285–c.1349		Dante (1265–1321), one of the earliest writers in Italian rather than Latin, writes *Divine Comedy*
		Black Death ravages Europe, killing one-third of English population 1347–51
		Boccaccio (1313–75) publishes *Decameron* 1348–53
		Chaucer (1340–1400) writes *The Canterbury Tales*
		Constantinople falls to Ottomans 1453, ending Byzantine era
Nicholas of Cusa c.1400–64		Caxton prints Chaucer's *Canterbury Tales* 1477
Marsilio Ficino 1433–99		Granada falls to Spanish, ending Moorish power in Spain, 1492
		Columbus crosses Atlantic 1492
		Leonardo da Vinci 1452–1519
		Raphael 1483–1520
		Michelangelo 1475–1564
Erasmus 1465–1536		Physician and alchemist Paracelsus 1493–1541
Machiavelli (1469–1527) writes *Il Principe* 1513		Luther (1483–1536) instigates Reformation at Wittenberg 1517
		Rabelais (1494–1553) publishes *Pantagruel* 1532
		St Ignatius Loyola founds Society of Jesus 1534
		Copernicus (1473–1543) publishes heliocentric theory 1541–3
		Calvin 1509–64
Suarez 1548–1607		Montaigne (1533–92)
		Queen Elizabeth I crowned 1558
		First microscope invented by Janssen 1590

Left margin dates: 1200, 1300, 1400, 1500

Right margin: BYZANTINE ERA / EUROPEAN RENAISSANCE / MOGUL EMPIRE IN ASIA

1600		Thermometer invented by Galileo
		Edict of Nantes, tolerating Huguenots, issued by Henri IV 1598
		Shakespeare (1564–1616) writes *Hamlet* c.1600

Francis Bacon (1561–1626) publishes *Advancement of Learning* 1605, *Novum Organum* 1620

Philosophy starts to be written in the vernacular rather than in Latin

Gassendi 1592–1655

Descartes (1596–1650) publishes *Meditations* 1641, *Principles of Philosophy* 1644

Hobbes (1588–1679) publishes *Leviathan* 1651

Spinoza (1632–77) publishes *Ethics* 1677

Cambridge Platonists (Whichcote (1609–83), More (1614–87), Cudworth (1617–88), *et al.*) active

Locke (1632–1704) publishes *Essay Concerning Human Understanding* 1690, *Two Treatises of Government* 1690

Malebranche (1628–1715) publishes *De la recherche de la vérité* 1674

Telescope invented by Dutch 1600

Bruno (born 1548) accused of heresy and burnt by Inquisition 1600

Kepler (1571–1630) discovers elliptical orbits of planets

Harvey discovers circulation of blood 1628

Galileo sentenced by Inquisition 1633

Harvard University founded 1636

English Civil War 1642–6

Louis XIV (1638–1715) becomes King of France 1643

Charles I executed 1649, inaugurating eleven-year Commonwealth period under Puritans in Britain

Fermat (1601–65) and Pascal (1633–62) inaugurate study of probability 1654

French drama flourishes with Corneille (1606–84), Molière (1622–73), Racine (1639–99)

Plague in England 1665

Great Fire of London 1666

Milton (1608–74) publishes *Paradise Lost* 1667

Decline of Latin as a language in which the educated are fluent

Bunyan (1628–88) publishes *The Pilgrim's Progress* 1678–84

Newton publishes *Principia* 1687

'Glorious Revolution' rids Britain of Stuart monarchs 1688

Dryden (1631–1700), poet, dramatist, and critic

1700

Leibniz 1646–1716

Vico 1668–1744

Shaftesbury (1671–1713) publishes *Characteristics* 1711

Berkeley (1685–1753) publishes *Principles of Human Knowledge* 1710, *Three Dialogues* 1713

Hutcheson (1694–1746/7) publishes *Inquiry into the Origin of our Ideas of Beauty and Virtue* 1725

Butler (1692–1752) publishes *Fifteen Sermons* 1726, *The Analogy of Religion* 1736

Jonathan Edwards 1703–58

Fahrenheit (1686–1736) constructs mercury thermometer 1714

Pope (1688–1744), poet and social critic

MOGUL EMPIRE IN ASIA

ERA OF EUROPEAN COLONIZATION

Hume (1711–76) publishes A *Treatise of Human Nature* 1739, *An Enquiry Concerning Human Understanding* 1748, *An Enquiry Concerning the Principles of Morals* 1751

Richard Price (1723–91) publishes *A Review of the Principal Questions in Morals* 1758

Adam Smith (1723–90) publishes *The Theory of Moral Sentiments* 1759, *Wealth of Nations* 1776

Rousseau (1712–78) publishes *Le Contrat social* 1762

Bentham (1748-1832) publishes *A Fragment on Government* 1776, *An Introduction to the Principles of Morals and Legislation* 1789

Condillac 1715–80

Kant (1724–1804) publishes *Critique of Pure Reason* 1781, *Fundamental Principles of the Metaphysic of Morals* 1785, *Critique of Practical Reason* 1788, *Critique of Judgement* 1790

Reid (1710–96) publishes *Essays on the Intellectual Powers of Man* 1785, *Essays on the Active Powers of Man* 1788

Condorcet 1743–94

Fichte 1762–1814

Diderot (1713–84) begins work on the *Encyclopédie* 1745

Mathematician d'Alembert (1717–83)

Montesquieu (1689–1755) publishes *De l'esprit des lois* 1748

Encyclopédie published 1751–80

Lisbon earthquake 1755 (referred to by Voltaire and others when discussing divine justice)

Voltaire (1694–1778) publishes *Candide* 1759

Süssmilch inaugurates study of statistics 1761

Benjamin Franklin (1706–90)

Samuel Johnson (1709–84) publishes *Dictionary of the English Language* 1755–73

Cook (1728–79) discovers Australia 1770

Boston Tea Party 1773

Watt (1738–1819) invents steam-engine, which pioneers Industrial Revolution

American Declaration of Independence 1776

Lavoisier (1743–94) analyses air into oxygen and nitrogen, opening the way for overthrow of phlogiston theory of combustion (dominant since early in the century) 1777

Mesmerism practised in Paris 1778

French Revolution 1789

Burke (1729–97) publishes *Reflections on the Revolution in France* 1790

Tom Paine (1737–1809) publishes *The Rights of Man* 1791–2, *The Age of Reason* 1794–5

French Reign of Terror 1793, followed by Napoleonic wars

Goethe 1749–1832

Schiller 1759–1805

Malthus (1766–1834) publishes *Essay on the Principle of Population* 1798

1800

Maine de Biran 1766–1824

Schleiermacher 1768–1834

Hegel (1770–1831) publishes *The Phenomenology of Mind* 180

James Mill 1773–1835

Schelling 1775–1854

Dalton (1766–1844) introduces atomic theory *c.*1800

Wordsworth 1770–1850

Coleridge 1772–1834

Thomas Jefferson (1743–1836), third President of USA 1801–9

Battle of Waterloo brings comparative stability to Europe 1815

Byron 1788–1824

Shelley 1792–1822

Ricardo writing on economics 1809–17

AGE OF ENLIGHTENMENT IN EUROPE

ERA OF EUROPEAN COLONIZATION

AGE OF REVOLUTION

Schopenhauer (1788–1860) publishes *The World as Will and Representation* 1819

John Austin (1790–1859) publishes *The Province of Jurisprudence Determined* 1832

Comte 1798–1857

Feuerbach 1804–72

Hamilton (1788–1856), philosopher criticized by J. S. Mill

Whewell 1794–1866

John Stuart Mill (1806–73) publishes A *System of Logic* 1843, *On Liberty* 1859, *Utilitarianism* 1863

Kierkegaard 1813–55

Engels (1820–95) publishes *The Condition of the Working Class in England* 1845

Marx (1818–83) publishes *Manifesto of the Communist Party* (with Engels) 1848, *Das Kapital* 1867, 1885, 1893

Emerson 1803–82

Spencer 1820–1903

Dilthey 1833–1911

Sidgwick (1838–1900) publishes *The Methods of Ethics* 1874

Mach (1838–1916) publishes *The Science of Mechanics* 1883, *Popular Scientific Lectures* 1894 (or 1896)

Brentano (1838–1917) publishes *Psychology from an Empirical Standpoint* 1874, *The Origin of our Knowledge of Right and Wrong* 1889

Peirce 1834–1914

Nietzsche (1844–1900) publishes *Thus Spake Zarathustra* 1883–5, *Beyond Good and Evil* 1886

Lamarck (1744–1829) propounds theory of inheritance of acquired characteristics

Non-Euclidean geometries developed by Lobachevsky (1793–1856) and Riemann (1826–66)

Faraday (1791–1867), experimental physicist

Carnot (1796–1832) propounds second law of thermodynamics

Carlyle (1795–1841) publishes *The French Revolution* 1837

British franchise widened to include male middle class 1832, and much of male working class 1867

Dickens 1812–70

Pre-Raphaelite Brotherhood founded by Hunt, Millais, Rossetti 1848

Major unrest in Paris. Louis-Philippe abdicates throne and Louis-Napoléon elected President 1848

Louis-Napoléon largely reverses reforms of 1848 in 1851

Great Exhibition in London 1851

Thoreau 1817–62

Dostoevsky 1821–81

Ruskin (1819–1900) publishes *Modern Painters* (1843–60)

Crimean War 1854–5

George Eliot 1819–80

Indian Mutiny repressed 1857

Darwin publishes *The Origin of Species* 1859

American Civil War 1861–5

Cardinal J. H. Newman (1801–90) publishes *Apologia pro vita mea* 1864

Courbet (1819–77) promotes realist movement in painting

Women get the vote in the American state of Wyoming 1869

Franco-Prussian War 1870–1

Matthew Arnold 1822–88

Tolstoy 1828–1910

William Thomson, Lord Kelvin (1824–1907), physicist

Maxwell (1831–74) unites electricity and magnetism 1873

Impressionist exhibitions in Paris 1874–86

AGE OF REVOLUTION

ERA OF COLONIAL EMPIRE

William James (1842–1910) publishes *The Principles of Psychology* 1890, *The Varieties of Religious Experience* 1902, *Pragmatism* 1907

Cantor, mathematician, 1845–1914

Bradley (1846–1924) publishes *Appearance and Reality* 1893

Frege (1848–1925) publishes *The Foundations of Arithmetic* 1884, 'On Sense and Reference' 1892

Michelson–Morley experiment shows that speed of light is unaffected by direction of travel, 1888 and after

Poincaré 1854–1912

Oscar Wilde 1854–1900

Husserl (1859–1938) publishes *Philosophy of Arithmetic* 1891, *Logical Investigations* 1900–1, *Cartesian Meditations* 1931

Bergson (1859–1941) publishes *Time and Free Will* 1889, *Matter and Memory* 1896, *Creative Evolution* 1907, *The Two Sources of Morality and Religion* 1932

Dewey 1859–1952

1900

Meinong (1853–1920) publishes *On Assumptions* 1902, 'On the Theory of Objects' 1904

Boer War 1899–1902

Croce (1866–1952) publishes *Aesthetic* 1902

Scheler 1874–1928

Freud (1856–1939) publishes *The Interpretation of Dreams* 1900, *The Psychopathology of Everyday Life* 1905, *Totem and Taboo* 1913

Moore (1873–1958) publishes *Principia Ethica* 1903, 'Refutation of Idealism' 1903

Russell (1872–1970) publishes *The Principles of Mathematics* 1903, *Principia Mathematica* (with Whitehead) 1910–13, *Our Knowledge of the External World* 1914

Bloomsbury Group of intellectuals including the Woolfs, the Bells, J. M. Keynes, Lytton Strachey, E. M. Forster, etc., influenced by Moore's *Principia Ethica* 1903, comes into existence c.1905

Duhem (1861–1916) publishes *The Aim and Structure of Physical Theory* 1906

Einstein (1879–1955) devises special relativity theory 1905

Bohr (1885–1962) publishes theory of hydrogen atom 1913

First World War 1914–18

Einstein (1879–1955) introduces general relativity theory 1915, confirmed by solar eclipse 1919

Jung, psychologist, 1875–1961

Santayana 1863–1952

Lenin (1870–1924) masterminds Bolshevik Revolution in Russia 1917, inaugurating communism there

Treaty of Versailles, imposing crippling war reparations on Germany 1919

Alexander (1859–1938) publishes *Space, Time and Deity* 1920

McTaggart (1866–1925) publishes *The Nature of Existence* 1921

J. M. Keynes (1883–1946) publishes *The Economic Consequences of the Peace* 1919; start of Keynesian economics

Wittgenstein (1889–1951) publishes *Tractatus Logico-Philosophicus* 1921

Mussolini (1883–1945) forms Fascist government in Italy 1922

Schlick 1882–1936

T. S. Eliot (1888–1965) publishes *The Waste Land* 1922

MODERNIST ERA IN ART AND LITERATURE

ERA OF COLONIAL EMPIRE

Ramsey 1903–30

Broad (1887–1971) publishes *The Mind and its Place in Nature* 1925, *Five Types of Ethical Theory* 1930

Heidegger (1889–1976) publishes *Sein und Zeit* 1927

Whitehead (1861–1947) publishes *Process and Reality* 1929

Carnap (1891–1970) publishes *Der Logische Aufbau der Welt* 1928, *The Unity of Science* 1932, *Meaning and Necessity* 1947, *Logical Foundations of Probability* 1950

Gödel (1906-78) publishes his incompleteness theorems 1931

Maritain 1882–1973

Jaspers 1883–1969

Bachelard 1884–1962

Marcel 1889–1973

Reichenbach 1891–1953

H. H. Price (1899–1984) publishes *Perception* 1932

Popper (1902–94) publishes *The Logic of Scientific Discovery* 1935, *The Open Society and its Enemies* 1945

Ayer (1910–89) publishes *Language, Truth and Logic* 1936

Collingwood (1889–1943) publishes *An Essay on Metaphysics* 1940

Merleau-Ponty (1908–61) publishes *La Structure du comportement* 1942, *La Phénoménologie de la perception* 1945

Sartre (1905–80) publishes *L'Être et le néant* 1943

Ryle (1900–76) publishes *The Concept of Mind* 1949

De Beauvoir publishes *Le Deuxième Sexe* 1949

James Joyce (1882–1941) publishes *Ulysses* (burnt by American Post Office) 1922, *Finnegan's Wake* 1939

General strike in Great Britain defeated 1926

Trotsky (1879–1940) expelled from Russian Communist Party 1927

Heisenberg's uncertainty principle 1927

Eddington (1882–1944) publishes *The Nature of the Physical World* 1928

Fleming (1881–1954) discovers penicillin 1928

Economic depression hits Europe and America 1929

Roosevelt elected US President 1932

Karl Barth, theologian, 1886–1968

Hitler (1889–1945) takes power 1933 and annexes Austria 1938, causing exodus of many intellectuals including philosophers

Alan Turing (1912–54) conceives universal digital computing machine

Franco (1892–1975) gains power in Spain after Civil War 1936–9

Munich Agreement offers 'peace in our time' 1938

German–Soviet pact 1939

Second World War, ended by atomic bombs, 1939–45

Orwell (1903–50) publishes *Animal Farm* 1945, *Nineteen Eighty-Four* (written in 1948) 1949

Labour government introduces socialist measures in Great Britain 1945–51

Camus (1913–60) publishes *L'Étranger* 1946

'Iron Curtain' named by Churchill 1946

First meeting of the General Assembly of the United Nations 1946

India given independence 1947

Mahatma Gandhi (born 1869) assassinated 1948

'Steady state' cosmology proposed 1948

ERA OF COLONIAL EMPIRE

MODERNIST ERA IN ART AND LITERATURE

Quine (1908–2000) publishes *Methods of Logic* 1950, *From a Logical Point of View* 1952, *Word and Object* 1960

Tarski 1902–83

Hare publishes *The Language of Morals* 1952

Wittgenstein's *Philosophical Investigations* published posthumously 1953

'Australian materialism' develops in 1950s

Goodman (1906–98) publishes *Fact, Fiction, and Forecast* 1955

Marcuse (1898–1979) publishes *Eros and Civilization* 1955

Church 1903–95

Chisholm (1916–99) publishes *The Philosophy of Perception* 1957

Adorno 1903–69

Ricœur 1913–

P. F. Strawson (born 1919) publishes *Individuals* 1959

Gadamer (1900–2002) publishes *Truth and Method* 1960

Foucault (1926–84) publishes *Histoire de la folie* 1961

Kuhn (1922–96) publishes *The Structure of Scientific Revolutions* 1962

Sense and Sensibilia and *How to Do Things with Words*, by J. L. Austin (1911–60), published 1962

Habermas (born 1929) publishes *Theorie und Praxis* 1963

Althusser (1918–90) publishes *Pour Marx* 1965

Derrida (1930–2004) publishes *L'Écriture et la différence* 1967

Davidson (1917–2003) publishes 'Truth and Meaning' 1967, 'Mental Events' 1970

Berlin (1909–97) publishes *Four Essays on Liberty* 1969

Putnam 1926–

Kripke (born 1940) publishes 'Naming and Necessity' 1972

Rawls (1921–2002) publishes *A Theory of Justice* 1972

Dummett (born 1925) publishes *Frege: Philosophy of Language* 1973

Mackie (1917–81) publishes *The Cement of the Universe* 1974

Nozick (1938–2002) publishes *Anarchy, State and Utopia* 1974

Searle (born 1932) publishes 'Minds, Brains, and Programs' 1980

Communists under Mao Tse-tung take over China 1949

Korean War 1950–3

Joseph McCarthy (1908–57) conducts campaign against Communists in USA, 1950–4

Stalin (born 1879) dies 1953

Russia suppresses Hungarian revolt 1956

Russia launches first Sputnik 1957

Chomsky (born 1928) publishes *Syntactic Structures* 1957

European Common Market established 1958

Castro becomes leader of Cuba 1959

Berlin Wall constructed 1961

Cuba crisis threatens nuclear war 1962

US 'military advisers' in Vietnam 1962

J. F. Kennedy assassinated 1963

Campaign for civil rights in USA

Russell active in campaign against British nuclear deterrent

Expansion of universities during 1960s

Arab–Israeli Six Day War 1967

Soviet forces suppress 'Prague Spring' 1968

Student riots in Paris and elsewhere 1968

Women get the vote in Switzerland 1971

Withdrawal of US troops from Vietnam 1971

Spain returns to democracy 1975

'Thatcherism' introduced in UK after Conservative election victory 1979

'COLD WAR' BETWEEN COMMUNIST BLOC AND WESTERN POWERS

Rorty (born 1931) publishes *Philosophy and the Mirror of Nature* 1980	War in Afghanistan between Soviet troops and Mujaheddin guerillas 1979–89
	Shipyard strike in Poland leads to the concession of workers' rights and the formation of the Solidarność union confederation
MacIntyre (born 1929) publishes *After Virtue* 1981	1980
Parfit (born 1942) publishes *Reasons and Persons* 1984	Deaths of IRA hunger strikers 1981
Bernard Williams (1929–2003) publishes *Ethics and the Limits of Philosophy* 1985	German Green party wins first parliamentary seats 1983
	John Paul II becomes the first pope to visit a synagogue
Thomas Nagel (born 1937) publishes *The View from Nowhere* 1986	Gorbachev campaigns for *glasnost* (openness) in the Soviet Union 1987
	Collapse of communism in Soviet Union and Eastern Europe 1989, followed by political fragmentation and intellectual liberation
	Series of wars in former Yugoslavia 1991–9
	100-day war against Iraq by UN (mainly US) forces 1991
	Nelson Mandela elected president in South Africa's first universally representative elections 1994
Brandom (born 1950) publishes *Making it Explicit* 1994	Demilitarization of Northern Ireland begins 1994, after 25 years
Scanlon (born 1940) publishes *What We Owe to Each Other* 1998	800,000 killed in Rwandan civil war 1994
	New York's World Trade Center destroyed 11 September 2001
	USA and allies invade Afghanistan 2001, Iraq 2003

2000

Chronological table by A. R. Lacey

Sources of Illustrations

The editor and publisher thank the following, who have kindly given permission to reproduce the illustrations listed:

page 25	Dewey	Camera Press
	Carnap	Bettman Corbis
	Quine	Courtesy of Prof. W. V. Quine, Harvard University Archives
	Goodman	Harvard University Press
page 35	Plato	Archivo Alinari
	Aristotle	Archivo Alinari
	Epicurus	Archivo Alinari
	Plotinus	Canali Photobank
page 121	Moore	National Portrait Gallery, London
	Russell	Hulton Getty Images
	Wittgenstein	Trinity College, Cambridge
	Collingwood	Reading University (Courtesy of Mrs Teresa Smith)
page 171	Husserl	Catholic University of Leyden; Husserl Archive
	Frege	Archiv für Kunst und Geschichte
	Ortega y Gassett	Archiv für Kunst und Geschichte
	Heidegger	Archiv für Kunst und Geschichte
page 243	Hobbes	National Portrait Gallery, London
	Locke	National Portrait Gallery, London
	Berkeley	National Portrait Gallery, London
	Hume	National Gallery of Scotland
page 249	Francis Bacon	National Portrait Gallery, London
	Reid	Hunterian Museum and Art Gallery, University of Glasgow
	Sidgwick	Hulton Getty Images
	Bradley	Merton College, Oxford (Thomas Photos)
page 278	Sartre	Archive Roger-Viollet
	de Beauvoir	Archive Roger-Viollet
	Foucault	Camera Press
	Althusser	Camera Press
page 320	Rousseau	National Gallery of Scotland
	Comte	Archive Roger-Viollet
	Bergson	Archive Roger-Viollet
	Merleau-Ponty	Archive Roger-Viollet
page 334	Fichte	Bildarchiv Preussischer Kulturbesitz
	Schopenhauer	Getty Images

Index and List of Entries

The headings in this index include all the headings of the entries in the book. So the index is also a list of the entries. To look up any subject, turn first to the main entry under the capitalized index heading (e.g. ABANDONMENT) and then to the entries under the following headings (e.g. authenticity).

Where an index heading is from an entry which is a bare cross-reference to another entry, the index indicates this by following the same form (e.g. ABSTRACT IDEAS *see* IDEAS).

In order not to submerge the significant entries on a subject in a host of others, the index does not include every mention of a subject in the book, but rather the more significant ones.

The few headings in the index which are not also headings of entries in the book are in large capitals. These are to AESTHETICS and so on—main parts of philosophy, which in the book are divided into one entry on the history of the part of philosophy and one on its problems. The few references in the index to such entries are also in large capitals.